THE SCRAMBLED WORD AND ANAGRAM FINDER

JOHN DAINTITH

THE SCRAMBLED WORD AND ANAGRAM FINDER

HarperPerennial

A Division of HarperCollinsPublishers

This book was originally published in Great Britain by Bloomsbury Publishing in 1994 under the title *Bloomsbury Anagram Finder*.

HarperCollins books may be purchased for educational, business, or sales promotional use. For information, please write: Special Markets Department, HarperCollins Publishers, Inc., 10 East 53rd Street, New York, NY 10022.

FIRST EDITION

Designed by Alma Hochhauser Orenstein

Library of Congress Cataloging-in-Publication Data
Daintith, John
    The scrambled word and anagram finder / John Daintith. — 1st ed.
      p. cm.
    Originally published under title: The Bloomsbury anagram finder : London : Bloomsbury, 1994

ISBN 0-06-273277-3
    1. Anagrams. I. Daintith, John. The Bloomsbury anagram finder.
    II. Title.
    GV1507.A5D35 1994
    793.73—dc20   93-34205

94 95 96 97 98 ❖/RRD 10 9 8 7 6 5 4 3 2 1

THE
SCRAMBLED
WORD AND
ANAGRAM
FINDER

TWO-LETTER WORDS

AB AB	**CD** CD	**EW** WE	**IN** IN	**NU** UN
AC AC	**CK** KC	**EX** EX	**IP** PI	**OP** OP
AD AD, DA	**CO** CO	**EY** YE	**IQ** IQ	**OR** OR
AF FA	**CP** PC	**FI** IF	**IT** IT, TI	**OS** SO
AH AH, HA	**CQ** QC	**FM** FM	**JO** JO	**OT** TO
AI AI	**CV** CV, VC	**FO** OF	**JP** JP	**OW** OW
AL AL, LA	**CW** WC	**GI** GI	**KO** KO	**OX** OX
AM AM, MA	**CY** CY	**GO** GO	**KU** UK	**PR** PR
AN AN	**DE** ED	**GP** GP	**LO** LO	**PS** PS
AP PA	**DI** ID	**GS** GS	**LP** LP	**PT** PT
AS AS	**DJ** DJ	**HI** HI	**MO** MO	**PU** UP
AT AT, TA	**DO** DO	**HM** H'M	**MP** MP, PM	**PX** PX
AX AX	**DV** VD	**HO** HO, OH	**MR** MR	**QT** QT
BC CB	**EH** EH, HE	**HP** PH	**MS** MS	**SU** US
BE BE	**EM** ME	**HQ** HQ	**MU** UM	**SV** VS
BO BO	**EP** PE	**HS** SH	**MY** MY	**TV** TV
BY BY	**ER** ER, RE	**IM** MI	**NO** NO, ON	

THREE-LETTER WORDS

AAB BAA	**ACP** CAP, CPA	**AEH** HAE	**AGO** AGO	**AJW** JAW
AAD ADA	**ACR** ARC, CAR	**AEL** ALE, LEA	**AGP** GAP	**AJY** JAY
AAH AHA	**ACS** SAC	**AEM** MAE	**AGR** RAG	**AKO** OAK
AAL À LA	**ACT** ACT, CAT	**AEN** ENA	**AGS** GAS, SAG	**AKR** ARK
AAS ASA	**ACV** VAC	**AEP** APE, PEA	**AGT** TAG	**AKS** ASK
AAV AVA	**ACW** CAW	**AER** EAR, ERA, RAE	**AGW** WAG	**AKU** AUK
ABB BAB	**ADD** ADD, DAD	**AES** SAE, SEA	**AGY** GAY	**AKY** KAY, YAK
ABC ABC, CAB	**ADE** EDA	**AET** ATE, EAT, TEA	**AHH** HAH	**AKZ** ZAK
ABD BAD, DAB	**ADF** FAD	**AEV** EVA	**AHL** HAL	**ALL** ALL
ABE ABE, BEA	**ADG** GAD	**AEW** AWE	**AHM** HAM	**ALN** LAN
ABF FAB	**ADH** HAD	**AEX** AXE	**AHN** HAN	**ALP** LAP, PAL
ABG BAG, GAB	**ADI** AID, DAI, IDA	**AEY** AYE, YEA	**AHP** HAP	**ALS** SAL
ABH BAH	**ADJ** ADJ	**AFG** FAG	**AHS** ASH, HAS	**ALV** VAL
ABJ JAB	**ADL** LAD	**AFL** ALF	**AHT** HAT	**ALW** AWL, LAW, WAL
ABL LAB	**ADM** DAM, MAD	**AFN** FAN	**AHW** HAW	**ALX** LAX
ABN BAN, NAB	**ADN** AND, DAN, DNA	**AFO** OAF	**AHY** HAY	**ALY** LAY
ABO ABO, BOA	**ADO** ADO	**AFR** FAR, RAF	**AIL** AIL	**AMM** MAM
ABR BAR, BRA, RAB	**ADP** PAD	**AFT** AFT, FAT	**AIM** AIM, MIA	**AMN** MAN
ABT BAT, TAB	**ADS** ADS, SAD	**AFX** FAX	**AIN** IAN, INA	**AMP** AMP, MAP, PAM
ABY BAY	**ADU** AUD	**AFY** FAY	**AIP** IPA, PIA	**AMR** ARM, MAR, RAM
ACD CAD	**ADV** ADV	**AGG** GAG	**AIR** AIR, IRA, RIA	**AMS** MAS, SAM
ACE ACE	**ADW** WAD	**AGH** HAG	**AIS** ISA	**AMT** MAT, TAM
ACI CAI, CIA	**ADY** DAY	**AGJ** JAG	**AIT** ITA	**AMW** MAW
ACM CAM, MAC	**AEG** AGE	**AGL** GAL, LAG	**AIV** VIA	**AMX** MAX
ACN CAN		**AGM** AGM, MAG	**AJM** JAM	
		AGN NAG	**AJN** JAN	
			AJR JAR, RAJ	

AMY AMY, MAY, YAM	**BDU** BUD, DUB	**CES** CSE, SEC	**DET** TED	**EES** SEE
ANN ANN, NAN	**BEE** BEE	**CET** ECT, ETC	**DEU** DUE	**EET** TEE
ANO ONA	**BEG** BEG	**CEU** CUE	**DEW** DEW, WED	**EEV** EVE
ANP NAP, PAN	**BEL** BEL	**CGO** COG	**DEY** DYE	**EEW** EWE, WEE
ANR RAN, RNA	**BEN** BEN	**CHI** HIC	**DEZ** ZED	**EEY** EYE
ANT ANT, NAT, TAN	**BES** SEB	**CIN** INC	**DGI** DIG	**EFF** EFF
ANU UNA	**BET** BET	**CIS** CIS, SIC	**DGO** DOG, GOD	**EFI** FIE
ANV VAN	**BEW** WEB	**CIT** TIC	**DGP** GDP	**EFL** ELF
ANW WAN	**BEY** BYE	**CIV** VIC	**DGU** DUG	**EFN** FEN
ANY ANY, NAY	**BFI** FBI, FIB	**CIY** ICY	**DHI** HID	**EFO** FOE
AOP OAP	**BFO** FOB	**CLM** LCM	**DHO** DOH, HOD	**EFR** REF
AOR OAR	**BGI** BIG	**CLO** COL	**DHP** PHD	**EFW** FEW
AOV OVA	**BGO** BOG, GOB	**CLP** PLC	**DIK** KID	**EFY** FEY
APP PAP	**BGU** BUG	**CMS** MSC	**DIL** LID	**EFZ** FEZ
APR PAR, RAP	**BHO** HOB	**CMU** CUM	**DIM** DIM, MID	**EGG** EGG
APS ASP, PAS, SAP, SPA	**BHU** HUB	**CMW** CWM	**DIN** DIN	**EGK** EKG, KEG
APT APT, PAT, PTA, TAP	**BIJ** JIB	**CNO** CON, NCO	**DIP** DIP	**EGL** GEL, LEG
APW PAW	**BIL** LIB	**COO** COO	**DIR** RID	**EGM** GEM, MEG
APY PAY, YAP	**BIN** BIN, NIB	**COP** COP	**DIS** IDS, SDI, SID	**EGN** GEN
APZ ZAP	**BIR** RIB	**COR** ROC	**DIU** IUD	**EGO** EGO
AQU QUA	**BIT** BIT	**COS** COS	**DIY** DIY, YID	**EGP** PEG
ART ART, RAT, TAR	**BJO** JOB	**COT** COT	**DJS** DJS	**EGR** ERG, REG
ARW RAW, WAR	**BLO** LOB	**COW** COW	**DLO** OLD	**EGT** GET
ARY RAY	**BMO** MOB	**COX** COX	**DLS** LSD	**EGV** VEG
ASS ASS	**BMU** BUM	**COY** COY	**DMO** MOD	**EHH** HEH
AST SAT	**BNO** NOB	**CPS** PCS	**DMU** MUD	**EHI** HIE
ASW SAW	**BNU** BUN, NUB	**CPU** CPU, CUP	**DNO** DON, NOD	**EHL** HEL
ASY SAY	**BOO** BOO	**CPV** PVC	**DNU** DUN	**EHM** HEM
ATT TAT	**BOP** BOP	**CPW** WPC	**DOO** ODO	**EHN** HEN
ATV VAT	**BOR** ORB, ROB	**CQS** QCS	**DOP** POD	**EHO** HOE
ATW WAT	**BOS** SOB	**CRU** CUR	**DOR** ROD	**EHP** HEP
ATX TAX	**BOW** BOW	**CRV** VCR	**DOS** DOS, SOD	**EHR** HER
AWX WAX	**BOX** BOX	**CRY** CRY	**DOT** DOT, TOD	**EHS** HE'S, SHE
AWY WAY, YAW	**BOY** BOY, YOB	**CSV** CVS, VCS	**DOU** DUO	**EHT** HET, THE
BBC BBC	**BPU** PUB	**CTU** CUT, TUC	**DPS** SDP	**EHU** HUE
BBE EBB	**BRU** BUR, RUB	**DDI** DID	**DPU** PUD	**EHW** HEW
BBI BIB	**BSU** BUS, SUB	**DDO** ODD	**DRY** DRY	**EHX** HEX
BBO BOB	**BTU** BUT, TUB	**DDT** DDT	**DST** D T'S, STD	**EHY** HEY
BBU BUB	**BUY** BUY	**DDU** DUD	**DSY** SYD	**EIK** IKE
BCO COB	**CDI** CID	**DEE** DEE	**DUV** VDU	**EIL** ELI, LEI, LIE
BCU CUB	**CDL** LCD	**DEF** FED	**EEF** FEE	**EIP** PIE
BDE BED, DEB	**CDN** CND	**DEH** HE'D	**EEG** GEE	**EIR** IRE
BDI BID	**CDO** COD, DOC	**DEI** DIE	**EEK** EEK	**EIT** TIE
BDO BOD	**CDS** CDS	**DEJ** JED	**EEL** EEL, LEE	**EIV** VIE
	CDU CUD	**DEL** DEL, LED	**EEN** NÉE	**EJM** JEM
	CEE EEC	**DEM** DEM	**EEP** PEE	**EJO** JOE
	CEG ECG, GCE	**DEN** DEN, END, NED	**EER** ERE	**EJT** JET
	CEI ICE	**DEO** DOE, ODE		**EJW** JEW
		DEP DEP		**EKL** ELK
		DER RED		**EKN** KEN
		DES DES		**EKY** KEY

ELM ELM, MEL
ELO LEO
ELT ELT, LET
ELW LEW
EMN MEN
EMT MET
EMU EMU
EMW MEW
ENO EON, ONE
ENP PEN
ENT NET, TEN
ENW NEW
ENY NYE, YEN
ENZ ZEN
EOR ORE, O'ER, ROE
EOT TOE
EOW OWE, WOE
EOZ ZOE
EPP PEP
EPR PER, REP
EPS ESP
EPT PET
EPW PEW
EQS ESQ
ERR ERR
ERU RUE
ERV REV
ERX REX
ERY RYE
EST SET
ESU SUE, USE
ESW SEW
ESX SEX
ESY YES
ETV VET
ETW WET
ETX TEX
ETY YET
EVX VEX
EWY YEW
FFO OFF
FGI FIG
FGO FOG
FGU FUG
FHU UHF
FHV VHF
FIN FIN
FIR FIR
FIS IFS
FIT FIT

FIX FIX
FLU FLU
FLY FLY
FNU FUN
FOO OOF
FOP FOP
FOR FOR, FRO
FOT OFT
FOU UFO
FOX FOX
FRU FUR
FRY FRY
GGI GIG
GHO HOG
GHU HUG, UGH
GIJ JIG
GIL GIL
GIN GIN
GIP PIG
GIR RIG
GIS GI'S
GIW WIG
GJO JOG
GJU JUG
GLO LOG
GLU LUG
GMU GUM, MUG
GMY GYM
GNP GNP
GNU GNU, GUN
GOO GOO
GOP GOP
GOT GOT, TOG
GOW WOG
GPS GPS
GPU PUG
GPY GYP
GRU RUG
GSU GUS
GTU GUT, TUG
GUV GUV
GUY GUY
HHU HUH
HIM HIM
HIN HIN
HIP HIP
HIS HIS, HSI
HIT HIT
HMO HOM, OHM

HMU HUM
HNS NHS
HNT NTH
HNU HUN
HOO HOO, OHO
HOP HOP
HOS SOH
HOT HOT
HOW HOW, WHO
HOY HOY
HPS PHS
HQS HQS
HSY SHY
HTU HUT
HTY THY
HUW HUW
HWY WHY
IJM JIM
IKL ILK
IKM KIM
IKN INK, KIN
IKP KIP
IKR IRK
IKS SKI
IKT KIT
ILL ILL
ILN NIL
ILO OIL
ILP LIP
ILT LIT
ILZ LIZ
IMP IMP
IMR RIM
IMS ISM, SIM
IMT TIM
IMV VIM
IMX MIX
INN INN
INO ION
INP NIP, PIN
INS SIN
INT NIT, TIN
INV VIN
INW WIN
INX NIX
INY YIN
IOU IOU
IOV IVO
IPP IPP
IPR RIP
IPS PIS, SIP
IPT PIT, TIP

IPV VIP
IPX PIX
IPZ ZIP
IQS IQS
IRS SIR
ISS SIS
IST ITS, SIT
ISX SIX
ITT TIT
ITV ITV
ITW WIT
IVV VIV
IVY IVY
IVZ VIZ
JNO JON
JOT JOT
JOY JOY
JPS JPS
JTU JUT
KOW WOK
KSY SKY
LNY LYN
LOO LOO
LOP LOP
LOS SOL
LOT LOT
LOU LOU
LOW LOW, OWL
LOX LOX
LPS LPS
LPY PLY
LSY SLY
LUV LUV
MMO MOM
MMU MUM
MOO MOO
MOP MOP
MOR ROM
MOS MOS
MOT MOT, TOM
MOW MOW
MPS MPS, PMS
MRS MRS
MRU RUM
MSU SUM
NNU NUN
NOR NOR, RON
NOS SON
NOT NOT, TON

NOW NOW, OWN, WON
NPU PUN
NRU RUN, URN
NSU SUN
NTT TNT
NTU NUT
OOT TOO
OOW WOO
OOZ ZOO
OPP POP
OPR PRO
OPS OPS, SOP
OPT OPT, POT, PTO, TOP
OPW POW, WOP
OPX POX
ORS ROS
ORT ROT, TOR
ORU OUR
ORW ROW
ORY ROY
OSS SOS
OST SOT
OSU SOU
OSW SOW
OSX SOX
OSY SOY
OTT TOT
OTU OUT
OTW TOW, TWO, WOT
OTY TOY
OUY YOU
OVW VOW
OWW WOW
PPS PPS
PPU PUP
PRU PRU
PRY PRY
PSU PUS, SUP
PSY SPY
PTU PUT
PXY PYX
RTU RUT
RTY TRY
RWY WRY
STV TVS
STY STY
TTU TUT

FOUR-LETTER WORDS

AABR ARAB
AABS BAAS
AACR CARA
AADH ADAH
AADL ALDA
AADM ADAM
AADN DANA, NADA
AADT DATA
AAER AREA
AAFH HAAF
AAFR AFAR, AFRA
AAGG GAGA
AAGL GALA
AAGR AGRA, RAGA
AAGS SAGA
AAGZ GAZA
AAHH HA-HA
AAHM HAMA
AAHR HAAR
AAHS HASA
AAHY AYAH
AAIR ARIA
AAIS ASIA
AAJR AJAR
AAKR KARA
AALM ALMA, LAMA
AALN ALAN, ANAL, LANA
AALS ALAS
AALV ALVA, LAVA
AAMM MAMA, MA'AM
AAMR MARA
AAMY MAYA
AANN ANNA
AANS NASA, SAN'A
AANY ANYA
AANZ ZANA
AAPP PAPA
AAQU AQUA
AARS SARA
AART TARA
AARU AURA
AARZ ZARA
AATT TA-TA
AAWY AWAY
ABBE BABE
ABBL BLAB
ABBR BARB
ABBS BABS

ABBU BABU
ABBY ABBY, BABY
ABCK BACK
ABCR CRAB
ABCS ABCS, CABS, SCAB
ABCU CUBA
ABDE ABED, BADE, BEAD
ABDL BALD
ABDN BAND
ABDR BARD, BRAD, DRAB
ABDS DABS
ABDU BAUD, DAUB
ABDW BAWD
ABEK BAKE, BEAK
ABEL ABEL, ABLE, BALE, ELBA
ABEM BEAM
ABEN BANE, BEAN
ABER BARE, BEAR, BRAE
ABES BASE
ABET ABET, BEAT, BETA
ABEU AUBE, BEAU
ABFL FLAB
ABGI GABI
ABGN BANG
ABGR BRAG, GARB, GRAB
ABGS BAGS
ABGY GABY
ABHL BLAH
ABHS BASH
ABHT BATH
ABHU HABU
ABIL BAIL, BALI
ABIM IAMB
ABIN BINA
ABIS BIAS
ABIT BAIT
ABJM JAMB
ABJS JABS
ABKL BALK
ABKN BANK
ABKR BARK
ABKS BASK
ABKU BAKU
ABLL BALL

ABLM BALM, LAMB
ABLS LABS, SLAB
ABLW BAWL
ABLY ABLY
ABMO AMBO
ABMR BRAM
ABNR BARN, BRAN
ABNS BANS
ABNU BUNA
ABOR BOAR
ABOS ABOS, BOAS
ABOT BOAT
ABOZ BOAZ
ABRS BARS, BRAS
ABRT BART, BRAT
ABRY BRAY
ABSS BASS
ABST BAST, BATS, STAB, TABS
ABSW SWAB
ABSY BAYS
ABTU ABUT, TUBA
ACCD AC/DC
ACCT ACCT
ACCU UCCA
ACDH CHAD
ACDI ACID
ACDL CLAD
ACDO CODA
ACDR CARD
ACDS CADS
ACEF CAFE, FACE
ACEG CAGE
ACEH ACHE, EACH
ACEK CAKE
ACEL ALEC, LACE
ACEM ACME, CAME, MACE
ACEN ACNE, CAEN, CANE
ACEP CAPE, PACE
ACER ACRE, CARE, RACE
ACES ACES, CASE
ACEV CAVE
ACFL CALF
ACFT FACT
ACGR CRAG
ACGS SCAG
ACHK HACK
ACHM MACH

ACHP CHAP
ACHR ARCH, CHAR
ACHS CASH, CHAS
ACHT CATH, CHAT
ACHY CHAY
ACIL CALI
ACIM MICA
ACIN INCA
ACIP PICA
ACIR RICA
ACJK JACK
ACKL CALK, LACK
ACKP PACK
ACKR RACK
ACKS CASK, SACK
ACKT TACK
ACKZ ZACK
ACLL CALL
ACLM CALM, CLAM
ACLN CLAN
ACLO COAL, COLA
ACLP CLAP
ACLR CARL
ACLT TALC
ACLU CAUL
ACLW CLAW
ACLX CALX
ACLY CLAY, LACY
ACMO COMA
ACMP CAMP
ACMR CRAM, MARC
ACMS CAMS, MACS, SCAM
ACNS CANS, SCAN
ACNT CANT
ACNY CYAN
ACOR CORA
ACOT COAT, TACO
ACOX COAX, COXA
ACPR CARP, CRAP
ACPS CAPS
ACPT PACT
ACRS ARCS, CARS, SCAR
ACRT CART
ACRY CARY, RACY
ACRZ CZAR
ACSS CASS, SACS

ACST ACTS, CAST, CATS, SCAT
ACSV VACS
ACSW CAWS
ACTT TACT
ACTY TACY
ACVY CAVY
ADDE DEAD
ADDO DADO
ADDS DADS
ADDY ADDY, DYAD, D-DAY
ADEF DEAF, FADE
ADEG AGED
ADEH HADE, HEAD
ADEI AIDE, IDEA
ADEJ JADE
ADEL ALED, DALE, DEAL, LADE, LEAD
ADEM DAME, EDAM, MADE, MEAD
ADEN ADEN, DANE, DEAN, EDNA
ADEP APED
ADER DARE, DEAR, READ
ADET DATE
ADEU AUDE
ADEV DAVE
ADEW AWED, WADE
ADEX AXED
ADEZ ADZE, DAZE
ADFF DAFF
ADFS FADS
ADFT DAFT
ADGL GLAD
ADGO DAGO, GOAD
ADGR DRAG, GARD
ADGY G'DAY
ADHJ HADJ
ADHK DHAK
ADHN HAND
ADHO DOHA, HOAD
ADHP DAPH
ADHR HARD
ADHS DASH, SHAD

ADIL DIAL, LAID
ADIM AMID, MAID
ADIP PAID
ADIR ARID, RAID
ADIS AIDS, DAIS, SAID
ADIV AVID, VIDA
ADIW WADI
ADKN DANK
ADKR DARK
ADLN LAND
ADLO ALDO, LOAD
ADLR LARD
ADLS LADS
ADLU DUAL, LAUD
ADLY LADY
ADMN DAMN
ADMP DAMP
ADMR DRAM
ADMS DAMS
ADMU MAUD
ADNR DARN, RAND
ADNS SAND
ADNW DAWN, WAND
ADNY ANDY
ADOR DORA, ROAD
ADOS SODA
ADOT TOAD
ADOW WOAD
ADPS PADS
ADQU QUAD
ADRT DART, DRAT, TRAD
ADRW DRAW, WARD
ADRY DRAY, YARD
ADSW WADS
ADSY DAYS
ADUV VAUD
ADVY DAVY
AEES EASE
AEFK FAKE
AEFL FLEA, LEAF
AEFM FAME
AEFR FARE, FEAR, RAFE
AEFS SAFE
AEFT FATE, FEAT
AEFY FAYE

AEFZ FAZE
AEGG GAGE
AEGL GALE
AEGM GAME
AEGP GAPE, PAGE
AEGR AREG, GEAR, RAGE
AEGS AGES, SAGE
AEGT GATE
AEGU AGUE
AEGV GAVE
AEGW WAGE
AEGY GAYE
AEGZ GAZE
AEHK HAKE
AEHL HALE, HEAL, HELA, LEAH
AEHM AHEM, HAEM, HAME
AEHP HEAP
AEHR HARE, HEAR, HERA, RHEA
AEHT HATE, HEAT, THEA
AEHV HAVE
AEHY YEAH
AEHZ HAZE
AEIL ELIA
AEIN AINE
AEIR EIRA
AEJK JAKE
AEJL JAEL
AEJN JANE, JEAN
AEJP JAPE
AEKL KALE, LAKE, LEAK
AEKM MAKE
AEKN KANE
AEKP PEAK
AEKR RAKE
AEKS SAKE
AEKT KATE, TAKE, TEAK
AEKW WAKE, WEAK
AELL ELLA, LELA
AELM ELMA, LAME, MALE, MEAL
AELN ÉLAN, LANE, LEAN, LENA, NEAL
AELO ALOE

AELP LEAP, PALE, PEAL, PLEA
AELR EARL, REAL
AELS ELSA, LEAS, SALE, SEAL
AELT ET AL, LATE, LETA, TALE, TEAL
AELV VALE, VEAL
AELW WEAL
AELX ALEX, AXEL, AXLE
AELZ LAZE, ZEAL
AEMM EMMA
AEMN AMEN, MANE, MEAN, NAME
AEMR MARE, REAM
AEMS SAME, SEAM
AEMT MATE, MEAT, META, TAME, TEAM
AEMX EXAM
AEMZ MAZE
AENN ANNE
AENO AEON
AENP NAPE, PANE
AENR EARN, NEAR, RENA
AENS SANE, SEAN
AENT ANTE, NEAT
AENV EVAN, NAVE, NEVA, VANE
AENW ANEW, EWAN, WANE, WEAN
AENZ ZANE, ZENA
AEPR PARE, PEAR, RAPE, REAP
AEPS APES, APSE, PEAS
AEPT PATE, PEAT, PETA, TAPE
AEPV PAVE
AEPX APEX
AEPY PAYE
AERR RARE, REAR
AERS ARSE, EARS, ERAS, SEAR, SERA
AERT RATE, TARE, TEAR
AERV AVER, RAVE, VERA
AERW WEAR

AERY YEAR
AERZ EZRA, RAZE
AESS SEAS
AEST EAST, EATS, SATE, SEAT, SETA, TEAS
AESU ESAU
AESV SAVE, VASE
AESX AXES
AESY AYES, EASY, YEAS
AETT ETTA, TEAT
AEUV UVEA
AEVW WAVE
AFFG GAFF
AFFN NAFF
AFGL FLAG
AFGN FANG
AFGS FAGS
AFHL HALF
AFHT HAFT
AFIL FAIL
AFIN FAIN
AFIR FAIR
AFIT FIAT
AFIW WAIF
AFKL FLAK
AFLL FALL
AFLN FLAN
AFLO FOAL, LOAF, OLAF
AFLP FLAP
AFLT FLAT
AFLW FLAW
AFLX FLAX
AFLY FLAY
AFMO FOAM
AFMR FARM
AFNS FANS
AFNU FAUN
AFNW FAWN
AFOR AFRO, FORA
AFOS OAFS, SOFA
AFPR FRAP
AFRT FART, RAFT
AFRU FRAU
AFRY FRAY
AFST FAST, FATS
AFTW WAFT
AGGN GANG
AGGO AGOG
AGGS GAGS
AGHI HAIG
AGHN HANG

AGHS GASH, HAGS, SHAG
AGHT GHAT
AGIL GAIL
AGIM MAGI
AGIN GAIN, GINA, INGA
AGIO IAGO
AGIT GAIT
AGIZ GIZA
AGJO JAGO
AGJS JAGS
AGKW GAWK
AGLL GALL
AGLO GAOL, GOAL, OLGA
AGLS GALS, LAGS, SLAG
AGLY ALGY
AGMR GRAM
AGMS AGMS, MAGS
AGMY GAMY
AGNP PANG
AGNR GRAN, RANG
AGNS NAGS, SANG, SNAG
AGNT GNAT, TANG
AGNW GNAW
AGNY YANG
AGOS SAGO
AGOT GOAT, TOGA
AGOY YOGA
AGPS GAPS, GASP
AGPW GAWP
AGRS RAGS
AGRY GARY, GRAY
AGSS SAGS
AGST STAG, TAGS
AGSW SWAG, WAGS
AGSY GAYS
AHHS HASH, SHAH
AHHT HATH
AHIK HAIK
AHIL HAIL
AHIR HAIR
AHIV IVAH
AHJJ HAJJ
AHKL LAKH
AHKN ANKH, HANK, KHAN
AHKR HARK

AHKS HASK
AHKT KATH
AHKW HAWK
AHLL HALL
AHLM HALM
AHLO HALO
AHLR HARL
AHLS LASH
AHLT HALT, LATH
AHLU HAUL, HULA
AHMO HAMO, HOMA
AHMR HARM
AHMS HAMS, MASH, SHAM
AHMW WHAM
AHNO NOAH
AHNS HANS
AHNT TANH, THAN
AHNW HWAN
AHOR HOAR, HORA
AHOS SHOA
AHOT OATH
AHOW WHOA
AHOX HOAX
AHOY AHOY, HOYA
AHPR HARP
AHPS HASP
AHPT PATH
AHRS RASH
AHRT HART
AHRZ HARZ
AHSS SASH
AHST HAST, HATS, SHAT
AHSW SHAW, WASH
AHSY ASHY
AHTT THAT
AHTU UTAH
AHTW THAW, WHAT
AHYZ HAZY
AIIN IAIN
AIJL JAIL
AIKN AKIN
AIKR RIKA
AILL LILA
AILM ILMA, LIAM, LIMA, MAIL, MALI

AILN LAIN, LINA, NAIL
AILO IOLA
AILP PAIL
AILR LAIR, LIAR, LIRA, RAIL, RIAL
AILS ISLA, LIAS, LISA, SAIL
AILT ALIT, LITA, TAIL
AILV VIAL
AILW WAIL
AILX ALIX
AILZ LIZA
AIMM IMAM, MAIM, MIMA
AIMN MAIN, MINA
AIMR AMIR, IRMA, MAIR, MIRA
AIMS AIMS
AINN NINA
AINO IONA
AINP PAIN
AINR IRAN, RAIN, RANI, RINA
AINS ANIS, SIAN
AINT NITA, TINA
AINU AINU
AINV IVAN, VAIN, VINA
AINZ NAZI
AIOT IOTA
AIOW IOWA
AIPR PAIR
AIPS PISA
AIQR IRAQ
AIRS AIRS, SARI
AIRT RITA
AIRY AIRY
AISV AVIS, VISA
AISX AXIS
AITV VITA
AITW WAIT
AITX TAXI
AITZ ZITA
AIVV VIVA
AJMS JAMS
AJNO JOAN
AJNU JUAN
AJRS JARS
AJRU JURA
AJSW JAWS
AJSY JAYS
AJZZ JAZZ

AKLN LANK	ALPY PLAY	ANOT NATO	ARTW WART
AKLR KARL, LARK	ALRS LARS	ANOV NOVA	ARTY ARTY, TRAY,
AKLT TALK	ALRY LYRA	ANPS NAPS, PANS,	TYRA
AKLW WALK	ALSS LASS	SNAP, SPAN	ARTZ TZAR
AKMO AMOK	ALST LAST, SALT,	ANPT PANT	ARVY VARY
AKMR MARK	SLAT	ANPW PAWN	ARWY AWRY,
AKMS MASK	ALSU SAUL	ANRT RANT, TARN	WARY
AKNP KNAP	ALSV SLAV	ANRW WARN	ARXY X-RAY
AKNR NARK,	ALSW AWLS, LAWS	ANRY RYAN, YARN	ASSS SASS
RANK	ALSY ALYS, LAYS,	ANST ANTS, STAN,	ASSW SAWS
AKNS SANK	SLAY	TANS	ASSY SAYS
AKNT TANK	ALTW WALT	ANSU ANUS	ASTT TATS
AKNW WANK	ALUW WAUL	ANSV VANS	ASTV VAST, VATS
AKNY YANK	ALWY YAWL	ANSW SAWN,	ASTW SWAT
AKOR OKRA	ALYZ LAZY	SWAN	ASTY STAY
AKOS OAKS, SOAK	AMMS MAMS	ANSY NAYS	ASWY SWAY, WAYS,
AKOY OKAY	AMNO MOAN,	ANTU AUNT,	YAWS
AKPR PARK	MONA	TUNA	ATTU TAUT
AKRS ARKS	AMNX MANX	ANTW WANT	ATTW TWAT, WATT
AKST TASK	AMNY MANY,	ANUY YUAN	AVWY WAVY
AKSU AUKS, SKUA	MYNA	ANVY NAVY	AWXY WAXY
AKSY YAKS	AMOR OMAR,	ANWY YAWN	BBES EBBS
AKTY KATY	ROAM, ROMA	ANYZ ZANY	BBIS BIBS
ALLM MALL	AMOS AMOS,	AOPS OAPS, SOAP	BBIY IBBY
ALLO LOLA	SOMA	AOPT ATOP	BBLO BLOB
ALLP PALL	AMOT ATOM,	AORR ROAR	BBLU BULB
ALLT TALL	MOAT	AORS OARS, ROSA,	BBMO BOMB
ALLW WALL	AMPR PRAM,	SOAR	BBOO BOOB
ALLY ALLY	RAMP	AORT ROTA, TARO	BBOS BOBS
ALMM MALM	AMPS AMPS, MAPS,	AORZ ZORA	BBOU BUBO
ALMO LOAM	SPAM	AOST OATS	BBSU BUBS
ALMP LAMP, PALM	AMPT TAMP	AOTU AUTO	BCEK BECK
ALMR MARL	AMPU PUMA	AOVW AVOW	BCEU CUBE
ALMS ALMS, SLAM	AMPV VAMP	APPS PAPS	BCIM ICBM
ALMT MALT	AMRS ARMS,	APPU PUPA	BCIR CRIB
ALMU ALUM,	MARS, RAMS	APRS PARS, RAPS,	BCKU BUCK
MAUL	AMRT TRAM	RASP, SPAR	BCLO BLOC
ALNO LOAN,	AMRW WARM	APRT PART, PRAT,	BCLU CLUB
NOLA	AMRY ARMY,	RAPT, TRAP	BCMO COMB
ALNP PLAN	MARY, MYRA	APRW WARP, WRAP	BCOS COBS
ALNU ALUN, ULNA	AMSS MASS	APRY PRAY	BCRU CURB
ALNW LAWN	AMST MAST, MATS	APSS ASPS, PASS,	BCSU CUBS
ALOP OPAL	AMSW MAWS,	SAPS, SPAS	BDEI BIDE
ALOR LORA, ORAL	SWAM	APST PAST, PATS,	BDEL BLED
ALOS ALSO, LAOS	AMSX XMAS	SPAT, TAPS	BDEN BEND
ALOT ALTO	AMSY MAYS, YAMS	APSW PAWS, SWAP,	BDEO BODE
ALOV OLAV, OVAL	AMTT MATT	WASP	BDES BEDS, DEBS
ALOW AWOL	AMYZ MAZY	APSY SPAY, YAPS	BDET DEBT
ALOZ ZOLA	ANNO ANON,	AQUY QUAY	BDII IBID
ALPP LAPP, PALP	NONA	ARST ARTS, RATS,	BDIN BIND
ALPS ALPS, LAPS,	ANOO OONA	STAR, TARS, TSAR	BDIR BIRD
PALS, SLAP	ANOR NORA,	ARSW WARS	BDIS BIDS
ALPU PAUL	ORAN, ROAN,	ARSY RAYS	BDLO BOLD
ALPW PAWL	RONA	ARTT TART	BDMU DUMB

BDNO BOND
BDOS BODS
BDOY BODY, BOYD
BDRU DRUB
BDSU BUDS
BEEF BEEF
BEEH HEBE
BEEL ELBE
BEEN EBEN
BEER BEER
BEES BEES
BEET BEET
BEGI GIBE
BEGY GYBE
BEHR HERB
BEHT BETH
BEIJ JIBE
BEIK BIKE
BEIL BILE
BEIN BE IN
BEIR BIER
BEIT BITE
BEIX IBEX
BEKO KOBE
BEKR BERK, KERB
BELL BELL
BELO BOLE, LOBE
BELP PLEB
BELT BELT
BELU BLUE
BELW BLEW
BENO BONE
BENR BERN
BENS BENS
BENT BENT
BEOO OBOE
BEOR BOER, BORE,
  ROBE
BEOY OBEY
BERT BERT, BRET
BERV VERB
BERY BYRE
BESS BESS
BEST BEST, BETS
BESW WEBS
BESY BYES
BETU TUBE
BETY BYTE
BEUZ ZEBU
BEVY BEVY
BFFI BIFF
BFFU BUFF
BFIS FIBS
BFMU BUMF

BFOS FOBS
BGIL GLIB
BGIN BING
BGIO GOBI
BGNU BUNG
BGOO GOBO
BGOS BOGS, GOBS
BGRU GRUB
BGSU BUGS
BHOO HOBO
BHOS BOSH, HOBS
BHOT BOTH
BHSU BUSH, HUBS
BIIS IBIS
BIJS JIBS
BIKL BILK
BIKS IKBS
BILL BILL
BILM LIMB
BILO BOIL
BILP BLIP
BIMR BRIM
BINS BINS, NIBS
BIOR BIRO
BIRS RIBS
BIRT BRIT
BIST BITS
BJOS JOBS
BKLU BULK
BKNO KNOB
BKNU BUNK
BKOO BOOK
BKRU BURK
BKSU BUSK
BLLO BOLL
BLLU BULL
BLOS LOBS, SLOB
BLOT BLOT, BOLT
BLOW BLOW,
  BOWL
BLRU BLUR
BLSU SLUB
BMNU NUMB
BMOO BOOM
BMOS MOBS
BMOT TOMB
BMOW WOMB
BMPU BUMP
BMSU BUMS
BNNO BONN
BNOO BOON
BNOR BORN,
  BRNO
BNOS NOBS, SNOB

BNOY BONY
BNRU BURN
BNRY BRYN
BNSU BUNS, NUBS,
  SNUB
BOOR BOOR
BOOS BOOS
BOOT BOOT
BOOZ BOZO
BOPS BOPS
BORS ORBS
BORT BORT
BORW BROW
BOSS BOSS, SOBS
BOSW BOWS
BOSY BOYS, YOBS
BOTU BOUT
BOTY TOBY
BOUY BUOY
BPRU BURP
BPSU PUBS
BRRU BURR
BRSU BURS, RUBS
BRTU BURT
BRUY BURY, RUBY
BSSU BUSS, SUBS
BSTU BUST, BUTS,
  STUB, TUBS
BSUY BUSY, BUYS
BTTU BUTT
BUZZ BUZZ
CCHI CHIC
CCIN C-IN-C
CCKO COCK
CDEE CEDE
CDEI DICE, ICED
CDEK DECK
CDEO CODE,
  COED
CDEU CUED
CDHI CHID
CDIK DICK
CDIS DISC
CDKO DOCK
CDKU DUCK
CDLO CLOD,
  COLD
CDOR CORD
CDOS CODS, DOCS
CDRU CURD
CDSU SCUD
CDTU DUCT
CEFH CHEF
CEFL CLEF

CEGS ECGS, GCES,
  GCSE
CEHK HECK
CEHO ECHO
CEHR CHER
CEHT ETCH
CEHW CHEW
CEIL LICE
CEIM MICE
CEIN NICE
CEIP EPIC
CEIR CERI, ERIC,
  RICE
CEIS ICES
CEIT CITE
CEIV VICE
CEKN NECK
CEKO COKE
CEKP PECK
CEKR RECK
CELL CELL
CELM CLEM
CELO CLEO
CELU CLUE, LUCE
CELW CLEW
CEMO COME
CENO CONE,
  ONCE
CENT CENT
CEOP COPE, OPEC
CEOR CORE
CEOV COVE
CEPS SPEC
CEPU PUCE
CERT CERT
CERU CURE, ECRU
CERW CREW
CESS CSES, SECS
CEST SECT
CESU CUES
CETU CUTE
CFFU CUFF
CFIO COIF, FOCI
CFKU FUCK
CGHU CHUG
CGLO CLOG
CGOS COGS
CHIK HICK
CHIN CHIN, INCH
CHIP CHIP
CHIR RICH
CHIT CHIT, ITCH
CHKO HOCK
CHLO LOCH

CHMU CHUM, MUCH
CHOP CHOP
CHOS COSH
CHOU CHOU, OUCH
CHOW CHOW
CHSU SUCH
CIKK KICK
CIKL LICK
CIKM MICK
CIKN NICK
CIKP PICK
CIKR RICK
CIKS SICK
CIKT TICK
CIKV VICK
CIKW WICK
CILO COIL, LOCI
CILP CLIP
CINO COIN, ICON
CINZ ZINC
CIOR COIR
CIPS SPIC
CIRU URIC
CISS CISS
CIST TICS
CITY CITY
CJKO JOCK
CKLO LOCK
CKLU LUCK
CKMO MOCK
CKMU MUCK
CKNO CONK
CKOO COOK
CKOR CORK, ROCK
CKOS SOCK
CKPU PUCK
CKRU RUCK
CKSU SUCK
CKTU TUCK
CKUY YUCK
CLLU CULL
CLMO COLM
CLMU CULM
CLOO COOL, LOCO
CLOP CLOP
CLOS COLS
CLOT CLOT, COLT
CLOW COWL
CLOY CLOY
CLRU CURL

CLTU CULT
CLUY LUCY
CMOR CORM
CMSU SCUM
CNNO CONN
CNOO COON
CNOR CORN
CNOS CONS, NCOS
CNOY CONY
CNSY SYNC
CNTU CUNT
COOP COOP
COOS COOS
COOT COOT
COPR CROP
COPS COPS
COPU COUP
COPY COPY
CORS ROCS
CORW CROW
COST COST, COTS
COSW COWS
COSY COSY
COYZ COZY
CPSU CUPS, CUSP
CPSW WPCS
CRSU CRUS, CURS
CRTU CURT
CRUX CRUX
CSSU CUSS
CSTU CUTS
CSTY CYST
DDEE DEED
DDEI DIED
DDEU DUDE
DDEY DYED, EDDY
DDJU JUDD
DDOO DODO
DDOS ODDS
DDOT TODD
DDSU DUDS
DEEF FEED
DEEG EDGE
DEEH HEED
DEEI EDIE
DEEL DELE
DEEM DEEM
DEEN EDEN, NEED
DEEP DEEP, PEED
DEER DEER, REED
DEES SEED
DEET TEED
DEEW WEED
DEEY EYED

DEFL FLED
DEFN FEND
DEFR FRED
DEFT DEFT
DEFU FEUD
DEFY DEFY
DEGL GELD
DEGO DOGE
DEGY EDGY
DEHI HIDE, HIED
DEHL HELD
DEHO HOED
DEHR HERD
DEHS SHED
DEHU HUED
DEHY HEDY, HYDE
DEIK DIKE
DEIL IDLE, LIED
DEIM DIME, IDEM
DEIN DINE, ENID
DEIP PIED
DEIR DIRE, RIDE
DEIS IDES, SIDE
DEIT DIET, EDIT, TIDE, TIED
DEIV DIVE, VIED
DEIW DEWI, WIDE
DEJN NEJD
DEJU JUDE
DEKS DESK
DEKU DUKE
DEKY DYKE
DELL DELL
DELN LEND
DELO DOLE, LODE
DELP PLED
DELS SLED
DELU DUEL
DELV VELD
DELW LEWD, WELD
DEMN MEND
DEMO DEMO, DOME, EDOM, MODE
DENO DONE, NODE
DENR NERD, REND
DENS DENS, ENDS, SEND
DENT DENT, TEND
DENU DUNE, NUDE

DENV VEND
DENW WEND
DENY DENY, DYNE
DEOP DOPE
DEOR DOER, REDO, RODE
DEOS DOES, DOSE, ODES
DEOT DOTE, TOED
DEOV DOVE
DEOW OWED
DEOZ DOZE
DEPS SPED
DEPU DUPE
DERS REDS
DERU RUDE, RUED
DERV DERV
DERW DREW
DERY DYER
DESU DUES, SUED, USED
DESY DYES
DESZ ZEDS
DETU DUET
DEWY DEWY
DFFO DOFF
DFFU DUFF
DFIN FIND
DFLO FOLD
DFNO FOND
DFNU FUND
DFOO FOOD
DFOR FORD
DGIL GILD
DGIR GIRD, GRID
DGIS DIGS
DGLO GOLD
DGNU DUNG
DGOO GOOD
DGOS DOGS, GODS
DGOU DOUG
DGRU DRUG
DGSU DUGS
DHIN HIND
DHIS DISH
DHLO HOLD
DHOO HOOD
DHOS HODS, SHOD
DHOW DHOW
DHTU THUD
DIIM MIDI
DIJO JODI
DIJU JUDI

DIKN KIND
DIKR DIRK
DIKS DISK, KIDS, SKID
DILL DILL
DILM MILD
DILO IDOL, LIDO
DILS LIDS, SLID
DILW WILD
DILY IDLY
DIMN MIND
DINO DION
DINR RIND
DINS DINS, SIND
DINT DINT
DINW WIND
DIOV VOID
DIPR DRIP
DIPS DIPS
DIQU QUID
DIRT DIRT
DIRU RUDI
DISU IUDS
DISY YIDS
DITY TIDY
DJOU JUDO
DJOY JODY
DJUY JUDY
DKNU DUNK
DKSU DUSK
DKUU KUDU
DLLO DOLL
DLLU DULL
DLMO MOLD
DLOP PLOD
DLOR LORD
DLOS SOLD
DLOT DOLT, TOLD
DLOU LOUD, LUDO
DLOW WOLD
DLOZ LODZ
DLUY DULY
DMOO DOOM, MOOD
DMOS MODS
DMPU DUMP
DMRU DRUM
DNOP POND
DNOS DONS, NODS
DNOU UNDO
DNOW DOWN
DNOZ ZOND

DNSU DUNS
DOOR DOOR, ROOD
DOOT TO-DO
DOOW WOOD
DOPR DROP, PROD
DOPS PODS
DOQU QUOD
DORS RODS
DORT TROD
DORU DOUR
DORW WORD
DORY DORY
DOSS DOSS, SODS
DOST DOTS, TODS
DOSU DUOS
DOYZ DOZY
DPSU PUDS, SPUD
DRSU SURD
DRTU TURD
DRUU URDU
DRUY RUDY
DSSU SUDS
DSTU DUST, STUD
DSUV VDUS
DTUY DUTY
EEEP ÉPÉE
EEFL FEEL, FLEE
EEFR FREE, REEF
EEFS FEES
EEFT FEET, FETE
EEGH GHEE
EEGL GLEE
EEGN GENE
EEHL HEEL
EEHR HERE
EEHT THEE
EEIR EIRE, ERIE
EEIV EVIE
EEJP JEEP
EEJR JEER
EEKL KEEL, LEEK
EEKM MEEK
EEKN KEEN, KNEE
EEKP KEEP, PEEK
EEKR REEK
EEKS SEEK
EEKW WEEK
EELP PEEL
EELR ERLE, LEER, REEL
EELS EELS, ELSE, LEES
EEMR MERE

EEMS ESME, SEEM, SEME
EEMT MEET, METE, TEEM
EENR NE'ER, RENÉ
EENS SEEN
EENV EVEN
EENW EWEN
EEPP PEEP
EEPR PEER
EEPS SEEP
EEPT PETE
EEPW WEEP
EERS ERSE, SEER, SERE
EERT TREE
EERU EURE
EERV EVER, VEER, VERE
EERW EWER
EESS SEES
EEST TEES
EESV EVES
EESW EWES
EESX EXES
EESY EYES
EETW TWEE
EFFI FIFE
EFFJ JEFF
EFHT HEFT
EFIK EFIK
EFIL FILE, LIEF, LIFE
EFIN FINE
EFIR FIRE, RIFE
EFIV FIVE
EFIW WIFE
EFLL FELL
EFLO FLOE
EFLS SELF
EFLT FELT, LEFT
EFLU FLUE, FUEL
EFLW FLEW
EFLX FLEX
EFMU FUME
EFNR FERN
EFNS FENS
EFOR FORE, FROE
EFOS FOES
EFRS REFS, SERF
EFRT FRET
EFSU FUSE
EFTW WEFT
EGGR GREG
EGGS EGGS

EGHU HUGE
EGIN INGE
EGIV GIVE
EGKS KEGS
EGLN GLEN
EGLO OGLE
EGLS GELS, LEGS
EGLU GLUE
EGMR GERM
EGMS GEMS
EGNO GONE
EGNT GENT
EGNU GENU
EGNW GWEN
EGOR ERGO, GOER, GORE, OGRE
EGOS EGOS, GOES
EGPS PEGS
EGRS ERGS
EGRT GERT
EGRU URGE
EGRW GREW
EGRY GREY
EHHT HETH
EHIK HIKE
EHIR HEIR, HIRE
EHIV HIVE
EHKO HOKE
EHLL HELL
EHLM HELM
EHLO HOLE
EHLP HELP
EHLR HERL
EHMO HOME
EHMP HEMP
EHMR HERM
EHMS HEMS, MESH, SHEM
EHMT THEM
EHMU HUME
EHNO HONE
EHNR HERN
EHNS HENS
EHNT HENT, THEN
EHNW HEWN, WHEN
EHOP HOPE
EHOR HERO, HOER
EHOS HOES, HOSE, SHOE
EHOT THEO
EHOV HOVE

EHOW HOWE
EHPW PHEW
EHPY HYPE
EHRR HERR
EHRS HERS
EHSS HESS
EHST HEST, SETH
EHSU HUES
EHSW SHEW
EHTW WHET
EHTY THEY
EHUY HUEY
EHWW WHEW
EHWY WHEY
EIJV JIVE
EIKK KIKE
EIKL KIEL, LIKE
EIKM MIKE
EIKN KINE
EIKP PIKE
EIKR ERIK, KEIR,
   KERI
EIKT KITE
EIKV KIEV
EILM EMIL, LIME,
   MILE
EILN LIEN, LINE,
   NEIL
EILP PILE
EILR LIRE, RILE
EILS ILSE, ISLE,
   LEIS, LIES, LISE,
   SILE
EILT TILE
EILU LIEU
EILV EVIL, LEVI,
   LIVE, VEIL, VILE
EILX ILEX
EILY EILY
EIMM MIME
EIMN MIEN, MINE
EIMR EMIR, MIRE,
   RIME
EIMS SEMI
EIMT EMIT, ITEM,
   MITE, TIME
EINN NINE
EINP PINE
EINR ERIN, REIN
EINS SINE
EINT TINE
EINV VEIN, VINE
EINW WINE
EINZ INEZ, ZEIN

EIPP PIPE
EIPR PIER, RIPE
EIPS PIES
EIPW WIPE
EIRS RISE, SIRE
EIRT RITE, TIER,
   TIRE
EIRV RIVE
EIRW WEIR, WIRE
EIST SITE, TIES
EISV IVES, VISE
EISW WISE
EISZ SIZE
EITX EXIT
EITY YETI
EIVW VIEW
EJKO JOKE
EJKR JERK
EJLL JELL
EJLO JOEL
EJNU JUNE
EJOS JOSÉ
EJOV JOVE
EJOY JOEY
EJSS JESS
EJST JEST, JETS
EJSW JEWS
EJTU JUTE
EKLP KELP
EKLS ELKS
EKLU LUKE
EKLY KYLE
EKMO MOKE
EKNR KERN
EKNS KENS
EKNT KENT
EKNU NUKE
EKNW KNEW
EKOP POKE
EKOW WOKE
EKOY YOKE
EKPR PERK
EKPT KEPT
EKPU PUKE
EKRT TREK
EKSW SKEW
EKSY KEYS, SKYE
ELLN NELL
ELLS SELL
ELLT TELL
ELLW WELL
ELLY LYLE, YELL
ELMO MOLE
ELMS ELMS

ELMT MELT
ELMU MULE
ELMY YLEM
ELNO LEON,
   LONE, NOEL
ELNS LENS
ELNT LENT
ELOP LOPE, POLE
ELOR LORE, ROLE
ELOS LEOS, LOSE,
   SLOE, SOLE
ELOV LOVE, VOLE
ELPT PELT
ELPY YELP
ELRU LURE, RULE
ELRY LYRE, RELY
ELSS LESS
ELST LEST, LETS
ELSU SLUE
ELSW SLEW
ELTU LUTE
ELTW WELT
ELUY YULE
ELVY LEVY
EMMO MEMO
EMNO OMEN
EMNU MENU
EMOP MOPE,
   POEM
EMOR MORE
EMOS SOME
EMOT MOTE,
   TOME
EMOV MOVE
EMOW MEOW
EMPR PERM
EMPT TEMP
EMRT TERM
EMRV MERV
EMSS MESS
EMST STEM
EMSU EMUS, MUSE
EMSW MEWS
EMTU MUTE
ENNO NEON,
   NONE
ENOP NOPE, OPEN
ENOS ENOS, EONS,
   NOES, NOSE,
   ONES
ENOT NOTE,
   TONE
ENOV OVEN
ENOW OWEN

ENOX OXEN
ENOZ ZONE
ENPS PENS
ENRT RENT, TERN
ENRU RUNE
ENRW WREN
ENST NEST, NETS,
   SENT, TENS
ENSW NEWS,
   SEWN
ENSY YENS
ENTT NETT, TENT
ENTU TUNE
ENTV VENT
ENTW NEWT,
   WENT
ENTX NEXT
ENVY ENVY
EOOZ OOZE
EOPP POPE
EOPR PORE, ROPE
EOPS PESO, POSE
EOPT POET
EORS ORES, ROES,
   ROSE, SORE
EORT ROTE, TORE
EORU ROUÉ
EORV OVER, ROVE
EORW WORE
EORY YORE
EORZ ZERO
EOST TOES
EOSW WOES
EOTT TOTE
EOTV VETO, VOTE
EOTY EYOT
EOVW WOVE
EOYZ OYEZ
EPPR PREP
EPRS REPS
EPRT PERT
EPRU PERU, PRUE,
   PURE
EPRY PREY, PYRE
EPST PEST, PETS,
   STEP
EPSW PEWS, SPEW
EPSY ESPY
EPTW WEPT
EPTY TYPE
ERST REST
ERSU RUSE, SUER,
   SURE, USER
ERSV REVS

ERSY RYES
ERTU TRUE
ERTY TYRE
ERVY VERY
ESST SETS, TESS
ESSU USES
ESTT STET, TEST
ESTU SUET
ESTV VEST, VETS
ESTW STEW, WEST,
  WETS
ESTZ ZEST
ESUZ SUEZ
ESVY YVES
ESWY YEWS
ESXY SEXY
ETTX TEXT
ETTY ETTY
FFGU GUFF
FFHU HUFF
FFII FIFI
FFIN NIFF
FFIR RIFF
FFIT TIFF
FFIY IFFY
FFLU LUFF
FFMU MUFF
FFOT TOFF
FFPU PUFF
FFRU RUFF
FGIS FIGS
FGIT GIFT
FGLO FLOG, GOLF
FGLU GULF
FGOO GOOF
FGOR FROG
FGOS FOGS
FGOY FOGY
FHII HI-FI
FHIS FISH
FHNO FOHN
FHOO HOOF
FHOW HOWF
FIIJ FIJI
FIJU FUJI
FILL FILL
FILM FILM
FILO FOIL
FILP FLIP
FILT FLIT, LIFT
FILW WILF
FIMR FIRM
FINN FINN
FINO INFO

FINS FINS
FIOR IFOR
FIRS FIRS
FIRT RIFT
FIST FIST, FITS, SIFT
FIZZ FIZZ
FKLO FOLK
FKNU FUNK
FKOR FORK
FLLU FULL
FLOO FOOL
FLOP FLOP
FLOR ROLF
FLOT LOFT
FLOU FOUL
FLOW FLOW,
  FOWL, WOLF
FLOY FLOY
FLRU FURL
FLUX FLUX
FMOR FORM,
  FROM
FMUY FUMY
FNOT FONT
FOOP POOF
FOOR ROOF
FOOT FOOT
FOOW WOOF
FOPR PROF
FOPS FOPS
FOPU POUF
FORT FORT
FORU FOUR
FOST SOFT
FOSU UFOS
FOXY FOXY
FRSU FURS, SURF
FRTU TURF
FRUY FURY
FSSU FUSS
FTTU TUFT
FUZZ FUZZ
GGHO HOGG
GGIS GIGS
GGNO GONG
GGOO GO-GO
GGOR GROG
GHHI HIGH
GHHU HUGH
GHIN NIGH
GHIS SIGH
GHIW WHIG
GHNO HONG
GHNU HUNG

GHOS GOSH,
  HOGS
GHOU HUGO
GHSU GUSH, HUGS
GHTU THUG
GIJS JIGS
GIKN KING
GILL GILL
GILN LING
GILR GIRL
GILT GILT
GIMP GIMP
GIMR GRIM
GINP PING
GINR GRIN, RING
GINS GINS, SIGN,
  SING
GINT TING
GINW WING
GIOR GIRO, IGOR
GIOY YOGI
GIPR GRIP, PRIG
GIPS PIGS
GIRS RIGS
GIRT GIRT, GRIT
GIST GIST
GISW SWIG, WIGS
GITW TWIG
GJOS JOGS
GJSU JUGS
GLLU GULL
GLMU GLUM
GLNO LONG
GLNU LUNG
GLNY GLYN
GLOO LOGO
GLOS LOGS, SLOG
GLOW GLOW
GLOY LOGY
GLPU GULP, PLUG
GLSU LUGS, SLUG
GLTU GLUT
GLUY UGLY
GMOS SMOG
GMSU GUMS,
  MUGS, SMUG
GMSY GYMS
GNOO GOON, NO
  GO
GNOP PONG
GNOS SNOG,
  SONG
GNOW GOWN
GNRU RUNG

GNSU GNUS,
  GUNS, SNUG,
  SUNG
GNWY GWYN
GOOT TOGO
GORW GROW
GORY GORY,
  ORGY
GOST TOGS
GOSW WOGS
GOTU GOUT
GPSU PUGS
GRSU RUGS
GRTU TRUG
GRUU GURU
GSTU GUST, GUTS,
  TUGS
GSUV GUVS
GSUY GUYS
HHSU HUSH
HIKS SIKH
HILL HILL
HILP PHIL
HILT HILT
HIMS SHIM
HIMW WHIM
HINS SHIN, SINH
HINT HINT, THIN
HIOO OHIO
HIOP HOPI, IPOH
HIPS HIPS, PISH,
  SHIP
HIPT PITH
HIPW WHIP
HIRW WHIR
HISS HISS
HIST HIST, HITS,
  SHIT, THIS
HISW WISH
HITW WHIT, WITH
HIWZ WHIZ
HJNO JOHN
HJOS JOSH
HKLO KOHL
HKLU HULK
HKNO HONK
HKNU HUNK
HKOO HOOK
HKSU HUSK
HLLU HULL
HLMO HOLM
HLOP HOLP
HLOS HOLS
HLOT HOLT, LOTH

HLOW HOWL	IINS NISI	ILST LIST, SILT, SLIT	IPSZ ZIPS
HLOY HOLY	IIRS IRIS	ILTT TILT	IPTY PITY
HLRU HURL	IJLL JILL	ILTW WILT	IQTU QUIT
HLSU LUSH	IJLT JILT	ILWY WILY	IQUZ QUIZ
HLWY HWYL	IJNN JINN	IMMY IMMY	IRSS SIRS
HMNY HYMN	IJNO JOIN	IMNT MINT	IRST STIR
HMOO HOMO	IJNX JINX	IMNX MINX	IRTW WRIT
HMOS HOMS,	IKKN KINK	IMOT OMIT	IRTX TRIX
OHMS	IKKR KIRK	IMPP PIMP	IRWY WIRY
HMOT MOTH,	IKLL KILL	IMPR PRIM	ISSY ISSY
THOM	IKLM MILK	IMPS IMPS	ISTT TITS
HMOW WHOM	IKLN KILN, LINK	IMPW WIMP	ISTU SUIT
HMOY HOMY	IKLO KILO	IMRS RIMS	ISTW WITS
HMPU HUMP	IKLS SILK	IMRT TRIM	ISTZ ZITS
HMSU HUMS,	IKLT KILT	IMRU MUIR	ITTW TWIT
MUSH	IKMN MINK	IMRY MIRY, RIMY	IYZZ IZZY
HMTY MYTH	IKMS SKIM	IMSS ISMS, MISS	IZZZ ZIZZ
HNOP PHON	IKNO IKON, OINK	IMST MIST	JJUU JUJU
HNOR HORN	IKNP PINK	IMSW SWIM	JKNU JUNK
HNOS NOSH	IKNR RINK	IMTT MITT	JLOT JOLT
HNOU HUON	IKNS INKS, SINK,	INNS INNS	JLOW JOWL
HNSU SHUN	SKIN	INOP PION	JLUY JULY
HNTU HUNT	IKNT KNIT	INOR IRON	JMPU JUMP
HOOP HOOP,	IKNW WINK	INOS IONS	JNOU JUNO
POOH	IKNY INKY	INOT INTO, TONI	JOSS JOSS
HOOS SHOO	IKPS KIPS, SKIP, SPIK	INOV VINO	JOSY JOYS
HOOT HOOT,	IKRS KRIS, RISK	INOZ ZION	JRUY JURY
OTHO	IKSS KISS, SKIS	INPS NIPS, PINS,	JSTU JUST
HOPS HOPS, POSH,	IKST KITS, SKIT	SNIP, SPIN	KKOO KOOK
SHOP	ILLM MILL	INPT PINT	KLOO LOOK
HOPT PHOT	ILLO LILO	INPY PINY	KLOY YOLK
HOPW WHOP	ILLP PILL	INQU QUIN	KLRU LURK
HOPY HYPO	ILLR RILL	INRU RUIN	KLSU SULK
HORU HOUR	ILLS ILLS, SILL	INSS SINS	KMNO MONK
HOST HOST, HOTS,	ILLT LILT, TILL	INST NITS, TINS	KMRU MURK
SHOT	ILLW WILL	INSW WINS	KMSU MUSK
HOSW SHOW	ILLY LILY	INTT TINT	KNOO NOOK
HOTU THOU	ILMN LIMN	INTU UNIT	KNOT KNOT
HPSU PUSH	ILMO MILO	INTW TWIN	KNOW KNOW
HPTU PHUT	ILMP LIMP	INTY TINY	KNPU PUNK
HRRU RUHR	ILMS SLIM	INWY WINY	KNSU SUNK
HRSU RUSH	ILMT MILT	IORT RIOT, TIRO,	KOOR ROOK
HRSY RHYS	ILMY LIMY	TRIO	KOOT TOOK
HRTU HURT,	ILNO LION, LOIN	IORV IVOR	KOPR PORK
RUTH, THRU	ILNT LINT	IOST OTIS	KOPY POKY
HSSU HUSS	ILNZ LINZ	IOSU IOUS	KORW WORK
HSTU HUTS, SHUT,	ILOO IOLO	IPPS PIPS	KOSW WOKS
THUS, TUSH	ILOR LORI	IPQU QUIP	KRSU RUSK
HSWY WHYS	ILOS LOIS, OILS,	IPRS RIPS	KRTU KURT
HTUU HUTU	SILO, SOIL	IPRT TRIP	KSTU TUSK
IIKW KIWI	ILOT TOIL	IPSS PISS, SIPS	LLLO LOLL
IILL LILI	ILOV VIOL	IPST PITS, SPIT, TIPS	LLLU LULL
IIMM MIMI	ILOY OILY	IPSV SPIV, VIPS	LLMO MOLL
IIMN MINI	ILPS LIPS, LISP, SLIP	IPSW WISP	LLMU MULL

LLNU NULL
LLOP POLL
LLOR ROLL
LLOT TOLL
LLPU PULL
LLUU LULU
LMOO LOOM
LMOT MOLT
LMPU LUMP, PLUM
LMSU SLUM
LNNY LYNN
LNOO LOON
LNOR LORN
LNOY LYON, ONLY
LNUY LUNY
LNXY LYNX
LOOP LOOP, POLO,
   POOL
LOOS LOOS, OSLO,
   SOLO
LOOT LOOT, TOOL
LOOW WOOL
LOPP PLOP
LOPS SLOP
LOPT PLOT
LOPW PLOW
LOPY PLOY, POLY
LORU LOUR
LORY ORLY, ROLY
LOSS LOSS
LOST LOST, LOTS,
   SLOT, STOL
LOSU SOUL
LOSW LOWS,
   OWLS, SLOW
LOTU LOUT
LOWY YOWL
LPPU PULP
LPRU PURL
LPSU PLUS
LRSU SLUR
LSTU LUST, SLUT
LSUV LUVS
LUUZ ZULU

MMOS MOMS
MMSU MUMS
MNOO MONO,
   MOON
MNOR MORN,
   NORM
MNOU MUON
MNOW MOWN
MOOR MOOR,
   ROOM
MOOS MOOS
MOOT MOOT
MOOZ ZOOM
MOPP POMP
MOPR PROM,
   ROMP
MOPS MOPS
MORS ROMS
MORT MORT
MORW WORM
MOSS MOSS
MOST MOST,
   MOTS
MOUV OVUM
MPPU PUMP
MPRU RUMP
MPSU SUMP
MRSU RUMS
MSSU MUSS, SUMS
MSTU MUST,
   SMUT, STUM
MSUW SWUM
MTTU MUTT
NNOO NOON
NNOU NON-U,
   NOUN
NNSU NUNS
NNWY WYNN
NOOS SOON
NOOT ONTO
NOPR PORN
NOPU UPON
NOPY PONY
NORT TORN

NORW WORN
NOSS SONS
NOST SNOT, TONS
NOSU NOUS, ONUS
NOSW SNOW,
   SOWN
NOSY NOSY
NOTU UNTO
NOTW TOWN,
   WONT
NOTY TONY
NOXY ONYX
NPSU PUNS, SPUN
NPTU PUNT
NPUY PUNY
NRSU RUNS, URNS
NRTU RUNT, TURN
NSSU SUNS
NSTU NUTS, STUN
OOPP POOP
OOPR POOR
OOPS OOPS
OORT ROOT
OOSS SO-SO
OOST SOOT
OOSZ ZOOS
OOTT OTTO,
   TOOT, TOTO
OOUZ OUZO
OOYY YOYO
OOYZ OOZY
OPPR PROP
OPPS POPS
OPRS PROS
OPRT PORT
OPRU POUR
OPRW PROW
OPRY ROPY
OPSS SOPS
OPST POST, POTS,
   SPOT, STOP, TOPS
OPSU OPUS, SOUP
OPSW POWS,
   SWOP, WOPS

OPSY POSY
OPTU POUT
ORRY RORY
ORSS ROSS
ORST ROTS, SORT,
   TORS
ORSU OURS, SOUR
ORSW ROWS
ORSY ROSY
ORTT TORT, TROT
ORTU ROUT, TOUR
ORTY TORY,
   TROY, TYRO
ORUX ROUX
ORUY YOUR
ORXY ORYX,
   ROXY
OSST SOTS, TOSS
OSSW SOWS
OSSY OSSY
OSTT TOTS
OSTU OUST
OSTW STOW,
   SWOT, TOWS,
   TWOS
OSTY TOYS
OSVW VOWS
OTTU TOUT
OYZZ OZZY
PPSU PUPS
PRRU PURR
PRSU SPUR
PRSY SPRY
PSST PSST
PSSU PUSS, SUPS
PTTU PUTT
RSSU RUSS
RSTU RUST, RUTS
SSSU SUSS
SUYZ SUZY
TTUU TUTU

FIVE-LETTER WORDS

AAABC ABACA
AAABQ AQABA
AAADN ADANA
AAAGM AGAMA
AAALN ALANA

AAAMT AMATA
AABCK ABACK
AABCL CABAL
AABDE BAAED
AABEM ABEAM, AMEBA

AABES ABASE
AABET ABATE, BEATA
AABFT ABAFT
AABGR BRAGA
AABHI BAHAI, BAHIA

AABHS ABASH, SABAH
AABLN ALBAN, BANAL, LABAN
AABLS BALAS, BALSA, BASAL
AABMM MAMBA
AABMR ABRAM
AABMS SAMBA
AABNW BWANA
AABRS ARABS, BASRA, SABRA
AABRT RABAT
AACCD DACCA
AACCO CACAO
AACCR ACCRA
AACEP APACE
AACER ARECA, CEARA
AACFI FACIA
AACHS SACHA
AACIS ISAAC
AACKL ALACK
AACLL CALLA
AACLN CANAL
AACLR CARLA, CLARA
AACMO MACAO
AACMW MACAW
AACNN CANNA
AACNZ ANZAC
AACRT CARAT
AADDX ADDAX
AADEG ADAGE
AADEH AHEAD
AADEL ADELA
AADFR DARAF, FARAD
AADGG DAGGA
AADGM MAGDA
AADGN GANDA
AADGR GARDA
AADHI HAIDA
AADHL HADAL
AADIL ADLAI
AADIN AIDAN, DIANA, NADIA, NAIAD
AADIR ADAIR
AADKR DAKAR
AADLS SALAD
AADLU DUALA
AADLV VALDA
AADMM MADAM
AADMN ADMAN, DAMAN
AADMR DRAMA
AADMS ADAMS
AADNP PANDA
AADNV VANDA

AADNW WANDA
AADPT ADAPT
AADPU PADUA
AADRR RADAR
AADRU AUDRA
AADRW AWARD
AAEGL ALGAE, GALEA
AAEGP AGAPE
AAEGT AGATE
AAEGV AGAVE
AAEHK HAKEA
AAEKP APEAK
AAEKW AWAKE
AAELP PALEA
AAELR AREAL
AAELT ALATE
AAELX ALEXA
AAEMZ AMAZE
AAENP PAEAN
AAENR ARENA
AAERS AREAS
AAERU AUREA
AAERW AWARE
AAFFJ JAFFA
AAFHI HAIFA
AAFIM MAFIA
AAFIN NAAFI
AAFLT FATAL
AAFNU FAUNA
AAGHL GALAH
AAGHN GHANA
AAGHR HAGAR
AAGIN AGAIN
AAGIS SAIGA
AAGIT TAIGA
AAGJN GANJA
AAGKN KANGA
AAGLL ALGAL, GALLA
AAGLN LAGAN
AAGLR ALGAR
AAGLS GALAS
AAGLV VAGAL
AAGMM GAMMA, MAGMA
AAGMR GRAMA
AAGNP PAGAN
AAGOR AGORA
AAGRS RAGAS
AAGRZ ZARGA
AAGSS SAGAS
AAGUV GUAVA
AAHHS HA-HAS
AAHJR RAJAH
AAHLL ALLAH, HALAL
AAHLM HALMA, HAMAL

AAHLP ALPHA
AAHLS LHASA
AAHLV ALVAH
AAHMO OMAHA
AAHMR MARAH
AAHMZ HAMZA
AAHNS HANSA
AAHPR APHRA
AAHPS PASHA
AAHRR HARAR
AAHRS SARAH
AAHSU HAUSA
AAHSW AWASH
AAHSY AYAHS
AAHWZ AHWAZ
AAIIL AALII
AAIKS KASAI, SAKAI
AAIKZ IZAAK
AAILN ALAIN, ALINA, LIANA
AAILS AILSA, ALIAS
AAILT ALTAI
AAILV AVAIL
AAILX AXIAL
AAIMN ANIMA, MANIA
AAIMR MARIA
AAIMS AMIAS, MASAI
AAIMZ ZAMIA
AAINP APIAN
AAINR ARIAN, RAINA
AAINS ASIAN
AAINT ANITA, TANIA
AAINV AVIAN
AAIRS ARIAS, SARAI
AAIRT ATRIA, TIARA
AAIRV VARIA
AAISS ASSAI
AAITW AWAIT
AAJLP JALAP
AAJNP JAPAN
AAKKY KAYAK
AAKLO KOALA
AAKLR KRAAL
AAKLT KALAT
AAKMR KARMA
AAKNZ KAZAN
AAKOS OSAKA
AAKPR PARKA
AAKRT KARAT
AALLM LLAMA
AALLN ALLAN
AALLV LAVAL
AALLY ALLAY
AALMO ALAMO

AALMP PALMA
AALMR ALARM, MALAR, MARLA
AALMS LAMAS
AALMT MALTA
AALMY MALAY
AALNN ANNAL
AALNS NASAL
AALNT NATAL
AALNU NUALA
AALNV NAVAL
AALNY NYALA
AALPP APPAL, PAPAL
AALPS SALPA
AALPU PAULA
AALPZ LA PAZ, PLAZA
AALRT ALTAR, RATAL
AALRU AURAL, LAURA
AALRV ALVAR, LARVA
AALRY ALARY
AALST ATLAS, SALTA
AALTY YALTA
AALUY AULAY
AAMMM MAMMA
AAMMN AMMAN
AAMMS MAMAS
AAMNN ANNAM, MANNA
AAMNS MASAN
AAMNT MANTA
AAMNY MAYAN
AAMOR AROMA
AAMOS SAMOA
AAMPR PARMA
AAMPT TAMPA
AAMRT MARTA, TAMAR
AAMRU MAURA
AAMSS AMASS, ASSAM
AAMSY AMYAS
AANNO ANONA
AANOR AARON
AANPP NAPPA
AANPT PATNA
AANRS SARAN
AANRV NAVAR, VARNA
AANRY ARYAN
AANST SATAN
AANSU SAUNA
AANSW ASWAN
AANTT TANTA
AANTY TANYA
AAORT AORTA
AAPPS PAPAS
AAPPU PAPUA
AAPPW PAPAW

AAPRS PARAS
AAPRT APART
AAPST PASTA
AAQRT QATAR
AARRS SARRA
AARRY ARRAY
AARST ASTRA
AARSU AURAS
AARTT ATTAR, TATAR, TATRA
AARTY TAYRA
AASSY ASSAY
AATZZ TAZZA
ABBCY CABBY
ABBEI ABBIE
ABBEK KEBAB
ABBEL BABEL
ABBEM BEMBA
ABBES BABES
ABBEY ABBEY
ABBGY GABBY
ABBIR RABBI
ABBLU BABUL, BUBAL
ABBNO NABOB
ABBOT ABBOT
ABBRS BARBS
ABBSU BABUS
ABBTY TABBY
ABCCY BACCY
ABCEH BEACH
ABCEI CEIBA
ABCEL CABLE, CALEB
ABCER BRACE, CABER
ABCHI CHIBA
ABCHT BATCH
ABCIN CABIN
ABCIO COBIA
ABCIR BARIC, RABIC
ABCIS BASIC
ABCJO JACOB
ABCKL BLACK
ABCKS BACKS
ABCLN BLANC
ABCNO BACON
ABCNU CUBAN
ABCOR CAROB, COBRA
ABCOV VOCAB
ABCRS CRABS
ABCRT BRACT
ABCSS SCABS
ABCSU SCUBA
ABDEG BADGE
ABDEI ABIDE
ABDEK BAKED

ABDEL BALED, BLADE
ABDEO ABODE, ADOBE
ABDER BARED, BEARD, BREAD, BREDA, DEBAR, DEBRA
ABDES BASED, BEADS
ABDET BATED
ABDEY BAYED, BEADY
ABDIL AD-LIB
ABDIR BRAID, RABID
ABDIU DUBAI
ABDLN BLAND
ABDLY BADLY
ABDNR BRAND, R AND B
ABDNS BANDS
ABDNY BANDY
ABDOR BOARD, BROAD
ABDRS BARDS, DRABS
ABDRY DARBY
ABDSU DAUBS
ABDSW BAWDS
ABDUY DAUBY
ABDWY BAWDY
ABDYY BY DAY
ABEEL ABELE
ABEFL FABLE
ABEGL BAGEL, GABLE
ABEGN BEGAN
ABEGR BARGE
ABEGS GABES
ABEGT BEGAT
ABEHO BOHEA
ABEHR HABER
ABEHS SHEBA
ABEHT BATHE
ABEIM I-BEAM
ABEIR BEIRA
ABEIS BASIE
ABEIZ BAIZE
ABEJZ JABEZ
ABEKL BLAKE, BLEAK
ABEKR BAKER, BRAKE, BREAK
ABEKS BEAKS
ABEKY BEAKY
ABELL BELLA, LABEL
ABELM AMBLE, BLAME, MABEL, MABLE, MELBA
ABELN BLANE
ABELR BALER, BLARE, BLEAR
ABELS BALES, BASEL, BLASE, SABLE
ABELT BLEAT, TABLE

ABELY BELAY
ABELZ BLAZE
ABEMR AMBER, BREAM
ABEMS BEAMS
ABEMY EMBAY, MAYBE
ABENO BEANO
ABENR ABNER
ABENS BANES, BEANS
ABEOV ABOVE
ABERR BARER
ABERS BASER, BEARS,
BRAES, SABER, SABRE
ABERV BRAVE
ABERY BARYE, BY EAR,
YERBA
ABERZ BRAZE, ZEBRA
ABESS BASES
ABEST BASTE, BEAST,
BEATS, BETAS, TABES
ABESU ABUSE, BEAUS
ABETU BEAUT
ABEUX BEAUX
ABFFN BANFF
ABFRY BY FAR
ABGGY BAGGY
ABGHN BHANG
ABGNO GABON
ABGNS BANGS
ABGRS GRABS
ABHIR BIHAR
ABHIS SAHIB
ABHIT HABIT
ABHMO ABOHM
ABHOR ABHOR
ABHRS BRASH
ABHST BATHS
ABIIL ALIBI
ABIIT TIBIA
ABIIZ IBIZA
ABIKT BATIK
ABILN ALBIN, BINAL,
BLAIN
ABILR BLAIR, BRAIL, LIBRA
ABILS BAILS, BASIL
ABILY LIBYA
ABIMS IAMBS
ABIMT AMBIT
ABINR BAIRN, BRAIN,
BRIAN
ABINS BASIN, SABIN
ABIOT BIOTA
ABIRR BRIAR
ABIRT BRITA
ABIRY BY AIR

ABISS BASIS
ABJMS JAMBS
ABJNO BANJO
ABJOT JABOT
ABKLN BLANK
ABKLS BALKS
ABKLU BAULK, KABUL
ABKNS BANKS
ABKRS BARKS
ABLLS BALLS
ABLLU BULLA
ABLLY BALLY
ABLMS BALMS, LAMBS
ABLMU ALBUM
ABLMY BALMY
ABLOP PABLO
ABLOR LOBAR
ABLOT BLOAT
ABLRW BRAWL
ABLSS SLABS
ABLST BLAST
ABLTU TUBAL
ABLWY BYLAW
ABLYY LAY-BY
ABMMO MAMBO
ABMRU BURMA, RUMBA,
UMBRA
ABMRY AMBRY, BARMY
ABMTU BATUM
ABNNS BANNS
ABNOR BARON, BONAR
ABNOT BATON
ABNRS BARNS
ABNRU UNBAR, URBAN
ABNRW BRAWN
ABNRY BRYAN
ABNTU BANTU
ABOOT TABOO
ABORR ARBOR
ABORS BOARS
ABORT ABORT, TABOR
ABORV BRAVO
ABORX BORAX
ABOSS BASSO
ABOST BOAST, BOATS,
SABOT
ABOTU ABOUT, U-BOAT
ABOUY BAYOU
ABQSU SQUAB
ABRRY BARRY
ABRSS BRASS
ABRST BRATS
ABRSU BURSA
ABRSY BRAYS

ABRXY BRAXY
ABSST STABS
ABSSW SWABS
ABSSY ABYSS
ABSTU TUBAS
ABTTY BATTY
ABWYY BYWAY
ACCDY CYCAD
ACCEH CACHE
ACCEM MECCA
ACCHO COACH
ACCHT CATCH
ACCIR CIRCA
ACCIT CACTI
ACCKL CLACK
ACCKR CRACK
ACCOO COCOA
ACCUY YUCCA
ACDDY CADDY
ACDEF FACED
ACDEG CADGE, CAGED
ACDEH ACHED
ACDEK CAKED
ACDEL CADEL, DECAL,
LACED
ACDEN CANED, DANCE
ACDEP PACED
ACDER CADRE, CARED,
CEDAR, RACED
ACDES CASED
ACDET ACTED, CADET
ACDEV CAVED
ACDEW CAWED
ACDEY DECAY
ACDHO AD HOC
ACDHR CHARD
ACDIR ACRID
ACDIS ACIDS, ASDIC
ACDIT DICTA
ACDIZ CADIZ
ACDLS SCALD
ACDLU CLAUD, DUCAL
ACDMO MADOC
ACDNY CANDY
ACDOS CODAS
ACDOT OCTAD
ACDRS CARDS
ACDRY DARCY
ACDSS SCADS
ACDTU DUCAT
ACEEK ACKEE
ACEEP PEACE
ACEES CEASE
ACEFH CHAFE

ACEFL FECAL
ACEFR FACER, FARCE
ACEFS CAFES, FACES
ACEFT FACET
ACEGL GLACÉ
ACEGR GRACE
ACEGS CAGES
ACEGY CAGEY
ACEHK HACEK
ACEHL CHELA, LEACH
ACEHN HANCE
ACEHP CHEAP, PEACH
ACEHR REACH
ACEHS ACHES, CHASE
ACEHT CHEAT, TEACH,
THECA
ACEIL ALICE, CELIA, ILEAC
ACEIM AMICE
ACEIR ERICA
ACEIV AVICE
ACEKL ALECK
ACEKR CRAKE, CREAK
ACEKS CAKES
ACELL CELLA
ACELM CAMEL, MACLE
ACELN ANCEL, CLEAN,
LANCE
ACELP PLACE
ACELR CLARE, CLEAR,
LACER
ACELS LACES, SCALE
ACELT CLEAT, ECLAT
ACELV CALVE
ACEMO CAMEO
ACEMR CREAM
ACEMS MACES
ACENN NANCE
ACENO CANOE, OCEAN
ACENP PECAN
ACENR CANER, CARNE,
CRANE, NACRE, RANCE
ACENS CANES
ACENT ENACT
ACEOR OCREA
ACEPR CAPER, CRAPE,
PACER, RECAP
ACEPS CAPES, PACES,
SCAPE, SPACE
ACEPT EPACT
ACERR RACER
ACERS ACRES, CARES,
RACES, SCARE, SERAC
ACERT CARET, CATER,
CRATE, REACT, TRACE

ACERV CARVE, CRAVE
ACERY CAREY
ACERZ CRAZE
ACESS CASES
ACEST CASTE
ACESU CAUSE, SAUCE
ACESV CAVES
ACESY CASEY
ACETT TACET
ACETU ACUTE
ACETX EXACT
ACETY TACEY
ACETZ AZTEC
ACFFH CHAFF
ACFHU CHUFA
ACFIR FARCI
ACFKL FLACK
ACFLO FOCAL
ACFNR FRANC
ACFNY FANCY
ACFRS SCARF
ACFRT CRAFT
ACFRY FARCY
ACFST FACTS
ACGIM GAMIC, MAGIC
ACGIR CIGAR, CRAIG
ACGLN CLANG
ACGNO CONGA
ACGOR CARGO
ACGOU GUACO
ACGRS CRAGS, SCRAG
ACHHT HATCH
ACHIL HALIC
ACHIM MICAH
ACHIN CHAIN, CHINA
ACHIR CHAIR
ACHIT AITCH, CHITA
ACHKL CHALK
ACHKS HACKS, SHACK
ACHKW WHACK
ACHLO LOACH
ACHLR LARCH
ACHLS CLASH
ACHLT LATCH
ACHMO MACHO, MOCHA
ACHMP CHAMP
ACHMR CHARM, MARCH
ACHMS CHASM
ACHMT MATCH
ACHNR RANCH
ACHNT CHANT
ACHNU NUCHA
ACHOP POACH
ACHOR ORACH, ROACH

ACHOS CHAOS
ACHOV HAVOC
ACHPR PARCH
ACHPS CHAPS
ACHPT PATCH
ACHRS CHARS, CRASH
ACHRT CHART
ACHRY ARCHY, CHARY
ACHST CHATS
ACHSW SCHWA
ACHTW WATCH
ACHTY CATHY, YACHT
ACIIL ILIAC
ACIIS ASCII
ACIKL ALICK
ACILL CILLA, LILAC
ACILM CLAIM
ACILP PLICA
ACILS SALIC
ACILT TICAL
ACILU LUCIA
ACILV CAVIL
ACILX CALIX
ACIMN MANIC
ACINP PANIC
ACINR CAIRN
ACINT ACTIN, ANTIC, CAN
IT!
ACIOR CAIRO
ACIOZ AZOIC
ACIPR CAPRI
ACIPS ASPIC, SPICA
ACIRU AURIC, CURIA
ACIRV VICAR
ACISU CAIUS
ACITT ATTIC, TACIT
ACJKS JACKS
ACJKY JACKY
ACJNU CAJUN
ACKKN KNACK
ACKLN CLANK
ACKLO CLOAK
ACKLR CLARK
ACKLS SLACK
ACKLU CAULK
ACKMS SMACK
ACKMU AMUCK
ACKNR CRANK
ACKNS SNACK
ACKOR CROAK
ACKPS PACKS
ACKQU QUACK
ACKRS RACKS
ACKRT TRACK

ACKRW WRACK
ACKSS CASKS, SACKS
ACKST STACK, TACKS
ACKTY TACKY
ACKWY WACKY
ACLLO LOCAL
ACLLS CALLS, SCALL
ACLMO COMAL
ACLMP CLAMP
ACLMS CLAMS
ACLMU CALUM
ACLNS CLANS
ACLOP COPAL
ACLOR CALOR, CARLO,
   CAROL, CLARO, CORAL
ACLOS COALS
ACLOT OCTAL
ACLOV VOCAL
ACLOX COXAL
ACLOY COALY
ACLOZ COLZA
ACLPS CLAPS, CLASP,
   SCALP
ACLPU CULPA
ACLRW CRAWL
ACLRY CARLY, CARYL,
   CLARY
ACLSS CLASS
ACLSU LUCAS
ACLSW CLAWS
ACLSY SCALY
ACLXY CALYX
ACMMO COMMA
ACMNO MACON
ACMOP CAMPO
ACMOR ARMCO,
   MARCO
ACMOS COMAS
ACMPR CRAMP
ACMPS CAMPS, SCAMP
ACMRS SCRAM
ACMRY CYMAR, MARCY
ACMSS SCAMS
ACNNO ANCON, CANON,
   CONAN
ACNNY CANNY, NANCY
ACNOP CAPON
ACNOR ACORN
ACNOT CANTO
ACNPU UNCAP
ACNSS SCANS
ACNST CANTS, SCANT
ACOPR COPRA
ACORS OSCAR

ACORT ACTOR, CROAT
ACOST ASCOT, COAST,
   COATS, COSTA, TACOS
ACOTT COTTA
ACPPU CUPPA
ACPRS CARPS, CRAPS,
   SCARP, SCRAP
ACPST PACTS
ACPSU SCAUP
ACPTU CAPUT
ACRRU CRURA
ACRRY CARRY
ACRSS CRASS, SCARS
ACRST CARTS
ACRSY CARYS, SCARY
ACRSZ CZARS
ACRTT TRACT
ACRTY TRACY
ACRYZ CRAZY
ACSST CASTS
ACSSU ASCUS
ACSTY STACY
ACSUY SAUCY
ACTTY CATTY
ADDDE ADDED
ADDDY DADDY
ADDEF FADED
ADDEH HEDDA
ADDEI ADDIE, AIDED
ADDEJ JADED
ADDEL ADDLE
ADDER ADDER, DARED,
   DREAD, DREDA
ADDET DATED
ADDEV VEDDA
ADDEW WADED
ADDEZ DAZED
ADDFY FADDY
ADDGI GADID
ADDIJ JIDDA
ADDIV DAVID
ADDMY MADDY
ADDNO ADD-ON
ADDNR R AND D
ADDNY DANDY
ADDPY PADDY
ADDRY DRYAD
ADEEL ADELE
ADEEM EDEMA
ADEER EARED
ADEES AEDES, EASED
ADEEV EVADE
ADEFK FAKED
ADEFM FAMED

ADEFR FADER, FARED,
   FREDA
ADEFT FATED
ADEFX FAXED
ADEFZ FAZED
ADEGG GAGED
ADEGL GLADE
ADEGM GAMED, MADGE
ADEGP GAPED, PAGED
ADEGR EDGAR, GERDA,
   GRADE, RAGED
ADEGS DEGAS
ADEGT GATED
ADEGW WADGE, WAGED
ADEGZ GAZED
ADEHK KEDAH
ADEHR HARED, HEARD
ADEHS HADES, HEADS,
   SHADE
ADEHT DEATH, HATED
ADEHX HEXAD
ADEHY HEADY
ADEHZ HAZED
ADEIL AILED, DELIA, IDEAL
ADEIM AIMED, AMIDE,
   MEDIA
ADEIN DIANE
ADEIP A PIED
ADEIR AIRED, REDIA
ADEIS AIDES, ASIDE, IDEAS,
   SADIE
ADEIU ADIEU
ADEIZ AZIDE
ADEJR JARED
ADEJS JADES
ADEJW JAWED
ADEKL KELDA
ADEKN KNEAD, NAKED
ADEKR DRAKE, RAKED
ADEKS ASKED
ADEKW WAKED
ADELL DELLA, LADLE
ADELM LAMED, MEDAL
ADELN ALDEN, ELAND,
   LADEN
ADELP PALED, PEDAL,
   PLEAD
ADELR ALDER, LADER
ADELS DALES, DEALS,
   LEADS
ADELT DEALT, DELTA
ADELV VELDA
ADELW WEALD
ADELY DELAY, LEADY

ADELZ LAZED, ZELDA
ADEMN ADMEN, AMEND, MANDE, MANED, MEDAN, NAMED
ADEMR AD REM, ARMED, DERMA, DREAM
ADEMS DAMES, MEADS
ADEMT MATED, TAMED
ADEMU MAUDE
ADENO ANODE
ADENR ANDRÉ, REDAN
ADENS ANDES, DEANS, SEDAN
ADENT ANTED, DANTE
ADENU DUANE
ADENV VENDA
ADENW WANED, WENDA
ADEOR ADORE, OARED
ADEPR DRAPE, PADRE, PARED, RAPED
ADEPS SPADE
ADEPT ADEPT, TAPED
ADEPV PAVED
ADEPW PAWED
ADERR DARER, DREAR
ADERS DARES, DEARS
ADERT DATER, RATED, TRADE, TREAD
ADERV RAVED
ADERW WADER
ADERY DEARY, READY
ADERZ RAZED
ADEST DATES, SATED, STEAD
ADESV SAVED
ADESW SAWED
ADESZ ADZES, DAZES
ADETX TAXED
ADEUX A DEUX
ADEVW WAVED
ADEWX WAXED
ADEWY YAWED
ADFFR DRAFF
ADFLO ADOLF
ADFRT DRAFT
ADFRU FRAUD
ADFRW DWARF
ADGIL ALGID, GILDA
ADGLN GLAND
ADGMO DOGMA
ADGNO GONAD
ADGNR GRAND
ADGOS DAGOS, GOADS
ADGOU GOUDA

ADGRS DRAGS
ADGRU GUARD
ADGUY GAUDY
ADHIJ HADJI, JIHAD
ADHIL HALID, HILDA
ADHIN DINAH
ADHIO IDAHO
ADHIP APHID
ADHJU JUDAH
ADHLU HULDA
ADHLY HYLDA
ADHNS HANDS
ADHNT HADN'T
ADHNY HANDY, HAYDN
ADHOR HOARD, RHODA
ADHRS HARDS, SHARD
ADHRY HARDY, HYDRA
ADHST HADST
ADHSU SADHU
ADHSY HYADS, SHADY
ADIIL ILIAD
ADIIN INDIA
ADIIR RADII
ADIKN DINKA
ADILN LINDA, NIDAL
ADILP PLAID
ADILR DRAIL, LAIRD
ADILS ALDIS, DIALS
ADILT TIDAL, TILDA
ADILU DULIA
ADILV VALID
ADILY DAILY, LYDIA
ADIMS MAIDS
ADIMT ADMIT
ADIMX ADMIX
ADINO DANIO
ADINR DINAR, DRAIN, NADIR
ADINV DIVAN, VIAND
ADIOP PODIA
ADIOR AROID, DORIA, RADIO
ADIOS ADIOS
ADIOU AUDIO
ADIOV AVOID
ADIOZ DIAZO
ADIPR RAPID
ADIPS SAPID
ADIPV VAPID
ADIRS RAIDS
ADIRT TRIAD
ADIRX RADIX
ADIRY DAIRY, DIARY
ADIST STAID

ADISW WADIS
ADISY DAISY
ADITU AUDIT
ADITV DAVIT
ADJOU OUJDA
ADJSU JUDAS
ADKLY ALKYD
ADKNR DRANK
ADKNY KANDY
ADKOV VODKA
ADKRS DARKS
ADKRY DARKY
ADLLO ALDOL
ADLLY DALLY
ADLMO MODAL
ADLMY MADLY
ADLNO DONAL, NODAL
ADLNS LANDS
ADLNY DYLAN, LYNDA
ADLOR ROALD
ADLOS LOADS
ADLOU ALOUD
ADLOW WALDO
ADLRW DRAWL
ADLRY DARYL
ADLSU ALDUS
ADLSY SADLY
ADLTU ADULT
ADLUY DYULA
ADMNO DAMON, MONAD, NOMAD
ADMNY MANDY
ADMOR RADOM
ADMRS DRAMS
ADMTU DATUM
ADNNO DONNA
ADNNY DANNY
ADNOR ADORN, DORAN, RADON
ADNRS DARNS
ADNRW DRAWN
ADNRY RANDY
ADNSS SANDS
ADNST STAND
ADNSU SUDAN
ADNSW DAWNS, WANDS
ADNSY SANDY
ADNTU DAUNT
ADOPT ADOPT
ADORR ARDOR
ADORS ROADS
ADOSS SODAS
ADOST TOADS
ADOTY TOADY, TODAY

ADQSU QUADS, SQUAD
ADRRU DURRA
ADRST DARTS
ADRSW DRAWS, SWARD,
   WARDS
ADRSY DRAYS, YARDS
ADRTY TARDY
ADUVZ VADUZ
AEEFZ FEAZE
AEEGL EAGLE
AEEGR AGREE, EAGER,
   EAGRE
AEEHV HEAVE
AEEIM AIMEE
AEELN ELENA
AEELS EASEL, LEASE
AEELT ELATE
AEELV LEAVE
AEEMN ENEMA
AEEMV MAEVE, MEAVE
AEENR RANEE
AEENT EATEN, ENATE
AEEPY PAYEE
AEERS EASER, ERASE
AEERT ARÊTE, EATER
AEEST TEASE
AEESV EAVES
AEEVW WEAVE
AEFFG GAFFE
AEFHS SHEAF
AEFIL ALFIE
AEFIR AFIRE, FERIA
AEFKL FLAKE
AEFKR FAKER, FREAK
AEFKS FAKES
AEFLM FLAME, FLEAM
AEFLR FARLE, FERAL,
   FLARE
AEFLS FALSE, FLEAS
AEFLT FETAL
AEFLY LEAFY
AEFMR FRAME
AEFOV FOVEA
AEFRR FARER
AEFRS FARES, FEARS, SAFER
AEFRT AFTER
AEFRW WAFER
AEFRY FAERY, FREYA
AEFSS SAFES
AEFST FATES, FEAST, FEATS
AEGGI AGGIE
AEGGR AGGER
AEGGS GAGES
AEGGU GAUGE

AEGHL HELGA
AEGHN HAGEN
AEGHU HAGUE
AEGIL AGILE, ALGIE
AEGIM IMAGE
AEGIN ANGIE
AEGIS AEGIS
AEGLL LEGAL
AEGLM GLEAM
AEGLN ANGEL, ANGLE,
   GLEAN
AEGLR ALGER, GLARE,
   LAGER, LARGE, REGAL
AEGLS GALES
AEGLT AGLET
AEGLV GAVEL, GÄVLE
AEGLY GAYLE
AEGLZ GLAZE
AEGMM GEMMA
AEGMN MANGE, MEGAN
AEGMO OMEGA
AEGMR MARGE
AEGMS GAMES
AEGMY GAMEY
AEGNO GENOA
AEGNR ANGER, RANGE
AEGNS AGNES, SENGA
AEGNT AGENT, TEGAN
AEGNV VEGAN
AEGPR GAPER, GRAPE
AEGPS GAPES, PAGES
AEGRS GEARS, RAGES,
   SARGE
AEGRT GRATE, GREAT,
   GRETA
AEGRU ARGUE, AUGER
AEGRV GRAVE
AEGRW WAGER
AEGRY GAYER
AEGRZ GAZER, GRAZE
AEGSS GASES, SAGES
AEGST GATES, STAGE
AEGSU AGUES, USAGE
AEGSW SWAGE, WAGES
AEGTU TAEGU
AEGUV VAGUE
AEGUZ GAUZE
AEHHT HEATH
AEHJZ HEJAZ
AEHKL HEKLA
AEHKS HAKES, SHAKE
AEHLR HALER
AEHLS LEASH, SHALE
AEHLT LATHE

AEHLV HALVE
AEHLW WHALE, WHEAL
AEHLZ HAZEL
AEHMN HE-MAN
AEHMR HAREM
AEHMS SHAME
AEHMT MEATH
AEHNN HENNA
AEHNS ASHEN, HANSE,
   SHANE, SHENA
AEHNT ETHAN, THANE,
   'NEATH
AEHNV HAVEN
AEHNY HYENA
AEHOR HORAE
AEHOS HOSEA
AEHPR RAPHE
AEHPS HEAPS, PHASE,
   SHAPE
AEHRS ASHER, HARES,
   RHEAS, SHARE, SHEAR
AEHRT EARTH, HEART,
   HERAT
AEHRV HAVER, HAVRE
AEHRZ HAZER
AEHSS ASHES
AEHST HASTE, HATES
AEHSV HAVES, SHAVE
AEHSW HAWES, HAWSE
AEHSZ HAZES
AEHTT THETA
AEHTX THE AX
AEHTW WHEAT
AEHVY HEAVY
AEIIL AILIE
AEIJM JAMIE
AEIJN JANIE
AEIKL ALIKE
AEIKR ERIKA
AEIKT KATIE
AEIKZ KEZIA
AEILL ALLIE, LEILA,
   LELIA
AEILN ALIEN, ALINE,
   ANILE, ELAIN
AEILR ARIEL
AEILS AISLE, ELIAS
AEILT EILAT
AEILV ALIVE, ALVIE
AEILX AXILE
AEILZ ELIZA
AEIMM MAMIE
AEIMN AMINE, MAINE,
   MENAI

AEIMR MAIRE, MARIE, RAMIE
AEINN ANNIE, INANE
AEINR ARIEN, RAINE
AEINS AISNE, ANISE, SIENA
AEINT TINEA
AEINV NAIVE
AEINX XENIA
AEINZ AZINE
AEIPS SEPIA
AEIPT PIETA
AEIRS ARIES, ARISE, RAISE
AEIRT ARTIE, IRATE
AEIRZ ZAIRE
AEITV EVITA
AEIVW WAIVE
AEJMM JEMMA
AEJMR AJMER
AEJMS JAMES
AEJNN JENNA
AEJNS JEANS
AEJNT JANET
AEJNY JANEY, JAYNE
AEJPR JAPER
AEJPS JAPES
AEKLN ANKLE
AEKLR KAREL, LAKER
AEKLS LAKES, LEAKS, SLAKE
AEKLW KWELA
AEKLY LEAKY
AEKMR MAKER
AEKMS MAKES
AEKNO OAKEN
AEKNR KAREN
AEKNS SNAKE, SNEAK
AEKNT TAKEN
AEKNV KNAVE
AEKNW WAKEN
AEKNY KENYA
AEKOR KOREA
AEKOW AWOKE
AEKPR PERAK
AEKPS PEAKS, SPEAK
AEKPY PEAKY
AEKQU QUAKE
AEKRR RAKER
AEKRS ASKER, RAKES, SAKER
AEKRT TAKER
AEKRW WAKER, WREAK
AEKSS SAKES
AEKST SKATE, STAKE, STEAK, TAKES, TEAKS

AEKSW ASKEW, WAKES
AEKTW TWEAK
AELLN ALLEN
AELLP LAPEL
AELLY ALLEY
AELMM LEMMA
AELMP AMPLE, MAPLE
AELMR LAMER, REALM
AELMS MALES, MEALS, SALEM, SELMA
AELMT METAL
AELMV MELVA, VELMA
AELMY MEALY
AELMZ ZELMA
AELNO ALONE, ANOLE, LEONA
AELNP NEPAL, PANEL, PENAL, PLANE
AELNR LEARN, RENAL
AELNS ANSEL, LANES
AELNT LEANT
AELNV NAVEL, VENAL
AELOV OLAVE
AELOZ AZOLE
AELPP APPEL, APPLE
AELPR PALER, PEARL
AELPS LAPSE, LEAPS, PALES, PEALS, PLEAS, SALEP, SEPAL
AELPT LEAPT, PETAL, PLATE, PLEAT
AELQU EQUAL, QUALE
AELRS EARLS, LASER
AELRT ALERT, ALTER, ARTEL, LATER, RATEL
AELRU UREAL
AELRV LAVER, RAVEL, VELAR
AELRX RELAX
AELRY EARLY, LAYER, RELAY
AELSS SALES, SEALS
AELST LEAST, SETAL, SLATE, STALE, STEAL, TALES, TESLA
AELSV SALVE, SELVA, SLAVE, VALES
AELSW WEALS
AELSX AXLES
AELTV VALET
AELTX EXALT, LATEX
AELUV UVEAL, VALUE
AELVV VALVE
AEMMY MAMEY

AEMNO EAMON
AEMNR MARNE
AEMNS MANES, MANSE, MEANS, NAMES
AEMNT AMENT, MEANT
AEMRR REARM
AEMRS MARES, MASER, REAMS, SMEAR
AEMRT MATER, TAMER
AEMSS SEAMS
AEMST MATES, SATEM, STEAM, TEAMS
AEMSU AMUSE
AEMSX EXAMS
AEMSY SAMEY, SEAMY
AEMSZ MAZES
AEMTT MATTE
AEMTY MATEY, MEATY
AEMUV MAUVE
AENNP PANNE, PENNA
AENNS SENNA
AENNW ANWEN
AENNX ANNEX
AENOP PAEON
AENOS AEONS
AENOT ATONE, OATEN
AENOV NOVAE
AENOW OWENA
AENPP NAPPE
AENPS ASPEN, NAPES, PANES
AENPT PATEN
AENPZ PENZA
AENRR RERAN
AENRS NARES, SANER, SNARE
AENRV RAVEN, VERNA
AENRY YEARN
AENSS NESSA
AENST ANTES, NATES, NESTA
AENSV AVENS, NAVES, VANES
AENSW WANES
AENSZ SENZA
AENTT NETTA
AENWX WAXEN
AENWY WANEY, WAYNE
AEOPR OPERA
AEORS AROSE
AEORT ORATE
AEOSS OASES
AEOTV OVATE
AEOTZ AZOTE

AEPPR PAPER	**AFFGS** GAFFS	**AFMRS** FARMS
AEPPU PUPAE	**AFFIX** AFFIX	**AFNNO** FANON
AEPRR PARER	**AFFLO** OFFAL	**AFNNY** FANNY
AEPRS ASPER, PARSE,	**AFFLU** LUFFA	**AFNOR** FARON
PEARS, PRASE, PRESA,	**AFFQU** QUAFF	**AFNRU** FURAN
RAPES, SPARE, SPEAR	**AFFST** STAFF	**AFNSU** FAUNS, SNAFU
AEPRT PATER, PETRA,	**AFFTY** TAFFY	**AFNSW** FAWNS
PRATE, TAPER	**AFGHU** FAUGH	**AFOOT** AFOOT
AEPRY APERY, REPAY	**AFGLS** FLAGS	**AFORS** AFROS, SOFAR
AEPSS APSES, PASSÉ	**AFGLU** FUGAL	**AFORY** FORAY
AEPST PASTE, PATES, PEATS,	**AFGNO** FANGO	**AFOSS** FOSSA, SOFAS
SPATE, TAPES	**AFGNS** FANGS	**AFOST** SOFTA
AEPSU PAUSE	**AFGRT** GRAFT	**AFRST** FARTS, RAFTS
AEPTU TAUPE	**AFHIT** FAITH	**AFRSW** SWARF
AEPTY PEATY	**AFHIZ** HAFIZ	**AFSST** FASTS
AERRR RARER	**AFHLS** FLASH	**AFSUV** FAVUS
AERRS REARS	**AFHRW** WHARF	**AFTTY** FATTY
AERRT TERRA	**AFHST** HAFTS, SHAFT	**AGGIN** AGING
AERRV RAVER	**AFIKR** FAKIR	**AGGLU** GULAG
AERRW RAWER	**AFILL** FLAIL	**AGGNS** GANGS
AERRZ RAZER	**AFILN** FINAL	**AGGOR** AGGRO
AERSS ARSES	**AFILP** PILAF	**AGGSY** SAGGY
AERST ASTER, RATES,	**AFILR** FILAR, FLAIR, FRAIL	**AGHHU** HAUGH
RESAT, STARE, TARES,	**AFILS** FAILS	**AGHLU** LAUGH
TEARS	**AFINO** FIONA	**AGHNO** HOGAN
AERSV SAVER	**AFINT** FAINT, FANTI	**AGHNS** GNASH
AERSW SAWER, SWEAR,	**AFIOS** SOFIA	**AGHNW** WHANG
WARES	**AFIRR** FRIAR	**AGHPR** GRAPH
AERSY SAYER, YEARS	**AFIRS** FAIRS	**AGHRT** GARTH
AERTT TETRA, TREAT	**AFIRY** FAIRY	**AGHSS** SHAGS
AERTU URATE	**AFIST** FIATS	**AGHST** GHATS
AERTV AVERT, TRAVE	**AFISW** WAIFS	**AGHTU** AUGHT
AERTW TAWER, WATER	**AFKLN** FLANK	**AGIKN** KIANG
AERTX EXTRA, TAXER	**AFKLS** FLASK	**AGILN** ALGIN, ALIGN
AERUZ AZURE	**AFKLY** FLAKY	**AGILR** ARGIL, GLAIR,
AERVV VARVE	**AFKNR** FRANK	GRAIL
AERVW WAVER	**AFKRT** KRAFT	**AGILS** SIGLA
AERVY AVERY	**AFLLO** ALL OF	**AGILY** GAILY
AERWX WAXER	**AFLLS** FALLS	**AGIMN** GAMIN
AERWY WEARY	**AFLMY** FLAMY	**AGIMO** IMAGO
AESSS ASSES	**AFLNS** FLANS	**AGIMS** AGISM, SIGMA
AESST ASSET, EASTS, SEATS,	**AFLOO** ALOOF	**AGINP** APING
TESSA	**AFLOR** FLORA	**AGINR** GRAIN
AESSV SAVES, VASES	**AFLOS** FOALS, SOL-FA	**AGINS** GAINS
AESSY ESSAY	**AFLOT** ALOFT, FLOAT	**AGINT** GIANT
AESTT STATE, TASTE,	**AFLOU** AFOUL	**AGINV** GAVIN
TEATS, TESTA	**AFLPS** FLAPS	**AGINX** AXING
AESTU SAUTÉ	**AFLST** FLATS	**AGIOS** GOIAS
AESTV STAVE, VESTA	**AFLSW** FLAWS	**AGIRV** VIRGA
AESTW SWEAT, WASTE	**AFLTU** FAULT	**AGIST** AGIST, GAITS
AESTX TAXES, TEXAS	**AFLUW** AWFUL	**AGISU** GAIUS
AESTY AS YET, YEAST	**AFLWY** FLAWY	**AGJLU** JUGAL
AESUV SUAVE	**AFMOX** OXFAM	**AGKWY** GAWKY
AESVW WAVES	**AFMOY** FOAMY	**AGLLO** ALGOL

AGLLS GALLS
AGLMU MULGA
AGLNO ALONG
AGLNR GNARL
AGLNS GLANS, SLANG
AGLOR ALGOR, ARGOL,
   GORAL, LARGO
AGLOS GAOLS, GOALS,
   LAGOS
AGLOT GLOAT
AGLOW AGLOW
AGLRU GULAR
AGLRY GLARY, GYRAL
AGLSS GLASS, SLAGS
AGMMU GUMMA
AGMMY GAMMY
AGMNO AMONG, MANGO
AGMNY MANGY
AGMOR MARGO, MORAG
AGMRS GRAMS
AGMSU MAGUS
AGMTU GAMUT
AGNOR ARGON, GROAN,
   ORGAN
AGNOT TANGO, TONGA
AGNOU GUANO
AGNOW WAGON
AGNOY AGONY
AGNPS PANGS
AGNRS GRANS
AGNRT GRANT
AGNRY ANGRY, RANGY
AGNSS SNAGS
AGNST ANGST, GNATS
AGNSU ANGUS
AGNTU GAUNT
AGNTW TWANG
AGNTY TANGY
AGORT ARGOT, GROAT
AGOST GOATS, TOGAS
AGPRS GRASP, SPRAG
AGPSS GASPS
AGRRY GARRY
AGRSS GRASS
AGRSU SUGAR
AGRSY GRAYS
AGRUU AUGUR
AGRVY GRAVY
AGSST STAGS
AGSSU GAUSS
AGSSY GASSY
AGSTU GUSTA
AGSTY STAGY
AGSUV VAGUS

AGTTU GUTTA
AGUYZ GAUZY
AHHOO HOO-HA
AHHRS HARSH
AHHSS SHAHS
AHIIT HAITI
AHIJJ HAJJI
AHIJZ HIJAZ
AHIKK KHAKI
AHIKM HAKIM
AHIKU HAIKU
AHILL HILLA
AHILP PHIAL
AHILR HILAR
AHILS HAILS
AHILT LAHTI
AHIMR HIRAM
AHINO HANOI
AHINS HSIAN, SHANI
AHINT HAIN'T
AHIPS APHIS, APISH
AHIRS HAIRS, SHARI
AHIRU URIAH
AHIRY HAIRY
AHIST TISHA
AHJNO JONAH
AHJTU THIJA
AHKNS KHANS, SHANK
AHKNT THANK
AHKNY HANKY
AHKOS SHAKO
AHKRS SHARK
AHKSW HAWKS
AHKSY SHAKY
AHKTY KATHY
AHLLO HALLO, HOLLA
AHLLS HALLS, SHALL
AHLMU HAULM
AHLOR HORAL
AHLOS HALOS, SHOAL
AHLOT ATHOL, LOATH
AHLPR RALPH
AHLPS PLASH
AHLPY HAPLY, PHYLA
AHLSS SLASH
AHLST HALTS, LATHS,
   SHALT
AHLSU HAULS
AHLSW SHAWL
AHLSY SHALY
AHMMY HAMMY
AHMNO HAMON
AHMNU HUMAN, NAHUM
AHMNY HYMAN, MYNAH

AHMRS MARSH
AHMSS SHAMS, SMASH
AHMSW WHAMS
AHMTY MY HAT
AHNNO HONAN
AHNNU HUNAN
AHNOR NORAH, RHONA
AHNOS SHONA
AHNST HANTS, HASN'T,
   SHAN'T, SNATH
AHNSU SHAUN
AHNSW SHAWN
AHNTU HAUNT
AHNUW WUHAN
AHOOW WAHOO
AHOOY YAHOO
AHORS HORSA
AHORT THORA, TORAH
AHORY HOARY
AHORZ ZORAH
AHOST HOSTA, OATHS,
   SHOAT
AHOSX XHOSA
AHPPY HAPPY
AHPRS HARPS, SHARP
AHPRY HARPY
AHPSS HASPS
AHPST PATHS
AHQSU QUASH
AHRRY HARRY
AHRST HARTS, RASHT,
   TRASH
AHRSU SURAH
AHRTW WRATH
AHRTY THYRA
AHSST STASH
AHSSW SWASH
AHSTW SWATH, THAWS
AHSTY HASTY
AHSWY WASHY
AHTTY HATTY
AIILS AILIS
AIIMM MIAMI
AIINS SINAI
AIIPU PIAUI
AIIQR IRAQI
AIIVV VIVIA
AIJLS JAILS
AIJLU JULIA
AIJNS JANIS
AIJOU OUIJA
AIKMU UMIAK
AIKNR KARIN
AIKNT TAKIN

AIKOP OKAPI
AIKRT KRAIT
AIKRU KAURI
AILLL LILLA
AILLN NIALL
AILLV VILLA
AILLW WILLA
AILMN MILAN
AILMS ISLAM
AILMV VILMA
AILMW WILMA
AILNO ALOIN, ILONA
AILNP PLAIN
AILNS NAILS, SLAIN, SNAIL
AILNT LATIN
AILNV ALVIN, ANVIL,
   NIVAL
AILNW IN-LAW
AILNY INLAY
AILOV OLIVA, VIOLA
AILPP PIPAL
AILPR APRIL
AILPS PAILS
AILPT PLAIT
AILQU QUAIL
AILRS LAIRS, LIARS, LIRAS,
   RAILS, RIALS
AILRT TRAIL, TRIAL
AILRU LAURI
AILRV AVRIL, RIVAL, VIRAL
AILRY RIYAL
AILSS SAILS, SILAS, SISAL
AILST TAILS
AILSV ALVIS, VIALS
AILTV VITAL
AILTY ITALY, LAITY
AIMMS IMAMS
AIMMX MAXIM
AIMNN MINNA
AIMNO AMINO, NAOMI
AIMNR ARMIN, MARNI
AIMNS MAINS
AIMNT MATIN
AIMNZ MAINZ
AIMOR MAORI, MARIO,
   MOIRA
AIMOW MIAOW
AIMOX AXIOM
AIMRS AMIRS
AIMRT MARTI
AIMRZ MIZAR
AIMSS AMISS
AIMSV MAVIS
AIMSW SWAMI

AIMSY ISMAY
AIMTY AMITY
AINNO ANION
AINNP PINNA
AINNS ANNIS
AINOP PIANO
AINOR ON-AIR
AINOS SONIA
AINOT TONIA
AINOW OWAIN
AINOZ ANZIO
AINPR PIRAN
AINPS PAINS, SPAIN
AINPT INAPT, PAINT, PINTA
AINRS RAINS
AINRT TRAIN, TRINA
AINRV INVAR
AINRY RAINY
AINST SAINT, SATIN, STAIN
AINSV SAVIN
AINSW SWAIN
AINSZ NAZIS
AINTT TAINT, TITAN
AINTU UNIAT
AINTW TWAIN
AINUX AUXIN
AIOPT PATIO
AIORT RATIO
AIORY ORIYA
AIOSS OASIS
AIOST IOTAS
AIPPP PIPPA
AIPRS PAIRS, PARIS
AIPRT ATRIP, TAPIR
AIPRU PIURA
AIPSS APSIS
AIPST TAPIS
AIPTT PATTI
AIPZZ PIZZA
AIRRS ARRIS
AIRSS ARSIS, SARIS
AIRST ASTIR, SITAR, STAIR,
   STRIA, TARSI
AIRSY SYRIA
AIRSZ SIZAR
AIRTT TRAIT
AIRVX VARIX
AISSV SIVAS, VISAS
AISTV VISTA
AISTW WAIST
AISTX TAXIS
AISWZ SWAZI
AISXX X-AXIS
AISXY Y-AXIS

AISXZ Z-AXIS
AITTV VITTA
AJLRU JURAL
AJMMU JAMMU
AJMMY JAMMY
AJMOR MAJOR
AJNOS JASON, JONAS,
   SONJA
AJNOU ANJOU
AJNTU JAUNT, JUNTA
AJRTU JURAT
AJRUU JURUA
AJYZZ JAZZY
AKKLU KULAK
AKKOP KAPOK
AKKPU PUKKA
AKLLY ALKYL
AKLNP PLANK
AKLNY LANKY
AKLOP POLKA
AKLOR KAROL
AKLRS LARKS
AKLST STALK, TALKS
AKLSW WALKS
AKMOU OAKUM
AKMRS MARKS
AKMSS MASKS
AKMUZ MUZAK
AKNOR KORAN, KRONA
AKNOY KONYA
AKNPR PRANK
AKNPS SPANK
AKNPU PUNKA
AKNRS NARKS, RANKS
AKNRY NARKY
AKNST STANK, TANKS
AKNSU KANSU
AKNSW SWANK
AKNSY SNAKY, YANKS
AKOOR KAROO
AKOOZ KAZOO
AKOPY YAPOK
AKOSS SOAKS
AKOSY OKAYS
AKOTY TOKAY
AKPRS PARKS, SPARK
AKPRY PARKY
AKPTU KAPUT
AKPWY PAWKY
AKQRU QUARK
AKQUY QUAKY
AKRST KARST, STARK
AKRSY SARKY
AKSST TASKS

AKSSU SKUAS
AKTUY YAKUT
ALLLY ALLYL
ALLMO MOLAL
ALLMS MALLS, SMALL
ALLNO LLANO
ALLOS SALOL
ALLOT ALLOT, ATOLL
ALLOW ALLOW
ALLOY ALLOY, LOYAL
ALLPS PALLS, SPALL
ALLPY PALLY
ALLRY RALLY
ALLST STALL
ALLSW WALLS
ALLSY SALLY
ALLTY TALLY
ALLWY WALLY
ALLXY LAXLY
ALMMO MALMO
ALMNO MONAL
ALMNY MANLY
ALMOR MOLAR, MORAL
ALMOY LOAMY
ALMPS LAMPS, PALMS,
  PLASM, PSALM
ALMPY AMPLY, PALMY
ALMQU QUALM
ALMRU MURAL
ALMST SMALT
ALMTY MALTY
ALNNO NOLAN
ALNNU ANNUL
ALNOP NOPAL
ALNOR LORAN, LORNA
ALNOS LOANS, SALON
ALNOT TALON, TOLAN,
  TONAL
ALNOZ ZONAL
ALNPS PLANS
ALNPT PLANT
ALNRS SNARL
ALNRU LUNAR, ULNAR
ALNST SLANT
ALNSU ULNAS
ALNSW LAWNS
ALNTY LANTY
ALNUY UNLAY, YULAN
ALNWY ALWYN, LAWNY,
  WANLY
ALNXY XYLAN
ALOOP PAOLO
ALOPR PAROL, POLAR
ALOPS OPALS, SALOP

ALORS LAROS, SOLAR
ALORU RAOUL
ALORV ORVAL, VOLAR
ALORY ROYAL
ALOSS LASSO
ALOST ALTOS
ALOSV OVALS, SALVO
ALOTT TOTAL
ALOTV LOVAT, VOLTA
ALOVV VOLVA
ALPPU PUPAL
ALPPY APPLY
ALPSS SLAPS
ALPST SPLAT
ALPSY PALSY, PLAYS, SPLAY
ALPTY APTLY, PLATY
ALRRU RURAL
ALRRY LARRY
ALRSU SURAL, URALS
ALRTW TRAWL
ALRWY RAWLY
ALSST LASTS, SALTS, SLATS
ALSSV SLAVS
ALSTU TALUS, TULSA
ALSTY SALTY, SLATY
ALSUU USUAL
ALSVY SYLVA
ALSWY YAWLS
ALTTY LYTTA
ALTUV VAULT
ALTWZ WALTZ
ALUUV UVULA
ALUVV VULVA
AMMMO MOMMA
AMMMY MAMMY
AMMOY MYOMA
AMMRS SMARM
AMMSY SAMMY
AMMTY TAMMY
AMNNU UNMAN
AMNNY MANNY
AMNOR MANOR, MORNA,
  NORMA, RAMON,
  ROMAN
AMNOS MASON, MOANS
AMNOW WOMAN
AMNOY MOYNA
AMNOZ MONZA
AMNRU NAMUR
AMNRY MYRNA
AMNSU MANUS
AMNTY MAYN'T
AMNUY YUMAN
AMORR ARMOR

AMORU AMOUR
AMORY MAYOR, MORAY,
  MOYRA
AMOST ATOMS, MOATS,
  STOMA
AMOTU OMUTA
AMPRS PRAMS, RAMPS
AMPRT TRAMP
AMPSS SPASM
AMPST STAMP
AMPSU PUMAS
AMPSV VAMPS
AMPSW SWAMP
AMRRY MARRY
AMRST SMART, TRAMS
AMRSU RAMUS
AMRSW SWARM
AMRTY MARTY, TRYMA
AMSST MASTS
AMSTY MAYST
AMTTY MATTY
ANNNY NANNY
ANNOR RONNA
ANNOT ANTON
ANNOY ANNOY
ANOOP POONA
ANOPR APRON, NO-PAR
ANOPW POWAN
ANORS ARSON, ROANS,
  SONAR
ANORT TRONA
ANORW ROWAN
ANORY RAYON
ANOSV NOVAS
ANOSX SAXON
ANOSY SONYA
ANOTT TANTO
ANOTX TAXON
ANOTY ATONY, TONYA
ANOWY NO WAY
ANPPY NAPPY
ANPRW PRAWN
ANPRY PYRAN
ANPSS SNAPS
ANPST PANTS
ANPSU PUSAN
ANPSW PAWNS, SPAWN
ANPSY PANSY
ANPTU UNAPT
ANPTY PANTY
ANQRU QUR'AN
ANQTU QUANT
ANRST TARNS
ANRSY YARNS

ANRUU NAURU	ARRTY TARRY	BCEKS BECKS
ANRUY UNARY	ARSST STARS, TRASS, TSARS	BCEKY BECKY
ANSSU SUSAN	ARSTT START, TARTS	BCEOY BOYCE
ANSSW SWANS	ARSTU SURAT	BCERU BRUCE
ANSTU AUNTS, TUNAS	ARSTW STRAW, WARTS	BCERY BRYCE
ANSTW WANTS	ARSTY SATYR, STRAY,	BCESU CUBES
ANSTY NASTY, TANSY	TRAYS	BCHIR BIRCH
ANSUY UNSAY	ARSTZ TZARS	BCHIT BITCH
ANSWY YAWNS	ARSUV VARUS	BCHNU BUNCH
ANTTU TAUNT	ARSUY SAURY	BCHOT BOTCH
ANTTY NATTY	ARSXY X-RAYS	BCHTU BUTCH
ANTUV VAUNT	ARTTY RATTY	BCHUU BUCHU
ANTWY TAWNY	ARTWY WARTY	BCIKR BRICK
ANVVY NAVVY	ASSSY SASSY	BCILM CLIMB
AOPPP POPPA	ASSTW SWATS	BCIOR BORIC
AOPRT APORT, OP ART,	ASSTY STAYS	BCIPU PUBIC
PRATO	ASTTW TWATS, WATTS	BCIRS CRIBS
AOPSS PSOAS, SOAPS	ASTTY TASTY	BCITU CUBIT
AOPSY SOAPY	ASVVY SAVVY	BCKLO BLOCK
AOPTZ TOPAZ	ATTTY TATTY	BCKOR BROCK
AOQTU QUOTA	ATTWY WYATT	BCKSU BUCKS
AORRS ROARS	BBBOY BOBBY	BCLOS BLOCS
AORRW ARROW	BBCEU CUBEB	BCLSU CLUBS
AORRZ RAZOR	BBDEE EBBED	BCMOO COMBO
AORSS SAROS	BBDOY DOBBY	BCMOS COMBS
AORST ROAST, ROTAS,	BBEII IBBIE	BCMRU CRUMB
TAROS	BBEIL BIBLE	BCRSU CURBS, SCRUB
AORSV SAVOR	BBEIR BRIBE	BDDEI BIDED
AORTT TAROT	BBEMO BOMBE	BDDEO BODED
AORVY OVARY	BBEOP BEBOP	BDDIY BIDDY
AOSSY SAY-SO	BBEWY WEBBY	BDDUY BUDDY
AOSTT STOAT, TOAST	BBHMO H-BOMB	BDEEL BLEED
AOSTU AUTOS	BBHOS HOBBS	BDEEM EMBED
AOSVY SAVOY	BBHOY HOBBY	BDEER BREED
APPPY PAPPY	BBHUY HUBBY	BDEGO BODGE
APPSU PUPAS	BBILY LIBBY	BDEGU BUDGE, DEBUG
APPSY SAPPY	BBISY SIBBY	BDEIJ JIBED
APPYZ ZAPPY	BBITY TIBBY	BDEIK BIKED
APRRY PARRY	BBLOS BLOBS	BDEIM IMBED
APRSS RASPS, SPARS	BBLOY LOBBY	BDEIP BIPED
APRST PARTS, PRATS,	BBLRU BLURB	BDEIR BRIDE
SPRAT, STRAP, TRAPS	BBLSU BULBS	BDEIS B-SIDE
APRSU SUPRA	BBMOS BOMBS	BDEIT BIDET, DEBIT
APRSW WARPS, WRAPS	BBOOS BOOBS	BDELN BLEND
APRSY SPRAY	BBOOY BOOBY	BDELO LOBED
APRTY PARTY	BBSUY BUSBY	BDEMO DEMOB
APSST PASTS, SPATS	BBTUY TUBBY	BDENO BONED
APSSW SWAPS, WASPS	BCCIU CUBIC	BDENS BENDS
APSTY PASTY, PATSY	BCDEU CUBED	BDEOO BOOED
APTTY PATTY	BCEEH BEECH	BDEOR BORED, ROBED
AQRTU QUART	BCEHL BELCH	BDEOW BOWED
AQSTU SQUAT	BCEHN BENCH	BDEOX BOXED
AQSUW SQUAW	BCEHO BOCHE	BDERY DERBY
AQSUY QUAYS	BCEIR BRICE	BDEST DEBTS

BDESU BUSED
BDETU DEBUT
BDFII BIFID
BDGIY DIGBY
BDIIR IRBID
BDILN BLIND
BDILU BUILD
BDINU IN BUD
BDIOP BIPOD
BDIOV BOVID
BDIRS BIRDS, DRIBS
BDLNO BLOND
BDLOO BLOOD
BDLOY DOLBY
BDNOS BONDS
BDNOU BOUND
BDNUU BUNDU
BDOOR BROOD, DOBRO
BDOSU DOUBS
BDOTU DOUBT
BEEFY BEEFY
BEEGI BEIGE
BEEGL GLEBE
BEEGR GREBE
BEEGT BEGET
BEEHP PHEBE
BEEHR HEBER
BEEIL BELIE
BEELL BELLE
BEELM BELEM
BEELP BLEEP
BEELR REBEL
BEELT BETEL
BEELV BEVEL
BEELZ BEZEL
BEEMR EMBER
BEENT BENET
BEEOS OBESE
BEERS BEERS
BEERT BERET
BEERV BREVE
BEERW WEBER
BEERY BEERY
BEEST BEETS, BESET
BEETT BETTE
BEFGO BEFOG
BEFIR BRIEF, FIBRE
BEFIT BEFIT
BEGIL BILGE
BEGIN BEGIN, BEING,
    BINGE
BEGIO BOGIE
BEGIR GIBER
BEGIS GIBES

BEGLO GLOBE
BEGLU BUGLE, BULGE
BEGMU BEGUM
BEGNU BEGUN
BEGOT BEGOT
BEGOY BOGEY
BEHOR HOREB
BEHRS HERBS
BEHRT BERTH
BEHRY HERBY
BEIJS JIBES
BEIKS BIKES
BEILL LIBEL
BEILR ERBIL
BEIMO BIOME
BEIMU IMBUE
BEINN BENIN
BEINR BRINE
BEIRR BRIER
BEIRS BIERS
BEIRT TRIBE
BEIST BITES
BEISV BEVIS, VIBES
BEITT TIBET
BEITZ ZIBET
BEJNY BENJY
BEKLO BLOKE
BEKOR BROKE
BEKRS BERKS, KERBS
BEKRU BURKE
BEKUZ UZBEK
BELLS BELLS
BELLY BELLY
BELMU UMBEL
BELNO NOBLE
BELOR ROBLE
BELOS BOLES, LOBES
BELOU BOULE
BELOW BELOW, BOWEL,
    ELBOW
BELPS PLEBS
BELRU BLUER, RUBLE
BELRY BERYL
BELSS BLESS
BELST BELTS, BLEST
BELSU BLUES
BELSY SELBY
BEMOR BROME
BEMOS BESOM
BEMOW EMBOW
BEMRU BRUME, UMBER
BEMSU SEBUM
BENNY BENNY
BENOR BORNE

BENOS BONES
BENOT T-BONE
BENOY EBONY
BENRT BRENT
BENRY BERNY
BENST BENTS
BEOOS OBOES
BEOOZ BOOZE
BEOPR PROBE
BEORR BORER
BEORS BOERS, BORES,
    ROBES, SOBER
BEORW BOWER
BEORX BOXER
BEOSU BOUSE
BEOSX BOXES
BEPSU PUBES
BERRY BERRY
BERST BREST
BERSU BURSE, REBUS
BERSV VERBS
BERSY BYRES
BERTT BRETT
BERTU BRUTE, REBUT,
    TUBER
BERUY BUYER
BESSU BUSES
BESSY BESSY
BESTU TUBES
BESTY BETSY, BYTES
BETTU BUTTE
BETTY BETTY
BFFIS BIFFS
BFFLU BLUFF
BFFSU BUFFS
BFLYY FLYBY
BGGOY BOGGY
BGGUY BUGGY
BGHIT BIGHT
BGHOU BOUGH
BGHRU BURGH
BGINO BINGO
BGINR BRING
BGIOT BIGOT
BGLUY BULGY
BGMOU GUMBO
BGNOO BONGO
BGNSU BUNGS
BGOOR BOGOR
BGOSU BOGUS
BGRSU GRUBS
BGRUY RUGBY
BHILU HUBLI
BHIRT BIRTH

BHLOO BOHOL
BHLSU BLUSH
BHMPU BUMPH
BHMRU RHUMB
BHMTU THUMB
BHOOS HOBOS
BHOOT BOOTH
BHORT BROTH, THROB
BHRSU BRUSH, SHRUB
BHSUY BUSHY
BIILN BLINI
BIIMN NIMBI
BIIOR ORIBI
BIISU SIBIU
BIJOU BIJOU
BIKLN BLINK
BIKNR BRINK
BIKRS BRISK
BIKRY KIRBY
BIKSY BIYSK
BILLR BRILL
BILLS BILLS
BILLY BILLY
BILMO LIMBO
BILMP BLIMP
BILMS LIMBS
BILOR BROIL
BILOS BOILS
BILPS BLIPS
BILSS BLISS
BILSY SIBYL, SYBIL
BILTU BUILT
BILTZ BLITZ
BINOR ROBIN
BINOS BISON
BINRU BRUIN, BURIN
BINRY BRINY
BIORS BIROS, BORIS
BIORT ORBIT
BIPSU PUBIS
BIQSU SQUIB
BIRST BRITS
BIRTT BRITT
BIRTU BRUIT
BITTY BITTY
BJMOU JUMBO
BJNOR BJORN
BKLSU BULKS
BKLUY BULKY
BKNOS KNOBS
BKNSU BUNKS
BKOOR BROOK
BKOOS BOOKS
BKOSY BOSKY

BKRSU BURKS
BLLOS BOLLS
BLLSU BULLS
BLLUY BULLY
BLMOO BLOOM
BLMPU PLUMB
BLNOW BLOWN
BLNOY NOBLY
BLNTU BLUNT
BLOSS SLOBS
BLOST BLOTS, BOLTS
BLOSU BOLUS
BLOSW BLOWS, BOWLS
BLOTY BY LOT
BLOWY BLOWY
BLRTU BLURT
BLRUY BURLY
BLTUY BUTYL
BMOOR BROOM
BMOOS BOOMS, BOSOM
BMOST TOMBS
BMOSW WOMBS
BMOTY BYTOM
BMOUX BUXOM
BMPSU BUMPS
BMPUY BUMPY
BNNOY BONNY
BNNUY BUNNY
BNOOR BORON
BNOOS BOONS, BOSON
BNORU BORNU, BOURN,
  BRUNO
BNORW BROWN
BNORX BRONX
BNORY BYRON, ROBYN
BNOSS SNOBS
BNOSU BONUS, BOSUN
BNRSU BURNS
BNRTU BRUNT, BURNT
BNSSU SNUBS
BOOPX PO BOX
BOORS BOORS
BOORT ROBOT
BOOST BOOST, BOOTS
BOOSZ BOZOS
BOOTY BOOTY
BOOWX OXBOW
BOOYZ BOOZY
BOPUW UP-BOW
BORRU BURRO
BORSW BROWS
BOSSY BOSSY
BOSTU BOUTS
BOSUY BUOYS

BPRSU BURPS
BRRSU BURRS
BRRUY BURRY
BRSTU BURST
BSSTU BUSTS, STUBS
BSTTU BUTTS
BSTUY BUSTY
BTTUY BUTTY
CCEHK CHECK
CCEHZ CZECH
CCEIL CECIL
CCEIR CERIC
CCELY CYCLE
CCEOS SECCO
CCESU CUSEC
CCHIK CHICK
CCHIN CINCH
CCHKO CHOCK
CCHKU CHUCK
CCHLU CULCH
CCHNO CONCH
CCHOU COUCH
CCHRU CURCH
CCIIT ICTIC
CCIIV CIVIC
CCIKL CLICK
CCIKR CRICK
CCILO COLIC
CCIMO COMIC
CCINO CONIC
CCINY CYNIC
CCIOS CISCO
CCKLO CLOCK
CCKLU CLUCK
CCKOR CROCK
CCKOS COCKS
CCKOY COCKY
CCORU OCCUR
CCOUZ CUZCO
CDDEE CEDED
CDDEI DICED
CDDEO CODED
CDDUY CUDDY
CDEEI DE-ICE
CDEER CEDER, CREED
CDEEU DEUCE, EDUCE
CDEHI CHIDE
CDEIM MEDIC
CDEIR CIDER, CRIED,
  DICER
CDEIT CITED, EDICT
CDEIV VEDIC
CDEIY DICEY
CDEKS DECKS

CDELO DOLCE
CDELU DULCE
CDELY CLYDE
CDEMO MEDOC
CDENS SCEND
CDENU DUNCE
CDEOO COOED
CDEOP COPED
CDEOR CODER, CORED,
    CREDO, DÉCOR
CDEOS CODES, COEDS
CDEOU COUDE
CDEOW COWED
CDEOX CODEX, COXED
CDEOY DECOY
CDERU CRUDE, CURED
CDERY CYDER, DECRY
CDETU EDUCT
CDHIL CHILD
CDHIT DITCH
CDHOR CHORD
CDHTU DUTCH
CDHUY DUCHY
CDIIN INDIC
CDIIO IODIC
CDIKS DICKS
CDIKY DICKY
CDILU LUCID
CDINY CINDY
CDIOR DORIC
CDIOS DISCO
CDIPU CUPID
CDISS DISCS
CDJOU JUDOC
CDKOS DOCKS
CDKSU DUCKS
CDKUY DUCKY
CDLOS CLODS, COLDS,
    SCOLD
CDLOU CLOUD, COULD
CDLWY CLWYD
CDMOR CD-ROM
CDNOO CODON
CDORS CORDS
CDORU DUROC
CDORW CROWD
CDRUY CURDY
CDSTU DUCTS
CEEEM EMCEE
CEEFN FENCE
CEEFS FECES
CEEHK CHEEK
CEEHL LEECH
CEEHN HENCE

CEEHP CHEEP
CEEHR CHEER
CEEIN NIECE
CEEIP PIECE
CEEJT EJECT
CEEKL CLEEK
CEEKR CREEK
CEELL CELLE
CEELR CREEL
CEELT ELECT
CEELX EXCEL
CEELY LYCÉE
CEEMR CREME
CEENP PENCE
CEENS CENSE, SCENE
CEEPR CREEP, CREPE,
    PERCE
CEERS CERES, SCREE
CEERT CRETE, ERECT
CEFHI CHIEF
CEFHS CHEFS
CEFHT FETCH
CEFIT FECIT
CEFKL FLECK
CEFLS CLEFS
CEFLT CLEFT
CEFOR FORCE
CEGIN GENIC
CEGKO GECKO
CEGNO CONGÉ
CEGSS GCSES
CEHIL CHILE
CEHIM CHIME
CEHIN CHINE, NICHE
CEHIR REICH
CEHIT ETHIC
CEHKO CHOKE
CEHKR KERCH
CEHKT KETCH
CEHLO CHLOE
CEHLW WELCH
CEHLY CHYLE
CEHMY CHYME
CEHNO ENOCH
CEHNT TENCH
CEHNW WENCH
CEHOP EPOCH
CEHOR CHORE, OCHRE
CEHOS CHOSE, SOCHE
CEHPR PERCH
CEHRT CHERT, RETCH
CEHRU RUCHE
CEHSS CHESS
CEHST CHEST

CEHSW CHEWS
CEHTU CHUTE
CEHTV VETCH
CEHTY TECHY
CEHWY CHEWY
CEIIR ICIER
CEIJU JUICE
CEILM CLIME
CEILN CLINE
CEILR RELIC
CEILS SLICE
CEILT TELIC
CEILU LUCIE
CEILV CLIVE
CEIMN MINCE
CEIMR CRIME
CEIMS MESIC
CEIMX CIMEX
CEINO ON ICE
CEINR NICER
CEINS SINCE
CEINV VINCE
CEINW WINCE
CEINZ ZENIC
CEIOV VOICE
CEIPR PRICE
CEIPS EPICS, SPICE
CEIPT TEPIC
CEIRR CRIER
CEIRS CRIES
CEIRT TRICE
CEIRU CURIE
CEIRX XERIC
CEISV VICES
CEITV CIVET, EVICT
CEITW TWICE
CEJOY JOYCE
CEKLR CLERK
CEKNS NECKS, SNECK
CEKNV V-NECK
CEKOS COKES
CEKPS PECKS, SPECK
CEKRW WRECK
CELLO CELLO
CELLS CELLS
CELNO CLONE
CELNU UNCLE
CELOS CLOSE, SOCLE
CELOV CLOVE
CELOY COLEY
CELPU CUPEL
CELRU CRUEL, LUCRE,
    ULCER
CELSU CLUES

CELSW CLEWS
CELTU CULET
CELUX CULEX
CEMOR COMER
CEMOT COMET
CEMRY MERCY
CENNO NONCE
CENOP PONCE
CENOR CRONE
CENOS CONES, SCONE
CENOT CENTO, CONTE
CENOU OUNCE
CENOV COVEN
CENOY CONEY
CENOZ COZEN
CENST CENTS, SCENT
CEOPS COPES, COPSE, SCOPE
CEOPU COUPÉ
CEORR CORER, CRORE
CEORS CORES, CORSE, SCORE
CEORT RECTO
CEORV COVER
CEORW COWER
CEORZ CROZE
CEOSV COVES
CEOSW COWES
CEOSX COXES
CEOTT OCTET
CEOTV COVET
CEOVY COVEY
CEPRT CREPT
CEPRY PERCY
CEPSS SPECS
CERRU RECUR
CERSS CRESS
CERST CERTS, CREST
CERSU CRUSE, CURES, CURSE
CERSW CREWS, SCREW
CERSY CERYS
CERTU CRUET, CURET, CUTER, ERUCT, TRUCE
CERUV CURVE
CESST SECTS
CESTU CETUS, SCUTE
CFFHU CHUFF
CFFIL CLIFF
CFFOS SCOFF
CFFSU CUFFS, SCUFF
CFHIL FILCH
CFHIN FINCH
CFHIT FITCH

CFHIU FICHU
CFIKL FLICK
CFIKU KUFIC
CFILO FOLIC
CFIOS COIFS
CFKLO FLOCK
CFKOR FROCK
CFKSU FUCKS
CFMOY COMFY
CFORT CROFT
CFOSU FOCUS
CFRSU SCURF
CFSUU FUCUS
CGHIN CHING
CGHLU GULCH
CGHOU COUGH
CGIIN ICING
CGILN CLING
CGILO LOGIC
CGINO COIGN
CGINU CUING
CGIOR CORGI
CGIOY YOGIC
CGIRU UGRIC
CGLNU CLUNG
CGLOS CLOGS
CGNOO COGON, CONGO
CHHIT HITCH
CHHIW WHICH
CHHNU HUNCH
CHHOO HOOCH
CHHTU HUTCH
CHIKN CHINK
CHIKO HOICK, KOCHI
CHIKS HICKS
CHIKT THICK
CHILL CHILL
CHILM MILCH
CHIMR CHIRM
CHIMT MITCH
CHIMU HUMIC
CHINP PINCH
CHINS CHINS
CHINW WINCH
CHIOR CHOIR
CHIOS SOCHI
CHIPR CHIRP
CHIPS CHIPS
CHIPT PITCH
CHIRR CHIRR
CHIRS CHRIS
CHIST CHITS, STICH
CHITW WITCH
CHITY ITCHY

CHIVY CHIVY, VICHY
CHKNU CHUNK
CHKOS HOCKS, SHOCK
CHKOY CHOKY
CHKSU SHUCK
CHKTU KUTCH
CHLMU MULCH
CHLNU LUNCH
CHLNY LYNCH
CHLOS LOCHS
CHLOT CLOTH
CHLRU CHURL, LURCH
CHMNU MUNCH
CHMOO MOOCH
CHMOP CHOMP
CHMPU CHUMP
CHMSU CHUMS
CHNOT NOTCH
CHNPU PUNCH
CHNRU CHURN
CHOOP POOCH
CHOPR PORCH
CHOPS CHOPS
CHOPU POUCH
CHORT TORCH
CHOSU HOCUS
CHOSW CHOWS
CHOTU TOUCH
CHOUV VOUCH
CHOUX CHOUX
CHPSY PSYCH
CHRSU CRUSH
CHSUY CUSHY
CIIKR RICKI
CIIKV VICKI
CIILT LICIT
CIILV CIVIL
CIILY ICILY
CIIMM MIMIC
CIINO IONIC
CIINR RICIN
CIINV VINIC
CIJUY JUICY
CIKKS KICKS
CIKLN CLINK
CIKLS LICKS, SLICK
CIKMS MICKS
CIKMY MICKY
CIKNS NICKS, SNICK
CIKNY NICKY
CIKPR PRICK
CIKPS PICKS
CIKPY PICKY
CIKQU QUICK

CIKRS RICKS	CKOST STOCK	CORWY COWRY
CIKRT TRICK	CKPSU PUCKS	COSST COSTS, SCOTS
CIKRY RICKY	CKRSU RUCKS	COSTT SCOTT
CIKST STICK, TICKS	CKRTU TRUCK	COSTU SCOUT
CIKSW WICKS	CKSTU STUCK, TUCKS	CPRTY CRYPT
CIKVY VICKY	CKUYY YUCKY	CPSSU CUSPS
CILNO COLIN, NICOL	CLLSU CULLS, SCULL	CPTUU CUT UP
CILNT CLINT	CLMOU COLUM, LOCUM	CRRUY CURRY
CILOS COILS	CLMPU CLUMP	CRSTU CRUST
CILOT LOTIC	CLMTU MULCT	CRSUY CYRUS
CILOW WILCO	CLNOO COLON	CSSTY CYSTS
CILPS CLIPS	CLNOW CLOWN	DDEEG EDGED
CILRU ULRIC	CLNUY CLUNY	DDEEI EDDIE
CILRY CYRIL, LYRIC	CLOOR COLOR	DDEEN ENDED
CILTY LYTIC	CLOOS COOLS	DDEES DEEDS
CIMNU CUMIN, MUCIN	CLOST CLOTS, COLTS	DDEFY DYFED
CIMOR MICRO	CLOSU LOCUS	DDEGO DODGE
CIMOS OSMIC	CLOSW COWLS, SCOWL	DDEIL IDLED
CIMPR CRIMP	CLOTU CLOUT	DDEIN DINED
CIMRS SCRIM	CLOYY COYLY	DDEIO DIODE, DODIE
CIMSU MUSIC	CLRSU CURLS	DDEIR DRIED, REDID
CINOS COINS, ICONS,	CLRUY CURLY	DDEIS SIDED
SCION, SONIC	CLSTU CULTS	DDEIT TIDED
CINOT TONIC	CMOOP COMPO	DDEIV DIVED
CINOV COVIN	CMOOS COSMO	DDELO DOLED
CINRU INCUR, RUNIC	CMORS CORMS	DDEMO DOMED
CINSU INCUS	CMORU MUCRO	DDENY NEDDY
CINTU CUTIN, TUNIC	CMPRU CRUMP	DDEOP DOPED
CIOPT OPTIC, PICOT, TOPIC	CMRSU SCRUM	DDEOR ODDER
CIORT TORIC	CMRYY CYMRY	DDEOS DOSED
CIORU CURIO	CMSUU MUCUS	DDEOT DOTED
CIOST STOIC	CNOOR CONOR, CROON	DDEOZ DOZED
CIOTX TOXIC	CNOOS COONS	DDEPU DUPED
CIPRS CRISP, SCRIP	CNOPY PONCY	DDERU UDDER
CIPRY PRICY	CNORS CORNS, SCORN	DDESU DUDES
CIPSS SPICS	CNORU CORNU	DDETY TEDDY
CIPSY SPICY	CNORW CROWN	DDGIY GIDDY
CISSY CISSY	CNORY CORNY, CRONY	DDGOY DODGY
CISTU CUTIS, ICTUS	CNOTU COUNT	DDILO DILDO
CJKOS JOCKS	CNOTY CYTON	DDILY LIDDY
CJNOU JUNCO	CNSTU CUNTS	DDIMY MIDDY
CKKNO KNOCK	CNSUU UNCUS	DDINU UNDID
CKLNU CLUNK	CNTUU UNCUT	DDIRU DRUID
CKLOS LOCKS	COOPS COOPS, SCOOP	DDLOY ODDLY
CKLPU PLUCK	COOPT CO-OPT	DDMUY MUDDY
CKLUY LUCKY	COOST COOTS, SCOOT	DDNOY NODDY
CKMOS MOCKS, SMOCK	COPRS CORPS, CROPS	DDOOS DODOS
CKMUY MUCKY	COPRU CROUP	DDORY RODDY
CKNOS CONKS	COPSU COUPS	DDOTY TODDY
CKOOR CROOK	COPUY COYPU	DDOWY DOWDY
CKOOS COOKS	CORSS CROSS	DDRUY RUDDY
CKORS CORKS, ROCKS	CORSU SCOUR	DEEFF EFFED
CKORY ROCKY	CORSW CROWS	DEEFR DEFER, FREED
CKOSS SOCKS	CORTU COURT	DEEFS FEEDS

DEEFT FETED
DEEGH HEDGE
DEEGK KEDGE
DEEGL LEDGE
DEEGO GEODE
DEEGR EDGER, GREED
DEEGS EDGES, SEDGE
DEEGW WEDGE
DEEHW HEWED
DEEHX HEXED
DEEIL ELIDE
DEEIR EIDER
DEEKN KNEED
DEEKR DEREK
DEEKY KEYED
DEELR ELDER
DEELU ELUDE
DEELV DELVE
DEEMN EMEND
DEEMT METED
DEEMW MEWED
DEENO DONEE
DEENR ENDER
DEENS DENSE, NEEDS
DEENU ENDUE
DEENY NEEDY
DEEOP EPODE
DEEOR ERODE
DEEPS SPEED
DEERR ERRED
DEERS REEDS
DEERT DETER
DEERY REEDY
DEESS SEEDS
DEEST STEED
DEESU SUEDE
DEESW SEWED, SWEDE,
    WEEDS
DEESX SEXED
DEESY SEEDY
DEETU ETUDE
DEETW TWEED
DEEUX EXUDE
DEEVX VEXED
DEEWY WEEDY
DEFGU FUDGE
DEFIL FIDEL, FIELD, FILED
DEFIN FIEND, FINED
DEFIR FIRED, FRIED
DEFIT FETID
DEFIX FIXED
DEFIY DEIFY, EDIFY
DEFJL FJELD
DEFLT DELFT

DEFLU FLUED
DEFLY FYLDE
DEFMU FUMED
DEFOX FOXED
DEFPU FED UP
DEFSU FEUDS, FUSED
DEGHY HEDGY
DEGIL GELID, GLIDE
DEGIM MIDGE
DEGIN DEIGN
DEGIO DOGIE, GEOID
DEGIR DIRGE, RIDGE
DEGIU GUIDE
DEGJU JUDGE
DEGLO LODGE, OGLED
DEGLU GLUED
DEGLY LEDGY
DEGNO OGDEN
DEGNU NUDGE
DEGOR GORED, RODGE
DEGOS DOGES
DEGRS DREGS
DEGRU URGED
DEGSY SEDGY
DEGUY GUYED
DEGWY WEDGY
DEHII HEIDI
DEHIK HIKED
DEHIL DELHI
DEHIR HIDER, HIRED
DEHIS HIDES, SHIED
DEHIT EDITH
DEHIV HIVED
DEHLO DHOLE
DEHNO HONED
DEHOP HOPED
DEHOR HEROD, HORDE
DEHOS HOSED, SHOED
DEHPT DEPTH
DEHPY HYPED
DEHRS HERDS, SHERD,
    SHRED
DEHSS SHEDS
DEHSY SHYED
DEIIM IMIDE
DEIIV IVIED
DEIIX DIXIE
DEIJO JODIE
DEIJV JIVED
DEIKL LIKED
DEIKN INKED
DEIKR IRKED
DEIKS DIKES, SKIED
DEILM LIMED

DEILN LINED
DEILO ODILE, OILED
DEILP PILED, PLIED
DEILR IDLER, RILED
DEILS SIDLE, SLIDE
DEILT TILDE, TILED
DEILV DEVIL, LIVED
DEILW WIELD
DEILY YIELD
DEIMM MIMED
DEIMN DENIM, MINED
DEIMR DIMER, MIRED
DEIMS DEISM, DIMES
DEIMT TIMED
DEIMX MIXED
DEINO DIONE
DEINP PINED
DEINR DINER, INDRE
DEINS DENIS, SNIDE
DEINU UDINE
DEINW EDWIN, WIDEN,
    WINED
DEINX INDEX, NIXED
DEIOV VIDEO
DEIOX OXIDE
DEIPP PIPED
DEIPR PRIDE, PRIED
DEIPS SPIED
DEIPT TEPID
DEIPW WIPED
DEIRR DIRER, DRIER,
    RIDER
DEIRS RIDES, SIRED
DEIRT TIRED, TRIED
DEIRV DIVER, DRIVE
DEIRW WEIRD, WIDER,
    WIRED, WRIED
DEISS SIDES
DEIST DEIST, DIETS, SITED,
    TIDES
DEISV DIVES
DEISW WIDES
DEISZ SIZED
DEITY DEITY
DEJKO JOKED
DEJOY JOYED
DEKKO DEKKO
DEKNU NUKED
DEKOP POKED
DEKOY YOKED
DEKPU PUKED
DEKRY DERYK
DEKSS DESKS
DEKSU DUKES

DEKSY DYKES
DELLS DELLS
DELLW DWELL
DELMO MODEL
DELNO ELDON, LODEN, OLDEN
DELOP LOPED, POLED
DELOR OLDER
DELOS DELOS, LODES, SOLED
DELOV LOVED
DELOW DOWEL, LOWED
DELOY YODEL
DELPU DUPLE
DELRU LURED, RULED
DELSS SLEDS
DELSU DUELS, DULSE, SLUED
DELSW WELDS
DELTW DWELT
DEMMO MODEM
DEMNO DEMON
DEMNS MENDS
DEMOO MOOED
DEMOP MOPED
DEMOR DROME
DEMOS DEMOS, DOMES, MODES
DEMOU ODEUM
DEMOV MOVED
DEMOW MOWED
DEMRU DEMUR
DEMSU MUSED, SEDUM
DEMTU MUTED
DENNY DENNY
DENOR DRONE
DENOS NODES, NOSED, SONDE
DENOT NOTED, TONED
DENOW ENDOW, OWNED
DENOY DOYEN
DENOZ DOZEN, ZONED
DENPS SPEND
DENPU UPEND
DENRS NERDS
DENRT TREND
DENRU UNDER
DENRY DERYN
DENST DENTS
DENSU DUNES, NUDES
DENSY DENYS
DENTU TUNED
DENUU UNDUE
DENWY EDWYN, WENDY

DEOOR RODEO
DEOOW WOOED
DEOOZ OOZED
DEOPR PEDRO, PORED, ROPED
DEOPS DOPES, POSED, SPODE
DEOPT DEPOT, OPTED
DEOPY DOPEY
DEORR ORDER
DEORS DOERS, DOSER
DEORT DOTER
DEORU UREDO
DEORV DROVE, ROVED
DEORW DOWER, ROWED
DEORZ DOZER
DEOSS DOSES
DEOSU DOUSE
DEOSV DOVES
DEOSW DOWSE, SOWED
DEOTT TOTED
DEOTV VOTED
DEOTW TOWED
DEOTY TOYED
DEOVW VOWED
DEOWW WOWED
DEPRU DRUPE, DUPER, PRUDE
DEPSU DUPES, PSEUD
DEPTY TYPED
DERRU RUDER
DERRY DERRY, DRYER
DERSS DRESS
DERSU DRUSE
DERSY DYERS
DERUX DUREX
DESTU DUETS
DETUV DUVET
DFFSU DUFFS
DFILU FLUID
DFINS FINDS
DFIOR FIORD
DFIRT DRIFT
DFJOR FJORD
DFLOO FLOOD, OF OLD
DFLOS FOLDS
DFLOY FLOYD
DFNOR FROND
DFNOU FOUND
DFNSU FUNDS
DFOOS FOODS
DFORS FORDS
DGGOO DOGGO
DGGOY DOGGY

DGHOU DOUGH
DGIIR RIGID
DGIIT DIGIT
DGILU GUILD
DGINO DINGO, DOING, GONDI
DGINR GRIND
DGINY DINGY, DYING
DGIOU GUIDO
DGIRS GRIDS
DGIRY RIDGY
DGLOS GOLDS
DGLOY GODLY
DGNUY DUNGY
DGOOR DROGO
DGOOS GOODS
DGOOY GOODY
DGOPY PODGY
DGORU GOURD
DGPUY PUDGY
DGRSU DRUGS
DHIIN HINDI
DHILP D PHIL
DHIMU HUMID
DHINS HINDS
DHINU HINDU
DHIOT DHOTI
DHIRT THIRD
DHISY DISHY
DHITW WIDTH
DHLOS HOLDS
DHNOO HONDO
DHNOU HOUND
DHOOS HOODS
DHORY HYDRO
DHOSW DHOWS
DHOWY HOWDY
DHRSU HURDS
DHSTU THUDS
DIILP LIPID
DIILV LIVID
DIIMO IDIOM
DIIMT TIMID
DIIOT IDIOT
DIIRS IDRIS
DIIVV VIVID
DIJNN DJINN
DIJNO DIJON
DIKNR DRINK
DIKNS KINDS
DIKNY DINKY
DIKRS DIRKS
DIKSS DISKS, SKIDS
DILLR DRILL

DILLY IDYLL
DILMY DIMLY
DILNY LINDY
DILOS IDOLS, LIDOS, SOLID
DILOY DOILY
DILRU LURID
DILRY DRILY
DILSW WILDS
DILSY DILYS
DIMNO MID-ON
DIMNS MINDS
DIMOU ODIUM
DIMST MIDST
DIMTU TUMID
DINRS RINDS
DINSU INDUS, NIDUS
DINSW WINDS
DINWY WINDY
DIOOT OOTID
DIOOV OVOID
DIOOZ ZOOID
DIOPY PYOID
DIORS DORIS
DIORT DROIT
DIOSV VOIDS
DIOTT DITTO
DIOTV DIVOT
DIOWW WIDOW
DIPRS DRIPS
DIQSU SQUID
DIRTU TRUDI
DIRTY DIRTY
DITTY DITTY
DIYZZ DIZZY
DKNRU DRUNK
DKNSU DUNKS
DKOSU KUDOS
DKSUY DUSKY
DKUUZ KUDZU
DLLOR DROLL
DLLOS DOLLS
DLLOY DOLLY, LLOYD
DLLUY DULLY
DLMOS MOLDS
DLMOU MOULD
DLMOY MOLDY
DLOOR DROOL, DOLOR
DLORS LORDS
DLORW WORLD
DLOST DOLTS
DLOSW WOLDS
DLOUW WOULD
DMMUY DUMMY
DMNOU MOUND

DMOOS DOOMS, MOODS
DMOOY MOODY
DMPSU DUMPS
DMPUY DUMPY
DMRSU DRUMS
DMRUU DURUM
DNNOY DONNY
DNOOR DONOR, RONDO
DNOOS SNOOD
DNOOT TONDO
DNOPS PONDS
DNOPU POUND
DNORU ROUND
DNORW DROWN
DNOSU NODUS, SOUND
DNOSW DOWNS
DNOSY SYNOD
DNOUW WOUND
DNOWY DOWNY
DOOPR DROOP
DOORS DOORS, ODORS, ROODS
DOORU DOURO, ODOUR
DOOST STOOD, TO-DOS
DOOSW WOODS
DOOTU OUTDO
DOOWY WOODY
DOPRS DROPS, PRODS
DOPRU PROUD
DORSS DROSS
DORSU SUDOR
DORSW SWORD, WORDS
DORTU TUDOR
DORWY DOWRY, ROWDY, WORDY
DOTTY DOTTY
DPSSU SPUDS
DRSSU SURDS
DRSTU TURDS
DRTUY TRUDY
DSSTU STUDS
DSSUY SUDSY
DSTUY DUSTY, STUDY
EEEGS GEESE
EEEIR EERIE
EEELM MELEE
EEELV LEVEE
EEEMS ESMEE
EEENR RENÉE
EEEPS ÉPÉES
EEEPT TEPEE
EEEPV PEEVE
EEEPW PEWEE
EEERV REEVE

EEFFI EFFIE
EEFLR FLEER
EEFLT FLEET
EEFRR FREER, REFER
EEFRS REEFS
EEFRV FEVER
EEFSS FESSE
EEFST FETES
EEFSU FUSEE
EEFSZ FEZES
EEGGR EGGER
EEGHL HEGEL
EEGHN HENGE
EEGIL LIEGE
EEGIN GENIE
EEGIR EIGER
EEGIS SIEGE
EEGKR GREEK
EEGLR LEGER
EEGLS GLEES
EEGLT GLEET
EEGLY ELEGY
EEGMR MERGE
EEGNR GENRE, GREEN
EEGNS GENES
EEGNT GENET
EEGNV NEGEV
EEGRS SERGE
EEGRT EGRET, GREET
EEGRV VERGE
EEGST EGEST, GEEST
EEHIN HENIE
EEHLL HELLE
EEHLN HELEN
EEHLS HEELS
EEHLT ETHEL
EEHLV HELVE
EEHLW WHEEL
EEHMN HE-MEN
EEHMT THEME
EEHNS SHEEN
EEHNT ETHNE
EEHPS SHEEP
EEHRS HERES, SHEER
EEHRT ETHER, THERE, THREE
EEHRV HERVÉ
EEHRW HEWER, WHERE
EEHRX HEXER
EEHSS HESSE
EEHST SHEET, THESE
EEHSX HEXES
EEHTT TEETH
EEILL ELLIE

EEILM   ELEMI, EMILE
EEILS   ELISE, ELSIE
EEILT   ELITE
EEILV   ELVIE
EEILX   EXILE
EEIMM   EMMIE
EEINR   ERNIE, IRENE,
   REINE, RENIE
EEINS   SEINE
EEIPP   EPPIE
EEIRS   ISERE
EEIRY   EYRIE
EEISS   ESSIE, SEISE
EEISV   SIEVE
EEISZ   SEIZE
EEITT   ETTIE
EEJLW   JEWEL
EEJPS   JEEPS
EEJRS   JEERS
EEJRZ   JEREZ
EEJSS   JESSE
EEKLN   KNEEL
EEKLS   KEELS, LEEKS, SLEEK
EEKLV   KEVEL
EEKNR   KEREN
EEKNS   KEENS, KNEES
EEKOP   PEKOE
EEKOV   EVOKE
EEKPS   KEEPS
EEKRS   ESKER
EEKRY   REEKY
EEKST   SKEET
EEKSW   WEEKS
EELLN   ELLEN
EELLV   LEVEL
EELMR   ELMER, MERLE
EELNO   NOELE
EELNW   NEWEL
EELOP   ELOPE
EELPR   LEPER, REPEL
EELPS   SLEEP
EELPX   EXPEL
EELRS   LEERS, REELS
EELRV   ELVER, LEVER,
   REVEL
EELRY   LEERY
EELST   SLEET, STEEL, STELE
EELSV   ELVES
EELTU   ELUTE
EELTX   TELEX
EEMMR   EMMER
EEMNS   MESNE, SEMEN
EEMNY   ENEMY, YEMEN
EEMOT   EMOTE

EEMRS   MERES
EEMRT   METER, METRE
EEMRX   REMEX
EEMRY   EMERY
EEMST   MEETS
EEMSU   MEUSE
EENPR   NEPER, PREEN
EENQU   QUEEN
EENRS   SNEER
EENRT   ENTER, RENTE,
   TERNE, TREEN
EENRU   ENURE
EENRV   NERVE, NEVER
EENRW   NEWER, RENEW
EENRY   NYREE
EENSS   ESSEN, SENSE
EENST   TEENS, TENSE
EENSU   ENSUE
EENSV   EVENS, SEVEN
EENTT   TENET
EENTV   EVENT
EENTW   'TWEEN
EENTY   TEENY
EENUV   VENUE
EENWY   WEENY
EEOPT   TOPEE
EEORS   EROSE
EEOXY   OXEYE
EEPPS   PEEPS
EEPRS   PEERS, PER SE, SPREE
EEPRT   PETER
EEPRU   PUREE, RUPEE
EEPST   STEEP
EEPSW   SWEEP
EEPWY   WEEPY
EEQRU   QUEER
EEQUU   QUEUE
EERSS   SEERS
EERST   ESTER, RESET,
   STEER, STERE, TERSE,
   TREES
EERSU   REUSE
EERSV   SERVE, SEVER,
   VERSE
EERSW   EWERS, SEWER
EERSX   REXES
EERTV   EVERT, REVET
EERTX   EXERT
EERUV   REVUE
EERVV   VERVE
EERVX   VEXER
EERVY   EVERY, VEERY
EESSX   SEXES
EESTV   STEVE

EESTW   SWEET
EETTU   TUTEE
EETTW   TWEET
EFFGO   GEOFF
EFFIR   FIFER
EFFIS   FIFES
EFFOR   OFFER
EFFRU   RUFFE
EFGIN   FEIGN
EFGIR   GRIEF
EFGOR   FORGE, GOFER
EFGUU   FUGUE
EFHIO   HOFEI
EFHIT   THIEF
EFHLS   FLESH, SHELF
EFHRS   FRESH
EFHTT   THEFT
EFHTY   HEFTY
EFIKN   KNIFE
EFILN   ELFIN
EFILR   FILER, FLIER, LIFER,
   RIFLE
EFILS   FILES, FLIES
EFILT   FILET
EFILX   FELIX
EFIMR   FERMI
EFINR   FINER, INFER
EFINS   FINES
EFINT   FEINT
EFIRR   FIRER, FRIER
EFIRS   FIRES, FRIES, FRISE,
   SERIF
EFIRT   REFIT
EFIRV   FIVER
EFIRX   FIXER
EFIRY   FIERY, REIFY
EFISV   FIVES
EFISX   FIXES
EFKLU   FLUKE
EFLLS   FELLS
EFLMU   FLUME
EFLNO   FELON
EFLOS   FLOES
EFLRU   FLEUR
EFLRY   FLYER
EFLSU   FLUES, FUELS, FUSEL
EFLSW   FLEWS
EFLTU   FLUTE
EFLTY   LEFTY
EFMOR   FORME
EFMRU   FEMUR, FUMER
EFMSU   FUMES
EFNNY   FENNY
EFNOR   FREON

EFNOT OFTEN
EFNRS FERNS
EFNRY FERNY
EFORT FETOR, FORTE
EFORY FOYER
EFORZ FROZE
EFOSS FOSSE
EFOSX FOXES
EFRRY FERRY, FRYER
EFRSS SERFS
EFRST FRETS
EFRUZ FURZE
EFSSU FUSES
EFSTU FETUS
EGGGR GREGG
EGGIU GIGUE
EGGLY LEGGY
EGGMY MEGGY
EGGNU GUNGE
EGGOP POGGE
EGGOR GORGE
EGGOU GOUGE
EGGPY PEGGY
EGHIL LEIGH
EGHIN HINGE, NEIGH
EGHIT EIGHT
EGHIW WEIGH
EGHNT GHENT, THEGN
EGHRU HUGER
EGIIN GENII
EGIJR REJIG
EGILN NIGEL
EGILR LIGER
EGILS GILES
EGILT GILET, LEGIT
EGILU GUILE
EGIMR GRIME
EGINR NIGER, REIGN
EGINS SINGE
EGINT TINGE
EGINV GIVEN
EGINW WINGE
EGINY EYING
EGIOV OGIVE
EGIPR GRIPE
EGIRT TIGER, TIGRE
EGIRV GIVER
EGISU GUISE
EGLMO GOLEM, GOMEL
EGLMU GLUME
EGLNN GLENN
EGLNS GLENS
EGLNU LUNGE
EGLOR OGLER

EGLOT LET GO
EGLOV GLOVE
EGLRU GLUER, GRUEL,
    LUGER
EGLSU GULES
EGLSY GYLES
EGLUY GLUEY
EGMNO GNOME
EGMRS GERMS
EGNOR GONER, NEGRO
EGNOS SEGNO
EGNOT GET ON
EGNPU UNPEG
EGNST GENTS
EGNSU GENUS, NEGUS
EGNTW GWENT
EGNUU ENUGU
EGOOS GOOSE
EGOOY GOOEY
EGOPR GROPE
EGORR ROGER
EGORS GOERS, GORES,
    GORSE, OGRES
EGORT ERGOT
EGORU ROGUE, ROUGE
EGORV GROVE
EGOSS GESSO
EGOUV VOGUE
EGPRU PURGE
EGPTU GETUP
EGPTY EGYPT
EGRRU URGER
EGRRY GERRY
EGRSU SURGE, URGES
EGRSY GREYS
EGSSU GUESS
EGSTU GUEST
EHHOP HOPEH
EHHPU HUPEH
EHIKR HIKER
EHIKS HIKES, SHEIK
EHIKT KEITH
EHILT ITHEL, LITHE
EHILU ELIHU
EHILW WHILE
EHILX HELIX
EHIMY HYMIE
EHINR HENRI, RHINE
EHINS HINES, SHINE
EHINT THINE
EHINW WHINE
EHIRR HIRER
EHIRS HEIRS, SHIER, SHIRE
EHIRT THEIR

EHISS SHIES
EHIST HEIST
EHISV HIVES, SHIVE
EHITT TITHE
EHITW WHITE, WITHE
EHJLO JEHOL
EHKLW WHELK
EHKMR KHMER
EHKOO HOOKE
EHLLO HELLO
EHLLS HELLS, SHELL
EHLMS HELMS
EHLMU HULME
EHLOS HOLES
EHLOT HELOT, HOTEL,
    THOLE
EHLOV HOVEL
EHLOW HOWEL, WHOLE
EHLOY HOLEY, HOYLE
EHLPS HELPS
EHLPW WHELP
EHLPY PHYLE
EHLSW WELSH
EHLTY ETHYL
EHLWY HYWEL
EHLXY HEXYL
EHMNY HYMEN
EHMOR HOMER, HORME
EHMOS HOMES, MOSHE
EHMOY HOMEY
EHMRT THERM
EHMRU RHEUM
EHMRY RHYME
EHMST METHS
EHMTY THYME
EHNNY HENNY
EHNOP PHONE
EHNOR HERON, RHONE
EHNOS SHONE
EHNOY HONEY
EHNRY HENRY
EHNSW SHEWN
EHNTT TENTH
EHOOY HOOEY
EHOPR HOPER
EHOPS HOPES
EHORS HORSE, SHORE
EHORT OTHER
EHORV HOVER
EHORW WHORE
EHOSS HOSES, SHOES
EHOST ETHOS, THOSE
EHOSU HOUSE
EHOSV SHOVE

EHOSW WHOSE
EHPRY HYPER
EHPSY HEPSY
EHPTU HET UP
EHRSU USHER
EHRSW SHREW
EHRSY SHYER
EHRTW THREW
EHRTZ HERTZ
EHSTW THEWS
EHTTY HETTY
EIILN LIE-IN
EIIMN IMINE
EIINT TIE-IN
EIIPX PIXIE
EIISV IVIES
EIJLU JULIE
EIJOS JOSIE
EIKKS KIKES
EIKLN INKLE, LIKEN
EIKLS LIKES
EIKLY KYLIE
EIKMS MIKES
EIKNO EIKON, KOINE
EIKNS SKEIN
EIKNV KEVIN
EIKPS PIKES, SPIKE
EIKRR KERRI
EIKRS SKIER
EIKRT TRIKE
EIKSS SKIES
EIKST KITES
EIKSV SKIVE
EIKTW KITWE
EILLL LILLE
EILLN NEILL
EILLO OLLIE
EILLS ELLIS, LIESL, LISLE
EILMN LIMEN
EILMP IMPEL
EILMR MILER
EILMS LIMES, MILES,
  SLIME, SMILE
EILMU ILEUM
EILMY EMILY, LIMEY
EILNN LINEN
EILNR LINER
EILNS LENIS, LIENS, LINES
EILNT INLET
EILNV ELVIN, LIVEN, NEVIL
EILOR LOIRE, OILER, ORIEL
EILOT ELIOT, TOILE
EILOU LOUIE
EILOV OLIVE, VOILE

EILPR PERIL, PLIER
EILPS PILES, SPIEL, SPILE
EILPX PIXEL
EILRT LITER, LITRE, TILER
EILRV LIVER, VILER
EILRY RILEY
EILSS ISLES
EILST ISLET, ISTLE, STILE,
  TILES
EILSU ILEUS, LIEUS
EILSV ELVIS, EVILS, LEVIS,
  LIVES, VEILS
EILSW LEWIS, WILES
EILSX LEXIS, SILEX
EILTT TITLE
EIMMR MIMER
EIMMS MIMES
EIMNR MINER
EIMNS MIENS, MINES,
  NIMES
EIMNV VIMEN
EIMOR MOIRE
EIMOV MOVIE
EIMOX OXIME
EIMPR PRIME
EIMPT TEMPI
EIMRS EMIRS, MIRES,
  MISER, REIMS
EIMRT MERIT, MITER,
  MITRE, REMIT, TIMER
EIMRX MIXER
EIMSS SEISM, SEMIS
EIMST ITEMS, MITES,
  SMITE, TIMES
EIMSX MIXES
EIMSY MYSIE
EINNR INNER, RENIN
EINNS NINES
EINNU ENNUI
EINNV VENIN
EINOP OPINE
EINOS EOSIN, NOISE
EINOT TIE-ON, TOE-IN
EINOV OVINE
EINPP PEPIN
EINPR RIPEN
EINPS PENIS, PINES, SNIPE,
  SPINE
EINPT INEPT
EINPY PINEY
EINRS REINS, RESIN, RINSE,
  RISEN, SERIN, SIREN
EINRT INERT, INTER,
  NITRE, TERNI, TRINE

EINRU INURE, URINE
EINRV RIVEN
EINRW ERWIN
EINSS SINES
EINST INSET, STEIN, TINES
EINSV VEINS, VINES
EINSW SINEW, SWINE,
  WINES
EINTU UNITE, UNTIE
EINTW TWINE
EINVX VIXEN
EINVY VEINY
EINWZ WINZE, WIZEN
EIOPS POISE
EIORS OSIER, ROSIE
EIORV VIREO
EIOSS OSSIE
EIOZZ OZZIE
EIPPR PIPER
EIPPS PIPES
EIPQU EQUIP, PIQUE
EIPRR PRIER, RIPER
EIPRS PIERS, PRISE, SPIRE
EIPRT TRIPE
EIPRV VIPER
EIPRW WIPER
EIPRZ PRIZE
EIPSS SPIES
EIPST PISTE, SPITE, STIPE
EIPSW SWIPE, WIPES
EIPTT PETIT
EIPTU TIE-UP
EIPTW PEWIT
EIPTY PIETY
EIPXY PYXIE
EIQRU QUIRE
EIQTU QUIET, QUITE
EIRRS RISER
EIRRT TERRI, TRIER
EIRRV RIVER
EIRRW WIRER, WRIER
EIRSS RISES, SIRES
EIRST RESIT, RITES, TIERS,
  TIRES, TRIES
EIRSW WEIRS, WIRES,
  WISER
EIRTT TITER, TITRE, TRITE
EIRTU UTERI
EIRTV RIVET
EIRTW WRITE
EISST SITES, STIES
EISSU ISSUE, SUSIE
EISSV VISES
EISSX SIXES

EISSZ SIZES	ELLSY YELLS	ELPSU PULSE
EISTU SUITE	ELLTU TULLE	ELPSY SLYPE, YELPS
EISTX EXIST, EXITS, SIXTE	ELLTY TELLY	ELPTU LETUP
EISTY YETIS	ELLWY WELLY	ELRRU LURER, RULER
EISTZ ZEIST	ELMMU LUMME	ELRSU LURES, RULES
EISVW VIEWS, WIVES	ELMMY LEMMY	ELRSY LYRES, SLYER
EITTW TWITE	ELMNO LEMON, MELON	ELRUX LUREX
EJKOR JOKER	ELMNU LUMEN	ELSSW SLEWS
EJKOS JOKES	ELMNY EMLYN	ELSTU LUTES
EJKRS JERKS	ELMOR MOREL	ELSTW WELTS
EJKRY JERKY	ELMOS MOLES	ELSTY STYLE
EJLLO JELLO	ELMOT METOL, MOTEL	ELTTY LETTY
EJLLY JELLY	ELMOU OLEUM	ELTUX EXULT
EJLOP POLJE	ELMPU PLUME	ELTWY WETLY
EJLOU JOULE	ELMRU LEMUR	EMMOS MEMOS, SOMME
EJLPU JULEP	ELMRY MERYL	EMNOS MESON, OMENS
EJLRU JUREL	ELMST SMELT	EMNOT MONTE
EJLSU JULES	ELMSU MULES	EMNOV VENOM
EJMMY JEMMY	ELMSY MYLES	EMNOW WOMEN
EJNNY JENNY	ELMUV VELUM	EMNOY MONEY
EJNOY ENJOY	ELMUY MULEY	EMNRU RUMEN
EJNSU JUNES	ELMXY XYLEM	EMNSU MENUS
EJOSV JOVES	ELNNY LENNY, LYNNE	EMOOR ROMEO
EJRRY JERRY	ELNOR ENROL, LONER,	EMOOS MOOSE
EJRWY JEWRY	LOREN, LORNE	EMOOT ME-TOO
EJSST JESTS	ELNOT ELTON, LENTO	EMOPR MOPER, PROEM
EJSSU JESUS	ELNOV NOVEL	EMOPS POEMS
EJTTY JETTY	ELNOW OLWEN	EMOPT TEMPO
EKLLN KNELL	ELNPZ PLZEN	EMOPY MYOPE
EKLLY KELLY	ELNWY ELWYN, NEWLY	EMORR ORMER
EKLNT KNELT	ELOOP POOLE	EMORS MORES
EKLOY YOKEL	ELOOS LOOSE	EMORT METRO
EKLPS SKELP	ELOPR LOPER, PROLE	EMORV MOVER, VOMER
EKMOS MOKES, SMOKE	ELOPS POLES, SLOPE	EMORW MOWER
EKNNY KENNY	ELOPU LOUPE	EMOSS MOSES
EKNOR KRONE	ELORR ERROL	EMOST MOTES, SMOTE,
EKNOT TOKEN	ELORS LOSER, ROLES	TOMES
EKNOW WOKEN	ELORV LOVER	EMOSU MOUSE
EKOPR POKER	ELORW LOWER, ROWEL	EMOSV MOVES
EKOPS POKES, SPOKE	ELORY ELROY, LEROY	EMOSW MEOWS
EKOST STOKE	ELOSS LOESS, SLOES, SOLES	EMOSY MOSEY
EKOSY YOKES	ELOST STOLE, TESOL	EMOTT MOTET, TOTEM
EKPRS PERKS	ELOSU LOUSE, SEOUL	EMOZZ MEZZO
EKPRY PERKY	ELOSV LOVES, SOLVE,	EMPRS SPERM
EKPSY PESKY	VOLES	EMPST TEMPS
EKRRY KERRY	ELOTW OWLET, TOWEL	EMPSU SPUME
EKRST TREKS	ELOTX EXTOL	EMPTT TEMPT
EKSSW SKEWS	ELOUV OVULE	EMPTY EMPTY
EKSUY SUKEY	ELOUZ OUZEL	EMRRY MERRY
ELLMS SMELL	ELOVW VOWEL	EMRST TERMS
ELLNY NELLY	ELOVY LOVEY	EMRSU MUSER, SERUM
ELLPS SPELL	ELPRU PULER	EMRSY EMRYS
ELLQU QUELL	ELPRY REPLY	EMRUX MUREX
ELLSW SWELL, WELLS	ELPST PELTS, SLEPT, SPELT	EMSST STEMS

EMSSU MUSES
EMSSY MESSY
EMSTU MUTES
ENNOO NO ONE
ENNOT TENON, TONNE
ENNOX XENON
ENNOY YONNE
ENNPY PENNY
ENNWY WYNNE
ENOOS NOOSE
ENOOZ OZONE
ENOPR PRONE
ENOPY PEONY
ENORS NORSE, SEÑOR,
  SNORE
ENORT TENOR, TONER
ENORU ROUEN
ENORW OWNER
ENOSS NOSES
ENOST NOTES, ONSET,
  STONE, TONES
ENOSV OVENS
ENOSZ ZONES
ENOVW WOVEN
ENOVY ENVOY
ENPRU PRUNE
ENPST SPENT
ENQRU QUERN
ENRRU RERUN
ENRST RENTS, STERN,
  TERNS
ENRSU NURSE, RUNES
ENRSW WRENS
ENRSY NERYS
ENRTU TUNER
ENRTY ENTRY
ENRVY NERVY
ENSST NESTS
ENSSU NEUSS
ENSTT TENTS
ENSTU TUNES, UNSET
ENSTV VENTS
ENSTW NEWTS
ENSUV VENUS
ENSUX NEXUS, UNSEX
ENSWY NEWSY
EOORW WOOER
EOPPS POPES
EOPRS PORES, POSER,
  PROSE, ROPES, SPORE
EOPRT TOPER, TROPE
EOPRV PROVE
EOPRW POWER
EOPRY ROPEY

EOPSS PESOS, POSES, POSSE
EOPST ESTOP, POETS,
  STOPE
EOPSX POXES
EOPSY POESY, SEPOY
EOPXY EPOXY
EOQTU QUOTE, TOQUE
EORRR ERROR
EORRV ROVER
EORRW ROWER
EORSS ROSES, SORES
EORST STORE
EORSU ROUÉS, ROUSE
EORSV OVERS, SERVO,
  VERSO
EORSW SEROW, SOWER,
  SWORE, WORSE
EORSZ ZEROS
EORTT OTTER, TOTER
EORTU OUTER, OUTRÉ,
  ROUTE
EORTV OVERT, TROVE,
  VOTER
EORTW TOWER, WROTE
EORTY TOYER
EORVW VOWER
EORXX XEROX
EOSSU SOUSE
EOSTT SET-TO, TOTES
EOSTV STOVE, VOTES
EOSTY EYOTS
EPPRS PREPS
EPPRU UPPER
EPRRU PURER
EPRRY PERRY
EPRSS PRESS
EPRSU PURSE, SPRUE,
  SUPER
EPRSY PYRES
EPRTU ERUPT
EPRTW TWERP
EPRXY PYREX
EPSST PESTS, STEPS
EPSTU SET-UP, STUPE,
  UPSET
EPSTW SWEPT
EPSTY TYPES
EPSXY PYXES
EPTTY PETTY
EQRUY QUERY
EQSTU QUEST
ERRSU SURER
ERRTU TRUER
ERRTY RETRY, TERRY

ERRWY WRYER
ERSST RESTS, TRESS
ERSSU RUSES, USERS
ERSTU TRUES
ERSTW STREW, TREWS,
  WREST
ERSTY TYRES
ERTTU UTTER
ESSTT TESTS
ESSTV VESTS
ESSTW STEWS
ESTTX TEXTS
ESTTY TESTY
ESTUY SUETY
ESTYZ ZESTY
ETTTY TETTY
FFFLU FLUFF
FFGRU GRUFF
FFHIT FIFTH
FFHIW WHIFF
FFHOU HOFUF
FFHUU HUFUF
FFHUY HUFFY
FFIJY JIFFY
FFIKS SKIFF
FFILO OLIFF
FFIMY MIFFY
FFINS SNIFF
FFINY NIFFY
FFIQU QUIFF
FFIRS RIFFS
FFIST STIFF, TIFFS
FFITY FIFTY
FFMSU MUFFS
FFNSU SNUFF
FFOST TOFFS
FFPSU PUFFS
FFPUY PUFFY
FFRSU RUFFS
FFSTU STUFF
FGGOY FOGGY
FGGUY FUGGY
FGHIT FIGHT
FGILN FLING
FGINO FINGO
FGINU FUNGI
FGIST GIFTS
FGLNO FLONG
FGLNU FLUNG
FGLSU GULFS
FGOOR FORGO
FGOOS GOOFS
FGOOY GOOFY
FGORS FROGS

FHIIS HI-FIS	FLOPS FLOPS	GHILT LIGHT
FHILT FILTH	FLORU FLOUR, FLUOR	GHIMT MIGHT
FHIRT FIRTH	FLORY FLORY	GHINT NIGHT, THING
FHIST SHIFT	FLOSS FLOSS	GHINY HYING
FHISY FISHY	FLOST LOFTS	GHIRT GIRTH, RIGHT
FHLSU FLUSH	FLOSU FOULS	GHISS SIGHS
FHORT FORTH, FROTH	FLOSW FOWLS	GHIST SIGHT
FIINS FINIS	FLOTU FLOUT	GHISW WHIGS
FIINX INFIX	FLOTY LOFTY	GHITT TIGHT
FIKRS FRISK	FLTUY FLUTY	GHITW WIGHT
FILLR FRILL	FMORS FORMS	GHLLY GHYLL
FILLY FILLY	FMORU FORUM	GHLOU GHOUL, LOUGH
FILMS FILMS	FMPRU FRUMP	GHLPY GLYPH
FILMU FILUM	FNNUY FUNNY	GHNOT THONG
FILMY FILMY	FNORS FRONS	GHORU ROUGH
FILNT FLINT	FNORT FRONT	GHOST GHOST
FILOO FOLIO	FNORW FROWN	GHOSU SOUGH
FILOR FORLI	FNOST FONTS	GHOTU OUGHT, TOUGH
FILOS FOILS	FNOTU FOUNT, FUTON	GHRSU SHRUG
FILPS FLIPS	FOOPR PROOF	GHSTU THUGS
FILRT FLIRT	FOOPS POOFS, SPOOF	GIILV VIGIL
FILST LIFTS	FOOPY POOFY	GIINO INIGO
FILSU FUSIL	FOORS ROOFS	GIINP PIING
FILTY FITLY	FOOST FOOTS	GIJNO GIJON, JINGO
FIMOS FOISM	FOOSW WOOFS	GIKNS KINGS
FIMOT MOTIF	FOPRS PROFS	GIKOR GORKI
FIMRS FIRMS	FOPSU POUFS	GILLR GRILL
FIMTU MUFTI	FORST FORTS, FROST	GILLS GILLS
FINNY FINNY	FORSU FOURS	GILNO LINGO
FINTU UNFIT	FORTY FORTY	GILNS SLING
FINTY NIFTY	FOSTY SOFTY	GILNT GLINT
FINUX UNFIX	FPRUY FRY-UP	GILNY LYING
FINUY UNIFY	FRRUY FURRY	GILOO IGLOO
FIOST FOIST	FRSTU TURFS	GILRS GIRLS
FIRRY FIRRY	FRSUU RUFUS	GILST GILTS
FIRST FIRST, RIFTS	FRSUY SURFY	GILTU GUILT
FIRTT FRITT	FRTUY TURFY	GILTZ GLITZ
FIRTU FRUIT	FRUYZ FURZY	GIMNY MINGY
FIRZZ FRIZZ	FSSUY FUSSY	GIMPY PIGMY
FISST FISTS	FSTTU TUFTS	GIMRY GRIMY
FISTW SWIFT	FSTUY FUSTY	GINNY GINNY
FIYZZ FIZZY	FTTUY TUFTY	GINOP PINGO
FKLNU FLUNK	FUYZZ FUZZY	GINOR GIRON, GROIN
FKLOS FOLKS	GGGLO GLOGG	GINOT INGOT, TIGON
FKLUY FLUKY	GGINO GOING	GINOW OWING
FKNSU FUNKS	GGIOT GIGOT	GINRS GRINS, RINGS
FKNUY FUNKY	GGIPY PIGGY	GINRU RUING, UNRIG
FKORS FORKS	GGMOY MOGGY	GINRW WRING
FLLOY FOLLY	GGMUY MUGGY	GINSS SIGNS
FLLUY FULLY, LYULF	GGNOS GONGS	GINST STING, TINGS
FLNOW FLOWN	GGOSY SOGGY	GINSU SUING, USING
FLOOR FLOOR	GHHIS HIGHS	GINSV V-SIGN
FLOOS FOOLS	GHHIT HIGHT, THIGH	GINSW SWING, WINGS
FLOOW WOLOF	GHHOU HOUGH	GINTY TYING

GINVY VYING	GOSTU GUSTO	HITWY WITHY
GINYZ ZINGY	GOTUY GOUTY, GUYOT	HIWZZ WHIZZ
GIORR RIGOR	GPPUY GUPPY	HKKOU HOKKU
GIORV VIRGO, VIGOR	GPSYY GYPSY	HKLSU HULKS
GIOSY YOGIS	GRSTU TRUGS	HKMOU HOKUM
GIPRS GRIPS, PRIGS, SPRIG	GRSUU GURUS	HKNOS HONKS
GIPSY GIPSY	GSSTU GUSTS	HKNOY HONKY
GIRST GRIST, GRITS	GSTUY GUSTY, GUTSY	HKNSU HUNKS
GIRUU UIGUR	HHLSU SHLUH	HKOOS HOOKS, SHOOK
GISSW SWIGS	HHMPU HUMPH	HKOOY HOOKY
GISTW TWIGS	HHSSU SHUSH	HKSSU HUSKS
GJMUU JUGUM	HIILN NIHIL	HKSUY HUSKY
GKNOO KONGO	HIIRS IRISH	HLLOO HOLLO
GLLOY GOLLY	HIKNT THINK	HLLOU HULLO
GLLSU GULLS	HIKRS SHIRK	HLLOY HOLLY
GLLUY GULLY	HIKSS SIKHS	HLLSU HULLS
GLMOO GLOOM	HIKSW WHISK	HLMPY LYMPH
GLMOU MOGUL	HILLS HILLS	HLOPR ROLPH
GLNSU LUNGS, SLUNG	HILLY HILLY	HLOPX PHLOX
GLOOS LOGOS	HILMU HILUM	HLORW WHORL
GLORW GROWL	HILOT THIOL	HLOSS SLOSH
GLORY GLORY	HILRS SHIRL	HLOST HOLST, SLOTH
GLOSS GLOSS, SLOGS	HILRW WHIRL	HLOSW HOWLS
GLOUV VOGUL	HILST HILTS	HLOTY HOTLY
GLPSU GULPS, PLUGS	HILSU HILUS	HLPSU PLUSH
GLRUY LURGY	HILSY SHILY	HLPSY SYLPH
GLSSU SLUGS	HILTT TILTH	HLSSU SLUSH
GLSTU GLUTS	HIMRT MIRTH	HLSYY SHYLY
GMMUY GUMMY	HIMST SMITH	HMNOT MONTH
GMNOU MUNGO	HIMSW WHIMS	HMNPY NYMPH
GMOOR GROOM	HINNT NINTH	HMNSY HYMNS
GMPYY PYGMY	HINNY HINNY	HMOOP OOMPH
GNOOS GOONS	HINOR RHINO	HMOPR MORPH
GNOPR PRONG	HINSS SHINS	HMORU HUMOR
GNOPS PONGS	HINST HINTS	HMOST MOTHS
GNOPY PONGY	HINSY SHINY	HMOTU MOUTH
GNORW GROWN, WRONG	HINWY WHINY	HMOTY MOTHY
GNOSS SNOGS, SONGS	HIOPP HIPPO	HMPSU HUMPS
GNOST TONGS	HIORU HOURI	HMPTU THUMP
GNOSW GOWNS	HIOST HOIST	HMPUY HUMPY
GNOUY YOUNG	HIPPY HIPPY	HMRRY MYRRH
GNRSU RUNGS	HIPSS SHIPS	HMRTU THRUM
GNRTU GRUNT	HIPSW WHIPS	HMSTU MUSTH
GNRUW WRUNG	HIPTY PITHY	HMSTY MYTHS
GNSSU SNUGS	HIRRS SHIRR	HMSUU HUMUS
GNSTU STUNG	HIRRW WHIRR	HMSUY MUSHY
GNSUW SWUNG	HIRST SHIRT	HNOOR HONOR
GOORS SORGO	HIRSW WHIRS	HNOOW NOHOW
GOOSY GOOSY	HISST SHITS	HNOPY PHONY
GOOTU OUTGO	HISSU SUSHI	HNORS HORNS, SHORN
GOPRU GROUP	HISSW SWISH	HNORT NORTH, THORN
GOPRY PORGY	HISTW WHIST, WHITS	HNORU HURON
GORSS GROSS	HISTX SIXTH	HNORY HORNY
GORTU GROUT	HISUW WUSIH	HNOSW SHOWN

HNSTU HUNTS, SHUNT
HOOPS HOOPS
HOOPT PHOTO
HOOPW WHOOP
HOOST HOOTS, SHOOT, SOTHO
HOOTT TOOTH
HOPSS SHOPS
HOPSY HYPOS, SOPHY
HOQTU QUOTH
HORRY HORRY
HORST HORST, SHORT
HORSU HORUS, HOURS
HORSY HORSY
HORTT TROTH
HORTW THROW, WORTH, WROTH
HOSST HOSTS, SHOTS
HOSSW SHOWS
HOSTT SHOTT
HOSTU SHOUT, SOUTH
HOSWY SHOWY
HOTUY YOUTH
HPSTU PHUTS
HPSUY PUSHY
HRRUY HURRY
HRSTU HURST, HURTS
HRSUY RUSHY
HRTTU TRUTH
HRUUU UHURU
HSSUY HUSSY
IIJNN JINNI
IIKKN NIKKI
IIKKR RIKKI
IIKKV VIKKI
IIKNN KININ
IIKNR KIRIN
IIKSW KIWIS
IILMT LIMIT
IILMU ILIUM
IILNN LININ
IIMMN MINIM
IIMNS MINIS
IIMRZ IZMIR
IIMST MITIS
IIMTZ IZMIT, MITZI
IINNO INION
IINRV IRVIN
IINRW IRWIN
IINST SIT-IN
IINTU INUIT
IIPPT PIPIT
IISTV VISIT
IJKNS JINKS

IJMMY JIMMY
IJNNY JINNY
IJNOS JOINS
IJNOT JOINT
IJOST JOIST
IKKNS KINKS, SKINK
IKKNY KINKY
IKKOS KIOSK
IKKRS KIRKS
IKKRU KUKRI
IKLLR KRILL
IKLLS KILLS, SKILL
IKLMY MILKY
IKLNS KILNS, LINKS, SLINK
IKLOS KILOS
IKLRS SKIRL
IKLRU KURIL
IKLSS SILKS
IKLST KILTS
IKLSY SILKY
IKMNS MINSK
IKMPS SKIMP
IKMRS SMIRK
IKNOP PINKO
IKNOS IKONS, OINKS
IKNPR PRINK
IKNPS PINKS
IKNRS RINKS
IKNSS SINKS, SKINS
IKNST SKINT, STINK
IKNSW WINKS
IKORV KIROV
IKPSS SKIPS, SPIKS
IKPSY SPIKY
IKQRU QUIRK
IKRSS RISKS
IKRST SKIRT, STIRK
IKRSY RISKY
IKRTU TURKI
IKSST SKITS
IKTTY KITTY
ILLMS MILLS
ILLMY MILLY
ILLOS LILOS
ILLPR PRILL
ILLPS PILLS, SPILL
ILLQU QUILL
ILLRS RILLS
ILLRT TRILL
ILLSS SILLS
ILLST LILTS, STILL, TILLS
ILLSW SWILL, WILLS
ILLSY SILLY, SLILY
ILLTW TWILL

ILLTY TILLY
ILLWY WILLY
ILMPY IMPLY
ILMSY SLIMY
ILNOR LORIN
ILNOS LIONS, LOINS
ILNPU LUPIN
ILNSY LYSIN
ILNTU UNTIL
ILNTY LINTY
ILNVY VINYL
ILOOP POLIO
ILOPS SPOIL
ILOPT PILOT
ILOPU POILU
ILOPX OXLIP
ILORS LORIS
ILORT TRIOL
ILOSS SILOS, SOILS
ILOST TOILS
ILOSU LOUIS
ILOSV VIOLS
ILPPU PUPIL
ILPSS SLIPS
ILPST SPILT, SPLIT
ILPTU TULIP
ILRSW SWIRL
ILRTW TWIRL
ILSST LISTS, SLITS
ILSSY LYSIS
ILSTT STILT, TILTS
ILSTY SILTY
ILYZZ LIZZY
IMMTY TIMMY
IMNOR MINOR
IMNOS SIMON
IMNST MINTS
IMNSU IN SUM, MINUS
IMNTY MINTY
IMOPR PRIMO
IMOPU OPIUM
IMOSS MOSSI
IMOST MOIST
IMOSX SIXMO
IMOTV VOMIT
IMPPR PRIMP
IMPPS PIMPS
IMPRS PRISM
IMPSW WIMPS
IMPUX MIX-UP
IMPWY WIMPY
IMRST TRIMS
IMSST MISTS

IMSSW swims
IMSSY missy
IMSTT mitts
IMSTY misty
INNNO ninon
INNNY ninny
INNOO onion
INNOU union
INNPU unpin
INNPY pinny
INNQU quinn
INNRU inurn, run-in
INNSU sunni
INNTY tinny
INNVY vinny
INOOR orion
INOPT pinto, piton, point
INOQU quoin
INORS irons, rosin
INORT intro
INORY irony
INOSW oswin
INOSY noisy
INOTW in tow, in two
INOTX toxin
INPPU pinup
INPPY nippy
INPRT print
INPRU unrip
INPSS snips, spins
INPST pints
INPSY spiny
INPTU input
INPUZ unzip
INQSU quins
INQTU quint
INRSU ruins
INRTU turin
INSSU nisus, sinus
INSTT stint, tints
INSTU suint, tunis, units
INSTW twins
INTTY nitty
INTUX x-unit
INTUY unity
IOPRR prior
IOPST posit
IOPSU pious
IOPTV pivot
IOQTU quito, quoit
IORRS orris
IORST riots, tiros, trios
IORSV visor

IORVY ivory
IOSUX sioux
IOTTW to wit
IPPYZ zippy
IPQSU quips
IPRST sprit, strip, trips
IPRSY spiry
IPRTW twirp
IPRVY privy
IPSST spits
IPSSV spivs
IPSSW wisps
IPSTU sit-up
IPSTY tipsy
IPSTZ spitz
IPSWY wispy
IPSXY pyxis
IQSTU quits
IRSST stirs
IRSTW wrist, writs
IRSUV virus
IRTUV virtu
IRTYZ ritzy
ISSSW swiss
ISSSY sissy
ISSTU situs, suits
ISTTU titus
ISTTW twist, twits
ISTUV vitus
ISTXY sixty
ITTTU tutti
ITTTY titty
ITTWX twixt
ITTWY witty
ITYZZ tizzy
JJSUU jujus
JKNSU junks
JLLOY jolly
JLOST jolts
JLOSW jowls
JMORU jorum
JMPSU jumps
JMPUY jumpy
JNOTU junto
JORRU juror
JOSTU joust
KKLSU skulk
KKNSU skunk
KKOOS kooks
KKOOY kooky
KKRSU kursk
KLLNO knoll
KLLSU skull
KLNOP plonk

KLNPU plunk
KLNRU knurl
KLNSU slunk
KLOOS looks
KLOSY yolks
KLOYY yolky
KLSSU sulks
KLSUY sulky
KMNOS monks
KMOOP mokpo
KMOST tomsk
KMOSY smoky
KMRUY murky
KMSUY musky
KNNOW known
KNOOR kroon
KNOOS nooks, snook
KNOST knots
KNOSW knows
KNOSY yonks
KNOUY yukon
KNOWY wonky
KNPSU punks, spunk
KNRTU trunk
KNSTU stunk
KOOPS spook
KOORS rooks
KOOST stook
KOOTY kyoto, tokyo
KOPRY porky
KOPSV pskov
KORST stork, torsk
KORSW works
KRSSU rusks
KRTUU turku
KSSTU tusks
LLLOY lolly
LLMOS molls
LLMOY molly
LLMSU mulls
LLOOR rollo
LLOPS polls
LLOPY polly
LLORS rolls
LLORT troll
LLORY rolly
LLOST tolls
LLOSY lysol, solly
LLOTY tolly, tolyl
LLOWY lowly
LLOXY xylol
LLPSU pulls
LLSTU stull
LLSUY sully

LLXYY XYLYL
LMOOS LOOMS
LMOOT MOLTO
LMOST MOLTS, SMOLT
LMOSU MOSUL, SOLUM
LMOTU MOULT
LMPPU PLUMP
LMPSU LUMPS, PLUMS,
   SLUMP
LMPUY LUMPY, PLUMY
LMSSU SLUMS
LNNOY NYLON
LNOOR ORLON
LNOOS LOONS
LNOOY LOONY
LNOPY PYLON·
LNOUZ LUZON
LNOWY OLWYN
LOOOV OVOLO
LOOPR ORLOP
LOOPS LOOPS, POOLS,
   SLOOP, SPOOL
LOOPY LOOPY
LOOSS SOLOS
LOOST STOOL, TOOLS
LOPPY POLYP
LOPRW PROWL
LOPSS SLOPS
LOPST PLOTS
LOPSW PLOWS
LOPSY PLOYS, POLYS
LOPTU PLUTO, POULT
LORRY LORRY
LORTY TYROL
LORUX LUXOR
LOSST SLOTS
LOSSU SOULS
LOSSY LOSSY
LOSTU LOTUS, LOUTS
LOSTV VOLTS
LOSUY LOUSY
LOSWY YOWLS
LOTTY LOTTY
LOTYZ ZLOTY
LPPSU PULPS
LPPUY PULPY
LPRSU SLURP
LPSUU LUPUS
LRSSU SLURS
LRSUY SURLY
LRTUY TRULY
LRWYY WRYLY
LSSTU LUSTS, SLUTS
LSTUY LUSTY

MMMOY MOMMY
MMMUY MUMMY
MMOPY POMMY
MMOTY TOMMY
MMPSU MUMPS
MMRUY RUMMY
MMTUY TUMMY
MNOOR MORON
MNOOS MOONS
MNOOY MOONY
MNORS MORNS, NORMS
MNORU MOURN
MNORY MYRON
MNOTU MOUNT, NOTUM
MNOTY MONTY
MOOPR PROMO
MOORS MOORS, ROOMS
MOORT MOTOR
MOORY ROOMY
MOOSS MOSSO
MOOTT MOTTO
MOPPU MOP-UP
MOPRS PROMS, ROMPS
MOPST STOMP
MORRU RUMOR
MORST STORM
MORSW WORMS
MORTU TUMOR
MORTY MORTY
MORWY WORMY
MOSSY MOSSY
MOSUY MOUSY
MPPSU PUMPS
MPRSU RUMPS
MPRTU TRUMP
MPSSU SUMPS
MPSTU STUMP
MRSTU STRUM
MSSTU SMUTS
MSTTU MUTTS
MSTUY MUSTY
MUYZZ MUZZY
NNOSU NOUNS
NNOSY SONNY
NNRUY RUNNY
NNSUY SUNNY
NNTUY TUNNY
NOOPR PORNO
NOOPS SNOOP, SPOON
NOORS ORSON
NOOSW SWOON
NOOTW ON TOW
NOPTU PUT-ON, TON-UP,
   UPTON

NORST SNORT
NORSW SWORN
NORTU TORUN
NORTY TRY-ON
NOSSW SNOWS
NOSTU SNOUT, TONUS
NOSTW TOWNS
NOSTY STONY
NOSWY SNOWY
NPRSU SPURN
NPRUU RUN-UP
NPSTU PUNTS
NPSUU SUN-UP
NPTUY PUNTY
NRSTU RUNTS, TURNS
NRTUU U-TURN
NRTUY RUNTY
NSTTU STUNT
NTTUY NUTTY
OOPPS POOPS
OOPRS SOPOR, SPOOR
OOPRT TROOP
OOPST STOOP, TOPOS
OOPSW SWOOP
OOPTT POTTO
OORRT ROTOR
OORRU ORURO
OORST ROOST, ROOTS,
   TORSO
OOSTT TOOTS
OOSTY SOOTY
OOSYY YOYOS
OOWYZ WOOZY
OPPPU POP-UP
OPPPY POPPY
OPPRS PROPS
OPPSY POPSY, SOPPY
OPRST PORTS, SPORT,
   STROP
OPRSW PROWS
OPRSY PROSY
OPRUY ROUPY
OPRXY PROXY
OPSST POSTS, SPOTS, STOPS
OPSSU SOUPS
OPSSW SWOPS
OPSTU POUTS, SPOUT,
   STOUP
OPSTY TOPSY
OPSUY SOUPY
OPTTU PUTTO
OPTTY POTTY
OPTUZ TZU-PO
ORRSY SORRY

ORRTU TRURO
ORRWY WORRY
ORSST SORTS
ORSSU SORUS
ORSTT TORTS, TROTS
ORSTU ROUST, ROUTS,
  TORUS, TOURS
ORSTW WORST
ORSTY STORY, TYROS
ORSUY YOURS
ORTTU TROUT, TUTOR
OSSST STOSS

OSSTW SWOTS
OSTTU STOUT, TOUTS
OSUYZ SOYUZ
OTTTY TOTTY
PPPUY PUPPY
PRRSU PURRS
PRSSU SPURS
PRSTU SPURT, TURPS
PRSUU USURP
PRSUY SYRUP
PSSUY PUSSY
PSTTU PUTTS

PTTUY PUTTY
RSSTU TRUSS
RSTTU STRUT, TRUST
RSTTY TRYST
RSTUW WURST
RSTUY RUSTY
RSUUY USURY
RTTUY RUTTY
STTUU TUTUS
TTTUY TUTTY

SIX-LETTER WORDS

AABCS CASABA
AAABDN ABADAN
AAABHN HABANA
AAABIR ARABIA
AAABLM AMBALA
AAABLT BALATA
AAABNN ANNABA,
  BANANA
AAABNS ANABAS
AAABRZ BAZAAR
AAACCI ACACIA
AAACDI ACADIA
AAACDN CANADA
AAACEH ACHAEA
AAACGI AGACIA
AAACJN JACANA
AAACLP ALPACA
AAACMR MARACA
AAACNR ARCANA
AAACOX OAXACA
AAADLM ALMADA
AAADMN AMANDA
AAADMR ARMADA,
  DAMARA
AAADNP PANADA
AAAELZ AZALEA
AAAGHT AGATHA
AAAGLM MALAGA
AAAGLT GALATA
AAAGNN NAGANA
AAAGRU AARGAU
AAAHLM MAHALA
AAAHLS AL HASA
AAAHMR AMHARA
AAAHNV HAVANA

AAAHRS SAHARA
AAAILM AMALIA
AAAITX ATAXIA
AAAJMP PAJAMA
AAAKLM KAMALA
AAAKLS ALASKA
AAAKNR ANKARA,
  KANARA
AAALMS SALAAM
AAALMY MALAYA
AAALNN ALANNA
AAAMMN MANAMA
AAAMNN MANANA
AAAMNP PANAMA
AAAMRS ASMARA,
  SAMARA
AAAMRT TAMARA
AAAMRY AYMARA
AAANPR PARANA
AAAPPY PAPAYA
AAARRT ARARAT
AAARTV AVATAR
AABBBO BAOBAB
AABBCY ABBACY
AABBLL LABLAB
AABBLO BALBOA
AABBRR BARBRA
AABBST SABBAT
AABCIN BIANCA
AABCIR ARABIC
AABCIU CUIABA
AABCJO JACOBA
AABCLS CABALS
AABCMN CABMAN
AABCRS SCARAB

AABCSU ABACUS
AABDER ABRADE
AABDES ABASED
AABDET ABATED
AABDEU AUBADE
AABDIN IBADAN
AABDLL BALLAD
AABDLM LAMBDA
AABDOR ABOARD,
  ABROAD, BARODA
AABDRT TABARD
AABEGT TEABAG
AABELM AMABEL
AABELR ARABLE
AABELZ ABLAZE
AABEMO AMOEBA
AABEMS AMEBAS
AABERZ ZAREBA
AABFIN FABIAN
AABFIR BIAFRA
AABGGR RAGBAG
AABGGS GASBAG
AABGIM GAMBIA
AABGIN BAAING
AABGRT RATBAG
AABHKS KASBAH
AABHKZ ABKHAZ
AABIKR KARIBA
AABILL LABIAL
AABILN ALBINA
AABILU ABULIA
AABIMZ ZAMBIA
AABINS SABINA
AABIST ABATIS
AABISW SWABIA

AABKLN BALKAN
AABKMO BAMAKO
AABLMS BALSAM
AABLNY ALBANY
AABLOR ABORAL
AABLOV LAVABO
AABLSS BALSAS
AABLST BASALT
AABLTU ABLAUT
AABMMS MAMBAS
AABMNR BARMAN
AABMNT BANTAM,
 BATMAN
AABMRS SAMBAR
AABMRY AMBARY
AABMSS SAMBAS
AABNNY BANYAN
AABORR ARROBA
AABORT ABATOR, RABATO
AABRSS SABRAS
AABTTW ABWATT
AACCDI CICADA
AACCHH CHA-CHA
AACCHM CHACMA
AACCLO CLOACA
AACCLP CALPAC
AACCLR CALCAR
AACCMO MACACO
AACCNN CANCAN
AACDDU CAUDAD
AACDEF FACADE
AACDER ARCADE
AACDIR ACARID
AACDLU CAUDAL
AACDMP MADCAP
AACDNR CANARD
AACEFL FAECAL
AACEFR CARAFE
AACEHN AACHEN
AACEHP APACHE
AACEHT CHAETA
AACELP PALACE
AACELS ALSACE
AACELT ACETAL
AACELY CELAYA
AACEMO CAEOMA
AACEMR CAMERA
AACENP CANAPÉ
AACENR ARCANE
AACENT CATENA
AACERS CAESAR
AACETV CAVEAT, VACATE
AACFIL FACIAL
AACFIR AFRICA

AACFIS FASCIA
AACFLU FACULA, FAUCAL
AACFNR FRANCA
AACFNT CAFTAN
AACFRS FRACAS
AACFTT FAT CAT
AACGIM AGAMIC
AACGIR AGARIC
AACHIT ITHACA
AACHKW KWACHA
AACHLS CALASH
AACHNO CHAOAN
AACHTT ATTACH
AACIIL ALICIA
AACIIM AMICIA
AACILL LAICAL
AACILP APICAL
AACILR ALARIC, RACIAL
AACILS CALAIS
AACILT ALTAIC
AACIMN MANIAC
AACIMR MARCIA
AACINR ARNICA, CARINA,
 CRANIA
AACIPS CAPIAS
AACIRT CARITA
AACIRV CAVIAR
AACISS CASSIA
AACITT ATTICA
AACITX ATAXIC
AACJKL JACKAL
AACJOU ACAJOU
AACKRR ARRACK
AACKTT ATTACK
AACLLO CALLAO
AACLMT LACTAM
AACLMU MACULA
AACLNR CARNAL
AACLNS CANALS
AACLNT CANTAL
AACLNU LACUNA
AACLOR CAROLA
AACLPR CARPAL
AACLPS PASCAL
AACLPU PAUCAL
AACLRS LASCAR, RASCAL,
 SACRAL, SCALAR
AACLSU CASUAL, CAUSAL
AACLTU ACTUAL
AACMNR CARMAN
AACMNU CUMANA
AACMNY CAYMAN
AACMOT TACOMA
AACMRT TARMAC

AACMSS CAMASS
AACMSW MACAWS
AACNNO ANCONA
AACNPT CATNAP
AACNRY CANARY
AACNSV CANVAS
AACNTV VACANT
AACPPY PAPACY
AACPRS CASPAR
AACRST CARATS
AACRSU ACARUS
AACRTV CRAVAT
AADDIL LA-DI-DA
AADDIV DAVIDA
AADDOU AOUDAD
AADEGL GELADA
AADEGM DAMAGE
AADEGN AGENDA
AADEGS ADAGES
AADEHN HADEAN
AADEJU JUDAEA
AADEKW AWAKED
AADEMM MADAME
AADEMN MAENAD
AADEMZ AMAZED
AADENN ANDEAN,
 DEANNA
AADENR ANDREA
AADENT ADNATE
AADENV NEVADA
AADEOR ORADEA
AADEPR PARADE
AADFIR AFRAID
AADGIO ADAGIO
AADGIR AGADIR
AADGMR DAGMAR
AADGNU UGANDA
AADGOP PAGODA
AADHIL DAHLIA
AADHIN HAIDAN
AADHLR HARALD
AADHRZ ADZHAR,
 HAZARD
AADILR RADIAL
AADILS DALASI
AADIMN DAMIAN
AADIMT MATADI
AADINR ADRIAN, RADIAN
AADINS NAIADS
AADINT DANITA
AADINV DAVINA
AADIST STADIA
AADKMS DAMASK
AADKNU KADUNA

AADKOT DAKOTA
AADKPU PADAUK
AADLLS DALLAS
AADLMY MALADY
AADLNR RANALD, RANDAL
AADLNS SANDAL
AADLNU LANDAU, LUANDA
AADLNV VANDAL
AADLOP APODAL
AADLOU DOUALA
AADLRU RADULA
AADLSS SALADS
AADMMN MADMAN
AADMMR DAMMAR
AADMMS MADAMS
AADMNR ARMAND
AADMOU AMADOU
AADMRS DRAMAS, MADRAS
AADMRU MARAUD
AADMYY MAY DAY
AADNNR RANDAN
AADNPS PANDAS
AADNRS SANDRA
AADNRU ARNAUD
AADNRW RWANDA
AADNRZ ZANDRA
AADNTU DANUTA
AADNTW WANT AD
AADPYY PAYDAY
AADRSW AWARDS
AADRTU DATURA
AADRTY DATARY
AAEEGN AEGEAN
AAEENS AENEAS
AAEERT AERATE
AAEEST AT EASE
AAEFLM AFLAME
AAEFLR RAFAEL
AAEFNZ FAENZA
AAEGGR GARAGE
AAEGGV GAVAGE
AAEGLL LALAGE
AAEGLN ANGELA, ANLAGE, GALENA, LAGENA
AAEGLR ALEGAR, LAAGER
AAEGLV LAVAGE
AAEGMN MANAGE
AAEGNT AGNATE, AGNETA
AAEGRV RAVAGE

AAEGST AGATES
AAEGSV SAVAGE
AAEGTU GÂTEAU
AAEHLM HAEMAL, MEHALA
AAEHLT ALTHEA
AAEHMT HAMATE
AAEHNT ANTHEA
AAEHNY HYAENA
AAEHRT EARTHA
AAEILM AMALIE, AMELIA
AAEILR AERIAL
AAEILX ALEXIA
AAEIMN ANEMIA
AAEINR ANEIRA, ARIANE
AAEITV AVIATE
AAEKLN ALKANE
AAEKLR KERALA
AAEKNW AWAKEN
AAEKRT KARATE
AAELLP PAELLA
AAELMP PAMELA
AAELMT MALATE
AAELNN ANNEAL
AAELNS SALENA
AAELNT LANATE
AAELNV LAVENA
AAELOR AREOLA
AAELPP APPEAL
AAELPT PALATE
AAELRV LARVAE
AAEMNP APEMAN
AAEMNS SEAMAN
AAENOP APNOEA
AAENPS PAEANS
AAENPV PAVANE
AAENRS ARENAS
AAENRT RENATA
AAENST ANSATE
AAENSU NAUSEA
AAEPPR APPEAR
AAERRT ERRATA
AAERWX EARWAX
AAESWY SEAWAY
AAFFIR AFFAIR, RAFFIA
AAFFJN JAFFNA
AAFFRY AFFRAY
AAFGHN AFGHAN
AAFIKS SIFAKA
AAFILV FLAVIA
AAFINR FARINA
AAFINS NAAFIS
AAFIRS SAFARI
AAFITU AU FAIT

AAFKNT KAFTAN
AAFLLL FALLAL
AAFLNU FAUNAL
AAFLOT AFLOAT
AAFNNT FAN-TAN
AAFNRR FARRAN
AAFNSU FAUNAS
AAGGHI HAGGAI
AAGGQU QUAGGA
AAGGRS SAGGAR
AAGGRT RAGTAG
AAGHMR ARMAGH, GRAHAM
AAGHNP PAHANG
AAGHNR HANGAR
AAGHST AGHAST
AAGILR ARGALI
AAGILT GALATI
AAGILV GAVIAL
AAGIMN MAGIAN
AAGINN ANGINA
AAGINR GRANIA
AAGINU GUIANA, IGUANA
AAGINV VAGINA
AAGINW GAWAIN
AAGJRU JAGUAR
AAGKLU KALUGA
AAGKLY GALYAK
AAGKNS KANGAS
AAGLLN LALANG
AAGLLP PLAGAL
AAGLMN MALANG
AAGLNO ANALOG, ANGOLA
AAGLNR RAGLAN
AAGLRT TRAGAL
AAGLST STALAG
AAGLWY GALWAY
AAGLXY GALAXY
AAGMMS GAMMAS
AAGMNR RAGMAN
AAGMNS GASMAN
AAGMRY MAGYAR, MARGAY
AAGNNO NAGANO
AAGNNY ANYANG
AAGNOR ANGORA, ARAGON
AAGNOY NAGOYA
AAGNPR PARANG
AAGNPS PAGANS
AAGNRY ANGARY
AAGNUY GUYANA
AAGPRS GASPAR

AAGRVY VAGARY
AAGSUV GUAVAS
AAHHLL HALLAH
AAHHLV HALVAH
AAHHNN HANNAH
AAHHPT APHTHA
AAHHWW HAWHAW
AAHIIS ISAIAH
AAHIIW HAWAII
AAHILT HIATAL
AAHINN HAINAN
AAHIPR PARIAH
AAHIRS SHARIA
AAHJRR JARRAH
AAHJRS RAJAHS
AAHKKZ KAZAKH
AAHKNO HAAKON
AAHLLW WALLAH
AAHLMT MALTHA
AAHLNT ANHALT
AAHLPS ALPHAS
AAHLRS ASHLAR
AAHLRT HARTAL
AAHMNS SHAMAN
AAHMRS MARSHA
AAHMRT MARTHA
AAHMST ASTHMA
AAHNNS ANSHAN
AAHNNT NATHAN
AAHNOV NAVAHO
AAHNPT PATHAN
AAHNSS HASSAN
AAHNSU SHAUNA
AAHNTU UTAHAN
AAHNTV HAVANT
AAHPPR PARAPH
AAHPTY APATHY
AAHRRR HARRAR
AAHRSS HARASS
AAHRSU AARHUS
AAHSSY SASHAY
AAIKLL ALKALI
AAIKLM KALMIA
AAIKNN ANNIKA
AAIKNR KARINA
AAILLX AXILLA
AAILMN ANIMAL,
    LAMINA, MANILA
AAILMP IMPALA
AAILMS SALAMI
AAILMW MALAWI
AAILNR NARIAL
AAILNS NASIAL, SALINA
AAILNV ALVINA, LAVINA

AAILPS PALAIS
AAILPU APULIA
AAILQU AQUILA
AAILRT ALTAIR, LARIAT,
    LATRIA
AAILSS ASSAIL
AAILSV SALIVA, SALVIA,
    VALAIS
AAILTU AU LAIT
AAILTV LATVIA
AAIMMR MARIAM
AAIMMS MIASMA
AAIMMX MAXIMA
AAIMNR AIRMAN,
    ARMINA, MARIAN,
    MARINA
AAIMNS MANIAS
AAIMNT AMINTA
AAIMRS MARISA
AAIMRT AMRITA, MARITA
AAINNT TAINAN
AAINOR ORIANA
AAINOX ANOXIA
AAINPP PAPAIN
AAINPR PARIAN
AAINPT PATINA, TAIPAN
AAINRS SARINA
AAINRT TIRANA
AAINRU ANURIA
AAINSS ASIANS
AAINTT ATTAIN
AAINTW TAIWAN
AAIPRU AU PAIR
AAIPRY APIARY
AAIPZZ PIAZZA
AAIQRT QATARI
AAIRST ARISTA, SARITA,
    TIARAS
AAIRVY AVIARY
AAIRWY AIRWAY
AAITUY YAUTIA
AAJNNO JOANNA
AAJPRU JAPURA
AAKKMR MARKKA
AAKKOP KAKAPO
AAKKSY KAYAKS
AAKLMU MAKALU
AAKLOS KOALAS
AAKLRS KRAALS
AAKLSU LUSAKA
AAKNOR ANORAK
AAKNSS KANSAS
AAKNSU KAUNAS
AAKPRS PARKAS

AAKRST KARATS
AALLMS LLAMAS
AALLPP APPALL
AALLPS PALLAS
AALLRV LARVAL
AALMMM MAMMAL
AALMMS LAMMAS
AALMNP NAPALM
AALMNU ALUMNA,
    MANUAL
AALMNY LAYMAN
AALMOR AMORAL
AALMOT AMATOL
AALMPR PALMAR
AALMPS LAMPAS, PLASMA
AALMRS ALARMS
AALMRT RATLAM
AALMTY AMYTAL
AALNNS ANNALS
AALNNU ANNUAL
AALNOT ALTONA,
    ATONAL
AALNPR PLANAR
AALNPT PLATAN
AALNRX LARNAX
AALNSS NASALS
AALNST ASLANT
AALOPY PAYOLA
AALOVW AVOWAL
AALPSZ PLAZAS
AALRST ALTARS, ASTRAL,
    TARSAL
AALRSY SALARY
AALSSV VASSAL
AALSWY ALWAYS
AALWYY WAYLAY
AAMNOR RAMONA
AAMNOS SAMOAN
AAMNOZ AMAZON
AAMNPS SAMPAN
AAMNST TASMAN
AAMNSU MANAUS
AAMNTX TAXMAN
AAMOPR PARAMO
AAMORS AROMAS
AAMOSS SAMOSA
AAMOTY TOYAMA
AAMPPS PAMPAS
AAMQSU SQUAMA
AAMRSU ASARUM
AAMRSW ASWARM
AAMRSY RAMSAY
AAMRTU TRAUMA
AANNOR ANNORA

AANNRU ANURAN
AANNTT NATANT
AANORV NOVARA
AANORX ROXANA
AANOST SONATA
AANPPU PAPUAN
AANPRT TARPAN
AANQTU QUANTA
AANRRT ARRANT
AANRTT RATTAN, TARTAN
AANRYZ RYAZAN
AANSSU NASSAU, SAUNAS
AANSTV SAVANT
AANSTW TSWANA
AANSTZ STANZA
AANWYY ANYWAY
AAOPST SAPOTA
AAORRU AURORA
AAORST AORTAS
AAOTTV OTTAVA
AAOTTW OTTAWA
AAPPWW PAWPAW
AAPRST PATRAS
AAPWXX PAXWAX
AAQRSU QUASAR
AARRSY ARRAYS
AARRTT TARTAR
AARSTT STRATA
AARSTY ASTRAY
AARSWW WARSAW
AARTTT RAT-TAT
AARTTY TATARY
AASSSY ASSAYS
ABBBEL BABBLE
ABBCOT BOBCAT
ABBCRY CRABBY
ABBCSY SCABBY
ABBDDE DABBED
ABBDEG GABBED
ABBDEI BABIED
ABBDEJ JABBED
ABBDEL DABBLE
ABBDEN NABBED
ABBDER BARBED, DABBER
ABBDET TABBED
ABBDEU BEDAUB
ABBEGI GABBIE
ABBEGL GABBLE
ABBEGR GABBER
ABBEIR BARBIE, RABBIE
ABBEIS BABIES
ABBEIU BAUBIE
ABBEJR JABBER
ABBEKS KEBABS

ABBELR BARBEL, RABBLE
ABBELU BAUBLE
ABBERR BARBER
ABBERT BARBET
ABBESS ABBESS
ABBESY ABBEYS
ABBFLY FLABBY
ABBGOR GABBRO
ABBHSY SHABBY
ABBILO BILBAO
ABBIRS RABBIS
ABBIRT RABBIT
ABBLRU BULBAR
ABBMOO BAMBOO
ABBMOY BOMBAY
ABBNOO BABOON
ABBNOS NABOBS
ABBORS ABSORB
ABBOST ABBOTS
ABBRSU BUSBAR
ABCCLU BUCCAL
ABCDEK BACKED
ABCDEL CABLED
ABCDER BRACED
ABCDIR BARDIC
ABCDTU ABDUCT
ABCEEM BECAME
ABCEHL BLEACH
ABCEHR BREACH
ABCEHU HECUBA
ABCEIM AMEBIC
ABCEJT ABJECT
ABCEKR BACKER
ABCELS CABLES
ABCELT CABLET
ABCEMR CAMBER
ABCENO BEACON
ABCENU CUBANE
ABCERR BRACER
ABCERS BRACES, CABERS
ABCEST BE CAST
ABCFIR FABRIC
ABCGIT BIG CAT
ABCHLN BLANCH
ABCHNR BRANCH
ABCHOR BROACH
ABCHPU HUBCAP
ABCIIM IAMBIC
ABCILT BALTIC
ABCILU ABULIC
ABCINS CABINS
ABCISS BASICS
ABCISY BISCAY
ABCKLS BLACKS

ABCKPU BACKUP
ABCLMY CYMBAL
ABCLOT COBALT
ABCMOR CRAMBO
ABCMOT COMBAT,
 TOMBAC
ABCNOR CARBON,
 CORBAN
ABCORS CAROBS, COBRAS
ABCORX BOXCAR
ABCORY CARBOY
ABCOSV VOCABS
ABCSSU SCUBAS
ABDDEE BEADED
ABDDEI ABIDED
ABDDEN BANDED
ABDDER BADDER
ABDDEU DAUBED
ABDDHU BUDDHA
ABDEEH BEHEAD
ABDEEL BEADLE
ABDEEM BEAMED
ABDEES DEBASE, SEABED
ABDEET DEBATE
ABDEFL FABLED
ABDEGG BAGGED
ABDEGL GABLED
ABDEGN BANGED
ABDEGO BODEGA
ABDEGR BADGER,
 BARGED, GARBED
ABDEGS BADGES
ABDEHS BASHED
ABDEHT BATHED
ABDEIL BAILED, BALDIE
ABDEIR ABIDER, AIRBED
ABDEIS BIASED
ABDEIT BAITED
ABDEKL BALKED
ABDEKN BANKED
ABDEKR BARKED,
 BRAKED, DEBARK
ABDEKS BASKED
ABDELM AMBLED,
 BEDLAM, BLAMED,
 LAMBED
ABDELO ALBEDO, DOABLE
ABDELR BLARED
ABDELS BLADES
ABDELT TABLED
ABDELW BAWLED
ABDELY DYABLE
ABDELZ BLAZED
ABDENN BANNED

ABDENP BEDPAN
ABDENR BRENDA
ABDENU DANUBE
ABDEOS ABODES
ABDEOT BOATED
ABDEPY PAYBED
ABDERR BARRED
ABDERS BEARDS
ABDERU DAUBER
ABDERV ADVERB, BRAVED
ABDERY BRAYED
ABDEST BASTED
ABDESU ABUSED
ABDETT BATTED
ABDFOR FORBAD
ABDHRY HARD BY
ABDIJM DJAMBI
ABDILR BRIDAL, RIBALD
ABDINT BANDIT
ABDIRS BRAIDS, DISBAR
ABDLLY BALDLY
ABDLNO BOLAND
ABDLRY DRABLY
ABDNOR ROBAND
ABDNOU ABOUND
ABDNRS BRANDS
ABDNRU DURBAN
ABDNRY BRANDY
ABDORS ADSORB,
  BOARDS, BROADS
ABDORY BYROAD
ABDOYY DAYBOY
ABDRRU DURBAR
ABDRSU ABSURD
ABEEGL BEAGLE
ABEEGR BARGEE
ABEEHV BEHAVE
ABEEIL BAILEE
ABEEKR BEAKER
ABEEKT BETAKE
ABEELN BALEEN, ENABLE
ABEENT BEATEN
ABEENU BEAUNE
ABEEOR AEROBE
ABEEOU EUBOEA
ABEERR BEARER
ABEERT BEATER, BERATE,
  REBATE
ABEERV BEAVER
ABEERW BEWARE
ABEFFL BAFFLE
ABEFHL BEHALF
ABEFLL BEFALL
ABEFLM FLAMBE

ABEFLR FABLER
ABEFLS FABLES
ABEFMR FERBAM
ABEFPR PREFAB
ABEGGR BEGGAR
ABEGIT GIBE AT
ABEGIU IBAGUE
ABEGLM GAMBLE
ABEGLN BANGLE, BENGAL
ABEGLR GARBLE
ABEGLS BAGELS, GABLES
ABEGLU BELUGA
ABEGMR BREGMA
ABEGNR BANGER,
  GRABEN
ABEGOR BORAGE
ABEGOZ GAZEBO
ABEGRS BARGES
ABEGRZ ZAGREB
ABEHIL HABILE
ABEHIT BETHIA
ABEHLR HERBAL
ABEHLU BEULAH
ABEHNT BETHAN
ABEHRT BATHER, BERTHA
ABEHSS BASHES
ABEIIR IBERIA
ABEIIT TIBIAE
ABEILL LABILE, LIABLE
ABEILN BLAINE
ABEILR BAILER
ABEILS ABSEIL, BLAISE,
  ISABEL
ABEILT ALBEIT, ALBITE
ABEILV VIABLE
ABEILW BEWAIL
ABEILY BAILEY
ABEINT BENITA, BINATE
ABEIRR BARRIE
ABEIRS BRAISE, RABIES,
  SERBIA
ABEISS BIASES
ABEJOR JERBOA
ABEJRU ABJURE
ABEKLR BALKER
ABEKLY KABYLE
ABEKMN EMBANK
ABEKMR EMBARK
ABEKNR BANKER
ABEKOU BOUAKE
ABEKRR BARKER
ABEKRS BAKERS, BRAKES,
  BREAKS
ABEKRY BAKERY

ABEKST BASKET
ABELLS LABELS
ABELLT BALLET
ABELMM EMBALM
ABELMR AMBLER,
  MARBLE, RAMBLE
ABELNU NEBULA, UNABLE
ABELOR BOREAL
ABELOT LOBATE, OBLATE
ABELPU PUEBLA
ABELRR BARREL
ABELRT ALBERT, BARTLE,
  LABRET
ABELRV VERBAL
ABELRW BAWLER, WARBLE
ABELRY BARELY, BARLEY,
  BLEARY
ABELRZ BLAZER
ABELSS SABLES
ABELST BLEATS, STABLE,
  TABLES
ABELSU SUABLE, USABLE
ABELSY BASELY
ABELSZ BLAZES
ABELTT BATTLE, TABLET
ABEMNO BEMOAN
ABEMNR BARMEN
ABEMNT BATMEN
ABENNR BANNER
ABENOR BORANE
ABENRR BARREN
ABENRT BANTER, BARNET
ABENRU URBANE
ABENRY BARNEY, NEARBY
ABENRZ BRAZEN
ABENST ABSENT
ABENTT BATTEN
ABENTU BUTANE
ABEORT BOATER, BORATE
ABEORZ BEZOAR
ABEOSS SASEBO
ABEPTU UPBEAT
ABEQRU BARQUE
ABEQSU BASQUE
ABERRT BARTER
ABERRV BRAVER
ABERRY BRAYER
ABERRZ BRAZER
ABERSS SABERS, SABRES
ABERST BAREST, BREAST
ABERSU ABUSER
ABERSV BRAVES
ABERSZ ZEBRAS
ABERTT BATTER

ABERTU AUBERT
ABERTY BETRAY
ABERUU BUREAU
ABERUY AUBREY
ABERZZ ZABRZE
ABESSS BASSES
ABESST BASEST, BASSET,
  BEASTS
ABESSU ABUSES
ABESTU BEAUTS
ABETTU BATTUE
ABETTY BEATTY
ABETUY BEAUTY
ABEUXY BAYEUX
ABFILU FIBULA
ABFISY BASIFY
ABGHTU HAGBUT
ABGIIL GALIBI
ABGIKN BAKING
ABGIKT KIT BAG
ABGILN BALING
ABGIMT GAMBIT
ABGIMY BIGAMY
ABGINO GABION, GOBIAN
ABGINR BARING
ABGINS BASING
ABGINU BANGUI
ABGINY BAYING
ABGLLO GLOBAL
ABGLMO GAMBOL
ABGOOT BOGOTA,
  TOBAGO
ABGRSU BURGAS
ABHIIR BIHARI
ABHINR HARBIN
ABHINS BANISH
ABHIOP PHOBIA
ABHISS SAHIBS
ABHIST HABITS
ABHLOP BHOPAL
ABHMSU AMBUSH
ABHNTU BHUTAN
ABHORR HARBOR
ABHORT HOBART
ABHOST BATHOS
ABHOTX HATBOX
ABHOXY HAYBOX
ABHRSY BRASHY
ABIILS ALIBIS
ABIIST TIBIAS
ABIJRU JABIRU
ABIKMO AKIMBO
ABILMT TIMBAL
ABILMU LABIUM

ABILNO ALBINO, ALBION
ABILNR LIBRAN
ABILNY LIBYAN
ABILOR BAILOR
ABILRT TRIBAL
ABILRU BURIAL
ABILRZ BRAZIL
ABILVY VIABLY
ABIMRU BARIUM, UMBRIA
ABIMST AMBITS
ABIMSU IAMBUS
ABINOR ROBINA
ABINOS BASION, BONSAI,
  BOSNIA
ABINOT BONITA, OBTAIN
ABINRS BAIRNS, BRAINS
ABINRU RUBINA
ABINRY BINARY, BRAINY
ABINSS BASINS
ABIORS ISOBAR
ABIOST TOBIAS
ABIRSU AIRBUS
ABIRTZ TABRIZ
ABISSU BISSAU
ABJNOS BANJOS
ABJNPU PUNJAB
ABKLNS BLANKS
ABKLSU BAULKS
ABKLSY SKYLAB
ABLLNO NO BALL
ABLLOT BALLOT
ABLLTU ALL BUT
ABLMOP APLOMB
ABLMOR BROMAL
ABLMRU BRUMAL,
  LABRUM, LUMBAR,
  UMBRAL
ABLMRY MARBLY
ABLMSU ALBUMS
ABLNOZ BLAZON
ABLNSU NABLUS
ABLOOR ROBALO
ABLORS LABORS
ABLORU LABOUR
ABLOST OBLAST
ABLOTT TALBOT
ABLOTV ABVOLT
ABLPRU BURLAP
ABLPYY BYPLAY
ABLRSU BURSAL
ABLRSW BRAWLS
ABLRTU BRUTAL
ABLSST BLASTS
ABLSTY STABLY

ABLSWY BYLAWS
ABLSYY LAY-BYS
ABLTTY TYBALT
ABMNOW BOWMAN
ABMNOY BONAMY
ABMNTU NUMBAT
ABMOTV TAMBOV
ABMOTW WOMBAT
ABMRSU RUMBAS
ABNORR BARRON
ABNORS BARONS
ABNORY BARONY,
  BARYON
ABNOST BATONS
ABNOTY BOTANY
ABNRTU TURBAN
ABNRUU AUBURN
ABNRWY BRAWNY
ABOOST TABOOS
ABORRS ARBORS
ABORRU ARBOUR
ABORRW BARROW
ABORSV BRASOV, BRAVOS
ABORTU RUBATO
ABORTW TOWBAR
ABORTY TORBAY
ABORUY YORUBA
ABOSST BOASTS
ABOSTU U-BOATS
ABOSUY BAYOUS
ABOSWW BOWSAW
ABPRTU ABRUPT
ABPSSY BYPASS
ABQSSU SQUABS
ABRRSU BURSAR
ABRSSY BRASSY
ABRTUY BURYAT
ABSUWY SUBWAY
ABSWYY BYWAYS
ACCCIL CALCIC
ACCDEE ACCEDE
ACCDEN DECCAN
ACCDII ACIDIC
ACCDOR ACCORD
ACCEHN CHANCE
ACCEHS CACHES
ACCEHT CACHET
ACCEIN CANICE
ACCEIP ICE CAP, IPECAC
ACCEIT ACETIC
ACCEKL CACKLE
ACCELN CANCEL
ACCELR CERCAL
ACCELS CALCES

ACCEMS MECCAS
ACCEMU CAECUM
ACCENR CANCER
ACCENT ACCENT
ACCEPT ACCEPT
ACCERS SCARCE
ACCERU ACCRUE
ACCESS ACCESS
ACCESU ACCUSE
ACCGNO COGNAC
ACCHNO CONCHA
ACCHNY CHANCY
ACCHOU CACHOU
ACCHTY CATCHY
ACCIIN ACINIC
ACCILO CALICO
ACCILT LACTIC
ACCIMM MICMAC
ACCINT CANTIC
ACCINY CYANIC
ACCIOS CAICOS
ACCIRT ARCTIC
ACCITT TACTIC
ACCKRS CRACKS
ACCLOU COUCAL
ACCMOR CORMAC
ACCORW CRACOW
ACCOST ACCOST
ACCRUY CURACY
ACCSTU CACTUS
ACCSUU CAUCUS
ACCSUY YUCCAS
ACCTUU CUCUTA
ACDDEE DECADE
ACDDEG CADGED
ACDDEI CADDIE
ACDDEN DANCED
ACDDER CARDED
ACDDEU ADDUCE
ACDDII DIACID
ACDDIN CANDID
ACDDIR DARDIC, ID CARD
ACDDIS CADDIS
ACDDIT ADDICT
ACDDIY DYADIC
ACDDTU ADDUCT
ACDEEF DEFACE
ACDEEN DECANE
ACDEER DECARE
ACDEES CEASED
ACDEFH CHAFED
ACDEGR CADGER,
   GRACED
ACDEGT GEDACT

ACDEHK HACKED
ACDEHR ARCHED,
   ECHARD
ACDEHS CASHED, CHASED
ACDEHT DETACH
ACDEIM DECIMA
ACDEIV ADVICE
ACDEJK JACKED
ACDEKL CALKED, LACKED
ACDEKP PACKED
ACDEKR RACKED
ACDEKS SACKED
ACDEKT TACKED
ACDELL CADELL, CALLED
ACDELM CALMED
ACDELN CANDLE,
   DECLAN, LANCED
ACDELO COALED
ACDELP PLACED
ACDELR CRADLE
ACDELS DECALS, SCALED
ACDELU CAUDLE, CLAUDE
ACDELV CALVED
ACDELW CLAWED
ACDEMP CAMPED,
   DECAMP
ACDENN CANNED
ACDENO ACNODE,
   CANOED, DEACON
ACDENR CRANED,
   DANCER, NACRED
ACDENS ASCEND, DANCES
ACDENT CADENT,
   CANTED, DECANT
ACDEOT COATED
ACDEOX COAXED
ACDEPP CAPPED
ACDEPR CARPED, REDCAP
ACDEPS SPACED
ACDERS CADRES, CEDARS,
   SACRED, SCARED
ACDERT CARTED,
   CRATED, REDACT,
   TRACED
ACDERV CARVED, CRAVED
ACDERZ CRAZED
ACDEST CADETS
ACDESU CAUSED, SAUCED
ACDEUX CAUDEX
ACDHMR DRACHM
ACDHRS CHARDS
ACDIIM AMIDIC
ACDIJU JUDAIC
ACDILP PLACID

ACDINO ANODIC
ACDINR RANCID
ACDIOZ ZODIAC
ACDIPS CAPSID
ACDLNU UNCLAD
ACDLSS SCALDS
ACDLTY DACTYL
ACDMTU MUDCAT
ACDNNU DUNCAN
ACDNOR CANDOR,
   CONRAD, DACRON
ACDORS DORCAS
ACDORW COWARD
ACDSTU DUCATS
ACEEFF EFFACE
ACEEFN ENFACE
ACEEFR REFACE
ACEEFS FAECES
ACEEGI ICE AGE
ACEEGN ENCAGE
ACEEHN ACHENE
ACEEHT HECATE
ACEEIP APIECE
ACEEJT EJECTA
ACEELN ENLACE
ACEELR CEREAL
ACEELV CLEAVE
ACEEMN MENACE
ACEEMR RACEME
ACEEMZ ECZEMA
ACEENR CAREEN
ACEENS ENCASE, SÉANCE,
   SENECA
ACEENT CETANE, TENACE
ACEEPS ESCAPE, PEACES
ACEERR CAREER
ACEERS CREASE
ACEERT CERATE, CREATE,
   ECARTE
ACEFFT AFFECT
ACEFHR CHAFER
ACEFIL FACILE
ACEFIN FIANCÉ
ACEFIR FIACRE
ACEFIS FACIES
ACEFLU FECULA
ACEFNR FRANCE
ACEFRS FARCES
ACEFST FACETS
ACEFSU FAUCES
ACEFSY CASEFY
ACEFTU FAUCET
ACEGHN CHANGE
ACEGHR CHARGE

ACEGHU GAUCHE

ACEGIL GAELIC

ACEGIR CAGIER, GRACIE

ACEGLN GLANCE

ACEGLY LEGACY

ACEGNY AGENCY

ACEGOS SOCAGE

ACEGOW COWAGE

ACEGRS GRACES

ACEHIM HAEMIC

ACEHIR ARCHIE, CAHIER

ACEHIS CHAISE

ACEHKL HACKLE

ACEHKR HACKER

ACEHLP CHAPEL, PLEACH

ACEHLR RACHEL

ACEHLS LACHES

ACEHLT CHALET, THECAL, THECLA

ACEHMN MANCHE

ACEHMR MARCHE

ACEHMS SCHEMA

ACEHNS ENCASH

ACEHOR CHOREA, HORACE

ACEHPR EPARCH, PREACH

ACEHPT HEPCAT

ACEHPY PEACHY

ACEHRR ARCHER

ACEHRS ARCHES, CHASER, ESCHAR, SEARCH

ACEHRX EXARCH

ACEHSS CHASES, CHASSE

ACEHST CHASTE, CHEATS, SACHET

ACEHSW CASHEW

ACEIJK JACKIE

ACEIJN JANICE

ACEILM MALEIC, MALICE

ACEILN CELINA

ACEILP PLAICE

ACEILR CLAIRE, ÉCLAIR, LACIER

ACEIMN ANEMIC, CINEMA, ICEMAN

ACEIMO MACEIO

ACEIMR CRIMEA, MARCIE, MERCIA

ACEIMS CAMISE

ACEIMU AECIUM

ACEINN ANNICE, CANINE

ACEINS CASEIN

ACEINT ENATIC

ACEINV CAVE-IN

ACEINX AXENIC

ACEIPS APICES

ACEIQU CAIQUE

ACEIRR CARRIE, RACIER

ACEIRS CARIES

ACEIRU CURIAE

ACEISS CASSIE

ACEISV VESICA

ACEITV ACTIVE

ACEIVV VIVACE

ACEJKT JACKET

ACEJLO CAJOLE

ACEKLM MACKLE

ACEKLS ALECKS

ACEKLT TACKLE

ACEKLY LACKEY

ACEKNR CANKER

ACEKPR PACKER

ACEKPT PACKET

ACEKRR RACKER

ACEKRS CREAKS, SACKER

ACEKRT RACKET, TACKER

ACEKRY CREAKY

ACEKST CASKET

ACELLO LOCALE

ACELLR CALLER, CELLAR, RECALL

ACELMR CALMER, CARMEL, MARCEL

ACELMS CAMELS, MASCLE, MESCAL

ACELMT CAMLET

ACELMU ALMUCE, CAELUM

ACELNN CANNEL

ACELNR LANCER

ACELNS LANCES

ACELNT CANTLE, CENTAL, LANCET

ACELNU CUNEAL, LAUNCE, UNLACE

ACELOR CAROLE, COALER, ORACLE

ACELOS SOLACE

ACELOT LOCATE

ACELOV ALCOVE, COEVAL

ACELPR CARPEL, PARCEL, PLACER

ACELPS PLACES

ACELPT PLACET

ACELQU CALQUE, CLAQUE

ACELRR CARREL

ACELRS SCALER, SCLERA

ACELRT CARTEL, CLARET, RECTAL

ACELRW CLAWER

ACELSS SCALES

ACELST CASTLE, CLEATS

ACELSU CLAUSE

ACELSV CALVES

ACELTT CATTLE

ACELTY ACETYL

ACELYY CLAYEY

ACEMNP ENCAMP

ACEMNR CARMEN

ACEMNU ACUMEN

ACEMOP POMACE

ACEMOS CAMEOS

ACEMOT COMATE

ACEMPR CAMPER

ACEMRS CREAMS, SCREAM

ACEMRY CREAMY

ACEMTU ACETUM

ACENNS CANNES

ACENNU NUANCE

ACENNY ANNECY

ACENOR CORNEA

ACENOS CANOES, OCEANS

ACENOT OCTANE

ACENPR PRANCE

ACENPS PECANS

ACENRS CARNES, CASERN, CRANES

ACENRT CANTER, CARNET, CRETAN, NECTAR, RECANT, TRANCE

ACENRV CAVERN, CRAVEN

ACENST ASCENT, SECANT, STANCE

ACENSU USANCE

ACEOPS PASCOE

ACEOPT CAPOTE, TOE CAP

ACEOPW COWPEA

ACEORS COARSE

ACEORX COAXER

ACEOTV AVOCET, OCTAVE

ACEPPR CAPPER

ACEPRS CAPERS, ESCARP, PARSEC, RECAPS, SCRAPE, SPACER

ACEPRT CARPET

ACEPRU APERCU

ACEPSS SPACES

ACEPST ASPECT

ACEPTU TEACUP

ACEQSU CASQUE
ACERRS RACERS, SCARER
ACERRT CARTER, CRATER,
  TRACER
ACERRU CURARE
ACERRV CARVER
ACERSS CARESS, SCARES
ACERST CARETS, CASTER,
  CRATES, RECAST, TRACES
ACERSU SAUCER
ACERSY SCAREY
ACERSZ CRAZES
ACERTU CURATE
ACERTY TRACEY
ACESST CASTES
ACESSU CAUSES, SAUCES
ACESTU CUESTA
ACESTY STACEY
ACFFHY CHAFFY
ACFFLS SCLAFF
ACFGIN FACING
ACFILO AFL-CIO
ACFILS FISCAL
ACFINT IN FACT
ACFIOS FIASCO
ACFIPY PACIFY
ACFLNO FALCON, FLACON
ACFLRU FULCRA
ACFMOR CORFAM
ACFNOR FRANCO
ACFNRS FRANCS
ACFORT FACTOR
ACFRSS SCARFS
ACFRST CRAFTS
ACFRTY CRAFTY
ACGGIN CAGING
ACGGIO AGOGIC
ACGGRY CRAGGY
ACGHIN ACHING, ICHANG
ACGHOU GAUCHO
ACGHTU CAUGHT
ACGIKN CAKING
ACGILL GALLIC
ACGILN LACING
ACGILR GARLIC
ACGILS GLACIS
ACGILY CAGILY
ACGINN CANING
ACGINO AGONIC
ACGINP PACING
ACGINR CARING, RACING
ACGINS CASING
ACGINT ACTING
ACGINV CAVING

ACGINW CAWING
ACGIRS CIGARS
ACGIRT TRAGIC
ACGIUU IGUACU
ACGNOR GAR*,CON
ACGNOS CONGAS,
  GASCON
ACGORS CARGOS
ACGORU COUGAR
ACGTTU CATGUT
ACHHNU HAUNCH
ACHHTT THATCH
ACHIIS ISCHIA
ACHIJK HIJACK
ACHIKW HAWICK
ACHILO LOCHIA
ACHILP CALIPH
ACHINR INARCH, RANCHI
ACHINS CHAINS
ACHIPS PHASIC
ACHIPT HAPTIC
ACHIRS CHAIRS, CHARIS,
  RACHIS
ACHKKU CHUKKA
ACHKLS CHALKS
ACHKLY CHALKY
ACHKRU CHUKAR
ACHKSS SHACKS
ACHKSW WHACKS
ACHKTW THWACK
ACHLLO CHOLLA
ACHLNU LAUNCH,
  NUCHAL
ACHLOR CHORAL
ACHLRY ARCHLY
ACHMNU MANCHU
ACHMOR CHROMA
ACHMPS CHAMPS
ACHMRS CHARMS
ACHMSS CHASMS
ACHMSU SUMACH
ACHNOR ANCHOR
ACHNOS NACHOS
ACHNPU PAUNCH
ACHNST CHANTS,
  SNATCH, STANCH
ACHNTU NAUTCH
ACHNTY CHANTY
ACHOPR CARHOP
ACHORS SORCHA
ACHPTY PATCHY
ACHRST CHARTS, STARCH
ACHSSW SCHWAS
ACHSTW SWATCH

ACHSTY YACHTS
ACHTTY CHATTY
ACIILS SIALIC, SILICA
ACIILT ITALIC
ACIIRT TRICIA
ACIJQU JACQUI
ACIKLN CALKIN
ACIKMR KARMIC
ACIKNP INK-CAP
ACIKNS INK SAC
ACIKNT CATKIN
ACIKPX PICKAX
ACILLN CALL-IN, CLINAL
ACILLP PLICAL
ACILLS LILACS, SCILLA
ACILLY LACILY
ACILMO COLIMA
ACILMS CLAIMS
ACILMX CLIMAX
ACILNO ALNICO, COLINA,
  NICOLA, OILCAN
ACILNT TINCAL
ACILNU LUCIAN, LUCINA,
  UNCIAL
ACILNV CALVIN
ACILOR LORICA
ACILOS SOCIAL
ACILOT COITAL
ACILRT CITRAL, RICTAL
ACILRU ULRICA, URACIL,
  URALIC
ACILRY RACILY
ACILSV SLAVIC
ACIMNO ANOMIC,
  CAMION, MONICA
ACIMNT MANTIC
ACIMOR ROMAIC
ACIMOS MOSAIC
ACIMOT ATOMIC
ACIMPS SCAMPI
ACIMPT IMPACT
ACIMRS RACISM
ACIMRY MYRICA
ACIMST MASTIC
ACINNT TANNIC
ACINOS CASINO
ACINOT ACTION, ATONIC,
  CATION
ACINOX ANOXIC
ACINPS PANICS
ACINPT CATNIP
ACINRS CAIRNS
ACINRT CATRIN
ACINRU URANIC

ACINST ANTICS
ACINSU ACINUS
ACINTT INTACT
ACINTU TUNICA
ACINUV VICUÑA
ACIORS SCORIA
ACIORT AORTIC
ACIOST SCOTIA
ACIOSV OVISAC
ACIOTZ AZOTIC
ACIPRS PRISCA
ACIPRY PIRACY
ACIQTU ACQUIT
ACIRSS CRASIS
ACIRST CRISTA, RACIST
ACIRSV VICARS
ACIRTU URATIC
ACISSS CASSIS
ACISTT ATTICS, STATIC
ACITUY ACUITY
ACITVY CAVITY
ACKLOS CLOAKS
ACKLSS SLACKS
ACKMSS SMACKS
ACKNPU UNPACK
ACKNRS CRANKS
ACKNRY CRANKY
ACKNSS SNACKS
ACKORS CROAKS
ACKPSY SKYCAP
ACKQSU QUACKS
ACKRST TRACKS
ACKSST STACKS
ACLLMU CALLUM
ACLLMY CALMLY
ACLLNO CLONAL
ACLLOR COLLAR
ACLLOS LOCALS
ACLLOW CALLOW
ACLLPU CALL-UP
ACLLSU CALLUS
ACLMMY CLAMMY
ACLMOP COPALM
ACLMOR CLAMOR
ACLMPS CLAMPS
ACLMTU TALCUM
ACLNOS CASLON
ACLNUY LUNACY
ACLOPU COPULA, CUPOLA
ACLORR CORRAL
ACLORS CARLOS, CAROLS,
CORALS
ACLORU OCULAR
ACLOST COSTAL

ACLOSV VOCALS
ACLOTU TOLUCA
ACLPSS CLASPS, SCALPS
ACLRRU CRURAL
ACLRSW CRAWLS, SCRAWL
ACLSSY CLASSY
ACMMOS COMMAS
ACMNNO CONMAN
ACMNOO MONACO
ACMNOR MACRON
ACMNOS MASCON,
SOCMAN
ACMNOW COWMAN
ACMOPS CAMPOS
ACMOST MASCOT
ACMOTT TOMCAT
ACMPRS CRAMPS
ACMPSS SCAMPS
ACMPSU CAMPUS
ACMRSU MARCUS,
SACRUM
ACMSTU MUSCAT
ACMUUV VACUUM
ACNNNO CANNON
ACNNOS CANONS
ACNNOT CANNOT,
CANTON
ACNNOY CANYON
ACNNRY CRANNY
ACNOOR CORONA,
RACOON
ACNOPS CAPONS
ACNOPY CANOPY
ACNORR RANCOR
ACNORS ACORNS
ACNORT CANTOR,
CARTON
ACNORY CRAYON
ACNOST CANTOS
ACNOTT OCTANT
ACNOTU TOUCAN
ACNOTX CAXTON
ACNSTU CANTUS, TUSCAN
ACNSTY SCANTY
ACOOTV OCTAVO
ACOPRT CAPTOR
ACOPTW COWPAT
ACORRT CARROT,
TROCAR
ACORSS ACROSS, OSCARS
ACORST ACTORS,
CASTOR, CO-STAR,
SCROTA
ACORTV CAVORT

ACORTX OXCART
ACORYZ CORYZA
ACOSST ASCOTS, COASTS
ACPPRY CRAPPY
ACPPSU CUPPAS
ACPRSS SCARPS, SCRAPS
ACPRSU CARPUS
ACPSTU CATSUP, UPCAST
ACRRWY WAR CRY
ACRSTT TRACTS
ACSTTY SCATTY
ADDDEG GADDED
ADDDEL ADDLED
ADDDEN ADDEND
ADDDEP PADDED
ADDDFY DAFYDD
ADDEEH HEADED
ADDEEN DEADEN
ADDEEV EVADED
ADDEGO GOADED
ADDEGR GADDER,
GRADED
ADDEHN HANDED
ADDEHS DASHED, SHADED
ADDEIL DIALED, LADDIE
ADDEIM DIADEM, MADDIE
ADDEIR RAIDED
ADDELL LADLED
ADDELN DANDLE,
LANDED
ADDELO LOADED
ADDELP PADDLE
ADDELR ALDRED,
LADDER, LARDED,
RADDLE
ADDELS SADDLE
ADDELU LAUDED
ADDELW DAWDLE,
WADDLE
ADDELY DEADLY
ADDEMM DAMMED
ADDEMN DAMNED,
DEMAND, MADDEN
ADDEMP DAMPED
ADDEMR MADDER
ADDENR DANDER,
DARNED
ADDENS SADDEN, SANDED
ADDENW DAWNED
ADDEOR ADORED,
DEODAR
ADDEOS DADOES
ADDEPP DAPPED
ADDEPR DRAPED

ADDERS ADDERS, DREADS,
    SADDER
ADDERT DARTED, TRADED
ADDERW EDWARD,
    WARDED
ADDGIN ADDING
ADDGIO GADOID
ADDGLU DUGALD
ADDGOO OGDOAD
ADDIMR MADRID
ADDIMY MIDDAY
ADDLNO DONALD
ADDNOS ADD-ONS
ADDNRU DURAND
ADDORS DORSAD
ADDORT DOTARD
ADDOST AT ODDS
ADDRSY DRYADS
ADEEFM DEFAME
ADEEFN DEAFEN
ADEEFR FEARED
ADEEFT DEFEAT
ADEEGG DEGAGE
ADEEGR AGREED,
    DRAGEE, GEARED
ADEEHI HAIDEE
ADEEHL HEALED
ADEEHP HEAPED
ADEEHR ADHERE,
    HEADER
ADEEHT HEATED
ADEEHV HEAVED
ADEEIL AEDILE
ADEEIT IDEATE
ADEEKL LEAKED
ADEEKP PEAKED
ADEELN LEADEN, LEANED
ADEELP LEAPED, PEALED
ADEELR DEALER, LEADER
ADEELS LEASED, SEALED
ADEELT ELATED
ADEELV LEAVED
ADEEMN DEMEAN
ADEEMO OEDEMA
ADEEMR REAMED,
    REMADE
ADEEMT TEAMED
ADEENN DEANNE,
    ENNEAD
ADEENR ANDRÉE,
    EARNED, ENDEAR,
    NEARED
ADEENT ANTEED
ADEENV EVADNE

ADEENW WEANED
ADEEPR REAPED
ADEEPS PESADE
ADEEPT PEDATE
ADEERR DEARER,
    READER, REARED,
    REREAD
ADEERS ERASED, RESEDA,
    SEARED
ADEERV EVADER
ADEERW DRAWEE
ADEERX EXEDRA
ADEEST SEATED, SEDATE,
    TEASED
ADEFGG FAGGED
ADEFGN FAG END,
    FANGED
ADEFIL AFIELD, FAILED
ADEFIN FADE-IN
ADEFIR FRIEDA
ADEFKL FLAKED
ADEFLM FLAMED
ADEFLO FOALED, LOAFED
ADEFLR ALFRED, FLARED
ADEFLU FEUDAL
ADEFLW FLAWED
ADEFLY FLAYED
ADEFMO FOAMED
ADEFMR FARMED,
    FRAMED
ADEFNN FANNED
ADEFNW FAWNED
ADEFOR FEDORA
ADEFRT DAFTER, FARTED,
    RAFTED
ADEFRY DEFRAY, FRAYED
ADEFST FASTED
ADEFTW WAFTED
ADEGGG GAGGED
ADEGGJ JAGGED
ADEGGL LAGGED
ADEGGN GANGED,
    NAGGED
ADEGGR DAGGER,
    RAGGED
ADEGGS SAGGED
ADEGGT GADGET,
    TAGGED
ADEGGU GAUGED
ADEGGW WAGGED
ADEGHS GASHED
ADEGII EGIDIA
ADEGIN GAINED
ADEGIY ADYGEI

ADEGKW GAWKED
ADEGLL GALLED
ADEGLN ANGLED,
    DANGLE, GLENDA
ADEGLO GAOLED, OLD
    AGE
ADEGLR GERALD, GLARED
ADEGLS GLADES
ADEGLZ GLAZED
ADEGMM GAMMED
ADEGNR DANGER,
    GANDER, GARDEN,
    RANGED
ADEGNU AUGEND
ADEGNW GNAWED,
    GWENDA
ADEGOR DOG-EAR
ADEGOS DAGOES,
    DOSAGE, SEA DOG
ADEGOT DOTAGE
ADEGPP GAPPED
ADEGPS GASPED
ADEGPW GAWPED
ADEGRR GERARD,
    GRADER, REGARD
ADEGRS GRADES
ADEGRT GRATED
ADEGRU ARGUED
ADEGRY GRAYED
ADEGRZ GRAZED
ADEGSS GASSED
ADEGST STAGED
ADEGSW WADGES
ADEHHS HASHED
ADEHIL HAILED, HALIDE
ADEHIR HARDIE
ADEHJS HADJES
ADEHJZ HEDJAZ
ADEHKR HARKED
ADEHKW HAWKED
ADEHLN HANDEL,
    HANDLE
ADEHLR HERALD
ADEHLS LASHED
ADEHLT HALTED
ADEHLU HAULED
ADEHLV HALVED
ADEHMM HAMMED
ADEHMR HARMED
ADEHMS MASHED,
    SHAMED
ADEHNO HEAD-ON
ADEHNP DAPHNE
ADEHNR HARDEN

ADEHNY HAYDEN
ADEHOX HOAXED
ADEHPR HARPED
ADEHPS PHASED, SHAPED
ADEHPT HEPTAD
ADEHRR HARDER
ADEHRS DASHER, SHARED
ADEHRT DEARTH,
  HATRED, THREAD
ADEHSS DASHES, SHADES
ADEHST DEATHS
ADEHSV SHAVED
ADEHSW WASHED
ADEHSY HYADES
ADEHTW THAWED
ADEHYY HEYDAY
ADEIIM MAIDIE
ADEIJL JAILED
ADEILL ALLIED
ADEILM MAILED, MEDIAL
ADEILN DANIEL, DELIAN,
  DENIAL, LEAD-IN, NAILED
ADEILP ALIPED, ELAPID,
  PLEIAD
ADEILR DERAIL, RAILED,
  RELAID
ADEILS IDEALS, LADIES,
  SAILED
ADEILT DETAIL, DILATE,
  TAILED
ADEILU AUDILE
ADEILW WAILED
ADEIMM MAIMED
ADEIMN DAMIEN,
  MAIDEN, MEDIAN,
  MEDINA
ADEIMR ADMIRE
ADEIMU MAUDIE
ADEINN DIANNE, NADINE
ADEINO IDONEA
ADEINP PAINED
ADEINR RAINED
ADEINS SANDIE, SENDAI,
  SINEAD
ADEINT DETAIN
ADEINV INVADE
ADEINW EDWINA
ADEIOT IODATE
ADEIPR DIAPER, PAIRED,
  REPAID
ADEIRR RAIDER
ADEIRS RAISED
ADEIRT TIRADE
ADEIRV VARIED

ADEISS ASIDES, DAISES
ADEISU ADIEUS
ADEISV ADVISE, VISAED
ADEITV DATIVE
ADEITW WAITED
ADEITX TAXIED
ADEIUX ADIEUX
ADEIVW WAIVED
ADEJMM JAMMED
ADEJRR JARRED
ADEJRU ADJURE
ADEJUV DÉJÀ VU
ADEJZZ JAZZED
ADEKKY YAKKED
ADEKLN KENDAL
ADEKLR LARKED
ADEKLS SLAKED
ADEKLT TALKED
ADEKLW WALKED
ADEKMR MARKED
ADEKMS MASKED
ADEKNR DANKER,
  DARKEN, KENDRA,
  NARKED, RANKED
ADEKNS SNAKED
ADEKNW WANKED
ADEKNY YANKED
ADEKOS SOAKED
ADEKOY OKAYED
ADEKPR PARKED
ADEKQU QUAKED
ADEKRR DARKER
ADEKRS DRAKES
ADEKST SKATED, STAKED
ADELLP PALLED
ADELLR LADLER
ADELLS LADLES
ADELLU ALLUDE, ALUDEL
ADELLW WALLED
ADELMP PALMED
ADELMR DERMAL,
  MEDLAR
ADELMS DAMSEL,
  MEDALS
ADELMT MALTED
ADELMU MAULED
ADELNO LOANED
ADELNP PLANED
ADELNR DARNEL
ADELNS ELANDS, LANDES
ADELNT DENTAL
ADELNU UNLEAD
ADELOR LOADER,
  ORDEAL, RELOAD

ADELOS ALDOSE
ADELPP DAPPLE, LAPPED
ADELPR PEDLAR
ADELPS LAPSED, PEDALS
ADELPT PLATED
ADELPW DEWLAP
ADELPY PLAYED
ADELRR DARREL, LARDER
ADELRU ALURED, LAUDER
ADELRY DEARLY
ADELST DELTAS, LASTED,
  SALTED, SLATED, STALED
ADELSV SALVED, SLAVED
ADELSY DELAYS
ADELUV VALUED
ADELZZ DAZZLE
ADEMMN MADMEN
ADEMMR RAMMED
ADEMNN MANNED
ADEMNO DAEMON,
  MENADO, MOANED,
  MODENA
ADEMNP DAMPEN
ADEMNR REMAND
ADEMNS AMENDS,
  DESMAN
ADEMNT TANDEM
ADEMNU UNMADE
ADEMOP POMADE
ADEMOR RADOME,
  ROAMED
ADEMOT MOATED
ADEMOW MEADOW
ADEMPP MAPPED
ADEMPR DAMPER
ADEMPT TAMPED
ADEMPU MADE-UP
ADEMRR MARRED
ADEMRS DREAMS
ADEMRT DREAMT
ADEMRW WARMED
ADEMRY DREAMY
ADEMSS MASSED
ADEMSU AMUSED
ADEMTT MATTED
ADENNP PANNED
ADENNT TANNED
ADENNU DUENNA
ADENNW WANNED
ADENOS ANODES
ADENOT ATONED,
  DONATE
ADENPP APPEND, NAPPED
ADENPR PANDER, REPAND

ADENPT PANTED, PEDANT, PENTAD
ADENPW PAWNED
ADENPX EXPAND
ADENRR DARNER, DARREN, ERRAND
ADENRS SANDER, SNARED
ADENRT ARDENT, RANTED
ADENRU UNREAD
ADENRW ANDREW, WANDER, WARDEN, WARNED
ADENRY DENARY, YARNED
ADENSS SEDANS
ADENSU SUNDAE
ADENTT ATTEND
ADENTV ADVENT
ADENTW WANTED
ADENWY DWAYNE, YAWNED
ADEOPS SOAPED
ADEORR ROARED
ADEORS SOARED
ADEORW REDOWA
ADEOSS ODESSA
ADEOSV VADOSE
ADEOTT TO DATE
ADEOVW AVOWED
ADEPPR DAPPER, RAPPED
ADEPPS SAPPED
ADEPPT TAPPED
ADEPPY YAPPED
ADEPPZ ZAPPED
ADEPRR DRAPER
ADEPRS DRAPES, PADRES, PARSED, RASPED, SPADER, SPARED, SPREAD
ADEPRT DEPART, PARTED, PETARD, PRATED
ADEPRW WARPED
ADEPRY PRAYED
ADEPSS PASSED, SPADES
ADEPST ADEPTS, PASTED
ADEPSU PAUSED
ADEPSY SPAYED
ADEPTT PATTED
ADEPTU UPDATE
ADERRT DARTER, RETARD, TARRED, TRADER
ADERRW DRAWER, REWARD, WARDER, WARRED

ADERRY DREARY
ADERST STARED, TRADES, TREADS
ADERSW SEWARD, WADERS
ADERTT RATTED, TETRAD
ADERTV ADVERT
ADERTW WARTED
ADERUY AUDREY
ADERXY X-RAYED
ADESSS SASSED
ADESST STEADS
ADESSU DESSAU
ADESTT STATED, TASTED
ADESTV STAVED
ADESTW WASTED
ADESTY STAYED, STEADY
ADESWY SWAYED
ADETTT TATTED
ADFFOR AFFORD
ADFFRY DRAFFY
ADFGIN FADING
ADFGLY GADFLY
ADFIRT ADRIFT
ADFIRY FRIDAY
ADFLTY DAFTLY
ADFNOU AU FOND
ADFRRU DARFUR
ADFRST DRAFTS
ADFRSU FRAUDS
ADFRSW DWARFS
ADFRTY DRAFTY
ADGGOT DOG TAG
ADGGRY DRAGGY
ADGIIN AIDING
ADGILN LADING, LIGAND
ADGILO ALGOID
ADGIMY DIGAMY
ADGINO GANOID
ADGINR DARING, GRADIN, IN DRAG
ADGINT DATING
ADGINW WADING
ADGINY GDYNIA
ADGINZ DANZIG, DAZING
ADGIRV GRAVID
ADGLLO OLD LAG
ADGLLY GLADLY
ADGLNS GLANDS
ADGLOP LAPDOG
ADGLOU DOUGAL
ADGLOY DAYGLO
ADGLSY GLADYS
ADGMOS DOGMAS

ADGNOR DRAGON
ADGNOS GONADS
ADGNRS GRANDS
ADGRSU GRADUS, GUARDS
ADHHIT HADITH
ADHHLU HULDAH
ADHHOW HOWDAH
ADHHWY WHYDAH
ADHIJS HADJIS, JIHADS
ADHIKU HAIDUK
ADHILO HALOID
ADHILT ALDITH
ADHIMR DIRHAM
ADHINS DANISH, SANDHI
ADHIOR HAIRDO
ADHIPS APHIDS
ADHIRS RADISH
ADHIRY HYDRIA, RIYADH
ADHLOP ADOLPH
ADHLOR HAROLD
ADHLOT OLD HAT
ADHLRY HARDLY
ADHMNO HODMAN
ADHNNU UNHAND
ADHNOR HADRON, HARD-ON, RHONDA
ADHNOU HOUDAN
ADHNOY HAYDON
ADHNSY SHANDY
ADHORS HOARDS
ADHORW HOWARD
ADHOSW SHADOW
ADHPRU HARD UP, PURDAH
ADHRSS SHARDS
ADHRSY HYDRAS
ADHSSU SADHUS
ADIIKO AIKIDO
ADIILN INLAID
ADIILO ODILIA
ADIIMR MIDAIR
ADIINN INDIAN
ADIINV AVIDIN
ADIIPR DIAPIR
ADIJMS MASJID
ADIJNO ADJOIN
ADIKMO MIKADO
ADIKNP INKPAD, KIDNAP
ADIKTT DIKTAT
ADILLP PALLID
ADILMO AMIDOL
ADILMS DISMAL
ADILMY MILADY
ADILNN INLAND

ADILNO LADINO
ADILNR ALDRIN
ADILNS ISLAND
ADILNU UNLAID
ADILNW ALDWIN
ADILOS ISOLDA
ADILOZ OZALID
ADILPS PLAIDS
ADILRS LAIRDS
ADILRZ LIZARD
ADILST DISTAL
ADILVY AVIDLY
ADIMNO DOMAIN
ADIMOT DIATOM
ADIMRS DISARM
ADIMRU RADIUM
ADIMRY MYRIAD
ADIMSS SADISM
ADIMST AMIDST
ADIMSY DISMAY
ADIMWY MIDWAY
ADINOR DORIAN,
   INROAD, ORDAIN
ADINOX DIOXAN
ADINPT PANDIT
ADINPU UNPAID
ADINRS DINARS, DRAINS,
   NADIRS
ADINRU DURIAN
ADINRW INWARD
ADINSU UNSAID
ADINSV DIVANS, VIANDS
ADINTY DAINTY
ADIORS RADIOS
ADIORT ADROIT, DORITA
ADIPPU PAID-UP
ADIPRS RAPIDS, SPARID
ADIPSX SPADIX
ADIRRY AIR-DRY
ADIRST ASTRID, TRIADS
ADIRSU RADIUS
ADIRWZ WIZARD
ADISST SADIST
ADISTU AUDITS
ADISTV DAVITS
ADJKOU JUDOKA
ADJNOR JORDAN
ADJORR JARROD
ADJSTU ADJUST
ADKKNO KOKAND
ADKLRY DARKLY
ADLLOR DOLLAR
ADLMNO ALMOND,
   DOLMAN, OLD MAN

ADLMOS DOLMAS
ADLMPY DAMPLY
ADLMTU TALMUD
ADLNOP POLAND
ADLNOR ARNOLD,
   LARDON, ROLAND,
   RONALD
ADLNOT DALTON
ADLNOU UNLOAD
ADLNPU UPLAND
ADLNWY ALDWYN
ADLORS DORSAL
ADLOSS DOSSAL
ADLOSU ALDOUS
ADLOSW OSWALD
ADLRRY DARRYL
ADLRSW DRAWLS
ADLRWY DRAWLY
ADLSTU ADULTS
ADMNOR RANDOM
ADMNOS DAMSON,
   NOMADS
ADMNOY DYNAMO,
   MONDAY
ADMNPY DYMPNA
ADMNUY MAUNDY
ADMORR RAMROD
ADMORU MADURO
ADNNOU ADNOUN
ADNOPR PARDON
ADNOPT DOPANT
ADNORU AROUND
ADNORW ONWARD
ADNOTY DAYTON
ADNRST STRAND
ADNRTU TUNDRA
ADNSST STANDS
ADNSTY DYNAST
ADNSUY SUNDAY
ADOPRY PARODY
ADORRU ARDOUR
ADPRUW UPWARD
ADQSSU SQUADS
ADRSSW SWARDS
ADRTWY TAWDRY
AEEFIR FAERIE
AEEFLM FEMALE
AEEFRR FEARER
AEEGGN ENGAGÉ
AEEGGR REGGAE
AEEGIR ARIEGE
AEEGLL ALLEGE
AEEGLP PELAGE
AEEGLR GALERE, REGALE

AEEGLS EAGLES
AEEGLT EAGLET, LEGATE
AEEGLU LEAGUE
AEEGMN MANEGE,
   MÉNAGE
AEEGMR GRAEME,
   MEAGRE
AEEGMT GAMETE,
   METAGE
AEEGNN ENNAGE
AEEGNR ENRAGE,
   GENERA
AEEGNS SENEGA
AEEGNT NEGATE
AEEGNV AVENGE, GENEVA
AEEGOP APOGEE
AEEGOT GOATEE
AEEGRS GREASE
AEEGST EGESTA
AEEGSW SEWAGE
AEEHHW HEE-HAW
AEEHJN JEHANE
AEEHKT HEKATE
AEEHLN HELENA
AEEHLR HEALER
AEEHLX EXHALE
AEEHLY HEALEY
AEEHMR HAREEM
AEEHMU HEAUME
AEEHNN HEENAN
AEEHNP PEAHEN
AEEHNS SHEENA
AEEHNT ATHENE,
   ETHANE
AEEHNV HEAVEN
AEEHNX HEXANE
AEEHPR HEAPER
AEEHRR HEARER, REHEAR
AEEHRS HAERES, HEARSE
AEEHRT AETHER, HEATER,
   HEREAT, REHEAT
AEEHRV HEAVER
AEEHSV HEAVES, SHEAVE
AEEHTX THE AXE
AEEIJN JEANIE
AEEILN AILEEN, ELAINE
AEEIRS EASIER
AEEJNN JEANNE
AEEKLN ALKENE
AEEKLR LEAKER
AEEKMR REMAKE
AEEKNW WEAKEN
AEEKNY YANKEE
AEEKRT RETAKE

AEEKRU EUREKA
AEEKRW WEAKER
AEELLL ALLELE
AEELLM MALLEE
AEELLS SALLEE
AEELLV A LEVEL
AEELMN ENAMEL
AEELMP EMPALE
AEELNN LEANNE
AEELNR ARLEEN, ARLENE,
   LEANER
AEELNS SELENA
AEELNT LATEEN
AEELNV LEAVEN
AEELOT OLEATE
AEELPR LEAPER, REPEAL
AEELPS ASLEEP, ELAPSE,
   PLEASE, SAPELE
AEELRS LEASER, RESALE,
   SEALER
AEELRT ELATER, RELATE
AEELRV LEAVER, REVEAL
AEELSS EASELS, LEASES
AEELST TEASEL
AEELSV LEAVES, SLEAVE
AEELSW WEASEL
AEELTV VELATE
AEELWY LEEWAY
AEEMNR MEANER,
   RENAME
AEEMNS ENEMAS,
   SEAMEN
AEEMNX EXAMEN
AEEMPR AMPERE
AEEMRR REAMER
AEEMRS SEAMER
AEEMSS SESAME
AEEMTX TAXEME
AEENNT NEATEN
AEENNX ANNEXE
AEENQU QUEENA
AEENRR EARNER, NEARER
AEENRS RANEES, SERENA
AEENRT NEATER
AEENRV VERENA
AEENST SATEEN, SENATE
AEENSU UNEASE
AEENUV AVENUE
AEEPRR REAPER
AEEPRS PARSEE
AEEPRT REPEAT
AEEPST PESETA
AEEPSX APEXES
AEEPSY PAYEES

AEEQTU EQUATE
AEERRR REARER
AEERRS ERASER
AEERRT TEARER
AEERRW WEARER
AEERST ARÊTES, EASTER,
   EATERS, RESEAT, SEATER,
   TEASER, TERESA
AEERSU RESEAU, UREASE
AEERSV AVERSE
AEERVW WEAVER
AEESST TEASES
AEESSW SEESAW
AEESTT ESTATE
AEESVW WEAVES
AEFFGR GAFFER
AEFFGS GAFFES
AEFFIN AFFINE
AEFFIP PIAFFE
AEFFLR RAFFLE
AEFFLW WAFFLE
AEFFRZ ZAFFER
AEFGLN FLANGE
AEFGOR FORAGE
AEFHRS AFRESH
AEFHRT FATHER, HAFTER
AEFILL FAILLE
AEFILN FINALE
AEFILR FERIAL
AEFILT FETIAL
AEFIMN FAMINE
AEFINN FENIAN
AEFIRR FAIRER
AEFIRY AERIFY
AEFIST FIESTA
AEFITX FIXATE
AEFJNT FANJET
AEFKLR FLAKER
AEFKLS FLAKES
AEFKRS FAKERS, FREAKS
AEFKRY FREAKY
AEFLLN FALLEN
AEFLLR FALLER
AEFLMR FLAMER
AEFLMS FLAMES
AEFLNX FLAXEN
AEFLOR LOAFER
AEFLOT FOETAL
AEFLOV FOVEAL
AEFLRS FALSER, FLARES
AEFLRT FALTER
AEFLRU EARFUL, FERULA
AEFLRY FLAYER
AEFLST FESTAL

AEFLSY SAFELY
AEFLTY FEALTY
AEFMOR FEMORA
AEFMRR FARMER,
   FRAMER
AEFMRS FRAMES
AEFMRT FERMAT
AEFNNR FANNER
AEFNRR FARREN
AEFNRU FRAUEN
AEFNRW FAWNER
AEFNST FASTEN
AEFNSU UNSAFE
AEFNTT FATTEN
AEFNZZ FEZZAN
AEFPPR FRAPPÉ
AEFRRS FRASER
AEFRRT FRATER, RAFTER
AEFRRY RAREFY
AEFRRZ FRAZER
AEFRST AFTERS, FASTER,
   STRAFE
AEFRSW WAFERS
AEFRTT FATTER
AEFRTW WAFTER
AEFSST FEASTS, SAFEST
AEFSTY SAFETY
AEGGGL GAGGLE
AEGGGR GAGGER
AEGGHL HAGGLE
AEGGIM MAGGIE
AEGGIN AGEING
AEGGLR GARGLE
AEGGLW WAGGLE
AEGGNR GANGER,
   GRANGE, NAGGER
AEGGNS GANGES
AEGGNU GANGUE
AEGGRT GARGET
AEGGRU GAUGER
AEGGSU GAUGES
AEGHIR HEGIRA
AEGHIS GEISHA
AEGHIW AWEIGH
AEGHMN MEGHAN
AEGHMO HOMAGE,
   OHMAGE
AEGHNO EOGHAN
AEGHNR HANGER
AEGHRT GARETH,
   GATHER
AEGHSS GASHES
AEGILN GENIAL, LINAGE
AEGILS GISELA, SILAGE

AEGILT LIGATE
AEGILZ EL GIZA
AEGIMN ENIGMA,
  GAMINE
AEGIMP MAGPIE
AEGIMR GAMIER,
  MARGIE, MIRAGE
AEGIMS AGEISM, IMAGES
AEGINR EARING, GAINER,
  REGAIN, REGINA
AEGINS EASING
AEGINT EATING
AEGINU GUINEA
AEGIPP PIPAGE
AEGIRT GAITER
AEGIRW EARWIG
AEGIRZ GEZIRA
AEGIST AGEIST
AEGISV VISAGE
AEGITU AUGITE
AEGITY GAIETY
AEGJLN JANGLE
AEGJLT JET LAG
AEGJTU JUGATE
AEGKRW GAWKER
AEGKST GASKET
AEGLLU ULLAGE
AEGLLY GALLEY
AEGLMN MANGLE
AEGLMS GLEAMS
AEGLMY GAMELY
AEGLNN GLENNA
AEGLNO ANGELO
AEGLNR ANGLER,
  ERLANG
AEGLNS ANGELS, ANGLES
AEGLNT TANGLE
AEGLNU LANGUE
AEGLNW WANGLE
AEGLOR GALORE,
  GAOLER
AEGLOT LEGATO
AEGLOV LOVAGE
AEGLPU PLAGUE
AEGLRR LARGER
AEGLRS GLARES, LAGERS
AEGLRT TERGAL
AEGLRV GRAVEL
AEGLRY ARGYLE
AEGLRZ GLAZER
AEGLSV GAVELS
AEGLSY SAGELY
AEGLSZ GLAZES
AEGMMR GRAMME

AEGMMS SMEGMA
AEGMNR ENGRAM,
  GERMAN, MANGER
AEGMNS GASMEN
AEGMNT MAGNET
AEGMOS OMEGAS
AEGMUY MAGUEY
AEGMUZ ZEUGMA
AEGNNO NONAGE
AEGNNP PENANG
AEGNNT GANNET
AEGNOR GAENOR,
  ONAGER, ORANGE
AEGNRR GARNER,
  RANGER
AEGNRS ANGERS, RANGES
AEGNRT ARGENT,
  GARNET
AEGNRV GRAVEN
AEGNRW GNAWER
AEGNRY ANERGY
AEGNST AGENTS
AEGNSV VEGANS
AEGOPT POTAGE
AEGORT ORGEAT
AEGORU AERUGO
AEGOTU OUTAGE
AEGOTW TOWAGE
AEGOVY VOYAGE
AEGPRS GASPER, GRAPES
AEGPRT PARGET
AEGPRU PRAGUE
AEGRRT GARRET,
  GARTER, GRATER
AEGRRU ARGUER
AEGRRV GRAVER
AEGRRY GRAYER
AEGRRZ GRAZER
AEGRSS GASSER, SARGES
AEGRST GRATES, GREATS,
  STAGER
AEGRSU AUGERS, SAUGER
AEGRSV GRAVES
AEGRSW SWAGER,
  WAGERS
AEGRSY GREASY
AEGRSZ GRAZES
AEGRTT TARGET
AEGRTU TUAREG
AEGRTY GYRATE
AEGSSS GASSES
AEGSST STAGES
AEGSSU USAGES
AEGSTY GAYEST, STAGEY

AEHHLT HEALTH
AEHHRS REHASH
AEHHRT HEARTH
AEHHSS HASHES
AEHHST HEATHS, SHEATH
AEHHTY HEATHY
AEHIJL ELIJAH
AEHIJR HEJIRA
AEHIKN HANKIE
AEHIKZ KEZIAH
AEHILL LEILAH
AEHILM HIEMAL
AEHILN INHALE
AEHILP PHILAE
AEHILR HAILER
AEHILS ELISHA, ILESHA,
  SHEILA
AEHILT HALITE
AEHILW AWHILE
AEHIMN HAEMIN
AEHIMR HERMIA
AEHIMS MASHIE
AEHIMT HAMITE
AEHINR HERNIA
AEHINT AITHNE, IANTHE
AEHINW ANHWEI
AEHIRS ASHIER, SHERIA
AEHIRZ HAZIER
AEHIST HESTIA, SAITHE
AEHITT HATTIE
AEHJJS HAJJES
AEHKLT THEKLA
AEHKNR HANKER,
  HARKEN
AEHKNS SHAKEN
AEHKRS SHAKER
AEHKRW HAWKER
AEHKSS SHAKES
AEHLLL HALLEL
AEHLLS HELLAS
AEHLLT LETHAL
AEHLLY HALLEY
AEHLMP PELHAM
AEHLMR HARLEM
AEHLMT HAMLET,
  THELMA
AEHLNS HANSEL
AEHLOR LAHORE
AEHLOS HALOES
AEHLOT LOATHE
AEHLRS LASHER
AEHLRT HALTER, LATHER
AEHLRU HAULER
AEHLRW WHALER

AEHLRY HARLEY

AEHLSS HASSLE, LASHES

AEHLST HALEST, HASLET, LATHES

AEHLSV HALVES

AEHLSW WHALES

AEHLSY ASHLEY

AEHLSZ HAZELS

AEHLTW WEALTH

AEHLYY HAYLEY

AEHMMR HAMMER

AEHMMY MAYHEM

AEHMNR ARNHEM, HERMAN

AEHMNT ANTHEM, HAMNET, HETMAN

AEHMNU HUMANE

AEHMOT AT-HOME

AEHMPR HAMPER

AEHMRR HARMER

AEHMRS HAREMS, MASHER

AEHMSS MASHES

AEHMST THAMES

AEHNNS HANSEN

AEHNPP HAPPEN

AEHNPT HAPTEN

AEHNRT ANTHER, THENAR

AEHNRY HARNEY

AEHNST ATHENS, HASTEN, THANES

AEHNSV HAVENS, SHAVEN

AEHNSY HYENAS

AEHNTV HAVEN'T

AEHNTX XANTHE

AEHORS ASHORE, HOARSE

AEHORX HOAXER

AEHOSX HOAXES

AEHPRR HARPER

AEHPRS PHRASE, SERAPH, SHERPA

AEHPSS PHASES, SHAPES

AEHPST SPATHE

AEHRRS RASHER, SHARER

AEHRRT RATHER

AEHRSS RASHES, SHARES, SHEARS

AEHRST EARTHS, HEARST, HEARTS, SARTHE

AEHRSV SHAVER

AEHRSW HAWSER, WASHER

AEHRTT HATTER, THREAT

AEHRTW THAWER, WREATH

AEHRTY EARTHY, HEARTY

AEHRVW WHARVE

AEHRVY HARVEY

AEHSSS SASHES

AEHSSV SHAVES

AEHSSW WASHES

AEHSTW SWATHE

AEIILM EMILIA

AEIILS LIAISE

AEIIMS MAISIE

AEIINR EIRIAN

AEIIPT TAIPEI

AEIIRR AIRIER

AEIJKR RIJEKA

AEIJLR JAILER

AEIJMM JEMIMA

AEIJNN JANINE

AEIKLS ALSIKE

AEIKLT TALKIE

AEIKNR KIERAN

AEIKNS KINASE

AEIKNT INTAKE

AEIKRS KAISER

AEILLN LIENAL, LINEAL

AEILLR ALLIER

AEILLS ALLIES

AEILLT TELIAL

AEILMN MENIAL

AEILMP IMPALE

AEILMR MAILER, MARIEL

AEILMS MALISE

AEILNN LIANNE

AEILNP ALPINE, NEPALI, PINEAL

AEILNR ARLINE, LARINE, LINEAR, NAILER

AEILNS ALIENS, SALINE, SELINA

AEILNT ENTAIL, TINEAL

AEILNV ALVINE, ELVINA, VALINE, VEINAL, VENIAL

AEILNX XENIAL

AEILOS ELOISA

AEILPS ESPIAL, LIPASE

AEILPT APLITE

AEILRR RAILER

AEILRS ISRAEL, SAILER, SERIAL

AEILRT RETAIL, RETIAL

AEILRU AURIEL, LAURIE

AEILRV AVERIL, ELVIRA

AEILRW LAWRIE, WAILER

AEILRX RAILEX

AEILRZ LAZIER

AEILSS AISLES, ELISSA

AEILSV VALISE

AEILSX ALEXIS

AEILSY EASILY

AEIMMN AMMINE

AEIMMR MAIMER

AEIMNN IN NAME

AEIMNO ANOMIE

AEIMNR AIRMEN, ARMINE, MARINE, MARNIE, REMAIN

AEIMNS AMIENS

AEIMNT INMATE

AEIMNX MAXINE

AEIMRS ARMIES

AEIMRT MARTIE

AEIMST SAMITE

AEIMTT MATTIE

AEINNR NERINA

AEINNS INSANE, SIENNA

AEINNT INNATE

AEINNV VIENNA

AEINPR RAPINE

AEINRR RAINER

AEINRS ARISEN, ARSINE, SARNIE

AEINRT RATINE, RETAIN, RETINA

AEINRV RAVINE, VAINER

AEINRZ ZANIER

AEINSS SANIES

AEINST TISANE

AEINSV NAVIES

AEINTV NATIVE

AEINTY YENTAI

AEIOPR PEORIA

AEIOPT OPIATE

AEIOSV SAVOIE

AEIPPT PEPITA

AEIPRR RAPIER, REPAIR

AEIPRS ASPIRE, PARIES, PERSIA, PRAISE

AEIPRT PIRATE

AEIPTT PATTIE

AEIRRS RAISER, SIERRA

AEIRRT ARTIER

AEIRRV ARRIVE

AEIRRW WARIER

AEIRSS RAISES

AEIRST SATIRE

AEIRTT ATTIRE, RATITE

AEIRTW WAITER

AEIRVW WAIVER, WAVIER
AEIRVX XAVIER
AEIRWX WAXIER
AEISST SIESTA
AEISSU AUSSIE
AEISSZ ASSIZE
AEJMMR JAMMER
AEJMRT RAMJET
AEJMST JETSAM
AEJNNO JOANNE
AEJNOT TAEJON
AEJNST SEJANT
AEJNUU JUNEAU
AEJPRS JASPER
AEJPRY JAPERY
AEKLNR LANKER, RANKLE
AEKLNS ANKLES
AEKLNT ANKLET
AEKLNW KNAWEL
AEKLNY ALKYNE
AEKLPS SPLAKE
AEKLRR LARKER
AEKLRS SLAKER
AEKLRT TALKER
AEKLRW WALKER
AEKLSS KASSEL
AEKLST LASKET
AEKLTU AUKLET
AEKLWY WEAKLY
AEKMNR KERMAN
AEKMNU UNMAKE
AEKMPU MAKE-UP
AEKMRR MARKER, REMARK
AEKMRS MAKERS, MASKER
AEKMRT MARKET
AEKNNY KENYAN
AEKNOR KOREAN
AEKNOW AWOKEN
AEKNRR RANKER
AEKNRT TANKER
AEKNRW NEWARK, WANKER
AEKNSS SNAKES, SNEAKS
AEKNSV KNAVES
AEKNSY SNEAKY
AEKOPT TOPEKA
AEKORS ARKOSE, SOAKER
AEKPRR PARKER
AEKPTU TAKEUP, UPTAKE
AEKQRU QUAKER
AEKQSU QUAKES, SQUEAK

AEKRST SKATER, STRAKE, STREAK, TAKERS, TASKER
AEKSST SKATES, STAKES, STEAKS
AEKSTW TWEAKS
AEKWYY KEYWAY
AELLLU LUELLA
AELLMT MALLET
AELLMY LAMELY
AELLNS ANSELL
AELLPS LAPELS
AELLPT L-PLATE, PALLET, TELPAL
AELLPY PALELY
AELLRT TALLER
AELLRU ALLURE, LAUREL
AELLRY REALLY
AELLST STELLA
AELLSY ALLEYS
AELLTU LUTEAL
AELLTW WALLET
AELLTY LATELY
AELLVY VALLEY
AELMNS ANSELM, LE MANS, MANSEL
AELMNT LAMENT, MANTEL, MANTLE, MENTAL
AELMNU MANUEL
AELMNY LAYMEN, MANLEY, MEANLY, NAMELY
AELMOR MORALE
AELMOS SALOME
AELMPR PALMER
AELMPS MAPLES, SAMPLE
AELMPU AMPULE
AELMRS REALMS
AELMRT ARMLET
AELMRU MAULER
AELMRV MARVEL
AELMRY AYLMER
AELMST LAMEST, METALS
AELMSU SAMUEL
AELMSY MEASLY
AELMTU AMULET
AELMTY TAMELY
AELNNR LANNER
AELNOR LOANER
AELNOT ETALON, LEAN-TO
AELNPP PEN PAL
AELNPR PARNEL, PLANER, REPLAN

AELNPS NAPLES, PANELS, PLANES
AELNPT PLANET, PLATEN
AELNRT ANTLER, LEARNT, RENTAL
AELNRU LAUREN, NEURAL, UNREAL
AELNRV VERNAL
AELNRY NEARLY
AELNSU UNSEAL
AELNSV NAVELS
AELNSY SANELY
AELNTT LATENT, LATTEN, TALENT
AELNTU LUNATE
AELNTV LEVANT
AELNTY NEATLY
AELOPP ALEPPO
AELOPR PAROLE
AELOPS EL PASO
AELOPT PELOTA
AELOPX POLEAX
AELOST OSTEAL
AELOSV LOAVES
AELOTZ ZEALOT
AELPPR LAPPER, RAPPEL
AELPPS APPLES
AELPPT LAPPET
AELPPU PAPULE
AELPQU PLAQUE
AELPRR PARREL
AELPRS LAPSER, PEARLS
AELPRT PALTER, PLATER
AELPRU PLEURA
AELPRY PARLEY, PEARLY, PLAYER, REPLAY
AELPSS LAPSES, SEPALS
AELPST PALEST, PASTEL, PETALS, PLATES, PLEATS, SEPTAL, STAPLE
AELPTU PETULA
AELQSU EQUALS, SQUEAL
AELRRY RARELY
AELRSS LASERS
AELRST ALERTS, LASTER, SALTER, SLATER, STALER, STELAR
AELRSV SALVER, SERVAL, SLAVER, VELARS
AELRSY LAYERS, RELAYS, SLAYER
AELRTT LATTER, RATTLE
AELRTV TRAVEL, VARLET
AELRTW WALTER

AELRTY LYRATE
AELRUV VALUER
AELRWY LAWYER
AELRYY YEARLY
AELRZZ RAZZLE
AELSSS LASSES
AELSST SLATES, TASSEL
AELSSV SALVES, SLAVES
AELSTT LATEST
AELSTU SALUTE
AELSTV VALETS, VESTAL
AELSUV VALUES
AELSUX SEXUAL
AELSVV VALVES
AELSYZ SLEAZY
AELTTT TATTLE
AELTTW WATTLE
AELTUX LUXATE
AELUUV UVULAE
AELUVV VULVAE
AEMMNR MERMAN
AEMMRR RAMMER
AEMMRY YAMMER
AEMNNO EAMONN
AEMNNP PENMAN
AEMNNR MANNER
AEMNOR ENAMOR,
    MOANER
AEMNOY YEOMAN
AEMNPU PNEUMA
AEMNQU MANQUÉ
AEMNRT MARTEN
AEMNRU MANURE
AEMNST STAMEN
AEMNSU UNSEAM
AEMNSY YES-MAN
AEMNTX TAXMEN
AEMORR REMORA,
    ROAMER
AEMORS RAMOSE
AEMORX XEROMA
AEMPPR PAMPER
AEMPRT TAMPER
AEMPRV REVAMP
AEMQRU MARQUE
AEMQSU MASQUE
AEMRRR MARRER
AEMRRU ARMURE
AEMRRW WARMER
AEMRSS MASERS, SMEARS
AEMRST MASTER,
    STREAM, TAMERS
AEMRSU MASERU,
    MAUSER

AEMRSY RAMSEY, SMEARY
AEMRTT MATTER
AEMRTU MATURE
AEMSSS MASSES
AEMSSU ASSUME, SEAMUS,
    SEUMAS
AEMSSX XMASES
AEMSTT TAMEST
AEMSTU MEATUS
AEMSTY STEAMY
AEMSYZ ZYMASE
AEMTTU MUTATE
AENNOY ANYONE
AENNRS SENNAR
AENNRT TANNER
AENNRW WANNER
AENNST NANTES
AENNTT TENANT
AENOPW WEAPON
AENOPY PAEONY
AENORS REASON, SEÑORA
AENORT ATONER,
    ORNATE
AENORV VERONA
AENORW ROWENA
AENORX ROXANE
AENOSS SEASON
AENOTZ ZONATE
AENOWY ONE-WAY
AENPPR NAPPER
AENPRT ENTRAP, PARENT,
    TREPAN
AENPRW ENWRAP
AENPRZ PANZER
AENPTT PATENT, PATTEN
AENPTU PEANUT
AENRRS SNARER
AENRRT ERRANT, RANTER
AENRRW WARNER,
    WARREN
AENRRY RAYNER
AENRSS SNARES
AENRST ASTERN, STERNA
AENRSV RAVENS
AENRSW ANSWER
AENRSY SENARY
AENRTT NATTER
AENRTU NATURE
AENRTV TAVERN
AENRTW WANTER
AENRWY YAWNER
AENSST ASSENT, SANEST
AENSSU ANUSES
AENSTU AUSTEN, UNSEAT

AENSTY ANSTEY
AENSUV NAEVUS
AENSUY UNEASY
AENTTU ATTUNE,
    TAUTEN, TETUAN
AENTTX EXTANT
AEOPPS APPOSE
AEOPQU OPAQUE
AEOPRS OPERAS
AEOPRT PROTEA
AEOPTT TEAPOT
AEOPTY TEAPOY
AEORRR ROARER
AEORRS SOARER
AEORRU AURORE
AEORSS SEROSA
AEORSU AROUSE
AEORSZ AZORES
AEORTT ROTATE
AEORVW AVOWER
AEPPRR RAPPER
AEPPRS PAPERS, SAPPER
AEPPRT TAPPER
AEPPRU PAUPER
AEPPRY PAPERY, PREPAY,
    YAPPER
AEPPTT TAPPET
AEPPTU PUPATE
AEPRRS PARSER, RASPER,
    SPARER
AEPRRT PRATER
AEPRRU PARURE, UPREAR
AEPRRW PREWAR, WARPER
AEPRRY PRAYER
AEPRSS SPARES, SPARSE,
    SPEARS
AEPRST PATERS, REPAST,
    TAPERS
AEPRSU PAUSER
AEPRTT PATTER
AEPRUV RAVE-UP
AEPSSS PASSES
AEPSST PASTES, STAPES
AEPSSU PAUSES
AEQRSU SQUARE
AEQRUV QUAVER
AEQSUY QUEASY
AERRST ARREST, RAREST,
    RASTER, STARER
AERRSV RAVERS
AERRTT RATTER
AERRTY ARTERY
AERSST ASSERT, STARES
AERSSU ASSURE

AERSSV SAVERS
AERSSW WRASSE
AERSTT AT REST, STATER,
TASTER, TREATS
AERSTV STARVE
AERSTW RAWEST, WASTER,
WATERS
AERSTX EXTRAS
AERSTY ESTRAY, STAYER
AERSTZ ERSATZ
AERSUU AUREUS
AERSWY SAWYER, SWAYER
AERTTT TATTER
AERTTU TAUTER
AERTTY TREATY
AERTUU AUTEUR
AERTWY WATERY
AESSSS ASSESS, SASSES
AESSST ASSETS
AESSSY ESSAYS
AESSTT STATES, TASTES
AESSTV STAVES
AESSTW SWEATS, WASTES
AESTTT ATTEST
AESTTU ASTUTE, STATUE
AESTWY SWEATY
AESTYY YEASTY
AFFFOR FAR-OFF
AFFGUW GUFFAW
AFFIKR KAFFIR
AFFIMR AFFIRM
AFFIRT TARIFF
AFFLOY LAY-OFF
AFFLUX AFFLUX
AFFOPY PAYOFF
AFFSST STAFFS
AFGGIO FOGGIA
AFGGLY FLAGGY
AFGGOT FAGGOT
AFGIKN FAKING
AFGILN FINGAL
AFGINR FARING
AFGINX FAXING
AFGINZ FAZING
AFGISY GASIFY
AFGLNO FLAGON
AFGLNU FUNGAL
AFGLRU FRUGAL
AFGOTU FUGATO
AFGRST GRAFTS
AFGSTU GUSTAF
AFHIIR HAIRIF
AFHIKL KHALIF
AFHIMS FAMISH

AFHIOS OAFISH
AFHIST FAITHS
AFHLOO LOOFAH
AFHLSY FLASHY
AFHMOT FATHOM
AFHRSW WHARFS
AFHSST SHAFTS
AFIIJN FIJIAN
AFIILL FILIAL
AFIILN FINIAL
AFIKRS FAKIRS
AFILLS FLAILS
AFILMY FAMILY
AFILNO FINOLA
AFILNS FINALS
AFILNU FULANI
AFILNV FLAVIN
AFILNY FINLAY
AFILOR FOLIAR
AFILPS PILAFS
AFILRY FAIRLY
AFILRZ FRAZIL
AFILSY SALIFY
AFIMNY INFAMY
AFIMRY RAMIFY
AFIMSS MASSIF
AFINNO FANION
AFINNT INFANT
AFINRU UNFAIR
AFINST FAINTS
AFINSU FUSAIN
AFIRRS FRIARS
AFIRRY FRIARY
AFIRTY RATIFY
AFKLNS FLANKS
AFKLSS FLASKS
AFLLOR FLORAL
AFLLOW FALLOW
AFLLTY FLATLY
AFLLUW LAWFUL
AFLMNU MANFUL
AFLMOR FORMAL
AFLMRU ARMFUL,
FULMAR
AFLMYY MAYFLY
AFLNOT FONTAL
AFLNTU FLAUNT
AFLORV FLAVOR
AFLOST FLOATS
AFLOTY FLOATY
AFLRTU ARTFUL
AFLSTU FAULTS, FLATUS
AFLSWY SAWFLY
AFLTUY FAULTY

AFMORT FORMAT
AFMOSU FAMOUS
AFNNRY FRANNY
AFNSSU SNAFUS
AFORRW FARROW
AFORSV FAVORS
AFORSY FORAYS
AFORTU FAR-OUT
AFORUV FAVOUR
AGGGIN GAGING
AGGHIS HAGGIS
AGGHSY SHAGGY
AGGILO LOGGIA
AGGIMN GAMING
AGGINP GAPING, PAGING
AGGINR RAGING
AGGINW WAGING
AGGINZ GAZING
AGGIWW WIGWAG
AGGIZZ ZIGZAG
AGGLSY SLAGGY
AGGLWY WAGGLY
AGGMOT MAGGOT
AGGNSY SNAGGY
AGGQUY QUAGGY
AGHILT ALIGHT
AGHINN HANG IN
AGHINR HARING
AGHINS HSIANG
AGHINT HATING
AGHINV HAVING
AGHINZ HAZING
AGHIRS GARISH
AGHIRT ARIGHT
AGHKRU GURKHA
AGHLLU GULLAH
AGHLOS GALOSH
AGHLSU LAUGHS
AGHNOO OONAGH
AGHNPU HANG-UP
AGHNTU NAUGHT
AGHNUV VAUGHN
AGHOQU QUAHOG
AGHPRS GRAPHS
AGHTTU TAUGHT
AGIILN AILING, NILGAI
AGIIMN AIMING
AGIINR AIRING
AGIJNW JAWING
AGIJSW JIGSAW
AGIKMN MAKING
AGIKNN ANKING
AGIKNR RAKING
AGIKNS ASKING, GASKIN

AGIKNT TAKING	AGJNOR JARGON	AGORSY ARGOSY
AGIKNW WAKING	AGKLNO KALONG	AGORTU RAGOUT
AGILLU LIGULA	AGKNOR ANGKOR	AGOSTU OUTGAS
AGILMM GIMMAL	AGKNRU KURGAN	AGOTTU TAUTOG
AGILMN LAMING,	AGKORT GO-KART	AGRSSU SUGARS
MALIGN	AGLLNO GALLON	AGRSSY GRASSY
AGILMO GLIOMA	AGLLOP GALLOP	AGRSTU TRAGUS
AGILNP PALING	AGLLRY ARGYLL	AGRSUY SUGARY
AGILNS SIGNAL	AGLNNO LONGAN	AGRUUY AUGURY
AGILNU LINGUA	AGLNOO LAGOON	AGSTUU AUGUST
AGILNY GAINLY, LAYING	AGLNOS SLOGAN	AGSTUV GUSTAV
AGILNZ LAZING	AGLNOU LANUGO	AHHIMS HAMISH
AGILOR GLORIA	AGLNOY LOYANG	AHHKOO HOOKAH
AGILOT GALIOT	AGLNRU LANGUR	AHHOOR HOORAH
AGILOV OGIVAL	AGLNSY SLANGY	AHHORT HATHOR
AGILRY GLAIRY	AGLNTY TANGLY	AHHORW HOWRAH
AGIMNN NAMING	AGLNUU UNGUAL,	AHHPPU HUPPAH
AGIMNR ARMING,	UNGULA	AHHRRU HURRAH
INGRAM, MARGIN	AGLORS LARGOS	AHHRST THRASH
AGIMNT MATING,	AGLOSS GLOSSA	AHHUZZ HUZZAH
TAMING	AGLOST GLOATS	AHIILT AILITH, LITHIA
AGIMST STIGMA	AGLPUY PLAGUY	AHIITT TAHITI
AGIMWW WIGWAM	AGLRUV VULGAR	AHIJJS HAJJIS
AGINNW AWNING,	AGLSSY GLASSY	AHIJNS JHANSI
WANING	AGLSUV VALGUS	AHIJOS JOSIAH
AGINOR ORIGAN	AGMMNO GAMMON	AHIKMO KOHIMA
AGINOS SAIGON	AGMMNU MAGNUM	AHIKMS HAKIMS
AGINPR PARING, RAPING	AGMNNU GUNMAN	AHIKRS RAKISH
AGINPT TAPING	AGMNOR MORGAN	AHILLL LILLAH
AGINPV PAVING	AGMNOS MANGOS	AHILLZ ZILLAH
AGINPW PAWING	AGMNSU MAGNUS	AHILMP IMPHAL
AGINPY PAYING	AGMOOY OOGAMY	AHILNR RHINAL
AGINRR RARING	AGMORS ORGASM	AHILNU INHAUL
AGINRS GRAINS	AGMORT MARGOT	AHILNY HYALIN
AGINRT RATING	AGMOYZ ZYGOMA	AHILPS PALISH, PHIALS
AGINRU AIRGUN, UGRIAN	AGMPUZ GAZUMP	AHILRY HILARY
AGINRV INGVAR, RAVING	AGNNOT TONGAN	AHILST LATISH
AGINRY GRAINY	AGNNRY GRANNY	AHILSV LAVISH
AGINRZ RAZING	AGNNTU ANTUNG	AHILTW WITHAL
AGINSS ASSIGN	AGNOQU QUANGO	AHILYZ HAZILY
AGINST GIANTS, SATING	AGNORS GROANS,	AHIMNT HIT MAN
AGINSV SAVING	ORGANS, SARONG	AHIMOR MOHAIR
AGINSW SAWING	AGNORY GAYNOR	AHIMPS MISHAP
AGINSY SAYING	AGNOST TANGOS,	AHINPT HATPIN
AGINTX TAXING	TSONGA	AHINRU UNHAIR
AGINVW WAVING	AGNOSW WAGONS	AHINSS SHANSI
AGINWX WAXING	AGNOTU NOUGAT	AHINSU HUSAIN
AGINWY YAWING	AGNPRS SPRANG	AHINSV VANISH
AGIORU GIAOUR	AGNPRU NAGPUR	AHINSW WASHIN
AGIORV VIRAGO	AGNRST GRANTS	AHINTT TANITH, TIN HAT
AGIOTU AGOUTI	AGNRTY GANTRY	AHIOPS SOPHIA
AGIRST GRATIS	AGNSTW TWANGS	AHIORT HOT AIR
AGIRTU GUITAR	AGNTWY TWANGY	AHIPRS PARISH
AGJLMO LOGJAM	AGORST ARGOTS, GROATS	AHIPRU RUPIAH

AHIRRS HARRIS, SIRRAH
AHIRST THIRSA, TRISHA
AHIRSV RAVISH
AHIRSZ SHIRAZ
AHIRTW WRAITH
AHIRTZ THIRZA, TIRZAH
AHISTU HIATUS
AHISTV VASHTI
AHJMOT JOTHAM
AHJOSU JOSHUA
AHKLNU KHULNA
AHKMOW MOHAWK
AHKNOW HANKOW
AHKNPU PUNKAH
AHKNRS SHRANK
AHKNSS SHANKS
AHKNST THANKS
AHKRSS SHARKS
AHLLMU MULLAH
AHLLOO HALLOO
AHLLOS HALLOS
AHLLOW HALLOW
AHLLRT THRALL
AHLLUX HALLUX
AHLMNY HAMLYN,
   HYMNAL
AHLMOS SHALOM
AHLNSU UNLASH
AHLOOP HOOP-LA
AHLORT HARLOT
AHLORW HARLOW
AHLOSS SHOALS
AHLOSY SHOALY
AHLPSS SPLASH
AHLPSU LASH-UP
AHLPSY PLASHY
AHLRSY RASHLY
AHLSSW SHAWLS
AHMMSY SHAMMY
AHMNOS HANSOM
AHMNPY NYMPHA
AHMNSU HUMANS
AHMNSY MYNAHS
AHMOST THOMAS
AHMOTU MAHOUT
AHMOWY HAYMOW
AHMRSY MARSHY
AHMRTW WARMTH
AHMSSU SHAMUS
AHNNSY SHANNY
AHNOOR HONORA
AHNOPR ORPHAN
AHNORS SHARON,
   SHORAN

AHNOSX XHOSAN
AHNOWY ANYHOW
AHNSTU HAUNTS
AHNSTY SHANTY
AHOORY HOORAY
AHOPST PASHTO, PATHOS,
   POTASH
AHOPTT TOP HAT
AHORRW HARROW
AHORRY HORARY
AHORTT THROAT
AHORTU AUTHOR
AHORTX THORAX
AHPRSS SHARPS
AHQSSU SQUASH
AHRRTU ARTHUR
AHRRUY HURRAY
AHRSSU HUSSAR
AHRSTY TRASHY
AHRTTW THWART
AHSSTU TUSSAH
AHSSTW SWATHS
AIIKLS LIKASI
AIILLN LILIAN
AIILLS LILIAS
AIILNS IN SAIL
AIILOV OLIVIA
AIILRY AIRILY
AIILSV SILVIA
AIIMMN MINIMA
AIIMMR MIRIAM
AIIMNR MAIRIN
AIIMNS SIMIAN
AIIMNT INTIMA
AIIMPR IMPAIR
AIINNN NINIAN
AIINNO IONIAN
AIINNZ ZINNIA
AIINRS RAISIN
AIINST ISATIN
AIINVV VIVIAN
AIIPTW WAPITI
AIIRST ISTRIA
AIIRTV TRIVIA
AIJJNU UJJAIN
AIJLNU JULIAN
AIJLOV JOVIAL
AIJOSS JOSIAS
AIJPRU JAIPUR
AIJRSV JARVIS
AIKLNO KAOLIN
AIKLNW WALK-IN
AIKLSU SALUKI
AIKMNR KIRMAN

AIKMOP MAIKOP
AIKMSU KUMASI
AIKNNP NAPKIN
AIKNPR PARKIN
AIKNRV NARVIK
AIKORT TROIKA
AIKTUW KUWAIT
AILLMU ALLIUM
AILLOT LOLITA
AILLPR PILLAR
AILLSV VILLAS
AILLSW WALLIS
AILLTW AT WILL
AILLYZ LAZILY
AILMNO OILMAN
AILMNR MARLIN
AILMNU ALUMNI
AILMNV MALVIN
AILMNY MAINLY
AILMOP LIPOMA
AILMOS SOMALI
AILMPR PRIMAL
AILMRT MITRAL, RAMTIL
AILMSS MISSAL
AILMSX SMILAX
AILMSY MISLAY
AILMTU LATIUM, ULTIMA
AILMUV VALIUM
AILMYZ MAZILY
AILNOS ALISON
AILNOT TALION
AILNPS PLAINS, SPINAL
AILNPT PLAINT, PLIANT
AILNRT TRINAL
AILNRU URINAL
AILNSS SNAILS
AILNST LATINS
AILNSU INSULA
AILNSV ANVILS, SILVAN
AILNSW IN-LAWS
AILNSY INLAYS
AILNTY LITANY
AILNVY VAINLY
AILNWY AYLWIN
AILNYZ ZANILY
AILORS SAILOR
AILORT RIALTO, TAILOR
AILORU AURIOL
AILOSU LOUISA
AILOSV VIOLAS
AILOSX OXALIS
AILOTX OXTAIL
AILPPS PIPALS
AILPRS APRILS, SPIRAL

AILPST PLAITS, SPITAL
AILQSU QUAILS
AILRRW WIRRAL
AILRST TRAILS, TRIALS
AILRSV RIVALS
AILRSY RIYALS
AILRTU RITUAL
AILRWY WARILY
AILSTV VITALS
AILSUV VISUAL
AILSVY SYLVIA
AILTXY LAXITY
AILVWY WAVILY
AILWXY WAXILY
AIMMOS MAOISM,
   MIMOSA
AIMMSX MAXIMS
AIMNNO AMNION,
   MINOAN
AIMNOR MARION
AIMNOS SIMONA
AIMNPT PITMAN
AIMNRT MARTIN
AIMNRV MARVIN
AIMNST MANTIS, MATINS,
   TAMSIN
AIMNSU ANIMUS
AIMNSY YASMIN
AIMNSZ NAZISM
AIMOPY MYOPIA
AIMOST MAOIST, TAOISM
AIMOSW MIAOWS
AIMOSX AXIOMS
AIMPRT ARMPIT, IMPART
AIMPSS PASSIM
AIMQSU MAQUIS
AIMRSU MARIUS
AIMRTU ATRIUM
AIMRTX MATRIX
AIMSSW SWAMIS
AIMSTU AUTISM
AINNNT TANNIN
AINNOS NASION
AINNOT ANOINT, NATION
AINNPW IN PAWN
AINNST TSINAN
AINOPS PIANOS
AINORS ROSINA
AINORT RATION
AINOSU SIOUAN
AINPRS SPRAIN
AINPST PAINTS, PINTAS,
   PTISAN
AINPSV SPAVIN

AINQRT QINTAR
AINQTU QUAINT
AINRST INSTAR, STRAIN,
   TRAINS
AINRSY SYRIAN
AINRTU IN A RUT, NUTRIA
AINRYZ ZYRIAN
AINSST SAINTS, STAINS
AINSSW SWAINS
AINSTT TITANS
AINSTU AUSTIN
AINSTY SANITY, SATINY
AINTVY VANITY
AIOORS ARIOSO
AIOPRT PORTIA
AIOPRV PAVIOR
AIOPST PATIOS, PATOIS
AIOPTU UTOPIA
AIORSS ORISSA
AIORST AORIST, ARTOIS,
   RATIOS, ROSITA
AIORSV SAVIOR
AIOSTT TAOIST
AIOSYZ ZOYSIA
AIPPRY PAPYRI
AIPPST PAPIST
AIPRST RAPIST, TAPIRS
AIPRSW RIPSAW
AIPRSX PRAXIS
AIPRTY PARITY
AIPRUY PYURIA
AIPSTW PITSAW
AIPSZZ PIZZAS
AIRRTY RARITY
AIRSST SITARS, STAIRS
AIRSSU RUSSIA
AIRSTT ARTIST, STRAIT,
   TRAITS
AIRSTV TRAVIS
AIRSTY STYRIA
AIRTTY YTTRIA
AISSST ASSIST, STASIS
AISSTV VISTAS
AISSTW WAISTS
AISTUW WATUSI
AJKORT RAJKOT
AJLOPY JALOPY
AJMORS MAJORS
AJNORT TROJAN
AJNSTU JAUNTS, JUNTAS
AJNTUY JAUNTY
AJPRTU RAJPUT
AKLLNY LANKLY
AKLMOY KOLYMA

AKLNOW WALK-ON
AKLNOX KLAXON
AKLNPS PLANKS
AKLNRY RANKLY
AKLOPS POLKAS
AKLOSV SLOVAK
AKLPUW WALK-UP
AKLSST STALKS
AKLSTY STALKY
AKMNSU UNMASK
AKMPRU MARKUP
AKNORU KORUNA
AKNPRS PRANKS
AKNPRU KANPUR
AKNPSS SPANKS
AKNSSW SWANKS
AKNSWY SWANKY
AKOTVY VOTYAK
AKPRSS SPARKS
AKQRSU QUARKS
AKQSUW SQUAWK
ALLMOS SLALOM
ALLMOW MALLOW
ALLMSS SMALLS
ALLNOP POLLAN
ALLNUU LUNULA
ALLOOP APOLLO
ALLOPR PALLOR
ALLOPW WALLOP
ALLORY ORALLY
ALLOST ATOLLS
ALLOSW SALLOW
ALLOSY ALLOYS
ALLOTW TALLOW
ALLOWW WALLOW
ALLPRU PLURAL
ALLQSU SQUALL
ALLSST STALLS
ALLSTY LASTLY
ALLUVV VULVAL
ALMMUY AMYLUM
ALMNOR NORMAL
ALMNOS SALMON
ALMNRY MARLYN
ALMNTU MULTAN
ALMORS MOLARS,
   MORALS
ALMORT MORTAL
ALMORU MORULA
ALMORY MALORY
ALMOST ALMOST,
   SMALTO
ALMPSS PSALMS
ALMQSU QUALMS

ALMRSU MURALS
ALMRWY WARMLY
ALMSUY ASYLUM
ALMTUU MUTUAL,
  UMLAUT
ALNNOU NOUNAL
ALNOOS ALONSO,
  SALOON
ALNOOZ ALONZO
ALNOSS SALONS
ALNOST TALONS
ALNOTV VOLANT
ALNOTY LAYTON
ALNPST PLANTS
ALNRSS SNARLS
ALNRSY SNARLY
ALNRUY URANYL
ALNRXY LARYNX
ALNSST SLANTS
ALNSTU SULTAN
ALNSVY SYLVAN
ALNTUW WALNUT
ALOOPS SALOOP
ALOPPR POPLAR
ALOPPT LAP-TOP
ALOPRR PARLOR
ALOPRT PATROL, PORTAL
ALOPST POSTAL
ALOQTU LOQUAT
ALORSV SALVOR
ALORSY ROYALS
ALORTY TAYLOR
ALORUV LOUVAR,
  OVULAR, VALOUR
ALOSSS LASSOS
ALOSSV SALVOS
ALOSTT TOTALS
ALOTUW OUTLAW
ALOTUY LAYOUT, OUTLAY
ALPPSU SLAP-UP
ALPRSU PULSAR
ALPRSW SPRAWL
ALPRTY PALTRY, PARTLY
ALPSSU LAPSUS
ALRSTW TRAWLS
ALRSTY STYLAR
ALRSUU URSULA
ALRSUW WALRUS
ALRTTY RATTLY, TARTLY
ALRUUV UVULAR
ALSSTU SALTUS
ALSTUV VAULTS
ALSTUY SALYUT
ALSTVY VASTLY

ALSUUV UVULAS
ALSUVV VULVAS
ALTTUY TAUTLY
AMMMNO MAMMON
AMMMOS MOMMAS
AMMORT MARMOT
AMMOSU OMASUM
AMMOXY MYXOMA
AMMPUW WAMPUM
AMMRSY SMARMY
AMMSTU SUMMAT
AMNNOR NORMAN
AMNOOR MAROON,
  ROMANO
AMNOPT TAMPON
AMNORR MARRON
AMNORS MANORS,
  RANSOM, ROMANS
AMNORT MATRON
AMNORY MORNAY,
  ROMANY
AMNOSS MASONS,
  SAMSON
AMNOTU AMOUNT,
  OUTMAN
AMNPTY TYMPAN
AMNRTU ANTRUM
AMNRTY MARTYN
AMNRVY MARVYN
AMNSSU SAMSUN
AMNTTU MUTANT
AMNTUU AUTUMN
AMOOTT TOMATO
AMOPRS PRO-AMS
AMORRT MORTAR
AMORRU ARMOUR
AMORRW MARROW
AMORRY ARMORY
AMORSS MORASS
AMORST STROMA
AMORSU AMOURS
AMORSY MAYORS
AMPRRU RAMPUR
AMPRST TRAMPS
AMPRUW WARM-UP
AMPSSS SPASMS
AMPSST STAMPS
AMPSSW SWAMPS
AMPSWY SWAMPY
AMRRTY MARTYR
AMRRUY MURRAY
AMRSSW SWARMS
AMRSTU STRUMA
ANNNUY YUNNAN

ANNOPZ POZNAN
ANNORT NATRON
ANNOST SONANT
ANNOSW WONSAN
ANNOTW WANTON
ANNOTY ANTONY,
  TANNOY
ANNPSU UNSNAP
ANNRTY TRANNY
ANNSTU SUNTAN
ANNTTU NUTANT
ANOOPS NO SOAP
ANOOPX A POX ON
ANOORS SONORA
ANOORT RATOON
ANOPRS APRONS,
  PARSON
ANOPRT PARTON,
  PATRON, TARPON
ANOPUY YAUPON
ANORRW NARROW
ANORRY RAYNOR
ANORSW ROWANS
ANORTT ATTORN
ANORTU OUTRAN
ANORTY NOTARY
ANORWY NORWAY
ANOSST SANTOS
ANOSSX SAXONS
ANOSXY SAXONY
ANPPSY SNAPPY
ANPRSW PRAWNS
ANPRTY PANTRY
ANPRUW UNWRAP
ANRSTU SATURN
ANRSUU URANUS
ANRSUY SUNRAY
ANRSYZ SYZRAN
ANRTTU TRUANT
ANRTTY TYRANT
ANRUWY RUNWAY,
  UNWARY
ANSTTU TAUNTS, TUTSAN
ANSTUV VAUNTS
ANSTWY WYSTAN
ANSTXY SYNTAX
ANSYZZ SNAZZY
ANVVYY VYVYAN
AOOPTT POTATO
AOOPTW PAOTOW
AOORRT ORATOR
AOOTTT TATTOO
AOPPPS POPPAS
AOPPRT POP ART

AOPRRT PARROT, RAPTOR
AOPRRU UPROAR
AOPRST PASTOR
AOPRSV VAPORS
AOPRUV VAPOUR
AOPTUY PAYOUT
AOQRTU QUARTO
AOQSTU QUOTAS
AORRST ROSTRA
AORRSW ARROWS
AORRSY ROSARY
AORRSZ RAZORS
AORRTY ROTARY
AORRWY YARROW
AORSST ASSORT, ROASTS
AORSTT STATOR, TAROTS
AORSTX STORAX
AORSUU AUROUS
AORSUV SAVOUR
AORSVY SAVORY
AORTVY VOTARY
AOSSTT STOATS, TOASTS
AOSSVY SAVOYS
AOSTWW SWATOW
AOTUWY WAY-OUT
AOTWWY TWO-WAY
APPPSU PAPPUS
APRRSY SPARRY
APRSST SPRATS, STRAPS
APRSSY SPRAYS
APRSTY PASTRY
AQRRUY QUARRY
AQRSTU QUARTS
AQRTUZ QUARTZ
AQSSTU SQUATS
AQSSUW SQUAWS
ARRSTY STARRY
ARSSTT STARTS
ARSSTU TARSUS
ARSSTW STRAWS
ARSSTY SATYRS, STRAYS
ARSTTU STUART
ARSTUU TAURUS
ARSTUX SURTAX
ARSTWY STRAWY
ARSTXY STYRAX
ASSTTU STATUS
BBBDEO BOBBED
BBBEIO BOBBIE
BBBELO BOBBLE
BBBELU BUBBLE
BBBHUU HUBBUB
BBBINO BOBBIN
BBBLUY BUBBLY

BBCDEU CUBBED
BBCELO COBBLE
BBCEOR COBBER
BBCEOW COBWEB
BBCHUY CHUBBY
BBCLUY CLUBBY
BBDDEI DIBBED
BBDDEU DUBBED
BBDEEI DEBBIE
BBDEEW WEBBED
BBDEFI FIBBED
BBDEFO FOBBED
BBDEGI GIBBED
BBDEGU BEDBUG
BBDEIJ JIBBED
BBDEIL DIBBLE
BBDEIR DIBBER, RIBBED
BBDEIY BIDE BY
BBDEJO JOBBED
BBDELO LOBBED
BBDEMO BOMBED,
   MOBBED
BBDEOO BOOBED
BBDEOR ROBBED
BBDEOS SOBBED
BBDERU RUBBED
BBDESU SUBBED
BBDETU TUBBED
BBDINO DOBBIN
BBDINU DUBBIN
BBEELP PEBBLE
BBEFIR FIBBER
BBEGIN EBBING
BBEGIR GIBBER
BBEGIT GIBBET
BBEGLO GOBBLE
BBEGOT GOBBET
BBEHLO HOBBLE
BBEHLU HUBBLE
BBEHOS HOBBES
BBEIIM IMBIBE
BBEIIS SIBBIE
BBEIJR JIBBER
BBEILN NIBBLE
BBEILR LIBBER
BBEILS BIBLES
BBEIOR ROBBIE
BBEIRR BRIBER
BBEJOR JOBBER
BBELMU BUMBLE
BBELNO NOBBLE
BBELNU NUBBLE
BBELOW WOBBLE
BBELPY PEBBLY, PLEBBY

BBELRU BURBLE, LUBBER,
   RUBBLE
BBEMNU BENUMB
BBEMOR BOMBER,
   MOBBER
BBEORR ROBBER
BBEORS SOBBER
BBERRU RUBBER
BBGINO GIBBON
BBGRUY GRUBBY
BBHMOS H-BOMBS
BBHNOO HOBNOB
BBIIIO IBIBIO
BBIKOS SKIBOB
BBILLU BULBIL
BBINOR RIBBON, ROBBIN
BBLLUU BULBUL
BBLNUY NUBBLY
BBLOWY BY-BLOW,
   WOBBLY
BBLRSU BLURBS
BBLRUY RUBBLY
BBNNOO BONBON
BBNSUY SNUBBY
BBORTU BURBOT
BBOSUY BUS BOY
BBRSUU SUBURB
BBSTUY STUBBY
BCDEEK BEDECK
BCDEIO BODICE
BCDEKU BUCKED
BCDEMO COMBED
BCDERU CURBED
BCDIOU CUBOID
BCEEHR BREECH
BCEEKT BECKET
BCEEMO BECOME
BCEEQU QUEBEC
BCEHLN BLENCH
BCEHOR BROCHE
BCEHRU CHERUB
BCEIKR BICKER
BCEIOX ICEBOX
BCEIPS BICEPS
BCEIRS SCRIBE
BCEIRT TERBIC
BCEIST BISECT
BCEJOT OBJECT
BCEKLU BUCKLE, LUBECK
BCEKNO BECKON
BCEKTU BUCKET
BCELNO EN BLOC
BCELOR CORBEL
BCELOU BOUCLE

BCEMOR COMBER	**BDEEOY** OBEYED	**BDENOY** BEYOND
BCEMRU CUMBER	**BDEEST** BESTED	**BDENRU** BURDEN,
BCENOU BOUNCE	**BDEETT** BETTED	BURNED
BCEOTT OBTECT	**BDEFFI** BIFFED	**BDENSU** SUNBED
BCGINU CUBING	**BDEFFU** BUFFED	**BDEOOT** BOOTED
BCHIOP PHOBIC	**BDEFIR** FIBRED	**BDEOOZ** BOOZED
BCHITY BITCHY	**BDEGGO** BOGGED	**BDEOPP** BOPPED
BCHLOT BLOTCH	**BDEGGU** BUGGED	**BDEOPR** PROBED
BCHMOU BOCHUM	**BDEGIN** BIG END	**BDEORR** BORDER ·
BCHNRU BRUNCH	**BDEGIR** BRIDGE	**BDEORS** DESORB
BCHNUY BUNCHY	**BDEGLU** BULGED	**BDEORT** DEBTOR
BCHOOR BROOCH	**BDEGNU** BUNGED	**BDEOSS** BOSSED
BCHOTY BOTCHY	**BDEGTU** BUDGET	**BDEOUY** BUOYED
BCIILM LIMBIC	**BDEHIN** BEHIND	**BDEPRU** BURPED
BCIINO BIONIC, NIOBIC	**BDEHLO** BEHOLD	**BDERRU** BURRED
BCIINU INCUBI	**BDEHOT** HOTBED	**BDESSU** BUSSED
BCIIOP BIOPIC	**BDEHSU** BUSHED	**BDESTU** BUSTED, DEBUTS
BCIIOT BIOTIC	**BDEIIR** BIRDIE, BRIDIE	**BDESUU** SUBDUE
BCILMS CLIMBS	**BDEIKL** BILKED	**BDETTU** BUTTED
BCILPU PUBLIC	**BDEILL** BILLED	**BDEUZZ** BUZZED
BCIMOR BROMIC	**BDEILO** BOILED, BOLIDE	**BDFIOR** FORBID
BCIMSU CUBISM	**BDEILR** BRIDLE	**BDGIIN** BIDING
BCINOR BICORN	**BDEIMU** IMBUED	**BDGIIR** BRIGID
BCIORS SORBIC	**BDEINN** BINNED	**BDGINO** BODING
BCIRRU RUBRIC	**BDEINR** BINDER, INBRED,	**BDHIRY** HYBRID
BCISTU CUBIST, CUBITS	REBIND	**BDIILO** LIBIDO
BCKLOS BLOCKS	**BDEINT** IN DEBT	**BDIIMR** MIDRIB
BCMOOS COMBOS	**BDEIOR** BORIDE	**BDIITT** TIDBIT
BCMORY CORYMB	**BDEIOS** BODIES	**BDIKNO** BODKIN
BCMRSU CRUMBS	**BDEIPS** BIPEDS	**BDILNS** BLINDS
BCMRUY CRUMBY	**BDEIRS** DEBRIS	**BDILNU** DUBLIN
BCNOOR BRONCO	**BDEIRU** BURIED	**BDILOY** BODILY
BCNOTU COBNUT	**BDEIRV** VERBID	**BDILSU** BUILDS
BCNOUY BOUNCY	**BDEIST** BIDETS, DEBITS	**BDIMOR** MORBID
BCOOWY COWBOY	**BDEISU** BUSIED	**BDINNU** UNBIND
BCRSSU SCRUBS	**BDEKLU** BULKED	**BDIOTU** OUTBID
BDDDEE BEDDED	**BDEKNU** BUNKED,	**BDIRTU** TURBID
BDDDEU BUDDED	DEBUNK	**BDLLOY** BOLDLY
BDDEER BEDDER	**BDEKOO** BOOKED	**BDLMUY** DUMBLY
BDDEGU BUDGED	**BDEKSU** BUSKED	**BDLNOS** BLONDS
BDDEIN BIDDEN	**BDELNO** BLONDE	**BDLNOY** BLODYN
BDDELU BUDDLE	**BDELNS** BLENDS	**BDLOOS** BLOODS
BDDENO BONDED	**BDELNU** BUNDLE	**BDLOOY** BLOODY, OLD
BDDERU REDBUD	**BDELOR** BOLDER	BOY
BDDIOR DO BIRD	**BDELOT** BOLTED	**BDLOUY** DOUBLY
BDDISU DISBUD	**BDELOU** DOUBLE	**BDNOOY** NOBODY
BDEEEF BEEFED	**BDELOW** BOWLED	**BDNOSU** BOUNDS
BDEEGG BEGGED	**BDEMMU** BUMMED	**BDOORS** BROODS
BDEEHL BEHELD	**BDEMNU** NUMBED	**BDOORY** BROODY
BDEEIL BELIED, EDIBLE	**BDEMOO** BOOMED	**BDORWY** BYWORD
BDEEIS BESIDE	**BDEMOY** EMBODY	**BDOSTU** DOUBTS
BDEEIT BETIDE	**BDEMPU** BUMPED	**BEEEFL** FEEBLE
BDEELN BLENDE	**BDEMRU** DUMBER	**BEEELT** BEETLE
BDEELT BELTED	**BDENNU** UNBEND	**BEEEMS** BESEEM

BEEERZ BREEZE
BEEFIL BELIEF
BEEFLL BEFELL
BEEFLY FEEBLY
BEEFOR BEFORE
BEEFRT BEREFT
BEEGLS GLEBES
BEEGNO BEGONE
BEEGNR BERGEN
BEEGRS GREBES
BEEGRT EGBERT
BEEGRU BURGEE
BEEHIR HERBIE
BEEHLT BETHEL
BEEHOP PHOEBE
BEEHOV BEHOVE
BEEHRW HEBREW
BEEHRY HEREBY
BEEHST BEHEST
BEEILR BELIER
BEEILZ BELIZE
BEEINR BERNIE
BEEIRT BERTIE
BEEISS BESSIE
BEEISV BEVIES
BEEISW BE WISE
BEEISX IBEXES
BEEKRU REBUKE
BEELLS BELLES
BEELMM EMBLEM
BEELNS BELSEN
BEELPS BLEEPS
BEELRS REBELS
BEELRT TREBLE
BEELSV BEVELS
BEEMMR MEMBER
BEEMNR BREMEN
BEEMRS EMBERS
BEEMSU BEMUSE
BEENNT BENNET
BEENOR ENROBE
BEENRU REUBEN
BEENTU BUTENE
BEEOOT BOOTEE
BEEOPP PEEPBO
BEEORY OBEYER
BEERRW BREWER
BEERST BERETS
BEERTT BETTER
BEERTV BREVET
BEERYZ BREEZY
BEFFRU BUFFER, REBUFF
BEFFTU BUFFET
BEFILM FIMBLE

BEFILO FOIBLE
BEFIRS FIBERS, FIBRES
BEFLMU FUMBLE
BEFLOO BEFOOL
BEFLOU BEFOUL
BEFLRY BELFRY
BEGGII BIGGIE
BEGGIR BIGGER
BEGGLO BOGGLE
BEGGRU BUGGER
BEGILO OBLIGE
BEGILR GERBIL
BEGILS BILGES
BEGINN BENIGN
BEGINO BIOGEN
BEGINR BERING
BEGINS BEINGS, BINGES
BEGIOS BOGIES
BEGIOU BOUGIE
BEGLNO BELONG
BEGLNU BLUNGE, BUNGLE
BEGLOS GLOBES
BEGLOT GOBLET
BEGLRU BUGLER, BURGLE
BEGLSU BUGLES, BULGES
BEGMSU BEGUMS
BEGNOY BYGONE
BEGOPX PEG BOX
BEGORU BROGUE
BEGOSY BOGEYS
BEGRRU BURGER
BEGRSU BRUGES
BEHILS ISHBEL
BEHILT BLITHE
BEHINT HENBIT
BEHKOR RHEBOK
BEHKRY KHYBER
BEHLMU HUMBLE
BEHLSU BUSHEL
BEHLTY BLYTHE
BEHMOR HOMBRE
BEHMRU HUMBER
BEHNOR HEBRON
BEHOOS HOBOES
BEHORT BOTHER
BEHRST BERTHS
BEHRTU HUBERT
BEHSSU BUSHES
BEIILL BILLIE
BEIISS IBISES
BEIKLR BILKER
BEIKOO BOOKIE
BEILLS LIBELS
BEILLT BILLET

BEILMN NIMBLE
BEILMO MOBILE
BEILMR LIMBER
BEILMW WIMBLE
BEILMY BLIMEY
BEILNR BERLIN
BEILNU NUBILE
BEILNY BY-LINE
BEILOR BOILER
BEILOS ISOBEL
BEIMOV B-MOVIE
BEIMOZ ZOMBIE
BEIMRT TIMBER, TIMBRE
BEIMRU ERBIUM, IMBRUE
BEINNO BENONI, BONNIE
BEINOR BONIER
BEINOT BENITO
BEINOV BOVINE
BEINRU BRUNEI
BEINTT BITTEN
BEIORS RIBOSE
BEIOTW BOW TIE
BEIQSU BISQUE
BEIRRU BURIER
BEIRRY BRIERY
BEIRST BESTIR, BISTRE, TRIBES
BEIRSU BRUISE, BUSIER, RUBIES
BEIRTT BITTER
BEIRTU BEIRUT
BEJJUU JUJUBE
BEJLMU JUMBLE
BEKLOS BLOKES
BEKNOR BROKEN
BEKNRU BUNKER
BEKOOT BETOOK
BEKORR BROKER
BEKOST BOSKET
BEKRSU BUSKER
BELLOU BOULLE, LOBULE
BELLOW BELLOW
BELLTU BULLET
BELMMU MUMBLE
BELMNY EMBLYN
BELMOY EMBOLY
BELMRU LUMBER, RUMBLE
BELMTU TUMBLE
BELNNY BLENNY
BELNOR NOBLER
BELNOS NOBLES
BELNOZ BENZOL
BELNTU UNBELT

BELNYZ BENZYL
BELOOR BOLERO
BELOPU PUEBLO
BELORT BOLTER
BELORU ROUBLE
BELORW BLOWER,
BOWLER
BELOSU BLOUSE, BOULES,
OBELUS
BELOSW BOWELS, ELBOWS
BELOTT BOTTLE
BELRRU BURLER
BELRSU RUBLES
BELRSY BERYLS
BELRTU BUTLER
BELRTY TREBLY
BELRUY BURLEY
BELSTU BLUEST, BUSTLE,
SUBLET, SUBTLE
BELTUU TUBULE
BEMNOT ENTOMB
BEMNOW BOWMEN,
ENWOMB
BEMNRU NUMBER
BEMORS SOMBRE
BEMORY EMBRYO
BEMOSS BESOMS, EMBOSS
BEMPRU BUMPER
BENNOT BONNET
BENNTU UNBENT
BENOOR BORNEO,
OBERON
BENORR REBORN
BENORT BRETON
BENORZ BONZER,
BRONZE
BENOST T-BONES
BENOTY BETONY
BENRRU BURNER
BENRTU BURNET
BEOORR OREBRO
BEOORZ BOOZER
BEOPRR PROBER
BEOPRS PROBES
BEORRS BORERS, RESORB
BEORRT ROBERT
BEORST OSBERT, SORBET,
STROBE
BEORSU BOURSE
BEORSW BOWERS,
BROWSE
BEORSX BOXERS
BEORTV OBVERT
BEORTY BY ROTE

BEORVV BOVVER
BEORWY BOWERY,
BOWYER
BEOSSS BOSSES, OBSESS
BEOSTU OBTUSE
BEOSTW BESTOW
BEPRSU SUPERB
BERSTU BRUTES, BUSTER,
TUBERS
BERSUX EXURBS
BERSUY BUYERS
BERTTU BUTTER
BERTWY WYBERT
BERUZZ BUZZER
BESSTU SUBSET
BESTTU BUTTES
BESUZZ BUZZES
BFFIIN BIFFIN
BFFINO BOFFIN
BFFLSU BLUFFS
BFGOOW FOGBOW
BFIILR FIBRIL
BFIINR FIBRIN
BFINOW BOWFIN
BFLOOT BOTOLF
BFLOTU BOTULF
BFLOTU BOTFLY
BFLSYY FLYBYS
BGGIIW BIGWIG
BGHIIL GHIBLI
BGHILT BLIGHT
BGHIRT BRIGHT
BGHIST BIGHTS
BGHMUU HUMBUG
BGHOSU BOUGHS
BGHOTU BOUGHT
BGHRSU BURGHS
BGIIJN JIBING
BGIIKN BIKING
BGIINT BITING
BGIIRT BIRGIT, BRIGIT
BGILLY GLIBLY
BGILNO GLOBIN, GOBLIN
BGINNO BONING
BGINOO BOOING
BGINOR BORING, ROBING
BGINOS BINGOS
BGINOW BOWING
BGINOX BOXING
BGINSU BUSING
BGINTU TUBING
BGINUY BUYING
BGIOPT BIG TOP
BGIOST BIGOTS

BGLNOO OBLONG
BGMOSU GUMBOS
BGNOOS BONGOS
BHIKOS KIBOSH
BHILSU BLUISH
BHIOPS BISHOP
BHIOSY BOYISH
BHIRST BIRTHS
BHIRSU HUBRIS
BHIRSY HYBRIS
BHLMUY HUMBLY
BHLOSY BOLSHY
BHMSTU THUMBS
BHOOOO BOOHOO
BHOOPS PHOBOS
BHOOST BOOTHS
BHORST THROBS
BHRSSU SHRUBS
BIIIKN BIKINI
BIINOT BIOTIN
BIIORV VIBRIO
BIISTV VIBIST
BIITTT TITBIT
BIKLNS BLINKS
BIKLNU IN BULK
BIKNSU BUSKIN
BILLNO BILLON
BILLNU LUBLIN
BILLOW BILLOW
BILLOY BILLY-O
BILMNY NIMBLY
BILMOS LIMBOS
BILMPS BLIMPS
BILMSU LIMBUS
BILNOS LISBON
BILNOY BONILY
BILNTZ BLINTZ
BILOOT LOBITO
BILOTW BLOW IT!
BILRTY TRILBY
BILRUW WILBUR
BILSSY SIBYLS
BILSUY BUSILY
BIMNSU NIMBUS
BIMSTU SUBMIT
BINNOR INBORN
BINNOU BUNION
BINOOT BONITO
BINORS ROBINS
BINORT BRITON
BINORY BRIONY
BINOSS BISONS
BIOORZ BORZOI
BIOOST OBOIST

BIOPSY BIOPSY	BSSSUY BYSSUS	CCIILT CLITIC
BIORST BISTRO, ORBITS	CCCDIO COCCID	CCIINO ICONIC
BIOSTU SUBITO	CCCILY CYCLIC	CCIINP PICNIC
BIOTTW TWO-BIT	CCCOSU COCCUS	CCIINZ ZINCIC
BIQSSU SQUIBS	CCCOXY COCCYX	CCIIRT CITRIC, CRITIC
BIRTTU TURBIT	CCDEIR CEDRIC, CERDIC	CCIISV CIVICS
BJLOOT JOB LOT	CCDEKO COCKED	CCIKLS CLICKS
BKMNUU BUNKUM	CCDELY CYCLED	CCIKRS CRICKS
BKNPUU BUNK-UP	CCDEOT DECOCT	CCILNO CLONIC
BKOORS BROOKS	CCEEHR CRECHE	CCILTU CULTIC
BKORTU TOBRUK	CCEEIL CECILE	CCIMOS COMICS, COSMIC
BLLORY BROLLY	CCEEOR COERCE	CCIMRY CYMRIC
BLMNUY NUMBLY	CCEHIL CHICLE, CLICHÉ	CCINOS CONICS
BLMOOS BLOOMS	CCEHIO CHOICE, ECHOIC	CCINSY CYNICS
BLMOSY SYMBOL	CCEHIT HECTIC	CCIOPT COPTIC
BLMRUY RUMBLY	CCEHKS CHECKS	CCIPRU CUPRIC
BLNOOS BOLSON	CCEHKY CHECKY	CCIRSU CIRCUS
BLNOTU UNBOLT	CCEHLN CLENCH	CCISTY CYSTIC
BLOOTT BLOTTO	CCEHLO CLOCHE	CCKLOO O'CLOCK
BLOPUW BLOW-UP	CCEHOS COSECH	CCKLOS CLOCKS
BLOWYZ BLOWZY	CCEIIL CILICE, ICICLE	CCKLSU CLUCKS
BLRRUY BLURRY	CCEILR CIRCLE, CLERIC	CCKOOU CUCKOO
BLSTUY SUBTLY	CCEILT CELTIC	CCKOPU COCK-UP
BMNOOT BON MOT	CCEILY CECILY, CICELY	CCKORS CROCKS
BMOORS BROOMS	CCEINS SCENIC	CCLOTU OCCULT
BMOOSS BOSOMS	CCEIOR CICERO	CCNOOO COCOON
BMOOSY BOSOMY	CCEIPT PECTIC	CCNORU CONCUR
BMOOTT BOTTOM	CCEIRS CERCIS	CCOOOR ROCOCO
BMOOTY TOMBOY	CCEIRT CRETIC	CCOPUY OCCUPY
BNNORU UNBORN	CCEKLO COCKLE	CCORSU CROCUS, SUCCOR
BNOORS OSBORN	CCELSY CYCLES	CCOSTU STUCCO
BNOOST BOSTON	CCENOS SCONCE	CCSSUU CUSCUS
BNORSU BOURNS, SUBORN	CCEORS SOCCER	CDDEEI DECIDE, DE-ICED
BNORSW BROWNS	CCERSU CERCUS	CDDEEK DECKED
BNORTU BURTON	CCHHII CHICHI	CDDEEO DECODE
BNORYY BRYONY	CCHHRU CHURCH	CDDEEU DEDUCE, DEUCED
BNORYZ BRONZY	CCHIKS CHICKS	CDDEHI CHIDED
BNOSSU BOSUNS	CCHILN CLINCH	CDDEIU CUDDIE
BNOSUW SUNBOW	CCHILY CHICLY	CDDEKO DOCKED
BNOTTU BUTTON	CCHINO COCHIN	CDDEKU DUCKED
BNOTUY BOUNTY	CCHIOR CHORIC	CDDELO CODDLE
BOOOTT TO BOOT	CCHIPU HICCUP	CDDELU CUDDLE
BOOPTY POTBOY	CCHKOS CHOCKS	CDDEOR CORDED
BOORRW BORROW	CCHKSU CHUCKS	CDDETU DEDUCT
BOORST ROBOTS	CCHLTU CLUTCH	CDDLOY CLODDY
BOOSST BOOSTS	CCHNOY CONCHY	CDDLUY CUDDLY
BOOWWW BOWWOW	CCHNRU CRUNCH	CDEEER DECREE, RECEDE
BORRSU BURROS	CCHORS SCORCH	CDEEES SECEDE
BORRUW BURROW	CCHORT CROTCH	CDEEEX EXCEED
BORSTU ROBUST	CCHORU CROUCH	CDEEFN FENCED
BORTTU TURBOT	CCHOST SCOTCH	CDEEFT DEFECT
BOTUUY BUYOUT	CCHRTU CRUTCH	CDEEHO ECHOED
BPSTUU BUST-UP	CCHSTU SCUTCH	CDEEHT ETCHED
BRSSTU BURSTS	CCIILN CLINIC	CDEEHW CHEWED

CDEEIL DECILE
CDEEIP PIECED
CDEEIR DE-ICER
CDEEIT DECEIT
CDEEIV DEVICE
CDEEJT DEJECT
CDEEKL DECKLE
CDEEKN NECKED
CDEEKO DECOKE
CDEEKP PECKED
CDEEKR RECKED
CDEENO ENCODE
CDEENT DECENT
CDEERS CREEDS, SCREED
CDEERU REDUCE
CDEERW CREWED
CDEESU SEDUCE
CDEETT DETECT
CDEFFU CUFFED
CDEFII DEIFIC
CDEFKU FUCKED
CDEFNU FECUND
CDEFOR FORCED
CDEGGO COGGED
CDEGIN CEDING
CDEGIO GEODIC
CDEGLU CUDGEL
CDEGOR CODGER
CDEHIM CHIMED
CDEHIN INCHED
CDEHIR CHIDER, HERDIC
CDEHIT ITCHED
CDEHIU HEIDUC
CDEHKO CHOKED,
  HOCKED
CDEHNR DRENCH
CDEHOS COSHED
CDEHOU DOUCHE
CDEIIK DICKIE
CDEIIR DICIER
CDEIJU JUICED
CDEIKK KICKED
CDEIKL LICKED
CDEIKM MEDICK
CDEIKN NICKED
CDEIKP PICKED
CDEIKR DICKER, RICKED
CDEIKS SICKED
CDEIKT TICKED
CDEIKW WICKED
CDEILO COILED, DOCILE
CDEILS SLICED
CDEILT DELICT
CDEILU DULCIE

CDEIMN MINCED
CDEIMO MEDICO
CDEIMR DERMIC
CDEIMS MEDICS
CDEINO COINED
CDEINR CINDER
CDEINU INDUCE
CDEINW WINCED
CDEIOP COPIED
CDEIOR DORICE
CDEIOV VOICED
CDEIPR PRICED
CDEIPS SPICED
CDEIPT DEPICT
CDEIRS CIDERS
CDEIRT CREDIT, DIRECT
CDEIRV CERVID
CDEIRY DRY ICE
CDEIST EDICTS
CDEKLO LOCKED
CDEKMO MOCKED
CDEKMU MUCKED
CDEKNO CONKED
CDEKOO COOKED
CDEKOP POCKED
CDEKOR CORKED,
  DOCKER, ROCKED
CDEKOS SOCKED
CDEKOT DOCKET
CDEKRU DUCKER,
  RUCKED
CDEKRY DERYCK
CDEKSU SUCKED
CDEKTU TUCKED
CDELLU CULLED
CDELOO COOLED
CDELOR COLDER
CDELOS CLOSED
CDELOY CLOYED
CDELRU CURDLE, CURLED
CDELTU DULCET
CDEMOO COMEDO
CDEMOY COMEDY
CDENNO CONNED
CDENOS SECOND
CDENOT DOCENT
CDENSU DUNCES, SECUND
CDEOOP COOPED
CDEOPP COPPED
CDEORR RECORD
CDEORS CREDOS,
  DÉCORS, SCORED
CDEORW CROWED
CDEOSU ESCUDO

CDEOSY DECOYS
CDEPPU CUPPED
CDERRU CRUDER
CDERSU CURSED
CDERSY CYDERS, DESCRY
CDERUV CURVED
CDESSU CUSSED
CDFINU FUNDIC
CDFIOU FUCOID
CDFIOY CODIFY
CDGIIN DICING
CDGINO CODING
CDHIOR ORCHID, RHODIC
CDHIRY HYDRIC
CDHORS CHORDS
CDIIIM IMIDIC
CDIIIR IRIDIC
CDIINT INDICT
CDIIOY IDIOCY
CDIISV VISCID
CDIKNO DICKON
CDIMOU MUCOID
CDIMOY CYMOID
CDIMSU MUSCID
CDIMTU DICTUM
CDINOO CONOID
CDINOR NORDIC
CDINSY SYNDIC
CDINTU INDUCT
CDIOSS DISCOS
CDIPSU CUPIDS, CUSPID
CDISSU DISCUS
CDJNOU JOCUND
CDLLOY COLDLY
CDLOSS SCOLDS
CDLOSU CLOUDS
CDLOUY CLOUDY
CDMNOO CONDOM,
  MOD CON
CDMORS CD-ROMS
CDNOOR CONDOR,
  CORDON
CDOORT DOCTOR
CDORSW CROWDS
CEEEFL FLEECE
CEEEGR GREECE
CEEEHS CHEESE
CEEENO EOCENE
CEEFFO COFFEE
CEEFFT EFFECT
CEEFHL FLECHE
CEEFIL FELICE
CEEFIR FIERCE, RECIFE
CEEFLY FLEECY

CEEFNN FENNEC
CEEFNR FENCER
CEEFNS FENCES
CEEFSU FESCUE
CEEHIR CHERIE
CEEHIS SEICHE
CEEHKL HECKLE
CEEHKS CHEEKS
CEEHKY CHEEKY
CEEHLR LECHER
CEEHLY LYCHEE
CEEHMS SCHEME
CEEHNT THENCE
CEEHNW WHENCE
CEEHOR COHERE,
   REECHO
CEEHOS ECHOES
CEEHPS CHEEPS, SPEECH
CEEHQU CHEQUE
CEEHRS CHEERS
CEEHRT ETCHER
CEEHRU EUCHRE
CEEHRW CHEWER
CEEHRY CHEERY
CEEHSW ESCHEW
CEEHSY CHEESY
CEEIKL KIELCE
CEEILN CELINE
CEEILS SIECLE
CEEIMN ICEMEN
CEEIMT EMETIC
CEEINS NIECES
CEEINT ENTICE
CEEINU EUNICE
CEEINV EVINCE, VENICE
CEEIPR PIECER, PIERCE,
   RECIPE
CEEIPS PIECES, SPECIE
CEEIRS CERISE
CEEIRT RECITE, TIERCE
CEEIRU ECURIE
CEEISS ECESIS
CEEISX EXCISE
CEEITX EXCITE
CEEJRT REJECT
CEEKNR NECKER
CEEKPR PECKER
CEEKRS CREEKS
CEELMO CLEOME
CEELNR CRENEL
CEELOR CREOLE
CEELOU COULEE
CEELOV VELOCE
CEELRS CREELS

CEELRT TERCEL
CEELRV CLEVER
CEELRW CREWEL
CEELRY CELERY
CEELST SELECT
CEELSY LYCÉES
CEEMNT CEMENT
CEEMNY CYMENE
CEEMRR MERCER
CEEMRT CERMET
CEENOR ENCORE
CEENPT PECTEN
CEENRS CENSER, SCREEN
CEENRT CENTER,
   CENTRE, RECENT,
   TENREC
CEENSS SCENES
CEEPRS CREEPS
CEEPRT RECEPT
CEEPRY CREEPY
CEEPTX EXCEPT, EXPECT
CEEPTY ECTYPE
CEERSS RECESS
CEERST RESECT, SECRET
CEERSU CEREUS, CERUSE,
   CREUSE, RESCUE, SECURE
CEERTT TERCET
CEESSX EXCESS
CEESUX EXCUSE
CEFFIO OFFICE
CEFFOR COFFER
CEFHIS CHIEFS
CEFHLT FLETCH
CEFHNR FRENCH
CEFIKL FICKLE
CEFINT INFECT
CEFINU UNICEF
CEFIRR FERRIC
CEFKLS FLECKS
CEFKRU FUCKER
CEFLOS FO'C'SLE
CEFLST CLEFTS
CEFNOR CONFER
CEFORR FORCER
CEFORS FORCES, FRESCO
CEFRUW CURFEW
CEGGPU EGGCUP
CEGHIO CHIGOE
CEGINR CRINGE
CEGKOS GECKOS
CEGLRY CLERGY
CEGNOR CONGER
CEGNOS CONGÉS
CEGNOT COGENT

CEGNTY CYGNET
CEGORR GROCER
CEHHIT HI-TECH
CEHIIR RICHIE
CEHIKY HICKEY
CEHILN LICHEN
CEHILS CHILES, CHISEL
CEHIMS CHIMES
CEHINP PENCHI
CEHINR ENRICH
CEHINS CHINES, INCHES,
   NICHES
CEHINT ETHNIC
CEHIOR COHEIR, HEROIC
CEHIPR CIPHER
CEHIQU QUICHE
CEHIRR RICHER
CEHIRS RICHES
CEHIRT THRICE
CEHIST ETHICS, ITCHES
CEHISV CHIVES
CEHITT THETIC
CEHKLU HUCKLE
CEHKOR CHOKER,
   HOCKER
CEHKOS CHOKES
CEHKOY HOCKEY
CEHKST SKETCH
CEHLOR CHOLER
CEHLOT CLOTHE
CEHLPS SCHLEP
CEHLRY CHERYL
CEHMOR CHROME
CEHNOS CHOSEN
CEHNOU COHUNE
CEHNQU QUENCH
CEHNRT TRENCH
CEHNRW WRENCH
CEHNST STENCH
CEHNUU EUNUCH
CEHOOS CHOOSE
CEHORS CHORES
CEHORT HECTOR,
   ROCHET, TROCHE
CEHOSS COSHES
CEHOTU TOUCHÉ
CEHPRY CYPHER
CEHPSY PSYCHE
CEHRRY CHERRY
CEHRTW WRETCH
CEHRTY CHERTY
CEHSST CHESTS
CEHSTU CHUTES, TUSCHE
CEHSTY CHESTY, SCYTHE

CEHTTY TETCHY
CEIIKV VICKIE
CEIILT ELICIT
CEIILX EXILIC
CEIINR IRENIC
CEIINS INCISE
CEIINT INCITE
CEIISS CISSIE
CEIIST CITIES, ICIEST
CEIISV CIVIES
CEIJNT INJECT
CEIJSU JUICES
CEIKKR KICKER
CEIKLN NICKEL
CEIKLP PICKLE
CEIKLR LICKER
CEIKLS SICKLE
CEIKLT KELTIC, TICKLE
CEIKMY MICKEY
CEIKNR NICKER
CEIKNS SICKEN
CEIKOO COOKIE
CEIKOS KOSICE
CEIKPR PICKER
CEIKPT PICKET
CEIKRS SICKER
CEIKRT TICKER
CEIKRW WICKER
CEIKRY CRIKEY
CEIKTT TICKET
CEIKTW WICKET
CEILLO COLLIE
CEILMS CLIMES
CEILNO CINEOL, NICOLE
CEILNP PENCIL
CEILNS CLINES
CEILNT CLIENT, LENTIC
CEILNU LUCIEN, NUCLEI
CEILNY NICELY
CEILOO COOLIE
CEILOP POLICE
CEILOR COILER, RECOIL
CEILPS SPLICE
CEILPV PELVIC
CEILQU CLIQUE
CEILRS RELICS, SLICER
CEILRT RELICT
CEILSS SLICES
CEILSU SLUICE
CEILSV CLEVIS
CEIMNO INCOME
CEIMNR MINCER
CEIMOX MEXICO
CEIMPU PUMICE

CEIMRS CRIMES
CEIMRT METRIC
CEIMRU CERIUM
CEIMSU MISCUE
CEINNO CONNIE
CEINOR COINER, ORCEIN
CEINOS CONIES, COSINE,
    OSCINE
CEINOT NOETIC, NOTICE
CEINOV NOVICE
CEINPR PINCER, PRINCE
CEINPT INCEPT, PECTIN
CEINQU CINQUE, QUINCE
CEINRT CRETIN
CEINRW WINCER
CEINST INCEST, INSECT,
    NICEST
CEINSU INCUSE
CEINSW WINCES
CEINTY NICETY
CEINWY WINCEY
CEIOOZ EOZOIC
CEIOPR COPIER
CEIOPS COPIES
CEIOPT POETIC
CEIORS COSIER
CEIORT EROTIC
CEIORV VOICER
CEIORW COWRIE
CEIORZ COZIER
CEIOSS COSIES
CEIOSV VOICES
CEIOSZ COZIES
CEIOTX EXOTIC
CEIPPT PEPTIC
CEIPRS CRIPES, PRÉCIS,
    PRICES, SPICER
CEIPRY PRICEY
CEIPSS PISCES, SPICES
CEIPST SEPTIC
CEIPTU CUP TIE
CEIQRU CIRQUE
CEIRRS CRIERS
CEIRSS CRISES
CEIRST STERIC, TRICES
CEIRSU CRUISE
CEIRTU URETIC
CEIRVX CERVIX
CEISTV CIVETS
CEJKOY JOCKEY
CEJNOU JOUNCE
CEJOOS JOCOSE
CEKKOP KOPECK
CEKLOR LOCKER

CEKLOT LOCKET
CEKLRS CLERKS
CEKLSU SUCKLE
CEKMOR MOCKER
CEKMRU MUCKER
CEKNOR CONKER,
    RECKON
CEKNSV V-NECKS
CEKOOR COOKER
CEKOPT POCKET
CEKORR CORKER,
    ROCKER
CEKORT ROCKET
CEKOST SOCKET
CEKPRU PUCKER
CEKPSS SPECKS
CEKRSU SUCKER
CEKRSW WRECKS
CEKRTU TUCKER
CELLOS CELLOS
CELLOT COLLET
CELLOU LOCULE
CELLOY COLLEY
CELLRU CULLER
CELLTU CULLET
CELMOO COELOM
CELMOP COMPEL
CELMOR CORMEL
CELMOY COMELY
CELMSU MUSCLE
CELMUY LYCEUM
CELNOR CORNEL
CELNOS CLONES
CELNOV CLOVEN
CELNOY CEYLON
CELNSU UNCLES
CELNTU LUCENT
CELOOR COOLER
CELOOT OCELOT
CELOPU COUPLE
CELORS CLOSER, CRESOL
CELORT LECTOR
CELORU COLURE
CELORV CLOVER, VELCRO
CELOSS CLOSES
CELOST CLOSET
CELOSU COLEUS
CELOSV CLOVES
CELOSX SCOLEX
CELOSY COLEYS
CELPUU CUPULE
CELRRU CURLER
CELRSU ULCERS
CELRTU CUTLER

CELRUW CURLEW	**CEORTX** CORTEX	**CGINOO** COOING
CELTTU CUTLET	**CEOSST** COSSET	**CGINOP** COPING
CELTUY CUTELY	**CEOSSU** SCOUSE	**CGINOR** CORING
CEMNNO CONMEN, NEM	**CEOSTT** OCTETS	**CGINOW** COWING
CON	**CEOSVY** COVEYS	**CGINOX** COXING
CEMNOO COME ON!	**CEPRSU** SPRUCE	**CGINRU** CURING
CEMNOW COWMEN	**CERSST** CRESTS	**CGINRY** CRYING
CEMNTU CENTUM	**CERSSU** CRUSES, CURSES	**CGIORS** CORGIS
CEMOOS COMOSE	**CERSSW** SCREWS	**CGLLOY** GLYCOL
CEMORS COMERS	**CERSTU** CRUETS, RECTUS,	**CGLNOU** UNCLOG
CEMOST COMETS	TRUCES	**CGNOOU** CONGOU
CEMOSY CYMOSE	**CERSUV** CURVES	**CGNSUY** CYGNUS
CEMOTU TEMUCO	**CERSUX** CRUXES	**CHHOOS** COHOSH
CEMRTU RECTUM	**CERSWY** SCREWY	**CHIILL** CHILLI
CENNOS NONCES	**CERTTU** CUTTER	**CHIILT** LITCHI, LITHIC
CENOPS PONCES	**CERTUV** CURVET	**CHIINT** CHITIN
CENOPU POUNCE	**CESSSU** CUSSES	**CHIKKO** HICKOK
CENOPY PONCEY	**CESTTU** CUTEST	**CHIKNO** IN HOCK
CENORR CORNER	**CFFILS** CLIFFS	**CHIKNS** CHINKS
CENORS CENSOR, CRONES	**CFFINO** COFFIN	**CHIKOS** HOICKS
CENORT CORNET	**CFFOSS** SCOFFS	**CHIKRS** KIRSCH
CENORY CORNEY	**CFFOTU** CUTOFF	**CHIKST** KITSCH
CENOSS SCONES	**CFFRSU** SCRUFF	**CHILLS** CHILLS
CENOSU OUNCES, UNESCO	**CFFSSU** SCUFFS	**CHILLY** CHILLY
CENOSV COVENS	**CFGINU** FUNGIC	**CHILMO** HOLMIC
CENOSY CONEYS	**CFHILN** FLINCH	**CHILOR** ORCHIL
CENOVX CONVEX	**CFHILT** FLITCH	**CHILRY** RICHLY
CENOVY CONVEY	**CFHLSY** FLYSCH	**CHIMNU** MUNICH
CENSST SCENTS	**CFHOUU** FU-CHOU	**CHIMOR** HORMIC
CENSSU CENSUS	**CFIILM** FILMIC	**CHIMRS** CHRISM, SMIRCH
CENSTY ENCYST	**CFIINN** FINNIC	**CHIMSS** SCHISM
CEOOPR COOPER	**CFIIST** FISTIC	**CHIMTY** THYMIC
CEOOTY COYOTE,	**CFIITY** CITIFY	**CHINNO** INCHON
OOCYTE	**CFIKLS** FLICKS	**CHINOP** PHONIC
CEOPPR COPPER	**CFILOR** FROLIC	**CHINOT** CHITON
CEOPRS CORPSE	**CFIMOR** FORMIC	**CHINRU** URCHIN
CEOPRU RECOUP	**CFIMOT** COMFIT	**CHINST** SNITCH
CEOPSS COPSES	**CFISTU** FUSTIC	**CHINTZ** CHINTZ
CEOPSU COUPÉS	**CFKLOS** FLOCKS	**CHIOPT** PHOTIC
CEOQTU COQUET	**CFKLOY** FLOCKY	**CHIORS** CHOIRS, ORCHIS
CEORRS CORERS, CRORES,	**CFKORS** FROCKS	**CHIORT** THORIC
SCORER	**CFKPUU** FUCK-UP	**CHIOST** SOTHIC
CEORRT RECTOR	**CFORST** CROFTS	**CHIPPY** CHIPPY
CEORRW CROWER	**CFRSUY** SCURFY	**CHIPRS** CHIRPS
CEORSS CORSES, CROSSE,	**CGGLOY** CLOGGY	**CHIPRY** CHIRPY
SCORES	**CGHHOU** CHOUGH	**CHIPSY** PHYSIC
CEORST CORSET, ESCORT,	**CGHILT** GLITCH	**CHIPTY** PITCHY
RECTOS, SCOTER, SECTOR	**CGHIOT** GOTHIC	**CHIRST** CHRIST
CEORSU CEROUS, COURSE,	**CGHORU** GROUCH	**CHIRUZ** ZURICH
SOURCE	**CGHOSU** COUGHS	**CHISST** SCHIST
CEORSV COVERS	**CGIINT** CITING	**CHISTT** STITCH
CEORSW ESCROW	**CGILNY** CLINGY	**CHISTW** SWITCH
CEORTT COTTER	**CGIMNO** COMING,	**CHITTW** TWITCH
CEORTV COVERT, VECTOR	GNOMIC	**CHITTY** TITCHY

CHJNOU CHONJU
CHKNSU CHUNKS
CHKNUY CHUNKY
CHKOSS SHOCKS
CHKSSU SHUCKS
CHLMOO MOLOCH
CHLOOS SCHOOL
CHLORS SCHORL
CHLOST CLOTHS
CHLOSU SLOUCH
CHLRSU CHURLS
CHMMUY CHUMMY
CHMOOS SMOOCH
CHMPSU CHUMPS
CHMSTU SMUTCH
CHNOOP PONCHO
CHNPUY PUNCHY
CHNRSU CHURNS
CHOORT COHORT
CHOOSY CHOOSY
CHOPPY CHOPPY
CHOPUY POUCHY
CHORSU CHORUS
CHOSUU SUCHOU
CHOTUY TOUCHY
CHPSTU PUTSCH
CHSSSU SCHUSS
CHSWYZ SCHWYZ
CIIIRT IRITIC
CIILMU CILIUM
CIILSY SICILY
CIIMMS MIMICS
CIIMOT MIOTIC
CIIMTV VICTIM
CIINOR IRONIC
CIINOT TICINO
CIINRT CITRIN, NITRIC
CIIRSS CRISIS
CIIRTV VITRIC
CIKLSS SLICKS
CIKLSY SICKLY
CIKNOT ON TICK
CIKNPU UNPICK
CIKNPY PYKNIC
CIKNSS SNICKS
CIKNTU TUCK-IN
CIKNYZ ZINCKY
CIKPPU PICK-UP
CIKPRS PRICKS
CIKRST STRICK, TRICKS
CIKRTU TURKIC
CIKRTY TRICKY
CIKSST STICKS
CIKSTY STICKY

CILLSU CULLIS
CILNOP CLIP-ON
CILNOU UNCOIL
CILOPU OILCUP
CILOPY POLICY
CILOSY COSILY
CILOYZ COZILY
CILRSY LYRICS
CILSUU LUCIUS
CIMMOS COMMIS
CIMMOT COMMIT
CIMNOR MICRON
CIMNOU CONIUM
CIMNRU CRINUM
CIMOOS COSIMO
CIMOPY MYOPIC
CIMORS MICROS
CIMORU CORIUM
CIMOST SITCOM
CIMOTY COMITY
CIMPRS SCRIMP
CIMRUU CURIUM
CIMSTY MYSTIC
CINNOU NUNCIO
CINOPT PONTIC
CINORT CITRON
CINORZ ZIRCON
CINOSS SCIONS
CINOST TOCSIN, TONICS
CINOSU COUSIN
CINQUY QUINCY
CINSTU TUNICS
CIOOPT OCTOPI
CIOPRT TROPIC
CIOPST OPTICS, TOPICS
CIORSU CURIOS
CIORTT TRICOT
CIORTV VICTOR
CIOSST STOICS
CIOSTU COITUS
CIPRSS CRISPS
CIPRST SCRIPT
CIPRSY CRISPY
CIRRSU CIRRUS
CIRSTT STRICT
CIRSTU CITRUS, CURTIS,
　　　 RICTUS, RUSTIC
CIRTTY YTTRIC
CKKNOS KNOCKS
CKLNOU UNLOCK
CKLOPU LOCKUP
CKLPSU PLUCKS
CKLPUY PLUCKY
CKMOPU MOCK-UP

CKMOSS SMOCKS
CKNORU UNCORK
CKNTUU UNTUCK
CKOORS CROOKS
CKOSST STOCKS
CKOSTY STOCKY
CKRSTU STRUCK, TRUCKS
CKRSUU RUCKUS
CLLOOY COOLLY
CLLORS SCROLL
CLMNOU COLUMN
CLMOPY COMPLY
CLMOSU LOCUMS
CLMPSU CLUMPS
CLMPUY CLUMPY
CLMSUY CLUMSY, MUSCLY
CLNOOS COLONS
CLNOOY COLONY
CLNOSU CLONUS, CONSUL
CLNOSW CLOWNS
CLNRUU UNCURL
CLOORS COLORS
CLOORU COLOUR
CLOSSW SCOWLS
CLOSTU CLOUTS, LOCUST
CLOSTY COSTLY
CLPSTU SCULPT
CLRTUY CURTLY
CLSSUU SULCUS
CMMNOO COMMON
CMMRUY CRUMMY
CMMSUY SCUMMY
CMNOSY SYNCOM
CMOOOR COMORO
CMOOSS COSMOS
CMOOSW MOSCOW
CMOSTU CUSTOM
CMOSUU MUCOUS
CMPRSU SCRUMP
CMRSSU SCRUMS
CMSTUU SCUTUM
CNNOOR CONNOR
CNOOPU COUPON
CNOORT CROTON
CNOOST NOSTOC,
　　　 ONCOST
CNOOTT COTTON
CNOOTY TYCOON
CNOOVY CONVOY
CNORSS SCORNS
CNORSW CROWNS
CNOSTU COUNTS,
　　　 TUCSON
CNOTUY COUNTY

COOPRS SCROOP
COOPSS SCOOPS
COOPTU COP-OUT
COOPWX COWPOX
COPRSU CORPUS, CROUPS
COPSUY COYPUS
CORRSU CURSOR
CORSTU COURTS
CORTUY OUTCRY
COSSTU SCOUTS
COTTUU CUTOUT
CPRSTY CRYPTS
CPRSUY CYPRUS
CPSTUU CUTUPS
CRRSUY SCURRY
CRSSTU CRUSTS
CRSTUY CRUSTY, CURTSY
CRSUVY SCURVY
CSUYZZ SCUZZY
DDDEEI EDDIED
DDDEEW WEDDED
DDDEGO DODGED
DDDEIK KIDDED
DDDEIL DIDDLE, LIDDED
DDDEIR RIDDED
DDDELO DODDLE
DDDEMU MUDDED
DDDENO NODDED
DDDEOP PODDED
DDDEOR DODDER
DDDEOS SODDED
DDEEEH HEEDED
DDEEEM DEEMED
DDEEEN NEEDED
DDEEES SEEDED
DDEEEW WEEDED
DDEEFI DEFIED
DDEEFN DEFEND, FENDED
DDEEFU FEUDED
DDEEGH HEDGED
DDEEGL GELDED
DDEEGR DREDGE
DDEEGW WEDGED
DDEEHL HEDDLE
DDEEHR HERDED
DDEEIL ELIDED
DDEEIN DENIED, INDEED,
  NEDDIE
DDEEIR DERIDE
DDEEIS EDDIES
DDEEIT DIETED, EDITED,
  TEDDIE
DDEELM MEDDLE
DDEELP PEDDLE

DDEELR ELDRED
DDEELU DELUDE, DUELED,
  ELUDED
DDEELV DELVED
DDEELW WELDED
DDEEMN MENDED
DDEEMO DÉMODÉ
DDEENN DENNED
DDEENP DEPEND
DDEENR REDDEN
DDEENT DENTED,
  TENDED
DDEENU DENUDE,
  DUDEEN, DUNDEE,
  ENDUED
DDEENV VENDED
DDEENW WENDED
DDEEOR ERODED
DDEERR REDDER
DDEERT TEDDER
DDEEUX EXUDED
DDEFFO DOFFED
DDEFGU FUDGED
DDEFIL FIDDLE
DDEFLO FOLDED
DDEFLU FUDDLE
DDEFNU FUNDED
DDEFOR FODDER,
  FORDED
DDEFRY FREDDY
DDEGGO DOGGED
DDEGIL GILDED, GLIDED
DDEGIR GIRDED, RIDGED
DDEGIU GUIDED
DDEGJU JUDGED
DDEGLO LODGED
DDEGMO DODGEM
DDEGNU NUDGED
DDEGOR DODGER
DDEGOS DODGES
DDEGRU DRUDGE
DDEHIN HIDDEN
DDEHIS DISHED
DDEHLU HUDDLE
DDEHNO HODDEN
DDEHOO HOODED
DDEIIK KIDDIE
DDEIIO IODIDE
DDEIIV DIVIDE
DDEIKR KIDDER
DDEILM MIDDLE
DDEILP PIDDLE
DDEILR RIDDLE
DDEILS SIDLED

DDEIMM DIMMED
DDEIMN MIDDEN,
  MINDED
DDEIMS DESMID
DDEINN DINNED
DDEINR RIDDEN
DDEINW WINDED
DDEIOV DEVOID, VOIDED
DDEIPP DIPPED
DDEIPR PRIDED
DDEIRR RIDDER
DDEITY TIDYED
DDEJRU JUDDER
DDEKNU DUNKED
DDELLO DOLLED
DDELLU DULLED
DDELMO MOLDED
DDELMU MUDDLE
DDELNO NODDLE
DDELOO DOODLE
DDELOR LORDED
DDELOT TODDLE
DDELPU PUDDLE
DDELRU RUDDLE
DDELUY DUDLEY
DDEMNO EDMOND
DDEMNU EDMUND
DDEMOO DOOMED
DDEMPU DUMPED
DDENNO DONNED
DDENNU DUNNED
DDENOR DRONED
DDENOS SODDEN
DDENOW DOWNED
DDENOY DYNODE
DDENSU SUDDEN
DDEOOS DODOES
DDEOOW WOODED
DDEORW WORDED
DDEOSS DOSSED
DDEOST ODDEST
DDEOSU DOUSED
DDEOSW DOWSED
DDEOTT DOTTED
DDERRU RUDDER
DDERSU UDDERS
DDESTU DUSTED
DDFILY FIDDLY
DDHINO HODDIN
DDHOSY SHODDY
DDIIKK DIK-DIK
DDILNR DIRNDL
DDILOS DILDOS
DDILTY TIDDLY

DDIOOS DO-SI-DO
DDIOPY DIPODY
DDIORS SORDID
DDIOTU OUTDID
DDIOTY ODDITY
DDIRSU DRUIDS
DDLPUY PUDDLY
DDMMUU DUMDUM
DDNOOS ODDS-ON
DEEEFR FEEDER, REEFED
DEEEGR DEGREE
DEEEHL HEELED
DEEEHR HEEDER
DEEEJR JEERED
DEEEKL KEELED
DEEEKN KEENED
DEEEKP PEEKED
DEEEKR REEKED
DEEELN NEEDLE
DEEELP PEELED
DEEELR LEERED, REELED
DEEELT DELETE
DEEEMR REDEEM
DEEEMS SEEMED
DEEEMT TEEMED
DEEENP DEEPEN
DEEENV VENDEE
DEEEPP PEEPED
DEEEPR DEEPER, PEERED
DEEEPS SEEPED
DEEEPV PEEVED
DEEERS SEEDER
DEEERV VEERED
DEEERW WEEDER
DEEFGL FLEDGE
DEEFIL DEFILE
DEEFIN DEFINE
DEEFIR DEFIER
DEEFLL FELLED
DEEFLU FUELED
DEEFLX FLEXED
DEEFNR FENDER
DEEFRT RED EFT
DEEFSU DEFUSE
DEEFZZ FEZZED
DEEGGL LEGGED
DEEGGP PEGGED
DEEGHR HEDGER
DEEGHS HEDGES
DEEGIR EDGIER
DEEGLL GELLED
DEEGLN LEGEND
DEEGLP PLEDGE
DEEGLR LEDGER

DEEGLS LEDGES, SLEDGE
DEEGLU DELUGE
DEEGMM GEMMED
DEEGMR MERGED
DEEGNO ON EDGE
DEEGNR GENDER
DEEGNU DENGUE
DEEGRV VERGED
DEEGRY GREEDY, GREYED
DEEGSW WEDGES
DEEGSZ SZEGED
DEEHLP HELPED
DEEHLY HEDLEY
DEEHMM HEMMED
DEEHMS MESHED
DEEHRR HERDER
DEEHRT THREE-D
DEEHSW SHEWED
DEEILN ELINED, LEIDEN
DEEILR RELIED
DEEILS DIESEL, SEDILE
DEEILV LEVIED, VEILED
DEEILX EXILED
DEEILY EYELID
DEEIMP IMPEDE
DEEIMS DEMISE
DEEINN DENNIE, INDENE
DEEINR DENIER, NEREID,
　REINED
DEEINS DENISE
DEEINV ENDIVE, ENVIED,
　VEINED
DEEIPP DIEPPE
DEEIPS ESPIED
DEEIRS DESIRE, RESIDE
DEEIRT DIETER
DEEIRU UREIDE
DEEIRV DERIVE
DEEIRW DEWIER
DEEISS SEISED
DEEISV DEVISE, SIEVED
DEEISZ SEIZED
DEEITX EXITED
DEEITY TIE-DYE
DEEIVW VIEWED
DEEJKR JERKED
DEEJLL JELLED
DEEJRU DE JURE
DEEJST JESTED
DEEJTT JETTED
DEEKNN KENNED
DEEKOV EVOKED
DEEKPR PERKED
DEEKSW SKEWED

DEELLW WELLED
DEELLY YELLED
DEELMT MELTED
DEELMY MEDLEY
DEELNR LENDER
DEELNU ELUNED
DEELNW DELWEN,
　WEDELN
DEELOP ELOPED
DEELPT PELTED
DEELPY DEEPLY, YELPED
DEELRS ELDERS
DEELRU ELUDER
DEELRV DELVER
DEELRW WELDER
DEELST ELDEST
DEELSW SLEWED
DEELTU TELEDU
DEELUX DE LUXE
DEEMNR MENDER
DEEMOT DEMOTE
DEEMOW MEOWED
DEEMPR PERMED
DEEMPT TEMPED
DEEMRT TERMED
DEEMRU DEMURE
DEEMRY REMEDY
DEEMSS MESSED
DEENNP PENNED
DEENNT NEEDN'T
DEENOP OPENED
DEENOR DOREEN,
　REDONE
DEENOS ODENSE
DEENOT DENOTE
DEENPX EXPEND
DEENRR RENDER
DEENRS DENSER, SENDER
DEENRT RENTED, TENDER
DEENRU ENDURE
DEENRV DENVER, NERVED
DEENSS SENSED
DEENST NESTED, TENSED
DEENSU ENSUED
DEENSW SWEDEN
DEENTT DETENT, NETTED
DEENTV VENTED
DEENTX DENTEX,
　EXTEND
DEEOPS DEPOSE
DEEORT TEREDO
DEEORZ ZEROED
DEEOTT ODETTE
DEEOTV DEVOTE, VETOED

DEEPPP PEPPED
DEEPRU PUREED
DEEPRY PREYED
DEEPSS SPEEDS
DEEPSW SPEWED
DEEPSY SPEEDY
DEEPTT PETTED
DEEPTU DEPUTE
DEEQUU QUEUED
DEERST DESERT, RESTED
DEERSU REUSED
DEERSV SERVED, VERSED
DEERTX DEXTER
DEERVV REVVED
DEESST STEEDS
DEESSW SWEDES
DEESTT DETEST, TESTED
DEESTV VESTED
DEESTW STEWED, TWEEDS
DEETTV VETTED
DEETTW WETTED
DEETWY TWEEDY
DEFFHU HUFFED
DEFFIM MIFFED
DEFFIR DIFFER
DEFFLU DUFFEL, LUFFED
DEFFMU MUFFED
DEFFNO OFFEND
DEFFOR DOFFER
DEFFPU PUFFED
DEFFRU DUFFER
DEFGGO FOGGED
DEFGIR FRIDGE
DEFGIT FIDGET, GIFTED
DEFGOO GOOFED
DEFGOR FORGED
DEFHIS FISHED
DEFHOO HOOFED
DEFIKN KNIFED
DEFILL FILLED
DEFILM FILMED
DEFILO FOILED
DEFILR RIFLED
DEFILS FIELDS
DEFILT LIFTED
DEFIMR FIRMED
DEFINN FINNED
DEFINR FINDER, FRIEND,
  REDFIN
DEFINS FIENDS
DEFIOO FOODIE
DEFIOT FOETID
DEFIRV FERVID
DEFIST SIFTED

DEFITT FITTED
DEFIZZ FIZZED
DEFKNU FUNKED
DEFKOR FORKED
DEFLNO ENFOLD, FONDLE
DEFLOO FOOLED
DEFLOR FOLDER
DEFLOT LOFTED
DEFLOU FOULED
DEFLOW FLOWED,
  WOLFED
DEFLRU FURLED
DEFLTU FLUTED
DEFLTY DEFTLY
DEFMOR DEFORM,
  FORMED
DEFNOR FONDER
DEFNOU FONDUE
DEFNRU REFUND
DEFOOR ROOFED
DEFRRU FURRED
DEFRSU SURFED
DEFRTU TURFED
DEFSSU FUSSED
DEFTTU TUFTED
DEFUZZ FUZZED
DEGGHO HOGGED
DEGGHU HUGGED
DEGGIJ JIGGED
DEGGIN EDGING
DEGGIP PIGGED
DEGGIR DIGGER, RIGGED
DEGGIU DUGGIE
DEGGIW WIGGED
DEGGJO JOGGED
DEGGJU JUGGED
DEGGLO DOGLEG,
  LOGGED
DEGGLU LUGGED
DEGGMU MUGGED
DEGGOR DOGGER,
  GORGED
DEGGOT TOGGED
DEGGOU GOUGED
DEGGPU PUGGED
DEGGRU GRUDGE,
  RUGGED
DEGGRY DREGGY
DEGGTU TUGGED
DEGHIN HINGED
DEGHIS SIGHED
DEGHIW HEDWIG
DEGHSU GUSHED
DEGILL GILLED

DEGILN DINGLE
DEGILO GOLDIE
DEGILR GILDER, GIRDLE,
  GLIDER
DEGILS GLIDES
DEGILY EDGILY
DEGIMS MIDGES
DEGIMT MIDGET
DEGINN ENDING
DEGINO GIDEON
DEGINP PINGED
DEGINR RINGED
DEGINS DESIGN, SIGNED,
  SINGED
DEGINT TINGED
DEGINW WINGED
DEGINY DYEING
DEGIOS DOGIES
DEGIOU DOUGIE
DEGIPR GRIPED
DEGIRR GIRDER
DEGIRS DIRGES, RIDGES
DEGIRU GUIDER
DEGIST DIGEST
DEGISU GUIDES
DEGITW WIDGET
DEGJRU JUDGER
DEGJSU JUDGES
DEGLLU GULLED
DEGLNO GOLDEN,
  LONGED
DEGLNU GULDEN,
  LUNGED
DEGLOR LODGER
DEGLOS LODGES
DEGLOV GLOVED
DEGLOW GLOWED
DEGLPU GULPED
DEGLSU SLUDGE
DEGMMU GUMMED
DEGMSU SMUDGE
DEGNNU GUNNED
DEGNOP PONGED
DEGNRU GERUND,
  NUDGER
DEGNSU NUDGES
DEGOPR GROPED
DEGORR RODGER
DEGORU DROGUE,
  ROUGED
DEGOST STODGE
DEGPPY GYPPED
DEGPRU PURGED
DEGRSU SURGED

DEGRTU TRUDGE
DEGSTU GUSTED
DEGTTU GUTTED
DEHHSU HUSHED
DEHILP DELPHI
DEHILS SHIELD
DEHILW WHILED
DEHINO HOIDEN, HONIED
DEHINR HINDER
DEHINT HINTED
DEHINW WHINED
DEHIOS HESIOD
DEHIPP HIPPED
DEHIRT DITHER
DEHISS DISHES, HISSED
DEHISW WISHED
DEHIUY YEHUDI
DEHJOS JOSHED
DEHKNO HONKED
DEHKOO HOOKED
DEHLLU HULLED
DEHLNO HOLDEN
DEHLOR HOLDER
DEHLOW HOWLED
DEHLPU UPHELD
DEHLRU HURDLE,
    HURLED
DEHLTY DELYTH
DEHMMU HUMMED
DEHMNY HYMNED
DEHMOT METHOD
DEHMPU HUMPED
DEHMRY RHYMED
DEHNOP PHONED
DEHNOR DEHORN,
    HORNED
DEHNOS NOSHED
DEHNOY HOYDEN
DEHNTU HUNTED
DEHOOP HOOPED
DEHOOS SHOOED
DEHOOT HOOTED
DEHOPP HOPPED
DEHORS HORDES,
    SHORED
DEHORT RED-HOT
DEHOST HOSTED
DEHOSU HOUSED
DEHOSV SHOVED
DEHOSW SHOWED
DEHPST DEPTHS
DEHPSU PUSHED
DEHRSS SHERDS, SHREDS
DEHRSW SHREWD

DEHRTY RHEYDT
DEIIKR KEDIRI
DEIINO IODINE
DEIINS INSIDE
DEIINT TINEID
DEIINV DIVINE
DEIIOS IODISE
DEIIOZ IODIZE
DEIIPT PITIED
DEIIRT TIDIER
DEIISS DIESIS
DEIISX DEIXIS
DEIJLT JILTED
DEIJNO JOINED
DEIJNX JINXED
DEIKLL KILLED
DEIKLM MILKED
DEIKLN KINDLE, LINKED
DEIKLO KELOID
DEIKLT KILTED
DEIKNO OINKED
DEIKNP PINKED
DEIKNR KINDER
DEIKNW WINKED
DEIKNY KIDNEY
DEIKPP KIPPED
DEIKPS SPIKED
DEIKRS RISKED
DEIKRU DUIKER
DEIKSS KISSED
DEIKSV SKIVED
DEIKTT KITTED
DEILLM MILLED
DEILLT TILLED
DEILLW WILLED
DEILMN LIMNED, MINDEL
DEILMO MELOID
DEILMP DIMPLE, LIMPED
DEILMR MILDER
DEILMS MISLED, SMILED
DEILMW MILDEW
DEILNN LINDEN
DEILNO DOLINE, INDOLE,
    LEONID
DEILNT DENTIL
DEILNZ DENZIL
DEILOP DIPLOE, DIPOLE,
    POLDIE
DEILOS ISOLDE, SOILED
DEILOT TOILED
DEILPS DISPEL, LISPED
DEILPX DIPLEX
DEILRS SIDLER
DEILRV DRIVEL

DEILRW WILDER
DEILSS SLIDES
DEILST IDLEST, LISTED,
    SILTED, TILDES
DEILSV DEVILS
DEILSY YIELDS
DEILTT TILTED, TITLED
DEILTU DILUTE
DEILTW WILTED
DEILWY DEWILY, WIDELY,
    WIELDY
DEIMMR DIMMER,
    RIMMED
DEIMMU MEDIUM
DEIMNP IMPEND
DEIMNR MINDER,
    REMIND
DEIMNS DENIMS
DEIMNT MINTED
DEIMOR DORMIE
DEIMOT DO TIME
DEIMPP PIMPED
DEIMPR PRIMED
DEIMPU MUD PIE
DEIMRS DERMIS
DEIMSS MISSED
DEIMST DEMIST, MISTED
DEIMTU TEDIUM
DEINNO DIONNE
DEINNP PINNED
DEINNR DINNER
DEINNS DENNIS, SINNED
DEINNT DENTIN, INDENT,
    INTEND, TINNED
DEINNW ENWIND
DEINOP OPINED
DEINOR INDORE, IRONED
DEINOS NO-SIDE, ONSIDE,
    SIDE-ON
DEINPP NIPPED
DEINPS SNIPED
DEINRS DINERS, RINSED,
    SNIDER
DEINRT TINDER
DEINRU INURED, RUINED
DEINRV DRIVEN, VERDIN
DEINRW REWIND, WINDER
DEINSU UNDIES
DEINSY SIDNEY
DEINTT TINTED
DEINTU DUNITE, UNITED,
    UNTIED
DEINTW TWINED
DEIOOR OROIDE

DEIOOV OVIEDO
DEIOPR DOPIER, PERIOD
DEIOPS POISED
DEIORR DORRIE
DEIORS DORIES
DEIORT EDITOR, RIOTED, TRIODE
DEIORV VOIDER
DEIORW WEIRDO
DEIORZ DOZIER
DEIOSV VIDEOS
DEIOSX OXIDES
DEIOTT DOTTIE
DEIPPP PIPPED
DEIPPR DIPPER, RIPPED
DEIPPS SIPPED
DEIPPT TIPPED
DEIPPZ ZIPPED
DEIPQU PIQUED
DEIPRS PRIDES, PRISED, SPIDER
DEIPRZ PRIZED
DEIPSS PISSED
DEIPST SPITED
DEIPSU UPSIDE
DEIPSV VESPID
DEIPSW SWIPED
DEIPTT PITTED
DEIRRS DERRIS, DRIERS, RIDERS
DEIRRV DRIVER
DEIRST DIREST, DRIEST, STRIDE
DEIRSU DISEUR
DEIRSV DIVERS, DRIVES
DEIRTU TRUDIE
DEIRTV DIVERT
DEISST DEISTS, DESIST
DEISSU DISUSE, ISSUED
DEISTU DUTIES, SUITED
DEISTV DIVEST
DEISTW WIDEST
DEJKNU JUNKED
DEJLOT JOLTED
DEJMPU JUMPED
DEJOTT JOTTED
DEJTTU JUTTED
DEKLOO LOOKED
DEKLRU LURKED
DEKLSU SULKED
DEKMOS SMOKED
DEKNOY DONKEY
DEKNOZ ZONKED
DEKNRU DUNKER

DEKOOR ROOKED
DEKORW WORKED
DEKOST STOKED
DELLLO LOLLED
DELLLU LULLED
DELLMU MULLED
DELLOP POLLED
DELLOR ROLLED
DELLOT TOLLED
DELLOU DUELLO
DELLPU PULLED
DELLRU DULLER
DELLWY LEWDLY
DELMNO DOLMEN
DELMOO LOOMED
DELMOR MOLDER, REMOLD
DELMOS MODELS, SELDOM
DELMOT MOLTED
DELMOU MODULE
DELMOY MELODY
DELMPU LUMPED, PLUMED
DELNOO NOODLE
DELNOR RONDEL
DELNOU LOUDEN, NODULE
DELNRU RUNDLE
DELNWY DELWYN
DELOOP LOOPED, POODLE, POOLED
DELOOS LOOSED, OODLES
DELOOT LOOTED, TOOLED
DELOPP LOPPED
DELOPR POLDER
DELOPS SLOPED
DELOPW PLOWED
DELOPY DEPLOY
DELORS SOLDER
DELORT RETOLD
DELORU LOUDER, LOURED
DELOST OLDEST
DELOSU LOUSED
DELOSV SOLVED
DELOSW SLOWED
DELOSY YODELS
DELOTT DOTTLE, LOTTED
DELOWY YOWLED
DELOYY DOYLEY
DELPPU PULPED
DELPRU PURLED

DELPSU PULSED
DELPTU DUPLET
DELPUX DUPLEX
DELRUY RUDELY
DELSTU LUSTED
DELSTY STYLED
DEMMOS MODEMS
DEMMSU SUMMED
DEMNOO MOONED
DEMNOR MODERN
DEMNOS DEMONS, ESMOND
DEMOOR MOORED, ROOMED
DEMOOT MOOTED
DEMOOZ ZOOMED
DEMOPP MOPPED
DEMOPR ROMPED
DEMOPS MOPEDS
DEMORR DORMER
DEMORT DERMOT
DEMORW WORMED
DEMOST MODEST
DEMPPU PUMPED
DEMPRU DUMPER
DEMRRU MURDER
DEMRSU DEMURS
DEMSSU MUSSED
DENNOT TENDON
DENNOU UNDONE
DENNPU PUNNED
DENNRU DUNNER
DENNSU SUNNED
DENOOS DO ONE'S, NODOSE
DENOOW WOODEN
DENOPR PERNOD, PONDER
DENORS DRONES, SNORED
DENORT RODENT
DENORU UNDOER
DENORV VENDOR
DENORW DOWNER, WONDER
DENORY RODNEY, YONDER
DENOST OSTEND, STONED
DENOSW SNOWED
DENOSY DOYENS
DENOSZ DOZENS
DENOTW WONTED
DENPRU PRUNED
DENPSU SEND-UP

DENPTU PUNTED
DENRST TRENDS
DENRSU NURSED, SUNDER
DENRTU TURNED
DENRTY TRENDY
DENSUU UNUSED
DENSUW SUNDEW
DENSYY SYDNEY
DENTTU NUTTED
DEOOPP POOPED
DEOORS RODEOS
DEOORT ROOTED
DEOORV OVERDO
DEOOTT TOOTED
DEOPPP POPPED
DEOPPS SOPPED
DEOPPT TOPPED
DEOPRT DEPORT, DE
    TROP, PORTED
DEOPRU POURED
DEOPRV PROVED
DEOPRW POWDER
DEOPST DEPOTS, DESPOT,
    POSTED
DEOPTT POTTED
DEOPTU POUTED
DEOQTU QUOTED
DEORRS ORDERS
DEORRU ORDURE
DEORRV DROVER
DEORRW REWORD
DEORSS DOSSER
DEORST SORTED, STORED,
    STRODE
DEORSU DOUSER,
    ROUSED, SOURED
DEORSV DROVES
DEORSW DOWSER,
    DROWSE
DEORTT DOTTER,
    ROTTED
DEORTU DETOUR,
    ROUTED, TOURED
DEORUV DEVOUR
DEOSST TOSSED
DEOSSU SOUSED
DEOSTU OUSTED
DEOSTW STOWED
DEOSUX EXODUS
DEOTTT TOTTED
DEOTTU TOUTED
DEOTUV DEVOUT
DEOTUX TUXEDO
DEPPPU PUPPED

DEPPSU SUPPED
DEPPTU TUPPED
DEPRRU PURRED
DEPRSU PRUDES, PURSED
DEPRUY DUPERY
DEPSSU PSEUDS
DEPSUY PSEUDY
DEPTTU PUTTED
DEPTUY DEPUTY
DERRSY DRYERS
DERSSU DURESS
DERSSY DRESSY
DERSTU DUSTER, RUDEST,
    RUSTED
DERTTU RUTTED
DESSSU SUSSED
DESTUV DUVETS
DFFIMO MID-OFF
DFGGOO FOGDOG
DFGIIR FRIGID
DFIINY NIDIFY
DFIIRT TRIFID
DFIKNO KIND OF
DFILOR FLORID
DFILSU FLUIDS
DFIMOY MODIFY
DFIORS FIORDS
DFIRST DRIFTS
DFIRTY DRIFTY
DFJORS FJORDS
DFLNOU UNFOLD
DFLNOY FONDLY
DFLOOS FLOODS
DFNORS FRONDS
DFNSUU FUNDUS
DGGNOU DUGONG,
    GUNDOG
DGHIIN HIDING
DGHINY DINGHY
DGHITW DWIGHT
DGHOOT HOT DOG
DGHOUY DOUGHY
DGIILN IDLING
DGIINN DINING
DGIINO INDIGO
DGIINP PIDGIN
DGIINR INGRID, RIDING
DGIINS SIDING
DGIINT TIDING
DGIINV DIVING
DGIIST DIGITS
DGIJOU JUDOGI
DGILNO DOLING
DGILOT DIGLOT

DGILSU GUILDS
DGIMTU MIDGUT
DGINOP DOPING, PONGID
DGINOS DOINGS, DOSING
DGINOT DOTING, TIN
    GOD
DGINOU GUIDON
DGINOW GODWIN
DGINOZ DOZING
DGINPU DUPING
DGINRS GRINDS
DGINRU DURING
DGINRY DRYING
DGIOTW GODWIT
DGIRTU TURGID
DGLOOY GOODLY
DGLSUY SLUDGY
DGMSUY SMUDGY
DGNOOR DRONGO,
    GORDON, GRODNO
DGNOOS GODSON
DGNORU GROUND
DGNOSU SUN GOD
DGOOPT TOP DOG
DGORSU GOURDS
DGOSTY STODGY
DGOTUU DUGOUT
DHIINS SINDHI
DHIIPS HISPID
DHIISW WIDISH
DHIJTU JUDITH
DHILOS OLDISH
DHIMOS MODISH
DHINOO HINDOO
DHINSU HINDUS
DHIORR HORRID
DHIOST DHOTIS
DHIOSV DOVISH
DHIRST THIRDS
DHISTW WIDTHS
DHLOPU HOLDUP,
    UPHOLD
DHLOSU SHOULD
DHLTUU DULUTH
DHNOSU HOUNDS,
    HUDSON
DHOOOO HOODOO
DHOORT HOT ROD
DHORSU SHROUD
DIILMP LIMPID
DIILOP LIPOID
DIILOS SOLIDI
DIILPS LIPIDS
DIILQU LIQUID

DIILST DISTIL
DIILTY TIDILY
DIIMNU INDIUM
DIIMOS IDIOMS, IODISM
DIIMOU OIDIUM
DIIMTW DIMWIT
DIIMTY DIMITY
DIINOX DIOXIN
DIINRS INDRIS
DIIOST IDIOTS
DIJNNS DJINNS
DIKLNY KINDLY
DIKMNU DINKUM
DIKNNU UNKIND
DIKNRS DRINKS
DILLMY MILDLY
DILLNO DILLON
DILLRS DRILLS
DILLSY IDYLLS
DILLWY WILDLY
DILMOR MILORD
DILMPY DIMPLY
DILNNU DUNLIN
DILNTU INDULT
DILOSS SOLIDS
DILOST STOLID
DILOXY XYLOID
DILOYZ DOZILY
DIMMSU DIM SUM
DIMNOO DOMINO
DIMNSU NUDISM
DIMOPU PODIUM
DIMOSU SODIUM
DIMOSW WISDOM
DIMSST MIDSTS
DINNUW UNWIND
DINOOR INDOOR
DINOPU UNIPOD
DINOSW DISOWN
DINOSY SIDONY
DINOWW WINDOW
DINPTU PUNDIT
DINPUW UPWIND
DINSTU DUSTIN, NUDIST
DINTUY NUDITY, UNTIDY
DIOOPS ISOPOD
DIOORT TOROID
DIOOSU IODOUS, ODIOUS
DIOOSV OVOIDS
DIOOTX TOXOID
DIOPRT TORPID, TRIPOD
DIORRT TORRID
DIOSTT DITTOS
DIOSTU STUDIO

DIOSWW WIDOWS
DIPPRY DRIPPY
DIPRTU PUTRID
DIPSTU STUPID
DIQSSU SQUIDS
DJNNOO DONJON
DKNRSU DRUNKS
DLLOOP DOLLOP
DLLORY DROLLY, LORDLY
DLLOUW LUDLOW
DLLOUY LOUDLY
DLMOSU MOULDS
DLMOUY MOULDY
DLNNOO LONDON
DLNNOY LYNDON
DLNOOS SOLD ON
DLNOTU UNTOLD
DLNUUY UNDULY
DLOOPZ PODZOL
DLOORU DOLOUR
DLORSW WORLDS
DLORUY DOURLY
DMNOOS OSMOND
DMNOSU MOUNDS, OSMUND
DMOOSY SODOMY
DMORSU DORSUM
DMRTUU UDMURT
DNOORS DONORS, RONDOS
DNOPSU POUNDS
DNORSU ROUNDS
DNORTU ROTUND
DNOSSU SOUNDS
DNOSSY SYNODS
DNOSUW WOUNDS
DNRSUY SUNDRY
DOOOOV VOODOO
DOOPRU UROPOD
DOOPRY DROOPY
DOORSU ODOURS
DOPRSY DROPSY
DORRTY DRY ROT
DORSSW SWORDS
DORSSY DROSSY
DORSTU STROUD
DORSWY DROWSY
DPSTUU DUSTUP
DRSTUY STURDY
EEEEGG GEE-GEE
EEEEPT TEEPEE
EEEEWW WEE-WEE
EEEFFT EFFETE
EEEFLR FEELER

EEEFRR REEFER
EEEFRZ FREEZE
EEEGMR EMERGE
EEEGNO EOGENE
EEEGNR RENEGE
EEEGNU EUGENE
EEEGRZ GEEZER
EEEHLN HELENE
EEEHLR HEELER
EEEHNT ETHENE
EEEHST SEETHE
EEEHTT TEETHE
EEEHWZ WHEEZE
EEEILN EILEEN
EEEJRR JEERER
EEEKLY KEELEY
EEEKMR MEEKER
EEEKNR KEENER
EEEKNT KETENE
EEEKPR KEEPER
EEEKRS SEEKER
EEELMS MELEES
EEELNV ELEVEN
EEELPR PEELER
EEELRR REELER
EEELSS LESSEE
EEELSV LEVEES, SLEEVE
EEELSY ELYSEE
EEELTY EYELET
EEEMMS SEMEME
EEEMRS SEEMER
EEEMRT METEER
EEEMST ESTEEM
EEENRS SERENE
EEENRT ENTRÉE, RETENE
EEENRV VENEER
EEENSZ SNEEZE
EEEOPP EPOPEE
EEEPPR PEEPER
EEEPRW WEEPER
EEEPST TEPEES
EEERRV REVERE
EEERSV REEVES, SEVERE
EEERTT TEETER, TERETE
EEERVW WEEVER
EEESTT SETTEE
EEESTV STEEVE
EEFFOT TOFFEE
EEFFSU EFFUSE
EEFGIR FERGIE
EEFGRU REFUGE
EEFHIR HEIFER
EEFHOR HEREOF
EEFHRT HEFTER

EEFILN FELINE
EEFILR RELIEF
EEFINR REFINE
EEFIRZ FRIEZE
EEFLLO FELLOE
EEFLLR FELLER
EEFLNN FENNEL
EEFLNS FLENSE
EEFLRT REFLET
EEFLRU FERULE, REFUEL
EEFLRX REFLEX
EEFLRY FREELY
EEFLST FLEETS
EEFLSX FLEXES
EEFLTT FETTLE
EEFLUY EYEFUL
EEFPRR PREFER
EEFPTY TEPEFY
EEFRRT FERRET
EEFRST FESTER, FREEST
EEFRSU REFUSE
EEFRTT FETTER
EEFRTU REFUTE
EEFSZZ FEZZES
EEGGIM MEGGIE
EEGGIR REGGIE
EEGGLP PEG LEG
EEGGOR GEORGE
EEGILS LIEGES
EEGILT ELEGIT
EEGIMR ÉMIGRÉ, REGIME
EEGINN ENGINE
EEGINP PEEING
EEGINS GENIES, SEEING
EEGINT TEEING
EEGINW WEEING
EEGINY EYEING
EEGIRS SERGEI
EEGIRT GERTIE
EEGIRV GRIEVE
EEGISS SIEGES
EEGLMU LEGUME
EEGLNT GENTLE
EEGLRS LEGERS
EEGLRT GRETEL, REGLET
EEGLTY GLEETY
EEGMNO GENOME
EEGMNR GERMEN
EEGMNT TEGMEN
EEGMRR MERGER
EEGNOP PONGEE
EEGNRS GENRES, GREENS
EEGNRT REGENT
EEGNRY ENERGY

EEGNTW TEGWEN
EEGRRT REGRET
EEGRRV VERGER
EEGRRY GREYER
EEGRSS EGRESS
EEGRST EGRETS
EEGRSV VERGES
EEGRSY GEYSER
EEGRTT GETTER
EEHIMP PHEMIE
EEHINN HENNIE
EEHINR HEREIN, INHERE
EEHINT EITHNE, THEINE
EEHIPS HEPSIE
EEHIRT EITHER
EEHITV THIEVE
EEHKLS SHEKEL
EEHLLN HELLEN
EEHLLR HELLER
EEHLLS HELLES
EEHLMT HELMET
EEHLNY HENLEY
EEHLPR HELPER
EEHLSV HELVES, SHELVE
EEHLSW WHEELS
EEHMMR HEMMER
EEHMNP HEMPEN
EEHMNS ENMESH
EEHMRS HERMES
EEHMSS MESHES
EEHMST THEMES
EEHMUX EXHUME
EEHNOR HEREON
EEHNOX HEXONE
EEHNPS SPHENE
EEHNPW NEPHEW
EEHNRR HERREN
EEHNRT NETHER
EEHNTY ETHYNE
EEHORR HERERO
EEHORS HEROES
EEHORT HERETO
EEHORW HOWE'ER
EEHOSX HEXOSE
EEHOTW TOWHEE
EEHPRS HERPES, SPHERE
EEHPSY HEPSEY
EEHRST ESTHER, HESTER,
   THREES
EEHRSW HEWERS
EEHRSY HERESY
EEHRTT TETHER
EEHRTW WETHER
EEHRVY HERVEY

EEHSST SHEETS, THESES
EEHWYY WHEYEY
EEHWYZ WHEEZY
EEIJNN JENNIE
EEIJSS JESSIE
EEIKLL KELLIE
EEIKLP KELPIE
EEIKRR KERRIE
EEILLN NELLIE
EEILLS LESLIE, LIESEL
EEILMR MERIEL
EEILNN LENNIE
EEILNO LEONIE
EEILNR LIERNE, RELINE
EEILNS ENSILE, SENILE
EEILNW EILWEN
EEILOS ELOISE
EEILPS ELSPIE
EEILPT PELITE
EEILRS RESILE
EEILRV EVILER, LEVIER,
   RELIVE, REVILE, VEILER
EEILRY EERILY
EEILSV LEVIES
EEILSX EXILES, ILEXES
EEILTT LETTIE
EEILVW WEEVIL
EEIMNR ERMINE
EEIMNY YEMENI
EEIMPR EMPIRE
EEIMRS MISERE, REMISE
EEIMRT MÉTIER
EEIMSS EMESIS
EEIMST SEMITE
EEINNP PINENE
EEINNV VIENNE
EEINPR REPINE
EEINQU EQUINE
EEINRS NEREIS, SEREIN,
   SERINE
EEINRT ENTIRE
EEINRV ENVIER, NIEVRE,
   VENIRE
EEINSS NESSIE, SEINES
EEINSV ENVIES
EEINTT NETTIE
EEINTX EXTINE
EEIORS SOIREE
EEIPPY YIPPEE
EEIPRR PIERRE
EEIPRS ESPIER
EEIPRX EXPIRE
EEIPTT PETITE
EEIPTW PEEWIT

EEIRRT RETIRE	EELMRY MERELY	EEMRSU RÉSUMÉ
EEIRRW REWIRE	EELMSY SEEMLY	EEMRTU MEERUT
EEIRSS SEISER, SERIES	EELMTT METTLE	EEMSSS MESSES
EEIRSV REVISE	EELNNT LENTEN	EEMSTU MUSTEE
EEIRSX SEXIER	EELNOR LENORE, LOREEN	EENNOR NOREEN
EEIRSY EYRIES	EELNOV ELEVON	EENNOV EVONNE
EEIRSZ SEIZER	EELNPS SPLEEN	EENNRS RENNES
EEIRVV REVIVE	EELNRT RELENT	EENNRT RENNET, TENNER
EEIRVW REVIEW, VIEWER	EELNSS LENSES, LESSEN	EENNSU UNSEEN
EEISST TESSIE	EELNST NESTLE	EENNUV UNEVEN
EEISSV SIEVES	EELNTT NETTLE	EENOPR OPENER,
EEISTV STEVIE	EELNUV VENULE	REOPEN, REPONE
EEJJNU JEJUNE	EELNVY EVELYN, EVENLY	EENOPT POTEEN
EEJKRR JERKER	EELNXY XYLENE	EENOSV VENOSE
EEJLNO JOLEEN, JOLENE	EELOPP PEOPLE	EENOTV VENETO
EEJLSW JEWELS	EELOPR ELOPER	EENOTW TOWNEE
EEJMOR JEROME	EELORS OR ELSE	EENOVZ EVZONE
EEJMRY JEREMY	EELORZ LOZERE	EENPRT REPENT
EEJNNT JENNET	EELOVV EVOLVE	EENPRY PYRENE
EEJRST JESTER	EELPPU PEEPUL	EENQSU QUEENS
EEJRSY JERSEY	EELPRS LEPERS	EENQUY QUEENY
EEJSSW JEWESS	EELPRT PELTER, PETREL	EENRRT RENTER
EEJSTT JET SET	EELPRY YELPER	EENRSS SNEERS
EEKLMN KENELM	EELPST PESTLE	EENRST ERNEST, NESTER,
EEKLMY MEEKLY	EELPSV PELVES	RESENT, TENSER
EEKLNN KENNEL	EELPSY SLEEPY	EENRSU ENSURE
EEKLNR KERNEL	EELQSU SEQUEL	EENRSV NERVES
EEKLNY KEENLY	EELRSS LESSER	EENRTT TENTER
EEKLTT KETTLE	EELRST LESTER	EENRTU NEUTER,
EEKLWY WEEKLY	EELRSV LEVERS	TENURE, TUREEN
EEKMNS MEKNES	EELRTT LETTER	EENRTV VENTER
EEKMRS KERMES	EELRTW WELTER	EENRTX EXTERN
EEKNOT KETONE	EELRUV VELURE	EENRVY VENERY
EEKORV EVOKER, REVOKE	EELSST STEELS	EENSSS SENSES
EEKOST KETOSE	EELSSV SELVES, VESSEL	EENSST TENSES
EEKPPU UPKEEP	EELSTT SETTLE	EENSSV SEVENS
EEKPRU PERUKE	EELSTV SVELTE	EENSTT TENETS
EEKRST KESTER	EELSTY SLEETY, STEELY	EENSTV EVENTS, STEVEN
EEKRSW SKEWER	EELSWY WESLEY	EENSTW NEWEST
EEKRSY KERSEY	EELTVV VELVET	EENSUV VENUES
EELLMU LEMUEL	EELTVW TWELVE	EENSWY SWEENY
EELLNO NOELLE	EEMNOR MOREEN	EENSYZ SNEEZY
EELLOV O LEVEL	EEMNOY YEOMEN	EENTTX EXTENT
EELLPT PELLET	EEMNSS MENSES	EENTUX EXEUNT
EELLRS SELLER	EEMNSY YES-MEN	EEOPRS REPOSE
EELLRT RETELL, TELLER	EEMNYZ ENZYME	EEOPRU EUROPE
EELLRY ELLERY, YELLER	EEMOPT METOPE	EEOPST TOPEES
EELLSV LEVELS	EEMORT EMOTER,	EEOPSX EXPOSÉ
EELLSY LESLEY	METEOR, REMOTE	EEOPTU TOUPEE
EELMNY EMELYN	EEMORV REMOVE	EEORST STEREO
EELMOT OMELET	EEMPRS SEMPRE	EEORSV SOEVER
EELMPT PELMET, TEMPLE	EEMPRT TEMPER	EEORSZ ZEROES
EELMRT MELTER	EEMPTX EXEMPT	EEORTV VETOER
EELMRW MEWLER	EEMRST METERS, METRES	EEORUV OEUVRE

EEOSST SETOSE
EEOSTV VETOES
EEPPPR PEPPER
EEPPST STEPPE
EEPRRY PREYER
EEPRSS SPREES
EEPRST PESTER, PETERS, PRESET
EEPRSU PERUSE, PUREES, RUPEES
EEPRSV VESPER
EEPRSW SPEWER
EEPRTT PETTER
EEPRTU REPUTE
EEPRTW PEWTER
EEPRTX EXPERT
EEPSSW SWEEPS
EEPSTT SEPTET
EEPTTU PUTTEE
EEQRSU QUEERS
EEQSUU QUEUES
EERRST RESTER
EERRSV REVERS, SERVER
EERRTT TERRET
EERRTU URETER
EERRTV REVERT
EERSST STEERS
EERSSV SERVES, SEVRES, VERSES
EERSSW SEWERS
EERSTT SETTER, STREET, TESTER
EERSTU RETUSE
EERSTV REVEST
EERSTW WESTER
EERSTX EXSERT
EERSUV REVUES
EERSVW SWERVE
EERTTT TETTER
EERTTW WETTER
EERTUY TUYERE
EERTVV VERVET
EERTVX VERTEX
EESSTT SESTET, TESTES
EESSTW SWEETS
EESTTU SUTTEE
EESTTW TWEETS
EESTTX SEXTET
EETTVY YVETTE
EFFFFO EFF OFF
EFFGIN EFFING
EFFGIR GRIFFE
EFFGIY EFFIGY
EFFGOR GOFFER

EFFILP PIFFLE
EFFILR RIFFLE
EFFLMU MUFFLE
EFFLRU RUFFLE
EFFLUX EFFLUX
EFFNOO ONE-OFF
EFFORS OFFERS
EFFORT EFFORT
EFFOST OFFSET, SET-OFF
EFFPRU PUFFER
EFFRSU SUFFER
EFFTTU TUFFET
EFGINR FINGER, FRINGE
EFGINT FETING
EFGIOS FOGIES
EFGIRU FIGURE
EFGLNU ENGULF
EFGLOR GOLFER
EFGOOR FOREGO
EFGORR FORGER
EFGORS FORGES, GOFERS
EFGORT FORGET
EFGRSU FERGUS
EFGSUU FUGUES
EFHILS ELFISH
EFHIRS FISHER
EFHISS FISHES
EFHIST FETISH
EFHLSY FLESHY
EFHRRU FUHRER
EFHSTT THEFTS
EFIINT FINITE
EFIKNR KNIFER
EFIKNU FUKIEN
EFILLR FILLER, REFILL
EFILLT FILLET
EFILNY FINELY
EFILOS FILOSE
EFILPP FIPPLE
EFILPR PILFER
EFILRR RIFLER
EFILRS FLIERS, LIFERS, RIFLES
EFILRT FILTER, LIFTER, TRIFLE
EFILRU IREFUL
EFILST FILETS, ITSELF, STIFLE
EFILSU FUSILE
EFILTU FUTILE
EFILWY WIFELY
EFILZZ FIZZLE
EFIMRR FIRMER
EFINRY FINERY

EFINST FEINTS, FINEST, INFEST
EFINSU INFUSE
EFIORX FOXIER
EFIOST SOFTIE
EFIPRX PREFIX
EFIRRS FRIERS
EFIRSS SERIFS
EFIRST REFITS, SIFTER, STRIFE
EFIRSU FURIES
EFIRSV FIVERS
EFIRSX FIXERS
EFIRTT FITTER, TITFER
EFIRVY VERIFY
EFIRZZ FIZZER
EFISTY FEISTY
EFKLSU FLUKES
EFKLUY FLUKEY
EFKNRU FUNKER
EFLLOW FELLOW
EFLLRU FULLER
EFLMSY MYSELF
EFLNNU FUNNEL
EFLNOS FELONS
EFLNOT TEFLON
EFLNOY FELONY
EFLNTU FLUENT
EFLOOT FOOTLE
EFLOOZ FOOZLE
EFLORT FLORET, LOFTER
EFLORU FOULER
EFLORW FLOWER, FOWLER
EFLORX FLEXOR
EFLOUW WOEFUL
EFLPRU PURFLE
EFLRRU FURLER
EFLRSY FLYERS
EFLRTU FLUTER
EFLRUU RUEFUL
EFLRUX REFLUX
EFLSTU FLUTES
EFLSUU USEFUL
EFMNOT FOMENT
EFMORR FORMER, REFORM
EFMRSU FEMURS
EFMTUY TUMEFY
EFNORS FRESNO
EFNORZ FROZEN
EFNOST SEFTON, SOFTEN
EFNRUZ FRUNZE
EFNRYZ FRENZY

EFOORT FOETOR, FOOTER
EFOORW WOOFER
EFORRT TREFOR
EFORRU FURORE
EFORRV FERVOR
EFORST FOREST, FORTES,
  FOSTER, SOFTER
EFORSY FOYERS
EFOSTU FOETUS
EFRRSU SURFER
EFRRSY FRYERS
EFRRTU ERFURT
EFRSSU FUSSER
EFRTTU TUFTER
EFRTUU FUTURE
EFSSSU FUSSES
EGGGIL GIGGLE
EGGGLO GOGGLE
EGGGNO EGGNOG
EGGHIL HIGGLE
EGGHOR HOGGER
EGGHRU HUGGER
EGGIJL JIGGLE
EGGIJR JIGGER
EGGILN NIGGLE
EGGILW WIGGLE
EGGINR GINGER, NIGGER
EGGIRR RIGGER
EGGJLO JOGGLE
EGGJLU JUGGLE
EGGJOR JOGGER
EGGLOR LOGGER
EGGLOT TOGGLE
EGGLRU GURGLE, LUGGER
EGGMRU MUGGER
EGGNTU NUGGET
EGGORR GORGER,
  GREGOR
EGGORS GORGES
EGGORU GOUGER
EGGOSU GOUGES
EGGRTU TUGGER
EGHHIR HIGHER
EGHHIT EIGHTH, HEIGHT
EGHHIU HUGHIE
EGHHSU HUGHES
EGHIIN HIEING
EGHILS SLEIGH
EGHINO HOEING
EGHINR HINGER
EGHINS HINGES, NEIGHS
EGHINT GETHIN
EGHINW HEWING,
  WHINGE

EGHINX HEXING
EGHIOT HOGTIE
EGHIRS SIGHER
EGHIST EIGHTS
EGHITW WEIGHT
EGHITY EIGHTY
EGHLMP PHLEGM
EGHLNT LENGTH
EGHLUY HUGELY
EGHMMO MEGOHM
EGHNOU ENOUGH
EGHNRU HUNGER
EGHNST THEGNS
EGHOPR GOPHER
EGHOTT GHETTO
EGHRSU GUSHER
EGHSTU HUGEST
EGIILL GILLIE
EGIILR GIRLIE
EGIIMN GEMINI
EGIINT IGNITE
EGIJLN JINGLE
EGIJRS REJIGS
EGIKNP PEKING
EGIKNY KEYING
EGILLR GRILLE
EGILLU LIGULE
EGILMN MINGLE
EGILMP MEGILP
EGILMT GIMLET
EGILNO LEGION
EGILNR LINGER
EGILNS GLENIS, SINGLE
EGILNT TINGLE
EGILOR LOGIER
EGILPT PIGLET
EGILRS GRILSE
EGILRU UGLIER
EGILRZ GRIZEL
EGILST LEGIST
EGIMNO IMOGEN
EGIMNT METING
EGIMNW MEWING
EGIMOS EGOISM
EGIMPU GUIMPE
EGINNS ENSIGN
EGINOP PIGEON
EGINOR IGNORE, REGION
EGINOS SOIGNÉ
EGINOT TOEING
EGINOW WIGEON
EGINRR ERRING, RINGER
EGINRS REIGNS, RESIGN,
  SIGNER, SINGER

EGINRW WINGER
EGINSS GNEISS, SINGES
EGINST INGEST, SIGNET
EGINSU GENIUS
EGINSW SEWING, SWINGE,
  WINGES
EGINSX SEXING
EGINTW TWINGE
EGINVX VEXING
EGIOOR GOOIER
EGIORR GORIER
EGIORS ORGIES, SERGIO
EGIORT GOITRE
EGIOST EGOIST
EGIPRR GRIPER
EGIPRS GRIPES
EGIRRT TRIGER
EGIRST TIGERS
EGIRTV GRIVET
EGISSU GUISES, GUSSIE
EGJLNU JUNGLE
EGKMNO MEKONG
EGKRRU KRUGER
EGLLTU GULLET
EGLNNU GUNNEL
EGLNOR LONGER
EGLNOU LOUNGE
EGLNPU PLUNGE
EGLNRU LUNGER
EGLNSU LUNGES
EGLNSY GLENYS
EGLNTU GLUTEN
EGLNTY GENTLY
EGLOPR PROLEG
EGLOPS GOSPEL
EGLORU REGULO
EGLORV GLOVER, GROVEL
EGLORW GLOWER
EGLOSV GLOVES
EGLOUY EULOGY
EGLPRU GULPER
EGLUZZ GUZZLE
EGMNNU GUNMEN
EGMNOR MONGER
EGMNOS GNOMES
EGMNTU NUTMEG
EGMORU MORGUE
EGMRTU TERGUM
EGNNOO NONEGO
EGNNOU GUENON
EGNNRU GUNNER
EGNOOR OREGON
EGNOPS SPONGE
EGNORS GONERS

EGNORV GOVERN
EGNORY ERYNGO,
  GROYNE
EGNOTU TONGUE
EGNOXY OXYGEN
EGNPPU PENGPU
EGNRTU GUNTER,
  URGENT
EGNRTY GENTRY
EGNRWY GERWYN
EGOORV GROOVE
EGOOST STOOGE
EGOPRR GROPER
EGOPRS GROPES
EGORRV GROVER
EGORRW GROWER
EGORSS OGRESS
EGORSU GROUSE,
  ROGUES, RUGOSE
EGORSV GROVES
EGORSY GYROSE
EGOSSV VOSGES
EGOSUV VOGUES
EGOSYZ ZYGOSE
EGOTYZ ZYGOTE
EGPRRU PURGER
EGPRSU PURGES, SPURGE
EGPSTU GETUPS
EGRRSU SURGER
EGRSSU SURGES
EGRTTU GUTTER
EGSSTU GUESTS, GUSSET
EHHIKS SHEIKH
EHHIRT HITHER
EHHNPY HYPHEN
EHHRST THRESH
EHIIJM HIMEJI
EHIIPP HIPPIE
EHIIST SHIITE
EHIJSW JEWISH
EHIKRS HIKERS, SHRIEK,
  SHRIKE
EHILLL HILLEL
EHILLR HILLER
EHILMU HELIUM
EHILOR HOLIER
EHILOS HELIOS, ISOHEL
EHILOT EOLITH
EHILRS RELISH
EHILRT HITLER, LITHER
EHIMNR MENHIR
EHIMNT HIT MEN
EHIMNU INHUME
EHIMOR HOMIER

EHIMRT HERMIT
EHIMST THEISM
EHINOR HEROIN, ON
  HIRE
EHINOT HOTIEN
EHINRS SHINER, SHRINE
EHINRT HINTER
EHINRW WHINER
EHINSS SHENSI
EHINSW NEWISH, WHINES
EHINTW WHITEN
EHINTZ ZENITH
EHIOPS SOPHIE
EHIOPT OPHITE
EHIORS HOSIER
EHIORT HERIOT
EHIOST HOSTIE
EHIOTT HOTTIE
EHIPPR HIPPER
EHIPRS PERISH, RESHIP
EHIRRS SHERRI
EHIRSS HISSER, SHIRES
EHIRST THEIRS
EHIRSV SHIVER, SHRIVE
EHIRSW WISHER
EHIRTT HITTER, TITHER
EHIRTU RUTHIE
EHIRTV THRIVE
EHIRTW WHITER,
  WITHER, WRITHE
EHIRTZ ZITHER
EHISSS HISSES
EHISST SHIEST, THESIS
EHISSW WISHES
EHISTT THEIST, TITHES
EHISTW WHITES
EHJOOR JOHORE
EHJOPS JOSEPH
EHJORT JETHRO
EHJOSS JOSHES
EHKLSW WHELKS
EHKNOR HONKER
EHKOOR HOOKER
EHKORS KOSHER
EHKRSU HUSKER
EHLLOR HOLLER
EHLLOS HELLOS
EHLLOW HOWELL
EHLLRU HULLER
EHLLSS SHELLS
EHLLSY SHELLY
EHLMMU HUMMEL
EHLMOO MOHOLE
EHLMOP PHLOEM

EHLMOS HOLMES
EHLMOY HOMELY
EHLMTY METHYL
EHLNOP HOLPEN,
  PHENOL
EHLNPY PHENYL
EHLOPP HOPPLE
EHLORW HOWLER
EHLOST HOSTEL, HOTELS
EHLOSU HOUSEL
EHLOSV HOVELS, SHOVEL
EHLOTW HOWLET
EHLPSW WHELPS
EHLRRU HURLER
EHLRSY SHERYL
EHLRTU HURTLE, LUTHER
EHLRUY HURLEY
EHLSSU LUSHES
EHLSTU HUSTLE, SLEUTH
EHLUXY HUXLEY
EHMMRU HUMMER
EHMNOR HERMON
EHMNSY HYMENS
EHMORT MOTHER
EHMRST THERMS
EHMRSY RHYMES
EHMRUY RHEUMY
EHMSSU MUSHES
EHNOPS PHONES
EHNOPY PHONEY
EHNORS HERONS
EHNORT HORNET,
  THRONE
EHNOST HONEST
EHNRTU HUNTER
EHNSTT TENTHS
EHOOOP HOOPOE
EHOOPR HOOPER
EHOOPY PHOOEY
EHOORT HOOTER
EHOORV HOOVER
EHOOST SOOTHE
EHOOSV HOOVES
EHOPPR HOPPER
EHOPRS POSHER
EHOPRT POTHER
EHOPRU UPHROE
EHORSS SHORES
EHORST OTHERS, THROES
EHORSV SHOVER
EHORSW SHOWER,
  WHORES
EHORTT HOTTER
EHORTV THROVE

EHORTX EXHORT
EHORTY THEORY
EHOSSU HOUSES
EHOSSV SHOVES
EHPRSU PUSHER
EHPRSY SYPHER
EHPRYZ ZEPHYR
EHPSSU PUSHES
EHRRSU RUSHER
EHRRSY SHERRY
EHRRTU HURTER
EHRRWY WHERRY
EHRSSU RHESUS, RUSHES, USHERS
EHRSSW SHREWS
EHRSTY THYRSE
EHSSTU TUSHES
EHSSTY SHYEST
EIIKNP PINKIE
EIIKNR INKIER
EIILLL LILLIE
EIILLM MILLIE
EIILLS LILIES
EIILLW WILLIE
EIILMR LIMIER
EIILMS SIMILE
EIILMU MILIEU
EIILNN IN LINE
EIILNR INLIER
EIILNS LIE-INS
EIILNU IN LIEU
EIILNV LIVE-IN
EIILOR OILIER
EIILRV VIRILE
EIILRW WILIER
EIILRX ELIXIR
EIILZZ LIZZIE
EIIMNN MINNIE
EIINNT INTINE
EIINNV VINNIE
EIINNW WINNIE
EIINOS IONISE
EIINOZ IONIZE
EIINPR PINIER
EIINPT PINITE, TIEPIN
EIINRT TINIER
EIINRV IRVINE
EIINSS SEISIN
EIINST TIE-INS
EIINTV INVITE
EIINVV VIVIEN
EIIPST PITIES
EIIPSX PIXIES
EIIRRW WIRIER

EIIRSS IRISES
EIIRTX TRIXIE
EIIRVZ VIZIER
EIISSS SISSIE
EIJKNR JERKIN
EIJKNU JUNKIE
EIJLRT JILTER
EIJLSU JULIES
EIJLTU JULIET
EIJNNO ENJOIN
EIJNOR JOINER, REJOIN
EIJNRU INJURE
EIJNSX JINXES
EIJRSU JURIES
EIJRTT JITTER
EIJSTU JESUIT
EIKLLR KILLER
EIKLLY LIKELY
EIKLMR MILKER
EIKLNS SILKEN
EIKLNT TINKLE
EIKLNU UNLIKE
EIKLNV KELVIN
EIKLNW WELKIN, WINKLE
EIKLRT KILTER
EIKMOS ESKIMO
EIKMST KISMET
EIKNOV INVOKE
EIKNPR PINKER
EIKNRS SINKER
EIKNRT TINKER
EIKNRW WINKER
EIKNSS SKEINS
EIKNSV KNIVES
EIKNTT KITTEN
EIKOOR ROOKIE
EIKOPR POKIER
EIKPPR KIPPER
EIKPSS SPIKES
EIKRRS RISKER
EIKRSS KISSER, KRISES, SKIERS
EIKRST STRIKE, TRIKES
EIKRSV SKIVER
EIKSSS KISSES
EILLMR MILLER
EILLMT MILLET
EILLNO LIONEL, NIELLO
EILLNT LENTIL, LINTEL
EILLOT ELLIOT
EILLPU PILULE
EILLRT RILLET, TILLER
EILLRW WILLER
EILLSU ILL-USE

EILLTT LITTLE
EILLTW WILLET
EILLVY EVILLY, LIVELY, VILELY
EILMNO OILMEN
EILMNR LIMNER, MERLIN
EILMNS SIMNEL
EILMNV MELVIN
EILMNY MYELIN
EILMOS MOLISE
EILMOT MOTILE
EILMPP PIMPLE
EILMPR LIMPER
EILMPS SIMPLE
EILMPT LIMPET
EILMPU PILEUM
EILMPW WIMPLE
EILMRS MILERS, SMILER
EILMRT MILTER
EILMRU MURIEL
EILMRW WILMER
EILMSS SMILES
EILMSU MUESLI
EILMSY LIMEYS
EILMTU TELIUM
EILMTY TIMELY
EILNNO LONNIE, ONLINE
EILNNT LINNET
EILNOR ELINOR
EILNOS INSOLE, LESION
EILNPP NIPPLE
EILNPS SPINEL, SPLINE
EILNPT PINTLE
EILNPU LINEUP, LUPINE
EILNRS LINERS
EILNRT LINTER
EILNST ENLIST, INLETS, LISTEN, SILENT, TINSEL
EILNSV SNIVEL
EILNSY LYSINE
EILNTY LENITY
EILNUV UNLIVE, UNVEIL
EILOOR ORIOLE
EILOOT OOLITE
EILOPS PILOSE
EILOPT POLITE
EILORT LOIRET, LOITER, TOILER
EILORV OLIVER
EILOSU LOUISE
EILOSV OLIVES
EILOSX ISOLEX
EILOTT LOTTIE, TOILET
EILOTV OLIVET, VIOLET

EILPPR RIPPLE
EILPPT TIPPLE
EILPPU PILEUP
EILPRS LISPER, PERILS, PERLIS, PLIERS
EILPRT TRIPLE
EILPSS PLISSE, SPIELS
EILPST STIPEL
EILPSU PILEUS
EILPSV PELVIS
EILPSX PIXELS
EILRST LITERS, LITRES, TILERS
EILRSV LIVERS, SILVER, SLIVER
EILRSY RILEYS
EILRTT LITTER, TILTER
EILRTU RUTILE
EILRVY LIVERY, VERILY
EILSST ISLETS, STILES
EILSSY SISLEY
EILSTT TITLES
EILSTU ISEULT
EILSTV VILEST
EILSVW SWIVEL
EILSVY SYLVIE
EILSWY WISELY
EILSXY SEXILY
EILSZZ SIZZLE
EILTTT TITTLE
EILTVY LEVITY
EIMMNU IMMUNE
EIMMOR MEMOIR
EIMMRS SIMMER
EIMMRU IMMURE
EIMNOR MERINO
EIMNOS EONISM, MONIES, SIMEON, SIMONE
EIMNPT PITMEN
EIMNRS MERSIN, MINERS
EIMNRT MINTER
EIMNRU MURINE
EIMNRV MERVIN, VERMIN
EIMNSX MINXES
EIMNTT MITTEN
EIMNTU MINUET, MINUTE
EIMNTY ENMITY
EIMNZZ MIZZEN
EIMOPS IMPOSE
EIMORS ISOMER, RIMOSE
EIMOST SOMITE
EIMOSV MOVIES
EIMOTV MOTIVE
EIMOTY MOIETY

EIMPRR PRIMER
EIMPRS PRIMES, SIMPER
EIMPRT PERMIT
EIMPRU IMPURE, UMPIRE
EIMPTU IMPUTE
EIMRRT TRIMER
EIMRRS MISERS, REMISS
EIMRST MERITS, MISTER, MITERS, MITRES, SMITER, TIMERS
EIMRSV VERISM, VERMIS
EIMRSX MIXERS
EIMRSY MISERY
EIMSSS MISSES
EIMSST TMESIS
EIMSSU MISUSE
EIMSSX SEXISM
EIMSTY STYMIE
EINNNR RENNIN
EINNOO IONONE
EINNOR RONNIE
EINNOT INTONE
EINNPR PINNER
EINNPT TENPIN
EINNRS SINNER
EINNRT INTERN
EINNRW WINNER
EINNST SENNIT, TENNIS
EINNTT INTENT
EINNTU IN TUNE
EINNTV INVENT
EINNTY NINETY
EINOPR ORPINE
EINOPS PONIES
EINOPT POINTE
EINORR IRONER
EINORS NOSIER, SENIOR
EINORT NORITE, ORIENT
EINORV RENVOI
EINOSS ENOSIS, NOESIS, NOISES, OSSEIN
EINOSW NOWISE
EINPPR NIPPER
EINPPS PEPSIN
EINPRS SNIPER
EINPRU PUNIER, PURINE, UNRIPE
EINPRY PINERY
EINPSS SNIPES, SPINES
EINPST INSTEP, SPINET
EINPSU SUPINE
EINQSU SEQUIN
EINQUU UNIQUE
EINRRS RINSER

EINRRU RUINER
EINRSS RESINS, RINSES, SIRENS
EINRST INSERT, SINTER
EINRSU INSURE, URSINE
EINRTU TRIUNE, UNITER
EINRTV INVERT
EINRTW TWINER, WINTER
EINRVY VINERY
EINSST INSETS, STEINS
EINSSW SINEWS, SWINES
EINSTV INVEST
EINSTZ ZENIST
EINSUW UNWISE
EINSUX UNISEX
EINSVX VIXENS
EINSWY SINEWY
EINTTY ENTITY
EIOORZ OOZIER
EIOOST OTIOSE
EIOPRR ROPIER
EIOPSS POSIES
EIOPST POSTIE
EIOPTT TIPTOE
EIORRS ROSIER
EIORRT RIOTER
EIORSS OSIERS
EIORST SORTIE, TORIES, TRIOSE
EIOSTV SOVIET
EIOTVV VOTIVE
EIPPRR RIPPER
EIPPRS PIPERS, SIPPER
EIPPRT TIPPER
EIPPRZ ZIPPER
EIPPST SIPPET
EIPPTT TIPPET
EIPPUY YUPPIE
EIPQSU PIQUES
EIPQTU PIQUET
EIPRRS SPRIER
EIPRSS PRISES, SPIRES
EIPRST ESPRIT, PRIEST, RIPEST, SPRITE, STRIPE
EIPRSU EPIRUS, UPRISE
EIPRSV VIPERS
EIPRSZ PRIZES
EIPRTV PRIVET
EIPRTY PYRITE
EIPRXY EXPIRY
EIPSSS PISSES, SEPSIS, SPEISS
EIPSST STIPES
EIPSSW SWIPES
EIPSTU TIE-UPS

EIPSTW PEWITS
EIQRSU QUIRES, RISQUÉ, SQUIRE
EIQRUV QUIVER
EIQTUY EQUITY
EIRRSS RISERS
EIRRST TRIERS
EIRRSV RIVERS
EIRRTW WRITER
EIRSST RESIST, RESITS, SISTER
EIRSSU ISSUER
EIRSTT SITTER
EIRSTV RIVETS, STRIVE, VERIST
EIRSTW WRIEST
EIRTTT TITTER
EIRTTV TRIVET
EIRTUV VIRTUE
EIRTVY VERITY
EISSSU ISSUES
EISSTT TESTIS
EISSTU SUITES, TISSUE
EISSTW WISEST
EISSTX SEXIST
EJKNTU JUNKET
EJKOPS SKOPJE
EJKORS JOKERS
EJLOST JOSTLE
EJLOSU JOULES
EJLPSU JULEPS
EJMPRU JUMPER
EJNOTT JETTON
EJOPRT PROJET
EJORTT JOTTER
EJRTTU JUTTER
EKLLNS KNELLS
EKLLSY SKELLY
EKLMMU KÜMMEL
EKLMOW WELKOM
EKLOOR LOOKER
EKLOSY YOKELS
EKLOWY LOW-KEY
EKLRRU LURKER
EKLRSU SULKER
EKMNOY MONKEY
EKMOOP MOPOKE
EKMORS SMOKER
EKMOSS SMOKES
EKMSTU MUSKET
EKNNOT KENTON, NEKTON
EKNNSU SUNKEN
EKNOPS SPOKEN

EKNORR KRONER
EKNORW KNOWER
EKNOST TOKENS
EKNOUY UNYOKE
EKOORT RETOOK
EKOPRR PORKER
EKOPRS POKERS
EKOPSS SPOKES
EKORRW REWORK, WORKER
EKORRY YORKER
EKORST STOKER, STROKE
EKOSST STOKES
EKRSTU TUSKER
EKRTUY TURKEY
ELLLOR LOLLER
ELLLOV LOVELL
ELLLOW LOWELL
ELLMOW MELLOW
ELLMRU MULLER
ELLMSS SMELLS
ELLMSY SMELLY
ELLMTU MULLET
ELLMUV VELLUM
ELLNOP POLLEN
ELLNOW NOWELL
ELLNOY LONELY
ELLNSU SULLEN
ELLNUW UNWELL
ELLOPX POLLEX
ELLORR ORRELL, ROLLER
ELLOSY SOLELY
ELLOVY LOVELY, VOLLEY
ELLOWY YELLOW
ELLPSS SPELLS
ELLPTU PULLET
ELLPUY PULLEY
ELLSSW SWELLS
ELMMOP POMMEL
ELMMOS MOSLEM
ELMMPU PUMMEL
ELMNOR MERLON
ELMNOS LEMONS, MELONS, SOLEMN
ELMNOT LOMENT, MELTON, MOLTEN
ELMNOY LEMONY
ELMNPU LUMPEN, PLENUM
ELMNVY MELVYN
ELMOPY EMPLOY
ELMORS MORSEL
ELMORT MOLTER
ELMOST MOLEST, MOTELS

ELMOTT MOTTLE
ELMOTY MOTLEY
ELMOUV VOLUME
ELMPPU PEPLUM
ELMPRU RUMPLE
ELMPSU PLUMES
ELMRSU LEMURS
ELMRTY MYRTLE, TERMLY
ELMSST SMELTS
ELMSSU MUSSEL
ELMTUU MUTULE
ELMTUY MUTELY
ELMUZZ MUZZLE
ELNNOS NELSON
ELNNOX LENNOX
ELNNRU RUNNEL
ELNNTU TUNNEL
ELNOOS LOOSEN
ELNOOY LOONEY
ELNOPT LEPTON
ELNOPY OPENLY, POLEYN
ELNORS LONERS
ELNOSS LESSON
ELNOST STOLEN, TELSON
ELNOSU ENSOUL
ELNOSV NOVELS, SLOVEN
ELNOUZ ZONULE
ELNOZZ NOZZLE
ELNPTU PENULT
ELNPTY PENTYL, PLENTY
ELNSSU UNLESS
ELNSWY SELWYN
ELNSXY LYNXES
ELNSYY LYNSEY
ELNTTU NUTLET
ELNTTY NETTLY
ELNUZZ NUZZLE
ELOOPR LOOPER
ELOORS LOOSER
ELOORT LOOTER, RETOOL, TOOLER
ELOOSS LOOSES
ELOOTT TOOTLE
ELOPPP POPPLE
ELOPPR LOPPER, PROPEL
ELOPPT TOPPLE
ELOPRS PROLES, SLOPER
ELOPRT PETROL
ELOPRV PLOVER
ELOPRX PLEXOR
ELOPSS SLOPES
ELOPTU TUPELO
ELORRS SORREL

ELORSS LESSOR, LOSERS
ELORST OSTLER, STEROL
ELORSV LOVERS, SOLVER
ELORSW SLOWER
ELORSY SORELY
ELORTV REVOLT
ELORTW TROWEL
ELORUV LOUVRE, VELOUR
ELORVW WOLVER
ELORVY OVERLY
ELORWY YOWLER
ELOSSS LOSSES
ELOSST STOLES
ELOSTU SOLUTE, TOUSLE
ELOSTW LOWEST,
   OWLETS, TOWELS
ELOSVW VOWELS, WOLVES
ELOSVY LOVEYS
ELOSXY XYLOSE
ELOTTU OUTLET
ELOTUV VOLUTE
ELOTWY OWELTY
ELPPRU PURPLE
ELPPSU SUPPLE
ELPRRU PURLER
ELPRTY PELTRY, PERTLY
ELPRUY PURELY
ELPSSU PLUSES, PULSES
ELPSTU LETUPS
ELPSUX PLEXUS
ELPUZZ PUZZLE
ELRRSU RULERS
ELRSSU RUSSEL
ELRSTU LUSTER, LUSTRE,
   RESULT, RUSTLE, ULSTER
ELRSTY STYLER
ELRSUY SURELY
ELRTTU TURTLE
ELRTTY TETRYL
ELSSTU TUSSLE
ELSSTY SLYEST, STYLES
ELSTTY STYLET
EMMMRU MUMMER
EMMNOT MOMENT
EMMORY MEMORY
EMMRRU RUMMER
EMMRSU SUMMER
EMMSUU MUSEUM
EMNNOT MENTON
EMNOPY EPONYM
EMNORS SERMON
EMNORT MENTOR,
   MERTON
EMNOSY MONEYS

EMNOTY ETYMON
EMNOXY EXONYM
EMNRVY MERVYN
EMNTUY TYUMEN
EMOORR ROOMER
EMOORS MOROSE,
   ROMEOS
EMOORT MOOTER
EMOOSS OSMOSE
EMOPPT MOPPET
EMOPRT PRO TEM,
   TROMPE
EMOPST TEMPOS
EMOQSU MOSQUE
EMORRT TERMOR,
   TREMOR
EMORRW WORMER
EMORST METROS
EMORSU MOUSER
EMORSV MOVERS
EMORSW MOWERS
EMORSY MYSORE
EMOSSU MOUSSE
EMOSTT MOTETS,
   TOTEMS
EMOSZZ MEZZOS
EMPRSS SPERMS
EMPSSU MESS-UP
EMPSTU SEPTUM
EMRSSU SERUMS
EMRSTU MUSTER, STUMER
EMRTTU MUTTER
EMSSTY SYSTEM
ENNNOP PENNON
ENNORU NEURON
ENNORV VERNON
ENNORW RENOWN
ENNOST SONNET,
   TENONS, TONNES
ENNOTW NEWTON
ENNOVY YVONNE
ENNPTU PUNNET
ENNRRU RUNNER
ENOOPR OPERON
ENOORS SOONER
ENOORT ENROOT
ENOOSS NOOSES
ENOOSZ SNOOZE
ENOPRR PERRON
ENOPRS PERSON
ENOPRV PROVEN
ENOPRY PYRONE
ENOPTT POTENT
ENORRS SNORER

ENORRY ORNERY
ENORSS SEÑORS, SENSOR,
   SNORES
ENORST STONER,
   TENORS, TENSOR
ENORSW OWNERS,
   WORSEN
ENORTT ROTTEN
ENORTY TYRONE
ENOSST STONES
ENOSTX SEXTON
ENOSUV VENOUS
ENOSVY ENVOYS
ENOTTU TENUTO,
   TEUTON
ENPPTU PENT UP
ENPRRU PRUNER
ENPRSU PRUNES
ENPRTU PUNTER
ENPRUY PENURY
ENPSTU UNSTEP
ENPTUU TUNE-UP
ENPTUW UNWEPT
ENRRSU RERUNS
ENRRTU RETURN,
   TURNER
ENRSST STERNS
ENRSSU NURSES
ENRSTU TUNERS, UNREST
ENRSTW STREWN
ENRSTY SENTRY
ENRSUU UNSURE
ENRTTU NUTTER
ENRTUU UNTRUE
ENRVWY WYVERN
ENSSTU SUNSET
ENTTWY TWENTY
EOOPPR POOPER
EOOPPS OPPOSE
EOOPRR POORER
EOORRT ROOTER,
   TORERO
EOORST TOROSE
EOORSW WOOERS
EOORTT TOOTER
EOOSTW SOWETO
EOPPPR POPPER
EOPPPT POPPET
EOPPRR PROPER
EOPPRT TOPPER
EOPPRY POPERY, PYROPE
EOPRRT PORTER,
   REPORT
EOPRRU POURER

EOPRSS POSERS, PROSES,
   SPORES
EOPRST POSTER, PRESTO,
   TROPES
EOPRSU POSEUR
EOPRSW POWERS
EOPRSY OSPREY
EOPRTT POTTER
EOPRTU POUTER, TROUPE
EOPRTX EXPORT
EOPRTY POETRY
EOPSSS POSSES
EOPSST POSSET
EOPSSU OPUSES, SPOUSE
EOPSTX SEXPOT
EOQRTU ROQUET,
   TORQUE
EOQSTU QUOTES
EORRRS ERRORS
EORRRT TERROR
EORRRY ORRERY
EORRST RESORT, ROSTER,
   SORTER
EORRSU ROUSER, SOURER
EORRSV ROVERS
EORRSW ROWERS
EORRTT RETORT, ROTTER
EORRTU ROUTER,
   TOURER
EORRTV TREVOR,
   TROVER
EORRZZ ROZZER
EORSST STORES, TOSSER
EORSSU SEROUS
EORSSV SERVOS, VERSOS
EORSSW SOWERS
EORSTT OTTERS
EORSTU OUSTER, ROUTES
EORSTV STOVER, STROVE,
   TROVES, VOTERS
EORSTW TOWERS
EORSTY OYSTER, STOREY
EORSTZ ZOSTER
EORTTT TOTTER
EORTTX EXTORT
EORTVX VORTEX
EORUVY VOYEUR
EOSSST TOSSES
EOSSTV STOVES
EOSTTU OUTSET
EPPPRY PREPPY
EPPPTU PUPPET
EPPRSU SUPPER, UPPERS
EPRRSU PURSER

EPRRTU RUPERT
EPRSSU PURSES
EPRSTU PUREST
EPRSTW TWERPS
EPRSUU PURSUE
EPRTTU PUTTER
EPRTTY PRETTY
EPRUVY PURVEY
EPSSSU PUSSES
EPSSTU SET-UPS, UPSETS
EQRTWY QWERTY
EQSSTU QUESTS
ERRSUU USURER
ERRSUY SURREY
ERRTTU TURRET
ERSSST STRESS
ERSSTU RUSSET, SUREST
ERSSTY TRESSY
ERSSUV VERSUS
ERSTTU TRUEST
ERSTUU SUTURE, UTERUS
ERSTUV TURVES
ERSTUY SURETY
ERSTVY VESTRY
ERSTWY WRYEST
ERSTXY XYSTER
ERSUVY SURVEY
ERTTUX URTEXT
ESSTUX SEXTUS
FFFLUY FLUFFY
FFGINO OFFING
FFHIST FIFTHS
FFHISW WHIFFS
FFHIWY WHIFFY
FFIINT TIFFIN
FFIKSS SKIFFS
FFILLU FULFIL
FFILTU FITFUL
FFIMNU MUFFIN
FFINPU PUFFIN
FFINSS SNIFFS
FFINSY SNIFFY
FFIOPR RIP-OFF
FFIOPT TIP-OFF
FFIOST SOFFIT
FFIQSU QUIFFS
FFISST STIFFS
FFISUX SUFFIX
FFLRUY RUFFLY
FFNORU RUN OFF
FFNSUY SNUFFY
FFOPTU PUT-OFF
FFRRUU FURFUR
FFSTUY STUFFY

FGGIIZ FIZGIG
FGGINU FUGING
FGGORY FROGGY
FGHILT FLIGHT
FGHIRT FRIGHT
FGHIST FIGHTS
FGHOTU FOUGHT
FGIILN FILING
FGIINN FINING
FGIINR FIRING
FGIINX FIXING
FGILNY FLYING
FGILUY UGLIFY
FGIMNU FUMING
FGINOX FOXING
FGINRY FRINGY, FRYING
FGINSU FUSING
FGKNUU KUNG FU
FGNSUU FUNGUS
FGOORT FORGOT
FHIINS FINISH
FHILTY FILTHY
FHIRST FIRTHS, SHRIFT
FHIRTT THRIFT
FHISST SHIFTS
FHISTU SHUFTI
FHISTY SHIFTY
FHNSUU FUSHUN
FHORST FROTHS
FHORTU FOURTH
FHORTY FROTHY
FHSTUY SHUFTY
FIIKNR FIRKIN
FIILLN FILL-IN
FIILLP FILLIP
FIILRU FRIULI
FIILST TIFLIS
FIILVY VILIFY
FIIMNR INFIRM
FIIMNY MINIFY
FIIMST MISFIT
FIINOR FIORIN
FIITXY FIXITY
FIIVVY VIVIFY
FIJLOR FRIJOL
FIKRSS FRISKS
FIKRSY FRISKY
FILLRS FRILLS
FILLRY FRILLY
FILLUW WILFUL
FILMOU FOLIUM
FILMRY FIRMLY
FILMSY FLIMSY
FILNOR FLORIN

FILNOW INFLOW
FILNST FLINTS
FILNSU SINFUL
FILNTY FLINTY
FILNUX INFLUX
FILOOS FOLIOS
FILORV FRIVOL
FILOSS FOSSIL
FILOXY FOXILY
FILPTU UPLIFT
FILRST FLIRTS
FIMNOR INFORM
FIMOST MOTIFS
FIMSTU MUFTIS
FINORX FORNIX
FINOSU FUSION
FINOTY NOTIFY
FIOOTT FOOT IT
FIOPRT PROFIT
FIORST FORTIS
FIOSSY OSSIFY
FIOTTU OUTFIT
FIPRUY PURIFY
FIPTYY TYPIFY
FIRSST FIRSTS
FIRSTU FRUITS
FIRTUY FRUITY
FIRYZZ FRIZZY
FISSTW SWIFTS
FJLOUY JOYFUL
FKLNUY FLUNKY
FKLOSY FOLKSY
FLLOOW FOLLOW
FLLOUY FOULLY
FLMOOS FOLSOM
FLMORY FORMYL
FLNRUU UNFURL
FLOORS FLOORS
FLOOYZ FLOOZY
FLOPPY FLOPPY
FLOPTU POTFUL
FLOPUU FOUL-UP
FLORUY FLOURY
FLOSSY FLOSSY
FLOSTY SOFTLY
FLRRUY FLURRY
FMORSU FORUMS
FMPRSU FRUMPS
FMPRUY FRUMPY
FNNRUU FUN RUN
FNORST FRONTS
FNORSW FROWNS
FNOSTU FOUNTS, FUTONS
FOOPRS PROOFS

FOOPSS SPOOFS
FOORST SORT OF
FOOTUX OUTFOX
FORRUW FURROW
FORSST FROSTS
FORSTY FROSTY
FORSUU RUFOUS
FORWYZ FROWZY
FPRSUY FRY-UPS
GGGILY GIGGLY
GGGORY GROGGY
GGHNOU GUNG-HO
GGIINP PIGGIN
GGIINV GIVING
GGIIRR GRIGRI
GGIJLY JIGGLY
GGIKNO GINKGO
GGILNO OGLING
GGILNU GLUING
GGILOO GIGOLO
GGILWY WIGGLY
GGINNO NOGGIN
GGINOR GORING,
   GRINGO
GGINRU URGING
GGINUY GUYING
GGITWY TWIGGY
GGLLOO LOGLOG
GGLOOO GOOGOL
GGLOOY GOOGLY
GGMOSY SMOGGY
GGNOOR GORGON
GGRRUU GRUGRU
GHHILY HIGHLY
GHHIST THIGHS
GHHOTU THOUGH
GHIIKN HIKING
GHIINR HIRING
GHIINV HIVING
GHIKNT KNIGHT
GHILPT PLIGHT
GHILST LIGHTS, SLIGHT
GHIMNO HOMING
GHIMTY MIGHTY
GHINNO HONING
GHINOP HOPING
GHINOS HOSING
GHINPY HYPING
GHINST NIGHTS, THINGS
GHINSY SHYING
GHIOPZ PHIZOG
GHIRST GIRTHS, RIGHTS
GHIRTW WRIGHT
GHISST SIGHTS

GHISTT TIGHTS
GHISTW WIGHTS
GHLLSY GHYLLS
GHLOPU PLOUGH
GHLOSU GHOULS,
   LOUGHS, SLOUGH
GHNORT THRONG
GHNOST THONGS
GHNOSU SHOGUN
GHNOTU HOGNUT,
   NOUGHT
GHNRUY HUNGRY
GHNSUY GUNSHY
GHORTU TROUGH
GHORTW GROWTH
GHOSST GHOSTS
GHOSSU SOUGHS
GHOSTU SOUGHT
GHRSSU SHRUGS
GIIJNV JIVING
GIIKLN LIKING
GIIKNN INKING
GIIKNR IRKING
GIIKNS SKIING
GIIKNV VIKING
GIILMN LIMING
GIILNN LIGNIN, LINING
GIILNO OILING
GIILNP PILING
GIILNR RILING
GIILNT TILING
GIILNV LIVING
GIILOR OILRIG
GIILRV VIRGIL
GIILSV VIGILS
GIIMMN MIMING
GIIMNN MINING
GIIMNR MIRING
GIIMNT TIMING
GIIMNX MIXING
GIINNN INNING
GIINNP PINING
GIINNS SINING
GIINNW WINING
GIINNX NIXING
GIINOR ORIGIN
GIINPP PIPING
GIINPW WIPING
GIINRS RISING, SIRING
GIINRT TIRING
GIINRV IRVING, VIRGIN
GIINRW WIRING
GIINST SITING
GIINSZ SIZING

GIIRST TIGRIS
GIJKNO JOKING
GIJLNY JINGLY
GIJNOY JOYING
GIKLNY KINGLY
GIKNNU NUKING
GIKNOP POKING
GIKNOY YOKING
GIKNPU PUKING
GILLRS GRILLS
GILMRY GRIMLY
GILMWY GWILYM,
　GWYLIM
GILNOO LOGION
GILNOP LOPING, POLING
GILNOS LOSING, SOLING
GILNOV LOVING
GILNOW LOWING
GILNPY PLYING
GILNRU LURING, RULING
GILNSS SLINGS
GILNST GLINTS
GILNSU SLUING
GILNSY GLINYS, GLYNIS,
　SINGLY
GILNTY TINGLY
GILOOS IGLOOS
GILORY GILROY, GORILY
GILRSY GRISLY
GILTUY GUILTY
GILTYZ GLITZY
GIMNNO MIGNON
GIMNOO MOOING
GIMNOP MOPING
GIMNOV MOVING
GIMNOW MOWING
GIMNPU IMPUGN
GIMNSU MUSING
GIMNTU MUTING
GIMOSY YOGISM
GIMOTU GOMUTI
GINNOO GONION
GINNOP NINGPO
GINNOS NOSING
GINNOT NOTING,
　TONING
GINNOW OWNING
GINNOZ ZONING
GINNTU TUNING
GINOOS ISOGON
GINOOW WOOING
GINOOZ OOZING
GINOPR PORING, ROPING
GINOPS POSING

GINOPT OPTING
GINORS GRISON, GROINS,
　SIGNOR
GINORV ROVING
GINORW ROWING
GINOSS GNOSIS
GINOST INGOTS
GINOSW SOWING
GINOTT TOTING
GINOTU OUTING
GINOTV VOTING
GINOTW TOWING
GINOTY TOYING
GINOVW VOWING
GINOWW WOWING
GINPRS SPRING
GINPRY PRYING
GINPSU PIGNUS
GINPSY SPYING
GINPTU PIGNUT
GINPTY TYPING
GINRST STRING
GINRTY TRYING
GINRWY WRYING
GINSST STINGS
GINSSV V-SIGNS
GINSSW SWINGS
GINSTY STINGY
GINSUU UNGUIS
GIOPSS GOSSIP
GIOPST SPIGOT
GIORRU RIGOUR
GIORSV VIRGOS
GIORTU RIG-OUT
GIORUV VIGOUR
GIOSTU GIUSTO
GIPRSS SPRIGS
GIPSTY PIGSTY
GIRSST GRISTS
GIRTTY GRITTY
GJLNUY JUNGLY
GJNRUU GURJUN
GLLMUY GLUMLY
GLLOOP GOLLOP
GLMNOO MONGOL
GLMOOY GLOOMY
GLMOSU MOGULS
GLMSUY SMUGLY
GLNOOO OOLONG
GLNPUU UNPLUG
GLNSUY SNUGLY
GLOOOY OOLOGY
GLOOPR PROLOG
GLOOSW GO-SLOW

GLOPTU PUTLOG
GLORSW GROWLS
GLOSSY GLOSSY
GMNNOO GNOMON
GMOOPR POGROM
GMOORS GROOMS
GMPRUY GRUMPY
GMPSUY GYPSUM
GNNOOS ON SONG
GNNSUU UNSUNG
GNOORT TROGON
GNOPPU OPPUGN,
　POPGUN
GNOPRS PRONGS
GNOPSY SPONGY
GNORST STRONG
GNORSW WRONGS
GNORUV GUVNOR
GNORYZ GROZNY
GNPRSU SPRUNG
GNRSTU GRUNTS, STRUNG
GNRTUU GUNTUR
GNSTUU TUNGUS
GOOPST STOP-GO
GOORTT GROTTO
GOORVY GROOVY
GOPRSU GROUPS
GORRTU TURGOR
GORSTU GROUTS
GORTTU ROTGUT
GORTTY GROTTY
GORTUY YOGURT
GSYYYZ SYZYGY
HHMRTY RHYTHM
HHNOSU HONSHU
HHOOSW WHOOSH
HHPSUU HUSH-UP
HHRSTU THRUSH
HIILLT LILITH
HIILPP PHILIP
HIIMPS IMPISH
HIIMST MISHIT
HIINTW WITHIN
HIKNRS SHRINK
HIKSSW WHISKS
HIKSWY WHISKY
HILLOY HOLILY
HILLPU UPHILL
HILLRS SHRILL
HILLRT THRILL
HILMOS HOLISM
HILMOY HOMILY
HILMSU MULISH
HILNPT PLINTH

HILNTY THINLY
HILOPS POLISH
HILOSW OWLISH
HILRSW WHIRLS
HILSTW WHILST
HIMMSU HUMISM
HIMNOY HOMINY
HIMPRS SHRIMP
HIMSST SMITHS
HIMSTY SMITHY
HIMSWY WHIMSY
HINNST NINTHS
HINNSY SHINNY
HINNWY WHINNY
HINOPS SIPHON
HINOST SHINTO
HINPSU PUNISH, UNSHIP
HINPSX SPHINX
HINRSU INRUSH
HIOPPS POPISH
HIOPST PITHOS
HIOPSY PHYSIO
HIORSU HOURIS
HIOSST HOISTS
HIPPSU UPPISH
HIPPWY WHIPPY
HIPRST THRIPS
HIQSSU SQUISH
HIRSST SHIRTS
HIRSTT THIRST, T-SHIRT
HIRSTY IRTYSH, SHIRTY
HIRTTY THIRTY
HISSTX SIXTHS
HISTTY SHITTY
HJNNOY JOHNNY
HJNOST ST JOHN
HKNOOU UNHOOK
HKNRSU SHRUNK
HKOOPU HOOKUP
HKSUUY KYUSHU
HLLOOW HOLLOW
HLLOSU HULLOS
HLLOWY WHOLLY
HLLPUY LYULPH
HLMOTY THYMOL
HLMPUY PHYLUM
HLNOUY UNHOLY
HLNSUU LU-SHUN
HLOOST SHOLTO, THOLOS
HLOPSS SPLOSH
HLORSW WHORLS
HLORUY HOURLY
HLOSST SLOTHS
HLOSSY SLOSHY

HLSSUY SLUSHY
HMNOST MONTHS
HMNPSY NYMPHS
HMOOST SMOOTH
HMORSU HUMORS
HMORUU HUMOUR
HMORUZ HORMUZ
HMOSTU MOUTHS
HMOSTY MYTHOS
HMPSTU THUMPS
HMPTUY HUMPTY
HMSTUY THYMUS
HNNOOP PHONON
HNOOPT PHOTON
HNOORS HONORS
HNOORT THORON
HNOORU HONOUR
HNOPSU NOSH-UP
HNOPSY SYPHON
HNOPTY PHYTON,
    PYTHON
HNORST NORTHS,
    THORNS
HNORSU ONRUSH
HNORTW THROWN
HNORTY RHYTON,
    THORNY
HNOSTU HUSTON
HNSSTU SHUNTS
HOOPST PHOTOS
HOOPSW WHOOPS
HOOPTT HOTPOT
HOORRR HORROR
HOOSST SHOOTS
HOOSSW SWOOSH
HOOTTY TOOTHY
HOPPSU HOPPUS
HOPRTY TROPHY
HOPSTU TOPHUS, UPSHOT
HORSST SHORTS
HORSTT TROTHS
HORSTW THROWS
HORSTY SHORTY
HORTWY WORTHY
HOSSTU SHOUTS
HOSTUY YOUTHS
HPPSUU PUSH-UP
HPSTUY TYPHUS
HRSTTU THRUST, TRUTHS
IIIMNR RIMINI
IIIRST IRITIS
IIKKMS SIKKIM
IIKNPP PIPKIN
IIKNSS SISKIN

IIKPST SKIP IT!
IILLOY OILILY
IILLSW WILLIS
IILMMU MILIUM
IILMST LIMITS
IILNNU INULIN
IILNOV VIOLIN
IILNST INSTIL
IILPST PISTIL
IILRWY WIRILY
IILTTW TWILIT
IIMMNS MINIMS
IIMMNU MINIUM
IIMNNO MINION
IIMOSS MIOSIS
IIMSSS MISSIS
IINNOP PINION
IINNTU INNUIT
IINORS ROISIN
IINOSV VISION
IINPPP PIPPIN
IINPTX PINXIT
IINSST INSIST, SIT-INS
IINSTU IN SITU, INUITS
IINTTU INTUIT
IINTTW NITWIT
IIOSTT OTITIS
IIPPST PIPITS
IIPRST SPIRIT
IIRSSU SIRIUS
IISSTV VISITS
IJLSUU JULIUS
IJNORU JUNIOR
IJNOST JOINTS
IJNRUY INJURY
IJNSTU JUSTIN
IJOSST JOISTS
IJRSTU JURIST
IKKKRU KIRKUK
IKKOSS KIOSKS
IKKRSU KUKRIS
IKKUUY KIKUYU
IKLLSS SKILLS
IKLNOO LOOK-IN
IKLNPU LINKUP
IKLNSY SLINKY
IKLNTY TINKLY
IKLOPY POKILY
IKLSSU SUSLIK
IKMNOO KIMONO
IKMPSY SKIMPY
IKMRSS SMIRKS
IKMSSU KUMISS
IKNNOT TONKIN

IKNNSY SKINNY	**ILORSY** ROSILY	**INORST** INTROS
IKNNTU UNKNIT	**ILPPRY** RIPPLY	**INORSY** ROSINY
IKNOPS PINKOS	**ILPPSU** PUPILS, SLIP-UP	**INORTT** TRITON
IKNSST STINKS	**ILPPSY** SLIPPY	**INORTU** TURION
IKQRSU QUIRKS	**ILPPTU** PULPIT	**INOSTX** TOXINS
IKQRUY QUIRKY	**ILPSST** SPLITS	**INOSUV** VINOUS
IKRSST SKIRTS	**ILPSTU** TULIPS	**INPPSU** PINUPS
IKRSTY KIRSTY	**ILPTTU** UPTILT	**INPPSY** SNIPPY
IKSVVY SKIVVY	**ILQSTU** QUILTS	**INPRST** PRINTS, SPRINT
ILLMPY LIMPLY	**ILRSSW** SWIRLS	**INPRTU** TURNIP
ILLMSY SLIMLY	**ILRSTW** TWIRLS	**INQSTU** SQUINT
ILLNOS LLINOS	**ILRSTY** LYRIST	**INQSUY** QUINSY
ILLNPU PULL-IN	**ILRSWY** SWIRLY	**INRSXY** SYRINX
ILLOPW PILLOW	**ILRTWY** TWIRLY	**INRTWY** WINTRY
ILLOWW WILLOW	**ILSSTT** STILTS	**INSSTT** STINTS
ILLPSS SPILLS	**IMMMOS** MOMISM	**IOPPTT** TIP-TOP
ILLQSU QUILLS, SQUILL	**IMMNOS** MONISM,	**IOPRRS** PRIORS
ILLRST TRILLS	NOMISM	**IOPRRY** PRIORY
ILLSST STILLS	**IMMOOS** SIMOOM	**IOPRST** TRIPOS
ILLSSW SWILLS	**IMMOSU** OSMIUM	**IOPSST** PTOSIS
ILLSTY STILLY	**IMMSTU** MUTISM, SUMMIT	**IOPSSY** PYOSIS
ILLSUV VILLUS	**IMNNOW** MINNOW	**IOPSTV** PIVOTS
ILMMSU MUSLIM	**IMNOOR** MORION	**IOQSTU** QUOITS
ILMNOT MILTON	**IMNOOT** MOTION	**IORSSV** VISORS
ILMNOU MOULIN	**IMNORS** MINORS	**IORSTU** SUITOR
ILMNSU MUSLIN	**IMNOST** INMOST, MONIST	**IOTTUW** OUTWIT
ILMOSS LISSOM	**IMNOSY** MYOSIN, SIMONY	**IPPPSU** PUPPIS
ILMOTW WILMOT	**IMNTUY** MUTINY	**IPPSSU** PISS-UP
ILMPPY PIMPLY	**IMOPRS** PORISM	**IPPTUY** UPPITY
ILMPRY PRIMLY	**IMOPRT** IMPORT	**IPRRTU** IRRUPT
ILMPSY SIMPLY	**IMOPST** IMPOST	**IPRSST** STIRPS, STRIPS
ILMRTY TRIMLY	**IMORRR** MIRROR	**IPRSSY** PRISSY
ILMSTU LITMUS	**IMORRS** MORRIS	**IPRSTU** PURIST
ILMTUU TUMULI	**IMOSTU** OSTIUM	**IPRSTW** TWIRPS
ILNOOT LOTION	**IMPRSS** PRISMS	**IPRSTY** STRIPY
ILNOPP POPLIN	**IMPRSU** PRIMUS, PURISM	**IPRTUY** PURITY
ILNOPS SLIP-ON	**IMPSUX** MIX-UPS	**IPSSTU** SIT-UPS
ILNOPT PONTIL	**IMQRSU** SQUIRM	**IPSTTY** TYPIST
ILNOQU QUINOL	**IMRSTU** TRUISM	**IPTTTU** TITTUP
ILNOST TONSIL	**IMSSSU** MISSUS	**IQRSTU** SQUIRT
ILNOSY NOSILY	**INNOOS** ONIONS	**IRSSTW** WRISTS
ILNPRU PURLIN	**INNOOT** NOTION	**IRSTWY** WRISTY
ILNPST SPLINT	**INNOPP** NIPPON	**ISSSTU** SUSS IT, TUSSIS
ILNPSU LUPINS	**INNOSU** UNIONS, UNISON	**ISSTTW** TWISTS
ILNSTU INSULT, SUNLIT	**INNOWW** WINNOW	**ISTTWY** TWISTY
ILNSVY VINYLS	**INNSSU** SUNNIS	**JLNOOY** JOLYON
ILOOYZ OOZILY	**INOOPS** POISON	**JLSTUY** JUSTLY
ILOPRX PROLIX	**INOOPT** OPTION, POTION	**JNOORU** JOURNO
ILOPRY ROPILY	**INOORS** ORISON	**JNSTUU** UNJUST
ILOPSS SPOILS	**INOOTT** IN TOTO	**JOOSUY** JOYOUS
ILOPST PILOTS, PISTOL,	**INOPRS** PRISON	**JORRSU** JURORS
POSTIL, SPOILT	**INOPST** PISTON, POINTS	**JOSSTU** JUST SO
ILOPTY POLITY	**INOPTT** TIN-POT	**KKLMUU** MUKLUK
ILOQRU LIQUOR	**INORRS** NORRIS	**KKNSSU** SKUNKS

KLLNOS KNOLLS
KLLSSU SKULLS
KLNNUU KUNLUN
KNOORR KRONOR
KNOTTY KNOTTY
KNPSUY SPUNKY
KNRSTU TRUNKS
KOOPSS SPOOKS
KOOPSY SPOOKY
KOORVV KOVROV
KOOSTV VOSTOK
KOOTWW KOWTOW
KORSST STORKS
LLLOOP LOLLOP
LLNOOR ROLL-ON
LLNOPU PULL-ON
LLNORU UNROLL
LLOOWY WOOLLY
LLOPUX POLLUX
LLORST STROLL, TROLLS
LLOSWY SLOWLY
LLOTUY TOLUYL
LMMOUX LUMMOX
LMMPUY PLUMMY
LMMSUY SLUMMY
LMOORU ORMOLU
LMOSTU MOULTS
LMOSTY MOSTLY
LMPRUY RUMPLY
LMPSSU SLUMPS
LMTTUU TUMULT
LNNOSY NYLONS
LNOOPY POLONY
LNOOST STOLON
LNOOTU TOULON
LNOPSY PYLONS
LNOPTU PLUTON
LNORSY ROSLYN
LNRUUY UNRULY
LOOPRY POORLY
LOOPSS SLOOPS, SPOOLS
LOOSST STOOLS
LOOVVX VOLVOX
LOPPRY PROPYL
LOPPSY POLYPS, SLOPPY
LOPRSW PROWLS
LOPRTY PORTLY
LOPTWY TWO-PLY

LORSUY SOURLY
LORTTY TROTYL
LPPSUY SUPPLY
LPRSYY SPRYLY
LRRSUY SLURRY
LRSTUY SULTRY
LRUUXY LUXURY
LSSTUY STYLUS
MMNOOR MORMON
MMNOSU SUMMON
MMOOPP POMPOM
MMOOTT MOTMOT,
       TOM-TOM
MMRRUU MURMUR
MNOOPP POMPON
MNOORS MORONS
MNOORU UNMOOR
MNOOTU MOUTON
MNOOTW MOTOWN
MNOSTU MOUNTS
MNOTTU MUTTON
MNSTTU MUSTN'T
MOOPRS PROMOS
MOORRW MORROW
MOORST MOTORS
MOOSSU OSMOUS
MOOSTT MOTTOS
MOPPRT PROMPT
MOPSSU POSSUM
MOQRUU QUORUM
MORRSU RUMORS
MORRUU RUMOUR
MORSST STORMS
MORSTU TUMORS
MORSTY STORMY
MORTUU TUMOUR
MOSTTU UTMOST
MPRSTU TRUMPS
MPRSUU RUMPUS
MPSSTU STUMPS
MPSTUU SPUTUM
MPSTUY STUMPY
MSTTUY SMUTTY
NNOORT NORTON
NNOOWW NOW NOW!
NNORTU TURN-ON
NOOPRT PRONTO,
       PROTON

NOOPSS SNOOPS, SPOONS
NOOPST SPOT-ON
NOOPSY SNOOPY
NOOSSW SWOONS
NOOSTY SNOOTY
NOOSYZ SNOOZY
NOPSTU PUT-ONS, UNSTOP
NOPTUW UPTOWN
NORSST SNORTS
NORTUU OUTRUN
NOSSTU SNOUTS
NOSTTY SNOTTY
NPRSUU RUN-UPS
NPRTUU TURN-UP,
       UPTURN
NRSTUU U-TURNS
NSSTTU STUNTS
OOOPRT OPORTO
OOPPRT TROPPO
OOPPVX VOX POP
OOPRRT TORPOR
OOPRSS SPOORS
OOPRST TROOPS
OOPRSU POROUS
OOPRTU UPROOT
OOPSSW SWOOPS
OOPWWW POWWOW
OORRST ROTORS
OORRSW SORROW
OORSST ROOSTS, TORSOS
OORSTV ROSTOV
OPRSST SPORTS, STROPS
OPRSTU SPROUT, STUPOR
OPRSTY SPORTY
OPSSTU SPOUTS, STOUPS,
       TOSS-UP
OPSTTY SPOTTY
OPTTUU OUTPUT
ORSTTU TROUTS, TUTORS
ORTTUY TRY-OUT
PRRSUY SPURRY
PRSSTU SPURTS
PRSUYY SYRUPY
RSSTTU STRUTS, TRUSTS
RSSTTY TRYSTS
RSTTUY TRUSTY
TTTTUU TUT-TUT

■ SEVEN-LETTER WORDS ■

AAAABLM ALABAMA
AAAADMW ADAMAWA
AAAALMT ALMA-ATA
AAABBCL CABBALA
AAABBMR BAMBARA
AAABBRR BARBARA
AAABCMR CARAMBA
AAABCOR CARABAO
AAABDFR ABFARAD
AAABDGN BAGANDA
AAABFIN FABIANA
AAABFLL FALBALA
AAABHMR ABRAHAM
AAABHMS BAHAMAS
AAABILN ALBANIA
AAABILX ABAXIAL
AAABINR ARABIAN
AAABIPR PARAIBA
AAABIRV BAVARIA
AAABKLR KARBALA
AAABLMR MALABAR
AAABNNS BANANAS
AAABNPR PAN-ARAB
AAABORR ARAROBA
AAABRSZ BAZAARS
AAACCIS ACACIAS
AAACCLM MALACCA
AAACCLR CARACAL
AAACCRS CARACAS,
   CASCARA
AAACDIN ACADIAN
AAACDIR ARCADIA
AAACDLU ACAUDAL
AAACDMM MACADAM
AAACEHN ACHAEAN
AAACENP PANACEA
AAACHLZ CHALAZA
AAACIJM JAMAICA
AAACIMR ARAMAIC
AAACINT CATANIA
AAACJMR JACAMAR
AAACJRU ARACAJU
AAACLLV CAVALLA
AAACLMN ALMANAC
AAACLNT CANTALA,
   CATALAN
AAACLPS ALPACAS
AAACLPT CATALPA
AAACLRZ ALCAZAR
AAACMRS MARACAS,
   MARASCA, MASCARA
AAACMRY MARACAY

AAACNRV CARAVAN
AAACNST CANASTA
AAACNTT CANTATA
AAACRWY CARAWAY
AAACSST CASSATA
AAACSSV CASSAVA
AAADFRY FARADAY
AAADGNR GRANADA
AAADHMN HAMADAN
AAADHWY HADAWAY
AAADILX ADAXIAL
AAADIMN ADAMINA
AAADINR ADRIANA
AAADKNN KANNADA
AAADMNN ADAMNAN
AAADMNR RAMADAN
AAADMNT ADAMANT
AAADMRS ARMADAS
AAAEFLR RAFAELA
AAAEGLT GALATEA
AAAEGNP PANGAEA
AAAEHLT ALTHAEA
AAAEIMN ANAEMIA
AAAENST ANATASE
AAAERWY AREAWAY
AAAFFLL ALFALFA
AAAFIRT RATAFIA
AAAFRSS AS FAR AS
AAAFRWY FARAWAY
AAAGHIP APHAGIA
AAAGHPR AGRAPHA
AAAGINR NIAGARA
AAAGKNT KATANGA
AAAGLMM AMALGAM
AAAGLNS LASAGNA
AAAGLOS ALAGOAS
AAAGMNR ANAGRAM
AAAGMNU MANAGUA
AAAHHKL HALAKAH
AAAHHLM MAHALAH
AAAHHLV HALAVAH
AAAHILM MAHALIA
AAAHIPS APHASIA
AAAHIRZ AZARIAH
AAAHMMT MAHATMA
AAAHMRT MARATHA
AAAHNRS SAHARAN
AAAHNRY HARYANA
AAAHNST NATASHA
AAAHOPR ARAPAHO
AAAHPPR HARAPPA
AAAILMR MALARIA

AAAILNT NATALIA
AAAILPS APLASIA
AAAILPT PATIALA
AAAIMNT AMANITA
AAAINNR ARIANNA
AAAINTT TATIANA
AAAIPRX APRAXIA
AAAIPSS ASPASIA
AAAIQRU AQUARIA
AAAJMPS PAJAMAS
AAAKLMP KAMPALA
AAAKLNS ALASKAN
AAAKLSS KASSALA
AAAKMOY OKAYAMA
AAAKMRS MAKASAR
AAAKRSW SARAWAK
AAALLPT PALATAL
AAALMNY MALAYAN
AAALMRS MARSALA
AAALMSS SALAAMS
AAALMTY MALATYA
AAALNNT LANTANA
AAALNTT ATLANTA
AAALRRY ARRAYAL
AAAMNPS PANAMAS
AAAMRTU TAMARAU
AAANNRS SARANNA
AAANNSV SAVANNA
AAAPPSY PAPAYAS
AAARRST TARRASA
AAARSTV AVATARS
AAARTTT RAT-A-TAT
AAARTTU TUATARA
AABBCEG CABBAGE
AABBEMN MBABANE
AABBERT BARBATE
AABBGGR GRAB BAG
AABBHST SABBATH
AABBMRU RUM
   BABA
AABBNRT BRABANT
AABBNRY BARNABY
AABBRRY BARBARY
AABBSSU BABASSU
AABBSTY BABY-SAT
AABCCET BACCATE
AABCDIR CARABID
AABCEFR FACEBAR
AABCELN BALANCE
AABCELP CAPABLE
AABCELT ACTABLE
AABCEMR MACABRE

AABCERT ABREACT,
   CABARET
AABCFKT FATBACK
AABCHNR BARCHAN
AABCILM CAMBIAL
AABCIMR CAMBRAI
AABCIMS CABIMAS
AABCIOP COPAIBA
AABCITX TAXICAB
AABCKNR CAB RANK
AABCKRR BARRACK
AABCKSW BACKSAW
AABCLPY CAPABLY
AABCLRY BARCLAY
AABCORT ACROBAT
AABCOST TABASCO
AABCOTT CATBOAT
AABCRSS SCARABS
AABDDER ABRADED
AABDDGH BAGHDAD
AABDDHN DAB HAND
AABDEFL FADABLE
AABDEGN BANDAGE
AABDEHS ABASHED
AABDEIS DIABASE
AABDELL BALLADE
AABDELR ALBREDA
AABDELT DATABLE
AABDELW WADABLE
AABDENU BANDEAU
AABDERR ABRADER
AABDFYZ FYZABAD
AABDGHN HANDBAG
AABDGLY BAG LADY
AABDGMO GAMBADO
AABDGNS SANDBAG
AABDGNU BUGANDA
AABDHIO OBADIAH
AABDHNT HATBAND
AABDIJN ABIDJAN
AABDIMR BARMAID
AABDINT TABANID
AABDIOT BIODATA
AABDJOZ BADAJOZ
AABDLLS BALLADS
AABDLRW BRADAWL
AABDMNR ARMBAND
AABDNNO ABANDON
AABDNNR BRANDAN
AABDNRR BARNARD
AABDNRS SANDBAR
AABDORV BRAVADO
AABDRRW DRAWBAR
AABDRST BASTARD

AABDSTU DATA BUS
AABEELT EATABLE
AABEEMO AMOEBAE
AABEFFL AFFABLE
AABEFGL FLEABAG
AABEGGG BAGGAGE
AABEGGR GARBAGE
AABEGLR ALGEBRA
AABEGRR BARRAGE
AABEGSS BAGASSE
AABEGST TEABAGS
AABEIKN IKEBANA
AABEILM AMIABLE
AABEILT LABIATE
AABEIRS AIRBASE
AABEKLT TAKABLE
AABELLM MABELLA
AABELLN BALNEAL
AABELLS SALABLE
AABELMN NAMABLE
AABELMT TAMABLE
AABELNN ANNABEL
AABELNO ABALONE
AABELPR PARABLE
AABELPY PAYABLE
AABELRT ALBERTA,
   RATABLE
AABELSV SAVABLE
AABELTU TABLEAU
AABELTX TAXABLE
AABEMOS AMOEBAS
AABEMST MASBATE
AABENTY ABEYANT
AABERST ABREAST
AABFFLY AFFABLY
AABFINS FABIANS
AABGGRS RAGBAGS
AABGGSS GASBAGS
AABGIIL ABIGAIL
AABGILM MAILBAG
AABGIMN GAMBIAN
AABGINR BARGAIN
AABGINS ABASING
AABGINT ABATING
AABGLOR AALBORG
AABGRST RATBAGS
AABHIMS BAHAISM
AABHINR BAHRAIN
AABHIST BAHAIST
AABHITT HABITAT,
   TABITHA
AABHKRU BUKHARA
AABHLTY BATHYAL
AABHMNR BRAHMAN

AABHMTT BATH MAT
AABHSUU BAUHAUS
AABIILN ALBINIA
AABIILS BASILIA
AABIILX BIAXIAL
AABIIMN NAMIBIA
AABIKNS BANKSIA
AABILLR BARILLA
AABILLS BASILLA, LABIALS
AABILMY AMIABLY
AABILRS BASILAR
AABIMMR MARIMBA
AABIMNZ ZAMBIAN
AABINOU OUABAIN
AABINRS SABRINA
AABINST ABSTAIN, BASTIAN
AABINSW SWABIAN
AABIRST ARABIST
AABIRSV BRAVAIS
AABKNRT TANBARK
AABKOOZ BAZOOKA
AABLLST BALLAST
AABLLWY WALLABY
AABLMOS ABSALOM
AABLMSS BALSAMS
AABLMSY ABYSMAL
AABLNOT BALATON
AABLNRU BARNAUL
AABLNTT BLATANT
AABLORT ABLATOR
AABLOTW AT A BLOW
AABLRTU TABULAR
AABLRTY RATABLY
AABLSSY ABYSSAL
AABLTTU ABUTTAL
AABMMOS MOMBASA
AABMNOT BOATMAN
AABMNOY AMBOYNA,
   BAYAMON
AABMNST BANTAMS,
   BATSMAN
AABMORU MARABOU
AABNNOZ BONANZA
AABNNSY BANYANS
AABORRS RASBORA
AABQSUU SUB-AQUA
AABRRUV BRAVURA
AABSSSY SASSABY
AABSTUX SAXTUBA
AACCDEN CANDACE
AACCDES CASCADE
AACCDIR CARDIAC
AACCDIS CICADAS
AACCDOR CARADOC

AACCEST SACCATE
AACCHHS CHA-CHAS
AACCHIR ARCHAIC
AACCHMP CHAMPAC
AACCIJO AJACCIO
AACCILM ACCLAIM
AACCILU ACICULA
AACCIOR CARIOCA
AACCITT ATACTIC
AACCLLO CLOACAL
AACCLLT CATCALL
AACCLRU ACCRUAL,
CARACUL
AACCNNS CANCANS
AACCNVY VACANCY
AACCORU CURACAO
AACCOTT TOCCATA
AACCRSS CARCASS
AACDDEL DECADAL
AACDDIN CANDIDA
AACDEFS FACADES
AACDEHL CHALDEA
AACDEHR CHARADE
AACDEHT CATHEAD
AACDELN CANDELA,
DECANAL
AACDELR CALDERA
AACDEMY ACADEMY
AACDENV ADVANCE
AACDENZ CADENZA
AACDERS ARCADES
AACDERV CADAVER
AACDERY DAY-CARE
AACDETU CAUDATE
AACDETV VACATED
AACDFIR FARADIC
AACDGOR CARADOG
AACDHMR DRACHMA
AACDIJU JUDAICA
AACDILR RADICAL
AACDILU CLAUDIA
AACDINT ANTACID
AACDINV VANADIC
AACDIOR ACAROID
AACDIRR RICARDA
AACDIRS ASCARID
AACDJKW JACKDAW
AACDLNO ACNODAL
AACDLNS SCANDAL
AACDLPR PLACARD
AACDNRS CANARDS
AACDOOV AVOCADO
AACDRSZ CZARDAS
AACEEGR ACREAGE

AACEEHR EARACHE
AACEEKT TEACAKE
AACEEPT AT PEACE
AACEERT ACERATE
AACEESS CASEASE
AACEEST CASEATE
AACEETT ACETATE
AACEFLT FALCATE
AACEFRR CARFARE
AACEFRS CARAFES
AACEGKP PACKAGE
AACEGNR CARNAGE
AACEGRT CARTAGE
AACEHLR RACHAEL
AACEHNP PANACHE
AACEHPU CHAPEAU
AACEHRT TRACHEA
AACEHTT ATTACHÉ
AACEHTU CHÂTEAU
AACEHWY EACH WAY
AACEIMN ANAEMIC
AACEIMR AMERICA
AACEINO OCEANIA
AACEIPP CAP-A-PIE
AACEIRV AVARICE
AACEKNP PANCAKE
AACEKNS ASKANCE
AACEKOT OATCAKE
AACELLN CANELLA
AACELLP CAPELLA,
LAPLACE
AACELLT LACTEAL
AACELLW WALLACE
AACELMN MANACLE
AACELMR CAMERAL,
CARAMEL, CARMELA
AACELNU LACUNAE
AACELNV VALANCE
AACELPR CARPALE
AACELPS PALACES,
PASCALE
AACELPT PLACATE
AACELRV CARAVEL
AACELST LACTASE
AACELTT LACTATE
AACELTV CLAVATE
AACEMMR MACRAMÉ
AACEMNV CAVEMAN
AACEMQU MACAQUE
AACEMRS CAMERAS
AACENPS CANAPÉS
AACENRS SARACEN
AACENTY CYANATE
AACEPRS PESCARA

AACEPRT RATE-CAP
AACERRT RAT RACE
AACERST CASERTA, CAT'S-
EAR
AACERSU CAESURA
AACERTU ARCUATE
AACESTV CAVEATS
AACETTU ACTUATE
AACFILS FACIALS,
FASCIAL
AACFINR AFRICAN
AACFINT FANATIC
AACFISS FASCIAS
AACFLLY FALLACY
AACFLRU FACULAR
AACFLTU FACTUAL
AACFNST CAFTANS
AACFSTT FAT CATS
AACGIIL GALICIA
AACGILL GLACIAL
AACGILM MAGICAL
AACGLOS COAL GAS
AACGLRY CALGARY
AACGNOU GUANACO
AACHHKR CHARKHA
AACHHLL CHALLAH
AACHIKL HALAKIC
AACHIKR KARACHI
AACHILM MALACHI
AACHILR RACHIAL
AACHIMN MAHICAN
AACHIMR AMHARIC
AACHIMS CHIASMA
AACHINS SANCHIA
AACHINT ITHACAN
AACHIPS CHIAPAS
AACHIRT CITHARA
AACHKRY HAYRACK
AACHKSW HACKSAW
AACHLLN LACHLAN
AACHLMS CHASMAL
AACHLMY MALACHY
AACHLPP CHAPPAL
AACHLPS PASCHAL
AACHNOP PANOCHA
AACHNPX PANCHAX
AACHNRY ANARCHY
AACHNSU ANCHUSA
AACHRRT CATARRH
AACHRWY ARCHWAY
AACHRYZ ZACHARY
AACIINT ACTINIA
AACIIST ASIATIC
AACIJLP JALAPIC

AACIJNT JACINTA
AACIKLL ALKALIC
AACIKLR CLARKIA
AACILLM CAMILLA
AACILLS CALLAIS
AACILNR ACRILAN, CRANIAL
AACILNT ACTINAL
AACILNU LUCIANA
AACILOS ASOCIAL
AACILOX COAXIAL
AACILPT CAPITAL
AACIMNS MANIACS
AACINOR OCARINA
AACINPS CASPIAN
AACINPT CAPTAIN
AACINRZ CZARINA
AACINST SATANIC
AACINTV VATICAN
AACIOPT TAPIOCA
AACIORT CROATIA
AACIORV CRAIOVA
AACIOTV OCTAVIA
AACIPRX APRAXIC
AACIQTU AQUATIC
AACISTT ASTATIC
AACJKLS JACKALS
AACJKMN MAN JACK
AACJKRT JACK TAR
AACJKSS JACKASS
AACJMOR MAJORCA
AACJOST JOCASTA
AACKLTW CATWALK
AACKNRS RANSACK
AACKPRR CAR PARK
AACKSTT ATTACKS
AACLLNT CALLANT
AACLLSU CLAUSAL
AACLMNT CLAMANT
AACLMRU MACULAR
AACLMSU CALAMUS
AACLNNO ANCONAL
AACLNNU CANNULA
AACLNPY CLAYPAN
AACLNRU LACUNAR
AACLNSU LACUNAS
AACLOPR CAPORAL
AACLORT COAL TAR
AACLOST COASTAL
AACLOTT CATTALO
AACLPSU SCAPULA
AACLPTY PLAY-ACT
AACLRSS RASCALS, SCALARS

AACLRVY CALVARY, CAVALRY
AACLSTU LUCASTA
AACLSUX LASCAUX
AACLTTU TACTUAL
AACMNNO MONACAN
AACMNRU ARCANUM
AACMNTX MANX CAT
AACMORS SARCOMA
AACMRRT TRAMCAR
AACMRSS SARCASM
AACMRST TARMACS
AACNNOZ CANZONA
AACNOST SACATON
AACNPST CAPSTAN, CATNAPS
AACNSSV CANVASS
AACNTUY YUCATAN
AACOPPR APOCARP
AACPSTW CAT'S PAW
AACRSTV CRAVATS
AACRTTT ATTRACT
AACRTUY ACTUARY
AACTUWY CUTAWAY
AADDDEN ADDENDA
AADDEFI DEAF-AID
AADDEGM DAMAGED
AADDEIL ALIDADE
AADDELR ALDREDA
AADDENP DEADPAN
AADDEPR PARADED
AADDEPT ADAPTED
AADDERW AWARDED
AADDGNR GRANDAD
AADDHKR KHADDAR
AADDIMS DADAISM
AADDIST DADAIST
AADDLNO DONALDA
AADDNVV DVANDVA
AADEELT DEALATE
AADEERT AERATED
AADEERW AWARDEE
AADEFHO AHEAD OF
AADEFHT FATHEAD
AADEFLR ALFREDA
AADEGGR AGGRADE, GARAGED
AADEGHO GO-AHEAD
AADEGMN MANAGED
AADEGMR DAMAGER
AADEGMS DAMAGES
AADEGNS AGENDAS
AADEGRT GRADATE
AADEGRV RAVAGED

AADEGRY YARDAGE
AADEGSV SAVAGED
AADEHLN HALDANE
AADEHMN HEADMAN
AADEHMS ASHAMED
AADEHRW WARHEAD
AADEHWY HEADWAY
AADEILN ADELINA
AADEILV AVAILED, VEDALIA
AADEIMR MADEIRA
AADEINR ARANEID, ARIADNE
AADEINS NAIADES
AADEINZ IN A DAZE
AADEIRT RADIATE
AADEITW AWAITED
AADEJNU JUDAEAN
AADELLY ALLAYED
AADELMO À LA MODE
AADELMR ALARMED
AADELNR ADRENAL
AADELRW RAW DEAL
AADELRY ALREADY
AADELTU ADULATE
AADEMMN MAN-MADE
AADEMNO ADENOMA
AADEMNS MAENADS
AADEMNT MANDATE
AADEMNY NAME DAY
AADEMSS AMASSED
AADENNT ANDANTE
AADENRS ANDREAS
AADENRV VERANDA
AADEPRR PARADER
AADEPRS PARADES
AADEPRT ADAPTER
AADEPSS PASSADE
AADERRW AWARDER
AADERRY ARRAYED
AADERSY DARESAY
AADESSY ASSAYED
AADFGLY FLAG DAY
AADGGHR HAGGARD
AADGGLR LAGGARD
AADGIMM DIGAMMA
AADGIMR DIAGRAM
AADGIOS ADAGIOS
AADGIPR PADRAIG
AADGLLW GADWALL
AADGLNO GONADAL
AADGLNR GARLAND
AADGLNT LANDTAG
AADGLNU LUGANDA
AADGLRU GRADUAL

AADGMNR GRANDMA
AADGNNU UGANDAN
AADGNPR GRANDPA
AADGOPR PODAGRA
AADGOPS PAGODAS
AADHHMS MASHHAD
AADHHNR DHAHRAN
AADHILS DAHLIAS
AADHINP DAPHNIA
AADHINR HADRIAN
AADHLRY HALYARD
AADHMNO DAHOMAN
AADHNPR HARDPAN
AADHNRS HANSARD
AADHNSW HANDSAW
AADHOSS SODA ASH
AADHRRV HARVARD
AADHRSZ HAZARDS
AADHRWY HAYWARD
AADHSWY WASHDAY
AADIINN INDIANA
AADIINO DIANOIA
AADIINV DAVINIA
AADIIRR AIR RAID
AADIISV ADIVASI
AADILMR ADMIRAL
AADILMT MATILDA
AADILNP PALADIN
AADILPS APSIDAL
AADILRS RADIALS
AADILTV DATIVAL
AADILWY WAYLAID
AADIMNR MIRANDA
AADIMOR DIORAMA
AADIMRS DAMARIS
AADIMRU MADURAI
AADINRT RADIANT
AADIORS ISADORA
AADKLNO OAKLAND
AADKNOT DAKOTAN
AADKNRT TANKARD
AADKRWW AWKWARD
AADLLMR MALLARD
AADLLMS SMALL AD
AADLLNP LAPLAND
AADLLNR RANDALL
AADLNOR RONALDA
AADLNOY YOLANDA
AADLNRY LANYARD
AADLNSS SANDALS
AADLNSU LANDAUS
AADLNSV VANDALS
AADLOPY PAYLOAD
AADLPPU APPLAUD

AADLRRU RADULAR
AADMNNO MADONNA
AADMNOR MADRONA,
MONARDA, ROADMAN
AADMNRS MANSARD
AADMNRY MAYNARD
AADMORT MATADOR
AADMRRY YARDARM
AADMRZZ MAZZARD
AADMSYY MAY DAYS
AADNOPR PANDORA
AADNORR ANDORRA
AADNRVW VANWARD
AADNSTW WANT ADS
AADOPRX PARADOX
AADORTX ROAD TAX
AADORWY ROADWAY
AADQRTU QUADRAT
AADRWWY WAYWARD
AAEEFGL LEAFAGE
AAEEFLT TEALEAF
AAEEGKL LEAKAGE
AAEEGLT GALEATE
AAEEGMT AGAMETE
AAEEGNO NEOGAEA
AAEEGRV AVERAGE
AAEEHLT ALETHEA
AAEEHRT HETAERA
AAEELLP PALE ALE
AAEELMT MALEATE
AAEELNS SEA-LANE
AAEELRZ ELEAZAR
AAEEMNT EMANATE,
MANATEE
AAEEPPS APPEASE
AAEERSW SEAWARE
AAEERTU AUREATE
AAEERTX EXARATE
AAEFFGR AGRAFFE
AAEFFIR AFFAIRE
AAEFFNR FANFARE
AAEFFTT TAFFETA
AAEFGLN FALANGE
AAEFGTW WAFTAGE
AAEFLPR EARFLAP
AAEFMRT FERMATA
AAEFNST SANTA FE
AAEFRRR FERRARA
AAEFRRW WARFARE
AAEFRST FAR EAST
AAEGGNO ANAGOGE
AAEGGOP APAGOGE
AAEGGRS GARAGES
AAEGHLU HAULAGE

AAEGHMR GRAHAME
AAEGILR ALGERIA,
REGALIA
AAEGISS ASSEGAI
AAEGITT AGITATE
AAEGKNT TANKAGE
AAEGKOS SOAKAGE
AAEGLLR ALLEGRA
AAEGLLT TALLAGE
AAEGLMN GAMELAN
AAEGLMT GAMETAL
AAEGLNS LASAGNE
AAEGLRR REALGAR
AAEGLSV SALVAGE
AAEGMNR MANAGER
AAEGMNT MAGENTA,
MAGNATE
AAEGMPR RAMPAGE
AAEGMRW WAR GAME
AAEGMSS MASSAGE
AAEGNNT TANNAGE
AAEGNPT PAGEANT
AAEGNPW PAWNAGE
AAEGNRR ARRANGE
AAEGNRT TANAGER
AAEGNSU GUANASE
AAEGNTV VANTAGE
AAEGPRW WARPAGE
AAEGPSS PASSAGE
AAEGQUY QUAYAGE
AAEGRRV RAVAGER
AAEGRST TEAR GAS
AAEGRSV RAVAGES
AAEGRTT REGATTA
AAEGSSU ASSUAGE,
SAUSAGE
AAEGSSV SAVAGES
AAEGSTW WASTAGE
AAEGTTW WATTAGE
AAEGTUX GÂTEAUX
AAEGTWY GATEWAY,
GETAWAY
AAEHHIL HIALEAH
AAEHHLM MEHALAH
AAEHILM MEHALIA
AAEHIMN ANAHEIM
AAEHIRT HETAIRA
AAEHKLN ELKANAH
AAEHKMY MAKE HAY
AAEHKNT KHANATE
AAEHLLL ALLHEAL
AAEHLPR RAPHAEL
AAEHLPX HEXAPLA
AAEHLRT TREHALA

AAEHNPR HANAPER
AAEHNPS SAPHENA
AAEHNSY HYAENAS
AAEHRSY HEARSAY
AAEHSTT HASTATE
AAEIKLS AS ALIKE
AAEIKMT TAKE AIM
AAEILLU EULALIA
AAEILMN MELANIA
AAEILMP PAMELIA
AAEILMR ALMERIA
AAEILMS MALAISE
AAEILNN ALANINE
AAEILNR AIRLANE,
    LARAINE
AAEILNT NATALIE
AAEILOT AETOLIA
AAEILRS AERIALS
AAEILRU AURELIA
AAEILRV VALERIA
AAEILSS ALIASES
AAEIMMT IMAMATE
AAEIMNR ARMENIA
AAEIMNS AMNESIA
AAEIMNT AMENTIA,
    ANIMATE
AAEIMPY PYAEMIA
AAEIMRU URAEMIA
AAEINNO AEONIAN
AAEINST ENTASIA
AAEIPRR PAREIRA
AAEIPRS SPIRAEA
AAEIPTT APATITE
AAEIRSU EURASIA
AAEIRTT ARIETTA
AAEIRTV VARIATE
AAEISTT SATIATE
AAEJNTT JANETTA
AAEKKRY KAYAKER
AAEKLNT ALKANET
AAEKMRR EARMARK
AAEKMRS SEAMARK
AAEKMWY MAKE WAY
AAEKPRT PARTAKE
AAEKSTT AT STAKE
AAELLLM LAMELLA
AAELLPT PATELLA
AAELLRS ALL EARS
AAELLRT LATERAL
AAELLSV SAVE-ALL
AAELLSW SEAWALL
AAELMNS ANSELMA
AAELMNU ALUMNAE,
    MANUELA

AAELMOT OATMEAL
AAELMPT PALMATE
AAELMST MALTASE
AAELMSY AMYLASE
AAELNNP ANNAPLE
AAELNRS ARSENAL
AAELNST SEALANT
AAELNSY ANALYSE
AAELORR AREOLAR
AAELORU AUREOLA
AAELOTX OXALATE
AAELPPR APPAREL
AAELPPS APPEALS
AAELPPT PALPATE
AAELPRT APTERAL
AAELPRV PALAVER
AAELPST PALATES
AAELPTT TAPETAL
AAELPTU PLATEAU
AAELPTY APETALY
AAELRTT ARLETTA
AAELSST ATLASES
AAELSUX ASEXUAL
AAELTVV VALVATE
AAEMMMR MAREMMA
AAEMNPP PAMPEAN
AAEMRSS AMASSER
AAEMRST ARTEMAS
AAEMRTU AMATEUR
AAENNNT ANTENNA
AAENNRV RAVENNA
AAENNST ANNATES
AAENNTT TANNATE
AAENPST ANAPEST,
    PEASANT
AAENPSV PAVANES
AAENRRT NARRATE
AAENRRV NAVARRE
AAENRTU TAUREAN
AAENRUW UNAWARE
AAENSSV VANESSA
AAENSSW SWANSEA
AAENSTV AVESTAN
AAEORRT AERATOR
AAEORRU AURORAE
AAEPPRT PARAPET
AAERRRS ARREARS
AAERSSY ASSAYER
AAESSWY SEAWAYS
AAFFINS SAFFIAN
AAFFIRS AFFAIRS
AAFFRSY AFFRAYS
AAFGHNS AFGHANS
AAFGLMN FLAGMAN

AAFGORR FARRAGO
AAFHILX HALIFAX
AAFHINS ISFAHAN
AAFHLMO HALF A MO
AAFHLWY HALFWAY
AAFHNST FATSHAN
AAFIILR FILARIA
AAFILNT FANTAIL
AAFIMRY MAYFAIR
AAFINNT INFANTA
AAFIPRT PARFAIT
AAFIRSS SAFARIS
AAFIRWY FAIRWAY
AAFKNST KAFTANS
AAFLLTY FATALLY
AAFLWYY FLYAWAY
AAFNSTT FANTAST
AAFNSTY FANTASY
AAFPSUX FAUX PAS
AAGGIUZ GAGAUZI
AAGGIZZ ZAGAZIG
AAGGNWY GANGWAY
AAGHILR ALIGARH
AAGHITU GAUHATI
AAGHKRS KASHGAR
AAGHMNN HANGMAN
AAGHNNY HANYANG
AAGHNRS HANGARS
AAGHNUV VAUGHAN
AAGIINO GOIANIA
AAGIINT NIIGATA
AAGIKNW AWAKING
AAGILMY MYALGIA
AAGILNN ANGINAL,
    ANGLIAN
AAGILNP PAGINAL
AAGILNV VAGINAL
AAGILTW WAGTAIL
AAGIMNO ANGIOMA
AAGIMNS SIAMANG
AAGIMNZ AMAZING
AAGINRR ARRAIGN
AAGINRS SANGRIA
AAGINRU GUARANI
AAGINST AGAINST
AAGINSU IGUANAS
AAGINSV VAGINAS
AAGINSY GAINSAY
AAGINTU ANTIGUA
AAGIOTT AGITATO
AAGJRSU JAGUARS
AAGJRTU GUJARAT
AAGKMSS GAS MASK
AAGKNRS ANGARSK

AAGLLNT GALLANT
AAGLNNO ANGOLAN
AAGLNOR GRANOLA
AAGLNOY ANALOGY
AAGLNRU ANGULAR
AAGLRUU AUGURAL
AAGMMRR GRAMMAR
AAGMNOR ROMAGNA
AAGMNRT TANGRAM
AAGMOPY APOGAMY
AAGMRUX MARGAUX
AAGNOPR PARAGON
AAGNORS ANGORAS
AAGNORZ ORGANZA
AAGNRRY GRANARY
AAGNRTV VAGRANT
AAGOPSS SAPSAGO
AAGORSU SAGUARO
AAGSTUU AUGUSTA
AAHHKKL KHALKHA
AAHHNPT NAPHTHA
AAHHOPR PHARAOH
AAHIINT HAITIAN
AAHIJNR HARIJAN
AAHIKRU HAURAKI
AAHILTT TALITHA
AAHIMNO MAHONIA
AAHIMRT MARATHI
AAHINNU HUAI-NAN
AAHINOP APHONIA
AAHINOR HONIARA
AAHINPR PIRANHA
AAHINST ASHANTI
AAHIORT HORATIA
AAHIPRS PARIAHS
AAHIPTY HYPATIA
AAHJNNO JOHANNA
AAHKKSS KHAKASS
AAHKMSY YASHMAK
AAHLLSW WALLAHS
AAHLLWY HALLWAY
AAHLMRS MARSHAL
AAHLMRU HAMULAR
AAHLNPX PHALANX
AAHLNRW NARWHAL
AAHLNTU NAHUATL
AAHLPRS PHRASAL
AAHLPST ASPHALT
AAHMNNU HANUMAN
AAHMNSS SHAMANS
AAHMOPR AMPHORA
AAHMRTU MATHURA
AAHNNOS HOSANNA
AAHNPST PATHANS

AAHNRTX ANTHRAX
AAHNRTY RHATANY
AAHPRTW WARPATH
AAHPTWY PATHWAY
AAHRSTY ASHTRAY
AAHRTTW ATHWART
AAIILMR AIRMAIL
AAIILNT ITALIAN
AAIILNV LAVINIA
AAIILOS ALOISIA
AAIILPT TILAPIA
AAIINNR IRANIAN
AAIINTT TITANIA
AAIINVV VIVIANA
AAIJLNU JULIANA
AAIJNTU JUANITA
AAIKLLS ALKALIS
AAIKMNN MANAKIN
AAIKNNT KANTIAN
AAIKNOW OKINAWA
AAIKNRT KATRINA
AAIKPPR PAPRIKA
AAILLMM MAMILLA
AAILLMX MAXILLA
AAILLNV VANILLA
AAILLPP PAPILLA
AAILLUV ALLUVIA
AAILMMN MAILMAN
AAILMMS LAMAISM,
    MIASMAL
AAILMMX MAXIMAL
AAILMNR LAMINAR
AAILMNS ANIMALS
AAILMNV MALVINA
AAILMOS SOMALIA
AAILMPR PALMIRA
AAILMPS IMPALAS
AAILMRT MARITAL,
    MARTIAL
AAILMST LAMAIST
AAILNOP PIANOLA
AAILNOS SINALOA
AAILNOT LAOTIAN
AAILNOV VALONIA
AAILNPT PLATINA
AAILNRU LAURINA
AAILNRY LANIARY
AAILNSV SILVANA
AAILNTV LATVIAN,
    VALIANT
AAILNWY WAYLAIN
AAILORS ROSALIA,
    SOLARIA
AAILORV VARIOLA

AAILOSY ALOYSIA
AAILPRT PARTIAL, PATRIAL
AAILPST SPATIAL
AAILRRV ARRIVAL
AAILRSS LARISSA
AAILRST LARIATS
AAILRTV TRAVAIL
AAILRWY RAILWAY
AAILSSW WASSAIL
AAILSTU LUSATIA
AAIMMNO AMMONIA
AAIMMSS MIASMAS
AAIMNOS ANOSMIA
AAIMNOT ANIMATO
AAIMNRS MARINAS
AAIMNRT MARTIAN,
    MARTINA, TAMARIN
AAIMNRU RUMANIA
AAIMNRX MARXIAN
AAIMNST STAMINA
AAIMORV MORAVIA
AAIMRSS MARISSA
AAIMRSU MASURIA,
    SAMURAI
AAIMSTV ATAVISM
AAINNOT ANTONIA
AAINNRU URANIAN
AAINNRV NIRVANA
AAINORV OVARIAN
AAINORZ ARIZONA
AAINRST ARTISAN,
    TSARINA
AAINRSU SAURIAN
AAINRTV VARIANT
AAINRTY NAYARIT
AAINRTZ TZARINA
AAINSVY VISAYAN
AAINTTT ATTAINT
AAINTUY TAIYUAN
AAIOPRR PAIR-OAR
AAIORTV AVIATOR
AAIPPTT PIT-A-PAT
AAIPRSU AU PAIRS
AAIPRTT PARTITA
AAIPSZZ PIAZZAS
AAIQSSU QUASSIA
AAIQTUV AQUAVIT
AAIRSSS SASSARI
AAIRSSY ASSYRIA
AAIRSTU AUSTRIA
AAIRSWY AIRWAYS
AAISTTV ATAVIST
AAITWXY TAXIWAY
AAJKLWY JAYWALK

AAJMPSY PYJAMAS	AAMNOTY ANATOMY	ABBDEGR GRABBED
AAJNNSU SAN JUAN	AAMNPRT RAMPANT	ABBDELR DABBLER,
AAJNRUY JANUARY	AAMNPSS SAMPANS	DRABBLE
AAKKLRU KARAKUL	AAMNPTY TYMPANA	ABBDERR DRABBER
AAKLMNW WALKMAN	AAMORSV SAMOVAR	ABBDEST STABBED
AAKMNUU MANUKAU	AAMORTY AMATORY	ABBDESW SWABBED
AAKMRUZ MAZURKA	AAMOSSS SAMOSAS	ABBDGIN DABBING
AAKNNTU NUNATAK	AAMOTTU AUTOMAT	ABBDINR RIBBAND
AAKNORS ANORAKS	AAMPRRT RAMPART	ABBDMOR BOMBARD
AAKNOSU ANOUSKA	AAMRSTU SUMATRA,	ABBDNOX BANDBOX
AAKNRSS SARANSK	TRAUMAS	ABBEETT BABETTE
AAKPRWY PARKWAY	AAMRTWY TRAMWAY	ABBEGLR GABBLER,
AAKRTUY AUTARKY	AAMSSTU SATSUMA	GRABBLE
AALLLNS LALLANS	AANNORS ROSANNA	ABBEGNU BUGBANE
AALLMPU AMPULLA	AANNORX ROXANNA	ABBEGRR GRABBER
AALLNPU PLANULA	AANNOTT ANNATTO	ABBEGRU BUGBEAR
AALLNSY NASALLY	AANNRUU NAURUAN	ABBEHMO HOBBEMA
AALLRST ALL-STAR	AANNSSU SUSANNA	ABBEIST TABBIES
AALLRUY AURALLY	AANNSUZ SUZANNA	ABBELLR BARBELL
AALMMMS MAMMALS	AANORTT TARANTO	ABBELMR BRAMBLE
AALMMNO AMMONAL	AANOSST SONATAS	ABBELOR BELABOR
AALMNOS SALAMON	AANPRST SPARTAN	ABBELRR RABBLER
AALMNOY ANOMALY	AANPRUU URUAPAN	ABBELRS RABBLES
AALMNSU MANUALS	AANPSST PASSANT	ABBELRU BARBULE
AALMORY MAYORAL	AANQRTU QUARTAN	ABBELSU BAUBLES
AALMPRY PALMYRA	AANRRTW WARRANT	ABBERRS BARBERS
AALNNRU ANNULAR	AANRSTT TARTANS	ABBERST STABBER
AALNNSU ANNUALS	AANRUWY RUNAWAY	ABBERSW SWABBER
AALNORS ALSO-RAN	AANSSTV SAVANTS	ABBESSU SUBBASE
AALNPRT PLANTAR	AANSSTZ STANZAS	ABBGGIN GABBING
AALNPST SALTPAN	AANSTTT STATANT	ABBGIJN JABBING
AALNQTU QUANTAL	AAOPRRT PRO RATA	ABBGINN NABBING
AALNRTU NATURAL	AAOQSSU OQUASSA	ABBGINT TABBING
AALNSTT SALTANT	AAORRSU AURORAS	ABBGINY BABYING
AALNSTU SULTANA	AAORSTV OSTRAVA,	ABBGOOU BUGABOO
AALNSTY ANALYST	SARATOV	ABBHISY BABYISH
AALOPRS PARASOL	AAOTTUY TATOUAY	ABBHRRU RHUBARB
AALOPTV POLTAVA	AAPPSWW PAWPAWS	ABBHTTU BATHTUB
AALORRU AURORAL	AAPRRTT RAT TRAP	ABBILOT BOBTAIL
AALORSU AROUSAL	AAQRSSU QUASARS	ABBIMNO BAMBINO
AALOSVW AVOWALS	AARRSTT TARTARS	ABBIRST RABBITS
AALPPSU UPPSALA	AARSSTT STRATAS	ABBISTY BABY-SIT
AALPSTU SPATULA	ABBBDEL BABBLED,	ABBKLOU BLAUBOK
AALRSTT STRATAL	BLABBED	ABBMOOS BAMBOOS
AALRSTU AUSTRAL	ABBBELR BABBLER,	ABBMOST BOMBAST
AALRSTY ASTYLAR	BLABBER	ABBMOTU BUMBOAT
AALRSUZ LAZARUS	ABBBITT BABBITT	ABBNOOS BABOONS
AALSSSV VASSALS	ABBCDER CRABBED	ABBOSTY BOBSTAY
AALSSTU ASSAULT	ABBCEIS CABBIES	ABBQSUY SQUABBY
AAMMMRY MAMMARY	ABBCELS SCABBLE	ABBSSSU SUBBASS
AAMMNNX MANXMAN	ABBCRYY CRYBABY	ABCCEER REBECCA
AAMNNOT MONTANA	ABBDDEL DABBLED	ABCCEIR ACERBIC,
AAMNORS OARSMAN	ABBDDET BAD DEBT	BRECCIA
AAMNOSZ AMAZONS	ABBDEGL GABBLED	ABCCILU CUBICAL

ABCCIMR CAMBRIC
ABCCIOR BORACIC
ABCCKTU CUTBACK
ABCCOOT TOBACCO
ABCDEEH BEACHED
ABCDEEL DÉBÂCLE
ABCDEHU DEBAUCH
ABCDEIK DIEBACK
ABCDEIR CARBIDE
ABCDEKL BLACKED
ABCDEMP CAMP BED
ABCDEOR BAR CODE,
  BROCADE
ABCDERU CUDBEAR
ABCDHIO ICHABOD
ABCDIIS DIBASIC
ABCDIRT CATBIRD
ABCDISU SUBACID
ABCDNOS ABSCOND
ABCDOOR CORDOBA
ABCEEHS BEACHES
ABCEEMR EMBRACE
ABCEENR CARBENE
ABCEENS ABSENCE
ABCEERR CEREBRA
ABCEESU BECAUSE
ABCEGIR RIB CAGE
ABCEGOS BOSCAGE
ABCEHIR HEBRAIC
ABCEHLN BLANCHE
ABCEHMR CHAMBER
ABCEHST BATCHES
ABCEILL ICEBALL
ABCEILM ALEMBIC
ABCEILR ALBERIC,
  CALIBRE
ABCEILT CITABLE
ABCEIMO AMOEBIC
ABCEINR CARBINE
ABCEINT CABINET
ABCEIOR AEROBIC
ABCEIRS ASCRIBE
ABCEISS ABSCISE, SCABIES
ABCEKLN BLACKEN
ABCEKLR BLACKER
ABCEKNR BRACKEN
ABCEKRS BACKERS
ABCEKRT BRACKET
ABCEKST SETBACK
ABCELLU BULLACE
ABCELMO CEMBALO
ABCELMR CLAMBER
ABCELOP PLACEBO
ABCELOV VOCABLE

ABCELRU CURABLE
ABCELRY CYBALER
ABCELSU BASCULE
ABCEMRS CAMBERS
ABCENOS BEACONS
ABCENOW COWBANE
ABCENOZ CABEZON
ABCENRU UNBRACE
ABCEOOS CABOOSE
ABCESSS ABSCESS
ABCFIKN FINBACK
ABCFILO BIFOCAL
ABCFIRS FABRICS
ABCFKLY FLYBACK
ABCGHKO HOGBACK
ABCGIKN BACKING
ABCGILN CABLING
ABCGINR BRACING
ABCGIST BIG CATS
ABCGKLO BACKLOG
ABCHHII HIBACHI
ABCHILS CHABLIS
ABCHILU BALUCHI
ABCHIOT COHABIT
ABCHKTU HACKBUT
ABCHPSU HUBCAPS
ABCIILL BACILLI
ABCIILN ALBINIC
ABCIILS BASILIC
ABCIILT ALBITIC
ABCIIMN MINICAB
ABCIIMS IAMBICS
ABCIJNO JACOBIN
ABCIKSY SICKBAY
ABCILRS SCRIBAL
ABCILTU CUBITAL
ABCIMMU CAMBIUM
ABCIMOR COIMBRA
ABCIMST CAMBIST
ABCINOR NICOBAR
ABCIORU CARIBOU
ABCIOUV BIVOUAC
ABCKLLY BLACKLY
ABCKMRU BUCKRAM
ABCKNNO BANNOCK
ABCKOTU OUTBACK
ABCKPSU BACKUPS
ABCKSUW BUCKSAW
ABCLLOX CALL BOX
ABCLLOY CALLBOY
ABCLMNU CLUBMAN
ABCLMOU COLUMBA
ABCLMSY CYMBALS
ABCLMUU BACULUM

ABCLNOY BALCONY
ABCLRUY CURABLY
ABCMNRW CWMBRAN
ABCMOST COMBATS
ABCNORS CARBONS
ABCORRW CROWBAR
ABCORSX BOXCARS
ABCORSY CARBOYS
ABDDEER BEARDED
ABDDEES DEBASED
ABDDEET DEBATED
ABDDEIN BANDIED
ABDDEIR BRAIDED
ABDDELR BLADDER
ABDDENR BRANDED
ABDDEOR BOARDED,
  ROADBED
ABDDEST BADDEST
ABDDINS DISBAND
ABDDLLO ODDBALL
ABDEEFG FEEDBAG
ABDEEFL FEEL BAD
ABDEEHV BEHAVED
ABDEEIL BEDELIA
ABDEEIR BEADIER
ABDEELL LABELED
ABDEELN ENABLED
ABDEELS BEADLES
ABDEELT BELATED,
  BLEATED
ABDEELY BELAYED
ABDEERS DEBASER
ABDEERT BERATED,
  DEBATER
ABDEEST DEBATES
ABDEETT ABETTED
ABDEFFL BAFFLED
ABDEFLT FLAT-BED
ABDEFOR FORBADE
ABDEGGR BRAGGED
ABDEGHI BIGHEAD
ABDEGIL BIG DEAL
ABDEGIN BEADING
ABDEGIR ABRIDGE,
  BRIGADE
ABDEGLM GAMBLED
ABDEGLR GARBLED
ABDEGNO BONDAGE,
  DOGBANE
ABDEGRS BADGERS
ABDEHIL HIDABLE
ABDEHIT HABITED
ABDEHLR HALBERD
ABDEHOR DEBORAH

ABDEHOW BOWHEAD
ABDEHRT BREADTH
ABDEILN BELINDA
ABDEILP PIEBALD
ABDEILR BEDRAIL
ABDEILS DISABLE
ABDEILU AUDIBLE
ABDEILY BEADILY
ABDEINR BANDIER,
   BRAINED
ABDEIRR BRAIDER
ABDEIRS AIRBEDS,
   BRAISED, SEABIRD
ABDEIRT TRIBADE
ABDEIRW BAWDIER
ABDEISS BIASSED
ABDEJRU ABJURED
ABDEKLU BAULKED
ABDELMR MARBLED,
   RAMBLED
ABDELMS BEDLAMS
ABDELNR BLANDER
ABDELOR LABORED
ABDELOT BLOATED
ABDELOW DOWABLE
ABDELPU DUPABLE
ABDELRU DURABLE
ABDELRW BRAWLED,
   WARBLED
ABDELRY BRADLEY,
   DRYABLE
ABDELST BLASTED,
   STABLED
ABDELTT BATTLED
ABDEMNO ABDOMEN
ABDEMRU BERMUDA
ABDENNR BRENDAN
ABDENOR BROADEN
ABDENPS BEDPANS
ABDENRR BERNARD
ABDENSS BADNESS
ABDEORR BOARDER,
   BROADER
ABDEORT ABORTED
ABDEOST BOASTED
ABDEPSY PAYBEDS
ABDERSV ADVERBS
ABDERUY DAUBERY
ABDETTU ABUTTED
ABDFIIR BID FAIR
ABDFMOR BAD FORM
ABDGIIN ABIDING
ABDGILN BALDING
ABDGINN BANDING

ABDGINR BRIGAND
ABDGINU DAUBING
ABDGINW WINDBAG
ABDGNNU BANDUNG
ABDHMTU MUD BATH
ABDHNSU HUSBAND
ABDHOSW BAD SHOW
ABDILNW BALDWIN
ABDILOO DIABOLO
ABDILOR LABROID
ABDILOT TABLOID
ABDILUY AUDIBLY
ABDILWY BAWDILY
ABDINOR INBOARD
ABDINOT BANTOID
ABDINST BANDITS
ABDIPRU UPBRAID
ABDIRSU SUBARID
ABDJORU DOBRUJA
ABDKNOU DO A BUNK
ABDKOOY DAYBOOK
ABDLLNY BLANDLY
ABDLLOR BOLLARD
ABDLMOR LOMBARD
ABDLORY BROADLY
ABDLRUY DURABLY
ABDLSUU SUBDUAL
ABDNNOR BRANDON
ABDNOSS DONBASS
ABDNOSX SANDBOX
ABDNOYY ANYBODY
ABDNSTY STANDBY
ABDOOWY BAYWOOD
ABDOSYY DAYBOYS
ABDRSTU BUSTARD
ABDRUZZ BUZZARD
ABEEEFT BEEF TEA
ABEEERV BEREAVE
ABEEGHR HERBAGE
ABEEGLS BEAGLES
ABEEGLT GETABLE
ABEEGRS BARGEES
ABEEGRU AUBERGE
ABEEGRW BREWAGE
ABEEHKR REBEKAH
ABEEHNN HENBANE
ABEEHNS BANSHEE, HAS-
   BEEN
ABEEHNT BENEATH
ABEEHRT BREATHE
ABEEHTY EYEBATH
ABEEINT BETAINE
ABEEITT BEATTIE
ABEEKLR BLEAKER

ABEEKNT BETAKEN
ABEEKPS BESPEAK
ABEEKRR BREAKER
ABEEKRS BEAKERS
ABEELLM MABELLE
ABEELLY EYEBALL
ABEELNR ENABLER
ABEELNT TENABLE
ABEELNU NEBULAE
ABEELOR EARLOBE
ABEELQU EQUABLE
ABEELRT BLEATER,
   RETABLE
ABEEMRS BESMEAR
ABEENOU EUBOEAN
ABEENRS BENARES
ABEENRV VERBENA
ABEERRS BEARERS
ABEERRT REBATER
ABEERST BEATERS,
   REBATES
ABEERSV BEAVERS
ABEESWX BEESWAX
ABEFFLR BAFFLER
ABEFFLS BAFFLES
ABEFFOT OFFBEAT
ABEFILN FINABLE
ABEFILR FRIABLE
ABEFILU FIBULAE
ABEFILX FIXABLE
ABEFITY BEATIFY
ABEFLLU BALEFUL
ABEFLLY FLYABLE
ABEFLNT FAN BELT
ABEFLNU BANEFUL
ABEFORR FORBEAR
ABEFPRS PREFABS
ABEGGIM BIG GAME
ABEGGIR BAGGIER
ABEGGMO GAMBOGE
ABEGGRR BRAGGER
ABEGGRS BEGGARS
ABEGGRY BEGGARY
ABEGHMR MAGHREB
ABEGHNS SHEBANG
ABEGHRU BEAR HUG
ABEGILN BELGIAN,
   BENGALI
ABEGILR GABRIEL
ABEGILV GIVABLE
ABEGIMN BEAMING, BIG
   NAME
ABEGIMR GAMBIER
ABEGINO BEGONIA

ABEGINR BEARING
ABEGINT BEATING
ABEGIPP BAGPIPE
ABEGLMR GAMBLER,
  GAMBREL
ABEGLNS BANGLES
ABEGLOT GLOBATE
ABEGLRR GARBLER
ABEGMOR BERGAMO,
  EMBARGO
ABEGMRU UMBRAGE
ABEGNOS NOSEBAG
ABEGNRS BANGERS
ABEGOPY PAGEBOY
ABEGORX GEARBOX
ABEGOSZ GAZEBOS
ABEGOTT TOTE BAG
ABEGOUY BUOYAGE
ABEHILR HIRABLE
ABEHIMO BOHEMIA
ABEHIRS BEARISH
ABEHITU HABITUÉ
ABEHKRU HAUBERK
ABEHLMS SHAMBLE
ABEHLRS HERBALS
ABEHLRT BLATHER
ABEHNRY ABHENRY
ABEHNTY BETHANY
ABEHRRS BRASHER
ABEHRST BATHERS
ABEHRTY BREATHY
ABEIILR LIBERIA
ABEIILS BASILIE
ABEIINR IBERIAN
ABEIINT BAINITE
ABEIIRS SIBERIA
ABEIJNS BASENJI
ABEIKLL LIKABLE
ABEIKLS SKIABLE
ABEIKNR BIKANER,
  BREAK-IN
ABEIKNT BEATNIK
ABEILLN LINABLE
ABEILLO LOBELIA
ABEILLP PLIABLE
ABEILLR BRAILLE, LIBERAL
ABEILLS SIBELLA
ABEILLV LIVABLE
ABEILMN MINABLE
ABEILMR BALMIER,
  MIRABEL
ABEILMT LIMBATE,
  TIMBALE
ABEILMX MIXABLE

ABEILNP BIPLANE
ABEILNS LESBIAN
ABEILRT LIBRATE,
  TRIABLE
ABEILST BESTIAL, STABILE
ABEILSY BAILEYS
ABEILSZ SIZABLE
ABEILVV BIVALVE
ABEIMNT AMBIENT
ABEIMRR BARMIER
ABEIMZZ ZAMBEZI
ABEINOZ ZENOBIA
ABEINRS SERBIAN
ABEINRW WINE BAR
ABEINSS BASSEIN
ABEINST ANTIBES
ABEINTT BETTINA,
  TIBETAN
ABEIOTV OBVIATE
ABEIPST BAPTISE
ABEIPTZ BAPTIZE
ABEIRRR BARRIER
ABEIRRT ARBITER,
  RAREBIT
ABEIRRZ BIZARRE,
  BRAZIER
ABEIRSS BRASSIE
ABEIRTT BATTIER,
  BIRETTA
ABEIRTV VIBRATE
ABEIRTX BEATRIX
ABEIRUX EXURBIA
ABEISTT BATISTE
ABEISUV ABUSIVE
ABEITUX BAUXITE
ABEJLUY BLUE JAY
ABEJNOW JAWBONE
ABEJRRU ABJURER
ABEKLLY BLEAKLY
ABEKLNT BLANKET
ABEKNRS BANKERS
ABEKRRS BARKERS
ABEKSST BASKETS
ABELLNT NETBALL
ABELLOS LOSABLE
ABELLOV LOVABLE
ABELLRU RUBELLA,
  RULABLE
ABELLST BALLETS
ABELLSY SYBELLA
ABELLTU BULLATE
ABELLUW BLUE LAW
ABELMNT LAMBENT
ABELMNU ALBUMEN

ABELMOV MOVABLE
ABELMRR MARBLER,
  RAMBLER
ABELMRS MARBLES,
  RAMBLES
ABELMRT LAMBERT
ABELMRY BRAMLEY
ABELMTU MUTABLE
ABELNNO LEBANON
ABELNOT NOTABLE
ABELNOY BALONEY
ABELNRU NEBULAR
ABELNRY BLARNEY
ABELNSU NEBULAS
ABELNTU TUNABLE
ABELOPT POTABLE
ABELORR LABORER
ABELORS ROSABEL
ABELORT BLOATER
ABELORU RUBEOLA
ABELOSV ABSOLVE
ABELOTV VOTABLE
ABELQUY EQUABLY
ABELRRS BARRELS
ABELRRW BRAWLER,
  WARBLER
ABELRSZ BLAZERS
ABELRTT BARTLET
ABELRVY BRAVELY
ABELSST STABLES
ABELSTT BATTLES
ABELSTY BEASTLY
ABELTWY BELTWAY
ABEMNOT BOATMEN
ABEMNST BATSMEN, BEST
  MAN
ABEMNSU SUNBEAM
ABEMORS AMBROSE
ABEMORT BROMATE
ABEMRRT BERTRAM
ABEMSSY EMBASSY
ABENNRS BANNERS
ABENNRW BRANWEN
ABENORT BARONET
ABENORU AUBERON
ABENOTY BAYONET
ABENOWX BONE WAX
ABENQTU BANQUET
ABENRST BARENTS
ABENRSY BARNEYS
ABENSTT BATTENS, TEST
  BAN
ABENTUZ BAUTZEN
ABEOOTV OBOVATE

ABEOPRS SAPROBE
ABEOPRT PROBATE
ABEOQRU BAROQUE
ABEORRT ROBERTA
ABEORST BAROTSE,
BOASTER, BOATERS
ABEORTT ABETTOR,
TABORET
ABEPRTY TYPEBAR
ABEQRSU BARQUES
ABERRTT BARRETT
ABERRVY BRAVERY
ABERSSS BRASSES
ABERSTT BATTERS
ABERSTV BRAVEST
ABERSTY BARYTES
ABERTTU ABUTTER
ABERTTY BATTERY
ABERUUX BUREAUX
ABESSST BASSETS
ABESSSY ABYSSES
ABFFIIL BAILIFF
ABFFLOU BUFFALO
ABFHIST BATFISH
ABFHLSU BASHFUL
ABFIILR BIFILAR
ABFIIMR FIMBRIA
ABFILRU FIBULAR
ABFILSU FIBULAS
ABFIMOR FIBROMA
ABFLOTY FLYBOAT
ABGGGIN BAGGING
ABGGILY BAGGILY
ABGGINN BANGING
ABGGINR BARGING,
GARBING
ABGHINS BASHING
ABGHINT BATHING
ABGHLRU BURGHAL
ABGHMRU HAMBURG
ABGIILN BAILING
ABGIINS BIASING
ABGIINT BAITING
ABGIKLN BALKING
ABGIKLT TALK BIG
ABGIKNN BANKING
ABGIKNR BARKING,
BRAKING
ABGIKNS BASKING
ABGIKST KIT BAGS
ABGILMN AMBLING,
BLAMING, LAMBING
ABGILMS GIMBALS
ABGILNR BLARING

ABGILNT TABLING
ABGILNW BAWLING
ABGILNZ BLAZING
ABGIMST GAMBITS
ABGINNN BANNING
ABGINOT BOATING
ABGINRR BARRING
ABGINRV BRAVING
ABGINRY BRAYING
ABGINST BASTING
ABGINSU ABUSING
ABGINTT BATTING
ABGINTW BATWING
ABGKKNO BANGKOK
ABGKORW WORKBAG
ABGLMOS GAMBOLS
ABGLMOU LUMBAGO
ABGLNOO BOLOGNA
ABGLRRU BURGLAR
ABGMORW BAGWORM
ABGNOPR PROBANG
ABGNOTU GUNBOAT
ABGOPST POSTBAG
ABHHIPT HIPBATH
ABHHOOP POOH-BAH
ABHHSUY HUSHABY
ABHIINT INHABIT
ABHIKRS BASHKIR
ABHILNO HOBNAIL
ABHILOS ABOLISH
ABHILTU HALIBUT
ABHINOS SIOBHAN
ABHINRS BAS-RHIN
ABHINST ABSINTH
ABHIOPS PHOBIAS
ABHIORS BOARISH
ABHIOST ISOBATH
ABHISTU HABITUS
ABHLRSY BRASHLY
ABHMNSU BUSHMAN
ABHOOST BASOTHO
ABHORRS HARBORS
ABHORRU HARBOUR
ABHOTUY HAUTBOY
ABHSTUW WASHTUB
ABIILLS SIBILLA
ABIILMU BULIMIA
ABIILOV BOLIVIA
ABIILRY BILIARY
ABIILTY ABILITY
ABIINOR NAIROBI
ABIIOSS ABIOSIS
ABIJNPU PUNJABI
ABIJPRU BIJAPUR

ABIKLLM KIMBALL
ABILLMY BALMILY
ABILLNP PINBALL
ABILLSW SAWBILL
ABILLSY SIBYLLA, SYBILLA,
SYLLABI
ABILLWX WAXBILL
ABILLWY WAYBILL
ABILMNU ALBUMIN
ABILMOX MAILBOX
ABILNOS ALBINOS
ABILOPR BIPOLAR,
PARBOIL
ABILORT ORBITAL
ABILORV BOLIVAR
ABILRRY LIBRARY
ABILRSU BURIALS
ABIMNRU UMBRIAN
ABIMOSS BIOMASS
ABIMPST BAPTISM
ABINNOS BOSNIAN
ABINORT TABORIN
ABINORW RAINBOW
ABINOST BASTION
ABINRTV VIBRANT
ABIORSS ISOBARS
ABIORTV VIBRATO
ABIORUX ROUBAIX
ABIPRTT BIT PART
ABIPSTT BAPTIST
ABIRUZZ ABRUZZI
ABISSST BASSIST
ABKLLNY BLANKLY
ABKLRUW BULWARK
ABKNRSY BRYANSK
ABLLLUY LULLABY
ABLLNOO BALLOON
ABLLNOS NO BALLS
ABLLORR ROLL BAR
ABLLORU LOBULAR
ABLLOST BALLOTS
ABLLOTY TALLBOY
ABLLPSU BALLS-UP
ABLMOOT TOMBOLA
ABLMOVY MOVABLY
ABLMSTU STAMBUL
ABLMTUY MUTABLY
ABLNOOZ BOLZANO
ABLNOSZ BLAZONS
ABLNOTU BUTANOL
ABLNOTY NOTABLY
ABLOPYY PLAYBOY
ABLORST BORSTAL
ABLORSU LABOURS

ABLOSTX SALTBOX
ABLRTUU TUBULAR
ABMORTU TAMBOUR
ABMOSTW WOMBATS
ABNOORZ BORAZON
ABNOOSS BASSOON
ABNORUY YORUBAN
ABNOTUY BOUYANT,
BUOYANT
ABNRSTU TURBANS
ABOOPSX SOAPBOX
ABOOTTU ABOUT TO
ABOOTTW TOWBOAT
ABORRSU ARBOURS
ABORRSW BARROWS
ABORSSU SUB ROSA
ABRRSSU BURSARS
ABRRSUY BURSARY
ABRRTUY TURBARY
ABRSTUU ARBUTUS
ABSSUWY SUBWAYS
ACCCILY ACYCLIC
ACCDDEE ACCEDED
ACCDEEN CADENCE
ACCDEER ACCEDER
ACCDEHN CHANCED
ACCDEHO COACHED
ACCDEIN CANDICE
ACCDEKL CACKLED,
CLACKED
ACCDEKO COCKADE
ACCDEKR CRACKED
ACCDENY CADENCY
ACCDERU ACCRUED
ACCDESU ACCUSED
ACCDFIL FLACCID
ACCDHIL CHALCID
ACCDINS SCANDIC
ACCDIOT OCTADIC
ACCDORS ACCORDS
ACCEELN CENACLE
ACCEERT ACCRETE
ACCEFLU FELUCCA
ACCEHIL CALICHE,
CHALICE
ACCEHIN CHICANE
ACCEHLN CHANCEL
ACCEHLO COCHLEA
ACCEHNR CHANCRE
ACCEHNS CHANCES
ACCEHOS COACHES
ACCEHRT CATCHER
ACCEHST CACHETS,
CATCHES

ACCEHTU CATECHU
ACCEIIL CECILIA
ACCEIKP ICE PACK, PACK
ICE
ACCEILN CALCINE
ACCEILO COELIAC
ACCEILR CLARICE
ACCEILT CALCITE
ACCEIMR CERAMIC,
RACEMIC
ACCEINO COCAINE,
OCEANIC
ACCEINV VACCINE
ACCEIPR CAPRICE
ACCEIPS ICE CAPS
ACCEIPV PECCAVI
ACCEIST ASCETIC
ACCEKLR CACKLER,
CRACKLE
ACCEKLS CACKLES
ACCEKOP PEACOCK
ACCEKOS SEACOCK
ACCEKPU CUP CAKE
ACCEKRR CRACKER
ACCELLY CALYCLE
ACCELNO CONCEAL
ACCELOR CORACLE
ACCELSU SACCULE
ACCELSY CALYCES
ACCENOV CONCAVE
ACCENPT PECCANT
ACCENRS CANCERS
ACCENST ACCENTS
ACCEPRY PECCARY
ACCERRS SCARCER
ACCERSU ACCUSER
ACCFIIP PACIFIC
ACCFILY CALCIFY
ACCGHIO CHICAGO
ACCGNOS COGNACS
ACCHINO CHICANO
ACCHIOT CHAOTIC
ACCHIOU ACOUCHI
ACCHKNO HANCOCK
ACCHKOY HAYCOCK
ACCHLNO CONCHAL
ACCHNUY CHAUNCY
ACCHOTW CHOCTAW
ACCHRST SCRATCH
ACCIINT ACTINIC
ACCIIST ASCITIC,
SCIATIC
ACCIKRR CARRICK
ACCIKRS CARSICK

ACCIKRT CRACK IT
ACCILLU CALCULI
ACCILMO COMICAL
ACCILMU CALCIUM
ACCILNO CONICAL,
LACONIC
ACCILNU CLUNIAC
ACCILNY CYNICAL
ACCILOR CALORIC
ACCILOS CALICOS
ACCILOV VOCALIC
ACCILRU CRUCIAL
ACCILRY ACRYLIC
ACCILSS CLASSIC
ACCILST CLASTIC
ACCIORS CORSICA
ACCISTT TACTICS
ACCISTU CAUSTIC
ACCKOSS CASSOCK
ACCKPRU CRACKUP
ACCKTTU CUTTACK
ACCMOOY COCOYAM
ACCMOPT COMPACT
ACCMRUU CURCUMA
ACCNOOR RACCOON
ACCNOTT CONTACT
ACCNOTU ACCOUNT
ACCOPTY COPYCAT
ACCOQSU SQUACCO
ACDDDEI CADDIED
ACDDDEU ADDUCED
ACDDEEF DEFACED
ACDDEES DECADES
ACDDEEY DECAYED
ACDDEHR CHEDDAR
ACDDEIN CANDIED
ACDDEIS CADDIES
ACDDEIU DECIDUA
ACDDELO CLADODE
ACDDELR CRADLED
ACDDELS SCALDED
ACDDEOP DECAPOD
ACDDHIS CADDISH
ACDDHKO HADDOCK
ACDDIRS DISCARD, ID
CARDS
ACDDIRY DRYADIC
ACDDIST ADDICTS
ACDDKOP PADDOCK
ACDEEES DECEASE
ACDEEFF EFFACED
ACDEEFR DEFACER,
REFACED
ACDEEHL LEACHED

ACDEEHR ARDECHE, REACHED
ACDEEHT CHEATED
ACDEEIR DECIARE
ACDEEJT DEJECTA
ACDEEKR CREAKED
ACDEELL CADELLE
ACDEELN CLEANED
ACDEELR CLEARED, CREEDAL, DECLARE
ACDEELS DESCALE
ACDEELV CLEAVED
ACDEEMN MENACED
ACDEEMR CREAMED
ACDEENS ENCASED
ACDEENT ENACTED
ACDEENV VENDACE
ACDEEPR CAPERED, RECAPED
ACDEEPS ESCAPED
ACDEERS CREASED
ACDEERT CATERED, CERATED, CREATED, REACTED
ACDEETU EDUCATE
ACDEETX EXACTED
ACDEFFH CHAFFED
ACDEFIN FANCIED
ACDEFOP PO-FACED
ACDEFOT DE FACTO
ACDEFRT CRAFTED
ACDEGHN CHANGED
ACDEGHR CHARGED
ACDEGKO DOCKAGE
ACDEGLN CLANGED, GLANCED
ACDEGNO DECAGON
ACDEGNU UNCAGED
ACDEGOR CORDAGE
ACDEGRS CADGERS
ACDEHHT HATCHED
ACDEHIN CHAINED, ECHIDNA
ACDEHIP EDAPHIC
ACDEHIR CHAIRED
ACDEHIX HEXADIC
ACDEHKL CHALKED
ACDEHKS SHACKED
ACDEHKW WHACKED
ACDEHLS CLASHED
ACDEHLT LATCHED
ACDEHMP CHAMPED
ACDEHMR CHARMED, MARCHED

ACDEHMT MATCHED
ACDEHNR ENDARCH
ACDEHNT CHANTED
ACDEHOP POACHED
ACDEHOT CATHODE
ACDEHPP CHAPPED
ACDEHPR PARCHED
ACDEHPT PATCHED
ACDEHRR CHARRED
ACDEHRS CRASHED
ACDEHRT CHARTED
ACDEHTT CHATTED
ACDEHTW WATCHED
ACDEILL CEDILLA
ACDEILM CLAIMED, DECIMAL, DECLAIM, MEDICAL
ACDEILN ICELAND
ACDEILR DECRIAL, RADICEL, RADICLE
ACDEILT CITADEL, DELTAIC, DIALECT, EDICTAL
ACDEILV CAVILED
ACDEIMY MEDIACY
ACDEINS CANDIES
ACDEINY CYANIDE
ACDEIPR PERACID
ACDEIRR CARRIED
ACDEIRS RADICES, SIDECAR
ACDEIST DIE-CAST
ACDEISV ADVICES
ACDEITT DICTATE
ACDEITY EDACITY
ACDEJLO CAJOLED
ACDEKLN CLANKED
ACDEKLO CLOAKED
ACDEKLS SLACKED
ACDEKLT TACKLED
ACDEKLU CAULKED
ACDEKMS SMACKED
ACDEKNR CRANKED
ACDEKNS SNACKED
ACDEKOR CROAKED
ACDEKQU QUACKED
ACDEKRT TRACKED
ACDEKST STACKED
ACDELMM CLAMMED
ACDELMP CLAMPED
ACDELNO CELADON
ACDELNR CANDLER
ACDELNS CALENDS, CANDLES
ACDELOP PEDOCAL

ACDELOR CAROLED
ACDELOS SOLACED
ACDELOT LOCATED
ACDELPP CLAPPED
ACDELPS CLASPED, SCALPED
ACDELRS CRADLES
ACDELRW CRAWLED
ACDELSS CLASSED, DECLASS
ACDELST CASTLED
ACDELWW DEWCLAW
ACDEMMR CRAMMED
ACDEMNO MACEDON
ACDEMOR COMRADE
ACDEMPR CRAMPED
ACDENNS SCANNED
ACDENOS DEACONS
ACDENOT TACNODE
ACDENPR PRANCED
ACDENPT PANDECT
ACDENRS DANCERS
ACDENRT TANCRED
ACDENRY ARDENCY
ACDENST DESCANT
ACDEORR CORRADE
ACDEORT ART DECO, CORDATE, REDCOAT
ACDEORU ECUADOR
ACDEOST COASTED
ACDEOUV COUVADE
ACDEPPR CRAPPED
ACDEPRS SCRAPED
ACDEQSU CASQUED
ACDERRS SCARRED
ACDERSU CRUSADE
ACDERTT DETRACT
ACDERTU TRADUCE
ACDESTT SCATTED
ACDFIIY ACIDIFY
ACDGGIN CADGING
ACDGHLO CLODAGH
ACDGINN DANCING
ACDGINR CARDING
ACDGKLO DAGLOCK
ACDGORT DOGCART
ACDHIIL CHILIAD
ACDHIIS HASIDIC
ACDHIRR RICHARD
ACDHIRY DIARCHY
ACDHLOR CHORDAL
ACDHMRS DRACHMS
ACDHNOW COWHAND
ACDHOPR POCHARD

ACDHORR ORCHARD
ACDHRYY DYARCHY
ACDIIIN INDICIA
ACDIINN INDICAN
ACDIIRT TRIACID,
TRIADIC
ACDIITY ACIDITY
ACDILMO DOMICAL
ACDILNO NODICAL
ACDILNU LUCINDA
ACDILOP PLACOID
ACDILOR CORDIAL
ACDILOT COTIDAL
ACDILTW WILDCAT
ACDIMMU CADMIUM
ACDIMNO MONADIC,
NOMADIC
ACDIMNY DYNAMIC
ACDINSU SUDANIC
ACDIOPR PARODIC,
PICADOR
ACDIORR CORRIDA,
RICARDO
ACDIORS SARCOID
ACDIORT CAROTID
ACDIOSZ ZODIACS
ACDIOXY OXYACID
ACDIPRY PICARDY
ACDIQRU QUADRIC
ACDIRST DRASTIC
ACDITUV VIADUCT
ACDJNTU ADJUNCT
ACDKLOP PADLOCK
ACDKMPU MUDPACK
ACDLLOR COLLARD
ACDLNOR CALDRON
ACDLORW COLD WAR
ACDLSTY DACTYLS
ACDMMNO COMMAND
ACDMOOW CAMWOOD
ACDNOOR CARDOON
ACDNORU CANDOUR
ACDORST COSTARD
ACDORSW COWARDS
ACDRSTU CUSTARD
ACEEEPS ESCAPEE
ACEEEUV EVACUEE
ACEEFFR EFFACER
ACEEFIN FAIENCE
ACEEFPR PREFACE
ACEEGIL ELEGIAC
ACEEGIS ICE AGES
ACEEHHT CHEETAH
ACEEHIV ACHIEVE

ACEEHLR LEACHER
ACEEHLT CHELATE
ACEEHMT MACHETE
ACEEHNN ENHANCE
ACEEHNP CHEAPEN
ACEEHPR CHEAPER
ACEEHPS PEACHES
ACEEHRR REACHER
ACEEHRS REACHES
ACEEHRT CHEATER,
HECTARE, TEACHER
ACEEILP CALIPEE
ACEEILT ELEATIC
ACEEINU EUCAINE
ACEEKNP KNEECAP
ACEELLN NACELLE
ACEELMP EMPLACE
ACEELNR CARLEEN,
CARLENE, CLEANER
ACEELNS CLEANSE,
SCALENE
ACEELNV ENCLAVE,
VALENCE
ACEELPR PERCALE,
REPLACE
ACEELRR CLEARER
ACEELRS CEREALS
ACEELRT TREACLE
ACEELRV CLEAVER
ACEELST CELESTA
ACEELVX EXCLAVE
ACEEMNR MENACER
ACEEMNS MENACES
ACEEMNV CAVEMEN
ACEEMNY MYCENAE
ACEEMRR CREAMER
ACEEMRT CREMATE
ACEENNP PENANCE
ACEENNT CANTEEN
ACEENNY CAYENNE
ACEENOT ACETONE
ACEENRT CRENATE
ACEENSS SÉANCES
ACEENTU CUNEATE
ACEEORS ACEROSE
ACEEORT OCREATE
ACEEOSS CASEOSE
ACEEPRS ESCAPER
ACEEPSS ESCAPES
ACEEPST PECTASE
ACEEPTT PECTATE
ACEERRS CAREERS
ACEERRT CATERER,
RETRACE, TERRACE

ACEERSS CREASES
ACEERTX EXCRETA
ACEESTU EUSTACE
ACEESTY CAT'S EYE
ACEFFFO FACE-OFF
ACEFFHR CHAFFER
ACEFHMR CHAMFER
ACEFIIL FELICIA
ACEFILL ICEFALL
ACEFILM MALEFIC
ACEFINN FINANCE
ACEFINR FANCIER,
FRANCIE
ACEFINS FANCIES,
FASCINE, FIANCÉS
ACEFITY ACETIFY
ACEFLRU CAREFUL
ACEFNRS FRANCES
ACEFNRU FURNACE
ACEFOTU OUTFACE
ACEFRRT REFRACT
ACEFRRU FARCEUR
ACEFRSU SURFACE
ACEFRTU FURCATE
ACEFSTU FAUCETS
ACEGHNR CHANGER
ACEGHNS CHANGES
ACEGHOU GOUACHE
ACEGHRR CHARGER
ACEGHRS CHARGES
ACEGILN ANGELIC,
GALENIC
ACEGILP PELAGIC
ACEGILR GLACIER,
GRACILE
ACEGIMR GRIMACE
ACEGINO COINAGE
ACEGINR ANERGIC,
GRECIAN
ACEGINS CEASING
ACEGIST CAGIEST
ACEGKLO LOCKAGE
ACEGKLR GRACKLE
ACEGKOR CORKAGE
ACEGLLO COLLAGE
ACEGLNO CONGEAL
ACEGLNR CLANGER
ACEGLNS GLANCES
ACEGLOU CAGOULE
ACEGNOR ACROGEN
ACEGNOT COGNATE
ACEGORS CARGOES,
CORSAGE, SOCAGER
ACEGORU COURAGE

ACEGOTT COTTAGE
ACEHHLT HATCHEL
ACEHHRT HATCHER
ACEHHRU HACHURE
ACEHHST HATCHES
ACEHHTT HATCHET
ACEHILL HELICAL
ACEHILM MICHAEL
ACEHILN CHILEAN
ACEHILR CHARLIE
ACEHILT ETHICAL
ACEHIMN MACHINE
ACEHIMP IMPEACH
ACEHIMR CHIMERA
ACEHINN ENCHAIN
ACEHINR ARCHINE
ACEHINT TEACH-IN
ACEHINY HYAENIC
ACEHIPT HEPATIC
ACEHIRR CHARIER
ACEHIRS CASHIER
ACEHIRT RHAETIC
ACEHIRV ARCHIVE
ACEHISS CHAISES
ACEHIST AITCHES
ACEHITT CHATTIE –
ACEHKLR HACKLER
ACEHKLS HACKLES,
    SHACKLE
ACEHKNY HACKNEY
ACEHKRS HACKERS
ACEHKRW WHACKER
ACEHLLS SHELLAC
ACEHLLT HELLCAT
ACEHLMY ALCHEMY
ACEHLNN CHANNEL
ACEHLNO CHALONE
ACEHLNR CHARNEL
ACEHLOP EPOCHAL
ACEHLOR CHOLERA,
    CHORALE, CHOREAL
ACEHLPS CHAPELS
ACEHLPT CHAPLET
ACEHLPY CHEAPLY
ACEHLRS CHARLES,
    CLASHER, LARCHES
ACEHLRY CHARLEY
ACEHLSS CLASHES
ACEHLST CHALETS,
    LATCHES, SATCHEL
ACEHLTT CHATTEL,
    LATCHET
ACEHMRR CHARMER,
    MARCHER

ACEHMRS MARCHES,
    MESARCH
ACEHMRT REMATCH
ACEHMST MATCHES
ACEHMTY ECTHYMA
ACEHNNT ENCHANT
ACEHNRR RANCHER
ACEHNRS RANCHES
ACEHNRT CHANTER
ACEHNST CHASTEN
ACEHOOT OOTHECA
ACEHOPR POACHER
ACEHORS ROACHES
ACEHOTY CHAYOTE
ACEHPRT CHAPTER,
    PATCHER
ACEHPRY EPARCHY
ACEHPST PATCHES
ACEHQUU QUECHUA
ACEHRRS ARCHERS
ACEHRRT CHARTER
ACEHRRX XERARCH
ACEHRRY ARCHERY
ACEHRSS CHASERS,
    CRASHES
ACEHRST CHASTER
ACEHRTT CHATTER,
    RATCHET
ACEHRTW WATCHER
ACEHSST SACHETS
ACEHSSW CASHEWS
ACEHSTW WATCHES
ACEIILS LAICISE
ACEIILT CILIATE
ACEIILZ LAICIZE
ACEIJSS JESSICA
ACEIKPX PICKAXE
ACEIKRT TACKIER
ACEIKSS SEASICK
ACEILLL ALLELIC
ACEILLM CAMILLE
ACEILLX LEXICAL
ACEILMN MELANIC
ACEILMR CLAIMER,
    MIRACLE, RECLAIM
ACEILMT CLIMATE
ACEILMX EXCLAIM
ACEILNP CAPELIN, IN
    PLACE, PANICLE, PELICAN
ACEILNR CARLINE
ACEILNS SANICLE
ACEILNU CAULINE
ACEILOR CALORIE,
    CARIOLE, CORALIE

ACEILOT ALOETIC
ACEILPR REPLICA
ACEILPS SPECIAL
ACEILPT PLICATE
ACEILRR CLARRIE
ACEILRS ÉCLAIRS, SCALIER
ACEILRT ARTICLE,
    RECITAL
ACEILRU AURICLE
ACEILRV CLAVIER,
    VALERIC
ACEILST CASTILE,
    ELASTIC, LACIEST
ACEILSV VESICAL
ACEILTT LATTICE,
    TACTILE
ACEIMNO ENCOMIA
ACEIMNR CARMINE,
    CRIMEAN
ACEIMNS CINEMAS
ACEIMNT NEMATIC
ACEIMNX MEXICAN
ACEIMPY PYAEMIC
ACEIMRU MAURICE,
    URAEMIC
ACEIMST SEMATIC
ACEIMSU CAESIUM
ACEINNP PINNACE
ACEINNR CANNIER
ACEINNS CANINES
ACEINNT ANCIENT
ACEINNY CYANINE
ACEINOT ACONITE
ACEINRS ARSENIC
ACEINRT CERTAIN
ACEINST ANSTICE
ACEINSV CAVE-INS
ACEINTT TETANIC
ACEINTV VENATIC
ACEINTX INEXACT
ACEINTY CYANITE
ACEINTZ ZINCATE
ACEINVZ VICENZA
ACEIOPT ECTOPIA
ACEIORT EROTICA
ACEIOTX EXOTICA
ACEIPPR CRAPPIE, EPICARP
ACEIPRT PARETIC,
    PICRATE
ACEIPSS CAPSISE
ACEIPST ASEPTIC,
    SPICATE
ACEIPSU AUSPICE
ACEIPSZ CAPSIZE

ACEIPTV CAPTIVE
ACEIQRU ACQUIRE
ACEIQSU CAIQUES
ACEIRRR CARRIER
ACEIRRS CARRIES, SCARIER
ACEIRRT CIRRATE,
ERRATIC
ACEIRRW AIRCREW
ACEIRRZ CRAZIER
ACEIRST RACIEST,
STEARIC
ACEIRSU SAUCIER
ACEIRSV VISCERA
ACEIRTT CATTIER,
CITRATE
ACEISST ASCITES
ACEJKST JACKETS
ACEJNOT JACONET
ACEJQSU JACQUES
ACEJRTT TRAJECT
ACEKLNS SLACKEN
ACEKLPT PLACKET
ACEKLRS SLACKER
ACEKLRT TACKLER
ACEKLRU CAULKER
ACEKLST TACKLES
ACEKLSY LACKEYS
ACEKMRS SMACKER
ACEKNRS CANKERS
ACEKORR CROAKER
ACEKPPR PREPACK
ACEKPRS PACKERS
ACEKPST PACKETS
ACEKRRT TRACKER
ACEKRST RACKETS,
STACKER
ACEKRTY RACKETY
ACEKSST CASKETS
ACELLMO CALOMEL
ACELLNY CLEANLY
ACELLOR OCELLAR
ACELLOS LOCALES
ACELLOT COLLATE
ACELLPS SCALPEL
ACELLPY CLYPEAL
ACELLRS CALLERS,
CELLARS, RECALLS
ACELLRU CURE-ALL
ACELLRY CLEARLY
ACELMOT CAMELOT
ACELMOU LEUCOMA
ACELMPR CLAMPER
ACELMST CALMEST
ACELNNU UNCLEAN

ACELNNY LYNCEAN
ACELNOP NO-PLACE
ACELNOR CORNEAL
ACELNOT LACTONE
ACELNPS SPANCEL
ACELNPU CLEANUP
ACELNRS LANCERS
ACELNRT CENTRAL
ACELNRU NUCLEAR,
UNCLEAR
ACELNRY LARCENY
ACELNST LANCETS
ACELNSU CENSUAL
ACELNTY LATENCY
ACELNVY VALENCY
ACELOPT POLECAT
ACELOQU COEQUAL
ACELORS ESCOLAR,
ORACLES, SOLACER
ACELORT LOCATER
ACELOSS SOLACES
ACELOST LACTOSE,
TALCOSE
ACELOSV ALCOVES,
COEVALS
ACELOTT CALOTTE
ACELOTY ACOLYTE
ACELOUV VACUOLE
ACELPPR CLAPPER
ACELPRS CLASPER,
PARCELS, SCALPER
ACELPRY PRELACY
ACELPSU CAPSULE
ACELPSY CYPSELA
ACELPTY ECTYPAL
ACELQRU LACQUER
ACELQSU CLAQUES
ACELRRW CRAWLER
ACELRST CARTELS,
SCARLET
ACELRSU SECULAR
ACELRTT CLATTER
ACELRTY TREACLY
ACELSSS CLASSES
ACELSST CASTLES
ACELSSU CLAUSES
ACELSTU SULCATE
ACELSUU ACULEUS
ACELSUX EXCUSAL
ACELSXY CALYXES
ACELTTU LUCETTA
ACELTUY ACUTELY
ACELTXY EXACTLY
ACEMMRR CRAMMER

ACEMNOR CAMERON,
ROMANCE
ACEMOPR COMPARE
ACEMORU MORCEAU
ACEMPRS CAMPERS,
SCAMPER
ACEMRSS SCREAMS
ACENNOS SONANCE
ACENNOT CONNATE
ACENNOZ CANZONE
ACENNRS SCANNER
ACENNRY CANNERY
ACENNST NASCENT
ACENNSU NUANCES
ACENNTY TENANCY
ACENOOR CORONAE
ACENORS COARSEN
ACENORT ENACTOR,
NOT CARE
ACENOST OCTANES
ACENOSZ COSENZA
ACENOTV CENTAVO
ACENPRR PRANCER
ACENPTY PATENCY
ACENRRY ERRANCY
ACENRST CANTERS,
TRANCES
ACENRSV CAVERNS
ACENRTU CENTAUR
ACENRTY NECTARY
ACENSST ASCENTS,
STANCES
ACENSTU NUTCASE
ACEOOPP APOCOPE
ACEOPSS SCAPOSE
ACEOPST TOE CAPS
ACEOPTZ ZAPOTEC
ACEORRS COARSER
ACEORRT ACROTER,
CREATOR, REACTOR
ACEORST COASTER
ACEORSU CAROUSE
ACEORTV OVERACT
ACEORTW EAT CROW
ACEORTX EXACTOR
ACEOSSU CASEOUS
ACEOSTT COSTATE
ACEOSTU ACETOUS
ACEOSTV OCTAVES
ACEOSTY TEA COSY
ACEOTTV CAVETTO
ACEOTUU AUTOCUE
ACEPRRS SCARPER,
SCRAPER

ACEPRSS SCRAPES
ACEPRST CARPETS, PRECAST, SPECTRA
ACEPRTU CAPTURE
ACEPSST ASPECTS
ACEPSTU CUSPATE, TEACUPS
ACEQRTU RACQUET
ACEQSSU CASQUES
ACERRST CARTERS, CRATERS, TRACERS
ACERRSV CARVERS
ACERRTT RETRACT
ACERRTY TRACERY
ACERRUV VERRUCA
ACERSST ACTRESS, CASTERS
ACERSSU SAUCERS, SUCRASE
ACERSSV SCARVES
ACERSTT SCATTER
ACERSTU CURATES
ACERSTY SECTARY
ACERTTX EXTRACT
ACERTTY CATTERY
ACERTUY CAUTERY
ACESSTY ECSTASY
ACESTTU SCUTATE
ACESTTY TESTACY
ACFFILT AFFLICT
ACFFIRT TRAFFIC
ACFFLTU FACTFUL
ACFFOST CAST-OFF
ACFGHIN CHAFING
ACFGINS FACINGS
ACFHIST CATFISH
ACFHISU FUCHSIA
ACFHLNU FLAUNCH, FUNCHAL
ACFILNO FOLACIN
ACFILNY FANCILY
ACFILRY CLARIFY
ACFILSS FISCALS
ACFIMOR FORMICA
ACFIMRU FUMARIC
ACFIMSS FASCISM
ACFINNY INFANCY
ACFINOT FACTION
ACFINRS FRANCIS
ACFINRT FRANTIC, INFARCT, INFRACT
ACFINRY CARNIFY
ACFIOSS FIASCOS
ACFIRSY SCARIFY

ACFISST FASCIST
ACFKLLU FUCK ALL
ACFLNOS FALCONS
ACFLRUU FURCULA
ACFLTTU TACTFUL
ACFLTUY FACULTY
ACFOQRT Q-FACTOR
ACFORST FACTORS
ACFORTY FACTORY
ACFRSTU FRACTUS
ACGGINR GRACING
ACGGRSY SCRAGGY
ACGHIKN HACKING
ACGHINR ARCHING, CHAGRIN
ACGHINS CASHING, CHASING
ACGHINT GNATHIC
ACGHINW CHINWAG
ACGHIPR GRAPHIC
ACGHOSU GAUCHOS
ACGIITU AUGITIC
ACGIJKN JACKING
ACGIKLN CALKING, LACKING
ACGIKNP PACKING
ACGIKNR RACKING
ACGIKNS SACKING
ACGIKNT TACKING
ACGIKRR GARRICK
ACGILLN CALLING
ACGILLO LOGICAL
ACGILMN CALMING
ACGILMY MYALGIC
ACGILNN LANCING
ACGILNO COALING
ACGILNP PLACING
ACGILNR CARLING
ACGILNS SCALING
ACGILNT CATLING
ACGILNV CALVING
ACGILNW CLAWING
ACGIMNO COAMING
ACGIMNP CAMPING
ACGINNN CANNING
ACGINNR CRANING
ACGINNT CANTING
ACGINOR ORGANIC
ACGINOT COATING, COTINGA
ACGINOX COAXING
ACGINPP CAPPING
ACGINPR CARPING
ACGINPS SPACING

ACGINRS SCARING
ACGINRT CARTING, CRATING, TRACING
ACGINRV CARVING, CRAVING
ACGINSS CASINGS
ACGINST CASTING
ACGINSU CAUSING, SAUCING
ACGIORT ARGOTIC
ACGIRST GASTRIC
ACGLNOR CLANGOR
ACGNOOT OCTAGON
ACGNORS GARÇONS
ACGNOSY GASCONY
ACGORSU COUGARS
ACHHIRW HARWICH
ACHHSUV CHUVASH
ACHIILS ISCHIAL
ACHIIMT HAMITIC
ACHIINT CHIANTI
ACHIITW WICHITA
ACHIJKS HIJACKS
ACHIJMO JOACHIM
ACHIJNT JACINTH
ACHIKLN NALCHIK
ACHILLO LOCHIAL
ACHILLP PHALLIC
ACHILLS CHALLIS
ACHILLT THALLIC
ACHILMR RICHMAL
ACHILNO NICHOLA
ACHILPS CALIPHS
ACHILRY CHARILY
ACHIMNO MOHICAN
ACHIMOS CHAMOIS
ACHINNU UNCHAIN
ACHINOP APHONIC
ACHINPS SPINACH
ACHINTX XANTHIC
ACHINTY CYNTHIA
ACHIOPT APHOTIC
ACHIORT CHARIOT, HARICOT
ACHIPST SPATHIC
ACHIQRU CHARQUI
ACHIRTU HAIRCUT
ACHIRTY CHARITY
ACHISSS CHASSIS
ACHISTT CATTISH
ACHITTW WATCH IT!
ACHKMMO HAMMOCK
ACHKOPS HOPSACK
ACHKOSS HASSOCK

ACHKSTW THWACKS
ACHLLOO ALCOHOL
ACHLLOR CHLORAL
ACHLNOW LANCHOW
ACHLNOY HALCYON
ACHLNTU UNLATCH
ACHLORS SCHOLAR
ACHLORT TROCHAL
ACHMNOR MONARCH
ACHMOPR CAMPHOR
ACHMOST STOMACH
ACHNNOS CHANSON
ACHNORS ANCHORS
ACHNOTY TACHYON
ACHNOVY ANCHOVY
ACHNPUY PAUNCHY
ACHNRTY CHANTRY
ACHNRUY RAUNCHY
ACHNSTU CANTHUS,
   STAUNCH
ACHNSTY SNATCHY
ACHOOST CAHOOTS
ACHOPRS CARHOPS
ACHOPRT TOPARCH
ACHOPRY CHARPOY
ACHRSTY STARCHY
ACIIKRS AIRSICK ·
ACIILMS ISLAMIC, LAICISM
ACIILNS SALICIN
ACIILNT CAITLIN
ACIILNV VICINAL
ACIILPT APLITIC
ACIILRY CILIARY
ACIILSS LIASSIC
ACIILST ITALICS
ACIIMRS CASIMIR
ACIINNO ANIONIC
ACIINOS NICOSIA
ACIINOV AVIONIC
ACIINPS PISCINA
ACIINTT TITANIC
ACIIPRT PIRATIC
ACIJLOS JALISCO
ACIJUZZ JACUZZI
ACIKLOR AIRLOCK
ACIKLTY TACKILY
ACIKNPY PANICKY
ACIKNST CATKINS
ACIKNTT TINTACK
ACIKPRT PATRICK
ACIKPSX SIX-PACK
ACIKPSY SICK PAY
ACIKRST KARSTIC
ACIKRWW WARWICK

ACIKUWZ ZWICKAU
ACILLLU LUCILLA
ACILLMS MISCALL
ACILLNS CALL-INS
ACILLRY LYRICAL
ACILMNO LIMACON
ACILMPS PSALMIC
ACILMSU MUSICAL
ACILNNY CANNILY
ACILNOR CLARINO,
   CLARION
ACILNOS NICOLAS,
   OILCANS
ACILNPY PLIANCY
ACILNTU LUNATIC
ACILOOR AIR-COOL
ACILOPT CAPITOL,
   OPTICAL, TOPICAL
ACILOSS SOCIALS
ACILOST STOICAL
ACILOTV VOLTAIC
ACILPST PLASTIC
ACILPTY TYPICAL
ACILRSS CRISSAL
ACILRTU CURTAIL
ACILRTY CLARITY
ACILRYZ CRAZILY
ACILSSS CLASSIS
ACILSUV CLAVIUS
ACILSUY SAUCILY
ACILTTY CATTILY,
   TACITLY
ACILTUV VICTUAL
ACIMMNO AMMONIC
ACIMNOP CAMPION
ACIMNOR MINORCA
ACIMNOS MASONIC
ACIMNRU CRANIUM
ACIMNTT CATMINT
ACIMOPT APOMICT,
   TAMPICO
ACIMOSS MOSAICS
ACIMOST SOMATIC
ACIMPRY PRIMACY
ACIMPST IMPACTS
ACIMSST MISCAST
ACINNOR CORINNA
ACINNOT ACTINON,
   CONTAIN
ACINNST STANNIC
ACINOPT CAPTION
ACINOQU COQUINA
ACINORR CARRION
ACINORS SARONIC

ACINOSS CAISSON,
   CASINOS, CASSINO
ACINOST ACTIONS
ACINOTU AUCTION,
   CAUTION
ACINOUV IN VACUO
ACINPRY CYPRIAN
ACINQTU QUANTIC
ACINRTU CURTAIN
ACINSUV VICUÑAS
ACIOPRS PROSAIC
ACIOPRT APRICOT,
   PAROTIC
ACIOPTY OPACITY
ACIORRS CORSAIR
ACIORSU CARIOUS,
   CURIOSA
ACIORTT RIOT ACT
ACIPRSY PISCARY
ACIPRVY PRIVACY
ACIPSST SPASTIC
ACIPTUY PAUCITY
ACIQRTU QUARTIC
ACIRSST RACISTS
ACIRSSU CUIRASS
ACIRSTY SATYRIC
ACISSTT STATICS
ACISSTU CASUIST
ACISTTU CATSUIT
ACITUVY VACUITY
ACJKKSY SKYJACK
ACJKLOW LOCKJAW
ACJKNOS JACKSON
ACJKOPT JACKPOT
ACJLORU JOCULAR
ACJMNTU MUNTJAC
ACJPTUU CAJUPUT
ACKKLMU KALMUCK
ACKLLOP POLLACK
ACKLLSY SLACKLY
ACKLNOU UNCLOAK
ACKLOOR OARLOCK
ACKLORW WARLOCK
ACKMOTT MATTOCK
ACKPSSY SKYCAPS
ACLLLOY LOCALLY
ACLLMMO MALCOLM
ACLLOOR COROLLA
ACLLOPS SCALLOP
ACLLORS COLLARS
ACLLORU LOCULAR
ACLLOSU CALLOUS
ACLLOVY VOCALLY
ACLLRYY ACRYLYL

ACLMNUY CALUMNY
ACLMORS CLAMORS
ACLMORU CLAMOUR
ACLNOOR CORONAL
ACLNOOT COOLANT
ACLNOOV VOLCANO
ACLNORT CARLTON
ACLNORU CORNUAL
ACLNORY CAROLYN
ACLNOTY CLAYTON
ACLNPSU UNCLASP
ACLOOPR CAR POOL
ACLOPRT CALTROP
ACLOPRU COPULAR
ACLOPSU CUPOLAS,
   SCOPULA
ACLOPSY CALYPSO
ACLORRS CORRALS
ACLORSU CAROLUS,
   OSCULAR
ACLORWW WROCLAW
ACLPRTY CRYPTAL
ACLRSSW SCRAWLS
ACLRSSY CRASSLY
ACLRSTU CRUSTAL
ACLRSTY CRYSTAL
ACLRSWY SCRAWLY
ACLSSTU CUTLASS
ACMNOPR CRAMPON
ACMNOPY COMPANY
ACMNORY ACRONYM
ACMNSTU SANCTUM
ACMNTUU TUCUMAN
ACMOOPT POTOMAC
ACMOOST SCOTOMA
ACMOPSS COMPASS
ACMOSST MASCOTS
ACMOSTT TOMCATS
ACMQTUU CUMQUAT
ACMSUUV VACUUMS
ACNNNOS CANNONS
ACNNNUY UNCANNY
ACNNORY CANONRY
ACNNOST CANTONS
ACNNOSY CANYONS
ACNOORS CORONAS,
   RACOONS
ACNOORT CARTOON
ACNOPSU CANOPUS
ACNOPSW SNOWCAP
ACNORRU RANCOUR
ACNORRY CARRY-ON
ACNORST CANTORS,
   CARTONS

ACNORSY CRAYONS
ACNOSTU CONATUS,
   TOUCANS
ACNPRSY SYNCARP
ACNRRTU CURRANT
ACNRSWY SCRAWNY
ACNRTUY TRUANCY
ACNSSTU SANCTUS
ACNSTUY TUSCANY
ACOOPRR CORPORA
ACOOPTT TOPCOAT
ACOORTU TOURACO
ACOPPRR PROCARP
ACOPRRT CARPORT
ACOPRST CAPTORS
ACOPSTW COWPATS
ACORRST CARROTS
ACORRTT TRACTOR
ACORRTU CURATOR
ACORRTY CARROTY
ACORSST CASTORS,
   CO-STARS
ACORSSU SARCOUS
ACORSTU SURCOAT
ACORSTX OXCARTS
ACORSUU RAUCOUS
ACOSTTU OUTCAST
ACOSUUV VACUOUS
ACPPRSY SCRAPPY
ADDDEEN DEAD END
ADDDEER DREADED
ADDDEIS DADDIES
ADDDELN DANDLED
ADDDELP PADDLED
ADDDELS SADDLED
ADDDELW DAWDLED,
   WADDLED
ADDEEEY DEADEYE
ADDEEFM DEFAMED
ADDEEGR DEGRADE
ADDEEHR ADHERED,
   REDHEAD
ADDEEIR READIED
ADDEEKN KNEADED
ADDEELP PEDALED,
   PLEADED
ADDEELR ELDREDA, RED
   DEAL
ADDEELY DELAYED
ADDEEMN AMENDED
ADDEEMR DREAMED
ADDEEST SEDATED
ADDEFRT DRAFTED
ADDEFRU DEFRAUD

ADDEFRW DWARFED
ADDEGGR DRAGGED
ADDEGHO GODHEAD
ADDEGJU ADJUDGE
ADDEGLN DANGLED,
   GLADDEN
ADDEGLR GLADDER
ADDEGRU GUARDED
ADDEHIO HODEIDA
ADDEHIR DIEHARD
ADDEHLN HANDLED
ADDEHOR HOARDED
ADDEILL DALLIED,
   DIALLED
ADDEILS LADDIES
ADDEILT DILATED
ADDEIMR ADMIRED
ADDEIMS DIADEMS
ADDEINO ADENOID
ADDEINR DANDIER,
   DRAINED
ADDEINS DANDIES
ADDEINU UNAIDED
ADDEINV INVADED
ADDEIOR RADIOED
ADDEIOT TOADIED
ADDEIOV AVOIDED
ADDEIPS PADDIES
ADDEISV ADVISED
ADDEITU AUDITED
ADDEJRU ADJURED
ADDELLU ALLUDED
ADDELNR DANDLER
ADDELPP DAPPLED
ADDELPR PADDLER
ADDELPS PADDLES
ADDELRS LADDERS,
   SADDLER
ADDELRW DAWDLER,
   DRAWLED, WADDLER
ADDELSS SADDLES
ADDELST STADDLE
ADDELSW SWADDLE,
   WADDLES
ADDELTW TWADDLE
ADDELYZ DAZEDLY
ADDELZZ DAZZLED
ADDEMNS DEMANDS
ADDEMST MADDEST
ADDENOR ADORNED
ADDENOT DONATED
ADDENOU DUODENA
ADDENPU PUDENDA
ADDENRS DANDERS

ADDENTU DAUNTED
ADDEOPT ADOPTED
ADDEPTU UPDATED
ADDERSS ADDRESS
ADDERTT DRATTED
ADDESST SADDEST
ADDFHIS FADDISH
ADDFIMS FADDISM
ADDFINY DANDIFY
ADDFIST FADDIST
ADDGGIN GADDING
ADDGINP PADDING
ADDGINW WADDING
ADDGMNO GODDAMN
ADDGOOY GOOD DAY
ADDGOSY DOG DAYS
ADDHITY HYDATID
ADDHLNO OLD HAND
ADDHNOR RHONDDA
ADDIINS DISDAIN
ADDIKTY KATYDID
ADDILMN MIDLAND
ADDILMO OLD MAID
ADDIMNO DIAMOND
ADDINOR ANDROID,
   DORINDA
ADDLLOY OLD LADY
ADDLLRU DULLARD
ADDLNRY DRY LAND
ADDLOSY LAY ODDS
ADEEESW SEAWEED
ADEEFKR FREAKED
ADEEFLR ELFREDA,
   FEDERAL
ADEEFLT DEFLATE
ADEEFMR DEFAMER
ADEEFRT DRAFTEE
ADEEFST DEFEATS,
   FEASTED
ADEEGGH EGGHEAD
ADEEGGN ENGAGED
ADEEGLL ALLEGED
ADEEGLM GLEAMED
ADEEGLN GLEANED
ADEEGLU LEAGUED
ADEEGLY GLAD EYE
ADEEGMN END GAME
ADEEGNR ANGERED,
   DERANGE, EN GARDE,
   ENRAGED, GRANDEE,
   GRENADE
ADEEGNT NEGATED
ADEEGNV AVENGED
ADEEGOT GOATEED

ADEEGRS GREASED
ADEEGRW RAGWEED,
   WAGERED
ADEEHIR HEADIER
ADEEHLX EXHALED
ADEEHMN HEADMEN
ADEEHNS DASHEEN
ADEEHRS HEADERS,
   SHEARED
ADEEHRT EARTHED
ADEEHST HEADSET
ADEEHSY HAYSEED
ADEEIJT JADEITE
ADEEILM LIMEADE
ADEEILN ADELINE,
   DELAINE
ADEEIMT MEDIATE
ADEEINN ADENINE
ADEEINS ANISEED
ADEEIRR READIER
ADEEIRS DEARIES,
   READIES
ADEEIRW WEARIED
ADEEISS DISEASE,
   SEASIDE
ADEEITV DEVIATE
ADEEKNP KNEEPAD
ADEEKNR KNEADER
ADEEKNS SNEAKED
ADEEKNW WAKENED
ADEEKRW WREAKED
ADEEKTW TWEAKED
ADEEKWY WEEKDAY
ADEELLS ALLSEED
ADEELMR EMERALD
ADEELMT METALED
ADEELMZ DEMELZA
ADEELNP PANELED
ADEELNR DARLENE,
   LEANDER, LEARNED
ADEELNT AL DENTE
ADEELNW ALEDWEN,
   NEW DEAL
ADEELNZ ZEELAND
ADEELPR PLEADER
ADEELPS ELAPSED,
   PLEASED
ADEELPT PLEATED
ADEELQU EQUALED
ADEELRS DEALERS,
   LEADERS
ADEELRT ALERTED,
   ALTERED, RELATED,
   TREADLE

ADEELRV RAVELED
ADEELRW LEEWARD
ADEELRX RELAXED
ADEELRY DELAYER,
   LAYERED, RELAYED
ADEELTX EXALTED
ADEELUV DEVALUE
ADEEMNR AMENDER,
   MEANDER, RENAMED
ADEEMRR DREAMER,
   REARMED
ADEEMRS SMEARED
ADEEMRT RED MEAT
ADEEMST STEAMED
ADEEMWY MAYWEED
ADEENNX ANNEXED
ADEENRY DEANERY,
   YEARNED
ADEENST EAST END
ADEENTT DANETTE,
   DENTATE
ADEEPPR PAPERED
ADEEPRS SPEARED
ADEEPRT PREDATE, RED
   TAPE, TAPERED
ADEEPRV DEPRAVE,
   PERVADE
ADEEQTU EQUATED
ADEERRS READERS
ADEERRT RETREAD,
   TREADER
ADEERRV AVERRED,
   EVERARD
ADEERST DEAREST
ADEERSV ADVERSE
ADEERTT TREATED
ADEERTV AVERTED
ADEERTW WATERED
ADEERVW WAVERED
ADEESSY ESSAYED
ADEESTU SAUTÉED
ADEESTW SWEATED
ADEFFIX AFFIXED
ADEFFLR RAFFLED
ADEFFLW WAFFLED
ADEFFST STAFFED
ADEFGGL FLAGGED
ADEFGLR RED FLAG
ADEFGNS FAG ENDS
ADEFGOR FORAGED
ADEFGRT GRAFTED
ADEFHLS FLASHED
ADEFHST SHAFTED
ADEFIIL FIDELIA

ADEFILL FLAILED
ADEFILR ELFRIDA
ADEFINT DEFIANT,
   FAINTED
ADEFITX FIXATED
ADEFKLN FLANKED
ADEFKNR FRANKED
ADEFLOT FLOATED
ADEFLPP FLAPPED
ADEFLTU DEFAULT,
   FAULTED
ADEFMNR MANFRED
ADEFOOR FEODORA
ADEFOOS SEAFOOD
ADEFORS FEDORAS
ADEFORY FORAYED
ADEFOTU FADEOUT
ADEFRRT DRAFTER,
   REDRAFT
ADEFRST STRAFED
ADEFSTT DAFTEST
ADEGGHL HAGGLED
ADEGGHS SHAGGED
ADEGGLR DRAGGLE,
   GARGLED
ADEGGLS SLAGGED
ADEGGLW WAGGLED
ADEGGNS SNAGGED
ADEGGRS DAGGERS
ADEGGST GADGETS
ADEGGTY GADGETY
ADEGHIN HEADING
ADEGHLU LAUGHED
ADEGHNS GNASHED
ADEGILN ALIGNED,
   DEALING, LEADING
ADEGINR READING
ADEGINV EVADING
ADEGINW WINDAGE
ADEGIRU GAUDIER
ADEGJLN JANGLED
ADEGLLU ULLAGED
ADEGLMN MANGLED
ADEGLNN ENGLAND
ADEGLNO DONEGAL
ADEGLNR DANGLER,
   GNARLED
ADEGLNS SLANGED
ADEGLNT TANGLED
ADEGLNW WANGLED
ADEGLOT GLOATED
ADEGLPU PLAGUED
ADEGLSS GLASSED
ADEGMNU AGENDUM

ADEGNNU DUNNAGE
ADEGNOR GROANED
ADEGNOS SONDAGE
ADEGNOT TANGOED
ADEGNOV DOGVANE
ADEGNPU UNPAGED
ADEGNRR GRANDER
ADEGNRS DANGERS,
   GANDERS, GARDENS
ADEGNRT DRAGNET,
   GRANTED
ADEGNTW TWANGED
ADEGNUW UNWAGED
ADEGORW DOWAGER,
   WORDAGE
ADEGOSS DOSAGES, SEA
   DOGS
ADEGOST DOTAGES
ADEGOVY VOYAGED
ADEGPRS GRASPED
ADEGPRU UPGRADE
ADEGRRR GERRARD
ADEGRRS REGARDS
ADEGRRU GUARDER
ADEGRSS GRASSED
ADEGRSU SUGARED
ADEGRTY GYRATED,
   TRAGEDY
ADEGRUU AUGURED
ADEGRUY GAUDERY
ADEGSSU DEGAUSS
ADEHHOP HOPHEAD
ADEHHOT HOTHEAD
ADEHILL DELILAH
ADEHILN HIELAND,
   INHALED
ADEHILY HEADILY
ADEHIMO HAEMOID
ADEHINP HEADPIN,
   PINHEAD
ADEHINR HANDIER
ADEHIPR RAPHIDE
ADEHIPS DIPHASE
ADEHIPT PITHEAD
ADEHIRR HARDIER,
   HARRIED
ADEHIRS SHADIER
ADEHIRW RAWHIDE
ADEHKNT THANKED
ADEHLLM ALDHELM
ADEHLMN HELMAND
ADEHLNR HANDLER
ADEHLNS HANDLES,
   HANDSEL

ADEHLOP ADOLPHE
ADEHLOT LOATHED
ADEHLRS HERALDS
ADEHLSS HASSLED,
   SLASHED
ADEHLTY DEATHLY
ADEHMMS SHAMMED
ADEHMNP HAMPDEN
ADEHMOY DAHOMEY
ADEHMSS SMASHED
ADEHNRU UNHEARD
ADEHNST HANDSET
ADEHNTU HAUNTED
ADEHOPX HEXAPOD
ADEHORR HOARDER
ADEHOTW TOWHEAD
ADEHPRS PHRASED
ADEHQSU QUASHED
ADEHRST HARDEST,
   THREADS, TRASHED
ADEHRTY HYDRATE,
   THREADY
ADEHSST STASHED
ADEHSTW SWATHED
ADEIILS DAILIES, LIAISED,
   SEDILIA
ADEIIMN DIAMINE
ADEIINZ DIAZINE
ADEIIRS DAIRIES, DIARIES
ADEIISS DAISIES
ADEIJSU JUDAISE
ADEIJUZ JUDAIZE
ADEIKLM LIKE MAD
ADEIKLR KILDARE
ADEIKRS DARKIES
ADEILLR DIALLER,
   RALLIED
ADEILLS SALLIED
ADEILLT TALLIED
ADEILLY IDEALLY
ADEILMM DILEMMA
ADEILMN MELINDA
ADEILMP IMPALED,
   IMPLEAD
ADEILMS MISDEAL,
   MISLEAD
ADEILNN ANNELID,
   LINDANE
ADEILNR IRELAND
ADEILNS DENIALS,
   LEAD-INS
ADEILNT TAIL END
ADEILNU ALIUNDE
ADEILOP OEDIPAL

ADEILOR DARIOLE
ADEILOZ DIAZOLE
ADEILPP APPLIED
ADEILPR LIP-READ
ADEILPS PALSIED
ADEILPT PLAITED,
TALIPED
ADEILQU QUAILED
ADEILRT TRAILED
ADEILRU UREDIAL
ADEILRV RIVALED
ADEILRY READILY
ADEILST DETAILS
ADEILSV DEVISAL
ADEILSY DIALYSE
ADEIMMR MERMAID
ADEIMNS MAIDENS,
MEDIANS
ADEIMNT MEDIANT
ADEIMOW MIAOWED
ADEIMRR ADMIRER,
MARRIED
ADEIMRS MISREAD,
SIDEARM
ADEIMRY MIDYEAR
ADEIMTU IDEATUM
ADEIMTY DAYTIME
ADEINOR ANEROID
ADEINOS ANODISE
ADEINOV NAEVOID
ADEINOZ ANODIZE
ADEINPT PAINTED
ADEINRR DRAINER,
RANDIER
ADEINRS SANDIER,
SARDINE
ADEINRT DETRAIN,
TRADE-IN, TRAINED
ADEINRU URANIDE
ADEINRV INVADER
ADEINST INSTEAD,
SAINTED, STAINED
ADEINTT TAINTED
ADEINTV DEVIANT
ADEIOPS ADIPOSE
ADEIORV AVOIDER
ADEIOST TOADIES
ADEIOSX OXIDASE
ADEIOTX OXIDATE
ADEIPPR PREPAID
ADEIPRR PARRIED
ADEIPRS ASPIRED,
DESPAIR, DIAPERS,
PRAISED

ADEIPRT PARTIED,
PERDITA, PIRATED
ADEIRRS RAIDERS
ADEIRRT TARDIER,
TARRIED
ADEIRRV ARRIVED
ADEIRST ASTRIDE,
DIASTER, DISRATE,
TIRADES
ADEIRSV ADVISER
ADEIRTT ATTIRED
ADEIRTY DIETARY
ADEISTV DATIVES,
VISTAED
ADEISTW WAISTED
ADEISWY WAYSIDE
ADEITUZ DEUTZIA
ADEITWY TIDEWAY
ADEJMOR MAJORED
ADEJNTU JAUNTED
ADEJRRU ADJURER
ADEJSSU JUDASES
ADEKLLN KENDALL
ADEKLNR RANKLED
ADEKLNS KALENDS
ADEKLNY NAKEDLY
ADEKLST STALKED
ADEKMNR DENMARK
ADEKNPS SPANKED
ADEKNST DANKEST
ADEKNSW SWANKED
ADEKPRS SPARKED
ADEKRST DARKEST
ADELLMU MEDULLA
ADELLOW ALLOWED
ADELLOY ALLOYED
ADELLRR DARRELL
ADELLRU ALLURED
ADELLST STALLED
ADELMMS SLAMMED
ADELMNR MANDREL
ADELMNT MANTLED
ADELMOR EARLDOM
ADELMPS SAMPLED
ADELMRS MEDLARS
ADELMSS DAMSELS
ADELNNP PLANNED
ADELNOR LEONARD
ADELNOY YOLANDE
ADELNPT PLANTED
ADELNRS SLANDER,
SNARLED
ADELNRU LAUNDER
ADELNST SLANTED

ADELNUU ULAN-UDE
ADELOPR LEOPARD,
PAROLED
ADELOPS DEPOSAL
ADELOPT TADPOLE
ADELORS ORDEALS
ADELORT LEOTARD
ADELOSS LASSOED
ADELOTT TOTALED
ADELOVY LOVEDAY
ADELPPS SLAPPED
ADELPRS PEDLARS
ADELPST STAPLED
ADELPSW DEWLAPS
ADELPSY SPLAYED
ADELPTY ADEPTLY
ADELRRS LARDERS
ADELRRU RUDERAL
ADELRRW DRAWLER
ADELRTT RATTLED
ADELRTW TRAWLED
ADELRTX DEXTRAL
ADELSTT SLATTED
ADELSTU SALUTED
ADELTTT TATTLED
ADELTUV VAULTED
ADELTWZ WALTZED
ADEMNNU MUNDANE,
UNNAMED
ADEMNOR ROADMEN
ADEMNOS DAEMONS
ADEMNOZ MENDOZA
ADEMNRS REMANDS
ADEMNRU MANURED,
MAUNDER, UNARMED
ADEMNSS MADNESS
ADEMNST TANDEMS
ADEMORR ARMORED
ADEMORS MODERAS
ADEMOSW MEADOWS
ADEMOSY SAMOYED,
SOMEDAY
ADEMPRS DAMPERS
ADEMPRT TRAMPED
ADEMPST DAMPEST,
STAMPED
ADEMPSW SWAMPED
ADEMRRU EARDRUM
ADEMRST SMARTED
ADEMRSW SWARMED
ADEMRTU MATURED
ADEMSSU ASSUMED
ADENNOY ANNOYED,
ANODYNE

ADENNPS SPANNED
ADENNPT PENDANT
ADENNSU DUENNAS
ADENNSW SWANNED
ADENOPR OPERAND,
PADRONE, PANDORE
ADENOPT NOTEPAD
ADENORR RED ROAN
ADENORU RONDEAU
ADENOUY YAOUNDE
ADENPPS SNAPPED
ADENPST PEDANTS
ADENPSW SPAWNED
ADENRRS ERRANDS
ADENRRY REYNARD
ADENRSS SANDERS
ADENRST STANDER
ADENRSU ASUNDER,
DANSEUR
ADENRSW WARDENS
ADENRTU DAUNTER
ADENRTV VERDANT
ADENRTX DEXTRAN
ADENRUY UNREADY
ADENSSS SADNESS
ADENSSU SUNDAES
ADENSTV ADVENTS
ADENSWY ENDWAYS
ADENTTU ATTUNED,
TAUNTED
ADENTUV VAUNTED
ADEOPST PODESTA
ADEORRW ARROWED
ADEORST ROASTED,
TORSADE
ADEORSU AROUSED
ADEORSV SAVORED
ADEORTT ROTATED
ADEORTU READOUT
ADEORTY YEAR DOT
ADEORYZ ZEDOARY
ADEOSTT TOASTED
ADEOTTU OUTDATE
ADEPPRT TRAPPED
ADEPPRW WRAPPED
ADEPPSW SWAPPED
ADEPRRS DRAPERS,
SPARRED
ADEPRRY DRAPERY
ADEPRSS SPREADS
ADEPRST PETARDS
ADEPRSY SPRAYED
ADEPRTU UPDATER
ADEPSTU UPDATES

ADEQRSU SQUARED
ADERRST STARRED,
TRADERS
ADERRSW DRAWERS,
REWARDS, WARDERS
ADERSSU ASSURED
ADERSTT STARTED
ADERSTV STARVED
ADERSTW STEWARD
ADERSTY STRAYED
ADERSUY DASYURE
ADERSVW DWARVES
ADESTTU STATUED
ADESTTW SWATTED
ADESTUY TUESDAY
ADFFHNO OFFHAND
ADFFIST DISTAFF
ADFFLOO OFF-LOAD
ADFHLNU HANDFUL
ADFHOOS SHADOOF
ADFIINO IN AID OF
ADFILLU FLUIDAL
ADFILNN FINLAND
ADFILOR FLORIDA
ADFILOT DO A FLIT
ADFIMNY DAMNIFY
ADFIRSY FRIDAYS
ADFLMPU MUDFLAP
ADFLMTU MUDFLAT
ADFLNOP PLAFOND
ADFLNSY SAND FLY
ADFLORU FOULARD
ADFNNOT FONDANT
ADFOOPT FOOTPAD
ADFORRW FORWARD,
FROWARD
ADFPRTU UPDRAFT
ADGGHNO HANGDOG
ADGGINO GOADING
ADGGINR GRADING,
NIGGARD
ADGGOST DOG TAGS
ADGHILO HIDALGO
ADGHINN HANDING
ADGHINR HARDING
ADGHINS DASHING,
SHADING
ADGHIPR DIGRAPH
ADGHNNU HANDGUN
ADGHOOR ROAD
HOG
ADGHRTU DRAUGHT
ADGIILN DIALING,
GLIADIN

ADGIILT DIGITAL
ADGIINR RAIDING
ADGILLN LADLING
ADGILNN LANDING
ADGILNO LOADING
ADGILNR DARLING,
LARDING
ADGILNS LADINGS
ADGILNU LANGUID,
LAUDING
ADGILUY GAUDILY
ADGIMMN DAMMING
ADGIMNN DAMNING
ADGIMNP DAMPING
ADGINNR DARNING
ADGINNS SANDING
ADGINNW DAWNING
ADGINOR ADORING
ADGINPP DAPPING
ADGINPR DRAPING
ADGINRT DARTING,
TRADING
ADGINRW DRAWING,
WARDING
ADGINWY GWYNIAD
ADGIRZZ GIZZARD
ADGKNOZ DZONGKA
ADGLLOS OLD LAGS
ADGLNOO GONDOLA
ADGLNOY DAYLONG
ADGLNRY GRANDLY
ADGLOOV VOLOGDA
ADGLOPS LAPDOGS
ADGLORY GAYLORD
ADGLOSU DOUGLAS
ADGLSWY GWLADYS
ADGMOOR MOGADOR
ADGNOOR DRAGOON,
GADROON
ADGNORS DRAGONS
ADGNORU AGROUND,
DURANGO
ADGNRRU GURNARD
ADHHMOS SHAHDOM
ADHHOSW HOWDAHS
ADHIIMS HASIDIM
ADHIKTZ TADZHIK
ADHILMO HALIDOM
ADHILNY HANDILY
ADHILOP HAPLOID
ADHILOY HOLIDAY,
HYALOID
ADHILRY HARDILY
ADHILSY SHADILY

ADHIMPS DAMPISH, PHASMID
ADHINPU DAUPHIN
ADHIORS HAIRDOS
ADHLLLO HOLDALL
ADHLLNO HOLLAND
ADHLNOW HOWLAND
ADHMMNO HAMMOND
ADHMNOO MANHOOD
ADHMNPY DYMPHNA
ADHMNWY WYNDHAM
ADHNNOS HANDS-ON
ADHNORS HARD-ONS
ADHNOTU HANDOUT
ADHNOVZ ZHDANOV
ADHNPSU HANDS UP
ADHNRTU HARD NUT
ADHNRTY HYDRANT
ADHOPRT HARDTOP
ADHOSSW SHADOWS
ADHOSWY SHADOWY
ADIIJNU JUNDIAI
ADIILMS MISLAID
ADIILNO LIANOID
ADIILNV INVALID
ADIILOS SIALOID
ADIINNS INDIANS
ADIINOS SIDONIA
ADIIORS ISIDORA
ADIIRST DIARIST
ADIIRTY ARIDITY
ADIITVY AVIDITY
ADIJMSU JUDAISM
ADIJNOT ADJOINT
ADIJSTU JUDAIST
ADIKMNN MANKIND
ADIKMOS MIKADOS
ADIKNPS INKPADS, SKIDPAN
ADILLMM MILLDAM
ADILLRW WILLARD
ADILLVY VALIDLY
ADILMNU MAUDLIN
ADILMOP DIPLOMA
ADILMOY AMYLOID
ADILMSU DUALISM
ADILNOR LORINDA, ORDINAL
ADILNRU DIURNAL
ADILNSS ISLANDS
ADILNSU SUNDIAL
ADILNSY LINDSAY
ADILOPR DIPOLAR
ADILORT DILATOR

ADILOUV OLDUVAI
ADILPRY PYRALID, RAPIDLY
ADILPST PLASTID
ADILPSY DISPLAY
ADILPTU PLAUDIT
ADILPVY VAPIDLY
ADILQSU SQUALID
ADILRSZ LIZARDS
ADILRTY TARDILY
ADILSTU DUALIST
ADILSTY STAIDLY
ADILTUY DUALITY
ADIMNOS DOMAINS, MADISON
ADIMORR MIRADOR
ADIMOST MASTOID
ADIMPRY PYRAMID
ADIMRSY MYRIADS
ADIMSST DISMAST
ADIMSTU STADIUM
ADINNOP DIPNOAN
ADINNOR ANDIRON
ADINNRS INNARDS
ADINNRW INDRAWN
ADINNST STAND-IN
ADINOPR PONIARD
ADINORS INROADS, SADIRON
ADINOTX OXIDANT
ADINPST PANDITS, SANDPIT
ADINRSW INWARDS
ADINSTT DISTANT
ADINTTY DITTANY
ADIOOSW WOODSIA
ADIOPRR AIRDROP
ADIOPRT PAROTID
ADIORST ASTROID
ADIORTU AUDITOR
ADIOSUV VAUDOIS
ADIOSVW DISAVOW
ADIPRTY PAY DIRT
ADIPRUU UDAIPUR
ADIRSSU SARDIUS
ADIRSTY SATYRID
ADIRSUY DYSURIA
ADIRSWZ WIZARDS
ADISSST SADISTS
ADJLNTU JUTLAND
ADJNNOU DON JUAN
ADJNORU ADJOURN
ADKORWY WORKDAY
ADLLLOR LOLLARD

ADLLMOY MODALLY
ADLLNOW LOWLAND
ADLLOPR POLLARD
ADLLORS DOLLARS
ADLMNOS ALMONDS
ADLMNUU ALUNDUM
ADLMORU MODULAR
ADLNOOR ORLANDO
ADLNOPU POUNDAL
ADLNORU NODULAR
ADLNORW ROWLAND
ADLNOSY SYNODAL
ADLNPSU UPLANDS
ADLNRUY LAUNDRY
ADLNTWY TYNWALD
ADLOPRU POULARD
ADLORRW WARLORD
ADLORUY OUR LADY
ADLOSSW SOD'S LAW
ADLRSTY DRY-SALT
ADMMNSU SUMMAND
ADMNOOR DOORMAN
ADMNOOW WOODMAN
ADMNOQU QUONDAM
ADMNORS RANDOMS
ADMNORT DORMANT, MORDANT
ADMNORY RAYMOND
ADMNOSS DAMSONS
ADMNOSU OSMUNDA
ADMNOSY DYNAMOS, MONDAYS
ADMNRUY RAYMUND
ADMNSTU DUSTMAN
ADMOORT DOORMAT
ADMOORY DAYROOM
ADMOPPU POPADUM
ADMOPST POTSDAM
ADMORRS RAMRODS
ADMORST STARDOM, TSARDOM
ADMORTW MADWORT
ADMRSTU DURMAST, MUSTARD
ADNNOOV DONOVAN
ADNNOOY NOONDAY
ADNNSTU DUNSTAN
ADNOORT DONATOR, TORNADO
ADNOOSS SO-AND-SO
ADNOPRS PARDONS
ADNORSW ONWARDS
ADNORTU ROTUNDA
ADNOSTU ASTOUND

ADNPPUU UP-AND-UP
ADNPSTU DUSTPAN,
  STAND-UP
ADNRSST STRANDS
ADNSSUY SUNDAYS
ADNSTYY DYNASTY
ADOOPSW SAPWOOD
ADOORWY DOORWAY
ADORSTW TOWARDS
ADORSUU ARDUOUS
ADORTUW OUTWARD
ADPRSUW UPWARDS
ADSSTUW SAWDUST
AEEEGLT LEGATEE
AEEEGNT TEENAGE
AEEEGPR PEERAGE
AEEEGPS SEEPAGE
AEEEGRT ETAGERE
AEEEILN ALIENEE
AEEELNR RAELENE
AEEELRS RELEASE
AEEELTV ELEVATE
AEEFHRT FEATHER
AEEFILR LEAFIER
AEEFIRS FREESIA
AEEFLLN FENELLA
AEEFLLT LEAFLET
AEEFLMS FEMALES
AEEFLRT REFLATE
AEEFLRW WELFARE
AEEFLSU EASEFUL
AEEFMNR FREEMAN
AEEFORS FAEROES
AEEFOTV FOVEATE
AEEFRRT FERRATE
AEEFRST FEASTER
AEEFRTU FEATURE
AEEFRTX TAX-FREE
AEEFRWY FREEWAY
AEEGGLM GAME LEG
AEEGGLT GATE-LEG
AEEGGNR ENGAGER
AEEGHNW WHANGEE
AEEGILL GALILEE
AEEGILM MILEAGE
AEEGILN LINEAGE
AEEGILP EPIGEAL
AEEGILW WEIGELA
AEEGINU EUGENIA
AEEGISS AEGISES
AEEGLLZ GAZELLE
AEEGLMN MÉLANGE
AEEGLMT MELTAGE
AEEGLNR ENLARGE,
  GENERAL, GLEANER

AEEGLNS SENEGAL
AEEGLNT ELEGANT
AEEGLNU EUGLENA
AEEGLNV EVANGEL
AEEGLOR AEROGEL
AEEGLRY EAGERLY
AEEGLSS AGELESS, SEA LEGS
AEEGLST EAGLETS,
  LEGATES
AEEGLSU LEAGUES
AEEGLSV SELVAGE
AEEGLTV VEGETAL
AEEGMMT GEMMATE,
  TAGMEME
AEEGMNR GERMANE
AEEGMNS MÉNAGES
AEEGMSS MESSAGE
AEEGNNV GENEVAN
AEEGNPP GENAPPE
AEEGNRT GRANTEE,
  REAGENT
AEEGNRV AVENGER,
  ENGRAVE, GENEVRA
AEEGNTT TENTAGE
AEEGNTV VENTAGE
AEEGOPS APOGEES
AEEGORV OVERAGE
AEEGOST GOATEES
AEEGPRS PRESAGE
AEEGRRS GREASER
AEEGRRT GREATER,
  REGRATE
AEEGRRW WAGERER
AEEGRSV GERVASE,
  GREAVES
AEEGSTT GESTATE
AEEGTTZ GAZETTE
AEEHHNT HEATHEN
AEEHHRT HEATHER
AEEHHST SHEATHE
AEEHIRV HEAVIER
AEEHISV HEAVIES
AEEHKNR HEARKEN
AEEHLPT HEELTAP
AEEHLRS HEALERS
AEEHLRT HALTERE,
  LEATHER
AEEHLRV LE HAVRE
AEEHLSS LEASHES
AEEHLSY EYELASH
AEEHLTT ATHLETE
AEEHMNT METHANE
AEEHNPS PEAHENS
AEEHNPT HAPTENE,
  HEPTANE

AEEHNRT EARTHEN,
  HEARTEN, TEHERAN
AEEHNSV HEAVENS
AEEHNSW SHAWNEE
AEEHNTW WHEATEN
AEEHPRS RESHAPE
AEEHPRT PREHEAT
AEEHPTT PET HATE
AEEHPUV UPHEAVE
AEEHRRS SHEARER
AEEHRSS HEARSES
AEEHRST HEATERS,
  THERESA
AEEHRSW WHEREAS
AEEHRTT THEATER,
  THEATRE, THREAT
AEEHRTW WEATHER,
  WHEREAT, WREATHE
AEEHSSV SHEAVES
AEEHSTT THE EAST
AEEHSWY EYEWASH
AEEIJNN JEANNIE
AEEIKLP APELIKE
AEEIKLR LEAKIER
AEEIKPR PEAKIER
AEEILLU EULALIE
AEEILMN MELANIE
AEEILMR MEALIER
AEEILMS SEA MILE
AEEILMT ELAMITE
AEEILNT LINEATE
AEEILNV AVELINE, EVELINA
AEEILPR PEARLIE
AEEILPT PILEATE
AEEILRR EARLIER
AEEILRS REALISE
AEEILRT ATELIER
AEEILRV VALERIE
AEEILRZ REALIZE
AEEILTV ELATIVE
AEEIMNT ETAMINE,
  MATINÉE
AEEIMNX EXAMINE
AEEIMRS SEAMIER,
  SERIEMA
AEEIMRT EMIRATE,
  MEATIER
AEEIMSS SIAMESE
AEEINRT ARENITE,
  RETINAE, TRAINEE
AEEINST ETESIAN
AEEINTV NAIVETE,
  VENETIA
AEEINVW INWEAVE
AEEIPRR PEREIRA

AEEIPTX EXPIATE
AEEIRRT ERITREA
AEEIRRW WEARIER
AEEIRST SERIATE
AEEIRSZ ZAIRESE
AEEIRTT ITERATE
AEEISST EASIEST
AEEISVV EVASIVE
AEEIUVX EXUVIAE
AEEJNTT JANETTE
AEEJRSW JEW'S-EAR
AEEKKNO KOKANEE
AEEKMRS REMAKES
AEEKMRT MEERKAT
AEEKNNN NANKEEN
AEEKNRS SNEAKER
AEEKNRT RETAKEN
AEEKNRW WAKENER
AEEKNSY YANKEES
AEEKPRS SPEAKER
AEEKRRT RETAKER
AEEKRRW WREAKER
AEEKRST RETAKES
AEEKSTW WEAKEST
AEELLST ESTELLA
AEELLSV A LEVELS
AEELLWY WALLEYE
AEELMNP EMPANEL
AEELMNR MARLENE
AEELMNU EMANUEL
AEELMNV VELAMEN
AEELMNY AMYLENE
AEELMPR EMPALER
AEELMPX EXAMPLE
AEELMSS MEASLES
AEELMST MALTESE
AEELMTU EMULATE
AEELNNP ENPLANE
AEELNOR ELEANOR
AEELNRR LEARNER
AEELNRT ETERNAL,
   TELERAN
AEELNRU LAUREEN
AEELNRV LAVERNE
AEELNRW RENEWAL
AEELNST LEANEST
AEELNSV ENSLAVE,
   LEAVENS
AEELOPX POLEAXE
AEELORU AUREOLE
AEELPRR PEARLER
AEELPRS PLEASER,
   RELAPSE
AEELPRT PLEATER,
   PRELATE

AEELPTT PALETTE,
   PELTATE
AEELPTU EPAULET
AEELQSU SEQUELA
AEELRRT RELATER
AEELRRX RELAXER
AEELRSS SEALERS
AEELRST STEALER
AEELRSV SEVERAL
AEELRSY SEALERY
AEELRTT ARLETTE
AEELRTX EXALTER
AEELRUV REVALUE
AEELSST TEASELS
AEELSSW WEASELS
AEELSTT SEATTLE
AEELTTY LAYETTE
AEELTVW WAVELET
AEEMMPY EMPYEMA
AEEMMRT AMMETER,
   METAMER
AEEMNNO ANEMONE
AEEMNNP PEN NAME
AEEMNNY MAYENNE
AEEMNPT PET NAME
AEEMNRU MAUREEN
AEEMNSS EN MASSE
AEEMNST MEANEST
AEEMORT EROTEMA
AEEMOSW AWESOME
AEEMPRT TAMPERE,
   TEMPERA
AEEMPTU AMPUTEE
AEEMQRU MARQUEE
AEEMRRS REAMERS,
   SMEARER
AEEMRST STEAMER
AEEMRSU MEASURE
AEENNOT NEONATE
AEENNPT PENNATE,
   PENTANE
AEENNRS ENSNARE
AEENNSX ANNEXES
AEENNTT ANNETTE,
   NANETTE
AEENOPU EUPNOEA
AEENPSX EXPANSE
AEENRRS EARNERS
AEENRRT TERRANE
AEENRRV RAVENER
AEENRRY YEARNER
AEENRST EARNEST,
   EASTERN, NEAREST
AEENRTT ENTREAT,
   TERNATE

AEENRTV NERVATE,
   VETERAN
AEENRVY YEREVAN
AEENRWY NEW YEAR
AEENSST SENATES,
   SENSATE
AEENSTT NEATEST
AEENSUV AVENUES
AEENVWW NEW WAVE
AEEOPRT OPERATE
AEEORST ROSEATE
AEEORVW OVERAWE
AEEPPRR PAPERER,
   PREPARE
AEEPRRS REAPERS,
   SPEARER
AEEPRRT TAPERER
AEEPRSS ASPERSE, PARSEES
AEEPRST REPEATS
AEEPRTX EX PARTE
AEEPRTZ TRAPEZE
AEEPSST PESETAS
AEEPSTT SEPTATE
AEERRSS ERASERS
AEERRST SERRATE
AEERRSU ERASURE
AEERRSW SWEARER
AEERRTT RETREAT,
   TREATER
AEERRTW WATERER
AEERRVW WAVERER
AEERSST EASTERS,
   TEASERS, TESSERA
AEERSTT ESTREAT,
   RESTATE
AEERSTU AUSTERE
AEERSTW SWEATER
AEERSVW WEAVERS
AEESSSW SEESAWS
AEESSTT ESTATES
AEESTTT TESTATE
AEFFGIL FIG LEAF
AEFFGIR GIRAFFE
AEFFGRS GAFFERS
AEFFIST TAFFIES
AEFFISX AFFIXES
AEFFKOP OFF-PEAK
AEFFKOR RAKE-OFF
AEFFKOT TAKEOFF
AEFFLLY FLYLEAF
AEFFLNS SNAFFLE
AEFFLRR RAFFLER
AEFFLRS RAFFLES
AEFFLRU FEARFUL
AEFFLSW WAFFLES

AEFFLTU FATEFUL
AEFFMRU EARMUFF
AEFFOVW WAVEOFF
AEFFQRU QUAFFER
AEFFRST STAFFER
AEFGGLR FLAGGER
AEFGIKN KAIFENG
AEFGILN FINAGLE
AEFGILO FOLIAGE
AEFGILR FRAGILE
AEFGINR FEARING
AEFGINU FUEGIAN
AEFGIRT FRIGATE
AEFGITU FATIGUE
AEFGLNR FLANGER
AEFGLNS FLANGES
AEFGLOT FLOTAGE
AEFGLOW FLOWAGE
AEFGNOR FAR GONE
AEFGNRT ENGRAFT
AEFGOOT FOOTAGE
AEFGORR FORAGER
AEFGORS FORAGES
AEFGORV FORGAVE
AEFGRRT GRAFTER
AEFGRSU FEARGUS
AEFHLRS FLASHER
AEFHLSS FLASHES
AEFHLTU HATEFUL
AEFHRRT FARTHER
AEFHRST FATHERS
AEFIILT FILIATE
AEFIIRS FAIRIES
AEFIKLR FLAKIER
AEFIKNR FRANKIE
AEFILLM FAMILLE
AEFILMN INFLAME
AEFILNS FINALES
AEFILNT INFLATE
AEFILOT FOLIATE
AEFILPT FLEAPIT
AEFILRR FRAILER
AEFILRU FAILURE
AEFILRV FAVRILE
AEFILSS FALSIES
AEFIMNR FIREMAN
AEFIMNS FAMINES
AEFIMOR FOAMIER
AEFIMRR FIREARM
AEFINNR FRANNIE
AEFINNS FANNIES
AEFINNT INFANTE
AEFINNZ FANZINE
AEFINPR FIREPAN

AEFINRR REFRAIN
AEFINRT FAINTER, FINE
    ART
AEFINTX ANTEFIX
AEFIQRU AQUIFER
AEFIRRR FARRIER
AEFIRST FAIREST
AEFIRSX FAIR SEX
AEFIRTT FATTIER
AEFISST FIESTAS
AEFISTT FATTIES
AEFKLNR FLANKER
AEFKLRT FARTLEK
AEFKLST FLASKET
AEFKLUW WAKEFUL
AEFKNRR FRANKER
AEFKORS FORSAKE
AEFLLNN FLANNEL
AEFLLSY FALSELY
AEFLLTT FLATLET
AEFLMOR FEMORAL
AEFLNOV FLAVONE
AEFLNRU FLANEUR,
    FUNERAL
AEFLNTT FLATTEN
AEFLOOV FOVEOLA
AEFLOPW PEAFOWL
AEFLORS LOAFERS,
    SAFROLE
AEFLORT FLOATER
AEFLPPR FLAPPER
AEFLPRS FELSPAR
AEFLPRU FLARE-UP
AEFLPRY PALFREY
AEFLRSU REFUSAL
AEFLRTT FLATTER
AEFLRTU TEARFUL
AEFLRZZ FRAZZLE
AEFLSST FALSEST
AEFMNOR FORAMEN,
    FOREMAN
AEFMNRU FRAENUM
AEFMORR FOREARM
AEFMORT FORMATE
AEFMPRU FRAME-UP
AEFMRRS FARMERS
AEFNOPR PROFANE
AEFNRSS FARNESS
AEFNSST FATNESS
AEFOPRW FOREPAW
AEFORRV FAVORER
AEFORRY FORAYER
AEFORSW FORESAW
AEFPPRS FRAPPÉS

AEFRRST RAFTERS,
    STRAFER
AEFRSTW FRETSAW
AEFSSTT FASTEST
AEFSTTT FATTEST
AEGGGLU LUGGAGE
AEGGHLR HAGGLER
AEGGINR GEARING
AEGGIOR GEORGIA
AEGGIOS ISAGOGE
AEGGIRS SAGGIER
AEGGJRY JAGGERY
AEGGLRR GARGLER
AEGGLRS GARGLES
AEGGLRY GREYLAG
AEGGLSW WAGGLES
AEGGNRS GANGERS,
    GRANGES, NAGGERS
AEGGRSS AGGRESS
AEGGRST STAGGER,
    TAGGERS
AEGGRSW SWAGGER
AEGGRTY GARGETY
AEGHHIT HIGH TEA
AEGHHLS SHELAGH
AEGHIKL HAGLIKE
AEGHILN HEALING
AEGHILR RALEIGH
AEGHINP HEAPING
AEGHINR HEARING
AEGHINT GAHNITE,
    HEATING
AEGHINV HEAVING
AEGHISS GEISHAS
AEGHLNO HALOGEN
AEGHLRU LAUGHER
AEGHMNN HANGMEN
AEGHNOX HEXAGON
AEGHNRS HANGERS
AEGHNSS GNASHES
AEGHOST HOSTAGE
AEGHRST GATHERS
AEGIIMN IMAGINE
AEGIINR NIGERIA
AEGIKLN LEAKING,
    LINKAGE
AEGIKNP PEAKING
AEGIKPR GARPIKE
AEGIKRW GAWKIER
AEGILLL ILLEGAL
AEGILLN GILLEAN
AEGILLP PILLAGE
AEGILLT TILLAGE
AEGILLV VILLAGE

AEGILLY AGILELY
AEGILMR GREMIAL
AEGILMT TIME LAG
AEGILNN LEANING
AEGILNP LEAPING, PEALING
AEGILNR ENGRAIL,
  REALIGN
AEGILNS LEASING,
  SEALING
AEGILNT GELATIN,
  GENITAL
AEGILNV LEAVING
AEGILOS SOILAGE
AEGILOU EULOGIA
AEGILRS ALGIERS
AEGILRZ GLAZIER
AEGIMNN MEANING
AEGIMNR GERMAIN,
  MANGIER, REAMING
AEGIMNS ENIGMAS
AEGIMNT MINTAGE,
  TEAMING
AEGIMPR EPIGRAM
AEGIMPS MAGPIES
AEGIMRR ARMIGER
AEGIMRS GISARME,
  MIRAGES
AEGIMRT MIGRATE,
  RAGTIME
AEGIMRY IMAGERY
AEGIMST GAMIEST,
  SIGMATE
AEGINNR EARNING,
  ENGRAIN, GRAINNE,
  NEARING
AEGINNT ANTEING,
  ANTIGEN, GENTIAN
AEGINNU ANGUINE,
  GUANINE, GUINEAN
AEGINNV ANGEVIN
AEGINNW WEANING
AEGINOR IRON AGE
AEGINOS AGONIES,
  AGONISE
AEGINOZ AGONIZE
AEGINPP GENIPAP
AEGINPR REAPING
AEGINRR ANGRIER,
  EARRING, GRAINER,
  REARING
AEGINRS ERASING,
  GAINERS, REGINAS,
  SEARING, SERINGA
AEGINRT GERAINT,

GRANITE, INGRATE,
  TANGIER, TEARING
AEGINRV GINEVRA,
  VINEGAR
AEGINRW WEARING
AEGINST EASTING,
  INGESTA, SEATING,
  TEASING
AEGINSU GUINEAS
AEGINTV VINTAGE
AEGINVW WEAVING
AEGIPRU PERUGIA
AEGIRRZ GRAZIER
AEGIRSS GASSIER
AEGIRST GAITERS, SEAGIRT
AEGIRSV GERVAIS
AEGIRSW EARWIGS
AEGIRTV VIRGATE
AEGIRUZ GAUZIER
AEGISST AGEISTS
AEGISSV VISAGES
AEGJLNR JANGLER
AEGKRSW GAWKERS
AEGKSST GASKETS
AEGLLLY LEGALLY
AEGLLNO GALLEON
AEGLLOR ALLEGRO
AEGLLRY ALLERGY,
  GALLERY, LARGELY,
  REGALLY
AEGLLSU SEAGULL,
  SULLAGE
AEGLLSY GALLEYS
AEGLLTU GLUTEAL
AEGLMNR MANGLER
AEGLMNS MANGLES
AEGLMPU PLUMAGE
AEGLNOT TANGELO
AEGLNPR GRAPNEL
AEGLNPS SPANGLE
AEGLNRS LANGRES
AEGLNRT TANGLER
AEGLNRU GRANULE
AEGLNRW WANGLER,
  WRANGLE
AEGLNST TANGLES
AEGLNSU ANGELUS
AEGLNSW WANGLES
AEGLNTT GANTLET
AEGLNUW GUNWALE
AEGLOPR PERGOLA
AEGLORS GAOLERS
AEGLORT GLOATER,
  LEGATOR

AEGLORV VORLAGE
AEGLOTV VOLTAGE
AEGLPPR GRAPPLE
AEGLPRU EARPLUG,
  GRAUPEL, PLAGUER
AEGLPSU PLAGUES
AEGLRRU REGULAR
AEGLRSS LARGESS
AEGLRST LARGEST
AEGLRSV VERGLAS
AEGLRTU TEGULAR
AEGLRTY GREATLY
AEGLRVY GRAVELY
AEGLSSS GLASSES
AEGLSTT GESTALT
AEGLTUV VULGATE
AEGLUUY GUAYULE
AEGLUVY VAGUELY
AEGMMRS GRAMMES
AEGMMRU RUMMAGE
AEGMNNO AGNOMEN
AEGMNOS MANGOES
AEGMNOT MAGNETO,
  MEGATON, MONTAGE
AEGMNRS GERMANS,
  MANGERS
AEGMNRT GARMENT
AEGMNRY GERMANY
AEGMNST MAGNETS
AEGMNTU AUGMENT,
  MUTAGEN
AEGMOOR MOORAGE
AEGMOXY EXOGAMY
AEGMRRY MARGERY
AEGNNOR ARGONNE,
  GARONNE
AEGNNOT TONNAGE
AEGNNRT REGNANT
AEGNNST GANNETS
AEGNNTT TANGENT
AEGNOOR OREGANO
AEGNORR GROANER
AEGNORS ORANGES
AEGNORT NEGATOR
AEGNORW WAGONER
AEGNOSY NOSEGAY
AEGNPRT TREPANG
AEGNRRS RANGERS
AEGNRRT GRANTER
AEGNRST GARNETS,
  STRANGE
AEGNSSY GAYNESS
AEGNTYZ YANGTZE
AEGOORT ROOTAGE

AEGOPRS GO SPARE
AEGOPRT PORTAGE
AEGOPST GESTAPO,
  POSTAGE
AEGOPTT POTTAGE
AEGORST STORAGE
AEGORTU OUTRAGE
AEGORVY VOYAGER
AEGOSSU GASEOUS
AEGOSTW STOWAGE
AEGOSVY VOYAGES
AEGOTTV GAVOTTE
AEGOTTW GET A TOW
AEGPRRS GRASPER
AEGPSTU UPSTAGE
AEGRRST GARRETS,
  GARTERS, GRATERS
AEGRRTT GARRETT
AEGRRUV GRAVURE
AEGRSSS GRASSES
AEGRSTT TARGETS
AEGRSTV GRAVEST
AEGRSTY GRAYEST
AEGSTUV GUSTAVE
AEGTTTU GUTTATE
AEHHILS SHEILAH
AEHHJOV JEHOVAH
AEHHJPT JAPHETH
AEHHLST HEALTHS
AEHHLTY HEALTHY
AEHHMSY HEYSHAM
AEHHRRS HARSHER
AEHHRST HEARTHS
AEHHSST SHEATHS
AEHIIRR HAIRIER
AEHIKLT HATLIKE
AEHIKNS HANKIES
AEHIKRS SHAKIER
AEHILMN HAMELIN
AEHILMO HEMIOLA
AEHILNR HERNIAL,
  INHALER
AEHILNY HYALINE
AEHILOP OPHELIA
AEHILPR HARELIP
AEHILPT HAPLITE
AEHILRU HAULIER
AEHILSS SHEILAS
AEHILTY HYALITE
AEHILVY HEAVILY
AEHIMNS HSIA-MEN
AEHIMPR EPHRAIM
AEHIMRS MISHEAR
AEHIMSS MESSIAH

AEHIMST ATHEISM
AEHINOT HIONATE
AEHINPR HEPARIN
AEHINPS IN PHASE,
  PHINEAS
AEHINRS HERNIAS
AEHINRT HAIRNET
AEHINSS HESSIAN
AEHIORR HOARIER
AEHIPPR HAPPIER
AEHIPPT EPITAPH
AEHIPRS HARPIES
AEHIPSS APHESIS
AEHIRRR HARRIER
AEHIRRT HARRIET
AEHIRST HASTIER
AEHIRWY HAYWIRE
AEHISST ASHIEST
AEHISTT ATHEIST
AEHISTZ HAZIEST
AEHJOPS JOSEPHA
AEHKLOY HOYLAKE
AEHKPSU SHAKE-UP
AEHKRSS SHAKERS
AEHKRSW HAWKERS
AEHKRTU KETURAH
AEHLLUV HELLUVA
AEHLMNO MANHOLE
AEHLMOR ARMHOLE
AEHLMRT THERMAL
AEHLMRU HUMERAL
AEHLMST HAMLETS
AEHLNOT ETHANOL
AEHLNRT ENTHRAL
AEHLNSU UNLEASH
AEHLOPT TAPHOLE
AEHLORT LOATHER
AEHLOSS ASSHOLE
AEHLPRS SPHERAL
AEHLPSS HAPLESS
AEHLPSY SHAPELY
AEHLRSS SLASHER
AEHLRST HALTERS,
  HARSLET
AEHLRSW WHALERS
AEHLRTY EARTHLY,
  HARTLEY, LATHERY
AEHLSSS HASSLES,
  SLASHES
AEHLSST HATLESS
AEHLSTT STEALTH
AEHLTWY WEALTHY
AEHMMRS HAMMERS,
  SHAMMER

AEHMNNR HERMANN
AEHMNST ANTHEMS
AEHMOPT APOTHEM
AEHMPRS HAMPERS
AEHMPTY EMPATHY
AEHMRSS MARSHES,
  SMASHER
AEHMRST HAMSTER
AEHMSSS SMASHES
AEHMTTW MATTHEW
AEHNNPY HA'PENNY
AEHNOPT PHAETON,
  PHONATE
AEHNORS HOARSEN
AEHNORT ANOTHER
AEHNORV HANOVER
AEHNOSX HEXOSAN
AEHNPRS SHARPEN
AEHNPRT PANTHER
AEHNRSS HARNESS
AEHNRST ANTHERS
AEHNRTU HAUNTER,
  UNEARTH
AEHNRTX NARTHEX
AEHOORT TOHEROA
AEHOPST TEASHOP
AEHORRS HOARSER
AEHORST EARSHOT
AEHORSX HOAXERS
AEHORTX OXHEART
AEHOSTT HOT SEAT
AEHPPRS PERHAPS
AEHPRRS SHARPER
AEHPRSS PHRASES,
  SERAPHS, SHERPAS
AEHPRTY THERAPY
AEHPSTT THE PAST
AEHRRSS RASHERS,
  SHARERS
AEHRRTU URETHRA
AEHRSST RASHEST
AEHRSSV SHAVERS
AEHRSSW HAWSERS,
  WASHERS
AEHRSTT HATTERS,
  SHATTER, THREATS
AEHRSTV HARVEST
AEHRSTW WREATHS
AEHRSVW WHARVES
AEHRSWY WASHERY
AEHRTUU HAUTEUR
AEHSSST STASHES
AEHSTUX EXHAUST
AEIIKNT KAINITE

AEIILNN ANILINE
AEIILNR AIRLINE
AEIILNS AINSLIE
AEIILRS ISRAELI
AEIILSS SILESIA
AEIILTT LETITIA
AEIIMTT IMITATE
AEIINNR ANEIRIN
AEIINNS ASININE
AEIINRR RAINIER
AEIINRT INERTIA
AEIIPRR PRAIRIE
AEIIRRV RIVIERA
AEIIRST AIRIEST
AEIITTV VITIATE
AEIJLNV JAVELIN
AEIJLRS JAILERS
AEIJMMR JAMMIER
AEIJMNS JASMINE
AEIJRZZ JAZZIER
AEIKLMN MALINKE,
  MANLIKE
AEIKLNR LANKIER
AEIKLOT KEITLOA
AEIKLRW WARLIKE
AEIKLST TALKIES
AEIKLSW WALKIES
AEIKLUZ ZULEIKA
AEIKLWX WAXLIKE
AEIKMNP PIKEMAN
AEIKMNR RAMEKIN
AEIKMST MISTAKE
AEIKNRR NARKIER
AEIKNRT KATRINE,
  KERATIN
AEIKNRU UKRAINE
AEIKNST INTAKES
AEIKNSY KYANISE
AEIKNYZ KYANIZE
AEIKPRR PARKIER
AEIKPRW PAWKIER
AEIKRRS SARKIER
AEIKRSS KAISERS
AEIKRSY KAYSERI
AEILLMT ALL-TIME
AEILLNR RALLINE
AEILLPR PALLIER
AEILLRR RALLIER
AEILLRS RALLIES, SALLIER
AEILLRT LITERAL, TALLIER
AEILLSS SALLIES
AEILLST TALLIES
AEILLSW WALLIES
AEILLUV ELUVIAL

AEILLVY VIYELLA
AEILMMN MAILMEN
AEILMMS MELISMA
AEILMNN LINEMAN,
  MELANIN
AEILMNP IMPANEL
AEILMNR MANLIER,
  MARLINE, MINERAL
AEILMNS MALINES,
  MENIALS, SEMINAL
AEILMNT AILMENT,
  ALIMENT
AEILMNV MELVINA
AEILMNY EL MINYA
AEILMOR MELIORA,
  MORELIA
AEILMPR IMPALER,
  PALMIER
AEILMRS REALISM
AEILMRT MARLITE
AEILMSS AIMLESS,
  MELISSA
AEILMTY MEATILY
AEILNNY INANELY
AEILNNZ LIZANNE
AEILNOP OPALINE
AEILNOR AILERON,
  ALIENOR, LORAINE
AEILNOS ANISOLE, SEA
  LION
AEILNOT ELATION,
  TOENAIL
AEILNPR PLAINER,
  PRALINE
AEILNPS SPANIEL
AEILNPT PANTILE
AEILNPU PAULINE
AEILNPX EXPLAIN
AEILNRT LATRINE,
  RATLINE, RELIANT,
  RETINAL
AEILNRV RAVELIN
AEILNRX RELAXIN
AEILNRY INLAYER
AEILNST ELASTIN,
  SALIENT
AEILNSY AINSLEY, ELYSIAN
AEILNTU ALUNITE
AEILNVY NAIVELY
AEILOPR PELORIA
AEILORS ROSALIE
AEILORV VARIOLE
AEILOST ISOLATE
AEILOTV VIOLATE

AEILPPR APPLIER
AEILPRV PREVAIL
AEILPST TALIPES
AEILPSY PAISLEY
AEILQTU LIQUATE,
  TEQUILA
AEILRRT RETRIAL,
  TRAILER
AEILRSS AIRLESS, SERIALS
AEILRST REALIST, SALTIER,
  SALTIRE
AEILRSV REVISAL
AEILRTT TERTIAL
AEILRTU URALITE
AEILRTY IRATELY,
  REALITY
AEILRVV REVIVAL
AEILRVY VIRELAY
AEILRWY WEARILY
AEILSST SET SAIL
AEILSSV VALISES
AEILSTZ LAZIEST
AEILTVV TEL AVIV
AEILUVX EXUVIAL
AEIMMMS MAMMIES
AEIMMRT MARMITE
AEIMNNT MANNITE
AEIMNOR MORAINE,
  ROMAINE
AEIMNPR PERMIAN
AEIMNRR MARINER
AEIMNRS MARINES,
  REMAINS, SEMINAR
AEIMNRT MARTINE,
  MINARET, RAIMENT
AEIMNRV MINERVA
AEIMNSS MESSINA,
  SAMISEN
AEIMNST INMATES
AEIMNTV VIETNAM
AEIMNTY AMENITY
AEIMOOP IPOMOEA
AEIMOPR EMPORIA
AEIMORR ARMOIRE
AEIMOST ATOMISE
AEIMOTZ ATOMIZE
AEIMPRS IMPRESA
AEIMPRT PRIMATE
AEIMPRV VAMPIRE
AEIMPSS IMPASSE
AEIMPST IMPASTE,
  PASTIME, SEPTIMA
AEIMRRR MARRIER
AEIMRST MAESTRI

AEIMRTW WARTIME
AEIMSST SEA MIST
AEIMSSV MASSIVE
AEIMSTZ MESTIZA
AEINNNS NANNIES
AEINNOT ANTOINE
AEINNPR PANNIER
AEINNPT PINNATE
AEINNRT ENTRAIN
AEINNRU ANEURIN
AEINOPR OPEN-AIR
AEINOPZ APIEZON
AEINORS ERASION
AEINOSV EVASION
AEINOXZ OXAZINE
AEINPPS NAPPIES
AEINPRS PERSIAN
AEINPRT PAINTER,
    PERTAIN, PETRINA
AEINPSS PANSIES
AEINPST PANTIES, SAPIENT
AEINPTT PATIENT
AEINPTU PETUNIA
AEINQTU ANTIQUE,
    QUINATE
AEINRRS SIERRAN
AEINRRT TERRAIN,
    TRAINER
AEINRSS NERISSA, SARNIES
AEINRST NASTIER,
    RETINAS, RETSINA,
    STAINER, STEARIN
AEINRSV RAVINES
AEINRTT ITERANT,
    NATTIER, NITRATE,
    TERTIAN
AEINRTU TAURINE,
    URANITE, URINATE
AEINRTW TINWARE
AEINRVV VERVAIN
AEINSST ENTASIS, SESTINA
AEINSSV VINASSE
AEINSTT INSTATE,
    SATINET
AEINSTU SINUATE
AEINSTV NATIVES,
    VAINEST
AEINSTW IN A STEW
AEINSTZ ZANIEST
AEINSVV NAVVIES
AEINSWY ANYWISE
AEINTVY NAIVETY
AEINTXY ANXIETY
AEIOPRS SOAPIER

AEIOPST OPIATES
AEIOQSU SEQUOIA
AEIORSV OVARIES
AEIOSST OSSETIA
AEIPPPS PAPPIES
AEIPPRS APPRISE, SAPPIER
AEIPPRZ ZAPPIER
AEIPRRS ASPIRER, PARRIES,
    PRAISER, RAPIERS,
    REPAIRS
AEIPRSS PARESIS, PRAISES
AEIPRST PARTIES, PASTIER,
    PIASTRE, PIRATES,
    TRAIPSE
AEIPRSU PIRAEUS, UPRAISE
AEIPRTT PARTITE
AEIPRTV PRIVATE
AEIPRTW WIRETAP
AEIPRXY PYREXIA
AEIPSSS ASEPSIS
AEIPSST PASTIES
AEIPSSV PASSIVE
AEIPSTT PATTIES
AEIPSTU IAPETUS
AEIPTXY EPITAXY
AEIRRRV ARRIVER
AEIRRSS RAISERS, SIERRAS
AEIRRST TARSIER
AEIRRTT RATTIER
AEIRRTU ETRURIA
AEIRSSS SASSIER
AEIRSST SATIRES
AEIRSTT ARTIEST,
    ARTISTE, STRIATE,
    TASTIER
AEIRSTW WAITERS,
    WARIEST
AEIRSVW WAIVERS
AEIRTTT TATTIER,
    TITRATE
AEIRTUZ AZURITE
AEIRTVY VARIETY
AEISSSS ASSISES
AEISSST SIESTAS
AEISSSU AUSSIES
AEISSSZ ASSIZES
AEISSUX AUXESIS
AEISTTU SITUATE
AEISTTV STATIVE
AEISTTY SATIETY
AEISTVW WAVIEST
AEISTWX WAXIEST
AEITTTV VITTATE
AEJJLNU JEJUNAL

AEJLOSU JEALOUS
AEJMSTY MAJESTY
AEJNOSS SAN JOSE
AEKLNST ANKLETS,
    LANKEST
AEKLOST SKATOLE
AEKLPPT PEP TALK
AEKLPRS SPARKLE
AEKLRST STALKER,
    TALKERS
AEKLRSW WALKERS
AEKMNRU UNMAKER
AEKMRRS MARKERS,
    REMARKS
AEKMRST MARKETS
AEKNOPS SPOKANE
AEKNPPR KNAPPER
AEKNPRS SPANKER
AEKNRRS RANKERS
AEKNRST TANKERS
AEKNRSW WANKERS
AEKNRVY KNAVERY
AEKOTTU OUT-TAKE,
    TAKEOUT
AEKPSSY PASSKEY
AEKPSTU TAKEUPS,
    UPTAKES
AEKQRSU QUAKERS
AEKQSSU SQUEAKS
AEKQSUY SQUEAKY
AEKRRST STARKER
AEKRSST STREAKS
AEKRSTY STREAKY
AELLLOU LOUELLA
AELLMNS MANSELL
AELLMNU LUMENAL
AELLMRS SMALLER
AELLMST MALLETS
AELLMSU MALLEUS
AELLMWX MAXWELL
AELLNOV NOVELLA
AELLNPR PARNELL
AELLNPY PENALLY
AELLNVY VENALLY
AELLORS ROSELLA
AELLORV ALL OVER,
    OVERALL
AELLPRU PLEURAL
AELLPST L-PLATES,
    PALLETS
AELLPTY PLAYLET
AELLQUY EQUALLY
AELLRRU ALLURER
AELLRST STELLAR

AELLRSU LAURELS
AELLRTY ALERTLY
AELLRVY RAVELLY
AELLSSW LAWLESS
AELLSTT TALLEST
AELLSTW WALLETS
AELLSVY VALLEYS
AELLTUU ULULATE
AELLUVV VALVULE
AELMMOY MYELOMA
AELMMRT TRAMMEL
AELMMST STAMMEL
AELMMSY MALMSEY
AELMNOR ALMONER
AELMNOT TELAMON
AELMNPR LAMPERN
AELMNRU NUMERAL
AELMNST LAMENTS,
MANTLES
AELMOPR PALERMO
AELMOPU AMPOULE
AELMOPY MAYPOLE
AELMORV REMOVAL
AELMOST MALTOSE
AELMOSY AMYLOSE
AELMPRS SAMPLER
AELMPRT TRAMPLE
AELMPRY LAMPREY
AELMPSS SAMPLES
AELMPTU PLUMATE
AELMRSS ARMLESS
AELMRSU SERUMAL
AELMRSV MARVELS
AELMRTU RELATUM
AELMSTU AMULETS
AELNNPR PLANNER
AELNNRT LANTERN
AELNNRU UNLEARN
AELNNTU ANNULET
AELNOOR LEONORA
AELNOPU APOLUNE
AELNORS ORLEANS,
SALERNO
AELNORV VERONAL
AELNOST LEAN-TOS
AELNPPS PEN PALS
AELNPPY PLAYPEN
AELNPRT PLANTER
AELNPRY PLENARY
AELNPST PLANETS
AELNPTX EXPLANT
AELNPTY APLENTY,
PENALTY
AELNQUU UNEQUAL

AELNRRS SNARLER
AELNRST ANTLERS,
RENTALS, SALTERN,
STERNAL
AELNRTU NEUTRAL
AELNRTV VENTRAL
AELNRUV UNRAVEL,
VENULAR
AELNSSU SENSUAL
AELNSSX LAXNESS
AELNSTT TALENTS
AELNSTY STANLEY
AELOORS AEROSOL,
ROSEOLA
AELOPRS PAROLES,
REPOSAL
AELOPRT PROLATE
AELOPRV OVERLAP
AELOPST APOSTLE,
PELOTAS
AELOPSX EXPOSAL
AELORRT REALTOR,
RELATOR
AELORSS LASSOER
AELORTT LORETTA
AELORTV LEVATOR
AELORUU ROULEAU
AELORVY OVERLAY
AELOSSV SALVOES
AELOSTV SOLVATE
AELOSTZ ZEALOTS
AELOSUZ ZEALOUS
AELOTTU TOLUATE
AELOTUV OVULATE
AELOTVV VOLVATE
AELPPRS SLAPPER
AELPPSU APPULSE
AELPQSU PLAQUES
AELPRST PLASTER,
PSALTER, STAPLER
AELPRSU PERUSAL
AELPRSY PARLEYS,
PARSLEY, PLAYERS,
REPLAYS
AELPRTT PLATTER,
PRATTLE
AELPRTY PTERYLA
AELPSSS SAPLESS
AELPSST PASTELS, STAPLES
AELPSSU PAS SEUL
AELPSTU PULSATE
AELQRRU QUARREL
AELQSSU SQUEALS
AELQTUZ QUETZAL

AELRRSU SURREAL
AELRRTW TRAWLER
AELRSST ARTLESS
AELRSSV SALVERS,
SLAVERS
AELRSSY SLAYERS
AELRSTT RATTLES,
STARLET, STARTLE,
TELSTAR
AELRSTU SALUTER
AELRSTV TRAVELS,
VARLETS, VESTRAL
AELRSTW WASTREL
AELRSUV VALUERS
AELRSVY SLAVERY
AELRSWY LAWYERS
AELRSZZ RAZZLES
AELRTTT TATTLER
AELRTUV VAULTER
AELRTWZ WALTZER
AELSSST TASSELS
AELSSTT STALEST
AELSSTU SALUTES
AELSTTW WATTLES
AELSTTY STATELY
AELSTWZ WALTZES
AELSUVY SUAVELY
AELTTUX TEXTUAL
AEMMNOT MOMENTA
AEMMRST STAMMER
AEMNNOS MANNOSE
AEMNNOT MONTANE
AEMNNRS MANNERS
AEMNNRT REMNANT
AEMNNTU UNMEANT
AEMNOPR MANROPE
AEMNORS MOANERS,
OARSMEN
AEMNORU ENAMOUR,
NEUROMA
AEMNORV OVERMAN
AEMNPTU PUTAMEN
AEMNPTY PAYMENT
AEMNRRU MANURER
AEMNRST MARTENS,
SMARTEN
AEMNRSU SURNAME
AEMNSST STAMENS
AEMNSTY AMNESTY
AEMOORT TEAROOM
AEMOORW WOOMERA
AEMOOST OSTEOMA
AEMOOSV VAMOOSE
AEMORRR ARMORER

AEMORRS ROAMERS
AEMORRV OVERARM
AEMORST MAESTRO
AEMORTU EURATOM
AEMOSWY SOMEWAY
AEMPRRT TRAMPER
AEMPRST STAMPER
AEMPTTT ATTEMPT
AEMPTTU TAPETUM
AEMQSSU MASQUES
AEMRRRY REMARRY
AEMRRST ARMREST,
 SMARTER
AEMRRTU ERRATUM
AEMRSST MASTERS,
 STREAMS
AEMRSSU ASSUMER,
 ERASMUS, MASSEUR
AEMRSTT MATTERS,
 SMATTER
AEMRSTU ARTEMUS
AEMRSTW WARMEST
AEMRSTY MASTERY
AENNNPT PENNANT
AENNORS ROSANNE,
 ROSEANN
AENNORX ROXANNE
AENNOTU TONNEAU
AENNPRS SPANNER
AENNRST TANNERS
AENNRTT ENTRANT
AENNRTY TANNERY
AENNSSU SUSANNE
AENNSSW WANNESS
AENNSTT TENANTS
AENNSTW WANNEST
AENNSUZ SUZANNE
AENOPPR PROPANE
AENOPRS PERSONA
AENOPRT OPERANT,
 PRONATE, PROTEAN
AENOPSW WEAPONS
AENORRV OVERRAN
AENORSS REASONS,
 SEÑORAS
AENORST ONE-STAR,
 SENATOR, TREASON
AENORSY REYNOSA
AENORVY AVEYRON
AENOSSS SEASONS
AENOSTU SOUTANE
AENPPRS SNAPPER
AENPRRT PARTNER
AENPRRW PRAWNER

AENPRST PARENTS,
 PASTERN
AENPRSW SPAWNER
AENPRSZ PANZERS
AENPRTT PATTERN,
 REPTANT
AENPRTW ANTWERP
AENPRUV PARVENU
AENPSST APTNESS
AENPSSY SYNAPSE
AENPSTT PATENTS,
 PATTENS
AENPSTU PEANUTS
AENRRST RANTERS
AENRRSW WARRENS
AENRRTY TERNARY
AENRSSW ANSWERS,
 RAWNESS
AENRSTU NATURES,
 SAUNTER
AENRSTV SERVANT,
 TAVERNS, VERSANT
AENRSUW UNSWEAR
AENRTTU TAUNTER
AENRTUV VAUNTER
AENSTTU TETANUS
AENSTTX SEXTANT
AEOOPPS PAPOOSE
AEOPPPS PAPPOSE
AEOPPRV APPROVE
AEOPRRV VAPORER
AEOPRST ESPARTO,
 SEAPORT
AEOPRVY OVERPAY
AEOPSTT TEAPOTS
AEOPSTZ TOPAZES
AEOQRTU EQUATOR,
 QUORATE
AEOQSUU AQUEOUS
AEORRST ROASTER
AEORRSU AROUSER
AEORSTT ROSETTA,
 TOASTER
AEORSVW OVERSAW
AEORTUW OUTWEAR
AEORTVX OVERTAX
AEPPRRT TRAPPER
AEPPRRW WRAPPER
AEPPRSS SAPPERS
AEPPRSU PAUPERS
AEPPRSW SWAPPER
AEPPSTT TAPPETS
AEPPSTU PASTE-UP
AEPQRTU PARQUET

AEPRRSS PARSERS,
 SPARSER
AEPRRSY PRAYERS,
 SPRAYER
AEPRRTU RAPTURE,
 RUPERTA
AEPRSST REPASTS
AEPRSSY PESSARY
AEPRSTT PATTERS,
 SPATTER
AEPRSTU PASTURE
AEPRSUV RAVE-UPS
AEQRRSU SQUARER
AEQRRTU QUARTER
AEQRSSU SQUARES
AEQRSTU T-SQUARE
AEQRSUV QUAVERS
AEQRTTU QUARTET
AEQRUVY QUAVERY
AERRSST ARRESTS
AERRSSU ASSURER
AERRSTT STARTER
AERRSTV STARVER,
 TRAVERS
AERRSTY STRAYER
AERSSTT TASTERS
AERSSTW WASTERS
AERSSTY STAYERS
AERSTTT STRETTA,
 TATTERS
AERSTTU STATURE
AERSTTW STEWART,
 SWATTER
AERSTUY ESTUARY
AESSTTU STATUES
AESSTUY EUSTASY
AESTTTU STATUTE,
 TAUTEST
AFFGSUW GUFFAWS
AFFHINU IN A HUFF
AFFHIRS RAFFISH
AFFHLLY FLY HALF
AFFHLUU AL HUFUF
AFFIKRS KAFFIRS
AFFILSY FALSIFY
AFFIMST MASTIFF
AFFINRU FUNFAIR,
 RUFFIAN
AFFINTY TIFFANY
AFFIRST TARIFFS
AFFLOPY PLAY-OFF
AFFLOSY LAY-OFFS
AFFNORS SAFFRON
AFFNORT AFFRONT

AFFNOSW SAWN-OFF
AFGGGIN FAGGING
AFGGOST FAGGOTS
AFGHHIS HAGFISH
AFGHIRS GARFISH
AFGHRTU FRAUGHT
AFGIILN FAILING
AFGIINR FAIRING
AFGIKLN FLAKING
AFGILLN FALLING
AFGILMN FLAMING
AFGILNO FOALING, LOAFING
AFGILNR FLARING
AFGILNT FATLING
AFGILNU GAINFUL
AFGILNW FLAWING
AFGILNY ANGLIFY, FLAYING
AFGILRU FIGURAL
AFGIMNO FOAMING
AFGIMNR FARMING, FRAMING
AFGIMNY MAGNIFY
AFGINNN FANNING
AFGINNW FAWNING
AFGINRT FARTING, RAFTING
AFGINRY FRAYING
AFGINST FASTING
AFGINTW WAFTING
AFGIRTY GRATIFY
AFGKORT KOFTGAR
AFGLLLY GALLFLY
AFGLLUY FALL GUY
AFGLMOP FOG LAMP
AFGLNOS FLAGONS
AFGMNOR FROGMAN
AFHIIRS FAIRISH
AFHIKLS KHALIFS
AFHILTW HALF-WIT
AFHIMNU HAFNIUM
AFHINOS FASHION
AFHIORS OARFISH
AFHISSW SAWFISH
AFHISTT FATTISH
AFHKORY HAYFORK
AFHLMRU HARMFUL
AFHLOOS LOOFAHS
AFHMOST FATHOMS
AFHORTW WHAT FOR
AFIILRT AIRLIFT
AFIINRS FRISIAN
AFIKNNU IN A FUNK

AFILLNY FINALLY
AFILLPT PITFALL
AFILLUV FLUVIAL
AFILLUW WAILFUL
AFILMOR ALIFORM
AFILMPY AMPLIFY
AFILNOR FLORIAN
AFILNPU PAINFUL
AFILNTY FAINTLY
AFILORW AIRFLOW
AFILOTX FOXTAIL
AFILQUY QUALIFY
AFILRTY FRAILTY
AFILSSY SALSIFY
AFILSTU FISTULA
AFILSTY FALSITY
AFILTTY FATTILY
AFIMOOS MAFIOSO
AFIMSSS MASSIFS
AFIMSUV FAUVISM
AFINNST INFANTS
AFINORS INSOFAR
AFINRTU UT INFRA
AFINSTU FUSTIAN
AFISSTY SATISFY
AFISTUV FAUVIST
AFITTUY FATUITY
AFKKOUU FUKUOKA
AFKLNRY FRANKLY
AFKRRTU FRAKTUR
AFLLOOY ALOOFLY
AFLLOTU FALLOUT, OUTFALL
AFLLPUY PLAYFUL
AFLLUWY AWFULLY
AFLMORU FORMULA
AFLMORW WOLFRAM
AFLMOST FLOTSAM
AFLMRSU ARMFULS, FULMARS
AFLNOOS ALFONSO
AFLNORT FRONTAL
AFLORSV FLAVORS
AFLORUV FLAVOUR
AFLPRTY FLYTRAP
AFLPSTY FLYPAST
AFMNOOT FOOTMAN
AFMNORT FORMANT
AFMNWYY MYFANWY
AFMOORS FORMOSA
AFMORST FORMATS
AFMOSTU SFUMATO
AFOORST OF A SORT
AFOOTWY FOOTWAY

AFORSUV FAVOURS
AFORUWY FOUR-WAY
AFOSTUU FATUOUS
AGGGGIN GAGGING
AGGGIJN JAGGING
AGGGILN LAGGING
AGGGINN GANGING, NAGGING
AGGGINR RAGGING
AGGGINS SAGGING
AGGGINT TAGGING
AGGGINU GAUGING
AGGGINW WAGGING
AGGHHIS HAGGISH
AGGHIMN GINGHAM
AGGHINN HANGING
AGGHINS GASHING
AGGHISW WAGGISH
AGGIINN GAINING
AGGIINV GINGIVA
AGGIKNW GAWKING
AGGILLN GALLING
AGGILNN ANGLING
AGGILNO GAOLING
AGGILNR GLARING
AGGILNZ GLAZING
AGGILOS LOGGIAS
AGGINNR RANGING
AGGINNW GNAWING
AGGINPP GAPPING
AGGINPS GASPING
AGGINPW GAWPING
AGGINRT GRATING
AGGINRU ARGUING
AGGINRY GRAYING
AGGINRZ GRAZING
AGGINSS GASSING
AGGINST STAGING
AGGISZZ ZIGZAGS
AGGKNOT GANGTOK
AGGLOSW GLASGOW
AGGMORR GROGRAM
AGGMOST MAGGOTS
AGGMOTY MAGGOTY
AGHHINS HASHING
AGHHIWY HIGHWAY
AGHHNOW HWANG HO
AGHHORT HOGARTH
AGHHOSW HOGWASH
AGHHTUY HAUGHTY
AGHIILN HAILING
AGHIKNN KHINGAN
AGHIKNR HARKING
AGHIKNS SHAKING

AGHIKNW HAWKING
AGHILNS LASHING
AGHILNT ALTHING,
  HALTING
AGHILNU HAULING
AGHILNV HALVING
AGHILNW WHALING
AGHILOT GOLIATH
AGHILRS LARGISH
AGHILRT ALRIGHT
AGHIMMN HAMMING
AGHIMNR HARMING
AGHIMNS MASHING,
  SHAMING
AGHINOX HOAXING
AGHINPR HARPING
AGHINPS PHASING,
  SHAPING
AGHINRS GARNISH,
  SHARING
AGHINSU ANGUISH
AGHINSV SHAVING
AGHINSW WASHING
AGHINTT AT NIGHT
AGHINTW THAWING
AGHJMNO MAH-JONG
AGHKOSW GOSHAWK
AGHLMPU GALUMPH
AGHLOSU GOULASH
AGHLSTY GHASTLY
AGHMNNU HUNGNAM
AGHMRTU MURTAGH
AGHNOTU HANGOUT
AGHNPSU HANG-UPS
AGHNRUY HUNGARY
AGHNTUY NAUGHTY
AGHORTW WARTHOG
AGHRTUU THURGAU
AGIIJLN JAILING
AGIIKNS KIANGSI
AGIILLN GILLIAN
AGIILMN MAILING
AGIILNN NAILING
AGIILNR RAILING
AGIILNS AISLING, SAILING
AGIILNT TAILING
AGIILNW WAILING
AGIILPT PIGTAIL
AGIILRU LIGURIA
AGIILTY AGILITY
AGIIMMN MAIMING
AGIIMMS IMAGISM
AGIIMOR ORIGAMI
AGIIMST IMAGIST

AGIINNP PAINING
AGIINNR INGRAIN,
  RAINING
AGIINPR PAIRING
AGIINRS AIRINGS,
  ARISING, RAISING
AGIINSV VISAING
AGIINTW WAITING
AGIINTX TAXIING
AGIINVW WAIVING
AGIJMMN JAMMING
AGIJNNU JUNGIAN
AGIJNRR JARRING
AGIJNZZ JAZZING
AGIJSSW JIGSAWS
AGIKKNY YAKKING
AGIKLNR LARKING
AGIKLNS SLAKING
AGIKLNT TALKING
AGIKLNW WALKING
AGIKMNR MARKING
AGIKMNS MAKINGS,
  MASKING
AGIKNNN NANKING
AGIKNNR NARKING,
  RANKING
AGIKNNS SNAKING
AGIKNNW WANKING
AGIKNNY YANKING
AGIKNOS SOAKING
AGIKNOY OKAYING
AGIKNPR PARKING
AGIKNQU QUAKING
AGIKNRT KARTING
AGIKNST SKATING,
  STAKING, TAKINGS
AGIKNSU KIANGSU
AGILLMU GALLIUM
AGILLNP PALLING
AGILLNU LINGUAL
AGILLNW WALLING
AGILLNY ALLYING
AGILLOR GORILLA
AGILLRU LIGULAR
AGILLSU LUGSAIL
AGILMNP PALMING
AGILMNT MALTING
AGILMNU MAULING
AGILMNY MANGILY
AGILNNO LOANING
AGILNNP PLANING
AGILNNS LANSING,
  LINSANG
AGILNPP LAPPING

AGILNPS LAPSING,
  PALINGS, SAPLING
AGILNPT PLATING
AGILNPW LAPWING
AGILNPY PLAYING
AGILNRY ANGRILY,
  RANGILY
AGILNSS SIGNALS
AGILNST LASTING,
  SALTING, SLATING,
  STALING
AGILNSV SALVING,
  SLAVING
AGILNSY SLAYING
AGILNUV VALUING
AGILOPT GALIPOT
AGILORS GIRASOL
AGILORW AIRGLOW,
  GWALIOR
AGILSTY STAGILY
AGIMMNR RAMMING
AGIMNNN MANNING
AGIMNNO MOANING
AGIMNOR ROAMING
AGIMNPP MAPPING
AGIMNPT TAMPING
AGIMNRR MARRING
AGIMNRS MARGINS
AGIMNRT MIGRANT
AGIMNRW WARMING
AGIMNSS MASSING
AGIMNSU AMUSING
AGIMNTT MATTING
AGIMORU GOURAMI
AGIMOSY ISOGAMY
AGIMSST STIGMAS
AGIMSWW WIGWAMS
AGINNNN NANNING
AGINNNP PANNING
AGINNNT TANNING
AGINNNW WANNING
AGINNOT ATONING
AGINNOV AVIGNON
AGINNPP NAPPING
AGINNPT PANTING
AGINNPW PAWNING
AGINNRS SNARING
AGINNRT RANTING
AGINNRW WARNING
AGINNRY YARNING
AGINNSW AWNINGS
AGINNTW WANTING
AGINNWY YAWNING
AGINOOP POGONIA

AGINOPS SOAPING
AGINOPT PAOTING
AGINORR ROARING
AGINORS SIGNORA,
  SOARING
AGINORV VIRGOAN
AGINOST AGONIST
AGINOVW AVOWING
AGINPPR RAPPING
AGINPPS SAPPING
AGINPPT TAPPING
AGINPPY YAPPING
AGINPPZ ZAPPING
AGINPRS PARINGS,
  PARSING, RASPING,
  SPARING
AGINPRT GIN TRAP,
  PARTING, PRATING
AGINPRW WARPING
AGINPRY PRAYING
AGINPSS PASSING
AGINPST PASTING
AGINPSU PAUSING
AGINPSV PAVINGS
AGINPSY SPAYING
AGINPTT PATTING
AGINRRT TARRING
AGINRRW WARRING
AGINRST GASTRIN,
  RATINGS, STARING
AGINRSU AIRGUNS
AGINRSV RAVINGS
AGINRSY SYRINGA
AGINRTT RATTING
AGINRVY VARYING
AGINRXY X-RAYING
AGINSSS SASSING
AGINSSV SAVINGS
AGINSSY SAYINGS
AGINSTT STATING,
  TASTING
AGINSTV STAVING
AGINSTW WASTING
AGINSTY STAYING,
  STYGIAN
AGINSWY SWAYING
AGINTTT TATTING
AGINWWX WAXWING
AGIORSV VIRAGOS
AGIRSTU GUITARS
AGIRTVY GRAVITY
AGJKNUW KWANGJU
AGJLMOS LOGJAMS
AGJLRUU JUGULAR

AGJNORS JARGONS
AGKORST GO-KARTS
AGLLNOO GALLOON
AGLLNOS GALLONS
AGLLNTU GALLNUT,
  NUTGALL
AGLLOPS GALLOPS
AGLLOSS GLOSSAL
AGLLOSU GALLOUS
AGLLOSW GALLOWS
AGLLOTT GLOTTAL
AGLMORU GLAMOUR
AGLNOOS LAGOONS
AGLNOOW OWN GOAL
AGLNOPS GOSPLAN
AGLNORU LANGUOR
AGLNOSS SLOGANS
AGLNPSY SPANGLY
AGLNRUU UNGULAR
AGLOOPY APOLOGY
AGMMNSU MAGNUMS
AGMNORU ORGANUM
AGMNOTU MONTAGU
AGMNSTU MUSTANG
AGMNSTY GYMNAST
AGMNSYY SYNGAMY
AGMOPRR PROGRAM
AGMORRW RAGWORM
AGMORSS ORGASMS
AGMPRSU GRAMPUS
AGNNNOO NONAGON
AGNNNTU NANTUNG
AGNNOOP GO NAP ON
AGNNOOR ORGANON,
  RANGOON
AGNOQSU QUANGOS
AGNORRT GRANTOR
AGNORSS SARONGS
AGNOSTU NOUGATS
AGOPPST STOPGAP
AGORRTW RAGWORT
AGORRTY GYRATOR
AGORSTU RAGOUTS
AGOSUYZ AZYGOUS
AGRUUUY URUGUAY
AHHHISS HASHISH
AHHIKSW HAWKISH
AHHKOOS HOOKAHS
AHHKSTY SHAKHTY
AHHLRSY HARSHLY
AHHOPRT HAP'ORTH
AHHORTW HAWORTH
AHIIKNT HAITINK
AHIILSW SWAHILI

AHIINPR HAIRPIN
AHIINRT THIN AIR
AHIIPRS AIRSHIP
AHIKLSY SHAKILY
AHIKMNS KHAMSIN
AHIKMRS KASHMIR
AHIKMSW MAWKISH
AHIKNOS KHOISAN
AHIKNRS KRISHNA
AHIKNSV KNAVISH
AHIKNSW HAWKINS
AHIKOSU HOKUSAI
AHILLNT ANTHILL
AHILLRY HILLARY
AHILLST TALLISH
AHILNPS PLANISH
AHILORY HOARILY
AHILPPY HAPPILY
AHILSSV SLAVISH
AHILSTY HASTILY
AHILTTZ HAZLITT
AHIMMRS RAMMISH
AHIMNNS MANNISH
AHIMNNU INHUMAN
AHIMPSS MISHAPS
AHIMRST MITHRAS
AHIMTUZ AZIMUTH
AHIMTVZ MITZVAH
AHINNTX XANTHIN
AHINOOR HONORIA
AHINOTZ HOATZIN
AHINPRS HARPINS
AHINPSS SPANISH
AHINPST HATPINS
AHINRST TARNISH
AHINRSV VARNISH
AHINSTT TIN HATS
AHIOORT HORATIO
AHIORRT HARRIOT
AHIPRST HARPIST
AHIPRSW WARSHIP
AHIPSSW WASPISH
AHIPSWW WHIPSAW
AHIPSWY SHIPWAY
AHIRRSS SIRRAHS
AHIRSTT RATTISH
AHIRSTW WRAITHS
AHISTTW WHATSIT
AHKKORV KHARKOV
AHKLTUY HAKLUYT
AHKMORR MARKHOR
AHKNPSU PUNKAHS
AHKNRTY KATHRYN
AHLLMSU MULLAHS

AHLLOPS SHALLOP
AHLLOST SHALLOT
AHLLOSW SHALLOW
AHLLOTY LOATHLY,
    TALLYHO
AHLLPSU PHALLUS
AHLLPYY APHYLLY
AHLLRST THRALLS
AHLLSTU THALLUS
AHLMNPY NYMPHAL
AHLMNSY HYMNALS
AHLMNUY HUMANLY
AHLMORU HUMORAL
AHLMOSW OHM'S LAW
AHLMSUU HAMULUS
AHLNOPR ALPHORN
AHLNORT ALTHORN
AHLORST HARLOTS
AHLOTUU OUTHAUL
AHLPRSY SHARPLY
AHLPSSU LASH-UPS
AHLPSSY SPLASHY
AHMMMOT MAMMOTH
AHMNNTU MANHUNT
AHMNOPT HAMPTON,
    PHANTOM
AHMNORU MANHOUR
AHMNORY HARMONY
AHMNOSS HANSOMS
AHMNOSU HOUSMAN
AHMNOSW SHOWMAN
AHMOOPS SHAMPOO
AHMOSTU MAHOUTS
AHMPSSU SMASH-UP
AHNNNOS SHANNON
AHNNOTY ANTHONY
AHNOOPR HARPOON
AHNOPRS ORPHANS
AHNORRS SHARRON
AHNORSX SAXHORN
AHNOTTW WHATNOT
AHNPPUY UNHAPPY
AHNPRXY PHARYNX
AHOORSY HOORAYS
AHOPRTY ATROPHY
AHOPSTT TOP HATS
AHOPTTW TOWPATH
AHORRSW HARROWS
AHORSTT THROATS
AHORSTU AUTHORS
AHORTTY THROATY
AHOSTUW OUTWASH,
    WASHOUT
AHPRRTY PHRATRY

AHQSSUY SQUASHY
AHRRSUY HURRAYS
AHRSSSU HUSSARS
AHRSTWY SWARTHY
AHRTUWY THRUWAY
AIIILMT MILITIA
AIIILNT INITIAL
AIIJLLN JILLIAN
AIIKLNN KALININ
AIIKMMS SKIMMIA
AIIKMNN MANIKIN
AIIKSTU KUTAISI
AIIKTUW KUWAITI
AIIILLLN LILLIAN
AIIILLLS LILLIAS
AIIILLMN LIMINAL
AIIILLMW WILLIAM
AIIILLNV VILLAIN
AIIILMMN MINIMAL
AIIILMNT INTIMAL
AIIILMRS SIMILAR
AIIILMRY MILIARY
AIIILNNS AISLINN
AIIILNOS LIAISON
AIIILNOV LIVONIA
AIIILNPT PINTAIL
AIIILNRY RAINILY
AIIILNTY ANILITY
AIIILORV RAVIOLI
AIIILOTT OTTILIA
AIIILQSU SILIQUA
AIIILRTV TRIVIAL
AIIMMNS ANIMISM
AIIMMNX MAXIMIN,
    MINIMAX
AIIMNPS PIANISM
AIIMNPT TIMPANI
AIIMNRT MARTINI
AIIMNSS SIMIANS
AIIMNST ANIMIST
AIIMNTV VITAMIN
AIIMSSY MYIASIS
AIINNTY INANITY
AIINPRS ASPIRIN
AIINPST PIANIST
AIINRSS RAISINS
AIINRST ISTRIAN
AIINRSY RAISINY
AIINRTV VITRAIN
AIINSTU TUNISIA
AIIOOTV VOIOTIA
AIIOPRR A PRIORI
AIIORTV VITORIA
AIIPSTW WAPITIS

AIISSVV VIS-À-VIS
AIJJMMS JIMJAMS
AIJLTTU JULITTA
AIJLYZZ JAZZILY
AIJNORT JANITOR
AIJNSTU JUSTINA
AIKLLNY LANKILY
AIKLMMN MILKMAN
AIKLMNN LINKMAN
AIKLNSY SNAKILY
AIKLOST SIALKOT
AIKLPWY PAWKILY
AIKLQUY QUAKILY
AIKLSSY SKYSAIL
AIKMNNS KINSMAN
AIKNNPS NAPKINS
AIKORST TROIKAS
AILLMOP PALM OIL
AILLMPU PALLIUM
AILLMSW SAWMILL
AILLNNO LANOLIN
AILLNNT TALLINN
AILLNOS ALLISON
AILLNPY PLAINLY
AILLNST INSTALL
AILLORZ ZORILLA
AILLPRS PILLARS
AILLPRU PILULAR
AILLPUV PLUVIAL
AILLQSU SQUILLA
AILLSTY SALTILY
AILLTVY VITALLY
AILMMOR IMMORAL
AILMNNO NOMINAL
AILMNOY ALIMONY
AILMNPS PLASMIN
AILMNPT IMPLANT
AILMNRS MARLINS
AILMNRY MARILYN
AILMOOV MOVIOLA
AILMOPT OPTIMAL
AILMOPY OLYMPIA
AILMOST SOMITAL
AILMPRU PRIMULA
AILMPST PALMIST
AILMPSY MISPLAY
AILMRST MISTRAL
AILMRSU SIMULAR
AILMSSS MISSALS
AILNNOT ANTLION
AILNORT ON TRIAL
AILNOUV LOUVAIN
AILNPST PLAINTS
AILNPSX SALPINX

AILNPTU NUPTIAL
AILNPTY INAPTLY,
   PTYALIN
AILNQTU QUINTAL
AILNRSU INSULAR,
   URINALS
AILNSTY NASTILY,
   SAINTLY
AILNTTY NATTILY
AILOPRS POLARIS
AILOPST APOSTIL, TOPSAIL
AILOPSY SOAPILY
AILOPTT TALIPOT
AILOPTV PIVOTAL
AILOQTU ALIQUOT
AILORSS SAILORS
AILORST TAILORS
AILORUX UXORIAL
AILORVY OLIVARY
AILOSSU SAO LUIS
AILPPSY PAYSLIP, SAPPILY
AILPRSS SPIRALS
AILPRSU SPIRULA
AILPSTU PAULIST
AILPSTY PASTILY
AILPSWY SLIPWAY,
   WASPILY
AILQTUY QUALITY
AILRRVY RIVALRY
AILRSTT STARLIT
AILRSTU RITUALS
AILRSTY TRYSAIL
AILRTTU TITULAR
AILRTTY RATTILY
AILRTUV VIRTUAL
AILSTTW SALT WIT
AILSTTY TASTILY
AILSTUV VISTULA
AILSTUW LAWSUIT
AILTTTY TATTILY
AIMMMUX MAXIMUM
AIMMORZ MIZORAM
AIMMOST ATOMISM
AIMMRSX MARXISM
AIMMSUX MAXIMUS
AIMNNOS MANSION
AIMNOPR RAMPION
AIMNOPT MAINTOP
AIMNOTU TINAMOU
AIMNPRU MANIPUR
AIMNRRU MURRAIN
AIMNRST MARTINS
AIMNRSU SURINAM
AIMNRTV VARMINT

AIMNRUU URANIUM
AIMNSTT MATTINS
AIMNSTU TSUNAMI
AIMOPRX PROXIMA
AIMOPST IMPASTO
AIMORST AMORIST
AIMOSST MAOISTS
AIMOSTT ATOMIST
AIMPRRY PRIMARY
AIMPRST ARMPITS
AIMQRSU MARQUIS
AIMRSTX MARXIST
AIMSSTT STATISM
AINNOOT ANTONIO
AINNOOX OXONIAN
AINNOPS SAPONIN
AINNOST NATIONS
AINNQTU QUINTAN
AINNRTU URINANT
AINNSTT INSTANT
AINNTUY ANNUITY
AINOORT ONTARIO,
   ORATION
AINOOTV OVATION
AINOOVV IVANOVO
AINOPPT APPOINT
AINOPSS PASSION
AINOPTU OPUNTIA,
   UTOPIAN
AINORST RATIONS
AINORTU RAINOUT
AINOSTT STATION
AINOSUX ANXIOUS
AINOSVY SYNOVIA
AINPPRS PARSNIP
AINPQTU PIQUANT
AINPRSS SPRAINS
AINPRST SPIRANT
AINPRTU PURITAN
AINQRTU TARQUIN
AINQRUY QUINARY
AINRRTY TRINARY
AINRRUY URINARY
AINRSST STRAINS
AINRSSU RUSSIAN
AINRSTT TRANSIT,
   TRISTAN
AINRSTU NUTRIAS
AINRTTT TITRANT
AINRTUY UNITARY
AINSSTU SUSTAIN
AIOORRS ROSARIO
AIOPRRT AIRPORT
AIOPRTT PATRIOT

AIOPRTY TOPIARY
AIOPRUV PAVIOUR
AIOPSTU UTOPIAS
AIORRRW WARRIOR
AIORRTT TRAITOR
AIORSSV SAVIORS
AIORSTV TRAVOIS
AIORSUV SAVIOUR,
   VARIOUS
AIOSSTT TAOISTS
AIPPSST PAPISTS
AIPRRTU TRIPURA
AIPRSST RAPISTS
AIPRSSU PRUSSIA
AIPRSSW RIPSAWS
AIPZZZZ PIZZAZZ
AIRSSTT ARTISTS, STRAITS,
   TSARIST
AIRSTVY VARSITY
AISSTTT STATIST
AISTTVY VASTITY
AISTUVY SUAVITY
AJLLMOR JAM ROLL
AJLNORU JOURNAL
AJMNRUY JURYMAN
AJNORST TROJANS
AKKLRSY SKYLARK
AKKSTUY YAKUTSK
AKLLNOW KNOW-ALL
AKLMNOO KOLOMNA
AKLNOSW WALK-ONS
AKLNOSX KLAXONS
AKLOPUV VOLAPUK
AKLOTTU OUTTALK
AKLOTUW WALKOUT
AKLPSUW WALK-UPS
AKLRSTY STARKLY
AKLUUWZ KWAZULU
AKMNORU RUN AMOK
AKMNORW WORKMAN
AKMORST OSTMARK
AKMPRSU MARKUPS
AKMQTUU KUMQUAT
AKMRSTU MUSKRAT
AKNORTU OUTRANK
AKOOPRT PARTOOK
AKORRTW ARTWORK
AKORWWX WAXWORK
AKQSSUW SQUAWKS
ALLLOYY LOYALLY
ALLMNOY ALLONYM
ALLMNPU PULLMAN
ALLMORY MALLORY,
   MORALLY

ALLMOSS SLALOMS
ALLMOSW MALLOWS
ALLNOOW WALLOON
ALLNOYZ ZONALLY
ALLNTUU ULULANT
ALLOOTX AXOLOTL
ALLOPRY PAYROLL
ALLOPSW WALLOPS
ALLOPTX POLL TAX
ALLORWY ROLLWAY
ALLORYY ROYALLY
ALLOSSW SALLOWS
ALLOSWW SWALLOW,
 WALLOWS
ALLOTTY TOTALLY
ALLOTYY LOYALTY
ALLPRSU PLURALS
ALLQSSU SQUALLS
ALLQSUY SQUALLY
ALLRSTU LUSTRAL
ALLSUUY USUALLY
ALMNNUY UNMANLY
ALMNOOP LAMPOON
ALMNOPS PLASMON
ALMNORU UNMORAL
ALMNOSS SALMONS
ALMNOSU SOLANUM
ALMNOWY WOMANLY
ALMNPSU SUNLAMP
ALMNSUU ALUMNUS
ALMORRU MORULAR
ALMORST MORTALS
ALMOTTU MULATTO
ALMRSTY SMARTLY
ALMRTUU TUMULAR
ALMSSUY ALYSSUM,
 ASYLUMS
ALMSTUU UMLAUTS
ALNNRSU UNSNARL
ALNNSUU ANNULUS
ALNOOPT PLATOON
ALNOORT ORTOLAN
ALNOOSS SALOONS
ALNOPPY PANOPLY
ALNOPYY POLYNYA
ALNORSY ROSALYN
ALNORUZ ZONULAR
ALNPRSU SNARL-UP
ALNSSTU SULTANS
ALNSTUW WALNUTS
ALNSUUU UNUSUAL
ALOOPRW POOR LAW
ALOPPRS POPLARS
ALOPPRU POPULAR

ALOPRRS PARLORS
ALOPRRU PARLOUR
ALOPRST PATROLS,
 PORTALS
ALOPRSU PARLOUS
ALOPSSU SPOUSAL
ALOPSTT SALTPOT
ALOPTUY OUTPLAY
ALOQRRU RORQUAL
ALOQRSU SQUALOR
ALOQSTU LOQUATS
ALORRST ROSTRAL
ALORTWW AWLWORT
ALORTYY ROYALTY
ALOSTTU OUTLAST
ALOSTUW OUTLAWS
ALOSTUY LAYOUTS,
 OUTLAYS
ALOSTXY OXYSALT
ALPRSSU PULSARS
ALPRSSW SPRAWLS
ALPRSWY SPRAWLY
ALRSTUU SUTURAL
ALRSUUV UVULARS
AMMNRUY NUMMARY
AMMORST MARMOTS
AMMRSUY SUMMARY
AMNNORS NORMANS
AMNNOSW SNOWMAN
AMNNOTY ANTONYM
AMNOOPP POMPANO
AMNOORS MAROONS
AMNOOTT OTTOMAN
AMNOOTY TOO MANY
AMNOPRY PARONYM
AMNOPSS SAMPSON
AMNOPST POSTMAN,
 TAMPONS
AMNOPTU PANTOUM
AMNORSS RAMSONS,
 RANSOMS
AMNORST MATRONS,
 TRANSOM
AMNORSY MASONRY
AMNOSTU AMOUNTS
AMNQTUU QUANTUM
AMNRTTU TANTRUM
AMNSTTU MUTANTS
AMNSTUU AUTUMNS
AMOOORS AMOROSO
AMOOPRT TAPROOM
AMOORSU AMOROUS
AMOPSTT TOPMAST
AMORRST MORTARS

AMORRSW MARROWS
AMORRUY ARMOURY
AMPRSUW WARM-UPS
AMRRSTY MARTYRS
AMRRTYY MARTYRY
AMRSTTU STRATUM
ANNRTYY TYRANNY
ANNSSTU SUNTANS
ANOOPRS SOPRANO
ANOPRRS SPORRAN
ANOPRSS PARSONS
ANOPRST PATRONS
ANORRSW NARROWS
ANORSUU ANUROUS,
 URANOUS
ANPRSTU SUNTRAP,
 UNSTRAP
ANRSSTU SUNSTAR
ANRSTTU TRUANTS
ANRSTTY TYRANTS
ANRSUWY RUNWAYS
AOOPPRS APROPOS,
 SAPPORO
AOOPRTT TAPROOT
AOORRST ORATORS
AOORRTT ROTATOR
AOORRTY ORATORY
AOOSTTT TATTOOS
AOPPRRT RAPPORT
AOPPRTU UP TO PAR
AOPRRST PARROTS
AOPRRSW SPARROW
AOPRRTY PORTRAY
AOPRSST PASTORS
AOPRSTW POSTWAR
AOPRSUV VAPOURS
AOPSTUY AUTOPSY,
 PAYOUTS
AOQRSTU QUARTOS
AOQRTUY TORQUAY
AORSSUY OSSUARY
AORSTTW AT WORST,
 TWO-STAR
AORSUVY SAVOURY
AOSTTUY OUTSTAY
APPRRUU PURPURA
APPRSUY PAPYRUS
APRSSSU SURPASS
APRSTTU UPSTART
APRSTUU UT SUPRA
ARSSTTU STRATUS
BBBDELU BUBBLED
BBBEIOS BOBBIES
BBBELOS BOBBLES

BBBELRU BLUBBER, BUBBLER
BBBELSU BUBBLES
BBBEORY BOBBERY
BBBGINO BOBBING
BBBINOS BOBBINS
BBCCIKO BIBCOCK
BBCDEIR CRIBBED
BBCDELO COBBLED
BBCDELU CLUBBED
BBCELOR CLOBBER, COBBLER
BBCEORS COBBERS
BBCEOSW COBWEBS
BBCGINU CUBBING
BBCINOU BUBONIC
BBCKLOU LUBBOCK
BBCRSUY SCRUBBY
BBDDEIL DIBBLED
BBDEEIT EBB TIDE
BBDEGLO GOBBLED
BBDEGRU GRUBBED
BBDEGSU BEDBUGS
BBDEHLO HOBBLED
BBDEIIM IMBIBED
BBDEILN NIBBLED
BBDEILO LOBBIED
BBDEILR DIBBLER, DRIBBLE
BBDEILS DIBBLES
BBDELMU BUMBLED
BBDELNO NOBBLED
BBDELOS BOBSLED
BBDELOW WOBBLED
BBDELRU BURBLED
BBDENSU SNUBBED
BBDERRU DRUBBER
BBDESTU STUBBED
BBDGIIN DIBBING
BBDGINU DUBBING
BBEEENT ENTEBBE
BBEELPS PEBBLES
BBEESTT BEST BET
BBEESUY BUSY BEE
BBEESYY BYE-BYES
BBEFILR FRIBBLE
BBEFIRS FIBBERS
BBEGILR GLIBBER, GRIBBLE
BBEGINW WEBBING
BBEGIST GIBBETS
BBEGLOR GOBBLER
BBEGLOS GOBBLES
BBEGOST GOBBETS

BBEGRRU GRUBBER
BBEHIOS HOBBIES
BBEHISU HUBBIES
BBEHLOR HOBBLER
BBEIIMR IMBIBER
BBEILNR NIBBLER
BBEILNS NIBBLES
BBEILOS BILBOES, LOBBIES
BBEILOT BIBELOT
BBEILQU QUIBBLE
BBEILRS LIBBERS
BBEIOOS BOOBIES
BBEIRRY BRIBERY
BBEIRTU TUBBIER
BBEISSU BUSBIES
BBEJORS JOBBERS
BBEJORY JOBBERY
BBEKLOS BLESBOK
BBELLOY BELLBOY
BBELMRU BUMBLER
BBELNOR NOBBLER
BBELORS SLOBBER
BBELORW WOBBLER
BBELORY LOBBYER
BBELOSW WOBBLES
BBELRRU BURBLER
BBELSTU STUBBLE
BBEMORS BOMBERS
BBENRSU SNUBBER
BBEORRS ROBBERS
BBEORRY ROBBERY
BBERRSU RUBBERS
BBERRUY RUBBERY
BBFGIIN FIBBING
BBFGINO FOBBING
BBGGIIN GIBBING
BBGIIJN JIBBING
BBGIINR RIBBING
BBGIJNO JOBBING
BBGILNO LOBBING
BBGIMNO BOMBING, MOBBING
BBGINOO BOOBING
BBGINOR ROBBING
BBGINOS GIBBONS, SOBBING
BBGINRU RUBBING
BBGINSU SUBBING
BBGINTU TUBBING
BBGIOSU GIBBOUS
BBHIMOS HOBBISM
BBHIOST HOBBIST
BBHIRSU RUBBISH
BBHRSUY SHRUBBY

BBIKOSS SKIBOBS
BBIKTUZ KIBBUTZ
BBINORS RIBBONS
BBKLNOY KNOBBLY
BBLOSUU BULBOUS
BBLSTUY STUBBLY
BBNNOOS BONBONS
BBNOORU BOURBON
BBOSSUY BUS BOYS
BBRSSUU SUBURBS
BCCEILO ECBOLIC
BCCEILU CUBICLE
BCCEILY BICYCLE
BCCIIMR CIMBRIC
BCCILOU BUCOLIC
BCCINOO OBCONIC
BCCISUU SUCCUBI
BCCMOOX COXCOMB
BCCMSUU SUCCUMB
BCCNOOR CORNCOB
BCDEEHL BELCHED
BCDEEIL DECIBEL
BCDEHIR BIRCHED
BCDEHIT BITCHED
BCDEHNU BUNCHED
BCDEHOT BOTCHED
BCDEHOU DEBOUCH
BCDEIIO BIOCIDE
BCDEIKS SICKBED
BCDEILM CLIMBED
BCDEIOS BODICES
BCDEKLO BLOCKED
BCDEKLU BUCKLED
BCDEKOR BEDROCK
BCDENOU BOUNCED
BCDIIRU RUBIDIC
BCDINOW COWBIND
BCDIORW COWBIRD
BCDKORU BURDOCK
BCDSTUU SUBDUCT
BCEEEHS BEECHES, BESEECH
BCEEELS CELEBES
BCEEGIR ICEBERG
BCEEHIT HEBETIC
BCEEHLS BELCHES
BCEEHNR BENCHER
BCEEHNS BENCHES
BCEEHOU BOUCHEE
BCEEINR BERNICE
BCEEKUY BUCKEYE
BCEENOS OBSCENE
BCEHIOR BRIOCHE
BCEHIRS BIRCHES

BCEHIST BITCHES
BCEHITW BEWITCH
BCEHNSU BUNCHES
BCEHORT BOTCHER
BCEHORW COWHERB
BCEHRSU CHERUBS
BCEHRTU BUTCHER
BCEILMO EMBOLIC
BCEILMR CLIMBER
BCEILOR BRICOLE,
    CORBEIL
BCEIMNO COMBINE
BCEIMOR MICROBE
BCEINOZ BENZOIC
BCEINRU BRUCINE
BCEIRRS SCRIBER
BCEIRSS SCRIBES
BCEJOST OBJECTS
BCEJSTU SUBJECT
BCEKLRU BUCKLER
BCEKLSU BUCKLES
BCEKORT BROCKET
BCEKORU ROEBUCK
BCEKSTU BUCKETS
BCELLOW COWBELL
BCELMRU CRUMBLE
BCELMSU SCUMBLE
BCELORS CORBELS
BCEMORS COMBERS
BCENORU BOUNCER
BCENOSU BOUNCES
BCEOORT OCTOBER
BCEORSU OBSCURE
BCFSSUU SUBFUSC
BCGIKNU BUCKING
BCGIMNO COMBING
BCGINRU CURBING
BCHIKOU CHIBOUK
BCHIMOR RHOMBIC
BCHINOR BRONCHI
BCHIOPR PIBROCH
BCHIOPS PHOBICS
BCHLOTY BLOTCHY
BCHOPTU BOTCH-UP
BCHORST BORSCHT
BCIINOS BIONICS
BCIIOPS BIOPICS
BCIIOPT BIOPTIC
BCIISTU BISCUIT
BCILMPU PLUMBIC
BCILOOR BICOLOR
BCINORU RUBICON
BCINORY BYRONIC
BCINSUU INCUBUS

BCIORST STROBIC
BCIRRSU RUBRICS
BCIRTUY BUTYRIC
BCKLLOU BULLOCK
BCKOTTU BUTTOCK
BCLMOOO COLOMBO
BCLMOOU COULOMB
BCLMRUY CRUMBLY
BCLOOSU COLOBUS
BCMOOTU COMB-OUT
BCMOSTU COMBUST
BCNOORS BRONCOS
BCOOSWY COWBOYS
BCOOTTY BOYCOTT
BDDEEES SEEDBED
BDDEEEW BEDEWED
BDDEEIS BEDSIDE
BDDEEIT BETIDED,
    DEBITED
BDDEELN BLENDED
BDDEFOR BEDFORD
BDDEGIN BEDDING
BDDEILN BLINDED
BDDEISU BUDDIES
BDDELNU BUNDLED
BDDELOO BLOODED
BDDELOU DOUBLED
BDDENOU BOUNDED
BDDEOOR BROODED
BDDEOTU DOUBTED
BDDESUU SUBDUED
BDDGIIN BIDDING
BDDGINU BUDDING
BDDGIOR BIRD DOG
BDEEELP BLEEPED
BDEEELR BLEEDER
BDEEELT BEETLED
BDEEELV BEVELED
BDEEERR BREEDER
BDEEERT RED BEET
BDEEFIR DEBRIEF
BDEEGUY BUG-EYED
BDEEHRT BERTHED
BDEEILL LIBELED
BDEEILV BEDEVIL
BDEEIMT BEDTIME
BDEEINR INBREED
BDEEIRS DERBIES
BDEEISS BESIDES
BDEEKRU REBUKED
BDEELNR BLENDER
BDEELOV BELOVED
BDEELOW ELBOWED
BDEELRT TREBLED

BDEELSS BLESSED
BDEEMSU BEMUSED
BDEENPR PREBEND
BDEEORS BEDSORE,
    SOBERED
BDEEOTW WEB-TOED
BDEERUW BURWEED
BDEFFLU BLUFFED
BDEFLMU FUMBLED
BDEGGLO BOGGLED
BDEGILO OBLIGED
BDEGINN BENDING
BDEGINS BIG ENDS
BDEGIOT BIGOTED
BDEGIRT BRIDGET
BDEGLNU BUNGLED
BDEGLRU BURGLED
BDEGOOY GOODBYE
BDEGSTU BUDGETS
BDEHINS BEHINDS
BDEHLMU HUMBLED
BDEHLSU BLUSHED
BDEHMTU THUMBED
BDEHOST HOTBEDS
BDEHRSU BRUSHED
BDEIIRS BIRDIES
BDEIKLN BLINKED
BDEILLR ILL-BRED
BDEILLU BULLIED
BDEILNR BRINDLE
BDEILOR BROILED
BDEILRT DRIBLET
BDEILRU BUILDER,
    REBUILD
BDEILTZ BLITZED
BDEIMOR BROMIDE
BDEINOU BEDOUIN
BDEINRS BINDERS
BDEINRY BINDERY
BDEINTW TWIN BED
BDEIORS DISROBE
BDEIORT ORBITED
BDEIORV OVERBID
BDEIOSY DISOBEY
BDEIOWY WIDE BOY
BDEIRST BESTRID
BDEIRSU BRUISED
BDEIRTU BRUITED
BDEISSU SUBSIDE
BDEISTU SUBEDIT
BDEITUY DUBIETY
BDEJLMU JUMBLED
BDEKNOO BOOKEND
BDEKOOR BROOKED

BDELMMU MUMBLED
BDELMOO BLOOMED
BDELMPU PLUMBED
BDELMRU RUMBLED
BDELMTU TUMBLED
BDELNOR BLONDER
BDELNOS BLONDES
BDELNOW BLODWEN
BDELNRU BLUNDER,
   BUNDLER
BDELNSU BUNDLES
BDELNTU BLUNTED
BDELORU BOULDER,
   DOUBLER
BDELOST BOLDEST
BDELOSU DOUBLES
BDELOTT BLOTTED,
   BOTTLED
BDELOTU DOUBLET
BDELOUW WOULD-BE
BDELRRU BLURRED
BDELRTU BLURTED
BDELSTU BUSTLED
BDEMOOR BEDROOM,
   BOREDOM
BDEMSTU DUMBEST
BDENNOU BOUNDEN,
   UNBONED
BDENORU BOUNDER,
   REBOUND
BDENORW BROWNED
BDENORY BONE-DRY
BDENORZ BRONZED
BDENOUW UNBOWED
BDENRSU BURDENS
BDENSSU SUNBEDS
BDENSTU SUBTEND
BDEOORR BROODER
BDEOOST BOOSTED
BDEOPST BEDPOST
BDEORRS BORDERS
BDEORRU BORDURE
BDEORST DEBTORS
BDEORSU ROSEBUD
BDEORSW BROWSED
BDEORTU DOUBTER,
   OBTRUDE, REDOUBT
BDFIIOR FIBROID
BDGGINU BUDGING
BDGHIIR BRIGHID
BDGIINN BINDING
BDGIIOO GOBIOID
BDGILOO GLOBOID
BDGINNO BONDING

BDGLLOU BULLDOG
BDHIRSY HYBRIDS
BDHOOOY BOYHOOD
BDIILOR OILBIRD
BDIILOS LIBIDOS
BDIISTT TIDBITS
BDIKNOS BODKINS
BDILLNY BLINDLY
BDILPUU BUILDUP,
   UPBUILD
BDINNOU INBOUND
BDINOOR BRIDOON
BDINOTU IN DOUBT
BDINRSU SUNBIRD
BDINRUU BURUNDI
BDINSTU DUSTBIN
BDIOOOV OBOVOID
BDIOORU BOUDOIR
BDIOSUU DUBIOUS
BDIRSTU DISTURB
BDISSUY SUBSIDY
BDLOOOT OLD BOOT
BDLOOOX OXBLOOD
BDLOOSY OLD BOYS
BDLORWY BLOW-DRY
BDNNOUU UNBOUND
BDNOORU BOURDON
BDNOOWW DOWN-BOW
BDNORUW RUBDOWN
BDOOOWX BOXWOOD
BDORSWY BYWORDS
BEEEFIR BEEFIER, FREEBIE
BEEEFLR FEEBLER
BEEEGIS BESIEGE
BEEEHIV BEEHIVE
BEEEHNS SHEBEEN
BEEEILN BEELINE
BEEEILV BELIEVE
BEEEJLW BEJEWEL
BEEEJLZ JEZEBEL
BEEEKLL BELLEEK
BEEELPR BLEEPER
BEEELPS PEEBLES
BEEELST BEETLES
BEEEMRS BERSEEM
BEEENNZ BENZENE
BEEENRS BERNESE
BEEENTW BETWEEN
BEEFGIN BEEFING
BEEFILR FEBRILE
BEEFILS BELIEFS
BEEFINT BENEFIT
BEEFIRS FRISBEE
BEEFLOR FROEBEL

BEEFLTY BEETFLY
BEEGILL LEGIBLE
BEEGILO OBLIGEE
BEEGILU BEGUILE
BEEGINR BIGENER
BEEGJRS ESBJERG
BEEHLLT BETHELL
BEEHLRT BLETHER
BEEHLST BETHELS
BEEHRRT HERBERT
BEEHRST SHERBET
BEEHRSW HEBREWS
BEEHRTY THEREBY
BEEHRWY WHEREBY
BEEIJLU JUBILEE
BEEILLR LIBELER
BEEILLS BELLIES
BEEILOS OBELISE
BEEILOZ OBELIZE
BEEIMST BETIMES
BEEINNZ BENZINE
BEEINOS EBONISE
BEEINOT EBONITE
BEEINOZ EBONIZE
BEEINRZ ZEBRINE
BEEIQUZ BEZIQUE
BEEIRRS BERRIES
BEEIRRV BREVIER
BEEIRST BISERTE
BEEIRTZ BIZERTE
BEEKNOT BETOKEN
BEEKOPS BESPOKE
BEEKRRS BERSERK
BEEKRRU REBUKER
BEEKRSU REBUKES
BEELMMS EMBLEMS
BEELMRT TREMBLE
BEELMSS BLESS ME!
BEELMWY WEMBLEY
BEELNNO ENNOBLE
BEELNOR BORNEEL
BEELNTY BENTLEY
BEELNUX BENELUX
BEELOTY EYEBOLT
BEELRST TREBLES
BEELRVY BEVERLY
BEEMMRS MEMBERS
BEEMNRU E NUMBER
BEEMRSU BURMESE
BEENNRR BRENNER
BEENNTT BENNETT
BEENORR ENROBER
BEENOST BONESET
BEEOOST BOOTEES

BEEORSV OBSERVE,
  OBVERSE, VERBOSE
BEEORWY EYEBROW
BEEQSTU BEQUEST
BEERRWY BREWERY
BEERSSU REBUSES
BEERSTT BETTERS
BEERSTW BESTREW
BEERTTU BURETTE
BEFFLRU BLUFFER
BEFFOST BEST-OFF
BEFFRSU BUFFERS,
  REBUFFS
BEFFSTU BUFFETS
BEFGIIL FILIBEG
BEFGIRU FIREBUG
BEFILOS FOIBLES
BEFILRT FILBERT
BEFILSU FUSIBLE
BEFINOR BONFIRE
BEFIORX FIREBOX
BEFIRVY VERBIFY
BEFITUX TUBIFEX
BEFLMRU FUMBLER
BEFLMSU FUMBLES
BEFLORT BELFORT
BEFLRTU FULBERT
BEFOORR FORBORE
BEFOOTW WEBFOOT
BEGGGIN BEGGING
BEGGIIS BIGGIES
BEGGIOR BOGGIER
BEGGIST BIGGEST
BEGGISU BUGGIES
BEGGRSU BUGGERS
BEGGRUY BUGGERY
BEGHRRU BURGHER
BEGIIMT BIG TIME
BEGIKNR KERBING
BEGILLY LEGIBLY
BEGILMU BELGIUM
BEGILNO GOBELIN,
  IGNOBLE
BEGILNT BELTING
BEGILNU BLUEING
BEGILNY BELYING
BEGILOR OBLIGER
BEGILRS GERBILS
BEGILRT GILBERT
BEGILRU BULGIER
BEGILST GIBLETS
BEGINOY OBEYING
BEGINRW BREWING
BEGINSS BIGNESS

BEGINST BESTING
BEGINTT BETTING
BEGKMOS GEMSBOK
BEGLLOU GLOBULE
BEGLMRU GRUMBLE
BEGLMUU BLUE GUM
BEGLNRU BLUNGER,
  BUNGLER
BEGLNSU BUNGLES
BEGLOOS GLOBOSE
BEGLOOT BOOTLEG
BEGLOST GOBLETS
BEGLOUY BEYOGLU
BEGLRSU BUGLERS
BEGNOOS BONGOES
BEGNORU BURGEON
BEGNOSY BYGONES
BEGORSU BROGUES
BEGRRSU BURGERS
BEGRSSU BURGESS
BEHIITX EXHIBIT
BEHIKLO HOBLIKE
BEHIKNT BETHINK
BEHILMS BLEMISH
BEHILMT THIMBLE
BEHILOS BOLSHIE
BEHILRT HILBERT
BEHILST LISBETH
BEHILTZ LIZBETH
BEHIMOR BIOHERM
BEHINOP HIPBONE
BEHIOTW HOWBEIT
BEHIRRT REBIRTH
BEHIRSU BUSHIER,
  BUSHIRE
BEHKKOO KOKOBEH
BEHKNOO HOBOKEN
BEHLLOX HELLBOX
BEHLMRU HUMBLER
BEHLORT BROTHEL
BEHLRSU BLUSHER
BEHLSSU BLUSHES,
  BUSHELS
BEHMOTT THE TOMB
BEHMRTU HUMBERT
BEHNOST BENTHOS
BEHNPRU HEPBURN
BEHNRTU BURTHEN
BEHOPRT POTHERB
BEHORRT BROTHER
BEHORTT BETROTH
BEHOSTY THE BOYS
BEHRRSU BRUSHER
BEHRSSU BRUSHES

BEIILLS BILLIES
BEIILRS RISIBLE
BEIILSV VISIBLE
BEIINOT NIOBITE
BEIINST STIBINE
BEIIOTT BIOTITE
BEIIRTT BITTIER
BEIKLNR BLINKER
BEIKLOS OBELISK
BEIKLRU BULKIER
BEIKRRS BRISKER
BEIKRST BRISKET
BEIKSTV VITEBSK
BEILLST BILLETS
BEILLSU BULLIES
BEILMNR NIMBLER
BEILMOR EMBROIL
BEILMOS MOBILES
BEILMRT TIMBREL
BEILMRU UMBRIEL
BEILMSU SUBLIME
BEILNOW BOWLINE
BEILNSY BY-LINES
BEILOPY EPIBOLY
BEILOQU OBLIQUE
BEILORR BROILER
BEILORS BOILERS
BEILORW BLOWIER
BEILRRU BURLIER
BEILRST BLISTER, BRISTLE
BEILRTT BRITTLE
BEILRTU REBUILT
BEILRTW WILBERT
BEILRTY LIBERTY
BEILSTW BLEWITS
BEILSTZ BLITZES
BEILTTU BLUETIT
BEIMMRR BRIMMER
BEIMNOR BROMINE
BEIMNTU BITUMEN
BEIMOSV B-MOVIES
BEIMOSZ ZOMBIES
BEIMPRU BUMPIER
BEIMRST TIMBERS,
  TIMBRES
BEIMRTU IMBRUTE,
  TERBIUM
BEINNOR BONNIER
BEINNOZ BENZOIN
BEINNSU BUNNIES
BEINOOT EOBIONT
BEINORT BORNITE
BEINORW BROWNIE
BEINOST BONIEST

BEINRSU SUBERIN
BEINRTT BITTERN
BEINRTU TRIBUNE,
TURBINE
BEIOOPT BIOTOPE
BEIOORZ BOOZIER
BEIOPTY BIOTYPE
BEIORSS BOSSIER
BEIOSTW BOW TIES
BEIOSTY OBESITY
BEIRRSU BRUISER
BEIRSSU BRUISES
BEIRSTT BITTERS
BEIRSTU BUSTIER
BEIRTTU TRIBUTE
BEIRTVY BREVITY
BEISSTU BUSIEST
BEISTTU BUTTIES
BEITTWX BETWIXT
BEJJSUU JUJUBES
BEJKOUX JUKEBOX
BEJLMRU JUMBLER
BEJLMSU JUMBLES
BEJLOSS JOBLESS
BEKLNOZ KOBLENZ
BEKLOOT BOOKLET
BEKLSUY BLUE-SKY, SKY-
BLUE
BEKNORS BONKERS
BEKNRSU BUNKERS
BEKORRS BROKERS
BEKRSSU BUSKERS
BELLOSU SOLUBLE
BELLOSW BELLOWS
BELLOUV VOLUBLE
BELLSTU BULLETS
BELMMRU MUMBLER
BELMNOU NELUMBO
BELMOOR BLOOMER
BELMOPR PROBLEM
BELMOSU EMBOLUS
BELMPRU PLUMBER
BELMRRU RUMBLER
BELMRSU RUMBLES,
SLUMBER
BELMRTU TUMBLER,
TUMBREL
BELMRTY TREMBLY
BELMSTU STUMBLE,
TUMBLES
BELNOOY BOLONEY
BELNOST NOBLEST
BELNOYZ BENZOYL
BELNSTU SUNBELT

BELOOPR BLOOPER
BELOORS BOLEROS
BELOOVY BYELOVO
BELORST BOLSTER,
LOBSTER
BELORSU ROUBLES
BELORSW BLOWERS,
BOWLERS
BELORSY SOBERLY
BELORTT BLOTTER
BELORTU TROUBLE
BELOSSU BLOUSES
BELOSTT BOTTLES
BELOSTU BOLETUS
BELRSTU BLUSTER,
BUSTLER, BUTLERS,
SUBTLER
BELRTUY BUTLERY
BELSSTU BUSTLES
BEMNRSU NUMBERS
BEMORST MOBSTER
BEMORSY EMBRYOS
BEMPRSU BUMPERS
BEMSSUU SUBSUME
BENNORW BRONWEN,
NEWBORN
BENNOST BONNETS
BENOORS OSBORNE
BENORRT NORBERT
BENORRW BROWNER
BENORSZ BRONZES
BENORTY RENT BOY
BENOSSU BONUSES
BENRRSU BURNERS
BEOOPSX PO BOXES
BEOOPUZ BOOZE-UP
BEOORSS SORBOSE
BEOORST BOOSTER
BEOORSZ BOOZERS
BEOPRRV PROVERB
BEOQTUU BOUQUET
BEORRSW BROWSER
BEORSST SORBETS
BEPRRTU PERTURB
BEPRTUY PUBERTY
BEPSTUY SUBTYPE
BEQRSUU BRUSQUE
BERRSTU BURSTER
BERSSTU BUSTERS
BERSTTY BETTRYS
BERSTUV SUBVERT
BERSUZZ BUZZERS
BERTTUY BUTTERY
BESSSTU SUBSETS

BFFGIIN BIFFING
BFFGINU BUFFING
BFFINOS BOFFINS
BFFLLUY BLUFFLY
BFFNOOU BUFFOON
BFGIORT FROG-BIT
BFHIRSU FURBISH
BFIINOR FIBROIN
BFILMRU BRIMFUL
BFIORSU FIBROUS
BFKLOOY FLYBOOK
BFLLOWY BLOWFLY,
FLYBLOW
BFOOOTY FOOTBOY
BGGGINO BOGGING
BGGGINU BUGGING
BGGIISW BIGWIGS
BGGILNU BULGING
BGGINNU BUNGING
BGHHIOY HIGHBOY
BGHILST BLIGHTS
BGHINOR BIGHORN
BGHINSU BUSHING
BGHINTY BY NIGHT
BGHIOST BIG SHOT
BGHIPSU BUSHPIG
BGHMORU HOMBURG
BGHMSUU HUMBUGS
BGHOOOS OSHOGBO
BGHOORU BOROUGH
BGIIKLN BILKING
BGIILLN BILLING
BGIILNO BOILING
BGIILNS SIBLING
BGIIMNU IMBUING
BGIINNN BINNING
BGIJNOY BY JINGO
BGIKLNU BULKING
BGIKNNU BUNKING
BGIKNOO BOOKING
BGIKNSU BUSKING
BGILMOU GUMBOIL
BGILMRU LIMBURG
BGILNOS GOBLINS
BGILNOT BILTONG,
BOLTING
BGILNOW BLOWING,
BOWLING
BGILNOY IGNOBLY
BGILOOR OBLIGOR
BGILOOY BIOLOGY
BGILRTU TILBURG
BGIMMNU BUMMING
BGIMNNU NUMBING

BGIMNOO BOOMING
BGIMNPU BUMPING
BGINNRU BURNING
BGINNTU BUNTING
BGINOOT BOOTING
BGINOOZ BOOZING
BGINOPP BOPPING
BGINOPR PROBING
BGINOSS BOSSING
BGINOUY BUOYING
BGINPRU BURPING
BGINRRU BURRING
BGINRUY BURYING
BGINSSU BUSSING
BGINSTU BUSTING
BGINSUY BUSYING
BGINTTU BUTTING
BGINUZZ BUZZING
BGIOPST BIG TOPS
BGIORTY BIGOTRY
BGJOTUY TOBY JUG
BGKLOOO LOGBOOK
BGLNOOS OBLONGS
BGLNOOW LONGBOW
BGLOSSU BUGLOSS
BGMOOTU GUMBOOT
BHIIINT INHIBIT
BHIIRST BRITISH
BHIKOOS BOOKISH
BHILLSU BULLISH
BHILOTU HOLIBUT
BHILPSU PUBLISH
BHIMOOS HOBOISM
BHIMOPR BIMORPH
BHIMSTU BISMUTH
BHINRSU BURNISH
BHIOORS BOORISH
BHIOPSS BISHOPS
BHIRSTU BRUTISH
BHISTTU BUSHTIT
BHLOOPT BOTOLPH
BHLRSUU BULRUSH
BHMORSU RHOMBUS
BHOOSTW BOWSHOT
BHPRSUU BRUSH-UP
BIIIKNS BIKINIS
BIIILTZ TBILIZI
BIILLNO BILLION
BIILNTU BUILT-IN
BIILOSU BILIOUS
BIILRSY RISIBLY
BIILSVY VISIBLY
BIIMNOU NIOBIUM
BIIMNSU MINIBUS

BIISTTT TITBITS
BIJNOSU SUBJOIN
BIKLLUY BULKILY
BIKLRSY BRISKLY
BIKMNPU BUMPKIN
BIKNRSY RYBINSK
BILLNOU BULLION
BILLOPX PILLBOX
BILLOSW BILLOWS
BILLOWY BILLOWY
BILLRWY WRYBILL
BILMNOO IN BLOOM
BILMNOR NOMBRIL
BILMNRU MILBURN
BILMPUY BUMPILY
BILNOTU BOTULIN
BILOOYZ BOOZILY
BILOSSU SUBSOIL
BILOSSY BOSSILY
BILPTUU BUILT-UP
BILRSTY BRISTLY
BIMMORS BROMISM
BIMNOSU OMNIBUS
BINNOSU BUNIONS
BINOOSU NIOBOUS
BINORST BRITONS
BINRTUY BUTYRIN
BIOORSZ BORZOIS
BIOOSST OBOISTS
BIOOSUV OBVIOUS
BIOPRTY PROBITY
BIORRTU BURRITO
BIORRTW RIBWORT
BIORSST BISTROS
BIORSTT BISTORT
BIORSUU RUBIOUS
BISSSTU SUBSIST
BJLOOST JOB LOTS
BJNOORU BONJOUR
BJORUXY JURY BOX
BKNOOTW BOWKNOT
BKNPSUU BUNK-UPS
BKOORWX WORKBOX
BLLNTUY BLUNTLY
BLLOUVY VOLUBLY
BLMOOOT TOMBOLO
BLMOOSS BLOSSOM
BLMOSSY SYMBOLS
BLNOORW LOWBORN
BLOOQUY OBLOQUY
BLOORWW LOWBROW
BLOOTUW BLOWOUT
BLOPSTU SUBPLOT
BLOPSUW BLOW-UPS

BMNOOSU UNBOSOM
BMOOORX BOXROOM
BMOOSTT BOTTOMS
BMOOSTY TOMBOYS
BMORSUU BRUMOUS
BNNORWY BRONWYN
BNNRSUU SUNBURN
BNORSTU BURTONS
BNORSUU BURNOUS
BNORTUU BURNOUT
BNOSTTU BUTTONS
BOOPRTT BOTTROP
BOOPSTX POSTBOX
BOPSSTU BUS STOP
BORRSUW BURROWS
BORSTTU TURBOTS
BOSTUUY BUYOUTS
BPSSTUU BUST-UPS
CCCDIOO COCCOID
CCCEHIO CHOC-ICE
CCCNOOT CONCOCT
CCCOOSU COCCOUS
CCDEEHK CHECKED
CCDEENO CONCEDE
CCDEENY DECENCY
CCDEEOR COERCED
CCDEESU SUCCEED
CCDEHIL CLICHÉD
CCDEHKO CHOCKED
CCDEHKU CHUCKED
CCDEHOU COUCHED
CCDEHRY CEDRYCH
CCDEIIL ICICLED
CCDEIIT DEICTIC
CCDEIKL CLICKED
CCDEIKR CRICKED
CCDEILO ICE-COLD
CCDEILR CIRCLED
CCDEIMO COMEDIC
CCDEIOS CODICES
CCDEKLO CLOCKED
CCDEKLU CLUCKED
CCDELOU OCCLUDE
CCDENOU CONDUCE
CCDHIIL CICHLID
CCDIILO CODICIL
CCDIILU CULICID
CCDIIOR CRICOID
CCDILOY CYCLOID
CCDKLOU CUCKOLD
CCDNOOR CONCORD
CCDNOTU CONDUCT
CCEEHHN CHECHEN
CCEEHOR ECORCHE

CCEEHRS CRECHES,
SCREECH
CCEEIIL CECILIE
CCEEILN LICENCE
CCEEINR ECCRINE
CCEEINS SCIENCE
CCEEIRV CREVICE
CCEELRU LUCRECE
CCEELRY RECYCLE
CCEERSY SECRECY
CCEFNOT CONFECT
CCEGNOY COGENCY
CCEHIKN CHECK-IN,
CHICKEN
CCEHILS CLICHÉS
CCEHINT TECHNIC
CCEHIOR CHOICER
CCEHIOS CHOICES
CCEHKLU CHUCKLE
CCEHKPU CHECKUP
CCEHLOS CLOCHES
CCEHNOS CONCHES
CCEHORT CROCHET
CCEHOSU COUCHES
CCEIIKP ICE PICK
CCEIILS ICICLES
CCEIIRT ICTERIC
CCEIKLR CLICKER
CCEIKOR COCKIER
CCEIKRT CRICKET
CCEILRR CIRCLER
CCEILRS CIRCLES, CLERICS
CCEILRT CIRCLET
CCEILTU CUTICLE
CCEIMST SMECTIC
CCEINOR CORNICE,
CROCEIN
CCEINOS CONCISE
CCEINOT CONCEIT
CCEINRT CENTRIC
CCEIOPP COPPICE
CCEIOPT ECTOPIC
CCEIORT ORECTIC
CCEIPST SCEPTIC
CCEKLOS COCKLES
CCEKNOY COCKNEY
CCEKOPT PETCOCK
CCEKORT CROCKET
CCELLOT COLLECT
CCELNOY CYCLONE
CCEMNOO COMECON
CCENNOR CONCERN
CCENNOT CONNECT
CCENOPT CONCEPT

CCENORT CONCERT
CCENOSS SCONCES
CCEOOTT COCOTTE
CCEORRT CORRECT
CCERTUW CREW CUT
CCESSSU SUCCESS
CCFIRUY CRUCIFY
CCFLOSU FLOCCUS
CCGHINO GNOCCHI
CCGIKNO COCKING
CCGILNY CYCLING
CCHHIKU CHUKCHI
CCHIIST STICHIC
CCHILOR CHLORIC
CCHIMOR CHROMIC
CCHINOR CHRONIC
CCHIORY CHICORY
CCHIPSU HICCUPS
CCHIPSY PSYCHIC
CCHKMSU SCHMUCK
CCHNRSU SCRUNCH
CCHNRUY CRUNCHY
CCIILS SILICIC
CCIILNS CLINICS
CCIILOT COLITIC
CCIINPS PICNICS
CCIIRST CRITICS
CCIIRTU CIRCUIT
CCIKLOW COWLICK
CCIKLOY COLICKY
CCIKOPT COCKPIT
CCILNOO COLONIC
CCILNOU COUNCIL
CCILOOP PICCOLO
CCILSTY CYCLIST
CCIMOTY MYCOTIC
CCINOTV CONVICT
CCIOORS SIROCCO
CCIOPTU OCCIPUT
CCIPRTY CRYPTIC
CCKOOSU CUCKOOS
CCKOPSU COCK-UPS
CCLOPSY CYCLOPS
CCMOOOR MOROCCO
CCNOOOS COCOONS
CCNOOPU PUCCOON
CCNOOTU COCONUT
CCNOSSU CONCUSS
CCORSUU SUCCOUR
CCSSSUU SUCCUSS
CDDDEEI DECIDED
CDDDEEO DECODED
CDDDEEU DEDUCED
CDDDELO CODDLED

CDDDELU CUDDLED
CDDDESU SCUDDED
CDDEEER DECREED,
RECEDED
CDDEEES SECEDED
CDDEEII DEICIDE
CDDEEIR DECIDER,
DECRIED
CDDEENO ENCODED
CDDEENS DESCEND
CDDEEOY DECOYED
CDDEERU REDUCED
CDDEESU SEDUCED
CDDEEUW CUDWEED
CDDEHIN CHIDDEN
CDDEHIT DITCHED
CDDEILM MIDDLE C
CDDEINU INDUCED
CDDELOS SCOLDED
CDDELOU CLOUDED
CDDELRU CURDLED
CDDEORW CROWDED
CDDIIOS DISCOID
CDDIIOY DIDICOY
CDDIIRU DRUIDIC
CDDIKOP PIDDOCK
CDDIORS DISCORD
CDDKORY DRY DOCK
CDEEEFL FLEECED
CDEEEFN DEFENCE
CDEEEHK CHEEKED
CDEEEHP CHEEPED
CDEEEHR CHEERED
CDEEEIV DECEIVE
CDEEEJT EJECTED
CDEEELT ELECTED
CDEEEPR PRECEDE
CDEEERR DECREER
CDEEERS DECREES,
SECEDER
CDEEERT ERECTED
CDEEFHT FETCHED
CDEEFII EDIFICE
CDEEFKL FLECKED
CDEEFLT DEFLECT
CDEEFOR DEFORCE
CDEEFST DEFECTS
CDEEHIS DEHISCE
CDEEHKL HECKLED
CDEEHLW WELCHED
CDEEHMS SCHEMED
CDEEHNW WENCHED
CDEEHOR COHERED
CDEEHPR PERCHED

CDEEHRT RETCHED
CDEEHST CHESTED
CDEEIIT EIDETIC
CDEEILN DECLINE
CDEEILP PEDICEL, PEDICLE
CDEEIMN ENDEMIC
CDEEINO CODEINE
CDEEINT ENTICED
CDEEINV EVINCED
CDEEIOS DIOCESE
CDEEIOV DEVOICE
CDEEIPR PIERCED
CDEEIRR DECRIER
CDEEIRT RECITED
CDEEISV DEVICES
CDEEISX EXCISED
CDEEITV EVICTED
CDEEITX EXCITED
CDEEKLR CLERKED
CDEEKNR REDNECK
CDEEKNV V-NECKED
CDEEKRW WRECKED
CDEELPU DECUPLE
CDEELSU SECLUDE
CDEELUX EXCLUDE
CDEENOR ENCODER
CDEENOZ COZENED
CDEENRT CENTRED,
CREDENT, RED CENT
CDEENST DESCENT,
SCENTED
CDEEOPR PROCEED
CDEEORV COVERED
CDEEORW COWERED
CDEEORY DECOYER
CDEEOST CESTODE
CDEEOTV COVETED
CDEERRU REDUCER
CDEERSS SCREEDS
CDEERST CRESTED
CDEERSU RESCUED,
SECURED, SEDUCER
CDEERSW SCREWED
CDEESUX EXCUSED
CDEFFHU CHUFFED
CDEFFOS SCOFFED
CDEFFSU SCUFFED
CDEFHIL FILCHED
CDEFIIT DEFICIT
CDEFIKL FLICKED
CDEFINO CONFIDE
CDEFIRR FREDRIC
CDEFKLO FLOCKED
CDEFKOR DEFROCK

CDEFNTU DEFUNCT
CDEFOSU FOCUSED
CDEGGHU CHUGGED
CDEGGLO CLOGGED
CDEGHOU COUGHED
CDEGIIN DE-ICING
CDEGIKN DECKING
CDEGINR CRINGED
CDEGLSU CUDGELS
CDEGORS CODGERS
CDEHHIT HITCHED
CDEHHNU HUNCHED
CDEHIIV CHIVIED
CDEHIKN CHINKED
CDEHILL CHILLED
CDEHILP DELPHIC
CDEHINO HEDONIC
CDEHINP PINCHED
CDEHINW WINCHED
CDEHIOW COWHIDE
CDEHIPP CHIPPED
CDEHIPR CHIRPED
CDEHIPT PITCHED
CDEHIRT DITCHER
CDEHIST DITCHES
CDEHISU DUCHIES
CDEHKOS SHOCKED
CDEHKSU SHUCKED
CDEHKUY HEYDUCK
CDEHLMU MULCHED
CDEHLNU LUNCHED
CDEHLNY LYNCHED
CDEHLOT CLOTHED
CDEHLRU LURCHED
CDEHMMU CHUMMED
CDEHMNU MUNCHED
CDEHMOO MOOCHED
CDEHMOP CHOMPED
CDEHNOT NOTCHED
CDEHNPU PUNCHED
CDEHNRU CHURNED
CDEHOPP CHOPPED
CDEHOPU POUCHED
CDEHORW CHOWDER,
COWHERD
CDEHOSU DOUCHES
CDEHOSW COWSHED
CDEHOTU TOUCHED
CDEHOUV VOUCHED
CDEHPSY PSYCHED
CDEHRSU CRUSHED
CDEHSSU DUCHESS
CDEHSTY SCYTHED
CDEIIKR DICKIER

CDEIIKS DICKIES
CDEIINR DINERIC
CDEIINS INCISED
CDEIINT IDENTIC, INCITED
CDEIIST DEISTIC, DICIEST
CDEIISU SUICIDE
CDEIJST DISJECT
CDEIKLN CLINKED
CDEIKLP PICKLED
CDEIKLS SLICKED
CDEIKLT TICKLED
CDEIKNS DICKENS,
SNICKED
CDEIKPR PRICKED
CDEIKRR DERRICK
CDEIKRT TRICKED
CDEIKSU DUCKIES
CDEILLO COLLIDE
CDEILMO MELODIC
CDEILNU INCLUDE,
NUCLIDE
CDEILOP POLICED
CDEILPP CLIPPED
CDEILPS SPLICED
CDEILPU CLUPEID
CDEILSU SLUICED
CDEILTU DUCTILE
CDEIMNO DEMONIC
CDEIMOR DORMICE
CDEIMOS MEDICOS
CDEIMOT DEMOTIC
CDEIMPR CRIMPED
CDEIMSU DECIMUS
CDEINOT CTENOID,
DEONTIC, D-NOTICE,
NOTICED
CDEINRS CINDERS,
DISCERN, RESCIND
CDEINRU INDUCER
CDEINRY CINDERY
CDEINSX EXSCIND
CDEIOPR PERCOID
CDEIOPZ ZIP CODE
CDEIORT CORDITE
CDEIORV DIVORCE
CDEIOST CESTOID
CDEIPRS CRISPED
CDEIPRT PREDICT
CDEIRRU CURRIED
CDEIRST CREDITS
CDEIRSU CRUISED
CDEIRTV VERDICT
CDEISST DISSECT
CDEISSY ECDYSIS

CDEKKNO KNOCKED
CDEKLOW WEDLOCK
CDEKLPU PLUCKED
CDEKLSU SUCKLED
CDEKOOR CROOKED
CDEKORS DOCKERS
CDEKOST DOCKETS,
STOCKED
CDEKRTU TRUCKED
CDELLOU COLLUDE
CDELLSU SCULLED
CDELMPU CLUMPED
CDELMSU MUSCLED
CDELMTU MULCTED
CDELNOO CONDOLE
CDELNOW CLOWNED
CDELNOY CONDYLE
CDELNWY CLEDWYN
CDELOOR COLORED,
DECOLOR
CDELOPP CLOPPED
CDELOPU COUPLED
CDELORS SCOLDER
CDELOST COLDEST
CDELOSW SCOWLED
CDELOTT CLOTTED
CDELOTU CLOUTED
CDELRUY CRUDELY
CDEMMNO COMMEND
CDEMMOO COMMODE
CDEMNNO CONDEMN
CDEMORU DECORUM
CDENNOO CONDONE
CDENNOT CONTEND
CDENOOR CROONED
CDENOOS SECONDO
CDENOPU POUNCED
CDENORS SCORNED
CDENORU CRUNODE
CDENORW CROWNED
CDENOSS SECONDS
CDENOTU COUNTED
CDEOOPP COPEPOD
CDEOOPS SCOOPED
CDEOOPT CO-OPTED
CDEOORR CORRODE
CDEOORT COTE-D'OR
CDEOOST SCOOTED
CDEOPPR CROPPED
CDEOPRU PRODUCE
CDEORRS RECORDS
CDEORSS CROSSED
CDEORSU COURSED,
SCOURED

CDEORTU COURTED
CDEOSTU SCOUTED
CDEPRSU SPRUCED
CDERSTU CRUDEST
CDFHIOS CODFISH
CDFIILU FLUIDIC
CDGHIIN CHIDING
CDGIKNO DOCKING
CDGIKNU DUCKING
CDGILNO CODLING,
LINGCOD
CDGINNO CONDIGN
CDGINOR CORDING
CDHIIST DISTICH
CDHILOS COLDISH
CDHIOOR CHOROID,
OCHROID
CDHIORS ORCHIDS
CDHIPTY DIPTYCH
CDHMORU MURDOCH
CDIIIOT IDIOTIC
CDIILLY IDYLLIC
CDIILNY DICLINY
CDIIMNO DOMINIC
CDIINOR CRINOID
CDIINOT DICTION
CDIINOV VIDICON
CDIIORS CIRSOID
CDIIOSS CISSOID
CDIIOSV VISCOID
CDIKLNO OLD NICK
CDIKNOR DORNICK
CDILLOO COLLOID
CDILLUY LUCIDLY
CDILOUV LUDOVIC
CDIMMOU MODICUM
CDIMOOS COSMOID
CDIMSTU DICTUMS
CDINOSY SYNODIC
CDINOTU CONDUIT,
NOCTUID
CDIOPRR RIPCORD
CDIOSTY CYSTOID
CDIOTUV OVIDUCT
CDIRSUY DYSURIC
CDIRTUY CRUDITY
CDISSSU DISCUSS
CDLNOTU COULDN'T
CDLOOPY LYCOPOD
CDLOSTU COULDST
CDMNOOS CONDOMS,
MOD CONS
CDNOORS CONDORS,
CORDONS

CDOOOPT OCTOPOD
CDOORST DOCTORS
CDOOTUW WOODCUT
CDOPRTU PRODUCT
CDOSTUY CUSTODY
CEEEFLS FLEECES
CEEEHLS LEECHES
CEEEHPR CHEEPER
CEEEHSS CHEESES
CEEEINP EPICENE
CEEEIRV RECEIVE
CEEEKNW EWE-NECK
CEEELRT RE-ELECT
CEEELST CELESTE
CEEENNO NEOCENE
CEEENRT TERENCE
CEEENSS ESSENCE
CEEEPRR CREEPER
CEEERRT ERECTER
CEEERST SECRETE
CEEERTX EXCRETE
CEEETUX EXECUTE
CEEFFNO OFFENCE
CEEFFST EFFECTS
CEEFHRT FETCHER
CEEFIRR FIERCER
CEEFKLR FRECKLE
CEEFLRT REFLECT
CEEFNOR ENFORCE
CEEFNRS FENCERS
CEEFPRT PERFECT,
PREFECT
CEEGINR GENERIC
CEEGINT GENETIC
CEEGINU EUGENIC
CEEGKOS GECKOES
CEEGLLO COLLEGE
CEEGLNT NEGLECT
CEEGLOU ECLOGUE
CEEGNRY REGENCY
CEEGORT CORTEGE
CEEHILM MICHELE
CEEHILS HELICES
CEEHILV VEHICLE
CEEHIMR CHIMERE
CEEHIMS CHEMISE
CEEHINS CHINESE
CEEHIOR CHEERIO
CEEHIRT ETHERIC,
HERETIC
CEEHIRW CHEWIER
CEEHKLR HECKLER
CEEHKNP HENPECK
CEEHKST KETCHES

CEEHLNO ECHELON
CEEHLRS LECHERS
CEEHLRY LECHERY
CEEHLSY LYCHEES
CEEHMRS SCHEMER
CEEHMSS SCHEMES
CEEHNRW WENCHER
CEEHNST TENCHES
CEEHNSW WENCHES
CEEHOPS EPOCHES
CEEHORT TROCHEE
CEEHPRR PERCHER
CEEHPRS PERCHES
CEEHPSU CEPHEUS
CEEHQRU CHEQUER
CEEHQSU CHEQUES
CEEHRST CHESTER,
    ETCHERS
CEEHSTV VETCHES
CEEIIPR EPEIRIC
CEEIJOR REJOICE
CEEIKNT NECKTIE
CEEILLM MICELLE
CEEILNR RECLINE
CEEILNS LICENSE,
    SELENIC, SILENCE
CEEILNU LEUCINE
CEEILPS ECLIPSE
CEEILRT RETICLE
CEEILST SECTILE
CEEILSV VESICLE
CEEILTT LETTICE
CEEILTU LEUCITE
CEEIMNO MIOCENE
CEEIMNT CENTIME
CEEIMRS MERCIES
CEEIMST EMETICS
CEEINNS INCENSE
CEEINNW CEINWEN
CEEINRS SINCERE
CEEINRT ENTERIC,
    ENTICER
CEEINRV CERVINE
CEEIOPT PICOTEE
CEEIORT COTERIE
CEEIORV REVOICE
CEEIPRR PIERCER
CEEIPRS PRECISE, RECIPES
CEEIPRT RECEIPT
CEEIPRU EPICURE
CEEIPSS SPECIES
CEEIPST PECTISE
CEEIPTZ PECTIZE
CEEIRRT RECITER

CEEIRSV SERVICE
CEEIRTX EXCITER
CEEJORT EJECTOR
CEEJRST REJECTS
CEEKLNT NECKLET
CEEKLPS SPECKLE
CEEKOSY SOCKEYE
CEEKPRS PECKERS
CEEKRRW WRECKER
CEELLLU CELLULE
CEELLNO COLLEEN
CEELMNT CLEMENT
CEELMOW WELCOME
CEELNOS ENCLOSE
CEELNRT LECTERN
CEELNRU LUCERNE
CEELORS CREOLES
CEELORT ELECTOR
CEELOTT COLETTE
CEELRSU RECLUSE
CEELRTU LECTURE
CEELRTY ERECTLY
CEELTTU LETTUCE,
    LUCETTE
CEEMNRU CERUMEN
CEEMOPR COMPEER,
    COMPERE
CEEMOPT COMPETE
CEENNOU ENOUNCE
CEENNOV CONVENE
CEENNRT CENTNER
CEENOOT ECOTONE
CEENORS ENCORES,
    NECROSE
CEENORZ COZENER
CEENPRS SPENCER
CEENPRT PER CENT
CEENRSS SCREENS
CEENRST CENTERS,
    CENTRES
CEENRSU CENSURE
CEENRSY SCENERY
CEEOPTY ECOTYPE
CEEORRT ERECTOR
CEEORRV COVERER,
    RECOVER
CEEORRZ CORREZE
CEEORTV COVETER
CEEPPRT PERCEPT,
    PRECEPT
CEEPPRU PREPUCE
CEEPRSS PRECESS
CEEPRST RESPECT,
    SCEPTRE, SPECTRE

CEEPRTX EXCERPT
CEERRSU RESCUER,
    SECURER
CEERRSW SCREWER
CEERRUV RECURVE
CEERSST CRESSET,
    SECRETS
CEERSSU RESCUES
CEESSUX EXCUSES
CEFFIOR OFFICER
CEFFIOS OFFICES
CEFFISU SUFFICE
CEFFLSU SCUFFLE
CEFFORS COFFERS,
    SCOFFER
CEFGINN FENCING
CEFHILR FILCHER
CEFHILY CHIEFLY
CEFHINS FINCHES
CEFIILT FICTILE
CEFIIOR ORIFICE
CEFIKLR FLICKER
CEFILNT INFLECT
CEFILNU FUNICLE
CEFILOR LEOFRIC
CEFILRU LUCIFER
CEFIMOR COMFIER
CEFINNO CONFINE
CEFINOR CONIFER
CEFINTU FINE-CUT
CEFIPSY SPECIFY
CEFIRTY CERTIFY, RECTIFY
CEFKLOT FETLOCK
CEFKRSU FUCKERS
CEFLNOU FLOUNCE
CEFLNUY FLUENCY
CEFLOSS FO'C'SLES
CEFMORY COMFREY
CEFNOSS CONFESS
CEFNOSU CONFUSE
CEFNOTU CONFUTE
CEFOPRS FORCEPS
CEFORRT CROFTER
CEFORSS FRESCOS
CEFORSU FOCUSER
CEFOSSU FOCUSES
CEFRSUW CURFEWS
CEGGHIR CHIGGER
CEGGIOR GEORGIC
CEGGPSU EGGCUPS
CEGHINO ECHOING
CEGHINT ETCHING
CEGHINW CHEWING
CEGHLSU GULCHES

CEGHNTU CHENGTU
CEGIILN CEILING
CEGIILW GLIWICE
CEGIINP PIECING
CEGIKNN NECKING
CEGIKNP PECKING
CEGIKNR RECKING
CEGILNR CLINGER,
   CRINGLE
CEGILNY GLYCINE
CEGINOS COGNISE
CEGINOZ COGNIZE
CEGINRW CREWING
CEGLNOO COLOGNE
CEGLOOY ECOLOGY
CEGLOSU GLUCOSE
CEGNORY CRYOGEN
CEGNOST CONGEST
CEGNRUY URGENCY
CEGNSTY CYGNETS
CEGOORS SCROOGE
CEGOOTY CETOOGY
CEGORRS GROCERS
CEGORRY GROCERY
CEGORSU SCOURGE
CEHHIRS CHERISH
CEHHIRT HITCHER
CEHHIST HITCHES
CEHHITU HUTCHIE
CEHHNSU HUNCHES
CEHHSTU HUTCHES
CEHIILS CHILIES
CEHIINR HIRCINE
CEHIINT ICHNITE
CEHIIRT ITCHIER
CEHIJOR JERICHO
CEHIKNT KITCHEN,
   THICKEN
CEHIKPS PECKISH
CEHIKRR HERRICK
CEHIKRT THICKER
CEHIKRW WHICKER
CEHIKTT THICKET
CEHILNO CHOLINE,
   HELICON
CEHILRV CHERVIL
CEHILSS CHISELS
CEHILTY ETHYLIC,
   TECHILY
CEHIMNY CHIMNEY
CEHIMOR HOMERIC
CEHIMOS ECHOISM
CEHIMRT THERMIC
CEHIMRU RHEUMIC

CEHIMST CHEMIST
CEHINOP PHOCINE
CEHINPR PHRENIC
CEHINPS PINCHES,
   SPHENIC
CEHINRW WINCHER
CEHINST STHENIC
CEHINSU ECHINUS
CEHINSW WINCHES
CEHIOPS HOSPICE
CEHIOPT POTICHE
CEHIORS HEROICS
CEHIOTV CHEVIOT
CEHIPPR CHIPPER
CEHIPRR CHIRPER
CEHIPRS CIPHERS
CEHIPRT PITCHER
CEHIPST PITCHES
CEHIQSU QUICHES
CEHIRST RICHEST
CEHIRSU CUSHIER
CEHISTW WITCHES
CEHKKRU CHUKKER
CEHKLMO HEMLOCK
CEHKNOY HOCKNEY
CEHKORS CHOKERS,
   SHOCKER
CEHKPTU KETCHUP
CEHKRSU SHUCKER
CEHKSTY SKETCHY
CEHLMWY WYCH-ELM
CEHLNRU LUNCHER
CEHLNRY LYNCHER
CEHLNSU LUNCHES
CEHLORT CHORTLE
CEHLOST CLOTHES
CEHLQSU SQUELCH
CEHLRRU LURCHER
CEHLRSU LURCHES
CEHMNRU MUNCHER
CEHMOOR MOOCHER
CEHMOOW HOW COME?
CEHNOOP HENCOOP
CEHNORV CHEVRON
CEHNOST NOTCHES
CEHNPRU PUNCHER
CEHNPSU PUNCHES
CEHNSUU EUNUCHS
CEHNTUY CHUTNEY
CEHOOPS POOCHES
CEHOORS CHOOSER
CEHOORT CHEROOT
CEHOPPR CHOPPER
CEHOPRS PORCHES

CEHOPSU POUCHES
CEHORST TORCHES
CEHORSZ SCHERZO
CEHORTU RETOUCH,
   TOUCHER
CEHORTW WOTCHER
CEHORUV VOUCHER
CEHOSTU TOUCHES
CEHPRSY CYPHERS
CEHPSSY PSYCHES
CEHRSSU CRUSHES
CEHRSTT STRETCH
CEHRTTU UTRECHT
CEHSSTY SCYTHES
CEIIJRU JUICIER
CEIIKNR ICE RINK
CEIIKNT KINETIC
CEIIKPR PICKIER
CEIIKQU QUICKIE
CEIILLS SILICLE
CEIILNN INCLINE
CEIILPP CLIPPIE
CEIILPT PELITIC
CEIIMMT MIMETIC
CEIIMOT MEIOTIC
CEIIMPR EMPIRIC
CEIIMSS SEISMIC
CEIIMST SEMITIC
CEIIMTT TITMICE
CEIINNO CONIINE
CEIINNR CINERIN
CEIINOS EOSINIC
CEIINOV INVOICE
CEIINPS PISCINE
CEIINRS IRENICS, SERICIN
CEIINRT CITRINE,
   CRINITE, INCITER,
   NERITIC
CEIINSS ICINESS
CEIINSU CUISINE
CEIINTZ CITIZEN, ZINCITE
CEIIOPZ EPIZOIC
CEIIPRR PRICIER
CEIIPRS SPICIER
CEIIPRT PICRITE
CEIIRST ERISTIC
CEIISSS CISSIES
CEIISVV CIVVIES
CEIITUV UVEITIC
CEIJSTU JUSTICE
CEIKKNR KENRICK
CEIKKSW KESWICK
CEIKLNR CLINKER,
   CRINKLE

CEIKLNS NICKELS
CEIKLPR PICKLER,
  PRICKLE
CEIKLPS PICKLES
CEIKLRS SLICKER
CEIKLRT TICKLER, TRICKLE
CEIKLRU LUCKIER
CEIKLRW LERWICK
CEIKLSS SICKLES
CEIKLST STICKLE, TICKLES
CEIKMRU MUCKIER
CEIKMSY MICKEYS
CEIKNOT KENOTIC,
  KETONIC
CEIKNQU QUICKEN
CEIKNRS SNICKER
CEIKOOS COOKIES
CEIKORR ROCKIER
CEIKORS ROCKIES
CEIKPRR PRICKER
CEIKPRS PICKERS
CEIKPRT PRICKET
CEIKPST PICKETS, SKEPTIC
CEIKQRU QUICKER
CEIKRRT TRICKER
CEIKRRT RICKETS,
  STICKER, TICKERS
CEIKRTY RICKETY
CEIKRUY YUCKIER
CEIKSST SICKEST
CEIKSTT TICKETS
CEIKSTW WICKETS
CEILLLU LUCILLE
CEILLOR COLLIER
CEILLOS COLLIES
CEILLST CELLIST
CEILMOP COMPILE,
  POLEMIC
CEILMPR CRIMPLE
CEILNNU NUCLEIN
CEILNOS INCLOSE
CEILNOT LECTION
CEILNOX LEXICON
CEILNPS SPLENIC
CEILNST CLIENTS,
  STENCIL
CEILNTU TUNICLE
CEILOOS COOLIES
CEILOSS OSSICLE
CEILPPR CLIPPER, CRIPPLE
CEILPRS SPLICER
CEILPSS SPLICES
CEILPSU SPICULE
CEILQSU CLIQUES

CEILQUY CLIQUEY
CEILRRU CURLIER
CEILRTU UTRICLE
CEILSSU CELSIUS, SLUICES
CEIMNOS COSMINE,
  INCOMES
CEIMNRS MINCERS
CEIMOPT METOPIC
CEIMOTT TOTEMIC
CEIMOTV VICOMTE
CEIMPRR CRIMPER
CEIMRST METRICS
CEINNOR CORINNE
CEINNOV CONNIVE
CEINNTV VINCENT
CEINOOT COONTIE
CEINOOZ NEOZOIC
CEINOPR PORCINE
CEINOPT ENTOPIC,
  NEPOTIC
CEINORR CORNIER
CEINORS COINERS,
  CRONIES
CEINORV CORVINE
CEINOSS CESSION,
  COSINES
CEINOST NOTICES,
  SECTION
CEINOSV NOVICES
CEINOTT TONETIC
CEINOTX EXCITON
CEINOUV UNVOICE
CEINPRS PINCERS,
  PRINCES
CEINPST INSPECT
CEINQSU QUINCES
CEINRST CISTERN,
  CRETINS
CEINRUV INCURVE
CEINSST INSECTS
CEINSTY CYSTINE
CEINTTX EXTINCT
CEIOPRS COPIERS
CEIOPST POETICS
CEIOPSU PICEOUS
CEIORRS CROSIER
CEIORRU COURIER
CEIORRZ CROZIER
CEIORSW COWRIES
CEIORTV EVICTOR
CEIORTX EXCITOR,
  XEROTIC
CEIORVY VICEROY
CEIOSST COSIEST, OSSETIC

CEIOSSV VISCOSE
CEIOSTV COSTIVE
CEIOSTX COEXIST
CEIOSTY SOCIETY
CEIOSTZ COZIEST
CEIPRST TRICEPS
CEIPRSY SPICERY
CEIPRTU CUPRITE,
  PICTURE
CEIPRTY PYRETIC
CEIPSST CESSPIT
CEIPSTU CUP TIES
CEIQRSU CIRQUES
CEIRRRU CURRIER
CEIRRSU CRUISER,
  CURRIES
CEIRRTT CRITTER
CEIRRTU RECRUIT
CEIRRTX RECTRIX
CEIRSSU CRUISES
CEIRSTT TRISECT
CEIRSTU ICTERUS
CEIRSUV CURSIVE
CEIRTTX TECTRIX
CEJKOSY JOCKEYS
CEJLNOY JOCELYN
CEJNORU CONJURE
CEJOPRT PROJECT
CEKKLNU KNUCKLE
CEKKNOR KNOCKER
CEKKOPS KOPECKS
CEKLORS LOCKERS
CEKLOST LOCKETS
CEKLPRU PLUCKER
CEKLRSU SUCKLER
CEKLRTU TRUCKLE
CEKMORS MOCKERS
CEKMORY MOCKERY
CEKNOOV CONVOKE
CEKNORS CONKERS
CEKNRWY WRYNECK
CEKOOPR PRECOOK
CEKOORS COOKERS
CEKOORY COOKERY
CEKOPST POCKETS
CEKORRS CORKERS,
  ROCKERS
CEKORRY ROCKERY
CEKORST RESTOCK,
  ROCKETS, STOCKER
CEKOSST SOCKETS
CEKPRSU PUCKERS
CEKRRTU TRUCKER
CEKRSSU SUCKERS

CELLNOO COLONEL
CELLOSU OCELLUS
CELLOSY CLOSELY
CELLRSU SCULLER
CELLRUY CRUELLY
CELMNOO MONOCLE
CELMOPX COMPLEX
CELMPRU CRUMPLE
CELMSSU MUSCLES
CELMTUU CUMULET
CELNNOU NUCLEON
CELNOOS CONSOLE
CELNOSU COUNSEL,
   UNCLOSE
CELNOTU NOCTULE
CELNSUU NUCLEUS
CELOORS COOLERS,
   CREOSOL
CELOOST COOLEST,
   OCELOTS
CELOPRU COUPLER
CELOPSU CLOSE-UP,
   COUPLES
CELOPTU COUPLET,
   OCTUPLE
CELORSU CLOSURE
CELORSW SCOWLER
CELORTU CLOTURE,
   COULTER
CELOSST CLOSEST,
   CLOSETS
CELPRSU SCRUPLE
CELPSUY CLYPEUS
CELRRSU CURLERS
CELRSTU CLUSTER,
   CUTLERS
CELRSUW CURLEWS
CELRTTU CLUTTER
CELRTUU CULTURE
CELRTUV CULVERT
CELRTUY CRUELTY,
   CUTLERY
CELSTTU CUTLETS,
   SCUTTLE
CEMMNOT COMMENT
CEMMNOU COMMUNE
CEMMOTU COMMUTE
CEMMRSU SCUMMER
CEMNNOT CONTEMN
CEMNOOY ECONOMY
CEMNOSU CONSUME
CEMNRTU CENTRUM
CEMOOPS COMPOSE
CEMOOPT COMPOTE

CEMOOTU OUTCOME
CEMOPTU COMPUTE
CEMOSTU COSTUME
CEMPRTU CRUMPET
CEMRRUY MERCURY
CEMRSTU RECTUMS
CENNOOT CONNOTE
CENNOST CONSENT
CENNOTT CONTENT
CENNOTV CONVENT
CENOORR CORONER,
   CROONER
CENOORT CORONET
CENOPSU POUNCES
CENOPSY SYNCOPE
CENOPTY POTENCY
CENOQRU CONQUER
CENORRS CORNERS,
   SCORNER
CENORSS CENSORS
CENORST CORNETS
CENORTU CORNUTE,
   COUNTER, RECOUNT,
   TROUNCE
CENORTV CONVERT
CENORUV UNCOVER
CENOSSY COYNESS
CENOSTT CONTEST
CENOSTU CONTUSE
CENOTTX CONTEXT
CENRRTU CURRENT
CENRSTU ENCRUST
CENRSUW UNSCREW
CENRTUY CENTURY
CEOOPRS COOPERS,
   SCOOPER
CEOORST SCOOTER
CEOOSTY COYOTES
CEOPPRR CROPPER
CEOPPRS COPPERS
CEOPPRY COPPERY
CEOPRRS SCORPER
CEOPRRU PROCURE
CEOPRSS CORPSES,
   PROCESS
CEOPRTT PROTECT
CEOPRUV COVER-UP
CEOQRTU CROQUET
CEORRSS CROSSER,
   SCORERS
CEORRST RECTORS
CEORRSU COURSER,
   SCOURER
CEORRSY SORCERY

CEORRTY RECTORY
CEORSSS CROSSES
CEORSST CORSETS,
   ESCORTS, SECTORS
CEORSSU COURSES,
   SOURCES, SUCROSE
CEORSTU SCOUTER
CEORSTV COVERTS,
   VECTORS
CEORTUU COUTURE
CEOSSSU SCOUSES
CEPPRRU CRUPPER
CEPPRSU SCUPPER
CEPRSSU PERCUSS,
   SPRUCES
CEPRSSY CYPRESS
CEPSSTU SUSPECT
CERSTTU CUTTERS
CERSTUY CURTESY
CFFGINU CUFFING
CFFHINO CHIFFON
CFFIKKO KICKOFF
CFFINOS COFFINS
CFFOSTU CUTOFFS
CFFRSSU SCRUFFS
CFFRSUY SCRUFFY
CFGIKNU FUCKING
CFGINOR FORCING
CFHINSU FUCHSIN
CFHIOSW COWFISH
CFHOOOW FOOCHOW
CFIIKNY FINICKY
CFIILNT INFLICT
CFIINOT FICTION
CFILNOT CLIFTON
CFILORS FROLICS
CFILORU FLUORIC
CFIMNOR CONFIRM
CFIMOST COMFITS
CFIORSY SCORIFY
CFKNORU UNFROCK
CFKOTTU FUTTOCK
CFKPSUU FUCK-UPS
CFLMRUU FULCRUM
CFLORWY CRY WOLF
CFMNOOR CONFORM
CFMOORT COMFORT
CFOSSUU FUSCOUS
CGGGINO COGGING
CGHIIMN CHIMING
CGHIINN INCHING
CGHIINT ITCHING
CGHIKNO CHOKING,
   HOCKING

CGHIKNU KUCHING
CGHILNU CHILUNG
CGHILPY GLYPHIC
CGHINNO CHIGNON
CGHINOS COSHING
CGHINRU RUCHING
CGHORUY GROUCHY
CGIIJNU JUICING
CGIIKKN KICKING
CGIIKLN LICKING
CGIIKMM GIMMICK
CGIIKNN NICKING
CGIIKNP PICKING
CGIIKNR RICKING
CGIIKNS SICKING
CGIIKNT TICKING
CGIIKNW WICKING
CGIILNO COILING
CGIILNS SLICING
CGIIMNN MINCING
CGIINNO COINING
CGIINNW WINCING
CGIINOV VOICING
CGIINPR PRICING
CGIINPS SPICING
CGIKLNO LOCKING
CGIKMNO MOCKING
CGIKMNU MUCKING
CGIKNNO CONKING
CGIKNOO COOKING
CGIKNOR CORKING,
  ROCKING
CGIKNOS SOCKING
CGIKNPU KINGCUP
CGIKNRU RUCKING
CGIKNSU SUCKING
CGIKNTU TUCKING
CGILLNU CULLING
CGILNOO COOLING
CGILNOS CLOSING
CGILNOW COWLING
CGILNOY CLOYING
CGILNRU CURLING
CGILORW COWGIRL
CGILOTT GLOTTIC
CGILPTY GLYPTIC
CGIMNOS COMINGS
CGINNNO CONNING
CGINNNU CUNNING
CGINNOS CONSIGN
CGINOPP COPPING
CGINOPS COPINGS
CGINOPY COPYING
CGINORS SCORING

CGINORW CROWING
CGINOST COSTING,
  GNOSTIC
CGINOSU CONGIUS
CGINPPU CUPPING
CGINRSU CURSING
CGINRUV CURVING
CGINSSU CUSSING
CGINTTU CUTTING
CGIOTYZ ZYGOTIC
CGKLNOU GUNLOCK
CHHOSUU HSU-CHOU
CHIILST LITCHIS
CHIIMSU ISCHIUM
CHIINOT THIONIC
CHIIOPT OPHITIC
CHIIPST PICTISH
CHIIPSW IPSWICH
CHIKLLO HILLOCK
CHIKLTY THICKLY
CHIKNOO CHINOOK
CHIKORY HICKORY
CHIKPSU PUCKISH
CHIKSTY KITSCHY
CHILLMU CHILLUM
CHILNSY LYCHNIS
CHILOOS COOLISH
CHILOST COLTISH
CHILPSY SYLPHIC
CHIMRUU URUMCHI
CHIMSSS SCHISMS
CHIMSTY TYCHISM
CHINOOR CHORION
CHINOPS PHONICS
CHINORS CORNISH
CHINORT CORINTH
CHINORW NORWICH
CHINOSU CUSHION
CHINOTU IN TOUCH
CHINQSU SQUINCH
CHINRSU URCHINS
CHINTYZ CHINTZY
CHIOORS ISOCHOR
CHIOPRT TROPHIC
CHIORST OSTRICH
CHIPRRU CHIRRUP
CHIPRRY PYRRHIC
CHIPSSY PHYSICS
CHIRRSU CURRISH
CHIRSSY CHRISSY
CHIRSTY CHRISTY
CHKMMOU HUMMOCK
CHLMORY CHROMYL
CHLOOSS SCHOOLS

CHLOSUY SLOUCHY
CHMOSUY CHYMOUS
CHMSTUY SMUTCHY
CHNNOOR CHRONON
CHNOOPS PONCHOS
CHNORSY SYNCHRO
CHNOTUU UNCOUTH
CHNPPUU PUNCH-UP
CHOOOSW SOOCHOW
CHOORST COHORTS
CHOORWZ CHORZOW
CIIILLT ILLICIT
CIIINPT INCIPIT
CIIINST SINITIC
CIIJLUY JUICILY
CIIKKLL KILLICK
CIILLVY CIVILLY
CIILNOP CIPOLIN
CIILNOS SILICON
CIILNOT NILOTIC
CIILNUV UNCIVIL
CIILOOT OOLITIC
CIILOPT POLITIC
CIILOST COLITIS,
  SOLICIT
CIILPSY SPICILY
CIIMMRY MIMICRY
CIIMOTT MITOTIC
CIIMRST TRISMIC
CIIMSTV VICTIMS
CIINORS INCISOR
CIINPRS CRISPIN
CIINQTU QUINTIC
CIIOSUV VICIOUS
CIIPRTY PYRITIC
CIJMORW JIM CROW
CIJNNOO CONJOIN
CIKLLOP PILLOCK
CIKLLOR ROLLICK
CIKLLSY SLICKLY
CIKLLUY LUCKILY
CIKLMOS MISKOLC
CIKLMUY MUCKILY
CIKLNRY CRINKLY
CIKLPRY PRICKLY
CIKLQUY QUICKLY
CIKLRTY TRICKLY
CIKMORR RIMROCK
CIKNOST STICK-ON
CIKNSTU UNSTICK
CIKPPSU PICK-UPS
CIKPSTU STICK-UP
CIKRSTY TRICKSY
CILLNNO LINCOLN

CILLOOR CRIOLLO
CILMNOP COMPLIN
CILMOOS LOCOISM
CILMOPY OLYMPIC
CILMSTU CULTISM
CILNNOT CLINTON
CILNOOR ORCINOL
CILNOTU LINOCUT
CILNPSU SCULPIN
CILNSTU LINCTUS
CILOOPT COPILOT
CILOORU COULOIR
CILOOSS COLOSSI
CILOPSW COWSLIP
CILOSTU OCULIST
CILPRSY CRISPLY
CILPRTU CULPRIT
CILSTTU CULTIST
CIMNOOR MORONIC,
  OMICRON
CIMNORS CRIMSON,
  MICRONS
CIMOOST OSMOTIC
CIMOSST SITCOMS
CIMOSSY MYCOSIS
CIMOTYZ ZYMOTIC
CIMPRSY SCRIMPY
CIMRSSU CRISSUM
CIMSSTY MYSTICS
CINNORU UNICORN
CINNOSU NUNCIOS
CINNOTU UNCTION
CINNSUU UNCINUS
CINOOOR ORINOCO
CINOOPS OPSONIC
CINORRT TRICORN
CINORSS INCROSS
CINORST CISTRON,
  CITRONS
CINORTU RUCTION
CINORTY TYRONIC
CINOSST CONSIST,
  TOCSINS
CINOSSU COUSINS
CINOSTU SUCTION
CIOOPRS SCORPIO
CIOOPRT PORTICO
CIOOPSU COPIOUS
CIOOQTU COQUITO
CIOPRST TROPICS
CIOPRTY CYPRIOT
CIOPSTY COPYIST
CIORSSS SCISSOR
CIORSTV VICTORS

CIORSUU CURIOUS
CIORTVY VICTORY
CIOSSSY SYCOSIS
CIOSSUV VISCOUS
CIPRSST SCRIPTS
CIPRTTY TRYPTIC
CIPSTTY STYPTIC
CIRSSTU RUSTICS
CKKLNUY KNUCKLY
CKKNNOO KNOCK-ON
CKKNOPU KNOCK-UP
CKLNOTU LOCKNUT
CKLNOUW LUCKNOW
CKLNUUY UNLUCKY
CKLOORW ROWLOCK
CKLOOTU LOCKOUT
CKLOPSU LOCKUPS
CKLOPTU POTLUCK
CKMOPSU MOCK-UPS
CKNOOOR ROCKOON
CKNSTUU UNSTUCK
CKOOOTU COOKOUT
CKOORST ROSTOCK
CKORTUW CUTWORK
CKOSSTU TUSSOCK
CKPSTUU STUCK-UP
CLLMOSU MOLLUSC
CLLOOPS SCOLLOP
CLLORSS SCROLLS
CLMNOSU COLUMNS
CLMOSUU OSCULUM
CLMPRUY CRUMPLY
CLMSUUU CUMULUS
CLNOORT CONTROL
CLNOOSS CONSOLS
CLNOSSU CONSULS
CLNOSTU CONSULT
CLOORSU COLOURS
CLORSSY CROSSLY
CLORTUY COURTLY
CLOSSTU LOCUSTS
CMMNOOS COMMONS
CMNOOPY COMPONY
CMOOPRT COMPORT
CMOOPST COMPOST
CMOORSU CORMOUS
CMORSTU SCROTUM
CMORTUW CUTWORM
CMOSSTU CUSTOMS
CMPRSUY SCRUMPY
CNNORTU NOCTURN
CNOOPPR POPCORN
CNOOPSU COUPONS,
  SOUPÇON

CNOORST CONSORT
CNOORTT CONTORT
CNOORTU CONTOUR,
  CROUTON
CNOOSTY TYCOONS
CNOOSVY CONVOYS
CNOOTTY COTTONY
CNORSSU UNCROSS
CNORTUY COUNTRY
COOPRRT PROCTOR
COOPRTU OUTCROP
COOPSTU COP-OUTS,
  OCTOPUS
COOSTTY OTOCYST
COPRRTU CORRUPT
COPRSUU CUPROUS
CORRSSU CURSORS
CORRSUY CURSORY
COSTTUU CUTOUTS
DDDDEIL DIDDLED
DDDEEGR DREDGED
DDDEEIR DERIDED
DDDEELM MEDDLED
DDDEELP PEDDLED
DDDEELS SLEDDED
DDDEELU DELUDED
DDDEENU DENUDED
DDDEFIL FIDDLED
DDDEFLU FUDDLED
DDDEGRU DRUDGED
DDDEHLU HUDDLED
DDDEHTU THUDDED
DDDEIIV DIVIDED
DDDEIKS SKIDDED
DDDEILP PIDDLED
DDDEILR RIDDLED
DDDEIMU MUDDIED
DDDEIOV VEDDOID
DDDELMU MUDDLED
DDDELOO DOODLED
DDDELOP PLODDED
DDDELOS DODDLES
DDDELOT TODDLED
DDDELPU PUDDLED
DDDEOPR PRODDED
DDDEORY DODDERY
DDDESTU STUDDED
DDEEELN NEEDLED
DDEEELT DELETED
DDEEEMN EMENDED
DDEEEPS SPEEDED
DDEEERR RED DEER
DDEEFII DEIFIED,
  EDIFIED

DDEEFIL DEFILED,
   FIELDED
DDEEFIN DEFINED
DDEEFIR FREDDIE
DDEEFSU DEFUSED
DDEEGIN DEIGNED
DDEEGLP PLEDGED
DDEEGLS SLEDGED
DDEEGLU DELUGED
DDEEGRR DREDGER
DDEEHRS SHEDDER
DDEEIIT TIE-DIED
DDEEILV DEVILED
DDEEILW WIELDED
DDEEILY YIELDED
DDEEIMP IMPEDED
DDEEIMS MISDEED
DDEEINW WIDENED
DDEEINX INDEXED
DDEEIOV VIDEOED
DDEEIPS DEPSIDE
DDEEIRR DEIRDRE,
   DERIDER
DDEEIRS DESIRED,
   RESIDED
DDEEIRV DERIVED
DDEEISV DEVISED
DDEELLU DUELLED
DDEELLW DWELLED
DDEELMO MODELED
DDEELMR MEDDLER
DDEELOY YODELED
DDEELPR PEDDLER
DDEELRS SLEDDER
DDEELRU DELUDER
DDEEMOT DEMOTED
DDEENOT DENOTED
DDEENOW ENDOWED
DDEENPU UPENDED
DDEENRS DRESDEN
DDEENRU DENUDER,
   ENDURED
DDEEOPS DEPOSED
DDEEORR ORDERED
DDEEOTV DEVOTED
DDEEPTU DEPUTED
DDEERSS DRESSED
DDEERST REDDEST
DDEERTU DETRUDE
DDEERYY DRY-EYED
DDEFILR FIDDLER
DDEFILS FIDDLES
DDEFIRT DRIFTED
DDEFLNO FONDLED

DDEFLOO FLOODED
DDEFLSU FUDDLES
DDEFNOR FRONDED
DDEFNOU FOUNDED
DDEGGRU DRUGGED,
   GRUDGED
DDEGIIR GIDDIER
DDEGILR GIRDLED,
   GRIDDLE
DDEGIMO DEMIGOD
DDEGINW WEDDING
DDEGINY EDDYING
DDEGIOR DODGIER
DDEGMOS DODGEMS
DDEGMSU SMUDGED
DDEGNOS GODSEND
DDEGNOU DUDGEON
DDEGNWY GWYNEDD
DDEGORS DODGERS
DDEGOSS GODDESS
DDEGRRU DRUDGER
DDEGRSU DRUDGES
DDEGRTU TRUDGED
DDEHIRS REDDISH
DDEHIRY HYDRIDE
DDEHLRU HUDDLER,
   HURDLED
DDEHLSU HUDDLES
DDEHNOU HOUNDED
DDEHNRU HUNDRED
DDEHRSU SHUDDER
DDEIIKS KIDDIES
DDEIINV DIVINED
DDEIIOX DIOXIDE
DDEIIRT DIRTIED
DDEIIRV DIVIDER
DDEIISV DIVIDES
DDEIKLN KINDLED
DDEIKNR KINDRED
DDEIKRS KIDDERS
DDEILLR DRILLED
DDEILMR MILDRED
DDEILNW DWINDLE
DDEILOS DILDOES
DDEILOT DELTOID
DDEILRR RIDDLER
DDEILRS RIDDLES
DDEILRT TIDDLER
DDEILTU DILUTED,
   LUDDITE
DDEILTW TWIDDLE
DDEILTY LYDDITE
DDEIMNS MIDDENS
DDEIMOR DERMOID

DDEIMOS DESMOID
DDEIMRU MUDDIER
DDEINOT DENTOID
DDEINST DISTEND
DDEIOOR DO-OR-DIE
DDEIORV OVERDID
DDEIORW DOWDIER
DDEIOST TODDIES
DDEIOWW WIDOWED
DDEIPPR DRIPPED
DDEIRRU RUDDIER
DDEISSU DISUSED
DDEISTU STUDIED
DDEKMOU DUKEDOM
DDELMOU MOULDED
DDELMRU MUDDLER
DDELMSU MUDDLES
DDELNOS NODDLES
DDELOOR DOODLER,
   DROOLED
DDELOOS DOODLES
DDELOPR PLODDER
DDELORT TODDLER
DDELPRU PUDDLER
DDELPSU PUDDLES
DDEMMRU DRUMMED
DDEMNOS DESMOND
DDEMNOT ODDMENT
DDENOPS DESPOND
DDENOPU POUNDED
DDENORT TRODDEN
DDENORU REDOUND,
   ROUNDED, UNDERDO
DDENORW DROWNED
DDENOSS ODDNESS
DDENOSU SOUNDED
DDENOUW WOUNDED
DDEOOPR DROOPED
DDEOORW REDWOOD
DDEOOWY DYEWOOD
DDEOPPR DROPPED
DDEOPRR PRODDER
DDEOPRW DEWDROP
DDEORSW DROWSED
DDERRSU RUDDERS
DDGGINO DODGING
DDGHOOO GODHOOD
DDGIIKN KIDDING
DDGIILY GIDDILY
DDGIINR RIDDING
DDGIMNU MUDDING
DDGINNO NODDING
DDGINOP PODDING
DDGINOS SODDING

DDGINPU PUDDING
DDGOOOW DOGWOOD
DDHIISY YIDDISH
DDHIORY HYDROID
DDHORSY DRY-SHOD
DDIILOP DIPLOID
DDILMUY MUDDILY
DDILNRS DIRNDLS
DDILOWY DOWDILY
DDILRUY RUDDILY
DDILTWY TWIDDLY
DDIMOOS DODOISM
DDIPRRY DRIP-DRY
DEEEFRS FEEDERS
DEEEFRV FEVERED
DEEEGMR EMERGED
DEEEGNR GREENED,
    RENEGED
DEEEGRS DEGREES
DEEEGRT DETERGE,
    GREETED
DEEEHLW WHEEDLE,
    WHEELED
DEEEHRS HEREDES,
    SHEERED
DEEEHST SEETHED
DEEEHWZ WHEEZED
DEEEILT LEE TIDE
DEEEINR NEEDIER
DEEEIPY PIE-EYED
DEEEIRR REEDIER
DEEEIRS DESIREE, SEEDIER
DEEEIRW WEEDIER
DEEEISV DEVISEE
DEEEKLN KNEELED
DEEEKLS SLEEKED
DEEEKNW WEEKEND
DEEELLV LEVELED
DEEELNS NEEDLES
DEEELPT DEPLETE
DEEELRV LEVERED,
    REVELED
DEEELST SLEETED,
    STEELED
DEEELTX TELEXED
DEEEMNS DEMESNE
DEEEMRS EMERSED
DEEEMRT METERED
DEEENPR PREENED
DEEENQU QUEENED
DEEENRS SNEERED
DEEENRT ENTERED
DEEENRW RENEWED
DEEENSZ SNEEZED

DEEENTT DÉTENTE
DEEEORR ROE DEER
DEEEOTV DEVOTEE
DEEEPRS SPEEDER
DEEEPST DEEPEST,
    STEEPED
DEEEQRU QUEERED
DEEERRV REVERED
DEEERST STEERED
DEEERSV DESERVE,
    SEVERED
DEEERTX EXERTED
DEEETTV VEDETTE
DEEETTW TWEETED
DEEFFOR OFFERED
DEEFGIN FEEDING,
    FEIGNED
DEEFHLS FLESHED
DEEFHLU HEEDFUL
DEEFIIR DEIFIER, EDIFIER
DEEFILR DEFILER,
    FIELDER
DEEFILS DEFILES
DEEFILT FILETED
DEEFINR DEFINER,
    REFINED
DEEFINT FEINTED
DEEFIRR FERRIED
DEEFKLR KREFELD
DEEFLLU FUELLED
DEEFLLW WELL-FED
DEEFLNU NEEDFUL
DEEFLOT FEEDLOT
DEEFMOR FREEDOM
DEEFNRS FENDERS
DEEFPRY DEEP FRY
DEEFRSU REFUSED
DEEFRTT FRETTED
DEEFRTU REFUTED
DEEGHIN HEEDING,
    NEIGHED
DEEGHIW WEIGHED
DEEGHOW HOGWEED
DEEGILS LEG SIDE
DEEGIMN DEEMING
DEEGINN NEEDING
DEEGINR ENERGID,
    REEDING, REIGNED
DEEGINS SEEDING
DEEGINW WEEDING
DEEGIOR GEORDIE
DEEGIPW PIGWEED
DEEGIRV DIVERGE,
    GRIEVED

DEEGIST EDGIEST
DEEGLNS LEGENDS
DEEGLOY GOLDEYE
DEEGLPR PLEDGER
DEEGLPS PLEDGES
DEEGLPT PLEDGET
DEEGLRS LEDGERS
DEEGLSS SLEDGES
DEEGLSU DELUGES
DEEGNRS GENDERS
DEEGOSY GEODESY
DEEGSSU GUESSED
DEEGSTU GUESTED
DEEHITV THIEVED
DEEHLLS SHELLED
DEEHLSV SHELVED
DEEHLSW WELSHED
DEEHMUX EXHUMED
DEEHNOY HONEYED
DEEHNRT DRENTHE
DEEHORV HOVERED
DEEHRSU USHERED
DEEHTTW WHETTED
DEEIINS SINE DIE
DEEIIRW WEIRDIE
DEEIIST DEITIES
DEEIJLL JELLIED
DEEIJMM JEMMIED
DEEIKLN LIKENED
DEEIKMW MIDWEEK
DEEILMO MELODIE
DEEILNR RELINED
DEEILNS LINSEED
DEEILNU EILUNED
DEEILNV LIVENED
DEEILNY DYELINE
DEEILPR REPLIED
DEEILRV DELIVER,
    EVERILD, RELIVED,
    REVILED
DEEILRW WIELDER
DEEILRY YIELDER
DEEILSS DIESELS
DEEILSY EYELIDS, SEEDILY
DEEILTU DILUTEE
DEEILWY WEEDILY
DEEIMNO DOMINEE
DEEIMPR IMPEDER, PER
    DIEM
DEEIMPT EMPTIED
DEEIMRT DEMERIT,
    DIMETER, MERITED
DEEIMTT EMITTED
DEEINNS DENISEN

DEEINNT DENTINE
DEEINNZ DENIZEN
DEEINPR DNIEPER,
  REPINED, RIPENED
DEEINRS DENIERS,
  NEREIDS
DEEINRW WIDENER
DEEINRX INDEXER
DEEINST DESTINE
DEEINSV ENDIVES
DEEINSW WISENED
DEEINSX INDEXES
DEEINTT DINETTE
DEEINTU DETINUE
DEEINTV EVIDENT
DEEINWZ WIZENED
DEEIOPS EPISODE
DEEIOPT EPIDOTE
DEEIPPT PEPTIDE
DEEIPRS DEPISER, PERSEID,
  PRESIDE
DEEIPRV DEPRIVE
DEEIPRX EXPIRED
DEEIPSS DESPISE
DEEIPST DESPITE
DEEIQRU QUERIED
DEEIRRS DESIRER,
  RESIDER, SERRIED
DEEIRRT RETIRED
DEEIRRV DERIVER
DEEIRRW REWIRED,
  WEIRDER
DEEIRSS DESIRES
DEEIRSU RESIDUE
DEEIRSV DEVISER,
  DIVERSE, REVISED
DEEIRTU ERUDITE
DEEIRTV RIVETED
DEEIRVV REVIVED
DEEISSU DISEUSE
DEEISTW DEWIEST
DEEISTX EXISTED
DEEJNOY ENJOYED
DEEKKRT TREKKED
DEEKNNY KENNEDY
DEEKORV REVOKED
DEEKPUY KEYED UP
DEELLMS SMELLED
DEELLNW WENDELL
DEELLPS SPELLED
DEELLQU QUELLED
DEELLRU DUELLER
DEELLRW DWELLER
DEELLRY ELDERLY

DEELLSW SWELLED
DEELMOR REMODEL
DEELMPU DEPLUME
DEELMST SMELTED
DEELMSY MEDLEYS
DEELNRS LENDERS,
  SLENDER
DEELNSS ENDLESS
DEELNST NESTLED
DEELNSY DENSELY
DEELNTT NETTLED
DEELOPP PEOPLED
DEELOPR DEPLORE
DEELOPV DEVELOP
DEELOPX EXPLODE
DEELORU URODELE
DEELORW LOWERED
DEELOSU DELOUSE
DEELOTW TOWELED
DEELOVV DEVOLVE,
  EVOLVED
DEELPRU PRELUDE
DEELRSW WELDERS
DEELSTT SETTLED
DEELTUX EXULTED
DEELVXY VEXEDLY
DEEMMST STEMMED
DEEMNOY MONEYED
DEEMNRS MENDERS
DEEMORV REMOVED
DEEMORX EXODERM
DEEMOSY MOSEYED
DEEMPTT TEMPTED
DEEMRRU DEMURER
DEEMRSU RESUMED
DEENNPT PENDENT
DEENOPS SPONDEE
DEENOPT PENTODE
DEENORS ENDORSE
DEENORT ERODENT
DEENORW ENDOWER
DEENPPR PERPEND
DEENPRS SPENDER
DEENPRT PRETEND
DEENRSS REDNESS,
  SENDERS
DEENRST TENDERS
DEENRSU END USER,
  ENSURED
DEENRTU DENTURE
DEENSST DENSEST
DEENSTW WEST
  END
DEEOPPY POP-EYED

DEEOPRS DEPOSER,
  REPOSED
DEEOPRW POWERED
DEEOPSX EXPOSED
DEEORRR ORDERER,
  REORDER
DEEORRS REREDOS
DEEORST OERSTED
DEEORTT DORETTE,
  TETRODE
DEEORTW TOWERED
DEEORUV OVERDUE
DEEORXX XEROXED
DEEPPST STEPPED
DEEPRSS DEPRESS,
  PRESSED
DEEPRSU PERUSED
DEEPRTU ERUPTED,
  REPUTED
DEEQSTU QUESTED
DEERRSS DRESSER,
  REDRESS
DEERRSV REDVERS
DEERRUV VERDURE
DEERSSS DRESSES
DEERSST DESERTS,
  DESSERT
DEERSTW STREWED,
  WRESTED
DEERSVW SWERVED
DEERTTU UTTERED
DEERTUX EXTRUDE
DEESSTU SUDETES
DEFFFLU FLUFFED
DEFFILR RIFFLED
DEFFINS SNIFFED
DEFFIOS OFFSIDE
DEFFISU DIFFUSE
DEFFLMU MUFFLED
DEFFLRU RUFFLED
DEFFNOS SEND-OFF
DEFFNSU SNUFFED
DEFFRSU DUFFERS
DEFFSTU STUFFED
DEFGGLO FLOGGED
DEFGINN FENDING
DEFGINR FRINGED
DEFGINU FEUDING
DEFGINY DEFYING
DEFGIOR FIREDOG
DEFGIRS FRIDGES
DEFGIRU FIGURED
DEFGIST FIDGETS
DEFGITY FIDGETY

DEFGORY GODFREY
DEFHIRS REDFISH
DEFHIST SHIFTED
DEFHLSU FLUSHED
DEFHORT FROTHED
DEFIILN INFIDEL,
INFIELD
DEFIIMS FIDEISM
DEFIIMW MIDWIFE
DEFIINU UNIFIED
DEFIIST FIDEIST
DEFIKRS FRISKED
DEFILLR FRILLED
DEFILPP FLIPPED
DEFILRT FLIRTED, TRIFLED
DEFILRU DIREFUL
DEFILRW WILFRED
DEFILST STIFLED
DEFILTT FLITTED
DEFILXY FIXEDLY
DEFIMOR DEIFORM
DEFINRS FRIENDS
DEFINRW WINFRED
DEFINSU INFUSED
DEFIOOS FOODIES
DEFIOST FOISTED
DEFIPRY PERFIDY
DEFIRRT DRIFTER
DEFIRTU FRUITED
DEFIRZZ FRIZZED
DEFKLNU FLUNKED
DEFLLOU DOLEFUL
DEFLNOR FONDLER
DEFLNOT TENFOLD
DEFLOOR FLOODER,
FLOORED
DEFLOPP FLOPPED
DEFLORS FOLDERS
DEFLORU FLOURED
DEFLOSS FLOSSED
DEFLOTU FLOUTED
DEFMORS SERFDOM
DEFNORT FRONTED
DEFNORU FOUNDER
DEFNORW FROWNED
DEFNOST FONDEST
DEFNOSU FONDUES
DEFNRSU REFUNDS
DEFOOPR PROOFED
DEFORST DEFROST,
FROSTED
DEGGGIL GIGGLED
DEGGGLO GOGGLED
DEGGHIN HEDGING

DEGGIJL JIGGLED
DEGGILN GELDING,
NIGGLED
DEGGILW WIGGLED
DEGGINS EDGINGS
DEGGINW WEDGING
DEGGIOS DOGGIES
DEGGIRS DIGGERS
DEGGISW SWIGGED
DEGGITW TWIGGED
DEGGJLO JOGGLED
DEGGJLU JUGGLED
DEGGLOS DOGLEGS,
SLOGGED
DEGGLPU PLUGGED
DEGGLRU GURGLED
DEGGLSU SLUGGED
DEGGNOO DOGGONE
DEGGNOS SNOGGED
DEGGNOU GUDGEON
DEGGORY DOGGERY
DEGGRRU GRUDGER
DEGGRSU GRUDGES
DEGGRTU DRUGGET
DEGHILT DELIGHT,
LIGHTED
DEGHINR HERDING
DEGHINW WHINGED
DEGHIRT RIGHTED
DEGHIST SIGHTED
DEGHOST GHOSTED
DEGHOSU SOUGHED
DEGIILN ELIDING
DEGIINR DINGIER
DEGIINT DIETING,
EDITING, IGNITED
DEGIISU EGIDIUS
DEGIJLN JINGLED
DEGIKLO GODLIKE
DEGILLR GRILLED
DEGILMN MINGLED
DEGILNN LENDING
DEGILNO GLENOID, ON-
GLIDE
DEGILNS DINGLES,
SINGLED
DEGILNT GLINTED,
TINGLED
DEGILNU DUELING,
ELUDING, INDULGE
DEGILNV DELVING
DEGILNW WELDING
DEGILOR GLORIED,
GODLIER

DEGILRR GIRDLER
DEGILRS GIRDLES,
GLIDERS
DEGILRU GUILDER
DEGILUV DIVULGE
DEGIMNN MENDING
DEGIMST MIDGETS
DEGINNN DENNING
DEGINNP PENDING
DEGINNR GRINNED,
RENDING
DEGINNS ENDINGS,
SENDING
DEGINNT DENTING,
TENDING
DEGINNU ENDUING
DEGINNV VENDING
DEGINNW WENDING
DEGINNY DENYING
DEGINOR ERODING,
GIRONDE, IGNORED,
NEGROID, REDOING
DEGINOS DINGOES
DEGINOW WIDGEON
DEGINRR GRINDER
DEGINRW REDWING
DEGINSS DESIGNS
DEGINUX EXUDING
DEGIOOS GOODIES
DEGIOPR PODGIER
DEGIPPR GRIPPED
DEGIPRU PUDGIER
DEGIRRS GIRDERS
DEGIRSS DIGRESS
DEGIRTT GRITTED
DEGISST DIGESTS
DEGLNOU LOUNGED
DEGLNPU PLUNGED
DEGLNSU GULDENS
DEGLOPR PLEDGOR
DEGLOPS SPLODGE
DEGLORS LODGERS
DEGLORW GROWLED
DEGLOSS GLOSSED,
GODLESS
DEGLTTU GLUTTED
DEGLUZZ GUZZLED
DEGMOOR GROOMED
DEGMSSU SMUDGES
DEGNNOU DUNGEON
DEGNOPS SPONGED
DEGNORU UNDERGO
DEGNORW WRONGED
DEGNRSU GERUNDS

DEGNRTU GRUNTED,
  TRUDGEN
DEGOORV GROOVED
DEGOPRU GROUPED
DEGORSS GROSSED
DEGORSU GROUSED
DEGRRTU TRUDGER
DEGRSTU TRUDGES
DEHHSSU SHUSHED
DEHIIRS DISHIER
DEHIKRS SHIRKED
DEHIKSW WHISKED
DEHILRW WHIRLED
DEHILSS SHIELDS
DEHIMOP HEMIPOD
DEHIMOR HEIRDOM
DEHIMOT ETHMOID
DEHINNS SHINNED
DEHINNT THINNED
DEHINOR HORDEIN
DEHINPT IN-DEPTH
DEHINRX HENDRIX
DEHINSW WENDISH
DEHIORT THEROID
DEHIOST HOISTED
DEHIOSU HIDEOUS
DEHIPPS SHIPPED
DEHIPPW WHIPPED
DEHIRRU HURRIED
DEHIRRW WHIRRED
DEHIRSV DERVISH
DEHIRTV THRIVED
DEHIRTW WRITHED
DEHISSW SWEDISH,
  SWISHED
DEHISTT SHITTED
DEHIWZZ WHIZZED
DEHJNOO JOHN DOE
DEHLMNO DENHOLM
DEHLNOS SHELDON
DEHLOOT TOEHOLD
DEHLORS HOLDERS
DEHLORW WHORLED
DEHLOSS SLOSHED
DEHLRRU HURDLER
DEHLRSU HURDLES
DEHLRTU HURTLED
DEHLSTU HUSTLED
DEHMORU HUMORED
DEHMOST METHODS
DEHMOTU MOUTHED
DEHMPTU THUMPED
DEHNNSU SHUNNED
DEHNOOR HONORED

DEHNOOW HOEDOWN
DEHNORU HOUNDER
DEHNOSY HOYDENS
DEHNOTZ DOZENTH
DEHNRTU THUNDER
DEHNSTU SHUNTED
DEHOOPW WHOOPED
DEHOOST SOOTHED
DEHOOWY HEYWOOD
DEHOPPS SHOPPED
DEHOPPW WHOPPED
DEHOQTU QUOTHED
DEHORST SHORTED
DEHOSTU SHOUTED
DEHPPUY HYPED UP
DEIIKLS DISLIKE
DEIIKNR DINKIER
DEIILMP IMPLIED
DEIILMT DELIMIT,
  LIMITED
DEIILOS DOILIES,
  IDOLISE
DEIILOZ IDOLIZE
DEIINOS IONISED, SIDONIE
DEIINOT EDITION
DEIINOZ IONIZED
DEIINRS INSIDER
DEIINRT NITRIDE
DEIINRU URIDINE
DEIINRV DIVINER, DRIVE-
  IN
DEIINRW WINDIER
DEIINSS INSIDES
DEIINTV INVITED
DEIIORS IODISER,
  ISIDORE
DEIIORT DIORITE
DEIIORZ IODIZER
DEIIOSX OXIDISE
DEIIOXZ OXIDIZE
DEIIPRT RIPTIDE
DEIIRRT DIRTIER
DEIIRZZ DIZZIER
DEIISTT DITTIES,
  TIDIEST
DEIISTV VISITED
DEIJLLO JOLLIED
DEIJNOR JOINDER
DEIJNOT JOINTED
DEIJNRU INJURED
DEIJORY JOYRIDE
DEIKLLS SKILLED
DEIKLNR KINDLER
DEIKLNT TINKLED

DEIKLNW WINKLED
DEIKLOR RODLIKE
DEIKMMS SKIMMED
DEIKMPS SKIMPED
DEIKMRS SMIRKED
DEIKNNS SKINNED
DEIKNOS DOESKIN,
  SEKONDI
DEIKNOV INVOKED
DEIKNRR DRINKER
DEIKNRS REDSKIN
DEIKNST KINDEST
DEIKNSY KIDNEYS
DEIKNTT KNITTED
DEIKPPS SKIPPED
DEIKRST SKIRTED
DEIKRSU DUSKIER
DEIKSVY SKYDIVE
DEILLOS DOLLIES
DEILLPS SPILLED
DEILLRR DRILLER
DEILLRT TRILLED
DEILLST STILLED
DEILLSU SULLIED
DEILLSW SWILLED
DEILMMS SLIMMED
DEILMOP IMPLODE
DEILMOR MOLDIER
DEILMOT OLDTIME
DEILMOY MYELOID
DEILMPP PIMPLED
DEILMPS DIMPLES
DEILMST MILDEST
DEILMWY MILDEWY
DEILNNS LINDENS
DEILNOO EIDOLON
DEILNOW LIE-DOWN
DEILNPS SPINDLE
DEILNRT TENDRIL
DEILNSW SWINDLE
DEILNSY LINDSEY,
  SNIDELY
DEILNTU DILUENT
DEILOPR LEPORID
DEILOPS DESPOIL,
  SPOILED
DEILOPT PILOTED
DEILOPU EUPLOID
DEILORS SOLDIER
DEILOTW LOW TIDE
DEILPPR RIPPLED
DEILPPS SLIPPED
DEILPRT TRIPLED
DEILPTY TEPIDLY

DEILQTU QUILTED
DEILRRV L-DRIVER
DEILRSW SWIRLED
DEILRTU DILUTER
DEILRTW TWIRLED
DEILRTY TIREDLY
DEILRVY DEVILRY
DEILRWY WEIRDLY
DEILRZZ DRIZZLE
DEILSTT SLITTED,
   STILTED
DEILSTW WILDEST
DEILSZZ SIZZLED
DEIMMRS DIMMERS
DEIMMRT MIDTERM,
   TRIMMED
DEIMMRU IMMURED
DEIMMST DIMMEST
DEIMMSU DUMMIES,
   MEDIUMS
DEIMNPS MENDIPS
DEIMNRS MINDERS
DEIMNSS DIMNESS
DEIMNTU MINUTED
DEIMOOR MOIDORE,
   MOODIER
DEIMOPS IMPOSED
DEIMOST MODISTE
DEIMOTT OMITTED
DEIMOTV VOMITED
DEIMPRU DUMPIER,
   UMPIRED
DEIMPSU MUD-PIES
DEIMPTU IMPUTED
DEIMPUX MIXED UP
DEIMRUU UREDIUM
DEIMSSU MISUSED
DEIMSTW MIDWEST
DEIMSTY STYMIED
DEINNOT INTONED
DEINNRS DINNERS
DEINNST INDENTS
DEINNTU DUNNITE
DEINNTW TWINNED
DEINOPT POINTED
DEINORS INDORSE,
   ROSINED
DEINORU DOURINE
DEINORW DOWNIER
DEINPPS SNIPPED
DEINPRT PRINTED
DEINPST STIPEND
DEINRSU INSURED
DEINRTT TRIDENT

DEINRTU INTRUDE,
   TURDINE, UNTRIED
DEINRTX DEXTRIN
DEINSST DISSENT, SNIDEST
DEINSTT DENTIST,
   STINTED
DEINSTY DENSITY,
   DESTINY
DEIOORW WOODIER
DEIOOST OSTEOID
DEIOPRS PERIODS
DEIOPRT DIOPTRE,
   PERIDOT
DEIOPRV PROVIDE
DEIOPSS DISPOSE
DEIOPST DEPOSIT,
   DOPIEST, POSITED,
   TOPSIDE
DEIOPTT TIPTOED
DEIOPTV PIVOTED
DEIORRW ROWDIER,
   WORDIER, WORRIED
DEIORSS DOSSIER
DEIORST EDITORS,
   STEROID, STORIED
DEIORSV DEVISOR,
   DEVOIRS
DEIORSW DOWRIES,
   WEIRDOS
DEIORTT DETROIT,
   DOTTIER
DEIORTU OUTRIDE
DEIORWW WIDOWER
DEIOSTU OUTSIDE,
   TEDIOUS
DEIOSTZ DOZIEST
DEIOSUV DEVIOUS
DEIPPQU QUIPPED
DEIPPRS DIPPERS
DEIPPRT TRIPPED
DEIPRSS SPIDERS
DEIPRST STRIPED
DEIPRSY SPIDERY
DEIPSTU DISPUTE
DEIQTTU QUITTED
DEIQUZZ QUIZZED
DEIRRST STIRRED
DEIRRSV DRIVERS
DEIRSST STRIDES
DEIRSTU DUSTIER
DEISSTU STUDIES
DEISTTW TWISTED
DEITTTW TWITTED
DEJLOST JOSTLED

DEJOSTU JOUSTED
DEKKLSU SKULKED
DEKLNOP PLONKED
DEKNNRU DRUNKEN
DEKNOST DONETSK
DEKNOSY DONKEYS
DEKNOTT KNOTTED
DEKNRRU DRUNKER
DEKOOPS SPOOKED
DEKOPST DESKTOP
DEKORST STROKED
DELLOOP LEOPOLD
DELLOPR REDPOLL
DELLORR DROLLER
DELLORT TROLLED
DELLSTU DULLEST
DELMMSU SLUMMED
DELMNOS DOLMENS
DELMORS REMOLDS,
   SMOLDER
DELMORU MOULDER,
   REMOULD
DELMOSU MODULES
DELMOTT MOTTLED
DELMOTU MOULTED
DELMOUV VOLUMED
DELMPPU PLUMPED
DELMPRU RUMPLED
DELMPSU SLUMPED
DELMUZZ MUZZLED
DELNOOS NOODLES
DELNORU ROUNDEL
DELNORY REYNOLD
DELNOSU NODULES
DELNOTW LETDOWN
DELNPRU PLUNDER
DELNRTU TRUNDLE
DELNUZZ NUZZLED
DELOOPS POODLES
DELOORS DOLORES
DELOOTT TOOTLED
DELOPPP PLOPPED
DELOPPS SLOPPED
DELOPPT TOPPLED
DELOPRT DROPLET
DELOPRW PROWLED
DELOPTT PLOTTED
DELORRY ORDERLY
DELORST OLDSTER
DELORSU LOURDES
DELOSTT SLOTTED
DELOSTU LOUDEST,
   TOUSLED
DELOSYY DOYLEYS

DELOSZZ SOZZLED
DELPRSU SLURPED
DELPUZZ PUZZLED
DELRRSU SLURRED
DELRSTU RUSTLED, STRUDEL
DELSSTU TUSSLED
DEMMRRU DRUMMER
DEMNOOR DOORMEN
DEMNORS MODERNS
DEMNORT MORDENT
DEMNORU MOURNED
DEMNOST ENDMOST
DEMNOTU DEMOUNT, MOUNTED
DEMNOUV UNMOVED
DEMNSTU DUSTMEN
DEMOOPP POPEDOM
DEMOORT MOTORED
DEMOPST STOMPED
DEMORRS DORMERS
DEMORST STORMED
DEMOSTY MODESTY
DEMPRSU DUMPERS
DEMPRTU TRUMPED
DEMPSTU STUMPED
DEMRRSU MURDERS
DENNOST TENDONS
DENNSTU DUNNEST, STUNNED
DENOOPS SNOOPED, SPOONED
DENOOSW SWOONED
DENOOSZ SNOOZED
DENOOTU DUOTONE, OUTDONE
DENOPPR PROPEND
DENOPRS RESPOND
DENOPRT PORTEND
DENOPRU POUNDER
DENOPUX EXPOUND
DENORRU RONDURE, ROUNDER
DENORRW DROWNER
DENORST RODENTS, SNORTED
DENORSU RESOUND, SOUNDER
DENORSV VENDORS
DENORSW DOWNERS, WONDERS
DENORUW WOUNDER
DENPRSU SPURNED
DENPRTU PRUDENT

DENPSSU SEND-UPS, SUSPEND
DENRSSU UNDRESS
DENRSSY DRYNESS
DENSTTU STUDENT, STUNTED
DENTUVY DUVETYN
DEOOPPS OPPOSED
DEOOPRT TORPEDO, TROOPED
DEOOPST STOOPED
DEOOPSW SWOOPED
DEOORRT REDROOT
DEOORST ROOSTED
DEOORTU OUTRODE
DEOPPPR PROPPED
DEOPPRR DROPPER
DEOPPST STOPPED
DEOPPSW SWOPPED
DEOPRRU PROUDER
DEOPRST SPORTED
DEOPRSW POWDERS
DEOPRWY POWDERY
DEOPSST DESPOTS
DEOPSTT SPOTTED
DEOPSTU SPOUTED
DEORRSV DROVERS
DEORSSS DOSSERS
DEORSSW DOWSERS
DEORSTU DETOURS
DEORSTW WORSTED
DEORSTY DESTROY
DEORTTT TROTTED
DEORTTU TUTORED
DEOSSYY ODYSSEY
DEOSTTW SWOTTED
DEOSTUX TUXEDOS
DEPRRSU SPURRED
DEPRRUY PRUDERY
DEPRSTU SPURTED
DEPRSUU PURSUED, USURPED
DERSSTU DUSTERS, TRUSSED
DERSTTU TRUSTED
DERSTUU SUTURED
DFFGINO DOFFING
DFFIIMR MIDRIFF
DFGGINU FUDGING
DFGHIOS DOGFISH
DFGIINN FINDING
DFGIINY DIGNIFY
DFGILNO FOLDING
DFGINNU FUNDING

DFGINOR FORDING
DFGINOU FUNGOID
DFGLOOY OLD FOGY
DFHILSU DISHFUL
DFHIMSU MUDFISH
DFIILRW WILFRID
DFIINRW WINFRID
DFILMNU MINDFUL
DFILNOO IN FLOOD
DFILNOP PINFOLD
DFILOSX SIXFOLD
DFILTUU DUTIFUL
DFLOOTU FOLDOUT
DFLOOTW TWOFOLD
DFNORUY FOUNDRY
DFNORWY WYNFORD
DGGGIIN DIGGING
DGGGINO DOGGING
DGGIILN GILDING, GLIDING
DGGIINR GIRDING, RIDGING
DGGIINU GUIDING
DGGIJNU JUDGING
DGGILNO LODGING
DGGINNU NUDGING
DGGIORY DIGGORY
DGGNOSU GUNDOGS
DGHIINS DISHING, HIDINGS, SHINDIG
DGHIKNO HODGKIN
DGHILNO HOLDING
DGHINTU HINDGUT
DGHIOOS GOODISH
DGHOOST HOT DOGS
DGHORTU DROUGHT
DGHOTUY DOUGHTY
DGIILNS SIDLING, SLIDING
DGIILNW WILDING
DGIILNY DINGILY
DGIILRY RIGIDLY
DGIIMMN DIMMING
DGIIMNN MINDING
DGIIMNS SMIDGIN
DGIIMOS SIGMOID
DGIINNN DINNING
DGIINNW WINDING
DGIINOV VOIDING
DGIINPP DIPPING
DGIINPR PRIDING
DGIINPS PIDGINS
DGIINPU PINGUID
DGIINRV DRIVING

DGIINSS SIDINGS
DGIINST TIDINGS
DGIINTY DIGNITY,
TIDYING
DGIKMNO KINGDOM
DGIKNNU DUNKING
DGILLNO DOLLING
DGILLNU DULLING
DGILMNO MOLDING
DGILNOR LORDING
DGILNOW GOLDWIN
DGILOPY PODGILY
DGILPUY PUDGILY
DGIMNOO DOOMING
DGIMNPU DUMPING
DGIMNSU SIGMUND
DGINNNO DONNING
DGINNNU DUNNING
DGINNOR DRONING
DGINNOU UNDOING
DGINNOW DOWNING
DGINNUY UNDYING
DGINORW WORDING
DGINOSS DOSSING
DGINOST TIN GODS
DGINOSU DOUSING
DGINOSW DOWSING
DGINOTT DOTTING
DGINSTU DUSTING
DGIOORR RODRIGO
DGIOPRY PRODIGY
DGIQSUY SQUIDGY
DGISSTU DISGUST
DGLNOUY UNGODLY
DGLNOWY GOLDWYN
DGLOOOW LOGWOOD
DGLOPSY SPLODGY
DGMOPRU GUMDROP
DGNORSU GROUNDS
DGNOSSU SUN GODS
DGOOPST TOP DOGS
DGOORTT DOGTROT
DGOSTUU DUGOUTS
DHIILOT LITHOID
DHIIMNO HOMINID
DHIINOU HOUDINI
DHIINRU HIRUDIN
DHIIOPX XIPHOID
DHIIORZ RHIZOID
DHIIOST HISTOID
DHIKRSU KURDISH
DHILLOS DOLLISH
DHILMUY HUMIDLY
DHILNOP DOLPHIN

DHILOST DOLTISH
DHILPSY SYLPHID
DHIMOPR DIMORPH
DHIMORU HUMIDOR,
RHODIUM
DHINNOS DONNISH
DHINORS DRONISH
DHIOPTY TYPHOID
DHIORTY THYROID
DHIPRSU PRUDISH
DHIPRSY SYRPHID
DHJOPRU JODHPUR
DHKORSY DROSHKY
DHLMOOU HOODLUM
DHLOOPR RODOLPH
DHLOPRU RUDOLPH
DHLOPSU HOLDUPS
DHMMRUU HUMDRUM
DHOOOOS HOODOOS
DHOORST HOT
RODS
DHOORTY DOROTHY
DHOPRSU PUSHROD
DHORSSU SHROUDS
DIIIMRU IRIDIUM
DIIINPS INSIPID
DIIJNOS DISJOIN
DIIKKNS KIDSKIN
DIIKNRU KIRUNDI
DIILLVY LIVIDLY
DIILMTY TIMIDLY
DIILNWY WINDILY
DIILQSU LIQUIDS
DIILRSU SILURID
DIILRTY DIRTILY
DIILVVY VIVIDLY
DIILYZZ DIZZILY
DIIMNOR MIDIRON
DIIMSSS DISMISS
DIIMSTW DIMWITS
DIIOPRS SPIROID
DIIORSV DIVISOR
DIIJOSTU JUDOIST
DIKKNRU DUNKIRK
DIKORSW SKID ROW
DILLOSY SOLIDLY
DILLPSY PSYLLID
DILLRUY LURIDLY
DILMNRU DRUMLIN
DILMOOY MOODILY
DILNOPT DIPLONT
DILNOXY INDOXYL
DILNPSY SPINDLY
DILOPVV PLOVDIV

DILORWY ROWDILY,
WORDILY
DILOSSU DULOSIS,
SOLIDUS
DILOSTY STYLOID
DILRYZZ DRIZZLY
DIMMOST MIDMOST
DIMNOPU IMPOUND
DIMNORV MORDVIN
DIMOPSU PODIUMS
DIMRTUU TRIDUUM
DINOORS INDOORS,
SORDINO
DINORSW WINDSOR
DINORWW WINDROW
DINOSTW SIT-DOWN
DINOSWW WINDOWS
DINPRSY SPIN-DRY
DINPSTU PUNDITS
DINSSTU NUDISTS
DIOORTT RIDOTTO
DIOPRST DISPORT,
TRIPODS
DIOPRTY TRIPODY
DIORRST STRIDOR
DIORSTT DISTORT
DIOSSTU STUDIOS
DIPRSTU DISRUPT
DKLOOPS PODOLSK
DLLOOPS DOLLOPS
DLLORWY WORLDLY
DLMOSUU MODULUS
DLNOOWW LOW-
DOWN
DLNORUY ROUNDLY
DLNOSUY SOUNDLY
DLNOTUW WOULDN'T
DLOOPPY POLYPOD
DLOOPWY PLYWOOD
DLOORRU OUR LORD
DLOOSTU OUTSOLD
DLOPRUY PROUDLY
DNNORUW RUN-DOWN
DNNOSUU UNSOUND
DNNOSUW SUNDOWN
DNNOUUW UNWOUND
DNOORTU OROTUND
DNOOTUW NUTWOOD
DNOPRUU ROUNDUP
DNOPTUW PUT-DOWN
DNOPUUW WOUND-UP
DOOORSU ODOROUS
DOOORTU OUTDOOR
DOOORWW WOODROW

DOOPRSY PROSODY
DOOPRTU DROPOUT
DPSSTUU DUSTUPS
EEEEFRR REFEREE
EEEEGGS GEE-GEES
EEEEGTX EXEGETE
EEEELNV EVELEEN
EEEEPST TEEPEES
EEEFGRU REFUGEE
EEEFLRS FEELERS
EEEFLRT FLEETER
EEEFMNR FREEMEN
EEEFORS FORESEE
EEEFRRS REEFERS
EEEFRRZ FREEZER
EEEGILS ELEGIES,
   ELEGISE
EEEGILZ ELEGIZE
EEEGINP EPIGENE
EEEGINU EUGENIE
EEEGIPR PERIGEE
EEEGLNT GENTEEL
EEEGNNO NEOGENE
EEEGNOS GENOESE
EEEGNPR EPERGNE
EEEGNRR GREENER,
   RENEGER
EEEGNRV REVENGE
EEEGRRT GREETER
EEEGRSZ GEEZERS
EEEGRUX EXERGUE
EEEHILW WHEELIE
EEEHLLN HELLENE
EEEHLNR HEERLEN
EEEHLRW WHEELER
EEEHRRS SHEERER
EEEHRST THÉRESE
EEEHRWZ WHEEZER
EEEHSTT ESTHETE
EEEHSWZ WHEEZES
EEEIKLL EEL-LIKE
EEEIKLZ EZEKIEL
EEEILMN EMELINE
EEEILNV EVELINE
EEEILRR LEERIER
EEEILRV RELIEVE
EEEILVY EVIL
   EYE
EEEIMNS ENEMIES
EEEIMNT EMETINE
EEEIMPR EPIMERE
EEEIMRT EREMITE
EEEINQU QUEENIE
EEEINRS ESERINE

EEEINRW WEENIER
EEEINST STEENIE
EEEIPST EPEEIST
EEEIRRV REVERIE
EEEISTW SWEETIE
EEEKLNX KLEENEX
EEEKLRS SLEEKER
EEEKMST MEEKEST
EEEKNPT KEEPNET
EEEKNST KEENEST
EEEKPRS KEEPERS
EEEKRSS SEEKERS
EEELLST ESTELLE
EEELMNT ELEMENT
EEELNNO NOELEEN
EEELNSV ELEVENS
EEELPRS SLEEPER
EEELPRT REPLETE
EEELPST STEEPLE
EEELRTV LEVERET
EEELSSS LESSEES
EEELSSV SLEEVES
EEELSSY EYELESS
EEELSTX TELEXES
EEELSTY EYELETS
EEEMNSS NEMESES
EEEMRTX EXTREME
EEENNPT PENTENE
EEENNTT ENTENTE
EEENPRR PREENER
EEENPRT TERPENE
EEENPST STEEPEN
EEENPSX EXPENSE
EEENRRS SNEERER
EEENRRT ENTERER, RE-
   ENTER, TERRENE
EEENRRW RENEWER
EEENRST ENTRÉES
EEENRSV VENEERS
EEENRSZ SNEEZER
EEENRUV REVENUE,
   UNREEVE
EEENSSZ SNEEZES
EEENSTW SWEETEN
EEEORSV OVERSEE
EEEORSY EYESORE
EEEPPRS PEEPERS
EEEPRSS PEERESS
EEEPRST STEEPER
EEEPRSW SWEEPER
EEEQRRU QUEERER
EEEQSUZ SQUEEZE
EEERRRV REVERER
EEERRST STEERER

EEERRSV RESERVE,
   REVERSE
EEERSTV EVEREST
EEERSTW SWEETER
EEERTTW TWEETER
EEESSTT SETTEES
EEFFFNO ENFEOFF
EEFFINT FIFTEEN
EEFFJRY JEFFERY, JEFFREY
EEFFORR OFFERER
EEFFOST TOFFEES
EEFGILN FEELING,
   FLEEING
EEFGINR FEIGNER,
   FREEING, REEFING
EEFGLLU GLEEFUL
EEFGLOR FORELEG
EEFGRSU REFUGES
EEFHIRS HEIFERS
EEFHIRT HEFTIER
EEFHISY FISH-EYE
EEFHITZ HEIFETZ
EEFHLRS FLESHER,
   HERSELF
EEFHLSS FLESHES
EEFHNRS FRESHEN
EEFHORT THEREOF
EEFHORW WHEREOF
EEFHRRS FRESHER,
   REFRESH
EEFHRST FRESHET
EEFIIRR FIERIER, REIFIER
EEFIJNR JENIFER
EEFILLX FLEXILE
EEFILNO OLEFINE
EEFILNS FELINES
EEFILOS FIESOLE
EEFILRS RELIEFS
EEFILRT FERTILE
EEFILST FELSITE, LEFTIES
EEFIMNR FIREMEN
EEFINRR REFINER
EEFINSS FINESSE
EEFIRRS FERRIES
EEFIRRT FERRITE, FIRTREE
EEFIRSZ FRIEZES
EEFISTV FESTIVE
EEFLLRS FELLERS
EEFLLRU FUELLER
EEFLNOS ONESELF
EEFLNRS FLENSER,
   FRESNEL
EEFLRRU FERRULE
EEFLRUX FLEXURE

EEFMNOR FOREMEN
EEFMNRT FERMENT
EEFMOTT MOFETTE
EEFMPRU PERFUME
EEFNRRY FERNERY
EEFNRTV FERVENT
EEFNSSW FEWNESS
EEFNSSY FEYNESS
EEFORRV FOREVER
EEFOTTU FOUETTE
EEFPRSU PERFUSE
EEFRRST FERRETS
EEFRRSU REFUSER
EEFRRTU REFUTER
EEFRRTY FERRETY
EEFRSTT FETTERS
EEFSSTU FETUSES
EEGGILR LEGGIER
EEGGIOR GEORGIE
EEGGLNO GEELONG
EEGGLPS PEG LEGS
EEGGNOR ENGORGE
EEGGNST NEST EGG
EEGHILN HEELING
EEGHINY HYGIENE
EEGHIRW WEIGHER
EEGHMNU HEGUMEN
EEGHNRY GREYHEN
EEGIJNR JEERING
EEGIKLN KEELING
EEGIKNN KEENING,
  KNEEING
EEGIKNP KEEPING,
  PEEKING
EEGIKNR REEKING
EEGIKNS SEEKING
EEGILLS GISELLE
EEGILNP PEELING
EEGILNR LEERING,
  REELING
EEGILNT GENTILE
EEGILRV VELIGER
EEGILST ELEGIST
EEGIMNR REGIMEN
EEGIMNS SEEMING
EEGIMNT MEETING,
  TEEMING
EEGIMRS ÉMIGRÉS,
  REGIMES
EEGINNS ENGINES
EEGINNTT ENGINES
EEGINNU GENUINE,
  INGENUE
EEGINNV EVENING
EEGINOP EPIGONE

EEGINPP PEEPING
EEGINPR PEERING
EEGINPS SEEPING
EEGINPV PEEVING
EEGINPW WEEPING
EEGINRS GREISEN
EEGINRT INTEGER
EEGINRV VEERING
EEGINSS GENESIS
EEGINTT GINETTE
EEGINTX EXIGENT
EEGIPRS SERGIPE
EEGIRRV GRIEVER
EEGISTV VESTIGE
EEGISTW GET WISE
EEGKNRU GERENUK
EEGLLSS LEGLESS
EEGLMMU GEMMULE
EEGLMSU LEGUMES
EEGLNOU EUGENOL
EEGLNOZ LOZENGE
EEGMNST SEGMENT
EEGMRRS MERGERS
EEGMRTU GUM TREE
EEGNORS NEGROES
EEGNPUX EXPUNGE
EEGNRSS NEGRESS
EEGNRST REGENTS
EEGOPRT PROTÉGÉ
EEGRRSS REGRESS
EEGRRST REGRETS
EEGRRSV VERGERS
EEGRRUY GRUYERE
EEGRSSU GUESSER
EEGRSSY GEYSERS
EEGRSTU GESTURE
EEGRSTY GREYEST
EEGSSSU GUESSES
EEHHRTW WHETHER
EEHIKLO HOELIKE
EEHILMN HEMLINE
EEHILOS HELOISE
EEHINOR HEROINE
EEHINOS HESIONE
EEHINRR ERRHINE
EEHINRT THEREIN
EEHINRW WHEREIN
EEHIPRT PRITHEE
EEHIPSV PEEVISH
EEHIPTT EPITHET
EEHIRSS HEIRESS
EEHIRST HEISTER
EEHISST HESSITE
EEHISTV THIEVES

EEHKLOY KEYHOLE
EEHKLSS SHEKELS
EEHKNNT KENNETH
EEHLLMP PHELLEM
EEHLLRY HELLERY
EEHLLSY SHELLEY
EEHLMST HELMETS
EEHLNUW HEULWEN
EEHLOSY HOLY SEE
EEHLPRT TELPHER
EEHLPST ELSPETH
EEHLRST SHELTER
EEHLRSV SHELVER
EEHLRSW WELSHER
EEHLSSV SHELVES
EEHMNOP PHONEME
EEHMNRY MYNHEER
EEHMORT THEOREM
EEHMRUX EXHUMER
EEHNNRY HENNERY
EEHNOPT POTHEEN
EEHNORT THEREON
EEHNORW NOWHERE,
  WHEREON
EEHNPST STEPHEN
EEHNPSW NEPHEWS
EEHNSTU ENTHUSE
EEHNSTV SEVENTH
EEHOOPW WHOOPEE
EEHOPRT THE ROPE
EEHOPRU EUPHROE
EEHOPST HEPTOSE
EEHORRV HOVERER
EEHORST HERE'S TO
EEHORSU REHOUSE
EEHORTT THERETO
EEHORTW WHERETO
EEHORVW HOWEVER,
  WHOEVER
EEHOSTY EYESHOT
EEHPRSS SPHERES
EEHRRST THREE R'S
EEHRSTT TETHERS
EEHRTTW WHETTER
EEHSTTW THE WEST
EEHSTUY SHUT-EYE
EEIIMST ITEMISE
EEIIMTZ ITEMIZE
EEIIPST PIETIES
EEIIRRV RIVIERE
EEIJKRR JERKIER
EEIJLLS JELLIES
EEIJMMS JEMMIES
EEIJNNS JENNIES

EEIJSTT JETTIES
EEIKMNP PIKEMEN
EEIKNPY PINKEYE
EEIKNRT KERNITE
EEIKPRR PERKIER
EEIKPRS PESKIER
EEIKTTT TEKTITE
EEILLNO LEOLINE
EEILLNS NELLIES
EEILLNV NEVILLE
EEILLOR LORELEI
EEILLPS ELLIPSE
EEILLRV EVILLER
EEILLST TELLIES
EEILLSV SEVILLE
EEILLSW WELLIES
EEILMNN LINEMEN
EEILMRV VERMEIL
EEILNNO LEONINE,
  NOELINE
EEILNNT LENIENT
EEILNNV ENLIVEN
EEILNPS PENSILE
EEILNRV LIVENER
EEILNST SETLINE,
  TENSILE
EEILNTT ENTITLE,
  LINETTE
EEILNTV VEINLET
EEILOPT PETIOLE
EEILORV OVERLIE
EEILOTZ ZEOLITE
EEILPRR REPLIER
EEILPRS REPLIES, SPIELER
EEILPRT PERLITE, REPTILE
EEILPRU PUERILE
EEILPST EPISTLE
EEILRRV REVILER
EEILRST LEISTER, STERILE
EEILRSU LEISURE
EEILRSV SERVILE
EEILSSS SESSILE
EEILSST TELESIS
EEILSSU ELEUSIS
EEILSTT LISETTE
EEILSTV EVILEST
EEILSTX SEXTILE
EEILSUV ELUSIVE
EEILSVW WEEVILS
EEILTTX TEXTILE
EEILVWY WEEVILY
EEIMMNS IMMENSE
EEIMMRS IMMERSE
EEIMNNO NOMINEE

EEIMNNT EMINENT
EEIMNOT ONETIME
EEIMNRS ERMINES
EEIMNSS MEISSEN,
  NEMESIS, SIEMENS
EEIMOPS EPISOME
EEIMOPT EPITOME
EEIMOTV EMOTIVE
EEIMPRR PREMIER
EEIMPRS EMPIRES,
  EPIMERS, PREMISE,
  SPIREME
EEIMPRT EMPTIER
EEIMPST EMPTIES,
  SEPTIME
EEIMQRU REQUIEM
EEIMRRR MERRIER
EEIMRRT TRIREME
EEIMRSS MESSIER
EEIMRST MÉTIERS
EEIMRTT EMITTER,
  TERMITE
EEINNPS PENNIES
EEINNRV INNERVE,
  NERVINE
EEINNST INTENSE
EEINNTT NINETTE
EEINNTW ENTWINE
EEINOPR PIONEER
EEINOPS PEONIES
EEINORT ORIENTE
EEINPRR RIPENER
EEINPRS EREPSIN
EEINPSS PENISES
EEINPSV PENSIVE, VESPINE
EEINQRU ENQUIRE
EEINQTU QUIETEN
EEINRRT RENTIER,
  TERRINE
EEINRRV NERVIER,
  VERNIER
EEINRST ENTRIES
EEINRSV INVERSE
EEINRTU RETINUE,
  REUNITE, UTERINE
EEINSTV TENSIVE
EEINSTX SIXTEEN
EEINSTY SYENITE
EEIORSS SOIREES
EEIORSV EROSIVE
EEIPPST PEPTISE
EEIPPTT PIPETTE
EEIPPTZ PEPTIZE
EEIPQRU PERIQUE

EEIPRRS REPRISE, RESPIRE
EEIPRRX EXPIRER
EEIPRST RESPITE
EEIPRTT PETTIER
EEIPRVW PREVIEW
EEIPRZZ PREZZIE
EEIPSTW PEEWITS
EEIQRRU REQUIRE
EEIQRSU ESQUIRE,
  QUERIES
EEIQRTU QUIETER,
  REQUITE
EEIRRRT RETIRER,
  TERRIER
EEIRRSV REVISER
EEIRRTV RIVETER
EEIRRTW REWRITE
EEIRRVV REVIVER
EEIRSSU REISSUE
EEIRSTT TESTIER, TRIESTE
EEIRSTV RESTIVE
EEIRSUZ SEIZURE
EEIRSVW REVIEWS,
  VIEWERS
EEIRTVV VETIVER
EEISSTX SEXIEST
EEJLRWY JEWELRY
EEJNORY ENJOYER
EEJNOSS JONESES
EEJOSTT JOSETTE
EEJPRRU PERJURE
EEJRSST JESTERS
EEJRSSY JERSEYS
EEKKRRT TREKKER
EEKLLSY SLEEKLY
EEKLLUU UKULELE
EEKLNNS KENNELS
EEKLNOS KEELSON
EEKLNRS KERNELS
EEKLRST KESTREL
EEKLSTT KETTLES
EEKNOTY KEYNOTE
EEKNSTU NETSUKE
EEKORRV REVOKER
EEKRSSW SKEWERS
EELLMOS MOSELLE
EELLNOV NOVELLE
EELLORV VELLORE
EELLOSV O LEVELS
EELLPRS SPELLER
EELLPST PELLETS
EELLQRU QUELLER
EELLRSS SELLERS
EELLRST TELLERS

EELLSTW WELL-SET
EELMORW EELWORM
EELMOST OMELETS
EELMPST PELMETS,
   TEMPLES
EELMRST SMELTER
EELNOPR PERONEL
EELNOPV ENVELOP
EELNOSV SLOVENE
EELNOTT NOTELET
EELNOTU TOLUENE
EELNPSS SPLEENS
EELNQUY QUEENLY
EELNRST NESTLER
EELNSTT NETTLES
EELNSTY TENSELY
EELNTTU LUNETTE
EELNTTY LYNETTE
EELOPPS PEOPLES
EELOPRS LEPROSE
EELOPRX EXPLORE
EELOPTU EELPOUT
EELORSV RESOLVE
EELORTT LORETTE
EELORVV EVOLVER,
   REVOLVE
EELOSTT TELEOST
EELOTUV EVOLUTE
EELPPRX PERPLEX
EELPRST PETRELS,
   SPELTER
EELPRSU REPULSE
EELPRTZ PRETZEL
EELPRVY REPLEVY
EELPSST PESTLES
EELPSTY STEEPLY
EELQRUY QUEERLY
EELQSSU SEQUELS
EELRRVY REVELRY
EELRSTT LETTERS,
   SETTLER, STERLET,
   TRESTLE
EELRSTW SWELTER,
   WRESTLE
EELRSTY RESTYLE,
   TERSELY
EELRSTZ SELTZER
EELSSSU USELESS
EELSSSV VESSELS
EELSSSX SEXLESS
EELSSTT SETTLES
EELSTVW TWELVES
EELSTWY SWEETLY
EELTVVY VELVETY

EEMMNOT MEMENTO
EEMMRST STEMMER
EEMNNOV ENVENOM
EEMNOOS SOMEONE
EEMNOOY MOONEYE
EEMNPTU UMPTEEN
EEMNSYZ ENZYMES
EEMOPRR EMPEROR
EEMOPRW EMPOWER
EEMORRS REMORSE
EEMORRT REMOTER
EEMORRV REMOVER
EEMORST METEORS
EEMORSV REMOVES
EEMPPRT PREEMPT
EEMPRSS EMPRESS
EEMPRST TEMPERS
EEMPRSU PRESUME,
   SUPREME
EEMPRTT TEMPTER
EEMPRTU PERMUTE
EEMPSTT TEMPEST
EEMRSSU RÉSUMÉS
EENNORT ENTERON,
   TENONER
EENNOSS ESSONNE,
   ONENESS
EENNOTY NEOTENY
EENNPTU NEPTUNE
EENNRST TENNERS
EENNRUV UNNERVE
EENNSSW NEWNESS
EENOPPR PROPENE
EENOPPT PEPTONE
EENOPRS OPENERS
EENOPST ONE-STEP,
   PENTOSE
EENOPTY NEOTYPE
EENORTU EN ROUTE
EENPRST PRESENT,
   SERPENT
EENPRTV PREVENT
EENQSTU SEQUENT
EENRRST RENTERS,
   STERNER
EENRRSU ENSURER
EENRRTY RE-ENTRY
EENRRUV NERVURE
EENRSTU TUREENS
EENRSTW WESTERN
EENRSTY STYRENE
EENRTUV VENTURE
EENSSTT TENSEST
EENSSTW WETNESS

EENSSUX NEXUSES
EENSTTX EXTENTS
EENSTVY SEVENTY
EEOPRRS REPOSER
EEOPRRV REPROVE
EEOPRSX EXPOSER
EEOPSST POETESS
EEOPSSU ESPOUSE
EEOPSSX EXPOSÉS
EEOPSTU TOUPEES
EEOPSTY EYESPOT
EEORRST RESTORE
EEORRTV EVERTOR
EEORRTW REWROTE
EEORSST STEREOS
EEORSTT ROSETTE
EEORSTV OVERSET
EEORSUV OVERUSE
EEORSVW OVERSEW
EEORSXX XEROXES
EEPPPRS PEPPERS
EEPPPRY PEPPERY
EEPPRST STEPPER
EEPPRSX PERSPEX
EEPPSST STEPPES
EEPPSUW UPSWEEP
EEPRRSS REPRESS
EEPRRSU PERUSER
EEPRRTV PERVERT
EEPRSSS PRESSES
EEPRSSV VESPERS
EEPRSSX EXPRESS
EEPRSTT PRETEST
EEPRSTX EXPERTS
EEPRTTX PRETEXT
EEPSSTT SEPTETS
EEPSTTY TYPESET
EEQRRUY EQUERRY
EEQRSTU QUESTER,
   REQUEST
EERRSSV SERVERS
EERRSTW STREWER,
   WRESTER
EERRSVW SWERVER
EERRSVY SERVERY
EERRTTU UTTERER
EERSSST TRESSES
EERSSTT SETTERS,
   STREETS, TESTERS
EERSSVW SWERVES
EERSTTU TRUSTEE
EERSTUV VESTURE
EERTTUX TEXTURE
EESSTTX SEXTETS

EESTTTW WETTEST
EESTTUZ SUZETTE
EFFGRRU GRUFFER
EFFHILW WHIFFLE
EFFHIRS SHERIFF
EFFHIRU HUFFIER
EFFHIRW WHIFFER
EFFHLSU SHUFFLE
EFFIIST FIFTIES
EFFIKLS SKIFFLE
EFFILNS SNIFFLE
EFFILRR RIFFLER
EFFILRY FIREFLY
EFFINRS SNIFFER
EFFINST STIFFEN
EFFIORT FORFEIT
EFFIORX FOXFIRE
EFFIPRU PUFFIER
EFFIRST STIFFER
EFFLLOW WELL-OFF
EFFLMRU MUFFLER
EFFLNSU SNUFFLE
EFFLOSU SOUFFLÉ
EFFLRRU RUFFLER
EFFLRSU RUFFLES
EFFLRTU FRETFUL,
  TRUFFLE
EFFNOOS ONE-OFFS
EFFNRSU SNUFFER
EFFOPRR PROFFER
EFFORST EFFORTS
EFFRSTU STUFFER
EFFSSUU SUFFUSE
EFGGIOR FOGGIER
EFGGIRU FUGGIER
EFGGLOR FLOGGER
EFGHIRT FIGHTER,
  FREIGHT
EFGILLN FELLING
EFGILMN FLEMING
EFGILNR FLINGER
EFGILNT FELTING
EFGILNU FUELING
EFGILNX FLEXING
EFGIMNT FIGMENT
EFGINNP PFENNIG
EFGINOR FOREIGN
EFGINRS FINGERS,
  FRINGES
EFGINRU GUNFIRE
EFGIOOR GOOFIER
EFGIORV FORGIVE
EFGIRRU FIGURER
EFGIRSU FIGURES

EFGLNTU FULGENT
EFGLORS GOLFERS
EFGMNOR FROGMEN
EFGNOOR FORGONE
EFGOORR FORGOER
EFGORRS FORGERS
EFGORRY FORGERY
EFGORTU FOREGUT
EFHIIRS FISHIER
EFHIJSW JEWFISH
EFHILMS FLEMISH,
  HIMSELF
EFHILSS SELFISH
EFHILTY HEFTILY
EFHINST FISHNET
EFHIORR FOR HIRE
EFHIRST SHIFTER
EFHIRSY FISHERY
EFHLLPU HELPFUL
EFHLLSY FLESHLY
EFHLOOX FOXHOLE
EFHLOPU HOPEFUL
EFHLRSU FLUSHER
EFHLRSY FRESHLY
EFHLSSU FLUSHES
EFHLSTY THYSELF
EFHLTTW TWELFTH
EFHRRTU FURTHER
EFHRTTU THE TURF
EFIILLS FILLIES
EFIILMR FILMIER
EFIILMS MISFILE
EFIILSS FISSILE
EFIIMRR RIM-FIRE
EFIIMRS MISFIRE
EFIINRT NIFTIER
EFIINRU UNIFIER
EFIIRZZ FIZZIER
EFIJLLY JELLIFY
EFIJLOT JETFOIL
EFIKLNU LIKE FUN
EFIKLOX FOXLIKE
EFIKNRU FUNKIER
EFIKRRS FRISKER
EFIKRST FRISKET
EFILLOS FOLLIES
EFILLOW LOW LIFE
EFILLRS REFILLS
EFILLST FILLETS
EFILMST FILMSET, LEFTISM
EFILNOX FLEXION
EFILOOS FOLIOSE
EFILOPR PROFILE, PRO-
  LIFE

EFILORR FLORRIE
EFILORT LOFTIER,
  TREFOIL
EFILOSS FLOSSIE
EFILPPR FLIPPER
EFILQUY LIQUEFY
EFILRRT FLIRTER,
  TRIFLER
EFILRRY RIFLERY
EFILRST FILTERS, STIFLER,
  TRIFLES
EFILRTT FLITTER
EFILRVV FLIVVER
EFILRZZ FRIZZLE
EFILSTT LEFTIST
EFIMMRU FERMIUM
EFIMNOR FERMION
EFIMNTT FITMENT
EFIMRST FIRMEST
EFIMRTY METRIFY
EFINNOR INFERNO
EFINNRU FUNNIER
EFINRST SNIFTER
EFINRSU INFUSER
EFINRUY REUNIFY
EFINSST FITNESS
EFIOOPR POOFIER
EFIOOST FOOTSIE
EFIORRT ROTIFER
EFIORRU FOURIER
EFIORST FORTIES
EFIOSST SOFTIES
EFIOSTX FOXIEST
EFIPRTY PETRIFY
EFIRRRU FURRIER
EFIRRSU FRISEUR
EFIRRTT FRITTER
EFIRRTU FRUITER
EFIRRTY TERRIFY
EFIRRZZ FRIZZER
EFIRSST SIFTERS
EFIRSSU FISSURE,
  FUSSIER
EFIRSTT FITTERS, TITFERS
EFIRSTU FUSTIER, SURFEIT
EFIRSTW SWIFTER
EFIRSVY VERSIFY
EFIRTUV FURTIVE
EFIRTUX FIXTURE
EFIRUZZ FUZZIER
EFISTTT FITTEST
EFISTTY TESTIFY
EFKLMNO MENFOLK
EFKLNUY FLUNKEY

EFLLOSW FELLOWS
EFLLSTU FULLEST
EFLMOSU FULSOME
EFLMSUU MUSEFUL
EFLNNSU FUNNELS
EFLNORU FLEURON
EFLNORY FELONRY
EFLNSSU FULNESS
EFLNTUU TUNEFUL
EFLOORY FOOLERY
EFLOORZ FOOZLER
EFLORSU OURSELF
EFLORSW FLOWERS
EFLORTU FLOUTER
EFLORTW FELWORT
EFLORVY FLYOVER,
    OVERFLY
EFLORWY FLOWERY
EFLOSTU FOULEST
EFLRSTU FLUSTER,
    RESTFUL
EFLRTTU FLUTTER
EFLSTUZ ZESTFUL
EFMNOOT FOOTMEN
EFMNORT FREMONT
EFMOPRR PERFORM
EFMORRS REFORMS
EFNOOST FESTOON
EFNORRU FORERUN
EFNORRW FROWNER
EFNORTU FORTUNE
EFNORTW FORWENT
EFNRSSU FURNESS
EFOOPRR REPROOF
EFOOPRS SPOOFER
EFOOPRT FORETOP
EFOORSW WOOFERS
EFOPPRY FOPPERY
EFOPRSS PROFESS
EFOPRSU PROFUSE
EFORRSU FERROUS
EFORRTY TORREFY
EFORRUV FERVOUR
EFORSST FORESTS
EFOSSTT SOFTEST
EFPRTUY PUTREFY
EFPSTUY STUPEFY
EFRRSSU SURFERS
EFRSTUU FUTURES
EGGGIKLO LEGGING
EGGGILR GIGGLER
EGGGILS GIGGLES
EGGGINP PEGGING
EGGGLOS GOGGLES

EGGIIPR PIGGIER
EGGIIPS PIGGIES
EGGIJLS JIGGLES
EGGIJRS JIGGERS
EGGILLN GELLING
EGGILNR NIGGLER
EGGILNS SNIGGLE
EGGILNU GLUEING
EGGILRW WIGGLER,
    WRIGGLE
EGGILSW WIGGLES
EGGIMMN GEMMING
EGGIMNR MERGING
EGGIMOS MOGGIES
EGGIMRU MUGGIER
EGGINNS GINSENG
EGGINRS NIGGERS,
    SNIGGER
EGGINRV VERGING
EGGINRY GINGERY,
    GREYING
EGGINTT GETTING
EGGIORS SOGGIER
EGGIPRY PIGGERY
EGGIRRT TRIGGER
EGGIRSW SWIGGER
EGGJLOR JOGGLER
EGGJLOS JOGGLES
EGGJLRU JUGGLER
EGGLLOR EGG ROLL
EGGLMSU SMUGGLE
EGGLNSU SNUGGLE
EGGLOOY GEOLOGY
EGGLORS LOGGERS,
    SLOGGER
EGGLOST TOGGLES
EGGLRSU LUGGERS
EGGMRSU MUGGERS,
    SMUGGER
EGGNSTU NUGGETS
EGGNTUY NUGGETY
EGGORRY GREGORY
EGGSSTU SUGGEST
EGHHHIO HEIGH-HO
EGHHIST EIGHTHS,
    HEIGHTS, HIGHEST
EGHIILL GHILLIE
EGHIINT NIGHTIE
EGHIINV INVEIGH
EGHIKLO HOGLIKE
EGHIKNR GHERKIN
EGHILNP HELPING
EGHILNS ENGLISH,
    SHINGLE

EGHILNT LIGHTEN
EGHILRT LIGHTER
EGHILSS SLEIGHS
EGHILST SLEIGHT
EGHIMMN HEMMING
EGHIMNS MESHING
EGHINNU UNHINGE
EGHINOS SHOEING
EGHINRR HERRING
EGHINST HENGIST
EGHINSW SHEWING
EGHINTT TIGHTEN
EGHIORS OGREISH
EGHIOTV EIGHTVO
EGHIRRT RIGHTER
EGHIRST SIGHTER
EGHIRSY GREYISH
EGHIRTT TIGHTER
EGHISTW WEIGHTS
EGHITWY WEIGHTY
EGHLLOU LUGHOLE
EGHLNOR LEGHORN
EGHLNST LENGTHS
EGHLNTY LENGTHY
EGHMORS GERSHOM
EGHMOSU GUMSHOE
EGHNOOS HOGNOSE
EGHNORU ROUGHEN
EGHNOTU TOUGHEN
EGHNRTU GUNTHER
EGHNSUY HUYGENS
EGHNTWY GWYNETH
EGHOPRS GOPHERS
EGHORRU ROUGHER
EGHORTU TOUGHER
EGHORTZ HERTZOG
EGHOSTT GHETTOS
EGHRSSU GUSHERS
EGHRTUY THEURGY
EGIILLS GILLIES
EGIILNT LIGNITE
EGIILNV VEILING
EGIILNX EXILING
EGIILPZ LEIPZIG
EGIIMNP IMPINGE
EGIIMNR MINGIER
EGIIMPS PIGMIES
EGIIMRR GRIMIER
EGIINNR REINING
EGIINNV VEINING
EGIINRT IGNITER
EGIINSV SIEVING
EGIINSZ SEIZING
EGIINTX EXITING

EGIINVW VIEWING
EGIIPRW PERIWIG
EGIIPSS GIPSIES
EGIJKNR JERKING
EGIJLLN JELLING
EGIJLNR JINGLER
EGIJLNS JINGLES
EGIJNST JESTING
EGIJNTT JETTING
EGIKNNN KENNING
EGIKNOV EVOKING
EGIKNPR PERKING
EGIKNRY KEY RING
EGIKNSW SKEWING
EGILLNS SELLING
EGILLNT TELLING
EGILLNW WELLING
EGILLNY YELLING
EGILLRR GRILLER
EGILLRS GRILLES
EGILLSU GULLIES
EGILMMN LEMMING
EGILMMR GLIMMER
EGILMNR GREMLIN
EGILMNT MELTING
EGILMNU LEGUMIN
EGILMOS LIMOGES
EGILMOV MOGILEV
EGILMPS GLIMPSE
EGILMST GIMLETS
EGILNOP ELOPING
EGILNOS LEGIONS,
LINGOES
EGILNOT LENTIGO
EGILNPS SPIGNEL
EGILNPT PELTING
EGILNPY YELPING
EGILNRS SLINGER
EGILNRT RINGLET,
TINGLER
EGILNRY RELYING
EGILNSS SINGLES
EGILNST GLISTEN,
SINGLET
EGILNSW SLEWING,
SWINGLE
EGILNTT LETTING
EGILNTW WINGLET
EGILNVY LEVYING
EGILORR GROLIER
EGILORS GLORIES
EGILOST LOGIEST
EGILPST PIGLETS
EGILRST GRISTLE

EGILRSU LURGIES
EGILRTT GLITTER
EGILRUV VIRGULE
EGILRZZ GRIZZEL,
GRIZZLE
EGILSTU UGLIEST
EGIMMRR GRIMMER
EGIMMRU GUMMIER
EGIMMTU GUMMITE
EGIMNOW MEOWING
EGIMNPR PERMING
EGIMNPT PIGMENT,
TEMPING
EGIMNRT TERMING
EGIMNSS MESSING
EGIMOST EGOTISM
EGIMPSY PYGMIES
EGINNNP PENNING
EGINNOP OPENING
EGINNPU PENGUIN
EGINNRR GRINNER
EGINNRT RENTING,
RINGENT
EGINNRV NERVING
EGINNSS ENSIGNS,
SENSING
EGINNST NESTING,
TENSING
EGINNSU ENSUING
EGINNTT NETTING
EGINNTV VENTING
EGINNVY ENVYING
EGINOPR PERIGON,
PONGIER
EGINOPS PIGEONS
EGINORR IGNORER
EGINORS REGIONS,
SIGNORE
EGINORT GENITOR,
NEGRITO
EGINORZ ZEROING
EGINOSU IGNEOUS
EGINOSY ISOGENY
EGINOTV VETOING
EGINOUV IN VOGUE
EGINPPP PEPPING
EGINPRS SPRINGE
EGINPRY PREYING
EGINPSW SPEWING
EGINPSY ESPYING
EGINPTT PETTING
EGINPYY EPIGYNY
EGINQUU QUEUING
EGINRRS RINGERS

EGINRRW WRINGER
EGINRSS INGRESS
EGINRST RESTING,
STINGER
EGINRSU REUSING
EGINRSV SERVING
EGINRSW SWINGER,
WINGERS
EGINRSY SYRINGE
EGINRTT GITTERN
EGINRVV REVVING
EGINSST SIGNETS
EGINSTT SETTING,
TESTING
EGINSTV VESTING
EGINSTW STEWING,
TWINGES, WESTING
EGINTTV VETTING
EGINTTW WETTING
EGIOOST GOOIEST
EGIOPRS SERPIGO
EGIOPRT EGO TRIP
EGIOPRU GROUPIE
EGIORST GORIEST
EGIORTV VERTIGO
EGIOSST EGOISTS
EGIOSTT EGOTIST
EGIPPRR GRIPPER
EGIPRRS GRIPERS
EGIPRUU GUIPURE
EGIPSSY GYPSIES
EGIRSST TIGRESS
EGIRSSU SERGIUS
EGIRSTU GUSTIER,
GUTSIER
EGIRTTU TURGITE
EGISUWY WISE GUY
EGJLNSU JUNGLES
EGKLORW LEGWORK
EGLLLPU LEG-PULL
EGLLOUY YULE LOG
EGLLSTU GULLETS
EGLMMRU GLUMMER
EGLMNOR MONGREL
EGLMOOR LEGROOM
EGLNNSU GUNNELS
EGLNORU LOUNGER
EGLNOST LONGEST
EGLNOSU LOUNGES
EGLNPRU PLUNGER
EGLOORS REGOSOL
EGLOPSS GOSPELS
EGLORRW GROWLER
EGLORSS GLOSSER

EGLORSU REGULOS
EGLPRSU SPLURGE
EGLRSUU REGULUS
EGLRUZZ GUZZLER
EGLSSTU GUTLESS
EGLSTUU GLUTEUS
EGMMORT GROMMET
EGMNOYZ ZYMOGEN
EGMNSTU NUTMEGS
EGMOORR GROOMER
EGMORSU MORGUES
EGMORTU GOURMET
EGNNORT RÖNTGEN
EGNNPTU PUNGENT
EGNNRSU GUNNERS
EGNNRUY GUNNERY
EGNNSTU STEN GUN
EGNNTUU UNGUENT
EGNOORY OROGENY
EGNOPRS SPONGER
EGNOPRY PROGENY,
   PYROGEN
EGNOPSS SPONGES
EGNORRW WRONGER
EGNORSS ENGROSS
EGNORSU SURGEON
EGNORSY GROYNES
EGNORUY YOUNGER
EGNOSTU TONGUES
EGNRRTU GRUNTER
EGNRSYY SYNERGY
EGOORSV GROOVES
EGOOSST STOOGES
EGOPRRU GROUPER,
   REGROUP
EGORRSS GROSSER
EGORRSU GROUSER
EGORRSW GROWERS
EGORRTU GROUTER
EGORRUY ROGUERY
EGORSSS GROSSES
EGORSSU GROUSES
EGORTUW OUTGREW
EGPRSUU UPSURGE
EGRRSUY SURGERY
EGRSTTU GUTTERS
EGSSSTU GUSSETS
EHHHOTU HUHEHOT
EHHIKSS SHEIKHS
EHHILLS HELLISH
EHHIRTT THITHER
EHHIRTW WHITHER
EHHMPTU THE HUMP
EHHNPSY HYPHENS

EHIIIKT HEITIKI
EHIIKLP HIPLIKE
EHIILLR HILLIER
EHIINRS SHINIER
EHIINRT INHERIT
EHIIPPS HIPPIES
EHIIPRT PITHIER
EHIISST SHIITES
EHIITTT HITTITE
EHIJNNO JOHNNIE
EHIKLNU HUNLIKE
EHIKLTU HUTLIKE
EHIKNOS HONKIES
EHIKNRT RETHINK
EHIKNST KENTISH
EHIKOOS HOOKIES
EHIKRRS SHIRKER
EHIKRSS SHRIEKS, SHRIKES
EHIKRSU HUSKIER
EHIKRSW WHISKER
EHIKSSU HUSKIES
EHIKSVZ IZHEVSK
EHIKSWY WHISKEY
EHILLNO HELLION
EHILLRY HILLERY
EHILLTY LITHELY
EHILNOP PINHOLE
EHILNOT HOT LINE,
   NEOLITH
EHILOPT HOPLITE
EHILOST HOLIEST,
   HOSTILE, THE SOIL
EHILPRT PHILTRE
EHILPSS HIPLESS
EHILRRW WHIRLER
EHILRST SLITHER
EHILRSV SHRIVEL
EHILRSY SHIRLEY
EHILSTT LITHEST, THISTLE
EHILSTW WHISTLE
EHILTTW WHITTLE
EHIMMPS MEMPHIS
EHIMMRS SHIMMER
EHIMNRU INHUMER,
   RHENIUM
EHIMNTY THYMINE
EHIMORS HEROISM,
   MOREISH
EHIMORZ RHIZOME
EHIMOST HOMIEST
EHIMPRW WHIMPER
EHIMRST HERMITS
EHIMRSU MUSHIER
EHIMRTT THERMIT

EHINNOP PHONE-IN
EHINNRT THINNER
EHINOPR PHONIER
EHINOPX PHOENIX
EHINORR HORNIER
EHINORS INSHORE
EHINOST HISTONE
EHINOSU HEINOUS, IN-
   HOUSE
EHINRSS SHRINES
EHINRSW WHINERS
EHINSSU HUSSEIN
EHINSTZ ZENITHS
EHIOPRS ROSE HIP
EHIORRS HORSIER
EHIORRT HERITOR
EHIORSS HOSIERS
EHIORST HOISTER,
   SHORTIE
EHIORSW SHOWIER
EHIORSY HOSIERY
EHIORTT THORITE
EHIOSTY ISOHYET
EHIPPRS SHIPPER
EHIPPRW WHIPPER
EHIPPST HIPPEST
EHIPPTW WHIPPET
EHIPRST HIPSTER
EHIPRSU PUSHIER
EHIPRSW WHISPER
EHIPSTT PETTISH
EHIRRSV SHRIVER
EHIRRTW WHERRIT,
   WRITHER
EHIRSSV SHIVERS
EHIRSSW SWISHER
EHIRSTU HIRSUTE
EHIRSTW WITHERS
EHIRSTZ ZITHERS
EHIRSVY SHIVERY
EHISSSU HUSSIES
EHISSSW SWISHES
EHISSTT THEISTS
EHISSTU HUSSITE
EHISTTW WETTISH,
   WHITEST
EHISWZZ WHIZZES
EHKNORS KHERSON
EHKNRSU HUNKERS
EHKOORS HOOKERS
EHLLORS HOLLERS
EHLMNOT MENTHOL
EHLOOPT POTHOLE
EHLOOST LESOTHO

EHLOPPR HOPPLER	**EHOPSTT** THE TOPS	**EIIMMSS** MIMESIS
EHLOPSX PHLOXES	**EHORRST** SHORTER	**EIIMMST** MISTIME
EHLORST HOLSTER,	**EHORRTW** THROWER	**EIIMNOR** MEIRION
HOSTLER	**EHORSSW** SHOWERS	**EIIMNPR** PRIMINE
EHLORSW HOWLERS	**EHORSTU** SHOUTER,	**EIIMNRT** INTERIM,
EHLORTY HELOTRY,	SOUTHER	TERMINI
THORLEY	**EHORSWY** SHOWERY	**EIIMNRV** MINIVER
EHLOSST HOSTELS	**EHOSSST** HOSTESS	**EIIMNTV** MINIVET
EHLOSSV SHOVELS	**EHOSTTT** HOTTEST	**EIIMOPP** POMPEII
EHLPRSU PLUSHER	**EHPRSSU** PUSHERS	**EIIMOSS** MEIOSIS
EHLRSTU HUSTLER	**EHPRSYZ** ZEPHYRS	**EIIMPSW** WIMPIES
EHLSSTU SLEUTHS	**EHPRTTU** TURPETH	**EIIMPTY** IMPIETY
EHLSTTU SHUTTLE	**EHRSSTY** SHYSTER	**EIIMSSS** MISSIES
EHMNOOR HORMONE,	**EHRSTTU** SHUTTER	**EIIMSSV** MISSIVE
MOORHEN	**EHRSTTW** STREWTH	**EIINNNP** NINEPIN
EHMNORU HOME RUN	**EIIILST** ILEITIS	**EIINNNS** NINNIES
EHMNOSW SHOWMEN	**EIIJMMS** JIMMIES	**EIINNPS** PINNIES
EHMNPTY NYMPHET	**EIIKKNR** KINKIER	**EIINNQU** QUININE
EHMNTTU HUTMENT	**EIIKLMR** MILKIER	**EIINNRT** TINNIER
EHMOOSW SOMEHOW	**EIIKLNW** KWEILIN	**EIINORS** IONISER,
EHMORST MOTHERS,	**EIIKLRS** SILKIER	IRONIES, NOISIER
SMOTHER, THERMOS	**EIIKNPS** PINKIES	**EIINORT** NITEROI
EHMORTU MOUTHER	**EIIKNST** INKIEST	**EIINORZ** IONIZER
EHMPRTU THUMPER	**EIIKPRS** SPIKIER	**EIINPPR** NIPPIER
EHMRSUU HUMERUS	**EIIKRRS** RISKIER	**EIINPRS** INSPIRE
EHNNOPR NEPHRON	**EIIKSTT** KITTIES	**EIINPST** PINIEST, TIEPINS
EHNNORW RHONWEN	**EIILLMN** MILLINE	**EIINQRU** INQUIRE
EHNNRSU SHUNNER	**EIILLNV** VILLEIN	**EIINQTU** INQUIET
EHNOORS ONSHORE	**EIILLRS** SILLIER	**EIINRTT** NITRITE
EHNOPSY PHONEYS	**EIILLSS** SILLIES	**EIINRTV** INVITER,
EHNOPUY EUPHONY	**EIILLSW** WILLIES	VITRINE
EHNORRY HERONRY	**EIILMPR** IMPERIL	**EIINRTW** WRITE-IN
EHNORST HORNETS,	**EIILMRS** SLIMIER	**EIINSTT** TINIEST
SHORTEN, THRONES	**EIILMRT** LEITRIM,	**EIINSTU** UNITIES
EHNORSU UNHORSE	LIMITER	**EIINTUV** UNITIVE
EHNOSST HOTNESS	**EIILMSS** MISSILE,	**EIIORSV** IVORIES
EHNOSTT SHOTTEN	SIMILES	**EIIOSTZ** ZOISITE
EHNOSTY HONESTY	**EIILMST** ELITISM, LIMIEST	**EIIPPRZ** ZIPPIER
EHNRSTU HUNTERS,	**EIILMSU** MILIEUS	**EIIPRRV** PRIVIER
SHUNTER	**EIILMUX** MILIEUX	**EIIPRST** TIPSIER
EHNSSSY SHYNESS	**EIILNOS** ELISION, ISOLINE,	**EIIPRSV** PRIVIES
EHOOPRW WHOOPER	LIONISE	**EIIPRSW** WISPIER
EHOOPTY OOPHYTE	**EIILNOV** OLIVINE	**EIIQUVV** QUI VIVE
EHOORST HOOTERS,	**EIILNOZ** LIONIZE	**EIIRSSS** SISSIER
SHOOTER, SOOTHER	**EIILNRT** NITRILE	**EIIRSST** TRISSIE
EHOORSV HOOVERS	**EIILNTU** INUTILE	**EIIRSTW** WIRIEST
EHOOSST SESOTHO	**EIILORV** OLIVIER	**EIIRSVZ** VIZIERS
EHOPPRS HOPPERS,	**EIILOST** OILIEST	**EIIRTTW** WITTIER
SHOPPER	**EIILOTT** OTTILIE	**EIISSSS** SISSIES
EHOPPRT PROPHET	**EIILRSX** ELIXIRS	**EIISSTX** SIXTIES
EHOPPRW WHOPPER	**EIILSTT** ELITIST	**EIISTTT** TITTIES
EHOPRRY ORPHREY	**EIILSTU** UTILISE	**EIISTUV** UVEITIS
EHOPRST STROPHE	**EIILSTW** WILIEST	**EIISTZZ** TIZZIES
EHOPSST POSHEST	**EIILTUZ** UTILIZE	**EIJKLRY** JERKILY

EIJKNRS JERKINS
EIJKNSU JUNKIES
EIJLLOR JOLLIER
EIJMPRU JUMPIER
EIJNORS JOINERS
EIJNORT JOINTER
EIJNORY JOINERY
EIJNPRU JUNIPER
EIJNRRU INJURER
EIJNSTU JUSTINE
EIJPRTU JUPITER
EIJRSTT JITTERS
EIJRTTY JITTERY
EIJSSTU JESUITS
EIJSSUV JUSSIVE
EIKKOOR KOOKIER
EIKKOPS KOPEISK
EIKLLNW INKWELL
EIKLLRS KILLERS
EIKLLST SKILLET
EIKLMMN MILKMEN
EIKLMNR KREMLIN
EIKLMRS MILKERS
EIKLNRU URNLIKE
EIKLNRW WRINKLE
EIKLNST TINKLES
EIKLNSV KELVINS
EIKLNSW WINKLES
EIKLNSY SKYLINE
EIKLNTW TWINKLE
EIKLOPS SKI POLE
EIKLPRY PERKILY
EIKLPST LIPETSK
EIKLRST KILTERS
EIKLRSU SULKIER
EIKLSTT SKITTLE
EIKMMRS SKIMMER
EIKMNNS KINSMEN
EIKMORS IRKSOME,
SMOKIER
EIKMOSS ESKIMOS
EIKMRRS SMIRKER
EIKMRRU MURKIER
EIKMRSU MUSKIER
EIKNNOR EINKORN
EIKNNRS SKINNER
EIKNOPS PINKOES
EIKNORV INVOKER
EIKNORW WONKIER
EIKNOSS KENOSIS
EIKNPRR PRINKER
EIKNPST PINKEST
EIKNRSS SINKERS
EIKNRST KIRSTEN,

KRISTEN, STINKER,
TINKERS
EIKNRSW WINKERS
EIKNRTT KNITTER,
TRINKET
EIKNSTT KITTENS
EIKNTUZ KUNZITE
EIKOORS ROOKIES
EIKOPPR PORK PIE
EIKOPRR PORKIER
EIKOPST POKIEST
EIKOSST KETOSIS
EIKPPRS KIPPERS, SKIPPER
EIKPPST SKIPPET
EIKRRST SKIRRET, STRIKER
EIKRSSS KISSERS
EIKRSST STRIKES
EIKRSSV SKIVERS
EIKRSTT SKITTER
EILLLOS LOLLIES
EILLLOW OIL WELL
EILLMNU MULLEIN
EILLMOT MELILOT
EILLMOU MOUILLE
EILLMRS MILLERS
EILLMTU MULLITE
EILLNSS ILLNESS
EILLNST LENTILS, LINTELS
EILLORV ORVILLE
EILLORW LOWLIER
EILLOTT ELLIOTT
EILLPPP PEP PILL
EILLPRS SPILLER
EILLRST STILLER, TILLERS,
TRELLIS
EILLRSW SWILLER
EILMMRS SLIMMER
EILMNRY MERILYN
EILMOPR IMPLORE
EILMPPS PIMPLES
EILMPRS PRELIMS,
SIMPLER
EILMPRU LUMPIER
EILMPST LIMPEST, LIMPETS
EILMPSU IMPULSE
EILMPSW WIMPLES
EILMPSX SIMPLEX
EILMPTY EMPTILY
EILMQSU QUILMES
EILMRRY MERRILY
EILMRSS RIMLESS
EILMRSU MISRULE
EILMRSY MISERLY
EILMSSY MESSILY

EILMSUY ELYSIUM
EILMUUV ELUVIUM
EILNNPU PINNULE
EILNNST LINNETS
EILNOOR LOONIER
EILNOOS LOONIES
EILNOPR PROLINE
EILNOPS EPSILON
EILNORT RETINOL
EILNOSS INSOLES,
LESIONS, LIONESS
EILNOSU ELUSION
EILNOTU LINE-OUT,
OUTLINE
EILNOTV VIOLENT
EILNOTW TOWLINE
EILNOVV INVOLVE
EILNPPS NIPPLES
EILNPRS PILSNER
EILNPSU LINEUPS, SPINULE
EILNPTY INEPTLY
EILNPUV VULPINE
EILNRTY INERTLY
EILNRVY NERVILY
EILNSSS SINLESS
EILNSST SILENTS
EILNSTU UTENSIL
EILOOST OSTIOLE
EILOPRS SPOILER
EILOPST PLOESTI
EILOPSU PILEOUS
EILOPSV PLOSIVE
EILOPTX EXPLOIT
EILORRS LORRIES
EILORSS RISSOLE
EILORSU LOUSIER
EILORSW LOW-RISE
EILORTT TRIOLET
EILORTU OUTLIER
EILOSTT LITOTES, TOILETS
EILOSTV VIOLETS
EILOTUV OUTLIVE
EILPPRR RIPPLER
EILPPRS RIPPLES, SLIPPER
EILPPRT RIPPLET, TIPPLER
EILPPRU PULPIER
EILPPST STIPPLE, TIPPLES
EILPPSU PILEUPS
EILPPSW SWIPPLE
EILPRTT TRIPLET
EILPRTX TRIPLEX
EILPRUU PURLIEU
EILPSTT SPITTLE
EILPSTU STIPULE

EILPTTY PETTILY
EILQRTU QUILTER
EILQRUU LIQUEUR
EILQTUY QUIETLY
EILRRSU SURLIER
EILRRTW TWIRLER
EILRSSV SILVERS, SLIVERS
EILRSTT LITTERS,
　SLITTER
EILRSVY SILVERY
EILRSZZ SIZZLER
EILRTTY TRITELY
EILRTUV RIVULET
EILSSTW WITLESS
EILSSTY STYLISE
EILSSVW SWIVELS
EILSTTY TESTILY
EILSTVY SYLVITE
EILSTYZ STYLIZE
EILSWZZ SWIZZLE
EIMMMOS MOMMIES
EIMMMSU MUMMIES
EIMMOPS POMMIES
EIMMORS MEMOIRS
EIMMPRR PRIMMER
EIMMPRU PREMIUM
EIMMRRT TRIMMER
EIMMRSW SWIMMER
EIMMSTU TUMMIES
EIMNNOT MENTION
EIMNOOS NOISOME
EIMNOOT EMOTION
EIMNOPT PIMENTO
EIMNOQU MONIQUE
EIMNORR MERRION
EIMNOST MOISTEN
EIMNOSW WINSOME
EIMNOTU MOUNTIE
EIMNPTU PINETUM
EIMNRST MINSTER
EIMNSSU MINUSES
EIMNSTT MITTENS,
　SMITTEN
EIMNSTU MINUETS,
　MINUTES
EIMNUZZ MUEZZIN
EIMOORR ROOMIER
EIMOPRS IMPOSER,
　PROMISE
EIMOPRV IMPROVE
EIMORRW WORMIER
EIMORSS MOSSIER
EIMORST MORTISE,
　TRISOME

EIMORSU MOUSIER
EIMORSV VERISMO
EIMORTT OMITTER
EIMORTV VOMITER
EIMOSTV MOTIVES
EIMOSTZ MESTIZO
EIMOTTW TWO-TIME
EIMPRRS PRIMERS
EIMPRSS IMPRESS,
　PREMISS, SIMPERS
EIMPRST IMPREST,
　PERMITS
EIMPRSU UMPIRES
EIMPRTU IMPUTER
EIMPSTU IMPETUS
EIMRSST MISTERS
EIMRSSU MISUSER,
　SURMISE
EIMRSTT METRIST
EIMRSTU MUSTIER
EIMRTUX MIXTURE
EIMRUZZ MUZZIER
EIMSSSU MISUSES
EINNOPS PENSION
EINNOPT PONTINE
EINNOQU QUINONE
EINNORT INTONER
EINNORU REUNION
EINNORV ENVIRON
EINNOST TENSION
EINNOSV VENISON
EINNOTT TONTINE
EINNPRS SPINNER
EINNPST TENPINS
EINNPSY SPINNEY
EINNQTU QUENTIN
EINNRRU RUNNIER
EINNRSS SINNERS
EINNRST INTERNS
EINNRSU SUNNIER
EINNRSW WINNERS
EINNRTV VINTNER
EINNSTU TUNNIES
EINOOPZ EPIZOON
EINOORS EROSION
EINOOST ISOTONE
EINOOSZ OZONISE
EINOOZZ OZONIZE
EINOPRT POINTER,
　PROTEIN
EINOPSS IN POSSE,
　SPINOSE
EINOQUX EQUINOX
EINORSS SENIORS

EINORST IN STORE,
　STONIER
EINORSV VERSION
EINORSW SNOWIER
EINORTT TRITONE
EINORTU ROUTINE
EINOSSS SESSION
EINOSST NOSIEST
EINOSUV ENVIOUS,
　NIVEOUS
EINPPRS NIPPERS
EINPPST SNIPPET
EINPRRT PRINTER,
　REPRINT
EINPRSS SNIPERS
EINPSST INSTEPS, SPINETS
EINPSTU PUNIEST
EINPTTY TINTYPE
EINQRUY ENQUIRY
EINQSSU SEQUINS
EINQSTU INQUEST
EINQTTU QUINTET
EINQTUU UNQUIET
EINRRSU INSURER
EINRSST INSERTS
EINRSSU SUNRISE
EINRSTT STINTER
EINRSTV STRIVEN
EINRSTW WINTERS
EINRTTU NUTTIER
EINRTTW WRITTEN
EINSSSU SINUSES
EINSSSY SYNESIS
EINSSTW WITNESS
EINSSUW SUNWISE
EINSTTW TWIN SET
EINTTUY TENUITY
EIOOPST ISOTOPE
EIOORST SOOTIER
EIOORWZ WOOZIER
EIOOSTT TOOTSIE
EIOOSTZ OOZIEST
EIOPPPS POPPIES
EIOPPRS SOPPIER
EIOPRRS PROSIER
EIOPRST REPOSIT,
　RIPOSTE, ROPIEST
EIOPRSX PROXIES
EIOPRTT POTTIER
EIOPSST POSTIES
EIOPSTT POTTIES, TIPTOES
EIOPSTU PITEOUS
EIORRRS SORRIER
EIORRRW WORRIER

EIORRST RIOTERS, ROISTER
EIORRSW WORRIES
EIORSST ROSIEST, SORITES, SORTIES, STORIES
EIORSSU SERIOUS
EIORSSX XEROSIS
EIOSSTU OUTSISE
EIOSSTV SOVIETS
EIOSTUZ OUTSIZE
EIPPPSU PUPPIES
EIPPRRT TRIPPER
EIPPRST TIPPERS
EIPPRSZ ZIPPERS
EIPPRTT TRIPPET
EIPPSUY YUPPIES
EIPRRST STRIPER
EIPRRSU UPRISER
EIPRRUV UPRIVER
EIPRSST PERSIST, PRIESTS, SPRIEST, SPRITES, STRIPES
EIPRSTT SPITTER, TIPSTER
EIPRSTY PYRITES, STRIPEY
EIPRSUU EURIPUS
EIPRTUW WRITE-UP
EIPRUVW PURVIEW
EIPSSSU PUSSIES
EIQRSSU SQUIRES
EIQRSTU QUERIST
EIQRSUV QUIVERS
EIQRTTU QUITTER
EIQRUVY QUIVERY
EIQRUZZ QUIZZER
EIQSTUU QUIETUS
EIQSUZZ QUIZZES
EIRRRST STIRRER
EIRRSTU RUSTIER
EIRRSTV STRIVER
EIRRSTW WRITERS
EIRSSST SISTERS
EIRSSTT SITTERS
EIRSSUV VIRUSES
EIRSTTT TITTERS
EIRSTTU TERTIUS
EIRSTTV TRIVETS
EIRSTTW TWISTER
EIRSTUV VIRTUES
EIRSUVV SURVIVE
EIRTTTW TWITTER
EISSSTU TISSUES
EISSSTX SEXISTS
EISSTUV TUSSIVE
EISTTUW WET SUIT
EJJMNUU JEJUNUM

EJKNSTU JUNKETS
EJLORST JOSTLER
EJLOSSY JOYLESS
EJMPRSU JUMPERS
EJNORUY JOURNEY
EJOORVY OVERJOY
EJOPRTT JETPORT
EJORSTT JOTTERS
EJORSTU JOUSTER
EJPRRUY PERJURY
EKKLRSU SKULKER
EKLNORS SNORKEL
EKLOORS LOOKERS
EKLOOTW WET-LOOK
EKMNORW WORKMEN
EKMNOSY MONKEYS
EKMNPTU UNKEMPT
EKMNRTU TURKMEN
EKMORSS SMOKERS
EKMSSTU MUSKETS
EKNOORS SNOOKER
EKNORSY ORKNEYS, YONKERS
EKNORTT KNOTTER
EKNORTW NETWORK
EKNORUY YUKONER
EKNRTUY TURNKEY
EKOOPRV PROVOKE
EKOORRY ROOKERY
EKOORST STOOKER
EKOPRRS PORKERS
EKORRSW WORKERS
EKORSST STOKERS, STROKES
EKORSWX EX-WORKS
EKRSSTU TUSKERS
EKRSTUY TURKEYS
ELLMOOR MORELLO
ELLMPUU PLUMULE
ELLMSTU MULLETS
ELLNOOW WOOLLEN
ELLNOSW SWOLLEN
ELLNSTU NULL SET
ELLOOSY LOOSELY
ELLOPTU POLLUTE
ELLORRS ROLLERS
ELLORTY TROLLEY
ELLOSTU OUTSELL, SELL-OUT
ELLOSVY VOLLEYS
ELLOSWY YELLOWS
ELLPSTU PULLETS
ELLPSUY PULLEYS
ELLRSSU RUSSELL

ELMMOPS POMMELS
ELMMORT TROMMEL
ELMMOSS MOSLEMS
ELMMPTU PLUMMET
ELMMRSU SLUMMER
ELMOORS MORELOS
ELMOORT TREMOLO
ELMOPRY POLYMER
ELMORSS MORSELS
ELMORTU MOULTER
ELMOSUU EMULOUS
ELMOSUV VOLUMES
ELMPPRU PLUMPER
ELMRSTY MYRTLES
ELMRUZZ MUZZLER
ELMSSSU MUSSELS
ELMSUZZ MUZZLES
ELNNRSU RUNNELS
ELNNSTU TUNNELS
ELNOORZ LORENZO
ELNOOSU UNLOOSE
ELNOPRU PLEURON
ELNOPTU OPULENT
ELNORSY ROSELYN
ELNORTY ELYTRON
ELNOSSS LESSONS
ELNOSSW LOWNESS
ELNOSTV SOLVENT
ELNOSZZ NOZZLES
ELNOTVY NOVELTY
ELNRSTY STERNLY
ELNSSSU SUNLESS
ELNSSSY SLYNESS
ELOORST LOOTERS
ELOORTT ROOTLET, TOOTLER
ELOOSST LOOSEST
ELOOSTT TOOTLES
ELOOSTU OUTSOLE
ELOPRRW PROWLER
ELOPRRY PYRROLE
ELOPRSU LEPROUS, PELORUS, SPORULE
ELOPRSV PLOVERS
ELOPRSY LEPROSY
ELOPRTT PLOTTER
ELOPRTY PROTYLE
ELOPSST TOPLESS
ELORSSS LESSORS
ELORSST OSTLERS
ELORSSV SOLVERS
ELORSTT SLOTTER
ELORSTV REVOLTS
ELORSTW TROWELS

ELORSUV LOUVRES,
  VELOURS
ELORTTY LOTTERY
ELORTVY OVERTLY
ELOSSTU LOTUSES
ELOSSTW SLOWEST
ELOSSTY SYSTOLE
ELOSTTU OUTLETS
ELOSTUU LUTEOUS
ELPPRSU PURPLES,
  SUPPLER
ELPRUZZ PUZZLER
ELPSTUU PUSTULE
ELPSUZZ PUZZLES
ELRRSTU RUSTLER
ELRRTTU TURTLER
ELRSSTU LUSTERS,
  LUSTRES, RESULTS
ELRSTTU TURTLES
ELRTTUY UTTERLY
ELRTUUV VULTURE
ELSSSTU TUSSLES
ELSSSUY ULYSSES
EMMMRSU MUMMERS
EMMMRUY MUMMERY
EMMNOOR MONOMER
EMMNOST MOMENTS
EMMNOTU OMENTUM
EMMNOTY METONYM
EMMOOTY MYOTOME
EMMRSSU SUMMERS
EMMRSTU RUMMEST
EMMRSUY SUMMERY
EMMSSUU MUSEUMS
EMNNOOW NEW MOON
EMNNOSW SNOWMEN
EMNOOST MOONSET
EMNOPST POSTMEN
EMNOPSU SPUMONE
EMNOPYY EPONYMY
EMNORRU MOURNER
EMNORSS SERMONS
EMNORST MENTORS,
  MONSTER
EMNORTT TORMENT
EMNORTU MOUNTER,
  REMOUNT
EMNORTV VERMONT
EMNOSST STEMSON
EMNRSTU MUNSTER,
  STERNUM
EMOOPRS OOSPERM
EMOOPRT PROMOTE
EMOORRS ROOMERS

EMOOSTT MOTTOES
EMOOSTW TWOSOME
EMOPPST MOPPETS
EMOPRRS ROMPERS
EMOPRST STOMPER
EMOPRSU SUPREMO
EMOQSSU MOSQUES
EMORRST TREMORS
EMORSSU MOUSERS
EMORSUY SEYMOUR
EMOSSSU MOUSSES
EMPRSTU STUMPER
EMPRTTU TRUMPET
EMPSSSU MESS-UPS
EMRRUUZ ERZURUM
EMRSSTU MUSTERS
EMRSTYY MYSTERY
EMSSSTY SYSTEMS
ENNNOPS PENNONS
ENNNRUY NUNNERY
ENNORTT TRENTON
ENNORTU NEUTRON
ENNOSST SONNETS
ENNOTWW NEW TOWN
ENNPSTU PUNNETS
ENNRRSU RUNNERS
ENNRSTU STUNNER
ENOOPRS SNOOPER
ENOORRT TORREON
ENOORSU ONEROUS
ENOORSZ SNOOZER
ENOOSSZ SNOOZES
ENOOTTW TWO-TONE
ENOOTXY OXYTONE
ENOPRSS PERSONS
ENOPRST POSTERN,
  PRESTON
ENOPRTT PORTENT
ENOPRTY ENTROPY
ENOPSST STEPSON
ENOQTUU UNQUOTE
ENORRSS SNORERS
ENORRST SNORTER
ENORRTT TORRENT
ENORRUV OVERRUN
ENORSSS SENSORS
ENORSSY SENSORY
ENORSTT STENTOR
ENORSTU TONSURE
ENORSUV NERVOUS
ENORTUY TOURNEY
ENOSSTT STETSON
ENOSSTX SEXTONS
ENOSTUU TENUOUS

ENPRRSU SPURNER
ENPRSTU PUNSTER,
  PUNTERS
ENRRSTU RETURNS,
  TURNERS
ENRRSUY NURSERY
ENRRTUU NURTURE
ENRRTUY TURNERY
ENRSSWY WRYNESS
ENRSTTU ENTRUST
ENRSVWY WYVERNS
ENSSSTU SUNSETS
EOOOPRS OOSPORE
EOOPPRS OPPOSER,
  POOPERS, PROPOSE
EOOPPRV POPOVER
EOOPRRS SPOORER
EOOPRRT TROOPER
EOOPRST POOREST,
  STOOPER
EOOPRTV OVERTOP
EOOPRTW TOWROPE
EOORRST ROOSTER
EOOSSSU OSSEOUS
EOOTTUV OUTVOTE
EOPPPRS POPPERS
EOPPPST POPPETS
EOPPRRS PROSPER
EOPPRSS OPPRESS
EOPPRST STOPPER,
  TOPPERS
EOPPRSU PURPOSE
EOPPSSU SUPPOSE
EOPRRSS PRESSOR
EOPRRST PORTERS,
  REPORTS, SPORTER
EOPRRTU TROUPER
EOPRSST POSTERS,
  PRESTOS
EOPRSSU POSEURS
EOPRSSW PROWESS
EOPRSSY OSPREYS
EOPRSTT POTTERS,
  PROTEST, SPOTTER
EOPRSTU PETROUS,
  POSTURE, SPOUTER,
  TROUPES
EOPRSTX EXPORTS
EOPRTTY POTTERY
EOPRTVY POVERTY
EOPSSSS POSSESS
EOPSSST POSSETS
EOPSSSU SPOUSES
EOPSSTX SEXPOTS

EOPSTTW TWO-STEP
EOQRSTU TORQUES
EORRRST TERRORS
EORRSST RESORTS,
ROSTERS
EORRSTT RETORTS,
ROTTERS, STERTOR
EORRSTU TROUSER
EORRSZZ ROZZERS
EORRTTT TROTTER
EORRTTU TORTURE
EORSSTU OESTRUS,
OUSTERS, SOUREST
EORSSTY OYSTERS,
STOREYS
EORSTTT STRETTO
EORSTTU STOUTER
EORSUVY VOYEURS
EORTTTY TOTTERY
EPPPSTU PUPPETS
EPPRRUU PURPURE
EPPRSSU PRESS-UP,
SUPPERS
EPRRSSU PURSERS
EPRRSUU PURSUER,
USURPER
EPRRTUU RUPTURE
EPRSTTU PUTTERS,
SPUTTER
ERRSSTU TRUSSER
ERRSSUU USURERS
ERRSSUY SURREYS
ERRSTTU TRUSTER,
TURRETS
ERRSTTY TRYSTER
ERSSSTU TRUSSES
ERSSTUU SUTURES
ERSSUVY SURVEYS
ERSTTTU STUTTER
FFFILOT LIFT-OFF
FFGHINU HUFFING
FFGIINR GRIFFIN
FFGILNU LUFFING
FFGIMNU MUFFING
FFGINOR GRIFFON
FFGINOS OFFINGS
FFGINPU PUFFING
FFGLRUY GRUFFLY
FFHHISU HUFFISH
FFHILSY FLY-FISH
FFHILUY HUFFILY
FFHOOSW SHOW-OFF
FFHOSTU SHUT-OFF
FFILPUY PUFFILY

FFILSTY STIFFLY
FFIMNSU MUFFINS
FFINOOT FINFOOT
FFINOPS SPIN-OFF
FFINOPT PONTIFF
FFINPSU PUFFINS
FFINSTU SNUFF IT
FFIOPRS RIP-OFFS
FFIOPST TIP-OFFS
FFIORTY FORTIFY
FFIQSUY SQUIFFY
FFJMOPU JUMP-OFF
FFKLORU FORKFUL
FFLNSUY SNUFFLY
FFNORSU RUN-OFFS
FFNORTU TURN-OFF
FFOPSTU PUT-OFFS
FGGGINO FOGGING
FGGHIIS FISHGIG
FGGILNO GOLFING
FGGILOY FOGGILY
FGGINOO GOOFING
FGGINOR FORGING
FGHHIOS HOGFISH
FGHIINS FISHING
FGHIIPS PIGFISH
FGHILST FLIGHTS
FGHILTY FLIGHTY
FGHIOSY FOGYISH
FGHIRST FRIGHTS
FGHNOOR FOGHORN
FGIIKNN KNIFING
FGIILLN FILLING
FGIILMN FILMING
FGIILNO FOILING
FGIILNR RIFLING
FGIILNS FILINGS
FGIILNT LIFTING
FGIILNY LIGNIFY
FGIIMNR FIRMING
FGIINNN FINNING
FGIINNS FININGS
FGIINST SIFTING
FGIINSY SIGNIFY
FGIINTT FITTING
FGIINZZ FIZZING
FGIKNNU FUNKING
FGIKNOR FORKING
FGILNOO FOOLING
FGILNOT LOFTING
FGILNOU FOULING
FGILNOW FLOWING,
FOWLING, WOLFING
FGILNRU FURLING

FGILNTU FLUTING
FGILOOY GOOFILY
FGILORY GLORIFY
FGIMNOR FORMING
FGINOOR ROOFING
FGINOOT FOOTING
FGINRRU FURRING
FGINRSU SURFING
FGINRTU TURFING
FGINSSU FUSSING
FGINUZZ FUZZING
FGIOORT GO FOR IT
FGIORTW FIGWORT
FGLNOOR FOR LONG
FGLNORU FURLONG
FGLNOSU SONGFUL
FGNORWY GWYNFOR
FGNOSUU FUNGOUS
FHIINNS FINNISH
FHIINPS PINFISH
FHIKLOS FOLKISH
FHILOOS FOOLISH
FHILOSW WOLFISH
FHILSUW WISHFUL
FHINRSU FURNISH
FHINSSU SUNFISH
FHIOPPS FOPPISH
FHIORRY HORRIFY
FHIRSST SHRIFTS
FHIRSTT THRIFTS
FHIRTTY THRIFTY
FHLRTUU HURTFUL
FHNOTUX FOXHUNT
FHOOOTT HOTFOOT
FHORSTU FOURTHS
FIIKLST SKI LIFT
FIILLMY FILMILY
FIILLNS FILL-INS
FIILLPS FILLIPS
FIILNOT TINFOIL
FIILNTY NIFTILY
FIILPTU PITIFUL
FIIMSST MISFITS
FIINOSS FISSION
FIINRTY NITRIFY
FIIOPST POSITIF
FIIRTVY VITRIFY
FIJLLOY JOLLIFY
FIJSTUY JUSTIFY
FIKKLNO KINFOLK
FIKLLSU SKILFUL
FIKLNSU SKINFUL
FILLMOY MOLLIFY
FILLNUY NULLIFY

FILLOTY LOFTILY
FILNNUY FUNNILY
FILNORS FLORINS
FILNOSW INFLOWS
FILNOUX FLUXION
FILORST FLORIST
FILORTU FLORUIT
FILOSSS FOSSILS
FILRSTY FIRSTLY
FILSSUY FUSSILY
FILSTTU FLUTIST
FILSTUW WISTFUL
FILSTWY SWIFTLY
FILUYZZ FUZZILY
FIMMMUY MUMMIFY
FIMNORU UNIFORM
FIMOORV OVIFORM
FIMORTY MORTIFY
FIMSTYY MYSTIFY
FINOPSU SOUPFIN
FINORSS FRISSON
FIOORSU FURIOSO
FIOPRST PROFITS
FIOPSTX POSTFIX
FIORSUU FURIOUS
FIORTYZ FITZROY
FIOSTTU OUTFITS
FIRRSTY STIR-FRY
FKLNOOR NORFOLK
FKOOORS FORSOOK
FLLOSUU SOULFUL
FLLSTUU LUSTFUL
FLMMOUX FLUMMOX
FLMNOOU MOUFLON
FLMOOOT TOMFOOL
FLMOORU ROOMFUL
FLNOORR FORLORN
FLOOTUW OUTFLOW
FLOPSTU POTFULS
FLOPSUU FOUL-UPS
FLOSUUV FULVOUS
FMOOPRR PRO-FORM
FMRSTUU FRUSTUM
FNNRSUU FUN RUNS
FNOOOTT FOOT-TON
FNOORSU SUNROOF
FNOPRTU UPFRONT
FNORSTY Y-FRONTS
FOOOPRT ROOFTOP
FOORSST OF SORTS
FOORTTX FOXTROT
FOPSSTU FUSSPOT
FORRSUW FURROWS
FORRUWY FURROWY

FORSTWY FROWSTY
GGGHINO HOGGING
GGGHINU HUGGING
GGGIIJN JIGGING
GGGIINP PIGGING
GGGIINR RIGGING
GGGIINW WIGGING
GGGIJNO JOGGING
GGGIJNU JUGGING
GGGILNO LOGGING
GGGILNU LUGGING
GGGIMNU MUGGING
GGGINNO NOGGING
GGGINOR GORGING
GGGINOT TOGGING
GGGINOU GOUGING
GGGINPU PUGGING
GGGINTU TUGGING
GGHHIOS HOGGISH
GGHIINN HINGING
GGHIINS SIGHING
GGHIIPS PIGGISH
GGHINSU GUSHING
GGIIILN GINGILI
GGIINNO INGOING
GGIINNP PINGING
GGIINNR RINGING
GGIINNS SIGNING,
  SINGING
GGIINNT TINGING
GGIINNW WINGING
GGIINPR GRIPING
GGILLNU GULLING
GGILMUY MUGGILY
GGILNNO LONGING
GGILNNU LUNGING
GGILNOS GOSLING
GGILNOW GLOWING
GGILNPU GULPING
GGILOOS GIGOLOS
GGILOSY SOGGILY
GGILRWY WRIGGLY
GGIMMNU GUMMING
GGIMNSU MUGGINS
GGINNNU GUNNING
GGINNOO ONGOING
GGINNOP PONGING
GGINNOS NOGGINS
GGINOPR GROPING
GGINORS GRINGOS
GGINORU ROUGING
GGINORW GROWING
GGINPPY GYPPING
GGINPRU PURGING

GGINRST G-STRING
GGINRSU SURGING
GGINSTU GUSTING
GGINTTU GUTTING
GGIPRSY SPRIGGY
GGNOORS GORGONS
GHHIKSY SKY-HIGH
GHHINSU HUSHING
GHHLOOY HOOGHLY
GHHORTU THROUGH
GHHOTTU THOUGHT
GHIIKRZ KIRGHIZ
GHIILNW WHILING
GHIILRS GIRLISH
GHIINNS HSINING,
  SHINING
GHIINNT HINTING
GHIINNW WHINING
GHIINSS HISSING
GHIINST INSIGHT
GHIINSW WISHING
GHIINTT HITTING,
  TITHING
GHIINTW WHITING
GHIJNOS JOSHING
GHIKLNU HULKING
GHIKNNO HONKING
GHIKNOO HOOKING
GHIKNST KNIGHTS
GHILLNU HULLING
GHILLTY LIGHTLY
GHILNOS LONGISH
GHILNOW HOWLING
GHILNRU HURLING
GHILNSY SHINGLY
GHILNTY NIGHTLY
GHILPST PLIGHTS
GHILRTY RIGHTLY
GHILSST SLIGHTS
GHILSTY SIGHTLY
GHILTTY TIGHTLY
GHIMMNU HUMMING
GHIMNNY HYMNING
GHIMNOS GNOMISH
GHIMNPU HUMPING
GHIMNRY RHYMING
GHIMNTT MIGHTN'T
GHINNOP PHONING
GHINNOS NOSHING
GHINNOT NOTHING
GHINNTU HUNTING
GHINOOS SHOOING
GHINOOT HOOTING
GHINOPP HOPPING

GHINORS SHORING
GHINOST HOSTING
GHINOSU HOUSING
GHINOSV SHOVING
GHINOSW SHOWING
GHINOTT TONIGHT
GHINOTU HOUTING
GHINPSU PUSHING
GHINRSU RUSHING
GHINRTU HURTING
GHIOPSZ PHIZOGS
GHIORSU ROGUISH
GHIPRTU UPRIGHT
GHIPTTU UPTIGHT
GHLMOOO HOMOLOG
GHLOPSU PLOUGHS
GHLORUY ROUGHLY
GHLOSSU SLOUGHS
GHLOSTY GHOSTLY
GHLOSUY SLOUGHY
GHLOTUY TOUGHLY
GHMORSU SORGHUM
GHMOSTU MUGSHOT
GHNOPRY GRYPHON
GHNORST THRONGS
GHNOSSU SHOGUNS
GHNOSTU GUNSHOT,
    NOUGHTS, SHOTGUN
GHNOTTU OUGHTN'T
GHORSTU TROUGHS
GHORSTW GROWTHS
GHORTUW WROUGHT
GHORTUY YOGHURT
GIIJLNT JILTING
GIIJNNO JOINING
GIIJNNX JINXING
GIIKLLN KILLING
GIIKLMN MILKING
GIIKLNN INKLING,
    LINKING
GIIKLNS LIKINGS
GIIKNNO OINKING
GIIKNNP KINGPIN, PINK
    GIN, PINKING
GIIKNNS SINKING
GIIKNNW WINKING
GIIKNPP KIPPING
GIIKNPS PIGSKIN, SPIKING
GIIKNRS RISKING
GIIKNSS KISSING
GIIKNSV SKIVING, VIKINGS
GIIKNTT KITTING
GIILLMN MILLING
GIILLNT LILTING, TILLING

GIILLNW WILLING
GIILMNN LIMNING
GIILMNP LIMPING
GIILMNS SMILING
GIILMPR PILGRIM
GIILNNS LININGS
GIILNNY LYING-IN
GIILNOR LIGROIN
GIILNOS SOILING
GIILNOT TOILING
GIILNPS LISPING
GIILNST LISTING, SILTING
GIILNSV LIVINGS
GIILNTT TILTING
GIILNTW WILTING
GIILORS OILRIGS
GIIMMNR RIMMING
GIIMNNT MINTING
GIIMNPP PIMPING
GIIMNPR PRIMING
GIIMNSS MISSING
GIIMNST MISTING,
    SMITING
GIINNNP PINNING
GIINNNS INNINGS,
    SINNING
GIINNNT TINNING
GIINNNW WINNING
GIINNOP OPINING
GIINNOR IRONING
GIINNPP NIPPING
GIINNPS SNIPING
GIINNRS RINSING
GIINNRU INURING,
    RUINING
GIINNSW INSWING
GIINNTT TINTING
GIINNTU UNITING
GIINNTW TWINING
GIINOPR PIG IRON
GIINOPS POISING
GIINORS ORIGINS
GIINORT RIOTING
GIINORV IN VIGOR
GIINPPP PIPPING
GIINPPR RIPPING
GIINPPS SIPPING
GIINPPT TIPPING
GIINPPZ ZIPPING
GIINPQU PIQUING
GIINPRS PRISING
GIINPRZ PRIZING
GIINPSS PISSING
GIINPST SPITING

GIINPSW SWIPING
GIINPTT PITTING
GIINPTY PITYING
GIINRSS RISINGS
GIINRSV VIRGINS
GIINRTW WRITING
GIINSSU ISSUING
GIINSTT SITTING
GIINSTU SUITING
GIJKNNU JUNKING
GIJLNOT JOLTING
GIJMNPU JUMPING
GIJNOTT JOTTING
GIJNTTU JUTTING
GIKLNOO LOOKING
GIKLNRU LURKING
GIKLNSU SULKING
GIKMNNU KUNMING
GIKMNOS SMOKING
GIKNNOO KONGONI
GIKNNOW KNOWING
GIKNOOR ROOKING
GIKNORW WORKING
GIKNOST STOKING
GIKNOWY YINGKOW
GILLLNO LOLLING
GILLLNU LULLING
GILLMNU MULLING
GILLNOP POLLING
GILLNOR ROLLING
GILLNOT TOLLING
GILLNPU PULLING
GILMNOO LOOMING
GILMNOT MOLTING
GILMNPU LUMPING,
    PLUMING
GILMPSY GYMSLIP
GILNNSU UNSLING
GILNOOP LOOPING,
    POOLING
GILNOOS LOOSING
GILNOOT LOOTING,
    TOOLING
GILNOPP LOPPING
GILNOPS SLOPING
GILNOPW PLOWING
GILNORU LOURING
GILNOSS LOSINGS
GILNOSU LOUSING
GILNOSV SOLVING
GILNOSW SLOWING
GILNOTT LOTTING
GILNOWY YOWLING
GILNPPU PULPING

GILNPRU PURLING
GILNPSU PULSING
GILNRSU RULINGS
GILNSTU LUSTING
GILNSTY STYLING
GILORTY TRILOGY
GILOSTT GLOTTIS
GILRSTY GRISTLY
GILRTUY LITURGY
GILRYZZ GRIZZLY
GILSTUY GUSTILY
GIMMMNU MUMMING
GIMMNSU SUMMING
GIMNNOO MOONING
GIMNNOR MORNING
GIMNOOR MOORING,
 ROOMING
GIMNOOT MOOTING
GIMNOOZ ZOOMING
GIMNOPP MOPPING
GIMNOPR ROMPING
GIMNORW WORMING
GIMNOSU MOUSING
GIMNOWY WYOMING
GIMNPPU PUMPING
GIMNSSU MUSSING
GINNNPU PUNNING
GINNNRU RUNNING
GINNNSU SUNNING
GINNOPS SPONGIN
GINNORS SNORING
GINNORW INGROWN
GINNORY GIRONNY
GINNOST STONING
GINNOSW SNOWING
GINNPRU PRUNING
GINNPTU PUNTING
GINNRSU NURSING
GINNRTU TURNING
GINNTTU NUTTING
GINNTUW WING NUT
GINNTUY UNTYING
GINOORT ROOTING
GINOOTT TOOTING
GINOOTW OWING TO
GINOPPP POPPING
GINOPPS SOPPING
GINOPPT TOPPING
GINOPRT PORTING
GINOPRU IN-GROUP,
 POURING
GINOPRV PROVING
GINOPST POSTING,
 STOPING

GINOPTT POTTING
GINOPTU POUTING
GINOQTU QUOTING
GINORSS SIGNORS
GINORST SORTING,
 STORING
GINORSU ROUSING,
 SOURING
GINORTT ROTTING
GINORTU ROUTING,
 TOURING
GINOSST TOSSING
GINOSSU SOUSING
GINOSTU OUSTING,
 OUTINGS
GINOSTW STOWING
GINOTTT TOTTING
GINOTTU TOUTING
GINPPPU PUPPING
GINPPSU SUPPING
GINPPTU TUPPING
GINPRRU PURRING
GINPRSS SPRINGS
GINPRSU PURSING
GINPRSY SPRINGY
GINPSUW UPSWING
GINPTTU PUTTING
GINRSST STRINGS
GINRSTU RUSTING
GINRSTY STRINGY
GINRTTU RUTTING
GINSSSU SUSSING
GIOPRRU PRURIGO
GIOPSSS GOSSIPS
GIOPSST SPIGOTS
GIOPSSY GOSSIPY
GIORSTU RIG-OUTS
GIOSSYZ ZYGOSIS
GJOORTT JOG TROT
GLMNOOS MONGOLS
GLMOOYY MYOLOGY
GLMORUW LUGWORM
GLNNOOR LORGNON
GLNNOOT LONG TON
GLNOOPR PROLONG
GLNOOPY POLYGON
GLNORWY WRONGLY
GLNOSUW SUNGLOW
GLNOTTU GLUTTON
GLOOORY OROLOGY
GLOOOTY OTOLOGY
GLOOOYZ ZOOLOGY
GLOORUY UROLOGY
GLOOSSW GO-SLOWS

GLORSSY GROSSLY
GMMPUUW MUGWUMP
GMOOPRS POGROMS
GMORSUU GRUMOUS
GMORTUW MUGWORT
GMRUYYZ ZYMURGY
GNOPPSU POPGUNS
GNOPRUW GROWN-UP
GNORSUV GUVNORS
GOORSTT GROTTOS
GOORTUW OUTGROW
HHINNSU HUNNISH
HHIORSW WHORISH
HHMRSTY RHYTHMS
HIIKNPS KINSHIP, PINKISH
HIILLPP PHILLIP
HIILLPS PHILLIS
HIILMTU LITHIUM
HIILPTY PITHILY
HIILSTT HIT LIST
HIIMNSX MINXISH
HIIMPSW WIMPISH
HIINSSW SWINISH
HIINSTW SWITHIN
HIKKOSU SHIKOKU
HIKLSUY HUSKILY
HIKMNOS MONKISH
HIKMSUU SUKHUMI
HIKNNTU UNTHINK
HIKNOPS HOPKINS
HIKNRSS SHRINKS
HIKRSTU TURKISH
HILLPSY PHYLLIS
HILLRST THRILLS
HILLRSY SHRILLY
HILMMOU HOLMIUM
HILMPSU LUMPISH
HILMSUY MUSHILY
HILMTUU THULIUM
HILNORY HORNILY
HILNOTY THIONYL
HILNPST PLINTHS
HILOOTT OTOLITH
HILORSY HORSILY
HILORTU UROLITH
HILOSTU LOUTISH
HILOSWY SHOWILY
HILOTWW WHITLOW
HILPSUY PUSHILY
HILSSTY STYLISH
HILSTTY THISTLY
HIMOORS MOORISH
HIMOPSS SOPHISM
HIMORTU THORIUM

HIMOTTY TIMOTHY
HIMPRSS SHRIMPS
HIMPRTU TRIUMPH
HIMSSSU HUSSISM
HIMSSTU ISTHMUS
HINNOOT HONITON
HINOORZ HORIZON
HINOOST IN SOOTH
HINOPSS SIPHONS
HINORSU NOURISH
HINORTT IN TROTH
HINORTW THROW-IN
HINRSTU RUNTISH
HINSTUW WHITSUN
HIOPRSW WORSHIP
HIOPSST SOPHIST
HIOPSSY PHYSIOS
HIORSTY HISTORY
HIOSSTT SOTTISH
HIOTTUW WITHOUT
HIQSSUY SQUISHY
HIRSSTT THIRSTS, T-
   SHIRTS
HIRSTTU RUTTISH
HIRSTTY THIRSTY
HKKLOOZ KOLKHOZ
HKNOOOS SHOOK ON
HKNOOWW KNOW-HOW
HKOOOPT POTHOOK
HKOOPSU HOOKUPS
HKOOSVZ SOVKHOZ
HKORSWY WORKSHY
HLLOOSW HOLLOWS
HLMNOTY MONTHLY
HLORSTY SHORTLY
HLPRSUU SULPHUR
HMMNOOY HOMONYM
HMOOOST MOSOTHO
HMOOSUU HOUMOUS
HMORSUU HUMOURS
HNOOPTY TYPHOON
HNOORSU HONOURS
HNOOSTU HOUSTON
HNOPSSY SYPHONS
HNOPSTY PYTHONS
HNRTTUU UNTRUTH
HOOPSTT HOTPOTS, HOT
   SPOT, POTSHOT
HOORRRS HORRORS
HOPRSTU HOTSPUR
HOPRTUW UPTHROW
HOPSTTU SHOT PUT
HOPSTUY TYPHOUS
HOSTTUU SHUTOUT

HPPSSUU PUSH-UPS
HRSSTTU THRUSTS
HRSSTUY THYRSUS
IIJNSUU SINUIJU
IIKKLNY KINKILY
IIKLLMY MILKILY
IIKLLSY SILKILY
IIKLMNP LIMPKIN
IIKLNOS OILSKIN
IIKLPSY SPIKILY
IIKLRSY RISKILY
IIKNRST KRISTIN
IILLLLW ILL WILL
IILLMNO MILLION
IILLMSY SLIMILY
IILLNOP PILLION
IILLNOZ ZILLION
IILMSTU STIMULI
IILMSTY MISTILY
IILNNSU INSULIN
IILNNTY TINNILY
IILNORS SIRLOIN
IILNOSV VIOLINS
IILNOSY NOISILY
IILNPPY NIPPILY
IILNSUV VILNIUS
IILOPRT TRIPOLI
IILORTV VITRIOL
IILOSTV VIOLIST
IILPRVY PRIVILY
IILPSST PISTILS
IILPSTY TIPSILY
IILPSWY WISPILY
IILTTUY UTILITY
IILTTWY WITTILY
IIMMMNU MINIMUM
IIMMNSU MINIMUS
IIMNNOS MINIONS
IIMNOSS MISSION
IIMNOSZ ZIONISM
IIMNPRT IMPRINT
IIMOPSU IMPIOUS
IIMOSST MITOSIS
IIMOSSU SIMIOUS
IIMOSTT TITOISM
IIMRTTU TRITIUM
IINNOOP OPINION
IINNOPS PINIONS
IINNORS IN IRONS
IINNQTU QUINTIN
IINORST IRONIST
IINORTT INTROIT
IINORTV IN VITRO
IINOSSV VISIONS

IINOSTZ ZIONIST
IINOTTU TUITION
IINPPPS PIPPINS
IINQRUY INQUIRY
IINRTTY TRINITY
IINSTTW NITWITS
IIORSTV VISITOR
IIOSTTT TITOIST
IIPRSST SPIRITS
IIPRTVY PRIVITY
IJJSTUU JUJITSU
IJKLLOY KILLJOY
IJKMPSU SKI JUMP
IJLLLOY JOLLILY
IJLLOTY JOLLITY
IJLMPUY JUMPILY
IJLNOQU JONQUIL
IJLNOTY JOINTLY
IJNORSU JUNIORS
IJRSSTU JURISTS
IKKRSTU IRKUTSK
IKLLSUY SULKILY
IKLMNRU MILK RUN
IKLMOPS MILKSOP
IKLMOSY SMOKILY
IKLMRUY MURKILY
IKLNOOT KILOTON
IKLNPSU LINKUPS
IKLNRWY WRINKLY
IKMNOOS KIMONOS
IKMNPPU PUMPKIN
IKMOOST MISTOOK
IKNOPRW PINWORK
IKNORTW TINWORK
IKNPSTU SPUTNIK
IKORSTY YORKIST
ILLMNOU MULLION
ILLMNRU MILLRUN
ILLMPUY LUMPILY
ILLMSUU LIMULUS
ILLNPSU PULL-INS
ILLNPUU LUPULIN
ILLNTUY NULLITY
ILLOPRY PILLORY
ILLOPSW PILLOWS
ILLOSUV VILLOUS
ILLOSUY LOUSILY
ILLOSWW WILLOWS
ILLOTUW WILL OUT
ILLOWWY WILLOWY
ILLRSUY SURLILY
ILLSTUY LUSTILY
ILMMSSU MUSLIMS
ILMNOOT MOONLIT

ILMNOOY MOONILY
ILMOOPP LIMPOPO
ILMOORY ROOMILY
ILMORTU TURMOIL
ILMOSTY MOISTLY
ILMSTUY MUSTILY
ILMUYZZ MUZZILY
ILNNSUY SUNNILY
ILNOOPS PLOSION
ILNOORV LIVORNO
ILNOOST LOTIONS
ILNOPRU PURLOIN
ILNOPSS SLIP-ONS
ILNOPSU UPSILON
ILNORST NOSTRIL
ILNOSST TONSILS
ILNOSTT STILTON
ILNOSTY STONILY
ILNOSWY SNOWILY
ILNPSST SPLINTS
ILNSSTU INSULTS
ILNTTUY NUTTILY
ILOOPST TOPSOIL
ILOOSST SOLOIST
ILOOSTY SOOTILY
ILOOWYZ WOOZILY
ILOPPSY SOPPILY
ILOPRSY PROSILY
ILOPSST PISTOLS
ILOPSTT SPOTLIT
ILOPSUY PIOUSLY
ILOQRTU TORQUIL
ILORRSY SORRILY
ILOSSTY TYLOSIS
ILPPSSU SLIP-UPS
ILPPSTU PULPITS
ILRSTUY RUSTILY
ILRTTUY RUTTILY
ILSSTTY STYLIST
IMMOPTU OPTIMUM
IMMSSTU SUMMITS
IMNNOSW MINNOWS
IMNOORT MONITOR
IMNOOST MOTIONS
IMNOOSU OMINOUS
IMNOOSY ISONOMY
IMNOPRW PINWORM
IMOOSSS OSMOSIS
IMOOSSU OSMIOUS
IMOPRST IMPORTS,
    TROPISM
IMOPRTU PROTIUM
IMORRRS MIRRORS
IMORSTU TOURISM

IMORSTY TORYISM
IMOSSYZ ZYMOSIS
IMOSTUV VOMITUS
IMQRSSU SQUIRMS
IMQRSUY SQUIRMY
IMRSSTU TRISMUS,
    TRUISMS
IMRTTUY YTTRIUM
INNNOOR NON-IRON
INNOOPS OPSONIN
INNOOST NOTIONS
INNOSTU NONSUIT
INNOSTW WINSTON
INOOPRT PORTION
INOOPSS POISONS
INOOPST OPTIONS,
    POTIONS
INOORSS ORISONS
INOORST ISOTRON,
    NITROSO, TORSION
INOORTT TORTONI
INOOSUX NOXIOUS
INOPPST TOPSPIN
INOPPTY PIT PONY
INOPRSS PRISONS
INOPSST PISTONS
INOPSSU SPINOUS
INORSTU NITROUS
INORSUU RUINOUS,
    URINOUS
INORTTY TRY IT ON
INOSSUU SINUOUS
INPRSST SPRINTS
INPRSTU TURNIPS
INPRSTY TRYPSIN
INQSSTU SQUINTS
INQSTUY SQUINTY
INRSTTU INTRUST
IOOPRRT PRIOR TO
IOOPRSV PROVISO
IOOPSTY ISOTOPY
IOORSSS SOROSIS
IOORSTT RISOTTO
IOORSTU RIOTOUS
IOOSSST OSTOSIS
IOPPPRT PIT PROP
IOPRSSY PYROSIS
IOPRSTT PROTIST
IOQRTTU QUITTOR
IORSSTU SUITORS
IORSTTU TOURIST
IPPSSSU PISS-UPS
IPRRSTU STIRRUP
IPRSSTU PURISTS

IPRSTUU PURSUIT
IPSSSTY STYPSIS
IPSSTTY TYPISTS
IQRSSTU SQUIRTS
JNOORSU JOURNOS,
    SOJOURN
KLNOOOW KOWLOON
KLOOOTU LOOKOUT,
    OUTLOOK
KNNNOUW UNKNOWN
KNNOOTW NOT KNOW
KNOOPTT TOPKNOT
KNOOSSS KNOSSOS
KNOPRTY KRYPTON
KOOPRTW WORKTOP
KOORTUW OUTWORK,
    WORKOUT
LLMOOPR ROLLMOP
LLNOORS ROLL-ONS
LLOOPRT ROLL-TOP,
    TROLLOP
LLOPTUU PULLOUT
LLORSST STROLLS
LMMPSUU LUMP SUM
LMNOOOS SOLOMON
LMOPSUY OLYMPUS
LMSTTUU TUMULTS
LMSTUUU TUMULUS
LNNOPSU NONPLUS
LNORSSY ROSSLYN
LOPPSUY POLYPUS
LOPRSUY PYLORUS
LOPRTUY POULTRY
LOPSSTY STYLOPS
LOSTTUY STOUTLY
LPRSSUU SURPLUS
MMNOORS MORMONS
MMNOSSU SUMMONS
MMOOPPS POMPOMS
MMOOSTT TOM-TOMS
MMOPSTY SYMPTOM
MMRRSUU MURMURS
MNNOOOS MONSOON
MNNOSYY SYNONYM
MNOOPTY TOPONYM
MNOOPRU NO-TRUMP
MNORSTU NOSTRUM
MNOTTUY MUTTONY
MOOOTYZ ZOOTOMY
MOOPPSU POMPOUS
MOOPSSU OPOSSUM
MOOPSTT TOPMOST
MOORRSW MORROWS
MOOSTTU OUTMOST

MOPPRST PROMPTS
MOPSSSU POSSUMS
MOPSSUU SPUMOUS
MOQRSUU QUORUMS
MORRSTU ROSTRUM
MORRSUU RUMOURS
MORSTUU TUMOURS
NNOOOOPT PONTOON
NNOOPRS NON-PROS
NNOOPRU PRONOUN
NNOOPSS SPONSON
NNOOPST NONSTOP
NNORSTU TURN-ONS
NOOOORTT TORONTO

NOOPRSS SPONSOR
NOOOPRST PROTONS
NOORSTY ROYSTON
NOORTUW OUTWORN,
    WORN-OUT
NOPPTUU PUT-UPON
NOPSSTU SUNSPOT
NORTTUU TURNOUT
NPRSTUU TURN-UPS,
    UPTURNS
NRSSTUU UNTRUSS
OOPPSVX VOX POPS
OOPRSSU SOURSOP
OOPRSTV PROVOST

OOPRTTU OUTPORT
OOPRTUU OUTPOUR
OOPSTTU OUTPOST
OOPSWWW POWWOWS
OORRSSW SORROWS
OORSTTU SORT-OUT
OPPRRTU PURPORT
OPPRSTU SUPPORT
OPPRSTY STROPPY
OPRSSTU SPROUTS,
    STUPORS
OPSSSTU TOSS-UPS
OPSTTUU OUTPUTS

EIGHT-LETTER WORDS

AAAABENN ANABAENA
AAAACCRR CARACARA
AAAACNRS ANASARCA
AAAADTVV AVADAVAT
AAAAGLRT AGARTALA
AAAAHJMR MAHARAJA
AAAAIMPR ARAPAIMA
AAAAIRTX ATARAXIA
AAAAKKNT KATAKANA
AAAAKMWY WAKAYAMA
AAAAKNRW ARAWAKAN
AAAAKNWZ KANAZAWA
AAAANNST SANTA ANA
AAABBILT ABBATIAL
AAABBNRS BARNABAS
AAABCCRT BACCARAT
AAABCHLS CALABASH
AAABCILR CALABRIA
AAABCINT ANABATIC
AAABCNRU CARNAUBA
AAABCPRY CAPYBARA
AAABDEST DATABASE
AAABDFIZ FAIZABAD
AAABDLNO BADALONA
AAABDNNN BANDANNA
AAABDNRS SARABAND
AAABDNRT ABRADANT
AAABEHNR HABANERA
AAABEHRT BARATHEA
AAABELLR ARABELLA
AAABGNST BATANGAS
AAABGRTU RUTABAGA
AAABHIKZ ABKHAZIA

AAABHIMN BAHAMIAN
AAABHLMR ALHAMBRA
AAABHPRT BHATPARA
AAABILNN ALBANIAN
AAABINRV BAVARIAN
AAABINSS ANABASIS
AAABLLRT BALLARAT
AAABLOPR PARABOLA
AAABRSUY SURABAYA
AAACCEPR CARAPACE
AAACCISU CAUCASIA
AAACCRTT CATARACT
AAACDEIM ACADEMIA
AAACDENR DRACAENA
AAACDIMM MACADMIA
AAACDINN CANADIAN
AAACDINR ARCADIAN
AAACDNNO ANACONDA
AAACDNPR PANDA CAR
AAACDNRS SANDARAC
AAACDOTV ADVOCAAT
AAACEHNR ARCHAEAN
AAACELRT À LA CARTE
AAACELST CATALASE
AAACENNP PANACEAN
AAACENPS PANACEAS
AAACGLSW SCALAWAG
AAACGMNP CAMPAGNA
AAACGMNR ARMAGNAC
AAACHLLZ CHALAZAL
AAACIJMN JAMAICAN
AAACILMN MANIACAL
AAACILRV CALVARIA

AAACILSY CALISAYA
AAACIMNP CAMPANIA
AAACINTV CAVATINA
AAACKMRT TAMARACK
AAACLLTX TLAXCALA
AAACLMNS ALMANACS
AAACLRTZ ALCATRAZ
AAACNOSV CASANOVA
AAACNRSV CARAVANS
AAACNSTT CANTATAS
AAACRSWY CARAWAYS
AAACSTWY CASTAWAY
AAADELMS SALAAMED
AAADELRW A RAW DEAL
AAADENTV VANADATE
AAADGGHH HAGGADAH
AAADGHNR ANGHARAD
AAADGLMY AMYGDALA
AAADGLNN NAGALAND
AAADHHSS HADASSAH
AAADHKNR KANDAHAR
AAADHRTZ AT HAZARD
AAADILMT DALMATIA
AAADILRS ALASDAIR
AAADILRU ADULARIA
AAADIMNY ADYNAMIA
AAADJKRT DJAKARTA
AAADKRRV AARDVARK
AAADLMNY MANDALAY
AAADLNRS SAARLAND
AAADMNTU TAMANDUA
AAAEGNPP APPANAGE
AAAEHLPR RAPHAELA

AAAEHMNT ANATHEMA	**AAAILNOT** ANATOLIA	**AABCDEIT** ABDICATE
AAAEHNPS ANAPHASE	**AAAILNST** ALSATIAN	**AABCDEKT** BACKDATE
AAAEKTWY TAKEAWAY	**AAAILRST** ALASTAIR	**AABCDELN** BALANCED
AAAELMMN ANALEMMA	**AAAIMNOR** MARIANAO	**AABCDHKN** BACKHAND
AAAELNPT PANATELA	**AAAIMNRT** ARAMINTA	**AABCDHKR** HARDBACK
AAAENPRV PARAVANE	**AAAIMNST** TASMANIA	**AABCDIIS** DIABASIC
AAAENPST ANAPAEST	**AAAIMRTV** AMRAVATI	**AABCDIKL** LAID-BACK
AAAERTWY TEARAWAY	**AAAINNTZ** TANZANIA	**AABCDIMO** CAMBODIA
AAAFGLNO FANAGALO	**AAAINOPR** PARANOIA	**AABCDKRW** BACKWARD,
AAAFHHRT HAFTARAH	**AAAINRSV** VARANASI	DRAWBACK
AAAFHILN HALAFIAN	**AAAINRTT** TATARIAN	**AABCDKRY** BACKYARD
AAAFINST FANTASIA	**AAAIPSSV** PIASSAVA	**AABCEEFL** FACEABLE
AAAFINUV AVIFAUNA	**AAAIRRSV** RARA AVIS	**AABCEENY** ABEYANCE
AAAGGLLN GALANGAL	**AAAKKMRU** KAMAKURA	**AABCEERT** ACERBATE
AAAGHINN GHANAIAN	**AAAKKORT** KRAKATOA	**AABCEGOT** CABOTAGE
AAAGHINR HIRAGANA	**AAAKLWWY** WALKAWAY	**AABCEHLS** CASHABLE
AAAGHIPR AGRAPHIA	**AAAKNRSS** ARKANSAS	**AABCEILM** AMICABLE
AAAGIKNS NAGASAKI	**AAALLPRX** PARALLAX	**AABCEILR** BALEARIC
AAAGINRR AGRARIAN	**AAALLPST** PALATALS	**AABCEIRT** BACTERIA
AAAGJMNR JAMNAGAR	**AAALMNTZ** MAZATLAN	**AABCEJNO** JACOBEAN
AAAGLMMS AMALGAMS	**AAALNRTT** TARLATAN	**AABCEKLM** CLAMBAKE
AAAGLMSY MALAGASY	**AAAMNOPR** PANORAMA	**AABCEKLP** PACKABLE
AAAGLNRW WARANGAL	**AAAMNOSZ** AMAZONAS	**AABCEKST** BACK SEAT
AAAGLRST ASTRAGAL	**AAAMOTTU** AUTOMATA	**AABCELLL** CALLABLE
AAAGMMRY GAMMA	**AAANNSSV** SAVANNAS	**AABCELLP** PLACABLE
RAY	**AAANOPRZ** PARAZOAN	**AABCELLS** SCALABLE
AAAGMNNN	**AAANQTUU** AQUANAUT	**AABCELNR** BALANCER,
NAMANGAN	**AAAPQRTU** PARAQUAT	BARNACLE
AAAGMNRS ANAGRAMS	**AABBCDRS** SCABBARD	**AABCELNS** BALANCES
AAAGMNRT RAMAT GAN	**AABBCEGS** CABBAGES	**AABCELOR** ALBACORE
AAAGORZZ ZARAGOZA	**AABBCEKR** BAREBACK	**AABCELRT** BRACTEAL
AAAGPRUY PARAGUAY	**AABBCINR** BARBICAN	**AABCELSU** CAUSABLE
AAAHHITW HIAWATHA	**AABBCIRR** BARBARIC	**AABCELWY** CABLEWAY
AAAHHTWY HATHAWAY	**AABBCIST** SABBATIC	**AABCEMRV** VAMBRACE
AAAHIINW HAWAIIAN	**AABBDHIU** ABU DHABI	**AABCENRR** CANBERRA
AAAHIKLR KALAHARI	**AABBDORS** BARBADOS	**AABCEPRS** SPACE-BAR
AAAHIMNR MAHARANI	**AABBEELR** BEARABLE	**AABCERST** CABARETS
AAAHINNY HINAYANA	**AABBEELT** BEATABLE	**AABCESSU** ABACUSES
AAAHJLMT TAJ MAHAL	**AABBEILL** BAILABLE	**AABCFHKL** HALFBACK
AAAHKNSW WAKASHAN	**AABBELLM** BLAMABLE	**AABCFIIL** BIFACIAL
AAAHMMST MAHATMAS	**AABBELLS** BASEBALL	**AABCFKST** FASTBACK
AAAHMNOR MARANHAO	**AABBELRY** BEARABLY	**AABCGIMO** CAMBOGIA
AAAHMNRT AMARANTH	**AABBGGRS** GRAB BAGS	**AABCHILR** BRACHIAL
AAAHMNST SAMANTHA	**AABBIILL** BILABIAL	**AABCHINR** BRANCHIA
AAAHNNSV SAVANNAH	**AABBIRSU** BABIRUSA	**AABCHKLS** BACKLASH
AAAHNOPR ANAPHORA	**AABBKLTY** BABY TALK	**AABCHKSW** BACKWASH
AAAHNPPR HARAPPAN	**AABCCEHK** BACKACHE	**AABCHMRY** CHAMBRAY
AAAIINPR APIARIAN	**AABCCELR** CABLE CAR	**AABCHRRT** BAR CHART
AAAIKKSW KAWASAKI	**AABCCHKT** BACKCHAT	**AABCIILR** BIRACIAL
AAAILLMR MALARIAL	**AABCCINN** CANNABIC	**AABCIILS** BASILICA
AAAILLPT PALATIAL	**AABCCKKP** BACKPACK	**AABCIJNO** JACOBIAN,
AAAILMSV MALVASIA	**AABCCKLP** BLACKCAP	JACOBINA
AAAILMSY MALAYSIA	**AABCCMOT** CATACOMB	**AABCIKLT** TAILBACK
AAAILNNS ANNALISA	**AABCDEIN** ABIDANCE	**AABCILLR** CABRILLA

AABCILMS BALSAMIC
AABCILMY AMICABLY
AABCILNN CANNIBAL
AABCILNO ANABOLIC
AABCIMNR CAMBRIAN
AABCINNN CANNABIN
AABCINNR CINNABAR
AABCINNS CANNABIS
AABCINRT BACTRIAN
AABCIRSS BRASSICA
AABCISSS ABSCISSA
AABCKKLT BACK TALK
AABCKLPY PLAYBACK
AABCKLRT BLACK ART
AABCKNPS SNAPBACK
AABCKNRS CAB RANKS,
   SNACK BAR
AABCKRRS BARRACKS
AABCKSTY BACKSTAY
AABCKSWY SWAY-BACK
AABCLLSY SCALABLY
AABCLNTY BLATANCY
AABCLOOR COOLABAR
AABCOORS SOROCABA
AABCORST ACROBATS
AABCRSTT ABSTRACT
AABDDEET DEAD BEAT
AABDDEGN BANDAGED
AABDDEHN HEADBAND
AABDDHNS DAB HANDS
AABDDLNS BADLANDS
AABDEELR READABLE
AABDEELT DATEABLE
AABDEELV EVADABLE
AABDEGIN BADINAGE
AABDEGLR GRADABLE
AABDEGNS BANDAGES
AABDEHKR HARDBAKE
AABDEKRY DAYBREAK
AABDELLS BALLADES,
   SABADELL
AABDELLU LAUDABLE
AABDELMN DAMNABLE
AABDELOR ADORABLE
AABDELPR DRAPABLE
AABDELRT TRADABLE
AABDELRW DRAWABLE
AABDELRY READABLY
AABDENOS A BAD NOSE
AABDENTU UNABATED
AABDENVW WAVE BAND
AABDEORS SEABOARD
AABDFHIT BAD FAITH
AABDFHLN FAHLBAND

AABDGHNS HANDBAGS
AABDGHOT GODTHAAB
AABDGINR ABRADING
AABDGNOV VAGABOND
AABDGNSS SANDBAGS
AABDGORR GARBOARD
AABDGOTU GADABOUT
AABDHLLN HANDBALL
AABDHLLR HARDBALL
AABDHNST HATBANDS
AABDHRUY BURAYDAH
AABDHRYZ BY HAZARD
AABDIILR BIRADIAL
AABDIILS BASIDIAL
AABDIMRS BARMAIDS
AABDINNR RAINBAND
AABDINNU DANUBIAN
AABDIOST BIODATAS
AABDKNNS SANDBANK
AABDLLRY BALLADRY
AABDLLUY LAUDABLY
AABDLMNU LABDANUM
AABDLMNY DAMNABLY
AABDLMRU ADUMBRAL
AABDLOOT BOATLOAD
AABDLOPR LAPBOARD
AABDLORR LABRADOR,
   LARBOARD
AABDLRSV SVALBARD
AABDLRSW BRADAWLS
AABDMNNS BANDSMAN
AABDMNRS ARMBANDS
AABDNNTU ABUNDANT
AABDNRRY BARNYARD
AABDNRSS SANDBARS
AABDORWY BROADWAY
AABDRRSS BRASSARD
AABDRSST BASTARDS
AABDRSTY BASTARDY
AABEEFLN FLEABANE
AABEEGKR BREAKAGE
AABEEGNT ABNEGATE
AABEEHLL HEALABLE
AABEEHLR HEARABLE
AABEEHLT HATEABLE
AABEEHMR HARAMBEE
AABEEKRT TEA BREAK
AABEELLS LEASABLE,
   SALEABLE, SEALABLE
AABEELMN AMENABLE
AABEELMT MATABELE,
   TAMEABLE
AABEELPR REAPABLE
AABEELRS ERASABLE

AABEELRT TEARABLE
AABEELRW WEARABLE
AABEEMPR ABAMPERE
AABEENOR ANAEROBE
AABEERST BASE RATE
AABEFGLS FLEABAGS
AABEFHKL HALFBEAK
AABEFLMR FARMABLE,
   FRAMABLE
AABEFLMU FLAMBEAU
AABEGGGS BAGGAGES
AABEGILN GAINABLE
AABEGLLL GLABELLA
AABEGLLM BALL GAME
AABEGLNW GNAWABLE
AABEGLRU ARGUABLE
AABEGMNY MANGABEY
AABEGNOR BARONAGE
AABEGORT ABROGATE
AABEGOST SABOTAGE
AABEGRRS BARRAGES
AABEHIMS MAEBASHI
AABEHKLS SHAKABLE
AABEHLMS SHAMABLE
AABEHLPS SHAPABLE
AABEHLPT ALPHABET
AABEHLRS SHARABLE
AABEHLSV SHAVABLE
AABEHLSW WASHABLE
AABEIKRR AIRBRAKE
AABEILLM MAILABLE
AABEILLS ISABELLA,
   SAILABLE
AABEILMN LIMA BEAN
AABEILRS RAISABLE
AABEILRV VARIABLE
AABEILST SATIABLE
AABEILTV ABLATIVE
AABEIRSS AIRBASES
AABEIRSV ABRASIVE
AABEISUV BEAUVAIS
AABEKLLS SLAKABLE
AABEKLLT TALKABLE
AABEKLLW WALKABLE
AABEKNRS NEBRASKA
AABEKNRT BANK RATE
AABEKOTU ABEOKUTA
AABELLMT MEATBALL
AABELLNO LOANABLE
AABELLOV ABOVE ALL
AABELLPP PALPABLE
AABELLPS LAPSABLE
AABELLPY PLAYABLE
AABELLSV SALVABLE

AABELLSY SALEABLY
AABELLUV VALUABLE
AABELMPP MAPPABLE
AABELMST BLASTEMA,
  LAMBASTE
AABELMTT TABLEMAT
AABELMTU AMBULATE
AABELNOT ATONABLE
AABELNPS ANABLEPS
AABELORR ARBOREAL
AABELOVW AVOWABLE
AABELPPT TAPPABLE
AABELPRS PARABLES,
  PARSABLE, SPARABLE
AABELPSS PASSABLE
AABELRTY BETRAYAL
AABELSTT STATABLE,
  TASTABLE
AABELSTU TABLEAUS
AABELSTW WASTABLE
AABELSWY SWAYABLE
AABELTTU TABULATE
AABELTUX TABLEAUX
AABENOSY SOYA BEAN
AABENRRT ABERRANT
AABENRST RATSBANE
AABENSTU ANTABUSE
AABFLOTT FALTBOAT,
  FLATBOAT
AABGGGNN GANG-BANG
AABGGRRT BRAGGART
AABGHKRS SHAGBARK
AABGHPRR BAR GRAPH
AABGILMS MAILBAGS
AABGILRU BULGARIA
AABGINRS BARGAINS
AABGLMNU GALBANUM
AABGLNPS SLAP-BANG
AABGLRUW WALBURGA
AABGLRUY ARGUABLY
AABGMORR BAROGRAM
AABHHORU BROUHAHA
AABHIINR BAHRAINI
AABHIINU BAUHINIA
AABHILLR HAIRBALL
AABHILNN HANNIBAL
AABHILTU HABITUAL
AABHIMNR BRAHMANI
AABHINTT HABITANT
AABHISTT HABITATS
AABHKKKU HABAKKUK
AABHMNRS BRAHMANS
AABHMSTT BATH MATS
AABHNOTU AUTOBAHN

AABHRSST BRASS HAT
AABIILRS BRASILIA
AABIIMNN NAMIBIAN
AABIKLNU KINABALU
AABILMNS BAILSMAN
AABILNNU BIANNUAL
AABILNOR BARONIAL
AABILNOT ABLATION
AABILNRU BINAURAL
AABILNTY BANALITY
AABILRRT ARBITRAL
AABILRSY BASILARY
AABILRVY VARIABLY
AABILSTY SATIABLY
AABIMMRS MARIMBAS
AABIMNOT MANITOBA
AABIMORS AMBROSIA
AABINNPR BRAINPAN
AABINORS ABRASION
AABINRTZ BARTIZAN
AABINRZZ ZANZIBAR
AABIORTT ABATTOIR
AABIOSSY BIO-ASSAY
AABISTUZ ZAIBATSU
AABJLPRU JABALPUR
AABKLLPR BALL PARK
AABKOOSZ BAZOOKAS
AABKOPRS SOAPBARK
AABLLMOR BALMORAL
AABLLPPY PALPABLY
AABLLSTU BLASTULA
AABLLSVY SALVABLY
AABLMNOR ABNORMAL
AABLMNTU AMBULANT
AABLOTUY LAYABOUT
ABLOUWY BULAWAYO
AABLPSSY PASSABLY
AABLSTTU ABUTTALS
AABMMOSU ABOMASUM
AABMMOSY MAMA'S BOY
AABMNRTU RAMBUTAN
AABMORSU MARABOUS
AABNNOSZ BONANZAS
AABNOSTW BOTSWANA
AABORRRT BARRATOR
AABORSTT BAROSTAT
AABRRRTY BARRATRY
AACCCHHU CACHUCHA
AACCCLOO COCA-COLA
AACCCRUY ACCURACY
AACCDDES CASCADED
AACCDEFR FACE CARD
AACCDEIM ACADEMIC
AACCDELO ACCOLADE

AACCDESS CASCADES
AACCDHRS CASH CARD
AACCDOVY ADVOCACY
AACCEENT CETACEAN
AACCEFKP FACE PACK
AACCEFLO COALFACE
AACCEHIX CACHEXIA
AACCEIRR CERCARIA
AACCEKRS SACK RACE
AACCELOR CARACOLE
AACCELTY CALYCATE
AACCENTU ACUTANCE
AACCERTU ACCURATE
AACCFILR FARCICAL
AACCGILT GALACTIC
AACCHHRT CARTHACH
AACCHINR ANARCHIC,
  CHARACIN
AACCHISV VISCACHA
AACCHLLT CATCH-ALL
AACCHLOR CHARCOAL
AACCHLOT CACHALOT
AACCHMNO COACHMAN
AACCIINV VACCINIA
AACCIIST SCIATICA
AACCILNU CULIACAN
AACCILNV VACCINAL
AACCILRU ACICULAR
AACCILTT TACTICAL
AACCIPTY CAPACITY
AACCLLST CATCALLS
AACCLOPU ACAPULCO
AACCLTTU CALCUTTA
AACCOPRS ASCOCARP
AACCOSTT STACCATO,
  TOCCATAS
AACCSSUU CAUCASUS
AACDDENV ADVANCED
AACDDETY TEA CADDY
AACDDINR RADICAND
AACDEEHH HEADACHE
AACDEEHR HEADRACE
AACDEELS ESCALADE
AACDEEOR AREA CODE
AACDEEPS ESCAPADE
AACDEGKP PACKAGED
AACDEHHY HEADACHY
AACDEHIN HACIENDA
AACDEHLP CEPHALAD
AACDEHMR DRACHMAE
AACDEHRS CHARADES
AACDEHRT CATHEDRA
AACDEHTT ATTACHED
AACDEIMN MAENADIC

AACDEINR RADIANCE
AACDEJNT ADJACENT
AACDEKTT ATTACKED
AACDELMN MANACLED
AACDELNR CALENDAR,
LANDRACE
AACDELNV VALANCED
AACDELPT PLACATED
AACDENPT TAP DANCE
AACDENRV ADVANCER
AACDENRW WAR DANCE
AACDENSV ADVANCES,
CANVASED
AACDENSZ CADENZAS
AACDEOTV ADVOCATE
AACDEQUY ADEQUACY
AACDERST CADASTER
AACDERSV CADAVERS
AACDETTU ACTUATED
AACDFIST ACID-FAST
AACDGGHI HAGGADIC
AACDGINR CARANGID,
CARDIGAN
AACDHHKR HARDHACK
AACDHHRS HARD CASH
AACDHINP HANDICAP
AACDHINR ARACHNID
AACDHKRT HARD TACK
AACDHLNP HANDCLAP
AACDHLRY CHARLADY
AACDHMRS DRACHMAS
AACDHNRT HANDCART
AACDIINR ACID RAIN
AACDIINS ASCIDIAN
AACDIIRT ADRIATIC
AACDILLP PALLADIC
AACDILMT DALMATIC
AACDILMU CALADIUM
AACDILNO DIACONAL
AACDILNR CARDINAL,
CLARINDA
AACDILNU DULCIANA
AACDILOZ ZODIACAL
AACDILRS RADICALS
AACDIMNY ADYNAMIC
AACDIMRT DRAMATIC
AACDIOTU AUTACOID
AACDIRTY CARYATID
AACDITUY AUDACITY
AACDJKSW JACKDAWS
AACDJQRU JACQUARD
AACDKLNU AUCKLAND
AACDLLUY CAUDALLY
AACDLNSS SCANDALS

AACDLOSV CALVADOS
AACDLPRS PLACARDS
AACDMMOR
CARDAMOM
AACDMSSU DAMASCUS
AACDNSST SAND-CAST
AACDOOSV AVOCADOS
AACDQRSU SQUAD CAR
AACEEFIT FACETIAE
AACEEFLP PALEFACE
AACEEGLV CLEAVAGE
AACEEGPS SPACE-AGE
AACEEHLR HERACLEA
AACEEIMT EMACIATE
AACEEINN ENCAENIA
AACEEIRT ACIERATE
AACEEKST TEACAKES
AACEELRT LACERATE
AACEELST ESCALATE
AACEELTU ACULEATE
AACEEMRT MACERATE
AACEEMST CASEMATE
AACEENNT CATENANE
AACEENRS CESAREAN
AACEENTT CATENATE
AACEEPSS SEASCAPE
AACEERTV ACERVATE
AACEETUV EVACUATE
AACEETVX EXCAVATE
AACEFFIN AFFIANCE
AACEFIST FASCIATE
AACEFRTT ARTEFACT
AACEGHRT CARTHAGE
AACEGILN ANGELICA
AACEGILT GLACIATE
AACEGINR CANAIGRE
AACEGIRR CARRIAGE
AACEGIRV VICARAGE
AACEGKPR PACKAGER
AACEGKPS PACKAGES
AACEGMUY CAMAGUEY
AACEHILL HELIACAL
AACEHILM MICHAELA
AACEHILN ACHENIAL
AACEHIMR CHIMAERA
AACEHIMT HAEMATIC
AACEHIPT HEPATICA
AACEHIRS ARCHAISE
AACEHIRZ ARCHAIZE
AACEHLRT TRACHEAL
AACEHLRX EXARCHAL
AACEHMRS MARCHESA
AACEHMST SCHEMATA
AACEHRST TRACHEAS

AACEHRTT ATTACHER
AACEHSTT ATTACHÉS
AACEIKMT KAMACITE
AACEILLM CAMELLIA
AACEILLN ALLIANCE,
CANAILLE
AACEILMN CALAMINE
AACEILMT CALAMITE
AACEILNS CANALISE
AACEILNT ALICANTE,
ANALCITE
AACEILNV VALENCIA,
VALIANCE
AACEILNZ CANALIZE
AACEILOP ALOPECIA
AACEILRT TAILRACE
AACEILRV CAVALIER
AACEIMNR AMERICAN,
CINERAMA, IN CAMERA
AACEIMNS AMNESIAC
AACEIMTT CATAMITE
AACEINNO OCEANIAN
AACEINPZ PIACENZA
AACEINRS CANARIES
AACEINRT CARINATE,
CRANIATE
AACEINRV VARIANCE
AACEINST ESTANCIA
AACEIPPS PAPACIES
AACEIPRS AIRSPACE
AACEIPTT APATETIC,
CAPITATE
AACEISTU EUSTACIA
AACEITTV ACTIVATE
AACEKKLW CAKEWALK
AACEKLST SALT CAKE
AACEKNPS PANCAKES
AACEKOST OATCAKES
AACEKRTT ATTACKER
AACELLLR ALL CLEAR
AACELLMR MARCELLA
AACELLOT ALLOCATE
AACELMNS MANACLES
AACELMPT PLACE MAT
AACELMPU MEA CULPA
AACELMRS CARAMELS
AACELNPR PARLANCE
AACELNPT PLACENTA
AACELNPY ANYPLACE
AACELNRT LACERANT
AACELNST ANALECTS
AACELNSV VALANCES
AACELRWY CLEARWAY
AACELSTY CATALYSE

AACELTTY CATTLEYA
AACEMNPS SPACEMAN
AACEMRRS ARMS RACE
AACEMRSS MASSACRE
AACENPRS PANCREAS
AACENPSU SAUCEPAN
AACENRSS SARACENS
AACENRTT REACTANT
AACENRTY CATENARY
AACENSSV CANVASES
AACENTUV EVACUANT
AACEORTV CAVEATOR
AACEOSST SEACOAST
AACERRTU ARCATURE
AACERSSU CAESURAS
AACERSTT CASTRATE
AACERTTT TRACTÁTE
AACESUWY CAUSEWAY
AACFHMST CAMSHAFT
AACFILLY FACIALLY
AACFINRS AFRICANS
AACFINST FANATICS
AACFIOPR A FAIR COP
AACFIRRT AIRCRAFT
AACFIRTT ARTIFACT
AACFJKLP FLAPJACK
AACFMNNY FANCY MAN
AACGGINO ANAGOGIC
AACGGIOP APAGOGIC
AACGHHNS CHANGSHA
AACGHNNN NANCHANG
AACGHOPZ GAZPACHO
AACGIILN GALICIAN
AACGIILR CAGLIARI
AACGIIMN MAGICIAN
AACGILNN ANGLICAN
AACGILNV GALVANIC
AACGILOU GUAIACOL
AACGILOX COXALGIA
AACGIMNN MANGANIC
AACGIMNP CAMPAIGN
AACGIMOP APOGAMIC
AACGIMRR MARGARIC
AACGIMUU GUAIACUM
AACGINTV VACATING
AACGISTY SAGACITY
AACGLMOU GLAUCOMA
AACGLORS CALOR GAS
AACGNRVY VAGRANCY
AACHHKNU CHANUKAH
AACHHTWY HATCHWAY
AACHILMS CHIASMAL
AACHILMT THALAMIC
AACHILNP CHAPLAIN

AACHILOU COAHUILA
AACHILPS CALIPASH
AACHILRV ARCHIVAL
AACHIMNN CHAINMAN,
   CHINAMAN
AACHIMNR CHAIRMAN,
   CHARMIAN
AACHIMRR ARMCHAIR
AACHIMRS ARCHAISM,
   CHARISMA
AACHINSW CHAIN SAW
AACHIPTT CHAPATTI
AACHIRSS CHARISSA
AACHIRST ARCHAIST
AACHKSSW HACKSAWS
AACHKSTY HAYSTACK
AACHLMNO MONACHAL
AACHLPRT LAP-CHART
AACHLSTU CALATHUS
AACHMNTW
   WATCHMAN
AACHMORT ACHROMAT,
   TRACHOMA
AACHMPRY PHARMACY
AACHNORT AT ANCHOR
AACHNRST TRASHCAN
AACHNSTU ACANTHUS
AACHOPPR APPROACH
AACHRSWY ARCHWAYS
AACHRTUY AUTARCHY
AACIILRV VICARIAL
AACIIPRT PATRICIA
AACIJLMO MAJOLICA
AACIJNOP JAPONICA
AACIKRTU AUTARKIC
AACILLMR LACRIMAL
AACILLRY RACIALLY
AACILMNT CALAMINT,
   CLAIMANT
AACILMTY CALAMITY
AACILNOR CAROLINA
AACILNRV CARNIVAL
AACILNTT ATLANTIC,
   TANTALIC
AACILNTU NAUTICAL
AACILNTY ANALYTIC
AACILOTT COAT-TAIL,
   TAILCOAT
AACILPRU PIACULAR
AACILPST APLASTIC,
   CAPITALS
AACILPTY ATYPICAL
AACILRSS CLARISSA
AACILRTY ALACRITY

AACILRUU AURICULA
AACILSTT STATICAL
AACILSTY SALACITY
AACIMMNO AMMONIAC
AACIMMRS MARASMIC
AACIMNOR MACARONI
AACIMNPS CAMPINAS
AACIMORT AROMATIC
AACINORS OCARINAS
AACINORT CATRIONA,
   RAINCOAT
AACINOTV OCTAVIAN,
   VACATION
AACINPST CAPTAINS
AACINQTU ACQUAINT
AACINRSZ CZARINAS
AACINSTZ STANZAIC
AACIPRTY RAPACITY
AACIQSTU AQUATICS
AACIRRTT TARTARIC
AACJKRST JACK TARS
AACJKSTY JACKSTAY
AACKKNPS KNAPSACK
AACKLSTW CATWALKS
AACKPRRS CAR PARKS
AACLLRRY CARRYALL
AACLLRSY RASCALLY
AACLLSUY CASUALLY,
   CAUSALLY
AACLLTUY ACTUALLY
AACLMNNS CLANSMAN
AACLMRRU MACRURAL
AACLNNOT CANTONAL
AACLNNOW CANON
   LAW
AACLNOPR COPLANAR
AACLNORU LA CORUNA
AACLNTVY VACANTLY
AACLORRU ORACULAR
AACLORSU CAROUSAL
AACLORTT CARLOTTA
AACLORUV VACUOLAR
AACLPPRT CLAPTRAP
AACLPRSU CAPSULAR,
   SCAPULAR
AACLPRTY CALYPTRA
AACLPSSU SCAPULAS
AACLPTTU CATAPULT
AACLRSUV VASCULAR
AACLSTTY CATALYST
AACLSTUY CASUALTY
AACMNOOR MACAROON
AACMNPRY RAMPANCY
AACMNRRU MACRURAN

AACMNSTX MANX CATS
AACNPSST CAPSTANS
AACNRSTT TRANSACT
AACOPRSU ACARPOUS
AACOPSTV POSTCAVA
AACORRTV VARACTOR
AACORSTT CASTRATO
AACORTTU ACTUATOR, AUTOCRAT
AACPSSTW CAT'S PAWS
AACSTUWY CUTAWAYS
AADDEEHT DEAD HEAT
AADDEEIL ADELAIDE
AADDEFIS DEAF-AIDS
AADDEFLL DEADFALL
AADDEHLN HEADLAND
AADDEHMN HANDMADE
AADDEHRW HEADWARD
AADDEHRZ HAZARDED
AADDEIRT RADIATED
AADDEMNT MANDATED
AADDEMRY DAYDREAM
AADDGHLN GLAD HAND
AADDGNRS GRANDADS
AADDHHIL LAH-DI-DAH
AADDLLNY LANDLADY
AADDLNRW LANDWARD
AADDNRST STANDARD
AADDOTYY DAY-TO-DAY
AADEEGHR HEADGEAR
AADEEGHT GET AHEAD
AADEEGMN ENDAMAGE
AADEEGRV AVERAGED
AADEEILR AIREDALE
AADEEIRT ERADIATE
AADEEKNW AWAKENED
AADEELNN ANNEALED
AADEELPP APPEALED
AADEELRW DELAWARE
AADEEMNT EMANATED
AADEEMRR DEMERARA
AADEENTT ANTEDATE
AADEEPPR APPEARED
AADEEPPS APPEASED
AADEEQTU ADEQUATE
AADEFHLT FLATHEAD
AADEFHST FATHEADS, HEADFAST
AADEFILR FAIRLEAD
AADEFIRS FARADISE
AADEFIRZ FARADIZE
AADEFLLR FALDERAL, LEAF-LARD
AADEFLRY DEFRAYAL

AADEGILL DIALLAGE, LEGAL AID
AADEGILT GLADIATE
AADEGINR DRAINAGE, GARDENIA
AADEGITT AGITATED
AADEGKRS DARK AGES
AADEGLMN MAGDALEN
AADEGLMY AMYGDALE
AADEGLSV SALVAGED
AADEGMPR RAMPAGED
AADEGMSS MASSAGED
AADEGNRR ARRANGED
AADEGNST DAGESTAN
AADEGPRT TRADE GAP
AADEGRRT RAG TRADE
AADEGRTU GRADUATE
AADEGSSU ASSUAGED
AADEHILN NAILHEAD
AADEHILR HEADRAIL, RAILHEAD
AADEHILS HEADSAIL
AADEHIWY HIDEAWAY
AADEHKOT HAKODATE
AADEHLNR ANHEDRAL
AADEHMNS HEADSMAN
AADEHMST MASTHEAD
AADEHRRW HARDWARE
AADEHRSS HARASSED
AADEHRSW WARHEADS
AADEHSSY SASHAYED
AADEHSWY HEADWAYS
AADEIIMV VIA MEDIA
AADEIKLP KLAIPEDA
AADEILLN DANIELLA
AADEILMN MADELINA
AADEILMS MALADIES
AADEILPR PRAEDIAL
AADEILPS PALISADE
AADEILRS SALARIED
AADEILSS ASSAILED
AADEILTV VALIDATE
AADEIMNR MARINADE
AADEIMNT ANIMATED, DIAMANTE
AADEIMST ADAMSITE, DIASTEMA
AADEINNR ADRIANNE
AADEINTT ATTAINED
AADEIPRS PARADISE
AADEIPSU DIAPAUSE
AADEIPTV ADAPTIVE
AADEISST DIASTASE
AADEISTT SATIATED

AADEJNNP JAPANNED
AADEKMNR MANDRAKE
AADELLPP APPALLED
AADELMNR ALDERMAN
AADELMNS DALESMAN, LEADSMAN
AADELNSY ANALYSED
AADELPPT PALPATED
AADELRSW RAW DEALS
AADEMNST MANDATES
AADEMNSY NAME DAYS
AADEMRRU MARAUDER
AADENNST ANDANTES
AADENRRT NARRATED
AADENRSV VERANDAS
AADEPRST ADAPTERS
AADEQRTU QUADRATE
AADERRRW REARWARD
AADERSSW SEAWARDS
AADERSTW EASTWARD
AADFGLSY FLAG DAYS
AADFGNNO FANDANGO
AADFHMNR FARMHAND
AADFHNST HANDFAST
AADFIMRS FARADISM
AADFKLLN FALKLAND
AADFLLLN LANDFALL
AADFLMNR FARMLAND
AADFLORW AARDWOLF
AADFLOTX TOADFLAX
AADFLOWY FOLDAWAY
AADFMRRY FARMYARD
AADGGIMN DAMAGING
AADGGLNN GANGLAND
AADGGLRS GLAD RAGS, LAGGARDS
AADGGRST STAGGARD
AADGHINN GANDHIAN
AADGHIPR DIAGRAPH
AADGIINS GAINSAID
AADGILLR GALLIARD
AADGILMR MADRIGAL
AADGILNO DIAGONAL
AADGIMPR PARADIGM
AADGIMRS DIAGRAMS
AADGINPR PARADING
AADGINPT ADAPTING
AADGINRU GUARDIAN
AADGINRW AWARDING
AADGLMNR GRAND MAL
AADGLNRS GARLANDS
AADGLOPR PODAGRAL
AADGMNOR
　DRAGOMAN, GARAMOND

AADGMNRS GRANDMAS
AADGNPRS GRANDPAS
AADGNRTU GUARDANT
AADGNRUV VANGUARD
AADHILLR HALLIARD
AADHILNR HANDRAIL
AADHILNT THAILAND
AADHILNU LUDHIANA
AADHILRV HAVILDAR
AADHINNZ ANDIZHAN
AADHINRR HARRIDAN
AADHLPSS SLAPDASH
AADHLRSY HALYARDS
AADHMNNY
  HANDYMAN
AADHMNRU DAMANHUR
AADHSSWY WASHDAYS
AADIIMRT DIARMAIT
AADIINRS SARDINIA
AADIIRRS AIR RAIDS
AADIKLLO ALKALOID
AADIKORT TAKORADI
AADILLLO ALLODIAL
AADILLRY RADIALLY
AADILMNN MAINLAND
AADILMOV MOLDAVIA
AADILMRS ADMIRALS
AADILNPR PRANDIAL
AADILNPS PALADINS
AADILNRU LAURINDA
AADILNTT DILATANT
AADILORR RAILROAD
AADILPRY LAPIDARY
AADILRST DIASTRAL
AADIMNNR MANDARIN
AADIMNOT MANATOID
AADIMNRT TAMARIND
AADIMNRY DAIRYMAN
AADIMNUV VANADIUM
AADIMSTZ SAMIZDAT
AADINOPR PARANOID
AADINOPS DIAPASON
AADINPRS SPANIARD
AADIOPRS DIASPORA
AADIORRT RADIATOR
AADIRRSY DISARRAY
AADJNTTU ADJUTANT
AADJNTUV ADJUVANT
AADJRTZZ TRAD JAZZ
AADKLMNR LANDMARK
AADKLNPR PARKLAND
AADKMNTU KATMANDU
AADKNRST TANKARDS
AADKORWY WORKADAY

AADLLMRS MALLARDS
AADLLMSS SMALL ADS
AADLMNOR MANDORLA
AADLMNRY MARYLAND
AADLMNSS LANDMASS
AADLMNUU LAUDANUM
AADLNOPR PARLANDO
AADLNRSY LANYARDS
AADLOPSY PAYLOADS
AADLORST LOADSTAR
AADLORSV SALVADOR
AADLORTU ADULATOR
AADMMNSU MANDAMUS
AADMNNOS MADONNAS
AADMNRSS MANSARDS
AADMORST MATADORS
AADMRRSY YARDARMS
AADNNORR ANDORRAN
AADNNPSU PANDANUS
AADNOPSS SANDSOAP
AADNOSUV VANADOUS
AADNOSWY NOWADAYS
AADNPRST SAND TRAP
AADNPSTT STAND PAT
AADNQRTU QUADRANT
AADNQRUY QUANDARY
AADOPPRR PARADROP
AADORSVY SAVOYARD
AADRSTUY SATURDAY
AAEEFLNW A NEW LEAF
AAEEFRRS SEAFARER
AAEEGILN ALIENAGE
AAEEGKLS LEAKAGES
AAEEGMPR AMPERAGE
AAEEGNNO NEOGAEAN
AAEEGNRS SANGAREE
AAEEGRRY GREY AREA
AAEEGRSV AVERAGES
AAEEGRTW WATERAGE
AAEEHHRR HEAR! HEAR!
AAEEHIMR HAEREMAI
AAEEHRTW AWEATHER,
  WHEATEAR
AAEEHTVW HEAT WAVE
AAEEILNT ALIENATE
AAEEJNPS JAPANESE
AAEEJNSV JAVANESE
AAEEKMNS NAMESAKE
AAEEKMRT TEA-MAKER
AAEEKNRS KANARESE
AAEEKNRW REAWAKEN
AAEEKPRT PARAKEET
AAEEKPTW TAKE A PEW
AAEEKQSU SEAQUAKE

AAEELLMR AMARELLE
AAEELMMT METAMALE
AAEELMNU EMANUELA
AAEELNNR ANNEALER
AAEELNOR ELEANORA
AAEELNPS SEAPLANE,
  SPELAEAN
AAEELPPR APPEALER
AAEELPRY LEAP YEAR
AAEELRTU LAUREATE
AAEELTUV EVALUATE
AAEEMMTT TEAM-MATE
AAEEMNRT MAN-EATER
AAEEMSSS ASSAMESE
AAEENNRZ NAZARENE
AAEENRST ARSENATE,
  NEAR EAST, SERENATA
AAEENRTT ANTEATER
AAEENSTU NAUSEATE
AAEEPPRR REAPPEAR
AAEEPRST SEPARATE
AAEERSTT STEARATE
AAEFFILS FAIL-SAFE
AAEFFNRS FANFARES
AAEFGHRW WHARFAGE
AAEFGIMR FAIR GAME
AAEFGLOT FLOATAGE
AAEFILTY FAYALITE
AAEFIMRR AIRFRAME
AAEFINNT FAINEANT
AAEFLMTT FLATMATE
AAEFLPSY PLAY SAFE
AAEFLRTW FLATWARE
AAEFRRWY WAYFARER
AAEGGIOT AGIOTAGE
AAEGGLNU LANGUAGE
AAEGGLNY LAY AN EGG
AAEGGNRY GARGANEY
AAEGGOPR PARAGOGE
AAEGHIRS HARGEISA
AAEGHLNP PHALANGE
AAEGHLPS SLAGHEAP
AAEGHMRX HEXAGRAM
AAEGHNRU HARANGUE
AAEGILLM GAMALIEL
AAEGILLN GALILEAN
AAEGILNN ANGELINA
AAEGILNR ALGERIAN,
  GERANIAL
AAEGILNT AGENTIAL,
  ALGINATE
AAEGILSX GALAXIES
AAEGILTT TAILGATE
AAEGIMNO EGOMANIA

AAEGIMNS MAGNESIA
AAEGIMNT AGMINATE
AAEGIMNZ MAGAZINE
AAEGIMRR MARRIAGE
AAEGINPS PAGANISE
AAEGINPT PAGINATE
AAEGINPZ PAGANIZE
AAEGINRT AERATING
AAEGINTV NAVIGATE,
VAGINATE
AAEGIRSV VAGARIES
AAEGIRTX EX GRATIA
AAEGISSS ASSEGAIS
AAEGIVWY GIVEAWAY
AAEGKTTT KATTEGAT
AAEGLLMN MAGELLAN
AAEGLLPR PELLAGRA
AAEGLLSS GALLEASS
AAEGLNOU ANALOGUE
AAEGLNTU ANGULATE
AAEGLRST AGRESTAL
AAEGLRSV SALVAGER
AAEGLSSV LAS VEGAS
AAEGLSVY SAVAGELY
AAEGMNRS MANAGERS,
SEMARANG
AAEGMNRV GRAVAMEN
AAEGMNST MAGNATES
AAEGMORR AEROGRAM
AAEGMPRR RAMPAGER
AAEGMRRT MARGARET
AAEGMRSS MASSAGER
AAEGMRSW WAR GAMES
AAEGMRTU AGERATUM
AAEGMSSS MASSAGES
AAEGMTTW MEGAWATT
AAEGNOOR NO-GO AREA
AAEGNOOT NOTOGAEA
AAEGNPST PAGEANTS
AAEGNRRR ARRANGER
AAEGNSTT STAGNATE
AAEGORRT ARROGATE
AAEGORTT AEGROTAT
AAEGPSSS PASSAGES
AAEGRSSU ASSUAGER
AAEGRSTT REGATTAS
AAEGRSTZ STARGAZE
AAEGRSVY SAVAGERY
AAEGSSSU SAUSAGES
AAEGSTWY GATEWAYS
AAEHHRST HEAT RASH
AAEHILNP APHELIAN
AAEHIMNT HAEMATIN
AAEHINNT ATHENIAN

AAEHINPT APHANITE
AAEHINRT RHAETIAN
AAEHINST ASTHENIA
AAEHKLST ALKAHEST
AAEHKMRY HAYMAKER
AAEHLMSY SEALYHAM
AAEHLNTX EXHALANT
AAEHLPRX HEXAPLAR
AAEHLPUV UPHEAVAL
AAEHMNSS MANASSEH
AAEHMOPR AMPHORAE
AAEHMORT ATHEROMA
AAEHNPST PHEASANT
AAEHNRTZ NAZARETH
AAEHNTTX XANTHATE
AAEHNTVX TAX HAVEN
AAEHPRSW PESHAWAR
AAEHRRSS HARASSER
AAEHRSTT HATTERAS
AAEHRSTU ARETHUSA
AAEIILTT LAETITIA
AAEIIPRS APIARIES
AAEIIRSV AVIARIES
AAEIJMNS JAMESINA
AAEIKKMZ KAMIKAZE
AAEIKLLN ALKALINE
AAEIKLLS ALKALIES,
ALKALISE
AAEIKLLZ ALKALIZE
AAEIKLMS MAKE SAIL
AAEIKLNR KARELIAN
AAEILLLU ALLELUIA
AAEILLNT ALLANITE
AAEILLPT PALLIATE
AAEILLRT ARILLATE
AAEILLRY AERIALLY
AAEILMNT LAMINATE
AAEILMRT MATERIAL
AAEILMSS MALAISES
AAEILNPR AIRPLANE
AAEILNPT PALATINE
AAEILNRR LARRAINE
AAEILNRS AIRLANES
AAEILNRU AURELIAN,
LAURAINE
AAEILNRV VALERIAN
AAEILNSS NASALISE
AAEILNSZ NASALIZE
AAEILNTT LATINATE
AAEILPRT PARIETAL
AAEILPRX PREAXIAL
AAEILPST STAPELIA
AAEILPSZ LA SPEZIA
AAEILRRT ARTERIAL

AAEILRSS ASSAILER,
SALARIES
AAEILRTV VARIETAL
AAEILSTV SALIVATE
AAEILTVX LAXATIVE
AAEIMMNR MARIAMNE
AAEIMNNR ARMENIAN,
MARIANNE
AAEIMNPR PEARMAIN
AAEIMNRT MARINATE
AAEIMNST TAMASINE
AAEIMOTX TOXAEMIA
AAEIMOTZ AZOTEMIA
AAEIMPRT PIA MATER
AAEIMRTT MARIETTA
AAEINORT AERATION
AAEINORX ANOREXIA
AAEINRST ARTESIAN
AAEINRSU EURASIAN
AAEINRSY ARYANISE
AAEINRYZ ARYANIZE
AAEINSTT ASTATINE, IN A
STATE
AAEINSTW IN A SWEAT
AAEINTTT TITANATE
AAEIPPRS APPRAISE
AAEIPQRU AREQUIPA
AAEIPRST ASPIRATE,
PARASITE
AAEIPRTZ TRAPEZIA
AAEIRSTT ARISTATE
AAEIRSVW AIRWAVES
AAEIRTTZ ZARATITE
AAEJORSV SARAJEVO
AAEKKRSY KAYAKERS
AAEKLMRY MALARKEY
AAEKLNNT KELANTAN
AAEKNPRT PARTAKEN
AAEKPRRT PARTAKER
AAELLLMR LAMELLAR
AAELLLPR PARALLEL
AAELLORV ALVEOLAR
AAELLPRT PATELLAR
AAELLPST PATELLAS
AAELLRST LATERALS
AAELLSSW SEAWALLS
AAELLTTV VALLETTA
AAELLWYY ALLEYWAY
AAELMMNO MELANOMA
AAELMNRT MATERNAL
AAELMNSS SALESMAN
AAELMNST TALESMAN
AAELMPTY PLAYMATE
AAELMRSY LAMASERY

AAELMRTT MALTREAT
AAELNNOT NEONATAL
AAELNNSU LAUSANNE
AAELNNTU ANNULATE
AAELNOSS SEASONAL
AAELNPRT PARENTAL,
PATERNAL, PRENATAL
AAELNPRW WARPLANE
AAELNPST PLEASANT
AAELNRSS ARSENALS
AAELNRST ASTERNAL
AAELNRSY ANALYSER
AAELNRTX RELAXANT
AAELNSSY ANALYSES
AAELOPRS PSORALEA
AAELORTY ALEATORY
AAELPPSU APPLAUSE
AAELPRSV PALAVERS
AAELPRSY PARALYSE
AAELPRUV PAR VALUE
AAELPRYZ PARALYZE
AAELRTTU LAURETTA
AAELRWYY WAYLAYER
AAELSSTX SALES TAX
AAEMMNRT ARMAMENT
AAEMNORT EMANATOR
AAEMNOTZ METAZOAN
AAEMNPRS PARMESAN
AAEMNPRT PARAMENT
AAEMNRST SANTAREM
AAEMNRTW WATERMAN
AAEMNSSS MANASSES
AAEMORTT TERATOMA
AAEMOTTU AUTOMATE
AAEMPTTU AMPUTATE
AAEMQSTU SQUAMATE
AAEMRRTU ARMATURE
AAEMRSTU AMATEURS
AAEMRTTU MATURATE
AAENNNST ANTENNAS
AAENNORS ROSEANNA
AAENNOTT ANNOTATE
AAENORTU AERONAUT
AAENPPRT APPARENT
AAENPSST PEASANTS
AAENRSUW UNAWARES
AAEOPSTT APOSTATE
AAEORSTT AEROSTAT
AAEPPRST PARAPETS
AAEPPSTT APPESTAT
AAEPRTTY TEA PARTY
AAEPRTXY TAXPAYER
AAERRTTT TARTRATE
AAERRTTW WATER RAT

AAERSSTV VASTERAS
AAERSTTU SATURATE
AAERTWWY WATERWAY
AAFFGILS GAFFSAIL
AAFFILRT TAFFRAIL
AAFFINPR PARAFFIN
AAFFLSTU AFFLATUS
AAFFMNST STAFFMAN
AAFFMORR FROM AFAR
AAFGLLNU LANGLAUF
AAFGLNRT FLAGRANT
AAFGNRRT FRAGRANT
AAFHLMST HALF-MAST
AAFHLSTY LAYSHAFT
AAFHQRRU FARQUHAR
AAFHRSUU HAUSFRAU
AAFIILLM FAMILIAL
AAFIILLR FILARIAL
AAFIILMR FAMILIAR
AAFIKLLY ALKALIFY
AAFILLNR RAINFALL
AAFILMST FATALISM
AAFILSTT FATALIST
AAFILTTY FATALITY
AAFINNOV FAVONIAN
AAFINNST INFANTAS
AAFINRRW WARFARIN
AAFINSTU FAUSTIAN,
FAUSTINA
AAFIRSWY FAIRWAYS
AAFLSTWY FLATWAYS
AAFMNORW MAN-OF-
WAR
AAGGGINR GARAGING
AAGGILLN GANGLIAL
AAGGIMNN MANAGING
AAGGINRV RAVAGING
AAGGINSV SAVAGING
AAGGNORT TAGANROG
AAGGNSWY GANGWAYS
AAGHHINS SHANGHAI
AAGHHINW HWANG HAI
AAGHHNUU HUANG HUA
AAGHILNN HANGNAIL
AAGHKMNY GYMKHANA
AAGHLNPY ANAGLYPH
AAGHMNOY
HOGMANAY, MAHOGANY
AAGHMRSS MARSH GAS
AAGHNNST TANGSHAN
AAGIILMN IMAGINAL
AAGIILNV AVAILING
AAGIINNU IGUANIAN
AAGIINTW AWAITING

AAGIJRTU GUJARATI
AAGIKLNO KAOLIANG
AAGIKNNW KINGWANA
AAGILLNY ALLAYING
AAGILMNO MAGNOLIA
AAGILMNR ALARMING,
MARGINAL
AAGILNOY LIAOYANG
AAGILNRR LARRIGAN
AAGILOOP APOLOGIA
AAGILSTT SAGITTAL
AAGILSTW WAGTAILS
AAGIMNNN MANGANIN
AAGIMNPR GRAMPIAN
AAGIMNPS PAGANISM
AAGIMNSS AMASSING
AAGIMPTU PATAGIUM
AAGIMSTT STIGMATA
AAGINNST SIANGTAN
AAGINOST SANTIAGO
AAGINPRU PAGURIAN
AAGINPST PAGANIST
AAGINRRS SRINAGAR
AAGINRRY ARRAYING
AAGINSST ASSIGNAT
AAGINSSY ASSAYING
AAGIORTT AGITATOR
AAGIRSTV GRAVITAS
AAGKMSSS GAS MASKS
AAGKNOOR KANGAROO
AAGLLMOY ALLOGAMY
AAGLLNST GALLANTS
AAGLLOPY POLYGALA
AAGLLOWY GALLOWAY
AAGLMNSS GLASSMAN
AAGLNQUU AQUALUNG
AAGLNRRU GRANULAR
AAGLRSTU GASTRULA
AAGMNORT MARTAGON
AAGMOTUY AUTOGAMY
AAGNNSTT STAGNANT
AAGNOPRS PARAGONS
AAGNOPRT TRAGOPAN
AAGNORRT ARROGANT,
TARRAGON
AAGNRSTV VAGRANTS
AAGNRTUY GUARANTY
AAGORSSS SARGASSO
AAGRSSTU SASTRUGA
AAHHKKNU HANUKKAH
AAHHNSSU SHUSHANA
AAHHOPRS PHARAOHS
AAHIIKRR HARA-KIRI,
HARIKARI

AAHIILRT HAIRTAIL
AAHIINPS HISPANIA
AAHIINTT TAHITIAN
AAHIKLNS SAKHALIN
AAHIKNSS KINSHASA
AAHILNNT INHALANT
AAHILNOT HALATION
AAHIMNRR HARRIMAN
AAHIMSTT MATTHIAS
AAHINORT HORATIAN
AAHINPRS PIRANHAS
AAHINPRT PARTHIAN
AAHIPPRS SAPPHIRA
AAHIPSXY ASPHYXIA
AAHITWWY AWAY WITH
AAHJNNOT JONATHAN
AAHKLLMR HALLMARK
AAHKLMOO OKLAHOMA
AAHKMOOY YOKOHAMA
AAHKMOTW
    TOMAHAWK
AAHKMSSY YASHMAKS
AAHKRSTV HRVATSKA
AAHLLLTU TALLULAH
AAHLLMRS MARSHALL
AAHLLOPT ALLOPATH
AAHLLSWY HALLWAYS
AAHLMRSS MARSHALS
AAHLMSTU THALAMUS
AAHMNNOT MARATHON
AAHMNOTX XANTHOMA
AAHMNPST PHANTASM
AAHMOPRS AMPHORAS
AAHNNOSS HOSANNAS
AAHNNSSU SUSANNAH
AAHNPSTY PHANTASY
AAHNRTTY HANRATTY
AAHPRSTW WARPATHS
AAHPSTWY PATHWAYS
AAHRSSTY ASHTRAYS
AAIIILMR MILIARIA
AAIIILMS ISMAILIA
AAIIJJPP JIPIJAPA
AAIILMNS MAINSAIL
AAIILNRZ ALIZARIN
AAIILNST ITALIANS
AAIILNUX UNIAXIAL
AAIILRST ALISTAIR
AAIILRTX TRIAXIAL
AAIIMNNT MAINTAIN
AAIIMNPX PANMIXIA
AAIIMNRS ARIANISM
AAIINOTV AVIATION
AAIINPRR RIPARIAN

AAIINPRS PARISIAN
AAIINRST INTARSIA
AAIIORRT AIR-TO-AIR
AAIIPRST APIARIST
AAIIRTVX AVIATRIX
AAIKLNRS SRI LANKA
AAIKLOSV SLOVAKIA
AAIKMRST TAMARISK
AAIKNNTT ANTITANK
AAIKNPST PAKISTAN
AAIKNRTX TAXI RANK
AAIKSSTW SWASTIKA
AAILLLUV ALLUVIAL
AAILLMNT MANTILLA
AAILLMOR AMARILLO
AAILLMRX MAXILLAR
AAILLRXY AXILLARY
AAILMMRS ALARMISM
AAILMNOR MANORIAL,
    MORAINAL
AAILMNOS SOMALIAN
AAILMNST STAMINAL,
    TALISMAN
AAILMORR ARMORIAL
AAILMRST ALARMIST
AAILMTTU ULTIMATA
AAILNNOT NATIONAL
AAILNNPT PLANTAIN
AAILNNST ANNALIST
AAILNOPP APPOLINA
AAILNOPS PIANOLAS
AAILNOPT TALAPOIN
AAILNORS ORINASAL
AAILNORT NOTARIAL,
    RATIONAL
AAILNOSV SLAVONIA
AAILNOTV LAVATION
AAILNOTX LAXATION
AAILNQTU ALIQUANT
AAILNSSY ANALYSIS
AAILNSTT ATLANTIS
AAILNSTU LUSATIAN
AAILNSTY NASALITY
AAILORRS RASORIAL
AAILORRV VARIOLAR
AAILPPRU PUPARIAL
AAILPRST PATRIALS
AAILRRSV ARRIVALS
AAILRSVY SALIVARY
AAILRSWY RAILWAYS
AAILSSTY STAYSAIL
AAIMMNST MAINMAST
AAIMMRSU SAMARIUM
AAIMNNRU RUMANIAN

AAIMNORT ANIMATOR
AAIMNORV MORAVIAN
AAIMNORW AIRWOMAN
AAIMNPRZ MARZIPAN
AAIMNRRT TRIMARAN
AAIMNRST MARTIANS
AAIMNRSU MASURIAN
AAIMNSST MANTISSA,
    SATANISM
AAIMNSTY MAINSTAY
AAIMOPRS MARIPOSA
AAIMPRST PASTRAMI
AAIMQRUU AQUARIUM
AAIMRRST AMRITSAR
AAIMRSSU SAMURAIS
AAINNNOT ANTONINA
AAINNOST SONATINA
AAINNOTT NATATION
AAINNRSV NIRVANAS
AAINNSST NAISSANT
AAINOPRV PAR AVION
AAINORRS ROSARIAN
AAINORRT ROTARIAN
AAINOTTX TAXATION
AAINPRST ASPIRANT,
    PARTISAN
AAINPRTW WAR PAINT
AAINQRTU QUATRAIN
AAINQTTU AQUATINT
AAINRSST ARTISANS,
    TSARINAS
AAINRSSY ASSYRIAN
AAINRSTU AUSTRIAN
AAINRSTV VARIANTS
AAINRSTY SANITARY
AAINRSTZ TZARINAS
AAINSSSS ASSASSIN
AAINSSTT SATANIST
AAIORSTV AVIATORS
AAIQRSTU AQUARIST
AAIQRSUU AQUARIUS
AAIRSSTU ASTURIAS
AAIRSTWY STAIRWAY
AAJMMORR MARJORAM
AAKLMNSW WALKMANS
AAKMMNRS MARKSMAN
AAKMOSSU MOUSSAKA
AAKMRSUZ MAZURKAS
AAKPRSWY PARKWAYS
AALLLLMP PALL MALL
AALLMNTY TALLYMAN
AALLMNUY MANUALLY
AALLMPRU AMPULLAR
AALLNNUY ANNUALLY

AALLNOTY ATONALLY
AALLNPRU PLANULAR
AALLOORW WALLAROO
AALLORWY ROLLAWAY
AALLPRST PLASTRAL
AALLRUVV VALVULAR
AALMNOPP PAMPLONA
AALMNORT MATRONAL
AALMNORU MONAURAL
AALMNORW ROMAN LAW
AALMNOWY LAYWOMAN
AALMNTTU TANTALUM
AALMNTUU AUTUMNAL
AALMOSTT STOMATAL
AALNNOST SONANTAL
AALNOPRT PATRONAL
AALNORSS ALSO-RANS
AALNPSST SALTPANS
AALNPTWX WAXPLANT
AALNRSTU NATURALS
AALNSSTU SULTANAS
AALNSSTY ANALYSTS
AALNSTTU TANTALUS
AALOOPSU SAO PAULO
AALOPPRV APPROVAL
AALOPRSS PARASOLS
AALOPRST PASTORAL
AALORTUV VALUATOR
AALORTVY LAVATORY
AALPRSTU SPATULAR
AALPSSTU SPATULAS
AALRSTTW STALWART
AALRSTUY SALUTARY
AALSSSTU ASSAULTS
AAMMNNOT MAN-TO-MAN
AAMMRSSU MARASMUS
AAMNRSTU SUMATRAN
AAMNRSTW STRAW MAN
AAMOPRRU PARAMOUR
AAMORSSV SAMOVARS
AAMOSTTU AUTOMATS
AAMPRRST RAMPARTS
AAMSSSTU SATSUMAS
AANNOSST ASSONANT
AANNRSTY STANNARY
AANOOSSS AS SOON AS
AANORRRT NARRATOR
AANRRSTW WARRANTS
AANRRTWY WARRANTY
AANRSTTU SATURANT
AANRSUWY RUNAWAYS
AAOPSSTY APOSTASY

AAOSTWWY STOWAWAY
AAPRRSTT RAT TRAPS
AARRSSTW STAR WARS
AARSTTUY STATUARY
ABBBEILR BRIBABLE
ABBBELRS BABBLERS
ABBBELUY BLUE BABY
ABBBGILN BABBLING, BLABBING
ABBBHSUY BUSHBABY
ABBCCKMO BACKCOMB
ABBCEERU BARBECUE
ABBCEGIR CRIBBAGE
ABBCEIKT BACKBITE
ABBCEILR BARBICEL
ABBCEIRR CRABBIER
ABBCEIRS SCABBIER
ABBCEKNO BACKBONE
ABBCEKNU BUCKBEAN
ABBCELRS SCRABBLE
ABBCGINR CRABBING
ABBCGIOR GABBROIC
ABBCIILL BIBLICAL
ABBCIKRT BRICKBAT
ABBCILSY SCABBILY
ABBCINOY CABIN BOY
ABBCKLOX BLACK BOX
ABBDDEEU BEDAUBED
ABBDDEIL AD-LIBBED, BIDDABLE
ABBDDEST BAD DEBTS
ABBDDLOO BAD BLOOD
ABBDEEER BEEBREAD
ABBDEEJR JABBERED
ABBDEILR AD-LIBBER
ABBDEINR BREAD BIN
ABBDEIRT RABBITED
ABBDELRS DABBLERS
ABBDEORS ABSORBED
ABBDERST DRABBEST
ABBDGILN DABBLING
ABBDHIRT BIRDBATH
ABBDHOOY BABYHOOD
ABBDOORX BOXBOARD
ABBEEJRR JABBERER
ABBEELVW EBBW VALE
ABBEESSS ABBESSES
ABBEFILR FLABBIER
ABBEGLRR GRABBLER
ABBEGRSU BUGBEARS
ABBEHIRS SHABBIER
ABBEHORT BATHROBE
ABBEILLO BOILABLE
ABBEILNU BUBALINE

ABBEILOT BILOBATE
ABBEIMWZ ZIMBABWE
ABBEINRS BRISBANE
ABBEIRRT RABBITER
ABBEKLOO BOOKABLE
ABBELMRS BRAMBLES
ABBELOPR PROBABLE
ABBELORU BELABOUR
ABBELQSU SQUABBLE
ABBENORY NABOBERY
ABBEORRS ABSORBER
ABBEORTW BROWBEAT
ABBERRRY BARBERRY
ABBERRYY BAYBERRY
ABBERSST STABBERS
ABBFILLY FLABBILY
ABBGGILN GABBLING
ABBGGINR GRABBING
ABBGHRSU HABSBURG
ABBGINST STABBING
ABBGINSW SWABBING
ABBGOOSU BUGABOOS
ABBHILSY SHABBILY
ABBHRRSU RHUBARBS
ABBHSTTU BATHTUBS
ABBILLSU SILLABUB
ABBILOST BOBTAILS
ABBIRRTY RABBITRY
ABBIRSUU SUBURBIA
ABBKKNOO BANKBOOK
ABBLLSUY SYLLABUB
ABBLOPRY PROBABLY
ABBMMOOT ATOM BOMB
ABBNRSUU SUBURBAN
ABCCDHIK DABCHICK
ABCCEELP PECCABLE
ABCCEIKL BLACK ICE
ABCCEILY CELIBACY
ABCCEKMO COMEBACK
ABCCHISU BACCHIUS
ABCCHNOO CABOCHON
ABCCIKKK KICKBACK
ABCCILOR CARBOLIC
ABCCILOT COBALTIC
ABCCINOR CARBONIC
ABCCIORS ASCORBIC
ABCCKLLO BALLCOCK
ABCCKSTU CUTBACKS
ABCCOOST TOBACCOS
ABCDDEOR BROCADED
ABCDDETU ABDUCTED
ABCDEEFK FEEDBACK
ABCDEEHL BLEACHED

ABCDEEHR BREACHED
ABCDEELM BECALMED
ABCDEELS DÉBÂCLES
ABCDEELU EDUCABLE
ABCDEEMR EMBRACED
ABCDEFLO BOLDFACE
ABCDEGIR BIRDCAGE
ABCDEHLN BLANCHED
ABCDEHNR BRANCHED
ABCDEHOR BROACHED
ABCDEIIT DIABETIC
ABCDEIKS BACKSIDE
ABCDEILR CALIBRED
ABCDEIRS ASCRIBED
ABCDEKLO BLOCKADE
ABCDEKNN NECKBAND
ABCDEKNU UNBACKED
ABCDELOO CABOODLE
ABCDEMNU DUMB-CANE
ABCDEMOT COMBATED
ABCDEMPS CAMP BEDS
ABCDENTU ABDUCENT
ABCDEORS BAR CODES
ABCDIILO BIOCIDAL, DIABOLIC
ABCDIIRT TRIBADIC
ABCDIKLS BACKSLID
ABCDKOOR BACK DOOR
ABCDKOPR BACKDROP
ABCDOPRU CUPBOARD
ABCDORUY OBDURACY
ABCEEEFK BEEFCAKE
ABCEEHLM BECHAMEL
ABCEEHLR BLEACHER
ABCEEHLW CHEWABLE
ABCEEHRS BREACHES
ABCEEILT CELIBATE
ABCEEIMN AMBIENCE
ABCEEIRT BEATRICE
ABCEEKLY BLACK EYE
ABCEELOV EVOCABLE
ABCEELRR CEREBRAL
ABCEELRT BRACELET
ABCEEMRR EMBRACER
ABCEEMRS EMBRACES
ABCEENSS ABSENCES
ABCEFIIT BEATIFIC
ABCEFIKR BACKFIRE, FIREBACK
ABCEFINO BONIFACE
ABCEFLSS BASS CLEF
ABCEGHIN BEACHING
ABCEGIRS RIB CAGES
ABCEGKLL BLACKLEG

ABCEGKLO BLOCKAGE
ABCEGKRY GREYBACK
ABCEHITT BATHETIC
ABCEHLOR BACHELOR
ABCEHLSU CHASUBLE
ABCEHMOT HECATOMB
ABCEHMRS CHAMBERS
ABCEHNRS BRANCHES
ABCEHOOT COHOBATE
ABCEHORR BROACHER
ABCEHORU BAROUCHE
ABCEIJOT JACOBITE
ABCEIKKL KICKABLE
ABCEIKLP PICKABLE
ABCEIKLT BLACK-TIE
ABCEIKWZ ZWIEBACK
ABCEILLR CLARIBEL
ABCEILNN BINNACLE
ABCEILOR CABRIOLE
ABCEILOS SOCIABLE
ABCEILRS CALIBRES
ABCEINRS BRISANCE, CARBINES
ABCEINRT BACTERIN
ABCEINST CABINETS
ABCEINTU INCUBATE
ABCEIORS AEROBICS
ABCEIORT BORACITE
ABCEIRSW CRABWISE
ABCEIRTT BRATTICE
ABCEIRTY ACERBITY
ABCEJKLT JET-BLACK
ABCEJLTY ABJECTLY
ABCEKKSW SKEWBACK
ABCEKLLO LOCKABLE
ABCEKLMO MOCKABLE
ABCEKLOO COOKABLE
ABCEKLSS BACKLESS
ABCEKLST BLACKEST
ABCEKOOS BOOKCASE
ABCEKRST BRACKETS
ABCEKSST SETBACKS
ABCELLMP CAMPBELL
ABCELLPU CULPABLE
ABCELMNY LAMBENCY
ABCELMRS SCRAMBLE
ABCELNUU NUBECULA
ABCELOOT BOOTLACE
ABCELOPS PLACEBOS
ABCELOST OBSTACLE
ABCEMORT COMBATER
ABCENNOS BESANCON
ABCEOOSS CABOOSES
ABCERRTU CARBURET

ABCERTUU CUBATURE
ABCESTUU SUBACUTE
ABCFHOTW FOB WATCH
ABCFIKLL BACKFILL
ABCFILOS BIFOCALS
ABCFKLLU FULLBACK
ABCFKLLY BLACKFLY
ABCGIKLN BLACKING
ABCGIKNS BACKINGS
ABCGILNO LOG CABIN
ABCGKLOS BACKLOGS
ABCHIKLS BLACKISH
ABCHIKRS BRACKISH
ABCHIMOR CHORIAMB
ABCHIMRU BRACHIUM
ABCHINOR BRONCHIA
ABCHIRRT TRIBRACH
ABCHKMPU HUMPBACK
ABCHKOOP CHAPBOOK
ABCHKOOS CASH-BOOK
ABCHLLUU CLUBHAUL
ABCHMOTX MATCHBOX
ABCIIKRR AIRBRICK
ABCIIMNR CIMBRIAN
ABCIIMNS MINICABS
ABCIIORS ISOBARIC
ABCIIRST TRIBASIC
ABCIIRTU CURITIBA
ABCIISTY BASICITY
ABCIKLST BACKLIST
ABCIKNPS BACKSPIN
ABCIKSSY SICKBAYS
ABCILLSU BACILLUS
ABCILLSY SYLLABIC
ABCILMOO COLOMBIA
ABCILMOU COLUMBIA
ABCILNPU PUBLICAN
ABCILOSY SOCIABLY
ABCILRRU RUBRICAL
ABCIMNRU CUMBRIAN
ABCINRVY VIBRANCY
ABCIOPRS SAPROBIC
ABCIORSU CARIBOUS
ABCIOSSU SCABIOUS
ABCIOSUV BIVOUACS
ABCJKOOT JACKBOOT
ABCKKOOR BOOKRACK
ABCKLOPT BLACKTOP
ABCKLOTU BLACKOUT
ABCKNNOS BANNOCKS
ABCKOORU BUCKAROO
ABCKOPST BACKSTOP
ABCLLPUY CULPABLY
ABCLNORY CARBONYL

ABCLPRUW PUB-CRAWL
ABCLSSSU SUBCLASS
ABCMOORT MOBOCRAT
ABCNOUYY BUOYANCY
ABCORRSS CROSSBAR
ABCORRSW CROWBARS
ABCORRTU TURBOCAR
ABCORSSU SCABROUS
ABCRSTTU SUBTRACT
ABDDEEEH BEHEADED
ABDDEEGR BADGERED
ABDDEEHT DEATHBED
ABDDEEKR DEBARKED
ABDDEERR DEBARRED
ABDDEEST BEDSTEAD
ABDDEGIR ABRIDGED
ABDDEHMO HEBDOMAD
ABDDEILS DISABLED
ABDDEILU BUDDLEIA
ABDDEINS SIDEBAND
ABDDELRS BLADDERS
ABDDENOU ABOUNDED
ABDDILMO LAMBDOID
ABDDILRY LADYBIRD
ABDDLLOS ODDBALLS
ABDEEEFL FEEDABLE
ABDEEEIW BIDE A WEE
ABDEEEKR BAEDEKER
ABDEEERV BEAVERED,
  BEREAVED
ABDEEFGS FEEDBAGS
ABDEEGGR BEGGARED
ABDEEGLR BELGRADE
ABDEEHLS SHEDABLE
ABDEEHNO BONEHEAD
ABDEEILN DENIABLE
ABDEEILS ABSEILED
ABDEEILW BEWAILED
ABDEEIST BEADIEST,
  DIABETES
ABDEEKMR EMBARKED
ABDEELLL LABELLED
ABDEELLW WELDABLE
ABDEELMM EMBALMED
ABDEELMN MENDABLE
ABDEELNS SENDABLE
ABDEELOR LEEBOARD
ABDEELPT BEDPLATE
ABDEELZZ BEDAZZLE
ABDEEMNO BEMOANED
ABDEEMNS BEAM-ENDS
ABDEENRT BANTERED
ABDEENRZ BRAZENED
ABDEENST ABSENTED

ABDEENTT BATTENED
ABDEERRT BARTERED
ABDEERST DEBATERS
ABDEERTT BATTERED
ABDEERTW WATERBED
ABDEERTY BETRAYED
ABDEESTT BEAD TEST
ABDEFILN FINDABLE
ABDEFINO BONA FIDE
ABDEFLLO FOLDABLE
ABDEFLOR FORDABLE
ABDEGHIS BIGHEADS
ABDEGILN BLINDAGE
ABDEGILU GUIDABLE
ABDEGIMX MIXED BAG
ABDEGINR BEARDING
ABDEGINS BEADINGS,
  DEBASING
ABDEGINT DEBATING
ABDEGIRR ABRIDGER
ABDEGLMO GAMBOLED
ABDEGOPR PEGBOARD
ABDEHINS BANISHED
ABDEHITU HABITUDE
ABDEHKLU BULKHEAD
ABDEHLLN HANDBELL
ABDEHLLO HOLDABLE
ABDEHLLU BULLHEAD
ABDEHLMS SHAMBLED
ABDEHLOT THEOBALD
ABDEHLRS HALBERDS
ABDEHMSU AMBUSHED
ABDEHNRR BERNHARD
ABDEHNSU DUSHANBE
ABDEHORR ABHORRED,
  HARBORED
ABDEHRST BREADTHS
ABDEIIRT DIATRIBE
ABDEILLS SLIDABLE
ABDEILMN MANDIBLE
ABDEILNO BODLEIAN
ABDEILNW WINDABLE
ABDEILOV VOIDABLE
ABDEILPS PIEBALDS
ABDEILRV DRIVABLE
ABDEILTU DUTIABLE
ABDEIMOO AMOEBOID
ABDEIMOR AMBEROID
ABDEINNR ENDBRAIN
ABDEINOR DEBONAIR
ABDEINOT OBTAINED
ABDEINRS BRANDIES
ABDEINST BANDIEST
ABDEINSU UNBIASED

ABDEIOTV OBVIATED
ABDEIPST BAPTISED
ABDEIPTZ BAPTIZED
ABDEIRSS SEABIRDS
ABDEIRTV VIBRATED
ABDEISSU DISABUSE
ABDEISTW BAWDIEST
ABDEKLSW SKEWBALD
ABDEKNSU SUNBAKED
ABDEKORY KEYBOARD
ABDELLMO MOLDABLE
ABDELLOT BALLOTED
ABDELNOR OBERLAND
ABDELNOZ BLAZONED
ABDELNRY BENADRYL
ABDELNSS BALDNESS
ABDELNST BLANDEST
ABDELORU LABOURED
ABDELOSV ABSOLVED
ABDELOSW DOWSABEL
ABDEMNNS BANDSMEN
ABDEMNOS ABDOMENS
ABDEMRTU DRUMBEAT
ABDENNOS NOSEBAND
ABDENNPY BAD PENNY
ABDENNRW BRAND-NEW
ABDENORW RAW-BONED
ABDENOTW DOWNBEAT
ABDENRRT BERTRAND
ABDENRRU UNBARRED
ABDENRSS DRABNESS
ABDENRTU BREADNUT,
  TURBANED
ABDEOPRT PROBATED
ABDEORRS BOARDERS
ABDEORRW DRAWBORE,
  WARDROBE
ABDEORST BROADEST
ABDEORSW SOWBREAD
ABDEORTU OBDURATE
ABDEORUX BORDEAUX
ABDEPSSY BYPASSED
ABDEPSTU BUDAPEST
ABDERSTW BEDSTRAW
ABDERTUW DRAWTUBE
ABDESTTU TASTE BUD
ABDFFLOY BADLY-OFF
ABDFLOOT FOLDBOAT
ABDGGGOY DOGGY BAG
ABDGHINR HANGBIRD
ABDGIINR BRAIDING
ABDGILOR GAOLBIRD
ABDGINNR BRANDING
ABDGINNY BANDYING

ABDGINOR BOARDING
ABDGINSW WINDBAGS
ABDHILLN HANDBILL
ABDHILNS BLANDISH
ABDHINRS BRANDISH
ABDHIRTY BIRTHDAY
ABDHKNOO HANDBOOK
ABDHLOPR BARDOLPH
ABDHLORW BLOWHARD
ABDHMOTU BAD-
    MOUTH
ABDHMSTU MUD BATHS
ABDHNSSU HUSBANDS
ABDIIJLR JAILBIRD
ABDIILLR BILLIARD
ABDIIMNR MIDBRAIN
ABDIIMSU BASIDIUM
ABDIINOS OBSIDIAN
ABDIIRTY RABIDITY
ABDILORW WILD BOAR
ABDILOST TABLOIDS
ABDILRRY RIBALDRY
ABDILRZZ BLIZZARD
ABDINOTY ANTIBODY
ABDINRTY BANDITRY
ABDJMOOR DOORJAMB
ABDLLORS BOLLARDS
ABDLMORY LOMBARDY
ABDLRSUY ABSURDLY
ABDNORUY BOUNDARY
ABDNSSTY STANDBYS
ABDOORTU OUTBOARD
ABDOOSSW BASSWOOD
ABDRSUZZ BUZZARDS
ABEEEERT BEE-EATER
ABEEEFRS FREE-BASE
ABEEEGRV BEVERAGE
ABEEEHTT HEBETATE
ABEEEELLR REELABLE
ABEEENST ABSENTEE
ABEEFILN FINEABLE
ABEEFILR AFEBRILE,
    FIREABLE
ABEEFILS FEASIBLE
ABEEFILT FLEABITE
ABEEFLLL FELLABLE
ABEEFLLN BEFALLEN
ABEEFORR FOREBEAR
ABEEGIRV VERBIAGE
ABEEGMRT BERGAMET
ABEEGNOS GABONESE
ABEEGTTU BAGUETTE
ABEEHINT THEBAINE
ABEEHIRS HEBRAISE

ABEEHIRZ HEBRAIZE
ABEEHLLL HEELBALL
ABEEHLLP HELPABLE
ABEEHLLR HAREBELL
ABEEHNNS HENBANES
ABEEHNSS BANSHEES,
    HAS-BEENS
ABEEHORS RHEOBASE
ABEEHQTU BEQUEATH
ABEEHRRT BREATHER
ABEEIKLT BAKELITE
ABEEIKRS BAKERIES
ABEEILLR RELIABLE
ABEEILLS ISABELLE
ABEEILLV LEVIABLE
ABEEILNP PLEBEIAN
ABEEILNS BALINESE,
    BASELINE
ABEEILNV ENVIABLE
ABEEILPX EXPIABLE
ABEEILRR BLEARIER
ABEEILRT LIBERATE
ABEEILRW BEWAILER
ABEEILSS SEISABLE,
    SISEABLE
ABEEILSZ SEIZABLE,
    SIZEABLE
ABEEISTU BEAUTIES
ABEEJMOR JAMBOREE
ABEEKLST BLEAKEST
ABEEKOOP PEEKABOO
ABEEKRRS BREAKERS
ABEELLLR LABELLER
ABEELLLT TELLABLE
ABEELLMT MELTABLE
ABEELLRY REELABLY
ABEELLSY EYEBALLS
ABEELMMR EMBALMER
ABEELMNO BONE MEAL
ABEELMPR PREAMBLE
ABEELMSS ASSEMBLE
ABEELMTT EMBATTLE
ABEELNOP BEANPOLE
ABEELNRT RENTABLE
ABEELOPR OPERABLE
ABEELORS EARLOBES
ABEELORX EXORABLE
ABEELRSU REUSABLE
ABEELRSV SERVABLE
ABEELSSS BASELESS
ABEELSSU SUBLEASE
ABEELSTT SEAT BELT,
    TESTABLE
ABEELTTW WETTABLE

ABEEMMNR MEMBRANE
ABEEMNST BASEMENT
ABEENNOT NOTA BENE
ABEENNTU UNBEATEN
ABEENORS SEABORNE
ABEENOTZ BENZOATE
ABEENRRT BANTERER
ABEENRSS BARENESS
ABEENRST ABSENTER
ABEENSSS BASENESS
ABEEORRV OVERBEAR
ABEERRRT BARTERER
ABEERRTT BARRETTE,
    BATTERER
ABEERRTV VERTEBRA
ABEERRTY BETRAYER,
    TEABERRY
ABEFHILS FISHABLE
ABEFILLL FALLIBLE
ABEFILLO FOILABLE
ABEFILLR FIREBALL
ABEFILLT LIFTABLE
ABEFILOT LIFEBOAT
ABEFILSY FEASIBLY
ABEFILTT FITTABLE
ABEFIORT FIREBOAT
ABEFIRRT FIREBRAT
ABEFITUY BEAUTIFY
ABEFLLMU BLAMEFUL
ABEFLLRU FURLABLE
ABEFLMOR FORMABLE
ABEFLNST FAN BELTS
ABEFLRSU SURFABLE
ABEFOORT BAREFOOT
ABEFORRS FORBEARS
ABEFRRUY FEBRUARY
ABEGGHLU HUGGABLE
ABEGGILN BEAGLING
ABEGGIST BAGGIEST
ABEGGLRY BEGGARLY
ABEGHIMR MAGHREBI
ABEGHINV BEHAVING
ABEGHINZ BENGHAZI
ABEGHRSU BEAR HUGS
ABEGIJTU BIJUGATE
ABEGIKNR BREAKING
ABEGIKNT BETAKING
ABEGILLN LABELING
ABEGILNN ENABLING
ABEGILNS SINGABLE
ABEGILNT BLEATING,
    TANGIBLE
ABEGILNY BELAYING
ABEGILOT OBLIGATE

ABEGILRT GILBERTA
ABEGIMNS BIG NAMES
ABEGINRS BEARINGS
ABEGINRT BERATING
ABEGINRW BEWARING
ABEGINST BEATINGS
ABEGINTT ABETTING
ABEGIPPS BAGPIPES
ABEGKORS GROSBEAK
ABEGLMRS GAMBLERS
ABEGLORW GROWABLE
ABEGLRSS GARBLESS
ABEGMNOY BOGEYMAN
ABEGMRSU UMBRAGES
ABEGNOOR GABORONE
ABEGNOSS NOSEBAGS
ABEGNSTU SUBAGENT
ABEGOSTT TOTE BAGS
ABEGSSTU SUBSTAGE
ABEHHIPZ HEPZIBAH
ABEHIINR HIBERNIA
ABEHILNR HIBERNAL
ABEHILPS SHIPABLE
ABEHILTT TITHABLE
ABEHIMMS MEMSAHIB
ABEHIMNO BOHEMIAN
ABEHIMRS HEBRAISM
ABEHINST ABSINTHE
ABEHIORV BEHAVIOR
ABEHIRST HEBRAIST
ABEHISTU HABITUÉS
ABEHLMSS SHAMBLES
ABEHMNOR HORNBEAM
ABEHMOOR REHOBOAM
ABEHMSSU AMBUSHES
ABEHNSTU SUNBATHE
ABEHORRR ABHORRER,
   HARBORER
ABEHRSST BRASHEST
ABEIILMT IMITABLE
ABEIILNN BIENNIAL
ABEIILNR BILINEAR,
   LIBERIAN
ABEIILNV INVIABLE
ABEIILPT PITIABLE
ABEIILST SIBILATE
ABEIILTV VITIABLE
ABEIINRR BRAINIER
ABEIINRS SIBERIAN
ABEIJLTU JUBILATE
ABEIJMNN BENJAMIN
ABEIKLLN LINKABLE
ABEIKLNS SINKABLE
ABEIKLSS KISSABLE

ABEIKNRS BEARSKIN,
   BREAK-INS
ABEIKNST BEATNIKS
ABEILLLM MILLABLE
ABEILLLT TILLABLE
ABEILLLW WILLABLE
ABEILLOS ISOLABLE
ABEILLOV VIOLABLE
ABEILLRS LIBERALS
ABEILLRY BAREILLY,
   BLEARILY, RELIABLY
ABEILLST BASTILLE,
   LISTABLE
ABEILMNT BAILMENT
ABEILMST BALMIEST
ABEILNNW WINNABLE
ABEILNPS BIPLANES
ABEILNPT PINTABLE
ABEILNRS RINSABLE
ABEILNRU RUINABLE
ABEILNSS LESBIANS
ABEILNTV BIVALENT
ABEILNVY ENVIABLY
ABEILORT LABORITE
ABEILPPR RIPPABLE
ABEILPPT TIPPABLE
ABEILPRT PARTIBLE
ABEILPSS PASSIBLE
ABEILPST EPIBLAST
ABEILRYY BIYEARLY
ABEILSSU ISSUABLE
ABEILSTU SUITABLE
ABEILSUX BISEXUAL
ABEILSVV BIVALVES
ABEIMRST BARMIEST
ABEIMRTV AMBIVERT,
   VERBATIM
ABEIMSSU IAMBUSES
ABEINORR AIRBORNE
ABEINORS BARONIES
ABEINORT BARITONE,
   OBTAINER
ABEINOST BOTANISE,
   OBEISANT
ABEINOTZ BOTANIZE
ABEINRRW BRAWNIER
ABEINRST BANISTER
ABEINRSU URBANISE
ABEINRSW WINE BARS
ABEINRTU BRAUNITE
ABEINRUZ URBANIZE
ABEINSST BASSINET
ABEINTTU INTUBATE
ABEIORTV ABORTIVE

ABEIPRRS SPARERIB
ABEIRRRS BARRIERS
ABEIRRSS BRASSIER
ABEIRRST ARBITERS
ABEIRRSZ BRAZIERS
ABEIRRVY BREVIARY
ABEIRSSU AIRBUSES
ABEIRSTT BIRETTAS
ABEIRSTY BESTIARY,
   SYBARITE
ABEIRTTY YTTERBIA
ABEISTTT BATTIEST
ABEJLMPU JUMPABLE
ABEJLSUY BLUE JAYS
ABEJMOOR JEROBOAM
ABEJNOSW JAWBONES
ABEKLMOS ABELMOSK,
   SMOKABLE
ABEKLNOW KNOWABLE
ABEKLNST BLANKETS
ABEKLORW WORKABLE
ABEKNNOT BANK NOTE
ABEKOORY YEARBOOK
ABEKORTU OUTBREAK
ABEKRSTY BASKETRY
ABELLLMU LABELLUM
ABELLLSY SYLLABLE
ABELLMRU UMBRELLA
ABELLNOT BALLONET
ABELLOSV SOLVABLE
ABELLRVY VERBALLY
ABELLSUW BLUE LAWS
ABELMNNO NOBLEMAN
ABELMNOP BELMOPAN
ABELMNOZ EMBLAZON
ABELMNTU NEMBUTAL
ABELMOSV MOVABLES
ABELMRRS RAMBLERS
ABELMSSY ASSEMBLY
ABELNORU BLUE ROAN
ABELNOST NOTABLES,
   STONABLE
ABELNPRU PRUNABLE
ABELNRTU TURNABLE
ABELNRUY URBANELY
ABELNRYZ BRAZENLY
ABELNSTU UNSTABLE
ABELNSTY ABSENTLY
ABELNSUU UNUSABLE
ABELNUVY NAVY BLUE
ABELOPRT PORTABLE
ABELOPRV PROVABLE
ABELOPRY OPERABLY
ABELOQTU QUOTABLE

ABELORRS LABORERS
ABELORRU LABOURER,
RUBEOLAR
ABELORST BLOATERS,
SORTABLE, STORABLE
ABELORSV ABSOLVER
ABELOSTU ABSOLUTE
ABELOSTW BESTOWAL
ABELOVWW BLOW-WAVE
ABELRRSW BRAWLERS,
WARBLERS
ABELRSTU BALUSTER
ABELRTTT BARTLETT
ABELRTTU REBUTTAL
ABELSTUU SUBULATE
ABELSTWY BELTWAYS
ABELTTUU TUBULATE
ABEMMNOO
MOONBEAM
ABEMNOTU UMBONATE
ABEMNPRU PENUMBRA
ABEMNSSU SUNBEAMS
ABEMNTTU ABUTMENT
ABENNOTU BUTANONE
ABENOPSU SUBPOENA
ABENORSS BARONESS
ABENORST BARONETS
ABENORTT BETATRON
ABENORTV BEVATRON
ABENOSSW SAWBONES
ABENOSTY BAYONETS
ABENQSTU BANQUETS
ABENRTTU BRUNETTA
ABENSSTT TEST BANS
ABEOPPRY PAPERBOY
ABEOPRST PROBATES
ABEORSST BOASTERS
ABEORSTT ABETTORS
ABEORSTU SABOTEUR
ABEORTUV OUTBRAVE
ABEOSSST ASBESTOS
ABEOSTWX SWEATBOX
ABEPRSSY PASSERBY
ABEPSSSY BYPASSES
ABERRWXY WAXBERRY
ABERSSTU ABSTRUSE
ABERTTUY BUTYRATE
ABFFGILN BAFFLING
ABFFIILS BAILIFFS
ABFFLLPU PUFFBALL
ABFFLOST BLAST-OFF
ABFFLOSU BUFFALOS
ABFFNOTU BOUFFANT
ABFGLLLO GOLF BALL

ABFGORUU FAUBOURG
ABFHIORS BOARFISH
ABFIILMR FIMBRIAL
ABFIILRR FIBRILAR
ABFILSTU FABULIST
ABFIRTTU FRUIT BAT
ABFLLOOT FOOTBALL
ABFLLORU FOUR-BALL
ABFLLOST SOFTBALL
ABFLOSTU BOASTFUL
ABFLOSUU FABULOUS
ABFNORTU TURBOFAN
ABFORSTU SURFBOAT
ABGGGINR BRAGGING
ABGGILMN GAMBLING
ABGGILNR GARBLING
ABGGNOOT TOBOGGAN
ABGGRSUU AUGSBURG
ABGHHILL HIGHBALL
ABGHINWZ WHIZ-BANG
ABGHMORU BROUGHAM
ABGHPRSU HAPSBURG
ABGIIMST BIGAMIST
ABGIINNO BIGNONIA
ABGIINNR BRAINING
ABGIINRS BRAISING
ABGIINSS BIASSING
ABGIIRTT BIRGITTA,
BRIGITTA
ABGIJNRU ABJURING
ABGIKLNU BAULKING
ABGILMNR MARBLING,
RAMBLING
ABGILNOR LABORING
ABGILNRW BRAWLING,
WARBLING
ABGILNST BLASTING,
STABLING
ABGILNTT BATTLING
ABGILNTY TANGIBLY
ABGIMOSU BIGAMOUS
ABGINORT ABORTING
ABGINOST BOASTING
ABGINTTU ABUTTING
ABGKORSW WORKBAGS
ABGLLLOY GLOBALLY
ABGLLORU GLOBULAR
ABGLMOPU PLUMBAGO
ABGLNOOT LONGBOAT
ABGLNOUW BUNGALOW
ABGLORSU GLABROUS
ABGLRRSU BURGLARS
ABGLRRUY BURGLARY
ABGLRSUZ SALZBURG

ABGNORSU OSNABURG
ABGNOSTU GUNBOATS
ABGOPSST POSTBAGS
ABHHIPST HIPBATHS
ABHIKLLW HAWKBILL
ABHIKLOR KOHLRABI
ABHILNOS HOBNAILS
ABHILNOT BIATHLON
ABHILOPS BASOPHIL
ABHILSTU HALIBUTS
ABHIMNOR MORBIHAN
ABHIOSTU HAUTBOIS
ABHIRRSU AIRBRUSH
ABHKOOOT BOAT
HOOK
ABHLLMOT MOTHBALL
ABHLLOOY BALLYHOO
ABHLOSWW WASHBOWL
ABHLSSTU SALTBUSH
ABHMNSUU SUBHUMAN
ABHMOORT BATHROOM
ABHOORST TARBOOSH
ABHOOSTW SHOWBOAT
ABHORRSU HARBOURS
ABHOSTUY HAUTBOYS
ABHRSTTU BATHURST
ABIIINOT AB INITIO
ABIIKLSS BASILISK
ABIILLMR MILLIBAR
ABIILLTY LABILITY
ABIILMNO BINOMIAL
ABIILMNS ALBINISM
ABIILNOT LIBATION
ABIILNOV BOLIVIAN
ABIILNRZ BRAZILIN
ABIILNST SIBILANT
ABIILPTY PITIABLY
ABIIMNOT AMBITION
ABIIRSSV VIBRISSA
ABIJLNTU JUBILANT
ABIKLMNS LAMBSKIN
ABIKNORR IRONBARK
ABILLLPY PLAYBILL
ABILLSWY WAYBILLS
ABILMNOU OLIBANUM
ABILMOPS BIOPLASM
ABILMORS LABORISM
ABILNOOT BOLTONIA,
OBLATION
ABILNOTU ABLUTION,
ABUTILON
ABILNRTU TRIBUNAL
ABILNRWY BRAWNILY
ABILNSTU ISTANBUL

ABILORST LABORIST,
   STROBILA
ABILRSSY BRASSILY
ABILSTUY SUITABLY
ABIMNOSU BIMANOUS
ABIMORSU BIRAMOUS
ABIMPSST BAPTISMS
ABINOORT ABORTION
ABINORSW RAINBOWS
ABINOSST BASTIONS
ABINOSTT BOTANIST
ABINRTTY BRITTANY
ABINRTUY URBANITY
ABIOPRSU BIPAROUS
ABIORRTV VIBRATOR
ABIORSTV VIBRATOS
ABIORTUY OBITUARY
ABIPRSTT BIT PARTS
ABIPRSUU UBI SUPRA
ABIPSSTT BAPTISTS
ABIRRSTU AIRBURST
ABISSSST BASSISTS
ABKKMOOR BOOKMARK
ABKLLNOR BANKROLL
ABKLRSUW BULWARKS
ABKNPRTU BANKRUPT
ABKOOPSS PASSBOOK
ABLLMOOR BALLROOM
ABLLMOPW BLOWLAMP
ABLLNOOS BALLOONS
ABLLNOSW SNOWBALL
ABLLORRS ROLL BARS
ABLLOSTY TALLBOYS
ABLLPSSU BALLS-UPS
ABLLRTUY BRUTALLY
ABLLSSUY SYLLABUS
ABLMNRUU LABURNUM
ABLNORYZ BLAZONRY
ABLOORTY OBLATORY
ABLOPRVY PROVABLY
ABLOPSYY PLAYBOYS
ABLORSST BORSTALS
ABLORSSU SUBSOLAR
ABLOSSUU SABULOUS
ABLOSTTU SUBTOTAL
ABLPRTUY ABRUPTLY
ABMORSTU TAMBOURS
ABNOORYZ BRYOZOAN
ABNOOSSS BASSOONS
ABNORTUU RUN-ABOUT
ABNOSSUU AUBUSSON
ABOPRSST TOP BRASS
ACCCENPY PECCANCY
ACCCFIIL CALCIFIC

ACCCIILT CALCITIC
ACCDDEOR ACCORDED
ACCDDIII DIACIDIC
ACCDDIIT DIDACTIC
ACCDEELN CANCELED
ACCDEENS CADENCES
ACCDEENT ACCENTED
ACCDEEPT ACCEPTED
ACCDEESS ACCESSED
ACCDEGIN ACCEDING
ACCDEILY DELICACY
ACCDEINO DECANOIC
ACCDEINT ACCIDENT
ACCDEIRT ACCREDIT
ACCDEKLR CRACKLED
ACCDEKOS COCKADES
ACCDELSU CUL-DE-SAC
ACCDELSY CYCLADES
ACCDEORR ACCORDER
ACCDEOST ACCOSTED
ACCDERSU ACCURSED
ACCDESUU CADUCEUS
ACCDHIIR DIARCHIC
ACCDHIOT CATHODIC
ACCDHIRY DYARCHIC
ACCDHPTU DUTCH CAP
ACCDIIOT ACIDOTIC
ACCDILTY DACTYLIC
ACCDINOR CANCROID,
   DRACONIC
ACCDIOOR CORACOID
ACCDITUY CADUCITY
ACCDOSUU CADUCOUS
ACCEEHLO COCHLEAE
ACCEEHMP CAMPECHE
ACCEEILR CELERIAC
ACCEEILS ECCLESIA
ACCEEIMR ICE CREAM
ACCEEKLN NECKLACE
ACCEELNR CLARENCE
ACCEELOS COALESCE
ACCEENNS NASCENCE
ACCEENST ACESCENT
ACCEESSS ACCESSES
ACCEFFIY EFFICACY
ACCEFILS FASCICLE
ACCEGKMO GAMECOCK
ACCEHIKP CHICKPEA
ACCEHILM ALCHEMIC,
   CHEMICAL
ACCEHILP CEPHALIC
ACCEHILS CHALICES
ACCEHIMN MECHANIC
ACCEHINO ANECHOIC

ACCEHINR ACRE-INCH,
   CHANCIER, CHICANER
ACCEHINT CATECHIN
ACCEHIRT CATCHIER
ACCEHKPY PAYCHECK
ACCEHLNS CHANCELS
ACCEHLOR COCHLEAR
ACCEHLOT CATECHOL
ACCEHMNO
   COACHMEN, COMANCHE
ACCEHNNO CHACONNE
ACCEHNOR ENCROACH
ACCEHNRY CHANCERY
ACCEHNUY CHAUNCEY
ACCEHOPT CACHEPOT
ACCEIKPS ICE PACKS
ACCEILLR CLERICAL
ACCEILLU CAULICLE
ACCEILLV CLAVICLE
ACCEILNT CANTICLE
ACCEILNY CALYCINE
ACCEILRV CERVICAL
ACCEIMRS CERAMICS
ACCEINRT ACENTRIC,
   NEARCTIC
ACCEINSV VACCINES
ACCEIOTV COACTIVE
ACCEIPRS CAPRICES
ACCEIPRT PRACTICE
ACCEIRTU CRUCIATE
ACCEISST ASCETICS
ACCEISTT ECSTATIC
ACCEKKOR ROCK CAKE
ACCEKLNR CRACKNEL
ACCEKLRS CACKLERS
ACCEKOPS PEACOCKS
ACCEKPSU CUP CAKES
ACCEKRRS CRACKERS
ACCELMNY CYCLAMEN
ACCELNOV CONCLAVE
ACCELNRU CARUNCLE
ACCELNTU CLEAN-CUT
ACCELORS CORACLES
ACCELRSY SCARCELY
ACCELRTU CLEAR-CUT
ACCENOPT CONCEPTA
ACCENORT ACCENTOR
ACCENOST COSECANT
ACCENOTT CONCETTA
ACCEOPRT ACCEPTOR
ACCEORST ECTOSARC
ACCERSST SCARCEST
ACCERSSU ACCUSERS
ACCESSTU CACTUSES

ACCESSUU CAUCUSES
ACCFHKLO HALF COCK
ACCFHLTY CATCHFLY
ACCFLNOO CONFOCAL
ACCGHINN CHANCING
ACCGHINO COACHING
ACCGHINT CATCHING
ACCGIKLN CACKLING,
CLACKING
ACCGIKMR GIMCRACK
ACCGIKNR CRACKING
ACCGILOX COXALGIC
ACCGINRU ACCRUING
ACCGINSU ACCUSING
ACCHHITT CHITCHAT
ACCHIIMS CHIASMIC
ACCHIIST CHIASTIC
ACCHILNY CHANCILY
ACCHILOT CATHOLIC
ACCHILOY CHICLAYO
ACCHILTY CATCHILY
ACCHIMOR ACHROMIC
ACCHINNO CINCHONA
ACCHINOS CHICANOS
ACCHINPU CAPUCHIN
ACCHIORT THORACIC,
TROCHAIC
ACCHKLOR CHARLOCK
ACCHKOSY HAYCOCKS
ACCHNOTU COUCHANT
ACCHOPRS CASH CROP
ACCHORTY OCTARCHY
ACCHORVY CRY HAVOC
ACCHRSTY SCRATCHY
ACCIILLN CLINICAL
ACCIILMT CLIMATIC
ACCIILRT CRITICAL
ACCIINOT ACONITIC,
CATIONIC
ACCIINTY CYANITIC
ACCIIRTX CICATRIX
ACCIKKNN NICKNACK
ACCIKKRR RICKRACK
ACCIKKTT TICKTACK
ACCIKLLS SICK CALL
ACCIKLOT COCKTAIL
ACCILMUU ACICULUM
ACCILNOT LACTONIC
ACCILNOV VOLCANIC
ACCILORT CORTICAL
ACCILRRU CIRCULAR
ACCILRSY ACRYLICS
ACCILSSS CLASSICS
ACCILTUU CUTICULA

ACCIMNOS MOCCASIN
ACCIMORU COUMARIC
ACCIMPSU CAPSICUM
ACCINOOS OCCASION
ACCINOOT COACTION
ACCINORT NARCOTIC
ACCINORV CAVICORN
ACCINOTY CYANOTIC
ACCIOPST SPICCATO
ACCIORST ACROSTIC,
SOCRATIC
ACCIORSY ISOCRACY
ACCIOSTU ACOUSTIC
ACCIRRTT TRICTRAC
ACCIRSTY SCARCITY
ACCKKRSU RUCKSACK
ACCKOOOT COCKATOO
ACCKOPRT CRACKPOT
ACCKORST STOCKCAR
ACCKOSSS CASSOCKS
ACCKPRSU CRACKUPS
ACCLLOSU OCCLUSAL
ACCLLSUU CALCULUS
ACCMNOOR MOROCCAN
ACCMOPST COMPACTS
ACCMOSTU ACCUSTOM
ACCNOORS RACCOONS
ACCNOPTU OCCUPANT
ACCNORTT CONTRACT
ACCNORTU ACCUTRON
ACCNOSTT CONTACTS
ACCNOSTU ACCOUNTS
ACCOPSTY COPYCATS
ACCORRTY CARRYCOT
ACDDDEIT ADDICTED
ACDDDEKU DEAD DUCK
ACDDEEES DECEASED
ACDDEEFR RED-FACED
ACDDEEHT DETACHED
ACDDEEIT DEDICATE
ACDDEELR DECLARED
ACDDEELS DESCALED
ACDDEEMP DECAMPED
ACDDEENS ASCENDED
ACDDEENT DECADENT,
DECANTED
ACDDEETU EDUCATED
ACDDEHKN DECKHAND
ACDDEIIL DEICIDAL
ACDDEIIM MEDICAID
ACDDEILU DECIDUAL
ACDDEINR RIDDANCE
ACDDEITT DICTATED
ACDDEKLO DEADLOCK

ACDDENTU ADDUCENT
ACDDERSU CRUSADED
ACDDERTU TRADUCED
ACDDGINU ADDUCING
ACDDGINY CADDYING
ACDDHIRY HYDRACID
ACDDHKOS SHADDOCK
ACDDIIOR CARDIOID
ACDDILNY CANDIDLY
ACDDIRSS DISCARDS
ACDDKLNO DOCKLAND
ACDDKOPS PADDOCKS
ACDDKORY DOCKYARD
ACDDORTU ADDUCTOR
ACDEEEFT DEFECATE
ACDEEENR CAREENED
ACDEEENT ANTECEDE
ACDEEERR CAREERED
ACDEEERS DECREASE
ACDEEESS SEEDCASE
ACDEEFFT AFFECTED
ACDEEFIN DEFIANCE
ACDEEFPR PREFACED
ACDEEGLY DELEGACY
ACDEEHIV ACHIEVED
ACDEEHMR DEMARCHE
ACDEEHNN ENHANCED
ACDEEHPR PREACHED
ACDEEHRS SEARCHED
ACDEEHRT DETACHER
ACDEEILT DELICATE
ACDEEIMR MEDICARE
ACDEEIMT DECIMATE,
MEDICATE
ACDEEINN ENNEADIC
ACDEEINU AUDIENCE
ACDEEINV DEVIANCE
ACDEEKPT TAPE DECK
ACDEELLR RECALLED
ACDEELNR CALENDER
ACDEELNS CLEANSED
ACDEELPR PARCELED,
REPLACED
ACDEELRR DECLARER
ACDEELRT DECRETAL
ACDEELSS DECLASSE
ACDEEMNP ENCAMPED
ACDEEMRS SCREAMED
ACDEEMRT CREMATED
ACDEENOT ANECDOTE
ACDEENRS ASCENDER
ACDEENRT CANTERED,
DECANTER, RECANTED
ACDEENRZ CREDENZA

ACDEEORT DECORATE
ACDEEPPR RECAPPED
ACDEEPRT CARPETED
ACDEERRT RETRACED
ACDEERSS CARESSED
ACDEFGIN DEFACING
ACDEFIIP PACIFIED
ACDEFILN CANFIELD
ACDEFILR FILECARD
ACDEFINN FINANCED
ACDEFIRR FREDRICA
ACDEFOTU OUTFACED
ACDEFOTW TWOFACED
ACDEFRSU SURFACED
ACDEFRTU FURCATED
ACDEGGRS SCRAGGED
ACDEGIMR GRIMACED
ACDEGINU GUIDANCE
ACDEGINY DECAYING
ACDEGIRS DISGRACE
ACDEHHNU HAUNCHED
ACDEHHTT THATCHED
ACDEHIJK HIJACKED
ACDEHILL HELLADIC
ACDEHILR HERALDIC
ACDEHIMN MACHINED
ACDEHINR RICHENDA
ACDEHIRT TRACHEID
ACDEHKLO HEADLOCK
ACDEHKLS SHACKLED
ACDEHKRU ARCHDUKE
ACDEHKSS CASH DESK
ACDEHKTW THWACKED
ACDEHLNR CHANDLER
ACDEHLNU LAUNCHED
ACDEHNOR ANCHORED
ACDEHNST SNATCHED,
  STANCHED
ACDEHORR HARD-CORE
ACDEHORT CHORDATE
ACDEHOST CATHODES
ACDEHOTT COT DEATH
ACDEHPST DESPATCH
ACDEHRRS CHRESARD
ACDEHRST STARCHED
ACDEIILN ALCIDINE
ACDEIINR ACRIDINE
ACDEIINS SCIAENID
ACDEIINT ACTINIDE,
  INDICATE
ACDEIJNU JAUNDICE
ACDEIKNP PANICKED
ACDEILLM MEDALLIC
ACDEILLS CEDILLAS

ACDEILLV CAVILLED
ACDEILMS DECIMALS,
  MEDICALS
ACDEILMX CLIMAXED
ACDEILNP PANICLED
ACDEILNU CLAUDINE
ACDEILOR CORDELIA
ACDEILPS DISPLACE
ACDEILRT ARTICLED
ACDEILST CITADELS,
  DIALECTS
ACDEILSY ECDYSIAL
ACDEIMNO COMEDIAN,
  DAEMONIC, DEMONIAC
ACDEIMNP PANDEMIC
ACDEIMOR MORDECAI
ACDEIMPT IMPACTED
ACDEIMRT TIMECARD
ACDEINNR CRANNIED
ACDEINOS DIOCESAN
ACDEINOT CATENOID
ACDEINOV VOIDANCE
ACDEINPT PEDANTIC
ACDEINRT DICENTRA
ACDEINSS ACIDNESS
ACDEINST DISTANCE
ACDEINTU INCUDATE
ACDEIOPS DIASCOPE
ACDEIORT CERATOID
ACDEIOSU EDACIOUS
ACDEIPSS CAPSISED
ACDEIPSZ CAPSIZED
ACDEIQRU ACQUIRED
ACDEIRSS CRESSIDA,
  SIDECARS
ACDEIRTT TETRACID
ACDEISTT ACID TEST,
  DICTATES
ACDEKLMU LAME DUCK
ACDEKNPU UNPACKED
ACDEKOST STOCKADE
ACDELLOR CAROLLED,
  COLLARED
ACDELLOS SO-CALLED
ACDELLOT COLLATED
ACDELMOR CLAMORED
ACDELMOS DAMOCLES
ACDELNOO CANOODLE
ACDELNOR COLANDER
ACDELNPU UNPLACED
ACDELNRY DRY-CLEAN
ACDELRSW SCRAWLED
ACDELRSY SACREDLY
ACDEMMRS SCRAMMED

ACDEMNOR ROMANCED
ACDEMOPR COMPARED
ACDEMORS COMRADES
ACDEMORT DEMOCRAT
ACDEMUUV VACUUMED
ACDENNNO CANNONED
ACDENNOR ORDNANCE
ACDENOPR ENDOCARP
ACDENORY CRAYONED,
  DEACONRY
ACDENRTU UNDERACT
ACDENRVY VERDANCY
ACDENSST DESCANTS
ACDEORRT REDACTOR
ACDEORST REDCOATS,
  SACRED TO
ACDEORSU CAROUSED
ACDEORTU EDUCATOR
ACDEORTV CAVORTED
ACDEPPRS SCRAPPED
ACDEPRTU CAPTURED
ACDEQTUU AQUEDUCT
ACDERRSU CRUSADER
ACDERRTU TRADUCER
ACDERSSU CRUSADES
ACDERSTT TEST CARD
ACDFFHNU HANDCUFF
ACDFFILR RADCLIFF
ACDFFIRT DIFFRACT
ACDFFLOS SCAFFOLD
ACDFGOOT ACT OF GOD
ACDFIILU FIDUCIAL
ACDFILOU FUCOIDAL
ACDGHOTW
  DOGWATCH, WATCHDOG
ACDGILNR CRADLING
ACDGILNS SCALDING
ACDGIMOT DOGMATIC
ACDGORST DOGCARTS
ACDHILPR PILCHARD
ACDHINOR HADRONIC
ACDHINSW SANDWICH
ACDHIPST DISPATCH
ACDHIQRU CHARQUID
ACDHKLRU HARD LUCK
ACDHKORS ROCK DASH
ACDHLNOR CHALDRON
ACDHMNTU DUTCHMAN
ACDHNOSW CASH
  DOWN, COWHANDS
ACDHOOTW WOODCHAT
ACDHOPRY HARD COPY
ACDHORRS ORCHARDS
ACDIIILN INDICIAL

ACDIIJLU JUDICIAL
ACDIILMS DISCLAIM
ACDIILNO CONIDIAL
ACDIILSU SUICIDAL
ACDIILTY DIALYTIC
ACDIIMNO DOMINICA
ACDIIMOR DIORAMIC
ACDIIMOT DIATOMIC
ACDIIMSU ASCIDIUM
ACDIINNT INDICANT
ACDIINOT ACTINOID,
  DIATONIC
ACDIIOSS ACIDOSIS
ACDIIOSX OXIDASIC
ACDIIRST CARDITIS
ACDIIRTY ACRIDITY
ACDIISST SADISTIC
ACDILLOT CLOTILDA
ACDILLPY PLACIDLY
ACDILMTU TALMUDIC
ACDILNOO CONOIDAL
ACDILNOR IRONCLAD
ACDILNOT DALTONIC
ACDILNSY SYNDICAL
ACDILNUU NUDICAUL
ACDILORS CORDIALS
ACDILOUV OVIDUCAL
ACDILSTW WILDCATS
ACDILSUU CLAUDIUS
ACDIMNOO CODOMAIN,
  MONOACID
ACDIMNSU SCANDIUM
ACDIMNSY DYNAMICS
ACDINOPS SPONDAIC
ACDINORS SARDONIC
ACDINORT TORNADIC
ACDINSTY DYNASTIC
ACDIOPRS PICADORS,
  SPORADIC
ACDIORTT DICTATOR
ACDIOSTX DOXASTIC
ACDIRSTT DISTRACT
ACDISTUV VIADUCTS
ACDJNSTU ADJUNCTS
ACDKLOPS PADLOCKS
ACDKMPSU MUDPACKS
ACDLNOPS COLD SNAP
ACDLNORS CALDRONS
ACDLNORU CAULDRON,
  COURLAND
ACDLNORY CONDYLAR
ACDLNOST SCOTLAND
ACDLOOOR COLORADO
ACDLOORT DOCTORAL

ACDLORWY COWARDLY
ACDMMNOO
  COMMANDO
ACDMMNOS COMMANDS
ACDMNORY DORMANCY,
  MORDANCY
ACDNOORT ACRODONT
ACDNOORV CORDOVAN
ACDNOSTW DOWNCAST
ACDOORST OSTRACOD
ACDOPRST POSTCARD
ACDRSSTU CUSTARDS
ACDRSTTU DUSTCART
ACEEEFRR CAREFREE
ACEEEGLN ELEGANCE
ACEEEIPR EARPIECE
ACEEEKPV KEEP CAVE
ACEEELMR CAMELEER
ACEEENSV EVANESCE
ACEEEPSS ESCAPEES
ACEEERRT RECREATE
ACEEERTX EXECRATE
ACEEESUV EVACUEES
ACEEFFIN CAFFEINE
ACEEFHWY WHEYFACE
ACEEFLPU PEACEFUL
ACEEFLSS FACELESS
ACEEFPRR PREFACER
ACEEFPRS PREFACES
ACEEFPTY TYPEFACE
ACEEFRSU FARCEUSE
ACEEGHNX EXCHANGE
ACEEGHRR RECHARGE
ACEEGILS LEGACIES
ACEEGIMY MAGIC EYE
ACEEGINS AGENCIES
ACEEGINT AGENETIC
ACEEGKRW WRECKAGE
ACEEGNOZ COZENAGE
ACEEGNSV SCAVENGE
ACEEGORV COVERAGE
ACEEHHST CHEETAHS
ACEEHINS EISENACH
ACEEHINT ECHINATE
ACEEHIPT PETECHIA
ACEEHIRT HETAERIC
ACEEHIRV ACHIEVER
ACEEHLNR CHARLENE
ACEEHLNT CATHLEEN
ACEEHLOS SHOELACE
ACEEHLRS HERACLES
ACEEHLSW ESCHEWAL
ACEEHMNP CAMPHENE
ACEEHMNR MENARCHE

ACEEHMRS CASHMERE,
  MARCHESE
ACEEHMST MACHETES
ACEEHNNR ENHANCER
ACEEHNRT CHARENTE
ACEEHPRR PREACHER
ACEEHPST CHEAPEST
ACEEHRRS RESEARCH,
  SEARCHER
ACEEHRSS SEARCHES
ACEEHRST HECTARES,
  TEACHERS
ACEEHRTT CATHETER
ACEEHRTY CYTHEREA
ACEEHSTT TEA CHEST
ACEEIKRR CREAKIER
ACEEIKST ICE SKATE
ACEEILNR RELIANCE
ACEEILNS SALIENCE
ACEEILPS ESPECIAL
ACEEIMRR CREAMIER
ACEEINNR NARCEINE
ACEEINPS SAPIENCE
ACEEINPT PATIENCE
ACEEINRS INCREASE
ACEEINRT CENTIARE,
  CREATINE
ACEEINST CINEASTE
ACEEINTV ENACTIVE
ACEEINTX EXITANCE
ACEEIRSU CAUSERIE
ACEEIRSW WISEACRE
ACEEIRTV CREATIVE,
  REACTIVE
ACEEIRTW ICE WATER,
  WATER ICE
ACEEISTV VESICATE
ACEEKLMR MACKEREL
ACEEKNPS KNEECAPS
ACEELLMR MARCELLE
ACEELLNS NACELLES
ACEELLNT LANCELET
ACEELLRR CELLARER
ACEELLRT CELLARET
ACEELNOR CAERLEON
ACEELNPT PENTACLE
ACEELNRS CLEANERS,
  CLEANSER
ACEELNRU CERULEAN,
  LAURENCE
ACEELNRW LAWRENCE
ACEELNST CLEANEST
ACEELNSU NUCLEASE
ACEELNSV ENCLAVES

ACEELNTT TENTACLE
ACEELNTU NUCLEATE
ACEELOPS ESCALOPE,
OPALESCE
ACEELORT RELOCATE
ACEELPRR REPLACER
ACEELPRV PERCEVAL
ACEELPTU PECULATE
ACEELRSS CARELESS
ACEELRST CLEAREST
ACEELRSV CLEAVERS
ACEELRTU ULCERATE
ACEELRTV CERVELAT
ACEELRTX EXCRETAL
ACEELSTT TELECAST
ACEEMNPS SPACEMEN
ACEEMNST CASEMENT
ACEEMORS RACEMOSE
ACEEMORV OVERCAME
ACEEMRRS CREAMERS,
SCREAMER
ACEEMRRY CREAMERY
ACEENNPS PENANCES
ACEENNPZ PENZANCE
ACEENNRT ENTRANCE
ACEENNST CANTEENS
ACEENORT CAROTENE
ACEENOST NOTECASE
ACEENPRR PARCENER
ACEENRRT RECANTER,
RECREANT
ACEENRTT ENTR'ACTE
ACEEPSTT SPECTATE
ACEERRSS CARESSER
ACEERRST TERRACES
ACEERRSU ECRASEUR
ACEERRTU CREATURE
ACEERRUV VERRUCAE
ACEERSSS CARESSES
ACEERSST CERASTES
ACEERSSV CREVASSE
ACEESSTT CASSETTE,
TEST CASE
ACEESSTY CAT'S EYES
ACEFFGIN EFFACING
ACEFFHRU CHAUFFER
ACEFFILT FACE-LIFT
ACEFFLRS SCLAFFER
ACEFGINR REFACING
ACEFGLNO LONG
FACE
ACEFGLRU GRACEFUL
ACEFHIKS FISHCAKE
ACEFHISV CAVEFISH

ACEFHORU FAROUCHE
ACEFIIPR PACIFIER
ACEFIIRT ARTIFICE
ACEFILLY FACILELY
ACEFILOP EPIFOCAL
ACEFILOS FOCALISE
ACEFILOZ FOCALIZE
ACEFIMPR CAMPFIRE
ACEFINNR FRANCINE
ACEFINNS FINANCES
ACEFINRS FANCIERS
ACEFINST FANCIEST
ACEFIORR AIRFORCE
ACEFIOSS FIASCOES
ACEFIRRT CRAFTIER
ACEFLLOV CALF
LOVE
ACEFLMNO FLAMENCO
ACEFLNOR FALCONER
ACEFLNOT CONFLATE,
FALCONET
ACEFLNRY CRANE FLY
ACEFLORS ALFRESCO
ACEFMNNY FANCY MEN
ACEFNORV CONFERVA
ACEFNRSU FURNACES
ACEFOOPT FOOTPACE
ACEFOORT ACRE-FOOT,
FOOTRACE
ACEFORST FORECAST
ACEFRRSU SURFACER
ACEFRRTU FRACTURE
ACEFRSSU SURFACES
ACEGGILN CAGELING
ACEGGIRR CRAGGIER
ACEGHHNT CHANGTEH
ACEGHIIT CHIGETAI
ACEGHIKN CHEKIANG
ACEGHILN LEACHING
ACEGHINR REACHING
ACEGHINT CHEATING,
TEACHING
ACEGHLTY LYCHGATE
ACEGHOSU GOUACHES
ACEGHRRS CHARGERS
ACEGIKNR CREAKING
ACEGILLR ALLERGIC
ACEGILMU MUCILAGE
ACEGILNN CLEANING
ACEGILNR CLEARING
ACEGILNV CLEAVING
ACEGILNW LACEWING
ACEGILRS GLACIERS
ACEGIMMT TAGMEMIC

ACEGIMNN MENACING
ACEGIMNR CREAMING,
GERMANIC
ACEGIMNT MAGNETIC
ACEGIMRR GRIMACER
ACEGIMRS GRAECISM,
GRIMACES
ACEGINNO CANOEING
ACEGINNS ENCASING
ACEGINNT ENACTING
ACEGINOS COINAGES
ACEGINPR CAPERING
ACEGINPS ESCAPING
ACEGINRS CREASING
ACEGINRT ARGENTIC,
CATERING, CREATING,
REACTING
ACEGINSS CAGINESS
ACEGINTX EXACTING
ACEGIOTT COGITATE
ACEGIPRT PRICE TAG
ACEGLLNO COLLAGEN
ACEGLLOS COLLAGES
ACEGLNRS CLANGERS
ACEGLOSU CAGOULES
ACEGMNOY GEOMANCY
ACEGNNOY CYANOGEN
ACEGNNTY TANGENCY
ACEGNOST COGNATES
ACEGORSS CORSAGES
ACEGORTT COTTAGER
ACEGORTY CATEGORY
ACEGOSTT COTTAGES
ACEHHIRR HIERARCH
ACEHHIRT THE CHAIR
ACEHHMNN HENCHMAN
ACEHHNRT ETHNARCH
ACEHHNSU HAUNCHES
ACEHHPRT HEPTARCH
ACEHHRTT THATCHER
ACEHHRTY HATCHERY,
THEARCHY
ACEHHSTT HATCHETS,
THATCHES
ACEHIIRT HIERATIC
ACEHIJKR HIJACKER
ACEHIKLR CHALKIER
ACEHILLS ACHILLES
ACEHILNP CEPHALIN
ACEHILPR PARHELIC
ACEHILRS CHARLIES
ACEHILTT ATHLETIC
ACEHIMNR CHAIRMEN
ACEHIMNS MACHINES

ACEHIMPT EMPATHIC, EMPHATIC
ACEHIMRS CHIMERAS
ACEHIMTT THEMATIC
ACEHINOT INCHOATE
ACEHINOX HEXANOIC
ACEHINST ASTHENIC, CHANTIES, TEACH-INS
ACEHIPRS SERAPHIC
ACEHIPRT PATCHIER, PHREATIC, PIE CHART
ACEHIPST PASTICHE
ACEHIPTT PATHETIC
ACEHIPTW WHITECAP
ACEHIRSS CASHIERS
ACEHIRST CHARIEST
ACEHIRSU EUCHARIS
ACEHIRSV ARCHIVES
ACEHIRTT CHATTIER
ACEHISST CHASTISE
ACEHISTX CATHEXIS
ACEHKLOV HAVELOCK
ACEHKLRS SHACKLER
ACEHKLSS SHACKLES
ACEHKLTY LATCHKEY
ACEHKMPU MUCKHEAP
ACEHKNSY HACKNEYS
ACEHKORV HAVOCKER
ACEHKRTW THWACKER
ACEHLLOO COALHOLE
ACEHLLST HELLCATS
ACEHLNNS CHANNELS
ACEHLNOU EULACHON
ACEHLNOY HALCYONE
ACEHLNPT PLANCHET
ACEHLNRU LAUNCHER
ACEHLNSU LAUNCHES
ACEHLOOT OOTHECAL
ACEHLORS CHORALES
ACEHLORT CHLORATE, TROCHLEA
ACEHLOTT TEA CLOTH
ACEHLPST CHAPLETS
ACEHLSSS CASHLESS
ACEHLSST SATCHELS
ACEHLSTT CHATTELS
ACEHLSTY CHASTELY
ACEHMNRT MERCHANT
ACEHMNSS CHESSMAN
ACEHMNTW WATCHMEN
ACEHMORT CHROMATE
ACEHMRRS CHARMERS, MARCHERS
ACEHMSTU MUSTACHE

ACEHNNPT PENCHANT
ACEHNOPR CHAPERON
ACEHNOPT CENOTAPH
ACEHNPSU PAUNCHES
ACEHNQUU QUECHUAN
ACEHNRRS RANCHERS
ACEHNRSS ARCHNESS
ACEHNRST SNATCHER, STANCHER
ACEHNSST SNATCHES
ACEHNSTU UNCHASTE
ACEHNSWZ SZECHWAN
ACEHOPRR REPROACH
ACEHOPRS POACHERS
ACEHORRV OVERARCH
ACEHORST THORACES
ACEHORTT THEOCRAT
ACEHORTU OUTREACH
ACEHOSSW SHOWCASE
ACEHOSTU SOUTACHE
ACEHPRST CHAPTERS
ACEHPRSU PURCHASE
ACEHRRST CHARTERS, STARCHER
ACEHRRTT TETRARCH
ACEHRSST STARCHES
ACEHRSSU CHASSEUR
ACEHRSTT RATCHETS
ACEHRTTY TRACHYTE
ACEHSSTT CHASTEST
ACEHSSTW SWATCHES
ACEIILMN LIMACINE
ACEIILMX MEXICALI
ACEIILST SILICATE
ACEIIMTU MAIEUTIC
ACEIINRT ANTI-ICER, ARENITIC, IN A TRICE
ACEIINTV INACTIVE
ACEIIPRS PIRACIES
ACEIIRRT CRITERIA
ACEIISTV CAVITIES
ACEIJMST MAJESTIC
ACEIKKLS SACKLIKE
ACEIKLLY CLAYLIKE
ACEIKLRY CREAKILY
ACEIKMNN NICKNAME
ACEIKMRV MAVERICK
ACEIKNPS CAPESKIN
ACEIKNRR CRANKIER
ACEIKOTW KATOWICE
ACEIKPPR PIPE RACK
ACEIKPSX PICKAXES
ACEIKSTT TACKIEST

ACEILLMR MICELLAR, MILLRACE
ACEILLMT METALLIC
ACEILLMY MYCELIAL
ACEILLNT CLIENTAL
ACEILLOP CALLIOPE
ACEILLOR ROCAILLE
ACEILLOS LOCALISE
ACEILLOT TEOCALLI
ACEILLOZ LOCALIZE
ACEILLPR CALLIPER
ACEILLPS ALLSPICE
ACEILLRS CARLISLE
ACEILLRV CAVILLER
ACEILMMO CAMOMILE
ACEILMMR CLAMMIER
ACEILMNO COALMINE
ACEILMNP MANCIPLE
ACEILMNS MESCALIN
ACEILMOS CAMISOLE
ACEILMPS MISPLACE
ACEILMRS MIRACLES
ACEILMRT METRICAL
ACEILMST CLEMATIS, CLIMATES
ACEILMSU MUSICALE
ACEILMSX CLIMAXES
ACEILNNP PINNACLE
ACEILNOR ACROLEIN, CAROLINE, CORNELIA
ACEILNPS PELICANS
ACEILNRT CLARINET
ACEILNSS LACINESS
ACEILOPR CAPRIOLE
ACEILOPT POETICAL
ACEILORS CALORIES
ACEILORT LORICATE
ACEILOST SOCIETAL
ACEILOSV VOCALISE
ACEILOTV LOCATIVE
ACEILOVZ VOCALIZE
ACEILPPY PIPECLAY
ACEILPRS CALIPERS, REPLICAS, SPIRACLE
ACEILPRT PARTICLE, PRELATIC
ACEILPRU PECULIAR
ACEILPRV PERCIVAL
ACEILPSS SLIPCASE, SPECIALS
ACEILPXY EPICALYX
ACEILRSS CLASSIER
ACEILRST ARTICLES, RECITALS

ACEILRSU AURICLES
ACEILRSV VISCERAL
ACEILRTT TRACTILE
ACEILRTU LUCRETIA
ACEILRTV VERTICAL
ACEILRTY LITERACY
ACEILRUZ LUCREZIA
ACEILSST SCALIEST
ACEILSTT LATTICES
ACEILTVY ACTIVELY
ACEIMMNP PEMMICAN
ACEIMMRS RACEMISM
ACEIMNRU MANICURE
ACEIMNST SEMANTIC
ACEIMNSY SYCAMINE
ACEIMOTX TOXAEMIC
ACEIMOTZ AZOTEMIC,
  METAZOIC
ACEIMPSS ESCAPISM
ACEIMPST CAMPSITE
ACEIMRRW WAR CRIME
ACEIMRST CERAMIST,
  MATRICES
ACEIMRTU MURICATE
ACEINNOS CANONISE
ACEINNOZ CANONIZE
ACEINNPS PINNACES
ACEINNRS CRANNIES
ACEINNST ANCIENTS,
  CANNIEST, INSTANCE
ACEINNSU NUISANCE
ACEINNTU UNCINATE
ACEINOPR APOCRINE,
  PROCAINE
ACEINOPS CANOPIES,
  CAPONISE
ACEINOPZ CAPONIZE
ACEINORS SCENARIO
ACEINORT CREATION,
  REACTION
ACEINORV VERONICA
ACEINOST CANOEIST
ACEINOTT TACONITE
ACEINOTV CONATIVE
ACEINOTX EXACTION
ACEINPTT PITTANCE
ACEINRRY CINERARY
ACEINRSS RACINESS
ACEINRST CANISTER,
  CISTERNA, SCANTIER
ACEINRTT INTERACT
ACEINRTV NAVICERT
ACEINRVY VICENARY
ACEINSSU ISSUANCE

ACEINSTV VESICANT
ACEINTTU TUNICATE
ACEINTTX EXCITANT
ACEINTTY TENACITY
ACEIOPRT OPERATIC
ACEIORSV VARICOSE
ACEIOTVV VOCATIVE
ACEIOVVV VIVA VOCE
ACEIPPRR CRAPPIER,
  PERICARP
ACEIPRRS PERISARC
ACEIPRST CRISPATE,
  PRACTISE
ACEIPRTY APYRETIC
ACEIPSST ESCAPIST
ACEIPSSU AUSPICES
ACEIPSTV CAPTIVES
ACEIQRRU ACQUIRER
ACEIRRRS CARRIERS
ACEIRRSU CURARISE
ACEIRRSW AIRCREWS,
  AIRSCREW, WAR CRIES
ACEIRRUZ CURARIZE
ACEIRSST SCARIEST
ACEIRSTT CRISTATE,
  SCATTIER
ACEIRSTU SURICATE
ACEIRSTZ CRAZIEST
ACEIRTTU URTICATE
ACEIRTTV TRACTIVE
ACEIRTUV CURATIVE
ACEIRTVY VERACITY
ACEISSTU SAUCIEST,
  SUITCASE
ACEISTTT CATTIEST
ACEISTTU EUSTATIC
ACEJLORY CAJOLERY
ACEKKMRU MUCKRAKE
ACEKLSST SLACKEST
ACEKMRSS SMACKERS
ACEKNORT ONE-TRACK
ACEKNPRU UNPACKER
ACEKNRRT RACK-RENT
ACEKORSW CASEWORK
ACEKQRUY QUACKERY
ACELLLRU CELLULAR
ACELLNOT LANCELOT
ACELLNRU NUCELLAR
ACELLOPS COLLAPSE
ACELLORV OVERCALL
ACELLOSW COLESLAW
ACELLPSS SCALPELS
ACELLRSU CURE-ALLS
ACELLRTY RECTALLY

ACELLSSU CALLUSES
ACELMNNS CLANSMEN
ACELMNSS CALMNESS
ACELMNSU UNCLE SAM
ACELMORS SCLEROMA
ACELMORY CLAYMORE
ACELMSTU MUSCATEL
ACELNOOT ECOTONAL
ACELNORT CARLETON
ACELNOSU LACUNOSE
ACELNOTV COVALENT
ACELNRVY CRAVENLY
ACELNSSU SCALENUS
ACELOPPU POPULACE
ACELOPRT PECTORAL
ACELOPST POLECATS
ACELOPTU COPULATE
ACELOQSU COEQUALS
ACELORSS LACROSSE
ACELORST SECTORAL
ACELORSU CAROUSEL
ACELORSY COARSELY
ACELORTU CLEAROUT
ACELOSTU OSCULATE
ACELOSTY ACOLYTES
ACELPPRS CLAPPERS
ACELPRSS SCALPERS
ACELPRST SPECTRAL
ACELPRSU SPECULAR
ACELPSSU CAPSULES
ACELPTUU CUPULATE
ACELRRSW CRAWLERS,
  SCRAWLER
ACELRSTT CLATTERS,
  SCARLETT
ACELRTTU CULTRATE
ACELRTTY CLATTERY
ACELSSTT TACTLESS
ACELSUUV VAUCLUSE
ACEMMOTY MYCETOMA
ACEMMRRS CRAMMERS
ACEMNOOR CAMEROON
ACEMNORS ROMANCES
ACEMNRUY NUMERACY
ACEMOOST COMATOSE
ACEMOPRR COMPARER
ACEMOPRS COMPARES,
  MESOCARP
ACEMORRT CREMATOR
ACEMORSY SYCAMORE
ACEMPSSU CAMPUSES
ACENNNOU ANNOUNCE
ACENNOSS CANONESS
ACENNOTT COTENANT

ACENNOTV COVENANT
ACENNOTZ CANZONET
ACENNRSS SCANNERS
ACENOPST CAPSTONE,
OPENCAST
ACENORRT TORRANCE
ACENORRW CAREWORN
ACENORST ANCESTOR
ACENORSU NACREOUS
ACENORTU COURANTE
ACENORTY ENACTORY
ACENOSTV CENTAVOS
ACENPTTU PUNCTATE
ACENRSTT TRANSECT
ACENRSTU CENTAURS,
ETRUSCAN, RECUSANT
ACENRSTY ANCESTRY
ACENRTTU TRUNCATE
ACENRTUY CENTAURY
ACENSSTU NUTCASES
ACENSSTW NEWSCAST
ACEOOPSU POACEOUS
ACEOORTV EVOCATOR,
OVERCOAT
ACEOPPRS COPPERAS
ACEORRST CREATORS,
REACTORS
ACEORRTT RETROACT
ACEORRTU EUROCRAT
ACEORSST COARSEST,
COASTERS
ACEORSTV OVERCAST
ACEOSSUY SOY SAUCE
ACEOSTTU OUTCASTE
ACEOSTUU AUTOCUES
ACEPRRSS SCRAPERS
ACEPRSTU CAPTURES
ACEPSTTY TYPECAST
ACEQRSTU RACQUETS
ACERRSUV VERRUCAS
ACERRUVZ VERACRUZ
ACERSSUY SYRACUSE
ACERSTTX EXTRACTS
ACERSTTY CYTASTER
ACERTTUW CUTWATER
ACFFGHIN CHAFFING
ACFFIILO OFFICIAL
ACFFILNU FANCIFUL
ACFGIIPR CAPRIFIG
ACFGINNY FANCYING
ACFGINRT CRAFTING
ACFGITUY FUGACITY
ACFHHINW HAWFINCH
ACFHIJKS JACKFISH

ACFHILNO FALCHION
ACFHILOS COALFISH
ACFHIRSW CRAWFISH
ACFHIRSY CRAYFISH
ACFHISSU FUCHSIAS
ACFHLOSW CASH FLOW
ACFHLTUW WATCHFUL
ACFHORRT RH FACTOR
ACFIILTY FACILITY
ACFIIMPS PACIFISM
ACFIIPST PACIFIST
ACFIKLNS CALFSKIN
ACFILLSY FISCALLY
ACFILNOR FORNICAL
ACFILNPU CUP FINAL
ACFILORT TRIFOCAL
ACFILRTY CRAFTILY
ACFILSSY CLASSIFY
ACFIMNRU FRANCIUM
ACFINORT FRACTION
ACFINOST FACTIONS
ACFINSTY SANCTIFY
ACFIOPRY FAIR COPY
ACFIOSTU FACTIOUS
ACFISSST FASCISTS
ACFKLLOR ROCKFALL
ACFKOORR ROOF RACK
ACFLLMRU CRAM-FULL
ACFLMNOO MOONCALF
ACFLNORY FALCONRY
ACFLOOPS FOOLSCAP
ACFLORSU SCROFULA
ACFMOTTU FACTOTUM
ACFOOSTT CAT'S-FOOT
ACGGHINN CHANGING
ACGGHINR CHARGING
ACGGIINT GIGANTIC
ACGGIIOS ISAGOGIC
ACGGILNN CLANGING,
GLANCING
ACGGLNOU GLUCAGON
ACGGLRSY SCRAGGLY
ACGHHIJK HIGHJACK
ACGHHINT HATCHING
ACGHHNOW
HANGCHOW
ACGHIIMN MICHIGAN
ACGHIINN CHAINING
ACGHIINR CHAIRING
ACGHIKLN CHALKING
ACGHIKNS SHACKING
ACGHIKNW WHACKING
ACGHILNS CLASHING
ACGHILNT LATCHING

ACGHILOR OLIGARCH
ACGHIMNP CHAMPING
ACGHIMNR CHARMING,
MARCHING
ACGHIMNT MATCHING
ACGHINNT CHANTING
ACGHINOP POACHING
ACGHINPP CHAPPING
ACGHINPR PARCHING
ACGHINPT NIGHTCAP,
PATCHING
ACGHINRR CHARRING
ACGHINRS CRASHING
ACGHINRT CHARTING
ACGHINST SCATHING
ACGHINTT CHATTING
ACGHINTU TAICHUNG
ACGHINTW WATCHING
ACGHINTY YACHTING
ACGHIPRS GRAPHICS
ACGHNRYY GYNARCHY
ACGIILMN CLAIMING
ACGIILNO LOGICIAN
ACGIILNV CAVILING
ACGIINRT GRANITIC
ACGIJLNO CAJOLING
ACGIKLNN CLANKING
ACGIKLNO CLOAKING
ACGIKLNS SLACKING
ACGIKLNT TACKLING
ACGIKLNU CAULKING
ACGIKLRY GARLICKY
ACGIKMNS SMACKING
ACGIKNNR CRANKING
ACGIKNNS SNACKING
ACGIKNOR CROAKING
ACGIKNQU QUACKING
ACGIKNRT TRACKING
ACGIKNST STACKING
ACGILLLR CALL GIRL
ACGILLNS CALLINGS
ACGILMMN CLAMMING
ACGILMNP CLAMPING
ACGILNOR CAROLING
ACGILNOS SOLACING
ACGILNOT LOCATING
ACGILNPP CLAPPING
ACGILNPS CLASPING,
SCALPING
ACGILNRW CRAWLING
ACGILNSS CLASSING
ACGILRSU SURGICAL
ACGIMMNR CRAMMING
ACGIMNPR CRAMPING

ACGIMNSY SYNGAMIC
ACGIMORS ORGASMIC
ACGINNNS SCANNING
ACGINNPR PRANCING
ACGINOST AGNOSTIC,
 COASTING, COATINGS
ACGINPPR CRAPPING
ACGINPRS SCRAPING
ACGINRRS SCARRING
ACGINRRY CARRYING
ACGINRST TRACINGS
ACGINRSV CARVINGS,
 CRAVINGS
ACGINSST CASTINGS
ACGINSTT SCATTING
ACGIORSU GRACIOUS
ACGJKLPU JACK PLUG
ACGJLNOU CONJUGAL
ACGLMOUU COAGULUM
ACGLOSUU GLAUCOUS
ACGLSSTU CUT GLASS
ACGNNOOT CONTANGO
ACGNOOST OCTAGONS
ACGNORST CONGRATS
ACHHILPT PHTHALIC
ACHHINTW WHINCHAT
ACHHINTY HYACINTH
ACHHIORT HATHORIC
ACHHIPPR HIPPARCH
ACHHLNOR RHONCHAL
ACHHNTTU NUTHATCH
ACHHOSTW CHAT SHOW
ACHHPTUZ CHUTZPAH
ACHHSTTU SUCH THAT
ACHIILMS CHILIASM
ACHIILPT HAPLITIC
ACHIILST CHILIAST
ACHIINPS HISPANIC
ACHIINRT TRICHINA
ACHIKKSW KICKSHAW
ACHIKOOW KIAOCHOW
ACHIKRSW RICKSHAW
ACHIKRTT HAT TRICK
ACHILLTY CITY HALL
ACHILMRS CHRISMAL
ACHILMTY MYTHICAL
ACHILNNS CLANNISH
ACHILNOS NICHOLAS
ACHILORT ACROLITH
ACHILPSY PHYSICAL
ACHILPTY PATCHILY
ACHILRVY CHIVALRY
ACHILTTY CHATTILY
ACHIMMOS MACHISMO

ACHIMMST MISMATCH
ACHIMNOP CHAMPION
ACHIMNOR HARMONIC
ACHIMNSU INASMUCH
ACHIMPSS SCAMPISH
ACHIMRST CHARTISM
ACHIMSSU CHIASMUS
ACHINOTZ HOACTZIN
ACHIOPRT ATROPHIC
ACHIORST CHARIOTS,
 HARICOTS
ACHIPRRT PHRATRIC
ACHIRRTY TRIARCHY
ACHIRSTT CHARTIST
ACHIRSTU HAIRCUTS
ACHISTTY CHASTITY
ACHKKORW HACKWORK
ACHKMMOS HAMMOCKS
ACHKMORS SHAMROCK
ACHKOSSS HASSOCKS
ACHLLNWY LYNCH LAW
ACHLLOOS ALCOHOLS
ACHLMSTZ SCHMALTZ
ACHLNORT CHARLTON
ACHLORSS SCHOLARS
ACHLRSTY CHRYSTAL
ACHMNORS MONARCHS,
 ROMANSCH
ACHMNORY MONARCHY
ACHMOSST STOMACHS
ACHMOSTY STOMACHY
ACHNOPRU UP-ANCHOR
ACHNPPSS SCHNAPPS
ACHNRSYY SYNARCHY
ACHOORTU COAUTHOR
ACHOPRTY TOPARCHY
ACHPRSTU PUSHCART
ACIIILMN INIMICAL
ACIIILNS SICILIAN
ACIIILNV CIVILIAN
ACIIINST ISATINIC,
 SINAITIC
ACIIKLNO KAOLINIC
ACIIKNNN CANNIKIN
ACIIKNPT PACK IT IN
ACIILLNV VANILLIC
ACIILLTV VILLATIC
ACIILLVW CIVIL LAW
ACIILMNR CRIMINAL
ACIILNPT PLATINIC
ACIILNRS SINCLAIR
ACIILRTU URALITIC
ACIILRVW CIVIL WAR
ACIILSST SILASTIC

ACIIMNNT MANNITIC
ACIIMNOS SIMONIAC
ACIIMNOT AMNIOTIC
ACIIMNST ACTINISM
ACIIMNSU MUSICIAN
ACIIMNTU ACTINIUM
ACIIMNTY INTIMACY
ACIIMOST IOTACISM
ACIIMOTT AMITOTIC
ACIIMPRV VAMPIRIC
ACIIMRST SCIMITAR
ACIIMSTV ACTIVISM
ACIIMTUV VIATICUM
ACIINNOT INACTION
ACIINNQU CINQUAIN
ACIINNRV NIRVANIC
ACIINOPT OPTICIAN
ACIINORZ ZIRCONIA
ACIINOSV AVIONICS
ACIINOTT CITATION
ACIINPRS CRISPIAN
ACIINRSS NARCISSI
ACIINRTU URANITIC
ACIIORST AORISTIC
ACIIORTV VICTORIA
ACIIRSST TRIASSIC
ACIIRSTT ARTISTIC
ACIISTTU AUTISTIC
ACIISTTV ACTIVIST
ACIITTVY ACTIVITY
ACIITVVY VIVACITY
ACIJKKPS SKIPJACK
ACIJRSSU JURASSIC
ACIJSUZZ JACUZZIS
ACIKLLST SALTLICK
ACIKLORS AIRLOCKS
ACIKLORY CROAKILY
ACIKNNPR CRANKPIN
ACIKNSTT TINTACKS
ACIKPSSX SIX-PACKS
ACILLLOP POLLICAL
ACILLMMY CLAMMILY
ACILLMOS LOCALISM
ACILLMSU CAMILLUS
ACILLNOO COLONIAL
ACILLNOR CARILLON
ACILLNOS SCALLION
ACILLORT CLITORAL
ACILLOST CALLISTO,
 LOCALIST
ACILLOSY SOCIALLY
ACILLOTY LOCALITY
ACILMNOP COMPLAIN
ACILMOPR PROCLAIM

ACILMOSV VOCALISM
ACILMSSS CLASSISM
ACILMSSU MUSICALS
ACILMSTY MYSTICAL
ACILNOOT LOCATION
ACILNOPS SALPICON
ACILNOPT PLATONIC
ACILNORS CLARIONS
ACILNORT CONTRAIL
ACILNOSU UNSOCIAL
ACILNOSV SLAVONIC
ACILNOUV UNIVOCAL
ACILNRSU CISLUNAR
ACILNRUY CULINARY,
  URANYLIC
ACILNSTU LUNATICS,
  SULTANIC
ACILNSTY SCANTILY
ACILOPRT TROPICAL
ACILORTV VORTICAL
ACILOSTV VOCALIST
ACILOTVY VOCALITY
ACILPSST PLASTICS
ACILRSTU RUSTICAL
ACILRTUV CULTIVAR
ACILSSST CLASSIST
ACILSTTY SCATTILY
ACILSTUV VICTUALS
ACILSTVY SYLVATIC
ACIMMTUY CYMATIUM
ACIMNNNO CINNAMON
ACIMNNOR MINORCAN
ACIMNOOR ACROMION
ACIMNORT ROMANTIC
ACIMNORU COUMARIN
ACIMNORY ACRIMONY
ACIMNOST MONASTIC
ACIMNPTY TYMPANIC
ACIMNRSU CRANIUMS
ACIMOSST MASSICOT
ACIMOSTT STOMATIC
ACIMRRSY MISCARRY
ACINNOOT CONATION
ACINNOSS SCANSION
ACINNOST CANONIST,
  SANCTION
ACINNOSU ASUNCION
ACINNOTU CONTINUA
ACINOOTV VOCATION
ACINOPPT PANOPTIC
ACINOPST CAPTIONS
ACINORSS NARCOSIS
ACINORST CAST-IRON
ACINORTT TRACTION

ACINOSSS CAISSONS
ACINOSSY CYANOSIS
ACINOSTT OSCITANT
ACINOSTU AUCTIONS,
  CAUTIONS
ACINOSTW WAINSCOT
ACINOSWX COXSWAIN
ACINOTTX TOXICANT
ACINPQUY PIQUANCY
ACINPSTY SYNAPTIC
ACINRSTU CURTAINS
ACINRTTU TACITURN
ACINSTTY SANCTITY
ACIOOPST SCOTOPIA
ACIOOPTX COTOPAXI
ACIOPRST APRICOTS
ACIOPSST POTASSIC
ACIOPSSU SPACIOUS
ACIOPSTU CAPTIOUS
ACIORRSS CORSAIRS
ACIORSSU SCARIOUS
ACIORSTT RIOT ACTS
ACIORTTY ATROCITY
ACIORTVY VORACITY
ACIOSTUU CAUTIOUS
ACIOSTUV OCTAVIUS
ACIPSSST SPASTICS
ACIRSSTY SACRISTY
ACISSSTU CASUISTS
ACISSTTU CATSUITS
ACJKOPST JACKPOTS
ACKKMOPR POCKMARK
ACKLLPSU SKULLCAP
ACKLOOPW WOOLPACK
ACKLOORS OARLOCKS
ACKLOOSW WOOLSACK
ACKLORST ROCK SALT
ACKLORSW WARLOCKS
ACKMNOST STOCKMAN
ACLLLLOR ROLL CALL
ACLLOORT COLLATOR
ACLLOOSS COLOSSAL
ACLLOPSS SCALLOPS
ACLLRTUU CULTURAL
ACLMMNOU
  COMMUNAL
ACLMNORU COLUMNAR
ACLMORSU CLAMOURS
ACLMRSUU MUSCULAR
ACLMSTUU CUSTUMAL
ACLMSUUV VASCULUM
ACLNOORT COLORANT
ACLNOOST COOLANTS
ACLNOOSV VOLCANOS

ACLNORSU CONSULAR
ACLNORTU CALUTRON
ACLNOSTU OSCULANT
ACLNPTUU PUNCTUAL
ACLOOPRR CORPORAL
ACLOOPRS CAR POOLS
ACLOOPRT COALPORT
ACLOPRRW PROWL CAR
ACLOPRXY XYLOCARP
ACLOPSSY CALYPSOS
ACLOSSTU OUTCLASS
ACLRSSTY CRYSTALS
ACMMNOSY SCAMMONY
ACMNOOPR MONOCARP
ACMNOORT MONOCRAT
ACMNOPRS CRAMPONS
ACMNORSY ACRONYMS
ACMNOSST SCOTSMAN
ACMNSSTU SANCTUMS
ACMOORRT MOTORCAR
ACMORSTW WORM CAST
ACMORSTY COSTMARY
ACMQSTUU CUMQUATS
ACNNNORY CANNONRY
ACNNORST SCRANTON
ACNNOSTT CONSTANT
ACNOORRY CORONARY
ACNOORST CARTOONS
ACNORRTY CONTRARY
ACNORSTT CONTRAST
ACNORTTU TURNCOAT
ACNPRSYY SYNCARPY
ACNRRSTU CURRANTS
ACOOPSTT TOPCOATS
ACOPRRST CARPORTS
ACOPRRTT PROTRACT
ACOPRTUY PAY COURT
ACORRSTT TRACTORS
ACORRSTU CURATORS
ACORRTUY CARRYOUT
ACORRTUZ RAZOR-CUT
ACORSSTU SURCOATS
ACORSSUW CURASSOW
ACORSTTY CRYOSTAT
ACOSSTTU OUTCASTS
ACRRSTUU ARCTURUS
ADDDEEEN DEADENED
ADDDEEGR DEGRADED
ADDDEELR LADDERED
ADDDEEMN DEMANDED,
  MADDENED
ADDDEENS DEAD ENDS,
  SADDENED
ADDDEGJU ADJUDGED

ADDDELSW SWADDLED
ADDDEMNU ADDENDUM
ADDDEOOW DEAD
WOOD
ADDEEEFN DEAFENED
ADDEEEFT DEFEATED
ADDEEEMN DEMEANED
ADDEEENR DEADENER,
ENDEARED
ADDEEFHN HANDFEED
ADDEEFLT DEFLATED
ADDEEFRY DEFRAYED
ADDEEGNR DERANGED,
GARDENED
ADDEEGOR DOG-EARED
ADDEEGRR DEGRADER,
REGARDED
ADDEEHIL ADELHEID
ADDEEHLR HERALDED
ADDEEHLY ALDEHYDE
ADDEEHNR HARDENED
ADDEEHRS REDHEADS
ADDEEHRT THREADED
ADDEEILN DEADLINE
ADDEEILP DEEP-LAID
ADDEEILR DEADLIER,
DERAILED
ADDEEILT DETAILED
ADDEEIMT MEDIATED
ADDEEINT DETAINED
ADDEEISS DISEASED
ADDEEIST STEADIED
ADDEEITV DEVIATED
ADDEEKNR DARKENED
ADDEELLP PEDALLED
ADDEELOR RELOADED
ADDEELUV DEVALUED
ADDEEMNP DAMPENED
ADDEEMNR DEMANDER,
REDEMAND, REMANDED
ADDEENPP APPENDED
ADDEENPR PANDERED
ADDEENPX EXPANDED
ADDEENRW WANDERED
ADDEENSS DEADNESS
ADDEENTT ATTENDED
ADDEENTU DENUDATE
ADDEEPRT DEPARTED,
PREDATED
ADDEEPRV DEPRAVED,
PERVADED
ADDEERRT RETARDED
ADDEERRW REWARDED
ADDEERTV ADVERTED

ADDEFFOR AFFORDED
ADDEFILY FIELD DAY
ADDEFLRU DREADFUL
ADDEFORW WORD-DEAF
ADDEGGLR DRAGGLED
ADDEGINR DREADING
ADDEGLST GLADDEST
ADDEGPRU UPGRADED
ADDEHIIJ JEDIDIAH
ADDEHILR DIHEDRAL
ADDEHINW HEADWIND
ADDEHIRS DIEHARDS
ADDEHMRU DRUMHEAD
ADDEHNNU UNHANDED
ADDEHORW HEADWORD
ADDEHOSW SHADOWED
ADDEHRTY HYDRATED
ADDEHSTU THADDEUS
ADDEIITV ADDITIVE
ADDEIJNO ADJOINED
ADDEIKNP KIDNAPED
ADDEIMOS SODAMIDE
ADDEIMRS DISARMED
ADDEIMSY DISMAYED
ADDEIMTT ADMITTED
ADDEINOR ORDAINED
ADDEINOS ADENOIDS
ADDEINST DANDIEST
ADDEIOPR PARODIED
ADDEIORS ROADSIDE
ADDEISSU DISSUADE
ADDEJSTU ADJUSTED
ADDELNOU DUODENAL,
UNLOADED
ADDELNSU UNSADDLE
ADDELOOR EL DORADO
ADDELRSS SADDLERS
ADDELRST STRADDLE
ADDELRSW DAWDLERS
ADDELRSY SADDLERY
ADDELRTW TWADDLER
ADDEMNPU UNDAMPED
ADDENNSU SAND DUNE
ADDENOPR PARDONED
ADDENRST STRANDED
ADDENRYY YARN-DYED
ADDEOTTU OUTDATED
ADDFFILO DAFFODIL
ADDFFNRU DANDRUFF
ADDGILNN DANDLING
ADDGILNP PADDLING
ADDGILNS SADDLING
ADDGILNW DAWDLING,
WADDLING

ADDGLORU OLD GUARD
ADDGMRUU MUDGUARD
ADDHHLNO HANDHOLD
ADDHIKRS HARD DISK
ADDHINSY DANDYISH
ADDHLNOS OLD HANDS
ADDHOORW
HARDWOOD
ADDIIMRU DIARMUID
ADDIINOT ADDITION
ADDIINRT TRINIDAD
ADDILMNS MIDLANDS
ADDILMOS OLD MAIDS
ADDIMNOS DIAMONDS
ADDIMNSY DANDYISM
ADDINNOR ORDINAND
ADDINORS ANDROIDS
ADDINRWW WINDWARD
ADDIORRT DIRT ROAD
ADDKNRRU DRUNKARD
ADDLLNOR LANDLORD
ADDLLRSU DULLARDS
ADDLNOOW
DOWNLOAD, WOODLAND
ADDMOOSY DOOMSDAY
ADDNORWW
DOWNWARD
ADEEEFRT DEFEATER,
FEDERATE
ADEEEGLT DELEGATE
ADEEEGNR RENEGADE
ADEEEGUW AGUEWEED
ADEEEHSY EYESHADE
ADEEEINT DETAINEE
ADEEEKNW WEAKENED
ADEEELMN ENAMELED
ADEEELNV LEAVENED
ADEEELPR REPEALED
ADEEELRS RELEASED
ADEEELRV REVEALED
ADEEELSW WEASELED
ADEEELTV ELEVATED
ADEEENRS SERENADE
ADEEENTT EDENTATE
ADEEEPRS RAPESEED
ADEEEPRT REPEATED
ADEEESSW SEESAWED
ADEEFHNR FREEHAND
ADEEFHOR FOREHEAD
ADEEFHRT FATHERED
ADEEFILN ENFILADE
ADEEFIRR RAREFIED
ADEEFLMS SELF-MADE
ADEEFLOR FREELOAD

ADEEFLPR PEDALFER
ADEEFLRT FALTERED,
  REFLATED
ADEEFLSS FADELESS
ADEEFLSX FLAXSEED
ADEEFMNR FREEDMAN
ADEEFMTU DEAF-MUTE
ADEEFNOT TONE-DEAF
ADEEFNSS DEAFNESS
ADEEFNST FASTENED
ADEEFNTT FATTENED
ADEEFRRY DEFRAYER
ADEEFRST DRAFTEES
ADEEFRTU FEATURED
ADEEGGHS EGGHEADS
ADEEGHRT GATHERED
ADEEGINN ENGADINE
ADEEGINR REGAINED
ADEEGIRS DISAGREE
ADEEGLLN GLENDALE
ADEEGLNR ENLARGED
ADEEGLRV GRAVELED
ADEEGMNR GENDARME
ADEEGMNS END
  GAMES
ADEEGMNY GANYMEDE
ADEEGNNR ENDANGER
ADEEGNRR GARDENER,
  GARNERED
ADEEGNRS GRANDEES,
  GRENADES
ADEEGNRU DUNGAREE,
  UNDERAGE
ADEEGNRV ENGRAVED
ADEEGORT DEROGATE
ADEEGPRS PRESAGED
ADEEGRSS DEGASSER,
  DRESSAGE
ADEEGRTT TARGETED
ADEEGSWY EDGEWAYS
ADEEHHRS REHASHED
ADEEHHST SHEATHED
ADEEHIKL HEADLIKE
ADEEHIKZ ZEDEKIAH
ADEEHILN HEADLINE
ADEEHIST HEADIEST
ADEEHISV ADHESIVE
ADEEHKNR HANKERED,
  HARKENED
ADEEHKWW HAWKWEED
ADEEHKWY HAWK-EYED
ADEEHLLW WELLHEAD
ADEEHLRT LATHERED
ADEEHLSS HEADLESS

ADEEHLTY HEATEDLY
ADEEHMMO HOMEMADE
ADEEHMMR HAMMERED
ADEEHMNN MENHADEN
ADEEHMPR HAMPERED
ADEEHMST STEMHEAD
ADEEHNPP HAPPENED
ADEEHNRR HARDENER
ADEEHNRT ADHERENT
ADEEHNST HASTENED
ADEEHORV OVERHEAD
ADEEHRRT THREADER
ADEEHRRW HEREWARD
ADEEHRST HEADREST
ADEEHRTW WREATHED
ADEEHSST HEADSETS
ADEEIILS IDEALISE
ADEEIILZ IDEALIZE
ADEEIITV IDEATIVE
ADEEIJMR JEREMIAD
ADEEILLN DANIELLE
ADEEILMN ENDEMIAL,
  MADELINE
ADEEILMR REMEDIAL
ADEEILMT LEAD TIME
ADEEILMV MEDIEVAL
ADEEILNT DATELINE,
  ENTAILED
ADEEILPS PLEIADES
ADEEILPT DEPILATE
ADEEILRS REALISED,
  SIDEREAL
ADEEILRT ELATERID,
  RETAILED
ADEEILRZ REALIZED
ADEEIMNR REMAINED
ADEEIMNT DEMENTIA
ADEEIMNX EXAMINED
ADEEIMRT DIAMETER
ADEEIMTT MEDITATE
ADEEINNR ADRIENNE
ADEEINNS ANDESINE
ADEEINPT NEAP TIDE
ADEEINRS ARSENIDE,
  NEARSIDE
ADEEINRT DETAINER,
  RETAINED
ADEEINST ANDESITE
ADEEIPRR REPAIRED
ADEEIPRS AIRSPEED
ADEEIPTX EXPIATED
ADEEIRRR DREARIER
ADEEIRST READIEST,
  STEADIER

ADEEISSS DISEASES
ADEEISST EAST SIDE
ADEEISTV SEDATIVE
ADEEKMRR REMARKED
ADEEKMRT MARKETED
ADEEKNPW KNAPWEED
ADEEKNRR DARKENER
ADEEKQSU SQUEAKED
ADEEKRST STREAKED
ADEEKSWY WEEKDAYS
ADEELLLP LAPELLED
ADEELLMT METALLED
ADEELLNP PANELLED
ADEELLPR PREDELLA
ADEELLPS SEPALLED
ADEELLQU EQUALLED
ADEELLRV RAVELLED
ADEELLRW WELL-READ
ADEELLWY WALLEYED
ADEELMMR MAL DE MER
ADEELMNO LEMONADE
ADEELMNR ALDERMEN
ADEELMNT LAMENTED
ADEELMRS DEMERSAL,
  EMERALDS
ADEELMRV MARVELED
ADEELMTU EMULATED
ADEELNOR OLEANDER
ADEELNPT ENDPLATE
ADEELNRV LAVENDER
ADEELNRY ALDERNEY
ADEELNSV ENSLAVED
ADEELNSW NEW DEALS
ADEELNTT TALENTED
ADEELOPR LOP-EARED
ADEELOPX POLEAXED
ADEELOST DESOLATE
ADEELPPT LAPPETED
ADEELPRS RELAPSED
ADEELPRY PARLEYED,
  REPLAYED
ADEELPST PEDESTAL
ADEELQSU SQUEALED
ADEELRRT RED ALERT,
  TREADLER
ADEELRST TREADLES
ADEELRSV SLAVERED
ADEELRTV TRAVELED
ADEELRUV REVALUED
ADEELSST TASSELED
ADEELSTY SEDATELY
ADEEMMRY YAMMERED
ADEEMMSS MESDAMES
ADEEMNNR MANNERED

ADEEMNOR DEMEANOR,
   ENAMORED
ADEEMNOT NEMATODE
ADEEMNPR DAMPENER
ADEEMNSS SEEDSMAN
ADEEMORT MODERATE
ADEEMPPR PAMPERED
ADEEMPRT TAMPERED
ADEEMPRV REVAMPED
ADEEMPST STAMPEDE
ADEEMRRS DREAMERS
ADEEMRST MASTERED,
   STREAMED
ADEEMRSU MADURESE,
   MEASURED
ADEEMRTT MATTERED
ADEEMRTW WET DREAM
ADEENNRS ARDENNES,
   ENSNARED
ADEENNRU UNEARNED
ADEENOPW WEAPONED
ADEENORS REASONED
ADEENORV ENDEAVOR
ADEENORY AERODYNE
ADEENOSS SEASONED
ADEENOTT DETONATE
ADEENPPR ENDPAPER
ADEENPRR PANDERER
ADEENPRX EXPANDER
ADEENPTT PATENTED
ADEENRRW WANDERER
ADEENRSS DEARNESS
ADEENRSU UNDERSEA
ADEENRSW ANSWERED
ADEENRTT NATTERED
ADEENRTU DENATURE
ADEENSST ASSENTED
ADEENSSU SUDANESE
ADEENSTU UNSEATED
ADEENTTU TAUTENED
ADEENTTV VENDETTA
ADEEOPRT OPERATED
ADEEORVW OVERAWED
ADEEPPRR PREPARED
ADEEPRRS SPREADER
ADEEPRRV DEPRAVER,
   PERVADER
ADEEPRST PEDERAST
ADEEPRSU PERSUADE
ADEEPRTT PATTERED
ADEEPRTU DEPURATE
ADEEPSWY SPEEDWAY
ADEEQRUV QUAVERED
ADEERRRT RETARDER

ADEERRRW REWARDER
ADEERRST ARRESTED,
   RETREADS, SERRATED
ADEERSST ASSERTED,
   DEARESTS
ADEERSTT RESTATED
ADEERTTT TATTERED
ADEERVYY EVERYDAY
ADEESSSS ASSESSED
ADEESTTT ATTESTED
ADEFFGUW GUFFAWED
ADEFFIMR AFFIRMED
ADEFFLNS SNAFFLED
ADEFFORT TRADE-OFF
ADEFGILR GARFIELD
ADEFGILS GADFLIES
ADEFGIMN DEFAMING
ADEFGIRT DRIFTAGE
ADEFGITU FATIGUED
ADEFGLLO GOLD LEAF
ADEFGLOT GATEFOLD
ADEFGLRS RED FLAGS
ADEFHILS DEALFISH
ADEFHILT HATFIELD
ADEFHIMS FAMISHED
ADEFHLNT LEFT-HAND
ADEFHMOT FATHOMED
ADEFHNOR FOREHAND
ADEFIILN FINIALED
ADEFIILR AIRFIELD
ADEFIIMR RAMIFIED
ADEFIIRT RATIFIED
ADEFIKRR FREDRIKA
ADEFILLT ILL-FATED
ADEFILMN INFLAMED
ADEFILNT INFLATED
ADEFILOT FOLIATED
ADEFILRW WILFREDA
ADEFIMPR FIREDAMP
ADEFINRR INFRARED
ADEFINRU FREUDIAN
ADEFINRW FINE-DRAW
ADEFIRRT DRAFTIER
ADEFLLMO LEAF MOLD,
   OLD FLAME
ADEFLNOR FORELAND
ADEFLNRS FLANDERS
ADEFLNTU FLAUNTED
ADEFLORT DEFLATOR
ADEFLORU FOUR-DEAL
ADEFLORV FLAVORED
ADEFLPRS FELDSPAR
ADEFLRTW LEFTWARD
ADEFLRZZ FRAZZLED

ADEFLSTU DEFAULTS
ADEFNNOR FERNANDO
ADEFNOPR PROFANED
ADEFNSST DAFTNESS
ADEFORRW FARROWED
ADEFORRY FOREYARD
ADEFORUV FAVOURED
ADEFOSTU FADEOUTS
ADEGGIRR DRAGGIER
ADEGGJLY JAGGEDLY
ADEGGLRY RAGGEDLY
ADEGGMOY DEMAGOGY
ADEGGOPY PEDAGOGY
ADEGGRTY GADGETRY
ADEGHHOS HOGSHEAD
ADEGHILT ALIGHTED,
   GILTHEAD
ADEGHINR ADHERING
ADEGHINS HEADINGS,
   SHEADING
ADEGHLNO HEADLONG
ADEGHORT GOATHERD
ADEGHRTU DAUGHTER
ADEGIILP DIPLEGIA
ADEGIIMN IMAGINED
ADEGIITT DIGITATE
ADEGIKNN KNEADING
ADEGILLP PILLAGED
ADEGILMN MALIGNED
ADEGILNP PEDALING,
   PLEADING
ADEGILNR DRAGLINE,
   REGINALD
ADEGILNS DEALINGS,
   SIGNALED
ADEGILNY DELAYING
ADEGILOU DIALOGUE
ADEGILRS GRISELDA
ADEGILSS GLISSADE
ADEGIMNN AMENDING
ADEGIMNR DREAMING
ADEGIMOR IDEOGRAM
ADEGIMRT MIGRATED
ADEGINOR ORGANDIE
ADEGINOS AGONISED,
   DIAGNOSE, SAN DIEGO
ADEGINOZ AGONIZED
ADEGINRS READINGS
ADEGINRT GRADIENT,
   RED GIANT, TREADING
ADEGINRY READYING
ADEGINSS ASSIGNED
ADEGINST SEDATING
ADEGISTU GAUDIEST

ADEGLLNU GLANDULE	**ADEHLLOW** HALLOWED	**ADEIKLLO** KELOIDAL
ADEGLLOP GALLOPED	**ADEHLLRS** HARD SELL	**ADEIKLLY** LADYLIKE
ADEGLNPS SPANGLED	**ADEHLMNO** HOMELAND	**ADEIKLSW** SIDEWALK
ADEGLNRS GLANDERS	**ADEHLNRS** HANDLERS	**ADEIKMRT** TIDEMARK
ADEGLNRW WRANGLED	**ADEHLNSS** HANDLESS	**ADEIKORT** KERATOID
ADEGLNSS GLADNESS	**ADEHLOPS** ASPHODEL	**ADEILLMY** MEDIALLY
ADEGLPPR GRAPPLED	**ADEHLPSS** SPLASHED	**ADEILLOR** ARILLODE
ADEGMMRU RUMMAGED	**ADEHLRRY** HERALDRY	**ADEILLRV** RIVALLED
ADEGMNOY ENDOGAMY	**ADEHMMMO**	**ADEILLSW** SIDEWALL
ADEGMPUZ GAZUMPED	MOHAMMED	**ADEILMMS** DILEMMAS
ADEGNNOR ANDROGEN	**ADEHMNNY** HANDYMEN	**ADEILMNN** LANDMINE
ADEGNOPU POUNDAGE	**ADEHMNOS** HANDSOME	**ADEILMNO** MELANOID
ADEGNORT DRAGONET	**ADEHMNRS** HERDSMAN	**ADEILMNY** MAIDENLY
ADEGNRRU GRANDEUR	**ADEHMOOR** HEADROOM	**ADEILMOX** ALDOXIME
ADEGNRST DRAGNETS,	**ADEHMORW** HOMEWARD	**ADEILMPS** MISPLEAD
GRANDEST	**ADEHMOST** HEADMOST	**ADEILMRY** DREAMILY
ADEGOPRR DRAGROPE	**ADEHMOSU** MADHOUSE	**ADEILMSV** MALDIVES
ADEGORSW DOWAGERS	**ADEHNOPR** ORPHANED	**ADEILNNR** INLANDER
ADEGORTU OUTRAGED	**ADEHNORV** HANDOVER,	**ADEILNNT** DENTINAL
ADEGPRRU UPGRADER	OVERHAND	**ADEILNOP** PALINODE
ADEGPSTU UPSTAGED	**ADEHNOSS** SANDSHOE	**ADEILNRS** ISLANDER
ADEHHIPS HEADSHIP	**ADEHNPRS** SHARP END	**ADEILNST** TAIL ENDS
ADEHHLOY HOLYHEAD	**ADEHNRSS** HARDNESS	**ADEILNTV** DIVALENT
ADEHHNTU HEADHUNT	**ADEHNRTU** UNTHREAD	**ADEILOPS** SEPALOID
ADEHHOST HOTHEADS	**ADEHNSSU** SUNSHADE	**ADEILOPT** PETALOID
ADEHHRST THRASHED	**ADEHNSUW** UNWASHED	**ADEILORT** IDOLATER,
ADEHIKLN HANDLIKE	**ADEHOORT** DOROTHEA,	TAILORED
ADEHIKNS SKINHEAD	THEODORA	**ADEILORV** OVERLAID
ADEHILLM HEIMDALL	**ADEHOPXY** HEXAPODY	**ADEILORX** EXORDIAL
ADEHILNP DELPHIAN	**ADEHORRW** HARROWED	**ADEILOST** DIASTOLE,
ADEHILNR HARD LINE	**ADEHORSW** SHADOWER	ISOLATED, SODALITE
ADEHILRY HYDER ALI	**ADEHORTU** AUTHORED	**ADEILOSV** VAL-D'OISE
ADEHILSV LAVISHED	**ADEHORTW** DEATH ROW	**ADEILOTT** DATOLITE
ADEHIMRS MISHEARD	**ADEHPSUW** WASHED-UP	**ADEILOTV** DOVETAIL,
ADEHINOP DIAPHONE	**ADEHQSSU** SQUASHED	VIOLATED
ADEHINOS ADHESION	**ADEHRSTY** HYDRATES	**ADEILPPP** PEDIPALP
ADEHINPS DEANSHIP,	**ADEHRTTW** THWARTED	**ADEILPRS** SPIRALED
PINHEADS	**ADEIILMS** IDEALISM	**ADEILPRT** DIPTERAL
ADEHINPU DAUPHINE	**ADEIILST** IDEALIST	**ADEILPRU** EPIDURAL
ADEHINRS SHERIDAN	**ADEIILTV** DILATIVE	**ADEILRRY** DREARILY
ADEHINSS SHANDIES	**ADEIILTY** IDEALITY	**ADEILRSU** RESIDUAL
ADEHINST HANDIEST	**ADEIIMNN** INDAMINE	**ADEILRSY** DIALYSER
ADEHINSV VANISHED	**ADEIIMNR** MERIDIAN	**ADEILRTT** DETRITAL
ADEHIORS HERODIAS,	**ADEIIMPR** IMPAIRED	**ADEILSTY** DIASTYLE,
RHODESIA	**ADEIIMRS** SEMIARID	STEADILY
ADEHIPRS SEPHARDI	**ADEIIMTT** IMITATED	**ADEILSXY** DYSLEXIA
ADEHIPST PITHEADS	**ADEIINOT** IDEATION	**ADEILTTU** ALTITUDE,
ADEHIRSS RADISHES	**ADEIINRT** DAINTIER	LATITUDE
ADEHIRST HARDIEST	**ADEIINST** ADENITIS,	**ADEIMMRS** MERMAIDS
ADEHIRSV RAVISHED	DAINTIES	**ADEIMNNT** IN TANDEM
ADEHIRSW RAWHIDES	**ADEIIPRS** PRESIDIA	**ADEIMNOT** DOMINATE
ADEHISST SHADIEST	**ADEIITTV** VITIATED	**ADEIMNRY** DAIRYMEN
ADEHKNRS REDSHANK	**ADEIJRSU** JUDAISER	**ADEIMNSS** MAN-SISED,
ADEHKORW HEADWORK	**ADEIJRUZ** JUDAIZER	SIDESMAN

ADEIMNSZ MAN-SIZED
ADEIMNTY DYNAMITE
ADEIMORT MEDIATOR
ADEIMOSS SESAMOID
ADEIMPRT IMPARTED
ADEIMRRS ADMIRERS,
   DISARMER, MARRIEDS
ADEIMRSS SIDEARMS
ADEIMRXY READY-MIX
ADEIMSTY DAYTIMES
ADEINNOT ANOINTED,
   ANTINODE
ADEINNOV DEVONIAN
ADEINNRZ RENDZINA
ADEINNTU INUNDATE
ADEINORR ORDAINER
ADEINORT ORDINATE,
   RATIONED
ADEINOST SEDATION
ADEINOTT ANTIDOTE
ADEINOTV DONATIVE
ADEINPPX APPENDIX
ADEINPRS SPRAINED
ADEINPRT DIPTERAN
ADEINPSS IN SPADES
ADEINRRS SERRANID
ADEINRSS SARDINES
ADEINRST RANDIEST,
   STRAINED
ADEINRSV INVADERS
ADEINRTU URINATED
ADEINRVY VINEYARD
ADEINSST SANDIEST
ADEINSSV AVIDNESS
ADEINSTV DEVIANTS
ADEIOPRS DIASPORE,
   PARODIES
ADEIOPRV OVERPAID
ADEIOPST DIOPTASE
ADEIOPTV ADOPTIVE
ADEIORST ASTEROID
ADEIORTT TERATOID
ADEIORTV DEVIATOR
ADEIPPRS APPRISED
ADEIPRST TRAIPSED
ADEIPRSY PRISE DAY
ADEIPRYZ PRIZE DAY
ADEIPTTU APTITUDE
ADEIQRRU QUARRIED
ADEIRRWW WIREDRAW
ADEIRSST DISASTER
ADEIRSSV ADVISERS
ADEIRSTT STRIATED,
   TARDIEST

ADEIRTUV DURATIVE
ADEIRVWY DRIVEWAY
ADEISSST ASSISTED
ADEISSTT DISTASTE
ADEISSWY SIDEWAYS
ADEISTTU SITUATED
ADEISTWY TIDEWAYS
ADEITTTU ATTITUDE
ADEJOPRY JEOPARDY
ADEJRSTU READJUST
ADEKLMRY MARKEDLY
ADEKLPRS SPARKLED
ADEKMNRU UNMARKED
ADEKMNSU UNMASKED
ADEKNNSS DANKNESS
ADEKNPTU TANKED UP
ADEKNRSS DARKNESS
ADEKQSUW SQUAWKED
ADELLNNU ANNULLED
ADELLOPW WALLOPED
ADELLOTT ALLOTTED,
   TOTALLED
ADELLOWW WALLOWED
ADELLQSU SQUALLED
ADELMOPS MALPOSED
ADELMORS EARLDOMS
ADELMOTU MODULATE
ADELMPRT TRAMPLED
ADELMRRU DEMURRAL
ADELMSSY MASSEDLY
ADELNORS SOLANDER
ADELNORU UNLOADER
ADELNORV OVERLAND
ADELNPRS SPANDREL
ADELNRSS SLANDERS
ADELNRTY ARDENTLY
ADELNRUY UNDERLAY
ADELNTUU UNDULATE
ADELNUUV UNVALUED
ADELOORV OVERLOAD
ADELOPRS LEOPARDS
ADELOPST TADPOLES
ADELOPTY PETALODY
ADELORST LEOTARDS,
   LODESTAR
ADELORTW LEADWORT
ADELOTUV OVULATED
ADELOTUW OUTLAWED
ADELPRSW SPRAWLED
ADELPRTT PRATTLED
ADELPSTT SPLATTED
ADELPSTU PULSATED
ADELRSTT STARTLED
ADELRTUY ADULTERY

ADEMNNNU UNMANNED
ADEMNOOR MAROONED
ADEMNOPR NAMEDROP,
   POMANDER
ADEMNORS RANSOMED
ADEMNORY RAYMONDE
ADEMNOTU AMOUNTED
ADEMNPSS DAMPNESS
ADEMNRRU UNDERARM
ADEMOORT MODERATO
ADEMOOSV VAMOOSED
ADEMOPRY PYODERMA
ADEMORRU ARMOURED
ADEMRRSU EARDRUMS
ADEMRRTY MARTYRED
ADENNOSY ANODYNES
ADENNPST PENDANTS
ADENOORW WANDEROO
ADENOPRR PARDONER
ADENOPST NOTEPADS
ADENOPSY DYSPNOEA
ADENORRW NARROWED
ADENORTW DANEWORT
ADENPPTU UNTAPPED
ADENPRTY PEDANTRY
ADENPRUY UNDERPAY
ADENQRSU SQUANDER
ADENRRWY WARDENRY
ADENRSTU TRANSUDE
ADENSTUY UNSTEADY
ADEOORRT TOREADOR
ADEOOTTT TATTOOED
ADEOPPRV APPROVED
ADEOPRRS EARDROPS
ADEOPRRT PARROTED,
   PREDATOR, TEARDROP
ADEOPRTT TETRAPOD
ADEOPSTT POSTDATE
ADEOPTTU UP-TO-DATE
ADEORRST ROADSTER
ADEORRVW OVERDRAW
ADEORSST ASSORTED
ADEORSTT ROAD TEST
ADEORSTU READOUTS
ADEORSTX EXTRADOS
ADEORSUV SAVOURED
ADEPPRST STRAPPED
ADEPRSTU PASTURED
ADEQSTTU SQUATTED
ADERRSSW WARDRESS
ADERRSTT REDSTART
ADERSSTW STEWARDS
ADERSTWW WESTWARD
ADESSTUY TUESDAYS

ADFFHNOS HANDS-OFF
ADFFISST DISTAFFS
ADFFOOST FAST FOOD
ADFFORST STAFFORD
ADFGIINR INFRA DIG
ADFGINRT DRAFTING
ADFGINRW DWARFING
ADFGLOUW GOD-AWFUL
ADFHIOST TOADFISH
ADFHIRSW DWARFISH
ADFHLNSU HANDFULS
ADFHLOST HOLDFAST
ADFHORRT HARTFORD
ADFIILRW WILFRIDA
ADFIIRST FIRST AID
ADFILLNW WINDFALL
ADFILMNO MANIFOLD
ADFILNOR FLORINDA
ADFIMRSW DWARFISM
ADFIORSV DISFAVOR
ADFIRSTY FIRST-DAY
ADFKNOOR KORDOFAN
ADFLLNOU ALL FOUND
ADFLLNOW DOWNFALL
ADFLMNOR LANDFORM
ADFLMSTU MUDFLATS
ADFMORST STAMFORD
ADFNNOST FONDANTS
ADFNOORT TO-AND-FRO
ADFNOORZ FORZANDO
ADFNORST STANFORD
ADFOOPST FOOTPADS
ADFORRSW FORWARDS
ADGGGINR DRAGGING
ADGGILNN DANGLING
ADGGINRS NIGGARDS
ADGGINRU GUARDING
ADGGLRSU SLUGGARD
ADGHHILN HIGHLAND
ADGHHIOR HIGH ROAD
ADGHILNN HANDLING
ADGHILTY DAYLIGHT
ADGHINOR HOARDING
ADGHINPR HANDGRIP
ADGHINSS SHADINGS
ADGHIPRS DIGRAPHS
ADGHLNNO LONGHAND
ADGHNNSU HANDGUNS
ADGHOORS ROAD HOGS
ADGHRSTU DRAUGHTS
ADGHRTUY DRAUGHTY
ADGIILLN DIALLING
ADGIILLO GLADIOLI
ADGIILNO GONIDIAL

ADGIILNT DILATING
ADGIILPY PYGIDIAL
ADGIIMNR ADMIRING
ADGIIMST DIGAMIST
ADGIINNR DRAINING
ADGIINNV INVADING
ADGIINOR RADIOING
ADGIINOV AVOIDING
ADGIINSV ADVISING
ADGIINTU AUDITING
ADGIJNRU ADJURING
ADGILLNU ALLUDING
ADGILLNW WINDGALL
ADGILLNY DALLYING
ADGILMOR MARIGOLD
ADGILNNS LANDINGS
ADGILNOS LOADINGS
ADGILNRS DARLINGS
ADGILNRW DRAWLING
ADGILNRY DARINGLY
ADGILNZZ DAZZLING
ADGILOOS SOLIDAGO
ADGILOPR PRODIGAL
ADGILOST DOG'S-TAIL
ADGIMOSU DIGAMOUS
ADGINNOR ADORNING
ADGINNOT DONATING
ADGINNST STANDING
ADGINNTU DAUNTING
ADGINOOR RIGADOON
ADGINOPT ADOPTING
ADGINORR RING ROAD
ADGINOTY TOADYING
ADGINPTU UPDATING
ADGINRSW DRAWINGS
ADGINRTT DRATTING
ADGIORTT TITOGRAD
ADGIRSZZ GIZZARDS
ADGLNOOS GONDOLAS
ADGMNOOR
   ONDOGRAM
ADGMNORU GOURMAND
ADGNNOQU QUANDONG
ADGNNORS GRANDSON
ADGNNRYY GYNANDRY
ADGNOORS DRAGOONS
ADHHINPW WHIP HAND
ADHHIPRS HARDSHIP
ADHHNRTY HYDRANTH
ADHIILLP PHILLIDA
ADHIILLR HILLIARD
ADHIIMSS HASIDISM
ADHIINOP OPHIDIAN
ADHIKKOO HOKKAIDO

ADHILLOT THALLOID
ADHILLOY HOLLIDAY
ADHILLPY PHYLLIDA
ADHILNOR RHODINAL
ADHILOOW HAILWOOD
ADHILOPS SHIPLOAD
ADHILOSY HOLIDAYS
ADHILPSY LADYSHIP
ADHIMNOS ADMONISH
ADHIMNOU HUMANOID
ADHIMOPP AMPHIPOD
ADHINOPY DIAPHONY
ADHINPSU DAUPHINS
ADHINSST STANDISH
ADHINSTU DIANTHUS
ADHIPRSW WARDSHIP
ADHIPRSY SHIPYARD
ADHIRTWW WITHDRAW
ADHLLLOS HOLDALLS
ADHLLNOS HOLLANDS
ADHLMNOO
   HANDLOOM
ADHLMORT THRALDOM
ADHLNOPR RANDOLPH
ADHLNOUW DOWNHAUL
ADHLOPSU ADOLPHUS
ADHNNORU HONDURAN
ADHNOPRU HARD UPON
ADHNORSU HONDURAS
ADHNOSTU HANDOUTS,
   THOUSAND
ADHNOSWW
   DOWNWASH
ADHNRSTU HARD NUTS
ADHNRSTY HYDRANTS
ADHOOPRS HOSPODAR
ADHOORSW ROADSHOW
ADHOPRST HARDTOPS
ADHOPRSY RHAPSODY
ADHORRTY HYDRATOR
ADHORSTY SHORT-DAY
ADHRSTUY THURSDAY
ADIIINRV VIRIDIAN
ADIIIQRU DAIQUIRI
ADIIKLMM MILKMAID
ADIIKLST TAILSKID
ADIILLMR MILLIARD
ADIILLOP LIPOIDAL
ADIILLUV DILUVIAL
ADIILMRV VLADIMIR
ADIILNOT DILATION
ADIILNSU INDUSIAL
ADIILNSV INVALIDS
ADIILNSW WINDSAIL

ADIILNTW TAILWIND
ADIILNTY DAINTILY
ADIILOPP DIPLOPIA
ADIILSSY DIALYSIS
ADIILTVY VALIDITY
ADIIMRST TRIADISM
ADIINOOT IODATION
ADIINOSY DIONYSIA
ADIINOTU AUDITION
ADIINRST DISTRAIN
ADIIPRTY RAPIDITY
ADIIPSTY SAPIDITY
ADIIPTVY VAPIDITY
ADIIRSST DIARISTS
ADIIRSTT DISTRAIT
ADIKNNST INKSTAND
ADIKNPSS SKIDPANS
ADILLLPY PALLIDLY
ADILLMNR MANDRILL
ADILLMOU ALLODIUM
ADILLMSY DISMALLY
ADILLNPS LANDSLIP
ADILLOSW DISALLOW
ADILLOSY DISLOYAL
ADILLRSU DRUSILLA
ADILMNNO MANDOLIN
ADILMOPS DIPLOMAS
ADILMOPT DIPLOMAT
ADILMOPY OLYMPIAD
ADILMOTY MODALITY
ADILNNOR LONDRINA
ADILNNSU DISANNUL
ADILNOOR DOORNAIL
ADILNORS ORDINALS,
ROSALIND
ADILNOTY NODALITY
ADILNRWY INWARDLY
ADILNSSU SUNDIALS
ADILNSSW WINDLASS
ADILOOPR POLAROID
ADILOORT TOROIDAL
ADILOPRS SLIP ROAD
ADILOPRT DIOPTRAL,
TRIPODAL
ADILOPSS DISPOSAL
ADILORSY SOLIDARY
ADILORTY ADROITLY,
DILATORY, IDOLATRY
ADILOSTW WILD OATS
ADILPSSY DISPLAYS
ADILPSTU PLAUDITS
ADILRTWY TAWDRILY
ADIMMNOS MONADISM,
NOMADISM

ADIMMNSY DYNAMISM
ADIMNNOT DOMINANT
ADIMNSTY DYNAMIST
ADIMOPRY MYRIAPOD
ADIMOSST MASTOIDS
ADIMOSTY TOADYISM
ADIMPRSY PYRAMIDS
ADIMSSTU STADIUMS
ADINNNTU INUNDANT
ADINNOOT DONATION
ADINNORS ANDIRONS
ADINNSST STAND-INS
ADINOOPS ISOPODAN
ADINOOPT ADOPTION
ADINOORT TANDOORI
ADINOOTT DOTATION
ADINOPRR RAINDROP
ADINOPRS PONIARDS
ADINORRY ORDINARY
ADINORST INTRADOS
ADINORSU DINOSAUR
ADINORTU DURATION
ADINPSST SANDPITS
ADIOOPRT PAROTOID
ADIOOPSS APODOSIS
ADIOPPST POSTPAID
ADIOPRST PARODIST,
PORT SAID
ADIOPRTY PODIATRY
ADIORSTU AUDITORS
ADIORSVY ADVISORY
ADIORTUY AUDITORY
ADIRRWYZ WIZARDRY
ADJKNRUY JUNKYARD
ADJNNOSU DON JUANS
ADKLOOPT POLKA DOT
ADKLOORW WOODLARK,
WORKLOAD
ADKMNORW
MARKDOWN
ADKMOORR DARKROOM
ADKOORRW ROADWORK
ADKORSWY WORKDAYS
ADKRSSWY SKYWARDS
ADLLLORY LOLLARDY
ADLLNORU ALL-ROUND
ADLLNOSW LOWLANDS
ADLLNUUZ ZULULAND
ADLLOPRS POLLARDS
ADLMNOOR MOORLAND
ADLMNOOW OLD
WOMAN
ADLMNORY RANDOMLY
ADLMOPSY PSALMODY

ADLNNTUU UNDULANT
ADLNOORW LOANWORD
ADLNOPWY DOWNPLAY
ADLOOPRU UROPODAL
ADLOPRWY WORDPLAY
ADLORRSW WARLORDS
ADLORSTW LAST WORD
ADMMNORU
OMDURMAN
ADMMNNORY
MONANDRY, NORMANDY
ADMNOORS ROSAMOND
ADMNOOST MASTODON
ADMNOOSW
WOODSMAN
ADMNORRU ROUND-
ARM
ADMNORSU ROSAMUND
ADMNORSW SANDWORM
ADMOOPPP POPPADOM
ADMOORRW
WARDROOM
ADMOORST DOORMATS
ADMOORSY DAYROOMS
ADMOPPSU POPADUMS
ADNNORTY DYNATRON
ADNOOQRU QUADROON
ADNOORST TORNADOS
ADNOOSSS SO-AND-SOS
ADNOQRSU SQUADRON
ADNORSTU ROTUNDAS
ADNORSTW SANDWORT
ADNORSXY SARDONYX
ADNORTUW UNTOWARD
ADNOSTTU OUTSTAND
ADNPPSUU UP-AND-UPS
ADNPSSTU DUSTPANS
ADNRSSUW SUNWARDS
ADOOPRRT TRAPDOOR
ADOOPRSU SAUROPOD
ADOORSWY DOORWAYS
ADOPRSSW PASSWORD
ADOPSSSU SOAPSUDS
ADORSTUW OUTWARDS
ADORSTUY SUDATORY
ADRSSTTU STARDUST
AEEEFORS FAEROESE
AEEEGGLU LEE GAUGE
AEEEGLLS LEGALESE
AEEEGLRT REGELATE,
RELEGATE
AEEEGLRV LEVERAGE
AEEEGLST LEGATEES
AEEEGNPR PEA GREEN

AEEEGNRT GENERATE, GREEN TEA, TEENAGER
AEEEGPRS PEERAGES
AEEEGRST STEERAGE
AEEEGRSW SEWERAGE
AEEEGTTV VEGETATE
AEEEHLRT ETHEREAL
AEEEHMPR EPHEMERA
AEEEHRRS REHEARSE
AEEEHRRT REHEATER
AEEEHSTT AESTHETE
AEEEIMNX EXAMINEE
AEEEJNTT JEANETTE
AEEEKKPS KEEPSAKE
AEEEKNRW WEAKENER
AEEELLPP APPELLEE
AEEELLSV SEA LEVEL
AEEELMNR ENAMELER
AEEELNPS NEPALESE
AEEELNRV VENEREAL
AEEELNST SELENATE
AEEELPRR REPEALER
AEEELRRS RELEASER
AEEELRRV REVEALER
AEEELRSS RELEASES
AEEELRTX AXLETREE
AEEEMMRT METAMERE
AEEEMNST EASEMENT
AEEEMPRT PERMEATE
AEEENPTT PATENTEE
AEEENRTV ENERVATE, VENERATE
AEEEPPRS PRAESEPE
AEEEPRRT REPARTEE, REPEATER
AEEEPSTW SWEET PEA
AEEERSST ESTERASE
AEEFFLLR FREE-FALL
AEEFFLTT FLAT FEET
AEEFFNRT AFFERENT
AEEFGILN FINE GAEL
AEEFGILR FILAGREE
AEEFGIRR FERRIAGE
AEEFGLSU FUSELAGE
AEEFHLLS SELFHEAL
AEEFHRST FEATHERS
AEEFHRTY FEATHERY
AEEFHRVY HAY FEVER
AEEFILNR FLANERIE
AEEFILST FETIALES, LEAFIEST
AEEFINST STEFANIE
AEEFIRRR RAREFIER
AEEFIRSS FREESIAS

AEEFISST SAFETIES
AEEFKOPR FOREPEAK
AEEFLLRW FAREWELL
AEEFLLST LEAFLETS
AEEFLMSS SELFSAME
AEEFLNRU FUNEREAL
AEEFLORV OVERLEAF
AEEFLRRR REFERRAL
AEEFLRRT FALTERER
AEEFLRSS FEARLESS
AEEFMNOR FORENAME
AEEFMORS FEARSOME
AEEFNRST FASTENER, FENESTRA
AEEFNRTT FATTENER
AEEFNSSS SAFENESS
AEEFPRSS FREE PASS
AEEFRSTU FEATURES
AEEFRSWY FREEWAYS
AEEGGIRV AGGRIEVE
AEEGGKOR OAK EGGER
AEEGGNNR GANGRENE
AEEGHHLS SHEELAGH
AEEGHILN HEGELIAN
AEEGHIRT HERITAGE
AEEGHMPR GRAPHEME
AEEGHNRS SHAGREEN
AEEGHRRT GATHERER
AEEGHTTX GET THE AX
AEEGILLS LEGALISE
AEEGILLZ LEGALIZE
AEEGILMS MILEAGES
AEEGILNN ANGELINE
AEEGILNR ALGERINE
AEEGILNS ENSILAGE, LINEAGES
AEEGILNT GELATINE, LEGATINE
AEEGILTV LEVIGATE
AEEGIMNR GERMAINE
AEEGIMNT GEMINATE
AEEGIMRT EMIGRATE
AEEGINPR PERIGEAN
AEEGINRR REGAINER
AEEGINSS AGENESIS, ASSIGNEE
AEEGINSU GUIANESE
AEEGINSV ENVISAGE
AEEGINTV AGENTIVE, NEGATIVE
AEEGIPQU EQUIPAGE
AEEGIRRS GREASIER
AEEGIRTT AIGRETTE
AEEGLLNR ALLERGEN

AEEGLLSZ GAZELLES
AEEGLMNS MÉLANGES
AEEGLMOS MESOGLEA
AEEGLMRT TELEGRAM
AEEGLMRY MEAGRELY
AEEGLNNO ANGELENO
AEEGLNNT ENTANGLE
AEEGLNOT ELONGATE
AEEGLNRR ENLARGER
AEEGLNRS GENERALS
AEEGLNRT REGENTAL
AEEGLNSY ANGLESEY
AEEGLORT ALTER EGO
AEEGLRSS EELGRASS, LARGESSE
AEEGLRTU REGULATE
AEEGLRUX EXERGUAL
AEEGLSSV SELVAGES
AEEGLSSY EYEGLASS
AEEGLTTU TUTELAGE
AEEGMNSS GAMENESS
AEEGMRST GAMESTER
AEEGMSSS MESSAGES
AEEGMSSU MESSUAGE
AEEGNNNO ENNEAGON
AEEGNOST STONE AGE
AEEGNRRV ENGRAVER
AEEGNRST ESTRANGE, REAGENTS, SERGEANT
AEEGNRSV AVENGERS
AEEGNRUV AUVERGNE
AEEGNSUY GUYANESE
AEEGPRRS PRESAGER
AEEGPRSS PRESAGES
AEEGRRRT REGRATER
AEEGRRSS GREASERS
AEEGRSTT GREATEST
AEEGSTTZ GAZETTES
AEEHHIKZ HEZEKIAH
AEEHHIMN NEHEMIAH
AEEHHLNZ HAZELHEN
AEEHHNST HEATHENS
AEEHHRSS REHASHES
AEEHHRTY HEATHERY
AEEHIJMR JEREMIAH
AEEHIKLR HARELIKE
AEEHILTV HELVETIA
AEEHIMPU EUPHEMIA
AEEHIPRS HESPERIA, PHARISEE
AEEHIRRT EARTHIER, HEARTIER
AEEHIRST THERESIA
AEEHISTT HESITATE

AEEHISTV HEAVIEST
AEEHKLNT KATHLEEN
AEEHKNRR HANKERER,
  HARKENER
AEEHLLRT HEAR TELL
AEEHLLSS SEASHELL
AEEHLMNY HYMENEAL
AEEHLMPT HELPMATE
AEEHLNOT ANETHOLE
AEEHLNPT ELEPHANT
AEEHLNSS HALENESS
AEEHLNVY HEAVENLY
AEEHLOSU ALEHOUSE
AEEHLRTY LEATHERY
AEEHLSST HEATLESS
AEEHLSTT ATHLETES
AEEHLTTY ETHYLATE
AEEHMMRR HAMMERER
AEEHMPRR HAMPERER
AEEHMPSS EMPHASES
AEEHMRTY ERYTHEMA
AEEHNNTX XANTHENE
AEEHNOPR EARPHONE
AEEHNRST HASTENER
AEEHNRTT THREATEN
AEEHNRTU URETHANE
AEEHNRTW ENWREATH
AEEHNRWY ANYWHERE
AEEHNSTW ENSWATHE
AEEHORRV OVERHEAR
AEEHORSS SEAHORSE,
  SEASHORE
AEEHORTV OVERHEAT
AEEHOSTU TEAHOUSE
AEEHPRRS REPHRASE
AEEHRSTT THEATERS,
  THEATRES
AEEHRTVW WHATEVER
AEEHSTVY HEAVY-SET
AEEIJMNR JERMAINE
AEEIJMRS JEREMIAS
AEEIJNNN JEANNINE
AEEIKLMU LEUKEMIA
AEEIKLST LEAKIEST
AEEIKLVW WAVELIKE
AEEIKNRS SNEAKIER
AEEIKNRT ANKERITE
AEEIKNTW KEEWATIN
AEEIKPST PEAKIEST
AEEILMMN MELAMINE
AEEILMNS MILANESE
AEEILMNT MELANITE
AEEILMRT MATERIEL,
  REAL-TIME

AEEILMSS SEA MILES
AEEILMST MEALIEST
AEEILNPS PENALISE
AEEILNPT PETALINE
AEEILNPZ PENALIZE
AEEILNRT ELATERIN,
  ENTAILER, TREENAIL
AEEILNSV VASELINE
AEEILORT AEROLITE
AEEILOTT ETIOLATE
AEEILPPP APPLE PIE
AEEILPRR PEARLIER
AEEILPRS ESPALIER
AEEILPRT PEARLITE
AEEILQSU EQUALISE
AEEILQUZ EQUALIZE
AEEILRRS REALISER
AEEILRRT RETAILER
AEEILRRZ REALIZER
AEEILRST EARLIEST
AEEILRSV VELARISE
AEEILRSZ SLEAZIER
AEEILRTT LATERITE,
  LITERATE
AEEILRTV RELATIVE
AEEILRVW LIVEWARE,
  REVIEWAL
AEEILRVZ VELARIZE
AEEILTTV LEVITATE
AEEIMMNT MEANTIME
AEEIMNRT ANTIMERE
AEEIMNRX EXAMINER
AEEIMNSS MESSENIA
AEEIMNST MATINÉES
AEEIMORV AVIEMORE
AEEIMRST EMIRATES,
  STEAMIER
AEEIMRTT MARIETTE
AEEIMSST SEAMIEST
AEEIMSTT ESTIMATE,
  MEATIEST
AEEINNRS ANSERINE
AEEINNTV VENETIAN
AEEINOPS PAEONIES
AEEINPRT APERIENT
AEEINRRT RETAINER
AEEINRSS ASNIERES
AEEINRST ARSENITE,
  RESINATE, TERESINA,
  TRAINEES
AEEINRSU UNEASIER
AEEINSSS EASINESS
AEEINSTT ANISETTE,
  TETANISE

AEEINTTZ TETANIZE
AEEIPPSU EUPEPSIA
AEEIPPTT APPETITE
AEEIPRRR REPAIRER
AEEIQRSU QUEASIER
AEEIRRST ARTERIES
AEEIRSTT TREATIES,
  TREATISE
AEEIRSTW AS IT WERE,
  SWEATIER, WEARIEST
AEEIRSVV AVERSIVE
AEEIRTTZ TREATIZE
AEEISTTT STEATITE
AEEITUVX EXUVIATE
AEEKLLST SKELETAL
AEEKLMRT TELEMARK
AEEKLSSW WAKELESS
AEEKLSTY EYESTALK
AEEKMRRR REMARKER
AEEKMRRT MARKETER
AEEKNPSW NEWSPEAK
AEEKNRSS SNEAKERS
AEEKNSSW WEAKNESS
AEEKORST KERATOSE
AEEKORTV OVERTAKE,
  TAKEOVER
AEEKPRSS SPEAKERS
AEEKQRSU SQUEAKER
AEEKRRST STREAKER
AEELLLTT TELLTALE
AEELLMNW MEAN WELL
AEELLNOT LET ALONE
AEELLOTT ALLOTTEE
AEELLPPY ALLEPPEY
AEELLPTT PLATELET
AEELLPTY TELEPLAY
AEELLRRV RAVELLER
AEELLSTT STELLATE
AEELLSWY WEASELLY
AEELMMNU EMMANUEL
AEELMNRT LAMENTER
AEELMNSS LAMENESS,
  MALENESS, NAMELESS,
  SALESMEN
AEELMPRX EXEMPLAR
AEELMPRY EMPYREAL
AEELMPSX EXAMPLES
AEELMPTT PALMETTE,
  TEMPLATE
AEELMSSS SEAMLESS
AEELNNRT LANNERET
AEELNNSS LEANNESS
AEELNOOR ELEONORA
AEELNOPR PERONEAL

AEELNOPT ANTELOPE
AEELNORS ROSALEEN
AEELNPSS PALENESS
AEELNQSU SQUALENE
AEELNRRS LEARNERS
AEELNRSS REALNESS
AEELNRSV ENSLAVER
AEELNRSW RENEWALS
AEELNRTV LEVANTER,
RELEVANT
AEELNRTX EXTERNAL
AEELNSST LATENESS
AEELNSWY WESLEYAN
AEELNTUV EVENTUAL
AEELORST OLEASTER
AEELORSU AUREOLES
AEELORTT TOLERATE
AEELORTV ELEVATOR
AEELOTTT TEETOTAL
AEELOTTW TEA TOWEL
AEELPRRS RELAPSER
AEELPRRT PALTERER
AEELPRRY PARLEYER
AEELPRSS RELAPSES
AEELPRST PRELATES
AEELPRSU PLEASURE
AEELPRSV VESPERAL
AEELPSTT PALETTES
AEELPSTU EPAULETS
AEELPTTU PAULETTE
AEELQRSU SQUEALER
AEELRRSV REVERSAL,
SLAVERER
AEELRRTU URETERAL
AEELRRTV TRAVELER
AEELRSST TESSERAL
AEELRSTT LETRASET
AEELRSTY EASTERLY
AEELRTTU LAURETTE
AEELSTTY LAYETTES
AEEMMRRY YAMMERER
AEEMMRST AMMETERS
AEEMMSST MESSMATE
AEEMNNOS ANEMONES
AEEMNNPS PEN NAMES
AEEMNNSS MEANNESS
AEEMNPRT PERMEANT
AEEMNPRY EMPYREAN
AEEMNPST PET NAMES
AEEMNPTV PAVEMENT
AEEMNRSW MENSWEAR
AEEMNRTU NUMERATE
AEEMNRTV AVERMENT
AEEMNRUV MANEUVER

AEEMNRVY EVERYMAN
AEEMNSSS SAMENESS
AEEMNSST TAMENESS
AEEMPPRR PAMPERER
AEEMPPRT TAMPERER
AEEMPRRV REVAMPER
AEEMPSTU AMPUTEES
AEEMPSTW SWAP MEET
AEEMQRRU REMARQUE
AEEMQRSU MARQUEES
AEEMQTTU MAQUETTE
AEEMRRST STREAMER
AEEMRRSU MEASURER
AEEMRSST MASSETER,
STEAMERS
AEEMRSSU MEASURES
AEEMRSTT TEAMSTER
AEENNORS ROSEANNE
AEENNPRY PYRENEAN
AEENNRRS ENSNARER
AEENNRSS NEARNESS
AEENNRTV REVENANT
AEENNSSS SANENESS
AEENNSST NEATNESS
AEENOPRU EUROPEAN
AEENORRS REASONER
AEENORSS SEASONER
AEENORST RESONATE
AEENORTV RENOVATE
AEENORVW OVENWARE
AEENRRSS RARENESS
AEENRRTV TAVERNER
AEENRSTV VETERANS
AEENRTTV ANTEVERT
AEENRTTY ENTREATY
AEENSVWW NEW WAVES
AEEOPRRT PERORATE
AEEOPRSW SEA POWER
AEEOPRTT OPERETTA
AEEORRTV OVERRATE
AEEORSSV OVERSEAS
AEEPPRTU PERPETUA
AEEPRRRT PARTERRE
AEEPRRSS ASPERSER
AEEPRRTU APERTURE
AEEPRSTZ TRAPEZES
AEEQRRUV QUAVERER
AEERRRST ARRESTER
AEERRSST ASSERTER
AEERRSSU ERASURES,
REASSURE
AEERRSTT RETREATS
AEERRSTU TREASURE
AEERRSTV TRAVERSE

AEERRSVW WAVERERS
AEERSSTW SWEATERS
AEFFGIIL EFFIGIAL
AEFFGILS FIG LEAFS
AEFFGIRS GIRAFFES
AEFFGOST OFFSTAGE
AEFFGRSU SUFFRAGE
AEFFHILL HALF-LIFE
AEFFIMRR AFFIRMER,
REAFFIRM
AEFFKORS RAKE-OFFS
AEFFKOST TAKEOFFS
AEFFLNSS SNAFFLES
AEFFLNTU AFFLUENT
AEFFLORU FOUR-LEAF
AEFFMRSU EARMUFFS
AEFFORST AFFOREST
AEFGIIRS GASIFIER
AEFGIKNR FREAKING
AEFGILNR FINAGLER
AEFGIMTU FUMIGATE
AEFGINST FEASTING
AEFGIORS FOIE GRAS
AEFGIRST FRIGATES
AEFGIRTU FIGURATE,
FRUITAGE
AEFGISTU FATIGUES
AEFGLLOP FLAGPOLE
AEFGLLPU FULL-PAGE
AEFGLMNU FUGLEMAN
AEFGLOOR FLOORAGE
AEFGLOPR LEAPFROG
AEFGLRTU GRATEFUL
AEFGMNRT FRAGMENT
AEFGNORT FRONTAGE
AEFGOORT FOOTGEAR
AEFGRRST GRAFTERS
AEFHIKRS FREAKISH
AEFHIKSW WEAKFISH
AEFHILMT HALF TIME
AEFHILRS FLASHIER
AEFHLMRT HALF TERM
AEFHLMSU SHAMEFUL
AEFHLNOT HALF NOTE,
HALFTONE
AEFHLRSS FLASHERS
AEFHLRTY FATHERLY
AEFHLSST FLASHEST
AEFHLSTU HASTEFUL
AEFHMNRS FRESHMAN
AEFHMORT FATHOMER
AEFHRSTT FARTHEST
AEFIILLN NAIL FILE
AEFIILMS FAMILIES

AEFIILNS FINALISE
AEFIILNZ FINALIZE
AEFIIMNS INFAMIES
AEFIINRS FRIESIAN
AEFIIPRT APERITIF
AEFIIRRS FRIARIES
AEFIIRRT RATIFIER
AEFIITVX FIXATIVE
AEFIKLMO FOAMLIKE
AEFIKLST FLAKIEST
AEFIKLTY FLY A KITE
AEFILLOT FELLATIO
AEFILMNR INFLAMER,
RIFLEMAN
AEFILMNT FILAMENT
AEFILMUY EL FAIYUM
AEFILNNR INFERNAL
AEFILNPS LIFESPAN
AEFILNRT INFLATER
AEFILNRU FRAULEIN
AEFILOOR AEROFOIL
AEFILORS FORESAIL
AEFILPRX PREFIXAL
AEFILPST FLEAPITS
AEFILRST FRAILEST
AEFILRSU FAILURES
AEFILRTT FILTRATE
AEFILRTU FAULTIER,
FILATURE
AEFILSTV FESTIVAL
AEFILTUU FAUTEUIL
AEFIMNST MANIFEST
AEFIMOST FOAMIEST
AEFIMRRS FIREARMS
AEFIMRRW FIRMWARE
AEFINNSZ FANZINES
AEFINOPR PINAFORE
AEFINORS FARINOSE
AEFINOTT FETATION
AEFINRRS REFRAINS
AEFINRRU UNFAIRER
AEFINRSS FAIRNESS
AEFINRST FINE ARTS
AEFINSTT FAINTEST
AEFIORTV FAVORITE
AEFIPRRT FIRETRAP
AEFIRRRS FARRIERS
AEFIRRRY FARRIERY
AEFIRSTV FIVE-STAR
AEFISTTT FATTIEST
AEFKLLOT FOLKTALE
AEFKNORS FORSAKEN
AEFKNRST FRANKEST
AEFKORRS FORSAKER

AEFLLNNS FLANNELS
AEFLLRUX FLEXURAL
AEFLLSSW FLAWLESS
AEFLLSTT FLATLETS
AEFLMORU FORMULAE,
FUMAROLE
AEFLMOTU FLAMEOUT
AEFLNORS FARNESOL
AEFLNRSU FUNERALS
AEFLNRTU FLAUNTER
AEFLNSST FLATNESS
AEFLOORV FOVEOLAR
AEFLOPRY FOREPLAY
AEFLOPSW PEAFOWLS
AEFLORRV FLAVORER
AEFLORST FLOATERS,
FORESTAL
AEFLORTT FLORETTA
AEFLORTW FLEAWORT
AEFLOSTT FALSETTO
AEFLPPRY FLYPAPER
AEFLPRSU FLARE-UPS
AEFLPRSY PALFREYS
AEFLRSSU REFUSALS
AEFLRTTU AFLUTTER
AEFLRTTY FLATTERY
AEFLSTTT FLATTEST
AEFLSTTU TASTEFUL
AEFLSTUW WASTEFUL
AEFMNORW MEN-OF-
WAR
AEFMNRRY FERRYMAN
AEFMORRS FOREARMS
AEFMORST FOREMAST
AEFMORVW WAVEFORM
AEFMPRSU FRAME-UPS
AEFNNSTU UNFASTEN
AEFNOPRR PROFANER
AEFNORRW FOREWARN
AEFNORST SEAFRONT
AEFNRRST TRANSFER
AEFNRRUY FUNERARY
AEFNSSST FASTNESS
AEFOORTW FOOTWEAR
AEFOPRRT FOREPART
AEFOPTUU POT-AU-FEU
AEFORRSW FORSWEAR
AEFORRUV FAVOURER
AEFORSTW SOFTWARE
AEFORSTY FORESTAY
AEFRSSTW FRETSAWS
AEGGGINN ENGAGING
AEGGHIRS SHAGGIER
AEGGHNNY HENG-YANG

AEGGHOPY GEOPHAGY
AEGGHORU ROUGHAGE
AEGGILLN ALLEGING
AEGGILLR GRILLAGE
AEGGILMN GLEAMING
AEGGILNN GLEANING
AEGGILNU LEAGUING
AEGGINNR ANGERING,
ENRAGING
AEGGINNT NEGATING
AEGGINNV AVENGING
AEGGINOR GEORGIAN,
GEORGINA
AEGGINOS SEAGOING
AEGGINRS GREASING
AEGGINRW WAGERING
AEGGIOPR ARPEGGIO
AEGGISST SAGGIEST
AEGGLNPT EGGPLANT
AEGGLORY GARGOYLE
AEGGLRST STRAGGLE
AEGGMMSU MUG'S
GAME
AEGGMORT MORTGAGE
AEGGNRST GANGSTER
AEGGOPRU AGE GROUP
AEGGRSST STAGGERS
AEGHHISS HIGH SEAS
AEGHILLT LIGHT ALE
AEGHILMT MEGALITH
AEGHILNX EXHALING
AEGHILRT LITHARGE
AEGHINRS HEARINGS,
SHEARING
AEGHINRT EARTHING,
INGATHER
AEGHINRV HAVERING
AEGHINRY HARINGEY
AEGHINTT GNATHITE
AEGHIPPR EPIGRAPH
AEGHIPRT GRAPHITE
AEGHLOSS GALOSHES
AEGHLRTU LAUGHTER
AEGHLRTY LETHARGY
AEGHNNOR HANGER-ON
AEGHNNSY SHENYANG
AEGHNOPT HEPTAGON,
PATHOGEN
AEGHNORV HANGOVER,
OVERHANG
AEGHNOSX HEXAGONS
AEGHOPPR PROPHAGE
AEGHOPPY APOPHYGE
AEGHORST SHORTAGE

AEGHOSST HOSTAGES
AEGIILLU AIGUILLE
AEGIILMR REMIGIAL
AEGIILTT LITIGATE
AEGIILTV LIGATIVE
AEGIIMNR IMAGINER,
 MIGRAINE
AEGIIMTT MITIGATE
AEGIINNR ARGININE,
 NIGERIAN
AEGIIRRT IRRIGATE
AEGIKLNS LINKAGES
AEGIKLNW WEAKLING
AEGIKMNR REMAKING
AEGIKNNS SNEAKING
AEGIKNNW WAKENING
AEGIKNPS SPEAKING
AEGIKNRT RETAKING
AEGIKNRW WREAKING
AEGIKNTW TWEAKING
AEGIKNWY KWEIYANG
AEGIKSTW GAWKIEST
AEGILLMS LEGALISM
AEGILLMU GULIELMA
AEGILLNO GOAL LINE
AEGILLNY GENIALLY
AEGILLPR PILLAGER
AEGILLPS SPILLAGE
AEGILLRV VILLAGER
AEGILLST LEGALIST
AEGILLSV VILLAGES
AEGILLTU LIGULATE
AEGILLTY LEGALITY
AEGILMNR GERMINAL,
 MALIGNER, MALINGER
AEGILMNS GALENISM
AEGILMNT LIGAMENT,
 METALING, TEGMINAL
AEGILMST TIME LAGS
AEGILNNP PANELING
AEGILNNR LEARNING
AEGILNNS LEANINGS
AEGILNNT GANTLINE
AEGILNNW WEANLING
AEGILNNY YEANLING
AEGILNOR GERANIOL,
 REGIONAL
AEGILNOS GASOLINE
AEGILNOT GELATION,
 LEGATION
AEGILNPS ELAPSING,
 PLEASING
AEGILNPT PLEATING
AEGILNQU EQUALING

AEGILNRS SIGNALER
AEGILNRT ALERTING,
 ALTERING, INTEGRAL,
 RELATING, TRIANGLE
AEGILNRV RAVELING
AEGILNRX RELAXING
AEGILNRY LAYERING,
 RELAYING, YEARLING
AEGILNSS GLASSINE
AEGILNST GALENIST,
 GENITALS, STEALING
AEGILNSV LEAVINGS
AEGILNTX EXALTING
AEGILOPS SPOILAGE
AEGILOPT PILOTAGE
AEGILORS GASOLIER,
 SERAGLIO
AEGILPPS SLIPPAGE
AEGILRSS GLASSIER
AEGILRSY GREASILY
AEGILRSZ GLAZIERS
AEGILRTU LIGATURE
AEGILRTY REGALITY
AEGILRVW LAWGIVER
AEGILRYZ GLAZIERY
AEGIMNNR RENAMING
AEGIMNNS MEANINGS
AEGIMNRR REARMING
AEGIMNRS SMEARING
AEGIMNRT EMIGRANT
AEGIMNRU GERANIUM
AEGIMNSS GAMINESS
AEGIMNST MANGIEST,
 STEAMING
AEGIMPRS EPIGRAMS
AEGIMQRU QUAGMIRE
AEGIMRST STERIGMA
AEGIMSSU MISUSAGE
AEGINNNX ANNEXING
AEGINNOS ANGINOSE
AEGINNOT NEGATION
AEGINNRS EARNINGS,
 GRANNIES
AEGINNRV RAVENING
AEGINNRY YEARNING
AEGINNST ANTIGENS,
 GENTIANS
AEGINNSU SANGUINE
AEGINORS ORGANISE
AEGINORZ ORGANIZE
AEGINOTV GO NATIVE
AEGINPPR PAPERING
AEGINPRS SPEARING
AEGINPRT TAPERING

AEGINPRY REPAYING
AEGINPTY EGYPTIAN
AEGINQTU EQUATING
AEGINRRS EARRINGS
AEGINRRV AVERRING
AEGINRSS ASSIGNER
AEGINRST ANGRIEST,
 GANISTER, GANTRIES,
 INGRATES
AEGINRSW SWEARING
AEGINRTT TREATING
AEGINRTV AVERTING,
 VINTAGER
AEGINRTW WATERING
AEGINRVW WAVERING
AEGINRVY VINEGARY
AEGINRWY WEARYING
AEGINSST GIANTESS
AEGINSSY ESSAYING
AEGINSTT TANGIEST
AEGINSTU SAUTÉING
AEGINSTV VINTAGES
AEGINSTW SWEATING
AEGIORSV VIRAGOES
AEGIOSTX GEOTAXIS
AEGIRRSS GRASSIER
AEGIRSST SEAGIRTS
AEGIRSUU AUGURIES
AEGISSST GASSIEST
AEGISTUZ GAUZIEST
AEGLLNOS GALLEONS
AEGLLOPR GALLOPER
AEGLLORY ALLEGORY
AEGLLOTT TOLLGATE
AEGLLRVY GRAVELLY
AEGLLSSU SEAGULLS
AEGLMNNO MANGONEL
AEGLMNTU GUNMETAL
AEGLMOTV MEGAVOLT
AEGLNNOR ALGERNON
AEGLNNPT PLANGENT
AEGLNNTU UNTANGLE
AEGLNORS SELANGOR
AEGLNORY YEARLONG
AEGLNOVW LONG WAVE
AEGLNPRS GRAPNELS
AEGLNPSS SPANGLES
AEGLNRRW WRANGLER
AEGLNRST STRANGLE
AEGLNRSU GRANULES
AEGLNRSW WRANGLES
AEGLNRSY LARYNGES
AEGLNSUW GUNWALES
AEGLNTTU GAUNTLET

AEGLNTUU UNGULATE
AEGLOOOZ ZOOGLOEA
AEGLOOPU APOLOGUE
AEGLOORY AEROLOGY
AEGLOPRS PERGOLAS
AEGLOPRY PLAYGOER
AEGLOSTV VOLTAGES
AEGLPPRR GRAPPLER
AEGLPRSU EARPLUGS
AEGLRRSU REGULARS
AEGLRSTU GESTURAL
AEGLSSTT GESTALTS
AEGMMNOR
  GAMMONER
AEGMMRRU RUMMAGER
AEGMMRSU RUMMAGES
AEGMNNOT MAGNETON
AEGMNORV MANGROVE
AEGMNOST MAGNETOS,
  MEGATONS, MONTAGES
AEGMNOTU MONTAGUE
AEGMNOXY XENOGAMY
AEGMNRST GARMENTS
AEGMNRTU ARGUMENT
AEGMOPRW GAPEWORM
AEGMORRW WORM
  GEAR
AEGMORSS GOSSAMER
AEGMPRUZ GAZUMPER
AEGNNOPT PENTAGON
AEGNNOST TONNAGES
AEGNNPRT PREGNANT
AEGNNSTT TANGENTS
AEGNORRY ORANGERY
AEGNORST ESTRAGON
AEGNORSX SEX ORGAN
AEGNOSSY NOSEGAYS
AEGNPPRU GUNPAPER
AEGNRRST STRANGER
AEGOPPST STOPPAGE
AEGOPSST GESTAPOS
AEGOPSTT GATEPOST
AEGORRTT GARROTTE
AEGORSTU GOAT'S-RUE,
  OUTRAGES
AEGORSVY VOYAGERS
AEGORTTU TUTORAGE
AEGOSTTV GAVOTTES
AEGRRSSY RYEGRASS
AEGRSTTY STRATEGY
AEHHHJPT JEPHTHAH
AEHHINPR HA-ERH-PIN
AEHHINPS PHINEHAS
AEHHRRST THRASHER

AEHHRSST HARSHEST
AEHIIKLR HAIRLIKE
AEHIILNR HAIRLINE
AEHIIMNT THIAMINE
AEHIINTZ THIAZINE
AEHIIOPT ETHIOPIA
AEHIIRST HAIRIEST
AEHIJNOV JEHOVIAN
AEHIKKLW HAWKLIKE
AEHIKLLO HALO-LIKE
AEHIKMNR KHMERIAN
AEHIKSST SHAKIEST
AEHILMSW LIMEWASH
AEHILNOP APHELION
AEHILNOT IOLANTHE
AEHILNRS INHALERS
AEHILNTX ANTHELIX
AEHILNTZ ZENITHAL
AEHILOTZ THIAZOLE
AEHILRSS HAIRLESS
AEHILRSU HAULIERS
AEHILRSV LAVISHER,
  SHRIEVAL
AEHILRTY EARTHILY,
  HEARTILY
AEHIMMNN MANNHEIM
AEHIMMSS SHAMMIES
AEHIMNNU INHUMANE
AEHIMNOR HOMERIAN
AEHIMNSU HUMANISE
AEHIMNUZ HUMANIZE
AEHIMOTT TIMOTHEA
AEHIMPRS SAMPHIRE,
  SERAPHIM
AEHIMPSS EMPHASIS,
  MISSHAPE
AEHIMPST SHIPMATE
AEHIMSSS MESSIAHS
AEHINNTX XANTHEIN,
  XANTHINE
AEHINORT ANTIHERO
AEHINPPY EPIPHANY
AEHINPRT PERIANTH
AEHINPST THESPIAN
AEHINRST HAIRNETS
AEHINRSV VANISHER
AEHINRTZ HERTZIAN
AEHINSSS HESSIANS
AEHINSST ANTHESIS,
  SHANTIES
AEHINSSZ HAZINESS
AEHINSTT HESITANT
AEHINTTW WHITE ANT
AEHINTWY IN THE WAY

AEHIOPRS APHORISE
AEHIOPRU EUPHORIA
AEHIOPRZ APHORIZE
AEHIORST HOARIEST
AEHIORTU THIOUREA
AEHIPPRS SAPPHIRE
AEHIPPST EPITAPHS,
  HAPPIEST
AEHIPRSS PARISHES
AEHIRRRS HARRIERS
AEHIRRST TRASHIER
AEHIRRSV RAVISHER
AEHIRRSY AYRSHIRE
AEHIRSTY HYSTERIA
AEHISSTT ATHEISTS,
  HASTIEST
AEHISSTU HIATUSES
AEHJNNOS JOHANNES
AEHJPRSW JEW'S HARP
AEHKLOOY HOLYOAKE
AEHKNSTT TASHKENT
AEHKOSTU SHAKEOUT
AEHKPSSU SHAKE-UPS
AEHLLLTY LETHALLY
AEHLLMTY METHYLAL
AEHLLNRT ENTHRALL,
  HARTNELL
AEHLLORW HALLOWER
AEHLMMNS HELMSMAN
AEHLMNNP HELPMANN
AEHLMNOS MANHOLES
AEHLMNOT METHANOL
AEHLMNUY HUMANELY
AEHLMORS ARMHOLES
AEHLMPPT PAMPHLET
AEHLMRSS HARMLESS
AEHLMRST THERMALS
AEHLNOPS ALPHONSE
AEHLNPRS SHRAPNEL
AEHLNPTY ENTHALPY
AEHLNRTU LUTHERAN
AEHLNTUZ HAZELNUT
AEHLOPRT PLETHORA
AEHLOPTT HOTPLATE
AEHLORSY HOARSELY
AEHLORUV OVERHAUL
AEHLOSSS ASSHOLES
AEHLPRSS SPLASHER
AEHLPSST PATHLESS
AEHLPSTU SULPHATE
AEHLRRTU URETHRAL
AEHLSSTY THESSALY
AEHLSTTY STEALTHY
AEHMNORS HORSEMAN

AEHMNOSU HOUSEMAN
AEHMOPRT METAPHOR
AEHMOSTW SOMEWHAT
AEHMPPTU HEAT PUMP
AEHMRSSS SMASHERS
AEHMRSST HAMSTERS
AEHMSTTY AMETHYST
AEHNNOPT PANTHEON
AEHNNPSU UNSHAPEN
AEHNNSUV UNSHAVEN
AEHNOPPY PAY PHONE
AEHNOPRT HAPTERON
AEHNOPST PHAETONS
AEHNORST SHERATON
AEHNOSTV HAVE-NOTS
AEHNPRST PANTHERS
AEHNPRTY HEN PARTY,
  TRYPHENA
AEHNRSSS RASHNESS
AEHNRTTU EARTHNUT
AEHNSTUW UNSWATHE
AEHOPPRS PROPHASE
AEHOPSTU PHASE-OUT
AEHOPSTW TWO-PHASE
AEHOPTVY TOP-HEAVY
AEHORRRW HARROWER
AEHORRSW WARHORSE
AEHORSST EARSHOTS,
  HOARSEST
AEHORSSW SAWHORSE
AEHORSTT RHEOSTAT
AEHORSTU SHARE-OUT
AEHORSTX THORAXES
AEHORTTW HOT WATER
AEHPRSST SHARPEST,
  SHARP-SET
AEHPRSUX HARUSPEX
AEHPRSUY EUPHRASY
AEHQRSSU SQUASHER
AEHQSSSU SQUASHES
AEHRRSTU URETHRAS
AEHRRTTW THWARTER
AEHRSSTV HARVESTS
AEHSSTUX EXHAUSTS
AEIIINTT INITIATE
AEIILLTV ILLATIVE
AEIILMNN MAIN LINE
AEIILMNS ALIENISM
AEIILMPR IMPERIAL
AEIILMTT MILITATE
AEIILNPR PLEIN-AIR
AEIILNQU AQUILINE
AEIILNRR AIRLINER
AEIILNRS AIRLINES

AEIILNRT INERTIAL
AEIILNST ALIENIST,
  LATINISE, LITANIES,
  TALIESIN
AEIILNTZ LATINIZE
AEIILPPT TAIL PIPE
AEIILRSS ISRAELIS
AEIILRTT LITERATI
AEIILSTV VITALISE
AEIILTVZ VITALIZE
AEIIMMRT MARITIME
AEIIMMSX MAXIMISE
AEIIMMXZ MAXIMIZE
AEIIMNTT INTIMATE
AEIIMNTU MINUTIAE
AEIIMPRR IMPAIRER
AEIIMRST SERIATIM
AEIINNRS SIRENIAN
AEIINRSS AIRINESS
AEIINRST RAINIEST
AEIINRTZ TRIAZINE
AEIINSST SANITISE
AEIINSTZ SANITIZE
AEIINSVV INVASIVE
AEIINTTT TITANITE
AEIIPRRS PRAIRIES
AEIIPRZZ PIZZERIA
AEIIPSST EPITASIS
AEIIRRST RARITIES
AEIIRRSV RIVIERAS
AEIIRRTT IRRITATE
AEIIRSST SATIRISE
AEIIRSTW WISTERIA
AEIIRSTZ SATIRIZE
AEIITTTV TITIVATE
AEIJLNNU JULIANNE
AEIJLNSV JAVELINS
AEIJLOPS JALOPIES
AEIJLOSU JALOUSIE
AEIJMMST JAMMIEST
AEIJMNSS JASMINES
AEIJMORR MARJORIE
AEIJNRTU JAUNTIER
AEIJORST JAROSITE
AEIJSTZZ JAZZIEST
AEIKLLLW WALL-LIKE
AEIKLNPS SKI PLANE
AEIKLNSS SEALSKIN
AEIKLNST LANKIEST
AEIKLNSY SNEAKILY
AEIKLRST STARLIKE
AEIKMNOS ESKIMOAN
AEIKMNRS RAMEKINS
AEIKMNST MISTAKEN

AEIKMSST MISTAKES
AEIKNRST NARKIEST,
  TRANSKEI
AEIKNRSW SWANKIER
AEIKNRTW KNITWEAR
AEIKPRSS APRES-SKI
AEIKPRST PARKIEST
AEIKPSST PISS-TAKE
AEIKPSTW PAWKIEST
AEIKRSST ASTERISK,
  SARKIEST
AEIKRSTW WATER-SKI
AEILLLMS ALLELISM
AEILLLNY LINEALLY
AEILLMNY MENIALLY
AEILLNPS SPLENIAL
AEILLNST ANTILLES
AEILLNUV LAEVULIN
AEILLOSS LOESSIAL
AEILLOTV VOLATILE
AEILLPRS PIS ALLER
AEILLPST PALLIEST,
  PASTILLE
AEILLRRY RAILLERY
AEILLRST LITERALS
AEILLRSY SERIALLY
AEILLRTT ILL-TREAT
AEILLSST TAILLESS
AEILLSUV ALLUSIVE
AEILLSYZ SLEAZILY
AEILLTUZ LAZULITE
AEILMMNS MELANISM
AEILMMOR MEMORIAL
AEILMMOT IMMOLATE
AEILMMRT TRILEMMA
AEILMNNS LINESMAN
AEILMNOS SEMOLINA
AEILMNRS MINERALS
AEILMNRT TERMINAL,
  TRAMLINE
AEILMNST AILMENTS,
  MANLIEST, MELANIST
AEILMOPR PROEMIAL
AEILMORS MORALISE
AEILMORZ MORALIZE
AEILMPRV PRIMEVAL
AEILMPST PALMIEST
AEILMPTT PETIT MAL
AEILMPTY PLAYTIME
AEILMRSY MISLAYER
AEILMSTT METALIST,
  SMALTITE
AEILMSTU SIMULATE
AEILMSTY STEAMILY

AEILMTTU MUTILATE, ULTIMATE
AEILNNRT INTERNAL
AEILNNSY INSANELY
AEILNNTY INNATELY
AEILNOPP APPOLINE
AEILNORR LORRAINE
AEILNORS AILERONS, ROSALINE
AEILNORT ORIENTAL, RELATION
AEILNORV OVERLAIN
AEILNOSS SEA LIONS
AEILNOST INSOLATE, TOENAILS
AEILNOSV SLOVENIA
AEILNOSX SILOXANE
AEILNPRS PRALINES
AEILNPRT TRIPLANE
AEILNPSS PAINLESS, SPANIELS
AEILNPST PANTILES, PLAINEST
AEILNPTT TINPLATE
AEILNRSS RAINLESS
AEILNRST ENTRAILS, LATRINES
AEILNRTU TENURIAL
AEILNRTV INTERVAL
AEILNRTY INTERLAY
AEILNSST SALIENTS
AEILNSSZ LAZINESS.
AEILNSTU INSULATE
AEILNSUY UNEASILY
AEILNTVY VENALITY
AEILNUVV UNIVALVE
AEILOPPT OPPILATE
AEILOPRS POLARISE
AEILOPRZ POLARIZE
AEILOPST SPOLIATE
AEILORSS SOLARISE
AEILORSV VALORISE
AEILORSZ SOLARIZE
AEILORTZ TRIAZOLE
AEILORVZ VALORIZE
AEILOSTT TOTALISE
AEILOTTV VIOLETTA
AEILOTTZ TOTALIZE
AEILPPQU APPLIQUÉ
AEILPPST SPLIT PEA
AEILPRRS REPRISAL
AEILPRRT PALTRIER
AEILPRST PILASTER
AEILPRTV LIVETRAP

AEILPRXY PYREXIAL
AEILPSUV PLAUSIVE
AEILQRTU QUARTILE, REQUITAL
AEILQSUY QUEASILY
AEILQTUY EQUALITY
AEILRRST RETRIALS, TRAILERS
AEILRRSU RURALISE
AEILRRTY LITERARY
AEILRRUZ RURALIZE
AEILRSST REALISTS
AEILRSVV REVIVALS
AEILRTUZ LAZURITE
AEILSSTT SALTIEST
AEILSTWY SWEATILY
AEILSTYY YEASTILY
AEIMMNNT IMMANENT
AEIMMNOT AMMONITE
AEIMMRRS SMARMIER
AEIMMRTU IMMATURE
AEIMNNNR INNER MAN
AEIMNNOT NOMINATE
AEIMNOPT PTOMAINE
AEIMNORS MORAINES, ROMANIES
AEIMNORW AIRWOMEN
AEIMNOSW WOMANISE
AEIMNOTZ MONAZITE
AEIMNOWZ WOMANIZE
AEIMNRRS MARINERS
AEIMNRSS NEAR MISS, SEMINARS
AEIMNRST MINARETS
AEIMNRSY SEMINARY
AEIMNRTT MARTINET
AEIMNRTU RUMINATE
AEIMNRTY TYRAMINE
AEIMNSST MANTISES
AEIMORRS ARMORIES
AEIMORST AMORTISE, ATOMISER
AEIMORTZ AMORTIZE, ATOMIZER
AEIMOTTV MOTIVATE
AEIMPRRT IMPARTER
AEIMPRST PRIMATES
AEIMPRSV VAMPIRES
AEIMPRTT PART-TIME
AEIMPSSS IMPASSES
AEIMPSST PASTIMES
AEIMQRSU MARQUISE
AEIMRSST ASTERISM
AEIMRSSY EMISSARY

AEIMRSTT MISTREAT, TERATISM
AEIMRSTX MATRIXES
AEIMSSST SEA MISTS
AEIMSSTT MISSTATE
AEINNOPV PAVONINE
AEINNORT ANOINTER
AEINNOST ESTONIAN
AEINNOTT INTONATE
AEINNOTV INNOVATE, VENATION
AEINNPRS PANNIERS
AEINNRST TRANNIES
AEINNSSV VAINNESS
AEINNSSZ ZANINESS
AEINNSTT STANNITE
AEINNSUV VENUSIAN
AEINOPRT ATROPINE
AEINOPST SAPONITE
AEINOQTU EQUATION
AEINORRT ANTERIOR
AEINORRW IRONWARE
AEINORST NOTARIES, NOTARISE, SEÑORITA
AEINORSV AVERSION
AEINORTU TOURAINE
AEINORTZ NOTARIZE
AEINOSSV EVASIONS
AEINOTVX VEXATION
AEINPPPS PANPIPES
AEINPPRS SNAPPIER
AEINPRRT TERRAPIN
AEINPRST PAINTERS, PANTRIES, PINASTER
AEINPRTT TRIPTANE
AEINPRUV PERUVIAN
AEINPSST STEAPSIN
AEINPSTT PATIENTS
AEINPSTU PETUNIAS, SUPINATE
AEINPSTY EPINASTY
AEINQSTU ANTIQUES, QUANTISE
AEINQTTU EQUITANT
AEINQTUZ QUANTIZE
AEINRRST RESTRAIN, STRAINER, TERRAINS, TRAINERS
AEINRSST ARTINESS
AEINRSSU ANURESIS
AEINRSSW WARINESS
AEINRSTT NITRATES, STRAITEN, TRAIN SET
AEINRSUZ SUZERAIN

AEINRSZZ SNAZZIER
AEINSSTT NASTIEST
AEINSSVW WAVINESS
AEINSSWX WAXINESS
AEINSTTT NATTIEST
AEINSUVV VESUVIAN
AEINTTUU AUTUNITE
AEIOPPST APPOSITE
AEIOPRRT PRETORIA,
    PRIORATE
AEIOPRSV VAPORISE
AEIOPRTX EXPIATOR
AEIOPRVZ VAPORIZE
AEIOPSST SOAPIEST
AEIOPTTV OPTATIVE
AEIOQSSU SEQUOIAS
AEIORRSS ROSARIES
AEIORRUV AU REVOIR
AEIORSSV SAVORIES
AEIORSTV VOTARIES
AEIORTTV ROTATIVE
AEIPPSST SAPPIEST
AEIPPSTZ ZAPPIEST
AEIPQRTU PRATIQUE
AEIPRRSU UPRAISER
AEIPRSST PASTRIES,
    PIASTRES
AEIPRSTV PRIVATES
AEIPRSTW WIRETAPS
AEIPRSTY ASPERITY
AEIPRSVY VESPIARY
AEIPRTVY VARITYPE
AEIPSSTT PASTIEST
AEIPTTUV PUTATIVE
AEIQRRRU QUARRIER
AEIQRRSU QUARRIES
AEIRRRST STARRIER
AEIRRTTY TERTIARY
AEIRSSST ASSISTER
AEIRSSTT ARTISTES
AEIRSSTW WAITRESS
AEIRSTTT RATTIEST
AEISSSST SASSIEST
AEISSSTY ESSAYIST
AEISSTTT TASTIEST
AEISTTTT TATTIEST
AEJLOSUY JEALOUSY
AEJMNSSY JESSAMYN
AEKKMNOO KAKEMONO
AEKLMORS LARKSOME
AEKLMRUW LUKEWARM
AEKLNNSS LANKNESS
AEKLNOSY ANKYLOSE
AEKLOPRW ROPEWALK

AEKLORVW WALKOVER
AEKLPPST PEP TALKS
AEKLPRRS SPARKLER
AEKLPRSS SPARKLES
AEKLRSST STALKERS
AEKMMNRS MARKSMEN
AEKMNRSU UNMASKER
AEKMORTW TEAMWORK
AEKMPRTU UP-MARKET
AEKNNRSS RANKNESS
AEKNOOTY KOOTENAY
AEKOSTTU OUT-TAKES,
    TAKEOUTS
AEKOSTVW TAKE VOWS
AEKPSSSY PASSKEYS
AEKQRSUW SQUAWKER
AEKRRSST STARKERS
AEKRSSTT STARKEST
AELLMNTY MENTALLY
AELLMORT MARTELLO
AELLMSST SMALLEST
AELLNOPV VOLPLANE
AELLNOSV NOVELLAS
AELLNPRU PRUNELLA
AELLNSST TALLNESS
AELLNTUU LUNULATE
AELLOPRW WALLOPER
AELLOPRY ROLE PLAY
AELLORSV OVERALLS
AELLORWW WALLOWER
AELLOSUV ALVEOLUS
AELLPPSU SELL A PUP
AELLQRSU SQUALLER
AELLRTTY LATTERLY
AELLSSTY TASSELLY
AELLSUXY SEXUALLY
AELMMORW MEALWORM
AELMMRST TRAMMELS
AELMNNOT NONMETAL
AELMNNRY MANNERLY
AELMNOPS NEOPLASM,
    PLEONASM
AELMNORS ALMONERS
AELMNORT MONTREAL
AELMNOSU MELANOUS
AELMNOWY LAYWOMEN
AELMNOYY YEOMANLY
AELMNRSU MENSURAL,
    NUMERALS
AELMOORS SALEROOM
AELMOPRR PREMOLAR
AELMOPRT TEMPORAL
AELMOPSU AMPOULES
AELMOPSY MAYPOLES

AELMOPTT PALMETTO
AELMORSU RAMULOSE
AELMORSV REMOVALS
AELMORTU EMULATOR
AELMOSSS MOLASSES
AELMPRRT TRAMPLER
AELMPRSS SAMPLERS
AELMPRSY LAMPREYS
AELMRSTT MALTSTER
AELMRSTY MASTERLY
AELMRTUY MATURELY
AELNNOOP NAPOLEON
AELNNOPP OPEN-PLAN
AELNNOSU ANNULOSE
AELNNPRS PLANNERS
AELNNRST LANTERNS
AELNOPRS PERSONAL
AELNORTT TOLERANT
AELNORTY ORNATELY
AELNOSSV OVALNESS
AELNPPSY PLAYPENS
AELNPRST PLANTERS
AELNPRSU PURSLANE,
    SUPERNAL
AELNPTTU PETULANT
AELNPTTY PATENTLY
AELNRSTT SLATTERN
AELNRSTU NEUTRALS
AELNRSXY LARYNXES
AELNSSST SALTNESS
AELNTTUX EXULTANT
AELOORRS ROSEOLAR
AELOORSS AEROSOLS
AELOORTW WATERLOO
AELOORTZ ZOOLATER
AELOPPRS PROLAPSE,
    SAPROPEL
AELOPPTU POPULATE
AELOPPXY APOPLEXY
AELOPQUY OPAQUELY
AELOPRRV REPROVAL
AELOPRST PETROSAL,
    POLE STAR
AELOPRSV OVERLAPS
AELOPRVY OVERPLAY
AELOPRYZ PYRAZOLE
AELOPSSS SOAPLESS
AELOPSST APOSTLES
AELOPSSU ESPOUSAL
AELORRST REALTORS
AELORSVY OVERLAYS
AELORTWW LOW WATER
AELORTYZ ZEALOTRY
AELOSTUY AUTOLYSE

AELPRRSW SPRAWLER
AELPRRTT PRATTLER
AELPRSST PLASTERS,
PSALTERS, STAPLERS
AELPRSSU PERUSALS
AELPRSSY SPARSELY
AELPRSTT PLATTERS,
SPLATTER
AELPRSTY PSALTERY
AELQRRSU QUARRELS
AELQRSUY SQUARELY
AELRRSTT STARTLER
AELRRSTW TRAWLERS
AELRSSST STARLESS
AELRSSTT STARLETS
AELRSSTW WASTRELS
AELRSSUW WALRUSES
AELRSTTT TATTLERS
AELRSTTU LUSTRATE
AELRSTUV VAULTERS,
VESTURAL
AELRTTUX TEXTURAL
AELRTTUY TUTELARY
AELSTTUY ASTUTELY
AEMMNRTU RAMENTUM
AEMMOORT ROOMMATE
AEMMORST MARMOSET
AEMMRSST STAMMERS
AEMNNORS NORSEMAN
AEMNNORT ORNAMENT
AEMNNORW
MORWENNA
AEMNNPRU PER ANNUM
AEMNNRST REMNANTS
AEMNOORT ANTEROOM
AEMNOPRW MANPOWER
AEMNORRS RANSOMER
AEMNORST ONSTREAM
AEMNORTY MONETARY
AEMNORYY YEOMANRY
AEMNOSTU SEAMOUNT
AEMNPRSS PRESSMAN
AEMNPRSU SUPERMAN
AEMNPSTY PAYMENTS
AEMNRRUY NUMERARY
AEMNRSSU SURNAMES
AEMNRSSW WARMNESS
AEMNRSTW STRAW MEN
AEMNRSUY ANEURYSM
AEMOORST TEAROOMS
AEMOORTT AMORETTO
AEMOOSST MAESTOSO
AEMOOSTT TOMATOES
AEMOOSTU AUTOSOME

AEMOPRTW TAPEWORM
AEMORRRS ARMORERS
AEMORRRU ARMOURER
AEMORRST REARMOST
AEMORRSY ROSEMARY
AEMORSSS MORASSES
AEMORSST MAESTROS
AEMORSSY MAYORESS
AEMORTTU TAUTOMER
AEMOTTZZ MOZZETTA
AEMPRRSY SPERMARY
AEMPRSTU UPSTREAM
AEMPSTTT ATTEMPTS
AEMQRSSU MARQUESS
AEMRSSSU MASSEURS
AEMRSSTT MATTRESS,
SMARTEST
AENNNPST PENNANTS
AENNOPST PENTOSAN
AENNORST RESONANT
AENNORSU UNREASON
AENNPRSS SPANNERS
AENNRSTT ENTRANTS
AENNRSWY SWANNERY
AENNRTTY TENANTRY
AENOOPST TEASPOON
AENOPRSS PERSONAS
AENOPRTT PATENTOR
AENOPRWY WEAPONRY
AENORRST ANTRORSE
AENORSST ASSENTOR,
SENATORS
AENORSUV RAVENOUS
AENORTTY ATTORNEY
AENOSSUU NAUSEOUS
AENPPRSS SNAPPERS
AENPRRST PARTNERS
AENPRSST PASTERNS,
RAPTNESS
AENPRSTT PATTERNS,
TRANSEPT
AENPRSUV PARVENUS
AENQRRTU QUARTERN
AENRRRTY ERRANTRY
AENRSSTT TARTNESS
AENRSSTU SAUNTERS
AENRSSTV SERVANTS
AENRSTWY STERNWAY
AENRTWYY ENTRYWAY
AENSSSTV VASTNESS
AENSSTTU TAUTNESS
AENSSTTX SEXTANTS
AEOOPPSS PAPOOSES
AEOOPRRT OPERATOR

AEOOPSTT POTATOES
AEOORRST SORORATE
AEOORTTT TATTOOER
AEOPRRUV VAPOURER
AEOPRRVW WRAPOVER
AEOPRSST SEAPORTS
AEOPRSSV OVERPASS,
PASSOVER
AEOPRSTT PROSTATE
AEOPRSTU APTEROUS
AEOPTTUY AUTOTYPE
AEOQRTTU TORQUATE
AEORRSST ASSORTER,
ROASTERS
AEORRTZZ TERRAZZO
AEORSSSS ASSESSOR
AEORSSTT TOASTERS
AEORSSTV VOTARESS
AEORSTTT TESTATOR
AEORSTTU OUTSTARE
AEORSTVY OVERSTAY
AEPPRRST TRAPPERS
AEPPRRSW WRAPPERS
AEPPSSTU PASTE-UPS
AEPRRSSY SPRAYERS
AEPRRSTU RAPTURES
AEPRSSST SPARSEST,
TRESPASS
AEPRSSTT SPATTERS
AEPRSSTU PASTURES
AEPRSTTY TAPESTRY
AEPRSTUX SUPERTAX
AEQRRSTU QUARTERS
AEQRSSTU SQUAREST, T-
SQUARES
AEQRSTTU QUARTETS,
SQUATTER
AERRSSTT STARTERS
AERRSTUY TREASURY
AERSSTTU STATURES
AERSSTTW SWATTERS
AERSTTVY TRAVESTY
AERTTUXY TEXTUARY
AESSSTTU STATUSES
AESSTTTU STATUTES
AFFFFIRR RIFFRAFF
AFFGIINX AFFIXING
AFFGIIRT GRAFFITI
AFFGILNR RAFFLING
AFFGILNW WAFFLING
AFFGINST STAFFING
AFFGIORT GRAFFITO
AFFGLNRU FAR-FLUNG
AFFHILLS FALLFISH

AFFHILST FLATFISH
AFFHILTU FAITHFUL
AFFHIMRS FISH FARM
AFFIINTY AFFINITY
AFFILLMM FLIMFLAM
AFFILSUX SUFFIXAL
AFFIMSST MASTIFFS
AFFINOSU AFFUSION
AFFINRSU FUNFAIRS,
  RUFFIANS
AFFIPSTT TIPSTAFF
AFFLLOOT FOOTFALL
AFFLOOTT FLATFOOT
AFFLOPSY PLAY-OFFS
AFFNORST AFFRONTS
AFFNRRUU FURFURAN
AFGGGILN FLAGGING
AFGGINOR FORAGING
AFGGINRT GRAFTING
AFGHILNS FLASHING
AFGHILNT FANLIGHT
AFGHILPS FLAGSHIP
AFGHINRT FARTHING
AFGHINST SHAFTING
AFGHLNSU FLASHGUN
AFGIILLN FLAILING
AFGIILNS FAILINGS
AFGIINNT FAINTING
AFGIINRS FAIRINGS
AFGIKLNN FLANKING
AFGIKNNR FRANKING
AFGIKORT KOFTGARI
AFGILMNO FLAMINGO
AFGILNOT FLOATING
AFGILNOW FOWLIANG
AFGILNPP FLAPPING
AFGILNTT FLATTING
AFGILNTU FAULTING
AFGIMNTU FUMIGANT
AFGIMORS GASIFORM
AFGINORV FAVORING
AFGINORY FORAYING
AFGINRST STRAFING
AFGINRTU FIGURANT
AFGIPRTW GIFT-WRAP
AFGJNRUU JUNGFRAU
AFGLLRUY FRUGALLY
AFGLLSUY FALL GUYS
AFGLMOPS FOG LAMPS
AFGNOORS FOR A SONG
AFGORTUW TUG-OF-WAR
AFHIILSS SAILFISH
AFHIILST FISHTAIL
AFHIINST FAINTISH

AFHIKLPS HIP FLASK
AFHIKNRS FRANKISH
AFHILLSY FLASHILY
AFHILOSY OAFISHLY
AFHILSTT FLATTISH
AFHILSTW HALF-WITS
AFHINOSS FASHIONS
AFHIRSST STARFISH
AFHKLNTU THANKFUL
AFHKORSY HAYFORKS
AFHLMNOO HALF MOON
AFHLRTUW WRATHFUL
AFHOOPTT FOOTPATH
AFIILLNU UNFILIAL
AFIILMNS FINALISM
AFIILNRU FRIULIAN
AFIILNST FINALIST
AFIILNTY FINALITY
AFIILRST AIRLIFTS
AFIINNOS SAINFOIN,
  SINFONIA
AFIINOTX FIXATION
AFIKLNNR FRANKLIN
AFIKMNNR FINNMARK
AFILLLOT FLOTILLA
AFILLPST PITFALLS
AFILLTUY FAULTILY
AFILMNOR FORMALIN,
  INFORMAL
AFILMNOS FOILSMAN
AFILMRST FILM STAR
AFILNPPT FLIPPANT
AFILNPST FLAT SPIN
AFILNRUY UNFAIRLY
AFILSTTU FLAUTIST
AFIMMNOY AMMONIFY
AFIMNOPR NAPIFORM
AFIMNOSU INFAMOUS
AFIMORRV VARIFORM
AFINNOOP ON PAIN OF
AFINNOTU FOUNTAIN
AFINNRTY INFANTRY
AFINOPSY SAPONIFY
AFINORUV IN FAVOUR
AFINQTUY QUANTIFY
AFINRSTX TRANSFIX
AFIRSTTY STRATIFY
AFKLNOTU OUTFLANK
AFKLOSWY FOLKWAYS
AFKMOORT FOOTMARK
AFLLLORY FLORALLY
AFLLLUWY LAWFULLY
AFLLMNUY MANFULLY
AFLLMORY FORMALLY

AFLLMRSY SMALL FRY
AFLLNOSW SNOWFALL
AFLLNUUW UNLAWFUL
AFLLOOTW FOOTWALL
AFLLOPUY FOUL PLAY
AFLLOSTU FALLOUTS,
  OUTFALLS
AFLLRTUY ARTFULLY
AFLMNOPR PLANFORM
AFLMOPRT PLATFORM
AFLMORSU FORMULAS
AFLMORTW FLATWORM
AFLMOSUY FAMOUSLY
AFLORSUV FLAVOURS
AFLPSSTY FLYPASTS
AFMNNORT FRONT MAN
AFMOOPRR PRO FORMA
AFMOORTZ FROM A TO
  Z
AFMORTUY FUMATORY
AFOOPSST SOFT SOAP
AFORRSTU FOUR-STAR
AFPPPTUY PUPPY FAT
AGGGHILN HAGGLING
AGGGHINS SHAGGING
AGGGILNN GANGLING
AGGGILNR GARGLING
AGGGILNS SLAGGING
AGGGILNW WAGGLING
AGGGINNS SNAGGING
AGGHILNU LAUGHING
AGGHILST GASLIGHT
AGGHILSY SHAGGILY
AGGHINNS GNASHING,
  HANGINGS
AGGHISTT GASTIGHT
AGGIILNN ALIGNING
AGGIILNV GINGIVAL
AGGIINNR GRAINING
AGGIJLNN JANGLING
AGGILMNN MANGLING
AGGILMNO GLOAMING
AGGILNNO GANGLION
AGGILNNS SLANGING
AGGILNNT TANGLING
AGGILNNW WANGLING
AGGILNOT GLOATING
AGGILNPU PLAGUING
AGGILNPY GAPINGLY
AGGILNRY GRAYLING
AGGILNSS GLASSING
AGGINNOR GROANING
AGGINNOT TANGOING
AGGINNRT GRANTING

AGGINNTW TWANGING	AGHMMOOY	AGIKNNSW SWANKING
AGGINOVY VOYAGING	HOMOGAMY	AGIKNOST GOATSKIN
AGGINPRS GRASPING	AGHMNPSU SPHAGNUM	AGIKNPRS SPARKING
AGGINRSS GRASSING	AGHMOPRY MYOGRAPH	AGILLMNY MALIGNLY
AGGINRST GRATINGS	AGHNNSTU SHANTUNG	AGILLMSU GAULLISM
AGGINRSU SUGARING	AGHNOSTU HANGOUTS	AGILLNOW ALLOWING
AGGINRTY GYRATING	AGHNTTUU UNTAUGHT	AGILLNOY ALLOYING
AGGINRUU AUGURING	AGHORSTW WARTHOGS	AGILLNRU ALLURING
AGGINSST STAGINGS	AGIIIKMR KIRIGAMI	AGILLNRY RALLYING
AGGLLOOY ALGOLOGY	AGIIILNS LIAISING	AGILLNST STALLING
AGGLMOOR LOGOGRAM	AGIIINNS INSIGNIA	AGILLNSY SALLYING,
AGGLOORY AGROLOGY	AGIIINRV VIRGINIA	SIGNALLY, SLANGILY
AGGLRSTY STRAGGLY	AGIILMNP IMPALING	AGILLNTY TALLYING
AGGNUWZZ ZUGZWANG	AGIILNNO LIAONING	AGILLOPT GALLIPOT
AGHHIILT HIGHTAIL	AGIILNNU INGUINAL	AGILLORS GORILLAS
AGHHIMSS HIGH MASS	AGIILNOR ORIGINAL	AGILLPUY PLAGUILY
AGHHINOP HAIPHONG	AGIILNOT INTAGLIO,	AGILLSSU LUGSAILS
AGHHISWY HIGHWAYS	LIGATION	AGILLSTU GAULLIST
AGHHLOTU ALTHOUGH	AGIILNOX GLOXINIA	AGILMMNS SLAMMING
AGHIILNN INHALING	AGIILNPT PLAITING	AGILMNNT MANTLING
AGHIINST TSINGHAI	AGIILNQU QUAILING	AGILMNOO MONGOLIA
AGHIIPRR HAIRGRIP	AGIILNRS RAILINGS	AGILMNPS SAMPLING
AGHIIRTT AIRTIGHT	AGIILNRT TRAILING	AGILMORS ALGORISM
AGHIJNRT NIGHTJAR	AGIILNRU LIGURIAN	AGILNNNP PLANNING
AGHIKLRU GURKHALI	AGIILNRV RIVALING,	AGILNNOP PANGOLIN
AGHIKNNT THANKING	VIRGINAL	AGILNNPT PLANTING
AGHILLRT ALL RIGHT	AGIILNSS SAILINGS	AGILNNRS SNARLING
AGHILMTY ALMIGHTY	AGIILNST TAILINGS	AGILNNST SLANTING
AGHILNOO HOOLIGAN	AGIILNTT LITIGANT	AGILNNUY UNGAINLY
AGHILNOT LOATHING	AGIILNTV VIGILANT	AGILNOOO OOGONIAL
AGHILNRS RINGHALS	AGIILORU OLIGURIA	AGILNOPR PAROLING
AGHILNSS HASSLING,	AGIILPST PIGTAILS	AGILNORT TRIGONAL
LASHINGS, SLASHING	AGIIMNOW MIAOWING	AGILNOSS LASSOING
AGHILNSU LANGUISH	AGIINNPT PAINTING	AGILNOTT TOTALING
AGHILOST GOLIATHS	AGIINNRT TRAINING	AGILNOTU LIAOTUNG
AGHILRSY GARISHLY	AGIINNST STAINING	AGILNOTW WAGON-LIT
AGHIMMNS SHAMMING	AGIINNTT TAINTING	AGILNPPS SLAPPING
AGHIMNSS SMASHING	AGIINORT RIGATONI	AGILNPPY APPLYING
AGHINNOT GNATHION	AGIINPRS ASPIRING,	AGILNPRS SPARLING
AGHINNTU HAUNTING	PRAISING	AGILNPSS SAPLINGS
AGHINNTY ANYTHING	AGIINPRT PIRATING	AGILNPST STAPLING
AGHINPRS HARPINGS,	AGIINRRV ARRIVING	AGILNPSW LAPWINGS
PHRASING	AGIINRTT ATTIRING	AGILNPSY SPLAYING
AGHINQSU QUASHING	AGIINRUU UIGURIAN	AGILNRST STARLING
AGHINRRY HARRYING	AGIINSTU IGNATIUS	AGILNRSU SINGULAR
AGHINRST TRASHING	AGIJLNPY JAPINGLY	AGILNRTT RATTLING
AGHINSST HASTINGS,	AGIJMNOR MAJORING	AGILNRTW TRAWLING
STASHING	AGIJNNTU JAUNTING	AGILNSTU SALUTING
AGHINSSV SHAVINGS	AGIKLMOR KILOGRAM	AGILNTTT TATTLING
AGHINSTW SWATHING	AGIKLNNP PLANKING	AGILNTTT TATTLING
AGHIPRRT TRIGRAPH	AGIKLNNR - RANKLING	AGILNTUV VAULTING
AGHIRSTT STRAIGHT	AGIKLNST STALKING	AGILNTWZ WALTZING
AGHLLNOU LONG-HAUL	AGIKMNRS MARKINGS	AGILNTXY TAXINGLY
AGHLMOOR HOLOGRAM	AGIKNNPS SPANKING	AGILOOPY APIOLOGY
		AGILOOXY AXIOLOGY

AGILSYYZ SYZYGIAL
AGIMMOSY MISOGAMY
AGIMNNRU MANURING
AGIMNORS ORGANISM
AGIMNORY AGRIMONY
AGIMNPPS MAPPINGS
AGIMNPRT TRAMPING
AGIMNPST STAMPING
AGIMNPSW SWAMPING
AGIMNRRY MARRYING
AGIMNRST MIGRANTS,
  SMARTING
AGIMNRSW SWARMING
AGIMNRTU MATURING
AGIMNSSU ASSUMING
AGIMORRT MIGRATOR
AGINNNOY ANNOYING
AGINNNPS SPANNING
AGINNNSW SWANNING
AGINNOPT POIGNANT
AGINNORT IGNORANT
AGINNPPS SNAPPING
AGINNPSW SPAWNING,
  WINGSPAN
AGINNRSW WARNINGS
AGINNTTU ATTUNING,
  TAUNTING
AGINNTUV VAUNTING
AGINOORT ROGATION
AGINORRS GARRISON
AGINORRW ARROWING
AGINORSS ASSIGNOR,
  SIGNORAS
AGINORST ORGANIST, .
  ROASTING
AGINORSU AROUSING
AGINORSV SAVORING
AGINORTT ROTATING
AGINORTV GRAVITON
AGINORTY GYRATION
AGINOSTT TANGOIST,
  TOASTING, TSINGTAO
AGINPPRT TRAPPING
AGINPPRW WRAPPING
AGINPPSW SWAPPING
AGINPRRS SPARRING
AGINPRRY PARRYING
AGINPRSS RASPINGS
AGINPRST GIN TRAPS,
  PARTINGS
AGINPRSY SPRAYING
AGINPRTY PARTYING
AGINPSST PASTINGS
AGINQRSU SQUARING

AGINRRST STARRING
AGINRRTY TARRYING
AGINRSST STAR SIGN
AGINRSSU ASSURING
AGINRSTT STARTING
AGINRSTV STARVING
AGINRSTY STINGRAY,
  STRAYING
AGINSTTW SWATTING
AGINSTUU AUGUSTIN
AGIOORTU AUTOGIRO
AGIOPPRT AGITPROP
AGIRTTUY GRATUITY
AGJLRSUU JUGULARS
AGKLOORV GORLOVKA
AGKORSSW GASWORKS
AGLLRUVY VULGARLY
AGLMOPYY POLYGAMY
AGLNOOSW OWN GOALS
AGLNOSWY LONGWAYS
AGLNSSSU SUNGLASS
AGLOOPST GOALPOST
AGLOPRTU PORTUGAL
AGLORSSY GLOSSARY
AGLOSUVY YUGOSLAV
AGLPSSSY SPYGLASS
AGLRTTUU GUTTURAL
AGLSTUUY AUGUSTLY
AGMMNOOR
  MONOGRAM
AGMMNOOY
  MONOGAMY
AGMMORSY MYOGRAMS
AGMNOORY AGRONOMY
AGMNORST ANGSTROM
AGMNSSTU MUSTANGS
AGMNSSTY GYMNASTS
AGMOOOSU OOGAMOUS
AGMOOTVY VAGOTOMY
AGMOPRRS PROGRAMS
AGNNOSSW SWANSONG
AGNOPRST PART-SONG
AGNORTUY NUGATORY
AGNPRSUY SPRAY GUN
AGOORRTY ROGATORY
AGOPPSST STOPGAPS
AGORRTYY GYRATORY
AGSSTUUU AUGUSTUS
AGSSTUUV GUSTAVUS
AHHILPSW WHIPLASH
AHHIMMSS MISHMASH
AHHIPRSS SHARPISH
AHHLNOPT NAPHTHOL
AHHLNPTY NAPHTHYL

AHHMPRRU HARRUMPH
AHHNORTW HAWTHORN
AHIIKMRS KASHMIRI
AHIILLPP PHILLIPA
AHIILPPP PHILIPPA
AHIILRTY HILARITY
AHIIMNOT HIMATION
AHIIMNRS IRISHMAN
AHIIMNST ISTHMIAN
AHIINPRS HAIRPINS
AHIIPRSS AIRSHIPS
AHIKLRSY RAKISHLY
AHIKNPRS PRANKISH
AHIKOSUZ SHIZUOKA
AHILLMSS SMALLISH
AHILLMTU THALLIUM
AHILLNST ANTHILLS
AHILLSVY LAVISHLY
AHILMNOT HAMILTON
AHILMOST MAILSHOT
AHILMQSU QUALMISH
AHILNOPS SIPHONAL
AHILNORT HORNTAIL
AHILOORT LOTHARIO
AHILOPSS ALPHOSIS,
  HAPLOSIS
AHILOPST HOSPITAL
AHILRSTY TRASHILY
AHIMMNSU HUMANISM
AHIMNOST THOMASIN
AHIMNOSW WOMANISH
AHIMNSTU HUMANIST
AHIMNTUY HUMANITY
AHIMOOSY YAHOOISM
AHIMOPRS APHORISM
AHIMORRW HAIRWORM
AHIMSSTU TSUSHIMA
AHIMSTUZ AZIMUTHS
AHINNNOR RHIANNON
AHINNOPT ANTIPHON
AHINORRS HARRISON
AHINOSST ASTONISH
AHINPPSS SNAPPISH
AHINQSUV VANQUISH
AHIOOPPT PHOTOPIA
AHIOPRST APHORIST
AHIOPRSV VAPORISH
AHIPRSST HARPISTS
AHIPRSSW WARSHIPS
AHIQRSSU SQUARISH
AHISSTTW WHATSITS
AHKLLOOY HOLLY
  OAK
AHKLOPRU KOLHAPUR

AHKLOPST SHOPTALK,
  TALK SHOP
AHKLOSTW TALK SHOW
AHKMORTU KHARTOUM
AHKNOTUY THANKYOU
AHLLNOOS SHALLOON
AHLLNOTW TOWN HALL
AHLLOSST SHALLOTS
AHLLOSSW SHALLOWS
AHLLOSTU THALLOUS
AHLMMOPY LYMPHOMA
AHLMNOOR HORMONAL
AHLMOOPS OMPHALOS
AHLMOPTY POLYMATH
AHLNOOPS ALPHONSO
AHLOPRSU SHOLAPUR
AHLORRTY HARLOTRY
AHMMMOST
  MAMMOTHS
AHMNNSTU HUNTSMAN,
  MANHUNTS
AHMNOPST PHANTOMS
AHMNORSU MANHOURS
AHMOOPPT PHOTOMAP
AHMOOPSS SHAMPOOS
AHMOORSW WASHROOM
AHMPSSSU SMASH-UPS
AHMPSTYY SYMPATHY
AHMQSSUU MUSQUASH
AHNOOPRS HARPOONS
AHNOORRY HONORARY
AHNOPPSW PAWNSHOP
AHNOPPSY PANSOPHY
AHNOPSST SNAPSHOT
AHNOSTTW WHATNOTS
AHNOSTUX XANTHOUS
AHNRSTTU THURSTAN
AHOOSSTY SOOTHSAY
AHOOSTTW SAWTOOTH
AHOPSTTW TOWPATHS
AHOPSTUW SOUTHPAW
AHORTTUW WATT-HOUR
AHOSSTUW WASHOUTS
AHRSTUWY THRUWAYS
AIIILMST MILITIAS
AIIILNST INITIALS
AIIKLNOR IRAKLION
AIIKMNNS MANIKINS
AIIKNNNP PANNIKIN
AIIKNRST KRISTINA
AIIILMRY MILLIARY
AIIILLNNV VANILLIN
AIIILLNSV VILLAINS
AIIILLNVY VILLAINY

AIIILLWWW WILLIWAW
AIIILMNPS ALPINISM
AIIILMNPT PALMITIN
AIIILMNST LATINISM
AIIILMNTT MILITANT
AIIILMRST MISTRIAL
AIIILMRTY LIMITARY,
  MILITARY
AIIILMSTV VITALISM
AIIILNNOV LIVONIAN
AIIILNOPT OIL PAINT
AIIILNOPV PAVILION
AIIILNOSS LIAISONS
AIIILNOSV VISIONAL
AIIILNPST ALPINIST,
  TAILSPIN
AIIILNRSU SILURIAN
AIIILNSTT LATINIST
AIIILNSTY SALINITY
AIIILNTTY LATINITY
AIIILSTTV VITALIST
AIIILTTVY VITALITY
AIIMNNOS INSOMNIA
AIIMNPSS SINAPISM
AIIMNRST MARTINIS
AIIMNSST ANIMISTS
AIIMNSTT TITANISM
AIIMNSTU UNIATISM
AIIMNSTV NATIVISM,
  VITAMINS
AIIMNTTU TITANIUM
AIIMOPSX APOMIXIS
AIIMORTT IMITATOR
AIIMOSST AMITOSIS
AIIMPPRS PRIAPISM
AIIMPRTY IMPARITY
AIIMRUVV VIVARIUM
AIIMSSTT MASTITIS
AIINNOSV INVASION
AIINNOTV NIVATION
AIINNSTU TUNISIAN
AIINNSTV VINNITSA
AIINNSTY INSANITY
AIINPRSS ASPIRINS
AIINPSST PIANISTS
AIINRRTT IRRITANT
AIINSTTV NATIVIST,
  VISITANT
AIINTTVY NATIVITY
AIIORSTV OVARITIS
AIIORTTV VITIATOR
AIIPRRST AIRSTRIP
AIIRSSTT SATIRIST,
  SITARIST

AIJKKNOU KINKAJOU
AIJKLMNU JUNK MAIL
AIJLLOVY JOVIALLY
AIJLNTUY JAUNTILY
AIJMORTY MAJORITY
AIJNOPPY POPINJAY
AIJNORST JANITORS
AIKLLSTY STALKILY
AIKLMWYY MILKY WAY
AIKLNSWY SWANKILY
AIKLOTTW KILOWATT
AIKMRSTZ SITZMARK
AIKNNOOS NAINSOOK
AIKNNSSW SWANSKIN
AIKNRSST SANSKRIT
AILLLNOO LINALOOL
AILLLOST SALTILLO
AILLLPSU LAPILLUS
AILLMOSS LIMASSOL
AILLMOSY LOYALISM
AILLMOTY MOLALITY
AILLMRTY MYRTILLA
AILLMRUY ARUM LILY
AILLMSSW SAWMILLS
AILLMUUV ALLUVIUM
AILLNOPP PAPILLON
AILLNOST STALLION
AILLNOSU ALLUSION
AILLNPTY PLIANTLY
AILLORSY SAILORLY
AILLORTT LITTORAL,
  TORTILLA
AILLOSTY LOYALIST
AILLPRTY PALTRILY
AILLPSWY SPILLWAY
AILLRTUY RITUALLY
AILLSUVY VISUALLY
AILMMNOO MONOMIAL
AILMMORS MORALISM
AILMMORT IMMORTAL
AILMMSTU SUMMITAL
AILMNNOT MANNITOL
AILMNOOP PALOMINO
AILMNOOR MONORAIL
AILMNOPY OLYMPIAN
AILMNPST IMPLANTS
AILMNPTU PLATINUM
AILMNRUY LUMINARY
AILMNSTU SIMULANT
AILMOPRX PROXIMAL
AILMORST MORALIST
AILMORSU SOLARIUM
AILMORSY ROYALISM
AILMORTY MORALITY

AILMOSTV VOLTAISM
AILMPPSY MISAPPLY
AILMPRSU PRIMULAS
AILMPSST PALMISTS,
PSALMIST
AILMPSTY PTYALISM
AILMRRSU RURALISM
AILMRSTU ALTRUISM,
MURALIST, ULTRAISM
AILNNOOT NOTIONAL
AILNNOSW SON-IN-LAW
AILNNOSY LYONNAIS
AILNNOTU LUNATION
AILNNSTU INSULANT
AILNOOPT OPTIONAL
AILNOPRU UNIPOLAR
AILNOPTY PONYTAIL
AILNOSUV AVULSION
AILNOSVY SYNOVIAL
AILNOTTY TONALITY
AILNOTUX LUXATION
AILNPPSY SNAPPILY
AILNPSTU NUPTIALS
AILNPSUU NAUPLIUS
AILNQRTU TRANQUIL
AILNQTUY QUAINTLY
AILNRRTU TRIAL RUN
AILNSSUV SILVANUS
AILNSTTU LUTANIST
AILNSTUU NAUTILUS
AILNSYZZ SNAZZILY
AILOORST ISOLATOR,
OSTIOLAR
AILOORTV VIOLATOR
AILOPRTU TROUPIAL
AILOPRTY POLARITY
AILOPRUY POLYURIA
AILORSTY ROYALIST,
SOLITARY
AILORTTU TUTORIAL
AILORTUV OUTRIVAL
AILOSSUY ALOYSIUS
AILOTTTY TOTALITY
AILPPSSY PAYSLIPS
AILPRSTU STIPULAR
AILPSSWY SLIPWAYS
AILPSTUY PLAYSUIT
AILRRSTU RURALIST
AILRRSTY STARRILY
AILRRTUY RURALITY
AILRSTTU ALTRUIST,
ULTRAIST
AILRSUVV SURVIVAL
AILSSTUW LAWSUITS

AIMMMNOU
AMMONIUM
AIMMMSUX MAXIMUMS
AIMMMNORT MORTMAIN
AIMNNOSS MANSIONS
AIMNNOTU MOUNTAIN
AIMNNOTY ANTIMONY,
ANTINOMY
AIMNNRTU RUMINANT
AIMNOORV MONROVIA
AIMNOOTY MYOTONIA
AIMNOQRU MAROQUIN
AIMNORTU MINOTAUR
AIMNORTY MINATORY
AIMNOTTU MUTATION
AIMNRRSU MURRAINS
AIMNRSTT TRANSMIT
AIMNRSTU NATURISM
AIMNRSTV VARMINTS
AIMOPRSS PROSAISM
AIMOPSSY SYMPOSIA
AIMORRUV VARIORUM
AIMORSTY RAMOSITY
AIMPPRUU PUPARIUM
AIMRRSTT TRISTRAM
AIMRSSTX MARXISTS
AIMRTTUY MATURITY
AINNNOST SANTONIN
AINNOOTT NOTATION
AINNOOTV NOVATION
AINNOOTZ ZONATION
AINNOTTU NUTATION
AINNRSTU NURISTAN
AINNSSTT INSTANTS
AINNSTTY NYSTATIN
AINOOPTT POTATION
AINOORST ORATIONS
AINOORTT ROTATION
AINOOSTT OSTINATO
AINOOSTV OVATIONS
AINOPPTU PUPATION
AINOPSSS PASSIONS
AINORSST ARSONIST
AINOSSTT STATIONS
AINOSTTU TITANOUS
AINPPRSS PARSNIPS
AINPRSSU PRUSSIAN
AINPRSTU PURITANS
AINPSSSY SYNAPSIS
AINPSSTU PUISSANT
AINQTTUY QUANTITY
AINRSSTT TRANSITS
AINRSTTU NATURIST
AIOOORRT ORATORIO

AIOPRRST AIRPORTS
AIOPRRTT PORTRAIT
AIOPRSST PROTASIS
AIOPRSTT PATRIOTS
AIORRRSW WARRIORS
AIORRSTT TRAITORS
AIORRSTV VARISTOR
AIORSSUV SAVIOURS
AIORSTTV VOTARIST
AIOSSSTY ISOSTASY
AIPPRSTT TRAPPIST
AIPPRSTY PAPISTRY
AIPRSSTU UPSTAIRS
AIRRSTTY ARTISTRY
AJLNORSU JOURNALS
AJORRTUY JURATORY
AKKLRSSY SKYLARKS
AKKORSTW TASKWORK
AKLLNOSW KNOW-ALLS
AKLNNOPT PLANKTON
AKLOSTUW WALKOUTS
AKLPRRSU LARKSPUR
AKMMNRSU MURMANSK
AKMMOOTU
KUMAMOTO
AKMNORTU TURKOMAN
AKMOORST KOSTROMA
AKMOPRST POSTMARK
AKMQSTUU KUMQUATS
AKOPRRTW PART WORK
AKORSWWX WAXWORKS
ALLLPRUY LYALLPUR
ALLMNORY NORMALLY
ALLMNPSU PULLMANS
ALLMOPSX SMALLPOX
ALLMORTY MORTALLY
ALLMTUUY MUTUALLY
ALLNOOPS PLANOSOL
ALLOPRSY PAYROLLS
ALLOSSWW SWALLOWS
ALMMNRUU NUMMULAR
ALMNOOPS LAMPOONS
ALMNORTY MATRONLY
ALMNPSSU SUNLAMPS
ALMOOPRY PLAYROOM
ALMOORTU ALUMROOT
ALMOPPST LAMPPOST
ALMOSTTU MULATTOS,
SUM TOTAL
ALNNOTWY WANTONLY
ALNOOPST PLATOONS
ALNOOPYZ POLYZOAN
ALNOPPTT POT PLANT
ALNOPRST PLASTRON

ALNORRWY NARROWLY
ALNPPSTU SUPPLANT
ALNPRSSU SNARL-UPS
ALNSSUVY SYLVANUS
ALOOPPRS PROPOSAL
ALOOPRSW POOR LAWS
ALOORSUV VALOROUS
ALOORTYZ ZOOLATRY
ALOPPRYY POLYPARY
ALOPPTUY PLAY UP TO
ALOPRRSU PARLOURS
ALOPRSTU POSTURAL,
   PULSATOR
ALOPSSTT LAST POST
ALOPSTUU PATULOUS
ALORSTTW SALTWORT
ALORTUWY OUTLAWRY
ALOSTTUZ ZLATOUST
ALPPSTUY PLATYPUS
ALPRSTUU PUSTULAR
AMMNOORT
   MOTORMAN
AMMNPTUY TYMPANUM
AMNNOSTW TOWNSMAN
AMNNOSTY ANTONYMS
AMNNSTTU STUNT MAN
AMNOOSTT OTTOMANS
AMNOOTUY AUTONOMY
AMNOOTXY TAXONOMY
AMNORSST TRANSOMS
AMNOTTUY TAUTONYM
AMNRSTTU TANTRUMS
AMOORRTY MORATORY
AMOORTWY MOTORWAY
AMOOTTUY AUTOTOMY
AMOPRSXY PAROXYSM
AMOQSSUU SQUAMOUS
AMORRTUY MORTUARY
AMORSTTU OUTSMART
ANNOORST SONORANT
ANNOSSTU STANNOUS
ANOOPRRT PRONATOR
ANOOPRSS SOPRANOS
ANOPRRSS SPORRANS
ANOPRTTU TRAPUNTO
ANORSUVY UNSAVORY
ANPRSSTU SUNTRAPS
ANPRSTUU PURSUANT
AOOOPRTZ PROTOZOA
AOOPPRSY APOSPORY
AOOPRSTT TAPROOTS
AOOPRSTW SOAPWORT
AOOPRSUV VAPOROUS
AOORRTTY ROTATORY

AOORSSUV SAVOROUS
AOPPRSST PASSPORT
AOPRRSSW SPARROWS
AOPRSTTY PYROSTAT
AOPTTUYY AUTOTYPY
AORRSTTW STARWORT
APRSSTTU UPSTARTS
BBBCEOWY COBWEBBY
BBBEILRU BUBBLIER
BBBEINOT BOBBINET
BBBGILNU BUBBLING
BBBINOPY BOBBY PIN
BBCDERSU SCRUBBED
BBCDIMOY BOMBYCID
BBCEHIRU CHUBBIER
BBCEILRS SCRIBBLE
BBCELORS COBBLERS
BBCERRSU SCRUBBER
BBCGIINR CRIBBING
BBCGILNO COBBLING
BBCGILNU CLUBBING
BBCHKSUU BUSHBUCK
BBCKLOOU BOOK CLUB
BBDDEEMO DEMOBBED
BBDDEILR DRIBBLED
BBDDEIRY BY-BIDDER
BBDEEGIR GIBBERED
BBDEEIST EBB TIDES
BBDEEMNU BENUMBED
BBDEHORT THROBBED
BBDEILLR BELLBIRD
BBDEILQU QUIBBLED
BBDEILRR DRIBBLER
BBDEILRS DRIBBLES
BBDEILRU BLUEBIRD
BBDEIMOV DIVE-BOMB
BBDELLMU DUMBBELL
BBDELSTU STUBBLED
BBDGIILN DIBBLING
BBDGINRU DRUBBING
BBDLOOWY BODY BLOW
BBDOSUYY BUSYBODY
BBEEHTYY BY THE BYE
BBEEIIRR BERIBERI
BBEEILPR PLEBBIER
BBEELLLU BLUEBELL
BBEFILRR FRIBBLER
BBEGIIST GIBBSITE
BBEGILNP PEBBLING
BBEGILST GLIBBEST
BBEGIRRU GRUBBIER
BBEHIOTW BOBWHITE
BBEILORW WOBBLIER
BBEILQRU QUIBBLER

BBEILQSU QUIBBLES
BBEILRRY BILBERRY
BBEIMMOT TIME BOMB
BBEIMOST BOMBSITE
BBEIRSTU STUBBIER
BBEISTTU TUBBIEST
BBEKLOOU BLUE BOOK
BBEKNOOT BONTEBOK
BBELLOSY BELLBOYS
BBELORSY SLOBBERY
BBENORSY SNOBBERY
BBEORRXY BOXBERRY
BBERRRUY BURBERRY
BBGGILNO GOBBLING
BBGGINRU GRUBBING
BBGHILNO HOBBLING
BBGIIIMN IMBIBING
BBGIILNN NIBBLING
BBGILMNU BUMBLING
BBGILNNO NOBBLING
BBGILNOW WOBBLING
BBGILNOY LOBBYING
BBGILNRU BURBLING
BBGILRUY GRUBBILY
BBGINNSU SNUBBING
BBGINRSU RUBBINGS
BBGINSTU STUBBING
BBHINOSS SNOBBISH
BBHIOSTY HOBBYIST
BBHIRSUY RUBBISHY
BBHRSSUU SUBSHRUB
BBIKLNOO BOBOLINK
BBILMOSY LOBBYISM
BBILOSTY LOBBYIST
BBILOSUU BIBULOUS
BBILSTUY STUBBILY
BBLLOUYY BULLYBOY
BBNORSTU STUBBORN
BCCCIILY BICYCLIC
BCCDEILY BICYCLED
BCCEEIRR CEREBRIC
BCCEHIRU CHERUBIC
BCCEIILO LIBECCIO
BCCEILOY BIOCYCLE
BCCEILRU CRUCIBLE
BCCEILSU CUBICLES
BCCEILSY BICYCLES
BCCEMRUU CUCUMBER
BCCIISTU CUBISTIC
BCCILMOU COLUMBIC
BCCILOOR BROCCOLI
BCCIRTUU CUCURBIT
BCCMOOSX COXCOMBS
BCCNOORS CORNCOBS

BCCSSUUU SUCCUBUS
BCDDEEEK BEDECKED
BCDEEEMR DECEMBER
BCDEEENR DEBRECEN
BCDEEHLN BLENCHED
BCDEEIKN BENEDICK
BCDEEIKR BICKERED
BCDEEILR CREDIBLE
BCDEEILS DECIBELS
BCDEEILU EDUCIBLE
BCDEEINT BENEDICT
BCDEEIRS DESCRIBE
BCDEEIST BISECTED
BCDEEJOT OBJECTED
BCDEEKNO BECKONED
BCDEEKRU REEDBUCK
BCDEEKTU BUCKETED
BCDEEMRU CUMBERED
BCDEIIRR RICEBIRD
BCDEIKRR REDBRICK
BCDEIKSS SICKBEDS
BCDEILRY CREDIBLY
BCDEIMNO COMBINED
BCDEINOU ICEBOUND
BCDELMRU CRUMBLED
BCDEORSU OBSCURED
BCDIIPSU BICUSPID
BCDILMOY MOLYBDIC
BCDILORU COLUBRID
BCDINRUU RUBICUND
BCEEEFIN BENEFICE
BCEEEHRS BREECHES
BCEEEINR BERENICE
BCEEERSU BERCEUSE
BCEEFLTU CLUBFEET
BCEEGIRS ICEBERGS
BCEEHHNT THE BENCH
BCEEHHSU BUCHSHEE
BCEEHKSU BUCKSHEE
BCEEHLNR BLENCHER
BCEEHNTU BEECHNUT
BCEEIILM IMBECILE
BCEEIKRR BICKERER
BCEEIOSX ICEBOXES
BCEEKNOR BECKONER
BCEELRTU TUBERCLE
BCEEMNRU ENCUMBER
BCEEMRRU CEREBRUM
BCEERTVY BREVETCY
BCEFFIIR FEBRIFIC
BCEFILOR FORCIBLE
BCEGHILN BELCHING
BCEGIMNO BECOMING
BCEHHIRT THE BIRCH

BCEHIIRT BITCHIER
BCEHILPU BLUE CHIP
BCEHIMOT CHIMBOTE
BCEHIMRS BESMIRCH
BCEHIORS BRIOCHES
BCEHIORT BOTCHIER
BCEHIRST BRITCHES
BCEHLOST BLOTCHES
BCEHNRSU BRUNCHES
BCEHOORS BROOCHES
BCEHORRU BROCHURE
BCEHORST BOTCHERS
BCEHRSTU BUTCHERS
BCEHRTTU CUTHBERT
BCEHRTUY BUTCHERY
BCEIIKLN ICEBLINK
BCEIILMS MISCIBLE
BCEIILOP EPIBOLIC
BCEIINRS INSCRIBE
BCEILMRS CLIMBERS
BCEILPRU REPUBLIC
BCEIMNOR COMBINER
BCEIMNOS COMBINES
BCEIMORS MICROBES
BCEINORU BOUNCIER
BCEINOVX BICONVEX
BCEIOOPS BIOSCOPE
BCEIOOVX VOICE BOX
BCEIORST BISECTOR
BCEJNOOT NO
   OBJECT
BCEJOORT OBJECTOR
BCEJSSTU SUBJECTS
BCEKLLNU BULLNECK
BCEKLNUU UNBUCKLE
BCEKLRSU BUCKLERS
BCEKORSU ROEBUCKS
BCELLOSW COWBELLS
BCELMRSU CRUMBLES
BCENORSU BOUNCERS
BCEOORST OCTOBERS
BCEOORTU CUBE ROOT
BCEORRWY COWBERRY
BCFGLLOU GOLF CLUB
BCFIIMOR MORBIFIC
BCFIIORT FIBROTIC
BCFILORY FORCIBLY
BCFIMORU CUBIFORM
BCFLOOTU CLUBFOOT
BCGHIINR BIRCHING
BCGHIINT BITCHING
BCGHINNU BUNCHING
BCGHINOT BOTCHING
BCGIIKST BIG STICK

BCGIILMN CLIMBING
BCGIKLNO BLOCKING
BCGIKLNU BUCKLING
BCGINNOU BOUNCING
BCHIILTY BITCHILY
BCHIISSU HIBISCUS
BCHILOTY BOTCHILY
BCHIOORY CHOIRBOY
BCHKNORU BUCKHORN
BCHKOSTU BUCKSHOT
BCHNOORS BRONCHOS
BCHNORSU BRONCHUS
BCHOPSTU BOTCH-UPS
BCIIIOTT BIOTITIC
BCIILOTY BIOLYTIC
BCIIMNOO BIONOMIC
BCIIMORU CIBORIUM
BCIINORV VIBRONIC
BCIIOPTY BIOTYPIC
BCIISSTU BISCUITS,
   CUBISIST
BCIKKNSU BUCKSKIN
BCIKOSTT BITSTOCK
BCILLPUY PUBLICLY
BCILMOSY SYMBOLIC
BCILNOUY BOUNCILY
BCILOORU BICOLOUR
BCINORSU RUBICONS
BCINOSSU SUBSONIC
BCINOSTU SUBTONIC
BCIOOPSY BIOSCOPY
BCIOORST ROBOTICS
BCKKOOOO COOKBOOK
BCKLLOOS BOLLOCKS
BCKLLOSU BULLOCKS
BCKOOOPY COPYBOOK
BCKOSTTU BUTTOCKS
BCLMOSUU COLUMBUS
BCOOORTW CROWBOOT
BCOORSSW CROSSBOW
BCOOSTTY BOYCOTTS
BCOOSTUY BOY SCOUT
BCORSTTU OBSTRUCT
BDDDEEEM EMBEDDED
BDDDEEIM IMBEDDED
BDDEEESS SEEDBEDS
BDDEEGGU DEBUGGED
BDDEEGTU BUDGETED
BDDEEIMM BEDIMMED
BDDEEIMO EMBODIED
BDDEEINT INDEBTED
BDDEEINW BINDWEED
BDDEEIRS BIRDSEED
BDDEEISS BEDSIDES

BDDEEKNU DEBUNKED
BDDEENRU BURDENED
BDDEEORR BORDERED
BDDEINNU UNBIDDEN
BDDEINOU UNBODIED
BDDEINRU UNDERBID
BDDEIORS DISROBED
BDDEISSU SUBSIDED
BDDELOOR BLOOD RED
BDDEORTU OBTRUDED
BDDEOTYY TEDDY BOY
BDDGIORS BIRD DOGS
BDDGOOSY DOGSBODY
BDDHIIRY DIHYBRID
BDDHIMSU BUDDHISM
BDDHISTU BUDDHIST
BDEEEGIS BESIEGED
BDEEEHTU HEBETUDE
BDEEEILV BELIEVED
BDEEELLR REBELLED
BDEEELLV BEVELLED
BDEEELRS BLEEDERS
BDEEERTT BETTERED
BDEEFFRU BUFFERED,
   REBUFFED
BDEEFFTU BUFFETED
BDEEFINR BEFRIEND
BDEEFITT BEFITTED
BDEEFOOR FOREBODE
BDEEFOOW BEEFWOOD
BDEEGGIW BEWIGGED
BDEEGGRU BEGRUDGE,
   BUGGERED
BDEEGILN BLEEDING
BDEEGILU BEGUILED
BDEEGINR BREEDING
BDEEGLNO BELONGED
BDEEHIRS HEBRIDES
BDEEHLNO BEHOLDEN
BDEEHLOR BEHOLDER
BDEEHMOR HOMEBRED
BDEEHORT BOTHERED
BDEEIILL ELIDIBLE
BDEEIILN INEDIBLE
BDEEILLL LIBELLED
BDEEILLT BILLETED
BDEEILNN BED LINEN
BDEEILNO BONE-IDLE
BDEEILNR RENDIBLE
BDEEILNV VENDIBLE
BDEEILRW BEWILDER
BDEEIMST BEDTIMES
BDEEINOT OBEDIENT
BDEEIRRV RIVERBED

BDEEIRST BESTRIDE
BDEEIRSY BIRD'S-EYE
BDEEKNRU DEBUNKER
BDEELLOW BELLOWED
BDEELLRW WELL-BRED
BDEELMNO EMBOLDEN
BDEELMRT TREMBLED
BDEELMRU LUMBERED
BDEELNNO ENNOBLED
BDEELNRS BLENDERS
BDEELORU REDOUBLE
BDEELOSV BELOVEDS
BDEEMNOT ENTOMBED
BDEEMNRU NUMBERED
BDEEMOSS EMBOSSED
BDEENPRS PREBENDS
BDEEORRR BORDERER
BDEEORSS BEDSORES
BDEEORST BESTRODE
BDEEORSV OBSERVED
BDEEORTU OUTBREED
BDEEOSSS OBSESSED
BDEEOSSY BOSS-EYED
BDEEOSTT BESOTTED
BDEEOSTW BESTOWED
BDEEPRRU PUREBRED
BDEERRWY DEWBERRY
BDEERTTU BUTTERED,
   REBUTTED
BDEGHILT BLIGHTED
BDEGIINT BETIDING,
   DEBITING
BDEGILNN BLENDING
BDEGIORX OXBRIDGE
BDEGLMRU GRUMBLED
BDEGLNOU BLUDGEON
BDEGOOSY GOODBYES
BDEGORRY DOGBERRY
BDEHLORT BERTHOLD
BDEHLSUV BUSHVELD
BDEHMOOY HOMEBODY
BDEHOOOO BOOHOOED
BDEIIKLR BIRDLIKE
BDEIIKRT DIRT BIKE
BDEIILMR BIRDLIME
BDEIILNY INEDIBLY
BDEIILTY DEBILITY
BDEILLMU BDELLIUM
BDEILLOW BILLOWED
BDEILNRS BLINDERS
BDEILNRU UNBRIDLE
BDEILORV LOVEBIRD
BDEILOSS BODILESS
BDEILRRY LYREBIRD

BDEILRST BRISTLED,
   DRIBLETS
BDEILRSU BUILDERS
BDEIMORS BROMIDES
BDEIMORY EMBRYOID
BDEINOOS NOBODIES
BDEINOOW WOODBINE
BDEINORV OVENBIRD
BDEINOSU BEDOUINS
BDEINSTW TWIN BEDS
BDEIOORR BROODIER
BDEIORRS DISROBER
BDEIORSV OVERBIDS
BDEIOSUX SUBOXIDE
BDEIOSWY WIDE BOYS
BDEIRSSU DISBURSE,
   SUBSIDER
BDEKNOOS BOOKENDS
BDELLOOR BORDELLO,
   DOORBELL
BDELLOUZ BULLDOZE
BDELMSTU STUMBLED
BDELNNOW END-BLOWN
BDELNOOW NEW BLOOD
BDELNOSS BOLDNESS
BDELNOST BLONDEST
BDELNOTU UNBOLTED
BDELNRSU BLUNDERS
BDELORSU BOULDERS
BDELORTU TROUBLED
BDELORUU DOUBLURE
BDELOSTU DOUBLETS
BDEMNSSU DUMBNESS
BDEMOORS BEDROOMS
BDEMOOSY SOMEBODY
BDEMSSUU SUBSUMED
BDENNOTU DUBONNET
BDENNRUU UNBURDEN
BDENOOTW BENTWOOD
BDENORSU BOUNDERS,
   REBOUNDS, SUBORNED
BDENOTTU BUTTONED
BDENRUUY UNDERBUY
BDEOORRS BROODERS
BDEOORRW BORROWED
BDEOPSST BEDPOSTS
BDEORRSU SUBORDER
BDEORRTU OBTRUDER
BDEORRUW BURROWED
BDEORSTU DOUBTERS,
   REDOUBTS
BDFFIPRU PUFFBIRD
BDFGNOOU FOGBOUND
BDFIIITY BIFIDITY

BDFILLLO BILLFOLD
BDFILNOO BLOODFIN
BDFIRRSU SURFBIRD
BDFLOTUU DOUBTFUL
BDGGIINR BRIDGING
BDGIIKNR KINGBIRD
BDGIILNN BLINDING
BDGIILNU BUILDING
BDGIINNS BINDINGS
BDGILNNU BUNDLING
BDGILNOO BLOODING
BDGILNOU DOUBLING
BDGINNOU BOUNDING
BDGINOOR BROODING
BDGINORS SONGBIRD
BDGINOTU DOUBTING
BDGINSUU SUBDUING
BDGIRSUU DUISBURG
BDGKOOOO GOOD BOOK
BDGLLOSU BULLDOGS
BDGNRUUY BURGUNDY
BDHIMOOR RHOMBOID
BDHLMOTU HUMBOLDT
BDHMOSUW DUMB
   SHOW
BDIIIORV VIBRIOID
BDIIJOTU DJIBOUTI
BDIIMRUU RUBIDIUM
BDILLOOY BLOODILY
BDILMORY MORBIDLY
BDILNPRU PURBLIND
BDILOORY BROODILY
BDILPSUU BUILDUPS
BDIMNORU MORIBUND
BDINNRUW WINDBURN
BDINORSW SNOWBIRD
BDINSSTU DUSTBINS
BDIOORSU BOUDOIRS
BDKNOOOR DOORKNOB
BDKOOORW WORDBOOK
BDKOORWY BODYWORK
BDKOOSTU STUDBOOK
BDLNOOOU DOUBLOON
BDLOSTUW DUSTBOWL
BDNOOPTU POTBOUND
BDNOOSUX SOUNDBOX
BDNOOTUU OUTBOUND
BDNORSUW RUBDOWNS
BDORUWZZ BUZZWORD
BEEEEFLN ENFEEBLE
BEEEENRT TEREBENE
BEEEENRZ EBENEZER
BEEEFIRS FREEBIES
BEEEFIST BEEFIEST

BEEEFLST FEEBLEST
BEEEGIRS BESIEGER
BEEEGNRR BERENGER
BEEEGRTT BEGETTER
BEEEHISV BEEHIVES
BEEEHNOY HONEYBEE
BEEEHNSS SHEBEENS
BEEEILLL LIBELLEE
BEEEILNS BEELINES
BEEEILRV BELIEVER
BEEEJLSZ JEZEBELS
BEEEKLRY BERKELEY
BEEELMNS ENSEMBLE
BEEELMRS RESEMBLE
BEEELMZZ EMBEZZLE
BEEELPRS BLEEPERS
BEEELRVY BEVERLEY
BEEEMMRR REMEMBER
BEEFFRTU BUFFETER
BEEFILLT LIFE BELT
BEEFILLX FLEXIBLE
BEEFILNU UNBELIEF
BEEFILRS BELFRIES
BEEFINST BENEFITS
BEEFIRSS FRISBEES
BEEFLORU BEFOULER
BEEFNORR FREEBORN
BEEFOORT FREEBOOT
BEEGHILW BIG WHEEL
BEEGHLTU THE BULGE
BEEGIILL ELIGIBLE
BEEGIILX EXIGIBLE
BEEGILNP BLEEPING
BEEGILNT BEETLING
BEEGILNV BEVELING
BEEGILRU BEGUILER
BEEGINNR BEGINNER
BEEGINSW BEESWING
BEEGLNOR GRENOBLE
BEEGMRSU SUBMERGE
BEEGNOTT BEGOTTEN
BEEHIKLR HERBLIKE
BEEHILMN BLENHEIM
BEEHIMOT BOEHMITE
BEEHLLNT HELL-BENT
BEEHLOOR BOREHOLE
BEEHLRSU BUSHELER
BEEHMORW HOME BREW
BEEHNRRT BRETHREN
BEEHRSST SHERBETS
BEEIILNZ ZIBELINE
BEEIJLSU JUBILEES
BEEIKLWY BIWEEKLY
BEEILLLR LIBELLER

BEEILLNO LOBELINE
BEEILLTT BELITTLE
BEEILMPR PERIBLEM
BEEILNNO BENNE OIL
BEEILNRY BERYLINE
BEEILNSS SENSIBLE
BEEILNST STILBENE,
   TENSIBLE
BEEILNSU NEBULISE
BEEILNUZ NEBULIZE
BEEILRRT TERRIBLE
BEEILRTU RUBELITE
BEEILRYZ BREEZILY
BEEIMRTT EMBITTER
BEEIRSSU SUBERISE
BEEIRSUZ SUBERIZE
BEEIRTVY EVERY BIT
BEEKNOPS BESPOKEN
BEELLORW BELLOWER
BEELLSUY BULL'S-EYE
BEELMNNO NOBLEMEN
BEELMRRT TREMBLER
BEELMRRU LUMBERER
BEELMRST TREMBLES
BEELNNOR ENNOBLER
BEELNOSS BONELESS
BEELNSSU BLUENESS
BEELOOST OBSOLETE
BEELRTUU TRUE-BLUE
BEELSSTU TUBELESS
BEEMNORV NOVEMBER
BEEMNRSU E NUMBERS
BEEMORRY RYE-BROME
BEEMORSS EMBOSSER
BEENORTV VERBOTEN
BEENRSTW BESTREWN
BEENRTTU BRUNETTE
BEEOORRT ROOT BEER
BEEOORRV OVERBORE
BEEOORTT BEETROOT
BEEORRSV OBSERVER
BEEORSSU SUBEROSE
BEEORSTU TUBEROSE
BEEORSTW BESTOWER
BEEORSWY EYEBROWS
BEEQSSTU BEQUESTS
BEERRTTU REBUTTER
BEERSSUV SUBSERVE
BEESTTTU TEST TUBE
BEFGIINR BRIEFING
BEFGILNU FUNGIBLE
BEFGIRRU FREIBURG
BEFGIRSU FIREBUGS
BEFHILSU BLUEFISH

BEFHINOS BONEFISH
BEFILLMU BLUE FILM
BEFILLXY FLEXIBLY
BEFILMOR FORELIMB
BEFILOUY LIFE BUOY
BEFINORS BONFIRES
BEFLLLUY BELLYFUL
BEFLORUW FURBELOW
BEFNOORR FORBORNE
BEGGIINN BEGINING
BEGGINOR INGEBORG
BEGGIOST BOGGIEST
BEGGOORT GOTEBORG
BEGHILRT BLIGHTER
BEGHINOR NEIGHBOR
BEGHINRT BERTHING,
BRIGHTEN
BEGHLNOU BUNGHOLE
BEGHOSTU BESOUGHT
BEGHRRSU BURGHERS
BEGIILLN LIBELING
BEGIIMRT BIG-TIMER
BEGIIRTT BRIGITTE
BEGIKNRU REBUKING
BEGILLLU BLUEGILL,
GULLIBLE
BEGILNNY BENIGNLY
BEGILNOW ELBOWING
BEGILNRT TREBLING
BEGILNSS BLESSING,
GLIBNESS
BEGILSTU BULGIEST
BEGINNOR RINGBONE
BEGINORS SOBERING
BEGLLOSU GLOBULES
BEGLMRRU GRUMBLER
BEGLMRSU GRUMBLES
BEGLMSUU BLUE GUMS
BEGLNOOU BOULOGNE
BEGLNRSU BUNGLERS
BEGLNRUU LUNEBURG
BEGNORRU ORENBURG
BEGNSSUU SUBGENUS
BEHIISTX EXHIBITS
BEHIKOSS KIBOSHES
BEHIKPSU PUSHBIKE
BEHILLOS SHOEBILL
BEHILLTY BLITHELY
BEHILMRW WHIMBREL
BEHILMST THIMBLES
BEHILNPY BIPHENYL
BEHILORR HORRIBLE
BEHILORS BOLSHIER
BEHILRTU THURIBLE

BEHIMNOO BONHOMIE
BEHINNOS SHINBONE
BEHINOSW WISHBONE
BEHISSTU BUSHIEST
BEHLLOOT BOLTHOLE
BEHLLOOW BLOWHOLE
BEHLMSTU HUMBLEST
BEHLORST BROTHELS
BEHLRSSU BLUSHERS
BEHMNOTU ON THE
BUM
BEHNOOPX PHONE BOX
BEHNRSTU BURTHENS
BEHOORSX HORSEBOX
BEHOOSUY HOUSEBOY
BEHORRST BROTHERS
BEHORSSU ROSEBUSH
BEIILMMO IMMOBILE
BEIILMOS MOBILISE
BEIILMOZ MOBILIZE
BEIILNNR BIN-LINER
BEIILRST TRILBIES
BEIILRSX EX LIBRIS
BEIILRTT LIBRETTI
BEIILSTT STILBITE
BEIINSTT STIBNITE
BEIIOPSS BIOPSIES
BEIISTTT BITTIEST
BEIKLMOT TOMBLIKE
BEIKLMOW WOMBLIKE
BEIKLMRY KIMBERLY
BEIKLNRS BLINKERS
BEIKLOSS OBELISKS
BEIKLOTY KILOBYTE
BEIKLSTU BULKIEST
BEIKNOST STEINBOK
BEIKNRRY INKBERRY
BEIKOORT BROOKITE
BEIKRSST BRISKEST
BEILLMSS LIMBLESS
BEILLNTU BULLETIN
BEILLORS BROLLIES
BEILLOSU LIBELOUS
BEILMMOS EMBOLISM
BEILMNOU NOBELIUM
BEILMNRU UNLIMBER
BEILMNST NIMBLEST
BEILMRST TIMBRELS
BEILNNTU BUNTLINE
BEILNSSY SENSIBLY
BEILOPPW BLOWPIPE
BEILOPSS POSSIBLE
BEILOQSU OBLIQUES
BEILORRS BROILERS

BEILORTT LIBRETTO
BEILORWZ BLOWZIER
BEILOSTW BLOWIEST
BEILRRTY TERRIBLY
BEILRSST BLISTERS,
BRISTLES
BEILRSTU BURLIEST
BEILRTTY BITTERLY
BEILSTTU SUBTITLE
BEIMNORY IN EMBRYO
BEIMNSSU NIMBUSES
BEIMOORS RIBOSOME
BEIMORTY BIOMETRY
BEIMPSTU BUMPIEST
BEINNOSS BONINESS
BEINNOST BONNIEST
BEINOQRU QUIBERON
BEINORSW BROWNIES
BEINOSTU BOUNTIES
BEINRSTT BITTERNS
BEINRSTU TRIBUNES,
TURBINES
BEINSSSU BUSINESS
BEIOOSTZ BOOZIEST
BEIOQTUU BOUTIQUE
BEIORSTY SOBRIETY
BEIOSSST BOSSIEST
BEIRRSSU BRUISERS
BEIRSTTU TRIBUTES
BEISSTTU BUSTIEST
BEJJMOTU JUMBO JET
BEJORTTU TURBOJET
BEKLNORY BROKENLY
BEKLOORU RULEBOOK
BEKLOOST BOOKLETS
BEKNNORU UNBROKEN
BEKNOOOT NOTEBOOK
BEKOOORV OVERBOOK
BEKOOTTX TEXTBOOK
BELLLLPU BELLPULL
BELLOPTY POTBELLY
BELLORTW BELLWORT
BELLOSWX SWELL BOX
BELMNOOU BLUE MOON
BELMOORS BLOOMERS
BELMOORY BLOOMERY
BELMOPRS PROBLEMS
BELMORSY SOMBERLY
BELMPRSU PLUMBERS
BELMPRUY PLUMBERY
BELMRRUY MULBERRY
BELMRSTU STUMBLER,
TUMBLERS, TUMBRELS
BELMSSTU STUMBLES

BELNOSUU NEBULOUS
BELNSSTU SUNBELTS
BELOOOSX LOOSEBOX
BELOOPRS BLOOPERS
BELOOPRT BOLTROPE
BELOOSST BOOTLESS
BELOOTUV OBVOLUTE
BELORRTU TROUBLER
BELORSST BOLSTERS,
  LOBSTERS
BELORSTT BLOTTERS
BELORSTU TROUBLES
BELOSSUY BLESS YOU!
BELOSTUY OBTUSELY
BELPRSUY SUPERBLY
BELRSSSU BRUSSELS
BELRSTUY BLUSTERY
BELSSTTU SUBTLEST
BELSTTUY SUBTLETY
BEMNNSSU NUMBNESS
BEMNOORT TROMBONE
BEMNOORW NEW
  BROOM
BEMNOOXY MONEYBOX
BEMOORRS SOMBRERO
BEMORSST MOBSTERS
BENNOORS SORBONNE
BENOORSU BURNOOSE
BENORRSU SUBORNER
BENORRTU TRUEBORN
BENORSTW BROWNEST
BENORSTY RENT BOYS
BENSSSUY BUSYNESS
BEOOPSUZ BOOZE-UPS
BEOORRRW BORROWER
BEOORSST BOOSTERS
BEOPRRSV PROVERBS
BEOPRSSX PRESS BOX
BEOQSTUU BOUQUETS
BEORRRUW BURROWER
BEORSTUU TUBEROUS
BERSSTTU BUTTRESS
BFFGILNU BLUFFING
BFFHORSU BRUSH-OFF
BFFLLOUY BULLY-OFF
BFFLMOPU OFF PLUMB
BFFLOTUU OUTBLUFF
BFFNOOSU BUFFOONS
BFFNOSUX SNUFFBOX
BFGILMNU FUMBLING
BFGIORRU FRIBOURG
BFGLLORU BULLFROG
BFHIILLS BILLFISH
BFHILOST FISHBOLT

BFHILOSW BLOWFISH,
  FISHBOWL
BFHIMNSU NUMBFISH
BFIIORSS FIBROSIS
BFILLSSU BLISSFUL
BFIMORTU TUBIFORM
BFLLNOWY FLYBLOWN
BFLOORSU SUBFLOOR
BGGGILNO BOGGLING
BGGIILNO OBLIGING
BGGIILNY GIBINGLY
BGGILNNU BUNGLING
BGGILNRU BURGLING
BGHHINOR HIGHBORN
BGHHIORW HIGHBROW
BGHHIOSY HIGHBOYS
BGHIIKNT THINK BIG
BGHILMNU HUMBLING
BGHILNSU BLUSHING
BGHIMNTU THUMBING
BGHINORT BRIGHTON
BGHINRSU BRUSHING
BGHIOSST BIG SHOTS
BGHMORSU HOMBURGS
BGHOORSU BOROUGHS
BGIIKLNN BLINKING
BGIILNOR BROILING
BGIILNRS BRISLING
BGIILNSS SIBLINGS
BGIILNTY BITINGLY
BGIILNTZ BLITZING
BGIINORT ORBITING
BGIINRSU BRUISING
BGIINRTU BRUITING
BGIJLMNU JUMBLING
BGIKLNOT KINGBOLT
BGIKNOOR BROOKING
BGIKNOOS BOOKINGS
BGILLLUY GULLIBLY
BGILLNOU GLOBULIN
BGILLNRU BULLRING
BGILLNUY BULLYING
BGILMMNU MUMBLING
BGILMNOO BLOOMING
BGILMNPU PLUMBING
BGILMNRU RUMBLING
BGILMNTU TUMBLING
BGILMOSU GUMBOILS
BGILMOTU GUMBOTIL
BGILNNTU BLUNTING
BGILNORT RINGBOLT
BGILNORY BORINGLY
BGILNOTT BLOTTING,
  BOTTLING

BGILNRRU BLURRING
BGILNRTU BLURTING
BGILNSTU BUSTLING
BGINNORW BROWNING
BGINNORZ BRONZING
BGINOOST BOOSTING
BGINORSW BROWSING
BGINRSTU BURSTING
BGJOSTUY TOBY JUGS
BGKLOOOS LOGBOOKS
BGKNOOOS SONGBOOK
BGLNOOSW LONGBOWS
BGLOORYY BRYOLOGY
BGMNOOOR
  GOMBROON
BGMOOSTU GUMBOOTS
BGOPRSUU SUBGROUP
BGRRUUWZ WURZBURG
BHIILMPS BLIMPISH
BHIIOPRT PROHIBIT
BHIKLLOO BILLHOOK
BHILLNOR HORNBILL
BHILLSTU BULLSHIT
BHILORRY HORRIBLY
BHILOSYY BOYISHLY
BHIMNORT THROMBIN
BHINORSW BROWNISH
BHINORTU THONBURI
BHJLLNOU JOHN BULL
BHKNOOOR HORNBOOK
BHKOOOPS BOOKSHOP
BHLLNORU BULLHORN
BHMNTTUU THUMBNUT
BHMORSTU THROMBUS
BHMPSTUU THUMBS UP
BHOOSSTW BOWSHOTS
BHPRSSUU BRUSH-UPS
BIIKNOUV BUKOVINI
BIILLNOS BILLIONS
BIILMOTY MOBILITY
BIILNOOV OBLIVION
BIILNOTY NOBILITY
BIILNTUY NUBILITY
BIILOSSY BIOLYSIS
BIIMMOSZ ZOMBIISM
BIIQTUUY UBIQUITY
BIIRSSTU BURSITIS
BIKMNPSU BUMPKINS
BIKMTTUU TIMBUKTU
BIKOOUUZ BOUZOUKI
BILLNOOU BOUILLON,
  BOULLION
BILLOWYZ BLOWZILY
BILMMPSU PLUMBISM

BILMOSTU BOTULISM
BILNNOOY LOONY BIN
BILOORST SORBITOL
BILOPSSY POSSIBLY
BIMNORSY BYRONISM
BIMNOSTY SYMBIONT
BIMNRUUV VIBURNUM
BIMOORST ROBOTISM
BIOOPSTT POST-OBIT
BIOPRSTW BOWSPRIT
BIORRSTU BURRITOS
BIORSTUY BISTOURY
BJOPPTUU PUT-UP JOB
BKKOOORW WORKBOOK
BKLNOORY BROOKLYN
BKMOOORW
    BOOKWORM
BLLLLOOY LOBLOLLY
BLLMOORW BOLLWORM
BLMOOOTY LOBOTOMY
BLMOOSSS BLOSSOMS
BLMOPSUU PLUMBOUS
BLOORSWW LOWBROWS
BLOOSTUW BLOWOUTS
BLOPSSTU SUBPLOTS
BLORSTUY ROBUSTLY
BLOSTUUU TUBULOUS
BMNOOSST BONS MOTS
BMOOORSX BOXROOMS
BMOORSSU SOMBROUS
BMOORSTU MOTORBUS
BMOORTTY BOTTOMRY
BNNORTUW NUT-
    BROWN
BNNOTTUU UNBUTTON
BNNRSTUU SUNBURNT
BNOOOSUY SONOBUOY
BNORSTUU BURNOUTS
BNRSSTUU SUNBURST
BOOPRSSU BOSPORUS
BOORSSTY SOB STORY
BOPSSSTU BUS STOPS
BORSTTUU OUTBURST
CCCEEILT ECLECTIC
CCCEGOSY COCCYGES
CCCEHIOS CHOC-ICES
CCCEILNY ENCYCLIC
CCCIINSU SUCCINIC
CCCILNOY CYCLONIC
CCCINSTU SUCCINCT
CCCKOORW COCKCROW
CCDDEENO CONCEDED
CCDDENOU CONDUCED
CCDEEENR CREDENCE

CCDEEHLN CLENCHED
CCDEEIOP CODPIECE
CCDEEKOY COCKEYED
CCDEELRY RECYCLED
CCDEHILN CLINCHED
CCDEHIPU HICCUPED
CCDEHKLU CHUCKLED
CCDEHLTU CLUTCHED
CCDEHNRU CRUNCHED
CCDEHORS SCORCHED
CCDEHORU CROUCHED
CCDEHOST SCOTCHED
CCDEIINO COINCIDE
CCDEINOT OCCIDENT
CCDEIOPU OCCUPIED
CCDELNOU CONCLUDE
CCDENOOO COCOONED
CCDENORU CONDUCER
CCDEORRU OCCURRED
CCDEORSU SUCCORED
CCDEOSTU STUCCOED
CCDHIILO CICHLOID
CCDHIIOR DICHROIC
CCDHINOO CONCHOID
CCDIILOS CODICILS
CCDIINOS SCINCOID
CCDIIORT DICROTIC
CCDKLOOR OLD CROCK
CCDKLOSU CUCKOLDS
CCDKOOOW
    WOODCOCK
CCDLOSTU COLD CUTS
CCEEELMN CLEMENCE
CCEEHKRS CHECKERS
CCEEHLNS CLENCHES
CCEEHRSY SCREECHY
CCEEILNR ENCIRCLE
CCEEILNS LICENCES
CCEEILNT ELENCTIC
CCEEILPY EPICYCLE
CCEEILRT ELECTRIC
CCEEIMNU ECUMENIC
CCEEINOR CICERONE
CCEEINOV CONCEIVE
CCEEINSS SCIENCES
CCEEIORV COERCIVE
CCEEIRSV CERVICES,
    CREVICES
CCEEITTU EUTECTIC
CCEEKLOR COCKEREL
CCEEKNRW CREW NECK
CCEELMNY CLEMENCY
CCEEMMNO COMMENCE
CCEEMMOR COMMERCE

CCEENNOS ENSCONCE
CCEENORT CONCRETE
CCEENRST CRESCENT
CCEFIIPS SPECIFIC
CCEFIRRU CRUCIFER
CCEFLLOU FLOCCULE
CCEFLOOS FLOCCOSE
CCEGHIKN CHECKING
CCEGILRY GLYCERIC
CCEGINOR COERCING
CCEHHRSU CHURCHES
CCEHIIMS ISCHEMIC
CCEHIKNS CHECK-INS,
    CHICKENS
CCEHILNR CLINCHER
CCEHILNS CLINCHES
CCEHILOR CHOLERIC
CCEHILOY CHOICELY
CCEHINOR CORNICHE
CCEHINOZ ZECCHINO
CCEHINST TECHNICS
CCEHIORT RICOCHET
CCEHIOST CHOICEST
CCEHKLRU CHUCKLER
CCEHKLSU CHUCKLES
CCEHKOTU CHECKOUT
CCEHKPSU CHECKUPS
CCEHLMOR CROMLECH
CCEHLNNU UNCLENCH
CCEHLSTU CLUTCHES
CCEHORRS SCORCHER
CCEHORSS SCORCHES
CCEHORST CROTCHES
CCEHORTT CROTCHET
CCEHRSTU CRUTCHES
CCEIIKLN NICKELIC
CCEIIKPS ICE PICKS
CCEIILNT ENCLITIC
CCEIILOR LICORICE
CCEIILPT ECLIPTIC
CCEIILST SCILICET
CCEIILTU LEUCITIC
CCEIKOST COCKIEST
CCEIKRST CRICKETS
CCEILNUY UNICYCLE
CCEILRRU CURRICLE
CCEILRST CIRCLETS
CCEILRSY CRESYLIC
CCEILRTY TRICYCLE
CCEILRUU CURLICUE
CCEILSTU CUTICLES
CCEIMNOO ECONOMIC
CCEIMOST COSMETIC
CCEIMRRU MERCURIC

CCEINNOV CONVINCE
CCEINOOR COERCION
CCEINOOZ CENOZOIC
CCEINORS CORNICES
CCEINORT NECROTIC
CCEINOST CONCEITS
CCEINOTT TECTONIC
CCEINPRT PRECINCT
CCEINRTU CINCTURE
CCEINSZZ SZCZECIN
CCEIOORT CROCOITE
CCEIOPRU OCCUPIER
CCEIOPTY ECOTYPIC
CCEIORST CORTICES
CCEIPRTU CUT-PRICE
CCEIPSST SCEPTICS
CCEIRSSU CIRCUSES
CCEKNOSY COCKNEYS
CCEKORRY CROCKERY
CCEKORSU COCKSURE
CCELLOST COLLECTS
CCELNOSY CYCLONES
CCENNORS CONCERNS
CCENOORT CONCERTO
CCENOPST CONCEPTS
CCENORST CONCERTS
CCENRRUY CURRENCY
CCEORRSU SUCCORER
CCEORSSU CROCUSES
CCERSTUW CREW CUTS
CCFFHKOU CHUCK OFF
CCFIIRUX CRUCIFIX
CCFILNOT CONFLICT
CCGHIKNO CHOCKING
CCGHIKNU CHUCKING
CCGHINOU COUCHING
CCGIIKLN CLICKING
CCGIIKNR CRICKING
CCGIILNR CIRCLING
CCGIKLNO CLOCKING
CCGIKLNU CLUCKING
CCGILLOY GLYCOLIC
CCGILOSU GLUCOSIC
CCHHIITY ICHTHYIC
CCHHINOU CHIN-CHOU
CCHHNRUU UNCHURCH
CCHHOOPP CHOP-CHOP
CCHHOOWW CHOW-
CHOW
CCHIINUZ ZUCCHINI
CCHIIORT ORCHITIC
CCHILMOW MILCH COW
CCHIPSSY PSYCHICS
CCHKMSSU SCHMUCKS

CCIILLRY CYRILLIC
CCIIMNSY CYNICISM
CCIINORZ ZIRCONIC
CCIIRSTU CIRCUITS
CCIIRTUY CIRCUITY
CCIKKLOP PICKLOCK
CCIKKOTT TICKTOCK
CCIKLOSW COWLICKS
CCIKOPST COCKPITS
CCILNOSU COUNCILS
CCILOOPS PICCOLOS
CCILORUU CURCULIO
CCILOSSY CYCLOSIS
CCILSSTY CYCLISTS
CCINOPSY SYNCOPIC
CCINORSY CRYONICS
CCINOSTV CONVICTS
CCIOOPST SCOTOPIC
CCIOORSS SIROCCOS
CCIOOTXY OXYTOCIC
CCJNNOTU CONJUNCT
CCKMOOOR MOORCOCK
CCKNORTU TURNCOCK
CCKOOPST STOPCOCK
CCKOPRSU COCKSPUR
CCNOOSTU COCONUTS
CCOOSSUU COUSCOUS
CCOOTTUU TUCOTUCO
CCORSSTU CROSSCUT
CDDDEETU DEDUCTED
CDDEEEEX EXCEEDED
CDDEEEFT DEFECTED
CDDEEEIV DECEIVED
CDDEEEJT DEJECTED
CDDEEEPR PRECEDED
CDDEEETT DETECTED
CDDEEGLU CUDGELED
CDDEEHIT CHEDDITE
CDDEEHNR DRENCHED
CDDEEIKR DICKERED
CDDEEILN DECLINED
CDDEEIPT DEPICTED
CDDEEIRS DESCRIED
CDDEEIRT CREDITED,
DIRECTED
CDDEEKOT DOCKETED
CDDEEKUW DUCKWEED
CDDEELSU SECLUDED
CDDEELUX EXCLUDED
CDDEELUY DEUCEDLY
CDDEENOS SECONDED
CDDEEORR RECORDED
CDDEERUV DECURVED
CDDEFIIO CODIFIED

CDDEFINO CONFIDED
CDDEGIIN DECIDING
CDDEGINO DECODING
CDDEGINU DEDUCING
CDDEIINT INDICTED
CDDEIKOS DOCKSIDE
CDDEILLO COLLIDED
CDDEILMS MIDDLE CS
CDDEILNU INCLUDED
CDDEILRU CUDDLIER
CDDEINTU INDUCTED
CDDEIORV DIVORCED
CDDELLOU COLLUDED
CDDELLOW COLD-WELD
CDDELNOO CONDOLED
CDDENNOO CONDONED
CDDENOOR CORDONED
CDDEOORR CORRODED
CDDEOORT DOCTORED
CDDEOPRU PRODUCED
CDDGHILO GODCHILD
CDDGILNO CODDLING
CDDGILNU CUDDLING
CDDGINSU SCUDDING
CDDHILOS CLODDISH
CDDIISTY DYTISCID
CDDIORSS DISCORDS
CDDKORSY DRY DOCKS
CDDOOORW
CORDWOOD
CDEEEERX EXCEEDER
CDEEEFFT EFFECTED
CDEEEFNS DEFENCES
CDEEEHNS ENSCHEDE
CDEEEHOR REECHOED
CDEEEHSW ESCHEWED
CDEEEINV EVIDENCE
CDEEEIRV DECEIVER,
RECEIVED
CDEEEJRT REJECTED
CDEEELLX EXCELLED
CDEEELST SELECTED
CDEEEMNT CEMENTED
CDEEEMRS MERCEDES
CDEEENRS SCREENED
CDEEENRT CENTERED
CDEEEPTX EXCEPTED,
EXPECTED
CDEEERSS RECESSED
CDEEERST SECRETED
CDEEERTT DETECTER
CDEEERTX EXCRETED
CDEEETUX EXECUTED
CDEEFFOR FORCE-FED

CDEEFIIS EDIFICES
CDEEFIIT FETICIDE
CDEEFINT INFECTED
CDEEFIRR FREDERIC
CDEEFKLR FRECKLED
CDEEFKOR FOREDECK
CDEEFLOT COLD FEET
CDEEFNOR ENFORCED
CDEEFORT DEFECTOR
CDEEGIIR REGICIDE
CDEEGINO GENOCIDE
CDEEGINR RECEDING
CDEEGINS SECEDING
CDEEGIOS GEODESIC
CDEEGIOT GEODETIC
CDEEHILS CHISELED
CDEEHINR ENRICHED
CDEEHIPR CIPHERED,
DECIPHER
CDEEHKST SKETCHED
CDEEHLSU SCHEDULE
CDEEHNQU QUENCHED
CDEEHNRR DRENCHER
CDEEHNRW WRENCHED
CDEEHORT HECTORED
CDEEHPRY CYPHERED
CDEEHRTW WRETCHED
CDEEIILT ELICITED
CDEEIIMN MEDICINE
CDEEIIMP EPIDEMIC
CDEEIINT INDICTEE
CDEEIIRT DIERETIC
CDEEIISV DECISIVE
CDEEIITT DIETETIC
CDEEIJNT INJECTED
CDEEIJOR REJOICED
CDEEIKLN NICKELED
CDEEIKNS SICKENED
CDEEIKPT PICKETED
CDEEIKTT TICKETED
CDEEILNP PENCILED
CDEEILNR DECLINER,
RECLINED
CDEEILNS DECLINES,
LICENSED, SILENCED
CDEEILNT DENTICLE
CDEEILOR RECOILED
CDEEILPS ECLIPSED
CDEEILRT DERELICT
CDEEIMNR ENDERMIC
CDEEIMOR MEDIOCRE
CDEEIMOS COMEDIES
CDEEINNS INCENSED
CDEEINNT INDECENT

CDEEINRW CERIDWEN
CDEEIORV DIVORCÉE
CDEEIOSS DIOCESES
CDEEIPRT DECREPIT,
DEPICTER
CDEEIPRU PEDICURE
CDEEIRRS DESCRIER
CDEEIRRT REDIRECT
CDEEIRST DISCREET,
DISCRETE
CDEEIRSV SERVICED
CDEEITUV EDUCTIVE
CDEEJKOY JOCKEYED
CDEEKLPS SPECKLED
CDEEKNOR RECKONED
CDEEKNRS REDNECKS
CDEEKOPT POCKETED
CDEEKORT ROCKETED
CDEEKORW ROCKWEED
CDEEKPRU PUCKERED
CDEEKRTU TUCKERED
CDEELMOW WELCOMED
CDEELNOS ENCLOSED
CDEELNPU PEDUNCLE
CDEELNTY DECENTLY
CDEELOOW LOCOWEED
CDEELOST CLOSETED
CDEELPRU PRECLUDE
CDEELRTU LECTURED
CDEELRUX EXCLUDER
CDEEMOPR COMPERED
CDEEMOPT COMPETED
CDEEMORT ECTODERM
CDEENNOS CONDENSE
CDEENNOU DENOUNCE
CDEENNOV CONVENED
CDEENNTY TENDENCY
CDEENORR CORNERED
CDEENORS CENSORED,
SECONDER, SEEDCORN
CDEENOSY ECDYSONE
CDEENOTX COEXTEND
CDEENOVY CONVEYED
CDEENPRU PRUDENCE
CDEENRSU CENSURED
CDEENSST DESCENTS
CDEEOOTV DOVECOTE
CDEEOPRS PROCEEDS
CDEEOPRU RECOUPED
CDEEORRR RECORDER
CDEEORST CORSETED,
ESCORTED
CDEEORTT DETECTOR
CDEERRRU RECURRED

CDEERSSU SEDUCERS
CDEFFISU SUFFICED
CDEFFLSU SCUFFLED
CDEFHILN FLINCHED
CDEFIIIL FILICIDE
CDEFIIIT CITIFIED
CDEFIIOR CODIFIER
CDEFIIST DEFICITS
CDEFIKRR FREDRICK
CDEFINNO CONFINED
CDEFINOR CONFIDER
CDEFLNOU FLOUNCED
CDEFNORU UNFORCED
CDEFNOSU CONFUSED
CDEFNOTU CONFUTED
CDEFOSSU FOCUSSED
CDEGHORU GROUCHED
CDEGIILO GOIDELIC
CDEGINNO ENCODING
CDEGINOY DECOYING
CDEGINRU REDUCING
CDEGINRY DECRYING
CDEGINSU SEDUCING
CDEGINSY DYSGENIC
CDEGORSU SCOURGED
CDEHIILO HELICOID
CDEHIIMO HOMICIDE
CDEHIINO ECHINOID
CDEHIIOS HESIODIC
CDEHIKOT HOCKTIDE
CDEHIKRW HERDWICK
CDEHILNR CHILDREN
CDEHILOR CHLORIDE
CDEHILRT ELDRITCH
CDEHIMRS SMIRCHED
CDEHINOS HEDONICS
CDEHINST SNITCHED
CDEHIOSW COWHIDES
CDEHISTT STITCHED
CDEHISTW SWITCHED
CDEHITTW TWITCHED
CDEHKLSU SHELDUCK
CDEHLOOS SCHOOLED
CDEHLORT CHORTLED
CDEHLOSU SLOUCHED
CDEHMOOS SMOOCHED
CDEHNOOP CHENOPOD
CDEHORSU CHORUSED
CDEHORSW COWHERDS
CDEHOSSW COWSHEDS
CDEIIILS SILICIDE
CDEIIIMT MITICIDE
CDEIIIOS IDIOCIES
CDEIIKKS SIDEKICK

CDEIIKMM MIMICKED
CDEIIKST DICKIEST
CDEIILMO DOMICILE
CDEIILNN INCLINED
CDEIILNO INDOCILE
CDEIILOT IDIOLECT
CDEIILPS DISCIPLE
CDEIILRU RIDICULE
CDEIIMRT DIMETRIC
CDEIINNT INCIDENT
CDEIINOS DECISION
CDEIINOV INVOICED
CDEIINRT INDIRECT
CDEIINTY CYTIDINE
CDEIIOPR PERIODIC
CDEIIOPS EPISODIC
CDEIIOPT EPIDOTIC
CDEIIRTU DIURETIC
CDEIISSU SUICIDES
CDEIKLNR CRINKLED
CDEIKLPR PRICKLED
CDEIKLRT TRICKLED
CDEIKLWY WICKEDLY
CDEIKNOS SOCKED IN
CDEIKNPU UNPICKED
CDEIKORR RODERICK
CDEIKOST DIESTOCK
CDEIKRRS DERRICKS
CDEILLOU CELULOID,
  LODICULE
CDEILLPU PELLUCID
CDEILMOP COMPILED,
  COMPLIED
CDEILMOY MYCELOID
CDEILMRU DULCIMER
CDEILNOS INCLOSED
CDEILNRY CYLINDER
CDEILOOW WOODLICE
CDEILOPU CLUPEOID
CDEILORS SCLEROID
CDEILORU CLOUDIER
CDEILOSS DISCLOSE
CDEILPPR CRIPPLED
CDEILRTY DIRECTLY
CDEILSTU DUCTILES
CDEILSXY DYSLEXIC
CDEIMOST DOMESTIC
CDEIMPRS SCRIMPED
CDEINNOU UNCOINED
CDEINNOV CONNIVED
CDEINORS CONSIDER
CDEINORT CENTROID,
  DOCTRINE
CDEINOST D-NOTICES

CDEINOTU EDUCTION
CDEINOUV UNVOICED
CDEINPRU UNPRICED
CDEINRRU INCURRED
CDEINSTY SYNDETIC
CDEIOPST DESPOTIC
CDEIOPSZ ZIP CODES
CDEIOPTY COPY-EDIT
CDEIORRT CREDITOR,
  DIRECTOR
CDEIORRV DIVORCER
CDEIORSV DISCOVER,
  DIVORCES
CDEIPRST SCRIPTED
CDEIPRTU PICTURED
CDEIRRSU SCURRIED
CDEIRSTU CRUDITÉS,
  CURTSIED
CDEIRSTV VERDICTS
CDEISSSU DISCUSES
CDEJNORU CONJURED
CDEKKLNU KNUCKLED
CDEKLMOR CLERKDOM
CDEKLNOU UNLOCKED
CDEKLRTU TRUCKLED
CDEKNOOV CONVOKED
CDEKNORU UNCORKED
CDELLORS SCROLLED
CDELLOTU CLOUDLET
CDELMNOU COLUMNED
CDELMPRU CRUMPLED
CDELNOOR CONDOLER
CDELNOOS CONSOLED
CDELNOSS COLDNESS
CDELNOSY SECONDLY
CDELOORS COLD SORE,
  COLOREDS
CDELOORU COLOURED,
  DECOLOUR
CDELORSS CORDLESS
CDELPRSU SCRUPLED
CDELRSUY CURSEDLY
CDELRTUU CULTURED
CDELSSUY CUSSEDLY
CDELSTTU SCUTTLED
CDEMMNOU
  COMMUNED
CDEMMOOS COMMODES
CDEMMOTU COMMUTED
CDEMNOOW
  COMEDOWN
CDEMNOSU CONSUMED
CDEMNOTU DOCUMENT
CDEMOOPS COMPOSED

CDEMOPTU COMPUTED
CDEMPRSU SCRUMPED
CDENNOOR CONDONER
CDENNOOT CONNOTED
CDENOORT CREODONT
CDENOOVY CONVOYED
CDENORTU TROUNCED
CDENOSTU CONTUSED
CDENRTUU UNDERCUT
CDEOOPST POSTCODE
CDEOORRR CORRODER
CDEOORSU DECOROUS
CDEOPRRU PROCURED,
  PRODUCER
CDEORRSS RED CROSS
CDERSTTU DESTRUCT
CDFFILOR CLIFFORD
CDFHILOS COLD FISH
CDFIILMS DISC FILM
CDFIILSU FLUIDICS
CDFNNOOU CONFOUND
CDGHIINT DITCHING
CDGHINOR CHORDING
CDGIINNU INDUCING
CDGIKLNU DUCKLING
CDGILNOS SCOLDING
CDGILNOU CLOUDING
CDGILNRU CURDLING
CDGINORW CROWDING
CDHHIILS CHILDISH
CDHIINNW CHINDWIN
CDHIIORT HIDROTIC,
  TRICHOID
CDHIIOSZ SCHIZOID
CDHILOOP CHILOPOD
CDHIOORT TROCHOID
CDHIOPRW WHIPCORD
CDHLOOPY COPYHOLD
CDHOORRU UROCHORD
CDIIIORT DIORITIC
CDIIKMNO DOMINICK
CDIIKPST DIPSTICK
CDIILOPP DIPLOPIC
CDIILOTY DOCILITY
CDIILTUY LUCIDITY
CDIIMNOU CONIDIUM
CDIINPRY CYPRINID
CDIINSTT DISTINCT
CDIIOPRT DIOPTRIC
CDIIORSU SCIUROID
CDIIPTUY CUPIDITY
CDIIRSTT DISTRICT
CDIJNSTU DISJUNCT
CDIKLPUY LUCKY DIP

CDIKNOSW WINDSOCK
CDILLOUY CLOUDILY
CDILOOPZ PODZOLIC
CDILOORS DISCOLOR
CDILOORT LORDOTIC
CDILOOTY COTYLOID
CDIMOORT MICRODOT
CDINNQUU QUIDNUNC
CDINORTU INDUCTOR
CDINOSTU CONDUITS,
   DISCOUNT
CDIOOPRS PROSODIC
CDIOORRR CORRIDOR
CDIOPRRS RIPCORDS
CDIOPRSU CUSPIDOR
CDKOOORW CORKWOOD
CDLOOSTW COTSWOLD
CDMNOOPU COMPOUND
CDMNORUU CORUNDUM
CDNNOOOT CONODONT
CDOORRUY CORDUROY
CDOOSTUW WOODCUTS
CDOPRSTU PRODUCTS
CEEEEIPY EYEPIECE
CEEEFFRT EFFECTER
CEEEFNOR CONFEREE
CEEEGITX EXEGETIC
CEEEGMNR MERGENCE
CEEEHIKR CHEEKIER
CEEEHIRR CHEERIER
CEEEHIST ICE SHEET
CEEEHKOR CHEROKEE
CEEEHNNY CHEYENNE
CEEEHPSS SPEECHES
CEEEHRSW ESCHEWER
CEEEIJTV EJECTIVE
CEEEILNS LICENSEE
CEEEILRT ERECTILE
CEEEILTV CLEVEITE,
   ELECTIVE
CEEEIMNN EMINENCE
CEEEINOP ONE-PIECE
CEEEIPRR CREEPIER
CEEEIPRV PERCEIVE
CEEEIPST SET PIECE
CEEEIRRV RECEIVER
CEEEIRSX EXERCISE
CEEEJRRT REJECTER
CEEELRTT ELECTRET
CEEEMNRT CEMENTER,
   CEREMENT
CEEEMORT ECTOMERE
CEEEMRTY CEMETERY
CEEEMSUX EXCUSE ME!

CEEENNST SENTENCE
CEEENNSV CEVENNES
CEEENPRS PRESENCE
CEEENPRT PRETENCE
CEEENQSU SEQUENCE
CEEENRRS SCREENER
CEEENRRT TERRENCE
CEEENSSS ESSENCES
CEEEPRRS CREEPERS
CEEERRTX EXCRETER
CEEERSSS RECESSES
CEEERTUX EXECUTER
CEEESSSX EXCESSES
CEEFFINT IN EFFECT
CEEFFNOS OFFENCES
CEEFFORT EFFECTOR
CEEFGILN FLEECING
CEEFHIKR KERCHIEF
CEEFHLRT FLETCHER
CEEFHLRU CHEERFUL
CEEFIKKR FREE KICK
CEEFILRY FIERCELY
CEEFINRT FRENETIC
CEEFIRRU FIRE-CURE
CEEFIRST FIERCEST
CEEFKLRS FRECKLES
CEEFKLSS FECKLESS
CEEFLNOR FLORENCE
CEEFLNTU FECULENT
CEEFLRUU FLUE-CURE
CEEFNORR CONFRERE,
   ENFORCER
CEEFNRVY FERVENCY
CEEFOPRR PERFORCE
CEEFORSS FRESCOES
CEEFORST SCOT-FREE
CEEFPRST PREFECTS
CEEGHIKN CHEEKING
CEEGHINP CHEEPING
CEEGHINR CHEERING
CEEGHLOW COGWHEEL
CEEGHNRT GRETCHEN
CEEGIJNT EJECTING
CEEGILNT ELECTING
CEEGILOT ECLOGITE
CEEGINPR CREEPING
CEEGINRT ERECTING
CEEGINST GENETICS
CEEGINSU EUGENICS
CEEGINXY EXIGENCY
CEEGIORX EXOERGIC
CEEGLLMR GERM CELL
CEEGLLOS COLLEGES
CEEGMNOY CYMOGENE

CEEGNNOR CONGENER
CEEGNORV CONVERGE
CEEGORST CORTEGES
CEEHHLRS HERSCHEL
CEEHHMNN HENCHMEN
CEEHIIST ETHICISE
CEEHIITZ ETHICIZE
CEEHIKLY CHEEKILY
CEEHILLM MICHELLE
CEEHILLN CHENILLE,
   HELLENIC
CEEHILRW CLERIHEW
CEEHILRY CHEERILY
CEEHILSV VEHICLES
CEEHILTV HELVETIC
CEEHIMRT HERMETIC
CEEHIMSS CHEMISES
CEEHINPR ENCIPHER
CEEHINPT PHENETIC
CEEHINRR ENRICHER
CEEHINTT ENTHETIC
CEEHIOSV COHESIVE
CEEHIPRT HERPETIC
CEEHIRRS CHERRIES
CEEHIRST CHESTIER,
   HERETICS
CEEHIRTT TETCHIER
CEEHISTW CHEWIEST
CEEHKLRS HECKLERS
CEEHKRST SKETCHER
CEEHKSST SKETCHES
CEEHLLOR ROCHELLE
CEEHLNOO HOLOCENE
CEEHLNOS ECHELONS
CEEHLNSU ELENCHUS
CEEHLRSU HERCULES
CEEHMRSS SCHEMERS
CEEHNNRT ENTRENCH
CEEHNORT COHERENT
CEEHNQRU QUENCHER
CEEHNRRT RETRENCH,
   TRENCHER
CEEHNRST TRENCHES
CEEHNRSW WRENCHES
CEEHNSST STENCHES
CEEHOPRY CORYPHEE
CEEHORRT TORCHERE
CEEHORST THE SCORE,
   TROCHEES
CEEHQRSU CHEQUERS
CEEHRSTW WRETCHES
CEEIIKLV VICELIKE
CEEIIMNP MINCE PIE
CEEIIMRT EREMITIC

CEEIINST NICETIES
CEEIINVV EVINCIVE
CEEIJNOT EJECTION
CEEIJORR REJOICER
CEEIJRUV VERJUICE
CEEIKLNN NECKLINE
CEEIKLPR PICKEREL
CEEIKNRS SICKENER
CEEIKNST NECKTIES
CEEIKPRT PICKETER
CEEILLLP PELLICLE
CEEILLNT LENTICEL
CEEILMNT MELICENT
CEEILMOR COMELIER
CEEILMPS SEMPLICE
CEEILNNU LUCIENNE
CEEILNNY LENIENCY
CEEILNOP PLIOCENE
CEEILNOT ELECTION
CEEILNOV VIOLENCE
CEEILNRR RECLINER
CEEILNRS LICENSER,
   SILENCER
CEEILNSS SILENCES
CEEILORR RECOILER
CEEILPRS ECLIPSER
CEEILPRY CREEPILY
CEEILPSS ECLIPSES
CEEILQSU LIQUESCE
CEEILRST SCLERITE
CEEILRSV VERSICLE
CEEILRTU RETICULE
CEEILRTY CELERITY
CEEILSSV VESICLES
CEEILSTT TESTICLE
CEEIMMPY EMPYEMIC
CEEIMMRS MESMERIC
CEEIMNPS SPECIMEN
CEEIMNST CENTIMES,
   TENESMIC
CEEIMORT CORE TIME,
   METEORIC
CEEINNPZ PINCE-NEZ
CEEINNSS NICENESS
CEEINNST NESCIENT
CEEINOPU EUPNOEIC
CEEINORT ERECTION,
   NEOTERIC
CEEINORX EXOCRINE
CEEINOTV EVECTION
CEEINPRT TERPENIC
CEEINPSX SIXPENCE
CEEINQRU QUERCINE
CEEINRST SECRETIN

CEEINRSU INSECURE,
   SINECURE
CEEINRTT RETICENT
CEEINRTU ENURETIC
CEEINSSX IN EXCESS
CEEINSTY CYSTEINE
CEEIOPPS EPISCOPE
CEEIOPTW TWO-PIECE
CEEIORST COTERIES,
   ESOTERIC
CEEIORSX EXORCISE
CEEIORTX EXOTERIC
CEEIORXZ EXORCIZE
CEEIPPTU EUPEPTIC
CEEIPRST RECEIPTS
CEEIPRSU EPICURES
CEEIRRST RECITERS
CEEIRRSW SCREWIER
CEEIRSSV SERVICES
CEEIRSTV VERTICES
CEEIRSVX CERVIXES
CEEKLNST NECKLETS
CEEKLPSS SPECKLES
CEEKLRSS RECKLESS
CEEKNORR RECKONER
CEEKOPRX OXPECKER
CEEKRRSW WRECKERS
CEELLMOU MOLECULE
CEELLNOS COLLEENS
CEELLRVY CLEVERLY
CEELLSSU CLUELESS
CEELMOPT COMPLETE
CEELMORW WELCOMER
CEELMOSW WELCOMES
CEELMRTU ELECTRUM
CEELNOPU OPULENCE
CEELNORS ENCLOSER
CEELNORT ELECTRON
CEELNRST LECTERNS
CEELNRTY RECENTLY
CEELNSTU ESCULENT
CEELORST CORSELET,
   ELECTORS, SELECTOR
CEELORTV COVERLET
CEELOSST CLOSE-SET
CEELRRTU LECTURER
CEELRSSU RECLUSES
CEELRSTU LECTURES
CEELRSTY SECRETLY
CEELRSUY SECURELY
CEELSTTU LETTUCES
CEEMMNTU CEMENTUM
CEEMNORW NEWCOMER
CEEMNORY CEREMONY

CEEMNOYZ COENZYME
CEEMOORV OVERCOME
CEEMOPRS COMPEERS,
   COMPERES
CEENNOOS NOSECONE
CEENNORS ON-SCREEN
CEENNORT CRETONNE
CEENNORU RENOUNCE
CEENNORV CONVENER
CEENNOORV ONCE-OVER
CEENOPRV PROVENCE
CEENOPTW TWOPENCE
CEENORSV CONSERVE,
   CONVERSE
CEENORTT CORNETTE
CEENORVY CONVEYER
CEENPPTU TUPPENCE
CEENRSSU CENSURES
CEENSSSU CENSUSES
CEENSSTU CUTENESS
CEEOORST CREOSOTE
CEEOPRRT RECEPTOR
CEEOPRTY CEROTYPE
CEEOQTTU COQUETTE
CEEORRRS SORCERER
CEEORRSU RECOURSE,
   RESOURCE
CEEORRVY RECOVERY
CEEORSSY CROSS-EYE
CEEORTTV CORVETTE
CEEORTUX EXECUTOR
CEEOSSTX TO EXCESS
CEEPPRST PRECEPTS
CEEPRSST RESPECTS,
   SCEPTERS, SCEPTRES,
   SPECTRES
CEEPRSTX EXCERPTS
CEERRSSU RESCUERS
CEERRSTU REST CURE
CEERSSTU SECUREST
CEERSSTW SETSCREW
CEFFIORS OFFICERS
CEFFIORU COIFFEUR,
   COIFFURE
CEFFIRSU SUFFICER
CEFFLORU FORCEFUL
CEFFLSSU SCUFFLES
CEFGHINT FETCHING
CEFGIKLN FLECKING
CEFHIIMS MISCHIEF
CEFHILNR FLINCHER
CEFIILNO OLEFINIC
CEFIILST FELSITIC
CEFIILTY FELICITY

CEFIIORS ORIFICES
CEFIIRRT TERRIFIC
CEFIKLRY FLICKERY
CEFILLLO FOLLICLE
CEFILMRU MERCIFUL
CEFILNOT FLECTION
CEFILOUV VOICEFUL
CEFIMOST COMFIEST
CEFINNOS CONFINES
CEFINORS CONIFERS,
FORENSIC
CEFINORT INFECTOR
CEFINOTT CONFETTI
CEFIORTY FEROCITY
CEFKLOOR FORELOCK
CEFKLOST FETLOCKS
CEFKLPSY FLYSPECK
CEFLNOSU FLOUNCES
CEFLNRUU FURUNCLE
CEFNORTU CONFUTER
CEFORRST CROFTERS
CEFORSTU FRUCTOSE
CEGGHIRS CHIGGERS
CEGGLNOY GLYCOGEN
CEGHHHIT HIGH TECH
CEGHIINY HYGIENIC
CEGHIKLN HECKLING
CEGHILNW WELCHING
CEGHILST GLITCHES
CEGHIMNS SCHEMING
CEGHINNW WENCHING
CEGHINOR COHERING
CEGHINPR PERCHING
CEGHINRT RETCHING
CEGHINST ETCHINGS
CEGHIRTU THEURGIC
CEGHMRUY CHEMURGY
CEGHNORS GROSCHEN
CEGHORSU GROUCHES
CEGIILNS CEILINGS
CEGIINNT ENTICING
CEGIINNV EVINCING
CEGIINPR PIERCING
CEGIINRT NEGRITIC,
RECITING
CEGIINSS GNEISSIC
CEGIINSX EXCISING
CEGIINTV EVICTING
CEGIINTX EXCITING
CEGIIOST EGOISTIC
CEGIKLNR CLERKING
CEGIKNRW WRECKING
CEGILNRY GLYCERIN
CEGILNTU CULTIGEN

CEGIMNOY MYOGENIC
CEGINNOZ COZENING
CEGINNRT CENTRING
CEGINNST SCENTING
CEGINOOP GEOPONIC
CEGINOOR OROGENIC
CEGINOPY PYOGENIC
CEGINORV COVERING
CEGINORW COWERING
CEGINOTV COVETING,
VIETCONG
CEGINOXY OXYGENIC
CEGINRST CRESTING
CEGINRSU RESCUING,
SECURING
CEGINRSW SCREWING
CEGINRSY SYNERGIC
CEGINSUX EXCUSING
CEGLLOOU COLLOGUE
CEGLLORY GLYCEROL
CEGLLRYY GLYCERYL
CEGLNOTY COGENTLY
CEGMNNOO
COGNOMEN
CEGNNPUY PUNGENCY
CEGNOOTY GONOCYTE
CEGNORSS CONGRESS
CEGNORSU SCROUNGE
CEGOORSS SCROOGES
CEGORRSU SCOURGER
CEGORSSU SCOURGES
CEHIILLR CHILLIER
CEHIILLS CHILLIES
CEHIILMO HEMIOLIC
CEHIILNN LICHENIN
CEHIILNT LECITHIN
CEHIILOT EOLITHIC
CEHIIMOS ISOCHEIM
CEHIIMPT MEPHITIC
CEHIIMRT HERMITIC
CEHIIOPT ETHIOPIC
CEHIIPPS CHIPPIES
CEHIIPRR CHIRPIER
CEHIIRSS CHRISSIE
CEHIIRST CHRISTIE
CEHIIRTT TITCHIER,
TRICHITE
CEHIISTT ETHICIST,
ITCHIEST, THEISTIC
CEHIKLNY HINCKLEY
CEHIKLSU SUCHLIKE
CEHIKMNT CHIMKENT
CEHIKMOS HOMESICK
CEHIKNRU CHUNKIER

CEHIKNST KITCHENS
CEHIKOWW KWEICHOW
CEHIKRSW WHICKERS
CEHIKSTT THICKEST,
THICKETS, THICKSET
CEHILLMT MITCHELL
CEHILLRS SCHILLER
CEHILMTY METHYLIC
CEHILNOP PHENOLIC,
PINOCHLE
CEHILNOR CHLORINE
CEHILNSS CHINLESS
CEHILORT CHLORITE,
CLOTHIER
CEHILOSU CHOISEUL
CEHILPTY PHYLETIC
CEHILSTY CHESTILY
CEHILTTY TETCHILY
CEHIMMRU CHUMMIER
CEHIMNOP PHONEMIC
CEHIMNOR NICHROME
CEHIMNOW CHOW MEIN
CEHIMNSY CHIMNEYS
CEHIMORT CHROMITE,
TRICHOME
CEHIMRRS SMIRCHER
CEHIMSST CHEMISTS
CEHINNRT INTRENCH
CEHINOOS COHESION
CEHINOPT PHONETIC
CEHINOPU EUPHONIC
CEHINPRU PUNCHIER
CEHINRSS RICHNESS
CEHINRST CHRISTEN
CEHINRSW SCHWERIN
CEHINRTU RUTHENIC
CEHINSST SNITCHES
CEHIOORS CHOOSIER
CEHIOPPR CHOPPIER
CEHIOPRU EUPHORIC
CEHIOPSS HOSPICES
CEHIOPST POSTICHE
CEHIOPTU EUPHOTIC
CEHIORRT RHETORIC,
TORCHIER
CEHIORTU TOUCHIER
CEHIPRSS SPHERICS
CEHIPRST PITCHERS
CEHIRSTT STITCHER
CEHIRSTW SWITCHER
CEHIRSTY HYSTERIC
CEHIRTTW TWITCHER
CEHIRTWY WITCHERY
CEHISSTT STITCHES

CEHISSTU CUSHIEST
CEHISSTW SWITCHES
CEHISTTW TWITCHES
CEHKKRSU CHUKKERS
CEHKLMOS HEMLOCKS
CEHKNPUY KEYPUNCH
CEHKORSS SHOCKERS
CEHKRSTU HUCKSTER
CEHLNNOU LUNCHEON
CEHLNOTU UNCLOTHE
CEHLORST CHORTLES
CEHLORSU SLOUCHER
CEHLQSUY SQUELCHY
CEHMNSSU MUCHNESS
CEHMORUV OVERMUCH
CEHNNOPU PUNCHEON
CEHNNOSU NONESUCH
CEHNOORS SCHOONER
CEHNORSV CHEVRONS
CEHNSTTU CHESTNUT
CEHOOORZ ZOOCHORE
CEHOORST CHEROOTS
CEHOORSU OCHREOUS
CEHOPPRS CHOPPERS
CEHOPPRY PROPHECY
CEHOPSUY CHOP SUEY
CEHORSSU CHORUSES
CEHORSSZ SCHERZOS
CEHORSUV VOUCHERS
CEHPSSTU PUTSCHES
CEHRSTTY STRETCHY
CEIIILSV CIVILISE
CEIIILVZ CIVILIZE
CEIIINSV INCISIVE
CEIIJSTU JESUITIC,
  JUICIEST
CEIIKLMR LIMERICK
CEIIKLRS SICKLIER
CEIIKMMR MIMICKER
CEIIKNRS ICE RINKS
CEIIKNST KINETICS
CEIIKPST PICKIEST
CEIIKQSU QUICKIES
CEIIKRRT TRICKIER
CEIIKRST STICKIER
CEIIKSST EKISTICS
CEIILMNT LIMNETIC
CEIILMNY MYELINIC
CEIILNNR INCLINER
CEIILNNS INCLINES
CEIILNOP PICOLINE
CEIILNOS ISOCLINE,
  SILICONE
CEIILOPS POLICIES

CEIILORT ELICITOR
CEIILOTZ ZEOLITIC
CEIILPPS CLIPPIES
CEIILPRT PERLITIC
CEIILPSS ECLIPSIS
CEIILPTX EXPLICIT
CEIILPTY PYELITIC
CEIILRTV VERTICIL
CEIILSSS SCISSILE
CEIIMOPT EPITOMIC
CEIIMORS ISOMERIC
CEIIMOST COMITIES,
  SEMIOTIC
CEIIMRST MERISTIC
CEIIMRTT TERMITIC
CEIIMSST SEMITICS
CEIINNOT NICOTINE
CEIINORS RECISION,
  SORICINE
CEIINOSV INVOICES
CEIINOSX EXCISION
CEIINOTV EVICTION
CEIINRSU INCISURE,
  SCIURINE
CEIINRTU NEURITIC
CEIINSST CITISENS
CEIINSTU CUTINISE
CEIINSTY SYENITIC
CEIINSTZ CITIZENS
CEIINTUZ CUTINIZE
CEIIOPRT PERIOTIC
CEIIOSTT OSTEITIC
CEIIPRRS CRISPIER
CEIIPRST PRICIEST
CEIIPSST SPICIEST
CEIIQRTU CRITIQUE
CEIIRSTV VERISTIC
CEIISTVV VIVISECT
CEIJLNOS JOSCELIN
CEIJNORT INJECTOR
CEIJSSTU JUSTICES
CEIKKNRS KNICKERS
CEIKLNRS CLINKERS,
  CRINKLES
CEIKLOSV LOVESICK
CEIKLPRS PRICKLES
CEIKLPRU PLUCKIER
CEIKLRSS SLICKERS
CEIKLRST STICKLER,
  STRICKLE
CEIKLSST SLICKEST
CEIKLSTU LUCKIEST
CEIKMPPU PICK-ME-UP
CEIKMSTU MUCKIEST

CEIKNNOT NEKTONIC
CEIKNRSS SNICKERS
CEIKNRST STRICKEN
CEIKNSSS SICKNESS
CEIKORST ROCKIEST,
  STOCKIER
CEIKPSST SKEPTICS
CEIKQSTU QUICKEST,
  QUICKSET
CEIKRRTY TRICKERY
CEIKRSST STICKERS
CEIKSTUY YUCKIEST
CEILLLOY ICE LOLLY
CEILLOQU COQUILLE
CEILLORS COLLIERS
CEILLORY COLLIERY
CEILLRTU TELLURIC
CEILLSST CELLISTS
CEILMMUY MYCELIUM
CEILMNOP COMPLINE
CEILMOPR COMPILER,
  COMPLIER
CEILMOPS POLEMICS
CEILMOSS SOLECISM
CEILMOSU COLISEUM
CEILMRSU CLUMSIER
CEILNNOT NON LICET
CEILNNSY SYNCLINE
CEILNOOS COLONIES,
  COLONISE, ECLOSION
CEILNOOZ COLONIZE
CEILNORV IN CLOVER
CEILNOST TELSONIC
CEILNOSX LEXICONS
CEILNPRY PRINCELY
CEILNRUV CULVERIN
CEILNSST STENCILS
CEILOPPS POPSICLE
CEILOPRT PETROLIC
CEILOPTU POULTICE
CEILOPTY EPICOTYL
CEILORST CLOISTER,
  COSTLIER
CEILORTY CRYOLITE
CEILOSST SOLECIST,
  SOLSTICE
CEILOSSU COULISSE
CEILOTVY VELOCITY
CEILPPRS CLIPPERS,
  CRIPPLES
CEILPRSS SPLICERS
CEILPRSU SURPLICE
CEILRSTU CURLIEST
CEIMMNNO MNEMONIC

CEIMMNOU ENCOMIUM,
  MECONIUM
CEIMMORT RECOMMIT
CEIMMRRU CRUMMIER
CEIMNNOY NEOMYCIN
CEIMNOPT PENTOMIC
CEIMNOPY EPONYMIC
CEIMNORS SERMONIC
CEIMNORT INTERCOM
CEIMNSSU MENISCUS
CEIMOOSZ MESOZOIC
CEIMOPRS COMPRISE
CEIMORSX EXORCISM
CEIMRRTU TURMERIC
CEIMSSTY SYSTEMIC
CEINNNOT INNOCENT
CEINNORU NEURONIC
CEINNORV CONNIVER
CEINNOTU CONTINUE
CEINOOTZ ENTOZOIC,
  ENZOOTIC
CEINOPRS CONSPIRE
CEINOPRT INCEPTOR
CEINOPRV PROVINCE
CEINORSS NECROSIS
CEINORST CORNIEST
CEINORSU COINSURE
CEINORSW IN ESCROW
CEINORTT CONTRITE
CEINORTU NEUROTIC
CEINORTV CONTRIVE
CEINOSSS CESSIONS,
  COSINESS
CEINOSST SECTIONS
CEINOSSZ COZINESS
CEINOSTT STENOTIC
CEINOSTU COUNTIES
CEINOSTY CYTOSINE
CEINOTTU TEUTONIC
CEINPRSS PRINCESS
CEINRSST CISTERNS
CEINRSTT CENTRIST
CEINRTTU TINCTURE
CEIOOTXX EXOTOXIC
CEIOPRRU CROUPIER
CEIOPRSU PRECIOUS
CEIOPSSU SPECIOUS
CEIORRSS CROSIERS
CEIORRSZ CROZIERS
CEIORRTU COURTIER
CEIORSTU CITREOUS,
  OUTCRIES
CEIORSTV VORTICES
CEIORSTX EXORCIST

CEIORSVY VICEROYS
CEIORTTU TOREUTIC
CEIPRRST RESCRIPT
CEIPRSTU PICTURES,
  PIECRUST
CEIPSSST CESSPITS
CEIRRRUY CURRIERY
CEIRRSSU CRUISERS
CEIRRSTT CRITTERS,
  RESTRICT, STRICTER
CEIRRSTU CRUSTIER,
  RECRUITS
CEIRSSTU CITRUSES,
  CURTSIES
CEIRSTUY SECURITY
CEJLOOSY JOCOSELY
CEJNORRU CONJURER
CEJNRTUU JUNCTURE
CEJOPRST PROJECTS
CEKKLNSU KNUCKLES
CEKKNORS KNOCKERS
CEKKNTUY KENTUCKY
CEKLLSSU LUCKLESS
CEKLNOOP POLO NECK
CEKMNOST STOCKMEN
CEKNOORV CONVOKER
CEKNOPST PENSTOCK
CEKOOORV OVERCOOK
CEKOORRS ROCKROSE
CEKOORRW CO-WORKER
CEKOPRST SPROCKET
CEKORRTY ROCKETRY
CEKRRSTU TRUCKERS
CEKRSSUU RUCKUSES
CELLNOOS COLONELS
CELLNSUU NUCELLUS
CELLRSSU SCULLERS
CELLRSUY SCULLERY
CELMNOOS MONOCLES
CELMNOTU UNCLE
  TOM
CELMPRTU PLECTRUM
CELMPSUU SPECULUM
CELNOORS CONSOLER
CELNOOSS CONSOLES,
  COOLNESS
CELNOPUU UNCOUPLE
CELNORWY CLOWNERY
CELNOSUV CONVULSE
CELNOSVY SOLVENCY
CELNOVXY CONVEXLY
CELOOPSS CESSPOOL
CELOPSSU CLOSE-UPS
CELOPSTU COUPLETS

CELORSST CROSSLET
CELORSSU CLOSURES,
  SCLEROUS
CELORSUU ULCEROUS
CELORTVY COVERTLY
CELOSTTU CULOTTES
CELPRSSU SCRUPLES
CELPRSUY SPRUCELY
CELRSSTU CLUSTERS
CELRSTUU CULTURES
CELRSTUV CULVERTS
CELRSTUY CLUSTERY
CELSSTTU SCUTTLES
CEMMNOOR
  COMMONER
CEMMNOOS CONSOMMÉ
CEMMNOST COMMENTS
CEMMNOSU COMMUNES
CEMMORTU COMMUTER
CEMNOOTY MONOCYTE
CEMNOPTT CONTEMPT
CEMNORSU CONSUMER
CEMOOPRS COMPOSER
CEMOOPST COMPOTES
CEMOOSTU OUTCOMES
CEMOPRSS COMPRESS
CEMOPRTU COMPUTER
CEMORSTU CUSTOMER
CEMOSSTU COSTUMES
CEMPRSTU CRUMPETS,
  SPECTRUM
CEMRSSTU SET SCRUM
CENNOOPR CORN PONE
CENNORTU NOCTURNE
CENNOSTT CONTENTS
CENNOSTV CONVENTS
CENOORRS CORONERS,
  CROONERS
CENOORST CORONETS
CENOORSU CORNEOUS
CENOORVY CONVEYOR
CENOQSTU CONQUEST
CENORSTU CONSTRUE,
  COUNTERS, RECOUNTS
CENORSTV CONVERTS
CENORSUU CERNUOUS,
  COENURUS
CENORSUY CYNOSURE
CENORTUY COURTNEY
CENORTVY COVENTRY
CENOSSTT CONTESTS
CENOSSTU COUNTESS
CENOSTTX CONTEXTS
CENPRTUU PUNCTURE

CENRRSTU CURRENTS
CENRSSTU CURTNESS
CEOOOPST OTOSCOPE
CEOOPRRV OVERCROP
CEOORSST SCOOTERS
CEOOSTUV COVETOUS
CEOPPRRS CROPPERS
CEOPPRST PROSPECT
CEOPRRRU PROCURER
CEOPRSTW SCREW TOP
CEOPRSUU CUPREOUS
CEOPRSUV COVER-UPS
CEOQRTUY COQUETRY
CEORRSSU SCOURERS
CEORRSTY CORSETRY
CEORSSST CROSSEST
CEORSTUY COURTESY
CEPPRSSU SCUPPERS
CEPPRTUU UPPERCUT
CEPRSTUU CUTPURSE
CEPSSSTU SUSPECTS
CERSSUUX EXCURSUS
CFFGINOS SCOFFING
CFFGINSU SCUFFING
CFFIKKOS KICKOFFS
CFFIKLNU CUFF LINK
CFFIRTUY FRUCTIFY
CFFLOOOR OFF COLOR
CFGHIILN FILCHING
CFGIIKLN FLICKING
CFGIKLNO FLOCKING
CFGIKNOR FROCKING
CFGINOSU FOCUSING
CFHIINOO FINOCHIO
CFHIIORR HORRIFIC
CFHIKORS ROCKFISH
CFIIILSY SILICIFY
CFIILMNU FULMINIC
CFIILOPR PROLIFIC
CFIINORT FRICTION
CFIINOST FICTIONS
CFIKLSTU STICKFUL
CFIMNORU UNCIFORM
CFINNOTU FUNCTION
CFKKLOOR FOLK-ROCK
CFLLOORU COLORFUL
CFLMRSUU FULCRUMS
CFLNORSU SCORNFUL
CFMOORST COMFORTS
CFNNOORT CONFRONT
CFOOORTW CROWFOOT
CFOOPSTY SOFT COPY
CFRSTUUU USUFRUCT
CGGGHINU CHUGGING

CGGGILNO CLOGGING
CGGHINOU COUGHING
CGGIILNN CLINGING
CGGIINNR CRINGING
CGHHIINT HITCHING
CGHHINNU HUNCHING
CGHIIKNN CHINKING
CGHIILLN CHILLING
CGHIINNP PINCHING
CGHIINNW WINCHING
CGHIINPP CHIPPING
CGHIINPR CHIRPING
CGHIINPT PITCHING
CGHIINTW WITCHING
CGHIINVY CHIVYING
CGHIJNNO CHONGJIN
CGHIKNOS SHOCKING
CGHIKNSU SHUCKING
CGHILMNU MULCHING
CGHILNNU LUNCHING
CGHILNNY LYNCHING
CGHILNOT CLOTHING
CGHILNRU LURCHING
CGHIMMNU CHUMMING
CGHIMNNU MUNCHING
CGHIMNOO MOOCHING
CGHIMNOP CHOMPING
CGHIMPSY SPHYGMIC
CGHINNOS CHIGNONS
CGHINNOT NOTCHING
CGHINNPU PUNCHING
CGHINNRU CHURNING
CGHINOPP CHOPPING
CGHINOTU TOUCHING
CGHINOUV VOUCHING
CGHINPSY PSYCHING
CGHINRSU CRUSHING
CGHINSTY SCYTHING
CGHNOOSU SOUCHONG
CGIIILNT LIGNITIC
CGIIINNS INCISING
CGIIINNT INCITING
CGIIKLNN CLINKING
CGIIKLNP PICKLING
CGIIKLNS LICKINGS,
   SLICKING
CGIIKLNT TICKLING
CGIIKMMS GIMMICKS
CGIIKMMY GIMMICKY
CGIIKNNS SNICKING
CGIIKNPR PRICKING
CGIIKNPS PICKINGS
CGIIKNRT TRICKING
CGIIKNST STICKING

CGIIKPST PIGSTICK
CGIILMOS LOGICISM
CGIILNOP POLICING
CGIILNPP CLIPPING
CGIILNPS SPLICING
CGIILNSU SLUICING
CGIILOST LOGISTIC
CGIIMNNO INCOMING
CGIIMNPR CRIMPING
CGIINNOT NOTICING
CGIINOOS ISOGONIC
CGIINPRS CRISPING
CGIINRSU CRUISING
CGIKKNNO KNOCKING
CGIKLNOR ROCKLING
CGIKLNPU PLUCKING
CGIKLNSU SUCKLING
CGIKMNOS SMOCKING
CGIKNOOR CROOKING
CGIKNOST STOCKING
CGIKNRTU TRUCKING
CGILLNSU SCULLING
CGILMNOO MONGOLIC
CGILMNPU CLUMPING
CGILMNSU MUSCLING
CGILMNTU MULCTING
CGILMNUU CINGULUM,
   GLUCINUM
CGILMOOY MYOLOGIC
CGILNNOW CLOWNING
CGILNOOR COLORING
CGILNOPP CLOPPING
CGILNOPU COUPLING
CGILNOSW COWLINGS,
   SCOWLING
CGILNOTT CLOTTING
CGILNOTU CLOUTING
CGILOORU UROLOGIC
CGILPSTY GLYPTICS
CGIMNNOO GNOMONIC,
   ONCOMING
CGIMNOPU UPCOMING
CGINNOOR CROONING
CGINNOPU POUNCING
CGINNORS SCORNING
CGINNORW CROWNING
CGINNOTU COUNTING
CGINOOPS SCOOPING
CGINOOPT COOPTING
CGINOOST SCOOTING
CGINOPPR CROPPING
CGINORSS CROSSING
CGINORSU COURSING,
   SCOURING

CGINORTU COURTING
CGINOSTU SCOUTING
CGINPRSU SPRUCING
CGINRRUY CURRYING
CGINSTTU CUTTINGS,
   TUNGSTIC
CGINSTUU TUNGUSIC
CGKNOSTU GUNSTOCK
CGLMOOYY MYCOLOGY
CGLNOOOY ONCOLOGY
CGLOOOTY TOCOLOGY
CGLOOTYY CYTOLOGY
CHHIIPST PHTHISIC
CHHILRSU CHURLISH
CHHIMRTY RHYTHMIC
CHHNORSU RHONCHUS
CHHOOPTT HOTCHPOT
CHIIKLST TICKLISH
CHIILNNP LINCHPIN
CHIILOPT HOPLITIC
CHIILOST HOLISTIC
CHIILPRY CHIRPILY
CHIILQSU CLIQUISH
CHIINORT ORNITHIC
CHIIORST HISTORIC,
   ORCHITIS
CHIIRSTT TRISTICH
CHIKLLOS HILLOCKS
CHIKMNPU CHIPMUNK
CHIKOPTY KYPHOTIC
CHILLOOT OILCLOTH
CHILMMUY CHUMMILY
CHILMOSU SCHOLIUM
CHILMPSU CLUMPISH
CHILNOSW CLOWNISH
CHILOOOZ HOLOZOIC
CHILOPPY CHOPPILY
CHILOTUY TOUCHILY
CHIMMORU CHROMIUM
CHIMNOSU INSOMUCH
CHIMNOSY CHYMOSIN
CHINOPTY HYPNOTIC,
   PYTHONIC, TYPHONIC
CHINOSSU CUSHIONS
CHINOSTZ SCHIZONT
CHINOSUY CUSHIONY
CHIOOPPT PHOTOPIC
CHIOOPTY OOPHYTIC
CHIOPRST STROPHIC
CHIOSSTT SCOTTISH
CHIPRRUY CHIRRUPY
CHIPRTTY TRIPTYCH
CHIRRSSU SCIRRHUS
CHKMMOSU HUMMOCKS

CHKMMOUY
   HUMMOCKY
CHLNOOOP COLOPHON
CHLOORSU CHLOROUS
CHMNORRU CRUMHORN
CHMOORSU CHROMOUS
CHNOOPTT TOP-NOTCH
CHNPPSUU PUNCH-UPS
CHORSTTU SHORT-
   CUT
CIIILMPT IMPLICIT
CIIILTVY CIVILITY
CIIINNOS INCISION
CIIINNOT COIN IT IN
CIIINTVY VICINITY
CIIJRSTU JURISTIC
CIIKLLOS OIL SLICK
CIIKLPST LIPSTICK
CIIKLRTY TRICKILY
CIIKLSTY STICKILY
CIIKNPPR PINPRICK
CIIKNPST STICKPIN
CIILLMTU TILLICUM
CIILLNOP POLLINIC
CIILMNOT MILTONIC
CIILMOPY IMPOLICY
CIILMRSY LYRICISM
CIILOOPT POLITICO
CIILOPST COLPITIS,
   POLITICS
CIILORST CLITORIS
CIILRSTY LYRICIST
CIIMNOST MONISTIC,
   NOMISTIC
CIIMORST TRISOMIC
CIIMOSST STOICISM
CIIMRTTU TRITICUM
CIINNSTT INSTINCT
CIINOOST ISOTONIC
CIINOPSU OPINICUS
CIINORSS INCISORS
CIINOSSS SCISSION
CIINOTTY TONICITY
CIINPSTU SINCIPUT
CIIOOPST ISOTOPIC
CIIOQTUX QUIXOTIC
CIIOTTXY TOXICITY
CIIPRRTU PRURITIC
CIIPRSTU PURISTIC
CIIRSTTU TRUISTIC
CIISSTTY CYSTITIS
CIJKOSTY JOYSTICK
CIJNNOOT CONJOINT
CIJNNOTU JUNCTION

CIJOOSTY JOCOSITY
CIKLLOPS PILLOCKS
CIKLLPUY PLUCKILY
CIKLNOST LINSTOCK
CIKLOSTY STOCKILY
CIKMOORS SICKROOM
CIKNNOOS COONSKIN
CIKNNOST NONSTICK
CIKOSSTT STOCKIST
CIKPSSTU STICK-UPS
CILLMSUY CLUMSILY
CILLNOSU SCULLION
CILLOOOT OCOTILLO
CILMNOPU PULMONIC
CILMNOUU INOCULUM
CILMNUUV VINCULUM
CILMPSUU SPICULUM
CILNOORU UNICOLOR
CILNOOST COLONIST
CILNOOTU LOCUTION
CILNOPTU PLUTONIC
CILNOSTU LINOCUTS
CILOOPST COPILOTS
CILOOPYZ POLYZOIC
CILOOORRT TRICOLOR
CILOORST COLORIST
CILOPRRY PYRROLIC
CILOPRUY POLYURIC
CILOPSSW COWSLIPS
CILOSSTU OCULISTS
CILOSSTY SYSTOLIC
CILOSSUU LUSCIOUS
CILPRSTU CULPRITS
CILPSSTU SCULPSIT
CILRSTTY STRICTLY
CILRSTUY CRUSTILY
CILRSUVY SCURVILY
CIMNOOTY MYOTONIC
CIMNORSS CRIMSONS
CIMNOSTU MISCOUNT
CIMNOSUU MUCINOUS
CIMNOSUY SYCONIUM
CIMOOOTZ ZOOTOMIC
CIMOSTUU MUTICOUS
CIMOSTUY MUCOSITY
CINNOOTU CONTINUO
CINNOOTX NONTOXIC
CINNOOVY IN CONVOY
CINNORSU UNICORNS
CINNOSTY SYNTONIC
CINNQUUX QUINCUNX
CINOOOPT COOPTION
CINOOPRS SCORPION
CINOOTXY OXYTOCIN

CINOPSTY SYNOPTIC	COOPRSUY UROSCOPY	DDEEILRV DRIVELED
CINOSTUV VISCOUNT	COORSSTU OUTCROSS	DDEEILWY WILD-EYED
CINRSTTU INSTRUCT	DDDDEEOR DODDERED	DDEEIMNR REMINDED
CINRSTUY SCRUTINY	DDDEEEFN DEFENDED	DDEEIMSS MISDEEDS
CIOOOPRS OOSPORIC	DDDEEENP DEPENDED	DDEEIMST DEMISTED
CIOOOTXZ ZOOTOXIC	DDDEEENR REDDENED	DDEEINNT INDENTED,
CIOOPRSS SCORPIOS	DDDEEHRS SHREDDED	INTENDED
CIOOPRST PORTICOS	DDDEEJRU JUDDERED	DDEEINOS ONE-SIDED
CIOPRSSU SCORPIUS	DDDEEORR DODDERER	DDEEINRT DENDRITE
CIOPSSTY COPYISTS	DDDEIINV DIVIDEND	DDEEINST DESTINED
CIORSSSS SCISSORS	DDDEILNW DWINDLED	DDEEIPRS PRESIDED
CIOTTTUU CUT IT OUT	DDDEILTW TWIDDLED	DDEEIPRV DEPRIVED
CIPRRUVY PYRRUVIC	DDDEINOR DENDROID	DDEEIPSS DESPISED
CIPSSTTY STYPTICS	DDDGIILN DIDDLING	DDEEIRTV DIVERTED
CKKNOOTU KNOCKOUT	DDEEEEMR REDEEMED	DDEEISST DESISTED
CKKNOPSU KNOCK-UPS	DDEEEENP DEEPENED	DDEEISTV DIVESTED
CKLOORSW ROWLOCKS	DDEEEFLX DEFLEXED	DDEELLMO MODELLED
CKLOOSTU LOCKOUTS	DDEEEFNR DEFENDER,	DDEELLOP DEED POLL
CKLOPSTU POTLUCKS	FENDERED	DDEELLOY YODELLED
CKMMORUW	DDEEEFRR DEFERRED	DDEELMOR MOLDERED,
.MUCKWORM	DDEEEHLW WHEEDLED	REMOLDED
CKNOOSTT STOCKTON	DDEEEIMR REMEDIED	DDEELMRS MEDDLERS
CKOOOSTU COOKOUTS	DDEEEIWY WIDE-EYED	DDEELOPR DEPLORED
CKOOPSTT STOCKPOT	DDEEELPT DEPLETED	DDEELOPX EXPLODED
CKOSSSTU TUSSOCKS	DDEEEMNT DEMENTED	DDEELOPY DEPLOYED
CKOSSTUY TUSSOCKY	DDEEENPX EXPENDED	DDEELORS SOLDERED
CLLMOSSU MOLLUSCS	DDEEENRR RENDERED	DDEELOSU DELOUSED
CLLOOPSS SCOLLOPS	DDEEENRT TENDERED	DDEELOVV DEVOLVED
CLLOOQUY COLLOQUY	DDEEENSU UNSEEDED	DDEELPRS PEDDLERS
CLLOSUUY CULOUSLY	DDEEENTX EXTENDED	DDEEMNOR ENDODERM
CLMMNOOY	DDEEERRT DETERRED	DDEEMRRU DEMURRED,
COMMONLY	DDEEERST DESERTED	MURDERED
CLMOOOTY COLOTOMY	DDEEERSV DESERVED	DDEENOPR PONDERED
CLMOSUUU CUMULOUS	DDEEESTT DETESTED	DDEENOPW PONDWEED
CLNOORST CONTROLS	DDEEEWYY DEWY-EYED	DDEENORS ENDORSED
CLOOOPRT PROTOCOL	DDEEFFIR DIFFERED	DDEENORW WONDERED
CLOOSSSU COLOSSUS	DDEEFFNO OFFENDED	DDEENRSU SUNDERED
CLOPRSSY CROSSPLY	DDEEFGIT FIDGETED	DDEEOPRT DEPORTED
CLOPRSTU SCULPTOR	DDEEFLNO ENFOLDED	DDEEOPRW POWDERED
CLOPSSTU COST-PLUS	DDEEFMOR DEFORMED	DDEEORRW REWORDED
CMMNNOOU	DDEEFNRU REFUNDED	DDEEORUV DEVOURED
UNCOMMON	DDEEGINS DESIGNED	DDEERTUX EXTRUDED
CMORSSTU SCROTUMS	DDEEGIRV DIVERGED	DDEFFISU DIFFUSED
CNOOOORT OCTOROON	DDEEGIST DIGESTED	DDEFIILM MIDFIELD
CNOORRTY CRYOTRON	DDEEGOPS GODSPEED	DDEFIIMO MODIFIED
CNOORSST CONSORTS	DDEEGOTW TWO-EDGED	DDEFLNOU UNFOLDED
CNOORSTU CONTOURS,	DDEEGRRS DREDGERS	DDEGGINR DREDGING
CROUTONS	DDEEHILS SHIELDED	DDEGGLOY DOGGEDLY
CNOSTUUU UNCTUOUS	DDEEHINR HINDERED	DDEGGNOO DOGGONED
COOOOPRRT ROOT	DDEEHIRT DITHERED	DDEGHINS SHEDDING
CROP	DDEEHRRS SHREDDER	DDEGIINR DERIDING
COOPRRST PROCTORS	DDEEIINT INEDITED	DDEGIIST GIDDIEST
COOPRSTU OUTCROPS	DDEEILLV DEVILLED	DDEGILMN MEDDLING
COOPRSUU CROUPOUS	DDEEILMW MILDEWED	DDEGILNP PEDDLING

DDEGILNS SLEDDING
DDEGILNU DELUDING,
  INDULGED
DDEGILOS DISLODGE
DDEGILRS GRIDDLES
DDEGILUV DIVULGED
DDEGIMOS DEMIGODS
DDEGINNU DENUDING
DDEGINSW WEDDINGS
DDEGIORT DOG-TIRED
DDEGIOST DODGIEST
DDEGIOSV GIVE ODDS
DDEGNOOR DORDOGNE
DDEGNORU GROUNDED,
  UNDERDOG
DDEGNOSS GODSENDS
DDEGOOOR DO-GOODER
DDEGOOWW
  WEDGWOOD
DDEGRRUY DRUDGERY
DDEHIISS SIDE DISH
DDEHILNY HIDDENLY
DDEHINOR DIHEDRON
DDEHIORS SHODDIER
DDEHNRSU HUNDREDS
DDEHOOSW WOODSHED
DDEHORSU SHROUDED
DDEHRSSU SHUDDERS
DDEHRSUY SHUDDERY
DDEIIKLS DISLIKED
DDEIILNR DIELDRIN
DDEIILOS IDOLISED
DDEIILOZ IDOLIZED
DDEIIOPS DIOPSIDE
DDEIIOST ODDITIES
DDEIIOSX DIOXIDES,
  OXIDISED
DDEIIOXZ OXIDIZED
DDEIIRSV DIVIDERS
DDEIIRUV REDUVIID
DDEIKNRS KINDREDS
DDEILMOP IMPLODED
DDEILNPS SPLENDID
DDEILNRU UNRIDDLE
DDEILNSW SWINDLED
DDEILOPS LOP-SIDED
DDEILRST TIDDLERS
DDEILRTW TWIDDLER
DDEILRZZ DRIZZLED
DDEILSTU LUDDITES
DDEILSTW TWIDDLES
DDEIMOSU MEDUSOID
DDEIMSTU MUDDIEST
DDEINORS INDORSED

DDEINOSW DISENDOW,
  DISOWNED
DDEINRST STRIDDEN
DDEINRTU INTRUDED
DDEIOPRS DROPSIED
DDEIOPRV PROVIDED
DDEIOPSS DISPOSED
DDEIORRS DISORDER
DDEIOSTW DOWDIEST,
  TWO-SIDED
DDEIPSTU DISPUTED
DDEIRSTU RUDDIEST
DDEKMOSU DUKEDOMS
DDELNRTU TRUNDLED
DDELNSUY SUDDENLY
DDELOPRS PLODDERS
DDELORST TODDLERS
DDEMNOST ODDMENTS
DDEMNOUU DUODENUM
DDEMNPUU PUDENDUM
DDEMOOTU OUTMODED
DDEOORSW REDWOODS
DDEOPRSW DEWDROPS
DDFGIILN FIDDLING
DDFGILNU FUDDLING
DDGGINNO DINGDONG
DDGGINRU DRUDGING
DDGHILNU HUDDLING
DDGHINTU THUDDING
DDGIIINO INDIGOID
DDGIIINV DIVIDING
DDGIIKNS SKIDDING
DDGIILMN MIDDLING
DDGIILNP PIDDLING
DDGIILNR RIDDLING
DDGILMNU MUDDLING
DDGILNOO DOODLING
DDGILNOP PLODDING
DDGILNOT TODDLING
DDGILNPU PUDDLING
DDGIMNUY MUDDYING
DDGINOPR PRODDING
DDGINPSU PUDDINGS
DDGINSTU STUDDING
DDGLOSTU GOLD DUST
DDGOOORW GOOD
  WORD
DDGOOOSW DOGWOODS
DDGOORSY DRY GOODS
DDHILOSY SHODDILY
DDIIIIVV DIVI-DIVI
DDIIMMUY DIDYMIUM
DDIIMRSU DRUIDISM
DDIIQTUY QUIDDITY

DDILOOPP DIPLOPOD
DDILORSY SORDIDLY
DDIMOSUY DIDYMOUS
DDINNOWW DOWNWIND
DDINOOOT ODONTOID
DDINOOWW WOODWIND
DDLLOORW OLD WORLD
DDLMORSU DOLDRUMS
DDMNORTU DORTMUND
DEEEEFRR REFEREED
DEEEEGKR KEDGEREE
DEEEEKNP KNEE-DEEP
DEEEEMRR REDEEMER
DEEEEMST ESTEEMED
DEEEENPR DEEPENER
DEEEENRV VENEERED
DEEEERTT TEETERED
DEEEFIIX IDEE FIXE
DEEEFIRW FIREWEED
DEEEFLRU REFUELED
DEEEFNRT DEFERENT
DEEEFRRR DEFERRER,
  REFERRED
DEEEFRRT FERRETED
DEEEFRST FESTERED
DEEEFRTT FETTERED
DEEEGIPR PEDIGREE
DEEEGIRR GREEDIER
DEEEGNNR ENGENDER
DEEEGNRV REVENGED
DEEEHLMT HELMETED
DEEEHLRT ETHELRED
DEEEHLRW WHEEDLER
DEEEHLSS HEEDLESS
DEEEHMNS ENMESHED
DEEEHRTT TETHERED
DEEEILRV RELIEVED
DEEEILST LEE TIDES
DEEEIMRS REMEDIES
DEEEINRR REINDEER
DEEEINST NEEDIEST
DEEEINTV EVENTIDE
DEEEIPRS SPEEDIER
DEEEIPTX EXPEDITE
DEEEIRSS DIERESES
DEEEIRST REEDIEST
DEEEIRVW REVIEWED
DEEEISST SEEDIEST,
  TEESSIDE
DEEEISTW WEEDIEST
DEEEJLLW JEWELLED
DEEEKLNN KENNELED
DEEEKNSW WEEKENDS
DEEEKOPW POKEWEED

DEEEKRSW SKEWERED
DEEELLLV LEVELLED
DEEELLPR REPELLED
DEEELLPX EXPELLED
DEEELLRV REVELLED
DEEELNRT RELENTED
DEEELNSS LESSENED,
  NEEDLESS
DEEELOSY SLOE-EYED
DEEELRTT LETTERED
DEEELSSS SEEDLESS
DEEEMNSS DEMESNES,
  SEEDSMEN
DEEEMPRT TEMPERED
DEEEMPTX EXEMPTED
DEEEMRST DEEMSTER
DEEENNRT ENTENDRE
DEEENOPR REOPENED
DEEENOPY OPEN-EYED
DEEENORS ENDORSEE
DEEENPRT REPENTED,
  REPETEND
DEEENPRX EXPENDER
DEEENPSS DEEPNESS
DEEENRRR RENDERER
DEEENRRT TENDERER
DEEENRRV REVEREND
DEEENRST RESENTED
DEEENRTU NEUTERED
DEEENRTX EXTENDER
DEEENRUV REVENUED
DEEENSTT DÉTENTES
DEEEOPRT DEPORTEE
DEEEOSTV DEVOTEES
DEEEPPPR PEPPERED
DEEEPRST PESTERED
DEEEQSUZ SQUEEZED
DEEERRST DESERTER
DEEERRSV DESERVER,
  RESERVED, REVERSED
DEEERRTV REVERTED
DEEERSTT DETESTER
DEEFFNOR OFFENDER
DEEFFRSU SUFFERED
DEEFGINR FINGERED
DEEFGLNU ENGULFED
DEEFGLUW GULFWEED
DEEFHLOR FREEHOLD
DEEFHORR HEREFORD
DEEFIINT DEFINITE
DEEFIIRS FIRESIDE
DEEFIIRV VERIFIED
DEEFILLR REFILLED
DEEFILLT FILLETED

DEEFILNX INFLEXED
DEEFILPR PILFERED
DEEFILRS DEFILERS,
  FIELDERS
DEEFILRT FILTERED
DEEFINRR INFERRED
DEEFINRW WINEFRED
DEEFINRZ FRENZIED
DEEFINST INFESTED
DEEFIORS FORESIDE
DEEFIPRX PREFIXED
DEEFIRTT REFITTED
DEEFLNNU FUNNELED
DEEFLNOR ENFOLDER
DEEFLORW DEFLOWER,
  FLOWERED
DEEFMNOT FOMENTED
DEEFMORR DEFORMER,
  REFORMED
DEEFMPRU PERFUMED
DEEFNOST SOFTENED
DEEFNRRU REFUNDER
DEEFNSST DEFTNESS
DEEFORST DEFOREST,
  FORESTED, FOSTERED
DEEFORUY FOUR-EYED
DEEFRTUY DUTY-FREE
DEEGGHHO HEDGEHOG
DEEGGIJR JIGGERED,
  REJIGGED
DEEGGINR GINGERED
DEEGGLOR DOGGEREL
DEEGHHOP HEDGEHOP
DEEGHITW WEIGHTED
DEEGHNRU HUNGERED
DEEGHOPS SHEEPDOG
DEEGHORW HEDGEROW
DEEGIINN INDIGENE
DEEGILNN NEEDLING
DEEGILNP IN PLEDGE
DEEGILNR LINGERED,
  REEDLING
DEEGILNS SEEDLING
DEEGILNT DELETING
DEEGILRY GREEDILY
DEEGILSS LEG SIDES
DEEGIMNN EMENDING
DEEGINPS SPEEDING
DEEGINRS DESIGNER,
  REDESIGN, RESIGNED
DEEGINSS EDGINESS
DEEGINST INGESTED
DEEGIORS GEORDIES
DEEGIRST DIGESTER

DEEGJPRU PREJUDGE
DEEGLNRY LEGENDRY
DEEGLORV GROVELED
DEEGLORW GLOWERED
DEEGNNOY ENDOGENY
DEEGNORV GOVERNED
DEEGNPUX EXPUNGED
DEEGOTUW GOUTWEED
DEEGRRTU GERTRUDE
DEEGRSTU GESTURED
DEEGRTTU GUTTERED
DEEHHPRS SHEPHERD
DEEHHRST THRESHED
DEEHIKRS SHRIEKED
DEEHILNP DELPHINE
DEEHILRS RELISHED,
  SHIELDER
DEEHILSS HIDELESS
DEEHILSV DISHEVEL
DEEHIMOP HEMIPODE
DEEHIMRT MEREDITH
DEEHINRR HINDERER
DEEHINTW WHITENED
DEEHIOTX ETHOXIDE
DEEHIPPS SHEEPDIP
DEEHIPRS PERISHED
DEEHIRRT DITHERER
DEEHIRSV SHIVERED
DEEHIRTW WITHERED
DEEHIRTY HEREDITY
DEEHKNOS KEESHOND
DEEHLLOR HOLLERED
DEEHLOSV SHOVELED
DEEHMNRS HERDSMEN
DEEHMORT MOTHERED
DEEHNORT DETHRONE
DEEHNOWY HONEYDEW
DEEHNSTU ENTHUSED
DEEHOORT THEODORE
DEEHOORV HOOVERED
DEEHORSU REHOUSED
DEEHORSW SHOWERED
DEEHORTX EXHORTED
DEEHRRSW SHREWDER
DEEIILNS SIDELINE
DEEIILRV LIVERIED
DEEIIMST ITEMISED
DEEIIMTZ ITEMIZED
DEEIIPRU PRIE-DIEU
DEEIIRSS DIERESIS
DEEIIRST SIDERITE
DEEIIRSV DERISIVE
DEEIISSS DISSEISE
DEEIJNNO ENJOINED

DEEIJNOR REJOINED
DEEIKLLR KILLDEER
DEEIKLMO DOMELIKE
DEEIKLMW MILKWEED
DEEIKLNN ENKINDLE
DEEIKLNR REKINDLE
DEEIKNPS SKIN-DEEP
DEEIKNRS DEERSKIN
DEEIKNRT TINKERED
DEEIKSTT DISKETTE
DEEILLMN MEDELLIN
DEEILLMP IMPELLED
DEEILLST LET SLIDE
DEEILLVY VEILEDLY
DEEILMNU DEMILUNE
DEEILMOS MELODIES,
 MELODISE
DEEILMOZ MELODIZE
DEEILNOT DELETION
DEEILNRU UNDERLIE
DEEILNSS IDLENESS
DEEILNST ENLISTED,
 LISTENED
DEEILNSV SNIVELED
DEEILNTT ENTITLED
DEEILNUV UNVEILED
DEEILOPT LEPIDOTE
DEEILORT DOLERITE,
 LOITERED
DEEILORV EVILDOER
DEEILPRX DIPLEXER
DEEILPSY SPEEDILY
DEEILRSU LEISURED
DEEILRSV SILVERED
DEEILRSW WIELDERS
DEEILRTT LITTERED
DEEILRVY DELIVERY
DEEILSUV DELUSIVE
DEEILSVW SWIVELED
DEEILTUY YULETIDE
DEEIMMNS ENDEMISM
DEEIMMOS SEMIDOME
DEEIMMRS IMMERSED,
 SIMMERED
DEEIMNOR DOMINEER
DEEIMNOS DEMONISE
DEEIMNOZ DEMONIZE
DEEIMNPT PEDIMENT
DEEIMNRR REMINDER
DEEIMNST SEDIMENT
DEEIMNSY MIND'S
 EYE
DEEIMPRR PERIDERM
DEEIMPRS SIMPERED

DEEIMRST DEMERITS,
 DEMISTER
DEEIMRTT REMITTED
DEEINNRT INDENTER,
 INTENDER, INTERNED
DEEINNSS DENISENS
DEEINNST DESINENT
DEEINNSZ DENIZENS
DEEINNTV INVENTED
DEEINNTW ENTWINED
DEEINOPW WIDE-OPEN
DEEINOSV NOSEDIVE
DEEINPSS DISPENSE
DEEINQRU ENQUIRED
DEEINQSU SEQUINED
DEEINRRT INTERRED,
 TRENDIER
DEEINRRW REWINDER
DEEINRST DNIESTER,
 INSERTED, RESIDENT,
 TRENDIES
DEEINRSX INDEXERS
DEEINRTU RETINUED,
 REUNITED
DEEINRTV INVERTED
DEEINRTW WINTERED
DEEINSSW DEWINESS,
 WIDENESS
DEEINSTT INSETTED
DEEINSTV INVESTED
DEEINSTY TYNESIDE
DEEIOPRX PEROXIDE
DEEIOPSS EPISODES
DEEIORRV OVERRIDE
DEEIORSV OVERSIDE
DEEIPPQU EQUIPPED
DEEIPRRS PRESIDER,
 RESPIRED
DEEIPRRV DEPRIVER
DEEIPRSS DISPERSE
DEEIPSST SIDESTEP
DEEIPSTU DEPUTIES,
 DEPUTISE
DEEIPTUZ DEPUTIZE
DEEIQRRU REQUIRED
DEEIQRTU REQUITED
DEEIQRUV QUIVERED
DEEIQTUU QUIETUDE
DEEIRRSS DRESSIER
DEEIRRTV DIVERTER
DEEIRSST RESISTED
DEEIRSSU REISSUED,
 RESIDUES
DEEIRSSV DISSEVER

DEEIRSTW WEIRDEST
DEEIRTTT TITTERED
DEEJPRRU PERJURED
DEEKMNOY MONKEYED
DEEKNOTW KNOTWEED
DEEKORRW REWORKED
DEELLMOR MODELLER
DEELLMOW MELLOWED
DEELLNOR ENROLLED
DEELLNOW WELL-DONE
DEELLORY YODELLER
DEELLOTW TOWELLED
DEELLOTX EXTOLLED
DEELLOVY VOLLEYED
DEELLOWY YELLOWED
DEELMMPU PUMMELED
DEELMNOO MELODEON
DEELMOPY EMPLOYED
DEELMOST MOLESTED
DEELMRUY DEMURELY
DEELNNTU TUNNELED
DEELNOOS LOOSE END,
 LOOSENED
DEELNORT REDOLENT,
 RONDELET
DEELNRTU UNDERLET
DEELNRTY TENDERLY
DEELNSSW LEWDNESS
DEELNWWY NEWLYWED
DEELOPRR DEPLORER
DEELOPRX EXPLODER,
 EXPLORED
DEELOPRY REDEPLOY
DEELORRS SOLDERER
DEELORSV RESOLVED
DEELORTT DOTTEREL
DEELORTV REVOLTED
DEELORVV REVOLVED
DEELPRRU PRELUDER
DEELPRSU PRELUDES,
 REPULSED
DEELPRTU DRUPELET
DEELPSUX DUPLEXES
DEELRSTU RESULTED
DEELRSTW WRESTLED
DEEMMORS MESODERM
DEEMMRSU SUMMERED
DEEMNOOS ENDOSOME,
 MOONSEED
DEEMNOQU QUEENDOM
DEEMNORT ENTODERM
DEEMOORT ODOMETER
DEEMORSW WORMSEED
DEEMPRST DEMPSTER

DEEMPRSU PRESUMED
DEEMPRTU PERMUTED
DEEMRRRU DEMURRER, MURDERER
DEEMRSTU DEMUREST, MUSTERED
DEEMRTTU MUTTERED
DEENNOPT DEPONENT
DEENNOPU UNOPENED
DEENNORW RENOWNED
DEENNRUV UNNERVED
DEENNSSU NUDENESS
DEENOORV OVERDONE
DEENOPRR PONDERER
DEENOPSS SPONDEES
DEENORRS ENDORSER
DEENORRW WONDERER
DEENORSW WORSENED
DEENORTU DEUTERON
DEENPRSS SPENDERS
DEENPSTU TENSED UP
DEENRRTU RETURNED
DEENRSSU END USERS, RUDENESS
DEENRSTU DENTURES, UNDERSET
DEENRSUV UNVERSED
DEENRTUV VENTURED
DEEOOORV OVERRODE
DEEOORSV OVERDOSE
DEEOPRRT REPORTED
DEEOPRRV REPROVED
DEEOPRRW POWDERER
DEEOPRTT POTTERED
DEEOPRTX EXPORTED
DEEOPSSU ESPOUSED
DEEORRST RESORTED, RESTORED
DEEORRTT RETORTED
DEEORRUV DEVOURER
DEEORRVW OVERDREW
DEEORSTX DEXTROSE
DEEORSTY STOREYED
DEEORTTT TOTTERED
DEEORTTX EXTORTED
DEEORTUV DEVOUTER
DEEPRTTU PUTTERED
DEEPRUVY PURVEYED
DEERRSSS DRESSERS
DEERRTTU TURRETED
DEERSSST DESSERTS, STRESSED
DEERSUVY SURVEYED
DEFFGILO OFF-GLIDE

DEFFHLSU SHUFFLED
DEFFILNS SNIFFLED
DEFFILOV FIVEFOLD
DEFFIRSU DIFFUSER
DEFFLNSU SNUFFLED
DEFFNOSS SEND-OFFS
DEFFSSUU SUFFUSED
DEFFSTUY DYESTUFF
DEFGIILN DEFILING, FIELDING
DEFGIINN DEFINING
DEFGIINY DEIFYING, EDIFYING
DEFGIIST DIGESTIF
DEFGINSU DEFUSING
DEFGIORS FIREDOGS
DEFGJORU FORJUDGE
DEFGLOOS GOOD SELF
DEFHIINS FIENDISH, FINISHED
DEFHLOOS SELFHOOD
DEFHORRT HERTFORD
DEFIIILV VILIFIED
DEFIILLO OILFIELD
DEFIILLW WILDLIFE
DEFIILNS INFIDELS
DEFIILOR OIL-FIRED
DEFIILPS FLIP SIDE
DEFIILRW WILDFIRE
DEFIILSU FLUIDISE
DEFIILTY FIDELITY
DEFIILUZ FLUIDIZE
DEFIIMOR MODIFIER
DEFIIMRS MISFIRED
DEFIINOT NOTIFIED
DEFIINRW WINIFRED
DEFIINTY IDENTIFY
DEFIIOSS OSSIFIED
DEFIIPRU PURIFIED
DEFIIPSS FISSIPED
DEFIIPTY TYPIFIED
DEFILNNO NINEFOLD
DEFILNRU UNRIFLED, URNFIELD
DEFILNRY FRIENDLY
DEFILOPR PROFILED
DEFILORU FLUORIDE
DEFILOTU OUTFIELD
DEFILPRU PRIDEFUL
DEFILPTU UPLIFTED
DEFILRRU FLURRIED
DEFILRVY FERVIDLY
DEFILRZZ FRIZZLED
DEFIMNOR INFORMED

DEFIMOPR PEDIFORM
DEFIMRRU DRUMFIRE
DEFINORW FOREWIND
DEFIOORW FIREWOOD
DEFIOPRT PROFITED
DEFIRRST DRIFTERS
DEFLLOOW FOLLOWED
DEFLNORU FLOUNDER, UNFOLDER
DEFLNRUU UNFURLED
DEFLOORT FORETOLD
DEFMNORU UNFORMED
DEFMOOOR FOREDOOM
DEFNNOSS FONDNESS
DEFNOOPS SPOON-FED
DEFNORRU FRONDEUR
DEFNORSU FOUNDERS
DEFNRRUU UNDERFUR
DEFOORRW FOREWORD
DEFOOTUX OUTFOXED
DEFORRUW FURROWED
DEGGHRSU SHRUGGED
DEGGIINN DEIGNING
DEGGILNP PLEDGING
DEGGILNS GELDINGS, SLEDGING
DEGGILNU DELUGING
DEGGILOO LIE DOGGO
DEGGILRW WRIGGLED
DEGGIORS DISGORGE
DEGGLMSU SMUGGLED
DEGGLNSU SNUGGLED
DEGGLORY GORGEDLY
DEGGLRUY RUGGEDLY
DEGGRSTU DRUGGETS
DEGHHIIT HIGH TIDE
DEGHHILV HIGHVELD
DEGHIINS DINGHIES
DEGHIKNT KNIGHTED
DEGHILPT PLIGHTED
DEGHILRT RED LIGHT
DEGHILST DELIGHTS, SLIGHTED
DEGHINNU UNHINGED
DEGHLOPU PLOUGHED
DEGHLOSU SLOUGHED
DEGHNORT THRONGED
DEGHNORY HYDROGEN
DEGHOOSU DOGHOUSE
DEGIIIST DIGITISE
DEGIIITZ DIGITIZE
DEGIILNT DILIGENT
DEGIILNV DEVILING
DEGIILNW WIELDING

DEGIILNY YIELDING
DEGIILTY GELIDITY
DEGIIMNP IMPEDING,
    IMPINGED
DEGIIMSU MISGUIDE
DEGIINNT INDIGENT
DEGIINNW WIDENING
DEGIINNX INDEXING
DEGIINOV VIDEOING
DEGIINRS DESIRING,
    RESIDING, RINGSIDE
DEGIINRV DERIVING
DEGIINST DINGIEST
DEGIINSV DEVISING
DEGIINTY TIE-DYING
DEGIISSU DISGUISE
DEGIJMSU MISJUDGE
DEGIKLOV KID-GLOVE
DEGIKNRY RING-DYKE
DEGILLNU DUELLING
DEGILLNW DWELLING
DEGILMNO GOLDMINE,
    MODELING
DEGILMPS GLIMPSED
DEGILNOS SIDELONG
DEGILNOY YODELING
DEGILNRU INDULGER
DEGILOOR GOODLIER
DEGILOOY IDEOLOGY
DEGILOST GODLIEST
DEGILRSU GUILDERS,
    SLUDGIER
DEGILRUV DIVULGER
DEGILRZZ GRIZZLED
DEGIMNOT DEMOTING
DEGIMNPU IMPUGNED
DEGINNNU UNENDING
DEGINNOT DENOTING
DEGINNOW ENDOWING
DEGINNPS SPENDING
DEGINNPU UPENDING
DEGINNRU ENDURING
DEGINOPS DEPOSING
DEGINORR ORDERING
DEGINORV RINGDOVE
DEGINOSW WIDGEONS
DEGINOTV DEVOTING
DEGINPTU DEPUTING
DEGINRRS GRINDERS
DEGINRRY GRINDERY
DEGINRSS DRESSING
DEGINRSY SYRINGED
DEGIOPRR PORRIDGE
DEGIOPSS GOSSIPED

DEGIOPST PODGIEST
DEGIORST STODGIER
DEGIPSTU PUDGIEST
DEGJMNTU JUDGMENT
DEGLMNOT LODGMENT
DEGLOOPY PEDOLOGY
DEGLOOUU DUOLOGUE
DEGLOPSS SPLODGES
DEGLPRSU SPLURGED
DEGNNOSU DUNGEONS
DEGNOOSS GOODNESS
DEHHILTW WITHHELD
DEHIILLS HILLSIDE
DEHIILSV DEVILISH
DEHIIMST DITHEISM
DEHIINNS SHINNIED
DEHIINNW WHINNIED
DEHIISST DISHIEST
DEHIISTT DITHEIST
DEHIJMNO DEMIJOHN
DEHIKLOO HOODLIKE
DEHIKMOS SHEIKDOM
DEHILLRT THRILLED
DEHILMOS DEMOLISH
DEHILNOY HONIEDLY
DEHILNPY DIPHENYL
DEHILOPS POLISHED
DEHILOTY HOLYTIDE
DEHILPSU SULPHIDE
DEHILSTW WHISTLED
DEHILTTW WHITTLED
DEHIMNOS HEDONISM
DEHINOPS SIPHONED,
    SPHENOID
DEHINOST HEDONIST
DEHINPSU PUNISHED
DEHINSUW UNWISHED
DEHIOPRS SPHEROID
DEHIOSSW SIDESHOW
DEHIQSSU SQUISHED
DEHIRTWW WITHDREW
DEHKLNOU ELKHOUND
DEHLLOOW HOLLOWED
DEHLLOPY PHYLLODE
DEHLMORY HYDROMEL
DEHLNTUY HUNTEDLY
DEHLOORV HOLDOVER
DEHLOOSS HOODLESS
DEHLOOST TOEHOLDS
DEHLOPRU UPHOLDER
DEHLOPSS SPLOSHED
DEHLORSU SHOULDER
DEHLRRSU HURDLERS
DEHLRSWY SHREWDLY

DEHLSTTU SHUTTLED
DEHMMRTU THRUMMED
DEHMOORW
    WHOREDOM
DEHMOOST SMOOTHED
DEHMORUU HUMOURED
DEHNOORU HONOURED
DEHNOPSY SYPHONED
DEHNORSU ENSHROUD,
    UNHORSED
DEHNORTY THRENODY
DEHNOSSW SNOWSHED
DEHNRSTU THUNDERS
DEHNRTUY THUNDERY
DEHOOPRT THEROPOD
DEHOORTU OUT-HEROD
DEHOPRST POTSHERD
DEIIINSV DIVINISE
DEIIINVZ DIVINIZE
DEIIISVV DIVISIVE
DEIIKLNR KINDLIER
DEIIKLSS DISLIKES
DEIIKMOS ESKIMOID
DEIIKNST DINKIEST
DEIIKNSV SKIN-DIVE
DEIIKSVV SKIVVIED
DEIILLMT ILL-TIMED
DEIILMRU DELIRIUM
DEIILNNU INDULINE
DEIILNOS LIONISED
DEIILNOT TOLIDINE
DEIILNOZ LIONIZED
DEIILNVY DIVINELY
DEIILNXY XYLIDINE
DEIILORS IDOLISER
DEIILORZ IDOLIZER
DEIILPSS SIDESLIP
DEIILSTU UTILISED
DEIILTUZ UTILIZED
DEIIMMRS DIMERISM
DEIIMMST MISTIMED
DEIIMNRT DIRIMENT
DEIIMNTU MUTINIED
DEIIMPRU PERIDIUM
DEIIMSVW MIDWIVES
DEIINNOP PINIONED
DEIINNPP PINNIPED
DEIINORS DERISION,
    RESINOID
DEIINOST EDITIONS,
    SEDITION
DEIINPPW WINDPIPE
DEIINPRS INSPIRED
DEIINPRT INTREPID

DEIINPRY PYRIDINE
DEIINQRU INQUIRED
DEIINRSS INSIDERS
DEIINRST DISINTER
DEIINRSV DIVINERS,
DRIVE-INS
DEIINSST INSISTED,
TIDINESS
DEIINSTU DISUNITE
DEIINSTW WINDIEST
DEIINTTU INTUITED
DEIINTTY IDENTITY
DEIIOPRS PRESIDIO
DEIIORSX OXIDISER
DEIIORTX TRIOXIDE
DEIIORXZ OXIDIZER
DEIIPRST RIPTIDES,
SPIRITED
DEIIPTTY TEPIDITY
DEIIQSTU DISQUIET
DEIIRSSU DIURESIS
DEIIRSTT DIRTIEST
DEIISTZZ DIZZIEST
DEIJORRY JOYRIDER
DEIJORSY JOYRIDES
DEIKKLNO KLONDIKE
DEIKLNRW WRINKLED
DEIKLNTW TWINKLED
DEIKMNOO KIMONOED
DEIKNNRU UNKINDER
DEIKNNSS KINDNESS
DEIKNRRS DRINKERS
DEIKNRSS REDSKINS
DEIKRSVY SKYDIVER
DEIKSSTU DUSKIEST
DEILLOPW PILLOWED
DEILLORR LORDLIER
DEILLSTU DUELLIST
DEILMNSS MILDNESS,
MINDLESS
DEILMOOT DOLOMITE
DEILMOPR IMPLORED
DEILMORT OLD-TIMER
DEILMORU LEMUROID,
MOULDIER
DEILMOST MELODIST,
MOLDIEST
DEILMOSU EMULSOID
DEILMOTV DEMIVOLT
DEILMPTU MULTIPED
DEILNNOT INDOLENT
DEILNOOS SOLENOID
DEILNOSU DELUSION
DEILNOSW LIE-DOWNS

DEILNOTU OUTLINED
DEILNOVV INVOLVED
DEILNPSS SPINDLES
DEILNPST SPLIT END
DEILNRST TENDRILS
DEILNRSW SWINDLER
DEILNRTY TRENDILY
DEILNSSW SWINDLES,
WILDNESS
DEILNSTU INSULTED,
UNLISTED
DEILNTTU UNTITLED
DEILNTUY UNITEDLY
DEILNUWY UNWIELDY
DEILOOPW WOODPILE
DEILORSS SOLDIERS
DEILORSY SOLDIERY
DEILORTY ELYTROID
DEILOSSV DISSOLVE
DEILOSTU SOLITUDE
DEILOSTW LOW
TIDES
DEILOTUV OUTLIVED
DEILPPST STIPPLED
DEILPPSU SUPPLIED
DEILPRSU SERPULID
DEILRRSV L-DRIVERS
DEILRSSY DRESSILY
DEILSSTY STYLISED
DEILSTUY SEDULITY
DEILSTWW WILD WEST
DEILSTYZ STYLIZED
DEIMMNOS DEMONISM
DEIMMOST IMMODEST
DEIMNOOS DOMINOES
DEIMNOOT DEMOTION,
MOTIONED
DEIMNOOX MONOXIDE
DEIMNOPT PIEDMONT
DEIMNOST DEMONIST
DEIMNOTW DOWNTIME
DEIMNPSS MISSPEND
DEIMNPTU IMPUDENT
DEIMNRTU RUDIMENT
DEIMOOST MOODIEST,
SODOMITE
DEIMOPRS PROMISED
DEIMOPRT IMPORTED
DEIMOPRV IMPROVED
DEIMORRR MIRRORED
DEIMORSU DIMEROUS,
SOREDIUM
DEIMORUX EXORDIUM
DEIMOSTT DEMOTIST

DEIMOTTW TWO-TIMED
DEIMPSTU DUMPIEST
DEIMQRSU SQUIRMED
DEIMRSSU SURMISED
DEIMRSUU RESIDUUM
DEINNNOU INNUENDO
DEINNOWW WINNOWED
DEINNPRU UNDERPIN
DEINNRSU IN SUNDER
DEINNRTV TV DINNER
DEINNRUW UNWINDER
DEINOOPS POISONED
DEINOOPW PINEWOOD
DEINOOTV DEVOTION
DEINOPPW DOWNPIPE
DEINOPRY PYRENOID
DEINOPSS DOPINESS
DEINORSU SOURDINE
DEINORSW DISOWNER
DEINORVW OVERWIND
DEINOSSZ DOZINESS
DEINOSTW DOWNIEST
DEINPPUZ UNZIPPED
DEINPRST SPRINTED
DEINPSST STIPENDS
DEINPTTU INPUTTED
DEINQSTU SQUINTED
DEINRRTU INTRUDER
DEINRSSU SUNDRIES
DEINRSTT STRIDENT,
TRIDENTS
DEINSSST DISSENTS
DEINSSSY SYNDESIS
DEINSTUU UNSUITED
DEIOORTV OVERDO IT
DEIOOSTW WOODIEST
DEIOPRRV PROVIDER
DEIOPRSS DISPOSER
DEIOPRST RIPOSTED
DEIOPRSV DISPROVE
DEIOPSST DEPOSITS
DEIOPTUW WIPED OUT
DEIORRSY DERISORY
DEIORRTU OUTRIDER
DEIORSSS DOSSIERS
DEIORSST STEROIDS
DEIORSSU DESIROUS
DEIORSTU OUTSIDER
DEIORSTV ROWDIEST,
WORDIEST
DEIORSWW WIDOWERS
DEIOSSTU OUTSIDES
DEIOSTTT DOTTIEST
DEIPPRST STRIPPED

DEIPRSTU DISPUTER,
  STUPIDER
DEIPSSTU DISPUTES
DEIQRSTU SQUIRTED
DEIRRSTU STURDIER
DEIRSSST DISTRESS
DEIRSTTU DETRITUS
DEIRSUVV SURVIVED
DEISSTTU DUSTIEST
DEISTTTU DUETTIST
DEJMPPUU JUMPED-UP
DEJNOORS SOJORNED
DEKKORSW DESKWORK
DEKNRSTU DRUNKEST
DEKOOPRV PROVOKED
DEKOOTWW
  KOWTOWED
DEKOPRUW WORKED UP
DELLLOOP LOLLOPED
DELLNOPU UNPOLLED
DELLNORU UNROLLED
DELLNSSU DULLNESS
DELLOOTW WELL-TO-DO
DELLOPTU POLLUTED
DELLORRY DROLLERY
DELLORST DROLLEST,
  STROLLED
DELMNOOW OLD
  WOMEN
DELMNOTW MELTDOWN
DELMNPUU PENDULUM
DELMORSU REMOULDS,
  SMOULDER
DELMOSTY MODESTLY
DELNNOOR LONDONER
DELNOOSU UNLOOSED
DELNOOWY WOODENLY
DELNOPRS SPLENDOR
DELNORSU ROUNDELS
DELNORWW NEW
  WORLD
DELNOSSU LOUDNESS
DELNOSTW LETDOWNS
DELOORRV OVERLORD
DELOORSS ODORLESS
DELOORSV OVERSOLD
DELOPRST DROPLETS
DELOPSTU POSTLUDE
DELOPSTW SPOT-WELD
DELORSST OLDSTERS
DELORSSW WORDLESS
DELORSUY DELUSORY
DELOSSUU SEDULOUS
DELOTUVY DEVOUTLY

DELRSSTU STRUDELS
DEMMNOSU SUMMONED
DEMMRRSU DRUMMERS
DEMMRRUU MURMURED
DEMMRSTU STRUMMED
DEMNNOOT EDMONTON
DEMNOOSW WOODSMEN
DEMNORSY SYNDROME
DEMNOSTU MUDSTONE
DEMOOPRR PRODROME
DEMOOPRT PROMOTED
DEMOORSU DORMOUSE
DEMOPPRT PROMPTED
DEMORRUU RUMOURED
DENNOORW NO
  WONDER
DENNOSTY SYNDETON
DENNOTUW UNWONTED
DENOOOTW WOODNOTE
DENOORRS ENDORSOR
DENOORTX NEXT-DOOR
DENORRSU ROUNDERS
DENORSSU DOURNESS
DENORSTU ROUNDEST
DENORSTY DRY-STONE
DENORTUW UNDERTOW
DENPRTUU UPTURNED
DENRRTUU NURTURED
DENSSTTU STUDENTS
DEOOORSW ROSEWOOD
DEOOPPRS PROPOSED
DEOOPPRT PTEROPOD
DEOOPRST DOORSTEP
DEOOPRTU UPROOTED
DEOORRSW SORROWED
DEOOTTUV OUTVOTED
DEOPPRRS DROPPERS
DEOPPRSU PURPOSED
DEOPPSSU SUPPOSED
DEOPRRTU PROTRUDE
DEOPRSST TOP-DRESS
DEOPRSTU POSTURED,
  PROUDEST, SPROUTED
DEORRTTU TORTURED
DEOSSSYY ODYSSEYS
DEPRRTUU RUPTURED
DERSTTTU STRUTTED
DFFIIMRS MIDRIFFS
DFFLOORU FOURFOLD
DFFOORUW WOODRUFF
DFGGHIOT DOGFIGHT
DFGHILOS GOLDFISH
DFGIILRY FRIGIDLY
DFGIINNS FINDINGS

DFGIINRT DRIFTING
DFGILNNO FONDLING
DFGILNOO FLOODING
DFGINNOU FOUNDING
DFHIIMUY HUMIDIFY
DFHILSSU DISHFULS
DFHIMRSU DRUMFISH
DFHLOOOT FOOTHOLD
DFHNOOUX FOXHOUND
DFIILMTU MULTIFID
DFIILOSY SOLIDIFY
DFIILTUY FLUIDITY
DFILLOOT FLOODLIT
DFILLORY FLORIDLY
DFILLOWW WILDFOWL
DFIMOOOR IODOFORM
DFIOOPRS DISPROOF
DFJKNOOU JUNK FOOD
DFNOOPRU PROFOUND
DFOOOSTW SOFTWOOD
DGGGIINS DIGGINGS
DGGGINRU DRUGGING,
  GRUDGING
DGGIILNR GIRDLING
DGGIINNR GRINDING
DGGILNOS LODGINGS
DGGIMNSU SMUDGING
DGGINRTU TRUDGING
DGGIRSTU DRUGGIST
DGHIIINN IN HIDING
DGHIIMNT MIDNIGHT
DGHIINSS SHINDIGS
DGHILLNU DUNGHILL
DGHILNOS HOLDINGS
DGHILNRU HURDLING
DGHILOOR GIRLHOOD
DGHINNOU HOUNDING
DGHLORSU GOLD RUSH
DGHNOTUU DOUGHNUT
DGHOOOSW GOOD
  SHOW
DGHOOOTT DOGTOOTH
DGHORRUY ROUGH-DRY
DGHORSTU DROUGHTS
DGHORTUY DROUGHTY
DGIIINNV DIVINING
DGIIIRTY RIGIDITY
DGIIKLNN KINDLING
DGIIKNNR DRINKING
DGIILLNR DRILLING
DGIILLOU LIGULOID
DGIILNTU DILUTING
DGIIMNOU GONIDIUM
DGIIMPUY PYGIDIUM

DGIINORR GRIDIRON
DGIINORT DIGITRON
DGIINPPR DRIPPING
DGIINRTY DIRTYING
DGIKMNOS KINGDOMS
DGIKNOOW KINGWOOD
DGILLOOW GOODWILL
DGILMNOS MOLDINGS
DGILMNOU MOULDING
DGILMNPU DUMPLING
DGILMSUY SMUDGILY
DGILNOOR DROOLING
DGILNOOY INDOLOGY
DGILNOTY DOTINGLY
DGILOSTY STODGILY
DGILRTUY TURGIDLY
DGIMMNRU DRUMMING
DGINNOPU POUNDING
DGINNORU ROUNDING
DGINNORW DROWNING
DGINNOSU SOUNDING
DGINNOUW WOUNDING
DGINOOPR DROOPING
DGINOOPS GOSPODIN
DGINOOTU OUTDOING
DGINOPPR DROPPING
DGINORSW DROWSING
DGINSTUY STUDYING
DGLOOOXY DOXOLOGY
DGMOPRSU GUMDROPS
DGNOOORV NOVGOROD
DGOORSTT DOGTROTS
DHHILOTW WITHHOLD
DHIIIMNS DIMINISH
DHIIKWZZ WHIZZ KID
DHIIMNOO HOMINOID
DHIIMNSU HINDUISM
DHIIMOST ISTHMOID
DHIIMTUY HUMIDITY
DHIIORSS HIDROSIS
DHIJOPRU JODHPURI
DHIKNOOW HOODWINK
DHILLNOW DOWNHILL
DHILLOPY PHYLLOID
DHILMOPY LYMPHOID
DHILMOSY MODISHLY
DHILNOPS DOLPHINS
DHILOPRS LORDSHIP
DHILOPSS SLIPSHOD
DHILORRY HORRIDLY
DHIMNOST HINDMOST
DHINOORS DISHONOR
DHINORSU ROUNDISH
DHINOTUW WHODUNIT

DHIOOPRZ RHIZOPOD
DHIORSTY THYROIDS,
   THYRSOID
DHJOPRSU JODHPURS
DHKMNOOO
   MONKHOOD
DHLMOOSU HOODLUMS
DHLNOSTU SHOULDN'T
DHMNOOOT
   HOMODONT
DHNOOSWW
   SHOWDOWN
DHNOSTUW SHUTDOWN
DHOOORTX ORTHODOX
DHOORSUW WOODRUSH
DIIILLQU ILLIQUID
DIIIMTTY TIMIDITY
DIIINOSV DIVISION
DIIINTVY DIVINITY
DIIIPRST DISPIRIT
DIIIRTVY VIRIDITY
DIIJNOST DISJOINT
DIILLMNW WINDMILL
DIILLMPY LIMPIDLY
DIILLSTY IDYLLIST
DIILNOTU DILUTION
DIILNTUY UNTIDILY
DIILOPRT TRIPLOID
DIILOPSS DIPLOSIS
DIILOSTY SOLIDITY
DIIMMNOU DOMINIUM
DIIMNNOO DOMINION
DIIMNOPT MIDPOINT
DIIMNSUU INDUSIUM
DIIMOPRS PRISMOID
DIIMPUXY PYXIDIUM
DIIMTTUY TUMIDITY
DIINNOSU DISUNION
DIINOOPS IODOPSIN
DIINOSSU SINUSOID
DIINSTUY DISUNITY
DIIORSST SISTROID
DIIORSSV DIVISORS
DIKLNNUY UNKINDLY
DILLMNOP MILLPOND
DILLOORS DOORSILL
DILLOSTY STOLIDLY
DILMOOSU MODIOLUS
DILOOPPY POLYPOID
DILOOPRY DROOPILY
DILOORSS LORDOSIS
DILOOSUY ODIOUSLY
DILOPRTY TORPIDLY
DILORRTY TORRIDLY

DILORSWY DROWSILY
DILPSTUY STUPIDLY
DILRSTUY STURDILY
DIMNOSTU DISMOUNT
DIMORSWY ROWDYISM
DINOOORW IRONWOOD
DINOOSTY NODOSITY
DINOSSTW SIT-DOWNS
DINRSTUY INDUSTRY
DIOSSTUU STUDIOUS
DIRSSTTU DISTRUST
DKOOORWW
   WOODWORK
DKORSTUW STUDWORK
DLNOOSWW SLOWDOWN
DLOOOORS DOLOROSO
DLOOORSU DOLOROUS
DLOOPPUW PULPWOOD,
   WOOD PULP
DLOOPPYY POLYPODY
DMMNRUUY DUMMY
   RUN
DMOOORWW
   WOODWORM,
   WORMWOOD
DNNOOTWW
   DOWNTOWN
DNNORSUW RUNDOWNS
DNNORTUW
   DOWNTURN
DNOOPPRU PROPOUND
DNOOPRSW SNOWDROP
DNOOPRUW DOWNPOUR
DNOORSUW WONDROUS
DNOPRSUU ROUNDUPS
DNOPSTUW PUT-DOWNS
DNORRSUU SURROUND
DOOOPRST DOORPOST,
   DOORSTOP
DOOORSTU OUTDOORS
DOOPRRTW DROPWORT
DOOPRSTU DROPOUTS
EEEEFRRS REFEREES
EEEEGQSU SQUEEGEE
EEEEGSSX EXEGESES
EEEEHTTY EYETEETH
EEEELLPX EXPELLEE
EEEENRRV VENEERER
EEEFFINT TENEFIFE
EEEFFNOR FREEFONE
EEEFFNRT EFFERENT
EEEFFORT FOREFEET
EEEFFRVW FEVERFEW
EEEFGRSU REFUGEES

EEEFILPR LIFE PEER
EEEFINRR FREE REIN
EEEFLRSX REFLEXES
EEEFLSTT FLEETEST
EEEFNORS FORESEEN
EEEFNRRT REFERENT,
RENT-FREE, TREE FERN
EEEFNRUZ UNFREEZE
EEEFORRS FORESEER
EEEFPRUZ FREEZE-UP
EEEFRRRR REFERRER
EEEFRRRT FERRETER
EEEFRRSZ FREEZERS
EEEFRRTT FETTERER
EEEGGILN NEGLIGEE
EEEGHINT EIGHTEEN
EEEGINNR ENGINEER
EEEGINRS ENERGISE
EEEGINRZ ENERGIZE
EEEGIPRS PERIGEES
EEEGISSX EXEGESIS
EEEGISTV EGESTIVE
EEEGLNRT GREENLET
EEEGMNRT EMERGENT
EEEGMORT GEOMETER
EEEGNRRV REVENGER
EEEGNRRY GREENERY
EEEGNRST GREENEST
EEEGOPRT PROTEGEE
EEEHILSW HELEWISE,
WHEELIES
EEEHIRSS HERESIES
EEEHIRST ETHERISE
EEEHIRTZ ETHERIZE
EEEHITWY WHITE-EYE
EEEHLLNS HELLENES
EEEHLLSS HEELLESS
EEEHLMPT HELPMEET
EEEHLNTV ELEVENTH
EEEHLNTY ETHYLENE
EEEHLOPP PEEPHOLE
EEEHLORS LEE
SHORE
EEEHMNTV VEHEMENT
EEEHNNPT NEPENTHE
EEEHNNQU HENEQUEN
EEEHNPRS ENSPHERE
EEEHNRVW WHENEVER
EEEHORST SHOETREE
EEEHRRVW WHEREVER
EEEHRSST SHEEREST
EEEHSSTT ESTHETES
EEEIKLSW WEEKLIES
EEEIKNPS PEKINESE

EEEILLRV REVEILLE
EEEILMMN EMMELINE
EEEILNRT TREELINE
EEEILNRY EYELINER
EEEILNST SELENITE
EEEILPRS SLEEPIER
EEEILRRV RELIEVER
EEEILRST LEERIEST,
STEELIER
EEEILSTV TELEVISE
EEEIMNRU MEUNIERE
EEEIMPRR PREMIERE
EEEIMRRS MISERERE
EEEIMRSZ MEZIERES
EEEINNNT NINETEEN
EEEINNRT INTERNEE,
RETINENE
EEEINNSV VIENNESE
EEEINPRT PINETREE
EEEINRSS EERINESS
EEEINRST ETERNISE
EEEINRTZ ETERNIZE
EEEINSTW WEENIEST
EEEINTUX EUXENITE
EEEIPRRV REPRIEVE
EEEIQSUX EXEQUIES
EEEIRRSV REVERIES
EEEIRRTV RETRIEVE
EEEIRRVW REVIEWER
EEEIRTVX EXERTIVE
EEEISSTW SWEETIES
EEEJKKNR KNEE-JERK
EEEJLLRW JEWELLER
EEEJLRSW JEWELERS
EEEKLSST SLEEKEST
EEEKMNSS MEEKNESS
EEEKNNSS KEENNESS
EEEKNORS KEROSENE
EEEKNSTV KESTEVEN
EEELLLRV LEVELLER
EEELLNOR ENROLLEE
EEELLPRR REPELLER
EEELLPRX EXPELLER
EEELLRRV REVELLER
EEELMNST ELEMENTS
EEELMOPY EMPLOYEE
EEELMOTT OMELETTE
EEELMRTU MULETEER
EEELNOPP PENELOPE
EEELNOPV ENVELOPE
EEELNRSW NEWSREEL
EEELNRSY SERENELY
EEELNRTY TERYLENE
EEELOPPR REPEOPLE

EEELPRSS PEERLESS,
SLEEPERS
EEELPSST STEEPLES
EEELPTTY TELETYPE
EEELRRTT LETTERER
EEELRSST TREELESS
EEELRSTT RESETTLE
EEELRSTV LEVERETS
EEELRSVY SEVERELY
EEELTTTX TELETEXT
EEEMMRUZ MEZEREUM
EEEMNNTT TENEMENT
EEEMNORZ MEZEREON
EEEMORRV EVERMORE
EEEMPRRT TEMPERER
EEEMRSST SEMESTER
EEEMRSTX EXTREMES
EEENNOPR NEOPRENE
EEENNSSV EVENNESS
EEENNSTT ENTENTES
EEENORSV OVERSEEN,
VERONESE
EEENORVY EVERYONE
EEENPPRS PREPENSE
EEENPRRT REPENTER
EEENPRST PRETENSE
EEENPRSY PYRENEES
EEENPSSX EXPENSES
EEENRRTV REVERENT
EEEORRSV OVERSEER
EEEORRSX XEROSERE
EEEORSSY EYESORES
EEEPRRST PESTERER
EEEPRRSV PERVERSE,
PRESERVE
EEEPRRTW PEWTERER
EEEPRSSW SWEEPERS
EEEPSSTT STEEPEST
EEEQRSTU QUEEREST
EEEQRSUZ SQUEEZER
EEEQSSUZ SQUEEZES
EEERRRSV RESERVER,
REVERSER
EEERRRTV REVERTER
EEERRSSV RESERVES,
REVERSES
EEERRSTT RESETTER
EEERSTTW TWEETERS
EEERSTVX VERTEXES
EEERSTWZ TWEEZERS
EEESSTTW SWEETEST
EEFFGIIS EFFIGIES
EEFFGORY GEOFFREY
EEFFISUV EFFUSIVE

EEFFLNTU EFFLUENT
EEFFRRSU SUFFERER
EEFGIILR FILIGREE
EEFGILNS FEELINGS
EEFGILNT FLEETING
EEFGINRR FINGERER
EEFGINRZ FREEZING
EEFGLNRY GREENFLY
EEFGLNUV VENGEFUL
EEFGLORS FORELEGS
EEFGNOOR FOREGONE
EEFGOORR FOREGOER
EEFHILLR HELLFIRE
EEFHILRS FLESHIER
EEFHIRSV FEVERISH
EEFHIRTY ETHERIFY
EEFHISST FETISHES
EEFHISTT HEFTIEST
EEFHLLPS SELF-HELP
EEFHLLWY FLYWHEEL
EEFHLSTY FLYSHEET
EEFHMNRS FRESHMEN
EEFHRSST FRESHEST
EEFIIKLL LIFELIKE
EEFIILLN LIFELINE
EEFIILMT LIFETIME
EEFIILSS LIFE-SISE
EEFIILSZ LIFE-SIZE
EEFIIMNN FEMININE
EEFIIMNS FEMINISE
EEFIIMNZ FEMINIZE
EEFIIRRV VERIFIER
EEFIIRST FIERIEST
EEFIJNNR JENNIFER
EEFIKNNP PENKNIFE
EEFILLRW FREE WILL
EEFILLSS LIFELESS
EEFILMST FISTMELE
EEFILNOS FELONIES
EEFILPRR PILFERER
EEFILRTU TRUE-LIFE
EEFIMORT FORETIME
EEFINNSS FINENESS
EEFINNTU FINE-TUNE
EEFINRRR INFERRER
EEFINRRY REFINERY
EEFINRSS RIFENESS
EEFINRST INFESTER
EEFIPRSX PREFIXES
EEFIRRST FIRTREES
EEFIRRSU SUREFIRE
EEFIRSTT FRISETTE
EEFIRSTY ESTERIFY
EEFKNORT REEF KNOT

EEFLLLNU FLUELLEN
EEFLLORT FORETELL,
   TOLL-FREE
EEFLLRSU SELF-RULE
EEFLLSSS SELFLESS
EEFLMSSU FUMELESS
EEFLNORU FLUORENE
EEFLNTUV EVENTFUL
EEFLORRW FLOWERER
EEFLORTT FLORETTE
EEFLORTV LEFTOVER
EEFLORVW OVERFLEW
EEFLORWW WEREWOLF
EEFLRRSU FERRULES
EEFLRSST FRETLESS
EEFMNORT FOMENTER
EEFMNRRY FERRYMEN
EEFMORRR REFORMER
EEFMPRRU PERFUMER
EEFMPRSU PERFUMES
EEFNORST SOFTENER
EEFNORTU FOURTEEN
EEFNORTW FOREWENT,
   FREETOWN
EEFNQRTU FREQUENT
EEFNRTTU UNFETTER
EEFOORRT ROOFTREE
EEFOPRRT FREE PORT
EEFOPRST FREEPOST,
   POST-FREE
EEFORRST FORESTER,
   FOSTERER, REFOREST
EEFORRSU FERREOUS
EEFORRTY FERETORY
EEFORSUY FOUREYES
EEFOSSTT FOSSETTE
EEFOSSTU FOETUSES
EEGGHLLS EGGSHELL
EEGGHNOR HONEGGER
EEGGILST LEGGIEST
EEGGIMNR EMERGING
EEGGIMRT EGG TIMER
EEGGINNR GREENING,
   RENEGING
EEGGINRT GREETING
EEGGNSST NEST
   EGGS
EEGGORTT GO-GETTER
EEGHHIKN KNEE-HIGH
EEGHHINT HEIGHTEN
EEGHIIST EIGHTIES
EEGHIKLY KEIGHLEY
EEGHILNW WHEELING
EEGHILRS SLEIGHER

EEGHINRS GREENISH,
   SHEERING
EEGHINST SEETHING,
   SHEETING
EEGHINTT TEETHING
EEGHINWZ WHEEZING
EEGHIOTT GOETHITE
EEGHIRTW WEIGHTER
EEGHISST SIGHTSEE
EEGHISTY EYESIGHT
EEGHLNNT LENGTHEN
EEGHMNOY HEGEMONY
EEGHNOPS PHOSGENE
EEGHNSSU HUGENESS
EEGHOPTY GEOPHYTE
EEGHORTT TOGETHER
EEGHOSTT GHETTOES
EEGIILNR LINGERIE
EEGIILNV INVEIGLE
EEGIINTV GENITIVE
EEGIJMNN NIJMEGEN
EEGIKLNN KNEELING
EEGIKLNS SLEEKING
EEGILLNV LEVELING
EEGILNPS PEELINGS,
   SLEEPING
EEGILNRR LINGERER
EEGILNRU REGULINE
EEGILNRV LEVERING,
   REVELING
EEGILNST GENTILES,
   SLEETING, STEELING
EEGILNSV SLEEVING
EEGILNTX TELEXING
EEGILOPU EPILOGUE
EEGILOSU EULOGIES,
   EULOGISE
EEGILOUZ EULOGIZE
EEGILRTV VERLIGTE
EEGIMNNS MENINGES
EEGIMNRS REGIMENS
EEGIMNRT METERING,
   REGIMENT
EEGIMNRU MERINGUE
EEGIMNST MEETINGS
EEGINNPR PREENING
EEGINNQU QUEENING
EEGINNRS SNEERING
EEGINNRT ENTERING
EEGINNRW RENEWING
EEGINNRY ENGINERY
EEGINNSU INGENUES,
   UNSEEING
EEGINNSV EVENINGS

EEGINNSZ SNEEZING
EEGINORR ERIGERON
EEGINOST EGESTION
EEGINPRU PUREEING
EEGINPST STEEPING
EEGINPSW SWEEPING
EEGINQRU QUEERING
EEGINRRS RESIGNER
EEGINRRV REVERING
EEGINRST INTEGERS,
  STEERING
EEGINRSU SEIGNEUR
EEGINRSV SEVERING
EEGINRTX EXERTING
EEGINSSU GENIUSES
EEGINTTV VIGNETTE
EEGINTTW TWEETING
EEGIPRST PRESTIGE
EEGIRRST REGISTER
EEGIRSTT GRISETTE
EEGISSTV VESTIGES
EEGLNOPY POLYGENE
EEGLNOSZ LOZENGES
EEGLNOTY TELEGONY
EEGLOOST TOGOLESE
EEGMNOST GEMSTONE
EEGMNSST SEGMENTS
EEGMORSU GRUESOME
EEGMORTY GEOMETRY
EEGMRSTU GUM TREES
EEGNNORT ROENTGEN
EEGNNOSV EVENSONG
EEGNOPTY GENOTYPE
EEGNORSU GENEROUS
EEGNOTYZ ZYGOTENE
EEGNPRUX EXPUNGER
EEGNRSSY GREYNESS
EEGNRSUY GUERNSEY
EEGOPRST PROTÉGÉS
EEGOPRSU SUPEREGO
EEGORRRU GUERRERO
EEGRRSTU GESTURER
EEGRSSTU GESTURES
EEHHIPSS SHEEPISH
EEHHIRST THIS HERE
EEHHIRTW HEREWITH
EEHHLLLO HELLHOLE
EEHHLMOP HOME HELP
EEHHLSTW THE WELSH
EEHHNOSU HEN HOUSE
EEHHRRST THRESHER
EEHHRSST THRESHES
EEHIIKLV HIVELIKE
EEHIILTV HELVETII

EEHIILTW WHITE LIE
EEHIITTW WHITE-TIE
EEHIKLMO HOMELIKE
EEHIKRRS SHRIEKER
EEHILMNS HEMLINES
EEHILMOR HOMELIER
EEHILNPW PINWHEEL
EEHILORT HOTELIER
EEHILRSS HEIRLESS,
  RELISHES
EEHILWYZ WHEEZILY
EEHIMNOR HERMIONE
EEHIMNRT THEREMIN
EEHIMRST ERETHISM
EEHIMRTT THERMITE
EEHINNRS ENSHRINE
EEHINNRT INHERENT
EEHINORT HEREINTO
EEHINPRT NEPHRITE,
  TREPHINE
EEHINRTT THIRTEEN
EEHINRTW WHITENER
EEHIORRT EITHER-OR
EEHIORST ISOTHERE,
  THEORIES; THEORISE
EEHIORTZ THEORIZE
EEHIPPST PSEPHITE
EEHIPPTY EPIPHYTE
EEHIPRRS PERISHER
EEHIPRTT TEPHRITE
EEHIPSTT EPITHETS
EEHIRRSV SHIVERER
EEHIRRTW WITHERER
EEHIRSTT TEE SHIRT
EEHIRTVY THIEVERY
EEHKLOSY KEYHOLES
EEHKLOWY HOLY WEEK
EEHLLMSS HELMLESS
EEHLLPSS HELPLESS
EEHLMMNS HELMSMEN
EEHLMORU HOME RULE
EEHLMOSS HOMELESS
EEHLNOSW HENSLOWE
EEHLOPSS HOPELESS
EEHLOPST HEELPOST,
  PESTHOLE
EEHLORSV SHOVELER
EEHLPRSU SPHERULE
EEHLPRTY THREE-PLY
EEHLRSST SHELTERS
EEHLRSSW WELSHERS
EEHMMOPR MORPHEME
EEHMMORT OHMMETER
EEHMNOPS PHONEMES

EEHMNORS HORSEMEN
EEHMNOSU HOUSEMEN
EEHMORST REST HOME,
  THEOREMS
EEHMORVW WHOMEVER
EEHNNOOT ETHONONE
EEHNNORT ENTHRONE
EEHNOORS ONE-HORSE
EEHNOPRU HEREUPON
EEHNOPTY NEOPHYTE
EEHNORST HORTENSE,
  THE NORSE
EEHNORTU HEREUNTO
EEHNSSTV SEVENTHS
EEHOOPRS OOSPHERE
EEHOOPSW WHOOPEES
EEHOORSV OVERSHOE
EEHOOTTY EYETOOTH
EEHOPPSW PEEPSHOW
EEHORRSV HOVERERS
EEHORRTX EXHORTER
EEHPRSSU HESPERUS
EEIIKLLR LIKELIER
EEIIKLSW LIKEWISE
EEIILLRV LIVELIER
EEIILMNT ILMENITE,
  MELINITE
EEIILMRT TIMELIER
EEIILNPP PIPELINE
EEIILNTV LENITIVE
EEIILRSV LIVERIES
EEIILRVW LIVE WIRE
EEIILSTW LEWISITE
EEIIMMTT MIMETITE
EEIIMOST MOIETIES
EEIIMRSS MISERIES
EEIIMSSV EMISSIVE
EEIINNST NINETIES
EEIINNVV VIVIENNE
EEIINPPR PIPERINE
EEIINPRV VIPERINE
EEIINRRV RIVERINE
EEIINRSS IN SERIES
EEIINRTT RETINITE
EEIINSSV INESSIVE
EEIINSTT ENTITIES
EEIIOPTZ EPIZOITE
EEIIQSTU EQUITIES
EEIIRSTV VERITIES
EEIJKRST JERKIEST
EEIJLNNU JULIENNE
EEIJLNRT JETLINER
EEIJLNUV JUVENILE
EEIJLTTU JULIETTE

EEIJNNOR ENJOINER
EEIKLNSS LIKENESS
EEIKLORT LORIKEET
EEIKLPST SPIKELET
EEIKMOTX KETOXIME
EEIKNRRT TINKERER
EEIKPRST PERKIEST
EEIKPSST PESKIEST
EEILLLMV MELVILLE
EEILLMPR IMPELLER
EEILLMRS SMELLIER
EEILLNOR LONELIER
EEILLORV LOVELIER
EEILLOSV LOVELIES
EEILLPSS ELLIPSES
EEILLPSY SLEEPILY
EEILLSTT STELLITE
EEILLSTV EVILLEST
EEILMNNO LIMONENE
EEILMNNS LINESMEN
EEILMNST MELISENT
EEILMNSU SELENIUM
EEILMSST TIMELESS
EEILMSUV EMULSIVE
EEILNNST SENTINEL
EEILNOPR LEPORINE
EEILNORS ROSELINE
EEILNPPZ ZEPPELIN
EEILNPRU PERILUNE
EEILNPRV REPLEVIN
EEILNRST ENLISTER,
LEINSTER, LISTENER
EEILNRTY ENTIRELY,
LIENTERY
EEILNSSV EVILNESS,
VILENESS
EEILNSVY YVELINES
EEILORRT LOITERER
EEILOSVW VOWELISE
EEILOTTT TOILETTE
EEILOTTV VIOLETTE
EEILOVWZ VOWELIZE
EEILPPSY EPILEPSY
EEILPRST EPISTLER,
REPTILES
EEILPSST EPISTLES
EEILPSSV PELVISES
EEILPSTY EPISTYLE
EEILRRSV REVILERS,
SILVERER, SLIVERER
EEILRSST TIRELESS
EEILRSSW WIRELESS
EEILSSVW VIEWLESS
EEILSTTX TEXTILES

EEIMMORS MEMORIES,
MEMORISE
EEIMMORZ MEMORIZE
EEIMMOST SOMETIME
EEIMMRST MERISTEM
EEIMNNOS NOMINEES
EEIMNORS EMERSION
EEIMNORV VOMERINE
EEIMNOST MONETISE,
SEMITONE
EEIMNOTZ MONETIZE,
TIME ZONE, ZONETIME
EEIMNPRS SPERMINE
EEIMNPRU PERINEUM
EEIMNRTU MUTINEER
EEIMOPRS REIMPOSE
EEIMORST TIRESOME
EEIMORTV OVERTIME
EEIMPRRS PREMIERS,
SIMPERER
EEIMPRSS PREMISES
EEIMPSTT EMPTIEST
EEIMQRSU REQUIEMS
EEIMQSTU MESQUITE
EEIMRRST MERRIEST,
TRIREMES
EEIMRRTT REMITTER,
TRIMETER
EEIMRSTT TERMITES
EEIMRSTU EMERITUS
EEIMRTTY TEMERITY
EEIMSSST MESSIEST
EEINNNPS PENNINES
EEINNPTT PENITENT
EEINNSTT SENTIENT
EEINOPRS ISOPRENE,
PIONEERS
EEINORST SEROTINE
EEINORSV EVERSION
EEINORTT TENORITE
EEINORTX EXERTION
EEINOSTT TEOSINTE
EEINPRSS RIPENESS
EEINPRTX INEXPERT
EEINQRRU ENQUIRER
EEINRRST INSERTER,
RENTIERS
EEINRRSU REINSURE
EEINRRTU REUNITER
EEINRRTV INVERTER
EEINRRTW WINTERER
EEINRRTX INTERREX
EEINRSST SENTRIES
EEINRSSU ENURESIS

EEINRSTT INSETTER,
INTEREST
EEINRSTU ESURIENT,
RETINUES
EEINRSTV NERVIEST,
REINVEST
EEINRSTX INTERSEX
EEINRSTY SERENITY
EEINRSUV UNIVERSE
EEINRTTY ENTIRETY,
ETERNITY
EEINSSSW WISENESS
EEINSSSX SEXINESS
EEINSSTX SIXTEENS
EEINSTTW TWENTIES
EEINSTTX EXISTENT
EEIOPRRT PORTIERE
EEIOPRRV OVERRIPE
EEIORRRS ORRERIES
EEIORRTV OVERTIRE
EEIORRTX EXTERIOR
EEIORSSV OVERSISE
EEIORSVZ OVERSIZE
EEIORVVW OVERVIEW
EEIORVWW WIRE-WOVE
EEIPPQRU EQUIPPER
EEIPPRRS PERSPIRE
EEIPPRST PEPTISER
EEIPPRTZ PEPTIZER
EEIPPSTT PIPETTES
EEIPRRSS REPRISES
EEIPRRTT PRETTIER
EEIPRSST RESPITES
EEIPRSTX PREEXIST
EEIPRSVW PREVIEWS
EEIPRSZZ PREZZIES
EEIPRTUV ERUPTIVE
EEIPSSTW STEPWISE
EEIPSTTT PETTIEST
EEIQRRRU REQUIRER
EEIQRRTU REQUITER
EEIQRRUV QUIVERER
EEIQSTTU QUIETEST
EFIRRRST TERRIERS
EEIRRSST RESISTER
EEIRRSSU REISSUER
EEIRRSSV REVISERS
EEIRRSTV RIVETERS
EEIRRSTW REWRITES
EEIRRTTT TITTERER
EEIRSSSU REISSUES
EEIRSSTU SURETIES
EEIRSSTV VESTRIES
EEIRSSUZ SEIZURES

EEIRSTVY SEVERITY
EEISSTTT TESTIEST
EEJKNRTU JUNKETER
EEJLPSTU PULSEJET
EEJPRRRU PERJURER
EEKLLSUU UKULELES
EEKLNNNU UNKENNEL
EEKLNOST SKELETON
EEKLRSST KESTRELS
EEKMNOYY KEY MONEY
EEKMOORV KEMEROVO
EEKNOSTY KEYNOTES,
KEYSTONE
EELLLLMP PELL-MELL
EELLLNWY LLEWELYN
EELLMNOY MELLONEY
EELLMORW MELLOWER
EELLNORR ENROLLER
EELLNPRU PRUNELLE
EELLNRSU SULLENER
EELLNSTU ENTELLUS
EELLOPTV TOP-LEVEL
EELLORSV OVERSELL
EELLORTX EXTOLLER
EELLORVY VOLLEYER
EELLOSSV LOVELESS
EELMMPUX EXEMPLUM
EELMNOOS LONESOME
EELMNSUY UNSEEMLY
EELMOPRY EMPLOYER,
RE-EMPLOY
EELMORST MOLESTER
EELMORTY REMOTELY
EELMOTVW TWELVEMO
EELMRRTU MURRELET
EELMRSST TERMLESS
EELMRSTY SMELTERY
EELNNRTU TUNNELER
EELNNTTY LYNNETTE
EELNNUVY UNEVENLY
EELNOORS LOOSENER
EELNOPPU UNPEOPLE
EELNOQTU ELOQUENT
EELNORST ENTRESOL
EELNOSST TONELESS
EELNOSTT NOTELETS
EELNSSTU TUNELESS
EELNSTTU UNSETTLE
EELOPPST ESTOPPEL
EELOPRRX EXPLORER
EELORRSV RESOLVER
EELORRTV REVOLTER
EELORRUV OVERRULE
EELORRVV REVOLVER

EELORSSV RESOLVES
EELORSTU RESOLUTE
EELORSTY TYROLESE
EELORTTU ROULETTE
EELORTUV REVOLUTE,
TRUELOVE
EELPPSTU SEPTUPLE
EELPRRSU REPULSER
EELPRSSU REPULSES
EELPRSTZ PRETZELS
EELPRTXY EXPERTLY
EELPSTUX SEXTUPLE
EELRRSTW WRESTLER
EELRSSST RESTLESS
EELRSSTT SETTLERS,
TRESTLES
EELRSSTU STREUSEL
EELRSTWY WESTERLY
EEMMNOST MEMENTOS
EEMMNOTV MOVEMENT
EEMNNORS NORSEMEN
EEMNOOPT TONE POEM
EEMNPRSS PRESSMEN
EEMNPRSU SUPERMEN
EEMNPRTU ERUMPENT
EEMNRSTU MUENSTER
EEMNSSTU MUTENESS,
TENESMUS
EEMNSTTV VESTMENT
EEMOORRT OROMETER
EEMOORRV MOREOVER
EEMOPRRS EMPERORS,
PREMORSE
EEMOQRSU MORESQUE
EEMOQTTU MOQUETTE
EEMORRSV REMOVERS
EEMORSST SOMERSET
EEMORSTT REMOTEST
EEMPRRSU PRESUMER
EEMPRSTT TEMPTERS
EEMPSSTT TEMPESTS
EEMRRTTU MUTTERER
EENNNOSS NONSENSE
EENNNOTV NON-EVENT
EENNOOOT ONE-TO-
ONE
EENNOORT ROTENONE
EENNOPSS OPENNESS
EENNOPTX EXPONENT
EENNORTT RONNETTE
EENOORST OESTRONE
EENOORTV OVERTONE
EENOPRSS RESPONSE
EENOPRTT ENTREPOT

EENOPRTU PURE TONE
EENOPRXY PYROXENE
EENORSSS SORENESS
EENORSSU NEUROSES
EENORSTX EXTENSOR
EENPRSST PERTNESS,
PRESENTS, SERPENTS
EENPRSSU PURENESS
EENPSSSU SUSPENSE
EENPSTTU PETUNTSE
EENRRRTU RETURNER
EENRRTUV VENTURER
EENRSSSU SURENESS
EENRSSTT STERNEST
EENRSSTU TRUENESS
EENRSSTW WESTERNS
EENRSTUV VENTURES
EENRSTUW WET NURSE
EEOOPRST PROTEOSE
EEOOPRSX EXOSPORE
EEOORRVV ROVE-OVER
EEOPRRRT REPORTER
EEOPRRRV REPROVER
EEOPRRTT POTTERER
EEOPRRTX EXPORTER,
RE-EXPORT
EEOPRSSS ESPRESSO
EEOPRSSU ESPOUSER,
REPOUSSE
EEOPRSTV OVERSTEP
EEOPRSUX EXPOSURE
EEOPSSTW SWEETSOP
EEORRRST RESORTER,
RESTORER, RETRORSE
EEORRRTT RETORTER
EEORRSTX EXTRORSE
EEORRTTT TOTTERER
EEORRTTX EXTORTER
EEORRTUV OVERTURE
EEORSSTT ROSETTES
EEORSSTV ESTOVERS
EEORSTVX VORTEXES
EEORTTTZ TERZETTO
EEPRRSSU PRESSURE
EEPRRSTV PERVERTS
EEPRSSUX SUPERSEX
EEPRSTTU UPSETTER
EEPRSTTX PRETEXTS
EEQRSSTU REQUESTS
EERRSSTU TRESSURE
EERSSSST STRESSES
EERSSTTU TRUSTEES
EERSSTUU UTERUSES
EERSTTUX TEXTURES

EFFFILRU FLUFFIER
EFFGINOR OFFERING
EFFGRSTU GRUFFEST
EFFHIILS FILEFISH
EFFHIIRW WHIFFIER
EFFHIISW FISHWIFE
EFFHIITT FIFTIETH
EFFHIOTW OFF-WHITE
EFFHIRSS SHERIFFS
EFFHISTU HUFFIEST
EFFHLRSU SHUFFLER
EFFHLSSU SHUFFLES
EFFHOORS OFFSHORE
EFFILNRS SNIFFLER
EFFILNSS SNIFFLES
EFFINOSU EFFUSION
EFFIORST FORFEITS
EFFIORTW WRITE-OFF
EFFIPSTU PUFFIEST
EFFIRSTU STUFFIER
EFFISSTT STIFFEST
EFFISSUX SUFFIXES
EFFLMRSU MUFFLERS
EFFLNRSU SNUFFLER
EFFLNSSU SNUFFLES
EFFLOSSU SOUFFLÉS
EFFLRSTU TRUFFLES
EFFNRSSU SNUFFERS
EFFOOORT FOREFOOT
EFFOORSW WORSE-OFF
EFGGIINN FEIGNING
EFGGIOST FOGGIEST
EFGGISTU FUGGIEST
EFGHHIIL HIGH LIFE
EFGHILNS FLESHING
EFGHINRT FRIGHTEN
EFGHIRST FIGHTERS
EFGIILNT FILETING
EFGIILRU UGLIFIER
EFGIINNR INFRINGE,
   REFINING
EFGIINNT FEINTING
EFGIINRU FIGURINE
EFGIITUV FUGITIVE
EFGILLNO LIFELONG,
   LONG-LIFE
EFGILLNU FUELLING
EFGILLUU GUILEFUL
EFGILNOR FLORIGEN
EFGILNTT FETTLING
EFGILNTW LEFT WING
EFGILPRU FIRE-PLUG
EFGIMNST FIGMENTS
EFGIMRUU REFUGIUM

EFGINNPS PFENNIGS
EFGINORV FORGIVEN
EFGINORW FOREWING
EFGINRRY FERRYING
EFGINRSU REFUSING
EFGINRTT FRETTING
EFGINRTU REFUTING
EFGINRTY GENTRIFY
EFGIOOST GOOFIEST
EFGIOPTT PETTIFOG
EFGIORRV FORGIVER
EFGIORTT FORGET IT!
EFGLOOVX FOXGLOVE
EFGNSSUU FUNGUSES
EFHIILRT FILTHIER
EFHIILST TILEFISH
EFHIINRS FINISHER,
   REFINISH
EFHIINSS FINISHES
EFHIIPPS PIPEFISH
EFHIIRST SHIFTIER
EFHIISST FISHIEST
EFHIKLOO HOOFLIKE
EFHIKSTY SHIFT KEY
EFHILTWY WHITEFLY
EFHINSST FISHNETS
EFHIORRT FROTHIER
EFHIORSS ROSEFISH
EFHIORTT FORTIETH
EFHIRRTU THURIFER
EFHLNORS HORNFELS
EFHLOOSS HOOFLESS
EFHLOOSX FOXHOLES
EFHLOPST FLESHPOT
EFHLOPSU HOPEFULS
EFHLORSY HORSEFLY
EFHLOSUU HOUSEFUL
EFHLOSUY HOUSEFLY
EFHLSTTW TWELFTHS
EFHRSTTU FURTHEST
EFIIILRV VILIFIER
EFIIINNT INFINITE
EFIIIRVV VIVIFIER
EFIIKRRS FRISKIER
EFIILLRR FRILLIER
EFIILMRS FLIMSIER
EFIILMST FILMIEST
EFIILNOU IN LIEU OF
EFIILNRT FLINTIER
EFIILNTY FELINITY,
   FINITELY
EFIILRSU FUSILIER
EFIIMMNS FEMINISM
EFIIMNST FEMINIST

EFIIMRSS MISFIRES
EFIINNNS SINN FEIN
EFIINORR INFERIOR
EFIINORT NOTIFIER
EFIINPSV FIVEPINS
EFIINPSX SPINIFEX
EFIINRRT FERRITIN
EFIINSTT NIFTIEST
EFIINSUV INFUSIVE
EFIIORSS OSSIFIER
EFIIPRRU PURIFIER
EFIIPRST SPITFIRE
EFIIRRTU FRUITIER
EFIIRRZZ FRIZZIER
EFIIRVVY REVIVIFY
EFIISTVW FIVE WITS
EFIISTZZ FIZZIEST
EFIJLOST JETFOILS
EFIKLLOW WOLFLIKE
EFIKLORW LIFE WORK
EFIKLRSU SURFLIKE
EFIKLRUY LIKE FURY
EFIKNORS FORESKIN
EFIKNSTU FUNKIEST
EFIKORRW FIREWORK
EFILLLSW SELF-WILL
EFILLMTU FULL-TIME
EFILLSTY STELLIFY
EFILMSUY EMULSIFY
EFILNNTU INFLUENT
EFILNORU FLUORINE
EFILNSUX INFLUXES
EFILOOSZ FLOOZIES
EFILOPPR FLOPPIER
EFILOPRS PROFILES
EFILORST TREFOILS
EFILOSTT LOFTIEST
EFILPPRS FLIPPERS
EFILPPST FLIPPEST
EFILPRTU UPLIFTER
EFILPSTU SPITEFUL
EFILPSTY SELF-PITY
EFILRRSU FLURRIES
EFILRRZZ FRIZZLER
EFILSSTT LEFTISTS
EFIMNORR INFORMER,
   RENIFORM
EFIMNORS ENSIFORM
EFIMNRSS FIRMNESS
EFIMNSTT FITMENTS
EFIMORST SETIFORM
EFIMPRRU FRUMPIER
EFIMRSTU FREMITUS

EFINNORS INFERNOS	EFLRSTUU FRUSTULE	EGGMSSTU SMUGGEST
EFINNPSU FINESPUN	EFLRTTUY FLUTTERY	EGGNOOSY GEOGNOSY
EFINNSTU FUNNIEST	EFMNNORT FRONT MEN	EGGNRSUY SNUGGERY
EFINOPTX PONTIFEX	EFMNORTY FROMENTY	EGGOORSU GORGEOUS
EFINORRT FRONTIER	EFMNRTUY FRUMENTY	EGHHIIMT HIGH TIME
EFINOSSX FOXINESS	EFMOORST FOREMOST	EGHHIIRS HIGH-RISE
EFINRSST SNIFTERS	EFMOORSU FOURSOME	EGHHINSS HIGHNESS
EFIOOPST POOFIEST	EFNNOOOR FORENOON	EGHHIPRU HIGHER-UP
EFIOOSST FOOTSIES	EFNOOOTT FOOTNOTE	EGHHIPTY TYPE-HIGH
EFIOPRRT PROFITER	EFNOOSST FESTOONS	EGHHORUW ROUGH-HEW
EFIORRST FROSTIER	EFNORSTU FORTUNES	EGHIILNR HIRELING
EFIORRTT RETROFIT	EFNOSSST SOFTNESS	EGHIILNS SHIELING
EFIORRWZ FROWZIER	EFOOOPRT FOOTROPE	EGHIIMRT MIGHTIER
EFIPPRRY FRIPPERY	EFOOORST FOOTSORE	EGHIINTV THIEVING
EFIPRSUX SUPERFIX	EFOOPRRS REPROOFS	EGHIKNRS GHERKINS
EFIPRTTY PRETTIFY	EFOOPSTT FOOTSTEP	EGHILLNS SHELLING
EFIRRRSU FURRIERS	EFOORRSW FORSWORE	EGHILLNW WELL-NIGH
EFIRRRUY FURRIERY	EFOORSTT FOOTREST	EGHILNOT LEIGHTON
EFIRRSTT FRITTERS	EFORRRUW FURROWER	EGHILNPS HELPINGS
EFIRRSTU FURRIEST	EFORRSST FORTRESS	EGHILNRS SHINGLER
EFIRSSSU FISSURES	EFORRSTY FORESTRY	EGHILNSS SHINGLES
EFIRSTUX FIXTURES	EGGGILNS LEGGINGS	EGHILNSV SHELVING
EFISSSTU FUSSIEST	EGGGIORR GROGGIER	EGHILNSW WELSHING
EFISSTTU FUSTIEST	EGGHIINN NEIGHING	EGHILPRT PLIGHTER
EFISSTTW SWIFTEST	EGGHIINW WEIGHING	EGHILRST LIGHTERS, SLIGHTER
EFISTUZZ FUZZIEST	EGGHIRWY WHIGGERY	EGHILSTT LIGHTEST
EFKLLOOR FOLKLORE	EGGHRTUY THUGGERY	EGHIMNUX EXHUMING
EFKLNSUY FLUNKEYS	EGGIINNR REIGNING	EGHINORV HOVERING
EFKNOORW FOREKNOW	EGGIINNS SINGEING	EGHINOST HISTOGEN
EFKORRTW FRETWORK	EGGIINRV GRIEVING	EGHINRRS HERRINGS
EFLLLLUW FULL WELL	EGGIIPST PIGGIEST	EGHINRRU HUNGRIER
EFLLNOOW LONE WOLF	EGGILNRS NIGGLERS, SNIGGLER	EGHINRSU USHERING
EFLLNSSU FULLNESS	EGGILNRY GINGERLY	EGHINTTW WHETTING
EFLLNTUY FLUENTLY	EGGILOOS GOOGLIES	EGHIOTUW OUTWEIGH
EFLLOORW FOLLOWER	EGGILQSU SQUIGGLE	EGHISTTT TIGHTEST
EFLLOSST SOFT SELL	EGGILRRW WRIGGLER	EGHLLNUW WELL-HUNG
EFLLOUWY WOEFULLY	EGGILRSW WRIGGLES	EGHLLOPU PLUGHOLE
EFLLRUUY RUEFULLY	EGGIMSTU MUGGIEST	EGHLLOSU LUGHOLES
EFLLSUUY USEFULLY	EGGINORR GORGERIN	EGHLOOOR HOROLOGE
EFLMMRUY FLUMMERY	EGGINRSS SNIGGERS	EGHLOORY RHEOLOGY
EFLMNRUU FRENULUM	EGGINSSU GUESSING	EGHLOOTY ETHOLOGY, THEOLOGY
EFLMORRY FORMERLY	EGGINSTU GUESTING	EGHLOPRU PLOUGHER
EFLMORSS FORMLESS	EGGIOSST SOGGIEST	EGHMNOOY HOMOGENY
EFLNORTT FRONTLET	EGGIPRRS SPRIGGER	EGHMOSSU GUMSHOES
EFLNOSSU FOULNESS	EGGIPRRY PRIGGERY	EGHNNTWY GWYNNETH
EFLNOSTY STONEFLY	EGGIRRST TRIGGERS	EGHNORUV HUNG OVER, OVERHUNG
EFLOORSS ROOFLESS	EGGJLRSU JUGGLERS	EGHNOTUU HUGUENOT
EFLOORVW OVERFLOW	EGGJLRUY JUGGLERY	EGHNRSTT STRENGTH
EFLOPRUW POWERFUL	EGGLLORS EGG ROLLS	EGHOOOSW HOOSEGOW
EFLOPSTW FOWL PEST	EGGLMOOY GEMOLOGY	
EFLORSUY YOURSELF	EGGLMRSU SMUGGLER	
EFLORSVY FLYOVERS	EGGLORSS SLOGGERS	
EFLOSUUX FLEXUOUS	EGGLRSTU STRUGGLE	
EFLRSTTU FLUTTERS		

EGHORRTW REGROWTH
EGHORSTU ROUGHEST
EGHOSTTU TOUGHEST
EGIIKLNN LIKENING
EGIIKLNR KINGLIER
EGIIKLNW WINGLIKE
EGIIKNSS KING-SISE
EGIIKNSZ KING-SIZE
EGIILNNR RELINING
EGIILNNV LIVENING
EGIILNOR RELIGION
EGIILNRS RIESLING
EGIILNRV RELIVING,
    REVILING
EGIILRRS GRISLIER
EGIILRTU GUILTIER
EGIILRTZ GLITZIER
EGIIMNPR IMPINGER
EGIIMNRT MERITING
EGIIMNST MINGIEST
EGIIMNTT EMITTING
EGIIMOPT IMPETIGO
EGIIMRST GRIMIEST
EGIINNPR REPINING,
    RIPENING
EGIINNPW WINNIPEG
EGIINOPR PEIGNOIR
EGIINPRX EXPIRING
EGIINRRT RETIRING
EGIINRRW REWIRING
EGIINRST STINGIER
EGIINRSV REVISING
EGIINRTU INTRIGUE
EGIINRTV RIVETING
EGIINRVV REVIVING
EGIINSTX EXISTING
EGIIPRSW PERIWIGS
EGIIPSST PIGSTIES
EGIIRRTT GRITTIER
EGIITUXY EXIGUITY
EGIJMMNY JEMMYING
EGIJNNOY ENJOYING
EGIKKNRT TREKKING
EGIKLNSY KINGSLEY
EGIKNORV REVOKING
EGIKNRSY KEY RINGS
EGILLMNS SMELLING
EGILLNOR NEGRILLO
EGILLNOV LIVELONG
EGILLNPS SPELLING
EGILLNQU QUELLING
EGILLNSW SWELLING
EGILLNTU GLUTELIN
EGILMMNS LEMMINGS

EGILMMRS GLIMMERS
EGILMNRS GREMLINS
EGILMNST SMELTING
EGILMOOR GLOOMIER
EGILMPRS GLIMPSER
EGILMPSS GLIMPSES
EGILNNOS SOLINGEN
EGILNNST NESTLING
EGILNNTT NETTLING
EGILNOPP PEOPLING
EGILNORW LOWERING
EGILNOSU LIGNEOUS
EGILNOTW TOWELING
EGILNOVV EVOLVING
EGILNPRY REPLYING
EGILNRST RINGLETS,
    STERLING
EGILNSST SINGLETS
EGILNSSU UGLINESS
EGILNSSW WINGLESS
EGILNSTT LETTINGS,
    SETTLING
EGILNTUX EXULTING
EGILNVXY VEXINGLY
EGILOOSU ISOLOGUE
EGILOOTY ETIOLOGY
EGILORSS GLOSSIER
EGILOSTU EULOGIST
EGILRRZZ GRIZZLER
EGILRSTT GLITTERS
EGILRTTY GLITTERY
EGIMMNST STEMMING
EGIMMRST GRIMMEST
EGIMMSTU GUMMIEST
EGIMNORS NEGROISM
EGIMNORV REMOVING
EGIMNOSY MOSEYING
EGIMNPRU IMPUGNER
EGIMNPST PIGMENTS
EGIMNPTT TEMPTING
EGIMNPTY EMPTYING
EGIMNRSS GRIMNESS
EGIMNRSU RESUMING
EGIMORST ERGOTISM
EGIMPRRU GRUMPIER
EGINNOPS OPENINGS
EGINNORT NITROGEN
EGINNPSU PENGUINS
EGINNRRU UNERRING
EGINNRSU ENSURING
EGINOPRS REPOSING,
    SPONGIER
EGINOPRW POWERING
EGINOPST PONGIEST

EGINOPSX EXPOSING
EGINORRY IRON-GREY
EGINORSS GORINESS
EGINORTW TOWERING
EGINORVW WINGOVER
EGINORXX XEROXING
EGINPPST STEPPING
EGINPRRS SPRINGER
EGINPRSS PRESSING
EGINPRSU PERUSING
EGINPRTU ERUPTING
EGINPRYY PERIGYNY
EGINQRUY QUERYING
EGINQSTU QUESTING
EGINRRST STRINGER
EGINRRSW WRINGERS
EGINRSST STINGERS
EGINRSSV SERVINGS
EGINRSSW SWINGERS
EGINRSSY SYRINGES
EGINRSTW STREWING,
    WRESTING
EGINRSVW SWERVING
EGINRTTU UTTERING
EGINSSTT SETTINGS
EGINSTTW WETTINGS
EGIOORRV GROOVIER
EGIOPRSS GOSSIPER
EGIOPRST EGO TRIPS
EGIOPRSU GROUPIES
EGIORRTT GROTTIER
EGIORSST STRIGOSE
EGIORSSU GRISEOUS
EGIORSUV GRIEVOUS
EGIOSSTT EGOTISTS
EGIOSUUX EXIGUOUS
EGIRRSTY REGISTRY
EGISSTTU GUSTIEST,
    GUTSIEST
EGISSUWY WISE GUYS
EGLLLPSU LEG-PULLS
EGLLMORW GROMWELL
EGLLOOPR GOLLOPER
EGLLOSUY YULE LOGS
EGLMMSTU GLUMMEST
EGLMNOOY MENOLOGY
EGLMNORS MONGRELS
EGLMNORT LONG-TERM
EGLMNSSU GLUMNESS
EGLMORSS GORMLESS
EGLNNOOR LONGERON
EGLNOOOY OENOLOGY
EGLNOOPY PENOLOGY
EGLNOORV OVERLONG

EGLNORSU LOUNGERS
EGLNORUU LONGUEUR
EGLNPRSU PLUNGERS
EGLNRTUY URGENTLY
EGLOOPRU PROLOGUE
EGLOOPTY LOGOTYPE
EGLOORSY SEROLOGY
EGLOOSXY SEXOLOGY
EGLORRSW GROWLERS
EGLPRSSU SPLURGES
EGLRSUZZ GUZZLERS
EGMNNOOY
  MONOGENY
EGMNOOOS MONGOOSE
EGMNSSSU SMUGNESS
EGMORSTU GOURMETS
EGNNOOTY ONTOGENY
EGNNORST RÖNTGENS
EGNNSSSU SNUGNESS
EGNNSSTU STEN GUNS
EGNNSTTU TUNGSTEN
EGNNSTUU UNGUENTS
EGNOOOPR GONOPORE
EGNOORRV GOVERNOR
EGNOOTUX OXTONGUE
EGNOPPRU OPPUGNER
EGNOPRSS SPONGERS
EGNORRST STRONGER
EGNORSST SONGSTER
EGNORSSU SURGEONS
EGNORSTU STURGEON
EGNOSTUY YOUNGEST
EGOOPRRU PROROGUE
EGOORRVW OVERGROW
EGOORSTT GROTTOES
EGOPRRSS PROGRESS
EGOPSSUY GYPSEOUS
EGORSSST GROSSEST
EGPRSSUU UPSURGES
EHHIIPRS HEIRSHIP
EHHIIRST THE IRISH
EHHIISTV THIEVISH
EHHILMNT HELMINTH
EHHIORTT HITHERTO
EHHIOTTW WHITE-HOT
EHHIRSSW SHREWISH
EHHMPRUY HUMPHREY
EHHNOORS SHOEHORN
EHHNORTT THE NORTH
EHHOOSSW WHOOSHES
EHHOOSTU HOTHOUSE
EHHOPRTW HEPWORTH
EHHOSTTU THE SOUTH
EHHRSSTU THRUSHES

EHIIKLNS HELSINKI
EHIIKLPW WHIPLIKE
EHIIKNSV KISHINEV
EHIIKSSW WHISKIES
EHIILLST HILLIEST
EHIILMOS HOMILIES
EHIILRSV LIVERISH
EHIIMNRS IRISHMEN
EHIIMNTV VIETMINH
EHIIMPST MEPHITIS
EHIIMSST SMITHIES
EHIIMSSW WHIMSIES
EHIINNOT THIONINE
EHIINNSW WHINNIES
EHIINSST SHINIEST
EHIINSVX VIXENISH
EHIIPSTT PITHIEST
EHIIRRST SHIRTIER
EHIIRSTT SHITTIER,
  THIRTIES
EHIISTTX SIXTIETH
EHIJNNOS JOHNNIES
EHIKKLOO HOOKLIKE
EHIKKLSU HUSKLIKE
EHIKLMPU HUMPLIKE
EHIKLNOR HORNLIKE
EHIKLNOS SINKHOLE
EHIKLOOP HOOPLIKE
EHIKLOSY YOKELISH
EHIKNRRS SHRINKER
EHIKRRSS SHIRKERS
EHIKRSSW WHISKERS
EHIKRSWY WHISKERY
EHIKSSTU HUSKIEST
EHILLLMO MOLEHILL
EHILLPTY PHYLLITE
EHILLRRS SHRILLER
EHILLRRT THRILLER
EHILMNOP PHILEMON
EHILMOOR HEIRLOOM
EHILMOST HELOTISM
EHILMPSY SYMPHILE
EHILNOSS HOLINESS
EHILNOST HOLSTEIN,
  HOT LINES
EHILNOTX XENOLITH
EHILOOPZ ZOOPHILE
EHILOPRS POLISHER
EHILOPRT HELIPORT
EHILOPSS POLISHES
EHILOPST ISOPLETH
EHILORTY RHYOLITE
EHILPRST PHILTRES
EHILPSTU SULPHITE

EHILRSSU SLUSHIER
EHILRSTW WHISTLER
EHILRSTY SLITHERY
EHILRTTW WHITTLER
EHILSSTT THISTLES
EHILSSTW WHISTLES
EHIMMRSY SHIMMERY
EHIMNOPR MORPHINE
EHIMNORT THERMION
EHIMNOSS HOMINESS
EHIMNOTT MONTEITH
EHIMNPST SHIPMENT
EHIMNRRU MURRHINE
EHIMOOST SMOOTHIE
EHIMORST ISOTHERM
EHIMORSZ RHIZOMES
EHIMPRRS SHRIMPER
EHIMPRSW WHIMPERS
EHIMPSUU EUPHUISM
EHIMRSTY SMITHERY
EHIMSSTU MUSHIEST
EHINNOPS PHONE-INS
EHINNOTW NONWHITE
EHINNSST THINNESS
EHINNSSU SUNSHINE
EHINNSTT THINNEST
EHINOOPS ISOPHONE
EHINOPPR HORNPIPE
EHINOPST PHONIEST
EHINORRT THORNIER
EHINORST HORNIEST
EHINORTY IN THEORY
EHINOSTU OUTSHINE
EHINPRSU PUNISHER
EHINPSSX SPHINXES
EHIOORTT TOOTHIER
EHIOPRSS ROSE HIPS
EHIOPRST TROPHIES
EHIORRTW IORWERTH,
  WORTHIER
EHIORSST HORSIEST,
  SHORTIES
EHIORSTT THEORIST
EHIORSTW WORTHIES
EHIORTWZ HOWITZER
EHIOSSTW SHOWIEST
EHIOTTUW WHITEOUT
EHIPPRSS SHIPPERS
EHIPPSTW WHIPPETS
EHIPQSUY PHYSIQUE
EHIPRSST HIPSTERS
EHIPRSSW WHISPERS
EHIPSSTU PUSHIEST
EHIPSTUU EUPHUIST

EHISSSTW SWISHEST
EHKLNOOT KNOTHOLE
EHKLOOSS HOOKLESS
EHKMMNOR MON-
  KHMER
EHKMOORW
  HOMEWORK
EHKNNRSU SHRUNKEN
EHKNOOOS HOOKNOSE
EHLLLSSU HULL-LESS
EHLLMOPY PHYLLOME
EHLLNSTU NUTSHELL
EHLLOOOP LOOPHOLE
EHLLOORW HOLLOWER
EHLLOPST TOP-SHELL
EHLMOORW WORMHOLE
EHLMORTY MOTHERLY
EHLMOSUU MULHOUSE
EHLNOPSU SULPHONE
EHLNORSS HORNLESS
EHLNOSTY HONESTLY,
  ON THE SLY
EHLNSSSU LUSHNESS
EHLOOPRT PORTHOLE,
  POTHOLER
EHLOOPST POTHOLES
EHLOOPTY HOLOTYPE
EHLOPSSS SPLOSHES
EHLORSST HOLSTERS,
  HOSTLERS
EHLORSTY HOSTELRY
EHLORTTT THROTTLE
EHLPSSTU PLUSHEST
EHLRSSTU HUSTLERS,
  RUTHLESS
EHLSSTTU SHUTTLES
EHMMOOPR ROMP
  HOME
EHMMRRTU THRUMMER
EHMNNSTU HUNTSMEN
EHMNOORS HORMONES,
  MOORHENS
EHMNOOST SMOOTHEN
EHMNOOTW
  HOMETOWN
EHMNOPSU HOMESPUN
EHMNORSU HOME RUNS
EHMNPSTY NYMPHETS
EHMOORST SMOOTHER
EHMOPRSU MORPHEUS
EHMORSTY SMOTHERY
EHMORTUV VERMOUTH
EHNNOPRT PENN'ORTH
EHNNORRT NORTHERN

EHNNORSY HENRYSON
EHNOOPPS OPEN SHOP
EHNOORRU HONOURER
EHNOORTW HONEWORT
EHNOORVZ VORONEZH
EHNOOSSW SNOWSHOE
EHNOOSTU OUTSHONE
EHNORSSU ONRUSHES
EHNORSTU SOUTHERN
EHNOSTUU NUTHOUSE
EHNRSSTU HUNTRESS,
  SHUNTERS
EHOOPRTY ORTHOEPY
EHOOPSTT PHOTOSET
EHOOPSTU HOUSETOP
EHOOPTYZ ZOOPHYTE
EHOORRUZ ZERO HOUR
EHOORSST SHOOTERS
EHOORSTV OVERSHOT
EHOORSUW ROW HOUSE
EHOOSTUU OUTHOUSE
EHOPPRSS SHOPPERS
EHOPPRST PROPHETS
EHOPPRSW WHOPPERS
EHOPPRSY PROPHESY
EHOPRSST STROPHES
EHOPRSUV PUSHOVER
EHORSSTT SHORTEST
EHRRSTTU THRUSTER
EHRSSSTY SHYSTERS
EHRSSTTU SHUTTERS
EIIIMMNS MINIMISE
EIIIMMNZ MINIMIZE
EIIJNRSU INJURIES
EIIKKNST KINKIEST
EIIKLLMN LIMEKILN
EIIKLMST MILKIEST
EIIKLNRS SLINKIER
EIIKLSST SILKIEST
EIIKMPRS SKIMPIER
EIIKNNRS SKINNIER
EIIKNNSS INKINESS
EIIKNNSW WINESKIN
EIIKNRST KRISTINE
EIIKPSST SPIKIEST
EIIKQRRU QUIRKIER
EIIKRSST RISKIEST
EIIKSSVV SKIVVIES
EIILLMNR MILLINER
EIILLNST NIELLIST
EIILLNSV VILLEINS
EIILLNTV VITELLIN
EIILLPSS ELLIPSIS
EIILLSST SILLIEST

EIILMMOT IMMOTILE
EIILMNNS LENINISM
EIILMNNT LINIMENT
EIILMNOT LIMONITE
EIILMNSS LIMINESS
EIILMOPT IMPOLITE
EIILMSSS MISSILES
EIILMSST SLIMIEST
EIILMSTY MYELITIS
EIILNNST LENINIST
EIILNORS LIONISER
EIILNORZ LIONIZER
EIILNOSS ELISIONS,
  OILINESS
EIILNQTU QUINTILE
EIILNSSW WILINESS
EIILNSTY SENILITY
EIILNTUV VITULINE
EIILOPST PISOLITE,
  POLITIES
EIILOTVV VOLITIVE
EIILPPRS SLIPPIER
EIILPSST PITILESS
EIILPSTY PYELITIS
EIILRSTU UTILISER
EIILRTUZ UTILIZER
EIILSSTT ELITISTS
EIIMMNNT IMMINENT
EIIMMNSU IMMUNISE
EIIMMNUZ IMMUNIZE
EIIMMPRU IMPERIUM
EIIMMSSS SEISMISM
EIIMNOPT PIMIENTO
EIIMNOSS EMISSION
EIIMNRST INTERIMS,
  MINISTER
EIIMNRTT INTERMIT
EIIMNRTX INTERMIX
EIIMNSTU MUTINIES
EIIMOPRX MIREPOIX
EIIMOPST OPTIMISE
EIIMOPSZ EPIZOISM
EIIMOPTZ OPTIMIZE
EIIMOTVV VOMITIVE
EIIMQSTU QUIETISM
EIIMRSTT METRITIS
EIIMSSSV MISSIVES
EIIMSSTT SEMITIST
EIINNNPS NINEPINS
EIINNOSU UNIONISE
EIINNOSV ENVISION
EIINNOUZ UNIONIZE
EIINNSTT TIENTSIN,
  TINNIEST

EIINOPTT PETITION	EIKLNSSS SKINLESS	EILMNTUY MINUTELY,
EIINORRT INTERIOR	EIKLNSSY SKYLINES	UNTIMELY
EIINORSS IONISERS	EIKLOORT ROOTLIKE	EILMOOST TOILSOME
EIINORSV REVISION	EIKLOPSS SKI POLES	EILMOPRR IMPLORER
EIINORSZ IONIZERS	EIKLSSTT SKITTLES	EILMOPST MILEPOST
EIINOSST NOISIEST	EIKLSSTU SULKIEST	EILMPSST MISSPELT,
EIINPPST NIPPIEST	EIKMMRSS SKIMMERS	SIMPLEST
EIINPRRS INSPIRER	EIKMNOST TOKENISM	EILMPSSU IMPULSES
EIINPRST PRISTINE	EIKMORTW TIMEWORK	EILMPSTU LUMPIEST
EIINPSST PINT-SISE	EIKMOSST SMOKIEST	EILMTTUU LUTETIUM
EIINPSTZ PINT-SIZE	EIKMPSST SKEPTISM	EILNNOST INSOLENT
EIINPTUV PUNITIVE	EIKMRSTU MURKIEST	EILNNOSW SNOWLINE
EIINQRRU INQUIRER	EIKMSSTU MUSKIEST	EILNNPTY IN PLENTY
EIINQTUY EQUINITY,	EIKNOPSS POKINESS	EILNNTTY INTENTLY
INEQUITY	EIKNORTT KNOTTIER	EILNOOST LOONIEST,
EIINRRTW WINTRIER	EIKNOSTW WONKIEST	OILSTONE
EIINRSST INSISTER,	EIKNPRSU SPUNKIER	EILNOPRT INTERPOL
SINISTER	EIKNPRTU TURNPIKE	EILNOPTY LINOTYPE
EIINRSSW WIRINESS	EIKNRSST STINKERS	EILNORTT TROTLINE
EIINRSTU NEURITIS	EIKNRSTT KNITTERS,	EILNORTV IN REVOLT
EIINRSTW WRITE-INS	TRINKETS	EILNORVV INVOLVER
EIIOPRRS PRIORIES	EIKOOPRS SPOOKIER	EILNOSTU OUTLINES
EIIOPSTV POSITIVE	EIKOPPRS PORK PIES	EILNOSTV NOVELIST
EIIOSSTT OSTEITIS	EIKOPRST PORKIEST	EILNOTUV INVOLUTE
EIIPPSTZ ZIPPIEST	EIKORRWW WIREWORK	EILNPRST SPLINTER
EIIPRRSS PRISSIER	EIKPPRSS SKIPPERS	EILNPSSU SPLENIUS
EIIPRRST STRIPIER	EIKRRSST STRIKERS	EILNPSUY SUPINELY
EIIPRRTW TRIPWIRE	EILLLOSW OIL	EILNQUUY UNIQUELY
EIIPRSTV PRIVIEST	WELLS	EILNRSTU INSULTER
EIIPSSTT TIPSIEST	EILLMNOU LINOLEUM	EILNRSUU URSULINE
EIIPSSTW WISPIEST	EILLMPSS MISSPELL	EILNRTUV VIRULENT
EIIQSTTU QUIETIST	EILLMPTU MULTIPLE	EILNSSTU UTENSILS
EIIRSTTW TWISTIER	EILLMUVX VEXILLUM	EILNSTTU LUTENIST
EIISSSST SISSIEST	EILLNOTU LUTEOLIN	EILOOPRR POORLIER
EIISTTTW WITTIEST	EILLNSTY SILENTLY,	EILOORST OESTRIOL
EIJKORRS SKIJORER	TINSELLY	EILOORWW WIRE WOOL
EIJLLOST JOLLIEST	EILLNSVY SNIVELLY	EILOPPRS SLOPPIER
EIJMPSTU JUMPIEST	EILLOORW WOOLLIER	EILOPRRT PORTLIER
EIJNORTU JOINTURE	EILLOOSW WOOLLIES	EILOPRSS SPOILERS
EIJNOSTT JETTISON	EILLOPTY POLITELY	EILOPRSU PERILOUS
EIJNPRSU JUNIPERS	EILLOSTW LOWLIEST	EILOPRTW PILEWORT
EIKKLNNY KILKENNY	EILLPPPS PEP PILLS	EILOPSSV PLOSIVES
EIKKLSTU TUSKLIKE	EILLSSST LISTLESS	EILOPSTX EXPLOITS
EIKKOOST KOOKIEST	EILLSSTT STILLEST	EILORRTU ULTERIOR
EIKLLNSW INKWELLS	EILMMNOU MOULMEIN	EILORSSS RISSOLES
EIKLLNTW WELL-KNIT	EILMMPRU PLUMMIER	EILORTTY TOILETRY
EIKLLNUY UNLIKELY	EILMMRSS SLIMMERS	EILOSSTU LOUSIEST
EIKLLORV OVERKILL	EILMMSST SLIMMEST	EILOSTTT STILETTO
EIKLLSST SKILLETS	EILMNOSU EMULSION	EILPPRSS SLIPPERS
EIKLMNOS MOLESKIN	EILMNOTY MYLONITE	EILPPRST STIPPLER,
EIKLMORW WORMLIKE	EILMNPSS LIMPNESS	TIPPLERS
EIKLNPRS SPRINKLE	EILMNRRY MERRILYN	EILPPRSU SUPPLIER
EIKLNRSW WRINKLES	EILMNRST MINSTREL	EILPPRSY SLIPPERY
EIKLNRTW TWINKLER	EILMNSSS SLIMNESS	EILPPSSU SUPPLIES

EILPPSTU PULPIEST
EILPRSTT SPLITTER,
    TRIPLETS
EILPRSTY PRIESTLY
EILPRSUU PURLIEUS
EILPRSUY PLEURISY
EILPRTTY PRETTILY
EILQRRSU SQUIRREL
EILQRSUU LIQUEURS
EILRRSTU SULTRIER
EILRRSTW TWIRLERS
EILRSSTU SURLIEST
EILRSSTY SISTERLY,
    STYLISER
EILRSSZZ SIZZLERS
EILRSTTW WRISTLET
EILRSTUV RIVULETS
EILRSTYZ STYLIZER
EILRSUUX LUXURIES
EIMMNNTU MUNIMENT
EIMMNORS MISNOMER
EIMMOPRU EMPORIUM
EIMMORRT MORTIMER
EIMMOSTT TOTEMISM
EIMMPRST PRIMMEST
EIMMPRSU PREMIUMS
EIMMRRST TRIMMERS
EIMMRSSW SWIMMERS
EIMMRSTT TRIMMEST
EIMNNOOT NOONTIME
EIMNNOPY PIN MONEY
EIMNNOST MENTIONS
EIMNNOTT OINTMENT
EIMNOORS MOONRISE
EIMNOORT MOTIONER
EIMNOORV OMNIVORE
EIMNOOST EMOTIONS
EIMNOPRT ORPIMENT
EIMNOPST NEPOTISM,
    PIMENTOS
EIMNOPTT IMPOTENT
EIMNORSU MONSIEUR
EIMNORTW TIMEWORN
EIMNORTY ENORMITY
EIMNOSTU MOUNTIES
EIMNPRSS PRIMNESS
EIMNPSST MISSPENT
EIMNRSST MINSTERS,
    TRIMNESS
EIMNRTTU TERMINUS
EIMNRSTY ENTRYISM
EIMNSUZZ MUEZZINS
EIMOORST MOTORISE,
    ROOMIEST

EIMOORTZ MOTORIZE
EIMOPPRR IMPROPER
EIMOPRRS PRIMROSE,
    PROMISER
EIMOPRRT IMPORTER,
    REIMPORT
EIMOPRRV IMPROVER
EIMOPRSS PROMISES
EIMOPRUU EUROPIUM
EIMOQSTU MISQUOTE
EIMORRST MORTISER,
    STORMIER
EIMORRWW WIREWORM
EIMORSST MORTISES
EIMORSTU MOISTURE
EIMORSTW WORMIEST
EIMORSTY ISOMETRY
EIMORTTW TWO-TIMER
EIMOSSST MOSSIEST
EIMOSSTU MOUSIEST
EIMOSSTZ MESTIZOS
EIMOSTTT TOTEMIST
EIMOSTTU TITMOUSE
EIMPRSSU PRIMUSES
EIMPRSTU STUMPIER
EIMPSSTU SEPTIMUS
EIMQRRSU SQUIRMER
EIMQSTUY MYSTIQUE
EIMRRSSU SURMISER
EIMRSSST MISTRESS
EIMRSSSU SURMISES
EIMRSTTU SMUTTIER
EIMRSTUX MIXTURES
EIMSSTTU MUSTIEST
EIMSTUZZ MUZZIEST
EINNOPSS PENSIONS
EINNORSU REUNIONS
EINNORSV ENVIRONS
EINNORTU NEUTRINO
EINNORTV INVENTOR
EINNORWW WINNOWER
EINNOSSS NOSINESS
EINNOSST TENSIONS
EINNPRSS SPINNERS
EINNPSSU PUNINESS
EINNPSSY SPINNEYS
EINNPSXY SIXPENNY
EINNRSTU RUNNIEST
EINNRSTV VINTNERS
EINNRTTU NUTRIENT
EINNSSTU SUNNIEST
EINOOPRS POISONER
EINOOPSS OPSONISE
EINOOPSZ OPSONIZE

EINOOPTT ON TIPTOE
EINOORST SNOOTIER
EINOORSZ OZONISER
EINOORZZ OZONIZER
EINOOSSZ OOZINESS
EINOOTXX EXOTOXIN
EINOPRRS PRISONER
EINOPRSS ROPINESS
EINOPRST POINTERS,
    PROTEINS
EINOPRSU PRUINOSE
EINOPRTU ERUPTION
EINOPSTT NEPOTIST, STEP
    ON IT
EINOPSWX SWINEPOX
EINOQSTU QUESTION
EINOQTTU QUOTIENT
EINORRST INTRORSE
EINORSSS ROSINESS
EINORSSU NEUROSIS,
    RESINOUS
EINORSSV VERSIONS
EINORSTT SNOTTIER
EINORSTU ROUTINES
EINORSTV INVESTOR
EINORSUV SOUVENIR
EINORTTU RITENUTO
EINOSSSS SESSIONS
EINOSSST STENOSIS
EINOSSTT STONIEST
EINOSSTW SNOWIEST
EINOSTVY VENOSITY
EINPPSST SNIPPETS
EINPRRST PRINTERS,
    REPRINTS, SPRINTER
EINPRRTU PRURIENT
EINPRSST SPINSTER
EINQRSTU SQUINTER
EINQSSTU INQUESTS
EINQSTTU QUINTETS
EINRRSSU INSURERS
EINRSSSU SUNRISES
EINSSTTW TWIN SETS
EINSTTTU NUTTIEST
EIOOPPRS PORPOISE
EIOOPPST OPPOSITE
EIOOPSST ISOTOPES
EIOORSTT TORTOISE
EIOOSSTT SOOTIEST,
    TOOTSIES
EIOOSTWZ WOOZIEST
EIOPPRTW PIPEWORT
EIOPPSST SOPPIEST
EIOPRRSS PRIORESS

EIOPRRST SPORTIER
EIOPRRSU SUPERIOR
EIOPRSST PROSIEST,
RIPOSTES, TRIPOSES
EIOPRSTT SPOTTIER
EIOPRSTV SPORTIVE
EIOPRSUV PERVIOUS,
PREVIOUS, VIPEROUS
EIOPSTTT POTTIEST
EIORRRSW WORRIERS
EIORRSST RESISTOR,
SORRIEST
EIORRSTV SERVITOR
EIORRSVY REVISORY
EIORSSTY SEROSITY
EIORSTUV VITREOUS
EIPPRRST STRIPPER,
TRIPPERS
EIPQRSTU QUIPSTER
EIPRRSSU SURPRISE
EIPRSSTT TIPSTERS
EIPRSTUW WRITE-UPS
EIQRRSTU SQUIRTER
EIQRSTTU QUITTERS
EIRRRSST STIRRERS
EIRRSTTU TRUSTIER
EIRSSTTU RUSTIEST,
TRUSTIES
EIRSSTTW TWISTERS
EIRSTTTW TWITTERS
EIRTTTWY TWITTERY
EISSTTUW WET SUITS
EISSUUVV VESUVIUS
EJMOSTTU MOT JUSTE
EJNOORRS SOJORNER
EJNORSUY JOURNEYS
EJNSSSTU JUSTNESS
EKKNSTUZ KUZNETSK
EKLMNOSS SMOLENSK
EKLNOOOR LOOKER-ON,
ONLOOKER
EKLNORSS SNORKELS
EKLOOORV OVERLOOK
EKMRSTUY MUSKETRY
EKNNOPSU UNSPOKEN
EKNOOPRW OPENWORK
EKNORSTW NETWORKS
EKNRSTUY TURNKEYS
EKOOORTV OVERTOOK
EKOORRVW OVERWORK
EKOORTWW KOWTOWER
EKOPRSTU UPSTROKE
ELLLMOWY MELLOWLY
ELLLNSUY SULLENLY

ELLMNOSY SOLEMNLY
ELLNOORV LOVELORN
ELLNOOSW WOOLLENS
ELLNORRT RENT-ROLL
ELLNORWW WELL-WORN
ELLNOSVY SLOVENLY
ELLNOUVY UNLOVELY
ELLNSSTU NULL SETS
ELLOPRST POLLSTER
ELLOPRTU POLLUTER
ELLOPRUV PULLOVER
ELLORRST STROLLER
ELLORSTY TROLLEYS
ELLOSSSU SOULLESS
ELLOSSTU SELL-OUTS
ELMNOOSS MOONLESS
ELMNOOSZ ZOOM LENS
ELMNUUZZ UNMUZZLE
ELMOORST TREMOLOS
ELMOORSY MOROSELY
ELMOOSSY LYSOSOME
ELMOPRSY POLYMERS
ELMOPSYY POLYSEMY
ELMOSTUU TUMULOSE
ELMOSYYZ LYSOZYME
ELMPPSTU PLUMPEST
ELNNOOSU UNLOOSEN
ELNOOSTZ SOLONETZ
ELNOPRVY PROVENLY
ELNOPSTU PLEUSTON
ELNOPTTY POTENTLY
ELNORSTU TURNSOLE
ELNORTTY ROTTENLY
ELNOSSSW SLOWNESS
ELNOSSTV SOLVENTS
ELNPRTUU PURULENT
ELOORSST ROOTLESS
ELOOSTUU TOULOUSE
ELOPPRRY PROPERLY
ELOPRRSW PROWLERS
ELOPRSTY PROSTYLE
ELOPSSST SPOTLESS
ELORSTUY UROSTYLE
ELPPSSTU SUPPLEST
ELPRSTTU SPLUTTER
ELPRSUZZ PUZZLERS
ELPSSTUU PUSTULES
ELRRSSTU RUSTLERS
ELRSTUUV VULTURES
ELSSSTUY STYLUSES
EMMMNOTU
MOMENTUM
EMMNNOTU
MONUMENT

EMMNOOOS
MONOSOME
EMMNOORS MEN'S
ROOM
EMMNOORT
MOTORMEN
EMMNOOSY MONOSEMY
EMMNOTTU
TOMENTUM
EMMNOTYY METONYMY
EMMRRRUU MURMURER
EMMRRSTU STRUMMER
EMMRSTYY SYMMETRY
EMNNOOOT
MONOTONE
EMNNOOSW NEW
MOONS
EMNNOSTW TOWNSMEN
EMNNSTTU STUNT MEN
EMNOOPTY MONOTYPE
EMNOORSU ENORMOUS
EMNOORSW NEWSROOM
EMNOOSUV VENOMOUS
EMNOOTTY TENOTOMY
EMNORRSU MOURNERS
EMNORSST MONSTERS
EMNORSTT TORMENTS
EMNORSTU REMOUNTS
EMNORSUU NUMEROUS
EMNOSUUY EUONYMUS
EMNOSUVY EVONYMUS
EMNRSSTU STERNUMS
EMOOPRRT PROMOTER
EMOOPRSZ ZOOSPERM
EMOORRST REST ROOM
EMOORTYZ ZOOMETRY
EMOOSSTW TWOSOMES
EMOPPRRT PROMPTER
EMOPRSSU SPERMOUS,
SUPREMOS
EMPRRTUY TRUMPERY
EMPRSTTU STRUMPET,
TRUMPETS
ENNOOOTZ ENTOZOON
ENNOOPPT OPPONENT
ENNOORTV NONVOTER
ENNOPRUV UNPROVEN
ENNOPTWY TWOPENNY
ENNORSST STERNSON
ENNORSTU NEUTRONS
ENNOSTWW NEW
TOWNS
ENNPPTUY TUPPENNY
ENNPRRUU RUNNER-UP

ENNRSSTU STUNNERS
ENOOPPST POSTPONE
ENOOPRSS POORNESS, SNOOPERS
ENOOPSTT POTSTONE
ENOPRSTT PORTENTS
ENOPSSSY SYNOPSES
ENORRSST SNORTERS
ENORRSTT TORRENTS
ENORRTUV OVERTURN, TURNOVER
ENORSSSU SOURNESS
ENORSSTU TONSURES
ENORSTUY TOURNEYS
ENOSSSTT STETSONS
ENOSSSUU SENSUOUS
ENPRSSSY SPRYNESS
ENPRSSTU PUNSTERS
ENRRRTUU NURTURER
EOOOPRSZ ZOOSPORE
EOOORRST ROSE-ROOT
EOOPPRRS PROPOSER
EOOPPRSV POPOVERS
EOOPPTTY TOPOTYPE
EOOPRRST TROOPERS
EOOPRRTU UPROOTER
EOOPRSTV STOPOVER
EOOPRSTW TOWROPES
EOORRRSW SORROWER
EOORRSST ROOSTERS
EOORRSTU OESTROUS
EOPPRRTY PROPERTY
EOPPRSST STOPPERS
EOPPRSSU PURPOSES, SUPPOSER
EOPRRSTU POSTURER, TROUPERS
EOPRRUVY PURVEYOR
EOPRSSTT PROTESTS, SPOTTERS
EOPRSSTU POSTURES, SPOUTERS
EOPSSTTW TWO-STEPS
EORRRTTU TORTURER
EORRSSTU TROUSERS
EORRSTTT TROTTERS
EORRSTTU TORTURES
EORRSUVY SURVEYOR
EOSSTTTU STOUTEST
EPPPRTUY PUPPETRY
EPPRSSTU PRESS-UPS, SUPPRESS
EPRRSSUU PURSUERS, USURPERS

EPRRSTUU RUPTURES
EPRSSTTU SPUTTERS
ERRSTTTU STRUTTER
ERSSTTTU STUTTERS
FFFGILNU FLUFFING
FFFILOST LIFT-OFFS
FFGHIIRT GRIFFITH
FFGHIORS FROGFISH
FFGHIRSU GRUFFISH
FFGIILNP PIFFLING
FFGIILNR RIFFLING
FFGIINNS SNIFFING
FFGIINRS GRIFFINS
FFGILMNU MUFFLING
FFGILNRU RUFFLING
FFGINNSU SNUFFING
FFGINSTU STUFFING
FFHILOSW WOLFFISH
FFHOOOST OFFSHOOT
FFHOOSSW SHOW-OFFS
FFHOSTTU HOT STUFF
FFIILMOR FILIFORM
FFIKLORT FORK-LIFT
FFILLOPP FLIP-FLOP
FFILLTUY FITFULLY
FFILRTUU FRUITFUL
FFILRTUY FRUIT FLY
FFILSTUY STUFFILY
FFIMORSU FUSIFORM
FFINOPRT OFFPRINT
FFINOPSS SPIN-OFFS
FFINOPST PONTIFFS
FFNORSTU TURN-OFFS
FFOORRUU FROUFROU
FFOORSTW WORST-OFF
FGGGIINR FRIGGING
FGGGILNO FLOGGING
FGGHIINT FIGHTING
FGGIILNN FLINGING
FGGIINNR FRINGING
FGGIINRU FIGURING
FGGINOOR FORGOING
FGGINORS FORGINGS
FGHIIKNS KINGFISH
FGHIILNT IN-FLIGHT
FGHIINST SHIFTING
FGHILNSU FLUSHING, LUNGFISH
FGHILRTU RIGHTFUL
FGHINORT FROTHING
FGHIOTTU OUTFIGHT
FGHLORUU FURLOUGH
FGHNOORS FOGHORNS
FGIIKNRS FRISKING

FGIILLNS FILLINGS
FGIILNPP FLIPPING
FGIILNRT FLIRTING, TRIFLING
FGIILNST STIFLING
FGIILNTT FLITTING
FGIINNSU INFUSING
FGIINNUY UNIFYING
FGIINOST FOISTING
FGIINRTU FRUITING
FGIINRZZ FRIZZING
FGIINSST SIFTINGS
FGIINSTT FITTINGS
FGIKLNNU FLUNKING
FGILMNUY FUMINGLY
FGILNNTU GUNFLINT
FGILNOOR FLOORING
FGILNOOT FOOTLING
FGILNOPP FLOPPING
FGILNORU FLOURING
FGILNOSS FLOSSING
FGILNOTU FLOUTING
FGILNPRU PURFLING
FGINNORT FRONTING
FGINNORW FROWNING
FGINOOPR PROOFING
FGINORST FROSTING
FGLLMOOU GLOOMFUL
FGLNORSU FURLONGS
FGLNORUW WRONGFUL
FGLOOOST FOOTSLOG
FHHIKOOS FISH-HOOK
FHHLOSTU HOT FLUSH
FHIIKLMS MILKFISH
FHIIKNSS FISHSKIN
FHIILLTY FILTHILY
FHIILMNT THIN-FILM
FHIILNOS LIONFISH
FHIILSTY SHIFTILY
FHIKLSWY FLYWHISK
FHIKMNOS MONKFISH
FHILLOOT FOOTHILL
FHILLORT HILLFORT
FHILMPSU LUMPFISH
FHILMRTU MIRTHFUL
FHILOPST SHOPLIFT
FHILORSU FLOURISH
FHILORTY FROTHILY
FHIMNOOS MOONFISH
FHIMPRSU FRUMPISH
FHIOOPTT PHOTOFIT
FHLLOSTU SLOTHFUL
FHLMORUU HUMORFUL
FHLMOTUU MOUTHFUL

FHLOTUUY YOUTHFUL	GGGIIJLN JIGGLING	GGILNUZZ GUZZLING
FHLRTTUU TRUTHFUL	GGGIILNN NIGGLING	GGILQSUY SQUIGGLY
FHNOSTUX FOXHUNTS	GGGIILNW WIGGLING	GGIMNOOR GROOMING
FHOOORST FORSOOTH	GGGIINSW SWIGGING,	GGINNOOS GOINGS-ON
FIIILNOP FILIPINO	WIGGINGS	GGINNOPP PING-PONG
FIIINNOX INFIXION	GGGIINTW TWIGGING	GGINNOPS SPONGING
FIIINNTY INFINITY	GGGIJLNO JOGGLING	GGINNORW WRONGING
FIIKLRSY FRISKILY	GGGIJLNU JUGGLING	GGINNOSS SINGSONG
FIIKLSST SKI LIFTS	GGGILNOS SLOGGING	GGINNRTU GRUNTING
FIILLMSY FLIMSILY	GGGILNPU PLUGGING	GGINOOTU OUTGOING
FIILMOPR PILIFORM	GGGILNRU GURGLING	GGINOPRU GROUPING
FIILMPSY SIMPLIFY	GGGILNSU SLUGGING	GGINORSS GROSSING
FIILTTUY FUTILITY	GGGILORY GROGGILY	GGINORSU GROUSING
FIIMOPRS PISIFORM	GGGIMNSU MUGGINGS	GGINRSST G-STRINGS
FIINNOSU INFUSION	GGGINNOS SNOGGING	GHHIJMPU HIGH JUMP
FIINORTU FRUITION	GGHHIISW WHIGGISH	GHHILOSU GHOULISH
FIKKLNOS KINSFOLK	GGHIILNT LIGHTING	GHHINSSU SHUSHING
FILLLUWY WILFULLY	GGHIINNW WHINGING	GHHIOPST HIGH SPOT
FILLNSUY SINFULLY	GGHIINRT RIGHTING	GHHOORTU THOROUGH
FILLOPPY FLOPPILY	GGHIINST SIGHTING	GHHOSTTU THOUGHTS
FILORSST FLORISTS	GGHIIPRS PRIGGISH	GHIIKNNS HSINKING
FILORSTY FROSTILY	GGHILSSU SLUGGISH	GHIIKNNT THINKING
FILSSTTU FLUTISTS	GGHINORU ROUGHING	GHIIKNPS KINGSHIP
FILSTTUY STULTIFY	GGHINOST GHOSTING	GHIIKNRS SHIRKING
FIMNORSU UNIFORMS	GGHINOSU SOUGHING	GHIIKNSW WHISKING
FIMOPRRY PYRIFORM	GGHKNNOO HONG	GHIILLNS SHILLING
FIMORTUY FUMITORY	KONG	GHIILMTY MIGHTILY
FIMRSTUU FUTURISM	GGIIINNT IGNITING	GHIILNRW WHIRLING
FINORSSS FRISSONS	GGIIJLNN JINGLING	GHIILTTW TWILIGHT
FIORTTUY FORTUITY	GGIILLNR GRILLING	GHIIMRST RIGHTISM
FIRSTTUU FUTURIST	GGIILMNN MINGLING	GHIINNNS SHINNING
FIRTTUUY FUTURITY	GGIILNNS GIN SLING,	GHIINNNT THINNING
FJLLOUYY JOYFULLY	SINGLING, SLINGING	GHIINOST HOISTING
FKMOORRW FORMWORK	GGIILNNT GLINTING,	GHIINPPS SHIPPING
FKNOORTX FORT KNOX	TINGLING	GHIINPPW WHIPPING
FKOOORTW FOOTWORK	GGIIMPRS PRIGGISM	GHIINRRS SHIRRING
FLLMNOOU FULL MOON	GGIINNNR GRINNING	GHIINRRW WHIRRING
FLLNOOOW FOLLOW-ON	GGIINNOR IGNORING	GHIINRST SHIRTING
FLLOOPUW FOLLOW-UP	GGIINNRW WRINGING	GHIINRTV THRIVING
FLLOPSTU FULL STOP	GGIINNSS SIGNINGS	GHIINRTW WRITHING
FLMNORUU MOURNFUL	GGIINNST STINGING	GHIINSST INSIGHTS
FLNOOPSU SPOONFUL	GGIINNSW SWINGING	GHIINSSW SWISHING
FLOOSTUW OUTFLOWS	GGIINPPR GRIPPING	GHIINSTT SHITTING
FLOPRSTU SPORTFUL	GGIINRTT GRITTING	GHIINSTW WHITINGS
FLRSTTUU TRUSTFUL	GGILLOOW GOLLIWOG	GHIINWZZ WHIZZING
FNOOORTW FOOTWORN	GGILNNOS LONGINGS	GHIIRSTT RIGHTIST
FNOORRSW FORSWORN	GGILNNOU LOUNGING	GHIKLNTY KNIGHTLY
FNOORSSU SUNROOFS	GGILNNPU PLUNGING	GHIKLSTY SKYLIGHT
FOOOPRST ROOFTOPS	GGILNORW GROWLING	GHILLSTY SLIGHTLY
FOOPSSTT SOFT SPOT	GGILNORY GLORYING	GHILNOPS LONGSHIP
FOORSTTX FOXTROTS	GGILNOSS GLOSSING,	GHILNOSS SLOSHING
FOPSSSTU FUSSPOTS	GOSLINGS	GHILNOTW NIGHT OWL
GGGGIILN GIGGLING	GGILNRUY URGINGLY	GHILNRTU HURTLING
GGGGILNO GOGGLING	GGILNTTU GLUTTING	GHILNRUY HUNGRILY

GHILNSTU HUSTLING, SUNLIGHT
GHILOPRS SHOPGIRL
GHILORSW SHOWGIRL
GHILPRTY TRIGLYPH
GHIMNORU HUMORING
GHIMNOTU MOUTHING
GHIMNPTU THUMPING
GHIMNSTU GUNSMITH
GHINNNSU SHUNNING
GHINNOOR HONORING
GHINNORT NORTHING
GHINNSTU SHUNTING
GHINOOPW WHOOPING
GHINOOST SHOOTING, SOOTHING
GHINOPPS SHOPPING
GHINOPPW WHOPPING
GHINOQTU QUOTHING
GHINORST SHORTING
GHINORTW INGROWTH, THROWING
GHINOSSU HOUSINGS
GHINOSSW SHOWINGS
GHINOSTU SHOUTING, SOUTHING
GHINOSUY YOUNGISH
GHINRRUY HURRYING
GHINSSTU HUSTINGS
GHINSTTU SHUTTING
GHIORTTU OUTRIGHT
GHLMOOOY HOMOLOGY
GHLNNOOR LONGHORN
GHLNOOST LONG SHOT
GHLOOORY HOROLOGY
GHLORTUU TURLOUGH
GHMNOOOY HOMOGONY
GHMOSSTU MUGSHOTS
GHNNOPUU HUNG UP ON
GHNOPRSY GRYPHONS
GHNOSSTU GUNSHOTS, SHOTGUNS
GHOPRTUW UPGROWTH
GIIILMNT LIMITING
GIIILOTV VITILIGO
GIIINNOT IGNITION
GIIINNOZ IONIZING
GIIINNTV INVITING
GIIINSTV VISITING
GIIJMNOS JINGOISM
GIIJNNOT JOINTING

GIIJNNRU INJURING
GIIJNOST JINGOIST
GIIKLLNS KILLINGS
GIIKLNNS SLINKING
GIIKLNNT TINKLING
GIIKLNNW WINKLING
GIIKMMNS SKIMMING
GIIKMNPS SKIMPING
GIIKMNRS SMIRKING
GIIKNNNS SKINNING
GIIKNNOV INVOKING
GIIKNNPS KINGPINS, PINK GINS
GIIKNNST STINKING
GIIKNNTT KNITTING
GIIKNPPS SKIPPING
GIIKNPSS PIGSKINS
GIIKNRST SKIRTING, STRIKING
GIILLNPS SPILLING
GIILLNRT TRILLING
GIILLNST STILLING
GIILLNSW SWILLING
GIILLPSW PIGSWILL
GIILLTUY GUILTILY
GIILMMNS SLIMMING
GIILMNPY IMPLYING
GIILMPRS PILGRIMS
GIILMPSU PUGILISM
GIILNNSY LYINGS-IN
GIILNOPS SPOILING
GIILNOPT PILOTING
GIILNPPR RIPPLING
GIILNPPS SLIPPING
GIILNPRT TRIPLING
GIILNQSU QUISLING
GIILNQTU QUILTING
GIILNRST STIRLING
GIILNRSW SWIRLING
GIILNRTW TWIRLING
GIILNSTT SLITTING
GIILNSTU LINGUIST
GIILNSTY STINGILY
GIILNSZZ SIZZLING
GIILPSTU PUGILIST
GIILRTTY GRITTILY
GIIMMNRT TRIMMING
GIIMMNRU IMMURING
GIIMMNSW SWIMMING
GIIMNNOY IGNOMINY
GIIMNNTU MINUTING
GIIMNOPS IMPOSING
GIIMNOTT OMITTING
GIIMNOTV VOMITING

GIIMNPRU UMPIRING
GIIMNPTU IMPUTING
GIIMNSSU MISUSING
GIIMORRS RIGORISM
GIINNNOT INTONING
GIINNNPS SPINNING
GIINNNSW WINNINGS
GIINNNTW TWINNING
GIINNOPT POINTING
GIINNORS ROSINING
GIINNORT IGNITRON
GIINNPPS SNIPPING
GIINNPRT PRINTING
GIINNRSU INSURING
GIINNRTU UNTIRING
GIINNSTT STINTING
GIINOPST POSITING
GIINOPTV PIVOTING
GIINORUV IN VIGOUR
GIINPPQU QUIPPING
GIINPPRT TRIPPING
GIINPRSU UPRISING
GIINPSTT SPITTING
GIINQTTU QUITTING
GIINQUZZ QUIZZING
GIINRRST STIRRING
GIINRSTW WRITINGS
GIINSSTT SITTINGS
GIINSTTW TWISTING
GIINTTTW TWITTING
GIIORRST RIGORIST
GIJKLNOY JOKINGLY
GIJLLNOY JOLLYING
GIJLNOST JOSTLING
GIJNOSTT JOTTINGS
GIJNOSTU JOUSTING
GIKKLNSU SKULKING
GIKLNNOP PLONKING
GIKNNOST KINGSTON
GIKNNOTT KNOTTING
GIKNOOPS SPOOKING
GIKNORST STROKING
GIKNORSW WORKINGS
GILLMOOY GLOOMILY
GILLNORT TROLLING
GILLNOVY LOVINGLY
GILLNOWY LOW-LYING
GILLNRUY LURINGLY
GILLNSUY SULLYING
GILLOSSY GLOSSILY
GILMMNSU SLUMMING
GILMNOPY MOPINGLY
GILMNOTU MOULTING
GILMNOVY MOVINGLY

GILMNPPU PLUMPING
GILMNPRU RUMPLING
GILMNPSU SLUMPING
GILMNSUY MUSINGLY
GILMNUZZ MUZZLING
GILMOOSY MISOLOGY
GILMPRUY GRUMPILY
GILMPSSY GYMSLIPS
GILNNRSU NURSLING
GILNNUZZ NUZZLING
GILNOOSY SINOLOGY
GILNOOTT TOOTLING
GILNOPPP PLOPPING
GILNOPPS SLOPPING
GILNOPPT TOPPLING
GILNOPRW PROWLING
GILNOPSY SPONGILY
GILNOPTT PLOTTING
GILNOSTT SLOTTING
GILNOSTU LONG SUIT,
 TOUSLING
GILNOTUY OUTLYING
GILNPRSU SLURPING
GILNPUZZ PUZZLING
GILNRRSU SLURRING
GILNRSTU RUSTLING
GILNSSTU TUSSLING
GILOOOST OOLOGIST
GILOORSU GLORIOUS
GILOORVY VIROLOGY
GILOOSSS ISOGLOSS
GILOOSTY SITOLOGY
GIMMNRUY GIN RUMMY
GIMMOSSU GUMMOSIS
GIMNNORS MORNINGS
GIMNNORU MOURNING
GIMNNOTU MOUNTING
GIMNOOOU OOGONIUM
GIMNOORS MOORINGS
GIMNOORT MOTORING
GIMNOPST STOMPING
GIMNOPTU GUMPTION
GIMNORRW RINGWORM
GIMNORST STORMING
GIMNOSYY MISOGYNY
GIMNPRTU TRUMPING
GIMNPSTU STUMPING
GIMNSTYY STYMYING
GINNNSTU STUNNING
GINNOOPS SNOOPING,
 SPOONING
GINNOOSW SWOONING
GINNOOSZ SNOOZING
GINNOPTU GUNPOINT

GINNORST SNORTING
GINNPRSU SPURNING
GINNRSTU TURNINGS,
 UNSTRING
GINNSTTU STUNTING
GINNSTUW WING NUTS
GINOOPPS OPPOSING
GINOOPRT TROOPING
GINOOPST STOOPING
GINOOPSW SWOOPING
GINOORST ROOSTING
GINOPPPR PROPPING
GINOPPST STOPPING,
 TOPPINGS
GINOPPSW SWOPPING
GINOPRST SPORTING
GINOPRSU IN-GROUPS
GINOPSST POSTINGS,
 SIGNPOST
GINOPSTT SPOTTING
GINOPSTU SPOUTING
GINORRWY WORRYING
GINORSTW WORSTING
GINORTTT TROTTING
GINORTTU TUTORING
GINOSTTW SWOTTING
GINOSTUW OUTSWING
GINPRRSU SPURRING
GINPRSTU SPURTING
GINPRSUU PURSUING,
 USURPING
GINPSSUW UPSWINGS
GINRSSTU TRUSSING
GINRSTTU TRUSTING
GINRSTUU SUTURING
GIOOORSV VIGOROSO
GIOORRSU RIGOROUS
GIOORSTU GOITROUS
GIOORSUV VIGOROUS
GIORSTUY RUGOSITY
GJLMNOPU LONG JUMP
GLLOOPTY POLYGLOT
GLMNOOOY
 MONOLOGY, NOMOLOGY
GLMNORUW
 LUNGWORM
GLMOOOPY POMOLOGY
GLMOORWW GLOW-
 WORM
GLMOOYYZ ZYMOLOGY
GLMORSUW LUGWORMS
GLNNOOST LONG TONS
GLNOOOSY NOSOLOGY
GLNOOOTY ONTOLOGY

GLNOOPSY POLYGONS
GLNOPYYY POLYGYNY
GLNORSTY STRONGLY
GLNORTUW LUNGWORT
GLNOSTTU GLUTTONS
GLNOTTUY GLUTTONY
GLOOOPSY POSOLOGY
GLOOOPTY TOPOLOGY
GLOOPTYY LOGOTYPY,
 TYPOLOGY
GMMNOTUY TOMMY
 GUN
GMMPSUUW MUGWUMPS
GMNNOOYY
 MONOGYNY
GNOOOTTW GO TO
 TOWN
GNOORTUW
 OUTGROWN
GNOPPUUY YOUNG PUP
GNOPRSUW GROWN-UPS
GNPRSTUU STRUNG-UP
GOOPRTUU OUT-GROUP
HHHHSSUU HUSH-HUSH
HHIIOORT HIROHITO
HHIIPSST PHTHISIS
HHKKSSUU KHUSKHUS
HHOOOOPP POOH-POOH
HHOOPPRS PHOSPHOR
HHORRSUU RUSH HOUR
HIIILMNS NIHILISM
HIIILNST NIHILIST
HIIILNTY NIHILITY
HIIINRST RHINITIS
HIIKMRSS SKIRMISH
HIIKSSTT SKITTISH
HIILMOST HOMILIST
HIILMPSY IMPISHLY
HIILMTUY HUMILITY
HIILOPST PISOLITH
HIILPSSY SYPHILIS
HIILSSTT HIT LISTS
HIIMNSTT TINSMITH
HIIMOPSS PHIMOSIS
HIIMORTU HIRI MOTU
HIIMORTZ ZHITOMIR
HIISSSSY SISSYISH
HIKNOOOR KOHINOOR
HIKOOPSS SPOOKISH
HIKOPSSY KYPHOSIS
HILLLOSU SOLIHULL
HILLMSUY MULISHLY
HILLOSWY OWLISHLY
HILMNOOT MONOLITH

HILNORTY THORNILY
HILOOTTY TOOTHILY
HILORSUU URUSHIOL
HILORTWY HOLY WRIT,
WORTHILY
HILOSTWW WHITLOWS
HILPPRSU PURPLISH
HILSSTTU SLUTTISH
HIMOOPRS ISOMORPH
HIMOPRRT TRIMORPH
HIMOPRSW SHIPWORM
HIMOPRWW WHIPWORM
HIMOPSSS SOPHISMS
HIMORSTU HUMORIST
HIMPRSTU TRIUMPHS
HINNSSUY SUNSHINY
HINOORSZ HORIZONS
HINOPRTW WINTHROP
HINOPSSY HYPNOSIS
HINOPSTW TOWNSHIP
HINORSTW THROW-INS
HIOORTWZ HOROWITZ
HIOPRSSW WORSHIPS
HIOPRSUZ RHIZOPUS
HIOPSSST SOPHISTS
HIPPPSUY PUPPYISH
HKMOOORW
HOOKWORM
HKOOPRSW WORKSHOP
HLLLOOWY HOLLOWLY
HLLMNOOU MONOHULL
HLLNOOUU HONOLULU
HLLPPSUU PUSH-PULL
HLMOOSTY SMOOTHLY
HLMOPTUY PLYMOUTH
HLNOOSUW HOUNSLOW
HMMMNOOSY
HOMONYMS
HMMOORSU
MUSHROOM
HMNOOOST MOON
SHOT
HMNOPSYY SYMPHONY
HMOOORSW
SHOWROOM
HMOORSUU HUMOROUS
HNNOORTT THORNTON
HNOOOSTT NOT SO HOT
HNOOPRST POST HORN
HNOOPSTY TYPHOONS
HNOORRTW
HORNWORT
HNORSTTU THURSTON
HNORTUWY UNWORTHY

HNRSTTUU UNTRUTHS
HOOOSTTU OUTSHOOT,
SHOOT-OUT
HOOPSSTT HOT SPOTS,
POTSHOTS
HOPPRRYY PORPHYRY
HPRSTTUU UPTHRUST
IIILLNOS ILLINOIS
IIILMRSV VIRILISM
IIILMUVX LIXIVIUM
IIILRTVY VIRILITY
IIINPRST INSPIRIT
IIINQTUY INIQUITY
IIJJSTUU JIUJITSU
IIKLLNSY SLINKILY
IIKLMPSY SKIMPILY
IIKLNOSS OILSKINS
IIKLQRUY QUIRKILY
IILLMNOS MILLIONS
IILLMRTU TRILLIUM
IILLMUUV ILLUVIUM
IILLNOPS PILLIONS
IILLNORT TRILLION
IILLNOSU ILLUSION
IILLNOSZ ZILLIONS
IILMMPSS SIMPLISM
IILMNOSU LIMOUSIN
IILMOTTY MOTILITY
IILNOOST INOSITOL
IILNOOTV VOLITION
IILNORSS SIRLOINS
IILNPPSY SNIPPILY
IILNRTWY WINTRILY
IILPRSSY PRISSILY
IILSTUUV UVULITIS
IILSTUVV VULVITIS
IIMMMNSU MINIMUMS
IIMMNTUY IMMUNITY
IIMMOPST OPTIMISM
IIMMOPSU OPIUMISM
IIMMSTTU MITTIMUS
IIMNNOOT MONITION
IIMNNOSU UNIONISM
IIMNNOTU MUNITION
IIMNOOSS OMISSION
IIMNOPRS IMPRISON
IIMNORTY MINORITY
IIMNOSSS MISSIONS
IIMNOSST SIMONIST
IIMNPRST IMPRINTS,
MISPRINT
IIMNPTUY IMPUNITY
IIMNRSTY MINISTRY
IIMOPSTT OPTIMIST

IIMORSSU MISSOURI
IIMORSTY RIMOSITY
IIMOTTVY MOTIVITY
IIMPRTUY IMPURITY
IIMSSTUW SWIMSUIT
IINNNOSU IN UNISON
IINNOOPS OPINIONS
IINNOPPT PINPOINT
IINNOSTU UNIONIST
IINNSTTU TINNITUS
IINOOPST POSITION
IINOSSTZ ZIONISTS
IINOSTVY VINOSITY
IINRTTUY TRIUNITY
IIOOPSTV OVIPOSIT
IIOOQRSU IROQUOIS
IIOOSTTY OTIOSITY
IIOPRRTY PRIORITY
IIORSSTV VISITORS
IIORSTUV VIRTUOSI
IJKLLOSY KILLJOYS
IJKMPSSU SKI JUMPS
IJLLORTU TRUJILLO
IJMPSTUU JUMPSUIT
IKKLNORW LINKWORK
IKKLNOSY KOLINSKY
IKLLOOTV KILOVOLT
IKLMNRSU MILK RUNS
IKLMOPSS MILKSOPS
IKLMORSW SILKWORM
IKLMORTW MILKWORT
IKLNOPST SLIPKNOT
IKLNOTTY KNOTTILY
IKLNPSUY SPUNKILY
IKLOOPSY SPOOKILY
IKMNPPSU PUMPKINS
IKNOOPRT PINKROOT
IKNOORRW IRONWORK
IKORSSTU KURTOSIS
ILLLMOPS PLIMSOLL
ILLLOOPP LOLLIPOP
ILLLOOWY WOOLLILY
ILLMNOSU MULLIONS
ILLMOSSY LISSOMLY
ILLMPTUY MULTIPLY
ILLOPPSY SLOPPILY
ILLORSUY ILLUSORY
ILLRSTUY SULTRILY
ILMNOOPU POLONIUM
ILMNOSUU LUMINOUS
ILMOPPSU POPULISM
ILMORSTY STORMILY
ILMSSTUU STIMULUS
ILMSTTUY SMUTTILY

ILNOOSTU SOLUTION
ILNOOSTY SNOOTILY
ILNOOTUV VOLUTION
ILNORSST NOSTRILS
ILNORSTY NITROSYL
ILNOSTTY SNOTTILY
ILNPSUUV PULVINUS
ILOOPPRS PROPOLIS
ILOOSSST SOLOISTS
ILOPPSTU POPULIST
ILOPRSTY SPORTILY
ILOPSTTY SPOTTILY
ILOPSUUV PLUVIOUS
ILOQRTUU LOQUITUR
ILRSTTUY TRUSTILY
ILSSSTTY STYLISTS
IMMNOORS MORONISM
IMNNOSUU NUMINOUS
IMNOORST MONITORS
IMNOORTY MONITORY
IMNOSTUU MUTINOUS
IMOOPRRS PROMISOR
IMOOPRST IMPOSTOR
IMOOQSTU MOSQUITO
IMOORSTT MOTORIST
IMOORSTU TIMOROUS
IMOORTVY VOMITORY
IMOOSSTY MYOSOTIS
IMRSSTTU MISTRUST
INNNNOOU NONUNION
INNNORTU TRUNNION
INNOOPSS SPONSION
INNOORST NOTORNIS
INOOOSSZ ZOONOSIS
INOOOTXZ ZOOTOXIN
INOOPRST PORTIONS,
  POSITRON, SORPTION
INOOPSTT SPITTOON
INOOPTTU OUTPOINT
INOORSTY SONORITY
INOPRTTU PRINTOUT
INOPSSSY SYNOPSIS
INORSSUV SUN VISOR
INPPRRUU PURPURIN

INPRRSTU SURPRINT
IOOPRSSV PROVISOS
IOOPRSTY ISOTROPY,
  POROSITY
IOORRSTY SORORITY
IOORSSTT RISOTTOS
IOORSSUV VOUSSOIR
IOORSTTU TORTIOUS
IOORSTUV VIRTUOSO
IOORSUUX UXORIOUS
IOPPPRST PIT PROPS
IOPRSSUU SPURIOUS
IOPRSTTU OUTSTRIP
IORRSUVV SURVIVOR
IORSSTTU TOURISTS
IORSSUUU USURIOUS
IORSTTUY TOURISTY
IORSTUUV VIRTUOUS
IPRRSSTU STIRRUPS
IPRRSTUU PRURITUS
IPRSSTUU PURSUITS
JLOOSUYY JOYOUSLY
JNNOORRU NONJUROR
JNOORSSU SOJOURNS
KLLMNSUU NUMSKULL
KLMMOOOS KOMSOMOL
KLNORSTY KLYSTRON
KLOOOSTU LOOKOUTS,
  OUTLOOKS
KLOOPRSW SLOPWORK
KMOOORRW
  WORKROOM
KNNNOSUW UNKNOWNS
KNOOPSTT TOPKNOTS
KOOPRSTW WORKTOPS
KOORSTUW OUTWORKS,
  WORKOUTS
LLMOOPRS ROLLMOPS
LLOOPRST TROLLOPS
LLOOPRYY ROLY-POLY
LLOPSTUU PULLOUTS
LLOSUUVV VOLVULUS
LMMPSSUU LUMP SUMS
LMNOOOPY MONOPOLY

LMOOPRTU PULMOTOR
LMOORSWW
  SLOWWORM
LMOOTXYY XYLOTOMY
LMOPPRTY PROMPTLY
LNOOOPRT POLTROON
LOOPPSUU POPULOUS
LOOPPSUY POLYPOUS
LORSSTUU LUSTROUS
MMOOPPRU PUMP ROOM
MMOORTTY
  TOMMYROT
MMOPSSTY SYMPTOMS
MNNOOOSS MONSOONS
MNNOOOTY
  MONOTONY
MNNOSSYY SYNONYMS
MNNOSYYY SYNONYMY
MNOOORTW
  MOONWORT
MNOOORXY
  OXYMORON
MNOOPTYY TOPONYMY
MNORSSTU NOSTRUMS
MNORSTUU SURMOUNT
MOOOORRTW
  MOORWORT,
  TOMORROW
MOOPSSSU OPOSSUMS
MOORSTUU TUMOROUS
MORRSSTU ROSTRUMS
NNOOOPST PONTOONS
NNOOPRSU PRONOUNS
NNOORTUU RUN OUT
  ON
NOOORSSU SONOROUS
NOOPRSSS SPONSORS
NOPSSSTU SUNSPOTS
NORSTTUU TURNOUTS
OOPRSSTV PROVOSTS
OOPSSTTU OUTPOSTS
OORSTTUU TORTUOUS
OPPRSSTU SUPPORTS
OPRSSSUU SOURPUSS

NINE-LETTER WORDS

AAAABCLLV BALACLAVA
AAAABDHLL ALLAHABAD
AAAABGNRU
GUANABARA
AAAABIKLL BALALAIKA
AAAABILMN ALABAMIAN
AAAABKLLV BALAKLAVA
AAAACCHMT
TACAMAHAC
AAAACDJNR JACARANDA
AAAACHSUY AYAHUASCA
AAAACINRU ARAUCANIA
AAAACIRRU ARAUCARIA
AAAACLMNS
SALAMANCA
AAAACMNRT
CATAMARAN
AAAADGKNR
KARAGANDA
AAAADILLM DALAI LAMA
AAAAEHKLL HALEAKALA
AAAAGIKMS AMAGASAKI
AAAAHHJMR
MAHARAJAH
AAAAHJMRS MAHARAJAS
AAAAILNPS ANAPLASIA
AAAAINSST ANASTASIA
AAAALLMMY
MALAYALAM
AAAAMPRTT
PARAMATTA
AAAABBDINR BARBADIAN
AAAABBINRR BARBARIAN
AAAABCCHLN
BACCHANAL
AAAABCCHNR
CHARABANC
AAAABCCITT CATABATIC
AAAABCDIIT ADIABATIC
AAAABCDRRU
BARRACUDA
AAAABCELTV VACATABLE
AAAABCEMRT
CARBAMATE
AAAABCIKTT KATABATIC
AAAABCILNT ABACTINAL
AAAABCIMOR MARACAIBO
AAAABCISST CATABASIS
AAAABCLNOT CANAL
BOAT
AAAABDDEHM
AHMEDABAD

AAAABDDMOR
MORADABAD
AAAABDELNR ALDEBARAN
AAAABDELPT ADAPTABLE
AAAABDELRW AWARDABLE
AAAABDESST DATABASES
AAAABDHHKS
ASHKHABAD
AAAABDILLS SABADILLA
AAAABDILMS ISLAMABAD
AAAABDINNT ANABANTID
AAAABDLLOR ALL
ABOARD!
AAAABDNNNS
BANDANNAS
AAAABDNRSS SARABANDS
AAAABEEMNO
AMOEBAEAN
AAAABEHLLV HAVE A
BALL
AAAABEILLV AVAILABLE
AAAABEKRWY BREAKAWAY
AAAABELLNN ANNABELLA
AAAABELLPT PALATABLE
AAAABELRST ALABASTER
AAAABELSSY ASSAYABLE
AAAABGHNRV
BHAVNAGAR
AAAABGLORR
ALGARROBA
AAAABGMNOZ
ZAMBOANGA
AAAABGRSTU RUTABAGAS
AAAABHIRTY BHARATIYA
AAAABHLRST BALTHASAR
AAAABHLRTZ BALTHAZAR
AAAABILLVY AVAILABLY
AAAABLLPTY PALATABLY
AAAABLOPRS PARABOLAS
AAAABLPRST PARABLAST
AAAACCCHHH CHA-CHA-
CHA
AAAACCDELV CAVALCADE
AAAACCELLN CALCANEAL
AAAACCEPRS CARAPACES
AAAACCESTZ ZACATECAS
AAAACCGIMU GUM
ACACIA
AAAACCIRTT ATARACTIC
AAAACCLMNO
CALAMANCO
AAAACCRSTT CATARACTS

AAAACDEHRS A HARD
CASE
AAAACDEHRZ
AZEDARACH
AAAACDNNOS
ANACONDAS
AAAACDNPRS PANDA CARS
AAAACDNRSS CASSANDRA
AAAACEENRS CAESAREAN
AAAACEGNRT
CARTAGENA
AAAACEGORT
ARCTOGAEA
AAAACEHLNV AVALANCHE
AAAACEIMNR AMERICANA
AAAACEIMNT CATAMENIA
AAAACEINNT CANAANITE
AAAACELNRV CANAVERAL
AAAACEMMNR
CAMERAMAN
AAAACENRTT AT A
CANTER
AAAACFILNT FANATICAL
AAAACGILSU CAUSALGIA
AAAACGINRU NICARAGUA
AAAACGLSSW SCALAWAGS
AAAACHHIRZ ZACHARIAH
AAAACHIRSZ ZACHARIAS
AAAACHKKMT
KAMCHATKA
AAAACHLNRT
CHARLATAN
AAAACHLRRT CATARRHAL
AAAACIIRSS ACARIASIS
AAAACILLNN ANACLINAL
AAAACILNOT CATALONIA
AAAACILNPT APLANATIC
AAAACILRTU ACTUARIAL
AAAACINOPR PARANOIAC
AAAACINOTT CATATONIA
AAAACINRSU CASUARINA
AAAACLMNPU
CAMPANULA
AAAACLMPST CATAPLASM
AAAACMRTUX
TARAXACUM
AAAACNOSSV CASANOVAS
AAAACSSTWY CASTAWAYS
AAAADDHMRY
HAMADRYAD
AAAADDLSSY SALAD
DAYS

AAADEGLMN
MAGDALENA
AAADEGNTV
ADVANTAGE
AAADELMMR
MARMALADE
AAADELNRX
ALEXANDRA
AAADEMNSU AD
NAUSEAM
AAADHHPRZ
HAPHAZARD
AAADHIILR HAIDAR ALI
AAADHMRSY
HAMADRYAS
AAADILLNP PALLADIAN
AAADILMNT DALMATIAN
AAADILNSU ANDALUSIA
AAADJJPRU DJAJAPURA
AAADKMNRS
SAMARKAND
AAADLMNTY
ADAMANTLY
AAADLNNSY
ANALYSAND, NYASALAND
AAADMNRTY
MANDATARY
AAAEELQRU EQUAL-
AREA
AAAEGGRTV AGGRAVATE
AAAEGILNS ANALGESIA
AAAEGLMNU
MALAGUENA
AAAEGLMTU
GUATEMALA
AAAEGLSSV VASSALAGE
AAAEGMNNT
MANGANATE
AAAEGMRRT
MARGARETA
AAAEHHLMR
HALMAHERA
AAAEHLNNT
NATHANAEL
AAAEHMMOT
HAEMATOMA
AAAEHMNST
ANATHEMAS
AAAEIMNOX
ANOXAEMIA
AAAEIMPRS SAPRAEMIA
AAAEKSTWY TAKEAWAYS
AAAELMMRT ALMA
MATER

AAAELNNTT
ANTENATAL, ATLANTEAN
AAAELNPQU AQUAPLANE
AAAELNPST PANATELAS
AAAELNTTT TANTALATE
AAAENPSST ANAPAESTS
AAAERSTWY TEARAWAYS
AAAFGLRRT TRAFALGAR
AAAFIILLR ALFILARIA
AAAFIKNRS AFRIKAANS
AAAFILNUV AVIFAUNAL
AAAFINORS AFRO-ASIAN
AAAFLORST SOLFATARA
AAAFRSSSS SASSAFRAS
AAAGGLOPS GALAPAGOS
AAAGHPPRR PARAGRAPH
AAAGILMNS SALAAMING
AAAGIMRRT MARGARITA
AAAGINNRV VARANGIAN
AAAGINOPT PATAGONIA
AAAGINSST AS AGAINST
AAAGMMRSY GAMMA
RAYS
AAAGPRSSU ASPARAGUS
AAAHHHPRT
HAPHTARAH
AAAHIKRTW KATHIAWAR
AAAHILMSY HIMALAYAS
AAAHIMNRS MAHARANIS
AAAHINRRT ANARTHRIA
AAAHJNRST RAJASTHAN
AAAHKNRST
ASTRAKHAN
AAAHLLOTY AYATOLLAH
AAAHLNNTU
NAHUATLAN
AAAHLNOPR
ANAPHORAL
AAAHMMSTU
HAMAMATSU
AAAHMNNTT
MANHATTAN
AAAHMNRTT
HARMATTAN
AAAHTTUYY
AYUTTHAYA
AAAIILMNR LAMINARIA
AAAIINRST SANITARIA
AAAIJMNRU MARIJUANA
AAAIKLLNT ANTALKALI
AAAILMMMN
MAMMALIAN
AAAILMNSY MALAYSIAN
AAAILNNOT ANATOLIAN

AAAILNNPR PLANARIAN
AAAILNSST ALSATIANS,
ASSAILANT
AAAILPPRS APPRAISAL
AAAILRSTU AUSTRALIA
AAAIMNNOZ
AMAZONIAN
AAAIMNNST TASMANIAN
AAAIMNORT
INAMORATA
AAAIMNRST SAMARITAN
AAAINNNTZ TANZANIAN
AAAINORST SANATORIA
AAAINPSTV VANASPATI
AAAIPPRZZ PAPARAZZI
AAAIPRSTX PARATAXIS
AAAKKMORR
KARAKORAM
AAAKLSWWY
WALKAWAYS
AAAKMSTTU
TAKAMATSU
AAAKRRSTU SURAKARTA
AAALLMPSS LAS PALMAS
AAALMPPRS PARAPLASM
AAALNPSTY ANAPLASTY
AAALNRSTV TRANSVAAL
AAALNRTTU TARANTULA
AAALOOPPS APPALOOSA
AAAMMNRST MAN-AT-
ARMS
AAAMMSTUY
MATSUYAMA
AAAMNOPRS
PANORAMAS
AAANNNPRU
ANNAPURNA
AAAOPPRZZ PAPARAZZO
AAAPPRSTU APPARATUS
AABBCCIRR BRIC-A-BRAC
AABBCDEIL ABDICABLE
AABBCDKOR
BACKBOARD
AABBCDRSS SCABBARDS
AABBCEHLL BEACH BALL
AABBCEINR CARIBBEAN
AABBCINRS BARBICANS
AABBCKLLL BLACKBALL
AABBDEELT DEBATABLE
AABBDENOR BROAD
BEAN
AABBDEORS BASEBOARD
AABBDNRSS BRASS BAND
AABBEEKLR BREAKABLE

AABBEELRT REBATABLE
AABBEHHST BATHSHEBA
AABBEHILT HABITABLE
AABBEIILT BILABIATE
AABBEINRT RABBINATE
AABBEIRRS BARBARISE
AABBEIRRZ BARBARIZE
AABBEKMMO MAKE A
BOMB
AABBELLSS BASEBALLS
AABBELLTU TABULABLE
AABBHILTY HABITABLY
AABBIILLS BILABIALS
AABBIMRRS BARBARISM
AABBIRRTY BARBARITY
AABBORRSU BARBAROUS
AABCCEHKS BACKACHES
AABCCEKPS BACKSPACE
AABCCELRS CABLE CARS
AABCCHHKT
HATCHBACK
AABCCHKKU
HUCKABACK
AABCCILOT CATABOLIC
AABCCIORT ACROBATIC
AABCCJKKL BLACKJACK
AABCCKKPS BACKPACKS
AABCCKKRT BACKTRACK
AABCCMOST
CATACOMBS
AABCDDEIT ABDICATED
AABCDDEKT BACKDATED
AABCDDORR
CARDBOARD
AABCDEEFR BAREFACED
AABCDEEHH
BEACHHEAD
AABCDEHKL BLACKHEAD
AABCDEILL CABLE-LAID
AABCDEIRR BARRICADE
AABCDEKLL BLACK LEAD
AABCDEKLP BACKPEDAL
AABCDEKRR BARRACKED
AABCDENNR BARN
DANCE
AABCDENNU
ABUNDANCE
AABCDENPS SPACEBAND
AABCDHILR ARCHIBALD
AABCDHKNS
BACKHANDS
AABCDHKRS HARDBACKS
AABCDIORS SCARABOID
AABCDIORT ABDICATOR

AABCDKLMP
BLACKDAMP
AABCDKRSW
BACKWARDS, DRAWBACKS
AABCDKRSY BACKYARDS
AABCDLOPR CLAPBOARD
AABCDNOOR
CARBONADO
AABCDORST BROADCAST
AABCEEELP PEACEABLE
AABCEEHLR REACHABLE
AABCEEHLT TEACHABLE
AABCEEHRW
BEACHWEAR
AABCEEKLS LEASEBACK
AABCEELLN CLEANABLE
AABCEELLR LACERABLE
AABCEELPS ESCAPABLE
AABCEELPY PEACEABLY
AABCEELRT TRACEABLE
AABCEELTX EXACTABLE
AABCEENRR ABERRANCE
AABCEERTT BRACTEATE
AABCEFIRT FABRICATE
AABCEFOSU FABACEOUS
AABCEGILR ALGEBRAIC
AABCEGKST BACKSTAGE
AABCEGLMR
CABLEGRAM
AABCEGPRT CARPETBAG
AABCEHHLT HATCHABLE
AABCEHIRT BRACHIATE
AABCEHITZ CHABAZITE
AABCEHLPT PATCHABLE
AABCEHLRT CHARTABLE
AABCEILLM CLAIMABLE
AABCEILMN IMBALANCE
AABCEILNP INCAPABLE
AABCEILNT CANTABILE
AABCEILRT BACTERIAL,
CALIBRATE
AABCEINOR ANAEROBIC
AABCEIORT AEROBATIC
AABCEJKMR AMBERJACK
AABCEKLMS CLAMBAKES
AABCEKLRT TRACKABLE
AABCEKPPR PAPERBACK
AABCEKRTW
BACKWATER
AABCEKSST BACK SEATS
AABCELLOR CABALLERO
AABCELLOT LOCATABLE
AABCELMNU
AMBULANCE

AABCELNNU
UNBALANCE
AABCELNOR BARCELONA
AABCELNRS BARNACLES
AABCELOOS CALABOOSE
AABCELORR BARCAROLE
AABCELORZ CARBAZOLE
AABCELPPR CRAB APPLE
AABCELPRS SCRAPABLE
AABCELRTT TRACTABLE
AABCELRTU TRABECULA
AABCENORT
CARBONATE
AABCFHKLS FLASHBACK,
HALFBACKS
AABCGILNN BALANCING
AABCHHIRT BATH CHAIR
AABCHILNR BRANCHIAL
AABCHRRST BAR
CHARTS
AABCIILNS BASILICAN
AABCIILSS BASILICAS
AABCIKLLM BLACKMAIL
AABCIKLLT BLACKTAIL
AABCIKLST TAILBACKS
AABCILLRY BACILLARY
AABCILLSY ASYLLABIC,
BASICALLY
AABCILNNS CANNIBALS
AABCILNOT BOTANICAL
AABCILNPY INCAPABLY
AABCILOPR PARABOLIC
AABCINNOR CARBANION
AABCKLLMP LAMP-
BLACK
AABCKLMSS BLACK MASS
AABCKLPSY PLAYBACKS
AABCKNRSS SNACK BARS
AABCKORRZ
RAZORBACK
AABCMNOTT
COMBATANT
AABCRSSTT ABSTRACTS
AABDDEEST DEADBEATS
AABDDEGLS SADDLEBAG
AABDDEHNS HEADBANDS
AABDDEHOR
HEADBOARD
AABDDEHRY
HYDERABAD
AABDDENNO
ABANDONED
AABDDHORR
HARDBOARD

AABDDHORS
DASHBOARD
AABDDNNST
BANDSTAND
AABDDORRT
DARTBOARD
AABDEELLP PLEADABLE
AABDEELMN
AMENDABLE
AABDEEMNO
ENDAMOEBA
AABDEERTT TRABEATED
AABDEFHKL HALF-BAKED
AABDEFLOR BROADLEAF
AABDEGILS BAG
LADIES
AABDEGINO GABIONADE
AABDEGINR BARGAINED,
GABARDINE
AABDEGLRU GUARDABLE
AABDEGORT
ABROGATED
AABDEGOST SABOTAGED
AABDEHKNR
HANDBRAKE
AABDEHLNR
HANDLEBAR
AABDEHLSY ABASHEDLY
AABDEHNSU UNABASHED
AABDEILLT DILATABLE
AABDEILMR ADMIRABLE
AABDEILNN LENINABAD
AABDEILNR DRAINABLE
AABDEILNV INVADABLE
AABDEILOV AVOIDABLE
AABDEILRV ADVERBIAL
AABDEILSV ADVISABLE
AABDEINNR BERNADINA
AABDEINST ABSTAINED
AABDELLNT TABLELAND
AABDELLST BALLASTED
AABDELMST LAMBASTED
AABDELTTU TABULATED
AABDELTWY TWAYBLADE
AABDEMNNR BRAND
NAME
AABDEMORT
DREAMBOAT
AABDEMRTU
ADUMBRATE
AABDENNPY A BAD
PENNY
AABDENSTW
SWEATBAND

AABDENSVW WAVE
BANDS
AABDEORSS SEABOARDS
AABDEORST ADSORBATE
AABDESSTU DATA BUSES
AABDFHLOR HALF
BOARD
AABDFILOT BIT OF A LAD
AABDFKNRT BANK
DRAFT
AABDGGINN BANDAGING
AABDGIILR GARIBALDI
AABDGNNOW
BANDWAGON
AABDGNOSV
VAGABONDS
AABDGOSTU
GADABOUTS
AABDHLORR HARD
LABOR
AABDHLRSU HASDRUBAL
AABDHORSW
WASHBOARD
AABDIJNOR JABORANDI
AABDIKORV KIROVABAD
AABDILMNO
ABDOMINAL
AABDILMRY ADMIRABLY
AABDILORS SAILBOARD
AABDILORT BROADTAIL,
TAILBOARD
AABDILSSU DISABUSAL
AABDINOST BASTINADO
AABDINSTW WAISTBAND
AABDKLORW
BOARDWALK
AABDKNNSS SANDBANKS
AABDLLORW
WALLBOARD
AABDLNSST SANDBLAST
AABDLNTWY WANT
BADLY
AABDLORRS LABRADORS
AABDLORUY LABOUR
DAY
AABDNRRSY BARNYARDS
AABDORRST STARBOARD
AABEEEGLR AGREEABLE
AABEEGGLU GAUGEABLE
AABEEGKRS BREAKAGES
AABEEGLLN GLEANABLE
AABEEGLLT BAGATELLE
AABEEGLRY AGREEABLY
AABEEGRRT GREAT BEAR

AABEEHLLX EXHALABLE
AABEEHRTT HEARTBEAT
AABEEILLN ALIENABLE
AABEEINRS BEARNAISE
AABEEKLPS SPEAKABLE
AABEEKRST TEA BREAKS
AABEELLLM MALLEABLE
AABEELLNN ANNABELLE
AABEELLNR LEARNABLE
AABEELLPS PLEASABLE
AABEELLRS RESALABLE
AABEELLRT ALTERABLE,
RELATABLE
AABEELLRX RELAXABLE
AABEELMST BASE METAL
AABEELNTU UNEATABLE
AABEELORT ELABORATE
AABEELPRR REPARABLE
AABEELPRS SEPARABLE
AABEELPRY REPAYABLE
AABEELQTU EQUATABLE
AABEELRTT TREATABLE
AABEELRTW TABLEWARE
AABEELRTY BETA LYRAE
AABEELTTX BATTLEAXE
AABEEMNOT
ENTAMOEBA
AABEEMNST ABASEMENT
AABEEMNTT
ABATEMENT
AABEEQRSU ARABESQUE
AABEERSST BASE
RATES
AABEFGILT FATIGABLE
AABEFKLNR FRANKABLE
AABEFKRST BREAKFAST
AABEFLLMM
FLAMMABLE
AABEFLLOT FLOATABLE
AABEFLORV FAVORABLE
AABEGGLUY GAUGEABLY
AABEGHLLU LAUGHABLE
AABEGHORR
HARBORAGE
AABEGILLR GABRIELLA
AABEGILNV NAVIGABLE
AABEGILRV BELGRAVIA
AABEGINRR BARGAINER
AABEGIRRT ARBITRAGE
AABEGIRRU BIGARREAU
AABEGLLLR GLABELLAR
AABEGLLMS BALL GAMES
AABEGLMNP
PALEMBANG

AABEGLNOR
BANGALORE
AABEGLNRT GRANTABLE
AABEGLPRS GRASPABLE
AABEGNORT
ABNEGATOR
AABEHILRR HERBARIAL
AABEHITTU HABITUATE
AABEHLMSS SMASHABLE
AABEHLOTW
WHALEBOAT
AABEHLPST ALPHABETS
AABEHLSTW SWATHABLE
AABEIILLS LABIALISE
AABEIILLZ LABIALIZE
AABEIIMNR BAIN-MARIE
AABEIIRTU AUBRIETIA
AABEIJKLR JAILBREAK
AABEIKLNS BALKANISE
AABEIKLNZ BALKANIZE
AABEIKNRR KARABINER
AABEIKRRS AIRBRAKES
AABEILLMN LAMINABLE
AABEILLMR MIRABELLA
AABEILLNR BALLERINA
AABEILLRT BILATERAL
AABEILLSW WALLABIES
AABEILMNS LIMA BEANS
AABEILNOT ANABOLITE
AABEILNRT ALBERTINA,
TRAINABLE
AABEILNST STAINABLE
AABEILPST BASIPETAL
AABEILRSV VARIABLES
AABEIMNOT ABOMINATE
AABEIMNZZ ZAMBEZIAN
AABEINORS ARABINOSE
AABEINRST ABSTAINER
AABEINRVW BRAINWAVE
AABEINSST SEBASTIAN
AABEIRRTT ARBITRATE
AABEIRSSV ABRASIVES
AABEKMNRS
BRAKESMAN
AABELLLOW ALLOWABLE
AABELLMST MEATBALLS
AABELLNPT PLANTABLE
AABELLOPR PAROLABLE
AABELLORS ROSABELLA
AABELLPPR PALPEBRAL
AABELLSUV VALUABLES
AABELMSSU ASSUMABLE
AABELMSTT TABLEMATS
AABELNPPS SNAPPABLE

AABELOPRR POLAR BEAR
AABELOPRV VAPORABLE
AABELORST ASTROLABE
AABELORTT ROTATABLE
AABELPRRY REPARABLY
AABELPRSY SEPARABLY
AABELRSSU ASSURABLE
AABELRSTU SATURABLE
AABELRSTY BETRAYALS
AABELRTTU TABLATURE
AABEMOSTT STEAMBOAT
AABEMRRSS EMBARRASS
AABENOSSY SOYA BEANS
AABEOPPRT APPROBATE
AABERSTUX BEAUX-ARTS
AABFIIMNS FABIANISM
AABFLORVY FAVORABLY
AABFORTTU FART
ABOUT
AABGGGNNS GANG-
BANGS
AABGGIMNO
GAMBOGIAN
AABGGRRST BRAGGARTS
AABGHLLUY LAUGHABLY
AABGHLPRU BHAGALPUR
AABGHOPRR
BAROGRAPH
AABGHPRRS BAR GRAPHS
AABGIINWY IN A BIG
WAY
AABGILNRU BULGARIAN
AABGILNVY NAVIGABLY
AABGILRRT GIBRALTAR
AABGINNOR BORN-
AGAIN
AABGOORRT
ABROGATOR
AABGORTVY GRAVY
BOAT
AABHIILRZ BILHARZIA
AABHIIMNP AMPHIBIAN
AABHIMMRU
HAMMURABI
AABHINRSW BRAINWASH
AABHINSSW WASHBASIN
AABHRSSST BRASS HATS
AABIILLMS LABIALISM
AABIILLTY LABIALITY
AABIILNRR LIBRARIAN
AABIILNRZ BRAZILIAN
AABIINNRT BRITANNIA
AABIINOSS ANABIOSIS
AABIINRZZ ZANZIBARI

AABIINSSY ABYSSINIA
AABILLORS ISALLOBAR
AABILMNOS ANABOLISM
AABILMNRU MANUBRIAL
AABILMOPY AMBLYOPIA
AABILMORS AMBROSIAL
AABILMPST BAPTISMAL
AABILNOTT BATTALION
ABILRRSU BURSARIAL
AABIMNORS AMBROSINA
AABIMORSU SIMAROUBA
AABINORSS ABRASIONS
AABINORTT BOAT TRAIN
AABINOSTW BOATSWAIN
AABIORSTT ABATTOIRS
AABIRRRTY ARBITRARY
AABJJLLNU LJUBLJANA
AABKLOTUW
WALKABOUT
AABKRSSSY SASSY BARK
AABLLLOWY ALLOWABLY
AABLLNTTY BLATANTLY
AABLLRSTU BLASTULAR
AABLLRSYY SYLLABARY
AABLMNORY
MYROBALAN
AABLNOORS SALOON
BAR
AABLNORTU ULAN
BATOR
AABLORSST ALBATROSS
AABLORTTU TABULATOR
AABLOSTUY LAYABOUTS
AABMMOSSY MAMA'S
BOYS
AABMNNOTU
MONTAUBAN
AABNNSTTU BANTUSTAN
AABRSSTTU SUBSTRATA
AACCCLOOS COCA-
COLAS
AACCDDINY CANDIDACY
AACCDEFRS FACE CARDS
AACCDEILM ACCLAIMED
AACCDEIMS ACADEMICS
AACCDEJNY ADJACENCY
AACCDELLT CATCALLED
AACCDELOS ACCOLADES
AACCDELPR PLACE CARD
AACCDGINS CASCADING
AACCDHLRU
ARCHDUCAL
AACCDHRSS CASH CARDS
AACCDIILM MALIC ACID

AACCDIINR CIRCADIAN

AACCDIOSU CAUCASOID

AACCDNORT

ACCORDANT

AACCEELNR CLEARANCE

AACCEENRT REACTANCE

AACCEENST CETACEANS

AACCEFKPS FACE PACKS

AACCEFLOS COALFACES

AACCEFNRS FRANCESCA

AACCEHJKP CHEAP-JACK

AACCEHRRT

CHARACTER

AACCEHSUZ ZACCHAEUS

AACCEIILN CAECILIAN

AACCEILNT ANALECTIC

AACCEILRR CERCARIAL

AACCEILTU ACICULATE

AACCEINRS SARACENIC

AACCEINRY CYRENAICA

AACCEINSV VACANCIES

AACCEINTV VACCINATE

AACCEKNRS CRANKCASE

AACCEKRRT RACETRACK

AACCEKRSS SACK RACES

AACCELLTU CALCULATE

AACCELMTY

CYCLAMATE

AACCELNSU CALCANEUS

AACCELNTU ACCENTUAL

AACCELSTU SACCULATE

AACCENPTT ACCEPTANT

AACCEORTT COARCTATE

AACCEPRTU CUT A

CAPER

AACCERSSS CARCASSES

AACCFINRS FRANCISCA

AACCHILMO

MAILCOACH

AACCHIMNO

MICHOACAN

AACCHINRS SACCHARIN

AACCHIPRR ARCHICARP

AACCHIRTT CATHARTIC

AACCHIRTU AUTARCHIC

AACCHLORS CHARCOALS

AACCIILNT ANACLITIC

AACCIILNV VACCINIAL

AACCIINPS CAPSAICIN

AACCIINTT TACTICIAN

AACCIIRSS CIRCASSIA

AACCILLSS CLASSICAL

AACCILMNU CACUMINAL

AACCILNNO CANONICAL

AACCILNRU CANICULAR

AACCILPRT PRACTICAL

AACCILTTY CATALYTIC

AACCIMNOR

CARCINOMA,

MACARONIC

AACCINOTT CATATONIC

AACCINPTY CAPTAINCY

AACCINRTT ANTARCTIC

AACCIOPRT CAPACITOR

AACCIOPSU CAPACIOUS

AACCIORST COSTA RICA

AACCIRSST SARCASTIC

AACCKMNRS

CRACKSMAN

AACCKRRTT CART

TRACK

AACCLMORY

CYCLORAMA

AACCLMSTY CATACLYSM

AACCMNOPY

ACCOMPANY

AACCOPRRS SARCOCARP

AACCORTUY

AUTOCRACY

AACDDEERT A DEAD

CERT

AACDDEHMR DEAD

MARCH

AACDDEINT CANDIDATE

AACDDELOP DECAPODAL

AACDDELPR PLACARDED

AACDDEOTV

ADVOCATED

AACDDGNOT CAT-AND-

DOG

AACDDIIST DADAISTIC

AACDEEFLT DEFALCATE

AACDEEHHR

HEADREACH

AACDEEHHS HEADACHES

AACDEEIMT ACETAMIDE,

EMACIATED

AACDEEIRT ERADICATE

AACDEELRS ESCALADER

AACDEELRT LACERATED

AACDEELST ESCALATED

AACDEEMNS

DAMASCENE

AACDEEMRT

DEMARCATE, MACERATED

AACDEEORS AREA CODES

AACDEEPSS ESCAPADES

AACDEETUV EVACUATED

AACDEETUX EXCAUDATE

AACDEETVX EXCAVATED

AACDEFFIN AFFIANCED

AACDEFHRS HEADSCARF

AACDEGLNO

DECAGONAL

AACDEHILN ENCHILADA

AACDEHINS HACIENDAS

AACDEHLRT CATHEDRAL

AACDEILLN DALLIANCE

AACDEILLT DIALECTAL

AACDEILNO LAODICEAN

AACDEILNS CANALISED

AACDEILNZ CANALIZED

AACDEILTU ACIDULATE

AACDEIMNY CYANAMIDE

AACDEIMPR PARAMEDIC

AACDEINOT DIACONATE

AACDEINOV AVOIDANCE

AACDEINPT CAPTAINED

AACDEINRS RADIANCES

AACDEINRT ERADICANT

AACDEITTV ACTIVATED

AACDEJKMP JAM-PACKED

AACDEKMRT

TARMACKED

AACDEKNRS RANSACKED

AACDELLNU CALENDULA

AACDELLOT ALLOCATED

AACDELMNS

CANDLEMAS

AACDELNOT

ANECDOTAL

AACDELNPS LANDSCAPE

AACDELNRS CALENDARS

AACDELNRT DECLARANT

AACDELPTY PLAY-ACTED

AACDEMRSS MASSACRED

AACDENNNO

CANNONADE

AACDENNST ASCENDANT

AACDENOTU

COADUNATE

AACDENPRT TAP

DANCER

AACDENPST TAP DANCES

AACDENRSW WAR

DANCES

AACDENSSV CANVASSED

AACDEOSTV ADVOCATES

AACDERSTT CASTRATED

AACDERTTT ATTRACTED

AACDFHNRT

HANDCRAFT

AACDGIMNW MAGIC
WAND
AACDGINNV ADVANCING
AACDGINRS CARDIGANS
AACDHIILL CHILIADAL
AACDHIILS DICHASIAL
AACDHINOR
ARACHNOID
AACDHINOT
ACANTHOID
AACDHINPS HANDICAPS
AACDHLNPS
HANDCLAPS, HANDCLASP
AACDHLNPU LAUNCH
PAD
AACDHLNRS CRASH-
LAND
AACDHNRST
HANDCARTS
AACDHPRRS CARDSHARP
AACDIIMNO AMINO
ACID
AACDIINNR CNIDARIAN
AACDIISST DIASTASIC
AACDIISTT DIASTATIC
AACDILLRY RADICALLY
AACDILNRS CARDINALS
AACDILNTY DILATANCY
AACDILORT CAROTIDAL
AACDIMRST DRAMATICS
AACDINNOR
DRACONIAN
AACDINOTU CAUDATION
AACDIOSUU AUDACIOUS
AACDIQRTU QUADRATIC
AACDIRSTY CARYATIDS
AACDJNTUY ADJUTANCY
AACDQRSSU SQUAD CARS
AACEEFINN FAINEANCE
AACEEFIRT CAFETERIA
AACEEFLPS PALEFACES
AACEEFLPT FACEPLATE
AACEEFLUV FACE VALUE
AACEEFRRT AFTERCARE
AACEEFRSV FACE-SAVER
AACEEGHNS SEA
CHANGE
AACEEGLLR CELLARAGE
AACEEGLSV CLEAVAGES
AACEEGNRR
CARRAGEEN
AACEEHHRT HEARTACHE
AACEEHLNR HERACLEAN
AACEEJLTU EJACULATE

AACEEKMPR PACEMAKER
AACEEKRRT CARETAKER
AACEELNPS PLEASANCE
AACEELNPT PLACENTAE
AACEELNST ELASTANCE
AACEELRTT ALTERCATE
AACEELTTY ACETYLATE
AACEEMMNR
CAMERAMEN
AACEEMNNY
MYCENAEAN
AACEEMRRT
MACERATER
AACEENRSS CESAREANS
AACEEOPRS AEROSPACE
AACEEPRSS CASSAREEP
AACEEPSSS SEASCAPES
AACEERSTT ESTATE CAR
AACEFFIRT AFFRICATE
AACEFGLNR FLAGRANCE
AACEFGNRR FRAGRANCE
AACEFGORT FACTORAGE
AACEFGOSU FAGACEOUS
AACEFHLST HALF-CASTE
AACEFILLS FALLACIES
AACEFINST FASCINATE
AACEFRSTT ARTEFACTS
AACEGHLNR
ARCHANGEL
AACEGHMNP
CHAMPAGNE
AACEGHNOR
ANCHORAGE
AACEGHRST GATECRASH
AACEGILLN ANGELICAL,
ENGLACIAL, GALENICAL
AACEGILNS ANALGESIC
AACEGILRS ALGECIRAS
AACEGILRT CARTILAGE
AACEGIMNO
EGOMANIAC
AACEGIRRS CARRIAGES
AACEGIRSV VICARAGES
AACEGISTT CASTIGATE
AACEGKPRS PACKAGERS
AACEGLOST GALACTOSE
AACEGLOSU COAGULASE
AACEGLOTU
CATALOGUE, COAGULATE
AACEGNORR
ARROGANCE
AACEGNRSU SUGARCANE
AACEGOPST SCAPEGOAT
AACEGORTT GREATCOAT

AACEHHIRZ ZECHARIAH
AACEHIIMS ISCHAEMIA
AACEHILLO ECHOLALIA
AACEHILMR CAMELHAIR
AACEHILMT MALACHITE
AACEHILNS SELACHIAN
AACEHILNT CHATELAIN
AACEHILNU ACHEULIAN
AACEHILPR EPARCHIAL
AACEHILPT CALIPHATE
AACEHIMNO
HEOMANIAC
AACEHIMNR
CHARMAINE
AACEHIMNT
MACHINATE
AACEHINNT ACANTHINE
AACEHINRT CATHARINE
AACEHINRW CHINAWARE
AACEHINST HANSEATIC
AACEHIPTT APATHETIC
AACEHIRRS ARCHAISER
AACEHIRRZ ARCHAIZER
AACEHIRSY EASY CHAIR
AACEHKMOR
HACKAMORE
AACEHKMRR
MARRAKECH
AACEHKRSV HAVERSACK
AACEHLRSU ARCHELAUS
AACEHLRTT CLATHRATE
AACEHMNRU HUMAN
RACE
AACEHNSSS SASSENACH
AACEHPPRS SCRAP HEAP
AACEHPRTU PARACHUTE
AACEHRSST CATHARSES
AACEIILNT LACINIATE
AACEIINRR CINERARIA
AACEIIRTV VICARIATE
AACEILLMS CAMELLIAS
AACEILLNS ALLIANCES
AACEILLRV VARICELLA
AACEILLTV VACILLATE
AACEILMNN ALEMANNIC
AACEILMNP CAMPANILE
AACEILMPS ECLAMPSIA
AACEILMRT CARMELITA
AACEILMTV CALMATIVE
AACEILNNR CARNELIAN
AACEILNNT LANCINATE
AACEILNPP APPLIANCE
AACEILNPT ANALEPTIC
AACEILNRS ARSENICAL

AACEILNRT LACERTIAN,
NECTARIAL
AACEILNRU LAURENCIA
AACEILPTU APICULATE
AACEILRSV CALVARIES,
CAVALIERS
AACEILSTU ACTUALISE
AACEILTUZ ACTUALIZE
AACEIMNOX
ANOXAEMIC
AACEIMNRS AMERICANS
AACEIMNSS AMNESIACS
AACEIMNTU ACUMINATE
AACEIMPRS SAPRAEMIC
AACEIMRST MARCASITE
AACEIMSTT MASTICATE
AACEINNRT INCARNATE
AACEINOST CASEATION
AACEINPST ANAPESTIC
AACEINRST ASCERTAIN,
CARTESIAN, SECTARIAN
AACEINRSV VARIANCES
AACEIOSST ASSOCIATE
AACEIPPRT PER CAPITA
AACEIPTTV CAPTIVATE
AACEIRSST STAIRCASE
AACEIRSTU ACTUARIES
AACEISTUV CAUSATIVE
AACEJKLPP APPLEJACK
AACEJKSSS JACKASSES
AACEJQTTU JACQUETTA
AACEKLPRT PLATE RACK
AACEKLPSW SPACEWALK
AACEKNRRS RANSACKER
AACEKPPTY PAY PACKET
AACEKRSTT ATTACKERS
AACELLLRU ACELLULAR
AACELLLUV VALLECULA
AACELLNOR OLECRANAL
AACELLNOW
ALLOWANCE
AACELLNPT PLACENTAL
AACELMNTT
CATTLEMAN
AACELMPST PLACE MATS
AACELMSST CLASSMATE
AACELNNTU
CANNULATE
AACELNPST PLACENTAS
AACELNRST ANCESTRAL,
LANCASTER
AACELOPRT ACROPETAL,
CLEOPATRA
AACELORST ESCALATOR

AACELOTUV
AUTOCLAVE, VACUOLATE
AACELPPRT APPLE CART
AACELPSTU CAPSULATE
AACELPSTY CATALEPSY
AACELPTXY CATAPLEXY
AACELRRTU CREATURAL
AACELRSTY CATALYSER
AACELRSWY CLEARWAYS
AACELRTUW
CATERWAUL
AACEMNNOR
CONNEMARA
AACEMNPRT
MERCAPTAN
AACEMNRST
SACRAMENT
AACEMRRSS ARMS
RACES, MASSACRER
AACEMRSSS MASSACRES
AACENNNOY
ANNOYANCE
AACENNOSS ASSONANCE
AACENOPTZ ZAPOTECAN
AACENPRRY PARCENARY
AACENPSSU SAUCEPANS
AACENRSSU ASSURANCE
AACENRSSV CANVASSER
AACENRTTU
CAUTERANT
AACENSSSV CANVASSES
AACENSSTT CASTANETS
AACEOOPPT APOCOPATE
AACEORTUV EVACUATOR
AACEORTVX EXCAVATOR
AACEOSTUX TAXACEOUS
AACESSUWY CAUSEWAYS
AACFGLNRY FLAGRANCY
AACFHJKST JACKSHAFT
AACFHMSST CAMSHAFTS
AACFIILNN FINANCIAL
AACFILNOT FACTIONAL
AACFILORT FACTORIAL
AACFINSTT FANTASTIC
AACFIRSTT ARTIFACTS
AACFJKLPS FLAPJACKS
AACFLLTUY FACTUALLY
AACFLOPSW SCAPA FLOW
AACFLRRTU FRACTURAL
AACFMNRST
CRAFTSMAN
AACGGHINN CHAIN
GANG
AACGGIKNP PACKAGING

AACGGIOPR PARAGOGIC
AACGHHIRY HAGIARCHY
AACGHIKUW
KAWAGUCHI
AACGHIMNP
CHAMPAIGN
AACGHINTT ATTACHING
AACGHMORT
TACHOGRAM
AACGHOPRR
ARCOGRAPH
AACGIIMNS MAGICIANS
AACGIKNTT ATTACKING
AACGILLMY MAGICALLY
AACGILLOS SCAGLIOLA
AACGILMNN
MANACLING
AACGILNNS ANGLICANS
AACGILNPT PLACATING
AACGIMNPS CAMPAIGNS
AACGIMPRT PRAGMATIC
AACGINTTU ACTUATING
AACGIOSSU SAGACIOUS
AACGLLSWY SCALLYWAG
AACGLNOOT
OCTAGONAL
AACGLNOTU
COAGULANT
AACGLOORY
ACAROLOGY
AACGMORRT
CARTOGRAM
AACGNNSTY
STAGNANCY
AACHHHIUU
CHIHUAHUA
AACHHINTY HYACINTHA
AACHHSTWY
HATCHWAYS
AACHIILMN CHAIN MAIL
AACHIILPT ALIPHATIC
AACHIINRT CARINTHIA
AACHIIPRS PHARISAIC
AACHIIRRV CHARIVARI
AACHILNPS CHAPLAINS
AACHILOPR PAROCHIAL
AACHILOPT CHIPOLATA
AACHILPST ASPHALTIC
AACHILSST THALASSIC
AACHIMNOR
HARMONICA
AACHIMNRS ANARCHISM
AACHIMNRU
MANCHURIA

AACHIMRRS ARMCHAIRS
AACHIMRRT MATRIARCH
AACHIMRSS ARCHAISMS
AACHIMSTT ASTHMATIC
AACHINRST ANARCHIST
AACHINSSW CHAIN SAWS
AACHIPRRT PATRIARCH
AACHIRSST CATHARSIS
AACHKMMRT
MATCHMARK
AACHKSSTY HAYSTACKS
AACHLLMRY
LACHRYMAL
AACHLLPTY CATAPHYLL
AACHLLRTW
WALLCHART
AACHLMNOR
MONARCHAL
AACHLMRSY
MARSHALCY
AACHLOPVY PLAY
HAVOC
AACHMNORW
CHARWOMAN
AACHMNSTY
YACHTSMAN
AACHMPRST MARCH-
PAST
AACHNOSTU
ACANTHOUS
AACHNOTTY
CHATOYANT
AACHNRSST TRASHCANS
AACHOPPRY APOCRYPHA
AACIILLRT ALTRICIAL
AACIILMRS RACIALISM
AACIILMST LAMAISTIC
AACIILNPT ANCIPITAL
AACIILNSS ANACLISIS
AACIILNST CASTILIAN
AACIILPRT PIRATICAL
AACIILRST RACIALIST,
SATIRICAL
AACIIMOTX AXIOMATIC
AACIINNOP POINCIANA
AACIINNOT NICOTIANA
AACIINPRT PATRICIAN
AACIIPRST PARASITIC
AACIIRRTU URTICARIA
AACIISTTV ATAVISTIC
AACIJNOPS JAPONICAS
AACIKMNNY
KANAMYCIN
AACILLNOT ALLANTOIC

AACILLNRY ANCILLARY
AACILLNTU LUNATICAL
AACILLNTV VACILLANT
AACILLPRY CAPILLARY
AACILMMNO
AMMONICAL
AACILMNST CLAIMANTS
AACILMRSU SIMULACRA
AACILNNUV VULCANIAN
AACILNOPT PLACATION
AACILNOTT LACTATION
AACILNOTY CLAYTONIA
AACILNPPT APPLICANT
AACILNRST CARNALIST
AACILNRSV CARNIVALS
AACILNRTY CARNALITY
AACILNRUV NAVICULAR
AACILNSTY ANALYTICS
AACILORTU AUCTORIAL
AACILOSSU SALACIOUS
AACILOSTT COAT TAILS,
TAILCOATS
AACILPRTU CAPITULAR
AACILPRTY PARALYTIC
AACILQTTU ACQUITTAL
AACILRRTU ARTICULAR
AACILRRUU AURICULAR
AACILRSTY RASCALITY
AACILSSTY CATALYSIS
AACILSTUY CAUSALITY
AACILTTUY ACTUALITY
AACIMNNNU
MANCUNIAN
AACIMNOPR PANORAMIC
AACIMNOST ANOSMATIC
AACIMORTU
AMAUROTIC
AACIMOTTU
AUTOMATIC
AACIMRRSU SACRARIUM
AACIMRTTU TRAUMATIC
AACINNORT CARNATION
AACINNOST SANTONICA
AACINOOTV AVOCATION
AACINOPRS CAPARISON
AACINORST RAINCOATS
AACINORTU ARCUATION
AACINOSST CASSATION
AACINOSTU CAUSATION
AACINOSTV VACATIONS
AACINOTTU ACTUATION
AACINRRTU ARCTURIAN
AACINRSST SACRISTAN
AACINRSSU ANACRUSIS

AACIOPRSU RAPACIOUS
AACIORTTV ACTIVATOR
AACIOSTTW WAISTCOAT
AACKKNPSS KNAPSACKS
AACLLOPRS COLLAPSAR
AACLLRRSY CARRYALLS
AACLNOPTU CANTALOUP
AACLNRUUV
AVUNCULAR
AACLOPRRR PARLOR
CAR
AACLOPRRT PATROL CAR
AACLOPRTU PORTULACA
AACLOPRTY PLACATORY
AACLORSSU CAROUSALS
AACLPSTTU CATAPULTS
AACLRRTUY CARTULARY
AACLSSTTY CATALYSTS
AACMNOORS
MACAROONS
AACMNOTTU
CATAMOUNT
AACNNOSTT
CONSTANTA
AACNORTUU AU
COURANT
AACNRSTUY SANCTUARY
AACNRSTUZ SANTA
CRUZ
AACORRSTT CASTRATOR
AACORRSTU TUSCARORA
AACORRTTT
ATTRACTOR
AACORSSWY CASSOWARY
AACORSTTU AUTOCRATS
AADDDGNRY
GRANDADDY
AADDEEFHT FATHEADED
AADDEEHST DEAD
HEATS
AADDEEMRY READY-
MADE
AADDEENRV
VERANDAED
AADDEENTT ANTEDATED
AADDEGLNR
GARLANDED
AADDEGRTU
GRADUATED
AADDEHHRS
HARDHEADS
AADDEHLNS HEADLANDS
AADDEHNST
HEADSTAND

AADDEHOST A DEAD
SHOT
AADDEHRSW
HEADWARDS
AADDEILNO ADENOIDAL
AADDEILTV VALIDATED
AADDEIMNW WAD
MEDANI
AADDEINRT ANDRADITE
AADDEINRW EDWARDIAN
AADDEKRST STARK DEAD
AADDELLNS SANDALLED
AADDELMNR
DREAMLAND
AADDELPPU APPLAUDED
AADDELRST ASTRADDLE
AADDEMNNT
DEMANDANT
AADDEMNOR
ANDROMEDA
AADDEMRSY
DAYDREAMS
AADDEMRYY
DAYDREAMY
AADDEORST ROADSTEAD
AADDHLNNO AN OLD
HAND
AADDHNNST
HANDSTAND
AADDIIMRY DAIRYMAID
AADDIINRV DRAVIDIAN
AADDILNNO
DONALDINA
AADDIRRWY IRRAWADDY
AADDLNRSW
LANDWARDS
AADDLRSTY DASTARDLY
AADDMRSTT
DARMSTADT
AADDNRSST STANDARDS
AADEEGHMT
MEGADEATH
AADEEGLMN
MAGDALENE
AADEEGNOR
ORANGEADE
AADEEGNPP APPENDAGE
AADEEGNRT GREAT
DANE, TEAGARDEN
AADEEHPRS SPEARHEAD
AADEEHRTT DEATH
RATE
AADEEIKWW WIDE-
AWAKE

AADEEILMV MEDIAEVAL
AADEEILNT ALIENATED
AADEEIMNT DEAMINATE
AADEEKMRR
EARMARKED
AADEELMRS ESMERALDA
AADEELNNR LEND AN
EAR
AADEELNPS ESPLANADE
AADEELNRX ALEXANDER
AADEELRRY LAY READER
AADEELTUV DEVALUATE,
EVALUATED
AADEEMNRT TRADE
NAME
AADEEMRSU ADMEASURE
AADEENSTU NAUSEATED
AADEEPRST PAEDERAST,
SEPARATED
AADEERRTT RETARDATE
AADEESTTV DEVASTATE
AADEFFILR FAR AFIELD
AADEFGLNN FANDANGLE
AADEFGRSU SAFEGUARD
AADEFILNT FAN-TAILED
AADEFIORS AFORESAID
AADEFIRRS FARADISER
AADEFIRRZ FARADIZER
AADEFLNOR FARANDOLE
AADEFMPRT AFTERDAMP
AADEFMRST FARMSTEAD
AADEFSSTT STEADFAST
AADEGHNRU
HARANGUED
AADEGHNRY
HYDRANGEA
AADEGHNST
STAGEHAND
AADEGILRT TALIGRADE
AADEGILTT TAILGATED
AADEGIMNT
DIAMAGNET
AADEGINRR ARRAIGNED
AADEGINRS GARDENIAS
AADEGINRT TRAGEDIAN
AADEGINTV NAVIGATED
AADEGIPRS DISPARAGE
AADEGLNNT LAND
AGENT
AADEGNRRT
REGARDANT
AADEGNSTT STAGNATED
AADEGORRT
ARROGATED

AADEGPRST TRADE GAPS
AADEGRRRU
REARGUARD
AADEGRRVY GRAVEYARD
AADEGRSTU GRADUATES
AADEHHKNS
HANDSHAKE
AADEHILRS RAILHEADS
AADEHIMOT
HAEMATOID
AADEHIORR DIARRHOEA
AADEHIPRT APARTHEID,
HIT PARADE
AADEHIRST STAIRHEAD
AADEHISWY HIDEAWAYS
AADEHKMST DEATH
MASK
AADEHLLST HEADSTALL
AADEHLMNN
MANHANDLE
AADEHLMPS LAMPSHADE
AADEHLMRS
MARSHALED
AADEHLMSY
ASHAMEDLY
AADEHLNNP
PANHANDLE
AADEHLNRT
HEARTLAND
AADEHLPST ASPHALTED
AADEHMNSU
UNASHAMED
AADEHMPST HAMPSTEAD
AADEHMSST MASTHEADS
AADEHORRW
ARROWHEAD
AADEHPRTT DEATH
TRAP
AADEHRRTW
EARTHWARD
AADEHRSTT HEAD
START
AADEIIPRS PRAESIDIA
AADEIIRRT IRRADIATE
AADEIIRTV RADIATIVE
AADEIKKVY KADIYEVKA
AADEILLPT PALLIATED
AADEILMNN
ALMANDINE
AADEILMNS LADIES'
MAN
AADEILMNT LAMINATED
AADEILMRT DIAMETRAL
AADEILNNN ANNELIDAN

AADEILNNR ADRENALIN
AADEILNOT DEALATION
AADEILNSV VANDALISE
AADEILNVZ VANDALIZE
AADEILPSS PALISADES
AADEILPST STAPEDIAL
AADEILRTV TRAVAILED
AADEILSTV SALIVATED
AADEILTVW TIDAL WAVE
AADEIMMNR
  DRAMAMINE
AADEIMMSS MASS MEDIA
AADEIMNRS MARINADES
AADEIMNRT MARINATED
AADEIMNSW ADAM'S
  WINE
AADEIMRST DRAMATISE
AADEIMRTZ DRAMATIZE
AADEINPRT PINTADERA
AADEINRST STERADIAN
AADEINRTT ATTAINDER
AADEIPPRS APPRAISED,
  DISAPPEAR
AADEIPRSS PARADISES
AADEIPRST ASPIRATED,
  DISPARATE
AADEJKLWY JAYWALKED
AADEKMMRU
  MARMADUKE
AADEKMNRS
  MANDRAKES
AADEKMRRT
  TRADEMARK
AADELLNOT LANOLATED
AADELLNPR LAPLANDER
AADELLNTU LANDAULET
AADELMMOR
  MELODRAMA
AADELMNRS
  MALANDERS
AADELMORV AD
  VALOREM
AADELNSTW
  WASTELAND
AADELPPRU APPLAUDER
AADELPRSY PARALYSED
AADELPRTW DRAWPLATE
AADELPRYZ PARALYZED
AADELRTTY LATTER-DAY
AADELSSTU ASSAULTED
AADEMMNOR
  MEMORANDA
AADEMMRST
  AMSTERDAM

AADEMNPRS
  AMPERSAND
AADEMNRST
  TRADESMAN
AADEMOTTU
  AUTOMATED
AADEMPTTU
  AMPUTATED
AADEMRRSU
  MARAUDERS
AADEMRRTU DURA
  MATER
AADENNOTT
  ANNOTATED
AADENNPPT APPENDANT
AADENNRST SANTANDER
AADENNTTT
  ATTENDANT
AADENPPRS SANDPAPER
AADENPRTU PANDURATE
AADENRRTT
  RETARDANT
AADENRRTW
  WARRANTED
AADEOPRSX PARADOXES
AADEORSTW SODA
  WATER
AADEORSTX ROAD
  TAXES
AADERRRSW
  REARWARDS
AADERRSVY ADVERSARY
AADERSSTW EASTWARDS
AADERSTTU SATURATED
AADFFIITV AFFIDAVIT
AADFGHRRT HARD
  GRAFT
AADFGNNOS
  FANDANGOS
AADFHMNRS
  FARMHANDS
AADFILNRY FAIRYLAND
AADFIMNRY MAN
  FRIDAY
AADFIMRRY DAIRY FARM
AADFLLLNS LANDFALLS
AADFMNRST
  DRAFTSMAN
AADFMRRSY FARMYARDS
AADGGHIST HAGGADIST
AADGGHLRY
  HAGGARDLY
AADGHIMPR
  DIAPHRAGM

AADGHINRZ
  HAZARDING
AADGHIPSY DYSPHAGIA
AADGIINRT RADIATING
AADGILMNY
  AMYGDALIN
AADGILMRS MADRIGALS
AADGILNOS DIAGONALS
AADGILORT GLADIATOR
AADGILRRU GUARDRAIL
AADGIMMNO
  GAMMADION
AADGIMNNT
  MANDATING
AADGIMNRU
  MARAUDING
AADGIMORR
  RADIOGRAM
AADGIMPRS PARADIGMS
AADGIMRRS MARDI
  GRAS
AADGINORT GRADATION
AADGINRSU GUARDIANS
AADGINRUZ DZUNGARIA
AADGLLNRU
  GLANDULAR
AADGLLRUY GRADUALLY
AADGLMNRS GRAND
  SLAM
AADGLNOOW
  WAGONLOAD
AADGLNRSS GRASSLAND
AADGMNORS
  DRAGOMANS
AADGMNRSU
  GUARDSMAN
AADGNRSUV GUARD'S
  VAN, VANGUARDS
AADGORRTU
  GRADUATOR
AADHILLNO HOLLANDIA
AADHILLRS HALLIARDS
AADHILLSS ALLIS SHAD
AADHILNRS HANDRAILS
AADHINRRS HARRIDANS
AADHIPSSY DYSPHASIA
AADHNSSTW
  WASHSTAND
AADHORRSU
  HADROSAUR
AADHORSUZ
  HAZARDOUS
AADIILLNP PLAIN-LAID
AADIILMNV MALDIVIAN

AADIILSUV VISUAL AID
AADIINNRS SARDINIAN
AADIINORT RADIATION
AADIINRRT IRRADIANT
AADIISSST DIASTASIS
AADIJNNOR JORDANIAN
AADILLMOR ARMADILLO
AADILLMPU PALLADIUM
AADILLNOT ALLANTOID
AADILLOPS SAPODILLA
AADILLPRY RADIAL-PLY
AADILMNNO
ADNOMINAL
AADILMNOV
MOLDAVIAN
AADILMNSV VANDALISM
AADILMNTU TAMIL
NADU
AADILMORT MALADROIT
AADILMPRY PYRAMIDAL
AADILMRTY ADMIRALTY
AADILNNOT ANTINODAL
AADILNOPT ANTIPODAL
AADILNORS ROSALINDA
AADILNOTU ADULATION,
LAUDATION
AADILNRTY RADIANTLY
AADILNSWZ SWAZILAND
AADILORRS RAILROADS
AADILOSVW DISAVOWAL
AADILPSSY DYSPLASIA
AADIMNNOT
DAMNATION
AADIMNNRS
MANDARINS
AADIMNRST TAMARINDS
AADIMRSTT DRAMATIST
AADINNNOT
ANDANTINO
AADINOORT ADORATION
AADINPRSS SPANIARDS
AADINSSTY SAINT'S
DAY
AADIORRST RADIATORS
AADJNSTTU ADJUTANTS
AADKLMNRS
LANDMARKS
AADKLRWWY
AWKWARDLY
AADKNORRS
KRASNODAR
AADLLNORU ALL-
AROUND
AADLLOPSU PALLADOUS

AADLMNPSW
SWAMPLAND
AADLORSST LOADSTARS
AADLORTUY
ADULATORY, LAUDATORY
AADMMNOOR
MONODRAMA
AADMNORTY
DAMNATORY,
MANDATORY
AADNNORSU
ANANDROUS
AADNPRSST SAND TRAPS
AADNQRSTU
QUADRANTS
AADRSSTUY SATURDAYS
AAEEEHLRT AETHEREAL
AAEEELSTV TEALEAVES
AAEEFHRTT AFTERHEAT
AAEEFKPRT AFTERPEAK
AAEEFLOTV FAVEOLATE
AAEEGGGRT AGGREGATE
AAEEGINTV EVAGINATE
AAEEGIRTV VARIEGATE
AAEEGKNST KATANGESE
AAEEGLMNT MENTAL
AGE
AAEEGLSVW WAGE SLAVE
AAEEGMNNS
MANGANESE
AAEEGMNST STAGE
NAME
AAEEGNORS ARAGONESE
AAEEGNPRT PARENTAGE
AAEEGNRRR
REARRANGE
AAEEGNRTU GUARANTEE
AAEEGPRUV AVERAGE UP
AAEEGRRSY GREY AREAS
AAEEHIMNT HAEMATEIN
AAEEHIMTT HAEMATITE
AAEEHISST AESTHESIA
AAEEHKMST MAKE
HASTE
AAEEHLRRS REHEARSAL
AAEEHMNTU
ATHENAEUM
AAEEHMNTX
EXANTHEMA
AAEEHMPST METAPHASE
AAEEHRRRT RARE
EARTH
AAEEHSTVW HEAT
WAVES

AAEEIKLMP MAKE A PILE
AAEEIKLMU LEUKAEMIA
AAEEILLMN EL ALAMEIN
AAEEILLST ILL AT EASE
AAEEILLTV ALLEVIATE
AAEEILMNS MELANESIA
AAEEILRTT RETALIATE
AAEEIMNRT REANIMATE
AAEEIMNTV EMANATIVE
AAEEIMNTX EXANIMATE
AAEEINSTW TAIWANESE
AAEEIPTTX EXPATIATE
AAEEISTTV AESTIVATE
AAEEKKMVY
MAKEYEVKA
AAEEKMNSS NAMESAKES
AAEEKPRST PARAKEETS
AAEEKPSSY SPEAKEASY
AAEELLOTV ALVEOLATE
AAEELLPPT APPELLATE
AAEELLPTT PATELLATE
AAEELLQRU AQUARELLE
AAEELLRWW WELL-
AWARE
AAEELMMNU
EMMANUELA
AAEELMMRT
METAMERAL
AAEELMNPT NAMEPLATE
AAEELMSST MATELASSE
AAEELMSTT STALEMATE
AAEELNOPR AEROPLANE
AAEELNPSS SEAPLANES
AAEELNRTT ALTERNATE
AAEELPPSX SEX APPEAL
AAEELPRSY LEAP YEARS
AAEELRRTT RETREATAL
AAEELRSTU LAUREATES
AAEEMMNTZ
AMAZEMENT
AAEEMNRST MAN-
EATERS
AAEEMPRRT PARAMETER
AAEENRRTW
WARRANTEE
AAEENRSSW AWARENESS
AAEENRSTT ANTEATERS
AAEENTTTU ATTENUATE
AAEEOPRSU AEROPAUSE
AAEEOPRTV EVAPORATE
AAEEPRRTY RATEPAYER
AAEEPRSST SEPARATES
AAEERRTTW WATER
RATE

AAEFFIILT AFFILIATE
AAEFFILRS RAFFLESIA
AAEFGHLMNR
FERMANAGH
AAEFGINRS SEAFARING
AAEFGIRSX SAXIFRAGE
AAEFGLLLR FLAGELLAR
AAEFGLRVW FLAG-
WAVER
AAEFGORRS FARRAGOES
AAEFHLPRT FLARE PATH
AAEFHMRTT
AFTERMATH
AAEFIKNRR AFRIKANER
AAEFILMRR FIRE
ALARM
AAEFILNTX ANTEFIXAL
AAEFILRTY FAIRY-TALE
AAEFIMMNR
MAINFRAME
AAEFINNRS SAFRANINE
AAEFINSST FANTASIES,
FANTASISE
AAEFINSTZ FANTASIZE
AAEFINTTU INFATUATE
AAEFKLLST LEAFSTALK
AAEFLLLRY FALLALERY
AAEFLLRTW WATERFALL
AAEFLMSTT FLATMATES
AAEFLNRRT FRATERNAL
AAEFLORTZ FORTALEZA
AAEFRRSWY WAYFARERS
AAEGGILLN GALINGALE
AAEGGILNW GALWEGIAN
AAEGGINOR GEORGIANA
AAEGGINRU RAIN GAUGE
AAEGGINRV AVERAGING
AAEGGLLNO
GALLONAGE
AAEGGLNSU LANGUAGES
AAEGHIILM HEMIALGIA
AAEGHLNOX
HEXAGONAL
AAEGHLNPR PHALANGER
AAEGHLNPS PHALANGES
AAEGHLPSS SLAGHEAPS
AAEGHMRSX
HEXAGRAMS
AAEGHNOPR
ORPHANAGE
AAEGHNRRU
HARANGUER
AAEGHNRSU
HARANGUES

AAEGHORRT
HARROGATE
AAEGIILQU AQUILEGIA
AAEGIKNNW
AWAKENING
AAEGILMRT METRALGIA
AAEGILNNN ANNEALING
AAEGILNNT GALANTINE
AAEGILNOS ANALOGIES,
ANALOGISE
AAEGILNOZ ANALOGIZE
AAEGILNPP APPEALING
AAEGILNRU NEURALGIA
AAEGILNSV GALVANISE
AAEGILNVZ GALVANIZE
AAEGILSTT TAILGATES
AAEGIMMNS
MISMANAGE
AAEGIMNNS MAGNESIAN
AAEGIMNNT
EMANATING,
MANGANITE, MAN-
EATING
AAEGIMNRR
MARGARINE
AAEGIMNRT MARGINATE
AAEGIMNSZ MAGAZINES
AAEGIMRRS MARRIAGES
AAEGIMRRT MARGARITE
AAEGINNRT ARGENTINA
AAEGINORT ARAGONITE
AAEGINPPR APPEARING
AAEGINPPS APPEASING
AAEGINPRS PAGANISER
AAEGINPRZ PAGANIZER
AAEGINPTZ GAZIANTEP
AAEGINRRR ARRAIGNER
AAEGINRRS GRANARIES
AAEGINRSY GAINSAYER
AAEGIRTTV GRAVITATE
AAEGISTTT SAGITTATE
AAEGISVWY GIVEAWAYS
AAEGKKRRS SKAGERRAK
AAEGLLMPS PLASMAGEL
AAEGLLNRY LARYNGEAL
AAEGLMNOR
MANGALORE
AAEGLNOSU ANALOGUES
AAEGLNRTU GRANULATE
AAEGLRSSW GLASSWARE
AAEGMNNOR
ORANGEMAN
AAEGMNORT
MATRONAGE

AAEGMNPRT
PENTAGRAM
AAEGMNRTT
TERMAGANT
AAEGMORRS
AEROGRAMS
AAEGMRRTT
TETRAGRAM
AAEGMRSTT STRATAGEM
AAEGNNOOT
NOTOGAEAN
AAEGNOORS NO-GO
AREAS
AAEGNOPRS PARSONAGE
AAEGNOPRT PATRONAGE
AAEGNPRTY PAGEANTRY
AAEGNRSTV STAVANGER
AAEGNRTTU GREAT-
AUNT
AAEGOPPRT PROPAGATE
AAEGPRSTU PASTURAGE
AAEGRRSTZ STARGAZER
AAEHHINPZ ZEPHANIAH
AAEHHLNOT
HALOTHANE
AAEHIKNRT KATHARINE
AAEHIKNSZ ASHKENAZI
AAEHILNNT NATHANIEL
AAEHILNTV LEVIATHAN
AAEHIMNOT
THEOMANIA
AAEHINPRS SERAPHINA
AAEHINPRT PARTHENIA
AAEHINRSV HAVERSIAN
AAEHJLLLU HALLELUJA
AAEHLLNOP ALLOPHANE
AAEHLMSSY SEALYHAMS
AAEHLNPSX PHALANXES
AAEHLNPSY SYNALEPHA
AAEHLNSTT ATHELSTAN
AAEHLOPPR PHALAROPE
AAEHLPSUV UPHEAVALS
AAEHMOSTT
HAEMOSTAT
AAEHMRSTU
SHAMATEUR
AAEHNPSST PHEASANTS
AAEHNSTVX TAX
HAVENS
AAEHRRSTT EARTHSTAR
AAEIIKNRT AIR-INTAKE
AAEIILMNS ANIMALISE
AAEIILMNZ ANIMALIZE
AAEIILMRT LATIMERIA

AAEIILNRT INTER ALIA
AAEIILPTX EPITAXIAL
AAEIIMNNT INANIMATE
AAEIIMRST ARTEMISIA
AAEIINQTU AQUITAINE
AAEIINSST TAENIASIS
AAEIJNRSU JANUARIES
AAEIKLNNN LENINAKAN
AAEIKLTTV TALKATIVE
AAEIKMNRR RAINMAKER
AAEIKNPST TAKE PAINS
AAEIKRSTU AUTARKIES
AAEILLLSU ALLELUIAS
AAEILLMMT MAMILLATE
AAEILLNPS SAILPLANE
AAEILLNPT TAILPLANE
AAEILLNTV ÉLAN VITAL
AAEILLPSS PAILLASSE,
  PALLIASSE
AAEILMNOS ANOMALIES
AAEILMNST LAMINATES
AAEILMNSZ MANIZALES
AAEILMNTU ALUMINATE
AAEILMPRV PRIMAEVAL
AAEILMPTT PALMITATE
AAEILMRST MATERIALS
AAEILNNTV VALENTINA
AAEILNORT ALIENATOR,
  RATIONALE
AAEILNPRS AIRPLANES
AAEILNPRT PERINATAL
AAEILNRTU LAURENTIA
AAEILNSTT TANTALISE
AAEILNTTT TANTALITE
AAEILNTTZ TANTALIZE
AAEILORTV VARIOLATE
AAEILPPTT PALPITATE
AAEILPRTZ TRAPEZIAL
AAEILRSSW WASSAILER
AAEILRSTU ESTUARIAL
AAEILSSSV VASSALISE
AAEILSSVZ VASSALIZE
AAEILSTVX LAXATIVES
AAEIMMNOT
  AMMONIATE
AAEIMMNNOT
  EMANATION
AAEIMNNSS ANAMNESIS
AAEIMNOPR POMERANIA
AAEIMNOST ANATOMIES,
  ANATOMISE
AAEIMNOTZ
  AMAZONITE, ANATOMIZE
AAEIMNPRR REPAIRMAN

AAEIMNPRS PEARMAINS
AAEIMNRTW WATER
  MAIN
AAEIMNSTT STAMINATE
AAEIMOPRT AMETROPIA
AAEIMORST AROMATISE
AAEIMORTZ AROMATIZE
AAEIMRRST AIRSTREAM
AAEINNRSW RAW SIENNA
AAEINPPRT APPERTAIN
AAEINPRST SEPTARIAN
AAEINQTTU ANTIQUATE
AAEINRRRS IN ARREARS
AAEINRRTV NARRATIVE
AAEINRRTW RAINWATER
AAEIPPRRS APPRAISER
AAEIPRSST ASPIRATES,
  PARASITES
AAEIRRSTT TARTARISE
AAEIRRTTZ TARTARIZE
AAEISSSUV ASSUASIVE
AAEJKLRWY JAYWALKER
AAEKLLSST SALES TALK
AAEKMRRTW
  WATERMARK
AAELLLMOR
  MALLEOLAR
AAELLLPRS PARALLELS
AAELLLRTY LATERALLY
AAELLNPPT APPELLANT
AAELLORSV ALVEOLARS
AAELLPPRW WALLPAPER
AAELLSUXY ASEXUALLY
AAELLSWYY ALLEYWAYS
AAELMMORR
  MARMOREAL
AAELMMPST METAPLASM
AAELMNOSU
  MAUSOLEAN
AAELMNRSU EL
  MANSURA
AAELMPSTY PLAYMATES
AAELNPRTY PLANETARY
AAELNRSTT TRANSLATE
AAELNRTUU AU
  NATUREL
AAELNSTTU SULTANATE
AAELOPRST PASTORALE
AAELOPSSU ASEPALOUS
AAELOPSTU APETALOUS
AAELORRSY SOLAR YEAR
AAELORSTV SALVATORE
AAELORTTZ LAZARETTO
AAELORTUV EVALUATOR

AAELPPRST STAR-APPLE
AAELPRRSY PARALYSER
AAELPRRYZ PARALYZER
AAELPRSSY PARALYSES
AAELPRSYZ PARALYZES
AAELPSTTU SPATULATE
AAELRRSTV TRAVERSAL
AAELRSSTU ASSAULTER,
  SALERATUS
AAELRSTTW SALTWATER
AAELSSTWY LEASTWAYS
AAEMMNRST
  ARMAMENTS, MEN-AT-
  ARMS
AAEMNORTY
  EMANATORY
AAEMNPRTT
  APARTMENT
AAEMNSSTT STATESMAN
AAEMPRSTY PAYMASTER
AAEMRRSTU ARMATURES
AAENNPSST EN PASSANT
AAENNTTTU
  ATTENUANT
AAENPRSTY PEASANTRY
AAENRRRTW
  WARRANTER
AAENSTTTT ATTESTANT
AAEOOPPRS SOAP OPERA
AAEOPRRST SEPARATOR
AAEOPRSTT PASTORATE
AAEOPSSTT APOSTATES
AAEPPRRST SPARE PART
AAEPRSTXY TAXPAYERS
AAERRSTTU SATURATER
AAERRSTTW. WATER
  RATS
AAERSTWWY
  WATERWAYS
AAFFFGLST FLAGSTAFF
AAFFGNRSU SUFFRAGAN
AAFGILMNS FALANGISM
AAFGILNRS FRANGLAIS
AAFGILNST FALANGIST
AAFGINRWY WAYFARING
AAFGORTTU
  AUTOGRAFT
AAFIILMRS FAMILIARS
AAFILLNOP FALLOPIAN
AAFILLNRS RAINFALLS
AAFILMMNY FAMILY
  MAN
AAFILMNOR FORAMINAL
AAFILNNOU FIONNUALA

AAFILNOOV OF NO AVAIL	**AAGILMNOS** MAGNOLIAS	**AAGNRUUUY**
AAFILNOTX AFLATOXIN	**AAGILMNSV** GALVANISM	URUGUAYAN
AAFILORUW RAUWOLFIA	**AAGILMNYZ** AMAZINGLY	**AAGOORRRT**
AAFILSSTT FATALISTS	**AAGILMRST** MAGISTRAL	ARROGATOR
AAFIOTTTU TOUT A FAIT	**AAGILNNSY** ANALYSING	**AAGPRSTTY** STAG PARTY
AAFKLOOST ASK A LOT	**AAGILNOST** ANALOGIST,	**AAHHNNSSU**
OF	NOSTALGIA	SHUSHANNA
AAFLORSWY FOR ALWAYS	**AAGILNPPT** PALPATING	**AAHIILNSW** SWAHILIAN
AAFMOPRRT APART	**AAGILNRUU** INAUGURAL	**AAHIILNTU** LITHUANIA
FROM	**AAGILNRUV** VULGARIAN	**AAHILMNOT**
AAFMORRTW	**AAGILNWYY** WAYLAYING	MALATHION
MARROWFAT	**AAGILOOPS** APOLOGIAS	**AAHILMTUZ** AZIMUTHAL
AAGGIINTT AGITATING	**AAGILQUUY** GUAYAQUIL	**AAHILNNST** INHALANTS
AAGGILNSV SALVAGING	**AAGIMMMST**	**AAHILNORT** INHALATOR
AAGGIMNPR RAMPAGING	MAGMATISM	**AAHILNSTU** AILANTHUS
AAGGIMNSS MASSAGING	**AAGIMNOSY**	**AAHILORTU** AUTHORIAL
AAGGINNRR	ANISOGAMY	**AAHILPSXY** ASPHYXIAL
ARRANGING	**AAGIMNPRT** PTARMIGAN	**AAHIMMNSS**
AAGGINSSU ASSUAGING	**AAGINNRRT** NARRATING	SHAMANISM
AAGGKLNNP	**AAGINOOTV**	**AAHIMNOST**
GANGPLANK	VAGOTONIA	THOMASINA
AAGHIKMNY	**AAGINORTV** NAVIGATOR	**AAHIMNSST** SHAMANIST
HAYMAKING	**AAGINSTUU** AUGUSTINA	**AAHIMNSTU** AMIANTHUS
AAGHIKMOS	**AAGIORSTT** AGITATORS	**AAHINOORR**
KAGOSHIMA	**AAGKMORYY**	HONORARIA
AAGHILNNS HANGNAILS	KARYOGAMY	**AAHINOPRT** PARATHION
AAGHILNRS SHANGRI-LA	**AAGKNOORS**	**AAHINORRV** HARROVIAN
AAGHIMOOP	KANGAROOS	**AAHINPTTY** ANTIPATHY
OMOPHAGIA	**AAGLLLNTY** GALLANTLY	**AAHINRRTU** ARTHURINA
AAGHINNRU	**AAGLLNRTY** GALLANTRY	**AAHIOPPSS** APOPHASIS
HUNGARIAN	**AAGLMMMOY**	**AAHJNRTUV** THANJAVUR
AAGHINRSS HARASSING	MAMMALOGY	**AAHKLLMRS**
AAGHINSSY SASHAYING	**AAGLMNORU**	HALLMARKS
AAGHKMNSY	GRANULOMA	**AAHKLMNOO**
GYMKHANAS	**AAGLNNNOO**	OKLAHOMAN
AAGHLLOPR ALLOGRAPH	NONAGONAL	**AAHKMOSTW**
AAGHOPRTU	**AAGLNOOSU**	TOMAHAWKS
AUTOGRAPH	ANALOGOUS	**AAHLLMOSW**
AAGIIKNNS KISANGANI	**AAGLNQSUU**	HALLOWMAS
AAGIILNSS ASSAILING	AQUALUNGS	**AAHLLOPTY** ALLOPATHY
AAGIIMNNT ANIMATING	**AAGLRRSTU** GASTRULAR	**AAHLLSTTT** HALLSTATT
AAGIIMNRY IMAGINARY	**AAGMNNOSU**	**AAHLMNNTU**
AAGIINNTT ATTAINING	MANGANOUS	LANTHANUM
AAGIINOTT AGITATION	**AAGMOOPSU**	**AAHLMPSTU** ASPHALTUM
AAGIINSTT SATIATING	APOGAMOUS	**AAHLPPPSY** SLAPHAPPY
AAGIJNNNP JAPANNING	**AAGMRSSSU** SARGASSUM	**AAHMNORST**
AAGIKNPRT PARTAKING	**AAGNNNOTY** NANNY	MARATHONS
AAGILLNTV GALLIVANT	GOAT	**AAHMNPSST** PHANTASMS
AAGILLORT ALLIGATOR	**AAGNNORTU** ORANG-	**AAHMOPPRR**
AAGILMNNO	UTAN	PARAMORPH
AGNOMINAL	**AAGNORRTU**	**AAHNNOOTZ**
AAGILMNNS SIGNALMAN	GUARANTOR	ANTHOZOAN
AAGILMNNT	**AAGNORSTU**	**AAHNNOSTU**
MALIGNANT	ANGOSTURA	ANANTHOUS

AAHNOTTXY
ANTHOTAXY
AAHORTWWY
THROWAWAY
AAIIKNNRU UKRAINIAN
AAIIKNPST PAKISTANI
AAIILMMNS ANIMALISM
AAIILMNSS MAINSAILS
AAIILMNST ANIMALIST
AAIILMNTY ANIMALITY
AAIILMPRT IMPARTIAL,
PRIMATIAL
AAIILNOSU LOUISIANA
AAIILRUXY AUXILIARY
AAIIMMNST ANIMATISM
AAIIMNNOT ANIMATION
AAIIMNRTU MAURITIAN
AAIIMORST TIMISOARA
AAIIMPPRR PRIMIPARA
AAIINNRTU UNITARIAN
AAIINNRTV INVARIANT
AAIINOPRT TOPIARIAN
AAIINORTV VARIATION
AAIINOSTT SATIATION
AAIINPRSS PARISIANS
AAIJNRSSY JANISSARY
AAIKLLOSS ALKALOSIS
AAIKLNOSV SLOVAKIAN
AAIKNNOPT PONTIANAK
AAIKNRSTX TAXI RANKS
AAIKSSSTW SWASTIKAS
AAILLLNOT LALLATION
AAILLMMRY MAMILLARY
AAILLMMXY
MAXIMALLY
AAILLMNST MANTILLAS
AAILLMOPP PAPILLOMA
AAILLMRSY AMARYLLIS
AAILLMRTY MARITALLY
AAILLMRXY MAXILLARY
AAILLNOOP APOLLONIA
AAILLNOPT ALTIPLANO
AAILLNOST ALLANTOIS
AAILLNOTV VALLATION
AAILLNPRU NULLIPARA
AAILLNTVY VALIANTLY
AAILLOPRT PALLIATOR
AAILLPPRY PAPILLARY
AAILLPRTY PARTIALLY
AAILLPSTY SPATIALLY
AAILMNNPS PLAINSMAN
AAILMNOPT PALMATION
AAILMNORT LAMINATOR
AAILMNOST ATONALISM

AAILMNSST TALISMANS
AAILMNTTU MATUTINAL
AAILMORTY AMORALITY
AAILMPRSU MARSUPIAL
AAILMPRTU MULTIPARA
AAILMRSST ALARMISTS
AAILNNOPT PLANATION
AAILNNOST NATIONALS
AAILNNOSV SLAVONIAN
AAILNNPQU PALANQUIN
AAILNNPRU UNIPLANAR
AAILNNPST PLANTAINS
AAILNNSST ANNALISTS
AAILNOOTV OVATIONAL
AAILNOPPT PALPATION
AAILNOPSS PASSIONAL
AAILNOPUW PAULOWNIA
AAILNOSTT SALTATION
AAILNOSTV SALVATION
AAILNOTTY ATONALITY
AAILNOTUV VALUATION
AAILNPRTU TARPAULIN
AAILNPSTU SAINT PAUL
AAILNSSST STANISLAS
AAILOPRRT RAPTORIAL
AAILOPSTX POSTAXIAL
AAILORRST SARTORIAL
AAILPRSSY PARALYSIS
AAIMMNNOO
MONOMANIA
AAIMMNRST
MARTINMAS
AAIMMNSST MAINMASTS
AAIMNNORS SAN
MARINO
AAIMNOPRY PYROMANIA
AAIMNOSTT ANATOMIST
AAIMNPRSZ MARZIPANS
AAIMNRRST TRIMARANS
AAIMNRSTT TARANTISM
AAIMNSSTY MAINSTAYS
AAIMOORRT
MORATORIA
AAIMORSSU AMAUROSIS
AAIMQRSUU AQUARIUMS
AAINNNTTU ANNUITANT
AAINNORRT NARRATION
AAINNPRSY SPIN A YARN
AAINNRSTU SATURNIAN
AAINORRST ROTARIANS
AAINPRSST ASPIRANTS,
PARTISANS
AAINPSTXY ANAPTYXIS
AAINQRSTU QUATRAINS

AAINQRTUY ANTIQUARY
AAINQSTTU AQUATINTS
AAINSSSSS ASSASSINS
AAINSSSTT ASSISTANT,
SATANISTS
AAIOPPRRT APPARITOR,
PRO PATRIA
AAIOPRRST ASPIRATOR
AAIORRTTT TRATTORIA
AAIPPRSSU PARI PASSU
AAJMORRSU URSA
MAJOR
AAKLLLMST SMALL TALK
AAKNOOSST SASKATOON
AALLLMMSS SMALL
SLAM
AALLLMOPS ALLOPLASM
AALLMMRSS SMALL
ARMS
AALLMOPSS PLASMASOL
AALLNNOPY POLLYANNA
AALLNRTUY NATURALLY
AALLORSVY YAROSLAVL
AALLPRTWY PARTY WALL
AALMNOOSU
ANOMALOUS
AALMNOPRT
PATROLMAN
AALMNPRTY
RAMPANTLY
AALMOOSTU
AUTOSOMAL
AALMOQSSU
SQUAMOSAL
AALMORTYY
MAYORALTY
AALNNRTUU
UNNATURAL
AALNOPSTT POSTNATAL
AALNOSTTU TANTALOUS
AALNPRTWY LAWN
PARTY
AALOPRRTY PORTRAYAL
AALOPRSST PASTORALS
AALRSSTTW LAST STRAW,
STALWARTS
AAMMOORST
MATAMOROS
AAMNNOTUY ANY
AMOUNT
AAMNOOTTU
AUTOMATON
AAMNOPRTU
PARAMOUNT

AAMOPRRSU
PARAMOURS
AANNOORTT
ANNOTATOR
AANORRRST
NARRATORS
AANORRRTW
WARRANTOR
AANORSTTU
ASTRONAUT
AANPRSSSU PARNASSUS
AAORRSTTU TARTAROUS
AAOSSTWWY
STOWAWAYS
ABBBCELLU CLUBBABLE
ABBBDEELR BLABBERED
ABBCCEHKN
BACKBENCH
ABBCCKKLU BLACKBUCK
ABBCDEERU BARBECUED
ABBCDELRS SCRABBLED
ABBCDELRY CRABBEDLY
ABBCDIKLR BLACKBIRD
ABBCDKORU
BUCKBOARD
ABBCEEIRS CARIBBEES
ABBCEERSU BARBECUES
ABBCEIKRT BACKBITER
ABBCEIRST CRABBIEST
ABBCEIRSY CRYBABIES
ABBCEISST SCABBIEST
ABBCEKLLT BLACK BELT
ABBCEKLLU BLUE-BLACK
ABBCEKLNO BONEBLACK
ABBCEKNOS BACKBONES
ABBCELRRS SCRABBLER
ABBCILPRU PUBLIC BAR
ABBCIMOST BOMBASTIC
ABBCINOSY CABIN BOYS
ABBCKLOOT
BOOTBLACK
ABBCLMOOU
ABCOULOMB
ABBDDEMOR
BOMBARDED
ABBDEELOR BELABORED
ABBDEELRU BLUEBEARD
ABBDEGINU BEDAUBING
ABBDEILOT BOBTAILED
ABBDEILTU DUBITABLE
ABBDEINRS BREAD BINS
ABBDEIRTT RABBITTED
ABBDELOTU DOUBTABLE
ABBDELQSU SQUABBLED

ABBDELSUU SUBDUABLE
ABBDGIILN AD-LIBBING
ABBDHLOOT
BLOODBATH
ABBDILLOR BILLBOARD,
BROADBILL
ABBDKLNOO BLOOD
BANK
ABBDMNOOR
BOMBARDON
ABBEEHTTY BABY
TEETH
ABBEEJRRS JABBERERS
ABBEEKLRU REBUKABLE
ABBEELMOT BE TO
BLAME
ABBEELOPR PROBEABLE
ABBEENORS BARE BONES
ABBEENRRY BANEBERRY
ABBEERRRY BEARBERRY
ABBEFILST FLABBIEST
ABBEGIJNR JABBERING
ABBEGILLO OBLIGABLE
ABBEHINOS HOBBESIAN
ABBEHISST SHABBIEST
ABBEHORST BATHROBES
ABBEILMSU ABU SIMBEL
ABBEIMNOZ BOMBAZINE
ABBEINORT BARBITONE
ABBEKLOOR BROOKABLE
ABBELLMPU PLUMBABLE
ABBELMOOZ
BAMBOOZLE
ABBELOPRS PROBABLES
ABBELOSTY STABLE BOY
ABBELQRSU SQUABBLER
ABBELQSSU SQUABBLES
ABBENORST ABSORBENT
ABBFHLLSU FLASHBULB
ABBGIINRT RABBITING
ABBGILMNR BRAMBLING
ABBGILOOT OBBLIGATO
ABBGINORS ABSORBING
ABBHOOTTY BABY
TOOTH
ABBILLSSU SILLABUBS
ABBJMRUUU BUJUMBURA
ABBKKNOOS
BANKBOOKS
ABBLLSSUY SYLLABUBS
ABBMMOOST ATOM
BOMBS
ABBOOPRTY BOOBY
TRAP

ABBOORRWY BARROW
BOY
ABCCCEFIO BECCAFICO
ABCCCKKLO BLACKCOCK
ABCCEEHKL CHECKABLE
ABCCEENRU BUCCANEER
ABCCEIIST SCABIETIC
ABCCEINOV BICONCAVE
ABCCEKMOS
COMEBACKS
ABCCELNRU CARBUNCLE
ABCCEMNRU
CUMBRANCE
ABCCEMNTU
ACCUMBENT
ABCCFIINO FIBONACCI
ABCCFIMOR BACCIFORM
ABCCGHLTU CLUTCH
BAG
ABCCHHKNU
HUNCHBACK
ABCCHKLOT
BACKCLOTH
ABCCIKKKS KICKBACKS
ABCCIKRST CRABSTICK
ABCCILORU CORBICULA
ABCCIRSTU SUBARCTIC
ABCCKLLOS BALLCOCKS
ABCCKORSS BACKCROSS
ABCCMOORY
MOBOCRACY
ABCDDEEHU
DEBAUCHED
ABCDDEEIL DECIDABLE
ABCDDEFLO BOLDFACED
ABCDDEKLO BLOCKADED
ABCDDENOS ABSCONDED
ABCDDKORU
DUCKBOARD
ABCDEEEHU DEBAUCHEE
ABCDEEHRU DEBAUCHER
ABCDEEHSU DEBAUCHES
ABCDEEILM MEDICABLE
ABCDEEINT DIABETICA
ABCDEEKLN BLACKENED
ABCDEEKRT BRACKETED
ABCDEELMR CLAMBERED
ABCDEFIKR BACKFIRED
ABCDEHIOT COHABITED
ABCDEHKLO
BLOCKHEAD
ABCDEIIST DIABETICS
ABCDEIJLU JUDICABLE
ABCDEIKLS BACKSLIDE

ABCDEIKRU RUDBECKIA
ABCDEIKSS BACKSIDES
ABCDEILMY MEDICABLY
ABCDEINTU INCUBATED
ABCDEIORT BACTEROID
ABCDEKLOR BLOCKADER
ABCDEKLOS BLOCKADES
ABCDEKNNS NECKBANDS
ABCDELLOS SCOLDABLE
ABCDELMRS SCRAMBLED
ABCDELOOS CABOODLES
ABCDEMOTT
 COMBATTED
ABCDENORR CORN
 BREAD
ABCDENORS ABSCONDER
ABCDENOSU
 CASEBOUND, SUBDEACON
ABCDEOORT
 OBCORDATE
ABCDGINOR BROCADING
ABCDGINTU ABDUCTING
ABCDHINRS DISBRANCH
ABCDHIOPR CHIPBOARD
ABCDHNRTU DUTCH
 BARN
ABCDIKRRY BRICKYARD
ABCDILMOR LOMBARDIC
ABCDILOPR CLIPBOARD
ABCDINOOT BANDICOOT
ABCDINOTU ABDUCTION
ABCDKLNOU
 CLOUDBANK
ABCDKLOOR
 ROADBLOCK
ABCDKOORR
 CORKBOARD
ABCDKOORS BACK
 DOORS
ABCDKOOSW
 BACKWOODS
ABCDKOPRS BACKDROPS
ABCDLNRSU SCRUBLAND
ABCDNOOXX BOX AND
 COX
ABCDOPRSU CUPBOARDS
ABCEEELRT CELEBRATE,
 ERECTABLE
ABCEEELRX EXECRABLE
ABCEEFFOR COFFEE BAR
ABCEEFIRS BRIEFCASE
ABCEEFLOR FORCEABLE
ABCEEFOSU BECAUSE OF
ABCEEGKNR GREENBACK

ABCEEHKLO CHOKEABLE
ABCEEHLLY BELLYACHE
ABCEEHLRS BLEACHERS
ABCEEILLS SLICEABLE
ABCEEILPR PIERCABLE
ABCEEILRT RECITABLE
ABCEEILST CELIBATES
ABCEEILSX EXCISABLE
ABCEEILTX EXCITABLE
ABCEEIMNS AMBIENCES
ABCEEINOS OBEISANCE
ABCEEINRR CARBINEER
ABCEEKKNR BREAKNECK
ABCEEKLSY BLACK EYES
ABCEEKPSW SWEEPBACK
ABCEELMNS SEMBLANCE
ABCEELNRT CELEBRANT
ABCEELNST ALBESCENT
ABCEELOPS PLACEBOES
ABCEELORT BRACTEOLE
ABCEELORV REVOCABLE
ABCEELRST BRACELETS
ABCEELRSU RESCUABLE,
 SECURABLE
ABCEELRXY EXECRABLY
ABCEELSUX EXCUSABLE
ABCEEMMRT
 CAMEMBERT
ABCEEMORR
 EMBRACEOR
ABCEEMORT
 EMBROCATE
ABCEEMRRY EMBRACERY
ABCEENRTY CYBERNATE
ABCEENSTT TABESCENT
ABCEEOSSU SEBACEOUS
ABCEEPRRU CUPBEARER
ABCEESSSS ABSCESSES
ABCEFFHNO OFFENBACH
ABCEFHLSU FLASHCUBE
ABCEFIRTU BIFURCATE
ABCEFLOSU FOCUSABLE
ABCEFLSSS BASS CLEFS
ABCEFOSTU OBFUSCATE
ABCEGHILN BLEACHING
ABCEGHINR BREACHING
ABCEGIMNR EMBRACING
ABCEGKLLS BLACKLEGS
ABCEGKLOS BLOCKAGES
ABCEHINNO BONE
 CHINA
ABCEHINOT AITCHBONE
ABCEHKLLO BLACK
 HOLE

ABCEHKLOS SHOCKABLE
ABCEHKMNR BENCH
 MARK
ABCEHKORS HORSEBACK
ABCEHKRRY HACKBERRY
ABCEHKTUW
 BUCKWHEAT
ABCEHLORS BACHELORS
ABCEHLOTU
 TOUCHABLE
ABCEHLSSU CHASUBLES
ABCEHOQRU
 QUEBRACHO
ABCEHRSTU BUCHAREST
ABCEIILNS SIBILANCE
ABCEIILRS IRASCIBLE
ABCEIIMRT IMBRICATE
ABCEIJLNU JUBILANCE
ABCEIJNOT ABJECTION
ABCEIJOST JACOBITES
ABCEILLOS OBELISCAL
ABCEILMOT METABOLIC
ABCEILMST BLASTEMIC
ABCEILNOS BALCONIES
ABCEILNOV INVOCABLE
ABCEILNRU BINUCLEAR,
 INCURABLE
ABCEILNVY BIVALENCY
ABCEILORS CARBOLISE
ABCEILORT CABRIOLET
ABCEILORZ CARBOLIZE
ABCEILOTT COBALTITE
ABCEILRTU LUBRICATE
ABCEILRUX EXCALIBUR
ABCEILSTU BISULCATE
ABCEIMOTV COMBATIVE
ABCEIMRTU BACTERIUM
ABCEINORS CARBONISE
ABCEINORZ CARBONIZE
ABCEIRRSU CARBURISE
ABCEIRRTU RUBRICATE
ABCEIRRUZ CARBURIZE
ABCEJNSTU SUBJACENT
ABCEKLNSS BLACKNESS
ABCEKLPRU PARBUCKLE
ABCEKOOSS BOOKCASES
ABCEKPSTW BACKSWEPT,
 SWEPT-BACK
ABCEKRTUW
 WATERBUCK
ABCELLOOR COLORABLE
ABCELLOSX CALL BOXES
ABCELLRSW SCREWBALL
ABCELMRRS SCRAMBLER

ABCELMRSS SCRAMBLES
ABCELNOST CONSTABLE
ABCELNOTU COUNTABLE
ABCELOOST BOOTLACES
ABCELORVY REVOCABLY
ABCELOSST OBSTACLES
ABCELOSTT ECTOBLAST
ABCELRTTY BATTLE CRY
ABCELRTUU LUCUBRATE
ABCELSUXY EXCUSABLY
ABCEMORSS CROSSBEAM
ABCENORTY
  BARONETCY
ABCENRRRY CRANBERRY
ABCENSSTU SUBSTANCE
ABCEOOPRS BAROSCOPE
ABCEOPRRY REPROBACY
ABCFHIKLS BLACKFISH
ABCFKLLSU FULLBACKS
ABCGGIKPY PIGGYBACK
ABCGHIKST BACKSIGHT
ABCGHILNN BLANCHING
ABCGHINNR BRANCHING
ABCGHINOR BROACHING
ABCGIINRS ASCRIBING
ABCGILNOS LOG CABINS
ABCGILNRY BRACINGLY
ABCGIMNOT
  COMBATING
ABCHIILLN CHILBLAIN
ABCHIIOST ISOBATHIC
ABCHILMOS SHAMBOLIC
ABCHILNOR BRONCHIAL
ABCHKMPSU
  HUMPBACKS
ABCHKMTTU
  THUMBTACK
ABCHKNORT
  THORNBACK
ABCHKORTW
  THROWBACK
ABCHLLNPU PUNCH
  BALL
ABCHLRWYZ
  WALBRZYCH
ABCIIIKLW BAILIWICK
ABCIIILPT BICIPITAL
ABCIIKNRS BRAINSICK
ABCIILLMU UMBILICAL
ABCIILLST BALLISTIC
ABCIILMOR MICROBIAL
ABCIILRSY IRASCIBLY
ABCIINNRT BRITANNIC
ABCIINRRU RUBRICIAN

ABCIIOSTT BIOSTATIC
ABCIIRSTY SYBARITIC
ABCIKLLST BLACKLIST
ABCILLMRU LUMBRICAL
ABCILLORU BILOCULAR
ABCILMNOO
  COLOMBIAN
ABCILMNOU
  COLUMBIAN, COLUMBINA
ABCILMOPY AMBLYOPIC
ABCILMSTY CYMBALIST
ABCILMSUX SUBCLIMAX
ABCILNNOU CONNUBIAL
ABCILNORU BINOCULAR
ABCILNPSU PUBLICANS
ABCILNRTU LUBRICANT
ABCILNRUY INCURABLY
ABCILOPSY POLYBASIC
ABCILORRU ORBICULAR
ABCILOSSU SUBSOCIAL
ABCIMNOOS MONOBASIC
ABCIMOSTU SUBATOMIC
ABCIMRSTY CAMBISTRY
ABCINORTU INCUBATOR
ABCINOSTY OBSTINACY
ABCIOPRRT PORTACRIB
ABCJKOOST JACKBOOTS
ABCKLLLOP BLACKPOLL
ABCKLOPST BLACK SPOT
ABCKLOSTU BLACKOUTS
ABCKNORSU
  OSNABRUCK
ABCKOOPRS SCRAPBOOK
ABCLMNNOT MONT
  BLANC
ABCLOORRU COLOUR
  BAR
ABCLOOSTU COBALTOUS
ABCLPRSUW PUB-CRAWLS
ABCMOSSUU
  SUBMUCOSA
ABCNOORSU
  CARBONOUS
ABCNORSTU
  OBSCURANT
ABCORRSSS CROSSBARS
ABDDDEINS DISBANDED
ABDDEEHIJ JIB-HEADED
ABDDEEHST DEATHBEDS
ABDDEELNY NEED BADLY
ABDDEENOR
  BROADENED
ABDDEEPRS BEDSPREAD
ABDDEERTY TEDDY BEAR

ABDDEESST BEDSTEADS
ABDDEHNSU
  HUSBANDED
ABDDEIILV DIVIDABLE
ABDDEILNT BLIND DATE
ABDDEIORS BROADSIDE,
  SIDEBOARD
ABDDEIPRU UPBRAIDED
ABDDEIRRS DISBARRED
ABDDEISSU DISABUSED
ABDDELOSW
  SADDLEBOW
ABDDGORUY
  BODYGUARD
ABDDHINTW
  BANDWIDTH
ABDDHNORU
  HARDBOUND
ABDDILNNS SAND-BLIND
ABDDILRSY LADYBIRDS
ABDDJMNOO ODD-JOB
  MAN
ABDDLMOOR
  MOLDBOARD
ABDEEEFRS FREE-BASED
ABDEEEGLL DELEGABLE
ABDEEELLY EYEBALLED
ABDEEELMN EMENDABLE
ABDEEEMRS BESMEARED
ABDEEFHLR HALF-BREED
ABDEEFIIT BEATIFIED
ABDEEFILN DEFINABLE
ABDEEFORR FREEBOARD
ABDEEGGLR BEDRAGGLE
ABDEEGHIN BEHEADING
ABDEEGINR GABERDINE
ABDEEGJLU JUDGEABLE
ABDEEGLLO LODGEABLE
ABDEEGMOR
  EMBARGOED
ABDEEGRRY GREYBEARD
ABDEEGRSY SAGE DERBY
ABDEEHINR HEBRIDEAN
ABDEEHLRT BLATHERED
ABDEEHNOS BONEHEADS
ABDEEIILR DIABLERIE
ABDEEILLW WIELDABLE
ABDEEILLY YIELDABLE
ABDEEILMS DEMISABLE
ABDEEILNR BREADLINE
ABDEEILNS DISENABLE
ABDEEILRS DESIRABLE
ABDEEILRT LIBERATED
ABDEEILRV DERIVABLE

ABDEEILSV DEVISABLE
ABDEEINNR BERNADINE
ABDEEINSS BEADINESS
ABDEEINSW WIESBADEN
ABDEEINTT BIDENTATE
ABDEEINTU BUTADIENE
ABDEEITTU BEATITUDE
ABDEEKLNT BLANKETED
ABDEEILLTY BELATEDLY
ABDEELMSS ASSEMBLED
ABDEELMTT EMBATTLED
ABDEELNOR
BANDEROLE, BANDOLEER
ABDEELNOT DENOTABLE
ABDEELNPR PREBENDAL
ABDEELNPS SPENDABLE
ABDEELNRU ENDURABLE
ABDEELNST STEEL BAND
ABDEELOPS DEPOSABLE
ABDEELRSS BEARDLESS
ABDEELSSU SUBLEASED
ABDEEMNOU BEAU
MONDE
ABDEEMNRT
DEBARMENT
ABDEENOTY BAYONETED
ABDEENQTU
BANQUETED
ABDEENRRT BARTENDER
ABDEENTTU DEBUTANTE
ABDEEOPST SPEEDBOAT
ABDEERRST REDBREAST
ABDEFFGLU DUFFEL BAG
ABDEFIISX BASIFIXED
ABDEFINOS BONA FIDES
ABDEFINRR FIREBRAND
ABDEFLLOO FLOODABLE
ABDEFORTY AFTERBODY
ABDEGGINR BADGERING
ABDEGGMRU
MAGDEBURG
ABDEGIINU BIGUANIDE
ABDEGIIRR BRIGADIER
ABDEGIKNR DEBARKING
ABDEGILOT OBLIGATED
ABDEGINRR DEBARRING
ABDEGNOTU ON A
BUDGET
ABDEGNSTU BUNDESTAG
ABDEGRTUY BUDGETARY
ABDEHIINT INHABITED
ABDEHILNO HOBNAILED
ABDEHILOS ABOLISHED
ABDEHKLSU BULKHEADS

ABDEHLOOT BLOOD
HEAT
ABDEHLOTW
DEATHBLOW
ABDEHNRSU HUSBANDER
ABDEHNSTU SUNBATHED
ABDEHORRU
HARBOURED
ABDEIILNU INAUDIBLE
ABDEIILNV DIVINABLE
ABDEIILOS DIABOLISE
ABDEIILOZ DIABOLIZE
ABDEIIRST DIATRIBES
ABDEIKLNR DRINKABLE
ABDEIKMRS DISEMBARK
ABDEIKNRW WINDBREAK
ABDEILLLO LABELLOID
ABDEILLLR DRILLABLE
ABDEILMNS MANDIBLES
ABDEILMOR BROMELIAD
ABDEILOPR PARBOILED
ABDEILORV OLIVE DRAB
ABDEILRRY EARLY BIRD
ABDEILRSY DESIRABLY
ABDEINOST BOTANISED
ABDEINOTZ BOTANIZED
ABDEINSSW BAWDINESS
ABDEIPRRU UPBRAIDER
ABDEIRRTW WATER BIRD
ABDEJORTT OBJET D'ART
ABDEKLSSW SKEWBALDS
ABDEKNORW
BREAKDOWN
ABDEKORRW
WORDBREAK
ABDEKORSY KEYBOARDS
ABDELLMOU
MOULDABLE
ABDELLNOO
BALLOONED
ABDELLORY LABOREDLY
ABDELMOTY
MOLYBDATE
ABDELNNSS BLANDNESS
ABDELNOST ENDOBLAST
ABDELNOSU SOUNDABLE
ABDELNOUW
WOUNDABLE
ABDELOOPS PASO DOBLE
ABDELORTX EXTRABOLD
ABDELORUV BOULEVARD
ABDEMRSTU DRUMBEATS
ABDENORSS BROADNESS
ABDENORST ADSORBENT

ABDENOSSX SANDBOXES
ABDENOSTU EASTBOUND
ABDENRRST ST BERNARD
ABDENRSTU BUNDESRAT
ABDENRSTY BYSTANDER
ABDEOORRT
BREADROOT
ABDEOORRV
OVERBOARD
ABDEOORWZ
ZEBRAWOOD
ABDEORRSW
WARDROBES
ABDEORTUV OUTBRAVED
ABDESSTTU TASTE BUDS
ABDFHORSU SHUFBOARD
ABDFIIKOR FABRIKOID
ABDFIIRRR FRIARBIRD
ABDFLLORU FULL BOARD
ABDFOOORT
FOOTBOARD
ABDFORRSU SURFBOARD
ABDGGGOSY DOGGY
BAGS
ABDGGIINR ABRIDGING
ABDGIILNS DISABLING
ABDGIILNY ABIDINGLY
ABDGILNNR BRANDLING
ABDGILORS GAOLBIRDS
ABDGINNOU
ABOUNDING
ABDGINORS SIGNBOARD
ABDGINOXY BOXING
DAY
ABDGLOPRU PLUGBOARD
ABDHIINNR HINDBRAIN
ABDHILLNS HANDBILLS
ABDHIMRTY
DITHYRAMB
ABDHIOPRS SHIPBOARD
ABDHIRSTY BIRTHDAYS
ABDHKNOOS
HANDBOOKS
ABDHLORSW
BLOWHARDS
ABDHNOORU
BOARHOUND
ABDHNRSUY
HUSBANDRY
ABDHOOSWX SHADOW-
BOX
ABDIIILLN LIBIDINAL
ABDIIJLRS JAILBIRDS
ABDIILLRS BILLIARDS

ABDIILMOS DIABOLISM

ABDIILNUY INAUDIBLY

ABDIILOST DIABOLIST,
IDIOBLAST

ABDIIMRST TRIBADISM

ABDILLMOR MILLBOARD

ABDILORSW WILD BOARS

ABDILRSZZ BLIZZARDS

ABDIMNNOT
BADMINTON

ABDIMPQSU DAMP SQUIB

ABDINOWWY BAY
WINDOW

ABDINRSTW WRISTBAND

ABDIRSTUY ABSURDITY

ABDJMOPRU BROAD
JUMP

ABDKLNORW WORLD
BANK

ABDKNOOST
BOOKSTAND

ABDLMOOOR
BROADLOOM

ABDMMNOSU
OMBUDSMAN

ABDMOOORR
BOARDROOM

ABDNNOSTY ON STAND-
BY

ABEEEEFRT BEEFEATER

ABEEEERSZ SEA BREEZE

ABEEEFKST BEEFSTEAK

ABEEEFLRR REFERABLE

ABEEEFLRZ FREEZABLE

ABEEEGLNR GENERABLE

ABEEEGLNS BENGALESE

ABEEEGLRU BELEAGUER

ABEEEGLTV VEGETABLE

ABEEEGNNR GREEN
BEAN

ABEEEGRSV BEVERAGES

ABEEEHLMT MEHETABEL

ABEEEHLSW WHEELBASE

ABEEEKNRV BREAKEVEN

ABEEELMPR PERMEABLE

ABEEELNRT ENTERABLE

ABEEELNRV VENERABLE

ABEEELNRW RENEWABLE

ABEEELRRV REVERABLE

ABEEELRST STEERABLE

ABEEELRSV SEVERABLE

ABEEENSST ABSENTEES

ABEEERRTV VERTEBRAE

ABEEERTUX EXUBERATE

ABEEFFILN INEFFABLE

ABEEFGLOR FORGEABLE

ABEEFIKRR FIREBREAK

ABEEFILNR INFERABLE,
REFINABLE

ABEEFILRS BAS-RELIEF

ABEEFILST FLEABITES

ABEEFLRSU REFUSABLE

ABEEFLRTU REFUTABLE

ABEEFLSSU SELF-ABUSE

ABEEFORRR FORBEARER

ABEEFORRS FOREBEARS

ABEEGGLOR GORGEABLE

ABEEGHILW WEIGHABLE

ABEEGHNOR
HABERGEON

ABEEGHRTU HAGBUTEER

ABEEGILLR GABRIELLE

ABEEGILLV GIVE A BELL

ABEEGILNN BENGALINE

ABEEGINRU AUBERGINE

ABEEGINRV BEAVERING,
BEREAVING

ABEEGKORR BROKERAGE

ABEEGLLRU REGULABLE

ABEEGLNPR PREGNABLE

ABEEGLOPR BARGE POLE,
PORBEAGLE

ABEEGLSSU GUESSABLE

ABEEGMORS EMBARGOES

ABEEGNORZ BRONZE
AGE

ABEEGORSX GEARBOXES

ABEEGRSTU SUGAR BEET

ABEEHILMT MEHITABEL

ABEEHILRT HERITABLE

ABEEHILST ELISABETH

ABEEHILTZ ELIZABETH

ABEEHIMSV MISBEHAVE

ABEEHINRT HIBERNATE

ABEEHIRRS HEBRAISER

ABEEHIRRZ HEBRAIZER

ABEEHKORS BRAKE SHOE

ABEEHLLRS HAREBELLS

ABEEHLMPS BLASPHEME

ABEEHLNOW
WHALEBONE

ABEEHNSTU BHUTANESE

ABEEHRSTT HARTBEEST

ABEEIINRT INEBRIATE

ABEEIKLRZ ZEBRA-LIKE

ABEEIKNST SNAKEBITE

ABEEILLMR MIRABELLE

ABEEILLRV RELIABLE

ABEEILMPT EMPTIABLE

ABEEILMRS MISERABLE

ABEEILMST ESTIMABLE

ABEEILMTT TIMETABLE

ABEEILNPS PLEBEIANS

ABEEILNRT ALBERTINE

ABEEILNSS BASELINES

ABEEILNTW TABLE WINE

ABEEILQTU EQUITABLE

ABEEILRRW REWIRABLE

ABEEILRST BEASTLIER,
BLEARIEST

ABEEILRSV REVISABLE,
VERBALISE

ABEEILRTT ALBERTITE,
BEAR TITLE

ABEEILRTV AVERTIBLE,
VERITABLE

ABEEILRVV REVIVABLE

ABEEILRVZ VERBALIZE

ABEEIMSSS EMBASSIES

ABEEIPSTT A BIT STEEP

ABEEIRRSS BRASSERIE,
BRASSIERE

ABEEIRRST BISERRATE

ABEEIRSTT BATTERIES

ABEEJLLNY JELLY BEAN

ABEEJLNOY ENJOYABLE

ABEEJLNSU BLUE JEANS

ABEEJMORS JAMBOREES

ABEEKLNNO ANKLEBONE

ABEEKLNSS BLEAKNESS

ABEEKLORV REVOKABLE

ABEELLLPS SPELLABLE

ABEELLMRS SMALL BEER

ABEELLMSS BLAMELESS

ABEELLMTU UMBELLATE

ABEELLORS ROSABELLE

ABEELLORT TOLERABLE

ABEELLORW LOWERABLE

ABEELLOVV EVOLVABLE

ABEELMMOR
MEMORABLE

ABEELMMRS EMBALMERS

ABEELMNRU
NUMERABLE

ABEELMORV REMOVABLE

ABEELMOSV MOVEABLES

ABEELMPRS PREAMBLES

ABEELMPTT TEMPTABLE

ABEELMRSS ASSEMBLER

ABEELMRSU RESUMABLE

ABEELNNTU UNTENABLE

ABEELOPSX EXPOSABLE

ABEELPRSU SUPERABLE
ABEELPRTU REPUTABLE
ABEELRRTV VERTEBRAL
ABEELRSVW SWERVABLE
ABEELRTTU UTTERABLE
ABEELSSSU SUBLEASES
ABEELSSTT SEAT BELTS
ABEEMMNRS
MEMBRANES
ABEEMMNTY
EMBAYMENT
ABEEMNSST BASEMENTS
ABEEMORRT
BAROMETER
ABEEMRRSU EMBRASURE
ABEEMRSTU A BUM
STEER
ABEENQTTU BANQUETTE
ABEENRSSV BRAVENESS
ABEENRTUX EXUBERANT
ABEEOPRRT PERBORATE,
REPROBATE
ABEEOPRSW POWER BASE
ABEEOSTUU BEAUTEOUS
ABEEPRSTT BESPATTER
ABEERRSTT BARRETTES
ABEERRSTY BETRAYERS
ABEFFILNY INEFFABLY
ABEFFLOSU BUFFALOES
ABEFGILLN BEFALLING
ABEFGILNR FRANGIBLE
ABEFGLOOR GABLE
ROOF
ABEFIILNU UNIFIABLE
ABEFIILOT BIFOLIATE
ABEFIIMRT FIMBRIATE
ABEFILLRS FIREBALLS
ABEFILOST LIFEBOATS
ABEFILTUU BEAUTIFUL
ABEFIMORS FRAMBOISE
ABEFINORR FOREBRAIN
ABEFLLLMU FLABELLUM
ABEFLLLUY BALEFULLY
ABEFLLNUY BANEFULLY
ABEFLNOSW WOLFSBANE
ABEFOORST BEAR'S-
FOOT
ABEFRTTTU BUTTERFAT
ABEGGGINR BEGGARING
ABEGGINSS BAGGINESS
ABEGGLLRU BUGGER ALL
ABEGGNOPS SPONGE BAG
ABEGHHILT HIGH TABLE
ABEGHILST SIGHTABLE

ABEGHINRR HARBINGER
ABEGHINRT BREATHING
ABEGHMRRU
HAMBURGER
ABEGHRSSU SAGEBRUSH
ABEGIILLT LITIGABLE
ABEGIILMT MITIGABLE
ABEGIILNS ABSEILING
ABEGIILNT IGNITABLE
ABEGIILNW BEWAILING
ABEGIILRR IRRIGABLE
ABEGIINOR ABORIGINE
ABEGIKMNR EMBARKING
ABEGILLLN LABELLING
ABEGILMMN
EMBALMING
ABEGIMNNO
BEMOANING
ABEGIMRRS AMBERGRIS
ABEGINNNT BENIGNANT
ABEGINNOW
WINNEBAGO
ABEGINNRT BANTERING
ABEGINNRZ BRAZENING
ABEGINNST ABSENTING
ABEGINNTT BATTENING
ABEGINRRT BARTERING
ABEGINRTT BATTERING
ABEGINRTY BETRAYING
ABEGJORTU OBJURGATE
ABEGJSTUU SUBJUGATE
ABEGKRSTU GRUBSTAKE
ABEGLNORU LOUNGE
BAR
ABEGLRSSU BLUEGRASS
ABEGMNOOR
BOOMERANG
ABEGMNOSY
MONEYBAGS
ABEGORSTU SUBROGATE
ABEHHHIPZ HEPHZIBAH
ABEHIINNR HIBERNIAN
ABEHIITTW WHITEBAIT
ABEHIKLNT THINKABLE
ABEHILMOP AMPHIBOLE
ABEHILORS ABOLISHER
ABEHILRST HERBALIST
ABEHILRSY BEARISHLY
ABEHILRTY BREATHILY,
HERITABLY
ABEHILSST ESTABLISH
ABEHIMMSS MEMSAHIBS
ABEHIMNOS BOHEMIANS
ABEHIMRRU HERBARIUM

ABEHIOPRU EUPHORBIA
ABEHIORUV BEHAVIOUR
ABEHIRRTT BIRTHRATE
ABEHLMPSY BLASPHEMY
ABEHLNNSU SHUNNABLE
ABEHLNOOR
HONORABLE
ABEHLOPRY HYPERBOLA
ABEHLORTT BETROTHAL
ABEHNORRT
ABHORRENT
ABEHNRRTU
HEARTBURN
ABEHNRSSS BRASHNESS
ABEHNRSTU SUNBATHER
ABEHOOSTU
BOATHOUSE,
HOUSEBOAT
ABEHORRRU
HARBOURER
ABEHQRSUU HARQUEBUS
ABEIIILST ABILITIES
ABEIILLLR ILLIBERAL
ABEIILLMT LIMITABLE
ABEIILNRZ BRAZILEIN
ABEIILRRS LIBRARIES
ABEIILRRT IRRITABLE
ABEIILRTV VIBRATILE
ABEIILSST STABILISE
ABEIILSTV VISITABLE
ABEIILSTZ STABILIZE
ABEIINNPT BIPINNATE
ABEIINNRT INEBRIANT
ABEIINRST BRAINIEST
ABEIIPRTT BIPARTITE
ABEIIRTVV VIBRATIVE
ABEIJLNRU INJURABLE
ABEIKLNTT KNITTABLE
ABEIKNORW WAKE-
ROBIN
ABEIKNRSS BEARSKINS
ABEILLLNT LIBELLANT
ABEILLLRY LIBERALLY
ABEILLLSU LULLABIES,
SULLIABLE
ABEILLPSU PLAUSIBLE
ABEILLRTX BELLATRIX
ABEILLSTY BESTIALLY
ABEILMMOV
IMMOVABLE
ABEILMMSW SWIMMABLE
ABEILMMTU IMMUTABLE
ABEILMNSS BALMINESS
ABEILMOPS IMPOSABLE

ABEILMORT BALTIMORE
ABEILMOSX MAILBOXES
ABEILMPTU IMPUTABLE
ABEILMRSV VERBALISM
ABEILMRSY MISERABLY
ABEILMSTU SUBLIMATE
ABEILNPRT PRINTABLE
ABEILNPST PINTABLES
ABEILNPSU SUBALPINE
ABEILNRSS BRAINLESS
ABEILNRSU INSURABLE
ABEILORRT LIBERATOR
ABEILORTT TRILOBATE
ABEILORTU LABOURITE
ABEILQTUY EQUITABLY
ABEILRRST STIRRABLE
ABEILRRYZ BIZARRELY
ABEILRSTU BRUTALISE
ABEILRSTV VERBALIST
ABEILRTUZ BRUTALIZE
ABEILRTVY VERITABLY
ABEILRVVY REVIVABLY
ABEILSSUX BISEXUALS
ABEILSTTW TWISTABLE
ABEILSUVY ABUSIVELY
ABEIMNORS AMBROSINE
ABEIMNORT BROMINATE
ABEIMNRST TRIBESMAN
ABEIMNRSU SUBMARINE
ABEIMNSTU SEMI-BANTU
ABEINNSTT ABSTINENT
ABEINNTYZ BYZANTINE
ABEINORST BARITONES
ABEINOSTT OBSTINATE
ABEINRSST BANISTERS
ABEINRSTW BRAWNIEST
ABEINRTTU TRIBUNATE,
   TURBINATE
ABEINSSST BASSINETS
ABEINSSTT BATTINESS
ABEIOPRTV PROBATIVE
ABEIPRRSS SPARERIBS
ABEIRRRST BARRISTER
ABEIRRSST ARBITRESS
ABEIRRSSU BURSARIES
ABEIRSSST BRASSIEST
ABEIRSSTY SYBARITES
ABEIRTTTU ATTRIBUTE
ABEJLNOYY ENJOYABLY
ABEJMOORS JEROBOAMS
ABEKKMOOR
   BOOKMAKER
ABEKLNNSS BLANKNESS
ABEKLOOPT BOOKPLATE

ABEKLORTW
   WORKTABLE
ABEKLORVY REVOKABLY
ABEKNNOST BANK
   NOTES
ABEKOORSY YEARBOOKS
ABEKORSTU OUTBREAKS
ABELLLSSY SYLLABLES
ABELLMRSU UMBRELLAS
ABELLORTY TOLERABLY
ABELLORUY ROYAL BLUE
ABELLOSWY BOYLE'S
   LAW
ABELMMNRU
   LUMBERMAN
ABELMMORY
   MEMORABLY
ABELMNOTU
   MOUNTABLE
ABELMNPRU
   PENUMBRAL
ABELMNRUY
   NUMERABLY
ABELMNSTU SUBMENTAL
ABELMORVY
   REMOVABLY
ABELNNORV
   NONVERBAL
ABELNOOTW AT ONE
   BLOW
ABELNOSTT ENTOBLAST
ABELNOSYZ LAZYBONES
ABELNRSTU SUBALTERN
ABELNRTTU TURNTABLE
ABELOOPPS OPPOSABLE
ABELOPPST STOPPABLE
ABELOPSTT SPOTTABLE
ABELORRSU LABOURERS
ABELORTTX RATTLEBOX
ABELOSTTY STYLOBATE
ABELPRTUY REPUTABLY
ABELRSTTU REBUTTALS,
   TRUSTABLE
ABEMMNOOS
   MOONBEAMS
ABEMNPRSU PENUMBRAS
ABEMNSTTU
   ABUTMENTS
ABEMOOPRR
   BROOMRAPE
ABEMOPRTY
   AMBROTYPE
ABEMORRTU
   ARBORETUM

ABENNSTTU SUBTENANT
ABENOPSSU SUBPOENAS
ABENORSTV OBSERVANT
ABEOOPRTW
   POWERBOAT
ABEOOPSSX SOAPBOXES
ABEOORRSU ARBOREOUS
ABEOPPRSY PAPERBOYS
ABEOPRRSY SOAPBERRY
ABEORSSTU SABOTEURS
ABEPRRRSY RASPBERRY
ABEPRSSSY PASSERSBY
ABERSSTTU SUBSTRATE
ABERTTTUW WATER
   BUTT
ABFGLLLOS GOLF BALLS
ABFHLLSUY BASHFULLY
ABFIILOTT BIT OF TAIL
ABFIIORSU BIFARIOUS
ABFILLSYY SYLLABIFY
ABFILMSUY SUBFAMILY
ABFIRSTTU FRUIT BATS
ABFLLOOST FOOTBALLS
ABGGIKNPY PIGGYBANK
ABGGILMNO
   GAMBOLING
ABGGNOOST
   TOBOGGANS
ABGHHILLS HIGHBALLS
ABGHIINNS BANISHING
ABGHILMNS SHAMBLING
ABGHIMNSU AMBUSHING
ABGHINORR
   ABHORRING, HARBORING
ABGHIOPRY BIOGRAPHY
ABGHMORSU
   BROUGHAMS
ABGIILLNU BILINGUAL
ABGIIMSST BIGAMISTS
ABGIIMTUY AMBIGUITY
ABGIINNOT OBTAINING
ABGIINOTV OBVIATING
ABGIINPTZ BAPTIZING
ABGIINRTV VIBRATING
ABGILLMOS GLOBALISM
ABGILLNOT BALLOTING
ABGILLOST GLOBALIST
ABGILLOTY BILLY GOAT
ABGILNNOZ BLAZONING
ABGILNORU LABOURING
ABGILNOSV ABSOLVING
ABGILNOSX SIGNAL BOX
ABGILOORT OBLIGATOR
ABGIMOSUU AMBIGUOUS

ABGINNRRU UNBARRING
ABGINOPRT PROBATING
ABGINPSSY BYPASSING
ABGLMNOOS
    BOOMSLANG
ABGLNOOST LONGBOATS
ABGLNOSUW
    BUNGALOWS
ABHHIIRUV BAHUVRIHI
ABHHILOTT BATHOLITH
ABHHIRRSU HAIRBRUSH
ABHIKLLSW HAWKSBILL
ABHIKMRRT BIRTHMARK
ABHILMNTU
    THUMBNAIL
ABHILMSTU BISMUTHAL
ABHILNOOT HALOBIONT
ABHILNRSU NAILBRUSH
ABHILNRTY LABYRINTH
ABHIOOOPZ ZOOPHOBIA
ABHKOOOST BOAT
    HOOKS
ABHLLMOST
    MOTHBALLS
ABHLLMSTU ALL
    THUMBS
ABHLNOORY
    HONORABLY
ABHLPRSUY SUBPHYLAR
ABHMOORST
    BATHROOMS
ABIIILLTY LIABILITY
ABIIILNTY INABILITY
ABIIILTVY VIABILITY
ABIIJMMUY MBUJIMAYI
ABIIKLSSS BASILISKS
ABIILLMRS MILLIBARS
ABIILLNRT BRILLIANT
ABIILMNOS BINOMIALS
ABIILMRST TRIBALISM
ABIILNOOT ABOLITION
ABIILNORT LIBRATION
ABIILNORY NOBILIARY
ABIILNOST LIBATIONS
ABIILNSST SIBILANTS
ABIILRRTY IRRITABLY
ABIILRSSV VIBRISSAL
ABIILRSTT TRIBALIST
ABIILSTTY STABILITY
ABIILSTUY SUABILITY,
    USABILITY
ABIIMNOST AMBITIONS
ABIIMORSS ISOBARISM
ABIIMOSTU AMBITIOUS

ABIINOOTV OBVIATION
ABIINORTV VIBRATION
ABIKLMNSS LAMBSKINS
ABIKLOSTY BIALYSTOK
ABILLMSSY SYLLABISM
ABILLNOPT BALLPOINT
ABILLOPRX PILLAR
    BOX
ABILLORRZ RAZORBILL
ABILLPSUY PLAUSIBLY
ABILMMOVY
    IMMOVABLY
ABILMMTUY IMMUTABLY
ABILMOORS RIBOSOMAL
ABILMORSU LABOURISM
ABILMSTTU SUBMITTAL
ABILNOOST OBLATIONS
ABILNOSTU ABLUTIONS
ABILNRSTU TRIBUNALS
ABILNRTVY VIBRANTLY
ABILOORSU LABORIOUS
ABILORRTY LIBRATORY
ABILORSTU LABOURIST
ABILRSSUY SALISBURY
ABILRTTUY BRUTALITY
ABIMMNRUU
    MANUBRIUM
ABIMNTUYZ
    BYZANTIUM
ABIMORSSU AMBROSIUS
ABINNOTVV BON
    VIVANT
ABINOOPRT PROBATION
ABINOORST ABORTIONS
ABINOSSTT BOTANISTS
ABINRRTUY TRIBUNARY
ABIOORRRT BRIARROOT
ABIORRSTV VIBRATORS
ABIRRTTUY TRIBUTARY
ABKKMOORS
    BOOKMARKS
ABKLLNORS BANKROLLS
ABKLLOOST BOOKSTALL
ABKNPRSTU BANKRUPTS
ABKOOPSSS PASSBOOKS
ABLLMOORS
    BALLROOMS
ABLLMOPSW
    BLOWLAMPS
ABLLNOSSW SNOWBALLS
ABLMNORSU
    SUBNORMAL
ABLMNRSUU
    LABURNUMS

ABLNOTUYY
    BUOYANTLY
ABLNRSUUY SUBLUNARY
ABLOOPPSY OPPOSABLY
ABLORTTUU TUBULATOR
ABLOSSTTU SUBTOTALS
ABMNORRST
    BARNSTORM
ABMOOORTT
    MOTORBOAT
ABNNSTUUY BUNYA
    NUTS
ABNORSTUU RUN-
    ABOUTS
ABNORTTUU ABOUT-
    TURN, TURNABOUT
ABOOPRSTT BOOTSTRAP
ACCCCEHIT CACHECTIC
ACCCDEEEN ACCEDENCE
ACCCDEEIN ACCIDENCE
ACCCDIIMU MUCIC ACID
ACCCEEENS ACESCENCE
ACCCEGLOY
    COCCYGEAL
ACCCEHIOT CACOETHIC
ACCCEIIRT CICATRICE
ACCCEILLO CALCICOLE
ACCCHKOOR
    COCKROACH
ACCCHOPRT CATCH
    CROP
ACCCIILLY ALICYCLIC
ACCCIILMT CLIMACTIC
ACCCIIOPR CAPRICCIO
ACCCNOPUY
    OCCUPANCY
ACCDDEEEN DECADENCE
ACCDDEILS DISCALCED
ACCDDIIST DIDACTICS
ACCDDIORS DISACCORD
ACCDEEHIK CHICKADEE
ACCDEEIST DESICCATE
ACCDEELLN CANCELLED
ACCDEELNO
    CONCEALED
ACCDEELOS COALESCED
ACCDEFIIL CALCIFIED
ACCDEFILS FASCICLED
ACCDEFILY DECALCIFY
ACCDEHIKR DECKCHAIR
ACCDEHKOT COCKED
    HAT
ACCDEHRST SCRATCHED
ACCDEIILN ICELANDIC

ACCDEIILT DIALECTIC
ACCDEINOT ANECDOTIC
ACCDEINST ACCIDENTS,
DESICCANT
ACCDEIORW COWARDICE
ACCDEIPRT PRACTICED
ACCDEKOSS CASSOCKED
ACCDELMOR COLD
CREAM
ACCDELSSU CUL-DE-SACS
ACCDEMNOO
CACODEMON
ACCDEMOPT
COMPACTED
ACCDEMORY
DEMOCRACY
ACCDENOTT
CONTACTED
ACCDENOTU
ACCOUNTED
ACCDENPSU DUNCE'S
CAP
ACCDEORRS SCORECARD
ACCDEORSW SACRED
COW
ACCDFILLY FLACCIDLY
ACCDGINOR
ACCORDING
ACCDHHRUY
ARCHDUCHY
ACCDHINOR
CHANCROID
ACCDHNPRU
CARDPUNCH
ACCDHORTW
CATCHWORD
ACCDHPSTU DUTCH
CAPS
ACCDIIINT DIACTINIC
ACCDIIIRT DIACRITIC
ACCDIIOPT APODICTIC
ACCDILLOY CYCLOIDAL
ACCDILSTY DACTYLICS
ACCDINOOR
ACCORDION
ACCDKNORW
CRACKDOWN
ACCDNOORT
CONCORDAT
ACCDORRTU COURT
CARD
ACCEEGLMY
MEGACYCLE
ACCEEHILR CHELICERA

ACCEEHIST CATECHISE
ACCEEHITY HAECCEITY
ACCEEHITZ CATECHIZE
ACCEEHKMT
CHECKMATE
ACCEEHLOT COCHLEATE
ACCEEHNPR PERCHANCE
ACCEEHOST CACOETHES
ACCEEIMRS ICE CREAMS
ACCEEIPRS PECCARIES
ACCEEIQSU ACQUIESCE
ACCEEIRTV ACCRETIVE
ACCEEISTX EXSICCATE
ACCEEKLNS NECKLACES
ACCEELLNR CANCELLER
ACCEELNPR PRECANCEL
ACCEELPST SPECTACLE
ACCEENNST CANESCENT
ACCEEORSU CERACEOUS
ACCEFGILU CALCIFUGE
ACCEFHLOT FACECLOTH
ACCEFIIRS SACRIFICE
ACCEFILSU FASCICULE
ACCEFNORS FRANCESCO
ACCEGILNN CANCELING
ACCEGINNT ACCENTING
ACCEGINOR ACROGENIC
ACCEGINPT ACCEPTING
ACCEGINSS ACCESSING
ACCEGIOTT GEOTACTIC
ACCEGKMOS
GAMECOCKS
ACCEHHIRT THEARCHIC
ACCEHIKNR RAIN CHECK
ACCEHIKPS CHICKPEAS
ACCEHILLO ECHOLALIC
ACCEHILMS CHEMICALS
ACCEHILNO COCHINEAL
ACCEHILNT TECHNICAL
ACCEHILOT CHICALOTE
ACCEHIMNS
MECHANICS, MISCHANCE
ACCEHIMST CATECHISM,
SCHEMATIC
ACCEHINRY CHICANERY
ACCEHINST CHANCIEST
ACCEHIRTT ARCHITECT
ACCEHISTT CATCHIEST,
CATECHIST
ACCEHKPSY PAYCHECKS
ACCEHLOOT
CHOCOLATE
ACCEHMNTT
CATCHMENT

ACCEHORTU
CARTOUCHE
ACCEHORTY
THEOCRACY
ACCEHRRST SCRATCHER
ACCEHRSST SCRATCHES
ACCEIILMN CALCIMINE
ACCEIIMNT CINEMATIC
ACCEIINOS COCAINISE
ACCEIINOZ COCAINIZE
ACCEIINRT CIRCINATE
ACCEIIPRT ACCIPITER
ACCEIIRST CICATRISE
ACCEIIRTZ CICATRIZE
ACCEIISTV SICCATIVE
ACCEIKLOT COCKATIEL
ACCEIKRSW WISECRACK
ACCEILLSV CLAVICLES
ACCEILMPT ECLAMPTIC
ACCEILNST CANTICLES
ACCEILNTU INCULCATE
ACCEILOPR PRECOCIAL
ACCEILPST SCEPTICAL
ACCEILRTU CIRCULATE
ACCEIMOSU MICACEOUS
ACCEINORT ACCRETION
ACCEINOSS ACCESSION
ACCEINSTU ENCAUSTIC,
SUCCINATE
ACCEIOTT CORTICATE
ACCEIPRST PRACTICES
ACCEISSTT ECSTATICS
ACCEKKORS ROCK
CAKES
ACCEKMNRS
CRACKSMEN
ACCEKNORR
CORNCRAKE
ACCELLLOS CLOSE
CALL
ACCELLOOT COLLOCATE
ACCELLTUU CUCULLATE
ACCELNOSV CONCLAVES
ACCELNOVY
COVALENCY
ACCEMNRTU
ACCRUMENT
ACCEMOPRT
COMPACTER
ACCEMORTY
MACROCYTE
ACCEMPRSU CREAMCUPS
ACCENNOST
CONSTANCE

ACCENNOTY
  COTENANCY
ACCENOORS
  COENOSARC
ACCENORSU CANCEROUS
ACCENRSUY RECUSANCY
ACCEORRSW
  SCARECROW
ACCEIINRSSY ACCESSORY
ACCEORSTU CORUSCATE
ACCFFHHIN CHAFFINCH
ACCFIILOR CALORIFIC
ACCFIISST FASCISTIC
ACCFINNOU CONFUCIAN
ACCFINORS FRANCISCO
ACCFKOORT FROCK
  COAT
ACCGHHNNU
  CHANGCHUN
ACCGHHNOW
  CHANGCHOW
ACCGHINRY GYNARCHIC
ACCGIKLNR CRACKLING
ACCGINOST ACCOSTING
ACCHHMNRU
  CHURCHMAN
ACCHIILRV CHIVALRIC
ACCHILLOO ALCOHOLIC
ACCHILLOT LACCOLITH
ACCHILORT HOLARCTIC
ACCHILOST CATHOLICS
ACCHILPSY PSYCHICAL
ACCHIMOPR
  CAMPHORIC
ACCHIMORT
  CHROMATIC
ACCHIMOST STOMACHIC
ACCHIRTTY TRACHYTIC
ACCHKLOST SACKCLOTH
ACCHKOOOP COCK-A-
  HOOP
ACCHKOORW
  COACHWORK
ACCHLOORT
  COLCOTHAR,
  OCHLOCRAT
ACCHLOOSW
  SLOWCOACH
ACCHLOOTY
  CHOCOLATY
ACCHNOOPY
  CACOPHONY
ACCHNORSU
  CHANCROUS

ACCHOPRSS CASH CROPS
ACCIIILNN CLINICIAN
ACCIILLVY CIVICALLY
ACCIILNOR CONCILIAR
ACCIILOPT OCCIPITAL
ACCIILRTU CIRCUITAL
ACCIILTVY ACCLIVITY
ACCIIMNOS COCAINISM
ACCIINRTY INTRICACY
ACCIIORST ISOCRATIC
ACCIIOSTT ISOTACTIC
ACCIISSTU CASUISTIC
ACCIKKNNS NICKNACKS
ACCIKLOST COCKTAILS
ACCILLMOY COMICALLY
ACCILLNOY CONICALLY
ACCILLNYY CYNICALLY
ACCILLRUY CRUCIALLY
ACCILNORV CLAVICORN
ACCILNOTU NOCTILUCA
ACCILRRSU CIRCULARS
ACCILRRUU CURRICULA
ACCILRTUU CUTICULAR
ACCIMNORY
  ACRONYMIC
ACCIMNOSS MOCCASINS
ACCIMNOSY SCIOMANCY
ACCIMORSY COSMIC
  RAY
ACCIMORTY
  TIMOCRACY
ACCIMPSSU CAPSICUMS
ACCINNOTT IN
  CONTACT
ACCINOOSS OCCASIONS
ACCINOPRR CAPRICORN
ACCINORST NARCOTICS
ACCINOSTY OSCITANCY
ACCINOTVY CONCAVITY
ACCINSTTY SYNTACTIC
ACCIOPRTT CATOPTRIC
ACCIORSST ACROSTICS
ACCIOSSTU ACOUSTICS
ACCKKRSSU RUCKSACKS
ACCKOOOST
  COCKATOOS
ACCKOPRST
  CRACKPOTS
ACCKORSST STOCKCARS
ACCLLOSUU CALCULOUS
ACCLMOPTY
  COMPACTLY
ACCMMOORS
  MACROCOSM

ACCMNOORY
  MONOCRACY,
  NOMOCRACY
ACCMNOTUY
  CONTUMACY
ACCMORSTY
  MACROCYST
ACCNNOOTU NO-
  ACCOUNT
ACCNNOSTY
  CONSTANCY
ACCNOORTT
  CONTACTOR
ACCNOPSTU OCCUPANTS
ACCNORSTT
  CONTRACTS
ACCOPRSTY CYSTOCARP
ACCORRSTY CARRYCOTS
ACDDEEIT DEDICATED
ACDDDEIRS DISCARDED
ACDDDEKSU DEAD
  DUCKS
ACDDEEEFT DEFECATED
ACDDEEEIT DEDICATEE
ACDDEEERS DECREASED
ACDDEEILM DECLAIMED
ACDDEEIMT DECIMATED,
  MEDICATED
ACDDEEORT DECORATED
ACDDEERTT DETRACTED
ACDDEFIII ACIDIFIED
ACDDEGIRS DISGRACED
ACDDEGNOO
  DODECAGON
ACDDEHIRR HARD CIDER
ACDDEHKNS
  DECKHANDS
ACDDEHNRU DUDE
  RANCH
ACDDEIINT INDICATED
ACDDEIITV ADDICTIVE
ACDDEIJNU JAUNDICED
ACDDEILPS DISPLACED
ACDDEINRS RIDDANCES
ACDDEINRX CARD
  INDEX
ACDDEINST DISTANCED
ACDDEIORT DEDICATOR
ACDDEIPRY RICE PADDY
ACDDEIRRS DISCARDER
ACDDEKLOP PADLOCKED
ACDDEKLOS
  DEADLOCKS
ACDDEKOST STOCKADED

ACDDELNOO
CANOODLED
ACDDEMMNO
COMMANDED
ACDDHHNSU
DACHSHUND
ACDDIILOS DISCOIDAL
ACDDIINOT ADDICTION
ACDDINOTU
ADDUCTION
ACDDKORSY
DOCKYARDS
ACDDLNORW COLD-
DRAWN
ACDEEEHIP HEADPIECE
ACDEEEHNP CHEAPENED
ACDEEEHNR
ADHERENCE
ACDEEELRY CLEAR-EYED
ACDEEEPRT DEPRECATE
ACDEEERRT RECREATED
ACDEEERSS DECREASES
ACDEEERST DESECRATE
ACDEEERTU RE-EDUCATE
ACDEEERTX EXECRATED
ACDEEFIRR FREDERICA
ACDEEFKRT AFTERDECK
ACDEEFNOP OPEN-FACED
ACDEEFNTU FECUNDATE
ACDEEFORT DEFECATOR
ACDEEFRRT REFRACTED
ACDEEGHNX
EXCHANGED
ACDEEGHRR
RECHARGED
ACDEEGLNO
CONGEALED
ACDEEGLOU DECALOGUE
ACDEEGNSV SCAVENGED
ACDEEGOPU DECOUPAGE
ACDEEHIMP IMPEACHED
ACDEEHINN ENCHAINED
ACDEEHIRS CASHIERED
ACDEEHKNY
HACKNEYED
ACDEEHLLN CHANDELLE
ACDEEHLNN
CHANNELED
ACDEEHLPT CHAPLETED
ACDEEHNNT
ENCHANTED
ACDEEHNST CHASTENED
ACDEEHPSY SPEECH DAY
ACDEEHRRT CHARTERED

ACDEEHRTT CHATTERED
ACDEEIIJTV ADJECTIVE
ACDEEIKST ICE-SKATED
ACDEEILMR DECLAIMER,
RECLAIMED
ACDEEILMX EXCLAIMED
ACDEEILNN CELANDINE,
DECENNIAL
ACDEEILNR ICELANDER
ACDEEILNT DECLINATE
ACDEEILNU EUCLIDEAN
ACDEEILTU ELUCIDATE
ACDEEILTY ACETYLIDE
ACDEEIMNO
MACEDOINE
ACDEEIMNP IMPEDANCE
ACDEEINRS INCREASED
ACDEEINSU AUDIENCES
ACDEEIOPR ADIPOCERE
ACDEEIPRT PREDICATE
ACDEEITUV EDUCATIVE
ACDEEKKNR
KNACKERED
ACDEEKLNS SLACKENED
ACDEEKPPR PREPACKED
ACDEEKPST TAPE DECKS
ACDEELLOT DECOLLATE,
OCELLATED
ACDEELLPR PARCELLED
ACDEELLTW WELL-
ACTED
ACDEELNRS CALENDERS
ACDEELORT RELOCATED
ACDEELPTU PECULATED
ACDEELQRU LACQUERED
ACDEELRTT CLATTERED
ACDEELRTU ULCERATED
ACDEELSTY DECASTYLE
ACDEELTTU CLAUDETTE
ACDEEMPRS SCAMPERED
ACDEENNRT
ENTRANCED
ACDEENNRU
ENDURANCE
ACDEENORS COARSENED
ACDEENOSS DEACONESS
ACDEENOST ANECDOTES
ACDEENRST DECANTERS,
DESCANTER
ACDEENRTU UNCREATED
ACDEEOPRR CROP-
EARED
ACDEEORTV OVERACTED
ACDEEPRRS SCARPERED

ACDEEPRRT RED CARPET
ACDEEPSTT SPECTATED
ACDEERRTT RETRACTED
ACDEERSTT SCATTERED
ACDEERSTU REDUCTASE
ACDEERTTX EXTRACTED
ACDEESSTU DECUSSATE
ACDEFFILR RADCLIFFE
ACDEFFILT AFFLICTED
ACDEFFIST DISAFFECT
ACDEFFLLU FULL-FACED
ACDEFFMOR
COFFERDAM
ACDEFHINR - ARCHFIEND
ACDEFIIIL EDIFICIAL
ACDEFIIIR ACIDIFIER
ACDEFIILR CLARIFIED
ACDEFIILT FETICIDAL
ACDEFIIRS SCARIFIED
ACDEFILLO COALFIELD
ACDEFINRT INFARCTED
ACDEFKLNO FOLK
DANCE
ACDEFLMOR COLD
FRAME
ACDEFLNOT CONFLATED
ACDEFMNOO MOON-
FACED
ACDEFRRTU FRACTURED
ACDEGGIMO
DEMAGOGIC
ACDEGGIOP PEDAGOGIC
ACDEGHINR CHAGRINED
ACDEGHINT DETACHING
ACDEGHIRS DISCHARGE
ACDEGHNRU
UNCHARGED
ACDEGIILR REGICIDAL
ACDEGILNO GENOCIDAL
ACDEGILNR DECLARING
ACDEGILNS DESCALING
ACDEGILOO LOGAOEDIC
ACDEGIMNP DECAMPING
ACDEGINNS ASCENDING
ACDEGINNT DECANTING
ACDEGINOY GYNAECOID
ACDEGINTU EDUCATING
ACDEGIOTT COGITATED
ACDEGIRRS DISGRACER
ACDEGIRRT CARTRIDGE
ACDEGLNOU
LANGUEDOC
ACDEGNNOU
UNDECAGON

ACDEHHIKT THICKHEAD
ACDEHHORX
HEXACHORD
ACDEHIITT DIATHETIC
ACDEHINNR HINDRANCE
ACDEHINSV CAVENDISH
ACDEHIOPX HEXAPODIC
ACDEHIPRS SEPHARDIC
ACDEHIPRT DIRT CHEAP
ACDEHIRSV CRASH-DIVE
ACDEHISST CHASTISED
ACDEHKMPU
CHEMPADUK
ACDEHKOST HEADSTOCK
ACDEHKPST SKETCHPAD
ACDEHKRSU ARCHDUKES
ACDEHKSSS CASH DESKS
ACDEHLNOR
CHLORDANE
ACDEHLNOT
DECATHLON
ACDEHLNRS CHANDLERS
ACDEHLNRY
CHANDLERY
ACDEHLRSU SCHEDULAR
ACDEHMNTU
UNMATCHED
ACDEHMOST
STOMACHED
ACDEHMPRY
PACHYDERM
ACDEHNRTU
UNCHARTED
ACDEHNRUY HUE AND
CRY
ACDEHNSTU
STAUNCHED, UNSCATHED
ACDEHNTUW
UNWATCHED
ACDEHOOPT
CHAETOPOD
ACDEHORRS HARD
CORES
ACDEHORRV
HARDCOVER
ACDEHORSS CROSSHEAD
ACDEHOSTT COT
DEATHS
ACDEHPRSU PURCHASED
ACDEIIINT DIETICIAN
ACDEIILMN ADMINICLE,
MEDICINAL
ACDEIILNT IDENTICAL
ACDEIILNX INDEXICAL

ACDEIILRV LARVICIDE,
VERIDICAL
ACDEIILTW TWICE-LAID
ACDEIIMMY IMMEDIACY
ACDEIIMNR AMERINDIC
ACDEIIMRT DIAMETRIC,
MATRICIDE
ACDEIINOT DIANOETIC
ACDEIINTV VINDICATE
ACDEIIOPR APERIODIC
ACDEIIPRR PARRICIDE
ACDEIIPRT PATRICIDE
ACDEIKMNN
NICKNAMED
ACDEIKRST SIDETRACK
ACDEILLMS MISCALLED
ACDEILLMY DECIMALLY,
MEDICALLY
ACDEILLOS LOCALISED
ACDEILLOZ LOCALIZED
ACDEILMPS MISPLACED
ACDEILNVY DIVALENCY
ACDEILOPT PETALODIC
ACDEILOST DISLOCATE
ACDEILPRS DISPLACER
ACDEILPRU PEDICULAR
ACDEILPTU DUPLICATE
ACDEILRTU CURTAILED
ACDEILTUV VICTUALED
ACDEIMNNO
DOMINANCE
ACDEIMNNT
MENDICANT
ACDEIMNOP COMPENDIA
ACDEIMNOS COMEDIANS
ACDEIMNPS PANDEMICS
ACDEIMNRU
MANICURED
ACDEIMNSU MUSCADINE
ACDEIMNTY MENDACITY
ACDEIMORT DECIMATOR
ACDEINNOR ORDINANCE
ACDEINNOS CANONISED
ACDEINNOT CONTAINED
ACDEINNOZ CANONIZED
ACDEINNST INSTANCED
ACDEINORR CORIANDER
ACDEINORS DINOCERAS
ACDEINORT REDACTION
ACDEINOTU
AUCTIONED, CAUTIONED,
EDUCATION
ACDEINOTV ADVECTION
ACDEINPRT PREDICANT

ACDEINRTU CURTAINED
ACDEINSST DISTANCES
ACDEINSTY ASYNDETIC,
SYNDICATE
ACDEIPRST PRACTISED
ACDEIPSTU CUSPIDATE
ACDEIQTTU ACQUITTED
ACDEIRTTX DIRECT TAX
ACDEISSTT ACID
TESTS
ACDEJKKSY SKYJACKED
ACDEKLMSU LAME
DUCKS
ACDEKOPTU PACKED-
OUT
ACDEKOSST STOCKADES
ACDELLOPS COLLAPSED,
SCALLOPED
ACDELLORR CORRALLED
ACDELMOPR
PLACODERM
ACDELMORU
CLAMOURED
ACDELMORY
COMRADELY
ACDELNNOO
COLONNADE
ACDELNNOR
CLARENDON
ACDELNNTU
CANDLENUT
ACDELNNUU
UNDULANCE
ACDELNOOW
LANCEWOOD
ACDELNORS COLANDERS
ACDELNRUY
UNDERCLAY
ACDELOPTU COPULATED,
CUPOLATED
ACDELOSTW COLD
SWEAT
ACDEMMMNO
COMMENDAM
ACDEMMNOR
COMMANDER
ACDEMNOPR
COMPANDER
ACDEMOORR
ACRODROME
ACDEMOORT
MOTORCADE
ACDEMORST
DEMOCRATS

ACDENNNOU
ANNOUNCED
ACDENNRST TRANSCEND
ACDENOOTT
COTTONADE
ACDENORSY SECONDARY
ACDENORTU
UNDERCOAT
ACDENRTTU
TRUNCATED
ACDEOORRT
DECORATOR
ACDEOORTT
DOCTORATE
ACDEOPSTU SPACED OUT
ACDEOPTTU COUP
D'ÉTAT
ACDEORRST CO-
STARRED
ACDEORRTT
DETRACTOR
ACDEORSTU
CERATODUS, EDUCATORS
ACDEORSUU RUDACEOUS
ACDEORTUY
EDUCATORY
ACDEORTUZ COTE
D'AZUR
ACDEQSTUU AQUEDUCTS
ACDERRSSU CRUSADERS
ACDERRSTU TRADUCERS
ACDERSSTT TEST CARDS
ACDESSTUY CASE STUDY
ACDFFHNSU HANDCUFFS
ACDFFLOSS SCAFFOLDS
ACDFGOOST ACTS OF
GOD
ACDFHILSS SCALDFISH
ACDFIIILL FILICIDAL
ACDFIIRUY FIDUCIARY
ACDFINNOT CONFIDANT
ACDFNTTUY
CANDYTUFT
ACDFOORTW
WOODCRAFT
ACDGHIIPR DIGRAPHIC
ACDGHIMOY
DICHOGAMY
ACDGHIPSY DYSPHAGIC
ACDGHOSTW
WATCHDOGS
ACDGIILNO GADOLINIC
ACDGIINNR DINING CAR
ACDGIINTT DICTATING

ACDGIIRST DIGASTRIC
ACDGIMOST DOGMATICS
ACDGINRSU CRUSADING
ACDGINRTU TRADUCING
ACDGLLOOR DOG
COLLAR
ACDHIILMO HOMICIDAL
ACDHIILOP ACIDOPHIL
ACDHIILST DISTICHAL
ACDHIIMSU DICHASIUM
ACDHIINNO INDOCHINA
ACDHIINOP DIAPHONIC
ACDHIKPRT PITCH-DARK
ACDHILNOO
CONHOIDAL
ACDHILPRS PILCHARDS
ACDHILRUY HYDRAULIC
ACDHILSTT LAST-DITCH
ACDHIMORT
CHROMATID
ACDHIOPRS RHAPSODIC
ACDHIORYZ HYDRAZOIC
ACDHIPSSY DYSPHASIC
ACDHLOOSY DAY
SCHOOL
ACDHMNOOR
CHONDROMA
ACDHMOOTW
MATCHWOOD
ACDHOOPPS SCAPHOPOD
ACDHORTWW
WATCHWORD
ACDIIILMT MITICIDAL
ACDIIIMOT IDIOMATIC
ACDIIJLRU JURIDICAL
ACDIIJRUY JUDICIARY
ACDIILMNO DOMINICAL
ACDIILMSX DISCLIMAX
ACDIILOST DIASTOLIC
ACDIILPTY PLACIDITY
ACDIILSTU DUALISTIC
ACDIIMNNO DOMINICAN
ACDIIMNTY DYNAMITIC
ACDIIMRTY MYDRIATIC
ACDIINORT INDICATOR
ACDIINOTT DICTATION
ACDIINRTY RANCIDITY
ACDIIOPRT DIATROPIC
ACDIJORTU JUDICATOR
ACDIKKLRY KIRKCALDY
ACDIKNQSU QUICKSAND
ACDIKRRTT DIRT TRACK
ACDIKRSTY YARDSTICK
ACDILLLOO COLLOIDAL

ACDILLOOR CORALLOID
ACDILLORY CORDIALLY
ACDILMOPS PSALMODIC
ACDILMOPY DIPLOMACY
ACDILMOTU COMATULID
ACDILNOOR COORDINAL
ACDILNORT DOCTRINAL
ACDILOPRS DROPSICAL
ACDILORSY CORYDALIS
ACDILOSTU CUSTODIAL
ACDILOSUU ACIDULOUS
ACDILRTTY TRIDACTYL
ACDIMOPSS SPASMODIC
ACDIMORRU
MACRUROID
ACDIMORTY
MORDACITY
ACDINOOPT ACTINOPOD
ACDINOSTU CUSTODIAN
ACDIORSTT DICTATORS
ACDJOORTU
COADJUTOR
ACDKLORTU
TRUCKLOAD
ACDKMNNOO
MONADNOCK
ACDKORSTY STOCKYARD
ACDLMNOOY
CONDYLOMA
ACDLMNOPW
CLAMPDOWN
ACDLNOPSS COLD SNAPS
ACDLNORSU
CAULDRONS
ACDLNSTYY SYNDACTYL
ACDLORSUW WAR
CLOUDS
ACDMMNOOS
COMMANDOS
ACDMOOSUV
MUSCOVADO
ACDMPRRTU TRUMP
CARD
ACDNOORRT
CORRODANT
ACDOPRSST POSTCARDS
ACDORRTUY
COURTYARD
ACDRSSTTU DUSTCARTS
ACEEEFIRS CEASE-FIRE
ACEEEFLNR FREELANCE
ACEEEGHPR REPECHAGE
ACEEEGNNV
VENGEANCE

ACEEEILMP PIECEMEAL
ACEEEIMPT PEACETIME
ACEEEIPPP PEACE PIPE
ACEEEIPRS EARPIECES
ACEEEKRRT RACKETEER
ACEEELNRV RELEVANCE
ACEEELNTU ENUCLEATE
ACEEELNTY ACETYLENE
ACEEELSSS CEASELESS
ACEEEMNNR
  REMANENCE
ACEEEMNPR PERMEANCE
ACEEENPPT APPETENCE
ACEEENRSV SEVERANCE
ACEEERSTT ETCETERAS
ACEEFFHRU RECHAUFFE
ACEEFFITV AFFECTIVE
ACEEFFLNU AFFLUENCE
ACEEFFLTU EFFECTUAL
ACEEFFNRY FANCY-FREE
ACEEFHLNP HALFPENCE
ACEEFHMRR
  CHAMFERER
ACEEFHORR FOREREACH
ACEEFIIRT ACETIFIER
ACEEFILPR FIREPLACE
ACEEFINNR REFINANCE
ACEEFINRT INTERFACE
ACEEFIRSS FRICASSEE
ACEEFKOPR POKER FACE
ACEEFLOTV VOLTE-FACE
ACEEFMORT FORCEMEAT
ACEEFPSTY TYPEFACES
ACEEFRRSU RESURFACE
ACEEGHIRU GAUCHERIE
ACEEGHLLN CHALLENGE
ACEEGHNRX
  EXCHANGER
ACEEGHNSX EXCHANGES
ACEEGILRS SACRILEGE
ACEEGILRV VICEGERAL,
  VICEREGAL
ACEEGIMSY MAGIC EYES
ACEEGINNR CAREENING
ACEEGINRR CAREERING
ACEEGINRV GRIEVANCE
ACEEGIRTT CIGARETTE
ACEEGKRWY
  GREYWACKE
ACEEGLLOU COLLEAGUE
ACEEGLNRT RECTANGLE
ACEEGLRSS GRACELESS
ACEEGMNOR
  GEOMANCER

ACEEGNORU
  ENCOURAGE
ACEEGNRSV SCAVENGER
ACEEGNRSY SERGEANCY
ACEEGOOPR COOPERAGE
ACEEGRTTU CURETTAGE
ACEEHHORT EACH
  OTHER
ACEEHHTUX
  HEXATEUCH
ACEEHIIPR HAIRPIECE
ACEEHILMS ALCHEMISE
ACEEHILMZ ALCHEMIZE
ACEEHILPT PETECHIAL
ACEEHILRT HERETICAL
ACEEHILRV CHEVALIER
ACEEHIMNS MECHANISE
ACEEHIMNZ MECHANIZE
ACEEHIMPR IMPEACHER
ACEEHINNV ENHANCIVE
ACEEHINPT PHENACITE
ACEEHINRT CATHERINE
ACEEHISTT AESTHETIC
ACEEHLMNO
  CHAMELEON
ACEEHLMOO
  HAEMOCOEL
ACEEHLMPV CHAMPLEVE
ACEEHLNNR
  CHANNELER
ACEEHLNRU HERCULEAN
ACEEHLNRW
  WALCHEREN
ACEEHLNSS SENESCHAL
ACEEHLNTU NEUCHATEL
ACEEHLOSS SHOELACES
ACEEHLRTW
  CARTWHEEL
ACEEHMMRT
  MACHMETER
ACEEHMNRY
  ARCHENEMY
ACEEHMOTY
  HAEMOCYTE
ACEEHMRSU
  CHARMEUSE
ACEEHNNRT
  ENCHANTER
ACEEHNPSS CHEAPNESS
ACEEHNPTY PACHYTENE
ACEEHNRST CHASTENER
ACEEHNRRT ENTRECHAT
ACEEHNSTU CHANTEUSE
ACEEHORRS RACEHORSE

ACEEHORRV
  OVERREACH
ACEEHOSTU THEACEOUS
ACEEHPRRS PREACHERS
ACEEHPRTY ARCHETYPE
ACEEHRRTT CHATTERER
ACEEHRRTY TREACHERY
ACEEHRSTT CATHETERS
ACEEHSSTT TEA CHESTS
ACEEIILPT TAILPIECE
ACEEIKLSV SICK LEAVE
ACEEIKRST CREAKIEST,
  ICE-SKATER
ACEEIKSST ICE SKATES
ACEEILLST CELESTIAL
ACEEILMNS MESCALINE
ACEEILMNT CLEMENTIA
ACEEILMRT CARMELITE
ACEEILMRX EXCLAIMER
ACEEILNPR PERCALINE
ACEEILNRS LARCENIES
ACEEILNRT INTERLACE,
  RECLINATE
ACEEILNST CELESTINA
ACEEILNSV VALENCIES
ACEEILPRS PERICLASE
ACEEILPRT REPLICATE
ACEEILPTX EXPLICATE
ACEEIMMNN
  IMMANENCE
ACEEIMMNT
  MINCEMEAT
ACEEIMMRT METAMERIC
ACEEIMNPR MEPACRINE
ACEEIMNSX EXCISEMAN
ACEEIMPRT IMPRECATE
ACEEIMPST SPACE-TIME
ACEEIMRRS CAREERISM
ACEEIMRSS CASSIMERE
ACEEIMRST CREAMIEST,
  MISCREATE
ACEEINNRS CANNERIES
ACEEINNRT NECTARINE
ACEEINNST INSECTEAN,
  TENANCIES
ACEEINNTU ENUNCIATE
ACEEINPRU EPICUREAN
ACEEINPTT PECTINATE
ACEEINRRS INCREASER
ACEEINRSS INCREASES
ACEEIORTX EXCORIATE
ACEEIOSST TEA COSIES
ACEEIOTVV EVOCATIVE
ACEEIPPRR RICE PAPER

ACEEIPRTT CREPITATE
ACEEIRRST CAREERIST
ACEEIRSTT CATTERIES
ACEEIRSTU CAUTERISE
ACEEIRSTW WATER ICES
ACEEIRSVV VICE VERSA
ACEEIRTTX EXTRICATE
ACEEIRTUZ CAUTERIZE
ACEEISSST ECSTASIES
ACEEKLMRS MACKERELS
ACEELLLSU CELLULASE
ACEELLORT ELECTORAL
ACEELMNPT PLACEMENT
ACEELMOPS SOMEPLACE
ACEELMORT LATECOMER
ACEELNNRU CANNELURE
ACEELNNSS CLEANNESS
ACEELNORT TOLERANCE
ACEELNPTU PETULANCE
ACEELNRSS CLEANSERS, CLEARNESS
ACEELNRTU CALENTURE, CRENULATE
ACEELNRVY RELEVANCY
ACEELNSTT TENTACLES
ACEELOOSU OLEACEOUS
ACEELOPRT PERCOLATE
ACEELOPSS ESCALOPES
ACEELORRT CORRELATE
ACEELORSS CASSEROLE
ACEELORSW LOWER CASE
ACEELORTT LECTORATE
ACEELORTU URCEOLATE
ACEELPSSS SPACELESS
ACEELPSTU SPECULATE
ACEELPTUX EXCULPATE
ACEELQRRU LACQUERER
ACEELRTUY ELECTUARY
ACEELSSTT TELECASTS
ACEEMMOOT AMMOCOETE
ACEEMNNTT ENACTMENT
ACEEMNRRY MERCENARY
ACEEMORTT OCTAMETER
ACEEMPRRS SCAMPERER
ACEEMRRTU MERCURATE
ACEENNOPR CAN OPENER

ACEENNORS RESONANCE
ACEENNOST CANTONESE
ACEENNRST ENTRANCES, RENASCENT
ACEENNRTY CENTENARY
ACEENPRRT CARPENTER
ACEENPTTX EXPECTANT
ACEENRRST RECREANTS
ACEENRSSY NECESSARY
ACEENRTTU UTTERANCE
ACEENSSTU ACUTENESS
ACEENSSTX EXACTNESS
ACEENTTUX EXECUTANT
ACEEOOPRT COOPERATE
ACEEOPRRT PROCREATE
ACEEORRRT RE-CREATOR
ACEEORRTT RECTORATE
ACEEORRTV OVERREACT
ACEEOSSTU SETACEOUS
ACEEPPRSU UPPER CASE
ACEEPRRTU RECAPTURE
ACEERRSTT SCATTERER, STREETCAR
ACEERRSTU CREATURES
ACEERRSTY SECRETARY
ACEERSSST ACTRESSES
ACEERSSSV CREVASSES
ACEERSSTT TESSERACT
ACEERSSTU SECATEURS
ACEESSSTT CASSETTES, TEST CASES
ACEFFGINT AFFECTING
ACEFFHRUU CHAUFFEUR
ACEFFIIOT OFFICIATE
ACEFFILST FACE-LIFTS
ACEFFINOT AFFECTION
ACEFFIORT FORFICATE
ACEFFOSTU SUFFOCATE
ACEFGINPR PREFACING
ACEFGLNOS LONG FACES
ACEFHIINT CHIEFTAIN
ACEFHIKLT THICKLEAF
ACEFHIKSS FISHCAKES
ACEFHINRS FRANCHISE
ACEFHIPRY PREACHIFY
ACEFHMNNR FRENCHMAN
ACEFHOSUV VOUCHSAFE
ACEFIILMS FACSIMILE
ACEFIILRR CLARIFIER
ACEFIINNR FINANCIER
ACEFIIPRS PACIFIERS
ACEFIIRRS SCARIFIER

ACEFIIRRT ARTIFICER
ACEFIIRST ARTIFICES
ACEFIIRTV FRICATIVE
ACEFIITTV FACTITIVE
ACEFIJKKN JACK KNIFE
ACEFIKRTU FRUITCAKE
ACEFILNNO FALCONINE
ACEFILORT FORTALICE
ACEFILSTU FACULTIES
ACEFIMPRS CAMPFIRES
ACEFINNSS FANCINESS
ACEFINORT FORNICATE
ACEFINSTU INFUSCATE
ACEFIORRS AIRFORCES
ACEFIORST FACTORIES, FACTORISE
ACEFIORTZ FACTORIZE
ACEFIOSTU FACETIOUS
ACEFIRSTT CRAFTIEST
ACEFKORST TASK FORCE
ACEFLLLSU FULL-SCALE
ACEFLLRUY CAREFULLY
ACEFLNORS FALCONERS
ACEFLNORV CONFERVAL
ACEFLTTUU FLUCTUATE
ACEFMNRST CRAFTSMEN
ACEFOORST FOOTRACES
ACEFORRRT REFRACTOR
ACEFORRRU CARREFOUR
ACEFORSST FORECASTS
ACEFRRSTU FRACTURES
ACEGGIRRS SCRAGGIER
ACEGGIRST CRAGGIEST
ACEGHHPTU HUGH CAPET
ACEGHIINV ACHIEVING
ACEGHILRT LETHARGIC
ACEGHINNN ENHANCING
ACEGHINPR PREACHING
ACEGHINRS SEARCHING
ACEGHLSTY LYCHGATES
ACEGHMNOS CHEONGSAM
ACEGHMORT HECTOGRAM
ACEGHOPRY CREOPHAGY
ACEGHOPTY PHAGOCYTE
ACEGHRRSU SURCHARGE
ACEGILLS GALLICISE
ACEGIILLZ GALLICIZE
ACEGIILNS ANGLICISE

ACEGIILNT GENITALIC
ACEGIILNV VIGILANCE
ACEGIILNZ ANGLICIZE
ACEGIIMNT ENIGMATIC
ACEGIINNT ANTIGENIC
ACEGIIRRT GERIATRIC
ACEGILLLO COLLEGIAL
ACEGILLNO COLLEGIAN
ACEGILLNR RECALLING
ACEGILLOT COLLIGATE
ACEGILNNO CONGENIAL
ACEGILNNS CLEANSING
ACEGILNPR PARCELING,
  REPLACING
ACEGILNRS CLEARINGS
ACEGILNRU NEURALGIC
ACEGILNRW CLEARWING
ACEGILNTU CINGULATE
ACEGILOOR AEROLOGIC
ACEGILRTU CURTILAGE,
  GRATICULE
ACEGIMMNR
  ENGRAMMIC
ACEGIMMRS SCRIMMAGE
ACEGIMMST TAGMEMICS
ACEGIMNNP ENCAMPING
ACEGIMNOT
  GEOMANTIC
ACEGIMNRS SCREAMING
ACEGIMNRT
  CENTIGRAM, CREMATING
ACEGIMNST MAGNETICS
ACEGIMNTU MUTAGENIC
ACEGIMTUZ ZEUGMATIC
ACEGINNOR IGNORANCE
ACEGINNRT CANTERING,
  RECANTING
ACEGINNSU UNCEASING
ACEGINPPR RECAPPING
ACEGINPRT CARPETING
ACEGINPRY PANEGYRIC
ACEGINRRT RETRACING
ACEGINRSS CARESSING
ACEGINRST RECASTING
ACEGIOPRR PAREGORIC
ACEGIOSTT GEOSTATIC
ACEGIPRST PRICE TAGS
ACEGIRSTT STRATEGIC
ACEGJNOTU CONJUGATE
ACEGLMNRY
  CLERGYMAN
ACEGLNNPY PLANGENCY
ACEGMMNOO
  COMMONAGE

ACEGMMRSU
  SCRUMMAGE
ACEGNNOTT
  COTANGENT
ACEGNNPRY
  PREGNANCY
ACEGORRTU
  CORRUGATE
ACEGORSTT COTTAGERS
ACEHHILPS CHELASHIP
ACEHHIRRY HIERARCHY
ACEHHISTX HEXASTICH
ACEHHLWYZ WYCH-
  HAZEL
ACEHHMNTT
  HATCHMENT
ACEHHNRTY
  ETHNARCHY
ACEHHOOTT
  TOOTHACHE
ACEHHPRTY HEPTARCHY
ACEHHRSTT THATCHERS
ACEHHSSTY HESYCHAST
ACEHIINOP PHOENICIA
ACEHIINPP EPIPHANIC
ACEHIIPPT EPITAPHIC
ACEHIIRST CHARITIES
ACEHIISTT ATHEISTIC
ACEHIJKRS HIJACKERS
ACEHIKLST CHALKIEST
ACEHIKORT ARTICHOKE
ACEHIKRST HEARTSICK
ACEHILLLY HELICALLY
ACEHILLTY ETHICALLY
ACEHILMMO
  CHAMOMILE
ACEHILMST ALCHEMIST
ACEHILNNO CHELONIAN
ACEHILNOO HOLOCAINE
ACEHILNOR ENCHORIAL
ACEHILNOT CHELATION
ACEHILNTU UNETHICAL
ACEHILNTY THYLACINE
ACEHILPRS SPHERICAL
ACEHILRUV VEHICULAR
ACEHILSTT ATHLETICS
ACEHIMMNS
  MECHANISM
ACEHIMNRY MACHINERY
ACEHIMNST MECHANIST
ACEHIMRTU RHEUMATIC
ACEHINNRY HERCYNIAN
ACEHINORT
  ANCHORITE, ANTECHOIR

ACEHINORX CHRONAXIE
ACEHINOSV ANCHOVIES
ACEHINPST CATHEPSIN
ACEHINRRU HURRICANE,
  RAUNCHIER
ACEHINRSS CHARINESS
ACEHINRSU SEA URCHIN
ACEHINRTT IN THE
  CART
ACEHINSST CAITHNESS
ACEHINSTY HESITANCY
ACEHINTTU AUTHENTIC
ACEHIPPSS SPACESHIP
ACEHIPRST PIE CHARTS
ACEHIPSST PASTICHES
ACEHIPSTT PATCHIEST
ACEHIPSTW WHITECAPS
ACEHIRRST STARCHIER
ACEHIRSTT THEATRICS
ACEHIRSTU EUCHARIST
ACEHISTTT CHATTIEST
ACEHKLNSU UNSHACKLE
ACEHKLSTY LATCHKEYS
ACEHKMPSU MUCKHEAPS
ACEHKNORT ON THE
  RACK
ACEHKOPRS PACKHORSE
ACEHKORST SHORTCAKE
ACEHLLLOR CHLORELLA
ACEHLLOOS COALHOLES
ACEHLMOST
  MOSCHATEL
ACEHLMSST MATCHLESS
ACEHLNPTY PHLYCTENA
ACEHLOOSU
  COALHOUSE
ACEHLOPSW
  SHOWPLACE
ACEHLORRT
  TROCHLEAR
ACEHLORSU HOUSECARL
ACEHLORTT
  CHARLOTTE
ACEHLOSTT TEA
  CLOTHS
ACEHLTTYY TACHYLYTE
ACEHMNOPY
  CYMOPHANE
ACEHMNORW
  CHARWOMEN
ACEHMNPRT
  PARCHMENT
ACEHMNRST
  MERCHANTS

ACEHMNSTY YACHTSMEN

ACEHMNTTU HUMECTANT

ACEHMOSTT CHEMOSTAT

ACEHMOSTU MOUSTACHE

ACEHMPRTY CHAMPERTY

ACEHMSSTU MUSTACHES

ACEHMSTTT TEST MATCH

ACEHNNPST PENCHANTS

ACEHNNRTT TRENCHANT

ACEHNOOTT ON THE COAT

ACEHNOPRS CHAPERONS

ACEHNOPST CENOTAPHS

ACEHNORSS ANCHORESS

ACEHNOSTT STONECHAT

ACEHNPRTY PENTARCHY

ACEHNRSTU STAUNCHER

ACEHNRSUZ SCHNAUZER

ACEHOOSTU HOUSECOAT

ACEHOPRRS SHARECROP

ACEHORRST CARTHORSE, ORCHESTRA

ACEHORSTY THEOCRASY

ACEHOSSSW SHOWCASES

ACEHPRRSU PURCHASER

ACEHPRSSU PURCHASES

ACEHPSTTY PETTY CASH

ACEHRRTTY TETRARCHY

ACEIIILST ITALICISE

ACEIIILTZ ITALICIZE

ACEIIKLST EKISTICAL

ACEIIKMNT KINEMATIC

ACEIILLOT CILIOLATE

ACEIILMPR EMPIRICAL

ACEIILMPT IMPLICATE

ACEIILNNT ANTICLINE

ACEIILNNV VICENNIAL

ACEIILNPR CIRALPINE

ACEIILNST INELASTIC, SCIENTIAL

ACEIILOSS SOCIALISE

ACEIILOST SOCIALITE

ACEIILOSZ SOCIALIZE

ACEIILPRT PEARLITIC

ACEIILRST ERISTICAL, REALISTIC

ACEIILRTT LATERITIC

ACEIILSST SILICATES

ACEIILSTV CALVITIES

ACEIIMMNR CIMMERIAN

ACEIIMMRU AMERICIUM

ACEIIMNRT ANTIMERIC

ACEIIMNSS MESSIANIC

ACEIIMRST ARMISTICE

ACEIINNTV VINCENTIA

ACEIINPRS PRECISIAN

ACEIINPST EPINASTIC

ACEIINRTT INTRICATE

ACEIINTTT NICTITATE

ACEIIPSTT EPISTATIC

ACEIIRSTV VARISCITE

ACEIISTTT STEATITIC

ACEIJKNPS JACKSNIPE

ACEIJMSST MAJESTICS

ACEIKLPST SKEPTICAL

ACEIKMNNS NICKNAMES

ACEIKMRSV MAVERICKS

ACEIKNRST CRANKIEST

ACEIKNSST TACKINESS

ACEIKNSSW WACKINESS

ACEIKOPRT AIRPOCKET

ACEIKOPSS SKIASCOPE

ACEIKPPRS PIPE RACKS

ACEIKPRRT PERITRACK

ACEIKRSTW WATER-SICK

ACEILLLXY LEXICALLY

ACEILLMOP POLEMICAL

ACEILLMOT COLLIMATE, LOCAL TIME

ACEILLMSY MESICALLY

ACEILLNOR COLLINEAR, CORALLINE

ACEILLORS LOCALISER

ACEILLORZ LOCALIZER

ACEILLOST OSCILLATE

ACEILLOTV COLLATIVE

ACEILLPSY SPECIALLY

ACEILLRSV CAVILLERS

ACEILLRXY XERICALLY

ACEILMMST CLAMMIEST

ACEILMNNU LUMINANCE

ACEILMNOP POLICEMAN

ACEILMNOS COALMINES

ACEILMNRU NUMERICAL

ACEILMNSU CALUMNIES, MASCULINE

ACEILMNTU CULMINATE

ACEILMOPT PTOLEMAIC

ACEILMOSS CAMISOLES, COSEISMAL

ACEILMOSV SEMIVOCAL

ACEILMRRU MERCURIAL

ACEILNNOR CORNELIAN

ACEILNNOT OCTENNIAL

ACEILNNPS PINNACLES

ACEILNOPR PORCELAIN

ACEILNORS CENSORIAL

ACEILNOST COASTLINE, SECTIONAL

ACEILNOSV VOLCANISE

ACEILNOTU INOCULATE

ACEILNOVZ VOLCANIZE

ACEILNPTU INCULPATE

ACEILNRST CLARINETS, LARCENIST

ACEILNRTU CENTURIAL

ACEILNRTY CERTAINLY

ACEILNSSS SCALINESS

ACEILNSUV VULCANISE

ACEILNTUV VULCANITE

ACEILNUVZ VULCANIZE

ACEILOPPS EPISCOPAL

ACEILOPST SCAPOLITE

ACEILOQUV EQUIVOCAL

ACEILORRT RECTORIAL

ACEILORST SECTORIAL

ACEILORSV VOCALISER

ACEILORTV VECTORIAL

ACEILORVZ VOCALIZER

ACEILOTVY COEVALITY

ACEILPPPR PAPER CLIP

ACEILPRST PARTICLES

ACEILPSSS SLIPCASES

ACEILPSTU EUPLASTIC, SPICULATE

ACEILPSTY SPECIALTY

ACEILRSUV VESICULAR

ACEILRTUV LUCRATIVE

ACEILSSST CLASSIEST

ACEILTTUV CULTIVATE

ACEIMMNNY IMMANENCY

ACEIMNOPS COMPANIES

ACEIMNORT CREMATION

ACEIMNOST ENCOMIAST

ACEIMNOTX INCOME TAX

ACEIMNPTU PNEUMATIC

ACEIMNRST MISCREANT

ACEIMNRSU MANICURES, MUSCARINE

ACEIMNSST SEMANTICS

ACEIMNTYZ ENZYMATIC
ACEIMORVW
  MICROWAVE
ACEIMOSTU AUTOECISM
ACEIMPRST SPERMATIC
ACEIMPSST CAMPSITES
ACEIMRRSW WAR
  CRIMES
ACEINNNRU UNCANNIER
ACEINNNSS CANNINESS
ACEINNOOV
  NOVOCAINE
ACEINNORT CONTAINER,
  CRENATION
ACEINNOSS ASCENSION
ACEINNRSU INSURANCE
ACEINNRTU RUNCINATE,
  UNCERTAIN
ACEINNSST INCESSANT,
  INSTANCES
ACEINNSSU NUISANCES
ACEINOOST ISOOCTANE
ACEINOOTV EVOCATION
ACEINOPRT RECAPTION
ACEINOPSU PINACEOUS
ACEINORRV CARNIVORE
ACEINORSS SCENARIOS
ACEINORST CREATIONS,
  NARCOTISE, REACTIONS
ACEINORTT CARNOTITE
ACEINORTU
  COINTREAU
ACEINORTZ NARCOTIZE
ACEINOSST CANOEISTS,
  CESSATION
ACEINOSTU TENACIOUS
ACEINOSUV VINACEOUS
ACEINOTTY TO A
  NICETY
ACEINPRTT CREPITANT
ACEINPRUY PECUNIARY
ACEINPSSU PUISSANCE
ACEINPSTT PITTANCES
ACEINQTTU QUITTANCE
ACEINRRSW SCRAWNIER
ACEINRSST CANISTERS,
  SCENARIST
ACEINRSSZ CRAZINESS
ACEINRTTY CERTAINTY
ACEINRTUV INCURVATE
ACEINSSSU SAUCINESS
ACEINSSTT CATTINESS,
  SCANTIEST, TACITNESS
ACEINSTTY INTESTACY

ACEIOPRRS ACROSPIRE
ACEIOPRTV PROACTIVE
ACEIOPTTT PETTICOAT
ACEIORRSV CORRASIVE
ACEIORSST OSTRACISE
ACEIORSTZ OSTRACIZE
ACEIORSUV VERACIOUS
ACEIOSTUV VITACEOUS
ACEIOSTVV VOCATIVES
ACEIOSVVV VIVA VOCES
ACEIPPRRS SCRAPPIER
ACEIPPRST CRAPPIEST
ACEIPSSST ESCAPISTS
ACEIPSSTU SPACESUIT
ACEIQRTTU ACQUITTER
ACEIQSTUY SEQUACITY
ACEIRSSSU CUIRASSES
ACEIRSTTU RUSTICATE
ACEIRSTUV CURATIVES
ACEISSSTU SUITCASES
ACEISSTTT SCATTIEST
ACEISTTTY CITY-STATE
ACEJKKRSY SKYJACKER
ACEJKLMST JACKSMELT
ACEJLMSUU MAJUSCULE
ACEJLNQUY JACQUELYN
ACEKKMRRU
  MUCKRAKER
ACEKLLMMU
  MALLEMUCK
ACEKLNSSS SLACKNESS
ACEKLOPRW
  WORKPLACE
ACEKLRSST TRACKLESS
ACEKNNTTU
  NANTUCKET
ACEKNORSU CANKEROUS
ACEKOPRRT RETROPACK
ACEKPRSSU SAPSUCKER
ACEKRSTUW AWESTRUCK
ACELLLMOU
  COLUMELLA
ACELLLORS SOLAR CELL
ACELLMORU
  MOLECULAR
ACELLMRSU MARCELLUS
ACELLNORU NUCLEOLAR
ACELLNOTU LAUNCELOT
ACELLNRTY CENTRALLY
ACELLOPRS SCALLOPER
ACELLOPSS COLLAPSES
ACELLOQUY COEQUALLY
ACELLORSS SCLEROSAL
ACELLORSV COVERALLS

ACELLRSTU SCUTELLAR
ACELLSSSS CLASSLESS
ACELMMNOS
  COMMENSAL
ACELMMNSU
  MUSCLEMAN
ACELMNTUU
  TENACULUM
ACELMOPST ECTOPLASM
ACELMORSY CLAYMORES
ACELMOSUU
  ULMACEOUS
ACELMSSTU MUSCATELS
ACELNNOOR
  OLECRANON
ACELNOOSV VOLCANOES
ACELNOPRV PROVENCAL
ACELNORSU LARCENOUS
ACELNORTU
  NUCLEATOR, RECOUNTAL
ACELNOSTU CONSULATE
ACELNOSTY CLAYSTONE
ACELNRTTU RELUCTANT
ACELOOPRR
  CORPORALE, CORPOREAL
ACELOORTW WATER-
  COOL
ACELOOSTT COELOSTAT
ACELOPRRU OPERCULAR
ACELOPRTU PECULATOR
ACELOPSTU SCOPULATE
ACELORSSU CAROUSELS
ACELOSSTU CASSOULET,
  LOST CAUSE
ACELPPRRU CURLPAPER
ACELSSSTU CUTLASSES
ACEMMOTTU
  COMMUTATE
ACEMNOOPS
  MOONSCAPE
ACEMNOPSS ENCOMPASS
ACEMNORTU
  MUCRONATE
ACEMOOPSU
  POMACEOUS
ACEMOORSU
  MORACEOUS
ACEMOPSSS COMPASSES
ACEMORRSU SOUR
  CREAM
ACEMORRTY
  CREMATORY
ACEMORSSY SYCAMORES
ACEMOSSUU MUSACEOUS

ACEMOSTVY
VASECTOMY
ACEMPRSUY SUPREMACY
ACENNNORU
ANNOUNCER
ACENNOSTV
COVENANTS
ACENNSSST SCANTNESS
ACENOPRRT
COPARTNER, PROCREANT
ACENOPSTW
TOWNSCAPE
ACENOPSTY SYNCOPATE
ACENOPTYY CYANOTYPE
ACENORRTU
RACONTEUR
ACENORSST ANCESTORS
ACENORSTU COURTESAN
ACENORSUV CAVERNOUS
ACENORTUY
COURTENAY
ACENORUVV
VANCOUVER
ACENOSTUU CUTANEOUS
ACENPRRTY CARPENTRY
ACENPRSUU PURSUANCE
ACENPTTUU PUNCTUATE
ACENRSSSS CRASSNESS
ACENRSSTU RECUSANTS
ACENRSTUU CENTAURUS
ACEOOPRRT CORPORATE
ACEOOPRSS ASCOSPORE
ACEOORSSU ROSACEOUS
ACEOORSTV OVERCOATS
ACEOPPRST SPACEPORT
ACEOPRSTT SPECTATOR
ACEORRRTT
RETRACTOR
ACEORRRVY CARRY-
OVER
ACEORRSTU CRATEROUS,
EUROCRATS
ACEORRTTX
EXTRACTOR
ACEORSTTY ASTROCYTE
ACEORSTUU RUTACEOUS
ACEOSSTTU OUTCASTES
ACERRTUUV CURVATURE
ACFFIILOS OFFICIALS
ACFFIINOT OFFICIANT
ACFFIIORY OFFICIARY
ACFGHMORR
FROGMARCH
ACFGIIMNO MAGNIFICO

ACFGIINNN FINANCING
ACFGIINPY PACIFYING
ACFGINORT FACTORING
ACFGINOTU OUTFACING
ACFGINRSU SURFACING
ACFGIOSUU FUGACIOUS
ACFGLNORY
GYRFALCON
ACFHIILRT CHAIR LIFT
ACFHKORST ROCKSHAFT
ACFHLMRSU SCRUMHALF
ACFHLNORW HALF
CROWN
ACFHLORTW
FLOWCHART
ACFHORRST RH
FACTORS
ACFIILNOT FICTIONAL
ACFIIMNOR ACINIFORM
ACFIIOPRV VAPORIFIC
ACFIIPSST PACIFISTS
ACFIJKRTU JACKFRUIT
ACFIKNRSS SCARFSKIN
ACFILMORU FORMULAIC,
FUMAROLIC
ACFILNNOR FRANCOLIN
ACFILNOOT OLFACTION
ACFILNPPY FLIPPANCY
ACFILNPSU CUP FINALS
ACFILNRUU FUNICULAR
ACFIMORRY FORMICARY
ACFINORRT INFRACTOR
ACFINORST FRACTIONS
ACFINORTU FURCATION
ACFIOOPST IPSO FACTO
ACFIORSTU FRACTIOUS
ACFJKORST JACK FROST
ACFKLLORS ROCKFALLS
ACFKMRRTU TRUCK
FARM
ACFKNORWY
FANCYWORK
ACFKOORRS ROOF
RACKS
ACFLLTTUY TACTFULLY
ACFLMNOOR
CONFORMAL
ACFLNTTUU FLUCTUANT
ACFLOORST COLORFAST
ACFLOORTY OLFACTORY
ACGGGINRS SCRAGGING
ACGGIIMNR GRIMACING
ACGGIIOSS ISAGOGICS
ACGGILRSY SCRAGGILY

ACGHHHIIR HIGH CHAIR
ACGHHILSS HIGH-CLASS
ACGHHINOT
HOATCHING
ACGHHINTT THATCHING
ACGHIIJKN HIJACKING
ACGHIIKNN CHINKIANG
ACGHIIMNN MACHINING
ACGHIIPRT GRAPHITIC
ACGHIKLNS SHACKLING
ACGHIKNSW
WHACKINGS
ACGHIKNTW
THWACKING
ACGHILNNU LAUNCHING
ACGHILORY OLIGARCHY
ACGHIMOOP
OMOPHAGIC
ACGHINNOR
ANCHORING
ACGHINNST SNATCHING,
STANCHING
ACGHINPST NIGHTCAPS
ACGHINRST STARCHING
ACGHINSTY YACHTINGS
ACGHLMOOY
LOGOMACHY
ACGHMOPRY
CYMOGRAPH
ACGHORSTU
ROUGHCAST
ACGIIIMST IMAGISTIC
ACGIIKNNP PANICKING
ACGIILLLO ILLOGICAL
ACGIILLMS GALLICISM
ACGIILLNV CAVILLING
ACGIILLOR CIGARILLO
ACGIILMNS ANGLICISM
ACGIILMNX CLIMAXING
ACGIILNOS GASOLINIC,
LOGICIANS
ACGIILNRT ARTICLING
ACGIIMNPT IMPACTING
ACGIIMSTT STIGMATIC
ACGIINNOR INORGANIC
ACGIINOST AGONISTIC
ACGIINPSZ CAPSIZING
ACGIINQRU ACQUIRING
ACGIIORST ORGIASTIC
ACGIIRSTT GASTRITIC
ACGIKNNPU
UNPACKING
ACGILLLOY LOGICALLY
ACGILLLRS CALL GIRLS

ACGILLNOR CAROLLING,
  COLLARING
ACGILLNOT COLLATING
ACGILLOOO OOLOGICAL
ACGILLOST COLLAGIST
ACGILMNOR
  CLAMORING
ACGILNNST SCANTLING
ACGILNOST NOSTALGIC
ACGILNOXY COAXINGLY
ACGILNRSW SCRAWLING
ACGILNRSY SCARINGLY
ACGIMMNRS
  SCRAMMING
ACGIMNNOR
  ROMANCING
ACGIMNOOR
  AGRONOMIC
ACGIMNOPR
  COMPARING
ACGIMNORR
  CAIRNGORM
ACGIMNOTU
  CONTAGIUM
ACGIMNSTY
  GYMNASTIC, NYSTAGMIC
ACGIMNUUV
  VACUUMING
ACGIMOTYZ
  ZYGOMATIC
ACGINNNNO
  CANNONING
ACGINNOOT
  COGNATION, CONTAGION
ACGINNOPY POIGNANCY
ACGINNORY CRAYONING
ACGINNOTZ
  COGNIZANT
ACGINORSU CAROUSING
ACGINORTV
  CAVORTING
ACGINOSST AGNOSTICS
ACGINPPRS SCRAPPING
ACGINPRSS SCRAPINGS
ACGINPRTU CAPTURING
ACGINPTUY PUGNACITY
ACGIOORTT COGITATOR
ACGJNNOTU
  CONJUGANT
ACGLOOPRY
  CARPOLOGY
ACGLOOSTY SCATOLOGY
ACGMOPRTY
  CRYPTOGAM

ACGORRSUY
  SURROGACY
ACHHILORT HAIRCLOTH
ACHHINNOT
  CHTHONIAN
ACHHINSTY HYACINTHS
ACHHIPRSU PUSHCHAIR
ACHHLOSTU SLOUCH
  HAT
ACHHLOSTW
  WASHCLOTH
ACHHOSSTW CHAT
  SHOWS
ACHIILMSW WHIMSICAL
ACHIIMNST MACHINIST
ACHIINPSY PHYSICIAN
ACHIINRST CHRISTIAN,
  CHRISTINA
ACHIIOPST PISTACHIO
ACHIIPRSV VICARSHIP
ACHIIRRTT ARTHRITIC
ACHIIRSTV ARCHIVIST
ACHIKLPTU CHALK IT UP
ACHIKRSSW RICKSHAWS
ACHIKRSTT HAT TRICKS
ACHILLMSU MUSIC HALL
ACHILLOST SAILCLOTH
ACHILLSTY CITY HALLS
ACHILMPTY ITCHY
  PALM, LYMPHATIC
ACHILNORT ANTICHLOR
ACHILNRUY RAUNCHILY
ACHILNSTY SNATCHILY
ACHILOPTU PATCHOULI
ACHILORTV ARCHIVOLT
ACHILOSST SCHOLIAST
ACHILPSSY PHYSICALS
ACHILRSSY CHRYSALIS
ACHILRSTY STARCHILY
ACHIMMNOS
  MONACHISM
ACHIMMOSS
  MASOCHISM
ACHIMNOPS CHAMPIONS
ACHIMNORS
  HARMONICS
ACHIMNORT
  CHROMATIN
ACHIMOOTX
  HOMOTAXIC
ACHIMORST RHOTACISM
ACHIMOSST MASOCHIST
ACHIMOSTU MUSTACHIO
ACHIMRSST CHRISTMAS

ACHIMRSSW SCRIMSHAW
ACHINNOST STANCHION
ACHINNOTW
  CHINATOWN
ACHINOPPS PANSOPHIC
ACHINPRST CHINSTRAP
ACHIOOPST SOCIOPATH
ACHIOPPRS HIPPOCRAS
ACHIORSTT RHOTACIST
ACHIPRSUY HARUSPICY
ACHKLNOOS
  SOLONCHAK
ACHKMORTU
  TOUCHMARK
ACHKOPRTW
  PATCHWORK
ACHKORRXY ROCK
  HYRAX
ACHLLORSY SCHOLARLY
ACHLMSTYZ
  SCHMALTZY
ACHLNSTUY STAUNCHLY
ACHLOOSTU
  HOLOCAUST
ACHNOPSTY SYCOPHANT
ACHOPSTTW
  STOPWATCH
ACHORSSST TROSSACHS
ACHORTTTU
  CUTTHROAT
ACHPRSSTU PUSHCARTS
ACIIILNOT CILIATION
ACIIILNSV CIVILIANS
ACIIIMNST ANIMISTIC
ACIIIMNTV VITAMINIC
ACIIINPST PIANISTIC
ACIIJRSTU JUSTICIAR
ACIIKMNRT MINITRACK
ACIILLNOS COLLINSIA,
  ISOCLINAL
ACIILLNST SCINTILLA
ACIILLOPT POLITICAL
ACIILLPRS PRISCILLA
ACIILMNPU MUNICIPAL
ACIILMNRS CRIMINALS
ACIILMNSV CALVINISM
ACIILMNTY MILITANCY
ACIILMOSS SOCIALISM
ACIILMOSU MALICIOUS
ACIILMQTU QUITCLAIM
ACIILNNOT CLINTONIA
ACIILNOOT COALITION
ACIILNOPT PLICATION
ACIILNOVV CONVIVIAL

ACIILNOVY INVIOLACY
ACIILNPPR PRINCIPAL
ACIILNRSU INCISURAL
ACIILNSTV CALVINIST
ACIILOPRT PICTORIAL
ACIILORST SORITICAL
ACIILORTZ TRIAZOLIC
ACIILOSST SOCIALIST
ACIILOSTY SOCIALITY
ACIILQUZZ QUIZZICAL
ACIILRSVW CIVIL WARS
ACIILTTTY TACTILITY
ACIIMMNOT
  AMMONITIC
ACIIMNNOS INSOMNIAC
ACIIMNNOT
  ANTIMONIC, ANTINOMIC
ACIIMNOPT IMPACTION
ACIIMNORT MORTICIAN
ACIIMNSSU MUSICIANS
ACIIMOPST SIMPATICO
ACIIMORTT TRIATOMIC
ACIIMOSST MOSAICIST
ACIIMOSTT ATOMISTIC
ACIIMOTTY ATOMICITY
ACIIMPRST PRISMATIC
ACIIMPSSS SIC PASSIM
ACIIMRSST SCIMITARS
ACIINNOTU INCAUTION
ACIINOPST OPTICIANS
ACIINORTV VICTORIAN
ACIINOSTT CITATIONS
ACIINOTTX ANTITOXIC
ACIINOTTY ATONICITY
ACIIOPRST PSORIATIC
ACIIOPRTT PATRIOTIC
ACIIOPTZZ PIZZICATO
ACIIORSSV VARICOSIS
ACIIORSTY CARIOSITY
ACIIORSUV VICARIOUS
ACIIOSSTT ISOSTATIC
ACIIOSUVV VIVACIOUS
ACIIPRSTT PATRISTIC
ACIIPTTVY CAPTIVITY
ACIISSTTT STATISTIC
ACIISSTTV ACTIVISTS
ACIJKNNOU UNION JACK
ACIKKNNOT ANTIKNOCK
ACIKLLSST SALTLICKS
ACIKLMSTU MAULSTICK
ACIKLOSTT TAILSTOCK
ACIKLPSST SLAPSTICK
ACIKOPSSY SKIASCOPY
ACIKRSTTU TRACKSUIT

ACILLLOUV COLLUVIAL
ACILLLRYY LYRICALLY
ACILLMSUY MUSICALLY
ACILLNNSY SYNCLINAL
ACILLNOOS COLONIALS
ACILLNOOT COLLATION
ACILLNORS CARILLONS
ACILLNOSS SCALLIONS
ACILLOPTY OPTICALLY,
  TOPICALLY
ACILLORST CLOISTRAL
ACILLORYZ ZIRCALLOY
ACILLOSTY CALLOSITY,
  STOICALLY
ACILLOTXY TOXICALLY
ACILLPTYY TYPICALLY
ACILMMOTT
  COMMITTAL
ACILMNNTU
  CULMINANT
ACILMNOPT COMPLAINT,
  COMPLIANT
ACILMNOSV VOLCANISM
ACILMNSUU UNMUSICAL
ACILMOPRS COMPRISAL
ACILMPTUU CAPITULUM
ACILNNNUY UNCANNILY
ACILNNOTU
  CONTINUAL
ACILNNQTU CLINQUANT
ACILNOOST LOCATIONS
ACILNOPRT PROLACTIN
ACILNORST CONTRAILS
ACILNOSTT CLINOSTAT
ACILNOSTU SUCTIONAL,
  SULCATION
ACILNPTUY UNTYPICAL
ACILNRSWY SCRAWNILY
ACILOOPRS ACROPOLIS
ACILOOPST APOSTOLIC
ACILOORST CASTOR OIL
ACILOQTUY LOQUACITY
ACILORRSU CURSORIAL
ACILORSSU OSSICULAR
ACILORSTU SUCTORIAL
ACILOSSTV VOCALISTS
ACILOTTUY AUTOLYTIC
ACILPPRSY SCRAPPILY
ACILPSTTY STYPTICAL
ACILRRTUU UTRICULAR
ACILSSTTY SYSTALTIC
ACIMMNOOT
  MONATOMIC
ACIMMORSS COMMISSAR

ACIMNNOOP
  COMPANION
ACIMNOOST
  ONOMASTIC
ACIMNOOTU
  AUTONOMIC
ACIMNOOTX
  TAXONOMIC
ACIMNOPRY PARONYMIC
ACIMNORST
  NARCOTISM, ROMANTICS
ACIMNOSUU
  ACUMINOUS
ACIMOOTTU
  AUTOTOMIC
ACIMOPSSY SYMPOSIAC
ACIMORSST OSTRACISM
ACIMORSTT STROMATIC
ACIMPRSTY SYMPATRIC
ACIMRSTTU STRUMATIC
ACINNORST CONSTRAIN,
  TRANSONIC
ACINNOSST SANCTIONS
ACINOORRS CORRASION
ACINOORST CONSORTIA
ACINOOSTV VOCATIONS
ACINORSST CROISSANT
ACINORSTY CRAYONIST
ACINOSSTW WAINSCOTS
ACINOSTTU SCUTATION
ACINRSSSU NARCISSUS
ACIOOPRSU PAROICOUS
ACIOOPRSZ SAPROZOIC
ACIOORSTU ATROCIOUS
ACIOORSUV VORACIOUS
ACIOOSTUU AUTOICOUS
ACIOOTTUX AUTOTOXIC
ACIOPRSSY CARYOPSIS
ACIOPRSTT PROSTATIC
ACIOPTTUY AUTOTYPIC
ACIRSSTUY CASUISTRY
ACJKOPRST JOCKSTRAP
ACJLLORUY JOCULARLY
ACKKMOPRS
  POCKMARKS
ACKLLNRTU TRUNK
  CALL
ACKLLPSSU SKULLCAPS
ACKLMOOOR
  CLOAKROOM
ACKLNOPRT ROCK
  PLANT
ACKLNORST CORNSTALK
ACKLORSST CROSS TALK

ACKLORSSW CROSSWALK
ACLLLLORS ROLL CALLS
ACLLLOSUY CALLOUSLY
ACLLMNOSU
  MOLLUSCAN
ACLLOORRY COROLLARY
ACLLOORST COLOSTRAL
ACLMMNOOW
  COMMON-LAW
ACLMNOORU
  MONOCULAR
ACLMOORSS
  CLASSROOM
ACLMOORSU
  CLAMOROUS
ACLMOPSTY CYTOPLASM
ACLNNORTU
  NOCTURNAL
ACLNOORTT
  CONTRALTO
ACLOOORRT
  CORALROOT
ACLOOPRRS CORPORALS
ACLOPPRYY POLYCARPY
ACLOPRRSW PROWL
  CARS
ACLOPRSUU CRAPULOUS
ACLOPRTTU PLUTOCRAT
ACLOPSTTY CYTOPLAST
ACLORSUUY RAUCOUSLY
ACLOSUUVY VACUOUSLY
ACMNOORRT
  CORMORANT
ACMNOOSTU
  COSMONAUT
ACMNOPRYY
  PYROMANCY
ACMOORRST
  MOTORCARS
ACMORRSUU
  MACRUROUS
ACMORSSTW WORM
  CASTS
ACMORSTUY
  CUSTOMARY
ACNNNOOST
  CONSONANT
ACNNOSSTT CONSTANTS
ACNOOPRST CORPOSANT
ACNOORRSU
  RANCOROUS
ACNORSSTT CONTRASTS
ACNORSTTU
  TURNCOATS

ACNORSTTY
  CONTRASTY
ACOOPPRRS SPOROCARP
ACOORSSTU AUTOCROSS
ACOPRRSST SPORTS CAR
ACOSSTTTY STATOCYST
ADDDEEEHR RED-
  HEADED
ADDDEEFRU DEFRAUDED
ADDDEEGLN
  GLADDENED
ADDDEEHNR RED-
  HANDED
ADDDEEKLS SKEDADDLE
ADDDEERSS ADDRESSED
ADDDEFIIN DANDIFIED
ADDDEGLOP DOG
  PADDLE
ADDDEIINS DISDAINED
ADDDEISSU DISSUADED
ADDDELNSU UNSADDLED
ADDDELRST STRADDLED
ADDEEEFRT FEDERATED
ADDEEEGLT DELEGATED
ADDEEEGRY DEGREE-
  DAY
ADDEEEMNR
  MEANDERED
ADDEEENRS SERENADED
ADDEEERRT RETREADED
ADDEEERSS ADDRESSEE
ADDEEFHIX FIXED-HEAD
ADDEEFILN ENFILADED
ADDEEFLTU DEFAULTED
ADDEEFNNT DEFENDANT
ADDEEFNSS FADEDNESS
ADDEEFRRU DEFRAUDER
ADDEEGHIP PIGHEADED
ADDEEGILM MIDDLE AGE
ADDEEGINN DEADENING
ADDEEGIRS DISAGREED
ADDEEGLNR
  GLADDENER, GLANDERED
ADDEEGNSW SAND
  WEDGE
ADDEEGORT
  DEROGATED
ADDEEHHOT
  HOTHEADED
ADDEEHILN HEADLINED
ADDEEHRSS HEADDRESS
ADDEEHRTY DEHYDRATE
ADDEEIILS IDEALISED
ADDEEIILZ IDEALIZED

ADDEEILNS DEADLINES
ADDEEILRV DAREDEVIL
ADDEEILST DEADLIEST
ADDEEIMTT MEDITATED
ADDEEINRT DETRAINED
ADDEEIPRR DRAPERIED
ADDEEIPRS DESPAIRED
ADDEELNRS SLANDERED
ADDEELNRU LAUNDERED
ADDEELOST DESOLATED
ADDEEMNOS
  DESDEMONA
ADDEEMNRU
  MAUNDERED
ADDEEMNST
  DAMNEDEST
ADDEEMORT
  MODERATED
ADDEEMPST STAMPEDED
ADDEENNPT DEPENDANT
ADDEENOST STONE-
  DEAD
ADDEENOTT
  DETONATED
ADDEENSST DATEDNESS
ADDEENSWY
  WEDNESDAY
ADDEEOPRS DESPERADO
ADDEEPRSU PERSUADED
ADDEEPSUX PAS DE DEUX
ADDEERRSS ADDRESSER,
  READDRESS
ADDEERSSS ADDRESSES
ADDEFFHNO
  OFFHANDED
ADDEFFLOO OFF-
  LOADED
ADDEFIIPT PEDATIFID
ADDEFILSY FIELD DAYS
ADDEFINNR FERDINAND
ADDEFINSS FADDINESS
ADDEFORRW
  FORWARDED
ADDEGGINR DEGRADING
ADDEGGOOT DOG-EAT-
  DOG
ADDEGHILR HILDEGARD
ADDEGHILT DEADLIGHT
ADDEGHINR HAG-
  RIDDEN
ADDEGILNR LADDERING
ADDEGIMNN
  DEMANDING,
  MADDENING

ADDEGINNS SADDENING
ADDEGINOS DIAGNOSED
ADDEGIRRS DISREGARD
ADDEGLLMO GOLD
  MEDAL
ADDEGLRUY
  GUARDEDLY
ADDEGNOOR
  DRAGOONED,
  GADROONED
ADDEGNORW
  DOWNGRADE
ADDEGNRUU
  UNGUARDED
ADDEHHOTY
  HYDATHODE
ADDEHILOY HOLIDAYED
ADDEHINRY ANHYDRIDE
ADDEHINSW HEADWINDS
ADDEHINSY HENDIADYS
ADDEHNNRU
  UNDERHAND
ADDEHNORS HARD-
  NOSED
ADDEHNORU
  ROUNDHEAD
ADDEHNOTW TWO-
  HANDED
ADDEHORSW
  HEADWORDS
ADDEHTTUY DEATH
  DUTY
ADDEIIIMT DIMIDIATE
ADDEIILNV INVALIDED
ADDEIILNX DIXIELAND
ADDEIIMNS DESMIDIAN
ADDEIINNR RED INDIAN
ADDEIISTV ADDITIVES
ADDEIKNPP KIDNAPPED
ADDEILLNS LANDSLIDE
ADDEILMMN
  MIDDLEMAN
ADDEILNNO DANDELION
ADDEILNSY DEADLY SIN
ADDEILPSY DISPLAYED
ADDEILSVY ADVISEDLY
ADDEIMNOT
  DEMANTOID,
  DOMINATED
ADDEIMNSY MANY-
  SIDED
ADDEIMNTY
  DYNAMITED
ADDEIMORT DERMATOID

ADDEIMSST DISMASTED
ADDEINNTU INUNDATED
ADDEINPRU UNDERPAID
ADDEINRTT DITTANDER
ADDEINRTW TRADE
  WIND
ADDEINSUV UNADVISED
ADDEIOSVW DISAVOWED
ADDEIRSSU DISSUADER
ADDEIRSSW SIDEWARDS
ADDEJNORU ADJOURNED
ADDELLOPR
  POLLARDED
ADDELMOTU
  MODULATED
ADDELNTUU
  UNDULATED
ADDELRRST STRADDLER
ADDEMORRY
  DROMEDARY
ADDENNRTU
  REDUNDANT
ADDENNSSU SAND
  DUNES
ADDENNTUU
  UNDAUNTED
ADDENOORT
  DEODORANT
ADDENOPTU
  UNADOPTED
ADDENORUY
  DUODENARY
ADDENOSTU
  ASTOUNDED
ADDEOPSTT POSTDATED
ADDEPPRSU SUPPERADD
ADDEPQRUU
  QUADRUPED
ADDFFILOS DAFFODILS
ADDFHILSY FADDISHLY
ADDFIIQRU QUADRIFID
ADDGGIJNU ADJUDGING
ADDGHNORU
  DRAGHOUND
ADDGILNSW SWADDLING
ADDGMRSUU
  MUDGUARDS
ADDHHIOOR
  HARDIHOOD
ADDHIKNRR HARD
  DRINK
ADDHIKRSS HARD DISKS
ADDHNNOSW HANDS
  DOWN

ADDHOORSW
  HARDWOODS
ADDIINOST ADDITIONS
ADDINORSU DIANDROUS
ADDIOPRTY ODD PARITY
ADDIORRST DIRT ROADS
ADDKNRRSU
  DRUNKARDS
ADDLLNORS LANDLORDS
ADDLNNOOP
  PONDOLAND
ADDMNOOTU ODD
  MAN OUT
ADDNNOPUW UP-AND-
  DOWN
ADDNORSWW
  DOWNWARDS
ADEEEEGLY EAGLE-EYED
ADEEEFHRT FEATHERED
ADEEEFLLT LEAFLETED
ADEEEFNRR REFERENDA
ADEEEFRRT FREE TRADE
ADEEEGHNR
  GREENHEAD
ADEEEGLRT RELEGATED
ADEEEGLST DELEGATES
ADEEEGNRS RENEGADES
ADEEEGNRT GENERATED
ADEEEGTTV VEGETATED
ADEEEHHRT HEATHERED
ADEEEHKNR
  HEARKENED
ADEEEHLST STEELHEAD
ADEEEHNRT HEARTENED
ADEEEHPRT PREHEATED
ADEEEHRRS REHEARSED
ADEEEHRTW
  WEATHERED
ADEEEILMN MADELEINE
ADEEEILNT DELINEATE
ADEEEINRS DEANERIES
ADEEEINST DETAINEES
ADEEEIRSS DIAERESES
ADEEEKKNW WEAK-
  KNEED
ADEEELLMN ENAMELLED
ADEEELLNS LEND-LEASE
ADEEELMNP EMPANELED
ADEEELNRZ ZEELANDER
ADEEELPRR REPLEADER
ADEEEMNRR
  MEANDERER
ADEEEMPRT PERMEATED
ADEEENRRS SERENADER

ADEEENRSS SERENADES
ADEEENRST EAST ENDER
ADEEENRTT ENTREATED
ADEEENRTV ENERVATED,
 VENERATED
ADEEEPRST DESPERATE
ADEEERRTT RETREATED
ADEEERTWW
 WATERWEED
ADEEFFILR FIELDFARE
ADEEFFLOT FLOAT-FEED
ADEEFGINN DEAFENING
ADEEFGINT DEFEATING
ADEEFHORS FOREHEADS
ADEEFIKRR FREDERIKA
ADEEFILNS ENFILADES
ADEEFILOT DEFOLIATE
ADEEFILSU FEUDALISE
ADEEFILUZ FEUDALIZE
ADEEFIMST DEFEATISM
ADEEFINRR REFRAINED
ADEEFISTT DEFEATIST
ADEEFLLNN FLANNELED
ADEEFLLST STALL-FEED
ADEEFLNTT FLATTENED
ADEEFLRTT FLATTERED
ADEEFLRTU DEFAULTER
ADEEFMNOR
 FORENAMED
ADEEFMORR
 FOREARMED
ADEEFMSTU DEAF-MUTES
ADEEFNOST STONE-
 DEAF
ADEEGGINS DISENGAGE
ADEEGGIRV AGGRIEVED
ADEEGGLNO GOLDEN
 AGE
ADEEGGMOU
 DEMAGOGUE
ADEEGGOPU PEDAGOGUE
ADEEGGRST STAGGERED
ADEEGGRSW
 SWAGGERED
ADEEGILLR GALLERIED
ADEEGILLS LEGALISED
ADEEGILLZ LEGALIZED
ADEEGILNR GERALDINE,
 REALIGNED
ADEEGILNW WIDE-
 ANGLE
ADEEGIMNN
 DEMEANING
ADEEGIMRT EMIGRATED

ADEEGINNR ENDEARING,
 GRENADINE
ADEEGINRR GRENADIER
ADEEGINRT DENIGRATE
ADEEGINST DESIGNATE
ADEEGINSV ENVISAGED
ADEEGINTV NEGATIVED
ADEEGIRST TRAGEDIES
ADEEGIUVW WAVEGUIDE
ADEEGLLLY ALLEGEDLY
ADEEGLLRV GRAVELLED
ADEEGLNNR
 GREENLAND
ADEEGLNNT
 ENTANGLED
ADEEGLNOT
 ELONGATED
ADEEGLNRY ENRAGEDLY,
 LEGENDARY
ADEEGLOOW
 EAGLEWOOD
ADEEGLRTU REGULATED
ADEEGMNRR
 GERMANDER
ADEEGMNRS
 GENDARMES
ADEEGMNTU
 AUGMENTED
ADEEGMRRU
 DEMURRAGE
ADEEGNNRS GREENSAND
ADEEGNRRS GARDENERS
ADEEGNRST ESTRANGED
ADEEGNRSU DUNGAREES
ADEEGORRZ RAZOR
 EDGE
ADEEGRRSS DEERGRASS
ADEEHIISV HEAVISIDE
ADEEHIKLT DEATHLIKE
ADEEHILNR HEADLINER
ADEEHILNS HEADLINES
ADEEHILNT ETHELINDA
ADEEHILTW WHITE
 DEAL, WHITE LEAD
ADEEHIMNV MIDHEAVEN
ADEEHINRT HERNIATED
ADEEHINSS HEADINESS
ADEEHIRRV RIVERHEAD
ADEEHISSV ADHESIVES
ADEEHISTT HESITATED
ADEEHLLOS LEASEHOLD
ADEEHLNSU UNLEASHED
ADEEHLOSU HEAD LOUSE
ADEEHLSST DEATHLESS

ADEEHMNOT
 METHADONE
ADEEHMOST
 HOMESTEAD
ADEEHNOST HEADSTONE
ADEEHNPPR APPREHEND
ADEEHNPRS SHARPENED
ADEEHNRSS HARNESSED
ADEEHNRST ADHERENTS
ADEEHNRTU
 UNEARTHED
ADEEHORRV
 OVERHEARD
ADEEHORSV OVERHEADS
ADEEHOSWY EYE
 SHADOW
ADEEHPRRS REPHRASED
ADEEHPRSY SHARP-EYED
ADEEHRSST HEADRESTS
ADEEHRSTT SHATTERED
ADEEHRSTV HARVESTED
ADEEHRSTW WATERSHED
ADEEHSTUX EXHAUSTED
ADEEIILRS IDEALISER
ADEEIILRZ IDEALIZER
ADEEIIMMT IMMEDIATE
ADEEIIMST MEDIATISE
ADEEIIMTV MEDIATIVE
ADEEIIMTZ MEDIATIZE
ADEEIIRSS DIAERESIS
ADEEIJMRS JEREMIADS
ADEEIKLMR DREAMLIKE
ADEEILMNN
 MENDELIAN
ADEEILMNS LADIES'
 MEN, MÉLISANDE
ADEEILMPR EPIDERMAL,
 IMPLEADER
ADEEILMRS MISDEALER,
 MISLEADER
ADEEILMST LEAD TIMES
ADEEILNPS PENALISED
ADEEILNPX EXPLAINED
ADEEILNPZ PENALIZED
ADEEILNST DATELINES
ADEEILOTT ETIOLATED
ADEEILPRR LIP-READER
ADEEILPRS PEARLISED
ADEEILPRV PREVAILED
ADEEILPRZ PEARLIZED
ADEEILPSS DISPLEASE
ADEEILQSU EQUALISED
ADEEILQUZ EQUALIZED
ADEEILTTV LEVITATED

ADEEIMNNO
MENADIONE
ADEEIMNOU
EUDEMONIA
ADEEIMNRR REMAINDER
ADEEIMNRT MINARETED
ADEEIMPPR PIPE DREAM
ADEEIMRRR REMARRIED
ADEEIMRST DIAMETERS
ADEEIMSST DEMITASSE
ADEEIMSTT ESTIMATED
ADEEINNOS ADENOSINE
ADEEINNRT ENTRAINED
ADEEINPRT PERTAINED
ADEEINPST NEAP TIDES
ADEEINRSS READINESS
ADEEINRST RESINATED
ADEEINRTT DENITRATE
ADEEINRUW UNWEARIED
ADEEINTVV ADVENTIVE
ADEEIOPRT PERIODATE
ADEEIOPTV VIDEOTAPE
ADEEIPPST PEPTIDASE
ADEEIPRRS DRAPERIES
ADEEIPRTU REPUDIATE
ADEEIRRST DREARIEST
ADEEIRSTV ADVERTISE
ADEEIRSTW WATERSIDE
ADEEIRTTW TIDEWATER
ADEEIRTTX EXTRADITE
ADEEISSTT STATESIDE,
STEADIEST
ADEEISSTV SEDATIVES
ADEEITUVX EXUDATIVE
ADEEKNNSS NAKEDNESS
ADEEKNRTU UNDERTAKE
ADEELLMRV MARVELLED
ADEELLNRY LEARNEDLY
ADEELLPSY PLEASEDLY
ADEELLRTV TRAVELLED
ADEELLRXY RELAXEDLY
ADEELLTXY EXALTEDLY
ADEELMRSS DREAMLESS
ADEELNNRU
UNLEARNED
ADEELNORS OLEANDERS
ADEELNORV OVERLADEN
ADEELNOST ENDOSTEAL
ADEELNQUU
UNEQUALED
ADEELNRRS SLANDERER
ADEELNRRU LAUNDERER
ADEELNRSU UNDERSEAL
ADEELNRTU UNRELATED

ADEELNRUV UNRAVELED
ADEELORST DESOLATER
ADEELORTT TOLERATED
ADEELPRST PLASTERED
ADEELPSST PEDESTALS
ADEELQRRU QUARRELED
ADEELRRST RED ALERTS
ADEELRRTT RED RATTLE
ADEELRRTU ADULTERER
ADEELRSTY STEELYARD
ADEELRSVY ADVERSELY
ADEEMMNNT
AMENDMENT
ADEEMMORT
DERMATOME
ADEEMMOXY
MYXOEDEMA
ADEEMMRST
STAMMERED
ADEEMNOPR
PROMENADE
ADEEMNORS
DEMEANORS
ADEEMNORT
EMENDATOR
ADEEMNORU
DEMEANOUR,
ENAMOURED
ADEEMNRRU
MAUNDERER
ADEEMNRST
SMARTENED, TRADESMEN
ADEEMNRTY
DYNAMETER
ADEEMOORR
AERODROME
ADEEMOPRR
MADREPORE
ADEEMORRX
XERODERMA
ADEEMORST
MODERATES
ADEEMORTT
TREMATODE
ADEEMOSTU
EDEMATOUS
ADEEMPRST STAMPEDER
ADEEMPSST STAMPEDES
ADEEMPSTU DESPUMATE,
STEAMED-UP
ADEEMPTTT ATTEMPTED
ADEEMRSTW WET
DREAMS
ADEENNPRT TREPANNED

ADEENORST RESONATED
ADEENORSV ENDEAVORS
ADEENORTV
RENOVATED
ADEENORUV
ENDEAVOUR
ADEENORVY OVEN-
READY
ADEENPPRT ENTRAPPED
ADEENPRRT PARTNERED
ADEENPRTT PATTERNED
ADEENRRSW
WANDERERS
ADEENRRTU UNDERRATE
ADEENRRUW
UNDERWEAR
ADEENRSTU SAUNTERED
ADEENRSTY SEDENTARY
ADEENRTTU UNTREATED
ADEENRTUV
ADVENTURE
ADEENSTTV VENDETTAS
ADEEOPRSV EAVESDROP
ADEEORRTV
OVERRATED, OVERTRADE
ADEEORTVX OVERTAXED
ADEEPPRSS APPRESSED
ADEEPPRST SPEED TRAP
ADEEPRRSU PERSUADER
ADEEPRRTU DEPARTURE
ADEEPRSST PEDERASTS
ADEEPRSTT SPATTERED
ADEEPRSTU DEPASTURE
ADEEPRSTY PEDERASTY
ADEEPSSWY SPEEDWAYS
ADEEQRRTU QUARTERED
ADEERRSSU REASSURED
ADEERRSTU TREASURED
ADEERRSTV TRAVERSED
ADEERSTYY YESTERDAY
ADEFFIILS FALSIFIED
ADEFFNORT AFFRONTED
ADEFFORST TRADE-OFFS
ADEFGHORT
GODFATHER
ADEFGIIMN MAGNIFIED
ADEFGIIRT GRATIFIED
ADEFGILNT DEFLATING
ADEFGILRU LIFEGUARD
ADEFGIMTU FUMIGATED
ADEFGINRY DEFRAYING
ADEFGIRRU FIREGUARD
ADEFGLOOT FLOODGATE
ADEFGLRRU REGARDFUL

ADEFHIMST HAM-FISTED
ADEFHINOS FASHIONED
ADEFHINRT THREADFIN
ADEFHIPSS SPADEFISH
ADEFHIRST HEADFIRST
ADEFHLOOS FALSEHOOD
ADEFHNORS FOREHANDS
ADEFHNORU UNHEARD-
 OF
ADEFIILMP AMPLIFIED
ADEFIILNS FINALISED
ADEFIILNZ FINALIZED
ADEFIILQU QUALIFIED
ADEFIILRS AIRFIELDS
ADEFIILRT AIRLIFTED
ADEFIIPRR RAPID-FIRE
ADEFIISST SATISFIED
ADEFIKNRW DRAWKNIFE
ADEFILLSU FUSILLADE
ADEFILMNS FIELDSMAN
ADEFILMSU FEUDALISM
ADEFILNOT DEFLATION,
 DEFOLIANT
ADEFILNRS FRIESLAND
ADEFILNSS SAND FLIES
ADEFILNTY DEFIANTLY
ADEFILORT FLORIATED
ADEFILSTU FEUDALIST
ADEFILTUY FEUDALITY
ADEFIMORS ASIDE FROM
ADEFINOST INSTEAD OF
ADEFIRSTT DRAFTIEST
ADEFIRSTX FIXED STAR
ADEFLLMOS OLD FLAMES
ADEFLLMOU LEAF
 MOULD
ADEFLLMSY DAMSELFLY
ADEFLMMOR
 MALFORMED
ADEFLOPST SOFT-PEDAL
ADEFLORUV FLAVOURED
ADEFLORWY
 DAYFLOWER
ADEFLRSTW LEFTWARDS
ADEFMNNTU
 FUNDAMENT
ADEFMNRST DRAFTSMEN
ADEFMOORR
 DOORFRAME
ADEFMORTT
 FORMATTED
ADEFOOPRR PROOFREAD
ADEFOOTTU OUT-OF-
 DATE

ADEFORRRW
 FORWARDER
ADEFORRTV OVERDRAFT
ADEFORRTW
 AFTERWORD
ADEFORTUY FEUDATORY
ADEGGGIZZ ZIGZAGGED
ADEGGHHIR HIGH-
 GRADE
ADEGGINNR GARDENING
ADEGGINRR REGARDING
ADEGGINUW WIND
 GAUGE
ADEGGIRST DRAGGIEST
ADEGGLORY
 GARGOYLED
ADEGGLRST STRAGGLED
ADEGGMORT
 MORTGAGED
ADEGGNORU
 GROUNDAGE
ADEGHHILT HEADLIGHT
ADEGHHOSS HOGSHEADS
ADEGHILNR HERALDING
ADEGHINNR
 HARDENING
ADEGHINRS GARNISHED
ADEGHINRT THREADING
ADEGHINSU ANGUISHED
ADEGHIRST SIGHT-READ
ADEGHLLNO
 HELGOLAND
ADEGHLMPU
 GALUMPHED
ADEGHLORS GASHOLDER
ADEGHMORU HOME
 GUARD
ADEGHNOPR HOP
 GARDEN
ADEGHNOUZ
 GAZEHOUND
ADEGHORST
 GOATHERDS
ADEGHRRTU
 DRAUGHTER
ADEGHRSTU DAUGHTERS
ADEGIILNR DERAILING,
 GRINDELIA
ADEGIILNT DETAILING
ADEGIILOS DIALOGISE
ADEGIILOZ DIALOGIZE
ADEGIILPT PIGTAILED
ADEGIILTT LITIGATED
ADEGIIMNT MEDIATING

ADEGIIMTT MITIGATED
ADEGIINNR INGRAINED
ADEGIINNT DETAINING
ADEGIINNU GUANIDINE
ADEGIINTV DEVIATING
ADEGIIRRT IRRIGATED
ADEGIKNNR DARKENING
ADEGILLNP PEDALLING
ADEGILLNS SIGNALLED
ADEGILNNR LENINGRAD
ADEGILNOR GIRANDOLE,
 RELOADING
ADEGILNOS ALONGSIDE
ADEGILNPS PLEADINGS
ADEGILNRU GERUNDIAL
ADEGILNUV DEVALUING
ADEGILNVY EVADINGLY
ADEGILORU DIALOGUER
ADEGILOSU DIALOGUES
ADEGILRSS GLISSADER
ADEGIMNNP
 DAMPENING
ADEGIMNNR
 REMANDING
ADEGIMNTU
 MAGNITUDE
ADEGIMORS IDEOGRAMS
ADEGIMOST DOGMATISE
ADEGIMOTZ
 DOGMATIZE
ADEGINNPP APPENDING
ADEGINNPR PANDERING
ADEGINNPX EXPANDING
ADEGINNRT INTEGRAND
ADEGINNRW
 WANDERING
ADEGINNTT ATTENDING
ADEGINORR RIO
 GRANDE
ADEGINORS GRANDIOSE,
 ORGANISED
ADEGINORZ ORGANIZED
ADEGINOSS DIAGNOSES
ADEGINPRS SPREADING
ADEGINPRT DEPARTING,
 PREDATING
ADEGINPRV DEPRAVING,
 PERVADING
ADEGINRRT RETARDING
ADEGINRRW REWARDING
ADEGINRST GRADIENTS,
 RED GIANTS
ADEGINRTV ADVERTING
ADEGINSSU GAUDINESS

ADEGINSTT DIGESTANT
ADEGINSTY STEADYING
ADEGIPRRT PARTRIDGE
ADEGIRTTU GRATITUDE
ADEGLLOPT GOLD PLATE
ADEGLNNTU
UNTANGLED
ADEGLNRST STRANGLED
ADEGLOOPY PAEDOLOGY
ADEGLORST OLD STAGER
ADEGMNRSU
GUARDSMEN
ADEGMOPRR
PROGRAMED
ADEGNNOPR
PENDRAGON
ADEGNNORW
DOWNRANGE
ADEGNNRSS GRANDNESS
ADEGNOOOS A GOOD
NOSE
ADEGNOORS
GOOSANDER
ADEGNOPRT
GODPARENT
ADEGNORSS DRAGONESS
ADEGNORSU
DANGEROUS
ADEGNOSTW
DOWNSTAGE
ADEGOORST STAGE
DOOR
ADEGORRTT
GARROTTED
ADEHHIPSS HEADSHIPS
ADEHHISTW DEATH
WISH
ADEHIILRS HAIR SLIDE
ADEHIISST DIATHESIS
ADEHIKNPS HANDSPIKE
ADEHIKNRT IN THE
DARK
ADEHIKNSS SKINHEADS
ADEHILLMR HEIMDALLR
ADEHILMNS MISHANDLE
ADEHILMOT ETHMOIDAL
ADEHILNNR RHINELAND
ADEHILNPR PHILANDER
ADEHILNRR HARD-LINER
ADEHILNRS HARD LINES
ADEHILRRT TRIHEDRAL
ADEHILRST HERALDIST
ADEHIMNOR
RHODAMINE

ADEHIMNSU HUMANISED
ADEHIMNUZ
HUMANIZED
ADEHIMOSU HOUSEMAID
ADEHIMPTW
WHITEDAMP
ADEHIMRTY DIATHERMY
ADEHINNSS HANDINESS
ADEHINOPU AUDIPHONE
ADEHINORS RHODESIAN
ADEHINOSS ADHESIONS
ADEHINRSS HARDINESS
ADEHINRST TARNISHED
ADEHINRSV VARNISHED
ADEHINRTY ANHYDRITE
ADEHINRYZ HYDRAZINE
ADEHINSSS SHADINESS
ADEHIOOST THEODOSIA
ADEHIOPRT ATROPHIED
ADEHIORSW
SHADOWIER
ADEHIPRST THERAPSID
ADEHIRRTT THIRD-RATE
ADEHIRSTW DISHWATER
ADEHKNOSW
SHAKEDOWN
ADEHKORRS DARK
HORSE
ADEHLLNOR
HOLLANDER
ADEHLLOSW
SHALLOWED
ADEHLLOTT DEATH
TOLL
ADEHLMNOS
HOMELANDS
ADEHMOOPS
SHAMPOOED
ADEHMORSW
HOMEWARDS
ADEHMOSSU
MADHOUSES
ADEHNOOPR
HARPOONED
ADEHNOPRS HORNED
ASP
ADEHNORSV
HANDOVERS
ADEHNOSSS SANDSHOES
ADEHNPPRU UPPER
HAND
ADEHNSSSU SUNSHADES
ADEHOORSU
ROADHOUSE

ADEHOORTW
HEARTWOOD
ADEHOOSTT
STATEHOOD
ADEHOPPPY POPPYHEAD
ADEHOSTUW WASHED-
OUT
ADEHTUVYY HEAVY-
DUTY
ADEIIILNT INITIALED
ADEIIINTT DIETITIAN,
INITIATED
ADEIILMNN MAINLINED
ADEIILMOZ IMIDAZOLE
ADEIILMTT MILITATED
ADEIILNRT DELIRIANT
ADEIILNST DISENTAIL
ADEIILORT EDITORIAL
ADEIILQTU LIQUIDATE
ADEIILSST IDEALISTS
ADEIIMMSX MAXIMISED
ADEIIMMXZ MAXIMIZED
ADEIIMNOT MEDIATION
ADEIIMNRS MERIDIANS
ADEIIMNRT AD INTERIM
ADEIIMNTT INTIMATED
ADEIIMOTT DIATOMITE
ADEIIMSSV ADMISSIVE,
MISADVISE
ADEIINNOS INDONESIA
ADEIINOTV DEVIATION
ADEIINPPR DRAINPIPE
ADEIINSST SANITISED
ADEIINSTT DAINTIEST
ADEIINSTZ SANITIZED
ADEIIOSTZ DIAZOTISE
ADEIIOTVX OXIDATIVE
ADEIIOTZZ DIAZOTIZE
ADEIIPRRS DISREPAIR
ADEIIPRSS DISPRAISE
ADEIIPSST DISSIPATE
ADEIIRRTT IRRITATED
ADEIIRSST SATIRISED
ADEIIRSTZ SATIRIZED
ADEIITTTV TITIVATED
ADEIKMORS KAISERDOM
ADEIKMRST TIDEMARKS
ADEIKNPPR KIDNAPPER
ADEIKNPRS SPIKENARD
ADEILLMNO MEDALLION
ADEILLMOT METALLOID
ADEILLMRT TREADMILL
ADEILLMST MEDALLIST
ADEILLNST INSTALLED

ADEILLPRS SPIRALLED
ADEILLPRU PRELUDIAL
ADEILLQRU QUADRILLE
ADEILMMOT
IMMOLATED
ADEILMNNS LANDMINES
ADEILMNPT IMPLANTED
ADEILMNST DISMANTLE
ADEILMNTU DENTALIUM
ADEILMOPT DIPLOMATE
ADEILMOPY POLYAMIDE
ADEILMORR MAIL
ORDER
ADEILMORS MORALISED
ADEILMORZ MORALIZED
ADEILMOTV MOLDAVITE
ADEILMPTU AMPLITUDE
ADEILMSTU SIMULATED
ADEILMTTU MUTILATED
ADEILNNRU UNDERLAIN
ADEILNOPP PANOPLIED
ADEILNOPT PLANETOID
ADEILNOPU ANEUPLOID
ADEILNRRT INTERLARD
ADEILNRSS ISLANDERS
ADEILNRSU LAUNDRIES
ADEILNRTU UITLANDER
ADEILNRUV UNRIVALED
ADEILNSSV VALIDNESS
ADEILNSTU INSULATED
ADEILOPRS POLARISED
ADEILOPRT DEPILATOR
ADEILOPRZ POLARIZED
ADEILOQSU ODALISQUE
ADEILORST IDOLATERS
ADEILOSTV DOVETAILS
ADEILPPRY REPLY-PAID
ADEILPRSS DISPERSAL
ADEILPRSU EPIDURALS
ADEILPRSY DISPLAYER
ADEILPTTU PLATITUDE
ADEILRTTU RUTILATED
ADEILSSTU LASSITUDE
ADEILSTTU ALTITUDES,
LATITUDES
ADEIMNNOT
NOMINATED
ADEIMNOPT ADEMPTION
ADEIMNORS RANDOMISE
ADEIMNORZ
RANDOMIZE
ADEIMNOST STAMINODE
ADEIMNOSW
WOMANISED

ADEIMNOWZ
WOMANIZED
ADEIMNPRR REPRIMAND
ADEIMNPRS SPIDERMAN
ADEIMNRRU
UNMARRIED
ADEIMNRSU NURSEMAID
ADEIMNRTU RUMINATED
ADEIMNRTY DYNAMITER
ADEIMORST AMORTISED,
MEDIATORS
ADEIMORTT MEDITATOR
ADEIMORTZ AMORTIZED
ADEIMOTTV MOTIVATED
ADEIMPRST SPERMATID
ADEIMRTUX ADMIXTURE
ADEIMRTXY TAXIDERMY
ADEIMSSTT MISSTATED
ADEINNNTT INTENDANT
ADEINNOTT DENTATION
ADEINNOTV INNOVATED
ADEINNRSS RANDINESS
ADEINNSSS SANDINESS
ADEINOOTX EXODONTIA
ADEINOPPT APPOINTED
ADEINOPRR PREORDAIN
ADEINOPRT PREDATION
ADEINOPST ANTIPODES
ADEINORST NOTARISED
ADEINORTY ARYTENOID
ADEINORTZ NOTARIZED
ADEINOSTT ANTIDOTES,
STATIONED
ADEINOTUX EXUDATION
ADEINPPRS SANDPIPER
ADEINPPST STANDPIPE
ADEINPRSS RAPIDNESS
ADEINPSSV VAPIDNESS
ADEINRSST TARDINESS
ADEINRSVY VINEYARDS
ADEINSSST STAIDNESS
ADEINSSTU SUSTAINED
ADEINSSTY DYNASTIES
ADEIOPRSV VAPORISED
ADEIOPRTZ TRAPEZOID
ADEIOPRVZ VAPORIZED
ADEIORSST ASTEROIDS
ADEIORSVW DISAVOWER
ADEIORTVY DEVIATORY
ADEIPPSSY DYSPEPSIA
ADEIPRSSY PRISE DAYS
ADEIPRSYZ PRIZE DAYS
ADEIPRTVY DEPRAVITY
ADEIPSTTU APTITUDES

ADEIRRSUY RESIDUARY
ADEIRSSST DISASTERS
ADEIRSTVY ADVERSITY
ADEIRSVWY DRIVEWAYS
ADEISTTTU ATTITUDES
ADEJLNRTU JUTLANDER
ADEKKLRSY SKYLARKED
ADEKLOTTU OUTTALKED
ADEKNORTU
OUTRANKED
ADEKOPRSW SPADEWORK
ADELLLOWY
ALLOWEDLY
ADELLMRUY
MEDULLARY
ADELLNORW
LOWLANDER
ADELLNOUY
UNALLOYED
ADELLOPRT PATROLLED
ADELLORRT TALL ORDER
ADELLOSWW
SWALLOWED
ADELMNNUY
MUNDANELY
ADELMNOOP
LAMPOONED
ADELMNOPS
ENDOPLASM
ADELMORST OLD
MASTER
ADELNNORW
LANDOWNER
ADELNOOPR
APELDOORN
ADELNOOST LOADSTONE
ADELNOPSY DYSPNOEAL
ADELNORRV LAND
ROVER
ADELNORSU UNLOADERS
ADELNORUY
ROUNDELAY
ADELNPRUY UNDERPLAY
ADELNRSSU LAUNDRESS
ADELNRSUY UNDERLAYS
ADELNSSTU DAUNTLESS
ADELOOPRT DOORPLATE
ADELOORSV
OVERLOADS
ADELOPPRS PROLAPSED
ADELOPPTU POPULATED
ADELOPTUY OUTPLAYED,
PLAYED-OUT
ADELORSST LODESTARS

ADELOSTTU OUTLASTED
ADELPQRUU QUADRUPLE
ADELRSSUY ASSUREDLY
ADEMMORST
MASTERDOM
ADEMNNORT
ADORNMENT
ADEMNOPRS
POMANDERS
ADEMNORSU
MEANDROUS
ADEMNRRSU SNARE
DRUM
ADEMNSSUU
UNASSUMED
ADEMOORRT
MODERATOR
ADEMOORST
ASTRODOME,
MODERATOS
ADEMORRTT
ROTTERDAM
ADENNNSTU
SUNTANNED
ADENNOPSS SENNA PODS
ADENNOSST SANDSTONE
ADENNOSTY
ASYNDETON
ADENNSSTW
NEWSSTAND
ADENOORST
TORNADOES
ADENOOORTT
DETONATOR
ADENOOSTT
TOADSTONE
ADENOPRRS PARDONERS
ADENOPRTV DAVENPORT
ADENORRVW
OVERDRAWN
ADENOTTWY
WYANDOTTE
ADENPRSSU UNDERPASS
ADEOOPRRST TOREADORS
ADEOPRRST PREDATORS,
TEARDROPS
ADEOPRRTU DEPURATOR
ADEOPRRTW TOP
DRAWER
ADEOPRRTY
PORTRAYED, PREDATORY
ADEOPRSTU OUTSPREAD
ADEOPRTTY TETRAPODY
ADEORRSST ROADSTERS

ADEORRSWW
SWEARWORD
ADEORSSTT ROAD TESTS
ADEORSTTU OUTSTARED
ADEOSTTUY OUTSTAYED
ADEPPPRUW WRAPPED
UP
ADEPRSSSU SURPASSED
ADERSSTWW
WESTWARDS
ADFFGINOR AFFORDING
ADFFIIMRS DISAFFIRM
ADFGHIOOT GOOD
FAITH
ADFGINORS SANGFROID
ADFGLNORY
DRAGONFLY
ADFHINRST FIRSTHAND
ADFHLOORY
FOOLHARDY
ADFILLNSW WINDFALLS
ADFILMNOS MANIFOLDS
ADFILRSTY FIRST LADY
ADFIORSUV DISFAVOUR
ADFLLNOSW DOWNFALLS
ADFLLOOST FALDSTOOL
ADFLORRWY
FORWARDLY
ADFMOOPST FOOD
STAMP
ADFNOORSZ
SFORZANDO
ADGGILNRY NIGGARDLY
ADGGINPRU UPGRADING
ADGGLOORV
VOLGOGRAD
ADGGLRSSU SLUGGARDS
ADGHHILNS HIGHLANDS
ADGHHINRT RIGHT-
HAND
ADGHHIORS HIGH
ROADS
ADGHIIMNS GANDHIISM
ADGHILLLU GUILDHALL
ADGHILNSY DASHINGLY
ADGHILSTY DAYLIGHTS
ADGHINNNU
UNHANDING
ADGHINORS
DRAGONISH, HOARDINGS
ADGHINOSW
SHADOWING
ADGHINRTU
INDRAUGHT

ADGHIRRTW
RIGHTWARD
ADGHLOPUY PLAY
DOUGH
ADGHNOOPR
ONDOGRAPH
ADGHNOSTU
STAGHOUND
ADGIIILNT DIGITALIN
ADGIIILST DIGITALIS
ADGIIJNNO ADJOINING
ADGIIKNNP KIDNAPING
ADGIILMOS DIALOGISM
ADGIILOST DIALOGIST
ADGIIMNRS DISARMING
ADGIIMNSY DISMAYING
ADGIIMNTT ADMITTING
ADGIINNNT INDIGNANT
ADGIINNOR ORDAINING
ADGIINOSS DIAGNOSIS
ADGIINRTY DIGNITARY
ADGIIRTVY GRAVIDITY
ADGIJNSTU ADJUSTING
ADGILLNUY LANGUIDLY
ADGILLOSU GLADIOLUS
ADGILMNSU GUILDSMAN
ADGILMORS MARIGOLDS
ADGILNNOU
UNLOADING
ADGILNOSS GLISSANDO
ADGILOORY
RADIOLOGY
ADGILOOUY AUDIOLOGY
ADGILOPRS PRODIGALS
ADGIMMOST
DOGMATISM
ADGIMOSTT DOGMATIST
ADGINNOOU
IGUANODON
ADGINNOPR PARDONING
ADGINOORS GRANDIOSO
ADGINOPRY PARODYING
ADGINORRS RING ROADS
ADGINPRRX GRAND PRIX
ADGJNRRUY GRAND
JURY
ADGMNORSU
GOURMANDS
ADGMOORRU
GUARDROOM
ADGNNORSS
GRANDSONS
ADGOOPRST GASTROPOD
ADHHIPRSS HARDSHIPS

ADHHNOORU
HOARHOUND
ADHHNORST
SHORTHAND
ADHIILORZ RHIZOIDAL
ADHIIMPSS AMIDSHIPS
ADHIIOPSU APHIDIOUS
ADHIIOPTY IDIOPATHY
ADHIIPSSY DIAPHYSIS
ADHIKMNNU
HUMANKIND
ADHIKNORW
HANDIWORK
ADHILMNPY NYMPHALID
ADHILOPTY TYPHOIDAL
ADHILPSSY LADYSHIPS
ADHIMNOSU
HUMANOIDS
ADHIMNOTU
ANTHODIUM
ADHIMSTYY DYSTHYMIA
ADHINNOTY
HYDANTOIN
ADHINNRTU HIT-AND-
RUN
ADHINNSTU HINDUSTAN
ADHINOOST SAINTHOOD
ADHINOPSY DYSPHONIA
ADHINORTY HYDRATION
ADHINRTWW
WITHDRAWN
ADHINSTTW WITHSTAND
ADHIOPRSY DYSPHORIA
ADHIPRSSY SHIPYARDS
ADHIRSSTY HYDRASTIS
ADHLLMORT
THRALLDOM
ADHLMNOOS
HANDLOOMS
ADHMNOOOW
WOMANHOOD
ADHNORRTW
NORTHWARD
ADHNORSUY
ANHYDROUS
ADHNOSSTU
THOUSANDS
ADHOOPRRT
ARTHROPOD
ADHOORSSW
ROADSHOWS
ADHORSTUW
SOUTHWARD
ADHRSSTUY THURSDAYS

ADIIIKNNN INDIAN INK
ADIIINOSZ ISONIAZID
ADIIIQRSU DAIQUIRIS
ADIIKLMMS MILKMAIDS
ADIILLNTU LUNITIDAL
ADIILLNVY INVALIDLY
ADIILMSSS DISMISSAL
ADIILNOPT PLATINOID
ADIILNOTU NAUTILOID
ADIILNSTW TAILWINDS
ADIILOORV VARIOLOID
ADIIMNOSS ADMISSION
ADIIMNOUZ
DIAZONIUM
ADIIMRSSY MYDRIASIS
ADIINOOTX OXIDATION
ADIINOQTU QUOTIDIAN
ADIINORTT TRADITION
ADIINOSST SOI-DISANT
ADIINOSTU AUDITIONS
ADIINRSTT DISTRAINT
ADIINRSTU SATURNIID
ADIIPRSTY DISPARITY
ADIISSTUY ASSIDUITY
ADIJNOOVV VOJVODINA
ADIKMNNOW
WOMANKIND
ADIKNNSST INKSTANDS
ADIKNRSTU KURDISTAN
ADILLMNRS MANDRILLS
ADILLNPSS LANDSLIPS
ADILLNRUY DIURNALLY
ADILLQSUY SQUALIDLY
ADILMMSTU TALMUDISM
ADILMNNOS
MANDOLINS
ADILMNOOS
SALMONOID
ADILMNOST DALTONISM
ADILMNRUU
DURALUMIN
ADILMOPST DIPLOMATS
ADILMOPSY OLYMPIADS,
SYMPODIAL
ADILMSTTU TALMUDIST
ADILNOORS DOORNAILS
ADILNORTW
ANTIWORLD
ADILNSTTY DISTANTLY
ADILOOPRS POLAROIDS
ADILOPRSS SLIP ROADS
ADILOPRSV DISPROVAL
ADILOPRXY PYRIDOXAL
ADILORSTW SWORDTAIL

ADIMNOORT
DOMINATOR
ADIMNOSTY STAMINODY
ADINNOOST DONATIONS
ADINNOOSW
SNOWDONIA
ADINNORTU
INUNDATOR
ADINNOSST DISSONANT
ADINOOPST ADOPTIONS
ADINOORST TANDOORIS
ADINOOSTW
SATINWOOD
ADINOPRRS RAINDROPS
ADINORSSU DINOSAURS
ADINPSTTU DISPUTANT
ADIOPRSST PARODISTS
ADIOSSSUU ASSIDUOUS
ADJMMOOOR
MAJORDOMO
ADJMMORRU DRUM
MAJOR
ADKLOOPST POLKA DOTS
ADKLOORSW
WORKLOADS
ADKMNORSW
MARKDOWNS
ADKMOORRS
DARKROOMS
ADKNORRTU TRUNK
ROAD
ADKNORSTT
KRONSTADT
ADKOORRSW ROAD
WORKS
ADLMNORTY
MORDANTLY
ADLMOOPRR
PRODROMAL
ADLMOORTU
MODULATOR
ADLNOORSW
LOANWORDS
ADLNOPRYY POLYANDRY
ADLNORTUU
UNDULATOR
ADLOOOSTT
TOADSTOOL
ADLOPRSWY
SWORDPLAY
ADLORSUUY ARDUOUSLY
ADLORTUWY
OUTWARDLY
ADLPQRUUY QUADRUPLY

ADMMNOOPW MOP
AND MOW
ADMMORRTY
MARTYRDOM
ADMNNORSU
ROUNDSMAN
ADMNOORTY
DYNAMOTOR
ADMNOOSST
MASTODONS
ADMNORSST
SANDSTORM
ADMNORSSW
SWORDSMAN
ADMOOPPRU
POMPADOUR
ADMOORRSW
WARDROOMS
ADNNORRUU RUN-
AROUND
ADNNOSSWW SWAN'S-
DOWN
ADNOOTTUU OUT-AND-
OUT
ADNOPRRTY
PROTANDRY
ADNOPSTTU STAND UP
TO
ADNOQRSSU
SQUADRONS
ADOOOORRWW
ARROWWOOD
ADOOPRRST TRAPDOORS
ADOPRSSSW PASSWORDS
ADOPSSSUY SOAPSUDSY
AEEEETTTT TÊTE-À-TÊTE
AEEEFGNRR FREE-RANGE
AEEEFGNRT FREE
AGENT
AEEEFHRRT HEREAFTER
AEEEFIRRT FIRE-EATER
AEEEGGGNR
GREENGAGE
AEEEGGRST EASTER EGG,
SEGREGATE
AEEEGHLRW
GEARWHEEL
AEEEGHTTX GET THE
AXE
AEEEGIMNR MENAGERIE
AEEEGLRRV GEAR
LEVER
AEEEGMNNP
EMPENNAGE

AEEEGMNRT
AGREEMENT
AEEEGNRSS EAGERNESS
AEEEGNRST TEENAGERS
AEEEGRTTZ GAZETTEER
AEEEHHSTV THE HEAVES
AEEEHKNRR HEARKENER
AEEEHLMPR EPHEMERAL
AEEEHLSSY EYELASHES
AEEEHMRTX
HEXAMETER
AEEEHRRRS REHEARSER
AEEEHRRTW
WEATHERER
AEEEHSSTT AESTHETES
AEEEILNNS ANNELIESE
AEEEILRTT ELATERITE
AEEEIMNRX RE-EXAMINE
AEEEIPPRT PAPETERIE
AEEEIRRTT REITERATE
AEEEJNNTT JEANNETTE
AEEEKKPSS KEEPSAKES
AEEEKLTTT TEAKETTLE
AEEEKMRRT MARKETEER
AEEEKRSWX WEAKER
SEX
AEEELLMNR ENAMELLER
AEEELLMNT ELEMENTAL
AEEELNPRT PLANE
TREE
AEEELNUVZ VENEZUELA
AEEELPSSY YES PLEASE
AEEEMNNRT
NEMERTEAN
AEEEMNRTU
ENUMERATE
AEEEMORRT
AEROMETER
AEEEMPRTT TEMPERATE
AEEEMRRTT ETRAMETER
AEEEMRTVW
WAVEMETER
AEEEMSTTW SWEETMEAT
AEEENNPRT PERENNATE
AEEENOPRW
WEAPONEER
AEEENORTX EXONERATE
AEEENPRTT PENETRATE
AEEENPSTT PATENTEES
AEEENRRST EASTERNER
AEEENRRTW
TREENWARE
AEEENTTUV EVENTUATE
AEEENTTUX EXTENUATE

AEEEPRRST REPARTEES,
REPEATERS
AEEEPSSTW SWEET PEAS
AEEFFILRT AFTERLIFE
AEEFGILPR PILFERAGE
AEEFGINPY FEE-PAYING
AEEFGINRS FAR-SEEING
AEEFGLLOT FLAGEOLET
AEEFGLORW FLOWERAGE
AEEFGLSSU FUSELAGES
AEEFGORST FOSTERAGE
AEEFHIKPT KEEP FAITH
AEEFHLRTT HEARTFELT
AEEFHOSSU SAFE HOUSE
AEEFIKLLM FLAMELIKE
AEEFILLMN EN FAMILLE
AEEFILMPR RELIEF MAP
AEEFILNRT INTERLEAF
AEEFILNSS LEAFINESS
AEEFILOTX EXFOLIATE
AEEFILRSV LIFE-SAVER
AEEFINRRR REFRAINER
AEEFIRRTW FIREWATER
AEEFLLOOS LOOSE-LEAF
AEEFLLRSW FAREWELLS
AEEFLLSVY FLYLEAVES
AEEFLMNRT FREMANTLE
AEEFLNORW ON
WELFARE
AEEFLNRST FENESTRAL
AAEFLNRTT FLATTENER
AEEFLNSSS FALSENESS
AEEFLOOTV FOVEOLATE
AEEFLRRRS REFERRALS
AEEFLRRTT FLATTERER
AEEFMNORS
FORENAMES, FREEMASON
AEEFMPTTT TEMPT FATE
AEEFNRSST FASTENERS
AEEFNSTTY SAFETY NET
AEEFOPRRT PERFORATE
AEEFORSTT FORETASTE
AEEGGILNR GINGER ALE
AEEGGINRR GREGARINE
AEEGGIRUW WIRE-
GAUGE
AEEGGLNOY
GENEALOGY
AEEGGMORT
MORTGAGEE
AEEGGNRSU GREASE
GUN
AEEGGRRST STAGGERER
AEEGGRRSW SWAGGERER

AEEGHIMRT HERMITAGE
AEEGHLPRT TELEGRAPH
AEEGHMNOP
  MEGAPHONE
AEEGHMNOT ON THE
  GAME
AEEGHMRTW WHEAT
  GERM
AEEGHMRTZ
  MEGAHERTZ
AEEGHOSTU GATEHOUSE
AEEGIKNNW
  WEAKENING
AEEGILLRS ALLERGIES,
  GALLERIES
AEEGILLRT TREILLAGE
AEEGILLST LEGISLATE
AEEGILMNN ENAMELING
AEEGILNNT EGLANTINE,
  INELEGANT
AEEGILNNV LEAVENING
AEEGILNPR REPEALING
AEEGILNQU ANGELIQUE
AEEGILNRS RELEASING
AEEGILNRV REVEALING
AEEGILNST ANGLESITE
AEEGILNSW WEASELING
AEEGILNTV ELEVATING
AEEGILPTT TITLE PAGE
AEEGILRTU GAULEITER
AEEGILUVY IVY LEAGUE
AEEGIMNNV GIVEN
  NAME
AEEGIMNRS GERMANISE
AEEGIMNRT
  GERMANITE, GERMINATE
AEEGIMNRZ GERMANIZE
AEEGIMNST MAGNESITE,
  MAGNETISE
AEEGIMNTT MAGNETITE
AEEGIMNTZ MAGNETIZE
AEEGIMOST ISOGAMETE
AEEGIMPTT PEGMATITE
AEEGINNRT ARGENTINE,
  TANGERINE
AEEGINOPS ESPIONAGE
AEEGINOTT NEGOTIATE
AEEGINPRT REPEATING
AEEGINPRV GRAPEVINE
AEEGINRTT ARGENTITE,
  INTEGRATE
AEEGINSSW SEESAWING
AEEGINSTV NEGATIVES
AEEGIORTV GIVE EAR TO

AEEGIRSST GREASIEST
AEEGLLNOR ORGANELLE
AEEGLLNRY GENERALLY
AEEGLLNTY ELEGANTLY
AEEGLMNNT
  GENTLEMAN
AEEGLMNST SEGMENTAL
AEEGLMORT
  ALGOMETER,
  GLOMERATE
AEEGLMRRW LEG-
  WARMER
AEEGLMRST TELEGRAMS
AEEGLNNRT ENTANGLER
AEEGLNRSS LARGENESS
AEEGLORST ALTER EGOS
AEEGLORVZ OVERGLAZE
AEEGMNRRS
  MERGANSER
AEEGMOPRS MEGASPORE
AEEGMORST
  GASOMETER
AEEGNNSTW
  NEWSAGENT
AEEGNOPRS PERSONAGE
AEEGNORRT
  GENERATOR
AEEGNORTU
  ENTOURAGE
AEEGNOTTW
  WAGONETTE
AEEGNOTXY
  OXYGENATE
AEEGNPRSS PASSENGER
AEEGNRRST ESTRANGER
AEEGNRRSV ENGRAVERS
AEEGNRSST GREATNESS,
  SERGEANTS
AEEGNRSSV GRAVENESS
AEEGNSSUV VAGUENESS
AEEGOPPST ESTOPPAGE
AEEGOPRRT PORTERAGE,
  REPORTAGE
AEEGPRTUX EXPURGATE
AEEGRSTTY GREY-STATE
AEEHHIKLT HEATHLIKE
AEEHHILRT HEALTHIER
AEEHHIMST HASHEMITE
AEEHHITTW WHITE
  HEAT
AEEHHLMTT AT THE
  HELM
AEEHHLOSW
  HAWSEHOLE

AEEHHNNPT
  NAPHTHENE
AEEHHNPTY HYPHENATE
AEEHHNSTU UNSHEATHE
AEEHIKNRT KATHERINE
AEEHILLNN HELLENIAN
AEEHILMNW
  MEANWHILE
AEEHILNSS SINHALESE
AEEHILNTV HELVETIAN
AEEHILPRS SHAPELIER
AEEHILRRT EARTHLIER
AEEHILRTW WEALTHIER
AEEHIMNST MAINSHEET
AEEHIMPSS EMPHASISE
AEEHIMPST EMPATHISE
AEEHIMPSZ EMPHASIZE
AEEHIMPTZ EMPATHIZE
AEEHIMRST HETAERISM
AEEHIMTTW WHITE
  MEAT
AEEHINNPZ PHENAZINE
AEEHINPRS HESPERIAN
AEEHINPST STEPHANIE
AEEHINRSV HAVERSINE
AEEHINRTT HENRIETTA
AEEHINRTU EUTHERIAN
AEEHINSSV HEAVINESS
AEEHIPPSW HAWSEPIPE
AEEHIPRSS APHERESIS,
  PHARISEES
AEEHIPRST THERAPIES
AEEHIRRST EARTHRISE
AEEHIRRTT HARRIETTE
AEEHIRSTT EARTHIEST,
  HEARTIEST, HESITATER,
  HETAERIST
AEEHKLPSW SHEEPWALK
AEEHKMMOR
  HOMEMAKER
AEEHKMORS
  SHOEMAKER
AEEHKMPRT THEME
  PARK
AEEHKMRTT THE
  MARKET
AEEHLLMOW
  WHOLEMEAL
AEEHLLNOW
  HALLOWE'EN
AEEHLLOSW WHOLESALE
AEEHLLSSS SEASHELLS
AEEHLMMNT
  EMMENTHAL

AEEHLMPST HELPMATES
AEEHLMRSY HAMERSLEY
AEEHLMSSS SHAMELESS
AEEHLMTTY
METHYLATE
AEEHLNOPS ANOPHELES
AEEHLNOPT PHENOLATE
AEEHLNOSW
HALESOWEN
AEEHLNPST ELEPHANTS
AEEHLNSSV HAVENLESS
AEEHLOPST TELOPHASE
AEEHLORST TREHALOSE
AEEHLORTW
WATERHOLE
AEEHLOSSU ALEHOUSES
AEEHLPSSS SHAPELESS
AEEHLPTTY TELEPATHY
AEEHLRSST HEARTLESS
AEEHLSTXY HEXASTYLE
AEEHMMORT
HAMMERTOE
AEEHMMPSY
EMPHYSEMA
AEEHMNNOP
PHENOMENA
AEEHMNOTT MOTH-
EATEN
AEEHMOPRS SEMAPHORE
AEEHMORST
HEARTSOME
AEEHMPRST PETERSHAM
AEEHNNOTW ON THE
WANE
AEEHNOOPR
AEROPHONE
AEEHNOPRS EARPHONES
AEEHNOPTX
TOXAPHENE
AEEHNPRRS SHARPENER
AEEHNRRSS HARNESSER
AEEHNRSSS HARNESSES
AEEHORSSS SEAHORSES
AEEHORSUW
WAREHOUSE
AEEHOSSTU TEAHOUSES
AEEHPRSTU, EUPHRATES,
SUPERHEAT
AEEHRRSTT SHATTERER,
THREE-STAR
AEEHRRSTV HARVESTER
AEEHRSTUX EXHAUSTER
AEEIILLOP AEOLIPILE
AEEIILMNT ELIMINATE

AEEIILRSS SERIALISE
AEEIILRST ISRAELITE,
REALITIES
AEEIILRSZ SERIALIZE
AEEIIMNST AMENITIES
AEEIINNTV VIENTIANE
AEEIINRTT ITINERATE
AEEIINSTV NAIVETIES
AEEIINSTX ANXIETIES
AEEIIRSTV VARIETIES
AEEIIRTTV ITERATIVE
AEEIJMNSS JESSAMINE
AEEIJMSST MAJESTIES
AEEIKLLPT PETAL-LIKE
AEEIKLMUW MILWAUKEE
AEEIKLNSS LEAKINESS
AEEIKMNSY YANKEEISM
AEEIKNRSV KNAVERIES
AEEIKNSST SNEAKIEST
AEEIKQRSU SQUEAKIER
AEEIKRRST STREAKIER
AEEILLMNT METALLINE
AEEILLMRS MARSEILLE
AEEILLMST METALLISE
AEEILLMTZ METALLIZE
AEEILLNOT LINEOLATE,
LINOLEATE
AEEILLPTT PAILLETTE
AEEILLSTT SATELLITE
AEEILLTVW WAVELLITE
AEEILLTVX VEXILLATE
AEEILMNNT LINEAMENT
AEEILMNRY MINELAYER
AEEILMNSS MESSALINE
AEEILMORT MELIORATE
AEEILMPST TIME-LAPSE
AEEILMRST SALIMETER
AEEILMRTT ALTIMETER
AEEILMRTU ELATERIUM
AEEILMRTW LIMEWATER
AEEILMTUV EMULATIVE
AEEILNNPP PENEPLAIN
AEEILNNPR PERENNIAL
AEEILNNSX SEXENNIAL
AEEILNNTV LEVANTINE,
VALENTINE
AEEILNOTV ELEVATION
AEEILNPPP PINEAPPLE
AEEILNPRX EXPLAINER
AEEILNPST PALESTINE,
PENALTIES
AEEILNPSX EXPANSILE
AEEILNRSS EARLINESS
AEEILNRSV VERNALISE

AEEILNRTW WATERLINE
AEEILNRVZ VERNALIZE
AEEILNSST ESSENTIAL
AEEILNTTV VENTILATE
AEEILOPTT PETIOLATE
AEEILORRT ARTERIOLE
AEEILPPPS APPLE PIES
AEEILPRRV PREVAILER
AEEILPRST PEARLIEST
AEEILQRSU EQUALISER
AEEILQRUZ EQUALIZER
AEEILRRST RETAILERS
AEEILRRTT AIRLETTER
AEEILRRTV RETRIEVAL
AEEILRSTV RELATIVES,
VERSATILE
AEEILRTTU ELUTRIATE
AEEILSSTZ SLEAZIEST
AEEILSVVY EVASIVELY
AEEIMMNST MEANTIMES
AEEIMNNZZ MEZZANINE
AEEIMNRSX EXAMINERS
AEEIMNRTT TERMINATE
AEEIMNSSS SEAMINESS
AEEIMNSST AMNESTIES,
MEATINESS
AEEIMNSTT ESTAMINET
AEEIMORRS ROSEMARIE
AEEIMORSW WEARISOME
AEEIMPRRT PRIME RATE
AEEIMPRTT IMPETRATE
AEEIMRSTT TASIMETER
AEEIMRSTV TIMESAVER
AEEIMRTTX TAXIMETER
AEEIMSSTT ESTIMATES,
STEAMIEST
AEEINNNPS APENNINES
AEEINNRST IN EARNEST,
TANNERIES
AEEINNRTT ENTERTAIN
AEEINNRTV INNERVATE
AEEINNSST INSENSATE
AEEINNSSV NAIVENESS
AEEINOPPT APPOINTEE
AEEINOPRT PERITONEA
AEEINORTT ORIENTATE
AEEINPPST PEPSINATE
AEEINPRSS PASSERINE
AEEINPRST SPARTEINE
AEEINPSVX EXPANSIVE
AEEINRRST RETAINERS
AEEINRRTT REITERANT
AEEINRRTV VERATRINE
AEEINRSSW WEARINESS

AEEINRSTT REINSTATE
AEEINRSTU ESTUARINE
AEEINRSTV INVERTASE
AEEINRSTY EYESTRAIN
AEEINSSTU UNEASIEST
AEEINSTTT ENSTATITE,
INTESTATE
AEEINSTTU AUSTENITE
AEEINTTTV ATTENTIVE,
TENTATIVE
AEEIOPRTV EVAPORITE,
OPERATIVE
AEEIPPRST APPETISER
AEEIPPRSU PAUPERISE
AEEIPPRTW WATER PIPE
AEEIPPRTZ APPETIZER
AEEIPPRUZ PAUPERIZE
AEEIPPSTT APPETITES
AEEIPRRTV PRIVATEER
AEEIPRSSS PESSARIES
AEEIPRSSV ASPERSIVE
AEEIPRSVV PERVASIVE
AEEIPRTTX EXTIRPATE
AEEIQSSTU QUEASIEST
AEEIRSSTT TREATISES
AEEIRSSTU ESTUARIES
AEEIRSSTV ASSERTIVE
AEEISSTTW SWEATIEST
AEEJLMRSU JERUSALEM
AEEJMORTT MAJORETTE
AEEJMRSTT JET STREAM
AEEKKOPRT KAPOK TREE
AEEKLLPSW SLEEPWALK
AEEKLSTTW SWEET TALK
AEEKMMRRY MAKE
MERRY
AEEKMRRST MARKETERS
AEEKMRSTY MASTER
KEY
AEEKNORTV OVERTAKEN
AEEKORSTV TAKEOVERS
AEEKQRSSU SQUEAKERS
AEEKRRSST STREAKERS
AEELLLSTT TELLTALES
AEELLMNTW WELL-
MEANT
AEELLNPPZ APPENZELL
AEELLNPTX EXPELLANT
AEELLNRTY ENTERALLY,
ETERNALLY
AEELLOPST SELLOTAPE
AEELLOSUV LAEVULOSE
AEELLPSTT PLATELETS
AEELLRRTV TRAVELLER

AEELLRSVY SEVERALLY
AEELLRTTU TELLURATE
AEELLSSUV VALUELESS
AEELLSSVV VALVELESS
AEELMMRRT
TRAMMELER
AEELMMTXY
METAXYLEM
AEELMORST ELASTOMER
AEELMPRXY EXEMPLARY
AEELMPSTT TEMPLATES
AEELMRSST SEMESTRAL
AEELMRTTW
MELTWATER
AEELNNNTU
ANTENNULE
AEELNOPST ANTELOPES
AEELNPRTV PREVALENT
AEELNRRUV UNRAVELER
AEELNRSST ALERTNESS
AEELNRSTX EXTERNALS
AEELNRSTY EARNESTLY
AEELNRTTV TERVALENT
AEELNSSST STALENESS
AEELNSSWY WESLEYANS
AEELORRTV REVELATOR
AEELORSTV ELEVATORS
AEELORTVW WATER
VOLE
AEELOSTTW TEA
TOWELS
AEELPPRRU PUERPERAL
AEELPPRTU PERPETUAL
AEELPRRST PLASTERER
AEELPRRTU PRELATURE
AEELPRSSU PLEASURES
AEELPRSTT SALTPETRE
AEELQRRRU
QUARRELER
AEELQRSSU SQUEALERS
AEELRRSSV REVERSALS
AEELRRSTU SERRULATE
AEELRRSTV TRAVELERS
AEELRRSTW WATERLESS
AEELRSTUY AUSTERELY
AEELRSTVY SEVERALTY
AEELSSSTT STATELESS,
TASTELESS
AEEMMNORT
MANOMETER
AEEMMNSTU
AMUSEMENT
AEEMMORTT
ATMOMETER

AEEMMPRUY
EMPYREUMA
AEEMMRRST
STAMMERER
AEEMNNORT
NANOMETER
AEEMNNOTT
ATONEMENT
AEEMNNPRT
PERMANENT
AEEMNOPRT
TREPONEMA
AEEMNOPSU MENOPAUSE
AEEMNOPYZ
APOENZYME
AEEMNORTW WORM-
EATEN
AEEMNORUV
MANOEUVRE
AEEMNPRTY REPAYMENT
AEEMNPSTV PAVEMENTS
AEEMNRSST MARE'S
NEST, STEERSMAN
AEEMNRSUV
MANEUVERS
AEEMNRTTT
TREATMENT
AEEMNSSTT MEANS
TEST, STATESMEN
AEEMNSSTY MATEYNESS
AEEMNSTTT STATEMENT,
TESTAMENT
AEEMOPRRT PERMEATOR
AEEMOPSSU MESOPAUSE
AEEMORRTT
ROTAMETER
AEEMORRTY
AEROMETRY
AEEMPRRTU PREMATURE
AEEMPRTTT ATTEMPTER
AEEMPSSTW SWAP
MEETS
AEEMRRSST STREAMERS
AEEMRRSTT SMATTERER
AEEMRSSTT SMEAR TEST,
TEAMSTERS
AEEMRSSTY EASY TERMS
AEEMRTTTW
WATTMETER
AEENNPRTT PENETRANT,
REPENTANT
AEENNRRTT
RE-ENTRANT
AEENOPPRT NOTEPAPER

AEENOPRST ESPERANTO,
PERSONATE
AEENOPTTT POTENTATE
AEENOQRSU SQUARE
ONE
AEENORRTV
ENERVATOR, VENERATOR
AEENORSTW
STONEWARE
AEENPPRRT ENTRAPPER
AEENPPRSW NEWSPAPER
AEENPRRTU ENRAPTURE
AEENPRSSS SPARENESS
AEENPRSTT AT PRESENT
AEENPRSTY SEPTENARY
AEENRRSTU SAUNTERER
AEENRSSTU SAUTERNES
AEENSSSUV SUAVENESS
AEEOOPRTZ AZEOTROPE
AEEOPPRSU PEA SOUPER
AEEOPRSSW SEA POWERS
AEEOPRSTT OPERETTAS,
POETASTER
AEEOQRRTU
QUERETARO
AEEORRSTW ROSEWATER
AEEORSTTV OVERSTATE
AEEORSTTW TWO-
SEATER
AEEPRRRST PARTERRES
AEEPRRSTU APERTURES
AEEPRRSTY SPARE TYRE
AEEQRSSTU SETSQUARE
AEEQRTUUX
EXEQUATUR
AEERRRSSU REASSURER
AEERRRSTU TREASURER
AEERRRSTV TRAVERSER
AEERRSSTU TREASURES
AEERRSSTV TRAVERSES
AEERRTTVX EXTRAVERT
AEESTTTTU STATUETTE
AEFFFLTUW LUFTWAFFE
AEFFGRSSU SUFFRAGES
AEFFHMOPT OFF THE
MAP
AEFFIILRS FALSIFIER
AEFFIKPST PIKESTAFF
AEFFILLUV EFFLUVIAL
AEFFINORS RAFFINOSE
AEFFIRTUX AFFIXTURE
AEFFKMNOU MAKE FUN
OF
AEFFLLRUY FEARFULLY

AEFFLLTUY FATEFULLY
AEFFLORSW SAFFLOWER
AEFFMORST OFF STREAM
AEFGHILNS ANGELFISH
AEFGHILST SAFELIGHT
AEFGHILTW WHITE FLAG
AEFGHINRT FATHERING
AEFGHORRT FORGATHER
AEFGIIMNR MAGNIFIER
AEFGIINNR FINE-GRAIN
AEFGIIRRT GRATIFIER
AEFGILMOR GALEIFORM
AEFGILNRT FALTERING,
REFLATING
AEFGILRUY LAY FIGURE
AEFGINNST FASTENING
AEFGINNTT FATTENING
AEFGINRTU FEATURING
AEFGIORSS OSSIFRAGE
AEFGIRSTT GAS FITTER
AEFGLLLMU FLAGELLUM
AEFGLLOPS FLAGPOLES
AEFGLNOST FLAGSTONE
AEFGLORTW
AFTERGLOW
AEFGMNRST FRAGMENTS
AEFGNOPRT FRONT-PAGE
AEFGNORST FRONTAGES
AEFHHISST SHEATFISH
AEFHHLLTU HEALTHFUL
AEFHHLOTW
HEATHFOWL
AEFHIKMST MAKESHIFT
AEFHILLSV HALF-LIVES
AEFHILPST FISHPLATE
AEFHILSST FAITHLESS,
FLASHIEST
AEFHIMNRS FISHERMAN
AEFHINORS FASHIONER
AEFHINRTW WAFER-
THIN
AEFHKNORS FORESHANK
AEFHLLSVY FLY HALVES
AEFHLLTUY HATEFULLY
AEFHLNNPY HALFPENNY
AEFHLNOST HALF
NOTES, HALFTONES
AEFHLORSV FLASHOVER
AEFHMORSU
FARMHOUSE
AEFHORRTU OUR
FATHER
AEFIIKLRY FAIRY-LIKE
AEFIILLNS NAIL FILES

AEFIILMNS SEMIFINAL
AEFIILMPR AMPLIFIER
AEFIILNNT INFANTILE
AEFIILQRU QUALIFIER
AEFIILRST FRAILTIES
AEFIILSST FALSITIES
AEFIINRSS FRIESIANS
AEFIINRTU INFURIATE
AEFIIPRST APERITIFS
AEFIIRSST SATISFIER
AEFIISTVX FIXATIVES
AEFIKLNSS FLAKINESS
AEFILLNOX FLEXIONAL
AEFILLOOT FOLIOLATE
AEFILMMNY FAMILY
MEN
AEFILMNST FILAMENTS
AEFILMNTU FULMINATE
AEFILMORS FORMALISE
AEFILMORZ FORMALIZE
AEFILNNUZ INFLUENZA
AEFILNORT REFLATION
AEFILNPSS LIFESPANS
AEFILORRT ROTIFERAL
AEFILSSTV FESTIVALS
AEFILSTTU FAULTIEST
AEFIMMNRT
FIRMAMENT
AEFIMNOSS FOAMINESS
AEFIMNOST MANIFESTO
AEFIMNRST FIRST NAME
AEFIMNSST MANIFESTS
AEFIMORTV FORMATIVE
AEFINNSST FAINTNESS
AEFINOOTT FOETATION
AEFINOPRR PORIFERAN
AEFINOPRS PINAFORES
AEFINORSS SANFORISE
AEFINORSU NEFARIOUS
AEFINORSZ SANFORIZE
AEFINPSTY SAFETY PIN
AEFINRSSS SANS SERIF
AEFINRSTU UNFAIREST
AEFINSSTT FATTINESS
AEFIORSTV FAVORITES
AEFIORTUV FAVOURITE
AEFIPRRST FIRETRAPS
AEFIRRSTT FIRST-RATE
AEFKLLOST FOLKTALES
AEFKLLUWY WAKEFULLY
AEFKLNOSW SNOWFLAKE
AEFKMORRW
FRAMEWORK
AEFKNNRSS FRANKNESS

AEFKNOPTU POKE FUN
AT
AEFLLNTTU FLATULENT
AEFLLORST FORESTALL
AEFLLRTUY TEARFULLY
AEFLLSSTU FAULTLESS
AEFLMORTU
FORMULATE
AEFLMORWY
MAYFLOWER
AEFLMRSTU MASTERFUL
AEFLNOOSS ALOOFNESS
AEFLNOPRY PROFANELY
AEFLNSSUW AWFULNESS
AEFLOOPTT FOOTPLATE
AEFLORRUV FLAVOURER
AEFLORTWW
WATERFOWL
AEFLPRRUY PRAYERFUL
AEFMNOORW
FOREWOMAN
AEFNNOORT
AFTERNOON
AEFNORSST SEAFRONTS
AEFNORTTU FORTUNATE
AEFNRRSST TRANSFERS
AEFNRRSTU TRANSFUER
AEFNRSSTU TRANSFUSE
AEFOOPRRW
WEARPROOF
AEFOPRRTY PREFATORY
AEFRRSTTU FRUSTRATE
AEGGGIRWW
WIGWAGGER
AEGGGIRZZ ZIGZAGGER
AEGGHINRT GATHERING
AEGGHIRTZ GIGAHERTZ
AEGGHISST SHAGGIEST
AEGGHOPRR
ERGOGRAPH
AEGGHOPRY
GEOGRAPHY
AEGGIINNR REGAINING
AEGGIINPU GUINEA PIG
AEGGILNNR ENLARGING
AEGGILNNS GLEANINGS
AEGGILNRV GRAVELING
AEGGINNRR GARNERING
AEGGINNRV ENGRAVING
AEGGINORR GREGORIAN
AEGGINOSY EASYGOING
AEGGINPRS PRESAGING
AEGGINPRT PARGETING
AEGGINRTT TARGETING

AEGGIOPRS ARPEGGIOS
AEGGLNNOR LONG-
RANGE
AEGGLNPST EGGPLANTS
AEGGLNRRY GLENGARRY
AEGGLORSY GARGOYLES
AEGGLRRST STRAGGLER
AEGGMORST
MORTGAGES
AEGGNNRTU
TRENGGANU
AEGGNOSUY
SYNAGOGUE
AEGGNPRSS PRESSGANG
AEGGNRSST GANGSTERS
AEGGOPRSU AGE GROUPS
AEGGORRSS AGGRESSOR
AEGHHINRS REHASHING
AEGHHINST SHEATHING
AEGHHIRTU HAUGHTIER
AEGHHIRTW HIGH
WATER
AEGHHRRTU
HEARTHRUG
AEGHIILNS GHISLAINE
AEGHIKNNR
HANKERING, HARKENING
AEGHIKNRS SHRINKAGE
AEGHILLNY HEALINGLY
AEGHILMST MEGALITHS
AEGHILNRS SHEARLING
AEGHILNRT EARTHLING,
LATHERING
AEGHILRST GHASTLIER
AEGHILRSV GRAVELISH
AEGHILRTY LIGHT YEAR
AEGHIMMNR
HAMMERING
AEGHIMNPR HAMPERING
AEGHIMNRT
NIGHTMARE
AEGHIMNWY
HEMINGWAY
AEGHIMORR
HIEROGRAM
AEGHIMPPR EPIPHRAGM
AEGHINNPP HAPPENING
AEGHINNRT NEAR
THING
AEGHINNST HASTENING
AEGHINOPS SIPHONAGE
AEGHINRRS GARNISHER
AEGHINRSS GARNISHES
AEGHINRTU NAUGHTIER

AEGHINRTW
NIGHTWEAR, WREATHING
AEGHIORWY GO
HAYWIRE
AEGHIPPRY EPIGRAPHY
AEGHIPRRS SERIGRAPH
AEGHIPSTT SPAGHETTI
AEGHLOOPR
OLEOGRAPH
AEGHLORTT
LARGHETTO
AEGHLRSTU SLAUGHTER
AEGHMNOPR
NEPHOGRAM
AEGHNNORS HANGERS-
ON
AEGHNOORR
GONORRHEA
AEGHNOPST HEPTAGONS
AEGHNORSV
HANGOVERS,
OVERHANGS
AEGHOPRST GRAPESHOT
AEGHOPSSU ESOPHAGUS
AEGHORSST SHORTAGES
AEGIILLRS GRISAILLE
AEGIILLRT ARGILLITE
AEGIILMSV VIGESIMAL
AEGIILNNT ENTAILING
AEGIILNRT RETAILING
AEGIILNRZ REALIZING
AEGIILNSS SIGNALISE
AEGIILNSZ SIGNALIZE
AEGIILNTV GENITIVAL,
VIGILANTE
AEGIILNTY GENIALITY
AEGIILSTV VESTIGIAL
AEGIIMMRT IMMIGRATE
AEGIIMNNR REMAINING
AEGIIMNNX EXAMINING
AEGIIMNRS MIGRAINES
AEGIINNRT RETAINING
AEGIINORT ORIGINATE
AEGIINOTT GONIATITE
AEGIINPRR REPAIRING
AEGIINPTX EXPIATING
AEGIINRTT GRANITITE
AEGIINSTT INSTIGATE
AEGIJNORS JARGONISE
AEGIJNORZ JARGONIZE
AEGIJNTUU UNIJUGATE
AEGIKKMNR
KINGMAKER
AEGIKLNSW WEAKLINGS

AEGIKMNRR
   REMARKING
AEGIKMNRT MARKETING
AEGIKNQSU SQUEAKING
AEGIKNRST STREAKING
AEGIKNSSW GAWKINESS
AEGILLLLY ILLEGALLY
AEGILLLNU GALLINULE
AEGILLMNT METALLING
AEGILLMRU MALGRE LUI
AEGILLNNP PANELLING
AEGILLNNW GWENLLIAN
AEGILLNOS GOAL LINES
AEGILLNOT NO-TILLAGE
AEGILLNQU EQUALLING
AEGILLNRS SIGNALLER
AEGILLNRV GRANVILLE,
   RAVELLING
AEGILLNTU LINGULATE
AEGILLNTY GENITALLY
AEGILLPPU PUPILLAGE
AEGILLPRS PILLAGERS
AEGILLRRU GUERRILLA
AEGILLRSS SALESGIRL
AEGILLRST ALLERGIST
AEGILLRSV VILLAGERS
AEGILMNNS SIGNALMEN
AEGILMNNT
   ALIGNMENT, LAMENTING
AEGILMNRV MARVELING
AEGILMNST LIGAMENTS
AEGILMNTU
   EMULATING, GLUTAMINE
AEGILMORR RIGMAROLE
AEGILMORS GLAMORISE
AEGILMORZ GLAMORIZE
AEGILNNSV ENSLAVING
AEGILNOPX POLEAXING
AEGILNORU NEUROGLIA
AEGILNORY LEGIONARY
AEGILNOST LEGATIONS
AEGILNPRS RELAPSING
AEGILNPRY PARLEYING,
   REPLAYING
AEGILNQSU SQUEALING
AEGILNRST TRIANGLES
AEGILNRSV SLAVERING
AEGILNRSY SYRINGEAL,
   YEARLINGS
AEGILNRTU GRANULITE
AEGILNRTV TRAVELING
AEGILNRTY TEARINGLY
AEGILNRUV REVALUING
AEGILNRWY WEARINGLY

AEGILNSSW WINEGLASS
AEGILNSTY TEASINGLY
AEGILOOPS APOLOGIES,
   APOLOGISE
AEGILOOPZ APOLOGIZE
AEGILOOTY AETIOLOGY
AEGILORSS SERAGLIOS
AEGILORSU GLAIREOUS
AEGILORTV LEVIGATOR
AEGILPPSS SLIPPAGES
AEGILRRRU IRREGULAR
AEGILRRTW WRIT LARGE
AEGILRSTU LIGATURES
AEGILRSUV VULGARISE
AEGILRTUV VIRGULATE
AEGILRUVZ VULGARIZE
AEGILSSST GLASSIEST
AEGIMMNOT
   GEMMATION
AEGIMMNRS
   GERMANISM
AEGIMMNRU
   GERMANIUM
AEGIMMNRY
   YAMMERING
AEGIMMNST
   MAGNETISM
AEGIMMNSU
   MAGNESIUM
AEGIMNNNU
   UNMEANING
AEGIMNNOR
   OMNIRANGE
AEGIMNNRT
   GERMINANT
AEGIMNNSS MANGINESS
AEGIMNORS ORANGEISM
AEGIMNORT
   MORGANITE
AEGIMNPPR PAMPERING
AEGIMNPRT TAMPERING
AEGIMNPRV REVAMPING
AEGIMNRST EMIGRANTS,
   MASTERING, STREAMING
AEGIMNRSU GERANIUMS,
   MEASURING
AEGIMNRTT MATTERING
AEGIMQRSU QUAGMIRES
AEGIMRSTY MAGISTERY
AEGINNNRS ENSNARING
AEGINNORS REASONING
AEGINNORW
   NORWEGIAN
AEGINNORZ ORGANZINE

AEGINNOSS SEASONING
AEGINNOST NEGATIONS
AEGINNOSU GUANOSINE
AEGINNOTT NEGOTIANT
AEGINNPPR PERPIGNAN
AEGINNPRT PARENTING
AEGINNPTT PATENTING
AEGINNRSS RANGINESS
AEGINNRSW ANSWERING
AEGINNRSY YEARNINGS
AEGINNRTT INTEGRANT,
   NATTERING
AEGINNSST ASSENTING
AEGINNSTU UNSEATING
AEGINNTTU TAUTENING
AEGINOPRS SINGAPORE
AEGINOPRT OPERATING
AEGINORRS ORGANISER
AEGINORRV GRANIVORE
AEGINORRZ ORGANIZER
AEGINORVW
   OVERAWING
AEGINOSTT GESTATION
AEGINPPRR PREPARING
AEGINPPRY PREPAYING
AEGINPRTT PATTERING
AEGINPSTY EGYPTIANS
AEGINQRUV
   QUAVERING
AEGINRRST ARRESTING
AEGINRRTU GARNITURE
AEGINRSST ASSERTING
AEGINRSTT RESTATING
AEGINRSTU SIGNATURE
AEGINSSSS ASSESSING,
   GASSINESS
AEGINSSST STAGINESS
AEGINSSUZ GAUZINESS
AEGINSTTT ATTESTING
AEGINSTUU AUGUSTINE
AEGIPRTUV PURGATIVE
AEGIRRRST REGISTRAR
AEGIRSSST GRASSIEST
AEGLLNOPW
   ALPENGLOW
AEGLLNOST GALLSTONE
AEGLLOOOZ
   ZOOGLOEAL
AEGLLOSTT TOLLGATES
AEGLLRRUY REGULARLY
AEGLMNOOY
   ANEMOLOGY
AEGLMNORW
   ANGLEWORM

AEGLMORTY
ALGOMETRY
AEGLNOSTU LANGOUSTE
AEGLNRRST STRANGLER
AEGLNRRSW
WRANGLERS
AEGLNRSST STRANGLES
AEGLNRSTY STRANGELY
AEGLNSTTU GAUNTLETS
AEGLOPPRU PROPAGULE
AEGLOPRSY PLAYGOERS
AEGLORRTU
REGULATOR
AEGLORTTY TETRALOGY
AEGMMOPRR
PROGRAMME
AEGMNNORT
MAGNETRON
AEGMNORRW
WARMONGER
AEGMNORSU
GERMANOUS
AEGMNORSV
MANGROVES
AEGMNORTU
AUGMENTOR
AEGMNOTTU
MANGETOUT
AEGMNRSTU
ARGUMENTS
AEGMOOSUX
EXOGAMOUS
AEGMOPRRR
PROGRAMER
AEGMOPRRS
PROGRAMES
AEGMORRSW WORM
GEARS
AEGMORSTY
GASOMETRY
AEGMPRSSU GRAMPUSES
AEGNNOPST PENTAGONS
AEGNNPRTU
REPUGNANT
AEGNNSSTU GAUNTNESS
AEGNORSSX SEX
ORGANS
AEGNORSTU
ARGENTOUS
AEGNRRSST STRANGERS
AEGNRSSTT STRANGEST
AEGNRSSTU ASSURGENT
AEGOPPSST STOPPAGES
AEGOPSSTT GATEPOSTS

AEGORRRTT
GARROTTER
AEGORRSTT GARROTTES
AEGORRSTU SURROGATE
AEGORSTTY GESTATORY
AEGPRRRUY PRAYER RUG
AEHHHITTY HIT THE
HAY
AEHHHOOTU HU-HO-
HAO-T'E
AEHHILLTW WHITEHALL
AEHHILLTY HEALTHILY
AEHHILNPT PHTHALEIN
AEHHILOPT THEOPHILA
AEHHIMPRS HAMPSHIRE
AEHHIORRS HORSEHAIR
AEHHIPPSS SHIPSHAPE
AEHHISTWW
WHITEWASH
AEHHLNTUY
UNHEALTHY
AEHHLOPTY HALOPHYTE
AEHHMOOPT
HOMEOPATH
AEHHNORTW
HAWTHORNE
AEHHNRSSS HARSHNESS
AEHHOPPST PHOSPHATE
AEHIILMTU HUMILIATE
AEHIILNRS HAIRLINES
AEHIIMNRT HERMITIAN
AEHIIMNST HISTAMINE
AEHIIMRST HETAIRISM
AEHIIMRTY HIMYARITE
AEHIINOPT ETHIOPIAN
AEHIINRSS HAIRINESS
AEHIIPSTT HEPATITIS
AEHIKKLMS MILK SHAKE
AEHIKLMNU HUMAN-
LIKE
AEHIKMOTT MAKE IT
HOT
AEHIKNOST SHAKE ON IT
AEHIKNSSS SHAKINESS
AEHILLNRT ALLETHRIN
AEHILLNSV NASHVILLE
AEHILLPTY PHILATELY
AEHILLTTY LETHALITY
AEHILLTWW WHITEWALL
AEHILLTWY WEALTHILY
AEHILMNOP PHILOMENA
AEHILNNOT ANTHELION
AEHILNOOZ HELIOZOAN
AEHILNOPR PARHELION

AEHILNOST HAILSTONE
AEHILNPRS PLANISHER
AEHILNQRU HARLEQUIN
AEHILORST HORSETAIL,
ISOTHERAL
AEHILOSTT HELIOSTAT
AEHILPRSS SPLASHIER
AEHILRSTY HAIRSTYLE
AEHIMNNOT
ANTHEMION
AEHIMNORS
HARMONIES, HARMONISE
AEHIMNORZ
HARMONIZE
AEHIMNOST THOMASINE
AEHIMNPSS MISSHAPEN
AEHIMNPST PANTHEISM
AEHIMNRSU HUMANISER
AEHIMNRUZ
HUMANIZER
AEHIMPSST SHIPMATES,
STEAMSHIP
AEHIMQSSU SQUEAMISH
AEHINNRSS IN HARNESS
AEHINNRTU RUTHENIAN
AEHINORSS HOARINESS
AEHINORST HORTENSIA
AEHINORTT ANORTHITE
AEHINPPSS HAPPINESS
AEHINPSSS APISHNESS
AEHINPSST THESPIANS
AEHINPSSY SISYPHEAN
AEHINPSTT PANTHEIST
AEHINRRST TARNISHER
AEHINRRSV VARNISHER
AEHINRRTU ARTHURINE
AEHINRSSV VARNISHES
AEHINSSST HASTINESS
AEHINSSSW WASHINESS
AEHINSTTW WHITE ANTS
AEHIORRTT THROATIER
AEHIORSTU AUTHORISE
AEHIORSTX RHEOTAXIS
AEHIORTTV HORTATIVE
AEHIORTUZ AUTHORIZE
AEHIPPRSS SAPPHIRES
AEHIPRSTT THERAPIST
AEHIQRSSU SQUASHIER
AEHIRRSTW SWARTHIER
AEHIRRSTT TRASHIEST
AEHJLLNOS HALL-JONES
AEHJPRSSW JEW'S HARPS
AEHKLNSST THANKLESS
AEHKLRRSU KARLSRUHE

AEHKORRTW
EARTHWORK
AEHKOSSTU SHAKEOUTS
AEHLLLNPU ALEPH-NULL
AEHLLNOOP
ALLOPHONE
AEHLLORSW
SHALLOWER
AEHLLPSSU PHALLUSES
AEHLLPSSY HAPLESSLY
AEHLMOOST
LOATHSOME
AEHLMOSSU ALMS-
HOUSE
AEHLMPPST PAMPHLETS
AEHLNRTUY UNEARTHLY
AEHLOPPSY POLYPHASE
AEHLOPRSY HORSEPLAY
AEHLOPSTT HOTPLATES
AEHLOPSUY PLAYHOUSE
AEHLORSUV OVERHAULS
AEHLPRRSU SPHERULAR
AEHLPSSTU SULPHATES
AEHMMOORT
HARMOTOME
AEHMNNRTU
MANHUNTER
AEHMNNSSU
HUMANNESS
AEHMNRRWY
WHERRYMAN
AEHMOOPRS
SHAMPOOER
AEHMOPRST
METAPHORS
AEHMORRTW
EARTHWORM,
HEARTWORM
AEHMORTWW
WHEATWORM
AEHMPPSTU HEAT PUMPS
AEHMSSTTY AMETHYSTS
AEHNNOPRT
PARTHENON
AEHNNOPST PANTHEONS
AEHNNRSSU UNHARNESS
AEHNOOPRR
HARPOONER
AEHNOOPSX
SAXOPHONE
AEHNOPPSY PAY
PHONES
AEHNOPRTU
NEUROPATH

AEHNOPRWY PHONEY
WAR
AEHNOPSSU SAPHENOUS
AEHNOPSTY PANTY
HOSE
AEHNORSTT
NORTHEAST
AEHNPRSSS SHARPNESS
AEHNPRSXY PHARYNXES
AEHOOPRRY
PYORRHOEA
AEHOOPSTT OSTEOPATH
AEHOOSSTU OAST
HOUSE
AEHOPSSTT POSTHASTE
AEHOPSSTU PHASE-OUTS
AEHOPSSTW SWEATSHOP
AEHOPTTUY
AUTOPHYTE
AEHORRSSW WARHORSES
AEHORSSTT RHEOSTATS
AEHORSSTU AUTHORESS
AEHORSTTW HOT
WATERS
AEHORSTVW SHORT
WAVE
AEHORSTWY
SEAWORTHY
AEHOSSTTU SOUTHEAST
AEHRSSTUU THESAURUS
AEIIILNRT INITIALER
AEIIILNTW LIE IN WAIT
AEIIIMTTV IMITATIVE
AEIIINNST INANITIES
AEIIINSTT INITIATES
AEIIJLNUV JUVENILIA
AEIIKKTTW KITTIWAKE
AEIIKLLNS SILKALINE
AEIIKLNOT KAOLINITE
AEIIKRSTT KERATITIS
AEIILLMNN MILLENNIA
AEIILLTTT TITILLATE
AEIILMNNS MAIN LINES
AEIILMNNT ELIMINANT
AEIILMNSU ALUMINISE
AEIILMNUZ ALUMINIZE
AEIILMOSV MALVOISIE
AEIILMRSS SERIALISM
AEIILMRTT LITERATIM
AEIILNNOT LINEATION
AEIILNNRT TRIENNIAL
AEIILNOTV INVIOLATE
AEIILNPRT REPTILIAN
AEIILNPST PLATINISE

AEIILNPTV PLAINTIVE
AEIILNPTZ PLATINIZE
AEIILNRRS AIRLINERS
AEIILNRRT TRILINEAR
AEIILNRST LATINISER
AEIILNRTY LINEARITY
AEIILNRTZ LATINIZER
AEIILNSTW WAISTLINE
AEIILNTVY VENIALITY
AEIILORST SOLITAIRE
AEIILORTV VARIOLITE
AEIILOSTV ISOLATIVE
AEIILOTVV VIOLATIVE
AEIILPPST TAIL PIPES
AEIILQSTU QUALITIES
AEIILRRST TRISERIAL
AEIILRRSV RIVALRIES
AEIILRSTU RITUALISE
AEIILRSTV VITALISER
AEIILRTUZ RITUALIZE
AEIILRTVZ VITALIZER
AEIILSSUV VISUALISE
AEIILSUVZ VISUALIZE
AEIIMMRSX MAXIMISER
AEIIMMRXZ MAXIMIZER
AEIIMNNRT NITRAMINE
AEIIMNPST IMPATIENS
AEIIMNPTT IMPATIENT
AEIIMNRTU MINIATURE
AEIIMNSTT INTIMATES
AEIIMPRRS PRIMARIES
AEIIMPSSV IMPASSIVE
AEIINNNTV ANTIVENIN
AEIINNPTT IN-PATIENT
AEIINNRSS RAININESS
AEIINNRSV NIVERNAIS
AEIINNRTT ITINERANT
AEIINNRTU URANINITE
AEIINNSTU ANNUITIES,
INSINUATE
AEIINOPTX EXPIATION
AEIINORTT ITERATION
AEIINOTTV NOVITIATE
AEIINRRTY ITINERARY
AEIINRTUV URINATIVE
AEIIPRSTV PRIVATISE
AEIIPRTTV PARTITIVE
AEIIPRTVV PRIVATIVE
AEIIPRTVZ PRIVATIZE
AEIIPSSST EPISTASIS
AEIIPSSTX EPISTAXIS
AEIIPSTTT STIPITATE
AEIIRRSST SATIRISER
AEIIRRSTT ARTERITIS

AEIIRRSTV ARRIVISTE
AEIIRRSTZ SATIRIZER
AEIIRSSTV VARSITIES
AEIIRTTTV ATTRITIVE
AEIJKKRVY REYKJAVIK
AEIJMNNSS JANSENISM
AEIJNNSST JANSENIST
AEIJNSTTU JAUNTIEST
AEIKKLLOO LOOK-ALIKE
AEIKKNNSS SNAKESKIN
AEIKLLNRY KILLARNEY
AEIKLMNOW WOMAN-
  LIKE
AEIKLNNSS LANKINESS
AEIKLNORT OIL TANKER
AEIKLNOVY NIKOLAYEV
AEIKLNPSS SKI PLANES
AEIKLRSTY STREAKILY
AEIKMQRSU QUAKERISM
AEIKNNPRS SPINNAKER
AEIKNNSSS SNAKINESS
AEIKNORTU KETONURIA
AEIKNPSSW PAWKINESS
AEIKNQSSU QUAKINESS
AEIKNSSTW SWANKIEST
AEIKORSST KERATOSIS
AEIKPPQSU PIPSQUEAK
AEIKPRSTY STRIKE PAY
AEIKPSSST PISS-TAKES
AEIKRSSST ASTERISKS
AEILLLRTY LITERALLY
AEILLMMST SMALL-TIME
AEILLMNRY MILLENARY
AEILLMRTW WATERMILL
AEILLMSSY AIMLESSLY
AEILLMSTT METALLIST
AEILLNOPT POLLINATE
AEILLNPRY PLENARILY
AEILLNPST PANELLIST
AEILLNRST INSTALLER,
  REINSTALL
AEILLNRTU TELLURIAN
AEILLOPPT PAPILLOTE,
  POPLITEAL
AEILLOSTY LOYALTIES
AEILLPRSU PLURALISE
AEILLPRUZ PLURALIZE
AEILLPSSS SALES SLIP
AEILLPSST PASTILLES
AEILLPSTU PULSATILE
AEILLQRSU SQUALLIER
AEILLRRTY ARTILLERY
AEILLRSTW STAIRWELL
AEILLRTWY WATER LILY

AEILLRVXY VEXILLARY
AEILMMNPS PELMANISM
AEILMMNST MENTALISM
AEILMMORS MEMORIALS
AEILMNNOT
  MELATONIN
AEILMNNSS MANLINESS
AEILMNOOT
  EMOTIONAL
AEILMNOPR PROLAMINE
AEILMNORS NORMALISE
AEILMNORT MENTORIAL
AEILMNORZ NORMALIZE
AEILMNOSS LOAMINESS,
  MELANOSIS
AEILMNOTU EMULATION
AEILMNPRT IMPLANTER
AEILMNRST TERMINALS,
  TRAMLINES
AEILMNRSU SEMILUNAR
AEILMNRVY LIVERYMAN
AEILMNSST MALTINESS
AEILMNTTY MENTALITY
AEILMORRS MORALISER
AEILMORRZ MORALIZER
AEILMOSTU MOUSETAIL
AEILMPRST PRELATISM
AEILMRSTY SALIMETRY
AEILMRTTY ALTIMETRY
AEILMSSVY MASSIVELY
AEILMSTTU STIMULATE
AEILMSTUU MUTUALISE
AEILMTUUZ MUTUALIZE
AEILNNOPR NONPAREIL
AEILNNOST TENSIONAL
AEILNNOSV SLOVENIAN
AEILNNOSY LYONNAISE
AEILNNPSS PLAINNESS
AEILNNPSU PENINSULA
AEILNNTUV UNIVALENT
AEILNOOPS POLONAISE
AEILNOORS EROSIONAL
AEILNOPPR PIPERONAL
AEILNOPST SEAL-POINT
AEILNOPSY POLYNESIA
AEILNOPTT PELTATION,
  POTENTIAL
AEILNORST ORIENTALS,
  RELATIONS, SEROTINAL,
  TENSORIAL
AEILNORSV VERSIONAL
AEILNORTT NATROLITE
AEILNOSSS SESSIONAL
AEILNPRTY INTERPLAY,

PAINTERLY, PARTY
  LINE
AEILNPSTY SAPIENTLY
AEILNPTTY PATIENTLY
AEILNPTUV PULVINATE
AEILNRSTT STERILANT
AEILNRSTV INTERVALS
AEILNRSUV UNIVERSAL
AEILNRTTV TRIVALENT
AEILNRTUV AVIRULENT
AEILNRTUY UNREALITY
AEILNSSST SALTINESS,
  SLATINESS, STAINLESS
AEILNSSTW SLANTWISE
AEILNSTVY SYLVANITE
AEILNSUUX UNISEXUAL
AEILOPRRS POLARISER
AEILOPRRZ POLARIZER
AEILOPRST SAPROLITE
AEILORSTT TOTALISER
AEILORSTY ROYALTIES
AEILORTTV LEVITATOR
AEILORTTZ TOTALIZER
AEILPPRTU PREPUTIAL
AEILPPSST SPLIT PEAS
AEILPPSUV APPULSIVE
AEILPRRSS REPRISALS
AEILPRSST PILASTERS
AEILPRSTT PALTRIEST,
  PRELATIST
AEILPRTVY PRIVATELY
AEILPSSVY PASSIVELY
AEILPSTTU STIPULATE
AEILPSTUV PULSATIVE
AEILQRRUY RELIQUARY
AEILRSSTY LAY SISTER
AEILRTUUX LUXURIATE
AEILSTUXY SEXUALITY
AEIMMNNRS
  MANNERISM
AEIMMNOPT
  PANTOMIME
AEIMMRSST SMARMIEST
AEIMMRSSU SUMMARIES,
  SUMMARISE
AEIMMRSUZ SUMMARIZE
AEIMNNNQU
  MANNEQUIN
AEIMNNOPU
  PNEUMONIA
AEIMMNNOST MINNESOTA
AEIMNNRST MANNERIST
AEIMNOPRT PROTAMINE
AEIMNORST STEAM IRON

AEIMNORSW
WOMANISER
AEIMNORTV NORMATIVE
AEIMNORWZ
WOMANIZER
AEIMNPRST SPEARMINT
AEIMNRSTT MARTINETS
AEIMNRSTU ANTISERUM
AEIMNRTTY MATERNITY
AEIMOPRTX PROXIMATE
AEIMORRSU ARMOURIES
AEIMORSST ATOMISERS
AEIMORSTT ESTIMATOR
AEIMORSTV MOVIE STAR
AEIMORSTZ ATOMIZERS
AEIMORTTU AUTOTIMER
AEIMPPRSU PAUPERISM
AEIMPRSTU SEPTARIUM
AEIMPRTUZ TRAPEZIUM
AEIMQRSSU MARQUISES
AEIMRRRTU TERRARIUM
AEIMRSTTY TASIMETRY
AEINNNOTW
NEWTONIAN
AEINNNPTU NEPTUNIAN
AEINNOPSX EXPANSION
AEINNORTV VERNATION
AEINNOSST SENSATION
AEINNOTTT ATTENTION,
TENTATION
AEINNPPSS NAPPINESS
AEINNPSST INAPTNESS
AEINNRSTT INSTANTER,
TRANSIENT
AEINNRSTU SATURNINE
AEINNRSTY TYRANNIES,
TYRANNISE
AEINNRTYZ TYRANNIZE
AEINNSSST NASTINESS
AEINNSSTT NATTINESS
AEINOOPRT OPERATION
AEINOOPSU IONOPAUSE
AEINOPPRT APPOINTER,
REAPPOINT
AEINOPRSS ASPERSION
AEINOPRST PATRONISE
AEINOPRSY AEPYORNIS
AEINOPRTZ PATRONIZE
AEINOPSSS SOAPINESS
AEINOQRTU
INQUORATE, ORTANIQUE
AEINOQSTU EQUATIONS
AEINOQTTU TOTAQUINE
AEINORRST SERRATION

AEINORSST ASSERTION,
SEÑORITAS
AEINORSSU ARSENIOUS
AEINORSSV AVERSIONS
AEINORSTT STATIONER
AEINOSTVX VEXATIONS
AEINPPSSS SAPPINESS
AEINPPSST SNAPPIEST
AEINPRRST TERRAPINS,
TRANSPIRE
AEINPRTTY PATERNITY
AEINPSSST PASTINESS
AEINPSSSW WASPINESS
AEINRRSST STRAINERS
AEINRRSTT RESTRAINT
AEINRSSTT RATTINESS,
RESISTANT, TRAIN SETS
AEINRSSTU SUSTAINER
AEINRSSUZ SUZERAINS
AEINRSTTT IN TATTERS
AEINSSSTT TASTINESS
AEINSSTTT TATTINESS
AEINSSTZZ SNAZZIEST
AEIOORRST ORATORIES
AEIOPRRSV VAPORISER
AEIOPRRVZ VAPORIZER
AEIOPRTTV PORTATIVE
AEIOPRTXY EXPIATORY
AEIOPSSTU AUTOPSIES
AEIORTUVV UVAROVITE
AEIOSTUVX VEXATIOUS
AEIPRRTVY VARITYPER
AEIPRSSTU PRUSSIATE
AEIPRSTUZ TRAPEZIUS
AEIQRTTUZ QUARTZITE
AEIRRSSTT STARRIEST
AEIRRTTTU TRITURATE
AEIRSSTTU TESSITURA
AEIRSTTTX TESTATRIX
AEIRSTTUY AUSTERITY
AEISSSSTY ESSAYISTS
AEJLLOSUY JEALOUSLY
AEJMPRTUW WATER
JUMP
AEJOPSTUX JUXTAPOSE
AEKKLRRSY SKYLARKER
AEKLMOORT TOOL-
MAKER
AEKLMORTW
METALWORK
AEKLORSVW WALKOVERS
AEKLPRRSS SPARKLERS
AEKMNOORR
MOONRAKER

AEKMNOPSS SPOKESMAN
AEKMNOPTW KEPT
WOMAN
AEKMOORSY
KARYOSOME
AEKMPRRSS PRESSMARK
AEKNOORST
SNAKEROOT
AEKNOOTTU TAKE OUT
ON
AEKNPRRST PRANKSTER
AEKNRSSST STARKNESS
AEKNRSTTU TURKESTAN
AEKOPPRRW PAPERWORK
AEKOPRTYY KARYOTYPE
AEKORRWWX
WAXWORKER
AEKQRSSUW SQUAWKERS
AELLLMOSU MALLEOLUS
AELLLPTUU PULLULATE
AELLLRSTU STELLULAR
AELLLSSWY LAWLESSLY
AELLMNOTT
ALLOTMENT
AELLMNSSS SMALLNESS
AELLMOPRY PERMALLOY
AELLMORTY
ALLOMETRY
AELLNNOTW
ALLENTOWN
AELLNOSTW STONEWALL
AELLNQUUY UNEQUALLY
AELLNRTUY NEUTRALLY
AELLOOPRT ALLOTROPE
AELLOPRRT PATROLLER
AELLOPRSY ROLE PLAYS
AELLOPSTX POLL TAXES
AELLOPTUV POLE VAULT
AELLORSWW
SWALLOWER
AELLOSUYZ ZEALOUSLY
AELLRSSTY ARTLESSLY
AELMMORST
MAELSTROM
AELMMOSUU
MAUSOLEUM
AELMNNNTU
ANNULMENT
AELMNNOOP
MONOPLANE
AELMNOOPR
LAMPOONER
AELMNOORT
MONOLATER

AELMNOORY
MONOLAYER
AELMNOPRT
PATROLMEN
AELMNOPSS PLEONASMS
AELMNOPTU
PULMONATE
AELMNORST
MESTRANOL
AELMNORWW
LAWNMOWER
AELMNRSTU
MENSTRUAL
AELMNRTTU
TREMULANT
AELMOORSS
SALEROOMS, SALESROOM
AELMOOSTT LOOM-
STATE
AELMOPSTT PALMETTOS
AELMOSTTU MULATTOES
AELMRSSTT MALTSTERS
AELNOOSSW LOW
SEASON
AELNOPRSS PERSONALS
AELNOPRSY LAYPERSON
AELNOPSTY NEOPLASTY
AELNORSTU SOLUTREAN
AELNOTUVV VOL-AU-
VENT
AELNRRUVY VULNERARY
AELNRSSTT SLATTERNS
AELNRSTTU RESULTANT
AELNSSSUU USUALNESS
AELOOPRTW WATER
POLO
AELOORRTT TOLERATOR
AELOPPRSS PROLAPSES
AELOPRSTU SPORULATE
AELOPSSSU ESPOUSALS
AELOPSTTU POSTULATE
AELPPRTUW WUPPERTAL
AELPRRSTT PRATTLERS
AELPRSSST STRAPLESS
AELPSTTUU PUSTULATE
AELQRRTUY
QUARTERLY
AEMMNORTY
MANOMETRY,
MOMENTARY
AEMMOORST
ROOMMATES
AEMMORSST
MARMOSETS

AEMMORTTY
ATMOMETRY
AEMMRSTYY
ASYMMETRY
AEMNNOORS ROMAN
NOSE
AEMNNORST
ORNAMENTS
AEMNNORTT
REMONTANT
AEMNOOPRT
PROTONEMA
AEMNOORST
ANTEROOMS
AEMNORRSS
RANSOMERS
AEMNORRTU
NUMERATOR
AEMNORSTY
MONASTERY
AEMNPRTUY
PRYTANEUM
AEMNRSSST SMARTNESS
AEMNRSTTU
TRANSMUTE
AEMNRSTVY
VESTRYMAN
AEMOORSTT
STATEROOM
AEMOPRRTY
TEMPORARY
AEMOPRSTU MOUSETRAP
AEMOPRSTW
TAPEWORMS
AEMOPSTTY ASYMPTOTE
AEMORRRSU
ARMOURERS
AEMQRRTUY
MARQUETRY
AENNORRST
RESNATRON
AENNPSSTU UNAPTNESS
AENNRSTTU
TRANSEUNT
AENOOPSST SOAPSTONE,
TEASPOONS
AENOORRST
RESONATOR
AENOORRTV
RENOVATOR
AENOPPRRT EN RAPPORT
AENOPRSST PATRONESS,
TRANSPOSE
AENOPRSUV SUPERNOVA

AENORRTWW
WATERWORN
AENORSSTU ANOESTRUS
AENORSTTY ATTORNEYS
AENPRSSTT TRANSEPTS
AENQSSSTU SQUATNESS
AENRSTWYY ENTRYWAYS
AEOOPRRST OPERATORS
AEOOPRTTV VAPORETTO
AEOPRRRTY PORTRAYER
AEOPRRSTT PROSTRATE
AEOPRRSTW SPEARWORT
AEOPRSSSV PASSOVERS
AEOPRSSTT PROSTATES
AEOQRRSSU SQUARROSE
AEORSSSSS ASSESSORS
AEORSSTTT TESTATORS
AEORSSTUU TROUSSEAU
AEPPRSSUY PAPYRUSES
AEPPRSTUU SUPPURATE
AEPQRRTUY PARQUETRY
AEPRRSSTU SUPERSTAR
AEQRSSTTU SQUATTERS
AEQSSTTTU SQUATTEST
AERRSSTUU SUSURRATE
AFFGGINUW GUFFAWING
AFFGIIMNR AFFIRMING
AFFGILNNS SNAFFLING
AFFGIORST SGRAFFITO
AFFHILRSY RAFFISHLY
AFFHILSTU FAITHFULS
AFFHIMRSS FISH FARMS
AFFIILNPT PLAINTIFF
AFFIILNRUY RUFFIANLY
AFFLLOOST FOOTFALLS
AFFLLORUV FLAVORFUL
AFFLOOTTU FOOT FAULT
AFFMNNRUY FUNNY
FARM
AFGGGINOT FAGGOTING
AFGGIINTU FATIGUING
AFGHHILLT HALF-LIGHT
AFGHILLNT NIGHTFALL
AFGHILNST FANLIGHTS
AFGHILPSS FLAGSHIPS
AFGHILSTT LIGHT-FAST
AFGHIMNOT
FATHOMING
AFGHINRST FARTHINGS
AFGHLNSSU FLASHGUNS
AFGHMOORT
HOMOGRAFT
AFGIILMNN INFLAMING
AFGIILNNT INFLATING

AFGIILNNU UNFAILING
AFGIILRTY FRAGILITY
AFGIIMNRY RAMIFYING
AFGIINRTY RATIFYING
AFGIKNORS FORSAKING
AFGIKNRST SKIN GRAFT
AFGILLNUY GAINFULLY
AFGILMNOS FLAMINGOS
AFGILNNTU FLAUNTING
AFGILNNWY FAWNINGLY
AFGILNORV FLAVORING
AFGILRTUY FRUGALITY
AFGIMORTU FUMIGATOR
AFGINNOPR PROFANING
AFGINNPRY FRYING PAN
AFGINORRW
    FARROWING
AFGINORUV FAVOURING
AFGINSTTU FUNGISTAT
AFGNNOOSU SON-OF-A-
    GUN
AFGNOPRSW
    FROGSPAWN
AFGORSTUW TUGS-OF-
    WAR
AFHHLRTTU HALF-
    TRUTH
AFHIILNTU HIFALUTIN
AFHIKLOTT OF THAT ILK
AFHIKLPSS HIP FLASKS
AFHIKMSUU FUKUSHIMA
AFHIORSTY FORSYTHIA
AFHLLMRUY
    HARMFULLY
AFHLLORST SHORTFALL
AFHLMNOOS HALF
    MOONS
AFHOOPSTT FOOTPATHS
AFHOORRST HOARFROST
AFIIILNOT FILIATION
AFIILNNOT INFLATION
AFIILNOOT FOLIATION
AFIILNSST FINALISTS
AFIILORRT TRIFORIAL
AFIIMNRRY INFIRMARY
AFIINOSTX FIXATIONS
AFIIOORRT A FORTIORI
AFIKLLMOT MILK FLOAT
AFILLLOST FLOTILLAS
AFILLNOUX FLUXIONAL
AFILLNPUY PAINFULLY
AFILLOOPR APRIL FOOL
AFILMMORS
    FORMALISM

AFILMNNTU FULMINANT
AFILMOPRS SALPIFORM
AFILMORST FORMALIST
AFILMORTY FORMALITY
AFILMRSST FILM STARS
AFILNOOTT FLOTATION
AFILNPSST FLAT SPINS
AFILOORSS FOSSORIAL
AFILSSTTU FLAUTISTS
AFIMNNORT
    INFORMANT
AFIMNOORT
    FORMATION
AFINNOSTU FOUNTAINS
AFINOOPRR RAINPROOF
AFINOPRTY PROFANITY
AFIORTTTT TIT FOR TAT
AFIOSTTUU FATUITOUS
AFKLOOSTT FOOTSTALK
AFLLLPUYY PLAYFULLY
AFLLNORTY FRONTALLY
AFLLNOSSW SNOWFALLS
AFLLOOSTT FOOTSTALL
AFLMOPRST PLATFORMS
AFLMORRUY
    FORMULARY
AFLOOPSTY SPLAYFOOT
AFLOORSUV FLAVOROUS
AFLOPRRSU FLUORSPAR
AFLOSTUUY FATUOUSLY
AFMNORRST
    TRANSFORM
AFMOORSTY
    STYROFOAM
AGGHHILSY HAGGISHLY
AGGHIILNT ALIGHTING
AGGHILOOY
    HAGIOLOGY
AGGHILSST GASLIGHTS
AGGHILSWY WAGGISHLY
AGGIIIMNN IMAGINING
AGGIIILLNP PILLAGING
AGGIILMNN MALIGNING
AGGIILNNS SIGNALING
AGGIILNNT TINGALING
AGGIILNVW LAWGIVING
AGGIIMNRT MIGRATING
AGGIIMNST GIGANTISM
AGGIINNOZ AGONIZING
AGGIINNSS ASSIGNING
AGGILLNOP GALLOPING
AGGILLNRY GLARINGLY
AGGILNNOS GANGLIONS
AGGILNNPS SPANGLING

AGGILNNRW
    WRANGLING
AGGILNOOY
    ANGIOLOGY
AGGILNPPR GRAPPLING
AGGILNPSY GASPINGLY
AGGILNRTY GRATINGLY
AGGIMMNRU
    RUMMAGING
AGGIMNPUZ
    GAZUMPING
AGGINNOOR
    GORGONIAN
AGGINORRS GROSGRAIN
AGGINORTU
    OUTRAGING
AGGINPSTU UPSTAGING
AGGKNNTUW
    KWANGTUNG
AGGMOORRT
    MORTGAGOR
AGGMOSTYY
    MYSTAGOGY
AGGNNOPYY
    PYONGYANG
AGHHIKNTW
    NIGHTHAWK
AGHHILTUY HAUGHTILY
AGHHINRST THRASHING
AGHHLOOPR
    HOLOGRAPH
AGHHMOOPR
    HOMOGRAPH
AGHIILLTT TAILLIGHT
AGHIILNSV LAVISHING
AGHIIMMMN
    IMMINGHAM
AGHIINNSV VANISHING
AGHIINRSV RAVISHING
AGHIINRTU THURINGIA
AGHIIPRRS HAIRGRIPS
AGHIKNOSU KAOHSIUNG
AGHILLNOW
    HALLOWING
AGHILLNSY LASHINGLY
AGHILLNTY HALTINGLY
AGHILLORY HOLY GRAIL
AGHILMORT
    ALGORITHM,
    LOGARITHM
AGHILNOOS HOOLIGANS
AGHILNORT GRANOLITH
AGHILNOTW ALONG
    WITH

AGHILNPSS SPLASHING
AGHILNPTY PLAYTHING
AGHILNTUY NAUGHTILY
AGHILRSTT STARLIGHT
AGHIMNRST HAMSTRING
AGHIMOPRY AMPHIGORY
AGHIMORST
HISTOGRAM
AGHINNOPR
ORPHANING
AGHINORRW
HARROWING
AGHINPSUW WASHING-
UP
AGHINQSSU SQUASHING
AGHINRTTW
THWARTING
AGHIRSSTT STRAIGHTS
AGHKMOPRY
KYMOGRAPH
AGHKOPRRU
GORAKHPUR
AGHLLOOPY
HAPLOLOGY
AGHLMNOPU
PLOUGHMAN
AGHLMOOPR
LAGOMORPH
AGHLMOORS
HOLOGRAMS
AGHLMOOTU
GOALMOUTH
AGHLNOOTY
ANTHOLOGY
AGHLNOSTU
ONSLAUGHT
AGHLOOPTY
PATHOLOGY
AGHLOPPRY POLYGRAPH
AGHLOPRXY
XYLOGRAPH
AGHLORSSU HOURGLASS
AGHMNOOPR
MONOGRAPH,
NOMOGRAPH,
PHONOGRAM
AGHMNOOPY
MONOPHAGY
AGHMNPSSU
SPHAGNUMS
AGHMNRSTU
HAMSTRUNG
AGHMOOPRT
PHOTOGRAM

AGHMOPRYY
MYOGRAPHY
AGHNNSTUU HSUAN
T'UNG
AGHNOPSSU SPHAGNOUS
AGHOOPRRY
OROGRAPHY
AGHOOPRYZ
ZOOGRAPHY
AGIIIMNPR IMPAIRING
AGIIIMNTT IMITATING
AGIIINNRV VIRGINIAN
AGIIINSTV VAGINITIS
AGIIINTTV VITIATING
AGIIKLMNR GRIMALKIN
AGIIKMNST MISTAKING
AGIILLLOP GALLIPOLI
AGIILLMMR MILLIGRAM
AGIILLNOR GORILLIAN
AGIILLNRV RIVALLING
AGIILLNWY WAILINGLY
AGIILMNSY MISLAYING
AGIILMNTY MALIGNITY
AGIILNORS ORIGINALS
AGIILNORT TAILORING
AGIILNOST INTAGLIOS,
ISOLATING
AGIILNOTV VIOLATING
AGIILNPRS SPIRALING
AGIILNRSV VIRGINALS
AGIILNSSS ISINGLASS
AGIILNSTT LITIGANTS
AGIILORTT LITIGATOR
AGIILOTTT TOGLIATTI
AGIIMMNRT IMMIGRANT
AGIIMNNRT INMIGRANT
AGIIMNNORT MIGRATION
AGIIMNOST SIGMATION
AGIIMNPRT IMPARTING
AGIIMORTT MITIGATOR
AGIINNNOT ANOINTING
AGIINNORS SIGNORINA
AGIINNORT RATIONING
AGIINNPRS SPRAINING
AGIINNPSS IN PASSING
AGIINNPST PAINTINGS
AGIINNRST STRAINING,
TRAININGS
AGIINNRTU URINATING
AGIINOORT IGNORATIO
AGIINPPRS APPRISING
AGIINPRST TRAIPSING
AGIINSSST ASSISTING
AGIINSTTU SITUATING

AGIIORRRT IRRIGATOR
AGIIRSSTT GASTRITIS
AGIIRSTTU GUITARIST
AGIKLMORS KILOGRAMS
AGIKLNOSY SOAKINGLY
AGIKLNOTT TALKING-TO
AGIKLNPRS SPARKLING
AGIKMNNSU
UNMASKING
AGIKNNPSS SPANKINGS
AGIKNOSST GOATSKINS
AGIKNQSUW
SQUAWKING
AGILLNNNU ANNULLING
AGILLNOPW WALLOPING
AGILLNOTT ALLOTTING,
TOTALLING
AGILLNOWW
WALLOWING
AGILLNQSU SQUALLING
AGILLNSTY LASTINGLY
AGILMNNOO
MONGOLIAN
AGILMNNOY
MOANINGLY
AGILMNPRT TRAMPLING
AGILMNSUY AMUSINGLY
AGILMRSUV VULGARISM
AGILNNOPS PLAINSONG
AGILNNOQU
ALGONQUIN
AGILNNRSY SNARINGLY
AGILNNRTY RANTINGLY
AGILNNWYY
YAWNINGLY
AGILNOPRT PATROLING
AGILNORSY SOARINGLY
AGILNORVY VAINGLORY
AGILNOTUV OVULATING
AGILNOTUW
OUTLAWING
AGILNOTUY OUTLAYING
AGILNPRSW SPRAWLING
AGILNPRSY RASPINGLY,
SPARINGLY
AGILNPRTT PRATTLING
AGILNPRTY PRATINGLY
AGILNPSTT SPLATTING
AGILNPSTU PULSATING
AGILNPSUY PAUSINGLY
AGILNRSST STARLINGS
AGILNRSSU SINGULARS
AGILNRSTT STARTLING
AGILNRVYY VARYINGLY

AGILNSWYY SWAYINGLY
AGILOOPST APOLOGIST
AGILOPRUY UROPYGIAL
AGILRRTUY GARRULITY
AGILRTUVY VULGARITY
AGIMMNSUY
GYMNASIUM
AGIMNNOOR
MAROONING
AGIMNNORS
RANSOMING
AGIMNNOTU
AMOUNTING
AGIMNNOVV MOVING
VAN
AGIMNOOSV
VAMOOSING
AGIMNORSS ORGANISMS
AGIMNORSU
IGNORAMUS
AGIMNRRTY
MARTYRING
AGIMOOSSU ISOGAMOUS
AGIMORRTY
MIGRATORY
AGINNORRW
NARROWING
AGINNPRSU UNSPARING
AGINNPSSW WINGSPANS
AGINNSTUU TUNGUSIAN
AGINOOPSS POISON GAS
AGINOOTTT
TATTOOING
AGINOPPRV APPROVING
AGINOPRRT PARROTING
AGINOPRTU PURGATION
AGINORRSS GARRISONS
AGINORSST ASSORTING,
ORGANISTS, ROASTINGS
AGINORSTY GYRATIONS,
SIGNATORY
AGINORSUV SAVOURING
AGINPPRST STRAPPING,
TRAPPINGS
AGINPPRSW WRAPPINGS
AGINPRSTU PASTURING
AGINQRRUY QUARRYING
AGINQSTTU SQUATTING
AGINRSSST STAR SIGNS
AGINRSSTY STINGRAYS
AGIOPRRSY SPIROGYRA
AGIQRSSTU GRASSQUIT
AGJKNORRU
KURRAJONG

AGKLLNOOO A LONG
LOOK
AGKLORSSW GLASSWORK
AGKLPPRSU SPARK PLUG
AGKNORSST KNOTGRASS
AGLLNOOPY
POLYGONAL
AGLMOORSU
GLAMOROUS
AGLOOPSST GOALPOSTS
AGLOORSTY ASTROLOGY
AGLOOTTUY
TAUTOLOGY
AGLOPPRUY PLAYGROUP
AGLORRSUU GARRULOUS
AGLORSSTW GLASSWORT
AGMMNOORS
GROOMSMAN,
MONOGRAMS
AGMMOSTUU
GUMMATOUS
AGMNORRST
STRONGARM
AGMNSSTUY
NYSTAGMUS
AGNNOSSSW
SWANSONGS
AGNOPRSST PART-SONGS
AGNPRSSUY SPRAY GUNS
AGNRRSTUY STRANGURY
AGOPRRTUY PURGATORY
AGORSTTUY GUSTATORY
AGRSTTTTU STUTTGART
AHHIIMORS HIROSHIMA
AHHIIRRST HAIR SHIRT
AHHLORSTU SHORT-
HAUL
AHHMOSTUW
MOUTHWASH
AHHNORRST
HARTSHORN
AHHNORSTW
HAWTHORNS
AHHOPPRUY HAPPY
HOUR
AHIIILSST LITHIASIS
AHIILLPPP PHILLIPPA
AHIILLTWW WITH A WILL
AHIILOOPZ ZOOPHILIA
AHIILORSU HILARIOUS
AHIILOSST HALITOSIS
AHIILRSTT SHIRTTAIL
AHIINORST HISTORIAN
AHIIPRSSZ SIZARSHIP

AHIIRRSTT ARTHRITIS
AHIKKNNTT THINK
TANK
AHIKKNRSS SHARKSKIN
AHIKLMSWY MAWKISHLY
AHIKLNSVY KNAVISHLY
AHILLPSSY SPLASHILY
AHILLPSTW WHIPSTALL
AHILLSSVY SLAVISHLY
AHILMNNSY MANNISHLY
AHILMOPSY SYPHILOMA
AHILMORST HAILSTORM
AHILMOSST MAILSHOTS
AHILMPRTU TRIUMPHAL
AHILNPPUY UNHAPPILY
AHILOPPTY HIPPOLYTA
AHILOPSST HOSPITALS
AHILORSTW SHOW TRIAL
AHILORTTY THROATILY
AHILOSTTT STATOLITH
AHILPSSWY WASPISHLY
AHILQSSUY SQUASHILY
AHILRSTWY SWARTHILY
AHIMMNORU
HARMONIUM
AHIMMOPRS
AMORPHISM
AHIMNNORY
INHARMONY
AHIMNORST
HARMONIST
AHIMNPSTY SYMPATHIN
AHIMNRTUU
ANTHURIUM
AHIMNSSTU HUMANISTS
AHIMOOSTX
HOMOTAXIS
AHIMOPRSS APHORISMS
AHIMOPRSY MAYORSHIP
AHIMOPSUX AMPHIOXUS
AHINNOOPT
PHONATION
AHINNOPTY
ANTIPHONY
AHINOOPRS SOPHRONIA
AHINOOSTU HOUSTONIA
AHINPRSST TRANSSHIP
AHIOPPSSY APOPHYSIS
AHIOPRSUV VAPOURISH
AHIORRTWY
AIRWORTHY
AHIORTTUY AUTHORITY
AHKLOOPYY PLAY
HOOKY

AHKLOSSTW TALK
SHOWS
AHKNOSTUY
THANKYOUS
AHKORSTUW
SOUTHWARK
AHLLLOSWY SHALLOWLY
AHLLMOOPR
ALLOMORPH
AHLLNOSTW TOWN
HALLS
AHLLOPSUY APHYLLOUS
AHLMOOOPR
HOMOPOLAR
AHLMOOPSY
HOMOPLASY
AHLMOPSTY POLYMATHS
AHLNOPSSU ALPHONSUS
AHMOOPRSU
AMORPHOUS
AHMOORSSW
WASHROOMS
AHMOPRTTU
MOUTHPART
AHNNNOOTY
HOOTNANNY
AHNOOPRTY
PHONATORY
AHNOPPSSW PAWNSHOPS
AHNOPSSSV SNAPSHOTS
AHNORRTTY
THYRATRON
AHOOOPTTT HOT
POTATO
AHOOPRRTX
PROTHORAX
AHOOPSTTT PHOTOSTAT
AHOORRTTY
HORTATORY
AHOPSSTUW SOUTHPAWS
AIIILLNTY INITIALLY
AIIILMNST LAMINITIS
AIIIMNOTT IMITATION
AIIINNNOT INANITION
AIIINNSTY ASININITY
AIIINORTT INITIATOR
AIIINOTTV VITIATION
AIIJLOTVY JOVIALITY
AIIKNNNPS PANNIKINS
AIIILLMMNY MINIMALLY
AIIILLMRSY SIMILARLY
AIIILLNSTY SAINTLILY
AIIILLPRRS SPIRILLAR
AIIILLRTVY TRIVIALLY

AIILMMNUU ALUMINIUM
AIILMNORT TRINOMIAL
AIILMNSST STALINISM
AIILMNSTT MILITANTS
AIILMOSST ALTISSIMO
AIILMPRRY PRIMARILY
AIILMRSST MISTRIALS
AIILMRSTU RITUALISM
AIILNOOST ISOLATION
AIILNOOTV VIOLATION
AIILNOPST OIL PAINTS
AIILNOPSV PAVILIONS
AIILNOQTU LIQUATION
AIILNORTT INTROITAL
AIILNOSTT SILTATION
AIILNOTTU TUITIONAL
AIILNPSST TAILSPINS
AIILNRSST SINISTRAL
AIILNSSTT STALINIST
AIILPRSST SPRITSAIL
AIILPRSTU SPIRITUAL
AIILRSTTU RITUALIST
AIIMMPRSV VAMPIRISM
AIIMNNTUY UNANIMITY
AIIMNOPRS PROSIMIAN
AIIMNOPSS IMPASSION
AIIMNOSTY ANIMOSITY
AIIMNPSTT TIMPANIST
AIIMORSTT IMITATORS
AIIMPSSSV PASSIVISM
AIIMRSTUU MAURITIUS
AIIMRSUVV VIVARIUMS
AIINNNOPT PINNATION
AIINNORTT NITRATION
AIINNORTU RUINATION,
URINATION
AIINNOSSV INVASIONS
AIINNOTTX ANTITOXIN
AIINNRSTT IN TRANSIT
AIINOOQRU IROQUOIAN
AIINOPRTT PARTITION
AIINOPRTV PRIVATION
AIINORSTT STRIATION
AIINORSVY VISIONARY
AIINORTTT ATTRITION,
TITRATION
AIINOSTTU SITUATION
AIINQTTUY ANTIQUITY
AIINRRSTT IRRITANTS
AIIOPRRTY APRIORITY
AIIOPRSSS PSORIASIS
AIIOPRSTT PAROTITIS,
TOPIARIST
AIIORRRTT IRRITATOR

AIIORTTTV TITIVATOR
AIIPPRRST PARTI PRIS
AIIPRRSST AIRSTRIPS
AIIPRTTUY PITUITARY
AIIPSSSTV PASSIVIST
AIIPSSTVY PASSIVITY
AIJMORSTU MAJOR SUIT
AIJNOPPSY POPINJAYS
AIKLNOSSY ANKYLOSIS
AIKLOSTTW KILOWATTS
AIKMNNOSW
KINSWOMAN
AIKNOPRTW PAINTWORK
AILLMMORY
IMMORALLY
AILLMNNOY
NOMINALLY
AILLMPRSU PLURALISM
AILLMSUUV ALLUVIUMS
AILLNORST TONSILLAR
AILLNORSU LUNISOLAR
AILLNOSST STALLIONS
AILLNOSSU ALLUSIONS
AILLNOTUU ULULATION
AILLORSTT LITTORALS,
TORTILLAS
AILLOSSTY LOYALISTS
AILLPPRUY PUPILLARY
AILLPRSTU PLURALIST
AILLPRTUY PLURALITY
AILLPSSWY SPILLWAYS
AILLRTUVY VIRTUALLY
AILMMOORT
IMMOLATOR
AILMMORST IMMORTALS
AILMMRSUY SUMMARILY
AILMMTTUU
ULTIMATUM
AILMNNOTY
ANTIMONYL
AILMNOOPS PALOMINOS
AILMNOORS MONORAILS
AILMNOPSY AMYLOPSIN,
OLYMPIANS
AILMNORST MORTAL SIN
AILMNORTY
NORMALITY
AILMNOSUU ALUMINOUS
AILMNSTTU STIMULANT
AILMORSST MORALISTS
AILMOORSU SOLARIUMS
AILMORSTU SIMULATOR
AILMORTTU MUTILATOR
AILMORTTY MORTALITY

AILMOSSTY ATMOLYSIS
AILMPRSTY PALMISTRY
AILMPSSST PSALMISTS
AILMTTUUY MUTUALITY
AILNNOSSW SONS-IN-
LAW
AILNNSTTY INSTANTLY
AILNOORST TONSORIAL,
TORSIONAL
AILNOOSTV SOLVATION
AILNOOTUV OVULATION
AILNOPSTU PLATINOUS,
PULSATION
AILNOPSTY PONYTAILS
AILNORSTU INSULATOR
AILNOSTUY AUTOLYSIN
AILNOSUXY ANXIOUSLY
AILNPPSTU SUPPLIANT
AILNPQTUY PIQUANTLY
AILNRRSTU TRIAL RUNS
AILNRTUUX LUXURIANT
AILNSSTTU LUTANISTS
AILOORSTV VIOLATORS
AILOORSUV VARIOLOUS
AILORRSUV RIVALROUS
AILORSSTY ROYALISTS
AILORSTTU TUTORIALS
AILORSUVY VARIOUSLY
AILOSSTUY AUTOLYSIS
AILRSSTTU ALTRUISTS
AILRSSUVV SURVIVALS
AIMMMMNOS
MAMMONISM
AIMMMNOST
MAMMONIST
AIMMNORTY
MATRIMONY
AIMMNOSTU
SUMMATION
AIMMPRSUU MARSUPIUM
AIMNNOORT
NOMINATOR
AIMNNOPST POINTSMAN
AIMNNOSTU
MOUNTAINS
AIMNNOSUU
UNANIMOUS
AIMNNOTYY
ANONYMITY
AIMNNRSTU RUMINANTS
AIMNOPRSY PARSIMONY
AIMNOPRTT IMPORTANT
AIMNOPRTY PATRIMONY
AIMNORRST RAINSTORM

AIMNORRTU
RUMINATOR
AIMNORSUU
UNIRAMOUS
AIMNOSTTU MUTATIONS
AIMNPSTTY TYMPANIST
AIMNRSSTU SATURNISM
AIMOPSSTU POTASSIUM
AINNOOPRS SOPRANINO
AINNOOPRT PRONATION
AINNOORTV
INNOVATOR
AINNOOSTT NOTATIONS
AINNORSTT STRONTIAN
AINOOPPRT APPOINTOR,
APPORTION
AINOOPSTT POTATIONS
AINOOQTTU
QUOTATION
AINOORSTT ROTATIONS
AINOOTTUX
AUTOTOXIN
AINOPRSTU PUT ON
AIRS, SUPINATOR
AINOPRSUU UNIPAROUS
AINORSSST ARSONISTS
AINRSSTTU NATURISTS
AIOOORRST ORATORIOS
AIOOPRSUV APIVOROUS,
OVIPAROUS
AIOOSTTTT TATTOOIST
AIOPRRSTT PORTRAITS
AIORRSSTU SARTORIUS
AIPPRSSTT TRAPPISTS
AJMMNNOPU
PANMUNJOM
AJMPRSTTU JUMP-START
AKKRSTVYY SYKTYVKAR
AKLNOOTUW WALK OUT
ON
AKLNOSUVY ULYANOVSK
AKLOPRRRY LORRY PARK
AKLORSSTW SALTWORKS
AKLPRRSSU LARKSPURS
AKMOPRSST POSTMARKS
AKNNORSYY
SYNKARYON
AKOPRRSTW PART
WORKS
ALLMOOSSY LYSOSOMAL
ALLNOOPTY POLYTONAL
ALLNOPTTU POLLUTANT
ALLNSUUUY UNUSUALLY
ALLOOPRTY ALLOTROPY

ALLOPPRUY POPULARLY
ALLOPRSTW STRAW POLL
ALLORSTTY TALL STORY
ALMNOORTY
MONOLATRY
ALMNOPRUY
PULMONARY
ALMOOPRSY
PLAYROOMS
ALMOORSUY
AMOROUSLY
ALMOPPSST LAMPPOSTS
ALNOPPRUU
UNPOPULAR
ALNOPPSTT POT PLANTS
ALNOPSTTU POSTULANT
ALNORTUVY
VOLUNTARY
ALNPSTTUU PUSTULANT
ALOOPPRSS PROPOSALS
ALOOPRSTV STAVROPOL
ALOOPSTYZ ZOOPLASTY
ALOPRSTUY PULSATORY
AMMNPSTUY
TYMPANUMS
AMMOOSTTU
MATSUMOTO
AMNNOOSUY
ANONYMOUS
AMNOORSTY
ASTRONOMY
AMNOPRSST SPORTSMAN
AMNOTTUYY
TAUTONYMY
AMOOORSTV
VASOMOTOR
AMOORRRWW
ARROWWORM
AMOORSTWY
MOTORWAYS
AMOPRSSXY PAROXYSMS
AMPRSTUUY SUMPTUARY
ANNOOPRSU
NONPAROUS
ANNORSTUY
TYRANNOUS
ANOOOPRSZ
SPOROZOAN
ANOOOPRTZ
PROTOZOAN
ANOPRRSTT TRANSPORT
ANORSUUVY
UNSAVOURY
ANRRSSTUU SUSURRANT

AOOORRRTW
ARROWROOT
AOOORRTTV
ROTOVATOR
AOOPRRSTT PROTOSTAR
AOPPRSSST PASSPORTS
AOPRRSTUU RAPTUROUS
AOQSSTTUU STATUS QUO
AORRRTWWY
WORRYWART
AORSTTTUY STATUTORY
BBBDEELRU BLUBBERED
BBBDEHNOO
HOBNOBBED
BBBEEELMU BUMBLEBEE
BBBEEELUZ BEELZEBUB
BBBEGLMUU BUBBLE
GUM
BBBEILSTU BUBBLIEST
BBBINOPSY BOBBY PINS
BBCDEELOR CLOBBERED
BBCDEILRS SCRIBBLED
BBCEHISTU CHUBBIEST
BBCEHLOUY CUBBYHOLE
BBCEILRRS SCRIBBLER
BBCEILRSS SCRIBBLES
BBCEIRRSU SCRUBBIER
BBCEIRSSU SUBSCRIBE
BBCERRSSU SCRUBBERS
BBCGINRSU SCRUBBING
BBCIIILOT BIBLIOTIC
BBCKLOOSU BOOK CLUBS
BBDDEELOU DOUBLE BED
BBDEELORS SLOBBERED
BBDEGIMNO
DEMOBBING
BBDEHIRSU RUBBISHED
BBDEILRSU BLUEBIRDS
BBDEIORRW BOWERBIRD
BBDELLMSU DUMBBELLS
BBDELLOOU BLUE
BLOOD
BBDGIILNR DRIBBLING
BBDGINRSU DRUBBINGS
BBDLOOSWY BODY
BLOWS
BBEEEEINR BEBEERINE
BBEEEHLMU HUMBLEBEE
BBEEEINRR BERBERINE
BBEEFLLUY BULLY BEEF
BBEEILPST PLEBBIEST
BBEEIORRS ROBBERIES
BBEEIRRSU RUBBERISE
BBEEIRRUZ RUBBERIZE

BBEELLLSU BLUEBELLS
BBEELORRS SLOBBERER
BBEELRRUY BLUEBERRY
BBEGGIINR GIBBERING
BBEGHIIRS GIBBERISH
BBEGHILOS BOBSLEIGH
BBEGIRSTU GRUBBIEST
BBEHKOOTY BY THE
BOOK
BBEHLLMOS BOMBSHELL
BBEHRRSUY SHRUBBERY
BBEIKLNOR KNOBBLIER
BBEIKSTUZ KIBBUTZES
BBEILOSTW WOBBLIEST
BBEILQRSU QUIBBLERS
BBEIMMOST TIME BOMBS
BBEIMOSST BOMBSITES
BBEINSSTU TUBBINESS
BBEISSTTU STUBBIEST
BBEKLOOSU BLUE BOOKS
BBEMNORUX BOX
NUMBER
BBERRTTUU BUTTERBUR
BBFMOOOPR
BOMBPROOF
BBGGINOPU GO PUBBING
BBGHILLTU LIGHT BULB
BBGHILNOO HOBGOBLIN
BBGHIMOST BOMBSIGHT
BBGHINORT THROBBING
BBGIILNQU QUIBBLING
BBGILNOSY SOBBINGLY
BBIIILNRU BILIRUBIN
BBIIKMTUZ KIBBUTZIM
BBIIKMNOST STINK-BOMB
BBLLOSUYY BULLYBOYS
BCCCKMOOS
COCKSCOMB
BCCDEHKOY
BODYCHECK
BCCDEMSUU
SUCCUMBED
BCCEEILOR COERCIBLE
BCCEHIKNP PINCHBECK
BCCEHKKOO
CHECKBOOK
BCCEILRSU CRUCIBLES
BCCEINNOU CONCUBINE
BCCEKLORU COCKLEBUR
BCCEKOSTU STOCK CUBE
BCCEMRSUU
CUCUMBERS, SUCCUMBER
BCCGIILNY BICYCLING
BCCIILSTY BICYCLIST

BCCIOOPRS BROSCOPIC
BCCIORSTU SCORBUTIC
BCCMOORXY
COXCOMBRY
BCCMORRUY
CURRYCOMB
BCCOSSTUU CUB SCOUTS
BCDDEEHOU
DEBOUCHED
BCDDEEILU DEDUCIBLE
BCDDEEIRS DESCRIBED
BCDDIIKRY DICKYBIRD
BCDEEEEHS BESEECHED
BCDEEEINO OBEDIENCE
BCDEEEMRS DECEMBERS
BCDEEGIKN BEDECKING
BCDEEHIIR HERBICIDE
BCDEEHITW BEWITCHED
BCDEEHRTU BUTCHERED
BCDEEILRU REDUCIBLE
BCDEEILSU SEDUCIBLE
BCDEEIORR CEREBROID
BCDEEIRRS DESCRIBER
BCDEEJSTU SUBJECTED
BCDEEMNTU
DECUMBENT
BCDEIILNU INDUCIBLE
BCDEIINRS INSCRIBED
BCDEIJSUU SUB JUDICE
BCDEIKORR BRODERICK
BCDEIKRRS REDBRICKS
BCDEKLNUU
UNBUCKLED
BCDEOOTTY
BOYCOTTED
BCDEORRSS CROSSBRED
BCDGOSYZZ BYDGOSZCZ
BCDHKNOUU
BUCKHOUND
BCDILMNOW CLIMB-
DOWN
BCDIMOORS SCOMBROID
BCDKLOOOW
WOODBLOCK
BCDKNOOOS
BOONDOCKS
BCDKNOORU
ROCKBOUND
BCDOPRTUY BY-
PRODUCT
BCEEEFINS BENEFICES
BCEEEGHIS BIG CHEESE
BCEEEHKNO CHEEKBONE
BCEEELQRU BECQUEREL

BCEEGHINR BREECHING
BCEEGIINR BIGENERIC
BCEEHKTTU BUCKTEETH
BCEEHORTT BROCHETTE
BCEEIIJTV BIJECTIVE
BCEEIILMS IMBECILES
BCEEIILNV EVINCIBLE
BCEEIIJOTV OBJECTIVE
BCEEILLOS BELLICOSE
BCEEILRTY CELEBRITY
BCEEINOOT COENOBITE
BCEEIOQSU QUEBECOIS
BCEEIPRRS PRESCRIBE
BCEEJNORT JOB CENTRE
BCEEJOSTX SEX OBJECT
BCEELNOSY OBSCENELY
BCEELOOSS OBSOLESCE
BCEEMNRTU
    RECUMBENT
BCEEMRRSU CEREBRUMS
BCEENPSTU PUBESCENT
BCEENRSTU RUBESCENT
BCEFFIOOX BOX OFFICE
BCEFFIOOY OFFICE BOY
BCEFIIKRR FIREBRICK
BCEFIIRTY FEBRICITY
BCEFIJOTY OBJECTIFY
BCEGHILNN BLENCHING
BCEGHORRU
    CHERBOURG
BCEGIIKNR BICKERING
BCEGIINST BISECTING
BCEGIJNOT OBJECTING
BCEGIKNNO BECKONING
BCEGIKNTU BUCKETING
BCEGIMNRU CUMBERING
BCEHIILPT PHLEBITIC
BCEHIISTT BITCHIEST
BCEHILORT BLOTCHIER
BCEHILPSU BLUE CHIPS
BCEHIMORS CHEMISORB
BCEHIOSTT BOTCHIEST
BCEHKNORW
    WORKBENCH
BCEHLOSUU CLUBHOUSE
BCEHMNOOY
    HONEYCOMB
BCEHORRSU BROCHURES
BCEIIJNOT BIJECTION
BCEIILPSU PUBLICISE
BCEIILPUZ PUBLICIZE
BCEIIMORT BIOMETRIC
BCEIINOST BISECTION
BCEIINRRS INSCRIBER

BCEIIRSTX BISECTRIX
BCEIJLOPU JOE PUBLIC
BCEIJNOOT OBJECTION
BCEILLMRU CRIBELLUM
BCEILMNOU COLUMBINE
BCEILMORY COR BLIMEY
BCEILMOTU COLUMBITE
BCEILMRRU CRUMBLIER
BCEILNOOT BOLECTION
BCEILNORU COLUBRINE
BCEILPRSU REPUBLICS
BCEIMNNTU
    INCUMBENT
BCEIMNORY EMBRYONIC
BCEINORRW BROWN
    RICE
BCEINOSTU BOUNCIEST
BCEINOSTY OBSCENITY
BCEINSSUU INCUBUSES
BCEIOPRRS PROSCRIBE
BCEIORSTT OBSTETRIC
BCEJOORST OBJECTORS
BCEKLOOTV BLOCK
    VOTE
BCELMOOTY
    LOBECTOMY
BCELORSUY OBSCURELY
BCEMOORSY
    CORYMBOSE
BCENOORTY CON BY
    ROTE
BCEOORSTU CUBE
    ROOTS
BCEOORRWY
    CROWBERRY
BCEORSTUX SUBCORTEX
BCEPRTTUU BUTTERCUP
BCFGLLOSU GOLF CLUBS
BCFHILLNU BULLFINCH
BCGHILNTU NIGHTCLUB
BCGIIMNNO COMBINING
BCGILMNRU
    CRUMBLING
BCGINORSU OBSCURING
BCHIIMSTU BISMUTHIC
BCHIIOPRS BISHOPRIC
BCHIIRSTU HUBRISTIC
BCHIIRSTY HYBRISTIC
BCHILLOTY BLOTCHILY
BCHILOPYY LYOPHOBIC
BCHINORTY BRYTHONIC
BCHIOORSY CHOIRBOYS
BCHKNORTU
    BUCKTHORN

BCHKOOTTU
    BUCKTOOTH
BCHLNOPUW PUNCH
    BOWL
BCHLOOOSY
    SCHOOLBOY
BCHMOOOTT
    TOOTHCOMB
BCIIIMRST BRITICISM
BCIILMSUU UMBILICUS
BCIILPSTU PUBLICIST
BCIILPTUY PUBLICITY
BCIILRTUY LUBRICITY
BCIIMNOOS BIONOMICS
BCIIMOSTY SYMBIOTIC
BCIISSSTU CUBISISTS
BCIKKORRW BRICKWORK
BCIKNNRSU INNSBRUCK
BCIKNRSUW BRUNSWICK
BCILLORSS CROSSBILL
BCILMMOUU
    COLUMBIUM
BCILMNOPU PLUMBICON
BCILORSUU LUBRICOUS
BCILPRSTU STRIP CLUB
BCIMNOOOS SONIC
    BOOM
BCIOOPRSS PROBOSCIS
BCIORSTUY OBSCURITY
BCIPRSSTU SUBSCRIPT
BCKOOOPSY COPYBOOKS
BCMNOOORR
    BROOMCORN
BCMOORSTU
    COMBUSTOR
BCOOORSSW CROSSBOWS
BCOOSSTUY BOY SCOUTS
BDDDEEINR BEDRIDDEN
BDDEEEFIR DEBRIEFED
BDDEEEILV BEDEVILED
BDDEEFOOR FOREBODED
BDDEEGGRU
    BEGRUDGED
BDDEEGIMN EMBEDDING
BDDEEIOSY DISOBEYED
BDDEEISTU SUBEDITED
BDDEELNRU BLUNDERED
BDDEELORU REDOUBLED
BDDEENORU
    REBOUNDED
BDDEENRRU
    UNDERBRED
BDDEENSTU SUBTENDED
BDDEFINOR FORBIDDEN

BDDEFIORR FORBIDDER	**BDEEFOORR** FOREBODER	**BDEGGGINU** DEBUGGING
BDDEFLOOU BLOOD	**BDEEFOOTW** WEB-	**BDEGGINTU** BUDGETING
FEUD	FOOTED	**BDEGGNUUY** DUNE
BDDEGIIMN IMBEDDING	**BDEEGGLOW** BOW-	BUGGY
BDDEGLOOU	LEGGED	**BDEGHILNO** BEHOLDING
DOODLEBUG	**BDEEGHINT** BENIGHTED	**BDEGHINRU** EDINBURGH
BDDEHINOU HIDEBOUND	**BDEEGMRSU** SUBMERGED	**BDEGIIILR** DIRIGIBLE
BDDEHLOOS BLOODSHED	**BDEEGNORU**	**BDEGIILOS** DISOBLIGE
BDDEIIMOR DIBROMIDE	BURGEONED	**BDEGIINNR** REBINDING
BDDEIISUV SUBDIVIDE	**BDEEHIITX** EXHIBITED	**BDEGIIPPR** BIG DIPPER
BDDEILNRU UNBRIDLED	**BDEEHILMS** BLEMISHED	**BDEGIKNNU** DEBUNKING
BDDEILORW BLOW-	**BDEEHLORS** BEHOLDERS	**BDEGIMNOY**
DRIED	**BDEEHNRTU**	EMBODYING
BDDEIMOSY DISEMBODY	BURTHENED	**BDEGINNNU** UNBENDING
BDDEINRSU DISBURDEN	**BDEEHORTT** BETROTHED	**BDEGINNRU** BURDENING
BDDEIRSSU DISBURSED	**BDEEIILLN** INDELIBLE	**BDEGINORR** BORDERING
BDDEIRSTU DISTURBED	**BDEEIILRS** DERISIBLE	**BDEGINORT** TONBRIDGE
BDDELLOUZ BULLDOZED	**BDEEIINNZ** BENZIDINE	**BDEGLNORU**
BDDELSUUY SUBDUEDLY	**BDEEIKLNR** BLINKERED	OLDENBURG
BDDENNOUU	**BDEEILLTT** BELITTLED	**BDEGLNOSU** BLUDGEONS
UNBOUNDED	**BDEEILMOR** EMBROILED	**BDEHIIINT** INHIBITED
BDDENORUY	**BDEEILMSS** DISSEMBLE	**BDEHIIRSY** HYBRIDISE
UNDERBODY	**BDEEILNNO** NONEDIBLE	**BDEHIIRYZ** HYBRIDIZE
BDDENOTUU	**BDEEILRST** BLISTERED	**BDEHILPSU** PUBLISHED
UNDOUBTED	**BDEEIMMRS** DISMEMBER	**BDEHINRSU** BURNISHED
BDDEOSTYY TEDDY	**BDEEIMORR** EMBROIDER	**BDEHIORSU** BIRDHOUSE
BOYS	**BDEEINRRT** INTERBRED	**BDEIIILSV** DIVISIBLE
BDDFILLNO BLINDFOLD	**BDEEIORSY** DISOBEYER	**BDEIIILTY** EDIBILITY
BDDFMNOUU	**BDEEIPRSW** SPIDERWEB	**BDEIIJNOS** INSIDE JOB
DUMBFOUND	**BDEEIRRST** BESTIRRED	**BDEIIKRST** DIRT BIKES
BDDHISSTU BUDDHISTS	**BDEEIRRSV** RIVERBEDS	**BDEIILLNY** INDELIBLY
BDDILLORY DOLLY BIRD	**BDEEIRSTT** BED-SITTER	**BDEIILMOS** MOBILISED
BDDINNOUW	**BDEEKNRSU** DEBUNKERS	**BDEIILMOZ** MOBILIZED
WINDBOUND	**BDEEKOORW**	**BDEIILNNO** BLENNIOID
BDEEEEFLN ENFEEBLED	BROOKWEED	**BDEIISSSU** SUBSIDIES,
BDEEEELRV BELVEDERE	**BDEELLSSY** BLESSEDLY	SUBSIDISE
BDEEEFILL BIELEFELD	**BDEELMRSU** SLUMBERED	**BDEIISSUZ** SUBSIDIZE
BDEEEFINT BENEFITED	**BDEELNRRU** BLUNDERER	**BDEIJNOSU** SUBJOINED
BDEEEGLUW BUGLEWEED	**BDEELNSSU** UNBLESSED	**BDEILLNPS** SPELLBIND
BDEEEHLRT BLETHERED	**BDEELORST** BOLSTERED	**BDEILMOOR** DORMOBILE
BDEEEIOTW WOE BETIDE	**BDEELRSTU** BLUSTERED	**BDEILNNSS** BLINDNESS
BDEEEKNOT BETOKENED	**BDEEMMOOS**	**BDEILOQTU** QUODLIBET
BDEEELMRS RESEMBLED	EMBOSOMED	**BDEILORSV** LOVEBIRDS
BDEEELMZZ EMBEZZLED	**BDEEORSTY** OYSTER BED	**BDEILORSW** BLOW-DRIES
BDEEELNOS NOSEBLEED	**BDEEORVYY** EVERYBODY	**BDEILORUV** OVERBUILD
BDEEELOSU SEE DOUBLE	**BDEEPRRSU** PUREBREDS	**BDEILPRUU** UPBUILDER
BDEEEMMNT	**BDEEPRRTU** PERTURBED	**BDEILRRSY** LYREBIRDS
EMBEDMENT	**BDEERSTUV** SUBVERTED	**BDEILSTTU** SUBTITLED
BDEEENRTU DEBENTURE	**BDEFFLORU** OLD BUFFER	**BDEIMSTTU** SUBMITTED
BDEEERSTW BESTREWED	**BDEFHIRSU** FURBISHED	**BDEINNORW** WIND-
BDEEFIILS DISBELIEF	**BDEFIILRR** RIFLEBIRD	BORNE
BDEEFLLOW BEDFELLOW	**BDEFILLOO** LIFEBLOOD	**BDEINORTX** TINDERBOX
BDEEFLORW FLOWERBED	**BDEFINORY** BOYFRIEND	**BDEIOORST** BROODIEST
BDEEFLOTT BOTTLE-FED	**BDEFLOSTU** SELF-DOUBT	**BDEIORSTU** SUBEDITOR

BDEIPRSTU BUPRESTID
BDEIRRSSU DISBURSER
BDEIRRSTU DISTURBER
BDEISSSTU SUBSISTED
BDELLOORS BORDELLOS,
DOORBELLS
BDELLOOSS BLOODLESS
BDELLORUZ BULLDOZER
BDELLRRUY BLURREDLY
BDELMNPUU
UNPLUMBED
BDELMOOSS BLOSSOMED
BDELMRTUY TUMBLE-
DRY
BDELNNOSS BLONDNESS
BDELNOOTU
DOUBLETON
BDELNOSSU BOUNDLESS
BDELOOPTY BLOOD
TYPE
BDELOOSUY BODY
LOUSE
BDELOSSTU DOUBTLESS
BDEMMNOSU
OMBUDSMEN
BDEMNOOSU
UNBOSOMED
BDENNOSSU SNUB-
NOSED
BDENNRSUU
SUNBURNED
BDENOSTUW
WESTBOUND
BDEOOOORRW
WOODBORER
BDFHIILNS BLINDFISH
BDFHNOOOU
HOOFBOUND
BDFILLLOS BILLFOLDS
BDFIOORST BIRD'S-FOOT
BDGIILNSU BUILDINGS
BDGIINNNU UNBINDING
BDGIINORS DISROBING
BDGIINSSU SUBSIDING
BDGINORSS SONGBIRDS
BDGINORTU OBTRUDING
BDHIIMRSY HYBRIDISM
BDHIIRTYY HYBRIDITY
BDHIMOORS
RHOMBOIDS
BDHLOOOST
BLOODSHOT
BDHMOSSUW DUMB
SHOWS

BDHOORSUW
BRUSHWOOD
BDIIMORTY MORBIDITY
BDIIRTTUY TURBIDITY
BDIKNORUV DUBROVNIK
BDILLORSW SWORDBILL
BDILNNOSW SNOW-
BLIND
BDILNNOWW
WINDBLOWN
BDILNOPST BLIND SPOT
BDILOSUUY DUBIOUSLY
BDINNOORU
IRONBOUND
BDINNRTUW
WINDBURNT
BDINOOWWW BOW
WINDOW
BDINOOWWX WINDOW
BOX
BDKNOOORS
DOORKNOBS
BDKOOSSTU STUDBOOKS
BDLLOOSTU BLOOD LUST
BDLMOOORW
BLOODWORM
BDLMOOSUY
MOLYBDOUS
BDLNOOOSU
DOUBLOONS
BDLOOOORT
BLOODROOT
BDLOSSTUW
DUSTBOWLS
BDNNOOSUW
SNOWBOUND
BDORSUWZZ
BUZZWORDS
BEEEEEKPR BEEKEEPER
BEEEEFLNR ENFEEBLER
BEEEFINSS BEEFINESS
BEEEGGRUZ ZEEBRUGGE
BEEEGLNOS BOLEGNESE
BEEEGLNRT GREEN BELT
BEEEGNOOW
WOEBEGONE
BEEEGNOTW GO-
BETWEEN
BEEEHHLMT
BETHLEHEM
BEEEHLLOR HELLEBORE
BEEEHLRTT ETHELBERT
BEEEHNOSY HONEYBEES
BEEEILMNT BELEMNITE

BEEEILRSV BELIEVERS,
EVERSIBLE
BEEEIMRSV SEMIBREVE
BEEEINORT BÊTE-
NOIRE
BEEEINRSS BEERINESS
BEEEELMNSS ENSEMBLES
BEEEELMRRS RESEMBLER
BEEEELMRZZ EMBEZZLER
BEEEELPRTU BLUE PETER
BEEEELSSSU SUBLESSEE
BEEEMPRST SEPTEMBER
BEEFFGIRU FEBRIFUGE
BEEFFORTT BETTER OFF
BEEFFOSTW WEB OFFSET
BEEFIILMS MISBELIEF
BEEFILLST LIFE BELTS
BEEFIORSX FIREBOXES
BEEGGIINS BESIEGING
BEEGGINTT BEGETTING
BEEGHILSW BIG WHEELS
BEEGHIRTY EYEBRIGHT
BEEGIILLL ILLEGIBLE
BEEGIILNV BELIEVING
BEEGILLNR REBELLING
BEEGILLNV BEVELLING
BEEGILLNW WELLBEING
BEEGILNRS INSELBERG
BEEGINNRS BEGINNERS
BEEGINRTT BETTERING
BEEGINSST BEESTINGS
BEEGINSTT BESETTING
BEEGKORRS GO BERSERK
BEEGMNRRU
NUREMBERG
BEEGMRRSU MERSEBURG
BEEGMSTUY BE MY
GUEST
BEEGRSSSU BURGESSES
BEEHILLMS EMBELLISH
BEEHILMRS BLEMISHER
BEEHILMSS BLEMISHES
BEEHINRTT TEREBINTH
BEEHIOPRS BIOSPHERE
BEEHIORRV HERBIVORE
BEEHLLRSU BUSHELLER
BEEHLOORS BOREHOLES
BEEHLOPRY HYPERBOLE
BEEHLOTTT THE BOTTLE
BEEHNOOPX
XENOPHOBE
BEEIIKNRZ BEREZNIKI
BEEIILNRT LIBERTINE
BEEIILRST LIBERTIES

BEEIINRTY INEBRIETY
BEEIKLMRU BERKELIUM
BEEIKLMRY KIMBERLEY
BEEILLNOR REBELLION
BEEILLNTU EBULLIENT
BEEILLRTT BELITTLER
BEEILMORR EMBROILER
BEEILNOPX EXPONIBLE
BEEILNRSU NEBULISER
BEEILNRUZ NEBULIZER
BEEILORTT BRIOLETTE
BEEILOTTU OUBLIETTE
BEEILPRTU ERUPTIBLE
BEEILRRSV VERS LIBRE
BEEILSTUV VESTIBULE
BEEIMNRST TENEBRISM,
 TRIBESMEN
BEEIMRRSU REIMBURSE
BEEINNOTT BENTONITE
BEEINNRTU INNER TUBE
BEEINRSTT TENEBRIST
BEEINRTTU BUTTERINE
BEEIOQSSU OBSEQUIES
BEEIOSSSV OBSESSIVE
BEEIQRTTU BRIQUETTE
BEEIRTTTY YTTERBITE
BEEJKOSUX JUKEBOXES
BEEKNORST KERBSTONE
BEEKOPRRY POKEBERRY
BEELLLMUU UMBELLULE
BEELLORSU RESOLUBLE
BEELLSSUY BULL'S-EYES
BEELMMNRU
 LUMBERMEN
BEELMNORU
 MELBOURNE
BEELMOORT
 BOLOMETER
BEELMRRSU SLUMBERER
BEELNNOSS NOBLENESS
BEELNOSTU BLUESTONE
BEELORRST BOLSTERER
BEELORSVY VERBOSELY
BEELORTTX LETTERBOX
BEELQRSUU BURLESQUE
BEELRRSTU BLUSTERER
BEEMMNOTW
 EMBOWMENT
BEEMNNORU NUMBER
 ONE
BEEMNNRTU NUMBER
 TEN
BEEMNORSV
 NOVEMBERS

BEENOORRV
 OVERBORNE
BEENOQSTU OBSEQUENT
BEENORRST RESORBENT
BEENORSSS SOBERNESS
BEENORSTU TENEBROUS
BEENRSTTU BRUNETTES
BEEOORSTT BEETROOTS
BEEORRSSV OBSERVERS
BEEORSTTU SOUBRETTE
BEEPRRSTY PRESBYTER
BEEQRSTUY BY REQUEST
BEERRSTUV SUBVERTER
BEESSTTTU TEST TUBES
BEFFGINRU BUFFERING,
 REBUFFING
BEFFGINTU BUFFETING
BEFFHINTU IN THE BUFF
BEFFIILLR FIBERFILL,
 FIBREFILL
BEFFLNSSU BLUFFNESS
BEFGIINTT BEFITTING
BEFHIRRSU FURBISHER,
 REFURBISH
BEFHKLOOS BOOKSHELF
BEFIILNSU INFUSIBLE
BEFIILRTY FEBRILITY
BEFILLMSU BLUE FILMS
BEFILLOSW BLOWFLIES
BEFILOSUY LIFE BUOYS
BEFIORSTT FROSTBITE
BEFLLLOPY BELLY FLOP
BEFLRTTUY BUTTERFLY
BEFNNNOUY FUNNY
 BONE
BEGGGINRU BUGGERING
BEGGGLOOX GOGGLE
 BOX
BEGGHMRUU
 HUMBUGGER
BEGGIILNU BEGUILING
BEGGIINNN BEGINNING
BEGGILNNO BELONGING
BEGGINOSS BOGGINESS
BEGHHINOT THIGHBONE
BEGHHOTTU
 BETHOUGHT
BEGHIINTW BEGIN WITH
BEGHILRST BLIGHTERS
BEGHINORT BOTHERING
BEGHINORU NEIGHBOUR
BEGHLNOSU BUNGHOLES
BEGIILLLN LIBELLING
BEGIILLLY ILLEGIBLY

BEGIILLNT BILLETING
BEGIIMRST BIG-TIMERS
BEGIINNTY BENIGNITY
BEGIJRTTU JITTERBUG
BEGILLNOW BELLOWING
BEGILMNRT TREMBLING
BEGILMNRU LUMBERING
BEGILNNNO
 ENNOBLING
BEGILNSSS BLESSINGS
BEGILNSSU BULGINESS
BEGIMNNOT
 ENTOMBING
BEGIMNNRU
 NUMBERING
BEGIMNOSS EMBOSSING
BEGINORSU SUBREGION
BEGINORSV OBSERVING
BEGINOSSS OBSESSING
BEGINOSTW BESTOWING
BEGINRTTU BUTTERING,
 REBUTTING
BEGIOORSU BOURGEOIS
BEGLMRRSU GRUMBLERS
BEHIIINRT INHIBITER
BEHIILPRT PHILIBERT
BEHIILPST PHLEBITIS
BEHIIMNOY YOHIMBINE
BEHIIORTX EXHIBITOR
BEHIIRRST BRITISHER
BEHIKLOSV BOLSHEVIK
BEHIKPSSU PUSHBIKES
BEHIKSUVY KUIBYSHEV
BEHILNOOT ON THE
 BOIL
BEHILOSST BOLSHIEST
BEHILPRSU PUBLISHER,
 REPUBLISH
BEHINNOSS SHINBONES
BEHINOSSW WISHBONES
BEHINRRSU BURNISHER
BEHINSSSU BUSHINESS
BEHKNOOOP PHONE
 BOOK
BEHKNOSUU
 BUNKHOUSE
BEHLLOOST BOLTHOLES
BEHLLOOSW
 BLOWHOLES
BEHLORRTY BROTHERLY
BEHLRSSUU BULRUSHES
BEHMORSSU RHOMBUSES
BEHNORSTU
 BUHRSTONE

BEHOOPTTU
  PHOTOTUBE
BEHOOSSUY HOUSEBOYS
BEHOPRTYY BRYOPHYTE
BEIIILNSV INVISIBLE
BEIIILLNSY SIBYLLINE
BEIILMOSS OMISSIBLE
BEIILNNRS BIN-LINERS
BEIILNRTT LITTERBIN
BEIILORTT TRILOBITE
BEIILSSTU SUBTILISE
BEIIJLSTUZ SUBTILIZE
BEIIMNSSU MINIBUSES
BEIINNRSS BRININESS
BEIINSSTT BITTINESS
BEIKLMOOR BROOKLIME
BEIKLNSSU BULKINESS
BEIKLOORT ROBOT-LIKE
BEIKLOSTY KILOBYTES
BEIKMOORT MOTORBIKE
BEIKNRSSS BRISKNESS
BEILLLOSU LIBELLOUS
BEILLMNPU PLUMB LINE
BEILLMRUY BERYLLIUM
BEILLMSUY SUBLIMELY
BEILLNOSU INSOLUBLE
BEILLNSTU BULLETINS
BEILLOPSX PILLBOXES
BEILMMOSS EMBOLISMS
BEILMNOSW WOMEN'S
  LIB
BEILMOSSY SYMBOLISE
BEILMOSYZ SYMBOLIZE
BEILNORTU IN TROUBLE
BEILNPRTU BLUEPRINT
BEILNRSSU BURLINESS
BEILOOPRT POTBOILER
BEILOPPSW BLOWPIPES
BEILOPSSS POSSIBLES
BEILORSSU SUBSOILER
BEILORSTT LIBRETTOS
BEILOSTWZ BLOWZIEST
BEILSSTTU SUBTITLES
BEIMMNORR
  MERBROMIN
BEIMNOORS BROMEOSIN
BEIMNORST BRIMSTONE
BEIMNOSSU OMNIBUSES
BEIMNPSSU BUMPINESS
BEIMOORST BIOSTROME
BEIMRSTTU SUBMITTER
BEIMRTTUY YTTERBIUM
BEINOOPRT OBREPTION
BEINOORSV OBVERSION

BEINOOSSS OBSESSION
BEINOOSSZ BOOZINESS
BEINOSSSS BOSSINESS
BEINRTTTU BITTERNUT
BEIOOPRRU POURBOIRE
BEIOPTTTU PITOT TUBE
BEIOQRSTU SOBRIQUET
BEIOQSTUU BOUTIQUES
BEIORSTUV OBTRUSIVE
BEIORSTVY VERBOSITY
BEIRSSSTU SUBSISTER
BEJJMOSTU JUMBO JETS
BEJORSTTU TURBOJETS
BEJORSUXY JURY BOXES
BEKKNOOOT BOOK
  TOKEN
BEKLOORSU RULEBOOKS
BEKLOOSTY STYLEBOOK
BEKNNNOUW
  UNBEKNOWN
BEKNOOOST
  NOTEBOOKS
BEKOOSTTX TEXTBOOKS
BELMOOORW
  ELBOWROOM
BELMOPSUU PLUMBEOUS
BELNNSSTU BLUNTNESS
BELNOORVW
  OVERBLOWN
BELNRTTUU TURBULENT
BELORSSSU SUBLESSOR
BELQRSUUY BRUSQUELY
BEMNOORST
  TROMBONES
BEMNOORSW NEW
  BROOMS
BEMNOOSTT
  TOMBSTONE
BEMNORTUU
  OUTNUMBER
BEMNOSSUX
  BUXOMNESS
BEMOORRSS SOMBREROS
BENOOSTUU
  BOUNTEOUS
BENORRSWY
  SNOWBERRY
BENORSSUU BURNOUSES
BENORSTTU OBSTRUENT
BENORSTXY SENTRY
  BOX
BENRTTTUU BUTTERNUT
BEOORRRSW
  BORROWERS

BFFHORSSU BRUSH-OFFS
BFFIIMORR FIBRIFORM
BFFLLOSUY BULLY-OFFS
BFGHILLTU BULLFIGHT
BFGLLORSU BULLFROGS
BFIILMORR LIBRIFORM
BFIINORSU FIBRINOUS
BFILNOTUU BOUNTIFUL
BFIMORRSU BURSIFORM
BFINORRST FIRSTBORN
BFLLLNOUW FULL-
  BLOWN
BFMMOOORR
  BROMOFORM
BFOORTUWY TWO-BY-
  FOUR
BGGHIILNT BLIGHTING
BGGILLNUY BULGINGLY
BGGILMNRU
  GRUMBLING
BGHHIORSW
  HIGHBROWS
BGHINOOOO
  BOOHOOING
BGHLOOPUY
  PLOUGHBOY
BGHMOOOOS
  OGBOMOSHO
BGIILLNOW BILLOWING
BGIILLNOY BOILINGLY
BGIILMOOR IMBROGLIO
BGIILNRST BRISTLING
BGIILOOST BIOLOGIST
BGIKNOPRS SPRINGBOK
BGILLNRSU BULLRINGS
BGILMNOOY
  MYOGLOBIN
BGILMNRSU RUMBLINGS
BGILMNSTU STUMBLING
BGILNNRUY BURNINGLY
BGILNOPRY PROBINGLY
BGILNORTU TROUBLING
BGILOORTY TRIBOLOGY
BGILOOSTY GLOBOSITY
BGILORSUU LOUISBURG
BGIMNSSUU SUBSUMING
BGINNORSU SUBORNING
BGINNORTU BINTURONG
BGINNOTTU BUTTONING
BGINOORRW
  BORROWING
BGINORRUW
  BURROWING
BGINORSTW BOWSTRING

BGKNOOOSS
SONGBOOKS
BGLMOOSYY
SYMBOLOGY
BGNOORSTX
STRONGBOX
BHIIINORT INHIBITOR
BHIILLLLY HILLBILLY
BHIILLNOT BILLIONTH
BHIIMORUZ RHIZOBIUM
BHIKLLOOS BILLHOOKS
BHILLLSUY BULLISHLY
BHILLNORS HORNBILLS
BHILLNORT THORNBILL
BHILMNOTY
BIMONTHLY
BHILOORSY BOORISHLY
BHILRSTUY BRUTISHLY
BHIMOOSTY TOMBOYISH
BHIOORRTT BIRTHROOT
BHIORRTTW
BIRTHWORT
BHKOOOPSS BOOKSHOPS
BHKORRSUW
BRUSHWORK
BHLLNORSU BULLHORNS
BHLLOOOTT
TOLLBOOTH
BHLMPSUUY SUBPHYLUM
BIIILNSVY INVISIBLY
BIILMSTUY SUBLIMITY
BIILOOSUV OBLIVIOUS
BIILOQTUY OBLIQUITY
BIIMNOOST BIONOMIST
BIIMOPRTY IMPROBITY
BIIMOSSSY SYMBIOSIS
BIISSTTYY ITSY-BITSY
BIKLNNOSW SNOWBLINK
BILLNOOPS SPOONBILL
BILLNOOSU BOUILLONS
BILLNORST STILLBORN
BILMMOSSY SYMBOLISM
BILMNOOSS IN BLOSSOM
BILMOSSTY SYMBOLIST
BILNNOOSY LOONY BINS
BILNOSTUU BOTULINUS
BILOOPRTU POLITBURO
BILOOSUVY OBVIOUSLY
BILORSSTU STROBILUS
BIMOPSTUU BUMPTIOUS
BINOOOSUX OBNOXIOUS
BINOORSTU OBTRUSION
BIOPRSSTW BOWSPRITS
BJOPPSTUU PUT-UP JOBS

BKKOOOORSW
WORKBOOKS
BKLLMNSUU
NUMBSKULL
BKMOOORSW
BOOKWORMS
BKOOOORSTY
STORYBOOK
BLOORSTUU TROUBLOUS
BOOPPRRTU TURBOPROP
BORSSTTUU OUTBURSTS
CCCDENOOT
CONCOCTED
CCCEEINRT ECCENTRIC
CCCEIILPY EPICYCLIC
CCCENOORT
CONCOCTER
CCCHHIKOT HITCHCOCK
CCCHIKNOP PINCHCOCK
CCCHILMOU
COLCHICUM
CCCHILOOT COCCOLITH
CCCIILRTY TRICYCLIC
CCDDEEESU SUCCEEDED
CCDDEIINO COINCIDED
CCDDEKLOU
CUCKOLDED
CCDDELNOU
CONCLUDED
CCDDENOTU
CONDUCTED
CCDEEEHKR CHECKERED
CCDEEEHRS SCREECHED
CCDEEEINS DECENCIES
CCDEEERSU SUCCEEDER
CCDEEHIKW CHICKWEED
CCDEEHKNU
UNCHECKED
CCDEEHORT
CROCHETED
CCDEEIINN INCIDENCE
CCDEEILNR ENCIRCLED
CCDEEILOW COLICWEED
CCDEEINNY INDECENCY
CCDEEINOT CONCEITED
CCDEEINOV CONCEIVED
CCDEEIOPS CODPIECES
CCDEELLOT COLLECTED
CCDEEMMNO
COMMENCED
CCDEENNOR
CONCERNED
CCDEENNOS
ENSCONCED

CCDEENNOT
CONNECTED
CCDEENORS CRESCENDO
CCDEENORT
CONCERTED, CONCRETED
CCDEEORRT CORRECTED
CCDEFIIRU CRUCIFIED
CCDEGINNO
CONCEDING
CCDEHNRSU
SCRUNCHED
CCDEIIKNP PICNICKED
CCDEILOOR CROCODILE
CCDEILSTY DYSLECTIC
CCDEINNOV CONVINCED
CCDEINOOT DECOCTION
CCDEINOTV CONVICTED
CCDEINOUV CONDUCIVE
CCDEKLOOR OLD
COCKER
CCDELNOTU
OCCLUDENT
CCDENORRU
CONCURRED
CCDENOSSU CONCUSSED
CCDEORSUU SUCCOURED
CCDGINNOU
CONDUCING
CCDHIILOR CHLORIDIC
CCDHIIMOR DICHROMIC
CCDHKOOUW
WOODCHUCK
CCDKOOOSW
WOODCOCKS
CCDNOORTU
CONDUCTOR
CCEEEFLNU FECULENCE
CCEEEHHRR RECHERCHÉ
CCEEEHNOR
COHERENCE
CCEEEHRRS SCREECHER
CCEEEHRSS SCREECHES
CCEEEIKNP NECKPIECE
CCEEEINNS NESCIENCE
CCEEEINRT RETICENCE
CCEEELORT RECTOCELE
CCEEFILLY LIFE CYCLE
CCEEGINOR CONCIERGE
CCEEHIKOY ICE HOCKEY
CCEEHILMY HEMICYCLE
CCEEHKORU
EUROCHECK
CCEEHKORV
OVERCHECK

CCEEHLORT CERECLOTH
CCEEHORRT
  CROCHETER
CCEEHOTTU
  COUCHETTE
CCEEIIPPR PRECIPICE
CCEEIKRRT CRICKETER
CCEEILNOR RECONCILE
CCEEILOST SCOLECITE
CCEEILPRY PERICYCLE
CCEEILRST ELECTRICS
CCEEIMORT ECTOMERIC
CCEEINNNO INNOCENCE
CCEEINORS CICERONES
CCEEKLORS COCKERELS
CCEEKNRSW CREW
  NECKS
CCEELLORT RECOLLECT
CCEELOSTY CYSTOCELE
CCEELOTUY LEUCOCYTE
CCEENNORT
  CONCENTER,
  CONCENTRE
CCEENOOTY
  COENOCYTE
CCEENRSST CRESCENTS
CCEESSSSU SUCCESSES
CCEFFIIIL FELICIFIC
CCEFIIPSS SPECIFICS
CCEFIIRRU CRUCIFIER
CCEFKNOYY
  COCKNEYFY
CCEGGHOST SCOTCH
  EGG
CCEGHHNOW
  CHENGCHOW
CCEGHILNN CLENCHING
CCEGHIMRU
  CHEMURGIC
CCEGILNRY RECYCLING
CCEHHNRTU THE
  CRUNCH
CCEHIILRS SCHLIERIC
CCEHIKLST CHECKLIST
CCEHILNOR CHRONICLE
CCEHILNRS CLINCHERS
CCEHINRRU CRUNCHIER
CCEHIORST RICOCHETS
CCEHKLNOT
  NECKCLOTH
CCEHKMOOR
  CHECKROOM
CCEHKOORS
  COCKHORSE

CCEHKOPST SPOT CHECK
CCEHKOSTU CHECKOUTS
CCEHLMORS
  CROMLECHS
CCEHNOSTU
  SCUTCHEON
CCEHORRSS SCORCHERS
CCEHORSTT CROTCHETS
CCEHORTTY
  CROTCHETY
CCEIIIPRT EPICRITIC
CCEIIIRST CRITICISE
CCEIIIRTZ CRITICIZE
CCEIIKNPR PICNICKER
CCEIILNOT NICCOLITE
CCEIILRST SCLERITIC
CCEIILSTT CELTICIST
CCEIINSTY CYSTEINIC
CCEIKLLOY KILOCYCLE
CCEIKLOSW CLOCKWISE
CCEIKNOSS COCKINESS
CCEILNNOU NUCLEONIC
CCEILNOSY CONCISELY
CCEILNOTY CYCLONITE
CCEILORST SCLEROTIC
CCEILOSUV OCCLUSIVE
CCEILRSTY TRICYCLES
CCEILRSUU CURLICUES
CCEIMNOOS ECONOMICS
CCEIMORTY MICROCYTE
CCEIMOSST COSMETICS
CCEINNORV CONVINCER
CCEINOOSS CONSOCIES
CCEINORRT INCORRECT
CCEINOSTT TECTONICS
CCEINPRST PRECINCTS
CCEINRSTU CINCTURES
CCEINRSTY SYNCRETIC
CCEINSSTY SYNECTICS
CCEIOORST CREOSOTIC
CCEIOPRST COST PRICE
CCEIOPRSU OCCUPIERS
CCEIOPRTY PRECOCITY
CCEKORRSW
  CORKSCREW
CCELLNOOY
  COLONELCY
CCELLOORT COLLECTOR
CCELMOOTY
  COLECTOMY
CCELNSTUU SUCCULENT
CCELOPRSU CORPUSCLE
CCELOPSSY CYCLOPSES
CCELORRTY CORRECTLY

CCENNNORU
  UNCONCERN
CCENNOORT
  CONNECTOR
CCENOORST
  CONCERTOS
CCENOORSU
  CONCOURSE
CCENOORTV
  CONVECTOR
CCENORRTU
  OCCURRENT
CCENORSTU SUCCENTOR
CCEOOPRSY CRYOSCOPE
CCEOOPRTT ECTOPROCT
CCEOORRRT
  CORRECTOR
CCEOPPRUY PREOCCUPY
CCEORRSUU SUCCOURER
CCEORSSSU SUCCESSOR
CCFGHIKOT COCKFIGHT
CCFHKLLOU CHOCK-
  FULL
CCFIILOOR COLORIFIC
CCFILNOST CONFLICTS
CCFIMORRU CRUCIFORM
CCFKOOOST COCKSFOOT
CCFLLOSUU FLOCCULUS
CCGHIILNN CLINCHING
CCGHIINPU HICCUPING
CCGHIKLNU CHUCKLING
CCGHILNTU CLUTCHING
CCGHILOOP CHOPLOGIC
CCGHINNRU
  CRUNCHING
CCGHINORS SCORCHING
CCGHINORU
  CROUCHING
CCGHINOST SCOTCHING
CCGINNOOO
  COCOONING
CCGINOPUY OCCUPYING
CCGINORRU OCCURRING
CCHHOOPST
  HOPSCOTCH
CCHIIIRTT TRICHITIC
CCHIILORT CHLORITIC
CCHIIMOPR MICROCHIP
CCHIIMORT TRICHOMIC
CCHIINOOR CHORIONIC
CCHIINSUZ ZUCCHINIS
CCHIIOORS ISOCHORIC
CCHIIORRT CIRRHOTIC,
  TRICHROIC

CCHIKOPST CHOPSTICK
CCHILMOSW MILCH
COWS
CCHILNRUY CRUNCHILY
CCHILOORT CHLOROTIC
CCHINRSTY STRYCHNIC
CCHIOPSTY PSYCHOTIC
CCHLNOOTY
COLOCYNTH
CCIIILNOP PICOLINIC
CCIIILNRT TRICLINIC
CCIIIMRST CRITICISM
CCIIINNOT NICOTINIC
CCIILNOTY CLONICITY
CCIILOOST SCOLIOTIC
CCIILOPRT PROCLITIC
CCIINNOOS CONCISION
CCIIORRTT TRICROTIC
CCIIRRTUY CIRCUITRY
CCILMOSTU OCCULTISM
CCILNOORU COUNCILOR
CCILNOOSU OCCLUSION
CCILOOORT COLICROOT
CCILOSTTU OCCULTIST
CCIMMOORS
MICROCOSM
CCIMNOOTY
MONOCYTIC
CCIMOOPRY MICROCOPY
CCINOOSSU CONSCIOUS
CCINOPRST CONSCRIPT
CCINORSTT CONSTRICT
CCIOOOPST OTOSCOPIC
CCIOOPRSU UROSCOPIC
CCIOOSTTY OTOCYSTIC
CCKKLOORW
CLOCKWORK
CCKNORSTU
TURNCOCKS
CCKOOPPPY POPPYCOCK
CCKOOPSST STOPCOCKS
CCLNOORTY
CYCLOTRON
CCNORSTTU
CONSTRUCT
CCOOPRSYY CRYOSCOPY
CDDDEEENS DESCENDED
CDDDEEILY DECIDEDLY
CDDDEEINU UNDECIDED
CDDEEEFLT DEFLECTED
CDDEEEIPY PIECE-DYED
CDDEEENRS DESCENDER
CDDEEEOPR PROCEEDED
CDDEEFKOR DEFROCKED

CDDEEGLLU CUDGELLED
CDDEEHLSU SCHEDULED
CDDEEINRS DISCERNED,
RESCINDED
CDDEEIPRT PREDICTED
CDDEEISST DISSECTED
CDDEEITUV DEDUCTIVE
CDDEELNPU PEDUNCLED
CDDEELPRU PRECLUDED
CDDEEMMNO
COMMENDED
CDDEEMNNO
CONDEMNED
CDDEEMNRU
CREDENDUM
CDDEENNOS
CONDENSED
CDDEENNOT
CONTENDED
CDDEENNOU
DENOUNCED
CDDEGINTU DEDUCTING
CDDEHORRT
DORDRECHT
CDDEIILMO DOMICILED
CDDEIILRU RIDICULED
CDDEIINRT DENDRITIC
CDDEIIOSV VIDEODISC
CDDEIIRST DISCREDIT
CDDEILOSS DISCLOSED
CDDEILSTU CUDDLIEST
CDDEIMOOU
DUODECIMO
CDDEINOTU DEDUCTION
CDDEIOSUU DECIDUOUS
CDDEISSSU DISCUSSED
CDDHHILOO
CHILDHOOD
CDDHIIORY HYDRIODIC
CDDIIILOP DIPLOIDIC
CDDILNOOY
CONDYLOID
CDEEEEFNR DEFERENCE
CDEEEELRT RE-ELECTED
CDEEEFFOR FORCE-FEED
CDEEEFITV DEFECTIVE
CDEEEFLRT REFLECTED
CDEEEFPRT PERFECTED
CDEEEGINR DECREEING
CDEEEGINX EXCEEDING
CDEEEGLNT NEGLECTED
CDEEEHKNP HENPECKED
CDEEEHQRU
CHEQUERED

CDEEEIMRT DECIMETRE
CDEEEINNS DESINENCE
CDEEEINPT CENTIPEDE
CDEEEINRS RESIDENCE
CDEEEINRT INTERCEDE
CDEEEINUV UNDECEIVE
CDEEEIPRV PERCEIVED
CDEEEIPTV DECEPTIVE
CDEEEIRSV DECEIVERS
CDEEEIRSX EXERCISED
CDEEEIRTV DECRETIVE
CDEEEITTV DETECTIVE
CDEEELLOT DÉCOLLETÉ
CDEEELNOR REDOLENCE
CDEEELORT ELECTRODE
CDEEEMNRT
DECREMENT
CDEEENNST SENTENCED
CDEEENPRT PRECEDENT
CDEEEOPRR PROCEEDER
CDEEEORRT RETROCEDE
CDEEEORRV RE-
COVERED
CDEEEPRST RESPECTED
CDEEFGINT DEFECTING
CDEEFIINT DEFICIENT
CDEEFIIOT FOETICIDE
CDEEFIIPS SPECIFIED
CDEEFIIRT CERTIFIED,
RECTIFIED
CDEEFIKLR FLICKERED
CDEEFIKRR FREDERICK
CDEEFILNT INFLECTED
CDEEFILTU DECEITFUL
CDEEFINOT DEFECTION
CDEEFLORT DEFLECTOR
CDEEFNORR CONFERRED
CDEEFNOSS CONFESSED
CDEEFORST DEFECTORS
CDEEGIILN DILIGENCE
CDEEGIIMR GERMICIDE
CDEEGIINN INDIGENCE
CDEEGIINT DIGENETIC
CDEEGIINV DECEIVING
CDEEGIIRS REGICIDES
CDEEGILRY GLYCERIDE
CDEEGINOR ENDOERGIC
CDEEGINPR PRECEDING
CDEEGINTT DETECTING
CDEEGLLRU CUDGELLER
CDEEGNORV
CONVERGED
CDEEGNOST CONGESTED
CDEEHHIRS CHERISHED

CDEEHIKNT THICKENED
CDEEHIKRW WHICKERED
CDEEHILLS CHISELLED
CDEEHIMRS REMSCHEID
CDEEHINST DEHISCENT
CDEEHKOSU DECKHOUSE
CDEEHLORY HYDROCELE
CDEEHLPPS SCHLEPPED
CDEEHLQSU SQUELCHED
CDEEHLSSU SCHEDULES
CDEEHORTU
RETOUCHED
CDEEHRSTT STRETCHED
CDEEHSSSU DUCHESSES
CDEEIILTV VIDELICET
CDEEIIMNS MEDICINES
CDEEIIMPS EPIDEMICS
CDEEIIMRV VERMICIDE
CDEEIIPRR CIRRIPEDE
CDEEIIPST PESTICIDE
CDEEIIPTV DEPICTIVE
CDEEIIRTV DIRECTIVE
CDEEIISTT DIETETICS
CDEEIJNOT DEJECTION
CDEEIJPRU PREJUDICE
CDEEIKLLN NICKELLED
CDEEIKNQU QUICKENED
CDEEIKNRS SNICKERED
CDEEIKSST STICKSEED
CDEEIKSTW STICKWEED
CDEEILLNP PENCILLED
CDEEILNNO INDOLENCE
CDEEILNPR RED-PENCIL
CDEEILNST STENCILED
CDEEILORS CREOLISED
CDEEILORZ CREOLIZED
CDEEILRST DERELICTS
CDEEILTXY EXCITEDLY
CDEEIMNOU
EUDEMONIC
CDEEIMNPU IMPUDENCE
CDEEINNOR ENDOCRINE
CDEEINNSU SECUNDINE
CDEEINOPT DECEPTION
CDEEINORT RECONDITE
CDEEINOST SECTIONED
CDEEINOTT DETECTION
CDEEINPST INSPECTED
CDEEINRRS DISCERNER,
RESCINDER
CDEEINRST STRIDENCE
CDEEINRSY RESIDENCY
CDEEIORSV DIVORCÉES
CDEEIORSX EXORCISED

CDEEIORXZ EXORCIZED
CDEEIOSTX COEXISTED
CDEEIPRSU PEDICURES
CDEEIPRTU DEPICTURE
CDEEIRRTU RECRUITED
CDEEIRSTT TRISECTED
CDEEIRTTU CERTITUDE,
RECTITUDE
CDEEISTUV SEDUCTIVE
CDEEJOPRT PROJECTED
CDEEKLNOW LOW-
NECKED
CDEEKOOPR PRECOOKED
CDEEKORST RESTOCKED
CDEELLMOP
COMPELLED
CDEELLNRU CULLENDER
CDEELLOST COLD STEEL
CDEELMNTU
DEMULCENT
CDEELMOPT COMPLETED
CDEELNOSU COUNSELED
CDEELORSS SCLEROSED
CDEELRSTU CLUSTERED
CDEELRTTU CLUTTERED
CDEEMMNOR
RECOMMEND
CDEEMMNOT
COMMENTED
CDEEMNNOR
CONDEMNER
CDEEMOOPS
DECOMPOSE
CDEEMOORS MORSE
CODE
CDEENNORS
CONDENSER
CDEENNORT
CONTENDER
CDEENNORU
DENOUNCER,
RENOUNCED
CDEENNOST CONSENTED
CDEENNOTT
CONTENTED
CDEENOOPS ENDOSCOPE
CDEENOQRU
CONQUERED
CDEENORSS SECONDERS
CDEENORSV
CONSERVED, CONVERSED
CDEENORTU
COUNTERED,
RECOUNTED

CDEENORTV
CONVERTED
CDEENORUV
UNCOVERED
CDEENOSTT CONTESTED
CDEENRRTU
DECURRENT
CDEENRSTU ENCRUSTED
CDEENRSUU UNSECURED
CDEENRSUW
UNSCREWED
CDEEOORST CREOSOTED
CDEEOOSTV DOVECOTES
CDEEOPRRR PRERECORD
CDEEOPRRU
PROCEDURE, REPRODUCE
CDEEOPRSS PROCESSED
CDEEOPRTT PROTECTED
CDEEOORRS RECORDERS
CDEEOORRTY DECRETORY
CDEEORSSY CROSS-EYED
CDEEORSTT DETECTORS
CDEEOSSTT COSSETTED
CDEEPPRSU SCUPPERED
CDEEPSSTU SUSPECTED
CDEFFIORU COIFFURED
CDEFGIINU FUNGICIDE
CDEFIIIST FIDEISTIC
CDEFIILNT INFLICTED
CDEFIINST DISINFECT
CDEFIKLOR FROLICKED
CDEFILNOR CORNFIELD
CDEFIMNOR CONFIRMED
CDEFINNOT CONFIDENT
CDEFINTUY FECUNDITY
CDEFKNORU
UNFROCKED
CDEFMNOOR
CONFORMED
CDEFMOORT
COMFORTED
CDEGGILNU CUDGELING
CDEGHINNR
DRENCHING
CDEGIIKNR DICKERING
CDEGIILNN DECLINING
CDEGIINPT DEPICTING
CDEGIINRT CREDITING,
DIRECTING
CDEGIKNOT DOCKETING
CDEGILNSU SECLUDING
CDEGILNUX EXCLUDING
CDEGILOSU GLUCOSIDE
CDEGILOSY GLYCOSIDE

CDEGINNOS CONSIGNED,
  SECONDING
CDEGINORR RECORDING
CDEGINRSY DESCRYING
CDEGINSSY DYSGENICS
CDEGLORST GOLDCREST
CDEGNORSU
  SCROUNGED
CDEHIIKLL CHILDLIKE
CDEHIILNO LICHENOID
CDEHIIMOS HOMICIDES
CDEHIIORT DICHROITE
CDEHIKLLO HILLOCKED
CDEHILLOV LOVECHILD
CDEHILLSS CHILDLESS
CDEHILOOR CHOLEROID
CDEHILORS CHLORIDES
CDEHILPST STEPCHILD
CDEHINORT CHONDRITE
CDEHINOSU CUSHIONED
CDEHIOORT THEODORIC
CDEHIORRS CIRRHOSED
CDEHIORTW
  DOWITCHER
CDEHKLSSU SHELDUCKS
CDEHLNORU
  CHONDRULE
CDEHNOOTT
  THECODONT
CDEHNOTUU
  UNTOUCHED
CDEHNOTUV DUTCH
  OVEN
CDEHOOOPS
  HODOSCOPE
CDEIIILSV CIVILISED
CDEIIILVZ CIVILIZED
CDEIIIRST SIDERITIC
CDEIIKKSS SIDEKICKS
CDEIIKMTW MID-WICKET
CDEIILLNO CELLOIDIN,
  DECILLION
CDEIILMOS DOMICILES
CDEIILMTU MULTICIDE
CDEIILNTU INDUCTILE
CDEIILORT DOLERITIC
CDEIILOST IDIOLECTS,
  SOLICITED
CDEIILOSU DELICIOUS
CDEIILPSS DISCIPLES
CDEIILRRU RIDICULER
CDEIILTVY DECLIVITY
CDEIIMNOS MENISCOID
CDEIIMNTU CTENIDIUM

CDEIIMRST MISDIRECT
CDEIINNST INCIDENTS
CDEIINOPT DEPICTION
CDEIINORT CRETINOID,
  DIRECTION
CDEIINOSS DECISIONS
CDEIINRTT INTERDICT
CDEIINTUV INDUCTIVE
CDEIIOOSU DIOECIOUS
CDEIIORST SIDEROTIC
CDEIIORUX UXORICIDE
CDEIIORVV DIVORCIVE
CDEIIRRTX DIRECTRIX
CDEIIRSTU CRUDITIES,
  DIURETICS
CDEIJNNOO CONJOINED
CDEIKNSTY STICKY END
CDEILLLOU CELLULOID
CDEILMRSU DULCIMERS
CDEILNNOU CLOUD
  NINE
CDEILNOOS COLONISED
CDEILNOOZ COLONIZED
CDEILNRSY CYLINDERS
CDEILORSS DISCLOSER
CDEILOSTU CLOUDIEST
CDEILOTTW TWICE-
  TOLD
CDEILRTUY CREDULITY
CDEIMMNOO
  INCOMMODE
CDEIMMOTT
  COMMITTED
CDEIMNNOT
  CONDIMENT
CDEIMNOPR PRINCEDOM
CDEIMNORS CRIMSONED
CDEIMNORU
  INDECORUM
CDEIMNOSU NICODEMUS
CDEIMOPRS COMPRISED
CDEIMOSST DOMESTICS
CDEINNOTU
  CONTINUED, UNNOTICED
CDEINOOTX ENDOTOXIC
CDEINOPRS CONSPIRED
CDEINORST DOCTRINES
CDEINORTU INTRODUCE,
  REDUCTION
CDEINORTV CONTRIVED
CDEINOSST CONSISTED
CDEINOSTU SEDUCTION
CDEINRSSU CURDINESS
CDEINRSTY STRIDENCY

CDEIOPRRT PREDICTOR
CDEIORRST CREDITORS,
  DIRECTORS
CDEIORRTY DIRECTORY
CDEIORSST DISSECTOR
CDEIORSSU DISCOURSE
CDEIORSTV DISCOVERT
CDEIORSVY DISCOVERY
CDEIPPSTY DYSPEPTIC
CDEKLOORY
  CROOKEDLY
CDELLOOPS SCOLLOPED
CDELLOSSU CLOUDLESS
CDELMNORU LEMON
  CURD
CDELMOOWY LOW
  COMEDY
CDELNOORT
  DECONTROL
CDELNOOST STONE-
  COLD
CDELNOOSW
  CLOSEDOWN
CDELNOOTY
  COTYLEDON
CDELNOPUU
  UNCOUPLED
CDELNORSU SCOUNDREL
CDELNOSTU CONSULTED
CDELNOSUV CONVULSED
CDELOORSS COLD SORES
CDELOORSU COLOUREDS
CDELOORUV
  OVERCLOUD
CDELORSUU CREDULOUS
CDEMMOOOR
  COMMODORE
CDEMNOORW
  DOWNCOMER
CDEMNOOSW
  COMEDOWNS
CDEMNOSTU
  DOCUMENTS
CDEMOOPRT
  COMPORTED
CDEMOOPST
  COMPOSTED
CDENNORUW
  UNCROWNED
CDENNOTUU
  UNCOUNTED
CDENOOPSY ENDOSCOPY
CDENOORST
  CONSORTED

CDENOORTT
CONTORTED
CDENOORTU
CONTOURED
CDENORSTU
CONSTRUED
CDENPRTUU PUNCTURED
CDEOOPRRT
PROCTORED
CDEOOPSST POSTCODES
CDEOORRVW
OVERCROWD
CDEOORSWW
WOODSCREW
CDEOPRRSU PRODUCERS
CDEOPRRTU CORRUPTED
CDFFIILTU DIFFICULT
CDFGHILNO GOLDFINCH
CDFGIINNO CONFIDING
CDFGIINOY CODIFYING
CDFHINORY CHONDRIFY
CDFIIMOST DISCOMFIT
CDFIIORSU SUDORIFIC
CDFIMOORR
CORDIFORM
CDFLNOORT COLD
FRONT
CDGIIINNT INDICTING
CDGIIINOT INDIGOTIC
CDGIILLNO COLLIDING
CDGIILNNU INCLUDING
CDGIILOTT DIGLOTTIC
CDGIINNTU INDUCTING
CDGIINORV DIVORCING
CDGIKLNSU DUCKLINGS
CDGILLNOU COLLUDING
CDGILNNOO
CONDOLING
CDGILNNOY CONDIGNLY
CDGILNOSS SCOLDINGS
CDGINNNOO
CONDONING
CDGINNOOR
CORDONING
CDGINOORR
CORRODING
CDGINOORT
DOCTORING
CDGINOPRU PRODUCING
CDHHIILTW WITH CHILD
CDHHIIOTY ICHTHYOID
CDHHILOST DISHCLOTH
CDHHIINOT CHITINOID
CDHIIMORS DICHROISM

CDHIIORRS SCIRRHOID
CDHIIPSTW DIPSWITCH
CDHIIRRTY TRIHYDRIC
CDHIMOOTY
DICHOTOMY
CDHIMSTYY DYSTHYMIC
CDHINOPSY DYSPHONIC
CDHIOOPRY CHIROPODY
CDHIOOPSZ SCHIZOPOD
CDHIOPRSY DYSPHORIC
CDHLLOOOS OLD
SCHOOL
CDHMNOOOR
MONOCHORD
CDHNOOORT
NOTOCHORD
CDHNOOTUW
TOUCHDOWN
CDHOOOORTW
TORCHWOOD
CDHOOOTUW
TOUCHWOOD
CDIIILMNS DICLINISM
CDIIISTVY VISCIDITY
CDIIJOSUU JUDICIOUS
CDIIKPSST DIPSTICKS
CDIILMOOT DOLOMITIC
CDIILNOSU DICLINOUS
CDIILPTUY DUPLICITY
CDIILTTUY DUCTILITY
CDIIMNPUY PYCNIDIUM
CDIIMORST DICROTISM
CDIINNOOT CONDITION
CDIINNOTU INDUCTION
CDIINOPRY CYPRINOID
CDIIOOPRS SCORPIOID
CDIIORRTT TORTRICID
CDIIPRSTU TRICUSPID
CDIIRSSTT DISTRICTS
CDIIJNOTUY JOCUNDITY
CDIKLPSUY LUCKY DIPS
CDIKMRSTU DRUMSTICK
CDIKNOSSW WINDSOCKS
CDILLNOOO COLLODION
CDILOORSU DISCOLOUR
CDILORSUU LUDICROUS
CDIMMNOOS
DISCOMMON
CDIMMOOTY
COMMODITY
CDIMNOORT
MICRODONT
CDIMNOORU
DORONICUM

CDIMNORSY
SYNDROMIC
CDINORSSW CROSSWIND
CDINOSSTU DISCOUNTS
CDINOSTUY IN CUSTODY
CDIOORRRS CORRIDORS
CDIOPRSSU CUSPIDORS
CDKKNNOOW
KNOCKDOWN
CDMNNORUU
CONUNDRUM
CDMNOOPSU
COMPOUNDS
CDNNOOTUW
COUNTDOWN
CDOORRSSW
CROSSWORD
CEEEEFFNR EFFERENCE
CEEEEFNRR REFERENCE
CEEEEGMNR
EMERGENCE
CEEEEHILP HEELPIECE
CEEEEHMNV
VEHEMENCE
CEEEEIPSY EYEPIECES
CEEEENRRV REVERENCE
CEEEFFITV EFFECTIVE
CEEEFFLNU EFFLUENCE
CEEEFINNR INFERENCE
CEEEFNORR FERROCENE,
RE-ENFORCE
CEEEFNQRU FREQUENCE
CEEEFPRRT PERFECTER
CEEEGILNT TELEGENIC
CEEEGINRS REGENCIES
CEEEGINRT ENERGETIC
CEEEGISTX EXEGETICS
CEEEGLNOR CONGER
EEL
CEEEGLNRT NEGLECTER
CEEEGMNRY
EMERGENCY
CEEEHIKST CHEEKIEST
CEEEHILST SCHEELITE
CEEEHINNR INHERENCE
CEEEHIRST CHEERIEST
CEEEHISST ICE SHEETS
CEEEHLNTY ENTELECHY
CEEEHLRSS CHEERLESS
CEEEHOPRS ECOSPHERE
CEEEHQRUX
EXCHEQUER
CEEEHRTTV CHEVRETTE
CEEEIIMPT TIMEPIECE

CEEEIINRV VICEREINE
CEEEIJRTV REJECTIVE
CEEEILLNT CLIENTELE
CEEEILNSS LICENSEES
CEEEILNST CELESTINE
CEEEILRST LEICESTER
CEEEILSTT CELESTITE
CEEEILSTV SELECTIVE
CEEEIMNNS EMINENCES
CEEEIMNTT CEMENTITE
CEEEIMRRS MERCERISE
CEEEIMRRZ MERCERIZE
CEEEINNPT PENITENCE
CEEEINNSS IN ESSENCE
CEEEINNST SENTIENCE
CEEEINPRT EPICENTRE
CEEEINRSU ESURIENCE
CEEEINSTX EXISTENCE
CEEEIPRRV PERCEIVER
CEEEIPRST CREEPIEST
CEEEIPRTV RECEPTIVE
CEEEIPSST SET PIECES
CEEEIPTVX EXCEPTIVE
CEEEIRRSV RECEIVERS
CEEEIRRSX EXERCISER
CEEEIRSSV RECESSIVE
CEEEIRSSX EXERCISES
CEEEIRSTV SECRETIVE
CEEEIRTVX EXCRETIVE
CEEEISSVX EXCESSIVE
CEEEITUVX EXECUTIVE
CEEEKORRT ROCKETEER
CEEELLNTX EXCELLENT
CEEELNOQU ELOQUENCE
CEEELOPST TELESCOPE
CEEEMNRRT
  RECREMENT
CEEEMNRTX
  EXCREMENT
CEEENNSST SENESCENT,
  SENTENCES
CEEENORTT ENTRECOTE
CEEENPRSS PRESENCES
CEEENPRST PRETENCES
CEEENQRSU SEQUENCER
CEEENQSSU SEQUENCES
CEEENRSST ERECTNESS
CEEEORRRV RECOVERER
CEEEPRRST RESPECTER
CEEEPRRTX EXCERPTER
CEEEPRSTU PERSECUTE
CEEFFFORT FOR EFFECT
CEEFFGINT EFFECTING
CEEFFIINT EFFICIENT

CEEFFOOPT COFFEEPOT
CEEFGLNTU GENUFLECT
CEEFHHNRT THE
  FRENCH
CEEFHIKRS KERCHIEFS
CEEFHIPSY SPEECHIFY
CEEFHITTY ITCHY FEET
CEEFHMNNR
  FRENCHMEN
CEEFIINTV INFECTIVE
CEEFIIPRS SPECIFIER
CEEFIIRRT RECTIFIER
CEEFIKKRS FREE KICKS
CEEFILNNU INFLUENCE
CEEFILRTY ELECTRIFY
CEEFIMPRT IMPERFECT
CEEFINORR REINFORCE
CEEFINORT REFECTION
CEEFINTTU FETTUCINE
CEEFIRRST FIRECREST
CEEFLOORS FORECLOSE
CEEFLORRT REFLECTOR
CEEFLORSU FLUORESCE
CEEFLPRTY PERFECTLY
CEEFNORRR CONFERRER
CEEFNORRS CONFRERES
CEEFNQRUY
  FREQUENCY
CEEFNRSTU RUFESCENT
CEEFORRTY REFECTORY
CEEFORSTW CROW'S
  FEET
CEEGHIMNO
  HEGEMONIC
CEEGHINOR RE-
  ECHOING
CEEGHINRW GREENWICH
CEEGHINSW ESCHEWING
CEEGHLOSW
  COGWHEELS
CEEGIINRV RECEIVING
CEEGIJNRT REJECTING
CEEGILLNX EXCELLING
CEEGILNOO OLIGOCENE
CEEGILNOT TELEGONIC
CEEGILNRY GLYCERINE
CEEGILNST SELECTING
CEEGIMNNT CEMENTING
CEEGIMORT GEOMETRIC
CEEGINNOS CONSIGNEE
CEEGINNRS SCREENING
CEEGINNRT CENTERING
CEEGINNST IGNESCENT
CEEGINOOT OOGENETIC

CEEGINORS CONGERIES,
  RECOGNISE
CEEGINORZ RECOGNIZE
CEEGINPTX EXCEPTING,
  EXPECTING
CEEGINRSS RECESSING
CEEGINRST SECRETING
CEEGINRTX EXCRETING
CEEGINTUX EXECUTING
CEEGIORRS GROCERIES
CEEGKNOOS
  GOOSENECK
CEEGLLMRS GERM CELLS
CEEGLMNRY
  CLERGYMEN
CEEGLNOOS CONGOLESE
CEEGORTTU COURGETTE
CEEHHIRRS CHERISHER
CEEHHIRVW WHICHEVER
CEEHHOPST HOPE
  CHEST
CEEHIILLN HELICLINE
CEEHIIPTT EPITHETIC
CEEHIKNNT IN THE
  NECK
CEEHIKNRT KITCHENER,
  THICKENER
CEEHIKPPR PIKEPERCH
CEEHIKRST SKETCHIER
CEEHILLRS CHISELLER
CEEHILNRS SCHLIEREN
CEEHILNTY ETHYLENIC
CEEHILPRT TELPHERIC
CEEHILRSS CHISELERS
CEEHILRSW CLERIHEWS
CEEHILSTT TELESTICH
CEEHINQTU TECHNIQUE
CEEHINRVY EVERY INCH
CEEHINSST TECHINESS
CEEHINSTU EUTHENICS
CEEHIOPSW SHOWPIECE
CEEHISSTT CHESTIEST,
  ESTHETICS
CEEHISTTT TETCHIEST
CEEHKRSST SKETCHERS
CEEHLORSU LECHEROUS
CEEHLPRSU SEPULCHRE
CEEHLQRSU SQUELCHER
CEEHMNORZ
  CHERNOZEM
CEEHNOPRR
  PERCHERON
CEEHNRRST TRENCHERS
CEEHOPTTY ECTOPHYTE

CEEHORRTU
  RETOUCHER
CEEHRRSTT STRETCHER
CEEHRSSTT STRETCHES
CEEIIJNTV INJECTIVE
CEEIIILNPR PERICLINE
CEEIILNRT LIENTERIC
CEEIILPPT EPILEPTIC
CEEIIMMNN IMMINENCE
CEEIIMNPS EPICENISM,
  MINCE PIES
CEEIIMNRS REMINISCE
CEEIIMPRS IMPRECISE
CEEIIMPST EPISTEMIC
CEEIIMRST METRICISE
CEEIIMRTZ METRICIZE
CEEIINNOR EIRENICON
CEEIINNRS INSINCERE
CEEIINNRT ENCRINITE
CEEIINNTV INCENTIVE
CEEIINPRT RECIPIENT
CEEIINPTV INCEPTIVE
CEEIINPTX EXCIPIENT
CEEIINRSV IN SERVICE
CEEIINTVV INVECTIVE
CEEIIOPST POETICISE
CEEIIOPTZ POETICIZE
CEEIIOSST SOCIETIES
CEEIJNORT REJECTION
CEEIJNRTT INTERJECT
CEEIKLNNS NECKLINES
CEEIKMORS MOCKERIES
CEEIKOPRW PIECEWORK,
  WORKPIECE
CEEIKORRS ROCKERIES
CEEILLNPR PENCILLER
CEEILLNTT INTELLECT
CEEILMNNT INCLEMENT
CEEILMNOP POLICEMEN
CEEILMNPR CRIMPLENE
CEEILMNSU LUMINESCE
CEEILMOST COMELIEST
CEEILMRSS MERCILESS
CEEILNNOS INSOLENCE
CEEILNORT CENTRIOLE
CEEILNOST ELECTIONS,
  SELECTION
CEEILNOTT NICOLETTE
CEEILNPST SPLENETIC
CEEILNRSS SILENCERS
CEEILNRST STENCILER
CEEILNRSY SINCERELY
CEEILNRTV VENTRICLE
CEEILNRUV VIRULENCE

CEEILORSX EXCELSIOR
CEEILOSSS ISOSCELES
CEEILOSSV VOICELESS
CEEILPRSS PRICELESS
CEEILPRSY PRECISELY
CEEILRSTU CRUELTIES,
  RETICULES
CEEILRSTW CREWELIST
CEEILRSUV RECLUSIVE
CEEILSSTT TESTICLES
CEEILSSUV SECLUSIVE
CEEILSUVX EXCLUSIVE
CEEIMMOTT
  COMMITTEE
CEEIMNNRT INCREMENT
CEEIMNOOS
  ECONOMIES, ECONOMISE
CEEIMNOOZ
  ECONOMIZE
CEEIMNOPT IMPOTENCE
CEEIMNORR MEROCRINE
CEEIMNPSS SPECIMENS
CEEIMNSTU INTUMESCE
CEEINNORS RECENSION
CEEINOPRS PRECONISE
CEEINOPRT RECEPTION
CEEINOPRZ PRECONIZE
CEEINOPTX EXCEPTION
CEEINORSS RECESSION
CEEINORST ERECTIONS,
  RESECTION, SECRETION
CEEINORSU CINEREOUS
CEEINORTX EXCRETION
CEEINOSSS SECESSION
CEEINOSTX EXSECTION
CEEINOTUX EXECUTION
CEEINPRRU PRURIENCE
CEEINPRST PRESCIENT
CEEINPRTT INTERCEPT
CEEINPSSX SIXPENCES
CEEINQRTU QUERCETIN
CEEINQSTU QUIESCENT
CEEINRSSU SINECURES
CEEINRSTT INTERSECT
CEEINRSTU CENTURIES
CEEINRSTV VIRESCENT
CEEINSSTY NECESSITY
CEEIOORTZ OZOCERITE
CEEIOORVV VOICE-OVER
CEEIOPPRS PERISCOPE
CEEIORRST RECTORIES
CEEIORRSX EXORCISER
CEEIORSSU SERICEOUS
CEEIPRSST TRICEPSES

CEEIRRRTU RECRUITER
CEEIRSSTU CERUSSITE
CEEIRSSTW SCREWIEST
CEEIRSUVX EXCURSIVE
CEEIRTUXX EXECUTRIX
CEELLLOSU CELLULOSE
CEELLMNTY CLEMENTLY
CEELLMOPR COMPELLER
CEELLMOSU MOLECULES
CEELLORTU COURTELLE
CEELMMNSU
  MUSCLEMEN
CEELMNOUW
  UNWELCOME
CEELMOPRT COMPLETER
CEELMOPSX COMPLEXES
CEELNORST ELECTRONS
CEELNORSU ENCLOSURE
CEELNOSSS CLOSENESS
CEELNPRUU PURULENCE
CEELNSSST SCENTLESS
CEELOPSTY TELESCOPY
CEELORSSS SCLEROSES
CEELORSST CORSELETS,
  SELECTORS
CEELORSSV COVERLESS
CEELORSTV COVERLETS
CEELRRSTU LECTURERS
CEEMMNORT
  COMMENTER
CEEMNNORT
  CONTEMNER
CEEMNOPTT
  COMPETENT
CEEMNORSW
  NEWCOMERS
CEEMNSTTU
  TUMESCENT
CEEMOOPRS RECOMPOSE
CEEMORRTY
  CRYOMETER
CEEMOSSTY ECOSYSTEM
CEENNOOSS NOSECONES
CEENNORRU
  RENOUNCER
CEENNORST CONSENTER
CEENNORSV CONVENERS
CEENNORTU
  ENCOUNTER
CEENOOPST COPESTONE
CEENOORSV ONCE-
  OVERS
CEENOORTV COVER
  NOTE

CEENOPRRT PRECENTOR
CEENOPSTT PENTECOST
CEENOPSTW TWOPENCES
CEENORRSV CONSERVER,
  CONVERSER
CEENORRTV
  CONVERTER, RECONVERT
CEENORSSV CONSERVES
CEENORSTT CONTESTER
CEENORSTW SWEET
  CORN
CEENORSVY CONVEYERS
CEENPPSTU TUPPENCES
CEENRRRTU RECURRENT
CEENRRTUX
  EXCURRENT
CEEOORRSV OVERSCORE
CEEOPPRRT PRECEPTOR
CEEOPRRSS REPROCESS
CEEOPRSSS PROCESSES
CEEOPRSTT TOP-SECRET
CEEOPRSTU PROSECUTE
CEEOQRTTU
  CROQUETTE
CEEOQSTTU COQUETTES
CEEORRRSS SORCERERS
CEEORRSSS SORCERESS
CEEORRSST CROSSTREE
CEEORRSSU RESOURCES
CEEORRSTW WORCESTER
CEEORRSTY SECRETORY
CEEORRSUV VERRUCOSE
CEEORRTUV COVERTURE
CEEORRTXY EXCRETORY
CEEORSTTV CORVETTES
CEEORSTUX EXECUTORS
CEEORTUXY EXECUTORY
CEEPRSSSY CYPRESSES
CEEPRSSTU SUSPECTER
CEERRRSTU RESURRECT
CEERRSSTU REST CURES
CEFFHINRY FRENCHIFY
CEFFIIOOX EX OFFICIO
CEFFIORSU COIFFEURS,
  COIFFURES
CEFFIRRSU SCRUFFIER
CEFGIINNT INFECTING
CEFGINNOR ENFORCING
CEFHIILSS FISH SLICE
CEFHIIMSS MISCHIEFS
CEFHIKRSW WRECKFISH
CEFHILMOR CHELIFORM
CEFHKOORS FORESHOCK
CEFHPRRSU SURFPERCH

CEFIILNRT INFLICTER
CEFIILNRU LUCIFERIN
CEFIINNOT INFECTION
CEFIIORRS SCORIFIER
CEFIKLORR FROLICKER
CEFILLLOS FOLLICLES
CEFILNORT INFLECTOR
CEFIMNORU CUNEIFORM
CEFINORSS FORENSICS
CEFINORTU CONFITURE
CEFIOORSU FEROCIOUS
CEFIORRSS CROSSFIRE
CEFKLOORS FORELOCKS
CEFKLOPTU POCKETFUL
CEFKOORRW
  WORKFORCE
CEFLNNOTU
  CONFLUENT
CEFMNOORR
  CONFORMER
CEFMOORRT
  COMFORTER
CEFNOORSS CONFESSOR
CEFOORRTU FORECOURT
CEGHIILNS CHISELING
CEGHIINNR ENRICHING
CEGHIINPR CIPHERING
CEGHIKNST SKETCHING
CEGHILLOU GUILLOCHE
CEGHILMTU GEMUTLICH
CEGHILNTV VETCHLING
CEGHILOOT ETHOLOGIC
CEGHINNQU
  QUENCHING
CEGHINNRW
  WRENCHING
CEGHINORT HECTORING
CEGHINPRY CYPHERING
CEGHIOPTY GEOPHYTIC
CEGHIORRU
  GROUCHIER
CEGHKNORU
  ROUGHNECK
CEGHMNOOR
  CHROMOGEN
CEGIIILNT ELICITING
CEGIIJNNT INJECTING
CEGIIJNOR REJOICING
CEGIIKLNN NICKELING
CEGIIKNNS SICKENING
CEGIIKNPT PICKETING
CEGIIKNTT TICKETING
CEGIILNNP PENCILING
CEGIILNNR RECLINING

CEGIILNNS LICENSING,
  SILENCING
CEGIILNOR RECOILING
CEGIILNPS ECLIPSING
CEGIINNNS INCENSING
CEGIINOTV COGNITIVE
CEGIINRSV SERVICING
CEGIIOSTT EGOTISTIC
CEGIJKNOY JOCKEYING
CEGIKNNOR RECKONING
CEGIKNOPT POCKETING
CEGIKNORT ROCKETING
CEGIKNPRU PUCKERING
CEGIKNRTU TUCKERING
CEGILLMOU COLLEGIUM
CEGILMMNO
  COMMINGLE
CEGILMNOW
  WELCOMING
CEGILNNOS ENCLOSING
CEGILNOST CLOSETING
CEGILNRSU SURCINGLE
CEGILNRTU LECTURING
CEGILOORS SEROLOGIC
CEGILOOST ECOLOGIST
CEGIMNNOO
  MONOGENIC
CEGIMNOOR
  ERGONOMIC
CEGIMNOPR COMPERING
CEGIMNOPT COMPETING
CEGIMNOUY
  GYNOECIUM
CEGIMNOYZ
  ZYMOGENIC
CEGINNNOV
  CONVENING
CEGINNOOT
  ONTOGENIC
CEGINNORR
  CORNERING
CEGINNORS CENSORING
CEGINNOVY CONVEYING
CEGINNRSU CENSURING
CEGINOOPS GEOPONICS
CEGINOPRU RECOUPING
CEGINOPRY PYROGENIC
CEGINOPTY GENOTYPIC
CEGINORST ESCORTING
CEGINORSV COVERINGS
CEGINRRRU RECURRING
CEGIOOPRT GEOTROPIC
CEGLNOORY
  NECROLOGY

CEGMNNOOS
COGNOMENS
CEGNNORTU
CONGRUENT
CEGNORRSU
SCROUNGER
CEGNORSUY
SURGEONCY
CEGOOPRSY GYROSCOPE
CEHHHIIKT HITCHHIKE
CEHHIIMST HEMISTICH
CEHHIMSTT HEMSTITCH
CEHHOOPSU
CHOPHOUSE
CEHIIKLTW WITCHLIKE
CEHIIKORS HICKORIES
CEHIILLST CHILLIEST
CEHIILMOT HOMILETIC
CEHIILNOT NEOLITHIC
CEHIIMSTY MYTHICISE
CEHIIMTYZ MYTHICIZE
CEHIINNOT ON THIN ICE
CEHIINPRT NEPHRITIC,
PHRENITIC
CEHIINRST CHRISTINE
CEHIINRTZ CHINTZIER
CEHIINSST ITCHINESS
CEHIINTWZ ZINC WHITE
CEHIIPPTY EPIPHYTIC
CEHIIPRST CHIRPIEST
CEHIIPRTT TEPHRITIC
CEHIIRSTU HEURISTIC
CEHIISTTT TITCHIEST
CEHIKLPRS CLERKSHIP
CEHIKLSTY SKETCHILY
CEHIKNSST THICKNESS
CEHIKNSTU CHUNKIEST
CEHIKOPPT HIP POCKET
CEHIKPRSW SHIPWRECK
CEHILNNPU PUNCH LINE
CEHILNOOR HOLOCRINE
CEHILNOSU LICHENOUS
CEHILNOTU TOUCHLINE
CEHILNSTZ SCHNITZEL
CEHILORST CLOTHIERS
CEHIMMOPR
MORPHEMIC
CEHIMMORS
MICROMESH
CEHIMMSTU
CHUMMIEST
CEHIMNNOU
ICHNEUMON
CEHIMNOPS PHONEMICS

CEHIMRSTY CHEMISTRY
CEHINOPRT NEPHROTIC
CEHINOPST PHONETICS
CEHINOPTY NEOPHYTIC
CEHINPRST SPHINCTER
CEHINPSTU PUNCHIEST
CEHINSSSU CUSHINESS
CEHINSTTY SYNTHETIC
CEHIOOPRT ORTHOEPIC
CEHIOOSST CHOOSIEST
CEHIOPPRT PROPHETIC
CEHIOPPST CHOPPIEST
CEHIOPRRT CHIROPTER
CEHIOPRTT PROTHETIC
CEHIOPRTU EUTROPHIC
CEHIOPRTY HYPOCRITE
CEHIORRST CHORISTER
CEHIORSST OSTRICHES
CEHIOSSST SCHISTOSE
CEHIOSTTU TOUCHIEST
CEHIPRRRU CHIRRUPER
CEHIRSSTY HYSTERICS
CEHKOOOSU
COOKHOUSE
CEHKRSSTU HUCKSTERS
CEHLLOOPT PHOTOCELL
CEHLOOPRS PRESCHOOL
CEHMOOPRT
ECTOMORPH
CEHMOORRU
UROCHROME
CEHNNORTU
TRUNCHEON
CEHNOOPPY
PHENOCOPY
CEHNOORSS SCHOONERS
CEHNSSTTU CHESTNUTS
CEHOOOPRS
HOROSCOPE
CEHOPRTYY CRYOPHYTE
CEHOPSSSY PSYCHOSES
CEHOPTTUY TOUCH-
TYPE
CEIIILRSV CIVILISER
CEIIILRVZ CIVILIZER
CEIIIMSTV VICTIMISE
CEIIIMTVZ VICTIMIZE
CEIIINNPT INCIPIENT
CEIIIPRSS EPICRISIS
CEIIJNNOT INJECTION
CEIIJNSSU JUICINESS
CEIIJNSTU INJUSTICE
CEIIKLMQU QUICKLIME
CEIIKLMRS LIMERICKS

CEIIKLMST KELTICISM
CEIIKLNRR CRINKLIER
CEIIKLPRR PRICKLIER
CEIIKLSST SICKLIEST
CEIIKLSTT KELTICIST
CEIIKNPRT NITPICKER
CEIIKNPSS PICKINESS
CEIIKRSTT TRICKIEST
CEIIKSSTT STICKIEST
CEIILLMNT MILLICENT
CEIILMNSU MINISCULE
CEIILNNOR CRINOLINE
CEIILNPPR PRINCIPLE
CEIILNSUV INCLUSIVE
CEIILOQRU LIQUORICE
CEIILOSSU SILICEOUS
CEIILPRST LIST PRICE
CEIILPRTU PLEURITIC
CEIILRSST SCLERITIS
CEIILSTTY SECTILITY
CEIIMNOST SEMITONIC
CEIIMNRST CRETINISM
CEIIMNSST SCIENTISM
CEIIMORST EROTICISM,
ISOMETRIC
CEIIMOSST SEMIOTICS
CEIIMOSTX EXOTICISM
CEIIMPRSU EPICURISM
CEIIMRRTT TRIMETRIC
CEIINNOPT INCEPTION
CEIINNORT INCRETION
CEIINNRTY INNER CITY
CEIINOPRS PRECISION
CEIINORRT CRITERION
CEIINORTT TRICOTINE
CEIINORTV VICTORINE
CEIINOSSX EXCISIONS
CEIINOSTV EVICTIONS
CEIINPRSS PRICINESS
CEIINPSSS SPICINESS
CEIINRSTX EXTRINSIC
CEIINRSTY CITISENRY,
SINCERITY
CEIINRSUV INCURSIVE
CEIINRTTY INTERCITY
CEIINRTYZ CITIZENRY
CEIINSSTT SCIENTIST
CEIIOOPTZ EPIZOOTIC
CEIIORSST ISOSTERIC
CEIIORSTV VICTORIES
CEIIPRSST CRISPIEST
CEIIPSTTY SEPTICITY
CEIIQRSTU CRITIQUES
CEIJNNOOR CONJOINER

CEIJNORTT INTROJECT
CEIKLNORT INTERLOCK
CEIKLNOST CLOSE-KNIT
CEIKLNOSU NICKELOUS
CEIKLNSSS SLICKNESS
CEIKLNSSU LUCKINESS
CEIKLOPST STOCKPILE
CEIKLOSTV LIVESTOCK
CEIKLPSTU PLUCKIEST
CEIKLRSST STICKLERS
CEIKMNSSU MUCKINESS
CEIKMPPSU PICK-ME-UPS
CEIKNORSS ROCKINESS
CEIKNOSTT STOCKINET
CEIKNQSSU QUICKNESS
CEIKORRTV OVERTRICK
CEIKOSSTT STOCKIEST
CEIKPQSTU QUICKSTEP
CEIKRRSTT TRICKSTER
CEILLLMTU CLITELLUM
CEILLNOOR COLOR LINE
CEILLNOUV INVOLUCEL
CEILLOPTU POLLUCITE
CEILLOSUV COLLUSIVE
CEILLPSTY SYLLEPTIC
CEILMNNOO
   MONOCLINE
CEILMNOOS SEMICOLON
CEILMNOTU MONTICULE
CEILMNSSU LEMNISCUS
CEILMNSUU MINUSCULE
CEILMOPRS COMPILERS
CEILMOPRY MICROPYLE,
   POLYMERIC
CEILMOSSS SOLECISMS
CEILMRTUU RETICULUM
CEILMSSTU CLUMSIEST
CEILNNOOS CLOISONNÉ
CEILNOOPS SCOPOLINE
CEILNOORS COLONISER
CEILNOORZ COLONIZER
CEILNOOTU ELOCUTION
CEILNOPRV PIN CLOVER
CEILNORSU CORNELIUS,
   INCLOSURE, RECLUSION
CEILNORUV INVOLUCRE
CEILNOSSU SECLUSION
CEILNOSUX EXCLUSION
CEILNRSSU CURLINESS
CEILNRUVY VIRULENCY
CEILOOPRT COPROLITE
CEILOPPRT PROLEPTIC
CEILOPPSS POPSICLES
CEILOPSTU POULTICES

CEILORRTU COURTLIER
CEILORSSS SCLEROSIS
CEILORSST CLOISTERS
CEILOSSST SOLSTICES
CEILOSSTT COSTLIEST
CEILPRSSU SURPLICES
CEILRSUVY CURSIVELY
CEIMMNNOS
   MNEMONICS
CEIMMNOOR
   MONOMERIC
CEIMMNOSU
   COMMUNISE,
   ENCOMIUMS
CEIMMNOTU
   COMMINUTE
CEIMMNOUZ
   COMMUNIZE
CEIMMOORS
   MICROSOME
CEIMMOORT
   MICROTOME
CEIMMORTT
   COMMITTER
CEIMMRSTU CRUMMIEST
CEIMNNOPU
   PNEUMONIC
CEIMNOORT
   MICROTONE
CEIMNOOST ECONOMIST
CEIMNORST INTERCOMS
CEIMNORTT METRIC
   TON
CEIMOOPRR POROMERIC
CEIMOOPST COMPOSITE
CEIMOORTZ
   ZOOMETRIC
CEIMOOSTX EXOSMOTIC
CEIMOPRST PRIME COST
CEIMOPSUU PUMICEOUS
CEIMORSSX EXORCISMS
CEIMORSTU COSTUMIER
CEIMOSSTU CUSTOMISE
CEIMOSTUV MUSCOVITE
CEIMOSTUZ CUSTOMIZE
CEINNNOTT CONTINENT
CEINNNOTV CONNIVENT
CEINNOPRT PRINCETON
CEINNORTU
   CENTURION, CONTINUER
CEINNRRTU INCURRENT
CEINOORST CORTISONE
CEINOOSSW SOSNOWIEC
CEINOPPRU PORCUPINE

CEINOPRRT INTERCROP
CEINOPRST INSPECTOR
CEINOPRSV PROVINCES
CEINOPRXY PYROXENIC
CEINORRTW TOWN
   CRIER
CEINORSTT CORNETIST
CEINORSTU COUNTRIES,
   CRETINOUS, NEUROTICS
CEINORSUX EXCURSION
CEINOSTUV CONTUSIVE
CEINOTVXY CONVEXITY
CEINPRSSS CRISPNESS
CEINRSSTT CENTRISTS
CEINRSTTU TINCTURES
CEIOOPRSS COREOPSIS
CEIOOPRST PORTICOES
CEIOOORSV CORROSIVE
CEIOPRRSU CROUPIERS
CEIORRSTT TRISECTOR
CEIORRSTU COURTIERS
CEIORRTUU COUTURIER
CEIORSSSW CROSSWISE
CEIORSSTX EXORCISTS
CEIORSTTU TOREUTICS
CEIPPRRST PRESCRIPT
CEIPRRSTU SCRIPTURE
CEIPRSSTU PIECRUSTS
CEIRRSTTU STRICTURE
CEIRSSTTT STRICTEST
CEIRSSTTU CRUSTIEST
CEJNORRSU CONJURERS
CEJNRSTUU JUNCTURES
CEJOOPRRT PROJECTOR
CEKKORSTY SKYROCKET
CEKLNOOPS POLO NECKS
CEKLNORTW TOWN
   CLERK
CEKOORRSW CO-
   WORKERS
CEKOORSTV OVERSTOCK
CEKOPRSST SPROCKETS
CELLMSTUU SCUTELLUM
CELLNOSUU NUCLEOLUS
CELLOOPTY COLLOTYPE
CELLOORSS COLORLESS
CELMNOTUY
   CONTUMELY
CELMOOPRY
   COPOLYMER
CELMOOTUY
   LEUCOTOMY
CELMOPRUU
   OPERCULUM

CELMPRSTU PLECTRUMS
CELNOOSTU CONSOLUTE
CELNOOTUV
CONVOLUTE
CELNOPRTU CORPULENT
CELNORSTU CONSULTER
CELNOSSTU COUNTLESS
CELNRRTUY CURRENTLY
CELNRTTUU TRUCULENT
CELOOPRSU SUPERCOOL
CELORSSUU SURCULOSE
CELPRSTUU SCULPTURE
CEMMNOORS
COMMONERS
CEMMORSTU
COMMUTERS
CEMNNOOPT
COMPONENT
CEMNOOOQU
MONOCOQUE
CEMNOORTY
NECROTOMY
CEMNORSSU
CONSUMERS
CEMNORTUY
EMUNCTORY
CEMOOPRSS COMPOSERS
CEMOOPRSU
COMPOSURE
CEMOPRSTU COMPUTERS
CEMORRSUU
MERCUROUS
CEMORRSWW
SCREWWORM
CEMORRTYY
CRYOMETRY
CEMORSSTU CUSTOMERS
CENNOOPPY
OPPONENCY
CENNOOPRU
PRONOUNCE
CENNORSTU
NOCTURNES
CENNOSSSU CONSENSUS
CENOOPRST STONECROP
CENOOQRRU
CONQUEROR
CENOORRST
CONSORTER
CENOQSSTU CONQUESTS
CENORRSTU CONSTRUER
CENORSSSS CROSSNESS
CENORSSTW CROW'S
NEST

CENORSSUY CYNOSURES
CENORSTXY XENOCRYST
CENPRRTUU PUNCTURER
CENPRSTUU PUNCTURES
CEOOOSTTV SOTTO
VOCE
CEOOPRRSS PROCESSOR
CEOOPRRST PROSECTOR
CEOOPRRTT PROTECTOR
CEOOPRSTY SPOROCYTE
CEOOPSSTU OCTOPUSES
CEOORRSSU SORCEROUS
CEOORRSSV CROSSOVER
CEOORSTUU COURTEOUS
CEOPPRSST PROSPECTS
CEOPRRRSU PRECURSOR,
PROCURERS
CEOPRRRTU CORRUPTER
CEOPRRSSU PERCUSSOR
CEOPRSSTW SCREW TOPS
CEPPRSTUU UPPERCUTS
CEPRSSTUU CUTPURSES
CERRSTTUU STRUCTURE
CFFGIINSU SUFFICING
CFFGILNSU SCUFFLING
CFFIIOOSU OFFICIOUS
CFFIKLNSU CUFF LINKS
CFFLOOORU OFF
COLOUR
CFGHIILNN FLINCHING
CFGHIILNS CLINGFISH
CFGIILLMN CLINGFILM
CFGIINNNO CONFINING
CFGILNNOU FLOUNCING
CFGILNORY FORCINGLY
CFGINNOSU CONFUSING
CFGINNOTU CONFUTING
CFGINOSSU FOCUSSING
CFHIIKSST FISH STICK
CFHIINOOR HONORIFIC
CFHIKOPRT PITCHFORK
CFHIKOSST STOCKFISH
CFHMNOOTU NOT
MUCH OF
CFHOOSTTU SOFT
TOUCH
CFIIKKLNS SKIN FLICK
CFIILMMOR MICROFILM
CFIILORST FLORISTIC
CFIIOOPRS SOPORIFIC
CFIIOPRRT TRPORIFIC
CFIKLLNOT FLINTLOCK
CFIKLLOOR FOLKLORIC
CFIKLMOST FILM STOCK

CFILNSUUU FUNICULUS
CFIMORSTU SCUTIFORM
CFINNOOSU CONFUSION
CFINNOSTU FUNCTIONS
CFLLOORUU COLOURFUL
CFLNOORRU
CORNFLOUR
CFLOOORRU FOUR-
COLOR
CFLOOOSTT COLTSFOOT
CFOOORSTW CROW'S
FOOT
CFORSTUUU FRUCTUOUS
CGGHIKNNU
CHUNGKING
CGGHINORU
GROUCHING
CGGINORSU SCOURGING
CGHHIORTU HIGH
COURT
CGHIILLNS SCHILLING
CGHIIMNRS SMIRCHING
CGHIIMOST GOTHICISM
CGHIINNST SNITCHING
CGHIINPPS CHIPPINGS
CGHIINSTT STITCHING
CGHIINSTW SWITCHING
CGHIINTTW TWITCHING
CGHILNOOS SCHOOLING
CGHILNOOY
ICHNOLOGY
CGHILNORT CHORTLING
CGHILNOSU SLOUCHING
CGHILOOOR
HOROLOGIC
CGHILORUY GROUCHILY
CGHIMNOOS
SMOOCHING
CGHINORSU CHORUSING
CGHIOPRTY COPYRIGHT
CGHKLOTUU TOUGH
LUCK
CGHLLNOOT
LONGCLOTH
CGHLOOORY
CHOROLOGY
CGHLOOPYY
PHYCOLOGY
CGIIIKMMN MIMICKING
CGIIILNNN INCLINING
CGIIINNOV INVOICING
CGIIKLNNR CRINKLING
CGIIKLNPR PRICKLING
CGIIKLNRT TRICKLING

CGIIKMMRY GIMMICKRY
CGIIKNNPU UNPICKING
CGIILMNNY MINCINGLY
CGIILMNOP COMPILING
CGIILNNOS INCLOSING
CGIILNNWY WINCINGLY
CGIILNPPR CRIPPLING
CGIILNPPS CLIPPINGS
CGIILOSST GLOSSITIC,
   LOGISTICS
CGIILRSTU LITURGICS
CGIIMNPRS SCRIMPING
CGIINNNOV CONNIVING
CGIINNOOT COGNITION,
   INCOGNITO
CGIINNRRU INCURRING
CGIINPRTU PICTURING
CGIJNNORU CONJURING
CGIKKLNNU KNUCKLING
CGIKLMNOY
   MOCKINGLY
CGIKLNNOU UNLOCKING
CGIKLNRTU TRUCKLING
CGIKLNSSU SUCKLINGS
CGIKNNOOV
   CONVOKING
CGIKNNORU
   UNCORKING
CGIKNOSST STOCKINGS
CGIKOOPST POGO STICK
CGILLNORS SCROLLING
CGILLNOYY CLOYINGLY
CGILMNOOO
   MONOLOGIC
CGILMNOPY COMPLYING
CGILMNPRU CRUMPLING
CGILMOOYZ
   ZYMOLOGIC
CGILNNNUY CUNNINGLY
CGILNNOOR
   LONGICORN
CGILNNOOS CONSOLING
CGILNOOOY
   ICONOLOGY
CGILNOORS COLORINGS
CGILNOORU COLOURING
CGILNOPSU COUPLINGS
CGILNOPUV LOVING CUP
CGILNPRSU SCRUPLING
CGILNSTTU SCUTTLING
CGILNTTUY CUTTINGLY
CGILOOOPT TOPOLOGIC
CGILOOOSY SOCIOLOGY
CGIMMNNOU

COMMUNING
CGIMMNOTU
   COMMUTING
CGIMNNOSU
   CONSUMING
CGIMNOOPS
   COMPOSING
CGIMNOPTU
   COMPUTING
CGIMNPRSU SCRUMPING
CGINNNOOT
   CONNOTING
CGINNOORS CONSIGNOR
CGINNOOTT COTTON
   GIN
CGINNOOVY
   CONVOYING
CGINNORTU
   TROUNCING
CGINNOSTU CONTUSING
CGINOPRRU PROCURING
CGINORSSS CROSSINGS
CGINORSSU SCOURINGS
CGINORTUY CONGRUITY
CGINRRSUY SCURRYING
CGINRSTUY CURTSYING
CGLMOOOSY
   COSMOLOGY
CGMNOOOSY
   COSMOGONY
CGNNOOTTU GUN
   COTTON
CGNOORSUU
   CONGRUOUS
CHHHIIMNO HO CHI
   MINH
CHHIMRSTY RHYTHMICS
CHHINTTUW WITCH-
   HUNT
CHHKLLOOY
   HOLLYHOCK
CHIIILPPP PHILIPPIC
CHIILLOPY LYOPHILIC
CHIILLPTY PHYLLITIC
CHIILNNPS LINCHPINS
CHIILOOPZ ZOOPHILIC
CHIILOOTT OTOLITHIC
CHIILORTU UROLITHIC
CHIILORTY RHYOLITIC
CHIILPSTU SULPHITIC
CHIILPTTY TYPHLITIC
CHIINOSTU CHITINOUS
CHIIOPSST SOPHISTIC
CHIIORRSS CIRRHOSIS

CHIIORSST TRICHOSIS
CHIIPSSTY PHYSICIST
CHIKLMOST LOCKSMITH
CHIKLPSUY PUCKISHLY
CHIKMNPSU CHIPMUNKS
CHIKOOPTT TOOTHPICK
CHIKOPSTW WHIPSTOCK
CHILLMOPY PHYLLOMIC
CHILLNOOT LOINCLOTH
CHILLOSTY COLTISHLY
CHILLOSUY SLOUCHILY
CHILMOOTY
   HOMOLYTIC
CHILOOPTY HOLOTYPIC
CHILOORSS CHLOROSIS
CHILORTUY ULOTRICHY
CHILOSTTY CYSTOLITH
CHIMMNOOY
   HOMONYMIC
CHIMNOOST
   MONOSTICH
CHIMNOPSY SYMPHONIC
CHIOOPRTT ORTHOPTIC
CHIOOPTYZ ZOOPHYTIC
CHIOPRSTU COURTSHIP
CHIOPRSYY HYPOCRISY
CHIOPSSSY PSYCHOSIS
CHIORRSSU SCIRRHOUS
CHIPRSTTY TRIPTYCHS
CHKLMOOST
   STOCKHOLM
CHLNOTUUY
   UNCOUTHLY
CHLOPPTYY POLYPTYCH
CHOOOPPTY
   PHOTOCOPY
CHOOOPRSY
   HOROSCOPY
CHORSSTTU SHORT CUTS
CIIILLLTY ILLICITLY
CIIILLSTV CIVIL LIST
CIIILMOPT IMPOLITIC
CIIILORTV VITRIOLIC
CIIILOSSS SILICOSIS
CIIIMSTTW WITTICISM
CIIINNOSS INCISIONS
CIIINNRST INTRINSIC
CIIINOSTZ ZIONISTIC
CIIJLNOPT CLIP JOINT
CIIKLLOSS OIL SLICKS
CIIKLPSST LIPSTICKS
CIIKNPPRS PINPRICKS
CIIKNPSST STICKPINS
CIILLNOOS COLLISION

CIILLNOOT COTILLION,
OCTILLION
CIILLOPTY LIPOLYTIC
CIILMPRSY SCRIMPILY
CIILMRSSY LYRICISMS
CIILNNOSU INCLUSION
CIILNOPTU PUNCTILIO,
UNPOLITIC
CIILOOPST POLITICOS
CIILOORST SOLICITOR
CIILOOSSS SCOLIOSIS
CIILOPRTY PYROLITIC
CIILOSUVY VICIOUSLY
CIILRSSTY LYRICISTS
CIILSSTTY STYLISTIC
CIIMMSSTY MYSTICISM
CIIMNORUZ ZIRCONIUM
CIIMOOSST ISOSMOTIC
CIIMORSTV VORTICISM
CIINNNOTU INUNCTION
CIINNORSU INCURSION
CIINNOSSW WISCONSIN
CIINNSSTT INSTINCTS
CIINOOPRT INOTROPIC
CIINOPSSU SUSPICION
CIINORSUU INCURIOUS
CIINOSTVY SYNOVITIC
CIIOOPRST ISOTROPIC
CIIOOSSTX TOXICOSIS
CIIOPRSTT TROPISTIC
CIIORSTTU TOURISTIC
CIIORSTTV VORTICIST
CIIORSTUV VIRTUOSIC
CIIORSTUY CURIOSITY
CIIOSSTVY VISCOSITY
CIIRSTTUY RUSTICITY
CIJKOSSST JOSS STICK
CIJKOSSTY JOYSTICKS
CIJNNOSTU JUNCTIONS
CIJNNOTTU T-JUNCTION
CIKKOOSSU KOSCIUSKO
CIKLLNUUY UNLUCKILY
CIKLNORSS CROSS-LINK
CIKLOOPST POLO STICK
CIKLOORSU COKULORIS
CIKLORSTW WRISTLOCK
CIKMOORSS SICKROOMS
CIKOSSSTT STOCKISTS
CILLMORUY COLLYRIUM
CILLMOUUV COLLUVIUM
CILLNOOSU COLLUSION
CILLNOSSU SCULLIONS
CILLOOOTY COYOTILLO
CILMNOSTU COLUMNIST

CILMOOPSY POLYSOMIC
CILMOSSUU SOUL MUSIC
CILMOTYYZ ZYMOLYTIC
CILNOORUU UNICOLOUR
CILNOOSST COLONISTS
CILNOOSTU LOCUTIONS
CILNOSTYY CYTOLYSIN
CILOOPSUY COPIOUSLY
CILOORRST TRICOLORS
CILOORRTU TRICOLOUR
CILOORSTU COLOURIST
CILOPPTYY POLYTYPIC
CILORRSUY CURSORILY
CILORSUUY CURIOUSLY
CILOSSTYY CYTOLYSIS
CILRSTTUU CULTURIST
CIMMMNOSU
COMMUNISM
CIMMNNOOU
COMMUNION
CIMMNOOOS
MONOSOMIC
CIMMNOOOT
COMMOTION
CIMMNOSTU
COMMUNIST
CIMMNOTUY
COMMUNITY
CIMMOORTY
MICROTOMY
CIMNNOOOT
MONOTONIC
CIMNNOSYY
SYNONYMIC
CIMNNOTUU
CONTINUUM
CIMNOOPTY
MONOTYPIC,
TOPONYMIC
CIMNOSSTU MISCOUNTS
CIMNSTUYY SYNCYTIUM
CINNOOSTU
CONTINUOS, CONTUSION
CINNOOSUU INNOCUOUS
CINOOOORRS CORROSION
CINOOPRSS SCORPIONS
CINOPRRTU INCORRUPT
CINOSSTUV VISCOUNTS
CIOOOPRSZ ZOOSPORIC
CIOOPSSTU POSTICOUS
CKKNOOSTU
KNOCKOUTS
CKLLNOORR ROCK 'N'
ROLL

CKMQOORST
STOCKROOM
CKNOORRWW
CROWNWORK
CKOOORSTT
ROOTSTOCK
CKOOPSSTT STOCKPOTS
CKOPRSTTU TRUCK STOP
CLMOOOOORT
LOCOMOTOR
CLMOOOSTY
COLOSTOMY
CLMOORSTU
COLOSTRUM
CLNOOPRSU PROCONSUL
CLOOOPRST PROTOCOLS
CLOPRRTUY CORRUPTLY
CLOPRSSTU SCULPTORS
CMNOOORST
COSMOTRON
CMOOOORRTU
COURTROOM
CMOOOORSST
MOTOCROSS
CMOOOSTTY
COSTOTOMY
CMOOSTTYY
CYSTOTOMY
CNNNOOTUU COUNT
NOUN
CNOPRTUUY UP-
COUNTRY
COOOOPRRST ROOT
CROPS
COOPRSSTY SPOROCYST
COORRSSTW
CROSSWORT
DDDEEHRSU SHUDDERED
DDDEEINST DISTENDED
DDDEENORU
REDOUNDED
DDDEEORRS DODDERERS
DDDEGILOS DISLODGED
DDDEGINOR
DODDERING
DDDEIINSV DIVIDENDS
DDDEIINUV UNDIVIDED
DDDEIIPRR DRIP-DRIED
DDEEEEKNW
WEEKENDED
DDEEEFIPR DEEP FRIED
DDEEEFNRS DEFENDERS
DDEEEFNRU UNDERFEED
DDEEEGIPR PEDIGREED

DDEEEILRV DELIVERED
DDEEEILTT TITLE DEED
DDEEEINRX DEXEDRINE
DDEEEIPTX EXPEDITED
DDEEEIRTU DEUTERIDE
DDEEELMOR
REMODELED
DDEEELOPV DEVELOPED
DDEEENNOP OPEN-
ENDED
DDEEENNPT DEPENDENT
DDEEENPRT PRETENDED
DDEEEPRSS DEPRESSED
DDEEERRSS REDRESSED
DDEEERSWY DYER'S-
WEED
DDEEESTUU DESUETUDE
DDEEFGINN DEFENDING
DDEEFGLNU
UNFLEDGED
DDEEFNORU
FOUNDERED
DDEEFORST DEFROSTED
DDEEGGGLO
DOGLEGGED
DDEEGGILT GILT-EDGED
DDEEGHILT DELIGHTED
DDEEGINNP DEPENDING
DDEEGINNR REDDENING
DDEEGIRSS DIGRESSED
DDEEGJPRU PREJUDGED
DDEEHIINT HIDDENITE
DDEEHNORT
DETHRONED
DDEEHNORU
DEERHOUND
DDEEHNRTU
THUNDERED
DDEEHRRSS SHREDDERS
DDEEIILMT DELIMITED
DDEEIILNS SIDELINED
DDEEIIOSX DEOXIDISE
DDEEIIOXZ DEOXIDIZE
DDEEIKLNR REKINDLED
DDEEIILLPS DISPELLED
DDEEIILLRV DRIVELLED
DDEEILMMN
MIDDLEMEN
DDEEILMSX MIDDLESEX
DDEEIILOPS DESPOILED
DDEEIILORS SOLDIERED
DDEEIMMNO
DEMIMONDE
DDEEIINNST INTENDEDS

DDEEINORW
EIDERDOWN
DDEEINOSV NOSEDIVED
DDEEINPSS DISPENSED
DDEEINRST DISTENDER
DDEEINRSU UNDERSIDE,
UNDESIRED
DDEEINSST DISSENTED
DDEEIOORS DEODORISE
DDEEIOORZ DEODORIZE
DDEEIOPST DEPOSITED
DDEEIORRS SIDE ORDER
DDEEIPRSS DISPERSED
DDEEIPSTU DEPUTISED
DDEEIPTUZ DEPUTIZED
DDEEIRSSS SIDE-DRESS
DDEELLOPS DEED POLLS,
DEEDS POLL
DEEELMORR
REMODELER
DDEELMORS
SMOLDERED
DDEELMORU
MOULDERED,
REMOULDED
DDEELNPRU PLUNDERED
DDEELOTVY DEVOTEDLY
DDEEMOPUY PUY DE
DOME
DDEENNORU
UNDERDONE
DDEENOPRS RESPONDED
DDEENOPRT PORTENDED
DDEENOPUX
EXPOUNDED
DDEENORSU RESOUNDED
DDEENOSTY EDDYSTONE
DDEENPSSU SUSPENDED
DDEENRSSU UNDRESSED
DDEEOOPRT TORPEDOED
DDEEOORSV OVERDOSED
DDEEOORSY DESTROYED
DDEFFIINT DIFFIDENT
DDEFGIIIN DIGNIFIED
DDEFGILLO GOLDFIELD
DDEFILOOT FLOOD TIDE
DDEFNNOUU
UNFOUNDED
DDEGGIORS DISGORGED
DDEGHINRS SHREDDING
DDEGIIIST DIGITISED
DDEGIIITZ DIGITIZED
DDEGIIMSU MISGUIDED
DDEGIINSS GIDDINESS

DDEGIISSU DISGUISED
DDEGIJMSU MISJUDGED
DDEGIJNRU JUDDERING
DDEGINORR DERRING-
DO
DDEGINRRU UNDERGIRD
DDEGIOOSS GOOD-SISED
DDEGIOOSZ GOOD-SIZED
DDEGISSTU DISGUSTED
DDEGLNOOR
GOLDENROD
DDEGNORSU
UNDERDOGS
DDEGOOORS DO-
GOODERS
DDEHHNRTU
HUNDREDTH
DDEHIOSST SHODDIEST
DDEHOOSSW
WOODSHEDS
DDEIIKNSV SKIN-DIVED
DDEIIKRSV DISK DRIVE
DDEIILLST DISTILLED
DDEIIMSSS DISMISSED
DDEIIMTTW DIM-WITTED
DDEIINPRS SPIN-DRIED
DDEIINSST DISSIDENT
DDEIINSTU DISUNITED
DDEILMNOW LOW-
MINDED
DDEILNRRU UNRIDDLER
DDEILORWW
WORLDWIDE
DDEILOSSV DISSOLVED
DDEIMNOPU
IMPOUNDED
DDEIMNSSU MUDDINESS
DDEINORTU OUTRIDDEN
DDEINOSSW DOWDINESS
DDEINRSSU RUDDINESS
DDEINSTUU UNSTUDIED
DDEIOPRST DISPORTED
DDEIOPRSV DISPROVED
DDEIORRSS DISORDERS
DDEIORSTT DISTORTED
DDEIPRSTU DISRUPTED
DDELNORSU
UNDERSOLD
DDEMNOOTU ODD MEN
OUT
DDEMNOSUU
DUODENUMS
DDENNORUU
UNROUNDED

DDENOOPRS DROPSONDE
DDENOORSW DO WONDERS
DDEOPRRTU PROTRUDED
DDFIOORTW DRIFTWOOD
DDGGINNOS DINGDONGS
DDGIILNNW DWINDLING
DDGIILNTW TWIDDLING
DDGOOORSW GOOD WORDS
DDHIOOOWW WIDOWHOOD
DEEEEKNRW WEEKENDER
DEEEEMRRS REDEEMERS
DEEEENPST STEEPENED
DEEEFGIKN KNIFE-EDGE
DEEEFHNRS FRESHENED
DEEEFHRRS REFRESHED
DEEEFINSV DEFENSIVE
DEEEFLLRU REFUELLED
DEEEFMNRT DEFERMENT, FERMENTED
DEEEFPRRR PREFERRED
DEEEFRRYZ FREEZE-DRY
DEEEGIMNR REDEEMING
DEEEGINNP DEEPENING
DEEEGINRS ENERGISED
DEEEGINRZ ENERGIZED
DEEEGIPRS PEDIGREES
DEEEGIRST GREEDIEST
DEEEGKLNT KENTLEDGE
DEEEGLNOY GOLDENEYE
DEEEGMNST SEGMENTED
DEEEGNRTT DETERGENT
DEEEGRRSS REGRESSED
DEEEGRRTT REGRETTED
DEEEHIMPR EPHEMERID
DEEEHINPR EPHEDRINE
DEEEHLRST SHELTERED
DEEEHNPRR REPREHEND
DEEEHNRRU HEREUNDER
DEEEHORSW HORSEWEED
DEEEILLMP MILLEPEDE
DEEEILNNV ENLIVENED
DEEEILPTV DEPLETIVE
DEEEILRRV DELIVERER, REDELIVER

DEEEILSSW EDELWEISS
DEEEILSTV TELEVISED
DEEEIMNRT DETERMINE
DEEEIMPRR PREMIERED
DEEEIMSST DISESTEEM
DEEEINNSS NEEDINESS
DEEEINOPR PIONEERED
DEEEINPTX EXPEDIENT
DEEEINQTU QUIETENED
DEEEINRSS REEDINESS
DEEEINRST TENDERISE
DEEEINRTZ TENDERIZE
DEEEINSSS SEEDINESS
DEEEINSSW WEEDINESS
DEEEIPRRV REPRIEVED
DEEEIPRTX EXPEDITER
DEEEIPRVW PREVIEWED
DEEEIPSST SPEEDIEST
DEEEIRRTV RETRIEVED
DEEEIRSTV DETERSIVE
DEEEIRUZZ ZUIDER ZEE
DEEEKLLNN KENNELLED
DEEELLPSW SPEEDWELL
DEEELNOPV ENVELOPED
DEEELNRWY RENEWEDLY
DEEELOPRV DEVELOPER, REDEVELOP
DEEELPPRX PERPLEXED
DEEELRSTT RESETTLED
DEEELRSTW SWELTERED
DEEEMNRTT DETERMENT
DEEEMOPRW EMPOWERED
DEEEMPPRT PRE-EMPTED
DEEENNRST ENTENDRES
DEEENNSSS DENSENESS
DEEENPRRT PRETENDER
DEEENPRST PRESENTED
DEEENPRTV PREVENTED
DEEENRRSV REVERENDS
DEEENRRTT DETERRENT
DEEENRSTT TENDEREST
DEEENSSVX VEXEDNESS
DEEEOPRST DEPORTEES
DEEEORRSS REREDOSES
DEEEORSTV STEVEDORE
DEEEORSVX OVERSEXED
DEEEPPPRR RED PEPPER
DEEEPRRSS REPRESSED
DEEEPRRSV PRESERVED
DEEEPRRTV PERVERTED
DEEEPRSST SPEEDSTER
DEEEPRSSU SUPERSEDE

DEEEPRSSX EXPRESSED
DEEEQRSTU REQUESTED
DEEERRRSS REDRESSER
DEEERRSST DESERTERS
DEEFFINRT DIFFERENT
DEEFFINST STIFFENED
DEEFFIORT FORFEITED
DEEFFNORS OFFENDERS
DEEFFOPRR PROFFERED
DEEFGHIRT FREIGHTED
DEEFGIIRS SIEGFRIED
DEEFGINNU UNFEIGNED
DEEFGINRR DEFERRING
DEEFGJORU FOREJUDGE
DEEFGLNNO DOG FENNEL
DEEFHLLUY HEEDFULLY
DEEFHLOPS SHEEPFOLD
DEEFHLORS FREEHOLDS
DEEFHLORT THREEFOLD
DEEFHRRTU FURTHERED
DEEFIILMN MINEFIELD
DEEFIILNR INFIELDER
DEEFIILQU LIQUEFIED
DEEFIINNS DEFINIENS
DEEFIIPRS PERFIDIES
DEEFIIPRT PETRIFIED
DEEFIIRRT TERRIFIED
DEEFIIRSS FIRESIDES
DEEFIISTT TESTIFIED
DEEFILMNS FIELDSMEN
DEEFILRSV SELF-DRIVE
DEEFILSTT FIELD-TEST
DEEFINNPR PEN FRIEND
DEEFINNRU UNREFINED
DEEFINNTU FINE-TUNED
DEEFIPRTU PUTREFIED
DEEFIPSTU STUPEFIED
DEEFIRRTT FRITTERED
DEEFIRSTU SURFEITED
DEEFLLNNU FUNNELLED
DEEFLLNUY NEEDFULLY
DEEFLNOSV SEVENFOLD
DEEFLNRTU UNDERFELT
DEEFLORRW FREE WORLD
DEEFLRSTU FLUSTERED
DEEFLRTTU FLUTTERED
DEEFMOPRR PERFORMED
DEEFNOOPS SPOON-FEED
DEEFNOOST FESTOONED
DEEFOPRSS PROFESSED
DEEFORRST DEFROSTER
DEEFRSTUY DUTY-FREES

DEEGGGILN LEGGINGED
DEEGGHHOS
HEDGEHOGS
DEEGGINRS SNIGGERED
DEEGGIRRT TRIGGERED
DEEGGSSTU SUGGESTED
DEEGHHIPS HIGH-SPEED
DEEGHIINV INVEIGHED
DEEGHILNT LIGHTENED
DEEGHILNW WHEEDLING
DEEGHILRT DELIGHTER
DEEGHINTT TIGHTENED
DEEGHINUW
UNWEIGHED
DEEGHNORU
ROUGHENED
DEEGHNOTU
TOUGHENED
DEEGHOPSS SHEEPDOGS
DEEGHORSW
HEDGEROWS
DEEGIILNU GUIDELINE
DEEGIILNV INVEIGLED
DEEGIINSS DIGENESIS
DEEGIINTY TIE-DYEING
DEEGIISTV DIGESTIVE
DEEGILLOR LIEGE LORD
DEEGILMMR
GLIMMERED
DEEGILNPT DEPLETING
DEEGILNSS SEEDLINGS
DEEGILNST GLISTENED
DEEGILOOU IDEOLOGUE
DEEGILOPR RIDGEPOLE
DEEGILOSU EULOGISED
DEEGILOUZ EULOGIZED
DEEGILRTT GLITTERED
DEEGIMNRY REMEDYING
DEEGIMORT GEOMETRID
DEEGINNPX EXPENDING
DEEGINNRR RENDERING
DEEGINNRT TENDERING
DEEGINNTX EXTENDING
DEEGINRRR DERRINGER
DEEGINRRT DETERRING
DEEGINRSS DESIGNERS
DEEGINRST DESERTING
DEEGINRSV DESERVING
DEEGINRTU NEGRITUDE
DEEGINRTV DIVERGENT
DEEGINRUV GERUNDIVE
DEEGINSTT DETESTING
DEEGIOSST GEODESIST
DEEGIPRST PREDIGEST

DEEGIRRSS DIGRESSER
DEEGIRRUU DE RIGUEUR
DEEGJMNTU
JUDGEMENT
DEEGJPRRU PREJUDGER
DEEGKLNOW
KNOWLEDGE
DEEGKOPRW POWDER
KEG
DEEGLLORV GROVELLED
DEEGLNNOU
GUENDOLEN
DEEGLNNOW
GWENDOLEN
DEEGNNORU
UNDERGONE
DEEGNNSSU DUNGENESS
DEEGNOORW
GREENWOOD
DEEGNORRU
UNDERGOER
DEEGNORSS ENGROSSED
DEEGOPRRU REGROUPED
DEEHHINST IN THE SHED
DEEHHIORS HORSEHIDE
DEEHHPRSS SHEPHERDS
DEEHIINRT INHERITED
DEEHIKRSW WHISKERED
DEEHILLRV HELLDIVER
DEEHILORU HIERODULE
DEEHILPRS ELDERSHIP
DEEHILRST SLITHERED
DEEHILRSV SHRIVELED
DEEHIMMRS SHIMMERED
DEEHIMOST METHODISE
DEEHIMOTX
METHOXIDE
DEEHIMOTZ METHODIZE
DEEHIMPRW WHIMPERED
DEEHINNOV EINDHOVEN
DEEHINNRS ENSHRINED
DEEHINNTU IN THE
NUDE
DEEHINOPX PHENOXIDE
DEEHINORT DINOTHERE
DEEHINPRT TREPHINED
DEEHINRSW SWINEHERD
DEEHIORST THEORISED
DEEHIORTZ THEORIZED
DEEHIOSTU TIED HOUSE
DEEHIPPSS SHEEPDIPS
DEEHIPRSW WHISPERED
DEEHIRSSV DERVISHES
DEEHLLOSV SHOVELLED

DEEHLNOYY
HONEYEDLY
DEEHLORST HOLSTERED
DEEHMNNOT ON THE
MEND
DEEHMOORT
HODOMETER
DEEHMORST
SMOTHERED
DEEHNNORT
ENTHRONED
DEEHNOPTY
ENDOPHYTE
DEEHNORRT
DETHRONER
DEEHNORST SHORTENED
DEEHNRRTU
THUNDERER
DEEHOORTX
HETERODOX
DEEHOPSTU DEEP SOUTH
DEEHRSSTW SHREWDEST
DEEHRSTTU SHUTTERED
DEEHSSTTU DUSTSHEET
DEEIIINPR PIERIDINE
DEEIILLMP MILLIPEDE
DEEIILMPR IMPERILED
DEEIILNSS SIDELINES
DEEIIMPRS EPIDERMIS
DEEIINSST DENSITIES,
DESTINIES
DEEIIPSSW SIDESWIPE
DEEIIRRSV RIVERSIDE
DEEIIRTVV DIVERTIVE
DEEIISSSU SIDE ISSUE
DEEIJNORR REJOINDER
DEEIKLNNR ENKINDLER
DEEIKNSTW STINKWEED
DEEIKPPRS SKIPPERED
DEEIKRSTT SKITTERED
DEEIKSSTT DISKETTES
DEEILLLNW WELL-LINED
DEEILLLOW WELL-OILED
DEEILLMNO ILL-OMENED
DEEILLMTW WELL-
TIMED
DEEILLNSV SNIVELLED
DEEILLPRS DISPELLER
DEEILLRRV DRIVELLER
DEEILLRSU SLIDE RULE
DEEILLRTU TELLURIDE
DEEILLRTW WELL-TRIED
DEEILLSVW SWIVELLED
DEEILMMNS MENDELISM

DEEILMNTV DEVILMENT
DEEILMORS MELODISER
DEEILMORZ MELODIZER
DEEILMRTY MERITEDLY
DEEILNNRU UNDERLINE
DEEILNOPT DEPLETION,
DIPLOTENE
DEEILNOST DELETIONS
DEEILNPTU PLENITUDE
DEEILNRRU UNDERLIER
DEEILNRTU INTERLUDE
DEEILNTVY EVIDENTLY
DEEILOPRS DESPOILER
DEEILOPTX EXPLOITED
DEEILORRS ORDERLIES
DEEILORSV EVILDOERS
DEEILRRSS RIDERLESS
DEEILRSVY DIVERSELY
DEEILRTUY ERUDITELY
DEEIMMORS MEMORISED
DEEIMMORZ
MEMORIZED
DEEIMNNOT
MENTIONED
DEEIMNNRU
UNDERMINE
DEEIMNORS MODERNISE
DEEIMNORZ
MODERNIZE
DEEIMNOSS DES MOINES
DEEIMNOST MOISTENED
DEEIMNPST PEDIMENTS
DEEIMNRRS REMINDERS
DEEIMNRTT DETRIMENT
DEEIMNSST SEDIMENTS
DEEIMOORT METEOROID
DEEIMORST DOSIMETER
DEEIMPRSS IMPRESSED
DEEIMPRST DISTEMPER
DEEIMPRTT PERMITTED
DEEIMRTUU DEUTERIUM
DEEINNOPS PENSIONED
DEEINNORT INTERNODE
DEEINNOTT DETENTION
DEEINNRTU INDENTURE
DEEINNSSS SNIDENESS
DEEINOPTX PENTOXIDE
DEEINORST DESERTION
DEEINORSW ROSINWEED
DEEINOSSV NOSEDIVES
DEEINPRRT REPRINTED
DEEINPRSS DISPENSER
DEEINPRST PRESIDENT
DEEINRRSU REINSURED

DEEINRSST DISSENTER,
RESIDENTS, TIREDNESS
DEEINRSSW WEIRDNESS
DEEINRSTT TRENDIEST
DEEINSSTW WITNESSED
DEEIOPRVW POWER DIVE
DEEIORRRV OVERRIDER
DEEIORRVV OVERDRIVE
DEEIORSSV OVERSISED
DEEIORSVZ OVERSIZED
DEEIORTTX TETROXIDE
DEEIPPRRS PERSPIRED
DEEIPRRSS DISPERSER
DEEIPRSST PERSISTED
DEEIPRSTU DISREPUTE
DEEIPSSST SIDESTEPS
DEEIRSSST DRESSIEST
DEEIRSTUV SERVITUDE
DEEIRTTTW TWITTERED
DEEIRTTXY DEXTERITY
DEEISTTTU DESTITUTE
DEEJNORUY JOURNEYED
DEEJOORVY OVERJOYED
DEEKNOORS
SNOOKERED
DEEKNORTW
NETWORKED
DEELLMMPU
PUMMELLED
DEELLMOOR ROLE
MODEL
DEELLNNTU TUNNELLED
DEELLNRSU UNDERSELL
DEELLNSSY ENDLESSLY
DEELLOPPR PROPELLED
DEELMMPTU
PLUMMETED
DEELMOORV
VELODROME
DEELNOOSS LOOSE ENDS
DEELNOOST LODESTONE
DEELNPRRU PLUNDERER
DEELNSTTU UNSETTLED
DEELNSWWY
NEWLYWEDS
DEELOPRSY REPOSEDLY
DEELORRUV OVERRULED
DEELPRTUY REPUTEDLY
DEEMNNOTW
ENDOWMENT
DEEMNNRUY
RUNNYMEDE
DEEMNOORT
ONDOMETER

DEEMNOPRS
ENDOSPERM
DEEMNOPSU
SPODUMENE
DEEMNORTT
TORMENTED
DEEMNORTU
REMOUNTED
DEEMNOSTU
ENDOSTEUM
DEEMOORST
ODOMETERS
DEEMPRTTU TRUMPETED
DEEMRRRSU MURDERERS
DEEMRRSSU MURDERESS
DEENNORTU
UNDERTONE
DEENNRTUW
UNDERWENT
DEENOOPRS ENDOSPORE
DEENOPRRS RESPONDER
DEENOPRRV PROVENDER
DEENOPRSV OVERSPEND
DEENOPRUX
EXPOUNDER
DEENPRSSU SUSPENDER
DEENRRRSU SURRENDER
DEENRSTTU ENTRUSTED
DEENRSTUW WET-
NURSED
DEENRSTYY DYSENTERY
DEEOOPRST TORPEDOES
DEEOOORSSV OVERDOSES
DEEOPPRRS PROSPERED
DEEOPPRSS OPPRESSED
DEEOPPRST STOPPERED
DEEOPRRSS DEPRESSOR
DEEOPSSSS POSSESSED
DEEORRSSV OVERDRESS
DEEORRSTX DEXTRORSE
DEEORRSTY DESTROYER
DEEORSTUX DEXTEROUS
DEEOSTTUV DEVOUTEST
DEEPRRSSU PRESSURED
DEEPRSTTU SPUTTERED
DEERSTTTU STUTTERED
DEFFGIINR DIFFERING
DEFFGINNO OFFENDING
DEFFIIORT FORTIFIED
DEFFIISUV DIFFUSIVE
DEFFILLLU FULFILLED
DEFFILSUY DIFFUSELY
DEFFLNRUU UNRUFFLED
DEFGGIINT FIDGETING

DEFGGILLN FLEDGLING
DEFGHILOT EIGHTFOLD
DEFGHIOSS DOGFISHES
DEFGIIINS SIGNIFIED
DEFGIILOR GLORIFIED
DEFGIINNR INFRINGED
DEFGIIRSU DISFIGURE
DEFGILNNO ENFOLDING
DEFGIMNOR
   DEFORMING
DEFGINNRU REFUNDING
DEFHIILSV DEVILFISH
DEFHIIORR HORRIFIED
DEFHINRSU FURNISHED
DEFHLOOOW
   WHOLEFOOD
DEFHOOOTT
   HOTFOOTED
DEFIIIRTV VITRIFIED
DEFIIJSTU JUSTIFIED
DEFIILLMO MOLLIFIED
DEFIILLNU NULLIFIED
DEFIILLOS OILFIELDS
DEFIILLRR FIRE DRILL
DEFIILMSU SEMIFLUID
DEFIILPRT FIELD TRIP
DEFIILRSU FLUIDISER
DEFIILRSW WILDFIRES
DEFIILRUZ FLUIDIZER
DEFIIMMMU MUMMIFIED
DEFIIMNNY INDEMNIFY
DEFIIMORS MODIFIERS
DEFIIMORT MORTIFIED
DEFIIMRWY MIDWIFERY
DEFIIMSTY MYSTIFIED
DEFIINNRW WINNIFRED
DEFIINRTY DENITRIFY
DEFIINSST DISINFEST
DEFIIRRST STIR-FRIED
DEFIIRSVY DIVERSIFY
DEFIIRTVY DEVITRIFY
DEFIKLORW FIELDWORK
DEFILLRUY DIREFULLY
DEFILMNRU REMINDFUL
DEFILMSUY DEMULSIFY
DEFILNOSW SNOWFIELD
DEFIMNORT DENTIFORM
DEFIMNORU UNIFORMED
DEFIMORTY DEFORMITY
DEFIMSTYY DEMYSTIFY
DEFINORSU FOUNDRIES
DEFIORSST DISFOREST
DEFIORTTU FORTITUDE
DEFIOTTTU OUTFITTED

DEFLLLOUY DOLEFULLY
DEFLLNOUW WELL-
   FOUND
DEFLLRSSU FULL DRESS
DEFLMMOUX
   FLUMMOXED
DEFLNORSU FLOUNDERS
DEFLNORUW
   WONDERFUL
DEFNOORTU
   UNDERFOOT
DEFOORRSW
   FOREWORDS
DEGGIILNR RIDGELING
DEGGIILRU GIRL GUIDE
DEGGIINNS DESIGNING
DEGGIINRV DIVERGING
DEGGIINST DIGESTING
DEGGIORRS DISGORGER
DEGGLRSTU STRUGGLED
DEGHHIIST HIGH TIDES
DEGHHINOT HIGH-
   TONED
DEGHIILNS SHIELDING
DEGHIILST SIDELIGHT
DEGHIINNR HINDERING
DEGHIINRT DITHERING
DEGHIJPSU JUDGESHIP
DEGHILMSU GUMSHIELD
DEGHILRST RED LIGHTS
DEGHIMNRU
   HUMDINGER
DEGHINSTU UNSIGHTED
DEGHIORTU
   DOUGHTIER
DEGHMOORT
   GODMOTHER
DEGHNNRUU
   UNDERHUNG
DEGHNORUY
   GREYHOUND
DEGHOOSSU
   DOGHOUSES
DEGIIIMRS SEMIRIGID
DEGIIINST DIGNITIES
DEGIIIRST DIGITISER
DEGIIIRTZ DIGITIZER
DEGIILLNV DEVILLING
DEGIILNOV EVILDOING
DEGIILNRV DRIVELING
DEGIIMNNP IMPENDING
DEGIIMNNR REMINDING
DEGIIMNST DEMISTING
DEGIIMRSU MISGUIDER

DEGIINNNT INDENTING,
   INTENDING
DEGIINNSS DINGINESS
DEGIINOST DIGESTION
DEGIINPRS PRESIDING
DEGIINPRV DEPRIVING
DEGIINPSS DESPISING
DEGIINRTU INTRIGUED
DEGIINRTV DIVERTING
DEGIINSST DESISTING
DEGIINSTU DISTINGUÉ
DEGIINSTV DIVESTING
DEGIIOPRS PRODIGIES
DEGIIQRSU SQUIDGIER
DEGIIRRSV VERDIGRIS
DEGIIRSSU DISGUISER
DEGIISSSU DISGUISES
DEGIJMRSU MISJUDGER
DEGIKLOSV KID GLOVES
DEGILLMNO MODELLING
DEGILLNOV LONG-LIVED
DEGILLNOY YODELLING
DEGILLNSW DWELLINGS
DEGILMNOR GOLD-
   MINER, MOLDERING,
   REMOLDING
DEGILMNOS GOLDMINES
DEGILNNRU UNDERLING
DEGILNNTU INDULGENT
DEGILNOOR GONDOLIER
DEGILNOPR DEPLORING
DEGILNOPX EXPLODING
DEGILNOPY DEPLOYING
DEGILNORS SOLDERING
DEGILNOSS GODLINESS
DEGILNOSU DELOUSING
DEGILNOTU LONGITUDE
DEGILNOVV DEVOLVING
DEGILOOST GOODLIEST
DEGILOSTT GLOTTIDES
DEGILSSTU SLUDGIEST
DEGIMNRRU
   DEMURRING,
   MURDERING
DEGINNOPR PONDERING
DEGINNORS ENDORSING
DEGINNORW
   WONDERING
DEGINNRSU SUNDERING
DEGINNRUW
   UNDERWING
DEGINOORV OVERDOING
DEGINOPRT DEPORTING
DEGINOPRW POWDERING

DEGINOPSS PODGINESS
DEGINORRW
REWORDING
DEGINORUV DEVOURING
DEGINPSSU PUDGINESS
DEGINRSSS DRESSINGS
DEGINRTUX EXTRUDING
DEGIOPRTY PTERYGOID
DEGIOPSTU GUIDEPOST
DEGIOSSTT STODGIEST
DEGJMNSTU JUDGMENTS
DEGLLOSSY GODLESSLY
DEGLNNOWY
GWENDOLYN
DEGLNOOPR
PROLONGED
DEGLNORSU GROUNDSEL
DEGLOOSUU
DUOLOGUES
DEGNOORRW
WRONGDOER
DEGNOPRUW
GUNPOWDER
DEGOOPRRU
PROROGUED
DEGORRSTU DRUGSTORE
DEHHIINOS HOIDENISH
DEHHIKMOS
SHEIKHDOM
DEHHILNOS HOLINSHED
DEHHINOSY HOYDENISH
DEHHIOPPS PHOSPHIDE
DEHHLLNOU
HELLHOUND
DEHHLOOSU
HOUSEHOLD
DEHHLORST THRESHOLD
DEHHNOORU
HOREHOUND
DEHIIINST HISTIDINE
DEHIIILLSS HILLSIDES
DEHIIILRSS DISRELISH
DEHIIMNTY THYMIDINE
DEHIINNRU HIRUNDINE
DEHIINOOP IDIOPHONE
DEHIISTWW WIDTHWISE
DEHIJMNOS DEMIJOHNS
DEHIKKOOZ KOZHIKODE
DEHILOORT RHODOLITE
DEHILORSW WILD HORSE
DEHILOSTW DISH TOWEL
DEHILOSUY HIDEOUSLY
DEHILPSSU SULPHIDES
DEHILRRUY HURRIEDLY

DEHIMMOST
METHODISM
DEHIMNOOT IN THE
MOOD
DEHIMNORT
TRONDHEIM
DEHIMNSSU HUMIDNESS
DEHIMOSTT METHODIST
DEHIMPRTU TRIUMPHED
DEHINOORT
RHODONITE
DEHINORRT TRIHEDRON
DEHINORSU NOURISHED
DEHINOSST DISHONEST,
HEDONISTS
DEHINRRUU UNHURRIED
DEHIOOTWW
HOWTOWDIE,
WHITEWOOD
DEHIOPRSS SPHEROIDS
DEHIOPRSW WORSHIPED
DEHIOSSSW SIDESHOWS
DEHKLOOST STOKEHOLD
DEHKNOOOS HOOK-
NOSED
DEHLMNOPY
ENDOLYMPH
DEHLOORSV
HOLDOVERS
DEHLOPRSU UPHOLDERS
DEHLORSSU SHOULDERS
DEHLORSYY HYDROLYSE
DEHLORTTT THROTTLED
DEHLORTYY HYDROLYTE
DEHMNOOPR
ENDOMORPH
DEHMOORTY
HODOMETRY
DEHNNOOPS
SPHENODON
DEHNNOSUW
NEWSHOUND
DEHNORSTU
UNDERSHOT
DEHOORSTU
HERODOTUS
DEHOOSSSU DOSSHOUSE
DEHOPRSST POTSHERDS
DEHORSSTU STUDHORSE
DEIIIKNTT IDENTIKIT
DEIIILQSU LIQUIDISE
DEIIILQUZ LIQUIDIZE
DEIIIMMNS MINIMISED
DEIIIMMNZ MINIMIZED

DEIIINNQU QUINIDINE
DEIIINSSS DISSEISIN
DEIIKLNST KINDLIEST
DEIIKNRSV SKIN DIVER
DEIILLNST INSTILLED
DEIILLOPR PILLORIED
DEIILLOPS ELLIPSOID
DEIILLRST DISTILLER
DEIILMNTU UNLIMITED
DEIILMOSS SEMISOLID
DEIILMRSU DELIRIUMS
DEIILNPRS SPINDLIER
DEIILNSSV LIVIDNESS
DEIILOPRT REPTILOID
DEIILORSU DELIRIOUS
DEIILPSSS SIDESLIPS
DEIILSUVV DIVULSIVE
DEIIMMNSU IMMUNISED
DEIIMMNUZ IMMUNIZED
DEIIMNNOS DIMENSION
DEIIMNNTY INDEMNITY
DEIIMNOQU DOMINIQUE
DEIIMNPRT IMPRINTED
DEIIMNRSS MINIDRESS
DEIIMNRTW MIDWINTER
DEIIMOPST OPTIMISED
DEIIMOPTZ OPTIMIZED
DEIIMPRSU PRESIDIUM
DEIINNNOT INDENTION
DEIINNORT RENDITION
DEIINNOSU UNIONISED
DEIINNOTT DENTITION
DEIINNOTV VENDITION
DEIINNOUZ UNIONIZED
DEIINNSSW WINDINESS
DEIINOPRT PERDITION
DEIINOPSS INDISPOSE
DEIINORSS IRONSIDES
DEIINORSV DIVERSION
DEIINORTT DETRITION
DEIINORTU ERUDITION
DEIINPPSW WINDPIPES
DEIINRSST DIRTINESS
DEIINSSVV VIVIDNESS
DEIINSSZZ DIZZINESS
DEIIORSSS DISSEISOR,
SIDEROSIS
DEIIOSSTU SEDITIOUS
DEIIRSTVY DIVERSITY
DEIJORRSY JOYRIDERS
DEIKLLNSU UNSKILLED
DEIKLNPRS SPRINKLED
DEIKNNSTU UNKINDEST
DEIKNSSSU DUSKINESS

DEIKRSSVY SKYDIVERS	**DEIMOORTZ**	**DELNOPRSU** SPLENDOUR
DEILLMNOU MULLIONED	MOTORIZED	**DELNOPRTU** UNDERPLOT
DEILLORRW WORLDLIER	**DEIMOOSST** SODOMITES	**DELNOPSUU** PENDULOUS
DEILLORST LORDLIEST	**DEIMOPSST** DESPOTISM	**DELNOSSSU** SOUNDLESS
DEILLORSY SOLDIERLY	**DEIMOQSTU** MISQUOTED	**DELNPRTUY** PRUDENTLY
DEILLSSTU DUELLISTS	**DEIMORSTY** DOSIMETRY	**DELOOOSUW**
DEILLSTTY STILTEDLY	**DEINNNOSU** INNUENDOS	WOODLOUSE
DEILMNOSS MOLDINESS	**DEINNOOTX**	**DELOORRSV** OVERLORDS
DEILMOOST DOLOMITES	ENDOTOXIN	**DELOORSSU** ODOURLESS
DEILMOOSU MELODIOUS	**DEINNOSTU** TENDINOUS	**DELORSTUY** DESULTORY
DEILMORST OLD-TIMERS	**DEINNRSTV** TV DINNERS	**DEMMNOSSU**
DEILMOSTU MOULDIEST	**DEINNRSUU** UNINSURED	SUMMONSED
DEILMTTUU MULTITUDE	**DEINNRTTU** UNDERTINT	**DEMNNORSU**
DEILNOPRU PURLOINED	**DEINOOPRT** PORTIONED	ROUNDSMEN
DEILNOPTY POINTEDLY	**DEINOOPSW** PINEWOODS	**DEMNOPSUY**
DEILNORSU UNDERSOIL	**DEINOOSSW** WOODINESS	PSEUDONYM
DEILNOSSS SOLIDNESS	**DEINOOSTV** DEVOTIONS	**DEMNORSSW**
DEILNOSSU DELUSIONS	**DEINOPRST** DRIPSTONE	SWORDSMEN
DEILNPSST SPLIT ENDS	**DEINOPRTV** PROVIDENT	**DEMNORSSY**
DEILNRSSU LURIDNESS	**DEINORRWW**	SYNDROMES
DEILNRSSW SWINDLERS	WINDROWER	**DEMNORSTU**
DEILORRWY WORRIEDLY	**DEINORSSW** ROWDINESS,	UNDERMOST
DEILORSSV DISSOLVER	WORDINESS	**DEMORRSUU**
DEILOSSTU DISSOLUTE	**DEINORSTU** DETRUSION	MURDEROUS
DEILOSTUY TEDIOUSLY	**DEINOSSTT** DOTTINESS	**DENNOOSTU** DO ONE'S
DEILOSUVY DEVIOUSLY	**DEINPRRSY** SPIN-DRYER	NUT
DEILPTUXY DUPLEXITY	**DEINPRSTU** UNSTRIPED	**DENNORSSU** ROUNDNESS
DEILSTTWY TWISTEDLY	**DEINPSTWW** WINDSWEPT	**DENNORSUW**
DEIMMMRSU	**DEINRRSTU** INTRUDERS	SUNDOWNER
MIDSUMMER	**DEINRSTTU** INTRUSTED	**DENNOSSSU** SOUNDNESS
DEIMMNORS	**DEINRSTTY** DENTISTRY	**DENOOPPST** POSTPONED
MODERNISM	**DEIOOPRST** DEPOSITOR	**DENOOPPSU** UNOPPOSED
DEIMMNOUY	**DEIOOPRTX** PROTOXIDE	**DENOOPRSS** SPONSORED
NEODYMIUM	**DEIOPRRSV** PROVIDERS	**DENOOPRSU** PONDEROUS
DEIMMOSTY	**DEIOPRSTU** DIPTEROUS	**DENOPPRRU**
IMMODESTY	**DEIORRSTT** DISTORTER	UNDERPROP
DEIMNOORT	**DEIORRSTU** OUTRIDERS	**DENOPPSTU** UNSTOPPED
MONITORED	**DEIORSSTU** DIOESTRUS,	**DENOPRSSU** PROUDNESS
DEIMNOOSS MOODINESS	OUTSIDERS	**DENOPSTTU** UNSPOTTED
DEIMNOOST DEMOTIONS	**DEIOTTTUW** OUTWITTED	**DENORTTUU**
DEIMNOOSX	**DEIPRRSSU** SURPRISED	UNTUTORED
MONOXIDES	**DEIPRRSTU** DISRUPTER	**DEOOPRSST** DOORSTEPS
DEIMNOPRU IMPOUNDER	**DEIPRTTUU** TURPITUDE	**DEOPPRRTU** PURPORTED
DEIMNORST MODERNIST	**DEIPSSTTU** STUPIDEST	**DEOPPRSTU** SUPPORTED
DEIMNORTY	**DEIRSSTTU** STURDIEST	**DEORRSUUV** VERDUROUS
MODERNITY	**DEJNOORSU** SOJOURNED	**DEPRSSSTU** PRESS-STUD
DEIMNPRTU IMPRUDENT	**DEKLNNRUY**	**DETTTTTUU**
DEIMNPSSU DUMPINESS	DRUNKENLY	TUT-TUTTED
DEIMNRSTU RUDIMENTS	**DEKNOORTU**	**DFFFOOSTU** FOODSTUFF
DEIMOOORT	UNDERTOOK	**DFFGIINSU** DIFFUSING
IDEOMOTOR	**DELLNORSS** DROLLNESS	**DFFIINOSU** DIFFUSION
DEIMOORST MOTORISED	**DELMNOSTW**	**DFGGHIOST** DOGFIGHTS
DEIMOORTY	MELTDOWNS	**DFGIIIRTY** FRIGIDITY
IODOMETRY	**DELMNPSUU** PENDULUMS	**DFGIIMNOY** MODIFYING

DFGILNNOU
FOUNDLING, UNFOLDING
DFHILOORY HYDROFOIL
DFHIORSSW SWORDFISH
DFHLNOOUW
WOLFHOUND
DFHLNSSUU SLUSH FUND
DFHLOOOST
FOOTHOLDS
DFHNOOSUX
FOXHOUNDS
DFIILORTY FLORIDITY
DFIINPRST SPINDRIFT
DFIKOOPRS SKIDPROOF
DFILLMOTU MULTIFOLD
DFILLTUUY DUTIFULLY
DFILMNNUU
UNMINDFUL
DFINORSTW SNOWDRIFT
DFNOOOPTU FOOT-
POUND
DFNOOORRT FRONT
DOOR
DFNRSTTUU TRUST
FUND
DFOOOSSTW
SOFTWOODS
DGGHINOOT
GOODNIGHT
DGGIILLNY GLIDINGLY
DGGIILNNU INDULGING
DGGIILNUV DIVULGING
DGGIILNUY GUIDINGLY
DGGIJLNUY JUDGINGLY
DGGINNORU
GROUNDING
DGGIRSSTU DRUGGISTS
DGHHIINST HINDSIGHT
DGHHINOPT
DIPHTHONG
DGHHOORSU
ROUGHSHOD
DGHIIMNST MIDNIGHTS
DGHILMOST GOLDSMITH
DGHILNOPU UPHOLDING
DGHILOPRT DROPLIGHT
DGHIMOPSY SPHYGMOID
DGHINORSU SHROUDING
DGHINORTW
DOWNRIGHT
DGHLOORYY
HYDROLOGY
DGHNOSTUU
DOUGHNUTS

DGIIIKLNS DISLIKING
DGIIILNOZ IDOLIZING
DGIIINNRT NITRIDING
DGIIINNTY INDIGNITY
DGIIINOTX DIGITOXIN
DGIIINOXZ OXIDIZING
DGIIJNORY JOYRIDING
DGIIKNSVY SKYDIVING
DGIILLOOR GORILLOID
DGIILMNOP IMPLODING
DGIILNNSW SWINDLING
DGIILNNWY WINDINGLY
DGIILNRZZ DRIZZLING
DGIIMNORS GIRONDISM
DGIIMNSSU SIGISMUND
DGIINNNUW
UNWINDING
DGIINNORS INDORSING
DGIINNOSW DISOWNING
DGIINNRTU INTRUDING
DGIINOPRV PROVIDING
DGIINOPSS DISPOSING
DGIINORRS GRIDIRONS
DGIINORST GIRONDIST
DGIINORTU OUTRIDING
DGIINPSTU DISPUTING
DGIIRTTUY TURGIDITY
DGILLNORW
WORLDLING
DGILMNOOO
MONGOLOID
DGILMNOSU MOULDINGS
DGILMNPSU DUMPLINGS
DGILNNRTU TRUNDLING
DGINNOPSU POUNDINGS
DGINNOSSU SOUNDINGS
DGINNOSWW
DOWNSWING
DGINOPPRS DROPPINGS
DGKLOOOOS GOOD
LOOKS
DGNNORTUU
GROUNDNUT
DHHIKNSUU HINDU
KUSH
DHIIIPSTY HISPIDITY
DHIIKSWZZ WHIZZ KIDS
DHIILNRWW WHIRLWIND
DHIILOPSY SYPHILOID
DHIIMNOOS HINDOOISM
DHIINOPTY TYPHOIDIN
DHILLOSTY DOLTISHLY
DHILNNOSY DONNISHLY
DHILOPRSS LORDSHIPS

DHILPRSUY PRUDISHLY
DHIMOOOOS
HOODOOISM
DHINOOPRS DONORSHIP,
RHODOPSIN
DHINOORSU DISHONOUR
DHINOPRUW WHIP-
ROUND
DHINOSTUW
WHODUNITS
DHIOOSTTW
WITHSTOOD
DHKMNOOOS
MONKSHOOD
DHKNORUYY HUNKY-
DORY
DHLLOOOWY
HOLLYWOOD
DHLMOOTUU
LOUDMOUTH
DHLNOOOTU HOLD
OUT ON
DHNOORTWW
DOWNTHROW
DHNOOSSWW
SHOWDOWNS
DHNOOSTUW
SOUTHDOWN
DHNOSSTUW
SHUTDOWNS
DHOOORTXY
ORTHODOXY
DHOOPPPUY
PUPPYHOOD
DHOPRSTYY DYSTROPHY
DIIILMPTY LIMPIDITY
DIIILNPSY INSIPIDLY
DIIILQTUY LIQUIDITY
DIIINOSSU INSIDIOUS
DIIINOSSV DIVISIONS
DIIINOSUV INVIDIOUS
DIILLMNOO MODILLION
DIILLMNSW WINDMILLS
DIILNOSTU DILUTIONS
DIILNOSUV DIVULSION
DIILOSTTY STOLIDITY
DIIMNNOOS DOMINIONS
DIIMNOPST MIDPOINTS
DIIMOORTY IRIDOTOMY
DIIMORSSY DIMISSORY
DIINNOOQU QUINONOID
DIINOSSUY DIONYSIUS
DIIOPRTTY TORPIDITY
DIIORRTTY TORRIDITY

DIIPRTTUY PUTRIDITY
DIIPSTTUY STUPIDITY
DIKNOOSTW
  STINKWOOD
DIKORRTWY DIRTY
  WORK
DILLMNOPS MILLPONDS
DILLOOPPY POLYPLOID
DILOOPTUW TULIPWOOD
DIMMOPSUY
  SYMPODIUM
DIMNORSTW
  WINDSTORM
DIMOOOOSV
  VOODOOISM
DIMOORRTY
  DORMITORY
DINOOPRTW
  WOODPRINT
DINOOPRRTU ROUND-TRIP
DINOPTTUY POINT DUTY
DINORTTUY ROTUNDITY
DIOOOOSTV VOODOOIST
DIOOPRSST PROSODIST
DJLLNRUUU JULLUNDUR
DKORSTUWY WORK-
  STUDY
DLLNORUWY
  UNWORLDLY
DLNOOSSWW
  SLOWDOWNS
DMMNRSUUY DUMMY
  RUNS
DMNOORRUW
  ROUNDWORM
DMORSSTTU DUST
  STORM
DNNORRTUU
  TURNROUND
DNNORSTUW
  DOWNTURNS
DNOOPRSSW
  SNOWDROPS
DNOOPRSUW
  DOWNPOURS
DNOOPSSTU SOUNDPOST
DNOOPSTUW
  DOWNSPOUT
DNOORTUWW
  WOUNDWORT
DNORRSSUU SURROUNDS
EEEEELRTY EYELETEER
EEEEFHLRW FREEWHEEL
EEEEFHRST FREESHEET

EEEEFRRSV FREE VERSE
EEEEGINVV GENEVIEVE
EEEEGNRRV EVERGREEN
EEEEGQSSU SQUEEGEES
EEEEHLRSW ELSEWHERE
EEEEKLNSX KLEENEXES
EEEELLMRS ELLESMERE
EEEELMRTT TELEMETER
EEEELNOPT ELEOPTENE
EEEELNSSV ELEVENSES
EEEELNTVV VELVETEEN
EEEENNSST TENNESSEE
EEEENNSTV SEVENTEEN
EEEENOPRY EYE-OPENER
EEEENPRST PRESENTEE
EEEENRSTW SWEETENER
EEEEPRRSV PERSEVERE
EEEEPRSSS PEERESSES
EEEFGKNRU FENUGREEK
EEEFHNOPR FREEPHONE
EEEFHNRRS FRESHENER
EEEFHORRT THEREFORE
EEEFHORRW
  WHEREFORE
EEEFHORST FORESHEET
EEEFHORSU FREE HOUSE
EEEFHRRRS REFRESHER
EEEFILPRS LIFE PEERS
EEEFILRRV FREE-LIVER
EEEFILRVX REFLEXIVE
EEEFINRRT INTERFERE
EEEFLNSST FLEETNESS
EEEFLRSTY FREESTYLE
EEEFLRTTU FLEURETTE
EEEFMNRRT FERMENTER
EEEFNORST FREESTONE
EEEFNRRST TREE FERNS
EEEGGILNS NEGLIGEES
EEEGGORTT GEORGETTE
EEEGHILNT GEHLENITE
EEEGHLRSS SHEERLEGS
EEEGIISSS EISEGESIS
EEEGIJNNT JET ENGINE
EEEGIKNPS PEKINGESE
EEEGIMNST ESTEEMING
EEEGINNRS ENGINEERS
EEEGINNRV VENEERING
EEEGINPRR PEREGRINE
EEEGINRRS ENERGISER
EEEGINRRZ ENERGIZER
EEEGINRTT TEETERING
EEEGINRUV GUINEVERE
EEEGIRSTY GEYSERITE
EEEGLLNTY GENTEELLY

EEEGLMNNT
  GENTLEMEN
EEEGLNSTX GENTLE SEX
EEEGMNNRU
  ENERGUMEN
EEEGMNRSS MESSENGER
EEEGMORRT
  ERGOMETER
EEEGNNRSS GREENNESS
EEEGRRRTT REGRETTER
EEEHILLNS HELLENISE
EEEHILLNZ HELLENIZE
EEEHILNNP NEPHELINE
EEEHIMPRS EPHEMERIS
EEEHIMPSU EUPHEMISE
EEEHIMPUZ EUPHEMIZE
EEEHIMSTT TIME SHEET
EEEHINRTT HENRIETTE
EEEHIRRST ETHERISER
EEEHIRRTZ ETHERIZER
EEEHIRSSS HEIRESSES
EEEHKLOSU HOUSELEEK
EEEHLMNTY
  METHYLENE
EEEHLNOPT PHENETOLE,
  TELEPHONE
EEEHLNSTV ELEVENTHS
EEEHLOPPS PEEPHOLES
EEEHLOPPT THE PEOPLE
EEEHLORSS LEE SHORES
EEEHLRRST SHELTERER
EEEHMMNTY
  ENTHYMEME
EEEHMNOPR
  EPHEMERON
EEEHMORRT
  RHEOMETER
EEEHMORST THREESOME
EEEHMORSW
  SOMEWHERE
EEEHNRSSS SHEERNESS
EEEHNSSTW NEWSSHEET
EEEHOPRSX EXOSPHERE
EEEHORSST SHOETREES
EEEHRSTTU USHERETTE
EEEIIKRST KIESERITE
EEEIKNNPR INNKEEPER
EEEIKNPSS PEKINESES
EEEILNNRV ENLIVENER
EEEILPRTV REPLETIVE
EEEILPSST SLEEPIEST
EEEILPTVX EXPLETIVE
EEEILRSTX EXSERTILE
EEEILSSTT STEELIEST

EEEIMMRSZ MESMERIZE
EEEIMORTT METEORITE
EEEIMPRRS PREMIERES
EEEIMPRRT PERIMETER
EEEINNNST NINETEENS
EEEINNRST ERNESTINE,
INTERNEES
EEEINNRTV INTERVENE
EEEINPRRS RESERPINE
EEEINPRST PINETREES
EEEINPSSW WEEPINESS
EEEINPSVX EXPENSIVE
EEEINRRST RE-ENTRIES
EEEINRRTW WERNERITE
EEEINRTTV RETENTIVE
EEEINSSTV SEVENTIES
EEEINSTVX EXTENSIVE
EEEIPRRRV REPRIEVER
EEEIPRRSV REPRIEVES
EEEIPRRTT PRETERITE
EEEIPRSTX EXPERTISE
EEEIQRRSU EQUERRIES
EEEIQTTTU ETIQUETTE
EEEIRRRTV RETRIEVER
EEEIRRRTW RETRIEVER
EEEIRRSSV SERVERIES
EEEIRRSVW REVIEWERS
EEEIRRTVV REVERTIVE
EEEIRSTTV SERVIETTE
EEEJLLRSW JEWELLERS
EEEJLLRWY JEWELLERY
EEEJRSTTT JET-SETTER
EEEKLNSSS SLEEKNESS
EEEKMRSTU MUSKETEER
EEEKNOSTY SYNOEKETE
EEELLLRSV LEVELLERS
EEELLNPRT REPELLENT
EEELLPSSS SLEEPLESS
EEELMNOPT ELOPEMENT
EEELMNRTV REVELMENT
EEELMOPSY EMPLOYEES
EEELMOSTT OMELETTES
EEELMRSTU MULETEERS
EEELMRTTY TELEMETRY
EEELMRTXY EXTREMELY
EEELNOPSV ENVELOPES
EEELNOPTT LEPTOTENE
EEELNOTTV NOVELETTE
EEELNRSSV NERVELESS
EEELNRSSW NEWSREELS
EEELNSSSS SENSELESS
EEELOPRSV OVERSLEEP
EEEMMNPRS PER
MENSEM
EEEMMNNSTT TENEMENTS

EEEMNORRV
NEVERMORE
EEEMNOXYZ
EXOENZYME
EEEMNRSST STEERSMEN
EEEMNRSTT ENTREMETS
EEEMNRSTY MESENTERY
EEEMNRTTV
REVETMENT
EEEMOPRTX EXTEMPORE
EEEMPRSSS EMPRESSES
EEEMRSSST SEMESTERS
EEENNORST SONNETEER
EEENNSSST TENSENESS
EEENPRRST PRESENTER,
REPRESENT
EEENPRRTV PREVENTER
EEENPRSUV SUPERVENE
EEENPSSST STEEPNESS
EEENQRSSU QUEERNESS
EEENRRSTW WESTERNER
EEENRRSUV UNRESERVE
EEENRSSST TERSENESS
EEENSSSTW SWEETNESS
EEEOPSSST POETESSES
EEEORRSSV OVERSEERS
EEEPPPRTU PUPPETEER
EEEPRRRSS REPRESSER
EEEPRRRSV PRESERVER
EEEPRRRTV PERVERTER
EEEPRRSSV PRESERVES
EEEPRRSSX EXPRESSER
EEEPRRSTT PRESETTER
EEEPRSSSX EXPRESSES
EEEQRRSTU REQUESTER
EEEQRSSTU SEQUESTER
EEEQRSSUZ SQUEEZERS
EEFFFKLRU KERFUFFLE
EEFFGLNTU EFFULGENT
EEFFHILLS SHELF LIFE
EEFFHINTT FIFTEENTH
EEFFHLRSU RESHUFFLE
EEFFIILRS FIREFLIES
EEFFINOSV OFFENSIVE
EEFFINRST STIFFENER
EEFFIORRT FORFEITER
EEFFJNORS JEFFERSON
EEFFLNSTU EFFLUENTS
EEFFOPRRR PROFFERER
EEFFORSTT OFF-STREET
EEFFRRSSU SUFFERERS
EEFGHIRRT FREIGHTER
EEFGILLNY FEELINGLY
EEFGILNNU UNFEELING

EEFGILNRU REFUELING
EEFGIMRUV VERMIFUGE
EEFGINORR FOREIGNER
EEFGINRRR REFERRING
EEFGINRRT FERRETING
EEFGINRST FESTERING
EEFGINRTT FETTERING
EEFGIORRS FORGERIES
EEFGIPRRU PREFIGURE
EEFGLLLUY GLEEFULLY
EEFGLNRTU REFULGENT
EEFGLRRTU REGRETFUL
EEFGORRTT FORGETTER
EEFHIIRSS FISHERIES
EEFHIJLSW JEWELFISH
EEFHILLRS SHELLFIRE
EEFHILSST FLESHIEST
EEFHIMNRS FISHERMEN
EEFHINSST HEFTINESS
EEFHIOSUW HOUSEWIFE
EEFHLLSWY FLYWHEELS
EEFHLORUW FOUR-
WHEEL
EEFHLSSTY FLYSHEETS
EEFHMORRT THE
FORMER
EEFHNRSSS FRESHNESS
EEFHOORRS FORESHORE
EEFHOORTT TO THE
FORE
EEFHRRRTU FURTHERER
EEFIILLNS LIFELINES
EEFIILMST LIFETIMES
EEFIILMTX FLEXITIME
EEFIILNRT INFERTILE,
INTERFILE
EEFIILQRU LIQUEFIER
EEFIILRST FERTILISE
EEFIILRTZ FERTILIZE
EEFIIMRRT METRIFIER
EEFIINRST FINISTERE
EEFIIPRRT PETRIFIER
EEFIIRRRT TERRIFIER
EEFIIRRSV VERSIFIER
EEFIIRSTT TESTIFIRE
EEFILLLOS FILOSELLE
EEFILLSTY LIFESTYLE
EEFILMPXY EXEMPLIFY
EEFILNTUW WULFENITE
EEFILOORS FOOLERIES
EEFILPRRS PILFERERS
EEFINORST FIRESTONE
EEFINPRSU SUPERFINE
EEFINRSTU INTERFUSE

EEFIOPRRT PROFITEER	EEGHINRTT TETHERING,	EEGIMNRST REGIMENTS
EEFIOPRRW FIREPOWER	TIGHTENER	EEGIMNRSU MERINGUES
EEFIORRRT RETROFIRE	EEGHIORVW OVERWEIGH	EEGINNOPR REOPENING
EEFIPRRTU PUTREFIER	EEGHIRSST SIGHTSEER	EEGINNPRT REPENTING
EEFIPRSTU STUPEFIER	EEGHLLNOP PHELLOGEN	EEGINNRST RESENTING
EEFIPRSUV PERFUSIVE	EEGHMNOST THEME	EEGINNRTU NEUTERING
EEFIRRRTT FRITTERER	SONG	EEGINOOSS OOGENESIS
EEFIRRRTU FRUITERER	EEGHMNOSU	EEGINOPRY EPIROGENY
EEFIRRSTU SURFEITER	HEGUMENOS	EEGINOPSU EPIGENOUS
EEFKNOORT FORETOKEN	EEGHNNORR	EEGINORSV SOVEREIGN
EEFKNORST REEF KNOTS	GREENHORN	EEGINORVY ROVING EYE
EEFLLNPSU SPLEENFUL	EEGHNNOTY	EEGINOSXY OXYGENISE
EEFLMRTUX FLUXMETER	ETHNOGENY	EEGINOXYZ OXYGENIZE
EEFLNRSTU RESENTFUL	EEGHNORTU	EEGINPPPR PEPPERING
EEFLNRTVY FERVENTLY	TOUGHENER	EEGINPRST PESTERING
EEFLOPRSU REPOSEFUL	EEGHRTTTU THE	EEGINPSSW SWEEPINGS
EEFLORRTX RETROFLEX	GUTTER	EEGINQSUZ SQUEEZING
EEFLORSTV LEFTOVERS	EEGIILNRV INVEIGLER,	EEGINRRSV RESERVING,
EEFLRRTTU FLUTTERER	RELIEVING	REVERSING
EEFLSSTTY TSETSE FLY	EEGIILORS RELIGIOSE	EEGINRRTV REVERTING
EEFLTTYZZ TZETZE FLY	EEGIILPRV PRIVILEGE	EEGINRSSU SEIGNEURS
EEFMNOORW	EEGIINRVW REVIEWING	EEGINRSTT RESETTING
FOREWOMEN	EEGIINSTV GENITIVES,	EEGINRSTW WESTERING
EEFMOPRRR PERFORMER	INGESTIVE	EEGINSTTV VIGNETTES
EEFMORRRS REFORMERS	EEGIISTTZ ZEITGEIST	EEGIORRSU ROGUERIES
EEFMPRRUY PERFUMERY	EEGIJLLNW JEWELLING	EEGIPRSST PRESTIGES
EEFOPRRST FREE PORTS	EEGIJLNRY JEERINGLY	EEGIRRSST REGISTERS
EEFOPRRTY FERROTYPE	EEGIKLNNN KENNELING	EEGIRRSSU SURGERIES
EEFORRSST FORESTERS	EEGIKLNRY REEKINGLY	EEGIRSSST TIGRESSES
EEFORRTVW FEVERWORT	EEGIKNNRT KENTIGERN	EEGLLMORU
EEGGHLLSS EGGSHELLS	EEGIKNRSW SKEWERING	GLOMERULE
EEGGIILNT GELIGNITE	EEGILLLNV LEVELLING	EEGLLOOTY TELEOLOGY
EEGGIIPRS PIGGERIES	EEGILLNPR REPELLING	EEGLLOPRS GOSPELLER
EEGGILNNR GREENLING	EEGILLNPX EXPELLING	EEGLLORRV GROVELLER
EEGGILNNT NEGLIGENT	EEGILLNRT RETELLING	EEGLMNNOU
EEGGILNSS LEGGINESS	EEGILLNRV GRENVILLE,	MELUNGEON
EEGGILOOS GEOLOGISE	REVELLING	EEGLNORTT LORGNETTE
EEGGILOOZ GEOLOGIZE	EEGILLNRY LEERINGLY	EEGLORRSV GROVELERS
EEGGIMRST EGG TIMERS	EEGILLSSU GUILELESS	EEGMNOORR
EEGGINNRV REVENGING	EEGILMMSU GELSEMIUM	GREENROOM
EEGGINRST GREETINGS	EEGILMNSY SEEMINGLY	EEGNNORST ROENTGENS
EEGGIORSU EGREGIOUS	EEGILNNRT RELENTING	EEGNOORST OESTROGEN
EEGGORSTT GO-GETTERS	EEGILNNSS LESSENING	EEGNOORSU
EEGGRSSTU SUGGESTER	EEGILNNUY GENUINELY	EROGENOUS
EEGHHIITT EIGHTIETH	EEGILNOOS NEOLOGISE	EEGNOOSUX
EEGHHILLV HIGH-LEVEL	EEGILNOOZ NEOLOGIZE	EXOGENOUS
EEGHIIKLN HINGELIKE	EEGILNPWY WEEPINGLY	EEGNORRSS ENGROSSER
EEGHIINRV INVEIGHER	EEGILNRRS LINGERERS	EEGNORSSV
EEGHIKNTW WEEKNIGHT	EEGILNRTT LETTERING	GOVERNESS
EEGHILNNT ENLIGHTEN	EEGILNRVY VEERINGLY	EEGNRRSTU RESURGENT
EEGHILNOR RHIGOLENE	EEGILOPSU EPILOGUES	EEGOOPSST GOOSESTEP
EEGHILNRT LENGTHIER	EEGILORST SORTILEGE	EEGOPRSSU SUPEREGOS
EEGHILNSS HINGELESS	EEGIMNPRT TEMPERING	EEGOQRSTU GROTESQUE
EEGHIMNNS ENMESHING	EEGIMNPTX EXEMPTING	EEGORRRSS REGRESSOR

EEHHHLNOO
HOHENLOHE
EEHHINOPT THIOPHENE
EEHHINOSS SHOESHINE
EEHHIOPTW WHITE
HOPE
EEHHIORTT THIO-ETHER
EEHHIRSST THE SHIRES
EEHHIRTTW THEREWITH
EEHHIRTWW
WHEREWITH
EEHHLMOPS HOME
HELPS
EEHHNOPPS PHOSPHENE
EEHHNOSSU HEN
HOUSES
EEHHOORSS HORSESHOE
EEHHRRSST THRESHERS
EEHIIKRSS ESKISEHIR
EEHIILSTW WHITE LIES
EEHIINNTT NINETIETH
EEHIIRTTW WITHERITE
EEHIJNOPS JOSEPHINE
EEHIKLNOY HONEY-LIKE
EEHIKLORS HORSELIKE
EEHIKNPSS SHEEPSKIN
EEHILLLMW MILLWHEEL
EEHILLMNS HELLENISM
EEHILLNST HELLENIST
EEHILMOST HOMELIEST
EEHILNNOO HOLE IN
ONE
EEHILNOPX XENOPHILE
EEHILNORS SHORELINE
EEHILNOSU HOUSELINE
EEHILNPRS REPLENISH
EEHILNPSS SPLEENISH
EEHILNPSW PINWHEELS
EEHILNSST LITHENESS
EEHILOPTY HELIOTYPE
EEHILORST HOTELIERS
EEHILPSST SLIPSHEET
EEHILPSVY PEEVISHLY
EEHILRSTW ERSTWHILE
EEHILSTUV HELVETIUS
EEHIMMOOV HOME
MOVIE
EEHIMMPSU EUPHEMISM
EEHIMOPRT HEMITROPE
EEHIMPRRW WHIMPERER
EEHIMPSTU EUPHEMIST
EEHINNORT THREONINE
EEHINOPSU EUPHONISE
EEHINOPSX PHOENIXES

EEHINOPUZ EUPHONIZE
EEHINORTT THEREINTO
EEHINOSST HESSONITE
EEHINPRST TREPHINES
EEHINSSTW WHITENESS
EEHINSTTU EUTHENIST
EEHINSTTX SIXTEENTH
EEHINTTTW TWENTIETH
EEHIORRST THEORISER
EEHIORRTZ THEORIZER
EEHIORSST HETEROSIS
EEHIORSTW OTHERWISE
EEHIPPRRY PERIPHERY
EEHIPRRSS PERISHERS
EEHIPRRSW WHISPERER
EEHIRRSST HERITRESS
EEHIRRTTY ERYTHRITE
EEHIRSSTT TEE SHIRTS
EEHKLOOST STOKEHOLE
EEHKLORWW
WHEELWORK
EEHLLLNVY HELVELLYN
EEHLLORST HOSTELLER
EEHLMOOSW
WHOLESOME
EEHLMORVW
OVERWHELM
EEHLMORWW WORM
WHEEL
EEHLNOOTW WHOLE
NOTE
EEHLNOPTY POLYTHENE,
TELEPHONY
EEHLNOSSW WHOLENESS
EEHLOPPTU UP THE POLE
EEHLORSSS HORSELESS,
SHORELESS
EEHLORSST HOSTELERS
EEHLOSSSU HOUSELESS
EEHMMOPRS
MORPHEMES
EEHMNOOPR
PHEROMONE
EEHMNORTY
HETERONYM
EEHMNOSSY
HOMEYNESS
EEHMNPTTU
UMPTEENTH
EEHMOPSTY MESOPHYTE
EEHMORRTY
RHEOMETRY
EEHMORSST REST
HOMES, THERMOSES

EEHMRRSTY RHYMESTER
EEHMRSSUU HUMERUSES
EEHMSSTTY THE SYSTEM
EEHNOOPSU OPEN
HOUSE
EEHNOPPTY PHENOTYPE
EEHNOPRTU
THEREUPON
EEHNOPRUW
WHEREUPON
EEHNOPSTU PENTHOUSE
EEHNOPSTY NEOPHYTES
EEHNOPTTY ENTOPHYTE
EEHNORRST SHORTENER
EEHNORSST OTHERNESS
EEHNOSTTW
WHETSTONE
EEHNPPRSU PEN PUSHER
EEHNSSSTY SYNTHESES
EEHOORSSV OVERSHOES
EEHOORSVW
HOWSOEVER,
WHOSOEVER
EEHOPRSTY HEY PRESTO
EEHOPRTXY XEROPHYTE
EEHORRTVW
OVERTHREW
EEHORSTTY SET THEORY
EEHOSSSST HOSTESSES
EEIIMPST IMPIETIES
EEIIKKMSS SIKKIMESE
EEIIKLLST LIKELIEST
EEIIKNNTZ ZINKENITE
EEIILLMRT MILLERITE
EEIILLMTW WILLEMITE
EEIILLNTV VITELLINE
EEIILLSTV LIVELIEST
EEIILMSTT TIMELIEST
EEIILNNRT INTERLINE
EEIILNORT TRIOELEIN
EEIILNOTV OLIVENITE
EEIILNPPS PIPELINES
EEIILNRST RESILIENT
EEIILOPST SEPIOLITE
EEIILRSST STERILISE
EEIILRSTU REUTILISE,
TUILERIES
EEIILRSTZ STERILIZE
EEIILRSVW LIVE WIRES
EEIILRTUZ REUTILIZE
EEIIMMPRT PRIME TIME
EEIIMMRST EREMITISM
EEIIMOPST EPITOMISE
EEIIMOPTZ EPITOMIZE

EEIIMORSS ISOMERISE
EEIIMORSZ ISOMERIZE
EEIIMRSSV REMISSIVE
EEIINNNPT PENNINITE
EEIINNSTT INTESTINE
EEIINNSTV INTENSIVE
EEIINNTVV INVENTIVE
EEIINQRSU ENQUIRIES
EEIINRRVV VIVERRINE
EEIINRSTT ENTERITIS
EEIINRSVV INVERSIVE
EEIINRTVW INTERVIEW
EEIINSSST SENSITISE
EEIINSSTV SENSITIVE
EEIINSSTZ SENSITIZE
EEIIOPQSU EQUIPOISE
EEIIOSSTV SOVIETISE
EEIIOSTVZ SOVIETIZE
EEIIQRSTU REQUISITE
EEIIQSTUX EXQUISITE
EEIIJKNRSS JERKINESS
EEIIJLNSUV JUVENILES
EEIIJPRRSU PERJURIES
EEIKLMORT KILOMETRE
EEIKLRTWY TRIWEEKLY
EEIKNNPSV PENKNIVES
EEIKNPRSS PERKINESS
EEIKOORRS ROOKERIES
EEILLMNOT EMOLLIENT
EEILLMNPT IMPELLENT
EEILLMOPR MILLEPORE
EEILLMSST SMELLIEST
EEILLNNTY LENIENTLY
EEILLNOST LONELIEST
EEILLNRSV SNIVELLER
EEILLNSSS ILLNESSES
EEILLOPTU PETIOLULE
EEILLORTT TITLE ROLE
EEILLOSTV LOVELIEST
EEILLRSST TRELLISES
EEILLRSTU TELLURISE
EEILLRSUY LEISURELY
EEILLRSVY SERVILELY
EEILLRTTU TELLURITE
EEILLRTUZ TELLURIZE
EEILLSUVY ELUSIVELY
EEILMMNPT IMPLEMENT
EEILMMNSY IMMENSELY
EEILMMORS SOMMELIER
EEILMMORT MILOMETER
EEILMNNTY EMINENTLY
EEILMNOSS SOLEMNISE
EEILMNOST LIMESTONE,
    MILESTONE

EEILMNOSZ SOLEMNIZE
EEILMNPPR PIMPERNEL
EEILMNRVY LIVERYMEN
EEILMNSTU MUSTELINE
EEILMORTT TREMOLITE
EEILMOSTT MISTLETOE
EEILMOSVW SEMIVOWEL
EEILMOTVY EMOTIVELY
EEILMRSST MERITLESS
EEILMRSTY LYSIMETER
EEILNNOPT LEPONTINE
EEILNNPSS PENNILESS
EEILNNSST SENTINELS
EEILNNSTY INTENSELY
EEILNOORS OLEORESIN
EEILNOPRT INTERLOPE,
    REPLETION, TERPINEOL
EEILNORVW WOLVERINE
EEILNOSSS NOISELESS
EEILNOSSU SELENIOUS
EEILNOSTV NOVELTIES
EEILNPPSZ ZEPPELINS
EEILNPSSS SPINELESS
EEILNPSTT PESTILENT
EEILNPSVY PENSIVELY
EEILNRSST LISTENERS
EEILNRSVY INVERSELY
EEILOPRTX EXPLOITER
EEILOPSST POLITESSE
EEILOPSVX EXPLOSIVE
EEILORRST LOITERERS
EEILORSTT LOTTERIES
EEILPRSTX TRIPLEXES
EEILPRSTY PERISTYLE
EEILPRSUV PRELUSIVE,
    PULVERISE, REPULSIVE
EEILPRUVZ PULVERIZE
EEILPSUVX EXPULSIVE
EEILRSSTV SILVESTER
EEILRSTVY RESTIVELY
EEILRSUVV REVULSIVE
EEIMMMRSS MESMERISM
EEIMMNRRT
    MERRIMENT
EEIMMORRS MEMORISER
EEIMMORRZ
    MEMORIZER
EEIMMOSST SOMETIMES
EEIMMRSST MESMERIST
EEIMMRSTW
    SWIMMERET
EEIMMRSTX EXTREMISM
EEIMNNORT
    MENTIONER

EEIMNNRTT INTERMENT
EEIMNNSTT SENTIMENT
EEIMNOOTV
    MOVIETONE
EEIMNOPTX EXEMPTION
EEIMNORSS SERMONISE
EEIMNORST MOISTENER
EEIMNORSZ SERMONIZE
EEIMNOSST SEMITONES
EEIMNOSTX SIXTEENMO
EEIMNOSTZ TIME ZONES
EEIMNPQTU EQUIPMENT
EEIMNPRSS PRIMENESS
EEIMNPSST EMPTINESS
EEIMNRRSS MERRINESS
EEIMNRSTU MUTINEERS
EEIMNSSSS MESSINESS
EEIMOOPRS MEIOSPORE
EEIMOORTZ MEROZOITE
EEIMOPRST PERISTOME,
    TEMPORISE
EEIMOPRTZ TEMPORIZE
EEIMPPRRS PERISPERM
EEIMPRRSS IMPRESSER
EEIMPRRTT PERMITTER
EEIMPRRTY PERIMETRY
EEIMPRSSS IMPRESSES
EEIMPSSTU IMPETUSES
EEIMQSTUU EQUISETUM
EEIMRRSTT TRIMESTER
EEIMRSSSU MESSIEURS
EEIMRSSTY MYSTERIES
EEIMRSTTX EXTREMIST
EEIMRTTXY EXTREMITY
EEINNNRSU NUNNERIES
EEINNOPPS NIPPONESE
EEINNOPRS PENSIONER
EEINNOPRT TIN OPENER
EEINNORTT RETENTION
EEINNOSTV VEINSTONE
EEINNOSTX EXTENSION
EEINNPRST SPINNERET
EEINNPRTT PERTINENT
EEINNPSST INEPTNESS
EEINNPSTT PENITENTS
EEINNPSWY PENNY-WISE
EEINNRSST INERTNESS
EEINNRSSV INVERNESS,
    NERVINESS
EEINNSSSW NEWSINESS
EEINOPPST PEPTONISE,
    PIPESTONE
EEINOPPTZ PEPTONIZE
EEINOPRST INTERPOSE

EEINOQRUV VÉRONIQUE
EEINOQSUX EQUINOXES
EEINORRSV REVERSION
EEINORSTX EXERTIONS,
EXSERTION
EEINORTVW INTERWOVE
EEINOSSTV OSTENSIVE
EEINPRRRT REPRINTER
EEINPRRTT INTERPRET
EEINPRSSW WINEPRESS
EEINPSSTT PETTINESS
EEINQRSTU IN REQUEST
EEINQSSTU QUIETNESS
EEINRRRSU REINSURER
EEINRRSSU NURSERIES
EEINRSSSY SYNERESIS
EEINRSSTT INTERESTS,
TRITENESS
EEINRSSTW WITNESSER
EEINRSSUV UNIVERSES
EEINSSSTT TESTINESS
EEINSSSTW WITNESSES
EEINSTTXY EXTENSITY
EEIOPPSTV STOVEPIPE
EEIOPRSTT POTTERIES
EEIOPRSTV POVERTIES
EEIOPRTTU PIROUETTE
EEIOQQUUV EQUIVOQUE
EEIORRRST ROISTERER,
TERRORISE
EEIORRRSV RESERVOIR
EEIORRRTZ TERRORIZE
EEIORRSTX EXTERIORS
EEIORRTVW OVERWRITE
EEIORSSUV OVERISSUE
EEIORSVVW OVERVIEWS
EEIORTTVX EXTORTIVE
EEIPRRSST PERSISTER
EEIPRSSST PRIESTESS
EEIPRSSUV SUPERVISE
EEIPRSTTT PRETTIEST
EEIPRTTWY TYPEWRITE
EEIQSSTUU QUIETUSES
EEIRRSSST RESISTERS
EEIRRSSTV RESERVIST
EEIRRTTTW TWITTERER
EEIRSTUVX EXTRUSIVE
EEJMNNOTY
ENJOYMENT
EEJMPQUUU QUEUE-
JUMP
EEJNOQSUU JUNOESQUE
EEJNORRUY JOURNEYER
EEJPRRRSU PERJURERS

EEKKORSTY KEYSTROKE
EEKLMOSSS SMOKELESS
EEKLNOSST SKELETONS
EEKLNPRSU SPELUNKER
EEKLORSTW STEELWORK
EEKMNOPTW KEPT
WOMEN
EEKNOSSTY KEYSTONES
EELLLLNWY LLEWELLYN
EELLMNOOS LEMON
SOLE
EELLMOSTW
MELLOWEST
EELLNNRTU TUNNELLER
EELLNSSTU SULLENEST
EELLOOSTW STEEL
WOOL
EELLOPPRR PROPELLER
EELLORRTW TROWELLER
EELLSSSTY STYLELESS
EELLSSSUY USELESSLY
EELMMNOTU
EMOLUMENT
EELMNNORT
ENROLMENT
EELMNOSSY MONEYLESS
EELMNOTTX
EXTOLMENT
EELMOOPST LEPTOSOME
EELMOOPTT TOTEM
POLE
EELMOPRSY EMPLOYERS
EELMOPRTU PETROLEUM
EELMORSST MOLESTERS
EELMORTTV
VOLTMETER
EELMORTUV
VOLUMETER
EELMPRSUY SUPREMELY
EELNNOOUV NUEVO
LEON
EELNNOPRS PERSONNEL
EELNNRSTU TUNNELERS
EELNOOSSS LOOSENESS
EELNOPSTU PLENTEOUS
EELNORSTV RESOLVENT
EELNORTUV VOLUNTEER
EELNOSSST STONELESS
EELNPRSTY PRESENTLY
EELNRSTTU NET RESULT
EELOPRRSX EXPLORERS
EELOPRRTU POULTERER
EELOPRSSW POWERLESS
EELOPRSTV OVERSLEPT

EELOPRSTY POLYESTER,
PROSELYTE
EELORRSUV REVELROUS
EELORRSVV REVOLVERS
EELORSSUV OURSELVES
EELORSTUV TRUELOVES
EELPPSTTU SEPTUPLET
EELPRSSXY EXPRESSLY
EELPRSTUU SEPULTURE
EELPSTTUX SEXTUPLET
EELRRSSTW WRESTLERS
EELRSSTTU UTTERLESS
EELRSSTVY SYLVESTER
EEMMNOORT
METRONOME,
MONOMETER,
MONOTREME
EEMMNOSTV
MOVEMENTS
EEMMOORST
OSMOMETER
EEMMORTYZ
ZYMOMETER
EEMNOOPST TONE
POEMS
EEMNOORTT
TONOMETER
EEMNORRTV
VERMONTER
EEMNORRTY
MONTERREY
EEMNSSTTV VESTMENTS
EEMOOOSTT
OSTEOTOME
EEMOOPRTT
OPTOMETER
EEMOPPRRT PRE-
EMPTOR
EEMOPRRTY
PYROMETER
EEMPRRTTU TRUMPETER
EEMPRSSTT TEMPTRESS
EEMRRSTTU MUTTERERS
EENNNOSTV NON-
EVENTS
EENNOOSTU
NEOTENOUS
EENNOPRSS PRONENESS
EENNOPSTX EXPONENTS
EENNORSTU ENTRE
NOUS
EENNRSSST STERNNESS
EENOOPPSS POPE'S NOSE
EENOORRSU ERRONEOUS

EENOORSTV OVERTONES
EENOPPRTT PREPOTENT
EENOPRRSS RESPONSER
EENOPRSSS RESPONSES
EENOPSTTY STENOTYPE
EENOQRSTU ON
  REQUEST
EENORTTTU
  NEUTRETTO
EENRRSTUV VENTURERS
EENRSSTUW WET NURSES
EEOOPRRVW
  OVERPOWER
EEOPPPPRT PEPPER POT
EEOPPRSSU SUPERPOSE
EEOPRRRST REPORTERS
EEOPRRRTY REPERTORY
EEOPRRSTT PROTESTER
EEOPRRSTX EXPORTERS
EEOPRSSSS ESPRESSOS,
  REPOSSESS
EEOPRSSSW PROWESSES
EEOPRSSUX EXPOSURES
EEORRRSST RESTORERS
EEORRSSTU RETROUSSÉ
EEORRSTUV OVERTURES
EEORRTTVX EXTROVERT
EEORSSTUW SOU'WESTER
EEPRRSSST PRESTRESS
EEPRRSSSU PRESSURES
EEPRRSTTU SPUTTERER
EERRSTTTU STUTTERER
EFFFILSTU FLUFFIEST
EFFFLORTU EFFORTFUL
EFFGINORS OFFERINGS
EFFGINRSU SUFFERING
EFFGLORTU FORGETFUL
EFFGNRSSU GRUFFNESS
EFFHIIKNS FISH KNIFE
EFFHIISTT FIFTIETHS
EFFHIISTW WHIFFIEST
EFFHIKSWW SKEW-WHIFF
EFFHILRSY FLY-FISHER
EFFHINSSU HUFFINESS
EFFHLRSSU SHUFFLERS
EFFIIMNSS MIFFINESS
EFFIIORRT FORTIFIER
EFFIIQRSU SQUIFFIER
EFFILLLRU FULFILLER
EFFILMUUV EFFLUVIUM
EFFILNRSS SNIFFLERS
EFFILORRS FLOS FERRI
EFFINOOSS NOISES OFF
EFFINOSSU EFFUSIONS

EFFINPSSU PUFFINESS
EFFINSSST STIFFNESS
EFFIOOPRR FIREPROOF
EFFIORSTW WRITE-OFFS
EFFIORTVY FORTY-FIVE
EFFISSTTU STUFFIEST
EFFISSUUV SUFFUSIVE
EFFLLRTUY FRETFULLY
EFFNOORRT FOREFRONT
EFFOORRTY OFFERTORY
EFGGIINNR FINGERING
EFGGILNNU ENGULFING
EFGGILOOS SOLFEGGIO
EFGGINOOR FOREGOING
EFGGINOSS FOGGINESS
EFGHHIILR HIGH-FLIER
EFGHIILNT NIGHTLIFE
EFGHIILRT FIRELIGHT,
  FLIGHTIER
EFGHIINRT INFIGHTER
EFGHILNSS FLESHINGS
EFGHILPRT PREFLIGHT
EFGHILTWY FLYWEIGHT
EFGHIORST FORESIGHT,
  GIFT HORSE
EFGHOOSTT GET SHOT
  OF
EFGHOSTTU GET SHUT
  OF
EFGIIINRS SIGNIFIER
EFGIILLNR REFILLING
EFGIILLNT FILLETING
EFGIILNPR PILFERING
EFGIILNRT FILTERING
EFGIILORR GLORIFIER
EFGIINNRR INFERRING,
  INFRINGER
EFGIINNST INFESTING
EFGIINPRT FINGERTIP
EFGIINPRX PREFIXING
EFGIINRSU FIGURINES
EFGIINRTT REFITTING
EFGIINRVY VERIFYING
EFGIISTUV FUGITIVES
EFGILNNNU FUNNELING
EFGILNORW FLOWERING
EFGILPRSU FIRE-PLUGS
EFGILRTUU FULGURITE
EFGIMNNOT
  FOMENTING
EFGIMNORR REFORMING
EFGIMNPRU PERFUMING
EFGINNOST SOFTENING
EFGINOOSS GOOFINESS

EFGINORST FOSTERING
EFGLOOSVX FOXGLOVES
EFGLOOTUV TUG-OF-
  LOVE
EFGNOORTT
  FORGOTTEN
EFGOOOOST
  GOOSEFOOT
EFHHIISTW WHITEFISH
EFHHILLSS SHELLFISH
EFHHNOOOT ON THE
  HOOF
EFHIILSTT FILTHIEST
EFHIIMSST FETISHISM
EFHIINPSS SNIPEFISH
EFHIINSSS FISHINESS
EFHIIRRTT THRIFTIER
EFHIISSTT FETISHIST,
  SHIFTIEST
EFHIJLLSY JELLYFISH
EFHIKSSTY SHIFT KEYS
EFHILLSSW SWELLFISH
EFHILLSSY SELFISHLY
EFHILNSSU UNSELFISH
EFHILSSST SHIFTLESS
EFHIMOPRZ PFORZHEIM
EFHINOOTT FINE-TOOTH
EFHINORRT FIRETHORN
EFHINOSST STONEFISH
EFHINRRSU FURNISHER
EFHIORSTT FORTIETHS,
  FROTHIEST
EFHLLLPUY HELPFULLY
EFHLLOPUY HOPEFULLY
EFHLLOSUU FULL HOUSE
EFHLOOPSU FLOPHOUSE
EFHLOPSST FLESHPOTS
EFHMNOORT HOME
  FRONT
EFHNORTUX
  FOXHUNTER
EFHOOOORTT
  FORETOOTH
EFIIJRSTU JUSTIFIER
EFIIKRSST FRISKIEST
EFIILLLST STILL LIFE
EFIILLMOR MOLLIFIER
EFIILLNRU NULLIFIER
EFIILLRST FILLISTER,
  FRILLIEST
EFIILMNSS FILMINESS
EFIILMSST FLIMSIEST
EFIILNSTT FLINTIEST
EFIILOSSS FOSSILISE

EFIILOSSZ FOSSILIZE
EFIILPRTT FILTER TIP
EFIILRTTY FERTILITY
EFIIMNSST FEMINISTS
EFIIMORRT MORTIFIER
EFIIMRSTY MYSTIFIER
EFIINNNOT NON-FINITE
EFIINNPRT FINE PRINT
EFIINNSST NIFTINESS
EFIINNSTY INTENSIFY
EFIINOPST IN SPITE OF
EFIINORRS FIRE IRONS,
INFERIORS
EFIINSSZZ FIZZINESS
EFIIPRRSU PURIFIERS
EFIIPRSST SPITFIRES
EFIIRSTTU FRUITIEST
EFIIRSTZZ FRIZZIEST
EFIISTTVY FESTIVITY
EFIKLNSSU FLUKINESS
EFIKNORSS FORESKINS
EFIKORRSW FIREWORKS
EFILLMOPU FILOPLUME
EFILLNPTU PLENTIFUL
EFILLORRV FRIVOLLER
EFILMNOSY SOLEMNIFY
EFILMOPRX PLEXIFORM
EFILNNOOS NO FLIES ON
EFILNNORT FRONT LINE
EFILNOORS SOLFERINO
EFILNOOSU FELONIOUS
EFILNOOTU OUT OF
LINE
EFILNOSST LOFTINESS
EFILOPPST FLOPPIEST
EFILORSTY LIFE STORY
EFILQRUUV QUIVERFUL
EFILRSSTU FRUITLESS
EFILRTUVY FURTIVELY
EFIMMORRS REFORMISM
EFIMMORRV
VERMIFORM
EFIMNORRS INFORMERS
EFIMNORST IN TERMS OF
EFIMORRRS SERRIFORM
EFIMORRST FIRESTORM,
REFORMIST, RESTIFORM
EFIMPRSTU FRUMPIEST
EFINNNSSU FUNNINESS
EFINNSSTU UNFITNESS
EFINOPRSU PERFUSION
EFINOPRSY PERSONIFY
EFINORRST FRONTIERS
EFINRRSSU FURRINESS

EFINRRTUU FURNITURE
EFINRSSTU TURFINESS
EFINSSSSU FUSSINESS
EFINSSSTU FUSTINESS
EFINSSSTW SWIFTNESS
EFINSSUZZ FUZZINESS
EFIOORSTX SIX-FOOTER
EFIOORSUV OVIFEROUS
EFIOPRTTU PETIT FOUR
EFIORRSTW FROWSTIER
EFIORSSTT FROSTIEST
EFIORSTWZ FROWZIEST
EFIORTTTU OUTFITTER
EFKLMNOOW
WOMENFOLK
EFKNOOPRS SPOKEN FOR
EFKORRSTW FRETWORKS
EFLLMOSUY FULSOMELY
EFLLNOOSW LONE
WOLFS
EFLLNTUUY TUNEFULLY
EFLLOORSW FOLLOWERS
EFLLRSTUY RESTFULLY
EFLLSTUYZ ZESTFULLY
EFLNOORVW
OVERFLOWN
EFLNOPRTU PROFLUENT
EFLNORSUW SUNFLOWER
EFLOOOOST FOOTLOOSE
EFLOOPRTW FLOWERPOT
EFLOORSVW OVERFLOWS
EFLOOSTTW LOWESTOFT
EFLOPRSUY PROFUSELY
EFLORRRTU TERRORFUL
EFLRSSSTU STRESSFUL
EFMOORSSU FOURSOMES
EFNOOOSTT FOOTNOTES
EFNOOTTUU OUT OF
TUNE
EFOOOPRRV OVERPROOF
EFOOPRRSS PROFESSOR
EFOOPSSTT FOOTSTEPS
EFOOQRRTU
ROQUEFORT
EGGGIIJNR REJIGGING
EGGGIINNR GINGERING
EGGGIORST GROGGIEST
EGGHIINTW WEIGHTING
EGGHINNRU
HUNGERING
EGGIILNNR LINGERING
EGGIINNRS RESIGNING
EGGIINNST INGESTING
EGGIINNSW SWINGEING

EGGILLNRU GRUELLING
EGGILNORV GROVELING
EGGILNORW
GLOWERING
EGGILOOST GEOLOGIST
EGGILQRSU SQUIGGLER
EGGILQSSU SQUIGGLES
EGGIMNNOR
MONGERING
EGGIMNSSU MUGGINESS,
MUGGINSES
EGGINNNOR
GRONINGEN
EGGINNORV GOVERNING
EGGINNOTT GOTTINGEN
EGGINNPTU TUNING PEG
EGGINNPUX EXPUNGING
EGGINNRTU GINGER
NUT
EGGINOORV GOING-
OVER
EGGINOSSS SOGGINESS
EGGINRSTU GESTURING
EGGINRTTU GUTTERING
EGGIORRTU OUTRIGGER
EGGJLMNUY JUNGLE
GYM
EGGLMRSSU SMUGGLERS
EGGLRRSTU STRUGGLER
EGGLRSSTU STRUGGLES
EGHHHIORS HIGH
HORSE
EGHHIIORS HIROSHIGE
EGHHIIRSS HIGH-RISES
EGHHINRST THRESHING
EGHHIPRSU HIGHER-UPS
EGHHNORUW ROUGH-
HEWN
EGHHORTTU
RETHOUGHT
EGHIIKNRS SHRIEKING
EGHIILLMT LIMELIGHT
EGHIILNRS HIRELINGS,
RELISHING
EGHIILTWY WEIGHTILY
EGHIIMNTT NIGHTTIME
EGHIIMSTT MIGHTIEST
EGHIINNTW WHITENING
EGHIINPRS PERISHING
EGHIINRSV SHIVERING
EGHIINRTW WITHERING
EGHIINSTY HYGIENIST
EGHILLNOR HOLLERING
EGHILLNTY LENGTHILY

EGHILNNOT NEON
LIGHT
EGHILNOSV SHOVELING
EGHILNSST LIGHTNESS
EGHILOORY HIEROLOGY
EGHILORST GHOSTLIER
EGHILRTVY VERY LIGHT
EGHILSSST SIGHTLESS
EGHILSSTT SLIGHTEST
EGHIMNORT
MOTHERING
EGHIMNOST SOMETHING
EGHIMPPSU PEMPHIGUS
EGHINNSTU ENTHUSING
EGHINOORV
HOOVERING
EGHINORSU REHOUSING
EGHINORSW
SHOWERING
EGHINORTV OVERNIGHT
EGHINORTX EXHORTING
EGHINOSTY HISTOGENY
EGHINPRSY SYPHERING
EGHINRSST RIGHTNESS
EGHINRSTU HUNGRIEST,
SURE THING
EGHINSSTT TIGHTNESS
EGHIOPRTT TIGHTROPE
EGHIORSTU RIGHTEOUS
EGHIORSTV OVERSIGHT
EGHIRSTTU THEURGIST
EGHLLOORY GLORY
HOLE
EGHLLOPSU PLUGHOLES
EGHLMNOPU
PLOUGHMEN
EGHLNOOPY
NEPHOLOGY,
PHENOLOGY
EGHLNOORS
LONGSHORE
EGHLNOOTY
ETHNOLOGY
EGHLNOPYY
PHYLOGENY
EGHMNOORW
HOMEGROWN
EGHNOOOPR
GONOPHORE
EGHNOOPRY
GYNOPHORE
EGHNORSSU ROUGHNESS
EGHNOSSTU TOUGHNESS
EGHNRSSTT STRENGTHS

EGHOPTYYZ
ZYGOPHYTE
EGIIIMNTZ ITEMIZING
EGIIJNNNO ENJOINING
EGIIJNNOR REJOINING
EGIIKLNST KINGLIEST
EGIIKLNSV KING'S EVIL
EGIIKNNRT TINKERING
EGIIKRSTZ SITZKREIG
EGIILLMNP IMPELLING
EGIILNNST ENLISTING,
LISTENING
EGIILNNSV SNIVELING
EGIILNNTT ENTITLING
EGIILNNUV UNVEILING
EGIILNORS RELIGIONS
EGIILNORT LOITERING
EGIILNOST GILSONITE
EGIILNRSV SILVERING
EGIILNRTT LITTERING
EGIILNSVW SWIVELING
EGIILNTTY GENTILITY
EGIILOPST EPILOGIST
EGIILORST TRILOGIES
EGIILORSU RELIGIOUS
EGIILRRST GRISTLIER
EGIILRSST GRISLIEST
EGIILRSTU LITURGIES
EGIILSTTU GUILTIEST
EGIILSTTZ GLITZIEST
EGIIMMNRS IMMERSING,
SIMMERING
EGIIMNPRS SIMPERING
EGIIMNRSS GRIMINESS
EGIIMNRTT REMITTING
EGIINNNRT INTERNING
EGIINNNTV INVENTING
EGIINNNTW ENTWINING
EGIINNORS NIGROSINE
EGIINNOST INGESTION
EGIINNOSU INGENIOUS
EGIINNQRU ENQUIRING
EGIINNRRT INTERRING
EGIINNRST INSERTING
EGIINNRSW INSWINGER
EGIINNRTU REUNITING
EGIINNRTV INVERTING
EGIINNRTW WINTERING
EGIINNSTT INSETTING
EGIINNSTV INVESTING
EGIINNTUY INGENUITY
EGIINPPQU EQUIPPING
EGIINPRRS RESPIRING,
SPRINGIER

EGIINQRRU REQUIRING
EGIINQRTU REQUITING
EGIINQRUV QUIVERING
EGIINRRST STRINGIER
EGIINRRTU INTRIGUER
EGIINRRTW REWRITING
EGIINRSST RESISTING
EGIINRSSU REISSUING
EGIINRSTT RESITTING
EGIINRSTU INTRIGUES
EGIINRTTT TITTERING
EGIINRTTY INTEGRITY
EGIINSSTT STINGIEST
EGIIRSTTT GRITTIEST
EGIJKLNRY JERKINGLY
EGIJKNNTU JUNKETING
EGIJLNSTY JESTINGLY
EGIJNPRRU PERJURING
EGIKLNNOO INGLENOOK
EGIKMNNOY
MONKEYING
EGIKNORRW
REWORKING
EGILLLNTY TELLINGLY
EGILLMNOW
MELLOWING
EGILLMNTY MELTINGLY
EGILLMOTU GUILLEMOT
EGILLNNOR ENROLLING
EGILLNOTT ILL-GOTTEN
EGILLNOTW TOWELLING
EGILLNOTX EXTOLLING
EGILLNOUU LONGUEUIL
EGILLNOVY VOLLEYING
EGILLNOWY YELLOWING
EGILLNPSS SPELLINGS
EGILLNSSW SWELLINGS
EGILLOSSY SYLLOGISE
EGILLOSYZ SYLLOGIZE
EGILLSSTU GUILTLESS
EGILMMNPU
PUMMELING
EGILMNOOS NEOLOGISM
EGILMNOPY EMPLOYING
EGILMNOST MOLESTING
EGILMOOST GLOOMIEST
EGILNNNTU TUNNELING
EGILNNOOS LOOSENING
EGILNNOST SINGLETON
EGILNNRSU NURSELING
EGILNNSST NESTLINGS
EGILNNSUY ENSUINGLY
EGILNNVYY ENVYINGLY
EGILNOOST NEOLOGIST

EGILNOOSU SINOLOGUE
EGILNOPRX EXPLORING
EGILNORSV RESOLVING
EGILNORTV REVOLTING
EGILNORVV REVOLVING
EGILNORVY OVERLYING
EGILNOTVY LONGEVITY
EGILNPRSU REPULSING
EGILNRSTU RESULTING
EGILNRSTW WRESTLING
EGILNSSTT SETTLINGS
EGILNSTTY TESTINGLY
EGILOSSST GLOSSIEST
EGILOSSTT GLOTTISES
EGILOSSTU EULOGISTS
EGIMMNRSU
  SUMMERING
EGIMMNSSU GUMMINESS
EGIMNORST GERMISTON
EGIMNORSV MISGOVERN
EGIMNPRSU PRESUMING
EGIMNPRTU PERMUTING
EGIMNRSSY SYNERGISM
EGIMNRSTU MUSTERING
EGIMNRTTU MUTTERING
EGIMPRSTU GRUMPIEST
EGINNNRRU RERUNNING
EGINNNRUV UNNERVING
EGINNORSW
  WORSENING
EGINNOSUU INGENUOUS
EGINNRRTU RETURNING
EGINNRSTT STRINGENT
EGINNRSTU INSURGENT
EGINNRTUV VENTURING
EGINOOSSS GOOSINESS
EGINOOSSU ISOGENOUS
EGINOPRRR PORRINGER
EGINOPRRT REPORTING
EGINOPRRV REPROVING
EGINOPRST PROGESTIN
EGINOPRTT POTTERING
EGINOPRTX EXPORTING
EGINOPSST SPONGIEST
EGINOPSSU ESPOUSING
EGINOPSUY EPIGYNOUS
EGINORRST RESORTING,
  RESTORING
EGINORRTT RETORTING
EGINORSTU GERONTIUS
EGINORTTT TOTTERING
EGINORTTX EXTORTING
EGINOSSTU GOUTINESS
EGINPRSSS PRESSINGS

EGINPRTTU PUTTERING
EGINPRUVY PURVEYING
EGINPSTTU UPSETTING
EGINPSTWW SWEPTWING
EGINRSSST STRESSING
EGINRSSTY SYNERGIST
EGINRSUVY SURVEYING
EGINSSSTU GUSTINESS
EGINSTTTU TUNGSTITE
EGIOORSTV GROOVIEST
EGIORSTTT GROTTIEST
EGKORSSUW GUESSWORK
EGLMNOOOU
  MONOLOGUE
EGLMOORTY
  METROLOGY
EGLMOOTYY
  ETYMOLOGY
EGLNNOSUU SUN
  LOUNGE
EGLNNPTUY PUNGENTLY
EGLNOOPRR
  PROLONGER
EGLNOORUY
  NEUROLOGY
EGLNOOSUV
  LONGEVOUS
EGLNORSTY STRONGYLE
EGLNORSUU LONGUEURS
EGLNOSTUU GLUTENOUS
EGLOOOSTY OSTEOLOGY
EGLOOPRSU PROLOGUES
EGLOOPRTY PETROLOGY
EGMNOOOSS
  MONGOOSES
EGMOORSTU
  GUESTROOM
EGNNNRRUU
  GUNRUNNER
EGNNORSSW
  WRONGNESS
EGNOOPRSS PROGNOSES
EGNOORRSV
  GOVERNORS
EGNOORRVW
  OVERGROWN
EGNOORSUU
  UROGENOUS
EGNORSSSS GROSSNESS
EGNORSSST SONGSTERS
EGNORSSTT STRONGEST
EGNORSSTU STURGEONS
EGNORSTUY
  YOUNGSTER

EGOOPRSYZ ZYGOSPORE
EHHIINSTT IN THE SHIT
EHHIIRTTT THIRTIETH
EHHILLLSY HELLISHLY
EHHILMOOP
  HOMOPHILE
EHHINOPPS PHOSPHINE
EHHIOPPST PHOSPHITE
EHHIOPRSW HORSEWHIP
EHHIORSST HORSESHIT
EHHIORTTT THITHERTO
EHHLOOPTY
  HOLOPHYTE
EHHMNNOPP PHNOM
  PENH
EHHMNOOOP
  HOMOPHONE
EHHMNOSUY HUSH
  MONEY
EHHMORTTU HOME
  TRUTH
EHHMRTUYY
  EURHYTHMY
EHHNOORSS
  SHOEHORNS
EHHOOPSTY THEOSOPHY
EHHOOSSTU HOTHOUSES
EHIIKNSTT KITTENISH
EHIILLTWY LILY-WHITE
EHIILMRST HITLERISM
EHIILRSTW WILTSHIRE
EHIINNORT ORNITHINE
EHIINNSSS SHININESS
EHIINORRT INHERITOR
EHIINPPRW WHIPPER-IN
EHIINPRST NEPHRITIS,
  PHRENITIS
EHIINPSST PITHINESS
EHIIORSST HISTORIES
EHIIPPSSY EPIPHYSIS
EHIIQRSSU SQUISHIER
EHIIRRSTT THIRSTIER
EHIIRSSTT SHIRTIEST
EHIIRSSTW IRISH STEW
EHIIRSTTZ ZITHERIST
EHIISSTTT SHITTIEST
EHIISSTTX SIXTIETHS
EHIKLLPSY SYLPHLIKE
EHIKLORTZ KILOHERTZ
EHIKNSSSU HUSKINESS
EHIKPRSSU SPIKE-RUSH
EHILLLMOS MOLEHILLS
EHILLOSTY HOSTILELY
EHILLOSWY YELLOWISH

EHILLRRST THRILLERS
EHILLRSST SHRILLEST
EHILMNOST MONTHLIES
EHILMOORS HEIRLOOMS
EHILMPPRY PERILYMPH
EHILMRSST MIRTHLESS
EHILMRSTU LUTHERISM
EHILMRSUV HILVERSUM
EHILNOOPT LITHOPONE,
  PHONOLITE
EHILNOSST HOLSTEINS
EHILNOSUY HEINOUSLY
EHILOPPTY HIPPOLYTE
EHILOPRST HELIPORTS
EHILOPRXY XEROPHILY
EHILPSTTY PETTISHLY
EHILRSTTW WHITTLERS
EHILSSSTU SLUSHIEST
EHIMNNOOS
  MOONSHINE
EHIMNOPUU
  EUPHONIUM
EHIMNORST HORSEMINT
EHIMNPSST SHIPMENTS
EHIMNPSSU HUMPINESS
EHIMNRTUU
  RUTHENIUM
EHIMNSSSU MUSHINESS
EHIMOOSST SMOOTHIES
EHIMOPPRR PERIMORPH
EHIMORSST ISOTHERMS
EHIMORSTT SHORT
  TIME
EHIMPRRTU TRIUMPHER
EHIMRRSTY ERYTHRISM
EHIMSSSTU ISTHMUSES
EHINNOPSS PHONINESS
EHINNORSS HORNINESS
EHINNOSST THONINESS
EHINNOSTW
  NONWHITES, WHINSTONE
EHINNSSTU NISSEN HUT
EHINOPPRS HORNPIPES
EHINOPRSS NEPHROSIS
EHINOPRSW OWNERSHIP,
  SHIPOWNER
EHINOPSTU IN THE SOUP
EHINOPSTY HYPNOTISE
EHINOPTYZ HYPNOTIZE
EHINORRSU NOURISHER
EHINORSSS HORSINESS
EHINORSTT THORNIEST
EHINORTXY THYROXINE
EHINOSSSW SHOWINESS

EHINOSTWW SNOW-
  WHITE
EHINPRRTY PYRETHRIN
EHINPSSSU PUSHINESS
EHINRSSSU RUSHINESS
EHINSSSTY SYNTHESIS
EHIOOPRTW POOR
  WHITE
EHIOOSTTT TOOTHIEST
EHIOPRSST PROTHESIS,
  SOPHISTER
EHIORSSTT THEORISTS
EHIORSTTW WORTHIEST
EHIORSTWZ HOWITZERS
EHIPQSSUY PHYSIQUES
EHIRSSSTU RUSSETISH
EHKNPRRSU PRESHRUNK
EHKOORRSW
  WORKHORSE
EHKOORSUW
  HOUSEWORK,
  WORKHOUSE
EHLLMOPSY MESOPHYLL
EHLLNSSTU NUTSHELLS
EHLLOOOPS LOOPHOLES
EHLLOOSTU TOLLHOUSE
EHLLOOSTW
  HOLLOWEST
EHLMOORSW
  WORMHOLES
EHLMORSSU HUMORLESS
EHLNOOPPY POLYPHONE
EHLNOOPRT NORTH
  POLE
EHLNOOPXY
  XYLOPHONE
EHLNOORSS HONORLESS
EHLNOOSTY
  HOLYSTONE
EHLNORRTY
  NORTHERLY
EHLNPSSSU PLUSHNESS
EHLOOPRST PORTHOLES,
  POTHOLERS
EHLOOPSTU SOUTH POLE
EHLOOSSTT TOOTHLESS
EHLOPRSTU UPHOLSTER
EHLORRTTT THROTTLER
EHLORSSTW WORTHLESS
EHLORSTTT THROTTLES
EHLORSTUY SOUTHERLY
EHLPRSTUU SULPHURET
EHMMOOPRS
  MESOMORPH

EHMMOORSU
  HUMORSOME
EHMNNOOOY
  HONEYMOON
EHMNOOSTW
  HOMETOWNS
EHMOOOPRS
  SOPHOMORE
EHMOOORSU
  HOUSEROOM
EHMOOOSTT
  TOOTHSOME
EHMOOSSTT
  SMOOTHEST
EHMORRSTT SHORT-
  TERM
EHMPRRTUY
  PYRETHRUM
EHNNOORST
  HORNSTONE
EHNNOOTTW ON THE
  TOWN
EHNNOPRST
  PENN'ORTHS
EHNOOPPSS OPEN
  SHOPS
EHNOOPPTY
  PHONOTYPE
EHNOORSSW
  SNOWSHOER
EHNOOSSSW
  SNOWSHOES
EHNOOSTUW TOWN
  HOUSE
EHNOOTTTT
  HOTTENTOT
EHNOPRTTU
  POTHUNTER
EHNORRTTU TRUE
  NORTH
EHNORSSST SHORTNESS
EHNORSTTW
  NORTHWEST
EHNOSSTUU NUTHOUSES
EHOOOPRSU
  POORHOUSE
EHOOORSTV
  OVERSHOOT
EHOOPPTTY PHOTOTYPE
EHOOPRRTT
  ORTHOPTER
EHOOPRRTV
  HOVERPORT
EHOOPSSTU HOUSETOPS

EHOORRTVW
  OVERTHROW
EHOORSSUW ROW
  HOUSES
EHOOSSTUU OUTHOUSES
EHOPRSTXY EXSTROPHY
EHORRSTTW
  THROWSTER
EHOSSTTUW
  SOUTHWEST
EHRRSSTTU THRUSTERS
EIIILMMTT TIME LIMIT
EIIILNNQU INQUILINE
EIIILSTTU UTILITIES
EIIIMMNRS MINIMISER
EIIIMMNRZ MINIMIZER
EIIIMPRTV PRIMITIVE
EIIINQRSU INQUIRIES
EIIINRSTT RETINITIS,
  TRINITIES
EIIINTTUV INTUITIVE
EIIJMSSTU JESUITISM
EIIKKNNSS KINKINESS
EIIKLLORT KILOLITER,
  KILOLITRE
EIIKLMNSS MILKINESS
EIIKLNNRT INTERLINK
EIIKLNSSS SILKINESS
EIIKLNSST SLINKIEST
EIIKMPSST SKIMPIEST
EIIKNNSST SKINNIEST
EIIKNPSSS SPIKINESS
EIIKNRSSS RISKINESS
EIIKQRSTU QUIRKIEST
EIIILLMNRS MILLINERS
EIIILLMNRY MILLINERY
EIIILLMSST LIMITLESS
EIIILLNRST INSTILLER
EIIILLNSSS SILLINESS
EIIILLNSTU NULLITIES
EIIILLOPRS PILLORIES
EIIILMMORS MELIORISM
EIIILMNORV VERMILION
EIIILMNOSU LIMOUSINE
EIIILMNSSS SLIMINESS
EIIILMOPSV IMPLOSIVE
EIIILMOTTV LEITMOTIV
EIIILMPRSU PUERILISM
EIIILMPSUV IMPULSIVE
EIIILMRSST LISTERISM
EIIILMRSSY MISSILERY
EIIILNNOQU QUINOLINE
EIIILNPSST SPLENITIS
EIIILNPSTY PENSILITY

EIIILNSTTY TENSILITY
EIIILOQSSU SILIQUOSE
EIIILPPSST SLIPPIEST
EIIILPRTUY PUERILITY
EIIILRSTTY STERILITY
EIIILRSTVY SERVILITY
EIIILSSSTY SESSILITY
EIIIMMNORS IMMERSION
EIIIMMNOSS MISONEISM
EIIIMMNRSU IMMUNISER
EIIIMMNRUZ IMMUNIZER
EIIIMMNSTY IMMENSITY
EIIIMMORSS ISOMERISM
EIIIMMOSTV EMOTIVISM
EIIIMMPSSS PESSIMISM
EIIIMMPSUY EPIMYSIUM
EIIIMNNRTU TRIENNIUM
EIIIMNORSS MISSIONER,
  REMISSION
EIIIMNOSSS EMISSIONS
EIIIMNOSST MISONEIST
EIIIMNOSUV VIMINEOUS
EIIIMNPRRT IMPRINTER
EIIIMNRSST MINISTERS
EIIIMNSSST MISTINESS
EIIIMOPRSU IMPERIOUS
EIIIMOPRSV IMPROVISE
EIIIMOPSTT EPITOMIST
EIIIMOSSTV SOVIETISM
EIIIMPSSST PESSIMIST
EIIINNNOST INTENSION
EIIINNNOTT INTENTION
EIIINNNOTV INVENTION
EIIINNNSST TINNINESS
EIIINNORST INSERTION
EIIINNORSV INVERSION
EIIINNOSSS NOISINESS
EIIINNPPSS NIPPINESS
EIIINNPSSS SPININESS
EIIINNRSTT INTERNIST
EIIINNSSTT INSISTENT
EIIINNSTTY INTENSITY
EIIINOPPST PIT PONIES
EIIINOPRSV PREVISION
EIIINOPSTT PETITIONS
EIIINOPTVW VIEWPOINT
EIIINORRST INTERIORS
EIIINORSSV REVISIONS
EIIINORSTY SENIORITY
EIIINPPRST PINSTRIPE
EIIINPSSST TIPSINESS
EIIINPSSSW WISPINESS
EIIINRSTTW WINTRIEST
EIIINRSTUV INTRUSIVE

EIIINRTTUV NUTRITIVE
EIIINSSSSY SYNIESIS
EIIINSSSYZ SYNIZESIS
EIIINSSTTW WITTINESS
EIIINSTTTU INSTITUTE
EIIOPSSTV POSITIVES
EIIOSSTTV SOVIETIST
EIIPRRSTW TRIPWIRES
EIIPRRTUV IRRUPTIVE
EIIPRSSST PRISSIEST
EIIPRSSTT STRIPIEST
EIIQSSTTU QUIETISTS
EIISSTTTW TWISTIEST
EIJLLNOSS JOLLINESS
EIJLMNPTU MINT JULEP
EIJMNPSSU JUMPINESS
EIJNORSST JOINTRESS
EIKKNOOSS KOOKINESS
EIKLLNOVX KNOXVILLE
EIKLMNOSS MOLESKINS
EIKLNPRRS SPRINKLER
EIKLNPRSS SPRINKLES
EIKLNSSSU SULKINESS
EIKMNOSSS SMOKINESS
EIKMNRRSU MURKINESS
EIKMNSSSU MUSKINESS
EIKNOPRSS PORKINESS
EIKNOSTTT KNOTTIEST
EIKNPRSTU TURNPIKES
EIKNPSSTU SPUNKIEST
EIKOOPSST SPOOKIEST
EIKORRSTV OVERSKIRT
EIKORRSWW
  WIREWORKS
EIKRRSTWY SKYWRITER
EILLMNOST MILLSTONE
EILLMNSSU SENSILLUM
EILLMOOPT MELITOPOL
EILLMPSTU MULTIPLES
EILLMPTTU MULTIPLET
EILLMPTUX MULTIPLEX
EILLMRTUU TELLURIUM
EILLNOPRU NULLIPORE
EILLNORTU TELLURION
EILLNOSSW LOWLINESS
EILLNOSTY STONE-LILY
EILLNOTVY VIOLENTLY
EILLNSSST STILLNESS
EILLOOPRV LIVERPOOL
EILLOOSTW WOOLLIEST
EILLOPRSV OVERSPILL
EILLOPRTY PELLITORY
EILLOPRWW WILLPOWER
EILLOSTTY STYLOLITE

EILLPSSSY SYLLEPSIS
EILLSSTWY WITLESSLY
EILMMNTUU
NUMMULITE
EILMMPSTU PLUMMIEST
EILMNOPST SIMPLETON
EILMNOPSU ON IMPULSE
EILMNORTT TORMENTIL
EILMNORTU MONTREUIL
EILMNOSSU EMULSIONS
EILMNOSTY SOLEMNITY
EILMNOSWY WINSOMELY
EILMNPSSU LUMPINESS
EILMNRSST MINSTRELS
EILMOOSTY ILEOSTOMY
EILNNOOSS LOONINESS
EILNNOSTV INSOLVENT
EILNOOPSS SLIPNOOSE
EILNOOPSX EXPLOSION
EILNOOTUV EVOLUTION
EILNOPRRU PURLOINER
EILNOPRSU PRELUSION,
REPULSION
EILNOPRTY LINOTYPER
EILNOPSST POINTLESS
EILNOPSSU SPINULOSE
EILNOPSUX EXPULSION
EILNORSTY STORY LINE
EILNORSUV REVULSION
EILNORTUY ROUTINELY
EILNOSSSU LOUSINESS
EILNOSSTV NOVELISTS
EILNOSUVY ENVIOUSLY
EILNPPSSU PULPINESS
EILNPQTUU QUINTUPLE
EILNPRSST SPLINTERS
EILNPRSTY SPLINTERY
EILNRSSSU SURLINESS
EILNRSTTU TURNSTILE
EILNRTUUV VULTURINE
EILNSSSTU LUSTINESS
EILOOPRST POORLIEST
EILOPPRSS PROLEPSIS
EILOPPRTY PROPYLITE
EILOPPSST SLOPPIEST
EILOPRSTT PORTLIEST
EILOPRSTU POULTRIES
EILOPSSTY STYLOPISE
EILOPSTTT TEST PILOT
EILOPSTUY PITEOUSLY
EILOPSTYZ STYLOPIZE
EILORRTVW LIVERWORT
EILORSSUY SERIOUSLY
EILOSSTTT STILETTOS

EILPPRRSU SUPPLIERS
EILQRRSSU SQUIRRELS
EILRSSTTU SULTRIEST
EILRSSTTW WRISTLETS
EIMMNNSTU
MUNIMENTS
EIMMNOPRS PERSIMMON
EIMMNORRS MORRIS
MEN
EIMMNORSS MISNOMERS
EIMMOPRSU EMPORIUMS
EIMMNOOSS MOONINESS
EIMNNOOTZ
MONZONITE
EIMNNOPRT PROMINENT
EIMNNORST INNERMOST
EIMNNOSTT OINTMENTS
EIMNNPTUU NEPTUNIUM
EIMNNRTTU
NUTRIMENT
EIMNOORRT
REMONTOIR
EIMNOORSS ROOMINESS
EIMNOPRTU IMPORTUNE
EIMNORSST MONITRESS
EIMNORSSU SENSORIUM
EIMNORSUV VERMINOUS
EIMNOSSSS MOSSINESS
EIMNOSSST MOISTNESS
EIMNOSSSU MOUSINESS
EIMNOSTTY TESTIMONY
EIMNOTTZZ
MEZZOTINT
EIMNSSSTU MUSTINESS
EIMNSSUZZ MUZZINESS
EIMOOPRTV PROMOTIVE
EIMOORRSW
WORRISOME
EIMOORSSU ISOMEROUS
EIMOOSSSX EXOSMOSIS
EIMOPRRSS PRIMROSES
EIMOPRRST IMPORTERS,
MISREPORT
EIMOPRSTU IMPOSTURE
EIMOPSTUU IMPETUOUS
EIMORRRST TERRORISM
EIMORRSTU TRIMEROUS
EIMORRSWW
WIREWORMS
EIMORRTTW
MITERWORT, MITREWORT
EIMORSSTT STORMIEST
EIMORSTTW TWO-
TIMERS

EIMORSUVY VOYEURISM
EIMPRSTUY SUPREMITY
EIMPSSTTU STUMPIEST
EIMQSSTUY MYSTIQUES
EIMSSTTTU SMUTTIEST
EINNNOTTY NONENTITY
EINNNSSSU SUNNINESS
EINNOOPST ON POINTES
EINNOORST IRONSTONE,
SEROTONIN
EINNORSTV INVENTORS
EINNORTVY INVENTORY
EINNOSSST STONINESS
EINNOSSSW SNOWINESS
EINNPRSTW NEWSPRINT
EINNRSSTU RUNTINESS
EINNRSTTU NUTRIENTS
EINNRTTUW
UNWRITTEN
EINNSSTTU NUTTINESS
EINOOPRSS POISONERS
EINOORRST RETORSION
EINOORRTT RETORTION
EINOORSST ROOTINESS
EINOORTTX EXTORTION
EINOORTTY NOTORIETY
EINOOSSST SOOTINESS
EINOOSSTT SNOOTIEST
EINOOSSWZ WOOZINESS
EINOPPSSS SOPPINESS
EINOPRRSS PRISONERS
EINOPRRTV OVERPRINT
EINOPRSSS PROSINESS
EINOPRSTU ERUPTIONS
EINOPRSUU PENURIOUS
EINOPSSSU PIOUSNESS
EINOPSSTT POTTINESS
EINOQSSTU QUESTIONS
EINOQSTTU QUOTIENTS
EINORRSSS SORRINESS
EINORRTTV INTROVERT
EINORSSUV SOUVENIRS
EINORSTUX EXTRUSION
EINOSSTTT SNOTTIEST
EINPRRSST SPRINTERS
EINPRRTTU INTERRUPT
EINPRSSST SPINSTERS
EINRSSSTU RUSTINESS
EINRSSTTU RUTTINESS
EIOOPPRSS PORPOISES
EIOOPPSST OPPOSITES
EIOOPRRST POSTERIOR
EIOOPRSTX EXPOSITOR
EIOORSSTT TORTOISES

EIOORSTTT TROOSTITE
EIOOSSSTX EXOSTOSIS
EIOOSSTTV OVOTESTIS
EIOPPRRST STROPPIER
EIOPPRRTY PROPRIETY
EIOPPRSUV PURPOSIVE
EIOPRRSSU SUPERIORS
EIOPRSSTT SPORTIEST
EIOPRSTTU PROUSTITE
EIOPRSTTY POSTERITY
EIOPSSTTT SPOTTIEST
EIOQRSTUU TURQUOISE
EIORRRSTT TERRORIST
EIORRRRTTY TERRITORY
EIORRSSST RESISTORS
EIORRSSTV SERVITORS
EIPPRRSST STRIPPERS
EIPRRRSSU SURPRISER
EIPRRSSSU SURPRISES
EIPRSSSTU PERTUSSIS
EIQRRSSTU SQUIRTERS
EIRSSTTTU TRUSTIEST
EJLLLLORY JELLY ROLL
EJLLOSSYY JOYLESSLY
EJNOORRSU SOJOURNER
EKKOOPRRW
   POKERWORK
EKLLNNOWW WELL-
   KNOWN
EKLMMNOSU
   MUSKMELON
EKLNOOORS
   ONLOOKERS
EKMNNOORS
   NONSMOKER
EKMNNOTUY MONKEY
   NUT
EKNOOPSTU OUTSPOKEN
EKNOORSTW
   STONEWORK
EKNORSSTU SUNSTROKE
EKOORRTUW
   OUTWORKER
EKOORSTTW TWO-
   STROKE
EKOPRRSSW PRESSWORK
ELLMORSTU ROSTELLUM
ELLNOPTUY OPULENTLY
ELLOPRSST POLLSTERS
ELLOPRSUV PULLOVERS
ELLORRSST STROLLERS
ELLORSTUU TELLUROUS
ELMNNOOST
   SOMNOLENT

ELMNPPSSU PLUMPNESS
ELMOOOPRW POWER
   LOOM
ELMOORSTW
   LOWERMOST
ELMORSTUU
   TREMULOUS
ELMORTUVY
   VOLUMETRY
ELMSSTUUU TUMULUSES
ELNOOOPRV
   PROVOLONE
ELNOORSUY ONEROUSLY
ELNORSUVY NERVOUSLY
ELNOSTUUY TENUOUSLY
ELOOORSTZ ZOOSTEROL
ELOORSTUW
   LOUSEWORT
ELOPPPUVY PUPPY
   LOVE
ELOPPRSUY PURPOSELY
ELOQRSUUU QUERULOUS
ELPRSSSUU SURPLUSES
ELPRSSTTU SPLUTTERS
EMMMMNOSTU
   MOMENTUMS
EMMNNOSTU
   MONUMENTS
EMMNOOOST
   MONOSTOME
EMMNOORSS MEN'S
   ROOMS
EMMNOOSTU
   MOMENTOUS
EMMNOSSSU
   SUMMONSES
EMMNRSTUU
   MENSTRUUM
EMMOORSTY
   OSMOMETRY
EMNNOOOST
   MOONSTONE
EMNOOPRTY
   MONOTYPER
EMNOOPSUY
   EPONYMOUS
EMNOORRTT
   TORMENTOR
EMNOORSSW
   NEWSROOMS
EMNOORTTY
   TONOMETRY
EMNOORTUY
   NEUROTOMY

EMNOORTWY
   MONEYWORT
EMNOPRSST SPORTSMEN
EMNORSSTT STERNMOST
EMOOORRST
   STOREROOM
EMOOOSTTY
   OSTEOTOMY
EMOOPRRSS PRESSROOM
EMOOPRRST
   PROMOTERS
EMOOPRTTY
   OPTOMETRY
EMOORRSST REST
   ROOMS
EMOORRSTU
   TREMOROUS
EMOORSTTU
   OUTERMOST
EMOPPRSTU UPPERMOST
EMOPRRTUV
   OVERTRUMP
EMOPRRTYY
   PYROMETRY
EMPRSSTTU STRUMPETS
ENNOOPPRT
   PROPONENT
ENNOOPPST OPPONENTS
ENNOPRTWY
   PENNYWORT
ENNORRTUU
   OUTRUNNER
ENNORSTTU
   TURNSTONE
ENNPRRSUU RUNNERS-
   UP, RUNNER-UPS
ENOOPPRST POSTPONER
ENOOPPRSU ON PURPOSE
ENOOPPRTU OPPORTUNE
ENOORSTTW
   STONEWORT
ENOOSSTTU SOSTENUTO
ENOPRSSSU SUSPENSOR
ENOPRSSTT STERNPOST
ENOPSTTYY STENOTYPY
ENORRSTUV TURNOVERS
ENORSSTUU STRENUOUS
ENOSSSTTU STOUTNESS
EOOOPRRTU
   EUROPOORT
EOOPPRRSS OPPRESSOR,
   PROPOSERS
EOOPPRTTY PROTOTYPE
EOOPRSSSS POSSESSOR

EOOPRSSTV STOPOVERS
EOPPRRSTU SUPPORTER
EOPPRSSST STOP PRESS
EOPRRSUVY PURVEYORS
EORRRSTTU TORTURERS
EORRSSUVY SURVEYORS
FFFOOPTUU OUT OF PUFF
FFGHILNSU SHUFFLING
FFGHILRTU FRIGHTFUL
FFGIILLNU IN FULL FIG
FFGIILNNS SNIFFLING
FFGILNNSU SNUFFLING
FFGILNOXY FLYING FOX
FFGIMNORU FUNGIFORM
FFGINOPRS OFFSPRING
FFGINSSUU SUFFUSING
FFHOOOSST OFFSHOOTS
FFIINOSUX SUFFIXION
FFILLOPPS FLIP-FLOPS
FFINOSSUU SUFFUSION
FFIORSTTU SOFT FRUIT
FFLOOOOPR FOOLPROOF
FFLOOOPRY POORLY OFF
FFNOPSTUU UP TO SNUFF
FGGGILNOS FLOGGINGS
FGGIINORV FORGIVING
FGHHILNOW HIGH-
  FLOWN
FGHHIOSTW SHOW
  FIGHT
FGHIIINNS FINISHING
FGHIILLTY FLIGHTILY
FGHILOPTT TOP-FLIGHT
FGHINORTT FORTNIGHT
FGHLORSUU FURLOUGHS
FGHMOORTU
  FROGMOUTH
FGHOOTTUU
  OUTFOUGHT
FGIIILNVY VILIFYING
FGIIIMNRS MISFIRING
FGIILMNOR LIGNIFORM
FGIILNOPR PROFILING
FGIILNPTU UPLIFTING
FGIILNRST FIRSTLING
FGIILNRZZ FRIZZLING
FGIIMNNOR INFORMING
FGIINNOTY NOTIFYING
FGIINOPRT PROFITING
FGIINOSSY OSSIFYING
FGIINPRUY PURIFYING
FGIINPTYY TYPIFYING
FGIKLLNOS GOLF LINKS
FGILLNOOW FOLLOWING

FGILLNOWY FLOWINGLY
FGILNNRUU UNFURLING
FGILNRRUY FLURRYING
FGINOOTUX OUTFOXING
FGINORRUW
  FURROWING
FGLLNORUW FULL-
  GROWN
FGLORSUUU FULGUROUS
FHHIORTTW
  FORTHWITH
FHIIIKLLS KILLIFISH
FHIILRTTY THRIFTILY
FHIKLSSWY FLYWHISKS
FHIKNRSTU TRUNKFISH
FHILLOOST FOOTHILLS
FHILLOOSY FOOLISHLY
FHIMORSTX SIXTH FORM
FHLLRTUUY HURTFULLY
FHLMORUUU
  HUMOURFUL
FHLMOSTUU
  MOUTHFULS
FHLOOOPRS SHOP
  FLOOR
FHLOOORSW FLOOR
  SHOW
FHMOOOPRT
  MOTHPROOF
FIIILSSTY FISSILITY
FIIIMNRTY INFIRMITY
FIIKLNNST SKINFLINT
FIILLMORV VILLIFORM
FIILLMOTU MULTIFOIL
FIILMORTU TRIFOLIUM
FIILMPRST FILMSTRIP
FIILORTVY FRIVOLITY
FIIMMNORS MISINFORM
FIIMNOSSU FUSIONISM
FIIMOPRST STIPIFORM
FIIMORRTU TRIFORIUM
FIIMORRTV VITRIFORM
FIINNOSSU INFUSIONS
FIINOSSTU FUSIONIST
FIKLLLSUY SKILFULLY
FIKLLNSUU UNSKILFUL
FILLLMORU FLOURMILL
FILLSTUWY WISTFULLY
FILMMORSU FORMULISM
FILMMORTU
  MULTIFORM
FILMNORUY UNIFORMLY
FILMORSTU FORMULIST
FILMORSTY STYLIFORM

FILMORUVV VULVIFORM
FILOOOPRT PORTFOLIO
FILOORSSU FLUOROSIS
FILOORSUV FRIVOLOUS
FILORSUUY FURIOUSLY
FILOSSTUU FISTULOUS
FINOOPRSU PROFUSION
FINOOPRTT FOOTPRINT
FIOPRSSTT FIRST POST
FIRSSTTUU FUTURISTS
FKOORRSTW
  FROSTWORK
FLLLOSUUY SOULFULLY
FLLLSTUUY LUSTFULLY
FLLMNOOSU FULL
  MOONS
FLLNOORRY FORLORNLY
FLLOOPSUW FOLLOW-UPS
FLLOPSSTU FULL STOPS
FLNOOPSSU SPOONFULS,
  SPOONSFUL
FLOOOOSTT FOOTSTOOL
FLOORRSUW
  SORROWFUL
FLOPRSSUU PLUS FOURS
FMNOOOORRT FRONT
  ROOM
FOOPRRSTU RUSTPROOF
FOOPSSSTT SOFT SPOTS
FOOPSSTUY PUSSYFOOT
GGGHINRSU SHRUGGING
GGGIILNRW WRIGGLING
GGGILMNSU SMUGGLING
GGGILNNSU SNUGGLING
GGHHHIILT HIGHLIGHT
GGHHILOSY HOGGISHLY
GGHIIILRW WHIRLIGIG
GGHIIKNNT KNIGHTING
GGHIILNNT LIGHTNING
GGHIILNPT PLIGHTING
GGHIILNST SLIGHTING
GGHIILPSY PIGGISHLY
GGHIINNNU UNHINGING
GGHIINRTW RIGHT
  WING
GGHIINSST SIGHTINGS
GGHILNNOT
  NIGHTLONG
GGHILNOPU PLOUGHING
GGHILNOSU SLOUGHING
GGHILNSUY GUSHINGLY
GGHILOOPR LOGOGRIPH
GGHINNORT
  THRONGING

GGHINNOTW
NIGHTGOWN
GGIIIMNNP IMPINGING
GGIIIMNSV MISGIVING
GGIILMNPS GLIMPSING
GGIILNNSS GIN SLINGS
GGIILNNSY SINGINGLY
GGIILNPRY GRIPINGLY
GGIILNRZZ GRIZZLING
GGIIMNNPU IMPUGNING
GGIINNORW INGROWING
GGIINNPRS SPRINGING
GGIINNRST STRINGING
GGIINNRSY SYRINGING
GGIINNSWW SWING-
WING
GGIINOPSS GOSSIPING
GGILLNNOY LONGINGLY
GGILLNOWY
GLOWINGLY
GGILLNPUY GULPINGLY
GGILLOOSW GOLLIWOGS
GGILNOPRY GROPINGLY
GGILNPRSU SPLURGING
GGINNOSSS SINGSONGS
GGINOOSTU OUTGOINGS
GGINOPRSU GROUPINGS
GHHIIJKNS HIGH JINKS
GHHIILPST LIGHTSHIP
GHHIINOPT HIGH POINT
GHHIJMPSU HIGH JUMPS
GHHILRSTU RUSHLIGHT
GHHIOPSST HIGH SPOTS
GHHLOOSTY HOLY
GHOST
GHIIKNNRS SHRINKING
GHIIKNSTT SKIN-TIGHT
GHIIKNTTT TIGHTKNIT
GHIILLNRT THRILLING
GHIILLNSS SHILLINGS
GHIILLRSY GIRLISHLY
GHIILNNWY WHININGLY
GHIILNOPS POLISHING
GHIILNOST NIGHT SOIL
GHIILNSTW WHISTLING
GHIILNTTW WHITTLING
GHIINNNSY SHINNYING
GHIINNNWY
WHINNYING
GHIINNOPS SIPHONING
GHIINNPSU PUNISHING
GHIINOPPT PIPING HOT
GHIINPPSW WHIPPINGS
GHIINQSSU SQUISHING

GHIIRSSTT RIGHTISTS
GHIKLSSTY SKYLIGHTS
GHILLNOOW
HOLLOWING
GHILLNOWY
HOWLINGLY
GHILLOOPY PHILOLOGY
GHILLOOTY LITHOLOGY
GHILMNOOT
MOONLIGHT
GHILNOOPT POTHOLING
GHILNOORY
RHINOLOGY
GHILNOPSS LONGSHIPS,
SPLOSHING
GHILNOSST SLINGSHOT
GHILNOSTW NIGHT
OWLS
GHILNPSUY PUSHINGLY
GHILNRSUY RUSHINGLY
GHILNSTTU SHUTTLING
GHILNSTUY UNSIGHTLY
GHILOOOPY OPHIOLOGY
GHILOOSTY HISTOLOGY
GHILOPSTT SPOTLIGHT,
STOPLIGHT
GHILORSSW SHOWGIRLS
GHILORSUY ROGUISHLY
GHILOSTTU LIGHTS-OUT
GHILPRSTY SPRIGHTLY
GHILPRTUY UPRIGHTLY
GHIMMNRTU
THRUMMING
GHIMNOOST
SMOOTHING
GHIMNORUU
HUMOURING
GHIMNSSTU GUNSMITHS
GHIMOOPSS GOMPHOSIS
GHINNOORU
HONOURING
GHINNOPSY SYPHONING
GHINNORSU
ONRUSHING, UNHORSING
GHINOOSST SHOOTINGS
GHINOTUWY WITH
YOUNG
GHINRSTTU THRUSTING
GHJLNNOOS LONG
JOHNS
GHLLOOOPY
HOPLOLOGY
GHLMOOTYY
MYTHOLOGY

GHLNOOOPY
PHONOLOGY
GHLNOOSST LONG
SHOTS
GHNNOOPRR
PRONGHORN
GHNOOSTTW GHOST
TOWN
GHOORTTUW
OUTGROWTH
GHOPRTUUW
WROUGHT-UP
GIIILNNOZ LIONIZING
GIIILNTUZ UTILIZING
GIIILOSTU LITIGIOUS
GIIIMMNST MISTIMING
GIIINNNOP PINIONING
GIIINNPRS INSPIRING
GIIINNQRU INQUIRING
GIIINNSST INSISTING
GIIINNTTU INTUITING
GIIINPRST SPIRITING
GIIINRTVY VIRGINITY
GIIJKNORS SKIJORING
GIIKLLLNY KILLINGLY
GIIKLNNOP LINKOPING
GIIKLNNRW WRINKLING
GIIKLNNTW TWINKLING
GIIKMMNSS SKIMMINGS
GIIKNSVVY SKIVVYING
GIILLLNWY WILLINGLY
GIILLMNPY LIMPINGLY
GIILLMNSY SMILINGLY
GIILLMRST GRISTMILL
GIILLNNUW UNWILLING
GIILLNOPW PILLOWING
GIILLNPSY LISPINGLY
GIILMNOPR IMPLORING
GIILMRSTU LITURGISM
GIILNNOTU OUTLINING
GIILNNOVV INVOLVING
GIILNNSTU INSULTING
GIILNOTUV OUTLIVING
GIILNPPST STIPPLING
GIILNPRST SPLIT RING,
STRIPLING
GIILNPRSY SPRINGILY
GIILNPSTT SPLITTING
GIILNPTYY PITYINGLY
GIILNQSSU QUISLINGS
GIILNRSTY STRINGILY
GIILNSSTU LINGUISTS
GIILNSTYZ STYLIZING
GIILOSSST GLOSSITIS

GIILPSSTU PUGILISTS
GIILRSTTU LITURGIST
GIIMMNRST TRIMMINGS
GIIMNNOOT
MOTIONING
GIIMNNTUY MUTINYING
GIIMNOPRS PROMISING
GIIMNOPRT IMPORTING
GIIMNOPRV IMPROVING
GIIMNORRR MIRRORING
GIIMNOTTW TWO-
TIMING
GIIMNQRSU SQUIRMING
GIIMNRSSU SURMISING
GIINNNOWW
WINNOWING
GIINNOOPS POISONING
GIINNPPUZ UNZIPPING
GIINNPRST PRINTINGS,
SPRINTING
GIINNPTTU INPUTTING
GIINNQSTU SQUINTING
GIINNTTUW UNWITTING
GIINOPRST RIPOSTING
GIINPPRST STRIPPING
GIINPRSSU UPRISINGS
GIINQRSTU SQUIRTING
GIINRSUVV SURVIVING
GIJKNNOOP JONKOPING
GIKLLNRUY LURKINGLY
GIKLNNOOO
ONLOOKING
GIKLNNOWY
KNOWINGLY
GIKLNOOOY
KONIOLOGY
GIKNNNOUW
UNKNOWING
GIKNNOSTW
KINGSTOWN
GIKNOOPRV PROVOKING
GIKNOOTWW
KOWTOWING
GILLLLNOY LOLLINGLY
GILLLLNUY LULLINGLY
GILLLNOOP LOLLOPING
GILLLNORY ROLLINGLY
GILLMNOOY
LIMNOLOGY
GILLMOORR
GRILLROOM
GILLMOSSY SYLLOGISM
GILLNNORU UNROLLING
GILLNOPSY SLOPINGLY

GILLNOPTU POLLUTING
GILLNORST STROLLING
GILLOOOPY OLIGOPOLY
GILMMNOOS
MONGOLISM
GILMNNQTY
LYMINGTON
GILMNOPRY ROMPINGLY
GILMOOSTY MYOLOGIST
GILNNOOSU UNLOOSING
GILNNRSSU NURSLINGS
GILNOPTUY POUTINGLY
GILNOSTUU GLUTINOUS
GILNPPSUY SUPPLYING
GILNSSTUU SINGULTUS
GILOOORST OROLOGIST
GILOOOSSU ISOLOGOUS
GILOOOSTT OTOLOGIST
GILOOOSTZ ZOOLOGIST
GILOORSTU UROLOGIST
GIMMNNOSU
SUMMONING
GIMMNPSUU SUMMING-
UP
GIMMNRRUU
MURMURING
GIMMNRSTU
STRUMMING
GIMMNNOORS
MONSIGNOR
GIMNOOPRT
PROMOTING
GIMNOPPRT PROMPTING
GIMOPRUUY
UROPYGIUM
GINNOSUUU UNGUINOUS
GINNRRTUU NURTURING
GINOOPPRS PROPOSING
GINOOPRSS PROGNOSIS
GINOOPRTU UPROOTING
GINOORRSW
SORROWING
GINOORSTU TRIGONOUS
GINOOTTUV
OUTVOTING
GINOPPRSU PURPOSING
GINOPPSSU SUPPOSING
GINOPRSTU POSTURING,
SPROUTING
GINOPSSST SIGNPOSTS
GINORRTTU TORTURING
GINPRRTUU RUPTURING
GINRSTTTU STRUTTING
GIOPRSTWY GIPSYWORT

GLLOOPSTY POLYGLOTS
GLMNOOPUY
POLYGONUM
GLMOORSWW GLOW-
WORMS
GLNOOOSTY
NOSTOLOGY
GLOOOPRTY
TROPOLOGY
GMMNOSTUY TOMMY
GUNS
GMNOORSSW MOSS-
GROWN
GNOOOPRSY
SPOROGONY
GNOOPRTYY
PROTOGYNY
GNORSTTUU STRUNG-
OUT
HHILNNSUY HUNNISHLY
HHLMOOPYY
HOMOPHYLY
HHMNOOOPY
HOMOPHONY
HHNOORRST
SHORTHORN
HHORRSSUU RUSH
HOURS
HIIILNSST NIHILISTS
HIILLMNOT MILLIONTH
HIILLOOOP HOI POLLOI
HIILNSSWY SWINISHLY
HIILOSTTY HOSTILITY
HIILPSTTY TYPHLITIS
HIILRSTTY THIRSTILY
HIIMOPSTU HOSPITIUM
HIIMORSST HIT-OR-MISS
HIKLMOOTT MILK
TOOTH
HIKNNORST STINKHORN
HILLLMTUU MULTIHULL
HILLOOPRW WHIRLPOOL
HILLSSTYY STYLISHLY
HILMNOOST
MONOLITHS
HILMOOSSY HOMOLYSIS
HILMOOTTY
LITHOTOMY
HILOOPTXY TOXOPHILY
HILORSSTT SHORT LIST
HIMNOPSTY HYPNOTISM
HIMOOPRSS MORPHOSIS
HIMOORTYZ
RHIZOTOMY

HIMORSSTU HUMORISTS
HIMPSSSYY SYMPHYSIS
HINOPPRRY PORPHYRIN
HINOPRSUU ONUPHRIUS
HINOPSSTW TOWNSHIPS
HINOPSTTY HYPNOTIST
HIOOPPRST TROOPSHIP
HIOPRSSTY SOPHISTRY
HIORRSTTY THYRISTOR
HKKNNOOTY HONKY-
TONK
HKMOOOORSW
HOOKWORMS
HKOOPRSSW
WORKSHOPS
HLLNOOOORR HONOR
ROLL
HLLPRSUUY SULPHURYL
HLMOOPPRY
POLYMORPH
HLNOOPPYY
POLYPHONY
HLNOORSTU
SOLOTHURN
HMMOORSSU
MUSHROOMS
HMNNOOOOPY
MONOPHONY
HMNOOOSST MOON
SHOTS
HMOOOPRSY
HOMOSPORY
HMOOORSSW
SHOWROOMS
HNOOPPTYY
PHONOTYPY
HNOOPRSST POST
HORNS
HNOOPRTTY
PHYTOTRON
HOOORTTTW
TOOTHWORT
HOOOSSTTU SHOOT-
OUTS
IIIKLLNPS SPILLIKIN
IIIKMNRST MINISKIRT
IIILNOSTV VIOLINIST
IIILNTTUY INUTILITY
IIINNOTTU INTUITION
IIINPRSSU NISI PRIUS
IIINSSSTU SINUSITIS
IIJNORSUU INJURIOUS
IIKLLMPST SPILT MILK
IIKNNNOOS ONIONSKIN

IILLMNOPU POLLINIUM
IILLMPRSU SPIRILLUM
IILLNNNOO NONILLION
IILLNORST TRILLIONS
IILLNOSSU ILLUSIONS
IILLOPSSY LIPOLYSIS
IILLOSTVY VILLOSITY
IILMMMSSU MUSLIMISM
IILMNOOPS IMPLOSION
IILMNOPSU IMPULSION
IILMOPSSS SOLIPSISM
IILMOPSUY IMPIOUSLY
IILNOOPST POSTILION
IILOPRTXY PROLIXITY
IILOPSSST SOLIPSIST
IILOSTVVZ SLIVOVITZ
IIMNNOSTU MUNITIONS
IIMNOOSSS OMISSIONS
IIMNORSTU MINOR SUIT,
ROUTINISM
IIMNPRSST MISPRINTS
IIMOPRTXY PROXIMITY
IIMOPSSTT OPTIMISTS
IIMOQSTUX QUIXOTISM
IIMORSTTU TUTIORISM
IINNOORST INTORSION
IINNOPPST PINPOINTS
IINNORSTU INTRUSION
IINNORTTU NUTRITION
IINNOSSTU UNIONISTS
IINOOPRSV PROVISION
IINOOPSST POSITIONS
IINOOPSVY POISON IVY
IINOORSTT SORTITION
IINOPRRTU IRRUPTION
IINOPSSTY SPINOSITY
IINORSTTU ROUTINIST
IINOSSTUY SINUOSITY
IINOSSTVY SYNOVITIS
IIOOPRSST SPIRITOSO
IIOPSTTTU SPIT IT OUT!
IIORSTTTU TUTIORIST
IJMNOORTW
JOINTWORM
IJMPSSTUU JUMPSUITS
IKLMORSSW SILKWORMS
IKLNOPSST SLIPKNOTS
IKNOORRSW
IRONWORKS
IKORSSTTU OUTSKIRTS
ILLLMOPSS PLIMSOLLS
ILLLOOPPS LOLLIPOPS
ILLLPSUUV PULVILLUS
ILLNOOPTU POLLUTION

ILLNOPVYY POLYVINYL
ILLOOQSUY SOLILOQUY
ILLOORSSW SLOW LORIS
ILLOQRTUW QUILLWORT
ILLORSSSW SWISS ROLL
ILMNOOSUY OMINOUSLY
ILMNOPTUU PLUTONIUM
ILMNOPXYY POLYMYXIN
ILMOSSYYZ ZYMOLYSIS
ILNOOPRSU PROLUSION
ILNOOSSTU SOLUTIONS
ILNOOSUXY NOXIOUSLY
ILNOPRXYY PYROXYLIN
ILNORSUUY RUINOUSLY
ILNOSSUUY SINUOUSLY
ILOOPPRSY ISOPROPYL
ILOORSTUY RIOTOUSLY
ILOPPSSTU POPULISTS
ILOPRSSYY PYROLYSIS
ILORSUUUX LUXURIOUS
IMMMNOORS
MORMONISM
IMMOPPRTU
IMPROMPTU
IMMOPSSUY SYMPOSIUM
IMNNOOPTW
TOPMINNOW
IMNOOOOPRT
PROMOTION
IMNOOOOPTT MOOT
POINT
IMNORSTTU STRONTIUM
IMOOOSTTZ
ZOOTOMIST
IMOOPPSTY POMPOSITY
IMOOPRSST IMPOSTORS
IMOOQSSTU MOSQUITOS
IMOORSSTT MOTORISTS
IMORSUVXY MYXOVIRUS
INNOOSSUU UNISONOUS
INOOOPSSU POISONOUS
INOOORSTU NOTORIOUS
INOOPPTTU PUT OPTION
INOOPRSST POSITRONS
INOOPSSTT SPITTOONS
INOPRSTTU PRINTOUTS
INORSSSUV SUN VISORS
INRSTTTUU UNIT TRUST
IOOPPRRTU POTPOURRI
IOOPPRSST PROPTOSIS
IOOPRRSVY PROVISORY
IOORSSTUV VIRTUOSOS
IORRSSUVV SURVIVORS
KLLMNSSUU NUMSKULLS

KMOOORRSW   MMOOPPRSU PUMP   MOOOORRSTW
  WORKROOMS   ROOMS   TOMORROWS
LMOOPPSUY POMPOUSLY   MNNOOOPSY   MOPSSTUUU SUMPTUOUS
LMOORSSWW   MONOPSONY   NOOOPPSSU SOUP SPOON
  SLOWWORMS   MNOORSSTU   OOPRSSTUU STUPOROUS
LNOOOPRST POLTROONS   MONSTROUS   OOPRTTTUY
LOOPRRSUY PROLUSORY   MNOORSSTW   PUTTYROOT
LORSTUUUV VULTUROUS   SNOWSTORM

TEN-LETTER WORDS

AAAAABCCRS ASARABACCA   AAABCEGGNR GARBAGE CAN
AAAABBDDIS ADDIS ABABA   AAABCEHLSS CALABASHES
AAAABCCLNS CASABLANCA   AAABCEHLTT ATTACHABLE
AAAABCLLSV BALACLAVAS   AAABCELLLR CLARABELLA
AAAABCNNTU CABANATUAN   AAABCERSSU SCARABAEUS
AAAABGKORY KABARAGOYA   AAABCIILST BASILICATA
AAAABHJRSY RAJYA SABHA   AAABCIKLMR BLACK MARIA
AAAABIKLLS BALALAIKAS   AAABCIKRSS CASSIA BARK
AAAACDGMNS MADAGASCAN   AAABCINNRT CANTABRIAN
AAAACDGMRS MADAGASCAR   AAABCLLMRU AMBULACRAL
AAAACGMNRT MAGNA CARTA   AAABCLNOST CANAL BOATS
AAAACHILPP APPALACHIA   AAABDEEGLM DAMAGEABLE
AAAACILPST CATAPLASIA   AAABDEHLRZ HAZARDABLE
AAAACINNRU ARAUCANIAN   AAABDEORVW ABOVE AWARD
AAAACLNRST SANTA CLARA   AAABDMNRRU BARRAMUNDA
AAAACMNRST CATAMARANS   AAABDMORSS AMBASSADOR
AAAADFNRWY FAR AND AWAY   AAABEEGLMN MANAGEABLE
AAAADIJVWY VIJAYAWADA   AAABEELLPP APPEALABLE
AAAADILLMS DALAI LAMAS   AAABEELMNS ABLE SEAMAN
AAAAEGLMMT AMALGAMATE   AAABEELPPS APPEASABLE
AAAAGGGGWW WAGGA WAGGA   AAABEGLMNY MANAGEABLY
AAAAGMSSSU MASSASAUGA   AAABEIJNRZ AZERBAIJAN
AAAAGNPRUY PARAGUAYAN   AAABEILLMR MARIABELLA
AAAAIMNNNP PANAMANIAN   AAABEILLSS ASSAILABLE
AAAAIMNRST SANTA MARIA   AAABEILNTT ATTAINABLE
AAAAKKKLPR KARA-KALPAK   AAABEKRSWY BREAKAWAYS
AAAALMNRSZ SALMANAZAR   AAABELLNSY ANALYSABLE
AAAAMNRSTT SANTA MARTA   AAABELLNYZ ANALYZABLE
AAABBCCHMO COCHABAMBA   AAABELNRRT NARRATABLE
AAABBCILST SABBATICAL   AAABELRSTW BASALTWARE
AAABBEIRSS BESSARABIA   AAABHIOPQU AQUAPHOBIA
AAABBINRRS BARBARIANS   AAABIKLNPP BALIKPAPAN
AAABCCHLNS BACCHANALS   AAABIKNNNS BANANA SKIN
AAABCCHNRS CHARABANCS   AAABILLNOS LABIONASAL
AAABCCKNSV CANVASBACK   AAABILRSTV BRATISLAVA
AAABCDEIRS SCARABAEID   AAABIMNPRS PAN-ARABISM
AAABCDELNR CANDELABRA   AAACCDELSV CAVALCADES
AAABCDRRSU BARRACUDAS   AAACCEHRSS SACCHARASE
AAABCEGGGR BAGGAGE CAR   AAACCEHRST SACCHARATE

AAACCEIPTT CAPACITATE
AAACCENRUV CUERNAVACA
AAACCILLNT CATACLINAL
AAACCILLRS CASCARILLA
AAACCINRTT ANTARCTICA
AAACCIPRTT PARATACTIC
AAACDEIMMS MACADAMISE
AAACDEIMMZ MACADAMIZE
AAACDEKNPY PANCAKE DAY
AAACDELMNR CALAMANDER
AAACDELMRS SALAD CREAM
AAACDGIILR CARDIALGIA
AAACDHINNR ARACHNIDAN
AAACDILNOP PIÑA COLADA
AAACDILRTY CARYATIDAL
AAACEENPPR APPEARANCE
AAACEENRSS CAESAREANS
AAACEFLQTU CATAFALQUE
AAACEGNORT ARCTOGAEAN
AAACEHLNSV AVALANCHES
AAACEILMNT CATAMENIAL
AAACEINNRT CATENARIAN
AAACEINPST ANAPAESTIC, SEA CAPTAIN
AAACEINRRS SARRACENIA
AAACEJKNPS JACKANAPES
AAACELLNPT APLACENTAL
AAACELMPRT METACARPAL
AAACGHNRTT TRAGACANTH
AAACGILLMY AGAMICALLY
AAACGILLNO ANALOGICAL
AAACGINNRU NICARAGUAN
AAACHINPRT CARPATHIAN
AAACHLNOTU TALCAHUANO
AAACHLNRST CHARLATANS
AAACHNPRTY PYRACANTHA
AAACIINNPR INCAPARINA
AAACIIRSSS ASCARIASIS
AAACIKLMNP PACK ANIMAL
AAACIKLMNR LAMARCKIAN
AAACILLMNY MANIACALLY
AAACILLRTU URAL-ALTAIC
AAACILMMNO AMMONIACAL
AAACILMNOT ANATOMICAL
AAACILNPST ANAPLASTIC
AAACILNRSS CARNASSIAL
AAACILNRST SCARLATINA
AAACINOPRS PARANOIACS
AAACISSSTT CATASTASIS
AAACLMNRVY CAVALRYMAN
AAACLNSSTU SANTA CLAUS
AAACNORSSU ANASARCOUS
AAADEELLNV AVELLANEDA
AAADEELNRW DELAWAREAN
AAADEFIOST ASAFOETIDA

AAADEGGRTV AGGRAVATED
AAADEGHMNR AHMEDNAGAR
AAADEGLMTY AMYGDALATE
AAADEGNRTV AVANT-GARDE
AAADEGNSTV ADVANTAGES
AAADEHLPRT HARD PALATE
AAADEILNRX ALEXANDRIA
AAADEIMNNT ADAMANTINE
AAADELMNRS SALAMANDER
AAADELMPPS ADAM'S APPLE
AAADELNPQU AQUAPLANED
AAADGIILLR GAILLARDIA
AAADGILLNR GRANADILLA
AAADGINNPT GIANT PANDA
AAADGLLNOR ALLARGANDO
AAADGNOPPR PROPAGANDA
AAADHHMRTU HADHRAMAUT
AAADHMMMNU MUHAMMADAN
AAADIILNPR LAPIDARIAN
AAADILMNST DALMATIANS
AAADILMORR RADIO ALARM
AAADILNOPS DIAPASONAL
AAADINOPTT ADAPTATION
AAADLNQRTU QUADRANTAL
AAADORSTTU AUTOSTRADA
AAAEEGGLRS GARAGE SALE
AAAEFLLMRS FALSE ALARM
AAAEFLMNST MALFEASANT
AAAEGHIOPR AEROPHAGIA
AAAEGHLLNP PHALANGEAL
AAAEGILMNR MANAGERIAL
AAAEGILNST EAST ANGLIA
AAAEGILPPR PARAPLEGIA
AAAEGINPRS ASPARAGINE
AAAEGLMTXY METAGALAXY
AAAEGMRRTT MARGARETTA
AAAEGNNTTT AT A TANGENT
AAAEGPSSWY PASSAGEWAY
AAAEHHLSSV HAVE A SLASH
AAAEHIMRTU HAEMATURIA
AAAEHINSTU EUTHANASIA
AAAEHKNOTT TAKE AN OATH
AAAEHPPRRS PARAPHRASE
AAAEIILNTT ITALIANATE
AAAEILLPST PALATALISE
AAAEILLPTZ PALATALIZE
AAAEILMPST METAPLASIA
AAAEILMRTU TULARAEMIA
AAAEILNPRT PLANETARIA
AAAEILNPTT PALATINATE
AAAEIMNPRS PARAMNESIA
AAAEIMNQRU AQUAMARINE
AAAEINNRTV TANANARIVE
AAAELLNRTT TARANTELLA

AAAELMMRST ALMA MATERS
AAAELNPQSU AQUAPLANES
AAAFFIILNN FIANNA FAIL
AAAFIKPRRS SAFARI PARK
AAAGGILLNO ALGOLAGNIA
AAAGGILRST GASTRALGIA
AAAGGNNRTU GARGANTUAN
AAAGHILRRT ARTHRALGIA
AAAGHIMNOP PHAGOMANIA
AAAGHNPSTU AGAPANTHUS
AAAGHPPRRS PARAGRAPHS
AAAGIILMNR MARGINALIA
AAAGIKNNTY TANGANYIKA
AAAGIMMNRR GRAMMARIAN
AAAGIMNSTT ANASTIGMAT
AAAGIMRRST MARGARITAS
AAAGJJKORT JOGJAKARTA
AAAGJLNRUW GUJRANWALA
AAAGJNOTUU GUANAJUATO
AAAGLNRSTU NATURAL GAS
AAAGLRSSTU ASTRAGALUS
AAAGMNNOTU GUANTANAMO
AAAHLLOSTY AYATOLLAHS
AAAHLMNPST PHANTASMAL
AAAHNPRRSU SAHARANPUR
AAAIIMNRTU MAURITANIA
AAAIINNRST SANITARIAN
AAAILLLPTY PALATIALLY
AAAILLMNNZ MANZANILLA
AAAILLMRTW MARTIAL LAW
AAAILLNOTV LAVATIONAL
AAAILLORTV LAVATORIAL
AAAILMPSTU TAMAULIPAS
AAAILMRRTT MARTIAL ART
AAAILNNOTT NATATIONAL
AAAILNOTTX TAXATIONAL
AAAILNRSTU AUSTRALIAN, SATURNALIA
AAAILNSSST ASSAILANTS
AAAILOPRSV VALPARAISO
AAAILPPRSS APPRAISALS
AAAIMNORST INAMORATAS
AAAIMNRSST SAMARITANS
AAAIPPRRSX PARAPRAXIS
AAALMNOPRR PARANORMAL
AAALNNOSST ASSONANTAL
AAALNRSTTU TARANTULAS
AAAMRTZZZZ RAZZMATAZZ
AABBBELORS ABSORBABLE
AABBCDKLOR BLACKBOARD
AABBCEEHLL BLEACHABLE
AABBCEHLLS BEACH BALLS
AABBCEILRS ASCRIBABLE
AABBCELMOT COMBATABLE
AABBCENORS ABSORBANCE

AABBCIILNR RABBINICAL
AABBCIJKRT JACKRABBIT
AABBDDEENN BADEN-BADEN
AABBDDEORR BREADBOARD
AABBDEGILR ABRIDGABLE
AABBDEIRRS BARBARISED
AABBDEIRRZ BARBARIZED
AABBDELORS ADSORBABLE
AABBDENORS BROAD BEANS
AABBDEOORV ABOVEBOARD
AABBDNRSSS BRASS BANDS
AABBEEIRTV ABBREVIATE
AABBEELLRT BARBELLATE
AABBEELNRU UNBEARABLE
AABBEELNTU UNBEATABLE
AABBEILMNO ABOMINABLE
AABBEILNOT OBTAINABLE
AABBEILRRT ARBITRABLE
AABBEKLLST BASKETBALL
AABBELLOSV ABSOLVABLE
AABBELNRUY UNBEARABLY
AABBILMNOY ABOMINABLY
AABBIMRRSS BARBARISMS
AABBMMNPYY NAMBY-PAMBY
AABBNNUUYY BUNYA-BUNYA
AABCCDELOR ACCORDABLE
AABCCEELPT ACCEPTABLE
AABCCEHHIR BEACHCHAIR
AABCCEKKPR BACKPACKER
AABCCEKPSS BACKSPACES
AABCCELLLU CALCULABLE
AABCCELOST ACCOSTABLE
AABCCELPTY ACCEPTABLY
AABCCGIKLM BLACK MAGIC
AABCCHHKST HATCHBACKS
AABCCIINRT BACITRACIN
AABCCIKNRR CRACKBRAIN
AABCCILNSS CABIN CLASS
AABCCIORST ACROBATICS
AABCCJKKLS BLACKJACKS
AABCDDEELU ADDUCEABLE
AABCDDEHKN BACKHANDED
AABCDDEIRR BARRICADED
AABCDDEKLS SADDLEBACK
AABCDEEEFL DEFACEABLE
AABCDEEHHS BEACHHEADS
AABCDEEHLT DETACHABLE
AABCDEEILR ERADICABLE
AABCDEELLR DECLARABLE
AABCDEFIRT FABRICATED
AABCDEHKLS BLACKHEADS
AABCDEHKLT BLACK DEATH
AABCDEHKNR BACKHANDER
AABCDEIITV ABDICATIVE

AABCDEILRT CALIBRATED
AABCDEIRRR BARRICADER
AABCDEIRRS BARRICADES
AABCDELNNU UNBALANCED
AABCDELORS SCALEBOARD
AABCDELORT CARBOLATED
AABCDENNRS BARN DANCES
AABCDENORT CARBONATED
AABCDERSTT ABSTRACTED
AABCDGIINT ABDICATING
AABCDGIKNT BACKDATING
AABCDGKLRU BLACKGUARD
AABCDHKLOR CHALKBOARD
AABCDHMORT MATCHBOARD
AABCDIILLO DIABOLICAL
AABCDIINOT ABDICATION
AABCDILMMS LAMBDACISM
AABCDKLRWY BACKWARDLY
AABCDNNORT CONTRABAND
AABCDORSST BROADCASTS
AABCEEEFFL EFFACEABLE
AABCEEEMRR MACEBEARER
AABCEEERTT EBRACTEATE
AABCEEERTX EXACERBATE
AABCEEGHLN CHANGEABLE
AABCEEGHLR CHARGEABLE
AABCEEHILV ACHIEVABLE
AABCEEHLMP PEACH MELBA
AABCEEHLNS ENCASHABLE
AABCEEHLRS SEARCHABLE
AABCEEHLTY CHALYBEATE
AABCEEIRTU EUBACTERIA
AABCEEKLSS LEASEBACKS
AABCEELLLR RECALLABLE
AABCEELLNS CLEANSABLE
AABCEELNRT TABERNACLE
AABCEESTTU SUBACETATE
AABCEFLORT FACTORABLE
AABCEGHLNY CHANGEABLY
AABCEGIRRR CARRIER BAG
AABCEGLLOU COAGULABLE
AABCEGLMNN BLANCMANGE
AABCEHILMN MACHINABLE
AABCEHILRT CHARITABLE
AABCEHINRT BRANCHIATE
AABCEHKLRT BLACKHEART
AABCEHKLSS BACKLASHES
AABCEHLNST STANCHABLE
AABCEHRRTT TETRABRACH
AABCEIINTU BEAUTICIAN
AABCEILLMP IMPLACABLE
AABCEILLPP APPLICABLE
AABCEILMNS IMBALANCES
AABCEILMST MASTICABLE

AABCEILNOT ACTIONABLE
AABCEILOSS ASSOCIABLE
AABCEILOTT CATABOLITE
AABCEILQRU ACQUIRABLE
AABCEINORT ABREACTION
AABCEIORST AEROBATICS
AABCEIRSTT TETRABASIC
AABCEKKLNS BLACKSNAKE
AABCEKPPRS PAPERBACKS
AABCEKRSTW BACKWATERS
AABCELMNSU AMBULANCES
AABCELMOPR COMPARABLE
AABCELMTUU ACETABULUM
AABCELNOTU OUTBALANCE
AABCELOOSS CALABOOSES
AABCELPPRS CRAB APPLES
AABCELRRTU TRABECULAR
AABCERRTUU BUREAUCRAT
AABCFHKLSS FLASHBACKS
AABCFIORRT FABRICATOR
AABCGIKNRR BARRACKING
AABCGILLSU SUBGLACIAL
AABCGKMMNO BACKGAMMON
AABCGLRRTU CAT BURGLAR
AABCHHIMPR AMPHIBRACH
AABCHHIRST BATH CHAIRS
AABCHHPSTY BATHYSCAPH
AABCHILRTY CHARITABLY
AABCHINOTT COHABITANT
AABCHIOOPR ACROPHOBIA
AABCHKLPSS SPLASHBACK
AABCHNRRUY BRACHYURAN
AABCIILLMY IAMBICALLY
AABCIILNOT ANABOLITIC
AABCIILPTY CAPABILITY
AABCIILTTY ACTABILITY
AABCIIOPRT PARABIOTIC
AABCIKRSST BACKSTAIRS
AABCILMOPR PROCAMBIAL
AABCILMOST CATABOLISM
AABCILNNUU INCUNABULA
AABCILNSUV SUBCLAVIAN
AABCILORRT CALIBRATOR
AABCILRRUV VIBRACULAR
AABCIQSTUU SUBAQUATIC
AABCKLMOOR BLACKAMOOR
AABCKRSSST BRASS TACKS
AABCLLNNNO CANNONBALL
AABCLMMRUU AMBULACRUM
AABCLMOPRY COMPARABLY
AABCLORUVY VOCABULARY
AABCMNOSTT COMBATANTS
AABCNORSST CONTRABASS
AABDDDEEHL BALDHEADED

AABDDEEEHR BAREHEADED
AABDDEEGLR DEGRADABLE
AABDDEELMN DEMANDABLE
AABDDEGGNS SANDBAGGED
AABDDEGLSS SADDLEBAGS
AABDDEHLMO HEBDOMADAL
AABDDEHLRS BALDERDASH
AABDDEHORS HEADBOARDS
AABDDEILRY DAILY BREAD
AABDDEMRTU ADUMBRATED
AABDDHORSS DASHBOARDS
AABDDNNSST BANDSTANDS
AABDDORRST DARTBOARDS
AABDEEELMS SEALED-BEAM
AABDEEFLRY DEFRAYABLE
AABDEEGLRR REGARDABLE
AABDEEHLLN HANDLEABLE
AABDEEHRRT THREADBARE
AABDEEILNT DETAINABLE
AABDEELNPX EXPANDABLE
AABDEELNRU UNREADABLE
AABDEELORT ELABORATED
AABDEELPRS SPREADABLE
AABDEELRRW REWARDABLE
AABDEFFLOR AFFORDABLE
AABDEGGGNN GANG-BANGED
AABDEGGNRS SANDBAGGER
AABDEGGORU BROAD GAUGE
AABDEGHLNS BANGLADESH
AABDEGINRS GABARDINES
AABDEGORST GOATSBEARD
AABDEHITTU HABITUATED
AABDEHKNRS HANDBRAKES
AABDEHLLNR HANDBALLER
AABDEHLNRS HANDLEBARS
AABDEIKNUZ ADZUKI BEAN
AABDEILLNR BANDERILLA
AABDEILLSY DIALYSABLE
AABDEILLYZ DIALYZABLE
AABDEILRSV ADVERBIALS
AABDEIMNOT ABOMINATED
AABDEINNRR BERNARDINA
AABDEIQRTU BIQUADRATE
AABDEIRRTT ARBITRATED
AABDEIRSST BASTARDISE
AABDEIRSTZ BASTARDIZE
AABDEJLSTU ADJUSTABLE
AABDEKLNRU DARK NEBULA
AABDEKORST SKATEBOARD
AABDELLNNO BELLADONNA
AABDELLNST TABLELANDS
AABDELNOPR PARDONABLE
AABDELNRUY UNREADABLY
AABDELRSTU BALUSTRADE

AABDEMNNNO ONE-MAN BAND
AABDEMNNRS BRAND NAMES
AABDEMNRST BANDMASTER
AABDEMORST DREAMBOATS
AABDENSSTW SWEATBANDS
AABDEOPPRR PAPERBOARD
AABDEOPRST PASTEBOARD
AABDFHIINT IN BAD FAITH
AABDFHLORS FLASHBOARD
AABDFKNRST BANK DRAFTS
AABDGIILNW LAW-ABIDING
AABDGIKNOS BAKING SODA
AABDGINNNO ABANDONING
AABDGNNOSW BANDWAGONS
AABDHLORRU HARD LABOUR
AABDHMNNSU HUSBANDMAN
AABDHNORRW HANDBARROW
AABDIIKRRY DIYARBAKIR
AABDIINNRR BRAIN DRAIN
AABDIJOORU OUIJA BOARD
AABDILOOPR PARABOLOID
AABDILORSS SAILBOARDS
AABDILORST TAILBOARDS
AABDINSSTW WAISTBANDS
AABDKLORSW BOARDWALKS
AABDLNNTUY ABUNDANTLY
AABDLNOPRY PARDONABLY
AABDLNOSTU BASUTOLAND
AABDLORSUY LABOUR DAYS
AABDORRSTW STRAWBOARD
AABEEELLPR REPEALABLE
AABEEELLRV REVEALABLE
AABEEELMNS ABLE SEAMEN
AABEEELPRT REPEATABLE
AABEEELRRT TALEBEARER
AABEEFHORT FEATHER BOA
AABEEFILRR RAREFIABLE
AABEEFLLLT FLABELLATE
AABEEFLNTT FATTENABLE
AABEEGHLRT GATHERABLE
AABEEGILNR REGAINABLE
AABEEGIMNS SENEGAMBIA
AABEEGINRR BERENGARIA
AABEEGLMSS ASSEMBLAGE
AABEEGNORT BARONETAGE
AABEEHKRRT HEARTBREAK
AABEEHRSTT HEARTBEATS
AABEEILLRZ REALIZABLE
AABEEILMNX EXAMINABLE
AABEEILNRT RETAINABLE
AABEEILPRR REPAIRABLE
AABEEJKRRW JAWBREAKER
AABEEKLMRR REMARKABLE
AABEEKLMRT MARKETABLE

AABEEKLRRW LAW-BREAKER
AABEEKRRTW BREAKWATER
AABEELLMNT LAMENTABLE
AABEELLNSU UNSEALABLE
AABEELLPRR PALLBEARER
AABEELMRSU MEASURABLE
AABEELMSST BASE METALS
AABEELMSTT METASTABLE
AABEELNORS REASONABLE
AABEELNOSS SEASONABLE
AABEELNPTT PATENTABLE
AABEELNRSW ANSWERABLE
AABEELOPRV EVAPORABLE
AABEELPPRT PALPEBRATE
AABEELPPRY PREPAYABLE
AABEELRTTW WATER TABLE
AABEELSSSS ASSESSABLE
AABEELSTTT ATTESTABLE
AABEELSTTX BATTLEAXES
AABEEQRSSU ARABESQUES
AABEFGIILS GASIFIABLE
AABEFGKLNR KLANGFARBE
AABEFHIKRT BREAK FAITH
AABEFHLMOT FATHOMABLE
AABEFIILLS SALIFIABLE
AABEFIILRT RATIFIABLE
AABEFILLNT INFLATABLE
AABEFINRRT AFTERBRAIN
AABEFKRSST BREAKFASTS
AABEFLORUV FAVOURABLE
AABEGHORRU HARBOURAGE
AABEGIILMN IMAGINABLE
AABEGILNSS ASSIGNABLE
AABEGILRST ALGEBRAIST
AABEGINNOT ABNEGATION
AABEGLOPPR PROPAGABLE
AABEHIILTT HABILITATE
AABEHILORV BEHAVIORAL
AABEHIOOPR AEROPHOBIA
AABEHKLNSU UNSHAKABLE
AABEIILNRV INVARIABLE
AABEIILNST BANALITIES, INSATIABLE
AABEIILPRT BIPARIETAL
AABEIILSST ASSIBILATE
AABEIIMOSS AMOEBIASIS
AABEIINNST IN ABSENTIA
AABEIIRRTT ABIRRITATE
AABEIJKLRS JAILBREAKS
AABEIJLOSU BEAUJOLAIS
AABEIKLMST MISTAKABLE
AABEILLMPP IMPALPABLE
AABEILLNRS BALLERINAS
AABEILLNUV INVALUABLE
AABEILLORV LABIOVELAR

AABEILLRYZ REALIZABLY
AABEILMMRU BARIUM MEAL
AABEILMNTU ALBUMINATE
AABEILMNTV AMBIVALENT
AABEILMPSS IMPASSABLE
AABEILNNTU BIANNULATE
AABEILOPRS PARABOLISE
AABEILOPRZ PARABOLIZE
AABEILRSTU TABULARISE
AABEILRSVY ABRASIVELY
AABEILRTTT TITRATABLE
AABEILRTUZ TABULARIZE
AABEIMPRTV VAMPIRE BAT
AABEINORRT ABERRATION
AABEINORTT TRABEATION
AABEINRSST ABSTAINERS
AABEINRSVW BRAINWAVES
AABEIRRTTT BITARTRATE
AABEKLMRRY REMARKABLY
AABEKLMRTY MARKETABLY
AABEKNNRRU RUN A BANKER
AABEKRSSTT BASKET-STAR
AABELLLNNU ANNULLABLE
AABELLMNTY LAMENTABLY
AABELLNPUY UNPLAYABLE
AABELLORSV SLAVE LABOR
AABELMPRRU PREAMBULAR
AABELMRSUY MEASURABLY
AABELNORSY REASONABLY
AABELNOSSY SEASONABLY
AABELNRSWY ANSWERABLY
AABELOORRT ELABORATOR
AABELOPRRS POLAR BEARS
AABELOPRUV VAPOURABLE
AABELSTTTU STATUTABLE
AABEMOSSTT STEAMBOATS
AABEMRSTTU MASTURBATE
AABFFIILTY AFFABILITY
AABFLMNOTY FLAMBOYANT
AABFLORUVY FAVOURABLY
AABGGIINNR BARGAINING
AABGGILNRZ GLAZING-BAR
AABGGINORT ABROGATING
AABGGINOST SABOTAGING
AABGHILOOP ALGOPHOBIA
AABGIILNOR ABORIGINAL
AABGIINNST ABSTAINING
AABGILLNST BALLASTING
AABGILMNST LAMBASTING
AABGILNTTU TABULATING
AABGINNOTW ANGWANTIBO
AABGINOORT ABROGATION
AABGIRSSTU BASS GUITAR
AABGORSTVY GRAVY BOATS

AABHIIMNPS AMPHIBIANS
AABHIINNTT INHABITANT
AABHIINOTT HABITATION
AABHIKLLRU RUB' AL KHALI
AABHILLTUY HABITUALLY
AABHIMMNRS BRAHMANISM
AABHIMRTVZ BAR MITZVAH
AABHINSSSW WASHBASINS
AABHKKORSV KHABAROVSK
AABHLLLOOU HULLABALOO
AABIIILMTY AMIABILITY
AABIILLNOT LIBATIONAL
AABIILLSTY SALABILITY
AABIILMTTY TAMABILITY
AABIILNRRS LIBRARIANS
AABIILNRVY INVARIABLY
AABIILNSTY INSATIABLY
AABIILRTTY RATABILITY
AABIILTTXY TAXABILITY
AABIINNSSY ABYSSINIAN
AABIINPRST BIPARTISAN
AABIINRRTT ABIRRITANT
AABIIOPRSS PARABIOSIS
AABIJNORTU ABJURATION
AABIKLMSTY MISTAKABLY
AABILLRUVV BIVALVULAR
AABILMNOTU AMBULATION
AABILMRSST STRABISMAL
AABILNOORT ABORTIONAL
AABILNOSTT BATTALIONS
AABILNOTTU TABULATION
AABILOPRST PARABOLIST
AABIMNOORT ABOMINATOR
AABINNORTY ANTIBARYON
AABINORSTT BOAT TRAINS
AABINOSSTW BOATSWAINS
AABIORRRTT ARBITRATOR
AABKKOORRU KOOKABURRA
AABKLOSTUW WALKABOUTS
AABLLMNORY ABNORMALLY
AABLMORTUY AMBULATORY
AABLNOORSS SALOON BARS
AABLOORRTY LABORATORY
AABLOPRRTY LABOR PARTY
AABLOSSTTT STATOBLAST
AABNOORRTW NARROW BOAT
AABORRRSTU BARRATROUS
AACCCDEIIT ACETIC ACID
AACCCDENOR ACCORDANCE
AACCCDIILT LACTIC ACID
AACCCEENPT ACCEPTANCE
AACCCEILTT CATALECTIC
AACCCEIORT CACCIATORE
AACCCEOSTU CACTACEOUS

AACCCINRUY INACCURACY
AACCDDEHKN CACK-HANDED
AACCDEGHRR CHARGE CARD
AACCDEHIRS SACCHARIDE
AACCDEHNOR ARCHDEACON
AACCDEIIPR EPICARDIAC
AACCDEILNT ACCIDENTAL
AACCDEINTV VACCINATED
AACCDELLTU CALCULATED
AACCDELNOR CLADOCERAN
AACCDELPRS PLACE CARDS
AACCDELRST CAT'S CRADLE
AACCDENNSY ASCENDANCY
AACCDERSTY SCAREDY CAT
AACCDGIILR CARDIALGIC
AACCDHIORS SACCHAROID
AACCDHPRST SCRATCHPAD
AACCDIISTU DIACAUSTIC
AACCEEELRT ACCELERATE
AACCEEFFOT FACE-TO-FACE
AACCEEGPRS SCAPEGRACE
AACCEEKMRS MAKE SCARCE
AACCEELLNT CANCELLATE
AACCEELNRS CLEARANCES
AACCEELNRT ACCELERANT
AACCEENTTU ACCENTUATE
AACCEEORTV COACERVATE
AACCEFPRST SPACECRAFT
AACCEGHOST STAGECOACH
AACCEHILMN MECHANICAL
AACCEHIMNN MAIN CHANCE
AACCEHINNT CACHINNATE
AACCEHINRS SACCHARINE
AACCEHINRT CHAIN-REACT
AACCEHLNOT COELACANTH
AACCEHMNNO COMANCHEAN
AACCEHORSS SACCHAROSE
AACCEHRRST CHARACTERS
AACCEIIPST CAPACITIES
AACCEIIPTV CAPACITIVE
AACCEILPTT CATALEPTIC
AACCEINNOT CANONICATE
AACCEINORV COVARIANCE
AACCEINPRT PANCREATIC
AACCEINRTT CANTATRICE
AACCEINRTU INACCURATE
AACCEIRRTU CARICATURE
AACCEISTUV ACCUSATIVE
AACCEKOPPT COP A PACKET
AACCEKRRST RACETRACKS
AACCELMSTY CYCLAMATES
AACCELMTUU ACCUMULATE
AACCELORSU CALCAREOUS
AACCELRTUY ACCURATELY

AACCENRSTU CRUSTACEAN	**AACDEEELST** DE-ESCALATE
AACCFGILLU CALCIFUGAL	**AACDEEFHMS** SHAMEFACED
AACCFHIRSY SACCHARIFY	**AACDEEFHNR** FACE-HARDEN
AACCFILLRY FARCICALLY	**AACDEEGNOT** ANECDOTAGE
AACCFILRSU FASCICULAR	**AACDEEHNRS** CASE-HARDEN
AACCFINNRS FRANCISCAN	**AACDEEHRTX** EX CATHEDRA
AACCGHIORY HAGIOCRACY	**AACDEEIINT** TAENIACIDE
AACCGHOPRY CACOGRAPHY	**AACDEEINRT** DERACINATE
AACCGIILMN ACCLAIMING	**AACDEEINRV** CADAVERINE
AACCGILLNT CATCALLING	**AACDEEIPTT** DECAPITATE
AACCHIIRST ARCHAISTIC	**AACDEEITTV** DEACTIVATE
AACCHILNPY CHAPLAINCY	**AACDEEJLTU** EJACULATED
AACCHIMORT ACHROMATIC	**AACDEENNTT** ATTENDANCE
AACCHKLLUW CHUCKWALLA	**AACDEEPPRT** RATE-CAPPED
AACCHLNORY ACRONYCHAL	**AACDEFINRU** FRICANDEAU
AACCHNORST CAST ANCHOR	**AACDEFINST** FASCINATED
AACCHNOTYY CHATOYANCY	**AACDEFLORT** DEFALCATOR
AACCIILORS SACROILIAC	**AACDEFPSTY** PASTY-FACED
AACCIILPRT ACCIPITRAL	**AACDEGHHNR** CHARGE HAND
AACCIINPTY INCAPACITY	**AACDEGIMNP** CAMPAIGNED
AACCIINSTT TACTICIANS	**AACDEGISTT** CASTIGATED
AACCILLRUV CLAVICULAR	**AACDEGLOTU** CATALOGUED,
AACCILLTTY TACTICALLY	COAGULATED
AACCILMMUY IMMACULACY	**AACDEHHTTW** DEATHWATCH
AACCILNNOT CLACTONIAN	**AACDEHILNR** HERACLIDAN
AACCILNOOS OCCASIONAL	**AACDEHILNS** ENCHILADAS
AACCILPRST PRACTICALS	**AACDEHILRS** CHARLADIES
AACCINORST COSTA RICAN	**AACDEHILRT** TRACHEIDAL
AACCINOSTU ACCUSATION, ANACOUSTIC	**AACDEHINRS** SEDAN CHAIR
AACCINPTTY ANAPTYCTIC	**AACDEHJKLT** JACK THE LAD
AACCINRSTU ANACRUSTIC	**AACDEHKPRT** PACKTHREAD
AACCIOPRST CAPACITORS	**AACDEHLMTY** CHLAMYDATE
AACCIORTTU AUTOCRATIC	**AACDEHLNNS** CLEAN HANDS
AACCKLLMOR ALARM CLOCK	**AACDEHLORT** OCTAHEDRAL
AACCKRRSTT CART TRACKS	**AACDEHLRST** CATHEDRALS
AACCLLORTU CALCULATOR	**AACDEHNTTU** UNATTACHED
AACCLMSSTY CATACLYSMS	**AACDEHOPPR** APPROACHED
AACCLNOTTU CONTACTUAL	**AACDEHPRTU** PARACHUTED
AACCLNRRUU CARUNCULAR	**AACDEIINRR** IRRADIANCE
AACCMNORTY CARTOMANCY	**AACDEIIPRT** PAEDIATRIC
AACCNNOTTU ACCOUNTANT	**AACDEIIRTV** DIVARICATE
AACCNORSST SACROSANCT	**AACDEIJLTV** ADJECTIVAL
AACDDEEHLR DECAHEDRAL	**AACDEIKPRS** SICK PARADE
AACDDEEIMP AIDE-DE-CAMP	**AACDEILLTV** VACILLATED
AACDDEEIRT ERADICATED	**AACDEILMNO** DEMONIACAL
AACDDEEIST TEA CADDIES	**AACDEILMNR** ALDERMANIC
AACDDEEMRT DEMARCATED	**AACDEILNNO** CALEDONIAN
AACDDEIJTU ADJUDICATE	**AACDEILNOR** ANDROECIAL
AACDDEINST CANDIDATES	**AACDEILNSS** SCANDALISE
AACDDEKLPS PACKSADDLE	**AACDEILNSZ** SCANDALIZE
AACDDELNPS LANDSCAPED	**AACDEIMNNO** MACEDONIAN
AACDDIKNOR ADIRONDACK	**AACDEIMNTT** ADMITTANCE
AACDEEEFNS DEFEASANCE	**AACDEIMPRS** PARAMEDICS
AACDEEEHNX HEXADECANE	**AACDEIMSTT** MASTICATED

AACDEINNRT INCARNATED
AACDEINORU ECUADORIAN
AACDEINOTV VACATIONED
AACDEINQTU ACQUAINTED
AACDEINQUY INADEQUACY
AACDEINRTX TAXI DANCER
AACDEIORRT ERADICATOR
AACDEIOSST ASSOCIATED
AACDEIPTTV CAPTIVATED
AACDELMRSU CLEAR AS MUD
AACDELNOPR ENDOCARPAL
AACDELNPSS LANDSCAPES
AACDELNSST SANDCASTLE
AACDELORST SACERDOTAL
AACDELPTTU CATAPULTED
AACDEMORRR ARMORED CAR
AACDEMORRT DEMARCATOR
AACDEMRRST MASTER CARD
AACDENNNOS CANNONADES
AACDENNSST ASCENDANTS
AACDENPRST TAP DANCERS
AACDENRSTT TRANSACTED
AACDEOPRRS RADARSCOPE
AACDEORSUV CADAVEROUS
AACDFHINRT HANDICRAFT
AACDFIINOO AFICIONADO
AACDGHHINR CHANDIGARH
AACDGHNORR DRAG ANCHOR
AACDGILNPR PLACARDING
AACDGIMNSW MAGIC WANDS
AACDGIMORR CARDIOGRAM
AACDGINNPT TAP DANCING
AACDGINOTV ADVOCATING
AACDGNNOPW CAP AND GOWN
AACDGORSTU COASTGUARD
AACDHINORT ANTHRACOID
AACDHLNPSU LAUNCH PADS
AACDHPRRSS CARDSHARPS
AACDIIILMR MIRACIDIAL
AACDIILLRV LARVICIDAL
AACDIILMRS RADICALISM
AACDIILMRT MATRICIDAL
AACDIILPRR PARRICIDAL
AACDIILPRT PATRICIDAL
AACDIILSTT DIASTALTIC
AACDIIMNOS AMINO ACIDS
AACDILMNNO CALAMONDIN
AACDILMORY MYOCARDIAL
AACDINOOTV ADVOCATION
AACDIQRSTU QUADRATICS
AACDJNOTTU COADJUTANT
AACDLNOSSU SCANDALOUS
AACDLOSTUY ADACTYLOUS
AACDMMNNOT COMMANDANT

AACDNOORST OSTRACODAN
AACDOORTVY ADVOCATORY
AACEEEHKPS CHESAPEAKE
AACEEEKMPR PEACEMAKER
AACEEELMNP ELECAMPANE
AACEEELNOP PALAEOCENE
AACEEFIRST CAFETERIAS
AACEEFLSUV FACE VALUES
AACEEFRSSV FACE-SAVERS
AACEEGHNSS SEA CHANGES
AACEEGILLN ALLEGIANCE
AACEEGKPPR PREPACKAGE
AACEEGKPTT GET A PACKET
AACEEGLLRS LARGE-SCALE
AACEEGNOST ACT ONE'S AGE
AACEEHIKLN HAECKELIAN
AACEEHILNT CHATELAINE
AACEEHINNP PHENACAINE
AACEEHKPST CHEAPSKATE
AACEEHLMNR MENARCHEAL
AACEEHMNRY AERENCHYMA
AACEEHNNRT ANTHRACENE
AACEEHPPRS PAPER CHASE
AACEEILMRS CARAMELISE
AACEEILMRZ CARAMELIZE
AACEEILPRT ALTARPIECE
AACEEILRTV CALAVERITE, LACERATIVE
AACEEIMNPT EMANCIPATE
AACEEIMRTV MACERATIVE
AACEEIMSST SIAMESE CAT
AACEEIPPRT APPRECIATE
AACEEIRTTV REACTIVATE
AACEEITUVV EVACUATIVE
AACEEKMPRS PACEMAKERS
AACEEKRRST CARETAKERS
AACEELLNOT LANCEOLATE
AACEELLNST CLEAN SLATE
AACEELLORT REALLOCATE
AACEELLPRT CARPELLATE
AACEELMSTU EMASCULATE
AACEELNTTU CATENULATE
AACEELOPRT CAPREOLATE
AACEELOPSU PALEACEOUS
AACEENORSU ARENACEOUS
AACEENPRSS PANCREASES
AACEEPRSTW WATERSCAPE
AACEERSSTT ESTATE CARS
AACEERSSTV STAVESACRE
AACEFFIRST AFFRICATES
AACEFGHNOR FOR A CHANGE
AACEFGINSV FACE-SAVING
AACEFGLMOU CAMOUFLAGE
AACEFGNRRS FRAGRANCES
AACEFGRSTT STAGECRAFT

AACEFHLLNP CHAPFALLEN
AACEFHLSST HALF-CASTES
AACEFIILTT FACILITATE
AACEFIIMPR PRIMA FACIE
AACEFIINST FANATICISE
AACEFIINTZ FANATICIZE
AACEFLMORT MALEFACTOR
AACEFRRTTW WATERCRAFT
AACEFRSTTT STATECRAFT
AACEGHLNRS ARCHANGELS
AACEGHMOPR MACROPHAGE
AACEGHNORS ANCHORAGES
AACEGHNORT COAT HANGER
AACEGILLPR PREGLACIAL
AACEGILNRT LACERATING
AACEGILNSS ANALGESICS
AACEGILNST ESCALATING
AACEGILPPR PARAPLEGIC
AACEGILRST CARTILAGES
AACEGIMNPR CAMPAIGNER
AACEGIMNRT MACERATING
AACEGINTUV EVACUATING
AACEGINTVX EXCAVATING
AACEGLMORY ACROMEGALY
AACEGLORTU CATALOGUER
AACEGLOSTU CATALOGUES
AACEGMNRTY TERMAGANCY
AACEGOPSST SCAPEGOATS
AACEGORSTT GREATCOATS
AACEHHILRR HIERARCHAL
AACEHHKLMS HAMSHACKLE
AACEHHMNTT HATCHET MAN
AACEHIIMNT HAEMATINIC
AACEHIIMTT HAEMATITIC
AACEHIKLMR LIKE A CHARM
AACEHILMMS MICHAELMAS
AACEHILNPT CHAINPLATE
AACEHILNRS LANCASHIRE
AACEHILOPT APOTHECIAL
AACEHILPST CALIPHATES
AACEHILRTT THEATRICAL
AACEHIMMPR AMPHIMACER
AACEHIMPRS PHARMACIES
AACEHIMPRT AMPHEATRIC
AACEHIMRTU HAEMATURIC
AACEHINNOU OUANANICHE
AACEHINRRT CATARRHINE
AACEHINRTT ANTHRACITE
AACEHINSTU EUSTACHIAN
AACEHIOPRX ECHOPRAXIA
AACEHIRRTV ARCHITRAVE
AACEHIRSSY EASY CHAIRS
AACEHIRSTU AUTARCHIES
AACEHJKMMR JACKHAMMER

AACEHKLMRS RAMSHACKLE
AACEHKMMRT MATCHMAKER
AACEHKMRTW WATCHMAKER
AACEHKRSSV HAVERSACKS
AACEHLOPSU ACEPHALOUS
AACEHLPRTY ARCHETYPAL
AACEHMNPRY PARENCHYMA
AACEHMNRRT CARMARTHEN
AACEHMNRTY ATHERMANCY
AACEHMNTTT ATTACHMENT
AACEHMOPRT CAMPHORATE
AACEHOPPRS APPROACHES
AACEHOPRTY APOTHECARY
AACEHPPRSS SCRAP HEAPS
AACEHPRSTU PARACHUTES
AACEIILMST CALAMITIES
AACEIILPST CAPITALISE
AACEIILPTZ CAPITALIZE
AACEIIMNOT EMACIATION
AACEIINNRV INVARIANCE
AACEIINORT ACIERATION
AACEIINPTT ANTICIPATE
AACEIINTTV INACTIVATE
AACEIIOPSS CASSIOPEIA
AACEIIPRTT PATRICIATE
AACEIIPTTV CAPITATIVE
AACEILLMNU ANIMALCULE
AACEILLMNY ANEMICALLY
AACEILLNRT CARNALLITE
AACEILLNTT CANTILLATE
AACEILLOSU ALLIACEOUS
AACEILLRRV VARICELLAR
AACEILLSTY SALICYLATE
AACEILMMTU IMMACULATE
AACEILMNPS CAMPANILES
AACEILMNRT RECLAIMANT
AACEILMNRU UNICAMERAL
AACEILMNSU MAIN CLAUSE
AACEILMNTU CALUMNIATE
AACEILMRTU TULARAEMIC
AACEILNNRS CARNELIANS
AACEILNORT CREATIONAL, LACERATION,
   REACTIONAL
AACEILNOST ESCALATION
AACEILNPPS APPLIANCES
AACEILNPSS SNAIL'S PACE
AACEILNPTU PANICULATE
AACEILOOPZ PALAEOZOIC
AACEILPRRS PERISARCAL
AACEILPTTU CAPITULATE
AACEILRTTU ARTICULATE
AACEILRTUU AURICULATE
AACEILSSTU CASUALTIES
AACEILSTTT STALACTITE

AACEIMMPRU PARAMECIUM	**AACELPPRST** APPLE CARTS
AACEIMNNRU UN-AMERICAN	**AACELPRTTY** CALYPTRATE
AACEIMNNST ANAMNESTIC	**AACELSTTUU** AUSCULTATE
AACEIMNORT MACERATION	**AACEMNOPSW** SPACEWOMAN
AACEIMNORU OCEANARIUM	**AACEMNORST** SACRAMENTO
AACEIMOPST APOSEMATIC	**AACEMNRSST** SACRAMENTS
AACEIMORRT CREMATORIA	**AACEMPRSTU** METACARPUS
AACEIMPRRT PARAMETRIC	**AACENNNOSY** ANNOYANCES
AACEIMSTTT METASTATIC	**AACENNSSTV** VACANTNESS
AACEINNNTU ANNUNCIATE	**AACENOTTUZ** UTO-AZTECAN
AACEINNOTT CATENATION	**AACENRRSTU** EARN A CRUST
AACEINNPRT PANCREATIN	**AACENRSSSU** ASSURANCES
AACEINORTU AERONAUTIC	**AACENRSSSV** CANVASSERS
AACEINORTV VACATIONER	**AACEORRTTT** TERRACOTTA
AACEINOTUV EVACUATION	**AACEORSTVX** EXCAVATORS
AACEINOTVX EXCAVATION	**AACEPPPRRS** SCRAP PAPER
AACEINPRST PERSIAN CAT	**AACFFIJMRT** TRAFFIC JAM
AACEINPRTY AT ANY PRICE	**AACFGILNRT** FLAT RACING
AACEINRSST INCRASSATE	**AACFHKNRST** CRANKSHAFT
AACEINSSST ASSISTANCE	**AACFHLNORW** HALF A CROWN
AACEIORSTT AEROSTATIC	**AACFIIILRT** ARTIFICIAL
AACEIOSSST ASSOCIATES	**AACFIILNOR** CALIFORNIA
AACEIRSSST STAIRCASES	**AACFIILSTT** FATALISTIC
AACEIRTTTV ATTRACTIVE	**AACFIIMNST** FANATICISM
AACEJKNRTT NATTERJACK	**AACFIINOST** FASCIATION
AACEJLORTU EJACULATOR	**AACFILLOSU** FALLACIOUS
AACEKKMRST MAKE TRACKS	**AACFILMSTU** FACTUALISM
AACEKLMRST SMART ALECK	**AACFILNORT** FRACTIONAL
AACEKLPRST PLATE RACKS	**AACFILORST** SOLFATARIC
AACEKLRRTY TRACKLAYER	**AACFILSTTU** FACTUALIST
AACEKPPSTY PAY PACKETS	**AACFINNNOR** FRANCONIAN
AACELLLMSS SMALL-SCALE	**AACFLNNOTU** NONFACTUAL
AACELLLORT COLLATERAL	**AACFMNNOWY** FANCY WOMAN
AACELLLRST SALTCELLAR	**AACFMOORST** COAT OF ARMS
AACELLLRUV VALLECULAR	**AACFNRSTTU** SURFACTANT
AACELLNOSW ALLOWANCES	**AACFRRTTYY** ARTY-CRAFTY
AACELLPRRY CARPELLARY	**AACGGHINNS** CHAIN GANGS
AACELLPSST CAST A SPELL	**AACGGIILOS** SIALAGOGIC
AACELMNRVY CAVALRYMEN	**AACGGILLNO** ALGOLAGNIC
AACELMOPSU PALMACEOUS	**AACGGILRST** GASTRALGIC
AACELMOSUV MALVACEOUS	**AACGHHOPRT** TACHOGRAPH
AACELMOSUY AMYLACEOUS	**AACGHILNPY** ANAGLYPHIC
AACELMPRST CAMPESTRAL	**AACGHILRRT** ARTHRALGIC
AACELMSSST CLASSMATES	**AACGHIOPRS** SARCOPHAGI
AACELNNOTV COVENANTAL	**AACGHMOPRR** MACROGRAPH
AACELNOPTU CANTALOUPE	**AACGIILLST** GLACIALIST
AACELNOTTV OCTAVALENT	**AACGIILNNZ** CANALIZING
AACELNRRUV VERNACULAR	**AACGIILNOT** GLACIATION
AACELNRTTU TENTACULAR	**AACGIIMSTT** ASTIGMATIC
AACELNSSSU CASUALNESS	**AACGIINNPT** CAPTAINING
AACELNTUUV AVUNCULATE	**AACGIINPST** PAGANISTIC
AACELOPPSY APOCALYPSE	**AACGIINTTV** ACTIVATING
AACELORSST ESCALATORS	**AACGIKMNRT** TARMACKING
AACELORSUU LAURACEOUS	**AACGIKMORY** KARYOGAMIC

AACGIKNNRS RANSACKING
AACGILLNOT ALLOCATING
AACGILLRTY TRAGICALLY
AACGILMNNY MALIGNANCY
AACGILNORS COR ANGLAIS
AACGILNPTY PLAY-ACTING
AACGIMNORT MORGANATIC
AACGIMNRSS MASSACRING
AACGIMPRST PRAGMATICS
AACGIMRSTY MAGISTRACY
AACGINNSSV CANVASSING
AACGINRSTT CASTRATING
AACGINRTTT ATTRACTING
AACGIORSTT CASTIGATOR
AACGLLMOOY MALACOLOGY
AACGLLSSWY SCALLYWAGS
AACGLNORTU OCTANGULAR
AACHHHISUU CHIHUAHUAS
AACHIINRST CHRISTIANA
AACHILLOPT ALLOPATHIC
AACHILNNPT PLAINCHANT
AACHILOPST CHIPOLATAS
AACHILPRSU HARUSPICAL
AACHIMMNRS RACHMANISM
AACHIMNNRU MANCHURIAN
AACHIMNOPR ANAMORPHIC
AACHIMNORS ANACHORISM,
HARMONICAS, MARASCHINO
AACHIMNORT ACHROMATIN,
MACHINATOR
AACHIMNORW CHAIRWOMAN
AACHIMPRST PHARMACIST
AACHIMRRST MATRIARCHS
AACHIMRRTY MATRIARCHY
AACHIMRSTT MAASTRICHT
AACHIMSSTT ASTHMATICS
AACHINRSST ANARCHISTS
AACHINRSTU CARTHUSIAN
AACHIPRRST PATRIARCHS
AACHIPRRTY PATRIARCHY
AACHIPRSTY PARASTICHY
AACHLLRSTW WALLCHARTS
AACHLMOPRS ARCHOPLASM
AACHLNNNOT NONCHALANT
AACHLOPPRY APOCRYPHAL
AACHMOOPRT APOCHROMAT
AACHMORTUY TAUROMACHY
AACHMPRSST MARCH-PASTS
AACHPRSTTW WATCHSTRAP
AACIILLNNT ANTICLINAL
AACIILLOPT APOLITICAL
AACIILMNOS SIMONIACAL
AACIILMNST TALISMANIC
AACIILMNTX ANTICLIMAX

AACIILMPST CAPITALISM
AACIILNNOR CAROLINIAN
AACIILNNST ANNALISTIC
AACIILNORS SALICORNIA
AACIILNOST ANTISOCIAL
AACIILPPST PAPISTICAL
AACIILPSTT CAPITALIST
AACIILRRTU URTICARIAL
AACIILRSST RACIALISTS
AACIIMNNRT MARTINICAN
AACIIMSSTT ASTATICISM
AACIINNPTT ANTICIPANT
AACIINOPTT CAPITATION
AACIINOTTV ACTIVATION, CAVITATION
AACIINPRST PATRICIANS
AACIINSTTT ANTISTATIC
AACIIORSUV AVARICIOUS
AACIKLMMRS LAMARCKISM
AACILLMNTY MANTICALLY
AACILLMORT MATRILOCAL
AACILLMOTY ATOMICALLY, LAY CLAIM
TO
AACILLNOOT ALLOCATION
AACILLNTUY NAUTICALLY
AACILLOOPR COPROLALIA
AACILLOPRT ALLOPATRIC, PATRILOCAL
AACILLORTV VACILLATOR
AACILLPTYY ATYPICALLY
AACILLRWXY WAX LYRICAL
AACILLTVWY CAVITY WALL
AACILMNOTU MACULATION
AACILMORRT LACRIMATOR
AACILMORSU MARLACIOUS
AACILMOSTU CALAMITOUS
AACILNNRTY TYRANNICAL
AACILNOOTV VOCATIONAL
AACILNOPTY NYCTALOPIA
AACILNORSS SCANSORIAL
AACILNORTT TRACTIONAL
AACILNPPST APPLICANTS
AACILOORRT ORATORICAL
AACILOPPRT APPLICATOR
AACILOPRTT OPTICAL ART
AACILORRTU CURATORIAL
AACILORSTU ALACRITOUS
AACILPRRSU SPIRACULAR
AACILPRRTU PARTICULAR
AACILPRSTT PLASTIC ART
AACILPRSTY PARALYTICS
AACILQSTTU ACQUITTALS
AACIMMNNOO MONOMANIAC
AACIMNNNSU MANCUNIANS
AACIMNOPRY PYROMANIAC
AACIMORSTT MASTICATOR

AACIMOSTTU AUTOMATICS
AACINNOOTZ ACTINOZOAN
AACINNORST CARNATIONS
AACINNOSTT CONSTANTIA
AACINOOPTT COAPTATION
AACINOOSTV AVOCATIONS, NOVA SCOTIA
AACINOPRSS CAPARISONS
AACINORSTT CASTRATION
AACINORTTT ATTRACTION
AACINORTUY CAUTIONARY
AACINRSSST SACRISTANS
AACIOOPPRT APOTROPAIC
AACIOPRTTV CAPTIVATOR
AACIORRSTT ARISTOCRAT
AACIOSSTTW WAISTCOATS
AACJLMRSUU MAJUSCULAR
AACLMNNOSW CLANSWOMAN
AACLNOPSTU CANTALOUPS
AACLOORRTU COLORATURA
AACLOPRRRS PARLOR CARS
AACLOPRRST PATROL CARS
AACMOOPRRT COMPARATOR
AACNNNOSTT CONSTANTAN
AACNORRSTT TRANSACTOR
AACOOPPRSU APOCARPOUS
AACORRSTTT STRATOCRAT
AADDDEEHHR HARDHEADED
AADDDEEMRY DAYDREAMED
AADDDGRSUY SUGAR DADDY
AADDEEHHST DEATH'S-HEAD
AADDEEHIMN MAIDENHEAD
AADDEEIRST DESIDERATA
AADDEEMRRY DAYDREAMER
AADDEESTTV DEVASTATED
AADDEFINRW FAR AND WIDE
AADDEGHNOR DRAGONHEAD
AADDEGIPRS DISPARAGED
AADDEGIRRT TARDIGRADE
AADDEGMNOR ARMAGEDDON
AADDEHIMNN HANDMAIDEN
AADDEHLMNN MANHANDLED
AADDEHLMOT THE OLD ADAM
AADDEHLNNP PANHANDLED
AADDEHQSTU DEATH SQUAD
AADDEIILPT DILAPIDATE
AADDEIIRRT IRRADIATED
AADDEILLNS LANDLADIES
AADDEILMRR RED ADMIRAL
AADDEILNSV VANDALISED
AADDEILNVZ VANDALIZED
AADDEILORR RAILROADED
AADDEIMRST DRAMATISED
AADDEIMRTZ DRAMATIZED
AADDEINRSW EDWARDIANS

AADDELMNRS DREAMLANDS
AADDELMRSS MALADDRESS
AADDGILMOY AMYGDALOID
AADDGNNRST GRANDSTAND
AADDHNNSST HANDSTANDS
AADDIILNOT ADDITIONAL
AADDIIMRSY DAIRYMAIDS
AADDILLLOV VALLADOLID
AADDINORRT RITARDANDO
AADDLNOOSW SANDALWOOD
AADEEEPPRR REAPPEARED
AADEEFGHOR FORGE AHEAD
AADEEFGLRT DEFLAGRATE
AADEEFHRRZ HAZARD-FREE
AADEEGGGRT AGGREGATED
AADEEGIRTV VARIEGATED
AADEEGNPPS APPENDAGES
AADEEGNRRR REARRANGED
AADEEGNRST GREAT DANES, TEAGARDENS
AADEEGNRTU GUARANTEED
AADEEHHLRX HEXAHEDRAL
AADEEHHMMR HAMMERHEAD
AADEEHLNVY HEAVY-LADEN
AADEEHLTWY LEAD THE WAY
AADEEHMRST HEADMASTER, HEADSTREAM
AADEEHNRVW HEAVENWARD
AADEEHPPRS PEAR-SHAPED
AADEEHPRSS SPEARHEADS
AADEEHQRSU HEADSQUARE
AADEEHRSTT DEATH RATES
AADEEHRSTW HEADWATERS
AADEEILLTV ALLEVIATED
AADEEILMNT DELAMINATE
AADEEILNNR ADRENALINE
AADEEILNST DESALINATE
AADEEILRTT RETALIATED
AADEEIMMNN MAIDEN NAME
AADEEIMNRT REANIMATED
AADEEIMPRT PREADAMITE
AADEEINQTU INADEQUATE
AADEEIPTTX EXPATIATED
AADEEIRSTT ASTERIATED
AADEEKKKOT TAKE A DEKKO
AADEELLLMT LAMELLATED
AADEELLLPR PARALLELED
AADEELLPPR APPARELLED
AADEELMNRV VAL-DE-MARNE
AADEELMRTT MALTREATED
AADEELMSTT STALEMATED
AADEELNNWZ NEW ZEALAND
AADEELNPSS ESPLANADES
AADEELNRTT ALTERNATED

AADEELQTUY ADEQUATELY
AADEELRRSY LAY READERS
AADEELRSTV SLAVE TRADE
AADEELRTTU ADULTERATE
AADEEMNRST TRADE NAMES
AADEEMQRSU MASQUERADE
AADEEMQSTU DESQUAMATE
AADEENTTTU ATTENUATED
AADEEOPRTV EVAPORATED
AADEEPPRWX WAXED PAPER
AADEEPRSST PAEDERASTS
AADEEPRSTY PAEDERASTY
AADEERRTTW TREAD WATER
AADEFFIILT AFFILIATED
AADEFFNORT FORE AND AFT
AADEFGRSSU SAFEGUARDS
AADEFHHIOR HEAD OF HAIR
AADEFHLNRT FATHERLAND
AADEFIKNRR AFRIKANDER
AADEFIMNOT DEFAMATION
AADEFINSST FANTASISED
AADEFINSTZ FANTASIZED
AADEFINTTU INFATUATED
AADEFLLMNO AN OLD FLAME
AADEFMORTY DEFAMATORY
AADEFMRSST FARMSTEADS
AADEFRRSTW AFTERWARDS
AADEGGINRS AGGRANDISE
AADEGGINRZ AGGRANDIZE
AADEGGNOOR DRAGOONAGE
AADEGGOSSU SAUSAGE DOG
AADEGHHINS SHANGHAIED
AADEGHIINR HEARING AID
AADEGHNRSY HYDRANGEAS
AADEGHNSST STAGEHANDS
AADEGILMNY AMYGDALINE
AADEGILNSV GALVANISED
AADEGILNVZ GALVANIZED
AADEGILRST SALTIGRADE
AADEGIMMNS MISMANAGED
AADEGIMRST SMARAGDITE
AADEGINNTT ANTEDATING
AADEGINRRS DISARRANGE
AADEGINRST TRAGEDIANS
AADEGIPRRS DISPARAGER
AADEGIRTTV GRAVITATED
AADEGLNNST LAND AGENTS
AADEGLNQRU QUADRANGLE
AADEGLNRTU GRANULATED
AADEGLNSTW SWEAT GLAND
AADEGMRRTU DRAMATURGE
AADEGNOPRR GRAND OPERA
AADEGOPPRT PROPAGATED
AADEGRRRSU REARGUARDS

AADEGRRSVY GRAVEYARDS
AADEHHKNSS HANDSHAKES, SHAKE
HANDS
AADEHIIMNR MAIDENHAIR
AADEHILNNT LANTHANIDE
AADEHILORR DIARRHOEAL
AADEHIPRST HIT PARADES
AADEHKLLMR HALLMARKED
AADEHKMSST DEATH MASKS
AADEHLLMRS MARSHALLED
AADEHLMPSS LAMPSHADES
AADEHLNNPR PANHANDLER
AADEHLNNPS PANHANDLES
AADEHMMMNO MOHAMMEDAN
AADEHORRSW ARROWHEADS
AADEHPRSTT DEATH TRAPS
AADEHRRSTW EARTHWARDS
AADEIILNNR DAIL EIRANN
AADEIILNOT IDEATIONAL
AADEIILNTV INVALIDATE
AADEIILPRS LAPIDARIES
AADEIIMNNR AMERINDIAN
AADEIIMNNT MAINTAINED
AADEIINNST EAST INDIAN
AADEIINNTV VANADINITE
AADEIINORT ERADIATION
AADEIINTTV ADVENTITIA
AADEIIRRTT TRIRADIATE
AADEILMNRV VINA DEL MAR
AADEILMNTY ANIMATEDLY
AADEILMORT TAILOR-MADE
AADEILMRTX TAXIDERMAL
AADEILNSTT TANTALISED
AADEILNSTU ANDALUSITE
AADEILNTTZ TANTALIZED
AADEILORST ASTEROIDAL
AADEILPPTT PALPITATED
AADEILSTVW TIDAL WAVES
AADEIMNRTV ANIMADVERT
AADEIMRRST DRAMATISER
AADEIMRRTZ DRAMATIZER
AADEINNOPT ANTIPODEAN
AADEINPQSU PASQUINADE
AADEINQRSU QUANDARIES
AADEINQTTU ANTIQUATED
AADEINRSTT ANTITRADES
AADEIOPQRU RADIOPAQUE
AADEKLMORW MEADOWLARK
AADEKMRRST TRADEMARKS
AADELLORSV EL SALVADOR
AADELMMORS MELODRAMAS
AADELMNSSS LANDMASSES
AADELMOOST STOMODAEAL
AADELMOPRR MADREPORAL

AADELNRSTT TRANSLATED
AADELNRTTU ADULTERANT
AADELNRTUY DAY-NEUTRAL
AADELNSSTW WASTELANDS
AADELRSTWY EASTWARDLY
AADEMNPRSS AMPERSANDS
AADENNRTTU DENATURANT
AADENNSTTT ATTENDANTS
AADENRSTTU TRANSUDATE
AADEORSTTV DEVASTATOR
AADEQRRTUU QUADRATURE
AADEQRRTUY QUARTER DAY
AADFFIISTV AFFIDAVITS
AADFILNRSY FAIRYLANDS
AADFILRSTU FRUIT SALAD
AADFIMNRSY MAN FRIDAYS
AADFIMRRSY DAIRY FARMS
AADFNORRTU FART AROUND
AADGGILNNR GARLANDING
AADGGINRTU GRADUATING
AADGHIMPRS DIAPHRAGMS
AADGHINSWY WASHING DAY
AADGHIOPRR RADIOGRAPH
AADGIILNTV VALIDATING
AADGIINNRT GRANT-IN-AID
AADGIJNORU JAGUARONDI
AADGILLNOY DIAGONALLY
AADGILMRSU GRADUALISM
AADGILNOOT ODONTALGIA
AADGILNPPU APPLAUDING
AADGILORST GLADIATORS
AADGILPSUV DAUGAVPILS
AADGILRRSU GUARDRAILS
AADGILRSTU GRADUALIST
AADGIMORRS RADIOGRAMS
AADGINNOPR GRAND PIANO
AADGINORST GRADATIONS
AADGINORTU GRADUATION
AADGLMNRSS GRAND SLAMS
AADGMRRTUY DRAMATURGY
AADGMRSSTU MUSTARD GAS
AADGNNOPRS SNAPDRAGON
AADGNRSSUV GUARD'S VANS
AADHIILPSY DIAPHYSIAL
AADHIIOPRS APHRODISIA
AADHILRTWW WITHDRAWAL
AADHINOPSU DIAPHANOUS
AADHNSSSTW WASHSTANDS
AADIILLNST TILLANDSIA
AADIILMMOT OMMATIDIAL
AADIILNOTT DILATATION
AADIILNOTV VALIDATION
AADIILNPRW RAWALPINDI
AADIILQRUV QUADRIVIAL

AADIILSSST DIASTALSIS
AADIILSSUV VISUAL AIDS
AADIIMNOPS DIPSOMANIA
AADIIMNORT ADMIRATION
AADIINORST RADIATIONS
AADIINORTX X-RADIATION
AADIIORRRT IRRADIATOR
AADIIPRSST ASPIDISTRA
AADIJNORTU ADJURATION
AADILLMNOS SOMALILAND
AADILLMORS ARMADILLOS
AADILNORTU DURATIONAL
AADILORSTU AUSTRALOID
AADILORTVY VALIDATORY
AADILOSSVW DISAVOWALS
AADIMNNOPR PRIMA DONNA
AADIMNOPRY MYRIAPODAN
AADIMOPPRU PARAPODIUM
AADIMRSSTT DRAMATISTS
AADINSSSTY SAINT'S DAYS
AADIOOPSSY OOPS-A-DAISY
AADJMNNPRU PANJANDRUM
AADJORRTUY ADJURATORY
AADLMNNNOS NO-MAN'S-LAND
AADLMNNRUY LAUNDRYMAN
AADLMNPSUY PALM SUNDAY
AADMNOORSU ANADROMOUS
AADNOOPPSW SAPPANWOOD
AAEEEFLMMT METAFEMALE
AAEEEGGMMT MEGAGAMETE
AAEEEGGRTX EXAGGERATE
AAEEEGLNOP PALAEOGENE
AAEEEHRSST HEARTSEASE
AAEEELMNRW ENAMELWARE
AAEEELNPRS PARASELENE
AAEEELRSTT REAL ESTATE
AAEEEMNNOS SEA ANEMONE
AAEEEPRSTX EXASPERATE
AAEEERSSTV ASSEVERATE
AAEEFGIMRT AFTERIMAGE
AAEEFGINTU TAENIAFUGE
AAEEFGLLLT FLAGELLATE
AAEEFHRSTV AFTERSHAVE
AAEEFKLMRT FLEA MARKET
AAEEFNRRST FAR EASTERN
AAEEFRSTTT AFTERTASTE
AAEEGGGRST AGGREGATES
AAEEGGHMOU HAEMAGOGUE
AAEEGHLLRT ALL THE RAGE
AAEEGHLNOT HALOGENATE
AAEEGHRRSV HARGREAVES
AAEEGILLTT TAGLIATELE
AAEEGILNNV EVANGELINA
AAEEGIMNRT EMARGINATE

AAEEGIMSSX SEXAGESIMA
AAEEGINRTV VEGETARIAN
AAEEGIRSSV SAVAGERIES
AAEEGLMNPS PLASMAGENE
AAEEGLMNST MENTAL AGES
AAEEGLSSVW WAGE SLAVES
AAEEGMMNNT MANAGEMENT
AAEEGMMORR AEROGRAMME
AAEEGMNRSS MANAGERESS
AAEEGMNRST EAST GERMAN
AAEEGMNRTV RAVAGEMENT
AAEEGMNSST STAGE NAMES
AAEEGNPRRR PREARRANGE
AAEEGNRRRR REARRANGER
AAEEGNRSTU GUARANTEES
AAEEGNRSXY SEXAGENARY
AAEEGNSSSV SAVAGENESS
AAEEGQRRTU QUARTERAGE
AAEEHHRSST HEAT RASHES
AAEEHILRTX EXHILARATE
AAEEHINSST ANESTHESIA
AAEEHKMOSU MAKE A HOUSE
AAEEHKQRTU EARTHQUAKE
AAEEHLNTTT LATENT HEAT
AAEEHLNTVX HEXAVALENT
AAEEHLRRSS REHEARSALS
AAEEHMNRTW WEATHERMAN
AAEEHMPRST METAPHRASE
AAEEHPTVWY PAVE THE WAY
AAEEHRRRST RARE EARTHS
AAEEHRRSTW SHEARWATER
AAEEHRTVWY HEAVY WATER
AAEEIKLMNS SEAMANLIKE
AAEEILLNST LATEEN SAIL
AAEEILLRTT ALLITERATE
AAEEILMNNS MELANESIAN
AAEEILMORT AMELIORATE
AAEEILMRSS LAMASERIES
AAEEILNPRT PENETRALIA
AAEEILRTTV ALTERATIVE
AAEEILTUVV EVALUATIVE
AAEEINPPRV PAPAVERINE
AAEEIPPRRS REAPPRAISE
AAEEIPRRTT REPATRIATE
AAEEIPRRTV REPARATIVE
AAEEIPRSTT TEA PARTIES
AAEEIPRSTV SEPARATIVE
AAEEIPRTTX EXPATRIATE
AAEEKKWWYY WAKEY WAKEY
AAEEKNQRSU NEAR SQUEAK
AAEELLPRTY PLATELAYER
AAEELMNPST NAMEPLATES
AAEELMQRSU SQUARE MEAL
AAEELMRRTT MALTREATER

AAEELMSSTT STALEMATES
AAEELNOPRS AEROPLANES
AAEELNPRRT PARENTERAL
AAEELNPRST PLEASANTER
AAEELPRSTY SEPARATELY
AAEELSSSTX SALES TAXES
AAEEMMNRRT REARMAMENT
AAEEMNNSSU AMANUENSES
AAEEMPRRST PARAMETERS
AAEEPPRSTW WASTE PAPER
AAEERRSTTW WATER RATES
AAEFFHRSTT AFTERSHAFT
AAEFFIILST AFFILIATES
AAEFFILORV LOVE AFFAIR
AAEFGIISTT FASTIGIATE
AAEFGLLLNT FLAGELLANT
AAEFGLLNRU LANGLAUFER
AAEFGLMNRT FRAGMENTAL
AAEFHLPRST FLARE PATHS
AAEFHMRSTT AFTERMATHS
AAEFIILSTT FATALITIES
AAEFIKNRRS AFRIKANERS
AAEFILLNRX FRAXINELLA
AAEFILMMNY FAMILY NAME
AAEFILMRRS FIRE ALARMS
AAEFILRSTY FAIRY TALES
AAEFIMMNRS MAINFRAMES
AAEFIMRRRT TERRA FIRMA
AAEFINPRST AFTERPAINS
AAEFKLMOOT MAKE A LOT OF
AAEFLLNSTU FUSTANELLA
AAEFLLRSTW WATERFALLS
AAEFLMPSTY SAFETY LAMP
AAEFLOPSTT SOFT PALATE
AAEFLORTZZ TO A FRAZZLE
AAEFLRSSTT FALSE START
AAEGGGLNUV LUGGAGE VAN
AAEGGILNSW GLASWEGIAN
AAEGGILOSU SIALAGOGUE
AAEGGINRSU RAIN GAUGES
AAEGHILLSS GALASHIELS
AAEGHILNPR NEPHRALGIA
AAEGHILORT HAGIOLATER
AAEGHILRTU GAULTHERIA
AAEGHINNNS SHENANIGAN
AAEGHLNOPT HEPTAGONAL
AAEGHLNPRY PHARYNGEAL
AAEGHLNRUX HEXANGULAR
AAEGHMNOPR ANEMOGRAPH,
  PHANEROGAM
AAEGHNOPRS ORPHANAGES
AAEGHOPRRY AEROGRAPHY,
  AREOGRAPHY
AAEGHPPPRR GRAPH PAPER

AAEGIILNNT ALIENATING
AAEGIILPRS PLAGIARISE
AAEGIILPRZ PLAGIARIZE
AAEGIINNTV INVAGINATE
AAEGIINRTT INGRATIATE
AAEGIKMNRR EARMARKING
AAEGIKNNSW AWAKENINGS
AAEGILLNOT ALLEGATION
AAEGILLORT LEGATORIAL
AAEGILMNRT MARTINGALE
AAEGILMSTT STALAGMITE
AAEGILNNTT TANGENTIAL
AAEGILNPPR APPARELING
AAEGILNRSV GALVANISER
AAEGILNRVZ GALVANIZER
AAEGILNSWX SEALING WAX
AAEGILNTUV EVALUATING
AAEGILPRTY APTERYGIAL
AAEGIMMNRS MISMANAGER
AAEGIMRRTU MARGUERITA
AAEGIMRSTT MAGISTRATE
AAEGINNOST ANTAGONISE
AAEGINNOTZ ANTAGONIZE
AAEGINNSTU NAUSEATING
AAEGINPRST SEPARATING
AAEGINRSTU GUARANTIES
AAEGINRTTV GRAVETTIAN
AAEGINRTUU INAUGURATE
AAEGIORRTV ARROGATIVE
AAEGIRRTTV GRAVITATER
AAEGKLMRSS GLASS-MAKER
AAEGLLPSST PLATE GLASS
AAEGLMOPRR PARLOR GAME
AAEGLNNOPT PENTAGONAL
AAEGLNORTT TETRAGONAL
AAEGMNPRST PENTAGRAMS
AAEGMNRSTT TERMAGANTS
AAEGMOPRSU RAMPAGEOUS
AAEGMRSSTT STRATAGEMS
AAEGNNNOTT ON A TANGENT
AAEGNOPRSS PARSONAGES
AAEGRRSSTZ STARGAZERS
AAEHHINOPT THEOPHANIA
AAEHHJLLLU HALLELUJAH
AAEHHKMNRS KERMANSHAH
AAEHIILMNS LEISHMANIA
AAEHIILNNT ANNIHILATE
AAEHIIMNNT AMIANTHINE
AAEHIKRRST HAIRSTREAK
AAEHILLOPT PALAEOLITH
AAEHILNOTX EXHALATION
AAEHILNRTX EXHILARANT
AAEHILNSST THESSALIAN
AAEHILNSTV LEVIATHANS

AAEHILPSTT ASPHALTITE
AAEHILPSTW WESTPHALIA
AAEHIMNPSS SEAMANSHIP
AAEHIMNSTY MYASTHENIA
AAEHIMOSST HAEMATOSIS
AAEHIMPRST AMPHIASTER
AAEHIMRSTU AMATEURISH
AAEHINNORV HANOVERIAN
AAEHINOPST ASTHENOPIA
AAEHINPSST PHANTASIES
AAEHIPSTXY ASPHYXIATE
AAEHKLRSST SALT SHAKER
AAEHLLMRRS MARSHALLER
AAEHMNRSST HARASSMENT
AAEHMNRSTV HARVESTMAN
AAEHMORTTX METATHORAX
AAEHMOSTTY STAY-AT-HOME
AAEHMPRSTT METAPHRAST
AAEHMRSSTU SHAMATEURS
AAEHOPPSTY APOPHYSATE
AAEHRRTTTU ARTHURETTA
AAEIILLPTV PALLIATIVE
AAEIILMMRT IMMATERIAL
AAEIILMNRS SEMINARIAL
AAEIILMSST ASSIMILATE
AAEIILNNOT ALIENATION
AAEIILNPST SAPIENTIAL
AAEIILNSTV INSALIVATE
AAEIIMNNNR RIEMANNIAN
AAEIIMNNRS SEMINARIAN
AAEIIMNNRT MAINTAINER
AAEIIPPRSV APPRAISIVE
AAEIIPRSST PARASITISE
AAEIIPRSTZ PARASITIZE
AAEIKMRSST SAMARSKITE
AAEIKNNRST TRANSKEIAN
AAEILLLLNV VILLANELLA
AAEILLLNPR IN PARALLEL
AAEILLMPRX PREMAXILLA
AAEILLMRTY MATERIALLY
AAEILLNORT RELATIONAL
AAEILLNPSS SAILPLANES
AAEILLNRTU UNILATERAL
AAEILLORTV ALLEVIATOR
AAEILLPSSS PAILLASSES, PALLIASSES
AAEILLRRTT TRILATERAL
AAEILMNNSU SEMIANNUAL
AAEILMNORT AMELIORANT
AAEILMNPRT PARLIAMENT
AAEILMNPTU MANIPULATE
AAEILMNRTY ALIMENTARY
AAEILMNSST ASSAILMENT
AAEILMPRRT PREMARITAL
AAEILNNOPT NEAPOLITAN

AAEILNNOTV VENATIONAL
AAEILNNRTU LAURENTIAN
AAEILNOORT AREOLATION
AAEILNOQTU EQUATIONAL
AAEILNORST RATIONALES, SENATORIAL
AAEILNORTT ALTERATION
AAEILNORTU LAUREATION
AAEILNORTX RELAXATION
AAEILNOTTX EXALTATION
AAEILNOTUV EVALUATION
AAEILNRSTT TANTALISER
AAEILNRSTU NATURALISE
AAEILNRTTZ TANTALIZER
AAEILNRTUZ NATURALIZE
AAEILOQRTU EQUATORIAL
AAEILORRTT RETALIATOR
AAEILORSTV LAVATORIES
AAEILSTUXY ASEXUALITY
AAEIMMNRST MAINSTREAM
AAEIMMPRTU AT A PREMIUM
AAEIMMRSTU AMATEURISM
AAEIMNNOPR POMERANIAN
AAEIMNNOST EMANATIONS
AAEIMNNOSY MAYONNAISE
AAEIMNNSSU AMANUENSIS
AAEIMNNTTT ATTAINMENT
AAEIMNOORT EROTOMANIA
AAEIMNORST ANATOMISER
AAEIMNORTZ ANATOMIZER
AAEIMNRSTW WATER MAINS
AAEIMNRTTT ANTIMATTER
AAEIMPRSST SEPARATISM
AAEIMQRSTU MARQUISATE
AAEIMRSTTU TRAUMATISE
AAEIMRTTUV MATURATIVE
AAEIMRTTUZ TRAUMATIZE
AAEIMSSSTT METASTASIS
AAEINNNOTX ANNEXATION
AAEINNOSTU NAUSEATION
AAEINNOTTV ANNOTATIVE
AAEINNQRTU QUARANTINE
AAEINOPRRT REPARATION
AAEINOPRST SEPARATION
AAEINOPSST PASSIONATE
AAEINRRSTV NARRATIVES
AAEINRRSTW WARRANTIES
AAEIOPRTTX EXPATIATOR
AAEIOPSSST APOSTASIES
AAEIOPSSTT APOSTATISE
AAEIOPSTTZ APOSTATIZE
AAEIORSTTV AESTIVATOR
AAEIPRRSTX SEPARATRIX
AAEIPRSSTT SEPARATIST
AAEJKLRSWY JAYWALKERS

AAEKKOSTTT TAKE TO TASK
AAEKMRRSTW WATERMARKS
AAEKMRSSTT TASKMASTER
AAEKRRSTUU SAUERKRAUT
AAELLLMNOS SALMONELLA
AAELLLORST SALTARELLO
AAELLMNRTY MATERNALLY
AAELLMORTT MARTELLATO
AAELLMORZZ MOZZARELLA
AAELLNOPRS SOLAR PANEL
AAELLNPRTY PATERNALLY, PRENATALLY
AAELLNPSTY PLEASANTLY
AAELLPPRSW WALLPAPERS
AAELLRSTTT TATTERSALL
AAELMNNORT ORNAMENTAL
AAELMNOPSU MENOPAUSAL
AAELMNORVV REMOVAL VAN
AAELMNOSSW SALESWOMAN
AAELMNRSUY ANEURYSMAL
AAELMOPRRT ARMOR PLATE
AAELMRRTUX EXTRAMURAL
AAELNNPSTU UNPLEASANT
AAELNORRTT ALTERNATOR
AAELNPPRTY APPARENTLY
AAELNPRRSU SUPRARENAL
AAELNPRSTT TRANSEPTAL
AAELNPRSTY PLEASANTRY
AAELNRSTUV TRANSVALUE
AAELNSSTTU SULTANATES, TANTALUSES
AAELOOPSTT APOSTOLATE
AAELORRSSY SOLAR YEARS
AAELPRRTTT RATTLETRAP
AAELSTTTUW STATUTE LAW
AAEMNNORTT TRAMONTANE
AAEMNNRSTV MANSERVANT
AAEMNOOSST ANASTOMOSE
AAEMNPRSTT APARTMENTS
AAEMPRSSTT PAST MASTER
AAEMPRSSTY PAYMASTERS
AAEMRSSTTU METATARSUS
AAENORTTTU ATTENUATOR
AAENORTUUV ART NOUVEAU
AAENQRRTUY QUATERNARY
AAENRRSTTU RESTAURANT
AAEOOPPRSS SOAP OPERAS
AAEOOPRRTV EVAPORATOR
AAEOPRRSST SEPARATORS
AAEOPRRTVW WATER VAPOR
AAEPPRRSST SPARE PARTS
AAEQRRSTUW QUARTERSAW
AAFFFGLSST FLAGSTAFFS
AAFFGIMNRU RAGAMUFFIN
AAFGGILNVW FLAG-WAVING
AAFGIINNPR FRANGIPANI

AAFGLLNRTY FLAGRANTLY
AAFGLNRRTY FRAGRANTLY
AAFHIINNOS IN A FASHION
AAFIIILRSS FILARIASIS
AAFIILLMRY FAMILIARLY
AAFIILMNRU UNFAMILIAR
AAFILNOOTT FLOATATION
AAFMNORSTW MAN OF STRAW
AAGGHINNRU HARANGUING
AAGGIILNTT TAILGATING
AAGGIINNRR ARRAIGNING
AAGGIINNSY GAINSAYING
AAGGIINNTV NAVIGATING
AAGGINNSTT STAGNATING
AAGGINORRT ARROGATING
AAGGINRSTZ STARGAZING
AAGGKLNNPS GANGPLANKS
AAGGLLLOSS GALLOGLASS
AAGGLLNNYY YLANG-YLANG
AAGGNNORTU ORANGUTANG
AAGHHIMNWY HIGHWAYMAN
AAGHHINORT HOGARTHIAN
AAGHIILMNP MALPIGHIAN
AAGHIILMNRS MARSHALING
AAGHILNPST ASPHALTING
AAGHILOPPY POLYPHAGIA
AAGHILORTY HAGIOLATRY
AAGHINPRSS SPRINGHAAS
AAGHNOPPRT PANTOGRAPH
AAGHOPRSTU AUTOGRAPHS
AAGHOPRSTY PYTHAGORAS
AAGHOPRTUY AUTOGRAPHY
AAGIIKMNNR RAINMAKING
AAGIILLNPT PALLIATING
AAGIILMNNT LAMINATING
AAGIILMPRS PLAGIARISM
AAGIILNNPS SALPINGIAN
AAGIILNNUV UNAVAILING
AAGIILNRTV TRAVAILING
AAGIILNSTV SALIVATING
AAGIILPRST PLAGIARIST
AAGIIMNNRT MARINATING
AAGIINNOPT PAGINATION
AAGIINNOTV NAVIGATION
AAGIINOSTT AGITATIONS
AAGIINPPRS APPRAISING
AAGIINPRST ASPIRATING
AAGIJKLNWY JAYWALKING
AAGILLMNRY ALARMINGLY, MARGINALLY
AAGILLORSS GLOSSARIAL
AAGILLORST ALLIGATORS
AAGILMNORS ORGANISMAL
AAGILMOPRS PARALOGISM
AAGILNNOQU ALGONQUIAN

AAGILNNOTU ANGULATION
AAGILNOORT GORNO-ALTAI
AAGILNOPRS SPORANGIAL
AAGILNPRSY PARALYSING
AAGILNPRYZ PARALYZING
AAGILNRRTU TRIANGULAR
AAGILNRTUY ANGULARITY
AAGILNSSTU ASSAULTING
AAGILOPRST PARALOGIST
AAGILOSUVY YUGOSLAVIA
AAGIMMPRST PRAGMATISM
AAGIMNNOST ANTAGONISM
AAGIMNNPRW WARMING PAN
AAGIMNOTTU AUTOMATING
AAGIMNPTTU AMPUTATING
AAGIMNSSTY GYMNASIAST
AAGIMPRSTT PRAGMATIST
AAGINNNOTT ANNOTATING
AAGINNOSTT ANTAGONIST, STAGNATION
AAGINNRRTW WARRANTING
AAGINNRSUY SANGUINARY
AAGINOORRT ARROGATION
AAGINORSTV NAVIGATORS
AAGINOSSTT GAS STATION
AAGINRRTVY GRAVY TRAIN
AAGINRSTTU ANTITRAGUS, SATURATING
AAGLLMOOSU ALLOGAMOUS
AAGLLNOPTT TOPGALLANT
AAGLMOOPRR POLAROGRAM
AAGLNNOOSX ANGLO-SAXON
AAGLNNSTTY STAGNANTLY
AAGLNORRTU GRANULATOR
AAGLNORRTY ARROGANTLY
AAGMOOSTUU AUTOGAMOUS
AAGNNNOSTY NANNY GOATS
AAGNORRSTU GUARANTORS
AAGOOPPRRT PROPAGATOR
AAHHILMOPT OPHTHALMIA
AAHHIMRRTY ARRHYTHMIA
AAHHLORSTT THROATLASH
AAHIIKMNRS KASHMIRIAN
AAHIILNNOT INHALATION
AAHIILNNTU LITHUANIAN
AAHIILNOPS HISPANIOLA
AAHIIMPRSS PHARISAISM
AAHIINNSTY HINAYANIST
AAHILMNSTU MALTHUSIAN
AAHILMTTUZ ALTAZIMUTH
AAHILNNOPT ANTIPHONAL
AAHILOPPSY APOPHYSIAL
AAHILORSTU HAUSTORIAL
AAHIMMNOTY MYTHOMANIA
AAHIMMNSSS SHAMANISMS
AAHIMNSSST SHAMANISTS

AAHINNOTTX XANTHATION
AAHINOPRTW ON A PAR WITH
AAHINPSTXY ASPHYXIANT
AAHIPPRSSY PARAPHYSIS
AAHKKNNPYY HANKY-PANKY
AAHKLOORSY YOSHKAR-OLA
AAHLLMOPSY HYALOPLASM
AAHNOPRTTU NATUROPATH
AAHNORRSTU ANARTHROUS
AAIIILLMNW WILLIAMINA
AAIIILMMNT MILITIAMAN
AAIIILMMNX MAXIMILIAN
AAIIILMNRT LIMITARIAN
AAIIJLNORT JANITORIAL
AAIIKLLNTY ALKALINITY
AAIIKMNNST KANTIANISM
AAIIKNPSST PAKISTANIS
AAIILLNOPT PALLIATION
AAIILMMRST MARTIALISM
AAIILMMSTX MAXIMALIST
AAIILMNNOT ANTIMONIAL, LAMINATION
AAIILMRSTT MARTIALIST
AAIILNORRT IRRATIONAL
AAIILNOSTV SALIVATION
AAIILNRSTY SANITARILY
AAIILPRTTY PARTIALITY
AAIILPSTTY SPATIALITY
AAIIMMNRSX MARXIANISM
AAIIMNNOPT IMPANATION
AAIIMNNORT MARINATION
AAIIMNRSTU SANITARIUM
AAIIMPRSST PARASITISM
AAIINNOSTT SANITATION
AAIINNRRTU RURITANIAN
AAIINNRSTU UNITARIANS
AAIINNRSTY INSANITARY
AAIINOPPRT APPARITION
AAIINOPRST ASPIRATION
AAIINOPRTT TRITANOPIA
AAIINORSTV VARIATIONS
AAIIRSSSTY SATYRIASIS
AAIKLLNOTY ALKYLATION
AAILLNNOTY NATIONALLY
AAILLNNOVV VILLANOVAN
AAILLNOPST SPALLATION
AAILLNORTY RATIONALLY
AAILLRSTUY SALUTARILY
AAILMNOTTU MUTATIONAL
AAILMNRRTU INTRAMURAL
AAILMNRSTU NATURALISM
AAILMOPPRX APPROXIMAL
AAILMPRSSU MARSUPIALS
AAILNNNOTU ANNULATION
AAILNNOOTT NOTATIONAL

AAILNNOPTT PLANTATION
AAILNNOTTU NUTATIONAL
AAILNNPQSU PALANQUINS
AAILNOORTT ROTATIONAL
AAILNOPPST PALPATIONS
AAILNOSTTU SALUTATION
AAILNOSTUV VALUATIONS
AAILNPPPTU AN APT PUPIL
AAILNPRSTU TARPAULINS
AAILNRSTTU NATURALIST
AAILNSSSTU STANISLAUS
AAIMMOSTTU AUTOMATISM
AAIMMRSTTU TRAUMATISM
AAIMNOOTTU AUTOMATION
AAIMNOPTTU AMPUTATION
AAIMNOQSTU SQUAMATION
AAIMNORSTU SANATORIUM
AAIMNORTTU MATURATION
AAIMNOSSTT ANATOMISTS
AAIMNPRSST SPARTANISM
AAIMOSTTTU AUTOMATIST
AAINNNOOST SAN ANTONIO
AAINNNOOTT ANNOTATION
AAINNORRST NARRATIONS
AAINNRSTUY UNSANITARY
AAINOOPPRT PROTANOPIA
AAINOPSTTY PAY STATION
AAINORSTTU SATURATION
AAINORSTTV STARVATION
AAINORSTTY STATIONARY
AAINSSSSTT ASSISTANTS
AAIOPRRSTY ASPIRATORY
AAKKMORRST KRAMATORSK
AAKLMOPRSY KARYOPLASM
AAKLNORSUY ANKYLOSAUR
AAKMMNORSW MARKSWOMAN
AALLLLOTWW WALL-TO-WALL
AALLMNTUUY AUTUMNALLY
AALLPRSTWY PARTY WALLS
AALLPSSWYY PALSY-WALSY
AALLRSTTWY STALWARTLY
AALMOOPPRS MALAPROPOS
AALMOOPRTY LAPAROTOMY
AALMOPRSXY PAROXYSMAL
AALNNOOPST PANTALOONS
AALNNPRSTT TRANSPLANT
AALNNRRSTU TRANSLUNAR
AALNOOPPRV ON APPROVAL
AALNOOPUZZ POZZUOLANA
AALNOPRRST TRANSPOLAR
AALNORRSTT TRANSLATOR
AALOPRRSTU AUSTRALORP
AALOPRRSTY PORTRAYALS
AALOPSTTUY AUTOPLASTY

AALORSTTUY SALUTATORY
AAMNNOTTTU TANTAMOUNT
AAMNOOSTTU AUTOMATONS
AAMOOSSTTU ASTOMATOUS
AAMOOSTTUU AUTOMATOUS
AANOOPRSTU ANATROPOUS
AANORSSTTU ASTRONAUTS
AAOOPPRRST PARATROOPS
ABBBDENRRU RUBBER BAND
ABBBEEILSU BLUE BABIES
ABBBEGILNR BLABBERING
ABBBEHISSU BUSHBABIES
ABBBELOPSU SOAP BUBBLE
ABBCCDEKMO BACKCOMBED
ABBCDEKLOU DOUBLE BACK
ABBCDEMRRU BREADCRUMB
ABBCDIKLRS BLACKBIRDS
ABBCDKORSU BUCKBOARDS
ABBCEGGHUY BEACH BUGGY
ABBCEGINRU BARBECUING
ABBCEIKRST BACKBITERS
ABBCEILMNO COMBINABLE
ABBCEILRSU SUBCALIBRE
ABBCEINSSS SCABBINESS
ABBCEKLLST BLACK BELTS
ABBCEKLOSX BLACK BOXES
ABBCEKLRRY BLACKBERRY
ABBCEKMNRU BACK NUMBER
ABBCENORSY ABSORBENCY
ABBCGIIKNT BACKBITING
ABBCGILNRS SCRABBLING
ABBCILPRSU PUBLIC BARS
ABBCKLOOST BOOTBLACKS
ABBDDEEILO ABLE-BODIED
ABBDEEGILR BRIDGEABLE
ABBDEEHLPS PEBBLEDASH
ABBDEEIRRW BARBED WIRE
ABBDEELNNU UNBENDABLE
ABBDEELORU BELABOURED
ABBDEELRSU BLUEBEARDS
ABBDEFIORR FIBREBOARD
ABBDEIMNRY BABY-MINDER
ABBDEIMORR BOMBARDIER
ABBDELLNRU LANDLUBBER
ABBDELMOOZ BAMBOOZLED
ABBDELORSY ABSORBEDLY
ABBDELOSSU DOUBLE BASS
ABBDGIMNOR BOMBARDING
ABBDHLOOST BLOODBATHS
ABBDILLORS BILLBOARDS
ABBDKLNOOS BLOOD BANKS
ABBDNORSSU BRASSBOUND
ABBEEEILLV BELIEVABLE
ABBEEILLVY BELIEVABLY

ABBEELORSV OBSERVABLE
ABBEELRTTU REBUTTABLE
ABBEENORST BREASTBONE
ABBEENORTW BROWBEATEN
ABBEENRTTU BUTTER BEAN
ABBEFILNSS FLABBINESS
ABBEFMORRU FOAM RUBBER
ABBEGILNOR BELABORING
ABBEGJLSUU SUBJUGABLE
ABBEHHIKSS SHISH KEBAB
ABBEHINSSS SHABBINESS
ABBEILLMSU SUBLIMABLE
ABBEILMOPR IMPROBABLE
ABBEIRSTTY BABY-SITTER
ABBEKLNOTT BOTTLE BANK
ABBELMOORZ BAMBOOZLER
ABBELMSSUU SUBSUMABLE
ABBELORSVY OBSERVABLY
ABBELOSSTY STABLE BOYS
ABBENORSST ABSORBENTS
ABBFHIIRST RABBITFISH
ABBFHLLSSU FLASHBULBS
ABBFILORST FIBROBLAST
ABBGIINRTT RABBITTING
ABBGILNQSU SQUABBLING
ABBHILMSUU LUBUMBASHI
ABBILMOPRY IMPROBABLY
ABBILORSTU SUBORBITAL
ABBOOPRSTY BOOBY TRAPS
ABBOORRSWY BARROW BOYS
ABCCCEMNUY ACCUMBENCY
ABCCDEEIRT BRECCIATED
ABCCEEELNS ALBESCENCE
ABCCEEENST TABESCENCE
ABCCEEILMP IMPECCABLE
ABCCEEILSS ACCESSIBLE
ABCCEENRSU BUCCANEERS
ABCCEHILRU CHERUBICAL
ABCCEHKKLN BLANK CHECK
ABCCEILMPY IMPECCABLY
ABCCEINOSU SUBOCEANIC
ABCCEJNSUY SUBJACENCY
ABCCELNRSU CARBUNCLES
ABCCGHLSTU CLUTCH BAGS
ABCCHHKNSU HUNCHBACKS
ABCCHIIMOR CHORIAMBIC
ABCCHIIRRT TRIBRACHIC
ABCCHIKLPT PITCH-BLACK
ABCCHIKSTT BACKSTITCH
ABCCHIKSTW SWITCHBACK
ABCCHIOOPR ACROPHOBIC
ABCCHKLOST BACKCLOTHS
ABCCIMOORT MOBOCRATIC
ABCCINORTU BUCCINATOR

ABCCMOPSTU SUBCOMPACT
ABCCNOOPRY CARBON COPY
ABCDDKORSU DUCKBOARDS
ABCDEEEELR DECREEABLE
ABCDEEEELX EXCEEDABLE
ABCDEEEHSU DEBAUCHEES
ABCDEEEILV DECEIVABLE
ABCDEEELLT DELECTABLE
ABCDEEELRT CELEBRATED
ABCDEEELTT DETECTABLE
ABCDEEHLLY BELLYACHED
ABCDEEHRUY DEBAUCHERY
ABCDEEILLN DECLINABLE
ABCDEEILNU INEDUCABLE
ABCDEEILPR PREDICABLE
ABCDEEILPS DESPICABLE
ABCDEEILRT CREDITABLE
ABCDEELLNY BELLY DANCE
ABCDEELLTY DELECTABLY
ABCDEELLUX EXCLUDABLE
ABCDEELORR RECORDABLE
ABCDEFIRTU BIFURCATED
ABCDEFOSTU OBFUSCATED
ABCDEGHINU DEBAUCHING
ABCDEHIILR HERBICIDAL
ABCDEHKLOS BLOCKHEADS
ABCDEHKMPU HUMPBACKED
ABCDEHLNUW BUCHENWALD
ABCDEHORSS CHESSBOARD
ABCDEIILNT INDICTABLE
ABCDEIILNV VINDICABLE
ABCDEIIMRT IMBRICATED
ABCDEIIORT ABORTICIDE
ABCDEIIRSS SACRED IBIS
ABCDEIKLRS BACKSLIDER
ABCDEIKOUV BIVOUACKED
ABCDEIKRSS DISC BRAKES
ABCDEILLLU DULCIBELLA
ABCDEILLNU INCLUDABLE
ABCDEILLPU DUPLICABLE
ABCDEILNUY INEDUCABLY
ABCDEILPSY DESPICABLY
ABCDEILRTU LUBRICATED, TRADUCIBLE
ABCDEILRTY CREDITABLY
ABCDEINORS CARBONISED
ABCDEINORZ CARBONIZED
ABCDELLORY LOCAL DERBY
ABCDELPRUW PUB-CRAWLED
ABCDEOORRS SCOREBOARD
ABCDERSTTU SUBTRACTED
ABCDGIKLNO BLOCKADING
ABCDGINNOS ABSCONDING
ABCDGKNORU BACKGROUND
ABCDHIILNR BRAINCHILD

ABCDHINNRU NUDIBRANCH
ABCDHIOOPR BRACHIOPOD
ABCDHLOORT BROADCLOTH
ABCDHNOPRU PUNCHBOARD
ABCDHNRSTU DUTCH BARNS
ABCDIIISTY DIBASICITY
ABCDIILLSY DISYLLABIC
ABCDIIMNOY BIODYNAMIC
ABCDIISTUY SUBACIDITY
ABCDIKLOWW BLACK WIDOW
ABCDIKOPRR DROP A BRICK
ABCDILLNOO BILL AND COO
ABCDILNOST CNIDOBLAST
ABCDILOPRS CLIPBOARDS
ABCDKLNOSU CLOUDBANKS
ABCDKLOORS ROADBLOCKS
ABCEEEHKRS SCHAERBEEK
ABCEEEIKRR ICEBREAKER
ABCEEEILRV RECEIVABLE
ABCEEEJLRT REJECTABLE
ABCEEELRR CEREBELLAR
ABCEEELNRS SCREENABLE
ABCEEELPTX EXCEPTABLE, EXPECTABLE
ABCEEELTUX EXECUTABLE
ABCEEENRUX EXUBERANCE
ABCEEFFORS COFFEE BARS
ABCEEFHNNR FRENCH BEAN
ABCEEFIILN BENEFICIAL
ABCEEFNORT BENEFACTOR
ABCEEGKNRS GREENBACKS
ABCEEHILNR HIBERNACLE
ABCEEHKLPS BLACK SHEEP
ABCEEHKLST SKETCHABLE
ABCEEHKRTU HACKBUTEER
ABCEEHLLSY BELLYACHES
ABCEEHLNQU QUENCHABLE
ABCEEHNORR ABHORRENCE
ABCEEHORSU HERBACEOUS
ABCEEIILLT ELICITABLE
ABCEEIJLNT INJECTABLE
ABCEEILLNR RECLINABLE
ABCEEILLNS LICENSABLE
ABCEEILLOT BIOCELLATE
ABCEEILLPX EXPLICABLE
ABCEEILMMT EMBLEMATIC
ABCEEILNNU ENUNCIABLE
ABCEEILNOT NOTICEABLE
ABCEEILNTU BINUCLEATE
ABCEEILPTZ PECTIZABLE
ABCEEILRTX EXTRICABLE
ABCEEINNOZ BENZOCAINE
ABCEEINNST ABSTINENCE
ABCEEINOSS OBEISANCES
ABCEEKLOPT POCKETABLE

ABCEEKRSTT BACK STREET
ABCEEKSTTU BUCKET SEAT
ABCEELLNOS ENCLOSABLE
ABCEELLORT BROCATELLE
ABCEELLPUX EXCULPABLE
ABCEELLRRY CEREBRALLY
ABCEELNNOV CONVENABLE
ABCEELNORS CENSORABLE
ABCEELNOVY CONVEYABLE
ABCEELNRSU CENSURABLE
ABCEELOPRU RECOUPABLE
ABCEELOPRW PACE BOWLER
ABCEELORRT CELEBRATOR
ABCEEMMRST CAMEMBERTS
ABCEEMOOTY AMOEBOCYTE
ABCEENORSV OBSERVANCE
ABCEENRRTY BARYCENTRE
ABCEEOPPRS SPACE PROBE
ABCEEPRRSU CUPBEARERS
ABCEFHLSSU FLASHCUBES
ABCEFHOSTW FOB WATCHES
ABCEFLNOSU CONFUSABLE
ABCEGIKLNN BLACKENING
ABCEGIKNRT BRACKETING
ABCEGILMNR CLAMBERING
ABCEGILNOZ COGNIZABLE
ABCEGINNNY BENIGNANCY
ABCEGJLNOU CONJUGABLE
ABCEGLNOOT CONGLOBATE
ABCEHHJOTT HATCHET JOB
ABCEHIIRST HEBRAISTIC
ABCEHILPRT BIRTHPLACE
ABCEHILRST CHRISTABEL
ABCEHILSTW SWITCHABLE
ABCEHINRRY CHINABERRY
ABCEHIOOPR AEROPHOBIC
ABCEHKLLOS BLACK HOLES
ABCEHKMNRS BENCH MARKS
ABCEHKORSY CHEBOKSARY
ABCEHLLOTT TABLECLOTH
ABCEHMMNRU MACH NUMBER
ABCEHMOPRT CHAMBER POT
ABCEHMOSTX MATCHBOXES
ABCEHORTTX CHATTERBOX
ABCEIILLMT BIMETALLIC
ABCEIILLNN INCLINABLE
ABCEIILLNR BRILLIANCE
ABCEIILMTU UMBILICATE
ABCEIILPST EPIBLASTIC
ABCEIINTUV INCUBATIVE
ABCEIIOORT AEROBIOTIC
ABCEIKLRRY BRICKLAYER
ABCEILLNOU INOCULABLE
ABCEILLNPU INCULPABLE

ABCEILLNRS CRANESBILL
ABCEILLPXY EXPLICABLY
ABCEILLSSU CASUS BELLI
ABCEILLTUV CULTIVABLE
ABCEILMOPT COMPATIBLE
ABCEILNOSU UNSOCIABLE
ABCEILNOTY NOTICEABLY
ABCEILNPRU REPUBLICAN
ABCEILNRRU INCURRABLE
ABCEILPRSU RES PUBLICA
ABCEIMOORT COIMBATORE
ABCEIMORRT BAROMETRIC
ABCEINRRST TRANSCRIBE
ABCEIORSUU RUBIACEOUS
ABCEJKLMRU LUMBERJACK
ABCEKKORST BACKSTROKE
ABCEKLLNOU UNLOCKABLE
ABCEKLNORU COALBUNKER
ABCEKLOPRW BLACK POWER
ABCEKLRTTU TURTLEBACK
ABCELLLORU BLUE-COLLAR
ABCELLNOOR COLLARBONE
ABCELLNOOS CONSOLABLE
ABCELLOORU COLOURABLE
ABCELLOOST BLASTOCOEL
ABCELLRSSW SCREWBALLS
ABCELMMNOO COMMONABLE
ABCELMMOTU COMMUTABLE
ABCELMNRSU UNSCRAMBLE
ABCELMOPTU COMPUTABLE
ABCELNORRY BARLEYCORN
ABCELNOSST CONSTABLES
ABCELRRTUU TUBERCULAR
ABCEMNOPRU PERNAMBUCO
ABCEMOOPRT AMBOCEPTOR
ABCENNSTUY SUBTENANCY
ABCENSSSTU SUBSTANCES
ABCERRSTTU SUBTRACTER
ABCFGIIKNR BACKFIRING
ABCFILMORU BACULIFORM
ABCGGIKPSY PIGGYBACKS
ABCGHIINOT COHABITING
ABCGHIIOPR BIOGRAPHIC
ABCGHLORYY BRACHYLOGY
ABCGIILLOO BIOLOGICAL
ABCGIINNTU INCUBATING
ABCGILMNRS SCRAMBLING
ABCGIMNOTT COMBATTING
ABCHHIOPRS ARCHBISHOP
ABCHIILLNS CHILBLAINS
ABCHIILMOP AMPHIBOLIC
ABCHIKLMST BLACKSMITH
ABCHIKLRST BLACKSHIRT
ABCHKLMORU BLACK HUMOR

ABCHKLNORT BLACKTHORN
ABCHKMSTTU THUMBTACKS
ABCHKORSTW THROWBACKS
ABCHLLNPSU PUNCH BALLS
ABCIIINOTT ANTIBIOTIC
ABCIIJMOST JACOBITISM
ABCIILLNRY BRILLIANCY
ABCIILLSST BALLISTICS
ABCIILMOPS BIOPLASMIC
ABCIILRTUY CURABILITY
ABCIINNOTU INCUBATION
ABCIINOSSS ABSCISSION
ABCIIOSSTT BIOSTATICS
ABCIKLLSST BLACKLISTS
ABCILMOPTY COMPATIBLY
ABCILMOSUX MUSICAL BOX
ABCILMRUUV VIBRACULUM
ABCILMSSTY CYMBALISTS
ABCILNORSU BINOCULARS
ABCILNRSTU LUBRICANTS
ABCILORRTU LUBRICATOR
ABCILPSTUY SUBTYPICAL
ABCIMMOPRU PROCAMBIUM
ABCINORSTU INCUBATORS
ABCIORRRTU RUBRICATOR
ABCKKNOOTU KNOCKABOUT
ABCKLOPSST BLACK SPOTS
ABCKNPRTUY BANKRUPTCY
ABCKOOPRSS SCRAPBOOKS
ABCLOORRSU COLOUR BARS
ABCLORRTUU LUCUBRATOR
ABCLORRTUY ROTARY CLUB
ABCLOSSTTY BLASTOCYST
ABCNORSTTY BY CONTRAST
ABDDEEEFLN DEFENDABLE
ABDDEEEHNO BONEHEADED
ABDDEEELNP DEPENDABLE
ABDDEEGGLR BEDRAGGLED
ABDDEEGHIR BRIDGEHEAD
ABDDEEHLLU BULLHEADED
ABDDEEKORY KEYBOARDED
ABDDEELNPY DEPENDABLY
ABDDEELOTU DOUBLE DATE
ABDDEEPRSS BEDSPREADS
ABDDEERSTY TEDDY BEARS
ABDDEGINRU UNABRIDGED
ABDDEGIRRW DRAWBRIDGE
ABDDEHHINN BEHINDHAND
ABDDEHILNR HILDEBRAND
ABDDEHILOR HARD-BOILED
ABDDEHINRS BRANDISHED
ABDDEHMOTU BAD-MOUTHED
ABDDEIIMRS BRIDESMAID
ABDDEILLLS SADDLEBILL

ABDDEILNST BLIND DATES
ABDDEIORSS BROADSIDES, SIDEBOARDS
ABDDELNORR BORDERLAND
ABDDELNRTU BLADDERNUT
ABDDGIINNS DISBANDING
ABDDGORSUY BODYGUARDS
ABDDLMOORU MOULDBOARD
ABDDOORRSW BROADSWORD
ABDEEEELMR REDEEMABLE
ABDEEEFHRT FEATHER BED
ABDEEEFILS DEFEASIBLE
ABDEEEFLRR DEFERRABLE
ABDEEEGGLR BARELEGGED
ABDEEEGGRW BEGGARWEED
ABDEEEHQTU BEQUEATHED
ABDEEEILMR REMEDIABLE
ABDEEEILRT DELIBERATE
ABDEEELLPT DEPLETABLE
ABDEEELMRY REDEEMABLY
ABDEEELNPX EXPENDABLE
ABDEEELNRR RENDERABLE
ABDEEELNRT TENDERABLE
ABDEEELSTT DETESTABLE
ABDEEEMNST DEBASEMENT
ABDEEENRTT BERNADETTE
ABDEEERSTW SWEETBREAD
ABDEEFFHLU BUFFLEHEAD
ABDEEFHLRS HALF-BREEDS
ABDEEFHNOR BEFOREHAND
ABDEEFIITU BEAUTIFIED
ABDEEFLMOR DEFORMABLE
ABDEEFLNRU REFUNDABLE
ABDEEFORRS FREEBOARDS
ABDEEGILNS DESIGNABLE
ABDEEGLORT GOLD-BEATER
ABDEEHIKNR BIRKENHEAD
ABDEEHILLS DÉSHABILLÉ
ABDEEHILRR HALBERDIER
ABDEEHIMRT TIMBERHEAD
ABDEEHIMSV MISBEHAVED
ABDEEHINRT HIBERNATED
ABDEEHLMPS BLASPHEMED
ABDEEHLOTT TABLE D'HÔTE
ABDEEHORST BROADSHEET
ABDEEIILTT DEBILITATE
ABDEEIINRT INEBRIATED
ABDEEIKNNY KIDNEY BEAN
ABDEEILMRY REMEDIABLY
ABDEEILMTT TIMETABLED
ABDEEILNNU UNDENIABLE
ABDEEILNRS BREADLINES
ABDEEILPRU REPUDIABLE
ABDEEILPRV DEPRIVABLE
ABDEEILRSV VERBALISED

ABDEEILRVZ VERBALIZED	**ABDEILMSTU** SUBLIMATED
ABDEEINNRR BERNARDINE	**ABDEILNNUW** UNWINDABLE
ABDEEIRRVW WEAVERBIRD	**ABDEILNNUY** UNDENIABLY
ABDEEISTTU BEATITUDES	**ABDEILOPSS** DISPOSABLE
ABDEEKLOTU DOUBLE TAKE	**ABDEILPSTU** DISPUTABLE
ABDEEKORRY KEYBOARDER	**ABDEILRRSY** EARLY BIRDS
ABDEELLOPR DEPLORABLE	**ABDEILRSTU** BRUTALISED
ABDEELLORS SOLDERABLE	**ABDEILRTTW** WATTLEBIRD
ABDEELLSTY SELL-BY DATE	**ABDEILRTUZ** BRUTALIZED
ABDEELMNOZ EMBLAZONED	**ABDEIMNRST** DISBARMENT
ABDEELMRRU DEMURRABLE	**ABDEIMNSTU** SUBMEDIANT
ABDEELNOPR PONDERABLE	**ABDEIMRRTY** TIMBERYARD
ABDEELNORS BANDOLEERS, ENDORSABLE	**ABDEIMRTUW** DUMBWAITER
ABDEELNSST STEEL BANDS	**ABDEINORSU** BOUNDARIES
ABDEELOPRT DEPORTABLE	**ABDEIRRSTW** WATER BIRDS
ABDEELORTT BATTLEDORE	**ABDEIRTTTU** ATTRIBUTED
ABDEELSTTY DETESTABLY	**ABDEJORSTT** OBJETS D'ART
ABDEEMRRSU EMBRASURED	**ABDEKLLNOR** BANKROLLED
ABDEENOPSU SUBPOENAED	**ABDEKLLOTU** DOUBLE-TALK
ABDEENPRRY PREBENDARY	**ABDEKLOPRU** DOUBLE-PARK
ABDEENRRST BARTENDERS	**ABDEKNORSW** BREAKDOWNS
ABDEENSTTU DEBUTANTES	**ABDEKNPRTU** BANKRUPTED
ABDEEOPSST SPEEDBOATS	**ABDELLNOSW** SNOWBALLED
ABDEERRSST REDBREASTS	**ABDELLOPRY** DEPLORABLY
ABDEFFGLSU DUFFEL BAGS	**ABDELLORUY** LABOUREDLY
ABDEFFORSS BRASSED OFF	**ABDELMORST** BLASTODERM
ABDEFIILMO MODIFIABLE	**ABDELMRRUY** LUMBERYARD
ABDEFILMOR FORMIDABLE	**ABDELNORTU** ROUND-TABLE
ABDEFINRRS FIREBRANDS	**ABDELOOORT** BOOTLOADER
ABDEFIRRTU BREADFRUIT	**ABDELORSUV** BOULEVARDS
ABDEGGIRRU BUDGERIGAR	**ABDELORTUY** OBDURATELY
ABDEGGNOOT TOBOGGANED	**ABDENRRSST** ST BERNARDS
ABDEGHINSU SUBHEADING	**ABDENRSSTY** BYSTANDERS
ABDEGIMNRT ABRIDGMENT	**ABDENSSTUY** SUNDAY BEST
ABDEGINNOR BROADENING	**ABDERRTTYY** DRY BATTERY
ABDEGJSTUU SUBJUGATED	**ABDFILMORY** FORMIDABLY
ABDEGLNNRU BURGENLAND	**ABDFILNORU** FLORIBUNDA
ABDEGNNRUU GRAUBUNDEN	**ABDFINSSTU** IFS AND BUTS
ABDEHIILLS DISHABILLE	**ABDFLOOORR** FLOORBOARD
ABDEHINRRS BRANDISHER	**ABDFORRSSU** SURFBOARDS
ABDEHINRTT HARD-BITTEN	**ABDGHINNSU** HUSBANDING
ABDEHIORTW WHITEBOARD	**ABDGIINPRU** UPBRAIDING
ABDEHLOSTW DEATHBLOWS	**ABDGIINRRS** DISBARRING
ABDEHMNNSU HUSBANDMEN	**ABDGIINSSU** DISABUSING
ABDEHNORTU EARTHBOUND	**ABDGINNRUU** BURGUNDIAN
ABDEHNRSTU SUBTRAHEND	**ABDGINORTU** GROUND BAIT
ABDEHORRST SHORTBREAD	**ABDHILMOOR** RHOMBOIDAL
ABDEIIKLLS DISLIKABLE	**ABDHIOPRSS** SHIPBOARDS
ABDEIILMSS ADMISSIBLE	**ABDIIILSTY** DISABILITY
ABDEIILSST STABILISED	**ABDIIILTUY** AUDIBILITY
ABDEIILSTZ STABILIZED	**ABDIIKNNRY** BRADYKININ
ABDEIINOST ANTIBODIES	**ABDIILMNOU** ALBUMINOID
ABDEIKNRSW WINDBREAKS	**ABDIILORRT** TAILORBIRD
ABDEILLLNY BLIND ALLEY	**ABDIILPTUY** DUPABILITY

ABDIILRTUY DURABILITY
ABDIINOTTU DUBITATION
ABDIIRSSUY SUBSIDIARY
ABDILNOOST BLOODSTAIN
ABDILNORSU SUBORDINAL
ABDILOORTY BOTRYOIDAL
ABDILPSTUY DISPUTABLY
ABDIMPQSSU DAMP SQUIBS
ABDINOSWWY BAY WINDOWS
ABDINRSSTW WRISTBANDS
ABDLMOORYY BLOODY MARY
ABDMOOORRS BOARDROOMS
ABDNOORTUU ROUNDABOUT
ABDOORRTUU TROUBADOUR
ABEEEEFRST BEEFEATERS
ABEEEERSSZ SEA BREEZES
ABEEEFLPRR PREFERABLE
ABEEEGGLRS SEGREGABLE
ABEEEGLSTV VEGETABLES
ABEEEGNNRS GREEN BEANS
ABEEEHITTV HEBETATIVE
ABEEEHLSSW WHEELBASES
ABEEEHQRTU BEQUEATHER
ABEEEHRSTT HARTEBEEST
ABEEEILLRV RELIEVABLE
ABEEEILRVW REVIEWABLE
ABEEELLLPX EXPELLABLE
ABEEELLNVY ABNEY LEVEL
ABEEELLSTT SETTLEABLE
ABEEELMPRT TEMPERABLE
ABEEELMRSS REASSEMBLE
ABEEELNPRT PENETRABLE
ABEEELQSUZ SQUEEZABLE
ABEEELRRSV RESERVABLE
ABEEENNOZZ AZOBENZENE
ABEEENNRTT BANNERETTE
ABEEEORSTT STEREOBATE
ABEEERRTTV VERTEBRATE
ABEEFFLMNT BAFFLEMENT
ABEEFFLRSU SUFFERABLE
ABEEFGINRS FREE-BASING
ABEEFIILRV VERIFIABLE
ABEEFIKRRS FIREBREAKS
ABEEFILLLR REFILLABLE
ABEEFILLRT FILTERABLE
ABEEFILNTT FLEA-BITTEN
ABEEFILRSS BAS-RELIEFS
ABEEFIRRSU FEBRUARIES
ABEEFLOPRR PERFORABLE
ABEEFLPRRY PREFERABLY
ABEEFLSTTY SAFETY BELT
ABEEGHNORU HAUBERGEON
ABEEGHNTTU BEAT THE GUN

ABEEGIKNPS BESPEAKING
ABEEGILLNY EYEBALLING
ABEEGILMNR GERMINABLE
ABEEGILNOT NEGOTIABLE
ABEEGILNRT INTEGRABLE
ABEEGIMNRS BESMEARING
ABEEGINRSU AUBERGINES
ABEEGLNORV GOVERNABLE
ABEEGLOPRS BARGE POLES
ABEEGNRSTT ABSTERGENT
ABEEHHRRTY HEATHBERRY
ABEEHILLRS RELISHABLE
ABEEHILPRS PERISHABLE
ABEEHIMRSV MISBEHAVER
ABEEHINOTT HEBETATION
ABEEHKNORS BONESHAKER
ABEEHKORSS BRAKE SHOES
ABEEHLMPRS BLASPHEMER
ABEEHMORTT BATHOMETER
ABEEHNORSU OBERHAUSEN
ABEEHOORRS SEBORRHOEA
ABEEHORSTU HEREABOUTS
ABEEHPRRSY BARYSPHERE
ABEEIILLMN ELIMINABLE
ABEEIILLRS LIBERALISE
ABEEIILLRZ LIBERALIZE
ABEEIILNPX INEXPIABLE
ABEEIILNTV INEVITABLE
ABEEIILSST BESTIALISE
ABEEIILSTZ BESTIALIZE
ABEEIINRST INEBRIATES
ABEEIIRSST BESTIARIES
ABEEILLMNR BELLARMINE
ABEEILLMOR MELIORABLE
ABEEILLNNT TABLE LINEN
ABEEILLNRU UNRELIABLE
ABEEILLNST LISTENABLE
ABEEILLNTV VENTILABLE
ABEEILLRTT LITTLE BEAR
ABEEILMNRT TERMINABLE
ABEEILMNSU ALBUMENISE
ABEEILMNUZ ALBUMENIZE
ABEEILMOST METABOLISE
ABEEILMOTT METABOLITE
ABEEILMOTZ METABOLIZE
ABEEILMRTT REMITTABLE
ABEEILMSSS ASSEMBLIES
ABEEILMSTT TIMETABLES
ABEEILNNUV UNENVIABLE
ABEEILNOPR INOPERABLE
ABEEILNORX INEXORABLE
ABEEILNPSX EXPANSIBLE
ABEEILNRSS BLEARINESS
ABEEILNRST EAST BERLIN, INSERTABLE

ABEEILNRTU REUNITABLE	ABEEOPRSSW POWER BASES
ABEEILNRWY BARLEY WINE	ABEFFGILRU FEBRIFUGAL
ABEEILNSTV INVESTABLE	ABEFFILLOR BILL OF FARE
ABEEILORTT OBLITERATE	ABEFGIINTY BEATIFYING
ABEEILPPTZ PEPTIZABLE	ABEFGILORV FORGIVABLE
ABEEILPRRS RESPIRABLE	ABEFGILRSS FIBREGLASS, GLASS FIBRE
ABEEILQRRU REQUIRABLE	ABEFGINORR FORBEARING
ABEEILQRTU REQUITABLE	ABEFHIRRTT AFTERBIRTH
ABEEILRRSV VERBALISER	ABEFIILLLN INFALLIBLE
ABEEILRRVZ VERBALIZER	ABEFIILNOT NOTIFIABLE
ABEEILRSST ASSERTIBLE	ABEFILLLOS BILL OF SALE
ABEEILRSSU REISSUABLE	ABEFILMORR MORAL FIBRE
ABEEILSSTT BEASTLIEST	ABEFILOPRT PROFITABLE
ABEEIRRSSS BRASSERIES, BRASSIERES	ABEFKNORRT BREAKFRONT
ABEEJLLMSU JUMBLE SALE	ABEFLLLOOW FOLLOWABLE
ABEEJLLNSY JELLY BEANS	ABEFLLLORW BALLFLOWER
ABEEJMMNNT ENJAMBMENT	ABEFLLOORT FOOTBALLER
ABEEKLNRSV BLANK VERSE	ABEFLLOSTU FAT-SOLUBLE
ABEEKLNTTW WET BLANKET	ABEFNNORUZ BENZOFURAN
ABEEKMMNNT EMBANKMENT	ABEGGIMNOR EMBARGOING
ABEEKMMNRT EMBARKMENT	ABEGGNOORT TOBOGGANER
ABEEKNOPST KEEP TABS ON	ABEGGNOPSS SPONGE BAGS
ABEELLMNTU ANTEBELLUM	ABEGHILNRT BLATHERING
ABEELLMOPY EMPLOYABLE	ABEGHINRRS HARBINGERS
ABEELLNRUV VULNERABLE	ABEGHIOPRR BIOGRAPHER
ABEELLORSV RESOLVABLE	ABEGHLLLUY BELLY LAUGH
ABEELLORVV REVOLVABLE	ABEGHLNOOP ANGLOPHOBE
ABEELLPRUV PULVERABLE	ABEGHMRRSU HAMBURGERS
ABEELMMMNT EMBALMMENT	ABEGHNRRSU BUSHRANGER
ABEELMNRST RESEMBLANT	ABEGHQSUUU USQUEBAUGH
ABEELMNRSU LEBENSRAUM,	ABEGIILNNT INTANGIBLE
MENSURABLE	ABEGIILNOR OIL-BEARING
ABEELMNTTT BATTLEMENT	ABEGIILNRT LIBERATING
ABEELMORST BLASTOMERE	ABEGIILOTV OBLIGATIVE
ABEELMPRSU PRESUMABLE	ABEGIINNRT BRIGANTINE
ABEELNOPRS PERSONABLE	ABEGIINORS ABORIGINES
ABEELNRRTU RETURNABLE	ABEGIINOST ABIOGENIST
ABEELNSSST STABLENESS	ABEGIKLNNT BLANKETING
ABEELOPRRT REPORTABLE	ABEGILLNTY BLEATINGLY
ABEELOPRRV REPROVABLE	ABEGILMNSS ASSEMBLING
ABEELOPRTX EXPORTABLE	ABEGILNSSU SUBLEASING
ABEELORRST RESTORABLE	ABEGILRRSU BURGLARIES
ABEELPSTTU UPSETTABLE	ABEGINNOTY BAYONETING
ABEELRSUVY SURVEYABLE	ABEGINNQTU BANQUETING
ABEEMORRST BAROMETERS	ABEGINNRST STRING BEAN
ABEEMRRSSU EMBRASURES	ABEGINRSTU GAS TURBINE
ABEENNNRRU RUNNER BEAN	ABEGKRSSTU GRUBSTAKES
ABEENNRRSS BARRENNESS	ABEGLLNOOY BALNEOLOGY
ABEENNRSSU URBANENESS	ABEGLNORRY LOGANBERRY
ABEENNRSSZ BRAZENNESS	ABEGLNORSU LOUNGE BARS
ABEENORRTW WATERBORNE	ABEGLOOSTZ GO TO BLAZES
ABEENORSSS BARONESSES	ABEGLORRRV VORARLBERG
ABEEOPRRRT REPROBATER	ABEGMNOORS BOOMERANGS
ABEEOPRRST REPROBATES	ABEGMORSUU UMBRAGEOUS

ABEGNNSTTU SUBTANGENT
ABEGNOORTU BATON ROUGE
ABEHHILLST SHEATHBILL
ABEHHIOOPT THEOPHOBIA
ABEHHMMRSU BUSHHAMMER
ABEHHORRTT HEARTTHROB
ABEHIILMNT HABILIMENT
ABEHIKLNRS SHRINKABLE
ABEHILNPSU PUNISHABLE
ABEHILOPST HOSPITABLE
ABEHILPSTT BATTLESHIP
ABEHILPSTU BISULPHATE
ABEHILRSST HERBALISTS
ABEHIMNNST BANISHMENT
ABEHINNORT ON THE BRAIN
ABEHINOOPX XENOPHOBIA
ABEHINOPRV VIBRAPHONE
ABEHINORRT HIBERNATOR
ABEHINRSSS BRASHINESS
ABEHIRRSTT BIRTH-RATES
ABEHKOOPRS PHRASEBOOK
ABEHLMOOST SMOOTHABLE
ABEHLNOORU HONOURABLE
ABEHLOPRSY HYPERBOLAS
ABEHLORRSS HARBORLESS
ABEHLORRTY LAY BROTHER
ABEHLORSTT BETROTHALS
ABEHLORTTU BLUETHROAT
ABEHMORTTY BATHOMETRY
ABEHMRSSTU BUSHMASTER
ABEHMRTTYY BATHYMETRY
ABEHNRSSTU SUNBATHERS
ABEHOOSSTU BOATHOUSES, HOUSEBOATS
ABEIIILMNT INIMITABLE
ABEIIILNSS SENSIBILIA
ABEIILLMRS LIBERALISM
ABEIILLNNY BIENNIALLY
ABEIILLNOV INVIOLABLE
ABEIILLRST LIBERALIST
ABEIILLRTY LIBERALITY
ABEIILLTUZ UTILIZABLE
ABEIILMNSS LESBIANISM
ABEIILMPRT IMPARTIBLE
ABEIILMRST BIMESTRIAL
ABEIILNORT LIBERATION
ABEIILNPRS INSPIRABLE
ABEIILNTTU INTUITABLE
ABEIILNTTY TENABILITY
ABEIILNTVY INEVITABLY
ABEIILQTUY EQUABILITY
ABEIILRSST STABILISER
ABEIILRSTZ STABILIZER
ABEIILSTTY BESTIALITY
ABEIINNRRT INTERBRAIN

ABEIINNRSS BRAININESS
ABEIINRRSV RIVER BASIN
ABEIIOORSS AEROBIOSIS
ABEIIORSTU OBITUARIES
ABEIKNSTUZ UZBEKISTAN
ABEILLMSTU STIMULABLE
ABEILLNOSV INSOLVABLE
ABEILLPPSU SUPPLIABLE
ABEILLPSTU STIPULABLE
ABEILLSUXY BISEXUALLY
ABEILMMOST METABOLISM
ABEILMNNRU MELBURNIAN
ABEILMNQRU LAMBREQUIN
ABEILMOOTU AUTOMOBILE
ABEILMOPRV IMPROVABLE
ABEILMRSSU SURMISABLE
ABEILMSSTU SUBLIMATES
ABEILNNOOW ON A BOWLINE
ABEILNORXY INEXORABLY
ABEILNSTUU UNSUITABLE
ABEILOPRRV PROVERBIAL
ABEILOPSTU BIPETALOUS
ABEILOPSTY POLYBASITE
ABEILORRST LIBERATORS
ABEILORTVY ABORTIVELY
ABEILRRTTU TRITURABLE
ABEILRSTUV VESTIBULAR
ABEILRSUVV SURVIVABLE
ABEIMMOQUZ MOZAMBIQUE
ABEIMNNOTT OBTAINMENT
ABEIMNORTU TAMBOURINE
ABEIMNRRSU SUBMARINER
ABEIMNRSSU SUBMARINES
ABEIMOSSTU ABSTEMIOUS
ABEINNORTU EBURNATION
ABEINNOSTT ABSTENTION
ABEINNRSSW BRAWNINESS
ABEINORTTX EXORBITANT
ABEINRSSSS BRASSINESS
ABEIOPPRSY PRESBYOPIA
ABEIOPRSTV ABSORPTIVE
ABEIOSSSST ASBESTOSIS
ABEIPRSTTY BAPTISTERY
ABEIRRRSST BARRISTERS
ABEIRRTTTU ATTRIBUTER
ABEIRSTTTU ATTRIBUTES
ABEKKMOORS BOOKMAKERS
ABEKKORSTW BASKETWORK,
    WORKBASKET
ABEKLLORWY YELLOWBARK
ABEKLNNOUW UNKNOWABLE
ABEKLNORUW UNWORKABLE
ABEKLOOPST BOOKPLATES
ABEKLOPRRR PORK BARREL

ABEKMNNOTU MOUNTEBANK
ABEKNOPRRW PAWNBROKER
ABEKORRSTW BREASTWORK
ABELLLLOVY VOLLEYBALL
ABELLNRUVY VULNERABLY
ABELLORVVY REVOLVABLY
ABELLOSTUY ABSOLUTELY
ABELLSSSUY SYLLABUSES
ABELMMNOSU SUMMONABLE
ABELMNORYZ EMBLAZONRY
ABELMOOPRT PROMOTABLE
ABELMPRSUY PRESUMABLY
ABELNNORUV VERBAL NOUN
ABELNOOPST TABLESPOON
ABELNOPRSY PERSONABLY
ABELNORSTU NEUROBLAST
ABELNRRTUU NURTURABLE
ABELNRSSTU SUBALTERNS
ABELNRSTTU TURNTABLES
ABELOOPPRS PROPOSABLE
ABELOOPRST BLASTOPORE
ABELOOSSTT OSTEOBLAST
ABELOPPSSU SUPPOSABLE
ABELPRRTUU RUPTURABLE
ABEMMNORSU MEMBRANOUS
ABEMNNOSTU SUBMONTANE
ABEMNOORRW BONE MARROW,
   MARROWBONE
ABENNSSTTU SUBTENANTS
ABENOPRRSS PRESS BARON
ABENOPRSTU BEANSPROUT
ABENORRRTW BARRENWORT
ABENPRSSTU ABRUPTNESS
ABEOOPRSTW POWERBOATS
ABEOPSTTUY BEAUTY SPOT
ABEOQSSUUU SUBAQUEOUS
ABERRRSTWY STRAWBERRY
ABERSTTTUW WATER BUTTS
ABFGILNOTY FLYING BOAT
ABFGILORVY FORGIVABLY
ABFGNOORRU GO FOR A BURN
ABFIIILRTY FRIABILITY
ABFIILLLNY INFALLIBLY
ABFIILNORV RIBOFLAVIN
ABFILOPRTY PROFITABLY
ABFLLOSTUY BOASTFULLY
ABFLLOSUUY FABULOUSLY
ABGGGILNRY BRAGGINGLY
ABGGIILNOT OBLIGATING
ABGGIKNPSY PIGGYBANKS
ABGHIIINNT INHABITING
ABGHIILNOS ABOLISHING
ABGHIJNORS JOBSHARING
ABGHINNSTU SUNBATHING

ABGHINORRU HARBOURING
ABGHIORTTU RIGHTABOUT
ABGHIRRRSU HARRISBURG
ABGHOORRUY YARBOROUGH
ABGIIILNNT NAIL-BITING
ABGIILLNSU BILINGUALS
ABGIILNNTY INTANGIBLY
ABGIILNOOT OBLIGATION
ABGIILNOPR PARBOILING
ABGIINNOTZ BOTANIZING
ABGILLNNOO BALLOONING
ABGILLNORY LABORINGLY
ABGILLNSUU SUBLINGUAL
ABGILLOSST GLOBALISTS
ABGILLOSTY BILLY GOATS
ABGILMOSUY BIGAMOUSLY
ABGILNOSTY BOASTINGLY
ABGILOORTY OBLIGATORY
ABGINNORRT BARRINGTON
ABGINOORTW ROWING BOAT
ABGINORTUV OUTBRAVING
ABGJOORRTU OBJURGATOR
ABGJORSTUU SUBJUGATOR
ABGLLORUUU LULUABOURG
ABGORRSSTU STRASBOURG
ABHHNORSSW HASH BROWNS
ABHIIMOPSU AMPHIBIOUS
ABHIKMRRST BIRTHMARKS
ABHILMNSTU THUMBNAILS
ABHILNRSTY LABYRINTHS
ABHILOPSTY HOSPITABLY
ABHILORTUW WHIRLABOUT
ABHIMNOOOP MONOPHOBIA
ABHINPRSTU PAINTBRUSH
ABHLLMSTTU THUMBSTALL
ABHLNOORUY HONOURABLY
ABHMNORRTU RHUMBATRON
ABIIILLPTY PLIABILITY
ABIIILLTVY LIVABILITY
ABIIILMNTY INIMITABLY
ABIIILMTXY MIXABILITY
ABIIILNOST SIBILATION
ABIIINOSST ANTIBIOSIS
ABIIJLNOTU JUBILATION
ABIILLMNSU SUBLIMINAL
ABIILLOTVY LOVABILITY
ABIILMOTVY MOVABILITY
ABIILMTTUY MUTABILITY
ABIILNOTTY NOTABILITY
ABIILOPTTY POTABILITY
ABIIMORSSV BRAVISSIMO
ABIINNOTTU INTUBATION
ABIINORSTV VIBRATIONS
ABIINOTTTU TITUBATION

ABIIORSTTU OBITUARIST
ABIJLLNTUY JUBILANTLY
ABIKKNSTUY AKTYUBINSK
ABIKLNNOPT POINT-BLANK
ABILLNOOST BALLOONIST
ABILLNOOTU LOBULATION
ABILLNOPST BALLPOINTS
ABILMNOSUU ALBUMINOUS
ABILMNOTUX TOXALBUMIN
ABILMOSSTU ABSOLUTISM
ABILNNOORU LABOR UNION
ABILNOOSTU ABSOLUTION
ABILNOTTUU TUBULATION
ABILORSSUU SALUBRIOUS
ABILOSSTUY SABULOSITY
ABILRSTTUU SUBTITULAR
ABILRTTUUY TUBULARITY
ABIMNORRST BRAINSTORM
ABIMRSSSTU STRABISMUS
ABINNOSTVV BON VIVANTS
ABINOOPRST ABSORPTION
ABINOOSSST BASSOONIST
ABINOSSTTU BUS STATION, SUBSTATION
ABKLLOOSST BOOKSTALLS
ABLOORSTUY ABSOLUTORY
ABMOOORSTT MOTORBOATS
ABMRSSTTUU SUBSTRATUM
ABNORSTTUU ABOUT-TURNS,
  TURNABOUTS
ABOOPRSSTT BOOTSTRAPS
ABOORSTTUU ROUSTABOUT
ACCCDEHKRS CHECK CARDS
ACCCDIIIPR PICRIC ACID
ACCCDIIIRT CITRIC ACID
ACCCEENRST ACCRESCENT
ACCCEFHKOR COCKCHAFER
ACCCEGINOS CACOGENICS
ACCCEHILOT CHALCOCITE
ACCCEHORTW COWCATCHER
ACCCEIILRT CICATRICLE
ACCCEIIRST CICATRICES
ACCCEILLNY ENCYCLICAL
ACCCEILMOP ACCOMPLICE
ACCCGLNOOO GONOCOCCAL
ACCCHINOOP CACOPHONIC
ACCCHKOPST SPATCHCOCK
ACCCHLOORY OCHLOCRACY
ACCCHOOTUU CAOUTCHOUC
ACCCHOPRST CATCH CROPS
ACCCILLLYY CYCLICALLY
ACCCILMORY CYCLORAMIC
ACCCIMORTY MACROCYTIC
ACCCINOPPU CAPPUCCINO
ACCDDEEIRT ACCREDITED

ACCDDEEIST DESICCATED
ACCDDEIRRT CREDIT CARD
ACCDEEHIST CATECHISED
ACCDEEHITZ CATECHIZED
ACCDEEHKMT CHECKMATED
ACCDEEHNOR ENCROACHED
ACCDEEHQRU CHEQUE CARD
ACCDEEIILS DELICACIES
ACCDEEINNS INCANDESCE
ACCDEEIQSU ACQUIESCED
ACCDEELPTY ACCEPTEDLY
ACCDEFIIRS SACRIFICED
ACCDEGHORT DOGCATCHER
ACCDEHIKRS DECKCHAIRS
ACCDEHKOST COCKED HATS
ACCDEHLNOY CHALCEDONY
ACCDEIILNY INDELICACY
ACCDEIILST DIALECTICS
ACCDEIKLNW CANDLEWICK
ACCDEILLOP PECCADILLO
ACCDEILNOT OCCIDENTAL
ACCDEILNTU INCULCATED
ACCDEILRTU CIRCULATED
ACCDEIMNNY MENDICANCY
ACCDEIMORT DEMOCRATIC
ACCDEINNTU INDUCTANCE
ACCDEINOOS OCCASIONED
ACCDEINSST DESICCANTS
ACCDEIORST DESICCATOR
ACCDELLOOT COLLOCATED
ACCDEMOSTU ACCUSTOMED
ACCDENORTT CONTRACTED
ACCDENPSSU DUNCE'S CAPS
ACCDEOPRST CADET CORPS
ACCDEORRSS SCORECARDS
ACCDEORSSW SACRED COWS
ACCDEORSTU CORUSCATED
ACCDFIILTY FLACCIDITY
ACCDFIIMOR FORMIC ACID
ACCDGIIILT TIGLIC ACID
ACCDHHRRUY CHURCHYARD
ACCDHIINOR DIACHRONIC
ACCDHILORV CLAVICHORD
ACCDHORSTW CATCHWORDS
ACCDIIINRT NITRIC ACID
ACCDIIIRST DIACRITICS
ACCDIILLPY PICCADILLY
ACCDIILOTU TOLUIC ACID
ACCDINOORS ACCORDIONS
ACCDINORTT CONTRADICT
ACCDKNORSW CRACKDOWNS
ACCDLOORSV VOCAL CORDS
ACCDNNOORT CONCORDANT
ACCDNOORST CONCORDATS

ACCDORRSTU COURT CARDS
ACCEEEEHKS CHEESECAKE
ACCEEEHRTY EYE-CATCHER
ACCEEELPRT RECEPTACLE
ACCEEHILLR CHELICERAL
ACCEEHILNP ENCEPHALIC
ACCEEHINRS CHANCERIES
ACCEEHISST CATECHESIS
ACCEEHKMST CHECKMATES
ACCEEHNORR ENCROACHER
ACCEEILLRT ELECTRICAL
ACCEEILMNU ECUMENICAL
ACCEEILNTY ACETYLENIC
ACCEEILORV VARICOCELE
ACCEEIMSST ACCESS TIME
ACCEEIORSU ERICACEOUS
ACCEEIRTUX EXCRUCIATE
ACCEELNOST COALESCENT
ACCEELNOSV CONVALESCE
ACCEELNPRU CRAPULENCE
ACCEELNRTU RELUCTANCE
ACCEELNSTT LACTESCENT
ACCEELNSTU CAULESCENT
ACCEELPSST SPECTACLES
ACCEEMNRST MARCESCENT,
  SCARCEMENT
ACCEEMOSTY ASCOMYCETE
ACCEENNNOV CONVENANCE
ACCEENNOVY CONVEYANCE
ACCEENOPRR COPARCENER
ACCEENORST CONSECRATE
ACCEENPTXY EXPECTANCY
ACCEENRSSS SCARCENESS
ACCEEOPPRS PEACE CORPS
ACCEEORRSU RACECOURSE
ACCEEORSTU CRETACEOUS
ACCEFFIINY INEFFICACY
ACCEFHLOST FACECLOTHS
ACCEFHLRTY FLYCATCHER
ACCEFIIRRS SACRIFICER
ACCEFIIRSS SACRIFICES
ACCEFILLOR CALCIFEROL
ACCEFILMOR CALCEIFORM
ACCEFINOST CONFISCATE
ACCEFLLOTU FLOCCULATE
ACCEGILLNN CANCELLING
ACCEGILLNO COLLAGENIC
ACCEGILLOO ECOLOGICAL
ACCEGILNNO CONCEALING
ACCEGILNOS COALESCING
ACCEGILNOT LACTOGENIC
ACCEGINNOR CARCINOGEN
ACCEGINNOZ COGNIZANCE
ACCEHHIPRT HEPTARCHIC

ACCEHIILMR CHIMERICAL
ACCEHIINNT TECHNICIAN
ACCEHIKNRS RAIN CHECKS
ACCEHILLMY CHEMICALLY
ACCEHILLTY HECTICALLY
ACCEHILNOS COCHINEALS
ACCEHIMNSS MISCHANCES
ACCEHIMSST CATECHISMS
ACCEHINNRY IN CHANCERY
ACCEHINNSS CHANCINESS
ACCEHINOPT CENOTAPHIC
ACCEHINSST CATCHINESS
ACCEHIORRY HIEROCRACY
ACCEHIORST ESCHAROTIC
ACCEHIORTT RHEOTACTIC, THEOCRATIC
ACCEHIRRST SCRATCHIER
ACCEHIRRTT TETRARCHIC
ACCEHIRSTT ARCHITECTS
ACCEHISSTT CATECHISTS
ACCEHLLNOR CHANCELLOR
ACCEHLMOOR HOMOCERCAL
ACCEHLOOST CHOCOLATES
ACCEHLOSUY CHYLACEOUS
ACCEHNNPTY CATCHPENNY
ACCEHNNRTY TRENCHANCY
ACCEHNOOTY CHOANOCYTE
ACCEHNORTT TECHNOCRAT, TRENCH
  COAT
ACCEHOPSTT SCOTCH TAPE
ACCEIILNOT CONCILIATE
ACCEIILRTT TECTRICIAL
ACCEIIMSST ASCETICISM
ACCEIINPRT IN PRACTICE
ACCEIINRST CISTERCIAN
ACCEIIRRST CICATRISER
ACCEIIRRTZ CICATRIZER
ACCEIIRSST SCARCITIES
ACCEIKRSSW WISECRACKS
ACCEILLLPS SCALPELLIC
ACCEILLLRY CLERICALLY
ACCEILLNSY SCENICALLY
ACCEILMMOR COMMERCIAL
ACCEILMNOO ECONOMICAL
ACCEILMNOP COMPLIANCE
ACCEILMOPT COMPLICATE
ACCEILMOST CACOMISTLE
ACCEILNRST CALCSINTER
ACCEILOPPT APOPLECTIC
ACCEILOPRR RECIPROCAL
ACCEILOPRV PREVOCALIC
ACCEIMNORS SCIOMANCER
ACCEIMOOPR COMIC OPERA
ACCEIMORST MESOCRATIC
ACCEINNNOV CONNIVANCE

ACCEINNORT CONCERTINA
ACCEINNSSY INCESSANCY
ACCEINOOST CONSOCIATE
ACCEINORST ACCRETIONS
ACCEINOSSS ACCESSIONS
ACCEIOORSU CORIACEOUS
ACCEIOPPSY EPISCOPACY
ACCEIORSTX EXSICCATOR
ACCEIOSSTU CISTACEOUS
ACCEJNOSUU JUNCACEOUS
ACCEKKLMOR CLOCKMAKER
ACCEKNORRS CORNCRAKES
ACCEKNRRTU NUTCRACKER
ACCELLLOSS CLOSE CALLS
ACCELLSSUU CALCULUSES
ACCELMNOPT COMPLACENT
ACCELNOPTU CONCEPTUAL
ACCELOOPST LACTOSCOPE
ACCEMNNORY NECROMANCY
ACCENNNOOS CONSONANCE
ACCENOORSU CORNACEOUS
ACCENORTTU COUNTERACT
ACCEORRSSW SCARECROWS
ACCEORSUUV CURVACEOUS
ACCFFFFHHI CHIFFCHAFF
ACCFGIILNY CALCIFYING
ACCFHIRTTW WITCHCRAFT
ACCFIINNOT FANTOCCINI
ACCFILSSUU FASCICULUS
ACCFKOORST FROCK COATS
ACCFLLNOTU FLOCCULANT
ACCGHIILOR OLIGARCHIC
ACCGHINRST SCRATCHING
ACCGHIOPTY PHAGOCYTIC
ACCGHORSSU COUCH GRASS
ACCGIILORT GO CRITICAL
ACCGIIMORT TRAGICOMIC
ACCGIINPRT PRACTICING
ACCGILNSUY ACCUSINGLY
ACCGIMNOPT COMPACTING
ACCGINNOTT CONTACTING
ACCGINNOTU ACCOUNTING
ACCHHIILLN CHINCHILLA
ACCHHORSST CROSSHATCH
ACCHIIILST CHILIASTIC
ACCHIIMSST SCHISMATIC
ACCHIKMSTT MATCHSTICK
ACCHILLOOS ALCOHOLICS
ACCHILMOPS ACCOMPLISH
ACCHILNNPS SPLANCHNIC
ACCHILNOOT CATHOLICON
ACCHILOSST SCHOLASTIC
ACCHILRSTY SCRATCHILY
ACCHILTTYY TACHYLYTIC

ACCHIMNORY CHIROMANCY
ACCHIMORST CHROMATICS
ACCHIOPRSZ SCHIZOCARP
ACCHIOSSTT STOCHASTIC
ACCHNORRST CORNSTARCH
ACCHOPRSST CROSSPATCH
ACCIIILLLP PICCALILLI
ACCIIINNNT CINCINNATI
ACCIILLLNY CLINICALLY
ACCIILLOST LOCALISTIC
ACCIILLRTY CRITICALLY
ACCIILMSSS CLASSICISM
ACCIILNNOT CALCITONIN
ACCIILNRTU UNCRITICAL
ACCIILORTY CALORICITY
ACCIILSSST CLASSICIST
ACCIIMNNNO CINNAMONIC
ACCIIMNOOT ICONOMATIC
ACCIIMNOST SCIOMANTIC
ACCIINNNPY PICCANINNY
ACCIINNOTY CANONICITY
ACCIIOPRSU CAPRICIOUS
ACCIIOTTVY COACTIVITY
ACCIKKKKNN KNICK-KNACK
ACCILLMOSY COSMICALLY
ACCILMNNOU COUNCILMAN
ACCILMNOOS ICONOCLASM
ACCILNOOST ICONOCLAST
ACCILNORTU INCULCATOR
ACCILNOSTV CONCLAVIST
ACCILNSSTY SYNCLASTIC
ACCILOPPRY POLYCARPIC
ACCILORRTU CIRCULATOR
ACCILRRRUU CURRICULAR
ACCIMNOOPR MONOCARPIC
ACCIMNOORT MONOCRATIC
ACCIMORSSY COSMIC RAYS
ACCINNOOOS ON OCCASION
ACCINOOPRU CORNUCOPIA
ACCINOOPTU OCCUPATION
ACCINOPRRS CAPRICORNS
ACCINOPRSY CONSPIRACY
ACCINSSTTY SYNTACTICS
ACCIOPRSTT CATOPTRICS
ACCKKNOOOS COCK A SNOOK
ACCKLMOORU COCKALORUM
ACCLLLOOOR LOCAL COLOR
ACCLOPRTUY PLUTOCRACY
ACCMMOORSS MACROCOSMS
ACCNNOOSTU NO-ACCOUNTS
ACCNOOORTV CONVOCATOR
ACCNOOPRRY PORNOCRACY
ACCNOORRTT CONTRACTOR
ACDDEEENOS DODECANESE

ACDDEEENRT DEAD CENTER, DEAD CENTRE
ACDDEEEPRT DEPRECATED
ACDDEEERST DESECRATED
ACDDEEERTU RE-EDUCATED
ACDDEEHLOO COOL-HEADED
ACDDEEHNOR DECAHEDRON
ACDDEEHPST DESPATCHED
ACDDEEIIPT DIAPEDETIC
ACDDEEILTU ELUCIDATED
ACDDEEIPRT PREDICATED
ACDDEELLSY CLYDESDALE
ACDDEELNRY DRY-CLEANED
ACDDEELNTY DECADENTLY
ACDDEENNST DESCENDANT
ACDDEENRTU UNDERACTED
ACDDEENTUU UNEDUCATED
ACDDEFFHNU HANDCUFFED
ACDDEFFIRT DIFFRACTED
ACDDEGHIRS DISCHARGED
ACDDEGIINT DEDICATING
ACDDEHIKNP HANDPICKED
ACDDEHINSW SANDWICHED
ACDDEHIPST DISPATCHED
ACDDEHIRRS HARD CIDERS
ACDDEHIRSV CRASH-DIVED
ACDDEHNNOS SECOND-HAND
ACDDEIILMS DISCLAIMED
ACDDEIINOT DEDICATION
ACDDEIINTV VINDICATED
ACDDEILMOU DUODECIMAL
ACDDEILOST DISLOCATED
ACDDEILPTU DUPLICATED
ACDDEILTTW WILDCATTED
ACDDEINSTY SYNDICATED
ACDDEIORTY DEDICATORY
ACDDEIRSTT DISTRACTED
ACDDEKLLNO LANDLOCKED
ACDDEKLORS DREADLOCKS
ACDDELNNOO COLONNADED
ACDDELNOOW CANDLEWOOD
ACDDENNRUY REDUNDANCY
ACDDENORSW SWORD DANCE
ACDDFHIORU CHAUDFROID
ACDDGHILNR GRANDCHILD
ACDDGIINRS DISCARDING
ACDDHHNSSU DACHSHUNDS
ACDDIINOST ADDICTIONS
ACDDINORST DISCORDANT
ACDEEEEHHS HEADCHEESE
ACDEEEELRT DECELERATE
ACDEEEEPRS PREDECEASE
ACDEEEFLNR FER-DE-LANCE, FREELANCED

ACDEEEFMNT DEFACEMENT
ACDEEEGNRY DEGENERACY
ACDEEEHIPS HEADPIECES
ACDEEEHRRS RESEARCHED
ACDEEEIPRT DEPRECIATE
ACDEEEKNPP KNEECAPPED
ACDEEENNTT ANTECEDENT
ACDEEENRTV ADVERTENCE
ACDEEEORRT REDECORATE
ACDEEFFHRT FARFETCHED
ACDEEFFLTY AFFECTEDLY
ACDEEFFNTU UNAFFECTED
ACDEEFGINT DEFECATING
ACDEEFINOT DEFECATION
ACDEEFINRT INTERFACED
ACDEEFKOPR POKER-FACED
ACDEEFOPRW FACE POWDER
ACDEEFORST FORECASTED
ACDEEFRRSU RESURFACED
ACDEEGHLLN CHALLENGED
ACDEEGHNNO HENDECAGON
ACDEEGINRR ADRENERGIC
ACDEEGINRS DECREASING
ACDEEGINRT CENTIGRADE
ACDEEGNORU ENCOURAGED
ACDEEHILNR CHANDELIER
ACDEEHIMNS MECHANISED
ACDEEHIMNZ MECHANIZED
ACDEEHIMRS ARCHIMEDES
ACDEEHLLNN CHANNELLED
ACDEEHLNRT ANDERLECHT
ACDEEHMNTT DETACHMENT
ACDEEHNOPR CHAPERONED
ACDEEHOPPR COPPERHEAD
ACDEEHOPRR REPROACHED
ACDEEHORRV OVERARCHED
ACDEEHPRST DESPATCHER
ACDEEHPSST DESPATCHES
ACDEEHPSSY SPEECH DAYS
ACDEEIILMP EPIDEMICAL
ACDEEIILMS DECIMALISE
ACDEEIILMZ DECIMALIZE
ACDEEIILNT INDELICATE
ACDEEIIMRT ACIDIMETER
ACDEEIIMTV MEDICATIVE
ACDEEIJSTV ADJECTIVES
ACDEEILLNR CINDERELLA
ACDEEILLOS DELOCALISE
ACDEEILLOZ DELOCALIZE
ACDEEILLRS ESCADRILLE
ACDEEILLTY DELICATELY
ACDEEILMPR PREMEDICAL
ACDEEILNPP APPENDICLE
ACDEEILNRT INTERLACED

ACDEEILOSV DEVOCALISE
ACDEEILOVZ DEVOCALIZE
ACDEEILPRT REPLICATED
ACDEEILPTU PEDICULATE
ACDEEILPTX EXPLICATED
ACDEEIMMNT MEDICAMENT
ACDEEIMNPS IMPEDANCES
ACDEEIMORT ACIDOMETER
ACDEEIMPRT MERCAPTIDE
ACDEEINNNT INTENDANCE
ACDEEINNTU DENUNCIATE, ENUNCIATED
ACDEEINPPS APPENDICES
ACDEEINRTT INTERACTED
ACDEEINSST DESISTANCE
ACDEEIORTV DECORATIVE
ACDEEIORTX EXCORIATED
ACDEEIOTTX DETOXICATE
ACDEEIPRRT TRADE PRICE
ACDEEIPRST PEDERASTIC, PREDICATES
ACDEEIRSTU CAUTERISED
ACDEEIRTTV DETRACTIVE
ACDEEIRTTX EXTRICATED
ACDEEIRTUZ CAUTERIZED
ACDEEITTUX EXACTITUDE
ACDEELMORT ECTODERMAL
ACDEELMORU LEUCODERMA
ACDEELNOST ADOLESCENT
ACDEELNRRY DRY CLEANER
ACDEELOPRT PERCOLATED
ACDEELORRT CORRELATED
ACDEELORTU EDULCORATE
ACDEELPSTU SPECULATED
ACDEELPTUX EXCULPATED
ACDEEMMNOR COMMANDEER
ACDEEMMNPT DECAMPMENT
ACDEEMNOTY ADENECTOMY
ACDEENNOST CONDENSATE
ACDEENNOTV COVENANTED
ACDEENORST SECOND-RATE
ACDEENRSSS SACREDNESS
ACDEENRTTU DETRUNCATE
ACDEEOOPRT COOPERATED
ACDEEOPRRT DEPRECATOR, PROCREATED
ACDEEORRST DESECRATOR
ACDEEPRRTU RECAPTURED
ACDEFFIIOT OFFICIATED
ACDEFFIKRT TRAFFICKED
ACDEFFLORS SCAFFOLDER
ACDEFFLOTU DUFFEL COAT
ACDEFFMORS COFFERDAMS
ACDEFFOSTU SUFFOCATED
ACDEFHILNS CANDLEFISH
ACDEFHINRS FRANCHISED
ACDEFHOSUV VOUCHSAFED

ACDEFIILSS CLASSIFIED
ACDEFIINST SANCTIFIED
ACDEFIIRRT FRATRICIDE
ACDEFIJKKN JACK-KNIFED
ACDEFILLOS COALFIELDS
ACDEFILSSY DECLASSIFY
ACDEFINORT FORNICATED
ACDEFIORST FACTORISED
ACDEFIORTZ FACTORIZED
ACDEFKLNOR FOLK DANCER
ACDEFKLNOS FOLK DANCES
ACDEFLMORS COLD FRAMES
ACDEFLNOOT FOOT-CANDLE
ACDEFLTTUU FLUCTUATED
ACDEFNORRU UNCARED-FOR
ACDEFNORTU FECUNDATOR
ACDEFNRSSY FANCY DRESS
ACDEGHIRRS DISCHARGER
ACDEGHIRSS DISCHARGES
ACDEGHRRSU SURCHARGED
ACDEGIILMN DECLAIMING
ACDEGIILMR GERMICIDAL
ACDEGIILNS ANGLICISED
ACDEGIILNZ ANGLICIZED
ACDEGIIMNT DECIMATING
ACDEGIINOR RADIOGENIC
ACDEGIINOU AUDIOGENIC
ACDEGIINST DIE-CASTING
ACDEGILNRW ARC WELDING
ACDEGILOOP LOGOPAEDIC
ACDEGILRTT CATTLE GRID
ACDEGIMMRS SCRIMMAGED
ACDEGIMNOY GEODYNAMIC
ACDEGINNOR ANDROGENIC
ACDEGINORR CORRIGENDA
ACDEGINORT DECORATING
ACDEGINRTT DETRACTING
ACDEGINRTY GARDEN CITY
ACDEGIORSU DISCOURAGE
ACDEGIRRST CARTRIDGES
ACDEGJNOTU CONJUGATED
ACDEGKNORR ROCK GARDEN
ACDEGMMRSU SCRUMMAGED
ACDEGORRTU CORRUGATED
ACDEHIIMRT DIATHERMIC
ACDEHILMOT METHODICAL
ACDEHIMMST MISMATCHED
ACDEHIMNOP CHAMPIONED
ACDEHIMORT DICHROMATE
ACDEHINNRS HINDRANCES
ACDEHINNST DISENCHANT
ACDEHINOPS DEACONSHIP
ACDEHINOPT DICTAPHONE
ACDEHINORT ACHONDRITE

ACDEHINSSW SANDWICHES
ACDEHIPSST DISPATCHES
ACDEHIRSSV CRASH-DIVES
ACDEHKPSST SKETCHPADS
ACDEHLNOST DECATHLONS
ACDEHLOOPP CEPHALOPOD
ACDEHMPRSY PACHYDERMS
ACDEHNOORT OCTAHEDRON
ACDEHNORST ON THE CARDS
ACDEHNORSZ SCHERZANDO
ACDEHORRTT TETRACHORD
ACDEHRTTTU DUTCH TREAT
ACDEIIILST IDEALISTIC, ITALICISED
ACDEIIILTZ ITALICIZED
ACDEIIINST DIETICIANS
ACDEIIINTV INDICATIVE
ACDEIIJTUV JUDICATIVE
ACDEIIKNNR KINCARDINE
ACDEIIKNNS DICKENSIAN
ACDEIILLOT IDIOLECTAL
ACDEIILMMT DILEMMATIC
ACDEIILMPT IMPLICATED
ACDEIILMRS DISCLAIMER
ACDEIILMRV VERMICIDAL
ACDEIILNNT INCIDENTAL
ACDEIILNOS DECISIONAL
ACDEIILOPR PERIODICAL
ACDEIILOSS SOCIALISED
ACDEIILOSZ SOCIALIZED
ACDEIILPST PESTICIDAL, SEPTICIDAL
ACDEIIMNOT DECIMATION, MEDICATION
ACDEIIMPRU EPICARDIUM
ACDEIIMRRS MISCARRIED
ACDEIIMRST MATRICIDES
ACDEIINNRY INCENDIARY
ACDEIINOSY ISOCYANIDE
ACDEIIORSU IRIDACEOUS
ACDEIIOSST DISSOCIATE
ACDEIIPRRS PARRICIDES
ACDEIIPRST PATRICIDES, PEDIATRICS
ACDEIIPRTY PERACIDITY
ACDEIJNTUV ADJUNCTIVE
ACDEIJRTUU JUDICATURE
ACDEIKRSST SIDETRACKS
ACDEILLORR CORDILLERA
ACDEILLOST OSCILLATED
ACDEILLTUV VICTUALLED
ACDEILMNNO NONMEDICAL
ACDEILMNOP COMPLAINED
ACDEILMOPR PROCLAIMED
ACDEILNNOR ENDOCRINAL
ACDEILNNPS CANDLEPINS
ACDEILNOTU INOCULATED
ACDEILNPTU INCULPATED

ACDEILNSUV VULCANISED
ACDEILNUVZ VULCANIZED
ACDEILORTU ELUCIDATOR
ACDEILOTTU COLATITUDE
ACDEILPSTU DUPLICATES
ACDEILTTUV CULTIVATED
ACDEIMMORT DERMATOMIC
ACDEIMMORY IMMODERACY
ACDEIMNNOT DEMICANTON
ACDEIMNNST MENDICANTS
ACDEIMNORU ANDROECIUM
ACDEIMNOSU MENDACIOUS
ACDEINNNTY INTENDANCY
ACDEINNORS ORDINANCES
ACDEINNOSS DISSONANCE
ACDEINNOST SANCTIONED
ACDEINNRSS RANCIDNESS
ACDEINOORT CAROTENOID,
   COORDINATE, DECORATION
ACDEINOPRS SCORPAENID
ACDEINORTT DETRACTION
ACDEINOSTT ANECDOTIST
ACDEINOTTX DETOXICANT
ACDEINPRST DISCREPANT
ACDEINSSTY SYNDICATES
ACDEINSTTU SANCTITUDE
ACDEIOOPRS RADIOSCOPE
ACDEIOPRSU PREDACIOUS
ACDEIOPRTT TETRAPODIC
ACDEIOPSSU SPADICEOUS
ACDEIORSST OSTRACISED
ACDEIORSTZ OSTRACIZED
ACDEIPQRSU QUADRICEPS
ACDEIPRSTU CUSTARD PIE
ACDEIQRSTU QUADRISECT
ACDEIRRSTT DISTRACTER
ACDEIRSSTT DICTATRESS
ACDEIRSTTU RUSTICATED
ACDEJKSTTU DUST JACKET
ACDEKKMOPR POCKMARKED
ACDELLOORT DECOLLATOR
ACDELNNOOS COLONNADES
ACDELNOORT DECOLORANT
ACDELNOOTY ACOTYLEDON
ACDELOPPTU CLAPPED-OUT
ACDELOPRRU PROCEDURAL
ACDELOSSTU OUTCLASSED
ACDEMMNORS COMMANDERS
ACDEMMOSTU CUSTOM-MADE
ACDEMOORST MOTORCADES
ACDEMOOTVY DEMY OCTAVO
ACDEMOPRSU DAMP COURSE
ACDENNNOOR ORDONNANCE
ACDENNNOOS NANOSECOND

ACDENOPPSW SNOW-CAPPED
ACDENOPSTY SYNCOPATED
ACDENORSTT CONTRASTED
ACDENORSTU UNDERCOATS
ACDENPTTUU PUNCTUATED
ACDENRRRTU REDCURRANT
ACDENRRSTU TRANSDUCER
ACDEOOORRST DECORATORS
ACDEOORRVW WOODCARVER
ACDEOORSTT DOCTORATES
ACDEOPPRSU PSEUDOCARP
ACDEOPRRTT PROTRACTED
ACDEOPRSUU DRUPACEOUS
ACDEOPSTTU COUPS D'ÉTAT
ACDEOORRSTT DETRACTORS
ACDFGIIINY ACIDIFYING
ACDFGIILNU FUNGICIDAL
ACDFINNOST CONFIDANTS
ACDFLNOSSY CANDYFLOSS
ACDFORRSTW SWORDCRAFT
ACDGGIINRS DISGRACING
ACDGHIOPRT DICTOGRAPH
ACDGHNOOTU TOUCH-AND-GO
ACDGIIIMNR GRAMICIDIN
ACDGIIINNT INDICATING
ACDGIILNPS DISPLACING
ACDGIIMOOS MOGADISCIO
ACDGIINNRS DINING CARS
ACDGIINNST DISTANCING
ACDGIINOST DIAGNOSTIC
ACDGIKLNOP PADLOCKING
ACDGIKNOST STOCKADING
ACDGILLOSU GLUCOSIDAL
ACDGILNNOO CANOODLING
ACDGILNOOT ODONTALGIC
ACDGILOORY CARDIOLOGY
ACDGIMMNNO COMMANDING
ACDGLLOORS DOG COLLARS
ACDGLOTYYZ ZYGODACTYL
ACDGMNOPRU CAMPGROUND
ACDHIIIOPT IDIOPATHIC
ACDHILLPSY CHILD'S PLAY
ACDHILMNOY MY OLD CHINA
ACDHILRSUY HYDRAULICS
ACDHIORRSW DISC HARROW
ACDHIORTTY TRACHYTOID
ACDHIRSSSW SWISS CHARD
ACDHLOORRU UROCHORDAL
ACDHLOORRY HYDROCORAL
ACDHLOOSSY DAY SCHOOLS
ACDHMNORYY HYDROMANCY
ACDHNOOPRR DROP ANCHOR
ACDHORSTWW WATCHWORDS
ACDIIIMMRU MIRACIDIUM

ACDIIIMNST DIACTINISM
ACDIIINNOT INDICATION
ACDIIJLLUY JUDICIALLY
ACDIILLSUY SUICIDALLY
ACDIILMOPT DIPLOMATIC
ACDIILORTY CORDIALITY
ACDIILORUX UXORICIDAL
ACDIIMNNOS DOMINICANS
ACDIIMNORT ANTIDROMIC
ACDIIMNOST MONADISTIC
ACDIIMNOSY ISODYNAMIC
ACDIIMNSTY DYNAMISTIC
ACDIINNNOR INDIAN CORN
ACDIINNORY INORDINACY
ACDIINOORV ORDOVICIAN
ACDIINORST INDICATORS
ACDIINORTV VINDICATOR
ACDIINORTY DICTIONARY, INDICATORY
ACDIINOSTT DICTATIONS
ACDIIOORTX RADIOTOXIC
ACDIJORTUY JUDICATORY
ACDIKNQSSU QUICKSANDS
ACDIKRRSTT DIRT TRACKS
ACDIKRSSTY YARDSTICKS
ACDILNOPRS SPINAL CORD
ACDILOPRTU DUPLICATOR
ACDILPSSTY DYSPLASTIC
ACDIMMORUY MYOCARDIUM
ACDIMOORSU MORDACIOUS
ACDINOSSTU CUSTODIANS
ACDINSSSTU DISCUSSANT
ACDIOOPRSY RADIOSCOPY
ACDJOORSTU COADJUTORS
ACDKLMOSSY LADY'S-SMOCK
ACDKLORSTU TRUCKLOADS
ACDKNORSTU SOUNDTRACK
ACDKORSSTY STOCKYARDS
ACDLLOOPSW CODSWALLOP
ACDLLOPTYY POLYDACTYL
ACDLLORSSW WORLD-CLASS
ACDLLORSTU COLLAR STUD
ACDLMNOPSW CLAMPDOWNS
ACDMPRRSTU TRUMP CARDS
ACDOOORRSS CROSSROADS
ACDORRSTUY COURTYARDS
ACEEEFFKTT TAKE EFFECT
ACEEEFFMNT EFFACEMENT
ACEEEFFTTU EFFECTUATE
ACEEEFIPRS FIRE ESCAPE
ACEEEFIPRT AFTERPIECE
ACEEEFIRSS CEASE-FIRES
ACEEEFLNRR FREELANCER
ACEEEFLNRS FREELANCES
ACEEEFMNNT ENFACEMENT

ACEEEGILNN INELEGANCE
ACEEEGINRT GREAT-NIECE
ACEEEGNNSV VENGEANCES
ACEEEGNNPRT PERCENTAGE
ACEEEGNRRY REGENERACY
ACEEEHIMRX HEXAEMERIC
ACEEEHRRRS RESEARCHER
ACEEEHRRSS RESEARCHES
ACEEEIMRRS CREAMERIES
ACEEEIPPPS PEACE PIPES
ACEEEIPPRV APPERCEIVE
ACEEEIRRST SECRETAIRE
ACEEEIRSTV EVISCERATE, TEA SERVICE
ACEEEIRTVX EXECRATIVE
ACEEEKRRST RACKETEERS
ACEEELLNRT CRENELLATE
ACEEELMNNT ENLACEMENT
ACEEELNPRV PREVALENCE
ACEEELNPSW CLEAN SWEEP
ACEEELORTT ELECTORATE
ACEEELRSTT TELECASTER
ACEEEMNNPR PERMANENCE
ACEEEMNNST ENCASEMENT
ACEEEMNPRT TEMPERANCE
ACEEEMNPST ESCAPEMENT
ACEEEMNRTT METACENTER,
  METACENTRE
ACEEEMORTT ACETOMETER
ACEEENNOTV COVENANTEE
ACEEENNPRT PENETRANCE, REPENTANCE
ACEEENNRRT RE-ENTRANCE
ACEEENNSTV EVANESCENT
ACEEENRSSV SEVERANCES
ACEEEPPPRR CREPE PAPER
ACEEEPRRTU RECUPERATE
ACEEFFIMNY EFFEMINACY
ACEEFFLOTY FEET OF CLAY
ACEEFFNRSU SUFFERANCE
ACEEFHHTTW CHEW THE FAT
ACEEFIILTT FELICITATE
ACEEFIJKLT LIFE JACKET
ACEEFILMNT MALEFICENT
ACEEFILNRS CRANE FLIES
ACEEFILNSS FACILENESS
ACEEFILPRS FIREPLACES
ACEEFINRST INTERFACES
ACEEFIOPSS PIECE OF ASS
ACEEFIORTV VOCIFERATE
ACEEFIRRTV REFRACTIVE
ACEEFIRSSS FRICASSEES
ACEEFLLNTU FLATULENCE
ACEEFLLORV CLOVERLEAF
ACEEFLLPUY PEACEFULLY
ACEEFLNSTV FLAVESCENT

ACEEFLORST FORECASTLE
ACEEFLOSTV VOLTE-FACES
ACEEFORRST FORECASTER
ACEEGGNORT CONGREGATE
ACEEGHHRTW CHEW THE RAG
ACEEGHINNP CHEAPENING
ACEEGHLLNR CHALLENGER
ACEEGHLLNS CHALLENGES
ACEEGHLNSS CHANGELESS
ACEEGHNNOP COPENHAGEN
ACEEGHNORV CHANGEOVER
ACEEGHNSSU GAUCHENESS
ACEEGHORRV OVERCHARGE
ACEEGIKTTW WICKET GATE
ACEEGILLNR ALLERGENIC
ACEEGILLOT COLLEGIATE
ACEEGILNTU GENICULATE
ACEEGILRSS SACRILEGES
ACEEGILSTU SLUICEGATE
ACEEGINNOS CASEINOGEN
ACEEGINNPT PANGENETIC
ACEEGINRRT RECREATING
ACEEGINRSV GRIEVANCES
ACEEGINRTX EXECRATING
ACEEGIOPTT COTTAGE PIE
ACEEGIORST CATEGORIES, CATEGORISE
ACEEGIORTZ CATEGORIZE
ACEEGIOTTX EXCOGITATE
ACEEGIRSTT CIGARETTES
ACEEGKNOPS SPONGE CAKE
ACEEGKORTT GET A ROCKET
ACEEGLLOSU COLLEAGUES
ACEEGLMNOR CAMERLENGO
ACEEGLNRST RECTANGLES
ACEEGLNRTU GREAT-UNCLE
ACEEGMMOSU GEMMACEOUS
ACEEGMOTTY GAMETOCYTE
ACEEGNNORV GOVERNANCE
ACEEGNNPRU REPUGNANCE
ACEEGNNSWY NEWS AGENCY
ACEEGNORRU ENCOURAGER
ACEEGNRSSV SCAVENGERS
ACEEHHILRW WHEELCHAIR
ACEEHHIRRS HERESIARCH
ACEEHHIRST HATCHERIES
ACEEHHLLRT HATCHELLER
ACEEHHMNTT HATCHET MEN
ACEEHHPTTU HEPTATEUCH
ACEEHIIPRS HAIRPIECES
ACEEHILMNN MANCHINEEL
ACEEHILPTT TELEPATHIC
ACEEHILRSV CHEVALIERS
ACEEHILSTT ESTHETICAL
ACEEHIMNPZ CHIMPANZEE

ACEEHIMNRS MECHANISER
ACEEHIMNRZ MECHANIZER
ACEEHIMRTX HEXAMETRIC
ACEEHIMSST SCHEMATISE
ACEEHIMSTZ SCHEMATIZE
ACEEHIMTTT METATHETIC
ACEEHINNPT PHENACETIN
ACEEHINPSS PEACHINESS
ACEEHINSTT ANESTHETIC
ACEEHIORRT CHARIOTEER
ACEEHISSTT AESTHETICS
ACEEHISTUW WHITE SAUCE
ACEEHKLNRT HALTERNECK
ACEEHLLNNR CHANNELLER
ACEEHLLNOP CELLOPHANE
ACEEHLMNOS CHAMELEONS
ACEEHLNNOP ENCEPHALON
ACEEHLNPRU LEPRECHAUN
ACEEHLNPTT PLANCHETTE
ACEEHLOPTY POLYCHAETE
ACEEHLOSSV CLOSE SHAVE
ACEEHLRSTW CARTWHEELS
ACEEHMMRSU MEERSCHAUM
ACEEHMNNST ENCASHMENT
ACEEHMNOOR ANEMOCHORE
ACEEHMNPRT PREACHMENT
ACEEHMORTT TACHOMETER
ACEEHMRTTY TACHYMETER
ACEEHMSSTT STEAM-CHEST
ACEEHNNRST ENCHANTERS
ACEEHNPTTU PENTATEUCH
ACEEHOPRRR REPROACHER
ACEEHOPRRS ARCHESPORE, REPROACHES
ACEEHORRSS RACEHORSES
ACEEHPRSTY ARCHETYPES
ACEEHPTTTX EXCEPT THAT
ACEEHRRSTT CHATTERERS
ACEEHRRSTU CHARTREUSE
ACEEIILMST ELEATICISM
ACEEIILNTT LICENTIATE
ACEEIILPSS SPECIALISE
ACEEIILPST TAILPIECES
ACEEIILPSZ SPECIALIZE
ACEEIILSST ELASTICISE
ACEEIILSTZ ELASTICIZE
ACEEIIMNPT IMPATIENCE
ACEEIINNRT CREATININE, INCINERATE
ACEEIIRTTV RECITATIVE
ACEEIITTVX EXCITATIVE
ACEEIJLNQU JACQUELINE
ACEEIJLRTT TRAJECTILE
ACEEIKLNRT TRANCELIKE
ACEEIKNOTT TAKE NOTICE
ACEEIKNRSS CREAKINESS

ACEEIKPRTT TICKERTAPE
ACEEIKRSST ICE-SKATERS
ACEEILLMTY EMETICALLY
ACEEILLPRX PRELEXICAL
ACEEILLPSY ESPECIALLY
ACEEILMNNT CLEMENTINA
ACEEILMNOR CEREMONIAL
ACEEILMNOT COLEMANITE
ACEEILMNOU LEUCOMAINE
ACEEILMNRT MERCANTILE
ACEEILMNST CENTESIMAL, LEMNISCATE
ACEEILMOSU MELIACEOUS
ACEEILNNNT CENTENNIAL
ACEEILNOPU LEUCOPENIA
ACEEILNOTV EVECTIONAL
ACEEILNPRS PRASELENIC
ACEEILNPRT EPICENTRAL
ACEEILNRST CENTRALISE, LINECASTER
ACEEILNRTV CANTILEVER
ACEEILNRTZ CENTRALIZE
ACEEILRRTT RETRACTILE
ACEEILRSSU SECULARISE
ACEEILRSUZ SECULARIZE
ACEEILRTTU RETICULATE
ACEEILRTUV ULCERATIVE
ACEEILRTVY CREATIVELY, REACTIVELY
ACEEILSTUV VESICULATE
ACEEIMNORT ACTINOMERE
ACEEIMNRSS CREAMINESS
ACEEIMNRSV SERVICEMAN
ACEEIMNRTT REMITTANCE
ACEEIMORRT AEROMETRIC
ACEEIMORTT EROTEMATIC
ACEEIMPRST SPERMACETI
ACEEIMRSST MASSETERIC
ACEEINNRST TRANSIENCE
ACEEINORRT RECREATION
ACEEINORSU ERINACEOUS
ACEEINORTU AUCTIONEER
ACEEINORTX EXECRATION
ACEEINPPRT APPRENTICE
ACEEINPRST INTERSPACE
ACEEINPRSU EPICUREANS
ACEEINRSST ANCESTRIES, RESISTANCE
ACEEINRTVY INVETERACY
ACEEINSSTV ACTIVENESS
ACEEIOOPRS AECIOSPORE
ACEEIOPPST EPISCOPATE
ACEEIOPSST CAESPITOSE
ACEEIOQTUV EQUIVOCATE
ACEEIORTVV OVERACTIVE, REVOCATIVE
ACEEIPPRTY PARTY PIECE
ACEEIPQRSU PICARESQUE
ACEEIQRSTU REQUIESCAT

ACEEIRRSST CAREERISTS
ACEEIRRTTV RETRACTIVE
ACEEIRTTUV ERUCTATIVE
ACEEIRTTVX EXTRACTIVE
ACEEKLLRSS SALESCLERK
ACEEKNRRRT RACK-RENTER
ACEEKNRTTV TRACK EVENT
ACEEKORRSW CASEWORKER
ACEELLNRSW ALLEN SCREW
ACEELLRSSY CARELESSLY
ACEELLSTTU SCUTELLATE
ACEELMNOTY MELANOCYTE
ACEELMNPST PLACEMENTS
ACEELMORST LATECOMERS
ACEELMORTT LACTOMETER
ACEELNOPRV PROVENÇALE
ACEELNOPST OPALESCENT
ACEELNOPSY CLAP EYES ON
ACEELNORTU ENUCLEATOR
ACEELNPRSY SCREENPLAY
ACEELORRST CORRELATES
ACEELORSSS CASSEROLES
ACEELPPRTU PERCEPTUAL
ACEELQRRUU CRAQUELURE
ACEEMMNNPT ENCAMPMENT
ACEEMMNOTT COMMENTATE
ACEEMMORSU COMMEASURE
ACEEMNNPRY PERMANENCY
ACEEMNNSTT ENACTMENTS
ACEEMNOOPS ANEMOSCOPE
ACEEMNOPST COMPENSATE
ACEEMNPRST ESCARPMENT
ACEEMOSTUZ ECZEMATOUS
ACEENNOPRS CAN OPENERS
ACEENNOPRV PROVENANCE
ACEENNORSS RESONANCES
ACEENNORTV CONTRAVENE,
COVENANTER
ACEENNRSSV CRAVENNESS
ACEENNSSTU SUSTENANCE
ACEENORSSS COARSENESS
ACEENPRRST CARPENTERS
ACEENPRUVY PURVEYANCE
ACEENRSSST ANCESTRESS
ACEENRSSTW NEWSCASTER
ACEENRSTTU UTTERANCES
ACEENSTTUX EXECUTANTS
ACEEOSSTTU TESTACEOUS
ACEEPRSTTY TYPECASTER
ACEERRSSTT STREETCARS
ACEERRSSTW WATERCRESS
ACEFFFILOT FACT OF LIFE
ACEFFHLNOR FRENCH LOAF
ACEFFHRSUU CHAUFFEURS

ACEFFIILTV AFFLICTIVE
ACEFFIKRRT TRAFFICKER
ACEFFINOST AFFECTIONS
ACEFFOSTUU TUFFACEOUS
ACEFGILNST SELF-ACTING
ACEFGINRRT REFRACTING
ACEFGLLRUY GRACEFULLY
ACEFHHIRRS ARCHERFISH
ACEFHIINST CHIEFTAINS
ACEFHILRTU ULTRAFICHE
ACEFHINRSS FRANCHISES
ACEFHIRSSY CRAYFISHES
ACEFHIRTTY CITY FATHER
ACEFHKMMOU MAKE MUCH OF
ACEFHKORST AFTERSHOCK
ACEFHORRTV HOVERCRAFT
ACEFHORSTU HOUSECRAFT
ACEFIIILST FACILITIES
ACEFIILMSS FACSIMILES
ACEFIILRSS CLASSIFIER
ACEFIINNRS FINANCIERS
ACEFIINRST SANCTIFIER
ACEFIIOPRS FAIR COPIES
ACEFIIRRST ARTIFICERS
ACEFIIRSTV FRICATIVES
ACEFIKLNPS CLASP KNIFE
ACEFIKRSTU FRUITCAKES
ACEFILLNOT FLECTIONAL
ACEFILNOST SELF-ACTION
ACEFILNTUU FUNICULATE
ACEFILOOSU FOLIACEOUS
ACEFINORRT FOR CERTAIN, REFRACTION
ACEFINORTV VOCIFERANT
ACEFINRSST CRAFTINESS
ACEFIRRTTU TRIFURCATE
ACEFKLNORS CORNFLAKES
ACEFKORSST TASK FORCES
ACEFLOOPTU OUT OF PLACE
ACEFMNNOWY FANCY WOMEN
ACEFORRRTY REFRACTORY
ACEFRRSSTU SURFCASTER
ACEGGHILNN CHANGELING
ACEGGHINNX EXCHANGING
ACEGGHINRR RECHARGING
ACEGGILLOO GEOLOGICAL
ACEGGILNNO CONGEALING
ACEGGINNOO OCEANGOING
ACEGGINNSV SCAVENGING
ACEGGIRSST SCRAGGIEST
ACEGHHIJKR HIGHJACKER
ACEGHHINOT HIGH-OCTANE
ACEGHHOPRT HECTOGRAPH
ACEGHIILMT MEGALITHIC
ACEGHIIMNP IMPEACHING

ACEGHIIMTW WHITE MAGIC
ACEGHIINNN ENCHAINING
ACEGHIINRS CASHIERING
ACEGHIIPPR EPIGRAPHIC
ACEGHILMPT PHLEGMATIC
ACEGHILNPR NEPHRALGIC
ACEGHIMNNU MACHINE GUN
ACEGHIMNOP MEGAPHONIC
ACEGHINNNT ENCHANTING
ACEGHINNST CHASTENING
ACEGHINOPT PATHOGENIC
ACEGHINRRT CHARTERING
ACEGHINRTT CHATTERING
ACEGHIOOPS HAGIOSCOPE
ACEGHIRSTW SWITCHGEAR
ACEGHOPRRY CEROGRAPHY
ACEGHOPSTY PHAGOCYTES
ACEGHRRRSU SURCHARGER
ACEGHRRSSU SURCHARGES
ACEGIIKNRY A GIN RICKEY
ACEGIIKNST ICE-SKATING
ACEGIILLRS GALLICISER
ACEGIILLRZ GALLICIZER
ACEGIILLST LEGALISTIC
ACEGIILMNR RECLAIMING
ACEGIILMNX EXCLAIMING
ACEGIILMTY LEGITIMACY
ACEGIILNNO LIGNOCAINE
ACEGIIMNTT MAGNETITIC
ACEGIIMOST ISOGAMETIC
ACEGIIMPTT PEGMATITIC
ACEGIINNRS INCREASING
ACEGIINORT IATROGENIC
ACEGIIOTTV COGITATIVE
ACEGIIPRST EPIGASTRIC
ACEGIIRRST GERIATRICS
ACEGIKLNNS SLACKENING
ACEGIKNPPR PREPACKING
ACEGILLNOO NEOLOGICAL
ACEGILLNPR PARCELLING
ACEGILLOOS OLIGOCLASE
ACEGILMNNY MENACINGLY
ACEGILNNOT CONGENITAL
ACEGILNOPY CLAY PIGEON
ACEGILNORT RELOCATING
ACEGILNOTU GLAUCONITE
ACEGILNPTU PECULATING
ACEGILNQRU LACQUERING
ACEGILNRTT CLATTERING
ACEGILNRTU ULCERATING
ACEGILNTXY EXACTINGLY
ACEGILOOPT APOLOGETIC
ACEGIMMRRS SCRIMMAGER
ACEGIMMRSS SCRIMMAGES

ACEGIMNPRS SCAMPERING
ACEGIMNRST CENTIGRAMS
ACEGIMOPRS MEGASPORIC
ACEGIMORST GASOMETRIC
ACEGINNNRT ENTRANCING
ACEGINNORS COARSENING
ACEGINOPRS SAPROGENIC
ACEGINORTV OVERACTING
ACEGINPRRS SCARPERING
ACEGINPRSY PANEGYRICS
ACEGINPSTT SPECTATING
ACEGINRRTT RETRACTING
ACEGINRSTT SCATTERING
ACEGINRTTX EXTRACTING
ACEGIOSSTT GEOSTATICS
ACEGIRSSTT STRATEGICS
ACEGLMOSUU GLUMACEOUS
ACEGLNOOOY OCEANOLOGY
ACEGLOOPSY ESCAPOLOGY
ACEGLOOTUY AUTECOLOGY
ACEGMMRRSU SCRUMMAGER
ACEGMMRSSU SCRUMMAGES
ACEGNNOSTT COTANGENTS
ACEGNRSTTU SCATTER-GUN
ACEGOORSUU COURAGEOUS
ACEGOPRRSU SUPERCARGO
ACEHHIKSTT HIT THE SACK
ACEHHILTWZ WITCH-HAZEL
ACEHHIPSTT HEPTASTICH
ACEHHNORSU RANCH HOUSE
ACEHHOOSTT TOOTHACHES
ACEHIILLPT PHILATELIC
ACEHIILMOS ISOCHEIMAL
ACEHIIMRTT ARITHMETIC
ACEHIINNOP PHOENICIAN
ACEHIINOTV INCHOATIVE
ACEHIIPRRT PERITRICHA
ACEHIIRSTT TRACHEITIS
ACEHIKLNSS CHALKINESS
ACEHIKMNOS CHAIN-SMOKE
ACEHIKMNSY HACKNEYISM
ACEHIKORST ARTICHOKES
ACEHILLNTY ETHNICALLY
ACEHILLOOS ALCOHOLISE
ACEHILLOOZ ALCOHOLIZE
ACEHILLORY HEROICALLY
ACEHILLPRY CAERPHILLY
ACEHILLTTY THETICALLY
ACEHILMMOS CHAMOMILES
ACEHILMMST MISCH METAL
ACEHILMNOR CHLORAMINE
ACEHILMOOP PHOCOMELIA
ACEHILMOTY HAEMOLYTIC
ACEHILMSST ALCHEMISTS

ACEHILNNOT NONETHICAL
ACEHILNORT CHLORINATE
ACEHILOORZ COLEORHIZA
ACEHILOPST TELOPHASIC
ACEHILORRT RHETORICAL
ACEHILPSST SALES PITCH
ACEHILRSTU HERACLITUS
ACEHILRSTY HYSTERICAL
ACEHIMMNSS MECHANISMS
ACEHIMMSST MISMATCHES, SCHEMATISM
ACEHIMNNOR ENHARMONIC
ACEHIMNORS MONARCHIES
ACEHIMNORW CHAIRWOMEN
ACEHIMNRSV REVANCHISM
ACEHIMNSTY MYASTHENIC
ACEHIMOPRS SEMAPHORIC
ACEHIMOPRT AMPHOTERIC,
  METAPHORIC
ACEHIMOPTU APOTHECIUM
ACEHIMOSTX CHEMOTAXIS
ACEHIMPSTY METAPHYSIC
ACEHIMRSTU RHEUMATICS
ACEHINOPST ASTHENOPIC
ACEHINORRT CHITARRONE
ACEHINORST ANCHORITES, CHAIN STORE
ACEHINORTV CHEVROTAIN
ACEHINPSST PATCHINESS
ACEHINPSTT PENTASTICH
ACEHINPSTU EPICANTHUS
ACEHINRRSU HURRICANES
ACEHINRSSU SEA URCHINS
ACEHINRSTU RAUNCHIEST
ACEHINRSTV REVANCHIST
ACEHIORSTT RHEOSTATIC
ACEHIPPSSS SPACESHIPS
ACEHIRSSTT STARCHIEST
ACEHIRSTTT TETRASTICH
ACEHLLMNOY MELANCHOLY
ACEHLLPRSU SEPULCHRAL
ACEHLMOOST SCHOOLMATE
ACEHLMORSY LACHRYMOSE
ACEHLNORST CHARLESTON
ACEHLOORST ORTHOCLASE
ACEHLOOSSU COALHOUSES
ACEHLOPXYY OXYCEPHALY
ACEHLORRST ORCHESTRAL
ACEHLPRTYY PHYLACTERY
ACEHMMNOOR CHROMONEMA
ACEHMNPRST PARCHMENTS
ACEHMOORUX AUXOCHROME
ACEHMORRTU ROUTE MARCH
ACEHMORTTY TACHOMETRY
ACEHMOSSTU MOUSTACHES
ACEHMRTTYY TACHYMETRY

ACEHNORRTT TROCHANTER
ACEHNSSTTU STAUNCHEST
ACEHOOPPRR CARPOPHORE
ACEHOOSSTU HOUSECOATS
ACEHOPPRTU TOUCHPAPER
ACEHORRSST CARTHORSES, ORCHESTRAS
ACEHORTTWW WATCHTOWER
ACEHPRRSSU PURCHASERS
ACEIIIMNST INTIMACIES
ACEIIISTTV ACTIVITIES
ACEIIJLSTU JESUITICAL
ACEIIKMNST KINEMATICS
ACEIIKRSTT RICKETTSIA
ACEIILLLPT ELLIPTICAL
ACEIILLNPR PERICLINAL
ACEIILLNRY IRENICALLY
ACEIILLOST LOCALITIES
ACEIILLOSU LILIACEOUS
ACEIILLRTY ILLITERACY
ACEIILLTXY LEXICALITY
ACEIILMMST MELISMATIC
ACEIILMNST MELANISTIC
ACEIILMOPT ATOMIC PILE
ACEIILMPSS SPECIALISM
ACEIILMRST SALIMETRIC
ACEIILNOTT ACTINOLITE
ACEIILNPST PLASTICINE
ACEIILNRST IN ARTICLES
ACEIILNTVY INACTIVELY
ACEIILORSS SOCIALISER
ACEIILORSZ SOCIALIZER
ACEIILOSST SOCIALITES
ACEIILOSTU TILIACEOUS
ACEIILPPRT PARTICIPLE
ACEIILPRTT TRIPLICATE
ACEIILPSST PLASTICISE, SPECIALIST
ACEIILPSTY SPECIALITY
ACEIILPSTZ PLASTICIZE
ACEIILSTTY ELASTICITY
ACEIIMNRRU CINERARIUM
ACEIIMRRST ERRATICISM
ACEIIMRSST ARMISTICES
ACEIIMRSTT TASIMETRIC
ACEIINNRTY ITINERANCY
ACEIINOPST SPECIATION
ACEIINORTT RECITATION
ACEIINOSTV VESICATION
ACEIINOTTX EXCITATION, INTOXICATE
ACEIINPSTT ANTISEPTIC, PSITTACINE
ACEIINRTVY INVERACITY
ACEIINSTTU AUSTENITIC
ACEIIORRRT CERTIORARI
ACEIIORSTT ATROCITIES
ACEIIPPSST EPISPASTIC

ACEIIRSSST SACRISTIES
ACEIIRTTVY CREATIVITY, REACTIVITY
ACEIJKKNSV JACK KNIVES
ACEIJNORTT TRAJECTION
ACEIKKNNTU KENTUCKIAN
ACEIKLRSTV TRAVELSICK
ACEIKMPRST STRIKE CAMP
ACEIKNORSS CROAKINESS
ACEIKNPSTT SEPTIC TANK
ACEIKOPRST AIRPOCKETS
ACEILLLPRU PELLICULAR
ACEILLMNSY MISCELLANY
ACEILLMORT ALLOMETRIC
ACEILLMRTY METRICALLY
ACEILLNNNO CANNELLONI
ACEILLNOOT OCELLATION
ACEILLNORT CITRONELLA
ACEILLNRTU LENTICULAR
ACEILLOPSW PILLOWCASE
ACEILLOPTY POETICALLY
ACEILLORTV VORTICELLA
ACEILLORTY EROTICALLY
ACEILLOTXY EXOTICALLY
ACEILLPRUY PECULIARLY
ACEILLPSTY SEPTICALLY
ACEILLRSTY STERICALLY
ACEILLRTUV VICTUALLER
ACEILLRTVY VERTICALLY
ACEILMMNSS CLAMMINESS
ACEILMNOPR COMPLAINER
ACEILMNORS SERMONICAL
ACEILMNRST CENTRALISM
ACEILMNRUW LAWRENCIUM
ACEILMRRUV VERMICULAR
ACEILMRSSU SECULARISM
ACEILMTUUV CUMULATIVE
ACEILNNOOP NAPOLEONIC
ACEILNNORS CORNELIANS
ACEILNNOTU NUCLEATION
ACEILNNUVY UNIVALENCY
ACEILNOORT ICONOLATER, RELOCATION
ACEILNOPPS SCALOPPINE
ACEILNOPRT PRATINCOLE
ACEILNOPST NEOPLASTIC, PLEONASTIC
ACEILNOPTU PECULATION
ACEILNORTU ULCERATION
ACEILNORTY LECTIONARY
ACEILNOSSS SOCIALNESS
ACEILNOSST COASTLINES
ACEILNOSTU INOSCULATE
ACEILNOTUV NOVACULITE
ACEILNPPSU SUPPLIANCE
ACEILNRSTU LACUSTRINE
ACEILNRSUV VULCANISER

ACEILNRTTY CENTRALITY
ACEILNRTVY TRIVALENCY
ACEILNRUUX LUXURIANCE
ACEILNRUVZ VULCANIZER
ACEILOOSUV OLIVACEOUS, VIOLACEOUS
ACEILOPPRS SAPROPELIC
ACEILOPRTX EXPLICATOR
ACEILOPTUV COPULATIVE
ACEILOQTUY COEQUALITY
ACEILPPPRS PAPER CLIPS
ACEILPPSTU SUPPLICATE
ACEILPRTUU APICULTURE
ACEILRSSTU SECULARIST
ACEILRSTTU TESTICULAR
ACEILRSTUY SECULARITY
ACEILRTUUV AVICULTURE
ACEIMMNORT MANOMETRIC
ACEIMMRSTY ASYMMETRIC
ACEIMNNOST CISMONTANE
ACEIMNNRUY INNUMERACY
ACEIMNOPRT IMPORTANCE
ACEIMNOPSU MENOPAUSIC
ACEIMNORST CREMATIONS
ACEIMNORUY AUREOMYCIN
ACEIMNPSTU PNEUMATICS
ACEIMNRRTY TERRAMYCIN
ACEIMNRSST MISCREANTS
ACEIMORSVW MICROWAVES
ACEIMORTTT TETRATOMIC
ACEIMORTTU TAUTOMERIC
ACEIMSSTTY SYSTEMATIC
ACEINNNSTU UNCANNIEST
ACEINNORST CONTAINERS, SANCTIONER
ACEINNORTU ENUNCIATOR
ACEINNRSSU INSURANCES
ACEINNRSTY TRANSIENCY
ACEINNRTUU NUNCIATURE
ACEINNSSST SCANTINESS
ACEINOORTV REVOCATION
ACEINOOSTV EVOCATIONS
ACEINOPRTU PRECAUTION
ACEINOPSTT CONSTIPATE
ACEINORRST CONTRARIES
ACEINORRSV CARNIVORES
ACEINORRTT RETRACTION
ACEINORSSY CESSIONARY
ACEINORTTU ERUCTATION
ACEINORTTW TONIC WATER
ACEINORTTX EXTRACTION
ACEINOSSST CESSATIONS
ACEINOSTTU UNICOSTATE
ACEINPSSSU PUISSANCES
ACEINQSTTU QUITTANCES
ACEINRSSTW SCRAWNIEST

ACEINSSSTT SCATTINESS
ACEIOOPRTZ AZEOTROPIC
ACEIOOPTTV COOPTATIVE
ACEIOOSTUU AUTOECIOUS
ACEIOPRRSU PRECARIOUS
ACEIOPSTTT PETTICOATS
ACEIOQSSUU SEQUACIOUS
ACEIORRSST OSTRACISER
ACEIORRSTZ OSTRACIZER
ACEIORSTTT TRICOSTATE
ACEIPPRSST SCRAPPIEST
ACEIPSSSTU SPACESUITS
ACEISSTTTY CITY-STATES
ACEJKKRSSY SKYJACKERS
ACEJKLPPSU SUPPLEJACK
ACEJKNOSST JACKSTONES
ACEJORRTTY TRAJECTORY
ACEKKMOSST SMOKESTACK
ACEKKMRRSU MUCKRAKERS
ACEKLLRSTU LACKLUSTER, LACKLUSTRE
ACEKLNOPST ALPENSTOCK
ACEKLOPRSW WORKPLACES
ACEKMNORRW CANKERWORM
ACEKPRRSSY SKYSCRAPER
ACELLLMORU COLUMELLAR
ACELLLORSS SOLAR CELLS
ACELLNOSSW CALLOWNESS
ACELLOPSTU LEUCOPLAST
ACELLOPTUY EUCALYPTOL
ACELLORSSW LOWER CLASS
ACELLPRUUV VULPECULAR
ACELLSSTTY TACTLESSLY
ACELMMNOOW COMMONWEAL
ACELMNNOTT MALCONTENT
ACELMNOORT MONTE CARLO
ACELNNOSSU CONSENSUAL
ACELNNOTUV CONVENTUAL
ACELNOPRRU PRONUCLEAR
ACELNOPRSY NARCOLEPSY
ACELNORRTY NECROLATRY
ACELNOSSTU CONSULATES
ACELNOTTUX CONTEXTUAL
ACELOOPRRT PERCOLATOR
ACELOORRTW WATERCOLOR
ACELOOSSTT OSTEOCLAST
ACELOPPRST PARCEL POST
ACELOPRSTU SPECULATOR
ACELOSSSTU LOST CAUSES
ACELPPRSSU UPPER CLASS
ACELPRSSSU SUPERCLASS
ACELPSTUUY EUCALYPTUS
ACELRSSTTY CRYSTAL SET
ACEMMNORTY COMMENTARY
ACEMMNOSTU CONSUMMATE

ACEMMOSTTY MASTECTOMY
ACEMNNNOTT CANTONMENT
ACEMNNORST MONSTRANCE
ACEMNOOPSS MOONSCAPES
ACEMNOOTYZ MYCETOZOAN
ACEMNOPRRY PYROMANCER
ACEMNOSTTY NEMATOCYST
ACEMOOPRRS MACROSPORE
ACEMOORSTU OCTAMEROUS
ACEMORSTUY MYRTACEOUS
ACENNNORSU ANNOUNCERS
ACENNOORTV COVENANTOR
ACENNORSTV CONVERSANT
ACENNOSTTT CONTESTANT
ACENNRSTTU ENCRUSTANT
ACENOPSSTW TOWNSCAPES
ACENORRSTU RACONTEURS
ACENORSSTU COURTESANS
ACENPRSSUU PURSUANCES
ACEOOOPRRT COOPERATOR
ACEOOPPRRS CARPOSPORE
ACEOOPRRRT PROCREATOR
ACEOOPSSTT STATOSCOPE
ACEOPRSSTT SPECTATORS
ACEORRRSVY CARRY-OVERS
ACEORRSTTX EXTRACTORS
ACEORSTUXY EXCUSATORY
ACERRSTUUV CURVATURES
ACFFGIILNT AFFLICTING
ACFFIILLOY OFFICIALLY
ACFFIILNOT AFFLICTION
ACFFIILNOU UNOFFICIAL
ACFFIIOORT OFFICIATOR
ACFFILLNUY FANCIFULLY
ACFGHINRSS GRASSFINCH
ACFGIILNRY CLARIFYING
ACFGIINRSY SCARIFYING
ACFGILNNOT CONFLATING
ACFGILOPRY PROFLIGACY
ACFGINRRTU FRACTURING
ACFHIILRST CHAIR LIFTS
ACFHIOPRST FACTORSHIP
ACFHLLTUWY WATCHFULLY
ACFHLNORSW HALF CROWNS
ACFHLORSTW FLOWCHARTS
ACFIILNOPT PONTIFICAL
ACFIILNORT FRICTIONAL
ACFIIMNORT ACTINIFORM
ACFIINNORS INFRASONIC
ACFIINNORT INFARCTION, INFRACTION
ACFIIOSTTU FACTITIOUS
ACFILLLORU FOLLICULAR
ACFILNNOOT CONFLATION
ACFILNNOTU FUNCTIONAL

ACFILNOOPT FOCAL POINT
ACFILNOOST TONIC SOL-FA
ACFILNRSUU FUNICULARS
ACFILRSSST FIRST-CLASS
ACFINOORRT FORNICATOR
ACFKMRRSTU TRUCK FARMS
ACFLLOOPRT PORT OF CALL
ACFLNOORTW CONTRAFLOW
ACFLNRRUUU FURUNCULAR
ACFLOORSTU COLOURFAST
ACFORRRUVY CURRY FAVOR
ACGGHIILOO HAGIOLOGIC
ACGGHIINNR CHAGRINING
ACGGHINOTT CHITTAGONG
ACGGIILLOT GLAGOLITIC
ACGGIILNNO GANGLIONIC
ACGGIINOTT COGITATING
ACGGILLNNY GLANCINGLY
ACGGILLOOY GLACIOLOGY
ACGGIMOSTY MYSTAGOGIC
ACGHHHIIRS HIGH CHAIRS
ACGHIIJKNS HIJACKINGS
ACGHIIMOPR AMPHIGORIC
ACGHIINSST CHASTISING
ACGHIIPRRT TRIGRAPHIC
ACGHILLOOP HAPLOLOGIC
ACGHILLOTY GOTHICALLY
ACGHILMNRY CHARMINGLY
ACGHILNSTY SCATHINGLY
ACGHIMNNOP CHAMPIGNON
ACGHIMNOOR HOMORGANIC
ACGHIMNOST STOMACHING
ACGHIMOPRR MICROGRAPH
ACGHIMOPRY MYOGRAPHIC
ACGHINNSTU STAUNCHING
ACGHINOPRZ ZINCOGRAPH
ACGHINPRSU PURCHASING
ACGHIOOPRR OROGRAPHIC
ACGHIOOPRZ ZOOGRAPHIC
ACGHIOPPRT PICTOGRAPH
ACGHMNOORR CHRONOGRAM
ACGHOOPPRY COPROPHAGY
ACGIIILLRT ARGILLITIC
ACGIIKMNNN NICKNAMING
ACGIILLMNS MISCALLING
ACGIILLNOZ LOCALIZING
ACGIILLOST LOGISTICAL
ACGIILLOTY LOGICALITY
ACGIILLRTU LITURGICAL
ACGIILMNPS MISPLACING
ACGIILMNSS ANGLICISMS
ACGIILMORS ALGORISMIC
ACGIILNRTU CURTAILING, GRANULITIC
ACGIILNRTY LARYNGITIC

ACGIILNTUV VICTUALING
ACGIIMNNRU MANICURING
ACGIIMNORR MARCONI RIG
ACGIIMNORS ORGANICISM
ACGIIMNRST SCINTIGRAM
ACGIIMNSST MISCASTING
ACGIINNNOT CONTAINING
ACGIINNNOZ CANONIZING
ACGIINNNST INSTANCING
ACGIINNOTU AUCTIONING, CAUTIONING
ACGIINNRTU CURTAINING
ACGIINOOTT COGITATION
ACGIINORST ORGANICIST
ACGIINPRST PRACTISING
ACGIINQTTU ACQUITTING
ACGIJKKNSY SKYJACKING
ACGIKKMNRU MUCKRAKING
ACGILLNOPS COLLAPSING, SCALLOPING
ACGILLNORR CORRALLING
ACGILLOOOR OROLOGICAL
ACGILLOOOT OTOLOGICAL
ACGILLOOOZ ZOOLOGICAL
ACGILLOPRY PYROGALLIC
ACGILLRSUY SURGICALLY
ACGILMNORU CLAMOURING
ACGILNNPRY PRANCINGLY
ACGILNOORY CRANIOLOGY
ACGILNOPTU COPULATING
ACGILORSUY GLYCOSURIA, GRACIOUSLY
ACGIMNOORS AGRONOMICS
ACGIMNOOSU ASCOGONIUM
ACGIMNSSTY GYMNASTICS
ACGINNNNOU ANNOUNCING
ACGINNOOST CONTAGIONS
ACGINNORRY CARRYING-ON
ACGINNRTTU TRUNCATING
ACGINOOSTU CONTAGIOUS
ACGINOPRTY AGRYPNOTIC
ACGINOPSUU PUGNACIOUS
ACGINORRST CO-STARRING
ACGIOOPRTV VAGOTROPIC
ACGIORSTTY GYROSTATIC
ACGJNOORTU CONJUGATOR
ACGLMNOOOS COSMOGONAL
ACGLNOORSU CLANGOROUS
ACHHIILPST PHTHISICAL
ACHHILMOPT OPHTHALMIC
ACHHILMRTY RHYTHMICAL
ACHHILOPTY HALOPHYTIC
ACHHINSTUY HYACINTHUS
ACHHIOPPST PHOSPHATIC
ACHHIPPRSU HIPPARCHUS
ACHHIPRSSU PUSHCHAIRS
ACHHLOSSTU SLOUCH HATS

ACHHLOSSTW WASHCLOTHS
ACHHNOOTTU AUTOCHTHON
ACHHOPPSTY PSYCHOPATH
ACHIIIMNOY ICHINOMIYA
ACHIIIMNST HISTAMINIC
ACHIIIMRTY HIMYARITIC
ACHIIIRSST TRICHIASIS
ACHIILLMPS PHALLICISM
ACHIILLPST PHALLICIST
ACHIILORST HISTORICAL
ACHIILORTU THIOURACIL
ACHIIMNNOR INHARMONIC
ACHIIMNSST MACHINISTS
ACHIIMNSTU HUMANISTIC
ACHIIMNSUV CHAUVINISM
ACHIINNOOT INCHOATION
ACHIINNORT CORINTHIAN
ACHIINNPQU CHINQUAPIN
ACHIINORTT ANORTHITIC
ACHIINPSSY PHYSICIANS
ACHIINRSST CHRISTIANS
ACHIINRSTT ANTICHRIST
ACHIINSTUV CHAUVINIST
ACHIIOPRST APHORISTIC
ACHIIOPSST PISTACHIOS
ACHIIPRSTY PHYSIATRIC
ACHIIRRSTT ARTHRITICS
ACHIIRSSTV ARCHIVISTS
ACHIKLOORW WORKAHOLIC
ACHIKMNOST MACKINTOSH
ACHILLMOOS ALCOHOLISM
ACHILLMSSU MUSIC HALLS
ACHILLNNSY CLANNISHLY
ACHILLNOOP ALLOPHONIC
ACHILLNOPY PHONICALLY
ACHILLOPRT PROTHALLIC
ACHILLPSYY PHYSICALLY
ACHILMOPTY POLYMATHIC
ACHILMPSTY ITCHY PALMS
ACHILNOORS ISOCHRONAL
ACHILNORUY HYALURONIC
ACHILORSUV CHIVALROUS
ACHIMMNORS MONARCHISM
ACHIMMNOPTT MATCH POINT
ACHIMNOPTY AMPHICTYON
ACHIMNORST MONARCHIST
ACHIMORRTT TRICHROMAT
ACHIMORRYZ MYCORRHIZA
ACHIMORSTT CHROMATIST
ACHIMOSSST MASOCHISTS
ACHIMOSSTU MUSTACHIOS
ACHINNOSST STANCHIONS
ACHINNOSTW CHINATOWNS
ACHINOOPSX SAXOPHONIC

ACHINPRSST CHINSTRAPS
ACHIOOPPTT POTATO CHIP
ACHIOOPSTY SOCIOPATHY
ACHIOPRSTY PHYSIOCRAT
ACHIOPTTUY AUTOPHYTIC
ACHIPRSTYY PSYCHIATRY
ACHIRSTTWW WRISTWATCH
ACHKOPRSTW PATCHWORKS
ACHLLOOPSY PLAYSCHOOL
ACHLMMOORS SCHOOLMARM
ACHLMNORUU HOMUNCULAR
ACHLOOSSTU HOLOCAUSTS
ACHNOOPSYZ SCYPHOZOAN
ACHNOPSSTY SYCOPHANTS
ACHORSTTTU CUTTHROATS
ACIIILNOPT POLITICIAN
ACIIILNPST SINCIPITAL
ACIIILORTV VARIOLITIC
ACIIILSTTV VITALISTIC
ACIIINNOTT INCITATION
ACIIINRSTT INARTISTIC
ACIIINSTTV NATIVISTIC
ACIIINTTVY INACTIVITY
ACIIJRSTUY JUSTICIARY
ACIIKNRSST SANSKRITIC
ACIILLMNRY CRIMINALLY
ACIILLNNOS SCILLONIAN
ACIILLNORY IRONICALLY
ACIILMORST MORALISTIC
ACIILNOOST COALITIONS
ACIILNOPRV PROVINCIAL
ACIILNORTT TINCTORIAL
ACIILNPPRS PRINCIPALS
ACIILNSSTV CALVINISTS
ACIILOPRST SAPROLITIC
ACIILOPTTY TOPICALITY
ACIILORSTY ROYALISTIC
ACIILOSSST SOCIALISTS
ACIILOSSUV LASCIVIOUS
ACIILPSTTY PLASTICITY
ACIILRSTTU ALTRUISTIC, ULTRAISTIC
ACIILRTTTY TRACTILITY
ACIIMMNOPT PANTOMIMIC
ACIIMMNSTU NUMISMATIC
ACIIMNNOSS INSOMNIACS
ACIIMNORST MORTICIANS
ACIIMNPTTY TYMPANITIC
ACIIMNRSSS NARCISSISM
ACIIMNRSTU MANICURIST
ACIIMOSTTT STOMATITIC
ACIINNOOTV INVOCATION
ACIINNOSTU INSOUCIANT
ACIINNOTTX INTOXICANT
ACIINOPRST ASCRIPTION, CRISPATION

ACIINOPRTT TRITANOPIC
ACIINORSTV VICTORIANS
ACIINORTTU URTICATION
ACIINOSTUU INCAUTIOUS
ACIINRSSST NARCISSIST
ACIIOPSSUU AUSPICIOUS
ACIIORSTVY VARICOSITY
ACIISSSTTT STATISTICS
ACIJLNNOTU JUNCTIONAL
ACIJLORTUY JOCULARITY
ACIKKLMNOR KILMARNOCK
ACIKLNNOPT PLANKTONIC
ACIKLOORSW SOCIAL WORK
ACIKLORTYY KARYOLYTIC
ACIKOPRTYY KARYOTYPIC
ACIKRSSTTU TRACKSUITS
ACILLLOOQU COLLOQUIAL
ACILLMNNOO MONOCLINAL
ACILLMOORT COLLIMATOR
ACILLMOPYY MYOPICALLY
ACILLMSTYY MYSTICALLY
ACILLNOOPT CALL OPTION
ACILLNOOST COLLATIONS
ACILLNOOTU ALLOCUTION, LOCULATION
ACILLNORUU UNILOCULAR
ACILLNORUV INVOLUCRAL
ACILLOOPRT ALLOTROPIC
ACILLOORST OSCILLATOR
ACILLOPRTY TROPICALLY
ACILLORRTU TRILOCULAR
ACILMMOORS MICROSOMAL
ACILMMOSTT COMMITTALS
ACILMMRSUU SIMULACRUM
ACILMNOORT MICROTONAL
ACILMNOPST COMPLAINTS
ACILMNOSUU CALUMNIOUS
ACILMNOTUU CUMULATION
ACILMNRSUU MINUSCULAR
ACILMOOPTY POLYATOMIC
ACILMOPRRY MICROPYLAR
ACILMORSUU MIRACULOUS
ACILNNOPTY NONTYPICAL
ACILNOOORT COLORATION
ACILNOOPTU COPULATION
ACILNOORST CONSORTIAL
ACILNOORTU INOCULATOR
ACILNOORTY ICONOLATRY
ACILNOOSTU OSCULATION
ACILNOOTTT COTTONTAIL
ACILNORRTU TRINOCULAR
ACILNORRTY CONTRARILY
ACILNORSTU ULTRASONIC
ACILNOSTUY LACUNOSITY
ACILNPPSTU SUPPLICANT

ACILNRTTUY TACITURNLY
ACILOOPRRT PROCTORIAL
ACILOOPSTZ ZOOPLASTIC
ACILOOQSUU LOQUACIOUS
ACILOOSSUX SAXICOLOUS
ACILOPSSUY SPACIOUSLY
ACILOPSTUY CAPTIOUSLY
ACILORTTUV CULTIVATOR
ACILOSTUUY CAUTIOUSLY
ACILPRRSTU SCRIPTURAL
ACIMMORSSS COMMISSARS
ACIMMORSSY COMMISSARY
ACIMNNOOPS COMPANIONS
ACIMNNOSTY SANCTIMONY
ACIMNOOPRS COMPARISON
ACIMNOOPSS COMPASSION
ACIMNOORTY CRANIOTOMY
ACIMNOOSST ONOMASTICS
ACIMNOOSTY ACTOMYOSIN
ACIMNOPPRS PRISON CAMP
ACIMNOPRTY PATRONYMIC,
PYROMANTIC
ACIMNOSTTY MYCOSTATIN
ACIMNOTTUY TAUTONYMIC
ACIMNPRSTU MANUSCRIPT
ACIMOOPRTT COMPATRIOT
ACIMOORTVY VARICOTOMY
ACIMOPSTTY ASYMPTOTIC
ACINNNOSTT INCONSTANT
ACINNNOTTU CONTINUANT
ACINNOOORT CORONATION
ACINNOPTTU PUNCTATION
ACINNORSTT CONSTRAINT
ACINNORTTU TRUNCATION
ACINNSTTYY NYCTINASTY
ACINOOOPTT COOPTATION
ACINOOPPRT PROTANOPIC
ACINOORSTT CARTOONIST
ACINOORTVY INVOCATORY
ACINORSSST CROISSANTS
ACINPRRSTT TRANSCRIPT
ACIOPRSTTY PYROSTATIC
ACIORRSTTU RUSTICATOR
ACJKOPRSST JOCKSTRAPS
ACKLLNRSTU TRUNK CALLS
ACKLMNOORS ROCK SALMON
ACKLMOOORS CLOAKROOMS
ACKLNOPRST ROCK PLANTS
ACKLORSSSW CROSSWALKS
ACLLLOOSSY COLOSSALLY
ACLLLRTUUY CULTURALLY
ACLLMRSUUY MUSCULARLY
ACLLNPTUUY PUNCTUALLY
ACLLPRSTUU SCULPTURAL

ACLMMNOOTY COMMONALTY
ACLMOORSSS CLASSROOMS
ACLNNOSTTU CONSULTANT
ACLNNOSTTY CONSTANTLY
ACLNNPTUUU UNPUNCTUAL
ACLNNRSUUU RANUNCULUS
ACLNOORSTT CONTRALTOS
ACLNOPSTUY POSTULANCY
ACLOORSTUY OSCULATORY
ACLOPRSTTU PLUTOCRATS
ACLRRSTTUU STRUCTURAL
ACMMOORTTU COMMUTATOR
ACMMPPUUUV VACUUM PUMP
ACMNNORTUY COUNTRYMAN
ACMNOORRST CORMORANTS
ACMNOOSSTU COSMONAUTS
ACNNNOOSST CONSONANTS
ACNOOPRSTY SYNCOPATOR
ACNOPRSSUY SYNCARPOUS
ACNOPRTTUU PUNCTUATOR
ACOOOPRRRT CORPORATOR
ACOOOPSTTV POST OCTAVO
ACOOPRRRTT PROTRACTOR
ACOOPRRRTU PROCURATOR
ACOPRRSSST SPORTS CARS
ADDDDEEKLS SKEDADDLED
ADDDEEFHIL FIDDLEHEAD
ADDDEEGILM MIDDLE-AGED
ADDDEEHNRU DUNDERHEAD
ADDDEEHRRU RUDDERHEAD
ADDDEEHRTY DEHYDRATED
ADDDEEILSS SIDESADDLE
ADDDEGNORW DOWNGRADED
ADDDELNOOW DOWNLOADED
ADDEEEEPST DEEP-SEATED
ADDEEEFHNR FREE-HANDED
ADDEEEFLOR FREELOADED
ADDEEEFNTU UNDEFEATED
ADDEEEGNNR ENDANGERED
ADDEEEHLRT ETHELDREDA
ADDEEEHNNV EVEN-HANDED
ADDEEEILNT DELINEATED
ADDEEEIRST DESIDERATE
ADDEEELNTT DEAD-NETTLE
ADDEEELRST SADDLETREE
ADDEEELRTT DEAD LETTER
ADDEEENORV ENDEAVORED
ADDEEERSSS ADDRESSEES
ADDEEFHLNT LEFT-HANDED
ADDEEFHOST SOFT-HEADED
ADDEEFILOT DEFOLIATED
ADDEEFNNST DEFENDANTS
ADDEEGGINS DISENGAGED
ADDEEGHILR HILDEGARDE

ADDEEGHLNO LONG-HEADED
ADDEEGILMS MIDDLE AGES
ADDEEGINRR DEAD RINGER
ADDEEGINRT DENIGRATED
ADDEEGINST DESIGNATED
ADDEEGLLNR GELDERLAND
ADDEEHHNTU HEADHUNTED
ADDEEHLNRU UNHERALDED
ADDEEHNNOP OPEN-HANDED
ADDEEIIPSS DIAPEDESIS
ADDEEIKMNW WEAK-MINDED
ADDEEILMMN MIDDLE NAME
ADDEEILMST MIDDLE EAST
ADDEEILNSS DEADLINESS
ADDEEILOTV DOVETAILED
ADDEEILPSS DISPLEASED
ADDEEILRSS SADDLERIES
ADDEEILRSV DAREDEVILS
ADDEEILRWY WIDELY READ
ADDEEIMNRR MIND READER
ADDEEIOPTV VIDEOTAPED
ADDEEIPRSW WIDESPREAD
ADDEEIPRTU REPUDIATED
ADDEEIRSTV ADVERTISED
ADDEEIRTTX EXTRADITED
ADDEEJRSTU READJUSTED
ADDEELLMTU MEDULLATED
ADDEELMNOR ENDODERMAL
ADDEELMOTU DEMODULATE
ADDEELOORV OVERLOADED
ADDEELOPRR ROPE LADDER
ADDEELORSS SADDLE-SORE
ADDEELPRST STEPLADDER
ADDEEMNNRU UNDERNAMED
ADDEEMNOPR PROMENADED
ADDEENNPST DEPENDANTS
ADDEENNTTU UNATTENDED
ADDEENQRSU SQUANDERED
ADDEENRRTU UNDERRATED
ADDEENSSWY WEDNESDAYS
ADDEEOPRSS DESPERADOS
ADDEEORSTT ROAD-TESTED
ADDEFGINRU DEFRAUDING
ADDEFHILPS PADDLEFISH
ADDEFHNORU FOUR-HANDED
ADDEFIIMNR FAIR-MINDED
ADDEFLLRUY DREADFULLY
ADDEGGILNN GLADDENING
ADDEGHHHIN HIGH-HANDED
ADDEGHLORT GOLDTHREAD
ADDEGILLNW WINDGALLED
ADDEGINRSS ADDRESSING
ADDEGIORRS DORSIGRADE
ADDEGLLMOS GOLD MEDALS

ADDEGLLOPT GOLD-PLATED
ADDEHIIMRS DIE-HARDISM
ADDEHILMNS MISHANDLED
ADDEHIMNOO MAIDENHOOD
ADDEHIMNOS ADMONISHED
ADDEHMNNOW HAND-ME-DOWN
ADDEHNORSU ROUNDHEADS
ADDEHORRTY DEHYDRATOR
ADDEIILLSV ILL-ADVISED
ADDEIILMPY EPIDIDYMAL
ADDEIILQTU LIQUIDATED
ADDEIINNRS RED INDIANS
ADDEIINOTU AUDITIONED
ADDEIINRST DISTRAINED
ADDEIIPSST DISSIPATED
ADDEILLNSS LANDSLIDES
ADDEILLOSW DISALLOWED
ADDEILMNST DISMANTLED
ADDEILMTTY ADMITTEDLY
ADDEILNNOS DANDELIONS
ADDEILNSSY DEADLY SINS
ADDEINNOOT ENDODONTIA
ADDEINNOPT ODD-PINNATE
ADDEINNOTU DENUDATION
ADDEINNRRU UNDERDRAIN
ADDEINOORS RADIOSONDE
ADDEINRSTW TRADE WINDS
ADDELMORRW DREAM WORLD
ADDELNNORW WONDERLAND
ADDELNOORW WOODLANDER
ADDELNOPWY DOWNPLAYED
ADDELPQRUU QUADRUPLED
ADDENNPRUU UP-AND-UNDER
ADDENNRSTU UNDERSTAND
ADDENOORST DEODORANTS
ADDEPQRSUU QUADRUPEDS
ADDFGIOORY GOOD FRIDAY
ADDFIILNSU DISDAINFUL
ADDGIIINNS DISDAINING
ADDGIINSSU DISSUADING
ADDGILLNWY WADDLINGLY
ADDGILNNSU UNSADDLING
ADDGILNRST STRADDLING
ADDHIILMOS OLD MAIDISH
ADDHILORSU SHROUD-LAID
ADDIIILNUV INDIVIDUAL
ADDIIINNOT IN ADDITION
ADDILLLLYY DILLYDALLY
ADDIMNOSUY DIDYNAMOUS
ADDIMOORSU DIADROMOUS
ADDNNOOTUW DOWN-AND-OUT
ADEEEEGNRT DEGENERATE
ADEEEFILRS FEDERALISE
ADEEEFILRZ FEDERALIZE

ADEEEFIRTV FEDERATIVE
ADEEEFLORR FREELOADER
ADEEEFRRRT FREE-TRADER
ADEEEGGRST SEGREGATED
ADEEEGLRSV EVERGLADES
ADEEEGLRTU DEREGULATE
ADEEEHHPSS SHEEPSHEAD
ADEEEHLPSY SLEEPYHEAD
ADEEEHLRTT LETTERHEAD
ADEEEHNRTT THREATENED
ADEEEHNSST HEATEDNESS
ADEEEIPRRT PIED-À-TERRE
ADEEEIRRTT REITERATED
ADEEEIRSTT EASTERTIDE
ADEEELLMNP EMPANELLED
ADEEELLNRW WELL-EARNED
ADEEELLRVY REVEALEDLY
ADEEELNNUV UNLEAVENED
ADEEELNSST ELATEDNESS
ADEEELPRTY REPEATEDLY
ADEEEMNNRT ENDEARMENT
ADEEEMNRTU ENUMERATED
ADEEEMNRUV MANEUVERED
ADEEENORRV ENDEAVORER
ADEEENORTX EXONERATED
ADEEENPRTT PENETRATED
ADEEENRRSW NEWSREADER
ADEEENRSST EAST ENDERS
ADEEENSSST SEDATENESS
ADEEENTTUX EXTENUATED
ADEEFFIMRR REAFFIRMED
ADEEFFORST AFFORESTED
ADEEFGHIRU FIGUREHEAD
ADEEFGINRT FEDERATING
ADEEFGLNNW NEWFANGLED
ADEEFGLRRS SELF-REGARD
ADEEFGMNRT FRAGMENTED
ADEEFHLNRT LEFT-HANDER
ADEEFHNRTU UNFATHERED
ADEEFILLNS SELF-DENIAL
ADEEFILMRS FEDERALISM
ADEEFILORR RELIEF ROAD
ADEEFILRST FEDERALIST
ADEEFIMNST MANIFESTED
ADEEFINORT FEDERATION
ADEEFIRSTU DISFEATURE
ADEEFISSTT DEFEATISTS
ADEEFLLLNN FLANNELLED
ADEEFLLORW FALLOW DEER
ADEEFLRSTU DEFAULTERS
ADEEFMNORW FREEDWOMAN
ADEEFNOPRR FREE PARDON
ADEEFNORRW FOREWARNED
ADEEFOPRRT PERFORATED

ADEEGGHLOR LOGGERHEAD
ADEEGGILNT DELEGATING
ADEEGGLNOS GOLDEN AGES
ADEEGGMOSU DEMAGOGUES
ADEEGGNRSS RAGGEDNESS
ADEEGGOPSU PEDAGOGUES
ADEEGGORUW OWE A GRUDGE
ADEEGIINSS DIAGENESIS
ADEEGIJLNR DARJEELING
ADEEGILLST LEGISLATED
ADEEGILMNR MALINGERED
ADEEGILNOT DELEGATION
ADEEGILNRR RINGLEADER
ADEEGIMNNR MEANDERING
ADEEGIMNRT GERMINATED
ADEEGIMNST MAGNETISED
ADEEGIMNTZ MAGNETIZED
ADEEGINNOT DENEGATION
ADEEGINNRS SERENADING
ADEEGINOTT NEGOTIATED
ADEEGINRRS GRENADIERS
ADEEGINRRT INTERGRADE, RETREADING
ADEEGINRTT INTEGRATED
ADEEGIORTV DEROGATIVE
ADEEGLLNOS GOLDENSEAL
ADEEGLLRUW WELL-ARGUED
ADEEGLMNNO GOLDEN MEAN
ADEEGLNRUZ UNDERGLAZE
ADEEGLOPUU GUADELOUPE
ADEEGLPPRY DAPPLE-GREY
ADEEGLRRSS REGARDLESS
ADEEGMNORT DERMATOGEN
ADEEGNOTXY OXYGENATED
ADEEGOORSV OVERDOSAGE
ADEEGOORSW GREASEWOOD
ADEEGORRRT RETROGRADE
ADEEGPRTUX EXPURGATED
ADEEHHILMR HEMIHEDRAL
ADEEHHILST HEAT SHIELD
ADEEHHLOSV SHOVELHEAD
ADEEHHMNOT HEATHENDOM
ADEEHHNOPS HEADPHONES
ADEEHHNORX HEXAHEDRON
ADEEHHNPTY HYPHENATED
ADEEHHNRTU HEADHUNTER
ADEEHIIRRW WIRE-HAIRED
ADEEHILNOT ETHANEDIOL
ADEEHILNTU HEULANDITE
ADEEHILPPR HARELIPPED
ADEEHILPRS DEALERSHIP, LEADERSHIP
ADEEHILSWY DAISY WHEEL
ADEEHIMNSU DEHUMANISE
ADEEHIMNUZ DEHUMANIZE
ADEEHIMPSS EMPHASISED

ADEEHIMPSZ EMPHASIZED
ADEEHINRST DISHEARTEN
ADEEHINRTT THENARDITE
ADEEHIPRRS READERSHIP
ADEEHIRRSS SHERARDISE
ADEEHIRRSZ SHERARDIZE
ADEEHIRRTY HEREDITARY
ADEEHKORRW HEADWORKER
ADEEHLLNRT ENTHRALLED
ADEEHLLNSS HANDLELESS
ADEEHLNOTW DOWN-AT-HEEL
ADEEHLORUV OVERHAULED
ADEEHMNPRU UNHAMPERED
ADEEHMOSST HOMESTEADS
ADEEHNNRTU UNDERNEATH
ADEEHNOSST HEADSTONES
ADEEHOSSWY EYE SHADOWS
ADEEHRSSTW WATERSHEDS
ADEEIIJNRR JARDINIERE
ADEEIILMNT ELIMINATED
ADEEIILNTV EVIDENTIAL
ADEEIILRSS SERIALISED
ADEEIILRSZ SERIALIZED
ADEEIILSTV DEVITALISE
ADEEIILTVZ DEVITALIZE
ADEEIIMTTV MEDITATIVE
ADEEIINRST DISTRAINEE
ADEEIINSST DESSIATINE, EAST INDIES
ADEEIIRTVV DERIVATIVE
ADEEIJMNRS RED JASMINE
ADEEIJOPRS JEOPARDISE
ADEEIJOPRZ JEOPARDIZE
ADEEIKLLWW WEAK-WILLED
ADEEIKRSST ASTERISKED
ADEEILLMNP IMPANELLED
ADEEILLMRY REMEDIALLY
ADEEILLPRS ESPADRILLE
ADEEILLRRU DERAILLEUR
ADEEILLRTT ILL-TREATED
ADEEILLUVV VAUDEVILLE
ADEEILMNPT PEDIMENTAL
ADEEILMNRT DERAILMENT
ADEEILMORS DEMORALISE
ADEEILMORZ DEMORALIZE
ADEEILMPRR PERIDERMAL
ADEEILNORT DELINEATOR
ADEEILNPRT INTERPLEAD
ADEEILNRTU ADULTERINE
ADEEILNTTT DILETTANTE
ADEEILNTTV VENTILATED
ADEEILOPRS DEPOLARISE
ADEEILOPRZ DEPOLARIZE
ADEEILPRRV PEARL DIVER
ADEEIMMORT IMMODERATE

ADEEIMMUVW MEDIUM WAVE
ADEEIMNNOT DENOMINATE,
  EMENDATION
ADEEIMNNTT DETAINMENT
ADEEIMNRRS REMAINDERS
ADEEIMNRSS DREAMINESS
ADEEIMNRTT TERMINATED
ADEEIMORRT RADIOMETER
ADEEIMORTU AUDIOMETER
ADEEIMOTTV DEMOTIVATE
ADEEIMPPRS PIPE DREAMS
ADEEINORTT ORIENTATED
ADEEINOTTV DENOTATIVE, DETONATIVE
ADEEINPPSX APPENDIXES
ADEEINPRST PEDANTRIES, PEDESTRIAN
ADEEINRRSS DREARINESS
ADEEINRRST RESTRAINED
ADEEINRSSV VARIEDNESS
ADEEINRSTT REINSTATED, STRAITENED
ADEEINRTTT TRIDENTATE
ADEEINSSST STEADINESS
ADEEIOPRSX PEROXIDASE
ADEEIOSXYY OXEYE DAISY
ADEEIPRSTT TAPESTRIED
ADEEIPRTTX EXTIRPATED
ADEEIPRTUV DEPURATIVE
ADEEIRRSTV ADVERTISER
ADEEJRRSTU READJUSTER
ADEEKMNRSS MARKEDNESS
ADEEKMRRSS DRESSMAKER
ADEEKNNRTU UNDERTAKEN
ADEEKNRRTU UNDERTAKER
ADEELLNQUU UNEQUALLED
ADEELLNRUV UNRAVELLED
ADEELLOPRY ROLE-PLAYED
ADEELLOPST SELLOTAPED
ADEELLORSS LOSS LEADER
ADEELLOSTY DESOLATELY
ADEELLQRRU QUARRELLED
ADEELMMORS MESODERMAL
ADEELMNORT ENTODERMAL
ADEELMNPUX UNEXAMPLED
ADEELMORTY MODERATELY
ADEELMRSUY MEASUREDLY
ADEELNNQSU QUEENSLAND
ADEELNOSSY SEASONEDLY
ADEELNRRSS SLANDERERS
ADEELNRUUV UNDERVALUE
ADEELOPPRV OVERLAPPED
ADEELOPPTU DEPOPULATE
ADEELOPRSS LEOPARDESS
ADEELOPRVY OVERPLAYED
ADEELPPRRY PREPAREDLY
ADEELPRSTT SPLATTERED

ADEELRRSTU ADULTERERS
ADEELRSSTU ADULTERESS
ADEEMMNNRT REMANDMENT
ADEEMMNNST AMENDMENTS
ADEEMNNNRU UNMANNERED
ADEEMNNORT ORNAMENTED
ADEEMNNORV OVERMANNED
ADEEMNOPRR PROMENADER
ADEEMNOPRS PROMENADES
ADEEMNORSU DEMEANOURS
ADEEMNORTY EMENDATORY
ADEEMNORUV MANOEUVRED
ADEEMNORYY READY MONEY
ADEEMNPRTT DEPARTMENT
ADEEMNRSUU UNMEASURED
ADEEMOORRS AERODROMES
ADEEMOOSTU OEDEMATOUS
ADEENNOSSU UNSEASONED
ADEENNPTTU UNPATENTED
ADEENORSUV ENDEAVOURS
ADEENPPRRU UNPREPARED
ADEENPRRTU ENRAPTURED
ADEENPRSST DEPRESSANT
ADEENPRSTY PRESENT-DAY
ADEENQRRSU SQUANDERER
ADEENRRTUV ADVENTURER
ADEENRRTUW UNDERWATER
ADEENRSTTU UNDERSTATE
ADEENRSTUV ADVENTURES
ADEEOPPRRR ORDER PAPER
ADEEORRTTU TRADE ROUTE
ADEEORSTTV OVERSTATED
ADEEORSTVY OVERSTAYED
ADEEPPRSST SPEED TRAPS
ADEEPPRRSTU DEPARTURES
ADEEPRSSST TRESPASSED
ADEERRSTYY STARRY-EYED
ADEERSSSTW STEWARDESS
ADEERSSTYY YESTERDAYS
ADEFFGGGIR GAFF-RIGGED
ADEFFLOOTT FLAT-FOOTED
ADEFGGINOR GOD-FEARING
ADEFGHIRST FARSIGHTED
ADEFGHORST GODFATHERS
ADEFGIILNN ENFILADING
ADEFGIINOR FOREIGN AID
ADEFGILNTU DEFAULTING
ADEFGILRSU LIFEGUARDS
ADEFGIRRSU FIREGUARDS
ADEFGLOOST FLOODGATES
ADEFGNOORR ROOF GARDEN
ADEFHHLOOT HEALTH FOOD
ADEFHHOORT FATHERHOOD
ADEFHILMSS DAMSELFISH

ADEFHILTTW HALF-WITTED	**ADEGHORSUU** GUARDHOUSE
ADEFHINPRT PATHFINDER	**ADEGIIILNZ** IDEALIZING
ADEFHIRTWW WHITE DWARF	**ADEGIIILST** DIGITALISE
ADEFHLOOSS FALSEHOODS	**ADEGIIILTZ** DIGITALIZE
ADEFHOORSW FORESHADOW	**ADEGIILMNS** MISLEADING
ADEFIILPSS FISSIPEDAL	**ADEGIILNOT** GADOLINITE, GELATINOID
ADEFIINQTU QUANTIFIED	**ADEGIILNPR** LIP-READING
ADEFIINRTU INFURIATED	**ADEGIILNRT** RING-TAILED
ADEFIIRSTT STRATIFIED	**ADEGIILNSS** SIGNALISED
ADEFILLLSU FULL-SAILED	**ADEGIILNSZ** SIGNALIZED
ADEFILLNTY INFLATEDLY	**ADEGIIMMRT** IMMIGRATED
ADEFILLORV ILL-FAVORED	**ADEGIIMNRS** MISREADING
ADEFILLSSU FUSILLADES	**ADEGIIMNTT** MEDITATING
ADEFILMNOR MANIFOLDER	**ADEGIINNRT** DETRAINING
ADEFILMNTU FULMINATED	**ADEGIINORT** ORIGINATED
ADEFILMORS FORMALISED	**ADEGIINPRS** DESPAIRING
ADEFILMORZ FORMALIZED	**ADEGIINSTT** INSTIGATED
ADEFILNOST DEFOLIANTS	**ADEGIIOPRR** PRAIRIE DOG
ADEFILOORT DEFOLIATOR	**ADEGILMNRY** DREAMINGLY
ADEFILORTU FLUORIDATE	**ADEGILMORS** GLAMORISED
ADEFIMRRRT DIRT FARMER	**ADEGILMORZ** GLAMORIZED
ADEFINOORR FOREORDAIN	**ADEGILNNNO** NONALIGNED
ADEFINORSS SANFORISED	**ADEGILNNNT** LANDING NET
ADEFINORSZ SANFORIZED	**ADEGILNNRS** SANDERLING, SLANDERING
ADEFINRSTX TRANSFIXED	**ADEGILNNRU** LAUNDERING
ADEFIRSSTX FIXED STARS	**ADEGILNOST** DESOLATING
ADEFKLNOTU OUTFLANKED	**ADEGILNOTT** GLOTTIDEAN
ADEFLMORTU FORMULATED	**ADEGILNRUV** GERUNDIVAL
ADEFLNRTUU FRAUDULENT	**ADEGILOOPS** APOLOGISED
ADEFNOORRW FOR A WONDER	**ADEGILOOPZ** APOLOGIZED
ADEFOOPSST SOFT-SOAPED	**ADEGILRSUV** VULGARISED
ADEFORRSTV OVERDRAFTS	**ADEGILRUVZ** VULGARIZED
ADEFRRSTTU FRUSTRATED	**ADEGIMNNRU** MAUNDERING
ADEGGHOSTU SHAGGED OUT	**ADEGIMNOPU** IMPOUNDAGE
ADEGGIMOPS PEDAGOGISM	**ADEGIMNORS** GORMANDISE
ADEGGINORT DEROGATING	**ADEGIMNORT** MODERATING
ADEGGINSUW WIND GAUGES	**ADEGIMNORZ** GORMANDIZE
ADEGGNOPTU GET-UP-AND-GO	**ADEGIMNPST** STAMPEDING
ADEGHHIKNT KNIGHTHEAD	**ADEGIMNSTU** MAGNITUDES
ADEGHHILNR HIGHLANDER	**ADEGIMORST** DOGMATISER
ADEGHHILST HEADLIGHTS	**ADEGIMORTZ** DOGMATIZER
ADEGHHINST NIGHTSHADE	**ADEGINNOTT** DETONATING
ADEGHIILNN HEADLINING	**ADEGINNRSW** WANDERINGS
ADEGHILLNO HELIGOLAND	**ADEGINOORT** DEROGATION
ADEGHILNOO HALOGENOID	**ADEGINORRS** GARRISONED
ADEGHILNOR LONGHAIRED	**ADEGINORRT** DENIGRATOR
ADEGHILNSU LANGUISHED	**ADEGINORST** DESIGNATOR
ADEGHINPRS HEADSPRING, SPRINGHEAD	**ADEGINPRSU** PERSUADING
ADEGHIOPRY IDEOGRAPHY	**ADEGIPRRST** PARTRIDGES
ADEGHLORSS GASHOLDERS	**ADEGJLMNTU** JUDGMENTAL
ADEGHLRTUY DAUGHTERLY	**ADEGKNRRRU** KRUGERRAND
ADEGHMOPRY DEMOGRAPHY	**ADEGLNORSU** GLANDEROUS
ADEGHMORSU HOME GUARDS	**ADEGMMOPRR** PROGRAMMED
ADEGHNORST HEADSTRONG	**ADEGMNOOSU** ENDOGAMOUS

ADEGNOOORW ORANGEWOOD
ADEGNOPRST GODPARENTS
ADEGNORSSU SANDGROUSE
ADEGOORRTY DEROGATORY
ADEGOORSST STAGE DOORS
ADEHHIIPRT DIPHTHERIA
ADEHHIRSSW DISHWASHER
ADEHHLLOOR HOLOHEDRAL
ADEHIILMTU HUMILIATED
ADEHIILNPR NEPHRIDIAL
ADEHIILRSS HAIR SLIDES
ADEHIINOPR HEPARINOID
ADEHIIPSUU EUPHAUSIID
ADEHILLORU LOUDHAILER
ADEHILNNRT HINTERLAND
ADEHILNOPS SPHENOIDAL
ADEHILNRRS HARD-LINERS
ADEHILNRST DISENTHRAL
ADEHILOPRS SPHEROIDAL
ADEHILPSTU DISULPHATE
ADEHIMNORS ADMONISHER,
  HARMONISED
ADEHIMNORZ HARMONIZED
ADEHIMORTU RHEUMATOID
ADEHIMOSSU HOUSEMAIDS
ADEHINOSST ASTONISHED
ADEHINQSUV VANQUISHED
ADEHINRSTY HYDRASTINE
ADEHIOPRSS RHAPSODIES, RHAPSODISE
ADEHIOPRSZ RHAPSODIZE
ADEHIORSTU AUTHORISED
ADEHIORTUZ AUTHORIZED
ADEHIOSSTW SHADOWIEST
ADEHIRRTTY TRIHYDRATE
ADEHIRRTWW WITHDRAWER
ADEHJMPRSU JAMSHEDPUR
ADEHKNORRW WORK-HARDEN
ADEHKNORST HANDSTROKE
ADEHKNOSSW SHAKEDOWNS
ADEHKORRSS DARK HORSES
ADEHLLNOUW UNHALLOWED
ADEHLLOPRY POLYHEDRAL
ADEHLLOSTT DEATH TOLLS
ADEHLMNOSY HANDSOMELY
ADEHLMOPTY METHYLDOPA
ADEHLRTTWY THWARTEDLY
ADEHMNNOSU UNHANDSOME
ADEHMOORST MASTERHOOD
ADEHMOORRTW THREADWORM
ADEHMORSTY MOTHER'S DAY
ADEHNOOPRT PARENTHOOD,
  THEROPODAN
ADEHOORSSU ROADHOUSES
ADEHOORSVW OVERSHADOW

ADEHORRSSW SHOREWARDS
ADEIIIKNSS DIAKINESIS
ADEIIILLNT INITIALLED
ADEIIIMNTT INTIMIDATE
ADEIILLMPX MAXILLIPED
ADEIILLSTT DISTILLATE
ADEIILLTTT TITILLATED
ADEIILMMTU MULTIMEDIA
ADEIILMNOR MERIDIONAL
ADEIILMPPS MISAPPLIED
ADEIILNOPT DEPILATION
ADEIILNRTT INTERTIDAL
ADEIILNTTT DILETTANTI
ADEIILORST EDITORIALS, IDOLATRISE
ADEIILORTZ IDOLATRIZE
ADEIILSSUV VISUALISED
ADEIILSUVZ VISUALIZED
ADEIIMNOTT MEDITATION
ADEIIMNOTV DOMINATIVE
ADEIIMNRST ADMINISTER
ADEIIMPRSU PRAESIDIUM
ADEIIMRSTT DERMATITIS
ADEIINNNOS INDONESIAN
ADEIINNORT INORDINATE
ADEIINNOTW NATIONWIDE
ADEIINNOTX INDEXATION
ADEIINNPPT PINNATIPED
ADEIINNSST DAINTINESS
ADEIINNSTU INSINUATED
ADEIINNSTW WEST INDIAN
ADEIINORTV DERIVATION
ADEIINOSTV DEVIATIONS
ADEIINPPRS DRAINPIPES
ADEIINPTTU INAPTITUDE
ADEIIPRRSS DISPRAISER
ADEIIPRSST DISSIPATER
ADEIIPRSTV PRIVATISED
ADEIIPRTVZ PRIVATIZED
ADEIISSSUV DISSUASIVE
ADEIJMMNRW WINDJAMMER
ADEIKLLLRY LADY-KILLER
ADEIKLLMMT MALTED MILK
ADEIKNPPRS KIDNAPPERS
ADEILLMNOS MEDALLIONS
ADEILLMRST TREADMILLS
ADEILLMSST MEDALLISTS
ADEILLNOOS SOLENOIDAL
ADEILLNOPT POLLINATED
ADEILLNOSU DELUSIONAL
ADEILLNPSS PALLIDNESS
ADEILLNRRT TENDRILLAR
ADEILLNRTU ILL-NATURED
ADEILLNRUV UNRIVALLED
ADEILLQRSU QUADRILLES

ADEILLRRST ILL-STARRED
ADEILMNOPR PALINDROME
ADEILMNORS NORMALISED
ADEILMNORZ NORMALIZED
ADEILMNRST DISMANTLER
ADEILMNSSS DISMALNESS
ADEILMOTUV MODULATIVE
ADEILMSTTU STIMULATED
ADEILNNORT INTERNODAL
ADEILNOOST DESOLATION
ADEILNOOTV DEVOTIONAL
ADEILNPRTU PRUDENTIAL
ADEILNSSSW WINDLASSES
ADEILNSTTU TESTUDINAL
ADEILNSTUY UNSTEADILY
ADEILOORST OESTRADIOL
ADEILOPRTT TETRAPLOID
ADEILOPRTY DEPILATORY
ADEILOPSSU DISEPALOUS
ADEILOPSTU DIPETALOUS
ADEILOQSSU ODALISQUES
ADEILORTUV OUTRIVALED
ADEILOSSTT SOLID-STATE
ADEILPSTTU PLATITUDES, STIPULATED
ADEILRSTTU STRIDULATE
ADEILRTTXY DEXTRALITY
ADEILRTUUX LUXURIATED
ADEIMMNRST MASTERMIND
ADEIMMRSSU SUMMARISED
ADEIMMRSUZ SUMMARIZED
ADEIMNOORT MODERATION
ADEIMNPRRS REPRIMANDS
ADEIMNRSSU NURSEMAIDS
ADEIMORRTY RADIOMETRY
ADEIMORSST DERMATOSIS
ADEIMORTUY AUDIOMETRY
ADEIMRSTUX ADMIXTURES
ADEINNOOTT DENOTATION,
  DETONATION
ADEINNOPWW WINDOWPANE
ADEINNORSW RAWINSONDE
ADEINNORTU TRADE UNION
ADEINNRSTU UNSTRAINED
ADEINNRSTY TYRANNISED
ADEINNRTYZ TYRANNIZED
ADEINOPRST PATRONISED
ADEINOPRTU DEPURATION
ADEINOPRTZ PATRONIZED
ADEINOPTTU DEPUTATION
ADEINORSST ADROITNESS
ADEINORSUV ADENOVIRUS
ADEINOSTVY VIDEO NASTY
ADEINPPRSS SANDPIPERS
ADEINPPSST STANDPIPES

ADEINPRRST TRANSPIRED
ADEINPRSSY DISPENSARY
ADEINRSSTW TAWDRINESS
ADEINRSTTU UNSTRIATED
ADEINSSSTU UNASSISTED
ADEIOPPRSV DISAPPROVE
ADEIOPRRTU REPUDIATOR
ADEIOPRSTY DEPOSITARY
ADEIOPRSTZ TRAPEZOIDS
ADEIORSSTT SIDEROSTAT
ADEIPPRRTY DAY-TRIPPER
ADEJMNSTTU ADJUSTMENT
ADEJOPSTUX JUXTAPOSED
ADEKMNORTW DOWN-MARKET
ADEKMOPRST POSTMARKED
ADEKNOPRST POND-SKATER
ADEKNRRSSS DRESS RANKS
ADELLLPTUU PULLULATED
ADELLNORRU ALL-ROUNDER
ADELLNORSW LOWLANDERS
ADELLOORRR ROAD ROLLER
ADELLOORRU EURODOLLAR
ADELMOPSTU DEUTOPLASM
ADELMORSST OLD MASTERS
ADELNOOSST LOADSTONES
ADELNORRSV LAND ROVERS
ADELNORSSU SLANDEROUS
ADELNPPSTU SUPPLANTED
ADELNRSTUW WANDERLUST
ADELOOPRST DOORPLATES
ADELOPSTTU POSTULATED
ADELORRWWY WORLD-WEARY
ADELORSTUU ADULTEROUS
ADELPQRTUU QUADRUPLET
ADELPQRUUX QUADRUPLEX
ADEMMMNORU MEMORANDUM
ADEMMOOSTU STOMODAEUM
ADEMNNORSS RANDOMNESS
ADEMNNORST ADORNMENTS
ADEMNORSTW DOWNSTREAM
ADEMNRRSSU SNARE DRUMS
ADEMNRSTTU TRANSMUTED
ADEMOORRST MODERATORS
ADEMOQRTUY DEMY QUARTO
ADEMORSTTU OUTSMARTED
ADENNORRRU ROADRUNNER
ADENNPRSTU UNDERPANTS
ADENNRRRSU RUN ERRANDS
ADENNSSSTW NEWSSTANDS
ADENOORSTT DETONATORS
ADENOPRSST TRANSPOSED
ADENPRSSUW UPWARDNESS
ADENRRSSTW STERNWARDS
ADENRRSUYY DAY NURSERY

ADEOPRRSTT PROSTRATED
ADEORRSSWW SWEARWORDS
ADEPPRSTUU SUPPURATED
ADFFGILNOO OFF-LOADING
ADFGIILRRY GIRL FRIDAY
ADFGINORRU FAIRGROUND
ADFGINORRW FORWARDING
ADFHILLORS DOLLARFISH
ADFHINNORU FOUR-IN-HAND
ADFHNOORST AND SO FORTH
ADFIIINNPT PINNATIFID
ADFIIKMNRU FAIR DINKUM
ADFIILMRSU DISULFIRAM
ADFIILQSUY DISQUALIFY
ADFIIOSSTU FASTIDIOUS
ADFIISSSTY DISSATISFY
ADFINNOOTU FOUNDATION
ADFLMNTUUU MUTUAL FUND
ADFMOOPSST FOOD STAMPS
ADFNOORTUY FOUDROYANT
ADFNOPRSTU STAND UP FOR
ADFNORRSTW FRONTWARDS
ADGGIINNOS DIAGNOSING
ADGGINNOOR DRAGOONING
ADGGINNORU GAIN GROUND
ADGHHOPRRY HYDROGRAPH
ADGHIILNOY HOLIDAYING
ADGHILLLSU GUILDHALLS
ADGHIMNOPP HOPPING MAD
ADGHINNPRS HANDSPRING
ADGHIRRSTW RIGHTWARDS
ADGHIRSTTU DISTRAUGHT
ADGHLPRSUU SULPHA DRUG
ADGIIILMST DIGITALISM
ADGIIILNNV INVALIDING
ADGIIIMNOR MIGRAINOID
ADGIIINOTT DIGITATION
ADGIIKNNPP KIDNAPPING
ADGIILMNOU GADOLINIUM
ADGIILMNRY ADMIRINGLY
ADGIILNPSY DISPLAYING
ADGIIMNNOT DOMINATING
ADGIIMNNTY DYNAMITING
ADGIIMNPRS RISING DAMP
ADGIIMNSST DISMASTING
ADGIINNNTU INUNDATING
ADGIINNPRW DRAWING PIN
ADGIINOSVW DISAVOWING
ADGIJNNORU ADJOURNING
ADGIKNORWY WORKING DAY
ADGIKOORRV KIROVOGRAD
ADGILLNOPR POLLARDING
ADGILLOPRY PRODIGALLY
ADGILMNOTU MODULATING

ADGILNNNTUU UNDULATING
ADGILNOOPW WADING POOL
ADGIMOSSTT DOGMATISTS
ADGINNOSTU ASTOUNDING
ADGINNPSTU UPSTANDING
ADGINOPSTT POSTDATING
ADGINPRRSX GRANDS PRIX
ADGINRRSTW DRAWSTRING
ADGIORSSWW GRASS WIDOW
ADGLMNOOOY MONADOLOGY
ADGLNNOPRU GROUND PLAN
ADGLNOPRUY PLAYGROUND
ADGMNNORSU GROUNDSMAN
ADGMNORSSU GROUNDMASS
ADGMOORRSU GUARDROOMS
ADGNNORSUY GYNANDROUS
ADGNOOORRT DRAGONROOT
ADHHNOSTTU THOUSANDTH
ADHIIKKNNT KITH AND KIN
ADHIILMNOT MIDLOTHIAN
ADHIIMMNPS MIDSHIPMAN
ADHIIMSTTU HUMIDISTAT
ADHIINNSTU HINDUSTANI
ADHIIPRTTY HIT PAY DIRT
ADHILLLOPY PHYLLODIAL
ADHILNOSTU OUTLANDISH
ADHILOOPRS DROSOPHILA
ADHILOQRRU HARD LIQUOR
ADHIMNORSY DISHARMONY
ADHINNOOOT NATIONHOOD
ADHINOOPRT ANTHROPOID
ADHINOOPRY RADIOPHONY
ADHINOOPRZ RHIZOPODAN
ADHINOSSWW SASH WINDOW
ADHIOPRSST RHAPSODIST
ADHIPRRTTY THIRD PARTY
ADHLNOPSSW SPLASHDOWN
ADHNORRSTW NORTHWARDS
ADHOORRTWY ROADWORTHY
ADHORSSTUW SOUTHWARDS
ADIIILMNSV INVALIDISM
ADIIILMRSS DISSIMILAR
ADIIILNOSV DIVISIONAL
ADIIILNTVY INVALIDITY
ADIIINNOTV DIVINATION
ADIIINOOST IODISATION
ADIIINOOTZ IODIZATION
ADIILMMNSU MAUDLINISM
ADIILMNOXY MIXOLYDIAN
ADIILMOPRR PRIMORDIAL
ADIILMOPRS PRISMOIDAL
ADIILMSSSS DISMISSALS
ADIILNORRY ORDINARILY
ADIILNOSSU SINUSOIDAL

ADIILNRSTU INDUSTRIAL
ADIILOPPSY POLYDIPSIA
ADIILOQRTU LIQUIDATOR
ADIILORSSY RADIOLYSIS
ADIILORSTY SOLIDARITY
ADIILQSTUY SQUALIDITY
ADIIMMMOTU OMMATIDIUM
ADIIMNNNOO ANNO DOMINI
ADIIMNNOOT ADMONITION,
  DOMINATION
ADIIMNNORV MORDVINIAN
ADIIMNOSSS ADMISSIONS
ADIIMOPRST DIATROPISM, PRISMATOID
ADIIMORTUU AUDITORIUM
ADIINNNOTU INUNDATION
ADIINNOORT ORDINATION
ADIINOPPST DISAPPOINT
ADIINOPSSS DISPASSION
ADIINORRST DISTRAINOR
ADIINORSTT TRADITIONS
ADIINORTVY DIVINATORY
ADIINOSSSU DISSUASION
ADIIOPRSTT PODIATRIST
ADILLLOSYY DISLOYALLY
ADILLNSSTT STANDSTILL
ADILLOSTYY DISLOYALTY
ADILMMOPSU PLASMODIUM
ADILMNOOOP MONOPODIAL
ADILMNOOTU MODULATION
ADILMOPSST PSALMODIST
ADILNNOTUU UNDULATION
ADILOORSTU IDOLATROUS
ADIMNOORTY ADMONITORY
ADIMNRRTUV TRIVANDRUM
ADINNOPSTT STANDPOINT
ADINNOSSTU INS AND OUTS
ADINOOPRST ADSORPTION
ADINOOSSTW SATINWOODS
ADINORSSTW DOWNSTAIRS
ADIORSSSTU DISASTROUS
ADJLOPRTUU PLAT DU JOUR
ADJMMOOORS MAJOR-DOMOS
ADJMMORRSU DRUM MAJORS
ADKNORRSTU TRUNK ROADS
ADLMOOORSU MALODOROUS
ADLNORSTUU ULTRASOUND
ADLNORTUUY UNDULATORY
ADLNORTUWY UNTOWARDLY
ADLOOOSSTT TOADSTOOLS
ADMNNOORSU MONANDROUS
ADMNORSSST SANDSTORMS
ADMOOOPSTT STOMATOPOD
ADNNORRTUU TURNAROUND
AEEEEGKMPR GAMEKEEPER

AEEEEGKPRT GATEKEEPER
AEEEEGLNSS SENEGALESE
AEEEEGNRRT REGENERATE
AEEEEGRTTV REVEGETATE
AEEEELNOPT ELAEOPTENE
AEEEENRTTX EXENTERATE
AEEEESTTTT TÊTE-À-TÊTES
AEEEFFIMNT EFFEMINATE
AEEEFGLNRU ENFLEURAGE
AEEEFGNRST FREE AGENTS
AEEEFHLSTT FALSE TEETH
AEEEFHRRTT THEREAFTER
AEEEFINRTZ ANTIFREEZE
AEEEFIRRST FIRE-EATERS
AEEEFLLNST FENESTELLA
AEEEFLMNSS FEMALENESS
AEEEFNRRST TRANSFEREE
AEEEFPRSSS FREE PASSES
AEEEGGGNRS GREENGAGES
AEEEGGMNNT ENGAGEMENT
AEEEGGRSST EASTER EGGS
AEEEGHLPRT TELPHERAGE
AEEEGHNRRT GREENHEART
AEEEGILNNV EVANGELINE
AEEEGILNRS GENERALISE
AEEEGILNRZ GENERALIZE
AEEEGILNSV EVANGELISE
AEEEGILNVZ EVANGELIZE
AEEEGIMNRS MENAGERIES
AEEEGINNOR AERO-ENGINE
AEEEGINRTV GENERATIVE
AEEEGITTVV VEGETATIVE
AEEEGKLOPR GOALKEEPER
AEEEGLMNRT REGALEMENT
AEEEGLNNOR GREEN ANOLE
AEEEGLNOST EAGLESTONE
AEEEGLRRSV GEAR LEVERS
AEEEGLSSSY EYEGLASSES
AEEEGMNNRT ENRAGEMENT
AEEEGMNRSS MEAGRENESS
AEEEGMNRST AGREEMENTS
AEEEGNPPRR GREEN PAPER
AEEEGPRSSX EXPRESSAGE
AEEEGQSTUU SQUETEAGUE
AEEEGRSTTZ GAZETTEERS
AEEEHHINST HEATHENISE
AEEEHHINTZ HEATHENIZE
AEEEHHPRST THREE-PHASE
AEEEHLLRTY ETHEREALLY
AEEEHLRTWW WATERWHEEL
AEEEHMNORX HEXAEMERON
AEEEHMNRTW WEATHERMEN
AEEEHMPRTT HEPTAMETER
AEEEHMRSTX HEXAMETERS

AEEEHNNNPT NEPENTHEAN
AEEEHNNSTV HEAVEN-SENT
AEEEHNORTY HONEY-EATER
AEEEHNRRTT THREATENER
AEEEHOPRRS AEROSPHERE
AEEEHRSTTW SWEETHEART
AEEEIIPPRT PERIPETEIA
AEEEILNRST ETERNALISE
AEEEILNRTV INTERLEAVE
AEEEILNRTZ ETERNALIZE
AEEEIMNRRX RE-EXAMINER
AEEEIMNSTV VIETNAMESE
AEEEIMPRTV PERMEATIVE
AEEEINRSTT ENTREATIES
AEEEINRTTV INVETERATE
AEEEINRTVV ENERVATIVE
AEEEINRTVW INTERWEAVE
AEEEJKRRRT TEARJERKER
AEEEJNRTUV REJUVENATE
AEEEKKPPRR PARK KEEPER
AEEEKMRRST MARKETEERS
AEEEKNSSSW WEAKNESSES
AEEEKPSSTW SWEEPSTAKE
AEEELLRTVW WATER LEVEL
AEEELLSSTT TESSELLATE
AEEELMMNPT EMPALEMENT
AEEELMMNRT EMMENTALER
AEEELMNNTT LENTAMENTE,
  TENEMENTAL
AEEELMNRTT MANTELTREE
AEEELMNRTV REVEALMENT
AEEELMNRTY ELEMENTARY
AEEELNNUVZ VENEZUELAN
AEEELNPRST PLANE TREES
AEEEMMNORT ANEMOMETER
AEEEMNOPSS OPEN SESAME
AEEEMNPRTT PENTAMETER
AEEEMNRRTU REMUNERATE
AEEEMSSTTW SWEETMEATS
AEEENNNSST TENNESSEAN
AEEENRRSST EASTERNERS
AEEEPPRRTT PERPETRATE
AEEEPPRTTU PERPETUATE
AEEERRSTYY YESTERYEAR
AEEERSSTTY EASY STREET
AEEFFHORRT FOREFATHER
AEEFFLLORR FREE-FOR-ALL
AEEFFORRST REAFFOREST
AEEFFSSTUY SAFETY FUSE
AEEFGGHIRT FREIGHTAGE
AEEFGHINRT FEATHERING
AEEFGHORRT FOREGATHER
AEEFGIINRT FIRE-EATING
AEEFGILLNT LEAFLETING

AEEFGILNRR RIFLE RANGE
AEEFGILPRS PERSIFLAGE
AEEFGLPRSU PRESAGEFUL
AEEFGORRRU FOURRAGERE
AEEFHHINRT FAHRENHEIT
AEEFHIKLRT FATHER-LIKE
AEEFHIKNST SNEAK THIEF
AEEFHINPRT PINFEATHER
AEEFHLOPPR LEAF-HOPPER
AEEFHLRSST FATHERLESS
AEEFHMORTT FATHOMETER
AEEFHOSSSU SAFE HOUSES
AEEFHPRSTT STEPFATHER
AEEFHRRSTW FRESHWATER
AEEFIIRRRS FIRE-RAISER
AEEFIKNPPR PAPER KNIFE
AEEFIKNRSS FREAKINESS
AEEFILMPRS RELIEF MAPS
AEEFILMRTY FAMILY TREE
AEEFILOPRT PERFOLIATE
AEEFILRSTV AFTERLIVES
AEEFIMNRRT FREEMARTIN
AEEFINRRST FRATERNISE
AEEFINRRTZ FRATERNIZE
AEEFLLNNOT FONTANELLE
AEEFLLNRUY FUNEREALLY
AEEFLLRSSY FEARLESSLY
AEEFLMOPRX FOR EXAMPLE
AEEFLRRSTT FLATTERERS
AEEFMNORSS FREEMASONS
AEEFNORRRW FOREWARNER
AEEFNSSSST FASTNESSES
AEEFNSSTTY SAFETY NETS
AEEFORRRSW FORSWEARER
AEEGGHILRT LIGHTERAGE
AEEGGHOPRR GEOGRAPHER
AEEGGILNRS GINGER ALES
AEEGGILNRT RELEGATING
AEEGGINNRT GENERATING
AEEGGINNRS GRANGERISE
AEEGGINRRZ GRANGERIZE
AEEGGINTTV VEGETATING
AEEGGIRSSV AGGRESSIVE
AEEGGMORST MORTGAGEES
AEEGGNRSSU GREASE GUNS
AEEGGORRST SEGREGATOR
AEEGGRRSSW SWAGGERERS
AEEGHHMORR HEMORRHAGE
AEEGHIILMP HEMIPLEGIA
AEEGHIKMTW MAKEWEIGHT
AEEGHIKNNR HEARKENING
AEEGHILNSS SINGHALESE
AEEGHILPST LEGATESHIP
AEEGHIMRST HERMITAGES

AEEGHINNRT HEARTENING
AEEGHINPRT PREHEATING
AEEGHINRRS REHEARSING
AEEGHINRTW WEATHERING
AEEGHIPPRR EPIGRAPHER
AEEGHKNNRS GREENSHANK
AEEGHLMORT GEOTHERMAL
AEEGHLNTVW WAVELENGTH
AEEGHLORTT ALTOGETHER
AEEGHLPRST TELEGRAPHS
AEEGHLPRTY TELEGRAPHY
AEEGHMNOOT HOMOGENATE
AEEGHMNOPS MEGAPHONES
AEEGHMORTY HETEROGAMY
AEEGHOSSTU GATEHOUSES
AEEGIILLLS ILLEGALISE
AEEGIILLLZ ILLEGALIZE
AEEGIILMTT LEGITIMATE
AEEGIILNST GELATINISE
AEEGIILNTZ GELATINIZE
AEEGIIMRTV EMIGRATIVE
AEEGIINRRT GARNIERITE
AEEGILLMNN ENAMELLING
AEEGILLORS ALLEGORIES, ALLEGORISE
AEEGILLORZ ALLEGORIZE
AEEGILMNNP EMPANELING
AEEGILMNRR MALINGERER
AEEGILMNRT REGIMENTAL
AEEGILMNSV EVANGELISM
AEEGILNNSV LEAVENINGS
AEEGILNORT REGELATION, RELEGATION
AEEGILNOTV ELONGATIVE
AEEGILNRST GENERALIST
AEEGILNRTU ARGENTEUIL
AEEGILNRTY GENERALITY
AEEGILNSTV EVANGELIST
AEEGILNTVY NEGATIVELY
AEEGILOSTY LAY SIEGE TO
AEEGILPSTT TITLE PAGES
AEEGILRRSU REGULARISE
AEEGILRRUZ REGULARIZE
AEEGILRTUV REGULATIVE
AEEGIMNNSV GIVEN NAMES
AEEGIMNPRT IMPREGNATE, PERMEATING
AEEGIMNRRS GERMANISER
AEEGIMNRRZ GERMANIZER
AEEGIMNRST MAGNETISER
AEEGIMNRTZ MAGNETIZER
AEEGIMPRRR GRIM REAPER
AEEGIMRRTU MARGUERITE
AEEGIMRRTV GRAVIMETER
AEEGINNNSU ENSANGUINE
AEEGINNORT GENERATION
AEEGINNPSS PANGENESIS

AEEGINNRRT INTERREGNA
AEEGINNRST TANGERINES
AEEGINNRTT ENTREATING
AEEGINNRTV ENERVATING, VENERATING
AEEGINNSUX EXSANGUINE
AEEGINORRS REORGANISE
AEEGINORRZ REORGANIZE
AEEGINORVY A ROVING EYE
AEEGINOTTV VEGETATION
AEEGINPRSV GRAPEVINES
AEEGINPRSY PANEGYRISE
AEEGINPRYZ PANEGYRIZE
AEEGINRRTT RETREATING
AEEGINRRTX GENERATRIX
AEEGINRSSS GREASINESS
AEEGINRSSV VERNISSAGE
AEEGIPPRRT PAPER TIGER
AEEGIRSSTT STRATEGIES
AEEGLLNOSS LOS ANGELES
AEEGLLORTT ALLEGRETTO
AEEGLMNNTT TANGLEMENT
AEEGLMRRSW LEG-WARMERS
AEEGLNORTU OUTGENERAL
AEEGLORTUV TRAVELOGUE
AEEGMNNOST MANGOSTEEN
AEEGMNOQSU MONEGASQUE
AEEGMNRSTY SEGMENTARY
AEEGMORRST STEREOGRAM
AEEGMORSST GASOMETERS
AEEGMPRTUU UP A GUMTREE
AEEGMPSTTU GET UP STEAM
AEEGMRRTTY GREY MATTER
AEEGMRSSTU GAUSSMETER
AEEGNNORSS SENSE ORGAN
AEEGNNSSTW NEWSAGENTS
AEEGNOPRSS PERSONAGES
AEEGNORRST GENERATORS
AEEGNORSTU ENTOURAGES
AEEGNORSTV GRAVESTONE
AEEGNPRSSS PASSENGERS
AEEGNPRSST PRESS AGENT
AEEHHHINST HEATHENISH
AEEHHILMOP HAEMOPHILE
AEEHHILSTT HEALTHIEST
AEEHHIMNST HEATHENISM
AEEHHINRST EARTHSHINE
AEEHHKNPSS SHEEPSHANK
AEEHHLMSTU METHUSELAH
AEEHHPSSTU HEPHAESTUS
AEEHIILLPT EPITHELIAL
AEEHIISTTV HESITATIVE
AEEHIKLLRT HALTER-LIKE
AEEHIKLMMR HAMMER-LIKE
AEEHILLORT HELIOLATER

AEEHILMRST THERMALISE
AEEHILMRTZ THERMALIZE
AEEHILMTTW WHITE METAL
AEEHILPPRR PERIPHERAL
AEEHILPPSY EPIPHYSEAL
AEEHILPRST SPHALERITE
AEEHILPSST SHAPELIEST
AEEHILRSTT EARTHLIEST, STEALTHIER
AEEHILSTTW WEALTHIEST
AEEHIMMRSX HEXAMERISM
AEEHIMNOPP EPIPHONEMA
AEEHIMNPRT HEMIPTERAN
AEEHIMSSTT METATHESIS
AEEHINORST ANTIHEROES
AEEHINPRST HEN PARTIES, INTERPHASE
AEEHINRSST EARTHINESS, HEARTINESS
AEEHIPPRTW WHITE PAPER
AEEHIRTTWW WHITEWATER
AEEHISTUVX EXHAUSTIVE
AEEHKLNPRS PLANK-SHEER
AEEHKMMORS HOMEMAKERS
AEEHKMPRST THEME PARKS
AEEHKOPSSV SPOKESHAVE
AEEHKORSTT HEATSTROKE
AEEHKOSSTU STEAKHOUSE
AEEHLLMRTY HEMELYTRAL
AEEHLLNRRT ENTHRALLER
AEEHLLORSW WHOLESALER
AEEHLMMRSS HAMMERLESS
AEEHLMNNOP PHENOMENAL
AEEHLMPRSW SPERM WHALE
AEEHLNOSTT ON THE SLATE
AEEHLNRSTT NETTLE RASH
AEEHLORSTW WATERHOLES
AEEHLRSTTX TAX SHELTER
AEEHMNNSSU HUMANENESS
AEEHMOPRRU AMPERE-HOUR
AEEHMOPRSS SEMAPHORES
AEEHMOPRST ATMOSPHERE
AEEHMORRRT ARTHROMERE
AEEHMORSUX HEXAMEROUS
AEEHMORTTY METATHEORY
AEEHNNOORT ONE ANOTHER
AEEHNORSSS HOARSENESS
AEEHNPPTVY HAPPY EVENT
AEEHNPRRSS SHARPENERS
AEEHOOPRRS HORSE OPERA
AEEHOOPRST PEASHOOTER
AEEHOOPSST APOTHEOSES
AEEHORSSUW WAREHOUSES
AEEHORSTVW WHATSOEVER
AEEHRRSSTV HARVESTERS
AEEIIKNRST KERATINISE
AEEIIKNRTZ KERATINIZE

AEEIILLRTT ILLITERATE
AEEIILMNRS MINERALISE
AEEIILMNRZ MINERALIZE
AEEIILNPRU EPINEURIAL
AEEIILRRTV IRRELATIVE
AEEIILRSST ISRAELITES
AEEIILRSTV REVITALISE
AEEIILRTVZ REVITALIZE
AEEIIMNNST INSEMINATE
AEEIIMNNTT TIEMANNITE
AEEIIMNRSS SEMINARIES
AEEIIMNSTT ANTI-SEMITE
AEEIIMPRTV IMPERATIVE
AEEIIMRSSS EMISSARIES
AEEIIMSTTV ESTIMATIVE
AEEIINPPRZ PIPERAZINE
AEEIIPRSST ASPERITIES, PATISSERIE
AEEIJLOSSU JEALOUSIES
AEEIJOPRTV PEJORATIVE
AEEIKLNNRT INTERLAKEN
AEEIKLNSSW WEAKLINESS
AEEIKNNSSS SNEAKINESS
AEEIKQSSTU SQUEAKIEST
AEEIKRRSTW WATER SKIER
AEEIKRSSTT STREAKIEST
AEEILLLLNV VILLANELLE
AEEILLMNST ENAMELLIST
AEEILLNSVV EVANSVILLE
AEEILLPSTT STIPELLATE
AEEILLRSSV VERSAILLES
AEEILLRTTY LITERATELY
AEEILLRTVY RELATIVELY
AEEILLSSTT SATELLITES
AEEILMMNPT IMPALEMENT
AEEILMNNST LINEAMENTS
AEEILMNNTT ENTAILMENT
AEEILMNPRT PLANIMETER
AEEILMNRST STREAMLINE
AEEILMNSSS MEASLINESS
AEEILMRSTT ALTIMETERS
AEEILNNPRS PERENNIALS
AEEILNNPST SEPTENNIAL
AEEILNNSTT SENTENTIAL
AEEILNNSTV VALENTINES
AEEILNNTTU LIEUTENANT
AEEILNOPRT PERITONEAL
AEEILNORTV REVELATION
AEEILNOSTV ELEVATIONS
AEEILNPPPS PINEAPPLES
AEEILNPRSS PEARLINESS
AEEILNPRST ALPESTRINE
AEEILNQSTU SEQUENTIAL
AEEILNQTUV EQUIVALENT
AEEILNRRTV IRRELEVANT

AEEILNRSTU NEUTRALISE	AEEINRSSTW WATERINESS
AEEILNRSTW IN A SWELTER	AEEINRSTTT INTERSTATE
AEEILNRTTY ETERNALITY	AEEINSSSTW SWEATINESS
AEEILNRTUZ NEUTRALIZE	AEEINSSSTY YEASTINESS
AEEILNSSST ESSENTIALS	AEEIOPRSTV OPERATIVES
AEEILNSSSZ SLEAZINESS	AEEIPPRSST APPETISERS
AEEILNSTVX SEXIVALENT	AEEIPPRSTW WATER PIPES
AEEILORTTV TOLERATIVE	AEEIPPRSTZ APPETIZERS
AEEILPPRRT PERIPTERAL	AEEIPRRSTV PRIVATEERS
AEEILPRSST PSALTERIES	AEEIPRSSTT STRIPTEASE, TAPESTRIES
AEEILPRSSY ERYSIPELAS	AEEIPRSSTU PASTEURISE
AEEILPSTTU ESTIPULATE	AEEIPRSSUV PERSUASIVE
AEEILQRSSU EQUALISERS	AEEIPRSTTX SEXPARTITE
AEEILQRSUZ EQUALIZERS	AEEIPRSTUZ PASTEURIZE
AEEILRRSTT AIR-LETTERS	AEEIPRTTUV VITUPERATE
AEEILRRSVW SILVERWARE	AEEIRRSSTU TREASURIES
AEEILRRTTU LITERATURE	AEEIRSSTTV TRAVESTIES
AEEIMMMRST METAMERISM	AEEIRSTUVY EASY VIRTUE
AEEIMMOPRT EMMETROPIA	AEEJLNORSU JOURNALESE
AEEIMNNPRT PINE MARTEN	AEEJMORSTT MAJORETTES
AEEIMNNRTT RETAINMENT	AEEKLMNORW ENAMELWORK
AEEIMNNRTU INNUMERATE	AEEKMMNORY MONEYMAKER
AEEIMNNSZZ MEZZANINES	AEEKMMRRRY MERRYMAKER
AEEIMNOPRT PERMEATION	AEEKMORRTU EUROMARKET
AEEIMNORTT MARIONETTE	AEEKMPRRTV VERKRAMPTE
AEEIMNOSTT MAISONETTE	AEEKMRSSTY MASTER KEYS
AEEIMNRSSS NEAR MISSES, SMEARINESS	AEELLMNOTV MALEVOLENT
AEEIMNRSTT MARTENSITE	AEELLMNRTU ALLUREMENT
AEEIMNRTUV NUMERATIVE	AEELLNOPRT PETRONELLA
AEEIMNSSST STEAMINESS	AEELLNRRUV UNRAVELLER
AEEIMORRTV VARIOMETER	AEELLNRTVY RELEVANTLY
AEEIMPRRST PRIME RATES	AEELLNRTXY EXTERNALLY
AEEIMQRSUV SEMIQUAVER	AEELLNTUVY EVENTUALLY
AEEIMRSTTX TAXIMETERS	AEELLORSTT ROSTELLATE
AEEINNNTVY IN ANY EVENT	AEELLORTTY TEA TROLLEY
AEEINNORTV ENERVATION, VENERATION	AEELLQRRRU QUARRELLER
AEEINNOTTT ANTOINETTE	AEELLRRSTV TRAVELLERS
AEEINNPQTU PENTAQUINE	AEELLRSTTW WALL STREET
AEEINNRTUV AVENTURINE	AEELMMNORU NEUROLEMMA
AEEINNSSSU UNEASINESS	AEELMMNRTV MARVELMENT
AEEINOPPST APPOINTEES	AEELMNNOTT MENTAL NOTE
AEEINOPRST PROTEINASE	AEELMNOPRT PLANOMETER
AEEINOPTTT POTENTIATE	AEELMNORTW WATERMELON
AEEINORTVV RENOVATIVE	AEELMNOSSW SALESWOMEN
AEEINPPRSS PAPERINESS	AEELMNSTTV VESTMENTAL
AEEINPRSTU RESUPINATE	AEELMOPRTV VOLT-AMPERE
AEEINPRTVY EVEN PARITY	AEELMOPSTT PALMETTOES
AEEINPSTTU UNISEPTATE	AEELNNPTTU ANTEPENULT
AEEINQRSTU EQUESTRIAN	AEELNPRTTW WENTLETRAP
AEEINQSSSU QUEASINESS	AEELORSTTU LOTUS-EATER
AEEINQSTTU TITANESQUE	AEELORSTVW WATER VOLES
AEEINRRRST RESTRAINER	AEELPRRSST PLASTERERS
AEEINRRTTV TRAVERTINE	AEELQRSSTU SEQUESTRAL
AEEINRRTVY VETERINARY	AEELRRSTUW LUSTERWARE, LUSTREWARE

AEEMMNORST MANOMETERS
AEEMMNORTT ANTE-MORTEM
AEEMMNORTY ANEMOMETRY
AEEMMNSSTU AMUSEMENTS
AEEMMRRSST STAMMERERS
AEEMNNPRST PERMANENTS
AEEMNNPRTT ENTRAPMENT
AEEMNOPPRY PAPER MONEY
AEEMNOQRSU ROMANESQUE
AEEMNORRTU ENUMERATOR
AEEMNORRUV MANOEUVRER
AEEMNORSST SARMENTOSE
AEEMNORSUV MANOEUVRES
AEEMNPPRTY PREPAYMENT
AEEMNPRRTU AMPERE-TURN
AEEMNPRSTY REPAYMENTS
AEEMNRSSST MARE'S NESTS
AEEMNRSTTT TREATMENTS
AEEMNRSTTU MENSTRUATE
AEEMNSSSST ASSESSMENT
AEEMNSSSTT MEANS TESTS
AEEMNSSTTT STATEMENTS, TESTAMENTS
AEEMORRSTV OVERMASTER
AEEMORRTTV OVERMATTER
AEEMORSSSY MAYORESSES
AEEMPRRTTU EAR TRUMPET
AEEMRSSSST SEAMSTRESS
AEEMRSSSTT MATTRESSES, SMEAR TESTS
AEENNOOPSS OPEN SEASON
AEENNORSST ORNATENESS
AEENNPPRRT TREPPANNER
AEENOORRTX EXONERATOR
AEENOPQSSU OPAQUENESS
AEENOPRRTT PENETRATOR
AEENOPSTTT POTENTATES
AEENORSTUX EXTRANEOUS
AEENORTTUX EXTENUATOR
AEENPPRSSW NEWSPAPERS
AEENPPRSTT STEPPARENT
AEENPRSSSS SPARSENESS
AEENQRSSSU SQUARENESS
AEENRRSSTV TRANSVERSE
AEENSSSSTV VASTNESSES
AEENSSSTTU ASTUTENESS
AEEOPPRSSU PEA SOUPERS
AEEOPRRSTT TETRASPORE
AEEOPRRTWW WATERPOWER
AEEOPRSSSV OVERPASSES
AEEOPRSSTT POETASTERS
AEEPRRSSST TRESPASSER
AEEPRRSSTY SPARE TYRES
AEEPRSSSST TRESPASSES
AEEPRSSWXY EXPRESSWAY
AEEQRSSSTU SETSQUARES

AEEQSSTTUU STATUESQUE
AEERRRSSTU TREASURERS
AEERRSTTVX EXTRAVERTS
AEESSTTTTU STATUETTES
AEFFHILSST FLATFISHES
AEFFHLLOTW OFF-THE-WALL
AEFFIIINST AFFINITIES
AEFFIIINTV AFFINITIVE
AEFFIKLLOW WALK OF LIFE
AEFFIKPSST PIKESTAFFS
AEFFILNSTU INSUFFLATE
AEFFLMOOPR FLAMEPROOF
AEFFLMOORW FOAMFLOWER
AEFFNRSSTU STAFF NURSE
AEFFOOSTTU AFFETTUOSO
AEFGHHLLNT HALF-LENGTH
AEFGHILSTW WHITE FLAGS
AEFGHINRRW WHARFINGER
AEFGHKNOUU HUA KUO-FENG
AEFGHNORTU FEARNOUGHT
AEFGIILNNR FINGERNAIL
AEFGIILNSV LIFE-SAVING
AEFGIIMNRS MAGNIFIERS
AEFGIINNRR REFRAINING
AEFGIINSTU IGNES FATUI
AEFGIIRTUV FIGURATIVE
AEFGILLNNN FLANNELING
AEFGILMNNU MEANINGFUL
AEFGILMNOS FLAMINGOES
AEFGILNNTT FLATTENING
AEFGILNOUW GUINEA FOWL
AEFGILNRTT FLATTERING
AEFGILOPRT PROFLIGATE
AEFGILRSUY LAY FIGURES
AEFGIMNORR FOREARMING
AEFGINNSST FASTENINGS
AEFGIPRRTU GRAPEFRUIT
AEFGIRSSTT GAS FITTERS
AEFGLLLOWY YELLOW FLAG
AEFGLLRTUY GRATEFULLY
AEFGLMRSTU GULF STREAM
AEFGLNOSST FLAGSTONES
AEFGLNRTUU UNGRATEFUL
AEFGLORSTW AFTERGLOWS
AEFHIKLRSY FREAKISHLY
AEFHIKMSST MAKESHIFTS
AEFHILNSSS FLASHINESS
AEFHILRSST HALF-SISTER
AEFHIMMNST FAMISHMENT
AEFHINOPTY IN THE PAY OF
AEFHINOSSS OAFISHNESS
AEFHIRSSST STARFISHES
AEFHLLLOVY HALF VOLLEY
AEFHLLMSUY SHAMEFULLY

AEFHLLSTUY HASTEFULLY
AEFHLMOSST FATHOMLESS
AEFHMORSSU FARMHOUSES
AEFHOOPSTU OUT OF PHASE, OUT OF
SHAPE
AEFIILLNSS FILIALNESS
AEFIILMNSS SEMIFINALS
AEFIILMPRS AMPLIFIERS
AEFIILNOTU UNIFOLIATE
AEFIILNRTT INFILTRATE
AEFIILORTT TRIFOLIATE
AEFIILQRSU QUALIFIERS
AEFIINOPRS SAPONIFIER
AEFIINQRTU QUANTIFIER
AEFIKNOPRS FAIR-SPOKEN
AEFILLNNRY INFERNALLY
AEFILLNNUZ INFLUENZAL
AEFILLRTVY RIFT VALLEY
AEFILMNSTY MANIFESTLY
AEFILMORRS FORMALISER
AEFILMORRZ FORMALIZER
AEFILMORTW WOLFRAMITE
AEFILNORSU LANIFEROUS
AEFILNORTU FLUORINATE
AEFILNSSTU FAULTINESS
AEFIILOQRTU QUATREFOIL
AEFILORSSU SALIFEROUS
AEFIMNOSST MANIFESTOS
AEFIMNRSST FIRST NAMES
AEFINNRSSU UNFAIRNESS
AEFINOOPRT FORTE-PIANO, PIANOFORTE
AEFINORRST RAIN FOREST
AEFINORTTU REFUTATION
AEFINPSSTY SAFETY PINS
AEFINRRTTY FRATERNITY
AEFIOPRSTU FETIPAROUS
AEFIORRSUU AURIFEROUS
AEFIORSTUV FAVOURITES
AEFKLNOSSW SNOWFLAKES
AEFKMORRSW FRAMEWORKS
AEFLLLOPWY PLAYFELLOW
AEFLLLORWW WALLFLOWER
AEFLLLPTTU AT FULL PELT
AEFLLLSSWY FLAWLESSLY
AEFLLNOSSW FALLOWNESS
AEFLLNSSUW LAWFULNESS
AEFLLORSSV FLAVORLESS
AEFLLSTTUY TASTEFULLY
AEFLLSTUWY WASTEFULLY
AEFLMNNSSU MANFULNESS
AEFLMOORSV FLAVORSOME
AEFLMORRSV SALVERFORM
AEFLNOPRRT PREFRONTAL
AEFLNRSSTU ARTFULNESS

AEFLOOPSTT FOOTPLATES
AEFLORRSTW STARFLOWER
AEFLORSTWW WATERFOWLS
AEFLRSTTWY FLYSWATTER
AEFMNORSTW MEN OF STRAW
AEFMNOSSSU FAMOUSNESS
AEFMOPRRST PERMAFROST
AEFNNOORST AFTERNOONS
AEFNOPPRRU RUN-OF-PAPER
AEFNORRRST TRANSFEROR
AEFNORRTTW WATERFRONT
AEFOOPRRRT PERFORATOR
AEFOOPRRTW WATERPROOF
AEFOORRSTT TORT-FEASOR
AEFOQRRSUU FOURSQUARE
AEFRRRSTTU FRUSTRATER
AEGGGILNNY ENGAGINGLY
AEGGGINRST STAGGERING
AEGGGINRSW SWAGGERING
AEGGHILNRT RIGHT ANGLE
AEGGHINRST GATHERINGS
AEGGHINSSS SHAGGINESS
AEGGHIOPST GEOPHAGIST
AEGGHOOPSU GEOPHAGOUS
AEGGIILLNZ LEGALIZING
AEGGIILMPR PILGRIMAGE
AEGGIILNNR REALIGNING
AEGGIILNVW LIVING WAGE
AEGGIIMNRT EMIGRATING
AEGGIINNSV ENVISAGING
AEGGIINNTV NEGATIVING
AEGGIINPSU GUINEA PIGS
AEGGIJMRST JIGGERMAST
AEGGILLMNY GLEAMINGLY
AEGGILLNRV GRAVELLING
AEGGILNNNT ENTANGLING
AEGGILNNOT ELONGATING
AEGGILNRTU REGULATING
AEGGILRRST STRAGGLIER
AEGGIMNNTU AUGMENTING
AEGGIMNRRS GRANGERISM
AEGGINNRST ESTRANGING
AEGGINNRSV ENGRAVINGS
AEGGINORSS AGGRESSION
AEGGIORRSU GREGARIOUS
AEGGJNRTUU JUGGERNAUT
AEGGLLNOOY ANGELOLOGY
AEGGLOORTY GERATOLOGY
AEGGLRRSST STRAGGLERS
AEGGMOSTUY MYSTAGOGUE
AEGGNNORSU GANGRENOUS
AEGGNOSSUY SYNAGOGUES
AEGGNPRSSS PRESSGANGS
AEGGORRSSS AGGRESSORS

AEGHHILLLS SHILLELAGH
AEGHHILOPR HELIOGRAPH
AEGHHILRTT EARTHLIGHT
AEGHHIMNWY HIGHWAYMEN
AEGHHIMSSS HIGH MASSES
AEGHHINOSS HIGH SEASON
AEGHHINSST SHEATHINGS
AEGHHISTTU HAUGHTIEST
AEGHHLORSU HORSELAUGH
AEGHHMOPPT APOPHTHEGM
AEGHHNOPPR NEPHOGRAPH
AEGHHRRSTU HEARTHRUGS
AEGHIILMRT ALMIGHTIER
AEGHIIMNRS MISHEARING
AEGHIINSTT HESITATING
AEGHIIPRST GRAPHITISE
AEGHIIPRTZ GRAPHITIZE
AEGHIKMMNO HOMEMAKING
AEGHIKMNOS SHOEMAKING
AEGHIKNNRS HANKERINGS
AEGHILLNOP ANGLOPHILE
AEGHILMNNS ENGLISHMAN
AEGHILMORT LITHOMARGE
AEGHILNNSU UNLEASHING
AEGHILNOOT THEOLOGIAN
AEGHILNRST EARTHLINGS
AEGHILNRSU LANGUISHER
AEGHILRSTY LIGHT YEARS
AEGHILSSTT GHASTLIEST
AEGHIMMOPR MIMEOGRAPH
AEGHIMNRST NIGHTMARES
AEGHIMSTTT STEAMTIGHT
AEGHINNPPS HAPPENINGS
AEGHINNPRS SHARPENING
AEGHINNRSS HARNESSING
AEGHINNRST NEAR THINGS
AEGHINNRTU UNEARTHING
AEGHINPRRS REPHRASING
AEGHINRSSS GARISHNESS
AEGHINRSTT SHATTERING, STRAIGHTEN
AEGHINRSTV HARVESTING
AEGHINSTTU NAUGHTIEST
AEGHINSTUX EXHAUSTING
AEGHIPRRSY SERIGRAPHY
AEGHIRRSTT STRAIGHTER
AEGHIRTTTW WATERTIGHT
AEGHLMOOOT HOMOLOGATE
AEGHLNNOOP ANGLOPHONE
AEGHLNOORS ALONGSHORE
AEGHLNOOSU HALOGENOUS
AEGHLNSTWY LENGTHWAYS
AEGHLOOORR LOGORRHOEA
AEGHLOOPRY OLEOGRAPHY
AEGHLOSSSU GLASSHOUSE

AEGHMMORRT THERMOGRAM
AEGHMNOOPR GRAMOPHONE
AEGHNOOOORR GONORRHOEA
AEGHNOPRRY GRANOPHYRE
AEGHNOPRST STENOGRAPH
AEGHNORRST SHORT-RANGE
AEGHOOPRRR OROGRAPHER
AEGHOOPRRZ ZOOGRAPHER
AEGHOOPSSU OESOPHAGUS
AEGHOPPRRU ROUGH PAPER
AEGHOPRRXY XEROGRAPHY
AEGIIILNTV INVIGILATE
AEGIIIMTTV MITIGATIVE
AEGIIIRRTV IRRIGATIVE
AEGIIKNOPP PIG IN A POKE
AEGIILLLTY ILLEGALITY
AEGIILMNRT TRIGEMINAL
AEGIILMNST TIME SIGNAL
AEGIILMNSX MAXISINGLE
AEGIILNNPX EXPLAINING
AEGIILNNPZ PENALIZING
AEGIILNNSS GAINLINESS
AEGIILNOTV LEVIGATION
AEGIILNPRV PREVAILING
AEGIILNQUZ EQUALIZING
AEGIILNRSS GLAIRINESS
AEGIILNSTV VIGILANTES
AEGIILNTTV LEVITATING
AEGIILRTTT GLITTERATI
AEGIIMNNOT GEMINATION
AEGIIMNORT EMIGRATION
AEGIIMNSTT ESTIMATING
AEGIIMNSTV NEGATIVISM, TIMESAVING
AEGIIMSSTT STIGMATISE
AEGIIMSTTZ STIGMATIZE
AEGIINNNRT ENTRAINING
AEGIINNOST ISOANTIGEN
AEGIINNPRT PERTAINING
AEGIINNRSS GRAININESS
AEGIINORTV INVIGORATE
AEGIINPPTZ APPETIZING
AEGIINSTTV NEGATIVIST
AEGIIRSTTU GRATUITIES
AEGIKKMNRS KINGMAKERS
AEGIKLMNOV LOVEMAKING
AEGIKLNNSY SNEAKINGLY
AEGIKNNSST TAKINGNESS
AEGILLMNRV MARVELLING
AEGILLNORY REGIONALLY
AEGILLNPSY PLEASINGLY
AEGILLNRTV TRAVELLING
AEGILLOPTT EPIGLOTTAL
AEGILLORST ALLEGORIST, LEGISLATOR
AEGILLPSSX PLEXIGLASS

AEGILLRRSU GUERRILLAS
AEGILLRSSS SALESGIRLS
AEGILMNNST ALIGNMENTS
AEGILMNOOP MONOPLEGIA
AEGILMNORS ROSEMALING
AEGILMNORY MINERALOGY
AEGILMORRS GLAMORISER, RIGMAROLES
AEGILMORRZ GLAMORIZER
AEGILMSTTU MULTISTAGE
AEGILNNNRU UNLEARNING
AEGILNNOOT ELONGATION
AEGILNNPSS GLANS PENIS
AEGILNNRUV UNRAVELING
AEGILNNSSS SLANGINESS
AEGILNNSUY SANGUINELY
AEGILNOOSU OLEAGINOUS
AEGILNORTT TOLERATING
AEGILNORTU REGULATION, UROGENITAL
AEGILNORVY OVERLAYING
AEGILNOSTU GELATINOUS
AEGILNPRST PLASTERING
AEGILNPRTY TAPERINGLY
AEGILNQRRU QUARRELING
AEGILNRSTV STARVELING
AEGILNRSWY SWEARINGLY
AEGILNRVWY WAVERINGLY
AEGILNRWYY WEARYINGLY
AEGILNSSSS GLASSINESS
AEGILOOPRS APOLOGISER
AEGILOOPRZ APOLOGIZER
AEGILOORST AEROLOGIST
AEGILOPRTT GRAPTOLITE
AEGILORRSS GRESSORIAL
AEGILORSSS GLOSSARIES
AEGILRRRSU IRREGULARS
AEGILRRSUV VULGARISER
AEGILRRTUY REGULARITY
AEGILRRUVZ VULGARIZER
AEGILRSTTZ SALZGITTER
AEGIMMNRST STAMMERING
AEGIMNNRST SMARTENING
AEGIMNNSST ASSIGNMENT
AEGIMNOPRS ANGIOSPERM
AEGIMNORRT GERMINATOR
AEGIMNORSU GRAMINEOUS
AEGIMNPRTY PIGMENTARY
AEGIMNPTTT ATTEMPTING
AEGIMNRRRY REMARRYING
AEGIMNNRRST RINGMASTER
AEGIMNRSTT SMATTERING
AEGIMRRTVY GRAVIMETRY
AEGINNNPRT TREPANNING
AEGINNORST RESONATING
AEGINNORTV RENOVATING

AEGINNOSSS SEASONINGS
AEGINNPPRT ENTRAPPING
AEGINNPRRT PARTNERING
AEGINNPRTT PATTERNING
AEGINNRSTT ASTRINGENT
AEGINNRSTU SAUNTERING
AEGINOORTT NEGOTIATOR
AEGINORRSS ORGANISERS
AEGINORRSZ ORGANIZERS
AEGINORRTT INTEGRATOR
AEGINORRTV OVERRATING
AEGINORTVX OVERTAXING
AEGINOSSTT GESTATIONS
AEGINPRSTT SPATTERING
AEGINPRSTU SUPERGIANT
AEGINPRSTY PANEGYRIST
AEGINQRRTU QUARTERING
AEGINRRSSU REASSURING
AEGINRRSTT REGISTRANT
AEGINRRSTU TREASURING
AEGINRRSTV TRAVERSING
AEGINRSSSS GRASSINESS
AEGINRSSSU SUGARINESS
AEGINRSSTU SIGNATURES
AEGINRSTWW WATERWINGS
AEGIPRSTUV PURGATIVES
AEGIRRRSST REGISTRARS
AEGIRSSTTT STRATEGIST
AEGKMNOSXY OXYGEN MASK
AEGLLMORRU GLOMERULAR
AEGLLMRTUY METALLURGY
AEGLLNNPTY PLANGENTLY
AEGLLNOSST GALLSTONES
AEGLLOPRSU PELLAGROUS
AEGLMOOSTY SEMATOLOGY
AEGLMOPRTU PROMULGATE
AEGLNNPRTY PREGNANTLY
AEGLNRRSST STRANGLERS
AEGLNRSSUV VULGARNESS
AEGLNSSSSU SUNGLASSES
AEGLOORRST ASTROLOGER
AEGLOORTTY TERATOLOGY
AEGLORRSTU REGULATORS
AEGLORRTUY REGULATORY
AEGLORSSUV GROSS VALUE
AEGLPRSSUU SURPLUSAGE
AEGLPSSSSY SPYGLASSES
AEGMMNOPRU PNEUMOGRAM
AEGMMNRTUU ARGUMENTUM
AEGMMOPRRR PROGRAMMER
AEGMMOPRRS PROGRAMMES
AEGMNOORST GASTRONOME
AEGMNOOSUX XENOGAMOUS
AEGMNORRSW WARMONGERS

AEGMOPRRRS PROGRAMERS
AEGNNRTUUY UNGUENTARY
AEGNOOSTUU AUTOGENOUS
AEGNRRSSST TRANSGRESS
AEGOORSTUU OUTRAGEOUS
AEGOPRRSSU SOUR GRAPES
AEGOPRRTUX EXPURGATOR
AEGORRSSTU SURROGATES
AEGPRRRSUY PRAYER RUGS
AEGPRRSSSU SUPERGRASS
AEHHIILMOP HEMOPHILIA
AEHHILNSTU HELIANTHUS
AEHHILPSSW WHIPLASHES
AEHHINOPRT HIEROPHANT
AEHHINPSST THE SPANISH
AEHHIOPSST HEPHAISTOS
AEHHMOOOPT HOMOEOPATH
AEHHMOOPST HOMEOPATHS
AEHHMOOPTY HOMEOPATHY
AEHHNOOPRT ANTHOPHORE
AEHHOPPSST PHOSPHATES
AEHHPSSTTU HATSHEPSUT
AEHIIILNNS SINHAILIEN
AEHIIKLRTW WRAITHLIKE
AEHIILLMNW WILHELMINA
AEHIILOSTX HELIOTAXIS
AEHIIMNSTU HUMANITIES
AEHIINORTT THORIANITE
AEHIINOSTT HESITATION
AEHIINPPRS SAPPHIRINE
AEHIINSSTT ANTITHESIS
AEHIIPPSTT EPITAPHIST
AEHIKKLMSS MILK SHAKES
AEHIKNRSSS RAKISHNESS
AEHILLOPSV SLAVOPHILE
AEHILLORTY HELIOLATRY
AEHILLSTTY STEALTHILY
AEHILMNNUY INHUMANELY
AEHILMNOPY ANEMOPHILY
AEHILMNOSY HAEMOLYSIN
AEHILMORST ISOTHERMAL, THIMEROSAL
AEHILMOSSY HAEMOLYSIS
AEHILNNOPS ALPHONSINE
AEHILNOSSS SHOALINESS
AEHILNOSST HAILSTONES
AEHILNOTTY ETHYLATION
AEHILNQRSU HARLEQUINS
AEHILNSSSV LAVISHNESS
AEHILNSTTY HESITANTLY
AEHILOPTVY TOP-HEAVILY
AEHILPSSST SPLASHIEST
AEHILRSSTY HAIRSTYLES
AEHILRSTVY SHRIEVALTY
AEHIMMPRRT TRIPHAMMER

AEHIMMRSTU RHEUMATISM
AEHIMNNPPS PENMANSHIP
AEHIMNNSTV VANISHMENT
AEHIMNORRS HARMONISER
AEHIMNORRZ HARMONIZER
AEHIMNOTUX EXHUMATION
AEHIMNRSSS MARSHINESS
AEHIMNRSTV RAVISHMENT
AEHIMNSSTU ENTHUSIASM
AEHIMOOPTY MYTHOPOEIA
AEHIMPRSST MASTERSHIP, SHIPMASTER
AEHIMPSSST STEAMSHIPS
AEHIMPSSTY SYMPATHIES, SYMPATHISE
AEHIMPSTYZ SYMPATHIZE
AEHINOPRTU EUPHORIANT
AEHINOPSTT ON THE TAPIS, TIP ONE'S
HAT
AEHINORRTV HOVERTRAIN
AEHINOSTUX EXHAUSTION
AEHINPSSTT PANTHEISTS
AEHINQRSUV VANQUISHER
AEHINRSSST TRASHINESS
AEHINSSTTU ENTHUSIAST
AEHIOOPSST APOTHEOSIS
AEHIORRSTU AUTHORISER
AEHIORRTUZ AUTHORIZER
AEHIORSSST AIR-HOSTESS
AEHIORSTTT THROATIEST
AEHIPRSSTT THERAPISTS
AEHIQSSSTU SQUASHIEST
AEHIRSSTTW SWARTHIEST, SWEATSHIRT
AEHKLOPRSW SHOPWALKER
AEHKMNOSTU SNAKEMOUTH
AEHKORRSTW EARTHWORKS
AEHLLMRSSY HARMLESSLY
AEHLLMSTUU HAUSTELLUM
AEHLLOOPRT HARTLEPOOL
AEHLLOPRXY PHYLLOXERA
AEHLLOSSTW SHALLOWEST
AEHLMOOSUX HOMOSEXUAL
AEHLMORTTY METHYLATOR
AEHLMOSSSU ALMS-HOUSES
AEHLNNOPTT PENTATHLON
AEHLNOPSTU HOUSEPLANT, SULPHONATE
AEHLOOPRRY PYORRHOEAL
AEHLOPSSUY PLAYHOUSES
AEHLPRSTUU SULPHURATE
AEHLRTTUUV TRUTH-VALUE
AEHMNOORSU MANOR HOUSE
AEHMNOORSW HORSEWOMAN
AEHMNORRTT MATTERHORN
AEHMNORRTW HARROWMENT
AEHMNPRSUU SUPERHUMAN
AEHMOORSTX MESOTHORAX

AEHMORRSTW EARTHWORMS
AEHMORSTTT THERMOSTAT
AEHNNNOOTY HOOTENANNY
AEHNOOPSSU SOUSAPHONE
AEHNOOPSSX SAXOPHONES
AEHNOPRSWY PHONEY WARS
AEHNOPRTUY NEUROPATHY
AEHOOPPRST APOSTROPHE
AEHOOPRYZZ ZAPOROZHYE
AEHOOPSSTT OSTEOPATHS
AEHOOPSTTT TOOTHPASTE
AEHOOPSTTY OSTEOPATHY
AEHOORSSTY SOOTHSAYER
AEHOOSSSTU OAST HOUSES
AEHOPPRSTY SAPROPHYTE
AEHOPRSTUY HOUSE PARTY
AEHOPSSSTW SWEATSHOPS
AEHORRRSTW RESTHARROW
AEIIIILNST INITIALISE
AEIIIILNTZ INITIALIZE
AEIIIINTTV INITIATIVE
AEIIILMRST MILITARISE
AEIIILMRTZ MILITARIZE
AEIIILRSTV TRIVIALISE
AEIIILRTVZ TRIVIALIZE
AEIIINSTTV NATIVITIES
AEIIIRRTTV IRRITATIVE
AEIIJMORST MAJORITIES
AEIIKKSTTW KITTIWAKES
AEIIKLLNPR PAINKILLER
AEIIILLLMMS MILLESIMAL
AEIIILLLMNN MILLENNIAL
AEIIILLMNOR MINERAL OIL
AEIIILLMNTU ILLUMINATE
AEIIILLMPRY IMPERIALLY
AEIIILLMRST LITERALISM
AEIIILLOSTV VOLATILISE
AEIIILLOTVZ VOLATILIZE
AEIIILLPRTT TRIPLETAIL
AEIIILLPSTT PISTILLATE
AEIIILLRRTT TRILITERAL
AEIIILLRRTY LITERARILY
AEIIILLRSTT LITERALIST
AEIIILMMMOR IMMEMORIAL
AEIIILMNORT ELIMINATOR
AEIIILMNRSU LUMINARIES
AEIIILMNSTY SEMINALITY
AEIIILMNTTY INTIMATELY
AEIIILMORST MORALITIES
AEIIILMOSSS ISOSEISMAL
AEIIILMRSTV RELATIVISM
AEIIILMRSVV REVIVALISM
AEIIILMSTUV SIMULATIVE
AEIIILMTTUV MUTILATIVE

AEIILNNORS ROSANILINE
AEIILNNSTT INTESTINAL
AEIILNQOTT ETIOLATION
AEIILNORST INTER ALIOS
AEIILNORSV REVISIONAL
AEIILNORTT LITERATION
AEIILNOSTT TONALITIES
AEIILNOTTV LEVITATION
AEIILNOTUV ELUVIATION
AEIILNPRST REPTILIANS
AEIILNQTUY INEQUALITY
AEIILNSSTW WAISTLINES
AEIILOPRST POLARITIES
AEIILORSST SOLITAIRES, SOLITARIES
AEIILRSSUV VISUALISER
AEIILRSTTV RELATIVIST
AEIILRSTTZ STRELITZIA
AEIILRSTVV REVIVALIST
AEIILRSUVZ VISUALIZER
AEIILRTTVY RELATIVITY
AEIIMMMNOR IN MEMORIAM
AEIIMMNPRT IMPAIRMENT
AEIIMMNRST ANTIMERISM
AEIIMNNNOT INNOMINATE
AEIIMNNOTV NOMINATIVE
AEIIMNOSTT ESTIMATION
AEIIMNPQRU PRIMAQUINE
AEIIMNQRTU MARTINIQUE
AEIIMNQTUY EQUANIMITY
AEIIMNRSTU MINIATURES
AEIIMNRTUV RUMINATIVE
AEIIMOPRRS IMPRESARIO
AEIIMOTTVV MOTIVATIVE
AEIIMPTTUV IMPUTATIVE
AEIINNOTVV INNOVATIVE
AEIINNPRTT TRIPINNATE
AEIINNPRTY ANTIPYRINE
AEIINNPSTT IN-PATIENTS
AEIINOPPST INAPPOSITE
AEIINOPRTX EXPIRATION
AEIINOPSTT POINSETTIA
AEIINOQTTU EQUITATION
AEIINOSTTV NOVITIATES
AEIINOTUVX EXUVIATION
AEIINPSSST ANTISEPSIS
AEIINQSTTU QUANTITIES
AEIINRSTTV TRANSITIVE
AEIINRTTTW IN A TWITTER
AEIIOPPRTT PROPITIATE
AEIIOPPSTV APPOSITIVE
AEIIPPSSSW PIPSISSEWA
AEIIPRRTTT TRIPARTITE
AEIIPRSTTV PARTITIVES
AEIJLNORSU JOURNALISE

AEIJLNORUZ JOURNALIZE	AEILMPRTUU PARI-MUTUEL
AEIJMNOSSS JAM SESSION	AEILMRRSSU SURREALISM
AEIJNNSSTU JAUNTINESS	AEILMRRSTT TRIMESTRAL
AEIJNOOPRT PEJORATION	AEILMSTTUX TEXTUALISM
AEIKKLLOOS LOOK-ALIKES	AEILNNNSTW LAWN TENNIS
AEIKLMNSTY MISTAKENLY	AEILNNOPRS NONPAREILS
AEIKLNORST OIL TANKERS	AEILNNOPSY POLYNESIAN
AEIKLNSSST STALKINESS	AEILNNOPTT ANTILEPTON
AEIKLNSSTU ESKILSTUNA	AEILNNORTT INTOLERANT
AEIKMNPRRT PRINTMAKER	AEILNNPRSU PENINSULAR
AEIKNNPRSS SPINNAKERS	AEILNNPSSU PENINSULAS
AEIKNNSSSW SWANKINESS	AEILNNRRTU INTERLUNAR
AEIKPPQSSU PIPSQUEAKS	AEILNOOPRT TROPAEOLIN
AEILLLMSTT LITTLE SLAM	AEILNOOPSS POLONAISES
AEILLLOTWY YELLOWTAIL	AEILNOORTT TOLERATION
AEILLLSUVY ALLUSIVELY	AEILNOPRST INTERPOSAL
AEILLMMORS ALLOMERISM	AEILNOPRTU ERUPTIONAL
AEILLMMRST MILLSTREAM, SMALL-TIMER	AEILNORRTT TORRENTIAL
AEILLMNPTU MULTIPLANE	AEILNORTTV VENTILATOR
AEILLMNRTY TERMINALLY	AEILNOTTUX EXULTATION
AEILLMRSTW WATERMILLS	AEILNPRSST PALTRINESS
AEILLMTTUY ULTIMATELY	AEILNPRSTY PARTY LINES
AEILLNNRTY INTERNALLY	AEILNRSTTU NEUTRALIST
AEILLNOPRT PETRONILLA	AEILNRTTUY NEUTRALITY
AEILLNOPTT POTENTILLA	AEILNSSSTU SENSUALIST
AEILLNPSST PANELLISTS	AEILNSSTUY SENSUALITY
AEILLNPSSY PAINLESSLY	AEILOOPTTZ TOPAZOLITE
AEILLPRRSU PLURALISER	AEILOPPRSU POPULARISE
AEILLPRRUZ PLURALIZER	AEILOPPRUZ POPULARIZE
AEILLPSSSS SALES SLIPS	AEILOPRSSU PLESIOSAUR
AEILLPSSTT PASTELLIST	AEILOPRSTY EPISTOLARY
AEILLQSSTU SQUALLIEST	AEILORRTTU ELUTRIATOR
AEILLRSSTW STAIRWELLS	AEILORSTTU STAUROLITE
AEILLRSTTU ILLUSTRATE	AEILPRRSTY PERISTYLAR
AEILMMRTUY IMMATURELY	AEILRRSSTU SURREALIST
AEILMNNOPR PRENOMINAL	AEILRSSSTY LAY SISTERS
AEILMNNSTT INSTALMENT	AEILRSTTUV LUSTRATIVE
AEILMNOPRS IMPERSONAL	AEILSTTTUX TEXTUALIST
AEILMNOPRT TRAMPOLINE	AEIMMNNRSS MANNERISMS
AEILMNORTU TOURMALINE	AEIMMNOPST PANTOMIMES
AEILMNOSTY MELANOSITY	AEIMMNORST MONETARISM
AEILMNPRTY PLANIMETRY	AEIMMNSTZZ MIZZENMAST
AEILMNRSTU NEUTRALISM	AEIMMPRSTU SPERMATIUM
AEILMNSSSU SENSUALISM	AEIMMRRSSU SUMMARISER
AEILMNSTTU LAST MINUTE	AEIMMRRSUZ SUMMARIZER
AEILMOORRT MELIORATOR	AEIMNNNOST MINNESOTAN
AEILMOPPSS AMPELOPSIS	AEIMNNNOTT ANOINTMENT
AEILMOPRST PERISTOMAL	AEIMNNNQSU MANNEQUINS
AEILMOPSTT PTOLEMAIST	AEIMNNORTU NUMERATION
AEILMORRSS MORALISERS	AEIMNOPRTT ARMIPOTENT
AEILMORRSZ MORALIZERS	AEIMNOPTTT TEMPTATION
AEILMPPSST PALIMPSEST	AEIMNOQSUU EQUANIMOUS
AEILMPRSST SLIPSTREAM	AEIMNORRTT TERMINATOR
AEILMPRSTU PSALTERIUM	AEIMNORSST STEAM IRONS

AEIMNORSSW WOMANISERS	AEIOPRRTXY EXPIRATORY
AEIMNORSTT MONETARIST	AEIPRSTUUV USURPATIVE
AEIMNORSWZ WOMANIZERS	AEJMNNORUY JOURNEYMAN
AEIMNPSTTY TYMPANITES	AEJMPRSTUW WATER JUMPS
AEIMNRRRTY INTERMARRY	AEKKLRTTUY TALK TURKEY
AEIMOOSTTU AUTOTOMISE	AEKMNORTTW MARKET TOWN
AEIMOOTTUV AUTOMOTIVE	AEKMORRSTW MASTERWORK
AEIMOOTTUZ AUTOTOMIZE	AEKMRRSSST STRESS MARK
AEIMOPRRTT IMPETRATOR	AEKNOPRRSY NOSY PARKER
AEIMOPRTUU EUPATORIUM	AEKNOQRSTU SQUARE KNOT
AEIMORRSTU MORTUARIES	AEKNPRRSST PRANKSTERS
AEIMORSSTT ESTIMATORS	AEKORRSTWW WATERWORKS
AEIMORSSTV MOVIE STARS	AELLMNOSTT ALLOTMENTS
AEIMPRSSTU PASTEURISM	AELLMOORSU ALLOMEROUS
AEIMPRSTUZ TRAPEZIUMS	AELLMOPSSY PLASMOLYSE
AEIMPSSTUV ASSUMPTIVE	AELLMORSUV MARVELLOUS
AEIMQRSTUZ QUIZMASTER	AELLNOPPRT PROPELLANT
AEINNNOQSU SINE QUA NON	AELLNOPRSY PERSONALLY
AEINNOORST RESONATION	AELLNOPTVY POLYVALENT
AEINNOORTV RENOVATION	AELLNORTTY TOLERANTLY
AEINNOPRSY PENSIONARY	AELLNOSSSW SALLOWNESS
AEINNOPSSX EXPANSIONS	AELLNPTTUY PETULANTLY
AEINNOQRTU QUATERNION	AELLNRSTTY SLATTERNLY
AEINNORSTT STENTORIAN	AELLNTTUXY EXULTANTLY
AEINNOSSST SENSATIONS	AELLOPPRSU ALL-PURPOSE
AEINNOSTTT ATTENTIONS	AELLOPSTUV POLE VAULTS
AEINNOSTTV NONSTATIVE	AELLRSSTVY SYLVESTRAL
AEINNPPSSS SNAPPINESS	AELLRTTUXY TEXTURALLY
AEINNQSSTU QUAINTNESS	AELMMNNOTU MONUMENTAL
AEINNRRSTY TYRANNISER	AELMMOOPSS PLASMOSOME
AEINNRRTYZ TYRANNIZER	AELMMORSST MAELSTROMS
AEINNSSSZZ SNAZZINESS	AELMMOSSUU MAUSOLEUMS
AEINOOPPRT PROPIONATE	AELMNNNRUY UNMANNERLY
AEINOOPRRT PERORATION	AELMNNNSTU ANNULMENTS
AEINOOPRST OPERATIONS	AELMNNOOPS MONOPLANES
AEINOPRRST PATRONISER	AELMNNOOTV MONOVALENT
AEINOPRRTZ PATRONIZER	AELMNOOPRT PROTONEMAL
AEINOPRSSS ASPERSIONS	AELMNOOPRY LAMPOONERY
AEINOPRSSU PERSUASION	AELMNOPRTY PLANOMETRY
AEINOPRTTU REPUTATION	AELMNORSWW LAWNMOWERS
AEINOPTTTU OUTPATIENT	AELMOOPRTU TROPAEOLUM
AEINORRSTT REINSTATOR	AELMOPPRUY PROPYLAEUM
AEINORSSST ASSERTIONS	AELMOPRTTU PETROLATUM
AEINORSSTT STATIONERS	AELMOPSSST EPSOM SALTS
AEINORSSTY TYROSINASE	AELMOQSSUU SQUAMULOSE
AEINORSTTY STATIONERY	AELMORSSTU SOMERSAULT
AEINPRRTTU PARTURIENT	AELMORSTTT LATTERMOST
AEINPRTTTW PATENT WRIT	AELNNOPRYY PENNYROYAL
AEINRRSSST STARRINESS	AELNNORSTY RESONANTLY
AEINRRSSTT RESTRAINTS	AELNNOSTWW NEWTON'S LAW
AEINRSSSTT STRAITNESS	AELNOPPRTW POWER PLANT
AEINRSTUYZ SUZERAINTY	AELNOPRSSY LAYPERSONS
AEIOPRRRST RESPIRATOR	AELNOPRSTY PERSONALTY
AEIOPRRTTX EXTIRPATOR	AELNORSUVY RAVENOUSLY

AELNOSSUUY NAUSEOUSLY
AELNOSTUVV VOL-AU-VENTS
AELNPPRSTU SUPPLANTER
AELNPRRSUU SUPERLUNAR
AELOOPSSTV SEVASTOPOL
AELOPPRRRU POURPARLER
AELOPPRTUV UPPER VOLTA
AELOPSSTTU POSTULATES
AELORRSSTT LAST RESORT
AELPPSSTUY PLATYPUSES
AEMMNORRTT MONTMARTRE
AEMNNNOPTY NONPAYMENT
AEMNNOORSS ROMAN NOSES
AEMNNOOSST STONEMASON
AEMNNORTTT ATTORNMENT
AEMNNORTTU TOURNAMENT
AEMNNRRSUY NURSERYMAN
AEMNOOPRTT PORTAMENTO
AEMNOORRST ASTRONOMER
AEMNORRSTU NUMERATORS
AEMNORSSTT ASSORTMENT
AEMNRRSTTU TRANSMUTER
AEMOOPSTTY SOMATOTYPE
AEMOORSSTT STATEROOMS
AEMOPRSSTT POSTMASTER
AEMOPRSSTU MOUSETRAPS
AEMORRSTTY ASTROMETRY
AENNNOSSTW WANTONNESS
AENNORRSSW NARROWNESS
AENNORRSTT NONSTARTER
AENOOPRRST PERSONATOR
AENOORRSST RESONATORS
AENOPRRSST TRANSPOSER
AENOPRSSUV SUPERNOVAS
AENOPRSTTT PROTESTANT
AENPRRSTTU TRANSPUTER
AEOOPPRSTU TROPOPAUSE
AEOOQRRSTU SQUARE ROOT
AEOPPRRRTU RAPPORTEUR
AEOPRRSSTW SPORTSWEAR
AEOPRSTTUW WATERSPOUT
AEORSSSTUU TROUSSEAUS
AEORSSTUUX TROUSSEAUX
AEPRRSSSTU SUPERSTARS
AFFGIILNSY FALSIFYING
AFFGIMRSSU SUFFRAGISM
AFFGINNORT AFFRONTING
AFFGIRSSTU SUFFRAGIST
AFFHILLTUY FAITHFULLY
AFFHILNTUU UNFAITHFUL
AFFIILNPST PLAINTIFFS
AFFIIMNRSU RUFFIANISM
AFFLLORUUV FLAVOURFUL
AFFLOOSTTU FOOT FAULTS

AFFMNNRSUY FUNNY FARMS
AFGGGILNNU UNFLAGGING
AFGGIIMNNY MAGNIFYING
AFGGIIMNTU FUMIGATING
AFGGIINRTY GRATIFYING
AFGHHILLST FLASHLIGHT
AFGHHILPTT FLIGHT PATH
AFGHIILRTY FAIRY LIGHT
AFGHIINNOS FASHIONING
AFGHIIRSTU GUITARFISH
AFGHIORTWY RIGHT OF WAY
AFGIIILNNZ FINALIZING
AFGIIILNRT AIR-LIFTING
AFGIILMNPY AMPLIFYING
AFGIILNNTY FAINTINGLY
AFGIILNQUY QUALIFYING
AFGIILOSTU FLAGITIOUS
AFGIIMNOTU FUMIGATION
AFGIINORTU FIGURATION
AFGIINSSTY SATISFYING
AFGIKMNORS KING-OF-ARMS
AFGIKNRSST SKIN GRAFTS
AFGILNORSV FLAVORINGS
AFGILNORUV FLAVOURING
AFGILNORVY FAVORINGLY
AFGIMNORSU AUSFORMING
AFGIMNORTT FORMATTING
AFGINNPRSY FRYING PANS
AFHHLRSTTU HALF-TRUTHS
AFHILNOPST FLASH POINT
AFHIOPRRST PARROTFISH
AFHKLLNTUY THANKFULLY
AFHKLNNTUU UNTHANKFUL
AFHLLORSST SHORTFALLS
AFHLLORSUY ROYAL FLUSH
AFHLLRTUWY WRATHFULLY
AFIILLRRTY FRITILLARY
AFIILNORSU INFUSORIAL
AFIILNORTT FILTRATION, FLIRTATION
AFIIMORSTV FAVORITISM
AFIKLLMOST MILK FLOATS
AFILLMNORY INFORMALLY
AFILLNOPRU PLAIN FLOUR
AFILLNPPTY FLIPPANTLY
AFILLOOPRS APRIL FOOLS
AFILMNORTU FULMINATOR
AFILMORSST FORMALISTS
AFILNOOSTT FLOTATIONS
AFILNORTTY FRONTALITY
AFIMMORTUU FUMATORIUM
AFIMNNORST INFORMANTS
AFIMNOORST FORMATIONS
AFIMORRSTT STRATIFORM
AFLLLNUUWY UNLAWFULLY

AFLLNOORSU ON ALL FOURS
AFLMOORRTU FORMULATOR
AFNORSTTUU FORTUNATUS
AGGGGIINZZ ZIGZAGGING
AGGGILLNWY WAGGLINGLY
AGGGILNRST STRAGGLING
AGGGIMNORT MORTGAGING
AGGHIINNRS GARNISHING
AGGHILLNUY LAUGHINGLY
AGGHILMNPU GALUMPHING
AGGHILNNSY GNASHINGLY
AGGHLOOPRY GRAPHOLOGY,
   LOGOGRAPHY
AGGIIILNTT LITIGATING
AGGIIIMNTT MITIGATING
AGGIIINRRT IRRIGATING
AGGIILLNNS SIGNALLING
AGGIILNNST TINGALINGS
AGGIILNNTU AGGLUTININ
AGGIINNORZ ORGANIZING
AGGILLNOTY GLOATINGLY
AGGILNNNTU UNTANGLING
AGGILNNORY GROANINGLY
AGGILNNRST STRANGLING
AGGIMNOPRR PROGRAMING
AGGINOORRT RARING TO GO
AGGINORRTT GARROTTING
AGGLNOOORY ORGANOLOGY
AGGLNOOORZ GORGONZOLA
AGGMOORRST MORTGAGORS
AGHHILOPRT LITHOGRAPH
AGHHLOOPRY HOLOGRAPHY
AGHHMOOPRS HOMOGRAPHS
AGHHNOOPPR PHONOGRAPH
AGHHOOPPRT PHOTOGRAPH
AGHHOPPTYY PHYTOPHAGY
AGHHORTUWY THROUGHWAY
AGHIIINNSU NINGSIA HUI
AGHIILLMTY ALMIGHTILY
AGHIILLSTT TAILLIGHTS
AGHIIMNNUZ HUMANIZING
AGHIINNRST TARNISHING
AGHIINNRSV VARNISHING
AGHIINNRTU THURINGIAN
AGHIINPRRS HAIRSPRING
AGHIINRTWW WAINWRIGHT
AGHILLNOSW SHALLOWING
AGHILLNSSY SLASHINGLY
AGHILMORST ALGORITHMS,
   LOGARITHMS
AGHILNNTUY HAUNTINGLY
AGHILNPSTY PLAYTHINGS
AGHILNRSTT STRINGHALT
AGHILNSSWY SWASHINGLY

AGHILOPPSY GYPSOPHILA
AGHILORSTT GASTROLITH
AGHILPRTWY PLAYWRIGHT
AGHIMNNOTT NOTTINGHAM
AGHIMNOOPS SHAMPOOING
AGHIMNRSST HAMSTRINGS
AGHIMORSST HISTOGRAMS
AGHINNOOPR HARPOONING
AGHINNOSTW WASHINGTON
AGHINOPRTY ATROPHYING
AGHIOPPRRS SPIROGRAPH
AGHLMOOSTU GOALMOUTHS
AGHLNOOORT ORTHOGONAL
AGHLNOSSTU ONSLAUGHTS
AGHLOPPRSY POLYGRAPHS
AGHLOPRSTY STYLOGRAPH
AGHLOPRXYY XYLOGRAPHY
AGHMMOOOSU HOMOGAMOUS
AGHMNOOPRS MONOGRAPHS
AGHMNOOPRY NOMOGRAPHY
AGHMNOORTU MOUTH ORGAN
AGHMOOPRTY TOMOGRAPHY
AGHNOOPRSY NOSOGRAPHY
AGHOOOPSUZ ZOOPHAGOUS
AGHOOPPRTY TOPOGRAPHY
AGHOPPRRYY PYROGRAPHY
AGHOPPRTYY TYPOGRAPHY
AGIIIILNNT INITIALING
AGIIIINNTT INITIATING
AGIIILMNNN MAINLINING
AGIIILMNTT MILITATING
AGIIILNOTT LITIGATION
AGIIIMMNXZ MAXIMIZING
AGIIIMNNTT INTIMATING
AGIIIMNOTT MITIGATION
AGIIINNSTZ SANITIZING
AGIIINORRT IRRIGATION
AGIIINRRTT IRRITATING
AGIIINRSTZ SATIRIZING
AGIIINTTTV TITIVATING
AGIIKNNNPR NAPKIN RING
AGIILLMMRS MILLIGRAMS
AGIILLNNST INSTALLING
AGIILLNORY ORIGINALLY
AGIILLNPRS SPIRALLING
AGIILLNRTU TRILINGUAL
AGIILLNRTY TRAILINGLY
AGIILLNTVY VIGILANTLY
AGIILMMNOT IMMOLATING
AGIILMNNPT IMPLANTING
AGIILMNORZ MORALIZING
AGIILMNOST ANTILOGISM
AGIILMNSTU SIMULATING
AGIILMNTTU MUTILATING

AGIILNNORU UNORIGINAL
AGIILNNSTU INSULATING
AGIILNOPRZ POLARIZING
AGIILNPRST SPRINGTAIL
AGIILNRSTY LARYNGITIS
AGIILNSSTV VITAL SIGNS
AGIILOOPST APIOLOGIST
AGIILOOSTX AXIOLOGIST
AGIIMMNRST IMMIGRANTS
AGIIMMORRT IMMIGRATOR
AGIIMMOSST MISOGAMIST
AGIIMMSSTT STIGMATISM
AGIIMNNNOT NOMINATING
AGIIMNNNOWZ WOMANIZING
AGIIMNNPRS MAINSPRING
AGIIMNNRTU RUMINATING
AGIIMNORST MIGRATIONS
AGIIMNORTZ AMORTIZING
AGIIMNOTTV MOTIVATING
AGIIMNSSTT MISSTATING
AGIIMNSSUV VAGINISMUS
AGIIMSSTTT STIGMATIST
AGIINNNOTV INNOVATING
AGIINNOPPT APPOINTING
AGIINNORSS SIGNORINAS
AGIINNORTZ NOTARIZING
AGIINNOSTT STATIONING
AGIINNSSTU SUSTAINING
AGIINOORRT ORIGINATOR
AGIINOPRRR RIP-ROARING
AGIINOPRVZ VAPORIZING
AGIINORSTT INSTIGATOR
AGIINORSUV VIRAGINOUS
AGIIRSSTTU GUITARISTS
AGIKKLNRSY SKYLARKING
AGIKLMNOOT TOOL-MAKING
AGIKLNOPRT PARKING LOT
AGIKLNOSTT TALKING-TOS
AGIKLNOTTU OUTTALKING
AGIKMNNORW WORKINGMAN
AGIKMNNOTU KUOMINTANG
AGIKNNORTU OUTRANKING
AGILLNNRSY SNARLINGLY
AGILLNNSTY SLANTINGLY
AGILLNOPRT PATROLLING
AGILLNOSWW SWALLOWING
AGILLNRSUY SINGULARLY
AGILLNTTTY TATTLINGLY
AGILLOOSSS ISOGLOSSAL
AGILMNNOOP LAMPOONING
AGILMNRSTY SMARTINGLY
AGILMOOSTU GLIOMATOUS
AGILMOPSTY POLYGAMIST
AGILNNNOPTY POIGNANTLY

AGILNNPPSY SNAPPINGLY
AGILNNTTUY TAUNTINGLY
AGILNNTUVY VAUNTINGLY
AGILNOPPRS PROLAPSING
AGILNOPPTU POPULATING
AGILNOPTUY OUTPLAYING
AGILNORSVY SAVORINGLY
AGILNOSSTW WAGONS-LITS
AGILNOSTTU OUTLASTING
AGILOOPSST APOLOGISTS
AGILORSSST GLOSSARIST
AGIMMNOOST MONOGAMIST
AGIMMNNSSUY GYMNASIUMS
AGIMNNOSVV MOVING VANS
AGIMNNSSUU UNASSUMING
AGIMNOORST AGRONOMIST
AGIMNOPRSU SPORANGIUM
AGINNOPTTU AT GUNPOINT
AGINNPPSUW SWAN-UPPING
AGINOPRRTY PORTRAYING
AGINORSTTU OUTSTARING
AGINOSTTUY OUTSTAYING
AGINPRSSSU SURPASSING
AGIORSTTUU GRATUITOUS
AGKLORSSSW GLASSWORKS
AGKLPPRSSU SPARK PLUGS
AGKNNNORTY GRANNY KNOT
AGLLLLOPPU GALLUP POLL
AGLLLOOPRY PYROGALLOL
AGLLNOOPYY PALYNOLOGY
AGLMOOOSTY SOMATOLOGY
AGLMOOPSUY POLYGAMOUS
AGLNOORSUU LANGUOROUS
AGLOPPRSUY PLAYGROUPS
AGMMNOOOSU MONOGAMOUS
AGMMNOPSUU MAGNUM OPUS
AGMNOORSTY GASTRONOMY
AGMOOORSST MATO GROSSO
AGMOORSTTY GASTROTOMY
AGOORRSSST GRASS ROOTS
AHHIIILNTW WITHIN HAIL
AHHIIRRSST HAIR SHIRTS
AHHIOPRSTU AUTHORSHIP
AHHISSWWYY WISHY-WASHY
AHHMORRSTW HARMSWORTH
AHHOPPRSUY HAPPY HOURS
AHIIIMMPSX AMPHIMIXIS
AHIIKMNRSS KRISHNAISM
AHIILMORTU HUMILIATOR
AHIILRSSTT SHIRTTAILS
AHIIMNNOTU INHUMATION
AHIIMNNTUY INHUMANITY
AHIIMNORSW IRISHWOMAN
AHIINORSST HISTORIANS

AHIKKNNSTT THINK TANKS
AHIKKSTUUY KITAKYUSHU
AHIKNPRRSW SHRINK-WRAP
AHILMORSST HAILSTORMS
AHILMPSSYY SYMPHYSIAL
AHILNOORTZ HORIZONTAL
AHILNOPPTY HIPPOLYTAN
AHILNOPSTU SULPHATION
AHILNPPSSY SNAPPISHLY
AHILORSSTW SHOW TRIALS
AHIMMNORSU HARMONIUMS
AHIMNOOOSU HOMOOUSIAN
AHIMNOORRU HONORARIUM
AHIMNOORSU HARMONIOUS
AHIMNPRTTU TRIUMPHANT
AHIMORSTUU HAUSTORIUM
AHIMPPPRSU PARISH-PUMP
AHINOPRSUX XIPHOSURAN
AHIOOPSTTX PHOTOTAXIS
AHKLMOPRYY KARYOLYMPH
AHLLMORSSU SMALL HOURS
AHLLOPRSTU PROTHALLUS
AHLMNNORTU LUNAR MONTH
AHLMNOORST SOLAR MONTH
AHLMOOPRTU PHOTOMURAL
AHLMOOPSTY HOMOPLASTY
AHLMPRSUWY MURPHY'S LAW
AHLNOPSTUY POLYANTHUS
AHLORRSTTU ULTRASHORT
AHMNNOOSTU MONANTHOUS
AHMNOOPRTU PROTOHUMAN
AHNNOSTTWY SHANTYTOWN
AHNOOPSTTY PHOTONASTY
AHNOOPPRTTY TRYPTOPHAN
AHOOPPRTTY PROTOPATHY
AHOOPSSTTT PHOTOSTATS
AIIIINNOTT INITIATION
AIIIILLMNTU ILLUMINATI
AIIIILLMRTY MILITARILY
AIIILMMNST MINIMALIST
AIIILMMRST MILITARISM
AIIILMNOTT LIMITATION, MILITATION
AIIILMRSTT MILITARIST
AIIILMRSTY SIMILARITY
AIIILORSTV VISITORIAL
AIIILRTTVY TRIVIALITY
AIIIMNNOTT INTIMATION
AIIIMNOPSS PIANISSIMO
AIIIMNOSTT IMITATIONS
AIIINNOOST IONISATION
AIIINNOOTZ IONIZATION
AIIINNOTTV INVITATION
AIIINORRTT IRRITATION
AIIINORTTY INITIATORY

AIIINOSTTV VISITATION
AIIINOTTTV TITIVATION
AIIIPRSSTY PITYRIASIS
AIIIPRTVVY VIVIPARITY
AIIILLMNNTU ILLUMINANT
AIIILLMNTTY MILITANTLY
AIIILLNOOTV VOLITIONAL
AIIILLNOSUV VILLAINOUS
AIIILLORSTY SOLITARILY
AIIILLOSSTT SOLSTITIAL
AIIILLOTTVY VOLATILITY
AIIILLSTUVV VALVULITIS
AIIILMMNNOS NOMINALISM
AIIILMMNOOT IMMOLATION
AIIILMMORST IMMORALIST
AIIILMMORTY IMMORALITY
AIIILMNNOST NOMINALIST
AIIILMNOORT MONITORIAL
AIIILMNORTY MINATORILY
AIIILMNOSTU SIMULATION
AIIILMNOTTU MUTILATION
AIIILMNRSSU INSULARISM
AIIILNNOOST INSOLATION
AIIILNNOSTU INSULATION
AIIILNOOPPT OPPILATION
AIIILNOOPST POSITIONAL, SPOLIATION
AIIILNOOSTV VIOLATIONS
AIIILNOSSTU SAINT LOUIS
AIIILNRSSUY URINALYSIS
AIIILNRSTUY INSULARITY
AIIILORSSTU SAILOR SUIT
AIIILPRSSTU SPIRITUALS
AIIILRTTUVY VIRTUALITY
AIIMMNNOTU AMMUNITION
AIIMMPRRTU IMPRIMATUR
AIIMMRTTUY IMMATURITY
AIIMNNNOOT NOMINATION
AIIMNNORTU RUMINATION
AIIMNNRSTT MINISTRANT
AIIMNOOTTV MOTIVATION
AIIMNOPRTV PROVITAMIN
AIIMNOPSTU UTOPIANISM
AIIMNOPTTU IMPUTATION
AIIMNORSSU MISSOURIAN
AIIMNORSSY MISSIONARY
AIIMNPRSTU PURITANISM
AIIMNPSSTT TIMPANISTS
AIIMNPSSTU IMPUISSANT
AIIMNPSTTY TYMPANITIS
AIIMOPRSTT PATRIOTISM
AIIMOSSTTT STOMATITIS
AIIINNNOOTT INTONATION
AIIINNNOOTV INNOVATION
AIIINNORSTT TRANSITION

AIINNORSTU INSINUATOR
AIINOOPPST APPOSITION
AIINOPRSTT PARTITIONS
AIINOPRSTV PRIVATIONS
AIINORSSTT STRIATIONS
AIINORTTVY INVITATORY
AIINOSSTTU SITUATIONS
AIIOPRSUVV VIVIPAROUS
AIIPRSTTVY VARITYPIST
AIJLMNORSU JOURNALISM
AIJLNORSTU JOURNALIST
AIJMORSSTU MAJOR SUITS
AIKLLLOPTW PILLOW TALK
AIKLOPSTUV VOLAPUKIST
AIKLORSSYY KARYOLYSIS
AILLMNOOPY POLYNOMIAL
AILLMNPRST SMALL PRINT
AILLMOSSYY AMYLOLYSIS
AILLNOOPRT POLLINATOR
AILLNOOPTY OPTIONALLY
AILLNQRTUY TRANQUILLY
AILLPRSSTU PLURALISTS
AILMMSTTUU ULTIMATUMS
AILMNNOOPR PRONOMINAL
AILMNORSST MORTAL SINS
AILMNORTUY UNMORALITY
AILMNSSTTU STIMULANTS
AILMOOPSTU LIPOMATOUS
AILMORSSTU SIMULATORS
AILMORSTTU STIMULATOR
AILNOOPPTU POPULATION
AILNOOPRSS SPONSORIAL
AILNOOSTUV OVULATIONS
AILNOPSSTU PULSATIONS
AILNORSSTU INSULATORS
AILNORSTTU LUSTRATION
AILNORSUVY UNSAVORILY
AILNOSTTUU USTULATION
AILNPPSSTU SUPPLIANTS
AILOPPRTUY POPULARITY
AILOPRSTTU STIPULATOR
AILRRSTUUV ULTRAVIRUS
AIMMNORSTU STRAMONIUM
AIMMNOSSTU SUMMATIONS
AIMMOORRTU MORATORIUM
AIMNNOOSTU ANTIMONOUS
AIMNOOSTTU AUTONOMIST
AIMNOOSTTX TAXONOMIST
AIMNOPSSTU ASSUMPTION
AIMNORRSST RAINSTORMS
AIMNRSTTUU NASTURTIUM
AIMOOOORTVY OVARIOTOMY
AINNOOPRTT ANTIPROTON
AINNOORSTV INNOVATORS

AINOOPRSTY ANISOTROPY
AINOOQSTTU QUOTATIONS
AINOOSTTTU OUTSTATION
AINOPRSTUU USURPATION
AINORRSSTT TRANSISTOR
AINORRSTTY TRANSITORY
AINPRSTUUV PURSUIVANT
AIOOPRRSUU UPROARIOUS
AIOORRSTTU TRAITOROUS
AIOOSSTTTT TATTOOISTS
AIOPPPRSUU PUPIPAROUS
AIORRRTTTU TRITURATOR
AKKKLLNUUX KU KLUX KLAN
AKKMMNORSU KOMMUNARSK
AKLOPRRRSY LORRY PARKS
ALLNOPSTTU POLLUTANTS
ALLOPRSSTW STRAW POLLS
ALMNOPRTUY POULTRYMAN
ALMOOPPRST PROTOPLASM
ALMOPPSSUY PLAY POSSUM
ALNOPSSTTU POSTULANTS
ALOOOORSTUZ ZOOLATROUS
ALOOPPRSTT PROTOPLAST
ALOOPPRTTY PROTOTYPAL
ALOOPRSTTU POSTULATOR
ALOPRTUUVY VOLUPTUARY
AMMOOSTUXY MYXOMATOUS
AMNNOOSTWW TOWNSWOMAN
AMNOOOSTUU AUTONOMOUS
AMNOOPRSUY PARONYMOUS
AMOPPRSTTU POSTPARTUM
ANOOOOPRSTZ PROTOZOANS
ANOPRRSSTT TRANSPORTS
AOOOORRSTTV ROTOVATORS
AOOPQRSTTU POST QUARTO
AORRRSTWWY WORRYWARTS
BBBCKOOSSY BOBBY SOCKS,
BBBEEELMSU BUMBLEBEES
BBBEEIINRW WINEBIBBER
BBBEGILNRU BLUBBERING
BBBGHINNOO HOBNOBBING
BBBHIINRSU RUBBISH BIN
BBBLLOOWWY BLOW-BY-BLOW
BBCDEIRSSU SUBSCRIBED
BBCEEKNRRU RUBBERNECK
BBCEELNOOU BUBONOCELE
BBCEGILNOR CLOBBERING
BBCEHINSSU CHUBBINESS
BBCEHLOSUY CUBBYHOLES
BBCEILRRSS SCRIBBLERS
BBCEIRRSSU SUBSCRIBER
BBCEIRSSTU SCRUBBIEST
BBCGIILNRS SCRIBBLING
BBCIIILOST BIBLIOTICS

BBDDEEIMOV DIVE-BOMBED
BBDDEELOSU DOUBLE BEDS
BBDDEILNOU DOUBLE BIND
BBDEEIMORV DIVE-BOMBER
BBDEIKNOOR BOOKBINDER
BBDEIOSSUY BUSYBODIES
BBDHIIOPRS BISHOPBIRD
BBEEERRRTU RUBBER TREE
BBEEIILRRS BILBERRIES
BBEEIRRRSU BURBERRIES
BBEELLOTTU BLUEBOTTLE
BBEELMORTT LETTER BOMB
BBEGHILOSS BOBSLEIGHS
BBEGHIORRT BIG BROTHER
BBEGILNORS SLOBBERING
BBEGINRSSU GRUBBINESS
BBEHHILOST SHIBBOLETH
BBEHHOORSY HOBBYHORSE
BBEHLLMOSS BOMBSHELLS
BBEIILLOOP BIBLIOPOLE
BBEIKLMOOO BOOKMOBILE
BBEIKLNOST KNOBBLIEST
BBEILNOSSW WOBBLINESS
BBEINSSSTU STUBBINESS
BBEIOOPRSY BOOBY PRISE
BBEIOOPRYZ BOOBY PRIZE
BBEKLORRUW RUBBLEWORK
BBEMNORSUX BOX NUMBERS
BBENORRSTU STUBBORNER
BBFHIINORS RIBBONFISH
BBGHIINRSU RUBBISHING
BBGHILLSTU LIGHT BULBS
BBGHILNOOS HOBGOBLINS
BBGILNNSUY SNUBBINGLY
BBHILNOSSY SNOBBISHLY
BBIIIMNOT IMBIBITION
BBIIILOSTT BIBLIOTIST
BBIKMNOSST STINK-BOMBS
BBJMMMOOUU MUMBO JUMBO
BBLMOORSUY BLOOMSBURY
BBLNORSTUY STUBBORNLY
BCCCKMOOSS COCKSCOMBS
BCCDEEEMNU DECUMBENCE
BCCDEILNOU CONDUCIBLE
BCCEEEMNRU RECUMBENCE
BCCEEENPSU PUBESCENCE
BCCEEENRSU RUBESCENCE
BCCEEINRTY CYBERNETIC
BCCEIMNNUY INCUMBENCY
BCCEINNOS CONCUBINES
BCCEKOSSTU STOCK CUBES
BCCGIMNSUU SUCCUMBING
BCCHHIINNY INCH BY INCH
BCCHIINORT BRONCHITIC

BCCIILSSTY BICYCLISTS
BCDDEEILTU DEDUCTIBLE
BCDDIIKRSY DICKYBIRDS
BCDEEEFNOR CORNED BEEF
BCDEEEIINT BENEDICITE
BCDEEEMNRU ENCUMBERED
BCDEEHIMRS BESMIRCHED
BCDEEHLOST BEDCLOTHES
BCDEEIILNR INCREDIBLE
BCDEEINSSU SUBSIDENCE
BCDEEIPRRS PRESCRIBED
BCDEEKLLNU BULLNECKED
BCDEENOSST SECOND BEST
BCDEEORRSS CROSSBREED
BCDEFLOOTU CLUBFOOTED
BCDEGHINOU DEBOUCHING
BCDEGIINRS DESCRIBING
BCDEHIILOR BICHLORIDE
BCDEHILNOU DOUBLE CHIN
BCDEIILNRY INCREDIBLY
BCDEIILPSU PUBLICISED
BCDEIILPUZ PUBLICIZED
BCDEILOORR CORRODIBLE
BCDEILOPRU PRODUCIBLE
BCDEILORTT BITTER COLD
BCDEIOPRRS PROSCRIBED
BCDEKLOOOS CLOSED BOOK
BCDELNOORU CORDON BLEU
BCDELORRUY CLOUDBERRY
BCDEMMNRUU CUMMERBUND
BCDEORSTTU OBSTRUCTED
BCDGIIOSTU DOG BISCUIT
BCDHHIILRT CHILDBIRTH
BCDHLNOOTU CLOTHBOUND
BCDIILMORU LUMBRICOID
BCDIIOPRRT TROPICBIRD
BCDILLNOOR COLOR-BLIND
BCDINOSTUU SUBDUCTION
BCDKLOOOST BLOODSTOCK
BCDKLOOOSW WOODBLOCKS
BCDKMRSTUU DUMBSTRUCK
BCDLNOOOTU BLOOD COUNT
BCDLORSTUU CLOUDBURST
BCDOPRSTUY BY-PRODUCTS
BCEEEEHLSU BLUE CHEESE
BCEEEFFILT EFFECTIBLE
BCEEEFINNT BENEFICENT
BCEEEFLLRT TREBLE CLEF
BCEEEGHINS BESEECHING
BCEEEHKNOS CHEEKBONES
BCEEEIILLNU EBULLIENCE
BCEEELLMRU CEREBELLUM
BCEEELQRSU BECQUERELS
BCEEENRSTU ERUBESCENT

BCEEFORRTU BRUTE FORCE	BCEHMNOOSY HONEYCOMBS
BCEEGIINOT BIOGENETIC	BCEHMRSTUW THUMBSCREW
BCEEGINRSU SUBGENERIC	BCEIIILMMS IMMISCIBLE
BCEEHKLNOU HUCKLEBONE	BCEIIILMTY IMBECILITY
BCEEHKOOQU CHEQUEBOOK	BCEIIILNNV INVINCIBLE
BCEEHKORRY CHOKEBERRY	BCEIIKLLLS SICKLEBILL
BCEEHMORUU EMBOUCHURE	BCEIILMMOS EMBOLISMIC
BCEEHNOOPR NECROPHOBE	BCEIJNOOST OBJECTIONS
BCEEHNORRX BRONX CHEER	BCEIJNOSTU SUBJECTION
BCEEIILPST PLEBISCITE	BCEILMNOSU COLUMBINES
BCEEIJOSTV OBJECTIVES	BCEILMOORT BOLOMETRIC
BCEEIJSTUV SUBJECTIVE	BCEILMRSTU CRUMBLIEST
BCEEILLNPU BLUE-PENCIL	BCEILNRTUU TUBERCULIN
BCEEILLOOS CELLOBIOSE	BCEIMNNSTU INCUMBENTS
BCEEILMOST COMESTIBLE	BCEINNOSSU BOUNCINESS
BCEEILNOTY BY-ELECTION	BCEINORTTU CONTRIBUTE
BCEEIOOSVX VOICE BOXES	BCEINOSSTU SUBSECTION
BCEEIPRRRS PRESCRIBER	BCEIOPPRSY PRESBYOPIC
BCEEIPRRSY SPICEBERRY	BCEIORSSTT OBSTETRICS
BCEEIPSSSU SUBSPECIES	BCEKKOOOPT POCKETBOOK
BCEEJNORST JOB CENTRES	BCEKLNRTUU TURNBUCKLE
BCEEJOSSTX SEX OBJECTS	BCEKLOORTW TOWER BLOCK
BCEEKLNOTT BOTTLENECK	BCEKLOOSTV BLOCK VOTES
BCEELNOTTU CUTTLEBONE	BCELRSTUUU SUBCULTURE
BCEELNRTUU TURBULENCE	BCEMNOPRTU PROCUMBENT
BCEEMMORSU CUMBERSOME	BCENOORSSS CROSSBONES
BCEEMMORTY EMBRECTOMY	BCEORRSTTU OBSTRUCTER
BCEFFIOOSX BOX OFFICES	BCEPRSTTUU BUTTERCUPS
BCEFFIOOSY OFFICE BOYS	BCFIIMORRR CRIBRIFORM
BCEFHNNORT FRONTBENCH	BCGHILNSTU NIGHTCLUBS
BCEFIIKRRS FIREBRICKS	BCGIIINNRS INSCRIBING
BCEFIJSTUY SUBJECTIFY	BCGIKLNNUU UNBUCKLING
BCEGHIINTW BEWITCHING	BCGINOOTTY BOYCOTTING
BCEGHIKNNS KING'S BENCH	BCHIINORST BRONCHITIS
BCEGHINRTU BUTCHERING	BCHIIOPRSS BISHOPRICS
BCEGIILORR CORRIGIBLE	BCHIIOPSSY BIOPHYSICS
BCEGIJNSTU SUBJECTING	BCHIMNOOOP MONOPHOBIC
BCEGILMNOY BECOMINGLY	BCHIMOORTT THROMBOTIC
BCEGILOOOY BIOECOLOGY	BCHIOPRTYY BRYOPHYTIC
BCEGIMNNOU UNBECOMING	BCHLNOPSUW PUNCH BOWLS
BCEHHNNOUY HONEYBUNCH	BCHMOOOSTT TOOTHCOMBS
BCEHIINSST BITCHINESS	BCIIILNNVY INVINCIBLY
BCEHIISSSU HIBISCUSES	BCIILNOPSY PSILOCYBIN
BCEHILNOOR BRONCHIOLE	BCIILORSUU LUBRICIOUS
BCEHILOPRY HYPERBOLIC	BCIILPSSTU PUBLICISTS
BCEHILOSTT BLOTCHIEST	BCIIMNOSTY SYMBIONTIC
BCEHILRRUV BUR CHERVIL	BCIKMOORST BROOMSTICK
BCEHINNSSU BUNCHINESS	BCILPRSSTU STRIP CLUBS
BCEHINOOPX XENOPHOBIC	BCIMNOOOSS SONIC BOOMS
BCEHINOSST BOTCHINESS	BCIMNOOSTU COMBUSTION
BCEHKKOOST SKETCHBOOK	BCIOPRSSTU SUBTROPICS
BCEHKLOOSU BLOCKHOUSE	BCKLLOOPSU BOLLOCKS-UP
BCEHKOPSTU BUCKET SHOP	BCKMOOORTT ROCK BOTTOM
BCEHLOSSUU CLUBHOUSES	BDDDEEINTW TWIN-BEDDED

BDDDEELOOR RED-BLOODED
BDDDEIISUV SUBDIVIDED
BDDEEEFINR BEFRIENDED
BDDEEEILLV BEDEVILLED
BDDEEEILRW BEWILDERED
BDDEEEELMNO EMBOLDENED
BDDEEEELORU DOUBLE-REED
BDDEEGLNOU BLUDGEONED
BDDEEILMSS DISSEMBLED
BDDEEINRST BESTRIDDEN
BDDEENNRUU UNBURDENED
BDDEFILLOU FULL-BODIED
BDDEFLOOSU BLOOD FEUDS
BDDEGIILOS DISOBLIGED
BDDEGIOOSS DOGSBODIES
BDDEHLNOOR BONDHOLDER
BDDEHLOOOT HOT-BLOODED
BDDEIIRSUV SUBDIVIDER
BDDEIISSSU SUBSIDISED
BDDEIISSUZ SUBSIDIZED
BDDEILMORW MIDDLEBROW
BDDFGIINOR FORBIDDING
BDDFILLNOS BLINDFOLDS
BDDGIINOTU OUTBIDDING
BDDHLNOOOU BLOODHOUND
BDDIKLNNRU BLIND DRUNK
BDDILLORSY DOLLY BIRDS
BDEEEEMMRR REMEMBERED
BDEEEFILNS DEFENSIBLE
BDEEEFLOTT BOTTLE-FEED
BDEEEGHILR HEIDELBERG
BDEEEHLLNR HELLBENDER
BDEEEHLSST THE BLESSED
BDEEEHMORW HOME-BREWED
BDEEEIILSV DISBELIEVE
BDEEEILNTX EXTENDIBLE
BDEEEILSTW WILDEBEEST
BDEEEIMRTT EMBITTERED
BDEEEINRRT INTERBREED
BDEEEIRTTW BITTERWEED
BDEEELMTUW TUMBLEWEED
BDEEELNOSS NOSEBLEEDS
BDEEELORTU DOUBLETREE
BDEEELRRRY ELDERBERRY
BDEEENRSTU DEBENTURES
BDEEFGIINR DEBRIEFING
BDEEFILNSY DEFENSIBLY
BDEEFLLOSW BEDFELLOWS
BDEEFLORSW FLOWERBEDS
BDEEFOORSS BED OF ROSES
BDEEGGLOOT BOOTLEGGED
BDEEGIILNV BEDEVILING
BDEEGIILST DIGESTIBLE
BDEEGIINNR INBREEDING

BDEEGIMOSU DISEMBOGUE
BDEEGLNORU BLUDGEONER
BDEEHIMOOS HOMEBODIES
BDEEHIMRSU HUMBERSIDE
BDEEHLNNOR HORNBLENDE
BDEEIILMOS DEMOBILISE
BDEEIILMOZ DEMOBILIZE
BDEEIILRTV DIVERTIBLE
BDEEIILSTV DIVESTIBLE
BDEEIILLNNR DINNER BELL
BDEEIILLOPT POTBELLIED
BDEEIILMOSW DISEMBOWEL
BDEEIILMOTU DOUBLE TIME
BDEEIILMRSS DISSEMBLER
BDEEIILNORR BORDERLINE
BDEEIILNOTY OBEDIENTLY
BDEEIILORSW BOWDLERISE
BDEEIILORWZ BOWDLERIZE
BDEEIMMNOT EMBODIMENT
BDEEIMORRY EMBROIDERY
BDEEIMRRSU REIMBURSED
BDEEINNORZ BENZODRINE
BDEEIPRSSW SPIDERWEBS
BDEEIRSSTT BED-SITTERS
BDEEKOOORV OVERBOOKED
BDEELLNRUY UNDERBELLY
BDEELMRRUU BLUE MURDER
BDEELNNOSS BLONDENESS
BDEELNRRSU BLUNDERERS
BDEELQRSUU BURLESQUED
BDEEMNNRUU UNNUMBERED
BDEEMNORSU BURDENSOME
BDEENORRUV OVERBURDEN
BDEEORSSTY OYSTER BEDS
BDEERSSTTU BUTTRESSED
BDEFFIILSU DIFFUSIBLE
BDEFFNOORW BROWNED-OFF
BDEFGINOOR FOREBODING
BDEFGIOORT FOOTBRIDGE
BDEFILOOST SOFT-BOILED
BDEFINORSY BOYFRIENDS
BDEFIOPRRY BIRD OF PREY
BDEGGGINRU BEGRUDGING
BDEGHHIINR HIGHBINDER
BDEGHINNRU HINDENBURG
BDEGHLNOUU DOUBLE-HUNG
BDEGIIILRS DIRIGIBLES
BDEGIILLNV DIVING BELL
BDEGIILNRU REBUILDING
BDEGIINNRR RING BINDER
BDEGIINOSY DISOBEYING
BDEGIINRST BESTRIDING
BDEGIINSTU SUBEDITING
BDEGIIPPRS BIG DIPPERS

BDEGIKORRW BRIDGEWORK
BDEGILNNRU BLUNDERING
BDEGILNORU REDOUBLING
BDEGIMOORR BRIDEGROOM
BDEGINNORU REBOUNDING
BDEGINNSTU SUBTENDING
BDEGIOPRRT BRIDGEPORT
BDEHIILPSU BISULPHIDE
BDEHIIOPRT PROHIBITED
BDEHIIRRSY HYBRIDISER
BDEHIIRRYZ HYBRIDIZER
BDEHNOOSUU HOUSEBOUND
BDEHNRRSUU UNDERBRUSH
BDEIIILNRV BILIVERDIN
BDEIIJNOSS INSIDE JOBS
BDEIIKLOOS OBELISKOID
BDEIILMORS DISEMBROIL
BDEIIRSSSU SUBSIDISER
BDEIIRSSUZ SUBSIDIZER
BDEIIRSTTU DISTRIBUTE
BDEIJLRRUY JERRY-BUILD
BDEIKNNORW WIND-BROKEN
BDEILLORWY YELLOWBIRD
BDEILLOSSU DISSOLUBLE
BDEILLOTUX BILLET-DOUX
BDEILMORSW BOWDLERISM
BDEILMOSSY SYMBOLISED
BDEILMOSYZ SYMBOLIZED
BDEILNNOST STONE-BLIND
BDEILNOOSS BLOODINESS
BDEIMNORSS MORBIDNESS
BDEINOORSS BROODINESS
BDEINOSSSU DO BUSINESS
BDEIOORTTW BITTERWOOD
BDEIORSSTU SUBEDITORS
BDEKNNOORW BROKEN-DOWN
BDELLNOPSU SPELLBOUND
BDELLORSUZ BULLDOZERS
BDELLORTUY TROUBLEDLY
BDELMMNOUY MOLYBDENUM
BDELMNOOOY BLOOD MONEY
BDELMNOTUW TUMBLEDOWN
BDELNOOOST BLOODSTONE
BDELOOPSTU DOUBLE-STOP
BDELOOPSTY BLOOD TYPES
BDENOPTTUU BUTTONED UP
BDFLLOTUUY DOUBTFULLY
BDFNOORSTU FROSTBOUND
BDGIINRSSU DISBURSING
BDGIINRSTU DISTURBING
BDGIKMNOSU SUBKINGDOM
BDGILLNOUZ BULLDOZING
BDGILNORWY BLOW-DRYING
BDGLOOOPRU BLOOD GROUP

BDHIILRRWY WHIRLYBIRD
BDHIMNOORY MONOHYBRID
BDHMNOSTUW THUMBS DOWN
BDHNNOORTU NORTHBOUND
BDHNOOSTUU SOUTHBOUND
BDIIILNOSU LIBIDINOUS
BDILNOPSST BLIND SPOTS
BDINNOORRU ROUND ROBIN
BDINOOSWWW BOW WINDOWS
BDKNNOOORY DONNYBROOK
BDLLOOSSTU BLOOD LUSTS
BDLMNOOTTU BUTTONMOLD
BDLOOOPRST BLOOD SPORT
BDMNOORSTU STORMBOUND
BDNNOOTTUW BUTTON-DOWN
BDNOOOTTUW BUTTONWOOD
BEEEEFLNSS FEEBLENESS
BEEEEGLSTU BETELGEUSE
BEEEEMMRRR REMEMBERER
BEEEFGILNN ENFEEBLING
BEEEFOORRT FREEBOOTER
BEEEGGINRR GINGER BEER
BEEEGHINRS HEISENBERG
BEEEGINRRR GREENBRIER
BEEEGLNRST GREEN BELTS
BEEEGNOSTW GO-BETWEENS
BEEEHLLRTW BELLWETHER
BEEEILMPTX EXEMPTIBLE
BEEEILNRUV UNBELIEVER
BEEEILNSTX EXTENSIBLE
BEEEILRRSV REVERSIBLE
BEEEILRRTV REVERTIBLE
BEEEIMRRTT EMBITTERER
BEEEIMRSSV SEMIBREVES
BEEEINRSSZ BREEZINESS
BEEEIRRSTW SWEETBRIER
BEEEKKOOPR BOOKKEEPER
BEEELLRSST BEST-SELLER
BEEELMMNST EMBLEMENTS
BEEELMRSZZ EMBEZZLERS
BEEELNNOTV BENEVOLENT
BEEEMNRTTT BETTERMENT
BEEEOQSUXZ SQUEEZEBOX
BEEFFNORUZ BUFFER ZONE
BEEFGIINNT BENEFITING
BEEFGRSTUU SUBTERFUGE
BEEFIILLNX INFLEXIBLE
BEEFIORSSU SEBIFEROUS
BEEFLMNOTU BEFOULMENT
BEEGGIILLN NEGLIGIBLE
BEEGGLOORT BOOTLEGGER
BEEGGNRRSU REGENSBURG
BEEGHILNRT BLETHERING
BEEGHINRRT BRIGHTENER

BEEGHMNRTU GREEN THUMB
BEEGIIILLN INELIGIBLE
BEEGIILNRT GILBERTINE
BEEGIILNST INGESTIBLE
BEEGIIINOSS BIOGENESIS
BEEGIKNNOT BETOKENING
BEEGILLNRR BELL-RINGER
BEEGILMNRS RESEMBLING
BEEGILMNZZ EMBEZZLING
BEEGINRSTW BESTREWING
BEEGMNORYY EMBRYOGENY
BEEGNOORRS GREENSBORO
BEEGOORRSY GOOSEBERRY
BEEHIIITVX EXHIBITIVE
BEEHILLMOR LIMBER HOLE
BEEHILMMOO MOBILE HOME
BEEHILMOST BLITHESOME
BEEHILNSST BLITHENESS
BEEHIMMPRS MEMBERSHIP
BEEHIORRSV HERBIVORES
BEEHKMNOOR BROKEN HOME
BEEHLMNSSU HUMBLENESS
BEEHLOPRSY HYPERBOLES
BEEHMOORST BOTHERSOME
BEEHMOORTT MOTHER-TO-BE
BEEHNOOPSX PHONE BOXES
BEEHOORSSX HORSEBOXES
BEEIIJORTU BIJOUTERIE
BEEIIKLMRT KIMBERLITE
BEEIILLLRV LIBREVILLE
BEEIILMMRS IMMERSIBLE
BEEIILMNRT TIMBERLINE
BEEIILMRSS REMISSIBLE
BEEIILNNSS INSENSIBLE
BEEIILNNTV INVENTIBLE
BEEIILNRST LIBERTINES
BEEIILNRTV INVERTIBLE
BEEIILSSTX BISSEXTILE
BEEIILLLNTU LUTINE BELL
BEEILLLOVW BOLL WEEVIL
BEEILLLOWY YELLOW BILE
BEEILLNORS REBELLIONS
BEEILLOPST POTBELLIES
BEEILLORSU REBELLIOUS
BEEIILLRSTT BELLETRIST
BEEILMNNSS NIMBLENESS
BEEILMRRSU MULBERRIES
BEEILNOPRS NOBEL PRISE
BEEILNOPRZ NOBEL PRIZE
BEEILNOSST OSTENSIBLE
BEEILOSTTU OUBLIETTES
BEEILSSTTU SUBTLETIES
BEEILSSTUV VESTIBULES
BEEIMRRRSU REIMBURSER

BEEINNRSTU INNER TUBES
BEEINORRTT TORBERNITE
BEEINRSSTT BITTERNESS
BEEINSSSSU BUSINESSES
BEEIOSSSSV OBSESSIVES
BEEIQRSTTU BRIQUETTES
BEEIRSSUVV SUBVERSIVE
BEEKLLOORS BOOKSELLER
BEEKNNORSS BROKENNESS
BEELMNRSSU NUMBERLESS
BEELMRRSSU SLUMBERERS
BEELNPRTUU PUBERULENT
BEELNSSSTU SUBTLENESS
BEELQRRSUU BURLESQUER
BEELQRSSUU BURLESQUES
BEELRRSSTU BLUSTERERS
BEEMMNNOTT ENTOMBMENT
BEEMMNOSST EMBOSSMENT
BEEMNOOSXY MONEYBOXES
BEEMNORSSS SOMBRENESS
BEENOSSSTU OBTUSENESS
BEENPRSSSU SUPERBNESS
BEENQSSTUU SUBSEQUENT
BEEOPRSSSX PRESS BOXES
BEEPRRSTYY PRESBYTERY
BEERSSSTTU BUTTRESSES
BEFFHILOOT OFF THE BOIL
BEFFNOORUY BUFFOONERY
BEFGIIINNOR FIBRINOGEN
BEFGILNORW FINGER BOWL
BEFGKOOORR GO FOR BROKE
BEFHILLMTU THIMBLEFUL
BEFHIRSTTU BUTTERFISH
BEFIILLNXY INFLEXIBLY
BEFIILRSTU FILIBUSTER
BEFLLLOPSY BELLY FLOPS
BEFNNNOSUY FUNNY BONES
BEGGHMRUUY HUMBUGGERY
BEGGIILLNY NEGLIGIBLY
BEGGIINNNS BEGINNINGS
BEGGILNNOS BELONGINGS
BEGGIMNRSU SUBMERGING
BEGGINNORU BURGEONING
BEGHIIINTX EXHIBITING
BEGHIIKNNT BETHINKING
BEGHIILMNS BLEMISHING
BEGHIILNRT BLITHERING
BEGHILMNOO HEMOGLOBIN
BEGHILNORY NEIGHBORLY
BEGHINNRTU BURTHENING
BEGHINORSU NEIGHBOURS
BEGHINORTT BETROTHING
BEGHINRSST BRIGHTNESS
BEGHMNOORT THROMBOGEN

BEGIIIILLTY LEGIBILITY
BEGIILLNTT BELITTLING
BEGIILMNOR EMBROILING
BEGIILNRST BLISTERING
BEGIILNRTT BITTERLING
BEGIINRRST BESTIRRING
BEGIJRSTTU JITTERBUGS
BEGIKLNRUY REBUKINGLY
BEGILMNRSU SLUMBERING
BEGILNORST BOLSTERING
BEGILNORSY SOBERINGLY
BEGILNRSTU BLUSTERING
BEGILNSTTU SUBLETTING
BEGILOOOXY EXOBIOLOGY
BEGINPRRTU PERTURBING
BEGINRSTUV SUBVERTING
BEGLMOORYY EMBRYOLOGY
BEGLMORUUX LUXEMBOURG
BEGNORRUYY YOUNGBERRY
BEHHIIRSTT THE BRITISH
BEHIIIINTV INHIBITIVE
BEHIIIINOTX EXHIBITION
BEHIILPSTU BISULPHITE
BEHIIOPRRT PROHIBITER
BEHIIORSTX EXHIBITORS
BEHIIORTXY EXHIBITORY
BEHIIRRSST BRITISHERS
BEHIKLOSSV BOLSHEVIKS
BEHILLORWW WILLOWHERB
BEHILMOSSV BOLSHEVISM
BEHILPRSSU PUBLISHERS
BEHIMSSSTU MISS THE BUS
BEHINORSTT BIRTHSTONE
BEHINOSSSY BOYISHNESS
BEHKNOOOPS PHONE BOOKS
BEHKNOSSUU BUNKHOUSES
BEHLMOOPTY PHLEBOTOMY
BEHLNOOTTU BUTTONHOLE
BEHMOOORST SMOOTHBORE
BEHMOORSST THROMBOSES
BEHMOORSTY MOTHER'S BOY
BEHMPRTTUU TUB-THUMPER
BEHNOOORTU ON THE BUROO
BEHOOPRSSU RUSSOPHOBE
BEHRRSSUWY SHREWSBURY
BEIIILMMOS IMMOBILISE
BEIIILMMOZ IMMOBILIZE
BEIIILNOST NOBILITIES
BEIIIMNSTU BITUMINISE
BEIIIMNTUZ BITUMINIZE
BEIIIOOPSS BIOPOIESIS
BEIIILLNOTU EBULLITION
BEIIILLOSSU SOLUBILISE
BEIIILLOSUZ SOLUBILIZE

BEIILMOPSS IMPOSSIBLE
BEIILMRTUY MULIEBRITY
BEIILNNSSY INSENSIBLY
BEIILNRSTT LITTERBINS
BEIILORSTT TRILOBITES
BEIILORSTU BOILER SUIT
BEIILRSSTU SUBTILISER
BEIILRSSTY RESISTIBLY
BEIILRSTTT LIBRETTIST
BEIILRSTUZ SUBTILIZER
BEIIMSSSUV SUBMISSIVE
BEIINORSTY INSOBRIETY
BEIJLRRTUY JERRY-BUILT
BEIKLMRTTU BUTTERMILK
BEIKMOORST MOTORBIKES
BEIKMORRTW TIMBERWORK
BEIKNOORUY ON YOUR BIKE
BEILLMNPSU PLUMB LINES
BEILMNOOSW SNOWMOBILE
BEILMNOOTT BOTTOM LINE
BEILMOOOST LOBOTOMIES
BEILNOSSTY OSTENSIBLY
BEILNOSSWZ BLOWZINESS
BEILNOSTUY NEBULOSITY
BEILNPRSTU BLUEPRINTS
BEILOOPRST POTBOILERS
BEILOOTUVV OBVOLUTIVE
BEIMMRSTYY BISYMMETRY
BEIMNNOOPT EMBONPOINT
BEIMNORSSU SUBMERSION
BEINNOSTUV SUBVENTION
BEINOOSSSS OBSESSIONS
BEINOPRSTU SUBREPTION
BEINORSSUV SUBVERSION
BEINORSTUU SUBROUTINE
BEINOSSTWX WITNESS BOX
BEINSSSTTU SUBSISTENT
BEIOOQSSUU OBSEQUIOUS
BEIOORSSST SOB STORIES
BEIOORSSTU BOISTEROUS
BEIOPSTTTU PITOT TUBES
BEIOQRSSTU SOBRIQUETS
BEIOQRSTUU SOUBRIQUET
BEIORRSTUY TUBEROSITY
BEISSTTTUU SUBSTITUTE
BEKKNOOOST BOOK TOKENS
BEKNOORSTY STONY BROKE
BELLMOPSTU POST-BELLUM
BELLNOSUUY NEBULOUSLY
BELLORSTUY TROLLEYBUS
BELMMOORRU LUMBER-ROOM
BELMOOSSTT BOTTOMLESS
BELMORSSUU SLUMBEROUS
BELOOPRSTT LOBSTERPOT

BEMNOOSSTT TOMBSTONES
BENNOORSTW BROWNSTONE
BENORSSSTU ROBUSTNESS
BEORRTTTUW BUTTERWORT
BFFFFILOTU BIT OF FLUFF
BFFFIOSTTU BIT OF STUFF
BFGHIINRSU FURBISHING
BFGHILLSTU BULLFIGHTS
BFGHILNTYY FLY-BY-NIGHT
BFGILLMNUY FUMBLINGLY
BFIIILSTUY FUSIBILITY
BFIIIORSST FIBROSITIS
BFIIKORSTT BIT OF SKIRT
BFIILMMORU UMBILIFORM
BFILLLNOUW IN FULL BLOW
BFILLLSSUY BLISSFULLY
BFLMOOPTUU OUT OF PLUMB
BGGIILLNOY OBLIGINGLY
BGGIINNPRU UPBRINGING
BGHHIIRRTT BIRTHRIGHT
BGHIIIINNT INHIBITING
BGHIILNPSU PUBLISHING
BGHIINNRSU BURNISHING
BGHIKNOORU KINBOROUGH
BGHIKORRTW BRIGHTWORK
BGHILLMNUY HUMBLINGLY
BGHILLNSUY BLUSHINGLY
BGHILLOUWY WILLOUGHBY
BGHILMOORU MILBOROUGH
BGHILNNSUU UNBLUSHING
BGHIPRSTTU PITTSBURGH
BGHLOOPSUY PLOUGHBOYS
BGIIILMNOZ MOBILIZING
BGIIILNOTY IGNOBILITY
BGIIJNNOSU SUBJOINING
BGIIKLNNNU UNBLINKING
BGIILMOORS IMBROGLIOS
BGIILOOSST BIOLOGISTS
BGIIMNSTTU SUBMITTING
BGIINORSUU RUBIGINOUS
BGIINSSSTU SUBSISTING
BGIJLLMNUY JUMBLINGLY
BGIKNOPRSS SPRINGBOKS
BGILLMMNUY MUMBLINGLY
BGILLMNRUY RUMBLINGLY
BGILMNOOSS BLOSSOMING
BGILOORSTY BRYOLOGIST
BGILORSUUU LUGUBRIOUS
BGIMNNOOSU UNBOSOMING
BGINNOOORU BUON GIORNO
BGINOORRSW BORROWINGS
BHHIMORSTY BIORHYTHMS
BHHOORSTTU TOOTHBRUSH
BHIIIINNOT INHIBITION

BHIILLNOST BILLIONTHS
BHIILLRSTT STILLBIRTH
BHIILMRTTU MULTIBIRTH
BHIMOORSST THROMBOSIS
BHIMOSSTUU BISMUTHOUS
BHKNOOOTTU BUTTONHOOK
BHLLOOOSTT TOLLBOOTHS
BHLLOOSSUU HOLUS-BOLUS
BHLLRRUUYY HURLY-BURLY
BHNOPSTTUU PUSH-BUTTON
BHOOOOPSUZ ZOOPHOBOUS
BIIIILRSTY RISIBILITY
BIIIILSTVY VISIBILITY
BIIILMMOTY IMMOBILITY
BIILLOSTUY SOLUBILITY
BIILLOTUVY VOLUBILITY
BIILMOPSSY IMPOSSIBLY
BIIMNOSSSU SUBMISSION
BIIMNOSTUU BITUMINOUS
BIIOQSTUUU UBIQUITOUS
BIKLLORSST STORKSBILL
BILMOORSWW LOWBROWISM
BILNOOOTUV OBVOLUTION
BILOOPRSTU POLITBUROS
BIMNOORSTT TROMBONIST
BIMOOPPRRU OPPROBRIUM
BKLLMNSSUU NUMBSKULLS
BKMOOOPPRT PROMPTBOOK
BMMOOOSTTT BOTTOMMOST
BOOPPRRSTU TURBOPROPS
CCCEEINNOS CONSCIENCE
CCCEEINRST CRESCENTIC, ECCENTRICS
CCCEELNSUU SUCCULENCE
CCCEENORRU OCCURRENCE
CCCEHIILMY HEMICYCLIC
CCCEHIILNO COLCHICINE
CCCEHKORSS CROSSCHECK
CCCEIILPRY PERICYCLIC
CCCEIIMRSU CIRCUMCISE
CCCEILOTUY LEUCOCYTIC
CCCEINNOOP CONCEPCION
CCCEINNORT CONCENTRIC
CCCEINOOTV CONCOCTIVE
CCCEINOOTY COENOCYTIC
CCCEKLNOOR CORNCOCKLE
CCCGINNOOT CONCOCTING
CCCGNOOOSU GONOCOCCUS
CCCHILMOOY HOMOCYCLIC
CCCIIMORTY MICROCYTIC
CCCILLOPYY POLYCYCLIC
CCCILMNOOY MONOCYCLIC
CCCILNSTUY SUCCINCTLY
CCCILOPSTY POST-CYCLIC
CCCINNOOOT CONCOCTION

CCCIOOPRSY CRYOSCOPIC
CCDDEELNOY CONCEDEDLY
CCDDEENNOS CONDESCEND
CCDEEEENPR PRECEDENCE
CCDEEEHINS DEHISCENCE
CCDEEENRST DECRESCENT
CCDEEERRSU RECRUDESCE
CCDEEFIINY DEFICIENCY
CCDEEFINNO CONFIDENCE
CCDEEGINSU SUCCEEDING
CCDEEHHTUW CHEW THE CUD
CCDEEHIORT RICOCHETED
CCDEEHNOSY SYNECDOCHE
CCDEEIIIPT EPIDEICTIC
CCDEEIILRT DIELECTRIC
CCDEEIIPPR PRECIPICED
CCDEEIKLRV CLEVER DICK
CCDEEILNOR RECONCILED
CCDEELNNOO CONDOLENCE
CCDEENORSS CRESCENDOS
CCDEFILNOT CONFLICTED
CCDEHILLOS COLD CHISEL
CCDEHILNOR CHRONICLED
CCDEHLNTUU DUTCH UNCLE
CCDEIIIRST CRITICISED
CCDEIIIRTZ CRITICIZED
CCDEIILOPY EPICYCLOID
CCDEIINNOR ENDOCRINIC
CCDEIINNOT COINCIDENT
CCDEIJKOSY DISC JOCKEY
CCDEILOORS CROCODILES
CCDEIMOOOT OCTODECIMO
CCDEINNOST DISCONNECT
CCDEINOOPS ENDOSCOPIC
CCDEINOOST DECOCTIONS
CCDEINOPUU UNOCCUPIED
CCDEINORST DISCONCERT
CCDEINOTUV CONDUCTIVE
CCDENOOPRU RED PUCCOON
CCDGIIINNO COINCIDING
CCDGIILOSY GLYCOSIDIC
CCDGIKLNOU CUCKOLDING
CCDGILNNOU CONCLUDING
CCDGINNOTU CONDUCTING
CCDHIINORT CHONDRITIC
CCDIMNOSTU MISCONDUCT
CCDINNOOTU CONDUCTION
CCDNOORSTU CONDUCTORS
CCEEEEHIKP CHEEKPIECE
CCEEEELLNX EXCELLENCE
CCEEEENNSS SENESCENCE
CCEEEFNNOR CONFERENCE
CCEEEFNRSU RUFESCENCE
CCEEEGINOS GEOSCIENCE

CCEEEIINPR RECIPIENCE
CCEEEINPRS PRESCIENCE
CCEEEINQSU QUIESCENCE
CCEEEINRSV VIRESCENCE
CCEEEIOPSS ECOSPECIES
CCEEELLNXY EXCELLENCY
CCEEEMMNOR RECOMMENCE
CCEEEMNOPT COMPETENCE
CCEEEMNSTU TUMESCENCE
CCEEENRRRU RECURRENCE
CCEEENRSTX EXCRESCENT
CCEEFFIINY EFFICIENCY
CCEEFFILNO OFF-LICENCE
CCEEFHHRRU FREE CHURCH
CCEEFILLSY LIFE CYCLES
CCEEFLNNOU CONFLUENCE
CCEEGHINRS SCREECHING
CCEEGINNOR CONGENERIC
CCEEGINORS CONCIERGES
CCEEGINORT EGOCENTRIC, GEOCENTRIC
CCEEGNNORU CONGRUENCE
CCEEHINOSS CHOICENESS
CCEEHKORSU EUROCHECKS
CCEEHNOSTU ESCUTCHEON
CCEEHOSTTU COUCHETTES
CCEEIIINNP INCIPIENCE
CCEEIILMRS SEMICIRCLE
CCEEIIPPRS PRECIPICES
CCEEIKRRST CRICKETERS
CCEEILLOTV COLLECTIVE
CCEEILMNNY INCLEMENCY
CCEEILNOPU LEUCOPENIC
CCEEILNORR RECONCILER
CCEEILNORT ELECTRONIC
CCEEILOPST TELESCOPIC
CCEEILORVY COERCIVELY
CCEEINNNOT CONTINENCE
CCEEINNOTV CONNECTIVE
CCEEINNRRU INCURRENCE
CCEEINNRST INCRESCENT
CCEEINOPRW CROWNPIECE
CCEEINOPTV CONCEPTIVE
CCEEINORST CONCRETISE
CCEEINORTV CONCRETIVE
CCEEINORTX EXOCENTRIC
CCEEINORTZ CONCRETIZE
CCEEINOSSV CONCESSIVE
CCEEINOTVV CONVECTIVE
CCEEINRRSU CURRENCIES
CCEEIOPRSS CROSSPIECE
CCEEIORRTV CORRECTIVE
CCEEISSSUV SUCCESSIVE
CCEEJNORTU CONJECTURE
CCEELMORTY CYCLOMETER

CCEELNOPRU CORPULENCE
CCEELNORTY CONCRETELY
CCEELNRTUU TRUCULENCE
CCEELOSTTU COS LETTUCE
CCEELOSTUY LEUCOCYTES
CCEEMNOPTY COMPETENCY
CCEENOPRRT PRECONCERT
CCEFHIIMOR MICROFICHE
CCEFIIINST SCIENTIFIC
CCEFIINPSU UNSPECIFIC
CCEFIIRSUX CRUCIFIXES
CCEFIKLSTT CLEFT STICK
CCEFILMRUX CIRCUMFLEX
CCEFIMRSUU CIRCUMFUSE
CCEFINNOOT CONFECTION
CCEFLLNOTU FLOCCULENT
CCEFLSSSUU SUCCESSFUL
CCEGGHOSST SCOTCH EGGS
CCEGGILNOY GLYCOGENIC
CCEGHHORRU CHURCHGOER
CCEGHIIIOP PICHICIEGO
CCEGHINORT CROCHETING
CCEGIILNNR ENCIRCLING
CCEGIINNOV CONCEIVING
CCEGILLNOT COLLECTING
CCEGIMMNNO COMMENCING
CCEGINNNOR CONCERNING
CCEGINNNOS ENSCONCING
CCEGINNNOT CONNECTING
CCEGINNORT CONCRETING
CCEGINORRT CORRECTING
CCEGINORSY CRYOGENICS
CCEHHILOTV CLOVE HITCH
CCEHIINNNO CINCHONINE
CCEHIINNOS CINCHONISE
CCEHIINNOZ CINCHONIZE
CCEHIKLSST CHECKLISTS
CCEHIKMOOR MOCK-HEROIC
CCEHIKNOPT CHECKPOINT
CCEHIKNOPX CHICKEN POX
CCEHILNORR CHRONICLER
CCEHILNORS CHRONICLES
CCEHIMOSSY ECCHYMOSIS
CCEHINRSTU CRUNCHIEST
CCEHKMOORS CHECKROOMS
CCEHKOORSS COCKHORSES
CCEHKOPSST SPOT CHECKS
CCEHKORTUU CHUCKER-OUT
CCEHMOORTY CYTOCHROME
CCEIIINNPY INCIPIENCY
CCEIIIRRST CRITICISER
CCEIIIRRTZ CRITICIZER
CCEIIIRSTV CERVICITIS
CCEIIKNPRS PICNICKERS

CCEIILMNOR MICROCLINE
CCEIILOSST SOLECISTIC
CCEIIMOORS SERIOCOMIC
CCEIIMPSST SCEPTICISM
CCEIINOTVV CONVICTIVE
CCEIINRTTY CENTRICITY
CCEIIOPPRS PERISCOPIC
CCEIIORTVY COERCIVITY
CCEIKKOPPT PICKPOCKET
CCEIKMNOSY COCKNEYISM
CCEILLLOSU CELLULOSIC
CCEILLNOOT COLLECTION
CCEILMNNOU COUNCILMEN
CCEILNNOSU NUCLEONICS
CCEILNOSUV CONCLUSIVE
CCEILOOQTU COQUELICOT
CCEIMNNOOU UNECONOMIC
CCEIMNRTUV CIRCUMVENT
CCEIMOOPRS MICROSCOPE
CCEINNNOOT CONNECTION
CCEINNOOPT CONCEPTION
CCEINNOORT CONCERTINO,
     CONCRETION
CCEINNOOSS CONCESSION
CCEINNOOTV CONVECTION
CCEINOOOPS ICONOSCOPE
CCEINOOORRT CORRECTION
CCEINOSSSU SUCCESSION
CCEINOSSUV CONCUSSIVE
CCEIOOPRSU PRECOCIOUS
CCEIOPRSST COST PRICES
CCEISSSUUV SUCCUSSIVE
CCEKLOORTW CLOCK TOWER
CCEKORRSSW CORKSCREWS
CCELLOORST COLLECTORS
CCELLOSTYY CYCLOSTYLE
CCELMOORTY MOTORCYCLE
CCELMOOSTY CYCLOSTOME
CCELMORTYY CYCLOMETRY
CCELNSSTUU SUCCULENTS
CCELOPRSSU CORPUSCLES
CCEMOSTTYY CYSTECTOMY
CCENNORRTU CONCURRENT
CCENOORSSU CONCOURSES
CCENOORSTV CONVECTORS
CCENOPSSTU CONSPECTUS
CCEOOPSSTY CYSTOSCOPE
CCEORSSSSU SUCCESSORS
CCFGHIKOST COCKFIGHTS
CCFGIINRUY CRUCIFYING
CCFILMORUU CUCULIFORM
CCGHHHHIRU HIGH CHURCH
CCGHINNRSU SCRUNCHING
CCGHLNOOOY CONCHOLOGY

CCGIIIKNNP PICNICKING
CCGIINNNOV CONVINCING
CCGIINNOTV CONVICTING
CCGILORSUY GLYCOSURIC
CCGIMNOOOS COSMOGONIC
CCGINNORRU CONCURRING
CCGINNOSSU CONCUSSING
CCGINORSUU SUCCOURING
CCGIOOPRSY GYROSCOPIC
CCHHHOOPTT HOTCHPOTCH
CCHHIIOTTY ICHTHYOTIC
CCHIIIRSTT TRISTICHIC
CCHIILNNOO CONCHIOLIN
CCHIILOPRY CRYOPHILIC
CCHIIMNNOS CINCHONISM
CCHIIMOPRS MICROCHIPS
CCHIINORTY CHRONICITY
CCHIKLOSTT LOCKSTITCH
CCHIKOPSST CHOPSTICKS
CCHIMOSSTT SCOTCH MIST
CCHINNORSY SYNCHRONIC
CCHIOOOPRS HOROSCOPIC
CCHIOPSSTY PSYCHOTICS
CCHIORSTTY TRICHOCYST
CCHKLNOSUU NO SUCH LUCK
CCHNOOSTUY COCONUT SHY
CCHOOPSSUU HOCUS-POCUS
CCIIIMRSST CRITICISMS
CCIILLNOPY POLYCLINIC
CCIILMNNOO MONOCLINIC
CCIILMOPTY COMPLICITY
CCIILNSTUY UNICYCLIST
CCIILOOPRT COPROLITIC
CCIILOORST COLORISTIC
CCIIMMOORT MICROTOMIC
CCIIMOPRST COMIC STRIP
CCIIMOSSTT SCOTTICISM
CCIINNNOTY CONCINNITY
CCIINNOOTV CONVICTION
CCIINOOPRS SCORPIONIC
CCIIOOPRTX PICROTOXIC
CCIIORSTUU CIRCUITOUS
CCIKNOOPTU CUCKOOPINT
CCILLNOORU COUNCILLOR
CCILLOOPTY COLLOTYPIC
CCILMRRUUU CURRICULUM
CCILNNOOSU CONCLUSION
CCILNOORSU COUNCILORS
CCIMMOORSS MICROCOSMS
CCIMOOPRSY MICROSCOPY
CCINNNOOSU CONCINNOUS
CCINNOOSSU CONCUSSION
CCINOPRSST CONSCRIPTS
CCINOSSSUU SUCCUSSION

CCINOSTUVY VISCOUNTCY
CCIOOPRTYZ CRYPTOZOIC
CCIOPPRRTY PROCRYPTIC
CCIORRSSSS CRISSCROSS
CCNOORRTUW CROWN COURT
CCNORSSTTU CONSTRUCTS
CCOOPSSTYY CYSTOSCOPY
CDDEEEENNP DEPENDENCE
CDDEEEHIPR DECIPHERED
CDDEEEINRT INTERCEDED
CDDEEEINUV UNDECEIVED
CDDEEEIRRT REDIRECTED
CDDEEEJLTY DEJECTEDLY
CDDEEENNPY DEPENDENCY
CDDEEENNST DESCENDENT
CDDEEFFIIN DIFFIDENCE
CDDEEGINNS DESCENDING
CDDEEIINSS DISSIDENCE
CDDEEIJPRU PREJUDICED
CDDEEIMNOR ENDODERMIC
CDDEEINORS CONSIDERED
CDDEEINRTU UNDIRECTED
CDDEEIORSV DISCOVERED
CDDEELMOSU CUDDLESOME
CDDEEMNOTU DOCUMENTED
CDDEEMOOPS DECOMPOSED
CDDEEOPRRU REPRODUCED
CDDEFNNOOU CONFOUNDED
CDDEHIILOR DICHLORIDE
CDDEIIOSSV VIDEODISCS
CDDEILOORS DISCOLORED
CDDEIMMNOO INCOMMODED
CDDEIMMOOS DISCOMMODE
CDDEINNOOT ENDODONTIC
CDDEINNOSW SECOND WIND
CDDEINORTU INTRODUCED
CDDEINOSTU DEDUCTIONS, DISCOUNTED
CDDEIORSSU DISCOURSED
CDDEMNOOPU COMPOUNDED,
   DECOMPOUND
CDDENOPRTU END PRODUCT
CDDEOORTUW CROWDED OUT
CDDHILLOSY CLODDISHLY
CDDIILNORY CYLINDROID
CDDILOOPSU DIPLODOCUS
CDDINNOOTY DICYNODONT
CDEEEEINPX EXPEDIENCE
CDEEEENRRT DETERRENCE
CDEEEENRRV REVERENCED
CDEEEFFHOS CHEESED OFF
CDEEEFFINR DIFFERENCE
CDEEEFFIST SIDE EFFECT
CDEEEFHIKR KERCHIEFED
CDEEEFILTV DEFLECTIVE

CDEEEFMNNS MEND FENCES	CDEEHKNPUY KEYPUNCHED
CDEEEGINRV DIVERGENCE	CDEEHLRTWY WRETCHEDLY
CDEEEGNRTY DETERGENCY	CDEEHMNOPR COMPREHEND
CDEEEHIPRR DECIPHERER	CDEEIIINSV INDECISIVE
CDEEEHLRSU RESCHEDULE	CDEEIILSVY DECISIVELY
CDEEEHNNRT ENTRENCHED	CDEEIIMNRS REMINISCED
CDEEEHNRRT RETRENCHED	CDEEIIMPRS SPERMICIDE
CDEEEIINNV IN EVIDENCE	CDEEIIMRST METRICISED
CDEEEIINRS DECREE NISI	CDEEIIMRTZ METRICIZED
CDEEEILOPV VELOCIPEDE	CDEEIINRST INDISCREET, INDISCRETE,
CDEEEILQSU DELIQUESCE	IRIDESCENT
CDEEEIMNNO COMEDIENNE	CDEEIIORRT CORDIERITE, DIRECTOIRE
CDEEEIMNNP IMPENDENCE	CDEEIIPRTV PREDICTIVE
CDEEEINNST TENDENCIES	CDEEIIPSST PESTICIDES
CDEEEINPST CENTIPEDES	CDEEIIRSSV DISSERVICE
CDEEEINPXY EXPEDIENCY	CDEEIIRSTV DIRECTIVES
CDEEEINRRT INTERCEDER	CDEEIJPRSU PREJUDICES
CDEEEINRSS RESIDENCES	CDEEIKNSSW WICKEDNESS
CDEEEINRSW WIDE-SCREEN	CDEEILLNST STENCILLED
CDEEEINRUV UNDECEIVER	CDEEILNNOS DECLENSION
CDEEEISTTV DETECTIVES	CDEEILNNSU UNLICENSED
CDEEELOPST TELESCOPED	CDEEILNNTY INDECENTLY
CDEEELORST ELECTRODES	CDEEILNOOS DECOLONISE
CDEEEMNNOT ENCODEMENT	CDEEILNOOZ DECOLONIZE
CDEEENNRSU UNSCREENED	CDEEILNOSU NUCLEOSIDE
CDEEENPRST PRECEDENTS	CDEEILNOTU NUCLEOTIDE
CDEEENPTUX UNEXPECTED	CDEEILOORS DECOLORISE
CDEEEPRSTU PERSECUTED	CDEEILOORZ DECOLORIZE
CDEEFGILNT DEFLECTING	CDEEILORST CLOISTERED
CDEEFIINRT DENTIFRICE	CDEEILRSTY DISCREETLY, DISCRETELY
CDEEFILNNU INFLUENCED	CDEEIMMOXY MYXOEDEMIC
CDEEFILNOT DEFLECTION	CDEEIMNNTU INDUCEMENT
CDEEFINORR REINFORCED	CDEEIMNOOS ECONOMISED
CDEEFINOST DEFECTIONS	CDEEIMNOOZ ECONOMIZED
CDEEFINTUV DEFUNCTIVE	CDEEIMNOSU EUDEMONICS
CDEEFKLPSY FLYSPECKED	CDEEIMNPRU IMPRUDENCE
CDEEFLNORT CENTER-FOLD, CENTRE-	CDEEINNRSW WINDSCREEN
FOLD	CDEEINNSSU SECUNDINES
CDEEFLNORY ENFORCEDLY	CDEEINOPRV PROVIDENCE
CDEEFLOORS FORECLOSED	CDEEINOPST DECEPTIONS
CDEEFNORSS FORCEDNESS	CDEEINORRS CONSIDERER, RECONSIDER
CDEEGHHITT GET HITCHED	CDEEINORTT CREDIT NOTE
CDEEGIIMRS GERMICIDES	CDEEINPRRU UNDERPRICE
CDEEGIKNNR RING-NECKED	CDEEINPRSY PRESIDENCY
CDEEGILNNU INDULGENCE	CDEEINRSST DIRECTNESS
CDEEGILNUV DIVULGENCE	CDEEINRSTY DYSENTERIC
CDEEGINOPR PROCEEDING	CDEEIORRSV DISCOVERER
CDEEGINORS RECOGNISED	CDEEIPRSST DISRESPECT
CDEEGINORZ RECOGNIZED	CDEEIRRSST DIRECTRESS
CDEEGINRVY DIVERGENCY	CDEEIRRSTT RESTRICTED
CDEEHIILOP OPHICLEIDE	CDEEKKKNNO KNOCK-KNEED
CDEEHIMNOR ECHINODERM	CDEEKOOPRW WOODPECKER
CDEEHINNRT INTRENCHED	CDEELLNOSU COUNSELLED
CDEEHINRST CHRISTENED	CDEELLNRSU CULLENDERS

CDEELNOSSY CLOYEDNESS
CDEEMNNOST SECONDMENT
CDEEMOOPRS DECOMPOSER
CDEEMOPRSS COMPRESSED, DECOMPRESS
CDEENNORSS CONDENSERS
CDEENNORST CONTENDERS
CDEENOORRS ROOD SCREEN
CDEENOOSTT COTTONSEED
CDEENORRSU UNDERSCORE
CDEENORRUV UNDERCOVER
CDEENOSTUU CONSUETUDE
CDEENSSSSU CUSSEDNESS
CDEEOPPRST PROSPECTED
CDEEOPRRRU REPRODUCER
CDEEOPRRSU PROCEDURES
CDEEOPRSTU PROSECUTED
CDEERSSSTU SEDUCTRESS
CDEFFIIRTU FRUCTIFIED
CDEFGHIKLT FLIGHT DECK
CDEFGIINSU FUNGICIDES
CDEFGIKNOR DEFROCKING
CDEFHILOSS COLD FISHES
CDEFILNOUU FLUID OUNCE
CDEFINNNOU UNCONFINED
CDEFINNOTU FUNCTIONED
CDEFINOORV CONFERVOID
CDEFLNOSUY CONFUSEDLY
CDEFNNOORT CONFRONTED
CDEFNNOORU CONFOUNDER
CDEFNORRTU UNDERCROFT
CDEGGILLNU CUDGELLING
CDEGHILNSU SCHEDULING
CDEGIINNRS DISCERNING, RESCINDING
CDEGIINPRT PREDICTING
CDEGIINSST DISSECTING
CDEGILNOPU DECOUPLING
CDEGILNPRU PRECLUDING
CDEGILNSUY SEDUCINGLY
CDEGIMMNNO COMMENDING
CDEGIMNNNO CONDEMNING
CDEGINNNOS CONDENSING
CDEGINNNOT CONTENDING
CDEGINNNOU DENOUNCING
CDEGINORRS RECORDINGS
CDEGMNORUU CURMUDGEON
CDEGNORRUW GROUND CREW
CDEHHHIIKT HITCHHIKED
CDEHHIIRRT THIRD REICH
CDEHIIISTT DITHEISTIC
CDEHIILOPS DISCOPHILE
CDEHIILORU HIERODULIC
CDEHIILPTY DIPHYLETIC
CDEHIINOST HEDONISTIC
CDEHILOPTW LOW-PITCHED

CDEHIMOPRY HYPODERMIC
CDEHINOPST DOCENTSHIP
CDEHINOPTY ENDOPHYTIC
CDEHINOSTW SWITCHED-ON
CDEHLNOOSU UNSCHOOLED
CDEHLOOPPR CLODHOPPER
CDEHLOOPRY COPYHOLDER
CDEHLOOPSS CLOSED SHOP
CDEHNOSTUV DUTCH OVENS
CDEHOPTTUY TOUCH-TYPED
CDEIIILNNS DISINCLINE
CDEIIILNPS DISCIPLINE
CDEIIIMRSV RECIDIVISM
CDEIIIMSTV VICTIMISED
CDEIIIMTVZ VICTIMIZED
CDEIIINNOS INDECISION
CDEIIINTVV VINDICTIVE
CDEIIIRSTV RECIDIVIST
CDEIILNPPR PRINCIPLED
CDEIILNRTY INDIRECTLY
CDEIILOSTU SOLICITUDE
CDEIIMNNTT INDICTMENT
CDEIIMNOST MIDSECTION
CDEIIMOORT IODOMETRIC
CDEIIMORRS MISERICORD
CDEIIMORST DOSIMETRIC
CDEIIMORTY IRIDECTOMY, MEDIOCRITY
CDEIIMPPSU PIPED MUSIC
CDEIINOPRT PREDICTION
CDEIINOPST DEPICTIONS
CDEIINORST DIRECTIONS, DISCRETION
CDEIINORTY TYROCIDINE
CDEIINOSST DISSECTION
CDEIINRSTT INTERDICTS
CDEIIOORRS SORORICIDE
CDEIIPRSTU PEDICURIST
CDEIIRSSUV DISCURSIVE
CDEIKLOPST STOCKPILED
CDEIKNRRTU UNDERTRICK
CDEIKNRSUW WINDSUCKER
CDEIKNSSTY STICKY ENDS
CDEILLLPUY PELLUCIDLY
CDEILNOSSU CLOUDINESS
CDEILOPSUU PEDICULOUS
CDEILORSSS CROSS-SLIDE
CDEILORSSU DISCLOSURE
CDEIMMNOPU COMPENDIUM
CDEIMNNOST CONDIMENTS
CDEIMNOOST ENDOSMOTIC
CDEIMNOPRS PRINCEDOMS
CDEIMNOSTU MISCOUNTED
CDEIMOOPSS DISCOMPOSE
CDEIMOSSTU CUSTOMISED
CDEIMOSTUZ CUSTOMIZED

CDEINNOSTT DISCONTENT
CDEINOORSU INDECOROUS
CDEINORRTU INTRODUCER
CDEINORSSX CROSS-INDEX
CDEINORSTU DISCOUNTER, REDISCOUNT,
  REDUCTIONS
CDEINPRSTU UNSCRIPTED
CDEINRSTTU INSTRUCTED
CDEIOPRTUV PRODUCTIVE
CDEIORRSSU DISCOURSER
CDEIORSSSU DISCOURSES
CDEKLORTUY COLD TURKEY
CDEKNORSTU UNDERSTOCK
CDELLNOORT CONTROLLED
CDELNOORUY EUROCLYDON
CDELNOOSSW CLOSEDOWNS
CDELNOOTUV CONVOLUTED
CDELNORSSU SCOUNDRELS
CDELOORSUY DECOROUSLY
CDELPRSTUU SCULPTURED
CDEMMOOORS COMMODORES,
  COSMODROME
CDEMNOOPRU COMPOUNDER
CDENNOOPRU PRONOUNCED
CDENOOPRRS CORRESPOND
CDEOORTTUW WOODCUTTER
CDEORRSTTU DESTRUCTOR
CDERRSTTUU STRUCTURED
CDFFIILTUY DIFFICULTY
CDFIMOORST DISCOMFORT
CDFLNOORST COLD FRONTS
CDGHIILMOU GLOCHIDIUM
CDGHILOORY HYDROLOGIC
CDGIIILNRU RIDICULING
CDGIIKNNOO IN GOOD NICK
CDGIILNOSS DISCLOSING
CDGIINSSSU DISCUSSING
CDGIKLLOOS GOLDILOCKS
CDGILLNOSY SCOLDINGLY
CDHHIILLSY CHILDISHLY
CDHHILOSST DISHCLOTHS
CDHIIINOOP IDIOPHONIC
CDHIINPSSY SYNDICSHIP
CDHIIOSSTU DISTICHOUS
CDHILORTYY HYDROLYTIC
CDHINOOPRY HYDROPONIC
CDHIOPRSTY DYSTROPHIC
CDHKNNPRUU PUNCH-DRUNK
CDHLLOOOSS OLD SCHOOLS
CDHNOOSTUW TOUCHDOWNS
CDIIILNOTY INDOCILITY
CDIIINNSTT INDISTINCT
CDIIKRRTTY DIRTY TRICK
CDIILNOOSU NIDICOLOUS

CDIILNSTTY DISTINCTLY
CDIILOPPSY POLYDIPSIC
CDIILORSUU RIDICULOUS
CDIIMNORST DOCTRINISM
CDIINNOOST CONDITIONS
CDIINNOSTU INDUCTIONS
CDIINOSSSU DISCUSSION
CDIKLLORST DRILLSTOCK
CDIKMRSSTU DRUMSTICKS
CDIKORSSTW SWORDSTICK
CDILLMOOSU MOLLUSCOID
CDILMOOORX LOXODROMIC
CDILMOOPUY LYCOPODIUM
CDIMMOOOSU COMMODIOUS
CDIMNOOOTY MONOCYTOID
CDINOOPRTU PRODUCTION
CDINORSSSW CROSSWINDS
CDLMOORSTU STORM CLOUD
CDMNNORSUU CONUNDRUMS
CDNNOOSTUW COUNTDOWNS
CDNOOOOTTW COTTONWOOD
CDOORRSSSW CROSSWORDS
CEEEEFFRSV EFFERVESCE
CEEEEFNPRR PREFERENCE
CEEEEFNRRR REFERENCER
CEEEEFNRRS REFERENCES
CEEEEGIPTX EPEXEGETIC
CEEEEHIPRT THREE-PIECE
CEEEEHNPRT THREEPENCE
CEEEEIMRST CEMETERIES
CEEEEINPRX EXPERIENCE
CEEEELLNPR REPELLENCE
CEEEENRRRV REVERENCER
CEEEENRRSV REVERENCES
CEEEFFGLNU EFFULGENCE
CEEEFFLORS EFFLORESCE
CEEEFGLNRU REFULGENCE
CEEEFILNSS FLEECINESS
CEEEFILRTV REFLECTIVE
CEEEFINNRS INFERENCES
CEEEFINRRT CENTER-FIRE, CENTRE-FIRE
CEEEFINRSS FIERCENESS
CEEEFIPRTV PERFECTIVE
CEEEFNORRR RE-ENFORCER
CEEEFPRRTU PREFECTURE
CEEEGGILNN NEGLIGENCE
CEEEGIINPT EPIGENETIC
CEEEGIINSX EXIGENCIES
CEEEGILNRT RE-ELECTING
CEEEGINORS RECOGNISEE
CEEEGINORZ RECOGNIZEE
CEEEGINRST ENERGETICS
CEEEGINRTV VICEGERENT
CEEEGLNORS CONGER EELS

CEEEGNRRSU RESURGENCE
CEEEHHLORS HORSELEECH
CEEEHIKNSS CHEEKINESS
CEEEHIMSTT CHEMISETTE
CEEEHINPRR ENCIPHERER
CEEEHINPTT EPENTHETIC
CEEEHINRSS CHEERINESS
CEEEHINSSS CHEESINESS
CEEEHKPRTU UP THE CREEK
CEEEHLLSSY SEYCHELLES
CEEEHLPSSS SPEECHLESS
CEEEHMMNSY MESENCHYME
CEEEHNNRRT ENTRENCHER
CEEEHOQRUU EUROCHEQUE
CEEEIILNRS RESILIENCE
CEEEIIMPST TIMEPIECES
CEEEIINRSV VICEREINES
CEEEILLMNO EMOLLIENCE
CEEEILLNST CLIENTELES
CEEEILMNNT CLEMENTINE
CEEEILMORT CEILOMETER
CEEEILMRTT TELEMETRIC
CEEEILNORT RE-ELECTION
CEEEILNPRT PERCENTILE
CEEEILNPST PESTILENCE
CEEEIMNNTT ENTICEMENT
CEEEIMNORS CEREMONIES
CEEEIMNRST MESENTERIC
CEEEIMNRSV SERVICEMEN
CEEEIMNRTT CENTIMETER, CENTIMETRE,
   REMITTENCE
CEEEIMNTTX EXCITEMENT
CEEEINNPRT PERTINENCE
CEEEINPRSS CREEPINESS
CEEEINPRST EPICENTERS, EPICENTRES
CEEEINSSTX EXISTENCES
CEEEINTTWY WINCEYETTE
CEEEIORRST CORSETIERE
CEEEIORRSV RECOVERIES
CEEEIPPRTV PERCEPTIVE, PRECEPTIVE
CEEEIPRSTV RESPECTIVE
CEEEISTUVX EXECUTIVES
CEEEJLORTT ELECTROJET
CEEEKKLOPR LOCK KEEPER
CEEEKRRSSU SEERSUCKER
CEEELNOORU NEUROCOELE
CEEELNRSSV CLEVERNESS
CEEELNSSST SELECTNESS
CEEELOPSST TELESCOPES
CEEEMNOPRS RECOMPENSE
CEEEMNORRT CENTROMERE
CEEEMNOTYZ ECTOENZYME
CEEEMNRSTU SECUREMENT
CEEENNRSST RECENTNESS

CEEENOPRST OPEN SECRET
CEEENRSSSU SECURENESS
CEEENRSSTT SCREEN TEST
CEEEPRRSST RESPECTERS
CEEFFHIMOO HOME OFFICE
CEEFFHOOPS COFFEE SHOP
CEEFFOOPST COFFEEPOTS
CEEFGHINNR GREENFINCH
CEEFGILNRT REFLECTING
CEEFGINPRT PERFECTING
CEEFGINRTU CENTRIFUGE
CEEFGLLNTU NEGLECTFUL
CEEFHHNORT HENCEFORTH
CEEFHLLRUY CHEERFULLY
CEEFHORTTU FOURCHETTE
CEEFIIILST FELICITIES
CEEFIILNTV INFLECTIVE
CEEFIIORST FEROCITIES
CEEFIIRRST RECTIFIERS
CEEFIKLNSS FICKLENESS
CEEFILNNRU INFLUENCER
CEEFILNNSU INFLUENCES
CEEFILNORT REFLECTION
CEEFINOPRT PERFECTION
CEEFKLLSSY FECKLESSLY
CEEFLNOORW CONEFLOWER
CEEFLORRST REFLECTORS
CEEFLPPRTU PLUPERFECT
CEEFLPRSTU RESPECTFUL
CEEFMNNORT CONFERMENT
CEEFNRSTTU FRUTESCENT
CEEFOORRSU FORECOURSE
CEEFORRRSS CROSS-REFER
CEEGGILNNT NEGLECTING
CEEGHIILMP HEMIPLEGIC
CEEGHIMOST GEOCHEMIST
CEEGHINNOT ETHNOGENIC
CEEGHKMNRU KREMENCHUG
CEEGHLOPST CLOTHES PEG
CEEGIINOPR EPIROGENIC
CEEGIINOTV GIVE NOTICE
CEEGIINPRV PERCEIVING
CEEGIINRSX EXERCISING
CEEGIINSTT GENETICIST
CEEGIINSTU EUGENICIST
CEEGINNNST SENTENCING
CEEGINNORU NEUROGENIC
CEEGINNOSS CONSIGNEES
CEEGINNQSU SEQUENCING
CEEGINNRSS SCREENINGS
CEEGINNRST NIGRESCENT
CEEGINNRSU INSURGENCE
CEEGINOORT EROTOGENIC
CEEGINORRS RECOGNISER

CEEGINORRV RE-COVERING
CEEGINORRZ RECOGNIZER
CEEGINOSTV CONGESTIVE
CEEGINPRST RESPECTING
CEEGINRSTY SYNERGETIC
CEEGNNORTV CONVERGENT
CEEGNOOSTU ECTOGENOUS
CEEGNORSSS CONGRESSES
CEEGNRSTTU TURGESCENT
CEEGORSTTU COURGETTES
CEEHHHIMOR HOCHHEIMER
CEEHHIMORT COME HITHER
CEEHHOPSST HOPE CHESTS
CEEHIIMRST ERETHISMIC
CEEHIKNRST THICKENERS
CEEHIKPPRS SCHIPPERKE
CEEHIKSSTT SKETCHIEST
CEEHILLRSS CHISELLERS
CEEHILNORU EUCHLORINE
CEEHILOPRT HELICOPTER
CEEHILORRT LOIR-ET-CHER
CEEHILOSVY COHESIVELY
CEEHILQRSU SQUELCHIER
CEEHIMNNRT ENRICHMENT
CEEHIMNTTU TECHNETIUM
CEEHIMOPTU MOUTHPIECE
CEEHIMORRT RHEOMETRIC
CEEHIMORTX EXOTHERMIC
CEEHIMSSTU SHEET MUSIC
CEEHINNORT INCOHERENT
CEEHINOPPR HIPPOCRENE
CEEHINQSTU TECHNIQUES
CEEHINRRST CHRISTENER, RECHRISTEN
CEEHINRSTW WINCHESTER
CEEHINSSST CHESTINESS
CEEHINSSTT TETCHINESS
CEEHIOPPRS PROPHECIES
CEEHIOPSSW SHOWPIECES
CEEHIORSTT THEORETICS
CEEHIRRSTT STRETCHIER
CEEHKKOOYY HOKEY COKEY
CEEHKNPRUY KEYPUNCHER
CEEHKNPSUY KEYPUNCHES
CEEHLLNOSW WELL-CHOSEN
CEEHLNORTY COHERENTLY
CEEHLPRSSU SEPULCHRES
CEEHMMOORR CHROMOMERE
CEEHNNOSSU NONESUCHES
CEEHNOOPPS NEPHOSCOPE
CEEHNOOPRT CTENOPHORE
CEEHRRSSTT STRETCHERS
CEEIIKLNPR PINCERLIKE
CEEIILLLOS ICE LOLLIES
CEEIILLMRV VERMICELLI

CEEIILLORS COLLIERIES
CEEIILNOSU ISOLEUCINE
CEEIILNRSY RESILIENCY
CEEIILNRTT CENTILITER, CENTILITRE
CEEIILOSTV VELOCITIES
CEEIILPPST EPILEPTICS
CEEIILPRSV LIP SERVICE
CEEIILRTTY ERECTILITY
CEEIILTTVY ELECTIVITY
CEEIIMNNTT INCITEMENT
CEEIIMORTT METEORITIC
CEEIIMPRRT PERIMETRIC
CEEIINNSST INSISTENCE
CEEIINNSTV INCENTIVES
CEEIINOPST CENTIPOISE
CEEIINPPRT PERCIPIENT
CEEIINPRST RECIPIENTS
CEEIINPSTV INSPECTIVE
CEEIINRSTT INTERSTICE
CEEIINTTVX EXTINCTIVE
CEEIIORRST ESCRITOIRE
CEEIIRSSTU SECURITIES
CEEIJLOPRT PROJECTILE
CEEIJNORST REJECTIONS
CEEIJOPRTV PROJECTIVE
CEEIJRSTUV SURJECTIVE
CEEIKLNRSS SILK SCREEN
CEEIKNPRTY PERNICKETY
CEEIKNSSSS SICKNESSES
CEEILLNRST STENCILLER
CEEILLNSTT INTELLECTS
CEEILLOOPT COLEOPTILE
CEEILLORSS RECOILLESS
CEEILLRSSU SCULLERIES
CEEILMNOPT INCOMPLETE
CEEILMNORT CLINOMETER
CEEILMNOSS COMELINESS
CEEILMOPTV COMPLETIVE
CEEILNOSST SELECTIONS
CEEILNQSTU LIQUESCENT
CEEILNRSTV VENTRICLES
CEEILNRSUY INSECURELY
CEEILNRTTY RETICENTLY
CEEILPRSTT TELESCRIPT
CEEILPRSUV PRECLUSIVE
CEEILSSUVX EXCLUSIVES
CEEIMMOPRT EMMETROPIC
CEEIMMORRT MICROMETER
CEEIMMOSTT COMMITTEES
CEEIMNNOPR PROMINENCE
CEEIMNNRST INCREMENTS
CEEIMNOORS ECONOMISER
CEEIMNOORZ ECONOMIZER
CEEIMORSTV VISCOMETER

CEEIMOSSTV VICOMTESSE
CEEINNNOTV CONVENIENT
CEEINNPSST SPINESCENT
CEEINOPPRT PERCEPTION
CEEINOPRSS PRECESSION
CEEINOPRST RECEPTIONS
CEEINOPSTX EXCEPTIONS
CEEINORRST CORRIENTES
CEEINORSSS RECESSIONS
CEEINORSST SECRETIONS
CEEINORSTV VENTRICOSE
CEEINORSTX EXCRETIONS
CEEINOSSTX EXOTICNESS
CEEINOSTTX COEXISTENT
CEEINOSTUX EXECUTIONS
CEEINPRSSS PRINCESSES
CEEINPRSTU PUTRESCINE
CEEINRRSTU SCRUTINEER
CEEINRSSTY SYNCRETISE
CEEINRSTTV VITRESCENT
CEEINRSTYZ SYNCRETIZE
CEEIOORSVV VOICE-OVERS
CEEIOPPRSS PERISCOPES
CEEIOPRTTV PROTECTIVE
CEEIOQRSTU COQUETRIES
CEEIORSSTU COURTESIES
CEEIPRSSUV PERCUSSIVE
CEEIPSSTUV SUSCEPTIVE
CEEKLLRSSY RECKLESSLY
CEEKLNRTTU TURTLENECK
CEEKLORRWW CREWELWORK
CEELLMOPTY COMPLETELY
CEELMMNOPT COMPLEMENT
CEELMNNOOS SOMNOLENCE
CEELMOORTU COULOMETER
CEELNORSSU ENCLOSURES
CEELNORSVY CONVERSELY
CEELORRSTY CLERESTORY
CEEMMOTXYY MYXOMYCETE
CEEMNNSTTY ENCYSTMENT
CEEMNOORST CENTROSOME
CEEMNOPRTU RECOUPMENT
CEEMNOPRTY PYCNOMETER
CEEMNORTUY NEURECTOMY
CEEMNPSSTU SPUMESCENT
CEEMOPRSSS COMPRESSES
CEEMOSSSTY ECOSYSTEMS
CEENNOQSTU CONSEQUENT
CEENNORSTU ENCOUNTERS
CEENNPRSSY PENNYCRESS
CEENOORSTV COVER NOTES
CEENOPPPRR PEPPERCORN
CEENOPPRTY PREPOTENCY
CEENOPRRST PRECENTORS

CEENORRSTV CONVERTERS
CEENORTTUX CONTEXTURE
CEENOSSSTU COUNTESSES
CEENPRSSSU SPRUCENESS
CEENPRSTTU PUTRESCENT
CEEOPRRSTT RETROSPECT
CEEOPRRSTU PERSECUTOR
CEEOQRSTTU CROQUETTES
CEEORRSSST CROSSTREES
CEFFFFHOTU OFF THE CUFF
CEFFHIINOR CHIFFONIER
CEFFIIKKLN FLICK KNIFE
CEFFIINSTU SUFFICIENT
CEFFIIRRTU FRUCTIFIER
CEFFIOOPST POST OFFICE
CEFFIRSSTU SCRUFFIEST
CEFFLLORUY FORCEFULLY
CEFGHILNST FLETCHINGS
CEFGHILNTY FETCHINGLY
CEFGIIKLNR FLICKERING
CEFGIILNNT INFLECTING
CEFGIINPSY SPECIFYING
CEFGIINRTY CERTIFYING, RECTIFYING
CEFGINNORR CONFERRING
CEFGINNOSS CONFESSING
CEFGLOORSU GOLF COURSE
CEFHHNNORR FRENCH HORN
CEFHIILSSS FISH SLICES
CEFHIIRRST FIRST REICH
CEFHIKNRSS FRENCH KISS
CEFHIKRSSU SUCKERFISH
CEFHILSTTU CUTTLEFISH
CEFIIILNTV INFLICTIVE
CEFIIILNTY INFELICITY
CEFIILNNOT INFLECTION
CEFIILNOQU CINQUEFOIL
CEFIILOSTU FELICITOUS
CEFIIMNNTU MUNIFICENT
CEFIINNOST INFECTIONS
CEFIINOPRT PROFICIENT
CEFIINOSTU INFECTIOUS
CEFILLMRUY MERCIFULLY
CEFILMNRUU UNMERCIFUL
CEFILMOORS FROLICSOME
CEFIMORSUY CYMIFEROUS
CEFINNOOSS CONFESSION
CEFINOORSU CONIFEROUS
CEFIOORSUV VOCIFEROUS
CEFKLOPSTU POCKETFULS
CEFLNOORRW CORNFLOWER
CEFMNOORRS CONFORMERS
CEFMOORRST COMFORTERS
CEFNNOORRT CONFRONTER
CEFNOORSSS CONFESSORS

CEFOORRSTU FORECOURTS
CEGGHIMNUW CHEWING GUM
CEGGILNOSS CLOGGINESS
CEGGINNORV CONVERGING
CEGGINOOST GEOGNOSTIC
CEGHHIINRS CHERISHING
CEGHIIKNNT THICKENING
CEGHIIKNRW WHICKERING
CEGHIILLNS CHISELLING
CEGHIILOOR HIEROLOGIC
CEGHIINNUY UNHYGIENIC
CEGHIINORZ RHIZOGENIC
CEGHILMNSY SCHEMINGLY
CEGHILNOOT ETHNOLOGIC
CEGHILNOPY PHYLOGENIC
CEGHILNOST CLOSE THING
CEGHILNPPS SCHLEPPING
CEGHILNQSU SQUELCHING
CEGHIMMNOO HOMECOMING
CEGHIMOOPR GEOMORPHIC
CEGHINOOPT PHOTOGENIC
CEGHINOORT ORTHOGENIC
CEGHINOPTY PHYTOGENIC, TYPHOGENIC
CEGHINORTU RETOUCHING
CEGHINORTY TRICHOGYNE
CEGHINOTUU HUGUENOTIC
CEGHINRSTT STRETCHING
CEGHIOPSSY GEOPHYSICS
CEGHIORSTU GROUCHIEST
CEGHKNORSU ROUGHNECKS
CEGHLNOOTY TECHNOLOGY
CEGIIIMNNT MENINGITIC
CEGIIKLLNN NICKELLING
CEGIIKNNQU QUICKENING
CEGIIKNNRS SNICKERING
CEGIIKPRST PIGSTICKER
CEGIILLNNP PENCILLING
CEGIILNNPR PRINCELING
CEGIILNNSS CLINGINESS
CEGIILNNST STENCILING
CEGIILNNTY ENTICINGLY
CEGIILNOSU GENIUS LOCI
CEGIILNPRY PIERCINGLY
CEGIILNTXY EXCITINGLY
CEGIILORTU OLIGURETIC
CEGIILOSTU EULOGISTIC
CEGIINNOST SECTIONING
CEGIINNPST INSPECTING
CEGIINORXZ EXORCIZING
CEGIINOSTX COEXISTING
CEGIINRRTU RECRUITING
CEGIINRSTT TRISECTING
CEGIJNOPRT PROJECTING
CEGIKNNORS RECKONINGS

CEGIKNOOPR PRECOOKING
CEGIKNORST RESTOCKING
CEGILLMNOP COMPELLING
CEGILLOOXY LEXICOLOGY
CEGILMNOOP MONOPLEGIC
CEGILMNOPT COMPLETING
CEGILNNOST CLINGSTONE
CEGILNRSTU CLUSTERING
CEGILNRTTU CLUTTERING
CEGILOOSST ECOLOGISTS
CEGILOOSTT CETOLOGIST
CEGIMMNNOT COMMENTING
CEGIMNOORS ERGONOMICS
CEGIMNOORV OVERCOMING
CEGINNNORU RENOUNCING
CEGINNNOST CONSENTING
CEGINNNOTT CONTENTING,
  CONTINGENT
CEGINNOOST CONGESTION
CEGINNOQRU CONQUERING
CEGINNORSV CONSERVING, CONVERSING
CEGINNORTU COUNTERING,
  RECOUNTING
CEGINNORTV CONVERTING
CEGINNORUV UNCOVERING
CEGINNOSTT CONTESTING
CEGINNRSTY STRINGENCY
CEGINNRSUW UNSCREWING
CEGINNRSUY INSURGENCY
CEGINOORRZ RECOGNIZOR
CEGINOORST CREOSOTING
CEGINOPRSS PROCESSING
CEGINOPRTT PROTECTING
CEGINOSSTT COSSETTING
CEGINPPRSU SCUPPERING
CEGINPSSTU SUSPECTING
CEGLNOOSYY SYNECOLOGY
CEGNORRSSU SCROUNGERS
CEGOOPRSSY GYROSCOPES
CEHHHIIKRT HITCHHIKER
CEHHIILMNT HELMINTHIC
CEHHILNRTU IN THE LURCH
CEHHIMRTUY EURHYTHMIC
CEHHIOOPST THEOSOPHIC
CEHHKLLOSS SHELLSHOCK
CEHHOOPSSU CHOPHOUSES
CEHIIINRST TRICHINISE
CEHIIINRTZ TRICHINIZE
CEHIILLNSS CHILLINESS
CEHIILMOST HOMILETICS, MESOLITHIC
CEHIILNOTX XENOLITHIC
CEHIILOPTY HELIOTYPIC
CEHIIMNORT THERMIONIC
CEHIIMNORY HIERONYMIC

CEHIIMOPPR EPIMORPHIC
CEHIIMOPRT HEMITROPIC
CEHIIMRSTY MYTHICISER
CEHIIMRTYZ MYTHICIZER
CEHIIMSTTW TIME SWITCH
CEHIINPRSS CHIRPINESS
CEHIINPSST PITCHINESS
CEHIINSSTT IN STITCHES
CEHIINSTTZ CHINTZIEST
CEHIIOSTTY HISTIOCYTE
CEHIIPPSST PSESPHITIC
CEHIIPRSTY SPHERICITY
CEHIIPSTUU EUPHUISTIC
CEHIIRRTTU URETHRITIC
CEHIIRSSTU HEURISTICS
CEHIKNNSSU CHUNKINESS
CEHIKOPPST HIP POCKETS
CEHIKPRSSW SHIPWRECKS
CEHILNNPSU PUNCH LINES
CEHILNOSTU TOUCHLINES
CEHILNSSTZ SCHNITZELS
CEHILOPRST LECTORSHIP
CEHILORSTY CHRYSOLITE, CHRYSOTILE
CEHIMMNSSU CHUMMINESS
CEHIMNOOPR MICROPHONE
CEHIMNOOTT NOMOTHETIC
CEHIMNOPTY CHIMNEYPOT
CEHIMOOORT HOMOEROTIC
CEHIMOOPTY HOMEOTYPIC,
  MYTHOPOEIC
CEHIMOPRTY MICROPHYTE
CEHIMOPSTY MESOPHYTIC
CEHIMRSTUY EURYTHMICS
CEHINNNPPY PINCHPENNY
CEHINNPSSU PUNCHINESS
CEHINNRSTY STRYCHNINE
CEHINOORRS RHINOCEROS
CEHINOPPRR PRONEPHRIC
CEHINOPPSS CHOPPINESS
CEHINOPPTY PHENOTYPIC
CEHINOPRSS CENSORSHIP
CEHINOPSTT PITCHSTONE
CEHINOPTTY ENPHYTOTIC, ENTOPHYTIC
CEHINOSSTU TOUCHINESS
CEHINPRSST SPHINCTERS
CEHIOOPRRT RHEOTROPIC
CEHIOORRRT RETROCHOIR
CEHIOPRSTT PROSTHETIC
CEHIOPRSTY HYPOCRITES
CEHIOPRTXY XEROPHYTIC
CEHIOQSTTU COQUETTISH
CEHIORRSST CHORISTERS
CEHKOOOSSU COOKHOUSES
CEHLMOOPRY POLYCHROME

CEHLMOPTYY LYMPHOCYTE
CEHLOOOOPRT TOCOPHEROL
CEHLOOPPRS PREP SCHOOL
CEHLOOPRSS PRESCHOOLS
CEHLORRTTY TERRYCLOTH
CEHMMNOOOR MONOCHROME
CEHMMOOORS CHROMOSOME
CEHMOOPRTY CORMOPHYTE,
  ECTOMORPHY
CEHNNORSTU TRUNCHEONS
CEHNOOOPPS PHONOSCOPE
CEHNOOSTTU TOUCHSTONE
CEHNOPRSTY PHENOCRYST
CEHNORSTVY CHERNOVTSY
CEHOOOPRSS HOROSCOPES
CEHOOORSTUU COURTHOUSE
CEHORSTTTU OUTSTRETCH
CEIIIILSTV CIVILITIES
CEIIIINSTV VICINITIES
CEIIILLMNO LIMICOLINE
CEIIILLNNP PENICILLIN
CEIIILNPTX INEXPLICIT
CEIIILNSVY INCISIVELY
CEIIILOPST POLITICISE
CEIIILOPTZ POLITICIZE
CEIIIMMPRS EMPIRICISM
CEIIIMPRST EMPIRICIST
CEIIIMRSTV VICTIMISER
CEIIIMRTVZ VICTIMIZER
CEIIINPPRT PRECIPITIN
CEIIIOPSST ISOPIESTIC
CEIIJNNOST INJECTIONS
CEIIJNNTUV INJUNCTIVE
CEIIJNSSTU INJUSTICES
CEIIKKLNPT TICKLE PINK
CEIIKLMORT KILOMETRIC
CEIIKLNRST CRINKLIEST
CEIIKLNSSS SICKLINESS
CEIIKLPRST PRICKLIEST
CEIIKNPRST NITPICKERS
CEIIKNRSST TRICKINESS
CEIIKNSSST STICKINESS
CEIILLLSTU CELLULITIS
CEIILLNNOT CENTILLION
CEIILLNRTU CITRULLINE
CEIILLOSSU SILICULOSE
CEIILLPTXY EXPLICITLY
CEIILMOPST POLEMICIST
CEIILNNORS CRINOLINES
CEIILNOSTU LICENTIOUS
CEIILNOSTV NOVELISTIC
CEIILNPPRS PRINCIPLES
CEIILOQRSU LIQUORICES
CEIILPRSST LIST PRICES

CEIIMMORSS MICROSEISM
CEIIMNNOST OMNISCIENT
CEIIMNRSSU SINECURISM
CEIIMORSST ISOMETRICS
CEIIMOSTTT TOTEMISTIC
CEIINNOPST INCEPTIONS, INSPECTION
CEIINNOTTX EXTINCTION
CEIINOPRSS PRECISIONS
CEIINOPRST ISENTROPIC
CEIINOPRSU PERNICIOUS
CEIINOPRTV VOICEPRINT
CEIINOPSTT NEPOTISTIC
CEIINORRST CRITERIONS
CEIINORSSS RESCISSION
CEIINPRSSS CRISPINESS
CEIINRSSTU SCRUTINIES, SCRUTINISE,
    SINECURIST
CEIINRSTUY INSECURITY
CEIINRSTUZ SCRUTINIZE
CEIINSSSTT SCIENTISTS
CEIIOORSTU TRIOECIOUS
CEIIOPRSTY PRECIOSITY
CEIIOPSSTY SPECIOSITY
CEIIORSTVV VIVISECTOR
CEIJNOOPRT PROJECTION
CEIJNORSTU SURJECTION
CEIKKORRWW WICKERWORK
CEIKLNNOST CLINKSTONE
CEIKLNPSSU PLUCKINESS
CEIKLOPRST STOCKPILER
CEIKLOPSST STOCKPILES
CEIKNOSSST STOCKINESS
CEIKPQSSTU QUICKSTEPS
CEIKRRSSTT TRICKSTERS
CEILLNOORS COLOR LINES
CEILLOOQSU COLLOQUIES
CEILMMNOPT COMPLIMENT
CEILMNOOPT COMPLETION
CEILMNOOPX COMPLEXION
CEILMNOOSS SEMICOLONS
CEILMNORTY CLINOMETRY
CEILMNSSSU CLUMSINESS
CEILMOOOTV LOCOMOTIVF
CEILMOOPSI LEPTOSOMIC
CEILMOPSUV COMPULSIVE
CEILMOPTXY COMPLEXITY
CEILMORSTU SCLEROTIUM
CEILMORTUV VOLUMETRIC
CEILMOSTUU METICULOUS
CEILNNNOTY INNOCENTLY
CEILNNOSVY INSOLVENCY
CEILNOOPRS NECROPOLIS
CEILNOORRS RESORCINOL
CEILNOORSS COLONISERS

CEILNOORSZ COLONIZERS
CEILNOPRSU PRECLUSION
CEILNORSSU INCLOSURES
CEILNORTTY CONTRITELY
CEILNOSSST COSTLINESS
CEILNOSUVV CONVULSIVE
CEILOORRSV VERSICOLOR
CEILOPRSTY PROSELYTIC
CEILOPRSUY PRECIOUSLY
CEILOPSSUY SPECIOUSLY
CEILORSTTU COURTLIEST
CEIMMMNOTT COMMITMENT
CEIMMNOORT METRONOMIC
CEIMMNOQUU COMMUNIQUÉ
CEIMMNORTY METRONYMIC
CEIMMOOPRS COMPROMISE
CEIMMOORST OSMOMETRIC
CEIMMORRTY MICROMETRY
CEIMMORSSU COMMISSURE
CEIMNOOOSU MONOECIOUS
CEIMNOORTT TONOMETRIC
CEIMNOOSST ECONOMISTS
CEIMNOPRSU PROSCENIUM
CEIMNORSTT METRIC TONS
CEIMNORSUU CERUMINOUS
CEIMNRSSTY SYNCRETISM
CEIMOOPRRS MICROSPORE
CEIMOOPRTT COMPETITOR,
    OPTOMETRIC
CEIMOOPSST COMPOSITES
CEIMOORSTY SOCIOMETRY
CEIMOPRRTY PYROMETRIC
CEIMORSSTU COSTUMIERS
CEIMORSTVY VISCOMETRY
CEIMOSSTUV MUSCOVITES
CEINNNOOTT CONTENTION
CEINNNOOTV CONVENTION
CEINNNOSTT CONTINENTS
CEINNOORSV CONVERSION
CEINNOPTUX EXPUNCTION
CEINNORSTU CENTURIONS
CEINNOSSTT CONSISTENT
CEINOOPRSS PROCESSION
CEINOOPRTT PROTECTION
CEINOORSSU CENSORIOUS
CEINOOSSUY SYNOECIOUS
CEINOPPRSU PORCUPINES
CEINOPRSST INSPECTORS
CEINOPRSSU PERCUSSION, SUPERSONIC
CEINOPRSTT INTROSPECT
CEINOPRSTU SUPERTONIC
CEINOPSTTY STENOTYPIC
CEINOQTUYZ QUEZON CITY
CEINORRSTW TOWN CRIERS

CEINORSSUX EXCURSIONS
CEINOSSTUU INCESTUOUS
CEINOSTTTU CONSTITUTE
CEINRSSSTT STRICTNESS
CEINRSSSTU CRUSTINESS
CEINRSSSUV SCURVINESS
CEINRSSTTY SYNCRETIST
CEIOOPRRTU PUERTO RICO
CEIOOPRRTY CORPOREITY
CEIOPRRTUV CORRUPTIVE
CEIOPRRTUY EURYTROPIC
CEIOPRRTWY COPYWRITER
CEIORRSSSY RESCISSORY
CEIORRSTUU COUTURIERS
CEIPPRRSST PRESCRIPTS
CEIPPRSTTY TYPESCRIPT
CEIRRSSTTU STRICTURES
CEJOOPRRST PROJECTORS
CEKKORSSTY SKYROCKETS
CEKLMOOORR LOCKER ROOM
CEKLNORSTW TOWN CLERKS
CELLNOORRT CONTROLLER
CELLNOORSU COUNSELLOR
CELLOORSSU COLOURLESS
CELMOORSSU LOOSE SCRUM
CELMOORSTY SCLEROTOMY
CELNOORSSU COUNSELORS
CELNOPRSUU PRONUCLEUS
CELOOSSSSU COLOSSUSES
CELOOSTUVY COVETOUSLY
CELPRSSSTU SCULPTRESS
CELPRSSTUU SCULPTURES
CEMMNNOOSS COMMONNESS
CEMMNNOOTW COMMON NEWT
CEMNNOOPST COMPONENTS
CEMNNORTUY COUNTRYMEN
CEMOOPRRSS COMPRESSOR
CENNOOPRRU PRONOUNCER
CENOOQRRSU CONQUERORS
CENOORRTTV CONTROVERT
CENOPRSTUY COUNTERSPY
CENORSSSTW CROW'S NESTS
CEOOPPRRST PROSPECTOR
CEOOPRRSSS PROCESSORS
CEOOPRRSTT PROTECTORS
CEOOPRRSTU PROSECUTOR
CEOOPRRTTY PROTECTORY
CEOPPRSSTU PROSPECTUS
CEOPRRRSSU PRECURSORS
CEOPRRRSUY PRECURSORY
CEPPRRSTUU UPPER CRUST
CERRSSTTUU STRUCTURES
CFFFIISSTU FISTICUFFS
CFFGIIKNOT TICKING OFF

CFFGILNOSY SCOFFINGLY
CFGIIILNNT INFLICTING
CFGIIKLNOR FROLICKING
CFGIIMNNOR CONFIRMING
CFGIINNORU FINNO-UGRIC
CFGIKNNORU UNFROCKING
CFGIMNNOOR CONFORMING
CFGIMNOORT COMFORTING
CFHIIKSSST FISH STICKS
CFHIIKSSTT SHIFT STICK, STICK SHIFT
CFHIINOORS HONORIFICS
CFHIKOPRST PITCHFORKS
CFHIMOPRSY SCYPHIFORM
CFHKOOOPRS SHOCKPROOF
CFHLLOOORT FLOOR CLOTH
CFHLMOOORR CHLOROFORM
CFIIILNNOT INFLICTION
CFIIINOSTT FICTIONIST
CFIIIOSTTU FICTITIOUS
CFIIKKLNSS SKIN FLICKS
CFIILLLNOU FOLLICULIN
CFIILMMORS MICROFILMS
CFIILORSST FLORISTICS
CFIINNNOOT NONFICTION
CFIIRSTTUU FUTURISTIC
CFIKLLNOST FLINTLOCKS
CFILMMORUU CUMULIFORM
CFIMNOORST CONFORMIST
CFIMNOORTY CONFORMITY
CFLLNORSUY SCORNFULLY
CFLOOORRUU FOUR-COLOUR
CFLOORSSUU SCROFULOUS
CGGIIKNPSU SUCKING PIG
CGGIINNNOS CONSIGNING
CGGINNORSU SCROUNGING
CGHHHILOOS HIGH SCHOOL
CGHHILORTT TORCHLIGHT
CGHHIORSTU HIGH COURTS
CGHIIKNSTT NIGHTSTICK
CGHIIKSTTT STICKTIGHT
CGHIILLOOT LITHOLOGIC
CGHIILOPST PHLOGISTIC
CGHIILPRTY TRIGLYPHIC
CGHIINNOSU CUSHIONING
CGHIKLNOSY SHOCKINGLY
CGHILLNRUY LURCHINGLY
CGHILLOORS SCHOOLGIRL
CGHILNOTUY TOUCHINGLY
CGHILOORTY TRICHOLOGY
CGHINOOOPR GONOPHORIC
CGHINOOPRY GYNOPHORIC
CGHINOOSYZ SCHIZOGONY
CGHIOPRSTY COPYRIGHTS
CGHLNOOORY CHRONOLOGY

CGHLOOPSYY PSYCHOLOGY
CGHOPRTUUU CUT UP ROUGH
CGIIIILNVZ CIVILIZING
CGIIIJNOST JINGOISTIC
CGIIIKNNPT NITPICKING
CGIIILNNTY INCITINGLY
CGIIILNOST SOLICITING
CGIIILNSTU LINGUISTIC
CGIIILPSTU PUGILISTIC
CGIIIORRST RIGORISTIC
CGIIJNNNOO CONJOINING
CGIIKLLNOR ROLLICKING
CGIIKLNRTY TRICKINGLY
CGIILNNOOZ COLONIZING
CGIILOOSTT ISOGLOTTIC
CGIIMMNOTT COMMITTING
CGIIMMNNORS CRIMSONING
CGIIMNOPRS COMPRISING
CGIINNNOTU CONTINUING
CGIINNOPRS CONSPIRING
CGIINNORTV CONTRIVING
CGIINNOSST CONSISTING
CGIINOTTUY CONTIGUITY
CGIKOOPSST POGO STICKS
CGILLNOOPS SCOLLOPING
CGILLNOSWY SCOWLINGLY
CGILLOSSYY GLYCOLYSIS
CGILMOOSTY MYCOLOGIST
CGILMOOSUY MUSICOLOGY
CGILNNOPUU UNCOUPLING
CGILNNORSY SCORNINGLY
CGILNNOSTU CONSULTING
CGILNNOSUV CONVULSING
CGILNOOOST NOSTOLOGIC,
    ONCOLOGIST
CGILNOORSU COLOURINGS
CGILNOPSUV LOVING CUPS
CGILOOOPRT TROPOLOGIC
CGILOOOTXY TOXICOLOGY
CGILOOSTTY CYTOLOGIST
CGIMNOOPRT COMPORTING
CGIMNOOPST COMPOSTING
CGINNOORSS CONSIGNORS
CGINNOORST CONSORTING
CGINNOORTT CONTORTING
CGINNOORTU CONTOURING
CGINNOOSTT COTTON GINS
CGINNORSTU CONSTRUING
CGINNPRTUU PUNCTURING
CGINOOPRST PROGNOSTIC
CGINOOSTUU CONTIGUOUS
CGINOPRRTU CORRUPTING
CGIOOPRSYZ ZYGOSPORIC
CGLOOOPRTY PROCTOLOGY

CHHIIOSSTY ICHTHYOSIS
CHHIIPSTTW WHIPSTITCH
CHHILLRSUY CHURLISHLY
CHHILOOPTY HOLOPHYTIC
CHHIMNOOOP HOMOPHONIC
CHHINSTTUW WITCH-HUNTS
CHHIOOPPRS PHOSPHORIC
CHHKLLOOSY HOLLYHOCKS
CHIIIILNST NIHILISTIC
CHIIILLOPP LIPOPHILIC
CHIIILPPPS PHILIPPICS
CHIIILPSTY SYPHILITIC
CHIIINORST HISTRIONIC
CHIIKLLSTY TICKLISHLY
CHIILMNOOT MONOLITHIC
CHIILMOOTT LITHOTOMIC
CHIILNOOPT PHONOLITIC
CHIILOSTTY HISTOLYTIC
CHIIMOOPRS ISOMORPHIC
CHIIMOPRRT TRIMORPHIC
CHIIMORRST TRICHROISM
CHIIMORSTU HUMORISTIC
CHIINNOPSU PINCUSHION
CHIINORSTU TRICHINOUS
CHIIOOOPRT OOPHORITIC
CHIIPSSSTY PHYSICISTS
CHIKLMOSST LOCKSMITHS
CHIKOOPSTT TOOTHPICKS
CHILLNOOST LOINCLOTHS
CHILLNOSWY CLOWNISHLY
CHILNOOPPY POLYPHONIC
CHILNOOPXY XYLOPHONIC
CHILNOPSSU CONSULSHIP
CHILOOPTTY PHOTOLYTIC
CHIMNNOOOP MONOPHONIC
CHIMOOOPRZ ZOOMORPHIC
CHIMOORTTY TRICHOTOMY
CHIMPSSTYY SYMPHYSTIC
CHINOOOPTT PHOTOTONIC
CHINOOPPTY PHONOTYPIC
CHINOOPRSY RHINOSCOPY
CHIOOORSSU ISOCHROOUS
CHIOOPPRRY PYROPHORIC
CHIOOPPTTY PHOTOTYPIC
CHIOPRSSTU COURTSHIPS
CHIORSTTTW STITCHWORT
CHKLOOORSW SCHOOLWORK
CHLMNOSUUU HOMUNCULUS
CHLMOOPRYY POLYCHROMY
CIIIILNTVY INCIVILITY
CIIILLMPTY IMPLICITLY
CIIILMPSST SIMPLISTIC
CIIILMPSTY SIMPLICITY
CIIILNTUVY UNCIVILITY

CIIILPRTTY TRIPLICITY
CIIIMNNOST NICOTINISM
CIIIMNPPRU PRINCIPIUM
CIIIMOPSTT OPTIMISTIC
CIIIMSSTTW WITTICISMS
CIIINNNOTT INTINCTION
CIIINNOSTU UNIONISTIC
CIIJLNOPST CLIP JOINTS
CIIJNNNOTU INJUNCTION
CIIKOSTTTU STICK IT OUT
CIILLMOOSU LIMICOLOUS
CIILLNOOSS COLLISIONS
CIILLNOOST COTILLIONS
CIILLNOOTU ILLOCUTION
CIILLOSTTY STYLOLITIC
CIILMMNTUU NUMMULITIC
CIILNNOSSU INCLUSIONS
CIILNOPSTU PUNCTILIOS
CIILOORSST SOLICITORS
CIILOOSSTU SOLICITOUS
CIILOPRTVY PROCLIVITY
CIILRRSTUY SCURRILITY
CIILSSSTTY STYLISTICS
CIIMMNOOSS COMMISSION
CIIMNNOOTZ MONZONITIC
CIIMNOPRRT MICROPRINT
CIIMORRSTT TRICROTISM
CIINNOORTT CONTRITION
CIINNORSSU INCURSIONS
CIINNOTTUY CONTINUITY
CIINOOPRTX PICROTOXIN
CIINOPSSSU SUSPICIONS
CIIOORSTUV VICTORIOUS
CIIOPSSSUU SUSPICIOUS
CIIPSTTTYY STYPTICITY
CIJKOSSSST JOSS STICKS
CIJLNNOOTY CONJOINTLY
CIJNNOSTTU T-JUNCTIONS
CIKLLOSSTT STOCK-STILL
CIKLNOOSTT SILK COTTON
CILLMOOQUU COLLOQUIUM
CILLOPRSTU PORTCULLIS
CILLOSSUUY LUSCIOUSLY
CILMNOOOOT LOCOMOTION
CILMNOOPSU COMPULSION
CILMNOSSTU COLUMNISTS
CILNNOOSUV CONVULSION
CILOORRSTU TRICOLOURS
CILORRSSUU SCURRILOUS
CIMMNNOOSU COMMUNIONS
CIMMNOOOST COMMOTIONS
CIMMNOSSTU COMMUNISTS
CIMNNOOOPP NINCOMPOOP
CIMNNOSTUU CONTINUUMS

CIMNOORSTU CONSORTIUM
CIMOOOOPRST COMPOSITOR
CIMOPSTTUU PUT TO MUSIC
CINNOOORTT CONTORTION
CINNOOSSTU CONTUSIONS
CINNOOSTUU CONTINUOUS
CINOOPRRTU CORRUPTION
CINOORSSTY CONSISTORY
CINORRSTTU INSTRUCTOR
CINOSTTUUY UNCTUOSITY
CIOOPRSSTU UROSCOPIST
CIOPPRSSTT POSTSCRIPT
CIPPRRSTUU STIRRUP CUP
CKLLOORRSW SCROLLWORK
CKMNOORSTU MOONSTRUCK
CKMOOORSST STOCKROOMS
CKOPRSSTTU TRUCK STOPS
CLMMNNOOUY UNCOMMONLY
CLMOOOORTU OCULOMOTOR
CLMOOPRSUY COMPULSORY
CLNOOOOTTW COTTON WOOL
CLNOOPRSSU PROCONSULS
CLNOSTUUUY UNCTUOUSLY
CLOOOOPRRTU PROLOCUTOR
CLOPRSSUUU SCRUPULOUS
CMMMNOOOOR COMMON ROOM
CMMNNNOOOU COMMON NOUN
CNNNOOSTUU COUNT NOUNS
CNNOOTTUWY COUNTY TOWN
DDDDDFUUYY FUDDY-DUDDY
DDDEEEFNNU UNDEFENDED
DDDEEFIOST EISTEDDFOD
DDDEEIOORS DEODORISED
DDDEEIOORZ DEODORIZED
DDDEEIORRS DISORDERED
DDDEFILOOW FIDDLEWOOD
DDEEEEGNNR ENGENDERED
DDEEEFLORW DEFLOWERED
DDEEEFORST DEFORESTED
DDEEEHHPRS SHEPHERDED
DDEEEHILSV DISHEVELED
DDEEEHNOWY HONEYDEWED
DDEEEILSTT TITLE DEEDS
DDEEEIMNOR DOMINEERED
DDEEEIMNRT DETERMINED
DDEEEINRST TENDERISED
DDEEEINRTZ TENDERIZED
DDEEELLMOR REMODELLED
DDEEELMMOS MEDDLESOME
DDEEELMNTY DEMENTEDLY
DDEEELOPRY REDEPLOYED
DDEEELRSVY DESERVEDLY
DDEEENRRTU UNDETERRED
DDEEENRSUX UNDERSEXED

DDEEEOOPRT DEEP-ROOTED
DDEEEPRSSU SUPERSEDED
DDEEFIIINT IDENTIFIED
DDEEFIINTU DEFINITUDE
DDEEFLNORU FLOUNDERED
DDEEFMOOOR FOREDOOMED
DDEEGGHOOP HODGEPODGE
DDEEGGNOSS DOGGEDNESS
DDEEGILNSY DESIGNEDLY
DDEEGJLLUW WELL-JUDGED
DDEEHIISSS SIDE DISHES
DDEEHILMOS DEMOLISHED
DDEEHINNSS HIDDENNESS
DDEEHLORSU SHOULDERED
DDEEHNORSU ENSHROUDED
DDEEHOORTU OUT-HERODED
DDEEIIKLMN LIKE-MINDED
DDEEIILMNV EVIL-MINDED
DDEEIINRSW SIDEWINDER
DDEEIIORSX DEOXIDISER
DDEEIIORXZ DEOXIDIZER
DDEEIIPSSW SIDESWIPED
DDEEIIQSTU DISQUIETED
DDEEILMSTW MIDDLE WEST
DDEEILNNRU UNDERLINED
DDEEILNOSY ONE-SIDEDLY
DDEEILNOTT DOTTED LINE
DDEEILRTVY DIVERTEDLY
DDEEIMNNOP OPEN-MINDED
DDEEIMNNRU UNDERMINED
DDEEIMNORS ENDODERMIS,
   MODERNISED
DDEEIMNORZ MODERNIZED
DDEEINNNTU UNINTENDED
DDEEINNRTU INDENTURED
DDEEINNSSW WINDEDNESS
DDEEINORRV OVERRIDDEN
DDEEINORSW DISENDOWER,
   EIDERDOWNS
DDEEINRSSU UNDERSISED
DDEEINRSUZ UNDERSIZED
DDEEIOORRS DEODORISER
DDEEIOORRZ DEODORIZER
DDEEIORRSS SIDE ORDERS
DDEEIRSSST DISTRESSED
DDEELLOORW OLDE WORLDE
DDEELLORWW WELL-WORDED
DDEELMORSU SMOULDERED
DDEELRRSSU RUDDERLESS
DDEENNOPST DESPONDENT
DDEENNOSSS SODDENNESS
DDEENNPRSU UNDERSPEND
DDEENNSSSU SUDDENNESS
DDEEFGIIRSU DISFIGURED

DDEFGILLOS GOLDFIELDS
DDEFHIIIMU HUMIDIFIED
DDEFHIIMUY DEHUMIDIFY
DDEFIIILOS SOLIDIFIED
DDEFILOOST FLOOD TIDES
DDEFIMNORR DENDRIFORM
DDEFLORSSU DUSSELDORF
DDEGGGILOR GOLD DIGGER
DDEGHHIIMN HIGH-MINDED
DDEGHINRSU SHUDDERING
DDEGIINNST DISTENDING
DDEGILLMNY MEDDLINGLY
DDEGILNNOW LONGWINDED
DDEGINNORU REDOUNDING
DDEGIOOPRR DO PORRIDGE
DDEGLLLOOR ROLLED GOLD
DDEGLNOORY DENDROLOGY
DDEHHNRSTU HUNDREDTHS
DDEHIIIMNS DIMINISHED
DDEHIILNSW WINDSHIELD
DDEHIILPSU DISULPHIDE
DDEHIKNOOW HOODWINKED
DDEHINOORS DISHONORED
DDEHINOSSS SHODDINESS
DDEHLNOSTU HUDDLESTON
DDEIIILQSU LIQUIDISED
DDEIIILQUZ LIQUIDIZED
DDEIIIMPSY EPIDIDYMIS
DDEIIIPRST DISPIRITED
DDEIIJNOST DISJOINTED
DDEIIKRSSV DISK DRIVES
DDEIIMNNOU DIMINUENDO
DDEIINOPSS INDISPOSED
DDEIINOSTU DUODENITIS
DDEIINSSST DISSIDENTS
DDEIIOPRSS DISPERSOID
DDEIKNNRUW WUNDERKIND
DDEILLNPSY SPLENDIDLY
DDEILORRSY DISORDERLY
DDEIMNOSTU DISMOUNTED
DDEINOPRUV UNPROVIDED
DDEINOPSUW UPSIDE DOWN
DDEINORSSS SORDIDNESS
DDEINPSTUU UNDISPUTED
DDEIRSSTTU DISTRUSTED
DDELNORRUW UNDERWORLD
DDENOOPPRU PROPOUNDED
DDENOORSTU UNDERSTOOD
DDENORRSUU SURROUNDED
DDENRSTUUY UNDERSTUDY
DDEOPRRSTU RUDDERPOST
DDGGIILNOS DISLODGING
DDGGOOOOYY GOODY-GOODY
DDGHRRUUYY HURDY-GURDY

DDGIINPRRY DRIP-DRYING
DDGILLMNUY MUDDLINGLY
DDGILLNOPY PLODDINGLY
DDHILORRTW THIRD WORLD
DDHINOOPTY DIPHYODONT
DDHOOOOUWY HOW DO YOU DO
DEEEEEFPRZ DFFP FREEZE
DEEEEFFLRS SELF-FEEDER
DEEEEFNRTT TENDERFEET
DEEEEGINNR ENGINEERED
DEEEEGNNRR ENGENDERER
DEEEEHLLLW WELL-HEELED
DEEEEKNRSW WEEKENDERS
DEEEEPRRSV PERSEVERED
DEEEFGIKNS KNIFE-EDGES
DEEEFHILNS NEEDLEFISH
DEEEFHLORR FREEHOLDER
DEEEFILMNT DEFILEMENT
DEEEFILNTV FIELD EVENT
DEEEFINRRT INTERFERED
DEEEFINRTW WINTERFEED
DEEEFINSSV DEFENSIVES
DEEEFLORRW DEFLOWERER
DEEEFMNRRU REFERENDUM
DEEEFMNRST DEFERMENTS
DEEEFNQRTU FREQUENTED
DEEEFNRTTU UNFETTERED
DEEEFORRST DEFORESTER, REFORESTED
DEEEGGGLOY GOGGLE-EYED
DEEEGHHINT HEIGHTENED
DEEEGHLNNT LENGTHENED
DEEEGHOOWZ GOOD WHEEZE
DEEEGIIMRV DEMIVIERGE
DEEEGIKNNW WEEKENDING
DEEEGILMTY GIMLET-EYED
DEEEGIMNRT REGIMENTED
DEEEGINRSS GREEDINESS
DEEEGIRRST REGISTERED
DEEEGNRSTT DETERGENTS
DEEEHIPRSS HESPERIDES
DEEEHLLSSY HEEDLESSLY
DEEEHLNOPT TELEPHONED
DEEEHNORTY HETERODYNE
DEEEHNRRTU THEREUNDER
DEEEIILRSV DELIVERIES
DEEEIKLLRW WEEDKILLER
DEEEILLMOS DEMOISELLE
DEEEILLMPS MILLEPEDES
DEEEILMRSS REMEDILESS
DEEEILNRSS SLENDERISE
DEEEILNRSZ SLENDERIZE
DEEEILNRUV UNRELIEVED
DEEEILRRVY REDELIVERY
DEEEILRSVW SILVERWEED

DEEEIMMRSS MESMERISED
DEEEIMMRSZ MESMERIZED
DEEEIMMNOST DEMONETISE
DEEEIMNOTZ DEMONETIZE
DEEEIMNRRT DETERMINER
DEEEIMNRST DENSIMETER
DEEEIMORTU EUDIOMETER
DEEEIMRSSY MERSEYSIDE
DEEEINNPTV PENDENTIVE
DEEEINNRTV INTERVENED
DEEEINPRST PREDESTINE
DEEEINPSSS SPEEDINESS
DEEEINPSTX EXPEDIENTS
DEEEINRRST TENDERISER
DEEEINRRTZ TENDERIZER
DEEEINRSTT INTERESTED
DEEEIPRSSV DEPRESSIVE
DEEEIPRSTX PREEXISTED
DEEEIRSSTT SIDE STREET
DEEEKLNORW NEEDLEWORK
DEEEKOOPRR DOORKEEPER
DEEELLMORR REMODELLER
DEEELLNORW NE'ER-DO-WELL
DEEELLNSSY NEEDLESSLY
DEEELLOWWY YELLOWWEED
DEEELNRTTU UNLETTERED
DEEELOPRSV DEVELOPERS
DEEELRRSVY RESERVEDLY
DEEEMNNOTT DENOTEMENT
DEEEMNNOTU DENOUEMENT
DEEEMNNOYZ ENDOENZYME
DEEEMNOTTV DEVOTEMENT
DEEEMNRSSU DEMURENESS
DEEEMNSTTV VESTMENTED
DEEENNRSST TENDERNESS
DEEENPRRST PRETENDERS
DEEENPRSUV SUPERVENED
DEEENRRSTT DETERRENTS
DEEENRRSUV UNRESERVED
DEEEOPPRRY EYEDROPPER
DEEEORSSTV STEVEDORES
DEEEPPPRRS RED PEPPERS
DEEEPRRSSU SUPERSEDER
DEEERSSUVX DEUX-SEVRES
DEEFFHLRSU RESHUFFLED
DEEFGHINRT FRIGHTENED
DEEFGINPRY DEEP FRYING
DEEFGINRTY GENTRIFYED
DEEFGINSST GIFTEDNESS
DEEFGIPRRU PREFIGURED
DEEFIIINNT INDEFINITE
DEEFIIINRT IDENTIFIER
DEEFIIINTV DEFINITIVE
DEEFIIIRVV REVIVIFIED

DEEFIILMNS MINEFIELDS
DEEFIILMSU EMULSIFIED
DEEFIILNRR FRIENDLIER
DEEFIILNRS FRIENDLIES, INFIELDERS
DEEFIILNTY DEFINITELY
DEEFIILRST FERTILISED
DEEFIILRTZ FERTILIZED
DEEFIINRVW VIEWFINDER
DEEFIIPRTT PRETTIFIED
DEEFILLLSW SELF-WILLED
DEEFILLRSU FLEUR-DE-LIS
DEEFILMOSU FIELDMOUSE
DEEFILNOST FIELDSTONE
DEEFILNRSS FRIENDLESS
DEEFILNRYZ FRENZIEDLY
DEEFILORTU OUTFIELDER
DEEFILSSTT FIELD-TESTS
DEEFINNPRS PEN FRIENDS
DEEFIORRRT FERRITE-ROD
DEEFKNORSS FORKEDNESS
DEEFLLSSTY SELF-STYLED
DEEFLMNNOT ENFOLDMENT
DEEFLOORVW OVERFLOWED
DEEFNOORTT TENDERFOOT
DEEFOORSTU SUREFOOTED
DEEFORRSST DEFROSTERS
DEEGGNRSSU RUGGEDNESS
DEEGGRSTUY GREEDY-GUTS
DEEGHINOPS DIPHOSGENE
DEEGHINRRR RED HERRING
DEEGHINSTU GESUNDHEIT
DEEGHIOTUW OUTWEIGHED
DEEGIILNRV DELIVERING
DEEGIILNSU GUIDELINES
DEEGIILOOS IDEOLOGIES
DEEGIILPRV PRIVILEGED
DEEGIINNRT INGREDIENT
DEEGIINPTX EXPEDITING
DEEGIIRSSV DIGRESSIVE
DEEGIISSTV DIGESTIVES
DEEGILMNOR REMODELING
DEEGILNNOW GWENDOLINE
DEEGILNOPV DEVELOPING
DEEGILNRSY RESIGNEDLY
DEEGILOOSU IDEOLOGUES
DEEGILOPRS RIDGEPOLES
DEEGINNPRT PRETENDING
DEEGINNRRS RENDERINGS
DEEGINOOPT PIGEON-TOED
DEEGINORSS DEGRESSION
DEEGINOTTU TONGUE-TIED
DEEGINPRSS DEPRESSING
DEEGINRRSS REDRESSING
DEEGKNOTTT GET KNOTTED!

DEEGKOPRSW POWDER KEGS
DEEGLLNORU GOLDEN RULE
DEEGNNOOSU ENDOGENOUS
DEEGOPRRSS PROGRESSED
DEEHHISSTW THE SWEDISH
DEEHIINPRS HESPERIDIN
DEEHIIRSTT HEREDITIST
DEEHILLRSV SHRIVELLED
DEEHILMORS DEMOLISHER
DEEHILOOTT THEODOLITE
DEEHIMORST METHODISER
DEEHIMORTZ METHODIZER
DEEHINOOPV VIDEOPHONE
DEEHINORST THRENODIES
DEEHINRSSW SWINEHERDS
DEEHIOPPRS PROPHESIED
DEEHIORSTV SHROVETIDE
DEEHIOSSTU TIED HOUSES
DEEHKNOOSS HOOKEDNESS
DEEHLLMOPR PHELLODERM
DEEHNNORSS HORNEDNESS
DEEHNOORTT HETERODONT
DEEHNRRSTU THUNDERERS
DEEHNRSSSW SHREWDNESS
DEEHOORTXY HETERODOXY
DEEHSSSTTU DUSTSHEETS
DEEIIINPPR PIPERIDINE
DEEIIINSTT IDENTITIES
DEEIIILLMPR IMPERILLED
DEEIIILLMPS MILLIPEDES
DEEIIILLNOS LINSEED OIL
DEEIIILLOPT LEPIDOLITE
DEEIIILMPST SPEED LIMIT
DEEIIILNNVY VINYLIDENE
DEEIIILNSTT DISENTITLE
DEEIIILOPPT EPILEPTOID
DEEIIILORST SIDEROLITE
DEEIIILPRRV PILE DRIVER
DEEIIILRSST STERILISED
DEEIIILRSTZ STERILIZED
DEEIIILRSVY DERISIVELY
DEEIIMMNPT IMPEDIMENT
DEEIIMNRST MINISTERED
DEEIIMOPST EPITOMISED
DEEIIMOPTZ EPITOMIZED
DEEIINNRTT TRIDENTINE
DEEIINNSTW DISENTWINE
DEEIINOPTT PETITIONED
DEEIINOPTX EXPEDITION
DEEIINPTTU INEPTITUDE
DEEIINQTUU INQUIETUDE
DEEIINSSST SENSITISED
DEEIINSSTZ SENSITIZED
DEEIIOPRTT PERIDOTITE

DEEIIPRSSV DISPERSIVE
DEEIIPRSSW SIDESWIPER
DEEIIPSSSW SIDESWIPES
DEEIISSSSU SIDE ISSUES
DEEIJNORRS REJOINDERS
DEEIJNOSTT JETTISONED
DEEIKNNSSS KINDNESSES
DEEIKORSST SIDESTROKE
DEEILLMPSS MISSPELLED
DEEILLORRS DROLLERIES
DEEILLRRSV DRIVELLERS
DEEILLRSSU SLIDE RULES
DEEILLSUVY DELUSIVELY
DEEILMNOSS SOLEMNISED
DEEILMNOSU EMULSIONED
DEEILMNOSZ SOLEMNIZED
DEEILNNORT TENDERLOIN
DEEILNNQTU DELINQUENT
DEEILNPRST SPLINTERED
DEEILNRSSW WILDERNESS
DEEILNRSTU INTERLUDES
DEEILPRSUV PULVERISED
DEEILPRUVZ PULVERIZED
DEEIMMNOSU EUDEMONISM
DEEIMNNNTT INTENDMENT
DEEIMNNRRU UNDERMINER
DEEIMNOOTV MONTEVIDEO
DEEIMNOPRT REDEMPTION
DEEIMNOPTT IDEMPOTENT
DEEIMNORRS MODERNISER
DEEIMNORRZ MODERNIZER
DEEIMNORSS SERMONISED
DEEIMNORSZ SERMONIZED
DEEIMNRRTU ERMINTRUDE
DEEIMNRSTT DETRIMENTS
DEEIMNRSTW MIDWESTERN, STEM-
 WINDER
DEEIMNRSTY DENSIMETRY
DEEIMNSTTV DIVESTMENT
DEEIMOPRST TEMPORISED
DEEIMOPRTZ TEMPORIZED
DEEIMORTUY EUDIOMETRY
DEEINNNOSU INNUENDOES
DEEINNRSST TRENDINESS
DEEINNRSSU INUREDNESS
DEEINNRSTU INDENTURES
DEEINNSSTU UNITEDNESS
DEEINOPRSS DEPRESSION
DEEINOPRST INTERPOSED
DEEINOQSTU QUESTIONED
DEEINORSST DESERTIONS
DEEINPRRST RINDERPEST
DEEINPRSSS DISPENSERS
DEEINPRSST PRESIDENTS

DEEINQRTUU UNREQUITED
DEEINRRTUW UNDERWRITE
DEEINRSSSS DRESSINESS
DEEINRSSST DISSENTERS
DEEINSTTTV VENDETTIST
DEEIOPPRRT PROPERTIED
DEEIOPPRSS PREDISPOSE
DEEIOPRSUX SUPEROXIDE
DEEIOPRSVW POWER DIVES
DEEIOPRTTU PIROUETTED
DEEIORRRST TERRORISED
DEEIORRRTZ TERRORIZED
DEEIPRRTUY EURYPTERID
DEEIPRSSUV SUPERVISED
DEEKLLNORS SNORKELLED
DEEKLMRTTU KETTLEDRUM
DEEKLOOORV OVERLOOKED
DEEKLRSSUU LESSER KUDU
DEEKOORRVW OVERWORKED
DEELLMOORS ROLE MODELS
DEELLNRTUW WELL-TURNED
DEELMMNOPU NOM DE PLUME
DEELMNOPTY DEPLOYMENT
DEELMNOPUY UNEMPLOYED
DEELMPRSUY PRESUMEDLY
DEELNNOOSU UNLOOSENED
DEELNNORWY RENOWNEDLY
DEELNOOSST LODESTONES
DEELNORSUV UNRESOLVED
DEELNOSTUU EDENTULOUS
DEELNPRRSU PLUNDERERS
DEELOPRRTY REPORTEDLY
DEELORTTUV TURTLEDOVE
DEELPRSTTU SPLUTTERED
DEEMNNORSS MODERNNESS
DEEMNNOSTW WONDERMENT
DEEMNNOSTW ENDOWMENTS
DEEMNOORRY MONEY ORDER
DEEMNOPRTT DEPORTMENT
DEEMNORSTU TREMENDOUS
DEEMNRRTUY ERMYNTRUDE
DEENNOOSSW WOODENNESS
DEENNOPRST RESPONDENT
DEENNORSTU UNDERTONES
DEENNORSVW NEWSVENDOR
DEENOQRTUU UNDERQUOTE
DEENORRTUV OVERTURNED
DEENORRTUW UNDERWROTE
DEENORSSSU ROUSEDNESS
DEENORSUVZ RENDEZVOUS
DEENOSSTUV DEVOUTNESS
DEENPRSSSU SUSPENDERS
DEENRRRSSU SURRENDERS
DEENRSSSTU UNSTRESSED

DEEOOPPRTV OVERTOPPED
DEEOOPRRSU UREDOSPORE
DEEOPRRRSU SUPERORDER
DEEORRSSTY DESTROYERS
DEEPPRRSUU SUPERDUPER
DEEPPRSSSU SUPPRESSED
DEFFGINOOR FINGER FOOD
DEFFINNOST SOFT-FINNED
DEFFOPPRUW POWDER PUFF
DEFGGILLNS FLEDGLINGS
DEFGGILLRU FULL-RIGGED
DEFGHILLTU DELIGHTFUL
DEFGHOOOSU HOUSE OF GOD
DEFGIILNRR GIRLFRIEND
DEFGIILNYY EDIFYINGLY
DEFGIINNUY UNEDIFYING
DEFGIIRRSU DISFIGURER
DEFGINNORU FOUNDERING
DEFGINORST DEFROSTING
DEFGNOORRU FOREGROUND
DEFHIIIMRU HUMIDIFIER
DEFHIILNSY FIENDISHLY
DEFHIINNSU UNFINISHED
DEFHIINPRS FRIENDSHIP
DEFHILOPST SHOPLIFTED
DEFHILORSU FLOURISHED
DEFHLNOSUW FLESH WOUND
DEFHLOOOSW WHOLEFOODS
DEFHNOOPRU UNHOPED-FOR
DEFHORRRTU RUTHERFORD
DEFIIILMPS SIMPLIFIED
DEFIIILNTY INFIDELITY
DEFIIILORS SOLIDIFIER
DEFIIINNOT DEFINITION
DEFIIINNTU INFINITUDE
DEFIILLNRY FRIENDLILY
DEFIILLRRS FIRE DRILLS
DEFIILOSSS FOSSILISED
DEFIILOSSZ FOSSILIZED
DEFIILPRST FIELD TRIPS
DEFIILSTTU STULTIFIED
DEFIINOPTX FIXED-POINT
DEFIIOPRSU PERFIDIOUS
DEFILLORWW WILDFOWLER
DEFILMNORY INFORMEDLY
DEFILNNRUY UNFRIENDLY
DEFILNORWW WINDFLOWER
DEFILNOSSW SNOWFIELDS
DEFILPRSUU SUPERFLUID
DEFIMNNORU UNINFORMED
DEFINRRSUW WIND-SURFER
DEFLNOORRU UNDERFLOOR
DEFNOOPRRU UNDERPROOF
DEGGHIILNT DELIGHTING

DEGGHIIPRS SHIP-RIGGED
DEGGIILRSU GIRL GUIDES
DEGGIINRSS DIGRESSING
DEGGIJNPRU PREJUDGING
DEGGIJRRUY JURY-RIGGED
DEGGINNORU UNDERGOING
DEGGINORUV GIVE GROUND
DEGHIILSST SIDELIGHTS
DEGHIMNRSU HUMDINGERS
DEGHINNORT DETHRONING
DEGHINNRTU THUNDERING
DEGHINRSST NIGHTDRESS
DEGHIORRRU ROUGHRIDER
DEGHIOSTTU DOUGHTIEST
DEGHLORSSU GOLD RUSHES
DEGHMOORST GODMOTHERS
DEGHNORSUY GREYHOUNDS
DEGIIILMNT DELIMITING
DEGIIILNNS SIDELINING
DEGIIIRSST DIGITISERS
DEGIIIRSTZ DIGITIZERS
DEGIIKLNNR REKINDLING
DEGIILLMRX MIXED GRILL
DEGIILLNPS DISPELLING
DEGIILLNRV DRIVELLING
DEGIILLNTY DILIGENTLY
DEGIILLNYY YIELDINGLY
DEGIILMNPY IMPEDINGLY
DEGIILNNUY UNYIELDING
DEGIILNOPS DESPOILING
DEGIILNORS SOLDIERING
DEGIILOOST IDEOLOGIST
DEGIINNOSU INDIGENOUS
DEGIINNOSV NOSEDIVING
DEGIINNPSS DISPENSING
DEGIINNSST DISSENTING
DEGIINOPST DEPOSITING
DEGIINORRV OVERRIDING
DEGIINORSS DIGRESSION
DEGIINOSST DIGESTIONS
DEGIINPRSS DISPERSING
DEGIINPRST SPRING TIDE
DEGIINPTUZ DEPUTIZING
DEGIIQSSTU SQUIDGIEST
DEGILLOOTY DELTIOLOGY
DEGILMNORS SMOLDERING
DEGILMNORU MOULDERING,
   REMOULDING
DEGILMNRSU MUDSLINGER
DEGILMNPRU PLUNDERING
DEGILNNRSU UNDERLINGS
DEGILNNRUY ENDURINGLY, UNDERLYING
DEGILNOORS GONDOLIERS
DEGILNOOSS GOODLINESS

DEGILNOSTU LONGITUDES
DEGILNRSTU DISGRUNTLE
DEGILOOPST PEDOLOGIST
DEGIMNSSSU SMUDGINESS
DEGINNOPRS RESPONDING
DEGINNOPRT PORTENDING
DEGINNOPUX EXPOUNDING
DEGINNORST GRINDSTONE, STRINGENDO
DEGINNORSU RESOUNDING
DEGINNPSSU SUSPENDING
DEGINNRSSU UNDRESSING
DEGINOOPRT TORPEDOING
DEGINOORSV OVERDOSING
DEGINOPSST SIGNPOSTED
DEGINORSTY DESTROYING
DEGINOSSST STODGINESS
DEGKLOOOOR GOOD LOOKER
DEGLMNOOOY DEMONOLOGY
DEGLMOOORT MOTOR LODGE
DEGLNNRSUU UNDERSLUNG
DEGLNOOOTY DEONTOLOGY
DEGLNOORSU LOSE GROUND
DEGLNORRUU GROUND RULE
DEGLNORSSU GROUNDLESS
DEGLOORTTY TROGLODYTE
DEGMNNORSU GROUNDSMEN
DEGNNORRTU GROUND RENT
DEGNNORRUW UNDERGROWN
DEGNOORRSW WRONGDOERS
DEGORRSSTU DRUGSTORES
DEHHIKMOSS SHEIKHDOMS
DEHHILOPRS HOLDERSHIP
DEHHILORTW WITHHOLDER
DEHHIMOORR HEMORRHOID
DEHHLOOSSU HOUSEHOLDS
DEHHLORSST THRESHOLDS
DEHHMOOORT MOTHERHOOD
DEHHOOOOPP POOH-POOHED
DEHIIINOTT DITHIONITE
DEHIIINRST DISINHERIT
DEHIIKLLOO LIKELIHOOD
DEHIIKMRSS SKIRMISHED
DEHIILLOOV LIVELIHOOD
DEHIILLSVY DEVILISHLY
DEHIILMNPU DELPHINIUM
DEHIILNPSY SYLPHIDINE
DEHIIMMNPS MIDSHIPMEN
DEHIIMNOPR PREHOMINID
DEHIIMNPRU NEPHRIDIUM
DEHIIOPRST EDITORSHIP
DEHIIRSTVW WHIST DRIVE
DEHIKNOORW HOODWINKER
DEHIKNRSZZ DZERZHINSK
DEHILNNOOP INDOPHENOL

DEHILOOPSS SHOPSOILED
DEHILORSTV SHORT-LIVED
DEHILOSSTW DISH TOWELS
DEHIMMNORR HORN-RIMMED
DEHIMNORST HINDERMOST
DEHIMNOSSS MODISHNESS
DEHIMOOPPR HIPPODROME
DEHIMOSSTT METHODISTS
DEHINNPSUU UNPUNISHED
DEHINOORRS DISHONORER
DEHINOPSTY HYPNOTISED
DEHINOPTYZ HYPNOTIZED
DEHINORRSS HORRIDNESS
DEHINOSSTY DISHONESTY
DEHINRRSTU UNDERSHIRT
DEHIOOPRST PRIESTHOOD
DEHIOORSST SISTERHOOD
DEHIOPPRSW WORSHIPPED
DEHKLOOSST STOKEHOLDS
DEHLLOOSSU DOLL'S HOUSE
DEHLNOOPRY POLYHEDRON
DEHLORRSYY HYDROLYSER
DEHLORRYYZ HYDROLYZER
DEHMMOORSU MUSHROOMED
DEHMNOOPRY ENDOMORPHY
DEHNNOSSUW NEWSHOUNDS
DEHNOORRSU HORRENDOUS
DEHNOORSTU UNDERSHOOT
DEHNOORSUU ROUNDHOUSE
DEHNORSTUU THUNDEROUS
DEHOOPRSUU HOUSE-PROUD
DEHOOSSSSU DOSSHOUSES
DEIIIINSTV DIVINITIES
DEIIIKNSTT IDENTIKITS
DEIIILMSTU SIMILITUDE
DEIIILQRSU LIQUIDISER
DEIIILQRUZ LIQUIDIZER
DEIIILSVVY DIVISIVELY
DEIIIMNPRY PYRIMIDINE
DEIIIMNTUV DIMINUTIVE
DEIIIMSSSV DISMISSIVE
DEIIJMNORS MISJOINDER
DEIIKLNNSS KINDLINESS
DEIIKNRSSV SKIN DIVERS
DEIILLMPTU MULTIPLIED
DEIILLNOTU TOLLUIDINE
DEIILLNUWY UNWIELDILY
DEIILLRSST DISTILLERS
DEIILLRSTY DISTILLERY
DEIILMNOOT DEMOLITION
DEIILNPRTY INTREPIDLY
DEIILNPSST SPINDLIEST
DEIILORRSY DERISORILY
DEIILPRSTY SPIRITEDLY

DEIIMNNOSS DIMENSIONS
DEIIMNOPRS IMPRISONED
DEIIMNPRST MISPRINTED
DEIIMOPRSV IMPROVISED
DEIIMORTXY OXIDIMETRY
DEIIMPRSSU PRESIDIUMS
DEIINNOPPT PINPOINTED
DEIINNORST RENDITIONS
DEIINNOSSS DISSENSION
DEIINNOSST DISTENSION
DEIINNPRSU UNINSPIRED
DEIINNSSTU UNTIDINESS
DEIINOOPST DEPOSITION, POSITIONED
DEIINOPRSS DISPERSION
DEIINOPRXY PYRIDOXINE
DEIINORSSV DIVERSIONS
DEIINPPRST PINSTRIPED
DEIINRSSTU INDUSTRIES
DEIINSTTTU INSTITUTED
DEIIORSTTV DISTORTIVE
DEIIPRSTUV DISRUPTIVE
DEIJNNNOOR NONJOINDER
DEIKMPPRSU MUDSKIPPER
DEIKNNNORR NONDRINKER
DEIKNNNSSU UNKINDNESS
DEIKNRRSTU UNDERSKIRT
DEILLMNSSY MINDLESSLY
DEILLNNOTY INDOLENTLY
DEILLNORSS LORDLINESS
DEILLORSTW WORLDLIEST
DEILMMOSTY IMMODESTLY
DEILMNOSSU MOULDINESS
DEILMNPTUY IMPUDENTLY
DEILMRSSUY SURMISEDLY
DEILMSTTUU MULTITUDES
DEILNNNTUW WIND TUNNEL
DEILNOOTUV DEVOLUTION
DEILNRSTTY STRIDENTLY
DEILOORRTV LORD IT OVER
DEILOSTTWW SLOW-WITTED
DEIMMNORSS MODERNISMS
DEIMNNOSTW DISOWNMENT
DEIMNOOSSS ENDOSMOSIS
DEIMNOPRTU IMPORTUNED
DEIMNOPRUV UNIMPROVED
DEIMNORSST MODERNISTS
DEIMOPRSSU DISPERMOUS
DEIMRSSTTU MISTRUSTED
DEINOOPRSS DROOPINESS
DEINOOPTTU OUTPOINTED
DEINOORSWW ROSE WINDOW
DEINOOSSST ENDOSTOSIS
DEINOOSSSU ODIOUSNESS
DEINOOSTTX EXODONTIST

DEINOPSSSU SUSPENSOID
DEINORSSSS DROSSINESS
DEINORSSSW DROWSINESS
DEINPSSSTU STUPIDNESS
DEINRSSSTU STURDINESS
DEIOOPRSST DEPOSITORS
DEIOOPRSTY DEPOSITORY
DEIOPRRSTW SPIDERWORT
DEIOPSSSSS DISPOSSESS
DEIRRSSTTU DISTRUSTER
DEKKNOORWY DONKEYWORK
DEKLORSSVV SVERDLOVSK
DEKNOOPRUV UNPROVOKED
DEKNOORRWW WONDERWORK
DEKOOORRWW WOODWORKER
DELLOOOWWY YELLOWWOOD
DELLORSSWY WORDLESSLY
DELLOSSUUY SEDULOUSLY
DELNNOPSSU NONPLUSSED
DELNOOPRTU PLEURODONT
DELNOPRSUU PLUNDEROUS
DELOOPRRWW WORLD POWER
DELOPPSSUY SUPPOSEDLY
DELORRTTUY TORTUREDLY
DEMMOORSUW SUMMERWOOD
DEMNOPPRTU UNPROMPTED
DEMNOPSSUY PSEUDONYMS
DEMNORSTUU SURMOUNTED
DEMNPRRTUU UNDERTRUMP
DEMOOOPRRW POWDER ROOM
DENNORSSUW SUNDOWNERS
DENOOPPRRU PROPOUNDER
DENOPRRTTU PROTRUDENT
DENOPSSTUU STUPENDOUS
DEOORRSSUU UREDOSORUS
DEPRSSSSTU PRESS-STUDS
DFFFOOSSTU FOODSTUFFS
DFGGIIINNY DIGNIFYING
DFGHILLOOT FLOODLIGHT
DFGIIIMORT DIGITIFORM
DFGIINOSUU NIDIFUGOUS
DFGILLNNOY FONDLINGLY
DFGILNNOSU FOUNDLINGS
DFHILOORSY HYDROFOILS
DFHLNOOSUW WOLFHOUNDS
DFHLNSSSUU SLUSH FUNDS
DFHLOOOOPT PHOTOFLOOD
DFHLOOORTU HOLD OUT FOR
DFIKLOPPSY FLOPPY DISK
DFINOPRTUY PROFUNDITY
DFINORSSTW SNOWDRIFTS
DFLNOOPRUY PROFOUNDLY
DFNOOOPRSU SOUNDPROOF
DFNOOOORRST FRONT DOORS

DFNRSSTTUU TRUST FUNDS
DFOOOORSTU OUT OF DOORS
DGGGIINORS DISGORGING
DGGGILNRUY GRUDGINGLY
DGGGINNRUU UNGRUDGING
DGGIIIINTZ DIGITIZING
DGGIIINSSU DISGUISING
DGGIIJMNSU MISJUDGING
DGGIILMNNO GOLD-MINING
DGGIINSSTU DISGUSTING
DGGILNNORU GROUNDLING
DGGINNOORW WRONGDOING
DGHHIKNOOT KNIGHTHOOD
DGHHINOPST DIPHTHONGS
DGHIILLNNO HILLINGDON
DGHILMOSST GOLDSMITHS
DGHINNNOTU HUNTINGDON
DGHLNOORST STRONGHOLD
DGIIIKNNSV SKIN DIVING
DGIIIILLNST DISTILLING
DGIIIMNSSS DISMISSING
DGIIIINNSTU DISUNITING
DGIIINPTUY PINGUIDITY
DGIILNOOST INDOLOGIST
DGIILNOSSV DISSOLVING
DGIIMNNOOR DINING ROOM
DGIIMNNOPU IMPOUNDING
DGIINNPRSY SPIN-DRYING
DGIINOPRST DISPORTING
DGIINOPRSV DISPROVING
DGIINORSTT DISTORTING
DGIINPRSTU DISRUPTING
DGIIOOPRSU PRODIGIOUS
DGILNNOUWY WOUNDINGLY
DGINOOPRSW SPRINGWOOD
DGINOPRRTU PROTRUDING
DGKNOORRUW GROUNDWORK
DGLNOOOOTY ODONTOLOGY
DGNNORSTUU GROUNDNUTS
DHIILNRSWW WHIRLWINDS
DHIIMMOPRS DIMORPHISM
DHILLOPSUY DIPHYLLOUS
DHILMMOOSU HOODLUMISM
DHILORSSYY HYDROLYSIS
DHIMOOPRSU DIMORPHOUS
DHINOOOPRT ORNITHOPOD
DHINOOPSWW WINDOW-SHOP
DHINOPRSUW WHIP-ROUNDS
DHIOOPPRRY PORPHYROID
DHLMOOSTUU LOUDMOUTHS
DHNNOSTUUW SHUNT-WOUND
DHNOOORTUX UNORTHODOX
DIIIINPSTY INSIPIDITY
DIIILSTTUY DISUTILITY

DIIIMMORSU OSMIRIDIUM
DIIIMNNOTU DIMINUTION
DIILLNOSWW WINDOWSILL
DIIMMOPRRU PRIMORDIUM
DIINOORSTT DISTORTION
DIINOPRSTU DISRUPTION
DILLLOSSTY LLOYD'S LIST
DILLOOPPYY POLYPLOIDY
DILORSSTUU STRIDULOUS
DILOSSTUUY STUDIOUSLY
DIMMNOOOPU MONOPODIUM
DIMNORSSTW WINDSTORMS
DIMOPRSSUY DYSPROSIUM
DINOPRRSTU ROUND TRIPS
DIOOPQQRUU QUID PRO QUO
DLLOOORSUY DOLOROUSLY
DLOOOPPSUY POLYPODOUS
DMORSSSTTU DUST STORMS
DNNORRSTUU TURNROUNDS
DNOOPSSTUW DOWNSPOUTS
DNOOSSTTUY NOT SO DUSTY
EEEEEHMTTY MEET THE EYE
EEEEFFNSST EFFETENESS
EEEEFGINRR REFEREEING
EEEEFKLRSS SELF-SEEKER
EEEEFLMSST SELF-ESTEEM
EEEEGHHLTT GET THE HEEL
EEEEGIPSSX EPEXEGESIS
EEEEGNRRSV EVERGREENS
EEEEHIMRSU EUHEMERISE
EEEEHIMRUZ EUHEMERIZE
EEEEHPSSSY SHEEP'S EYES
EEEEHRRVWY EVERYWHERE
EEEEIKMPRT TIMEKEEPER
EEEEKMRRSY KERSEYMERE
EEEELLSSSV SLEEVELESS
EEEENNRRVV NEVER-NEVER
EEEENNRSSS SERENENESS
EEEENNTWYY TEENY WEENY
EEEENOPRSY EYE-OPENERS
EEEENRSSSV SEVERENESS
EEEENRSSTW SWEETENERS
EEEERRRTTV TERRE-VERTE
EEEFGIINNR FIRE ENGINE
EEEFGILNRS GREENFLIES
EEEFGIMRSU REFUGEEISM
EEEFGINORS FORESEEING
EEEFGLNRUV REVENGEFUL
EEEFHOORRT HERETOFORE
EEEFHORRSW WHEREFORES
EEEFHORSSU FREE HOUSES
EEEFIINRRS REFINERIES
EEEFILRSVX REFLEXIVES
EEEFIMNNRT REFINEMENT

EEEFINRRRT INTERFERER
EEEFKNOPRS FREE-SPOKEN
EEEFLLORRT FORETELLER
EEEFMNPRRT PREFERMENT
EEEFNNORSU UNFORESEEN
EEEFNQRRTU FREQUENTER
EEEGHHINRT HEIGHTENER
EEEGHHINTT EIGHTEENTH
EEEGHIMNOT EIGHTEENMO
EEEGHKLNNT KNEE-LENGTH
EEEGHLNNRT LENGTHENER
EEEGHNNOST STONEHENGE
EEEGHNORSU GREENHOUSE
EEEGHNORTW GET NOWHERE
EEEGIINPSS EPIGENESIS
EEEGIJNNST JET ENGINES
EEEGIMORST GEOMETRISE
EEEGIMORTZ GEOMETRIZE
EEEGINNPST STEEPENING
EEEGINNSTW SWEETENING
EEEGINOPRY EPEIROGENY
EEEGINORSV OVERSEEING
EEEGINORTY EROGENEITY
EEEGIRRRST REGISTERER
EEEGIRRSSV REGRESSIVE
EEEGLNNSST GENTLENESS
EEEGMNRSSS MESSENGERS
EEEGNNORST GREENSTONE
EEEHHIMPRS HEMISPHERE
EEEHHLOSUW WHEELHOUSE
EEEHHOTTTT TO THE TEETH
EEEHIKLLMT HELMET-LIKE
EEEHILLNRS HELLENISER
EEEHILLNRZ HELLENIZER
EEEHILMORT HELIOMETER
EEEHILNPRS PREHENSILE
EEEHILPSSS LESSEESHIP
EEEHIMMRSU EUHEMERISM
EEEHIMPRSU EUPHEMISER
EEEHIMPRUZ EUPHEMIZER
EEEHIMRSTU EUHEMERIST
EEEHIMSSTT TIME SHEETS
EEEHINNNTT NINETEENTH
EEEHINNTTV IN THE EVENT
EEEHINPSST EPENTHESIS
EEEHINSSWZ WHEEZINESS
EEEHINSTTV SEVENTIETH
EEEHJNOSST THE JONESES
EEEHKLOPTT KEEL THE POT
EEEHKOPPRS SHOPKEEPER
EEEHLMNTVY VEHEMENTLY
EEEHLMSSTV THEMSELVES
EEEHLNOPRT TELEPHONER
EEEHLNOPST TELEPHONES

EEEHMOPRSS MESOSPHERE
EEEHMORSST THREESOMES
EEEHNORSSS HORSE SENSE
EEEHNORSVW WHENSOEVER
EEEHNPRSTT THE PRESENT
EEEHNSSSTW NEWSSHEETS
EEEHOPPRRT TREEHOPPER
EEEHORRTVY EVERY OTHER
EEEHRSSTTU USHERETTES
EEEIINRSTT ETERNITIES
EEEIIPRTTV REPETITIVE
EEEIIRSSTV SEVERITIES
EEEIJLMRSS IJSSELMEER
EEEIKLMSWY SEMIWEEKLY
EEEIKLNSSS LIKENESSES
EEEIKNNPRS INNKEEPERS
EEEILMMORT MILEOMETER
EEEILMNRST RESILEMENT
EEEILMNRTV REVILEMENT
EEEILMNSSS SEEMLINESS
EEEILMNSTY MESITYLENE
EEEILNPRRT TERREPLEIN
EEEILNPSSS SLEEPINESS
EEEILNSSST STEELINESS
EEEILORRTU EURE-ET-LOIR
EEEILPSTVX EXPLETIVES
EEEILRRTTW TELEWRITER
EEEILRSSSW WIRELESSES
EEEILRSSTW WESTERLIES
EEEIMMRRSS MESMERISER
EEEIMMRRSZ MESMERIZER
EEEIMNNPRT PRE-EMINENT
EEEIMNORST REMONETISE
EEEIMNORTZ REMONETIZE
EEEIMNPRTX EXPERIMENT
EEEIMNRRTT RETIREMENT
EEEIMNRSTT TENSIMETER
EEEIMORSTT METEORITES
EEEIMPPRTV PRE-EMPTIVE
EEEIMPRRST PERIMETERS
EEEIMRRSTV TIMESERVER
EEEINNPRSS PERSIENNES
EEEINNPRST SERPENTINE
EEEINNPRTV PREVENIENT
EEEINNRRTV INTERVENER
EEEINNRSST ENTIRENESS
EEEINPRRST ENTERPRISE
EEEINPRSTV VESPERTINE
EEEINPRTVV PREVENTIVE
EEEINRRRTV IRREVERENT
EEEINRSSTW WESTERNISE
EEEINRSTWZ WESTERNIZE
EEEINSSTWY EYEWITNESS
EEEIOPRRRT REPERTOIRE

EEEIPRRSSV REPRESSIVE
EEEIPRSSVX EXPRESSIVE
EEEIRRRSTV RETRIEVERS
EEEIRSSTTV SERVIETTES
EEEIRSSTTW STREETWISE
EEEJRSSTTT JET-SETTERS
EEEKLNRSUV LEVERKUSEN
EEEKMRSSTU MUSKETEERS
EEELLNPRST REPELLENTS
EEELLNPSUV ELEVEN-PLUS
EEELLNRSST RELENTLESS
EEELMMOSTT METTLESOME
EEELMNOPST ELOPEMENTS
EEELMNOSTT NETTLESOME
EEELMNOTVV EVOLVEMENT
EEELMNSTTT SETTLEMENT
EEELNOPRTT OPEN LETTER
EEELNOSTTV NOVELETTES
EEELNOTTVW TWELVE-TONE
EEELNRRTVY REVERENTLY
EEELNRSTTW NEWSLETTER
EEELORSVWW WEREWOLVES
EEELPRRSVY PERVERSELY
EEEMNNORST MESENTERON
EEEMNNRSTT RESENTMENT
EEEMNORSST REMOTENESS
EEEMNRSTTV REVETMENTS
EEENNNSSUV UNEVENNESS
EEENORSTWZ SNEEZEWORT
EEENPRRSST PRESENTERS
EEENPRSSTX EXPERTNESS
EEENRRSSTW WESTERNERS
EEEOOPRSVX OVEREXPOSE
EEEOPRRRTX RE-EXPORTER
EEEOPRSTTY STEREOTYPE
EEEORRRSTV RETROVERSE
EEEPPPRSTU PUPPETEERS
EEEPRRRSSV PRESERVERS
EEEPRSTTTY TYPESETTER
EEEFFFKLRSU KERFUFFLES
EEFFGIINRV FIVE-FINGER
EEFFGINORR FOREFINGER
EEFFHINSTT FIFTEENTHS
EEFFHLRRSU REFRESHFUL
EEFFHLRSSU RESHUFFLES
EEFFILSUVY EFFUSIVELY
EEFFINOSSV OFFENSIVES
EEFFINRSST STIFFENERS
EEFFIORRST FORFEITERS
EEFFIORRTU FORFEITURE
EEFFLORSST EFFORTLESS
EEFFNORRTY EFFRONTERY
EEFGHHIILR HIGH RELIEF
EEFGHINNRS FRESHENING

EEFGHINRRS REFRESHING
EEFGHINRRT FRIGHTENER
EEFGHIRRST FREIGHTERS
EEFGHLOOSS GOOSEFLESH
EEFGIILLNS SINGLE FILE
EEFGIILNRV FREE-LIVING
EEFGILLNRU REFUELLING
EEFGILLNTY FLEETINGLY
EEFGILNRTW LEFT-WINGER
EEFGIMNNRT FERMENTING
EEFGINNRRT REFRINGENT
EEFGINORRS FOREIGNERS
EEFGINPRRR PREFERRING
EEFGKLLNOT GENTLEFOLK
EEFGLLMNOR FELLMONGER
EEFGLLNUVY VENGEFULLY
EEFGLMNNTU ENGULFMENT
EEFHHLORSS HORSEFLESH
EEFHIINRRS REFINISHER
EEFHILLSSV SHELF LIVES
EEFHILNSSS FLESHINESS
EEFHILORSS HORSEFLIES
EEFHILOSSU HOUSEFLIES
EEFHILRSVY FEVERISHLY
EEFHLNOORS HOLOFERNES
EEFHNORTTU FOURTEENTH
EEFIILLMPS SIMPLE LIFE
EEFIILMRSU EMULSIFIER
EEFIILNSSW WIFELINESS
EEFIILRRST FERTILISER
EEFIILRRTZ FERTILIZER
EEFIIMNNNU UNFEMININE
EEFIINNNRS SINN FEINER
EEFIINRRST FINISTERRE
EEFIKLLORW FLOWER-LIKE
EEFIKLORST FOREST-LIKE
EEFILLLSSY LIFELESSLY
EEFILLNOTU FEUILLETON
EEFILLSSTY LIFESTYLES
EEFILMRSTT FILMSETTER
EEFILNNORT FLORENTINE
EEFILNPPTT FELT-TIP PEN
EEFILNRTUV INTERFLUVE
EEFINNORRT INTERFERON
EEFINNQRTU INFREQUENT
EEFIOPRRST PROFITEERS
EEFIORRRTX FOX TERRIER
EEFIORRSTT FORSTERITE
EEFIRRRSTU FRUITERERS
EEFKLNOOST FOLKESTONE
EEFLLLSSSY SELFLESSLY
EEFLLNTUVY EVENTFULLY
EEFLLORSSW FLOWERLESS
EEFLMORRSU REMORSEFUL

EEFLNNTUUV UNEVENTFUL
EEFLNOSSUW WOEFULNESS
EEFLNQRTUY FREQUENTLY
EEFLNRSSUU RUEFULNESS
EEFLNSSSUU USEFULNESS
EEFMOPRRRS PERFORMERS
EEFNNORRRU FORERUNNER
EEFNNORSSZ FROZENNESS
EEFNOOPRRS FOR OPENERS
EEFNOORSTY FESTOONERY
EEFORRSSST FORTRESSES
EEGGHILNRT GREEN LIGHT
EEGGIINNRZ ENERGIZING
EEGGIMNNST SEGMENTING
EEGGINOTUV GIVE TONGUE
EEGGINRRSS REGRESSING
EEGGINRRTT REGRETTING
EEGGISSTUV SUGGESTIVE
EEGHHIISTT EIGHTIETHS
EEGHHILNST THE ENGLISH
EEGHHINOTT EIGHTH NOTE
EEGHHINSSS HIGHNESSES
EEGHHIRSTT HIGH STREET
EEGHHORSTU SEE-THROUGH
EEGHIKLRSU KIESELGUHR
EEGHIKNSTW WEEKNIGHTS
EEGHILMNNS ENGLISHMEN
EEGHILNOOP PIGEONHOLE
EEGHILNRST SHELTERING
EEGHILNSTT LENGTHIEST
EEGHILNSTY SEETHINGLY
EEGHILNWYZ WHEEZINGLY
EEGHILOOST THEOLOGIES, THEOLOGISE
EEGHILOOTZ THEOLOGIZE
EEGHILSSTW WEIGHTLESS
EEGHIMNOOS HOMOGENISE
EEGHIMNOOZ HOMOGENIZE
EEGHINOPST PHOSGENITE
EEGHINPRST REGENTSHIP
EEGHINRTVY EVERYTHING
EEGHIORTVW OVERWEIGHT
EEGHIRSSST SIGHTSEERS
EEGHLOORTY HETEROLOGY
EEGHMNOSST THEME SONGS
EEGHNNORRS GREENHORNS
EEGHNNRSTT STRENGTHEN
EEGHNOORTY HETEROGONY
EEGHOSSTUU GUESTHOUSE
EEGIIILMST LEGITIMISE
EEGIIILMTZ LEGITIMIZE
EEGIIKLPRS KRIEGSPIEL
EEGIILNNNV ENLIVENING
EEGIILNSTV TELEVISING
EEGIILPRSV PRIVILEGES

EEGIINNOPR PIONEERING
EEGIINNQTU QUIETENING
EEGIINPRRV REPRIEVING
EEGIINPRVW PREVIEWING
EEGIINRRTV RETRIEVING
EEGIINRSSV INGRESSIVE
EEGIIRRSST REGISTRIES
EEGIKLLNNN KENNELLING
EEGILMNORS MONGRELISE
EEGILMNORZ MONGRELIZE
EEGILNNOPV ENVELOPING
EEGILNNRSY SNEERINGLY
EEGILNNSSS SINGLENESS
EEGILNNSUY UNSEEINGLY
EEGILNOSST TELEGNOSIS
EEGILNPPRX PERPLEXING
EEGILNPSWY SWEEPINGLY
EEGILNRSTT RESETTLING
EEGILNRSTW SWELTERING
EEGIMNNOTT MIGNONETTE
EEGIMNNTTU INTEGUMENT
EEGIMNOORT GONIOMETER
EEGIMNOPPT PEEPING TOM
EEGIMNOPRW EMPOWERING
EEGIMNPPRT PRE-EMPTING
EEGINNOOTT OTTO ENGINE
EEGINNOPPS PEPSINOGEN
EEGINNPRST PRESENTING
EEGINNPRTV PREVENTING
EEGINOPSSY PYOGENESIS
EEGINORRSS REGRESSION
EEGINORSSV SOVEREIGNS
EEGINORSTY GENEROSITY
EEGINORSXY OXYGENISER
EEGINORXYZ OXYGENIZER
EEGINPRRSS REPRESSING
EEGINPRRSV PRESERVING
EEGINPRRTV PERVERTING
EEGINPRSSX EXPRESSING
EEGINPRSTT PRESETTING
EEGINQRSTU REQUESTING
EEGLLLOSWY YELLOWLEGS
EEGLLNOOSY SELENOLOGY
EEGLLOOPSY SPELEOLOGY
EEGLLORRSV GROVELLERS
EEGLMORSUY GRUESOMELY
EEGLNORSTT LORGNETTES
EEGLNORSUY GENEROUSLY
EEGLOORRST ERGOSTEROL
EEGMNNOORT MONTENEGRO
EEGMNNORTV GOVERNMENT
EEGNNORSUU UNGENEROUS
EEGNNOTTXY OXYGEN TENT
EEGOOPSSST GOOSESTEPS

EEGOPRRSSS PROGRESSES
EEGOPRSTUU PORTUGUESE
EEGOQRSSTU GROTESQUES
EEGORRRSST RETROGRESS
EEHHILMPTT PITH HELMET
EEHHILPSSY SHEEPISHLY
EEHHIMNOST HENOTHEISM
EEHHINOSSS SHOESHINES
EEHHINOSTT HENOTHEIST
EEHHINRTTT THIRTEENTH
EEHHIOPSTW WHITE HOPES
EEHHIORRSS SHIRE HORSE
EEHHIORSTW WHITE HORSE
EEHHIOSTUW WHITE HOUSE
EEHHOORSSS HORSESHOES
EEHHOORSUW WHOREHOUSE
EEHHOPSSTY HYPOTHESES
EEHIILMPTU EPITHELIUM
EEHIILNOPR PERIHELION
EEHIIMNNOT METHIONINE
EEHIINNSTT NINETIETHS
EEHIJRSTTT THE JITTERS
EEHIKNPSSS SHEEPSKINS
EEHIKOSSTT TO THE SKIES
EEHIKPPTUW KEEP UP WITH
EEHILLLMSW MILLWHEELS
EEHILLRSWW WELL-WISHER
EEHILMNOSS HOMELINESS
EEHILMOPRT THERMOPILE
EEHILMORTY HELIOMETRY
EEHILNNOOS HOLES IN ONE
EEHILNNRTY INHERENTLY
EEHILNOSSS HOLINESSES
EEHILOOPRT HELIOTROPE
EEHILOPRST PRIEST-HOLE
EEHILORSST HOSTELRIES
EEHILOSTTU SILHOUETTE
EEHILPRSTU SPHERULITE
EEHIMMOOSV HOME MOVIES
EEHIMMPSSU EUPHEMISMS
EEHIMNNOTY IN THE MONEY
EEHIMNOPPS HIPPOMENES
EEHIMNOPRT HEMIPTERON
EEHIMNPRST RESHIPMENT
EEHINNOPRS PREHENSION
EEHINNOPRT INTERPHONE
EEHINNORST RHINESTONE
EEHINOOPRS IONOSPHERE
EEHINSSSTX SIXTH SENSE
EEHINSSSTY SYNTHESISE
EEHINSSTTX SIXTEENTHS
EEHINSSTYZ SYNTHESIZE
EEHINSTTTW TWENTIETHS
EEHIOPPRRS PROPHESIER

EEHIOPPRSS PROPHESIES
EEHIOSSUVW HOUSEWIVES
EEHIPRRSSW WHISPERERS
EEHKKOOPYY HOKEY-POKEY
EEHKMOOSSU SMOKEHOUSE
EEHKNOORTT TENTERHOOK
EEHLLLPSSY HELPLESSLY
EEHLLMNOOP MELLOPHONE
EEHLLNOOPS HENLE'S LOOP
EEHLLNOPST HELLESPONT
EEHLLOPSSY HOPELESSLY
EEHLLORSST HOSTELLERS
EEHLMNOOYZ HOLOENZYME
EEHLMNORTY HEMELYTRON
EEHLMORSST MOTHERLESS
EEHLNOOSSV SHOVELNOSE
EEHLNOOSTW WHOLE NOTES
EEHLLOORSUW LOWER HOUSE
EEHMNNNOOP PHENOMENON
EEHMNOOPRT PHONOMETER
EEHMNOORSW HORSEWOMEN
EEHMNOORTY HETERONOMY
EEHMNORSTT NETHERMOST
EEHMNPSTTU UMPTEENTHS
EEHMOOPRTT PHOTOMETER
EEHMOPRSSU MORPHEUSES
EEHMOPRSTT STEPMOTHER
EEHMOQRSUU HUMORESQUE
EEHMRRSSTY RHYMESTERS
EEHNNOPSSY PHONEYNESS
EEHNNORRRT NORTHERNER
EEHNNOSSST HONESTNESS
EEHNOORTTU ON THE OUTER
EEHNOPSSTU PENTHOUSES
EEHNOPSTUY HYPOTENUSE
EEHNORRSTU SOUTHERNER
EEHNOSSTTW WHETSTONES
EEHNPPRSSU PEN PUSHERS
EEHNRSSSTU HUNTRESSES
EEHOOPRRSW HORSEPOWER
EEHOOPRSUW POWERHOUSE
EEHOOPRTTY HETEROTOPY
EEHOOPSTTY OSTEOPHYTE
EEHOORSSTU STOREHOUSE
EEHOOSTTTW SWEET TOOTH
EEHOPPRSUU UPPER HOUSE
EEHOPRRSTV SHREVEPORT
EEIIINQSTU INEQUITIES
EEIIKLNPRW PERIWINKLE
EEIILLMMRT MILLIMETER, MILLIMETRE
EEIILLNSSV LIVELINESS
EEIILMNSST TIMELINESS
EEIILNNRRT INTERLINER
EEIILNOSTV TELEVISION

EEIIILORSTT TOILETRIES
EEIIILPRRST PRIESTLIER
EEIIILRRSST STERILISER
EEIIILRRSTZ STERILIZER
EEIIMNNPTT IMPENITENT
EEIIMNORST ENORMITIES
EEIIMNPRUU EPINEURIUM
EEIIMNRSTX IN EXTREMIS
EEIIMNRTTW WINTERTIME
EEIIMNRTZZ INTERMEZZI
EEIIMOPRST EPITOMISER
EEIIMOPRTZ EPITOMIZER
EEIIMPRSSV IMPRESSIVE, PERMISSIVE
EEIINNNNTY NINETY-NINE
EEIINNNSTU INSENTIENT
EEIINNRTTW INTERTWINE
EEIINNSSSW SINEWINESS
EEIINNSSTT INTESTINES
EEIINNSTTX INEXISTENT
EEIINOPRTT PETITIONER, REPETITION
EEIINRSSST SENSITISER
EEIINRSSTZ SENSITIZER
EEIINRSTVW INTERVIEWS
EEIIORRSST ROTISSERIE
EEIIPQRSTU PERQUISITE
EEIIQRSSTU REQUISITES
EEIIJLORSSV OVERIJSSEL
EEIIJMNNNOT ENJOINMENT
EEIKLMORST KILOMETERS, KILOMETRES
EEIKMORRTW TIMEWORKER
EEIKMRSSTU MUSKETRIES
EEIKNRRSTT RENT STRIKE
EEIKORRRWW WIREWORKER
EEILLLPSTV SPLIT-LEVEL
EEILLMMORT IMMORTELLE
EEILLMNOST EMOLLIENTS
EEILLMNSSS SMELLINESS
EEILLMPPPR PEPPER MILL
EEILLMSSTY TIMELESSLY
EEILLNNOSS LONELINESS
EEILLNOSSV LOVELINESS
EEILLNRSSV SNIVELLERS
EEILLORSTT TITLE ROLES
EEILLRSSTY TIRELESSLY
EEILMMNPST IMPLEMENTS
EEILMMORST MILOMETERS
EEILMNNSTT ENLISTMENT
EEILMNORSS SOLEMNISER
EEILMNORSZ SOLEMNIZER
EEILMNOSST MILESTONES
EEILMNOSSU MOUSSELINE
EEILMNPPRS PIMPERNELS
EEILMNPSSS SIMPLENESS
EEILMOPRSY POLYMERISE

EEILMOPRYZ POLYMERIZE
EEILMORSTY TIRESOMELY
EEILMOSSTV MOTIVELESS
EEILMOSSVW SEMIVOWELS
EEILMPRSTU PULSIMETER
EEILNNOQTU INELOQUENT
EEILNNPTTY PENITENTLY
EEILNNSSST SILENTNESS
EEILNOPRRT INTERLOPER
EEILNOPSST POLITENESS
EEILNPRTXY INEXPERTLY
EEILOOPRST TELIOSPORE
EEILOPRSTX EXPLOITERS
EEILOPSSVX EXPLOSIVES
EEILORRSTU IRRESOLUTE
EEILORRTTW ROTTWEILER
EEILPPRTXY PERPLEXITY
EEILPPSTUV SUPPLETIVE
EEILPRRSTY SPERRYLITE
EEILPRRSUV PULVERISER
EEILPRRUVZ PULVERIZER
EEILPRSSTY PERISTYLES
EEILRSSSST RESISTLESS
EEIMMMRSTU SUMMERTIME
EEIMMOPRRV PRIME MOVER
EEIMMRSSST MESMERISTS
EEIMMRSSTY SYMMETRISE
EEIMMRSTYZ SYMMETRIZE
EEIMNNNRTT INTERNMENT
EEIMNNOPTT PENTIMENTO
EEIMNNORST MINESTRONE
EEIMNNRSTT INTERMENTS
EEIMNNSSTT SENTIMENTS
EEIMNNSSTU MINUTENESS
EEIMNNSTTV INVESTMENT
EEIMNOPPRT PRE-EMPTION
EEIMNOPRTU PERITONEUM
EEIMNOPSTX EXEMPTIONS
EEIMNORRSS SERMONISER
EEIMNORRSZ SERMONIZER
EEIMNORRTT NITROMETER
EEIMNORTZZ INTERMEZZO
EEIMNPPPRT PEPPERMINT
EEIMNPRSTU EPISTERNUM
EEIMNRSSSS REMISSNESS
EEIMNRSSTU TERMINUSES
EEIMNRSSTW WESTERNISM
EEIMOPRRST SPIROMETER, TEMPORISER
EEIMOPRRTZ TEMPORIZER
EEIMOPRSTU PERIOSTEUM
EEIMPPRRUU PUERPERIUM
EEIMPRSTUV RESUMPTIVE
EEIMRRSSTT TRIMESTERS
EEIMRSSSST MISTRESSES

EEIMRSSSTY SYSTEMISER
EEIMRSSTYZ SYSTEMIZER
EEINNNSSTT INTENTNESS
EEINNOPRSS PENSIONERS
EEINNOPRST PRETENSION, TIN OPENERS
EEINNOPRTV PREVENTION
EEINNORTVW INTERWOVEN
EEINNOSSTX EXTENSIONS
EEINNPRTTU TURPENTINE
EEINNPSSSU SUPINENESS
EEINNQSSUU UNIQUENESS
EEINOPPRST PEPTONISER
EEINOPPRTZ PEPTONIZER
EEINOPQTTU EQUIPOTENT
EEINOPRRSS REPRESSION
EEINOPRRST INTERPOSER
EEINOPRRSV PERVERSION
EEINOPRSSV RESPONSIVE
EEINOPRSSX EXPRESSION
EEINOPRSXY EPOXY RESIN
EEINOPRTXY PYROXENITE
EEINOQRSTU QUESTIONER
EEINOSSTVV VOTIVENESS
EEINPRSSTT PERSISTENT, PRETTINESS
EEINPSSSUV SUSPENSIVE
EEIOPPRRST PROPERTIES
EEIOPPRSSV OPPRESSIVE
EEIOPRRSTV RESORPTIVE
EEIOPRSSST STEREOPSIS
EEIOPRSTTT OPERETTIST
EEIOPRSTTU PIROUETTES
EEIOPSSSSV POSSESSIVE
EEIORRRRST TERRORISER
EEIORRRRTZ TERRORIZER
EEIORRRSST ROISTERERS
EEIORRRSSV RESERVOIRS
EEIPPRTTUY PERPETUITY
EEIPRRSSSU PRESSURISE
EEIPRRSSUZ PRESSURIZE
EEIPRRSTVY PERVERSITY
EEIPRRTTWY TYPEWRITER
EEIPRSSSTT STEPSISTER
EEIRRSSSTV RESERVISTS
EEJMNNORUY JOURNEYMEN
EEJMNNOSTY ENJOYMENTS
EEKLLNOPSW WELL-SPOKEN
EEKLOOPPRW WORKPEOPLE
EEKLORSSTW STEELWORKS
EELLMNOOSS LEMON SOLES
EELLMNOSSW MELLOWNESS
EELLNNSSSU SULLENNESS
EELLNOPPRT PROPELLENT
EELLNOQTUY ELOQUENTLY
EELLNOSSTY TONELESSLY

EELLNSSTUY TUNELESSLY
EELLOPPRRS PROPELLERS
EELLORSTUY RESOLUTELY
EELLRSSSTY RESTLESSLY
EELMMNOPTY EMPLOYMENT
EELMMNOSTU EMOLUMENTS
EELMNNORST ENROLMENTS
EELMNNOSSS SOLEMNNESS
EELMNOOSSZ ZOOM LENSES
EELMNPPSTU SUPPLEMENT
EELMNPTUZZ PUZZLEMENT
EELMOOPSTT TOTEM POLES
EELNOPRSTW SPLEENWORT
EELNORSTUV VOLUNTEERS
EELNPPRSSU PURPLENESS
EELNPPSSSU SUPPLENESS
EELOOPRSTT PROTOSTELE
EELOPRRSTU POULTERERS
EELOPRSSTY PROSELYTES
EELORSSUVY YOURSELVES
EELPRRSTTU SPLUTTERER
EELPSSTTUX SEXTUPLETS
EEMMNOORST METRONOMES
EEMNNOPSTT PENTSTEMON
EEMNNRRSUY NURSERYMEN
EEMNOORSSS MOROSENESS
EEMNOORTTY ENTEROTOMY
EEMOOPPRRT PRO TEMPORE
EEMOORSTTY STEREOTOMY
EEMOPPRRTY PEREMPTORY, PRE-
EMPTORY
EEMORSSTTU METOESTRUS
EEMPRRSTTU TRUMPETERS
EEMQRSSTUU SEQUESTRUM
EENNNNOOSS NO-NONSENSE
EENNOOOSST ON ONE'S TOES
EENNOPSSTT POTENTNESS
EENNORSSTT ROTTENNESS
EENNOSSSUV VENOUSNESS
EENOOPPSSS POPE'S NOSES
EENOPPRRSS PROPERNESS
EEOPPPPRST PEPPER POTS
EEOPPPRRTW PEPPERWORT
EEOPPPRSSU PRESUPPOSE
EEOPPRRSUW SUPERPOWER
EEOPPRSSSS PREPOSSESS
EEOPPRRSTT PROTESTERS
EEOPRSTTYY STEREOTYPY
EEORRSTTVX EXTROVERTS
EEORSSSTUW SOU'WESTERS
EERRSSTTTU STUTTERERS
EFFFILNSSU FLUFFINESS
EFFGHIINRS FISH FINGER
EFFGIINNST STIFFENING

EFFGIINORT FORFEITING
EFFGILLNOT TELLING-OFF
EFFGINOPRR PROFFERING
EFFGINOSTT OFFSETTING
EFFGINRSSU SUFFERINGS
EFFIIKLOSS KISS OF LIFE
EFFIILRSTU FRUIT FLIES
EFFIIORRST FORTIFIERS
EFFIIQSSTU SQUIFFIEST
EFFILLMNTU FULFILMENT
EFFINNSSSU SNUFFINESS
EFFINSSSTU STUFFINESS
EFFNNOOSTU OFF ONE'S NUT
EFGGHIINRT FREIGHTING
EFGGIILNNR FINGERLING
EFGGIILNNY FEIGNINGLY
EFGGIINNRR RING FINGER
EFGGINOORS FOREGOINGS
EFGGINORTT FORGETTING
EFGHHIILRS HIGH-FLIERS
EFGHIIKNRS KINGFISHER
EFGHIILSTT FLIGHTIEST
EFGHIIPRST PRISEFIGHT
EFGHIIPRTZ PRIZEFIGHT
EFGHILLSST FLIGHTLESS
EFGHILORTV OVERFLIGHT
EFGHILSTWY FLYWEIGHTS
EFGHIMNORS FISHMONGER
EFGHINRRTU FURTHERING
EFGHIORSST GIFT HORSES
EFGHLLLNTU FULL-LENGTH
EFGHLLNORU FLUGELHORN
EFGHOOPPRR FROGHOPPER
EFGIIILNNR FIRING LINE
EFGIIILNQUY LIQUEFYING
EFGIIMNORS FOREIGNISM
EFGIINNNTU FINE-TUNING
EFGIINPRST FINGERTIPS
EFGIINPRSY PRESIGNIFY
EFGIINPRTY PETRIFYING
EFGIINRRTT FRITTERING
EFGIINRRTY TERRIFYING
EFGIINRSTU SURFEITING
EFGIINSTTY TESTIFYING
EFGILLLUUY GUILEFULLY
EFGILLNNNU FUNNELLING
EFGILLORRW FLOWER GIRL
EFGILNORST FOSTERLING
EFGILNORVY OVERFLYING
EFGILNRSTU FLUSTERING
EFGILNRTTU FLUTTERING
EFGIMNOPRR PERFORMING
EFGINNOOST FESTOONING
EFGINNORUV UNFORGIVEN

EFGINOPRSS PROFESSING
EFGINPRTUY PUTREFYING
EFGINPSTUY STUPEFYING
EFGLOOSTUV TUGS-OF-LOVE
EFHHIOORTT HIT THE ROOF
EFHHLOSSTU HOT FLUSHES
EFHIIKNSSV FISH KNIVES
EFHIILNSST FILTHINESS
EFHIILRSSV SILVERFISH
EFHIINSSST SHIFTINESS
EFHIIRSTTT THRIFTIEST
EFHIISSSTT FETISHISTS
EFHILLOPSW FELLOWSHIP
EFHILOPRST SHOPLIFTER
EFHILORRSU FLOURISHER
EFHILORSSU FLOURISHES
EFHILRSSTT THRIFTLESS
EFHIMNNOPR PHENFORMIN
EFHINORSST FROTHINESS
EFHLLOOPRS SHELLPROOF
EFHLLOSSUU FULL HOUSES
EFHLOOPSSU FLOPHOUSES
EFHNORSTUX FOXHUNTERS
EFIIIINNTV INFINITIVE
EFIIILMPRS SIMPLIFIER
EFIIILNNTY INFINITELY
EFIIIMNNTY FEMININITY
EFIIKNRSSS FRISKINESS
EFIILLLSST STILL LIFES
EFIILLNRSS FRILLINESS
EFIILMNSSS FLIMSINESS
EFIILNNSST FLINTINESS
EFIILOPRSU PILIFEROUS
EFIILPRSTT FILTER TIPS
EFIILRSTTU STULTIFIER
EFIIMORRSU FOURIERISM
EFIINORSUV VINIFEROUS
EFIINRSSTU FRUITINESS
EFIINRSSZZ FRIZZINESS
EFIIORRSTU FOURIERIST
EFIKLNOSSS FOLKSINESS
EFILLMORST STELLIFORM
EFILLNSSUW WILFULNESS
EFILLOOPRW LOW PROFILE
EFILLPSTUY SPITEFULLY
EFILMNPTTU UPLIFTMENT
EFILMOOPRS SIMFEROPOL
EFILNNSSSU SINFULNESS
EFILNOPPSS FLOPPINESS
EFILNORTWW TWINFLOWER
EFILOPRSST PROFITLESS
EFIMNORSTU MISFORTUNE
EFIMOOPRSU POMIFEROUS
EFIMORRSST FIRESTORMS

EFINNORRTY FORTY-NINER
EFINOOPRSS PROFESSION
EFINOORSSU SONIFEROUS
EFINORSSST FROSTINESS
EFINORSSWZ FROWZINESS
EFINORSTTU STONE FRUIT
EFIOOPRRSU PORIFEROUS
EFIOORSSSU OSSIFEROUS
EFIOORSSTX SIX-FOOTERS
EFIOPRSTTU PETIT FOURS
EFIORSTTTU OUTFITTERS
EFJLNOSSUY JOYFULNESS
EFKNOOPSST SOFT-SPOKEN
EFKOORRSTU FOUR-STROKE
EFLLMORSSY FORMLESSLY
EFLLOPRUWY POWERFULLY
EFLMNOOORW MOONFLOWER
EFLMOOORTY TOMFOOLERY
EFLNORSSUW SUNFLOWERS
EFLOOPRSTW FLOWERPOTS
EFLOPPRSUU PURPOSEFUL
EFNNOORRSU NONFERROUS
EFOOPRRSSS PROFESSORS
EFOOPRRSTU FOUR-POSTER
EGGGIINNRS SNIGGERING
EGGGIINRRT TRIGGERING
EGGGINORSS GROGGINESS
EGGGINSSTU SUGGESTING
EGGHHIPRSU HIPHUGGERS
EGGHIIINNV INVEIGHING
EGGHIILNNT LIGHTENING
EGGHIINNTT TIGHTENING
EGGHINNORU ROUGHENING
EGGHINNOTU TOUGHENING
EGGIIILNNV INVEIGLING
EGGIILMMNR GLIMMERING
EGGIILNNST GLISTENING
EGGIILNOUZ EULOGIZING
EGGIILNRTT GLITTERING
EGGIILNRVY GRIEVINGLY
EGGIINNTTV VIGNETTING
EGGILLNORV GROVELLING
EGGILMOOST GEMOLOGIST
EGGILNSSUY GUESSINGLY
EGGILOOSST GEOLOGISTS
EGGINNORSS ENGROSSING
EGGINNPSTU TUNING PEGS
EGGINNRSTU GINGER NUTS
EGGINOORSV GOINGS-OVER
EGGINOPRRU REGROUPING
EGGINOSSTU SUGGESTION
EGGIOPRSTT GET TO GRIPS
EGGIORRSTU OUTRIGGERS
EGGLLOOOPX GOOGOLPLEX

EGGLOOPTYY EGYPTOLOGY
EGGLOORSUY GORGEOUSLY
EGHHHIORSS HIGH HORSES
EGHHIINRTT IN THE RIGHT
EGHHIIPRST HIGH PRIEST
EGHHIJMPRU HIGH JUMPER
EGHHILOPRY HIEROGLYPH
EGHHILOSTU LIGHTHOUSE
EGHHINORTU IN THE ROUGH
EGHHOORSUU ROUGHHOUSE
EGHIIINNRT INHERITING
EGHIIKNNRT RETHINKING
EGHIILNRST SLITHERING
EGHIILNRSV SHRIVELING
EGHIILNTVY THIEVINGLY
EGHIIMMNRS SHIMMERING
EGHIIMNPRW WHIMPERING
EGHIIMNSST MIGHTINESS
EGHIINNNRS ENSHRINING
EGHIINNPRT TREPHINING
EGHIINNPSS ENSIGNSHIP
EGHIINORTZ THEORIZING
EGHIINPRSW WHISPERING
EGHIINSSTY HYGIENISTS
EGHIINSTUX EXTINGUISH
EGHILLNOST HOSTELLING
EGHILLNOSV SHOVELLING
EGHILMOOOS HOMOLOGISE
EGHILMOOOZ HOMOLOGIZE
EGHILNNOST NEON LIGHTS
EGHILNORVY HOVERINGLY
EGHILNSSST SLIGHTNESS
EGHILOOPPT PHLOGOPITE
EGHILOORST RHEOLOGIST
EGHILOOSTT ETHOLOGIST
EGHILOSSTT GHOSTLIEST
EGHILRSTVY VERY LIGHTS
EGHIMNORST SMOTHERING
EGHINNNORT ENTHRONING
EGHINNORST SHORTENING
EGHINNRSSU HUNGRINESS
EGHINORSST SHOESTRING
EGHINRSTTU SHUTTERING
EGHIOPRSTT TIGHTROPES
EGHIORSSTV OVERSIGHTS
EGHIORSTTW GHOSTWRITE
EGHIORTTWY TROY WEIGHT
EGHJMNPTUU JUMP THE GUN
EGHLLOORSY GLORY HOLES
EGHLNOOPRY PHRENOLOGY
EGHLOOPPSY PSEPHOLOGY
EGHLOPPRTY PETROGLYPH
EGHMNOOOSU HOMOGENOUS
EGHMOOOTYZ HOMOZYGOTE

EGIIILMMST LEGITIMISM
EGIIILMNPR IMPERILING
EGIIILMSTT LEGITIMIST
EGIIILNORR IRRELIGION
EGIIIMNNOS IGNOMINIES
EGIIIMNNST MENINGITIS
EGIIKLNNSS KINGLINESS
EGIIKNPPRS SKIPPERING
EGIIKNRSTT SKITTERING
EGIILLNNSV SNIVELLING
EGIILLNOTU GUILLOTINE
EGIILLNRVY REVILINGLY
EGIILLNSVW SWIVELLING
EGIILNOPTX EXPLOITING
EGIILNRSSS GRISLINESS
EGIILNRVVY REVIVINGLY
EGIILNSSTU GUILTINESS
EGIILOPSTT EPIGLOTTIS
EGIILRSSTT GRISTLIEST
EGIIMMNORZ MEMORIZING
EGIIMNNNOT MENTIONING
EGIIMNNOST MOISTENING
EGIIMNPRSS IMPRESSING
EGIIMNPRST SPRINGTIME
EGIIMNPRTT PERMITTING
EGIINNNOPS PENSIONING
EGIINNORSS INGRESSION
EGIINNPRRT REPRINTING
EGIINNRRSU REINSURING
EGIINNSSTT STINGINESS
EGIINNSSTW WITNESSING
EGIINPPRRS PERSPIRING
EGIINPRSST PERSISTING, SPRINGIEST
EGIINRSSTT GRITTINESS, STRINGIEST
EGIINRTTTW TWITTERING
EGIINSTTTV VIGNETTIST
EGIJKNNSTU JUNKETINGS
EGIJNNORUY JOURNEYING
EGIKLNNOOS INGLENOOKS
EGIKLNNORS SNORKELING
EGIKLNNPSU SPELUNKING
EGIKLNORVY REVOKINGLY
EGIKNNOORS SNOOKERING
EGIKNNORTW NETWORKING
EGILLMMNPU PUMMELLING
EGILLMOSTU GUILLEMOTS
EGILLNNNTU TUNNELLING
EGILLNNOTW WELLINGTON
EGILLNOPPR PROPELLING
EGILLNORWY LOWERINGLY
EGILLNOSTU OUTSELLING
EGILLNPRSW WELLSPRING
EGILLNTUXY EXULTINGLY
EGILLORSSY SYLLOGISER

EGILLORSYZ SYLLOGIZER
EGILMMNORS MONGRELISM
EGILMMNPTU PLUMMETING
EGILMNOOSS GLOOMINESS, NEOLOGISMS
EGILMNOPTT MELTING POT
EGILMNOSUU LEGUMINOUS
EGILMNPTTY TEMPTINGLY
EGILMOOSSY SEISMOLOGY
EGILNNOSST SINGLETONS
EGILNNRRUY UNERRINGLY
EGILNNRSSU NURSELINGS
EGILNNSTTU UNSETTLING
EGILNOOOST OENOLOGIST
EGILNOOPST PENOLOGIST
EGILNORRUV OVERRULING
EGILNOSSSS GLOSSINESS
EGILNOSTUU LOUNGE SUIT
EGILNPRSSY PRESSINGLY
EGILNQSTUY QUESTINGLY
EGILNRSVWY SWERVINGLY
EGILOORSST SEROLOGIST
EGILOOSSTX SEXOLOGIST
EGILORSUVY GRIEVOUSLY
EGILOSUUXY EXIGUOUSLY
EGIMNNOORR IRONMONGER
EGIMNNORTT TORMENTING
EGIMNNORTU REMOUNTING
EGIMNOORTY GONIOMETRY
EGIMNPRSSU GRUMPINESS
EGIMNPRTTU TRUMPETING
EGIMOOPRST GEOTROPISM
EGINNOPSSS SPONGINESS
EGINNRSSTU INSURGENTS
EGINNRSSTY TRYINGNESS
EGINNRSTTU ENTRUSTING
EGINNRSTUW WET-NURSING
EGINNRSUVW UNSWERVING
EGINOOPRRT PROGENITOR
EGINOPPRRS PROSPERING
EGINOPPRSS OPPRESSING
EGINOPPRST STOPPERING
EGINOPRRTU INTERGROUP
EGINOPRSUY PERIGYNOUS
EGINOPSSSS POSSESSING
EGINORRSTW SONGWRITER
EGINORSSTT GROTTINESS
EGINORSTUW OUTSWINGER
EGINPRRSSU PRESSURING
EGINPRSTTU SPUTTERING
EGINRSTTTU STUTTERING
EGJLLOORRY JOLLY ROGER
EGJLMNOPRU LONG-JUMPER
EGLLMORSSY GORMLESSLY
EGLLMORSUU GLOMERULUS

EGLMNOOOSU MONOLOGUES
EGLMNOOOTY ENTOMOLOGY
EGLMNOORUY NUMEROLOGY
EGLMNOOYYZ ENZYMOLOGY
EGLNNOSSUU SUN LOUNGES
EGLOOOORRWW WOOLGROWER
EGMMNOORTY MONTGOMERY
EGMMNOPRSY GYMNOSPERM
EGMNNOOOSU MONOGENOUS
EGMOORSSTU GUESTROOMS
EGNNNRRSUU GUNRUNNERS
EGNNORSSST STRONGNESS
EGNORRSTUV OVERSTRUNG
EGNORSSSST SONGSTRESS
EGNORSSTUY YOUNGSTERS
EHHIILSTVY THIEVISHLY
EHHIIMSTTW WHITESMITH
EHHIIRSTTT THIRTIETHS
EHHILOPRSU HEROPHILUS
EHHILOPSTU THEOPHILUS
EHHILOPTTY LITHOPHYTE
EHHILORTWW WORTHWHILE
EHHILRSSWY SHREWISHLY
EHHIMORSTT HITHERMOST
EHHIOPSSTY HYPOTHESIS
EHHLOOOOPPR LOPHOPHORE
EHHMNOOOPS HOMOPHONES
EHHMORSTTU HOME TRUTHS
EHHOOOOPPRT PHOTOPHORE
EHIIILNPPP PHILIPPINE
EHIIILNPST PHILISTINE
EHIIKMRRSS SKIRMISHER
EHIIKMRSSS SKIRMISHES
EHIIILLOOPS HELIOPOLIS
EHIIILLOPSY LYOPHILISE
EHIIILLOPYZ LYOPHILIZE
EHIIILNOOPS EOSINOPHIL
EHIIILNQRSU RELINQUISH
EHIIILPRTTY TRIPHYLITE
EHIIMNPSSS IMPISHNESS
EHIIMOPRSV IMPOVERISH
EHIIMPPRSU UMPIRESHIP
EHIINNPRST INTERNSHIP
EHIIQSSSTU SQUISHIEST
EHIIRRSTTU URETHRITIS
EHIIRSSSTW IRISH STEWS
EHIIRSSTTT THIRSTIEST
EHIKNORSTW IN THE WORKS
EHILLNRSSS SHRILLNESS
EHILLNSTUV HUNTSVILLE
EHILMNOOOS HOMOLOSINE
EHILMNSSSU MULISHNESS
EHILMOPSTY POLYTHEISM
EHILNNOSSU UNHOLINESS

EHILNOPRTU NEUTROPHIL
EHILNSSSSU SLUSHINESS
EHILOPRSSU RUSSOPHILE
EHILOPSTTY POLYTHEIST
EHILORRTTY ERYTHRITOL
EHILPRSSUU SULPHURISE
EHILPRSUUZ SULPHURIZE
EHIMMNOOST MONOTHEISM
EHIMMOPRTU PROMETHIUM
EHIMNNPSTU PUNISHMENT
EHIMNOOSTT MONOTHEIST
EHIMNOPSSY SYMPHONIES
EHIMNOPSUU EUPHONIUMS
EHIMNORSUY HIERONYMUS
EHIMNSSTTY SYNTHETISM
EHIMORRSTT THERMISTOR
EHINNORSST THORNINESS
EHINNSSSTU NISSEN HUTS
EHINOOPSUU EUPHONIOUS
EHINOOSSTT TOOTHINESS
EHINOPPRTY PERIPHYTON
EHINOPPSSS POPISHNESS
EHINORSSTW WORTHINESS
EHINORSTUU RUTHENIOUS
EHINPPSSSU UPPISHNESS
EHINSSSTTY SYNTHESIST
EHINSSTTTY SYNTHETIST
EHIOOPRSTW POOR WHITES
EHIOORSSTX SIX-SHOOTER
EHIOPPRSSW WORSHIPPER
EHIOPRRSTY PREHISTORY
EHIOPRRTTY PYRRHOTITE
EHIOPRSSST PROSTHESIS
EHJMOPRSUW SHOW JUMPER
EHKOORRSSW WORKHORSES
EHLLNOOSSW HOLLOWNESS
EHLLRSSTUY RUTHLESSLY
EHLMNOPPTY NYMPHOLEPT
EHLMORSSUU HUMOURLESS
EHLNOOPRST NORTH POLES
EHLNOOPSXY XYLOPHONES
EHLNOORSSU HONOURLESS
EHLOORRRTY HOLY TERROR
EHLOPRSTUY UPHOLSTERY
EHMMOOPRSY MESOMORPHY
EHMMOORSUU HUMOURSOME
EHMNNOOOSY HONEYMOONS
EHMNOOPRTY NEPHROTOMY
EHMNOOSSST SMOOTHNESS
EHMNOPSTTU ON THE STUMP
EHMOOOPRSS SOPHOMORES
EHMOOPRTTY PHOTOMETRY
EHMOORRTTW MOTHERWORT
EHNNOPRTWY PENNYWORTH

EHNOOPPRRS PRONEPHROS
EHNOORRTVW OVERTHROWN
EHNOORTTWY NOTEWORTHY
EHNOOSSTUW TOWN HOUSES
EHNOPRSTTU POTHUNTERS
EHNOQSTTUU QUONSET HUT
EHNORSTWWY NEWSWORTHY
EHOOOPPRRS SPOROPHORE
EHOOOPRSSU POORHOUSES
EHOOPPRSTY SPOROPHYTE
EHOOPPRTTY TROPOPHYTE
EHOORRSTVW OVERTHROWS
EHOPPSTTUU UP THE SPOUT
EHORRSTTUV OVERTHRUST
EIIIINQSTU INIQUITIES
EIIILLLMRT MILLILITER, MILLILITRE
EIIILMMSTT TIME LIMITS
EIIILORSTV VITRIOLISE
EIIILORTVZ VITRIOLIZE
EIIIMNORST MINORITIES
EIIIMNPSTU IMPUNITIES
EIIIMNRSST MINISTRIES
EIIIMPRSTU IMPURITIES
EIIIMPRSTV PRIMITIVES
EIIIMSSTVY EMISSIVITY
EIIINPRRST INSPIRITER
EIIIOPRRST PRIORITIES, PRIORITISE
EIIIOPRRTZ PRIORITIZE
EIIJLNTUVY JUVENILITY
EIIJMNRTUY INJURY TIME
EIIKLLORST KILOLITERS, KILOLITRES
EIIKLNNSSS SLINKINESS
EIIKLNORST TRISKELION
EIIKMNPSSS SKIMPINESS
EIIKNNNSSS SKINNINESS
EIIKNQRSSU QUIRKINESS
EIIILLLOSUV LOUISVILLE
EIIILLMMNNU MILLENNIUM
EIIILLMOPTY IMPOLITELY
EIIILLMPRTU MULTIPLIER
EIIILLNOPST SEPTILLION
EIIILLNOSTX SEXTILLION
EIIILLPSSTY PITILESSLY
EIIILMMNNTY IMMINENTLY
EIIILMNNSTT INSTILMENT
EIIILMNOSST LENTISSIMO
EIIILMNOSSU LIMOUSINES
EIIILMNPPSS PIMPLINESS
EIIILMOSTTV LEITMOTIVS
EIIILNPPSSS SLIPPINESS
EIIILNPTUVY PUNITIVELY
EIIILOPSTVY POSITIVELY
EIIILPRSSST SPIRITLESS
EIIIMMPRSUY PERIMYSIUM

EIIMNNORSU REUNIONISM
EIIMNOPRRS IMPRISONER
EIIMNOPRSS IMPRESSION, PERMISSION
EIIMNORSSS REMISSIONS
EIIMOOPSTY EPISIOTOMY
EIIMOPRRSV IMPROVISER
EIIMOPRSUV IMPERVIOUS
EIIMORSSTU MOISTURISE
EIIMORSTUZ MOISTURIZE
EIIMPSSSST PESSIMISTS
EIIINNNOSTT INTENTIONS
EIIINNNOSTV INVENTIONS
EIIINNORSST INSERTIONS
EIIINNORSSV INVERSIONS
EIIINNORSTU REUNIONIST
EIIINNPPSSS SNIPPINESS
EIIINNRSSTW WINTRINESS
EIIINOOPRST REPOSITION
EIIINOOPSTX EXPOSITION
EIIINOPPTTT PETIT POINT
EIIINOPRSSV PREVISIONS
EIIINOPSTVW VIEWPOINTS
EIIINORTTWZ ZWITTERION
EIIINPPRSST PINSTRIPES
EIIINPRSSSS PRISSINESS
EIIINRSTUVY UNIVERSITY
EIIINSSTTTU INSTITUTES
EIIIOORRSST SORORITIES
EIIIOPPSSTT PETITS POIS
EIIIPRTTUVY ERUPTIVITY
EIJLMNPSTU MINT JULEPS
EIJLMPPRTU TRIPLE JUMP
EIKLNPRRSS SPRINKLERS
EIKNNORRST NON-STRIKER
EIKNNOSSTT STINKSTONE
EIKNNPSSSU SPUNKINESS
EIKNOOPSSS SPOOKINESS
EIKORSTTTY TROTSKYITE
EILLLOORTT TOILET ROLL
EILLLSSSTY LISTLESSLY
EILLMNOSST MILLSTONES
EILLMORSTU LUMISTEROL
EILLNNOSTY INSOLENTLY
EILLNOORRT RITORNELLO
EILLNOOSSW WOOLLINESS
EILLNRTUVY VIRULENTLY
EILLOOPRSY ROLY-POLIES
EILLOPRSSV OVERSPILLS
EILLOPRSUY PERILOUSLY
EILLORTTTU LITTERLOUT
EILMMOPRSY POLYMERISM
EILMNOOOPS MONOPOLIES,
    MONOPOLISE
EILMNOOOPZ MONOPOLIZE

EILMNOOSST MOTIONLESS
EILMNOPSST SIMPLETONS
EILMNOPTTY IMPOTENTLY
EILMNOSSSS LISSOMNESS
EILMNRSSTY MINSTRELSY
EILMOOPRST METROPOLIS
EILMOPPRRY IMPROPERLY
EILNNNOOTV NONVIOLENT
EILNNOOSTW LOW-TENSION
EILNNOSSTV INSOLVENTS
EILNNRSSUU UNRULINESS
EILNOOPSSX EXPLOSIONS
EILNOORSTU RESOLUTION
EILNOORTUV REVOLUTION
EILNOPPRTW NIPPLEWORT
EILNOPPSSS SLOPPINESS
EILNOPPSTU SUPPLETION
EILNOPRSST PORTLINESS
EILNOPRSSU REPULSIONS
EILNOPSSUX EXPULSIONS
EILNORSSTY STORY LINES
EILNOSTUUV VELUTINOUS
EILNPQTTUU QUINTUPLET
EILNPRRTUY PRURIENTLY
EILNRSSSTU SULTRINESS
EILNRSSTTU TURNSTILES
EILOOPPRST PETROPOLIS
EILOORSSTT SITOSTEROL
EILOPPRSUV PROPULSIVE
EILOPRRSTU PROTRUSILE
EILOPRSTUY PYROLUSITE
EILOPRSTVY SPORTIVELY, VERY PISTOL
EILOPRSUVY PREVIOUSLY
EILOPSSTTT TEST PILOTS
EIMMNOPRSS PERSIMMONS
EIMNNOOPTT OMNIPOTENT
EIMNNOSSYY SYNONYMISE
EIMNNOSYYZ SYNONYMIZE
EIMNNRSTTU INSTRUMENT
EIMNOOPRSS SPOONERISM
EIMNOOSTTT TENOTOMIST
EIMNOPRRTU IMPORTUNER
EIMNOPRSTU RESUMPTION
EIMNORSSST STORMINESS
EIMNOSTTZZ MEZZOTINTS
EIMNPSSSTU STUMPINESS
EIMNSSSTTU SMUTTINESS
EIMOOQSSTU MOSQUITOES
EIMOPPSSSU MISSUPPOSE
EIMOPRRSTY SPIROMETRY
EIMOPRSSTU IMPOSTURES
EIMORSSTUY MYSTERIOUS
EIMRRSSTTU MISTRUSTER
EINNOOSSST SNOOTINESS

EINNOPSSSU SUSPENSION
EINNOSSSTT SNOTTINESS
EINNOSSTTU SUSTENTION
EINOOPPRSS OPPRESSION
EINOOPPRTW POWER POINT
EINOOPRRST RESORPTION
EINOOPSSSS POSSESSION
EINOOPTTTT TOTIPOTENT
EINOORSTTX EXTORTIONS
EINOPPRSTY PROPENSITY
EINOPRSSST SPORTINESS
EINOPSSSTT SPOTTINESS
EINOQRTTUU TOURNIQUET
EINORRSTTV INTROVERTS
EINORSSTUX EXTRUSIONS
EINRSSSTTU TRUSTINESS
EIOOOPRSTZ SPOROZOITE
EIOOPPRRRT PROPRIETOR
EIOOPRRSST POSTERIORS
EIOOPRRSTY REPOSITORY
EIOOPRSTXY EXPOSITORY
EIOORRSSTU ROISTEROUS
EIOORRTVWY IVORY TOWER
EIOPPRRSTY PROSPERITY
EIOPPRSSTT STROPPIEST
EIOPPRSTUV SUPPORTIVE
EIOPRRSSUV SUPERVISOR
EIOPRRSTTU TRIPTEROUS
EIOPRRSTUV PROTRUSIVE
EIOPRSTTTU PROSTITUTE
EIOQRSSTUU TURQUOISES
EIORRRSSTT TERRORISTS
EIPPRRSUVY PRIVY PURSE
EJLLLLORSY JELLY ROLLS
EJMOSSSTTU MOTS JUSTES
EJNNSSSTUU UNJUSTNESS
EJNOORRSSU SOJOURNERS
EJNOOSSSUY JOYOUSNESS
EKLOOPRRSW SLOPWORKER
EKLOORRTUW WORK-TO-RULE
EKMNNOORSS NONSMOKERS
EKMNNOSTUY MONKEY NUTS
EKNORRTTUU TRUNK ROUTE
EKOORRSTUW OUTWORKERS
ELLLOSSSUY SOULLESSLY
ELLOPSSSTY SPOTLESSLY
ELMNOORSUY ENORMOUSLY
ELMNOOSUVY VENOMOUSLY
ELMNORSUUY NUMEROUSLY
ELMOOPRSUY POLYMEROUS
ELMOOPRTUY PLEUROTOMY
ELMOOPRTXY PROTOXYLEM
ELMOOPSSUY POLYSEMOUS
ELNOSSSUUY SENSUOUSLY

ELOPPRSTUY SUPPLETORY
EMMNOOORSU MONOMEROUS
EMMOOPRSTT POSTMORTEM
EMNNOOORTU MOTONEURON
EMNNOOOSST MOONSTONES
EMNOOOPRST MONOPTEROS
EMNOORRSTT TORMENTORS
EMNOPPRSST PROMPTNESS
EMNORRSTUU SURMOUNTER
EMNORSSTUU MENSTRUOUS
EMOOOORSST STOREROOMS
EMOOOORRSTV SERVOMOTOR
ENNOOPPRRU PROPER NOUN
ENNOOPPRST PROPONENTS
ENOOPRRSSY RESPONSORY
ENOOPRSSSU POROUSNESS
ENOOPRSTTU PORTENTOUS
ENOPRSSSUY SUSPENSORY
EOOOPRSSUX EXOSPOROUS
EOOPPRRSSS OPPRESSORS
EOOPPRRSSU PROSPEROUS
EOOPPRSTTY PROTOTYPES
EOOPRRSSTU PRO-OESTRUS
EOOPRSSSSS POSSESSORS
EOOPRSSSSY POSSESSORY
EOORRSSTTU STERTOROUS
EOPPRRSSSU SUPPRESSOR
EOPPRRSSTU SUPPORTERS
EOPRSSSSUU SOURPUSSES
FFFFIITTYY FIFTY-FIFTY
FFGHHIOSTY FIGHT SHY OF
FFGHIILNSY FLYING FISH, FLY-FISHING
FFGHIIOPPR HIPPOGRIFF
FFGHORSTUU ROUGH STUFF
FFGIILLLNU FULFILLING
FFGIILNNSY SNIFFINGLY
FFGIINORTY FORTIFYING
FFGILNNSUY SNUFFINGLY
FFGINOPTTU OFF-PUTTING
FFILLRTUUY FRUITFULLY
FFILNRTUUU UNFRUITFUL
FFILOORRST FIRST FLOOR
FFIORSSTTU SOFT FRUITS
FGGHHIILNY HIGH-FLYING
FGGHIIINNT INFIGHTING
FGGIIINNNR INFRINGING
FGGIIINNSY SIGNIFYING
FGGIILNORY GLORIFYING
FGHHIINSTT NIGHT SHIFT
FGHHIORRTT FORTHRIGHT
FGHHLOTTUU THOUGHTFUL
FGHIILNSTU INSIGHTFUL
FGHIILNSTY SHIFTINGLY
FGHIINNRSU FURNISHING

FGHIINORRY HORRIFYING
FGHIINRSTT FIRST NIGHT
FGHIIOTTTU FIGHT IT OUT
FGHILLRTUY RIGHTFULLY
FGHILOOSTT FOOTLIGHTS
FGHINNOTUX FOXHUNTING
FGHINOOOTT HOTFOOTING
FGHINORSTT FORTNIGHTS
FGIIINRTVY VITRIFYING
FGIIJNSTUY JUSTIFYING
FGIILLMNOY MOLLIFYING
FGIILLNNUY NULLIFYING
FGIILLNRTY FLIRTINGLY, TRIFLINGLY
FGIILLNSTY STIFLINGLY
FGIILMNORU LINGUIFORM
FGIILNOSUU FULIGINOUS
FGIIMMMNUY MUMMIFYING
FGIIMNORTY MORTIFYING
FGIIMNSTYY MYSTIFYING
FGIIMORRST STRIGIFORM
FGIINOTTTU OUTFITTING
FGIINRRSTY STIR-FRYING
FGIKNNORTU TUNING FORK
FGILLNOOSW FOLLOWINGS
FGILLNOTUY FLOUTINGLY
FGILMMNOUX FLUMMOXING
FGILNNORWY FROWNINGLY
FGLLNORUWY FULLY-GROWN,
     WRONGFULLY
FGLOORTUUY FUTUROLOGY
FGNNOOSSSU SONS-OF-GUNS
FHILLMRTUY MIRTHFULLY
FHILMOORRR HORROR FILM
FHILOPRSUW WORSHIPFUL
FHIMORSSTX SIXTH FORMS
FHINORRSTT SHIRTFRONT
FHLLLOSTUY SLOTHFULLY
FHLLOTUUYY YOUTHFULLY
FHLLRTTUUY TRUTHFULLY
FHLNRTTUUU UNTRUTHFUL
FHLOOORSSW FLOOR SHOWS
FHMOOORTUU OUT OF HUMOR
FIIKLNNSST SKINFLINTS
FIILMMNOOR MONILIFORM
FIILMPRSST FILMSTRIPS
FIIMNORTUY UNIFORMITY
FIIMOORSST FORTISSIMO
FIIMORSTTU FORTUITISM
FIIORSTTTU FORTUITIST
FIKLLOORST FOLKLORIST
FIKNORSTWY FORTY WINKS
FILLLMORSU FLOURMILLS
FILLOOSTUW FOLLOW SUIT
FILOOOPRST PORTFOLIOS

FINOOOPSTT SOFT OPTION
FINOOPRSTT FOOTPRINTS
FIOORSTTUU FORTUITOUS
FLLMNORUUY MOURNFULLY
FLLRSTTUUY TRUSTFULLY
FLOOOOSSTT FOOTSTOOLS
FMNOOORRST FRONT ROOMS
FMOOOPRRST STORMPROOF
FOOORSSTTU OUT OF SORTS
GGGILLNRUY GURGLINGLY
GGGILNRSTU STRUGGLING
GGHHHIILST HIGHLIGHTS
GGHHIILNTT NIGHTLIGHT
GGHHINRSTU HIGH-STRUNG
GGHIIILRSW WHIRLIGIGS
GGHIILNNST LIGHTNINGS
GGHIILPRSY PRIGGISHLY
GGHILLSSUY SLUGGISHLY
GGIIIINSTV GINGIVITIS
GGIIIMNSSV MISGIVINGS
GGIIINNRTU INTRIGUING
GGIILLNNTY TINGLINGLY
GGIILNNSTY STINGINGLY
GGIILNNSWY SWINGINGLY
GGIILNPPRY GRIPPINGLY
GGILLLNOOR LOGROLLING
GGILLNTTUY GLUTTINGLY
GGILNNOOPR PROLONGING
GGILNNRTUY GRUNTINGLY
GGINNNNRUU GUNRUNNING
GGINOOPRRU PROROGUING
GGINOORTUW OUTGROWING
GGLLNNOOOW WOLLONGONG
GHHIILPSST LIGHTSHIPS
GHHIINOPST HIGH POINTS
GHHIINRSTT NIGHTSHIRT
GHHIIPRSTW SHIPWRIGHT
GHHILRSSTU RUSHLIGHTS
GHHINOPRTT TRIPHTHONG
GHHLOORTUY THOROUGHLY
GHHNORRTUU RUN-THROUGH
GHHOORTTUU THROUGHOUT
GHHOOTTTUU THOUGHT-OUT
GHHOPRTTUU THROUGHPUT
GHIIKNNNTU UNTHINKING
GHIILLMRTW MILLWRIGHT
GHIILLNRWY WHIRLINGLY
GHIILLOPTT PILOT LIGHT
GHIILNRTWY WRITHINGLY
GHIILNSSWY SWISHINGLY
GHIILNSTTW WHITTLINGS
GHIIMNPRTU TRIUMPHING
GHIINNORSU NOURISHING
GHIINNOSTU OUTSHINING

GHIINOPRSW WORSHIPING
GHILMNPTUY THUMPINGLY
GHILMOOORU HOROLOGIUM
GHILNOOPST PHLOGISTON
GHILNOOSTY SOOTHINGLY
GHILNORTTT THROTTLING
GHILNOSSST SLINGSHOTS
GHILNRRUYY HURRYINGLY
GHILOOORST HOROLOGIST
GHILOOPSYY PHYSIOLOGY
GHILOPSSTT SPOTLIGHTS
GHLLOOPTYY TYPHLOLOGY
GHLMOOOOSU HOMOLOGOUS
GHLMOOOPRY MORPHOLOGY
GHLNOOPSUW SNOWPLOUGH
GHMNOOOOSU HOMOGONOUS
GHMOOOSUYZ HOMOZYGOUS
GHNOOSSTTW GHOST TOWNS
GHOORSTTUW OUTGROWTHS
GIIIIMMNNZ MINIMIZING
GIIILLNNST INSTILLING
GIIILNNTVY INVITINGLY
GIIIMMNNUZ IMMUNIZING
GIIIMNNPRT IMPRINTING
GIIIMNOPTZ OPTIMIZING
GIIINNNOUZ UNIONIZING
GIIKLLNNSY SLINKINGLY
GIIKLMNRSY SMIRKINGLY
GIIKLNNPRS SPRINKLING
GIIKLNNSTW TWINKLINGS
GIIKLNNSTY STINKINGLY
GIIKLNRSTY STRIKINGLY
GIIKNRSTWY SKYWRITING
GIILLNNOPR ROLLING PIN
GIILLNOPRY PILLORYING
GIILLNPPRY RIPPLINGLY
GIILLNPPSY SLIPPINGLY
GIILLNRSWY SWIRLINGLY
GIILMMNSWY SWIMMINGLY
GIILMNOORV LIVING ROOM
GIILMNOPSY IMPOSINGLY
GIILMOOSST MISOLOGIST
GIILNNOPRU PURLOINING
GIILNNRTUY UNTIRINGLY
GIILNOORSU INGLORIOUS
GIILNOOSST SINOLOGIST
GIILNPPRTY TRIPPINGLY
GIILNPRSST SPLIT RINGS, STRIPLINGS
GIILNRRSTY STIRRINGLY
GIILNSTTWY TWISTINGLY
GIILOORSTV VIROLOGIST
GIIMNNNORU IN MOURNING
GIIMNNOORT MONITORING
GIIMNNOPSU UNIMPOSING

GIIMNOORTZ MOTORIZING
GIIMNOQSTU MISQUOTING
GIIMNOSSTY MISOGYNIST
GIINNNSTTU UNSTINTING
GIINNOOPRT PORTIONING
GIINNOPRST PISTON RING
GIINNRSTTU INTRUSTING
GIINOTTTUW OUTWITTING
GIINPRRSSU SURPRISING
GIJNNOORSU SOJOURNING
GIKMNNNOOS NONSMOKING
GIKNNOOPRR NORRKOPING
GILLMOSSSY SYLLOGISMS
GILLNOPRRS SPRING ROLL
GILLNPUYZZ PUZZLINGLY
GILLNRSTUY RUSTLINGLY
GILLOORSUY GLORIOUSLY
GILMMNOOUY IMMUNOLOGY
GILMNOOOST MONOLOGIST,
 NOMOLOGIST
GILMOOOPST POMOLOGIST
GILMOOSTYZ ZYMOLOGIST
GILNNNSTUY STUNNINGLY
GILNNOOSWY SWOONINGLY
GILNNORSTY SNORTINGLY
GILNOOOPSY OLIGOPSONY
GILNOOOSST NOSOLOGIST
GILNOOPPSY OPPOSINGLY
GILNOOPPTY TYPING POOL
GILNOOPSTY STOOPINGLY
GILNOPSTYY POLYGYNIST
GILNORRWYY WORRYINGLY
GILNPRSUUY USURPINGLY
GILOOOPSTT TOPOLOGIST
GILOOOSSTZ ZOOLOGISTS
GILOOPRSTT PROGLOTTIS
GILOOPSTTY TYPOLOGIST
GILOORRSUY RIGOROUSLY
GILOORSUVY VIGOROUSLY
GIMMNNOSSU SUMMONSING
GIMMNPSSUU SUMMINGS-UP
GIMMPPTUYY GIPPY TUMMY
GIMNNOORSS MONSIGNORS
GIMNNOOSTY MONOGYNIST
GIMNOOSSUY MISOGYNOUS
GINNNORTUU OUTRUNNING
GINNOOPPST POSTPONING
GINNOOPRSS SPONSORING
GINNOPPSTU UNSTOPPING
GINOOPRTUU OUTPOURING
GINOPPRRTU PURPORTING
GINOPPRSTU SUPPORTING
GINTTTTTUU TUT-TUTTING

GLNOOPSUYY POLYGYNOUS
GLNOOSTTUU GLUTTONOUS
GMNNOOOSUY MONOGYNOUS
GMNOOORRST STRONG ROOM
GNNOOSTUWY YOUNGSTOWN
HHILOOPPSY PHILOSOPHY
HHILOOPPTY PHOTOPHILY
HHIMOOPRRZ RHIZOMORPH
HHLMOPRTYY POLYRHYTHM
HHOOPPRSSU PHOSPHORUS
HIIKLSSTTY SKITTISHLY
HIILLMNOST MILLIONTHS
HIILLNORTT TRILLIONTH
HIILMOOPSZ ZOOPHILISM
HIILOPRSTY HOLY SPIRIT
HIILORTTTY LITHOTRITY
HIILOSSSTY HISTOLYSIS
HIIMMNOPRS MORPHINISM
HIINOORSST ORNITHOSIS
HIIOOOPRST OOPHORITIS
HIIOOTTTYY HOITY-TOITY
HIKLMOOSTT MILK TOOTHS
HILLOOPRSW WHIRLPOOLS
HILMNORTTY TRIMONTHLY
HILNOORSST HONORS LIST
HILNORTUWY UNWORTHILY
HILOOOPSUZ ZOOPHILOUS
HILOOPSSTY PHOTOLYSIS
HILOPPSTUY HIPPOLYTUS
HILORSSSTT SHORT LISTS
HIMMNOOTYY HOMONYMITY
HIMNOPSSTY SYMPHONIST
HINOOPTTXY PHYTOTOXIN
HINOPSSTTY HYPNOTISTS
HIOOOSTTTU SHOOT IT OUT
HIOOPPRSST TROOPSHIPS
HIOOPRTTXY THIXOTROPY
HIORSSTTUU STRUTHIOUS
HLLOOPPRSY SPOROPHYLL
HLMOORSUUY HUMOROUSLY
HLOPRSSUUU SULPHUROUS
HMOOPSSTUU POSTHUMOUS
HNOOOPSTTU PHOTOTONUS
HOORRSSTTY SHORT STORY
IIILLMMNSU ILLUMINISM
IIILLMNSTU ILLUMINIST
IIILMMOTTY IMMOTILITY
IIILNOSSTV VIOLINISTS
IIIMNOOPST IMPOSITION
IIIMNOPRSS MISPRISION
IIIMOPSSTV POSITIVISM
IIINNOSTTU INTUITIONS
IIINOQRSTU INQUISITOR
IIINOQSTUU INIQUITOUS

IIIOPSSTTV POSITIVIST
IILLLLNWYY WILLY-NILLY
IILLLORSUY ILLUSORILY
IILLNOOPSS POLLINOSIS
IILMNOOPSS IMPLOSIONS
IILMNOPSSU IMPULSIONS
IILMNOPSTY POSTLIMINY
IILMNOSTUY LUMINOSITY
IILNNOOSTU IN SOLUTION
IILNNOOTUV INVOLUTION
IILNOOPSST POSTILIONS
IIMNNOOOUX OXONIUM ION
IIMNNOOSSU INSOMNIOUS
IIMNORSSTU MINOR SUITS
IINNORSSTU INTRUSIONS
IINOOOOPPST OPPOSITION
IINOOPRSSV PROVISIONS
IINOPRRSTU IRRUPTIONS
IINORSSSTU SINISTROUS
IINORSTTTU INSTITUTOR
IINORSTTUU NUTRITIOUS
IIOOOPRSTV OVIPOSITOR
IIOOPPRSTU PROPITIOUS
IIOPRSSTUU SPIRITUOUS
IIORSTTUVY VIRTUOSITY
IKLOOPPRSU PRUSIK LOOP
IKMORSSTTY TROTSKYISM
IKORSSTTTY TROTSKYIST
ILLMNOSUUY LUMINOUSLY
ILLNOORSSU ROUSSILLON
ILLOOSSSVY SOLVOLYSIS
ILMMNOOOPS MONOPOLISM
ILMNOOOPST MONOPOLIST
ILMNOOOSTW SLOW MOTION
ILMNOOSUUV VOLUMINOUS
ILMNOSTUUY MUTINOUSLY

ILMOORSTUY TIMOROUSLY
ILMOOSTTXY XYLOTOMIST
ILMOSTTUUY TUMULOSITY
ILNOOOSSYZ OZONOLYSIS
ILNOOPPRSU PROPULSION
ILOOPPRSST SPOILSPORT
ILOPRSSUUY SPURIOUSLY
ILORSTUUVY VIRTUOUSLY
IMMOOPRSTU PROSTOMIUM
IMMOPSSSUY SYMPOSIUMS
IMNNOSTYYY SYNONYMITY
IMNOOOPRST PROMOTIONS
IMNOOOPSTT MOOT POINTS
IMNOOORSUV OMNIVOROUS
IMOOPRRSSY PROMISSORY
IMOOPRSSTU IMPOSTROUS
INOOOPPRRT PROPORTION
INOOPRRSTU PROTRUSION
INRSSTTTUU UNIT TRUSTS
IOOOPRSSTU ISOTROPOUS
IOOPPRRSTU POTPOURRIS
IOOPPRSSTU PROPOSITUS
IOORSTTTUY TORTUOSITY
LLORSSTUUY LUSTROUSLY
LMOOOSTUXY XYLOTOMOUS
LMOSTTUUUU TUMULTUOUS
LNOOORSSUY SONOROUSLY
LOOPSTUUUV VOLUPTUOUS
LOORSTTUUY TORTUOUSLY
MMOOPRRSUU RUMPUS ROOM
MNNOOOOSTU MONOTONOUS
MNNOOSSUYY SYNONYMOUS
MNOOOPRRTY PROMONTORY
MNOORSSTTW SNOWSTORMS
NOOOPPSSSU SOUP SPOONS
OPRSTTUVYY TOPSY-TURVY

ELEVEN-LETTER WORDS

AAAAABBCDRR ABRACADABRA
AAAAABBCHILN BAHIA BLANCA
AAAAABBCORSS CABORA BASSA
AAAAABBINRST SABBATARIAN
AAAAABCCHILN BACCHANALIA
AAAABDIIRSU SAUDI ARABIA
AAAABEKMSTT MAKE A STAB AT
AAAACHHKKLM MAKHACHKALA
AAAADEGLMMT AMALGAMATED
AAAADELMRSS DAR ES SALAAM
AAAAFGNOSTT ANTOFAGASTA

AAAAFINRRST RASTAFARIAN
AAAAGHIPPRR PARAGRAPHIA
AAAAGJNNNRY NARAYANGANJ
AAAAGORRSTZ STARA ZAGORA
AAAAHHMRRST MAHARASHTRA
AAAAILRSSTU AUSTRALASIA
AAABBCEELLN BALANCEABLE
AAABBCILSST SABBATICALS
AAABCDDIRRY BRADYCARDIA
AAABCDEIORS SCARABAEOID
AAABCEEIMRT BACTERAEMIA

AAABCEGGGRS BAGGAGE CARS	**AAACEGIRRWY** CARRIAGEWAY
AAABCEGGNRS GARBAGE CANS	**AAACEHKRTTT** HEART ATTACK
AAABCEGILLR ALGEBRAICAL	**AAACEHLMNNP** PANCHEN LAMA
AAABCEGKPSS BACK PASSAGE	**AAACEHLMRST** STEAL A MARCH
AAABCEHINRT ABRANCHIATE	**AAACEILLMNR** ALL-AMERICAN
AAABCELRTTT ATTRACTABLE	**AAACEIMNNPR** PAN-AMERICAN
AAABCIKLMRS BLACK MARIAS	**AAACEINPSST** SEA CAPTAINS
AAABDDENORW DRAW A BEAD ON	**AAACELMNPTU** CAMPANULATE
AAABDEGGNOV VAGABONDAGE	**AAACELMNRST** SACRAMENTAL
AAABDMORSSS AMBASSADORS	**AAACELMOPRT** PARACETAMOL
AAABEEGLLSV SALVAGEABLE	**AAACENOPRRT** NOT CARE A RAP
AAABEHIMNPS AMPHISBAENA	**AAACERRSTTU** TARTAR SAUCE
AAABEIILNRS RABELAISIAN	**AAACFIIORST** AFRO-ASIATIC
AAABEIKLLLZ ALKALIZABLE	**AAACFILLNTY** FANATICALLY
AAABEILLNUV UNAVAILABLE	**AAACFIMNRRT** AIRCRAFTMAN
AAABELLNPTU UNPALATABLE	**AAACGHIMNOP** PHAGOMANIAC
AAABELNRRTW WARRANTABLE	**AAACGHIMNSU** AS MUCH AGAIN
AAABGHIOOPR AGORAPHOBIA	**AAACGHIPPRR** PARAGRAPHIC
AAABHIOPRST ASTRAPHOBIA	**AAACGHNOOTT** CHATTANOOGA
AAABHMPRRTU BRAHMAPUTRA	**AAACGIINNRU** AURIGNACIAN
AAABIKNNNSS BANANA SKINS	**AAACGILMMRT** GRAMMATICAL
AAACCCEINPT CAPACITANCE	**AAACGINNNRV** CARAVANNING
AAACCCILSTT CATACLASTIC	**AAACHIKPPRT** APPARATCHIK
AAACCCISTTU CATACAUSTIC	**AAACHILMRRT** MATRIARCHAL
AAACCDEIIMN ACADEMICIAN	**AAACHILNOTU** ANACOLUTHIA
AAACCDEILMS ACADEMICALS	**AAACHILPRRT** PATRIARCHAL
AAACCDHIRTY TACHYCARDIA	**AAACIKLMNPS** PACK ANIMALS
AAACCEEHSTT ATTACHÉ CASE	**AAACILLMNRU** ANIMALCULAR
AAACCEILLOR CALCEOLARIA	**AAACILLMORT** CLAMATORIAL
AAACCEILPRT PALAEARCTIC	**AAACILLNOTT** LACTATIONAL
AAACCHILLRY ARCHAICALLY	**AAACILLNRST** SCARLATINAL
AAACCILLNRU CANALICULAR	**AAACILLNSTY** SATANICALLY
AAACCILLPRT PARALLACTIC	**AAACILLQTUY** AQUATICALLY
AAACCILMNOT ACCLAMATION	**AAACILNNRST** LANCASTRIAN
AAACCILPSTT CATAPLASTIC	**AAACILPPRST** PARAPLASTIC
AAACCLMORTY ACCLAMATORY	**AAADDFHNRST** HARD-AND-FAST
AAACDEEGKLP PACKAGE DEAL	**AAADEELQRSU** A SQUARE DEAL
AAACDEEIKMR MADEIRA CAKE	**AAADEENRRTW** WEAR AND TEAR
AAACDEEIMRR CAMARADERIE	**AAADEGILMNN** MAGDALENIAN
AAACDEEMRRY CAMERA-READY	**AAADEGMNORR** ROAD MANAGER
AAACDEERSWY CARAWAY SEED	**AAADEGMNPRR** RAMP AND RAGE
AAACDEILMPR PARAMEDICAL	**AAADEGNOTTV** TO ADVANTAGE
AAACDEILNRT CARDINALATE	**AAADEHLPRST** HARD PALATES
AAACDEILPSS PAS-DE-CALAIS	**AAADEHPPRRS** PARAPHRASED
AAACDEIMMRS MACADAMISER	**AAADEILMRRR** REAR ADMIRAL
AAACDEIMMRZ MACADAMIZER	**AAADEILNNRX** ALEXANDRINA
AAACDIINNSV SCANDINAVIA	**AAADEILNRSS** ALESSANDRIA
AAACDILNOPS PIÑA COLADAS	**AAADEILRRSV** ADVERSARIAL
AAACDILOPRX PARADOXICAL	**AAADELLMPRT** MAR DEL PLATA
AAACEEFLMNS MALFEASANCE	**AAADELLOSTV** VALLE D'AOSTA
AAACEENPPRS APPEARANCES	**AAADELMNRSS** SALAMANDERS
AAACEFLQSTU CATAFALQUES	**AAADELMPPSS** ADAM'S APPLES
AAACEGILLNN GALLINACEAN	**AAADENNPRST** TRANSPADANE
AAACEGILMNO EGOMANIACAL	**AAADGGINORT** AGGRADATION

AAADGIILMNR MADRIGALIAN
AAADGILNORT GRADATIONAL
AAADGINNPST GIANT PANDAS
AAADHHLPRYZ HAPHAZARDLY
AAADHILNRSS HARD AS NAILS
AAADHMMMNSU MUHAMMADANS
AAADIILNORR RADIOLARIAN
AAADIILNORT RADIATIONAL
AAADILLLNOT ALLANTOIDAL
AAADILMORRS RADIO ALARMS
AAADILNORSV SALVADORIAN
AAADINOPSTT ADAPTATIONS
AAADLLNRSTW WARTS AND ALL
AAADLNORSSV SAN SALVADOR
AAAEEGGLRSS GARAGE SALES
AAAEEGGMNST STAGE-MANAGE
AAAEEGMSSTU SAUSAGE MEAT
AAAEEGRTTVX EXTRAVAGATE
AAAEEHINSST ANAESTHESIA
AAAEELNPRTY PENALTY AREA
AAAEERSTTVX EXTRAVASATE
AAAEFHHKMOS MAKE A HASH OF
AAAEFLLMRSS FALSE ALARMS
AAAEGGILMNT GAMETANGIAL
AAAEGIILNRT EGALITARIAN
AAAEGILMMNO MEGALOMANIA
AAAEGILNNST EAST ANGLIAN
AAAEGKLPTTU TAKE A PLUG AT
AAAEGNRTTVX EXTRAVAGANT
AAAEHILNOPR AEOLIAN HARP
AAAEHIMNNRT AMARANTHINE
AAAEHIMOSST HAEMOSTASIA
AAAEHKLMPSS MAKE A SPLASH
AAAEHPPRRSS PARAPHRASES
AAAEIKLLNNT ANTALKALINE
AAAEILMNNOT EMANATIONAL
AAAEILNPSTT PALATINATES
AAAEILPPRRS REAPPRAISAL
AAAEIMNQRSU AQUAMARINES
AAAEIMOPRRT AMOR PATRIAE
AAAEINSSSST ASSASSINATE
AAAEKNPTTTU TAKE A PUNT AT
AAAELLNRSTT TARANTELLAS
AAAELNRRSTV TRANSVAALER
AAAEPPRSSTU APPARATUSES
AAAFGHINNST AFGHANISTAN
AAAFIKPRRSS SAFARI PARKS
AAAGGGINRTV AGGRAVATING
AAAGGHHIOPR HAGIOGRAPHA
AAAGGINORTV AGGRAVATION
AAAGIIMNRRS AGRARIANISM
AAAGIINRSTT SAGITTARIAN
AAAGILNNPQU AQUAPLANING
AAAGIMMNRRS GRAMMARIANS

AAAGMMRRRSS MARRAM GRASS
AAAGMPPRSSS PAMPAS GRASS
AAAHILNPSXY ANAPHYLAXIS
AAAIILNORTV VARIATIONAL
AAAIIMNNRTU MAURITANIAN
AAAIINNQRTU ANTIQUARIAN
AAAILLNOSTV SALVATIONAL
AAAILLNOTUV VALUATIONAL
AAAILLORSTT SALTATORIAL
AAAILMNOPPR MALAPROPIAN
AAAILMRRSTT MARTIAL ARTS
AAAILNNOSTY ANALYSATION
AAAILNRSSTU AUSTRALIANS,
    SATURNALIAS
AAAINNNNOST SAN ANTONIAN
AAAINNOOPST PIANO SONATA
AABBBEHRSTY BABY'S-BREATH
AABBCDEINRT BRACE AND BIT
AABBCDEKLLL BLACKBALLED
AABBCDKLORS BLACKBOARDS
AABBCEEELMR EMBRACEABLE
AABBCEINORT BICARBONATE
AABBCIJKRST JACKRABBITS
AABBDDDENOR BED AND BOARD
AABBDDEORRS BREADBOARDS
AABBDEEIRTV ABBREVIATED
AABBDEEKRST BREADBASKET
AABBDEEORRV BEAVERBOARD
AABBEEIRRTV REBARBATIVE
AABBEEKLNRU UNBREAKABLE
AABBEFGLRST FLABBERGAST
AABBEGILLNR BALL BEARING
AABBEHIILNT INHABITABLE
AABBEHNRSUW BHUBANESWAR
AABBEIILLNV ABBEVILLIAN
AABBEIIRRST BARBARITIES
AABBEIORRTV ABBREVIATOR
AABBEIRRTTU BARBITURATE
AABBGIINRRZ BARBARIZING
AABBIIILMNO BIBLIOMANIA
AABBLORRSUY BARBAROUSLY
AABCCDDIRRY BRADYCARDIC
AABCCDEIIIT ABIETIC ACID
AABCCDEKKRT BACKTRACKED
AABCCEHHIRS BEACHCHAIRS
AABCCEILPRT PRACTICABLE
AABCCEKKPRS BACKPACKERS
AABCCELLMUU ACCUMULABLE
AABCCELNOTU ACCOUNTABLE
AABCCERRUUY BUREAUCRACY
AABCCGIKKNP BACKPACKING
AABCCILPRTY PRACTICABLY
AABCCKNNOTU BANK ACCOUNT
AABCCLNRRUU CARBUNCULAR

AABCDDEEKLP BACKPEDALED
AABCDDIKMNO DIAMONDBACK
AABCDEEERTX EXACERBATED
AABCDEEFLRY BAREFACEDLY
AABCDEFIIIL ACIDIFIABLE
AABCDEHIMMR CHAMBERMAID
AABCDEHKNRS BACKHANDERS
AABCDEIILNT INDICATABLE
AABCDEIKLLM BLACKMAILED
AABCDEILNST ELASTIC BAND
AABCDEINOOR RADIO BEACON
AABCDEKNRRS BANKER'S CARD
AABCDELMNRU CANDELABRUM
AABCDELNOTU OUTBALANCED
AABCDEORRST BROADCASTER
AABCDGGIOOR BRAGGADOCIO
AABCDGIINRR BARRICADING
AABCDGKLRSU BLACKGUARDS
AABCDHKLORS CHALKBOARDS
AABCDHMNORY RHABDOMANCY
AABCDIINOST ABDICATIONS
AABCDIIQRTU BIQUADRATIC
AABCDINOORR RADIOCARBON
AABCEEELLPR REPLACEABLE
AABCEEELRRT RETRACEABLE
AABCEEFLRRT REFRACTABLE
AABCEEFNORR FORBEARANCE
AABCEEHILMP IMPEACHABLE
AABCEEHKLRT LEATHERBACK
AABCEEHLMPS PEACH MELBAS
AABCEEHMNRT ANTECHAMBER
AABCEEILLMR RECLAIMABLE
AABCEEILMNV AMBIVALENCE
AABCEEILNPS INESCAPABLE
AABCEEILNRS INCREASABLE
AABCEEILPPR APPRECIABLE
AABCEELNORV OVERBALANCE
AABCEELNRST TABERNACLES
AABCEELORTT BRACTEOLATE
AABCEELRRTT RETRACTABLE
AABCEELRSTT SCATTERABLE
AABCEELRTTX EXTRACTABLE
AABCEFIIRTV FABRICATIVE
AABCEFLMNOY FLAMBOYANCE
AABCEFLNOTU CONFABULATE
AABCEFLRRTU FRACTURABLE
AABCEGIRRRS CARRIER BAGS
AABCEGLMNNS BLANCMANGES
AABCEHILLRY HEBRAICALLY
AABCEHILMNR CHAMBERLAIN
AABCEHILSST CHASTISABLE
AABCEHLNPUX BLUE PANCHAX
AABCEHLNSTU STAUNCHABLE
AABCEHLPRSU PURCHASABLE

AABCEHMRRST STAR CHAMBER
AABCEHNOOTV A NOTCH ABOVE
AABCEIILNNS CANNIBALISE
AABCEIILNNZ CANNIBALIZE
AABCEIINSTU BEAUTICIANS
AABCEIKLLMR BLACKMAILER
AABCEILLLOZ LOCALIZABLE
AABCEILMNRY CARBYLAMINE
AABCEILNPSY INESCAPABLY
AABCEILNRTT INTRACTABLE
AABCEILPPRY APPRECIABLY
AABCEIMNPRR PRECAMBRIAN
AABCEIRSTTV ABSTRACTIVE
AABCEKKLMRT BLACK MARKET
AABCEKLMSSS BLACK MASSES
AABCEKLPPRS BACKSLAPPER
AABCEKNRRSU SAARBRUCKEN
AABCELLOORT COLLABORATE
AABCELLQRTU RACQUETBALL
AABCELMOPSS COMPASSABLE
AABCELORSXY CARBOXYLASE
AABCELORTXY CARBOXYLATE
AABCENOPPRR CARBON PAPER
AABCENOPRST ABSORPTANCE
AABCEOORTTZ AZOTOBACTER
AABCERRSTUU BUREAUCRATS
AABCFGIINRT FABRICATING
AABCFIINORT FABRICATION
AABCGHIOOPR AGORAPHOBIC
AABCGHIOPRR BAROGRAPHIC
AABCGIILNRT CALIBRATING
AABCGILNNNU UNBALANCING
AABCGINRSTT ABSTRACTING
AABCGLRRSTU CAT BURGLARS
AABCHIINNTY INHABITANCY
AABCHIINORT BRACHIATION
AABCHILNSTU BALUCHISTAN
AABCHIOPRST ASTRAPHOBIC
AABCIIILMTY AMICABILITY
AABCIILLPTY PLACABILITY
AABCIILMNNS CANNIBALISM
AABCIILNORT CALIBRATION
AABCIILSTUY CAUSABILITY
AABCILLMNTU LACTALBUMIN
AABCILLNOTY BOTANICALLY
AABCILNNRUU INCUNABULAR
AABCILNRTTY INTRACTABLY
AABCILOSTTY BIOCATALYST
AABCINNOORT CARBONATION
AABCINORSTT ABSTRACTION
AABCKLMOORS BLACKAMOORS
AABCLLLRSTY CRYSTAL BALL
AABCLLNNNOS CANNONBALLS
AABCLPRSSUU SUBSCAPULAR

AABDDDEFMNU DEAF-AND-DUMB
AABDDEGGORR DAGGERBOARD
AABDDEGLLLR GALL BLADDER
AABDDEHHNRT HANDBREADTH
AABDDEHMORY HEBDOMADARY
AABDDEILSSU DISSUADABLE
AABDDEINOST BASTINADOED
AABDDEIRSST BASTARDISED
AABDDEIRSTZ BASTARDIZED
AABDDELNNOY ABANDONEDLY
AABDDELNSST SANDBLASTED
AABDDNRSSTU SUBSTANDARD
AABDEEFKRST BREAKFASTED
AABDEEHHRRS HABERDASHER
AABDEEHINRR HAREBRAINED
AABDEEILLMP IMPLEADABLE
AABDEELNSST DATABLENESS
AABDEELPRSU PERSUADABLE
AABDEEMRRSS EMBARRASSED
AABDEGGORSU BROAD GAUGES
AABDEGHILNS BANGLADESHI
AABDEGILNOS DIAGNOSABLE
AABDEHHIRRT HAIRBREADTH
AABDEHINRSW BRAINWASHED
AABDEHRSTWY BREADTHWAYS
AABDEIILLNT DENTILABIAL
AABDEIILNSV INADVISABLE
AABDEIILRTY READABILITY
AABDEIKNORT DEBARKATION
AABDEILLNOT LABIODENTAL
AABDEILLRVY ADVERBIALLY
AABDEILNOUV UNAVOIDABLE
AABDEILORRT LABRADORITE
AABDEIMRTUV ADUMBRATIVE
AABDEINOSST BASTINADOES
AABDEKORSST SKATEBOARDS
AABDELLNSTU UNBALLASTED
AABDELNORST BAROTSELAND
AABDELNRSST SANDBLASTER
AABDELNRSTU SALAD BURNET
AABDELRSSTU BALUSTRADES
AABDEMNNNOS ONE-MAN BANDS
AABDEMNNNOT ABANDONMENT
AABDEMNRSST BANDMASTERS
AABDEMRSTTU MASTURBATED
AABDEOPRSST PASTEBOARDS
AABDFIIINPS SPINA BIFIDA
AABDGGGINNS SANDBAGGING
AABDGIILRTY GRADABILITY
AABDGIMNOSV VAGABONDISM
AABDGIMNRTU ADUMBRATING
AABDHIILNTU HABITUDINAL
AABDHIKLNOY BANK HOLIDAY
AABDHINNOPS ABANDON SHIP

AABDHIOSTTV BODHISATTVA
AABDHLOPRSS SPLASHBOARD
AABDHMMOORY RHABDOMYOMA
AABDIILLTUY LAUDABILITY
AABDIILMNTY DAMNABILITY
AABDIILMQRU LIQUIDAMBAR
AABDIINNRRS BRAIN DRAINS
AABDIJOORSU OUIJA BOARDS
AABDIMNORTU ADUMBRATION
AABDLLMOOPS BLOOD PLASMA
AABDMOORRRT MORTARBOARD
AABDNOOPRSX PANDORA'S BOX
AABEEEEGRRV EAGER BEAVER
AABEEEFKRRS SAFEBREAKER
AABEEEGLLNR ENLARGEABLE
AABEEELRRST TALEBEARERS
AABEEFHORST FEATHER BOAS
AABEEFLLRTT FLATTERABLE
AABEEGINNRT ANNABERGITE
AABEEGLMNTU AUGMENTABLE
AABEEGLMSSS ASSEMBLAGES
AABEEHILNTZ ELIZABETHAN
AABEEHILPST ALPHABETISE
AABEEHILPTZ ALPHABETIZE
AABEEHKLNSU UNSHAKEABLE
AABEEHLRSTY BREATHALYSE
AABEEHLRTYZ BREATHALYZE
AABEEIILLNN INALIENABLE
AABEEIILLNPX EXPLAINABLE
AABEEIILLNRT INALTERABLE
AABEEIILNPRS INSEPARABLE
AABEEILORTV ELABORATIVE
AABEEILPRRR IRREPARABLE
AABEEINRRRT TRAINBEARER
AABEEINRRST BRAINTEASER
AABEEINSSTT BASTNAESITE
AABEEJKRRSW JAWBREAKERS
AABEEKLNPSU UNSPEAKABLE
AABEEKLRRSW LAW-BREAKERS
AABEELLMNOT BALLETOMANE
AABEELLNRTU UNALTERABLE
AABEELLORTY ELABORATELY
AABEELLPRRS PALLBEARERS
AABEELLPRSU PLEASURABLE
AABEELMNSST TAMABLENESS
AABEELMPRTU PERAMBULATE
AABEELMPTTT ATTEMPTABLE
AABEELNORST TREASONABLE
AABEELNRTTU ENTABLATURE
AABEELNSSSV SAVABLENESS
AABEELPRSTT BREASTPLATE
AABEELRRSTU TREASURABLE
AABEELRRSTV TRAVERSABLE
AABEELRRTWY BARLEY WATER

AABEELRSTTW WATER TABLES
AABEEMMOPRT MEPROBAMATE
AABEFFIILLS FALSIFIABLE
AABEFGIILMN MAGNIFIABLE
AABEFHILNOS FASHIONABLE
AABEFIILLMP AMPLIFIABLE
AABEFIILLQU QUALIFIABLE
AABEFIILSST SATISFIABLE
AABEFILLMMN INFLAMMABLE
AABEFILLRTT FILTRATABLE
AABEFLLNPPU UNFLAPPABLE
AABEFLNORUV UNFAVORABLE
AABEGGGMOOR BAGGAGE ROOM
AABEGIILNNV INVAGINABLE
AABEGIKLNRW LAWBREAKING
AABEGILNORT ELABORATING
AABEGIRRRTU ARBITRAGEUR
AABEGLLMOST MEGALOBLAST
AABEGLNORRR BARREL ORGAN
AABEGLRRSUY BARLEY SUGAR
AABEHIILLNN ANNIHILABLE
AABEHILNRST TARNISHABLE
AABEHILORUV BEHAVIOURAL
AABEHINRRSW BRAINWASHER
AABEHLPRRSV PHRASAL VERB
AABEIILLMSS ASSIMILABLE
AABEIILLSTY SALEABILITY
AABEIILMMOR MEMORABILIA
AABEIILMNTY AMENABILITY
AABEIILNRRT LIBERTARIAN
AABEIILRTWY WEARABILITY
AABEIKMNORT EMBARKATION
AABEILLLRTY BILATERALLY
AABEILLOPRZ POLARIZABLE
AABEILLRRST LIBERAL ARTS
AABEILLRRTZ TRAILBLAZER
AABEILLRVZZ BRAZZAVILLE
AABEILMMRSU BARIUM MEALS
AABEILMORTZ AMORTIZABLE
AABEILNOORT ELABORATION
AABEILNPRSY INSEPARABLY
AABEILNRSTT TRANSITABLE
AABEILNSSTU SUSTAINABLE
AABEILOPRVZ VAPORIZABLE
AABEILPRRRY IRREPARABLY
AABEILPRTUU BUILT-UP AREA
AABEIMNRRTT ARBITRAMENT
AABEIMPRSTV VAMPIRE BATS
AABEINOPSTT BE AT PAINS TO
AABEINORRST ABERRATIONS
AABEIOPPRTV APPROBATIVE
AABEKLMORRT LABOR MARKET
AABEKLNPSUY UNSPEAKABLY
AABELLLOSWW SWALLOWABLE

AABELLORSUV SLAVE LABOUR
AABELLORTTY BATTLE ROYAL
AABELLPRSUY PLEASURABLY
AABELMMNSSY ASSEMBLYMAN
AABELNORSTY TREASONABLY
AABELOPRRTY PORTRAYABLE
AABELORSSST ALBATROSSES
AABELPRSSSU SURPASSABLE
AABFLLNPPUY UNFLAPPABLY
AABFLNORUVY UNFAVORABLY
AABGGGGINNN GANG-BANGING
AABGHHIOOPP PHAGOPHOBIA
AABGHIINTTU HABITUATING
AABGHILNOOP ANGLOPHOBIA
AABGIILNORS ABORIGINALS
AABGIILNOST SAILING BOAT
AABGIIMNNOT ABOMINATING
AABGIINRRTT ARBITRATING
AABGIKNNSSV SAVINGS BANK
AABGILMNRSU SUBMARGINAL
AABGILNORSV LABORSAVING
AABGINOORST ABROGATIONS
AABGIRSSSTU BASS GUITARS
AABGKLOOTUW GO WALKABOUT
AABGLLMORSY SYLLABOGRAM
AABHIILORTT HABILITATOR
AABHIILSTWY WASHABILITY
AABHIINNSTT INHABITANTS
AABHIINOSTT HABITATIONS
AABHIINOTTU HABITUATION
AABHIMNPSST BATSMANSHIP
AABHIMRSTVZ BAR MITZVAHS
AABHLLLOOSU HULLABALOOS
AABIIILRTVY VARIABILITY
AABIIILSTTY SATIABILITY
AABIIKLLTTY TALKABILITY
AABIILLNORT LIBRATIONAL
AABIILLPPTY PALPABILITY
AABIILLSTVY SALVABILITY
AABIILMNRUU ALBUMINURIA
AABIILNORTV VIBRATIONAL
AABIILRRRTY ARBITRARILY
AABIIMNNOOT ABOMINATION
AABIINORRTT ARBITRATION
AABILLRSUXY SUBAXILLARY
AABILMNORTY ABNORMALITY
AABILNOOPRT PROBATIONAL
AABILNORTUY ABLUTIONARY
AABILNOSTTU TABULATIONS
AABILNSSTTU SUBSTANTIAL
AABINOOPPRT APPROBATION
AABIORRRSTT ARBITRATORS
AABKKOORRSU KOOKABURRAS
AABLOPRRTUY LABOUR PARTY

AABNOORRSTW NARROW BOATS
AABNOORSTTY ASTROBOTANY
AACCCDENORS ACCORDANCES
AACCCDEOSUY CYCADACEOUS
AACCCEENPST ACCEPTANCES
AACCCEJKKRR CRACKERJACK
AACCCGHIOPR CACOGRAPHIC
AACCCIIILRT CICATRICIAL
AACCCILMSTY CATACLYSMIC
AACCCNNOTUY ACCOUNTANCY
AACCDDEIINS CANDIDACIES
AACCDEEEELRT ACCELERATED
AACCDEELNOR ACCELERANDO
AACCDEENTTU ACCENTUATED
AACCDEGHRRS CHARGE CARDS
AACCDEHNORS ARCHDEACONS
AACCDEIILLT DIALECTICAL
AACCDEIIMMS ACADEMICISM
AACCDEIMNOP ACCOMPANIED
AACCDEIRRTU CARICATURED
AACCDELMTUU ACCUMULATED
AACCDEMMOOT ACCOMMODATE
AACCDEORSUU CARDUACEOUS
AACCDERSSTY SCAREDY CATS
AACCDGIIILN ALGINIC ACID
AACCDHILNOR CHANCROIDAL
AACCDHPRSST SCRATCHPADS
AACCDIIILRT DIACRITICAL
AACCDIILMNO MALONIC ACID
AACCDIOSSTU CAUSTIC SODA
AACCEEFILNT CALEFACIENT
AACCEEINRRT INCARCERATE
AACCEELLNOT COLLECTANEA
AACCEELNSTU ACAULESCENT
AACCEELORRT ACCELERATOR
AACCEENNOTT CONCATENATE
AACCEFHSTTY SAFETY CATCH
AACCEFILNOT CALEFACTION
AACCEFLORTY CALEFACTORY
AACCEGHILNR ARCHANGELIC
AACCEGHNRTT GNATCATCHER
AACCEGIKNPS PACKING CASE
AACCEGILMOR ACROMEGALIC
AACCEGILORT CATEGORICAL
AACCEGORRTY ERGATOCRACY
AACCEHHMOST STOMACHACHE
AACCEHHPRST CATCHPHRASE
AACCEHIIMNN MECHANICIAN
AACCEHILLNT CHALCANLITE
AACCEHILMOT MACHICOLATE
AACCEHILMST CATECHISMAL
AACCEHIOORZ ARCHAEOZOIC
AACCEHIRSST CATACHRESIS
AACCEHLNNNO NONCHALANCE

AACCEIILMST ACCLIMATISE
AACCEIILMTZ ACCLIMATIZE
AACCEILLSTY ASCETICALLY
AACCEILMPRT MALPRACTICE
AACCEILNNOT CANCELATION
AACCEILNOSS ACCESSIONAL
AACCEILORSS ACCESSORIAL
AACCEILOSSU SALICACEOUS
AACCEIMNOPR ACCOMPANIER
AACCEINOPTT ACCEPTATION
AACCEINQTTU ACQUITTANCE
AACCEIORSTU AUTOCRACIES
AACCEIRRSTU CARICATURES
AACCEISSTUV ACCUSATIVES
AACCEKLLNOY CYCLOALKANE
AACCEKMNOTT MAKE CONTACT
AACCELNRTUU CARUNCULATE
AACCELPRSTU SPECTACULAR
AACCELRTTUU ACCULTURATE
AACCENOPRRY COPARCENARY
AACCENRSSTU CRUSTACEANS
AACCFIIILRS SACRIFICIAL
AACCFIILLPY PACIFICALLY
AACCFIILRTY FARCICALITY
AACCFIIMNOR ACINACIFORM
AACCFINNRSS FRANCISCANS
AACCGHIMOPR MACROPHAGIC
AACCGIINNTV VACCINATING
AACCGILLNTU CALCULATING
AACCHIIMRST CHARISMATIC
AACCHIINRST ANARCHISTIC
AACCHIINRTT ANTHRACITIC
AACCHILLOTY CHAOTICALLY
AACCHILMNOR MONARCHICAL
AACCHILMOST STOMACHICAL
AACCHILNOTU ANACOLUTHIC
AACCHLNOOTY CHOANOCYTAL
AACCIIILLNTY ACTINICALLY
AACCIIILMPRT IMPRACTICAL
AACCIILNNOT CALCINATION
AACCIILNSTT ANTICLASTIC
AACCIILORSS SACROILIACS
AACCIILSTTT STALACTITIC
AACCIINNOTV VACCINATION
AACCIINOSTU ACOUSTICIAN
AACCIINRTTZ CICATRIZANT
AACCILLLNOY LACONICALLY
AACCILLNOTU CALCULATION
AACCILLNRTU CURTAIN CALL
AACCILLNSUU CANALICULUS
AACCILLPRTY PRACTICALLY
AACCILLSTUY CAUSTICALLY
AACCILNOSST CLASS ACTION
AACCILNOSTU SACCULATION

AACCILNPRTU UNPRACTICAL
AACCILOPPTY APOCALYPTIC
AACCILOPSUY CAPACIOUSLY
AACCILRRSUW CIRCULAR SAW
AACCIMNOPST ACCOMPANIST
AACCINOORTT COARCTATION
AACCINOSSTU ACCUSATIONS
AACCIORRSTY ARISTOCRACY
AACCKLLMORS ALARM CLOCKS
AACCLLORSTU CALCULATORS
AACCLMORTUU ACCUMULATOR
AACCLNORTTU CONTRACTUAL
AACCNNOSTTU ACCOUNTANTS
AACCOOPRRSU ACROCARPOUS
AACCORRSTTY STRATOCRACY
AACDDDEIJTU ADJUDICATED
AACDDEEEHLR CLEAR-HEADED
AACDDEEELST DE-ESCALATED
AACDDEEHMRS DEAD MARCHES
AACDDEEIMPS AIDES-DE-CAMP
AACDDEEIPTT DECAPITATED
AACDDEGLNOO DODECAGONAL
AACDDEHINPP HANDICAPPED
AACDDEHLNRS CRASH-LANDED
AACDDEILNOR ENDOCARDIAL
AACDDEILNSS SCANDALISED
AACDDEILNSZ SCANDALIZED
AACDDIJORTU ADJUDICATOR
AACDEEGHRST GATECRASHED
AACDEEHILMX HEXADECIMAL
AACDEEHNRTU HARDECANUTE
AACDEEIILNT ACETANILIDE
AACDEEIIRTV ERADICATIVE
AACDEEILRTV DECLARATIVE
AACDEEIMNPT EMANCIPATED
AACDEEINRST ASCERTAINED
AACDEEIPPRT APPRECIATED
AACDEEIRTTV REACTIVATED
AACDEELLSTT CASTELLATED
AACDEELMSTU EMASCULATED
AACDEELRTUW CATERWAULED
AACDEEMNNTV ADVANCEMENT
AACDEENNSTT ATTENDANCES
AACDEENQRSU SQUARE DANCE
AACDEFGLMOU CAMOUFLAGED
AACDEFIILTT FACILITATED
AACDEFILNOT DEFALCATION
AACDEGHHNNS CHANGE HANDS
AACDEGHHNRS CHARGE HANDS
AACDEGIIMNT DIAMAGNETIC
AACDEGIINRT ERADICATING
AACDEGIMNRT DEMARCATING
AACDEHILLPY EDAPHICALLY
AACDEHILORS ICOSAHEDRAL

AACDEHINOTT ANTICATHODE
AACDEHINPPR HANDICAPPER
AACDEHINRSS SEDAN CHAIRS
AACDEHINRST CANTHARIDES
AACDEHINRTU HARDICANUTE
AACDEHMOORR CHOREODRAMA
AACDEIILPST CAPITALISED
AACDEIILPTZ CAPITALIZED
AACDEIINNRT INCARDINATE
AACDEIINORT ERADICATION
AACDEIINPTT ANTICIPATED
AACDEIIORTV RADIOACTIVE
AACDEIIPRST PAEDIATRICS
AACDEILMNOT DECLAMATION
AACDEILMNTU CALUMNIATED
AACDEILNORT DECLARATION, REDACTIONAL
AACDEILNOTU EDUCATIONAL
AACDEILNRSS RADICALNESS, SCANDALISER
AACDEILNRSZ SCANDALIZER
AACDEILPTTU CAPITULATED
AACDEILRSTT STRAITLACED
AACDEILRTTU ARTICULATED
AACDEILRTTY DAIRY CATTLE
AACDEIMNNOP PANDEMONIAC
AACDEIMNORT DEMARCATION
AACDEIMNORY AERODYNAMIC
AACDEINOTUV COADUNATIVE
AACDEIOPRTT DECAPITATOR
AACDEIORRST ERADICATORS
AACDEIORTTV DEACTIVATOR
AACDELMNNOR ROMAN CANDLE
AACDELMORTY DECLAMATORY
AACDELNPTTY PENTADACTYL
AACDELNSSST SANDCASTLES
AACDELORRTY DECLARATORY
AACDEMORRRS ARMORED CARS
AACDEMORRRU ARMOURED CAR
AACDEMRRSST MASTER CARDS
AACDFHINRST HANDICRAFTS
AACDFIILRRT FRATRICIDAL
AACDFIINOOS AFICIONADOS
AACDGGHIIST HAGGADISTIC
AACDGHIOPRR CARDIOGRAPH
AACDGILNNPS LANDSCAPING
AACDGILNNVY ADVANCINGLY
AACDGILNPRY PLAYING CARD
AACDGIMRRTU DRAMATURGIC
AACDGINNSST SAND-CASTING
AACDGORSSTU COASTGUARDS
AACDHIIOPRS APHRODISIAC
AACDHLNOSYY HALCYON DAYS
AACDHMOPRSY PSYCHODRAMA

AACDIILNOTT DICTATIONAL
AACDIILNOTU ACIDULATION
AACDIILNSTV VANDALISTIC
AACDIILORTT DICTATORIAL
AACDIIMNOPS DIPSOMANIAC
AACDIINNOTY CYANIDATION
AACDIIOPRTY RADIOPACITY
AACDIIORRTV DIVARICATOR
AACDILLMNOY NOMADICALLY
AACDILLMNYY DYNAMICALLY
AACDILLRSTY DRASTICALLY
AACDILNOSTY ANISODACTYL
AACDILNPSST LANDSCAPIST
AACDILORTTY ARTIODACTYL
AACDILOSUUY AUDACIOUSLY
AACDIMOORST SARCOMATOID
AACDINNOOTU COADUNATION
AACDMMNNOST COMMANDANTS
AACDMOORSTU CATADROMOUS
AACEEEHLMOT HAEMATOCELE
AACEEEHPRST SPACE HEATER
AACEEFFMNRT RAMAN EFFECT
AACEEFIMNSS MISFEASANCE
AACEEFLLPTT CLEFT PALATE
AACEEFNNNOS NONFEASANCE
AACEEGHLMPY MEGACEPHALY
AACEEGHNOPR CHAPERONAGE
AACEEGHRRST GATECRASHER
AACEEGILLLY ELEGIACALLY
AACEEGILLNS ALLEGIANCES
AACEEGILLNV EVANGELICAL
AACEEGINPRT PARAGENETIC
AACEEGMMORT MACROGAMETE
AACEEHHLTUX HEXATEUCHAL
AACEEHHMMOR HAEMACHROME
AACEEHILNST CHATELAINES
AACEEHIMPPR PAPIER-MACHÉ
AACEEHINSTT ANAESTHETIC
AACEEHKPSST CHEAPSKATES
AACEEHLMNOP ENCEPHALOMA
AACEEHLNNSV CLEAN-SHAVEN
AACEEHMPRST SPERMATHECA
AACEEHPPRSS PAPER CHASES
AACEEHRRTTT TETRARCHATE
AACEEIIMNRS AMERICANISE
AACEEIIMNRZ AMERICANIZE
AACEEIIMPST SEPTICAEMIA
AACEEIJLTUV EJACULATIVE
AACEEIKLMNR AMERICAN ELK
AACEEILLMNS MESALLIANCE,
  MISCELLANEA
AACEEILLRTV VARICELLATE
AACEEILNRTT INTERCALATE
AACEEILPRST ALTARPIECES

AACEEILRRST SECRETARIAL
AACEEILSSTT ATELECTASIS
AACEEIMNNNT MAINTENANCE
AACEEIMSSST SIAMESE CATS
AACEEINNNRT CENTENARIAN
AACEEINNRRT REINCARNATE
AACEEINNRSS RENAISSANCE
AACEEIPRRTV PREVARICATE
AACEEIRRSTT SECRETARIAT
AACEEKLMPRT MARKETPLACE
AACEELNPSTU ENCAPSULATE
AACEENRRSSU REASSURANCE
AACEFFHINRS AFFRANCHISE
AACEFFIIRTV AFFRICATIVE
AACEFFILNOT AFFECTIONAL
AACEFFINOTT AFFECTATION
AACEFGHINRR FAR-REACHING
AACEFGLMOSU CAMOUFLAGES
AACEFGLOOTT COTTAGE LOAF
AACEFHMSTTY SAFETY MATCH
AACEFIILNRV ACRIFLAVINE
AACEFIINSTV FASCINATIVE
AACEFILMNOT MALEFACTION
AACEFILTTUV FACULTATIVE
AACEFIMNRRT AIRCRAFTMEN
AACEFINORRT RAREFACTION
AACEFINORSU FARINACEOUS
AACEFINORTT FRACTIONATE
AACEFLMORST MALEFACTORS
AACEFLNSSTU FACTUALNESS
AACEFMNRTUU MANUFACTURE
AACEGGGKLRU LUGGAGE RACK
AACEGGILPTU TEGUCIGALPA
AACEGGINRRU GUN CARRIAGE
AACEGGINRSV SAVING GRACE
AACEGHHNOTT CHAETOGNATH
AACEGHILOPR ARCHIPELAGO
AACEGHLLMNS SMALL CHANGE
AACEGHLLSSV CHEVAL GLASS
AACEGHLOORY ARCHAEOLOGY
AACEGHNORST COAT HANGERS
AACEGHNORTU AUTOCHANGER
AACEGHPRTTU GUTTA-PERCHA
AACEGIIMRRS MISCARRIAGE
AACEGIJLNTU EJACULATING
AACEGILLLNY ANGELICALLY
AACEGILLLOR ALLEGORICAL
AACEGILLOPS PLAGIOCLASE
AACEGILMNPS PLASMAGENIC
AACEGILNPRY PANEGYRICAL
AACEGILOTUV COAGULATIVE
AACEGILPPRS PARAPLEGICS
AACEGIMNPRS CAMPAIGNERS
AACEGINNRTW WATERING CAN

AACEGINPPRT RATE-CAPPING
AACEGKOPRTU PACKAGE TOUR
AACEGLNRRTU RECTANGULAR
AACEGMNOORR GRAECO-ROMAN
AACEGNOORSU ONAGRACEOUS
AACEGRRSSTU CASTER SUGAR
AACEHHIKNNV NAKHICHEVAN
AACEHIILMPT EPITHALAMIC
AACEHIILSTT ATHEISTICAL
AACEHIIMMNS MANICHAEISM
AACEHILLMNO MELANCHOLIA
AACEHILLNTU HALLUCINATE
AACEHILLPTY APHETICALLY
AACEHILRSTT THEATRICALS
AACEHIMMSTT MATHEMATICS
AACEHIMNNOY HAEMOCYANIN
AACEHIMORST ACHROMATISE
AACEHIMORTT HAEMATOCRIT
AACEHIMORTZ ACHROMATIZE
AACEHIMOSTT HAEMOSTATIC
AACEHINOTTY THIOCYANATE
AACEHJKMMRS JACKHAMMERS
AACEHKMMRST MATCHMAKERS
AACEHKMRSTW WATCHMAKERS
AACEHMMNNRT MERCHANTMAN
AACEHMNORSU RHAMNACEOUS
AACEHMNSTTT ATTACHMENTS
AACEHMSSSTU MASSACHUSET
AACEHNNORST ANTHRACNOSE
AACEHOPRSTT CATASTROPHE
AACEHOPSSTU SPATHACEOUS
AACEHPRRSTY SEARCH PARTY
AACEHPRSTUX PURCHASE TAX
AACEIILLMNS MISALLIANCE
AACEIILLNRS ANCILLARIES
AACEIILLNRT LACERTILIAN
AACEIILLPRS CAPILLARIES
AACEIILMRSV CAVALIERISM
AACEIILNPRR PERICRANIAL
AACEIILNRRT INTERRACIAL
AACEIILPPRR PERICARPIAL
AACEIILPPTV APPLICATIVE
AACEIILSTTU ACTUALITIES
AACEIIMMNRS AMERICANISM
AACEIIMNRTV CARMINATIVE
AACEIIMQSTU SEMIAQUATIC
AACEIINORTT RATIOCINATE
AACEIIOSSTV ASSOCIATIVE
AACEIIPPRTT PARTICIPATE
AACEIJLNOTU EJACULATION
AACEILLLSTY ELASTICALLY
AACEILLMPRY MIRACLE PLAY
AACEILLMPUX AMPLEXICAUL
AACEILLNTTY TETANICALLY

AACEILLPRRT CATERPILLAR
AACEILLPTVY CAPITAL LEVY
AACEILLRRTY ERRATICALLY
AACEILMMPST METAPLASMIC
AACEILMNORT RECLAMATION
AACEILMNOTX EXCLAMATION
AACEILMNSSU MAIN CLAUSES
AACEILMRRTU MATRICULATE
AACEILNNOSS ASCENSIONAL
AACEILNNRTU ANTINUCLEAR
AACEILNORST LACERATIONS
AACEILNORTT ALTERCATION
AACEILNOTTY ACETYLATION
AACEILNPSTU INCAPSULATE
AACEILNRRTU RETINACULAR
AACEILNRRTY INTERCALARY
AACEILPRSTU SPIRACULATE
AACEILPRTTU PARTICULATE
AACEILSSTTT STALACTITES
AACEILSTUVY CAUSATIVELY
AACEIMMNOST SCAMMONIATE
AACEIMNNOTT CONTAMINATE
AACEIMNOORT EROTOMANIAC
AACEIMNOPRT EMANCIPATOR
AACEIMOPRTV COMPARATIVE
AACEINNORTT RECANTATION
AACEINORRTY REACTIONARY
AACEINORSTU AERONAUTICS
AACEINORSTV VACATIONERS
AACEINOSTUV EVACUATIONS
AACEINOSTVX EXCAVATIONS
AACEINPRSST PERSIAN CATS
AACEINRSSTU SANCTUARIES
AACEIORSSTT AEROSTATICS
AACEJLORTUY EJACULATORY
AACEKLLNOPR PANCAKE ROLL
AACEKLMRSST SMART ALECKS
AACEKLMRSTY SMART ALECKY
AACEKLRRSTY TRACKLAYERS
AACELLLRSST SALTCELLARS
AACELLNOOST CELLO SONATA
AACELLOPRSU ACARPELLOUS
AACELMMRSUU MARE CLAUSUM
AACELMORSTU EMASCULATOR
AACELMORTXY EXCLAMATORY
AACELNOOSSU SOLANACEOUS
AACELNORSTT TRANSLOCATE
AACELNRRSUV VERNACULARS
AACELOPPSSY APOCALYPSES
AACELPRSSTT PLASTER CAST
AACELQRTUUU AQUACULTURE
AACENNNORTW WATER CANNON
AACENOOPSSU SAPONACEOUS
AACENORRTVY CONTRAYERVA

AACEOOPSSTU SAPOTACEOUS
AACEOPPRSUY PAPYRACEOUS
AACFFIJMRST TRAFFIC JAMS
AACFFIORRTT TRAFFICATOR
AACFFMORRTY FACTORY FARM
AACFGIINNST FASCINATING
AACFHKNRSST CRANKSHAFTS
AACFHMORSSU FORASMUCH AS
AACFIILLNNY FINANCIALLY
AACFIILORTT FACILITATOR
AACFIINNOST FASCINATION
AACFILLNRTY FRANTICALLY
AACFILMORRS SCALARIFORM
AACFILNORST INFRACOSTAL
AACFINORRTY FRACTIONARY
AACFKLMSUUV VACUUM FLASK
AACFMNORTUY MANUFACTORY
AACFMOORSST COATS OF ARMS
AACFNORSTUU ANFRACTUOUS
AACGGIIMNNP CAMPAIGNING
AACGGIINSTT CASTIGATING
AACGGILLOOR AGROLOGICAL
AACGGILNOSY SYNAGOGICAL
AACGGILNOTU CATALOGUING,
  COAGULATING
AACGHHOPRST TACHOGRAPHS
AACGHIKMMNT MATCHMAKING
AACGHIKMNTW WATCHMAKING
AACGHILLOPR ALLOGRAPHIC
AACGHILLPRY CALLIGRAPHY,
  GRAPHICALLY
AACGHINOPPR APPROACHING
AACGHINPRTU PARACHUTING
AACGHIOPRTU AUTOGRAPHIC
AACGHKNNOWW KWANGCHOWAN
AACGHLMOORU CHAULMOOGRA
AACGHNOOPRR CORONAGRAPH
AACGHOPRRTY CARTOGRAPHY
AACGHOPRSSU SARCOPHAGUS
AACGIILLNPY CALLIPYGIAN
AACGIILLNTV VACILLATING
AACGIILLOOX AXIOLOGICAL
AACGIILMNNS ANGLICANISM
AACGIILMSTT STALAGMITIC,
  STIGMATICAL
AACGIILNNOR CAROLINGIAN
AACGIIMNSTT MASTICATING
AACGIINNNRT INCARNATING
AACGIINNOTV VACATIONING
AACGIINNQTU ACQUAINTING
AACGIINOSST ASSOCIATING
AACGIINOSTT CASTIGATION
AACGIINPTTV CAPTIVATING
AACGILLNORY ORGANICALLY

AACGILLOPST POSTGLACIAL
AACGILNOOPR CARPOGONIAL
AACGILNOOTU COAGULATION
AACGILNORSS CORS ANGLAIS
AACGILNPTTU CATAPULTING
AACGILOSSUY SAGACIOUSLY
AACGINNRSTT TRANSACTING
AACGINPRVYZ CRAZY PAVING
AACGLMNOOPY CAMPANOLOGY
AACGORRSSTU CASTOR SUGAR
AACHHIIMPRT AMPHITRICHA
AACHHILMOPT OPHTHALMIAC
AACHIIINRST CHRISTIANIA
AACHIIMNNOT MACHINATION
AACHIIMNSST SHAMANISTIC
AACHIINRSSU SAURISCHIAN
AACHIKMNORV MARKOV CHAIN
AACHIKMNPRU KANCHIPURAM
AACHILLOPRY PAROCHIALLY
AACHILMNOOS MONOCHASIAL
AACHILMOPPP HIPPOCAMPAL
AACHIMMNOTY MYTHOMANIAC
AACHIMMORST ACHROMATISM
AACHIMNNORS ANACHRONISM
AACHIMNORSS MARASCHINOS
AACHIMOPPRR PARAMORPHIC
AACHIMPRSST PHARMACISTS
AACHINNNOTY ANTHOCYANIN
AACHIPRSTTU PARACHUTIST
AACHLLOOSTU HOLOCAUSTAL
AACHLNNOOTU ANACOLUTHON
AACHMMRRSUU HARUM-SCARUM
AACHMNOSTWY YACHTSWOMAN
AACHMOORSTU ACHROMATOUS
AACHPRSSTTW WATCHSTRAPS
AACIIILNNOT LACINIATION
AACIIILNOST LAICISATION
AACIIILNOTZ LAICIZATION
AACIIILPPRT PARTICIPIAL
AACIIJNOTTT JACTITATION
AACIILLMRTU MULTIRACIAL
AACIILLNOOT COALITIONAL
AACIILLNOTV VACILLATION
AACIILLNTTY TITANICALLY
AACIILLPRTY CAPILLARITY, PIRATICALLY
AACIILLRSTY SATIRICALLY
AACIILMNORT LACRIMATION
AACIILMNOST ANOMALISTIC
AACIILNNNOT LANCINATION
AACIILNOPPT APPLICATION
AACIILNPRTU PURITANICAL
AACIILOPRST PISCATORIAL
AACIILPSSTT CAPITALISTS
AACIILSSTTT STATISTICAL

AACIIMNNOTU ACUMINATION
AACIIMNORTT INTRA-ATOMIC
AACIIMNOSTT MASTICATION
AACIIMORTTY AROMATICITY
AACIINNNORT INCARNATION
AACIINNNOTT INCANTATION
AACIINOOSST ASSOCIATION
AACIINOPRTT ANTICIPATOR
AACIINOPSTT CAPITATIONS
AACIINOPTTV CAPTIVATION
AACIINPPRTT PARTICIPANT
AACILLLMOPS ALLOPLASMIC
AACILLLPSTY PLASTICALLY
AACILLMNOSY MASONICALLY
AACILLMOSTY SOMATICALLY
AACILLNOOST ALLOCATIONS
AACILLNOPRS RAPSCALLION
AACILLOPRSY PROSAICALLY
AACILLOSSUY SALACIOUSLY
AACILLPRTUU APICULTURAL
AACILLPSSTY SPASTICALLY
AACILLSTVWY CAVITY WALLS
AACILMNNOPT COMPLAINANT
AACILMNOPST COMPLAISANT
AACILMNRTTU MATRICULANT
AACILMORRTY LACRIMATORY
AACILNOOTUV VACUOLATION
AACILNOPRTY COPLANARITY
AACILNOPSTU CAPSULATION
AACILNORSTT INTRACOSTAL
AACILNORTVY CLAIRVOYANT
AACILOPPRTY APPLICATORY
AACILOPRSUY RAPACIOUSLY
AACILOPRTTU CAPITULATOR
AACILOPSTTU AUTOPLASTIC
AACILORRTTU ARTICULATOR
AACILPRRSTU PARTICULARS
AACILPRSSTT PLASTIC ARTS
AACILRSTUVY VASCULARITY
AACIMMNNOOS MONOMANIACS
AACIMNNNOTT CONTAMINANT
AACIMNOORST ARONOMASTIC
AACIMNOOSTT ANASTOMOTIC
AACIMNOPRSY PYROMANIACS
AACIMORSTTY MASTICATORY
AACINNNORTU ANNUNCIATOR
AACINNORSTT TRANSACTION
AACINNRRSTU TRANSURANIC
AACINOOOPPT APOCOPATION
AACINORSTTT ATTRACTIONS
AACINORSTTU ASTRONAUTIC
AACIORRSSTT ARISTOCRATS
AACLLNRUUVY AVUNCULARLY
AACLNNNOOST CONSONANTAL

AACLOOOORTVY ROYAL OCTAVO
AACLOOPPRSY LAPAROSCOPY
AACLOORRSTU COLORATURAS
AACLORSTTUU AUSCULTATOR
AACMNOPRTUY PARAMOUNTCY
AADDDEGINRS GRANDADDIES
AADDDEIILPT DILAPIDATED
AADDDEILRRT TARRADIDDLE
AADDEEEHPRS SPEARHEADED
AADDEEFGRSU SAFEGUARDED
AADDEEHHNVY HEAVY-HANDED
AADDEEHHRRT HARD-HEARTED
AADDEEHHSST DEATH'S-HEADS
AADDEEHIMNS MAIDENHEADS
AADDEEHLPRY PARALDEHYDE
AADDEEILNST DESALINATED
AADDEEIPPRS DISAPPEARED
AADDEELLNRS DARDANELLES
AADDEELLPTW WELL-ADAPTED
AADDEELRTTU ADULTERATED
AADDEEMQRSU MASQUERADED
AADDEEMRRSY DAYDREAMERS
AADDEENPPRS SANDPAPERED
AADDEGILLNY LEADING LADY
AADDEGIMNRY DAYDREAMING
AADDEGINORT DEGRADATION
AADDEGINRRS DISARRANGED
AADDEHIMNNS HANDMAIDENS
AADDEHNORTY READY TO HAND
AADDEHQSSTU DEATH SQUADS
AADDEIILNTV INVALIDATED
AADDEILMRRS RED ADMIRALS
AADDEINRSST STANDARDISE
AADDEINRSTZ STANDARDIZE
AADDEJLMSTU MALADJUSTED
AADDELPQRUU QUADRUPEDAL
AADDGNNRSST GRANDSTANDS
AADDIIINNRT TRINIDADIAN
AADDIILOPRT DILAPIDATOR
AADDNNNORST NONSTANDARD
AADEEEGGRTX EXAGGERATED
AADEEEGLPRS SPREAD-EAGLE
AADEEEHLNNR ENNEAHEDRAL
AADEEEPRSTX EXASPERATED
AADEEERSSTV ASSEVERATED
AADEEFGLLLT FLAGELLATED
AADEEFHHLRT HALF-HEARTED
AADEEGIKNTV GIVE-AND-TAKE
AADEEGILOPR A RIPE OLD AGE
AADEEGNORVW AVERAGE DOWN
AADEEGNPRRR PREARRANGED
AADEEHHLPRT HEPTAHEDRAL
AADEEHHRTXY HEXAHYDRATE
AADEEHILRTX EXHILARATED

AADEEHINRRV RAVEN-HAIRED
AADEEHLNNRT NEANDERTHAL
AADEEHLRRTT TETRAHEDRAL
AADEEHLRTTT DEATH RATTLE
AADEEHMRRTW WARM-HEARTED
AADEEHMRSST HEADMASTERS
AADEEHNRSVW HEAVENWARDS
AADEEIILNNR DAIL EIREANN
AADEEILMORT AMELIORATED
AADEEIMMNNS MAIDEN NAMES
AADEEIMRRRS SIERRA MADRE
AADEEINPPRT APPERTAINED
AADEEIPPRRS REAPPRAISED
AADEEIPRRTT REPATRIATED
AADEEIPRTTX EXPATRIATED
AADEEIRRSSV ADVERSARIES
AADEEIRRTTV RETARDATIVE
AADEEIRSTVV ADVERSATIVE
AADEEISTTVV DEVASTATIVE
AADEEKOPRTW TAKE A POWDER
AADEELLLLPR PARALLELLED
AADEELLNPTT DENTAL PLATE
AADEELLPPRW WALLPAPERED
AADEEMORTWW WATER MEADOW
AADEEMQRRSU MASQUERADER
AADEEMQRSSU MASQUERADES
AADEEMRRSTU ESTREMADURA
AADEENRSTVY VETERANS DAY
AADEENRSWYY NEW YEAR'S DAY
AADEEORRTWY READY-TO-WEAR
AADEFGHNRRT GRANDFATHER
AADEFGMNNSU FUN AND GAMES
AADEFHLNRST FATHERLANDS
AADEFIKLNNR RANK AND FILE
AADEFIMRRRY DAIRY FARMER
AADEFLMNNTU FUNDAMENTAL
AADEFLSSTTY STEADFASTLY
AADEGGGHLNU HAND LUGGAGE
AADEGGHNRSS HAGGARDNESS
AADEGGILNNR LANDING GEAR
AADEGGINRRS AGGRANDISER
AADEGGINRRZ AGGRANDIZER
AADEGGOSSSU SAUSAGE DOGS
AADEGHIINRS HEARING AIDS
AADEGHINRRW HARDWEARING
AADEGHOPRTU AUTOGRAPHED
AADEGIILNTT INTAGLIATED
AADEGIILPRS PLAGIARISED
AADEGIILPRZ PLAGIARIZED
AADEGIINRTT INGRATIATED
AADEGILLNNP PINEAL GLAND
AADEGILLNTV GALLIVANTED
AADEGILNNRS GARDEN SNAIL
AADEGILNPRT PLANTIGRADE

AADEGINNOST ANTAGONISED
AADEGINNOTZ ANTAGONIZED
AADEGINRTUU INAUGURATED
AADEGINSTTV DEVASTATING
AADEGLNQRSU QUADRANGLES
AADEGLNRSSU GRADUALNESS
AADEGLNSSTW SWEAT GLANDS
AADEGMNRRST GRAND MASTER
AADEGNNPRRT GRANDPARENT
AADEGNOPRRS GRAND OPERAS
AADEGNPRRTY GARDEN PARTY
AADEHIILNNT ANNIHILATED
AADEHIILNRT ANTHERIDIAL
AADEHILLNOS HOLLANDAISE
AADEHILMNNT THE MAINLAND
AADEHIPSTXY ASPHYXIATED
AADEHLNNPRS PANHANDLERS
AADEHMMMNOS MOHAMMEDANS
AADEIIIRRTV IRRADIATIVE
AADEIILMNST MEDIASTINAL
AADEIILMSST ASSIMILATED
AADEIILNRRT INTERRADIAL
AADEIILPRTY PRAEDIALITY
AADEIIMNNOT DEAMINATION
AADEIINORRT RERADIATION
AADEILLLMOT METALLOIDAL
AADEILLNOPT PLANETOIDAL
AADEILMNPTU MANIPULATED
AADEILMNRRT INTRADERMAL
AADEILNNQRU QUADRENNIAL
AADEILNORTY ARYTENOIDAL
AADEILNOTUV DEVALUATION
AADEILNRSTU NATURALISED
AADEILNRTUZ NATURALIZED
AADEILPRSTY DISPARATELY
AADEIMMNRST DISARMAMENT
AADEIMNRSTV MAIDSERVANT
AADEIMRSTTU TRAUMATISED
AADEIMRTTUZ TRAUMATIZED
AADEINNQRTU QUARANTINED
AADEINOPRTV DEPRAVATION
AADEINORRTT RETARDATION
AADEINORSST DIATESSARON
AADEINOSTTV DEVASTATION
AADEINPQRSU PASQUINADER
AADEKNRSSWW AWKWARDNESS
AADELLNNORT RALLENTANDO
AADELMMOPSS PLASMODESMA
AADELMOPRRT ARMOR-PLATED
AADELORRTTU ADULTERATOR
AADEMNORSTW TRADESWOMAN
AADENNRRTUW UNWARRANTED
AADENRSSWWY WAYWARDNESS
AADENRSTTUU UNSATURATED

AADEQRRSTUY QUARTER DAYS
AADFFORRSTW FAST-FORWARD
AADFGHINNST HANDFASTING
AADFHHILLOY HALF-HOLIDAY
AADFILRSSTU FRUIT SALADS
AADFLLLOOSY ALL FOOLS' DAY
AADGGIINPRS DISPARAGING
AADGGOOOUUU OUAGADOUGOU
AADGHHOPRSW SHADOWGRAPH
AADGHILMNNN MANHANDLING
AADGHILNNNP PANHANDLING
AADGHINOSSW WASHING SODA
AADGHINRSWW WASH DRAWING
AADGHINSSWY WASHING DAYS
AADGHIOPRRY RADIOGRAPHY
AADGHLPRSSU SPLASH GUARD
AADGHMNRSTU DRAUGHTSMAN
AADGIIINRRT IRRADIATING
AADGIIKLNNR KALININGRAD
AADGIILMRST MADRIGALIST
AADGIILNNNO ANGLO-INDIAN
AADGIILNNVZ VANDALIZING
AADGIILNORR RAILROADING
AADGIIMNRTZ DRAMATIZING
AADGINNOPRS GRAND PIANOS
AADGINORSTU GRADUATIONS
AADGNNOPRSS SNAPDRAGONS
AADGNOOPRST GASTROPODAN
AADHHINSTTT THIS AND THAT
AADHIIMOPRS ADIAPHORISM
AADHIIOPRST ADIAPHORIST
AADHILRSTWW WITHDRAWALS
AADHIOOPRSU ADIAPHOROUS
AADHIOPPRTY PARATYPHOID
AADHIOPRRTY PARATHYROID
AADHLORSUYZ HAZARDOUSLY
AADHORRSSUU HADROSAURUS
AADIIINNNOR INDO-IRANIAN
AADIIINORRT IRRADIATION
AADIIJNOSTU JUDAISATION
AADIIJNOTUZ JUDAIZATION
AADIILLNTTU ALTITUDINAL,
    LATITUDINAL
AADIILNOOTX OXIDATIONAL
AADIILNOPSS ANADIPLOSIS
AADIILNORTT TRADITIONAL
AADIILNORTV INVALIDATOR
AADIILNOSTV VALIDATIONS
AADIILNOSTY DIALYSATION
AADIILNOTYZ DIALYZATION
AADIILNTTTU ATTITUDINAL
AADIILOSUUV AUDIO-VISUAL
AADIIMNORST ADMIRATIONS
AADIINNORSU DINOSAURIAN

AADIINNOTTX ANTIOXIDANT
AADIIPRSSST ASPIDISTRAS
AADILLMNOOT AMONTILLADO
AADILLMORTY MALADROITLY
AADILMNORTY MANDATORILY
AADILOORSTV VASODILATOR
AADILOPPRSV DISAPPROVAL
AADIMNNOPRS PRIMA DONNAS
AADJMNNPRSU PANJANDRUMS
AADJNNORRST TRANS-JORDAN
AADLMNNNOSS NO-MAN'S-LANDS
AAEEEFFLMMT FEMME FATALE
AAEEEGNSTTT ESTATE AGENT
AAEEEGRSTWY STEERAGEWAY
AAEEEHNRRTW EARTHENWARE
AAEEEHNRTVW WEATHER VANE
AAEEEIKPSSS SPEAKEASIES
AAEEEMNNOSS SEA ANEMONES
AAEEEMNPPST APPEASEMENT
AAEEEMPRSTU TAPE MEASURE
AAEEENNRRST NEAR EASTERN
AAEEEPRRSTX EXASPERATER
AAEEFGMRRRW GERM WARFARE
AAEEFHHILRT FAITH HEALER
AAEEFHIRRTW FAIR-WEATHER
AAEEFHLMTWY MEET HALFWAY
AAEEFHRSSTV AFTERSHAVES
AAEEFKLMRST FLEA MARKETS
AAEEFLSTVVY SAFETY VALVE
AAEEFNRRSST TRANSFERASE
AAEEFRSSTTT AFTERTASTES
AAEEGGLMORT AGGLOMERATE
AAEEGGORRTX EXAGGERATOR
AAEEGHHMORR HAEMORRHAGE
AAEEGHLOOPS OESOPHAGEAL
AAEEGHNPPRR PAPERHANGER
AAEEGIKLNTV LEAVE TAKING
AAEEGILLLNS SELAGINELLA
AAEEGILLLTT TAGLIATELLE
AAEEGILLNNT GENTIANELLA
AAEEGILMSSX SEXAGESIMAL
AAEEGILNPPT EATING APPLE
AAEEGILPRTT TETRAPLEGIA
AAEEGINNNRT ARGENTINEAN
AAEEGINPPRR REAPPEARING
AAEEGINPRSS PARAGENESIS
AAEEGINPRST GREASEPAINT
AAEEGINRRTW GRANITEWARE
AAEEGINRSTV VEGETARIANS
AAEEGLMMRSU RUMMAGE SALE
AAEEGLMNOPT PLANOGAMETE
AAEEGLNNPTT PLANTAGENET
AAEEGLNRTTV TRAVEL AGENT
AAEEGLORTVY LAEVOGYRATE

AAEEGLPRSTY PEARLY GATES
AAEEGMMNNST MANAGEMENTS
AAEEGMMORRS AEROGRAMMES
AAEEGMNNRRT ARRANGEMENT
AAEEGMNOPRT POMEGRANATE
AAEEGMNRSTY EAST GERMANY
AAEEGMNSSTU ASSUAGEMENT
AAEEGNPRRRR PREARRANGER
AAEEHHLNNPT NAPHTHALENE
AAEEHILMOPR HEMERALOPIA
AAEEHIMMNPT AMPHETAMINE
AAEEHIMNRTT METATHERIAN
AAEEHIPRSST PARESTHESIA
AAEEHKMOPTY TAKE-HOME PAY
AAEEHKQRSTU EARTHQUAKES
AAEEHLLOSTW AT WHOLESALE
AAEEHLLSTTU HAUSTELLATE
AAEEHLNPTTV HEPTAVALENT
AAEEHMNOORR AMENORRHOEA
AAEEIIILLTVV ALLEVIATIVE
AAEEIILMRST MATERIALISE
AAEEIILMRTZ MATERIALIZE
AAEEIILRRST ARTERIALISE
AAEEIILRRTZ ARTERIALIZE
AAEEIILRTTV RETALIATIVE
AAEEIINRSSV SANSEVIERIA
AAEEIKLLMRT ALKALIMETER
AAEEIILLMNNT LINEAMENTAL
AAEEIILLPPTV APPELLATIVE
AAEEIILLQRTU EQUILATERAL
AAEEIILMMPST SEMIPALMATE
AAEEIILNNPRT PENETRALIAN
AAEEIILNRTTV ALTERNATIVE
AAEEIMNNRSS SAN MARINESE
AAEEIMSSSTT METASTASISE
AAEEIMSSTTZ METASTASIZE
AAEEIOPRTVV EVAPORATIVE
AAEEIPPRRTV PREPARATIVE
AAEEIPRSTTX EXPATRIATES
AAEEKLNRSTT RATTLESNAKE
AAEELLNRTTY ALTERNATELY
AAEELLNSTTV AT ALL EVENTS
AAEELLOOSST A SLATE LOOSE
AAEELLPRSTY PLATELAYERS
AAEELMNSTTT TESTAMENTAL
AAEELMQRSSU SQUARE MEALS
AAEELNNPTTV PENTAVALENT
AAEELNPSSTT PLEASANTEST
AAEELNPSTTV SEPTAVALENT
AAEELNRTTTV TETRAVALENT
AAEELOPRTTX EXTRAPOLATE
AAEEMNORTUX AUXANOMETER
AAEEMQRSSTU MARQUESSATE
AAEENNRSSUW UNAWARENESS

AAEFFIIMRTV AFFIRMATIVE
AAEFFILORSV LOVE AFFAIRS
AAEFGHILNRT FARTHINGALE
AAEFGILPRST SEPTIFRAGAL
AAEFGLLLNST FLAGELLANTS
AAEFGLSSSTY SAFETY GLASS
AAEFGMNRRTY FRAGMENTARY
AAEFHILNRTW FATHER-IN-LAW
AAEFIIILMRS FAMILIARISE
AAEFIIILMRZ FAMILIARIZE
AAEFIIORRSV SAVOIR-FAIRE
AAEFILMMNRT FIRMAMENTAL
AAEFILMMNSY FAMILY NAMES
AAEFILMNRTY FILAMENTARY
AAEFLLNRRTY FRATERNALLY
AAEFLMPSSTY SAFETY LAMPS
AAEFLOPSSTT SOFT PALATES
AAEFLRSSSTT FALSE STARTS
AAEFORRSTYZ SAFETY RAZOR
AAEGGGGINRT AGGREGATING
AAEGGGINORT AGGREGATION
AAEGGGLNSUV LUGGAGE VANS
AAEGGIIMNTW WAITING GAME
AAEGGILNTTU AGGLUTINATE
AAEGGIMMNTU GAMETANGIUM
AAEGGINNRRR REARRANGING
AAEGGLRRUUY A REGULAR GUY
AAEGGNORRUW NARROW GAUGE
AAEGHHIIKST HIGH AS A KITE
AAEGHIINRVW HAIRWEAVING
AAEGHIMNORR MENORRHAGIA
AAEGHINNNSS SHENANIGANS
AAEGHLLNOXY HEXAGONALLY
AAEGHLMOOTY HAEMATOLOGY
AAEGHLNPRTU HEPTANGULAR
AAEGHLOPPRY PALEOGRAPHY
AAEGHMNOPRY ANEMOGRAPHY
AAEGHMOPRRS PHRASEOGRAM
AAEGHNOPRTY PYTHAGOREAN
AAEGHNPRRST STRAPHANGER
AAEGHNSTTTU SET AT NAUGHT
AAEGIIIMNTV IMAGINATIVE
AAEGIILLNTV ALLEVIATING
AAEGIILMRST MAGISTERIAL
AAEGIILNRTT RETALIATING
AAEGIILPRRS PLAGIARISER
AAEGIILPRRZ PLAGIARIZER
AAEGIIMNNRT REANIMATING
AAEGIIMNRSS MINAS GERAIS
AAEGIINNOTV EVAGINATION
AAEGIINORTV VARIEGATION
AAEGIINPTTX EXPATIATING
AAEGIIRTTVV GRAVITATIVE
AAEGIKMNPST MASKING TAPE

AAEGILLLNPR PARALLELING
AAEGILLNNST SAINT GALLEN
AAEGILLNOST ALLEGATIONS
AAEGILLNPPR APPARELLING
AAEGILLNPPY APPEALINGLY
AAEGILLNRST GALLANTRIES
AAEGILMMNOS MAGLEMOSIAN
AAEGILMNRTT MALTREATING
AAEGILMNSTT STALEMATING
AAEGILMSSTT STALAGMITES
AAEGILNNRTT ALTERNATING
AAEGILNORTY LEGATIONARY
AAEGILNOSTT GESTATIONAL
AAEGILNQRUU EQUIANGULAR
AAEGILNRTTU TRIANGULATE
AAEGILNRTUV GRANULATIVE
AAEGIMNNRRT ARRAIGNMENT
AAEGIMRSSTT MAGISTRATES
AAEGINNOPRS SINGAPOREAN
AAEGINNTTTU ATTENUATING
AAEGINOPRTV EVAPORATING
AAEGIOPPRTV PROPAGATIVE
AAEGIOPSTTY STEATOPYGIA
AAEGIPRSSTT STAG PARTIES
AAEGLLNNSST GALLANTNESS
AAEGLLOPRTY PYROGALLATE
AAEGLLORSSU SAUSAGE ROLL
AAEGLMOPRRS PARLOR GAMES
AAEGLMOPRRU PARLOUR GAME
AAEGLNNPRTU PENTANGULAR
AAEGLNRSTTU STRANGULATE
AAEGNNRSSTV VAGRANTNESS
AAEHHIILMOP HAEMOPHILIA
AAEHHOPPSST PHOSPHATASE
AAEHHOTUVWY WHAT HAVE YOU
AAEHIIMNOPS HEMIANOPSIA
AAEHIIMNSST HISTAMINASE
AAEHIIINPSTT ANTIPATHIES
AAEHILLMTTY I'LL EAT MY HAT
AAEHILNPSTW WESTPHALIAN
AAEHILORRTX EXHILARATOR
AAEHIMOSSST HAEMOSTASIS
AAEHKLORSTT HOLKAR STATE
AAEHKLRSSST SALT SHAKERS
AAEHLNOPPRY ALPHA PYRONE
AAEHLNPRSTY PHALANSTERY
AAEHMNOOOTZ HAEMATOZOON
AAEHMNORSTU ATHERMANOUS
AAEHMNORSWW WASHERWOMAN
AAEHMOPRTTU THAUMATROPE
AAEHMOSSTTY STAY-AT-HOMES
AAEIIIKNNOS ANISEIKONIA
AAEIIILRSUX AUXILIARIES
AAEIIJNRSSS JANISSARIES

AAEIILLMNNR MILLENARIAN
AAEIILLMNRT MATRILINEAL
AAEIILLNOTV ALLEVIATION
AAEIILLNPRT PATRILINEAL
AAEIILLPSTV PALLIATIVES
AAEIILMMRST MATERIALISM
AAEIILMNRRT AIR TERMINAL
AAEIILMRSTT MATERIALIST
AAEIILMRTTY MATERIALITY
AAEIILNNOST NATIONALISE
AAEIILNNOTZ NATIONALIZE
AAEIILNNPST PALESTINIAN
AAEIILNORST RATIONALISE, REALISATION
AAEIILNORTT RETALIATION
AAEIILNORTZ RATIONALIZE,
    REALIZATION
AAEIILPPRSS PARALEIPSIS
AAEIILQTTUV QUALITATIVE
AAEIIMNNORT REANIMATION
AAEIIMNNOTX EXAMINATION,
    EXANIMATION
AAEIIMNRSST ERASTIANISM
AAEIINNPPRT PARIPINNATE
AAEIINOPTTX EXPATIATION
AAEIINOSTTV AESTIVATION
AAEIKLLMRTY ALKALIMETRY
AAEIKLMNOPT KLEPTOMANIA
AAEILLLMNOT LAMELLATION
AAEILLLMPRS PARALLELISM
AAEILLLOSTV SAL VOLATILE
AAEILLLPRST PARALLELIST
AAEILLNNPTY TIN PAN ALLEY
AAEILLNOOTV ALVEOLATION
AAEILLNOPPT APPELLATION
AAEILLQRSTU AQUARELLIST
AAEILMMNRST MATERNALISM
AAEILMMNNOTT LAMENTATION
AAEILMNORST MONASTERIAL
AAEILMNPRST PARLIAMENTS,
    PATERNALISM
AAEILMNPRTU PLANETARIUM
AAEILMNRRTU ULTRAMARINE
AAEILMOORRT AMELIORATOR
AAEILMOPTTT TOTIPALMATE
AAEILNNOPTX EXPLANATION
AAEILNNORTT ALTERNATION
AAEILNNOSST SENSATIONAL
AAEILNNPRST TRANSALPINE
AAEILNOOPRT OPERATIONAL
AAEILNOPPRY PLAYER PIANO
AAEILNOPRRT PROLETARIAN
AAEILNORSTT ALTERATIONS
AAEILNORSTX RELAXATIONS
AAEILNORTUV REVALUATION

AAEILNOSTUV EVALUATIONS
AAEILNPRSST PARTIALNESS
AAEILNPRSTT PATERNALIST
AAEILNPRSTW LAWN PARTIES
AAEILNRRSTU SERTULARIAN
AAEILNRSTTV AT INTERVALS
AAEILNOPRRTT PROLETARIAT
AAEILORRTTY RETALIATORY
AAEILORSSSS ASSESSORIAL
AAEIMMOOPST MESOPOTAMIA
AAEIMNNOSSY MAYONNAISES
AAEIMNNSTTT ATTAINMENTS
AAEIMOPPRTX APPROXIMATE
AAEINNNOSTX ANNEXATIONS
AAEINNOSSTT ASSENTATION
AAEINNOSTTT NATION STATE
AAEINNOTTTU ATTENUATION
AAEINNRRSVY ANNIVERSARY
AAEINOOPRTV EVAPORATION
AAEINOORSTT AEROSTATION
AAEINOPPRRT PREPARATION
AAEINOPRRST REPARATIONS
AAEINOPRSST SEPARATIONS
AAEINORSSTU AUSTRONESIA
AAEINOSTTTT ATTESTATION
AAEIOPPPRRT APPROPRIATE
AAEIORSSTTV ASSORTATIVE
AAEIPRSSSTT SEPARATISTS
AAEKMRSSSTT TASKMASTERS
AAELLNOPRSS SOLAR PANELS
AAELLOPSSTT ELASTOPLAST
AAELLORRSTT STELLARATOR
AAELMNORSVV REMOVAL VANS
AAELMNPQTUU QUANTUM LEAP
AAELMOPRRTU ARMOUR PLATE
AAELNNRSSTU NATURALNESS
AAELNOPRTXY EXPLANATORY
AAELNORRSTT ALTERNATORS
AAELNRRSSTV TRANSVERSAL
AAELNRRSTUV TRANSVALUER
AAELPRRSTTT RATTLETRAPS
AAEMNNRSSTV MANSERVANTS
AAEMNOPRTTU PORTMANTEAU
AAEMNOSSTTW STATESWOMAN
AAEMOOPRSTZ SPERMATOZOA
AAEMORSSTTT TOASTMASTER
AAEMPRSSSTT PAST MASTERS
AAENNPPRTTU APPURTENANT
AAENNPRRSTT TRANSPARENT
AAENNPRSTTU SUPERNATANT
AAENRRSSTTU RESTAURANTS
AAEOOPPRRRT PARATROOPER
AAEOPPRRRTY PREPARATORY
AAEOPRRTUVW WATER VAPOUR

AAEOPRSSTTU STRATOPAUSE
AAEPPRSSTTY A PRETTY PASS
AAFFGIIILNT AFFILIATING
AAFFGILOPST GAFF-TOPSAIL
AAFFGIMNRSU RAGAMUFFINS
AAFFIIILNOT AFFILIATION
AAFFIIMNORT AFFIRMATION
AAFGHILNNOU FIONNGHUALA
AAFGHIMNOSV SHAVING FOAM
AAFGIINNSTZ FANTASIZING
AAFGILLNRST FALLING STAR
AAFGINORRSU FARRAGINOUS
AAFIIILMRTY FAMILIARITY
AAFIINNOTTU INFATUATION
AAFILLMNORW LAMINAR FLOW
AAFILMNOORT FORMATIONAL
AAFILNOOSTT FLOATATIONS
AAFIMNNNRTY INFANTRYMAN
AAFINNOOPRT PROFANATION
AAFLNNOORST NASOFRONTAL
AAFNOOPRRTY PROFANATORY
AAGGGHILNSU LAUGHING GAS
AAGGHHIINNS SHANGHAIING
AAGGHHIOPRY HAGIOGRAPHY
AAGGHIIJMNT THINGAMAJIG
AAGGIILNNVZ GALVANIZING
AAGGIIMMNNS MISMANAGING
AAGGIINRTTV GRAVITATING
AAGGIKLMNSS GLASS-MAKING
AAGGILLNOST ALGOLAGNIST
AAGGILLNNTTU AGGLUTINANT
AAGGINOPPRT PROPAGATING
AAGGNNORSTU ORANGUTANGS
AAGHHLOPPRY HAPLOGRAPHY
AAGHIIINRRS HAIR-RAISING
AAGHIILLNOP ANGLOPHILIA
AAGHIKLLMNR HALLMARKING
AAGHILLMNPY LYMPHANGIAL
AAGHILLMNRS MARSHALLING
AAGHILNRSSY HARASSINGLY
AAGHIRSTTWY STRAIGHTWAY
AAGHLNOPPRY PLANOGRAPHY
AAGHLOOPPRR POLAROGRAPH
AAGHNOPPRST PANTOGRAPHS
AAGHNOPPRTY PANTOGRAPHY
AAGHNOPRRUY URANOGRAPHY
AAGIIILMNRY IMAGINARILY
AAGIIIMNNNT MAINTAINING
AAGIIIMNNOT IMAGINATION
AAGIIKNNPST PAINSTAKING
AAGIILMNORT MIGRATIONAL
AAGIILMNRTY MARGINALITY
AAGIILMPRSS PLAGIARISMS
AAGIILNNTTZ TANTALIZING

AAGIILNPPTT PALPITATING
AAGIILOPRRT GLORIA PATRI
AAGIILPRSST PLAGIARISTS
AAGIIMMNNTY MAGNANIMITY
AAGIIMMSSTT ASTIGMATISM
AAGIIMNNORT MARGINATION
AAGIIMSSSSU MISSISSAUGA
AAGIINNOSST ASSIGNATION
AAGIINORTTV GRAVITATION
AAGIIRSSTTU SAGITTARIUS
AAGIJKNOPRT JOKING APART
AAGILLLNPPY APPALLINGLY .
AAGILLLOOSS GLOSSOLALIA
AAGILLMNNTY MALIGNANTLY
AAGILLMRSTY MAGISTRALLY
AAGILLNRTUV VULGAR LATIN
AAGILMMMOST MAMMALOGIST
AAGILNNORTU GRANULATION
AAGILNNRSTT TRANSLATING
AAGILNOSUVY YUGOSLAVIAN
AAGILNRRTUY GRANULARITY
AAGILOPRRTU PURGATORIAL
AAGIMMNNOSU MAGNANIMOUS
AAGIMNNOSST ANTAGONISMS
AAGIMNNPRSW WARMING PANS
AAGIMNOOSSU ANISOGAMOUS
AAGIMNOOSTU ANGIOMATOUS
AAGIMPRSSTT PRAGMATISTS
AAGINNOSSTT ANTAGONISTS
AAGINOOPPRT PROPAGATION
AAGINORRTUU INAUGURATOR
AAGINOSSSTT GAS STATIONS
AAGLLMNRTUU MULTANGULAR
AAGLNNOOSSX ANGLO-SAXONS
AAGLNOOPRTW PATROL WAGON
AAGOOPPRRST PROPAGATORS
AAHIILMNNOT HAMILTONIAN
AAHIILNNORT ANNIHILATOR
AAHIILNNOST INHALATIONS
AAHIILNNRSV NAIL VARNISH
AAHIINPRSST ANTIPHRASIS
AAHILMPRSTY AMPHISTYLAR
AAHIMMNNOPY NYMPHOMANIA
AAHIMMNOPRS ANAMORPHISM
AAHIMNOPRSS OARSMANSHIP
AAHINNOPRTY ANTIPHONARY
AAHIOPRSTXY ASPHYXIATOR
AAHKOPRRSWW SPARROWHAWK
AAHLLMMORSW MARSHMALLOW
AAHMNNRSTTU TRANSHUMANT
AAHNNOPRSXY NASOPHARYNX
AAHNNRRSTUY THYRSANURAN
AAHNOPRSTTU NATUROPATHS
AAHNOPRTTUY NATUROPATHY

AAIIILMNOTT IMITATIONAL
AAIIILNRTTU UTILITARIAN
AAIIJKLMNOR KILIMANJARO
AAIIKNNOSTY KYANISATION
AAIIKNNOTYZ KYANIZATION
AAIILLLPSUZ LAPIS LAZULI
AAIILLMPRTY IMPARTIALLY
AAIILMMNORT MATRIMONIAL
AAIILMNNOST NATIONALISM
AAIILMNOPRT PATRIMONIAL
AAIILMNOPST MAINTOPSAIL
AAIILMNORST RATIONALISM
AAIILNNOSTT NATIONALIST
AAIILNNOTTY NATIONALITY
AAIILNOORTV VARIOLATION
AAIILNOPPTT PALPITATION
AAIILNORSTT RATIONALIST
AAIILNORTTT ATTRITIONAL
AAIILNORTTY RATIONALITY
AAIILNOSTTU SITUATIONAL
AAIIMMNNOOT AMMONIATION
AAIIMMNORSV MORAVIANISM
AAIIMNOOSTT ATOMISATION
AAIIMNOOTTZ ATOMIZATION
AAIIMNOPRTT IMPARTATION
AAIIMNOPSTT IMPASTATION
AAIIMNORRST ROTARIANISM
AAIIMNRSSTU SANITARIUMS
AAIINOPPRST APPARITIONS
AAIINOPRSST ASPIRATIONS
AAILLLOSTWW SWALLOWTAIL
AAILLORRSTY SARTORIALLY
AAILMMNOSTU SUMMATIONAL
AAILMMOPPRS MALAPROPISM
AAILMNOPRTU MANIPULATOR
AAILMNRSTTT TRANSMITTAL
AAILNNOPSTT PLANTATIONS
AAILNNORSTT TRANSLATION
AAILNOPPSSY PASSION PLAY
AAILNOSSTTU SALUTATIONS
AAILNRSSTTU NATURALISTS
AAILOORTTTZ TOTALIZATOR
AAILOPRRTUV VAPOUR TRAIL
AAIMMNOPSTT MAIN-TOPMAST
AAIMMNOSSUY IMMUNOASSAY
AAIMNOOSSST ANASTOMOSIS
AAIMNOPSTTU AMPUTATIONS
AAIMNORSSTU SANATORIUMS
AAINNNOOSTT ANNOTATIONS
AAINNNOPRST NONPARTISAN
AAINNOPRSTT PATRON SAINT
AAINOPSSTTY PAY STATIONS
AAKKNORRSSY KRASNOYARSK
AAKLLMPRUUU KUALA LUMPUR

AALLMNOOSUY ANOMALOUSLY
AALLNNRTUUY UNNATURALLY
AALMMOOPSST SOMATOPLASM
AALNNPRSSTT TRANSPLANTS
AALNORRSSTT TRANSLATORS
AALOOQRRTUY ROYAL QUARTO
AALORSSTTTU ALTOSTRATUS
AAMNPRSSTTY SMARTY-PANTS
ABBBDENRRSU RUBBER BANDS
ABBBELOPSSU SOAP BUBBLES
ABBCCEEHKNR BACKBENCHER
ABBCCEEHKNS BACKBENCHES
ABBCCEEHMOR BEACHCOMBER
ABBCCGIKMNO BACKCOMBING
ABBCDEEFIKO BIOFEEDBACK
ABBCDEEILRS DESCRIBABLE
ABBCDEENRSS CRABBEDNESS
ABBCDEMRRSU BREADCRUMBS
ABBCEEEHRRS BEAR'S-BREECH
ABBCEEJLSTU SUBJECTABLE
ABBCEHIILOT BIBLIOTHECA
ABBCEIILNRS INSCRIBABLE
ABBCEKMNRSU BACK NUMBERS
ABBCHHIRTTU RABBIT HUTCH
ABBCHINPRTU RABBIT PUNCH
ABBCIILMNOY BIBLIOMANCY
ABBCKMOOORY BACKROOM BOY
ABBDDEGIORR BRIDGEBOARD
ABBDDEIINRR BIRD-BRAINED
ABBDEELORTU REDOUBTABLE
ABBDEGNNRRU BRANDENBURG
ABBDEIILNTU INDUBITABLE
ABBDEIINRRU INDIA RUBBER
ABBDEILRSSU DISBURSABLE
ABBDEIMNRSY BABY-MINDERS
ABBDEIMORRS BOMBARDIERS
ABBDELLNRSU LANDLUBBERS
ABBDELORTUY REDOUBTABLY
ABBDEMMNORT BOMBARDMENT
ABBDGIIINNS BIAS BINDING
ABBDHIINORZ BIROBIDZHAN
ABBDIILNTUY INDUBITABLY
ABBEELPRRTU PERTURBABLE
ABBEEMNSSTU SUBBASEMENT
ABBEENRSTTU BUTTER BEANS
ABBEGIKLMOO GO LIKE A BOMB
ABBEGILNORU BELABOURING
ABBEGINORTW BROWBEATING
ABBEHHIKSSS SHISH KEBABS
ABBEHIIILNT INHIBITABLE
ABBEHILLPSU PUBLISHABLE
ABBEHILNRSU BURNISHABLE
ABBEIILLMOZ MOBILIZABLE
ABBEILMSTTU SUBMITTABLE

ABBEINRSTUU SUBURBANITE
ABBEIRSSTTY BABY-SITTERS
ABBEKLNOSTT BOTTLE BANKS
ABBELMSSSUY SUBASSEMBLY
ABBELNPRRTU RUBBER PLANT
ABBELPRRTUY PERTURBABLY
ABBEMPRRSTU RUBBER STAMP
ABBGIINSTTY BABY-SITTING
ABBGILMNOOZ BAMBOOZLING
ABBGILNORSY ABSORBINGLY
ABBIILLORTY BIBLIOLATRY
ABBIILMOPRS PROBABILISM
ABBIILOPRST PROBABILIST
ABBIILOPRTY PROBABILITY
ABCCCHKKLOO CHOCK-A-BLOCK
ABCCDEEELSU SUCCEEDABLE
ABCCDEEIIRT BACTERICIDE, TEREBIC
  ACID
ABCCDEHHKNU HUNCHBACKED
ABCCDEKLMOY BLACK COMEDY
ABCCDENNORT CONCERT BAND
ABCCEEILNOV CONCEIVABLE
ABCCEEKLOPU PEACOCK BLUE
ABCCEELLLOT COLLECTABLE
ABCCEELORRT CORRECTABLE
ABCCEEMNNRU ENCUMBRANCE
ABCCEFILNOS CONFISCABLE
ABCCEFIORSU BACCIFEROUS
ABCCEGINNOU CONCUBINAGE
ABCCEHHKKLNS BLANK CHECKS
ABCCEIILPTY PECCABILITY
ABCCEIKKLST STICKLEBACK
ABCCEILNOTV CONVICTABLE
ABCCEILNOVY CONCEIVABLY
ABCCEILOSTT ECTOBLASTIC
ABCCEINORRT CENTROBARIC
ABCCELMOOST CLOSE COMBAT
ABCCELORSUU SUCCOURABLE
ABCCHIKSSTW SWITCHBACKS
ABCCIIMOORT MACROBIOTIC
ABCCIINOTVY BICONCAVITY
ABCCILLLOUY BUCOLICALLY
ABCCILORSTU SUBCORTICAL
ABCCINOOSTT TOBACCONIST
ABCCIOORSUV BACCIVOROUS
ABCCKNORTUY BACK COUNTRY
ABCCMOPSSTU SUBCOMPACTS
ABCCNORSTTU SUBCONTRACT
ABCDDEEELNS DESCENDABLE
ABCDDEEFIIN BID DEFIANCE
ABCDDEEFLOU DOUBLE-FACED
ABCDDEEILRS SLICED BREAD
ABCDDEFINOR FORBIDDANCE
ABCDDEKLORS BADDERLOCKS

ABCDEEEERRT DECEREBRATE
ABCDEEEILPR DEPRECIABLE
ABCDEEFHNRR FRENCH BREAD
ABCDEEGGKLL BLACKLEGGED
ABCDEEIILMM IMMEDICABLE
ABCDEEILLMN CLEAN-LIMBED
ABCDEEILNRS RESCINDABLE
ABCDEEILORV DIVORCEABLE
ABCDEEILPRT PREDICTABLE
ABCDEEINORS DECARBONISE
ABCDEEINORZ DECARBONIZE
ABCDEELLNRY BELLY DANCER
ABCDEELLNSY BELLY DANCES
ABCDEELLPRU PRECLUDABLE
ABCDEELMMNO COMMENDABLE
ABCDEELMNNO CONDEMNABLE
ABCDEELMORU DOUBLE CREAM
ABCDEELNNOS CONDENSABLE
ABCDEELNRRY CANDLEBERRY
ABCDEELOPSU DOUBLE-SPACE
ABCDEENORRT CENTERBOARD
ABCDEENORRT CENTREBOARD
ABCDEHILSTW SWITCHBLADE
ABCDEHIRRTW BIRD-WATCHER
ABCDEHORSSS CHESSBOARDS
ABCDEIILOSS DISSOCIABLE
ABCDEIILTUY EDUCABILITY
ABCDEIIORTT OBITER DICTA
ABCDEIKLLST BLACKLISTED
ABCDEIKLRSS BACKSLIDERS
ABCDEILNOST ENDOBLASTIC
ABCDEILPRTY PREDICTABLY
ABCDEINOORT NOTICE BOARD
ABCDEINRRST TRANSCRIBED
ABCDEINRSTU DISTURBANCE
ABCDELMMNOY COMMENDABLY
ABCDELMNRSU UNSCRAMBLED
ABCDEOORRSS SCOREBOARDS
ABCDGIIKLNS BACKSLIDING
ABCDGKNORSU BACKGROUNDS
ABCDHIIMRTY DITHYRAMBIC
ABCDHIIRSTU HUDIBRASTIC
ABCDHINOOPR BRANCHIOPOD
ABCDHIOPSTX DISPATCH BOX
ABCDHIORSTW SWITCHBOARD
ABCDHNOORRY HYDROCARBON
ABCDIIILOST IDIOBLASTIC
ABCDIILLSSY DISSYLLABIC
ABCDIILORUV VIBRACULOID
ABCDIIMNOSY BIODYNAMICS
ABCDIKLOSWW BLACK WIDOWS
ABCDMNORRUU CARBORUNDUM
ABCEEEFFKOR COFFEE BREAK
ABCEEEFFLOT COFFEE TABLE

ABCEEEFLNOR ENFORCEABLE
ABCEEEHIKRT BREAK THE ICE
ABCEEEIKRRS ICEBREAKERS
ABCEEEILPRV PERCEIVABLE
ABCEEEILRSV RECEIVABLES, SERVICEABLE
ABCEEEILRSX EXERCISABLE
ABCEEEILRTV CELEBRATIVE
ABCEEELMNRS RESEMBLANCE
ABCEEELORRV RECOVERABLE
ABCEEELPRST RESPECTABLE
ABCEEEMMNRR REMEMBRANCE
ABCEEEMMNRT EMBRACEMENT
ABCEEFHNNRS FRENCH BEANS
ABCEEFIILPS SPECIFIABLE
ABCEEFIILRT CERTIFIABLE, RECTIFIABLE
ABCEEFIINRY BENEFICIARY
ABCEEFILLMR LEAF-CLIMBER
ABCEEFINNOT BENEFACTION
ABCEEFINRTU RUBEFACIENT
ABCEEFNORST BENEFACTORS
ABCEEGIINOT ABIOGENETIC
ABCEEGILNRT CELEBRATING
ABCEEHHILRS CHERISHABLE
ABCEEHKLNQU BLANK CHEQUE
ABCEEHLORTU RETOUCHABLE
ABCEEHLRSTT STRETCHABLE
ABCEEHORRRT TORCHBEARER
ABCEEILLNTU INELUCTABLE
ABCEEILNORT CELEBRATION
ABCEEILNPST INSPECTABLE
ABCEEILNSUX INEXCUSABLE
ABCEEILORRV IRREVOCABLE
ABCEEILRRSU IRRECUSABLE
ABCEEILRRTU RECRUITABLE
ABCEEILRSTT BATTLE CRIES
ABCEEILRSVY SERVICEABLY
ABCEEINNRTY BICENTENARY
ABCEEINORRT CEREBRATION
ABCEEINORST BARONETCIES
ABCEEINORTX EXORBITANCE
ABCEEINRRRS CRANBERRIES
ABCEEKLPPPR BLACK PEPPER
ABCEEKLRRRW KERB CRAWLER
ABCEEKRSSTT BACK STREETS
ABCEEKSSTTU BUCKET SEATS
ABCEELNORSV CONSERVABLE, CONVERSABLE
ABCEELOPRSW PACE BOWLERS
ABCEELOSTUU BETULACEOUS
ABCEELPRSTY RESPECTABLY
ABCEELRTTUU TUBERCULATE
ABCEENORRST ARBORESCENT
ABCEENORSSV OBSERVANCES
ABCEEOPPRSS SPACE PROBES

ABCEFHNOOPR FRANCOPHOBE
ABCEFIMNORY BY MAIN FORCE
ABCEFINORTU RUBEFACTION
ABCEFLMNOOR CONFORMABLE
ABCEFLMOORT COMFORTABLE
ABCEGHILLNY BELLYACHING
ABCEGHORRTU TURBOCHARGE
ABCEGILNNOS CONSIGNABLE
ABCEGILNOST BLASTOGENIC
ABCEHHIOOPT THEOPHOBIAC
ABCEHHJOSTT HATCHET JOBS
ABCEHHKRSUW BUSHWHACKER
ABCEHIILPRT BLEPHARITIC
ABCEHIKLNSY CHELYABINSK
ABCEHILNORV OLIVE BRANCH
ABCEHILOPSU BICEPHALOUS
ABCEHILPRST BIRTHPLACES
ABCEHIMORTT BATHOMETRIC
ABCEHIMRTTY BATHYMETRIC
ABCEHINOOPR NECROPHOBIA
ABCEHKNOORS ON HORSEBACK
ABCEHKPSSTU PASS THE BUCK
ABCEHLLOSTT TABLECLOTHS
ABCEHLNOTUU UNTOUCHABLE
ABCEHLNRSUU UNCRUSHABLE
ABCEHMOPRST CHAMBER POTS
ABCEIIJLSTU JUSTICIABLE
ABCEIILNOTX INTOXICABLE
ABCEIILRTUV LUBRICATIVE
ABCEIIMNOTV COMBINATIVE
ABCEIKNORTW CABINETWORK
ABCEILLLOPS COLLAPSIBLE
ABCEILLMORU BIMOLECULAR
ABCEILLNOOZ COLONIZABLE
ABCEILLNTUY INELUCTABLY
ABCEILLRTUV CARVEL-BUILT
ABCEILMOPRS COMPRISABLE
ABCEILMOPRT PROBLEMATIC
ABCEILMORST BLASTOMERIC,
   MEROBLASTIC
ABCEILMOTVY COMBATIVELY
ABCEILNOSTT ENTOBLASTIC
ABCEILNPRSU REPUBLICANS
ABCEILNRSTU INSCRUTABLE
ABCEILNSUXY INEXCUSABLY
ABCEILORRVY IRREVOCABLY
ABCEIMNOORT EMBROCATION
ABCEINNORTY CYBERNATION
ABCEINRRRST TRANSCRIBER
ABCEIRSTTUV SUBTRACTIVE
ABCEJKLMRSU LUMBERJACKS
ABCEKKORSST BACKSTROKES
ABCEKLNORSU COALBUNKERS
ABCELLLMNOO COLLEMBOLAN

ABCELLNOORS COLLARBONES
ABCELMNRRSU UNSCRAMBLER
ABCELNNOTUU UNCOUNTABLE
ABCELNPRTUU PUNCTURABLE
ABCEOOOORRRT CORROBORATE
ABCEORRRTTU CARBURETTOR
ABCEORSTUUY BUTYRACEOUS
ABCFGIINRTU BIFURCATING
ABCFGINOSTU OBFUSCATING
ABCFHINOOST SON-OF-A-BITCH
ABCFIILLMOR BACILLIFORM
ABCFIINORTU BIFURCATION
ABCFINOOSTU OBFUSCATION
ABCFLMNOORY CONFORMABLY
ABCFLMOORTY COMFORTABLY
ABCGHHIOOPP PHAGOPHOBIC
ABCGIIKNOUV BIVOUACKING
ABCGIILNRTU LUBRICATING
ABCGIINNORZ CARBONIZING
ABCGILLOORY BRYOLOGICAL
ABCGILNPRUW PUB-CRAWLING
ABCGINRSTTU SUBTRACTING
ABCHHIILOTT BATHOLITHIC
ABCHHILOOOP OCHLOPHOBIA
ABCHHIOPRSS ARCHBISHOPS
ABCHHLNOOPR LOPHOBRANCH
ABCHIIIMOPT AMPHIBIOTIC
ABCHIILOPSY BIOPHYSICAL
ABCHIKLMSST BLACKSMITHS
ABCHIKLRSST BLACKSHIRTS
ABCHILLOOST HOLOBLASTIC
ABCHILNOORR BRONCHIOLAR
ABCHINOOPTY NYCTOPHOBIA
ABCHINORRSY CHRYSAROBIN
ABCHKLMORUU BLACK HUMOUR
ABCHKOOSSUY YAH BOO SUCKS
ABCIIILOSTY SOCIABILITY
ABCIIIMNORT IMBRICATION
ABCIIINOSTT ANTIBIOTICS
ABCIILLMRSU LUMBRICALIS
ABCIILLPTUY CULPABILITY
ABCIILNOPTU PUBLICATION
ABCIILNORTU LUBRICATION
ABCIIMNNOOT COMBINATION
ABCIINORRTU RUBRICATION
ABCIINORSTT ABSTRICTION
ABCIKLLMMSU BLACK MUSLIM
ABCILMMORUU COLUMBARIUM
ABCILNORTUU LUCUBRATION
ABCILNRSTUY INSCRUTABLY
ABCILOOPRST BLASTOPORIC
ABCILOPRSTU SUBTROPICAL
ABCILORRSTU LUBRICATORS
ABCINNOORTU CONURBATION

ABCINOORSTU OBSCURATION
ABCINORSTTU SUBTRACTION
ABCLLRSTUUU SUBCULTURAL
ABCNORRSTUY SUBCONTRARY
ABDDDEEELOTU DOUBLE DATED
ABDDDEIMNOR BROADMINDED
ABDDEEEILRT DELIBERATED
ABDDEEENSSS DEBASEDNESS
ABDDEEIILTT DEBILITATED
ABDDEEIKMRS DISEMBARKED
ABDDEEELOSTU DOUBLE DATES
ABDDEFFILNN EFF AND BLIND
ABDDEGIRRSW DRAWBRIDGES
ABDDEHKLNNU BUNDELKHAND
ABDDEHLLNOO LO AND BEHOLD
ABDDEHOOSWX SHADOW-BOXED
ABDDEIMNNST DISBANDMENT
ABDDELMOORW WARM-BLOODED
ABDDELNORRS BORDERLANDS
ABDDELORRTW BLADDERWORT
ABDDGIINORV DIVINGBOARD
ABDDOORRSSW BROADSWORDS
ABDEEEEGLRU BELEAGUERED
ABDEEEFHRST FEATHER BEDS
ABDEEEFRRST FAST-BREEDER
ABDEEEHILRT HEREDITABLE
ABDEEEHLLVW WELLBEHAVED
ABDEEEILLRV DELIVERABLE
ABDEEELLOPV DEVELOPABLE
ABDEEEELMNRU DENUMERABLE
ABDEEEELNSST BELATEDNESS
ABDEEEELRRSS REDRESSABLE
ABDEEEMNSST DEBASEMENTS
ABDEEEPRSTT BESPATTERED
ABDEEERSSTW SWEETBREADS
ABDEEFGIIRR FIRE BRIGADE
ABDEEFIILNN INDEFINABLE
ABDEEFILLTT BATTLEFIELD
ABDEEGGINRR GINGERBREAD
ABDEEGLLOUZ DOUBLE-GLAZE
ABDEEGLNOTU DOUBLE AGENT
ABDEEGMNOOR BOOMERANGED
ABDEEHILRTY HEREDITABLY
ABDEEHILSST ESTABLISHED
ABDEEHORSST BROADSHEETS
ABDEEIILLRS LIBERALISED
ABDEEIILLRZ LIBERALIZED
ABDEEIILRST DETRIBALISE
ABDEEIILRTZ DETRIBALIZE
ABDEEIILSST DESTABILISE
ABDEEIILSTZ DESTABILIZE
ABDEEIKNNSY KIDNEY BEANS
ABDEEILMNNO DENOMINABLE
ABDEEILMNST DISABLEMENT

ABDEEILMSSS DISASSEMBLE
ABDEEILNNRT DINNER TABLE
ABDEEILNPSS DISPENSABLE
ABDEEILNRSU UNDESIRABLE
ABDEEILORRT DELIBERATOR
ABDEEILORTT OBLITERATED
ABDEEINNRRW BREADWINNER
ABDEEKLOSTU DOUBLE TAKES
ABDEEKNORSZ BAKER'S DOZEN
ABDEEKORRSY KEYBOARDERS
ABDEELLNPRU PLUNDERABLE
ABDEELLSSTY SELL-BY DATES
ABDEELMNORZ BRONZE MEDAL
ABDEELMNOTU DEMOUNTABLE
ABDEELORRTW WORLD-BEATER
ABDEELORSTY DESTROYABLE
ABDEFGINORR FINGERBOARD
ABDEFGIRSSU FIGURED BASS
ABDEFIILNNY INDEFINABLY
ABDEFIRRSTU BREADFRUITS
ABDEFLLOTUU DOUBLE FAULT
ABDEGGILNOT GOLD-BEATING
ABDEGGIRRSU BUDGERIGARS
ABDEGHINSSU SUBHEADINGS
ABDEGIILNNT DINING TABLE
ABDEGIILSSU DISGUISABLE
ABDEGIKNORY KEYBOARDING
ABDEGIMNRST ABRIDGMENTS
ABDEGLNNOOU GO A BUNDLE ON
ABDEGOOORRV GO OVERBOARD
ABDEHIINNPR HAIRPIN BEND
ABDEHIINNTU UNINHABITED
ABDEHIORSTW WHITEBOARDS
ABDEHLNSSSU HUSBANDLESS
ABDEIIJLNOS DISJOINABLE
ABDEIILLLST DISTILLABLE
ABDEIILLTWY WELDABILITY
ABDEIILMNOT INDOMITABLE
ABDEIIRSSTU ABSURDITIES
ABDEIKLNNRU UNDRINKABLE
ABDEILLLNSY BLIND ALLEYS
ABDEILLLSSY DISSYLLABLE
ABDEILLOSSV DISSOLVABLE
ABDEILMOTTU TOLBUTAMIDE
ABDEILMSSSY DISASSEMBLY
ABDEILNRSUY UNDESIRABLY
ABDEILOPRSV DISPROVABLE
ABDEIMRSTUW DUMBWAITERS
ABDEINORSTU SUBORDINATE
ABDELMOORST BLOODSTREAM
ABDELMRRSUY LUMBERYARDS
ABDELOPRRTU PROTRUDABLE
ABDEMNORRST BARNSTORMED
ABDENOPRSUU SUPERABOUND

ABDFILMOORR DOLABRIFORM
ABDFLOOOORRS FLOORBOARDS
ABDGHIINNRS BRANDISHING
ABDGHIMNOTU BAD-MOUTHING
ABDGINOPRRS SPRINGBOARD
ABDGINORRST STRINGBOARD
ABDGMOORRSS SMORGASBORD
ABDHHIOOPRY HYDROPHOBIA
ABDHINOOPRS ON SHIPBOARD
ABDIIILTTUY DUTIABILITY
ABDIIILLMOTY MOULDABILITY
ABDIILMNOTY INDOMITABLY
ABDIINOSTUU SUBAUDITION
ABDILNOOSST BLOODSTAINS
ABDIMNNOSTU SUBDOMINANT
ABDINORRSUY SUBORDINARY
ABDLNOOOSTT ODONTOBLAST
ABDNOORSTUU ROUNDABOUTS
ABDOORRSTUU TROUBADOURS
ABEEEEEFLORS FORESEEABLE
ABEEEEGLNRR REGENERABLE
ABEEEEIKLMV MAKE-BELIEVE
ABEEEEMNRTV BEREAVEMENT
ABEEEERRRTV REVERBERATE
ABEEEEFLMNRT FERMENTABLE
ABEEEGLORSW ELBOW GREASE
ABEEEGLRRTT REGRETTABLE
ABEEEHHINPR HEBEPHRENIA
ABEEEHMNRRV BREMERHAVEN
ABEEEHRSSTT HARTEBEESTS
ABEEEIKRRST TIEBREAKERS
ABEEEILLPRV REPLEVIABLE
ABEEEILMMPR IMPERMEABLE
ABEEEILMMST EMBLEMATISE
ABEEEILMMTZ EMBLEMATIZE
ABEEEILPRRV REPRIEVABLE
ABEEEILRRTV RETRIEVABLE
ABEEEIMNSST ABSENTEEISM
ABEEELMNNTT ENTABLEMENT
ABEEELMNRRU REMUNERABLE
ABEEELNPRST PRESENTABLE
ABEEELNPRTV PREVENTABLE
ABEEELPRRSV PRESERVABLE
ABEEELPSTUY BEAUTY SLEEP
ABEEENQTUUY BEAUTY QUEEN
ABEEENRRRTV REVERBERANT
ABEEERRSTTV VERTEBRATES
ABEEFFILORT FORFEITABLE
ABEEFFRSTTU BUFFER STATE
ABEEFGILNRR REFRANGIBLE
ABEEFGLORTT FORGETTABLE
ABEEFIILLQU LIQUEFIABLE
ABEEFIILNRT ANTIFEBRILE
ABEEFILPRTU PUTREFIABLE

ABEEFILRRTU IRREFUTABLE
ABEEFLLNSSU BALEFULNESS
ABEEFLMOPRR PERFORMABLE
ABEEFLSSTTY SAFETY BELTS
ABEEFNRRRTU AFTERBURNER
ABEEGGILNPS SLEEPING BAG
ABEEGHINQTU BEQUEATHING
ABEEGIINOSS ABIOGENESIS
ABEEGILMNPR IMPREGNABLE
ABEEGILRRST REGISTRABLE
ABEEGINORRV OVERBEARING
ABEEGINRRTU TRUE BEARING
ABEEGLLLNSU ANGELUS BELL
ABEEGLRRTTY REGRETTABLY
ABEEHHPRSTY BATHYSPHERE
ABEEHIILNRT INHERITABLE
ABEEHILMPSS BLASPHEMIES
ABEEHILPRSS PERISHABLES
ABEEHILRSST ESTABLISHER
ABEEHILSTUX EXHAUSTIBLE
ABEEHINRSSS BEARISHNESS
ABEEHINRSST BREATHINESS
ABEEHKNORRT HEARTBROKEN
ABEEHKNORSS BONESHAKERS
ABEEHLMPRSS BLASPHEMERS
ABEEHLOORRS SEBORRHOEAL
ABEEHLORRWW WHEELBARROW
ABEEHORSTTU THEREABOUTS
ABEEHORSTUW WHEREABOUTS
ABEEIIILRRS LIBERALISER
ABEEIILLRRZ LIBERALIZER
ABEEIILMNPS PLEBEIANISM
ABEEIILMNST INESTIMABLE
ABEEIILNQTU INEQUITABLE
ABEEIILQRTU EQUILIBRATE
ABEEIKLLNSS LIKABLENESS
ABEEIKLLRSV BASKERVILLE
ABEEIKLMORR BOILERMAKER
ABEEIKLNNST LINEN BASKET
ABEEILLNORT INTOLERABLE
ABEEILLNRSS LIBERALNESS
ABEEILLNSSV LIVABLENESS
ABEEILLOPRT BOILERPLATE
ABEEILLOPTX EXPLOITABLE
ABEEILLRUVZ ULVERIZABLE
ABEEILMMORZ MEMORIZABLE
ABEEILMMRRU MARE LIBERUM
ABEEILMNNOT MENTIONABLE
ABEEILMNNRU INNUMERABLE
ABEEILMORRV IRREMOVABLE
ABEEILMORST STEAM-BOILER
ABEEILNNOPS PENSIONABLE
ABEEILNNSTT TABLE TENNIS
ABEEILNPRSU INSUPERABLE

ABEEILNRRTV INVERTEBRAL
ABEEILNRSST TRIABLENESS
ABEEILNSSST BEASTLINESS
ABEEILNSSSZ SIZABLENESS
ABEEILNSSTW WITNESSABLE
ABEEILORSTT BITTER ALOES
ABEEILRRSST LIBERATRESS
ABEEILRRTVY RETRIEVABLY
ABEEINNQRTU BARQUENTINE
ABEEINORSSU BUENOS AIRES
ABEEINRSSTW BEAR WITNESS
ABEEINRSTUX EXURBANITES
ABEEINSSSUV ABUSIVENESS
ABEEIOPRRTV REPROBATIVE
ABEEIPRRRSS RASPBERRIES
ABEEJLLMSSU JUMBLE SALES
ABEEKLNSTTW WET BLANKETS
ABEEKMMNNST EMBANKMENTS
ABEELLLMSSY BLAMELESSLY
ABEELLLMTUU UMBELLULATE
ABEELMMNSSY ASSEMBLYMEN
ABEELMNPRTU NUMBERPLATE
ABEELMNSTTT BATTLEMENTS
ABEELNNOOPR NONOPERABLE
ABEELNNOSST NOTABLENESS
ABEELNPRSTY PRESENTABLY
ABEELNPRTVY PREVENTABLY
ABEELNRTTUU UNUTTERABLE
ABEELNRTUXY EXUBERANTLY
ABEELOSTUUY BEAUTEOUSLY
ABEELPRRSTY PRESBYTERAL
ABEELQQRUUU ALBUQUERQUE
ABEEMNRSSTU SURBASEMENT
ABEENNNRRSU RUNNER BEANS
ABEFFIILORT FORTIFIABLE
ABEFFILLORS BILLS OF FARE
ABEFFLNORRU BARREL OF FUN
ABEFGIIILNS SIGNIFIABLE
ABEFGIILLOR GLORIFIABLE
ABEFGIILNNR INFRANGIBLE
ABEFGIINTUY BEAUTIFYING
ABEFHHLORRT HALF-BROTHER
ABEFHIRRSTT AFTERBIRTHS
ABEFHLNSSSU BASHFULNESS
ABEFIIILNRT NITRIFIABLE
ABEFIIILRTV VITRIFIABLE
ABEFIIILSTY FEASIBILITY
ABEFIIJLSTU JUSTIFIABLE
ABEFIILLLMO MOLLIFIABLE
ABEFIILLOOT BIFOLIOLATE
ABEFIILNOSS FISSIONABLE
ABEFILLLOSS BILLS OF SALE
ABEFILLTUUY BEAUTIFULLY
ABEFILRRTUY IRREFUTABLY

ABEFLLOOORV LABOR OF LOVE
ABEFLLOORST FOOTBALLERS
ABEFLMOORTT FOOT-LAMBERT
ABEFLMOOSTT FALSE BOTTOM
ABEGGHRSSTU STAGGERBUSH
ABEGGIILNOR GLOBIGERINA
ABEGHIIMNSV MISBEHAVING
ABEGHIINNRT HIBERNATING
ABEGHIIOPRS BIOGRAPHIES
ABEGHILMNOO HAEMOGLOBIN
ABEGHILMNPS BLASPHEMING
ABEGHIOPRRS BIOGRAPHERS
ABEGHLLLSUY BELLY LAUGHS
ABEGHLNOOPS ANGLOPHOBES
ABEGIIINNRT INEBRIATING
ABEGIILMNTT TIMETABLING
ABEGIILNRVZ VERBALIZING
ABEGIILRTUV GIVE IT A
  BURL
ABEGIIRRSTU SUBIRRIGATE
ABEGILMNNOZ EMBLAZONING
ABEGILMNOTY AMBLYGONITE
ABEGILMNPRY IMPREGNABLY
ABEGILNNRTY BANTERINGLY
ABEGILNORSU SUBREGIONAL
ABEGILNOSSX SIGNAL BOXES
ABEGILRRYZZ GRIZZLY BEAR
ABEGINNOPSU SUBPOENAING
ABEGINNORRT INTERROBANG
ABEGINNRSST STRING BEANS
ABEGINRSSTU GAS TURBINES
ABEGLLORSSW GLASSBLOWER
ABEGMORRSTU BURGOMASTER
ABEHHIRRSSU HAIRBRUSHES
ABEHHORRSTT HEARTTHROBS
ABEHIILMOPT AMPHIBOLITE
ABEHIILPSTT BLEPHATITIS
ABEHIIMORSV BEHAVIORISM,
  MISBEHAVIOR
ABEHIINNORT HIBERNATION
ABEHIIORSTV BEHAVIORIST
ABEHIKLNNTU UNTHINKABLE
ABEHILMNOST ABOLISHMENT
ABEHILNRSSU NAILBRUSHES
ABEHILOOPRU AILUROPHOBE
ABEHILOPRSW WORSHIPABLE
ABEHILPSSTT BATTLESHIPS
ABEHINOORTT BOTHERATION
ABEHINOPRSV VIBRAPHONES
ABEHKOOPRSS PHRASEBOOKS
ABEHLMOORTW BARTHOLOMEW
ABEHLMOPSSU BLASPHEMOUS
ABEHLMORTWY BLAMEWORTHY
ABEHLORRSSU HARBOURLESS

ABEHLORRSTY LAY BROTHERS
ABEHNNOOTTY ETHNOBOTANY
ABEIIIILLST LIABILITIES
ABEIIIILLLMT ILLIMITABLE
ABEIIIILLNOR BILLIONAIRE
ABEIIIILLRTY RELIABILITY
ABEIIINNORT INEBRIATION
ABEIILLLLRY ILLIBERALLY
ABEIILLMMST BIMETALLISM
ABEIILLMPSU IMPLAUSIBLE
ABEIIILLMTTY MELTABILITY
ABEIIILLRSTT BRISTLETAIL
ABEIIILMNSTY INESTIMABLY
ABEIIILMSSUX BISEXUALISM
ABEIILNQRTU EQUILIBRANT
ABEIILNQTUY INEQUITABLY
ABEIIILNRRTT INTERTRIBAL
ABEIIILNRTTY RENTABILITY
ABEIIILOPPRT PROPITIABLE
ABEIIILOPRTY OPERABILITY
ABEIIILORTXY EXORABILITY
ABEIIILRSSST STABILISERS
ABEIIILRSSTZ STABILIZERS
ABEIIILRSTTU BRUTALITIES
ABEIIILRSTUY REUSABILITY
ABEIIILSTTTY TESTABILITY
ABEIIILSTUXY BISEXUALITY
ABEIIILTTTWY WETTABILITY
ABEIINNOSTT SINO-TIBETAN
ABEIINRRSSV RIVER BASINS
ABEIIRRSTTU TRIBUTARIES
ABEIIRTTTUV ATTRIBUTIVE
ABEILLMORTU RAMBOUILLET
ABEILLNORTY INTOLERABLY
ABEILLNRSSY BRAINLESSLY
ABEILLOPRSX PILLAR BOXES
ABEILMMOSST METABOLISMS
ABEILMOOSTU AUTOMOBILES
ABEILNNPRTU UNPRINTABLE
ABEILNOOSSS OBSESSIONAL
ABEILNOSTTY OBSTINATELY
ABEILNPRSUY INSUPERABLY
ABEILOORRTT OBLITERATOR
ABEILORSSTW BELOW STAIRS
ABEILQRRTUY BIQUARTERLY
ABEILRRSTTT BRITTLE-STAR
ABEIMNNSSSU BUSINESSMAN
ABEIMNORSTU TAMBOURINES
ABEIMNRRSSU SUBMARINERS
ABEINNNRSTU BURNT SIENNA
ABEINNORSTV INOBSERVANT
ABEINNOSSTT ABSTENTIONS
ABEINOOPRRT PROBATIONER,
  REPROBATION

ABEINOORSTV OBSERVATION
ABEINORSTUV SUBORNATIVE
ABEINOSSTTU ABSTENTIOUS
ABEINSSTTUV SUBSTANTIVE
ABEIRSSTTUV SUBSTRATIVE
ABEKKORSSTW WORKBASKETS
ABEKLOPRRRS PORK BARRELS
ABEKMNNOSTU MOUNTEBANKS
ABEKNOPRRSW PAWNBROKERS
ABEKOOSTTTU STATUTE BOOK
ABELLNNORVY NONVERBALLY
ABELMNORRSY SALMONBERRY
ABELNNORSUV VERBAL NOUNS
ABELNOOPPST POSTPONABLE
ABELNOOPSST TABLESPOONS
ABELNOPPSTU UNSTOPPABLE
ABELNRTTUUY UNUTTERABLY
ABELOPPRSTU SUPPORTABLE
ABELRRSTTUU SURREBUTTAL
ABEMNOORRSW BONE MARROWS,
  MARROWBONES
ABEMNORRRST BARNSTORMER
ABENOPRRSSS PRESS BARONS
ABENOPRRTTU PROTUBERANT
ABENOPRSSTU BEANSPROUTS
ABEOORRSTVY OBSERVATORY
ABEOPSSTTUY BEAUTY SPOTS
ABFGHNOORRU FARNBOROUGH
ABFGILNOSTY FLYING BOATS
ABFIIILLLTY FALLIBILITY
ABFIIIMNORT FIMBRIATION
ABFIIJLSTUY JUSTIFIABLY
ABFILMNSTUU FUNAMBULIST
ABFIMOORSTU FIBROMATOUS
ABGGGINNOOT TOBOGGANING
ABGGIIMTUUY AMBIGUGUITY
ABGGIJNSTUU SUBJUGATING
ABGGILOOORY AGROBIOLOGY
ABGHIINRSTT BRATTISHING
ABGHIINSTTU BATHING SUIT
ABGHIKPRRST BRIGHT SPARK
ABGHILMOOPY AMPHIBOLOGY
ABGHINNTTUY ANYTHING BUT
ABGHLMOORRU MARLBOROUGH
ABGIIILNSTZ STABILIZING
ABGIIILNTTY TANGIBILITY
ABGIILMNSTU SUBLIMATING
ABGIILNOOST OBLIGATIONS
ABGIILNRTUZ BRUTALIZING
ABGIILNRTVY VIBRATINGLY
ABGIILNRTTTU ATTRIBUTING
ABGIJNOORTU OBJURGATION
ABGIJNOSTUU SUBJUGATION
ABGIKLLNNOR BANKROLLING

ABGIKNNOPRW PAWNBROKING
ABGIKNNPRTU BANKRUPTING
ABGILLNNOSW SNOWBALLING
ABGILLNORUY LABOURINGLY
ABGILMOSUUY AMBIGUOUSLY
ABGIMNOSUUU UNAMBIGUOUS
ABGINOORSTU SUBROGATION
ABGINOORSTW ROWING BOATS
ABGJOORRTUY OBJURGATORY
ABHHIKRSTTU TURKISH BATH
ABHHIOOOPPT PHOTOPHOBIA
ABHILMMNOPT PHANTOM LIMB
ABHIMNORRTU NORTHUMBRIA
ABHIOOPRSSU RUSSOPHOBIA
ABHLLMOPSTY LYMPHOBLAST
ABHLOOPRSTT TROPHOBLAST
ABIIIILMTTY IMITABILITY
ABIIIILNTVY INVIABILITY
ABIIIILLOSTY ISOLABILITY
ABIIIILLOTVY VIOLABILITY
ABIIIILNRSTY RINSABILITY
ABIIIILNSTTY INSTABILITY
ABIIIILPSSTY PASSIBILITY
ABIIIILRTTVY VIBRATILITY
ABIIIILSTTUY SUITABILITY
ABIIINOPRTT BIPARTITION
ABIIKLORTWY WORKABILITY
ABIIILLMPSUY IMPLAUSIBLY
ABIIILLOSTVY SOLVABILITY
ABIILMNOSTU SUBLIMATION
ABIILMOSTUY AMBITIOUSLY
ABIILNORTTU TRIBULATION
ABIILNRSTUY INSALUBRITY
ABIILOPRTTY PORTABILITY
ABIILOPRTVY PROVABILITY
ABIILOQTTUY QUOTABILITY
ABIILRRTTUY TRIBUTARILY
ABIIMNNOORT BROMINATION
ABIIMNOSTUU UNAMBITIOUS
ABIINNORTTU TURBINATION
ABIINOOPSTT OBSTIPATION
ABIINOORSTT ABORTIONIST
ABIINORTTTU ATTRIBUTION
ABILLNOOSST BALLOONISTS
ABILLOORSUY LABORIOUSLY
ABILLORSTTU SUBLITTORAL
ABILNNOORSU LABOR UNIONS
ABIMNORRSST BRAINSTORMS
ABINNOOOPRT ON PROBATION
ABINNOORSTU SUBORNATION
ABINOORRSTU BRONTOSAURI
ABINOOSSSST BASSOONISTS
ABINOSSSTTU BUS STATIONS,
    SUBSTATIONS

ABINRRSSTTU BRAINS TRUST
ABOORSSTTUU ROUSTABOUTS
ACCCDEHILNO CHALCEDONIC
ACCCDEIILNU NUCLEIC ACID
ACCCDENNOOR CONCORDANCE
ACCCDENNOTU CONDUCTANCE
ACCCDILLOOP DIPLOCOCCAL
ACCCDIMOPST COMPACT DISC
ACCCEEELNOS COALESCENCE
ACCCEEELNST LACTESCENCE
ACCCEEEMNRS MARCESCENCE
ACCCEEHILRS ECCLESIARCH
ACCCEELMNOP COMPLACENCE
ACCCEELNOPT CONCEPTACLE
ACCCEFHKORS COCKCHAFERS
ACCCEHIISTT CATECHISTIC
ACCCEHIMOTT CHEMOTACTIC
ACCCEHIOPRT ECHOPRACTIC
ACCCEHKOORS COCKROACHES
ACCCEHNORTY TECHNOCRACY
ACCCEHORSTW COWCATCHERS
ACCCEIILMRT CLIMACTERIC
ACCCEIILLNSY ENCYCLICALS
ACCCEILMOPS ACCOMPLICES
ACCCEILORTU LEUCOCRATIC
ACCCELMNOPY COMPLACENCY
ACCCHIILLOT LACCOLITHIC
ACCCHILOORT OCHLOCRATIC
ACCCHOOPRTY PTOCHOCRACY
ACCCIIOOPRS CAPRICCIOSO
ACCCILLOOSU CALCICOLOUS
ACCCIMMOORS MACROCOSMIC
ACCCIMOOPRS MACROSCOPIC
ACCCIOPRSTY CYSTOCARPIC
ACCDDEEIINO DECANEDIOIC
ACCDDEHNPRU PUNCHED CARD
ACCDDEIIRST DISACCREDIT
ACCDDEINORS DISCORDANCE
ACCDDEIRRST CREDIT CARDS
ACCDDELLMOU MALOCCLUDED
ACCDDELOPPU CLOUD-CAPPED
ACCDDIIIMST DIDACTICISM
ACCDEEEENNT ANTECEDENCE
ACCDEEEFNRT FACE-CENTRED
ACCDEEELNOS ADOLESCENCE
ACCDEEELNST DECALESCENT
ACCDEEFIILR DECALCIFIER
ACCDEEFNORY CONFEDERACY
ACCDEEGOPRU COUP DE GRACE
ACCDEEHIMNO MACHINE CODE
ACCDEEHIORS ARCHDIOCESE
ACCDEEHQRSU CHEQUE
    CARDS
ACCDEEIISTV DESICCATIVE

ACCDEEIKRSW WISECRACKED
ACCDEEIMORS DEMOCRACIES
ACCDEEIORTT DECORTICATE
ACCDEELNOSV CONVALESCED
ACCDEELOOPR CAPE COLORED
ACCDEEMNSUU SUCCEDANEUM
ACCDEENORST CONSECRATED
ACCDEFINOST CONFISCATED
ACCDEFNOSTU SAFE-CONDUCT
ACCDEGHORST DOGCATCHERS
ACCDEGIINST DESICCATING
ACCDEHHITTT CHITCHATTED
ACCDEHHRSSU ARCHDUCHESS
ACCDEHILPRY DIPHYCERCAL
ACCDEHNPRSU CARDPUNCHES
ACCDEHNRSTU UNSCRATCHED
ACCDEHOPSTT SCOTCH TAPED
ACCDEIIIMRT ACIDIMETRIC
ACCDEIILLTY DEICTICALLY
ACCDEIILNOT CONCILIATED
ACCDEIINOST DESICCATION
ACCDEIKLNST CANDLESTICK
ACCDEIKLNSW CANDLEWICKS
ACCDEILLOPS PECCADILLOS
ACCDEILMOPT COMPLICATED
ACCDEILNOST OCCIDENTALS
ACCDEINOOTU COEDUCATION
ACCDEINPRSY DISCREPANCY
ACCDEIPRRTU PICTURE CARD
ACCDEKORRRT TRACK RECORD
ACCDELMOPTY COMPACTEDLY
ACCDELNOSSS SECOND-CLASS
ACCDENNOTUU UNACCOUNTED
ACCDFIIINOP INDO-PACIFIC
ACCDGILNORY ACCORDINGLY
ACCDHHNSSUU SUCH AND SUCH
ACCDHHRRSUY CHURCHYARDS
ACCDHIIILOP ACIDOPHILIC
ACCDHIIMORT DICHROMATIC
ACCDHIINORT ACHONDRITIC
ACCDHILORSV CLAVICHORDS
ACCDHINOPRY HYDNOCARPIC
ACCDHINORYY HYDROCYANIC
ACCDIILLNRY CYLINDRICAL
ACCDIILLORY CODICILLARY
ACCDIILNOOR CROCODILIAN
ACCDIIOOPRS RADIOSCOPIC
ACCDIIPRSSU PRUSSIC ACID
ACCDIMOSSTU DISACCUSTOM
ACCDNNOOTTY COTTON CANDY
ACCEEEEHKSS CHEESECAKES
ACCEEEEHMRS CREAM CHEESE
ACCEEEENNSV EVANESCENCE
ACCEEEFIKOP PIECE OF CAKE

ACCEEEFILMN MALEFICENCE
ACCEEEFLNRT REFLECTANCE
ACCEEEHILRT CHELICERATE
ACCEEEIKKLO COCK-A-LEEKIE
ACCEEEELNOPS OPALESCENCE
ACCEEEELNRST RECALESCENT
ACCEEEELPRST RECEPTACLES
ACCEEFIIRTT CERTIFICATE
ACCEEFIKRRR FIRECRACKER
ACCEEFINORV VOCIFERANCE
ACCEEGHILMO GEOCHEMICAL
ACCEEGHINTY EYE-CATCHING
ACCEEGHORRV COVER CHARGE
ACCEEGILRRT GREAT CIRCLE
ACCEEHHIRST CHESHIRE CAT
ACCEEHIINRS CHICANERIES
ACCEEHILMNO CHAMELEONIC
ACCEEHILNRT CHANTICLEER
ACCEEHINRRT ARCHENTERIC
ACCEEHKORTW WEATHERCOCK
ACCEEHLLNRY CHANCELLERY
ACCEEHLNOXY CYCLOHEXANE
ACCEEIILNRT ELECTRICIAN
ACCEEIIMPST SEPTICAEMIC
ACCEEIISTVX EXSICCATIVE
ACCEEIKNPRS SCIENCE PARK
ACCEEIKRRSW WISECRACKER
ACCEEILNNST INCALESCENT
ACCEEIMNOPS CINEMASCOPE
ACCEEIMNRTT METACENTRIC
ACCEEINQSTU ACQUIESCENT
ACCEEIOPRRT RECIPROCATE
ACCEEIORSSS ACCESSORIES
ACCEELMNNOT CONCEALMENT
ACCEEMNNORR NECROMANCER
ACCEEMNOPPU COME-UPPANCE
ACCEENNNOTU COUNTENANCE
ACCEENNORSV CONVERSANCE
ACCEENNORTT CONCENTRATE,
   CONCERTANTE
ACCEENNORVY CONVEYANCER
ACCEENNOSVY CONVEYANCES
ACCEENPSSTU SUSCEPTANCE
ACCEEOPRSUY CYPERACEOUS
ACCEEORRSSU RACECOURSES
ACCEFFHHINS CHAFFINCHES
ACCEFFIIOSU EFFICACIOUS
ACCEFHLRSTY FLYCATCHERS
ACCEFIINRRY FERRICYANIC
ACCEFILORSU CALCIFEROUS
ACCEFINORRY FERROCYANIC
ACCEFMNNOOR CONFORMANCE
ACCEGGIKNRT GET CRACKING
ACCEGHHITTW CATCHWEIGHT

ACCEGHIINTZ CATECHIZING
ACCEGHIKMNT CHECKMATING
ACCEGHIKNQU QUICK-CHANGE
ACCEGHINNOR ENCROACHING
ACCEGHIOPRR CEROGRAPHIC
ACCEGIINQSU ACQUIESCING
ACCEGILLOOT CETOLOGICAL
ACCEGILLOPY CYCLOPLEGIA
ACCEGINNORS CARCINOGENS
ACCEGINNOSZ COGNIZANCES
ACCEHHHHIIR CHICHIHAERH
ACCEHHIISTX HEXASTICHIC
ACCEHHISSTY HESYCHASTIC
ACCEHIILOST CATHOLICISE
ACCEHIILOTT HELIOTACTIC
ACCEHIILOTZ CATHOLICIZE
ACCEHIIMNST MECHANISTIC
ACCEHIINNST TECHNICIANS
ACCEHIIORRT HIEROCRATIC
ACCEHIIRSTU EUCHARISTIC
ACCEHILLMNO MELANCHOLIC
ACCEHILLNTY TECHNICALLY
ACCEHILMOOZ ZOOCHEMICAL
ACCEHILOPPR PROCEPHALIC
ACCEHILOPXY OXYCEPHALIC
ACCEHIMNNOR CHROMINANCE
ACCEHIMORTT TACHOMETRIC
ACCEHIMORTU EUCHROMATIC
ACCEHIMRTTY TACHYMETRIC
ACCEHIRSSTT SCRATCHIEST
ACCEHKOPPTT PATCH POCKET
ACCEHLLMNOY COLLENCHYMA
ACCEHLLNORS CHANCELLORS
ACCEHLOOSSW SLOWCOACHES
ACCEHNORSTT TECHNOCRATS, TRENCH
COATS
ACCEHOOSTWZ CZESTOCHOWA
ACCEIIILLNN ACLINIC LINE
ACCEIIILSTV ACCLIVITIES
ACCEIIINPRT ACCIPITRINE
ACCEIIINRST INTRICACIES
ACCEIIILLNPR PRECLINICAL
ACCEIIILMOSV SEMIVOCALIC
ACCEIIILPRRT PRECRITICAL
ACCEIIILPRST PERICLASTIC
ACCEIIILRRSU CIRCULARISE
ACCEIIILRRUZ CIRCULARIZE
ACCEIIILRTUV CIRCULATIVE
ACCEIIMNOST COSMETICIAN,
ENCOMIASTIC
ACCEIIINNOSU INSOUCIANCE
ACCEIINOSTV CONCAVITIES
ACCEIINOSTX EXSICCATION
ACCEIKKOTTT TICK-TACK-TOE

ACCEIKNRSSS CARSICKNESS
ACCEILLPSTY SCEPTICALLY
ACCEILMMORS COMMERCIALS
ACCEILMOPST ECTOPLASMIC
ACCEILNNOTY ANTICYCLONE
ACCEILNOPRT NARCOLEPTIC
ACCEILNORTT CONTRACTILE
ACCEILNORTU CORNICULATE
ACCEILOPRST CEROPLASTIC
ACCEILORSSY ACCESSORILY
ACCEIMMNOTU COMMUNICATE
ACCEIMNNORT NECROMANTIC
ACCEIMOOPRS COMIC OPERAS
ACCEIMORRTY MERITOCRACY
ACCEINNNOTU CONTINUANCE
ACCEINNORST CONCERTINAS
ACCEINNORSU COINSURANCE
ACCEINNORTV CONTRIVANCE
ACCEINOORRY COERCIONARY
ACCEINOOTVV CONVOCATIVE
ACCEINORTTV CONTRACTIVE
ACCEINSSSTU CAUSTICNESS
ACCEIOORSSU SCORIACEOUS
ACCEIORSTUU URTICACEOUS
ACCEJLNORTU CONJECTURAL
ACCEKNRRSTU NUTCRACKERS
ACCELLOSTTU COALSCUTTLE
ACCELMMNOOP COMMONPLACE
ACCELNNOSTT CONTACT LENS
ACCELORSSSU SUCCESSORAL
ACCELPRRSUU CREPUSCULAR
ACCEMNOPSST COMPACTNESS
ACCENNNOOSS CONSONANCES
ACCENNORSVY CONSERVANCY
ACCENOOPRTU POCOCURANTE
ACCENOORRST CONSECRATOR
ACCENOPRRTT PRECONTRACT
ACCENORRTTU CONTRACTURE
ACCENPRTUUU ACUPUNCTURE
ACCEOOORSSTU ECTOSARCOUS
ACCEORSSTUU CRUSTACEOUS
ACCFGIIINRS SACRIFICING
ACCFGILOSUU CALCIFUGOUS
ACCFIIMOORR CORACIIFORM
ACCFINOORST CONFISCATOR
ACCGHIIOOPS HAGIOSCOPIC
ACCGIILNNTU INCULCATING
ACCGIILNOTU GLAUCONITIC
ACCGIILNRTU CIRCULATING
ACCGIINNOOS OCCASIONING
ACCGILLMOOY MYCOLOGICAL
ACCGILLNOOO ONCOLOGICAL
ACCGILLNOOT COLLOCATING
ACCGILLOOTY CYTOLOGICAL

ACCGIMNOSTU ACCUSTOMING
ACCGIMOPRTY CRYPTOGAMIC
ACCGINNORTT CONTRACTING
ACCGINORSTU CORUSCATING
ACCHHIILLNS CHINCHILLAS
ACCHHIIMOPR AMPHICHROIC
ACCHHIINSTT CHAIN STITCH
ACCHHMNORUW CHURCHWOMAN
ACCHIILLSTY STICHICALLY
ACCHIILMOST CATHOLICISM
ACCHIILOSST SCHOLIASTIC
ACCHIILOTTY CATHOLICITY
ACCHIIMNORT CHROMATINIC
ACCHIIMOSST MASOCHISTIC
ACCHIIMSSST SCHISMATICS
ACCHIIOOPST SOCIOPATHIC
ACCHIIOPPRT HIPPOCRATIC
ACCHIIORSTT RHOTACISTIC
ACCHIIPRSTY PSYCHIATRIC
ACCHIKMSSTT MATCHSTICKS
ACCHILLNORY CHRONICALLY
ACCHILLPSYY PSYCHICALLY
ACCHILMOTYY CYCLOTHYMIA
ACCHILOPTTY PHYLOTACTIC
ACCHINOPSTY SYCOPHANTIC
ACCHIOOPTTT PHOTOTACTIC
ACCHIOORRSU CHIAROSCURO
ACCHNOOOPSU CACOPHONOUS
ACCIIIKKNPW PICKWICKIAN
ACCIIILNSTV CALVINISTIC
ACCIIILOSST SOCIALISTIC
ACCIILNNOTU INCULCATION
ACCIILNNQUU QUINCUNCIAL
ACCIILNOORT CONCILIATOR
ACCIILNORTU CIRCULATION
ACCIILNOTVY VOLCANICITY
ACCIILOSTUV ACCLIVITOUS
ACCIILRRTUY CIRCULARITY
ACCIILSSSST CLASSICISTS
ACCIIMNNOTY ACTINOMYCIN
ACCIINNSTTY NYCTINASTIC
ACCIINOORTT CORTICATION
ACCIJNNOTUV CONJUNCTIVA
ACCIKKKKNNS KNICK-KNACKS
ACCILLNOOOT COLLOCATION
ACCILLPRTYY CRYPTICALLY
ACCILMNRRUU CIRCUMLUNAR
ACCILMOPRRU CIRCUMPOLAR
ACCILMOPSTY CYTOPLASMIC
ACCILNOOSST ICONOCLASTS
ACCILNOOTTU OCCULTATION
ACCILOPRSTY PYROCLASTIC
ACCILOPRTTU PLUTOCRATIC
ACCILORRTUY CIRCULATORY

ACCIMMNNOTU COMMUNICANT
ACCIMNNOOTT CONCOMITANT
ACCINNNOSTY INCONSTANCY
ACCINNOOOTV CONVOCATION
ACCINNOORTT CONTRACTION
ACCINOOPRSU CORNUCOPIAS
ACCINOOPSTU OCCUPATIONS
ACCINOORRRW CARRION CROW
ACCINOORSTU CORUSCATION
ACCINOPRRSU CAPRICORNUS
ACCIORSSSTY SYSSARCOTIC
ACCLLLOOORU LOCAL COLOUR
ACCLNNOSTUY CONSULTANCY
ACCLOPRRSUU CORPUSCULAR
ACCNOORRSTT CONTRACTORS
ACDDDEEILTY DEDICATEDLY
ACDDDEEINRTU CUT-AND-DRIED
ACDDEEEELRT DECELERATED
ACDDEEEEPRS PREDECEASED
ACDDEEEIPRT DEPRECIATED
ACDDEEEORRT REDECORATED
ACDDEEFFIST DISAFFECTED
ACDDEEGIKLR GRIDDLECAKE
ACDDEEHHIKT THICKHEADED
ACDDEEHHKOS SHOCKHEADED
ACDDEEHLORT COLD-HEARTED
ACDDEEHNORW CROWNED HEAD
ACDDEEHNRSU DUDE RANCHES
ACDDEEIILMS DECIMALISED
ACDDEEIILMZ DECIMALIZED
ACDDEEIIPRS RICE PADDIES
ACDDEEIKRST SIDETRACKED
ACDDEEINRSX CARD INDEXES
ACDDEENNRST TRANSCENDED
ACDDEENNSST DESCENDANTS
ACDDEGIILNO DIALING CODE
ACDDEGIORSU DISCOURAGED
ACDDEHLLOST SADDLECLOTH
ACDDEHNNOSS SECOND HANDS
ACDDEHNOOPY DODECAPHONY
ACDDEIINOST DEDICATIONS
ACDDEIIOSST DISSOCIATED
ACDDEILLMSS MIDDLE CLASS
ACDDEIMNORU ENDOCARDIUM
ACDDEINOORT COORDINATED
ACDDENORRSW SWORD DANCER
ACDDENORSSW SWORD DANCES
ACDEEEEHLRR CHEERLEADER
ACDEEEFFTTU EFFECTUATED
ACDEEEFILNR ILE-DE-FRANCE
ACDEEEFNORT CONFEDERATE
ACDEEEGLLOT DÉCOLLETAGE
ACDEEEHLRTW CARTWHEELED
ACDEEEHORRV OVERREACHED

ACDEEEILNRV DELIVERANCE
ACDEEEIPRTT DECREPITATE
ACDEEEIPRTV DEPRECATIVE
ACDEEEIRSTV EVISCERATED
ACDEEELLNRT CRENELLATED
ACDEEELORRT DECELERATOR
ACDEEENNSTT ANTECEDENTS
ACDEEEORRTV OVERREACTED
ACDEEEPRRTV RECUPERATED
ACDEEFFHRUU CHAUFFEURED
ACDEEFHLSTT FLAT-CHESTED
ACDEEFIILTT FELICITATED
ACDEEFIORTV VOCIFERATED
ACDEEFLNRUU FRAUDULENCE
ACDEEFMORRS ARMED FORCES
ACDEEGGNORT CONGREGATED
ACDEEGHNRRU UNDERCHARGE
ACDEEGHORRV OVERCHARGED
ACDEEGINPRT DEPRECATING
ACDEEGINRST DESECRATING
ACDEEGINRTU RE-EDUCATING
ACDEEGIORST CATEGORISED
ACDEEGIORTZ CATEGORIZED
ACDEEGIOTTT TIED COTTAGE
ACDEEGKLNOW ACKNOWLEDGE
ACDEEHIINOT ETHANEDIOIC
ACDEEHILNOT ENDOTHECIAL
ACDEEHILNPP CHIPPENDALE
ACDEEHILNRS CHANDELIERS
ACDEEHILPSY PSYCHEDELIA
ACDEEHIMNRS MERCHANDISE
ACDEEHIMSST SCHEMATISED
ACDEEHIMSTZ SCHEMATIZED
ACDEEHINRTW WINDCHEATER
ACDEEHIORTT OCTAHEDRITE
ACDEEHLLOSU CLOSE-HAULED
ACDEEHMNORW REACH-ME-DOWN
ACDEEHMNSTT DETACHMENTS
ACDEEHNRRTU UNCHARTERED
ACDEEIIILLTY EIDETICALLY
ACDEEIILMTV MALEDICTIVE
ACDEEIILPSS SPECIALISED
ACDEEIILPSZ SPECIALIZED
ACDEEIILTUV ELUCIDATIVE
ACDEEIIMMNN MEDICINE MAN
ACDEEIINNRT INCINERATED
ACDEEIIOPPS EPIDIASCOPE
ACDEEIIPRTV PREDICATIVE
ACDEEILLMNY ENDEMICALLY
ACDEEILLNRS CINDERELLAS
ACDEEILNNST CLANDESTINE
ACDEEILNOTT DELECTATION
ACDEEILNRST CENTRALISED,
CREDENTIALS

ACDEEILNRSY INCREASEDLY
ACDEEILNRTZ CENTRALIZED
ACDEEILNTTU DENTICULATE
ACDEEILPRTU REDUPLICATE
ACDEEILRSSU SECULARISED
ACDEEILRSTT DECRETALIST
ACDEEILRSUZ SECULARIZED
ACDEEILRTTU RETICULATED
ACDEEIMMNST MEDICAMENTS
ACDEEIMNPRT PREDICAMENT
ACDEEIMORRR MICROREADER
ACDEEIMORST DEMOCRATISE
ACDEEIMORTZ DEMOCRATIZE
ACDEEIMOSTT DOMESTICATE
ACDEEINOPRT DEPRECATION
ACDEEINORST CONSIDERATE,
DESECRATION
ACDEEINORTU RE-EDUCATION
ACDEEINPPRT APPRENTICED
ACDEEIOPRRT DEPRECIATOR
ACDEEIOQTUV EQUIVOCATED
ACDEEIORRSV SERVICE ROAD
ACDEEIORRTT DIRECTORATE
ACDEEIPRRST TRADE PRICES
ACDEEIRSTTX DIRECT TAXES
ACDEEISSSTU CASE STUDIES
ACDEEKQRRTU QUARTERDECK
ACDEELLMORU LEUCODERMAL
ACDEELMORRS SCLERODERMA
ACDEELNOPRW CANDLEPOWER
ACDEELNOSST ADOLESCENTS
ACDEELNPTUU PEDUNCULATE
ACDEELNRRSY DRY CLEANERS
ACDEEMMNOTT COMMENTATED
ACDEEMNOPSS ENCOMPASSED
ACDEEMNOPST COMPENSATED
ACDEEMNRTTU TRADUCEMENT
ACDEENNORTV CONTRAVENED
ACDEENORRST SECOND-RATER
ACDEEOPRRTY DEPRECATORY
ACDEFFIIRTV DIFFRACTIVE
ACDEFFLOSTU DUFFEL COATS
ACDEFGHMORR FROGMARCHED
ACDEFGILRSU DISGRACEFUL
ACDEFHILPST FELDSPATHIC
ACDEFHLORTW FLOWCHARTED
ACDEFHMOOST SMOOTH-FACED
ACDEFIIINNT INFANTICIDE
ACDEFIIINOT DEIFICATION, EDIFICATION
ACDEFIILSTU FEUDALISTIC
ACDEFIIORTY EDIFICATORY
ACDEFIIRRST FRATRICIDES
ACDEFINNOTU FECUNDATION
ACDEFKLNORS FOLK DANCERS

ACDEFLLNORU UNCALLED-FOR
ACDEFLMMNOS SELF-COMMAND
ACDEFNORTUY FECUNDATORY
ACDEGHHIOWY HIGHWAY CODE
ACDEGHIILOT GLOCHIDIATE
ACDEGHIIMNR MICHIGANDER
ACDEGHILLNT CANDLELIGHT
ACDEGHIMOPR DEMOGRAPHIC
ACDEGHINPST DESPATCHING
ACDEGHLOORS GRADE SCHOOL
ACDEGIILLOO IDEOLOGICAL
ACDEGIILNTU ELUCIDATING
ACDEGIIMNSU MISGUIDANCE
ACDEGIINPRT PREDICATING
ACDEGIINSST DIE-CASTINGS
ACDEGILLOOP PEDOLOGICAL
ACDEGILNNRY DRY-CLEANING
ACDEGILOOPS LOGOPAEDICS
ACDEGILRSTT CATTLE GRIDS
ACDEGIMNOSY GEODYNAMICS
ACDEGIMORTY TRAGICOMEDY
ACDEGINNOQU QUINDECAGON
ACDEGINNRTU UNDERACTING
ACDEGIORRSU DISCOURAGER
ACDEGKNORRS ROCK GARDENS
ACDEGLOORST COLD STORAGE
ACDEHIILMPS DICEPHALISM
ACDEHIIOPRT DIAPHORETIC
ACDEHIKMNOS CHAIN-SMOKED
ACDEHILNORT CHLORINATED
ACDEHILOPSU DICEPHALOUS
ACDEHIMOPRS COMRADESHIP
ACDEHIMOSTU MUSTACHIOED
ACDEHINOORS ICOSAHEDRON
ACDEHINOPST DICTAPHONES
ACDEHIOOPRT ORTHOPAEDIC
ACDEHKMRSTU DEUTSCHMARK
ACDEHLLLOPY PHYLLOCLADE
ACDEHLMOSUY CHLAMYDEOUS
ACDEHLNPRTU THUNDERCLAP
ACDEHLRSTTY STRATHCLYDE
ACDEHMNNOOR ENCHONDROMA
ACDEHMNORRY HYDROMANCER
ACDEHOORRTU UROCHORDATE
ACDEHORRTWW DRAW THE CROW
ACDEHORRTYY CRYOHYDRATE
ACDEHRSTTTU DUTCH TREATS
ACDEIIILMOT DOMICILIATE
ACDEIIINSTV INDICATIVES
ACDEIIJLPRU PREJUDICIAL
ACDEIIKNRST INSIDE TRACK
ACDEIILLMNY MEDICINALLY
ACDEIILLNTY IDENTICALLY
ACDEIILLORV VARICELLOID

ACDEIILMNOT MALEDICTION
ACDEIILMRSS DISCLAIMERS
ACDEIILNNOT DECLINATION
ACDEIILNNST INCIDENTALS
ACDEIILNORT DIRECTIONAL
ACDEIILNOST SLIDE-ACTION
ACDEIILNOTU ELUCIDATION
ACDEIILNOTV VALEDICTION
ACDEIILNPTU INDUPLICATE
ACDEIILOPRS PERIODICALS
ACDEIILORRT DIRECTORIAL
ACDEIILPTUV DUPLICATIVE
ACDEIIMNOST MEDICATIONS
ACDEIIMORRT RADIOMETRIC
ACDEIIMORTU AUDIOMETRIC
ACDEIIMPRRU PERICARDIUM
ACDEIINNRTY TYRANNICIDE
ACDEIINOPRT PREDICATION
ACDEIINORRT DOCTRINAIRE
ACDEIINOTTX INTOXICATED
ACDEIIRSTTV DISTRACTIVE
ACDEIJRSTUU JUDICATURES
ACDEIKRSTTU TRACKSUITED
ACDEILLLMOY MELODICALLY
ACDEILLMNOY DEMONICALLY
ACDEILLNOOT DECOLLATION
ACDEILLORRS CORDILLERAS
ACDEILMNOPS ENDOPLASMIC
ACDEILMOPRR DIMERCAPROL
ACDEILNOOST CONSOLIDATE
ACDEILNORSY SECONDARILY
ACDEILNORTU RADIOLUCENT,
REDUCTIONAL
ACDEILNORTY DECLINATORY
ACDEILOORRV VARICOLORED
ACDEILORTUY ELUCIDATORY
ACDEILORTVY VALEDICTORY
ACDEILPPSTU SUPPLICATED
ACDEIMNNORU ENDOCRANIUM
ACDEIMNORRS MORRIS DANCE
ACDEINNORST CONSTRAINED
ACDEINNORTU DENUNCIATOR
ACDEINNOSSS DISSONANCES
ACDEINOOPRS SCORPAENOID
ACDEINOORST COORDINATES,
DECORATIONS
ACDEINOPSTT CONSTIPATED
ACDEINOSSTU DECUSSATION
ACDEINOSTTU OUTDISTANCE
ACDEINOSTTW WAINSCOTTED
ACDEINPRSTU UNPRACTISED
ACDEIOOPRSU ADIPOCEROUS
ACDEIOPRRTY PREDICATORY
ACDEIPRSSTU CUSTARD PIES

ACDEJKSSTTU DUST JACKETS
ACDELLNOOTY COTYLEDONAL
ACDELOPRTTY PTERODACTYL
ACDEMMMNNOT COMMANDMENT
ACDEMMNOSTU CONSUMMATED
ACDEMNNORTU COUNTERMAND
ACDEMNORTUY DOCUMENTARY
ACDEMOORRST OSTRACODERM
ACDEMOPRSSU DAMP COURSES, MASS-
    PRODUCE
ACDENNNNOUU UNANNOUNCED
ACDENRRRSTU REDCURRANTS
ACDEORRSSST STAR-CROSSED
ACDFFGHINNU HANDCUFFING
ACDFFGIINNT FACT-FINDING
ACDFFGIINRT DIFFRACTING
ACDFFGILNOS SCAFFOLDING
ACDFFIILMOO OFFICIALDOM
ACDFFIINORT DIFFRACTION
ACDFGHHIINS CHAFING DISH
ACDFGIIMNOR ACID-FORMING
ACDGGHIINRS DISCHARGING
ACDGHIIIOPR IDIOGRAPHIC
ACDGHIINNSW SANDWICHING
ACDGHIINPST DISPATCHING
ACDGHIINRSV CRASH-DIVING
ACDGHIMOOSU DICHOGAMOUS
ACDGHIOPRSY DISCOGRAPHY
ACDGHIRRRYY HYDRARGYRIC
ACDGIIILMNS DISCLAIMING
ACDGIIILOST DIALOGISTIC
ACDGIIINNTV VINDICATING
ACDGIILNOST DISLOCATING
ACDGIILNPTU DUPLICATING
ACDGIINNSTY SYNDICATING
ACDGIINOSST DIAGNOSTICS
ACDGIINRSTT DISTRACTING
ACDGILLOOOX DOXOLOGICAL
ACDGILNRTUY TRADUCINGLY
ACDGIMNNOPU UP AND COMING
ACDGINOORVW WOODCARVING
ACDGLLOOTYY DACTYLOLOGY
ACDGMNOPRSU CAMPGROUNDS
ACDHHIMOTUW WITH MUCH ADO
ACDHHIOPRRS HARPSICHORD
ACDHIIIMRTT MITHRIDATIC
ACDHIILLMOY HOMICIDALLY
ACDHIILOPSU ACIDOPHILUS
ACDHIINOOPR RADIOPHONIC
ACDHIIOPRST DIASTROPHIC
ACDHIMNOORT TRICHOMONAD
ACDHIMNORTY HYDROMANTIC
ACDHINNORYY CYANOHYDRIN
ACDHIORRSSW DISC HARROWS

ACDHIRSSSSW SWISS CHARDS
ACDHLLOOOOW WOOD ALCOHOL
ACDHLNOOORT NOTOCHORDAL
ACDIIILLNPS DISCIPLINAL
ACDIIILLOTY IDIOTICALLY
ACDIIILMORY DOMICILIARY
ACDIIIMNOST DIATONICISM
ACDIIIMOTTY DIATOMICITY
ACDIIINNOST INDICATIONS
ACDIIINNOTV VINDICATION
ACDIILLLLYY IDYLLICALLY
ACDIILLORST CLOSTRIDIAL
ACDIILMNNRU CLINANDRIUM
ACDIILMNOPR PALINDROMIC
ACDIILMNSSY SYNDICALISM
ACDIILNNOOT CONDITIONAL
ACDIILNNOTU INDUCTIONAL
ACDIILNOOST DISLOCATION
ACDIILNOPTU DUPLICATION
ACDIILNSSTY SYNDICALIST
ACDIILOORRS SORORICIDAL
ACDIILPRSTU TRICUSPIDAL
ACDIIMNORSS SARDONICISM
ACDIIMORSTY MYOCARDITIS
ACDIINNOSTY SYNDICATION
ACDIINOPSTU CUSPIDATION
ACDIINORSTT DISTRACTION
ACDIINORTVY VINDICATORY
ACDIKKPSTUU KICK UP A DUST
ACDILLORSTY CRYSTALLOID
ACDILNOPRSS SPINAL CORDS
ACDILOPRSTU DUPLICATORS
ACDINNNOOOT CONDONATION
ACDINOOORRT COORDINATOR
ACDKLLNOORR ROCK-AND-ROLL
ACDKNORSSTU SOUNDTRACKS
ACDLLORSSTU COLLAR STUDS
ACDLNOOOORTY CONDOLATORY
ACDNNOOPRSS PROS AND CONS
ACDOOORSSTU OSTRACODOUS
ACEEEFFFRTT AFTEREFFECT
ACEEEFFKNOT TAKE OFFENCE
ACEEEFHLNRV FRENCH LEAVE
ACEEEFIOPPP PIPE OF PEACE
ACEEEFIPRSS FIRE ESCAPES
ACEEEFLNRRU NUCLEAR-FREE
ACEEEGHHRST CHARGE SHEET
ACEEEGIMNRT RACE MEETING
ACEEEGIMNTT METAGENETIC
ACEEEGNPRST PERCENTAGES
ACEEEGNRSTT SECRET AGENT
ACEEEHIMNRS ARCHENEMIES
ACEEEHIMNTV ACHIEVEMENT
ACEEEHINNTT CANINE TEETH

ACEEEHIORVV OVERACHIEVE
ACEEEHIRRST TREACHERIES
ACEEEHIRSTT CATHETERISE
ACEEEHIRTTZ CATHETERIZE
ACEEEHLLNRT CHANTERELLE
ACEEEHLLRSV SACHEVERELL
ACEEEHMNNNT ENHANCEMENT
ACEEEHMORTT TACHEOMETER
ACEEEHRRRSS RESEARCHERS
ACEEEILMNPT MANTELPIECE
ACEEEILNPPR PIPE CLEANER
ACEEEILNQUV EQUIVALENCE
ACEEEILNRRV IRRELEVANCE
ACEEEIMNRRS MERCENARIES
ACEEEIMPRST MASTERPIECE
ACEEEINNRST CENTENARIES
ACEEEINRSSS NECESSARIES
ACEEEINSSTT NECESSITATE
ACEEEIPTTVX EXPECTATIVE
ACEEEIRRSST SECRETARIES
ACEEEIRSSTV TEA SERVICES
ACEEEJKLPST STEEPLEJACK
ACEEEJORSTT EJECTOR SEAT
ACEEELLMNOT METALLOCENE
ACEEELLMNOV MALEVOLENCE
ACEEELLSSSY CEASELESSLY
ACEEELMMNPT EMPLACEMENT
ACEEELMNPRT REPLACEMENT
ACEEELMNRRT RECREMENTAL
ACEEELMNRTX EXCREMENTAL
ACEEELNPSSW CLEAN SWEEPS
ACEEELORSTT ELECTORATES
ACEEEMNPSST ESCAPEMENTS
ACEEEMNRRTT RETRACEMENT
ACEEEOPRTTX EXPECTORATE
ACEEFFIILOS OFFICIALESE
ACEEFFILNTU INEFFECTUAL
ACEEFFLLTUY EFFECTUALLY
ACEEFGILNNR FREELANCING
ACEEFHINNRS ENFRANCHISE
ACEEFHNRRTU FURTHERANCE
ACEEFIILOPT PIECE OF TAIL
ACEEFIJKLST LIFE JACKETS
ACEEFILRSTV SERVICE FLAT
ACEEFIMNORS FREEMASONIC
ACEEFIMNTTU TUMEFACIENT
ACEEFINOPTT TEPEFACTION
ACEEFLLNRST CRESTFALLEN
ACEEFLNRSSU CAREFULNESS
ACEEFLORSUU FERULACEOUS
ACEEFLPRRTU PREFECTURAL
ACEEFMNOPRR PERFORMANCE
ACEEFORRSST FORECASTERS
ACEEFPPRSTT PAST PERFECT

ACEEGGIMMNO EMMENAGOGIC
ACEEGGIMNOT GAMETOGENIC,
GAMOGENETIC, GEOMAGNETIC
ACEEGHILOOT OLIGOCHAETE
ACEEGHILPRT TELEGRAPHIC
ACEEGHINNRT INTERCHANGE
ACEEGHINRRS RESEARCHING
ACEEGHLLNRS CHALLENGERS
ACEEGHLNOOS LOOSE CHANGE
ACEEGHNORSV CHANGEOVERS
ACEEGHNRRSU CHARGE NURSE
ACEEGHORRSV OVERCHARGES
ACEEGHPRRSU SUPERCHARGE
ACEEGIILNNT GEANTICLINE
ACEEGIKNNPP KNEECAPPING
ACEEGIKSTTW WICKET GATES
ACEEGILLNRY GENERICALLY
ACEEGILLNTY GENETICALLY
ACEEGILLNUY EUGENICALLY
ACEEGILNPRS SLEEPING CAR
ACEEGILNPSS SINGLE-SPACE
ACEEGILSTTU GESTICULATE
ACEEGIMMORT MICROGAMETE
ACEEGINNPRS PREGNANCIES
ACEEGINORTT TERATOGENIC
ACEEGINOTTU AUTOGENETIC
ACEEGIRRRTY CERARGYRITE
ACEEGKNOPSS SPONGE CAKES
ACEEGLLRSSY GRACELESSLY
ACEEGLMNNOT CONGEALMENT
ACEEGMNORRS SCAREMONGER
ACEEGNPRSSY PRESS AGENCY
ACEEHHIIRRS HIERARCHIES
ACEEHHIKLTT HATCHET-LIKE
ACEEHHILRSW WHEELCHAIRS
ACEEHHLMRST CRASH HELMET
ACEEHHMMOOR HAEMOCHROME
ACEEHHMMSTU MUCH THE SAME
ACEEHHNORST SHEET ANCHOR
ACEEHIILNST LECITHINASE
ACEEHIINNRT INHERITANCE
ACEEHIIRSTT HETAERISTIC
ACEEHIKNRTW KITCHENWARE
ACEEHILLNNP PANHELLENIC
ACEEHILLRTY HERETICALLY
ACEEHILMOPR HEMERALOPIC
ACEEHILMPRT HALTEMPRICE
ACEEHILNRTT CHAIN LETTER
ACEEHILNSST ETHICALNESS
ACEEHILORTT THEORETICAL
ACEEHIMMNPT IMPEACHMENT
ACEEHIMNNNT ENCHAINMENT
ACEEHIMNPSZ CHIMPANZEES
ACEEHIMORTT THEOREMATIC

ACEEHIMRTTY ERYTHEMATIC	ACEEILMPSTU TIME CAPSULE
ACEEHINNSTZ NIETZSCHEAN	ACEEILMRTUV VERMICULATE
ACEEHINPRTT PARENTHETIC	ACEEILNNNST CENTENNIALS
ACEEHINSSTT ANESTHETICS	ACEEILNNORT INTOLERANCE
ACEEHIOPRST SPIROCHAETE	ACEEILNNOTU ENUCLEATION
ACEEHIORRST CHARIOTEERS	ACEEILNNTUY LIEUTENANCY
ACEEHIPRSTT PARESTHETIC	ACEEILNOPTX EXCEPTIONAL
ACEEHIPRTTU THERAPEUTIC	ACEEILNORSS RECESSIONAL
ACEEHIPRTVY HYPERACTIVE	ACEEILNORST RESECTIONAL
ACEEHKLNRST HALTERNECKS	ACEEILNOSSS SECESSIONAL
ACEEHLLNTTU CALL THE TUNE	ACEEILNOSST COESSENTIAL
ACEEHLMMNSY MESENCHYMAL	ACEEILNPRTT CENTRIPETAL
ACEEHLMNRUU HERCULANEUM	ACEEILNPSSS SPECIALNESS
ACEEHLMOPSY MESOCEPHALY	ACEEILNPSST PLICATENESS
ACEEHLNOPSU ENCEPHALOUS	ACEEILNQUVY EQUIVALENCY
ACEEHLNPRSU LEPRECHAUNS	ACEEILNRSST TREACLINESS
ACEEHLOORRU LEUCORRHOEA	ACEEILNRSSY NECESSARILY
ACEEHLOPRRT PERCHLORATE	ACEEILNRSTV CANTILEVERS
ACEEHLOSSSV CLOSE SHAVES	ACEEILNSTTT CLIENT STATE
ACEEHMMNNRT MERCHANTMEN	ACEEILOORVV CAVO-RELIEVO
ACEEHMMRSSU MEERSCHAUMS	ACEEILOPRTV PERCOLATIVE
ACEEHMNNNTT ENCHANTMENT	ACEEILOPSTT POLICE STATE
ACEEHMNNRRT TRENCHERMAN	ACEEILORRTV CORRELATIVE
ACEEHMNOSTU MENTHACEOUS	ACEEILORTUX EXECUTORIAL
ACEEHMORSTT TACHOMETERS	ACEEILPRRTY PRELITERACY
ACEEHMSSTTT TEST MATCHES	ACEEILPSTUV SPECULATIVE
ACEEHNNORRT ARCHENTERON	ACEEILRRSSU SECULARISER
ACEEHNNRSST ENCHANTRESS	ACEEILRRSUZ SECULARIZER
ACEEHNOPRTT ON THE CARPET	ACEEILSTTTU TESTICULATE
ACEEHORRSTT ORCHESTRATE	ACEEIMMNORT ANEMOMETRIC
ACEEHORRSTU TREACHEROUS	ACEEIMMORST COMMISERATE
ACEEIILLNPT PENICILLATE	ACEEIMMNOTT CEMENTATION
ACEEIILNRRT RECTILINEAR	ACEEIMNOPRT ARMIPOTENCE
ACEEIILNSTT LICENTIATES	ACEEIMNORRT CRANIOMETER
ACEEIILPRTV REPLICATIVE	ACEEIMNORTT ACTINOMETER
ACEEIILPTVX EXPLICATIVE	ACEEIMNOSTX INCOME TAXES
ACEEIIMNRRT RECRIMINATE	ACEEIMNQRTU ACQUIREMENT
ACEEIINNTUV ENUNCIATIVE	ACEEIMNRSTT REMITTANCES
ACEEIINRSST RESISTENCIA	ACEEIMOSSTV VASECTOMIES
ACEEIINRSTT CERTAINTIES	ACEEINNNSST ANCIENTNESS
ACEEIINRTTV INTERACTIVE	ACEEINNORTV NONCREATIVE
ACEEIIPPRTT PERIPATETIC, PRECIPITATE	ACEEINNRRSU REINSURANCE
ACEEIIRSSTT CASSITERITE	ACEEINNSSTX INEXACTNESS
ACEEIIRSTTV RECITATIVES	ACEEINOPTTX EXPECTATION
ACEEIKMPRRT MARKET PRICE	ACEEINORRST RECREATIONS
ACEEIKNSSSS SEASICKNESS	ACEEINORSTU AUCTIONEERS
ACEEILLNNSS CLEANLINESS	ACEEINORSTX EXECRATIONS
ACEEILLNPST SPLENETICAL	ACEEINPPRST APPRENTICES
ACEEILMNNRT INCREMENTAL	ACEEINPRRST TRANSPIERCE
ACEEILMNORS CEREMONIALS	ACEEINRRSTV TRANSCEIVER
ACEEILMNRRY MERCENARILY	ACEEINRSSST RESISTANCES
ACEEILMORRT CALORIMETER	ACEEIOOPRTV COOPERATIVE
ACEEILMORST ELASTOMERIC	ACEEIOPPRSU PIPERACEOUS
ACEEILMPSST ESEMPLASTIC	ACEEIORRSTV EVISCERATOR

ACEEIORRTTV RETROACTIVE
ACEEIPPRSTY PARTY PIECES
ACEEIRSSTTU RESUSCITATE
ACEEJNPRSTU SUPERJACENT
ACEEKLLRSSS SALESCLERKS
ACEEKNRSTTV TRACK EVENTS
ACEEKORRSSW CASEWORKERS
ACEELLMNRSS SMALL SCREEN
ACEELLNOSTT CONSTELLATE
ACEELMNNOOV MONOVALENCE
ACEELMNOPTT CONTEMPLATE
ACEELMOPRRU COME A PURLER
ACEELNNNSSU UNCLEANNESS
ACEELNOOPRT COLEOPTERAN
ACEELNOOSSS CLOSE SEASON
ACEELNOPSTT PENTECOSTAL
ACEELNORRTX RENAL CORTEX
ACEELNPRSSY SCREENPLAYS
ACEELNPTTXY EXPECTANTLY
ACEELOPPPRT COPPERPLATE
ACEELORSTTW WATER CLOSET
ACEEMMMOORT COMMEMORATE
ACEEMMNNPST ENCAMPMENTS
ACEEMNOOSWY COME ONE'S WAY
ACEEMNPRSST ESCARPMENTS
ACEENNOPRTU COUNTERPANE
ACEENNORRTV CONTRAVENER
ACEENNORSTT CONSTERNATE
ACEENNRSSUY UNNECESSARY
ACEENOORSTT COTONEASTER
ACEENOPRSTV VAPORESCENT
ACEENOPRTTX EXPECTORANT
ACEENRSSSTW NEWSCASTERS
ACEEOPRRRTU RECUPERATOR
ACEEORRSTUW WATERCOURSE
ACEEPPRRTTU PAPER-CUTTER
ACEFFFILOST FACTS OF LIFE
ACEFFGHILNR CLIFFHANGER
ACEFFGILNTY AFFECTINGLY
ACEFFIITTVY AFFECTIVITY
ACEFFIKRRST TRAFFICKERS
ACEFFIOSTUV SUFFOCATIVE
ACEFGHLLNOT FOCAL LENGTH
ACEFGIIMNNT MAGNIFICENT
ACEFGIINNRT INTERFACING
ACEFGILNRTU CENTRIFUGAL
ACEFGINORST FORECASTING
ACEFGINRRSU RESURFACING
ACEFHILNOPR FRANCOPHILE
ACEFHIRSTTY CITY FATHERS
ACEFHLOPRRU REPROACHFUL
ACEFHMNNORW FRENCHWOMAN
ACEFHNNOOPR FRANCOPHONE
ACEFHNORSTT FRENCH TOAST

ACEFHORRSTV HOVERCRAFTS
ACEFIIINORT REIFICATION
ACEFIILORTT FELICITATOR
ACEFIILPRSU SUPERFICIAL
ACEFIINOPTT PONTIFICATE
ACEFIINORST FRACTIONISE
ACEFIINORTZ FRACTIONIZE
ACEFILLLOTU FOLLICULATE
ACEFILLORUW CAULIFLOWER
ACEFILMMOTU COMME IL FAUT
ACEFILORSTU LACTIFEROUS
ACEFILOSTUY FACETIOUSLY
ACEFIMNOTTU TUMEFACTION
ACEFINNORST FOR INSTANCE
ACEFINOTTUV CONFUTATIVE
ACEFIOORRTV VOCIFERATOR
ACEFIPRRSTT PRIESTCRAFT
ACEFLNSSTTU TACTFULNESS
ACEFOOPSTTX EX POST FACTO
ACEGGHILLNN CHALLENGING
ACEGGHILNNS CHANGELINGS
ACEGGILLMOO GEMOLOGICAL
ACEGGILOORT GERATOLOGIC
ACEGGINNORU ENCOURAGING
ACEGGINRSSS SCRAGGINESS
ACEGGLNOOYY GYNAECOLOGY
ACEGGNOORRT CONGREGATOR
ACEGHHILOPR HELICOGRAPH
ACEGHHILRST SEARCHLIGHT
ACEGHHINORW WEIGH ANCHOR
ACEGHHMNRRU HUNGER MARCH
ACEGHHNORST SHORT-CHANGE
ACEGHHOOPRR CHOREOGRAPH
ACEGHHOPRTY HECTOGRAPHY
ACEGHIIIMNT MICHIGANITE
ACEGHIILORS OLIGARCHIES
ACEGHIIMNNZ MECHANIZING
ACEGHIKLLNS SHELLACKING
ACEGHIKMNOP EPOCH-MAKING
ACEGHILLNNN CHANNELLING
ACEGHILLOOR RHEOLOGICAL
ACEGHILLOOT THEOLOGICAL
ACEGHILNRSY SEARCHINGLY
ACEGHILOOPR OLEOGRAPHIC
ACEGHILOPSY GEOPHYSICAL
ACEGHIMNNSU MACHINEGUNS
ACEGHIMNORR MENORRHAGIC
ACEGHIMNORU ARCHEGONIUM
ACEGHIMNRSY CRYING SHAME
ACEGHINNOPR CHAPERONING
ACEGHINOPRR REPROACHING
ACEGHINORRV OVERARCHING
ACEGHIOPRRX XEROGRAPHIC
ACEGHLNOPTT PLECTOGNATH

ACEGHLOOSTY ESCHATOLOGY
ACEGHNOPRSY SCENOGRAPHY
ACEGHOOPRSU CREOPHAGOUS
ACEGHORRSTU ROUGHCASTER
ACEGIIKNPRS ASKING PRICE
ACEGIILLOOT ETIOLOGICAL
ACEGIILLOTV COLLIGATIVE
ACEGIILNNRT INTERLACING
ACEGIILNPRT REPLICATING
ACEGIILNPTX EXPLICATING
ACEGIILOSTT EGOTISTICAL
ACEGIILRSST SACRILEGIST
ACEGIIMNOST ISOMAGNETIC
ACEGIIMRRTV GRAVIMETRIC
ACEGIINNNTU ENUNCIATING
ACEGIINNRTT INTERACTING
ACEGIINORTX EXCORIATING
ACEGIINRTTX EXTRICATING
ACEGIINRTUZ CAUTERIZING
ACEGIJNOTUV CONJUGATIVE
ACEGIKLNRST SINGLE-TRACK
ACEGILLMRTU METALLURGIC
ACEGILLNNOY CONGENIALLY
ACEGILLNOOO OENOLOGICAL
ACEGILLNOOP PENOLOGICAL
ACEGILMNRSY SCREAMINGLY
ACEGILMOSTY CLEISTOGAMY
ACEGILNNOOT CONGELATION
ACEGILNNPRS SPRING-CLEAN
ACEGILNOPRT PERCOLATING
ACEGILNOPSY CLAY PIGEONS
ACEGILNORRT CORRELATING
ACEGILNPSTU SPECULATING
ACEGILNPTUX EXCULPATING
ACEGILNRSSY CARESSINGLY
ACEGILNTUUU UNGUICULATE
ACEGILOOPST APOLOGETICS
ACEGILOORTT TERATOLOGIC
ACEGILRRTUU AGRICULTURE
ACEGIMNOTVY VAGINECTOMY
ACEGIMORSST MESOGASTRIC
ACEGINNNOTV COVENANTING
ACEGINNRSTY ASTRINGENCY
ACEGINOOPRT COOPERATING
ACEGINOPRRT PROCREATING
ACEGINOSTTV CASTING VOTE
ACEGINPRRTU RECAPTURING
ACEGINPSTTY TYPECASTING
ACEGIOORTTX EXCOGITATOR
ACEGIOPSTTY STEATOPYGIC
ACEGKRSSTTU STAGESTRUCK
ACEGLNOPRTY CALYPTROGEN
ACEGLNORTUY GRANULOCYTE
ACEGLRSSTTU GLASSCUTTER

ACEGMNNORSS CONGRESSMAN
ACEGMOPRRST SPECTROGRAM
ACEGMORSTTY GASTRECTOMY
ACEGNORRSST CROSS-GARNET
ACEGOOPRSST GASTROSCOPE
ACEHHIILMOP HAEMOPHILIC,
    HEMOPHILIAC
ACEHHIIMRRS HIERARCHISM
ACEHHIINNTY HYACINTHINE
ACEHHIMOOPT HOMEOPATHIC
ACEHHINOSTX HEXASTICHON
ACEHHNORSSU RANCH HOUSES
ACEHIIINPSS HISPANICISE
ACEHIIINPSZ HISPANICIZE
ACEHIILLOPT PALEOLITHIC
ACEHIILLOST ISOLECITHAL
ACEHIILMSTT ATHLETICISM
ACEHIILNOPR NECROPHILIA
ACEHIILOSTT CHIASTOLITE, HELIOSTATIC
ACEHIILSTWW WELWITSCHIA
ACEHIINNOPT PHONETICIAN
ACEHIINORRT RHETORICIAN
ACEHIINPSTT PANTHEISTIC
ACEHIKKLMMO HAMMOCK-LIKE
ACEHIKLPRRS PARISH CLERK
ACEHIKLPRTY PRICKLY HEAT
ACEHIKMNORS CHAIN-SMOKER
ACEHIKMRTUY RHEUMATICKY
ACEHILLMORY HOMERICALLY
ACEHILLORTW WHITE-COLLAR
ACEHILMNOOT MACHINE TOOL
ACEHILMNOST SLOT MACHINE
ACEHILNPRST SPHINCTERAL
ACEHILNSTTY SYNTHETICAL
ACEHILRSSSY CHRYSALISES
ACEHIMMOPRT METAMORPHIC
ACEHIMNORSS MARCHIONESS
ACEHIMNORTU EUCHROMATIN
ACEHIMOOSTT HOMEOSTATIC
ACEHIMOPRST ATMOSPHERIC
ACEHIMORRRT ARTHROMERIC
ACEHIMORRST CHOIRMASTER
ACEHIMORTTX THERMOTAXIC
ACEHIMPSSTY METAPHYSICS
ACEHIMPSTTY SYMPATHETIC
ACEHIMRSSST CHRISTMASES
ACEHINNOOTT CANINE TOOTH
ACEHINNPSSU PAUNCHINESS
ACEHINNRSSU RAUNCHINESS
ACEHINOOPRZ PHANEROZOIC
ACEHINOPRRS CHAIRPERSON
ACEHINOPRRT CHIROPTERAN
ACEHINOPRTU NEUROPATHIC
ACEHINORSST CHAIN STORES

ACEHINRSSST STARCHINESS
ACEHIOOPSTT OSTEOPATHIC
ACEHIOOPTTV PHOTOACTIVE
ACEHIOPPRST HIPPOCRATES
ACEHIORSSTY CASE HISTORY
ACEHIQRRSUY SQUIREARCHY
ACEHKMRRSTT STRETCHMARK
ACEHLLMSSTY MATCHLESSLY
ACEHLMMNOOR CHROMONEMAL
ACEHLMOOSST SCHOOLMATES
ACEHLMRSSUV SCRUMHALVES
ACEHLNNRTTY TRENCHANTLY
ACEHLORSTUY LYTHRACEOUS
ACEHMNOPRSY PROSENCHYMA
ACEHMOORTTY TRACHEOTOMY
ACEHMOPRSTU CHAMPERTOUS
ACEHNNOOPRT CTENOPHORAN
ACEHNNSSSTU STAUNCHNESS
ACEHOPPRSTU TOUCHPAPERS
ACEHOPRRSSY CHRYSOPRASE
ACEHOPRRTYY CRYOTHERAPY
ACEHOPSSTTW STOPWATCHES
ACEHORSTTWW WATCHTOWERS
ACEIIIKNNOS ANISEIKONIC
ACEIIILMPTV IMPLICATIVE
ACEIIILNOTT ELICITATION
ACEIIIMNNRT INCRIMINATE
ACEIIIMNOST SEMIOTICIAN
ACEIIIMNSTT ANTI-SEMITIC
ACEIIIQSTUV ACQUISITIVE
ACEIIKLLNTY KINETICALLY
ACEIIKLRSTT RICKETTSIAL
ACEIIKNOTTU AUTOKINETIC
ACEIIKNRSSS AIRSICKNESS
ACEIILLMMTY MIMETICALLY
ACEIILLMNNU ILLUMINANCE
ACEIILLMOTY MEIOTICALLY
ACEIILLMPRY EMPIRICALLY
ACEIILLMSSY SEISMICALLY
ACEIILLNSTT SCINTILLATE
ACEIILMNPRT PLANIMETRIC
ACEIILMNSTT MENTALISTIC
ACEIILMOPST ATOMIC PILES
ACEIILMORST ISOMETRICAL
ACEIILMOTTU ITACOLUMITE
ACEIILMPSSS SPECIALISMS
ACEIILNNORT RECLINATION
ACEIILNOPPR PILOCARPINE
ACEIILNOPRT REPLICATION
ACEIILNOPTX EXPLICATION
ACEIILNOQTU EQUINOCTIAL
ACEIILNOTUV INOCULATIVE
ACEIILNPRUY PECUNIARILY
ACEIILNRRUV CURVILINEAR

ACEIILNRSTT CLARINETIST
ACEIILNRSTU UNREALISTIC
ACEIILNRTTY INTRICATELY
ACEIILOPRST TROPICALISE
ACEIILOPRTZ TROPICALIZE
ACEIILPPRST PARTICIPLES
ACEIILPRSST PLASTICISER
ACEIILPRSTT PERISTALTIC, TRIPLICATES
ACEIILPRSTZ PLASTICIZER
ACEIILPRTUY PECULIARITY
ACEIILPSSST SPECIALISTS
ACEIILRTTVY VERTICALITY
ACEIIMNNRST MANNERISTIC
ACEIIMNOPRT IMPRECATION
ACEIIMNORST ANISOMETRIC,
    MISCREATION, REACTIONISM,
    ROMANTICISE
ACEIIMNORTT INTERATOMIC,
    METRICATION
ACEIIMNORTZ ROMANTICIZE
ACEIIMNPRRU PERICRANIUM
ACEIIMNPSSU IMPUISSANCE
ACEIIMNRSTT MARTENSITIC
ACEIIMNRSTU INSECTARIUM
ACEIIMNSSTT SEMANTICIST
ACEIINNNOTU ENUNCIATION
ACEIINNOPTT PECTINATION
ACEIINNORRT INCINERATOR
ACEIINNORTT INTERACTION
ACEIINNPSTT PINNATISECT
ACEIINOORTX EXCORIATION
ACEIINOPRTT CREPITATION
ACEIINOPSTT PECTISATION
ACEIINOPTTZ PECTIZATION
ACEIINORSTT RECITATIONS
ACEIINORTTX EXTRICATION
ACEIINPPRTT PRECIPITANT
ACEIINPRTTY ANTIPYRETIC, PERTINACITY
ACEIINPSSTT ANTISEPTICS
ACEIIOOPPST APOSIOPETIC
ACEIKKLNPTY PENALTY KICK
ACEIKLLPSTY SKEPTICALLY
ACEIKLNPSSV CLASP KNIVES
ACEIKLPPRRY PRICKLY PEAR
ACEIKNPSSTT SEPTIC TANKS
ACEILLLMNOR LAMELLICORN
ACEILLLMOPY POLEMICALLY
ACEILLLNORT CITRONELLAL
ACEILLLNRUU UNICELLULAR
ACEILLMNNOT NONMETALLIC
ACEILLMNRUY NUMERICALLY
ACEILLMOTTY TOTEMICALLY
ACEILLMRRUY MERCURIALLY
ACEILLNNOOO NEOCOLONIAL

ACEILLNOPTU CUPELLATION
ACEILLNRSTY CRYSTALLINE
ACEILLOORRS COROLLARIES
ACEILLOPSSW PILLOWCASES
ACEILLOQUVY EQUIVOCALLY
ACEILLRSSTY CRYSTALLISE
ACEILLRSTTY CRYSTALLITE
ACEILLRSTYZ CRYSTALLIZE
ACEILLRTUVY LUCRATIVELY
ACEILMMNOSU COMMUNALISE
ACEILMMNOTY METONYMICAL
ACEILMMNOUZ COMMUNALIZE
ACEILMMRSTY SYMMETRICAL
ACEILMNOOPS SCOPOLAMINE
ACEILMNOOPW POLICEWOMAN
ACEILMNOPRS COMPLAINERS
ACEILMNOPRT PLANOMETRIC
ACEILMNOPTY AMYLOPECTIN
ACEILMNRTTU CURTAILMENT
ACEILMNRTUU RETINACULUM
ACEILMNSSSU MUSICALNESS
ACEILMORRTY CALORIMETRY
ACEILMRRTUU MARICULTURE
ACEILNNNOSS NONSENSICAL
ACEILNNNOTT CONTINENTAL
ACEILNNNOTU ANTINUCLEON
ACEILNNORTU CRENULATION
ACEILNNRTUY UNCERTAINLY
ACEILNNSSTY INCESSANTLY
ACEILNOOPRR INCORPOREAL
ACEILNOOPRT PERCOLATION
ACEILNOORRT CORRELATION
ACEILNOORSU ARENICOLOUS
ACEILNOPRST INSPECTORAL
ACEILNOPSTU PECULATIONS,
  SPECULATION
ACEILNOPTUX EXCULPATION
ACEILNOQUUV UNEQUIVOCAL
ACEILNORSTT INTERCOSTAL
ACEILNORTUV COUNTERVAIL,
  INVOLUCRATE
ACEILNOSSST STOICALNESS
ACEILNOSTUY TENACIOUSLY
ACEILNPSSTY TYPICALNESS
ACEILNRRTUV VENTRICULAR
ACEILOOPPRS POLARISCOPE
ACEILOOSSST OSTEOCLASIS
ACEILOPRRTT PROTRACTILE
ACEILORSUVY VERACIOUSLY
ACEILORTVYY VICEROYALTY
ACEILPRSTTY SPECTRALITY
ACEILQRTUUU AQUICULTURE
ACEILRRTTUU TURRICULATE
ACEIMMOOSSU MIMOSACEOUS

ACEIMMORRTU CREMATORIUM
ACEIMMOTTUV COMMUTATIVE
ACEIMNNNOTT CONTAINMENT
ACEIMNOPRRS MARINE CORPS
ACEIMNORRTU MERCURATION
ACEIMNORRTY CRANIOMETRY
ACEIMNORRTY ACTINOMETRY
ACEIMOPRRTY IMPRECATORY
ACEIMORRSTT ASTROMETRIC
ACEIMPRSSTU SUPREMACIST
ACEIMSSSTTY SYSTEMATICS
ACEINNNOSTT CONSTANTINE
ACEINNOOTTV CONNOTATIVE
ACEINNORRST CONSTRAINER
ACEINNORSTT TRANSECTION
ACEINNPTUUV NUNCUPATIVE
ACEINNRSSSW SCRAWNINESS
ACEINNRTTUY UNCERTAINTY
ACEINOOOPRT COOPERATION
ACEINOOPRRT INCORPORATE,
  PROCREATION
ACEINOOPRTU APONEUROTIC
ACEINOORRTT RETROACTION
ACEINOORSTV REVOCATIONS
ACEINOPRRTU PUERTO RICAN
ACEINOPRSSS PROSAICNESS
ACEINOPRSTU PRECAUTIONS
ACEINORRSTT RETRACTIONS
ACEINORRTTY CONTRARIETY
ACEINORSTTU ERUCTATIONS
ACEINORSTTV CONTRASTIVE
ACEINORSTTX EXTRACTIONS
ACEINPPRSSS SCRAPPINESS
ACEINPRRTUY PARTURIENCY
ACEINRRTUUV INCURVATURE
ACEINRSSSSU NARCISSUSES
ACEIOOPRRTV CORPORATIVE
ACEIOOPRTVV PROVOCATIVE
ACEIOPRRSTT TETRASPORIC,
  TRICERATOPS
ACEIOPRRTTV PROTRACTIVE
ACEIOPRSTUU PRECAUTIOUS
ACEKKLOPTTU TAKE POTLUCK
ACEKKMORSTT STOCK MARKET
ACEKKMOSSST SMOKESTACKS
ACEKNNORSTU COUNTERSANK
ACEKNOPPRRS COPPER'S NARK
ACEKPRRSSSY SKYSCRAPERS
ACELLMNOPSU NUCLEOPLASM
ACELLNOPRUY POLYNUCLEAR
ACELLNOPVYY POLYVALENCY
ACELLNOSSSU CALLOUSNESS
ACELLNRTTUY RELUCTANTLY
ACELLOOPRRY CORPOREALLY

ACELMNNOORT NOMENCLATOR
ACELMNNOORU MONONUCLEAR
ACELMNNOSTT MALCONTENTS
ACELMRSTUUU MUSCULATURE
ACELNNOOPVX PLANO-CONVEX
ACELNNRSTTU TRANSLUCENT
ACELNORSUVY CAVERNOUSLY
ACELNORTTUX CONTEXTURAL
ACELNOSTTTU TALENT SCOUT
ACELOOPRRST PERCOLATORS
ACELOOPRRTT PROTECTORAL
ACELOOPRRTY CORPORATELY
ACELOORRSTW WATERCOLORS
ACELOORRTUW WATERCOLOUR
ACELOPRSSTU SPECULATORS
ACELOPRTUXY EXCULPATORY
ACELRSSSTTY CRYSTAL SETS
ACEMMNOORTT COMMENTATOR
ACEMMNOPRTT COMPARTMENT
ACEMNNORSST MONSTRANCES
ACEMNOOPRST COMPENSATOR
ACEMORSSTTU SCOUTMASTER
ACENNOSSTTT CONTESTANTS
ACENOORRSTV CONSERVATOR
ACENOPRRSTU PROCRUSTEAN
ACENOPRRTTU COUNTERPART
ACENORSSSUU RAUCOUSNESS
ACENORSTTUY COUNTRY SEAT
ACENOSSSUUV VACUOUSNESS
ACEOOOPRRST COOPERATORS
ACEOOPRSSTU STAUROSCOPE
ACFFGIIINOT OFFICIATING
ACFFGIIKNRT TRAFFICKING
ACFFGINOSTU SUFFOCATING
ACFFIIINOOT OFFICIATION
ACFFIILNOST AFFLICTIONS
ACFFILMNOOR FALCONIFORM
ACFFINOOSTU SUFFOCATION
ACFGHIINNRS FRANCHISING
ACFGHINOSUV VOUCHSAFING
ACFGIIINNST SIGNIFICANT
ACFGIIJKKNN JACK-KNIFING
ACFGIILNSSY CLASSIFYING
ACFGIINNORT FORNICATING
ACFGIINNSTY SANCTIFYING
ACFGIINORTZ FACTORIZING
ACFGIINSTTU FUNGISTATIC
ACFGIKNORRV CARVING FORK
ACFGILNTTUU FLUCTUATING
ACFGINRSSTU SURFCASTING
ACFIIINNOTU UNIFICATION
ACFIIINORTV VINIFICATOR
ACFIILLNOTY FICTIONALLY
ACFIILMNORU CALIFORNIUM

ACFIILMORST FORMALISTIC
ACFIILNOPST PONTIFICALS
ACFIIMNOORT FORMICATION
ACFIINNOORT FORNICATION
ACFIINNORST INFRACTIONS
ACFIIOPRRTU PURIFICATOR
ACFILLMORUY FORMULAICLY
ACFILMNNOTU MALFUNCTION
ACFILNNOOST CONFLATIONS
ACFILNOTTUU FLUCTUATION
ACFILORSTUY FRACTIOUSLY
ACFINNOOTTU CONFUTATION
ACFINNORTUY FUNCTIONARY
ACFLLOOPRST PORT OF CALLS
ACFLNOORSTW CONTRAFLOWS
ACFORRRUUVY CURRY FAVOUR
ACGGHILOOPR GRAPHOLOGIC
ACGGHINRRSU SURCHARGING
ACGGIIILNNZ ANGLICIZING
ACGGIILMNRY GRIMACINGLY
ACGGIIMMNRS SCRIMMAGING
ACGGIJNNOTU CONJUGATING
ACGGIMMNRSU SCRUMMAGING
ACGHHILOOPR HOLOGRAPHIC
ACGHHIMOOPR HOMOGRAPHIC
ACGHHINOPRY ICHNOGRAPHY
ACGHHIOPRRY CHIROGRAPHY
ACGHHNOOPRR CHRONOGRAPH
ACGHHOOPRRY CHOROGRAPHY
ACGHHOPPRSY PSYCHOGRAPH
ACGHIILMNPT ITCHING PALM
ACGHIILMORT ALGORITHMIC,
  LOGARITHMIC
ACGHIILNORT GRANOLITHIC
ACGHIIMMNST MISMATCHING
ACGHIIMNNOP CHAMPIONING
ACGHIIPRSST SPHRAGISTIC
ACGHIKMOPRY KYMOGRAPHIC
ACGHILLMOOO HOMOLOGICAL
ACGHILMOOPR LAGOMORPHIC
ACGHILMOORT COLOGARITHM
ACGHILMOOST LOGOMACHIST
ACGHILOPPRY POLYGRAPHIC
ACGHILOPRXY XYLOGRAPHIC
ACGHIMNOOPR MONOGRAPHIC,
  NOMOGRAPHIC, PHONOGRAMIC
ACGHIMOPRRY MICROGRAPHY
ACGHINOOPRS NOSOGRAPHIC
ACGHINOOPRY ICONOGRAPHY
ACGHINOPRRY GRANOPHYRIC
ACGHINOPRYZ ZINCOGRAPHY
ACGHIOOPPRT TOPOGRAPHIC
ACGHIOPPRRY PYROGRAPHIC
ACGHIOPPRTY TYPOGRAPHIC

ACGHIORRSTT GASTROTRICH
ACGHOPPRRTY CRYPTOGRAPH
ACGIIILNTZ ITALICIZING
ACGIIILMNPT IMPLICATING
ACGIIILNOST LOGISTICIAN
ACGIIILNOSZ SOCIALIZING
ACGIIILNPST SALPINGITIC
ACGIIILLLOY ILLOGICALLY
ACGIIILLNOOS SINOLOGICAL
ACGIIILLNOOT COLLIGATION
ACGIIILLNOST OSCILLATING
ACGIIILLNTUV VICTUALLING
ACGIIILLOORV VIROLOGICAL
ACGIILMNNOP COMPLAINING
ACGIILMNOPR PROCLAIMING
ACGIILLNNOTU INOCULATING
ACGIILLNNPTU INCULPATING
ACGIILLNNUVZ VULCANIZING
ACGIILLNTTUV CULTIVATING
ACGIIMNOSST AGNOSTICISM
ACGIIMNRRSY MISCARRYING
ACGIINNNOST SANCTIONING
ACGIINNNOTZ INCOGNIZANT
ACGIINNOSTW WAINSCOTING
ACGIINOOSTT COGITATIONS
ACGIINORSTZ OSTRACIZING
ACGIINRSTTU RUSTICATING
ACGIJKKNSSY SKYJACKINGS
ACGIJLNOTUY CONJUGALITY
ACGIJNNOOTU CONJUGATION
ACGIKKNOSTT STOCKTAKING
ACGILLMNOOO NOMOLOGICAL
ACGILLMOOOP POMOLOGICAL
ACGILLMOORS OSCILLOGRAM
ACGILLMOOTY CLIMATOLOGY
ACGILLNOOOS NOSOLOGICAL
ACGILLNOOOT ONTOLOGICAL
ACGILLOOPTY TYPOLOGICAL
ACGILLOTYYZ ZYGOTICALLY
ACGILMOOOST SOMATOLOGIC
ACGILNOSSTU OUTCLASSING
ACGILOOPRST CARPOLOGIST
ACGILOOSSTT SCATOLOGIST
ACGIMNNOORT MORNING COAT
ACGIMNOOPRU CARPOGONIUM
ACGIMNOORST GASTRONOMIC
ACGINNOPSTY SYNCOPATING
ACGINNORSTT CONTRASTING
ACGINNPTTUU PUNCTUATING
ACGINOORRTU CORRUGATION
ACGINOORSTY COSIGNATORY
ACGINOPRRTT PROTRACTING
ACGIORSSTTY GYROSTATICS
ACGLLNOOOVY VOLCANOLOGY

ACGLMNNOOUY AGONY COLUMN
ACGMOOPRSSY GYROCOMPASS
ACGOOPRSSTY GASTROSCOPY
ACHHIILLPTY ITHYPHALLIC
ACHHILLMOOT HOMOTHALLIC
ACHHILOPRSS SCHOLARSHIP
ACHHOPPSSTY PSYCHOPATHS
ACHHOPPSTYY PSYCHOPATHY
ACHIIIMNPSS HISPANICISM
ACHIIINPSST HISPANICIST
ACHIILLMSWY WHIMSICALLY
ACHIILMPSSY PHYSICALISM
ACHIILOOPPR COPROPHILIA
ACHIILOSTTT STATOLITHIC
ACHIILPSSTY PHYSICALIST
ACHIIMNORST HARMONISTIC
ACHIINNRSTU UNCHRISTIAN
ACHIINSSTUV CHAUVINISTS
ACHIIPRSSTY PHYSIATRICS
ACHIKLOORSW WORKAHOLICS
ACHILLMOOPR ALLOMORPHIC
ACHILLOPRTY TROPHICALLY
ACHILMOOPST HOMOPLASTIC
ACHILMOPSUY POLYCHASIUM
ACHILMORRYZ MYCORRHIZAL
ACHILNOORRT CHLORINATOR
ACHIMMNOOSU MONOCHASIUM
ACHIMNNNOOR NONHARMONIC
ACHIMNOPSTT MATCH POINTS
ACHIMNOPTYY AMPHICTYONY
ACHIMNORSST MONARCHISTS
ACHIMOPPPSU HIPPOCAMPUS
ACHIMOPSSTY SCYPHISTOMA
ACHIMORRSTY CHRISMATORY
ACHINNOOPTY APOCYNTHION
ACHINOOPSTT PHOTONASTIC
ACHIOOPPRTT PROTOPATHIC
ACHIOOPPSTT POTATO CHIPS
ACHIOOPRTTU AUTOTROPHIC
ACHIOOPSTTT PHOTOSTATIC
ACHIOPPRSTY SAPROPHYTIC
ACHIOPRRSTU CURATORSHIP
ACHLLOOPRST CHLOROPLAST
ACHLLOOPSSY PLAYSCHOOLS
ACHLMMOOORS CHROMOSOMAL
ACHLMMOOPRS CHROMOPLASM
ACHLMMOORSS SCHOOLMARMS
ACHLMOOPRST CHROMOPLAST
ACHMMNOOORT MONOCHROMAT
ACHMMOPPSTU STOMACH PUMP
ACHMOOORTTY THORACOTOMY
ACIIILMNOPT IMPLICATION
ACIIILMNRTY CRIMINALITY
ACIIILNNNOT INCLINATION

ACIIILNOPST POLITICIANS
ACIIILRSTTU RITUALISTIC
ACIIINNOTTT NICTITATION
ACIIINOQSTU ACQUISITION
ACIIILLLOPTY POLITICALLY
ACIILLMNOOS COLONIALISM
ACIILLMNOOT COLLIMATION
ACIILLMNPUY MUNICIPALLY
ACIILLMOSUY MALICIOUSLY
ACIILLMOTTY MITOTICALLY
ACIILLNOOST COLONIALIST,
  OSCILLATION
ACIILLNOPTU UNPOLITICAL
ACIILLNOVVY CONVIVIALLY
ACIILLNPPRY PRINCIPALLY
ACIILLOPRTY PICTORIALLY
ACIILLPRSTU PLURALISTIC
ACIILLQUYZZ QUIZZICALLY
ACIILMNNOPT INCOMPLIANT
ACIILMNNOTU CULMINATION
ACIILMNOOPT COMPILATION
ACIILMNORTU TOURMALINIC
ACIILMNSTUY MASCULINITY
ACIILNNOOTU INOCULATION
ACIILNNOPTU INCULPATION
ACIILNOPRSV PROVINCIALS
ACIILNOPSSU SUSPICIONAL
ACIILNOTTUV CULTIVATION
ACIILOPRTTY TROPICALITY
ACIILORSTTU STAUROLITIC
ACIILORSUVY VICARIOUSLY
ACIILOSUVVY VIVACIOUSLY
ACIIMMMNOST MAMMONISTIC
ACIIMMNNOOT COMMINATION
ACIIMMNORST ROMANTICISM
ACIIMMNOSST MONASTICISM
ACIIMMNNSSTU NUMISMATICS
ACIIMNOORSU ACRIMONIOUS
ACIIMNORSTT ROMANTICIST
ACIIMNRSSTU MANICURISTS
ACIIMOPRSTT TROPISMATIC
ACIINNOOSTV INVOCATIONS
ACIINNORRTU IRON CURTAIN
ACIINNORTUV INCURVATION
ACIINNOSTTX INTOXICANTS
ACIINOOPRST ANISOTROPIC
ACIINOORTTX INTOXICATOR
ACIINOPRTTU UNPATRIOTIC
ACIINORSTTU RUSTICATION
ACIINRSSSST NARCISSISTS
ACIINRTTTUY TACITURNITY
ACIIOPSSSTT PSITTACOSIS
ACIJNNOORTU CONJURATION
ACIKNNORSYY SYNKARYONIC

ACILLMNOORY MORONICALLY
ACILLMNOPTY COMPLIANTLY
ACILLMOOSTY OSMOTICALLY
ACILLMOPSTY PLASMOLYTIC
ACILLMOTYYZ ZYMOTICALLY
ACILLNNOTUY CONTINUALLY
ACILLNOOOPT LOCAL OPTION
ACILLOORRTT TORTICOLLAR
ACILLOORSST OSCILLATORS
ACILLOORSTY OSCILLATORY
ACILMMMNOSU COMMUNALISM
ACILMMNNOOU COMMUNIONAL
ACILMMNOOOT COMMOTIONAL
ACILMMNOSTU COMMUNALIST
ACILMMNOTUY COMMUNALITY
ACILMMORSSU COMMISSURAL
ACILMMRSSUU SIMULACRUMS
ACILMOOPSTX TOXOPLASMIC
ACILMORSTUY CUSTOMARILY
ACILMRSTUUY MUSCULARITY
ACILNNOOOST CONSOLATION
ACILNOOSTTT COTTONTAILS
ACILNORSSTU ULTRASONICS
ACILNPPSSTU SUPPLICANTS
ACILNPTTUUY PUNCTUALITY
ACILOOPRRTY CORPORALITY
ACILOOORSTUY ATROCIOUSLY
ACILOORSUVY VORACIOUSLY
ACILORSTTUV CULTIVATORS
ACIMMNOORTY COMMINATORY
ACIMMNOOTTU COMMUTATION
ACIMMOPSTTY SYMPTOMATIC
ACIMNNOORTU MUCRONATION
ACIMNOOPRSS COMPARISONS
ACIMNOOPTTU COMPUTATION
ACIMNOPPRSS PRISON CAMPS
ACIMNOPRSTY PATRONYMICS
ACIMNPRSSTU MANUSCRIPTS
ACIMOOPRSTT COMPATRIOTS
ACINNNNOOST INCONSONANT
ACINNNOOOTT CONNOTATION
ACINNOOORST CORONATIONS
ACINNOOPRTT CONTRAPTION
ACINNOOPSTY SYNCOPATION
ACINNOORTTU CONTINUATOR
ACINNOPTTUU PUNCTUATION
ACINNORSSTT CONSTRAINTS
ACINOOOPRRT CORPORATION
ACINOOOPRTV PROVOCATION
ACINOOPRSST CONSPIRATOR
ACINOOPRRTT PROTRACTION
ACINOOPRRTU PROCURATION
ACINOORRSUV CARNIVOROUS
ACINOORSSTT CARTOONISTS

ACINPRRSSTT TRANSCRIPTS
ACIOOPPRSTT POTATO CRISP
ACIORSSSSSY SYSSARCOSIS
ACLLMOSTUUU ALTOCUMULUS
ACLLNNORTUY NOCTURNALLY
ACLNNOSSTTU CONSULTANTS
ACLNOOORSTY CONSOLATORY
ACLNOOPRRSU PROCONSULAR
ACLNOORRSUY RANCOROUSLY
ACLOOPRSUXY XYLOCARPOUS
ACMMNOORSTU CONSUMMATOR
ACMMOORSTTU COMMUTATORS
ACMMPPSUUUV VACUUM PUMPS
ACMOOOSSTTU SCOTOMATOUS
ACOOPRRRSTT PROTRACTORS
ADDDDENNOSS ODDS AND ENDS
ADDDEEERRSS READDRESSED
ADDDEEGIRRS DISREGARDED
ADDDEEHNRSU DUNDERHEADS
ADDDEEILSSS SIDESADDLES
ADDDEGIKLNS SKEDADDLING
ADDDERSSTTU STAR-STUDDED
ADDEEEEGNRT DEGENERATED
ADDEEEEHLLV LEVEL-HEADED
ADDEEEGLRTU DEREGULATED
ADDEEEHIKNS HIDE-AND-SEEK
ADDEEEHMPTY EMPTY-HEADED
ADDEEEHNPPR APPREHENDED
ADDEEEHRSSS HEADDRESSES
ADDEEEIMNRR REMAINDERED
ADDEEELRSTT DEAD LETTERS
ADDEEENORUV ENDEAVOURED
ADDEEEOPRSS DESPERADOES
ADDEEFHLRUY FURALDEHYDE
ADDEEFLOPST SOFT-PEDALED
ADDEEFMNORU UNDREAMED-OF
ADDEEFMNRTU DEFRAUDMENT
ADDEEGHHILT LIGHT-HEADED
ADDEEGHILPY PIGHEADEDLY
ADDEEGHNORW WRONGHEADED
ADDEEGILMNR LARGE-MINDED
ADDEEGINRRS DEAD RINGERS
ADDEEGIRRRS DISREGARDER
ADDEEGNRSSU GUARDEDNESS
ADDEEHHLOTY HOTHEADEDLY
ADDEEHIKNRT KIND-HEARTED
ADDEEHIMNSU DEHUMANISED
ADDEEHIMNUZ DEHUMANIZED
ADDEEHISTTU DEATH DUTIES
ADDEEHMNPTY EMPTY-HANDED
ADDEEHNORTW DOWNHEARTED
ADDEEHPRRSS HARD-PRESSED
ADDEEIILSTV DEVITALISED
ADDEEIILTVZ DEVITALIZED

ADDEEIINNNW WINE AND DINE
ADDEEIJOPRS JEOPARDISED
ADDEEIJOPRZ JEOPARDIZED
ADDEEILLSVW WELL-ADVISED
ADDEEILMMNS MIDDLE NAMES
ADDEEILNRRT INTERLARDED
ADDEEILRRVY DAREDEVILRY
ADDEEIMNNOT DENOMINATED
ADDEEIMNPRR REPRIMANDED
ADDEEIMNRRS MIND READERS
ADDEEIMORRS DROMEDARIES
ADDEEIMOTTV DEMOTIVATED
ADDEEIMRSTU DESIDERATUM
ADDEEINOPRR PREORDAINED
ADDEEINOPRT DEPREDATION
ADDEEIRTTWY READY-WITTED
ADDEELNNSTU SUDETENLAND
ADDEELNPRUY UNDERPLAYED
ADDEELNRUUV UNDERVALUED
ADDEELOPPTU DEPOPULATED
ADDEELOPRRS ROPE LADDERS
ADDEELPRSST STEPLADDERS
ADDEEMNNNRU UNDERMANNED
ADDEEMNOPPR NAMEDROPPED
ADDEENORTWW WATERED-DOWN
ADDEENRSTTU UNDERSTATED
ADDEFFHLNOY OFFHANDEDLY
ADDEFILORTU FLUORIDATED
ADDEGGHORTU GODDAUGHTER
ADDEGGIIIRT DIGITIGRADE
ADDEGHHINRT RIGHT-HANDED
ADDEGHINRTY DEHYDRATING
ADDEGHNORTU DREADNOUGHT
ADDEGIIMNNR MIND READING
ADDEGIKNRRS KIND REGARDS
ADDEGILLNRW GRINDELWALD
ADDEGILMNNY MADDENINGLY
ADDEGILNNSY SADDENINGLY
ADDEGIMNNNU UNDEMANDING
ADDEGIMNORS GORMANDISED
ADDEGIMNORZ GORMANDIZED
ADDEGJMNTUY JUDGMENT DAY
ADDEGNOORTU GOOD-NATURED
ADDEHHNORST SHORTHANDED
ADDEHIILMOT THALIDOMIDE
ADDEHILNORS RHODE ISLAND
ADDEHILOPSU DIADELPHOUS
ADDEHINORTY DEHYDRATION
ADDEHINOSWW WINDOW SHADE
ADDEHIOPRSS RHAPSODISED
ADDEHIOPRSZ RHAPSODIZED
ADDEHMNNOSW HAND-ME-DOWNS
ADDEHMORSUY HYDROMEDUSA
ADDEIIIMNTT INTIMIDATED

ADDEIIINOOR RADIOIODINE
ADDEIIINTUV INDIVIDUATE
ADDEILLMMNS SMALL-MINDED
ADDEILNSUVY UNADVISEDLY
ADDEILOSVWY DISAVOWEDLY
ADDEILRSTTU STRIDULATED
ADDEIOPPRSV DISAPPROVED
ADDELMOORTU DEMODULATOR
ADDELMORRSW DREAM WORLDS
ADDELNNORSW WONDERLANDS
ADDELNNRTUY REDUNDANTLY
ADDEMNOOORT RODOMONTADE
ADDGGINNORW DOWNGRADING
ADDGHILNOOR ROADHOLDING
ADDGILNNOOW DOWNLOADING
ADDIIIIMNOT DIMIDIATION
ADDIIIILNSUV INDIVIDUALS
ADDILLNNOUV NULL AND VOID
ADDILMNORTY DIRTY OLD MAN
ADDNNOOSTUW DOWN-AND-OUTS
ADDNNOPSSUW UPS AND DOWNS
ADEEEEFGHRT FEATHEREDGE
ADEEEEFHRRT FREE-HEARTED
ADEEEEGGRST DESEGREGATE
ADEEEEGNRRT REGENERATED
ADEEEEGNRST DEGENERATES
ADEEEEHKNTY THE NAKED EYE
ADEEEFILNRT DEFERENTIAL
ADEEEFLORRS FREELOADERS
ADEEEFNRSTT FENESTRATED
ADEEEGGLLNO GOLDEN EAGLE
ADEEEGHLPRT TELEGRAPHED
ADEEEGILMNR LEGERDEMAIN
ADEEEGILNRS GENERALISED
ADEEEGILNRZ GENERALIZED
ADEEEGILNSV EVANGELISED
ADEEEGILNVZ EVANGELIZED
ADEEEGIMNRR GENDARMERIE
ADEEEGIMNST DEMAGNETISE
ADEEEGIMNTZ DEMAGNETIZE
ADEEEGINNRT TRAGEDIENNE
ADEEEGLLNRT LEGAL TENDER
ADEEEGLNNRR GREENLANDER
ADEEEGMNNRT DERANGEMENT
ADEEEGNOTXY DEOXYGENATE
ADEEEHLLORS LEASEHOLDER
ADEEEHLPSSY SLEEPYHEADS
ADEEEHLRSTT LETTERHEADS
ADEEEHMORST HOMESTEADER
ADEEEHNNNOR ENNEAHEDRON
ADEEEHNOPRT OPENHEARTED
ADEEEHNRRSU UNREHEARSED
ADEEEHPRSST SPREADSHEET
ADEEEHRRTTU TRUEHEARTED

ADEEEIILNTV DELINEATIVE
ADEEEIIMMOR AIDE-MEMOIRE
ADEEEILSSUX DESEXUALISE
ADEEEILSUXZ DESEXUALIZE
ADEEEIMNRTT DETERMINATE
ADEEEIMPRTT PREMEDITATE
ADEEEINNRTT ENTERTAINED
ADEEEIORRTT DETERIORATE
ADEEEIPRRST PIEDS-À-TERRE
ADEEEJNRTUV REJUVENATED
ADEEEKLLPSW SLEEPWALKED
ADEEEKLRRST DEERSTALKER
ADEEEKLSTTW SWEET-TALKED
ADEEELLNSWY WENSLEYDALE
ADEEELLSSTT TESSELLATED
ADEEELMNNOW NEEDLEWOMAN
ADEEELNNRSS LEARNEDNESS
ADEEELNRSST RELATEDNESS
ADEEELNRTTU LAUNDERETTE
ADEEELNSSTX EXALTEDNESS
ADEEELPRSTY DESPERATELY
ADEEEMNNRST ENDEARMENTS
ADEEEMNRRTU REMUNERATED
ADEEEMOSTWW MEADOWSWEET
ADEEENOPRTU DEUTERANOPE
ADEEENORRUV ENDEAVOURER
ADEEENRRSSW NEWSREADERS
ADEEEPPRRTT PERPETRATED
ADEEEPPRTTU PERPETUATED
ADEEEPRSSSU SUPERSEDEAS
ADEEFFIINRT DIFFERENTIA
ADEEFFORSTV OVERSTAFFED
ADEEFGGLOPR LEAPFROGGED
ADEEFGHIRSU FIGUREHEADS
ADEEFGHORRT FORGATHERED
ADEEFGIINNR FINE-GRAINED
ADEEFGILNOR FREELOADING
ADEEFGINNRR RANGE FINDER
ADEEFHLNRST LEFT-HANDERS
ADEEFHORSTT SOFTHEARTED
ADEEFILORRS RELIEF ROADS
ADEEFILRSST FEDERALISTS
ADEEFINORST FEDERATIONS
ADEEFINRRST FRATERNISED
ADEEFINRRTZ FRATERNIZED
ADEEFIOPSST SAFE-DEPOSIT
ADEEFLLORST FORESTALLED
ADEEFLLORVW WELL-FAVORED
ADEEFLRSSSU SELF-ASSURED
ADEEFNOPRRS FREE PARDONS
ADEEFNRRRST TRANSFERRED
ADEEFOOPRRR PROOFREADER
ADEEGGHLORS LOGGERHEADS
ADEEGGIINRS DISAGREEING

ADEEGGILRVY AGGRIEVEDLY
ADEEGGINNNR ENDANGERING
ADEEGGLORTW WATERLOGGED
ADEEGGMORUY DEMAGOGUERY
ADEEGGNPRSS PRESSGANGED
ADEEGHINRST NEARSIGHTED
ADEEGHIRRST SIGHT-READER
ADEEGHLRSTU SLAUGHTERED
ADEEGHMOPRR DEMOGRAPHER
ADEEGHNORTY HYDROGENATE
ADEEGIILNNT DELINEATING
ADEEGIINSTV DESIGNATIVE
ADEEGIIRSST GREAT DIESIS
ADEEGILNNRY ENDEARINGLY
ADEEGILNNST DISENTANGLE
ADEEGILNOST DELEGATIONS
ADEEGILNRRS RINGLEADERS
ADEEGILNTTU DEGLUTINATE
ADEEGILRRSU REGULARISED
ADEEGILRRUZ REGULARIZED
ADEEGIMNNRS MEANDERINGS
ADEEGIMNPRT IMPREGNATED
ADEEGINNORV ENDEAVORING
ADEEGINORRS REORGANISED
ADEEGINORRZ REORGANIZED
ADEEGKRRTUU GREATER KUDU
ADEEGLPPRSY DAPPLE-GREYS
ADEEGMNNORY DANGER MONEY
ADEEGMNRRRY GERRYMANDER
ADEEGMORTUY DEUTEROGAMY
ADEEHHILSST HEAT SHIELDS
ADEEHHIMRTY HEMIHYDRATE
ADEEHHISTWW WHITEWASHED
ADEEHHLORRS SHAREHOLDER
ADEEHHNOPRT HEPTAHEDRON
ADEEHHNRSTU HEADHUNTERS
ADEEHIINPRS HESPERIDIAN
ADEEHIIOPRS ISODIAPHERE
ADEEHILLNOT ENDOTHELIAL
ADEEHILNOPT ELEPHANTOID
ADEEHILNORT LION-HEARTED
ADEEHILNPRR PHILANDERER
ADEEHILNSST DEATHLINESS
ADEEHILPRSS DEALERSHIPS
ADEEHILSSWY DAISY WHEELS
ADEEHINRSST THREADINESS
ADEEHIPRRSS READERSHIPS
ADEEHIRRRSS HAIRDRESSER
ADEEHIRRSTW HARRIS TWEED
ADEEHKLORST STAKEHOLDER
ADEEHLLNOSW SWOLLEN HEAD
ADEEHLLSSTY DEATHLESSLY
ADEEHLMNOTT MENTHOLATED
ADEEHLNNRST NETHERLANDS

ADEEHLOORTW LEATHERWOOD
ADEEHNNOPRT PENTAHEDRON
ADEEHNORRTT TETRAHEDRON
ADEEIILMMSV MEDIEVALISM
ADEEIILMMTY IMMEDIATELY
ADEEIILMNOT MATINÉE IDOL
ADEEIILMSTV MEDIEVALIST
ADEEIILNNOT DELINEATION
ADEEIILNRST RESIDENTIAL
ADEEIILRSTV REVITALISED
ADEEIILRTVZ REVITALIZED
ADEEIIMMNPT IMPEDIMENTA
ADEEIIMNNST INSEMINATED
ADEEIIMNSST DISSEMINATE
ADEEIINRRTV VERATRIDINE
ADEEIIPRSTV DEPRAVITIES
ADEEIIPRTUV REPUDIATIVE
ADEEIIRSSTV ADVERSITIES
ADEEIIRSTVV DERIVATIVES
ADEEILLMNNR ILL-MANNERED
ADEEILLMRSV SILVER MEDAL
ADEEILMNNST ENLISTED MAN
ADEEILMNORT ENDOMETRIAL
ADEEILMNRST DERAILMENTS,
    STREAMLINED
ADEEILMNRTT DETRIMENTAL
ADEEILMNRVY DELIVERYMAN
ADEEILMORRS DEMORALISER
ADEEILMORRZ DEMORALIZER
ADEEILMORST DILATOMETER
ADEEILNNPTT PENTLANDITE
ADEEILNNPUX UNEXPLAINED
ADEEILNNRTT INTERDENTAL
ADEEILNRSTU NEUTRALISED
ADEEILNRSTY SEDENTARILY
ADEEILNRTUZ NEUTRALIZED
ADEEILNSTTT DILETTANTES
ADEEILOPRRS DEPOLARISER
ADEEILOPRRZ DEPOLARIZER
ADEEILPRRSV PEARL DIVERS
ADEEILPRSSU DISPLEASURE
ADEEILRRSVV SLAVE DRIVER
ADEEIMMNORS MISDEMEANOR
ADEEIMNNOST EMENDATIONS
ADEEIMNNPTU ANTEPENDIUM
ADEEIMNNRTT DETERMINANT,
    DETRAINMENT
ADEEIMNOPRT PREDOMINATE
ADEEIMNPRRR REPRIMANDER
ADEEIMNRSTY SEDIMENTARY
ADEEIMORSTT STADIOMETER
ADEEIMRTTTY TETRADYMITE
ADEEINNRTTV INADVERTENT
ADEEINOPRST DESPERATION

ADEEINORRST RAISON D'ETRE
ADEEINOSTTT DETESTATION
ADEEINPRSST PEDESTRIANS
ADEEIPRSSTU PASTEURISED
ADEEIPRSTUZ PASTEURIZED
ADEEIRRSSTV ADVERTISERS
ADEEKLOPRSU LOUDSPEAKER
ADEEKMRRSSS DRESSMAKERS
ADEEKNRRSTU UNDERTAKERS
ADEELLMNSSW MENDEL'S LAWS
ADEELLMRSSY DREAMLESSLY
ADEELLNOSTW STONEWALLED
ADEELLNRTUV UNTRAVELLED
ADEELLOPTUV POLE VAULTED
ADEELLORSSS LOSS LEADERS
ADEELMMNRTU UNTRAMMELED
ADEELMNOORT DEMONOLATER
ADEELNNRTUW UNTERWALDEN
ADEELNOORST ALDOSTERONE
ADEELNRRUUV UNDERVALUER
ADEELNRTTVY ADVERTENTLY
ADEELRRSSUY REASSUREDLY
ADEEMMNORTY DYNAMOMETER
ADEEMNNNSSU MUNDANENESS
ADEEMNNOOOW WOOD ANEMONE
ADEEMNOPPRR NAMEDROPPER
ADEEMNORSTT DEMONSTRATE
ADEEMNPRSTT DEPARTMENTS
ADEEMNRSTTU MENSTRUATED
ADEENNNPPSY SPEND A PENNY
ADEENPRSSSU UNDERPASSES
ADEENQRRSSU SQUANDERERS
ADEENRRSTUV ADVENTURERS
ADEENRSSSSU ASSUREDNESS
ADEENRSSTUV ADVENTURESS
ADEEOPPRRRS ORDER PAPERS
ADEEORRSTTU TRADE ROUTES
ADEFFILNRTU FAULT-FINDER
ADEFFIMMNOR FRAME OF MIND
ADEFFINRSST FAST FRIENDS
ADEFFIORSST DISAFFOREST
ADEFFLOOTTU FOOT FAULTED
ADEFGHLOORT HEART OF GOLD
ADEFGIILNOT DEFOLIATING
ADEFGIILLNOS SELF-LOADING
ADEFGILNORS DRAGONFLIES
ADEFGIPPRTW GIFT-WRAPPED
ADEFGKNOORS GODFORSAKEN
ADEFGNOORRS ROOF GARDENS
ADEFHHLOOST HEALTH FOODS
ADEFHIKOSST KISS OF DEATH
ADEFHINPRST PATHFINDERS
ADEFHINRRTY FIRE HYDRANT
ADEFHIRSTWW WHITE DWARFS

ADEFIILNNRS LINDISFARNE
ADEFIILNOOT DEFOLIATION
ADEFIILNQUU UNQUALIFIED
ADEFIILNRTT INFILTRATED
ADEFIIMNRSU FREUDIANISM
ADEFIINSSTU UNSATISFIED
ADEFILLORUV ILL-FAVOURED
ADEFILNOORT DEFLORATION
ADEFILSSTTU DISTASTEFUL
ADEFIMNOORT DEFORMATION
ADEFIMRRRST DIRT FARMERS
ADEFLLNOSST DENTAL FLOSS
ADEFLNOORRS FOOL'S ERRAND
ADEFLOOPSTY SPLAYFOOTED
ADEFMNORRST TRANSFORMED
ADEFNORRSSW FORWARDNESS
ADEGGGIINNS DISENGAGING
ADEGGHILNRT RIGHT-ANGLED
ADEGGIINNRT DENIGRATING
ADEGGIINNST DESIGNATING
ADEGGILNRUU UNGULIGRADE
ADEGHHILNNP HELPING HAND
ADEGHHILNRS HIGHLANDERS
ADEGHHINNTU HEADHUNTING
ADEGHHINRRT RIGHT-HANDER
ADEGHHINSST NIGHTSHADES
ADEGHHORRTU READ-THROUGH
ADEGHINOORT IN GOOD HEART
ADEGHMNORRT GRANDMOTHER
ADEGHMNRSTU DRAUGHTSMEN
ADEGHORRTUV OVERDRAUGHT
ADEGHORSSUU GUARDHOUSES
ADEGIIILNTV INVIGILATED
ADEGIIINRST DIGNITARIES
ADEGIILNNOT DIALING TONE
ADEGIILNNRW LINE DRAWING
ADEGIILNNRY INGRAINEDLY
ADEGIILNOST DIGESTIONAL
ADEGIILNOTV DOVETAILING
ADEGIILNPSS DISPLEASING
ADEGIIMNTTU UNMITIGATED
ADEGIIMSSTT STIGMATISED
ADEGIIMSTTZ STIGMATIZED
ADEGIINNORT DENIGRATION
ADEGIINNOST DESIGNATION
ADEGIINOPRR PERIGORDIAN
ADEGIINOPTV VIDEOTAPING
ADEGIINORSS DISORGANISE
ADEGIINORSZ DISORGANIZE
ADEGIINORTV INVIGORATED
ADEGIINPRTU REPUDIATING
ADEGIINRSTV ADVERTISING
ADEGIINRTTU INGRATITUDE
ADEGIINRTTX EXTRADITING

ADEGIIOPRRS PRAIRIE DOGS
ADEGIJNRRSU GRAND JURIES
ADEGIJNRSTU READJUSTING
ADEGIKMNRSS DRESSMAKING
ADEGIKNNRTU UNDERTAKING
ADEGILLOSSU GLADIOLUSES
ADEGILLPTUY PLEAD GUILTY
ADEGILNNNST LANDING NETS
ADEGILNNRWY WANDERINGLY
ADEGILNOORV OVERLOADING
ADEGILNORST TSELINOGRAD
ADEGILNRRTY RETARDINGLY
ADEGILOOPST PAEDOLOGIST
ADEGIMNNOPR PROMENADING
ADEGIMNORRS GORMANDISER
ADEGIMNORRZ GORMANDIZER
ADEGIMNORSU GOURMANDISE
ADEGINNORSU UNORGANISED
ADEGINNORUZ UNORGANIZED
ADEGINNPRUY UNDERPAYING
ADEGINNQRSU SQUANDERING
ADEGINNRRTU UNDERRATING
ADEGINORRVW OVERDRAWING
ADEGINORSTT ROAD TESTING
ADEGKNRRRSU KRUGERRANDS
ADEGLMOORTY DERMATOLOGY
ADEGLMOPRTU PROMULGATED
ADEGLNORSUY DANGEROUSLY
ADEGMMMNOOR MONOGRAMMED
ADEGNNOORSU ANDROGENOUS
ADEHHIORRSS HORSERADISH
ADEHHIRSSSW DISHWASHERS
ADEHIIMNRTU ANTHERIDIUM
ADEHIIOPRSS DIAPHORESIS
ADEHIIORSTT HISTORIATED
ADEHILLNRST DISENTHRALL
ADEHILLORSU LOUDHAILERS
ADEHIMMPPUY HAPPY MEDIUM
ADEHIMORRTY RADIOTHERMY
ADEHIMPSSTY SYMPATHISED
ADEHIMPSTYZ SYMPATHIZED
ADEHINNRSUV UNVARNISHED
ADEHINNRTTW HANDWRITTEN
ADEHINOORTZ ANTHEROZOID
ADEHINOSSSW SHADOWINESS
ADEHINQRRTU HINDQUARTER
ADEHINRSTTW WITHSTANDER
ADEHIPRSSTW STEWARDSHIP
ADEHIPRSTTW SHARP-WITTED
ADEHLLLMORS SMALLHOLDER
ADEHLLLORST STALLHOLDER
ADEHLORSTYY HYDROLYSATE
ADEHMNOORTY MONOHYDRATE
ADEHNNOPSTU OPEN-AND-SHUT

ADEHNOORTTW DOWN-TO-EARTH
ADEHOPRSSTW SHOP STEWARD
ADEIIILMRST MILITARISED
ADEIIILMRTZ MILITARIZED
ADEIIILMSST DISSIMILATE
ADEIIILRSTV TRIVIALISED
ADEIIILRTVZ TRIVIALIZED
ADEIIIMOSTT OTITIS MEDIA
ADEIIIMRSTY SEMIARIDITY
ADEIIINNTTU UNINITIATED
ADEIIIPRSST DISPARITIES
ADEIIIPSSTV DISSIPATIVE
ADEIILLLOPS ELLIPSOIDAL
ADEIILLMNTU ILLUMINATED
ADEIILLORTY EDITORIALLY
ADEIILMNNOS DIMENSIONAL
ADEIILMNRSU SEMIDIURNAL
ADEIILMSSTU DISSIMULATE
ADEIILNORSV DIVERSIONAL
ADEIILORRST IDOLATRISER
ADEIILORRTZ IDOLATRIZER
ADEIIMMNSTU MEDIASTINUM
ADEIIMNOPSS IMPASSIONED
ADEIIMNOSTT MEDITATIONS
ADEIIMPRSSU PRAESIDIUMS
ADEIIMRSTTX TAXIDERMIST
ADEIINNNOTT INDENTATION
ADEIINNOOPT OPINIONATED
ADEIINNORTT DENITRATION
ADEIINNOSTT DESTINATION
ADEIINOPRTT PARTITIONED, TREPIDATION
ADEIINOPRTU REPUDIATION
ADEIINOPRTV DEPRIVATION
ADEIINOPSST PASSIONTIDE
ADEIINORSTV DERIVATIONS
ADEIINORSTY SEDITIONARY
ADEIINORTTX EXTRADITION
ADEIINPRSTY STIPENDIARY
ADEIINQSTTU EQUIDISTANT
ADEIINRSTVY VINEYARDIST
ADEIIOPPRTT PROPITIATED
ADEIJMMNRSW WINDJAMMERS
ADEIKLLLRSY LADY-KILLERS
ADEIKLLMMST MALTED MILKS
ADEILLMRRST DRILLMASTER
ADEILLORSST ILL-ASSORTED
ADEILLORTUV OUTRIVALLED
ADEILLOSVWW SWALLOW DIVE
ADEILLRSTTU ILLUSTRATED
ADEILMMOOTY MYELOMATOID
ADEILMNNSSU MAUDLINNESS
ADEILMNOPRS PALINDROMES
ADEILMNOPTU DEPLUMATION

ADEILMORTTY DILATOMETRY
ADEILNOOPRT PERIODONTAL
ADEILNRSTWZ SWITZERLAND
ADEILNSSTUY SUSTAINEDLY
ADEILOPPRSS PREDISPOSAL
ADEILOPPRSU POPULARISED
ADEILOPPRUZ POPULARIZED
ADEILOPRRTY PREDATORILY
ADEIMMNNOPU PANDEMONIUM
ADEIMMNRSST MASTERMINDS
ADEIMMNSSTT DISMASTMENT
ADEIMNNOORT DENOMINATOR
ADEIMNNOPRT PREDOMINANT
ADEIMNNQRUU QUADRENNIUM
ADEIMNOPSTU DESPUMATION
ADEIMNRRTUY RUDIMENTARY
ADEIMNRSTTT TRANSMITTED
ADEIMNRSTUV ADVENTURISM
ADEINNOOSTT DENOTATIONS,
   DETONATIONS
ADEINNOPSWW WINDOWPANES
ADEINNORSTU TRADE UNIONS
ADEINOOPPRT APPORTIONED
ADEINOOPRTT DEPORTATION
ADEINOPSTTU DEPUTATIONS
ADEINRSTTUV ADVENTURIST
ADEIOPPRRSV DISAPPROVER
ADEIOPRRTUY REPUDIATORY
ADEJMNNORTU ADJOURNMENT
ADEJMNSSTTU ADJUSTMENTS
ADELLMNORSW SMALL WONDER
ADELLNNNOOP LONDON PLANE
ADELLNORRSU ALL-ROUNDERS
ADELLNSSTUY DAUNTLESSLY
ADELLOOPRRT PETRODOLLAR
ADELLOORRRS ROAD ROLLERS
ADELLOORRSU EURODOLLARS
ADELMNOORTY DEMONOLATRY
ADELMNORRTU ULTRAMODERN
ADELOOPRRST POSTAL ORDER
ADELOPPRSUU DUAL-PURPOSE
ADELOPRRRSY LORD'S PRAYER
ADELPQRSTUU QUADRUPLETS
ADEMMMNORSU MEMORANDUMS
ADEMMNNOUYY MAUNDY MONEY
ADEMMNORTYY DYNAMOMETRY
ADEMNNOPTWY DOWN PAYMENT
ADENNOPRRST TRANSPONDER
ADENOPRRSTT TRANSPORTED
ADENORSSSUU ARDUOUSNESS
ADENORSTUUV ADVENTUROUS
ADENPRSSSUU UNSURPASSED
ADFFFFHNPUU HUFF AND PUFF
ADFFGNORSTU GROUND STAFF

ADFFHINOSST STANDOFFISH
ADFGHIINNPT PATHFINDING
ADFGHIINOOT IN GOOD FAITH
ADFGIILRRSY GIRL FRIDAYS
ADFGIINQRSU FIRING SQUAD
ADFGILNNOST SOFT LANDING
ADFGILNQSUY FLYING SQUAD
ADFGINORRSU FAIRGROUNDS
ADFHHNOOSSW SHOW OF HANDS
ADFHIMNOOOR MAID OF HONOR
ADFIIILLNNU NULLIFIDIAN
ADFIIIMNNTU AD INFINITUM
ADFINNOOSTU FOUNDATIONS
ADFLMNSTUUU MUTUAL FUNDS
ADFLNOOOPTU FOOT-POUNDAL
ADGGGHIILNN HANG GLIDING
ADGGLNORSSU GROUND GLASS
ADGHHIINRTT HARD-HITTING
ADGHHILNOPT DIPHTHONGAL
ADGHHOPRRYY HYDROGRAPHY
ADGHIILMNNS MISHANDLING
ADGHIIMNNOS ADMONISHING
ADGHIINNRTW HANDWRITING
ADGHIINRTWW WITHDRAWING
ADGHIOPRTTY DITTOGRAPHY
ADGHLPRSSUU SULPHA DRUGS
ADGHMRRRUYY HYDRARGYRUM
ADGHNOOOPRT ODONTOGRAPH
ADGIIILNQTU LIQUIDATING
ADGIIINNNOT INDIGNATION
ADGIIINNOTU AUDITIONING
ADGIIINNRST DISTRAINING
ADGIIINPSST DISSIPATING
ADGIILLNOSW DISALLOWING
ADGIILMNNST DISMANTLING
ADGIILNNNTY INDIGNANTLY
ADGIILOORST RADIOLOGIST
ADGIILOOSTU AUDIOLOGIST
ADGIILOPRTY PRODIGALITY
ADGIINNPRSW DRAWING PINS
ADGIINOPTUY AUDIOTYPING
ADGIINORSTY GRANDIOSITY
ADGIKNNOORT GORDIAN KNOT
ADGIKNORSWY WORKING DAYS
ADGILNNOPWY DOWNPLAYING
ADGILNOOPSW WADING POOLS
ADGILNPQRUU QUADRUPLING
ADGIMMNORSU GOURMANDISM
ADGIMNOORRW DRAWING ROOM
ADGINNOSTTU OUTSTANDING
ADGINOPRSTT TRADING POST
ADGINRRSSTW DRAWSTRINGS
ADGIORSSSWW GRASS WIDOWS
ADGLNNOPRSU GROUND PLANS

ADGLNOPRSUY PLAYGROUNDS
ADGNNOORSUY ANDROGYNOUS
ADHHNOSSTTU THOUSANDTHS
ADHIIOPPSSY DIAPOPHYSIS
ADHIIORRSST DIARTHROSIS
ADHILMNOOSW OLD-WOMANISH
ADHINNOPRSX ANDROSPHINX
ADHINOSSSWW SASH WINDOWS
ADHLNOPSSSW SPLASHDOWNS
ADIIILNOOST IDOLISATION
ADIIILNOOTZ IDOLIZATION
ADIIILNOQTU LIQUIDATION
ADIIIMNORTT INTIMIDATOR
ADIIIMOSSTT MASTOIDITIS
ADIIINNOSTV DIVINATIONS
ADIIINOOSTX OXIDISATION
ADIIINOOTXZ OXIDIZATION
ADIIINOPSST DISSIPATION
ADIIILLMNOOT TOIL AND MOIL
ADIILLNOQRU QUADRILLION
ADIILMNNOST MANDOLINIST
ADIILMOPSTT DIPLOMATIST
ADIILOQRSTU LIQUIDATORS
ADIIMNNOOST ADMONITIONS
ADIIMNOOPST ADOPTIONISM
ADIIMORSTUU AUDITORIUMS
ADIINNNOSTU INUNDATIONS
ADIINNOORST ORDINATIONS
ADIINOOPSTT ADOPTIONIST
ADIINOPSTTU DISPUTATION
ADIIOOPRSUV AVOIRDUPOIS
ADIIOPRSSTT PODIATRISTS
ADIIOPSTTUY AUDIOTYPIST
ADIKLOOSTVV VLADIVOSTOK
ADILLLOOPPY POLYPLOIDAL
ADILMNOOSTU MODULATIONS
ADILNNOSTUU UNDULATIONS
ADILOOSSTWW SOW WILD OATS
ADILORRSTTU STRIDULATOR
ADILOSSSUUY ASSIDUOUSLY
ADIMOOPRSUY MYRIAPODOUS
ADINNOPSSTT STANDPOINTS
ADJLOPRSTUU PLATS DU JOUR
ADLNOOPRSUY POLYANDROUS
ADLNOOPRSWY PLAY ON WORDS
ADNNORRSTUU TURNAROUNDS
ADNOOPRRSTU PROTANDROUS
ADOOOPRSSUU SAUROPODOUS
AEEEEGKMPRS GAMEKEEPERS
AEEEEGKPRST GATEKEEPERS
AEEEEHILRST ETHEREALISE
AEEEEHILRTZ ETHEREALIZE
AEEEEHLRTTT LEATHERETTE
AEEEENRSVWY NEW YEAR'S EVE

AEEEFFLOPPT TOFFEE APPLE
AEEEFFLORRT FREE-FLOATER
AEEEFGIKNPS SAFEKEEPING
AEEEFGIRRRT REFRIGERATE
AEEEFHINRRT HEREINAFTER
AEEEFILNRRT REFERENTIAL
AEEEFLLNNTT FLANNELETTE
AEEEFLNSSSU EASEFULNESS
AEEEFLRSSTU FEATURELESS
AEEEFPRSTTU SUPERFETATE
AEEEGGHIMTV GIVE THE GAME
AEEEGGIKMNP GAMEKEEPING
AEEEGGILNOS GENEALOGIES
AEEEGGIRSTV SEGREGATIVE
AEEEGGMMNOU EMMENAGOGUE
AEEEGGMNNST ENGAGEMENTS
AEEEGHLPRRT TELEGRAPHER
AEEEGHNPRTW GREAT-NEPHEW
AEEEGHNRTWY GET ANYWHERE
AEEEGHORRTT THEATREGOER
AEEEGILNRRS GENERALISER
AEEEGILNRRZ GENERALIZER
AEEEGILNRSV EVANGELISER
AEEEGILNRVZ EVANGELIZER
AEEEGIMNNST STEAM-ENGINE
AEEEGIMNSST METAGENESIS
AEEEGINORTT RENEGOTIATE
AEEEGINPRRT PEREGRINATE
AEEEGKLOPRS GOALKEEPERS
AEEEGKLPRRU KEEP REGULAR
AEEEGLMNNRT ENLARGEMENT
AEEEGLNNRSS GENERALNESS
AEEEGLNSSSS AGELESSNESS
AEEEGMNNRSS GERMANENESS
AEEEGNPPRRS GREEN PAPERS
AEEEHHNNSST HEATHENNESS
AEEEHILNNPT ELEPHANTINE
AEEEHILRTTY ETHEREALITY
AEEEHIMSSTT METATHESISE
AEEEHIMSTTZ METATHESIZE
AEEEHINSSTT ANESTHETISE
AEEEHINSTTZ ANESTHETIZE
AEEEHIRSTWW WEATHER-WISE
AEEEHKMOOPW MAKE WHOOPEE
AEEEHLLMPRY EPHEMERALLY
AEEEHLMPPRT PAMPHLETEER
AEEEHLPRRWY PRAYER WHEEL
AEEEHLRSTWW WATERWHEELS
AEEEHNNORRW NOWHERE NEAR
AEEEHNPRSST PARENTHESES
AEEEHRSSTTW SWEETHEARTS
AEEEIILNRRT INERTIA REEL
AEEEIINPPRT PERIPETEIAN
AEEEIIRRTTV REITERATIVE

AEEEILNORRS SIERRA LEONE
AEEEILNRRTT INTERRELATE
AEEEILNRRTV REVERENTIAL
AEEEILNRSTX EXTERNALISE
AEEEILNRTXZ EXTERNALIZE
AEEEILPRRTT PRELITERATE
AEEEIMNPRTT INTEMPERATE
AEEEIMNRTTX EXTERMINATE
AEEEIMNRTUV ENUMERATIVE
AEEEINNRRTT ENTERTAINER
AEEEINOPRSU EUROPEANISE
AEEEINOPRUZ EUROPEANIZE
AEEEINORTVX EXONERATIVE
AEEEINPRRTTV PENETRATIVE
AEEEINRRTVW INTERWEAVER
AEEEINSSSVV EVASIVENESS
AEEEJKRRRST TEARJERKERS
AEEEJLMSSTY LESE-MAJESTY
AEEEKKPPRRS PARK KEEPERS
AEEEKLLOSTX EXOSKELETAL
AEEEKLLPRSW SLEEPWALKER
AEEEKPSSSTW SWEEPSTAKES
AEEELLOPPSS SALESPEOPLE
AEEELLORTTT TEETOTALLER
AEEELLRSTVW WATER LEVELS
AEEELMMNNPT EMPANELMENT
AEEELMNNSTV ENSLAVEMENT
AEEELMRSSSU MEASURELESS
AEEELNOPPVY PAY ENVELOPE
AEEELRSTTUV STREET VALUE
AEEEMMNORST ANEMOMETERS
AEEEMMNPRTT TEMPERAMENT
AEEEMMNRSTU MEASUREMENT
AEEEMNNNRST ENSNAREMENT
AEEEMNNRTTT ENTREATMENT
AEEEMNOPSSS OPEN SESAMES
AEEEMNOSSSW AWESOMENESS
AEEEMNPRSTT PENTAMETERS
AEEEMNRSTTT RESTATEMENT
AEEEMPRRTTU TEMPERATURE
AEEENNRSSST EARNESTNESS
AEEENOPRSTT STEAROPTENE
AEEENPRRSTV PERSEVERANT
AEEENRSSSTU AUSTERENESS
AEEEQRSSTTU SEQUESTRATE
AEEFFGRSTTU SUFFRAGETTE
AEEFFHORRST FOREFATHERS
AEEFFILMRTU FEATURE FILM
AEEFFLLORRS FREE-FOR-ALLS
AEEFFLNRSSU FEARFULNESS
AEEFFLNSSTU FATEFULNESS
AEEFGHORRTT HETEROGRAFT
AEEFGILLNSS SELF-SEALING
AEEFGILNPRT FINGERPLATE

AEEFGILNRRS RIFLE RANGES
AEEFGINRRRT REFRIGERANT
AEEFHHIKNST SHEATH KNIFE
AEEFHHORSTU HOUSEFATHER
AEEFHILNNPS HALFPENNIES
AEEFHLLMNST MANTELSHELF
AEEFHLNSSTU HATEFULNESS
AEEFIILNNRT INFERENTIAL
AEEFIILOTVX EXFOLIATIVE
AEEFIIRRRSS FIRE-RAISERS
AEEFILLNRST SELF-RELIANT
AEEFILMRSTY FAMILY TREES
AEEFILOPRRT PROLIFERATE
AEEFIMNNRRT REFRAINMENT
AEEFIMNOSST MANIFESTOES
AEEFIMOPRRT IMPERFORATE
AEEFIMORRTV REFORMATIVE
AEEFINRRRST FRATERNISER
AEEFINRRRTZ FRATERNIZER
AEEFIOPRRTV PERFORATIVE
AEEFKLNSSUW WAKEFULNESS
AEEFLLORRST FORESTALLER
AEEFLLPRSUU PLEASUREFUL
AEEFLNRSSTU TEARFULNESS
AEEFLRRSSTT SELF-STARTER
AEEFMNORRSY FREEMASONRY
AEEFNNOPRSS PROFANENESS
AEEFNORRSVW WAR OF NERVES
AEEFOQRRRTU FOREQUARTER
AEEGGGINRST SEGREGATING
AEEGGHIOPRS GEOGRAPHIES
AEEGGHOPRRS GEOGRAPHERS
AEEGGIINORS SEIGNIORAGE
AEEGGIKLNOP GOALKEEPING
AEEGGILNOST GENEALOGIST
AEEGGIMNOSS GAMOGENESIS
AEEGGINORST SEGREGATION
AEEGGINQSTU GIGANTESQUE
AEEGGINRRRS GRANGERISER
AEEGGINRRRZ GRANGERIZER
AEEGGIRRTTU REGURGITATE
AEEGGORSTTY GEOSTRATEGY
AEEGHHITVWY HEAVYWEIGHT
AEEGHHMORRS HEMORRHAGES
AEEGHIILMNS HEGELIANISM
AEEGHILNPRS GENERALSHIP
AEEGHILNPSS SINGLE-PHASE
AEEGHINNRTT THREATENING
AEEGHINORRV OVERHEARING
AEEGHINORVZ HERZEGOVINA
AEEGHIPPRTW PAPERWEIGHT
AEEGHLNOPRS SELENOGRAPH
AEEGHLNSTVW WAVELENGTHS
AEEGHLORSTT ALTOGETHERS

AEEGHLRRSTU SLAUGHTERER
AEEGHMOOPRT GAMETOPHORE
AEEGHMOPTTY GAMETOPHYTE
AEEGHOPRRRX XEROGRAPHER
AEEGHOPRRST STEREOGRAPH
AEEGHOPSSSU ESOPHAGUSES
AEEGIILLSTV LEGISLATIVE
AEEGIILNNOR LEGIONNAIRE
AEEGIILNORS LEGIONARIES
AEEGIILNRST GELATINISER
AEEGIILNRTZ GELATINIZER
AEEGIINRRTT REITERATING
AEEGIINRTTV INTEGRATIVE,
  VINAIGRETTE
AEEGIINSTTV INVESTIGATE
AEEGILLMNNP EMPANELLING
AEEGILLMNNW WELL-MEANING
AEEGILLNNTY INELEGANTLY
AEEGILLNRVY REVEALINGLY
AEEGILLRSTU LEGISLATURE
AEEGILMNNRT ENGRAILMENT,
  REALIGNMENT
AEEGILMNNSS MEANINGLESS
AEEGILMNRRS MALINGERERS
AEEGILMNRST REGIMENTALS
AEEGILNNRRT INTERREGNAL
AEEGILNRSTV EVERLASTING
AEEGILNSSTV EVANGELISTS
AEEGIMNNRTU ENUMERATING
AEEGIMNNRUV MANEUVERING
AEEGIMSSTTU GUESSTIMATE
AEEGINNORST GENERATIONS
AEEGINNORTX EXONERATING
AEEGINNPRTT PENETRATING
AEEGINNRSTV EVENING STAR
AEEGINNTTUX EXTENUATING
AEEGINORRRS REORGANISER
AEEGINORRRZ REORGANIZER
AEEGINORRTT INTERROGATE
AEEGINOSSTU AUTOGENESIS
AEEGIOPRRTV PREROGATIVE
AEEGIPPRRST PAPER TIGERS
AEEGLLMNNTY GENTLEMANLY
AEEGLLMORTU GLOMERULATE
AEEGLLOPSWY YELLOW PAGES
AEEGLMNNOTW GENTLEWOMAN
AEEGLMNOOPR PROLEGOMENA
AEEGLOOPRRT PORTO ALEGRE
AEEGLORSTUV TRAVELOGUES
AEEGMNNNORT MONTENEGRAN
AEEGMNORRTV OVERGARMENT
AEEGNNORSSS SENSE ORGANS
AEEGNNRSSST STRANGENESS
AEEGNORSSTV GRAVESTONES

AEEGNOSSSSU GASEOUSNESS
AEEGNPRSSST PRESS AGENTS
AEEHHHOSTTV HAVE THE HOTS
AEEHHILNSST HEALTHINESS
AEEHHILRTWW WHEREWITHAL
AEEHHIPRSTW WEATHER SHIP
AEEHHISSTWW WHITEWASHER
AEEHHISSTWW WHITEWASHES
AEEHHMORSTV HARVEST HOME
AEEHHNORSTT HEARTHSTONE
AEEHIILMOPT EPITHELIOMA
AEEHIKLLLRW KILLER WHALE
AEEHIKLNRSS HARNESS-LIKE
AEEHIKNSTTV HAVE KITTENS
AEEHIKPPRSS SPEAKERSHIP
AEEHIKPSSTT TAKE THE PISS
AEEHILLMOST MESOTHELIAL
AEEHILLMRTY HEMIELYTRAL
AEEHILMMNTY METHYLAMINE
AEEHILMSTTW WHITE METALS
AEEHILNNOST STENOHALINE
AEEHILNPPRS PLANISPHERE
AEEHILNPSSS SHAPELINESS
AEEHILNRSST EARTHLINESS
AEEHILNSSTW WEALTHINESS
AEEHILPPRRS PERIPHERALS
AEEHILPSTTT TELEPATHIST
AEEHILRSTVW WHITE-SLAVER
AEEHILSSTTT STEALTHIEST
AEEHIMMNRST HAMMERSTEIN
AEEHIMNSTTY AMETHYSTINE
AEEHINPRSST PARENTHESIS
AEEHINSSTTT ANESTHETIST
AEEHIOOPRTT HETEROTOPIA
AEEHIOOPSST APOTHEOSISE
AEEHIOOPSTZ APOTHEOSIZE
AEEHIORSTTX HETEROTAXIS
AEEHIORTTVX EXHORTATIVE
AEEHIPPRRSS PERIPHRASES
AEEHIPPRSTW WHITE PAPERS
AEEHKMPRRTY HYPERMARKET
AEEHLLMSSSY SHAMELESSLY
AEEHLLORSSW WHOLESALERS
AEEHLLPSSSY SHAPELESSLY
AEEHLLRSSTY HEARTLESSLY
AEEHLMNNRTT ENTHRALMENT
AEEHLMORSTY HEARTSOMELY
AEEHLMOSSTV STEAM SHOVEL
AEEHLMOSTTY STATELY HOME
AEEHLMPRSSW SPERM WHALES
AEEHLMRRTUY EURYTHERMAL
AEEHLNPSSSS HAPLESSNESS
AEEHLNRSSSS HARNESSLESS
AEEHLOOPRRT HETEROPOLAR

AEEHLPPRRTU PURPLE HEART	AEEIILLMMNPT IMPLEMENTAL
AEEHLRSSSTV HARVESTLESS	AEEIILLMNOPS PSILOMELANE
AEEHLRSSTTX TAX SHELTERS	AEEIILLMPRXY EXEMPLARILY
AEEHMNOPRST METANEPHROS	AEEIILLNNPRY PERENNIALLY
AEEHMNORSWW WASHERWOMEN	AEEIILLNOPPT EN PAPILLOTE
AEEHMOPRSST ATMOSPHERES	AEEIILLNRSST LITERALNESS
AEEHMOPRSTU HEPTAMEROUS	AEEIILLNSSTY ESSENTIALLY
AEEHMORSSTU HOUSEMASTER	AEEIILLPRSTV SILVER PLATE
AEEHNOPRSTU HOUSEPARENT	AEEIILMNNSTT SENTIMENTAL
AEEHNORRSTT NORTHEASTER	AEEIILMNORST SALINOMETER
AEEHNPPSTVY HAPPY EVENTS	AEEIILMNPRST SEMPITERNAL
AEEHOOPRRSS HORSE OPERAS	AEEIILMNPTTU PENULTIMATE
AEEHOOPRSST PEASHOOTERS	AEEIILMNRSTX EXTERNALISM
AEEHOPRRSST ASTROSPHERE	AEEIILMNSSSS AIMLESSNESS
AEEHORRSSTU HOUSE ARREST	AEEIILMNSSWY WESLEYANISM
AEEHORSSTTU SOUTHEASTER	AEEIILMOPRRT POLARIMETER
AEEHRSSSTUU THESAURUSES	AEEIILMORRST SOLARIMETER
AEEIIILMNTV ELIMINATIVE	AEEIILMOSTTT TEETOTALISM
AEEIIINNNST EINSTEINIAN	AEEIILMPPRRS PERISPERMAL
AEEIIINRRST ITINERARIES	AEEIILNNOPTX EXPONENTIAL
AEEIILLRRST ARTILLERIES	AEEIILNNOSTX EXTENSIONAL
AEEIILLRSTW WATER LILIES	AEEIILNNSSST SALIENTNESS
AEEIILMMORS MEMORIALISE	AEEIILNNSSTU UNESSENTIAL
AEEIILMMORZ MEMORIALIZE	AEEIILNNSTTU LIEUTENANTS
AEEIILMNRRS MINERALISER	AEEIILNOPRSS PERSONALISE
AEEIILMNRRZ MINERALIZER	AEEIILNOPRSZ PERSONALIZE
AEEIILMNSTT MENTALITIES	AEEIILNOPRTT INTERPOLATE
AEEIILMORTV MELIORATIVE	AEEIILNORSTV REVELATIONS
AEEIILMRRST SEMITRAILER	AEEIILNPSTTV SEPTIVALENT
AEEIILNNPTT PENITENTIAL	AEEIILNPSVXY EXPANSIVELY
AEEIILNNRRT INTERLINEAR	AEEIILNQSTUV EQUIVALENTS
AEEIILNNRST INTERNALISE	AEEIILNRRSTU NEUTRALISER
AEEIILNNRTZ INTERNALIZE	AEEIILNRRTUZ NEUTRALIZER
AEEIILNNSST INESSENTIAL	AEEIILNRSSSS AIRLESSNESS
AEEIILNORST ORIENTALISE	AEEIILNRSTTX EXTERNALIST
AEEIILNORTZ ORIENTALIZE	AEEIILNRSTUX INTERSEXUAL
AEEIILNSTTX EXISTENTIAL	AEEIILNRTTXY EXTERNALITY
AEEIILNTTVV VENTILATIVE	AEEIILNSSSTT STATELINESS
AEEIILQRRSU RELIQUARIES	AEEIILNTTTVY ATTENTIVELY,
AEEIIMNRTTV TERMINATIVE	TENTATIVELY
AEEIIMNSSTT ANTI-SEMITES	AEEIILNTTUVY EVENTUALITY
AEEIIMNSSTW SIAMESE TWIN	AEEIILOPPRTT TOILET PAPER
AEEIIMPRSTV IMPERATIVES	AEEIILOPRRRT REPERTORIAL
AEEIIMPRTTV IMPETRATIVE	AEEIILORTTTW TOILET WATER
AEEIINNTTTV INATTENTIVE	AEEIILPPRRSV SILVER PAPER
AEEIINOPRTV INOPERATIVE	AEEIILPRSTUV SUPERLATIVE
AEEIINORRTT REITERATION	AEEIILPRSVVY PERVASIVELY
AEEIIPRSSST PATISSERIES	AEEIILPSTTUX EXSTIPULATE
AEEIIPRTTVX EXTIRPATIVE	AEEIILQRRSTU QUARTERLIES
AEEIIRSSTTU AUSTERITIES	AEEILRRRSTT TERRESTRIAL
AEEIKMNSTTU MINUTE STEAK	AEEILRSTTU LITERATURES
AEEIKNPPRSV PAPER KNIVES	AEEILRRTTTU LITTERATEUR
AEEIKNRSSST STREAKINESS	AEEILRSSTVY ASSERTIVELY
AEEIKRRSSTW WATER SKIERS	AEEIMMNNPRT IMPERMANENT

AEEIMMRRSTT TETRAMERISM
AEEIMNNNOQU MENAQUINONE
AEEIMNNNRTT ENTRAINMENT
AEEIMNNORTU ENUMERATION,
   MOUNTAINEER
AEEIMNNPRST PINE MARTENS
AEEIMNNSTTT INSTATEMENT
AEEIMNOPRST IMPERSONATE
AEEIMNOPRSU EUROPEANISM
AEEIMNORSST MONASTERIES
AEEIMNORSTT MARIONETTES
AEEIMNOSSTT MAISONETTES
AEEIMNRSTUV MENSURATIVE
AEEIMNSSSSV MASSIVENESS
AEEIMOPRRTV VAPORIMETER
AEEIMORRSTU TEMERARIOUS
AEEIMQRSSUV SEMIQUAVERS
AEEIMQRSTTU MARQUISETTE
AEEIMSSSTTY SYSTEMATISE
AEEIMSSTTYZ SYSTEMATIZE
AEEINNOORTX EXONERATION
AEEINNOPRTT PENETRATION
AEEINNORSTV ANTEVERSION
AEEINNOTTUV EVENTUATION
AEEINNOTTUX EXTENUATION
AEEINOPRSTV PERSONATIVE
AEEINORRSTV RESERVATION
AEEINPSSSSV PASSIVENESS
AEEIOPPRRTX EXPROPRIATE
AEEIORRSTTV RESTORATIVE
AEEIORSSTTX STEREOTAXIS
AEEIPRRSSTU PASTEURISER
AEEIPRRSTUZ PASTEURIZER
AEEIPRSSSTT SPESSARTITE, STRIPTEASES
AEEJNORRTUV REJUVENATOR
AEEKLLORRST ROLLER SKATE
AEEKLMORRTW METALWORKER
AEEKMMNORSY MONEYMAKERS
AEEKMMRRRSY MERRYMAKERS
AEEKMPRRSTU SUPERMARKET
AEEKNPRRSTU SUPERTANKER
AEELLMNRSTU ALLUREMENTS
AEELLMORRST STEAMROLLER
AEELLNORRTT RETROLENTAL
AEELLNORSTW STONEWALLER
AEELLNPRTVY PREVALENTLY
AEELLNSSSSW LAWLESSNESS
AEELLOPRTUV POLE VAULTER
AEELLORSTTY TEA TROLLEYS
AEELLPPRTUY PERPETUALLY
AEELLSSSTTY TASTELESSLY
AEELMMORTTV VOLTAMMETER
AEELMNNOSTT MENTAL NOTES
AEELMNNPRTY PERMANENTLY

AEELMNNRTUV UNRAVELMENT
AEELMNORSTW WATERMELONS
AEELMOPRSTT PLASTOMETER
AEELMOQRRSU QUARRELSOME
AEELMPRRTUY PREMATURELY
AEELNNPRTTY REPENTANTLY
AEELNNQSSUU UNEQUALNESS
AEELNNSSSSU SENSUALNESS
AEELNOPRSSS SALESPERSON
AEELNOPRSST PROLATENESS
AEELNOSSSUZ ZEALOUSNESS
AEELNRSSSST ARTLESSNESS
AEELOPSTTUX EXPOSTULATE
AEELORSSTTU LOTUS-EATERS
AEEMNOPRRTY PYRANOMETER
AEEMNOPRSTU PENTAMEROUS
AEEMNORRRTU REMUNERATOR
AEEMNORRSTT REMONSTRATE
AEEMNORSSTT EASTERNMOST
AEEMNSSSSST ASSESSMENTS
AEEMORRSTTU TETRAMEROUS
AEEMPRRSTTU EAR TRUMPETS
AEENNOOPSSS OPEN SEASONS
AEENNOPRRTU NEUROPTERAN
AEENOPRRSTT PATERNOSTER
AEENOQRRTTU QUARTER NOTE
AEENORTTUXY EXTENUATORY
AEENPPRSSTT STEPPARENTS
AEENQRSSTTU SEQUESTRANT
AEEOOPSTTTW SWEET POTATO
AEEOPPRRRTT PERPETRATOR
AEEPRSSSWXY EXPRESSWAYS
AEFFGIIMNRR REAFFIRMING
AEFFGIMSTUU SUFFUMIGATE
AEFFGINORST AFFORESTING
AEFFHHILTTU THE FAITHFUL
AEFFHIKMOTW MAKE OFF WITH
AEFFHINRSSS RAFFISHNESS
AEFFIIMNORR FORAMINIFER
AEFFIKLLOSW WALKS OF LIFE
AEFFIRSSTTY SAFETY-FIRST
AEFFKNRRRTU FRANKFURTER
AEFFNRSSSTU STAFF NURSES
AEFGGHIRSTT STAGE FRIGHT
AEFGGIMNNRT FRAGMENTING
AEFGHORSTTU SOUGHT-AFTER
AEFGIIINRRS FIRE-RAISING
AEFGIILNNRS FINGERNAILS
AEFGIIMNNST MANIFESTING
AEFGILLLNNN FLANNELLING
AEFGILLNRST FINGERSTALL
AEFGILLNRTY FALTERINGLY
AEFGILNNRTU UNFALTERING
AEFGILNNSSU GAINFULNESS

AEFGILOPRST PROFLIGATES
AEFGINNNSSW FAWNINGNESS
AEFGINNORRW FOREWARNING
AEFGINOPRRT PERFORATING
AEFGINORRSW FORSWEARING
AEFGINRRSTU TRANSFIGURE
AEFGIPRRSTU GRAPEFRUITS
AEFHHLLLTUY HEALTHFULLY
AEFHILLSSTY FAITHLESSLY
AEFHILRSSST HALF-SISTERS
AEFHIMNOPRS FOREMANSHIP
AEFHKOORTTU OUT OF THE ARK
AEFHLLLOSVY HALF VOLLEYS
AEFHLMNRSSU HARMFULNESS
AEFHMORRSTT FARTHERMOST
AEFHOOTTUWY OUT-OF-THE-WAY
AEFIIIMNRRS INFIRMARIES
AEFIIKLNNRT FRANKLINITE
AEFIILLNNTU INFLUENTIAL
AEFIILMORST FORMALITIES
AEFIILNNRTY INFERNALITY
AEFIILNOOTX EXFOLIATION
AEFIILOPRRW PRAIRIE WOLF
AEFIIMNORTV INFORMATIVE
AEFIINNOSTT FESTINATION,
    INFESTATION, SINFONIETTA
AEFIINNRSTT TRANSFINITE
AEFIINOPRST PROFANITIES
AEFIINORSTT FIRE STATION
AEFIINQRSTU QUANTIFIERS
AEFILLLMMOR LAMELLIFORM
AEFILLMOPRT PATELLIFORM
AEFILLRRTTU ULTRAFILTER
AEFILLRSTVY RIFT VALLEYS
AEFILMORRSU FORMULARISE
AEFILMORRUZ FORMULARIZE
AEFILMORTVY FORMATIVELY
AEFILMPRSUY SUPERFAMILY
AEFILNNPSSU PAINFULNESS
AEFILNORSUY NEFARIOUSLY
AEFILOOPRST FORE-TOPSAIL
AEFILOOPSTY PLAY FOOTSIE
AEFILOPRRTY PREFATORILY
AEFIMMMORSU MAMMIFEROUS
AEFIMNNNRTY INFANTRYMEN
AEFIMNNOOTT FOMENTATION
AEFIMNOORRT REFORMATION
AEFINNNOPTU FOUNTAIN PEN
AEFINNRRRST TRANSFERRIN
AEFINOOPRRT PERFORATION
AEFINOORSTT FORESTATION
AEFINORRSST RAIN FORESTS
AEFINORSTTU REFUTATIONS
AEFINRSSTUV TRANSFUSIVE

AEFKLLOORRW FLOORWALKER
AEFLLLOPRUW ALL-POWERFUL
AEFLLLOPSWY PLAYFELLOWS
AEFLLLORSWW WALLFLOWERS
AEFLLLSSTUY FAULTLESSLY
AEFLLMRSTUY MASTERFULLY
AEFLLNPSSUY PLAYFULNESS
AEFLLORSSUV FLAVOURLESS
AEFLMOORSUV FLAVOURSOME
AEFLNORTTUY FORTUNATELY
AEFLORRSTWW STRAWFLOWER
AEFLRSSTTWY FLYSWATTERS
AEFMNORRRST TRANSFORMER
AEFMOOPRSTT FORE-TOPMAST
AEFMOORRRTY REFORMATORY
AEFNNORTTUU UNFORTUNATE
AEFNORRSTTW WATERFRONTS
AEFNOSSSTUU FATUOUSNESS
AEFOOPRRSTW WATERPROOFS
AEGGGNORSTU GO GREAT GUNS
AEGGHHINSSS HAGGISHNESS
AEGGHIILNNT NIGHTINGALE
AEGGHIIRRRT HAIR TRIGGER
AEGGHILNRST RIGHT ANGLES
AEGGHINSSSW WAGGISHNESS
AEGGHLOOPRR LOGOGRAPHER
AEGGIILLNST LEGISLATING
AEGGIILMNNR MALINGERING
AEGGIILMPRS PILGRIMAGES
AEGGIIMNNRT GERMINATING
AEGGIIMNNTZ MAGNETIZING
AEGGIINNOTT NEGOTIATING
AEGGIINNRTT INTEGRATING
AEGGIINRTTU INGURGITATE
AEGGILNNORW LONGWEARING
AEGGILNNRSS GLARINGNESS
AEGGILRSSTT STRAGGLIEST
AEGGIMNOSST MAGGOTINESS
AEGGINNOTXY OXYGENATING
AEGGINPRTUX EXPURGATING
AEGGINRRTTU REGURGITANT
AEGGJNRSTUU JUGGERNAUTS
AEGHHILOPRS HELIOGRAPHS
AEGHHILOPRY HELIOGRAPHY
AEGHHINNPTY HYPHENATING
AEGHHINORST HIGH TREASON
AEGHHINSSTU HAUGHTINESS
AEGHHLOPRSU PLOUGHSHARE
AEGHHLORSSU HORSELAUGHS
AEGHHMOPRRT THERMOGRAPH
AEGHHNOPRTY ETHNOGRAPHY
AEGHHNOSTTU THAT'S ENOUGH!
AEGHIIKMNNT IN THE MAKING
AEGHIILMSTT ALMIGHTIEST

AEGHIIMNPSZ EMPHASIZING
AEGHIIMNRST TIME-SHARING
AEGHIIPPRST EPIGRAPHIST
AEGHILLNNRT ENTHRALLING
AEGHILLNOPS ANGLOPHILES
AEGHILNNSST HALTINGNESS
AEGHILNOOST ANTHOLOGIES,
   ANTHOLOGISE, THEOLOGIANS
AEGHILNOOTZ ANTHOLOGIZE
AEGHILNORUV OVERHAULING
AEGHILNOTTU GLUTATHIONE
AEGHILNSSST GHASTLINESS
AEGHIMMOPRS MIMEOGRAPHS
AEGHIMNNRST GARNISHMENT
AEGHIMOPRSS SEISMOGRAPH
AEGHINNSSTU NAUGHTINESS
AEGHIRSSTTT STRAIGHTEST
AEGHLNOOORR GONORRHOEAL
AEGHLOOPRSY PHRASEOLOGY
AEGHLOPPRYY PYELOGRAPHY
AEGHLOPRRXY XYLOGRAPHER
AEGHLORSSSU HOURGLASSES
AEGHLOSSSSU GLASSHOUSES
AEGHMNOOPRR MONOGRAPHER,
   NOMOGRAPHER
AEGHMNOOPRS GRAMOPHONES
AEGHMNOPPRU PNEUMOGRAPH
AEGHNOOPRRS NOSOGRAPHER
AEGHNOPRSTY STENOGRAPHY
AEGHNOPSSTU STENOPHAGUS
AEGHOOPPRRT TOPOGRAPHER
AEGHOPPRRRY PYROGRAPHER,
   REPROGRAPHY
AEGHOPPRRSS GRASSHOPPER
AEGHOPPRRTY PETROGRAPHY,
   TYPOGRAPHER
AEGIIILMNNT ELIMINATING
AEGIIILNRSZ SERIALIZING
AEGIIINSTTV INSTIGATIVE
AEGIIKLLNRT GIANT KILLER
AEGIIKNRSST ASTERISKING
AEGIIKNRSTW WATER SKIING
AEGIILLMNNP IMPANELLING
AEGIILLNOST LEGISLATION
AEGIILLNRTT ILL-TREATING
AEGIILLSTVY VESTIGIALLY
AEGIILMNORS REGIONALISM
AEGIILMNSST TIME SIGNALS
AEGIILNNRTU INTERLINGUA
AEGIILNNTTV VENTILATING
AEGIILNORST REGIONALIST
AEGIILNRSSU SINGULARISE
AEGIILNRSUZ SINGULARIZE
AEGIILOOSTT AETIOLOGIST

AEGIILRSTUV VULGARITIES
AEGIIMMMNUW MINIMUM WAGE
AEGIIMMORRR MIRROR IMAGE
AEGIIMNNORT GERMINATION
AEGIIMNNRTT TERMINATING
AEGIIMNORST EMIGRATIONS
AEGIIMPRSTU EPIGASTRIUM
AEGIIMRSSTT STIGMATISER
AEGIIMRSTTZ STIGMATIZER
AEGIINNOOTT NEGOTIATION
AEGIINNORST RESIGNATION
AEGIINNORTT INTEGRATION,
   ORIENTATING
AEGIINNRRST RESTRAINING
AEGIINNRSTT REINSTATING
AEGIINORSST SIGNATORIES
AEGIINPPRTW WIRE-TAPPING
AEGIINPRTTX EXTIRPATING
AEGIJLNRUUV JUGULAR VEIN
AEGIKMMNNOY MONEYMAKING
AEGIKMMNRRY MERRYMAKING
AEGILLMNNTY LAMENTINGLY
AEGILLMOOPS MEGALOPOLIS
AEGILLNNRUV UNRAVELLING
AEGILLNOPRY ROLE PLAYING
AEGILLNOPST SELLOTAPING
AEGILLNQRRU QUARRELLING
AEGILLORSST LEGISLATORS
AEGILLPRSSU ASPERGILLUS
AEGILLRRRUY IRREGULARLY
AEGILMMNOTU GEMMULATION
AEGILMNOORT GLOMERATION
AEGILMNOPRU PELARGONIUM
AEGILMNOSTU LIGAMENTOUS
AEGILMOOSSY SEMASIOLOGY
AEGILNNOOST ELONGATIONS
AEGILNOOSSX XENOGLOSSIA
AEGILNOPPRV OVERLAPPING
AEGILNOPRVY OVERPLAYING
AEGILNORSTU REGULATIONS
AEGILNPRSTT SPLATTERING
AEGILNQRUVY QUAVERINGLY
AEGILNRRSTY ARRESTINGLY
AEGILNRSSTV STARVELINGS
AEGILOOSTTU TAUTOLOGIES,
   TAUTOLOGISE
AEGILOOTTUZ TAUTOLOGIZE
AEGILRSTTUU GUTTURALISE
AEGILRTTUUZ GUTTURALIZE
AEGIMMOPRSU GEMMIPAROUS
AEGIMNNNORT ORNAMENTING
AEGIMNNNORV OVERMANNING
AEGIMNNNRTU RUNNING MATE
AEGIMNNORUV MANOEUVRING

AEGIMNNSSST ASSIGNMENTS
AEGIMNOPRRT IMPREGNATOR
AEGIMNORSSU IGNORAMUSES
AEGIMNRRSST RINGMASTERS
AEGIMNRSSTT SMATTERINGS
AEGINNNORSU UNREASONING
AEGINNOORRV VINEGARROON
AEGINNOOTXY OXYGENATION
AEGINNOPSTV PAVING STONE
AEGINNOSSUU SANGUINEOUS
AEGINNPRRTU ENRAPTURING
AEGINNPRSSS SPARINGNESS
AEGINNRSSTT ASTRINGENTS
AEGINOORSTT NEGOTIATORS
AEGINOPRTUX EXPURGATION
AEGINOQSTTU QUESTION TAG
AEGINORSTTV OVERSTATING
AEGINORSTVY OVERSTAYING
AEGINPRSSST TRESPASSING
AEGIPRRRTYY PYRARGYRITE
AEGIRSSSTTT STRATEGISTS
AEGKLORRSSW GLASS-WORKER
AEGKMNOSSXY OXYGEN MASKS
AEGLOORRSST ASTROLOGERS
AEGMMOPRRRS PROGRAMMERS
AEGMNOORSST GASTRONOMES
AEGNOOPRSSY GREASY SPOON
AEGOORRRTUV ROTOGRAVURE
AEGOPRRTUXY EXPURGATORY
AEHHIIILNNS HSIN-HAI-LIEN
AEHHIKNSSSW HAWKISHNESS
AEHHILLNTUY UNHEALTHILY
AEHHIMMMRST HAMMERSMITH
AEHHIMOPRTY HYPOTHERMIA
AEHHINNOPTY HYPHENATION
AEHHIOPPSST PHOSPHATISE
AEHHIOPPSTZ PHOSPHATIZE
AEHHIORTTTW WHITETHROAT
AEHHLLOPTTY THALLOPHYTE
AEHHLMMOORT HOMOTHERMAL
AEHHMOOOPST HOMOEOPATHS
AEHHMOOOPTY HOMOEOPATHY
AEHHMOSSTUW MOUTHWASHES
AEHHNOPRRTY TENORRHAPHY
AEHHOOPPRST PHOSPHORATE
AEHIIILMTUV HUMILIATIVE
AEHIIILLOPRU AILUROPHILE
AEHIIILLPSTT PHILATELIST
AEHIILOPSST HOSPITALISE
AEHIILOPSTZ HOSPITALIZE
AEHIIMNRSTT MARTINETISH
AEHIINOPRRS PARISHIONER
AEHIINOSSTT HESITATIONS
AEHIIORSTTU AUTHORITIES

AEHIIPPRRSS PERIPHRASIS
AEHIKLNOOPR HARPOON-LIKE
AEHIKLNRSSS LARKISHNESS
AEHIKMNSSSW MAWKISHNESS
AEHILLOPPTY APOPHYLLITE
AEHILLOPRST HOSPITALLER
AEHILMNNOOP AMINOPHENOL
AEHILMNORTW MOTHER-IN-LAW
AEHILMNOTTY METHYLATION
AEHILMNRSTU LUTHERANISM
AEHILMQSSUY SQUEAMISHLY
AEHILMRRSTY ERYTHRISMAL
AEHILNPRRTY PLATYRRHINE
AEHILNPSSSS SPLASHINESS
AEHILNSSSSV SLAVISHNESS
AEHIMNNNSSS MANNISHNESS
AEHIMNOOPPR APOMORPHINE
AEHIMNOOPSS HOMO SAPIENS
AEHIMNOPRST MISANTHROPE
AEHIMNOSTUX EXHUMATIONS
AEHIMNSSSTU ENTHUSIASMS
AEHIMOOSSST HOMEOSTASIS
AEHIMOPSSTY HAEMOPTYSIS
AEHIMORSTTX THERMOTAXIS
AEHIMPPRSTU HIPPEASTRUM
AEHIMPRSSTY SYMPATHISER
AEHIMPRSTYZ SYMPATHIZER
AEHINNPPSSU UNHAPPINESS
AEHINOORSTT ANORTHOSITE
AEHINOORTTX EXHORTATION
AEHINOPSSTT STEPHANOTIS
AEHINORRSST ENARTHROSIS
AEHINORSSTT THROATINESS
AEHINPPRRST PARTNERSHIP
AEHINPSSSSW WASPISHNESS
AEHINQSSSSU SQUASHINESS
AEHINRSSSTW SWARTHINESS
AEHINSSSTTU ENTHUSIASTS
AEHIRSSSTTW SWEATSHIRTS
AEHJNOORRST TROJAN HORSE
AEHKLLNSSTY THANKLESSLY
AEHKLOPRSSW SHOPWALKERS
AEHLLMOOSTY LOATHSOMELY
AEHLLNOSSSW SHALLOWNESS
AEHLMNOQSSU LEMON SQUASH
AEHLMOOSSUX HOMOSEXUALS
AEHLMOPPRRY LAMPROPHYRE
AEHLNNOPSTT PENTATHLONS
AEHLNOPSSTU HOUSEPLANTS
AEHLOPPRSXY PROPHYLAXES
AEHMMOOOPRT OMMATOPHORE
AEHMNOORSSU MANOR HOUSES
AEHMNOORSTV HARVEST MOON
AEHMORSSTTT THERMOSTATS

AEHNOOPRRTT ORTHOPTERAN
AEHNOOPSSSU SOUSAPHONES
AEHOOOOPSTTT HOT POTATOES
AEHOOPPRSST APOSTROPHES
AEHOOPRRRST ARTHROSPORE
AEHOOPRRSTT TRAPSHOOTER
AEHOORSSSTY SOOTHSAYERS
AEHOQRRRTUU QUARTER-HOUR
AEIIIINSTTV INITIATIVES
AEIIIILLMNOR MILLIONAIRE
AEIIIILLMNST SILLIMANITE
AEIIIILLTTTV TITILLATIVE
AEIIIILMMPRS IMPERIALISM
AEIIIILMNNOT ELIMINATION
AEIIIILMNRST MINISTERIAL
AEIIIILMNSST ANTIMISSILE
AEIIIILMPRST IMPERIALIST
AEIIIILMRRSV VERISIMILAR
AEIIIILMTTVY IMITATIVELY
AEIIIIMNOSST ANIMOSITIES
AEIIIIMNOSTT ITEMISATION
AEIIIIMNOTTZ ITEMIZATION
AEIIIIMNRSTU MINIATURISE
AEIIIIMNRTUZ MINIATURIZE
AEIIIINNORTT ITINERATION
AEIIIINNSTUV INSINUATIVE
AEIIIINORSSV VISIONARIES
AEIIIINPRSTV INSPIRATIVE
AEIIIINQSTTU ANTIQUITIES
AEIIIINRSSTT INITIATRESS
AEIIIIPRSTTU PITUITARIES
AEIIKLLNPRS PAINKILLERS
AEIIKLLOPRT REALPOLITIK
AEIIILLMNORS MINERAL OILS
AEIIILLMSTTU SATELLITIUM
AEIIILLNPTVY PLAINTIVELY
AEIIILLNTUUX LUXULIANITE
AEIIILLPRSTU PLURALITIES
AEIIILMMORST IMMORTALISE,
   MEMORIALIST
AEIIILMMORTZ IMMORTALIZE
AEIIILMNNOPS MINNEAPOLIS
AEIIILMNOORT MELIORATION
AEIIILMNORST ORIENTALISM
AEIIILMNOSTT TESTIMONIAL
AEIIILMNPRRY PRELIMINARY
AEIIILMNPTTY IMPATIENTLY
AEIIILMORSTT MORTALITIES
AEIIILMPSSVY IMPASSIVELY
AEIIILMSTTUV STIMULATIVE
AEIIILNNNOST INTENSIONAL
AEIIILNNNOTT INTENTIONAL
AEIIILNNNOTV INVENTIONAL
AEIIILNNORST INSERTIONAL

AEIIILNNORTV INVENTORIAL
AEIIILNNOTTV VENTILATION
AEIIILNNRRST LINERTRAINS
AEIIILNNRTTY INTERNALITY
AEIIILNNSSST SAINTLINESS
AEIIILNORSSS INSESSORIAL
AEIIILNORSTT ORIENTALIST
AEIIILNORTTU ELUTRIATION
AEIIILNRSSTW SISTER-IN-LAW
AEIIILORRRTT TERRITORIAL
AEIIILPRSSST PERISTALSIS
AEIIILPRTTVY PARTITIVELY
AEIIILRSSTVV REVIVALISTS
AEIIILRSTTVY VERSATILITY
AEIIIMMNRSTT MARTINETISM
AEIIMNNOPRY AMINOPYRINE
AEIIIMNNORST INSEMINATOR,
   NITROSAMINE
AEIIMNNORTT TERMINATION
AEIIMNNORTV VERMINATION
AEIIMNNOSTV NOMINATIVES
AEIIMNOPRTT IMPETRATION
AEIIMOOPRST ISOMETROPIA
AEIIMOPPRRT IMPROPRIATE
AEIIMOPRRSS IMPRESARIOS
AEIIMRRTTUV TRIUMVIRATE
AEIINNNORTV INNERVATION
AEIINNNOTTT INATTENTION
AEIINNOORTT ORIENTATION
AEIINOPPSTT PEPTISATION
AEIINOPPTTZ PEPTIZATION
AEIINOPRRST RESPIRATION
AEIINOPRRTT PARTITIONER,
   REPARTITION
AEIINOPRTTX EXTIRPATION
AEIINOPRTTY PETITIONARY
AEIINOPSSTT POINSETTIAS
AEIINPRSSTY ANTIPYRESIS
AEIINRSSTTV TRANSITIVES
AEIINSSTTUV ANTITUSSIVE
AEIIOOPPSSS APOSIOPESIS
AEIIOOPRRST A POSTERIORI
AEIJLNORRSU JOURNALISER
AEIJLNORRUZ JOURNALIZER
AEIJMNOSSSS JAM SESSIONS
AEIKKLMNORW WORKMANLIKE
AEIKLNNOPPS PLAINSPOKEN
AEIKLNOPSTT KINETOPLAST
AEILLLMOSTY LAMELLOSITY
AEILLMMRSST SMALL-TIMERS
AEILLMNOOTY EMOTIONALLY
AEILLMNOSTY SEMITONALLY
AEILLMNOTTW LITTLE WOMAN
AEILLMNTTUV MULTIVALENT

AEILLNOPTTY POTENTIALLY
AEILLNOSSSY SILLY SEASON
AEILLNRSTUV SURVEILLANT
AEILLNRSUVY UNIVERSALLY
AEILLORSSTT TALL STORIES
AEILLORTTUV ULTRAVIOLET
AEILMMNORTY MOMENTARILY
AEILMNNNSSU UNMANLINESS
AEILMNNOPRT MINOR PLANET
AEILMNNOSSW WOMANLINESS
AEILMNNSSTT INSTALMENTS
AEILMNOOSTT MOLESTATION
AEILMNOPRRT TRAMPOLINER
AEILMNOPRSS PERSONALISM
AEILMNOPRST TRAMPOLINES
AEILMNORSTY SALINOMETRY
AEILMOPRRSU LEPROSARIUM
AEILMOPRRTY POLARIMETRY,
TEMPORARILY
AEILMOPRTTY TEMPORALITY
AEILMOPRTXY PROXIMATELY
AEILMPPSSST PALIMPSESTS
AEILMPRSSST SLIPSTREAMS
AEILMPRSTUU PARI-MUTUELS
AEILNNOPRSU UNIPERSONAL
AEILNOOPRTX EXPLORATION
AEILNOPPTTY PLATINOTYPE
AEILNOPRSST PERSONALIST ?
AEILNOPRSTY PERSONALITY
AEILNOPSSSS PASSIONLESS
AEILNORRSTU SERRULATION
AEILNORSTTV VENTILATORS
AEILNORSTUV VOLUNTARIES
AEILNORTTVY VENTILATORY
AEILNSSSSTU SENSUALISTS
AEILOPPRRSU POPULARISER
AEILOPPRRUZ POPULARIZER
AEILOSSSTTY STEATOLYSIS
AEILOSTUVXY VEXATIOUSLY
AEILRRSSSTU SURREALISTS
AEIMMNRSSSU SUMMARINESS
AEIMMORSTTU TAUTOMERISM
AEIMMPRSSTU SUPREMATISM
AEIMMSSSTTY SYSTEMATISM
AEIMNNNOSTT ANOINTMENTS
AEIMNNOPPTT APPOINTMENT
AEIMNNORSTU MENSURATION,
NUMERATIONS
AEIMNNSSTTU SUSTAINMENT
AEIMNOORSSU ANISOMEROUS
AEIMNNOPRTTU IMPORTUNATE,
PERMUTATION
AEIMNOPSTTT TEMPTATIONS
AEIMNORRTTY TERMINATORY

AEIMNORSSTT MONETARISTS
AEIMNRRSTTT TRANSMITTER
AEIMPRSSTTU SUPREMATIST
AEIMQRSSTUZ QUIZMASTERS
AEIMSSSTTTY SYSTEMATIST
AEINNNOQSSU SINE QUA NONS
AEINNNORTTU ANTINEUTRON
AEINNOOPRST PERSONATION
AEINNOORSTV RENOVATIONS
AEINNOOSTTT OSTENTATION
AEINNOPSTTY SPONTANEITY
AEINNORSTUV INTRAVENOUS
AEINNOSSSUX ANXIOUSNESS
AEINOOPPRRT APPORTIONER,
REAPPORTION
AEINOOPRRST PERORATIONS
AEINOOPRSSU APONEUROSIS
AEINOOPRTTX EXPORTATION
AEINOORRSTT RESTORATION
AEINOORSUVX OVERANXIOUS
AEINOPPRSTT POSTER PAINT
AEINOPRSSSU PERSUASIONS
AEINOPRSSSV VASOPRESSIN
AEINOPRSTTU REPUTATIONS
AEINOPSTTTU OUTPATIENTS
AEINOQRSTUY QUESTIONARY
AEINORSSSUV VARIOUSNESS
AEIOPPRRRTY PROPRIETARY
AEIOPRRRSST RESPIRATORS
AEIOPRRRSTY RESPIRATORY
AEIOPRRRTTU PORTRAITURE
AEIOPRRTTUV VITUPERATOR
AEIPPRSTUUV SUPPURATIVE
AEKMNOOPSSW SPOKESWOMAN
AEKMNORSTTW MARKET TOWNS
AEKMORRSSTW MASTERWORKS
AEKMRRSSSST STRESS MARKS
AEKNOPRRSSY NOSY PARKERS
AEKNOQRSSTU SQUARE KNOTS
AELLMORSUVY MARVELOUSLY
AELLNOPPRST PROPELLANTS
AELLNPRSTUU NE PLUS ULTRA
AELLOPRSSUX SOLAR PLEXUS
AELMNOPRRSU SUPERNORMAL
AELMOPRSTTY PLASTOMETRY
AELMOPSSTUY SYMPETALOUS
AELMORSSSTU SOMERSAULTS
AELMORSSSTY SOLAR SYSTEM
AELMPRSTYYY MYSTERY PLAY
AELNNNOPRTW TOWN PLANNER
AELNOPPRSTW POWER PLANTS
AELNOPPSTTY PENALTY SPOT
AELNPRRSUUY SUPERLUNARY
AELOOPRRTXY EXPLORATORY

AELOOPSSTTY OSTEOPLASTY	**AFGINRRSTTU** FRUSTRATING
AELPPRSTUWY WATER SUPPLY	**AFHILNOPSST** FLASH POINTS
AEMNNOOSSST STONEMASONS	**AFIIIILNNTV** INFINITIVAL
AEMNNORRSTT REMONSTRANT	**AFIIILMNNST** INFANTILISM
AEMNNORSTTU TOURNAMENTS	**AFIIILNNTTY** INFANTILITY
AEMNOOPRSTY TRYPANOSOME	**AFIIINNORTU** INFURIATION
AEMNOORRSST ASTRONOMERS	**AFIILMNNOTU** FULMINATION
AEMNOORSSSU AMOROUSNESS	**AFIILMNORTY** INFORMALITY
AEMNOORSTUU NEUROMATOUS	**AFIILNORRTT** INFILTRATOR
AEMNORSSSTT ASSORTMENTS	**AFIILNORSTT** FLIRTATIONS
AEMNOSTTTUX MANTOUX TEST	**AFIILORSTTU** FLIRTATIOUS
AEMOOPPRRRU AMOUR-PROPRE	**AFIIMNNOORT** INFORMATION
AEMOPRSSSTT POSTMASTERS	**AFIIMNOORSU** OMNIFARIOUS
AENNOOPRSSS PARSON'S NOSE	**AFIIMORSTUV** FAVOURITISM
AENNOOPSSTU SPONTANEOUS	**AFIINNORSTX** TRANSFIXION
AENNORRSSTT NONSTARTERS	**AFIIOPRSSSU** FISSIPAROUS
AENOPRRRSTT TRANSPORTER	**AFILMNOORTU** FORMULATION
AENOPRSSTTT PROTESTANTS	**AFILMNORTUY** FULMINATORY
AENORRSTTTU STERNUTATOR	**AFINNORSSTU** TRANSFUSION
AENPRRSSTTU TRANSPUTERS	**AFINORRSTTU** FRUSTRATION
AEOOPPPRRTY PARTY POOPER	**AGGHHIIKNNR** HIGH-RANKING
AEOOQRRSSTU SQUARE ROOTS	**AGGHHLOPPRY** GLYPHOGRAPH
AEOPPRRTTVY POVERTY TRAP	**AGGHIILNNSU** LANGUISHING
AEOPRSSTTUW WATERSPOUTS	**AGGHIILOOST** HAGIOLOGIST
AFFGHIIMNRS FISH FARMING	**AGGHINORRTW** RIGHT A WRONG
AFFGHLOPSTU PLOUGHSTAFF	**AGGHMMOPRSY** SPHYGMOGRAM
AFFILNORSTU INSUFFLATOR	**AGGIIILNNSZ** SIGNALIZING
AFFOOORTUUV OUT OF FAVOUR	**AGGIIIMMNRT** IMMIGRATING
AFGGILNRTUU FULGURATING	**AGGIIINNORT** ORIGINATING
AFGHHIILNTU HIGHFALUTIN	**AGGIIINNSTT** INSTIGATING
AFGHHILLSST FLASHLIGHTS	**AGGIILMNORZ** GLAMORIZING
AFGHHILPSTT FLIGHT PATHS	**AGGIILNNOYZ** AGONIZINGLY
AFGHIILRSTY FAIRY LIGHTS	**AGGIILNOOPZ** APOLOGIZING
AFGHILMOPRY FILMOGRAPHY	**AGGIILNRUVZ** VULGARIZING
AFGHIORSTWY RIGHTS OF WAY	**AGGIINNORRS** GARRISONING
AFGHIPPTTUU PUT UP A FIGHT	**AGGIINORTTU** GURGITATION
AFGIIINNRTU INFURIATING	**AGGIMMNOPRR** PROGRAMMING
AFGIILLMNNY INFLAMINGLY	**AGGINOPSSTT** STAGING POST
AFGIILLNNUY UNFAILINGLY	**AGGLLNOORYY** LARYNGOLOGY
AFGIILMNNTU FULMINATING	**AGGLOOORSTY** AGROSTOLOGY
AFGIILMNORZ FORMALIZING	**AGHHIIMNRST** NIGHTMARISH
AFGIILNNOTU ANTIFOULING	**AGHHILOPRST** LITHOGRAPHS
AFGIINNNQTUY QUANTIFYING	**AGHHILOPRTY** LITHOGRAPHY
AFGIINNRSTX TRANSFIXING	**AGHHIMNRSTU** HUMAN RIGHTS
AFGIINRSTTY STRATIFYING	**AGHHNOOPPRS** PHONOGRAPHS
AFGIINSSTUU IGNIS FATUUS	**AGHHNOOPPRY** PHONOGRAPHY
AFGIKLNNOTU OUTFLANKING	**AGHHOOPPRST** PHOTOGRAPHS
AFGILLNNTUY FLAUNTINGLY	**AGHHOOPPRTY** PHOTOGRAPHY
AFGILMNORTU FORMULATING	**AGHHOOPRRTY** ORTHOGRAPHY
AFGILNORSUV FLAVOURINGS	**AGHHOPPRTYY** PHYTOGRAPHY
AFGILNORTUU FULGURATION	**AGHHORSTUWY** THROUGHWAYS
AFGILNORUVY FAVOURINGLY	**AGHIIILMNTU** HUMILIATING
AFGILNRSTTY FLYING START	**AGHIILMNOOS** HOOLIGANISM
AFGINOOPSST SOFT-SOAPING	**AGHIILNNSVY** VANISHINGLY

AGHIILNRSVY RAVISHINGLY
AGHIIMNNORZ HARMONIZING
AGHIIMOSTTX THIGMOTAXIS
AGHIINNOSST ASTONISHING
AGHIINNQSUV VANQUISHING
AGHIINORTUZ AUTHORIZING
AGHIINPRRSS HAIRSPRINGS
AGHIINPRSTY PHARYNGITIS
AGHILNOOSTT ANTHOLOGIST
AGHILNORRWY HARROWINGLY
AGHILOOPSTT PATHOLOGIST
AGHILPRSTWY PLAYWRIGHTS
AGHIMNOPRST PROGNATHISM
AGHINOPRSTT PARTING SHOT
AGHIORSTTTU STRAIGHT-OUT
AGHLOOPSUXY XYLOPHAGOUS
AGHLOPRSTYY STYLOGRAPHY
AGHMNOOOPSU MONOPHAGOUS
AGHMNOORSTU MOUTHORGANS
AGHMOOOPRRT GRAPHOMOTOR
AGHNOOPPRRY PORNOGRAPHY
AGHNOOPRSTU PROGNATHOUS
AGIIIIILLNNT INITIALLING
AGIIIILLMNST MAILING LIST
AGIIILLNTTT TITILLATING
AGIIILNNOPT OIL PAINTING
AGIIILNNORS ORIGINAL SIN
AGIIILNORTV INVIGILATOR
AGIIILNORTY ORIGINALITY
AGIIILNPSST SALPINGITIS
AGIIILNSTTW WAITING LIST
AGIIILNSUVZ VISUALIZING
AGIIIMMNORT IMMIGRATION
AGIIINNNSTU INSINUATING
AGIIINNOORT ORIGINATION
AGIIINNOSTT INSTIGATION
AGIIINPRTVZ PRIVATIZING
AGIIKNNNPRS NAPKIN RINGS
AGIILLNNOPT POLLINATING
AGIILMNNORZ NORMALIZING
AGIILMNPPSY MISAPPLYING
AGIILMNSTTU STIMULATING
AGIILNNRSTY STRAININGLY
AGIILNORTUV OUTRIVALING
AGIILNPSTTU STIPULATING
AGIILNRSTUY SINGULARITY
AGIILNRTUUX LUXURIATING
AGIIMMNRSUZ SUMMARIZING
AGIIMNNOPTU IMPUGNATION
AGIIMNNPRSS MAINSPRINGS
AGIIMNOORTW WAITING ROOM
AGIINNNRTYZ TYRANNIZING
AGIINNOPRTZ PATRONIZING
AGIINNPRRST TRANSPIRING

AGIINOORRST ORIGINATORS
AGIINOORRTV INVIGORATOR
AGIINORSSTT INSTIGATORS
AGIJNOPSTUX JUXTAPOSING
AGIKLNOPRST PARKING LOTS
AGIKMNOPRST POSTMARKING
AGILLLNPTUU PULLULATING
AGILLMNNOOU MONOLINGUAL
AGILLNPRTTY PRATTLINGLY
AGILLNRSTTY STARTLINGLY
AGILMOOPRTY PRIMATOLOGY
AGILMOPSSTY POLYGAMISTS
AGILNNPPSTU SUPPLANTING
AGILNNPRSUY UNSPARINGLY
AGILNOOOPRS SPOROGONIAL
AGILNOPPRVY APPROVINGLY
AGILNOPSTTU POSTULATING
AGILNORSUVY SAVOURINGLY
AGILOORSSYY ASSYRIOLOGY
AGIMNNORRST MORNING STAR
AGIMNNRSTTU TRANSMUTING
AGIMNOOPRST PROTAGONISM
AGIMNORSTTU OUTSMARTING
AGINNOPRSST TRANSPOSING
AGINOOOPRRT PROROGATION
AGINOOPRSTT PROTAGONIST
AGINOORRSTU SURROGATION
AGINOORRSUV GRANIVOROUS
AGINOPRRSTT PROSTRATING
AGINPPRSTUU SUPPURATING
AGKNNNORSTY GRANNY KNOTS
AGLLLLOPPSU GALLUP POLLS
AGLLMOORSUY GLAMOROUSLY
AGLLOOPSTTT GLOTTAL STOP
AGLLORRSUUY GARRULOUSLY
AGLMNOORTYY LARYNGOTOMY
AGLMOOOSTTY STOMATOLOGY
AGLMOOPRRTU PROMULGATOR
AGLMOORRTYY MARTYROLOGY
AGMOORSSTTY GASTROSTOMY
AHHIIIPRSST PHTHIRIASIS
AHHILMOPSTY HALOPHYTISM
AHHILNOORTU HOLOTHURIAN
AHHIMNOPSSW SHOWMANSHIP
AHHLLNOPTXY XANTHOPHYLL
AHIIIILMNOTU HUMILIATION
AHIIIMNNOSY NISHINOMIYA
AHIILLORSUY HILARIOUSLY
AHIILMORTUY HUMILIATORY
AHIILOPSTTY HOSPITALITY
AHIILRSSTTY HAIRSTYLIST
AHIIMNNRRTU ANTIRRHINUM
AHIIMNOOOSU HOMOIOUSIAN
AHIIMOOPPPT HIPPOPOTAMI

AHIKKOORRSW KWASHIORKOR
AHIKLMOORSW WORKAHOLISM
AHIKLOTTUWW WALK OUT WITH
AHIKMNOPRSW WORKMANSHIP
AHILLOPSTXY PHYLLOTAXIS
AHILLOTUWWY WHAT YOU WILL
AHILNOORSTZ HORIZONTALS
AHILNOPRSTY RHINOPLASTY
AHILOORRTTY HORTATORILY
AHILOPPRSXY PROPHYLAXIS
AHILOPRRUXY PYRRHULOXIA
AHIMNOORRSU HONORARIUMS
AHIMNOPRSTY MISANTHROPY
AHIMOORSTUZ RHIZOMATOUS
AHINOOPSSTX SAXOPHONIST
AHINORSTTTT THAT'S TORN IT
AHKNNOPSSSY SHANKS'S PONY
AHLMNNORSTU LUNAR MONTHS
AHLMNOTUXYZ ZANTHOXYLUM
AHLMOOPRSUY AMORPHOUSLY
AHMNNOOPRTT NORTHAMPTON
AHMNOOPSTTU SOUTHAMPTON
AHNNOSSTTWY SHANTYTOWNS
AIIIINNOSTT INITIATIONS
AIIILLLNPTU LILLIPUTIAN
AIIILLNOTTT TITILLATION
AIIILLNOTUV ILLUVIATION
AIIILMNOSST IN ALTISSIMO
AIIILMNOSTT LIMITATIONS
AIIILMNPRTT TRIPALMITIN
AIIILMRSSTT MILITARISTS
AIIILNNOOST LIONISATION
AIIILNNOOTZ LIONIZATION
AIIILNNOTTU INTUITIONAL
AIIILNOSTTU UTILISATION
AIIILNOTTUZ UTILIZATION
AIIIMNNOSTT INTIMATIONS
AIIIMNRSTTU MINIATURIST
AIIIMPPRRTY PRIMIPARITY
AIIIMPSSTVY IMPASSIVITY
AIIINNNOSTU INSINUATION
AIIINNNOPRST INSPIRATION
AIIINNOSTTV INVITATIONS
AIIINORRSTT IRRITATIONS
AIIINOSSTTV VISITATIONS
AIIKLRSTUVV SURVIVAL KIT
AIIKNRSSSTT SANSKRITIST
AIIILLMMNOTU MULTINOMIAL
AIIILLMNORTU ILLUMINATOR
AIIILLNNOOPT POLLINATION
AIIILLNORSUY ILLUSIONARY
AIIILLPRSTUY SPIRITUALITY
AIIILLPSTTUY PULSATILITY
AIIILMMORTTY IMMORTALITY

AIILMNOOPRT IMPLORATION
AIILMNOOPST MALPOSITION
AIILMNOOSST SOLMISATION
AIILMNOOSTZ SOLMIZATION
AIILMNOSSTU SIMULATIONS
AIILMNOSTTU MUTILATIONS,
  STIMULATION
AIILMNOSTUY ALUMINOSITY
AIILMPRTTUY MULTIPARITY
AIILNNORSTU INTRUSIONAL
AIILNNORTTU NUTRITIONAL
AIILNOOPRSV PROVISIONAL
AIILNOPRTUY UNIPOLARITY
AIILNOPSTTU STIPULATION
AIILNORTUUX LUXURIATION
AIILNOSSTTY STYLISATION
AIILNOSTTYZ STYLIZATION
AIILNQRTTUY TRANQUILITY
AIILNQRTTUY TRANQUILITY
AIILORSSSTU SAILOR SUITS
AIIMMNOPSTT PANTOMIMIST
AIIMMNSSTTU NUMISMATIST
AIIMMPRRSTU IMPRIMATURS
AIIMNNNOOST NOMINATIONS
AIIMNNORSTU RUMINATIONS
AIIMNNRSSTT MINISTRANTS
AIIMNOOPRTT IMPORTATION
AIIMNOOPRTX PROXIMATION
AIIMNOPSTTU IMPUTATIONS
AIIMOPPRRSU PRIMIPAROUS
AIINNNOOSTT INTONATIONS
AIINNNOOSTV INNOVATIONS
AIINNNORRTT NONIRRITANT
AIINNOOOSTZ OZONISATION
AIINNOOOTZZ OZONIZATION
AIINNOORRST IRON RATIONS
AIINNORSSTT TRANSITIONS
AIINOPRRSTY INSPIRATORY
AIINOPRRTTU PARTURITION
AIINORRTTTU TRITURATION
AIIOOPPRRTT PROPITIATOR
AIIOPRRSTTT PORTRAITIST
AIIOPRSSTTT PROSTATITIS
AIJLNORSSTU JOURNALISTS
AIKNOORSTTW WORKSTATION
AILLLMNOOPP LOLLIPOP MAN
AILLLNOOPRU ALLOPURINOL
AILLLNOPTUU PULLULATION
AILLMOPSSSY PLASMOLYSIS
AILLNOPRSUU NULLIPAROUS
AILLNORTUVY VOLUNTARILY
AILLNRTUUXY LUXURIANTLY
AILLORRSTTU ILLUSTRATOR
AILMNNOSUUY UNANIMOUSLY

AILMNOOOPRT PROMOTIONAL
AILMNOPPSSS SIMPLON PASS
AILMNOPRTTY IMPORTANTLY
AILMNORSTUV VOLUNTARISM
AILMOOPRRTY IMPLORATORY
AILMOOPRUYZ POLYZOARIUM
AILMOPRSTUU MULTIPAROUS
AILNNORTUVY INVOLUNTARY
AILNOOPPSTU POPULATIONS
AILNOOPRSTU SPORULATION
AILNOOPSTTU POSTULATION
AILNOPPSTTU POSTNUPTIAL
AILNOPSTTUU PUSTULATION
AILNORSTTUV VOLUNTARIST
AILNORSUUVY UNSAVOURILY
AILNRSSTUUU LAURUSTINUS
AILOPRSTTUY STIPULATORY
AILORSTTTUY STATUTORILY
AIMMOOSSTXY MYXOMATOSIS
AIMNNOOPTTU MOUNTAINTOP
AIMNNOOSTUU MOUNTAINOUS
AIMNOPSSSTU ASSUMPTIONS
AIMNRSSTTUU NASTURTIUMS
AINNNOOOORTT TORONTONIAN
AINOOPRRSTT PROSTRATION
AINOPPRSTUU SUPPURATION
AINORRSSSTT TRANSISTORS
AINORRSSTUU SUSURRATION
AKLNNOOOPTZ ZOOPLANKTON
ALLNOOOPPRR PROPRANOLOL
ALLOORSTWWW SWALLOWWORT
ALMNNOOSUYY ANONYMOUSLY
ALMNOOORSTU MONOLATROUS
ALMNOORSTTU SALMON TROUT
ALOPRRSTUUY RAPTUROUSLY
AMNOOPRSSTW SPORTSWOMAN
BBBEGIIINNW WINEBIBBING
BBBHIINRSSU RUBBISH BINS
BBCCEEHKLOR BREECHBLOCK
BBCDEHIRRTU BUTCHERBIRD
BBCEELNOOST COBBLESTONE
BBCEILMOSTU COMBUSTIBLE
BBCEINRSSSU SCRUBBINESS
BBCEIRRSSSU SUBSCRIBERS
BBCEJKOORST STOCKJOBBER
BBCEKLORSTU BLOCKBUSTER
BBCELMORSTU CLUSTER BOMB
BBCGIINRSSU SUBSCRIBING
BBDDEELLOOU BLUE-BLOODED
BBDDEILLNOU DOUBLE-BLIND
BBDDEILNOSU DOUBLE BINDS
BBDEEELOUYY BLUE-EYED BOY
BBDEEGHILOS BOBSLEIGHED
BBDEEHHLOOY HOBBLEDEHOY

BBDEEILLLOW I'LL BE BLOWED
BBDEEIMORSV DIVE-BOMBERS
BBDEFFLLOUU DOUBLE BLUFF
BBDEGIIMNOV DIVE-BOMBING
BBDEIKNOORS BOOKBINDERS
BBDEIKNOORY BOOKBINDERY
BBDELNRSSUU BLUNDERBUSS
BBDGIIKNNOO BOOKBINDING
BBEEEILRRSU BLUEBERRIES
BBEEERRRSTU RUBBER TREES
BBEEGIILLNR GIBBERELLIN
BBEEHIRRSSU SHRUBBERIES
BBEEILMRSSU SUBMERSIBLE
BBEELLOSTTU BLUEBOTTLES
BBEELMORSTT LETTER BOMBS
BBEENORRSYY BOYSENBERRY
BBEFILORSUU BULBIFEROUS
BBEGIINSSSU BIG BUSINESS
BBEGINOSSSU GIBBOUSNESS
BBEHHILOSST SHIBBOLETHS
BBEHHOORSSY HOBBYHORSES
BBEHIIILLOP BIBLIOPHILE
BBEHINRSSSU SHRUBBINESS
BBEIKLMOOOS BOOKMOBILES
BBEIOOPRSSY BOOBY PRISES
BBEIOOPRSYZ BOOBY PRIZES
BBELLMOOSTT BELL-BOTTOMS
BBELLNOTTUY BELLY BUTTON
BBEMNNOORTU NEUTRON BOMB
BBENORSSTTU STUBBORNEST
BBGHILNORTY THROBBINGLY
BBGIILLNQUY QUIBBLINGLY
BBHIIILMOPS BIBLIOPHISM
BCCDEEHKLOU DOUBLE-CHECK
BCCDEILNOTU CONDUCTIBLE
BCCEEEEFINN BENEFICENCE
BCCEEEENRSU ERUBESCENCE
BCCEEIILNOR INCOERCIBLE
BCCEEILNNOT CONNECTIBLE
BCCEEILNOSS CONCESSIBLE
BCCEEINRSTY CYBERNETICS
BCCEFFIKLOO OFFICE BLOCK
BCCEFIIPSSU SUBSPECIFIC
BCCEHINOOPR NECROPHOBIC
BCCEIILNNOV CONVINCIBLE
BCCEIINOORT NECROBIOTIC
BCCHHOORSTT SCOTCH BROTH
BCCHINOOPTY NYCTOPHOBIC
BCCLNORTUUY COUNTRY CLUB
BCDDDELLOOO COLD-BLOODED
BCDDEEEILNS DESCENDIBLE
BCDDEEIIRTT DIRECT DEBIT
BCDDEENORTY BODY-CENTRED
BCDDEHLOTUU DOUBLE-DUTCH

BCDEEEIINNT BENEDICTINE	**BCEEHKNORSW** WORKBENCHES
BCDEEEIORRS CEREBROSIDE	**BCEEHNORRSX** BRONX CHEERS
BCDEEHILNPT PITCHBLENDE	**BCEEIILPSST** PLEBISCITES
BCDEEHMNOOY HONEYCOMBED	**BCEEIILRSSS** RESCISSIBLE
BCDEEHMNOTU DEBOUCHMENT	**BCEEIINOSST** OBSCENITIES
BCDEEIIILRT LIBERTICIDE	**BCEEIJLOTVY** OBJECTIVELY
BCDEEIILNRS DISCERNIBLE	**BCEEILMNNOT** CONTEMNIBLE
BCDEEIILRRU IRREDUCIBLE	**BCEEILMOSST** COMESTIBLES
BCDEEIILSST DISSECTIBLE	**BCEEILNORTV** CONVERTIBLE
BCDEEIINNOT BENEDICTION	**BCEEILNOSTY** BY-ELECTIONS
BCDEEIMNRSU DISENCUMBER	**BCEEILPPRTY** PERCEPTIBLY
BCDEEINORTY BENEDICTORY	**BCEEILPSSTU** SUSCEPTIBLE
BCDEEINSSSU SUBSIDENCES	**BCEEINSSSTU** SUBSISTENCE
BCDEEORRSSS CROSSBREEDS	**BCEEIPRRSSU** SUPERSCRIBE
BCDEGHNRRSU BERGSCHRUND	**BCEEKKLNNOU** KNUCKLEBONE
BCDEHILNNOR HORNBLENDIC	**BCEEKLNOSTT** BOTTLENECKS
BCDEHILNOSU DOUBLE CHINS	**BCEELMMOOTY** EMBOLECTOMY
BCDEHILORSU SUBCHLORIDE	**BCEELNOOSST** OBSOLESCENT
BCDEIIILRTY CREDIBILITY	**BCEEMMORTYY** EMBRYECTOMY
BCDEIILNRSY DISCERNIBLY	**BCEFFKORSTU** BUFFER STOCK
BCDEIILRRUY IRREDUCIBLY	**BCEFHILLNSU** BULLFINCHES
BCDEIILSSSU DISCUSSIBLE	**BCEFIIOPRST** FIBER OPTICS
BCDEIKLOQUU DOUBLE-QUICK	**BCEFIIOPRST** FIBRE OPTICS
BCDEINORTTU CONTRIBUTED	**BCEGHHIMOWY** HIGH WYCOMBE
BCDEIOOPRSS PROBOSCIDES	**BCEGHIIMNRS** BESMIRCHING
BCDEKLOORSU BLOODSUCKER	**BCEGHILLNNY** BLENCHINGLY
BCDELMNOSUU MUSCLE-BOUND	**BCEGIINPRRS** PRESCRIBING
BCDELOORSSU DOUBLE-CROSS	**BCEGILNOOOY** BIOCENOLOGY
BCDEMMNRSUU CUMMERBUNDS	**BCEHIIIMNRS** HIBERNICISM
BCDGIIKMNOR MOCKINGBIRD	**BCEHIILRRSV** SILVER BIRCH
BCDGIIOSSTU DOG BISCUITS	**BCEHILMOOPT** PHLEBOTOMIC
BCDGILLLOPU BULLDOG CLIP	**BCEHILNOSST** BLOTCHINESS
BCDIILOOPTY BODY POLITIC	**BCEHILOPSUU** PUBLIC HOUSE
BCDIINRTUUY RUBICUNDITY	**BCEHKLOOSSU** BLOCKHOUSES
BCDILLNOORU COLOUR-BLIND	**BCEHKOPSSTU** BUCKET SHOPS
BCDLNOOOSTU BLOOD COUNTS	**BCEHLORRSYY** CHRYSOBERYL
BCDLORSSTUU CLOUDBURSTS	**BCEHMOORTTY** THROMBOCYTE
BCEEEEHLSSU BLUE CHEESES	**BCEHMRSSTUW** THUMBSCREWS
BCEEEELNNOV BENEVOLENCE	**BCEIIJMOSTV** OBJECTIVISM
BCEEEFILPRT PERFECTIBLE	**BCEIIJOSTTV** OBJECTIVIST
BCEEEFLLRST TREBLE CLEFS	**BCEIIJOTTVY** OBJECTIVITY
BCEEEHHINPR HEBEPHRENIC	**BCEIILLOSTY** BELLICOSITY
BCEEEHHNNQSU QUEEN'S BENCH	**BCEIIMMRSTY** BISYMMETRIC
BCEEEIILRST CELEBRITIES	**BCEIINOORSS** NECROBIOSIS
BCEEEILPPRT PERCEPTIBLE	**BCEIIORSSTU** OBSCURITIES
BCEEEILPRTX EXCERPTIBLE	**BCEIJNSTUUV** SUBJUNCTIVE
BCEEENQSSUU SUBSEQUENCE	**BCEIKQOPRTU** PICTURE BOOK
BCEEFKLNRRU BUCKLER-FERN	**BCEILLORSSU** BRUCELLOSIS
BCEEGILNOST CONGESTIBLE	**BCEILOPRRTU** CORRUPTIBLE
BCEEGIMNNRU ENCUMBERING	**BCEINOSSSTU** SUBSECTIONS
BCEEGIMNORY EMBRYOGENIC	**BCEIOOPRSSS** PROBOSCISES
BCEEGKLMNRU MECKLENBURG	**BCEIORSTTUV** OBSTRUCTIVE
BCEEHJKLOWY CHEEK BY JOWL	**BCEKKOOOORY** COOKERY BOOK
BCEEHKLRRUY HUCKLEBERRY	**BCEKKOOOPST** POCKETBOOKS

BCEKKOORRST STOCKBROKER
BCEKLOORSTW TOWER BLOCKS
BCELORSTUUU TUBERCULOUS
BCELRSSTUUU SUBCULTURES
BCEOOOPRSST STROBOSCOPE
BCGIIILNPUZ PUBLICIZING
BCGIINOPRRS PROSCRIBING
BCGILOOORYY CRYOBIOLOGY
BCGINORSTTU OBSTRUCTING
BCHHIOOOPPT PHOTOPHOBIC
BCHIIIPSSTU SHIP BISCUIT
BCHIOOPRSSU RUSSOPHOBIC
BCHMOOOTTTU TOUCH BOTTOM
BCHNOORSSTU HOT-CROSS BUN
BCIIIILMSTY MISCIBILITY
BCIILMOSSTY SYMBOLISTIC
BCIJNNOSTUU SUBJUNCTION
BCIKLOPRSUW PUBLIC WORKS
BCIKMOORSST BROOMSTICKS
BCILMOSTTUU CUSTOM-BUILT
BCINOORRTTU CONTRIBUTOR
BCINOORSTTU OBSTRUCTION
BCKLLOOPSSU BOLLOCKS-UPS
BDDDEEEGLOU DOUBLE-EDGED
BDDDEEEINRT INTERBEDDED
BDDDEEIIMOS DISEMBODIED
BDDDEEINRRU UNDERBIDDER
BDDDEFILLNO BLINDFOLDED
BDDDEFMNOUU DUMBFOUNDED
BDDEEEIILSV DISBELIEVED
BDDEEEIMMRS DISMEMBERED
BDDEEEIMNRT DEBRIDEMENT
BDDEEEIMORR EMBROIDERED
BDDEEIINOST DISOBEDIENT
BDDEEILMRTU TUMBLE-DRIED
BDDEEILORSW BOWDLERISED
BDDEEILORWZ BOWDLERIZED
BDDEELOOPRU PUREBLOODED
BDDEENSSSUU SUBDUEDNESS
BDDEFLLLOOU FULL-BLOODED
BDDEFMNORUU DUMBFOUNDER
BDDEGIIMNNN MIND-BENDING
BDDEGIINORV OVERBIDDING
BDDEHINRRTU THUNDERBIRD
BDDEEHLNOORS BONDHOLDERS
BDDEIIRSTTU DISTRIBUTED
BDDEILMORSW MIDDLEBROWS
BDDELNOTUUY UNDOUBTEDLY
BDDGIIINSUV SUBDIVIDING
BDDHIIIMRSY DIHYBRIDISM
BDDHLNOOOSU BLOODHOUNDS
BDEEEEIIMRR BIEDERMEIER
BDEEEHILLMS EMBELLISHED
BDEEEHILMTW THIMBLEWEED

BDEEEIILRSV DISBELIEVER
BDEEEILMNTV BEDEVILMENT
BDEEEILPRSS DEPRESSIBLE
BDEEEILSSTW WILDEBEESTS
BDEEEIMMRRS DISMEMBERER
BDEEEIMORRR EMBROIDERER
BDEEELNSSSS BLESSEDNESS
BDEEFGIINNR BEFRIENDING
BDEEFHIRRSU REFURBISHED
BDEEGGHIIRW WEIGHBRIDGE
BDEEGGINSUU DUNE BUGGIES
BDEEGHILNTY BENIGHTEDLY
BDEEGIILLNV BEDEVILLING
BDEEGIILNRW BEWILDERING
BDEEGILMNNO EMBOLDENING
BDEEHILMNSU UNBLEMISHED
BDEEIIILNSST DISTENSIBLE
BDEEILLNNRS DINNER BELLS
BDEEILLNPRS SPELLBINDER
BDEEILMNOTY MOLYBDENITE
BDEEILMRSSS DISSEMBLERS
BDEEILNORRS BORDERLINES
BDEEILNPSSU SUSPENDIBLE
BDEEIMNORST DISROBEMENT
BDEEINNSSSU BUSINESS END
BDEEINORSTX TINDERBOXES
BDEEIOORSXY DEOXYRIBOSE
BDEELLOOSSV BLOOD VESSEL
BDEELMRRSUU BLUE MURDERS
BDEELMRRTUY TUMBLE-DRYER
BDEELNRRSSU BLURREDNESS
BDEEMNORTUU OUTNUMBERED
BDEENPRRTUU UNPERTURBED
BDEFGINOORS FOREBODINGS
BDEFGIOORST FOOTBRIDGES
BDEFHNOOORT DEBT OF HONOR
BDEFIOPRRSY BIRDS OF PREY
BDEGGILNNOU BLUDGEONING
BDEGIILLNNS SINGLE-BLIND
BDEGIILLNSV DIVING BELLS
BDEGIILMNSS DISSEMBLING
BDEGIINNRRS RING BINDERS
BDEGIMORRSY DOGBERRYISM
BDEGINNNRUU UNBURDENING
BDEHHOOOORRT BROTHERHOOD
BDEHIIIILNTY INHIBITEDLY
BDEHIIINNTU UNINHIBITED
BDEHIILPRSU SHIPBUILDER
BDEHIINNPTU NIP IN THE BUD
BDEHIKLNOTU DOUBLETHINK
BDEHILLSTTU BULLSHITTED
BDEHILNPSUU UNPUBLISHED
BDEHLNOOTTU BUTTONHOLED
BDEHLNORTTU THUNDERBOLT

BDEIIIILNSV INDIVISIBLE
BDEIIIILNTY INEDIBILITY
BDEIIILMMOS IMMOBILISED
BDEIIILMMOZ IMMOBILIZED
BDEIIILMSSS DISMISSIBLE
BDEIIILNTVY VENDIBILITY
BDEIILMRSUU SUBDELIRIUM
BDEIINNRTUW WIND TURBINE
BDEIIRSSSSU SUBSIDISERS
BDEIIRSSSUZ SUBSIDIZERS
BDEIKNORSTU STRIKEBOUND
BDEILLLNORR ROLLER BLIND
BDEILLOSTUX BILLETS-DOUX
BDEILNNOOOS IN ONE'S BLOOD
BDEILNORSTY BLINDSTOREY
BDEIMMNOPRU PREMIUM BOND
BDEINOOSWWX WINDOW BOXES
BDEINOSSSUU DUBIOUSNESS
BDEISSTTTUU SUBSTITUTED
BDELLLOOSSY BLOODLESSLY
BDELLNOSSUY BOUNDLESSLY
BDELMNOOSUY MOLYBDENOUS
BDGGIIILNOS DISOBLIGING
BDGHIIMMNRU HUMMINGBIRD
BDGIIINSSUZ SUBSIDIZING
BDGIILMNNOW MIND-BLOWING
BDGIILNOTUU OUTBUILDING
BDGLOOOPRSU BLOOD GROUPS
BDHIILRRSWY WHIRLYBIRDS
BDIIIIILNSVY INDIVISIBLY
BDIIINOSSUV SUBDIVISION
BDIIMNORTUY MORIBUNDITY
BDIIORRSTTU DISTRIBUTOR
BDINNOORRSU ROUND ROBINS
BDLMNOOTTUU BUTTONMOULD
BDLOOOPRSST BLOOD SPORTS
BEEEFHINRSS FINES HERBES
BEEEFOORRST FREEBOOTERS
BEEEGGINRRS GINGER BEERS
BEEEGIINNOR BIOENGINEER
BEEEGILLNRT BELLIGERENT
BEEEGILMNTU BEGUILEMENT
BEEEGIMMNRR REMEMBERING
BEEEGLNORTT BOTTLE GREEN,
  GREENBOTTLE
BEEEHILLMRS EMBELLISHER
BEEEHILLNOR HELLEBORINE
BEEEIILNRSUV UNBELIEVERS
BEEEIILPRRSS REPRESSIBLE
BEEEIILPRRTV PERVERTIBLE
BEEEILPRSSX EXPRESSIBLE
BEEEIMMMRRS MISREMEMBER
BEEEINORSST BÊTES-NOIRES
BEEEIRSTTTW BITTERSWEET

BEEEKKOOPRS BOOKKEEPERS
BEEELLRSSST BEST-SELLERS
BEEELMNNNOT ENNOBLEMENT
BEEELORSTTX LETTERBOXES
BEEENOPPRTY TEENYBOPPER
BEEFFNORSUZ BUFFER ZONES
BEEFGLLOORW GLOBEFLOWER
BEEFGRSSTUU SUBTERFUGES
BEEFILRSTTU BUTTERFLIES
BEEGGILSSTU SUGGESTIBLE
BEEGGLOORST BOOTLEGGERS
BEEGHINNORR HERRINGBONE
BEEGIIMNRTT EMBITTERING
BEEGIIOORSU BOURGEOISIE
BEEGIKKNOOP BOOKKEEPING
BEEGILLNSST BEST-SELLING
BEEGIMNOSTT MISBEGOTTEN
BEEGKLNTTUU TELUKBETUNG
BEEHILMMOOS MOBILE HOMES
BEEHILPRRSU REPUBLISHER
BEEHIMMPRSS MEMBERSHIPS
BEEHIMNOORT THEOBROMINE
BEEHKNOORSU HOUSEBROKEN
BEEHLMNORUW WHOLE NUMBER
BEEHMNOOSST MESOBENTHOS
BEEHMOORSTT MOTHERS-TO-BE
BEEHOPRRSTT STEPBROTHER
BEEIILMPRSS IMPRESSIBLE, PERMISSIBLE
BEEIILNSSSV VISIBLENESS
BEEIIRRTTUV RETRIBUTIVE
BEEILLLNTUY EBULLIENTLY
BEEILLLOSVW BOLL WEEVILS
BEEILLORRSU IRRESOLUBLE
BEEILLRRRTU BULL TERRIER
BEEILMMNORT EMBROILMENT
BEEILNNOSTW TENNIS ELBOW
BEEILNOPRSS NOBEL PRISES, RESPONSIBLE
BEEILNOPRSZ NOBEL PRIZES
BEEILNRSSTT BRITTLENESS
BEEIMMNPRRU PRIME NUMBER
BEEIMNNSSSU BUSINESSMEN
BEEINORSTTY TENEBROSITY
BEEINRSSTUV SUBSERVIENT
BEEIRSSSUVV SUBVERSIVES
BEEJOORTTUV OBJET TROUVE
BEEKLLOORSS BOOKSELLERS
BEEKOOPRRRW POWER BROKER
BEELLNOSSSU SOLUBLENESS
BEELMOORSTU TROUBLESOME
BEEMMMNNOSTT ENTOMBMENTS
BEENORSSTXY SENTRY BOXES
BEENQRSSSUU BRUSQUENESS
BEERRRSTTUU SURREBUTTER
BEFGHILLRTU BULLFIGHTER

BEFGIIILNTTY BEFITTINGLY
BEFGILNORSW FINGER BOWLS
BEFHIIILLLLT FILL THE BILL
BEFHILLMSTU THIMBLEFULS
BEFHILLOOTT FOOT THE BILL
BEFHLMORTUU RULE OF THUMB
BEFIIIILLTXY FLEXIBILITY
BEFIILNORRU NEUROFIBRIL
BEFIILRSSTU FILIBUSTERS
BEFINORSSSU FIBROUSNESS
BEFINORSTTT FROSTBITTEN
BEFLLOOPRTU BULLETPROOF
BEGGGILNOOT BOOTLEGGING
BEGGHIINNOR NEIGHBORING
BEGGIIILLNNR BELL-RINGING
BEGGIIILLNUY BEGUILINGLY
BEGHILNORUY NEIGHBOURLY
BEGHILORSTT STROBE LIGHT
BEGIIIILLTY ELIGIBILITY
BEGIIMNRRSU REIMBURSING
BEGIKNOOORV OVERBOOKING
BEGILLMNRTY TREMBLINGLY
BEGILLMNRUY LUMBERINGLY
BEGILLNNNOY ENNOBLINGLY
BEGILNQRSUU BURLESQUING
BEGINRSSTTU BUTTRESSING
BEGNOORSSTX STRONGBOXES
BEHIIILLLLS HILLBILLIES
BEHIIINOSTX EXHIBITIONS
BEHIIIOPRTV PROHIBITIVE
BEHIKNOOSSS BOOKISHNESS
BEHILLNSSSU BULLISHNESS
BEHINOORSSS BOORISHNESS
BEHINRSSSTU BRUTISHNESS
BEHIOORRSUV HERBIVOROUS
BEHLNOOSTTU BUTTONHOLES
BEHLOORRSTU SOUL BROTHER
BEHMNOORTUU BOURNEMOUTH
BEHMOORSSTY MOTHER'S BOYS
BEHMPRSTTUU TUB-THUMPERS
BEIIILMMORS IMMOBILISER
BEIIILMMORZ IMMOBILIZER
BEIIILMNRST LIBERTINISM
BEIIILMQRUU EQUILIBRIUM
BEIIILNSSTY SENSIBILITY
BEIIILNSTTY TENSIBILITY
BEIIILQRSTU EQUILIBRIST
BEIIILLNOSSW BILLOWINESS
BEIIILLORTUV BLUE VITRIOL
BEIILMPRSSY PERMISSIBLY
BEIILNOSSSU BILIOUSNESS
BEIILORSSTU BOILER SUITS
BEIILRSSTTT LIBRETTISTS
BEIINORRTTU RETRIBUTION

BEILLLLOSUY LIBELLOUSLY
BEILLMPSTUU SUBMULTIPLE
BEILLNOSTTU BLUE STILTON
BEILMNOOSSW SNOWMOBILES
BEILNOPRSSY RESPONSIBLY
BEILORSTUVY OBTRUSIVELY
BEIMPSSTUUV SUBSUMPTIVE
BEINNOSSTUV SUBVENTIONS
BEINOOSSSUV OBVIOUSNESS
BEINORSSTUU SUBROUTINES
BEINORSTUUV UNOBTRUSIVE
BEINSSTTTUU SUBSTITUENT
BEIOQRSSTUU SOUBRIQUETS
BEISSSTTTUU SUBSTITUTES
BELLNRTTUUY TURBULENTLY
BELMMOORRSU LUMBER-ROOMS
BELNOOSTUUY BOUNTEOUSLY
BELOOPRSSTT LOBSTERPOTS
BELOOPRSTTU TROUBLE SPOT
BENNOORSSTW BROWNSTONES
BFFFFILOSTU BIT OF FLUFFS
BFGIIILNTUY FUNGIBILITY
BFILLLMNOOU IN FULL BLOOM
BGGILLMNRUY GRUMBLINGLY
BGHHIIRRSTT BIRTHRIGHTS
BGHIIINOPRT PROHIBITING
BGHIIINRRTV VIRGIN BIRTH
BGHIINOPPWY WHIPPING BOY
BGHIMNPTTUU TUB-THUMPING
BGIIILLLTUY GULLIBILITY
BGIILMNOSYZ SYMBOLIZING
BGILLMNSTUY STUMBLINGLY
BGILLNORTUY TROUBLINGLY
BGILMOOSSTY SYMBOLOGIST
BHIIIINNOST INHIBITIONS
BHIIINOOPRT PROHIBITION
BHIILLRSSTT STILLBIRTHS
BHIIOOPRRTY PROHIBITORY
BHILMOOSTYY TOMBOYISHLY
BHIMNOOPRRT PROTHROMBIN
BIIILOPSSTY POSSIBILITY
BIIILORSTTY TORSIBILITY
BIIKNOORSSV NOVOSIBIRSK
BIILLOOSUVY OBLIVIOUSLY
BIILOOQSTUU OBLIQUITOUS
BIIMNOSSSSU SUBMISSIONS
BILMOPSTUUY BUMPTIOUSLY
BILNOOOSUXY OBNOXIOUSLY
BIMNOORSSTT TROMBONISTS
BIMNOPSSTUU SUBSUMPTION
BIMORSSTUUU RUMBUSTIOUS
BIOOOPPRRSU OPPROBRIOUS
CCCCIMOORSU MICROCOCCUS
CCCCKKLOOOU CUCKOO CLOCK

CCCDEEEENRS DECRESCENCE	**CCDEHIOOPRS** DICHROSCOPE
CCCDEEIINNO COINCIDENCE	**CCDEHLNSTUU** DUTCH UNCLES
CCCDEHINOSY SYNECDOCHIC	**CCDEIILOORT** CROCIDOLITE
CCCDEIIMRSU CIRCUMCISED	**CCDEIJKOSSY** DISC JOCKEYS
CCCDGINOOOO GONOCOCCOID	**CCDEIMNOORS** MICROSECOND
CCCDIIIOOSS COCCIDIOSIS	**CCDEINNNOUV** UNCONVINCED
CCCDILOOPSU DIPLOCOCCUS	**CCDEINOPRST** CONSCRIPTED
CCCEEEEENRSX EXCRESCENCE	**CCDEINORSTT** CONSTRICTED
CCCEEEENRSXY EXCRESCENCY	**CCDELLOSTYY** CYCLOSTYLED
CCCEEFIIOPS ECOSPECIFIC	**CCDENORSSTU** CONDUCTRESS
CCCEEFLLNOU FLOCCULENCE	**CCDENORSTTU** CONSTRUCTED
CCCEEFOORSS FRESCO SECCO	**CCDFLMOOORT** COLD COMFORT
CCCEEIILMST ECLECTICISM	**CCDHHILLOOS** SCHOOLCHILD
CCCEEIINNOSS CONSCIENCES	**CCDHIOORTTW** WITCHDOCTOR
CCCEEENNORRU CONCURRENCE	**CCDHIOOSTUU** STUDIO COUCH
CCCEEENORRSU OCCURRENCES	**CCDKMOSUUVY** MUSCOVY DUCK
CCCEEFIINOPS CONSPECIFIC	**CCEEEEILRTY** ELECTRIC EYE
CCCEEFIOORSU COCCIFEROUS	**CCEEEEINPRT** CENTREPIECE
CCCEEIMPRSTU CIRCUMSPECT	**CCEEEFHIKNR** NECKERCHIEF
CCCEEINNOTTU CONNECTICUT	**CCEEEFHIRTV** HECTIC FEVER
CCCEEIRSSTUY CYSTICERCUS	**CCEEEFLNORS** FLORESCENCE
CCCHILMOTYY CYCLOTHYMIC	**CCEEEFNNORS** CONFERENCES
CCCIIMMOORS MICROCOSMIC	**CCEEEFNRSTU** FRUTESCENCE
CCCIIMOOPRS MICROSCOPIC	**CCEEEGINNRS** NIGRESCENCE
CCCINNOOOST CONCOCTIONS	**CCEEEGINRVY** VICEGERENCY
CCCIOOOPPST POCTOSCOPIC	**CCEEEGNNORV** CONVERGENCE
CCCIOOPSSTY CYSTOSCOPIC	**CCEEEGNRSTU** TURGESCENCE
CCDDELNNOUU UNCONCLUDED	**CCEEEHHLOST** CHEESECLOTH
CCDEEEEINNR NICENE CREED	**CCEEEHINNOR** INCOHERENCE
CCDEEEFHIKN CHICKENFEED	**CCEEEIINPPR** PERCIPIENCE
CCDEEEGINOT GENETIC CODE	**CCEEEILNORT** COELENTERIC
CCDEEEIINRS IRIDESCENCE	**CCEEEILNQSU** LIQUESCENCE
CCDEEEELLORT RECOLLECTED	**CCEEEINNNOV** CONVENIENCE
CCDEEENRRST RED CRESCENT	**CCEEEINNPSS** SPINESCENCE
CCDEEFINNOS CONFIDENCES	**CCEEEINOPRV** PRECONCEIVE
CCDEEHHMOSY ECHCHYMOSED	**CCEEEINOPSS** CENOSPECIES
CCDEEHILPSY PSYCHEDELIC	**CCEEEINOSTX** COEXISTENCE
CCDEEHINORS SECOND REICH	**CCEEEINRRST** CIRENCESTER
CCDEEHIORTT RICOCHETTED	**CCEEEINRSTV** VITRESCENCE
CCDEEHKOPST SPOT CHECKED	**CCEEELORTTU** ELECTROCUTE
CCDEEIIINST INSECTICIDE	**CCEEEMNPSSU** SPUMESCENCE
CCDEEIKLRSV CLEVER DICKS	**CCEEENNOQSU** CONSEQUENCE
CCDEEILNOTY CONCEITEDLY	**CCEEENPRSTU** PUTRESCENCE
CCDEEILRRSS DRESS CIRCLE	**CCEEENRRRSU** RECURRENCES
CCDEEINNORT ENDOCENTRIC	**CCEEFFIINOT** COEFFICIENT
CCDEEIOPPRU PREOCCUPIED	**CCEEFFILNOS** OFF-LICENCES
CCDEEJNORTU CONJECTURED	**CCEEFIIMNNU** MUNIFICENCE
CCDEELLLOTY COLLECTEDLY	**CCEEFLNNOSU** CONFLUENCES
CCDEELNNOOS CONDOLENCES	**CCEEFLNOPST** SELF-CONCEPT
CCDEELNNORY CONCERNEDLY	**CCEEGINNNOT** CONTINGENCE
CCDEELNORTY CONCERTEDLY	**CCEEGINOOTT** GEOTECTONIC
CCDEENNNORU UNCONCERNED	**CCEEGNNORVY** CONVERGENCY
CCDEENNNOTU UNCONNECTED	**CCEEGNOORRT** CONCERTGOER
CCDEHILLOSS COLD CHISELS	**CCEEHHKORRY** CHOKECHERRY

CCEEHINORTT THEOCENTRIC
CCEEHKLLLOS COCKLESHELL
CCEEHLMOORS COLOR SCHEME
CCEEHMOPTYY PHYCOMYCETE
CCEEHNOSSTU ESCUTCHEONS
CCEEIILMRSS SEMICIRCLES
CCEEIILORST ISOELECTRIC
CCEEIILRTTY ELECTRICITY
CCEEIIMNNOS OMNISCIENCE
CCEEIIMNOSV MISCONCEIVE
CCEEIINOPTV NOCICEPTIVE
CCEEIILLOSTV COLLECTIVES
CCEEILNNOTV CONVENTICLE
CCEEILNORST ELECTRONICS
CCEEILPPRTU PEPTIC ULCER
CCEEIMNOORT ECONOMETRIC
CCEEIMNORRT CENTROMERIC
CCEEIMNRSTU MUSIC CENTRE
CCEEINOSTUV CONSECUTIVE
CCEEIOPRSSS CROSSPIECES
CCEEIORRSTV CORRECTIVES
CCEEJNORRTU CONJECTURER
CCEEJNORSTU CONJECTURES
CCEELOSSTTU COS LETTUCES
CCEENORRSST CORRECTNESS
CCEFFIINSUY SUFFICIENCY
CCEFHHILSTU HECTIC FLUSH
CCEFHIIMORS MICROFICHES
CCEFIIIPSTY SPECIFICITY
CCEFIILNOTV CONFLICTIVE
CCEFIINOPRY PROFICIENCY
CCEFIKLSSTT CLEFT STICKS
CCEFINNOOST CONFECTIONS
CCEFIORRSUU CRUCIFEROUS
CCEGHHORRSU CHURCHGOERS
CCEGHIILNOR CHOLINERGIC
CCEGHIINORT RICOCHETING
CCEGHIMNOOR CHROMOGENIC
CCEGHINOPSY PSYCHOGENIC
CCEGIILNNOR RECONCILING
CCEGIINOOTX TOXICOGENIC
CCEGILNOORY ECCRINOLOGY
CCEGILNOOSY SYNECOLOGIC
CCEGINNNOTY CONTINGENCY
CCEGINNOOST COGNOSCENTI
CCEGINOPRTY CRYPTOGENIC
CCEHHKOOORT CROCHET HOOK
CCEHIILNOPR NECROPHILIC
CCEHIKNOPST CHECKPOINTS
CCEHILNOORT TECHNICOLOR
CCEHILNOPTY POLYTECHNIC
CCEHILNORRS CHRONICLERS
CCEHIMMOOST CHEMOSMOTIC
CCEHIMNOORT HOMOCENTRIC

CCEHIMOOPRT CHEMOTROPIC,
  ECTOMORPHIC
CCEHINNRSSU CRUNCHINESS
CCEHINOOSTZ ZOOTECHNICS
CCEHINOPRTY PYROTECHNIC
CCEHKLOSTTU SHUTTLECOCK
CCEHNOOOPRS CHRONOSCOPE
CCEIIINSSTT SCIENTISTIC
CCEIIKLRSTY CITY SLICKER
CCEIIKNSSTT STICK INSECT
CCEIILMNORT CLINOMETRIC
CCEIIMMORRT MICROMETRIC
CCEIIMOORST SOCIOMETRIC
CCEIIMORSTV VISCOMETRIC
CCEIINOORST COERCIONIST
CCEIIOPRRTY RECIPROCITY
CCEIJNNOTUV CONJUNCTIVE
CCEIKKOPPST PICKPOCKETS
CCEIKLNOPRU CUPRONICKEL
CCEILLNOOST COLLECTIONS
CCEILNNOTTU NOCTILUCENT
CCEILNORRTY INCORRECTLY
CCEIMNOORST CENTROSOMIC
CCEIMNOPRTY PYCNOMETRIC
CCEIMOOPRSS MICROSCOPES
CCEINNNOOST CONNECTIONS
CCEINNOOPST CONCEPTIONS
CCEINNOOSSS CONCESSIONS
CCEINNOOSTU CONSECUTION
CCEINNOPRRW CROWN PRINCE
CCEINNOSSTY CONSISTENCY
CCEINOORRST CORRECTIONS
CCEINOSSSSU SUCCESSIONS
CCEJNNORTUU CONJUNCTURE
CCEKLOORSTW CLOCK TOWERS
CCEKMNOSTUU COME UNSTUCK
CCELMOORSTY MOTORCYCLES
CCENORRSTTU RECONSTRUCT
CCEOOOOPPRST PROCTOSCOPE
CCFGIILNNOT CONFLICTING
CCFIIINORUX CRUCIFIXION
CCFIILNNOOT CONFLICTION
CCGGHHINORU CHURCHGOING
CCGHIILNNOR CHRONICLING
CCGIIIINRTZ CRITICIZING
CCGIOOPRSSY GYROSCOPICS
CCHHILOOORS CHOIR SCHOOL
CCHIIILNOPS SILICON CHIP
CCHIIIOSTTY HISTIOCYTIC
CCHIILORSTY CHRYSOLITIC
CCHIIMNOOPR MICROPHONIC
CCHIIMNOOST MONOSTICHIC
CCHIIMOORTT TRICHOTOMIC
CCHIIMOPRTY MICROPHYTIC

CCHIINOOPRS RHINOSCOPIC
CCHILMOPTYY LYMPHOCYTIC
CCHIMMNOOOR MONOCHROMIC
CCHIMOOPRTY CORMOPHYTIC
CCHIMOSSSTT SCOTCH MISTS
CCHIOOOOPRST ORTHOSCOPIC
CCHIORSSSTT CROSS-STITCH
CCIILOORSTU COLOURISTIC
CCIIMMNOSTU COMMUNISTIC
CCIIMOOPRRS MICROSPORIC
CCIIMOPRSST COMIC STRIPS
CCIINNOOSTV CONVICTIONS
CCIINOPRTTY NYCTITROPIC
CCIJNNNOOTU CONJUNCTION
CCIKLMNOOTU COCONUT MILK
CCILLNOORSU COUNCILLORS
CCILMRRSUUU CURRICULUMS
CCILNNOOSSU CONCLUSIONS
CCILNOOSSUY CONSCIOUSLY
CCIMNNOOPTU COMPUNCTION
CCINNOOSSUU UNCONSCIOUS
CCINOOPSSUU CONSPICUOUS
CCINOORRSTT CONSTRICTOR
CCLNNOOOORWY CROWN COLONY
CCNOORRSTTU CONSTRUCTOR
CCNOORRSTUW CROWN COURTS
CCNOORTTUUY COUNTY COURT
CCOOOOPPRSTY PROCTOSCOPY
CDDDEEEEGKL DECKLE-EDGED
CDDDEEIIRST DISCREDITED
CDDDEEILNUY UNDECIDEDLY
CDDDEIMMOOS DISCOMMODED
CDDEEEHLRSU RE-SCHEDULED
CDDEEEIPRTU DECREPITUDE
CDDEEEMMNOR RECOMMENDED
CDDEEEOPRRR PRERECORDED
CDDEEFIINST DISINFECTED
CDDEEFILNSU SELF-INDUCED
CDDEEHLNSUU UNSCHEDULED
CDDEEHNNRSU SUNDRENCHED
CDDEEIIMRST MISDIRECTED
CDDEEIINORT RODENTICIDE
CDDEEILNOOS DECOLONISED
CDDEEILNOOZ DECOLONIZED
CDDEEILTUVY DEDUCTIVELY
CDDEELOORUV OVERCLOUDED
CDDEENNOPSY DESPONDENCY
CDDEENORRSU UNDERSCORED
CDDEENORSSW CROWDEDNESS
CDDEEOORRVW OVERCROWDED
CDDEFIIMOST DISCOMFITED
CDDEGHILNOR GODCHILDREN
CDDEHIILMNR CHILDMINDER
CDDEIIIILNNS DISINCLINED

CDDEIIILNPS DISCIPLINED
CDDEIILPPSS SLIPPED DISC
CDDEIINNOOT CONDITIONED
CDDEIINOSUU INDECIDUOUS
CDDEIKOPSTT SPOTTED DICK
CDDEILNOOTY DICOTYLEDON
CDDEILNOSSU UNDISCLOSED
CDDEILOORSU DISCOLOURED
CDDEIMOOPSS DISCOMPOSED
CDDEINNOOST ENDODONTICS
CDDELLLMOOY MOLLYCODDLE
CDDENOORSTU COTES-DU-NORD
CDDENOPRSTU END PRODUCTS
CDEEEEFFLNS SELF-DEFENCE
CDEEEEFFRSV EFFERVESCED
CDEEEEFLNSS DEFENCELESS
CDEEEEINPRX EXPERIENCED
CDEEEFFFILT FIELD-EFFECT
CDEEEFFINRS DIFFERENCES
CDEEEFFISST SIDE EFFECTS
CDEEEFGLNTU GENUFLECTED
CDEEEFHIIPS SPEECHIFIED
CDEEEFHORUV CHEF D'OEUVRE
CDEEEFIILNS FIN DE SIECLE
CDEEEFIILRT ELECTRIFIED
CDEEEFILTVY DEFECTIVELY
CDEEEFLNRST SELF-CENTRED
CDEEEFLNRTU UNREFLECTED
CDEEEFMNORT DEFORCEMENT
CDEEEGILNXY EXCEEDINGLY
CDEEEGINRSV DIVERGENCES
CDEEEIIMMNN MEDICINE MEN
CDEEEIINNRS IN-RESIDENCE
CDEEEIIOPPR PERIOD PIECE
CDEEEIJNRTT INTERJECTED
CDEEEILNSTT DELITESCENT
CDEEEILOPSV VELOCIPEDES
CDEEEILORTT LIE DETECTOR
CDEEEILPTVY DECEPTIVELY
CDEEEINPRTT INTERCEPTED
CDEEEINRSTT INTERSECTED
CDEEEINSSTX EXCITEDNESS
CDEEEMMNORR RECOMMENDER
CDEEEMNOPRS RECOMPENSED
CDEEENNOPRS RESPONDENCE
CDEEENNORTU ENCOUNTERED
CDEEEOPRRSS PREDECESSOR,
  REPROCESSED
CDEEERRRSTU RESURRECTED
CDEEFFIKNST STIFF-NECKED
CDEEFHIKLOY FIELD HOCKEY
CDEEFIILNTY DEFICIENTLY
CDEEFIINPSU UNSPECIFIED
CDEEFILLTUY DECEITFULLY

CDEEFILNOST DEFLECTIONS
CDEEFILOSST CLOSEFISTED
CDEEFLLOORS SELF-COLORED
CDEEFLNORST CENTER-FOLDS
CDEEFLNORST CENTRE-FOLDS
CDEEFLNOSSY CONFESSEDLY
CDEEFNNORST FRONDESCENT
CDEEFOORRTU TOUR DE FORCE
CDEEFOPRRTW WORD-PERFECT
CDEEGGINTTU CUTTING EDGE
CDEEGGLORSS CROSS-LEGGED
CDEEGHIINPR DECIPHERING
CDEEGIINNRT INTERCEDING
CDEEGIINNUV UNDECEIVING
CDEEGIINRRT REDIRECTING
CDEEGILNNSU INDULGENCES
CDEEGINOPRS PROCEEDINGS
CDEEGNOSSSU SECOND-GUESS
CDEEHIINNOS INDOCHINESE
CDEEHIINNST INDEHISCENT
CDEEHIKPRSW SHIPWRECKED
CDEEHILOPRR PERCHLORIDE
CDEEHIMNORT ENDOTHERMIC
CDEEHIMNOTU ENDOTHECIUM
CDEEHIOQSTU DISCOTHEQUE
CDEEHPRSTTU UPSTRETCHED
CDEEIIILSTV DECLIVITIES
CDEEIIKLNSS SLICKENSIDE
CDEEIILNORT DERELICTION
CDEEIIMNRST DENSIMETRIC
CDEEIIMORTU EUDIOMETRIC
CDEEIIMPRSS SPERMICIDES
CDEEIINORRT REDIRECTION
CDEEIINRSTV VIRIDESCENT
CDEEIINRTTU INCERTITUDE
CDEEIIORRST DIRECTORIES
CDEEIIORSSV DISCOVERIES
CDEEIIPRSTV DESCRIPTIVE
CDEEIKLNNOO NICKELODEON
CDEEIKLNORT INTERLOCKED
CDEEILMOOSW LOW COMEDIES
CDEEILNNOSS DECLENSIONS
CDEEILNNQUY DELINQUENCY
CDEEILSTUVY SEDUCTIVELY
CDEEIMNNRST DISCERNMENT,
RESCINDMENT
CDEEIMNNSTU INDUCEMENTS
CDEEIMNOPRS ENDOSPERMIC
CDEEIMNORTV DIVORCEMENT
CDEEIMOOSTX SEXTODECIMO
CDEEINNRSSW WINDSCREENS
CDEEINOPRSV PROVIDENCES
CDEEINOPRTV OPEN VERDICT
CDEEINORRTU REINTRODUCE

CDEEINORSTT CREDIT NOTES
CDEEINPRSUU SUPERINDUCE
CDEEIORRSSV DISCOVERERS
CDEEIORRTXY EX-DIRECTORY
CDEEIRRRSVW SCREWDRIVER
CDEEIRSTTUV DESTRUCTIVE
CDEEKKORSTY SKYROCKETED
CDEEKNOORSS CROOKEDNESS
CDEEKOOPRSW WOODPECKERS
CDEEKOORSTV OVERSTOCKED
CDEELNNOTTY CONTENTEDLY
CDEELOOORRS ROSE-COLORED
CDEEMNNOSST SECONDMENTS
CDEENNORTUV UNCONVERTED
CDEENNOSTTU UNCONTESTED
CDEENOORRRT TROCORNERED
CDEENOORRSS ROOD SCREENS
CDEENPSSTUU UNSUSPECTED
CDEEOOPPRRV OVERCROPPED
CDEEOOPRRUV OVERPRODUCE
CDEEOPRRRSU REPRODUCERS
CDEFFGIOOOS GOOD OFFICES
CDEFGHIKLST FLIGHT DECKS
CDEFGHILNOS GOLDFINCHES
CDEFHIKOPRT PITCHFORKED
CDEFHNOORRS FRENCH DOORS
CDEFIIILMSU SEMIFLUIDIC
CDEFIILMMOR MICROFILMED
CDEFIIMORST DISCOMFITER
CDEFIINORST DISINFECTOR
CDEFIINORTU COUNTRIFIED
CDEFILNNOTY CONFIDENTLY
CDEFILNOSUU FLUID OUNCES
CDEGHHHIIPT HIGH-PITCHED
CDEGHINOSST SECOND SIGHT
CDEGIIJNPRU PREJUDICING
CDEGIINNORS CONSIDERING
CDEGIINORSV DISCOVERING
CDEGIMNNOTU DOCUMENTING
CDEGIMNOOPS DECOMPOSING
CDEGIMNORRU CORRIGENDUM
CDEGINOPRRU REPRODUCING
CDEGMNORSUU CURMUDGEONS
CDEGNORRSUW GROUND CREWS
CDEHHNOOOPR CHORDOPHONE
CDEHIIKTTTW THICK-WITTED
CDEHIILLNOT DECILLIONTH
CDEHIILOOTT THEODOLITIC
CDEHIILORRT TRICHLORIDE
CDEHIIMOOST DICHOTOMIES,
DICHOTOMISE
CDEHIIMOOTZ DICHOTOMIZE
CDEHIINOOPV VIDEOPHONIC
CDEHIIPSSTW DIPSWITCHES

CDEHILPRTUU PULCHRITUDE
CDEHIMNOOPR ENDOMORPHIC
CDEHIMNORST CHRISTENDOM
CDEHIMOPRSY HYPODERMICS
CDEHINOPRRY PONDICHERRY
CDEHIOOOPPT PHOTOCOPIED
CDEHKLOORST STOCKHOLDER
CDEHLOOPPRS CLODHOPPERS
CDEHLOOPSSS CLOSED SHOPS
CDEIIILNPRS DISCIPLINER
CDEIIILNPSS DISCIPLINES
CDEIIILNSUV UNCIVILISED
CDEIIILNUVZ UNCIVILIZED
CDEIIILOPST POLITICISED
CDEIIILOPTZ POLITICIZED
CDEIIIMORTX OXIDIMETRIC
CDEIIINNORT INDIRECTION
CDEIIINSTTV DISTINCTIVE
CDEIIIOPRTT PERIDOTITIC
CDEIIIOPRTY PERIODICITY
CDEIIIRSSTV RECIDIVISTS
CDEIIISSTUV VICISSITUDE
CDEIIJNSTUV DISJUNCTIVE
CDEIIKQTTUW QUICK-WITTED
CDEIILLMNOS MILLISECOND
CDEIILLOORV COD-LIVER OIL
CDEIILLOSUY DELICIOUSLY
CDEIILLPTUY PELLUCIDITY
CDEIILNRTUY INCREDULITY
CDEIILNTUVY INDUCTIVELY
CDEIILOORST SCLEROTIOID
CDEIILOPSSU PEDICULOSIS
CDEIILOSTUV DECLIVITOUS
CDEIIMMOOST COMMODITIES
CDEIIMNNSTT INDICTMENTS
CDEIIMNORST MODERNISTIC
CDEIIMOSTTY DOMESTICITY
CDEIIMPPRUY CYPRIPEDIUM
CDEIINNOORT CONDITIONER,
    RECONDITION
CDEIINNOSTU DISCONTINUE
CDEIINOOPRT PERIODONTIC
CDEIINOPRST DESCRIPTION, PREDICTIONS
CDEIINORRTT INTERDICTOR
CDEIINOSSST DISSECTIONS
CDEIINRSSTU SCRUTINISED
CDEIINRSTUZ SCRUTINIZED
CDEIIPRSSTU PEDICURISTS
CDEIJLNNOOY CONJOINEDLY
CDEIJNRSTUU DISJUNCTURE
CDEIJOOSTTU DO JUSTICE TO
CDEILNNNOOU ON CLOUD NINE
CDEILNOPSST SPLIT SECOND
CDEILNORSUU INCREDULOUS

CDEILORSSSU DISCLOSURES
CDEIMMNOPSU COMPENDIUMS
CDEIMMNOTTU UNCOMMITTED
CDEIMMOOPRS COMPROMISED
CDEIMNNOOPSU COMPENDIOUS
CDEIMNOSSTY SYNDESMOTIC
CDEINNOORSU ENDOCRINOUS
CDEINNOOSTU CONTUSIONED
CDEINNOPRST NONDESCRIPT
CDEINNORSTU DSCONTINUER
CDEINOOPSST ENDOSCOPIST
CDEINORSTTU DESTRUCTION
CDEINORSTUY COUNTRYSIDE
CDEINOSTTTU CONSTITUTED
CDEIORSSTUY DISCOURTESY
CDEKKNOOORR DOORKNOCKER
CDELLORSUUY CREDULOUSLY
CDENOORRTUW COUNTERWORD
CDEOOORSTTUW WOODCUTTERS
CDEOPRRRUWY CURRY POWDER
CDFGIILNNOY CONFIDINGLY
CDFGINNNOOU CONFOUNDING
CDFIMOORSST DISCOMFORTS
CDFINNOSTUY DYSFUNCTION
CDGIIKNNSUW WIND-SUCKING
CDGIIKNSTTU SITTING DUCK
CDGIILNOORS DISCOLORING
CDGIIMMNNOO INCOMMODING
CDGIINNORTU INTRODUCING
CDGIINNOSTU DISCOUNTING
CDGIINORSSU DISCOURSING
CDGILOORTTY TROGLODYTIC
CDGIMNNOOPU COMPOUNDING
CDGINOOTTUW WOODCUTTING
CDGINOPRSTU CROP-DUSTING
CDHIIIMOOPR IDIOMORPHIC
CDHIILPRSUU DISULPHURIC
CDHIIMOOSTT DICHOTOMIST
CDHIIOOPRST CHIROPODIST
CDHIMOOOSTU DICHOTOMOUS
CDHINOOORTT ORTHODONTIC
CDHINOOPRSY HYDROPONICS
CDIIIJNOSUU INJUDICIOUS
CDIIILNTTUY INDUCTILITY
CDIIINNNOOT IN CONDITION
CDIIINNOSTT DISTINCTION
CDIIJLOSUUY JUDICIOUSLY
CDIIJNNOSTU DISJUNCTION
CDIIKRRSTTY DIRTY TRICKS
CDIILMORSTU CLOSTRIDIUM
CDIIMMNNOOU CONDOMINIUM
CDIINOSSSSU DISCUSSIONS
CDIIOOOOSTV VOODOOISTIC
CDILLORSUUY LUDICROUSLY

CDILMOOORSX LOXODROMICS
CDILOOORUUU DOUROUCOULI
CDINNOOPRTY CYPRINODONT
CDINOOPRSTU PRODUCTIONS
CDLMOORSSTU STORM CLOUDS
CDOORRSSSSW CROSS SWORDS
CEEEEFNPRRS PREFERENCES
CEEEEGIMNRS EMERGENCIES
CEEEEHHRRST THREE CHEERS
CEEEEHNPRST THREEPENCES
CEEEEILNORT ELECTIONEER
CEEEEIMNNPR PRE-EMINENCE
CEEEEIMNNSS MISE-EN-SCENE
CEEEEINPRSX EXPERIENCES
CEEEEINRRRV IRREVERENCE
CEEEEENNRRTV NERVE CENTER
CEEEEENNRRTV NERVE CENTRE
CEEEEFFGINOV GIVE OFFENCE
CEEEFFHOOSU COFFEE HOUSE
CEEEFFIINTV INEFFECTIVE
CEEEFFILTVY EFFECTIVELY
CEEEFHIIPRS SPEECHIFIER
CEEEFIILRRT ELECTRIFIER
CEEEFIKQRUZ QUICK-FREEZE
CEEEFILRSSV SELF-SERVICE
CEEEFINQRSU FREQUENCIES
CEEEFIORRST REFECTORIES
CEEEFLPRSST SELF-RESPECT
CEEEFMNNORT ENFORCEMENT
CEEEFPRRSTU PREFECTURES
CEEEGGHINNS GEGENSCHEIN
CEEEGGNORRR GREENGROCER
CEEEGIKNORT GREENOCKITE
CEEEGINNOTX XENOGENETIC
CEEEGINNRRV REVERENCING
CEEEGINOSST ECTOGENESIS
CEEEHHKLNOP HECKELPHONE
CEEEHHMOPRS CHEMOSPHERE
CEEEHHNRSTT THE TRENCHES
CEEEHIKNTTT KITCHENETTE
CEEEHILORTT HETEROCLITE
CEEEHIMNRTU HERMENEUTIC
CEEEHIMORST HETEROECISM
CEEEHISSSSW SWISS CHEESE
CEEEHLLRSSY CHEERLESSLY
CEEEHMNNRRT TRENCHERMEN
CEEEHOQRSUU EUROCHEQUES
CEEEHRRSTWY SWEET CHERRY
CEEEIIKLNTT TELEKINETIC
CEEEIIMNNPT IMPENITENCE
CEEEIINNNRT INTERNECINE
CEEEIINNNST INSENTIENCE
CEEEIINNSTX INEXISTENCE
CEEEIINSSST NECESSITIES

CEEEIILLSTVY SELECTIVELY
CEEEEILNNOQU INELOQUENCE
CEEEEILNOPST PLEISTOCENE
CEEEEILNORST RE-ELECTIONS
CEEEEILNPSST PESTILENCES
CEEEEILPRTVY RECEPTIVELY
CEEEEILRSTVY SECRETIVELY
CEEEEILSSVXY EXCESSIVELY
CEEEEIMMNRTX CEMENT MIXER
CEEEEIMMPSUU MUSEUM PIECE
CEEEEIMNNSTT ENTICEMENTS
CEEEEIMNRSTT CENTIMETERS
CEEEEIMNRSTT CENTIMETRES
CEEEEIMNSTTX EXCITEMENTS
CEEEEINNOSTV VENESECTION
CEEEEINORTUX EXECUTIONER
CEEEEINOSTVX COEXTENSIVE
CEEEEINPRSSS PRECISENESS
CEEEEINPRSST PERSISTENCE
CEEEEIPPRSTV PERSPECTIVE
CEEEEIPRSTUV PERSECUTIVE
CEEEEJNNSTUV JUVENESCENT
CEEEEKKLOPRS LOCK KEEPERS
CEEEEKMNORSS SMOKESCREEN
CEEEELLLNTXY EXCELLENTLY
CEEEELLORSTY ELECTROLYSE
CEEEELLORTTY ELECTROLYTE
CEEEELMNOSSW WELCOMENESS
CEEEELMORRST ELECTROMERS,
    SCLEROMETER
CEEEELNNOORT COELENTERON
CEEEELOPRTTY ELECTROTYPE
CEEEELORSTVW SWEET CLOVER
CEEEEMNOPRRS RECOMPENSER
CEEEENNORRTU ENCOUNTERER
CEEEENOPRSST OPEN SECRETS
CEEEENRSSSTT SCREEN TESTS
CEEEEOOPRSST STEREOSCOPE
CEEEFFHIIORS IRISH COFFEE
CEEEFFHINRRS FRENCH FRIES
CEEEFFHOOPSS COFFEE SHOPS
CEEEFFIIINNT INEFFICIENT
CEEEFFIILLOS SLICE OF LIFE
CEEEFFIILNTY EFFICIENTLY
CEEEFGIMOORT COME TO GRIEF
CEEEFGINNRRY REFRINGENCY
CEEEFGINRSTU CENTRIFUGES
CEEEFGLNORTU GENUFLECTOR
CEEEFHHNORTT THENCEFORTH
CEEEFHILMRST FLETCHERISM
CEEEFHILORSU CHELIFEROUS
CEEEFIKKNOPT POCKETKNIFE
CEEEFIKOOPRW PIECE OF WORK
CEEEFILMPRTY IMPERFECTLY

CEEFILNORST REFLECTIONS
CEEFILNORSU FLUORESCEIN
CEEFIMNNNOT CONFINEMENT
CEEFIMOPRSS FORM SPECIES
CEEFINNQRUY INFREQUENCY
CEEFINOPRST IN RESPECT OF
CEEFINORTTU COUNTERFEIT
CEEFINOSSTY OF NECESSITY
CEEFLMOORRT ELECTROFORM
CEEFLNORSTU FLUORESCENT
CEEFLOORRSU FORECLOSURE
CEEFLORRSUU RESOURCEFUL
CEEFMNNORST CONFERMENTS
CEEGHILLNOP PHELLOGENIC
CEEGHINNNRT ENTRENCHING
CEEGHINNRRT RETRENCHING
CEEGHINRSST SIGHTSCREEN
CEEGHLOPSST CLOTHES PEGS
CEEGIINPRST STRINGPIECE
CEEGIINSSTT GENETICISTS
CEEGIIOOTVV GIVE VOICE TO
CEEGILNNOSY GEOSYNCLINE
CEEGILNOPST TELESCOPING
CEEGILNOPTY POLYGENETIC
CEEGILNOSTT TELEGNOSTIC
CEEGIMNNOOT MONOGENETIC
CEEGIMNORST EGOCENTRISM
CEEGINOORST OESTROGENIC
CEEGINOSSTY CYTOGENESIS
CEEGINPRSTU PERSECUTING
CEEGMNNORSS CONGRESSMEN
CEEHHIIMPRS HEMISPHERIC
CEEHHILMOOR HELIOCHROME
CEEHHIMRSTT HEMSTITCHER
CEEHHKMOORV CHEREMKHOVO
CEEHHMORSTT HOME STRETCH
CEEHIIINORS CHINOISERIE
CEEHIILLNST HELLENISTIC
CEEHIILMORT HELIOMETRIC
CEEHIIMPRTU PERITHECIUM
CEEHIIMPSTU EUPHEMISTIC
CEEHIKNSSST SKETCHINESS, THICKNESSES
CEEHILLNOPU NUCLEOPHILE
CEEHILLNOST CLOTHESLINE
CEEHILMNORT THERMOCLINE
CEEHILOPRST ELECTORSHIP,
 HELICOPTERS
CEEHILORTTY HETEROLYTIC
CEEHILPRSTU LECTURESHIP
CEEHILQSSTU SQUELCHIEST
CEEHIMNOPRS MESONEPHRIC
CEEHIMOPRSS MESOSPHERIC
CEEHIMOPRTT PITCHOMETER
CEEHIMOPSTU MOUTHPIECES

CEEHIOOPRTT HETEROTOPIC
CEEHIOPRTTY HETEROTYPIC
CEEHIRSSTTT STRETCHIEST
CEEHKLNOSUY HONEYSUCKLE
CEEHKNORSUY HONEYSUCKER
CEEHKNPRSUY KEYPUNCHERS
CEEHLLOORST CHOLESTEROL
CEEHLLORSUY LECHEROUSLY
CEEHLNOOPRR CHLOROPRENE
CEEHMNOORRT CHRONOMETER
CEEHMNOPRTY NEPHRECTOMY
CEEHMOOPRST THERMOSCOPE
CEEHNOORRTT ORTHOCENTER
CEEHNOORRTT ORTHOCENTRE
CEEHOOPSSTT STETHOSCOPE
CEEHORRTTYY ERYTHROCYTE
CEEIIINNRST INNER CITIES
CEEIIKNRSST RICKETINESS
CEEIILMRTUV VERMICULITE
CEEIILNNRSY INSINCERELY
CEEIILSTTVY SELECTIVITY
CEEIIMMPRST METEMPIRICS
CEEIIMNNRST REMINISCENT
CEEIIMOPRTZ PIEZOMETRIC
CEEIIMOPTTV COMPETITIVE
CEEIIMORSST ESOTERICISM
CEEIIMORSTX EXOTERICISM
CEEIINORSTV INSECTIVORE
CEEIINOSTVX CONVEXITIES
CEEIINRSSTT INTERSTICES
CEEIIPRTTVY RECEPTIVITY
CEEIIRRSTTV RESTRICTIVE
CEEIJLOPRST PROJECTILES
CEEIJNORRTT INTERJECTOR
CEEIKLNORRT INTERLOCKER
CEEIKMMOSUY MICKEY MOUSE
CEEIKNPRSTY PERSNICKETY
CEEILLMRSSY MERCILESSLY
CEEILLSUVXY EXCLUSIVELY
CEEILMNNSTU LUMINESCENT
CEEILMNOOPW POLICEWOMEN
CEEILMNOSTU CONTUMELIES
CEEILMNRSTU MULTISCREEN
CEEILMOORRT COLORIMETER
CEEILMOOSTU LEUCOTOMIES
CEEILNNNOOV NONVIOLENCE
CEEILNQSTUY QUIESCENTLY
CEEILRRSTUU SERICULTURE
CEEIMMORRST MICROMETERS
CEEIMNNOOPT OMNIPOTENCE
CEEIMNNOPRS PROMINENCES
CEEIMNNOPTT INCOMPETENT
CEEIMNNORTU COUNTERMINE
CEEIMNNSTTU INTUMESCENT

CEEIMNOORSU CEREMONIOUS
CEEIMNRRTTU RECRUITMENT
CEEIMOOPSSS SEISMOSCOPE
CEEIMOORRSV ROOM SERVICE
CEEIMOPRSSV COMPRESSIVE
CEEIMOPRSTU COMPUTERISE
CEEIMOPRTUZ COMPUTERIZE
CEEINNNOSTT CONSENTIENT
CEEINNOORRT RECONNOITRE
CEEINNOOSTX COEXTENSION
CEEINOOPRST RETINOSCOPE
CEEINOPPRSS SNIPERSCOPE
CEEINOPRRTT INTERCEPTOR
CEEINOPRSSS PRECESSIONS
CEEINOPRSTU PERSECUTION
CEEINOPRTTX EXCERPTTION
CEEINORRSST INTERCESSOR
CEEINORRSTU INTERCOURSE
CEEINOSSSTU NECESSITOUS
CEEINRRSSTU SCRUTINEERS
CEEIOPPRSTV PROSPECTIVE
CEEIOPRRTTY STEREOTYPIC
CEEIPQRSTUU PICTURESQUE
CEEIRSTTVVY CIVVY STREET
CEEJLNORSWW CROWN JEWELS
CEEKLNRSTTU TURTLENECKS
CEEKMNOOPTY POCKET MONEY
CEEKOORRRTT RETRO-ROCKET
CEELMMNOPST COMPLEMENTS
CEELMNNOSTU LOCUM TENENS
CEELMNOPSTY SPLENECTOMY
CEELMNOPTTY COMPETENTLY
CEELNRRRTUY RECURRENTLY
CEEMMNNOOSS COMMON SENSE
CEEMMNOPTUY PNEUMECTOMY
CEEMMOOPRTT COMPTOMETER
CEEMMOORSTT COME TO TERMS
CEEMNNNOTTT CONTENTMENT
CEEMNOORTUV COUNTERMOVE
CEEMNOPRRTU PROCUREMENT
CEEMNOPRSTT CONTRETEMPS
CEENNOORRST CORNERSTONE
CEENNOSSSSU CONSENSUSES
CEENOPPPRRS PEPPERCORNS
CEENOPRTTUY COUNTERTYPE
CEENORSTTTU STONECUTTER
CEEOOPRRTTV OVERPROTECT
CEEOOPRSSTY STEREOSCOPY
CEEOPRRSSTT PROTECTRESS
CEEOPRRSSTU PERSECUTORS
CEERRRSTTUU RESTRUCTURE
CEFFHIINORS CHIFFONIERS
CEFFHIRSSTT FESTSCHRIFT
CEFFIOOPSST POST OFFICES

CEFGIILNNNU INFLUENCING
CEFGIINNORR REINFORCING
CEFGIKLLNOS SELF-LOCKING
CEFGILNOORS FORECLOSING
CEFGLOORSSU GOLF COURSES
CEFHHNNORRS FRENCH HORNS
CEFHIIISSTT FETISHISTIC
CEFHILLRTUY FILTHY LUCRE
CEFHOOSSTTU SOFT TOUCHES
CEFIIKKLNSV FLICK KNIVES
CEFIILNNOST INFLECTIONS
CEFIINORSUZ ZINCIFEROUS
CEFILMORSUU CULMIFEROUS
CEFILNOORTU COUNTERFOIL
CEFILOORSUY FEROCIOUSLY
CEFINNOOSSS CONFESSIONS
CEFIOPRRSUU CUPRIFEROUS
CEFLLNOORST SELF-CONTROL
CEFLMOORSST COMFORTLESS
CEFLNOORRSW CORNFLOWERS
CEFLOOOPRSU FLUOROSCOPE
CEFNOPRRTUY PERFUNCTORY
CEGGIINNORZ RECOGNIZING
CEGHIIINNRT INTRENCHING
CEGHIIINNRST CHRISTENING
CEGHIMMNOOS HOMECOMINGS
CEGHINORSSU GROUCHINESS
CEGHIOOPRST GEOSTROPHIC
CEGIIIMNNRS REMINISCING
CEGIIIMNRTZ METRICIZING
CEGIIKLNNSY SICKENINGLY
CEGIILLNNST STENCILLING
CEGIILLNORY RECOILINGLY
CEGIILMNOST CLOSING TIME
CEGIILMOOSS SEISMOLOGIC
CEGIILNOOST NEOLOGISTIC
CEGIILNORST CLOISTERING
CEGIILNOTVY COGNITIVELY
CEGIILOOPST GEOPOLITICS
CEGIIMMNNOU IMMUNOGENIC
CEGIIMNNOOZ ECONOMIZING
CEGIIMNOORT GONIOMETRIC
CEGIINNOORT RECOGNITION
CEGIINORSTU CONGRUITIES
CEGIINRRSTT RESTRICTING
CEGILLNNOSU COUNSELLING
CEGILNNOSSY CLOYINGNESS
CEGILNOORST NECROLOGIST
CEGILNOOSTY SCIENTOLOGY
CEGILNORSSS SINGLE-CROSS
CEGILNRRRUY RECURRINGLY
CEGIMNNNOST CONSIGNMENT
CEGIMNOOOSS COSMOGONIES
CEGIMNOPRSS COMPRESSING

CEGIMOOOORRV MICROGROOVE
CEGIMOOPRST COME TO GRIPS
CEGINNNOSTT CONTINGENTS
CEGINNORSTU COUNTERSIGN
CEGINOPPRST PROSPECTING
CEGINOPRSTU PROSECUTING
CEGLMMOORYY MYRMECOLOGY
CEGLMOOSSTY GLOSSECTOMY
CEGLNNORTUY CONGRUENTLY
CEGORRRSUYY CRYOSURGERY
CEHHHIIKRST HITCHHIKERS
CEHHIIILLOT HELIOLITHIC
CEHHIIMMOPR HEMIMORPHIC
CEHHILMRSUY HELICHRYSUM
CEHHIMRSTUY EURHYTHMICS
CEHHINRTTUW WITCH-HUNTER
CEHHIOPRRST CHRISTOPHER
CEHHIOPSTYZ SCHIZOPHYTE
CEHHLOOOSSU SCHOOLHOUSE
CEHHMNORSSY SYNCHROMESH
CEHHMOOOPRR CHROMOPHORE
CEHHOOOOPRRT TROCHOPHORE
CEHIIINPSST CITISENSHIP
CEHIIINPSTZ CITIZENSHIP
CEHIIJPSSTU JUSTICESHIP
CEHIIJSTTUW WITH JUSTICE
CEHIIKLNOPS PICK HOLES IN
CEHIIKNSSTT IN THE STICKS
CEHIILOOPRT HELIOTROPIC
CEHIILPRSTU SPHERULITIC
CEHIIMNORST THERMIONICS
CEHIIMOPPRR PERIMORPHIC
CEHIIMOSSUV MISCHIEVOUS
CEHIINOOPRS IONOSPHERIC
CEHIINOORSS ISOCHRONISE
CEHIINOORSZ ISOCHRONIZE
CEHIIOPPTTY EPIPHYTOTIC
CEHIIOPRRST PREHISTORIC
CEHIIOPRSVY VICEROYSHIP
CEHIIOSSSVY VICHYSSOISE
CEHIKMRSSTU HUCKSTERISM
CEHIKNOPSTU SOUP KITCHEN
CEHIKNPSSSU PUCKISHNESS
CEHILLMOPSY MESOPHYLLIC
CEHILMOOPPR PLEOMORPHIC
CEHILMOOPRS PLEOCHROISM
CEHILMORTTY THERMOLYTIC
CEHILNOOQRU CHLOROQUINE
CEHILNOSSST COLTISHNESS
CEHILNOSSSU SLOUCHINESS
CEHIMMOOPRS MESOMORPHIC
CEHIMMOOSSS CHEMOSMOSIS
CEHIMNOOPRS MICROPHONES
CEHIMNOOPRT PHONOMETRIC

CEHIMNOOPRX XENOMORPHIC
CEHIMNOPSTY CHIMNEYPOTS
CEHIMOOPRRX XEROMORPHIC
CEHIMOOPRTT PHOTOMETRIC
CEHIMOOSSST SCHISTOSOME
CEHIMOPPRST COPPERSMITH
CEHIMORSTTY STICHOMETRY
CEHINNORSSY SYNCHRONISE
CEHINNORSYZ SYNCHRONIZE
CEHINOOPRRS CORONERSHIP
CEHIOOOPPRT PHOTOCOPIER
CEHIOOOPPST PHOTOCOPIES
CEHIOOPSTTY OSTEOPHYTIC
CEHIOPRSSTT PROSTHETICS
CEHKNOOSSTT ON THE STOCKS
CEHLOOPPRSS PREP SCHOOLS
CEHMMNOORSW COMMON SHREW
CEHMMOOORSS CHROMOSOMES
CEHMMOOORSX X CHROMOSOME
CEHMMOOORSY Y CHROMOSOME
CEHMNOORRTY CHRONOMETRY
CEHMOPRSTYY PSYCHOMETRY
CEHNNOSSTUU UNCOUTHNESS
CEHNOOSSTTU TOUCHSTONES
CEHOOPSSTTY STETHOSCOPY
CEHOORSSTUU COURTHOUSES
CEIIILLMNPU PENICILLIUM
CEIIILLPTTY ELLIPTICITY
CEIIILNNPTY INCIPIENTLY
CEIIIMNOPRS IMPRECISION
CEIIIMNOSST MISONEISTIC
CEIIIMPSSST PESSIMISTIC
CEIIINNRSTY INSINCERITY
CEIIINNSTTV INSTINCTIVE
CEIIINOPRTT PERITONITIC
CEIIINOSTVV VIVISECTION
CEIIINPRSTV INSCRIPTIVE
CEIIIOPRSTT PERIOSTITIC
CEIIIORSSTU CURIOSITIES
CEIIIOSSTTV SOVIETISTIC
CEIIKLLPSTT LICKSPITTLE
CEIIKLNNRSS CRINKLINESS
CEIIKLNPRSS PRICKLINESS
CEIIKLQRSUV QUICKSILVER
CEIIKNOSSTY CYTOKINESIS
CEIIKNRSSST TRICKSINESS
CEIIKPRSSTT SPITSTICKER
CEIILLNSUVY INCLUSIVELY
CEIILNRTUUV VINICULTURE
CEIILRTTUUV VITICULTURE
CEIILRTTUVY RELUCTIVITY
CEIIMMNOSTU COMMUNITIES
CEIIMNOOPTT COMPETITION
CEIIMNOPSUU IMPECUNIOUS

CEIIMNORRTT NITROMETRIC
CEIIMNORSTU NEUROTICISM
CEIIMNPRSSS SCRIMPINESS
CEIIMOPRRST SPIROMETRIC
CEIIMOPRSST SEMITROPICS
CEIINNNNOTT INCONTINENT
CEIINNNNORTU INTERNUNCIO
CEIINNOPSST INSPECTIONS
CEIINORRSTT RESTRICTION
CEIINOSSSUV VICIOUSNESS
CEIINRRSSTU SCRUTINISER
CEIINRRSTUZ SCRUTINIZER
CEIINRSTTUV INSTRUCTIVE
CEIIOPPRSTU PRECIPITOUS
CEIIORRRSTT TERRORISTIC
CEIIORSTUVY VOYEURISTIC
CEIIPPRSTUY PERSPICUITY
CEIJNOOPRST PROJECTIONS
CEIKLLMOORS ROLLICKSOME
CEIKLMOORST MORTISE LOCK
CEIKLNNSSUU UNLUCKINESS
CEIKLNOORRT CRINKLEROOT
CEIKNNORSTU COUNTERSINK
CEILLLNOOOV VIOLONCELLO
CEILLNOPRSU CURL ONE'S LIP
CEILMMNOPST COMPLIMENTS
CEILMMOPRUY PROMYCELIUM
CEILMNOOPSX COMPLEXIONS
CEILMNOTYYZ ENZYMOLYTIC
CEILMOOOPST COSMOPOLITE
CEILMOOOSTV LOCOMOTIVES
CEILMOPRTUU POMICULTURE
CEILNOOPRTU PERLOCUTION
CEILNORSSTU COURTLINESS
CEILNRSTUUV VENTRICULUS
CEILOOPRSTT PROTOSTELIC
CEILOOPRTTY PROTEOLYTIC
CEILOORRSTU TERRICOLOUS
CEILOORRSUV VERSICOLOUR
CEILOORRSVY CORROSIVELY
CEIMMMNOSTT COMMITMENTS
CEIMMNOQSUU COMMUNIQUÉS
CEIMMNORSSU CONSUMERISM
CEIMMOOPRRS COMPROMISER
CEIMMOOPRSS COMPROMISES
CEIMNOOPRSS COMPRESSION
CEIMNOOPRTU MUCOPROTEIN
CEIMNOORSTU COTERMINOUS
CEIMNOPRSSU PROSCENIUMS
CEIMNOPSTUV CONSUMPTIVE
CEIMNORSSTU MISCONSTRUE
CEIMOOPRSTT COMPETITORS
CEIINNNOOSTT CONTENTIONS
CEIINNNOOSTV CONVENTIONS

CEINNOORSSU CONNOISSEUR
CEINNOORSSV CONVERSIONS
CEINNOOSTTU CONTENTIOUS
CEINNOSTTTU CONSTITUENT
CEINOOPRSSS PROCESSIONS
CEINOOPRSTT PROTECTIONS,
STENOTROPIC
CEINOOPRSTU PROSECUTION
CEINOOPRSTY RETINOSCOPY
CEINOOPTTTY TOTIPOTENCY
CEINOPRSSSU SUPERSONICS
CEINORSSSUU CURIOUSNESS
CEINORSTTTU CONSTITUTER
CEINOSSSSUV VISCOUSNESS
CEINOSSSTUV VISCOUNTESS
CEIOOOPRRTZ PROTEROZOIC
CEIOOPRTTYZ CRYPTOZOITE
CEIOPPRSSUU PERSPICUOUS
CEIOPRRSTWY COPYWRITERS
CEIORRSTUVY VERRUCOSITY
CEIPPRRSSTU SUPERSCRIPT
CEIPPRSSTTY TYPESCRIPTS
CEKLMOOORRS LOCKER ROOMS
CEKNNORSTUU COUNTERSUNK
CEKNOORRTUW COUNTERWORK
CELLLOORSSY COLORLESSLY
CELLMOOPRRT COMPTROLLER
CELLNNOOPTU POLLEN COUNT
CELLNOORRST CONTROLLERS
CELLNOORSSU COUNSELLORS
CELLNRTTUUY TRUCULENTLY
CELMNOORTUU MONOCULTURE
CELMOOPRTYY PYLORECTOMY
CELNOOPRTTU COUNTERPLOT
CELOOOPRRST POSTER COLOR
CELOORSTUUY COURTEOUSLY
CEMMNOOPRTT COMPORTMENT
CEMOOPRRSSS COMPRESSORS
CENOORRSTVY CONTROVERSY
CENOPRRSSTU CORRUPTNESS
CENORSTTUWY WEST COUNTRY
CEOOPPRRSST PROSPECTORS
CEOOPRRSSTU PROSECUTORS
CEPRRSSTTUU SUPERSTRUCT
CFFGIIKNOST TICKINGS OFF
CFFGIINRTUY FRUCTIFYING
CFFHILMNOTU FIFTH COLUMN
CFFIIINOOSU INOFFICIOUS
CFFIILOOSUY OFFICIOUSLY
CFGHIILLNNY FLINCHINGLY
CFGHIILNNNU UNFLINCHING
CFGHIMNOORT FORTHCOMING
CFGIINNNOTU FUNCTIONING
CFGILNNOSUY CONFUSINGLY

CFGINNNOORT CONFRONTING
CFGINOSTUUY YOUNG FUSTIC
CFHHIKMNOTU THINK MUCH OF
CFHIIKSSSTT SHIFT STICKS, STICK SHIFTS
CFHLLOOOORST FLOOR CLOTHS
CFIIILNNOST INFLICTIONS
CFIILMORSTU FORMULISTIC
CFIINORSSTU FIRST COUSIN
CFIMNOORSST CONFORMISTS
CFINNOORSTU INNS OF COURT
CFLOOOOPRSUY FLUOROSCOPY
CGGHIILOOPR LOGOGRIPHIC
CGGIIIKNPST PIGSTICKING
CGGIIKNPSSU SUCKING PIGS
CGGILNORSUY SCOURGINGLY
CGHHHIIIKNT HITCHHIKING
CGHHHILOOSS HIGH SCHOOLS
CGHHILNOOST NIGHT SCHOOL
CGHHILOOTYY ICHTHYOLOGY
CGHIIIILRSTV CIVIL RIGHTS
CGHIIKNSSTT NIGHTSTICKS
CGHIILNTTWY TWITCHINGLY
CGHILLNOSUY SLOUCHINGLY
CGHILMOOOPR MORPHOLOGIC
CGHILOOPSTY PHYCOLOGIST
CGHILOORSTY CHRISTOLOGY
CGHIMNOORST SHORTCOMING
CGHIMOOOTYZ HOMOZYGOTIC
CGHIMOOPRYZ ZYGOMORPHIC
CGHINOPTTUY TOUCH-TYPING
CGIIIIMNTVZ VICTIMIZING
CGIIIKLNOPT POLITICKING
CGIIILNSSTU LINGUISTICS
CGIIILRSTTU LITURGISTIC
CGIIKLLNORS ROLLICKINGS
CGIIKLLNRTY TRICKLINGLY
CGIIKLNOPST STOCKPILING
CGIILLOSSTY SYLLOGISTIC
CGIILMMNOOU IMMUNOLOGIC
CGIILMNOORY CRIMINOLOGY
CGIILNNNSUU CUNNILINGUS
CGIILNOOOST ICONOLOGIST
CGIILOOOSST SOCIOLOGIST
CGIIMNNOSTU MISCOUNTING
CGIIMNOSTUZ CUSTOMIZING
CGIINNORTUY INCONGRUITY
CGIINNRSTTU INSTRUCTING
CGILLNNOORT CONTROLLING
CGILMOOOSST COSMOLOGIST
CGILNPRSTUU SCULPTURING
CGILOOSSTTY CYTOLOGISTS
CGIMNOOOSST COSMOGONIST
CGINNNOOPRU PRONOUNCING
CGINNOORSUU INCONGRUOUS

CGINRRSTTUU STRUCTURING
CHHIILOPTTY LITHOPHYTIC
CHHIIMORSTY ISORHYTHMIC
CHHIIMRTTYY RHYTHMICITY
CHHILLMOOPY HOMOPHYLLIC
CHHILMOOOPR HOLOMORPHIC
CHHIMMOOOPR HOMOMORPHIC
CHHIOORSTTY ORTHOSTICHY
CHHLLLOOPRY CHLOROPHYLL
CHIIILPSSTY SYPHILITICS
CHIIIMORSST HISTORICISM
CHIIINORSST HISTRIONICS, TRICHINOSIS
CHIIIORSSTT HISTORICIST
CHIIIORSTTY HISTORICITY
CHIILLNOOTT OCTILLIONTH
CHIILOOPRTT PROTOLITHIC
CHIINNOPSSU PINCUSHIONS
CHIINORRTTY TYROTHRICIN
CHIIOOPRTTX THIXOTROPIC
CHIIOPPRRTY PORPHYRITIC
CHIIORRSSTY SCIRRHOSITY
CHIIORSSTTU TRISTICHOUS
CHIIOSSSTTY SCHISTOSITY
CHILNOPSSSU CONSULSHIPS
CHILOOPPRTY POLYTROPHIC
CHILOORSTUU ULOTRICHOUS
CHIMMNOOOPR MONOMORPHIC
CHIMNNORSSY SYNCHRONISM
CHIMNOOPRRS PROCHRONISM
CHIOOOPPRTT PHOTOTROPIC
CHIOOOPRRTT ORTHOTROPIC
CHIOOPPRSTY SPOROPHYTIC
CHIOOPPRTTY TROPOPHYTIC
CHIOPSTTTUY TOUCH-TYPIST
CHKOOOOPRSST SHOCK TROOPS
CHMNOOPSTTU MUTTONCHOPS
CHMNOOPTTUU NOT UP TO MUCH
CHMOOOOPRSTY PSYCHOMOTOR
CHNNOORRSTY SYNCHROTRON
CHNNOORSSUY SYNCHRONOUS
CIIIILLMMNOR MILLIMICRON
CIIILOPSSST SOLIPSISTIC
CIIILRSTTUU UTRICULITIS
CIIINNOPRST INSCRIPTION
CIIINOOSTTY ISOTONICITY
CIIINORSTUY INCURIOSITY
CIIJNNNOSTU INJUNCTIONS
CIILLOORSTT TORTICOLLIS
CIILMMNNOOS MONOCLINISM
CIILNOPSTUU PUNCTILIOUS
CIIMMNNOOTU COMMINUTION
CIIMMNOOSSS COMMISSIONS
CIIMMOORSTT MICROTOMIST
CIIMNOOOPST COMPOSITION

CIIMOPRRSTU SCRIPTORIUM
CIIMOPRSTUY PROMISCUITY
CIINNORSTTU INSTRUCTION
CIIOOPRSSUV PISCIVOROUS
CILMNNOOOSU MONOCLINOUS
CILMNOOPSSU COMPULSIONS
CILNNOOOTUV CONVOLUTION
CILNNOOSSUV CONVULSIONS
CILNNOOSUUY INNOCUOUSLY
CIMNNOOOPPS NINCOMPOOPS
CIMNNOOPSTU CONSUMPTION
CIMNOORSSTU CONSORTIUMS
CIMNOPPSTUU SUCTION PUMP
CIMOOOOPRSST COMPOSITORS
CIMOOPRSSUU PROMISCUOUS
CIMOPRSSTUU SCRUMPTIOUS
CINNOOORSTT CONTORTIONS
CINOOPRRSTU CORRUPTIONS
CINORRSSTTU INSTRUCTORS
CIOPPRSSSTT POSTSCRIPTS
CIPPRRSSTUU STIRRUP CUPS
CIRRSSTTTUU STRUCTURIST
CLLNOOSUUVV CONVOLVULUS
CMMMNOOOORS COMMON ROOMS
CMMNNNOOOSU COMMON NOUNS
CNNOOSTTUWY COUNTY TOWNS
DDDEEFIOSST EISTEDDFODS
DDDEEIILMSS MIDDLE-SISED
DDDEEIILMSZ MIDDLE-SIZED
DDDEELMNSSU MUDDLEDNESS
DDDEGILNORY DODDERINGLY
DDDENNOORTW DOWNTRODDEN
DDEEEEFIRRZ FREEZE-DRIED
DDEEEEHNPRR REPREHENDED
DDEEEELOPRV REDEVELOPED
DDEEEFILLNW WELL-DEFINED
DDEEEFILSTT FIELD-TESTED
DDEEEGHIRRT THIRD-DEGREE
DDEEEGIPRST PREDIGESTED
DDEEEHILLSV DISHEVELLED
DDEEEILNRSS SLENDERISED
DDEEEILNRSZ SLENDERIZED
DDEEEIMNOST DEMONETISED
DDEEEIMNOTZ DEMONETIZED
DDEEEIMPRST DISTEMPERED
DDEEEINNNPT INDEPENDENT
DDEEEINPRST PREDESTINED
DDEEEIPPSST SIDESTEPPED
DDEEEELLNOWW WELL-ENDOWED
DDEEELNOPUV UNDEVELOPED
DDEEELNPRTY PRETENDEDLY
DDEEENOSSTV DEVOTEDNESS
DDEEENRRRSU SURRENDERED
DDEEEORRSSV OVERDRESSED

DDEEFFGLLLU FULL-FLEDGED
DDEEFHILNOT ON THE FIDDLE
DDEEFIIIMNN INDEMNIFIED
DDEEFIIIRSV DIVERSIFIED
DDEEFIIMNNU DEFINIENDUM
DDEEFIIMSTY DEMYSTIFIED
DDEEFIORSST DISFORESTED
DDEEFLLNOUW WELL-FOUNDED
DDEEGINNRSU UNDERSIGNED
DDEEGNOPRSU GROUNDSPEED
DDEEHIILRSS DISRELISHED
DDEEHNNORSW SEND HER DOWN
DDEEIIILPPSS SIDESLIPPED
DDEEIINRRST DISINTERRED
DDEEIIQSTUU DISQUIETUDE
DDEEIKNNRSS KINDREDNESS
DDEEIILNOSTT DOTTED LINES
DDEEINNNPRU UNDERPINNED
DDEEINSSSTU STUDIEDNESS
DDEEIOPPRSS PREDISPOSED
DDEELLNORUW WELL-ROUNDED
DDEENNORSSU ROUNDEDNESS
DDEFFIILNTY DIFFIDENTLY
DDEGGGILORS GOLD DIGGERS
DDEGGIINNRW WEDDING RING
DDEGHIIMNRT RIGHT-MINDED
DDEGHMOOORU GOOD-HUMORED
DDEGIILMSUY MISGUIDEDLY
DDEGIINOORZ DEODORIZING
DDEGIINORRS DISORDERING
DDEGILMNOST DISLODGMENT
DDEGILNRSTU DISGRUNTLED
DDEGILSSTUY DISGUSTEDLY
DDEGNNORRUU UNDERGROUND
DDEHHIIOPRT DIPHTHEROID
DDEHIILNSSW WINDSHIELDS
DDEHINOORSU DISHONOURED
DDEHINORSTW SHORT-WINDED
DDEHLMOOTUU LOUDMOUTHED
DDEIIMNNOSU DIMINUENDOS
DDEIILMNORTY DIRTY OLD MEN
DDEINNOOSTT ENDODONTIST
DDELNNOORRY LONDONDERRY
DDGGGGIILNO GOLD-DIGGING
DDGIILNOORS SLIDING DOOR
DDGILMNPPUU PLUM PUDDING
DDHOOOOSUWY HOW DO YOU DOS
DDIIKLNSTWY TIDDLYWINKS
DDINOOOPRTT DIPROTODONT
DEEEEFHLRW FREEWHEELED
DEEEEEFPRSZ DEEP FREEZES
DEEEEHILRSW SIDE-WHEELER
DEEEEHNPRRR REPREHENDER
DEEEELMNNOW NEEDLEWOMEN

DEEEELOPRRV REDEVELOPER
DEEEEMOPRST SPEEDOMETER
DEEEENPRRST REPRESENTED
DEEEEQRSSTU SEQUESTERED
DEEEFFGHIRT FIFTH-DEGREE
DEEEFFNOOST TOFFEE-NOSED
DEEEFGIRRST FIRST-DEGREE
DEEEFHLNSSU HEEDFULNESS
DEEEFHLORRS FREEHOLDERS
DEEEFIILMPX EXEMPLIFIED
DEEEFILNSTV FIELD EVENTS, SELF-
  EVIDENT
DEEEFILNSVY DEFENSIVELY
DEEEFIOPRRT PROFITEERED
DEEEFLNNSSU NEEDFULNESS
DEEEFMNRRSU REFERENDUMS
DEEEGGINNNR ENGENDERING
DEEEGHHOPPR HEDGEHOPPER
DEEEGHILNNT ENLIGHTENED
DEEEGLORRSU GUELDER-ROSE
DEEEHHPRSSS SHEPHERDESS
DEEEHIINNPT PHENETIDINE
DEEEHILNPRS REPLENISHED
DEEEHIMRRSU RUDESHEIMER
DEEEHLMORVW OVERWHELMED
DEEEHMOPRTT HOT-TEMPERED
DEEEIIJORVV JOIE DE VIVRE
DEEEIIMPRSS EPIDERMISES
DEEEIINNPTX INEXPEDIENT
DEEEIINRTVW INTERVIEWED
DEEEIINSSST DESENSITISE
DEEEIINSSTZ DESENSITIZE
DEEEILLMPRT ILL-TEMPERED
DEEEILMMNPT IMPLEMENTED
DEEEILMMNUV MENDELEVIUM
DEEEILMNNST ENLISTED MEN
DEEEILMNRVY DELIVERYMEN
DEEEILNNOPT NEEDLEPOINT
DEEEILNPTXY EXPEDIENTLY
DEEEILORSTU DELETERIOUS
DEEEIMNRRST DETERMINERS
DEEEINPRRTT INTERPRETED
DEEEINPRTUX EXPENDITURE
DEEEINRRSSV VINEDRESSER
DEEEINRSSTW DESSERT WINE,
  WESTERNISED
DEEEINRSTWZ WESTERNIZED
DEEEIPPRSST SIDESTEPPER
DEEEIRSSSTT SIDE STREETS
DEEEJLOPPRT JET-PROPELED
DEEEJMPQUUU QUEUE-JUMPED
DEEEKOOPRRS DOORKEEPERS
DEEELLNORSW NE'ER-DO-WELLS
DEEELLNRRSU UNDERSELLER

DEEELLPPRXY PERPLEXEDLY
DEEELMNNORY MONEYLENDER
DEEELMNOPTV DEVELOPMENT
DEEELMNOTVV DEVOLVEMENT
DEEELNNPRST RESPLENDENT
DEEELNNRSSS SLENDERNESS
DEEELNNSSSS ENDLESSNESS
DEEELNORTUV VOLUNTEERED
DEEELNRRTTU UNDERLETTER
DEEELOOPRVV OVERDEVELOP
DEEELPRRTVY PERVERTEDLY
DEEEMNNORST ENDORSEMENT
DEEEMNNOSTU DENOUEMENTS
DEEEMPRTTUW TRUMPETWEED
DEEEMRRSSSU MURDERESSES
DEEENOPRSUX UNDEREXPOSE
DEEENOPSSSX EXPOSEDNESS
DEEENPRSSUX UNEXPRESSED
DEEENRRRRSU SURRENDERER
DEEENRRSTTT TRENDSETTER
DEEEOOPRRVW OVERPOWERED
DEEEOOPRSVX OVEREXPOSED
DEEEOPPRSTV OVERSTEPPED
DEEEOPRSSSS REPOSSESSED
DEEEOPRSTTY STEREOTYPED
DEEEORRRTTV RETROVERTED
DEEEORRTTVX EXTROVERTED
DEEEPRRSSST PRESTRESSED
DEEEPRRSSUU SUPERSEDURE
DEEFFIINNRT INDIFFERENT
DEEFFILNRTY DIFFERENTLY
DEEFFINSSSU DIFFUSENESS
DEEFFIOOPRR FIREPROOFED
DEEFFORSTUV OVERSTUFFED
DEEFGHIORST FORESIGHTED
DEEFGIINNRX INDEX FINGER
DEEFGILNNSY SELF-DENYING
DEEFGILNORW DEFLOWERING
DEEFGINORST DEFORESTING
DEEFHILLLOR FIELD-HOLLER
DEEFIIIMNNR INDEMNIFIER
DEEFIIINNST INTENSIFIED
DEEFIIIRRSV DIVERSIFIER
DEEFIILMRSU DEMULSIFIER
DEEFIILNRST FRIENDLIEST
DEEFIIMORST DEFORMITIES
DEEFIINOPRS PERSONIFIED
DEEFIINRSVW VIEWFINDERS
DEEFIKLORRW FIELDWORKER
DEEFILLRSSU FLEURS-DE-LIS
DEEFILMOPSS SELF-IMPOSED
DEEFILORSTU OUTFIELDERS
DEEFLLNOSSU DOLEFULNESS
DEEFLOPRSSY PROFESSEDLY

DEEFNOORSTT TENDERFOOTS
DEEFNOPRSSU UNPROFESSED
DEEGGINNOOV GOOD EVENING
DEEGHHINPRS SHEPHERDING
DEEGHHINRST RING THE SHED
DEEGHHIOPRW HIGH-POWERED
DEEGHILLNWY WHEEDLINGLY
DEEGHILNOOP PIGEONHOLED
DEEGHIMNOOS HOMOGENISED
DEEGHIMNOOZ HOMOGENIZED
DEEGHINORSY HYDROGENISE
DEEGHINORYZ HYDROGENIZE
DEEGHINRRRS RED HERRINGS
DEEGHINRTUW UNDERWEIGHT
DEEGHNORSTU GROUNDSHEET
DEEGIIILMST LEGITIMISED
DEEGIIILMTZ LEGITIMIZED
DEEGIIINSTV INDIGESTIVE
DEEGIIMNNOR DOMINEERING
DEEGIIMNNRT DETERMINING
DEEGIINNRST INGREDIENTS
DEEGIINNRTZ TENDERIZING
DEEGILLMNOR REMODELLING
DEEGILNOPRY REDEPLOYING
DEEGILNORUV OVERINDULGE
DEEGILNRSVY DESERVINGLY
DEEGILNRTVY DIVERGENTLY
DEEGINPRSSU SUPERSEDING
DEEGJMNPRTU PREJUDGMENT
DEEGLLMOORW WELL-GROOMED
DEEGLNORSSY ENGROSSEDLY
DEEGLNOSSSS GODLESSNESS
DEEHHLOORSU HOUSEHOLDER
DEEHIIMPRSU HESPERIDIUM
DEEHILLORTT TITLEHOLDER
DEEHILMNOTU ENDOTHELIUM
DEEHILOOSTT THEODOLITES
DEEHILOSTTU SILHOUETTED
DEEHIMNOORT TIME-HONORED
DEEHIMOSTTW WISDOM TEETH
DEEHINOSSSU HIDEOUSNESS
DEEHINRRSSU HURRIEDNESS
DEEHINSSSTY SYNTHESISED
DEEHINSSTYZ SYNTHESIZED
DEEHLOPRSTU UPHOLSTERED
DEEHMNNOOOY HONEYMOONED
DEEHMNOOPTU OPEN-MOUTHED
DEEHMOORRTY HYDROMETEOR
DEEHOORRSUV HORS D'OEUVRE
DEEIIMMNNST INDEMNITIES
DEEIIKLLMSS SEMISKILLED
DEEIIKLNNRT INTERLINKED
DEEIILLLRVY LILY-LIVERED
DEEIILMNSSU DISSEMINULE

DEEIILMPSST SPEED LIMITS
DEEIILNOPRS LEPIDOSIREN
DEEIILOPRSY ERYSIPELOID
DEEIILPRRSV PILE DRIVERS
DEEIIMMNPST IMPEDIMENTS
DEEIIMMNRST DETERMINISM
DEEIIMNOPTT PIEDMONTITE
DEEIIMNPSST DISSEPIMENT
DEEIIMNRRST IRREDENTISM
DEEIIMNRSTT DETERMINIST
DEEIINNRTTW INTERTWINED
DEEIINNSSTT DISSENTIENT
DEEIINOPSTX EXPEDITIONS
DEEIINPRSTY SERENDIPITY
DEEIINRRSTT IRREDENTIST
DEEIINRSSTT DISINTEREST
DEEIIOPSTUX EXPEDITIOUS
DEEIIOQSSUX SESQUIOXIDE
DEEIIRSTTUV DIVESTITURE
DEEIKMNPPSU PUMPKINSEED
DEEILMNOPST DESPOILMENT
DEEILNNQSTU DELINQUENTS
DEEILNORRSS ORDERLINESS
DEEILNSSSTT STILTEDNESS
DEEILOPPPTY POLYPEPTIDE
DEEILORRSSW WORLD SERIES
DEEILQRRRSU RED SQUIRREL
DEEIMMMNORTU ENDOMETRIUM
DEEIMNNORUU ENDONEURIUM
DEEIMNOSSTU SEDIMENTOUS
DEEIMOOPRTT DIOPTOMETER
DEEIMOPRRST MISREPORTED
DEEINNNORST NONRESIDENT
DEEINNOPSST POINTEDNESS
DEEINNOSTTU TENDENTIOUS
DEEINNPRSTU SUPERINTEND
DEEINNSSTUW UNWITNESSED
DEEINOPRSSS DEPRESSIONS
DEEINORRRVW OWNER-DRIVER
DEEINORRTTV INTROVERTED
DEEINORSSUW SERIES-WOUND
DEEINOSSSTU TEDIOUSNESS
DEEINOSSSUV DEVIOUSNESS
DEEINPRRTTU INTERRUPTED
DEEINRRRTUW UNDERWRITER
DEEIPRRSSSU PRESSURISED
DEEIPRRSSUZ PRESSURIZED
DEEKLMRSTTU KETTLEDRUMS
DEEKNNNRSSU DRUNKENNESS
DEELMMNOPSU NOMS DE PLUME
DEELMNOOTTU TOUT LE MONDE
DEELMNORTTY TORMENTEDLY
DEELORSTTUV TURTLEDOVES
DEELORSTUXY DEXTEROUSLY

DEEMNOORRSY MONEY ORDERS
DEENNOPRSST RESPONDENTS
DEENNORSSVW NEWSVENDORS
DEENNPRSSTU PRUDENTNESS
DEENNSSSTTU STUNTEDNESS
DEEOPPPRSSU PRESUPPOSED
DEFFIINORSU REDIFFUSION
DEFFILLLNUU UNFULFILLED
DEFFOPPRSUW POWDER PUFFS
DEFGGIILNTY FIDGETINGLY
DEFGGLOOOST FOOTSLOGGED
DEFGHIISTTT TIGHTFISTED
DEFGHILOOTT LIGHT-FOOTED
DEFGIIINNTY IDENTIFYING
DEFGIILNNSW SELF-WINDING
DEFGIILNPRS SPRINGFIELD
DEFGIILNRRS GIRLFRIENDS
DEFGILNNORU FLOUNDERING
DEFGJMNORTU FORJUDGMENT
DEFGNOORRSU FOREGROUNDS
DEFHHLOORTT HOLD THE FORT
DEFHIIIMRSU HUMIDIFIERS
DEFHIINPRSS FRIENDSHIPS
DEFHINPRSTT SPENDTHRIFT
DEFHIORSSSW SWORDFISHES
DEFHLLMOTUU FULL-MOUTHED
DEFHLMOOTUU FOUL-MOUTHED
DEFHLNOSSUW FLESH WOUNDS
DEFHMOOOPRT MOTHPROOFED
DEFIIINNOST DEFINITIONS
DEFIIJNSTUU UNJUSTIFIED
DEFIILMSTYY MYSTIFIEDLY
DEFIIMMNORS MISINFORMED
DEFIIMORRSV DIVERSIFORM
DEFIINNNPSY SPINY-FINNED
DEFIINORRRU FOURDRINIER
DEFILMNNSSU MINDFULNESS
DEFILNSSTUU DUTIFULNESS
DEFILRSSSTU DISTRESSFUL
DEFINRRSSUW WIND-SURFERS
DEFIOOORRSU ODORIFEROUS
DEFKLNOOORU UNLOOKED-FOR
DEFLLNORUWY WONDERFULLY
DEFOOPRRSTU RUSTPROOFED
DEFOOPSSTUY PUSSYFOOTED
DEGGHHHIILT HIGHLIGHTED
DEGGHILNOST LONGSIGHTED
DEGGIINNNSU UNDESIGNING
DEGGILOOPRS SLOOP-RIGGED
DEGGKLRSUUY SKULDUGGERY
DEGHIIINRTV DIVINE RIGHT
DEGHIILMNOS DEMOLISHING
DEGHIILNNRY HINDERINGLY
DEGHIILPPTT TIGHT-LIPPED

DEGHILNORSU SHOULDERING
DEGHINNORSU ENSHROUDING
DEGHINOORTU OUT-HERODING
DEGHINOPSTT POTTING SHED
DEGHLMOOOTY METHODOLOGY
DEGHNOORSUY HYDROGENOUS
DEGHNOORXYY OXYHYDROGEN
DEGHNORRTUW UNDERGROWTH
DEGIIIINNST INDIGNITIES
DEGIIINNOST INDIGESTION
DEGIIINPSSW SIDESWIPING
DEGIIINQSTU DISQUIETING
DEGIIKNRSTW WRITING DESK
DEGIILLMRSX MIXED GRILLS
DEGIILLNOTU GUILLOTINED
DEGIILNNNRU UNDERLINING
DEGIILNOTTU DEGLUTITION
DEGIILNRTVY DIVERTINGLY
DEGIIMNNNRU UNDERMINING
DEGIIMNNORZ MODERNIZING
DEGIIMNNPSS MISSPENDING
DEGIINNNRTU INDENTURING
DEGIINORSSS DIGRESSIONS
DEGIINPRSST SPRING TIDES
DEGIINRSSST DISTRESSING
DEGIJMMNSTU MISJUDGMENT
DEGILLNNTUY INDULGENTLY
DEGILLNOPRY DEPLORINGLY
DEGILMNORSU SMOULDERING
DEGILNNORWY WONDERINGLY
DEGILNNOSSU UNGODLINESS
DEGILNORUVY DEVOURINGLY
DEGILOOPRTY PTERIDOLOGY
DEGINNORSST GRINDSTONES
DEGINOPRSST TOPDRESSING
DEGKLOOOORS GOOD LOOKERS
DEGLLNORSUW GROUNDSWELL
DEGLMOOORST MOTOR LODGES
DEGLNOOOPTT GOLDEN POTTO
DEGLNOPRSUY GOLDEN SYRUP
DEGLNORRSUU GROUND RULES
DEGLOORSTTY TROGLODYTES
DEGNNOORSTU STONE-GROUND
DEGNNORRSTU GROUND RENTS
DEHHIILMNOT HELMINTHOID
DEHHILMOORS HOLOHEDRISM
DEHHILNOOSW HINSHELWOOD
DEHHIMOORRS HEMORRHOIDS
DEHHLNOSTUU SLEUTHHOUND
DEHIIINOTTT INDO-HITTITE
DEHIIKNNNST THIN-SKINNED
DEHIILLOOSV LIVELIHOODS
DEHIILMNPSU DELPHINIUMS
DEHIILPRSTU TRISULPHIDE

DEHIINSTTUW WHITSUNTIDE
DEHIIRSSTVW WHIST DRIVES
DEHILNOSSTY DISHONESTLY
DEHILNOSTTW THISTLEDOWN
DEHILOPSUXY OXYSULPHIDE
DEHILORSSTT SHORT-LISTED
DEHINOORRSU DISHONOURER
DEHINOPRRST THIRD PERSON
DEHINPRSSSU PRUDISHNESS
DEHINPSSTTU STUDENTSHIP
DEHINRRSSTU UNDERSHIRTS
DEHIOOOPPRT PHOTOPERIOD
DEHIOORSSST SISTERHOODS
DEHLLOOSSSU DOLL'S HOUSES
DEHLNNOOOSW HOLD ONE'S OWN
DEHMMNRSSUU HUMDRUMNESS
DEHMMORSTUW MUM'S THE WORD
DEHMOOPPRSU PSEUDOMORPH
DEHNOOOOPRT ODONTOPHORE
DEHNRRSTTUU UNDERTHRUST
DEHOOOPRTTW TOOTH POWDER
DEIIILLSSUV DISILLUSIVE
DEIIILQRSSU LIQUIDISERS
DEIIILQRSUZ LIQUIDIZERS
DEIIIMNORSS MINOR DIESIS
DEIIIMNSTUV DIMINUTIVES
DEIIINPRTTY INTREPIDITY
DEIIIOPRRST PRIORITISED
DEIIIOPRRTZ PRIORITIZED
DEIIIPSSTTU STUPIDITIES
DEIIKKLMMMS SKIMMED MILK
DEIILLORSUY DELIRIOUSLY
DEIILMNOOST DEMOLITIONS
DEIILMPRSTW LIMP-WRISTED
DEIILNOORWW ORIEL WINDOW
DEIILNOPRRY PYRROLIDINE
DEIILOPRSTW LOW-SPIRITED
DEIILOSSTUV DISSOLUTIVE
DEIILOSSTUY SEDITIOUSLY
DEIIMNOPRTV IMPROVIDENT
DEIIMOORRST DORMITORIES
DEIIMORSSTU MOISTURISED
DEIIMORSTUZ MOISTURIZED
DEIIMQRTTUU TERTIUM QUID
DEIINNNOOTW DOWN IT IN ONE
DEIINNOSSSS DISSENSIONS
DEIINOOPRSV PROVISIONED
DEIINOOPSST DEPOSITIONS
DEIINORSTTU ROTUNDITIES
DEIINOSSSTU DISSENTIOUS
DEIINOSTTTU DESTITUTION
DEILLMOOSUY MELODIOUSLY
DEILLNORSSW WORLDLINESS
DEILLORSTUY DESULTORILY

DEILLORSWWY WORLDLY-WISE
DEILLOSSTUY DISSOLUTELY
DEILMNOOOPS MONOPOLISED
DEILMNOOOPZ MONOPOLIZED
DEILMNPRTUY IMPRUDENTLY
DEILMOORRTY DOLORIMETRY
DEILNNNSTUW WIND TUNNELS
DEILNOPRTVY PROVIDENTLY
DEILPRRSSUY SURPRISEDLY
DEIMMRSSTYY DISSYMMETRY
DEIMNOSSSSY SYNDESMOSIS
DEIMOOPRTTY DIOPTOMETRY
DEIMOPPRTTU PROMPTITUDE
DEINNPSSUUY SUNNY-SIDE UP
DEINOORSSWW ROSE WINDOWS
DEIOPPRSTTU OUTSTRIPPED
DEIOPRSTTTU PROSTITUTED
DEKLLOOPRST ROLLTOP DESK
DEKNOORRSWW WORK WONDERS
DELLNOPSUUY PENDULOUSLY
DELLNOSSSUY SOUNDLESSLY
DELMORRSUUY MURDEROUSLY
DELNOOPRSSU SPLENDOROUS
DELNOOPRSUY PONDEROUSLY
DELOOPRRSWW WORLD POWERS
DEMOOOPRRSW POWDER ROOMS
DENNOOOOPSW WOODEN SPOON
DENOOOPRSSU ENDOSPOROUS
DENOOOORSSSU ODOROUSNESS
DEOOOOPPRRST DOORSTOPPER
DFFIIISTUVY DIFFUSIVITY
DFGGIIINRSU DISFIGURING
DFGHIIIMNUY HUMIDIFYING
DFGHILLOOST FLOODLIGHTS
DFGIIILNOSY SOLIDIFYING
DFGIIKNNNSU SINKING FUND
DFGIILLNOWW WILDFOWLING
DFGIINNRSUW WIND-SURFING
DFGLNOOOORRU GROUND FLOOR
DFIKLOPPSSY FLOPPY DISKS
DFILRSSTTUU DISTRUSTFUL
DGGIIILLNRR DRILLING RIG
DGGIIILLNNUY INDULGINGLY
DGGIILMNNSU MUDSLINGING
DGGIKLNOOOO GOOD-LOOKING
DGGILNNORSU GROUNDLINGS
DGGIMNNOOOR GOOD MORNING
DGGINNOORSW WRONGDOINGS
DGHHHIOOPTU UP TO HIGH DOH
DGHHIILNOTW WITHHOLDING
DGHHIKNOOST KNIGHTHOODS
DGHIIIIMNNS DIMINISHING
DGHIIINSSTU DISTINGUISH
DGHIIKNNOOW HOODWINKING

DGHIIMNNSTU MIDNIGHT SUN	EEEFFHILRTW WHIFFLETREE
DGHIINNOORS DISHONORING	EEEFFILORTW EIFFEL TOWER
DGHILOORSTY HYDROLOGIST	EEEFGIINNRS FIRE ENGINES
DGHLNOORSST STRONGHOLDS	EEEFGIKLNSS SELF-SEEKING
DGHLNOORUUY UNGODLY HOUR	EEEFGLLNSSU GLEEFULNESS
DGIIIILNQUZ LIQUIDIZING	EEEFHIKNRRT FREETHINKER
DGIIIINPRST DISPIRITING	EEEFHILNSSY FISH-EYE LENS
DGIILLNNSWY SWINDLINGLY	EEEFHILRRSW FERRIS WHEEL
DGIILNNRTUY INTRUDINGLY	EEEFHMNRRST REFRESHMENT
DGIIMNNOORS DINING ROOMS	EEEFHOORRTT THERETOFORE
DGIIMNNOSTU DISMOUNTING	EEEFIILMPRX EXEMPLIFIER
DGIINRSSTTU DISTRUSTING	EEEFILSSSTT TSETSE FLIES
DGIKNOOORWW WOODWORKING	EEEFILSTTZZ TZETZE FLIES
DGINNOOPPRU PROPOUNDING	EEEFIMMRRSW FREE-SWIMMER
DGINNORRSUU SURROUNDING	EEEFIMNNRST REFINEMENTS
DHHMNOOOSTU SMOOTH HOUND	EEEFLLORVWY YELLOW FEVER
DHIIIORSTTY THYROIDITIS	EEEFNNRSSTV FERVENTNESS
DHILLNOOPPY PODOPHYLLIN	EEEGGHORTTT GET-TOGETHER
DHIMOOOSTTW WISDOM TOOTH	EEEGGIINNNR ENGINEERING
DHIOOOPRSUZ RHIZOPODOUS	EEEGGIINNRV VEREENIGING
DHLOOPRXYYY POLYHYDROXY	EEEGGMNNORT ENGORGEMENT
DHMNOOORXYY MONOHYDROXY	EEEGHHINSTT EIGHTEENTHS
DIIIIMNOSSV DIVISIONISM	EEEGHILNNRT ENLIGHTENER
DIIIINOSSTV DIVISIONIST	EEEGHNORSSU GREENHOUSES
DIIIILLNOSSU DISILLUSION	EEEGIINPSST EPIGENESIST
DIIILNOSSUY INSIDIOUSLY	EEEGILLLNST TELESELLING
DIIILNOSUVY INVIDIOUSLY	EEEGINNNSSU GENUINENESS
DIIIMNNOSTU DIMINUTIONS	EEEGINNORVW OVERWEENING
DIIINOOPSST DISPOSITION	EEEGINNOSSX XENOGENESIS
DIILLNOSSWW WINDOWSILLS	EEEGINNRRTW WINTERGREEN
DIILNOOSSTU DISSOLUTION	EEEGINPRRSV PERSEVERING
DIILNOPSSTY SPONDYLITIS	EEEGLMNNOTW GENTLEWOMEN
DIINOORSSTT DISTORTIONS	EEEGLNOORVY VENEREOLOGY
DIINOPRSSTU DISRUPTIONS	EEEGLNOPRRV GREEN PLOVER
DIINORSSTUU INDUSTRIOUS	EEEGNORSSSV GOVERNESSES
DILMOOPSTUY STYLOPODIUM	EEEHHILLLNP PHILHELLENE
DIOOPQQRSUU QUID PRO QUOS	EEEHHILPPTW HEPPLEWHITE
EEEEFKLRSSS SELF-SEEKERS	EEEHHIMPRSS HEMISPHERES
EEEEFLRSTTT FLEET STREET	EEEHHLOSSUW WHEELHOUSES
EEEEGLNNSST GENTEELNESS	EEEHHOPRTTY HETEROPHYTE
EEEEGNPPPRR GREEN PEPPER	EEEHIILNNPT NEPHELINITE
EEEEHIMNPRT HEMITERPENE	EEEHIIPPRRS PERIPHERIES
EEEEHKOPRSU HOUSEKEEPER	EEEHILNPRRS REPLENISHER
EEEEHNNSTTV SEVENTEENTH	EEEHILRSSTV SHIRTSLEEVE
EEEEHORRSVW WHERESOEVER	EEEHIMNRSST SMITHEREENS
EEEEIINRTVW INTERVIEWEE	EEEHINNNSTT NINETEENTHS
EEEEIKMPRST TIMEKEEPERS	EEEHINPSSSV PEEVISHNESS
EEEEIMNPRSW MINESWEEPER	EEEHINSSTTV SEVENTIETHS
EEEEKOPRRST STOREKEEPER	EEEHIPPPRTW WHITE PEPPER
EEEELNPRSST REPLETENESS	EEEHKOPPRSS SHOPKEEPERS
EEEELRRSTTT TRESTLETREE	EEEHLNNOSST NONETHELESS
EEEEMNRSSTX EXTREMENESS	EEEHMMORRTT THERMOMETER
EEEENNRRSVV NEVER-NEVERS	EEEHMNOQRTU QUEEN MOTHER
EEEEPPPRSTW SWEET PEPPER	EEEHMOPRRST SPHEROMETER

EEEIIKLNSST TELEKINESIS
EEEIIMRSTTX EXTREMITIES
EEEIINNPSVX INEXPENSIVE
EEEIINRRTTV IRRETENTIVE
EEEIINRRTVW INTERVIEWER
EEEIIORRSTX EXTERIORISE
EEEIIORRTXZ EXTERIORIZE
EEEIIPRRTTV PRETERITIVE
EEEIKLNOSST SKELETONISE
EEEIKLNOSTZ SKELETONIZE
EEEILMMNPRT IMPLEMENTER
EEEILMNNNTV ENLIVENMENT
EEEILMNNTTT ENTITLEMENT
EEEILNNQSSU QUEENLINESS
EEEILNPRRTT TELEPRINTER
EEEILNPSVXY EXPENSIVELY
EEEILNRTTVY RETENTIVELY
EEEILNSSSUV ELUSIVENESS
EEEILNSTVXY EXTENSIVELY
EEEIMNNNTTW ENTWINEMENT
EEEIMNORSTT TENSIOMETER
EEEIMNOSSTV EMOTIVENESS
EEEIMNPRSTX EXPERIMENTS
EEEIMNQRRTU REQUIREMENT
EEEIMNQRTTU REQUITEMENT
EEEIMNRRSTT RETIREMENTS
EEEIMOPRSTX EXTEMPORISE
EEEIMOPRTXZ EXTEMPORIZE
EEEIMRRSSTV TIMESERVERS
EEEINNPRSTT PRESENTIENT
EEEINNPSSSV PENSIVENESS
EEEINORRRSV REVERSIONER
EEEINORSSSV EROSIVENESS
EEEINPRRRST ENTERPRISER
EEEINPRRRTT INTERPRETER
EEEINPRRSST ENTERPRISES, INTERSPERSE
EEEINPRSTTX PRE-EXISTENT
EEEINPRSTVV PREVENTIVES
EEEINRSSSTV RESTIVENESS
EEEIOPRRRST REPERTOIRES, REPERTORIES
EEEJMPQRUUU QUEUE-JUMPER
EEEKKLNOSTY SKELETON KEY
EEEKLNOOSTX EXOSKELETON
EEEKLORRSTW STEELWORKER
EEELLLPSSSY SLEEPLESSLY
EEELLNRSSVY NERVELESSLY
EEELLNSSSSY SENSELESSLY
EEELMNNOPTV ENVELOPMENT
EEELMNSSTTT SETTLEMENTS
EEELMORRSSS REMORSELESS
EEELNNOOPPS PELOPONNESE
EEELNOPRSTT OPEN LETTERS
EEELNRSSTTW NEWSLETTERS
EEELNSSSSSU USELESSNESS

EEELNSSSSSX SEXLESSNESS
EEELPRRSSTT LETTERPRESS
EEEMMNOPRTW EMPOWERMENT
EEEMMNNPRSTT PRESENTMENT
EEEMNORSTUV VENTURESOME
EEEMNPRSSSU SUPREMENESS
EEEMORRSTTY STEREOMETRY
EEEMPRSSSTT TEMPTRESSES
EEEOPRRSTTY STEREOTYPER
EEEOPRSSTTY STEREOTYPES
EEEPRSSTTTY TYPESETTERS
EEFFGHIIRRT FIRE FIGHTER
EEFFGILNRSU GLUE-SNIFFER
EEFFGINORRS FOREFINGERS
EEFFHLNSSTU THE SNUFFLES
EEFFIILLORY LIFE OF RILEY
EEFFIILMOPR PRIME OF LIFE
EEFFIINNOSV INOFFENSIVE
EEFFILNOSVY OFFENSIVELY
EEFFIOORRST OFFERTORIES
EEFFIORRRSU FERRIFEROUS
EEFFLNRSSTU FRETFULNESS
EEFGGIOPRTT PETTIFOGGER
EEFGHIILRRT FIRELIGHTER
EEFGIINNRRT INTERFERING
EEFGILLNORT FORETELLING
EEFGILNRSTW LEFT-WINGERS
EEFGINNQRTU FREQUENTING
EEFGINORRST REFORESTING
EEFGINORSSV FORGIVENESS
EEFGLLRRTUY REGRETFULLY
EEFGMNOORTT FORGET-ME-NOT
EEFHIJLLSSY JELLYFISHES
EEFHILLNSSS FLESHLINESS
EEFHILNSSSS SELFISHNESS
EEFHILOSUWY HOUSEWIFELY
EEFHIORSUWY HOUSEWIFERY
EEFHLLNPSSU HELPFULNESS
EEFHLNOPSSU HOPEFULNESS
EEFHMORRRTU FURTHERMORE
EEFHNOORRST FORESHORTEN
EEFHNORSTTU FOURTEENTHS
EEFHOORRSTW FOR THE WORSE
EEFIIINNRST INTENSIFIER
EEFIILORSST LIFE STORIES
EEFIILRRSST FERTILISERS
EEFIILRRSTZ FERTILIZERS
EEFILLLMRSU MILLEFLEURS
EEFILLMORSU MELLIFEROUS
EEFILNORSSW FLOWERINESS
EEFILNPPSTT FELT-TIP PENS
EEFILOOPRRT PROFITEROLE
EEFILOORSST LOOSESTRIFE
EEFINRSSTUV FURTIVENESS

EEFIOPRSSTU PESTIFEROUS	EEGILLLNPRY REPELLINGLY
EEFIORRRSTX FOX TERRIERS	EEGILLLSSUY GUILELESSLY
EEFLLNRSTUY RESENTFULLY	EEGILLMOOST TELEOLOGISM
EEFLMNOSSSU FULSOMENESS	EEGILLNORSV OVERSELLING
EEFLMOORRTU FLUOROMETER	EEGILLOOSTT TELEOLOGIST
EEFLNNSSTUU TUNEFULNESS	EEGILMOOSTY ETYMOLOGIES
EEFLNPSSSUU SUSPENSEFUL	EEGILNNNRTU UNRELENTING
EEFLNRSSSTU RESTFULNESS	EEGILNOPSSY POLYGENESIS
EEFLNSSSTUZ ZESTFULNESS	EEGILNPRSTY PESTERINGLY
EEFMOOPRTTU OUT OF TEMPER	EEGILOPRSTT POLTERGEIST
EEFNNORRRSU FORERUNNERS	EEGIMNNOOSS MONOGENESIS
EEFNOPRSSSU PROFUSENESS	EEGIMNNORSU MONSEIGNEUR
EEGGHHIINNT HEIGHTENING	EEGIMNNRRTU INTERREGNUM
EEGGHIINSST SIGHTSEEING	EEGIMNNSTTU INTEGUMENTS
EEGGHILNNNT LENGTHENING	EEGIMNOPPST PEEPING TOMS
EEGGIIMNNRT REGIMENTING	EEGIMNOSSYZ ZYMOGENESIS
EEGGIINNPRW WINNIPEGGER	EEGINNPRSUV SUPERVENING
EEGGIINRRST REGISTERING	EEGINORRSTU TERRIGENOUS
EEGGILLNNTY NEGLIGENTLY	EEGINORSTVY SOVEREIGNTY
EEGGILNNRVY REVENGINGLY	EEGINPRSTTU GUTTERSNIPE
EEGGILORSUY EGREGIOUSLY	EEGIOPRRSSV PROGRESSIVE
EEGHHHLOOTW THE WHOLE HOG	EEGKLLMNSUU MUSKELLUNGE
EEGHHILRTWW WHEELWRIGHT	EEGKORRSTUW GUEST WORKER
EEGHIINSSTW WEIGHTINESS	EEGLMOOORTY METEOROLOGY
EEGHILNNOPT TELEPHONING	EEGLNSSSSTU GUTLESSNESS
EEGHILNNSST LENGTHINESS	EEGLOPPPTUV GLOVE PUPPET
EEGHILNOOPS PIGEONHOLES	EEGLOQRSTUY GROTESQUELY
EEGHILOORST THEOLOGISER	EEGMNNORSST ENGROSSMENT
EEGHILOORTZ THEOLOGIZER	EEGMNNORSTV GOVERNMENTS
EEGHILRSTTT STREETLIGHT	EEGNNOSTTXY OXYGEN TENTS
EEGHIMNOORS HOMOGENISER	EEGOOQRRSTUY GROTESQUERY
EEGHIMNOORZ HOMOGENIZER	EEGPRRSSTTU GUTTER PRESS
EEGHIMNOOTY HOMOGENEITY	EEHHIKLOTTW THE WHOLE KIT
EEGHIMOORST ISOGEOTHERM	EEHHILLNSSS HELLISHNESS
EEGHINNOSTT ETHNOGENIST	EEHHILMPSTT PITH HELMETS
EEGHINNPTWY PENNYWEIGHT	EEHHILOPRST LITHOSPHERE
EEGHINOORTV IN THE GROOVE	EEHHINRSTTT THIRTEENTHS
EEGHLOOPRTY HERPETOLOGY	EEHHIOPRRSZ RHIZOSPHERE
EEGHMNOOOSU HOMOGENEOUS	EEHHIORRSSS SHIRE HORSES
EEGHOSSSTUU GUESTHOUSES	EEHHIORSSTW WHITE HORSES
EEGIIILLNNTT INTELLIGENT	EEHHMOORSTU HOUSEMOTHER
EEGIIILMNNRT INTERMINGLE	EEHHMOPRTUV OVER THE HUMP
EEGIIMMNNPT IMPINGEMENT	EEHHNOOPRTY HETEROPHONY
EEGIIMMNRSZ MESMERIZING	EEHHNOORRTW WHETHER OR NO
EEGIIMNNOPT OPENING TIME	EEHHOOPPRST PHOTOSPHERE
EEGIIMNRSTV TIMESERVING	EEHHOORSSUW WHOREHOUSES
EEGIIINNNRTV INTERVENING	EEHHIIKNPSTY PIE IN THE SKY
EEGIINNORST NITROGENISE	EEHHIILNOPRS PERIHELIONS
EEGIINNORTZ NITROGENIZE	EEHHIIMNRSTT THEREMINIST
EEGIINNRSTT INTERESTING	EEHHIIMPPRRS PREMIERSHIP
EEGIINNRTTW WIRE NETTING	EEHHILLRSSWW WELL-WISHERS
EEGIINOPRTV PROGENITIVE	EEHHILMMOSTU MESOTHELIUM
EEGIINPRSTX PRE-EXISTING	EEHHILMNORTY HEMIELYTRON
EEGIKKNORWW WORKING WEEK	EEHHILMOORTT LITHOMETEOR

EEHILMOPPRS SPERMOPHILE
EEHILNOPRRT LEPTORRHINE
EEHILNOPSTT TELEPHONIST
EEHILOOPRST HELIOTROPES
EEHILORSSTY HETEROLYSIS
EEHILOSSTTU SILHOUETTES
EEHIMOPPRRS EMPERORSHIP
EEHIMOPRSTU HEMIPTEROUS
EEHINNORSST RHINESTONES
EEHINNOSSSU HEINOUSNESS
EEHINPSSSTT PETTISHNESS
EEHINRSSSTU HIRSUTENESS
EEHINRSSSTY SYNTHESISER
EEHINRSSTYZ SYNTHESIZER
EEHIPRSSTTU TRUSTEESHIP
EEHKNOORSTT TENTERHOOKS
EEHKOORRSUW HOUSEWORKER
EEHLMNOOSUW UNWHOLESOME
EEHLMNOTTVW TWELVEMONTH
EEHLOPRRSTU REUPHOLSTER,
UPHOLSTERER
EEHLORSTTYY HETEROSTYLY
EEHMMORRTTY THERMOMETRY
EEHMMORSSUU SUMMERHOUSE
EEHMNNOOOORY HONEYMOONER
EEHMNOOOORTV OVER THE MOON
EEHMNOOPRSS MESONEPHROS
EEHNNORRRST NORTHERNERS
EEHNNORSSTT HORNET'S NEST
EEHNOOOPRSZ OZONOSPHERE
EEHNORRSSTU SOUTHERNERS
EEHNORRSTTW NORTHWESTER
EEHOOPPRRST TROPOSPHERE
EEHOOPRRSTU PORTERHOUSE
EEHOOPRRSTY HETEROSPORY
EEHOOPRSSUW POWERHOUSES
EEHOOPRSTTT PHOTOSETTER
EEHOORSSSTU STOREHOUSES
EEHORSSTTUW SOUTHWESTER
EEIIIMNNSTU EINSTEINIUM
EEIIINNSSTV INSENSITIVE
EEIIINSTTVV INVESTITIVE
EEIIKLLNNNS ENNISKILLEN
EEIIKLNPRSW PERIWINKLES
EEIILLLMMRST MILLIMETERS
EEIILLMMRST MILLIMETRES
EEIILLNRSTY RESILIENTLY
EEIILLPPRST PIPISTRELLE
EEIILLPRSTV SPIRIT LEVEL
EEIILMNOSST SOLEMNITIES
EEIILMNRSSS MISERLINESS
EEIILNNPRRT LINE PRINTER
EEIILNNSTVY INTENSIVELY
EEIILNNTVVY INVENTIVELY

EEIIILNOSSTV TELEVISIONS
EEIIILNRSSSV SILVERINESS
EEIIILNSSTVY SENSITIVELY
EEIIILPRSSTT PRIESTLIEST
EEIIILQSTUXY EXQUISITELY
EEIIILRRSSST STERILISERS
EEIIILRRSSTZ STERILIZERS
EEIIMNNPRTT IMPERTINENT
EEIIMNNOSSTT TESTIMONIES
EEIIMNPRRUU PERINEURIUM
EEIIINNNNSTY NINETY-NINES
EEIIINNNOSTT NONENTITIES
EEIIINNOOPRT POINTE-NOIRE
EEIIINNORSTV INVENTORIES
EEIINOPRRTT PRETERITION
EEIINOPRSTT PETITIONERS, REPETITIONS
EEIINRSTTUV INVESTITURE
EEIINRTTTVY RETENTIVITY
EEIIOPPRRST PROPRIETIES
EEIIOPPRSTV PREPOSITIVE
EEIIOPRSSTT POSTERITIES
EEIIOPRSTTU REPETITIOUS
EEIIORRRSTT TERRITORIES
EEIIORRSSST ROTISSERIES
EEIIPQRSSTU PERQUISITES
EEIIRSTTTUV RESTITUTIVE
EEIKNRRSSTT RENT STRIKES
EEIILLMNOPRT MONTPELLIER
EEILLMOOPRT TROMPE L'OEIL
EEILLMPPPRS PEPPER MILLS
EEILLMPRTUX MULTIPLEXER
EEILLNOPQTU EQUIPOLLENT
EEILLNOSSSY NOISELESSLY
EEILLNPSSSY SPINELESSLY
EEILLOPSVXY EXPLOSIVELY
EEILLPRSUVY REPULSIVELY
EEILMNNOTVV INVOLVEMENT
EEILMNNSSTT ENLISTMENTS
EEILMNOOSST EMOTIONLESS
EEILMOPRTUV PLUVIOMETER
EEILNNPRTTY PERTINENTLY
EEILNNSSSSS SINLESSNESS
EEILNOPRRST INTERLOPERS
EEILNSSSSTW WITLESSNESS
EEILOPRSSTY PROSELYTISE
EEILOPRSTYZ PROSELYTIZE
EEIMMNOPRTV IMPROVEMENT
EEIMMNPRSST IMPRESSMENT
EEIMMNRSSSU SUMMERINESS
EEIMMOPRRSV PRIME MOVERS
EEIMNNNORTV ENVIRONMENT
EEIMNNNRSTT INTERNMENTS
EEIMNNOOSSS NOISOMENESS
EEIMNNOPRST OMNIPRESENT

EEIMNNORSSV MONS VENERIS
EEIMNNOSSSW WINSOMENESS
EEIMNNSSTTV INVESTMENTS
EEIMNOPRSTU PERITONEUMS
EEIMNORSTZZ INTERMEZZOS
EEIMNPPPRST PEPPERMINTS
EEIMNRSSTTW WESTMINSTER
EEIMOPPRSSU SUPERIMPOSE
EEIMPPRSTUV PRESUMPTIVE
EEINNNORRTU INTERNEURON
EEINNNOSTTX NONEXISTENT
EEINNOPRSST PRETENSIONS
EEINNOSSSUV ENVIOUSNESS
EEINNOSSTTU SENTENTIOUS
EEINOPRRSSS REPRESSIONS
EEINOPRRSSV PERVERSIONS
EEINOPRSSSX EXPRESSIONS
EEINOPRSTTU PRETENTIOUS
EEINOPSSSTU PITEOUSNESS
EEINOQRSSTU QUESTIONERS
EEINORRSTUV ENTEROVIRUS
EEINORSSSSU SERIOUSNESS
EEINPRRRTTU INTERRUPTER
EEINPRTTTWY TYPEWRITTEN
EEIOPSSSSSV POSSESSIVES
EEIPPRSSSUV SUPPRESSIVE
EEIPRRRSSSU PRESSURISER
EEIPRRRSSUZ PRESSURIZER
EEIPRRSTTWY TYPEWRITERS
EEIPRSSSSTT STEPSISTERS
EEJLNOSSSSY JOYLESSNESS
EEKKOORRRTV VOORTREKKER
EEKLORRSSTW TRESTLEWORK
EEKMNNPSSTU UNKEMPTNESS
EEKNOORRSTW STONEWORKER
EELLLLOPSTU LULL TO SLEEP
EELLLOORRTW ROLLER TOWEL
EELLNNOSSSW SWOLLENNESS
EELLNOOSTWY YELLOWSTONE
EELLNOPSTUY PLENTEOUSLY
EELLNPRTUUV PULVERULENT
EELLOPRSSWY POWERLESSLY
EELLORRSTTY STORYTELLER
EELMMNOPSTY EMPLOYMENTS
EELMNOSSSUU EMULOUSNESS
EELMNPPSSTU SUPPLEMENTS
EELNNSSSSSU SUNLESSNESS
EELNOOPPSTW TOWNSPEOPLE
EELNOORRSUY ERRONEOUSLY
EELNOPRSTYY POLYSTYRENE
EELOPPRSSSU PURPOSELESS
EELOPRRSSUW LOW-PRESSURE
EEMNNRSTTTU ENTRUSTMENT
EEMNOORSTTY ENTEROSTOMY

EEMNORSSTTW WESTERNMOST
EEMOORRSTTU TORTURESOME
EEMOPSSTTUU TEMPESTUOUS
EENNOORSSSU ONEROUSNESS
EENNOORSTTT ROTTENSTONE
EENNORSSSUV NERVOUSNESS
EENNOSSSTUU TENUOUSNESS
EENNPPRTTYY PRETTY PENNY
EEOOPRRSSSS REPOSSESSOR
EEOPQRSSTTU REQUEST STOP
EFFGHHHIIRS HIGH SHERIFF
EFFGHIINNOT IN THE OFFING
EFFGHIINOTT IN THE GIFT OF
EFFGHIINRSS FISH FINGERS
EFFGHILNRSU RESHUFFLING
EFFGILLNOST TELLING-OFFS
EFFGILNOSXY FLYING FOXES
EFFGILNRSUY SUFFERINGLY
EFFGLLORTUY FORGETFULLY
EFFHOOOOPSTT PHOTO-OFFSET
EFFIOORRSTT FIRST-FOOTER
EFGGHIINNRT FRIGHTENING
EFGGHIIRRST TRIGGERFISH
EFGGIINNRRS RING FINGERS
EFGGIINNRTY GENTRIFYING
EFGGIINPRRU PREFIGURING
EFGHHIILOPR HIGH PROFILE
EFGHHOORTTU FORETHOUGHT
EFGHIIKNRSS KINGFISHERS
EFGHIILNOST LINE OF SIGHT
EFGHIILNSST FLIGHTINESS
EFGHIIPRSST PRISEFIGHTS
EFGHIIPRSTZ PRIZEFIGHTS
EFGHILOOSST LOSE SIGHT OF
EFGHIMNORSS FISHMONGERS
EFGHINORSSU SURGEONFISH
EFGIIILLNNR FRINGILLINE
EFGIIILNRTZ FERTILIZING
EFGIIINRVVY REVIVIFYING
EFGIILLMORU FLORILEGIUM
EFGIILMNSTT FILMSETTING
EFGIILMNSUY EMULSIFYING
EFGIILNPSTY SELF-PITYING
EFGIINNPRRT FINGERPRINT
EFGIINPRTTY PRETTIFYING
EFGILLLORWY GILLYFLOWER
EFGILLORRSW FLOWER GIRLS
EFGILNOORVW OVERFLOWING
EFGILNORSTY FOSTERINGLY
EFGINORRSUU FERRUGINOUS
EFGIOPRSSUY GYPSIFEROUS
EFGLNNOSSSU SONGFULNESS
EFHIINRSSTT THRIFTINESS
EFHILLOPSSW FELLOWSHIPS

EFHILLOSTWW WOLF WHISTLE
EFHILLSSSTY SHIFTLESSLY
EFHILNOOSSS FOOLISHNESS
EFHILNOSSSW WOLFISHNESS
EFHILNSSSUW WISHFULNESS
EFHILOPRSST SHOPLIFTERS
EFHIMORRSTX SIXTH-FORMER
EFHINOPPSSS FOPPISHNESS
EFHLNOOOPRR FORLORN HOPE
EFHLNRSSTUU HURTFULNESS
EFHMORRSTTU FURTHERMOST
EFHOOOPRRSW SHOWERPROOF
EFIIIIMNRST INFIRMITIES
EFIIIINNSTV INFINITIVES
EFIIILNRTTY INFERTILITY
EFIIILORSTV FRIVOLITIES
EFIIIMNNNSS SINN FEINISM
EFIIINORRTY INFERIORITY
EFIIKRRSSTT FIRST STRIKE
EFIILNPSSTU PITIFULNESS
EFIINNORSTU INTERFUSION
EFIINOOPTVW POINT OF VIEW
EFIINOPRSSU SPINIFEROUS
EFIINORRSUU URINIFEROUS
EFIIOPRRSSU SPIRIFEROUS
EFIKLLNSSSU SKILFULNESS
EFIKLOORTTU OUT OF KILTER
EFILLLMOSUU MELLIFLUOUS
EFILLLNPTUY PLENTIFULLY
EFILLOOPRSW LOW PROFILES
EFILLRSSTUY FRUITLESSLY
EFILNSSSTUW WISTFULNESS
EFILOOPRRSU PROLIFEROUS
EFILPRSTUUY SUPERFLUITY
EFIMNNORSSU UNIFORMNESS
EFIMNORSSTU MISFORTUNES
EFINNORRRTU IN RETURN FOR
EFINOOORSUZ OZONIFEROUS
EFINOOPRSSS PROFESSIONS
EFINOPRRSST FIRST PERSON
EFINORSSSUU FURIOUSNESS
EFINORSSTTU STONE FRUITS
EFIORRSTTUY YTTRIFEROUS
EFLLNOSSSUU SOULFULNESS
EFLLNSSSTUU LUSTFULNESS
EFLMOORRTUY FLUOROMETRY
EFLNNOORRSS FORLORNNESS
EFLNNORTUUX NEUTRON FLUX
EFLOPRSSUUU SUPERFLUOUS
EFNNNORRRTU FRONT-RUNNER
EFNOOPPRRTY PORT OF ENTRY
EFOOOPRRSSTU FOUR-POSTERS
EGGGINOPRRU GINGER GROUP
EGGHHIILTTW LIGHTWEIGHT

EGGHHINOSSS HOGGISHNESS
EGGHIINOTUW OUTWEIGHING
EGGHIINPSSS PIGGISHNESS
EGGHIINRRTW RIGHT-WINGER
EGGHLNOORSW HORNSWOGGLE
EGGIILLNNRY LINGERINGLY
EGGIILQSSTU SQUIGGLIEST
EGGIINNRTWW WRINGING WET
EGGILLLNRUY GRUELLINGLY
EGGILLNORVY GROVELINGLY
EGGILLNORWY GLOWERINGLY
EGGINOPRRSS PROGRESSING
EGGINOSSSTU SUGGESTIONS
EGGLNOOOORTY GERONTOLOGY
EGHHIIKNTTW WHITE KNIGHT
EGHHIINNOST HIGH-TENSION
EGHHIIPRSST HIGH PRIESTS
EGHHIJMPRSU HIGH JUMPERS
EGHHILNNORS ENGLISH HORN
EGHHILOPRSY HIEROGLYPHS
EGHHILOSSTU HOUSE LIGHTS,
  LIGHTHOUSES
EGHHLOSSTTU THOUGHTLESS
EGHIILLNRSV SHRIVELLING
EGHIILLNRSY RELISHINGLY
EGHIILLNSWW WELL-WISHING
EGHIILNPRSY PERISHINGLY
EGHIILNRSSS GIRLISHNESS
EGHIILNRSVY SHIVERINGLY
EGHIILNSSST SIGHTLINESS
EGHIILOORST HIEROLOGIST
EGHIINNOPSS SPHINGOSINE
EGHIIOPPRSU HIPPO REGIUS
EGHIIRSSSTU RIGHTS ISSUE
EGHILMNOORT MOONLIGHTER
EGHILMOOORS HOMOLOGISER
EGHILMOOORZ HOMOLOGIZER
EGHILMOOSTY MYTHOLOGIES,
  MYTHOLOGISE
EGHILMOOTYZ MYTHOLOGIZE
EGHILNOOPST NEPHOLOGIST,
  PHENOLOGIST
EGHILNOOSTT ETHNOLOGIST
EGHILNOOSST GHOSTLINESS
EGHILORSTUY RIGHTEOUSLY
EGHIMNNORSU NURSING HOME
EGHIMNOSTUU HUGUENOTISM
EGHIMOOTTUV GIVE MOUTH TO
EGHINNNOSST NOTHINGNESS
EGHINNPSSSU PUSHINGNESS
EGHINOPPRSY PROPHESYING
EGHINORSSST SHOESTRINGS
EGHINORSSSU ROGUISHNESS
EGHINORSTUU UNRIGHTEOUS

EGHINPRSSTU UPRIGHTNESS
EGHIORRSTTW GHOSTWRITER
EGHKNOOPRSU ROUGH-SPOKEN
EGHLLLPPTUU PULL THE PLUG
EGHOORRTUVW OVERWROUGHT
EGIIILLMNPR IMPERILLING
EGIIILMNORS RELIGIONISM
EGIIILNNNRT INTERLINING
EGIIILNRSTZ STERILIZING
EGIIILORRSU IRRELIGIOUS
EGIIILORSTY RELIGIOSITY
EGIIIMNNRST MINISTERING
EGIIIMNOPTZ EPITOMIZING
EGIIINNOPRT PRE-IGNITION
EGIIINNOPTT PETITIONING
EGIIINNSSTZ SENSITIZING
EGIIJNNOSTT JETTISONING
EGIIKNPRSTT SPIRKETTING
EGIIILMNPSS MISSPELLING
EGIIILNNSSW WILLINGNESS
EGIIILNORTU GUILLOTINER
EGIIILLNORTY LOITERINGLY
EGIIILLNOSTU GUILLOTINES
EGIIILORSUY RELIGIOUSLY
EGIIILMMNRSY SIMMERINGLY
EGIIILMNNOSU EMULSIONING
EGIIILMNNOSZ SOLEMNIZING
EGIIILMNNSSS SMILINGNESS
EGIIILMNPRSY SIMPERINGLY
EGIIILNNOSTU LENTIGINOUS
EGIIILNNOSUY INGENIOUSLY
EGIIILNNPRST SPLINTERING
EGIIILNPRUVZ PULVERIZING
EGIIILNQRUVY QUIVERINGLY
EGIIILNRSSST GRISTLINESS
EGIIILNRSSTY RESISTINGLY
EGIIILNRTTTY TITTERINGLY
EGIIMNNORSZ SERMONIZING
EGIIMNNRTTU UNREMITTING
EGIIMNOPRTZ TEMPORIZING
EGIIINNNNSSW WINNINGNESS
EGIIINNOPRST INTERPOSING
EGIIINNOQSTU QUESTIONING
EGIIINNPRSSS SPRINGINESS
EGIIINNRSSST STRINGINESS
EGIINOPRSSU SERPIGINOUS
EGIINOPRTTU PIROUETTING
EGIINORRRTZ TERRORIZING
EGIINORSTUV VERTIGINOUS
EGIINPRSSUV SUPERVISING
EGIINPRTTWY TYPEWRITING
EGIIOPRSSTU PRESTIGIOUS
EGIKLLNNORS SNORKELLING
EGIKLNOOORV OVERLOOKING

EGIKNOORRVW OVERWORKING
EGILLLNOTXY EXTOLLINGLY
EGILLLOOVXY VEXILLOLOGY
EGILLLSSTUY GUILTLESSLY
EGILLNNOSTW WELLINGTONS
EGILLNORTVY REVOLTINGLY
EGILLNORVVY REVOLVINGLY
EGILLNPRSSW WELLSPRINGS
EGILMNOORTY TERMINOLOGY
EGILMNOPSTT MELTING POTS
EGILMNPRSUY PRESUMINGLY
EGILMNRTTUY MUTTERINGLY
EGILMOORSTT METROLOGIST
EGILMOOSTTY ETYMOLOGIST
EGILNNNOOSU UNLOOSENING
EGILNNOPSSS SLOPINGNESS
EGILNNOSUUY INGENUOUSLY
EGILNNRSTTY STRINGENTLY
EGILNOOOPST STOOLPIGEON
EGILNOORSTU NEUROLOGIST
EGILNOPRRVY REPROVINGLY
EGILNOSSTUU LOUNGE SUITS
EGILNPRSTTU SPLUTTERING
EGILOOOSSTT OSTEOLOGIST
EGILOOPRSTT PETROLOGIST
EGILOOSSSTX SEXOLOGISTS
EGIMNNOORRS IRONMONGERS
EGIMNNOORRY IRONMONGERY
EGIMNNOORSV MISGOVERNOR
EGIMNOORRTT TRIMETROGON
EGINNNORRUV OVERRUNNING
EGINNOORSTU NITROGENOUS
EGINNOPRSTY TRYPSINOGEN
EGINNORRTUV OVERTURNING
EGINOOPPRTV OVERTOPPING
EGINOOPRRSS PROGRESSION
EGINOOPRRST PROGENITORS
EGINPPRSSSU SUPPRESSING
EGJLMNOPRSU LONG JUMPERS
EGLMNNOOPRT PROLONGMENT
EGMMNOORRRU RUMORMONGER
EGNOOOPRSSU SPOROGENOUS
EHHILOOPPRS PHILOSOPHER
EHHIMOOPRRT THERIOMORPH
EHHIMOOPSST THEOSOPHISM
EHHINNNSSSU HUNNISHNESS
EHHIOOPPRST PHOSPHORITE
EHHIOOPRRSW HERO WORSHIP
EHHIOOPSSTT THEOSOPHIST
EHHLOOSTTUY YOUTH HOSTEL
EHIIILNPPPS PHILIPPINES
EHIIILNPSST PHILISTINES
EHIIILOSSTT HOSTILITIES
EHIIIPRSTTW WHITE SPIRIT

EHIIKLNSTTY KITTENISHLY
EHIIKMNOOSS SHIMONOSEKI
EHIIKMRRSSS SKIRMISHERS
EHIILMRSSTV SILVERSMITH
EHIILNOOPRT HELIOTROPIN
EHIILOOPTTX TOXOPHILITE
EHIIMMOPRST HEMITROPISM
EHIIMNOSSTT SMITHSONITE
EHIINNPRSST INTERNSHIPS
EHIINNSSSSW SWINISHNESS
EHIINPRSSST SPINSTERISH
EHIINRSSSTT THIRSTINESS
EHIIOPRSSST SOPHISTRIES
EHILLMRSSTY MIRTHLESSLY
EHILMMNOSTY SEMIMONTHLY
EHILMNOOPTY ENTOMOPHILY
EHILMOOPRSU HERMOUPOLIS
EHILMORSSTY THERMOLYSIS
EHILNOORSSZ HORIZONLESS
EHILNOSSSTU LOUTISHNESS
EHILNSSSSTY STYLISHNESS
EHILOOPRSUX XEROPHILOUS
EHILOPSSTTY POLYTHEISTS
EHIMMOOOORST HOMOEROTISM
EHIMMOOPSTY MYTHOPOEISM
EHIMMOORSTU MESOTHORIUM
EHIMNNORSTU NOURISHMENT
EHIMNNPSSTU PUNISHMENTS
EHIMNOORTTU NOTOTHERIUM
EHIMNOOSSTT MONOTHEISTS
EHIMNORRSTU MOTHER'S RUIN
EHIMOOPRRST RHEOTROPISM
EHIMOOPSTTY MYTHOPOEIST
EHIMOPRSTXY XEROPHYTISM
EHINNRSSSTU RUNTISHNESS
EHINOOPRRTT ORNITHOPTER
EHINOSSSSTT SOTTISHNESS
EHINRSSSTTU RUTTISHNESS
EHIOOOPRTTZ TROPHOZOITE
EHIOORSSSTX SIX-SHOOTERS
EHIOPPRRSSW WORSHIPPERS
EHJMOPRSSUW SHOW JUMPERS
EHKNOOPRSST SHORT-SPOKEN
EHLLORSSTWY WORTHLESSLY
EHLMNOPPSYY NYMPHOLEPSY
EHLOPRSSUUU SULPHUREOUS
EHMNOOOOPRST MONOSTROPHE
EHMOOOPRSTU HOMOPTEROUS
EHNNOPRSTWY PENNYWORTHS
EHNOORSSTTW STONE'S THROW
EHNOQSSTTUU QUONSET HUTS
EHOOPPRSSTW SHOWSTOPPER
EIIIINQSTUV INQUISITIVE
EIIILLLMRST MILLILITERS

EIIILLLMRST MILLILITRES
EIIILMPRTVY PRIMITIVELY
EIIILNTTUVY INTUITIVELY
EIIIMMNRSTU MINISTERIUM
EIIIMNORSSV REVISIONISM
EIIINOPRSTT PERITONITIS
EIIINOQRSTU REQUISITION
EIIINORSSTV REVISIONIST
EIIINOSSSTU SINUOSITIES
EIIINSSTTVY SENSITIVITY
EIIINSTTTUV INSTITUTIVE
EIIIOPRSSTT PERIOSTITIS
EIIIRSSTTVY RESISTIVITY
EIIILLLMSSTY LIMITLESSLY
EIIILLMPSUVY IMPULSIVELY
EIIILLOOQSSU SOLILOQUIES, SOLILOQUISE
EIIILLOOQSUZ SOLILOQUIZE
EIIILMOPRSUY IMPERIOUSLY
EIIILNNSSTTY INSISTENTLY
EIIILNOOPPRT LIPOPROTEIN
EIIILNOPRSTV SILVERPOINT
EIIIMNNOOPRT PREMONITION
EIIIMNNOPRTU PREMUNITION
EIIIMNOPRSSS IMPRESSIONS
EIIIMNOPSSSU IMPIOUSNESS
EIIIMNORRTTT INTERMITTOR
EIIIMOORRSTU MERITORIOUS
EIIIMOPPRRTY IMPROPRIETY
EIIIMOPRSSST PRESTISSIMO
EIIIMOPSTTUY IMPETUOSITY
EIIIMORRSSTU MOISTURISER
EIIIMORRSTUZ MOISTURIZER
EIIINOOPPRST PREPOSITION
EIIINOOPRRSV PROVISIONER
EIIINOOPSSTX EXPOSITIONS
EIIINOPRSSUV SUPERVISION
EIIINORRSSST SINISTRORSE
EIIINORSTTTU RESTITUTION
EIIIOPPSSTUV SUPPOSITIVE
EIIIOPRRSTUY SUPERIORITY
EIKLLORRSTW TRELLISWORK
EILLLMNOOPP LOLLIPOP MEN
EILLLOORSTT TOILET ROLLS
EILLNOPSSTY POINTLESSLY
EILLORSTTTU LITTERLOUTS
EILMNNOPRTY PROMINENTLY
EILMNOOOPRS MONOPOLISER
EILMNOOOPRZ MONOPOLIZER
EILMNOSSYYZ ENZYMOLYSIS
EILMOPRSSTY PROSELYTISM
EILMOPRTUVY PLUVIOMETRY
EILMOPSTUUY IMPETUOUSLY
EILMORSTTUY MULTISTOREY
EILNOORSSTU RESOLUTIONS

EILNOORSTUV REVOLUTIONS
EILNOPRSUUY PENURIOUSLY
EILNPQSTTUU QUINTUPLETS
EILOOPRSSTY PROTEOLYSIS
EIMNNOOSSSU OMINOUSNESS
EIMNNRSSTTU INSTRUMENTS
EIMNOOPRRTY PREMONITORY
EIMNOOPRSSS SPOONERISMS
EIMNOOQSTTU MOSQUITO NET
EIMNOORSTTU NEUROTOMIST
EIMNOPPRSTU PRESUMPTION
EIMOOPRSTTT OPTOMETRIST
EIMOORRSUVV VERMIVOROUS
EINNOOPPRTU INOPPORTUNE
EINNOOPRSSS RESPONSIONS
EINNOOSSSUX NOXIOUSNESS
EINNOPSSSSU SUSPENSIONS
EINNOQRSTUU NON SEQUITUR
EINNOSSSSUU SINUOUSNESS
EINOOPPRSTW POWER POINTS
EINOOPSSSSS POSSESSIONS
EINOORSSSTU RIOTOUSNESS
EINOPPRSSSU SUPPRESSION
EINOPSSTTTY STENOTYPIST
EINOQRSTTUU TOURNIQUETS
EINORSSTTUY STRENUOSITY
EIOOPPRRRST PROPRIETORS
EIOORRSTVWY IVORY TOWERS
EIOPRRSSSUV SUPERVISORS
EIOPRRSSUVY SUPERVISORY
EIOPRSSTTTU PROSTITUTES
EIOQRRSTTUU TRIQUETROUS
EKKOOPPRSVY PROKOPYEVSK
EKLNOOPSTUY OUTSPOKENLY
EKNNNNOSSUW UNKNOWNNESS
EKNORRSTTUU TRUNK ROUTES
ELLMNNOOSTY SOMNOLENTLY
ELLMORSTUUY TREMULOUSLY
ELLOQRSUUUY QUERULOUSLY
ELMNOPPSUYY MONEY SUPPLY
ELNOOORTTUY ONLY TOO TRUE
ELNOOPPRTUY OPPORTUNELY
ELNORSSTUUY STRENUOUSLY
EMMOOPRSSTT POSTMORTEMS
EMNOOPPSSSU POMPOUSNESS
EMOOORRSSTV SERVOMOTORS
EMORRSTTUYY MYSTERY TOUR
ENNOOPPRRSU PROPER NOUNS
EOPPRRSSSSU SUPPRESSORS
FFGHILLRTUY FRIGHTFULLY
FGGHIINOTTU OUTFIGHTING
FGGIILNORVY FORGIVINGLY
FGHHIINSSTT NIGHT SHIFTS
FGHIILNOPST SHOPLIFTING

FGHIILNORSU FLOURISHING
FGHIINNRSSU FURNISHINGS
FGHIINRSSTT FIRST NIGHTS
FGHILNORTTY FORTNIGHTLY
FGHILOPTTTU PUT TO FLIGHT
FGIIILMNPSY SIMPLIFYING
FGIIILNOSSZ FOSSILIZING
FGIILLNOORT ROOT FILLING
FGIILMNNORY INFORMINGLY
FGIILNSTTUY STULTIFYING
FGIINRRSSTT FIRST-STRING
FGIKNNORSTU TUNING FORKS
FGIOORRSUUV FRUGIVOROUS
FHHIINOOPST PHOTO FINISH
FHHIORRSSTT SHORT SHRIFT
FHILMOORRRS HORROR FILMS
FHINORRSSTT SHIRTFRONTS
FHLLNOOOORR ROLL OF HONOR
FHMOOORTUUU OUT OF HUMOUR
FIIIMNNOSSU INFUSIONISM
FIIINNOSSTU INFUSIONIST
FIIOOPPRRST PROOF SPIRIT
FIIRTTTTTUU TUTTI FRUTTI
FILLOORSUVY FRIVOLOUSLY
FILMRSSTTUU MISTRUSTFUL
FILNOORSSTY FRONTOLYSIS
FINOOOPSSTT SOFT OPTIONS
FLLOORRSUWY SORROWFULLY
GGGIILLNRWY WRIGGLINGLY
GGHHIILNSTT NIGHTLIGHTS
GGHIILLNSTY SLIGHTINGLY
GGHIIMNNSTU GUNSMITHING
GGIILNOPSSY GOSSIPINGLY
GGIINNOPSST SIGNPOSTING
GGILNOOORWW WOOLGROWING
GHHHIORTTUW THROUGH WITH
GHHIINRSSTT NIGHTSHIRTS
GHHIIPRSSTW SHIPWRIGHTS
GHHINOOOOPP POOH-POOHING
GHHINOOPRTU THOROUGHPIN
GHHMNNOOOPT MONOPHTHONG
GHHNORRSTUU RUN-THROUGHS
GHHOPRSTTUU HROUGHPUTS
GHIIKMNRSS SKIRMISHING
GHIIKLNNRSY SHRINKINGLY
GHIILLLNRTY THRILLINGLY
GHIILLOOPST PHILOLOGIST
GHIILLOOSTT LITHOLOGIST
GHIILLOPSTT PILOT LIGHTS
GHIILNNPSUY PUNISHINGLY
GHIILNOORST RHINOLOGIST
GHIILOOOPST OPHIOLOGIST
GHIILOOSSTT HISTOLOGIST
GHIINNOPTYZ HYPNOTIZING

GHIIINOPPRSW WORSHIPPING
GHIIINOPTTUW WHITING POUT
GHIJMNOPSUW SHOW JUMPING
GHILLOOOPST HOPLOLOGIST
GHILLOOPSYY SYPHILOLOGY
GHILMOOSTTY MYTHOLOGIST
GHILNOOOOPST PHONOLOGIST
GHILNOOOORTY ORNITHOLOGY
GHILOOOPRTY OLIGOTROPHY
GHIMMNOORSU MUSHROOMING
GHIMNOOPSYY PHYSIOGNOMY
GHIMOOOSSYZ HOMOZYGOSIS
GHINOORRTUW WROUGHT IRON
GHLNOOPSSUW SNOWPLOUGHS
GIIIKLMNNSS MISSING LINK
GIIIKNNNPRT PRINTING INK
GIIILLNNORT ROLLING IN IT
GIIILNNPRSY INSPIRINGLY
GIIILNNQRUY INQUIRINGLY
GIIIMNNOOSU IGNOMINIOUS
GIIIMNNOPRS IMPRISONING
GIIIMNNPRST MISPRINTING, STRIP
  MINING
GIIIMNOPRSV IMPROVISING
GIIINNNOPPT PINPOINTING
GIIINNNPRSU UNINSPIRING
GIIINNOOPST POSITIONING
GIIINNSTTTU INSTITUTING
GIIKLNNPRSS SPRINKLINGS
GIILLLLMNOR ROLLING MILL
GIILLLNNUWY UNWILLINGLY
GIILLMNOOST LIMNOLOGIST
GIILLMNOPRY IMPLORINGLY
GIILLMNPTUY MULTIPLYING
GIILLNNOPRS ROLLING PINS
GIILMNOORSV LIVING ROOMS
GIILMNOPRSY PROMISINGLY
GIILMNOPRVY IMPROVINGLY
GIILMNQRSUY SQUIRMINGLY
GIILNNTTUWY UNWITTINGLY
GIILNOOSSST SINOLOGISTS
GIIMNNOPRSU UNPROMISING
GIIMNNOPRTU IMPORTUNING
GIIMNOORSTT SITTING ROOM
GIIMNOSSSTY MISOGYNISTS
GIIMNRSSTTU MISTRUSTING
GIIMOORRRST RIGOR MORTIS
GIINNNOOPRS SPRING ONION
GIINNNOPSTW WINNING POST
GIINNOOPTTU OUTPOINTING
GIINNOPRSST PISTON RINGS
GIINOORSTUV VORTIGINOUS
GIINRTTTTYY NITTY-GRITTY
GIJMNNNPRUU RUNNING JUMP

GIKLNNNOUWY UNKNOWINGLY
GIKLNOOPRVY PROVOKINGLY
GILLMOOPSTY POLYGLOTISM
GILLNOPRRSS SPRING ROLLS
GILMMNRRUUY MURMURINGLY
GILNNNOPSSU NONPLUSSING
GILNOOPPSTY TYPING POOLS
GILNORRTTUY TORTURINGLY
GILNRSTTTUY STRUTTINGLY
GIMNNORSTUU SURMOUNTING
GIMNOOOPRSU SPOROGONIUM
GINNOOPRSTT STRONG POINT
GINOOPRSTUU OUTPOURINGS
GMNOOORRSST STRONG ROOMS
GNOOOPRSTUY PROTOGYNOUS
HHIMOOPPRSS PHOSPHORISM
HHMNOOOOPSU HOMOPHONOUS
HHOOOPPRSSU PHOSPHOROUS
HIILLNNNOOT NONILLIONTH
HIILLNORSTT TRILLIONTHS
HIILMOOSTTT LITHOTOMIST
HIILNORTTYY HOLY TRINITY
HIIMMOOPRSS ISOMORPHISM
HIIMMOPRRST TRIMORPHISM
HIIMNOOPRST MONITORSHIP
HILNOOPSTXY XYLOPHONIST
HILNOORSSTU HONOURS LIST
HIMMOOOPRSZ ZOOMORPHISM
HIMNOOPSSUY SYMPHONIOUS
HINOOPPRSSS SPONSORSHIP
HINOOPPSTTY PHONOTYPIST
HINOOPRRTTY THYROTROPIN
HLNOOOPPSUY POLYPHONOUS
HMOOOOPRSSU HOMOSPOROUS
HORRSTTTUWY TRUSTWORTHY
IIIILMNNQSU INQUILINISM
IIIIMMPRSTV PRIMITIVISM
IIIIMNSTTUV INTUITIVISM
IIIIMPPSSSS MISSISSIPPI
IIIIMPRSTTV PRIMITIVIST
IIIINNOQSTU INQUISITION
IIIINSTTTUV INTUITIVIST
IIIILLMNOPST POINTILLISM
IIIILLMNOSSU ILLUSIONISM
IIIILLNNOQTU QUINTILLION
IIIILLNOPSTT POINTILLIST
IIIILLNOSSTT TONSILLITIS
IIIILLNOSSTU ILLUSIONIST
IIIILNNOQSUU INQUILINOUS
IIIMNOOPSST IMPOSITIONS
IIINNNORRTTU INNUTRITION
IIINNOSTTTU INSTITUTION
IIINOOOPSTV OVIPOSITION
IIINOQRSSTU INQUISITORS

IIIOPSSSTTV POSITIVISTS
IIJLNORSUUY INJURIOUSLY
IILLNNOOOPP OPINION POLL
IILLOOQSSTU SOLILOQUIST
IILLORSSTUU ILLUSTRIOUS
IILMOORTTUY UTILITY ROOM
IILOOPRRSVY PROVISORILY
IILOSSSTTXY STYLOSTIXIS
IIMNOOPRSTU POSITRONIUM
IIMNOPRTTUY IMPORTUNITY
IINOOOOPPRST PROPOSITION
IINOOOOPPSST OPPOSITIONS
IINOOPPSSTU SUPPOSITION
IINOPPQRTUY PROPINQUITY
IKORSSSTTTY TROTSKYISTS
ILLOPSSUWWY PUSSY WILLOW
ILLORSUUUXY LUXURIOUSLY
ILMNOOOPSST MONOPOLISTS

ILNOOOPSSUY POISONOUSLY
ILNOOOORSTUY NOTORIOUSLY
ILOOPPRSSST SPOILSPORTS
IMNOOPPRSTU OPPORTUNISM
IMNOORSSTTY MONSTROSITY
IMPPPRRSTUU STIRRUP PUMP
INOOOOPPRRST PROPORTIONS
INOOPPRSTTU OPPORTUNIST
INOOPPRTTUY OPPORTUNITY
INOOPRRSSTU PROTRUSIONS
IOOPPRSSTUY SUPPOSITORY
IOOPRRSTTTU PROSTITUTOR
LMNOOOSSTUY MONOSTYLOUS
LMNOORSSTUY MONSTROUSLY
LMOPSSTUUUY SUMPTUOUSLY
LOORRSTTUUY TORTUROUSLY
MMOOPRRSSUU RUMPUS ROOMS

TWELVE-LETTER WORDS

AAAAAALMRSTT TARAMASALATA
AAAAABBCDRRS ABRACADABRAS
AAAAABBINRSST SABBATARIANS
AAAABCCHILNN BACCHANALIAN
AAAABDIINRSU SAUDI ARABIAN
AAAACCCCIRTU ACCIACCATURA
AAAACDIILPRS PARADISIACAL
AAAACDIMMNTU MACADAMIA NUT
AAAACEHHKTVW HAVE A WHACK AT
AAAACEHKMSTV HAVE A SMACK AT
AAAACEINRRSV CARAVANSERAI
AAAACGIMMNRT ANAGRAMMATIC
AAAACHILNPPS APPALACHIANS
AAAACIMNRSST ANTIMACASSAR
AAAADEHMRSTT MAD AS A HATTER
AAAAEGGLNPRU PARALANGUAGE
AAAAEGNRTVXZ EXTRAVAGANZA
AAAAFINRRSST RASTAFARIANS
AAAAGGILMMNT AMALGAMATING
AAAAGILMMNOT AMALGAMATION
AAAAILLPRRSS SARSAPARILLA
AAAAILMNPRTY MALAYAN TAPIR
AAAAILNNRSTV TRANSVAALIAN
AAAAILNRSSTU AUSTRALASIAN
AAABBCEGIRRY BABY CARRIAGE
AAABBCILLRRY BARBARICALLY
AAABBIIMNRRS BARBARIANISM
AAABCCDERRSS SACRED SCARAB

AAABCDEHLNNU BECHUANALAND
AAABCEGKPSSS BACK PASSAGES
AAABCEHILLPT ALPHABETICAL
AAABCEHILNPT ANALPHABETIC
AAABCEHLOPPR APPROACHABLE
AAABCEILLRWY CABLE RAILWAY
AAABCELNRRTU TABERNACULAR
AAABCGIINNRT CANTABRIGIAN
AAABDDJNNORY DARBY AND JOAN
AAABDEELLMNT MATABELELAND
AAABDEILMRTZ DRAMATIZABLE
AAABDEMRSSSS AMBASSADRESS
AAABDGHMNRSS SMASH-AND-GRAB
AAABDIILPTTY ADAPTABILITY
AAABDIJMNNRS BANDJARMASIN
AAABDILLOOPR PARABOLOIDAL
AAABEEGILMRR MARRIAGEABLE
AAABEEGLMNNU UNMANAGEABLE
AAABEELLNPPU UNAPPEALABLE
AAABEHIKPPPT PHI BETA KAPPA
AAABEHLMOSTT HAEMATOBLAST
AAABEIILMNNT MAINTAINABLE
AAABEILLNSSU UNASSAILABLE
AAABEILNNTTU UNATTAINABLE
AAABEINNSSST SAN SEBASTIAN
AAABELLLPRRS PARALLEL BARS
AAABELLNRSTT TRANSLATABLE
AAABELNOOPTY PALAEOBOTANY

AAABGIILNRRT GIBRALTARIAN
AAABGLLMRRRU BURGLAR ALARM
AAABHIILNOTT HABITATIONAL
AAABIIILLTVY AVAILABILITY
AAABIILLPTTY PALATABILITY
AAABILLNQRRU BARRANQUILLA
AAACCCDHIRTY TACHYCARDIAC
AAACCCEHKPTT CATCH A PACKET
AAACCDEIIMNS ACADEMICIANS
AAACCDEILLMY ACADEMICALLY
AAACCDEILMNO DECALCOMANIA
AAACCDHNRRSY CASH AND CARRY
AAACCDIINRRT INTRACARDIAC
AAACCDIIRRTT TARTARIC ACID
AAACCEEHSSTT ATTACHÉ CASES
AAACCEGILMTT METAGALACTIC
AAACCEGIORSU AGARICACEOUS
AAACCEHNOSTU ACANTHACEOUS
AAACCEIINPTT INCAPACITATE
AAACCEINNQTU ACQUAINTANCE
AAACCHILLNRY ANARCHICALLY
AAACCHILNPTY ANAPHYLACTIC
AAACCIILMRST MARCASITICAL
AAACCIINOPTT CAPACITATION
AAACCILMNOST ACCLAMATIONS
AAACCILORSTU ACCUSATORIAL
AAACDEEGKLPS PACKAGE DEALS
AAACDEELNRRY CALENDAR YEAR
AAACDEGILMOR MEGALOCARDIA
AAACDEGIMPRS PARADIGM CASE
AAACDEINRSTT TRADESCANTIA
AAACDENNOPSU PANDANACEOUS
AAACDGIIMMRT DIAGRAMMATIC
AAACDGIIMPRT PARADIGMATIC
AAACDIINNNSV SCANDINAVIAN
AAACDILLMRTY DRAMATICALLY
AAACEEENPPRR REAPPEARANCE
AAACEEFLMNSS MALFEASANCES
AAACEEGNRTVX EXTRAVAGANCE
AAACEESSSTVW SWEET CASSAVA
AAACEFIMNORR AFRO-AMERICAN
AAACEGGGLOTU GALACTAGOGUE
AAACEGILMMNO MEGALOMANIAC
AAACEGIMNPRT PARAMAGNETIC
AAACEGIRRSWY CARRIAGEWAYS
AAACEHHNRTTU HARTHACANUTE
AAACEHILMMTT MATHEMATICAL
AAACEHIPRRTT PATRIARCHATE
AAACEHKNSSTW SASKATCHEWAN
AAACEHKRSTTT HEART ATTACKS
AAACEHLMORTY HAEMATOCRYAL
AAACEILMOOST OSTEOMALACIA
AAACEILNORTU AERONAUTICAL
AAACELNOSSTU SANTALACEOUS

AAACFGILNNRU LINGUA FRANCA
AAACFIINRRTT ANTI-AIR-CRAFT
AAACFLMNRTUU MANUFACTURAL
AAACGGILLNOY ANAGOGICALLY
AAACGGILLOPY APAGOGICALLY
AAACGIILNPST CAPITAL GAINS
AAACGIIMNSTT ANASTIGMATIC
AAACGILLLNVY GALVANICALLY
AAACGILLMMMO MAMMALOGICAL
AAACHIKPPRST APPARATCHIKS
AAACHILLLMTY THALAMICALLY
AAACHILMNRST CHARLATANISM
AAACHIMNORTU TAUROMACHIAN
AAACHIPPRRST PARAPHRASTIC
AAACIILNNOST CANALISATION
AAACIILNNOTZ CANALIZATION
AAACIILNNRRT INTRACRANIAL
AAACILLLNTYY ANALYTICALLY
AAACILLMNOTY ANATOMICALLY
AAACILLMORTY AROMATICALLY
AAACILMMNNOO MONOMANIACAL
AAACILMNOPRY PYROMANIACAL
AAACILNSTTTY ANTICATALYST
AAADDEGINSTV DISADVANTAGE
AAADDFHLLOOO ALL OF A DOODAH
AAADDGILLMOY AMYGDALOIDAL
AAADDLMNPRST STANDARD LAMP
AAADEEGGMNST STAGE-MANAGED
AAADEEGINNRV EVER AND AGAIN
AAADEEINRRSV SIERRA NEVADA
AAADEGIMQRSU QUADRAGESIMA
AAADEGMNORRS ROAD MANAGERS
AAADEGNOSTUV ADVANTAGEOUS
AAADEHNRRTTW DEATH WARRANT
AAADEILMNNRS SALAMANDRINE
AAADEILMRRRS REAR ADMIRALS
AAADEINSSSST ASSASSINATED
AAADEMNNSSWY WAYS AND MEANS
AAADFIINORST FARADISATION
AAADFIINORTZ FARADIZATION
AAADGIILLORT GLADIATORIAL
AAADGLNQRRUU QUADRANGULAR
AAADGLOORSVW AVOGADRO'S LAW
AAADGMNNNOOR MOAN AND GROAN
AAADHIINOPRS ANAPHRODISIA
AAADIILLNOTT DILATATIONAL
AAAEEGGLMNTU METALANGUAGE
AAAEEGGMNRST STAGE MANAGER
AAAEEGINNRSX SEXAGENARIAN
AAAEEGMNNPRT PERMANGANATE
AAAEEHIMNSTT ANATHEMATISE
AAAEEHIMNTTZ ANATHEMATIZE
AAAEEHIPRSST PARAESTHESIA
AAAEEKRRSTTT STEAK TARTARE

AAAAEELNPRSTY PENALTY AREAS
AAAAEGHLOPPRY PALAEOGRAPHY
AAAAEGILLMNRY MANAGERIALLY
AAAAEGINNNNOR NONAGENARIAN
AAAAEGNOPRRST PERSONA GRATA
AAAAEIILNQRTU EQUALITARIAN
AAAAEILLLNPRT ANTIPARALLEL
AAAAEILLNPSST PALATIALNESS
AAAAEILMRRTTX EXTRAMARITAL
AAAAEILNNNOTX ANNEXATIONAL
AAAAEILPPRRSS REAPPRAISALS
AAAAELQQRSUUV QUAQUAVERSAL
AAAAEMMRRSSTT MASTER-AT-ARMS
AAAAGGINORSTV AGGRAVATIONS
AAAAGGIOPPRTU APPOGGIATURA
AAAAGHINPPRRS PARAPHRASING
AAAAGHIRSTTWY STRAIGHTAWAY
AAAAGIILNNOTV NAVIGATIONAL
AAAAGIINNOPST PAGANISATION
AAAAGIINNOPTZ PAGANIZATION
AAAAGIINNOSTV GAVANISATION
AAAAGIINNOTVZ GAVANIZATION
AAAAGILLLORRT GRALLATORIAL
AAAAHHHJNPRSU SHAHJAHANPUR
AAAAHIILNNOTT ANTIHALATION
AAAAHIIMNNRTU HUMANITARIAN
AAAAHIKLTWWWY WALK AWAY WITH
AAAAHILLNSTTT HALLSTATTIAN
AAAAHLLLMNPRS MARSHALL PLAN
AAAAIILMNPRSU MARSUPIALIAN
AAAAIILMPRRTY PARAMILITARY
AAAAIILNNOSST NASALISATION
AAAAIILNNOSTZ NASALIZATION
AAAAIILNORTTT TOTALITARIAN
AAAAIIMMNRSST SAMARITANISM
AAAAIINNQRSTU ANTIQUARIANS
AAAAIKLNNOPRT NATIONAL PARK
AAAAILMNORTTU MATURATIONAL
AAAAILNNRSTVY TRANSYLVANIA
AAAAILNOPRSTY PARALYSATION
AAAAINOOPPSST APPASSIONATO
AABBCCEMOOSU BOMBACACEOUS
AABBCDEKLLNU BLACK AND BLUE
AABBCEGIKKNR BACKBREAKING
AABBCGIKLLLN BLACKBALLING
AABBCIIILMNO BIBLIOMANIAC
AABBDEEFLOTU FEEL BAD ABOUT
AABBEGIINRTV ABBREVIATING
AABBEGILLNRS BALL BEARINGS
AABBEIIKLLOS BIELSKO-BIALA
AABBEIINORTV ABBREVIATION
AABBEILRTTTU ATTRIBUTABLE
AABBEIMMNPSY NAMBY-PAMBIES
AABBEINRRRTW RABBIT WARREN

AABBEIRRSTTU BARBITURATES
AABBHIIILTTY HABITABILITY
AABCCDEIILRT BACTERICIDAL
AABCCDEIKNRR CRACKBRAINED
AABCCDEILLSY DECASYLLABIC
AABCCEEHLNRT CARTE BLANCHE
AABCCEELNPTU UNACCEPTABLE
AABCCEILLLNU INCALCULABLE
AABCCEILMNOR MICROBALANCE
AABCCEIRRTUU BUREAUCRATIC
AABCCENOORSU CARBONACEOUS
AABCCGIKKNRT BACKTRACKING
AABCCHHIIMPR AMPHIBRACHIC
AABCCIILOTTY BIOCATALYTIC
AABCCILLLNUY INCALCULABLY
AABCCINRSTTU SUBANTARCTIC
AABCCKLNRRTU BLACKCURRANT
AABCCKNNOSTU BANK ACCOUNTS
AABCDDEEILNT BALANCED DIET
AABCDDEEKLLP BACKPEDALLED
AABCDDEHKLNY BACKHANDEDLY
AABCDDEKLRRW BLADDERWRACK
AABCDDGINORR BOARDING CARD
AABCDEEHKLRT BLACK-HEARTED
AABCDEEIILNR INERADICABLE
AABCDEEIILLPS DISPLACEABLE
AABCDEELLLNW WELL-BALANCED
AABCDEELLLSY DECASYLLABLE
AABCDEELNORV OVERBALANCED
AABCDEENOSTU SUBDEACONATE
AABCDEFLNOTU CONFABULATED
AABCDEGIKLNP BACKPEDALING
AABCDEHIINRT DIBRANCHIATE
AABCDEHIMMRS CHAMBERMAIDS
AABCDEHORRTY CARBOHYDRATE
AABCDEIILNNS CANNIBALISED
AABCDEIILNNZ CANNIBALIZED
AABCDEIILNRY INERADICABLY
AABCDEILNSST ELASTIC BANDS
AABCDEINOORS RADIO BEACONS
AABCDEINOSTU SUBDIACONATE
AABCDEKNRRSS BANKER'S CARDS
AABCDEKNRSSW BACKWARDNESS
AABCDELLOORT COLLABORATED
AABCDELMNRSU CANDELABRUMS
AABCDELOPPRR CLAPPERBOARD
AABCDELRSTTY ABSTRACTEDLY
AABCDENOPRSW BOW AND SCRAPE
AABCDEORRSST BROADCASTERS
AABCDGINNORT CARBON DATING
AABCDGINORST BROADCASTING
AABCDGKLLRUY BLACKGUARDLY
AABCDIILLLOY DIABOLICALLY
AABCDKMNOOSW BACKWOODSMAN

AABCEEEFFILN INEFFACEABLE
AABCEEEGHLNX EXCHANGEABLE
AABCEEEHLNST BALANCE SHEET
AABCEEEHLRRS RESEARCHABLE
AABCEEFIPRRT PREFABRICATE
AABCEEGGPRRT CARPETBAGGER
AABCEEGINRTX EXACERBATING
AABCEEHLMNRT MERCHANTABLE
AABCEEHLNRSU UNSEARCHABLE
AABCEEHLOPRR REPROACHABLE
AABCEEHMNRST ANTECHAMBERS
AABCEEIKMNRT CABINET-MAKER
AABCEEINORTX EXACERBATION
AABCEELLNOOT OBLANCEOLATE
AABCEELLNSSS SCALABLENESS
AABCEFHKMOOT MAKE A BOTCH OF
AABCEFIILLSS CLASSIFIABLE
AABCEFIILLTY BEATIFICALLY
AABCEFIILNST SANCTIFIABLE
AABCEFLNRSTU BLAST FURNACE
AABCEGGKRRTU GARBAGE TRUCK
AABCEHIIMNPS AMPHISBAENIC
AABCEHILMNRS CHAMBERLAINS
AABCEHILNRTU UNCHARITABLE
AABCEHIRRRRS CRASH BARRIER
AABCEHKLNPRT BLACK PANTHER
AABCEHKMNNRT MERCHANT BANK
AABCEHLLORTT CALL TO THE BAR
AABCEHLMNORS ELASMOBRANCH
AABCEHLOPRRY REPROACHABLY
AABCEHMRRSST STAR CHAMBERS
AABCEHOPRSSU HABEAS CORPUS
AABCEIIILPST CAPABILITIES
AABCEIIILLNPP INAPPLICABLE
AABCEIIILLOSZ SOCIALIZABLE
AABCEIIILRTY LACERABILITY
AABCEIIILRTTY TRACEABILITY
AABCEIIILRTUU BIAURICULATE
AABCEIKLLMRS BLACKMAILERS
AABCEILLLORT BICOLLATERAL
AABCEILLNUVZ VULCANIZABLE
AABCEILMNOPR INCOMPARABLE
AABCEILNNOST SANCTIONABLE
AABCEILORSTZ OSTRACIZABLE
AABCEILORSUV VOCABULARIES
AABCEINRRSTT SCATTERBRAIN
AABCEKLPPRSS BACKSLAPPERS
AABCENOPPRRS CARBON PAPERS
AABCENORSSST CONTRABASSES
AABCFIINORST FABRICATIONS
AABCFLNOORTU CONFABULATOR
AABCGHIILOPR BIOGRAPHICAL
AABCGHIOOPRS AGORAPHOBICS
AABCGHKLLNOY BY A LONG CHALK

AABCGIIKLLMN BLACKMAILING
AABCGIKLNPPS BACKSLAPPING
AABCGILNNOTU OUTBALANCING
AABCHIIMORTT MICROHABITAT
AABCHIINOOTT COHABITATION
AABCHILNRTUY UNCHARITABLY
AABCIIILNPTY INCAPABILITY
AABCIILLNPPY INAPPLICABLY
AABCIILLPRSY PARISYLLABIC
AABCIILNNOTU INCUBATIONAL
AABCIILNORST CALIBRATIONS
AABCIILRTTTY TRACTABILITY
AABCILLLLSYY SYLLABICALLY
AABCILMNOPRY INCOMPARABLY
AABCILRRSUUU SUBAURICULAR
AABCINORSSTT ABSTRACTIONS
AABCLLLRSSTY CRYSTAL BALLS
AABCLLOOOORRT COLLABORATOR
AABCLNORSTUY CONSTABULARY
AABCMNNNOOTT NONCOMBATANT
AABDDEEELMNR REDEMANDABLE
AABDDEGLLLRS GALL BLADDERS
AABDDEHLLMOY HEBDOMADALLY
AABDDGHORRTU DRAUGHTBOARD
AABDDGINORRW DRAWING BOARD
AABDEEEGILRS DISAGREEABLE
AABDEEGILRSY DISAGREEABLY
AABDEEHHRRSS HABERDASHERS
AABDEEHHRRSY HABERDASHERY
AABDEEHORRTW WEATHERBOARD
AABDEEILRTTX EXTRADITABLE
AABDEEJLRSTU READJUSTABLE
AABDEELMPRTU PERAMBULATED
AABDEELNOPRS LEOPARD'S-BANE
AABDEGGLNOUY BODY LANGUAGE
AABDEGIIMSTU DISAMBIGUATE
AABDEHHIRRST HAIR'S BREADTH
AABDEHILRTWW WITHDRAWABLE
AABDEIILNRST DISTRAINABLE
AABDEIKNORST DEBARKATIONS
AABDEILLLOSW DISALLOWABLE
AABDEILNNOTT NATIONAL DEBT
AABDEIMRRSSS DISEMBARRASS
AABDELOPRRST PLASTERBOARD
AABDGIINNOST BASTINADOING
AABDGIINRSTZ BASTARDIZING
AABDGILNNSST SANDBLASTING
AABDHIKLNOSY BANK HOLIDAYS
AABDIIILLTTY DILATABILITY
AABDIIILSTVY ADVISABILITY
AABDIILMNRTY MILITARY BAND
AABDIMNORSTU ADUMBRATIONS
AABDINOOTTUY AUTOANTIBODY
AABDMOORRRST MORTARBOARDS

AABEEEEGRRSV EAGER BEAVERS
AABEEEFKRRSS SAFEBREAKERS
AABEEEHKRRRT HEARTBREAKER
AABEEEILMNRX RE-EXAMINABLE
AABEEELMNRUV MANEUVERABLE
AABEEFGILLLT BIFLAGELLATE
AABEEFGILRRR IRREFRAGABLE
AABEEFHINRRT FEATHERBRAIN
AABEEFILMNST MANIFESTABLE
AABEEFLMOSTV MOVABLE FEAST
AABEEFLNRRST TRANSFERABLE
AABEEGGLMORT MORTGAGEABLE
AABEEGILMNTZ MAGNETIZABLE
AABEEGMMORRU OBERAMMERGAU
AABEEHIILRTT REHABILITATE
AABEEHILNSTZ ELIZABETHANS
AABEEHILPRST ALPHABETISER
AABEEHILPRTZ ALPHABETIZER
AABEEHLMQRSU ALHAMBRESQUE
AABEEHLRRTYZ BREATHALYZER
AABEEILMMRSU IMMEASURABLE
AABEEILNRRST RESTRAINABLE
AABEEINRRRST TRAINBEARERS
AABEEINRRSST BRAINTEASERS
AABEELLNSSUV VALUABLENESS
AABEELMNNRST TABLE MANNERS
AABEELMNORUV MANOEUVRABLE
AABEELMNRSUU UNMEASURABLE
AABEELNNORSU UNREASONABLE
AABEELNNOSSU UNSEASONABLE
AABEELNNRSUW UNANSWERABLE
AABEELNRSTTU SUBALTERNATE
AABEELORUVYY A BY-YOUR-LEAVE
AABEENNRRSTU SUBTERRANEAN
AABEENNRTUUV BUENAVENTURA
AABEFFLORTUW WATER BUFFALO
AABEFGIKNRST BREAKFASTING
AABEFHLMNOTU UNFATHOMABLE
AABEFIILNOPS SAPONIFIABLE
AABEFIILNQTU QUANTIFIABLE
AABEFLLMMNNO NONFLAMMABLE
AABEFLNORUUV UNFAVOURABLE
AABEGGGMOORS BAGGAGE ROOMS
AABEGGILLNTU AGGLUTINABLE
AABEGHIKNRTT BREATHTAKING
AABEGHILLOSU HELIOGABALUS
AABEGHIMNTTW BANTAMWEIGHT
AABEGIILMNNU UNIMAGINABLE
AABEGILNOPRU ABELIAN GROUP
AABEGIMNRRSS EMBARRASSING
AABEGIMNRRTT BATTERING RAM
AABEGIRRRSTU ARBITRAGEURS
AABEGLLRSSTU GLAUBER'S SALT
AABEGLMMOPRR PROGRAMMABLE

AABEGLNORRRS BARREL ORGANS
AABEGLRRSSUY BARLEY SUGARS
AABEHIINORST HEBRAISATION
AABEHIINORTZ HEBRAIZATION
AABEHILLORVY BEHAVIORALLY
AABEHILMNNOT HAMBLETONIAN
AABEHILMNORZ HARMONIZABLE
AABEHILNQSUV VANQUISHABLE
AABEHILNSSTU HABITUALNESS
AABEHLPRRSSV PHRASAL VERBS
AABEIIILLNTY ALIENABILITY
AABEIIILLLMTY MALLEABILITY
AABEIIILLRTTY ALTERABILITY
AABEIILNRRST LIBERTARIANS
AABEIILPRRTY REPARABILITY
AABEIILPRSTY SEPARABILITY
AABEIILQTTUY EQUATABILITY
AABEIKLMNSTU UNMISTAKABLE
AABEIKMNORST EMBARKATIONS
AABEIKNORSTT STATION BREAK
AABEILLMNTVY AMBIVALENTLY
AABEILLNRRTU TURBELLARIAN
AABEILLPRRTY LIBERAL PARTY
AABEILMMRSUY IMMEASURABLY
AABEILMMRSUZ SUMMARIZABLE
AABEILNOORST ELABORATIONS
AABEILNPRRST TRANSPIRABLE
AABEILOORRST LABORATORIES
AABEILOPPPRR APPROPRIABLE
AABEINSSTTTU SUBSTANTIATE
AABEKLMORRTU LABOUR MARKET
AABELLORSTTY BATTLE ROYALS
AABELMMNOSTU SOMNAMBULATE
AABELMNRSTTU TRANSMUTABLE
AABELMOPRRTU PERAMBULATOR
AABELNNORSUY UNREASONABLY
AABELNNOSSUY UNSEASONABLY
AABELNOPRSST TRANSPOSABLE
AABELOPRRTUY BEAUTY PARLOR
AABFGIIILTTY FATIGABILITY
AABFHLMNOTUY UNFATHOMABLY
AABFIILLMMTY FLAMMABILITY
AABFIILLOTTY FLOATABILITY
AABFLLMNOTYY FLAMBOYANTLY
AABFLNORUUVY UNFAVOURABLY
AABGHIINNRSW BRAINWASHING
AABGIIILNTVY NAVIGABILITY
AABGIILLNOOT OBLIGATIONAL
AABGIILLNRTZ TRAILBLAZING
AABGIILNOSST SAILING BOATS
AABGIKNNSSSV SAVINGS BANKS
AABGILNORSUV LABOURSAVING
AABGIMNRSTTU MASTURBATING
AABHIIILNOTT HABILITATION

AABHIIILRSSZ BILHARZIASIS
AABHIIINNOTT INHABITATION
AABHIILOOPRU AILUROPHOBIA
AABIIILNOSST ASSIBILATION
AABIIILNSTTY STAINABILITY
AABIILNOORTY ABOLITIONARY
AABIILOPRTVY VAPORABILITY
AABIILRSTTUY SATURABILITY
AABIIMNNOOST ABOMINATIONS
AABIINNORSTU URBANISATION
AABIINNORTUZ URBANIZATION
AABIINOORRST ARBORISATION
AABIINOORRTZ ARBORIZATION
AABIKLMNSTUY UNMISTAKABLY
AABILLMRSUXY SUBMAXILLARY
AABILNSSTTUV SUBSTANTIVAL
AABILOPRRSTU SUPRAORBITAL
AABIMNORSTTU MASTURBATION
AABINOOPRRTY PROBATIONARY
AABLMMNNOSTU SOMNAMBULANT
AABMNNOOTTUW MAN-ABOUT-TOWN
AACCCEEHILTT CATECHETICAL
AACCCEGNORYY GYNAECOCRACY
AACCCEHIRSTT CATACHRESTIC
AACCCEIINRSU INACCURACIES
AACCDDEHIIRS DISACCHARIDE
AACCDDEMMOOT ACCOMMODATED
AACCDDIILLTY DIDACTICALLY
AACCDDIILOPR DIPLOCARDIAC
AACCDEEFHHTT HATCHET-FACED
AACCDEEHHIKS SICK HEADACHE
AACCDEEIMORS ICE-CREAM SODA
AACCDEEINRRT INCARCERATED
AACCDEENNOTT CONCATENATED
AACCDEHINORS ARCHDIOCESAN
AACCDEHNORRY ARCHDEACONRY
AACCDEIIILNT DIALECTICIAN
AACCDEIILMST ACCLIMATISED
AACCDEIILMTZ ACCLIMATIZED
AACCDEIILLNTY ACCIDENTALLY
AACCDEKMPUUV VACUUM-PACKED
AACCDGINRRRY CARD-CARRYING
AACCDIIILRST RADICALISTIC
AACCDIILNOTU CLAUDICATION
AACCDILLLTYY DACTYLICALLY
AACCDILLNORY DRACONICALLY
AACCEEEILRTV ACCELERATIVE
AACCEEGHILMP MEGACEPHALIC
AACCEEGHOSST STAGECOACHES
AACCEEGILNRT ACCELERATING
AACCEEHIMNOR AEROMECHANIC
AACCEEHIRRST CHARACTERISE
AACCEEHIRRTZ CHARACTERIZE
AACCEEIIILPR CAPERCAILLIE

AACCEEILNORT ACCELERATION
AACCEELORRST ACCELERATORS
AACCEFHLRRTU CHARACTERFUL
AACCEGHIILPR ARCHIPELAGIC
AACCEGIKNPSS PACKING CASES
AACCEGINNTTU ACCENTUATING
AACCEHHIILRR HIERARCHICAL
AACCEHHMOSST STOMACHACHES
AACCEHHPRSST CATCHPHRASES
AACCEHIILNPS CHAPLAINCIES
AACCEHIIMNRV VICE-CHAIRMAN
AACCEHILLMNO MELANCHOLIAC
AACCEHILLMNY MECHANICALLY
AACCEHILNPRT PENTARCHICAL
AACCEHILPRTY ARCHETYPICAL
AACCEHIMORTT METATHORACIC
AACCEHINOOSX HEXACOSANOIC
AACCEHPPRRST SCRATCH PAPER
AACCEIILLNRT ANTICLERICAL
AACCEIILMRST ACCLIMATISER
AACCEIILMRTZ ACCLIMATIZER
AACCEILLMSTU MISCALCULATE
AACCEILLNNOT CANCELLATION
AACCEILLNOSS NEOCLASSICAL
AACCEILLOPSU CAPILLACEOUS
AACCEILLSTTY ECSTATICALLY
AACCEILMMORT MACROCLIMATE
AACCEILMNOPS COMPLAISANCE
AACCEILMOSSU SMILACACEOUS
AACCEILMPRST MALPRACTICES
AACCEILMTUUV ACCUMULATIVE
AACCEILNNOST CANCELATIONS
AACCEILNORVY CLAIRVOYANCE
AACCEILNRRTT RECALCITRANT
AACCEILNRTUY INACCURATELY
AACCEINNORST TRANSOCEANIC
AACCEINNOTTU ACCENTUATION
AACCEINOORTV COACERVATION
AACCEINORRRT INCARCERATOR
AACCEIOPRTVY OVERCAPACITY
AACCELLRRSTY CRYSTAL CLEAR
AACCELNNOOPV PLANO-CONCAVE
AACCELPRSSTU SPECTACULARS
AACCENOOPSUY APOCYNACEOUS
AACCEORSSTUY STYRACACEOUS
AACCFIIINOPT PACIFICATION
AACCFIILMOPT FAIT ACCOMPLI
AACCFIILSTTU FACTUALISTIC
AACCFIIORRST SCARIFICATOR
AACCFINNORSS SAN FRANCISCO
AACCGHHIKNOW CHANGCHIAKOW
AACCGHHLOPRY CHALCOGRAPHY
AACCGHIILLPR CALLIGRAPHIC
AACCGHIMOPRR MACROGRAPHIC

AACCGHIOPRRT CARTOGRAPHIC
AACCGIINRRTU CARICATURING
AACCGILLOOPR CARPOLOGICAL
AACCGILLOOST SCATOLOGICAL
AACCGILMNTUU ACCUMULATING
AACCGIMNNOPY ACCOMPANYING
AACCHIIINRTT ANTIRACHITIC
AACCHIINNNOT CACHINNATION
AACCHIINRSTY SACCHARINITY
AACCHILLORTY TROCHAICALLY
AACCHILLOSST SCHOLASTICAL
AACCHILMOPRS ARCHOPLASMIC
AACCHIMNOPRT PANCHROMATIC
AACCHIMOOPRT APOCHROMATIC
AACCHINOOSTT COACH STATION
AACCHIOPRSTT CATASTROPHIC
AACCIILLLMTY CLIMATICALLY
AACCIILLSSTY CLASSICALITY
AACCIILPRTTY PRACTICALITY
AACCIINNOSTV VACCINATIONS
AACCIINRSTTU TRACUCIANIST
AACCIIORRSTT ARISTOCRATIC
AACCIIRRSTTU CARICATURIST
AACCILLLNOVY VOLCANICALLY
AACCILLNOOSY OCCASIONALLY
AACCILLNORTY NARCOTICALLY
AACCILLNOSTU CALCULATIONS
AACCILLNRSTU CURTAIN CALLS
AACCILLORSTY ACROSTICALLY
AACCILLOSTUY ACOUSTICALLY
AACCILMNOTUU ACCUMULATION
AACCILNOOPTU OCCUPATIONAL
AACCILNOSSST CLASS ACTIONS
AACCILRRSSUW CIRCULAR SAWS
AACCIMNOPSST ACCOMPANISTS
AACCINOPRSTY PANTISOCRACY
AACCIORRSTTT STRATOCRATIC
AACCLMORSTUU ACCUMULATORS
AACDDDEEHLOR DODECAHEDRAL
AACDDEEEHLTY ACETALDEHYDE
AACDDEFIILSS CLASSIFIED AD
AACDDEGNNNOS SONG AND DANCE
AACDDGIIJNTU ADJUDICATING
AACDDIIJNOTU ADJUDICATION
AACDDIJORSTU ADJUDICATORS
AACDDIKMNNRU MANDARIN DUCK
AACDDLNORSTY SCOTLAND YARD
AACDEEFHLMSY SHAMEFACEDLY
AACDEEGHIMNT MAGNETIC HEAD
AACDEEGHLNNO HENDECAGONAL
AACDEEGILNST DE-ESCALATING
AACDEEIIMNRS AMERICANISED
AACDEEIIMNRZ AMERICANIZED
AACDEEIINQSU INADEQUACIES

AACDEEILMMNT MEDICAMENTAL
AACDEEILMRVY DEVIL-MAY-CARE
AACDEEILNOST DE-ESCALATION
AACDEEINNRRT REINCARNATED
AACDEEIPRRTV PREVARICATED
AACDEENQRSSU SQUARE DANCES
AACDEFILNSTY FASCINATEDLY
AACDEFMNRTUU MANUFACTURED
AACDEGIINPTT DECAPITATING
AACDEGILLOOP PAEDOLOGICAL
AACDEGILMORY CARDIOMEGALY
AACDEGLNOPRR DROP A CLANGER
AACDEHILLLRY HERALDICALLY
AACDEHILLNTU HALLUCINATED
AACDEHIMNRTY DIATHERMANCY
AACDEHINORRT RIDE AT ANCHOR
AACDEHLMOSUY ACHLAMYDEOUS
AACDEHLNOOPP CEPHALOPODAN
AACDEHLOPRRT PROCATHEDRAL
AACDEHLORRTT TETRACHORDAL
AACDEHNOPRTY HYDNOCARPATE
AACDEIIINPRT PEDIATRICIAN
AACDEIIIPRST PARASITICIDE
AACDEIINNORT DERACINATION
AACDEIINOPTT DECAPITATION
AACDEIINOTTV DEACTIVATION
AACDEIIOSSST DISASSOCIATE
AACDEIIPPRTT PARTICIPATED
AACDEIJLLTVY ADJECTIVALLY
AACDEILLMNOY DAEMONICALLY,
DEMONIACALLY
AACDEILLNOSW DISALLOWANCE
AACDEILLNPTY PEDANTICALLY
AACDEILMMORT MELODRAMATIC
AACDEILMNOST DECLAMATIONS
AACDEILMRTTU MATRICULATED
AACDEILNORST DECLARATIONS
AACDEILNPPRU APPENDICULAR
AACDEIMNNOTT CONTAMINATED
AACDEIMNORSY AERODYNAMICS
AACDEIMOOSTU DIATOMACEOUS
AACDEINNOPRS CAPARISONNED
AACDEINNOSSY ASCENSION DAY
AACDEINNQTUU UNACQUAINTED
AACDEINOPSSU SAPINDACEOUS
AACDEKKNRRSY KNACKER'S YARD
AACDELMNNORS ROMAN CANDLES
AACDELMOPRSU CAMELOPARDUS
AACDEMORRRSU ARMOURED CARS
AACDFGILNNRT LANDING CRAFT
AACDFHIKNSTT THICK AND FAST
AACDFIIILNNT INFANTICIDAL
AACDGHIINNPP HANDICAPPING
AACDGHIIOPRR RADIOGRAPHIC

AACDGHILNNRS CRASH LANDING
AACDGHIOPRRY CARDIOGRAPHY
AACDGIILLOOR RADIOLOGICAL
AACDGIILLOOU AUDIOLOGICAL
AACDGIILNNSZ SCANDALIZING
AACDGIILRSTU GRADUALISTIC
AACDGILLMOTY DOGMATICALLY
AACDGILNPRSY PLAYING CARDS
AACDHHILORRY ACHLORHYDRIA
AACDHIIOPRSS APHRODISIACS
AACDHINOPQRU QUADRAPHONIC
AACDIIINORTV DIVARICATION
AACDIIJLORTU JUDICATORIAL
AACDIILLLTYY DIALYTICALLY
AACDIILLNOTY DIATONICALLY
AACDIILLSSTY SADISTICALLY
AACDIILMNOST DISCLAMATION
AACDIILNNRTY TYRANNICIDAL
AACDIIMNNORS DRACONIANISM
AACDIIMNOPSS DIPSOMANIACS
AACDIIMNRSTU TRADUCIANISM
AACDIINNORRT DOCTRINARIAN
AACDIKNNPPSS SPICK-AND-SPAN
AACDILLNORSY SARDONICALLY
AACDILLOPRSY SPORADICALLY
AACDIMMNOORT MONODRAMATIC
AACDLLNOSSUY SCANDALOUSLY
AACEEEGHNRTX EXCHANGE RATE
AACEEEGNSTTY ESTATE AGENCY
AACEEEHPRSST SPACE HEATERS
AACEEENPRSVY SEVERANCE PAY
AACEEFFIMNRR REAFFIRMANCE
AACEEFFINOTT AFFECTIONATE
AACEEFLLPSTT CLEFT PALATES
AACEEFLMRSST MALEFACTRESS
AACEEGGILLNO GENEALOGICAL
AACEEGGIMNOT AGAMOGENETIC
AACEEGHIMNOT HAEMATOGENIC
AACEEGHNPRTX PART EXCHANGE
AACEEGHRRSST GATECRASHERS
AACEEGIMNPTT MAGNETIC TAPE
AACEEGIMNRST EAST GERMANIC
AACEEGINORSU GERANIACEOUS
AACEEGLMORTT GALACTOMETER
AACEEGLNRTVY TRAVEL AGENCY
AACEEHHIKRTT TAKE THE CHAIR
AACEEHIINSTT AESTHETICIAN
AACEEHINSSTT ANAESTHETICS
AACEEHINTTTU AUTHENTICATE
AACEEHIOPRST APOTHECARIES
AACEEHIPRSTT PARAESTHETIC
AACEEHKMNRRS SNAKE CHARMER
AACEEHLMPRST SPERMATHECAL
AACEEHLMRTTY METHACRYLATE

AACEEHNNPPST HAPPENSTANCE
AACEEIILPRST RECAPITALISE
AACEEIILPRTZ RECAPITALIZE
AACEEIIMNPTV EMANCIPATIVE
AACEEIIMNRRS AMERICANISER
AACEEIIMNRRZ AMERICANIZER
AACEEIIPPRTV APPRECIATIVE
AACEEIKLNNRS RANKINE SCALE
AACEEILMMMNY MECAMYLAMINE
AACEEILMPPRS PRE-ECLAMPSIA
AACEEILMSTUV EMASCULATIVE
AACEEILNORRT RECREATIONAL
AACEEILPRTTU RECAPITULATE
AACEEINNNRST CENTENARIANS
AACEEINNRSSS RENAISSANCES
AACEEIOPRSTT ECTOPARASITE
AACEEIRRSSTT SECRETARIATS
AACEEKLMPRST MARKETPLACES
AACEELMRRSUU RÉAUMUR SCALE
AACEELNRRTUX EXTRANUCLEAR
AACEELNRTTVY TETRAVALENCY
AACEEMNORSTU RAMENTACEOUS
AACEEMOPRTTV CAVEAT EMPTOR
AACEENNPPRTU APPURTENANCE
AACEENRRSSSU REASSURANCES
AACEFFHHNSSU SCHAFFHAUSEN
AACEFFINOSTT AFFECTATIONS
AACEFFMORTTT MATTER-OF-FACT
AACEFIIILTTV FACILITATIVE
AACEFIIINORT AERIFICATION
AACEFILNORRT REFRACTIONAL
AACEFIORRSTU SURFACE-TO-AIR
AACEFLLNORTU CALL OF NATURE
AACEFLNNORRT CONFRATERNAL
AACEFMNRRTUU MANUFACTURER
AACEGGGKLRSU LUGGAGE RACKS
AACEGGHILOPR GEOGRAPHICAL
AACEGGHINRST GATECRASHING
AACEGGINRRSU GUN CARRIAGES
AACEGGINRSSV SAVING GRACES
AACEGHHIMORR HAEMORRHAGIC
AACEGHILLPRR CALLIGRAPHER
AACEGHILMOOT HAEMATOLOGIC
AACEGHILOPRS ARCHIPELAGOS
AACEGHIMNOPR ANEMOGRAPHIC,
  PHANEROGAMIC
AACEGHIMNRSV SHAVING CREAM
AACEGHNOOPRY OCEANOGRAPHY
AACEGHOPRRRT CARTOGRAPHER
AACEGIIINRRT GERIATRICIAN
AACEGIILLNNT GEANTICLINAL
AACEGIILLNRT INTERGLACIAL
AACEGIILLOOT AETIOLOGICAL
AACEGIILMNNS MALIGNANCIES

AACEGIIMMPRT EPIGRAMMATIC	AACEIILNOSTT ELASTICATION
AACEGIIMNNPT EMANCIPATING	AACEIILNPRTT ANTIPARTICLE
AACEGIIMNNTT ANTIMAGNETIC	AACEIILNRTTU INARTICULATE
AACEGIIMRRSS MISCARRIAGES	AACEIIMMNRSS AMERICANISMS
AACEGIIMRSST MAGISTRACIES	AACEIIMNNOPT EMANCIPATION
AACEGIINNRST ASCERTAINING	AACEIIMNORST RACEMISATION
AACEGIINPPRT APPRECIATING	AACEIIMNORTZ RACEMIZATION
AACEGIINRTTV REACTIVATING	AACEIIMNRSST SECTARIANISM
AACEGILLMNTY MAGNETICALLY	AACEIINNNTUV ANNUNCIATIVE
AACEGILLNOSU GALLINACEOUS	AACEIINOPPRT APPRECIATION
AACEGILLORSU ARGILLACEOUS	AACEIINORTTV REACTIVATION
AACEGILLPRSU SUPERGLACIAL	AACEIIPRSSTT SEPARATISTIC
AACEGILMNNRT MAGIC LANTERN	AACEIJKRSTTT STRAITJACKET
AACEGILMNSTU EMASCULATING	AACEIJLLMSTY MAJESTICALLY
AACEGILNOOSU LOGANIACEOUS	AACEIJLNOSTU EJACULATIONS
AACEGILNRTUW CATERWAULING	AACEIKLMNOPT KLEPTOMANIAC
AACEGINNOORT OCTOGENARIAN	AACEILLLLMTY METALLICALLY
AACEGINNRSTW WATERING CANS	AACEILLMMTUY IMMACULATELY
AACEGINPPRRT TRACING PAPER	AACEILLMNSTY SEMANTICALLY
AACEGKOPRSTU PACKAGE TOURS	AACEILLMPRSY MIRACLE PLAYS
AACEGLMORTTY GALACTOMETRY	AACEILLNOORT REALLOCATION
AACEGLNOOPSV GALVANOSCOPE	AACEILLNOSTT CASTELLATION
AACEGLNORTTU CONGRATULATE	AACEILLOPRTY OPERATICALLY
AACEGLRRSTYZ CRYSTAL GAZER	AACEILLPRRST CATERPILLARS
AACEHHIILMOP HAEMOPHILIAC	AACEILLRTTUY ARTICULATELY
AACEHIILLOPT PALAEOLITHIC	AACEILLSTTUY EUSTATICALLY
AACEHIILLRTY HIERATICALLY	AACEILMMNORT COMMENTARIAL
AACEHIILNTTT ANTITHETICAL	AACEILMNOSTU EMASCULATION
AACEHIIMRRST MATRIARCHIES	AACEILMNOSTX EXCLAMATIONS
AACEHIINPTTT ANTIPATHETIC	AACEILNNOPTT PLACENTATION
AACEHIINRRST CHRISTIAN ERA	AACEILNNRRTU INTRANUCLEAR
AACEHIIPRRST PATRIARCHIES	AACEILNORSTT ALTERCATIONS
AACEHILLLTTY ATHLETICALLY	AACEILRSTTTU STRATICULATE
AACEHILLMPTY EMPATHICALLY,	AACEILRTTTVY ATTRACTIVELY
EMPHATICALLY	AACEIMNNOOPT COMPANIONATE
AACEHILLMTTY THEMATICALLY	AACEIMNOPRTY EMANCIPATORY
AACEHILLPTTY PATHETICALLY	AACEINNNORST NONSECTARIAN
AACEHILLRTTY THEATRICALLY	AACEINNORSTT RECANTATIONS
AACEHILMNPRU ALPHANUMERIC	AACEINOPSSTT SPACE STATION
AACEHILMOPRT METAPHORICAL	AACEINRTTTUV UNATTRACTIVE
AACEHILMOTXY HAEMATOXYLIC	AACEIOPRRRTV PREVARICATOR
AACEHILMPSTY METAPHYSICAL	AACEJKLNNORT JACK-O'-LANTERN
AACEHILOPRRS ARCHESPORIAL	AACEKLLNOPRS PANCAKE ROLLS
AACEHIMPRSTT METAPHRASTIC	AACEKNNORSTU CANTANKEROUS
AACEHMNNRSTU TRANSHUMANCE	AACELLMOPSUU AMPULLACEOUS
AACEHMNNRTVY MERCHANT NAVY	AACELMNORSTW SCARLET WOMAN
AACEHOPRSSTT CATASTROPHES	AACELPRSSSTT PLASTER CASTS
AACEIIINPTTV ANTICIPATIVE	AACENNNORSTW WATER CANNONS
AACEIIKLLMRT ALKALIMETRIC	AACENNPRRSTY TRANSPARENCY
AACEIILLMNSS MISALLIANCES	AACFFIORRSTT TRAFFICATORS
AACEIILLMNTU NAUTICAL MILE	AACFFMORRSTY FACTORY FARMS
AACEIILLMRTT ALTIMETRICAL	AACFGGILMNOU CAMOUFLAGING
AACEIILMNSTX ANTICLIMAXES	AACFGIIILNTT FACILITATING
AACEIILNOPPS EPISCOPALIAN	AACFGIIINOST GASIFICATION

AACFIIILLRTY ARTIFICIALLY
AACFIIILNOST SALIFICATION
AACFIIILNOTT FACILITATION
AACFIIIMNORT RAMIFICATION
AACFIIINORTT RATIFICATION
AACFIILMNOST FACTIONALISM
AACFIILNOOST FOCALISATION
AACFIILNOOTZ FOCALIZATION
AACFIILNOSTT FACTIONALIST
AACFIINOSSTT SATISFACTION
AACFILLLOSUY FALLACIOUSLY
AACFILLNORTY FRACTIONALLY
AACFILMORSTT STALACTIFORM
AACFINOORRTT FRACTIONATOR
AACFIORSSTTY SATISFACTORY
AACFKLMSSUUV VACUUM FLASKS
AACGGHHIIOPR HAGIOGRAPHIC
AACGGIILLNTY GIGANTICALLY
AACGHIILLNOP ANGLOPHILIAC
AACGHILLNOOT ANTHOLOGICAL
AACGHILLOOPT PATHOLOGICAL
AACGHILNOPPR PLANOGRAPHIC
AACGHINOPPRT PANTOGRAPHIC
AACGHINOPRRU URANOGRAPHIC
AACGHLMOOPRY PHARMACOLOGY
AACGHMMOORRT CHROMATOGRAM
AACGHOOPPRSU CARPOPHAGOUS
AACGIIILNPTZ CAPITALIZING
AACGIIILPRST PLAGIARISTIC
AACGIIINNPTT ANTICIPATING
AACGIILLMOPX PLAGIOCLIMAX
AACGIILMNNTU CALUMNIATING
AACGIILNPTTU CAPITULATING
AACGIILNRTTU ARTICULATING
AACGIILOPRST PARALOGISTIC
AACGIIMPRSTT PRAGMATISTIC
AACGIINNOSTT ANTAGONISTIC
AACGILLMOOST MALACOLOGIST
AACGILLOORST ASTROLOGICAL
AACGILLOOTTU TAUTOLOGICAL
AACGILLRRTUU AGRICULTURAL
AACGILNNOOTV LONG VACATION
AACGIMMNNOOU COMMON IGUANA
AACGIMMOPRRT PROGRAMMATIC
AACGINOPPRTU GROUP CAPTAIN
AACGLMOOSTUU GLAUCOMATOUS
AACGLNOOPSVY GALVANOSCOPY
AACHHIIMNPRS CHAIRMANSHIP
AACHIIINNSTY HINAYANISTIC
AACHIILMOPRS PAROCHIALISM
AACHIIMNNOST MACHINATIONS
AACHILLMNORY HARMONICALLY
AACHILLMOPSY HYALOPLASMIC
AACHILLNORTU HALLUCINATOR

AACHILMNNOSU NO SUCH ANIMAL
AACHIMMMNNOPY NYMPHOMANIAC
AACHIMNNORSS ANACHRONISMS
AACHIMNOPRRS PARACHRONISM
AACHINOPRTTU NATUROPATHIC
AACHIPRSSTTU PARACHUTISTS
AACHLLNNNOTY NONCHALANTLY
AACHMOORSTTU TRACHOMATOUS
AACIIINNOPTT ANTICIPATION
AACIIINNOTTV INACTIVATION
AACIIINNRSSU UNCINARIASIS
AACIIINSSTTT STATISTICIAN
AACIILLMOTTY AMITOTICALLY
AACIILLNOOST LOCALISATION
AACIILLNOOTZ LOCALIZATION
AACIILLNOSTV VACILLATIONS
AACIILLORSTY AORISTICALLY
AACIILLRSTTY ARTISTICALLY
AACIILLSTTUY AUTISTICALLY
AACIILMMORSS COMMISSARIAL
AACIILMNNOTU CALUMNIATION
AACIILNNOOTV INVOCATIONAL
AACIILNOOSTV VOCALISATION
AACIILNOOTVZ VOCALIZATION
AACIILNOPPST APPLICATIONS
AACIILNOPTTU CAPITULATION
AACIILNORTTU ARTICULATION
AACIILNRSTTU NATURALISTIC
AACIILORSUVY AVARICIOUSLY
AACIIMMORSST COMMISSARIAT
AACIINNNNOTU ANNUNCIATION
AACIINNNOOST CANONISATION
AACIINNNOOTZ CANONIZATION
AACIINNNORST INCARNATIONS
AACIINNNOSTT INCANTATIONS
AACIINNORSST INCRASSATION
AACIINOORRTT RATIOCINATOR
AACIINOOSSST ASSOCIATIONS
AACIINOPRTTY ANTICIPATORY
AACIINORRSTU CURARISATION
AACIINORRTUZ CURARIZATION
AACIINPPRSTT PARTICIPANTS
AACIIOPPRRTT PARTICIPATOR
AACIKLMOPRSY KARYOPLASMIC
AACILLLNOPTY PLATONICALLY
AACILLLNOSVY SLAVONICALLY
AACILLMNORTY ROMANTICALLY
AACILLMNOSTY MONASTICALLY
AACILLMOSTUY CALAMITOUSLY
AACILLNNRTYY TYRANNICALLY
AACILLNOPPTY PANOPTICALLY
AACILLNOPRSS RAPSCALLIONS
AACILLNPSTYY SYNAPTICALLY
AACILLOORRTY ORATORICALLY

AACILLPRRTUY PARTICULARLY
AACILLQRTUUU AQUICULTURAL
AACILMNNOPST COMPLAINANTS
AACILMNOOPRT PROCLAMATION
AACILMNOORST ASTRONOMICAL
AACILMNORSTY MICROANALYST
AACILMORRTTU COURT-MARTIAL,
  MATRICULATOR
AACILNORSTVY CLAIRVOYANTS
AACILNOSTTUU AUSCULTATION
AACILORRTTUY ARTICULATORY
AACIMMOPSTTY ASYMPTOMATIC
AACIMNNNOSTT CONTAMINANTS
AACIMNNOOPWY COMPANIONWAY
AACIMNNOORTT CONTAMINATOR
AACIMNNOOSTT ANTONOMASTIC
AACIMOORSSST SARCOMATOSIS
AACINNORSSTT TRANSACTIONS
AACINORSSTTU ASTRONAUTICS
AACLNNOPRTTU CONTRAPUNTAL
AACLNPRSTTYY CRYPTANALYST
AACMOOPRSSST ASTROCOMPASS
AADDDEGIRSSU SUGAR DADDIES
AADDDEINRSST STANDARDISED
AADDDEINRSTZ STANDARDIZED
AADDDGLNORST GOLD STANDARD
AADDEEEGLPRS SPREAD-EAGLED
AADDEEEHHMMR HAMMERHEADED
AADDEEHHRTXY HEXAHYDRATED
AADDEEHNSSWY ASH WEDNESDAY
AADDEEIMNRTV ANIMADVERTED
AADDEFFIILST FIT AS A FIDDLE
AADDEFINORTU DEFRAUDATION
AADDEFLLNOSU ALL OF A SUDDEN
AADDEGINORST DEGRADATIONS
AADDEGNOPRRU PARADE GROUND
AADDEIMNRSTT STANDARD TIME
AADDEINRRSST STANDARDISER
AADDEINRRSTZ STANDARDIZER
AADDELNOORTV VOLTA REDONDA
AADDHIILORRT DIARTHRODIAL
AADDIIILNOPT DILAPIDATION
AADDIIILLNOTY ADDITIONALLY
AADDLLNNRSUY ALL AND SUNDRY
AADEEEGMMNNT ENDAMAGEMENT
AADEEEHHRTVY HEAVYHEARTED
AADEEEHIRSST HEART DISEASE
AADEEELNNRWZ NEW ZEALANDER
AADEEFFNORRT FORE-AND-AFTER
AADEEFHINRTT FAINT-HEARTED
AADEEFILLMRT FLEET ADMIRAL
AADEEGGLMORT AGGLOMERATED
AADEEGHINPRS SPEARHEADING
AADEEGKMNRRT MARKET GARDEN

AADEEGKNOPTW TAKE DOWN A PEG
AADEEHILNQRU HARLEQUINADE
AADEEHIMNOTZ DIAZOMETHANE
AADEEHLNNRST NEANDERTHALS
AADEEHLRSTTT DEATH RATTLES
AADEEHQRRSTU HEADQUARTERS
AADEEIIKMTVW TAKE A DIM VIEW
AADEEIILMRST MATERIALISED
AADEEIILMRTZ MATERIALIZED
AADEEIIMNNRT ANTEMERIDIAN
AADEEILNQTUY INADEQUATELY
AADEEILNRSTU DENATURALISE
AADEEILNRTUZ DENATURALIZE
AADEEIMMMNNRR REMAINDERMAN
AADEEIMMNNST MISDEMEANANT
AADEEINOPRST ENDOPARASITE
AADEEINOPRTU DEUTERANOPIA
AADEEJLNNRTW LANTERN-JAWED
AADEELLLNPRU UNPARALLELED
AADEELLNPSTT DENTAL PLATES
AADEELLRZZZZ RAZZLE-DAZZLE
AADEELMNPRTT DEPARTMENTAL
AADEELOPRTTX EXTRAPOLATED
AADEEMNNRTUX EXTRAMUNDANE
AADEEMORSTWW WATER MEADOWS
AADEEMQRRSSU MASQUERADERS
AADEFFHLNOTT FAT OF THE LAND
AADEFFIIILST DISAFFILIATE
AADEFGGINRSU SAFEGUARDING
AADEFGHNRRST GRANDFATHERS
AADEFGILNORT DEFLAGRATION
AADEFHILLMRS FIELD MARSHAL
AADEFHINNOTU FOUNTAINHEAD
AADEFIIILMRS FAMILIARISED
AADEFIIILMRZ FAMILIARIZED
AADEFIKMNORR AFRIKANERDOM
AADEFILMORTY DEFAMATORILY
AADEFILNORTY DEFLATIONARY
AADEFILNSSTY SAFETY ISLAND
AADEFILNTTUY INFATUATEDLY
AADEFIMRRRSY DAIRY FARMERS
AADEFLMNNSTU FUNDAMENTALS
AADEFLOOSSST A DOSE OF SALTS
AADEGGILNNST LANDING STAGE
AADEGHIMMORX HEXAGRAMMOID
AADEGHIOPRRR RADIOGRAPHER
AADEGHNOPRRY PARAHYDROGEN
AADEGIILNNST DESALINATING
AADEGIILPQRU QUADRIPLEGIA
AADEGIIMMNST DIAMAGNETISM
AADEGIINPPRS DISAPPEARING
AADEGILLNNPS PINEAL GLANDS
AADEGILNRTTU ADULTERATING
AADEGILNSSST STAINED GLASS

AADEGIMNQRSU MASQUERADING
AADEGINNPPRS SANDPAPERING
AADEGINOPPRS PROPAGANDISE
AADEGINOPPRZ PROPAGANDIZE
AADEGLLNNSUY AULD LANG SYNE
AADEGLNPRSST STAR-SPANGLED
AADEGLNRSTTU STRANGULATED
AADEGMNRRSST GRAND MASTERS
AADEGNNPRRST GRANDPARENTS
AADEGOPRSTTU POSTGRADUATE
AADEHHIILLPP PHILADELPHIA
AADEHIKLMORY HOLIDAYMAKER
AADEHILNORRT ENARTHRODIAL
AADEHINOPRST HEROD ANTIPAS
AADEHIOPRRTY RADIOTHERAPY
AADEHMNNRSTT HERMANNSTADT
AADEHPRRSTTU UTTAR PRADESH
AADEIIILNOST IDEALISATION
AADEIIILNOTZ IDEALIZATION
AADEIIILNUVV VAUDEVILLIAN
AADEIILMNNOT DELAMINATION
AADEIILNNOST DESALINATION,
  NATIONALISED
AADEIILNNOTZ NATIONALIZED
AADEIILNNTUV ANTEDILUVIAN
AADEIILNORST RATIONALISED
AADEIILNORTV DERIVATIONAL
AADEIILNORTZ RATIONALIZED
AADEIILNRSTT INTERSTADIAL
AADEIIMNRSTT ADMINISTRATE
AADEIINNORST TARDENOISIAN
AADEILNNSSTT STATEN ISLAND
AADEILNORTTU ADULTERATION
AADEILNOSTUV DEVALUATIONS
AADEILNQRTUV QUADRIVALENT
AADEIMNOQSTU DESQUAMATION
AADEIMNRSSTV MAIDSERVANTS
AADEIMOPPRTX APPROXIMATED
AADEIMPRRSTY TRYPARSAMIDE
AADEINNORTTU DENATURATION
AADEIOPPPRRT APPROPRIATED
AADELLNNORST RALLENTANDOS
AADELMNNRTUU ULTRAMUNDANE
AADELMOPRRTU ARMOUR-PLATED
AADELNNPRSTT TRANSPLANTED
AADEMNNNRSTU TRANSMUNDANE
AADEMNOPPRTU PUT A DAMPER ON
AADFFFHLNOST STANDOFF HALF
AADFHHILLOSY HALF-HOLIDAYS
AADFILNNOOTU FOUNDATIONAL
AADFINNOOSTU SODA FOUNTAIN
AADGGIINNRRS DISARRANGING
AADGHHIMNNRT RIGHT-HAND MAN
AADGHIINPRSU GUARDIANSHIP

AADGHILNORSZ LOSING HAZARD
AADGHINRSSWW WASH DRAWINGS
AADGHLPRSSSU SPLASH GUARDS
AADGIIILNNTV INVALIDATING
AADGIILMRTUV MULTIGRAVIDA
AADGIILNNNOS ANGLO-INDIANS
AADGIILQRUUV GUADALQUIVIR
AADGILLNPPUY APPLAUDINGLY
AADGIMNOPPRS PROPAGANDISM
AADGIMNPRSTT TRADING STAMP
AADGINOPPRST PROPAGANDIST
AADHIIKNSTTZ TADZHIKISTAN
AADHIILOPPSY DIAPOPHYSIAL
AADHILNOOPRT ANTHROPOIDAL
AADHINPRSSTY DANISH PASTRY
AADHIOPRRSTY PARATHYROIDS
AADHJKLMMORS HAMMARSKJOLD
AADIIIILNNOPS INDIANAPOLIS
AADIIILNNOTV INVALIDATION
AADIIINORRST IRRADIATIONS
AADIIKNNRSST KRISTIANSAND
AADIILMNOQRU QUADRINOMIAL
AADIILMOPRST PRISMATOIDAL
AADIILNOOSTV VASODILATION
AADIINOOTTUX AUTOXIDATION
AADIIRRSSTUV STRADIVARIUS
AADILNOPPRST POSTPRANDIAL
AADLMNNORUWY LAUNDRYWOMAN
AADMNOQRSUUU QUADRUMANOUS
AADNORRSTTUY TRANSUDATORY
AAEEEFLRSTTW WELFARE STATE
AAEEEGGHRTUW WEATHER GAUGE
AAEEEGGIRTVX EXAGGERATIVE
AAEEEGMNRSSS MANAGERESSES
AAEEEGNSSTTT ESTATE AGENTS
AAEEEHILRTTY AETHEREALITY
AAEEEHILSSTT TELAESTHESIA
AAEEEHIMMSST HAEMATEMESIS
AAEEEHINSSTT ANAESTHETISE
AAEEEHINSTTZ ANAESTHETIZE
AAEEEHLNPRST ELEPHANT'S-EAR
AAEEEHLPQRSU RAPHAELESQUE
AAEEEHNRSTVW WEATHER VANES
AAEEELMNPSTX SET AN EXAMPLE
AAEEELOPRTTU POET LAUREATE
AAEEEMNPPSST APPEASEMENTS
AAEEEMPRSSTU TAPE MEASURES
AAEEENPRSSST SEPARATENESS
AAEEFFGLNRST GENERAL STAFF
AAEEFHHILRST FAITH HEALERS
AAEEFHILRRTU HEART FAILURE
AAEEFHLMRSSU HALF MEASURES
AAEEFIILRSSZ LAISSEZ-FAIRE
AAEEFLSSTVVY SAFETY VALVES

AAEEFMNNRRTT TENANT FARMER
AAEEFNNPRSST SNAP FASTENER
AAEEGGGINRTX EXAGGERATING
AAEEGGIMNOSS AGAMOGENESIS
AAEEGGIMNRTV GRAM-NEGATIVE
AAEEGGINNRTU GUARANTEEING
AAEEGGINORTX EXAGGERATION
AAEEGGLNNOTU TONE LANGUAGE
AAEEGHLOPPRR PALEOGRAPHER
AAEEGHLRSSTW WEATHERGLASS
AAEEGHNPPRRS PAPERHANGERS
AAEEGIKLNSTV LEAVE TAKINGS
AAEEGILNOTTV VEGETATIONAL
AAEEGILNPPST EATING APPLES
AAEEGILRSSUV LIVER SAUSAGE
AAEEGIMNORST MÉNAGE À TROIS
AAEEGIMNTTUV AUGMENTATIVE
AAEEGIMPSSTU SEPTUAGESIMA
AAEEGINPRSTX EXASPERATING
AAEEGINRSSTV ASSEVERATING
AAEEGJLMNORR MAJOR GENERAL
AAEEGLMMRSSU RUMMAGE SALES
AAEEGLMNORTV GALVANOMETER
AAEEGLNRSTTV TRAVEL AGENTS
AAEEGLOPRSSS OPERA GLASSES
AAEEGMNNRRST ARRANGEMENTS
AAEEGMNOPRST POMEGRANATES
AAEEHHIMPRTT AMPHITHEATER,
  AMPHITHEATRE
AAEEHHORRTTT HEART-TO-HEART
AAEEHIIKNSST KINAESTHESIA
AAEEHIILRTVX EXHILARATIVE
AAEEHIIMPRST HEMIPARASITE
AAEEHIKNOSTT TAKE A SHINE TO
AAEEHILPRSTU LAUREATESHIP
AAEEHIMMNPST AMPHETAMINES
AAEEHINNRSTU NEURASTHENIA
AAEEHINPPRRT HEIR APPARENT
AAEEHINSSSTY SYNAESTHESIA
AAEEHINSSTTT ANAESTHETIST
AAEEHLNOPPRS APLANOSPHERE
AAEEHMNORSUW WAREHOUSEMAN
AAEEHOORRSTT STEATORRHOEA
AAEEIIKKLLTW WALKIE-TALKIE
AAEEIILLMRSS MARSEILLAISE
AAEEIILLRTTV ALLITERATIVE
AAEEIILMNTTV ALIMENTATIVE
AAEEIILMORTV AMELIORATIVE
AAEEIILMRRST MATERIALISER
AAEEIILMRRTZ MATERIALIZER
AAEEIILNQSTU ITALIANESQUE
AAEEIILLMNPST PLANETESIMAL
AAEEIILLNORTV REVELATIONAL
AAEEIILLNRSTW ARTESIAN WELL

AAEEIILLPRSTT SEPTILATERAL
AAEEIILMNRRTW MINERAL WATER
AAEEIILNNORTV VENERATIONAL
AAEEIILNPRSST PLEASANTRIES
AAEEIILNRSTTV ALTERNATIVES
AAEEIILQRSSTU SESQUIALTERA
AAEEINOPRSTX EXASPERATION
AAEEINORSSTV ASSEVERATION
AAEEKLNRSSTT RATTLESNAKES
AAEELMMNRTTT MALTREATMENT
AAEELNNOSSSS SEASONALNESS
AAEELNNPSSST PLEASANTNESS
AAEEMNNPPRSW NEWSPAPERMAN
AAEEMNNPRTWY PERMANENT WAY
AAEEMNRSTTTY TESTAMENTARY
AAEENNPPRSST APPARENTNESS
AAEENNPRSTUU SUPERANNUATE
AAEERRRSTTUU RESTAURATEUR
AAEFFIIMRSTV AFFIRMATIVES
AAEFFQRRSTTU QUARTERSTAFF
AAEFGGILLLNT FLAGELLATING
AAEFGHHIILNT FAITH HEALING
AAEFGILLLNOT FLAGELLATION
AAEFGINNORTT ENGRAFTATION
AAEFHHLOSUWY HALFWAY HOUSE
AAEFHIKLNSUV HAVE A SKINFUL
AAEFHILNRSTW FATHERS-IN-LAW
AAEFIIILMRRS FAMILIARISER
AAEFIIILMRRZ FAMILIARIZER
AAEFIILMNRSS FAMILIARNESS
AAEFIILMPSST FISSIPALMATE
AAEFILLNSSSY SELF-ANALYSIS
AAEFILMNRRST FRATERNALISM
AAEFILNORRTY REFLATIONARY
AAEFILNQRRTU QUARTERFINAL
AAEFILORSSTY FORESTAYSAIL
AAEFLLNOPSTU PULL A FAST ONE
AAEFMORRSSTT MASTER OF ARTS
AAEFORRSSTYZ SAFETY RAZORS
AAEGGGILNNSU SIGN LANGUAGE
AAEGGGINORST AGGREGATIONS
AAEGGHHIOPRR HAGIOGRAPHER
AAEGGHINNPPR PAPERHANGING
AAEGGHMNOPRT MAGNETOGRAPH
AAEGGINNPRRR PREARRANGING
AAEGGINRSTTT STARTING GATE
AAEGGNORRSUW NARROW GAUGES
AAEGHHIKNRST EARTHSHAKING
AAEGHHOPPRRS PHRASEOGRAPH
AAEGHIILNRTX EXHILARATING
AAEGHILNNOOT HALOGENATION
AAEGHIMMNPSS GAMESMANSHIP
AAEGHIMMNSTT METAGNATHISM
AAEGHIMNRRTW HEARTWARMING

AAEGHIMORRRT METRORRHAGIA
AAEGHLLNNOTT TEN-GALLON HAT
AAEGHLMNRSTU MANSLAUGHTER
AAEGHLOPRTTU TELAUTOGRAPH
AAEGHMNOSTTU METAGNATHOUS
AAEGHNOPPRRT PANTOGRAPHER
AAEGHNOPRRRU URANOGRAPHER
AAEGHNPRRSST STRAPHANGERS
AAEGIIKKLLMN MAKE A KILLING
AAEGIILLNOST LEGALISATION
AAEGIILLNOTZ LEGALIZATION
AAEGIILMNORT AMELIORATING,
  EMIGRATIONAL
AAEGIILNRSTU ANGULARITIES
AAEGIIMMNNORT EMARGINATION
AAEGIINNPPRT APPERTAINING
AAEGIINOQSTU GIANT SEQUOIA
AAEGIINPPRRS REAPPRAISING
AAEGIINPRRTT REPATRIATING
AAEGIINPRTTX EXPATRIATING
AAEGILLLLNPR PARALLELLING
AAEGILLNNTTY TANGENTIALLY
AAEGILLNPPRW WALLPAPERING
AAEGILNNSTUY NAUSEATINGLY
AAEGIMNNOTTU AUGMENTATION
AAEGIMNNRRST ARRAIGNMENTS
AAEGIMNRRSTT TRANSMIGRATE
AAEGIMRRSTTU MAGISTRATURE
AAEGINNOPTTV VANTAGEPOINT
AAEGLLORSSSU SAUSAGE ROLLS
AAEGLMNORTVY GALVANOMETRY
AAEGLMOOPSSU GAMOSEPALOUS
AAEGLMOOPSTU GAMOPETALOUS
AAEGLMOPRRSU PARLOUR GAMES
AAEGLMOPRSST ERGASTOPLASM
AAEGMOPPSSTT POSTAGE STAMP
AAEHHNOPRTTW ON THE WARPATH
AAEHIIILNNTV ANNIHILATIVE
AAEHIILMMPTU EPITHALAMIUM
AAEHIILNORTX EXHILARATION
AAEHIINOPRTZ AZATHIOPRINE
AAEHILLMORSV VILLAHERMOSA
AAEHILMNOTXY HAEMATOXYLIN
AAEHILMNPSSS SALESMANSHIP
AAEHILMOSSTY HAEMATOLYSIS
AAEHILMRSTUY AMATEURISHLY
AAEHILNNOPTY PAY ON THE NAIL
AAEHIMMRSSTU SHAMATEURISM
AAEHIMNPRSTW WATERMANSHIP
AAEHKKLLNPTW WALK THE PLANK
AAEHLMNOOTXY HAEMATOXYLON
AAEHLRSSTTTW THE LAST STRAW
AAEHMOORSTTU ATHEROMATOUS
AAEHMOPRSSTY MASSOTHERAPY

AAEIIILMSSTV ASSIMILATIVE
AAEIIILPRSTT PARTIALITIES
AAEIILLLNOSV LEVALLOISIAN
AAEIILLMNNRS MILLENARIANS
AAEIILLNORTT ALLITERATION
AAEIILMMPRST MARITIME ALPS
AAEIILMNNOTT ALIMENTATION
AAEIILMNNRRT INTERLAMINAR
AAEIILMNOORT AMELIORATION
AAEIILMNPTUV MANIPULATIVE
AAEIILMNRRST AIR TERMINALS
AAEIILMNRSST INERTIAL MASS
AAEIILMRSSTT MATERIALISTS
AAEIILNNOPST PENALISATION
AAEIILNNOPTZ PENALIZATION
AAEIILNOQSTU EQUALISATION
AAEIILNOQTUZ EQUALIZATION
AAEIILNORRST RATIONALISER
AAEIILNORRTZ RATIONALIZER
AAEIILNORSST REALISATIONS
AAEIILNORSTV VELARISATION
AAEIILNORSTZ REALIZATIONS
AAEIILNORTVZ VELARIZATION
AAEIILNPRSTT INTERSPATIAL
AAEIIMNNOSTX EXAMINATIONS
AAEIINNOSTTT TETANISATION
AAEIINNOTTTZ TETANIZATION
AAEIINNRSSST SANITARINESS
AAEIINOPRRTT REPATRIATION
AAEIINOPRTTX EXPATRIATION
AAEIINQTTTUV QUANTITATIVE
AAEIKMNPPSTY MAKE IT SNAPPY
AAEILLLMPRSS PARALLELISMS
AAEILLLMRTTU MULTILATERAL
AAEILLLNRTUY UNILATERALLY
AAEILLMNRRTY ARTILLERYMAN
AAEILLMPRRTY PREMARITALLY
AAEILLMPRRXY PREMAXILLARY
AAEILLNOPPST APPELLATIONS
AAEILMNNOSTT LAMENTATIONS
AAEILMNPRSTU PLANETARIUMS
AAEILNNNPSVY PENNSYLVANIA
AAEILNNOPSTX EXPLANATIONS
AAEILNNOPTTX EXPLANTATION
AAEILNNORSTT ALTERNATIONS
AAEILNOPPRSY PLAYER PIANOS
AAEILNOPRRST PROLETARIANS
AAEILNOPSSTY PASSIONATELY
AAEILNORSTUV REVALUATIONS
AAEILNPRSSTT PATERNALISTS
AAEILNRSSSTU SALUTARINESS
AAEIMMMOSSTT METASOMATISM
AAEIMMNOOPST MESOPOTAMIAN
AAEIMNOOOOPT ONOMATOPOEIA

AAEINNOPRSXY EXPANSIONARY
AAEINNORSSTU AUSTRONESIAN
AAEINNOSSTTT NATION STATES
AAEINOPPRRST PREPARATIONS
AAEINOSSTTTT ATTESTATIONS
AAEIPPRRSTTV PRIVATE PARTS
AAEKLMORRTWW LOW-WATER MARK
AAEKLOPRSTTY KERATOPLASTY
AAEKNOQRRSUW NARROW SQUEAK
AAELLMNNORTY ORNAMENTALLY
AAELLNNPSTUY UNPLEASANTLY
AAELMMNNORRU ROMAN NUMERAL
AAELMNNORTTU ULTRAMONTANE
AAELMNPQSTUU QUANTUM LEAPS
AAELMOOPRSTZ SPERMATOZOAL
AAELNNPRRSTT TRANSPLANTER
AAELNPRRSTUU SUPERNATURAL
AAELNRSSSTTW STALWARTNESS
AAELOOPRRTTX EXTRAPOLATOR
AAEMNNOPRSST MONTPARNASSE
AAEMNOPRSTTU PORTMANTEAUS
AAEMNOPRTTUX PORTMANTEAUX
AAEMORSSSTTT TOASTMASTERS
AAEOOPPRRRST PARATROOPERS
AAEOPPRSSTTU PASSE-PARTOUT
AAFFIIILNOST AFFILIATIONS
AAFFIIMNORST AFFIRMATIONS
AAFGILLNRSST FALLING STARS
AAFHLMOSTUUY SAY A MOUTHFUL
AAFIIILNNOST FINALISATION
AAFIIILNNOTZ FINALIZATION
AAFIIILNRTTU FUTILITARIAN
AAFIILMMNNOT INFLAMMATION
AAFIILNNORTY INFLATIONARY
AAFIINNOSTTU INFATUATIONS
AAFILMMNOORT MALFORMATION
AAFILMMNORTY INFLAMMATORY
AAFINNOOPRST PROFANATIONS
AAGGHIIJMNST THINGAMAJIGS
AAGGHINNPRST STRAPHANGING
AAGGHINOPRTU AUTOGRAPHING
AAGGHNOOPRRY ORGANOGRAPHY
AAGGIIILNPRZ PLAGIARIZING
AAGGIIINNRTT INGRATIATING
AAGGIIILLNNTV GALLIVANTING
AAGGIINNNOTZ ANTAGONIZING
AAGGIINNRTUU INAUGURATING
AAGGLMMOORTY GRAMMATOLOGY
AAGHIIILNNNT ANNIHILATING
AAGHIINPSTXY ASPHYXIATING
AAGHILOORSTU HAGIOLATROUS
AAGHIPRRSTTY STRATIGRAPHY
AAGHLMOOTTUY THAUMATOLOGY
AAGHLOOPPRRY POLAROGRAPHY

AAGHOOPPRSSU SAPROPHAGOUS
AAGIIILLNNPS PLAIN SAILING
AAGIIILMNSST ASSIMILATING
AAGIIILNORRT IRRIGATIONAL
AAGIIIMNNOST IMAGINATIONS
AAGIIINNNOTV INVAGINATION
AAGIIINNORTT INGRATIATION
AAGIILLNNPTW WALL PAINTING
AAGIILMNNPTU MANIPULATING
AAGIILNNRSUY SANGUINARILY
AAGIILNNRTUZ NATURALIZING
AAGIILNPPRSY APPRAISINGLY
AAGIIMNRTTUZ TRAUMATIZING
AAGIINNNQRTU QUARANTINING
AAGIINNOORST ORGANISATION
AAGIINNOORTZ ORGANIZATION
AAGIINNORTUU INAUGURATION
AAGIINNOSSST ASSIGNATIONS
AAGILLMNTUWY MULLIGATAWNY
AAGILLNOUVVV VULVOVAGINAL,
  APPALLING
AAGILMNNNNOT NONMALIGNANT
AAGILNORSTTU GASTRULATION
AAGILOOPRSTY PARASITOLOGY
AAGIMNNRRSTT TRANSMIGRANT
AAGINNOOSTTW STATION WAGON
AAGLLOPRSTTU SUPRAGLOTTAL
AAGLNOOPRSTW PATROL WAGONS
AAHHIOPPRSTU PHOSPHATURIA
AAHHIPRSSTTW ATHWARTSHIPS
AAHIIILLOPRU AILUROPHILIA
AAHIIILNNNOT ANNIHILATION
AAHIIMNNOSTU HUMANISATION
AAHIIMNNOTUZ HUMANIZATION
AAHIINOPSTXY ASPHYXIATION
AAHIINPPRSST PARTISANSHIP
AAHIKMMNPRSS MARKSMANSHIP
AAHILLMOOTXY HOMOTAXIALLY
AAHILLMOPRSX MORPHALLAXIS
AAHILLOPRSTX TROPHALLAXIS
AAHILMNOOPRT PROTHALAMION
AAHIMMOPPRRS PARAMORPHISM
AAHIMNOOPRSS ANAMORPHOSIS
AAHLLMMORSSW MARSHMALLOWS
AAIIILMNOSST ASSIMILATION
AAIIILMPRTTY IMPARTIALITY
AAIIILNNOSTT LATINISATION
AAIIILNNOSTV INSALIVATION
AAIIILNNOTTZ LATINIZATION
AAIIILNOPRTT TRIPOLITANIA
AAIIILNOSTTV VISITATIONAL,
  VITALISATION
AAIIILNOTTVZ VITALIZATION
AAIIILORSTTV VISITATORIAL

AAIIIMMNOSTX MAXIMISATION
AAIIIMMNOTXZ MAXIMIZATION
AAIIIMNNRSTU UNITARIANISM
AAIIIMNOSSTV AVITAMINOSIS
AAIIINORSSTT SATIRISATION
AAIIINORSTTZ SATIRIZATION
AAIILLLPSSUZ LAPIS LAZULIS
AAIILLMMNRTU MULTILAMINAR
AAIILLMNPRSU SUPRALIMINAL
AAIILLNNOSTT INSTALLATION
AAIILLNORRTY IRRATIONALLY
AAIILMNNOPTT IMPLANTATION
AAIILMNNOPTU MANIPULATION
AAIILMNOORST MORALISATION
AAIILMNOORTZ MORALIZATION
AAIILMNOOTTV MOTIVATIONAL
AAIILMNOSSTV SALVATIONISM
AAIILNNNOOTT INTONATIONAL
AAIILNNNOOTV INNOVATIONAL
AAIILNNOOSTV VIOLIN SONATA
AAIILNNORSTT TRANSITIONAL
AAIILNNOSSTT NATIONALISTS
AAIILNOOPRST POLARISATION
AAIILNOOPRTZ POLARIZATION
AAIILNOORSST SOLARISATION
AAIILNOORSTV VALORISATION
AAIILNOORSTZ SOLARIZATION
AAIILNOORTVZ VALORIZATION
AAIILNOPPSTT PALPITATIONS
AAIILNORRSTU RURALISATION
AAIILNORRTUZ RURALIZATION
AAIILNORSSTT RATIONALISTS
AAIILNORSTTY STATIONARILY
AAIILNOSSTTV SALVATIONIST
AAIILNPTTVYY NATIVITY PLAY
AAIIMNOORSTT AMORTISATION
AAIIMNOORTTZ AMORTIZATION
AAIINNOQSTTU QUANTISATION
AAIINNOQTTUZ QUANTIZATION
AAIINOOPRSTV VAPORISATION
AAIINOOPRTVZ VAPORIZATION
AAILLMNOPRTT ALL-IMPORTANT
AAILLMOPRTYY MORALITY PLAY
AAILLORSTTUY SALUTATORILY
AAILMMOPPRSS MALAPROPISMS
AAILMNOPRTUY MANIPULATORY
AAILNNORSSTT TRANSLATIONS
AAILNOPPSSSY PASSION PLAYS
AAILOORSTTTZ TOTALIZATORS
AAILOPRRSTUV VAPOUR TRAILS
AAINNOPRSSTT PATRON SAINTS
AAINNORSTTUU UNSATURATION
AAINOOORTTTU AUTOROTATION
AAKLNNNNOOPT NANOPLANKTON

AALMNOOPRSTY TRYPANOSOMAL
ABBBCEHLOPSY PSYCHOBABBLE
ABBBCGINNOUY BOUNCING BABY
ABBBDEEIILSS SIDI-BEL-ABBES
ABBBEESTTTUY TEST-TUBE BABY
ABBBEHLMORTU BLABBERMOUTH
ABBCCEEHKNRS BACKBENCHERS
ABBCCEEHMORS BEACHCOMBERS
ABBCDEFKNOOY BACK OF BEYOND
ABBCEEGGHISU BEACH BUGGIES
ABBCEEIKLRRS BLACKBERRIES
ABBCFIILORST FIBROBLASTIC
ABBCKMOOORSY BACKROOM BOYS
ABBDEEFLORSS SELF-ABSORBED
ABBDEELOSSSU DOUBLE BASSES
ABBDEHIILRYZ HYBRIDIZABLE
ABBDEIILSSUZ SUBSIDIZABLE
ABBDEILOPSYY PLAY BOBSY-DIE
ABBDELLLNRUY LANDLUBBERLY
ABBDEMMNORST BOMBARDMENTS
ABBDEOOPPRTY BOOBY-TRAPPED
ABBEEEHNORST THE BARE BONES
ABBEEEILLNUV UNBELIEVABLE
ABBEEILLNUVY UNBELIEVABLY
ABBEEILMRRSU REIMBURSABLE
ABBEELORRRSU RABBLE-ROUSER
ABBEHIJMNNSU BENJAMIN BUSH
ABBEINRSSTUU SUBURBANITES
ABBELNPRRSTU RUBBER PLANTS
ABBEMPRRSSTU RUBBER STAMPS
ABBGHIILOPRY BIBLIOGRAPHY
ABBHLOORTWWY THROW A WOBBLY
ABBHMOOOOSST BAMBOO SHOOTS
ABCCCIILMSTU SUBCLIMACTIC
ABCCDEEELPST BESPECTACLED
ABCCDEEHKORR CHECKERBOARD
ABCCDEHILORU COACHBUILDER
ABCCDHILNSUW CLUB SANDWICH
ABCCDIILORXY DICARBOXYLIC
ABCCEEEELRSU CAUSE CÉLEBRE
ABCCEEEHLNRT TREBLE CHANCE
ABCCEEELNORT CONCELEBRATE
ABCCEEENORRS ARBORESCENCE
ABCCEEIILNSS INACCESSIBLE
ABCCEEIILLNOR RECONCILABLE
ABCCEEILOSST ACCESSIBLE TO
ABCCEEMNNRRU ENCUMBRANCER
ABCCEEMNNRSU ENCUMBRANCES
ABCCEHILLRUY CHERUBICALLY
ABCCEHIMMRSU CHAMBER MUSIC
ABCCEHOPRSST BATCH PROCESS
ABCCEIILNSSY INACCESSIBLY
ABCCEIINRRSU CABIN CRUISER
ABCCEIKKLSST STICKLEBACKS

ABCCEILLNORY RECONCILABLY	ABCDIILLOPST DIPLOBLASTIC
ABCCEILMMNOU COMMUNICABLE	ABCEEEFFKORS COFFEE BREAKS
ABCCEILNNOOS CONSCIONABLE	ABCEEEFFLOST COFFEE TABLES
ABCCEILNORTT CONTRACTIBLE	ABCEEEFNRSST BENEFACTRESS
ABCCEILORSTU SCROBICULATE	ABCEEEHLNRRT RETRENCHABLE
ABCCEINOOPRS CARBON COPIES	ABCEEELMNRSS RESEMBLANCES
ABCCEKLMNOOY BLACK ECONOMY	ABCEEEMMNRRR REMEMBRANCER
ABCCELRRRSUW CURB CRAWLERS	ABCEEEMMNRRS REMEMBRANCES
ABCCGILNRRUW CURB CRAWLING	ABCEEENORSUV VERBENACEOUS
ABCCHILLMORU CHLORAMBUCIL	ABCEEFFIINRT FEBRIFACIENT
ABCCILLOOSTY OCTOSYLLABIC	ABCEEFIILLNY BENEFICIALLY
ABCCILMMNOUY COMMUNICABLY	ABCEEFINNOST BENEFACTIONS
ABCCINOOSSTT TOBACCONISTS	ABCEEFLLOORS FORECLOSABLE
ABCCKLNORTUY BLACK COUNTRY	ABCEEGILNORZ RECOGNIZABLE
ABCDDGIKLNPU BLACK PUDDING	ABCEEHKLNQSU BLANK CHEQUES
ABCDEEEHILPR DECIPHERABLE	ABCEEHLORSUY HERBACEOUSLY
ABCDEEEHIRSU DEBAUCHERIES	ABCEEHMMNNRT EMBRANCHMENT
ABCDEEEHLORR BREECHLOADER	ABCEEHORSTTX CHATTERBOXES
ABCDEEEILNUV UNDECEIVABLE	ABCEEIILLNPX INEXPLICABLE
ABCDEEHOQRRU CHEQUERBOARD	ABCEEIILNRTX INEXTRICABLE
ABCDEEIILLNN INDECLINABLE	ABCEEIILLSSTU SUBCELESTIAL
ABCDEEIILLORS LOCAL DERBIES	ABCEEILNORST CELEBRATIONS
ABCDEEILMNSS DISSEMBLANCE	ABCEEILNORSU RIBONUCLEASE
ABCDEEILMOST DOMESTICABLE	ABCEEILRSSTU RESUSCITABLE
ABCDEEILNORS CONSIDERABLE	ABCEEINNORSV INOBSERVANCE
ABCDEEILORSV DISCOVERABLE	ABCEEINRRTVY INVERTEBRACY
ABCDEEIMNNTY AMBITENDENCY	ABCEEJKLMRTU LUMBERJACKET
ABCDEEINORRS DECARBONISER	ABCEEKLNNORU UNRECKONABLE
ABCDEEINORRZ DECARBONIZER	ABCEEKLRRRSW KERB CRAWLERS
ABCDEELLNRSY BELLY DANCERS	ABCEELOPRSTU PROSECUTABLE
ABCDEELMOOPS DECOMPOSABLE	ABCEENOPRRTU PROTUBERANCE
ABCDEGHIILNR CHILDBEARING	ABCEEORRSSUU BURSERACEOUS
ABCDEGHORRTU TURBOCHARGED	ABCEGGGIKLLN BLACKLEGGING
ABCDEGILNOTU DOUBLE-ACTING	ABCEGHIKLLNS BLACK ENGLISH
ABCDEHILSSTW SWITCHBLADES	ABCEGHORRRTU TURBOCHARGER
ABCDEHIRRSTW BIRD-WATCHERS	ABCEGIKLNRRW KERB CRAWLING
ABCDEHMOORST HORS DE COMBAT	ABCEGILMNOST SINGLE COMBAT
ABCDEHNORSTY BODY SNATCHER	ABCEGILNORYZ RECOGNIZABLY
ABCDEIIILLRT LIBERTICIDAL	ABCEGILOORTY BACTERIOLOGY
ABCDEIIILRSTT DISTRACTIBLE	ABCEHIJKNOTX JACK-IN-THE-BOX
ABCDEIINNSST CITISENS' BAND	ABCEHIKNRSSS BRACKISHNESS
ABCDEIINNSTZ CITIZENS' BAND	ABCEHILMNRUU HIBERNACULUM
ABCDEILMORST BLASTODERMIC	ABCEHILSTTTY CHASTITY BELT
ABCDEILNORSY CONSIDERABLY	ABCEHIRRRRSU CRUSH BARRIER
ABCDEILNOSTU DISCOUNTABLE	ABCEHKLRSSUW SWASHBUCKLER
ABCDEINOOPRS PROBOSCIDEAN	ABCEHLNOSTUU UNTOUCHABLES
ABCDEINOORST NOTICE BOARDS	ABCEIIILLRST LIBERALISTIC
ABCDEINRSSTU DISTURBANCES	ABCEIIILTTXY EXCITABILITY
ABCDEKMNOOSW BACKWOODSMEN	ABCEIIILLNPXY INEXPLICABLY
ABCDEKNORRTU ROUND BRACKET	ABCEIILMNOPT INCOMPATIBLE
ABCDELOOPRUV CUPBOARD LOVE	ABCEIILNRTXY INEXTRICABLY
ABCDEOOOORRRT CORROBORATED	ABCEIILOORST BOROSILICATE
ABCDHIORSSTW SWITCHBOARDS	ABCEIILORTVY REVOCABILITY
ABCDHNOORRSY HYDROCARBONS	ABCEIINORSTT OBSTETRICIAN

ABCEIIRSTTUW WATER BISCUIT
ABCEIKNPRSTU BANKRUPTCIES
ABCEILLNNOOS INCONSOLABLE
ABCEILMMNOTU INCOMMUTABLE
ABCEILMNNOSU INCONSUMABLE
ABCEILMNOPTU INCOMPUTABLE
ABCEILMOSSUX MUSICAL BOXES
ABCEILNOOPRR INCORPORABLE
ABCEILOOSSTT OSTEOBLASTIC
ABCEIMNOORST EMBROCATIONS
ABCELLLNOORT CONTROLLABLE
ABCELLLOOSTY OCTOSYLLABLE
ABCELMNOSTTU MESCAL BUTTON
ABCELNORSTTU COUNTERBLAST
ABCENOSSTUUU SUBCUTANEOUS
ABCEORRRSTTU CARBURETTORS
ABCFIILLMORY MORBIFICALLY
ABCFIINORSTU BIFURCATIONS
ABCFLNOOORRU FLUOROCARBON
ABCGHLOORSUY BRACHYLOGOUS
ABCGIIKLLNST BLACKLISTING
ABCGIILLLOOY BIOLOGICALLY
ABCGIINNRRST TRANSCRIBING
ABCGILLMOOSY SYMBOLOGICAL
ABCGILMNNRSU UNSCRAMBLING
ABCGILNNOOOT CONGLOBATION
ABCHIIKLOSTY SHOCKABILITY
ABCHIMORSSTX CHRISTMAS BOX
ABCIIIILRSTY IRASCIBILITY
ABCIIILMNOTU UMBILICATION
ABCIIILNRTUY INCURABILITY
ABCIILLMNOOY BIONOMICALLY
ABCIILMNOPTY INCOMPATIBLY
ABCIILNNOTUY CONNUBIALITY
ABCIILNOPPRY PRINCIPAL BOY
ABCIILNOPSTU PUBLICATIONS
ABCIILNPPRSU SUBPRINCIPAL
ABCIILORRTUY ORBICULARITY
ABCIIMNNOOST COMBINATIONS
ABCIJKNNOORS JACK ROBINSON
ABCIKLLMMSSU BLACK MUSLIMS
ABCILLLMOSYY SYMBOLICALLY
ABCILLLOPSYY POLYSYLLABIC
ABCILLMNOOSY MONOSYLLABIC
ABCILLNNOOSY INCONSOLABLY
ABCILMMNOSTU NOCTAMBULISM
ABCILMNNOOSU NO-CLAIM BONUS
ABCILMNOSTTU NOCTAMBULIST
ABCIMNORSSTU OBSCURANTISM
ABCIMNORSTUU RAMBUNCTIOUS
ABCINNOORSTU CONURBATIONS
ABCINORSSTTU OBSCURANTIST,
SUBTRACTIONS
ABCOOOOORRRRT CORROBORATOR

ABDDEEEEHLLTU BULLET-HEADED
ABDDEEEEHLNYZ BENZALDEHYDE
ABDDEEEEHLORU DOUBLE-HEADER
ABDDEEEELLORU DOUBLE-DEALER
ABDDEEEGLLOUZ DOUBLE-GLAZED
ABDDEEEHLLLUY BULLHEADEDLY
ABDDEEEIILSST DESTABILISED
ABDDEEEIILSTZ DESTABILIZED
ABDDEEEIMNNST ABSENT-MINDED
ABDDEEEKLLOTU DOUBLE-TALKED
ABDDEEEKLOPRU DOUBLE-PARKED
ABDDEEGILNOTU DOUBLE-DATING
ABDDEEILNOOST BLOODSTAINED
ABDDEEINORSTU SUBORDINATED
ABDDEEKMOOOSY DOMESDAY BOOK
ABDDGIINORSV DIVINGBOARDS
ABDDGIMNNPRU BUMP AND GRIND
ABDEEEEILMRR IRREDEEMABLE
ABDEEEERRRTV REVERBERATED
ABDEEEFIILNS INDEFEASIBLE
ABDEEEIILMRR IRREMEDIABLE
ABDEEEIILRTV DELIBERATIVE
ABDEEEIILRTY DELIBERATELY
ABDEEEILMNRT DETERMINABLE
ABDEEEILMRRY IRREDEEMABLY
ABDEEEINPRRS PREBENDARIES
ABDEEEELMNTZZ BEDAZZLEMENT
ABDEEEELPRSSU SUPERSEDABLE
ABDEEFGIIRRS FIRE BRIGADES
ABDEEFHILMRT HALF-TIMBERED
ABDEEFIIILNT IDENTIFIABLE
ABDEEFILLSTT BATTLEFIELDS
ABDEEFINSTUU SUBINFEUDATE
ABDEEGIILNRT DELIBERATING
ABDEEGLNOSTU DOUBLE AGENTS
ABDEEHNORTUW WEATHER-BOUND
ABDEEIIILTTV DÉBILITATIVE
ABDEEIILMRRY IRREMEDIABLY
ABDEEIILNORT DELIBERATION
ABDEEIILLNORR BANDERILLERO
ABDEEILMNOPR IMPONDERABLE
ABDEEILMNSST DISABLEMENTS
ABDEEILNOSSV VOIDABLENESS
ABDEEILNRSSU UNDESIRABLES
ABDEEILPRSTU DISREPUTABLE
ABDEEINNRRSW BREADWINNERS
ABDEEINNRSTU NUBIAN DESERT
ABDEEINNSSSU UNBIASEDNESS
ABDEEIRRSTTY DRY BATTERIES
ABDEEKNORRRS BANKER'S ORDER
ABDEELMNORST DEMONSTRABLE
ABDEELMNORSZ BRONZE MEDALS
ABDEELORRSTW WORLD-BEATERS
ABDEEOORRSTT BORED TO TEARS

ABDEFFHLORSU SHUFFLEBOARD
ABDEFGINORRS FINGERBOARDS
ABDEFIIILLOS SOLIDIFIABLE
ABDEFLLOSTUU DOUBLE FAULTS
ABDEGIIILNTT DEBILITATING
ABDEGIIKMNRS DISEMBARKING
ABDEGIILNNST DINING TABLES
ABDEGIKNOPRW BAKING POWDER
ABDEGILLLNNY BELLY-LANDING
ABDEGILNORTW WORLD-BEATING
ABDEGINNPSTU BE UPSTANDING
ABDEHHLMOORR RHOMBOHEDRAL
ABDEHHNOSSUU HOUSE HUSBAND
ABDEHIIILMNS DIMINISHABLE
ABDEHIILSSST DISESTABLISH
ABDEHIINNPRS HAIRPIN BENDS
ABDEHILNOORS DISHONORABLE
ABDEHLLORSYY HYDROLYSABLE
ABDEHNNORSSU RUB ONE'S HANDS
ABDEIIIILSST DISABILITIES
ABDEIIILMNSS INADMISSIBLE
ABDEIIILMTXY MIXED-ABILITY
ABDEIIILNOTT DEBILITATION
ABDEIIILRSTY DESIRABILITY
ABDEIIIRSSSU SUBSIDIARIES
ABDEIILNPSTU INDISPUTABLE
ABDEIILNRTUY ENDURABILITY
ABDEIIOOPRSS BASIDIOSPORE
ABDEILMNOSTU DISMOUNTABLE
ABDEILPRSTUY DISREPUTABLY
ABDEIMORSTUX AMBIDEXTROUS
ABDEINORRRSU SOUND BARRIER
ABDEINORSSTU SUBORDINATES
ABDELMNORSTY DEMONSTRABLY
ABDELMOORSST BLOODSTREAMS
ABDEMOORRTTW BOTTOM DRAWER
ABDENOQRRTUU QUARTER-BOUND
ABDFGIILLLNO BILL OF LADING
ABDFIILNNRUU INFUNDIBULAR
ABDFIILNOOOV BIOFLAVONOID
ABDGHINOOSWX SHADOW-BOXING
ABDGIILOOORY RADIOBIOLOGY
ABDGIINNOORR IRONING BOARD
ABDGINOPRRSS SPRINGBOARDS
ABDGMOORRSSS SMORGASBORDS
ABDHILNOORSY DISHONORABLY
ABDIIIILNTUY INAUDIBILITY
ABDIIILMNSSY INADMISSIBLY
ABDIIILRSSUY SUBSIDIARILY
ABDIIIMORSST TROMBIDIASIS
ABDIILLMOTUY MODULABILITY,
  MOULDABILITY
ABDIILNPSTUY INDISPUTABLY
ABDIIRRSTTUY DISTRIBUTARY

ABDLNNOSSTTU NUTS AND BOLTS
ABEEEEMNRSTV BEREAVEMENTS
ABEEEFLNQRTU FREQUENTABLE
ABEEEGGILNRU BELEAGUERING
ABEEEGILNORT RENEGOTIABLE
ABEEEHILMPTU EAT HUMBLE PIE
ABEEEHKORRSU HOUSEBREAKER
ABEEEHLOPRST OBLATE SPHERE
ABEEEIILLRRV IRRELIEVABLE
ABEEEILMNPRT IMPENETRABLE
ABEEEILMNRTX EXTERMINABLE
ABEEEILNNSSV ENVIABLENESS
ABEEEILNRRST EAST BERLINER
ABEEEIMNQSTU MESQUITE BEAN
ABEEEINRRTTV INVERTEBRATE
ABEEELOOPTTT POTATO BEETLE
ABEEELQRSSTU SEQUESTRABLE
ABEEEMPRSTTU SUBTEMPERATE
ABEEENQSTUUY BEAUTY QUEENS
ABEEEORRRRTV REVERBERATOR
ABEEEPRRSTTY PRESBYTERATE
ABEEFFIILNRSU INSUFFERABLE
ABEEFFRSSTTU BUFFER STATES
ABEEFGHILNRT FRIGHTENABLE
ABEEFIIILLMSU EMULSIFIABLE
ABEEFIILLRTZ FERTILIZABLE
ABEEFKLNOORW FOREKNOWABLE
ABEEFLLMNSSU BLAMEFULNESS
ABEEFLLMSSSY SELF-ASSEMBLY
ABEEGGILNPSS SLEEPING BAGS
ABEEGGILNRSS BEGGARLINESS
ABEEGHMNOOPR GERMANOPHOBE
ABEEGIILNSTV INVESTIGABLE
ABEEGIKNPSTU SPEAKING TUBE
ABEEGILNORRS LOGANBERRIES
ABEEGILNOXYZ OXYGENIZABLE
ABEEGLNNORUV UNGOVERNABLE
ABEEHHPRSSTY BATHYSPHERES
ABEEHIILMPRS IMPERISHABLE
ABEEHILLMORT THERMOLABILE
ABEEHILOPPRS PROPHESIABLE
ABEEHILRRSTW WELSH RAREBIT
ABEEHIQRRSUU HARQUEBUSIER
ABEEHKLNNOTT ON THE BLANKET
ABEEHLMORSTT THERMOSTABLE
ABEEHLOPRSST BLASTOSPHERE
ABEEHLORRSWW WHEELBARROWS
ABEEIIILLRST LIBERALITIES
ABEEIILLRSTZ STERILIZABLE
ABEEIILMMMOR IMMEMORIABLE
ABEEIILMNNRT INTERMINABLE
ABEEIILMNRTX INTERMIXABLE
ABEEIILMPRTY PERMEABILITY
ABEEIILNPRTX INEXTIRPABLE

ABEEIILNPSST PITIABLENESS
ABEEIILNRTVY VENERABILITY
ABEEIILNRTWY RENEWABILITY
ABEEIILORTTV OBLITERATIVE
ABEEIILPRRRS IRRESPIRABLE
ABEEIKLNNSST LINEN BASKETS
ABEEILLMNSSY ASSEMBLY LINE
ABEEILLNNRUV INVULNERABLE,
  VILLEURBANNE
ABEEILLORRSV IRRESOLVABLE
ABEEILLRSTVY LIVERY STABLE
ABEEILMMOORS AEROEMBOLISM
ABEEILMNRRSU SERIAL NUMBER
ABEEILNOPRST INTERPOSABLE
ABEEILNOQSTU QUESTIONABLE
ABEEILNSSSTU SUITABLENESS
ABEEILOPPRRX EXPROPRIABLE
ABEEILPRRSTY PRESBYTERIAL
ABEEINORRTTV VERTEBRATION
ABEEINPRRSTY PRESBYTERIAN
ABEEIRRRSSTW STRAWBERRIES
ABEEKLMORRTU TROUBLEMAKER
ABEEKMRRSTUY BUYER'S MARKET
ABEEKORRSSTT BREASTSTROKE
ABEELLMNOPUY UNEMPLOYABLE
ABEELLMNOTTT BALLOTTEMENT
ABEELMMNNOTZ EMBLAZONMENT
ABEELMNPRSTU NUMBERPLATES
ABEELNNNOSTT NANSEN BOTTLE
ABEELNOSSSTU ABSOLUTENESS
ABEELNOSSTUV SOLVENT ABUSE
ABEELOORSTUZ ABSOLUTE ZERO
ABEELOPPRSSU SUPERPOSABLE
ABEENPRTTTUU PEANUT BUTTER
ABEENRSSSSTU ABSTRUSENESS
ABEFFIIILNTY INEFFABILITY
ABEFFILNRSUY INSUFFERABLY
ABEFGILNORRY FORBEARINGLY
ABEFGILNORUV UNFORGIVABLE
ABEFGINNRRTU AFTERBURNING
ABEFHHILLLOT BILL OF HEALTH
ABEFHHLORRST HALF-BROTHERS
ABEFIIILLOSSZ FOSSILIZABLE
ABEFIILRTTUY REFUTABILITY
ABEFILNOPRTU UNPROFITABLE
ABEFILNRSSTU TRANSFUSIBLE
ABEFLLOOORSV LABORS OF LOVE
ABEFLLOOORUV LABOUR OF LOVE
ABEFLMOOSSTT FALSE BOTTOMS
ABEFLNOSSSTU BOASTFULNESS
ABEFLNOSSSUU FABULOUSNESS
ABEGGHIOOPRY BIOGEOGRAPHY
ABEGGIMNNOOR BOOMERANGING
ABEGHIILNSST ESTABLISHING

ABEGHJNNORSU JOHANNESBURG
ABEGIIILLNRZ LIBERALIZING
ABEGIILNORTT OBLITERATING
ABEGIILNPRTY PREGNABILITY
ABEGIKLNNOOR BOOK-LEARNING
ABEGILLLNOWY BOWLING ALLEY
ABEGILLNOOST BALNEOLOGIST
ABEGILNNRTTU TABLE-TURNING
ABEGILRRSSST BRISTLE-GRASS
ABEGILRRSYZZ GRIZZLY BEARS
ABEGLLORSSSW GLASSBLOWERS
ABEGLNORSSSU GLABROUSNESS
ABEHIIILNNSU HUSEIN IBN-ALI
ABEHIIILRTTY HERITABILITY
ABEHIIIMNNRS HIBERNIANISM
ABEHIILNNRTY LABYRINTHINE
ABEHIILNOPST INHOSPITABLE
ABEHIIMORSUV BEHAVIOURISM,
  MISBEHAVIOUR
ABEHIIORSSTV BEHAVIORISTS
ABEHIIORSTUV BEHAVIOURIST
ABEHILNORRTW BROTHER-IN-LAW
ABEHINPRSSTU PAINTBRUSHES
ABEHLORRSTTY ERYTHROBLAST
ABEIIILLLRTY ILLIBERALITY
ABEIIIILLNNRT BRILLIANTINE
ABEIIILLNSTY ENSILABILITY
ABEIIILRSTVY REVISABILITY
ABEIIILRTVVY REVIVABILITY
ABEIIKLORTVY REVOKABILITY
ABEIILLLMPTU MULTIPLIABLE
ABEIILMMORTY MEMORABILITY
ABEIILMNNRTY INTERMINABLY
ABEIILMORTVY REMOVABILITY
ABEIILNNOSTU NEBULISATION
ABEIILNNOTUZ NEBULIZATION
ABEIILNNTTUY UNTENABILITY
ABEIILNOORTT OBLITERATION
ABEIILOQRRTU EQUILIBRATOR
ABEIILPRSTUY SUPERABILITY
ABEIILPRTTUY REPUTABILITY
ABEIIMOQRSTU BARQUISIMETO
ABEIINORSSTU SUBERISATION
ABEIINORSTUZ SUBERIZATION
ABEILLNNRUVY INVULNERABLY
ABEILLNOPPRT BIPROPELLANT
ABEILLOPRRVY PROVERBIALLY
ABEILMOSSTUY ABSTEMIOUSLY
ABEILNOQSTUY QUESTIONABLY
ABEILNORSSUY BYELORUSSIAN
ABEILNORTTXY EXORBITANTLY
ABEILNPRSSUU PRUSSIAN BLUE
ABEINOOPRRST PROBATIONERS
ABEINOORSSTV OBSERVATIONS

ABEINOPRRTTU PERTURBATION
ABEINSSSTTUV SUBSTANTIVES
ABELLLLOPSYY POLYSYLLABLE
ABELLLMNOOSY MONOSYLLABLE
ABELMNORSTUU SURMOUNTABLE
ABEMNNOOTTUW MEN-ABOUT-TOWN
ABEMNORRRSST BARNSTORMERS
ABFGIIILNRTY FRANGIBILITY
ABFIIILLNORT FIBRILLATION
ABGGILLNOSSW GLASS-BLOWING
ABGHIIMMNSTW SWIMMING BATH
ABGHIINSSTTU BATHING SUITS
ABGIIIILNTTY IGNITABILITY
ABGIIILLMNSU BILINGUALISM
ABGIIILLOORTY OBLIGATORILY
ABGILNOOPSST SPONGIOBLAST
ABGILOOOORSTY ASTROBIOLOGY
ABGIMNNORRST BARNSTORMING
ABHHIKRSSTTU TURKISH BATHS
ABHIIKMNNPRS BRINKMANSHIP
ABHIILNOPSTY INHOSPITABLY
ABHIINOPRSTV VIBRAPHONIST
ABHIMNNORRTU NORTHUMBRIAN
ABIIIILRRTTY IRRITABILITY
ABIIIILLPSTUY PLAUSIBILITY
ABIIILMMOTVY IMMOVABILITY
ABIIILMMTTUY IMMUTABILITY
ABIIILMNOOST ABOLITIONISM,
  MOBILISATION
ABIIILMNOOTZ MOBILIZATION
ABIIILMPTTUY IMPUTABILITY
ABIIILNOOSTT ABOLITIONIST
ABIIILNPRTTY PRINTABILITY
ABIIILNRSTUY INSURABILITY
ABIIILSTTTWY TWISTABILITY
ABIILMOOSTTU AUTOMOBILIST
ABIILNOORSTT STROBILATION
ABIILNORSSUU INSALUBRIOUS
ABIILNORSTTU TRIBULATIONS
ABIILOOPPSTY OPPOSABILITY
ABIILRSTTTUY TRUSTABILITY
ABIIMNORSTTU TAMBOURINIST
ABIINOORSSTT ABORTIONISTS
ABIIOPRSTTVY ABSORPTIVITY
ABILMMMNOSSU SOMNAMBULISM
ABILMMNOSSTU SOMNAMBULIST
ABILMNORSTUY SUBNORMALITY
ABIMNORSSTTU NIMBOSTRATUS
ABINRRSSSTTU BRAINS TRUSTS
ABNOORRSSTUU BRONTOSAURUS
ACCCCEIILRRT ARCTIC CIRCLE
ACCCDEEEELNS DECALESCENCE
ACCCDENNOORS CONCORDANCES
ACCCDIMOPSST COMPACT DISCS

ACCCEEEELNRS RECALESCENCE
ACCCEEEILNNS INCALESCENCE
ACCCEEEINQSU ACQUIESCENCE
ACCCEEIILSST ECCLESIASTIC
ACCCEEILLLTY ECLECTICALLY
ACCCEGIINNOR CARCINOGENIC
ACCCEHILMOTY CYTOCHEMICAL
ACCCEEIILMRST CLIMACTERICS
ACCCEIMNNOOT CONCOMITANCE
ACCCEEIMNRSTU CIRCUMSTANCE
ACCCHIIOPRRT CHIROPRACTIC
ACCCIIILLOSS LOCI CLASSICI
ACCCIIILSSST CLASSICISTIC
ACCCIILNNOTY ANTICYCLONIC
ACCCIILNOOST ICONOCLASTIC
ACCDDEHINOOP DODECAPHONIC
ACCDDEHNPRSU PUNCHED CARDS
ACCDDEIINORT ENDOCARDITIC
ACCDDEINORTT CONTRADICTED
ACCDEEEEFNRT FACE-CENTERED
ACCDEEFIIRTT CERTIFICATED
ACCDEEFLLOTU DEFLOCCULATE
ACCDEEGOPRSU COUPS DE GRACE
ACCDEEHIILNP DIENCEPHALIC
ACCDEEHIMNOS MACHINE CODES
ACCDEEHIORSS ARCHDIOCESES
ACCDEEIILNOT INDOLEACETIC
ACCDEEIILLOPS PECCADILLOES
ACCDEEILNOPY ENCYCLOPEDIA
ACCDEEINNNST INCANDESCENT
ACCDEEINNORT CONCERTINAED
ACCDEEIOPRRT RECIPROCATED
ACCDEELMORTT CLOTTED CREAM
ACCDEELOOPRS CAPE COLOREDS
ACCDEELOOPRU CAPE COLOURED
ACCDEENNNOTU COUNTENANCED
ACCDEENNORTT CONCENTRATED
ACCDEENORTTU COUNTERACTED
ACCDEENOSSUU SUCCEDANEOUS
ACCDEGHORTUU DUTCH COURAGE
ACCDEGIILRSY LYSERGIC ACID
ACCDEGNNORRT CONCERT GRAND
ACCDEHHNRRUW CHURCHWARDEN
ACCDEHILMOPS ACCOMPLISHED
ACCDEHILOOPP CEPHALOPODIC
ACCDEHIOORSU ORCHIDACEOUS
ACCDEHNRRRUY HARD CURRENCY
ACCDEIIILNST INSECTICIDAL
ACCDEIIIPRRT PERICARDITIC
ACCDEIILLOPY EPICYCLOIDAL
ACCDEIILNNOT COINCIDENTAL
ACCDEIILRRSU CIRCULARISED
ACCDEIILRRUZ CIRCULARIZED
ACCDEIKLNSST CANDLESTICKS

ACCDEILNOPTU CONDUPLICATE
ACCDEIMMNOTU COMMUNICATED
ACCDEIMNORTU UNDEMOCRATIC
ACCDEINORRTT CONTRADICTER
ACCDEIOORRTT DECORTICATOR
ACCDEIPRRSTU PICTURE CARDS
ACCDEKORRRST TRACK RECORDS
ACCDEMNOSTUU UNACCUSTOMED
ACCDENNORTUY COUNTRY DANCE
ACCDFIIINOOT CODIFICATION
ACCDHIIINORTW IN ACCORD WITH
ACCDHINOTTUU DUTCH AUCTION
ACCDIINOORST ACCORDIONIST
ACCDIINOSTTY SYNDIOTACTIC
ACCEEEGINNOT CAENOGENETIC
ACCEEEHILNPP EPENCEPHALIC
ACCEEEHLORRT HETEROCERCAL
ACCEEENOPRSV VAPORESCENCE
ACCEEFFHKLOT COFFEE KLATCH
ACCEEFGIIMNN MAGNIFICENCE
ACCEEFHIMSTU FACE THE MUSIC
ACCEEFHMNORT FRANCHE-COMTÉ
ACCEEFIIRSTT CERTIFICATES
ACCEEFIKRRRS FIRECRACKERS
ACCEEGHIMNOS GEOMECHANICS
ACCEEGHNNORX CORN EXCHANGE
ACCEEGHORRSV COVER CHARGES
ACCEEGILRRST GREAT CIRCLES
ACCEEGINNORZ RECOGNIZANCE
ACCEEHHIRSST CHESHIRE CATS
ACCEEHIILNPT ENCEPHALITIC
ACCEEHILMOPS MESOCEPHALIC
ACCEEHILRRST RICHTER SCALE
ACCEEHIMORTT TACHEOMETRIC
ACCEEHIORTTT HETEROTACTIC
ACCEEHIRRTTU ARCHITECTURE
ACCEEHKORSTW WEATHERCOCKS
ACCEEHLMNRSY SCLERENCHYMA
ACCEEHLMORTY THE REAL MCCOY
ACCEEHMNNORT ENCROACHMENT
ACCEEIILNRST ELECTRICIANS
ACCEEIINPPRT PRECIPITANCE
ACCEEIKNPRSS SCIENCE PARKS
ACCEEILLLRTY ELECTRICALLY
ACCEEILLMNUY ECUMENICALLY
ACCEEILNPTTU CENTUPLICATE
ACCEEILNRTTY TETRACYCLINE
ACCEEIMNOTTY ACTINOMYCETE
ACCEEIORSTTT STEREOTACTIC
ACCEELLOORTT COLLECTORATE
ACCEELMNOPTU ACCOUPLEMENT
ACCEELNNOPTY CYCLOPENTANE
ACCEELNNOSTV CONVALESCENT
ACCEELNNRSTU TRANSLUCENCE

ACCEELPRRWYY CREEPY-CRAWLY
ACCEEMNNORRS NECROMANCERS
ACCEEMNOPPSU COME-UPPANCES
ACCEEMNORTTU ACCOUTREMENT
ACCEEMOOPPRR COME A CROPPER
ACCEENNNOSTU COUNTENANCES
ACCEENNORSTT CONCENTRATES
ACCEFGIIINNS SIGNIFICANCE
ACCEFIILLMRY FAMILY CIRCLE
ACCEFIILLPSY SPECIFICALLY
ACCEGHHIOPRT HECTOGRAPHIC
ACCEGHINOPRS SCENOGRAPHIC
ACCEGIIKNRSW WISECRACKING
ACCEGIINNNOZ INCOGNIZANCE
ACCEGIINRTUX EXCRUCIATING
ACCEGILLLOOY ECOLOGICALLY
ACCEGILLNOOR NECROLOGICAL
ACCEGILNNOSV CONVALESCING
ACCEGINNNOVY CONVEYANCING
ACCEGINNORST CONSECRATING
ACCEGNOORRTY GERONTOCRACY
ACCEHHLMNORY CHLORENCHYMA
ACCEHIILLNST CALLISTHENIC
ACCEHIILNOPR NECROPHILIAC
ACCEHIILNSST CALISTHENICS
ACCEHIILNTTY TECHNICALITY
ACCEHIIRSTTT TETRASTICHIC
ACCEHIKMNSTY CHIMNEYSTACK
ACCEHILLLORY CHOLERICALLY
ACCEHILMOPRS ACCOMPLISHER
ACCEHILMOPRY MICROCEPHALY,
PYROCHEMICAL
ACCEHILNNNOT NONTECHNICAL
ACCEHILNOOOT ECHOLOCATION
ACCEHILOPRTY CHALCOPYRITE
ACCEHIMOORST MESOTHORACIC
ACCEHINNNOPT PANTECHNICON
ACCEHINRSSST SCRATCHINESS
ACCEHIOPSTVY PSYCHOACTIVE
ACCEHKLOOSVZ CZECHOSLOVAK
ACCEHKOPPSTT PATCH POCKETS
ACCEHLOOPRTY PYROCATECHOL
ACCEHLOORSSU SCHORLACEOUS
ACCEHMNOOORT COME TO ANCHOR
ACCEHOPRSSST CROSSPATCHES
ACCEIIILPSST SPECIALISTIC
ACCEIIINNNPS PICCANINNIES
ACCEIIKKMNRS CAMI-KNICKERS
ACCEIILLLNTY ENCLITICALLY
ACCEIILLLPTY ECLIPTICALLY
ACCEIILMMORT MICROCLIMATE
ACCEIILMNNOP INCOMPLIANCE
ACCEIILMORRT CALORIMETRIC
ACCEIILMRRSU SEMICIRCULAR

ACCEIILNORTV INTERVOCALIC
ACCEIILORRTV OVERCRITICAL
ACCEIILRRRSU CIRCULARISER
ACCEIILRRRUZ CIRCULARIZER
ACCEIILRSSTU SECULARISTIC
ACCEIIMNORRT CRANIOMETRIC
ACCEIIMNORTT ACTINOMETRIC
ACCEIIMNOSST COSMETICIANS
ACCEIINOPRSS CONSPIRACIES
ACCEIINORTUX EXCRUCIATION
ACCEIIPPRSTY PERSPICACITY
ACCEILLMMORY COMMERCIALLY
ACCEILLMNOOY ECONOMICALLY
ACCEILLMOSTY COSMETICALLY
ACCEILLNNORT CENTROCLINAL
ACCEILLNOTTY TECTONICALLY
ACCEILLOPRRY RECIPROCALLY
ACCEILLOPTYY ECOTYPICALLY
ACCEILMMNORU UNCOMMERCIAL
ACCEILMNNOOU UNECONOMICAL
ACCEILMNORTU COUNTERCLAIM
ACCEILNNNOOT CONNECTIONAL
ACCEILNNOOPT CONCEPTIONAL
ACCEILNNOOTV CONVECTIONAL
ACCEILNNOSTY ANTICYCLONES
ACCEILNOSSSU SUCCESSIONAL
ACCEILOOSSTT OSTEOCLASTIC
ACCEILOPRSTU PLUTOCRACIES
ACCEIMNOSTTY NEMATOCYSTIC
ACCEIMNRTTUU CIRCUMNUTATE
ACCEINNNNOOS INCONSONANCE
ACCEINNOORST CONSECRATION
ACCEINNORSTV CONTRIVANCES
ACCEIOOPRRRT RECIPROCATOR
ACCELLMNOPTY COMPLACENTLY
ACCELLNOPTUY CONCEPTUALLY
ACCELLOOORSU COROLLACEOUS
ACCELLOSSTTU COALSCUTTLES
ACCELMMNOOPS COMMONPLACES
ACCELMNORSUU MACRONUCLEUS
ACCELMOOSTTY CYCLOSTOMATE
ACCELNNRSTUY TRANSLUCENCY
ACCELORSUUVY CURVACEOUSLY
ACCEMOOSSTUY ASCOMYCETOUS
ACCENNOORRTT CONCENTRATOR
ACCENOORRSTY CONSECRATORY
ACCFGHHIOSTT CATCH SIGHT OF
ACCFGIINNOST CONFISCATING
ACCFIIMNNOSU CONFUCIANISM
ACCFIINNOOST CONFISCATION
ACCFIINNOSTU CONFUCIANIST
ACCFILLNOOTU FLOCCULATION
ACCFINOORSTY CONFISCATORY
ACCGGHHIKNOU HACKING COUGH

ACCGHHIINOPR ICHNOGRAPHIC
ACCGHHIINTTT CHITCHATTING
ACCGHHIIOPRR CHIROGRAPHIC
ACCGHHIOOPRR CHOROGRAPHIC
ACCGHIIKNORR ROCKING CHAIR
ACCGHIILLNOO ICHNOLOGICAL
ACCGHIIMOPRR MICROGRAPHIC
ACCGHIIMOTTT THIGMOTACTIC
ACCGHIINOOPR ICONOGRAPHIC
ACCGHIINOPRZ ZINCOGRAPHIC
ACCGHILLOOPY PHYCOLOGICAL
ACCGHINOPSTT SCOTCH TAPING
ACCGIIILNNOT CONCILIATING
ACCGIIINORST ORGANICISTIC
ACCGIILLMOOT CLIMATOLOGIC
ACCGIILLNOOO ICONOLOGICAL
ACCGIILLOOOS SOCIOLOGICAL
ACCGIILMNOPT COMPLICATING
ACCGILLMOOOS COSMOLOGICAL
ACCGILNORTUY GRANULOCYTIC
ACCGIOOPRSST GASTROSCOPIC
ACCHHIOPPSTY PSYCHOPATHIC
ACCHIIINSTUV CHAUVINISTIC
ACCHIILLOOTY ALCOHOLICITY
ACCHIILOPRTY HYPOCRITICAL
ACCHIIMMORST CHROMATICISM
ACCHIIMNOPTY AMPHICTYONIC
ACCHIIMNORST MONARCHISTIC
ACCHIIMOORST ISOCHROMATIC
ACCHIIMORRTT TRICHROMATIC
ACCHIIMORTTY CHROMATICITY
ACCHIINOOPTT PHOTOACTINIC
ACCHIIOPRSTY PHYSIOCRATIC
ACCHILOOPSSY PSYCHOSOCIAL
ACCHILOPPRTY PROPHYLACTIC
ACCHIMOPRSSY MACROPHYSICS
ACCHINOOPSTT PHONOTACTICS
ACCHIOOPRRRT CHIROPRACTOR
ACCHIOORRSSU CHIAROSCUROS
ACCIIILNNOOT CONCILIATION
ACCIIINRSSST NARCISSISTIC
ACCIILLNRTUY UNCRITICALLY
ACCIILLRSTTY CRYSTALLITIC
ACCIILMNOOPT COMPLICATION
ACCIILNOORST CONCILIATORS
ACCIILNOORTY CONCILIATORY
ACCIILOPRSUY CAPRICIOUSLY
ACCIIMOOPRTT COMPATRIOTIC
ACCIINNOOOST CONSOCIATION
ACCIJLNNOTUV CONJUNCTIVAL
ACCILLMNOOSU MALOCCLUSION
ACCILLNOOOST COLLOCATIONS
ACCIMMNNOSTU COMMUNICANTS
ACCIMMNOORTU COMMUNICATOR

ACCIMNNOOSTT CONCOMITANTS
ACCIMNOOSTUU CONTUMACIOUS
ACCIMOORSSTY MACROCYTOSIS
ACCINNOOOSTV CONVOCATIONS
ACCINNOORSTT CONTRACTIONS
ACCJLNNORTUU CONJUNCTURAL
ACDDDEEHNOOR DODECAHEDRON
ACDDDEGINOOR GOOD RIDDANCE
ACDDEEEFLSTU SELF-EDUCATED
ACDDEEEFNORT CONFEDERATED
ACDDEEEHIMST SEMIDETACHED
ACDDEEELLTUW WELL-EDUCATED
ACDDEEEMMNOR COMMANDEERED
ACDDEEFIILSS DECLASSIFIED
ACDDEEGHNRRU UNDERCHARGED
ACDDEEGKLNOW ACKNOWLEDGED
ACDDEEHIMNRS MERCHANDISED
ACDDEEHINNST DISENCHANTED
ACDDEEHNORSW CROWNED HEADS
ACDDEEILPRTU REDUPLICATED
ACDDEEIMORST DEMOCRATISED
ACDDEEIMORTZ DEMOCRATIZED
ACDDEEIMOSTT DOMESTICATED
ACDDEEINNRSU REDUNDANCIES
ACDDEFIRSTUV FIVE-CARD STUD
ACDDEFNNNOOR CANNON FODDER
ACDDEGHINRSU UNDISCHARGED
ACDDEGIILLNO DIALLING CODE
ACDDEGIILNOS DIALING CODES
ACDDEIILNORU RADIONUCLIDE
ACDDEIINORST ENDOCARDITIS
ACDDEIINRTTY IDENTITY CARD
ACDDEILNOOST CONSOLIDATED
ACDDEILRSTTY DISTRACTEDLY
ACDDEINOSTTU OUTDISTANCED
ACDDEINPRSTY CANDY-STRIPED
ACDDEMOPRSSU MASS-PRODUCED
ACDDENORRSSW SWORD DANCERS
ACDDHIMNORYY HYDRODYNAMIC
ACDDILNORSTY DISCORDANTLY
ACDDOOORRRUY CORDUROY ROAD
ACDEEEEHLRRS CHEERLEADERS
ACDEEEFFNSST AFFECTEDNESS
ACDEEEFNORST CONFEDERATES
ACDEEEGILNRT DECELERATING
ACDEEEGINOPT PAEDOGENETIC
ACDEEEGINPRS PREDECEASING
ACDEEEGLLOST DÉCOLLETAGES
ACDEEEHINRUV UNDERACHIEVE
ACDEEEILNORT DECELERATION
ACDEEEILNPRT PRECEDENTIAL
ACDEEEILNRST DECENTRALISE
ACDEEEILNRTZ DECENTRALIZE

ACDEEEILNSST DELICATESSEN
ACDEEEINNRTV INADVERTENCE
ACDEEEINRSSV DISSEVERANCE
ACDEEEINSSTT NECESSITATED
ACDEEEOPRRRT TAPE RECORDER
ACDEEEOPRTTX EXPECTORATED
ACDEEFFLNTUY UNAFFECTEDLY
ACDEEFFNORRT FORT-DE-FRANCE
ACDEEFHHIKNR HANDKERCHIEF
ACDEEFHINNRS ENFRANCHISED
ACDEEFIILRST FEDERALISTIC
ACDEEFIINRRY FERRICYANIDE
ACDEEFILMTTU MULTIFACETED
ACDEEFILOPPR PRIDE OF PLACE
ACDEEFINORRY FERROCYANIDE
ACDEEFNOSSTW TWO-FACEDNESS
ACDEEFNRRSUU UNDERSURFACE
ACDEEGHILRST CLEAR-SIGHTED
ACDEEGHINNRT INTERCHANGED
ACDEEGHLLNNU UNCHALLENGED
ACDEEGHPRRSU SUPERCHARGED
ACDEEGIINPRT DEPRECIATING
ACDEEGIINRST GARDEN CITIES
ACDEEGILNORS CLOSE-GRAINED
ACDEEGILSTTU GESTICULATED
ACDEEGINORRT REDECORATING
ACDEEGIOSTTT TIED COTTAGES
ACDEEGKLNORW ACKNOWLEDGER
ACDEEGNNOSTT DECONGESTANT
ACDEEGNOORVW COVERED WAGON
ACDEEHHIMORT HEMICHORDATE
ACDEEHILMNOR ECHINODERMAL
ACDEEHILNNOP DIENCEPHALON
ACDEEHIMNRRS MERCHANDISER
ACDEEHINNRST DISENCHANTER
ACDEEHINRSTW WINDCHEATERS
ACDEEHKMRSTU DEUTSCHE MARK
ACDEEHLORTTY HETERODACTYL
ACDEEHMNORSW REACH-ME-DOWNS
ACDEEHORRSTT ORCHESTRATED
ACDEEIILLNTY INDELICATELY
ACDEEIILLTTY DIETETICALLY
ACDEEIIMNRRT RECRIMINATED
ACDEEIIMNRTY INTERMEDIACY
ACDEEIINOPRT DEPRECIATION
ACDEEIINOPRT DEPRECIATION
ACDEEIINQSTU EQUIDISTANCE
ACDEEIINTTUX INEXACTITUDE
ACDEEIIPPRTT PRECIPITATED
ACDEEIJKNNRT DINNER JACKET
ACDEEIKLOOPS KALEIDOSCOPE
ACDEEILLNNOS DECLENSIONAL
ACDEEILLNRTY INTERLACEDLY
ACDEEILMNPST DISPLACEMENT
ACDEEILNPQTU QUINDECAPLET

ACDEEILNRSTT DECENTRALIST
ACDEEILORTVY DECORATIVELY
ACDEEIMMORST COMMISERATED
ACDEEIMNNOPR PREDOMINANCE
ACDEEIMNPRST PREDICAMENTS
ACDEEIMORRTX XERODERMATIC
ACDEEINOORST AERODONETICS
ACDEEINOPRTU DEUTERANOPIC
ACDEEINOSSSU EDACIOUSNESS
ACDEEIOPPRTU PROPAEDEUTIC
ACDEEIOPRRTY DEPRECIATORY
ACDEEIORRSSV SERVICE ROADS
ACDEEIORRSTT DIRECTORATES
ACDEEIRSSTTU RESUSCITATED
ACDEEJKKNOTY DONKEY JACKET
ACDEELMNOPTT CONTEMPLATED
ACDEELNOOSSS CLOSED SEASON
ACDEELOPRRRY RECORD PLAYER
ACDEEMMMOORT COMMEMORATED
ACDEEMNOPPTY APPENDECTOMY
ACDEENNNOTUV UNCOVENANTED
ACDEENNNRSTT TRANSCENDENT
ACDEENNORSTU SECOND NATURE
ACDEFFIINOST DISAFFECTION
ACDEFHIINRSS DISFRANCHISE
ACDEFHOORSSU HOUSE OF CARDS
ACDEFIIINNST INFANTICIDES
ACDEFIILNNOT CONFIDENTIAL
ACDEFIILNSSU UNCLASSIFIED
ACDEFIINNSTT DISINFECTANT
ACDEFIINOPTT PONTIFICATED
ACDEFILRTTUX FLUIDEXTRACT
ACDEGHHNORST SHORT-CHANGED
ACDEGHIILRSY RAYLEIGH DISC
ACDEGHIOPRRS DISCOGRAPHER
ACDEGHLOORSS GRADE SCHOOLS
ACDEGIIILMNZ DECIMALIZING
ACDEGIIKNRST SIDETRACKING
ACDEGIILLNSS SLIDING SCALE
ACDEGIILLOOO IDEOLOOGICAL
ACDEGIILPQRU QUADRIPLEGIC
ACDEGIIOOPRT DIAGEOTROPIC
ACDEGILLOOTY DIALECTOLOGY
ACDEGILNNOST LONG-DISTANCE
ACDEGINNNRST TRANSCENDING
ACDEGINORRSS CROSS-GRAINED
ACDEHHHNOTTW DOWN THE HATCH
ACDEHHLOPRYY HYDROCEPHALY
ACDEHHOOOPTT PHOTOCATHODE
ACDEHIILLLOY HELICOIDALLY
ACDEHIILMMOT IMMETHODICAL
ACDEHIIMNNOT INDOMETHACIN
ACDEHIIMORST RADIOCHEMIST
ACDEHILLMOTY METHODICALLY

ACDEHINNOPSW OPEN SANDWICH
ACDEHINOPTTU PUT THE ACID ON
ACDEHIOOPRST ORTHOPAEDICS
ACDEHKMRSSTU DEUTSCHMARKS
ACDEHLNPRSTU THUNDERCLAPS
ACDEIIILNTVY INDICATIVELY
ACDEIIILRTVY VERIDICALITY
ACDEIIIMNNOT NICOTINAMIDE
ACDEIIIMNNRS INCENDIARISM
ACDEIIIMNNRT INCRIMINATED
ACDEIIIMNRST DISCRIMINATE
ACDEIIIMORST ISODIAMETRIC
ACDEIIINOPRT ANTIPERIODIC
ACDEIIINORST DICTIONARIES
ACDEIIINPPST APPENDICITIS
ACDEIIIOPRTY APERIODICITY
ACDEIIIOSSTV DISSOCIATIVE
ACDEIIIPRRST PERICARDITIS
ACDEIIILLNNTY INCIDENTALLY
ACDEIILLNSTT SCINTILLATED
ACDEIILLOPRY PERIODICALLY
ACDEIILLOPSY EPISODICALLY
ACDEIILLRTUY DIURETICALLY
ACDEIILMNOST MALEDICTIONS
ACDEIILMORTT DILATOMETRIC
ACDEIILNNNOT NONIDENTICAL
ACDEIILNNOST DECLINATIONS
ACDEIILNOSTV VALEDICTIONS
ACDEIILRRTUV DIVERTICULAR
ACDEIIMNORST ROMANTICISED
ACDEIIMNORTZ ROMANTICIZED
ACDEIINNNOTU DENUNCIATION
ACDEIINNOORT INCOORDINATE
ACDEIINNORTT INDOCTRINATE
ACDEIINOOTTX DETOXICATION
ACDEIIORSSTT SIDEROSTATIC
ACDEIKMNNORT ONE-TRACK MIND
ACDEIKNORSTT STOCK-IN-TRADE
ACDEILLMOSTY DOMESTICALLY
ACDEILLNSTYY SYNDETICALLY
ACDEILLOPSTY DESPOTICALLY
ACDEILLRSSTY CRYSTALLISED
ACDEILLRSTYZ CRYSTALLIZED
ACDEILMNOSUY MENDACIOUSLY
ACDEILMOPSTU DEUTOPLASMIC
ACDEILNOOORT DECOLORATION
ACDEILNOORTU EDULCORATION
ACDEILNOORTY COORDINATELY
ACDEILNOOSST DISCONSOLATE
ACDEILNORSSW COWARDLINESS
ACDEILOORRUV VARICOLOURED
ACDEIMMNNOOT COMMENDATION
ACDEIMMNORTY DYNAMOMETRIC
ACDEIMMOOORR AIR COMMODORE

ACDEIMNNNOOT CONDEMNATION
ACDEIMNORRRS MORRIS DANCER
ACDEIMNORRSS MORRIS DANCES
ACDEIMOORSTT DOMESTICATOR
ACDEINNNOOST CONDENSATION
ACDEINNNOSTU UNSANCTIONED
ACDEINNORTTU DETRUNCATION
ACDEINNORTUY DENUNCIATORY
ACDEINOOPRRT INCORPORATED
ACDELMOPRTUW TALCUM POWDER
ACDELNOORTYY COTYLEDONARY
ACDELOORRSTW STRAW-COLORED
ACDELOPRRTTY PROTRACTEDLY
ACDELOPRSTTY PTERODACTYLS
ACDEMMMNNOST COMMANDMENTS
ACDEMMNOORTY COMMENDATORY
ACDEMNNOORTY CONDEMNATORY
ACDEMOPRRSSU MASS-PRODUCER
ACDEOPRSTTUW WASTE PRODUCT
ACDFIIIINNOT NIDIFICATION
ACDFIIIMNOOT MODIFICATION
ACDFIIMOORTY MODIFICATORY
ACDFILMOORTY FAMILY DOCTOR
ACDGGIINORSU DISCOURAGING
ACDGHHIOPRRY HYDROGRAPHIC
ACDGHIIOPRTT DITTOGRAPHIC
ACDGIIINOSST DISSOCIATING
ACDGIIINRSTV VISITING CARD
ACDGIILOORST CARDIOLOGIST
ACDGIINNOORT COORDINATING
ACDHHINOOPRY HYPOCHONDRIA
ACDHHIOPRRSS HARPSICHORDS
ACDHIIMMORST DICHROMATISM
ACDHIIOPRSST RHAPSODISTIC
ACDHIIOPRSTT DICTATORSHIP
ACDHILLOORTY TROCHOIDALLY
ACDHIMNOOPTY PHOTODYNAMIC
ACDHLNOOSSUY SUNDAY SCHOOL
ACDHNRSTTTUU CUT AND THRUST
ACDIIILNPRSY DISCIPLINARY
ACDIIIMNNOOT NONIDIOMATIC
ACDIIIMNNRST DISCRIMINANT
ACDIIINNOORT AIR-CONDITION
ACDIIINOOSST DISSOCIATION
ACDIIIOSSTTU ADSCITITIOUS
ACDIIILLLOOTY COLLOIDALITY
ACDIIILLMNPTU MULTIPLICAND
ACDIIILLOPRTY DIOPTRICALLY
ACDIILNOOSST DISLOCATIONS
ACDIILNORTTY DOCTRINALITY
ACDIILNOSSSU DISCUSSIONAL
ACDIILNSSSTY SYNDICALISTS
ACDIINNOOORT COORDINATION
ACDIINORSSTT DISTRACTIONS

ACDIINORSSYY IDIOSYNCRASY
ACDILMNSSTYY SYNDACTYLISM
ACDILNOOOORST CONSOLIDATOR
ACDILNOOPRTU PRODUCTIONAL
ACDINNORSTTU TRANSDUCTION
ACDINOOQRSTU CONQUISTADOR
ACDLOOOPRSTT POSTDOCTORAL
ACEEEEFJKRRT REEFER JACKET
ACEEEEHLPSST STEEPLECHASE
ACEEEELMNRTT TRACE ELEMENT
ACEEEELNORTT COELENTERATE
ACEEEENPRRSV PERSEVERANCE
ACEEEFFFRSTT AFTEREFFECTS
ACEEEFILLNRS SELF-RELIANCE
ACEEEFIOPPPS PIPES OF PEACE
ACEEEFLNPSSU PEACEFULNESS
ACEEEFLNSSSS FACELESSNESS
ACEEEFLORRST STEER CLEAR OF
ACEEEFLRRSTV SCARLET FEVER
ACEEEFNNRRST TRANSFERENCE
ACEEEGHHRSST CHARGE SHEETS
ACEEEGHINPRS CHEESEPARING
ACEEEGIIMNNR ANCIEN RÉGIME
ACEEEGILLTXY EXEGETICALLY
ACEEEGIMNRST RACE MEETINGS
ACEEEGINNOSS CAENOGENESIS
ACEEEGINNSSW NEWS AGENCIES
ACEEEGNNRRUY UNREGENERACY
ACEEEGNRSSTT SECRET AGENTS
ACEEEHHILLLS ACHILLES' HEEL
ACEEEHHILNOT ACE IN THE HOLE
ACEEEHILSTTT TELAESTHETIC
ACEEEHIMNQTU CINEMATHEQUE
ACEEEHIMNSTV ACHIEVEMENTS
ACEEEHINOSST COENESTHESIA
ACEEEHLMOPRT CEPHALOMETER
ACEEEHLNNOPP EPENCEPHALON
ACEEEHMNNNST ENHANCEMENTS
ACEEEILLLNTT LENTICELLATE
ACEEEILLNPST LICENSE PLATE
ACEEEILMNPST MANTELPIECES
ACEEEILNNNSV VALENCIENNES
ACEEEILNPPRS PIPE CLEANERS
ACEEEILNRRSV IRRELEVANCES
ACEEEIMMNNPR IMPERMANENCE
ACEEEIMNNPRT INTEMPERANCE
ACEEEIMNRSVX EX-SERVICEMAN
ACEEEIMPRSST MASTERPIECES
ACEEEINRSSTV REACTIVENESS
ACEEEIPPPRTV APPERCEPTIVE
ACEEEIPRRTUV RECUPERATIVE
ACEEEJKLPSST STEEPLEJACKS
ACEEEJORSSTT EJECTOR SEATS
ACEEELLOPRTT ELECTROPLATE

ACEEELLORSVV CLOVERLEAVES
ACEEELMMNPST EMPLACEMENTS
ACEEELMNPRST REPLACEMENTS
ACEEELNOTXYY OXYACETYLENE
ACEEELNRSSSS CARELESSNESS
ACEEEMNNNRTT ENTRANCEMENT
ACEEENNRRTTY TERCENTENARY
ACEEENNRSTXY SEXCENTENARY
ACEEEOPPRRRT PRECEPTORATE
ACEEFFFGILNS SELF-EFFACING
ACEEFFGHILNO CHANGE OF LIFE
ACEEFFGINTTU EFFECTUATING
ACEEFFHOTTTT TO THAT EFFECT
ACEEFFILTTUY EFFECTUALITY
ACEEFFINOTTU EFFECTUATION
ACEEFFNNORSU ON SUFFERANCE
ACEEFGILNRST SELF-CATERING
ACEEFGLNRSSU GRACEFULNESS
ACEEFGNNOOST AGE OF CONSENT
ACEEFHINNRRS ENFRANCHISER
ACEEFHLNORSV FRENCH LOAVES
ACEEFHLOPRRS SELF-REPROACH
ACEEFHMORTTY AT THE MERCY OF
ACEEFHNOPRTU PUT HER FACE ON
ACEEFHNORSTU ON THE SURFACE
ACEEFHOPPRST PART OF SPEECH
ACEEFIIIRTVV VERIFICATIVE
ACEEFIILNQTU LIQUEFACIENT
ACEEFIILQTUV LIQUEFACTIVE
ACEEFIKNNNRS FRANKINCENSE
ACEEFILLNORT REFLECTIONAL
ACEEFILLNRTY FRENETICALLY
ACEEFILNNORT CONFERENTIAL
ACEEFILNNOST LINE OF ASCENT
ACEEFILOPRRT PREFECTORIAL
ACEEFILRSSTV SERVICE FLATS
ACEEFINPSTTU STUPEFACIENT
ACEEFIPRTTUV PUTREFACTIVE
ACEEFKMORRST MARKET FORCES
ACEEFMNOPRRS PERFORMANCES
ACEEFPPRSSTT PAST PERFECTS
ACEEGGINORTV CONGREGATIVE
ACEEGHILNOSU CHAISE LONGUE
ACEEGHILNRTW CARTWHEELING
ACEEGHILOORS ARCHEOLOGIES
ACEEGHINNRST INTERCHANGES
ACEEGHINOPTT PATHOGENETIC
ACEEGHINORRV OVERREACHING
ACEEGHIRRSST CASH REGISTER
ACEEGHLLNSSY CHANGELESSLY
ACEEGHLOPRRT ELECTROGRAPH
ACEEGHMNNORY MONEYCHANGER
ACEEGHNOPRRS SCENOGRAPHER
ACEEGHNRRSSU CHARGE NURSES

ACEEGHPRRRSU SUPERCHARGER
ACEEGIILNNPT PALINGENETIC
ACEEGIILNSTV EVANGELISTIC
ACEEGIINRSTV EVISCERATING
ACEEGIIOTTVX EXCOGITATIVE
ACEEGIKNNRRV NERVE-RACKING
ACEEGILLLNTY TELGENICALLY
ACEEGILLLOOT TELEOLOGICAL
ACEEGILMNOPT MAGNETIC POLE
ACEEGILNPRSS SLEEPING CARS
ACEEGILNPSTT PLACE SETTING
ACEEGIMNORTY ATOMIC ENERGY
ACEEGINNSSTX EXACTINGNESS
ACEEGINORRTV OVERREACTING
ACEEGINPRRTU RECUPERATING
ACEEGLMNOORT CONGLOMERATE
ACEEGMNORRSS SCAREMONGERS
ACEEHHIPRRSU HIRE PURCHASE
ACEEHHKNPPRU KERENHAPPUCH
ACEEHHLMRSST CRASH HELMETS
ACEEHHLNORSU CHARNEL HOUSE
ACEEHHMOPRTY CHEMOTHERAPY
ACEEHHNORSST SHEET ANCHORS
ACEEHHOPRSTU CHAPTERHOUSE
ACEEHHOPRTTY TRACHEOPHYTE
ACEEHIIKNSTT KINAESTHETIC
ACEEHIILNPST ENCEPHALITIS
ACEEHIIMOOPT HAEMOPOIETIC
ACEEHIIMSSTT AESTHETICISM
ACEEHIINNRST INHERITANCES
ACEEHIINNORT THEORETICIAN
ACEEHIINSTUU HAUTE CUISINE
ACEEHILLLLNY HELLENICALLY
ACEEHILLMRTY HERMETICALLY
ACEEHILLSTTY ESTHETICALLY
ACEEHILNORSS HEROICALNESS
ACEEHILNRSTT CHAIN LETTERS
ACEEHILPSSST SALES PITCHES
ACEEHIMMNTTY ENTHYMEMATIC
ACEEHIMNSSTT CHASTISEMENT
ACEEHIMOPRTV OVEREMPHATIC
ACEEHIMRSSTV CHRISTMAS EVE
ACEEHINNRSTU NEURASTHENIC
ACEEHINORUUV NOUVEAU RICHE
ACEEHINSSTTY SYNAESTHETIC
ACEEHIOSTTUW WITHOUT CEASE
ACEEHIPRSTTU THERAPEUTICS
ACEEHLLOORRU LEUCORRHOEAL
ACEEHLLOORSV SCHOOL-LEAVER
ACEEHLMOPRTY CEPHALOMETRY
ACEEHLPSSTTU SPACE SHUTTLE
ACEEHMNNNSTT ENCHANTMENTS
ACEEHMORRSTU ROUTE MARCHES
ACEEHNNSSSTU UNCHASTENESS

ACEEHOPPRRRS SHARECROPPER
ACEEHORTTUUU HAUTE COUTURE
ACEEIIILPSST SPECIALITIES
ACEEIIILLMNSS MISCELLANIES
ACEEIILLRTTV VERTICILLATE
ACEEIILMMPRT METEMPIRICAL
ACEEIILMRRSU MERCURIALISE
ACEEIILMRRUZ MERCURIALIZE
ACEEIIILNOSST SECTIONALISE
ACEEIILNOSTZ SECTIONALIZE
ACEEIIMMRSTT MERISTEMATIC
ACEEIIMNPRSU EPICUREANISM
ACEEIINNORST CONTAINERISE
ACEEIINNORTZ CONTAINERIZE
ACEEIINNRTUV RENUNCIATIVE
ACEEIINORSTV EVISCERATION
ACEEIIPPRSTT PRECIPITATES
ACEEIJORRSTT TRAJECTORIES
ACEEIKKNOPST TAKE ONE'S PICK
ACEEIKMPRRST MARKET PRICES
ACEEIKNOSSTT SEASON TICKET
ACEEILLLNTTU INTELLECTUAL
ACEEILLMMRSY MESMERICALLY
ACEEILLMNORY CEREMONIALLY
ACEEILLMORTY METEORICALLY
ACEEILLNNORT CRENELLATION
ACEEILLNORTY NEOTERICALLY
ACEEILLNOTUV INVOLUCELATE
ACEEILLNRSUV SURVEILLANCE
ACEEILLORSTY ESOTERICALLY
ACEEILLORTXY EXOTERICALLY
ACEEILMMNPST MISPLACEMENT
ACEEILMPSSTU TIME CAPSULES
ACEEILNOPPRT PERCEPTIONAL
ACEEILNOPRRT PRECENTORIAL
ACEEILNOPRSS PRECESSIONAL
ACEEILNORSSS RECESSIONALS
ACEEILNPRTTY PETIT LARCENY
ACEEILNSSTTT CLIENT STATES
ACEEILOPPRRT PRECEPTORIAL
ACEEILOPSSTT POLICE STATES
ACEEILORRSTV CORRELATIVES
ACEEILPPSTTU SEPTUPLICATE
ACEEILPSTTUX SEXTUPLICATE
ACEEIMMMNOTT COMMITTEEMAN
ACEEIMMNORST COMMENTARIES
ACEEIMMOSSTT MASTECTOMIES
ACEEIMNOPSTV COMPENSATIVE
ACEEIMNORSSX CROSS-EXAMINE
ACEEINOORRTV OVERREACTION
ACEEINOPPPRT APPERCEPTION
ACEEINOPRRTU RECUPERATION
ACEEINOPRSTT INSPECTORATE
ACEEINOPSTTX EXPECTATIONS

ACEEINORRSTY SECRETIONARY
ACEEINORSTVV CONSERVATIVE
ACEEIOOPRSTV COOPERATIVES
ACEELLORSSSW LOWER CLASSES
ACEELMNNORTU NOMENCLATURE
ACEELMNOOSTU LOMENTACEOUS
ACEELMNORSTW SCARLET WOMEN
ACEELMORSSST MALTESE CROSS
ACEELNOOSSSS CLOSE SEASONS
ACEELNPRTTYY PETTY LARCENY
ACEELNSSSSTT TACTLESSNESS
ACEELOOPPPPT POPOCATEPETL
ACEELORSSTTW WATER CLOSETS
ACEELPSSTUUY EUCALYPTUSES
ACEEMMNORSTU COMMENSURATE
ACEEMNNNNOTU ANNOUNCEMENT
ACEEMNNORRST REMONSTRANCE
ACEEMOPRSTTY SPERMATOCYTE
ACEENNOPRSTU COUNTERPANES
ACEENOPRSTUU PERCUTANEOUS
ACEEOOPRRTTT PROTECTORATE
ACEEOOPRRTTX EXPECTORATOR
ACEEORRSSTUW WATERCOURSES
ACEFFFFHIOST CHIEF OF STAFF
ACEFFFFIORST STAFF OFFICER
ACEFFGHILNRS CLIFFHANGERS
ACEFFGHINRUU CHAUFFEURING
ACEFFILNNSSU FANCIFULNESS
ACEFFILOSSUU USUAL OFFICES
ACEFFORRSUUU FURFURACEOUS
ACEFGIIILNTT FELICITATING
ACEFGIIKNNRV CARVING KNIFE
ACEFGIINORTV VOCIFERATING
ACEFGILNRSUY FLYING SAUCER
ACEFHIIMNRTU FRUIT MACHINE
ACEFHLNSSTUW WATCHFULNESS
ACEFHNORSTTU COUNTERSHAFT
ACEFHORRSSTU RHESUS FACTOR
ACEFIIILNOST FICTIONALISE
ACEFIIILNOTT FELICITATION
ACEFIIILNOTZ FICTIONALIZE
ACEFIIINORTV VERIFICATION
ACEFIILLNNOT INFLECTIONAL
ACEFIILLRRTY TERRIFICALLY
ACEFIILNOQTU LIQUEFACTION
ACEFIILORSTU LATICIFEROUS
ACEFIINOORTV VOCIFERATION
ACEFIINOPRTT PETRIFACTION
ACEFIINOPSTT PONTIFICATES
ACEFIIPRRSUY SUPERFICIARY
ACEFILLNORSY FORENSICALLY
ACEFILLORSUW CAULIFLOWERS
ACEFILNNOOSS CONFESSIONAL
ACEFILORRRTY REFRACTORILY

ACEFINOORRTT TORREFACTION
ACEFINOPRTTU PUTREFACTION
ACEFINOPSTTU STUPEFACTION
ACEFINOSSSTU FACTIOUSNESS
ACEFLLMOOPRW CAMP FOLLOWER
ACEGGGINNORT CONGREGATING
ACEGGHINORRV OVERCHARGING
ACEGGIILNNST SINGLE-ACTING
ACEGGIINNSST GIGANTICNESS
ACEGGIINORTZ CATEGORIZING
ACEGGILLLOOY GEOLOGICALLY
ACEGGIMNORTY GYROMAGNETIC
ACEGGINNOORT CONGREGATION
ACEGHHIILOPR HELIOGRAPHIC
ACEGHHILRSST SEARCHLIGHTS
ACEGHHINOPRT ETHNOGRAPHIC
ACEGHHIOPRRR CHIROGRAPHER
ACEGHHNOPRTY TECHNOGRAPHY
ACEGHHNORRST SHORT-CHANGER
ACEGHHOOPRRR CHOROGRAPHER
ACEGHHOOPRRS CHOREOGRAPHS
ACEGHHOOPRRY CHOREOGRAPHY
ACEGHIILLNYY HYGIENICALLY
ACEGHIIMNSTZ SCHEMATIZING
ACEGHIKLLNSS SHELLACKINGS
ACEGHILLNNOU HALLUCINOGEN
ACEGHILLNOOP NEPHOLOGICAL,
  PHENOLOGICAL
ACEGHILLNOOT ETHNOLOGICAL
ACEGHILLRTUY THEURGICALLY
ACEGHILOPPRY PYELOGRAPHIC
ACEGHILOPRXY LEXICOGRAPHY
ACEGHIMOOPRT GAMETOPHORIC
ACEGHIMOPRRR MICROGRAPHER
ACEGHIMOPTTY GAMETOPHYTIC
ACEGHINOOPRR ICONOGRAPHER
ACEGHINOPRRZ ZINCOGRAPHER
ACEGHINOPRST STENOGRAPHIC
ACEGHINORRSU HARE COURSING
ACEGHIOPPRRR REPROGRAPHIC
ACEGHIOPPRRT PETROGRAPHIC
ACEGHIOPRRST CEROGRAPHIST
ACEGHLMNOOUY HUMAN ECOLOGY
ACEGHOPPRRST SPECTROGRAPH
ACEGIIILLMTY ILLEGITIMACY
ACEGIIILNPSZ SPECIALIZING
ACEGIIINNNRT INCINERATING
ACEGIIINSTTV NEGATIVISTIC
ACEGIIKNPRSS ASKING PRICES
ACEGIILLOOPT GEOPOLITICAL
ACEGIILLOSTY EGOISTICALLY
ACEGIILNNOST SINGLE-ACTION
ACEGIILNNOTU GENICULATION
ACEGIILNNOTY CONGENIALITY

ACEGIILNNRSY INCREASINGLY
ACEGIILNNRTZ CENTRALIZING
ACEGIILNRSUZ SECULARIZING
ACEGIILORSSU SACRILEGIOUS
ACEGIINNPPRT APPRENTICING
ACEGIINOOTTX EXCOGITATION
ACEGIINOQTUV EQUIVOCATING
ACEGIKLNOOPP COOKING APPLE
ACEGILLLNOOY NEOLOGICALLY
ACEGILLMOORT METROLOGICAL
ACEGILLMOOTY ETYMOLOGICAL
ACEGILLNNOSY GEOSYNCLINAL
ACEGILLNNOTY CONGENITALLY
ACEGILLNOORU NEUROLOGICAL
ACEGILLNOORY OROGENICALLY
ACEGILLOOOST OSTEOLOGICAL
ACEGILLOOPRT PETROLOGICAL
ACEGILMMOPSY OLYMPIC GAMES
ACEGILNNNRTY ENTRANCINGLY
ACEGILNNOTTU CONGLUTINATE
ACEGILNOOPRT ORGANOLEPTIC
ACEGILOOPSST ESCAPOLOGIST
ACEGILORSTTU GESTICULATOR
ACEGIMMMNOTT COMMENTATING
ACEGIMNNOPSS ENCOMPASSING
ACEGIMNNOPST COMPENSATING
ACEGINNNORTV CONTRAVENING
ACEGINNNORTT NONSTRATEGIC
ACEGINORSSSU GRACIOUSNESS
ACEGINOSSTTV CASTING VOTES
ACEGIOOOOPRT APOGEOTROPIC
ACEGLNOOPRSY LARYNGOSCOPE
ACEGLOOORSUY COURAGEOUSLY
ACEGLRSSSTTU GLASSCUTTERS
ACEHHIILMOPS HEMOPHILIACS
ACEHHIIMMPTU AMPHITHECIUM
ACEHHIINOPRT HIEROPHANTIC
ACEHHILMOPTX EXOPHTHALMIC
ACEHHILOPTTY HYPOTHETICAL
ACEHHINOPRTT THEANTHROPIC
ACEHHLLLOOTY ETHYL ALCOHOL
ACEHHLOOPRTY ORTHOCEPHALY
ACEHIIINRSST CHRISTIANISE
ACEHIIINRSTZ CHRISTIANIZE
ACEHIILLMPTY MEPHITICALLY
ACEHIILLMRTY HERMITICALLY
ACEHIILLSTTY THEISTICALLY
ACEHIILNPPRS PLANISPHERIC
ACEHIINNOPPR HIPPOCRENIAN
ACEHIINNOPST PHONETICIANS
ACEHIINORRST RHETORICIANS
ACEHIINSSTTU ENTHUSIASTIC
ACEHIINTTTUY AUTHENTICITY
ACEHIIOPSSTT SOPHISTICATE

ACEHIIPPRRST PERIPHRASTIC
ACEHIKLPRRSS PARISH CLERKS
ACEHIKMNORSS CHAIN-SMOKERS
ACEHIKMNOSST MACKINTOSHES
ACEHILLLMNOY MELANCHOLILY
ACEHILLLPTYY PHYLETICALLY
ACEHILLMNNTU MULTICHANNEL
ACEHILLMNOPY PHONEMICALLY
ACEHILLNOPST PLAIN-CLOTHES
ACEHILLNOPTY PHONETICALLY
ACEHILLNOPUY EUPHONICALLY
ACEHILLOPRUY EUPHORICALLY
ACEHILLORRTY RHETORICALLY
ACEHILLRSTYY HYSTERICALLY
ACEHILMNOOST MACHINE TOOLS
ACEHILMNOSST SLOT MACHINES
ACEHILMOOPSU AMPHICOELOUS
ACEHILMOPTYY POLYCYTHEMIA
ACEHILNNNSSS CLANNISHNESS
ACEHILNPSSSY PHYSICALNESS
ACEHIMOPRSST ATMOSPHERICS
ACEHIMORRSST CHOIRMASTERS
ACEHIMORSTTT THERMOSTATIC
ACEHINNOOPRT NEOANTHROPIC
ACEHINOPRRSS CHAIRPERSONS
ACEHINOPRRTT TRICHOPTERAN
ACEHIOPRRSTT ORCHESTRA PIT
ACEHIRSSTTWW WRISTWATCHES
ACEHKMRRSSTT STRETCHMARKS
ACEHLMMNOOTW COMMONWEALTH
ACEHLMOORSST SCHOOLMASTER
ACEHLNOOPRTU PHOTONUCLEAR
ACEHLOOPSTUY POLYCHAETOUS
ACEHLOPSSUXY PSYCHOSEXUAL
ACEHMOORSTTY TRACHEOSTOMY
ACEHNNOOPRRS ANCHORPERSON
ACEIIILLRSTT LITERALISTIC
ACEIIILMNNSS INIMICALNESS
ACEIIILMNPSU MUNICIPALISE
ACEIIILMNPUZ MUNICIPALIZE
ACEIIILNNOPT PENICILATION
ACEIIILNNOTT LICENTIATION
ACEIIILNSTTY INELASTICITY
ACEIIILRSTTV RELATIVISTIC
ACEIIILRSTVV REVIVALISTIC
ACEIIIMNOSST SEMIOTICIANS
ACEIIIMNPRSS PRECISIANISM
ACEIIINNNORT INCINERATION
ACEIIINOTTVX INTOXICATIVE
ACEIIKKNORTY KARYOKINETIC
ACEIILLLLPTY ELLIPTICALLY
ACEIILLLNSUV ALL-INCLUSIVE
ACEIILLMNSST MISCELLANIST
ACEIILLMPTTU MULTIPLICATE

ACEIILMMNRST MERCANTILISM
ACEIILMNORST SALINOMETRIC
ACEIILMNOSST SECTIONALISM
ACEIILMNRSTT MERCANTILIST
ACEIILMOPPSS EPISCOPALISM
ACEIILMOPRRT POLARIMETRIC
ACEIILMOPRST SEMITROPICAL
ACEIILNNNRTU INTERNUNCIAL
ACEIILNNOPST INSPECTIONAL
ACEIILNOPRST REPLICATIONS
ACEIILNORTTU RETICULATION
ACEIILNOSSTT SECTIONALIST
ACEIILNOSTUV VESICULATION
ACEIILNRSTTT CLARINETTIST
ACEIILNRSTVV CIVIL SERVANT
ACEIILOQSSUU SILIQUACEOUS
ACEIILOQTUVY EQUIVOCALITY
ACEIILPRRSUY SUPERCILIARY
ACEIILRRSSTU SURREALISTIC
ACEIILRRTTTY RETRACTILITY
ACEIIMMNORST CREMATIONISM
ACEIIMMORSSS COMMISSARIES
ACEIIMNOPRST IMPRECATIONS
ACEIIMNORRRT RECRIMINATOR
ACEIIMNORSTT CREMATIONIST
ACEIINNNORTU RENUNCIATION
ACEIINNORRST INCINERATORS
ACEIINNORRTY INCRETIONARY
ACEIINNORSTT INTERACTIONS
ACEIINNOTTUV CONTINUATIVE
ACEIINOOQTUV EQUIVOCATION
ACEIINOORSTX EXCORIATIONS
ACEIINOPRRTT PRACTITIONER
ACEIINOPRSTU PERTINACIOUS
ACEIINORRSTW CONTRARIWISE
ACEIIOPPRRTT PRECIPITATOR
ACEIJKLLNOSV JACKSONVILLE
ACEIJLNOOPRT PROJECTIONAL
ACEIKKNORRST NOT A SKERRICK
ACEIKLOORRSW SOCIAL WORKER
ACEIKLPPRRSY PRICKLY PEARS
ACEIKNNORSST IN ONE'S TRACKS
ACEIKORRRTTT TRICK OR TREAT
ACEILLMMNNOY MNEMONICALLY
ACEILLMMNOOT MONOMETALLIC
ACEILLMNRTUU MULTINUCLEAR
ACEILLMNTUVY MULTIVALENCY
ACEILLMORRTU TRIMOLECULAR
ACEILLMSSTYY SYSTEMICALLY
ACEILLMTUUVY CUMULATIVELY
ACEILLNNORRU CARILLONNEUR
ACEILLNOOTYZ ENZOOTICALLY
ACEILLNORTUY NEUROTICALLY
ACEILLNOSTTU SCUTELLATION

ACEILLNOTTUY TEUTONICALLY
ACEILLRRSTUU SERICULTURAL
ACEILMMMNOSS COMMENSALISM
ACEILMMNOORT MONOMETRICAL
ACEILMNNOOPT COMPONENTIAL
ACEILMNOORTU NEUROTOMICAL
ACEILMNRSTTU CURTAILMENTS
ACEILMOPRSTT PLASTOMETRIC
ACEILMOPRSUU PRIMULACEOUS
ACEILNNNOOTT CONTENTIONAL
ACEILNNNOOTV CONVENTIONAL
ACEILNNNOSTT CONTINENTALS
ACEILNNOORSV CONVERSIONAL
ACEILNOOPRSS PROCESSIONAL
ACEILNOOPRST PERCOLATIONS
ACEILNOOPRTT LACTOPROTEIN
ACEILNOORRST CORRELATIONS
ACEILNOORTUY ELOCUTIONARY
ACEILNOPSSTU SPECULATIONS
ACEILNORSUXY EXCLUSIONARY
ACEILNOSTTUV CONSULTATIVE
ACEILOOPRRTY CORPOREALITY
ACEILOOPSSTT OSTEOPLASTIC
ACEILOPRRSUY PRECARIOUSLY
ACEIMMNOSTUV CONSUMMATIVE
ACEIMMOORRST COMMISERATOR
ACEIMMORRSTU CREMATORIUMS
ACEIMNNOOPST COMPENSATION
ACEIMNOOOOPT ONOMATOPOEIC
ACEIMNORSSTV CONSERVATISM
ACEIMOOPRSTZ ZOOSPERMATIC
ACEIMPRRRSTW WRITER'S CRAMP
ACEIMPRSSSTU SUPREMACISTS
ACEINNOORSTV CONSERVATION,
   CONVERSATION
ACEINNOOSTTT CONTESTATION
ACEINNORRSST CONTRARINESS
ACEINNORSTTU ENCRUSTATION
ACEINOPPRRTU PORT-AU-PRINCE
ACEINOPSSSSU SPACIOUSNESS
ACEINOPSSSTU CAPTIOUSNESS
ACEINOSSSTUU CAUTIOUSNESS
ACEIOOPRRRRT TROOP CARRIER
ACEIOOQRTUVY EQUIVOCATORY
ACEIOORSTUUV OVERCAUTIOUS
ACEIORRSSTTU RESUSCITATOR
ACEKKMORSSTT STOCK MARKETS
ACEKMMMNOORT COMMON MARKET
ACELLNOTTUXY CONTEXTUALLY
ACELMMMNOSTUY CONSUMMATELY
ACELMNOOPRTT CONTEMPLATOR
ACELNOOPRSTU PROCONSULATE
ACELNOSSTTTU TALENT SCOUTS
ACELOORRSTUW WATERCOLOURS

ACEMMMOOORRT COMMEMORATOR
ACEMMNOORSTT COMMENTATORS
ACEMMNOPRSTT COMPARTMENTS
ACEMMPRSSSTU MASS SPECTRUM
ACEMNOOPRRTY CONTEMPORARY
ACEMNOOPRSTY COMPENSATORY
ACEMOOPRRSTU MACROPTEROUS
ACEMORSSSTTU SCOUTMASTERS
ACENNRRRSTTU TRANSCURRENT
ACENOORRSTVY CONSERVATORY
ACENOPRRSTTU COUNTERPARTS
ACENORSSTTUY COUNTRY SEATS
ACFFGGHIILNN CLIFFHANGING
ACFFGHIILRTT TRAFFIC LIGHT
ACFFIILLNOUY UNOFFICIALLY
ACFGGHIMNORR FROGMARCHING
ACFGHILNORTW FLOWCHARTING
ACFGIIILNOTU UGLIFICATION
ACFGIKNORRSV CARVING FORKS
ACFHHLNORSSY SYNCHROFLASH
ACFHIILLORRY HORRIFICALLY
ACFHKMOOOSTU ASK TOO MUCH OF
ACFIIIILNOTV VILIFICATION
ACFIIIIMNNOT MINIFICATION
ACFIIIINOTVV VIVIFICATION
ACFIIINNOOTT NOTIFICATION
ACFIIINOOSST OSSIFICATION
ACFIIINOPRTU PURIFICATION
ACFIIINOPTTY TYPIFICATION
ACFIILLLOPRY PROLIFICALLY
ACFIILNNNOOT NONFICTIONAL
ACFIIMNNOORT CONFIRMATION
ACFIINORRTTU TRIFURCATION
ACFIIOPRRTUY PURIFICATORY
ACFILLNNOTUY FUNCTIONALLY
ACFILMNNOSTU MALFUNCTIONS
ACFILNOSTTUU FLUCTUATIONS
ACFIMNNOOORT CONFORMATION
ACFIMNOORRTY CONFIRMATORY
ACFINNOOSTTU CONFUTATIONS
ACFRRSTUUUUY USUFRUCTUARY
ACGGHIMNNOOR CHANGING ROOM
ACGGIILLOOST GLACIOLOGIST
ACGHHHIOPTYY ICHTHYOPHAGY
ACGHHIILOPRT LITHOGRAPHIC
ACGHHIOOPPRT PHOTOGRAPHIC
ACGHHIOOPRRT ORTHOGRAPHIC
ACGHHNOOPRRS CHRONOGRAPHS
ACGHHOPPRSYY PSYCHOGRAPHY
ACGHIIKMNNOS CHAIN-SMOKING
ACGHIILLLOOP PHILOLOGICAL
ACGHIILLNOOR RHINOLOGICAL
ACGHIILLOOOP OPHIOLOGICAL
ACGHIILLOOST HISTOLOGICAL

ACGHIILMNPTY LYMPHANGITIC
ACGHIILNNORT CHLORINATING
ACGHIILNORTY TRICHOGYNIAL
ACGHIIOPPRRS SPIROGRAPHIC
ACGHIIPRSSST SPHRAGISTICS
ACGHIKNOOSTW WHAT'S COOKING??
ACGHILLMOOTY MYTHOLOGICAL
ACGHILLNOOOP PHONOLOGICAL
ACGHILLOOPRS OSCILLOGRAPH
ACGHILOPRSTY STYLOGRAPHIC
ACGHINOOPPRR PORNOGRAPHIC
ACGHIOOPSSTY PHAGOCYTOSIS
ACGHKLOPPUYY HAPPY-GO-LUCKY
ACGHOOOPPRSU COPROPHAGOUS
ACGHOPPRRTYY CRYPTOGRAPHY
ACGIIILLLOTY ILLOGICALITY
ACGIIINNOTTX INTOXICATING
ACGIIKKLNSTW WALKING STICK
ACGIILLLMNOO LIMNOLOGICAL
ACGIILLLOSTY LOGISTICALLY
ACGIILLLRTUY LITURGICALLY
ACGIILMNOSUU MUCILAGINOUS
ACGIILNOORST CRANIOLOGIST
ACGIILNPPSTU SUPPLICATING
ACGIIMMNOOST MONOGAMISTIC
ACGIINNNOOST CONSIGNATION
ACGIINNNORST CONSTRAINING
ACGIJNNOOSTU CONJUGATIONS
ACGIKLNORSSW WORKING CLASS
ACGILLLOOORY OROLOGICALLY
ACGILLMNNOOY GNOMONICALLY
ACGILNNNOTTU CONGLUTINANT
ACGILNOOSTUY CONTAGIOUSLY
ACGILNOPSUUY PUGNACIOUSLY
ACGIMMNNOSTU CONSUMMATING
ACGIMMOPRRSU PROGRAM MUSIC
ACGIMNNOORST MORNING COATS
ACGINOORRSTU CORRUGATIONS
ACGINOPPRRSY CROP-SPRAYING
ACGLLNOORSUY CLANGOROUSLY
ACGLMNNOOSUY AGONY COLUMNS
ACGLNOOPRSYY LARYNGOSCOPY
ACHHIILMNOPR PHILHARMONIC
ACHHIIMNOPPS CHAMPIONSHIP
ACHHIIMOSTYZ SCHIZOTHYMIA
ACHHILLMRTYY RHYTHMICALLY
ACHHILLOPTTY THALLOPHYTIC
ACHHILOOPRST HOLOPHRASTIC
ACHHILOPRSSS SCHOLARSHIPS
ACHHIOPPRSTU PHOSPHATURIC
ACHHNNOOOPRY ONYCHOPHORAN
ACHIIIINRSST TRICHINIASIS
ACHIIILMSTWY WHIMSICALITY
ACHIIIMNPSSU MUSICIANSHIP

ACHIIINRSTTY CHRISTIANITY
ACHIILLLOSTY HOLISTICALLY
ACHIILLNOSSU HALLUCINOSIS
ACHIILLORSTY HISTORICALLY
ACHIILNNOORT CHLORINATION
ACHIILNOPRST RHINOPLASTIC
ACHIIMNOPRST MISANTHROPIC
ACHIIPRSSTTY PSYCHIATRIST
ACHILLNOPTYY HYPNOTICALLY
ACHILLORSUVY CHIVALROUSLY
ACHILMORSTYY LACHRYMOSITY
ACHILOOPPRRS CORPORALSHIP
ACHIMNNORSSY ASYNCHRONISM
ACHINOOPTTUY AUTOHYPNOTIC
ACHINOPRSSTY CORNISH PASTY
ACHIOOPRRRST ARTHROSPORIC
ACHIOOPRRSUZ RHIZOCARPOUS
ACHIOPRRSSTU CURATORSHIPS
ACHIOPRSSSTY ASTROPHYSICS
ACHMMOPPSSTU STOMACH PUMPS
ACHNNOORSSUY ASYNCHRONOUS
ACHOOPRRRTTU PORT HARCOURT
ACIIIILMRSTT MILITARISTIC
ACIIIILNOSTV CIVILISATION
ACIIIILNOTVZ CIVILIZATION
ACIIILMNNOST NOMINALISTIC
ACIIILMNOPST IMPLICATIONS
ACIIILMNPTUY MUNICIPALITY
ACIIILNNNOST INCLINATIONS
ACIIILNOOSTT COALITIONIST,
  SOLICITATION
ACIIILNOPRTT TRIPLICATION
ACIIILNOTVVY CONVIVIALITY
ACIIILNPPRTY PRINCIPALITY
ACIIILQTUYZZ QUIZZICALITY
ACIIIMNNORRT INCRIMINATOR
ACIIIMNORSTV VICTORIANISM
ACIIINNOOTTX INTOXICATION
ACIIINOPSSUU INAUSPICIOUS
ACIIINOQSSTU ACQUISITIONS
ACIIJLNORSTU JOURNALISTIC
ACIIKKPRSSTU KICK UPSTAIRS
ACIILLMNOSTY MONISTICALLY
ACIILLNNOOPT NONPOLITICAL
ACIILLNOOSST COLONIALISTS,
  OSCILLATIONS
ACIILLNOPRVY PROVINCIALLY
ACIILLNORSTT SCINTILLATOR
ACIILLNRTUUV VINICULTURAL
ACIILLOOPSTY ISOTOPICALLY
ACIILLOQTUXY QUIXOTICALLY
ACIILLOSSUVY LASCIVIOUSLY
ACIILLPRSTUY PURISTICALLY
ACIILLRTTUUV VITICULTURAL

ACIILMMNOOSS COMMISSIONAL
ACIILMNNOOTU COLUMNIATION
ACIILMNOOPST COMPILATIONS
ACIILMNORSTU MATRICLINOUS
ACIILMOPRTUV VICTORIA PLUM
ACIILNNOOOST COLONISATION
ACIILNNOOOTZ COLONIZATION
ACIILNNOOSTU INOCULATIONS,
  INOSCULATION
ACIILNNOTTUY CONTINUALITY
ACIILNOORSST CONSISTORIAL
ACIILNOPPSTU SUPPLICATION
ACIILNOPRSTU PATRICLINOUS
ACIILNORSSSS NAIL SCISSORS
ACIILNOSTUUY INCAUTIOUSLY
ACIILOPSSUUY AUSPICIOUSLY
ACIILPRSTTUU APICULTURIST
ACIILRSTTUUV AVICULTURIST
ACIIMNOPRTTU PROTACTINIUM
ACIIMNORSSTT ROMANTICISTS
ACIINNNOOTTU CONTINUATION
ACIINNOOPSTT CONSTIPATION
ACIINNORSTTU INCRUSTATION
ACILLLLOOQUY COLLOQUIALLY
ACILLMOOOTYZ ZOOTOMICALLY
ACILLNNOSTYY SYNTONICALLY
ACILLNOOOPST LOCAL OPTIONS
ACILLNOPSTYY SYNOPTICALLY
ACILLOOQSUUY LOQUACIOUSLY
ACILMMNNOOTT NONCOMMITTAL
ACILMNOOOPST COSMOPOLITAN
ACILMOOPPRST PROTOPLASMIC
ACILMOOPRRRY PRIMARY COLOR
ACILNNOOOORTT CONTORTIONAL
ACILNNOOOSST CONSOLATIONS
ACILNNOOSTTU CONSULTATION
ACILNNORTTUY NOCTURNALITY
ACILNOOORSTU ICONOLATROUS
ACILOOPPRSTT PROTOPLASTIC
ACILOPPRSTUY SUPPLICATORY
ACILORSSSTTU TOURIST CLASS
ACIMMNNOOSTU CONSUMMATION
ACIMMNOOSTTU COMMUTATIONS
ACIMNOOPPSST COMPASS POINT
ACIMNOOPSTTU COMPUTATIONS
ACINNNOOOSTT CONNOTATIONS
ACINNOOPRSTT CONTRAPTIONS
ACINNOORSTTT IN CONTRAST TO
ACINOOOPRRRT INCORPORATOR
ACINOOOPRRST CORPORATIONS
ACINOOOPRSTV PROVOCATIONS
ACINOOPRRSST CONSPIRATORS
ACINOOPRRSTT STRIP CARTOON
ACIOOPPRSSTT POTATO CRISPS

ACIORRRSSTTU CIRROSTRATUS
ACKLNNOOPRTY CRYOPLANKTON
ACLLRRSTTUUY STRUCTURALLY
ACMNOOOTTXYY CYTOTAXONOMY
ADDDDEEEHLMU MUDDLE-HEADED
ADDDDEEFFILL FIDDLE-FADDLE
ADDDEEEHNOOW WOODENHEADED
ADDDEIILLLLY DILLYDALLIED
ADDEEEEGGRST DESEGREGATED
ADDEEEGIMNST DEMAGNETISED
ADDEEEGIMNTZ DEMAGNETIZED
ADDEEEIIRSTV DESIDERATIVE
ADDEEEIMPRTT PREMEDITATED
ADDEEEIORRTT DETERIORATED
ADDEEELLNTTW WELL-ATTENDED
ADDEEELRRTTY RED-LETTER DAY
ADDEEENPRSSV DEPRAVEDNESS
ADDEEEOPPRSV EAVESDROPPED
ADDEEFFNRSTU UNDERSTAFFED
ADDEEFHLMORY FORMALDEHYDE
ADDEEFHOORSW FORESHADOWED
ADDEEFINOORR FOREORDAINED
ADDEEFLLOPST SOFT-PEDALLED
ADDEEFLNRSSU DREADFULNESS
ADDEEGHILNNS SINGLE-HANDED
ADDEEGILNNST DISENTANGLED
ADDEEGINPPSU PEASE PUDDING
ADDEEGINRRSS READDRESSING
ADDEEHHIMRTY HEMIHYDRATED
ADDEEHLLOOWY WOOLLY-HEADED
ADDEEHLNNOPY OPEN-HANDEDLY
ADDEEHOORSVW OVERSHADOWED
ADDEEIIMMNNO DEMIMONDAINE
ADDEEIIMNRST ADMINISTERED
ADDEEIIMNSST DISSEMINATED
ADDEEIINORST DESIDERATION
ADDEEIMMNRST MASTERMINDED
ADDEEIMNOPRT PREDOMINATED
ADDEEINOPRST DEPREDATIONS
ADDEEJLLSTUW WELL-ADJUSTED
ADDEELNOSSTT STADDLESTONE
ADDEEMNORSTT DEMONSTRATED
ADDEFGIILLNN LANDING FIELD
ADDEFGILRRSU DISREGARDFUL
ADDEFHILNOOS OLD-FASHIONED
ADDEFIIILQSU DISQUALIFIED
ADDEFIIISSST DISSATISFIED
ADDEFLNNNOUW NEWFOUNDLAND
ADDEGGIINRRS DISREGARDING
ADDEGHHHILNY HIGH-HANDEDLY
ADDEGHNORSTU DREADNOUGHTS
ADDEGIINORSS DISORGANISED
ADDEGIINORSZ DISORGANIZED
ADDEHHLORRSU HARD SHOULDER

ADDEHINOSSWW WINDOW SHADES
ADDEHMNORSUY HYDROMEDUSAN
ADDEIILMSSTU DISSIMULATED
ADDEIINOPPST DISAPPOINTED
ADDEILMNOOTU DEMODULATION
ADDEILMNOPRS PROMISED LAND
ADDEIMMMRSUY MIDSUMMER DAY
ADDEIMNNORRW NARROW-MINDED
ADDFIILLNSUY DISDAINFULLY
ADDGHIMNOORU ROUGH DIAMOND
ADDGIILNSSTU STUDDINGSAIL
ADDGILLNOOPP PADDLING POOL
ADDHIIILMOPP AMPHIDIPLOID
ADDIIILLNUVY INDIVIDUALLY
ADDIIINORTUV INDIVIDUATOR
ADEEEEGINRTV DEGENERATIVE
ADEEEEGLRSST EASTER-LEDGES
ADEEEEHHNRRT HERE AND THERE
ADEEEFFORRST REAFFORESTED
ADEEEFGIRRRT REFRIGERATED
ADEEEFIMTUUX FAUTE DE MIEUX
ADEEEFMNSSTU DEAF-MUTENESS
ADEEEGGILNRT LATEENRIGGED
ADEEEGGINNRT DEGENERATING
ADEEEGGLLNOS GOLDEN EAGLES
ADEEEGGNRSTU UNSEGREGATED
ADEEEGHLMMRS SLEDGEHAMMER
ADEEEGIMNRST DEMAGNETISER,
  DISAGREEMENT
ADEEEGIMNRTZ DEMAGNETIZER
ADEEEGINNORT DEGENERATION
ADEEEGINNRST TRAGEDIENNES
ADEEEGINOPSS PAEDOGENESIS
ADEEEGINRRTT REDINTEGRATE
ADEEEGLNORTU OUTGENERALED
ADEEEGMNNNRT ENDANGERMENT
ADEEEGMNNRST DERANGEMENTS
ADEEEHHLORTW WHOLE-HEARTED
ADEEEHIMNRTT HEREDITAMENT
ADEEEHINSSSV ADHESIVENESS
ADEEEHINSSTT ANESTHETISED
ADEEEHINSTTZ ANESTHETIZED
ADEEEHIRRTTT TETRAHEDRITE
ADEEEHLLORSS LEASEHOLDERS
ADEEEHLNNRRT NETHERLANDER
ADEEEHMNPRSS HAMPEREDNESS
ADEEEHMORSTV MOHAVE DESERT
ADEEEHPRSSST SPREADSHEETS
ADEEEIILNPTX EXPEDIENTIAL
ADEEEIIMMNRT ANTE MERIDIEM
ADEEEIIMMRST SEMIDIAMETER
ADEEEIIMNRTT INTERMEDIATE
ADEEEILLMMOS MADEMOISELLE
ADEEEILMNORT RADIOELEMENT

ADEEEILNPRRT INTERPLEADER
ADEEEILNRSTX EXTERNALISED
ADEEEILNRTXZ EXTERNALIZED
ADEEEIMNRTTX EXTERMINATED
ADEEEINPRSTT PREDESTINATE
ADEEEIOPPSTX EXOPEPTIDASE
ADEEEKLLNOST ENDOSKELETAL
ADEEEKLRRSST DEERSTALKERS
ADEEELLMNNRW WELL-MANNERED
ADEEELLNSSWY WENSLEYDALES
ADEEELNRSTTU LAUNDERETTES
ADEEELOPPRST TRADESPEOPLE
ADEEEMNORSST MODERATENESS
ADEEEMORRSTV OVERMASTERED
ADEEENOPPRRT PREPONDERATE
ADEEENPPRRSS PREPAREDNESS
ADEEENPRRTUV PERADVENTURE
ADEEEOPPRRSV EAVESDROPPER
ADEEEQRSSTTU SEQUESTRATED
ADEEFFIILNRT DIFFERENTIAL
ADEEFGHILNRS HARD FEELINGS
ADEEFGILLSSS FIELD GLASSES
ADEEFGINNRRS RANGE FINDERS
ADEEFGINNRST FREESTANDING
ADEEFHLOPSST FELDSPATHOSE
ADEEFHOORRSW FORESHADOWER
ADEEFILOPRRT PROLIFERATED
ADEEFLLORUVW WELL-FAVOURED
ADEEFNOPRRTU UNPERFORATED
ADEEFOOPRRRS PROOFREADERS
ADEEFOOPRRTW WATERPROOFED
ADEEGGHIRSTT STRAIGHTEDGE
ADEEGGILNRTU DEREGULATING
ADEEGGIQRRSU SQUARE-RIGGED
ADEEGGIRRTTU REGURGITATED
ADEEGHHILRTT LIGHT-HEARTED
ADEEGHIMMOPR MIMEOGRAPHED
ADEEGHINNPPR APPREHENDING
ADEEGHINNRRT HEARTRENDING
ADEEGHINRSTT STRAIGHTENED
ADEEGHIRRSST SIGHT-READERS
ADEEGHMOPRRS DEMOGRAPHERS
ADEEGHOPRRSW HEDGE SPARROW
ADEEGHPRSTTU STEPDAUGHTER
ADEEGIIMNNRR REMAINDERING
ADEEGIINRSTT DISINTEGRATE
ADEEGIINSTTV INVESTIGATED
ADEEGIKNNRRT KINDERGARTEN
ADEEGIKNRRST RING-STREAKED
ADEEGILMNNRY MEANDERINGLY
ADEEGILNORTU DEREGULATION
ADEEGINNORUV ENDEAVOURING
ADEEGINORRTT INTERROGATED
ADEEGMNNRRTU UNDERGARMENT

ADEEGNPRTUUX UNEXPURGATED
ADEEGNRRSSST TRANSGRESSED
ADEEGORRTTXY DEXTROGYRATE
ADEEHHIKNRRS HEADSHRINKER
ADEEHHLORRSS SHAREHOLDERS
ADEEHHNNPTUY UNHYPHENATED
ADEEHIILRRTY HEREDITARILY
ADEEHILMNOOT ENDOTHELIOMA
ADEEHILMORTT MAITRE D'HOTEL
ADEEHILNPRRS PHILANDERERS
ADEEHIMNPPRS MISAPPREHEND
ADEEHINORSTU HOUSE-TRAINED
ADEEHIRRRSSS HAIRDRESSERS
ADEEHKLORSST STAKEHOLDERS
ADEEHLLLMOPR PHELLODERMAL
ADEEHLLNOSSW HALLOWEDNESS
ADEEHLMMOTUY MEALY-MOUTHED
ADEEHMNNOSSS HANDSOMENESS
ADEEHMOPRTTY DERMATOPHYTE
ADEEHNOPSTTY SPOTTED HYENA
ADEEHNORSTTY STONY-HEARTED
ADEEHOPRRTTW THE TOP DRAWER
ADEEHORSTTTU STOUTHEARTED
ADEEIIILMRST DEMILITARISE
ADEEIIILMRTZ DEMILITARIZE
ADEEIIILMTTV DELIMITATIVE
ADEEIIILORST EDITORIALISE
ADEEIIILORTZ EDITORIALIZE
ADEEIIJNOORR RIO DE JANEIRO
ADEEIILMMNPT IMPEDIMENTAL
ADEEIILMNNSS MAIDENLINESS
ADEEIILMNOST MATINÉE IDOLS
ADEEIILMTTVY MEDITATIVELY
ADEEIILNNRST INTERNALISED
ADEEIILNNRTZ INTERNALIZED
ADEEIILNPRST PRESIDENTIAL
ADEEIILOPRST DEPILATORIES
ADEEIILRTVVY DERIVATIVELY
ADEEIIMNNOTV DENOMINATIVE
ADEEIIMNRRRT INTERMARRIED
ADEEIIMNRRTY INTERMEDIARY
ADEEIINORSTT DISORIENTATE
ADEEIINOSSTV VIDEO NASTIES
ADEEIINPRSSS DISPENSARIES
ADEEIINRRSTY RESIDENTIARY
ADEEIKLMSTTT ATTESTED MILK
ADEEILLMRSSV SILVER MEDALS
ADEEILLNNRST LANTERNSLIDE
ADEEILLOSTVW OLD WIVES' TALE
ADEEILLSTTUW WELL-SITUATED
ADEEILMMORTY IMMODERATELY
ADEEILMNOPRT REDEMPTIONAL
ADEEILMPRSST SLIPSTREAMED
ADEEILNOPPRT LEPIDOPTERAN

ADEEIILNOPRSS PERSONALISED
ADEEILNOPRSZ PERSONALIZED
ADEEIILNOPRTT INTERPOLATED
ADEEILNRRSTY RESTRAINEDLY
ADEEILRRSSVV SLAVE DRIVERS
ADEEIMMNORSS MISDEMEANORS
ADEEIMMNORSU MISDEMEANOUR
ADEEIMNNRSTT DETERMINANTS
ADEEIMNOPRST IMPERSONATED
ADEEIMNRSTUV MISADVENTURE
ADEEIMOPRRTT PREMEDITATOR
ADEEIMSSSTTY SYSTEMATISED
ADEEIMSSTTYZ SYSTEMATIZED
ADEEINNOOPRU INDO-EUROPEAN
ADEEINNRRSTU UNRESTRAINED
ADEEINNRSSST STRAINEDNESS
ADEEINNSSSTU UNSTEADINESS
ADEEINORRSST RAISON D'ETRES
ADEEINRRSSUY DAY NURSERIES
ADEEIOPPRRTX EXPROPRIATED
ADEEJMNRSTTU READJUSTMENT
ADEEKLLORRST ROLLER SKATED
ADEEKLOPRSSU LOUDSPEAKERS
ADEEKNORSSYY DONKEY'S YEARS
ADEELLMMNRTU UNTRAMMELLED
ADEELLORSSTW WELL-ASSORTED
ADEELMNOSTTT OLD TESTAMENT
ADEELMORSSTU SOMERSAULTED
ADEELOPSTTUX EXPOSTULATED
ADEEMNNPRTUY UNDERPAYMENT
ADEEMNOPPRRS NAMEDROPPERS
ADEEMNORRSTT REMONSTRATED
ADEENNOORRST ANDROSTERONE
ADEENNOPPRRT PREPONDERANT
ADEENOPSSTTU UP-TO-DATENESS
ADEENORSSTUW SWEET-AND-SOUR
ADEFFIMMNORS FRAMES OF MIND
ADEFGHHIOORT HAIR OF THE DOG
ADEFGHILNSUW LUDWIGSHAFEN
ADEFGHILRSTY FARSIGHTEDLY
ADEFGIILLNPY PLAYING FIELD
ADEFGIIMMNRX MIXED FARMING
ADEFGILNOPST SOFT-PEDALING
ADEFGILNRSSY LADY'S FINGERS
ADEFGINOOPRR PROOFREADING
ADEFGINRRSTU TRANSFIGURED
ADEFHILLTTWY HALF-WITTEDLY
ADEFHINRRSTY FIRE HYDRANTS
ADEFHINRSSSW DWARFISHNESS
ADEFIIILNNOT DEFINITIONAL
ADEFIIILQRSU DISQUALIFIER
ADEFIILNOSTT DEFLATIONIST
ADEFIILNPRSU FREUDIAN SLIP
ADEFIINRSTTU UNSTRATIFIED

ADEFILORRSST FIRST SEA LORD
ADEFILOSSSTV FAST DISSOLVE
ADEFIMNOORST DEFORMATIONS
ADEFLLNRTUUY FRAUDULENTLY
ADEGGHIILLNT LEADING LIGHT
ADEGGHIINRST SIGHT-READING
ADEGGINNORRR ORGAN GRINDER
ADEGGLNRSSSU SLUGGARDNESS
ADEGHHILNNPS HELPING HANDS
ADEGHHILOPRT LITHOGRAPHED
ADEGHHIMNNRT RIGHT-HAND MEN
ADEGHHINRRST RIGHT-HANDERS
ADEGHHIPRSST SHARP-SIGHTED
ADEGHHOOPPRT PHOTOGRAPHED
ADEGHHOPRRRY HYDROGRAPHER
ADEGHIILNNPR PHILANDERING
ADEGHIIMNNUZ DEHUMANIZING
ADEGHIINRRSS HAIRDRESSING
ADEGHINORRST HORSE-TRADING
ADEGHIORRTTW WITH REGARD TO
ADEGHLLNORST STRANGLEHOLD
ADEGHLNORSTY HEADSTRONGLY
ADEGHMNORRST GRANDMOTHERS
ADEGHNOORRTY HYDROGENATOR
ADEGHNOPRSTU SHARP-TONGUED
ADEGIIILNTVZ DEVITALIZING
ADEGIIJNOPRZ JEOPARDIZING
ADEGIIILLMNSY MISLEADINGLY
ADEGIIILLNNOT DIALLING TONE
ADEGIILNNTU DENTILINGUAL
ADEGIILMNTTY MEDITATINGLY
ADEGIILNNOST DIALING TONES
ADEGIILNNRRT INTERLARDING
ADEGIILNNRSW LINE DRAWINGS
ADEGIILNORSS DIGRESSIONAL
ADEGIILNPRSY DESPAIRINGLY
ADEGIIMNNNOT DENOMINATING
ADEGIIMNNPRR REPRIMANDING
ADEGIIMNOTTV DEMOTIVATING
ADEGIINNOPRR PREORDAINING
ADEGIINNOSST DESIGNATIONS
ADEGIINOORRT GRANODIORITE
ADEGIINORRSS DISORGANISER
ADEGIINORRSZ DISORGANIZER
ADEGIKNNRSTU UNDERTAKINGS
ADEGILNNPRUY UNDERPLAYING
ADEGILNNRUUV UNDERVALUING
ADEGILNOPPTU DEPOPULATING
ADEGILOORRTY DEROGATORILY
ADEGIMNNOPPR NAMEDROPPING
ADEGINNRSTTU UNDERSTATING
ADEGJLMNSTTU LAST JUDGMENT
ADEHHILLPPSU PHILADELPHUS
ADEHHIMOORRS HAEMORRHOIDS

ADEHHOPRRTYY HYDROTHERAPY
ADEHIILNSTTT DILETTANTISH
ADEHIILOPSST HOSPITALISED
ADEHIILOPSTZ HOSPITALIZED
ADEHIINNRSTY HYDRASTININE
ADEHIIPRRSTT THIRD PARTIES
ADEHILMNOPSU SULPHONAMIDE
ADEHILMNORSU MALNOURISHED
ADEHIMMPPSUY HAPPY MEDIUMS
ADEHINQRRSTU HINDQUARTERS
ADEHIOOPRSTT ORTHOPAEDIST
ADEHIORSSTTW SHORT-WAISTED
ADEHLLLMORSS SMALLHOLDERS
ADEHLLLORSST STALLHOLDERS
ADEHLMNOOPSU MONADELPHOUS
ADEHLNNOPSTY SHETLAND PONY
ADEHOOPSTTTT PHOTOSTATTED
ADEHOPRSSSTW SHOP STEWARDS
ADEIIILMNOTT DELIMITATION
ADEIIILORSTT EDITORIALIST
ADEIIIMNOSTV DEVIATIONISM
ADEIIINNORRV VIN ORDINAIRE
ADEIIINOSTTV DEVIATIONIST
ADEIIINSTTTU ATTITUDINISE
ADEIIINTTTUZ ATTITUDINIZE
ADEIILLMNOST MEDALLIONIST
ADEIILLNPRUV LIVERPUDLIAN
ADEIILLOSSTY DISLOYALTIES
ADEIILLSTUVV VAUDEVILLIST
ADEIILMMNPRT MALIMPRINTED
ADEIILMMORST IMMORTALISED
ADEIILMMORTZ IMMORTALIZED
ADEIILMNSTTT DILETTANTISM
ADEIILNNORTY INORDINATELY
ADEIILNOOPST DESPOLIATION
ADEIILNOPRTV PROVIDENTIAL
ADEIILNORSST DILATORINESS
ADEIIMMNNRSU INDIAN SUMMER
ADEIIMMNOORT IMMODERATION
ADEIIMNNNOOT DENOMINATION
ADEIIMNNOSTU MOUNTAINSIDE
ADEIIMNNRSTT DISTRAINMENT
ADEIIMNOOTTV DEMOTIVATION
ADEIIMNOPRST POSTMERIDIAN
ADEIIMNOPRXY PYRIDOXAMINE
ADEIIMNORSST DISSEMINATOR
ADEIIMORSTTU AUDIOMETRIST
ADEIIMRSSTTX TAXIDERMISTS
ADEIINNNOSTT INDENTATIONS
ADEIINNOPSST DISPENSATION
ADEIINNORRSS ORDINARINESS
ADEIINNOSSTT DESTINATIONS
ADEIINOOPRST DISOPERATION
ADEIINOPPRST DISAPPOINTER

ADEIINOPRSTV DEPRIVATIONS
ADEIINORRSVY DIVERSIONARY
ADEIINORSSTT DISSERTATION
ADEIINORSTTX EXTRADITIONS
ADEIINOSTTUV ADVENTITIOUS
ADEIIOOOPRST RADIOISOTOPE
ADEILLNOPPRT DIPROPELLANT
ADEILLNPRTUY PRUDENTIALLY
ADEILLOSSVWW SWALLOW DIVES
ADEILLPPRSSY LADY'S-SLIPPER
ADEILMNNNSTU DISANNULMENT
ADEILNOOPPTU DEPOPULATION
ADEILNORRSTV DORSIVENTRAL
ADEIMMNNOPSU PANDEMONIUMS
ADEIMMOPRSUY PRASEODYMIUM
ADEIMNNOORST DENOMINATORS
ADEIMNOOPRRT PREDOMINATOR
ADEIMOOPRSTZ SPERMATOZOID
ADEINOOPRSTT DEPORTATIONS
ADEINOPRSSTY DISPENSATORY
ADEINOPRTTTY POTTY-TRAINED
ADEJLORSSSTU LOSS ADJUSTER
ADEJMNNORSTU ADJOURNMENTS
ADEKOOPRSTVZ PETROZAVODSK
ADELLNORSSUY SLANDEROUSLY
ADELLOOPRRST PETRODOLLARS
ADELNOORRSTV DORSOVENTRAL
ADELOOPRRSST POSTAL ORDERS
ADEMNNOPSTWY DOWN PAYMENTS
ADEMNOORRSTT DEMONSTRATOR
ADENNOPRRSST TRANSPONDERS
ADENNORSSTUW UNTOWARDNESS
ADFFGIILNNTU FAULT-FINDING
ADFFGNORSSTU GROUND STAFFS
ADFGIILNORTU FLUORIDATING
ADFGIINQRSSU FIRING SQUADS
ADFGILNNOSST SOFT LANDINGS
ADFGILNQSSUY FLYING SQUADS
ADFHIMNOOORS MAIDS OF HONOR
ADFHIMNOOORU MAID OF HONOUR
ADFHMNOOOTTU FOOT-AND-MOUTH
ADFIIILNNOST DISINFLATION
ADFIIILNOSTU FLUIDISATION
ADFIIILNOTUZ FLUIDIZATION
ADFIILNOORTU FLUORIDATION
ADFIILOSSTUY FASTIDIOUSLY
ADGGIIMNNORZ GORMANDIZING
ADGGILNNNOST LONG-STANDING
ADGHIINNSTTW WITHSTANDING
ADGHIINOPRSZ RHAPSODIZING
ADGHIKLNORSW WORLDSHAKING
ADGHILLLMNOS SMALLHOLDING
ADGHNOOOPRTY ODONTOGRAPHY
ADGIIIIMNNTT INTIMIDATING

ADGIIIINOSTT DIGITISATION
ADGIIIINOTTZ DIGITIZATION
ADGIILLNNOTU LONGITUDINAL
ADGIILNNPRST LANDING STRIP
ADGIILNRSTTU STRIDULATING
ADGIILOORSST RADIOLOGISTS
ADGIINOPPRSV DISAPPROVING
ADGIKNNORRRU ROARING DRUNK
ADGILNNOSTUY ASTOUNDINGLY
ADGIMNNOOOST SANTO DOMINGO
ADGIMNNOORST STANDING ROOM
ADGIMNOORRSW DRAWING ROOMS
ADGINNOOOPRT GONADOTROPIN
ADGINOPRSSTT TRADING POSTS
ADGLNNOORTUW LONG-DRAWN-OUT
ADGOOOPRSSTU GASTROPODOUS
ADHIIIMMRSTT MITHRIDATISM
ADHIIMOPRSST DIASTROPHISM
ADHILLNOSTUY OUTLANDISHLY
ADHILMMOOPTY LYMPHOMATOID
ADHLNOOOOPRT ODONTOPHORAL
ADHOOOPRRSTU ARTHROPODOUS
ADIIIIMNNOTT INTIMIDATION
ADIIIINNOSTV DIVINISATION
ADIIIINNOTVZ DIVINIZATION
ADIIIILLMRSSY DISSIMILARLY
ADIIIILLNOSTT DISTILLATION
ADIIINORSTTT TRADITIONIST
ADIILLMOPRRY PRIMORDIALLY
ADIILLNOQRSU QUADRILLIONS
ADIILLNRSTUY INDUSTRIALLY
ADIILLOPSTUV POSTDILUVIAL
ADIILLORSTTY DISTILLATORY
ADIILMOPSSTT DIPLOMATISTS
ADIILMORSSTU DISSIMULATOR
ADIILNOORSTT DISTORTIONAL
ADIILNOPSTUV POSTDILUVIAN
ADIILNORSTTU STRIDULATION
ADIINOPSSTTU DISPUTATIONS
ADIIOPSSTTUU DISPUTATIOUS
ADILLOORSTUY IDOLATROUSLY
ADILORRSTTUY STRIDULATORY
ADILORSSSTUY DISASTROUSLY
ADLNOOPRSSWY PLAYS ON WORDS
AEEEEGHLPRST TELEGRAPHESE
AEEEEGHMORTT HETEROGAMETE
AEEEEGINRRTV REGENERATIVE
AEEEEGNNRRTU UNREGENERATE
AEEEEHHPRRSS SHEEPSHEARER
AEEEEIMNNRST SEINE-ET-MARNE
AEEEEKLNNNOV ON AN EVEN KEEL
AEEEELPRRSSS PRESS RELEASE
AEEEFFILMNTY EFFEMINATELY
AEEEFFLOPPST TOFFEE APPLES

AEEEFHINRRTT THEREINAFTER
AEEEFIKLNPTT PALETTE KNIFE
AEEEFILNPRRT PREFERENTIAL
AEEEFIMNRTTV FERMENTATIVE
AEEEFLNRSSSS FEARLESSNESS
AEEEFMNORSSS FEARSOMENESS
AEEEGGINNRRT REGENERATING
AEEEGHLPRRST TELEGRAPHERS
AEEEGHORRSTT THEATERGOERS,
  THEATREGOERS
AEEEGIILNRST GENERALITIES
AEEEGIKLNNNW WANKEL ENGINE
AEEEGILNNRRV LINE-ENGRAVER
AEEEGILNOPTV NEGATIVE POLE
AEEEGIMNNSTV ENVISAGEMENT
AEEEGINNORRT REGENERATION
AEEEGINNSSTV NEGATIVENESS
AEEEGINORTTV REVEGETATION
AEEEGIRRSTTV TERGIVERSATE
AEEEGLMNNNTT ENTANGLEMENT
AEEEGLMNNRST ENLARGEMENTS
AEEEGMMNORTT MAGNETOMETER
AEEEGMNNRSTT ESTRANGEMENT
AEEEHHNNNPRT PHENANTHRENE
AEEEHHNOTTXY ETHOXYETHANE
AEEEHIKNSSTV SNEAK THIEVES
AEEEHILMPRTY EPHEMERALITY
AEEEHILNNSSV HEAVENLINESS
AEEEHILNRSST LEATHERINESS
AEEEHINPPRSV APPREHENSIVE
AEEEHINPRSST PARENTHESISE
AEEEHINPRSTZ PARENTHESIZE
AEEEHLMPPRST PAMPHLETEERS
AEEEHLNRSSTT NETTLE RASHES
AEEEHLORSTUX HETEROSEXUAL
AEEEHLPRRSWY PRAYER WHEELS
AEEEHLRRSTTY HARLEY STREET
AEEEHMORTTTX METHOTREXATE
AEEEHQRRRTTU THREE-QUARTER
AEEEIILMNORT MAINE-ET-LOIRE
AEEEIILNPRTX EXPERIENTIAL
AEEEIILNRRST INERTIA REELS
AEEEIINNNSTT SAINT-ÉTIENNE
AEEEIKNNORST ENTEROKINASE
AEEEIKNPRSVW SNEAK PREVIEW
AEEEIILNPRTT INTERPELLATE
AEEEILMNPRTX EXPERIMENTAL
AEEEILNOORST SAONE-ET-LOIRE
AEEEILNRSSTT LITERATENESS
AEEEIMNRRTUV REMUNERATIVE
AEEEIMOPRRTV EVAPORIMETER
AEEEIMORSTTV OVERESTIMATE
AEEEINNORTTX EXENTERATION
AEEEINNRRSTT ENTERTAINERS

AEEEINPRSTTV PRESENTATIVE
AEEEINRRTTUX EXTRAUTERINE
AEEEIPRRSTVV PRESERVATIVE
AEEEKLLPRSSW SLEEPWALKERS
AEEEKLRRSTTW STREETWALKER
AEEELLORSTTT TEETOTALLERS
AEEELMNORSYY ELEEMOSYNARY
AEEELNOPPSVY PAY ENVELOPES
AEEELRSSTTUV STREET VALUES
AEEEMMNPRSTT TEMPERAMENTS
AEEEMMNRSSTU MEASUREMENTS
AEEEMNNSTTTW NEW TESTAMENT
AEEEMNRSSTTT RESTATEMENTS
AEEEMPRRSTTU TEMPERATURES
AEEEMRSSSSST SEAMSTRESSES
AEEFFGHIRRTU FATHER FIGURE
AEEFFGILNORT FREE-FLOATING
AEEFFGRSSTTU SUFFRAGETTES
AEEFFHKOORST FOR THE SAKE OF
AEEFFILMRSTU FEATURE FILMS
AEEFFGIKRRSTU FIGURE SKATER
AEEFGILNORRT FORETRIANGLE
AEEFGILNPRST FINGERPLATES
AEEFGINRRRST REFRIGERANTS
AEEFGIORRRRT REFRIGERATOR
AEEFGLNRSSTU GRATEFULNESS
AEEFHHORSSTU HOUSEFATHERS
AEEFHIKNRSSS FREAKISHNESS
AEEFHILNRSST FATHERLINESS
AEEFHIOORRST RAISE THE ROOF
AEEFHLLOOSTW FOLLOW THE SEA
AEEFHLLRRSTU FULLER'S EARTH
AEEFHLMNSSSU SHAMEFULNESS
AEEFHLMORRTW FLAME-THROWER
AEEFHLLOOSTTT ATHLETE'S FOOT
AEEFHMNORRWY ANYWHERE FROM
AEEFHOOPRRTW WEATHERPROOF
AEEFHORSTTTU FOURTH ESTATE
AEEFIILMPPRR PREAMPLIFIER
AEEFIINRRSTT FRATERNITIES
AEEFIKLLMOTT MAKE LITTLE OF
AEEFILOPRSTU PETALIFEROUS
AEEFIMNNORTT FERMENTATION
AEEFIMOPRRTV PERFORMATIVE
AEEFINNORSTT FENESTRATION
AEEFLMNORSTT FORESTALMENT, MAN
  OF LETTERS
AEEFLNSSSTTU TASTEFULNESS
AEEFLNSSSTUW WASTEFULNESS
AEEFLOPQRSUW PASQUEFLOWER
AEEFLRRSSSTT SELF-STARTERS
AEEFNORRSSVW WARS OF NERVES
AEEGGGINNNSS ENGAGINGNESS
AEEGGHILNPRT TELEGRAPHING

AEEGGIILNNRZ GENERALIZING
AEEGGIILNNVZ EVANGELIZING
AEEGGILNOSST GENEALOGISTS
AEEGGILRSSVY AGGRESSIVELY
AEEGGIMMNOST GEOMAGNETISM
AEEGGINNTTTW WETTING AGENT
AEEGGIQRRRSU SQUARE-RIGGER
AEEGHHILOPRR HELIOGRAPHER
AEEGHHISTVWY HEAVYWEIGHTS
AEEGHHNOPRRT ETHNOGRAPHER
AEEGHHOPRRTY HETEROGRAPHY
AEEGHILLMMRT HELLGRAMMITE
AEEGHILMNOPR GERMANOPHILE
AEEGHILNNRTY HEARTENINGLY
AEEGHILNORTW WATERING HOLE
AEEGHILORRUV HELIOGRAVURE
AEEGHINOPSST PATHOGENESIS
AEEGHINPTTVY HEAVY PETTING
AEEGHINRRSTT STRAIGHTENER
AEEGHIPPRSTW PAPERWEIGHTS
AEEGHIPRSSTW STAGE WHISPER
AEEGHLNOPRSY SELENOGRAPHY
AEEGHLOORRTW WOOLGATHERER
AEEGHMOOPRRT METEOROGRAPH
AEEGHMOORSTU HETEROGAMOUS
AEEGHNOOPRTV PHOTOENGRAVE
AEEGHNOPRRST STENOGRAPHER
AEEGHOOPSSSU OESOPHAGUSES
AEEGHOPPRRRT PETROGRAPHER
AEEGHOPRRSTY STEREOGRAPHY
AEEGIIILLLST ILLEGALITIES
AEEGIIILLMTT ILLEGITIMATE
AEEGIIILMSTT LEGITIMATISE
AEEGIIILMTTZ LEGITIMATIZE
AEEGIILLMTTY LEGITIMATELY
AEEGIILNNORS LEGIONNAIRES
AEEGIILNNPSS PALINGENESIS
AEEGIINNNRTT ENTERTAINING
AEEGIINNRTVW INTERWEAVING
AEEGIJNNRTUV REJUVENATING
AEEGIKLLNPSW SLEEPWALKING
AEEGIKLNSTTW SWEET-TALKING
AEEGIKMNPRRT PARKING METER
AEEGIKNNNSSS SNEAKINGNESS
AEEGIKNRSTUY KEY SIGNATURE
AEEGILLRSSST LEGISLATRESS
AEEGILLRSSTU LEGISLATURES
AEEGILMNNRST REALIGNMENTS
AEEGILNNPSSS PLEASINGNESS
AEEGILNNRTTY ENTREATINGLY
AEEGIMNNOSTT SEGMENTATION
AEEGIMNNRRTU REMUNERATING
AEEGIMSSSTTU GUESSTIMATES
AEEGINNNSSSU SANGUINENESS

AEEGINOPRRRT PEREGRINATOR
AEEGINPPRRTT PERPETRATING
AEEGINPPRTTU PERPETUATING
AEEGIOPRRSTV PREROGATIVES
AEEGKNOORSTU KERATOGENOUS
AEEGLLMNOOPR PROLEGOMENAL
AEEGLLMNOPSY SPLENOMEGALY
AEEGLLMNRUWZ MANGEL-WURZEL
AEEGLLPRRSSY PRESS GALLERY
AEEGLMNNORTV GOVERNMENTAL
AEEGLNNOORTT LOT-ET-GARONNE
AEEGMMNORTTY MAGNETOMETRY
AEEGPRRSSSSU SUPERGRASSES
AEEHHHILNSTY HEATHENISHLY
AEEHHHIKNSSTV SHEATH KNIVES
AEEHHILMNSTY MYELIN SHEATH
AEEHHILOPRTY HELIOTHERAPY
AEEHHILRSTWW WHEREWITHALS
AEEHHIPRSSTW WEATHER SHIPS
AEEHHLOSSTTW STEAL THE SHOW
AEEHHMORSSTV HARVEST HOMES
AEEHHNOPPRTY PHANEROPHYTE
AEEHIIMOOPSS HAEMOPOIESIS
AEEHIINORSTT ETHERISATION
AEEHIINORTTZ ETHERIZATION
AEEHIKLLLRSW KILLER WHALES
AEEHIKLNNPPT PINK ELEPHANT
AEEHILLMNNPS PANHELLENISM
AEEHILLNNPST PANHELLENIST
AEEHILLPPRRY PERIPHERALLY
AEEHILNSSSTT STEALTHINESS
AEEHILORRSTU TRAILER HOUSE
AEEHILRSTVWY WHITE SLAVERY
AEEHILSTUVXY EXHAUSTIVELY
AEEHIMNNORTT NITROMETHANE
AEEHINNOPPRS APPREHENSION
AEEHINOORSTU HETEROOUSIAN
AEEHINOPSSTV TOP-HEAVINESS
AEEHINSSSTTT ANESTHETISTS
AEEHIOPPSTTV STOVEPIPE HAT
AEEHIOPRSSTU HOUSE PARTIES
AEEHIORRRRST HAIR-RESTORER
AEEHIORSSSST AIRHOSTESSES
AEEHKMPRRSTY HYPERMARKETS
AEEHLLMMORWY YELLOWHAMMER
AEEHLLMNNOPY PHENOMENALLY
AEEHLLNORSTY LONELY HEARTS
AEEHLMNORSTT STENOTHERMAL
AEEHLMNRSSSS HARMLESSNESS
AEEHLMOSSSTV STEAM SHOVELS
AEEHLMOSSTTY STATELY HOMES
AEEHLNOPRTUY POLYURETHANE
AEEHLOPRSTTY HETEROPLASTY
AEEHLPPRRSTU PURPLE HEARTS

AEEHMMOOPRST METAMORPHOSE
AEEHMNORRTTU MOTHER NATURE
AEEHMORSSSTU HOUSEMASTERS
AEEHNNORRSTT NORTHEASTERN
AEEHNOPRSSTU HOUSEPARENTS
AEEHNORRSSTT NORTHEASTERS
AEEHNORSSTTU SOUTHEASTERN
AEEHOPRRSSTT STRATOSPHERE
AEEHORRSSSTU HOUSE ARRESTS
AEEIIILNQSTU INEQUALITIES
AEEIIJNOQSSU JE NE SAIS QUOI
AEEIIKLMNPRS MARLINESPIKE
AEEIIKMNNSSY KEYNESIANISM
AEEIIILLLRTTY ILLITERATELY
AEEIIILLNOSTV TELEVISIONAL
AEEIIILLNPSTT PESTILENTIAL
AEEIIILMMORRS MEMORIALISER
AEEIIILMMORRZ MEMORIALIZER
AEEIIILMNOOST EMOTIONALISE
AEEIIILMNOOTZ EMOTIONALIZE
AEEIIILMNSSST ESSENTIALISM
AEEIIILMPRTVY IMPERATIVELY
AEEIIILNNSSST INESSENTIALS
AEEIIILNRRSST LITERARINESS
AEEIIILNRRSSUV UNIVERSALISE
AEEIIILNRSUVZ UNIVERSALIZE
AEEIIILNSSSTT ESSENTIALIST
AEEIIILNSSTTY ESSENTIALITY
AEEIIILOPTTVX EXPLOITATIVE
AEEIIMNSSSTW SIAMESE TWINS
AEEIINNORSTT ETERNISATION
AEEIINNORTTZ ETERNIZATION
AEEIINNPRTTY PENITENTIARY
AEEIINNRRTTU INTRAUTERINE
AEEIINORRSTT REITERATIONS
AEEIIPRTTUVV VITUPERATIVE
AEEIJLOPRTVY PEJORATIVELY
AEEIJNNORTUV REJUVENATION
AEEIKMNSSTTU MINUTE STEAKS
AEEILLMNRTTT ILL-TREATMENT
AEEIILLNNPRTT INTERPELLANT
AEEIILLNOSSTT TESSELLATION
AEEIILLNQSTUY SEQUENTIALLY
AEEIILLNQTUVY EQUIVALENTLY
AEEIILLNRRSTT INTERSTELLAR
AEEIILLNRRTVY IRRELEVANTLY
AEEIILLNSSSUV ALLUSIVENESS
AEEIILLTTTTTT TITTLE-TATTLE
AEEILMNNNRSS MANNERLINESS
AEEIILMNNPTTU PENNULTIMATE
AEEILMNRSSST MASTERLINESS
AEEILNNNOSST NONESSENTIAL
AEEIILNNOPRTV OPEN INTERVAL
AEEIILNOPRRTT INTERPOLATER

AEEIILNOPRSSX EXPRESSIONAL
AEEIILNPRRRST LASER PRINTER
AEEIILPRSSTUV SUPERLATIVES
AEEIILPRSSUVY PERSUASIVELY
AEEIILRRSTTTU LITTERATEURS
AEEIMMNORSTT AMORTISEMENT
AEEIMMNORTTZ AMORTIZEMENT
AEEIMMNRSTTT MISTREATMENT
AEEIMMNSSTTT MISSTATEMENT
AEEIMNNORRTU REMUNERATION
AEEIMNNORSTT SENARMONTITE
AEEIMNNORSTU ENUMERATIONS,
  MOUNTAINEERS
AEEIMNORRTTX EXTERMINATOR
AEEIMRSSSTTY SYSTEMATISER
AEEIMRSSTTYZ SYSTEMATIZER
AEEINNOOPRTV NONOPERATIVE
AEEINNOPRSTT PRESENTATION
AEEINOORRSSU AERONEUROSIS
AEEINOORTTTX EXTORTIONATE
AEEINOPPRRTT PERPETRATION
AEEINOPPRTTU PERPETUATION
AEEINOPRRSTV PRESERVATION
AEEINOPRRSTY ARSENOPYRITE
AEEINORRRSVY REVERSIONARY
AEEINORRSSTV RESERVATIONS
AEEINRSSTTTV TRANSVESTITE
AEEINRSTTTUV STERNUTATIVE
AEEIORRSSTTV RESTORATIVES
AEEIPPRRTTTT PITTER-PATTER
AEEKLLORRRST ROLLER-SKATER
AEEKLLORRSST ROLLER SKATES
AEEKLMORRSTW METALWORKERS
AEEKMORRSSTT MASTERSTROKE
AEEKMPRRSSTU SUPERMARKETS
AEEKNPRRSSTU SUPERTANKERS
AEELLLMNOTVY MALEVOLENTLY
AEELLLORTTWY YELLOW RATTLE
AEELLMNPPSTU SUPPLEMENTAL
AEELLMORRSST STEAMROLLERS
AEELLNORSSTW STONEWALLERS
AEELLOPRSTUV POLE VAULTERS
AEELMNPRRSTU PREMENSTRUAL
AEELMOOPRSTU SOMATOPLEURE
AEELNORSTUXY EXTRANEOUSLY
AEELNRRSSTVY TRANSVERSELY
AEELOOPPRTUV OVERPOPULATE
AEELOPPRRRTY REAL PROPERTY
AEEMNOORTUUV OUTMANOEUVRE
AEENNORSSSUV RAVENOUSNESS
AEENNOSSSSUU NAUSEOUSNESS
AEENOPRRSSTT PATERNOSTERS
AEENOQRRSTTU QUARTER NOTES
AEENORRSSTXY EXTRASENSORY

AEEOOPSSTTTW	SWEET POTATOS
AEEOPPRRRSTT	PERPETRATORS
AEEOPRRSTTTU	TETRAPTEROUS
AEEOQRRSSTTU	SEQUESTRATOR
AEFFGILLLMOR	FLAGELLIFORM
AEFFHILNSSTU	FAITHFULNESS
AEFFILRRSSTU	FIRST REFUSAL
AEFFKNRRRSTU	FRANKFURTERS
AEFGGGILNOPR	LEAPFROGGING
AEFGGHINORRT	FORGATHERING
AEFGHHOORRTU	THOROUGHFARE
AEFGHHOORTTU	AFORETHOUGHT
AEFGHHORTTTU	AFTERTHOUGHT
AEFGIILRTUVY	FIGURATIVELY
AEFGIINNRRTZ	FRATERNIZING
AEFGIINPPSWW	WIFE SWAPPING
AEFGILLMNNUY	MEANINGFULLY
AEFGILLNORST	FORESTALLING
AEFGILLNRSST	FINGERSTALLS
AEFGILLNRTTY	FLATTERINGLY
AEFGILLNSSUW	WINEGLASSFUL
AEFGILNNRTTU	UNFLATTERING
AEFGINNRRRST	TRANSFERRING
AEFGLLNRTUUY	UNGRATEFULLY
AEFHKLMORSST	THERMOS FLASK
AEFHKLNNSSTU	THANKFULNESS
AEFHKNOOSTTV	VOTE OF THANKS
AEFHLLORSSUY	ROYAL FLUSHES
AEFHLNRSSTUW	WRATHFULNESS
AEFHOOPRRSTT	SHATTERPROOF
AEFIIILMNSST	SEMIFINALIST
AEFIIILNRTTV	INFILTRATIVE
AEFIIIMNNOST	FEMINISATION
AEFIIIMNNOTZ	FEMINIZATION
AEFIILLMOTTU	MULTIFOLIATE
AEFIILLNOOTU	UNIFOLIOLATE
AEFIILLNRTUV	INTERFLUVIAL
AEFIILMNORUV	FLUVIOMARINE
AEFIILNOOPRT	PERFOLIATION
AEFIINNOSSTT	INFESTATIONS
AEFIINORSSTT	FIRE STATIONS
AEFIINORSTTU	TITANIFEROUS
AEFILMMNNOOT	MONOFILAMENT
AEFILMORRRSU	FORMULARISER
AEFILMORRRUZ	FORMULARIZER
AEFILNOOPRSS	PROFESSIONAL
AEFILNOOPRTV	FLAVOPROTEIN
AEFILOOPRRSS	PROFESSORIAL
AEFILOPPRSUU	PAPULIFEROUS
AEFILOPRRSTT	SELF-PORTRAIT
AEFIMNNORRST	FRONTIERSMAN
AEFIMNOOPRRT	PREFORMATION
AEFIMNOORRST	REFORMATIONS
AEFINNNOPSTU	FOUNTAIN PENS
AEFINNORSSTU	STANNIFEROUS
AEFINOOPRRST	PERFORATIONS
AEFKLLOORRSW	FLOORWALKERS
AEFLLMNORSTU	SMALL FORTUNE
AEFLLNNSSUUW	UNLAWFULNESS
AEFLLOOPRSSY	FOOL'S-PARSLEY
AEFMNORRRSST	TRANSFORMERS
AEFNNORSTTUU	UNFORTUNATES
AEGGGILNNOTU	AGGLUTINOGEN
AEGGGILNRSTY	STAGGERINGLY
AEGGGILNRSWY	SWAGGERINGLY
AEGGGINNPRSS	PRESSGANGING
AEGGHIIKLNNU	HEILUNGKIANG
AEGGHIILNNST	NIGHTINGALES
AEGGHIIRRRST	HAIR TRIGGERS
AEGGHILNRSTU	SLAUGHTERING
AEGGHINSSSTT	GASTIGHTNESS
AEGGHIPPRRTY	TRIGGER-HAPPY
AEGGHLNOOSTT	SNAGGLETOOTH
AEGGHOOOOPRYZ	ZOOGEOGRAPHY
AEGGIILNRRUZ	REGULARIZING
AEGGIIMNNPRT	IMPREGNATING
AEGGIINNORRZ	REORGANIZING
AEGGILORRSUY	GREGARIOUSLY
AEGGIMNNORRW	WARMONGERING
AEGGLOOORSTY	ASTROGEOLOGY
AEGHHIINSTWW	WHITEWASHING
AEGHHILOPRRT	LITHOGRAPHER
AEGHHLOPRSSU	PLOUGHSHARES
AEGHHMOPRRTY	THERMOGRAPHY
AEGHHNOOPPRR	PHONOGRAPHER
AEGHHOOPPRRT	PHOTOGRAPHER
AEGHHOOPPRRT	ORTHOGRAPHER
AEGHIIKLNNTY	LIKE ANYTHING
AEGHIILMNSST	ALMIGHTINESS
AEGHIILNSTTY	HESITATINGLY
AEGHIINNSTTU	UNHESITATING
AEGHIKNNRRTT	KNIGHT-ERRANT
AEGHILLPRSTU	SUGAR THE PILL
AEGHILMNNOSW	ENGLISHWOMAN
AEGHILMNNSTU	LANGUISHMENT
AEGHILNRSTTY	SHATTERINGLY
AEGHILQRRTTU	QUARTERLIGHT
AEGHIMMNOSST	MESOGNATHISM
AEGHIMNORSUW	HOUSEWARMING
AEGHIMOOPRST	MASTIGOPHORE
AEGHIMOPRSSS	SEISMOGRAPHS
AEGHIMOPRSSY	SEISMOGRAPHY
AEGHINNOPPPT	PHONE-TAPPING
AEGHINOOOTTV	NOT GIVE A HOOT
AEGHINRRRTUY	TEARING HURRY
AEGHINRRSSTT	HEARTSTRINGS
AEGHINRSSSTT	STRAIGHTNESS
AEGHLMNNOORS	LONGSHOREMAN

AEGHLORSSTUU SLAUGHTEROUS
AEGHMNOOOPTT PHOTOMONTAGE
AEGHMNOOSSTU MESOGNATHOUS
AEGHMNOPSSUW HUMP ONE'S SWAG
AEGHNOOPPRRR PORNOGRAPHER
AEGHOOPPRRST TOPOGRAPHERS
AEGHOOPRRTUV PHOTOGRAVURE
AEGHOPPRRSSS GRASSHOPPERS
AEGHOPPRRSTY TYPOGRAPHERS
AEGHOPPRRTUY GROUP THERAPY
AEGIIILMNOTT LEGITIMATION
AFGIIILNRTVZ REVITALIZING
AEGIIIMNNNST INSEMINATING
AEGIIINNPRSW AWE-INSPIRING
AEGIIINORTVV INVIGORATIVE
AEGIIKLLNRST GIANT KILLERS
AEGIILLMRRSU GUERRILLAISM
AEGIILLNPRVY PREVAILINGLY
AEGIILMMNNST MISALIGNMENT
AEGIILMNNRST STREAMLINING
AEGIILMNORST MINERALOGIST
AEGIILNNNSSU UNGAINLINESS
AEGIILNNORTU URINOGENITAL
AEGIILNNRTUZ NEUTRALIZING
AEGIILNPPTYZ APPETIZINGLY
AEGIILNPRSTT EARSPLITTING
AEGIILNRSTVV VESTAL VIRGIN
AEGIILRRRTUY IRREGULARITY
AEGIIMMMMNSUW MINIMUM WAGES
AEGIIMMORRRS MIRROR IMAGES
AEGIIMNNOPRT IMPREGNATION
AEGIIMNNOPTT PIGMENTATION
AEGIIMOPRSTV GRAM-POSITIVE
AEGIINNNRSTT INTRANSIGENT
AEGIINNOOSTT NEGOTIATIONS
AEGIINNORSST RESIGNATIONS
AEGIINNSTUXY EXSANGUINITY
AEGIINORRSTT REGISTRATION
AEGIINORSTTV INVESTIGATOR
AEGIINPPRRTW WRITING PAPER
AEGIINPRSTUZ PASTEURIZING
AEGIJLNRSUUV JUGULAR VEINS
AEGIJLPSUWZZ JIGSAW PUZZLE
AEGIKLMNORTW METALWORKING
AEGIKMMNOPRT TEMPO MARKING
AEGILLMRSTTU METALLURGIST
AEGILLNNOSTW STONEWALLING
AEGILLNOPTUV POLE VAULTING
AEGILMMNRSTY STAMMERINGLY
AEGILMNNNNOT NONALIGNMENT
AEGILMNNOQTU MAGNILOQUENT
AEGILMORSSTT STIGMASTEROL
AEGILNNNOSTU SANGUINOLENT
AEGILNNRSSSU SINGULARNESS

AEGILNNRSTTY ASTRINGENTLY
AEGILNRRSSUY REASSURINGLY
AEGILOORSTTT TERATOLOGIST
AEGILORRSSTU GROSSULARITE
AEGIMMORSSTU MESOGASTRIUM
AEGIMNNNRSTU RUNNING MATES
AEGIMNNRSTTU MENSTRUATING
AEGINNOPSSTV PAVING STONES
AEGINOORRRTT INTERROGATOR
AEGINOPRSTUX EXPURGATIONS
AEGINOPRSTWY STAYING POWER
AEGINOQSSTTU QUESTION TAGS
AEGLLNOOOPTY PALEONTOLOGY
AEGLNRSSTTUU GUTTURALNESS
AEGLOORSTUUY OUTRAGEOUSLY
AEGMMNOPSSUU MAGNUM OPUSES
AEGNOOPRSSSY GREASY SPOONS
AEGNORRRSSST TRANSGRESSOR
AEGOOPSSTTUY STEATOPYGOUS
AEHHILOPSTTU THIOSULPHATE
AEHHIMNOPRSS HORSEMANSHIP
AEHHIMOOPSTT HOMEOPATHIST
AEHHLMOOPSTX EXOPHTHALMOS
AEHHLOOOPPRT LOPHOPHORATE
AEHHOOPPRTTY PHOTOTHERAPY
AEHHOOPRRSST SHARPSHOOTER
AEHIIIMNNOST THIOSINAMINE
AEHIIIMNNSTU INHUMANITIES
AEHIIILPSSTT PHILATELISTS
AEHIILNOPRST RELATIONSHIP
AEHIILPRRSTT HAIRSPLITTER
AEHIINNOPRTT TREPHINATION
AEHIINOORSTT THEORISATION
AEHIINOORTTZ THEORIZATION
AEHIINOPRRSS PARISHIONERS
AEHIIRRSSTTW SHIRTWAISTER
AEHILLOORSTU HELIOLATROUS
AEHILMNOOPSU ANEMOPHILOUS
AEHILMNORSTW MOTHERS-IN-LAW
AEHIMMMOPRST METAMORPHISM
AEHIMNNOOPRT ENANTIOMORPH
AEHIMNNOPPSU ONE-UPMANSHIP
AEHIMNNOSSSW WOMANISHNESS
AEHIMNNOSSTT ASTONISHMENT
AEHIMNNQSTUV VANQUISHMENT
AEHIMNOPRSST MISANTHROPES
AEHIMNOPRSTW WITH OPEN ARMS
AEHIMNPRSSST TRAMPISHNESS
AEHIMPRSSSTY SYMPATHISERS
AEHIMPRSSTYZ SYMPATHIZERS
AEHINNNOSTTT ON THE INSTANT
AEHINNPPSSSS SNAPPISHNESS
AEHINOOPRRTT PROTOTHERIAN
AEHINOORSTTX EXHORTATIONS

AEHINOOSSTTU STATION HOUSE
AEHINOPRSSSV VAPORISHNESS
AEHINPPRRSST PARTNERSHIPS
AEHIOOPPRSST APOSTROPHISE
AEHIOOPPRSTZ APOSTROPHIZE
AEHIOPRRSTWY PRAISEWORTHY
AEHJNOORRSST TROJAN HORSES
AEHLMPRSTTTU THE LAST TRUMP
AEHLNOPSSTUY POLYANTHUSES
AEHLOPPRSTUY PYROSULPHATE
AEHMNOOPRTUX PNEUMOTHORAX
AEHMNOORSSTV HARVEST MOONS
AEHOOPRRSSUW HOUSE SPARROW
AEIIILMRSST SIMILARITIES
AEIIILRSTTV TRIVIALITIES
AEIIILLMNORS MILLIONAIRES
AEIIILLMNTUV ILLUMINATIVE
AEIIILMMORST IMMORALITIES
AEIIILMPRSST IMPERIALISTS
AEIIILNRSTTT INTERSTITIAL
AEIIILPRSSTU SPIRITUALISE
AEIIILPRSTUZ SPIRITUALIZE
AEIIIMMNSSTT ANTI-SEMITISM
AEIIIMNNNOST INSEMINATION
AEIIIMNORSSS MISSIONARIES
AEIIIMNRSTTV MINISTRATIVE
AEIIINNRSTTV INTRANSITIVE
AEIIIOPPRTTV PROPITIATIVE
AEIIKKNORSSY KARYOKINESIS
AEIIILLNQRSTU TRANQUILLISE
AEIIILLNQRTUZ TRANQUILLIZE
AEIIILLRSTTUV ILLUSTRATIVE
AEIILMMNOOST EMOTIONALISM
AEIILMMORRST IMMORTALISER
AEIILMMORRTZ IMMORTALIZER
AEIILMNOOSTT EMOTIONALIST
AEIILMNOOTTY EMOTIONALITY
AEIILMNOPRSS IMPRESSIONAL
AEIILMNOSSTT TESTIMONIALS
AEIILMNRSSUV UNIVERSALISM
AEIILMNRTUVY RUMINATIVELY
AEIILMNSTTUY SIMULTANEITY
AEIILMPRTTTU MULTIPARTITE
AEIILNNNQQUU QUINQUENNIAL
AEIILNOOPSTX EXPOSITIONAL
AEIILNOOPTTX EXPLOITATION
AEIILNOOSTVW VOWELISATION
AEIILNOOTVWZ VOWELIZATION
AEIILNOPTTTY POTENTIALITY
AEIILNORSSST SOLITARINESS
AEIILNORSSTT ORIENTALISTS
AEIILNRSSSTW SISTERS-IN-LAW
AEIILNRSSTUV UNIVERSALIST
AEIILNRSTUVY UNIVERSALITY

AEIIILNSTUUXY UNISEXUALITY
AEIIILORRRSTT TERRITORIALS
AEIIMMNOORST MEMORISATION
AEIIMMNOORTZ MEMORIZATION
AEIIMNNOOSTT MONETISATION
AEIIMNNOOTTZ MONETIZATION
AEIIMNNOPSSX EXPANSIONISM
AEIIMNNORSTT TERMINATIONS
AEIIMNRSSSTV TRANSMISSIVE
AEIIMRRSTTUV TRIUMVIRATES
AEIINNNORTTU ANTINEUTRINO
AEIINNOORSTT ORIENTATIONS
AEIINNOPRSTU RESUPINATION
AEIINNOPSSTX EXPANSIONIST
AEIINNORSTTT STRONTIANITE
AEIINOPPRRST PERSPIRATION
AEIINOPRTTUV VITUPERATION
AEIKMNOQRSTU QUESTION MARK
AEILLMMMSSTY SYMMETALLISM
AEILLMNOPRSY IMPERSONALLY
AEILLNNORTTY INTOLERANTLY
AEILLNOOSTTW WOLLASTONITE
AEILLORRRTTY ROTARY TILLER
AEILMNNOPRST MINOR PLANETS
AEILMNNORSST MATRONLINESS
AEILMNNOSSTW WINSTON-SALEM
AEILMNNRSTTU INSTRUMENTAL
AEILMNOOPRTT METROPOLITAN
AEILMNOSSTUU SIMULTANEOUS
AEILMOORSTTT STROMATOLITE
AEILNNRTTUWW UNWRITTEN LAW
AEILNOOOPRRT POOR RELATION
AEILNOOPRSTX EXPLORATIONS
AEILNOORTUVY EVOLUTIONARY
AEILNORRSUVY REVULSIONARY
AEILOPRSTUUV VOLUPTUARIES
AEIMNNOPPSTT APPOINTMENTS
AEIMNNORSTTU MENSTRUATION
AEIMNOOPRRST IMPERSONATOR
AEIMNOPRSTTU PERMUTATIONS
AEIMNRRSSTTT TRANSMITTERS
AEIMNRSSSTTV TRANSVESTISM
AEINNNORSSTT NONRESISTANT
AEINNNOOPRSTU PUT ONE'S OAR IN
AEINNORSSSUV UNSAVORINESS
AEINNORSTTTU STERNUTATION
AEINOOPRSTTT PROTESTATION
AEINOOPRSTTW POWER STATION
AEINOORRSSTT RESTORATIONS
AEINOORRTTXY EXTORTIONARY
AEINOOSSTTTU OSTENTATIOUS
AEINOPPRSSTT POSTER PAINTS
AEINOPRRSTTV TRANSPORTIVE
AEINORRSTVWY WINTER SAVORY

AEIOOOOPPPRS	PROSOPOPOEIA
AEIOOPPRRRTX	EXPROPRIATOR
AEIOPPRRRSTY	PERSPIRATORY
AEKLLPPSSTUU	PULL UP STAKES
AEKLMNNOOPRT	MEROPLANKTON
AELLLMORSUVY	MARVELLOUSLY
AELLMMNNOTUY	MONUMENTALLY
AELLOOPPSSUY	POLYSEPALOUS
AELLOOPPSTUY	POLYPETALOUS
AELMNOOOPSSU	MONOSEPALOUS
AELMNOOOPSTU	MONOPETALOUS
AELMORSSSSTY	SOLAR SYSTEMS
AELMPRSSTYYY	MYSTERY PLAYS
AELNNNOPRSTW	TOWN PLANNERS
AELOOPRSTTUX	EXPOSTULATOR
AEMMORRSSUVY	SUMMER SAVORY
AEMNNOORSSTY	STONEMASONRY
AEMNOOOPRSTZ	SPERMATOZOON
AEMNOOOPRSZZ	MEZZO-SOPRANO
AEMNOORRRSTT	REMONSTRATOR
AEMNOQSSSSUU	SQUAMOUSNESS
AEMPRRSSTTUU	SUPERSTRATUM
AENNOOPRSSSS	PARSON'S NOSES
AENOOPRSSSUV	VAPOROUSNESS
AENOPRRRSSTT	TRANSPORTERS
AENORRSTTTUY	STERNUTATORY
AEOOOPPPRRSTY	PARTY POOPERS
AEOPPRRSSTTU	SUPRAPROTEST
AEOPPRRSTTVY	POVERTY TRAPS
AFFGILNOOTTU	FOOT FAULTING
AFFHILLNTUUY	UNFAITHFULLY
AFFIILNNOSTU	INSUFFLATION
AFGGGILLNNUY	UNFLAGGINGLY
AFGGIILNRTYY	GRATIFYINGLY
AFGGIINPPRTW	GIFT-WRAPPING
AFGIIILNNRTT	INFILTRATING
AFGIILLMNORU	ANGUILLIFORM
AFGIILLNQUYY	QUALIFYINGLY
AFGIILNSSTYY	SATISFYINGLY
AFGIIMNOPRRT	PROFIT MARGIN
AFGIKNOORSTT	TOASTING FORK
AFGIMNNORRST	TRANSFORMING
AFGIMNORRSTY	TRANSMOGRIFY
AFIIILMNNOST	INFLATIONISM
AFIIILNNORTT	INFILTRATION
AFIIILNNOSTT	INFLATIONIST
AFIILMNNOSTU	FULMINATIONS
AFIILMORSTUU	MULTIFARIOUS
AFIILNNOORTU	FLUORINATION
AFIILNORRSTT	INFILTRATORS
AFIILORRSSST	FISSIROSTRAL
AFIIMMNNORST	MISINFORMANT
AFILMNOORSTU	FORMULATIONS
AFIMMNORRSST	TRANSFORMISM
AFIMNORRSSTT	TRANSFORMIST
AFINNORSSSTU	TRANSFUSIONS
AFINORRSSTTU	FRUSTRATIONS
AGGGILLNRSTY	STRAGGLINGLY
AGGHHLOPPRYY	GLYPHOGRAPHY
AGGHHMOPPRSY	SPHYGMOGRAPH
AGGHIIKLNPRT	PARKING LIGHT
AGGHIIKNNSTV	THANKSGIVING
AGGHIIMNNRST	HAMSTRINGING
AGGHILMNNRSY	RHYMING SLANG
AGGHILOOPRST	GRAPHOLOGIST
AGGHLNOOPRYY	PHARYNGOLOGY
AGGHLOOPRSSY	GLOSSOGRAPHY
AGGHLOPPRTYY	GLYPTOGRAPHY
AGGIIILLNNTV	INVIGILATING
AGGIIIMNSTTZ	STIGMATIZING
AGGIIINNORTV	INVIGORATING
AGGIINNOPRSW	GROWING PAINS
AGGIKLLNOOSS	LOOKING GLASS
AGGIKMNOORST	MAGNITOGORSK
AGGILMNOPRTU	PROMULGATING
AGGILNOOORST	ORGANOLOGIST
AGGINOPSSSTT	STAGING POSTS
AGHHILNOPRTT	TRIPHTHONGAL
AGHHIOPPRSYY	PHYSIOGRAPHY
AGHHOOPPSTUY	PHYTOPHAGOUS
AGHIILMNPSTY	LYMPHANGITIS
AGHIIMNPSTYZ	SYMPATHIZING
AGHIINOPPRTU	UPRIGHT PIANO
AGHILMNOOOOT	HOMOLOGATION
AGHILNOOSSTT	ANTHOLOGISTS
AGHILOOPSSTT	PATHOLOGISTS
AGHINOOPRSTT	TRAPSHOOTING
AGHINOORSSTT	SHOOTING STAR
AGHINOPRSSTT	PARTING SHOTS
AGHIOPPSSYYZ	ZYGAPOPHYSIS
AGHLLMOOPSUY	GAMOPHYLLOUS
AGHLLMOORSUW	GALLOWS HUMOR
AGHLNOOOOPRTY	ANTHROPOLOGY
AGHMNOOPRTYY	PHARYNGOTOMY
AGIIIILMNRTZ	MILITARIZING
AGIIIILNNOTV	INVIGILATION
AGIIIILNRTVZ	TRIVIALIZING
AGIIILLMNNTU	ILLUMINATING
AGIIILLMNSST	MAILING LISTS
AGIIILLNNOPST	OIL PAINTINGS
AGIIILNORSTV	INVIGILATORS
AGIIILNSSTTW	WAITING LISTS
AGIIINNOORTV	INVIGORATION
AGIIINNOPRTT	PARTITIONING
AGIIINOPPRTT	PROPITIATING
AGIIKLNNOPTT	TALKING POINT
AGIILLLMNTUU	MULTILINGUAL
AGIILLLNRTUY	TRILINGUALLY

AGIIILLMNORYZ MORALIZINGLY
AGIIILLNORTUV OUTRIVALLING
AGIIILLNRSTTU ILLUSTRATING
AGIIILLOPSSSS SALPIGLOSSIS
AGIIILMNNRTUY RUMINATINGLY
AGIIILNNSSTUY SUSTAININGLY
AGIIILNOORSUV VAINGLORIOUS
AGIIILNOPPRUZ POPULARIZING
AGIIMNNRSTTT TRANSMITTING
AGIIMNOORSTW WAITING ROOMS
AGIIINNOOPPRT APPORTIONING
AGIKMNNOORWW WORKINGWOMAN
AGIKNOPRRTWY WORKING PARTY
AGILLNOOPSTY PALYNOLOGIST
AGILMNNSSUUY UNASSUMINGLY
AGILMNOOOOSY ONOMASIOLOGY
AGILMNOOPRTU PROMULGATION
AGILMOOOSSTT SOMATOLOGIST
AGILNNNNOPTW TOWN PLANNING
AGILNNOOOOPRT PROLONGATION
AGILNPRSSSUY SURPASSINGLY
AGILORSTTUUY GRATUITOUSLY
AGIMNOORSSTT GASTRONOMIST
AGINNOPRRSST APRON STRINGS
AGINNOPRRSTT TRANSPORTING
AGINNRRSSSTU SATURN'S RINGS
AGINOOOOPRRST PROROGATIONS
AGINOOPRSSTT PROTAGONISTS
AGINOPRSSTTT STARTING POST
AGLLNOORSUUY LANGUOROUSLY
AGLLOOPSSTTT GLOTTAL STOPS
AGLMMNOOOSUY MONOGAMOUSLY
AGLMOOPRRSTU PROMULGATORS
AHHIILMOPSTT OPHTHALMITIS
AHHILLLLSSYY SHILLY-SHALLY
AHHILLMMOOST HOMOTHALLISM
AHHILNOPPRTY PHILANTHROPY
AHHINNOPRSTT STROPHANTHIN
AHHNOPRSSTTU STROPHANTHUS
AHIIILMNOSTU HUMILIATIONS
AHIIMNNOORSU INHARMONIOUS
AHIKLOORTTUW KILOWATT-HOUR
AHILLMMOOPRS ALLOMORPHISM
AHILLNOORTYZ HORIZONTALLY
AHILMNOORSUY HARMONIOUSLY
AHILMNPRTTUY TRIUMPHANTLY
AHILMOOOPRTY HOMOPOLARITY
AHILNOPRSTUU SULPHURATION
AHIMOOPPPSTU HIPPOPOTAMUS
AHIMOOPPRSTT HAPTOTROPISM
AHIMOOPPRSTU AMPHITROPOUS
AHINNOPRSSTU SINANTHROPUS
AHINOOPSSSTU SOUSAPHONIST
AHINOOPSSSTX SAXOPHONISTS

AHINOOPSSTUY AUTOHYPNOSIS
AHINORRSSSTY SYNARTHROSIS
AHKLLNNOOOPT HOLOPLANKTON
AHNOOOOPRRTTY PROTHONOTARY
AIIIIMMNNOST MINIMISATION
AIIIIMMNNOTZ MINIMIZATION
AIIIILLMNNOTU ILLUMINATION
AIIIILLNNOSTT INSTILLATION
AIIILMNOOSST ISOLATIONISM
AIIILMPRSSTU SPIRITUALISM
AIIILNOOSSTT ISOLATIONIST
AIIILPRSSTTU SPIRITUALIST
AIIILPRSTTUY SPIRITUALITY
AIIIMMNNOSTU IMMUNISATION
AIIIMMNNOTUZ IMMUNIZATION
AIIIMNNORSTT MINISTRATION
AIIIMNOOPSTT OPTIMISATION
AIIIMNOOPTTZ OPTIMIZATION
AIIIMNRSSTTU MINIATURISTS
AIIINNNOOSTU UNIONISATION
AIIINNNOOTUZ UNIONIZATION
AIIINNNOSSTU INSINUATIONS
AIIINNOPRSST INSPIRATIONS
AIIINOOPPRTT PROPITIATION
AIIINOPRRTTT TRIPARTITION
AIIKLRSSTUVV SURVIVAL KITS
AIILLNNOOTUV INVOLUTIONAL
AIILLNORSTTU ILLUSTRATION
AIILLNQRTTUY TRANQUILLITY
AIILMNNNOOTU MOUNTAIN LION
AIILMNNORTTU MALNUTRITION
AIILNNOTTUUV INVULTUATION
AIILNOOOOPPST OPPOSITIONAL
AIILNOPSSTTU STIPULATIONS
AIILNORRSSST SINISTRORSAL
AIILNORRSTTY TRANSITORILY
AIIMMNSSSTTU NUMISMATISTS
AIIMNNORSSST TRANSMISSION
AIIMNOOORSTT MOTORISATION
AIIMNOOORTTZ MOTORIZATION
AIIMNOOPRSSU PARSIMONIOUS
AIIMNOOPRSTT IMPORTATIONS
AIIMNOOQSTTU MISQUOTATION
AIIMOOPPRRRT IMPROPRIATOR
AIINNOOOPSST OPSONISATION
AIINNOOOPSTZ OPSONIZATION
AIIOOPPRRTTY PROPITIATORY
AIKNOORSSTTW WORKSTATIONS
AILLMNNOOPRY PRONOMINALLY
AILLNOOPSTTY POLYTONALIST
AILLNOOPTTYY POLYTONALITY
AILLORRSSTTU ILLUSTRATORS
AILMNORSTUVY VOLUNTARYISM
AILNOOOPPRRT PROPORTIONAL

AILNOPPRTUUY UNPOPULARITY
AILNORSTTUVY VOLUNTARYIST
AILOOPRRSUUY UPROARIOUSLY
AILOORRSTTUY TRAITOROUSLY
AIMNNOOPRSSU PONS ASINORUM
AIMNNOOPSTTU MOUNTAINTOPS
AIMOORRRTWWY TWO-WAY MIRROR
AINOOPRRSSTT PROSTRATIONS
ALMNOOOSTUUY AUTONOMOUSLY
ALMNOORSSTTU SALMON TROUTS
BBBBBEEHLLUU HUBBLE-BUBBLE
BBCDEEEEKNRRU RUBBERNECKED
BBCEELNOOSST COBBLESTONES
BBCEILMOSSTU COMBUSTIBLES
BBCEJKOORSST STOCKJOBBERS
BBCEJKOORSTY STOCKJOBBERY
BBCEKLORSSTU BLOCKBUSTERS
BBCELLLOOSWY COLLYWOBBLES
BBCELMORSSTU CLUSTER BOMBS
BBCENOORRSTU BRONCOBUSTER
BBDDDDEEELOU DOUBLE-BEDDED
BBDEEEGGKLOOO GOBBLEDEGOOK
BBDEEHHLOOSY HOBBLEDEHOYS
BBDEFFLLOSUU DOUBLE BLUFFS
BBDEGGKLOOOY GOBBLEDYGOOK
BBDEGHINRRUY RUBBER DINGHY
BBDEGHMNOORY HYDROGEN BOMB
BBDEHLOOORRT BLOOD BROTHER
BBEEEHLLOTTW BELOW THE BELT
BBEEGMNORRUY MONEY-GRUBBER
BBEEILMRSSSU SUBMERSIBLES
BBEENNNRRSUU BUNSEN BURNER
BBEGGHIILNOS BOBSLEIGHING
BBEHIIILLOPS BIBLIOPHILES
BBEHIIILLOTY BOIL THE BILLY
BBEHINNOSSSS SNOBBISHNESS
BBELLNOSTTUY BELLY BUTTONS
BBEMNNOORSTU NEUTRON BOMBS
BBENNORSSSTU STUBBORNNESS
BBHJNNOOOOSS HOBSON-JOBSON
BCCCEIIMRRSU CIRCUMSCRIBE
BCCDEEIJORTT DIRECT OBJECT
BCCEEEHKRRRY CHECKERBERRY
BCCEEELNOOSS OBSOLESCENCE
BCCEEHKLMOOR CHECKERBLOOM
BCCEEHNORRSS CROSSBENCHER
BCCEEHNORSSS CROSSBENCHES
BCCEEIIMNNSU INCUMBENCIES
BCCEFFIKLOOS OFFICE BLOCKS
BCCEEHNOOOPRS BRONCHOSCOPE
BCCEHORSTTTU BUTTERSCOTCH
BCCEILOPRSTU PUBLIC SECTOR
BCCHILLOOPSU PUBLIC SCHOOL

BCCHIMOORTTY THROMBOCYTIC
BCCHNOOOPRSY BRONCHOSCOPY
BCCINOOSSSUU SUBCONSCIOUS
BCCIOOOPRSST STROBOSCOPIC
BCCLNORSTUUY COUNTRY CLUBS
BCDDEEEIINOS DISOBEDIENCE
BCDDEEEKLORU DOUBLE-DECKER
BCDDEEENORTY BODY-CENTERED
BCDDEEIIRSTT DIRECT DEBITS
BCDDEELLLOOR RED BLOOD CELL
BCDDEIIILTUY DEDUCIBILITY
BCDEEEIINNST BENEDICTINES
BCDEEEIILLNPU BLUE-PENCILED
BCDEEEKORRST STOCKBREEDER
BCDEEFHIILNT CHILD BENEFIT
BCDEEIINNOST BENEDICTIONS
BCDEEILOPRRU REPRODUCIBLE
BCDEEILRSTTU DESTRUCTIBLE
BCDEIIILRTUY REDUCIBILITY
BCDEIILNORTU INTRODUCIBLE
BCDEIIMORTTU OBITER DICTUM
BCDEKLOORSSU BLOODSUCKERS
BCDGHHIIILTW BIG WITH CHILD
BCDGIIKMNORS MOCKINGBIRDS
BCDGIKNOOSTY BODY STOCKING
BCDGILLLOPSU BULLDOG CLIPS
BCEEEEEHKNRS KNEE BREECHES
BCEEEEGHRRSU CHEESEBURGER
BCEEEEGILLNR BELLIGERENCE
BCEEEFILNNTY BENEFICENTLY
BCEEEGILLNRY BELLIGERENCY
BCEEEINRSSUV SUBSERVIENCE
BCEEEIRRRSVY SERVICEBERRY
BCEEELNORTVY CONVEYER BELT
BCEEFHNNORRT FRONTBENCHER
BCEEFHNNORST FRONTBENCHES
BCEEFILNORSS FORCIBLENESS
BCEEIIIILMST IMBECILITIES
BCEEIIILLRSTT BELLETRISTIC
BCEEIJLSTUVY SUBJECTIVELY
BCEEILMNOPTT CONTEMPTIBLE
BCEEILMOPRSS COMPRESSIBLE
BCEEILNORSTV CONVERTIBLES
BCEEIMMOSTTU SUBCOMMITTEE
BCEEJLNOOSST OBJECT LESSON
BCEEKLLORSTT BLOCK LETTERS
BCEFFKORSSTU BUFFER STOCKS
BCEFGIIINNOR FIBRINOGENIC
BCEFIMNNOORU UNCIFORM BONE
BCEFIMOPRTTU BIT OF CRUMPET
BCEFOORSTUYY BY COURTESY OF
BCEGHIILNTWY BEWITCHINGLY
BCEGIIILNORR INCORRIGIBLE
BCEGIILOOOST BIOECOLOGIST

BCEGIKLNOSTU BLUESTOCKING
BCEHIIMORSTY BIOCHEMISTRY
BCEHIINOSTTY BIOSYNTHETIC
BCEHILOPSSUU PUBLIC HOUSES
BCEIIILLRTVY CIVIL LIBERTY
BCEIIJMSSTUV SUBJECTIVISM
BCEIIJSSTTUV SUBJECTIVIST
BCEIIJSTTUVY SUBJECTIVITY
BCEIIKLLNRTU CLINKER-BUILT
BCEIILNRSTTU INSTRUCTIBLE
BCEIINORTTUV CONTRIBUTIVE
BCEIIPRSSTUV SUBSCRIPTIVE
BCEIJNSSTUUV SUBJUNCTIVES
BCEIKNNRSUWW NEW BRUNSWICK
BCEIKOOPRSTU PICTURE BOOKS
BCEILLOOPSUY EBULLIOSCOPY
BCEILMNOPTTY CONTEMPTIBLY
BCEILORSSTUU TUBERCULOSIS
BCEINNNOSTTU SUBCONTINENT
BCEKKOOOORSY COOKERY BOOKS
BCEKKOORRSST STOCKBROKERS
BCEOOOPRSSST STROBOSCOPES
BCERRSSTTUUU SUBSTRUCTURE
BCFIIILNORTY FIBRINOLYTIC
BCGIIILMNNOR CLIMBING IRON
BCGIIILNORRY INCORRIGIBLY
BCGIILMOOORY MICROBIOLOGY
BCGIINNORTTU CONTRIBUTING
BCGIINOOOSTT GNOTOBIOTICS
BCHHIMOOORRT ORTHORHOMBIC
BCHIIIOPSSTY BIOPHYSICIST
BCHILNOORRTT BIRTH CONTROL
BCHNOORSSSTU HOT-CROSS BUNS
BCIIILPPRSTU PUBLIC SPIRIT
BCIINNOORTTU CONTRIBUTION
BCIINOPRSSTU SUBSCRIPTION
BCILMMNOSUUU CUMULONIMBUS
BCINOORRSTTU CONTRIBUTORS
BCINOORRTTUY CONTRIBUTORY
BCINOORSSTTU OBSTRUCTIONS
BDDDEEFIILNR BLIND FREDDIE
BDDDEELOOTTU DOUBLE-DOTTED
BDDDEILMNOOY BLOODY-MINDED
BDDEEEEFILMN FEEBLEMINDED
BDDEEEEGNNRR GENDER-BENDER
BDDEEEILMOSW DISEMBOWELED
BDDEEEINNSST INDEBTEDNESS
BDDEEENORRUV OVERBURDENED
BDDEEILMOSUX MIXED DOUBLES
BDDFGIILLNNO BLINDFOLDING
BDDFGIILNORY FORBIDDINGLY
BDDFGIMNNOUU DUMBFOUNDING
BDEEEFIILNNS INDEFENSIBLE
BDEEEIILRSSV DISBELIEVERS

BDEEEIIMNOST BIDE ONE'S TIME
BDEEEIIMORRS EMBROIDERIES
BDEEEIIRSVWY BIRD'S-EYE VIEW
BDEEEILLNRSU UNDERBELLIES
BDEEEILMNRTW BEWILDERMENT
BDEEFIILNNSY INDEFENSIBLY
BDEEFIILRSTU FILIBUSTERED
BDEEGGHIIRSW WEIGHBRIDGES
BDEEGHHIINRS DENBIGHSHIRE
BDEEGIIILNST INDIGESTIBLE
BDEEGIIILNSV DISBELIEVING
BDEEGIIMMNRS DISMEMBERING
BDEEGIIMNORR EMBROIDERING
BDEEGLNOOTUU DOUBLE-TONGUE
BDEEHINOSTUU HEBETUDINOUS
BDEEIIMRRTTU TURBIDIMETER
BDEEIIRRSTTU REDISTRIBUTE
BDEEIILLNPRSS SPELLBINDERS
BDEEIMNRSSTU DISBURSEMENT
BDEEIINNORSTV INVERTED SNOB
BDEELLOOSSSV BLOOD VESSELS
BDEELMRRSTUY TUMBLE-DRYERS
BDEFHNOOOORST DEBTS OF HONOR
BDEFHNOOORTU DEBT OF HONOUR
BDEGGGILNRUY BEGRUDGINGLY
BDEGHHIINOOOR NEIGHBORHOOD
BDEGHHOORRTU THOROUGHBRED
BDEGIIILNSTY INDIGESTIBLY
BDEGIIILLNNPS SPELLBINDING
BDEGIILNORWZ BOWDLERIZING
BDEGILLNNRUY BLUNDERINGLY
BDEGILLNOOTT BLOODLETTING
BDEGILMNRTUY TUMBLE-DRYING
BDEHHMNOOOORR RHOMBOHEDRON
BDEHHOOOORRST BROTHERHOODS
BDEHIILPRSSU SHIPBUILDERS
BDEHLNORSTTU THUNDERBOLTS
BDEHMOOOORRTU MOUTHBROODER
BDEIIIILLNTY INDELIBILITY
BDEIIIRSTTUV DISTRIBUTIVE
BDEIILLNOSSU INDISSOLUBLE
BDEIINNRSTUW WIND TURBINES
BDEILLLNORRS ROLLER BLINDS
BDEIMMNOPRSU PREMIUM BONDS
BDFGHILLOOSW GOLDFISH BOWL
BDFIILMNNUUU INFUNDIBULUM
BDGGGIILMNNO MIND-BOGGLING
BDGHIIILNPSU SHIPBUILDING
BDGHIIMMNRSU HUMMINGBIRDS
BDGIIIIILRTY DIRIGIBILITY
BDGIIINRSTTU DISTRIBUTING
BDGIILNOSTUU OUTBUILDINGS
BDHILOORSTTY BLOODTHIRSTY
BDIIIIILLSTVY DIVISIBILITY

BDIIIILLNOSUY LIBIDINOUSLY	**BEEEINNNOOQUZ** BENZOQUINONE
BDIIINORSTTU DISTRIBUTION	**BEEINNORRTUW** WINTERBOURNE
BDIIINOSSSUV SUBDIVISIONS	**BEEINOSSSTWX** WITNESS BOXES
BDIIILLNOSSUY INDISSOLUBLY	**BEEKOOPRRRSW** POWER BROKERS
BDIIORRSSTTU DISTRIBUTORS	**BEELLORSSTUY** TROLLEYBUSES
BDKNNNOOOSUW KNOW NO BOUNDS	**BEELNNOSSSUU** NEBULOUSNESS
BEEEEEFLMNNT ENFEEBLEMENT	**BEELNQSSTUUY** SUBSEQUENTLY
BEEEEFHINORR HEREINBEFORE	**BEEOOPRRSSTU** OBSTREPEROUS
BEEEELMMNTZZ EMBEZZLEMENT	**BEFGHIINRRSU** REFURBISHING
BEEEEOQSSUXZ SQUEEZEBOXES	**BEFGHILLRSTU** BULLFIGHTERS
BEEEGILLNRST BELLIGERENTS	**BEFHINNOOORS** ONE FOR HIS NOB
BEEEGIMNPRSU SUPREME BEING	**BEFHLMORSTUU** RULES OF THUMB
BEEEGIOORRSS GOOSEBERRIES	**BEFILLNSSSSU** BLISSFULNESS
BEEEEHHRRSTTU THERE'S THE RUB	**BEFILMOPRSUU** PLUMBIFEROUS
BEEEHIINNRTT TEREBINTHINE	**BEGGHIINNORU** NEIGHBOURING
BEEEEHLNOOPTX TELEPHONE BOX	**BEGHILORSSTT** STROBE LIGHTS
BEEEHNNNOOPZ BENZOPHENONE	**BEGIIIILLLTY** ILLEGIBILITY
BEEEIILLNNSTX INEXTENSIBLE	**BEGIIILLLNTY** INTELLIGIBLY
BEEEIILRRRSV IRREVERSIBLE	**BEGIILLLNTTY** BELITTLINGLY
BEEEILLMNTTT BELITTLEMENT	**BEGIILLNRSTY** BLISTERINGLY
BEEEILNNSSSS SENSIBLENESS	**BEGIILOOOSTX** EXOBIOLOGIST
BEEEILNRRSST TERRIBLENESS	**BEGIINORRSVW** VIRGIN'S-BOWER
BEEEIMMNRTTT EMBITTERMENT	**BEGILLMNRSUY** SLUMBERINGLY
BEEEINNNORTZ NITROBENZENE	**BEGILLNORSTY** BOLSTERINGLY
BEEEIPRRSSTY PRESBYTERIES	**BEGILLNRSTUY** BLUSTERINGLY
BEEEELLNNOTVY BENEVOLENTLY	**BEGILMOORSTY** EMBRYOLOGIST
BEEEELMNOSTTU TOUT ENSEMBLE	**BEGILNPRRTUY** PERTURBINGLY
BEEEELNOOSSST OBSOLETENESS	**BEGIMNNORTUU** OUTNUMBERING
BEEENOPPRSTY TEENYBOPPERS	**BEGIMNORRSTT** BRING TO TERMS
BEEFGIINNRRT BIREFRINGENT	**BEHHOORSSTTU** TOOTHBRUSHES
BEEFIILRRSTU FILIBUSTERER	**BEHIIIMNSTTU** BISMUTHINITE
BEEFILMNNOOT BLOEMFONTEIN	**BEHIINOSSSTY** BIOSYNTHESIS
BEEGGILNNORW BOWLING GREEN	**BEHILMOOPSTT** PHLEBOTOMIST
BEEGHHILLRST SHE'LL BE RIGHT	**BEHINOSSSSUW** SHOW BUSINESS
BEEGHIILLMNS EMBELLISHING	**BEHLOORRSSTU** SOUL BROTHERS
BEEGHINNORRS HERRINGBONES	**BEIIILRRSSTY** IRRESISTIBLY
BEEGHOOPRRTU PETERBOROUGH	**BEIILLORSTUY** RESOLUBILITY
BEEGIIILLLNT INTELLIGIBLE	**BEIILMMMOPRU** PRIMUM MOBILE
BEEGIINNSSTT BESETTING SIN	**BEIILMSSSUVY** SUBMISSIVELY
BEEGLOORRTTT GLOBETROTTER	**BEIINNOOPRTW** BROWNIE POINT
BEEHIIINORTX EXHIBITIONER	**BEIINSSSSTUU** BUSINESS SUIT
BEEHILNORRSS HORRIBLENESS	**BEIISSTTTUUV** SUBSTITUTIVE
BEEHLMNORSUW WHOLE NUMBERS	**BEILLOORSSTT** STILBOESTROL
BEEHLORRRTWY WHORTLEBERRY	**BEILOOQSSUUY** OBSEQUIOUSLY
BEEHOPRRSSTT STEPBROTHERS	**BEILOORSSTUY** BOISTEROUSLY
BEEIIILLMRRSS IRREMISSIBLE	**BEILOPPRSTUU** PURPOSE-BUILT
BEEIIILRRSST IRRESISTIBLE	**BELMNOOPRYYY** POLYEMBRYONY
BEEIIKLNSSSU BUSINESSLIKE	**BELOOPRSSTTU** TROUBLE SPOTS
BEEIILRRRSVY IRREVERSIBLY	**BFFIIILLMORR** FIBRILLIFORM
BEEILLLORSUY REBELLIOUSLY	**BFGGHIILLNTU** BULLFIGHTING
BEEILLRRRSTU BULL TERRIERS	**BFGHIILLORST** BILL OF RIGHTS
BEEILPPRSSSU SUPPRESSIBLE	**BFIIIILNSTUY** INFUSIBILITY
BEEILRSSUVVY SUBVERSIVELY	**BFIIILNNORSY** FIBRINOLYSIN
BEEIMMNPRRSU PRIME NUMBERS	**BFIIILNORSSY** FIBRINOLYSIS

BGGHHLOOORUU LOUGHBOROUGH
BGHIILLNSTTU BULLSHITTING
BGHIINOPPSWY WHIPPING BOYS
BGHILLNOOOPT POLLING BOOTH
BGHILNNOOTTU BUTTONHOLING
BGIIIILMMNOZ IMMOBILIZING
BGIIIILNNOOPT BOILING POINT
BGIIILMNSTTUY SUBMITTINGLY
BGIIILNSSSTUY SUBSISTINGLY
BGIINSSTTTUU SUBSTITUTING
BGILLORSUUUY LUGUBRIOUSLY
BHIIINOOPRST PROHIBITIONS
BIIIIILNSTVY INVISIBILITY
BIIIILLNOSTUY INSOLUBILITY
BIIKOOORSSTV VISITORS' BOOK
BIILOQSTUUUY UBIQUITOUSLY
BIINOSSTTTUU SUBSTITUTION
CCCCEEENNORS CONCRESCENCE
CCCCEHINOOSU ECHINOCOCCUS
CCCCHHIOPRTU COPTIC CHURCH
CCCCKKLOOOSU CUCKOO CLOCKS
CCCDEEHKORSS CROSSCHECKED
CCCDEEIINNOS COINCIDENCES
CCCDEEIILNOPY ENCYCLOPEDIC
CCCDEIIORSTY CYSTICERCOID
CCCDHIIOOPRS DICHROSCOPIC
CCCEEEEENRSSX EXCRESCENCES
CCCEEHILORTY HETEROCYCLIC
CCCEEHKNORTU COUNTERCHECK·
CCCEEIINRTTY ECCENTRICITY
CCCEEILMNOTY METONIC CYCLE
CCCEEILNNOTU NOCTILUCENCE
CCCEENNORRSU CONCURRENCES
CCCEHINOPRTT CONCERT PITCH
CCCEILOOTTUY LEUCOCYTOTIC
CCCEINNOPSTU CONCUPISCENT
CCCEINNSSSTU SUCCINCTNESS
CCCEIOOPRSTT STREPTOCOCCI
CCCEMNOOPSUU PNEUMOCOCCUS
CCCGIIIMNRSU CIRCUMCISING
CCCHHHIRRSTU CHRISTCHURCH
CCCHIIORSTTY TRICHOCYSTIC
CCCHINOOOPRS CHRONOSCOPIC
CCCIIIMNORSU CIRCUMCISION
CCCIIIMORRTU MICROCIRCUIT
CCDDDEEENNOS CONDESCENDED
CCDDEEINNOST DISCONNECTED
CCDDEEINORST DISCONCERTED
CCDDEIMNOSTU MISCONDUCTED
CCDEEEEILNST DELITESCENCE
CCDEEEEMNSTU DETUMESCENCE
CCDEEEFIIINS DEFICIENCIES
CCDEEEFIILNV CIVIL DEFENCE
CCDEEEFNNORS FRONDESCENCE

CCDEEEHIINNS INDEHISCENCE
CCDEEEHIPRST DIRECT SPEECH
CCDEEEHNOSTU ESCUTCHEONED
CCDEEEIINRSV VIRIDESCENCE
CCDEEEINOPRV PRECONCEIVED
CCDEEELORTTU ELECTROCUTED
CCDEEFIINNNO IN CONFIDENCE
CCDEEGILNSUY SUCCEEDINGLY
CCDEEIIINSST INSECTICIDES
CCDEEIIMNOSV MISCONCEIVED
CCDEEILRRSSS DRESS CIRCLES
CCDEEIMNRTUV CIRCUMVENTED
CCDEEINNORST DISCONNECTER
CCDEEIORRTTU CORRECTITUDE
CCDEELOOPPRS CLOSE-CROPPED
CCDEGIMNNOOS SECOND COMING
CCDEHIIINNNO CINCHONIDINE
CCDEIIIIRSTV RECIDIVISTIC
CCDEIMNOORSS MICROSECONDS
CCDEINNOOSSU SECOND COUSIN
CCDEIORRSSSS CRISSCROSSED
CCDHHILOORRY HYDROCHLORIC
CCDHIOORSTTW WITCHDOCTORS
CCDIINOTTUVY CONDUCTIVITY
CCDNNNOOORTU NONCONDUCTOR
CCEEEEILLNSX EXCELLENCIES
CCEEEEILRSTY ELECTRIC EYES
CCEEEEINPRST CENTERPIECES,
 CENTREPIECES
CCEEEEJNNSUV JUVENESCENCE
CCEEEFHHRRSU FREE CHURCHES
CCEEEFHIKNRS NECKERCHIEFS
CCEEEFLNORSU FLUORESCENCE
CCEEEGIIMNST MISCEGENETIC
CCEEEGNNORSV CONVERGENCES
CCEEEHIIMNPY CHIMNEYPIECE
CCEEEHINOSTT COENESTHETIC
CCEEEHOOPRRT PORTE-COCHERE
CCEEEIIMNNRS REMINISCENCE
CCEEEIILLORTV RECOLLECTIVE
CCEEEIILMNNRT ENCIRCLEMENT
CCEEEIILMNNSU LUMINESCENCE
CCEEEIILOPRST SECRET POLICE
CCEEEIMNNOPT INCOMPETENCE
CCEEEIMNNSTU INTUMESCENCE
CCEEEINNNOST CONSENTIENCE
CCEEEINNNOSV CONVENIENCES
CCEEEINORSSV COERCIVENESS
CCEEELOOPRST ELECTROSCOPE
CCEEEMMMNNOT COMMENCEMENT
CCEEENNOQSSU CONSEQUENCES
CCEEFFIIINNY INEFFICIENCY
CCEEFFIINOST COEFFICIENTS
CCEEFHIIJSTU CHIEF JUSTICE

CCEEFINNOORT CONFECTIONER
CCEEGGILNOTU GLUCOGENETIC
CCEEGGILNOTY GLYCOGENETIC
CCEEGILLNORT RECOLLECTING
CCEEGILLOOSY ECCLESIOLOGY
CCEEGINOSTTY CYTOGENETICS
CCEEGNOORRST CONCERTGOERS
CCEEHHILOSTV CLOVE HITCHES
CCEEHHIMOPRS CHEMOSPHERIC
CCEEHIILNORT HELIOCENTRIC
CCEEHIMOSTYZ SCHIZOMYCETE
CCEEHINNORTT ETHNOCENTRIC
CCEEHINNOSTU INESCUTCHEON
CCEEHKLLLOSS COCKLESHELLS
CCEEHKLOORST ELECTROSHOCK
CCEEHLMOORSS COLOR SCHEMES
CCEEHLMOORSU COLOUR SCHEME
CCEEIIILRSVV CIVIL SERVICE
CCEEIIILLOSTV COLLECTIVISE
CCEEIIILLOTVZ COLLECTIVIZE
CCEEIILOOPTU LEUCOPOIETIC
CCEEIIMNORSV MISCONCEIVER
CCEEIINNNNOT INCONTINENCE
CCEEIILLLOTVY COLLECTIVELY
CCEEIILLNOORT RECOLLECTION
CCEEIILLORTTY ELECTROLYTIC
CCEEIILMORRST SCLEROMETRIC
CCEEIILNNOSTV CONVENTICLES
CCEEIILNOORTT ELECTROTONIC
CCEEIILOPRRTY PYROELECTRIC
CCEEIILORRTVY CORRECTIVELY
CCEEIILPPRSTU PEPTIC ULCERS
CCEEIILSSSUVY SUCCESSIVELY
CCEEIIMNOORST ECONOMETRICS
CCEEIIMNRRTUV CIRCUMVENTER
CCEEIIMNRSSTU MUSIC CENTERS, MUSIC
CENTRES
CCEEIINNNORTT INTERCONNECT
CCEEIIOOPRSST STEREOSCOPIC
CCEEENOPSSSTU CONSPECTUSES
CCEEEOOPPRSST SPECTROSCOPE
CCEFFHINOORSU CONCHIFEROUS
CCEFIIINNSTU UNSCIENTIFIC
CCEFLLSSSUUY SUCCESSFULLY
CCEFLNSSSUUU UNSUCCESSFUL
CCEGGINNNOOR GOING CONCERN
CCEGHIINORTT RICOCHETTING
CCEGHIKNOPST SPOT-CHECKING
CCEGIILNOPRS CLOSING PRICE
CCEGIJNNORTU CONJECTURING
CCEGINOPPRUY PREOCCUPYING
CCEHHIILMOOR HELIOCHROMIC
CCEHIILLNOPU NUCLEOPHILIC
CCEHIIMORSTT STICHOMETRIC

CCEHIINOORRT RHINOCEROTIC
CCEHIKLOSSTT LOCKSTITCHES
CCEHILNOPSTY POLYTECHNICS
CCEHIMNOORRT CHRONOMETRIC
CCEHIMOOPRST THERMOSCOPIC
CCEHIMOPRSTY PSYCHOMETRIC
CCEHINOOSSTU COCONUT SHIES
CCEHINOPRSTY PYROTECHNICS
CCEHIOOPSSTT STETHOSCOPIC
CCEHIORRTTYY ERYTHROCYTIC
CCEHKLOSSTTU SHUTTLECOCKS
CCEHLOOSTTUY HECTOCOTYLUS
CCEHNOOPRSSY SYNCHROSCOPE
CCEIIIMMORSS MICROSEISMIC
CCEIIINOORRT ONEIROCRITIC
CCEIIKKSTTWY STICKY WICKET
CCEIIKNSSSTT STICK INSECTS
CCEIIILLMOSTV COLLECTIVISM
CCEIIILLOSTTV COLLECTIVIST
CCEIIILLOTTVY COLLECTIVITY
CCEIIILMOORRT COLORIMETRIC
CCEIIILNNOSUV INCONCLUSIVE
CCEIIILPRSTUU PISCICULTURE
CCEIIILRRTTUU CITRICULTURE
CCEIIMOOPSSS SEISMOSCOPIC
CCEIINNOSSSU IN SUCCESSION
CCEIINOOPRST RETINOSCOPIC
CCEIINORSTTV CONSTRICTIVE
CCEIINOSSTUV VISCOUNTCIES
CCEIJNNOSTUV CONJUNCTIVES
CCEILLNOSUVY CONCLUSIVELY
CCEILLOOOPSS OSCILLOSCOPE
CCEILMNORSUU MICRONUCLEUS
CCEILOOPRSUY PRECOCIOUSLY
CCEILOOSSTUY LEUCOCYTOSIS
CCEINNOPRRSW CROWN PRINCES
CCEINNOSTTUY CONSTITUENCY
CCEINOOPRSSU PRECONSCIOUS
CCEINOORSSST CROSS-SECTION
CCEINORSTTUV CONSTRUCTIVE
CCEIORRSSSSS CRISSCROSSES
CCEJNNORSTUU CONJUNCTURES
CCELNNORRTUY CONCURRENTLY
CCENORRRSSTU CROSSCURRENT
CCEOOPPRSSTY SPECTROSCOPY
CCFGGHIIKNOT COCKFIGHTING
CCFIIMNORSUU CIRCUMFUSION
CCFILMORSUUU CIRCUMFLUOUS
CCFILOOOPRSU FLUOROSCOPIC
CCGHHIILOOTY ICHTHYOLOGIC
CCGHILNOOOST CONCHOLOGIST
CCGIILNNNOVY CONVINCINGLY
CCGIINNNNOUV UNCONVINCING
CCGIINNOPRST CONSCRIPTING

CCGIINNORSTT CONSTRICTING
CCGILLNOSTYY CYCLOSTYLING
CCGINNORSTTU CONSTRUCTING
CCHHIIMOSTYZ SCHIZOTHYMIC
CCHHIIOPSTYZ SCHIZOPHYTIC
CCHHIKOSSTWY SCOTCH WHISKY
CCHHILOOORSS CHOIR SCHOOLS
CCHHIMOOOPRR CHROMOPHORIC
CCHIILNOPSS SILICON CHIPS
CCHIILNOOPRR CHLOROPICRIN
CCHIIMOPRSSY MICROPHYSICS
CCHIIORRSTTU SHORT CIRCUIT
CCHIORSSSTUU HORTUS SICCUS
CCIILNNNOOSU IN CONCLUSION
CCIILNOPRUVY PRIVY COUNCIL
CCIILORSTUUY CIRCUITOUSLY
CCIIMOOPRSST MICROSCOPIST
CCIINNOOPRST CONSCRIPTION
CCIINNOORSTT CONSTRICTION
CCIJNNNOOSTU CONJUNCTIONS
CCILMOORSTTY MOTORCYCLIST
CCILMORRSUUU CIRROCUMULUS
CCIMNOOPSTUU COMPUNCTIOUS
CCINNOORSTTU CONSTRUCTION
CCINOORRSSTT CONSTRICTORS
CCNOORRSSTTU CONSTRUCTORS
CCNOORRSSTUY CROSS-COUNTRY
CCNOORSTTUUY COUNTY COURTS
CDDDEEFIIOST EISTEDDFODIC
CDDDELLLMOOY MOLLYCODDLED
CDDEEEEGNORS SECOND-DEGREE
CDDEEEEINNNP INDEPENDENCE
CDDEEEEINNPS DEPENDENCIES
CDDEEEEJNSST DEJECTEDNESS
CDDEEEHMNOPR COMPREHENDED
CDDEEEINNNPY INDEPENDENCY
CDDEEEINORRS RECONSIDERED
CDDEEEIRRSTT DERESTRICTED
CDDEEELNSSSU SECLUDEDNESS
CDDEEEMOPRSS DECOMPRESSED
CDDEEHLNNOSU NONSCHEDULED
CDDEEIJNPRUU UNPREJUDICED
CDDEEILMORSU MIDDLE COURSE
CDDEEINNORSU UNCONSIDERED
CDDEEINNOSTT DISCONTENTED
CDDEEELLNOORT DECONTROLLED
CDDEENOOPRRS CORRESPONDED
CDDEFIIKLSST FIDDLESTICKS
CDDEFLNNOOUY CONFOUNDEDLY
CDDEGIIINRST DISCREDITING
CDDEHIILMNRS CHILDMINDERS
CDDEHILLMOOS MIDDLE SCHOOL
CDDEHILNOSSS CLODDISHNESS
CDDEHLLOORSU COLD SHOULDER

CDDEHLNORTUU THUNDERCLOUD
CDDEIINNOSTU DISCONTINUED
CDDEIKOPSSTT SPOTTED DICKS
CDDEILNOOPRS SCOLOPENDRID
CDDGHIIILMNN CHILDMINDING
CDDGHIILOPRY CHILD PRODIGY
CDDGIIMMNOOS DISCOMMODING
CDDIIMMOOSTY DISCOMMODITY
CDEEEEFLNRST SELF-CENTERED
CDEEEEIINNPX INEXPEDIENCE
CDEEEEIKLPRW PICKERELWEED
CDEEEEILLRVW WELL-RECEIVED
CDEEEEELNNPRS RESPLENDENCE
CDEEEEFFGINOR FORCE-FEEDING
CDEEEEFFIINNR INDIFFERENCE
CDEEEFFHILRST CHESTERFIELD
CDEEEFHORSUV CHEFS D'OEUVRE
CDEEEGIKLNRS SINGLE-DECKER
CDEEEHIMNPRT DECIPHERMENT
CDEEEHNRSSTW WRETCHEDNESS
CDEEEIINNSST DISSENTIENCE
CDEEEIINPRSS PRESIDENCIES
CDEEEIINSSSV DECISIVENESS
CDEEEIIOPPRS PERIOD PIECES
CDEEEILMNORT DECLINOMETER
CDEEEILNQSTU DELIQUESCENT
CDEEEILORRST CLERESTORIED
CDEEEILORSTT LIE DETECTORS
CDEEEIMNORTT MINE DETECTOR
CDEEEINNNORS NONRESIDENCE
CDEEEINRSSST DISCREETNESS,
   DISCRETENESS
CDEEELMMNOPT COMPLEMENTED
CDEEEMNNNOTU DENOUNCEMENT
CDEEEOPRRSSS PREDECESSORS
CDEEFFHILOOR OFFICEHOLDER
CDEEFFHOORRT OFF-THE-RECORD
CDEEFFIMNOOT DOMINO EFFECT
CDEEFFNOSSTU SOUND EFFECTS
CDEEFILNNNUU UNINFLUENCED
CDEEFLLOORSU SELF-COLOURED
CDEEFLRSSTTU SELF-DESTRUCT
CDEEGHILNRSU RESCHEDULING
CDEEGIILRRTY TRIGLYCERIDE
CDEEGIKNOPRR PECKING ORDER
CDEEGIMMNNOR RECOMMENDING
CDEEGINNORSU UNRECOGNISED
CDEEGINNORUZ UNRECOGNIZED
CDEEGINOPRRR PRERECORDING
CDEEHHKLLOSS SHELLSHOCKED
CDEEHILLNORV LOVECHILDREN
CDEEHILNPRST STEPCHILDREN
CDEEHIOQSSTU DISCOTHEQUES
CDEEHKLNOSUY HONEYSUCKLED

CDEEEHLNORSTU UNDERCLOTHES
CDEEHORSTTTU OUTSTRETCHED
CDEEIIILNSVY INDECISIVELY
CDEEIIILOPST DEPOLITICISE
CDEEIIILOPTZ DEPOLITICIZE
CDEEIIIMORST MEDIOCRITIES
CDEEIIINNOST DENICOTINISE
CDEEIIINNOTZ DENICOTINIZE
CDEEIIINNSTV DISINCENTIVE
CDEEIIINRTTV INTERDICTIVE
CDEEIIILNOPRT PREDILECTION
CDEEIIILNORST DERELICTIONS
CDEEIIILNRSTY INDISCREETLY
CDEEIIILPRTVY PREDICTIVELY
CDEEIIIMNOPRV IMPROVIDENCE
CDEEIIINNRSST INDIRECTNESS
CDEEILMMNOPT COMPLIMENTED
CDEEILNOOOTV DO VIOLENCE TO
CDEEILRRSTTY RESTRICTEDLY
CDEEIMMNOOXY MIXED ECONOMY
CDEEIMOPRSTU COMPUTERISED
CDEEIMOPRTUZ COMPUTERIZED
CDEEINNOORRT RECONNOITRED
CDEEINOPRSTV OPEN VERDICTS
CDEEINRRSTTU UNRESTRICTED
CDEEIOPRRTUV REPRODUCTIVE
CDEEIORRSTUV DISCOVERTURE
CDEEIRRRSSVW SCREWDRIVERS
CDEELOOOORRSU ROSE-COLOURED
CDEENNOOPRSS SECOND PERSON
CDEENNOOPRST CORESPONDENT
CDEENNRRRTUU UNDERCURRENT
CDEEORRRSSSS CROSS-DRESSER
CDEERRRSTTUU RESTRUCTURED
CDEFFIIILSTU DIFFICULTIES
CDEFGIIINNST DISINFECTING
CDEFHLMOOOORR CHLOROFORMED
CDEFIIINNOST DISINFECTION
CDEFIIMORSTU DISCOMFITURE
CDEFKLOOOTUW OUT OF WEDLOCK
CDEGIIIMNRST MISDIRECTING
CDEGIILNNOOZ DECOLONIZING
CDEGILNOORUV OVERCLOUDING
CDEGINNORRSU UNDERSCORING
CDEGINNORSST SECOND-STRING
CDEGINNRTTUU UNDERCUTTING
CDEGINOORRVW OVERCROWDING
CDEGLMNORUUY CURMUDGEONLY
CDEHHIIIPRTT DIPHTHERITIC
CDEHHIILNSSS CHILDISHNESS
CDEHIIILPPSS DISCIPLESHIP
CDEHIIKKNNST THICK-SKINNED
CDEHIIKNORTY HYDROKINETIC
CDEHIINOOOPR CONIDIOPHORE

CDEHIIOPRRST DIRECTORSHIP
CDEHILLOOOST OLD SCHOOL TIE
CDEHILLOOOPRY POLICYHOLDER
CDEHILMNOOOR MONOCHLORIDE
CDEHIMNOOORS CHONDRIOSOME
CDEHINNORSSY SYNCHRONISED
CDEHINNORSYZ SYNCHRONIZED
CDEHKLOORSST STOCKHOLDERS
CDEIIIILNNPS INDISCIPLINE
CDEIIIJRSTUV JURISDICTIVE
CDEIIILNTVVY VINDICTIVELY
CDEIIIMNORST MISDIRECTION
CDEIIINNORST INDISCRETION
CDEIIINNORTT INTERDICTION
CDEIIISSSTUV VICISSITUDES
CDEIILMRTUUV DIVERTICULUM
CDEIILNNPPRU UNPRINCIPLED
CDEIILRSSUVY DISCURSIVELY
CDEIIMMNOOSS COMMISSIONED
CDEIIMMRSSTY DISSYMMETRIC
CDEIINNOOPRT PRECONDITION
CDEIINNOORST CONDITIONERS
CDEIINNSSSTT DISTINCTNESS
CDEIINOOPRST PERIODONTICS
CDEIINOPRSST DESCRIPTIONS
CDEILLMOORTU MULTICOLORED
CDEILNOORSUY INDECOROUSLY
CDEILNOPSSST SPLIT SECONDS
CDEILOPRTUVY PRODUCTIVELY
CDEIMNORSSTU MISCONSTRUED
CDEIMOOPRSSU DISCOMPOSURE
CDEINOOPRRTU REPRODUCTION
CDEINOPRTUUV UNPRODUCTIVE
CDEIOOORSSTUU DISCOURTEOUS
CDEKKNOOOORRS DOORKNOCKERS
CDEKLNNOOORT LONDON ROCKET
CDELLNOOTUVY CONVOLUTEDLY
CDELNNOOPRUY PRONOUNCEDLY
CDELNOOOSTUY COTYLEDONOUS
CDENRRSTTUUU UNSTRUCTURED
CDFGIIIMNOST DISCOMFITING
CDFGILNOORTY FLYING DOCTOR
CDFHILOORRUY HYDROFLUORIC
CDGGIKLLNUUY UGLY DUCKLING
CDGIIIILNNPS DISCIPLINING
CDGIIINNNOOT CONDITIONING
CDGIIKNSSTTU SITTING DUCKS
CDGIILNOORSU DISCOLOURING
CDGIIMNOOPSS DISCOMPOSING
CDGIKLNOOSTU DUCKING STOOL
CDGINNNOOORR NONCORRODING
CDHHILNOORRY CHLOROHYDRIN
CDHIIOOPRSST CHIROPODISTS
CDHIMNNOOSTY SYNODIC MONTH

CDHINOOORSTT ORTHODONTICS
CDIIIJNORSTU JURISDICTION
CDIIILNNSTTY INDISTINCTLY
CDIIINNOSSTT DISTINCTIONS
CDIILLORSUUY RIDICULOUSLY
CDIIMMNNOOSU CONDOMINIUMS
CDIIMMNOOOSU INCOMMODIOUS
CDIINNOORTTU INTRODUCTION
CDIIOPRTTUVY PRODUCTIVITY
CDILMMOOOSUY COMMODIOUSLY
CDINOORRTTUY INTRODUCTORY
CEEEEFFNRSTV EFFERVESCENT
CEEEEFHNORTV OVER THE FENCE
CEEEEFINNRRT INTERFERENCE
CEEEEHNORSVW WHENCESOEVER
CEEEEIINNPRX INEXPERIENCE
CEEEEIKKPRTW WICKET KEEPER
CEEEEIMNNSSS MISE-EN-SCENES
CEEEEIMNRSVX EX-SERVICEMEN
CEEEEINPRSTX PRE-EXISTENCE
CEEEELMORRTT ELECTROMETER
CEEEENNRRSTV NERVE CENTERS, NERVE
  CENTRES
CEEEFFGINRSV EFFERVESCING
CEEEFFHOOSSU COFFEE HOUSES
CEEEFFLNORST EFFLORESCENT
CEEEFGHIIOPT PIECE OF EIGHT
CEEEFHINRSST SCENESHIFTER
CEEEFHLNRSSU CHEERFULNESS
CEEEFIIMPRTV IMPERFECTIVE
CEEEFILNRTUV UNREFLECTIVE
CEEEFKLNSSSS FECKLESSNESS
CEEEGGNORRRS GREENGROCERS
CEEEGGNORRRY GREENGROCERY
CEEEGIILLNNT INTELLIGENCE
CEEEGIINNPRX EXPERIENCING
CEEEGIINRSTT ENERGETICIST
CEEEHHIINSTW CHINESE WHITE
CEEEHIIMRSTU EUHEMERISTIC
CEEEHIIPRRSV RECEIVERSHIP
CEEEHIKNSTTT KITCHENETTES
CEEEHIMNNPRT ENCIPHERMENT
CEEEHIMNPSWY CHIMNEYSWEEP
CEEEHIMNRSTU HERMENEUTICS
CEEEHINOSSST COENESTHESIS
CEEEHINOSSSV COHESIVENESS
CEEEHIOORSTU HETEROECIOUS
CEEEHLLPSSSY SPEECHLESSLY
CEEEHLNNOTTU LUNCHEONETTE
CEEEHLNOOPRT ELECTROPHONE
CEEEHLOQQSUU QUELQUE CHOSE
CEEEHMNNNRTT ENTRENCHMENT
CEEEHHIINSTW CHINESE WHITE
CEEEHMNNRRTT RETRENCHMENT

CEEEHMOORRST STEREOCHROME
CEEEHNOPRRST CENTROSPHERE
CEEEIILLNTTV INTELLECTIVE
CEEEIIMNNPRT IMPERTINENCE
CEEEIIMPPRTV IMPERCEPTIVE
CEEEIINPRTTV INTERCEPTIVE
CEEEIIPRRSTV IRRESPECTIVE
CEEEIILLNOPQU EQUIPOLLENCE
CEEEEILORRSST CLERESTORIES
CEEEILPPRTVY PERCEPTIVELY
CEEEILPRSTVY RESPECTIVELY
CEEEIMMMNOTT COMMITTEEMEN
CEEEIMMNRSTX CEMENT MIXERS
CEEEIMMPSSUU MUSEUM PIECES
CEEEIMNNOPRS OMNIPRESENCE
CEEEIMNNORST MESENTERONIC
CEEEIMORRSTT STEREOMETRIC
CEEEINNNOSTX NONEXISTENCE
CEEEINNQSSTU QUINTESSENCE
CEEEINORSTUX EXECUTIONERS
CEEEIORRSSTV RETROCESSIVE
CEEEIPPRSSTV PERSPECTIVES
CEEEIPRRSSUV REPERCUSSIVE
CEEEKLNRSSSS RECKLESSNESS
CEEEKMNORSSS SMOKESCREENS
CEEELLNPRUUV PULVERULENCE
CEEELLORRSTY ELECTROLYSER
CEEELLORSTTY ELECTROLYTES
CEEELMNOPSST COMPLETENESS
CEEELMORRTTY ELECTROMETRY
CEEELOPRRTTY ELECTROTYPER
CEEELORRSSSU RESOURCELESS
CEEEMNNNORTU RENOUNCEMENT
CEEEMOPRRSTT SPECTROMETER
CEEEOOPRRTTX EXTEROCEPTOR
CEEFFHIIORSS IRISH COFFEES
CEEFFIOPRTTY PETTY OFFICER
CEEFFLNORSSU FORCEFULNESS
CEEFGGILNNTU GENUFLECTING
CEEFGHIINPSY SPEECHIFYING
CEEFGIILNRTY ELECTRIFYING
CEEFGILLNRTY REFLECTINGLY
CEEFGILNNOTU GENUFLECTION
CEEFGLLLNTUY NEGLECTFULLY
CEEFHIKNRSSS FRENCH KISSES
CEEFHILSSTTU CUTTLEFISHES
CEEFIIMNOPRT IMPERFECTION
CEEFIINOPRST FRONTISPIECE
CEEFIKOOPRSW PIECES OF WORK
CEEFILMNRSSU MERCIFULNESS
CEEFILNNORST INFLORESCENT
CEEFIMNNNOST CONFINEMENTS
CEEFLLPRSTUY RESPECTFULLY
CEEFLOORRSSU FORECLOSURES

CEEGGILNOSSU GLUCOGENESIS
CEEGGILNOSSY GLYCOGENESIS
CEEGHIINOSTT HISTOGENETIC
CEEGHILNOOST TECHNOLOGIES
CEEGHILOOPRT HERPETOLOGIC
CEEGHIMORSTY GEOCHEMISTRY
CEEGHINOORTT ORTHOGENETIC
CEEGHINOPTTY PHYTOGENETIC
CEEGIIJNNRTT INTERJECTING
CEEGIINNNSST ENTICINGNESS
CEEGIINNPRTT INTERCEPTING
CEEGIINNRSSU INSURGENCIES
CEEGIINNRSTT INTERSECTING
CEEGIINOPRTV PRECOGNITIVE
CEEGIKLLNOPS GLOCKENSPIEL
CEEGIKNNOSTV EVENING STOCK
CEEGIMNNOPRS RECOMPENSING
CEEGINNNORTU ENCOUNTERING
CEEGINNOPTTX NOT EXCEPTING
CEEGINOPRRSS REPROCESSING
CEEGINRRRSTU RESURRECTING
CEEGMNOORRST COSTERMONGER
CEEHHIINOSTT HENOTHEISTIC
CEEHHLOORSST CLOTHESHORSE
CEEHHMOOPRRS CHROMOSPHERE
CEEHHOOPPRSS PHOSPHORESCE
CEEHIIMNSSTZ NIETZSCHEISM
CEEHIIMSSTTW TIME SWITCHES
CEEHIINNNPPS PINCH PENNIES
CEEHIKMNOSSS HOMESICKNESS
CEEHILLNOSST CLOTHESLINES
CEEHILMMOPRY MYRMECOPHILE
CEEHILNNORTY INCOHERENTLY
CEEHILPRSSTU LECTURESHIPS
CEEHIMMORRTT THERMOMETRIC
CEEHIMNOOSTU HOME COUNTIES
CEEHIMNORSTT THEOCENTRISM
CEEHINNNPPRY PENNY PINCHER
CEEHINOOPRST STEREOPHONIC
CEEHINOORRSS RHINOCEROSES
CEEHINRSSSTT STRETCHINESS
CEEHIOPRSTUX EXECUTORSHIP
CEEHKLNOSSUY HONEYSUCKLES
CEEHKMNNORWY MONKEY WRENCH
CEEHLLMOORWY CHROME YELLOW
CEEHLMOOPRTU THERMOCOUPLE
CEEHLOPRSSST CLOTHES-PRESS
CEEHMNOORRST CHRONOMETERS
CEEHMNORSTUX HERSTMONCEUX
CEEHMOORRSTY STEREOCHROMY
CEEHMOPRRSTY PSYCHROMETER
CEEHMORSTTYY HYSTERECTOMY
CEEHOOPPRRSTU URETHROSCOPE
CEEHOOPSSSTT STETHOSCOPES

CEEIIINNSSSV INCISIVENESS
CEEIIINPRRTU PERINEURITIC
CEEIIJNNORTT INTERJECTION
CEEIIJNORTTV INTROJECTIVE
CEEIIILLNNOTT INTELLECTION
CEEIIILMNNORT INCLINOMETER
CEEIIILMOPSTX COMPLEXITIES
CEEIIILNNPRSS PRINCELINESS
CEEIIILNPSSTX EXPLICITNESS
CEEIIILOOPSSU LEUCOPOIESIS
CEEIIMNOPPRT IMPERCEPTION
CEEIIMNOSSSS SECESSIONISM
CEEIIMOPRSSU SEMIPRECIOUS
CEEIIMORRSTU MERETRICIOUS
CEEIINNNNOTV INCONVENIENT
CEEIINNOPRTT INTERCEPTION
CEEIINNORSST INTERCESSION
CEEIINNORSTT INTERSECTION
CEEIINOPRSTT RECEPTIONIST
CEEIINORSSTV INSECTIVORES
CEEIINOSSSST SECESSIONIST
CEEIIPPRRSTV PRESCRIPTIVE
CEEIIPPRTTVY PERCEPTIVITY
CEEIIJNORRTTY INTERJECTORY
CEEIKLMNPPRU PUMPERNICKEL
CEEIKNNOOPST IN ONE'S POCKET
CEEILLMNOPTY INCOMPLETELY
CEEILLORSSTY ELECTROLYSIS
CEEILMOOPRSY COPOLYMERISE
CEEILMOOPRYZ COPOLYMERIZE
CEEILNNNOTVY CONVENIENTLY
CEEILNOOPRSS NECROPOLISES
CEEILOPRTTVY PROTECTIVELY
CEEIMMMNORTT RECOMMITMENT
CEEIMNNOPSTT INCOMPETENTS
CEEIMNOOPRST CONTEMPORISE
CEEIMNOOPRTZ CONTEMPORIZE
CEEINNNOQSTU INCONSEQUENT
CEEINNOORRRT RECONNOITRER
CEEINNOORRSV RECONVERSION
CEEINNPRTUUV VENIPUNCTURE
CEEINNRRRTTU INTERCURRENT
CEEINOOPRRTT INTEROCEPTOR
CEEINOOPRSTT STEREOPTICON
CEEINOOPRSTU COUNTERPOISE
CEEINOORRSST RETROCESSION
CEEINOPRRSSU REPERCUSSION
CEEINOPRRSTT INTERCEPTORS
CEEINOPRSSSU PRECIOUSNESS
CEEINOPRSSTU PERSECUTIONS
CEEINOPSSSSU SPECIOUSNESS
CEEINORRRSTU RESURRECTION
CEEINORRSSTY INTERCESSORY
CEEINORSTTTU RECONSTITUTE

CEEIOOPRRSTT STEREOTROPIC
CEEKOORRRSTT RETRO-ROCKETS
CEELLNOORTTV ELECTRONVOLT
CEELNNOQSTUY CONSEQUENTLY
CEELNOORSTTU ELECTROTONUS
CEELOOOPRSTU COLEOPTEROUS
CEEMOPRRSTTY SPECTROMETRY
CEEMOPRRSTUU SUPREME COURT
CEENNOOQRSTU QUEEN CONSORT
CEENNOORRSST CORNERSTONES
CEENNOORRTTU COUNTERTENOR
CEENOOOPPRSS SNOOPERSCOPE
CEENOORRRTTV CONTROVERTER
CEENOOSSSTUV COVETOUSNESS
CEEOPPRSSSTU PROSPECTUSES
CEFFHMNOOPSU OFF ONE'S CHUMP
CEFFIIINNSTU INSUFFICIENT
CEFFIILOOPRT PILOT OFFICER
CEFFIORRSTUU FRUCTIFEROUS
CEFFIORSSTUU SUFFRUTICOSE
CEFGIIKLLNRY FLICKERINGLY
CEFGIIKLNPTY FLYING PICKET
CEFHHILNOPRS FRENCH POLISH
CEFHILMNNOUY ICHNEUMON FLY
CEFHLLLOOOSW SCHOOLFELLOW
CEFIIILNOSTU INFELICITOUS
CEFIIILORSSU SILICIFEROUS
CEFIIIORRSTU FOURIERISTIC
CEFIILLOSTUY FELICITOUSLY
CEFIILMNNTUY MUNIFICENTLY
CEFIILNOORRS FERROSILICON
CEFIILNOPRSS PROLIFICNESS
CEFIILNOPRTY PROFICIENTLY
CEFIILNOSTUY INFECTIOUSLY
CEFILLORRTUU FLORICULTURE
CEFILMOORRTU FLUOROMETRIC
CEFILNOORSTU COUNTERFOILS
CEFILOORSUVY VOCIFEROUSLY
CEFKKLOORRSW CLERK OF WORKS
CEFLNNORSSSU SCORNFULNESS
CEFNOOOOPRRTU COUNTERPROOF
CEGHHIILOPRY HIEROGLYPHIC
CEGHIIKNPRSW SHIPWRECKING
CEGHIILNRSTT CHITTERLINGS
CEGHIIINNRSST CHRISTENINGS
CEGHIIOPSSTY GEOPHYSICIST
CEGHIKNNOSSS SHOCKINGNESS
CEGHIKNOORRS ROCKING HORSE
CEGHILLNQSUY SQUELCHINGLY
CEGHILNOOORS CHRONOLOGIES
CEGHILNOOSTT TECHNOLOGIST
CEGHILOOPSSY PSYCHOLOGIES,
   PSYCHOLOGISE
CEGHILOOPSYZ PSYCHOLOGIZE

CEGIIIILMSTT LEGITIMISTIC
CEGIIKLLMNRY MERCY KILLING
CEGIIKLNNORT INTERLOCKING
CEGIIKLNNRSY SNICKERINGLY
CEGIILLOOSTX LEXICOLOGIST
CEGIILMNOSST CLOSING TIMES
CEGIILNNPSTY INSPECTINGLY
CEGIINNOOPRT PRECOGNITION
CEGIINNOORST RECOGNITIONS
CEGIINOPTTYY GENOTYPICITY
CEGIKKNORSTY SKYROCKETING
CEGIKLNNOSSU KING'S COUNSEL
CEGIKNOORSTV OVERSTOCKING
CEGILLLMNOPY COMPELLINGLY
CEGILNNNOTTY CONTINGENTLY
CEGILNNORSTU CURLING STONE
CEGILNOOPRTY GLYCOPROTEIN
CEGIMNNNOSST CONSIGNMENTS
CEGINNNNOSTU UNCONSENTING
CEGINNNOORTW CONNING TOWER
CEGINNORSSTU COUNTERSIGNS
CEGINNOSTTTU STONECUTTING
CEGINNPSSTUU UNSUSPECTING
CEGINOOPPRRV OVERCROPPING
CEGINPRSSTTU PRESS CUTTING
CEHHILNRSSSU CHURLISHNESS
CEHHIMMOOOPR HOMEOMORPHIC
CEHHIMOOPRTT PHOTOTHERMIC
CEHHIMOOPSTT PHOTOCHEMIST
CEHHIOOPPRST PHOTOSPHERIC
CEHHLOOOSSSU SCHOOLHOUSES
CEHIIILNOOPS EOSINOPHILIC
CEHIIKLNSSST TICKLISHNESS
CEHIIKNOOPTT PHOTOKINETIC
CEHIILMNOPRS NECROPHILISM
CEHIILNQSSSU CLIQUISHNESS
CEHIILOPSTTY POLYTHEISTIC
CEHIIMNOOSTT MONOTHEISTIC
CEHIIMNOPRUY PERIONYCHIUM
CEHIINNOPRTY PERICYNTHION
CEHIIOPRRSTU PERITRICHOUS
CEHIKLMORSTY LOCKSMITHERY
CEHIKNOPSSTU SOUP KITCHENS
CEHILLOPPTYY POLYPHYLETIC
CEHILMNOOPTY MONOPHYLETIC
CEHILMNOPPTY NYMPHOLEPTIC
CEHILNNOSSSW CLOWNISHNESS
CEHILOQSTTUY COQUETTISHLY
CEHILORRTTUU HORTICULTURE
CEHIMMOOPRST CHEMOTROPISM
CEHIMNORRTYY ERYTHROMYCIN
CEHIMOOPRRTT THERMOTROPIC
CEHIMOORSTYZ ZOOCHEMISTRY
CEHINNORRSSY SYNCHRONISER

CEHINNORRSYZ SYNCHRONIZER
CEHIOOOPPRST PHOTOCOPIERS
CEHLMMOOORSSU SUMMER SCHOOL
CEHMMOOORSSX X CHROMOSOMES
CEHMMOOORSSY Y CHROMOSOMES
CEHMNORSTUUX HURSTMONCEUX
CEHMOOOOPPST PHOTOCOMPOSE
CEHMOOOOPRTY OOPHORECTOMY
CEHNOOPRRTTU PHOTOCURRENT
CEHOOPRRSTUY URETHROSCOPY
CEIIIIILNSTV INCIVILITIES
CEIIILMNPSST IMPLICITNESS
CEIIILOPRSTV PROCLIVITIES
CEIIIMNOPRSS PRECISIONISM
CEIIINNORSTU REUNIONISTIC
CEIIINNOSSTW WISCONSINITE
CEIIINOPRSST PRECISIONIST
CEIIINORTTWZ ZWITTERIONIC
CEIIINOSSTVV VIVISECTIONS
CEIIJNNOORTT INTROJECTION
CEIIKLSSTWZZ SWIZZLE STICK
CEIIKRRSSTUY SECURITY RISK
CEIILLNOSTUY LICENTIOUSLY
CEIILLRSTUUV SILVICULTURE
CEIILMOPRTUV PLUVIOMETRIC
CEIILNOOSTTU ELOCUTIONIST
CEIILNOPRSUY PERNICIOUSLY
CEIILOPRSSUU SUPERCILIOUS
CEIILRRTTUUV VITICULTURER
CEIIMMNOORSS COMMISSIONER
CEIIMMNOPRTU MINICOMPUTER
CEIIMNOOPSTT COMPETITIONS
CEIIMOOPRSTT PROTOSEMITIC
CEIIMOORSSTT SOCIOMETRIST
CEIINNNOSSTT INCONSISTENT
CEIINNORRSTU INSURRECTION
CEIINOOPRRTY INCORPOREITY
CEIINOPPRRST PRESCRIPTION
CEIINORRSSTT RESTRICTIONS
CEIINORSSTUX EXCURSIONIST
CEIINORSTTVY VENTRICOSITY
CEIINOSTTTUV CONSTITUTIVE
CEIIOPPRRSTV PROSCRIPTIVE
CEIIPRRRSTTW SCRIPTWRITER
CEIIPSSTTUVY SUSCEPTIVITY
CEIKLMOORSST MORTISE LOCKS
CEILLLNOOOSV VIOLONCELLOS
CEILLMOPSUVY COMPULSIVELY
CEILLMOSTUUY METICULOUSLY
CEILLNOSUVVY CONVULSIVELY
CEILLOPRSSTU PORTCULLISES
CEILMNOOSTUU CONTUMELIOUS
CEILMNOPRSTY POLYCENTRISM
CEILNNOSSTTY CONSISTENTLY

CEILNOORRTTU INTERLOCUTOR
CEILNOORSSUY CENSORIOUSLY
CEILNOSSSSUU LUSCIOUSNESS
CEILNOSSTUUY INCESTUOUSLY
CEIMMNOOPSST COMPOS MENTIS
CEIMNNOOPRSU MISPRONOUNCE
CEIMNNOORSTU CONTERMINOUS
CEIMNOPRSTTY STREPTOMYCIN
CEIMNOPSSTUV CONSUMPTIVES
CEIMOOORRSTV VISCEROMOTOR
CEINNOOPRTTU COUNTERPOINT
CEINNOORSSSU CONNOISSEURS
CEINNOSSTTTU CONSTITUENTS
CEINOOPRSSTU PROSECUTIONS
CEINPSSSTTUU INTUSSUSCEPT
CEJNOORRRSUY CORONER'S JURY
CELLLOORSSUY COLOURLESSLY
CELLMOOPRRST COMPTROLLERS
CELLNNOOPSTU POLLEN COUNTS
CELMNOPRTUUU MUCOPURULENT
CELOOOPRRSST POSTER COLORS
CELOOOPRRSTU POSTER COLOUR
CEMMNNNOOSSU UNCOMMONNESS
CEMMOOSTUXYY MYXOMYCETOUS
CEMNOOPSTTUU CONTEMPTUOUS
CEMOOOOORRSTT MOTOR SCOOTER
CENNOSSSTUUU UNCTUOUSNESS
CFFHILMNOSTU FIFTH COLUMNS
CFGHIIKNOPRT PITCHFORKING
CFGIIILMMNOR MICROFILMING
CFGIILNOOSTV COST OF LIVING
CFGILLNOORSY FLYING COLORS
CFGILMNOORTY COMFORTINGLY
CFIIILOSTTUY FICTITIOUSLY
CFIIKLLOORST FOLKLORISTIC
CFIILLNOOSTU SOLIFLUCTION
CFIIMNNOORTY INCONFORMITY
CFIINORSSSTU FIRST COUSINS
CFILNORSSUUU FURUNCULOSIS
CFIMNNOORTUY UNCONFORMITY
CGHHIINNTTUW WITCH-HUNTING
CGHHIINORTUW WITCHING HOUR
CGHIIKKNNOPS SHOCKING PINK
CGHIILOOOPRT OLIGOTROPHIC
CGHIILOOOSTY STOICHIOLOGY
CGHIILOORSTT TRICHOLOGIST
CGHIIMNOOPSY PHYSIOGNOMIC
CGHIIMOOPRTT THIGMOTROPIC
CGHILMOOPSSY PSYCHOLOGISM
CGHILNOOOORST CHRONOLOGIST
CGHILOOPSSTY PSYCHOLOGIST
CGHIMMNOORSST SHORTCOMINGS
CGHINOOOOPPTY PHOTOCOPYING
CGHINOOPSSSY PSYCHOGNOSIS

CGIIIILNOPTZ POLITICIZING	DDDDDEFISUUY FUDDY-DUDDIES
CGIIINNRSTUZ SCRUTINIZING	DDDEEEGINNOP PODDED ENGINE
CGIIKLLLNORY ROLLICKINGLY	DDDEEENRRSSU UNDERDRESSED
CGIILMOOSSTU MUSICOLOGIST	DDDEEFHILRSU HUDDERSFIELD
CGIILNNNOTUY CONTINUINGLY	DDDEEINRSTUU UNDERSTUDIED
CGIILOOOSSST SOCIOLOGISTS	DDDEHNNOOORR RHODODENDRON
CGIILOOOSTTX TOXICOLOGIST	DDEEEELLRSVW WELL-DESERVED
CGIIMMNOOPRS COMPROMISING	DDEEEEMNNSST DEMENTEDNESS
CGIINNOSTTTU CONSTITUTING	DDEEEENNSSTX EXTENDEDNESS
CGIKLLNOORST ROLLING STOCK	DDEEEENRSSSV DESERVEDNESS
CGILNOOSTUUY CONTIGUOUSLY	DDEEEFHLNOTU DO THE NEEDFUL
CGILOOOPRSTT PROCTOLOGIST	DDEEEFMNORSS DEFORMEDNESS
CGILOOPRSTTY CRYPTOLOGIST	DDEEEIINSSST DESENSITISED
CGINOOPRSSTY PYROGNOSTICS	DDEEEIINSSTZ DESENSITIZED
CHHIIOOPPRST PHOSPHORITIC	DDEEEIMNNRTU UNDETERMINED
CHHILMOPRTYY POLYRHYTHMIC	DDEEEINNNPST INDEPENDENTS
CHHIMOOOOPRRT ORTHOMORPHIC	DDEEEINNOSSS ONE-SIDEDNESS
CHHINORRSSTT CHRIST'S-THORN	DDEEEELNOPRUV UNDERDEVELOP
CHHMMOOOORSU HOMOCHROMOUS	DDEEEENOPRSUX UNDEREXPOSED
CHIIILOOPTTX TOXOPHILITIC	DDEEFFGLLLUY FULLY-FLEDGED
CHIIMNNRSSTY STRYCHNINISM	DDEEFGIILMNR MIDDLE FINGER
CHIJLNOOORSU JUNIOR SCHOOL	DDEEFHIIIMRU DEHUMIDIFIER
CHILOOOPPRSU COPROPHILOUS	DDEEFIIINNTU UNIDENTIFIED
CHIMMNOOORST MONOCHROMIST	DDEEGHIILMTW MIDDLEWEIGHT
CHIMNOOOPRST MONOSTROPHIC	DDEEGHIINTWW WHITE WEDDING
CHIMNOOORSTU MONOTRICHOUS	DDEEGIILMNNS SINGLE-MINDED
CHIMNOPRSTYY CHYMOTRYPSIN	DDEEGILMNOST DISLODGEMENT
CHIMOOOPPRRT PROTOMORPHIC	DDEEGILNORUV OVERINDULGED
CHIOOOPPRRTT PROTOTROPHIC	DDEEGLLNORUW WELL-GROUNDED
CHMMNOOORSST SHORT COMMONS	DDEEHIINNRST DISINHERITED
CIIIIOPSSTTV POSITIVISTIC	DDEEHIILNOOT ENDOTHELIOID
CIIIILMPTTUY MULTIPLICITY	DDEEIILMMNPS SIMPLE-MINDED
CIIINNOPRSST INSCRIPTIONS	DDEEIILQSTUY DISQUIETEDLY
CIIILLOOSSTUY SOLICITOUSLY	DDEEIINPRRST PRIEST-RIDDEN
CIILMNNORSUY SYNCLINORIUM	DDEEILLOPRVW WELL-PROVIDED
CIILMNOOOPST MONOPOLISTIC	DDEEILLOPSSW WELL-DISPOSED
CIILOORSTUVY VICTORIOUSLY	DDEEILMNNOPY OPEN-MINDEDLY
CIILOPSSSUUY SUSPICIOUSLY	DDEEILNNORUW LIE DOWN UNDER
CIIMMNNOOSTU COMMUNIONIST	DDEEILNNPSSS SPLENDIDNESS
CIIMNOOOPSST COMPOSITIONS	DDEEIMNNOSTW DISENDOWMENT
CIIMNOPRSTTY NYCTITROPISM	DDEEINRSSTUU UNDERSTUDIES
CIINNOOSTTTU CONSTITUTION	DDEEIOPSSSSS DISPOSSESSED
CIINNORSSTTU INSTRUCTIONS	DDEELNNOPSTY DESPONDENTLY
CIINOOPPRRST PROSCRIPTION	DDEFNOOOPRSU SOUNDPROOFED
CIJLNORSSTUU JURISCONSULT	DDEGGIINNRSW WEDDING RINGS
CILLMOOPRSUY COMPULSORILY	DDEGGIOOOOSY GOODY-GOODIES
CILLORRSSUUY SCURRILOUSLY	DDEGHHIILMNY HIGH-MINDEDLY
CILNNOOOSTUV CONVOLUTIONS	DDEGHILNRSUY SHUDDERINGLY
CILNNOOSTUUY CONTINUOUSLY	DDEGHIRRSUUY HURDY-GURDIES
CIMMOOORSSTU MICROSTOMOUS	DDEGHMOOORUU GOOD-HUMOURED
CIMNNOOPSSTU CONSUMPTIONS	DDEGILLNNOWY LONGWINDEDLY
CIMNOPPSSTUU SUCTION PUMPS	DDEGILNNOPSS PLODDINGNESS
CLLOPRSSUUUY SCRUPULOUSLY	DDEGILNOORST DENDROLOGIST
CLNOPRSSUUUU UNSCRUPULOUS	DDEGIMNNORST STRONG-MINDED

DDEGINNORSSW DRESSING-DOWN
DDEGNNORRSUU UNDERGROUNDS
DDEHILNNOOPR PHILODENDRON
DDEHINOORSTU RIDE TO HOUNDS
DDEIIILPRSTY DISPIRITEDLY
DDEIIJLNOSTY DISJOINTEDLY
DDEIILNNOORR LIRIODENDRON
DDEIIMNOSUVV MODUS VIVENDI
DDEIMOOPPSUU PSEUDOPODIUM
DDELNORRSUUY SURROUNDEDLY
DDGIILNOORSS SLIDING DOORS
DDGILMNPPSUU PLUM PUDDINGS
DEEEEEMNPRTV EVEN-TEMPERED
DEEEEGIILNNS DIESEL ENGINE
DEEEEGMNNNRT ENGENDERMENT
DEEEEHILRSSW SIDE-WHEELERS
DEEEEHLNSSSS HEEDLESSNESS
DEEEEILNNPTT PENDENTE LITE
DEEEEIMNPRRT PREDETERMINE
DEEEEIMNPRTX EXPERIMENTED
DEEEELLMPRTW WELL-TEMPERED
DEEEELNNSSSS NEEDLESSNESS
DEEEEMOPRSST SPEEDOMETERS
DEEEENRRSSSV RESERVEDNESS
DEEEFGHORRTU FOURTH-DEGREE
DEEEFGINRRYZ FREEZE-DRYING
DEEEFIINNSST DEFINITENESS
DEEEFLLMOPSY SELF-EMPLOYED
DEEEFNNQRTUU UNFREQUENTED
DEEEGHINNPRR REPREHENDING
DEEEGHNNRSTT STRENGTHENED
DEEEGIINNRRV ENGINE DRIVER
DEEEGILNOPRV REDEVELOPING
DEEEGINNRSSS RESIGNEDNESS
DEEEGINNRSSV EVENING DRESS
DEEEGJMNPRTU PREJUDGEMENT
DEEEGOOPPSST GOOSESTEPPED
DEEEGORRRSST RETROGRESSED
DEEEHHIPPRSS SHEPHERD'S PIE
DEEEHIILRTVW WHITE-LIVERED
DEEEHILMNSTV DISHEVELMENT
DEEEHINPRRSV REVERENDSHIP
DEEEHINRSSTW WITHEREDNESS
DEEEHMNNORTT DETHRONEMENT
DEEEIILNORRT INDRE-ET-LOIRE
DEEEIINRSSST DESENSITISER
DEEEIINRSSSV DERISIVENESS
DEEEIINRSSTZ DESENSITIZER
DEEEILLPPQUW WELL-EQUIPPED
DEEEILNRSSSW WILDERNESSES
DEEEILNRSTTY INTERESTEDLY
DEEEIMNORSTT DENSITOMETER
DEEEIMNRRSTW MIDWESTERNER
DEEEIMOPRSTX EXTEMPORISED

DEEEIMOPRTXZ EXTEMPORIZED
DEEEEINNRSTTU UNINTERESTED
DEEEEINPRRSST INTERSPERSED
DEEEINRSSSTW DESSERT WINES
DEEEJLLOPPRT JET-PROPELLED
DEEEKLNNOOST ENDOSKELETON
DEEELMNNORSY MONEYLENDERS
DEEELMNOPRTY REDEPLOYMENT
DEEELMNOPSTV DEVELOPMENTS
DEEELMNPPSTU SUPPLEMENTED
DEEELNORSSSV RESOLVEDNESS
DEEELNRRSUVY UNRESERVEDLY
DEEEMNNORSST ENDORSEMENTS
DEEENRRSSTTT TRENDSETTERS
DEEEOPPRSSSS PREPOSSESSED
DEEFFHINRRSU UNDERSHERIFF
DEEFGIILNSTT FIELD-TESTING
DEEFGIINNRSX INDEX FINGERS
DEEFGINNOOPS SPOON-FEEDING
DEEFGKNOORTU FORKED TONGUE
DEEFHIINNSSS FIENDISHNESS
DEEFIIIILNST INFIDELITIES
DEEFIIILNNTY INDEFINITELY
DEEFIIILNTVY DEFINITIVELY
DEEFIILNNRSS FRIENDLINESS
DEEFIILPPRTT FILTER-TIPPED
DEEFIKLORRSW FIELDWORKERS
DEEFILLMNORW WELL-INFORMED
DEEFILNRRSUY USER-FRIENDLY
DEEFLOORSTUY SUREFOOTEDLY
DEEGGHHINOPP HEDGEHOPPING
DEEGGIINPRST PREDIGESTING
DEEGGIMNORST DISGORGEMENT
DEEGHIINNSTW WINDING SHEET
DEEGHIINSTUX EXTINGUISHED
DEEGHINRSSST NIGHTDRESSES
DEEGHNORSSTU GROUNDSHEETS
DEEGIILMNNRT INTERMINGLED
DEEGIILMOOPY EPIDEMIOLOGY
DEEGIILNNRSZ SLENDERIZING
DEEGIILNNSSY YIELDINGNESS
DEEGIILOPSTT EPIGLOTTIDES
DEEGIIMNNOTZ DEMONETIZING
DEEGIIMNPRST DISTEMPERING
DEEGIINNPRST PREDESTINING
DEEGIINOPRST PREDIGESTION
DEEGIINPPSST SIDESTEPPING
DEEGIINPRSTW SPEEDWRITING
DEEGIJMMNSTU MISJUDGEMENT
DEEGILLNNRSU UNDERSELLING
DEEGILLNOOOR GOLDEN ORIOLE
DEEGILMNNNOY MONEYLENDING
DEEGILNPRSSY DEPRESSINGLY
DEEGINNRRRSU SURRENDERING

DEEGINNRSTTT TRENDSETTING
DEEGINORRSSV OVERDRESSING
DEEGJMNPRSTU PREJUDGMENTS
DEEGLLOOSTYY DYSTELEOLOGY
DEEGLNOOOSTU LOOSE-TONGUED
DEEHHIIMOPRS HEMISPHEROID
DEEHHIOPPRSW HORSEWHIPPED
DEEHHLOORSSU HOUSEHOLDERS
DEEHIILNQRSU RELINQUISHED
DEEHIILNSSSV DEVILISHNESS
DEEHIIMOPRSV IMPOVERISHED
DEEHIIINPRSST RESIDENTSHIP
DEEHILLORSTT TITLEHOLDERS
DEEHILMMNOST DEMOLISHMENT
DEEHIMMNORST ENDOTHERMISM
DEEHIMNOORTU TIME-HONOURED
DEEHINNSSTUY THE SUNNY SIDE
DEEHIOPPRTTY PTERIDOPHYTE
DEEHNNORSTTU THUNDERSTONE
DEEHOORRSSUV HORS D'OEUVRES
DEEIIIILLRSST DISTILLERIES
DEEIIINSSSVV DIVISIVENESS
DEEIILNNSSUW UNWIELDINESS
DEEIIMMOPRST POST MERIDIEM
DEEIIMNNRSTT DISINTERMENT
DEEIIMNORTTV DIVERTIMENTO
DEEIIMORRTTU DUMORTIERITE
DEEIINPRSSST SPIRITEDNESS
DEEIIOOPRSST DEPOSITORIES
DEEIJLNOOOST LOOSE-JOINTED
DEEIJNORRRSU SURREJOINDER
DEEILLNORRSS SLENDER LORIS
DEEILMNNSSSS MINDLESSNESS
DEEILNOOPPRT LEPIDOPTERON
DEEILOPRSSTY PROSELYTISED
DEEILOPRSTYZ PROSELYTIZED
DEEIMMNNOOSS SOMEONE'S MIND
DEEIMNORSTTY DENSITOMETRY
DEEIMOPPRRST PTERIDOSPERM
DEEIMOPPRSSU SUPERIMPOSED
DEEINNNORSST NONRESIDENTS
DEEINNOQSTUU UNQUESTIONED
DEEINNRRTTUW UNDERWRITTEN
DEEINORRRSVW OWNER-DRIVERS
DEEINRRRSTUW UNDERWRITERS
DEEKNOORRRWW WONDER-WORKER
DEELMNORSTUY TREMENDOUSLY
DEELNORSSSSW WORDLESSNESS
DEELNOSSSSUU SEDULOUSNESS
DEENOOPRSSST DESSERTSPOON
DEENOPRRSTTU UNDER PROTEST
DEFFHIRSSTTU STUFFED SHIRT
DEFFHLNOOPSU POUND OF FLESH
DEFGGINORRUU FIGURE-GROUND

DEFGHHIIILTY HIGH FIDELITY
DEFGHILLLTUY DELIGHTFULLY
DEFGIIMNNNY INDEMNIFYING
DEFGIIINRSVY DIVERSIFYING
DEFGIIMNSTYY DEMYSTIFYING
DEFGIINORSST DISFORESTING
DEFHINPRSSTT SPENDTHRIFTS
DEFHLOOORSSU HOUSE OF LORDS
DEFIIIILMSTUY SEMIFLUIDITY
DEFIILOPRSUY PERFIDIOUSLY
DEFIINOPRSTU PROFUNDITIES
DEFILOORSTUY DO-IT-YOURSELF
DEFINOOOPRRT POINT OF ORDER
DEFIOORRSSUU SUDORIFEROUS
DEFNNOOPRSSU PROFOUNDNESS
DEGGHILNOOSU LODGING HOUSE
DEGGINNORSSW DRESSING GOWN
DEGHHIIIPRST HIGH-SPIRITED
DEGHHIINOPST DIPHTHONGISE
DEGHHIINOPTZ DIPHTHONGIZE
DEGHHIORSSTT SHORTSIGHTED
DEGHIIIILNRSS DISRELISHING
DEGHILNNRTUY THUNDERINGLY
DEGHINOORSTV OVERDO THINGS
DEGHINOPSSTT POTTING SHEDS
DEGIIILNPPSS SIDESLIPPING
DEGIIINNRRST DISINTERRING
DEGIIKNRSSTW WRITING DESKS
DEGIILLOOSTT DELTIOLOGIST
DEGIILNNOSUY INDIGENOUSLY
DEGIINNNNPRU UNDERPINNING
DEGIINNOSSUU DISINGENUOUS
DEGIINNRRTUW UNDERWRITING
DEGIINOPPRSS PREDISPOSING
DEGIJMMNSSTU MISJUDGMENTS
DEGIKNOORRRW WORKING ORDER
DEGILLNORSTW STRONG-WILLED
DEGILMNOOOST DEMONOLOGIST
DEGILNNORSUY RESOUNDINGLY
DEGILNOOOSTT DEONTOLOGIST
DEGIMNNORSS MORNING DRESS
DEGIMNOORRSS DRESSING ROOM
DEGINOOPPRST DOORSTEPPING
DEGINOPRSSST TOPDRESSINGS
DEGKNOORRSTU GROUND STROKE
DEGLLNORSSUW GROUNDSWELLS
DEGLLNORSSUY GROUNDLESSLY
DEGMNOORRRUY MERRY-GO-ROUND
DEHHHMMORTTY RHYTHM METHOD
DEHIIIMMNNST DIMINISHMENT
DEHIIKLLNOOU UNLIKELIHOOD
DEHILLOPPSUY POLYSULPHIDE
DEHIMMNOOPRS ENDOMORPHISM
DEHINNORRSUU UNDERNOURISH

DEHINOOPRSST SPINSTERHOOD
DEHLLOORRTWY OTHERWORLDLY
DEHLNOORRSUY HORRENDOUSLY
DEHLNORSTUUY THUNDEROUSLY
DEHLOOOSTTTW TWO-TOED SLOTH
DEHMNORRSTTU THUNDERSTORM
DEHNOOORSTUW SOUTHERNWOOD
DEIIKLNNNSSU UNKINDLINESS
DEIILLOOQSSU SOLILOQUISED
DEIILLOOQSUZ SOLILOQUIZED
DEIILNOORSWW ORIEL WINDOWS
DEIILPRSTUVY DISRUPTIVELY
DEIIOOPPRRST POOR-SPIRITED
DEIJNPRRSTUU JURISPRUDENT
DEILLOOSSSVW SLOW DISSOLVE
DEIMNOPSTUYY PSEUDONYMITY
DEINOOOOPPRRT PROPORTIONED
DEINOSSSSTUU STUDIOUSNESS
DEIOOPRSSSSS DISPOSSESSOR
DEKLLOOPRSST ROLLTOP DESKS
DELNNOOPSTYY POLYSYNDETON
DELNOPSSTUUY STUPENDOUSLY
DEMNOOPSSUUY PSEUDONYMOUS
DENNOORSSSUW WONDROUSNESS
DEOOOOPPRRSST DOORSTOPPERS
DFGHIINOPSSY SPINY DOGFISH
DFGIIKNNNSSU SINKING FUNDS
DFGLNOOOORRSU GROUND FLOORS
DFHILNOOOPSU POUND-FOOLISH
DGGHHIINNOSU HIGH-SOUNDING
DGGHIINNNOOT NOTHING DOING
DGGIILNSSTUY DISGUSTINGLY
DGHIINNOORSU DISHONOURING
DGIIILNNOOSV LONG DIVISION
DGIILOOPRSUY PRODIGIOUSLY
DGILNOOOOSTT ODONTOLOGIST
DGINNORRSSUU SURROUNDINGS
DHHIILOOPPPS PHOSPHOLIPID
DHIIIMMOOPRS IDIOMORPHISM
DHLNOOOPPTYY POLYPHYODONT
DHMMPPTTUUYY HUMPTY DUMPTY
DIIIINOQSSTU DISQUISITION
DIIIINOOPSSST DISPOSITIONS
DIILNOOSSSTU DISSOLUTIONS
DIILNOOSSTUU SOLITUDINOUS
EEEEEHHLRRTW THREE-WHEELER
EEEEFGHILNRW FREEWHEELING
EEEEGHMORSTW GET SOMEWHERE
EEEEGIILNPSS SPIEGELEISEN
EEEEGNPPPRRS GREEN PEPPERS
EEEEHINPRRSV REPREHENSIVE
EEEEHKOPRSSU HOUSEKEEPERS
EEEEHLMNOPRT NEPHELOMETER
EEEEHLNRSSTV NEVERTHELESS

EEEEHNNSSTTV SEVENTEENTHS
EEEEIINRSTVW INTERVIEWEES
EEEEIMNPRRTX EXPERIMENTER
EEEEIMNPRSSW MINESWEEPERS
EEEEINNQRSTU EQUESTRIENNE
EEEEINSSSTWY EYEWITNESSES
EEEEKOPRRSST STOREKEEPERS
EEEELMNRSTTT RESETTLEMENT
EEEELNOPRRTT LETTER OPENER
EEEELNRSSSST TREELESSNESS
EEEEMNORSTTX EXTENSOMETER
EEEENNPRRRTU ENTREPRENEUR
EEEENNRRSSTV REVERENTNESS
EEEENPRRSSSV PERVERSENESS
EEEEORRTTTTT TEETER-TOTTER
EEEEPPPRSSTW SWEET PEPPERS
EEEFFIILNNTT IN FINE FETTLE
EEEFFIMORSTU EFFUSIOMETER
EEEFFINSSSUV EFFUSIVENESS
EEEFFLLNNORW FENNELFLOWER
EEEFGGINNRRS GREEN FINGERS
EEEFGLNNSSUV VENGEFULNESS
EEEFGNNOORSS FOREGONENESS
EEEFHHINOTTT IN THE TEETH OF
EEEFHIKNRRST FREETHINKERS
EEEFHILRRSSW FERRIS WHEELS
EEEFHINNOTTV IN THE EVENT OF
EEEFHINRSSSV FEVERISHNESS
EEEFHMNRRSST REFRESHMENTS
EEEFIILLLLMU MILLEFEUILLE
EEEFIILMMPRR FILM PREMIERE
EEEFIILNRRTT INTERFERTILE
EEEFILLNSSSS LIFELESSNESS
EEEFILNRSSTT SELF-INTEREST
EEEFJLNNOOSY ENJOY ONESELF
EEEFLLNSSSSS SELFLESSNESS
EEEFLMNORSTT MEN OF LETTERS
EEEFLNNSSTUV EVENTFULNESS
EEEGGHORSTTT GET-TOGETHERS
EEEGHIKNOPSU HOUSEKEEPING
EEEGHILRTTWW WELTERWEIGHT
EEEGHIMNOSTU MEETINGHOUSE
EEEGHINSTTVY SEVENTY-EIGHT
EEEGHNNRRSTT STRENGTHENER
EEEGHNOORSTU HETEROGENOUS
EEEGHNORSSTT TOGETHERNESS
EEEGHOORTTYZ HETEROZYGOTE
EEEGIIMNNPSW MINESWEEPING
EEEGIINNORRT ORIENTEERING
EEEGIINORSST GENEROSITIES
EEEGIKMNNNOY MONKEY ENGINE
EEEGIKNOPRST STOREKEEPING
EEEGILNOPRSV OVERSLEEPING
EEEGINNPRRST REPRESENTING

EEEGINNPSSSW SWEEPINGNESS
EEEGMNORSSSU GRUESOMENESS
EEEGNNORSSSU GENEROUSNESS
EEEGNOOPRRST PROGESTERONE
EEEGNOORRSUV OVERGENEROUS
EEEHHINPSSSS SHEEPISHNESS
EEEHHLNORTUV ELEVENTH HOUR
EEEHHMOPRRST THERMOSPHERE
EEEHILLOSTTT STILETTO HEEL
EEEHILMNORST HERMOTENSILE
EEEHILRSSSTV SHIRTSLEEVES
EEEHIMNNNRST ENSHRINEMENT
EEEHIMNRSTTU HERMENEUTIST
EEEHINNOPRRS REPREHENSION
EEEHINNORSTW NONE THE WISER
EEEHJMPQTUUU JUMP THE QUEUE
EEEHLLNOPTYY POLYETHYLENE
EEEHLLNPSSSS HELPLESSNESS
EEEHLMNOSSSS HOMELESSNESS
EEEHLNOPSSSS HOPELESSNESS
EEEHLOPRSTTW POTTER'S WHEEL
EEEHMMORRSTT THERMOMETERS
EEEHMNNNORTT ENTHRONEMENT
EEEHMNNOQRSTU QUEEN MOTHERS
EEEHMOORRSTU HETEROMEROUS
EEEHNOPRRRSY REPREHENSORY
EEEHNORSSTTT ON THE STREETS
EEEHNOSSSTUY SHUT ONE'S EYES
EEEHOPRRSSTZ HERPES ZOSTER
EEEIILPPRSTX PERPLEXITIES
EEEIIMNRSSTT MESENTERITIS
EEEIINPRRTTV INTERPRETIVE
EEEIINPRSSVX INEXPRESSIVE
EEEIINRRSTVW INTERVIEWERS
EEEIIPPRSTTU PERPETUITIES
EEEIIPQRRSTU PREREQUISITE
EEEIIPRRSSTV PERVERSITIES
EEEIILLLOPPTT LITTLE PEOPLE
EEEILMNNPRTY PRE-EMINENTLY
EEEILMNNSSSU UNSEEMLINESS
EEEILMNORSTU SON ET LUMIERE
EEEILMNSSSST TIMELESSNESS
EEEILMOORVZZ MEZZO-RELIEVO
EEEILMPPRTVY PRE-EMPTIVELY
EEEILNPRRSTT TELEPRINTERS
EEEILNPRTVVY PREVENTIVELY
EEEILNRRRTVY IRREVERENTLY
EEEILNRSSSST TIRELESSNESS
EEEILNRSSSTW WESTERLINESS
EEEILPRRSSVY REPRESSIVELY
EEEILPRSSVXY EXPRESSIVELY
EEEIMNNPRSTT PRESENTIMENT
EEEIMNNPRSTU SUPEREMINENT
EEEIMNNRSTTV REINVESTMENT

EEEIMNORSSST TIRESOMENESS
EEEIMNORSSTT SENSITOMETER
EEEIMNPRRSST MISREPRESENT
EEEIMNQRRSTU REQUIREMENTS
EEEIMOORRSST STEREOISOMER
EEEIMOPRRSTX EXTEMPORISER
EEEIMOPRRTXZ EXTEMPORIZER
EEEIMOPRSTUX TIME EXPOSURE
EEEINNPRSSTX INEXPERTNESS
EEEINNPRSTUV SUPERVENIENT
EEEINPRRRSTT INTERPRETERS
EEEINPRSSUVX UNEXPRESSIVE
EEEINRRTTTUX INTERTEXTURE
EEEIORRSTVVX EXTROVERSIVE
EEEJMPQRSUUU QUEUE-JUMPERS
EEEKKLNOSSTY SKELETON KEYS
EEEKLOOPPPSS SPOKESPEOPLE
EEELLLNRSSTY RELENTLESSLY
EEELLMORRTTU TELLUROMETER
EEELLOPPPRWY YELLOW PEPPER
EEELMMNOPRTY RE-EMPLOYMENT
EEELMNNOOSSS LONESOMENESS
EEELMNNOOSTT ON ONE'S METTLE
EEELMNNSTTTU UNSETTLEMENT
EEELMNPPRSTU SUPPLEMENTER
EEELMOPPRRTT TELEPROMPTER
EEELNNOQSSTU ELOQUENTNESS
EEELNNOSSSST TONELESSNESS
EEELNNSSSSTU TUNELESSNESS
EEELNORSSSTU RESOLUTENESS
EEELNRSSSSST RESTLESSNESS
EEELOOPRSTTU TELEUTOSPORE
EEEMPRSSTTXY EXPERT SYSTEM
EEENOORSSTTT TESTOSTERONE
EEEOPRRTTTVY REVERT TO TYPE
EEFFGHIIRRST FIRE FIGHTERS
EEFFGILNRSSU GLUE-SNIFFERS
EEFFIIILLORX ELIXIR OF LIFE
EEFFLLORSSTY EFFORTLESSLY
EEFGHIIKNNRT FREETHINKING
EEFGHIILNRRT FREIGHTLINER
EEFGHIILRRST FIRELIGHTERS
EEFGHIILRTTW WEIGHT LIFTER
EEFGHIIPRRST PRISEFIGHTER
EEFGHIIPRRTZ PRIZEFIGHTER
EEFGHILNRRSY REFRESHINGLY
EEFGIILLNRTT LITTLE FINGER
EEFGIILMNPXY EXEMPLIFYING
EEFGIIMMNRSW FREE-SWIMMING
EEFGIIMNNNRT INFRINGEMENT
EEFGIINOPRRT PROFITEERING
EEFGMNOORSTT FORGET-ME-NOTS
EEFHHMMMOOOR HOME FROM HOME
EEFHIILRSSSV SILVERFISHES

EEFIIINNRSST INTENSIFIERS
EEFIIMNORSSU SEMINIFEROUS
EEFIINORRSSU RESINIFEROUS
EEFILLORSSTU STELLIFEROUS
EEFILMOOORST TOMFOOLERIES
EEFILMORSTTU FLITTERMOUSE
EEFILNNQRTUY INFREQUENTLY
EEFILNOORRTX RETROFLEXION
EEFILNPSSSTU SPITEFULNESS
EEFIMNNORRST FRONTIERSMEN
EEFLLMORRSUY REMORSEFULLY '
EEFLLNNTUUVY UNEVENTFULLY
EEFLLNOOOPSW ONE FELL SWOOP
EEFLMNORSSSS FORMLESSNESS
EEFLNOPRSSUW POWERFULNESS
EEGGGGHMRRUU .HUGGER-MUGGER
EEGGHIILNNNT ENLIGHTENING
EEGGHIINTTUV GIVE IT THE GUN
EEGGIILNNRSS GINGERLINESS
EEGGILSSTUVY SUGGESTIVELY
EEGGNOORSSSU GORGEOUSNESS
EEGHHILRSTWW WHEELWRIGHTS
EEGHHIPRRSSU HIGH-PRESSURE
EEGHIILNNPRS REPLENISHING
EEGHIINOSSST HISTOGENESIS
EEGHIINPRRTZ THE PRIZE RING
EEGHIINRSTUX EXTINGUISHER
EEGHIKNRRSTU HUNGER STRIKE
EEGHILLSSTWY WEIGHTLESSLY
EEGHILMNORVW OVERWHELMING
EEGHINOORSST ORTHOGENESIS
EEGHINOPSSTY PHYTOGENESIS
EEGHLLOOPRST HOT-GOSPELLER
EEGHLMNNOORS LONGSHOREMEN
EEGHLOOORSTU HETEROLOGOUS
EEGHMNOORSTU THERMOGENOUS
EEGHMNOORTTU MOTHER TONGUE
EEGHNOOORSTU HETEROGONOUS
EEGHNOORSTUY HETEROGYNOUS
EEGHOORSTUYZ HETEROZYGOUS
EEGIIINNRTVW INTERVIEWING
EEGIILLLNPPS SLEEPING PILL
EEGIILLNNNVY ENLIVENINGLY
EEGIILMMNNPT IMPLEMENTING
EEGIILNORRTV GREEN VITRIOL
EEGIILOPSSTT EPIGLOTTISES
EEGIIMNNOPST OPENING TIMES
EEGIINNPRRST ENTERPRISING
EEGIINNPRRTT INTERPRETING
EEGIINNRSTWZ WESTERNIZING
EEGIJMNPQUUU QUEUE-JUMPING
EEGIKKNORSWW WORKING WEEKS
EEGILLNOOSST SELENOLOGIST
EEGILLNRSTWY SWELTERINGLY

EEGILLOOPSST SPELEOLOGIST
EEGILLOOSSTT TELEOLOGISTS
EEGILMNOOOST ENTOMOLOGISE
EEGILMNOOOTZ ENTOMOLOGIZE
EEGILMOOPPSS GOOSE PIMPLES
EEGILMOOPSTY EPISTEMOLOGY
EEGILNNORTUV VOLUNTEERING
EEGILNNSSSSW WINGLESSNESS
EEGILNOPRTTU TRIPLE-TONGUE
EEGILOPRSSTT POLTERGEISTS
EEGILQRRRSUY GREY SQUIRREL
EEGIMNNRRSTU INTERREGNUMS
EEGINNPRSSSS PRESSINGNESS
EEGINOOPRRVW OVERPOWERING
EEGINOOPRSSS SPOROGENESIS
EEGINOOPRSVX OVEREXPOSING
EEGINOPPRSTV OVERSTEPPING
EEGINOPPRSSS REPOSSESSING
EEGINOPRSTTY STEREOTYPING
EEGINORSSSUV GRIEVOUSNESS
EEGINOSSSUUX EXIGUOUSNESS
EEGINPRSSTTU GUTTERSNIPES
EEGIOPRRSSSV PROGRESSIVES
EEGKORRSSTUW GUEST WORKERS
EEGLMNNOOOPR PROLEGOMENON
EEGLOPPPSTUV GLOVE PUPPETS
EEGNNOORRSUU NEUROSURGEON
EEGNORRRSUUY NEUROSURGERY
EEHHIIMMOPRT HEMIMORPHITE
EEHHIINSSSTV THIEVISHNESS
EEHHILLNOPTY THEOPHYLLINE
EEHHINRSSSSW SHREWISHNESS
EEHHIOPPRRSW HORSEWHIPPER
EEHHLLNNOORZ HOHENZOLLERN
EEHHLLOPRTYY HETEROPHYLLY
EEHHMOORSSTU HOUSEMOTHERS
EEHHOOOSSTUU HOUSE-TO-HOUSE
EEHHOOSSUUYY HOUSEY-HOUSEY
EEHIIIIMNNRTT IN THE INTERIM
EEHIILNQRRSU RELINQUISHER
EEHIIMNPPRRU PERINEPHRIUM
EEHIIMOPRRSV IMPOVERISHER
EEHIIMPPRRSS PREMIERSHIPS
EEHIINNSSSVX VIXENISHNESS
EEHILMNORSST MOTHERLINESS
EEHILNNPSTWY PENNY WHISTLE ,
EEHILNOOPSST SIPHONOSTELE
EEHILNOPSSTT TELEPHONISTS
EEHIMOPRSTTY MORE'S THE PITY
EEHINRSSSSTY SYNTHESISERS
EEHINRSSSTYZ SYNTHESIZERS
EEHIPRSSSTTU TRUSTEESHIPS
EEHLNRSSSSTU RUTHLESSNESS
EEHLOORRSTTU RULE THE ROOST

EEHLOPRRSSTU UPHOLSTERERS
EEHMMORSSSUU SUMMERHOUSES
EEHMNNOOORSY HONEYMOONERS
EEHMNOOORSTU HETERONOMOUS
EEHMNOORSTUY HETERONYMOUS
EEHMNRRRSUYY NURSERY RHYME
EEHNNORRSTTW NORTHWESTERN
EEHNNORSSSTT HORNET'S NESTS
EEHNORSSTTUW SOUTHWESTERN
EEHOOPRRSSTU PORTERHOUSES
EEIIIMNRSSTV INTERMISSIVE
EEIIINPRRSTU PERINEURITIS
EEIIINRSSTUV UNIVERSITIES
EEIIIKLLNNSSU UNLIKELINESS
EEIIILLPRSSTV SPIRIT LEVELS
EEIIILMNNPTTY IMPENITENTLY
EEIIILMNNSSTU UNTIMELINESS
EEIIILMNOPSST IMPOLITENESS
EEIIILMPRSSVY IMPRESSIVELY,
    PERMISSIVELY
EEIIILNNPRRST LINE PRINTERS
EEIIILNPPRSSS SLIPPERINESS
EEIIILNPRSSST PRIESTLINESS
EEIIILNPSSSST PITILESSNESS
EEIIILNRSSSST SISTERLINESS
EEIIILOOPPSTV POSITIVE POLE
EEIIIMNNRTTTT INTERMITTENT
EEIIIMNOPRRSS REIMPRESSION
EEIIIMNOQSTTU QUESTION TIME
EEIIIMNPRRSTT MISINTERPRET
EEIIIMNPRSSUV UNIMPRESSIVE
EEIIIMNPRSTTY SEMPITERNITY
EEIIIMNRRTTUX INTERMIXTURE
EEIIIMORSSTUV SEMIVITREOUS
EEIIINNNORTTV INTERVENTION
EEIIINNPSSTUV PUNITIVENESS
EEIIINNRSSSST SINISTERNESS
EEIIINOORSSTV STEREOVISION
EEIIINOPPRSST PROPENSITIES
EEIIINOPRRSSV IRRESPONSIVE
EEIIINOPSSSTV POSITIVENESS
EEIIINORRSTVV INTROVERSIVE
EEIIINPRRTTUV INTERRUPTIVE
EEIIINRSSTTUV INVESTITURES
EEIIIOOPRRSST REPOSITORIES
EEIIIPRSSTVXY EXPRESSIVITY
EEIKLMNNOSTY MILTON KEYNES
EEIKOPRRRSTW WORKER-PRIEST
EEILLNNOSSSV SLOVENLINESS
EEILLNSSSSST LISTLESSNESS
EEILLORRSTUY IRRESOLUTELY
EEILMMNNOPTY IN EMPLOYMENT
EEILMOOPRSST METROPOLISES
EEILMOPPRRTY PEREMPTORILY

EEILNNOOPSVX NONEXPLOSIVE
EEILNOOORSSU OLEORESINOUS
EEILNOOPPRSY POLYISOPRENE
EEILNOORRSTU RESOLUTIONER
EEILNOPRSSSU PERILOUSNESS
EEILNOPRSSVY RESPONSIVELY
EEILNPRSSTTY PERSISTENTLY
EEILOPPRSSVY OPPRESSIVELY
EEILOPRRSSTY PROSELYTISER
EEILOPRRSTYZ PROSELYTIZER
EEILOPSSSSVY POSSESSIVELY
EEIMMMNSSTUY IMMUNE SYSTEM
EEIMMNOPRSTV IMPROVEMENTS
EEIMNNNOPRSY MONEY-SPINNER
EEIMNNNORSTV ENVIRONMENTS
EEIMNORSSTTY SENSITOMETRY
EEINNOPRSSUV UNRESPONSIVE
EEINNORRSSSU RESINOUSNESS
EEINOOPPSSST OPPOSITENESS
EEINOOPRSSSS REPOSSESSION
EEINOORRRSTV RETROVERSION
EEINOORRSTVX EXTROVERSION
EEINOPRSSSSU SUPERSESSION
EEINOPRSSSTV SPORTIVENESS
EEINOPRSSSUV PERVIOUSNESS,
    PREVIOUSNESS
EEINORSSSTUV VITREOUSNESS
EEKLMNOPUYZZ MONKEY-PUZZLE
EEKNOOPPRSSS SPOKESPERSON
EELLLOORRSTW ROLLER TOWELS
EELLNNNOOSSV NOLENS VOLENS
EELLNOSSSSSU SOULLESSNESS
EELLORRSSTTY STORYTELLERS
EELMMNNOPTUY UNEMPLOYMENT
EELMOPRRSTTY STORMY PETREL
EELNOORSSSST ROOTLESSNESS
EELNOPSSSSST SPOTLESSNESS
EEMNNOOPPSTT POSTPONEMENT
EEMNNOORSSSU ENORMOUSNESS
EEMNNORSSSUU NUMEROUSNESS
EENNOOPPRSSU ON ONE'S UPPERS
EENNOSSSSSUU SENSUOUSNESS
EENOOPRRSTUU NEUROPTEROUS
EEOOPPRRSSTU PREPOSTEROUS
EEOOPQRSSSTTU REQUEST STOPS
EEOPRRRSSSTU TROUSER PRESS
EEPPRRTTTTYY PRETTY-PRETTY
EFFGGHIIINRT FIRE FIGHTING
EFFGGIILNNSU GLUE-SNIFFING
EFFGHHHIIRSS HIGH SHERIFFS
EFFGIINOOPRR FIREPROOFING
EFFILNRSSTUU FRUITFULNESS
EFGGGIINOPTT PETTIFOGGING
EFGHHIILOPRS HIGH PROFILES

EFGHIILNOSST LINES OF SIGHT
EFGHIIINNSSST SHIFTINGNESS
EFGHIINRRSTT FIRST-NIGHTER
EFGHILNRSSTU RIGHTFULNESS
EFGHLNOOPUUY YOUNG HOPEFUL
EFGIIINNNSTY INTENSIFYING
EFGIILNRRTYY TERRIFYINGLY
EFGIINNOPRSY PERSONIFYING
EFGIINNPRRST FINGERPRINTS
EFGILLNRTTUY FLUTTERINGLY
EFGILNPSTUYY STUPEFYINGLY
EFGLNNORSSUW WRONGFULNESS
EFHHILLOOOSY HOLY OF HOLIES
EFHIILQRRSSU SQUIRRELFISH
EFHILLMNORTU RUN-OF-THE-MILL
EFHILLOSSTWW WOLF WHISTLES
EFHILMNRSSTU MIRTHFULNESS
EFHIMNPRSSSU FRUMPISHNESS
EFHLLNOSSSTU SLOTHFULNESS
EFHLNNOOPRTY HORN OF PLENTY
EFHLNOSSTUUY YOUTHFULNESS
EFHLNRSSTTUU TRUTHFULNESS
EFIILMOPRSVY OVERSIMPLIFY
EFIINOOPSTVW POINTS OF VIEW
EFILLOPRSSTY PROFITLESSLY
EFIOOOPRRSSU SOPORIFEROUS
EFLLOPPRSUUY PURPOSEFULLY
EFLMNNORSSUU MOURNFULNESS
EFLNOPRSSSTU SPORTFULNESS
EFLNRSSSTTUU TRUSTFULNESS
EFNNNORRRSTU FRONT-RUNNERS
EFNOOPRRSTTY PORTS OF ENTRY
EGGGIILNNRSY SNIGGERINGLY
EGGGILNSSTUY SUGGESTINGLY
EGGGINOPRRSU GINGER GROUPS
EGGHHIILSTTW LIGHTWEIGHTS
EGGHHIINSSSW WHIGGISHNESS
EGGHIIKLNNSS KING'S ENGLISH
EGGHIILNNOOP PIGEONHOLING
EGGHIIMNNOOZ HOMOGENIZING
EGGHIINPRSSS PRIGGISHNESS
EGGHIINRRSTW RIGHT-WINGERS
EGGHILNSSSSU SLUGGISHNESS
EGGHLOOOOPTY PHOTOGEOLOGY
EGGIIIILMNTZ LEGITIMIZING
EGGIILLMMNRY GLIMMERINGLY
EGGIILLNNSTY GLISTENINGLY
EGGIILLNRTTY GLITTERINGLY
EGGILLLNORVY GROVELLINGLY
EGGILNNORSSY ENGROSSINGLY
EGGILOOPSTTY EGYPTOLOGIST
EGGIMNOOPRSS GOSSIPMONGER
EGHHIIKNSTTW WHITE KNIGHTS
EGHHILNNORSS ENGLISH HORNS

EGHHILNOSSSU GHOULISHNESS
EGHHNOORSSTU THOROUGHNESS
EGHIILMMNRSY SHIMMERINGLY
EGHIILMNPRWY WHIMPERINGLY
EGHIILNOSTTU SILHOUETTING
EGHIILOOPSSY PHYSIOLOGIES
EGHIINNSSTYZ SYNTHESIZING
EGHIIRSSSSTU RIGHTS ISSUES
EGHILMNOORST MOONLIGHTERS
EGHILMOOOPRS MORPHOLOGIES
EGHILMOORSTY MYTHOLOGISER
EGHILMOORTYZ MYTHOLOGIZER
EGHILNOOPRST PHRENOLOGIST
EGHILNOOSSTT ETHNOLOGISTS
EGHILNOPRSTU UPHOLSTERING
EGHILOOPPSST PSEPHOLOGIST
EGHIMNNNOOOY HONEYMOONING
EGHIMNNORSSU NURSING HOMES
EGHIMNOOORSU ROOMING HOUSE
EGHINNOOSSST SOOTHINGNESS
EGHINOOORSTV OVERSHOOTING
EGHINOOPRRSV GOVERNORSHIP
EGHINOORRTVW OVERTHROWING
EGIIIKLNNNRT INTERLINKING
EGIIILNNNPRT LINE PRINTING
EGIIIMNOPSTU IMPETIGINOUS
EGIIINNNRTTW INTERTWINING
EGIIKLNPPRRS KLIPSPRINGER
EGIIKNNNSSST STINKINGNESS
EGIIKNNRSSST STRIKINGNESS
EGIIKNOPPPRS SKIPPING-ROPE
EGIIILLMNPSS MISSPELLINGS
EGIIILLNNOPST SELLING POINT
EGIILMMNORVY LIVING MEMORY
EGIILMNNOPTT MELTING POINT
EGIILMOOSSST SEISMOLOGIST
EGIILNNPPSSS SLIPPINGNESS
EGIILNPPRRSY PERSPIRINGLY
EGIIMNOOPRRT PRIMOGENITOR
EGIIMNOPRRST MISREPORTING
EGIINNPRRTTU INTERRUPTING
EGIINPRRSSUZ PRESSURIZING
EGIKKNNOPRTY PONY-TREKKING
EGILLNNOORST ROLLING STONE
EGILLNORSTTY STORYTELLING
EGILMNNORTTY TORMENTINGLY
EGILMNOOOSTT ENTOMOLOGIST
EGILMNOOSTYZ ENZYMOLOGIST
EGILMOOSSTTY ETYMOLOGISTS
EGILNOOOPSST STOOLPIGEONS
EGILNOOPRSUY PYROLIGNEOUS
EGILNOORSSSU GLORIOUSNESS
EGILNOORSSTU NEUROLOGISTS
EGILNOPPRSSY OPPRESSINGLY

EGILNOPRSTTY PROTESTINGLY
EGILNRSTTTUY STUTTERINGLY
EGILOOPRSSTT PETROLOGISTS
EGIMMNOOPRSU SPERMOGONIUM
EGIMNOORRTTY TRIGONOMETRY
EGINOOPRRSSS PROGRESSIONS
EGINOORRSSSU RIGOROUSNESS
EGINOORSSSUV VIGOROUSNESS
EGINOPPPRSSU PRESUPPOSING
EGINPRRSSSTU PURSE STRINGS
EGMMNOORRRSU RUMORMONGERS
EGMMNOORRRUU RUMOURMONGER
EHHIILOOPPSS PHILOSOPHIES,
  PHILOSOPHISE
EHHIILOOPPSZ PHILOSOPHIZE
EHHIIMMMOPRS HEMIMORPHISM
EHHILOOPPRSS PHILOSOPHERS
EHHIMNOOPRST THERMOSIPHON
EHHINOOOOPPRS SIPHONOPHORE
EHHLOOSSTTUY YOUTH HOSTELS
EHHMNOOOOPRTY PHYTOHORMONE
EHIIILNNOPTW WHIP INTO LINE
EHIIILORTTVW WHITE VITRIOL
EHIIKNOOPSST PHOTOKINESIS
EHIIKNSSSSTT SKITTISHNESS
EHIILLNOPSTT SEPTILLIONTH
EHIILLNOSTTX SEXTILLIONTH
EHIILLOPSTWW WILL-O'-THE-WISP
EHIILMOOPRST HELIOTROPISM
EHIILMRSSSTV SILVERSMITHS
EHIILNOOSTTTW WHITE STILTON
EHIIMMOPPRRS PERIMORPHISM
EHIIMNPRSTUX XIPHISTERNUM
EHIIMOOPPRSS EPIMORPHOSIS
EHILLOPPRTYY PYROPHYLLITE
EHILMMOOPPRS PLEOMORPHISM
EHILNOOORTTWY NOTEWORTHILY
EHILNSSSSTTU SLUTTISHNESS
EHIMMMOOPRSS MESOMORPHISM
EHIMOOPPRRTY PYROMORPHITE
EHIMOOPRSTTT PHOTOMETRIST
EHINNORSSTUW UNWORTHINESS
EHIOORRSSSTT SHORT STORIES
EHIOPRRSSUVY SURVEYORSHIP
EHKMNOOOPSST SMOOTH-SPOKEN
EHLMOOOPPRTY PHOTOPOLYMER
EHMMOOOOPRSSU MESOMORPHOUS
EHMNNOORRSTT NORTHERNMOST
EHMNOORSSSSUU HUMOROUSNESS
EHMNOORSSTTU SOUTHERNMOST
EHNNOOOOPRTTU PHOTONEUTRON
EHOOOPRRSSTTU ORTHOPTEROUS
EHOOPPRSSSTW SHOWSTOPPERS
EIIIMMMMNORSS IMMERSIONISM

EIIIMMNORSST IMMERSIONIST
EIIIMNNORSST INTERMISSION
EIIIMNNPRSTT INSPIRITMENT
EIIIMNOOPRST REIMPOSITION
EIIIMPRTTTVY PERMITTIVITY
EIIINOQRSSTU REQUISITIONS
EIIINORSSSTV REVISIONISTS
EIIILLLLMNOPS PLIMSOLL LINE
EIILLNORSSSU ILLUSORINESS
EIILMNOOSTUV EVOLUTIONISM
EIILMOOPPRST PLEIOTROPISM
EIILNNNOSTUV TUNNEL VISION
EIILNOOOOPPST POLE POSITION
EIILNOORRSTU IRRESOLUTION
EIILNOOSTTUV EVOLUTIONIST
EIILOOPRSTXY EXPOSITORILY
EIIMMNNOPRST IMPRISONMENT
EIIMNNNQQUUU QUINQUENNIUM
EIIMNNOOPRST PREMONITIONS
EIIINNOORRSTV INTROVERSION
EIIINNOPRRTTU INTERRUPTION
EIIINOOPPRSST PREPOSITIONS
EIIINOORSTTTX EXTORTIONIST
EIIINOPRSSTTU SUPERSTITION
EIIOOPPSSTTV POSTPOSITIVE
EIILLMNOOSSTY MOTIONLESSLY
EIILLNNNOOTVY NONVIOLENTLY
EIILLOPPRSTUY SUPPLETORILY
EILMOPPRSTUU MULTIPURPOSE
EILMORSSTUYY MYSTERIOUSLY
EIMMNNNOOOTTT NOT TO MENTION
EIMNNNOSSSUU NUMINOUSNESS
EIMNOOOOPRRST PROMONTORIES
EIMNOOOORRSST SENSORIMOTOR
EIMNOOQSSTTU MOSQUITO NETS
EIMNOORSSSTU TIMOROUSNESS
EIMNOPPRSSTU PRESUMPTIONS
EINNOPRSSSUW WIN ONE'S SPURS
EINNOQRSSTUU NON SEQUITURS
EINOORSSSUUX UXORIOUSNESS
EINOPRRSSTTW WINTER SPORTS
EINOPRSSSSUU SPURIOUSNESS
EINORSSSSUUU USURIOUSNESS
EINORSSSTUUV VIRTUOUSNESS
EKKNNOOSTUVZ NOVOKUZNETSK
ELNOOPPSSSUU POPULOUSNESS
ELNOOPRSTTUY PORTENTOUSLY
ELOOPPRRSSUY PROSPEROUSLY
ELOOPPRRSTTY LOST PROPERTY
ELOORRSSTTUY STERTOROUSLY
EMMNOOOOPRSSU MONOSPERMOUS
EMOOOOPRRRSTT STORM TROOPER
EMOPPRSSTUUU PRESUMPTUOUS
EMORRSSTTUYY MYSTERY TOURS

ENNOOORSSSSU SONOROUSNESS
ENOORSSSTTUU TORTUOUSNESS
FFGIINOORSTT FIRST-FOOTING
FFHJLOORTUUY FOURTH OF JULY
FGGGILNOOOST FOOTSLOGGING
FGHHLLOTTUUY THOUGHTFULLY
FGHIILNORRYY HORRIFYINGLY
FGHIMNOOOPRT MOTHPROOFING
FGIIILLNOSSV LIVING FOSSIL
FGIIIMMNNNORS MISINFORMING
FGIIJLNSTUYY JUSTIFYINGLY
FGIILLLLMNOYY MOLLIFYINGLY
FGIILMNORTYY MORTIFYINGLY
FGIILMNSTYYY MYSTIFYINGLY
FGILOORSTTUU FUTUROLOGIST
FGINOOPRRSTU RUSTPROOFING
FGINOOPSSTUY PUSSYFOOTING
FHLLNOOOORRS ROLL OF HONORS
FHLLNOOOORRU ROLL OF HONOUR
FIILMMORTTUY MULTIFORMITY
FILLMNOSUUUX LUMINOUS FLUX
FILOORSTTUUY FORTUITOUSLY
FMNNOORSSTUU FROM SUN TO SUN
GGGHHHIIILNT HIGHLIGHTING
GGGILLNRSTUY STRUGGLINGLY
GGHHILNRSTUY HIGHLY STRUNG
GGHIILMNNOOT MOONLIGHTING
GGHIILNOPSTT SPOTLIGHTING
GGIIILLNNOTU GUILLOTINING
GGIIILNNRTUY INTRIGUINGLY
GGIILMMNOSWY GO SWIMMINGLY
GGILMNNOORRY MORNING GLORY
GHHMNNOOOOPST MONOPHTHONGS
GHIIKLNNNTUY UNTHINKINGLY
GHIILLOOPSST PHILOLOGISTS
GHIILNNORSUY NOURISHINGLY
GHIILNORSSTT SHORT-LISTING
GHIILOOPSSTY PHYSIOLOGIST
GHILMOOOOPRST MORPHOLOGIST
GHILMOOSSTTY MYTHOLOGISTS
GHILNOOOPSST PHONOLOGISTS
GHIMMOOOPRSYZ ZYGOMORPHISM
GHINOOPPSSTW SHOWSTOPPING
GHLMNOOOOSUY HOMOGONOUSLY
GHLMOOOOSUYYZ HOMOZYGOUSLY
GIIIINOPRRTZ PRIORITIZING
GIIIKLMNNSSS MISSING LINKS
GIIIMNNPRSST STRIP MININGS
GIIIMNORSTUZ MOISTURIZING
GIIINNOOPRSV PROVISIONING
GIILLLLMNORS ROLLING MILLS
GIILLNOORSUY INGLORIOUSLY
GIILMMNOOPSW SWIMMING POOL
GIILMMNOOSTU IMMUNOLOGIST

GIILMNNOOOPZ MONOPOLIZING
GIILNPRRSSUY SURPRISINGLY
GIIMNOORSSTT SITTING ROOMS
GIINNNOOPRSS SPRING ONIONS
GIINNNOPRTTU TURNING POINT
GIINOPPRSTTU OUTSTRIPPING
GIINOPRSTTTU PROSTITUTING
GIJMNNNPRSUU RUNNING JUMPS
GINNOOPRSSTT STRONG POINTS
GLLNOOSTTUUY GLUTTONOUSLY
GLOOOOOPRTYZ PROTOZOOLOGY
HHILOOOPPSTU PHOTOPHILOUS
HHIMMMOOOPRS HOMOMORPHISM
HHIOOTTTUUWW TU-WHIT TU-WHOO
HHMMOOOTTTUU MOUTH-TO-MOUTH
HIIIILMNPSST PHILISTINISM
HIILLOOPPRWW WHIPPOORWILL
HIKLMMOORSTW SILKWORM MOTH
HILMMOOPPRSY POLYMORPHISM
HILOOOPPRSTU TROPOPHILOUS
HIMMMMNOOOPRS MONOMORPHISM
HIMOOOOPPRSTT PHOTOTROPISM
HIMOOOPRRSTT ORTHOTROPISM
HINOOPPPRRSY PORPHYROPSIN
HIOOOPRRSTTY PROTOHISTORY
HLLMNOOOOPSUY MONOPHYLLOUS
HLMOOOOPPRSUY POLYMORPHOUS
HLMOOPSSTUUY POSTHUMOUSLY
HMOOOPSSSTUY PHYSOSTOMOUS
HOOOOPRRSTTU ORTHOTROPOUS
IIIIMNNOSTTU INTUITIONISM
IIIINNOQSSTU INQUISITIONS
IIIINNOSTTTU INTUITIONIST
IIILLNOPSSTT POINTILLISTS
IIILLNOSSSTU ILLUSIONISTS
IIILNOQSTUUY INIQUITOUSLY
IIIMNOORTTUV VOMITURITION
IIINNORSTTTU NUTRITIONIST
IIINNORSTTUU INNUTRITIOUS
IIINNOSTTTTU INSTITUTIONS
IIIOPRSSTTUY SPIRITUOSITY
IILLNNOOOPPS OPINION POLLS
IILMNOOSTUVY VOLUMINOSITY
IILMOORSTTUY UTILITY ROOMS
IILNORSTTUUY NUTRITIOUSLY
IILOOPPRSTUY PROPITIOUSLY
IINNOOOPPTTT POINT-TO-POINT
IINOOOPPRSST PROPOSITIONS
IINOOOPPSSTT POSTPOSITION
IINOOPPSSSTU SUPPOSITIONS
IINOOPRSTTTU PROSTITUTION
IIOOPPSSSTUU SUPPOSITIOUS
ILLMNOOOSTTY TONSILLOTOMY
ILLMNOOSUUVY VOLUMINOUSLY

ILLOPSSSUWWY PUSSY WILLOWS
IMPPPRRSSTUU STIRRUP PUMPS
INNNOOOOPSSU NONPOISONOUS
INOOPPRSSTTU OPPORTUNISTS
LLMOSTTUUUUY TUMULTUOUSLY

LLOOPSTUUUVY VOLUPTUOUSLY
LMNNOOOOSTUY MONOTONOUSLY
LMNNOOSSUYYY SYNONYMOUSLY
MNPPRRSTTUUU TURN UP TRUMPS

▚▚▚ THIRTEEN-LETTER WORDS ▚▚▚

AAAAACINNRSTT SANTA CATARINA
AAAAADGGIINNN AGAIN AND AGAIN
AAAABCCEELRTU BACCALAUREATE
AAAABCCHILMRR HAMILCAR BARCA
AAAABCEEKKSTT TAKE A BACK SEAT
AAAABDILMORSS AMBASSADORIAL
AAAACCDIIKLLS LACKADAISICAL
AAAACCINRSSTU TRANSCAUCASIA
AAAACCLMNORST MALACOSTRACAN
AAAACEINRRSSV CARAVANSERAIS
AAAACILLLNPTY APLANATICALLY
AAAACILLNOPRY PARANOIACALLY
AAAACIMNRSSST ANTIMACASSARS
AAAADEGHLMNOP ALPHA AND OMEGA
AAAAEGIMMNRST ANAGRAMMATISE
AAAAEGIMMNRTZ ANAGRAMMATIZE
AAAAEGNRSTVXZ EXTRAVAGANZAS
AAAAEHILNPPRR PARAPHERNALIA
AAAAGILMMNOST AMALGAMATIONS
AAAAGIMMMNRST ANAGRAMMATISM
AAAAGIMMNRSTT ANAGRAMMATIST
AAAAILNRSSSTU AUSTRALASIANS
AAAABBCEGIRRSY BABY CARRIAGES
AAAABCCILLORTY ACROBATICALLY
AAAABCCILMNOTY BY ACCLAMATION
AAABCDEHINRTU CHATEAUBRIAND
AAAABCDIKNORTW BACKWARDATION
AAAABCEEILNRST ASCERTAINABLE
AAAABCEGILLLRY ALGEBRAICALLY
AAAABCEILLNORY ANAEROBICALLY
AAAABCEILLRSWY CABLE RAILWAYS
AAAABCEILMNRRU ARABIC NUMERAL
AAAABCEIRSSTTV BITTER CASSAVA
AAAABCILLLOPRY PARABOLICALLY
AAAABDDELNTTUW WATTLE AND DAUB
AAAABDEGIILMTY DAMAGEABILITY
AAAABDEGMNNNOR RAG-AND-BONE
 MAN
AAAABEEELLRTUV RATEABLE VALUE
AAAABEGIILMNTY MANAGEABILITY
AAAABEGILNNOTZ ANTAGONIZABLE

AAAABEHIKPPPST PHI BETA KAPPAS
AAAABEILLMNPTU MANIPULATABLE
AAAABELNNRRTUW UNWARRANTABLE
AAABGLLMRRRSU BURGLAR ALARMS
AAABHILLMPSTU AMPHIBLASTULA
AAAABIIILLNOST LABIALISATION
AAAABIIILLNOTZ LABIALIZATION
AAAABIIILNTTTY ATTAINABILITY
AAAABIIKLNNOST BALKANISATION
AAAABIIKLNNOTZ BALKANIZATION
AAACCCEGIKNPR A CRACKING PACE
AAACCDEIINPTT INCAPACITATED
AAAACCDHIILNOR ARCHIDIACONAL
AAAACCEEELLNRS CLEARANCE SALE
AAAACCEEHMNRTT CATCHMENT AREA
AAAACCEGILRTTX EXTRAGALACTIC
AAAACCEINNQSTU ACQUAINTANCES
AAAACCFINNNRSS SAN FRANCISCAN
AAAACCGILLLMOO MALACOLOGICAL
AAAACCHILLRTTY CATHARTICALLY
AAAACCHLORSSTY THALASSOCRACY
AAAACCILLMNORY MACARONICALLY
AAAACCILLRSSTY SARCASTICALLY
AAAACDDIILLSTY DADAISTICALLY
AAAACDEEINPPRS DISAPPEARANCE
AAAACDEELNRRSY CALENDAR YEARS
AAAACDEFGNORRV GRACE-AND-FAVOR
AAAACDEGINRRSS AIRS AND GRACES
AAAACDEIIINPRT PAEDIATRICIAN
AAAACDEIIORTTV RADIOACTIVATE
AAAACDELNPPRRT PART AND PARCEL
AAAACDFNRRSSTT ARTS AND CRAFTS
AAAACDGHIIMPRT DIAPHRAGMATIC
AAAACDHIINOPRS ANAPHRODISIAC
AAAACDIIILPRST PARASITICIDAL
AAAACDIILMNOPS DIPSOMANIACAL
AAAACDILLOPRXY PARADOXICALLY
AAAACEEGNRSTVX EXTRAVAGANCES
AAAACEELNRSTTY SCALY ANTEATER
AAAACEENNNOPPR NONAPPEARANCE
AAAACEENOPRRSW A NARROW ESCAPE

AAACEEOPPRSUV PAPAVERACEOUS
AAACEFIILNNRY FINANCIAL YEAR
AAACEFILNORRT RAREFACTIONAL
AAACEFMORRRTT CREAM OF TARTAR
AAACEGHILOPPR PALAEOGRAPHIC
AAACEGIINNRSS CASSEGRAINIAN
AAACEGILMMNOS MEGALOMANIACS
AAACEGILMNNOR ANGLO-AMERICAN
AAACEHIILLMNV MACHIAVELLIAN
AAACEHIIMMNTT MATHEMATICIAN
AAACEHILLPTTY APATHETICALLY
AAACEHIMOOPPR PHARMACOPOEIA
AAACEHNRRRSTW SEARCH WARRANT
AAACEIILMNNRT LATIN AMERICAN
AAACEIKLMOSTT STAKE A CLAIM TO
AAACEILLMNOTX EXCLAMATIONAL
AAACEILLMOOST OSTEOMALACIAL
AAACEILNNSSST SATANICALNESS
AAACELRRSTUVX EXTRAVASCULAR
AAACENRRRSTTU RESTAURANT CAR
AAACENRSTTTTX SEX ATTRACTANT
AAACFGILNNRSU LINGUA FRANCAS
AAACFILLNSTTY FANTASTICALLY
AAACFIMNORRTW AIRCRAFTWOMAN
AAACGGILLOPRY PARAGOGICALLY
AAACGIIMNPRTT ANTIPRAGMATIC
AAACGILLMMRTY GRAMMATICALLY
AAACGILLMPRTY PRAGMATICALLY
AAACHILLMSTTY ASTHMATICALLY
AAACHILLNOPRY ANAPHORICALLY
AAACHILNRSSSU HALICARNASSUS
AAACIILLMOTXY AXIOMATICALLY
AAACIILLPRSTY PARASITICALLY
AAACIILLSTTVY ATAVISTICALLY
AAACIILNNNOTT INCANTATIONAL
AAACIILNOSTTU ACTUALISATION
AAACIILNOTTUZ ACTUALIZATION
AAACIIORSSTTU AUSTRO-ASIATIC
AAACIKOPRRSST SICK AS A PARROT
AAACILLLPRTYY PARALYTICALLY
AAACILLMNOPRY PANORAMICALLY
AAACILLMOTTUY AUTOMATICALLY
AAACILLMRTTUY TRAUMATICALLY
AAACILNNORSSY NARCOANALYSIS
AAACILNNORSTT TRANSACTIONAL
AAACILNNRSTTT TRANSATLANTIC
AAACILOSSTTUY AUTOCATALYSIS
AAADDDEELTUVX VALUE-ADDED TAX
AAADDDEGINSTV DISADVANTAGED
AAADDEGINSSTV DISADVANTAGES
AAADDEHHNPRRS ANDHRA PRADESH
AAADDLMNPRSST STANDARD LAMPS
AAADEEEINNNRS SEANAD EIREANN
AAADEEFHNRRTT TAR AND FEATHER

AAADEEGMRRRSU DEMERARA SUGAR
AAADEEHHLNRTY HALE AND HEARTY
AAADEEHIMNSTT ANATHEMATISED
AAADEEHIMNTTZ ANATHEMATIZED
AAADEGGILNNRU GUARDIAN ANGEL
AAADEGINORRRT A ROARING TRADE
AAADEHHNPRSSZ HAPHAZARDNESS
AAADEHNRRSTTW DEATH WARRANTS
AAADEILLQRRTU QUADRILATERAL
AAADEINOPPRTT PREADAPTATION
AAADGIMNOORST GOOD SAMARITAN
AAADHHILNRRSU HARUN AL-RASHID
AAADHIMMMMNSU MUHAMMADANISM
AAADIIMNORSTT DRAMATISATION
AAADIIMNORTTZ DRAMATIZATION
AAADKLMRRSTTX KARL-MARX-STADT
AAAEEEHKNPRSS SHAKESPEAREAN
AAAEEGGLMNSTU METALANGUAGES
AAAEEGGMNRSST STAGE MANAGERS
AAAEEGINNRSSX SEXAGENARIANS
AAAEEGINNRTTT GIANT ANTEATER
AAAEEJLNRSTTW SERJEANT AT LAW
AAAEFFHINORST AFTER A FASHION
AAAEFGMOPRSSS PASSAGE OF ARMS
AAAEFGNPRRSSU ASPARAGUS FERN
AAAEFIILMMRST MATERFAMILIAS
AAAEFIILMPRST PATERFAMILIAS
AAAEGGGIKNPRR PARKING GARAGE
AAAEGGGIMNNST STAGE-MANAGING
AAAEGIILMMNOR EMILIA-ROMAGNA
AAAEGILNNPRTT GREAT PLANTAIN
AAAEGIMMNPRST PARAMAGNETISM
AAAEGINNNNORS NONAGENARIANS
AAAEGINORTTVX EXTRAVAGATION
AAAEGLLLMOPRR PARALLELOGRAM
AAAEGLMOPRRSS MASSAGE PARLOR
AAAEGLNRTTVXY EXTRAVAGANTLY
AAAEHIMNRSSTT THE SAMARITANS
AAAEIILMNNOTX EXAMINATIONAL
AAAEILMNPRRTY PARLIAMENTARY
AAAEINORSTTVX EXTRAVASATION
AAAEMMRRSSSTT MASTERS-AT-ARMS
AAAFILMNNOSTW TASMANIAN WOLF
AAAGGGILNRTVY AGGRAVATINGLY
AAAGIILNORTTV GRAVITATIONAL
AAAGIINNSSSST ASSASSINATING
AAAGILNOOPPRT PROPAGATIONAL
AAAHIIMNNRSTU HUMANITARIANS
AAAHIINORRTTU AUTHORITARIAN
AAAIIILMNNOST ANIMALISATION
AAAIIILMNNOTZ ANIMALIZATION
AAAIILNNOSTTT TANTALISATION
AAAIILNNOTTTZ TANTALIZATION
AAAIIMNNOOSTT ANATOMISATION

AAAIIMNNOOTTZ ANATOMIZATION
AAAIIMNOORSTT AROMATISATION
AAAIIMNOORTTZ AROMATIZATION
AAAIINNORSTTV INTRAVASATION
AAAIINNOSSSST ASSASSINATION
AAAIINORRSTTT TARTARISATION
AAAIINORRTTTZ TARTARIZATION
AAAIKLNNOPRST NATIONAL PARKS
AAAILLNNORSTT TRANSLATIONAL
AAAILLNNORTTU ULTRANATIONAL
AAAILLNORRSTT TRANSLATORIAL
AAAILMNORSTVY SALVATION ARMY
AAAILNNNRSTVY TRANSYLVANIAN
AAAILNNOPRSTU SUPRANATIONAL
AABBBIILORSTY ABSORBABILITY
AABBCEEHILNOS BELISHA BEACON
AABBCEGINPRTU TURNIP CABBAGE
AABBCEHIKNSTT STAB IN THE BACK
AABBCEILNRRST TRANSCRIBABLE
AABBCILLMOSTY BOMBASTICALLY
AABBDDEEGILOR BIODEGRADABLE
AABBDEEFGLRST FLABBERGASTED
AABBDIILORSTY ADSORBABILITY
AABBEEILLMOTZ METABOLIZABLE
AABBEHIILNNTU UNINHABITABLE
AABBEIILLOSSU BOUILLABAISSE
AABBEIINORSTV ABBREVIATIONS
AABBEINRRRSTW RABBIT WARRENS
AABBENORRSSSU BARBAROUSNESS
AABBIIILNOTTY OBTAINABILITY
AABCCEEFIILRS SACRIFICEABLE
AABCCEEIRRSUU BUREAUCRACIES
AABCCEHHLPRYY BRACHYCEPHALY
AABCCEHILNPRS SPECIAL BRANCH
AABCCEIILMPRT IMPRACTICABLE
AABCCEIILPTTY ACCEPTABILITY
AABCCEIORSSSU BRASSICACEOUS
AABCCELNNOTUU UNACCOUNTABLE
AABCCIIILNNST CANNIBALISTIC
AABCCIILLLTUY CALCULABILITY
AABCCIILMPRTY IMPRACTICABLY
AABCCILLLOSTU LACTOBACILLUS
AABCCKLNRRSTU BLACKCURRANTS
AABCCLNNOTUUY UNACCOUNTABLY
AABCDDEEILNST BALANCED DIETS
AABCDDGINORRS BOARDING CARDS
AABCDDHINORSW SANDWICH BOARD
AABCDEEEFNRSS BAREFACEDNESS
AABCDEEFIPRRT PREFABRICATED
AABCDEEGHILRS DISCHARGEABLE
AABCDEELRRSTT BATTLE-SCARRED
AABCDEENNORUV OVERABUNDANCE
AABCDEGIKLLNP BACKPEDALLING
AABCDEHIILTTY DETACHABILITY

AABCDEHIKLNTW BLACK AND WHITE
AABCDEHORRSTY CARBOHYDRATES
AABCDELLMNOOR BALLROOM DANCE
AABCDELOPPRRS CLAPPERBOARDS
AABCDGIKLMRSU BLACKGUARDISM
AABCDINNORSTT CONTRABANDIST
AABCEEEELNPSS PEACEABLENESS
AABCEEEGHLLLN CHALLENGEABLE
AABCEEEHLNSST BALANCE SHEETS
AABCEEEILLPRR IRREPLACEABLE
AABCEEGGPRRST CARPETBAGGERS
AABCEEGHIOPRT BACTERIOPHAGE
AABCEEGHLNORX LABOR EXCHANGE
AABCEEHILMNPU UNIMPEACHABLE
AABCEEIILLMRR IRRECLAIMABLE
AABCEEIKMNRST CABINET-MAKERS
AABCEEILMNRSV VRAISEMBLANCE
AABCEEKQRRSTU SQUARE BRACKET
AABCEFGIMOTTU COMBAT FATIGUE
AABCEFIIINOTT BEATIFICATION
AABCEFIINORTT ABORTIFACIENT
AABCEFIOPRRRT PREFABRICATOR
AABCEFLNRSSTU BLAST FURNACES
AABCEGGKRRSTU GARBAGE TRUCKS
AABCEGHIILNTY CHANGEABILITY
AABCEGHIILRTY CHARGEABILITY
AABCEGHINORRS A CRASHING BORE
AABCEGILLLNOO BALNEOLOGICAL
AABCEGILLMOST MEGALOBLASTIC
AABCEGILNORV OVERBALANCING
AABCEGINOORSU BORAGINACEOUS
AABCEHILLLMNR LAMELLIBRANCH
AABCEHILMNPUY UNIMPEACHABLY
AABCEHIRRRRSS CRASH BARRIERS
AABCEHKMNNRST MERCHANT BANKS
AABCEIINORRTT NITROBACTERIA
AABCEIIRSTTTY TETRABASICITY
AABCEILLLMOTY METABOLICALLY
AABCEILLOORTV COLLABORATIVE
AABCEILLRSTTY TETRASYLLABIC
AABCEILMNNOOP COMPANIONABLE
AABCEIMRRSTUU BUREAUCRATISM
AABCEINOORRST SERBO-CROATIAN
AABCEINRRSSTT SCATTERBRAINS
AABCELMMNNOSU SOMNAMBULANCE
AABCFGILNNQTU CONFABULATING
AABCFIILORTTY FACTORABILITY
AABCFIKMNOORT BACK FORMATION
AABCFILNNOOTU CONFABULATION
AABCFILORRSUV FIBROVASCULAR
AABCFLNOORTUY CONFABULATORY
AABCGIIILNNNZ CANNIBALIZING
AABCGILLNOORT COLLABORATING
AABCHIIILMNTY MACHINABILITY

AABCIIILLMPTY IMPLACABILITY
AABCIIILLPPTY APPLICABILITY
AABCIILLLLSTY BALLISTICALLY
AABCIILLNORTU LUBRICATIONAL
AABCIILLOSTTY BIOSTATICALLY
AABCIILLRSTTY SYBARITICALLY
AABCIILMOPRTY COMPARABILITY
AABCIINNOORST CARBONISATION
AABCIINNOORTZ CARBONIZATION
AABCIINORRSTU CARBURISATION
AABCIINORRTUZ CARBURIZATION
AABCILLNOOOORT COLLABORATION
AABCILMNNNOOPY COMPANIONABLY
AABCINORSSSTT CONTRABASSIST
AABCLLOOOORRST COLLABORATORS
AABCMNNNOOSTT NONCOMBATANTS
AABCNNOOORSST CONTRABASSOON
AABDDEEGINNPRS BANDSPREADING
AABDDEHIILNNR HILDEBRANDIAN
AABDDGHILORTY BROAD DAYLIGHT
AABDDGIINNORR DRAINING BOARD
AABDDGINORRSW DRAWING BOARDS
AABDEEFGIILNT INDEFATIGABLE
AABDEEHIILRTT REHABILITATED
AABDEEHORRSTW WEATHERBOARDS
AABDEFGIILNTY INDEFATIGABLY
AABDEFGIOPRSS BIRD OF PASSAGE
AABDEFGKORSST DOG'S BREAKFAST
AABDEGIINNRRT GRIN AND BEAR IT
AABDEIILNRTUY UNREADABILITY
AABDEILNNOSTT NATIONAL DEBTS
AABDEINNNORRS SAN BERNARDINO
AABDEINSSTTTU SUBSTANTIATED
AABDEKLNRSTUY LAUNDRY BASKET
AABDENNPRSTUU SUPERABUNDANT
AABDENOOPRSSX PANDORA'S BOXES
AABDHIMNORSTT RHABDOMANTIST
AABDIIILLSTYY DIALYSABILITY
AABEEEEGLNRSS AGREEABLENESS
AABEEEEHNRTTW WEATHER-BEATEN
AABEEEFLMNSST SELF-ABASEMENT
AABEEEELNORSST ELABORATENESS
AABEEEELOORRTV OVERELABORATE
AABEEFILNNOTU FONTAINEBLEAU
AABEEFLMOSSTV MOVABLE FEASTS
AABEEFLNORSSV FAVORABLENESS
AABEEGHIKNRRT HEARTBREAKING
AABEEIILLRTVY REVEALABILITY
AABEEIILPRTTY REPEATABILITY
AABEELLLRSTTY TETRASYLLABLE
AABEEMMNRRSST EMBARRASSMENT
AABEFFLORSTUW WATER BUFFALOS
AABEFHILNNOSU UNFASHIONABLE
AABEFIILLNQUU UNQUALIFIABLE

AABEFILLNOPTU FALLOPIAN TUBE
AABEFILMORSSU BALSAMIFEROUS
AABEFLMNORRST TRANSFORMABLE
AABEGHIMNOOPR GERMANOPHOBIA
AABEGHIMNSTTW BANTAMWEIGHTS
AABEGHINQRSSU SQUARE-BASHING
AABEGIILLNOUV BOUGAINVILLEA
AABEGILMNPRTU PERAMBULATING
AABEGILNORRTU GUBERNATORIAL
AABEGILNRRSTT SABRE-RATTLING
AABEGIMNRRSTT BATTERING RAMS
AABEHILLORUVY BEHAVIOURALLY
AABEIIILNRTTY RETAINABILITY
AABEIIKLMRTTY MARKETABILITY
AABEIILLLOTVZ VOLATILIZABLE
AABEIILMNORST ABNORMALITIES
AABEIILMRSTUY MEASURABILITY
AABEIILMSTTTY METASTABILITY
AABEIILNORSTV VERBALISATION
AABEIILNORTVZ VERBALIZATION
AABEIILNRSTWY ANSWERABILITY
AABEIILOPRTVY EVAPORABILITY
AABEIILRRUVXY AUXILIARY VERB
AABEIIMNNRSTU ANTISUBMARINE
AABEIINRRRSST ARBITRARINESS
AABEIKNORSSTT STATION BREAKS
AABEILMNOPRTU PERAMBULATION
AABEILNOOPPRT APPORTIONABLE
AABEILNOORSTV OBSERVATIONAL
AABEILOQRSTUU SUBEQUATORIAL
AABELMOPRRSTU PERAMBULATORS
AABELMOPRRTUY PERAMBULATORY
AABELNOPRRSTT TRANSPORTABLE
AABELOPRRSTUY BEAUTY PARLORS
AABELOPRRTUUY BEAUTY PARLOUR
AABGGILLMMNOU GAMMA GLOBULIN
AABGHIOOPRTUY AUTOBIOGRAPHY
AABGHLLOPRSYY SYLLABOGRAPHY
AABGIIILNSSTY ASSIGNABILITY
AABGIILOPPRTY PROPAGABILITY
AABHIIILNPRRS LIBRARIANSHIP
AABIIIILNRTVY INVARIABILITY
AABIIIILNSTTY INSATIABILITY
AABIIILLMPPTY IMPALPABILITY
AABIIILMPSSTY IMPASSABILITY
AABIIILNOSSTT STABILISATION
AABIIILNOSTTZ STABILIZATION
AABIILNNNRTTU TINTINNABULAR
AABIILNNSSTTU INSUBSTANTIAL
AABIILNORSTTU BRUTALISATION
AABIILNORTTUZ BRUTALIZATION
AABIILOPRTUVY VAPOURABILITY
AABIILOSTTTUY AUTOSTABILITY
AABILLNSSTTUY SUBSTANTIALLY

AABILNNSSTTUU UNSUBSTANTIAL
AABINORSSTTTU SUBSTANTIATOR
AABLMMNOORSTU SOMNAMBULATOR
AACCCEEILNRRT RECALCITRANCE
AACCCEGHNORTU CHARGE ACCOUNT
AACCCEGINORTY GYNAECOCRATIC
AACCCEIILLMRT CLIMACTERICAL
AACCCFIIILNOT CALCIFICATION
AACCCGHHILOPR CHALCOGRAPHIC
AACCCIIILMNTT ANTICLIMACTIC
AACCCIILMMORT MACROCLIMATIC
AACCDEEHHIKSS SICK HEADACHES
AACCDEEHINOPT HEPTADECANOIC
AACCDEEHIRRST CHARACTERISED
AACCDEEHIRRTZ CHARACTERIZED
AACCDEEIILNRU CLAIRAUDIENCE
AACCDEEIMORSS ICE-CREAM SODAS
AACCDEGHHNNOP CHOP AND CHANGE
AACCDEHIILMOR RADIOCHEMICAL
AACCDEHIIRRST TRISACCHARIDE
AACCDEIIILNST DIALECTICIANS
AACCDEIILNOST DIATONIC SCALE
AACCDEIINNOPT PENTANOIC ACID
AACCDEIINORTT ACCREDITATION
AACCDEILLMSTU MISCALCULATED
AACCDEILNOOTU COEDUCATIONAL
AACCDEIMMOOTV ACCOMMODATIVE
AACCDEIMNNOPU UNACCOMPANIED
AACCDFIIIINOT ACIDIFICATION
AACCDGHIIOPRR CARDIOGRAPHIC
AACCDGIILLOOR CARDIOLOGICAL
AACCDGIMMNOOT ACCOMMODATING
AACCDHIMRRSST CHRISTMAS CARD
AACCDIILLOPTY APODICTICALLY
AACCDIIMNOORT CARCINOMATOID
AACCDIMMNOOOT ACCOMMODATION
AACCEEFHSSTTY SAFETY CATCHES
AACCEEFIRSTUV SURFACE-ACTIVE
AACCEEHHIMNNT THE MAIN CHANCE
AACCEEHILMNOT CATECHOLAMINE
AACCEEHIMNORS AEROMECHANICS
AACCEEHIMRRST SACCHARIMETER
AACCEEHLMNPRY MACRENCEPHALY
AACCEEHLRRSST CHARACTERLESS
AACCEEHMORRST SACCHAROMETER
AACCEELMNRUUV VACUUM CLEANER
AACCEFIIINOTT ACETIFICATION
AACCEFILORRSU CALCARIFEROUS
AACCEGHHLOPRR CHALCOGRAPHER
AACCEGHINOOPR OCEANOGRAPHIC
AACCEGIILNRTT INTERGALACTIC
AACCEGIINNRRT INCARCERATING
AACCEGILLOOTU AUTECOLOGICAL
AACCEGILLORTY CATEGORICALLY

AACCEGILLOTTY GEOTACTICALLY
AACCEGINNNOTT CONCATENATING
AACCEEHHLNPRTY CHANTRY CHAPEL
AACCEHIINNORT CHAIN REACTION
AACCEHIINOSTT CATECHISATION
AACCEHIINOTTZ CATECHIZATION
AACCEHIKMRSST CHRISTMAS CAKE
AACCEHILLMSTY SCHEMATICALLY
AACCEHILOSSTT SCHOLASTICATE
AACCEHILRRTTU ARCHITECTURAL
AACCEHIMMORTT METACHROMATIC
AACCEHIMPRSTU PHARMACEUTICS
AACCEHIPPRRST SHARP PRACTICE
AACCEIILLMNTY CINEMATICALLY
AACCEIINNORRT INCARCERATION
AACCEIIOPRSTT ECTOPARASITIC
AACCEIIORRSST ARISTOCRACIES
AACCEIJKLOPRT PRACTICAL JOKE
AACCEILLMRTUV CIRCUMVALLATE
AACCEILLNNOST CANCELLATIONS
AACCEILLNSTUY ENCAUSTICALLY
AACCEIMMNNOPT ACCOMPANIMENT
AACCEINNNOOTT CONCATENATION
AACCEINNOSTTU ACCENTUATIONS
AACCEINOPSSSU CAPACIOUSNESS
AACCEKNORTTTU COUNTERATTACK
AACCELLNOOPRR LANCE CORPORAL
AACCELLPRSTUY SPECTACULARLY
AACCELORSSSUU CRASSULACEOUS
AACCFIIILLRSY SACRIFICIALLY
AACCFIIILNORT CLARIFICATION
AACCFIIINNORT CARNIFICATION
AACCFIIINOPRT CAPRIFICATION
AACCFIIINORST SCARIFICATION
AACCFIIILLORY CALORIFICALLY
AACCFIILLSSTY FASCISTICALLY
AACCFIILNOSTU FASCICULATION
AACCGGIILLLOO GLACIOLOGICAL
AACCGHILLNOOT ANGLO-CATHOLIC
AACCGIIILMNTZ ACCLIMATIZING
AACCGIILLNOOR CRANIOLOGICAL
AACCGILNOOPSV GALVANOSCOPIC
AACCHIILMNOOT MACHICOLATION
AACCHIILMRSSU MUSICAL CHAIRS
AACCHIIMNNORT ANTIMONARCHIC
AACCHIINNORST ANACHRONISTIC
AACCHILLLLOOY ALCOHOLICALLY
AACCHILLMORTY CHROMATICALLY
AACCHILLOPRTT TROPHALLACTIC
AACCHILMNOORT ROMAN CATHOLIC
AACCHINOOSSTT COACH STATIONS
AACCIIINNOOST COCAINISATION
AACCIIINNOOTZ COCAINIZATION
AACCIIINORSTT CICATRISATION

AACCIIINORTTZ CICATRIZATION
AACCIILLMPRTY IMPRACTICALLY
AACCIILLSSTUY CASUISTICALLY
AACCIILMNOOSS OCCASIONALISM
AACCIILMNORTY MICROANALYTIC
AACCIIRRSSTTU CARICATURISTS
AACCILLNSTTYY SYNTACTICALLY
AACCILMNOSTUU ACCUMULATIONS
AACCILNNOOOTV CONVOCATIONAL
AACCILNNOORTT CONTRACTIONAL
AACCILNORTTUU ACCULTURATION
AACCILNPRTTYY CRYPTANALYTIC
AACCINORSSTTY SACROSANCTITY
AACCLLNORTTUY CONTRACTUALLY
AACDDEEEHLLRY CLEAR-HEADEDLY
AACDDEEELLNVV ADVANCED LEVEL
AACDDEFIILSSS CLASSIFIED ADS
AACDDEIIOSSST DISASSOCIATED
AACDDFIIINNOT DANDIFICATION
AACDDIKMNNRSU MANDARIN DUCKS
AACDEEGHIMNST MAGNETIC HEADS
AACDEEGINRRRU UNDERCARRIAGE
AACDEEHINTTTU AUTHENTICATED
AACDEEILPRTTU RECAPITULATED
AACDEEIMNNOTT DECONTAMINATE
AACDEEIQRSTTU ACQUIRED TASTE
AACDEENNNNOTT NONATTENDANCE
AACDEFFIIMNRS DISAFFIRMANCE
AACDEFFINRRTW TRAFFIC WARDEN
AACDEFGHIRSTT STRAIGHT-FACED
AACDEFLLNNOOR ONCE AND FOR ALL
AACDEGGILLMOY DEMAGOGICALLY
AACDEGGILLOPY PEDAGOGICALLY
AACDEGHIOPRRR CARDIOGRAPHER
AACDEGJLNOSUU JUGLANDACEOUS
AACDEGLMNNORS SCANDALMONGER
AACDEGLNORTTU CONGRATULATED
AACDEHIIMNRRT ARCHIMANDRITE
AACDEHLMNNORT CALENDAR MONTH
AACDEIIINPRST PEDIATRICIANS
AACDEIIJLRTUX EXTRAJUDICIAL
AACDEIILLMRTY DIAMETRICALLY
AACDEIILLOPRY APERIODICALLY
AACDEIILOPPRR PERICARPOIDAL
AACDEIILRSTTU DISARTICULATE
AACDEIINNRSTT TRANSACTINIDE
AACDEIINOPRST ENDOPARASITIC
AACDEIINOPSTT DECAPITATIONS
AACDEIKLLNPST SLAP AND TICKLE
AACDEILLMORTY DECLAMATORILY
AACDEILLNSTYY ASYNDETICALLY
AACDEILLORRTY DECLARATORILY
AACDEILNQRUVY QUADRIVALENCY
AACDEILPQRTUU QUADRUPLICATE

AACDEIMNNNOTT DECONTAMINANT
AACDEINNORSUU ARUNDINACEOUS
AACDEINOSSSUU AUDACIOUSNESS
AACDELNOPRSSY PLAY ONE'S CARDS
AACDFFIILNRST TRAFFIC ISLAND
AACDFIIIMNNOT DAMNIFICATION
AACDFMNOORSTW WOODCRAFTSMAN
AACDGHILNNRSS CRASH LANDINGS
AACDGIIINNOST DIAGNOSTICIAN
AACDHIIIOPRST ADIAPHORISTIC
AACDHILLLRUYY HYDRAULICALLY
AACDHILLOPRSY RHAPSODICALLY
AACDHILMNOORT TRICHOMONADAL
AACDHIMMOOSSS SADOMASOCHISM
AACDHIMOOSSST SADOMASOCHIST
AACDIIILLMOTY IDIOMATICALLY
AACDIIILPQRTU QUADRICIPITAL
AACDIIINNNORT INCARDINATION
AACDIIIORTTVY RADIOACTIVITY
AACDIIKNNNOPR RACK-AND-PINION
AACDIILLLSTUY DUALISTICALLY
AACDIILLORTTY DICTATORIALLY
AACDIILNNOPRT CARDINAL POINT
AACDIIMNOPSST ANTISPASMODIC
AACDIIMNORRTY DRAMATIC IRONY
AACDILLMOPSSY SPASMODICALLY
AACDIMNORSSTY ASTRODYNAMICS
AACEEEGHNRSTX EXCHANGE RATES
AACEEEHJKLRTT LEATHERJACKET
AACEEFHMSSTTY SAFETY MATCHES
AACEEFLNRSSSU SELF-ASSURANCE
AACEEGHILOPRS ARCHIPELAGOES
AACEEGHLLSSSV CHEVAL GLASSES
AACEEGHLMNOPR ENCEPHALOGRAM
AACEEGHLMOPSU MEGACEPHALOUS
AACEEGHNOOPRR OCEANOGRAPHER
AACEEGHNPRSTX PART EXCHANGES
AACEEGIILLNPR ALPINE GLACIER
AACEEGILNPRTW WATERING PLACE
AACEEGIMNPSTT MAGNETIC TAPES
AACEEGINNOSTU GENTIANACEOUS
AACEEGLOOSTTV COTTAGE LOAVES
AACEEHIILNPST ELEPHANTIASIC
AACEEHILLSTTY AESTHETICALLY
AACEEHILMPRTT HEPTAMETRICAL
AACEEHILNPRTT PARENTHETICAL
AACEEHIPRRSST SEARCH PARTIES
AACEEHKMNRRSS SNAKE CHARMERS
AACEEHMNOPSUY NYMPHAEACEOUS
AACEEIILLPSTV CAPITAL LEVIES
AACEEIILNRTTV INTERCALATIVE
AACEEIINNRSST NECESSITARIAN
AACEEIINORRST REACTIONARIES
AACEEILLMMRTY METAMERICALLY

AACEEILMMNORT ANEMOMETRICAL
AACEEILNNRSTW SAINT LAWRENCE
AACEEILNNSUUV NUISANCE VALUE
AACEEIMNNRSTT ASCERTAINMENT
AACEELLLRRTUX EXTRACELLULAR
AACEENNPPRSTU APPURTENANCES
AACEFGILNORTV CONFLAGRATIVE
AACEFIILLNRTY INTERFACIALLY
AACEFILLMNRUY NUCLEAR FAMILY
AACEFILMNRSST MASSIF CENTRAL
AACEFINRSTTUY SAFETY CURTAIN
AACEFMNRRSTUU MANUFACTURERS
AACEFNOPRRSTT TRANSPORT CAFE
AACEGGHJKNNNU KANGCHENJUNGA
AACEGHILLLRTY LETHARGICALLY
AACEGHILLMPRY GRAPHEMICALLY
AACEGHILNPRSS GRAPHICALNESS
AACEGHILOORST ARCHAEOLOGIST
AACEGHIMNOPRT CINEMATOGRAPH
AACEGHOPRRRST CARTOGRAPHERS
AACEGHOPRSSSU SARCOPHAGUSES
AACEGIIIMNNRZ AMERICANIZING
AACEGIIINRRST GERIATRICIANS
AACEGIILLMNOR MINERALOGICAL
AACEGIILLMNTY ENIGMATICALLY
AACEGIILLNNTY ANTIGENICALLY
AACEGIINNNRRT REINCARNATING
AACEGIINPRRTV PREVARICATING
AACEGILLLLORY ALLEGORICALLY
AACEGILLLMRTU METALLURGICAL
AACEGILLRSTTY STRATEGICALLY
AACEGILMNNRST MAGIC LANTERNS
AACEGILMNOOSU MAGNOLIACEOUS
AACEGILMNORTV GALVANOMETRIC
AACEGIMNOPSTU COME UP AGAINST
AACEGINNOORST OCTOGENARIANS
AACEGINOSSSSU SAGACIOUSNESS
AACEGLLMMORRU GRAM-MOLECULAR
AACEGLLOOPSUY POLYGALACEOUS
AACEGLMNORRSS MARRONS GLACÉS
AACEGLRRSSTYZ CRYSTAL GAZERS
AACEHHILNOPRZ RHIZOCEPHALAN
AACEHHLOOPRTX CEPHALOTHORAX
AACEHIIIMNRTT ARITHMETICIAN
AACEHIILLSTTY ATHEISTICALLY
AACEHIILNOPST CEPHALISATION
AACEHIILNOPTZ CEPHALIZATION
AACEHIILRTTTY THEATRICALITY
AACEHIIMNNOST MECHANISATION
AACEHIIMNNOTZ MECHANIZATION
AACEHIIMNNRST CHRISTIAN NAME
AACEHIIMNPSTY METAPHYSICIAN
AACEHILLNTTUY AUTHENTICALLY

AACEHILMNPRRU HURRICANE LAMP
AACEHINOPRTTY ACTINOTHERAPY
AACEHINORTTTU AUTHENTICATOR
AACEHLNOPSSYY PSYCHOANALYSE
AACEHLNOPSYYZ PSYCHOANALYZE
AACEHMSSSSTTU MASSACHUSETTS
AACEHNOPPRRTY PARTHENOCARPY
AACEIIILMRSTT MATERIALISTIC
AACEIIIMPRSST SEMIPARASITIC
AACEIIKLLMNTY KINEMATICALLY
AACEIILLLRSTY REALISTICALLY
AACEIILLMNSSY MESSIANICALLY
AACEIILLMNSTU NAUTICAL MILES
AACEIILLNRRTY INTERCALARILY,
    INTERRACIALLY
AACEIILMMNRSU UNICAMERALISM
AACEIILMNRSTT MATERNALISTIC
AACEIILMNRSTU UNICAMERALIST
AACEIILNNORTT INTERACTIONAL,
    INTERCALATION
AACEIILNNOSTT CAT-O'-NINE-TAILS
AACEIILNOPPSS EPISCOPALIANS
AACEIILNPRSTT PATERNALISTIC
AACEIILNRSSST SATIRICALNESS
AACEIILPRRSTU PARTICULARISE
AACEIILPRRTUZ PARTICULARIZE
AACEIIMMOSTTU SEMIAUTOMATIC
AACEIIMOPRRST MICROPARASITE
AACEIINNNORRT REINCARNATION
AACEIINOPPRST APPRECIATIONS
AACEIINOPRRTV PREVARICATION
AACEIINORSTTU CAUTERISATION
AACEIINORTTUZ CAUTERIZATION
AACEIINRRRSTU CURTAIN RAISER
AACEIJKRSSTTT STRAITJACKETS
AACEIKLMNOPST KLEPTOMANIACS
AACEIKLOPRSTT KERATOPLASTIC
AACEILLLNRRTU INTRACELLULAR
AACEILLMNPTUY PNEUMATICALLY
AACEILLMORTXY EXCLAMATORILY
AACEILLMPRSTY SPERMATICALLY
AACEILMNRRSUV VERNACULARISM
AACEILMOPRTVY COMPARATIVELY
AACEILNNOPSTU ENCAPSULATION
AACEILNOSSSSU SALACIOUSNESS
AACEILNRRSTUU CRANIAL SUTURE
AACEILOOPPRSS LAPAROSCOPIES
AACEILRSSTTTU TRUCIAL STATES
AACEIMNNRSTTT TRANSMITTANCE
AACEIMNOOPSST COMPASSIONATE
AACEINNOOTTTV CONNOTATATIVE
AACEINOPRRSTT PROCRASTINATE
AACEINOPRRTUY PRECAUTIONARY
AACEINOPSSSTT SPACE STATIONS

AACEIOPRRRSTV PREVARICATORS
AACEJKLNNORST JACK-O'-LANTERNS
AACELMMNOPRTT COMPARTMENTAL
AACELNORRSUUV NEUROVASCULAR
AACELNRSSTTUU SUSTENTACULAR
AACELORSSSTUU ASSAULT COURSE
AACEMNNOORSTT ENTOMOSTRACAN
AACEMNNOPPRTY PARENT COMPANY
AACFFIIILNOST FALSIFICATION
AACFGHIILRRTT LIGHT AIRCRAFT
AACFGIIIMNNOT MAGNIFICATION
AACFGIIINORTT GRATIFICATION
AACFGIILNNSTY FASCINATINGLY
AACFGILNNOORT CONFLAGRATION
AACFGIMNNRTUU MANUFACTURING
AACFHIMNPRSST CRAFTSMANSHIP
AACFIIIILRTTY ARTIFICIALITY
AACFIIIILMNOPT AMPLIFICATION
AACFIIIILNOQTU QUALIFICATION
AACFIIIIMNORST RAMIFICATIONS
AACFIILOQRTUY QUALIFICATORY
AACFIINNOORTT FRACTIONATION
AACFIINOORSTT FACTORISATION
AACFIINOORTTZ FACTORIZATION
AACFIINOSSSTT SATISFACTIONS
AACFINORSTTUY ANFRACTUOSITY
AACFORRSSTTTU FRACTOSTRATUS
AACGGHIKNNSUW KWANGSI-CHUANG
AACGGHINOOPRR ORGANOGRAPHIC
AACGGILLNOOOR ORGANOLOGICAL
AACGGILMMOORT LOGOGRAMMATIC
AACGGILNRSTYZ CRYSTAL GAZING
AACGHHIMNNTTW NIGHT WATCHMAN
AACGHIILLNNTU HALLUCINATING
AACGHIILLPRST CALLIGRAPHIST
AACGHIIPRRSTT STRATIGRAPHIC
AACGHILMNOOPR NOMOGRAPHICAL
AACGHILOOPPRT TOPOGRAPHICAL
AACGHILOPPRTY TYPOGRAPHICAL
AACGHLMMOORRS GRAMMAR SCHOOL
AACGHMNOOPRSY PHARMACOGNOSY
AACGIIILLMSTY IMAGISTICALLY
AACGIIILLNOST GALLICISATION
AACGIIILLNOTZ GALLICIZATION
AACGIIILNNOST ANGLICISATION
AACGIIILNNOTZ ANGLICIZATION
AACGIIIMSSTTT ASTIGMATISTIC
AACGIIINPPRTT PARTICIPATING
AACGIILLLNTVY VACILLATINGLY
AACGIILLNNORY INORGANICALLY
AACGIILMNRTTU MATRICULATING
AACGIILNORSTU CARTILAGINOUS
AACGIIMNNNOTT CONTAMINATING
AACGIINNNOPRS CAPARISONNING

AACGIJLNNOOTU CONJUGATIONAL
AACGILLLNOOPY PALYNOLOGICAL
AACGILLLNOSTY NOSTALGICALLY
AACGILMNOOPST CAMPANOLOGIST
AACGILNNOOSTV LONG VACATIONS
AACGILNOOPRTV GALVANOTROPIC
AACGIMMMNOORT MONOGRAMMATIC
AACGINOPPRSTU GROUP CAPTAINS
AACGKNOOORRTU KANGAROO COURT
AACGLNOORRTTU CONGRATULATOR
AACHHIIMNPRSS CHAIRMANSHIPS
AACHHILPSTXYY TACHYPHYLAXIS
AACHHIMNPSSTY YACHTSMANSHIP
AACHIILLNNOTU HALLUCINATION
AACHILLLMPTYY LYMPHATICALLY
AACHILLNOPPSY PANSOPHICALLY
AACHILLNORTUY HALLUCINATORY
AACHILOPRSSTY ASTROPHYSICAL
AACHIMMNNOPSY NYMPHOMANIACS
AACHIMMNOPRST PANCHROMATISM
AACHIMMOOPRST APOCHROMATISM
AACHIMOPRSSTT CATASTROPHISM
AACHIOPRSSTTT CATASTROPHIST
AACHLNOPSSTYY PSYCHOANALYST
AACHLOOPRSTTY THORACOPLASTY
AACIIIILNOSTT ITALICISATION
AACIIIILNOTTZ ITALICIZATION
AACIIILLNNNOT INCLINATIONAL
AACIIILLPPRTY PARTICIPIALLY
AACIIILNNOSTT NATIONALISTIC
AACIIILNOOSST SOCIALISATION
AACIIILNOOSTZ SOCIALIZATION
AACIIILNORSTT RATIONALISTIC
AACIIINNOORTT RATIOCINATION
AACIIINOPPRTT PARTICIPATION
AACIIINSSSTTT STATISTICIANS
AACIILLMNNOTY ANTINOMICALLY
AACIILLMORTTY MATRILOCALITY,
  TRIATOMICALLY
AACIILLMOSTTY ATOMISTICALLY
AACIILLNPRTUY PURITANICALLY
AACIILLOPRTTY PATRIOTICALLY
AACIILLPRSTTY PATRISTICALLY
AACIILLSSTTTY STATISTICALLY
AACIILMNORSSY MICROANALYSIS
AACIILMNORTTU MATRICULATION
AACIILMPRRSTU PARTICULARISM
AACIILNNOOSTV VOLCANISATION
AACIILNNOOTVZ VOLCANIZATION
AACIILNNOPSTU INCAPSULATION
AACIILNNOSTUV VULCANISATION
AACIILNNOTUVZ VULCANIZATION
AACIILNOPSTTU CAPITULATIONS
AACIILNORSTTU ARTICULATIONS

AACIILPRRSTTU PARTICULARIST
AACIILPRRTTUY PARTICULARITY
AACIIMMNNORTU COMMUNITARIAN
AACIIMMORSSST COMMISSARIATS
AACIIMNNNOOTT CONTAMINATION
AACIIMNNORTUU ACTINOURANIUM
AACIINNNOOSST CANONISATION
AACIINNNOOSTZ CANONIZATIONS
AACIINNNOORSTT NARCOTISATION
AACIINNNOORTTZ NARCOTIZATION
AACIINNNOPSSTT PANIC STATIONS
AACILLMNOOTUY AUTONOMICALLY
AACILLMNOOTXY TAXONOMICALLY
AACILLMNOPSTY COMPLAISANTLY
AACILLMPRSTYY SYMPATRICALLY
AACILMNOOPRST PROCLAMATIONS
AACILMNOOPTTU COMPUTATIONAL
AACILMNRRSTUU INTRAMUSCULAR
AACILMOOPSSTT SOMATOPLASTIC
AACILMORRSTTU COURT MARTIALS,
  COURTS-MARTIAL
AACILNNOORSTT TRANSLOCATION
AACILNPRSSTYY CRYPTANALYSIS
AACIMNNOOPSWY COMPANIONWAYS
AACIMNNOORSTT CONTAMINATORS
AACIMNNRSTTTY TRANSMITTANCY
AADDDELNOORSW RED SANDALWOOD
AADDEEEFHNSST FATHEADEDNESS
AADDEEEHIRRTW READ-WRITE HEAD
AADDEEEELMPRST PADDLE STEAMER
AADDEEGIILLNS LEADING LADIES
AADDEEGINNRRU UNDERDRAINAGE
AADDEEGNRRTUU UNDERGRADUATE
AADDEEHHINNST HEAD IN THE SAND
AADDEEHHLRRTY HARD-HEARTEDLY
AADDEELNRTTUU UNADULTERATED
AADDEFFIIILST DISAFFILIATED
AADDEGGHNRRTU GRANDDAUGHTER
AADDEGHNORRUY ROUGH-AND-READY
AADDEGHOPRRSS ADDRESSOGRAPH
AADDEGILNRSSS SALAD DRESSING
AADDEGINOPPRS PROPAGANDISED
AADDEGINOPPRZ PROPAGANDIZED
AADDEGNOPRRSU PARADE GROUNDS
AADDEILNRSSST DASTARDLINESS
AADDGIINNRSTZ STANDARDIZING
AADDIIILNOPST DILAPIDATIONS
AADEEEGGLRTXY EXAGGERATEDLY
AADEEEHINSSTT ANAESTHETISED
AADEEEHINSTTZ ANAESTHETIZED
AADEEEHIRSSST HEART DISEASES
AADEEEIKNSSWW WIDE-AWAKENESS
AADEEEIMNNRRT MEDITERRANEAN
AADEEEELPRSTXY EXASPERATEDLY

AADEEEMMNRSTU ADMEASUREMENT
AADEEEMMORSTU MADE-TO-MEASURE
AADEEFHHLLRTY HALF-HEARTEDLY
AADEEFILLMRST FLEET ADMIRALS
AADEEFNSSSSTT STEADFASTNESS
AADEEGGILNPRS SPREAD-EAGLING
AADEEGILMORRT RADIOTELEGRAM
AADEEGILMQRSU MADRIGALESQUE
AADEEGIMNPRST DISPARAGEMENT
AADEEGINPRRST GARDEN PARTIES
AADEEGINRSTTT TRADING ESTATE
AADEEGKMNRRST MARKET GARDENS
AADEEGLLMNRRW WALL GERMANDER
AADEEHLMRRTWY WARM-HEARTEDLY
AADEEHLOPRRTZ TRAPEZOHEDRAL
AADEEHLORRTTT TETARTOHEDRAL
AADEEHMNNSSSU UNASHAMEDNESS
AADEEIILNNOST DENATIONALISE
AADEEIILNNOTZ DENATIONALIZE
AADEEILNNNORR NORADRENALINE
AADEELNPPPRST PEPPER-AND-SALT
AADEENNPRSTUU SUPERANNUATED
AADEFFMNOORSW MEADOW SAFFRON
AADEFGHHINORR HARD OF HEARING
AADEFHILLMRSS FIELD MARSHALS
AADEFIILNOSTU FEUDALISATION
AADEFIILNOTUZ FEUDALIZATION
AADEFILNSSSTY SAFETY ISLANDS
AADEFILOOPRSS FOOL'S PARADISE
AADEFLLMNNTUY FUNDAMENTALLY
AADEGGILNNSST LANDING STAGES
AADEGHILNRTUW DAUGHTER-IN-LAW
AADEGHIOPRRRS RADIOGRAPHERS
AADEGIIMNNRTV ANIMADVERTING
AADEGILNSTTVY DEVASTATINGLY
AADEGOPRSSTTU POSTGRADUATES
AADEHHILMOORR HAEMORRHOIDAL
AADEHIILMOSSY HAEMODIALYSIS
AADEHIILNPSUZ SULPHADIAZINE
AADEHIKLMORSY HOLIDAYMAKERS
AADEHILNORSUY HYALURONIDASE
AADEHIMMMMNOS MOHAMMEDANISM
AADEHIMNNORSTU DIATHERMANOUS
AADEHNORRSTTW NORTHEASTWARD
AADEHNORSSSUZ HAZARDOUSNESS
AADEHORSSTTUW SOUTHEASTWARD
AADEIIILNOSST IDEALISATIONS
AADEIIILNOSTZ IDEALIZATIONS
AADEIIIMNOSTT MEDIATISATION
AADEIIIMNOTTZ MEDIATIZATION
AADEIIILLMORTY MEDIATORIALLY
AADEIIILLMPRXY MAXILLIPEDARY
AADEIILMMNRST MALADMINISTER
AADEIIMNNORSV ANIMADVERSION

AADEIINOPSSST DISPASSIONATE
AADEIIPQRRTTU QUADRIPARTITE
AADEILMMORSTT MELODRAMATIST
AADEILMNORSST MALADROITNESS
AADEIMNNRSSSU RUSSIAN DESMAN
AADEINORRRTXY EXTRAORDINARY
AADEINRRSTTWW WITWATERSRAND
AADEJLMMNSTTU MALADJUSTMENT
AADELMOPRSTTY DERMATOPLASTY
AADEMNORSTTUY TETRADYNAMOUS
AADFFIKNRSSTT STIFF AND STARK
AADFILLOOPRSY APRIL FOOLS' DAY
AADFINNOORTUY FOUNDATIONARY
AADFINNOOSSTU SODA FOUNTAINS
AADGGIILNPRSY DISPARAGINGLY
AADGHIIKLMNOY HOLIDAYMAKING
AADGHIINNNRWZ WINNING HAZARD
AADGIIILNNTWY LADY-IN-WAITING
AADGIIMNOOSTT DOGMATISATION
AADGIIMNOOTTZ DOGMATIZATION
AADGILNNOPRST PROSTAGLANDIN
AADGIMNPRSSTT TRADING STAMPS
AADGINOPPRSST PROPAGANDISTS
AADHILNORRSTY SYNARTHRODIAL
AADHMNNOORTTW NOT WORTH A
  DAMN
AADIIINOOSTTZ DIAZOTISATION
AADIIINOOTTZZ DIAZOTIZATION
AADIILLNORTTY TRADITIONALLY
AADIIMNNOORST RANDOMISATION
AADIIMNNOORTZ RANDOMIZATION
AADIIMNORRSTT ADMINISTRATOR
AAEEEFFLMMSST FEMMES FATALES
AAEEEFGHMMNOT NAME OF THE
  GAME
AAEEEFLRSSTTW WELFARE STATES
AAEEEGHLMPRST GREASE THE PALM
AAEEEGLMMNRSS GERMAN MEASLES
AAEEEGMNNRRRT REARRANGEMENT
AAEEEHIILLSSS HAILE SELASSIE
AAEEEHILPPRRT PRE-RAPHAELITE
AAEEEILNNORRS SIERRA LEONEAN
AAEEELMMNPRTT TEMPERAMENTAL
AAEEELOPRSTTU POETS LAUREATE
AAEEEMNNPRTVW PERMANENT WAVE
AAEEEFFGNRSSTT STAFF SERGEANT
AAEEEFGILLNNNS SELF-ANNEALING
AAEEEFHORSTTTT STATE-OF-THE-ART
AAEEEFKKMMNOOY MAKE A MONKEY
  OF
AAEEEFMNNRRSTT TENANT FARMERS
AAEEEFNNPRSSST SNAP FASTENERS
AAEEGGILMNRST MARAGING STEEL

AAEEGGILMORTV AGGLOMERATIVE
AAEEGGILNORST SEGREGATIONAL
AAEEGGINNOPRT GENERATION GAP
AAEEGGINORSTX EXAGGERATIONS
AAEEGGLNNOSTU TONE LANGUAGES
AAEEGHLOPPRRS PALEOGRAPHERS
AAEEGHMNOOSTU HAEMATOGENOUS
AAEEGIILMNRRS MARRIAGE LINES
AAEEGIILMPRTX EXEMPLI GRATIA
AAEEGIIMMPRST EPIGRAMMATISE
AAEEGIIMMPRTZ EPIGRAMMATIZE
AAEEGIIMNRRRT INTERMARRIAGE
AAEEGIIMNRSTV VEGETARIANISM
AAEEGIMMMNNST MISMANAGEMENT
AAEEGIMNRTTUV ARGUMENTATIVE
AAEEGINOPRSTU EUSPORANGIATE
AAEEGJLMNORRS MAJOR GENERALS
AAEEGJMNORRST SERGEANT MAJOR
AAEEGLPPPRSSU PURPLE PASSAGE
AAEEGNNNORRTT TARN-ET-GARONNE
AAEEHHIMPRSTT AMPHITHEATERS,
  AMPHITHEATRES
AAEEHHMOPPSTT METAPHOSPHATE
AAEEHHORRSTTT HEART-TO-HEARTS
AAEEHIILNPSST ELEPHANTIASIS
AAEEHILLNNNPY PHENYLALANINE
AAEEHINPPRRST HEIRS APPARENT
AAEEHINSSSTTT ANAESTHETISTS
AAEEHLLLLOSVW ALLHALLOWS EVE
AAEEHMNOSTTUX EXANTHEMATOUS
AAEEHNORSSTTT EAST-NORTHEAST
AAEEHOSSSTTTU EAST-SOUTHEAST
AAEEIIILMMRST IMMATERIALISE
AAEEIIILMMRTZ IMMATERIALIZE
AAEEIIKKLLSTW WALKIE-TALKIES
AAEEIIILMNNRTT INTERLAMINATE
AAEEIIMNNORTX RE-EXAMINATION
AAEEIINNRRSSV ANNIVERSARIES
AAEEIKLMNSSTT STATESMANLIKE
AAEEIKLNSSTTV TALKATIVENESS
AAEEILLNRSSTW ARTESIAN WELLS
AAEEIILLNRTTVY ALTERNATIVELY
AAEEIILMNRRSTW MINERAL WATERS
AAEEILNNNOPPT PENEPLANATION
AAEEIILNOPRSTX EXPLANATORIES
AAEEIILNRRSTTT TRANSLITERATE
AAEEIILOPRTTVX EXTRAPOLATIVE
AAEEIINNPRSTTY SPINY ANTEATER
AAEEINNORRSTTU EURASIAN OTTER
AAEEINORSSSTV ASSEVERATIONS
AAEEKMMNPRSTU AMUSEMENT PARK
AAEELNPRRRTTU PRETERNATURAL
AAEEMNNPRSTWY PERMANENT WAYS
AAEEMPPRRSSTU SEMPER PARATUS

AAEEMQRRRSTTU QUARTERMASTER
AAEEQRRSSTTUV QUARTERSTAVES
AAEERRRSSTTUU RESTAURATEURS
AAEFFIILMNORR FORAMINIFERAL
AAEFFIILMRTVY AFFIRMATIVELY
AAEFFIIMNORRT REAFFIRMATION
AAEFFINOORSTT AFFORESTATION
AAEFFQRRSSTTU QUARTERSTAFFS
AAEFGILLLMNST FLAGELLANTISM
AAEFGIMNNORTT FRAGMENTATION
AAEFHHLOSSUWY HALFWAY HOUSES
AAEFIIIILMRST FAMILIARITIES
AAEFIIMNNOSTT MANIFESTATION
AAEFILMNOORRT REFORMATIONAL
AAEFILNQRRSTU QUARTERFINALS
AAEFLLNOPRRRU FUNERAL PARLOR
AAEFMORRSSSTT MASTERS OF ARTS
AAEGGGILMNORT AGGLOMERATING
AAEGGHHIIOPRS HAGIOGRAPHIES
AAEGGHHILNNUY LAUGHING HYENA
AAEGGIILNTTUV AGGLUTINATIVE
AAEGGILMNOORT AGGLOMERATION
AAEGGIMNNOORT AGGIORNAMENTO
AAEGGINRSSTTT STARTING GATES
AAEGGLNOOPRTU PROTOLANGUAGE
AAEGHHIKMRRTW HIGH-WATER MARK
AAEGHHOPPRRSY PHRASEOGRAPHY
AAEGHIILMNOPR GERMANOPHILIA
AAEGHILMOOSTT HAEMATOLOGIST
AAEGHIPRRRSTT STRATIGRAPHER
AAEGHLLMOPRTY METALLOGRAPHY
AAEGHLLNNOSTT TEN-GALLON HATS
AAEGHLOPPSYYZ ZYGAPOPHYSEAL
AAEGHLOPRTTUY TELAUTOGRAPHY
AAEGHNOOPRRTY ORGANOTHERAPY
AAEGIIILMNRTZ MATERIALIZING
AAEGIIILMNTVY IMAGINATIVELY
AAEGIILLLORST LEGISLATORIAL
AAEGIILLMRSTY MAGISTERIALLY
AAEGIILNNTTTY TANGENTIALITY
AAEGIIMMMPRST EPIGRAMMATISM
AAEGIIMMPRSTT EPIGRAMMATIST
AAEGIIMNNORST GERMANISATION
AAEGIIMNNORTZ GERMANIZATION
AAEGIIMNNOSTT MAGNETISATION
AAEGIIMNNOTTZ MAGNETIZATION
AAEGIIMNQQSUU QUINQUAGESIMA
AAEGIKLNPPRSW WALKING PAPERS
AAEGILLMNOOPT MEGALOPOLITAN
AAEGILNOPRTTX EXTRAPOLATING
AAEGIMNNORTTU ARGUMENTATION
AAEGIMNNOSTTU AUGMENTATIONS
AAEGINNOPSTTV VANTAGE POINTS
AAEGINOORSTTY GEOSTATIONARY

AAEGLLNOOOPTY PALAEONTOLOGY
AAEGLLOOOOPYZ PALAEOZOOLOGY
AAEGMOPPSSSTT POSTAGE STAMPS
AAEHHILLNORTY A ROLL IN THE HAY
AAEHHILMOPRTX XEROPHTHALMIA
AAEHIIILMNSSS LEISHMANIASIS
AAEHIIIMNNSTT ANTIHISTAMINE
AAEHIIORTTTUV AUTHORITATIVE
AAEHIMNPSSSTT STATESMANSHIP
AAEHINNNOQRTU ANTHRAQUINONE
AAEHINPRSSSTY PARASYNTHESIS
AAEHNNOPRSTTY PARASYNTHETON
AAEIIILMMMRST IMMATERIALISM
AAEIIILMMRSTT IMMATERIALIST
AAEIIILMMRTTY IMMATERIALITY
AAEIIILNNOSTT NATIONALITIES
AAEIIILNORSST SERIALISATION
AAEIIILNORSTZ SERIALIZATION
AAEIIIMNNPPRT IMPARIPINNATE
AAEIIKLMNPSST SEMIPALATINSK
AAEIILLMNOSTT METALLISATION
AAEIILLMNOTTZ METALLIZATION
AAEIILLMNRSTU UNILATERALISM
AAEIILLQTTUVY QUALITATIVELY
AAEIILMNNORTT TERMINATIONAL
AAEIILNNNORTT INTERNATIONAL
AAEIILNNOORTT ORIENTATIONAL
AAEIILNNORSTV VERNALISATION
AAEIILNNORTVZ VERNALIZATION
AAEIILNOPRRST RESPIRATIONAL
AAEIILNORRTTT TRILATERATION
AAEIIMNNNOSTX ANNEXATIONISM
AAEIIMNOOPRST ANISOMETROPIA
AAEIINNNOSTTX ANNEXATIONIST
AAEIINOPPPRRT INAPPROPRIATE
AAEILLNNOSSTY SENSATIONALLY
AAEILLNOOPRTY OPERATIONALLY
AAEILLNOPRTXY EXPLANATORILY
AAEILMNNORSTU MENSURATIONAL
AAEILMNOPRTTU PERMUTATIONAL
AAEILMOPPRTXY APPROXIMATELY
AAEILNNNNPSVY PENNSYLVANIAN
AAEILNNOPRRST INTRAPERSONAL
AAEILNOOORTTV LAEVOROTATION
AAEILNOOPRTTX EXTRAPOLATION
AAEILNORSTTWY SANITARY TOWEL
AAEILOPPPRRTY APPROPRIATELY
AAEILOPPRRRTY PREPARATORILY
AAEIMNNNOORTT ORNAMENTATION
AAEIMNORSSTTT STATIONMASTER
AAEINNNOSSTTU INSTANTANEOUS
AAEINNOPRSTTU SUPERNATATION
AAEKLMORRSTWW LOW-WATER MARKS
AAEKNOQRRSSUW NARROW SQUEAKS

AAELLMOOPRSTU SOMATOPLEURAL
AAELMMNNORRSU ROMAN NUMERALS
AAELNNNRSSTUU UNNATURALNESS
AAELNNPRRSTTY TRANSPARENTLY
AAELOOOORRTTVY LAEVOROTATORY
AAFFGHINPRSSU SUFFRAGANSHIP
AAFFIINNOPRRT NITROPARAFFIN
AAFGIIIILMNRZ FAMILIARIZING
AAFHINOOPRRST PARROT-FASHION
AAFIIILMNRTUY UNFAMILIARITY
AAFIILMMNNOST INFLAMMATIONS
AAFIILMNNOORT INFORMATIONAL
AAFIILMNOORST FORMALISATION
AAFIILMNOORTZ FORMALIZATION
AAFILMMNNOORST MALFORMATIONS
AAGGIILNNOTTU AGGLUTINATION
AAGGILNNRSTTU STRANGULATING
AAGHHINOOPPRT ANTHROPOPHAGI
AAGHIILMNORTT ANTILOGARITHM
AAGHIINNNOSTW WASHINGTONIAN
AAGHIMNOOPRST MASTIGOPHORAN
AAGIIILMMNORT IMMIGRATIONAL
AAGIIILNNNOTZ NATIONALIZING
AAGIIILNNORTZ RATIONALIZING
AAGIIJNNOORST JARGONISATION
AAGIIJNNOORTZ JARGONIZATION
AAGIIKLNNPSTY PAINSTAKINGLY
AAGIIILLNNPSTW WALL PAINTINGS
AAGIIILLNNTTYZ TANTALIZINGLY
AAGIILMNOORST GLAMORISATION
AAGIILMNOORTZ GLAMORIZATION
AAGIILNNORTTU TRIANGULATION
AAGIILNORSTUV VULGARISATION
AAGIILNORTUVZ VULGARIZATION
AAGIILNRRTTUY TRIANGULARITY
AAGIIMNNPRSTY PRAYING MANTIS
AAGIIMNOPPRTX APPROXIMATING
AAGIINNOORSST ORGANISATIONS
AAGIINNOORSTZ ORGANIZATIONS
AAGIINNORSTUU INAUGURATIONS
AAGIINOPPPRRT APPROPRIATING
AAGILMMNNOSUY MAGNANIMOUSLY
AAGILNNNPRSTT TRANSPLANTING
AAGILNNORSTTU STRANGULATION
AAGILNOOOPRSZ ZOOSPORANGIAL
AAGIMNORRRSTT TRANSMIGRATOR
AAGINNOOSSTTW STATION WAGONS
AAGLMNOORSTUU GRANULOMATOUS
AAHHNOOPPRTTY ANTHROPOPATHY
AAHIILMMNSSTU MALTHUSIANISM
AAHIIMNNOORST HARMONISATION
AAHIIMNNOORTZ HARMONIZATION
AAHIINOORSTTU AUTHORISATION
AAHIINOORTTUZ AUTHORIZATION

AAHINOPSSSSTT SHOP ASSISTANT
AAIIILNNOPRST INSPIRATIONAL
AAIIILNNOPRTT TRIPOLITANIAN
AAIIILNNOPSTT PLATINISATION
AAIIILNNOPTTZ PLATINIZATION
AAIIILNOORSTV VARIOLISATION
AAIIILNOORTVZ VARIOLIZATION
AAIIILNORRTTY IRRATIONALITY
AAIIILNOSSTUV VISUALISATION
AAIIILNOSTUVZ VISUALIZATION
AAIIINOPRSTTV PRIVATISATION
AAIIINOPRTTVZ PRIVATIZATION
AAIIINOPSSSTV PASSIVISATION
AAIIINOPSSTVZ PASSIVIZATION
AAIILLMNNOTTU MULTINATIONAL
AAIILLNNOSSTT INSTALLATIONS
AAIILLNOPRSTU PLURALISATION
AAIILLNOPRTUZ PLURALIZATION
AAIILMNNOORST NORMALISATION
AAIILMNNOORTZ NORMALIZATION
AAIILMNNOPSTU MANIPULATIONS
AAIILMNOOPTTT TOTIPALMATION
AAIILNOSSSTTV SALVATIONISTS
AAIILNPSTTVYY NATIVITY PLAYS
AAIIMMNORSSTU SUMMARISATION
AAIIMMNORSTUZ SUMMARIZATION
AAIIMNOOPPRTX APPROXIMATION
AAIIMNORRSTTY MARTYRISATION
AAIIMNORRTTYZ MARTYRIZATION
AAIINNOPRRSTT TRANSPIRATION
AAIINOOPPPRRT APPROPRIATION
AAIJLMMOORRTY MORAL MAJORITY
AAIKLNNOPRSSW PARKINSON'S LAW
AAIKMNOOQRTTU QUOTATION MARK
AAILLMOOPPSTU PAPILLOMATOUS
AAILLMOPRSTYY MORALITY PLAYS
AAILNNOPPSTTU SUPPLANTATION
AAILNNORSTTTU NATIONAL TRUST
AAIMNNORSTTTU TRANSMUTATION
AAINOPRRRSTTY TRANSPIRATORY
AALMOOPSSTTTY STOMATOPLASTY
AANNORRSSTUUY TYRANNOSAURUS
ABBBEHLMORSTU BLABBERMOUTHS
ABBCDEEIILNRS INDESCRIBABLE
ABBCDEIILNRSY INDESCRIBABLY
ABBCEEIJLNOOT OBJECTIONABLE
ABBCEGIKLNRRY BLACKBERRYING
ABBCEGILNOPUU BUBONIC PLAGUE
ABBCEHHIRSTTU RABBIT HUTCHES
ABBCEHILNORTU BRONCHIAL TUBE
ABBCEHINPRSTU RABBIT PUNCHES
ABBCEHKOORRSS SHOCK ABSORBER
ABBCEIJLNOOTY OBJECTIONABLY
ABBCGHIIILOPR BIBLIOGRAPHIC

ABBCIIILOPRST PROBABILISTIC
ABBDEEFNORSTU BEAST OF BURDEN
ABBDEEMPRRSTU RUBBER-STAMPED
ABBDEIILRSTTU DISTRIBUTABLE
ABBDEILLNORTU BULLETIN BOARD
ABBDFFILMNNSU BLIND MAN'S BUFF
ABBEEHILLPRSU REPUBLISHABLE
ABBEEILLMNRTY BLANTYRE-LIMBE
ABBEEILMPRRTU IMPERTURBABLE
ABBEELMMNOOTZ BAMBOOZLEMENT
ABBEGGHINORTY BIG BANG THEORY
ABBEGHIILOPRR BIBLIOGRAPHER
ABBEGILNORRSU RABBLE-ROUSING
ABBEIIILOPRST PROBABILITIES
ABBEIILLMORRY MOBILE LIBRARY
ABBEILMPRRTUY IMPERTURBABLY
ABBEILSSTTTUU SUBSTITUTABLE
ABBGINOOPPRTY BOOBY TRAPPING
ABBIIILMOPRTY IMPROBABILITY
ABCCDEEIKLMOS BLACK COMEDIES
ABCCDEHILORSU COACHBUILDERS
ABCCDENORSTTU SUBCONTRACTED
ABCCDIILLMORU UMBILICAL CORD
ABCCEEIILNNOV INCONCEIVABLE
ABCCEGIILLOOO BIOECOLOGICAL
ABCCEIIILMPTY IMPECCABILITY
ABCCEIIILSSTY ACCESSIBILITY
ABCCEIILLMORS SOCIAL CLIMBER
ABCCEIILNNOVY INCONCEIVABLY
ABCCEIILORTTY BACTERIOLYTIC
ABCCEIIMMNRTU CIRCUMAMBIENT
ABCCEIINRRSSU CABIN CRUISERS
ABCCEIMMORTUY MYCOBACTERIUM
ABCCHHIIOPRRS ARCHBISHOPRIC
ABCCILMNOPPUY PUBLIC COMPANY
ABCCNOOORRSTTU SUBCONTRACTOR
ABCDDEEIILRST DISCREDITABLE
ABCDDEEILTTUX TAX-DEDUCTIBLE
ABCDDEIILRSTY DISCREDITABLY
ABCDDEIINOORX CARBON DIOXIDE
ABCDDGIKLNPSU BLACK PUDDINGS
ABCDEEEGHNRST BERCHTESGADEN
ABCDEEEINORRT DECEREBRATION
ABCDEEELMMNOR RECOMMENDABLE
ABCDEEHILPTTT PITCHED BATTLE
ABCDEEIILOPRT PERIODIC TABLE
ABCDEEIIMOSTY BASIDIOMYCETE
ABCDEEILNNNOS INCONDENSABLE
ABCDEEILNPRTU UNPREDICTABLE
ABCDEELLOPRST CORPS DE BALLET
ABCDEEMNOOPRY BEYOND COMPARE
ABCDEHIOPSSTX DISPATCH BOXES
ABCDEHNORSSTY BODY SNATCHERS
ABCDEIIILLNPS DISCIPLINABLE

ABCDEIIILMRTU MIRABILE DICTU
ABCDEIIILNTUY INEDUCABILITY
ABCDEIIILPRTY PREDICABILITY
ABCDEIIILPSTY DESPICABILITY
ABCDEIILLOQTU QUODLIBETICAL
ABCDEIILLTUXY EXCLUDABILITY
ABCDEILORRRRY RECORD LIBRARY
ABCDEKNORRSTU ROUND BRACKETS
ABCDIIIILNTVY VINDICABILITY
ABCDIIILLPTUY DUPLICABILITY
ABCDILNOOOSTT ODONTOBLASTIC
ABCEEEELNRSSX EXECRABLENESS
ABCEEEFIIINRS BENEFICIARIES
ABCEEEFIILLRT ELECTRIFIABLE
ABCEEEFILLNNU INFLUENCEABLE
ABCEEEHMMRRRT CHARTER MEMBER
ABCEEEIINNRST BICENTENARIES
ABCEEEILNOPTX EXCEPTIONABLE
ABCEEEILNRSUV UNSERVICEABLE
ABCEEEILORRRV IRRECOVERABLE
ABCEEELMNOPRS RECOMPENSABLE
ABCEEELNSSSUX EXCUSABLENESS
ABCEEHILLPTUW THE PUBLIC WEAL
ABCEEHILNORSV OLIVE BRANCHES
ABCEEHIMNRSTY CHIMNEYBREAST
ABCEEIILNPRSU REPUBLICANISE
ABCEEIILNPRUZ REPUBLICANIZE
ABCEEILMOORSU BROMELIACEOUS
ABCEEILNNOSTT INCONTESTABLE
ABCEEILNOPRRS CEREBROSPINAL
ABCEEILORRRVY IRRECOVERABLY
ABCEEILRRSTTU BATTLE CRUISER
ABCEEJMRSTTTU SUBJECT MATTER
ABCEELMMNORSU COMMENSURABLE
ABCEELNNOOPRU PRONOUNCEABLE
ABCEENOORRSSS BEAR ONE'S CROSS
ABCEENOPRRSTU PROTUBERANCES
ABCEFGIIILNNT FILING CABINET
ABCEFGIILMMNR CLIMBING FRAME
ABCEFHIILLMRU LIEBFRAUMILCH
ABCEFIIINORTV VERBIFICATION
ABCEFINOORRSU CARBONIFEROUS
ABCEFLMNNOORU UNCONFORMABLE
ABCEFLMNOORTU UNCOMFORTABLE
ABCEGHIMNNSUU SUBMACHINE GUN
ABCEGHORRRSTU TURBOCHARGERS
ABCEGIINNOOSU BIGNONIACEOUS
ABCEGILLMOORY EMBRYOLOGICAL
ABCEGINORRSSZ ZEBRA CROSSING
ABCEHILSSTTTY CHASTITY BELTS
ABCEHIRRRRSSU CRUSH BARRIERS
ABCEHLOOPRSTU CLAUSTROPHOBE
ABCEHOPRRSTUY BRACHYPTEROUS
ABCEIIILNNTUY ENUNCIABILITY

ABCEIIILNOTTY NOTICEABILITY
ABCEIIILLMORTY BIOMETRICALLY
ABCEIILMNPRSU REPUBLICANISM
ABCEIILNOPRTU REPUBLICATION
ABCEIILORSSTY BACTERIOLYSIS
ABCEIIMNNOORT RECOMBINATION
ABCEIINORSSTT OBSTETRICIANS
ABCEIIRSSTTUW WATER BISCUITS
ABCEILLLPSTTU PLASTIC BULLET
ABCEILLMNORYY EMBRYONICALLY
ABCEILLORSTTY OBSTETRICALLY
ABCEILNNOSTTY INCONTESTABLY
ABCEILNORTTUU TUBERCULATION
ABCEILNSSSSSU BUSINESS CLASS
ABCEILOORSSTU STROBILACEOUS
ABCEILORRRTUU ARBORICULTURE
ABCEIOOORRRTV CORROBORATIVE
ABCEKKLNRSSSU BRASS KNUCKLES
ABCELNORSSTTU COUNTERBLASTS
ABCFLMNOORTUY UNCOMFORTABLY
ABCGGHINORRTU TURBOCHARGING
ABCGHIKLNSSUW SWASHBUCKLING
ABCGIKLNORSTT STARTING BLOCK
ABCGINOOORRRT CORROBORATING
ABCHHINOOPRST OPISTHOBRANCH
ABCHILLMOPSTY LYMPHOBLASTIC
ABCHILOOPRSTT TROPHOBLASTIC
ABCIIIILLNOTUY INOCULABILITY
ABCIIILLNPTUY INCULPABILITY
ABCIIILMOPTTY COMPATIBILITY
ABCIIILNOSTUY UNSOCIABILITY
ABCIILLOPRSTT TRIPLOBLASTIC
ABCIILMOPTTUY COMPUTABILITY
ABCIILNOPPRSY PRINCIPAL BOYS
ABCILNOORSTTU OBSTRUCTIONAL
ABCIMNNNOOOOP BOON
  COMPANION
ABCINOOOORRRT CORROBORATION
ABCLRRSSTTUUU SUBSTRUCTURAL
ABCOOOORRRRST CORROBORATORS
ABDDDEEEEFHRT FEATHERBEDDED
ABDDDEILMNORY BROADMINDEDLY
ABDDEEEGHINSS BIGHEADEDNESS
ABDDEEEELLORSU DOUBLE-DEALERS
ABDDEEFILNNOY BADLY IN NEED OF
ABDDEEGILLNOU DOUBLE-DEALING
ABDDEEHIILNNR HILDEBRANDINE
ABDDEEHLLORSU SHOULDER BLADE
ABDDEEHLRTUYY BUTYRALDEHYDE
ABDDEEIILNPTY DEPENDABILITY
ABDDEFHLLNOOS FLESH AND BLOOD
ABDDEILNNNSSS SAND-BLINDNESS
ABDDGINNOORSU SOUNDING BOARD
ABDEEEEHLNPRR REPREHENDABLE

ABDEEEEFLORTUU DOUBLE FEATURE
ABDEEEGKLLNOW KNOWLEDGEABLE
ABDEEEHKNORRT BROKEN-HEARTED
ABDEEEHLNOPTY BEYOND THE PALE
ABDEEEIILMRTY REDEEMABILITY
ABDEEEILMNNST DISENABLEMENT
ABDEEFGIRSSSU FIGURED BASSES
ABDEEFGLMOORR GAMBREL-ROOFED
ABDEEFIIILRSV DIVERSIFIABLE
ABDEEGIILNRST DISINTEGRABLE
ABDEEGILNRST DRESSING TABLE
ABDEEGKLLNOWY KNOWLEDGEABLY
ABDEEIILNNNTV VENETIAN BLIND
ABDEEIILNNPSS INDISPENSABLE
ABDEEIILNORST DELIBERATIONS
ABDEEIILNPTXY EXPENDABILITY
ABDEEIILSTTTY DETESTABILITY
ABDEEIIMRTTXY AMBIDEXTERITY
ABDEEILMNOPRS IMPONDERABLES
ABDEEKNORRRSS BANKER'S ORDERS
ABDEFIILLORRT DEFIBRILLATOR
ABDEGGILLNOUZ DOUBLE-GLAZING
ABDEGHINOORSU BOARDINGHOUSE
ABDEGIIILNSTZ DESTABILIZING
ABDEGIKLLNOTU DOUBLE-TALKING
ABDEGIKLNOPRU DOUBLE-PARKING
ABDEGILLLNNSY BELLY-LANDINGS
ABDEHHNOSSSUU HOUSE HUSBANDS
ABDEHILMNNSST BLANDISHMENTS
ABDEHILNOORSU DISHONOURABLE
ABDEIILNNPSSY INDISPENSABLY
ABDEIILNOPRTY PONDERABILITY
ABDEIINNORSTU INSUBORDINATE
ABDEIINNORSTUV SUBORDINATIVE
ABDEILLNOOOORT BLOOD RELATION
ABDEMOORRSTTW BOTTOM DRAWERS
ABDFGIILLLNOS BILLS OF LADING
ABDFIIIILMOTY MODIFIABILITY
ABDFIIILMORTY FORMIDABILITY
ABDGIIKNORRST SKIRTING BOARD
ABDGIINNOORRS IRONING BOARDS
ABDGIINNORSTU SUBORDINATING
ABDHIIINORSTY HYBRIDISATION
ABDHIIINORTYZ HYBRIDIZATION
ABDHILNOORSUY DISHONOURABLY
ABDIIIILMSSTY ADMISSIBILITY
ABDIIILNOSSUV SUBDIVISIONAL
ABDIIILOPSSTY DISPOSABILITY
ABDIIILPSTTUY DISPUTABILITY
ABDIIINOSSSTU SUBSIDISATION
ABDIIINOSSTUZ SUBSIDIZATION
ABDIINNOORSTU SUBORDINATION
ABDILLMNNOPTU PLATINUM-BLOND
ABDMOOOORRTTU OUTBOARD MOTOR

ABEEEEFLNORSU	UNFORESEEABLE	ABEEILNNSTTUU	SUBLIEUTENANT
ABEEEEILMMPRS	SEMIPERMEABLE	ABEEILNOORTTX	EXTORTIONABLE
ABEEEEIRRRTVV	REVERBERATIVE	ABEEINPRRSSTY	PRESBYTERIANS
ABEEEELNPRRST	REPRESENTABLE	ABEEIOORRSSTV	OBSERVATORIES
ABEEEFIILLMPX	EXEMPLIFIABLE	ABEEKLMORRSTU	TROUBLEMAKERS
ABEEEGINRRRTV	REVERBERATING	ABEEKMNNORTUY	MOUNTEBANKERY
ABEEEHILNPPRS	APPREHENSIBLE	ABEELNNNORRTU	NONRETURNABLE
ABEEEHKORRSSU	HOUSEBREAKERS	ABEFGLNORTTUY	UNFORGETTABLY
ABEEEHLOPRSST	OBLATE SPHERES	ABEFHHILLLOST	BILLS OF HEALTH
ABEEEIILLPRRV	IRREPLEVIABLE	ABEFHOOOPRSTT	A SPOT OF BOTHER
ABEEEIILRRRTV	IRRETRIEVABLE	ABEFIIILLRTTY	FILTERABILITY
ABEEEIKKRRRST	STRIKEBREAKER	ABEFIILNORRRU	NEUROFIBRILAR
ABEEEILMNRSSS	MISERABLENESS	ABEFLLOOORSUV	LABOURS OF LOVE
ABEEEILMNSSST	ESTIMABLENESS	ABEGGIIIMSTUU	AMBIGUGUITIES
ABEEEILNPRRTT	INTERPRETABLE	ABEGIIILNOTTY	NEGOTIABILITY
ABEEEILNQSSTU	EQUITABLENESS	ABEGIIILNRTTY	INTEGRABILITY
ABEEEILNRSSTV	VERITABLENESS	ABEGIILNORTVY	GOVERNABILITY
ABEEEIMMPRRTV	PRIVATE MEMBER	ABEGILLLNOSWY	BOWLING ALLEYS
ABEEEINORRRTV	REVERBERATION	ABEGILNOPPRTT	BLOTTING PAPER
ABEEEINRRSTTV	INVERTEBRATES	ABEGIMNOSSSUU	AMBIGUOUSNESS
ABEEELLMNSSSS	BLAMELESSNESS	ABEHHINNOORST	HEATH ROBINSON
ABEEELLNORSST	TOLERABLENESS	ABEHIIILPRSTY	PERISHABILITY
ABEEELNRSSTTU	UTTERABLENESS	ABEHIILNSTUXY	INEXHAUSTIBLY
ABEEELOOPSTTT	POTATO BEETLES	ABEHIIORSSTUV	BEHAVIOURISTS
ABEEEORRRRTVY	REVERBERATORY	ABEHILNORRSTW	BROTHERS-IN-LAW
ABEEFFIMMORRT	FAR BE IT FROM ME	ABEHLLMOPSSUY	BLASPHEMOUSLY
ABEEFGIILNRRR	IRREFRANGIBLE	ABEIIIILLNSSTT	INSTABILITIES
ABEEFGLNORTTU	UNFORGETTABLE	ABEIIIILLNTTVY	INEVITABILITY
ABEEFHOPRSTTT	THE BEST PART OF	ABEIIIILLNRTUY	UNRELIABILITY
ABEEFIILNOPRS	PERSONIFIABLE	ABEIIIILMNRTTY	TERMINABILITY
ABEEFIILPRRTY	PREFERABILITY	ABEIIIILNOPRTY	INOPERABILITY
ABEEGHHLPRSTU	BUSH TELEGRAPH	ABEIIILNOQRTU	EQUILIBRATION
ABEEGHIKNORSU	HOUSEBREAKING	ABEIIILNORTXY	INEXORABILITY
ABEEGHLORSTTT	GHETTO BLASTER	ABEIIILNPSTXY	EXPANSIBILITY
ABEEGIILMNNRS	NEGRI SEMBILAN	ABEIIILPRRSTY	RESPIRABILITY
ABEEGIKNPSSTU	SPEAKING TUBES	ABEIIILMOPTYY	EMPLOYABILITY
ABEEGILNORRVY	OVERBEARINGLY	ABEIIILLNRTUVY	VULNERABILITY
ABEEGILNOSSST	BLASTOGENESIS	ABEIIILLORSTVY	RESOLVABILITY
ABEEHIILNSTUX	INEXHAUSTIBLE	ABEIILMNRSSST	TRANSMISSIBLE
ABEEHILMNSSTT	ESTABLISHMENT	ABEIILNRRTTUY	RETURNABILITY
ABEEHILRRSSTW	WELSH RAREBITS	ABEIILOPRTTXY	EXPORTABILITY
ABEEHKLNORRTY	HEARTBROKENLY	ABEIILRTTTUVY	ATTRIBUTIVELY
ABEEHLNNOORSS	HONORABLENESS	ABEIIMNOSSSTU	AMBITIOUSNESS
ABEEIIILLRRSUV	AUBERVILLIERS	ABEIIMOORSTUV	OVERAMBITIOUS
ABEEIIILMPRTTY	TEMPERABILITY	ABEIINSSSTTUV	SUBSTANTIVISE
ABEEIIILNNORTV	INVENTORIABLE	ABEIINSSTTUVZ	SUBSTANTIVIZE
ABEEIIILNPRTTY	PENETRABILITY	ABEILNOORSSSU	LABORIOUSNESS
ABEEIIILRRRTVY	IRRETRIEVABLY	ABEILNOPPRSTU	INSUPPORTABLE
ABEEIIOOPRRRT	RIBEIRAO PRETO	ABEILNSSTTUVY	SUBSTANTIVELY
ABEEIILLMNSSSY	ASSEMBLY LINES	ABEIMNNOSSSUW	BUSINESSWOMAN
ABEEIILLRSSTVY	LIVERY STABLES	ABEINNORSTUVY	SUBVENTIONARY
ABEEIILMNNNOTU	UNMENTIONABLE	ABELLLLOPSSYY	POLYSYLLABLES
ABEEIILMNRRSSU	SERIAL NUMBERS	ABELLLMNOOSSY	MONOSYLLABLES
ABEEIILNNRSSSS	BRAINLESSNESS	ABELNOPRRTTUY	PROTUBERANTLY

ABFGHIILLORTT BIT OF ALL RIGHT
ABFIIIILLLNTY INFALLIBILITY
ABFIIILOPRTTY PROFITABILITY
ABFLLLOOOOPST FOOTBALL POOLS
ABGGIILOOORST AGROBIOLOGIST
ABGHIIMMNSSTW SWIMMING BATHS
ABGIIIILNNTTY INTANGIBILITY
ABGIIINORRSTU SUBIRRIGATION
ABGIIMNNORRST BRAINSTORMING
ABHIIILNPSTUY PUNISHABILITY
ABHIIINOORSTV VASOINHIBITOR
ABIIIIILMNTTY INIMITABILITY
ABIIIILLNOTVY INVIOLABILITY
ABIIIILMPRTTY IMPARTIBILITY
ABIIIILLNOSTVY INSOLVABILITY
ABIIILMNOOSST MOBILISATIONS
ABIIILMNOOSTZ MOBILIZATIONS
ABIIILMOPRTVY IMPROVABILITY
ABIIILNOOSSTT ABOLITIONISTS
ABIIILNOSSTTU SUBTILISATION
ABIIILNOSTTUZ SUBTILIZATION
ABIIILNSTTUUY UNSUITABILITY
ABIIILRSTUVVY SURVIVABILITY
ABIILMNNNTTUU TINTINNABULUM
ABIILMNOOSSTY SYMBOLISATION
ABIILMNOOSTYZ SYMBOLIZATION
ABIILMORRTTUV MULTIVIBRATOR
ABILLMMNOOSSY MONOSYLLABISM
ABILMMNOSSSTU SOMNAMBULISTS
ABILNOOPPSTUU SUBPOPULATION
ACCCDEEEINNNS INCANDESCENCE
ACCCDEINORTTU CREDIT ACCOUNT
ACCCEEEELNNOSV CONVALESCENCE
ACCCEEHIILRRT ELECTRIC CHAIR
ACCCEEIILNOSS SOCIAL SCIENCE
ACCCEEIILSSST ECCLESIASTICS
ACCCEEILLNRTY ECCENTRICALLY
ACCCEFFIILRRT TRAFFIC CIRCLE
ACCCEHIILMMOR MICROCHEMICAL
ACCCEHIILMOPR MICROCEPHALIC
ACCCEHIINORTT ARCHITECTONIC
ACCCEIMMNOOOR MACROECONOMIC
ACCCEIMNRSSTU CIRCUMSTANCES
ACCCELOOPRSTT STREPTOCOCCAL
ACCCENNOOOVVX CONCAVO-CONVEX
ACCCGHILLNOOO CONCHOLOGICAL
ACCCHILOOPSTY STAPHYLOCOCCI
ACCCIIILMMORT MICROCLIMATIC
ACCCIIKKLOSTT COCKTAIL STICK
ACCCIIMNOOTTY ACTINOMYCOTIC
ACCCILOPRSTTY CRYPTOCLASTIC
ACCDDEEHRRSTU STARCH-REDUCED
ACCDEEEFINORS CONFEDERACIES
ACCDEEEENNNRST TRANSCENDENCE

ACCDEEGHNORRR RECORD-CHANGER
ACCDEEHHORRST SCORCHED EARTH
ACCDEEIILNOST OCCIDENTALISE
ACCDEEIIILNOTZ OCCIDENTALIZE
ACCDEEIINPRSS DISCREPANCIES
ACCDEEILNOPSY ENCYCLOPEDIAS
ACCDEEINNOPRT ACCIDENT-PRONE
ACCDEELOOPRSU CAPE COLOUREDS
ACCDEENNNRSTY TRANSCENDENCY
ACCDEGNNORRST CONCERT GRANDS
ACCDEHHIKLLTY LATCHKEY CHILD
ACCDEHHILOPRY HYDROCEPHALIC
ACCDEHHNRRSUW CHURCHWARDENS
ACCDEHINOORTW WITH ONE ACCORD
ACCDEIIKLOOPS KALEIDOSCOPIC
ACCDEIILMNOST OCCIDENTALISM
ACCDEIILNNOOT CODECLINATION
ACCDEIILNOSTT OCCIDENTALIST
ACCDEIINOORTT DECORTICATION
ACCDEIINORTTV CONTRADICTIVE
ACCDEILLMOPTY COMPLICATEDLY
ACCDEILMNOPTU UNCOMPLICATED
ACCDENNORSTUY COUNTRY DANCES
ACCDFIINOOST CODIFICATIONS
ACCDGIINNORTT CONTRADICTING
ACCDHHINOOPRY HYPOCHONDRIAC
ACCDHIILORSTV CLAVICHORDIST
ACCDHIILPRSUU SULPHURIC ACID
ACCDHIMNOPSYY PSYCHODYNAMIC
ACCDHINOSTTUU DUTCH AUCTIONS
ACCDIIILNSSTY SYNDICALISTIC
ACCDIIINORSTY IDIOSYNCRATIC
ACCDIILLLNRYY CYLINDRICALLY
ACCDIIMMNNOOU INCOMMUNICADO
ACCDIINNOORTT CONTRADICTION
ACCDILNOORRTU CONDUCTOR RAIL
ACCDINOORRTTY CONTRADICTORY
ACCEEEEGHOSTT COTTAGE CHEESE
ACCEEEELLNPRX PAR EXCELLENCE
ACCEEEELMORRT ACCELEROMETER
ACCEEEGHIRRSV SERVICE CHARGE
ACCEEEHILLNPT TELENCEPHALIC
ACCEEEHILLNRS CHANCELLERIES
ACCEEEHILMNPS MESENCEPHALIC
ACCEEEHILMNPT METENCEPHALIC
ACCEEEILLORST ECCLESIOLATER
ACCEEFFIILRSS SELF-SACRIFICE
ACCEEFIIIPSTV SPECIFICATIVE
ACCEEGHILNTYY EYE-CATCHINGLY
ACCEEGHKNOSTX STOCK EXCHANGE
ACCEEGHNNORSX CORN EXCHANGES
ACCEEGHNORRTU COUNTERCHARGE
ACCEEHHLOORST SCHOOLTEACHER
ACCEEHILLNOTY ACETYLCHOLINE

ACCEEHILMOPRT CEPHALOMETRIC,
PETROCHEMICAL
ACCEEHMNNORST ENCROACHMENTS
ACCEEHORRSTTY OYSTERCATCHER
ACCEEIILLNRTV INTERCLAVICLE
ACCEEIILMMNSU ECUMENICALISM
ACCEEIILMMORS COMMERCIALISE
ACCEEIILMMORZ COMMERCIALIZE
ACCEEIILORSSV SOCIAL SERVICE
ACCEEIIMORRST MERITOCRACIES
ACCEEIIOPRRTV RECIPROCATIVE
ACCEEIKLNOPRS COCKER SPANIEL
ACCEEILLORSTY ECCLESIOLATRY
ACCEEILNOPSTU CONCEPTUALISE
ACCEEILNOPTUZ CONCEPTUALIZE
ACCEEILNPSSST SCEPTICALNESS
ACCEEILNQSTUY ACQUIESCENTLY
ACCEEILORSTTT ELECTROSTATIC
ACCEEIMMNOTUX EXCOMMUNICATE
ACCEEINNORSSV CONSERVANCIES
ACCEEINNORTTV CONCENTRATIVE
ACCEEINOPRTTV CONTRACEPTIVE
ACCEEINORSSSS ACCESSORINESS
ACCEEINORTTUV COUNTERACTIVE
ACCEELLMMOORU MACROMOLECULE
ACCEELNNOSSTT CONTACT LENSES
ACCEELNNOSSTV CONVALESCENTS
ACCEEMNORSTTU ACCOUTREMENTS
ACCEEOOORRSSTU STERCORACEOUS
ACCEFFIIINOSU INEFFICACIOUS
ACCEFFIILOSUY EFFICACIOUSLY
ACCEFIIINOPST SPECIFICATION
ACCEFIIINORTT - CERTIFICATION,
RECTIFICATION
ACCEFIIORRTTY CERTIFICATORY
ACCEFINNOORTY CONFECTIONARY
ACCEFIOOPRTTU OUT OF PRACTICE
ACCEGHHIOOPRR CHOREOGRAPHIC
ACCEGHIILOPRX LEXICOGRAPHIC
ACCEGHILLNOOT TECHNOLOGICAL
ACCEGHILNNORY ENCROACHINGLY
ACCEGIILLLOOX LEXICOLOGICAL
ACCEGIINNNORT CONCERTINAING
ACCEGIINOPRRT RECIPROCATING
ACCEGILMNOORT CONGLOMERATIC
ACCEGINNNNOTU COUNTENANCING
ACCEGINNNORTT CONCENTRATING
ACCEGINNORTTU COUNTERACTING
ACCEGINOORRTT GERONTOCRATIC
ACCEGIOPPRRTU GROUP PRACTICE
ACCEHHIILMOST HISTOCHEMICAL
ACCEHHIINSSTT CHAIN STITCHES
ACCEHHILMOOPT PHOTOCHEMICAL
ACCEHHILOOPRT ORTHOCEPHALIC

ACCEHHORRSSTT RORSCHACH TEST
ACCEHIILLNSST CALLISTHENICS
ACCEHIILNOPRS NECROPHILIACS
ACCEHIILPRRTY HYPERCRITICAL
ACCEHIKLLMOOT MILK CHOCOLATE
ACCEHIKMNSSTY CHIMNEYSTACKS
ACCEHILLOOPSS SPECIAL SCHOOL
ACCEHIMNORSST CHROMATICNESS
ACCEHINNNOPST PANTECHNICONS
ACCEHIOOPSSTT TACHISTOSCOPE
ACCEIIKLNOSTW ANTICLOCKWISE
ACCEIIKNNPRST PANIC-STRICKEN
ACCEIILMMMORS COMMERCIALISM
ACCEIILMMORST COMMERCIALIST
ACCEIILMMORTY COMMERCIALITY
ACCEIILMNOSSS NEOCLASSICISM
ACCEIILNOSSST NEOCLASSICIST
ACCEIILOPRRTY RECIPROCALITY
ACCEIIMMNOTUV COMMUNICATIVE
ACCEIINNNOSST INCONSTANCIES
ACCEIINOOPRRT RECIPROCATION
ACCEIIOPPRSSU PERSPICACIOUS
ACCEILLLNNOUY NUCLEONICALLY
ACCEILLMNOPSU NUCLEOPLASMIC
ACCEILMNNNOOP NONCOMPLIANCE
ACCEILMNOPSTU CONCEPTUALISM
ACCEILMNORSTU COUNTERCLAIMS
ACCEILNNOSSTU CONSULTANCIES
ACCEILNOPSTTU CONCEPTUALIST
ACCEINNNOORTT CONCENTRATION
ACCEINNOOPRTT CONTRACEPTION
ACCEINNOORRTY CONCRETIONARY
ACCEINNOORSSY CONCESSIONARY
ACCEINNOORTTU COUNTERACTION
ACCEINOOPPRTU PREOCCUPATION
ACCEINOPPRSSU PERCUSSION CAP
ACCELOOPRRSST PECTORAL CROSS
ACCFGIIILNRSY SACRIFICINGLY
ACCFIIINOORST SCORIFICATION
ACCFIINNOOSST CONFISCATIONS
ACCFLMORSTUUU FRACTOCUMULUS
ACCGGHHIKNOSU HACKING COUGHS
ACCGHHHHIMNRU HIGH CHURCHMAN
ACCGHHINOOPRR CHRONOGRAPHIC
ACCGHHINORSST CROSS-HATCHING
ACCGHHIOPPRSY PSYCHOGRAPHIC
ACCGHIIKNORRS ROCKING CHAIRS
ACCGHIILMNOPS ACCOMPLISHING
ACCGHILLNOOOR CHRONOLOGICAL
ACCGHILLOOPSY PSYCHOLOGICAL
ACCGHIOPPRRTY CRYPTOGRAPHIC
ACCGIIILNRRUZ CIRCULARIZING
ACCGIILLMOOSU MUSICOLOGICAL
ACCGIILLOOOTX TOXICOLOGICAL

ACCGIIMMNNOTU COMMUNICATING
ACCGILLOOOPRT PROCTOLOGICAL
ACCGILNOOPRSY LARYNGOSCOPIC
ACCHHIMMOOORT HOMOCHROMATIC
ACCHIIILPSSTY PHYSICALISTIC
ACCHIILMOPRSY MICROPHYSICAL
ACCHIILMOSSST SCHOLASTICISM
ACCHIIMNOOPRT ACTINOMORPHIC
ACCHIIMORRSSU CHIAROSCURISM
ACCHIIORRSSTU CHIAROSCURIST
ACCHILLOOPRST CHLOROPLASTIC
ACCHILLOPSTYY PSYCHOTICALLY
ACCHILMMOOPRS CHROMOPLASMIC
ACCHILMOOPRTY POLYCHROMATIC
ACCHILOPPRSTY PROPHYLACTICS
ACCHIMMNOOORT MONOCHROMATIC
ACCHIMOOPSSTY PSYCHOSOMATIC
ACCHIOOPRRRST CHIROPRACTORS
ACCHIOOPRSSUZ SCHIZOCARPOUS
ACCIIILNNORTU IN CIRCULATION
ACCIIIMMNOOST ICONOMATICISM
ACCIIINNOPSTW IT WAS NO PICNIC
ACCIILLPRSTUU PISCICULTURAL
ACCIILMMNOSTU COMMUNALISTIC
ACCIILMNOOPST COMPLICATIONS
ACCIILNORTTTY CONTRACTILITY
ACCIIMMNNOOTU COMMUNICATION
ACCIIMNOOSSTY ACTINOMYCOSIS
ACCIIOORRSSTV VICTORIA CROSS
ACCIJLNNNOOTU CONJUNCTIONAL
ACCILMNNOOTTY CONCOMITANTLY
ACCIMMNOORTUY COMMUNICATORY
ACCIMNOOOTTXY CYTOTAXONOMIC
ACDDEEEGSSTUU EDUCATED GUESS
ACDDEEEHHNNOR HENDECAHEDRON
ACDDEEEHIMSST SEMIDETACHEDS
ACDDEEEHINRUV UNDERACHIEVED
ACDDEEEILNRST DECENTRALISED
ACDDEEEILNRTZ DECENTRALIZED
ACDDEEEKMNOPR PROMENADE DECK
ACDDEEENOPRTT TOP DEAD CENTRE
ACDDEEFFILSTY DISAFFECTEDLY
ACDDEEGIKNNOR DEAD RECKONING
ACDDEEHHIITTW DICE WITH DEATH
ACDDEEHLLORTY COLD-HEARTEDLY
ACDDEEIMNOOTY ADENOIDECTOMY
ACDDEELNOORSS SECOND SEA LORD
ACDDEEMNNORTU COUNTERMANDED
ACDDEENRSSTUV SEVEN-CARD STUD
ACDDEFHIINRSS DISFRANCHISED
ACDDEGHILNNRR GRANDCHILDREN
ACDDEGIILLNOS DIALLING CODES
ACDDEGILLNOOR DENDROLOGICAL
ACDDEGLLNSSTU DUCTLESS GLAND

ACDDEHIILMOSU DICHLAMIDEOUS
ACDDEHIMNOOPS DODECAPHONISM
ACDDEHINOOPST DODECAPHONIST
ACDDEIIIMNRST DISCRIMINATED
ACDDEIILLNRTY DENDRITICALLY
ACDDEIINNORTT INDOCTRINATED
ACDDEIINRSTTY IDENTITY CARDS
ACDDEINNOORTU UNCOORDINATED
ACDDELMMMNOOU COMMAND MODULE
ACDDHIMNORSYY HYDRODYNAMICS
ACDDOOOORRSUY CORDUROY ROADS
ACDEEEHINNSTT INDECENT HASTE
ACDEEEHINRRUV UNDERACHIEVER
ACDEEEHLNOOPS HOLD ONE'S PEACE
ACDEEEHORRSTU TERRACED HOUSE
ACDEEEILNSSST DELICATESSENS
ACDEEELNOPRST PREADOLESCENT
ACDEEELNPRRSU SUPERCALENDER
ACDEEENNOPPRR PREPONDERANCE
ACDEEEOPRRRST TAPE RECORDERS
ACDEEFGIILMNT MAGNETIC FIELD
ACDEEFGINNORT CONFEDERATING
ACDEEFHHIKNRS HANDKERCHIEFS
ACDEEFHNORRTW THENCEFORWARD
ACDEEFIIILMRT CERTIFIED MAIL
ACDEEFILNNOST SELF-CONTAINED
ACDEEFINNOORT CONFEDERATION
ACDEEFNORRRTW CENTER FORWARD,
  CENTRE FORWARD
ACDEEGHHOOPRR CHOREOGRAPHED
ACDEEGHIKNNRT KITCHEN GARDEN
ACDEEGHIMNNNU MACHINEGUNNED
ACDEEGIIMORST TRAGICOMEDIES
ACDEEGILNNPRS SPRING-CLEANED
ACDEEGILNPRTY DEPRECATINGLY
ACDEEGIMMNNOR COMMANDEERING
ACDEEGNNOSSTT DECONGESTANTS
ACDEEGNOORSVW COVERED WAGONS
ACDEEHIIKMNNY KIDNEY MACHINE
ACDEEHIKLOTTT TICKLE TO DEATH
ACDEEHILORRTT TETRACHLORIDE
ACDEEHINPRSSS CASH DISPENSER
ACDEEHLNNOORR HOLE-AND-CORNER
ACDEEIIILMSTV MEDIEVALISTIC
ACDEEIILNNNQU QUINDECENNIAL
ACDEEIILPRTUV REDUPLICATIVE
ACDEEIILPRTVY PREDICATIVELY
ACDEEIIMNNRTY INDETERMINACY
ACDEEIIMNOPRT PREMEDICATION
ACDEEIIMOSTTV DOMESTICATIVE
ACDEEIINNORST CONTAINERISED,
  INCONSIDERATE
ACDEEIINNORTZ CONTAINERIZED
ACDEEIINOPRTT DECREPITATION

ACDEEIJKNNRST DINNER JACKETS
ACDEEIKLOOPSS KALEIDOSCOPES
ACDEEILLNNSTY CLANDESTINELY
ACDEEILMNPSST DISPLACEMENTS
ACDEEILNORSTY CONSIDERATELY
ACDEEILNPPRRU PERPENDICULAR
ACDEEILOPRRTY DEPRECATORILY
ACDEEIMMNORTV INVERTED COMMA
ACDEEIMNORSSX CROSS-EXAMINED
ACDEEIMNORSTU DOCUMENTARIES
ACDEEINNORSSS SECONDARINESS
ACDEEJKKNOSTY DONKEY JACKETS
ACDEELNOOSSSS CLOSED SEASONS
ACDEELOPRRRSY RECORD PLAYERS
ACDEEMNNOPSTU UNCOMPENSATED
ACDEFGHHIINSS CHAFING DISHES
ACDEFGIILNSSY DECLASSIFYING
ACDEFGILLRSUY DISGRACEFULLY
ACDEFHLLOTTUY THE CALL OF DUTY
ACDEFHOORSSSU HOUSES OF CARDS
ACDEFIIILNOST FICTIONALISED
ACDEFIIILNOTZ FICTIONALIZED
ACDEFIINNSSTT DISINFECTANTS
ACDEFILMNNOTU MALFUNCTIONED
ACDEGGHIINPRS GRAPHIC DESIGN
ACDEGGHINNRRU UNDERCHARGING
ACDEGGIKLNNOW ACKNOWLEDGING
ACDEGGINORSS GRADE CROSSING
ACDEGHHOOPRTU THOROUGHPACED
ACDEGHIIMNNRS MERCHANDISING
ACDEGIILLLOOY IDEOLOGICALLY
ACDEGIILLNSSS SLIDING SCALES
ACDEGIILNPRTU REDUPLICATING
ACDEGIIMNORTZ DEMOCRATIZING
ACDEGIIMNOSTT DOMESTICATING
ACDEGIIMNOSTY GEODYNAMICIST
ACDEGILLMNOOO DEMONOLOGICAL
ACDEGILLNOOOT DEONTOLOGICAL
ACDEGIMMNNORW WING
  COMMANDER
ACDEHHIILNPRSS SHIP'S CHANDLER
ACDEHHLOPRSUY HYDROCEPHALUS
ACDEHIIMRSSTT CHRISTMASTIDE
ACDEHIIOPSSTT SOPHISTICATED
ACDEHILMNOPTY ENDOLYMPHATIC
ACDEHIMMNOPRS COMMANDERSHIP
ACDEHIMMNORTY THERMODYNAMIC
ACDEHIMOPRTTY DERMATOPHYTIC
ACDEHLMOOPRSY CHLAMYDOSPORE
ACDEHMRSTTTUU CUT THE MUSTARD
ACDEHOOOPRRTT PROTOCHORDATE
ACDEIIILLNNTTW IDENTICAL TWIN
ACDEIIIMNORST DOSIMETRICIAN
ACDEIIKLRSTTW WILDCAT STRIKE

ACDEIILNNOTTU DENTICULATION
ACDEIILNOPRTU REDUPLICATION
ACDEIIMNOOSTT DOMESTICATION
ACDEIINNNOSTU DENUNCIATIONS
ACDEIINNOORST CONSIDERATION
ACDEIINOQRSTU QUADRISECTION
ACDEIINORRSTY DISCRETIONARY
ACDEIKMNNORST ONE-TRACK MINDS
ACDEIKNNNORTT DARK CONTINENT
ACDEILLMMOUWY CADMIUM YELLOW
ACDEILMNORTUY DOCUMENTARILY
ACDEILNNOPTUU PEDUNCULATION
ACDEILNNORSTY CONSTRAINEDLY
ACDEILOOPRRTU PARTI-COLOURED
ACDEILOPRSSTY PERISSODACTYL
ACDEIMMNNOOST COMMENDATIONS
ACDEIMMOOORRS AIR COMMODORES
ACDEIMMOOSTTY MASTOIDECTOMY
ACDEIMNNNOOST CONDEMNATIONS
ACDEIMNNOOTTU DOCUMENTATION
ACDEIMNORRRSS MORRISDANCERS
ACDEINNNORSTU UNCONSTRAINED
ACDEKLLNOORRR ROCK-AND-ROLLER
ACDELNOOOSTUY ACOTYLEDONOUS
ACDELOORRSTUW STRAW-COLOURED
ACDEMMNNOSTUU UNCONSUMMATED
ACDEOPRSSTTUW WASTE PRODUCTS
ACDFIIIMNOOST MODIFICATIONS
ACDFILMOORSTY FAMILY DOCTORS
ACDGHINOOOPRT ODONTOGRAPHIC
ACDGIIINRSSTV VISITING CARDS
ACDGIILNNOOST CONSOLIDATING
ACDGIINNOSTTU OUTDISTANCING
ACDGILLNOOOOT ODONTOLOGICAL
ACDGILMOSTYYZ ZYGODACTYLISM
ACDGIMNOPRSSU MASS-PRODUCING
ACDGLOOOSTUYZ ZYGODACTYLOUS
ACDHIIKKNPSUY KICK UP A SHINDY
ACDHIILMNOORT MITOCHONDRIAL
ACDHIINOPSSTU CUSTODIANSHIP
ACDHIIOPRSSTT DICTATORSHIPS
ACDHILMNOOORS CHONDRIOSOMAL
ACDHIMNOOPSTY PHOTODYNAMICS
ACDHKLORRSTUY HARD-LUCK STORY
ACDHLNOOSSSUY SUNDAY SCHOOLS
ACDHMNOOORSTU CHONDROMATOUS
ACDIIILNNOPTU INDUPLICATION
ACDIIIMNORRST DISCRIMINATOR,
  DOCTRINAIRISM
ACDIIIOOOPRST RADIOISOTOPIC
ACDIILLLNSSSY SCILLY ISLANDS
ACDIILLNNOOTY CONDITIONALLY
ACDIILNNNOOTU UNCONDITIONAL
ACDIILNNOOOST CONSOLIDATION

ACDIILNOOORST DISCOLORATION
ACDIILPQRTUUY QUADRUPLICITY
ACDIINNOOORRTT INDOCTRINATOR
ACDINOOQRSSTU CONQUISTADORS
ACDLLOOPSTUYY POLYDACTYLOUS
ACDLMNOOOSTUY CONDYLOMATOUS
ACEEEEEKNOPPS KEEP ONE'S PEACE
ACEEEEFJKRRST REEFER JACKETS
ACEEEEHLPRSST STEEPLECHASER
ACEEEEHLPSSST STEEPLECHASES
ACEEEELMNRSTT TRACE ELEMENTS
ACEEEENNPPPRY CAYENNE PEPPER
ACEEEEPPRRSTW CARPET SWEEPER
ACEEEFFGINOPR PEACE OFFERING
ACEEEFGGNNOOS EGG ON ONE'S FACE
ACEEEFHHITTVY HAVE ITCHY FEET
ACEEEFMORRRTT REFRACTOMETER
ACEEEGILLNRTY ENERGETICALLY
ACEEEGINPRSSS PRESS AGENCIES
ACEEEGLMNORTT ELECTROMAGNET
ACEEEGLNNRRUY NUCLEAR ENERGY
ACEEEGLNRSSSS GRACELESSNESS
ACEEEGMNNORTU ENCOURAGEMENT
ACEEEHHILLLSS ACHILLES' HEELS
ACEEEHHPPRSTY SPEECH THERAPY
ACEEEHIKMNSTY SMACK IN THE EYE
ACEEEHINRSTVY SEVEN-YEAR ITCH
ACEEEHLLNNOPT TELENCEPHALON
ACEEEHLMNNOPS MESENCEPHALON
ACEEEHLMNNOPT METENCEPHALON
ACEEEHNNRSSST ENCHANTRESSES
ACEEEIINNRSTV INTENSIVE CARE
ACEEEIINSSTTV NECESSITATIVE
ACEEEIKNOPTTX TAKE EXCEPTION
ACEEEILLNPSST LICENSE PLATES
ACEEEILMNNRTT INTERLACEMENT
ACEEEILNRSSVY NECESSARY EVIL
ACEEEIMNNRRSS MERCENARINESS
ACEEEIMNORSVY YEOMAN SERVICE
ACEEEINNOPRVX AIX-EN-PROVENCE
ACEEEINOSSTVV EVOCATIVENESS
ACEEELLNORTTV ELECTROVALENT
ACEEELLOPRRTT ELECTROPLATER
ACEEFFHINNPRS AFFENPINSCHER
ACEEFFILLNTUY INEFFECTUALLY
ACEEFGIIMNRRT FERRIMAGNETIC
ACEEFGIMNORRT FERROMAGNETIC
ACEEFHHIRSTTT FEATHERSTITCH
ACEEFHIMNNRST FRANCHISEMENT
ACEEFHMNOSTUV VOUCHSAFEMENT
ACEEFHOPPRSST PARTS OF SPEECH
ACEEFINOSSSTU FACETIOUSNESS
ACEEFMNORSTUU FRUMENTACEOUS
ACEEFMORRRTTY REFRACTOMETRY

ACEEGGINNOORT ORGANOGENETIC
ACEEGHHIOPRRT HETEROGRAPHIC
ACEEGHHLNORST CLOTHES HANGER
ACEEGHHMNRRRU HUNGER MARCHER
ACEEGHHMNRRSU HUNGER MARCHES
ACEEGHHOOPRRR CHOREOGRAPHER
ACEEGHIIMNNSW SEWING MACHINE
ACEEGHILNOPRS SELENOGRAPHIC
ACEEGHILNORSU CLEARINGHOUSE
ACEEGHILNOSSU CHAISE LONGUES
ACEEGHILOPRRX LEXICOGRAPHER
ACEEGHIOPRRST STEREOGRAPHIC
ACEEGHIRRSSST CASH REGISTERS
ACEEGHLOPRRTY ELECTROGRAPHY
ACEEGHMNNORSY MONEYCHANGERS
ACEEGHPRRRSSU SUPERCHARGERS
ACEEGIILSTTUV GESTICULATIVE
ACEEGIIMNNOST MISCEGENATION
ACEEGIINNNRST INTRANSIGENCE
ACEEGIINNSSTT NECESSITATING
ACEEGIINOPRRR CARRIER PIGEON
ACEEGILLLOOPS SPELEOLOGICAL
ACEEGILLMORTY GEOMETRICALLY
ACEEGILMNNOQU MAGNILOQUENCE
ACEEGILMNOPST MAGNETIC POLES
ACEEGILNPSSTT PLACE SETTINGS
ACEEGIMMNORTT MAGNETOMETRIC
ACEEGINNNSSSU UNCEASINGNESS
ACEEGINOPRTTX EXPECTORATING
ACEEGLMNOORST CONGLOMERATES
ACEEHHILLORTT HETEROTHALLIC
ACEEHHIRVWWYY EVERY WHICH WAY
ACEEHHLNORSSU CHARNEL HOUSES
ACEEHIILMMNPS SIMPLE MACHINE
ACEEHIIORSSST CASE HISTORIES
ACEEHIIQRRSSU SQUIREARCHIES
ACEEHIKNRSSST HEARTSICKNESS
ACEEHILLORTTY THEORETICALLY
ACEEHILNPRSSS SPHERICALNESS
ACEEHILOPRSTT HETEROPLASTIC
ACEEHIMNORSSS MARCHIONESSES
ACEEHIMNSSSTT CHASTISEMENTS
ACEEHIMRRSSTT CHRISTMAS TREE
ACEEHINOPRRST TERPSICHOREAN
ACEEHIPRRSSTY SECRETARYSHIP
ACEEHLLMOOORT ALCOHOLOMETER
ACEEHLLOORSSV SCHOOL-LEAVERS
ACEEHLLOPPSTU LEPTOCEPHALUS
ACEEHLMMNOOTW THE COMMON
  WEAL
ACEEHLMNORRTU THERMONUCLEAR
ACEEHLMNSSSST MATCHLESSNESS
ACEEHLORRSTUY TREACHEROUSLY
ACEEHLPPRSTUY SUPPLY TEACHER

ACEEHLPSSSTTU SPACE SHUTTLES
ACEEHMNOPPRRT RAPPROCHEMENT
ACEEIIILPRSTU PECULIARITIES
ACEEIIIMNRRTV RECRIMINATIVE
ACEEIIIPPRTTV PRECIPITATIVE
ACEEIILLLPPTY EPILEPTICALLY
ACEEIILMMNORS CEREMONIALISM
ACEEIILMNOPRS SEMIPORCELAIN
ACEEIILMNORST CEREMONIALIST
ACEEIILMNPRSS EMPIRICALNESS
ACEEIILNNNRTT TRICENTENNIAL
ACEEIILNRTTVY INTERACTIVELY
ACEEIILPPRTTY PRECIPITATELY
ACEEIIMMORSTV COMMISERATIVE
ACEEIIMNNOSST AMNIOCENTESIS
ACEEIIMNORRST MERCERISATION
ACEEIIMNORRTZ MERCERIZATION
ACEEIINNOSSTT NECESSITATION
ACEEIINORSSVV VARICOSE VEINS
ACEEIIRSSTTUV RESUSCITATIVE
ACEEIKNOSSSTT SEASON TICKETS
ACEEILLLNRRTU INTERCELLULAR
ACEEILLLNSTTU INTELLECTUALS
ACEEILLMNNRTY INCREMENTALLY
ACEEILLMNOSSU MISCELLANEOUS
ACEEILLMOQRUU EQUIMOLECULAR
ACEEILLNNNSSU UNCLEANLINESS
ACEEILLNOPTXY EXCEPTIONALLY
ACEEILLPSTUVY SPECULATIVELY
ACEEILLRRSSTY RECRYSTALLISE
ACEEILLRRSTYZ RECRYSTALLIZE
ACEEILMNOPTTV CONTEMPLATIVE
ACEEILMNRRSSU MERCURIALNESS
ACEEILMOPRSTU PRECIOUS METAL
ACEEILNNOPRTV CONVERTIPLANE
ACEEILNNOPTUX UNEXCEPTIONAL
ACEEILNNOQSTU CONSEQUENTIAL
ACEEILNNRRTUW NUCLEAR WINTER
ACEEILNNRSSUY UNNECESSARILY
ACEEILNORSTTU INTEROSCULATE
ACEEILNOSTTUX CONTEXTUALISE
ACEEILNOTTUXZ CONTEXTUALIZE
ACEEILNRTTUUV ENCULTURATIVE
ACEEILOOPRTVY COOPERATIVELY
ACEEILOPPRSSW SPECIAL POWERS
ACEEILOPRSTTY STEREOTYPICAL
ACEEILORRTTVY RETROACTIVELY
ACEEILORTTUVV OVERCULTIVATE
ACEEIMMMOORTV COMMEMORATIVE
ACEEIMNORRSSX CROSS-EXAMINER
ACEEIMNPRTTUY PNEUMATIC TYRE
ACEEINNNRSSTU UNCERTAINNESS
ACEEINNOORSVZ CONVERSAZIONE
ACEEINNOSSSTU TENACIOUSNESS

ACEEINOOPRSTU PROTEINACEOUS
ACEEINOOPRTTX EXPECTORATION
ACEEINOORRSTV CONSERVATOIRE,
    OVERREACTIONS
ACEEINOPRSSTT INSPECTORATES
ACEEINORSSSUV VERACIOUSNESS
ACEEINORSSTVV CONSERVATIVES
ACEEIOPRRSTTV PRIVATE SECTOR
ACEELLNOOPRSU PORCELLANEOUS
ACEELLNSSSSSS CLASSLESSNESS
ACEELLOORRRST ROLLER COASTER
ACEELMMNOPRTY COMPLEMENTARY
ACEELMNNORSTU NOMENCLATURES
ACEEMMNNOPSST ENCOMPASSMENT
ACEEMNNNNOSTU ANNOUNCEMENTS
ACEEMNNORRSST REMONSTRANCES
ACEEOOPRRSTTT PROTECTORATES
ACEFFFFHIOSST CHIEFS OF STAFF
ACEFFFFIORSST STAFF OFFICERS
ACEFGHIINNNRS ENFRANCHISING
ACEFGIIIINSTV SIGNIFICATIVE
ACEFGIILMNNTY MAGNIFICENTLY
ACEFGIILNNRTU LUNATIC FRINGE
ACEFGIKKOOTTU GET A KICK OUT OF
ACEFGILNRSSUY FLYING SAUCERS
ACEFHHIIINPST CHIEFTAINSHIP
ACEFHIIMNRSTU FRUIT MACHINES
ACEFHLLOPRRUY REPROACHFULLY
ACEFIIIJLLNOT JELLIFICATION
ACEFIIIILNOSTT FELICITATIONS
ACEFIIINNORTU REUNIFICATION
ACEFIIINORSTV VERSIFICATION
ACEFIIINOSTTT TESTIFICATION
ACEFIILLPRSUY SUPERFICIALLY
ACEFIILNORSTY FORENSICALITY
ACEFIINNORSTU FUNCTIONARIES
ACEFIINOORSTV VOCIFERATIONS
ACEFILNNOOSSS CONFESSIONALS
ACEFILNOOPRSS FALSE SCORPION
ACEFINNOORSSY CONFESSIONARY
ACEFINNORRTTY CONFRATERNITY
ACEFINORSSSTU FRACTIOUSNESS
ACEFJKKLNOORT NORFOLK JACKET
ACEFLLMOOPRSW CAMP FOLLOWERS
ACEFLNOORSSST COLORFASTNESS
ACEFOOOORRTTWW WATER CROWFOOT
ACEGGGHIINNNR CHANGE RINGING
ACEGGHIINNNRT INTERCHANGING
ACEGGHINPRRSU SUPERCHARGING
ACEGGHIOOOPRZ ZOOGEOGRAPHIC
ACEGGIILNSTTU GESTICULATING
ACEGGILLOOPTY EGYPTOLOGICAL
ACEGGILNNORUY ENCOURAGINGLY
ACEGGILNOOSTY GYNAECOLOGIST

ACEGGINNOORST CONGREGATIONS
ACEGGLLRSSSTU CLASS STRUGGLE
ACEGHHIMOPRRT THERMOGRAPHIC
ACEGHHNOOPRRR CHRONOGRAPHER
ACEGHIIMNNRTU TURING MACHINE
ACEGHIIMOPRSS SEISMOGRAPHIC
ACEGHILLLOOTY ETHOLOGICALLY,
  THEOLOGICALLY
ACEGHILLNOOPR PHRENOLOGICAL
ACEGHILLOOPPS PSEPHOLOGICAL
ACEGHILNOPRRY REPROACHINGLY
ACEGHILNORSSU SOUL-SEARCHING
ACEGHILOOSSTT ESCHATOLOGIST
ACEGHIMNNORTT MAGNETIC NORTH
ACEGHINORRSTT ORCHESTRATING
ACEGHNOOPPRSY PHARYNGOSCOPE
ACEGHOPPRRRTY CRYPTOGRAPHER
ACEGHOPPRRSTY SPECTROGRAPHY
ACEGIIILNOOPT GEOPOLITICIAN
ACEGIIIMNNRRT RECRIMINATING
ACEGIIINORTTY IATROGENICITY
ACEGIIINPPRTT PRECIPITATING
ACEGIIKNNRSVV CARVING KNIVES
ACEGIILLLOOTY ETIOLOGICALLY
ACEGIILLNNSSW LICENSING LAWS
ACEGIILLOSTTY EGOTISTICALLY
ACEGIILNNOORT RECOGNITIONAL
ACEGIILNOSTTU GESTICULATION
ACEGIIMMNORST COMMISERATING
ACEGIINOORSST COSIGNATORIES
ACEGIINOPRSTY SAPROGENICITY
ACEGIINPRRSTT STARTING PRICE
ACEGIINRSSTTU RESUSCITATING
ACEGIKLNOOPPS COOKING APPLES
ACEGILLMNOOOT ENTOMOLOGICAL
ACEGILLMNOORU NUMEROLOGICAL
ACEGILLMNOORY ERGONOMICALLY
ACEGILLMNOOYZ ENZYMOLOGICAL
ACEGILLNNOOTY ONTOGENICALLY
ACEGILLOOPRTY GEOTROPICALLY
ACEGILLSTYYYZ SYZYGETICALLY
ACEGILMNNOPTT CONTEMPLATING
ACEGILMNOPSTY SALPINGECTOMY
ACEGILMOOSSTU CLEISTOGAMOUS
ACEGILNNNOSUY SANGUINOLENCY
ACEGILNNOORSS CONGRESSIONAL
ACEGILNORRSUU NEUROSURGICAL
ACEGILOOPSSST ESCAPOLOGISTS
ACEGIMMMNOORT COMMEMORATING
ACEGIMNOPRSTU PNEUMOGASTRIC
ACEGINOOPRSTT PROGNOSTICATE
ACEGLNOOOPSUY POLYGONACEOUS
ACEGMNNOORSSW CONGRESSWOMAN
ACEHHIINOPRSX HIERACOSPHINX

ACEHHIINOPRSZ SCHIZOPHRENIA
ACEHHILMOPRTX XEROPHTHALMIC
ACEHHLLLMOOTY METHYL ALCOHOL
ACEHHMMNRSTUY CHRYSANTHEMUM
ACEHHMOOOPRRT CHROMATOPHORE
ACEHHOPPRSTYY PSYCHOTHERAPY
ACEHIIINRRSST CHRISTIANISER
ACEHIIINRRSTZ CHRISTIANIZER
ACEHIILLLMOTY HOMILETICALLY
ACEHIILLPPTYY EPIPHYTICALLY
ACEHIILLRSTUY HEURISTICALLY
ACEHIILMNSSSW WHIMSICALNESS
ACEHIILOOPPRT APHELIOTROPIC
ACEHIIMMRSSTT CHRISTMASTIME
ACEHIIOPSSSTT SOPHISTICATES
ACEHIJKLPRSSY PHYSICAL JERKS
ACEHILLMMOPRY MORPHEMICALLY
ACEHILLNORSSS SCHOLARLINESS
ACEHILLNSTTYY SYNTHETICALLY
ACEHILLOOPRTY ORTHOEPICALLY
ACEHILLOPPRTY PROPHETICALLY
ACEHILLOPRTTY PROTHETICALLY
ACEHILMOPRSTT THERMOPLASTIC
ACEHILOOPRSTV PRIVATE SCHOOL
ACEHILPPRSSUY SUPERPHYSICAL
ACEHIMOORSTTT TRACHEOTOMIST
ACEHIMORSSTTT THERMOSTATICS
ACEHINOORRSTT ORCHESTRATION
ACEHIOPRRSSTT ORCHESTRA PITS,
  STRATOSPHERIC
ACEHIORSSTTTU TETRASTICHOUS
ACEHLMOORSSST SCHOOLMASTERS
ACEHMMOPSTTYY SYMPATHECTOMY
ACEHNNOOPRRSS ANCHORPERSONS
ACEHNNOORRTTY ON THE CONTRARY
ACEHNOORRTTTY TO THE CONTRARY
ACEIIIILMPRST IMPERIALISTIC
ACEIIILLNNOPT PENICILLATION
ACEIIILNORSTT ORIENTALISTIC
ACEIIILNOSTVV VIVISECTIONAL
ACEIIILQSTUVY ACQUISITIVELY
ACEIIIMNNORRT RECRIMINATION
ACEIIINOPPRTT PRECIPITATION
ACEIIINRTTTVY INTERACTIVITY
ACEIIKLMOSTTU STICK OUT A MILE
ACEIILLNORRTY ACRYLONITRILE
ACEIILLNRRTTU INTRATELLURIC
ACEIILLNRSTXY EXTRINSICALLY
ACEIILLOOPTYZ EPIZOOTICALLY
ACEIILMNOPSST NEOPLASTICISM
ACEIILMNORTUV VERMICULATION
ACEIILMNOSSSU MALICIOUSNESS
ACEIILNOOPSTT POLICE STATION
ACEIILNOPRRTT INTERTROPICAL

ACEIIILNOPRSST PERSONALISTIC
ACEIIILNORSTTU RETICULATIONS
ACEIIILNPQTTUU QUINTUPLICATE
ACEIIILNRSSTTT CLARINETTISTS
ACEIIILNRSSTVV CIVIL SERVANTS
ACEIIMMNOORST COMMISERATION
ACEIIMNNOOOST ECONOMISATION
ACEIIMNNOOOTZ ECONOMIZATION
ACEIIMNORRRTY RECRIMINATORY
ACEIINNNORSTU RENUNCIATIONS
ACEIINNOOPRST PRECONISATION
ACEIINNOOPRTZ PRECONIZATION
ACEIINOOPRRTV INCORPORATIVE
ACEIINOOQSTUV EQUIVOCATIONS
ACEIINOPRRSTT PRACTITIONERS
ACEIINORSSSUV VICARIOUSNESS
ACEIINORSSTTU RESUSCITATION
ACEIINOSSSUVV VIVACIOUSNESS
ACEIIORRTTTVY RETROACTIVITY
ACEIKLOORRSSW SOCIAL WORKERS
ACEILLLLMRTUU MULTICELLULAR
ACEILLLLPSTYY SYLLEPTICALLY
ACEILLLOPPRTY PROLEPTICALLY
ACEILLMMRSTYY SYMMETRICALLY
ACEILLNNNOSSY NONSENSICALLY
ACEILLNNOOSTT CONSTELLATION
ACEILLNOOPRRY INCORPOREALLY
ACEILLNOQUUVY UNEQUIVOCALLY
ACEILLOPSTUUY EUCALYPTUS OIL
ACEILMMNOPRTY COMPLIMENTARY
ACEILMMNNOOPTT CONTEMPLATION
ACEILMNNORRTU INTERCOLUMNAR
ACEILMNNSSSUU UNMUSICALNESS
ACEILMNOOPRSS COMPRESSIONAL
ACEILMNOPRVYY LIVERY COMPANY
ACEILNNORTTUU ENCULTURATION
ACEILNOORRSTV CONTROVERSIAL
ACEILOOPRTVVY PROVOCATIVELY
ACEIMMMNOOORT COMMEMORATION
ACEIMNNORRTTU MACRONUTRIENT
ACEINNNOORSTT CONSTERNATION
ACEINNNOORTTV CONTRAVENTION
ACEINNOORSSTV CONVERSATIONS
ACEINOORSSSTU ATROCIOUSNESS
ACEINOPRRSSST CONSPIRATRESS
ACEIOOPRRRRST TROOP CARRIERS
ACELLMMNOOORU MONOMOLECULAR
ACELLNOORSTTY CONSTELLATORY
ACELMNOPRRSUU SUPERCOLUMNAR
ACELMNORRSUUU NEUROMUSCULAR
ACELNOOPRSSTU PROCONSULATES
ACELOOPRSSSVY SOLVAY PROCESS
ACEMOOPRSTTTY PROSTATECTOMY
ACENNOOOOPRRT NONCOOPERATOR

ACENNOORRSSSU RANCOROUSNESS
ACFFGHIILRSTT TRAFFIC LIGHTS
ACFFGILNOSTUY SUFFOCATINGLY
ACFFIIINOORTT FORTIFICATION
ACFFIINNOOPTT IN POINT OF FACT
ACFGIIIILNNOT LIGNIFICATION
ACFGIIIINNNST INSIGNIFICANT
ACFGIIIINNOST SIGNIFICATION
ACFGIIILNNSTY SIGNIFICANTLY
ACFGIIILNOORT GLORIFICATION
ACFGIIINNOPTT PONTIFICATING
ACFGIINNOORTU CONFIGURATION
ACFHIIINOORRT HORRIFICATION
ACFHIILLNOORY HONORIFICALLY
ACFIIIILNOSTV VILIFICATIONS
ACFIIIINNORTT NITRIFICATION
ACFIIIINORTTV VITRIFICATION
ACFIIIJLLNOOT JOLLIFICATION
ACFIIIJNOSTTU JUSTIFICATION
ACFIIILLMNOOT MOLLIFICATION
ACFIIILLNNOTU NULLIFICATION
ACFIIIMMMNOTU MUMMIFICATION
ACFIIIMNOORTT MORTIFICATION
ACFIIIMNOSTTY MYSTIFICATION
ACFIIINNOOSTT NOTIFICATIONS
ACFIIJORSTTUY JUSTIFICATORY
ACFIIILLLORSTY FLORISTICALLY
ACFIIILLOOPRSY SOPORIFICALLY
ACFIILMNNOSTU FUNCTIONALISM
ACFIILNNOSTTU FUNCTIONALIST
ACFIIMNNOOSTT CONFIRMATIONS
ACFILLLORRTUU FLORICULTURAL
ACFIMNNOOORST CONFORMATIONS
ACFINNNOOORTT CONFRONTATION
ACGGHHILOPPRY GLYPHOGRAPHIC
ACGGHHINNORST SHORT-CHANGING
ACGGHIKLNOSTU LAUGHINGSTOCK
ACGGHILOPPRTY GLYPTOGRAPHIC
ACGGHIMNNOORS CHANGING ROOMS
ACGGHHIIOPPRSY PHYSIOGRAPHIC
ACGGHHILMOOOPR HOMOLOGRAPHIC
ACGGHHIMNOOSTT SHOOTING MATCH
ACGGHIILLOOPSY PHYSIOLOGICAL
ACGGHILLLMOOOY HOMOLOGICALLY
ACGGHILLMOOOPR MORPHOLOGICAL
ACGGHILLOOPRSY OSCILLOGRAPHY
ACGGHIMNNOOOPT PATHOGNOMONIC
ACGGHNOOPPRSYY PHARYNGOSCOPY
ACGIIIIMNNNRT INCRIMINATING
ACGIIILLNNSTT SCINTILLATING
ACGIIIMNNORTZ ROMANTICIZING
ACGIIKKLNSSTW WALKING STICKS
ACGIILLLOSSTY SYLLOGISTICAL
ACGIILLMNNOPY COMPLAININGLY

ACGIILLMOOSTT CLIMATOLOGIST
ACGIIILLNRSTYZ CRYSTALLIZING
ACGIILMNNNOPU UNCOMPLAINING
ACGIILRRSTTUU AGRICULTURIST
ACGIIMMNOORRS MICROORGANISM
ACGIINNNOSTUY CONSANGUINITY
ACGIINNNOOPRRT INCORPORATING
ACGILLLMNOOOY NOMOLOGICALLY
ACGILLLNOOOSY NOSOLOGICALLY
ACGILLLNOOOTY ONTOLOGICALLY
ACGILLLOOOPTY TOPOLOGICALLY
ACGILLNOOOSTV VOLCANOLOGIST
ACGINNNOOOSTU NONCONTAGIOUS
ACGIOOPRSSSTT GASTROSCOPIST
ACHHIIINNORST ORNITHISCHIAN
ACHHIILLLOOPPS PHILOSOPHICAL
ACHHIILNOPPRT PHILANTHROPIC
ACHHIIMNOPPSS CHAMPIONSHIPS
ACHHIIMOPRSTU AMPHITRICHOUS
ACHHIINOOSTTW IN CAHOOTS WITH
ACHHILMMOORSS SCHOOLMARMISH
ACHHIMNOORSTX XANTHOCHROISM
ACHHIMNOOSTTU AUTOCHTHONISM
ACHHLLNOOOSTU ALLOCHTHONOUS
ACHHNOOOSTTUU AUTOCHTHONOUS
ACHIIIJPRSSTU JUSTICIARSHIP
ACHIIIMNOSTTY MYTHICISATION
ACHIIIMNOTTYZ MYTHICIZATION
ACHIILLLOPSSTY SOPHISTICALLY
ACHIIMMORRSTT TRICHROMATISM
ACHIIMNNOOPPS COMPANIONSHIP
ACHIIOOPRSSTT SOPHISTICATOR
ACHIIPRSSSTTY PSYCHIATRISTS
ACHILLMNOPSYY SYMPHONICALLY
ACHILLMPSSYYY SYMPHYSICALLY
ACHILLORRTTUU HORTICULTURAL
ACHILMOOPRRSY PRIMARY SCHOOL
ACHILMOORSSTY CHROMATOLYSIS
ACHILMOPSTTYY SYMPATHOLYTIC
ACIIIILNOSSTV CIVILISATIONS
ACIIIILNOSTVZ CIVILIZATIONS
ACIIIIMNNNORT INCRIMINATION
ACIIIIMNOSTTV VICTIMISATION
ACIIIIMNOTTVZ VICTIMIZATION
ACIIILLLORTVY VITRIOLICALLY
ACIIILLNNOSTT SCINTILLATION
ACIIILLNNRSTY INTRINSICALLY
ACIIILMNNORTU ANTICLINORIUM
ACIIILMNOPRSV PROVINCIALISM
ACIIILNNOPRST INSCRIPTIONAL
ACIIILNOOSSTT SOLICITATIONS
ACIIILNOPRTVY PROVINCIALITY
ACIIIMNNORRTY INCRIMINATORY
ACIIILLLMOOQSU COLLOQUIALISM

ACIILLLLRSTUUV SILVICULTURAL
ACIILLLSSTTYY STYLISTICALLY
ACIILLNOORTUY ILLOCUTIONARY
ACIILLNRSTTYY CRYSTALLINITY
ACIILMNOOOPST COMPOSITIONAL
ACIILMNOORSUY ACRIMONIOUSLY
ACIILMNOORTTY MICROTONALITY
ACIILMOORSTTT STROMATOLITIC
ACIILMOPRSTUV VICTORIA PLUMS
ACIILNNORSTTU INSTRUCTIONAL
ACIILNOPPSSTU SUPPLICATIONS
ACIILNORSTTUV VOLUNTARISTIC
ACIILQRSTTUUU AQUICULTURIST
ACIIMMNNOOSTU COMMUNISATION
ACIIMMNNOOTUZ COMMUNIZATION
ACIIMMOOPRSTT COMPATRIOTISM
ACIIMNNOOSSTU SANCTIMONIOUS
ACIINNNOOPRTU PRONUNCIATION
ACIINNNOOSTTU CONTINUATIONS
ACIINNOOOPRRT INCORPORATION
ACIINNOPRRSTT TRANSCRIPTION
ACIINNORSSTTU INCRUSTATIONS
ACILMMOOPSSSY MYCOPLASMOSIS
ACILMNOOOPSST COSMOPOLITANS
ACILMOOPRRRSY PRIMARY COLORS
ACILMOOPRRRUY PRIMARY COLOUR
ACILMRRSSTTUU STRUCTURALISM
ACILNNOOSSTTU CONSULTATIONS
ACILRRSSTTTUU STRUCTURALIST
ACIMMNNOOSSTU CONSUMMATIONS
ACIMNOOPPSSST COMPASS POINTS
ACINNNOPRSTTU CONTRAPUNTIST
ACINOOPRRSSTT STRIP CARTOONS
ACKKMNNOOPSST POSTMAN'S KNOCK
ACLMORSSTTUUU CUMULOSTRATUS,
    STRATOCUMULUS
ADDDEEEEFLRSSS SELF-ADDRESSED
ADDDEEEHLNNRUY UNDERHANDEDLY
ADDDEGGLLNOSY DADDY LONGLEGS
ADDEEEEHNRRTT TENDERHEARTED
ADDEEEGHINPSS PIGHEADEDNESS
ADDEEEGHNORSY DEHYDROGENASE
ADDEEEGHNORTY DEHYDROGENATE
ADDEEEGMNRRRY GERRYMANDERED
ADDEEEHHNOSST HOT-HEADEDNESS
ADDEEEHLLNOSW SWOLLEN HEADED
ADDEEEILMNRST MIDDLE EASTERN
ADDEEEINOPPST ENDOPEPTIDASE
ADDEEELRRSTTY RED-LETTER DAYS
ADDEEENOPPRRT PREPONDERATED
ADDEEFFHNNOSS OFFHANDEDNESS
ADDEEFFIORSST DISAFFORESTED
ADDEEFLNNPRUY PENNY-DREADFUL
ADDEEGHHILLTY LIGHT-HEADEDLY

ADDEEGHLNORWY WRONGHEADEDLY
ADDEEGIINRSTT DISINTEGRATED
ADDEEGNNRSSUU UNGUARDEDNESS
ADDEEHIKLNRTY KIND-HEARTEDLY
ADDEEHLNORTWY DOWNHEARTEDLY
ADDEEIIILMRST DEMILITARISED
ADDEEIIILMRTZ DEMILITARIZED
ADDEEIINORSTT DISORIENTATED
ADDEEIMNNSSSY MANY-SIDEDNESS
ADDEEINNSSSUV UNADVISEDNESS
ADDEFGIILLNNS LANDING FIELDS
ADDEGHILNOOTU GO INTO A HUDDLE
ADDEGINNNRSTU UNDERSTANDING
ADDEGINNORRST STANDING ORDER
ADDEGLNOORTUY GOOD-NATUREDLY
ADDEEHHLORRSSU HARD SHOULDERS
ADDEHILNORTUY THE DAILY ROUND
ADDEIIIILNSUV INDIVIDUALISE
ADDEIIIILNUVZ INDIVIDUALIZE
ADDEIIINOOSTX DEOXIDISATION
ADDEIIINOOTXZ DEOXIDIZATION
ADDEIILNNOTTY AN OLD IDENTITY
ADDEIINOOORST DEODORISATION
ADDEIINOOORTZ DEODORIZATION
ADDEIINOPRSTU SUPERADDITION
ADDEIKMNOOSST IT MAKES NO ODDS
ADDEILMNOPRSS PROMISED LANDS
ADDEIMNNRSSTU MISUNDERSTAND
ADDEIMNOOPRSU MODUS OPERANDI
ADDGHIMNOORSU ROUGH DIAMONDS
ADDGIILLLLNYY DILLYDALLYING
ADDGILLNOOPPS PADDLING POOLS
ADDIIIILMNSUV INDIVIDUALISM
ADDIIIILNSTUV INDIVIDUALIST
ADDIIIILNTUVY INDIVIDUALITY
ADDIIIINNOTUV INDIVIDUATION
ADEEEEEHLLRRW WHEELER-DEALER
ADEEEEFHINRTV FEATHER-VEINED
ADEEEEGHHNOTV HAVE THE EDGE ON
ADEEEEGHKLPTT TAKE THE PLEDGE
ADEEEEHHLORSV HEAD OVER HEELS
ADEEEEHNRTTVY THREE-DAY EVENT
ADEEEFFGILNST SELF-DEFEATING
ADEEEFFIINRTT DIFFERENTIATE
ADEEEFILLNRTY DEFERENTIALLY
ADEEEGGGINRST DESEGREGATING
ADEEEGGIMNNST DISENGAGEMENT
ADEEEGGINORST DESEGREGATION
ADEEEGHLMMRSS SLEDGEHAMMERS
ADEEEGIMNRSST DISAGREEMENTS
ADEEEGLLNORTU OUTGENERALLED
ADEEEGOPRRTUY DAGUERREOTYPE
ADEEEHIMNRSTT HEREDITAMENTS
ADEEEHLNOPRTY OPENHEARTEDLY

ADEEEIIMNNRTT INDETERMINATE
ADEEEIIMNRTTV DETERMINATIVE
ADEEEIIMPRTTV PREMEDITATIVE
ADEEEIINPRSST PEDESTRIANISE
ADEEEIINPRSTZ PEDESTRIANIZE
ADEEEIIORRTTV DETERIORATIVE
ADEEEILNNNRUV INLAND REVENUE
ADEEEILNOPRSS DEPERSONALISE
ADEEEILNOPRSZ DEPERSONALIZE
ADEEEILOPRTTY RADIOTELETYPE
ADEEEILORSSTW LOWER EAST SIDE
ADEEEIMNRSTTU UNDERESTIMATE
ADEEEIMNRSTTV ADVERTISEMENT
ADEEEIMORSTTV OVERESTIMATED
ADEEEINNRSSST SEDENTARINESS
ADEEEINOPQRTU EQUIPONDERATE
ADEEELLMNOPTV DEVELOPMENTAL
ADEEELLMORRST STEAMROLLERED
ADEEEENRSSSTUV ADVENTURESSES
ADEEEOPPRRSSV EAVESDROPPERS
ADEEFFIILNRST DIFFERENTIALS
ADEEFFIILSSST SELF-SATISFIED
ADEEFGLNRRSSU REGARDFULNESS
ADEEFIILLLQUW WELL-QUALIFIED
ADEEFILLNOORV OIL OF LAVENDER
ADEEFILNOPPST SELF-APPOINTED
ADEEFINOORSTT DEFORESTATION
ADEEGGGINSSZZ ZIGZAGGEDNESS
ADEEGGHIRSSTT STRAIGHTEDGES
ADEEGGIIMNNTZ DEMAGNETIZING
ADEEGGLNNPRSU GELANDESPRUNG
ADEEGHHNORVYY HEAVY HYDROGEN
ADEEGHILNRSTY NEARSIGHTEDLY
ADEEGHLMNORST GOLDEN HAMSTER
ADEEGHOPRRSSW HEDGE SPARROWS
ADEEGIINNNRSS INGRAINEDNESS
ADEEGIINNRRTT INTERGRADIENT
ADEEGIINORRTT DETERIORATING
ADEEGIKNNRRST KINDERGARTENS
ADEEGILNNOOPS OLD AGE PENSION
ADEEGIMORSTTU DEUTEROGAMIST
ADEEGINNOOTXY DEOXYGENATION
ADEEGINOPPRSV EAVESDROPPING
ADEEGJLMNTUUV VALUE JUDGMENT
ADEEGLNNORSTU DENTAL SURGEON
ADEEGMNNRRSTU UNDERGARMENTS
ADEEGOPRRTUYY DAGUERREOTYPY
ADEEHHIKNRRSS HEADSHRINKERS
ADEEHHILNOOTT TOAD-IN-THE-HOLE
ADEEHHIMOPRRT HERMAPHRODITE
ADEEHHLMNOOSU HOUSEHOLD NAME
ADEEHIILMNNPY DIPHENYLAMINE
ADEEHIIMNORTT TRIMETHADIONE
ADEEHILMNORST SIDEREAL MONTH

ADEEHIMMOPRTX   MIXED METAPHOR
ADEEHIMNSSTUU   HUMANE STUDIES
ADEEHMMOOPRST   METAMORPHOSED
ADEEHMNOORRSY   DYSMENORRHOEA
ADEEHNOOPRRTZ   TRAPEZOHEDRON
ADEEHORSSTUVY   SHROVE TUESDAY
ADEEIIILORRST   EDITORIALISER
ADEEIIILORRTZ   EDITORIALIZER
ADEEIIIMMNPRR   PRIME MERIDIAN
ADEEIIIMNSSTV   DISSEMINATIVE
ADEEIIINPRSST   STIPENDIARIES
ADEEIIILMNNSTT   DISENTAILMENT
ADEEIIILMNPSST   DISSEPIMENTAL
ADEEIIILMNRSTY   SEDIMENTARILY
ADEEIIILNORTTT   TOILET-TRAINED
ADEEIIMNNORTT   DETERMINATION
ADEEIIMNNOSTT   SEDIMENTATION
ADEEIIMNOPRTT   PREMEDITATION
ADEEIIMNORRTT   INTERMEDIATOR
ADEEIIINNORSTT   TENDERISATION
ADEEIIINNORTTZ   TENDERIZATION
ADEEIIINOORRTT   DETERIORATION
ADEEIIINOPRTXY   EXPEDITIONARY
ADEEIILLMNRTTY   DETRIMENTALLY
ADEEIILLNNRSST   LANTERNSLIDES
ADEEIILLNOPPTW   WELL-APPOINTED
ADEEIILLNORRVY   ORDINARY LEVEL
ADEEIILLOSSTVW   OLD WIVES' TALES
ADEEIILLTTTTTT   TITTLE-TATTLED
ADEEIILMMNNSTT   DISMANTLEMENT
ADEEIILMNOORTZ   METRONIDAZOLE
ADEEIILNNRTTVY   INADVERTENTLY
ADEEIMMNORSSU   MISDEMEANOURS
ADEEIMNORSTTV   DEMONSTRATIVE
ADEEIMNPRRTTT   PRINTED MATTER
ADEEIMNRSSTUV   MISADVENTURES
ADEEINNOPQRTU   EQUIPONDERANT
ADEEINNOSSTTW   AT ONE'S WITS' END
ADEEINOPRRSST   PREDATORINESS
ADEEINOPRRSTU   SUPERORDINATE
ADEEJMMORRTTU   DRUM MAJORETTE
ADEEJMNRSSTTU   READJUSTMENTS
ADEELOOPPRTUV   OVERPOPULATED
ADEEMNOORTUUV   OUTMANOEUVRED
ADEEMNRSTTTUU   MATURE STUDENT
ADEFFHILLNOSU   FULL-FASHIONED
ADEFGHHILNOST   SLEIGHT OF HAND
ADEFGHINOORSW   FORESHADOWING
ADEFGIILLNPSY   PLAYING FIELDS
ADEFGIINNOORR   FOREORDAINING
ADEFGILLNOPST   SOFT-PEDALLING
ADEFGNNOOOORT   GOOD AFTERNOON
ADEFHILNOORSS   FOOLHARDINESS
ADEFIIILNPRSSU   FREUDIAN SLIPS

ADEFILLSSTTUY   DISTASTEFULLY
ADEFLLOOPSTYY   SPLAYFOOTEDLY
ADEGGHIILLNST   LEADING LIGHTS
ADEGGIILNNNST   DISENTANGLING
ADEGGIILNNRSS   NIGGARDLINESS
ADEGGINNORRRS   ORGAN GRINDERS
ADEGHIKNNORRW   WORK-HARDENING
ADEGHINNNOSTT   ONE-NIGHT STAND
ADEGHINNOORTY   HYDROGENATION
ADEGHINOORSVW   OVERSHADOWING
ADEGHLLNORSST   STRANGLEHOLDS
ADEGIIIMNNRST   ADMINISTERING
ADEGIIIMNNSST   DISSEMINATING
ADEGIIKNNRRTW   DRINKING WATER
ADEGIIILNNOST   DIALLING TONES
ADEGIILNNOTTU   DEGLUTINATION
ADEGIIMMNNRST   MASTERMINDING
ADEGIIMNNOPRT   PREDOMINATING
ADEGIIMOOPRST   DIAGEOTROPISM
ADEGIINNNPRTU   UNDERPAINTING
ADEGIINORRSTT   DISINTEGRATOR
ADEGIKLNNOTWY   TAKE LYING DOWN
ADEGILMOORSTT   DERMATOLOGIST
ADEGILNNOQRTU   GRANDILOQUENT
ADEGILNNQRSUY   SQUANDERINGLY
ADEGIMNNORSTT   DEMONSTRATING
ADEGIMNORRSUY   YOUNG MARRIEDS
ADEHHIIILMOOP   HAEMOPHILIOID
ADEHIILMNPSTY   LYMPHADENITIS
ADEHIIMNOOSTT   METHODISATION
ADEHIIMNOOTTZ   METHODIZATION
ADEHILNNOPRSW   LANDOWNERSHIP
ADEHINNRSSTWW   WITHDRAWNNESS
ADEHINRSTUVYY   HEAVY INDUSTRY
ADEHIOOPPRSST   APOSTROPHISED
ADEHIOOPPRSTZ   APOSTROPHIZED
ADEHLLOOPPSUY   POLYADELPHOUS
ADEHLOPRRSSTU   SHOULDER STRAP
ADEHNORRSTTWW   NORTHWESTWARD
ADEHORSSTTUWW   SOUTHWESTWARD
ADEIIIILMSSTV   DISSIMILATIVE
ADEIIILMSSTUV   DISSIMULATIVE
ADEIIILNPSTTU   PLATITUDINISE
ADEIIILNPTTUZ   PLATITUDINIZE
ADEIIILNRSSTU   INDUSTRIALISE
ADEIIILNRSTUZ   INDUSTRIALIZE
ADEIIIMNNOSST   DISSEMINATION
ADEIIINOSSTTV   DEVIATIONISTS
ADEIIINRSSTTV   DITRANSITIVES
ADEIIINRSTTTU   ATTITUDINISER
ADEIIINRTTTUZ   ATTITUDINIZER
ADEIIKPRRSTTY   STRIKE PAY DIRT
ADEIIILLNQRSTU   TRANQUILLISED
ADEIIILLNQRTUZ   TRANQUILLIZED

ADEIILMNOPSSY IMPASSIONEDLY	ADIILNNNORSTU NONINDUSTRIAL
ADEIILNOOTTVY DEVOTIONALITY	ADIILNOPSTTUU PLATITUDINOUS
ADEIIMMNNNOOTT TIME-AND-MOTION	ADIMNNOORSSWY IN SO MANY WORDS
ADEIIMMNNRSSU INDIAN SUMMERS	AEEEEEINPRRRS ARRIERE-PENSÉE
ADEIIMNNNOOST DENOMINATIONS	AEEEEFHNRTTTV AFTER THE EVENT
ADEIIMNNOOPRT PREDOMINATION	AEEEEHHNNSTVV SEVENTH HEAVEN
ADEIIMNNOORST MODERNISATION	AEEEEILNRRSST RENSSELAERITE
ADEIIMNNOORTZ MODERNIZATION	AEEEEIMNPRSST PASSEMENTERIE
ADEIIMNNORSTU TRADE UNIONISM	AEEEELPRRSSSS PRESS RELEASES
ADEIIMNNOSSTU MOUNTAINSIDES	AEEEEMNPRSSTT TEMPERATENESS
ADEIINNNOSTTU UNITED NATIONS	AEEEFGHHIRTTW FEATHERWEIGHT
ADEIINNOOPRRT PREORDINATION	AEEEFGHLNRTTU FEATURE-LENGTH
ADEIINNOPSSST DISPENSATIONS	AEEEFGIIRRRTV REFRIGERATIVE
ADEIINNORSTTU TRADE UNIONIST	AEEEFILRSSSTV SELF-ASSERTIVE
ADEIINORSSSTT DISSERTATIONS	AEEEFINQRTTUV FREQUENTATIVE
ADEIILNRSTTUU UNILLUSTRATED	AEEEFNORRSTTW WATER SOFTENER
ADEIILMNNOPRTY PREDOMINANTLY	AEEEGGIMNOSST GAMETOGENESIS
ADEIILNOORTUVY DEVOLUTIONARY	AEEEGHHINPRSS SHEEPSHEARING
ADEIMNNOORSTT DEMONSTRATION	AEEEGHLLOPPRT TELEGRAPH POLE
ADEINOSSSSSUU ASSIDUOUSNESS	AEEEGHLNOPRRS SELENOGRAPHER
ADEJLORSSSSTU LOSS ADJUSTERS	AEEEGHMNOPRST MAGNETOSPHERE
ADELNOPRRSTTY TRANSPORTEDLY	AEEEGIKLMNRTT TELEMARKETING
ADELNORSTUUVY ADVENTUROUSLY	AEEEGIKLNRRST GENERAL STRIKE
ADEMNOORRSSTT DEMONSTRATORS	AEEEGILMNNORT NOLI-ME-TANGERE
ADENNORSTUUUV UNADVENTUROUS	AEEEGILNOPSTV NEGATIVE POLES
ADFFHILNOSSTY STANDOFFISHLY	AEEEGIMNPRRTY PRAYER MEETING
ADFGGHHIILLNN HIGHLAND FLING	AEEEGLMNNNSTT ENTANGLEMENTS
ADFGIIILNQSUY DISQUALIFYING	AEEEGMNNRSSTT ESTRANGEMENTS
ADFGIIINSSSTY DISSATISFYING	AEEEGNOOPRRST OPERATOR GENES
ADFGIIINNOPRTY INFANT PRODIGY	AEEEHHHILNPTTW WHITE ELEPHANT
ADFHIMNOOORSU MAIDS OF HONOUR	AEEEHHNOPRSST ASTHENOSPHERE
ADGGHHHIIMNTY HIGH-AND-MIGHTY	AEEEHHOPPRSTU PAPER THE HOUSE
ADGHIILMNNOSY ADMONISHINGLY	AEEEHIIMMNNTT IN THE MEANTIME
ADGHILLLMNOSS SMALLHOLDINGS	AEEEHILMNNOPP EPIPHENOMENAL
ADGHMNNOOPRRY GYNANDROMORPH	AEEEHIMOPRSSV OVEREMPHASISE
ADGIIILMNSSTU DISSIMULATING	AEEEHIMOPRSVZ OVEREMPHASIZE
ADGIIINNOPPST DISAPPOINTING	AEEEHLLMNSSTV MANTELSHELVES
ADGIILNNPRSST LANDING STRIPS	AEEEHLMNSSSSS SHAMELESSNESS
ADGIIMNNOSTUU MAGNITUDINOUS	AEEEHLNPSSSSS SHAPELESSNESS
ADGILNNOSTTUY OUTSTANDINGLY	AEEEHLNRSSSST HEARTLESSNESS
ADHIILLNOOQRTU QUADRILLIONTH	AEEEHLORSSTUX HETEROSEXUALS
ADHIILNOPPSST SPIT AND POLISH	AEEEHMNORSSST HEARTSOMENESS
ADHIIMNOORSSU DISHARMONIOUS	AEEEIIILLLNTV ILLE-ET-VILAINE
ADHILNOORSTYY HYDROLYSATION	AEEEIIIMMNRST SEINE-MARITIME
ADHIMNOPRSSSW SWORDSMANSHIP	AEEEIILNSTTUV EVENTUALITIES
ADIIIILMNOSST DISSIMILATION	AEEEIIMNRTTVX EXTERMINATIVE
ADIIIILMNPRTU PLATINIRIDIUM	AEEEIKLLOPPST SLEEP LIKE A TOP
ADIIIILMRSSTY DISSIMILARITY	AEEEIKLNPSTTV PALETTE KNIVES
ADIIIILLNOSSTT DISTILLATIONS	AEEEIKNPRSSVW SNEAK PREVIEWS
ADIIILMNOSSTU DISSIMULATION	AEEEILLNRRTVY REVERENTIALLY
ADIIILMNRSSTU INDUSTRIALISM	AEEEILMNPRSSX EXEMPLARINESS
ADIIILMORSSTY DISSIMILATORY	AEEEILMNPRTTY INTEMPERATELY
ADIIILNOOPSST DISPOSITIONAL	AEEEILNPRTTVY PENETRATIVELY
ADIIILNRSSTTU INDUSTRIALIST	AEEEIMNNNRTTT ENTERTAINMENT

AEEEIMNNRSTTT REINSTATEMENT
AEEEIMNORSSSW WEARISOMENESS
AEEEIMORSSTTV OVERESTIMATES
AEEEINNPSSSVX EXPANSIVENESS
AEEEINNSSTTTV ATTENTIVENESS,
  TENTATIVENESS
AEEEINOPRRSTV PERSEVERATION
AEEEINOPRSSTV OPERATIVENESS
AEEEINPRSSSVV PERVASIVENESS
AEEEINRSSSSTV ASSERTIVENESS
AEEEIPRRSSTVV PRESERVATIVES
AEEEKLLMRRSST SELLER'S MARKET
AEEEKLRRSSTTW STREETWALKERS
AEEEELLNSSSSUV VALUELESSNESS
AEEEELNPRSTTTT LETTERS PATENT
AEEEELNSSSSSTT STATELESSNESS,
  TASTELESSNESS
AEEEMMNOPRTTU PNEUMATOMETER
AEEEMNORSTTTV OVERSTATEMENT
AEEEMNPRRSSTU PREMATURENESS
AEEEENOPRSSTTT POSTE RESTANTE
AEEEEORRRSTTUV TREASURE TROVE
AEEFFGHIRRSTU FATHER FIGURES
AEEFFGINORRST REAFFORESTING
AEEFFHIMOPPTW WIPE OFF THE MAP
AEEFGGIINRRRT REFRIGERATING
AEEFGIINORRRT REFRIGERATION
AEEFGIIPRRTUV PREFIGURATIVE
AEEFGIKRRSSTU FIGURE SKATERS
AEEFGINORRSTU ARGENTIFEROUS
AEEFGIORRRRST REFRIGERATORS
AEEFHHLLNSSTU HEALTHFULNESS
AEEFHILNSSSST FAITHLESSNESS
AEEFHKMMOOSTT MAKE THE MOST OF
AEEFHLMOOPRRT MOTHER-OF-PEARL
AEEFHLMORRSTW FLAME-THROWERS
AEEFHLNOOPSTT ELEPHANT'S-FOOT
AEEFIILLNNRTY INFERENTIALLY
AEEFIILOPRRTV PROLIFERATIVE
AEEFILLMORSTU METALLIFEROUS
AEEFILNORSSST SELF-ASSERTION
AEEFILNRRSSTT SELF-RESTRAINT
AEEFIMNORSSTV FORMATIVENESS
AEEFIMOORRRST REFORMATORIES
AEEFINNOQRTTU FREQUENTATION
AEEFINNORSSSU NEFARIOUSNESS
AEEFINOORRSTT REFORESTATION
AEEFINOPRSTTU SUPERFETATION
AEEFIOOPRRSST PROFESSORIATE
AEEFLLNSSSSTU FAULTLESSNESS
AEEFLMNRSSSTU MASTERFULNESS
AEEGGHOOOPRRZ ZOOGEOGRAPHER
AEEGGIILNNNRV LINE-ENGRAVING
AEEGGILNNORTU OUTGENERALING

AEEGGINNOORSS ORGANOGENESIS
AEEGGINNSTTTW WETTING AGENTS
AEEGGLLORRSUY ROGUES' GALLERY
AEEGHHMOPRRRT THERMOGRAPHER
AEEGHHMPRSTUV HAVE THE GRUMPS
AEEGHHNOPRRST ETHNOGRAPHERS
AEEGHIINNSTTZ ANESTHETIZING
AEEGHILMOORST ISOGEOTHERMAL
AEEGHILNNRTTY THREATENINGLY
AEEGHILNORSTW WATERING HOLES
AEEGHIMOPRRSS SEISMOGRAPHER
AEEGHIPRSSSTW STAGE WHISPERS
AEEGHNOOPRRTV PHOTOENGRAVER
AEEGHNOPRRSST STENOGRAPHERS
AEEGIINNSTTVV INVESTIGATIVE
AEEGIILMNORSS GENERALISSIMO
AEEGIILNNRTXZ EXTERNALIZING
AEEGIIMNNORTT REGIMENTATION
AEEGIIMNNRTTX EXTERMINATING
AEEGIIMNRSTTU TIME SIGNATURE
AEEGIINNOORTT RENEGOTIATION
AEEGIINNOPRRT PEREGRINATION
AEEGIINORRTTV INTERROGATIVE
AEEGIKMNPRRST PARKING METERS
AEEGIKNRSSTUY KEY SIGNATURES
AEEGILLLNPRST SELLING-PLATER
AEEGILLMNNSSY MEANINGLESSLY
AEEGILLNRSTVY EVERLASTINGLY
AEEGILNNPRTTY PENETRATINGLY
AEEGILNNTTUXY EXTENUATINGLY
AEEGIMMNOOTTV MAGNETOMOTIVE
AEEGIMNNRTTUY INTEGUMENTARY
AEEGIMNORRSTV OVERMASTERING
AEEGINNRSTTUU SIGNATURE TUNE
AEEGINQRSSTTU SEQUESTRATING
AEEGINRRSSSTV TRANSGRESSIVE
AEEGIORRRSTTV TERGIVERSATOR
AEEGLLMNRSUWZ MANGEL-WURZELS
AEEHHIINNOPTZ PHENOTHIAZINE
AEEHHILLMNSVW WILHELMSHAVEN
AEEHHILMMNNTT NEMATHELMINTH
AEEHHILNNSSTU UNHEALTHINESS
AEEHHMOPRRTTY THERMOTHERAPY
AEEHIILLNNOST HELLENISATION
AEEHIILLNNOTZ HELLENIZATION
AEEHIKLNNPPST PINK ELEPHANTS
AEEHILMMNNOPS PHENOMENALISM
AEEHILMNNOPST PHENOMENALIST
AEEHILNNRSSTU UNEARTHLINESS
AEEHILORRSSTU TRAILER HOUSES
AEEHIMNQSSSSU SQUEAMISHNESS
AEEHINNOPPRSS APPREHENSIONS
AEEHINORSSSTW SEAWORTHINESS
AEEHIOPPSSTTV STOVEPIPE HATS

AEEHIORRRRSST HAIR-RESTORERS
AEEHIPRRRSSTU TREASURERSHIP
AEEHKLNNSSSST THANKLESSNESS
AEEHLMNOOSSST LOATHSOMENESS
AEEHLNORRSTTY NORTHEASTERLY
AEEHLORSSTTUY SOUTHEASTERLY
AEEHMMOOPRSST METAMORPHOSES
AEEHMMOPSSTUY EMPHYSEMATOUS
AEEHMNOOPPRTU PNEUMATOPHORE
AEEHMOOPPRRST SPERMATOPHORE
AEEHMOPPRSTTY SPERMATOPHYTE
AEEIIILMNPRRS PRELIMINARIES
AEEIIIMNSSTTV IMITATIVENESS
AEEIIILLNNPTTY PENITENTIALLY
AEEIILMNOPRSS IMPERSONALISE
AEEIILMNOPRSZ IMPERSONALIZE
AEEIILNNORRTT INTERRELATION
AEEIILNNPSSTV PLAINTIVENESS
AEEIILNNTTTVY INATTENTIVELY
AEEIILNOPQTTU EQUIPOTENTIAL
AEEIILNOPRSST PERSONALITIES
AEEIILNOPRTTV INTERPOLATIVE
AEEIILNORSTTV REVELATIONIST
AEEIILNORSTVY TELEVISIONARY
AEEIILNQSTTUY SEQUENTIALITY
AEEIILORRRTTX EXTERRITORIAL
AEEIIMMNORSST MESMERISATION
AEEIIMMNORSTZ MESMERIZATION
AEEIIMNNORTTX EXTERMINATION
AEEIIMNPSSSSV IMPASSIVENESS
AEEIIMNQRSSTU EQUESTRIANISM
AEEIINNOQRSTU QUESTIONNAIRE
AEEIKNOPRSSTT STREPTOKINASE
AEEIILLMNNSTTY SENTIMENTALLY
AEEIILLNNOPTXY EXPONENTIALLY
AEEIILLNOPRRTT INTERPELLATOR
AEEIILLPRSTUVY SUPERLATIVELY
AEEIILLRRRSTTY TERRESTRIALLY
AEEIILLRTTTTTT TITTLE-TATTLER
AEEIILMNNNORTV ENVIRONMENTAL
AEEIILMOPRRTXY EXTEMPORARILY
AEEIILNNNOOPPS PELOPONNESIAN
AEEIILNNNOPRST ANTIPERSONNEL
AEEIILNNOPRRST INTERPERSONAL
AEEIILNNPRRSTT SILENT PARTNER
AEEIILNNQQTUUV QUINQUEVALENT
AEEIILNNRSSSUV UNIVERSALNESS
AEEIILNOORRSTV LATEROVERSION
AEEIILNPRRRSST LASER PRINTERS
AEEIILOPRSSTUY ERYSIPELATOUS
AEEIILPPRSSTUW WATER SUPPLIES
AEEIMMNSSSTTT MISSTATEMENTS
AEEIMNNOPPRTT REAPPOINTMENT
AEEIMNOPRRSST TEMPORARINESS

AEEIMNOPRSSTX PROXIMATENESS
AEEIMNORRSTTV REMONSTRATIVE
AEEIMNORRSTTX EXTERMINATORS
AEEINNNRSSSTU SATURNINENESS
AEEINNOPRSSTT PRESENTATIONS
AEEINOOPRRTTX RE-EXPORTATION
AEEINOORRSTUV ARTERIOVENOUS
AEEINOQRSSTTU SEQUESTRATION
AEEINOSSSTUVX VEXATIOUSNESS
AEEINRSSSTTTV TRANSVESTITES
AEEIOOPPRSTTV POSTOPERATIVE
AEEIPPRRSSSTT ASSET-STRIPPER
AEEKLLORRRSST ROLLER-SKATERS
AEEKMORRSSSTT MASTERSTROKES
AEELMNPPRSTUY SUPPLEMENTARY
AEELNOOPSSTTU STENOPETALOUS
AEEMMNOPRTTUY PNEUMATOMETRY
AEEMNOOPRSTTU TREPONEMATOUS
AEEMNPRRRSUUY SUPERNUMERARY
AEFFGIMRSSTTU SUFFRAGETTISM
AEFGGIIKNRSTU FIGURE-SKATING
AEFGHHOORRSTU THOROUGHFARES
AEFGHHORSTTTU AFTERTHOUGHTS
AEFGHIKMNNOOT MAKE NOTHING OF
AEFGHINNNPRTY PENNY-FARTHING
AEFGIILLORRSU ARGILLIFEROUS
AEFGIILNOPRRT PROLIFERATING
AEFGIINOPRRTU PREFIGURATION
AEFGILLNNRTUY UNFALTERINGLY
AEFGILNNORRWY FOREWARNINGLY
AEFGILNOORTTV FLOATING VOTER
AEFGINOOPRRTW WATERPROOFING
AEFHKLMORSSST THERMOS FLASKS
AEFHKNOOSSTTV VOTES OF THANKS
AEFHLOOSTTUUU OUT OF THE USUAL
AEFIIIILMNNST INFINITESIMAL
AEFIIILMNSSST SEMIFINALISTS
AEFIIILNORSTT FERTILISATION
AEFIIILNORTTZ FERTILIZATION
AEFIILLLNNTUY INFLUENTIALLY
AEFIILMNORSUU ALUMINIFEROUS
AEFIILMNORTVY INFORMATIVELY
AEFIILNOOPRRT PROLIFERATION
AEFIILNOPRSTU PLATINIFEROUS
AEFIIMNOOPRRT IMPERFORATION
AEFIIMNORSSTU STAMINIFEROUS
AEFIINRRSTTTY INTERSTRATIFY
AEFILLOPRSSTW LOW-PASS FILTER
AEFILMNOPRSTT SELF-IMPORTANT
AEFILNOOPRSSS PROFESSIONALS
AEFILNOOPRSSW PASSIONFLOWER
AEFILNOOQSTUW QUESTION OF LAW
AEFINOOPRRRSW PRISONER OF WAR
AEFIOQRRSTUUZ QUARTZIFEROUS

AEFLLMNORSSTU SMALL FORTUNES
AEFLNNORTTUUY UNFORTUNATELY
AEGGGIINRRTTU REGURGITATING
AEGGHHLOPPRRY GLYPHOGRAPHER
AEGGHIILNRRTT RIGHT TRIANGLE
AEGGHIIMMNOPR MIMEOGRAPHING
AEGGHIINNRSTT STRAIGHTENING
AEGGHILNOORTW WOOLGATHERING
AEGGHLOOPRRSS GLOSSOGRAPHER
AEGGHLOPPRRTY GLYPTOGRAPHER
AEGGIIIMNPSTT SPITTING IMAGE
AEGGIIINNSTTV INVESTIGATING
AEGGIIINNORRTT INTERROGATING
AEGGIINORRTTU REGURGITATION
AEGGIINRSTTTT SITTING TARGET
AEGGINNNOORSS NONAGGRESSION
AEGGINNRRSSST TRANSGRESSING
AEGHHILNORSSY ROYAL HIGHNESS
AEGHHIOPPRRSY PHYSIOGRAPHER
AEGHHOOPPRRST PHOTOGRAPHERS
AEGHIIKNNPRSS PINKING SHEARS
AEGHIINNSTTUX EXTINGUISHANT
AEGHIIPRRRSST REGISTRARSHIP
AEGHIKNNRRSTT KNIGHTS-ERRANT
AEGHILLLNNRTY ENTHRALLINGLY
AEGHILNORSTUV VAULTING HORSE
AEGHILOOPRSST PHRASEOLOGIST
AEGHIMNORSSUW HOUSEWARMINGS
AEGHIMNORTTUW MOUTH-WATERING
AEGHINNOORSST ON A SHOESTRING
AEGHIOPRRSSTU SURROGATESHIP
AEGHLMMOORTTY THREMMATOLOGY
AEGHMNOOOPSTU ENTOMOPHAGOUS
AEGHNNOOPTTUY PUT ON THE AGONY
AEGHNOOPPRRRS PORNOGRAPHERS
AEGIIILNNNRTZ INTERNALIZING
AEGIIILNRSSTU SINGULARITIES
AEGIIINNOSTTV INVESTIGATION
AEGIIILLOPRSS ASPERGILLOSIS
AEGIILMNORSST MINERALOGISTS
AEGIILMNORSYY SYRINGOMYELIA
AEGIILMNPRSST SLIPSTREAMING
AEGIILMOOSSST SEMASIOLOGIST
AEGIILNNOPRSZ PERSONALIZING
AEGIILNNOPRTT INTERPOLATING
AEGIILNNRRSTY RESTRAININGLY
AEGIILNRSSTVV VESTAL VIRGINS
AEGIIMNNOPRST IMPERSONATING
AEGIIMNNRRRTY INTERMARRYING
AEGIIMNSSTTYZ SYSTEMATIZING
AEGIINNOORRTT INTERROGATION
AEGIINOPPRRTX EXPROPRIATING
AEGIINORRSSTT REGISTRATIONS
AEGIINORSSTTV INVESTIGATORS

AEGIJLPSSUWZZ JIGSAW PUZZLES
AEGIKLLNORRST ROLLER SKATING
AEGILLLMNSSST SMELLING SALTS
AEGILLMNOORSS LEMON GRASS OIL
AEGILLMRSSTTU METALLURGISTS
AEGILMNORSSTU SOMERSAULTING
AEGILNOOPRRSS PROGRESSIONAL
AEGILNOPSTTUX EXPOSTULATING
AEGIMNNOPRRRY MORNING PRAYER
AEGIMNNORRSTT REMONSTRATING
AEGIMNNOOPRSSU ANGIOSPERMOUS
AEGIMOOOPPRST APOGEOTROPISM
AEGINNORRSSST TRANSGRESSION
AEGINOORRRSTT INTERROGATORS
AEGINOORRRTTY INTERROGATORY
AEGLMNOORSSSU GLAMOROUSNESS
AEGLMOOSSTTYY SYSTEMATOLOGY
AEGLNORRSSSUU GARRULOUSNESS
AEGNORRRSSSST TRANSGRESSORS
AEHHHINOPRRRY HERNIORRHAPHY
AEHHIIILMNSST HELMINTHIASIS
AEHHIINORSTTW WITHIN EARSHOT
AEHHILLMNPTTY PLATYHELMINTH
AEHHIMMNOPRST THEANTHROPISM
AEHHINOPRSTTT THEANTHROPIST
AEHHIOPPRSTYY PHYSIOTHERAPY
AEHHLLMORSSTU THE SMALL HOURS
AEHHLNORRTUUY UNEARTHLY HOUR
AEHHLOOPPRSSY PHOSPHORYLASE
AEHHOOPPPRSTY PYROPHOSPHATE
AEHHOOPRRSSTT SHARPSHOOTERS
AEHIILNOPRSST RELATIONSHIPS
AEHIIILNORSSSU HILARIOUSNESS
AEHIINORRSSTW AIRWORTHINESS
AEHIIRRSSSTTW SHIRTWAISTERS
AEHILMMNORTUY ALUMINOTHERMY
AEHILMOOSTUXY HOMOSEXUALITY
AEHILMOPPRSTY AMPHIPROSTYLE
AEHIMMNOPRTUY IMMUNOTHERAPY
AEHIMMOOPRSST METAMORPHOSIS
AEHIMNNPRSSTT TRANSSHIPMENT
AEHIMNPRSTUUY SUPERHUMANITY
AEHINNOORSSTT NORTH OSSETIAN
AEHINOOSSSTTU STATION HOUSES
AEHINOPRSSSUV VAPOURISHNESS
AEHLMNOOPRTVW WOLVERHAMPTON
AEHMNOOPRRTTY ANTHROPOMETRY
AEHMNOOPRSSSU AMORPHOUSNESS
AEHMNOQRTTUUY QUANTUM THEORY
AEHOOPRRSSSUW HOUSE SPARROWS
AEIIILLLMNNST MILLENNIALIST
AEIIILLMNORSS MILLIONAIRESS
AEIIILLMNPRRY PRELIMINARILY
AEIIILLMNRSTY MINISTERIALLY

AEIIILNORSSTT STERILISATION
AEIIILNORSTTU REUTILISATION
AEIIILNORSTTZ STERILIZATION
AEIIILNORTTUZ REUTILIZATION
AEIIILPRRSSTU SPIRITUALISER
AEIIILPRRSTUZ SPIRITUALIZER
AEIIIMNOOPSTT EPITOMISATION
AEIIIMNOOPTTZ EPITOMIZATION
AEIIIMNOORSST ISOMERISATION
AEIIIMNOORSTZ ISOMERIZATION
AEIIINNORSSSV VISIONARINESS
AEIIINNOSSSTT SENSITISATION
AEIIINNOSSTTZ SENSITIZATION
AEIIINOOSSTTV SOVIETISATION
AEIIINOOSTTVZ SOVIETIZATION
AEIIILNNNOTTY INTENTIONALLY
AEIIILNOQRTUV VENTRILOQUIAL
AEIIILNQRRSTU TRANQUILLISER
AEIIILNQRRTUZ TRANQUILLIZER
AEIIILMNNOOPRS PRONOMINALISE
AEIIILMNNOOPRZ PRONOMINALIZE
AEIIILMNNOOSST SOLEMNISATION
AEIIILMNNOOSTZ SOLEMNIZATION
AEIIILMNNOPSTU EMULSION PAINT
AEIIILMNOORSTT TOLERATIONISM
AEIIILMNOPRSTY IMPERSONALITY
AEIIILNNNNOTTU UNINTENTIONAL
AEIIILNNNORTTU INTERLUNATION
AEIIILNNOOPRTT INTERPOLATION
AEIIILNOOPPRST PREPOSITIONAL
AEIIILNOOPSTTX SEXPLOITATION
AEIIILNOORSTTT TOLERATIONIST
AEIIILNOPRSTUV PULVERISATION
AEIIILNOPRTUVZ PULVERIZATION
AEIIILOOPPRRRT PROPRIETORIAL
AEIIILOPPRRRTY PROPRIETARILY
AEIIIMNNOOPRST IMPERSONATION
AEIIIMNOOPRRTT REIMPORTATION
AEIIIMNOOPRSTT TEMPORISATION
AEIIIMNOOPRTTZ TEMPORIZATION
AEIIIMNOSSSTTY SYSTEMISATION
AEIIIMNOSSTTYZ SYSTEMIZATION
AEIIINNOOPPSTT PEPTONISATION
AEIIINNOOPPTTZ PEPTONIZATION
AEIIINNOPSSSTX EXPANSIONISTS
AEIIINOOPPRRTX EXPROPRIATION
AEIIINOOPRSSTT ESPIRITO SANTO
AEIIINOOPRSTTX EXTRAPOSITION
AEIIINOORRRSTT TERRORISATION
AEIIINOORRRTTZ TERRORIZATION
AEIIINORRSSTTT TRANSISTORISE
AEIIINORRSSTTZ TRANSISTORIZE
AEIKLMNOPRSST SPORTSMANLIKE
AEIKMNOQRSSTU QUESTION MARKS

AEILLLMNOOSSS SALMONELLOSIS
AEILLMMMNOOST MONOMETALLISM
AEILLMMNOOSTT MONOMETALLIST
AEILLNOPRTTWW WILLOW PATTERN
AEILLNOPSSSSY PASSIONLESSLY
AEILLORRRSTTY ROTARY TILLERS
AEILMMNNOTTUY MONUMENTALITY
AEILMNOOPRSTT METROPOLITANS
AEILMNOPRTTUY IMPORTUNATELY
AEILMNOPSSTUY PNEUMATOLYSIS
AEILNNORSSTUV VOLUNTARINESS
AEILNNORSTUVY INTRAVENOUSLY
AEILNNRSTTUWW UNWRITTEN LAWS
AEILNOOOOPRRST POOR RELATIONS
AEILNOOPRSTTT PETROL STATION
AEILNOOPSTTUX EXPOSTULATION
AEILNOORRTUVY REVOLUTIONARY
AEILOOOOPPPRS PROSOPOPOEIAL
AEIMNNOOPPRTT APPORTIONMENT
AEIMNNOORRSTT REMONSTRATION
AEIMNNORSSTTU MENSTRUATIONS
AEIMNOOPRRSST IMPERSONATORS
AEIMNOPRSSTTT PROTESTANTISM
AEIMPRRRSSSTY PRIMARY STRESS
AEINNORSSSUUV UNSAVOURINESS
AEINOOOPPRRTT PROPORTIONATE
AEINOOPRSSTTT PROTESTATIONS
AEINOOPRSSTTW POWER STATIONS
AEIOOPPRRRSTX EXPROPRIATORS
AEKLOOPPRSTVV PETROPAVLOVSK
AELNNOOPSSTUY SPONTANEOUSLY
AELOOPRSTTUXY EXPOSTULATORY
AEMMNOOORSTTU MONOTREMATOUS
AEMNOOOPRSSZZ MEZZO-SOPRANOS
AENNNORSSSTUY TYRANNOUSNESS
AENOOOPPRRTXY PROPAROXYTONE
AENOPRRSSSTUU RAPTUROUSNESS
AFFGIIMNOSTUU SUFFUMIGATION
AFGGHHIIRSTTT STRAIGHT FIGHT
AFGGIINNRRSTU TRANSFIGURING
AFGHIINOPRRST PROFIT SHARING
AFGHIKNOORTUW FOR AUGHT I KNOW
AFGIIILNNRTUY INFURIATINGLY
AFGIILNNOOPPT FLOATING-POINT
AFGIIMNOPRRST PROFIT MARGINS
AFGIKNOORSSTT TOASTING FORKS
AFIIILNNORSTT INFILTRATIONS
AFIIILNOOSSST FOSSILISATION
AFIIILNOOSSTZ FOSSILIZATION
AFIILLNOOOPRS FLORIANOPOLIS
AFIILLORSTTUY FLIRTATIOUSLY
AFILNOPPRRUUV FLAVOPURPURIN
AGGHHIILNOPRT LITHOGRAPHING
AGGHHINOOPPRT PHOTOGRAPHING

AGGHHMOPPRSYY SPHYGMOGRAPHY
AGGHIIKLNPRST PARKING LIGHTS
AGGHIIKNNSSTV THANKSGIVINGS
AGGHILOOPRSST GRAPHOLOGISTS
AGGIIILNNOSTU ISOAGGLUTININ
AGGIIILNNSTTY INSTIGATINGLY
AGGIIINNORTTU INGURGITATION
AGGIILNNOPPRR GRAPPLING IRON
AGGILLNOORSTY LARYNGOLOGIST
AGHHIILMNRSTY NIGHTMARISHLY
AGHHILMNOPPSU PLOUGHMANSHIP
AGHHIMNOORSTT ORTHOGNATHISM
AGHHLLMOOOPTY OPHTHALMOLOGY
AGHHLMNNOOOPT MONOPHTHONGAL
AGHHNOOORSTTU ORTHOGNATHOUS
AGHIIILLMNTUY HUMILIATINGLY
AGHIIILNOPSTZ HOSPITALIZING
AGHIIILNPRSTT HAIR-SPLITTING
AGHIILNNOSSTY ASTONISHINGLY
AGHIINOPPRSTU UPRIGHT PIANOS
AGHINOOPSTTTT PHOTOSTATTING
AGHINOORSSSTT SHOOTING STARS
AGHLLMOORSUUW GALLOWS HUMOUR
AGIIILLLNTTTY TITILLATINGLY
AGIIIILMNRSTU TRILINGUALISM
AGIIIILMMNNPRT MALIMPRINTING
AGIIIILMMNORTZ IMMORTALIZING
AGIIILNNNOOPT NO OIL PAINTING
AGIIILNNQRTUZ TRANQUILIZING
AGIIKLNNOPSTT TALKING POINTS
AGIILLMNSTTUY STIMULATINGLY
AGIIILNOOSSTY SYLLOGISATION
AGIIILNOOSTYZ SYLLOGIZATION
AGIILMOOPPRST PLAGIOTROPISM
AGIILNNNRTYYZ TYRANNIZINGLY
AGIILNNOPRTYZ PATRONIZINGLY
AGIILOORSSSTY ASSYRIOLOGIST
AGIIMNOORRSUV GRAMINIVOROUS
AGIINNOPRTTTY POTTY-TRAINING
AGILMMNOOSTUY NUMISMATOLOGY
AGILMOORRSTTY MARTYROLOGIST
AGILNNOOOOPRST PROLONGATIONS
AGIMNOOOOPRSUZ ZOOSPORANGIUM
AHHNOOOPPRSTY ANTHROPOSOPHY
AHIIILNOOPRRT HORRIPILATION
AHIIILNOPSTTY INHOSPITALITY
AHIIMMNOOOSSU HOMOOUSIANISM
AHIJNNOPRSTUZ ZINJANTHROPUS
AHIMNOPPRSSST SPORTSMANSHIP
AHKLNNOOPPTTY PHYTOPLANKTON
AHLLMMMOOOTWY WOOLLY
    MAMMOTH
AHMMOOOOPRSTU OMMATOPHOROUS
AIIIILNNOQSTU INQUISITIONAL

AIIIILNOQRSTU INQUISITORIAL
AIIIIMNPPSSSS MISSISSIPPIAN
AIIILLMNNOSTU ILLUMINATIONS
AIIILLMNPSTUY PUSILLANIMITY
AIIILNNOSTTTU INSTITUTIONAL
AIIILNOOSSSTT ISOLATIONISTS
AIIILPRSSSTTU SPIRITUALISTS
AIIIMMNNOSSTU IMMUNISATIONS
AIIIMMNNOSTUZ IMMUNIZATIONS
AIIIMNOOPPRRT IMPROPRIATION
AIIIMNOOPRSTV IMPROVISATION
AIIINNNOOSTTV INNOVATIONIST
AIIIOOPPRSTTU PROPITIATIOUS
AIIJNOOPSTTUX JUXTAPOSITION
AIILLMNOPSSUU PUSILLANIMOUS
AIILLNNORTUVY INVOLUNTARILY
AIILLNOOPRSVY PROVISIONALLY
AIILLNORSSTTU ILLUSTRATIONS
AIILMNNNOOSTU MOUNTAIN LIONS
AIILNOOOPPRST PROPOSITIONAL
AIILNOOPPSSTU SUPPOSITIONAL
AIILNOOPSSSTU SAN LUIS POTOSI
AIIMNNNORSSST TRANSMISSIONS
AIIMNOOQSSTTU MISQUOTATIONS
AIINNOOPRSSTT TRANSPOSITION
AIIOOOOPRSUVVV OVOVIVIPAROUS
AILMOOOPSSSTX TOXOPLASMOSIS
AIMOORRRSTWWY TWO-WAY MIRRORS
BBCDEELMORSTU CLUSTER-BOMBED
BBCDGIIKLLNOU BUILDING BLOCK
BBCEEGIKNNRRU RUBBERNECKING
BBCEEIORRSSUV OVERSUBSCRIBE
BBCEHMOORRSTU BUTCHER'S-BROOM
BBCEIILMNOSTU INCOMBUSTIBLE
BBCGGHIILNNTU NIGHTCLUBBING
BBDEELNRSSSUU BLUNDERBUSSES
BBDEGHMNOORSY HYDROGEN BOMBS
BBDEHLOOORRST BLOOD BROTHERS
BBDIIILNOOSVY DIVISION LOBBY
BBEEEEEEHIIJS HEEBIE-JEEBIES
BBEEFGHIMORRT FIGHTER-BOMBER
BBEEGMNORRSUY MONEY-GRUBBERS
BBEENNNRRSSUU BUNSEN BURNERS
BBEGGIMNNORUY MONEY-GRUBBING
BBINNOOORRSTT TORN TO RIBBONS
BCCCDEIIMRRSU CIRCUMSCRIBED
BCCCHINOOOPRS BRONCHOSCOPIC
BCCDDEEEHKLOU DOUBLE-CHECKED
BCCDEEIJORSTT DIRECT OBJECTS
BCCEEHIKKKTTU KICK THE BUCKET
BCCEEHNNORRSSS CROSSBENCHERS
BCCEEIILORRTT TRIBOELECTRIC
BCCEEIINRSTTY CYBERNETICIST
BCCEEILORRTTU TURBO-ELECTRIC

BCCEHHINOOOSS HOBSON'S CHOICE
BCCEIIIJOSTTV OBJECTIVISTIC
BCCEIIILNNNOV INCONVINCIBLE
BCCEILNORSTTU CONSTRUCTIBLE
BCCHILLOOPSSU PUBLIC SCHOOLS
BCDDDELLLOOOY COLD-BLOODEDLY
BCDDEEEKLORSU DOUBLE-DECKERS
BCDDEEELLLOORS RED BLOOD CELLS
BCDDEELOORSSU DOUBLE-CROSSED
BCDDEIIILTTUY DEDUCTIBILITY
BCDDGILLNOORU BLOODCURDLING
BCDEEEILLLNPU BLUE-PENCILLED
BCDEEEKORRSST STOCKBREEDERS
BCDEEGIKNORST STOCKBREEDING
BCDEEGINORRSS CROSSBREEDING
BCDEEIIILNNNS INDISCERNIBLE
BCDEELOORRSSU DOUBLE-CROSSER
BCDEELOORSSSU DOUBLE-CROSSES
BCDEIIIILNRTY INCREDIBILITY
BCDEIILNORTUY INDOLEBUTYRIC
BCDGHIIKKRRTU KIRKCUDBRIGHT
BCDGIKNOOSSTY BODY STOCKINGS
BCDIIILOORRTY CORRODIBILITY
BCDIIILOPRTUY PRODUCIBILITY
BCEEEEFFILRSV EFFERVESCIBLE
BCEEEEFKNOORR REFERENCE BOOK
BCEEEFGIINNRR BIREFRINGENCE
BCEEEGIINORST BIOENERGETICS
BCEEEGILLNORT COBELLIGERENT
BCEEEHIKLRRSU HUCKLEBERRIES
BCEEEHLNNOORZ CHLOROBENZENE
BCEEEIILMPPRT IMPERCEPTIBLE
BCEEEIJNOSSTV OBJECTIVENESS
BCEEEIILNOPRWY EYEBROW PENCIL
BCEEEELNORSTVY CONVEYER BELTS
BCEEFHNNORRST FRONTBENCHERS
BCEEGILMNNRUY ENCUMBERINGLY
BCEEHIILRRSSV SILVER BIRCHES
BCEEIILMPPRTY IMPERCEPTIBLY
BCEEIIILNNORTV INCONVERTIBLE
BCEEIIILNPSSTU INSUSCEPTIBLE
BCEEIIILPPRRST PRESCRIPTIBLE
BCEEIMMOSSTTU SUBCOMMITTEES
BCEEJLNOOSSST OBJECT LESSONS
BCEFFIOOOOPSTX POST OFFICE BOX
BCEFHIMNOOOTT FINE-TOOTH COMB
BCEFHINOOSSST SONS-OF-BITCHES
BCEFJMOOOORRST JOB'S COMFORTER
BCEGHILNOOOTY BIOTECHNOLOGY
BCEGIKLNOSSTU BLUESTOCKINGS
BCEIIIILQRSTU EQUILIBRISTIC
BCEIILNOPRRTU INCORRUPTIBLE
BCEILMNOOPRYY POLYEMBRYONIC
BCEILORSTTUVY OBSTRUCTIVELY

BCEINNNOSSTTU SUBCONTINENTS
BCERRSSSTTUUU SUBSTRUCTURES
BCFGIIMMNNOOR COMBINING FORM
BCGHILNOOOORY CHRONOBIOLOGY
BCGHILOOOPSYY PSYCHOBIOLOGY
BCGIIIILORRTY CORRIGIBILITY
BCGIIILMNNORS CLIMBING IRONS
BCGILOOORSTY CRYOBIOLOGIST
BCIIIIILMMSTY IMMISCIBILITY
BCIIIIILNNTVY INVINCIBILITY
BCIILNOPRRTUY INCORRUPTIBLY
BCIINNOORSTTU CONTRIBUTIONS
BCIINOPRSSSTU SUBSCRIPTIONS
BDDEEEEGNNRRS GENDER-BENDERS
BDDEEEGINNRRU UNDERBREEDING
BDDEEEILLMOSW DISEMBOWELLED
BDDEEIILNOSTY DISOBEDIENTLY
BDDEEIIMMNOST DISEMBODIMENT
BDDEEIIRRSTTU REDISTRIBUTED
BDDEEIJLNOOTU DOUBLE-JOINTED
BDDEEILNOOPRX PEROXIDE BLOND
BDDEEIMNNRSTU DISBURDENMENT
BDDEGHILMORSU MIDDLESBROUGH
BDDEIILMMORSW MIDDLEBROWISM
BDDEIINRSTTUU UNDISTRIBUTED
BDDEILNNORSSW WORD BLINDNESS
BDEEEEFILNOSS BESIDE ONESELF
BDEEEFGIKRRRS FREDERIKSBERG
BDEEEFGILNOTT BOTTLE-FEEDING,
                FEEDING BOTTLE
BDEEEGIINNRRT INTERBREEDING
BDEEEGIJLLNOU GOLDEN JUBILEE
BDEEEIIRSSVWY BIRD'S-EYE VIEWS
BDEEEIMMMNRST DISMEMBERMENT
BDEEEELNNSSSSU UNBLESSEDNESS
BDEEFGILORSUU DOUBLE FIGURES
BDEEFIIILNSTY DEFENSIBILITY
BDEEGIILLNRWY BEWILDERINGLY
BDEEGIILMNOSW DISEMBOWELING
BDEEGIILMNSSX MIXED BLESSING
BDEEGIINORSUW BROWNIE GUIDES
BDEEGINNNNSSU UNBENDINGNESS
BDEEGINNORRUV OVERBURDENING
BDEEIIILNTTXY EXTENDIBILITY
BDEEIMNRSSSTU DISBURSEMENTS
BDEEINNORSSTV INVERTED SNOBS
BDEELLNOOSSSS BLOODLESSNESS
BDEELNNOSSSSU BOUNDLESSNESS
BDEELOOPRRSSU BLOOD PRESSURE
BDEFFNOOOOPRRU BURDEN OF PROOF
BDEFHNOOORSTU DEBTS OF HONOUR
BDEGHHINOOORS NEIGHBORHOODS
BDEGHHINOOORU NEIGHBOURHOOD
BDEGHHOORRSTU THOROUGHBREDS

BDEGIIIILSTTY DIGESTIBILITY
BDEHIIIILNNTUY UNINHIBITEDLY
BDEHNOOOPRSTU BOUSTROPHEDON
BDEILNNNOSSSW SNOW BLINDNESS
BDEKLNOOOORTWY OLD-BOY NETWORK
BDFFIIIILSTUY DIFFUSIBILITY
BDFGHILLOOSSW GOLDFISH BOWLS
BDGGIIIILLNOSY DISOBLIGINGLY
BDIIIILLOSSTUY DISSOLUBILITY
BDIIINORSSTTU DISTRIBUTIONS
BEEEEHILNPRRS REPREHENSIBLE
BEEEELLLRSSTT BELLES-LETTRES
BEEEFFGIINNRT FRINGE BENEFIT
BEEEHILLMMNST EMBELLISHMENT
BEEEHILNPRRSY REPREHENSIBLY
BEEEIIJLLRSUV SILVER JUBILEE
BEEEIIILNPRSSX INEXPRESSIBLE
BEEEIIILPRRRSS IRREPRESSIBLE
BEEEILNPRSSSU SUPERSENSIBLE
BEEEIMMNRRSTU REIMBURSEMENT
BEEEINOSSSSSV OBSESSIVENESS
BEEFGINRRSTTU BUTTERFINGERS
BEEFHIMNRRSTU REFURBISHMENT
BEEFILLMORSUU UMBELLIFEROUS
BEEGGILNNORSW BOWLING GREENS
BEEGHNRRSTTTU BRUTE STRENGTH
BEEGIIILLNNUVY UNBELIEVINGLY
BEEGLOORRSTTT GLOBETROTTERS
BEEHILMRRTUWY WHITE MULBERRY
BEEHILNOOORTZ BELO HORIZONTE
BEEHILNORRSST BROTHERLINESS
BEEIIILMMPRSS IMPERMISSIBLE
BEEIIILNSTTXY EXTENSIBILITY
BEEIIILRRSTVY REVERSIBILITY
BEEIILNOPRRSS IRRESPONSIBLE
BEEIILNPRRTTU INTERRUPTIBLE
BEEIILNPRSSXY INEXPRESSIBLY
BEEIILPRRRSSY IRREPRESSIBLY
BEEILNRSSTUVY SUBSERVIENTLY
BEEINORSSSTUV OBTRUSIVENESS
BEENNOOSSSTUU BOUNTEOUSNESS
BEFFGINNORRTU BURNT OFFERING
BEFGIIILNRSTU FILIBUSTERING
BEFGIILNOOPRS BE SPOILING FOR
BEFGILLOORSUU GLOBULIFEROUS
BEFIIIILLNTXY INFLEXIBILITY
BEFILNNOSSTUU BOUNTIFULNESS
BEFINNNSSSUUY FUNNY BUSINESS
BEGGIIIILLNTY NEGLIGIBILITY
BEGGILNOORTTT GLOBETROTTING
BEGHNOOOORRTTU ROTTEN BOROUGH
BEGIIIIILLNTY INELIGIBILITY
BEGIILNNNOPTW TENPIN BOWLING
BEHIIIIMNOSTX EXHIBITIONISM

BEHIIIINOSTTX EXHIBITIONIST
BEHIIIILOPRTVY PROHIBITIVELY
BEHILOORRSUVY HERBIVOROUSLY
BEIIIILMRSSTY REMISSIBILITY
BEIIIILNNSSTY INSENSIBILITY
BEIIIILNRTTVY INVERTIBILITY
BEIIIILOPSSST POSSIBILITIES
BEIIIILRSSTTY RESISTIBILITY
BEIIILNOSSTTY OSTENSIBILITY
BEIILNOOSSSUV OBLIVIOUSNESS
BEIILNOPRRSSY IRRESPONSIBLY
BEIINNOOPRSTW BROWNIE POINTS
BEIINSSSSSTUU BUSINESS SUITS
BEIIOPRSSTTUU SUBREPTITIOUS
BEILNORSTUUVY UNOBTRUSIVELY
BEIMNOPSSSTUU BUMPTIOUSNESS
BEINNOOOSSSUX OBNOXIOUSNESS
BFGHIIILLORSST BILLS OF RIGHTS
BFILLLMNOOSSU IN FULL BLOSSOM
BFILLOORSTUUU TUBULIFLOROUS
BGHILLNOOOPST POLLING BOOTHS
BGIIILNNOOPST BOILING POINTS
BIIIILMOPSSTY IMPOSSIBILITY
BIIKOOORSSSTV VISITORS' BOOKS
BIINOSSSTTTUU SUBSTITUTIONS
BILOOOPPRRSUY OPPROBRIOUSLY
CCCCEEINNOPSU CONCUPISCENCE
CCCDEEEENRRSU RECRUDESCENCE
CCCDEIILORSTU CLOSED-CIRCUIT
CCCDEIIMNRSUU UNCIRCUMCISED
CCCEEEFIMNRRU CIRCUMFERENCE
CCCEEEIILNOPT POETIC LICENCE
CCCEEEIILOOPRST ELECTROSCOPIC
CCCEEGHIKNORSS CROSSCHECKING
CCCEEHIIMOSTYZ SCHIZOMYCETIC
CCCEIIILORSUV VICIOUS CIRCLE
CCCEIIMNOOOOS SOCIOECONOMIC
CCCEIINNORTTY CONCENTRICITY
CCCEILMPRSTUY CIRCUMSPECTLY
CCCEIOOPPRSST SPECTROSCOPIC
CCCEOOPRSSTTU STREPTOCOCCUS
CCCIIIMNORSSU CIRCUMCISIONS·
CCCILNNOOTUUY COUNTY COUNCIL
CCDDEEELLMNNO CONDEMNED CELL
CCDDEEGINNNOS CONDESCENDING
CCDDENOORTTUU CONDUCTED TOUR
CCDEEEEIILNQSU DELIQUESCENCE
CCDEEELLNNOTW WELL-CONNECTED
CCDEEHILORRTY HYDROELECTRIC
CCDEEIINNOSTV DISCONNECTIVE
CCDEEILMNOPSY ENCYCLOPEDISM
CCDEEILNOPSTY ENCYCLOPEDIST
CCDEEIMOORRTT MICRODETECTOR
CCDEEINNNOOSS CONDESCENSION

CCDEEINNOSSUV CONDUCIVENESS
CCDEEINOOPRUW OWNER-OCCUPIED
CCDEEINRRRTTU DIRECT CURRENT
CCDEELNNNORUY UNCONCERNEDLY
CCDEENNOOPRSY CO-RESPONDENCY
CCDEENORRSTTU RECONSTRUCTED
CCDEGIINNNNOST DISCONNECTING
CCDEGIINNORST DISCONCERTING
CCDEGINNNOORT CONNECTING ROD
CCDEHIOOSSTUU STUDIO COUCHES
CCDEHKLNOORTU ROUND THE CLOCK
CCDEIINNNOOST DISCONNECTION
CCDEIINNOORST DISCONCERTION
CCDEIMNOORSTU SEMICONDUCTOR
CCDEINNOOSSSU SECOND COUSINS
CCDGIIMNNOSTU MISCONDUCTING
CCDNNNOOORSTU NONCONDUCTORS
CCEEEEEFFNRSV EFFERVESCENCE
CCEEEEFFLNORS EFFLORESCENCE
CCEEEEHIKNRSV NECKERCHIEVES
CCEEEEIRRSSTV SECRET SERVICE
CCEEEFFIOSTTV COST-EFFECTIVE
CCEEEFILNNORS INFLORESCENCE
CCEEEFILORRRT FERROELECTRIC
CCEEEFNOORRRT FERROCONCRETE
CCEEEHIIMNPSY CHIMNEYPIECES
CCEEEHMOOPRRT CHEMORECEPTOR
CCEEEIIILOPRTZ PIEZOELECTRIC
CCEEEIIMNNRSS REMINISCENCES
CCEEEIINNNNOV INCONVENIENCE
CCEEEILMNNORT RECONCILEMENT
CCEEEILMORRTT ELECTROMETRIC
CCEEEIMNORRTX CONCRETE MIXER
CCEEEINNNOQSU INCONSEQUENCE
CCEEEINNRRRTU INTERCURRENCE
CCEEEMMMNNOST COMMENCEMENTS
CCEEFFIIINSSU SUFFICIENCIES
CCEEFFIILOOPR POLICE OFFICER
CCEEFHIIJSSTU CHIEF JUSTICES
CCEEFINNOORST CONFECTIONERS
CCEEFINNOORTY CONFECTIONERY
CCEEGHIINOSTZ SCHIZOGENETIC
CCEEGHINOPSTY PSYCHOGENETIC
CCEEGIINNNOST CONTINGENCIES
CCEEGIINORTTY EGOCENTRICITY
CCEEGILNORTTU ELECTROCUTING
CCEEHIILLOPRT ELECTROPHILIC
CCEEHILNOOPRT ELECTROPHONIC
CCEEHILOOPRTT PHOTOELECTRIC
CCEEHILOOPRTU HEROIC COUPLET
CCEEHIMMNOOOS HOME ECONOMICS
CCEEHIMNNORRY CHIMNEY CORNER
CCEEHLMOORSSU COLOUR SCHEMES
CCEEHMMOORRRU MERCUROCHROME

CCEEIIIORRSTV OVERCRITICISE
CCEEIIIORRTVZ OVERCRITICIZE
CCEEIIJOPSTTU POETIC JUSTICE
CCEEIILNOORST ISOELECTRONIC
CCEEIINNOSSST CONSISTENCIES
CCEEIILLNOORST RECOLLECTIONS
CCEEIILNOORTTU ELECTROCUTION
CCEEILNOSSSUV OCCLUSIVENESS
CCEEILNOSTUVY CONSECUTIVELY
CCEEIMOPRRSTT SPECTROMETRIC
CCEEINNOOPPRT PRECONCEPTION
CCEEINNORRSST INCORRECTNESS
CCEEINOOPRRUW OWNER-OCCUPIER
CCEENNOOOVVXX CONVEXO-CONVEX
CCEEOOPPRSSST SPECTROSCOPES
CCEFFIIINNSUY INSUFFICIENCY
CCEFIILMNORUX CIRCUMFLEXION
CCEFILNOOSSSU SELF-CONSCIOUS
CCEGHIIKNNPRS SPRING CHICKEN
CCEGIIIMNNOSV MISCONCEIVING
CCEGIILLNNORY RECONCILINGLY
CCEGIILNNRRTU TURNING CIRCLE
CCEGIILNOPRSS CLOSING PRICES
CCEGIIMNNRTUV CIRCUMVENTING
CCEHHIINOPRSZ SCHIZOPHRENIC
CCEHHIMOOPRRS CHROMOSPHERIC
CCEHIIKNOPSTY PSYCHOKINETIC
CCEHILMNOORTY CHLOROMYCETIN
CCEHIMOPRSSTY PSYCHOMETRICS
CCEHIMORSTTYY CYTOCHEMISTRY
CCEHIOOPRRSTU URETHROSCOPIC
CCEHIORSSSSTT CROSS-STITCHES
CCEHMOOPSTUYY PHYCOMYCETOUS
CCEIIILLOSTTV COLLETIVISTIC
CCEIIMNNOOPST MISCONCEPTION
CCEIIMNNORTUV CIRCUMVENTION
CCEIIMNOOSSSU SEMICONSCIOUS
CCEIINNNOSSTY INCONSISTENCY
CCEIINNOOSSTU CONSCIENTIOUS
CCEIKKKLLOORW LIKE CLOCKWORK
CCEILNNOOORSW CROWN COLONIES
CCEIMMOOPRRTU MICROCOMPUTER
CCEINNOOPRRST PRINCE CONSORT
CCEINNOOSSSSU CONSCIOUSNESS
CCEINNOPRRSSW CROWN PRINCESS
CCEINOORSSSST CROSS-SECTIONS
CCENNNNOORRTU NONCONCURRENT
CCENOORRRSTTU RECONSTRUCTOR
CCENORRRSSSTU CROSSCURRENTS
CCGHILNOOOSST CONCHOLOGISTS
CCGHINOOPSSTY PSYCHOGNOSTIC
CCGIIKNNOOPTT COTTON-PICKING
CCGIINORRSSSS CRISSCROSSING
CCHHIILOPPRSY PSYCHROPHILIC

CCHHIOPPSSSYY PSYCHOPHYSICS
CCHIINNORSSTY SYNCHRONISTIC
CCHIIORRSSTTU SHORT CIRCUITS
CCHILMOOPTTYY LYMPHOCYTOTIC
CCIINNOOPSSUU INCONSPICUOUS
CCIINNOORSSTT CONSTRICTIONS
CCILMOORSSTTY MOTORCYCLISTS
CCILNNOOSSUUY UNCONSCIOUSLY
CCILNOOPSSUUY CONSPICUOUSLY
CCINNOORSSTTU CONSTRUCTIONS
CCINNOORSTUUY COUNTRY COUSIN
CDDDEEEINNSSU UNDECIDEDNESS
CDDEEEEENNPRTU UNPRECEDENTED
CDDEEEGNOSSSU SECOND-GUESSED
CDDEEEHIORRTT OTHER-DIRECTED
CDDEEIIILLNORS ILL-CONSIDERED
CDDEEIINNOORT RECONDITIONED
CDDEEIKLMNNOS CONDENSED MILK
CDDEHHILOORRY HYDROCHLORIDE
CDDEHILLMOOSS MIDDLE SCHOOLS
CDDEHLNORSTUU THUNDERCLOUDS
CDDEIIILNNPSU UNDISCIPLINED
CDDEIINNNOOTU UNCONDITIONED
CDDEILMOOPSSY DISCOMPOSEDLY
CDDGILLLMNOOY MOLLYCODDLING
CDDIIMMOOOSSU DISCOMMODIOUS
CDEEEEEHMMNRT CREME DE MENTHE
CDEEEEFILPSTV SELF-DECEPTIVE
CDEEEEFINSSTV DEFECTIVENESS
CDEEEEHNORRRT THREE-CORNERED
CDEEEEIINNPRX INEXPERIENCED
CDEEEEINNPRUX UNEXPERIENCED
CDEEEEINPSSTV DECEPTIVENESS
CDEEEEIQRSTUZ CREDIT SQUEEZE
CDEEEFFLNOSSS SELF-CONFESSED
CDEEEFHILRSST CHESTERFIELDS
CDEEEFILNNSST INFLECTEDNESS
CDEEEFILNOPST SELF-DECEPTION
CDEEEFILNSSTU DECEITFULNESS
CDEEEFINORTTU COUNTERFEITED
CDEEEFORRRRSS CROSS-REFERRED
CDEEEGHINOPST PIGEON-CHESTED
CDEEEGIIKNNSV KING'S EVIDENCE
CDEEEGIKLNRSS SINGLE-DECKERS
CDEEEIIILNNQSU DELINQUENCIES
CDEEEIINNRRSV DINNER SERVICE
CDEEEIINPRSTV VICE PRESIDENT
CDEEEIKMPQRTU QUICK-TEMPERED
CDEEEIMNORSTT MINE DETECTORS
CDEEEIMOPRSSV DECOMPRESSIVE
CDEEEINNORSST RECONDITENESS
CDEEEINSSSTUV SEDUCTIVENESS
CDEEFFHILOORS OFFICEHOLDERS
CDEEFFIILLNST SELF-INFLICTED

CDEEFFILNNOST SELF-CONFIDENT
CDEEFIIIKLMRT CERTIFIED MILK
CDEEFIIILMRSS MID-LIFE CRISES
CDEEFIILNSTUV SELF-INDUCTIVE
CDEEFILPRSSTU DISRESPECTFUL
CDEEFINNOORTV OVERCONFIDENT
CDEEGGHIINPTW PITCHING WEDGE
CDEEGHIMNNOPR COMPREHENDING
CDEEGIINNORRS RECONSIDERING
CDEEGIKNOPRRS PECKING ORDERS
CDEEGIMNOPRSS DECOMPRESSING
CDEEGINNORSTU COUNTERSIGNED
CDEEGLOORSTUX DEXTROGLUCOSE
CDEEHIINOPRTY DRYOPITHECINE
CDEEHILLNSSSS CHILDLESSNESS
CDEEIIIMNRSTT DETERMINISTIC
CDEEIIIMOSSTT DOMESTICITIES
CDEEIIINNSSTV DISINCENTIVES
CDEEIILNOPRST PREDILECTIONS
CDEEIILNOSSSU DELICIOUSNESS
CDEEIILPRSTVY DESCRIPTIVELY
CDEEIIMNORSTT DENSITOMETRIC
CDEEIINNOORRT RECONDITIONER
CDEEIIORSSSTU DISCOURTESIES
CDEEIJNPRRSUU JURISPRUDENCE
CDEEILNNOOPRS SCOLOPENDRINE
CDEEIILRSTTUVY DESTRUCTIVELY
CDEEIMNOOPRSS DECOMPRESSION
CDEEINOOPRSTU COUNTERPOISED
CDEEINORSTTTU RECONSTITUTED
CDEEIOPPRRSST ESPRIT DE CORPS
CDEEKKLNRSTUU KNUCKLE-DUSTER
CDEENNOOPRRST CORRESPONDENT
CDEENNOOPRSST CO-RESPONDENTS
CDEENNRRRSTUU UNDERCURRENTS
CDEEORRRSSSSS CROSS-DRESSERS
CDEFHINNORSWW FRENCH WINDOWS
CDEFIIIILMRSS MID-LIFE CRISIS
CDEFIILNNOSTU SELF-INDUCTION
CDEFOOOOPRRSS FOOD PROCESSOR
CDEGHHILOORY HIGHLY COLORED
CDEGHHNOOSTTU SECOND THOUGHT
CDEGIIMOOOPSS SIGMOIDOSCOPE
CDEGIINNNOSTT DISCONTENTING
CDEGIKNNNORUW UNCROWNED KING
CDEGILLNNOORT DECONTROLLING
CDEGILNNOOORY ENDOCRINOLOGY
CDEGINNOOPRRS CORRESPONDING
CDEGINORRSSSS CROSS-DRESSING
CDEHHIOOORRST RHODOCHROSITE
CDEHIIIOPRSTY SPHEROIDICITY
CDEHIIKMNSTTU STICK-IN-THE-MUD
CDEHIIKNORSTY HYDROKINETICS
CDEHIIMNOPRRU PERICHONDRIUM

CDEHIIOOOPPRT PHOTOPERIODIC
CDEHIIOPPRTTY PTERIDOPHYTIC
CDEHIIOPRRSST DIRECTORSHIPS
CDEHILLOOOSST OLD SCHOOL TIES
CDEHIMOOPPRSU PSEUDOMORPHIC
CDEHIMOORTTYY THYROIDECTOMY
CDEHKNRRSTTUU THUNDERSTRUCK
CDEIIIINNSTTV INDISTINCTIVE
CDEIIILNSTTVY DISTINCTIVELY
CDEIIIMPRSSTV DESCRIPTIVISM
CDEIIINNORSST INDISCRETIONS
CDEIIJNOSSSUU JUDICIOUSNESS
CDEIIMNOOOPST DECOMPOSITION
CDEIINNOOPRST PRECONDITIONS
CDEIINOPRTUWW PICTURE WINDOW
CDEILLMOORTUU MULTICOLOURED
CDEILLNORSUUY INCREDULOUSLY
CDEILMNOOPSUY COMPENDIOUSLY
CDEILNORSSSUU LUDICROUSNESS
CDEINNOOPRTUV NONPRODUCTIVE
CDEINOOPRRSTU REPRODUCTIONS
CDEINOORSSTTU DISCOUNT STORE
CDELLNOOOPTYY POLYCOTYLEDON
CDELMNNOOOOTY MONOCOTYLEDON
CDEOOOPRRRSSW WORD PROCESSOR
CDFGILNOORSTY FLYING DOCTORS
CDFIIMNOORSTY DISCONFORMITY
CDGGIKLLNSUUY UGLY DUCKLINGS
CDGIIINNNOSTU DISCONTINUING
CDGIIMOOOPSSY SIGMOIDOSCOPY
CDGIKLNOOSSTU DUCKING STOOLS
CDHIIMNNOOORT MITOCHONDRION
CDIIIJLNOSUUY INJUDICIOUSLY
CDIIINNOSTTUY DISCONTINUITY
CDIINNOORSTTU INTRODUCTIONS
CDIINNOOSSTUU DISCONTINUOUS
CEEEEEILNORRT ELECTIONEERER
CEEEEFFILPRTT PELTIER EFFECT
CEEEEFFINSSTV EFFECTIVENESS
CEEEEFLPRRTTT LETTER-PERFECT
CEEEEFMNNNORRT RE-ENFORCEMENT
CEEEEGHINORTT HETEROGENETIC
CEEEEGIIMNNRS ÉMINENCE GRISE
CEEEEHLNRSSSS CHEERLESSNESS
CEEEEIKKPRSTW WICKET KEEPERS
CEEEEILNSSSTV SELECTIVENESS
CEEEEIMNNPRSU SUPEREMINENCE
CEEEEINNPRSUV SUPERVENIENCE
CEEEEINRSSSSV RECESSIVENESS
CEEEEINRSSSTV SECRETIVENESS
CEEEEINSSSSVX EXCESSIVENESS
CEEEEIOPRTTVX EXTEROCEPTIVE
CEEEEJNNRSTUV REJUVENESCENT
CEEEFFIILNTVY INEFFECTIVELY

CEEEFFPRRTTUU FUTURE PERFECT
CEEEFGHIIOPST PIECES OF EIGHT
CEEEFHINRSSST SCENESHIFTERS
CEEEFIINNSSTV INFECTIVENESS
CEEEFIMNNORRT REINFORCEMENT
CEEEFINORRTTU COUNTERFEITER
CEEEFNOORSTUV VOTE OF CENSURE
CEEEGGINORRTU GEIGER COUNTER
CEEEGHIKLNNRS GELSENKIRCHEN
CEEEGHILLNOPT PHELLOGENETIC
CEEEGIIILNNRV CIVIL ENGINEER
CEEEGIIKNNRTY KINETIC ENERGY
CEEEHIILNNSTT LIECHTENSTEIN
CEEEHILLLMOSU HEMICELLULOSE
CEEEHILLOPRST ELECTROPHILES
CEEEHIMNOPRSV COMPREHENSIVE
CEEEHIMNPSSWY CHIMNEYSWEEPS
CEEEHLNNOSTTU LUNCHEONETTES
CEEEHLNORSSSU LECHEROUSNESS
CEEEHNSSTTTUW SWEET CHESTNUT
CEEEIIMNNRTTT INTERMITTENCE
CEEEIINOPRTTV INTEROCEPTIVE
CEEEILMMORRST ELECTROMERISM
CEEEILMNRSSSS MERCILESSNESS
CEEEILMOORTTV ELECTROMOTIVE
CEEEILNOSSSSV VOICELESSNESS
CEEEILNPRSSSS PRICELESSNESS
CEEEILNSSSSUV SECLUSIVENESS
CEEEILNSSSUVX EXCLUSIVENESS
CEEEINRSSSUVX EXCURSIVENESS
CEEEIOPRRSTTV RETROSPECTIVE
CEEELNNOQSSUU QUEEN'S COUNSEL
CEEEOPRRRSSSV PROCESS-SERVER
CEEFFFGIINOOR FOREIGN OFFICE
CEEFFIIILNNTY INEFFICIENTLY
CEEFFIOPRSTTY PETTY OFFICERS
CEEFGILNNOSTU GENUFLECTIONS
CEEFIIKLNORSU NICKELIFEROUS
CEEFIIMNOPRST IMPERFECTIONS,
  PERFECTIONISM
CEEFIINOPRSST FRONTISPIECES
CEEFIINOPRSTT PERFECTIONIST
CEEFINOORSSSU FEROCIOUSNESS
CEEFLLORRSUUY RESOURCEFULLY
CEEGHIINOSSSZ SCHIZOGENESIS
CEEGHIIRRSTUW CRUISERWEIGHT
CEEGHIMNOOPRT MORPHOGENETIC
CEEGHINOPSSSY PSYCHOGENESIS
CEEGHINORTTUW COUNTERWEIGHT
CEEGHLNNOOTWY NEW TECHNOLOGY
CEEGIIMMNNOTU IMMUNOGENETIC
CEEGIKLLNOPSS GLOCKENSPIELS
CEEGILLNORSSV LEVEL CROSSING
CEEGILMMNNOPT COMPLEMENTING

CEEGMNOORRSST COSTERMONGERS
CEEHHIMMORSTT THERMOCHEMIST
CEEHHIMOOPRRT HETEROMORPHIC
CEEHHIOOPRRTT HETEROTROPHIC
CEEHHLOORSSST CLOTHESHORSES
CEEHHNORSSTTU HORSE CHESTNUT
CEEHIMNNOOPRS COMPREHENSION
CEEHIMNNORSTT ETHNOCENTRISM
CEEHINNNNPPRSY PENNY-PINCHERS
CEEHIOPPPRRST PRECEPTORSHIP
CEEHIOPRSTTTW WITH RESPECT TO
CEEHLNOOOOPRTT PHOTOELECTRON
CEEHHLOORRSSTU ELECTROPHORUS
CEEHNOORSSTTW STONE THE CROWS
CEEHOOOOPPRRTT PHOTORECEPTOR
CEEIIILMRSSSU CRUISE MISSILE
CEEIIIMMPRSTT METEMPIRICIST
CEEIIINNORSST SENIOR CITISEN
CEEIIINNORSTZ SENIOR CITIZEN
CEEIIJNNORSTT INTERJECTIONS
CEEIILMOPTTVY COMPETITIVELY
CEEIILRRSTTVY RESTRICTIVELY
CEEIIMNOPTTUV UNCOMPETITIVE
CEEIIMPPRSSTV PERSPECTIVISM
CEEIINNOPRSTT INTERCEPTIONS
CEEIINNORSSST INTERCESSIONS
CEEIINNORSSTT INTERSECTIONS
CEEIINOPRSSTT RECEPTIONISTS
CEEIINOPRSTTV INTROSPECTIVE
CEEIINOSSSSST SECESSIONISTS
CEEIKLNNOSTUU KINETONUCLEUS
CEEILMNNOPTTY INCOMPETENTLY
CEEILMNOORSUY CEREMONIOUSLY
CEEILNNOOPRTU NUCLEOPROTEIN
CEEILNOOPRRST SCLEROPROTEIN
CEEILNOSSSTUY NECESSITOUSLY
CEEILOOPRSTTU TELEUTOSPORIC
CEEILPQRSTUUY PICTURESQUELY
CEEIMNNOORSUU UNCEREMONIOUS
CEEIMNOOOPRRT RECEPTION ROOM
CEEINNORSTTTU RECONSTITUENT
CEEINOOPRRSTT RETROSPECTION
CEEINOOPRSSTU COUNTERPOISES,
  PRECIOUS STONE
CEEINOORRSSSV CORROSIVENESS
CEEINOORRSSTV CONTROVERSIES
CEEINOPRRSSSU REPERCUSSIONS
CEEINORRRSSTU RESURRECTIONS
CEEINOSSSSTUV VISCOUNTESSES
CEEIOOPRSSSTT STEREOSCOPIST
CEELLNOORSSSS COLORLESSNESS
CEELMNOOORRTT REMOTE CONTROL
CEELPQRSSTUUU SCULPTURESQUE
CEEMMNNOOPTUY PNEUMONECTOMY

CEEMNNNOOPRTU PRONOUNCEMENT
CEENNNOOQRSSTU QUEENS CONSORT
CEENNOORRSTTU COUNTERTENORS
CEENOORSSSTUU COURTEOUSNESS
CEFFFGIILNORY FLYING OFFICER
CEFFIILOOPRST PILOT OFFICERS
CEFFIINOOSSSU OFFICIOUSNESS
CEFGIIKLNPSTY FLYING PICKETS
CEFHIMMOORRRU FERROCHROMIUM
CEFHLLLOOOSSW SCHOOLFELLOWS
CEFIINNNOOSTU NONINFECTIOUS
CEFILNOPRRTUY PERFUNCTORILY
CEFKKLOORRSSW CLERKS OF WORKS
CEGGGHLNOOOORY GEOCHRONOLOGY
CEGHHIILOPRSY HIEROGLYPHICS
CEGHIIILLNNPS SPINE-CHILLING
CEGHIINNNNPPY PENNY-PINCHING
CEGHIKNOORRSS ROCKING HORSES
CEGHILNOOSSTT TECHNOLOGISTS
CEGHINNOOSTUU COUNTINGHOUSE
CEGHOPRRSSUYY PSYCHOSURGERY
CEGIIILNOORST CORELIGIONIST
CEGIIINNORSTU INCONGRUITIES
CEGIIKLLMNRSY MERCY KILLINGS
CEGIILMMNNOPT COMPLIMENTING
CEGIILMNORSYY SYRINGOMYELIC
CEGIILNNORRTY NITROGLYCERIN
CEGIILNOOSSTT SCIENTOLOGIST
CEGIIMMNNOSTU TIME-CONSUMING
CEGIIMNOORRTT TRIGONOMETRIC
CEGIIMNOPRTUV MOVING PICTURE
CEGIIMNOPRTUZ COMPUTERIZING
CEGIINNNOORRT RECONNOITRING
CEGIKLNNOSSSU KING'S COUNSELS
CEGILMMOORSTY MYRMECOLOGIST
CEGIMNNNNOOST ON CONSIGNMENT
CEGINNNOORSTW CONNING TOWERS
CEGINPRSSSTTU PRESS CUTTINGS
CEGINRRRSTTUU RESTRUCTURING
CEHHIIMMOOORT HOMOIOTHERMIC
CEHHIIMOOPRRT THERIOMORPHIC
CEHHOOPRTTTTU PUT TO THE TORCH
CEHHOOPTTTTUU PUT TO THE TOUCH
CEHIIKNOPSSSY PSYCHOKINESIS
CEHIILMOOPPTY LYMPHOPOIETIC
CEHIILMOSSUVY MISCHIEVOUSLY
CEHIILNOOPSST SIPHONOSTELIC
CEHIIMMOOORST HOMOEROTICISM
CEHIIMNOOPRST CHEMISORPTION
CEHIIMOORSTTY STOICHIOMETRY
CEHIINOPPRSST INSPECTORSHIP
CEHIMMMNOOTUY COMMUNITY
  HOME
CEHIMNOOOPRRT CHROMOPROTEIN

CEHLMMOORSSSU SUMMER SCHOOLS
CEHLNOORRSSUY NURSERY SCHOOL
CEHMNOORRTTUY MOTHER COUNTRY
CEHMOOOOPPRST PHOTOCOMPOSER
CEIIILNNSTTVY INSTINCTIVELY
CEIIJNOOPRSTT PROJECTIONIST
CEIIKLSSSTWZZ SWIZZLE STICKS
CEIIKRRSSSTUY SECURITY RISKS
CEIILLLNOOSTV VIOLONCELLIST
CEIILMNOPSUUY IMPECUNIOUSLY
CEIILNNOORTTU INTERLOCUTION
CEIILNRSTTUVY INSTRUCTIVELY
CEIILOOPPRSTW POWER POLITICS
CEIILOPPRSTUY PRECIPITOUSLY
CEIILRRSSTTUU SERICULTURIST
CEIIMMNOORSSS COMMISSIONERS
CEIIMMNOPRSTU MINICOMPUTERS
CEIIMNNORRTTU MICRONUTRIENT
CEIIMNOOOPRST RECOMPOSITION
CEIIMNOOPRSTT PROTECTIONISM
CEIIMNOOPRTTU MOTION PICTURE
CEIINNOOPRSTT INTROSPECTION
CEIINNORRSSTU INSURRECTIONS
CEIINOOPRSSTT RETINOSCOPIST
CEIINOOPRSTTT PROTECTIONIST
CEIINOORSSTUV INSECTIVOROUS
CEIINOPPRRSST PRESCRIPTIONS
CEIINOPRSSSTU PERCUSSIONIST
CEIIPRRRSSTTW SCRIPTWRITERS
CEILLMNOOSTTY TONSILLECTOMY
CEILMNNOOOSSU MONONUCLEOSIS
CEILMNOORSTUY COTERMINOUSLY
CEILNNOOSTTUY CONTENTIOUSLY
CEILNOORRSTTU INTERLOCUTORS
CEILNOORRTTUY INTERLOCUTORY
CEINNNOOSSSUU INNOCUOUSNESS
CEINNOOPRSTTU COUNTERPOINTS
CEINOOQRSSSTU CROSS-QUESTION
CEIOOOPPPRRRT PROPRIOCEPTOR
CELLNOOSSUUVV CONVOLVULUSES
CELOOOPRRSSTU POSTER COLOURS
CEMOOOORRSSTT MOTOR SCOOTERS
CEOOPPRRSSSSU CROSS-PURPOSES
CFFIKKLORRTTU FORKLIFT TRUCK
CFGHIILLNNNUY UNFLINCHINGLY
CFGHILMNOOORR CHLOROFORMING
CFGILLNOORSUY FLYING COLOURS
CFHINNORTTTUU TRUTH-FUNCTION
CFIMMNNNOOORS NONCONFORMISM
CFIMNNNOOORST NONCONFORMIST
CFIMNNNOOORTY NONCONFORMITY
CGGHHINOOOPUW WHOOPING COUGH
CGGILNNOORRWY CROWNING GLORY
CGHHIILOOSTTY ICHTHYOLOGIST

CGHIIKNOOSSTT SHOOTING STICK
CGHIILOORSSTT CHRISTOLOGIST,
TRICHOLOGISTS
CGHIINNNORSYZ SYNCHRONIZING
CGHILOOPSSSTY PSYCHOLOGISTS
CGIIIKNNOPSTT STICKING POINT
CGIIILLOOOPST OLIGOPOLISTIC
CGIIILMNOORST CRIMINOLOGIST
CGIIILNOOSSTU SOCIOLINGUIST
CGIIIMMNNOOSS COMMISSIONING
CGIIINPRRSTTW SCRIPTWRITING
CGIILOOOSSTTX TOXICOLOGISTS
CGIIMNNORSSTU MISCONSTRUING
CGILNNOORSUUY INCONGRUOUSLY
CHHIOOOORSSTTU ORTHOSTICHOUS
CHHIOOPRSSTYY PSYCHOHISTORY
CHIIILOOPRSST SOLICITORSHIP
CHIIOOOPRRSTT PROTOHISTORIC
CHIJLNOOORSSU JUNIOR SCHOOLS
CHILMMNNOOOUY HOLY
COMMUNION
CHILMOOPSSTYY LYMPHOCYTOSIS
CHILOOPSSSTUY PHYSOCLISTOUS
CIIIIMPRSTTV PRIMITIVISTIC
CIIIILLNOSSTU ILLUSIONISTIC
CIIILNRSTTUUV VINICULTURIST
CIILLNOPSTUUY PUNCTILIOUSLY
CIILMMOOOPSST COSMOPOLITISM
CIIMNNOOOPSST MONOPSONISTIC
CIINNOOORSTTT CONTORTIONIST
CIINNOOSSTTTU CONSTITUTIONS
CIINOOPPRRSST PROSCRIPTIONS
CIINOOPPRSTTU OPPORTUNISTIC
CIINOOPRRSTTU CORRUPTIONIST
CILMOOPRSSUUY PROMISCUOUSLY
DDDEEGGILNNOW GOLDEN WEDDING
DDDEHNNOOORRS RHODODENDRONS
DDEEEEIMNPRRT PREDETERMINED
DDEEEEELLLOPVW WELL-DEVELOPED
DDEEEEELOOPRVV OVERDEVELOPED
DDEEEGHINORSY DEHYDROGENISE
DDEEEGHINORYZ DEHYDROGENIZE
DDEEEIIMPRRST RED SPIDER MITE
DDEEEIINRSSTT DISINTERESTED
DDEEEIILMNRSTW MIDDLE WESTERN
DDEEEIILNNNPTY INDEPENDENTLY
DDEEEEINNPRSTU SUPERINTENDED
DDEEELMNOPRUY UNDEREMPLOYED
DDEEFGIILMNRS MIDDLE FINGERS
DDEEFNNNOSSUU UNFOUNDEDNESS
DDEEGHHINRTUW HUNDREDWEIGHT
DDEEGHIILMSTW MIDDLEWEIGHTS
DDEEGHIINSTWW WHITE WEDDINGS
DDEEGIIILMSSU GUIDED MISSILE

DDEEGIILNRSVW SILVER WEDDING
DDEEHILNOOTWY DYED-IN-THE-WOOL
DDEEIIKMNRRST KIDDERMINSTER
DDEEIIMNSSTTW DIM-WITTEDNESS
DDEEINORRSSWW WINDOW-DRESSER
DDEFINOOPRRUV UNPROVIDED FOR
DDEGHHIOORRSU RIDE ROUGHSHOD
DDEGHIIINSSTU DISTINGUISHED
DDEGHLMOOORUY GOOD-
    HUMOREDLY
DDEGINNRSTUUY UNDERSTUDYING
DDEGLNNOOOOTY ENDODONTOLOGY
DDEHIIKNOORZZ ORDZHONIKIDZE
DDEHINOOPPSWW WINDOW-SHOPPED
DDEIIIILMSSTU DISSIMILITUDE
DDEIIIILLNOSSU DISILLUSIONED
DDEIMNOORSSTU MISUNDERSTOOD
DDEMNNOORSSWY DOWN'S
    SYNDROME
DEEEEFFGIRRRZ FRIDGE-FREEZER
DEEEEFGGINNRR GREEN-FINGERED
DEEEEFINNSSSV DEFENSIVENESS
DEEEEGIILNNSS DIESEL ENGINES
DEEEEHHPRSSSS SHEPHERDESSES
DEEEEIMNPRRRT PREDETERMINER
DEEEELLPRRSVW WELL-PRESERVED
DEEEELMNOPRTV REDEVELOPMENT
DEEEENNPRRSTU UNREPRESENTED
DEEEENPRRSSTV PERVERTEDNESS
DEEEFGJMNORTU FOREJUDGEMENT
DEEEFGKLLNOSW SELF-KNOWLEDGE
DEEEFGKLNOORW FOREKNOWLEDGE
DEEEFHHIORRRS HEREFORDSHIRE
DEEEFHNOORRST FORESHORTENED
DEEEFIILMPRSS SEMPER FIDELIS
DEEEFILLNSTVY SELF-EVIDENTLY
DEEEFLLLOPPRS SELF-PROPELLED
DEEEFLNORSSUW SUNFLOWER SEED
DEEEFLOPSSSSS SELF-POSSESSED
DEEEGGHILNPST SIGN THE PLEDGE
DEEEGHILNNNTU UNENLIGHTENED
DEEEGIINNRRSV ENGINE DRIVERS
DEEEGJMNPRSTU PREJUDGEMENTS
DEEEHLMNNOOWY HONEYDEW
    MELON
DEEEHMOPRRSTT SHORT-TEMPERED
DEEEILLORSTUY DELETERIOUSLY
DEEEINOQSTUVX VEXED QUESTION
DEEEKLMMRRTTU KETTLEDRUMMER
DEEELLNNORRSU ENROLLED NURSE
DEEELLNNPRSTY RESPLENDENTLY
DEEENOPRRSUUX UNDEREXPOSURE
DEEENORSSSTUX DEXTEROUSNESS
DEEFFFINORRST FIRST OFFENDER

DEEFFIILNNRTY INDIFFERENTLY
DEEFFLNNRSSUU UNRUFFLEDNESS
DEEFFOORSTUWW SWEET WOODRUFF
DEEFGGHIILNRT LIGHT-FINGERED
DEEFGIIMNRSTU DISFIGUREMENT
DEEFGIIMNNPRRT FINGERPRINTED
DEEFGILLNNSTU SELF-INDULGENT
DEEFHHIORRRST HERTFORDSHIRE
DEEFILNOPRSSU SPLENDIFEROUS
DEEFLNNORSSUW WONDERFULNESS
DEEGHHIPRRSSU HIGH-PRESSURED
DEEGHIINNSSTW WINDING SHEETS
DEEGHILLNOSUW DWELLING HOUSE
DEEGHILMOOOST METHODOLOGIES
DEEGIIINNSSTZ DESENSITIZING
DEEGIJMMNSSTU MISJUDGEMENTS
DEEGILMNOOSTY SEDIMENTOLOGY
DEEGILNORSTUV SILVER-TONGUED
DEEGIMNNNOPSY SPENDING MONEY
DEEGINNOPRSUX UNDEREXPOSING
DEEGINNORSTTW DOWNING STREET
DEEHHIINNOSSS HOIDENISHNESS
DEEHHINNOSSSY HOYDENISHNESS
DEEHHNORRSTUW THUNDERSHOWER
DEEHIINNPRSTU INDENTURESHIP
DEEIIIMMNNRST INDETERMINISM
DEEIIIMMNNRSTT INDETERMINIST
DEEIIINOQRSTU REQUISITIONED
DEEIIILLNORSSS SOLDIERLINESS
DEEIIILMNNOSSS DIMENSIONLESS
DEEIIILNORSSSU DELIRIOUSNESS
DEEIIILOPPRSTT LEPIDOPTERIST
DEEIIILOPSTUXY EXPEDITIOUSLY
DEEIIMNNRSSTT DISINTERMENTS
DEEIIMNNSSTTV DISINVESTMENT
DEEIIMNOORSST ENDOMETRIOSIS
DEEIIMOORRSTU DEMERITORIOUS
DEEIINOSSSSTU SEDITIOUSNESS
DEEIILMNOOSSSU MELODIOUSNESS
DEEIILNNOSTTUY TENDENTIOUSLY
DEEIILNORSSSTU DESULTORINESS
DEEIILNOSSSSTU DISSOLUTENESS
DEEIILOOPPRSTU LEPIDOPTEROUS
DEEIIMNOSSSTUW WOMEN'S STUDIES
DEEIINNPRRTTUU UNINTERRUPTED
DEELLOPPRSTUW WELL-SUPPORTED
DEELNNOSSSSSU SOUNDLESSNESS
DEEMNORRSSSUU MURDEROUSNESS
DEEMOOOOPRRSST DEPRESSOMOTOR
DEENNOOPRSSSU PONDEROUSNESS
DEENOOPRSSSST DESSERTSPOONS
DEFFHIRSSSTTU STUFFED SHIRTS
DEFFIIILNOOSV FIELD OF VISION
DEFHILMRRTTYY MERTHYR TYDFIL

DEFIILPRSTUUY SUPERFLUIDITY
DEFIMNNOOOSTU OUT OF ONE'S MIND
DEFINOOOPPRRST POINTS OF ORDER
DEGGHILNOOSSU LODGING HOUSES
DEGGIILNNORUV OVERINDULGING
DEGGINNORSSSW DRESSING GOWNS
DEGHHNOOORRTY ORTHOHYDROGEN
DEGHIIIINNRST DISINHERITING
DEGHIIINRSSTU DISTINGUISHER
DEGHILMOOOSTT METHODOLOGIST
DEGHIMNOOOSTT DO SOMETHING TO
DEGHMNOOOSTTU SMOOTH-TONGUED
DEGIIILNPSSTT SIDESPLITTING
DEGIILMNNNRUY UNDERMININGLY
DEGIILNNOORRS SOLDERING IRON
DEGIILNRSSSTY DISTRESSINGLY
DEGIILOOPRSTT PTERIDOLOGIST
DEGIINNNNPRSU UNDERPINNINGS
DEGIINOPSSSSS DISPOSSESSING
DEGIKNNOORRWW WONDER-WORKING
DEGIMNOORRSSS DRESSING ROOMS
DEGKNOORRSSTU GROUND STROKES
DEGMNOORRRSUY MERRY-GO-ROUNDS
DEHHIILOOPPSS PHILOSOPHISED
DEHHIILOOPPSZ PHILOSOPHIZED
DEHINOOPPRSWW WINDOW-SHOPPER
DEHMNORRSSTTU THUNDERSTORMS
DEIIILMNOOSTT DEMOLITIONIST
DEIIINNOSSSSU INSIDIOUSNESS
DEIIINNOSSSUV INVIDIOUSNESS
DEIIIOPSSSTTU UTI POSSIDETIS
DEIIILMNOPRTVY IMPROVIDENTLY
DEIINOOOPPRST PROPOSITIONED
DEIINOOPSSSSS DISPOSSESSION
DEILNNNOPRSSU SUN IN SPLENDOR
DEINNNOSSTTUU STUDENTS' UNION
DEIOOPRSSSSSY DISPOSSESSORY
DFGGHIILLNOOT FLOODLIGHTING
DFGHHIMOOOSST SMOOTH DOGFISH
DFGIINNOOOOPS FOOD POISONING
DFGINNOOOPRSU SOUNDPROOFING
DFIINOORSTTUU FORTITUDINOUS
DFILLRSSTTUUY DISTRUSTFULLY
DGGHINNNORTUU HUNTING GROUND
DGGINNOOPRRUV PROVING GROUND
DGLMNOOOOSSTU ODONTOGLOSSUM
DHIIIMMOOPRSS ISODIMORPHISM
DHIIMOOOPRSSU ISODIMORPHOUS
DIIIINNOOPSST INDISPOSITION
DIIIINOQSSSTU DISQUISITIONS
DIILMNOSTTUUU MULTITUDINOUS
DIILNORSSTUUY INDUSTRIOUSLY
DIINOOOPPRRST DISPROPORTION
DILNOOOPSSSUY ISOSPONDYLOUS

DLNOOOOPPRTTY POLYPROTODONT
EEEEFHILNSSSY FISH-EYE LENSES
EEEEFILNRSSVX REFLEXIVENESS
EEEEFILPRRRSV LIFE PRESERVER
EEEEFKLNOOPST KEEP TO ONESELF
EEEEFLNOOPSSX EXPOSE ONESELF
EEEEGHILNRSTW STEERING WHEEL
EEEEGHINORSST HETEROGENESIS
EEEEGHINORTTY HETEROGENEITY
EEEEGHNOORSTU HETEROGENEOUS
EEEEGNOPRRRSS REPRESSOR GENE
EEEEHKLLRRSTT HELTER-SKELTER
EEEEINNPSSSVX EXPENSIVENESS
EEEEINNRSSTTV RETENTIVENESS
EEEEINNSSSTVX EXTENSIVENESS
EEEELLNPSSSSS SLEEPLESSNESS
EEEELNNRSS$SV NERVELESSNESS
EEEELNNSSSSSS SENSELESSNESS
EEEELNOPRRSTT LETTER OPENERS
EEEELPRRSSSTT LETTERPRESSES
EEEENNPRRRSTU ENTREPRENEURS
EEEEORRSTTTTT TEETER-TOTTERS
EEEFFGILLLNOW FELLOW FEELING
EEEFFINNOSSSV OFFENSIVENESS
EEEFGILNNNSSU UNFEELINGNESS
EEEFGIMNPRRTU PREFIGUREMENT
EEEFGLNRRSSTU REGRETFULNESS
EEEFIILMMPRRS FILM PREMIERES
EEEFLLNORRTTU FORTUNE-TELLER
EEEFLNNRSSSTU RESENTFULNESS
EEEFLNOPRSSSU REPOSEFULNESS
EEEGGINORSSSU EGREGIOUSNESS
EEEGHILMNNNTT ENLIGHTENMENT
EEEGHILNNQSSU QUEEN'S ENGLISH
EEEGHILRSTTWW WELTERWEIGHTS
EEEGHIMNORSST THERMOGENESIS
EEEGHIMNOSSTU MEETINGHOUSES
EEEGIIMNNPRTX EXPERIMENTING
EEEGILLNNPRSS REPELLINGNESS
EEEGILLNSSSSU GUILELESSNESS
EEEGILNNORVWY OVERWEENINGLY
EEEGILNOORSTV VENEREOLOGIST
EEEGINOPRRSTW POWER STEERING
EEEGIORRRSSTV RETROGRESSIVE
EEEGNOQRSSSTU GROTESQUENESS
EEEHHIILNPRTW THREE-LINE WHIP
EEEHHNOOSSTTW SHOW ONE'S TEETH
EEEHIIILNNPPT IN THE PIPELINE
EEEHILLOSSTTT STILETTO HEELS
EEEHILMNNPRST REPLENISHMENT
EEEHILMOPRRTY PYRHELIOMETER
EEEHILMPPRSSX HERPES SIMPLEX
EEEHIMNNNOOPP EPIPHENOMENON
EEEHINNOSTTTX SIXTEENTH NOTE

EEEEHLLNOOPSTT TELEPHOTO LENS
EEEEHLMNOOSSSW WHOLESOMENESS
EEEEHLOPRSSTTW POTTER'S WHEELS
EEEEHMNNNORSTT ENTHRONEMENTS
EEEEHOOPRRSTTU HETEROPTEROUS
EEEIILLNRSSSU LEISURELINESS
EEEIILLNNPSVXY INEXPENSIVELY
EEEIINNNSSTVV INVENTIVENESS
EEEIINNSSSSTV SENSITIVENESS
EEEIINQSSSTUX EXQUISITENESS
EEEIINRSSSSTV RESISTIVENESS
EEEIIPQRRSSTU PREREQUISITES
EEEIILNNNPSSSS PENNILESSNESS
EEEILNNOSSSSS NOISELESSNESS
EEEILNNPSSSSS SPINELESSNESS
EEEILNOPSSSVX EXPLOSIVENESS
EEEILNPRSSSUV REPULSIVENESS
EEEIMNNORSSSV MONS VENERISES
EEEIMNNPRSSTT PRESENTIMENTS
EEEIMNOOPRTTT POTENTIOMETER
EEEIMOPRSSTUX TIME EXPOSURES
EEELLMORRSSSY REMORSELESSLY
EEELMOPPRRSTT TELEPROMPTERS
EEELNNOPSSSTU PLENTEOUSNESS
EEELNOPRSSSSW POWERLESSNESS
EEEMPRSSSTTXY EXPERT SYSTEMS
EEENNOORRSSSU ERRONEOUSNESS
EEFFGGHIIORTU FIGURE OF EIGHT
EEFFGLNORSSTU FORGETFULNESS
EEFFIILNNOSVY INOFFENSIVELY
EEFGHIILNRRST FREIGHTLINERS
EEFGHIILRSTTW WEIGHT LIFTERS
EEFGHIIPRRSST PRISEFIGHTERS
EEFGHIIPRRSTZ PRIZEFIGHTERS
EEFGHILORSSTU SELF-RIGHTEOUS
EEFGIILLNRSTT LITTLE FINGERS
EEFGIILNNRRTY INTERFERINGLY
EEFGIIMNNNRST INFRINGEMENTS
EEFGIINNOPRTZ FREEZING POINT
EEFGINNOORSST FRONTOGENESIS
EEFGINOORRRRT REIGN OF TERROR
EEFHHINOORSTT IN THE THROES OF
EEFHILNNSSSUU UNSELFISHNESS
EEFHILNSSSSST SHIFTLESSNESS
EEFHNNORRTTUU FORTUNE HUNTER
EEFIILLMNOSTU FEUILLETONISM
EEFIILLNOSTTU FEUILLETONIST
EEFILLNNPSSTU PLENTIFULNESS
EEFILNNOOSSSU FELONIOUSNESS
EEFILNRSSSSTU FRUITLESSNESS
EEGGHHHLOOOTW GO THE WHOLE
  HOG
EEGGHINNNRSTT STRENGTHENING
EEGGIJKOPRRYY JIGGERY-POKERY

EEGGINOOPPSST GOOSESTEPPING
EEGGINORRRSST RETROGRESSING
EEGHHIILOPSVX HIGH EXPLOSIVE
EEGHIILNNNPSW SPINNING WHEEL
EEGHIINNRSSTW WITHERINGNESS
EEGHIINRSSTUX EXTINGUISHERS
EEGHIKNOOSSTT SKEET SHOOTING
EEGHIKNRRRSTU HUNGER STRIKER
EEGHIKNRRSSTU HUNGER STRIKES
EEGHILNSSSSST SIGHTLESSNESS
EEGHILOOPRSTT HERPETOLOGIST
EEGHIMNOOPRSS MORPHOGENESIS
EEGHIMNORSTTT THERMOSETTING
EEGHINNOSSTTW SWEET NOTHINGS
EEGHINORSSSTU RIGHTEOUSNESS
EEGHIOORSSTYZ HETEROZYGOSIS
EEGHLLOOPRSST HOT-GOSPELLERS
EEGHLMNNOOOPY PHENOMENOLOGY
EEGHLMNOOOSUY HOMOGENEOUSLY
EEGHMNOORSTTU MOTHER TONGUES
EEGIIILLLNNTTY INTELLIGENTLY
EEGIIILLLNPPSS SLEEPING PILLS
EEGIILLNNNTTU UNINTELLIGENT
EEGIILMNOORST TERMINOLOGIES
EEGIILNNRSTTY INTERESTINGLY
EEGIILNORSSSU RELIGIOUSNESS
EEGIIMNOPRRTU PRIMOGENITURE
EEGIIMNOPRTXZ EXTEMPORIZING
EEGIINNPRRSST INTERSPERSING
EEGILLNNNRTUY UNRELENTINGLY
EEGILLNSSSSTU GUILTLESSNESS
EEGILLOOPSSST SPELEOLOGISTS
EEGILMNNPPSTU SUPPLEMENTING
EEGILMOOORSTT METEOROLOGIST
EEGILOPRRSSVY PROGRESSIVELY
EEGIMMNNORSTV MISGOVERNMENT
EEGINNNOSSSUU INGENUOUSNESS
EEGINNOPPSSTT STEPPING-STONE
EEGINOORRRSST RETROGRESSION
EEGINOPPRSSSS PREPOSSESSING
EEGINOPRRSTTU INTEREST GROUP
EEGINORSTTTUW TONGUE TWISTER
EEGOPPRRRSSUU PRESSURE GROUP
EEHHIILLLMNPS PHILHELLENISM
EEHHIMNNNOOPP PHI-PHENOMENON
EEHHMMNOOOOPPR MORPHOPHONEME
EEHIIMOOPSSTV PHOTOEMISSIVE
EEHILLOORSSTT TORTOISESHELL
EEHILMNRSSSST MIRTHLESSNESS
EEHILNNPSSTWY PENNY WHISTLES
EEHILNORSSSTU SOUTHERLINESS
EEHIMNOPTTTUU UP-TO-THE-MINUTE
EEHIMORSSSSTU HOUSEMISTRESS
EEHKNNOOORSTT ON TENTERHOOKS

EEHLMNORSSSSU HUMORLESSNESS
EEHLNORRSTTWY NORTHWESTERLY
EEHLNORSSSSTW WORTHLESSNESS
EEHLOORSSTTUY HETEROSTYLOUS
EEHLORSSTTUWY SOUTHWESTERLY
EEHMNOOOSSSTT TOOTHSOMENESS
EEHMNRRRSSUYY NURSERY RHYMES
EEHNORSSTTTWW WEST-NORTHWEST
EEHOOOOPRRSSTU HETEROSPOROUS
EEHOSSSTTTUWW WEST-SOUTHWEST
EEIIILNNSSTVY INSENSITIVELY
EEIIIMMNPRRST PRIME MINISTER
EEIIIMNPRSSTV PRIMITIVENESS
EEIIIMOPPRRST IMPROPRIETIES
EEIIINNSSTTUV INTUITIVENESS
EEIIINOQRRSTU REQUISITIONER
EEIIILLMNSSSST LIMITLESSNESS
EEIIILMNNPRTTY IMPERTINENTLY
EEIIILMNPSSSUV IMPULSIVENESS
EEIIILMOOSSTTY OSTEOMYELITIS
EEIIILNOORSTUV REVOLUTIONISE
EEIIILNOORTUVZ REVOLUTIONIZE
EEIIILNOQRSTUV VENTRILOQUISE
EEIIILNOQRTUVZ VENTRILOQUIZE
EEIIILOOPPSSTV POSITIVE POLES
EEIIMNOPRSSSU IMPERIOUSNESS
EEIIMNOPRSSSX EXPRESSIONISM
EEIIINNNORSTTV INTERVENTIONS
EEIIINNPRRSST INTERSPERSION
EEIIINOPRSSSTX EXPRESSIONIST
EEIILLMNOOSSTY EMOTIONLESSLY
EEIILLMOPRSTTU MULTIPLE STORE
EEIILLNOOPQRSU NOLLE PROSEQUI
EEIILMPPRSTUVY PRESUMPTIVELY
EEIILNNOPSSSST POINTLESSNESS
EEIILNNOSSTTUY SENTENTIOUSLY
EEIILNOPRSTTUY PRETENTIOUSLY
EEIILOPRRSSSTY PROSELYTISERS
EEIILOPRRSSTYZ PROSELYTIZERS
EEIMNNNOPRSST PROMINENTNESS
EEIMNNNOPRSSY MONEY-SPINNERS
EEIMNNORSSSUV VERMINOUSNESS
EEIMNOOPRSSTV PROMOTIVENESS
EEIMNOPSSSTUU IMPETUOUSNESS
EEIMOOPRRSSTT STEREOTROPISM
EEINNOPRSTTUU UNPRETENTIOUS
EEINOOPPRSSSS PREPOSSESSION
EEINOPPRRSSTU PRESSURE POINT
EEINOPPRSSSUV PURPOSIVENESS
EEKLMNOPSUYZZ MONKEY-PUZZLES
EEKNNOOPSSSTU OUTSPOKENNESS
EELLNOOPPPRYY POLYPROPYLENE
EELLOPPRSSSUY PURPOSELESSLY
EELMNORSSSTUU TREMULOUSNESS

EELMOPRRSSTTY STORMY PETRELS
EELMOPSSTTUUY TEMPESTUOUSLY
EELNOQRSSSUUU QUERULOUSNESS
EEMNNOOPPSSTT POSTPONEMENTS
EEMNORSSSTUVY NERVOUS SYSTEM
EENNOOPPRSSTU OPPORTUNENESS
EENNORSSSSTUU STRENUOUSNESS
EFFGGILNNORSU LONGSUFFERING
EFFGHILNRSSTU FRIGHTFULNESS
EFFIILOORSSSU FOSSILIFEROUS
EFFIILPPPRSTU STIFF UPPER LIP
EFGGHIIILNTTW WEIGHT LIFTING
EFGGHIIINPRST PRISEFIGHTING
EFGGHIIINPRTZ PRIZEFIGHTING
EFGGHIILNNRTY FRIGHTENINGLY
EFGGIINNORSSV FORGIVINGNESS
EFGHHLLOOTTUW WELL-THOUGHT-OF
EFGIILLNPSTYY SELF-PITYINGLY
EFGIKLNNOORWY FOREKNOWINGLY
EFHHIINOOPSST PHOTO FINISHES
EFHIOOPPRRSSS PROFESSORSHIP
EFHLNNOOPRSTY HORNS OF PLENTY
EFHMMNOORTTTU MOMENT OF
  TRUTH
EFHOOOOPPRTTTU PUT TO THE PROOF
EFIILLNOOPRSU POLLINIFEROUS
EFILNOOOORSSTU STOLONIFEROUS
EFILNOORSSSUV FRIVOLOUSNESS
EFLLOPRSSUUUY SUPERFLUOUSLY
EFLNOORRSSSUW SORROWFULNESS
EGGHIIINNSTUX EXTINGUISHING
EGGHILLNOOPST HOT-GOSPELLING
EGGHLMOOOOPRY GEOMORPHOLOGY
EGGIIILMNNNRT INTERMINGLING
EGGILNOOORSTT GERONTOLOGIST
EGHHIILOPRSTY HIEROGLYPHIST
EGHHIINOPPRSW HORSEWHIPPING
EGHHILLMNOOTY HELMINTHOLOGY
EGHHLLOSSTTUY THOUGHTLESSLY
EGHIIILNNQRSU RELINQUISHING
EGHIIIMNOPRSV IMPOVERISHING
EGHIILMNNOPSY SPHINGOMYELIN
EGHIILNNSSSTU UNSIGHTLINESS
EGHIILNPRSSST SPRIGHTLINESS
EGHIIMNOOPSSY PHYSIOGNOMIES
EGHIIMNOPSSTY PHYSOSTIGMINE
EGHILOOPPSSST PSEPHOLOGISTS
EGHIMNOOORSSU ROOMING HOUSES
EGIIIILNORRST IRRELIGIONIST
EGIIILNOSSSTU LITIGIOUSNESS
EGIIJNNNNNPSY SPINNING JENNY
EGIILLLOOSTVX VEXILLOLOGIST
EGIILLNNNSSUW UNWILLINGNESS
EGIILLNNOPSST SELLING POINTS

EGIILMNNOPSTT MELTING POINTS
EGIILMNNRTTUY UNREMITTINGLY
EGIILMNOORSTT TERMINOLOGIST
EGIILMNOPRTYZ TEMPORIZINGLY
EGIILMOOSSSST SEISMOLOGISTS
EGIILNNOPRSTY INTERPOSINGLY
EGIILNNOQSTUY QUESTIONINGLY
EGIILNOPRSTYZ PROSELYTIZING
EGIIMMNNOPRSSS PROMISINGNESS
EGIIMNOPPRSSU SUPERIMPOSING
EGIIMOPRRSSSV PROGRESSIVISM
EGIIINNNOQSTUU UNQUESTIONING
EGIIINNOORRSST INTROGRESSION
EGIIINNPPRRSST PRINTING PRESS
EGIIINPRSTTTTY SITTING PRETTY
EGIIOPRRSSSTV PROGRESSIVIST
EGILLNNOORSST ROLLING STONES
EGILMNOOOSSTT ENTOMOLOGISTS
EGILNNOSSSTUU GLUTINOUSNESS
EGILNOPPRRSTU SPLINTER GROUP
EGIMMMMNOPRSSY GYMNOSPERMISM
EGMMNOOPRSSUY GYMNOSPERMOUS
EGMMNOORRRSUU RUMOURMONGERS
EHHIILOOPPRSS PHILOSOPHISER
EHHIILOOPPRSZ PHILOSOPHIZER
EHHIMMMOOOPRS HOMEOMORPHISM
EHIILLOPSSTWW WILL-O'-THE-WISPS
EHIILMOOPPSSY LYMPHOPOIESIS
EHIIMNOOOPSST PHOTOEMISSION
EHILLNNOOPQUY PHYLLOQUINONE
EHILMNOOOPSTU ENTOMOPHILOUS
EHILNOPSSSTYY POLYSYNTHESIS
EHIMMOOPRRSTT THERMOTROPISM
EHLLLOOPPSTUY LEPTOPHYLLOUS
EHLLNOOPSSTUY STENOPHYLLOUS
EIIIIILNQSTUVY INQUISITIVELY
EIIIINNSSTTVY INSENSITIVITY
EIIILLMOOPSTY POLIOMYELITIS
EIIIMMNOPRSSS IMPRESSIONISM
EIIIMNNORSSST INTERMISSIONS
EIIIMNOPRSSST IMPRESSIONIST
EIIINNOOPRSTT INTERPOSITION
EIILLLLLMNOPSS PLIMSOLL LINES
EIILMNOQRSTUV VENTRILOQUISM
EIILMOORRSTUY MERITORIOUSLY
EIILNOOOPPSST POLE POSITIONS
EIILNOORSTTUV REVOLUTIONIST
EIILNOQRSTTUV VENTRILOQUIST

EIIMNOORSSSTT MONSTROSITIES
EIIINNOPRRSTTU INTERRUPTIONS
EIINOOPPRSSTU SUPERPOSITION
EIINOOPPRSTTU OPPORTUNITIES
EIINOORSSTTTX EXTORTIONISTS
EIINOPRSSSTTU SUPERSTITIONS
EIIOOPPRSSSTU SUPPOSITORIES
EIIOPRRSSTTUU SURREPTITIOUS
EIIOPRSSSTTUU SUPERSTITIOUS
EIJLNOOPPRSTU JET PROPULSION
EILNNOOPPRTUY INOPPORTUNELY
EINNOOOPSSSSU POISONOUSNESS
EINNOOORSSSTU NOTORIOUSNESS
EMNOPSSSSTUUU SUMPTUOUSNESS
EMOOOPRRRSSTT STORM TROOPERS
FFIIINNOOSSSU FISSION-FUSION
FFLLLLNOOOORR ROLL-ON ROLL-OFF
FGHHLLOOOORTUW FOLLOW-THROUGH
FGHIILLMNOOTT MOONLIGHT FLIT
FGHIILLNORSUY FLOURISHINGLY
FGIIILLNOSSSV LIVING FOSSILS
FHLLNOOOORRSU ROLL OF HONOURS
FILLMRSSTTUUY MISTRUSTFULLY
GGGHHINOOORTU THOROUGHGOING
GGHIIILNPRSTT STRIP LIGHTING
GHIILLOOPSSTY SYPHILOLOGIST
GHIILNOOORSTT ORNITHOLOGIST
GHIILNOPPRSWY WORSHIPPINGLY
GHIILOOPSSSTY PHYSIOLOGISTS
GHIIMMOOPRSTT THIGMOTROPISM
GHIIMNOOPSSTY PHYSIOGNOMIST
GIIIILNNPRSTY INSPIRITINGLY
GIIIILNOOQSUZ SOLILOQUIZING
GIIILMNNOOSUY IGNOMINIOUSLY
GIILMMNOOPSSW SWIMMING POOLS
GIILMNRSSTTUY MISTRUSTINGLY
GIINNNOPRSTTU TURNING POINTS
GIINNOOOPPRRT PROPORTIONING
GILLLMOOPSSYY POLYSYLLOGISM
HHIMOOOPRRSUZ RHIZOMORPHOUS
HIIILLNNOQTTU QUINTILLIONTH
HIILLOOPPRSWW WHIPPOORWILLS
HILORRSTTTUWY TRUSTWORTHILY
IIINOOOPPSSTT OPPOSITIONIST
IIINOOPRRSSTV PRISON VISITOR
IILLLORSSTUUY ILLUSTRIOUSLY
IIMNOOOOPPRRST MISPROPORTION
IINNOOOOPPSTTT POINT-TO-POINTS

FOURTEEN-LETTER WORDS

AAAABCCEELRSTU BACCALAUREATES
AAAABEHKLLLMRU MAHALLA EL KUBRA
AAAACCDEINORSU ANACARDIACEOUS
AAAACCILLPRTTY PARATACTICALLY
AAAACCINNRSSTU TRANSCAUCASIAN
AAAACDIIMMNOST MACADAMISATION
AAAACDIIMMNOTZ MACADAMIZATION
AAAACEGILLMMNO MEGALOMANIACAL
AAAACEHMNORSTU AMARANTHACEOUS
AAAACEIMNNRRST SACRAMENTARIAN
AAAACHIILNNRSS HALICARNASSIAN
AAAADEGINNQRRU QUADRAGENARIAN
AAAADELLLNORRV ANDORRA LA VELLA
AAAAEGLNRSTTUW NATURAL WASTAGE
AAAAEHILNPPRRS PARAPHERNALIAS
AAAAFIILNNPRRS INFRALAPSARIAN
AAAAFIIMNRRSST RASTAFARIANISM
AAAAGHIMNOPRST PHANTASMAGORIA
AAAAHHIKMNPSTV VISHAKHAPATNAM
AAAAIIILLNOPSTT PALATALISATION
AAAAIIILLNOPTTZ PALATALIZATION
AAAABBCEILNNPRU BANANA REPUBLIC
AAAABCCDHILRTYY BRACHYDACTYLIA
AAAABCCEIILLMTZ ACCLIMATIZABLE
AAAABCCILMNNOOY CYANOCOBALAMIN
AAAABCDEEFLNORT BALANCE OF TRADE
AAAABCDEGINOSTU SANTIAGO DE CUBA
AAAABCEFLMNRTUU MANUFACTURABLE
AAAABCEHILLLPTY ALPHABETICALLY
AAAABCEHILMOSTT HAEMATOBLASTIC
AAAABCEHILNOPPR INAPPROACHABLE
AAAABCEHLNOPPRU UNAPPROACHABLE
AAAABCEILMNOSSU BALSAMINACEOUS
AAAABCEILMNRRSU ARABIC NUMERALS
AAAABDDEEEHORST BEAT A DEAD HORSE
AAAABDDEELLLLNN BE-ALL AND END-ALL
AAAABDDEENRRRST STANDARD-BEARER
AAAABDEEELMPSTX SET A BAD EXAMPLE
AAAABDEEMRSSSSS AMBASSADRESSES
AAAABDHIMOPRSSS AMBASSADORSHIP
AAAABDIINORSSTT BASTARDISATION
AAAABDIINORSTTZ BASTARDIZATION
AAAABEEELLRSTUV RATEABLE VALUES
AAAABEGGIILNNPR PLEA BARGAINING
AAAABEIILLMNPRR PRIMA BALLERINA
AAAABEILNOOPSTT PALAEOBOTANIST

AAAABELLNNPRSTT TRANSPLANTABLE
AAAABIILNOOPRST PARABOLISATION
AAAABIILNOOPRTZ PARABOLIZATION
AAAABIILNRRTTWY WARRANTABILITY
AAAACCDEHIINORT ARCHIDIACONATE
AAAACCDEHINRSS CASH AND CARRIES
AAAACCDEIMNNOOR ADENOCARCINOMA
AAAACCDEIOPPRSU CAPPARIDACEOUS
AAAACCDILORRSUV CARDIOVASCULAR
AAAACCEEELLNRSS CLEARANCE SALES
AAAACCEEFHHKLTT AT THE CHALKFACE
AAAACCEEHILMNOR AEROMECHANICAL
AAAACCEEHMNRSTT CATCHMENT AREAS
AAAACCEGHILLOOR ARCHAEOLOGICAL
AAAACCEHILMPRTU PHARMACEUTICAL
AAAACCEILNNORTX EXTRACANONICAL
AAAACCELMNOPSUU CAMPANULACEOUS
AAAACCGHILOPRRT CARTOGRAPHICAL
AAAACCGIIINNPTT INCAPACITATING
AAAACCHIILNRSTT CHARLATANISTIC
AAAACCHILLMORTY ACHROMATICALLY
AAAACCIIINNOPTT INCAPACITATION
AAAACCILLORTTUY AUTOCRATICALLY
AAAACCLMOORSSTU MALACOSTRACOUS
AAAACDDEGGKLNOR CLOAK-AND-DAGGER
AAAACDEEGHILNRR HEGIRA CALENDAR
AAAACDEEINPPRSS DISAPPEARANCES
AAAACDEFGNORRUV GRACE-AND-FAVOUR
AAAACDEGIKLNNNP PANCAKE LANDING
AAAACDEIIIMNNNR AMERICAN INDIAN
AAAACDEIIINPRST PAEDIATRICIANS
AAAACDFHIMNNRST HANDICRAFTSMAN
AAAACDHILNOOPRS ACHONDROPLASIA
AAAACDHINNRSTTU TRISTAN DA CUNHA
AAAACDIILNNOSST SCANDALISATION
AAAACDIILNNOSTZ SCANDALIZATION
AAAACEEGILNSSTU AGUASCALIENTES
AAAACEEILLNNORRS ALSACE-LORRAINE
AAAACEEILNORSUV VALERIANACEOUS
AAAACEFGIORSSUX SAXIFRAGACEOUS
AAAACEFIILNNRSY FINANCIAL YEARS
AAAACEFILLLNSTY SELF-ANALYTICAL
AAAACEGILMNNORS ANGLO-AMERICANS
AAAACEHIILMRRSV AIR VICE-MARSHAL
AAAACEHIIMMNSTT MATHEMATICIANS
AAAACEHILLMMTTY MATHEMATICALLY
AAAACEHILMOOPPR PHARMACOPOEIAL
AAAACEHILNOPPRT PALAEANTHROPIC

AAACEHIMOOPPRS PHARMACOPOEIAS
AAACEHNRRRSSTW SEARCH WARRANTS
AAACEIIMMNNPRS PAN-AMERICANISM
AAACEILLMNNSTY ANAMNESTICALLY
AAACEILLMSTTTY METASTATICALLY
AAACEILMMNRSST SACRAMENTALISM
AAACEILMNRSSTT SACRAMENTALIST
AAACEILMNRSTTY SACRAMENTALITY
AAACENRRRSSTTU RESTAURANT
   CARS
AAACFIILLLSTTY FATALISTICALLY
AAACFIILNOSSTT SATISFACTIONAL
AAACGHIKLNSSTT SLASHING ATTACK
AAACGHIMNOPRST PHANTASMAGORIC
AAACGIILLMSTTY ASTIGMATICALLY
AAACGIILLNPSTY PAGANISTICALLY
AAACGIILMMRTTY GRAMMATICALITY
AAACGIILLMNORTY MORGANATICALLY
AAACGLORRSSTUV GASTROVASCULAR
AAACHILLLLOPTY ALLOPATHICALLY
AAACHILMMNNOPY
   NYMPHOMANIACAL
AAACHILMOPRTTU THAUMATROPICAL
AAACIIILNOPSTT CAPITALISATION
AAACIIILNOPTTZ CAPITALIZATION
AAACILLLLOPRTY ALLOPATRICALLY
AAADEEGHHMSTTW WHAT'S THE
   DAMAGE?
AAADEEHLLORTTT LEAD TO THE ALTAR
AAADEEHLMNNNRT NEANDERTHAL
   MAN
AAADEGGILNNRSU GUARDIAN ANGELS
AAADEGLNOSTUVY ADVANTAGEOUSLY
AAADEHMNPSTTYY TEA AND
   SYMPATHY
AAADEIILNNRTUV VALETUDINARIAN
AAADEILLQRRSTU QUADRILATERALS
AAADEIMNNORRSY ORDINARY SEAMAN
AAADFIILLMORRY FAIRY ARMADILLO
AAADGHIOOPRRTU AUTORADIOGRAPH
AAADGIILLMNORT GIANT ARMADILLO
AAADGIMNOORSST GOOD SAMARITANS
AAADIIILNNRTTU LATITUDINARIAN
AAADIIMNORSSTT DRAMATISATIONS
AAADIIMNORSTTZ DRAMATIZATIONS
AAADIJNNNORRST TRANS-JORDANIAN
AAAEEFGIKMOPRS MAKE A PIG'S EAR OF
AAAEEGINNPRSTU SEPTUAGENARIAN
AAAEEGMNRRSSTT SERGEANT-AT-ARMS
AAAEEHHLMMORTT
   HAEMATOTHERMAL
AAAEEHIIMNRRTT HENRIETTA MARIA
AAAEEHMNRRSTWX MANX
   SHEARWATER

AAAEEIILLPRTXY EPITAXIAL LAYER
AAAEEJMNRRSSTT SERJEANT-AT-ARMS
AAAEGGGIKNPRRS PARKING GARAGES
AAAEGHIIMNNTTZ ANATHEMATIZING
AAAEGHLNNOPRSY NASOPHARYNGEAL
AAAEGIIILMNRST EGALITARIANISM
AAAEGLLLMOPRRS PARALLELOGRAMS
AAAEGLMOPRRSSS MASSAGE PARLORS
AAAEGLMOPRRSSU MASSAGE PARLOUR
AAAEHILMNNNOTT NATIONAL
   ANTHEM
AAAGIILNNOORST ORGANISATIONAL
AAAGIILNNOORTZ ORGANIZATIONAL
AAAGIIMMNPRSTT ANTIPRAGMATISM
AAAGIINNNOOSTT ANTAGONISATION
AAAGIINNNOOSTT ANTAGONISATION
AAAGIINNNOOTTZ ANTAGONIZATION
AAAGINOORRSTTV ASTRONAVIGATOR
AAAHIINORRSTTU AUTHORITARIANS
AAAIILNNORSTTU NATURALISATION
AAAIILNNORTTUZ NATURALIZATION
AAAIILNORSTTWY RAILWAY STATION
AAAIIMNORSTTTU TRAUMATISATION
AAAIIMNORTTTUZ TRAUMATIZATION
AAAIINNOSSSSST ASSASSINATIONS
AAAILNNORSTTUV TRANSVALUATION
AABBCEEFINORST ABSORBEFACIENT
AABBCEEHILNOSS BELISHA BEACONS
AABBDDEEGILORS BIODEGRADABLES
AABBDDEENRRTTU BREAD-AND-
   BUTTER
AABBDEEHIMNORT BROAD IN THE
   BEAM
AABBEEELNNRSSU UNBEARABLENESS
AABBEFGGILNRST FLABBERGASTING
AABBEIILLOSSSU BOUILLABAISSES
AABBELOPRRRSWY BLOW A RASPBERRY
AABBHIIIILNTTY INHABITABILITY
AABCCCDHILRTYY BRACHYDACTYLIC
AABCCCEHHILPRY BRACHYCEPHALIC
AABCCDEKKLLNOT BLOCK AND
   TACKLE
AABCCEELNNORTU COUNTERBALANCE
AABCCEGHIIOPRT BACTERIOPHAGIC
AABCCEHILLMOPS ACCOMPLISHABLE
AABCCEHNOOORSU
   OROBANCHACEOUS
AABCCEIIORSTTT BACTERIOSTATIC
AABCCEILMMRTUU CIRCUMAMBULATE
AABCCIIILPRTTY PRACTICABILITY
AABCCIILNOTTUY ACCOUNTABILITY
AABCDDEEHKNNSS BACKHANDEDNESS
AABCDDHINORSSW SANDWICH BOARDS
AABCDEEEGHNRUU BUREAU DE
   CHANGE

AABCDEEEMMNRRY REMEMBRANCE DAY
AABCDEEFIILLSS DECLASSIFIABLE
AABCDEEHLOTTTU CHATEAU BOTTLED
AABCDEEHNNRUZZ NEBUCHADNEZZAR
AABCDEEHORTTUY CATHODE RAY TUBE
AABCDEEIKRRSTV BACK-SEAT DRIVER
AABCDEEINRRSTT SCATTERBRAINED
AABCDEEKMNOPPY KEEP BAD COMPANY
AABCDEENNPRSUU SUPERABUNDANCE
AABCDEENRSSSTT ABSTRACTEDNESS
AABCDEGIILLNNV ADVANCE BILLING
AABCDEGIKLNRRT BLANK CARTRIDGE
AABCDEHOORRSST ACROSS-THE-BOARD
AABCDEIILLNOSS DIABOLICALNESS
AABCEEEEFLNOSV LEAVE OF ABSENCE
AABCEEEGHLNNSS CHANGEABLENESS
AABCEEEHKNRTTT THE BEATEN TRACK
AABCEEEKKLMRRT BLACK MARKETEER
AABCEEFLNOOPRW BALANCE OF POWER
AABCEEGHLNORSX LABOR EXCHANGES
AABCEEGHLNORUX LABOUR EXCHANGE
AABCEEGILNRTXY EXACERBATINGLY
AABCEEHIKLMNNS BLACKEN HIS NAME
AABCEEHILNRSST CHARITABLENESS
AABCEEHILOPRRR IRREPROACHABLE
AABCEEHINSTTUU EUSTACHIAN TUBE
AABCEEIIILLPRTY REPLACEABILITY
AABCEEILLLMMTY EMBLEMATICALLY
AABCEEKQRRSSTU SQUARE BRACKETS
AABCEFGIINPRRT PREFABRICATING
AABCEFIIINOSTT BEATIFICATIONS
AABCEFIIINOTTU BEAUTIFICATION
AABCEFIINOPRRT PREFABRICATION
AABCEGHHIIMNNT BATHING MACHINE
AABCEHIIILMPTY IMPEACHABILITY
AABCEHIIILLRSTY HEBRAISTICALLY
AABCEHILOPRRRY IRREPROACHABLY
AABCEIILLORSST AEROBALLISTICS
AABCEIILNNPRTU ANTIREPUBLICAN
AABCEIILRRTTTY RETRACTABILITY
AABCEIILRTTTXY EXTRACTABILITY
AABCEIIORSSSTT BACTERIOSTASIS
AABCEILLMORRTY BAROMETRICALLY
AABCEILNORSSTU CONSTABULARIES
AABCEIMOORSSUU SIMAROUBACEOUS
AABCFIKMNOORST BACK FORMATIONS

AABCFILNNOOSTU CONFABULATIONS
AABCGGIILLOOOR AGROBIOLOGICAL
AABCGHIILLMOOP AMPHIBOLOGICAL
AABCGHIILLOPRY BIOGRAPHICALLY
AABCGHIIOOPRTU AUTOBIOGRAPHIC
AABCGHIMOOPRRR MICROBAROGRAPH
AABCHIILPRSTUY PURCHASABILITY
AABCHILOOPRSTU CLAUSTROPHOBIA
AABCIIILLMPRSY IMPARISYLLABIC
AABCIIILNRTTTY INTRACTABILITY
AABCIIMNORSSTT ABSTRACTIONISM
AABDDEEIMNNORT ONE-ARMED BANDIT
AABDDEELNNRSTU UNDERSTANDABLE
AABDDEFIIOPRRS BIRD OF PARADISE
AABDDELNNRSTUY UNDERSTANDABLY
AABDDGIINNORRS DRAINING BOARDS
AABDEEEFHINRRT FEATHERBRAINED
AABDEEEHHIRRSS HABERDASHERIES
AABDEEEHILNNNR BANNER HEADLINE
AABDEFGIOPRSSS BIRDS OF PASSAGE
AABDEFIIILLQSU DISQUALIFIABLE
AABDEIIKMNORST DISEMBARKATION
AABDEIILPRSTUY PERSUADABILITY
AABDEKLNRSSTUY LAUNDRY BASKETS
AABDHHNPRSSUUW WASH AND BRUSH-UP
AABDHILMNOSSUY BUSMAN'S HOLIDAY
AABDIIIILNSTVY INADVISABILITY
AABDIIILNOTUVY UNAVOIDABILITY
AABDIINOOPPRST DISAPPROBATION
AABEEEFMNNOOST BEMOAN ONE'S FATE
AABEEEINORRSWY RAISE AN EYEBROW
AABEEEKLMNRRSS REMARKABLENESS
AABEEELNNORSSS REASONABLENESS
AABEEELNNOSSSS SEASONABLENESS
AABEEFGILNNOST SELF-ABNEGATION
AABEEFLNORSSUV FAVOURABLENESS
AABEEGIKMNORRR BROKEN MARRIAGE
AABEEHIIILRTTV REHABILITATIVE
AABEEHIIILLPRSS HERPES LABIALIS
AABEEHIILRTTWY WEATHERABILITY
AABEEHJKMNORST JAM ON THE BRAKES
AABEEIMNNORTUV MOUNTAIN BEAVER
AABEEMMNRRSSST EMBARRASSMENTS
AABEFGHLLORRSU BARREL OF LAUGHS
AABEFILLMMNNNO NONINFLAMMABLE
AABEFILLNOPSTU FALLOPIAN TUBES
AABEGHIIILNRTT REHABILITATING
AABEGHIOOPRRTU AUTOBIOGRAPHER
AABEGIIILLNOSUV BOUGAINVILLEAS

AABEGILMNRRSSY EMBARRASSINGLY
AABEHIIILNORTT REHABILITATION
AABEIIIILLNNTY INALIENABILITY
AABEIIIILLNORST LIBERALISATION
AABEIIIILLNORTZ LIBERALIZATION
AABEIIIILLNRTTY INALTERABILITY
AABEIIIILMNRRST LIBERTARIANISM
AABEIIIILNPRSTY INSEPARABILITY
AABEIIIILPRRRTY IRREPARABILITY
AABEIIILRRSUVXY AUXILIARY VERBS
AABEIINSSTTTUV SUBSTANTIATIVE
AABEILMNOPRSTU PERAMBULATIONS
AABEILNNORSTTU SUBALTERNATION
AABEKMRRRRSTWY STRAWBERRY
MARK
AABELOPRRSTUUY BEAUTY PARLOURS
AABENORRRRSTWY STRAWBERRY
ROAN
AABFIIILLMMNTY INFLAMMABILITY
AABFIIILLNPPTUY UNFLAPPABILITY
AABGIINNSSTTTU SUBSTANTIATING
AABHIIINPPRSST BIPARTISANSHIP
AABIIIILLMNPTUY MANIPULABILITY
AABIILMNSSSTTU SUBSTANTIALISM
AABIILNSSSTTTU SUBSTANTIALIST
AABIILNSSTTTUY SUBSTANTIALITY
AABIINNOSSTTTU SUBSTANTIATION
AABILMMNNOOSTU
SOMNAMBULATION
AACCCCENNOOOVV CONCAVO-
CONCAVE
AACCCDHIIINOTY THIOCYANIC ACID
AACCCEEHILLTTY CATECHETICALLY
AACCCEEIIILLSST ECCLESIASTICAL
AACCCEGHNORSTU CHARGE
ACCOUNTS
AACCCEHIIRRSTT CHARACTERISTIC
AACCCHLLOOPSTY STAPHYLOCOCCAL
AACCDDDEEHHNRT CATCH RED-
HANDED
AACCDDEMMNOOTU
UNACCOMMODATED
AACCDEHILOPRSY POLYSACCHARIDE
AACCDEHIMNOORS MONOSACCHARIDE
AACCDEIINNORTT CONTRAINDICATE
AACCDEILLMORTY DEMOCRATICALLY
AACCDHIMOPRSTY PSYCHODRAMATIC
AACCDHIMRRSSST CHRISTMAS
CARDS
AACCDIIINRSTTU TRADUCIANISTIC
AACCDIINNNORTT CONTRAINDICANT
AACCDIMMNOOOST
ACCOMMODATIONS
AACCEEGHILLMOP MEGALOCEPHALIC

AACCEEGIILNTTT TELANGIECTATIC
AACCEEILNNOPRT PRECANCELATION
AACCEEILNNRSTU NATURAL SCIENCE
AACCEEINNNORSS RECONNAISSANCE
AACCEELMNRSUUV VACUUM CLEANERS
AACCEELNORRRTU NUCLEAR REACTOR
AACCEGGHINRRRY CARRYING CHARGE
AACCEGGILLNOOY GYNAECOLOGICAL
AACCEGHIINRRTZ CHARACTERIZING
AACCEGHILLOOST ESCHATOLOGICAL
AACCEGIILOOPTT GALACTOPOIETIC
AACCEGIIMNRTUV CIRCUMNAVIGATE
AACCEGINNOSTUY NYCTAGINACEOUS
AACCEHHIILLRRY HIERARCHICALLY
AACCEHHLNPRSTY CHANTRY CHAPELS
AACCEHIILOPPRS ARCHIEPISCOPAL
AACCEHIINNORST CHAIN REACTIONS
AACCEHIKLOOSSV CSECHOSLOVAKIA
AACCEHIKMRSSST CHRISTMAS CAKES
AACCEHILLNOOPT PLAIN CHOCOLATE
AACCEHILLORTTY THEOCRATICALLY
AACCEHILLPRTYY ARCHETYPICALLY
AACCEHINOPPRRT PARTHENOCARPIC
AACCEIIILPRSTT PRACTICALITIES
AACCEIIILRRTUUV CURRICULA VITAE
AACCEIJKLOPRST PRACTICAL JOKES
AACCEILLLOPPTY APOPLECTICALLY
AACCEILLMTUUVY ACCUMULATIVELY
AACCEIMMNNOPST ACCOMPANIMENTS
AACCEINNNOOSTT CONCATENATIONS
AACCEKNORSTTTU COUNTERATTACKS
AACCELLMMOORRU
MACROMOLECULAR
AACCELLNOOPRRS LANCE CORPORALS
AACCELNNORSUUU RANUNCULACEOUS
AACCELOOPRSTUU PORTULACACEOUS
AACCFHOORRRRTY CARRY A TORCH
FOR
AACCFIIILNORST CLARIFICATIONS
AACCFIIILNOSST CLASSIFICATION
AACCFIIINNOSTT SANCTIFICATION
AACCFIILMOPSST FAITS ACCOMPLIS
AACCFIILORSSTY CLASSIFICATORY
AACCFLOOOOPSTV FOOLSCAP OCTAVO
AACCFNNORTTTUU TURF
ACCOUNTANT
AACCGHHHHIINSU SHIHCHIACHUANG
AACCGHIIILLORY OLIGARCHICALLY
AACCGHILLNOOST ANGLO-CATHOLICS
AACCGIILLMNSTU MISCALCULATING
AACCGIILLMORTY TRAGICOMICALLY
AACCGILLLNOOOV VOLCANOLOGICAL
AACCGINNOSSTUV SAVINGS ACCOUNT
AACCHIILLMSSTY SCHISMATICALLY

AACCHILLOSSTTY STOCHASTICALLY
AACCHILMNOORST ROMAN CATHOLICS
AACCHILNOPSTYY PSYCHOANALYTIC
AACCIIILMPRTTY IMPRACTICALITY
AACCIIIMOPRRST MICROPARASITIC
AACCIILLMNOSTU MISCALCULATION
AACCIILLNNOORR CONRAIL, CONRAIL
AACCIILMNRSTTU CIRCUMSTANTIAL
AACCIILNPRTTUY UNPRACTICALITY
AACCIIMNOORSST CARCINOMATOSIS
AACCILLNOOPTUY OCCUPATIONALLY
AACCKLNNNOPSTT PLANCK CONSTANT
AACDDDEKKNRSSU DUCKS AND DRAKES
AACDDEEELLNSVV ADVANCED LEVELS
AACDDEEILOSTVV DEVIL'S ADVOCATE
AACDDEEIMNNOTT DECONTAMINATED
AACDDEILNOTTUU ADULT EDUCATION
AACDEEEFHMNSSS SHAMEFACEDNESS
AACDEEEGHHNORST CHASE THE
  DRAGON
AACDEEGIILLNRT LEADING ARTICLE
AACDEEGINRRRSU UNDERCARRIAGES
AACDEEGIPPRRRT CARTRIDGE PAPER
AACDEEIILLNQTUW WELL-ACQUAINTED
AACDEEILOPPRTU PROPAEDEUTICAL
AACDEEIQRSSTTU ACQUIRED TASTES
AACDEELNNNRSTT TRANSCENDENTAL
AACDEENORSSSUV CADAVEROUSNESS
AACDEFFINRRSTW TRAFFIC WARDENS
AACDEGILLMOORT DERMATOLOGICAL
AACDEGINOPRSST DATA PROCESSING
AACDEGLMNNORSS SCANDALMONGERS
AACDEHIIMNRRST ARCHIMANDRITES
AACDEHILORRSTT TRISOCTAHEDRAL
AACDEHLMNNORST CALENDAR
  MONTHS
AACDEHLNOPSSYY PSYCHOANALYSED
AACDEHMOPRSTUY PACHYDERMATOUS
AACDEIIILLLSTY IDEALISTICALLY
AACDEIIILMNOST DECIMALISATION
AACDEIIILMNOTZ DECIMALIZATION
AACDEIILLNOOST DELOCALISATION
AACDEIILLNOOTZ DELOCALIZATION
AACDEIILMMNOST DOMESTIC ANIMAL
AACDEIILNNOPTY PLATINOCYANIDE
AACDEIILNOSTTU EDUCATIONALIST
AACDEIILPRRSTU PARTICULARISED
AACDEIILPRRTUZ PARTICULARIZED
AACDEIINORTTTX DIRECT TAXATION
AACDEILMOPRSTT DERMATOPLASTIC
AACDEILMORRTTU COURT-MARTIALED
AACDEILNOPRSSS SPORADICALNESS
AACDEIMNNNOTTU
  UNCONTAMINATED

AACDEIMNNOORTT
  DECONTAMINATOR
AACDEINOPRRSTT PROCRASTINATED
AACDELNNOSSSSU SCANDALOUSNESS
AACDFFIILNRSST TRAFFIC ISLANDS
AACDGHIMOOPRRY
  MYOCARDIOGRAPH
AACDGIIINOSSST DISASSOCIATING
AACDGIILLNOSTY DIAGNOSTICALLY
AACDHIMOOSSSST SADOMASOCHISTS
AACDIIIILNNPRS DISCIPLINARIAN
AACDIIINOOSSST DISASSOCIATION
AACDIILLLMOPTY DIPLOMATICALLY
AACDIILNNOPRST CARDINAL POINTS
AACDIILORRSTTU DISARTICULATOR
AACDIKNNPQRSSU QUIPS AND CRANKS
AACDILNOOSSTUY ANISODACTYLOUS
AACDILOORSTTUY ARTIODACTYLOUS
AACEEEEGINSSTT ESTATE AGENCIES
AACEEEFGHNORTX RATE OF
  EXCHANGE
AACEEEFHINRSTT STARE IN THE FACE
AACEEEGILNRSTV TRAVEL AGENCIES
AACEEEGIPPRRTT CIGARETTE PAPER
AACEEEHIMNNOST IN THE SAME
  CANOE
AACEEEHKMRRRST MARKET RESEARCH
AACEEEHLMOSTUY THYMELAEACEOUS
AACEEEHMMORTTY
  HAEMACYTOMETER
AACEEEIILLRSTUV RELATIVE CLAUSE
AACEEFFILNOTTY AFFECTIONATELY
AACEEGGILLLNOY GENEALOGICALLY
AACEEGHHLNOPPR ENCEPHALOGRAPH
AACEEGHILNNRTT CENTRAL HEATING
AACEEGHNOOPRRS OCEANOGRAPHERS
AACEEGIILLMNSV EVANGELICALISM
AACEEGIILNSSTT TELANGIECTASIS
AACEEGIIPRSVWY GIVEAWAY PRICES
AACEEGILLNNPTY PANGENETICALLY
AACEEGILNPRSTW WATERING PLACES
AACEEHHMNOPRTY
  MECHANOTHERAPY
AACEEHHNOPPRST ON THE SCRAPHEAP
AACEEHIIMOOPTT HAEMATOPOIETIC
AACEEHILLLPTTY TELEPATHICALLY
AACEEHILMNPSST EMPHATICALNESS
AACEEHILRRTUVX EXTRAVEHICULAR
AACEEHIMNNRSTV MERCHANT NAVIES
AACEEHIPRSSTTY CRYPTAESTHESIA
AACEEIIINPPRTV INAPPRECIATIVE
AACEEIIILOPRSTV OVERCAPITALISE
AACEEIIILOPRTVZ OVERCAPITALIZE
AACEEIILPPRTVY APPRECIATIVELY

AACEEIILPRTTUV RECAPITULATIVE
AACEEIINPPRTUV UNAPPRECIATIVE
AACEEILNPPPRRT RICE-PAPER PLANT
AACEEILNPRTTUV VENTURE CAPITAL
AACEEILNRSSTTU ARTICULATENESS
AACEEINNPRRSST TRANSPARENCIES
AACEEINRSSTTTV ATTRACTIVENESS
AACEFFINORRRTW WARRANT OFFICER
AACEFFLMORTTTY MATTER-OF-FACTLY
AACEFIINPRRTTU PARTURIFACIENT
AACEFILLNOSSSU FALLACIOUSNESS
AACEFINRSSTTUY SAFETY CURTAINS
AACEFNOPRRSSTT TRANSPORT CAFES
AACEGGHILLOPRY GEOGRAPHICALLY
AACEGGHINNORRT GREGORIAN
   CHANT
AACEGGILNNOORT CONGREGATIONAL
AACEGHHIIMNNSW WASHING-MACHINE
AACEGHHIOPPRRS PHRASEOGRAPHIC
AACEGHIILLPPRY EPIGRAPHICALLY
AACEGHIILMOPSU MALPIGHIACEOUS
AACEGHIINNTTTU AUTHENTICATING
AACEGHIJKRSTTT STRAIGHTJACKET
AACEGHILLLMPTY PHLEGMATICALLY
AACEGHILLMNOPY MEGAPHONICALLY
AACEGHILLMOPRT METALLOGRAPHIC
AACEGHILLOOPRS PHRASEOLOGICAL
AACEGHILOORSST ARCHAEOLOGISTS
AACEGHILOPRTTU TELAUTOGRAPHIC
AACEGHIMNOPRTY CINEMATOGRAPHY
AACEGIILLLLSTY LEGALISTICALLY
AACEGIILLMOOSS SEMASIOLOGICAL
AACEGIILNPRTTU RECAPITULATING
AACEGIILOOPSST GALACTOPOIESIS
AACEGIINNOPRST ANGINA PECTORIS
AACEGIINOORSTT CATEGORISATION
AACEGIINOORTTZ CATEGORIZATION
AACEGILLLOOPTY APOLOGETICALLY
AACEGILLMNOORT ORGANOMETALLIC
AACEGILNRRTTUY RECTANGULARITY
AACEHHILNNOPTY PHTHALOCYANINE
AACEHIIIMNRSTT ARITHMETICIANS
AACEHIILLLLPTY PHILATELICALLY
AACEHIILLMRTTY ARITHMETICALLY
AACEHIILLNTTTY ANTITHETICALLY
AACEHIILMNSTUV MALE CHAUVINIST
AACEHIIMNNRSST CHRISTIAN NAMES
AACEHIIMNOSSTT SCHEMATISATION
AACEHIIMNOSTTZ SCHEMATIZATION
AACEHIINNOTTTU AUTHENTICATION
AACEHILLLNNOUY UNHOLY ALLIANCE
AACEHILLMNNORY ENHARMONICALLY
AACEHILLMOPRSY SEMAPHORICALLY
AACEHILLMOPRTY METAPHORICALLY

AACEHILLMPSTYY METAPHYSICALLY
AACEHILMNPRRSU HURRICANE LAMPS
AACEHIMMMORSTT
   METACHROMATISM
AACEHIMOOPPRST PHARMACOPOEIST
AACEHLNOPRSYYZ PSYCHOANALYZER
AACEHMNOOOPPRS
   ANAMORPHOSCOPE
AACEHMNOPRSTUY PARENCHYMATOUS
AACEIIILNOPSST SPECIALISATION
AACEIIILNOPSTZ SPECIALIZATION
AACEIILLMNNOOT CALAMINE LOTION
AACEIILLNPSTTY ANTISEPTICALLY
AACEIILLNRTTUY INARTICULATELY
AACEIILMOOPRTV IMPERIAL OCTAVO
AACEIILNNORSTT CENTRALISATION
AACEIILNNORTTZ CENTRALIZATION
AACEIILNOPRTTU RECAPITULATION
AACEIILNORSSTU SECULARISATION
AACEIILNORSTUZ SECULARIZATION
AACEIILPPPRSTT PAST PARTICIPLE
AACEIILPRRRSTU PARTICULARISER
AACEIILPRRRTUZ PARTICULARIZER
AACEIINNNORRST REINCARNATIONS
AACEIINOPRRSTV PREVARICATIONS
AACEIINRRRSSTU CURTAIN RAISERS
AACEILLLNOPSTY PLEONASTICALLY
AACEILLMMNORTY MANOMETRICALLY
AACEILLMMRSTYY ASYMMETRICALLY
AACEILLMNORRTU INTRAMOLECULAR
AACEILLMSSTTYY SYSTEMATICALLY
AACEILNNNRSSTY TYRANNICALNESS
AACEILNNOORSTV CONSERVATIONAL,
   CONVERSATIONAL
AACEILNNOPSSTU ENCAPSULATIONS
AACEILNORSTTUX EXCLAUSTRATION
AACEIMNOPRSTTU STORM IN A TEACUP
AACEINNORSTTUU INTRACUTANEOUS
AACEINOPRSSSST CAST ASPERSIONS
AACEKLNNORSTUY CANTANKEROUSLY
AACELLLOPPRRYY POLYCARPELLARY
AACELLMNOOPRRY MONOCARPELLARY
AACELLMOPRRSUU SUPRAMOLECULAR
AACELORSSSSTUU ASSAULT COURSES
AACFFGIMNORRTY FACTORY FARMING
AACFFIIILNOSST FALSIFICATIONS
AACFGHIILRRSTT LIGHT AIRCRAFTS
AACFGIIIMNNOST MAGNIFICATIONS
AACFGIIINORSTT GRATIFICATIONS
AACFGILNNOORST CONFLAGRATIONS
AACFGILNORRTUV VULGAR
   FRACTION
AACFIIIILNOQSTU QUALIFICATIONS
AACFIIIMMNNOOT AMMONIFICATION

AACFIIINNOOPST SAPONIFICATION
AACFIIINNOQTTU QUANTIFICATION
AACFIIINORSTTT STRATIFICATION
AACFIIILLMORTTU MULTIFACTORIAL
AACFIIILORSSTTY SATISFACTORILY
AACFINORSSTTUY UNSATISFACTORY
AACFLOOOPQRSTU FOOLSCAP QUARTO
AACGGILLLNOORY LARYNGOLOGICAL
AACGGILLMOSTYY MYSTAGOGICALLY
AACGGILNNORTTU CONGRATULATING
AACGHHILOOPRRT ORTHOGRAPHICAL
AACGHHIMNNSTTW NIGHT
WATCHMANS
AACGHHMOOPRRTY
CHROMATOGRAPHY
AACGHIILLPRSST CALLIGRAPHISTS
AACGHILLLOOPTY PATHOLOGICALLY
AACGHILLMOPRYY MYOGRAPHICALLY
AACGHILLOOPRRY OROGRAPHICALLY
AACGHILMOOPRST PHARMACOLOGIST
AACGHLMMOORRSS GRAMMAR
SCHOOLS
AACGHLOOPPRSYY 'PARAPSYCHOLOGY
AACGILLLOORSTY ASTROLOGICALLY
AACGILLLOOTTUY TAUTOLOGICALLY
AACGILLMOORRTY MARTYROLOGICAL
AACGILMNOOPSST CAMPANOLOGISTS
AACGILNNOORTTU CONGRATULATION
AACGKNOOOORRSTU KANGAROO
COURTS
AACGLNOORRTTUY
CONGRATULATORY
AACHHINOOPPRTT ANTHROPOPATHIC
AACHIILLNNOSTU HALLUCINATIONS
AACHIILLNOOOST ALCOHOLISATION
AACHIILLNOOOTZ ALCOHOLIZATION
AACHIIMNNORSTT ANTIMONARCHIST
AACHILLOORTTUY LOCAL AUTHORITY
AACHILLOPTTUYY AUTOPHYTICALLY
AACHILNOPSSSYY PSYCHOANALYSIS
AACHLLLMOOPSUY MALACOPHYLLOUS
AACHLNOPSSSTYY PSYCHOANALYSTS
AACIIILLNRSTTY INARTISTICALLY
AACIIILMNOPPST MISAPPLICATION
AACIIILNOPRTTY ANTICIPATORILY
AACIIILNOPSSTT PLASTICISATION
AACIIILNOPSTTZ PLASTICIZATION
AACIIIMNOOSSST ASSOCIATIONISM
AACIILLLMORSTY MORALISTICALLY
AACIILLLRSTTUY ALTRUISTICALLY
AACIILMOOPTTTU AUTOMATIC PILOT
AACIILNOOPRRST CONSPIRATORIAL
AACIILNORSTTTU STRATICULATION
AACIILNPPPRRST PRINCIPAL PARTS

AACIILOPRSSTTY SOCIALIST PARTY
AACIINNOOSSTTT ACTION STATIONS
AACILLLLOOPRTY ALLOTROPICALLY
AACILLLNORSTUY ULTRASONICALLY
AACILLMNOORSTY ASTRONOMICALLY
AACILLMOPSTTYY ASYMPTOTICALLY
AACINOOPRRSTTX CORPORATION TAX
AACINOOPRRRSTT PROCRASTINATOR
AACLLNNOPRTTUY CONTRAPUNTALLY
AADDDEEEHHNRSS HARD-HEADEDNESS
AADDEEELMPRSST PADDLE STEAMERS
AADDEEFGHLOORS FLOG A DEAD
HORSE
AADDEEGNRRSTUU UNDERGRADUATES
AADDEEIILNNOST DENATIONALISED
AADDEEIILNNOTZ DENATIONALIZED
AADDEELNOQRRSU SQUADRON LEADER
AADDEGGHNRRSTU
GRANDDAUGHTERS
AADDEGILNRSSSS SALAD DRESSINGS
AADDEGINNRSTVW GRANDSTAND VIEW
AADDHMNRSTUUYY MAUNDY
THURSDAY
AADEEEFGIOPRST PÂTÉ DE FOIE
GRAS
AADEEEGKMNRRRT MARKET
GARDENER
AADEEEHLLRTTTY TETRAETHYL LEAD
AADEEEHLRRRSSS DRESS REHEARSAL
AADEEEILLLPPPR PARALLELEPIPED
AADEEELMNRSSTT ELDER STATESMAN
AADEEEMNNNPRSY PYRENEAN DESMAN
AADEEFGHILMNRY FLYING HEAD MARE
AADEEFGILLLNOT DINOFLAGELLATE
AADEEFGLLNRRUV GLANDULAR FEVER
AADEEFHILNRTTY FAINT-HEARTEDLY
AADEEFIILNORST FEDERALISATION
AADEEFIILNORTZ FEDERALIZATION
AADEEGGIMNNRST AGGRANDISEMENT
AADEEGGIMNNRTZ AGGRANDIZEMENT
AADEEGHILOPRRT RADIOTELEGRAPH
AADEEGIMNNRRST DISARRANGEMENT
AADEEGIMNPRSST DISPARAGEMENTS
AADEEGINRSSTTT TRADING ESTATES
AADEEHHIMPRSST HEADMASTERSHIP
AADEEIILNPQSSU SESQUIPEDALIAN
AADEEIINNPRRST PREDESTINARIAN
AADEEIKLMOPRTV EVAPORATED MILK
AADEEILNRRSTTT TRANSLITERATED
AADEEINNPRSSTT ANTIDEPRESSANT
AADEEINNQSSTTU ANTIQUATEDNESS
AADEEPRRSSTTUU SUPERSATURATED
AADEFFHLNOSSTV STANDOFF HALVES
AADEFFIILNSTUV DIVINE AFFLATUS

AADEFILMMNNSTU FUNDAMENTALISM
AADEFILMNNSTTU FUNDAMENTALIST
AADEFILMNNTTUY FUNDAMENTALITY
AADEGHILNRSTUW DAUGHTERS-IN-
LAW
AADEGIINNORRTT INTERGRADATION
AADEGINOORRRTT RETROGRADATION
AADEGOORRRRTTY RETROGRADATORY
AADEHHKLLNNOOV HOEK VAN
HOLLAND
AADEHIILLMNPSU SULPHANILAMIDE
AADEHIIMNNOSTU DEHUMANISATION
AADEHIIMNNOTUZ DEHUMANIZATION
AADEHIINORRSST SHERARDISATION
AADEHIINORRSTZ SHERARDIZATION
AADEHIINPRSSST DANISH PASTRIES
AADEHIIOPRRSTT RADIOTHERAPIST
AADEHINNOPSSSU DIAPHANOUSNESS
AADEHORSSSTTUW SOUTHEASTWARDS
AADEIIILNOSTTV DEVITALISATION
AADEIIILNOTTVZ DEVITALIZATION
AADEIIIMNRSTTV ADMINISTRATIVE
AADEIIKLRSSTTW SIDEWALK ARTIST
AADEIILMNNNOOT DENOMINATIONAL
AADEIILMNOORST DEMORALISATION
AADEIILMNOORTZ DEMORALIZATION
AADEIILNNOPSST DISPENSATIONAL
AADEIILNOOPRST DEPOLARISATION
AADEIILNOOPRTZ DEPOLARIZATION
AADEIILNORSSTT DISSERTATIONAL
AADEIIMNNORSSV ANIMADVERSIONS
AADEILNNORTUUV UNDERVALUATION
AADEILNOOPSSST AT ONE'S DISPOSAL
AADEINOPPPRRTU UNAPPROPRIATED
AADELLOPSSTTTU SLOTTED SPATULA
AADELMPRRSSTTU MUSTARD PLASTER
AADFFGIIIILNST DISAFFILIATING
AADFFIIIILNOST DISAFFILIATION
AADGGIIINNOPPRZ PROPAGANDIZING
AADGIIIILNOSTT DIGITALISATION
AADGIIIILNOTTZ DIGITALIZATION
AADIIIILMNORSTT TRADITIONALISM
AADIIILNORSTTT TRADITIONALIST
AADIIIMNNORSTT ADMINISTRATION
AADIIIMNRRSTTX ADMINISTRATRIX
AADIIMNORRSSTT ADMINISTRATORS
AAEEEFGMNNORRS FERROMANGANESE
AAEEEGGGHINRTT IN THE AGGREGATE
AAEEEGHIMNOSST HAEMATOGENESIS
AAEEEGMNNPRRRT PREARRANGEMENT
AAEEEGMNNRRRST REARRANGEMENTS
AAEEEHHIMRSSTT THERMAESTHESIA
AAEEEHILPPRRST PRE-RAPHAELITES
AAEEEINPRSSSTV SEPARATIVENESS

AAEEELNOPRSSTT PERSONAL ESTATE
AAEEEMNNPRSTVW PERMANENT WAVES
AAEEFFGNRSSSTT STAFF SERGEANTS
AAEEFFHIIMRTTV THE AFFIRMATIVE
AAEEFFFILLNOOSV AVAIL ONESELF OF
AAEEFGIMNNORRS FERROMAGNESIAN
AAEEFHHLORSTTT SALT OF THE EARTH
AAEEFILNNRRSTT TRANSFERENTIAL
AAEEGGGILNRTXY EXAGGERATINGLY
AAEEGHIINNSTTZ ANAESTHETIZING
AAEEGHLLMOPRRT METALLOGRAPHER
AAEEGHLLNOOPTY PALAEETHNOLOGY
AAEEGHLMNNOOPX HAPAX
LEGOMENON
AAEEGIILNNORST GENERALISATION
AAEEGIILNNORTZ GENERALIZATION
AAEEGIILNNOSTV EVANGELISATION
AAEEGIILNNOTVZ EVANGELIZATION
AAEEGILNPRSTXY EXASPERATINGLY
AAEEGJMNORRSST SERGEANT MAJORS
AAEEGLMNPRSSTU SUPRASEGMENTAL
AAEEGLPPPRSSSU PURPLE PASSAGES
AAEEGMNOPRSSSU RAMPAGEOUSNESS
AAEEGOPRRRSTTW GREAT SPEARWORT
AAEEHIIMOOPSST HAEMATOPOIESIS
AAEEHIMNRSSSTU AMATEURISHNESS
AAEEHINORSTTTW WEATHER STATION
AAEEHMNOPRSTTU APARTMENT HOUSE
AAEEHMOOPRRRST SPERMATORRHOEA
AAEEIILLLRTTVY ALLITERATIVELY
AAEEIILMMPRSST ALPES MARITIMES
AAEEIILNNNORTT INTERNATIONALE
AAEEIILNNORSTT ETERNALISATION
AAEEIILNNORTTZ ETERNALIZATION
AAEEIKLNRRSSTU KAISERSLAUTERN
AAEEILNNOPRSTT PRESENTATIONAL
AAEEILNNPRRTTY INTERPLANETARY
AAEEIMNPRSTTTV PAVEMENT ARTIST
AAEEINNOPSSSST PASSIONATENESS
AAEEINRRSSTTTW WATER-RESISTANT
AAEEKMMNNPRSSTU AMUSEMENT PARKS
AAEELNNNPSSSTU UNPLEASANTNESS
AAEEMQRRRSSTTU QUARTERMASTERS
AAEFFFGIINORRS FOREIGN AFFAIRS
AAEFFIIMNORRST REAFFIRMATIONS
AAEFGLLNOOPRTT FORE-TOPGALLANT
AAEFHHMMOOTTTU FOAM AT THE
MOUTH
AAEFHINNORRRST FINSTERAARHORN
AAEFIIMNNOSSTT MANIFESTATIONS
AAEFIINNORRSTT FRATERNISATION
AAEFIINNORRTTZ FRATERNIZATION
AAEFILOPPRRSST PLASTER OF PARIS
AAEFIMNORRSTTV TRANSFORMATIVE

AAEFLLNOPRRRSU FUNERAL PARLORS
AAEFLLNOPRRRUU FUNERAL PARLOUR
AAEGGGGLNNORSTU STRONG
LANGUAGE
AAEGGHIILMNNTU HAEMAGGLUTININ
AAEGGIINNORRST GRANGERISATION
AAEGGIINNORRTZ GRANGERIZATION
AAEGGILMNOORST AGGLOMERATIONS
AAEGGILMNOSSYZ GLOSSY MAGAZINE
AAEGHHIKMRRSTW HIGH WATER
MARKS
AAEGHIILLNRTXY EXHILARATINGLY
AAEGHILMNRRTWY HEARTWARMINGLY
AAEGIIILLLNOST ILLEGALISATION
AAEGIIILLLNOTZ ILLEGALIZATION
AAEGIIIILNNOSTT GELATINISATION
AAEGIIIILNNOTTZ GELATINIZATION
AAEGIIILLNOORST ALLEGORISATION
AAEGIIILLNOORTZ ALLEGORIZATION
AAEGIIILNORRSTT REGISTRATIONAL
AAEGIIILNORRSTU REGULARISATION
AAEGIIILNORRTUZ REGULARIZATION
AAEGIIIMNRRSTTV TRANSMIGRATIVE
AAEGIIINNNRSSSU SANGUINARINESS
AAEGIIINNOORRST REORGANISATION
AAEGIIINNOORRTZ REORGANIZATION
AAEGILMNOOPRST SPERMATOGONIAL
AAEGILNOOPRSTT PROGESTATIONAL
AAEGIMNNRRTTTY MATERNITY GRANT
AAEHHILLOPSTUZ SULPHATHIAZOLE
AAEHIIIMNNSSTT ANTIHISTAMINES
AAEHILLMNOPSTT MENTAL HOSPITAL
AAEHIMOPRSSSTT MASSOTHERAPIST
AAEHLMOOOPPRRST SPERMATOPHORAL
AAEIIIKNNORSTT KERATINISATION
AAEIIIKNNORTTZ KERATINIZATION
AAEIIIILLMMNNRS MILLENARIANISM
AAEIIILMNNORST MINERALISATION
AAEIIILMNNORTZ MINERALIZATION
AAEIIIILNORSSST SERIALISATIONS
AAEIIILNORSSTZ SERIALIZATIONS
AAEIIILNORSTTV REVITALISATION
AAEIIILNORTTVZ REVITALIZATION
AAEIIIMMPRSSST SEMIPARASITISM
AAEIIINNNRSSST INSANITARINESS
AAEIIINNPPRTTT PINNATIPARTITE
AAEIIILLNNORSTT REINSTALLATION
AAEIIILMNNOSSST SENSATIONALISM
AAEIIILMNOOPRST OPERATIONALISM
AAEIIILMNOPRRST PROLETARIANISM
AAEIIILMNSSTYZZ MIZZEN STAYSAIL
AAEIIILMOPQRRTU IMPERIAL QUARTO
AAEIIILNNNORSTT INTERNATIONALS
AAEIIILNNORSTTU NEUTRALISATION

AAEIIILNNORTTUZ NEUTRALIZATION
AAEIIILNNOSSSTT SENSATIONALIST
AAEIIILNQTTTUVY QUANTITATIVELY
AAEIIMOPPPRRST MISAPPROPRIATE
AAEIINNORSSSTT STATIONARINESS
AAEIINNPPRRSTT ANTIPERSPIRANT
AAEIINOPRSSTTU PASTEURISATION
AAEIINOPRSTTUZ PASTEURIZATION
AAEIKKKLMNRSSU KAMENSK-URALSKI
AAEILLLLMORRST LAMELLIROSTRAL
AAEILLLLMRTTUY MULTILATERALLY
AAEILMOOPPRSTT SPATIOTEMPORAL
AAEILNORRRSTTT TRANSLITERATOR
AAEILNORSSTTWY SANITARY TOWELS
AAEIMNORSSSTTT STATIONMASTERS
AAEINNNOPRSTUU SUPERANNUATION
AAELLNPRRSTUUY SUPERNATURALLY
AAELMNSSSSTTYY SYSTEMS ANALYST
AAENNNOPPRSSST NANSEN PASSPORT
AAFGIILLMNNNPY FAMILY PLANNING
AAFIIIMNNORRTU UNIFORMITARIAN
AAFIILLMMNORTY INFLAMMATORILY
AAFIMNNOORRSTT TRANSFORMATION
AAGGHINOOPRRST ORGANOGRAPHIST
AAGGIIILNNRTTY INGRATIATINGLY
AAGGILMMOORSTT GRAMMATOLOGIST
AAGHIIINOPRSTT GRAPHITISATION
AAGHIIINOPRTTZ GRAPHITIZATION
AAGHIILMNORSTT ANTILOGARITHMS
AAGIIIMNOSSTTT STIGMATISATION
AAGIIIMNOSTTTZ STIGMATIZATION
AAGIIILNORSSTUV VULGARISATIONS
AAGIIILNORSTUVZ VULGARIZATIONS
AAGIILOOPRSSTT PARASITOLOGIST
AAGIIMNNORRSTT TRANSMIGRATION
AAGILMNOOPRSTV GALVANOTROPISM
AAGIMNORRRSTTY TRANSMIGRATORY
AAHHIIMOPRRSST AMPHIARTHROSIS
AAHIIINOORSSTTU AUTHORISATIONS
AAHIIINOORSTTUZ AUTHORIZATIONS
AAHILMOPPRRSTY AMPHIPROSTYLAR
AAHILNOOOPRRTT PROTHONOTARIAL
AAHILNORRSTTUY NATURAL HISTORY
AAHINOPSSSSSTT SHOP ASSISTANTS
AAHLLOPPSSTTYY STAPHYLOPLASTY
AAIIIIILNNOSTT INITIALISATION
AAIIIIILNNOTTZ INITIALIZATION
AAIIIILMNORSTT MILITARISATION
AAIIIILMNORTTZ MILITARIZATION
AAIIIILMNRSTTU UTILITARIANISM
AAIIIILNORSTTV TRIVIALISATION
AAIIIILNORTTVZ TRIVIALIZATION
AAIIILLNOOSTTV VOLATILISATION
AAIIILLNOOTTVZ VOLATILIZATION

AAIIINNOOOSTTU AUTOIONISATION
AAIIINNOOOTTUZ AUTOIONIZATION
AAIIJLNNOORSTU JOURNALISATION
AAIIJLNNOORTUZ JOURNALIZATION
AAIILLLNORSTTU ILLUSTRATIONAL
AAIILLMNNOSTTU MULTINATIONALS
AAIILLMOOPPSST PAPILLOMATOSIS
AAIILLNNORSTTY TRANSITIONALLY
AAIILNOOPPRSTU POPULARISATION
AAIILNOOPPRTUZ POPULARIZATION
AAIIMNOOPPRSTX APPROXIMATIONS
AAIINOOPPPRRST APPROPRIATIONS
AAIKMNOOQRSTTU QUOTATION
  MARKS
AAILMMNNORSTTU ULTRAMONTANISM
AAILMNNORSTTTU ULTRAMONTANIST
AAIMNNORSSTTTU TRANSMUTATIONS
AAINNOOPRRSTTT TRANSPORTATION
ABBBEEEISSTTTU TEST-TUBE BABIES
ABBCDEEEIORRSU BERBERIDACEOUS
ABBCEHILNORSTU BRONCHIAL TUBES
ABBCEHKOORRSSS SHOCK ABSORBERS
ABBCEIIJLSTTUY SUBJECTABILITY
ABBCEIKLLLRRYY BLACKBERRY LILY
ABBCGHILLNOORU RUBBING ALCOHOL
ABBDDEEELORSTU DOUBLE-BREASTED
ABBDEEFNORSSTU BEASTS OF BURDEN
ABBDEILLNORSTU BULLETIN BOARDS
ABBDIIIILNTTUY INDUBITABILITY
ABBEEEFHLLLLOT BELLE OF THE BALL
ABBEEELNORSSSV OBSERVABLENESS
ABBEEFHNORRTTU BEAR THE BRUNT
  OF
ABBEEHINNOOPRT PHENOBARBITONE
ABBEGHIIILOPRS BIBLIOGRAPHIES
ABBEGHIIILOPRRS BIBLIOGRAPHERS
ABBEGIMNPRRSTU RUBBER-STAMPING
ABCCCEEIIMMNRU CIRCUMAMBIENCE
ABCCCEIORSTUUU CUCURBITACEOUS
ABCCDEEHOPRSST BATCH PROCESSED
ABCCDEHILNSSUW CLUB SANDWICHES
ABCCDIILLMORSU UMBILICAL CORDS
ABCCEEEELRSSSU CAUSES CÉLEBRES
ABCCEEELORRRTX CEREBRAL CORTEX
ABCCEEFHILNOST CHIEF CONSTABLE
ABCCEEIIKRRRTU CIRCUIT BREAKER
ABCCEEIIILLNORR IRRECONCILABLE
ABCCEEIILLNRTYY CYBERNETICALLY
ABCCEEILMMNOUX EXCOMMUNICABLE
ABCCEEILNNOORT CONCELEBRATION
ABCCEHIINORSST BRONCHIECTASIS
ABCCEHIKLNPSST PITCH-BLACKNESS
ABCCEIILLMORSS SOCIAL CLIMBERS
ABCCEIIILLNORRY IRRECONCILABLY

ABCCEIILMMNNOU INCOMMUNICABLE
ABCCEIILNNPSUU PUBLIC NUISANCE
ABCCEILNNNOOSU UNCONSCIONABLE
ABCCGINNORSTTU SUBCONTRACTING
ABCCHHIIOPRRSS ARCHBISHOPRICS
ABCCHILOOPRSTU CLAUSTROPHOBIC
ABCCILNNNOOSUY UNCONSCIONABLY
ABCCNOORRSSTTU SUBCONTRACTORS
ABCDEEEEFHMMMR FEMME DE
  CHAMBRE
ABCDEEEEEILNSSV DECEIVABLENESS
ABCDEEEELLNSST DELECTABLENESS
ABCDEEEHIILNPR INDECIPHERABLE
ABCDEEEIILRSSV DISSERVICEABLE
ABCDEEEILNRSST CREDITABLENESS
ABCDEEEILPRSST DISRESPECTABLE
ABCDEEELLOOORT COLORADO BEETLE
ABCDEEGIKNORRR RECORD-BREAKING
ABCDEEHIILNPRY INDECIPHERABLY
ABCDEEHILPSTTT PITCHED BATTLES
ABCDEEIIILNNORS INCONSIDERABLE
ABCDEGIIIILPRTY CREDIBILITY GAP
ABCDEIIILPRTTY PREDICTABILITY
ABCDEIILNNOSTY CONDENSABILITY
ABCDEIMNNOOORX CARBON
  MONOXIDE
ABCDENOOORRRTU
  UNCORROBORATED
ABCDGHILNOOORS BOARDING SCHOOL
ABCDIIIILOSSTY DISSOCIABILITY
ABCEEEHMMRRRST CHARTER
  MEMBERS
ABCEEFIILNORTY ENFORCEABILITY
ABCEEGHIKLOORT GLOBE ARTICHOKE
ABCEEGIIILLNOTY BIOGENETICALLY
ABCEEGIINORSUZ ZINGIBERACEOUS
ABCEEGILNNORUZ UNRECOGNIZABLE
ABCEEGKKOORRST STOCKBROKERAGE
ABCEEGKNNOOSTW GET ONE'S OWN
  BACK
ABCEEHHHRTTTUY BURY THE
  HATCHET
ABCEEHIIKSTTTU TAKE THE BISCUIT
ABCEEHIJKNOSTX JACK-IN-THE-BOXES
ABCEEHIMNRSSTY CHIMNEYBREASTS
ABCEEHIOOPRSUU EUPHORBIACEOUS
ABCEEIIILPRTVY PERCEIVABILITY
ABCEEIIILRSTVY SERVICEABILITY
ABCEEIIILORRTVY RECOVERABILITY
ABCEEIIILPRSTTY RESPECTABILITY
ABCEEILNNSTUUY SUBLIEUTENANCY
ABCEEILRRSSTTU BATTLE CRUISERS
ABCEEMMMNORSUU MUCOUS
  MEMBRANE

ABCEFGIIILNNST FILING CABINETS
ABCEFGIILMMNRS CLIMBING FRAMES
ABCEGHIMNNSSUU SUBMACHINE GUNS
ABCEGIIJNRSSTU SUBJECT-RAISING
ABCEGIILOORSTT BACTERIOLOGIST
ABCEGILNNORSWW BROWN
  LACEWINGS
ABCEGINORRSSSZ ZEBRA CROSSINGS
ABCEHIILRSTTTY STRETCHABILITY
ABCEHILLLOPRYY HYPERBOLICALLY
ABCEHILORRSTTY ERYTHROBLASTIC
ABCEHIMORSSSTX CHRISTMAS BOXES
ABCEIIILLNTTUY INELUCTABILITY
ABCEIIIILNSTUXY INEXCUSABILITY
ABCEIIILORRTVY IRREVOCABILITY
ABCEIINOOPSSUV ABOVE SUSPICION
ABCEILLLMOORTY BOLOMETRICALLY
ABCEILLLPSSTTU PLASTIC BULLETS
ABCEILLMNOPSUU PNEUMOBACILLUS
ABCEILLMNOSSSY SYMBOLICALNESS
ABCEILMNNOOSSU NO-CLAIM BONUSES
ABCEILNNNOSTTU SUBCONTINENTAL
ABCELLLNNOOORTU UNCONTROLLABLE
ABCELNOSSTUUUY SUBCUTANEOUSLY
ABCEMMMNOORSUU
  MUCOMEMBRANOUS
ABCFFFLMOOOORTY COMFORTABLY OFF
ABCFIILMNOORTY CONFORMABILITY
ABCGIILLMOOOTY BIOCLIMATOLOGY
ABCGIILNOOPSST SPONGIOBLASTIC
ABCGIKLNORSSTT STARTING BLOCKS
ABCHIILNOTTUUY UNTOUCHABILITY
ABCHILMOOPRSTT THROMBOPLASTIC
ABCIIIIJLSTTUY JUSTICIABILITY
ABCIIILLLOPSTY COLLAPSIBILITY
ABCIIILNRSTTUY INSCRUTABILITY
ABCIILLMNOSTYY SYMBIONTICALLY
ABCIILMMNOSSTU SOMNAMBULISTIC
ABCIILNOORRTTU CONTRIBUTORIAL
ABCILMNORSTUUY RAMBUNCTIOUSLY
ABCIMNNNOOOOPS BOON
  COMPANIONS
ABDDEEEEFGHINRT FEATHERBEDDING
ABDDEEEHLLNSSU BULLHEADEDNESS
ABDDEEHIILSSST DISESTABLISHED
ABDDEEHLLORSSU SHOULDER BLADES
ABDDEEHLNOOSTU DOUBLET AND
  HOSE
ABDDEEIIJLMNOU DIAMOND JUBILEE
ABDDEEILMNNSTY ABSENT-MINDEDLY
ABDDEEMNNOSSTU METES AND
  BOUNDS
ABDDGINNOORSSU SOUNDING BOARDS
ABDEEEEILNRSST DELIBERATENESS

ABDEEEFFIILNRT DIFFERENTIABLE
ABDEEEFLORSTUU DOUBLE FEATURES
ABDEEEGHIIRTVW GIVE A WIDE BERTH
ABDEEEGILNRSST SINGLE-BREASTED
ABDEEEIILMNNRT INDETERMINABLE
ABDEEEIMNNOOTV ABOVE-
  MENTIONED
ABDEEEELLNOPRSS DEPLORABLENESS
ABDEEFIIILNNTU UNIDENTIFIABLE
ABDEEFIOOPSSTX SAFE-DEPOSIT BOX
ABDEEGHIOSTWYY GO BY THE WAYSIDE
ABDEEGILNRSSST DRESSING TABLES
ABDEEHIIILRTTY HEREDITABILITY
ABDEEIIILLRSSTU LIBERAL STUDIES
ABDEEIILMNNRTY INDETERMINABLY
ABDEEIILNNNSTV VENETIAN BLINDS
ABDEFIINNOSTUU SUBINFEUDATION
ABDEFINORSTUUY SUBINFEUDATORY
ABDEFMOOOORRSTW FROM BAD TO
  WORSE
ABDEGHINOOORSSU BOARDINGHOUSES
ABDEGHLMNORTUU ROUGH-AND-
  TUMBLE
ABDEGIIILLNNRRY LENDING LIBRARY
ABDEHHLMNRSTUY RHYTHM AND
  BLUES
ABDEHLMNNORRTU
  NORTHUMBERLAND
ABDEIIILMNOOST DEMOBILISATION
ABDEIIILMNOOTZ DEMOBILIZATION
ABDEIIILNPSSTY DISPENSABILITY
ABDEIIILNRSTUY UNDESIRABILITY
ABDEIIINRSSSSU SUBSIDIARINESS
ABDEIILNOORSTW BOWDLERISATION
ABDEIILNOORTWZ BOWDLERIZATION
ABDEILLMNNOPTU PLATINUM BLONDE
ABDEILLMOPRUWY UPWARDLY-MOBILE
ABDEILLNOOORST BLOOD RELATIONS
ABDEILMORSTUXY AMBIDEXTROUSLY
ABDEILRRRSTWWY WILD STRAWBERRY
ABDGHIMNOOSTTU DOUBTING
  THOMAS
ABDGIIILOOOORST RADIOBIOLOGIST
ABDGIIKNORRSST SKIRTING BOARDS
ABDIIIILMNOTTY INDOMITABILITY
ABDIIIILLOSSTVY DISSOLVABILITY
ABDIIILNORSTTU DISTRIBUTIONAL
ABDIIOOOPRSSSU BASIDIOSPOROUS
ABDILLMNNOPSTU PLATINUM BLONDS
ABDMOOOOORRSTTU OUTBOARD
  MOTORS
ABEEEEFGIKLNTV VEGETABLE KNIFE
ABEEEFFILNNOOS BANE OF ONE'S LIFE
ABEEEFILNNRRTT ENFANT TERRIBLE

ABEEEGHHIMNSTV MIGHT-HAVE-BEENS
ABEEEHLNRSSSST BREATHLESSNESS
ABEEEIKKRRRSST STRIKEBREAKERS
ABEEEIMMPRRSTV PRIVATE MEMBERS
ABEEEINORRRSTV REVERBERATIONS
ABEEELNNOPRSS PERSONABLENESS
ABEEFIILMNRTTY FERMENTABILITY
ABEEGHIILNSTUX EXTINGUISHABLE
ABEEGHILMMNOOT
METHAEMOGLOBIN
ABEEGHLORSSTTT GHETTO BLASTERS
ABEEGIIKKNRRST STRIKEBREAKING
ABEEGILNRRSSST TRANSGRESSIBLE
ABEEGNOORRRTTU TURBOGENERATOR
ABEEEHILMNSSSTT ESTABLISHMENTS
ABEEHILNOPSSST HOSPITABLENESS
ABEEEHLNNOORSSU HONOURABLENESS
ABEEHLOORTTTTW HOT-WATER
BOTTLE
ABEEIIILMMPRTY IMPERMEABILITY
ABEEIIILRRTTVY RETRIEVABILITY
ABEEIILMNNOSSU EMISSION NEBULA
ABEEIILMNOPRSS IMPRESSIONABLE
ABEEIILMNRRTUY REMUNERABILITY
ABEEIILPRRSTVY PRESERVABILITY
ABEEILMNNNOSTU UNMENTIONABLES
ABEEILNNOQSTUU UNQUESTIONABLE
ABEEILNNSSTTUU SUBLIEUTENANTS
ABEEILRRRSSTTU SUBTERRESTRIAL
ABEEIMNOSSSSTU ABSTEMIOUSNESS
ABEEKLNNNOSSUW UNKNOWABLENESS
ABEFGIIILNRRTY REFRANGIBILITY
ABEFIIILRRTTUY IRREFUTABILITY
ABEFILNOOPRSST SELF-ABSORPTION
ABEGGHHINORRTU ROUGH BREATHING
ABEGHILMNOOOXY
OXYHAEMOGLOBIN
ABEGHLMNRRSSTU BREMSSTRAHLUNG
ABEGIIILMNPRTY IMPREGNABILITY
ABEGIILORRSSTY GYROSTABILISER
ABEGIILORRSTYZ GYROSTABILIZER
ABEHIIIILNRTTY INHERITABILITY
ABEHIIILSTTUXY EXHAUSTIBILITY
ABEIIIILMNSTTY INESTIMABILITY
ABEIIIILLNORTTY INTOLERABILITY
ABEIIILMNNRTUY INNUMERABILITY
ABEIIILMORRTVY IRREMOVABILITY
ABEIIILNPRSTUY INSUPERABILITY
ABEIILMNOPRSSY IMPRESSIONABLY
ABEIIMNOPRRTTU IMPERTURBATION
ABEIINNORTTTUV NONATTRIBUTIVE
ABEILMNNORSTUU INSURMOUNTABLE
ABEILNNOQSTUUY UNQUESTIONABLY
ABEILNORSSSSUU SALUBRIOUSNESS

ABFGIIIILNNRTY INFRANGIBILITY
ABFIIIIILRTTVY VITRIFIABILITY
ABFIIIIJLSTTUY JUSTIFIABILITY
ABFIIIILNOSSTY FISSIONABILITY
ABHIIIKLNNTTUY UNTHINKABILITY
ABHIIINOOPRRTY PROHIBITIONARY
ABHIIINOORSTVY VASOINHIBITORY
ABHILLMNOPSTTU PUT IN MOTHBALLS
ABHILMNOOPRSTT THROMBOPLASTIN
ABIIIIILLLMTTY ILLIMITABILITY
ABIIIILLMPSTUY IMPLAUSIBILITY
ABIIIILMMNOOST IMMOBILISATION
ABIIIILMMNOOTZ IMMOBILIZATION
ABIIIIMNNOSTTU BITUMINISATION
ABIIIIMNNOTTUZ BITUMINIZATION
ABIILOPPRSTTUY SUPPORTABILITY
ACCCDEIIIILNOR RICINOLEIC ACID
ACCCDEINORSTTU CREDIT ACCOUNTS
ACCCEEEIIILLNPS SPECIAL LICENCE
ACCCEEHILLNORV VICE-CHANCELLOR
ACCCEEIIILNOSSS SOCIAL SCIENCES
ACCCEENNOOOVVX CONVEXO-
CONCAVE
ACCCEFFIILRRST TRAFFIC CIRCLES
ACCCEFINOOPRRT TROPIC OF
CANCER
ACCCEHHILMOPSY PSYCHOCHEMICAL
ACCCEHIINORSTT ARCHITECTONICS
ACCCEIMMNOOORS
MACROECONOMICS
ACCCENNORRTTUU CURRENT
ACCOUNT
ACCCHIIOOPSSTT TACHISTOSCOPIC
ACCCHLOOPSSTUY STAPHYLOCOCCUS
ACCCIIKKLOSSTT COCKTAIL STICKS
ACCCILLOSSSSUU LOCUS CLASSICUS
ACCCILNOOSSSSU CLASS-CONSCIOUS
ACCDDDEKLOOOOO COCK-A-DOODLE-
DOO
ACCDEEEELNOPRS PREADOLESCENCE
ACCDEEEHHIKNRT CHICKENHEARTED
ACCDEEFILNNSTU SELF-INDUCTANCE
ACCDEEHINRRRSU HARD CURRENCIES
ACCDEEIIILLLRTY DIELECTRICALLY
ACCDEEIILMMORS COMMERCIALISED
ACCDEEIILMMORZ COMMERCIALIZED
ACCDEEILMNORTY DYNAMOELECTRIC,
ELECTRODYNAMIC
ACCDEEILNNNSTY INCANDESCENTLY
ACCDEEILNOPSTU CONCEPTUALISED
ACCDEEILNOPTUZ CONCEPTUALIZED
ACCDEEILOORRST CROCODILE TEARS
ACCDEEIMMNOTUX
EXCOMMUNICATED

ACCDEEIMNOPPTY APPENDICECTOMY
ACCDEEINNNOSTU DISCOUNTENANCE
ACCDEELLMOSTUW WELL-
ACCUSTOMED
ACCDEFILLNOOTU DEFLOCCULATION
ACCDEFNNOORTUU UNACCOUNTED-
FOR
ACCDEHHIMNORSY HYDROMECHANICS
ACCDEHILMNOPSU UNACCOMPLISHED
ACCDEHINORSSUW SANDWICH COURSE
ACCDEHKLNOORTU AROUND THE
CLOCK
ACCDEIILLNNOTY COINCIDENTALLY
ACCDEIINNNOSTU DISCONTINUANCE
ACCDEINOOPSTTU DEPOSIT ACCOUNT
ACCDHHINOOPRSY HYPOCHONDRIACS
ACCDHIIIMMORST DICHROMATICISM
ACCDHIMNOPSSYY PSYCHODYNAMICS
ACCDIILNNOOPTU CONDUPLICATION
ACCDIINNOORSTT CONTRADICTIONS
ACCDILNOORRSTU CONDUCTOR RAILS
ACCEEEFFHKLOST COFFEE KLATCHES
ACCEEEFILNPTXY LIFE EXPECTANCY
ACCEEEGHIRRSSV SERVICE CHARGES
ACCEEEHILLMNPY MYELENCEPHALIC
ACCEEEHKLRRSTV TRAVELER'S CHECK
ACCEEEILOPSTVY ESCAPE VELOCITY
ACCEEEILPRRSWY CREEPY-CRAWLIES
ACCEEEELLMOPRTX ELECTRA COMPLEX
ACCEEELLNORTVY ELECTROVALENCY
ACCEEENNOPSTUX EXPENSE ACCOUNT
ACCEEEORRSSTUW WORCESTER SAUCE
ACCEEFFFHHNNOOT ON THE OFF
CHANCE
ACCEEFILLMORTV COLLECTIVE FARM
ACCEEFIMORRRTT REFRACTOMETRIC
ACCEEGHILOPRRT ELECTROGRAPHIC
ACCEEGHKNOSSTX STOCK EXCHANGES
ACCEEGILLNORTY EGOCENTRICALLY,
GEOCENTRICALLY
ACCEEHHIILNNPR RHINENCEPHALIC
ACCEEHHILMMORT
THERMOCHEMICAL
ACCEEHHLOORSST SCHOOLTEACHERS
ACCEEHIIILNSTT TECHNICALITIES
ACCEEHILMOPRST PETROCHEMICALS
ACCEEHKLNORRTU ROCKET-
LAUNCHER
ACCEEHORRSSTTY OYSTERCATCHERS
ACCEEIILORSSSV SOCIAL SERVICES
ACCEEIIMNNOORT ECONOMETRICIAN
ACCEEIINNOORSS CONCESSIONAIRE
ACCEEIKLNOPRSS COCKER SPANIELS
ACCEEILLLNORTY ELECTRONICALLY

ACCEEILLLOPSTY TELESCOPICALLY
ACCEEILORSSTTT ELECTROSTATICS
ACCEEILORSSTUU STERCULIACEOUS
ACCEEINOPRSTTV CONTRACEPTIVES
ACCEFGGHHIINNT FIGHTING CHANCE
ACCEFGIIIINNNS INSIGNIFICANCE
ACCEFIIIILLNSTY SCIENTIFICALLY
ACCEFIIINOPSST SPECIFICATIONS
ACCEFIIINORSTT RECTIFICATIONS
ACCEGHIILLNNOU HALLUCINOGENIC
ACCEGHIIMNNPRR PRINCE CHARMING
ACCEGHIOPPRRST SPECTROGRAPHIC
ACCEGIILNRTUXY EXCRUCIATINGLY
ACCEGIKLLNOOTU COCKTAIL LOUNGE
ACCEGILLMMOORY MYRMECOLOGICAL
ACCEGIOPPRRSTU GROUP PRACTICES
ACCEHHORRSSSTT RORSCHACH TESTS
ACCEHIKLLMOORY MOCK-HEROICALLY
ACCEHILLOOPSSS SPECIAL SCHOOLS
ACCEHILMMNOPST ACCOMPLISHMENT
ACCEHILMOOPRSU MICROCEPHALOUS
ACCEHILOORSSTU HORATIUS COCLES
ACCEIIILNNOORT RECONCILIATION
ACCEIIIILNOORT ONEIROCRITICAL
ACCEIIILLMOORSY SERIOCOMICALLY
ACCEIIILLOPPRSY PERISCOPICALLY
ACCEIILNOORRTY RECONCILIATORY
ACCEIILORSSTUY SOCIAL SECURITY
ACCEIINNOORSTT CONCRETISATION
ACCEIINNOORTTZ CONCRETIZATION
ACCEIINOPRSSSU CAPRICIOUSNESS
ACCEILLMNNOOUY UNECONOMICALLY
ACCEILNOORSSST CROSS-SECTIONAL
ACCEIMMNOORTUX
EXCOMMUNICATOR
ACCEINNNOORSTT CONCENTRATIONS
ACCEINNOORSTTU COUNTERACTIONS
ACCEINOOPPRSTU PREOCCUPATIONS
ACCEINOPPRSSSU PERCUSSION CAPS
ACCFFIIINORTTU FRUCTIFICATION
ACCFIIIIILNOST SILICIFICATION
ACCFIMMNNOOORT COMMON
FRACTION
ACCGHIILLOOPRS OSCILLOGRAPHIC
ACCGHIILLOORST CHRISTOLOGICAL
ACCGHILOPRSSUY PSYCHOSURGICAL
ACCGHINOOPPRSY PHARYNGOSCOPIC
ACCGIIILLMNOOR CRIMINOLOGICAL
ACCGIILLLOOOSY SOCIOLOGICALLY
ACCHHILOPPSSYY PSYCHOPHYSICAL
ACCHHIMOOOPRRT
CHROMATOPHORIC
ACCHHIMOOOORRTT
ORTHOCHROMATIC

ACCHIIILNORSTT ANTICHLORISTIC
ACCHIIINNNOOST CINCHONISATION
ACCHIIINNNOOTZ CINCHONIZATION
ACCHIILLOPRTYY HYPOCRITICALLY
ACCHILLNNORSYY SYNCHRONICALLY
ACCHIMOOPSSSTY PSYCHOSOMATICS
ACCIIILLOOOPST SOCIOPOLITICAL
ACCIILNNOOPRST CONSCRIPTIONAL
ACCIIMMNNOOSTU COMMUNICATIONS
ACCIIMNNORTTUU CIRCUMNUTATION
ACCILLOPPRRTYY PROCRYPTICALLY
ACCILMNOOSTUUY CONTUMACIOUSLY
ACCILNNOORSTTU CONSTRUCTIONAL
ACDDDEEIILMNST MIDDLE-DISTANCE
ACDDEEEKMNOPRS PROMENADE DECKS
ACDDEEGILNNNOR ENDOCRINE GLAND
ACDDEGLLNSSSTU DUCTLESS GLANDS
ACDDEIIINNOORT AIR-CONDITIONED
ACDDELMMMNOOSU COMMAND
  MODULES
ACDEEEEINSSTTV STATE'S EVIDENCE
ACDEEEHINRRSUV UNDERACHIEVERS
ACDEEEHNORSSTY DO THE NECESSARY
ACDEEEHORRSSTU TERRACED HOUSES
ACDEEEIIMNNPTT PATENT MEDICINE
ACDEEEILOOPRST RADIO TELESCOPE
ACDEEEIMNOPPST APPENDECTOMIES
ACDEEEINNOPQRU EQUIPONDERANCE
ACDEEENRRRSTUY UNDERSECRETARY
ACDEEFFIMORRTT DIFFRACTOMETER
ACDEEFGIILMNST MAGNETIC FIELDS
ACDEEFHIINNRSS DISENFRANCHISE
ACDEEFHORRSSTW CHEST OF DRAWERS
ACDEEFINNOORST CONFEDERATIONS
ACDEEFINOQRRUY RADIO FREQUENCY
ACDEEFNORRRSTW CENTER
  FORWARDS, CENTRE FORWARDS
ACDEEGHIIMNNNV VENDING MACHINE
ACDEEGHIINNRUV UNDERACHIEVING
ACDEEGHIKNNRST KITCHEN GARDENS
ACDEEGHILLRSTY CLEAR-SIGHTEDLY
ACDEEGHILOOSSW WILD-GOOSE CHASE
ACDEEGIILNNRTZ DECENTRALIZING
ACDEEGIIMNORRS ORGANISED CRIME
ACDEEGIIMNORRZ ORGANIZED CRIME
ACDEEGIINORSTT STAGE DIRECTION
ACDEEGILNNOQRU GRANDILOQUENCE
ACDEEGIMNORSTU DISCOURAGEMENT
ACDEEGKLMNNOTW
  ACKNOWLEDGMENT
ACDEEHIIINNRST DISINHERITANCE
ACDEEHIIKMNNSY KIDNEY MACHINES
ACDEEHILMNOSST METHODICALNESS
ACDEEHIMNNNSTT DISENCHANTMENT

ACDEEHINNOPSSW OPEN SANDWICHES
ACDEEHINPRSSSS CASH DISPENSERS
ACDEEIILNRSSTU DIURETICALNESS
ACDEEIKORRRTTT TRICK OR TREATED
ACDEEILLLNNOSY DECLENSIONALLY
ACDEEILLNORSTV CLOSED INTERVAL
ACDEEILNPPRRSU PERPENDICULARS
ACDEEIMMNNOORT
  RECOMMENDATION
ACDEEIMMNORSTV INVERTED
  COMMAS
ACDEEIMNNOSSSU MENDACIOUSNESS
ACDEEIMNNOSTWW CASEMENT
  WINDOW
ACDEEINOPRSSSU PREDACIOUSNESS
ACDEELNNNRSTTY TRANSCENDENTLY
ACDEEMMNOORRTY
  RECOMMENDATORY
ACDEENNORRSUVY ORDNANCE SURVEY
ACDEENOPRRSSTT PROTRACTEDNESS
ACDEFGHILMNORR FRENCH MARIGOLD
ACDEFGIKNNOORY DAY OF
  RECKONING
ACDEFIIIINNOTT IDENTIFICATION
ACDEFIIILLNNOTY CONFIDENTIALLY
ACDEGGINORRSSS GRADE
  CROSSINGS
ACDEGHILLMOOOT METHODOLOGICAL
ACDEGHIMNORRRS MARCHING
  ORDERS
ACDEGHIMNORSTY HYDROMAGNETICS
ACDEGHINNORSTU COUNTERSHADING
ACDEGIILLLOOOY IDEOLOOGICALLY
ACDEGIILLOOPRT PTERIDOLOGICAL
ACDEGIILLOOSTT DIALECTOLOGIST
ACDEGILNNNRSTY TRANSCENDINGLY
ACDEGIMMNNORSW WING
  COMMANDERS
ACDEGIMNNNORTU
  COUNTERMANDING
ACDEGINOOPRSTT PROGNOSTICATED
ACDEGMMNNOOORR COMMON-OR-
  GARDEN
ACDEHHIILOORTZ CHLOROTHIAZIDE
ACDEHHIIMOPRRT HERMAPHRODITIC
ACDEHHILNPRSSS SHIP'S CHANDLERS
ACDEHIILLMMOTY IMMETHODICALLY
ACDEHIILLOPRSY SPHEROIDICALLY
ACDEHIIMORRSTY RADIOCHEMISTRY
ACDEHILLMOPRYY HYPODERMICALLY
ACDEHILLNOPTYY ENDOPHYTICALLY
ACDEHILMOOPPRR CHLORPROPAMIDE
ACDEHIMMNORSTY
  THERMODYNAMICS

ACDEHINOORRSTT TRISOCTAHEDRON
ACDEHLOOOOPPRSV APPROVED SCHOOL
ACDEIIIIMNNRST INDISCRIMINATE
ACDEIIILNNORTU UNIDIRECTIONAL
ACDEIIILNNSTTW IDENTICAL TWINS
ACDEIIILNORTTY DIRECTIONALITY
ACDEIIINORSSSY IDIOSYNCRASIES
ACDEIIKLRSSTTW WILDCAT STRIKES
ACDEIILLMNPRTU PNEUMATIC DRILL
ACDEIILLMOORTY IODOMETRICALLY
ACDEIILNNOOOST DECOLONISATION
ACDEIILNNOOOTZ DECOLONIZATION
ACDEIILNOOORST DECOLORISATION
ACDEIILNOOORTZ DECOLORIZATION
ACDEIINNOORSST CONSIDERATIONS
ACDEILLMNOOSTY ENDOSMOTICALLY
ACDEILLNOOSSTY DISCONSOLATELY
ACDEIMMNNOPSUY PNEUMODYNAMICS
ACDEINNOOPRRTU UNINCORPORATED
ACDEINNORSTUUY CONSUETUDINARY
ACDEINOOQRSSTU CONQUISTADORES
ACDFGHIIINNRSS DISFRANCHISING
ACDFHIIIIMNOTU HUMIDIFICATION
ACDFIIIILNOOST SOLIDIFICATION
ACDGGIILNORSUY DISCOURAGINGLY
ACDGHILLLOORYY HYDROLOGICALLY
ACDGHILMNNOOPY HOLDING
  COMPANY
ACDGIIIIMNNRST DISCRIMINATING
ACDGIIINNNORTT INDOCTRINATING
ACDHHIIOPRRSST HARPSICHORDIST
ACDHIIOOOPPRTT DIAPHOTOTROPIC
ACDIIIILNNNOST DISINCLINATION
ACDIIIIMNNORST DISCRIMINATION
ACDIIIJLNORSTU JURISDICTIONAL
ACDIIILNNOOTTY CONDITIONALITY
ACDIIIMNNORSTY DISCRIMINATORY
ACDIIINNNOOORT INCOORDINATION
ACDIIINNNOORTT INDOCTRINATION
ACDIILNNOOOSST CONSOLIDATIONS,
  DISCONSOLATION
ACDIILNOOORSST DISCOLORATIONS
ACDILLLMOOORXY LOXODROMICALLY
ACDIMNOOPRSSTU MASS PRODUCTION
ACEEEEFFFLMNST SELF-EFFACEMENT
ACEEEEFHHLNPRT THREE-HALFPENCE
ACEEEEFLNPRSST FALSE PRETENCES
ACEEEEGILLPTXY EPEXEGETICALLY
ACEEEEHHILNRTW CATHERINE WHEEL
ACEEEEILMNPPRS MALICE PREPENSE
ACEEEEINNNRRST TERCENTENARIES
ACEEEEPPRRSSTW CARPET SWEEPERS
ACEEEFFGINOPRS PEACE OFFERINGS
ACEEEFHIMRRTUV RHEUMATIC FEVER

ACEEEFINRRSSTV REFRACTIVENESS
ACEEEGGILNNRSW GREEN LACEWINGS
ACEEEGHNNNOSTU CHANGE ONE'S
  TUNE
ACEEEGIIILNPTY EPIGENETICALLY
ACEEEGIMMOSTTT COMMITTEE STAGE
ACEEEGMNNORSTU
  ENCOURAGEMENTS
ACEEEHHILLORTT HETEROLECITHAL
ACEEEHILNNNRST CHINESE LANTERN
ACEEEHILNORSST CHOLINESTERASE
ACEEEHLLMNNOPY MYELENCEPHALON
ACEEEHLLMORRTT ELECTROTHERMAL
ACEEEHMMOORTTY
  HAEMOCYTOMETER
ACEEEHNORTTTTU TO THE
  UTTERANCE
ACEEEHOORRSTUV HAVE RECOURSE TO
ACEEEIILMNNNST SEMICENTENNIAL
ACEEEILLLMRTTY TELEMETRICALLY
ACEEEILMNORTTU ROMAINE LETTUCE
ACEEEILMORRSTT STEREOMETRICAL
ACEEEILNNNOQUV NONEQUIVALENCE
ACEEEILNPRSTTY PETTY LARCENIES
ACEEELMORSSSST MALTESE CROSSES
ACEEEMNOOPRSTV OVERCOMPENSATE
ACEEEMNORRSTUU COUNTERMEASURE
ACEEFFGLNNORSU LONG-SUFFERANCE
ACEEFFIILNTTUY INEFFECTUALITY
ACEEFFHIIINORT ETHERIFICATION
ACEEFHILORSSTW AS THE CROW FLIES
ACEEFIIINORSTT ESTERIFICATION
ACEEFILMNOPRST SELF-IMPORTANCE
ACEEFILMPRRSTU SIMPLE FRACTURE
ACEEFINORRRSST REFRACTORINESS
ACEEGHHLNORSST CLOTHES HANGERS
ACEEGHHMNRRRSU HUNGER
  MARCHERS
ACEEGHHOOPRRRS CHOREOGRAPHERS
ACEEGHIIMNNSSW SEWING MACHINES
ACEEGHIKLNNRSU RECKLINGHAUSEN
ACEEGHILNORSSU CLEARINGHOUSES
ACEEGHILNOSSSU CHAISES LONGUES
ACEEGHILOPRRSX LEXICOGRAPHERS
ACEEGHIMMNORTT
  THERMOMAGNETIC
ACEEGHIMOOPRRT METEOROGRAPHIC
ACEEGIINNNORTT TRACTION ENGINE
ACEEGIINOPRRRS CARRIER PIGEONS
ACEEGILLLLOOTY TELEOLOGICALLY
ACEEGILLMOOORT METEOROLOGICAL
ACEEGILLNRSTYY SYNERGETICALLY
ACEEGLNRRSTTUU STRUCTURAL GENE
ACEEGNOORSSSUU COURAGEOUSNESS

ACEEHHIIKSSTTV THICK AS THIEVES
ACEEHHILNNNNOPR RHINENCEPHALON
ACEEHHIMOPRSTT CHEMOTHERAPIST
ACEEHIIILNPSTT LICENTIATESHIP
ACEEHIIINSTTTU AUTHENTICITIES
ACEEHIIILLNNPST PANHELLENISTIC
ACEEHIILMMNPSS SIMPLE MACHINES
ACEEHIINPPPRST APPRENTICESHIP
ACEEHILLMNNOSS MELANCHOLINESS
ACEEHILLMORTXY EXOTHERMICALLY
ACEEHILNNNOPSSU EUPHONICALNESS
ACEEHIMMNORSSV SERVOMECHANISM
ACEEHIMRRSSSTT CHRISTMAS TREES
ACEEHINORSUUVX NOUVEAUX RICHES
ACEEHKMNORSTTT SHOCK
  TREATMENT
ACEEHLNNOOPPRS PROSENCEPHALON
ACEEHLPPRSSTUY SUPPLY TEACHERS
ACEEHMNOPPRRST RAPPROCHEMENTS
ACEEHPRRRSTTTY STRETCHER PARTY
ACEEIIIILLLMPST SEMIELLIPTICAL
ACEEIIJLNNORTT INTERJECTIONAL
ACEEIIILLNPSST ELLIPTICALNESS
ACEEIIILLMPRRTY PERIMETRICALLY
ACEEIIILLRRSTTV VERTICILLASTER
ACEEIIILNNNOPTT EPICONTINENTAL
ACEEIIILNNORSST INTERCESSIONAL
ACEEIIILNNORSTT INTERSECTIONAL
ACEEIIILNOPTTXY EXCEPTIONALITY
ACEEIIILNOSSTTY COESSENTIALITY
ACEEIIILNPRSTTT PETIT LARCENIST
ACEEIINORSSTTV SERVICE STATION
ACEEIKLNRSSSTV TRAVELSICKNESS
ACEEILLLLNTTUY INTELLECTUALLY
ACEEIILLMNORRTU INTERMOLECULAR
ACEEILMNOOOPSU POLEMONIACEOUS
ACEEILMOPRSSTU PRECIOUS METALS
ACEEILNNQQUUVY QUINQUEVALENCY
ACEEILNNRRSTUW NUCLEAR WINTERS
ACEEILNORRRSTU RESURRECTIONAL
ACEEILNORSTVVY CONSERVATIVELY
ACEEIMMNNORSTU INCOMMENSURATE
ACEEIMNOOORRRT RECREATION
  ROOM
ACEEIMNOOPRRST CONTEMPORARIES
ACEEIMNOPPRRTU MERCAPTOPURINE
ACEEIMNORRSSSX CROSS-EXAMINERS
ACEEINNOOOPRTV NONCOOPERATIVE
ACEEINOORRSSTV CONSERVATOIRES,
  CONSERVATORIES
ACEEINOPRRSSSU PRECARIOUSNESS
ACEELLOORRRSST ROLLER COASTERS
ACEFFIIOSSTTUY SUFFICE IT TO SAY
ACEFFINOOQSTTU QUESTION OF FACT

ACEFGIIINNORTT GENTRIFICATION
ACEFGIINNORTTU CENTRIFUGATION
ACEFHHIIINPSST CHIEFTAINSHIPS
ACEFHIIIOTTVVY HIVE OF ACTIVITY
ACEFIIIILMPSTV SIMPLIFICATIVE
ACEFIIIINORTVV REVIVIFICATION
ACEFIIILMNOSTU EMULSIFICATION
ACEFIIILPRSTUY SUPERFICIALITY
ACEFIINOSSSTTU FACTITIOUSNESS
ACEFINOOPPRRRT PROPER FRACTION
ACEFINRRRSTTUU INFRASTRUCTURE
ACEFJKKLNOORST NORFOLK JACKETS
ACEFLNOORSSSTU COLOURFASTNESS
ACEGGHHINOOPRR CHOREOGRAPHING
ACEGGHIIMNNNNU MACHINEGUNNING
ACEGGIILNNNPRS SPRING-CLEANING
ACEGGILLNOOORT GERONTOLOGICAL
ACEGGILNOOSSTY GYNAECOLOGISTS
ACEGHILLLNOOTY ETHNOLOGICALLY
ACEGHILLNOOPTY PHOTOGENICALLY
ACEGHILLNOORTY ORTHOGENICALLY
ACEGHLMOOPSTYY METAPSYCHOLOGY
ACEGHMMOOPRSUY
  MYRMECOPHAGOUS
ACEGHOPPRRRSTY CRYPTOGRAPHERS
ACEGIIINNNNORTZ CONTAINERIZING
ACEGIILLLOSTUY EULOGISTICALLY
ACEGIILLMNOORT TERMINOLOGICAL
ACEGIILLORSSUY SACRILEGIOUSLY
ACEGIILNNORTUV COUNTERVAILING
ACEGIILNNOTTUV CONGLUTINATIVE
ACEGIILNOQTUVY EQUIVOCATINGLY
ACEGIILNOSSTTU GESTICULATIONS
ACEGIIMNNORSSX CROSS-EXAMINING
ACEGIINPRRSSTT STARTING PRICES
ACEGILLLMOOTYY ETYMOLOGICALLY
ACEGILLLOOOSTY OSTEOLOGICALLY
ACEGILMNNOOORT
  CONGLOMERATION
ACEGILNOPRSSTU PLASTIC SURGEON
ACEGILPRRSSTUY PLASTIC SURGERY
ACEGIMMMOPRRSU PROGRAMME
  MUSIC
ACEGINNNOOSSUU CONSANGUINEOUS
ACEGINNOOSSSTU CONTAGIOUSNESS
ACEGINNOPSSSUU PUGNACIOUSNESS
ACEHHIIINOPRRTT THERIANTHROPIC
ACEHHILLOOPSTY THEOSOPHICALLY
ACEHHILLOPTTYY HYPOTHETICALLY
ACEHHILOOPRSUZ RHIZOCEPHALOUS
ACEHHLMOOOPPST OPHTHALMOSCOPE
ACEHHMMNRSSTUY
  CHRYSANTHEMUMS
ACEHIIIILMSSTW WHIMSICALITIES

ACEHIILLPSTUUY EUPHUISTICALLY
ACEHIILNORSSST HISTORICALNESS
ACEHIIMNNOOPRT ENANTIOMORPHIC
ACEHIINNSSTTUU UNENTHUSIASTIC
ACEHIINOOPRTTU EUTROPHICATION
ACEHIINOPPRSST SPINTHARISCOPE
ACEHIINOPRSSST CORNISH PASTIES
ACEHIIOOPRSSST SPIROCHAETOSIS
ACEHIIOORRSTTT OSTEOARTHRITIC
ACEHILLNOPPTYY PHENOTYPICALLY
ACEHILLOPRSTTY PROSTHETICALLY
ACEHILLOPRTXYY XEROPHYTICALLY
ACEHILMNOOPRRZ CHLORPROMAZINE
ACEHILMOPRSSTT THERMOPLASTICS
ACEHILOOPRSSTV PRIVATE SCHOOLS
ACEHIMNOOPRRTT ANTHROPOMETRIC
ACEHIMOPPRSTTY SPERMATOPHYTIC
ACEHINNORSSSTY NARCOSYNTHESIS
ACEHINOORRSSTT ORCHESTRATIONS
ACEIIIILMNPSTU MUNICIPALITIES
ACEIIIILNPPRST PRINCIPALITIES
ACEIIIILLMOPRTY MILITARY POLICE
ACEIIIILLMPTTUV MULTIPLICATIVE
ACEIIIILLNORTTV VERTICILLATION
ACEIIIILLOPSSTY ISOPIESTICALLY
ACEIIIILMNOOSTT EMOTIONALISTIC
ACEIIIILNRRTUVY CURVILINEARITY
ACEIIIILNRSSTUV UNIVERSALISTIC
ACEIIIMMNOORSS COMMISSIONAIRE
ACEIIIMNNORRST RECRIMINATIONS
ACEIIINOPSSTX EXPANSIONISTIC
ACEIIINOPPRSTT PRECIPITATIONS
ACEIILLLNRTUUY UNICELLULARITY
ACEIILLMNNOOOS NEOCOLONIALISM
ACEIILLNNOOOST NEOCOLONIALIST
ACEIILMNNNOSTT CONTINENTALISM
ACEIILNNNOSTTT CONTINENTALIST
ACEIILNNNOTTTY CONTINENTALITY
ACEIILNNOOPRST IN LOCO PARENTIS
ACEIILNNORRSTU INSURRECTIONAL
ACEIILNOOPSSTT POLICE STATIONS
ACEIILNOPRSTUY PERTINACIOUSLY
ACEIILNOSSSSUV LASCIVIOUSNESS
ACEIIMMNNOORTU IMMUNOREACTION
ACEIIMMNOORSST COMMISERATIONS
ACEIINNOOORSVZ CONVERSAZIOONI
ACEIINNORSSTTY SYNCRETISATION
ACEIINNORSTTYZ SYNCRETIZATION
ACEIINNOSSSTUU INCAUTIOUSNESS
ACEIINOPSSSSUU AUSPICIOUSNESS
ACEILLLMORTUVY VOLUMETRICALLY
ACEILLMMOORSTY OSMOMETRICALLY
ACEILLMNOORRSS CRIMSON ROSELLA
ACEILLMOPRRTYY PYROMETRICALLY

ACEILLNNNOOTVY CONVENTIONALLY
ACEILLNNOOSSTT CONSTELLATIONS
ACEILLNOOPRSST CROSS-POLLINATE
ACEILLNOPRSSUY SUPERSONICALLY
ACEILMNOOORTUV MACROEVOLUTION
ACEILMNOOPRRTY CONTEMPORARILY
ACEILNNNNOOTUV UNCONVENTIONAL
ACEILNNNOOPRST CONSTANTINOPLE
ACEILNNOOOPRST SPIRONOLACTONE
ACEILNOOOPRRTUY PERLOCUTIONARY
ACEILNOPRRRTUV PROVENTRICULAR
ACEILOORRSTTUW WATERCOLOURIST
ACEIMMNNOORSTU
    COMMENSURATION
ACEINNNOOOOPRT NONCOOPERATION
ACEINNNOORSTTV CONTRAVENTIONS
ACELLMNNOOPRSU PERSONAL
    COLUMN
ACELNOPRSSSSWY LAWSON'S CYPRESS
ACELRRRSTTTUUU ULTRASTRUCTURE
ACEMNOOORSSTTU
    ENTOMOSTRACOUS
ACFFIIINOOORSTT FORTIFICATIONS
ACFGIIIILNNOTZ FICTIONALIZING
ACFGIIIINNOSST SIGNIFICATIONS
ACFGIIIILNOORST GLORIFICATIONS
ACFGIILMNNNOTU MALFUNCTIONING
ACFGIINNOORSTU CONFIGURATIONS
ACFIIIILMNOPST SIMPLIFICATION
ACFIIIJLLNOOST JOLLIFICATIONS
ACFIIILNOSTTTU STULTIFICATION
ACFIILLRSTTUUY FUTURISTICALLY
ACFIILNNOSSTTU FUNCTIONALISTS
ACFIMNOOOORSTTT COMFORT STATION
ACFINNNOOOORSTT CONFRONTATIONS
ACGGHHIMOPPRSY SPHYGMOGRAPHIC
ACGGHIKLNOSSTU LAUGHINGSTOCKS
ACGHHHIOOPSTUY ICHTHYOPHAGOUS
ACGHIIILNOPSTT ANTIPHLOGISTIC
ACGHIIKNNOSTTT STICK AT NOTHING
ACGHIILLLLOOPY PHILOLOGICALLY
ACGHIILLLLOOTY LITHOLOGICALLY
ACGHIILLLOOSTY HISTOLOGICALLY
ACGHIILLNOOORT ORNITHOLOGICAL
ACGHILLLNOOOPY PHONOLOGICALLY
ACGIIILLLNSTUY LINGUISTICALLY
ACGIIILLLPSTUY PUGILISTICALLY
ACGIIILNNOTTXY INTOXICATINGLY
ACGIIILPRRSSTU SURGICAL
    SPIRIT
ACGILRRSSTTUU AGRICULTURISTS
ACGIIMMNOORRSS MICROORGANISMS
ACGILNOOPRSSTY LARYNGOSCOPIST
ACGINOOOPRRSTT PROGNOSTICATOR

ACHHILLMNOOOPY
  HOMOPHONICALLY
ACHHIMMMOOOORST
  HOMOCHROMATISM
ACHHINOOOPPRST ANTHROPOSOPHIC
ACHHLMOOOOPPSTY
  OPHTHALMOSCOPY
ACHIIIINNORSTT TRICHINISATION
ACHIIIINNORTTZ TRICHINIZATION
ACHIIILLLPSTYY SYPHILITICALLY
ACHIIILLNORSTY HISTRIONICALLY
ACHIIIMNOORSST TRICHOMONIASIS
ACHIIINOOPSSTT SOPHISTICATION
ACHIILLLMNOOTY MONOLITHICALLY
ACHIILLLOSTTYY HISTOLYTICALLY
ACHIIOPRSSSTTY ASTROPHYSICIST
ACHILLLNOOOPPYY POLYPHONICALLY
ACHILLOOPPTTYY PHOTOTYPICALLY
ACHILMMOOPRSTY POLYCHROMATISM
ACHILMOOPRRSSY PRIMARY SCHOOLS
ACHIMMMNOOOORST
  MONOCHROMATISM
ACIIIILNOOPSTT POLITICISATION
ACIIIILNOOPTTZ POLITICIZATION
ACIIIILPRSSTTU SPIRITUALISTIC
ACIIILLLMPSSTY SIMPLISTICALLY
ACIIILLMNOPTTU MULTIPLICATION
ACIIILLMOPSTTY OPTIMISTICALLY
ACIIILMNOPRSSV PROVINCIALISMS
ACIIILNOPSSUUY INAUSPICIOUSLY
ACIILLLMOOQSSU COLLOQUIALISMS
ACIILNNOOSTTTU CONSTITUTIONAL
ACIINNNOOPRSTU PRONUNCIATIONS
ACIINNOOOPRSTT CONTRAPOSITION
ACIINNOPRRSSTT TRANSCRIPTIONS
ACIKMNNOORSTUY ROCKY
  MOUNTAINS
ACILLMMNNOOTTY
  NONCOMMITTALLY
ACILMOOPRRRSUY PRIMARY COLOURS
ACIMMOOORSSTTU MICROSTOMATOUS
ACIMNOOOSTTTXY CYTOTAXONOMIST
ADDDDEGIIMNNOW DIAMOND
  WEDDING
ADDDEIIIILNSUV INDIVIDUALISED
ADDDEIIIILNUVZ INDIVIDUALIZED
ADDEEEEHNNNSSV EVEN-HANDEDNESS
ADDEEEFFIINRTT DIFFERENTIATED
ADDEEEFHLNNSST LEFT-HANDEDNESS
ADDEEEFILMNTXY EXTENDED FAMILY
ADDEEEHIMNPPRS MISAPPREHENDED
ADDEEEHNNNOPSS OPEN-HANDEDNESS
ADDEEEIKMNNSSW WEAK-MINDEDNESS
ADDEEEILMPRTTY PREMEDITATEDLY

ADDEEEILNNNPSS PINS AND NEEDLES
ADDEEEIMNPRTTU UNPREMEDITATED
ADDEEEIMNRSTTU UNDERESTIMATED
ADDEEFFHLRRUUY FURFURALDEHYDE
ADDEEFIIMNNRSS FAIR-MINDEDNESS
ADDEEFLNNNORUW
  NEWFOUNDLANDER
ADDEEFLNNPRSUY PENNY DREADFULS
ADDEEGHHHINNSS HIGH-HANDEDNESS
ADDEEHIIMMNNRTY DIMENHYDRINATE
ADDEEILMNNPRSU NIL DESPERANDUM
ADDEEINNNORSWY NINE DAYS'
  WONDER
ADDEGILNOORRSU RIO GRANDE DO
  SUL
ADDEGINNNRSSTU UNDERSTANDINGS
ADDEGINNNORRSST STANDING ORDERS
ADDEIIIILNRSUV INDIVIDUALISER
ADDEIIIILNRUVZ INDIVIDUALIZER
ADDEIIIILNRSSTU INDUSTRIALISED
ADDEIIIILNRSTUZ INDUSTRIALIZED
ADDEIIILLNNOPTW WIND-POLLINATED
ADDEIILNOPPSTY DISAPPOINTEDLY
ADDIIIILNSSTUV INDIVIDUALISTS
ADEEEEEGNNRSST DEGENERATENESS
ADEEEEEHLLRRSW WHEELER-DEALERS
ADEEEEFHINRSUW AUF WIEDERSEHEN
ADEEEEGHILLNRW WHEELER-DEALING
ADEEEEHHLMMPST HEMEL HEMPSTEAD
ADEEEEHNRSTTVY THREE-DAY EVENTS
ADEEEEIMNPRRTT PREDETERMINATE
ADEEEELMNRSSTT ELDER STATESMEN
ADEEEELNNNRRVV NEVER-NEVER
  LAND
ADEEEFGILORRTU TIERRA DEL FUEGO
ADEEEFHOOPRRTW WEATHERPROOFED
ADEEEFIMNNOORT AFOREMENTIONED
ADEEEFIMNRSTTU DISFEATUREMENT
ADEEEFINNORSTT DEFENESTRATION
ADEEEGHHMNPRRS GERMAN
  SHEPHERD
ADEEEGHNOORRRY HONORARY
  DEGREE
ADEEEGIILMNRST LEGERDEMAINIST
ADEEEGIINRRTTV REDINTEGRATIVE
ADEEEGIKNNRRRT KINDERGARTENER
ADEEEGLNRRSSSS REGARDLESSNESS
ADEEEGOPRRRTUY DAGUERREOTYPER
ADEEEGOPRRSTUY DAGUERREOTYPES
ADEEEHHLLORTWY WHOLE-
  HEARTEDLY
ADEEEHIINRRSST HEREDITARINESS
ADEEEHIKMNOSSU HOUSEMAID'S KNEE
ADEEEHILNOOPRT RADIOTELEPHONE

ADEEEHIMNNRSTT DISHEARTENMENT
ADEEEHIRRSSTTV THE DRIVER'S SEAT
ADEEEIIMNNRRST INTERMEDIARIES
ADEEEIIMMQRSUV DEMISEMIQUAVER
ADEEEIIMNSSTTV MEDITATIVENESS
ADEEEILMORRTTY RADIOTELEMETRY
ADEEEIMNRSSTTU UNDERESTIMATES
ADEEEMNNRSTTTU UNDERSTATEMENT
ADEEEENNPPRRSSU UNPREPAREDNESS
ADEEFFIINORRTT DIFFERENTIATOR
ADEEFGHINRSSST FARSIGHTEDNESS
ADEEFGINNOSTTU DETONATING FUSE
ADEEFGLLOOPRSU GOLD-OF-PLEASURE
ADEEFHILLNOSTU THE LIFE AND SOUL
ADEEFHILNSSTTW HALFWITTEDNESS
ADEEFIMNNOORRT FOREORDAINMENT
ADEEFLLLLMOORWY FOLLOW-MY-
    LEADER
ADEEGGIMNNRRRY GERRYMANDERING
ADEEGHHNOOOSTV HAVE THE GOODS
    ON
ADEEGHILNNRRTY HEARTRENDINGLY
ADEEGHILNRSSTU DAUGHTERLINESS
ADEEGHNNORSSST HEADSTRONGNESS
ADEEGIIINRSTTV DISINTEGRATIVE
ADEEGIINNORRTT REDINTEGRATION
ADEEGINNOPPRRT PREPONDERATING
ADEEGINOORRSST DEROGATORINESS
ADEEGJLMNSTUUV VALUE JUDGMENTS
ADEEGLNNORSSTU DENTAL SURGEONS
ADEEHHIILMOPRS HEMISPHEROIDAL
ADEEHHIMOPRRST HERMAPHRODITES
ADEEHHLMNOOSSU HOUSEHOLD
    NAMES
ADEEHILMNNRSTT DISENTHRALMENT
ADEEHILNNOPSST SHETLAND PONIES
ADEEHILNOOPRTY RADIOTELEPHONY
ADEEHIMMOPRSTX MIXED METAPHORS
ADEEHLMNOORRSY
    DYSMENORRHOEAL
ADEEHMNNNOSSSU UNHANDSOMENESS
ADEEIIINORSSTV RADIOSENSITIVE
ADEEIIILNNNORST NONRESIDENTIAL
ADEEIIILOPRRSTV PRIVATE SOLDIER
ADEEIIMNNOOSTT DEMONETISATION
ADEEIIMNNOOTTZ DEMONETIZATION
ADEEIINNOPRSTT PREDESTINATION
ADEEIINSSSSSUV DISSUASIVENESS
ADEEIILLNORRSVY ORDINARY LEVELS
ADEEEILNNRRSTUY UNRESTRAINEDLY
ADEEIILNORRSSWW WORLD-WEARINESS
ADEEIMNNORRSST ARRONDISSEMENT
ADEEINNOOPPRRT PREPONDERATION
ADEEJMMORRSTTU DRUM MAJORETTES

ADEELNNOPPRRTY PREPONDERANTLY
ADEELNNORSSSSU SLANDEROUSNESS
ADEEMNRSSTTTUU MATURE STUDENTS
ADEFFGHINNORTU FOUNDING FATHER
ADEFFGIINORSST DISAFFORESTING
ADEFFHILLNOSUY FULLY-FASHIONED
ADEFGHIMOORRTY FAIRY GODMOTHER
ADEFGIIMNORRST TRANSMOGRIFIED
ADEFIIINNOSSTT DISINFESTATION
ADEFIINOORSSTT DISFORESTATION
ADEFIINOSSSSTU FASTIDIOUSNESS
ADEGGIIINNRSTT DISINTEGRATING
ADEGGILLNRSSSU SLUGGARDLINESS
ADEGHIKNNOORTT THE GORDIAN
    KNOT
ADEGHINNNOSSTT ONE-NIGHT STANDS
ADEGIIIILMNRTZ DEMILITARIZING
ADEGIIIINNORSTT DISINTEGRATION,
    DISORIENTATING
ADEGIILLMNPRSY PYRAMID SELLING
ADEGIILMNNPRRY REPRIMANDINGLY
ADEGILMOORSSTT DERMATOLOGISTS
ADEGINNNPSSSTU UPSTANDINGNESS
ADEHHIILLLLSSY SHILLY-SHALLIED
ADEHHIMOPRRSTU HERMAPHRODITUS
ADEHILNNOSSSTU OUTLANDISHNESS
ADEHIMOOOPPRSS PAEDOMORPHOSIS
ADEHIMOOOORTTUW WITHOUT MORE
    ADO
ADEHINOORRSSTW ROADWORTHINESS
ADEHLOPRRSSSTU SHOULDER STRAPS
ADEHORSSSTTUWW SOUTHWESTWARDS
ADEIIILMNNORST TRIDIMENSIONAL
ADEIIILMNNOSTY DIMENSIONALITY
ADEIIILNPRSTTU PLATITUDINISER
ADEIIILNPRTTUZ PLATITUDINIZER
ADEIIINNOORSTT DISORIENTATION
ADEIIILLMNRRTUY RUDIMENTARILLY
ADEIIILLNOPRTVY PROVIDENTIALLY
ADEIIILMNNNOOSX MASON-DIXON LINE
ADEIILMNNOOSTW TWO-DIMENSIONAL
ADEIIMNNOORSST MODERNISATIONS
ADEIIMNNOORSTZ MODERNIZATIONS
ADEIIMNNOPPSTT DISAPPOINTMENT
ADEIINNOOPRRST PREORDINATIONS
ADEIINNORSSTTU TRADE UNIONISTS
ADEIINORRSSSTT TRANSISTORISED
ADEIINORRSSTTZ TRANSISTORIZED
ADEILMMNORRSTU ULTRAMODERNISM
ADEILMNORRSTTU ULTRAMODERNIST
ADEIMNNOORSSTT DEMONSTRATIONS
ADEINOOORRTTTX DEXTROROTATION
ADEOOOORRRTTTXY
    DEXTROROTATORY

ADFGGHHIILLNNS HIGHLAND FLINGS
ADFGGIINNNOORT TO-ING AND FRO-ING
ADFGIKLNOOORRW FORWARD-LOOKING
ADFHNNOOOORRST AND SO ON OR FORTH
ADGGGHOORSSTYY SHAGGY-DOG STORY
ADGGIMNNOPRSTU STAMPING GROUND
ADGHILOOORRSVV VOROSHILOVGRAD
ADGIILLLNNOTUY LONGITUDINALLY
ADGIILNOPPRSVY DISAPPROVINGLY
ADIIILMNOSSSTU DISSIMULATIONS
ADIIILNRSSSTTU INDUSTRIALISTS
ADIILOPSSTTUUY DISPUTATIOUSLY
AEEEEFHNOPSTTX AT THE EXPENSE OF
AEEEEFLNOOPPSY APPLE OF ONE'S EYE
AEEEEGINSSTTVV VEGETATIVENESS
AEEEEILMNNRSST ELEMENTARINESS
AEEEEINNPRRTTT INTERPENETRATE
AEEEEINPRRSTTV REPRESENTATIVE
AEEEELLNPRRTTW WATER-REPELLENT
AEEEFGHHIRSTTW FEATHERWEIGHTS
AEEEFHOQRSTTTU AT THE REQUEST OF
AEEEFIILNNRRTT INTERFERENTIAL
AEEEFILLNPRRTY PREFERENTIALLY
AEEEFLLLORRTVW FELLOW TRAVELER
AEEEFNORRSSTTW WATER SOFTENERS
AEEEGGGIMNNNRT ENGAGEMENT RING
AEEEGGINRSSSSV AGGRESSIVENESS
AEEEGHLLOPPRST TELEGRAPH POLES
AEEEGHLNPRSTTT GRASP THE NETTLE
AEEEGIILNNRSTT LARGE INTESTINE
AEEEGIKLNRRSST GENERAL STRIKES
AEEEGILLPRRSSS PRESS GALLERIES
AEEEGIMNPRRSTY PRAYER MEETINGS
AEEEGNNOOPQRTU ROENTGENOPAQUE
AEEEGNNOORRSTT ENTEROGASTRONE
AEEEHHHILRTTWW THE WHEREWITHAL
AEEEHHHINNSSST HEATHENISHNESS
AEEEHHILNPSTTW WHITE ELEPHANTS
AEEEHIINNPPRSV INAPPREHENSIVE
AEEEHILNPPRSVY APPREHENSIVELY
AEEEHIMNNRSTTT MAN IN THE STREET
AEEEHINSSSTUVX EXHAUSTIVENESS
AEEEHLLORSTUXY HETEROSEXUALLY
AEEEIIINNPRSTT PENITENTIARIES
AEEEIILMNNSSTT SENTIMENTALISE
AEEEIILMNNSSTTZ SENTIMENTALIZE
AEEEIINPRRTTTV INTERPRETATIVE

AEEEIILLMNPRTXY EXPERIMENTALLY
AEEEIILMMRSSTTY REAL-TIME SYSTEM
AEEEIILMNRRTUVY REMUNERATIVELY
AEEEIILNOPRSTUV SUPERELEVATION
AEEEIMNNNRSTTT ENTERTAINMENTS
AEEEIMNNRSSTTT REINSTATEMENTS
AEEEINNNPRRTTT INTERPENETRANT
AEEEINNOPRRSTT REPRESENTATION
AEEEINPRSSSSUV PERSUASIVENESS
AEEEIOOPRRRTTV RETRO-OPERATIVE
AEEELLNOOPRRRU EUROPEAN ROLLER
AEEELMNNNRSSSS MANNERLESSNESS
AEEELNOOPRRSST PERSONAL STEREO
AEEEMNOOPRSTUX EXTEMPORANEOUS
AEEEMNORSSTTTV OVERSTATEMENTS
AEEENNORSSSTUX EXTRANEOUSNESS
AEEENNRRSSSSTV TRANSVERSENESS
AEEENQSSSSTTUU STATUESQUENESS
AEEEORRRSSTTUV TREASURE TROVES
AEEFGGHILNRSTT FLIGHT SERGEANT
AEEFGHJLLNOTUW LAW OF THE JUNGLE
AEEFGIIMMNNRST FERRIMAGNETISM
AEEFGIINRSSTUV FIGURATIVENESS
AEEFGILMNNNSSU MEANINGFULNESS
AEEFGIMMNORRST FERROMAGNETISM
AEEFGLNNRSSTUU UNGRATEFULNESS
AEEFHINNOSTTTT NOT THE FAINTEST
AEEFHLNNNNPPYY PENNY-HALFPENNY
AEEFIILNOQQTUU QUINQUEFOLIATE
AEEFNOOPRRSSTW WATERPROOFNESS
AEEGGHLNORSTTT TO GREAT LENGTHS
AEEGGIINORSSTT SEGREGATIONIST
AEEGGILLNNORTU OUTGENERALLING
AEEGGINORRSSSU GREGARIOUSNESS
AEEGGIOSSTTUUV AUTOSUGGESTIVE
AEEGHHLORSSTUU SLAUGHTERHOUSE
AEEGHILNNOOPTY PILE ON THE AGONY
AEEGHIMNSSSTTT STEAMTIGHTNESS
AEEGHINRSSTTTW WATERTIGHTNESS
AEEGIIILLLMTTY ILLEGITIMATELY
AEEGIIILLNNRST INERTIA SELLING
AEEGIIILLNNSTT INTELLIGENTSIA
AEEGIIILRRRSTU IRREGULARITIES
AEEGIILMNORSSS GENERALISSIMOS
AEEGIILNNNRTTY ENTERTAININGLY
AEEGIIMNNNORTU MOUNTAINEERING
AEEGIIMNORSTTV OVERESTIMATING
AEEGIIMNRSSTTU TIME SIGNATURES
AEEGIINNOPRRST PEREGRINATIONS
AEEGIINORRSTTV INTERROGATIVES, TERGIVERSATION
AEEGILLMNORRST STEAMROLLERING

AEEGINNRSSTTUU SIGNATURE TUNES
AEEGIORRRSTTVY TERGIVERSATORY
AEEGNOORSSSTUU OUTRAGEOUSNESS
AEEHHLMNNOPSTU
SULPHONMETHANE
AEEHHOPPPRSSTU SUPERPHOSPHATE
AEEHIKNOOPRRUY KEEP YOUR HAIR
ON!
AEEHILLMNOTTTW THE LITTLE
WOMAN
AEEHILLNOPRVXY VINE PHYLLOXERA
AEEHILOOPRRTTY HETEROPOLARITY
AEEHIMNORSSTUV OVERENTHUSIASM
AEEHINPPPPRRSW WHIPPERSNAPPER
AEEIIILMMMMORT TIME IMMEMORIAL
AEEIIILMNSSTTX EXISTENTIALISM
AEEIIILNNSSTTY INESSENTIALITY
AEEIIILNOPSTTT POTENTIALITIES
AEEIIILNSSTTTX EXISTENTIALIST
AEEIIILORRRSTT TERRITORIALISE
AEEIIILORRRTTZ TERRITORIALIZE
AEEIIILLMNNSSTT SMALL INTESTINE
AEEIIILLNNOPRTT INTERPELLATION
AEEIILMMNNOPTT IMPLEMENTATION
AEEIIILMMNNSSTT SENTIMENTALISM
AEEIILMNNSSTTT SENTIMENTALIST
AEEIILMNNSTTTY SENTIMENTALITY
AEEIILNNNORTTV INTERVENTIONAL
AEEIILNNORRSTT INTERRELATIONS
AEEIILNNOSTTXY EXTENSIONALITY
AEEIILNNQSSTTU QUINTESSENTIAL
AEEIILNRSTTUXY INTERSEXUALITY
AEEIILPRTTUVVY VITUPERATIVELY
AEEIIMNNOORSTT REMONETISATION
AEEIIMNNOORTTZ REMONETIZATION
AEEIIMNOORSTTV OVERESTIMATION
AEEIINNOPRRTTT INTERPRETATION
AEEIINNOQRSSTU QUESTIONNAIRES
AEEIINNORSSTTW WESTERNISATION
AEEIINNORSTTWZ WESTERNIZATION
AEEIINNRSSSTTV TRANSITIVENESS
AEEIINPQQRTTUU QUINQUEPARTITE
AEEIILLNNRSSSTT SLATTERNLINESS
AEEIILNNPRRSSTT SILENT PARTNERS
AEEILNOORTTTXY EXTORTIONATELY
AEEIIMNOQRSSTTU QUESTION MASTER
AEEINOQRSSSTTU SEQUESTRATIONS
AEFFHILNNSSTUU UNFAITHFULNESS
AEFFHLNOOOORRUW FLOWER-OF-AN-
HOUR
AEFGGHIKNSTUWY GUY FAWKES NIGHT
AEFGHIILMPRRST PILGRIM FATHERS
AEFGHINNNPRSTY PENNY-FARTHINGS
AEFGIINOORRRST ROARING FORTIES

AEFGIINOPRRSTU PREFIGURATIONS
AEFGILNOORSTTV FLOATING VOTERS
AEFHHLNNOPRTWY
HALFPENNYWORTH
AEFHKLNNNSSTUU UNTHANKFULNESS
AEFIILNOOPRRST PROLIFERATIONS
AEFILLNOOPRSSY PROFESSIONALLY
AEFILLOOPRRSSY PROFESSORIALLY
AEFILNNOOPRSSU UNPROFESSIONAL
AEFILNOOPRSSSW PASSIONFLOWERS
AEFINOOPRRRSSW PRISONERS OF WAR
AEGGHHOOPPRTYY PHYTOGEOGRAPHY
AEGGHIILNRRSTT RIGHT TRIANGLES
AEGGHINNOOPRTV PHOTOENGRAVING
AEGGIIIMNPSSTT SPITTING IMAGES
AEGGIILLNNOSTT ILL-GOTTEN GAINS
AEGGIINRSSTTTT SITTING TARGETS
AEGGIKLLNOOSSS LOOKING GLASSES
AEGGINOOSSTTUU AUTOSUGGESTION
AEGHHLMOPPRSTY PLETHYSMOGRAPH
AEGHIILNOOOSTT THEOLOGISATION
AEGHIILNOOOTTZ THEOLOGIZATION
AEGHIIMNNOOOST HOMOGENISATION
AEGHIIMNNOOOTZ HOMOGENIZATION
AEGHIKNNRRRTTY KNIGHT-ERRANTRY
AEGHILNORSSTUV VAULTING HORSES
AEGHIMMNOOPRST
METAMORPHOSING
AEGHLLMOOPPRSY MEGASPOROPHYLL
AEGHLNOOOOPRTUY
NEUROPATHOLOGY
AEGHMMOOPRRTTY
PHOTOGRAMMETRY
AEGHNNNOORTTUY TURN ON THE
AGONY
AEGIIIILMNOSTT LEGITIMISATION
AEGIIIILMNOTTZ LEGITIMIZATION
AEGIIILLNNORTT TOILET TRAINING
AEGIIILLNNPRSWY AWE-INSPIRINGLY
AEGIIIMNNORRTT INTERMIGRATION
AEGIIINNORSTTT INTEGRATIONIST
AEGIIINNOSSTTV INVESTIGATIONS
AEGIIKMNOPSSSV PASSIVE SMOKING
AEGIIKNOPRRSTW WORKING
PARTIES
AEGIIILLLNNRSTW ALL-IN WRESTLING
AEGIILLNTTTTTT TITTLE-TATTLING
AEGIILMNNOORST MONGRELISATION
AEGIILMNNOORTZ MONGRELIZATION
AEGIILNNNRSTTY INTRANSIGENTLY
AEGIINNOORRSTT INTERROGATIONS
AEGIINPPRRSSSTT ASSET-STRIPPING
AEGILLNOOOPSTT PALEONTOLOGIST
AEGIMMNNOOPRSTU SPERMATOGONIUM

AEGIMNNOORTUUV OUTMANOEUVRING
AEGINNORRSSSST TRANSGRESSIONS
AEGINNPRSSSSSU SURPASSINGNESS
AEGINORSSSTTUU GRATUITOUSNESS
AEGKKMNOORSSTU UST-KAMENOGORSK
AEGLLMOPRRTUYY PYROMETALLURGY
AEHHHILNOORTTU HOLIER-THAN-THOU
AEHHHOOOPPRSTT ORTHOPHOSPHATE
AEHHIILLLLRSSY SHILLYSHALLIER
AEHHNNOORRSTTT NORTH-NORTHEAST
AEHHOOSSSTTTUU SOUTH-SOUTHEAST
AEHIIKLLMOOPRT POIKILOTHERMAL
AEHIILOPRRSTWY PRAISEWORTHILY
AEHIINNOSSSTTY SYNTHESISATION
AEHIINNOSSTTTY SYNTHETISATION
AEHIINNOSSTTYZ SYNTHESIZATION
AEHIINNOSTTTYZ SYNTHETIZATION
AEHIIOORRSSTTT OSTEOARTHRITIS
AEHIJKMOOOOSTV KOSOVO-METOHIJA
AEHILLOOPSSUXZ SULPHISOXAZOLE
AEHILNNOORSSTZ HORIZONTALNESS
AEHIMNNOORSSSU HARMONIOUSNESS
AEHIMOOPPPSSTU HIPPOPOTAMUSES
AEIIILMORRRSTT TERRITORIALISM
AEIIILNNNOTTTY INTENTIONALITY
AEIIILNNRSTTVY INTRANSITIVELY
AEIIILORRRSTTT TERRITORIALIST
AEIIILORRRTTTY TERRITORIALITY
AEIIINOQRRSTUY REQUISITIONARY
AEIIIJLNNORSTUV UNIVERSAL JOINT
AEIILLLMNNOPST POSTMILLENNIAL
AEIILLLRSTTUVY ILLUSTRATIVELY
AEIILLMNOPRSSY IMPRESSIONALLY
AEIILLNNOSSSUV VILLAINOUSNESS
AEIILLNQRRSSTU TRANQUILLISERS
AEIILLNQRRSTUZ TRANQUILLIZERS
AEIILMNNOPSSTU EMULSION PAINTS
AEIILMNOOPRSTY POLYMERISATION
AEIILMNOOPRTYZ POLYMERIZATION
AEIILNNOOPRSTT INTERPOLATIONS
AEIILNNOPRSTUY UNIPERSONALITY
AEIIMMNORSSTTY SYMMETRISATION
AEIIMMNORSTTYZ SYMMETRIZATION
AEIIMNNOOPRSST IMPERSONATIONS
AEIINNORRSSSTT TRANSITORINESS
AEIINOOPPRRSTX EXPROPRIATIONS
AEIINOPRRSSSTU PRESSURISATION
AEIINOPRRSSTUZ PRESSURIZATION
AEILLMNOSSTUUY SIMULTANEOUSLY
AEILLOOPPRRRTY PROPRIETORALLY

AEILMNOPRRSTUY SUPERNORMALITY
AEILNOOOPPRTUV OVERPOPULATION
AEILNOOPRSSTTT PETROL STATIONS
AEILNOOPSSTTUX EXPOSTULATIONS
AEILNOOSSTTTUY OSTENTATIOUSLY
AEIMNNOOPPRSTT APPORTIONMENTS
AEINOORRSSSTTU TRAITOROUSNESS
AELLMNNOOOPPRT MONOPROPELLANT
AFFGHNNOOSSTUW SAWN-OFF SHOTGUN
AFGGHHIIRSSTTT STRAIGHT FIGHTS
AFGIIILLNNOSTT FILLING STATION
AFIIIMMNNOORST MISINFORMATION
AFIILLMORSTUUY MULTIFARIOUSLY
AGGHIIKNNRSSUU SINKIANG-UIGHUR
AGGHILNOOPRSTY PHARYNGOLOGIST
AGGIIILNNORTVY INVIGORATINGLY
AGGIILNNOPPRRS GRAPPLING IRONS
AGGLLNOOOOORTYY OTOLARYNGOLOGY
AGHHIIOOPRRSTY HISTORIOGRAPHY
AGHHILOOOPSTTY HISTOPATHOLOGY
AGHHLOOOPPTTYY PHYTOPATHOLOGY
AGHIILMNPSTYYZ SYMPATHIZINGLY
AGHIINOOPPRSTZ APOSTROPHIZING
AGHILNOOOOPRSTT ANTHROPOLOGIST
AGIIIILLNNQRTUZ TRANQUILLIZING
AGIIILNOSTUVVV VULVOVAGINITIS
AGIILLNNOOPSTT POLLING STATION
AGIILMNNNOSTTU NONSTIMULATING
AGINOPPPRRSTTU SUPPORTING PART
AGLMMOOOOPSTTYY SYMPTOMATOLOGY
AHHIILNOPPRSTT PHILANTHROPIST
AHHLLNOOPSTUXY XANTHOPHYLLOUS
AHIIMMNOOOSSU HOMOIOUSIANISM
AHIILMNNOORSUY INHARMONIOUSLY
AHIILMOOPSSSST HISTOPLASMOSIS
AHIILNOPRSSTUU SULPHURISATION
AHIILNOPRSTUUZ SULPHURIZATION
AIIIILNOORSTTV VITRIOLISATION
AIIIILNOORTTVZ VITRIOLIZATION
AIIIMNOOPRSSTV IMPROVISATIONS
AIIIMNRSSSTTVY TRANSMISSIVITY
AIIINNNOOSTTUW NO-WIN SITUATION
AIIINNORSTTTUY INSTITUTIONARY
AIILMNNOOOOOPST MONOPOLISATION
AIILMNNOOOOPTZ MONOPOLIZATION
AIILMNOOPRSSUY PARSIMONIOUSLY
AIILNOOOPPSSTT POSTPOSITIONAL
AIINNOOPRSSSTT TRANSPOSITIONS
AILLNOOOPPRRTY PROPORTIONALLY
BBBCGHINRRSSUU SCRUBBING BRUSH

BBBDEHLLLMNOOS BLOND BOMBSHELL
BBCDEEIORRSSUV OVERSUBSCRIBED
BBCDGIIKLLNOSU BUILDING BLOCKS
BBCEGILMNORSTU CLUSTER BOMBING
BBCGIKLLMNOSTU STUMBLING BLOCK
BBCIIILMOSTTUY COMBUSTIBILITY
BBCILNOOOOPPRU PRO BONO PUBLICO
BBDEEGHIINRRSU RUBBER DINGHIES
BBDEEGILNOOOSU BOIS DE BOULOGNE
BBEEEGILLNOOSS NOBLESSE OBLIGE
BBEIIILMRSSTUY SUBMERSIBILITY
BCCCGIIIMNRRSU CIRCUMSCRIBING
BCCCIIMOOPRSSU SUBMICROSCOPIC
BCCDEEEGHIKLNOU DOUBLE-CHECKING
BCCDEEIIJNORTT INDIRECT OBJECT
BCCEEEEGILRTTU ICEBERG LETTUCE
BCCEEIKKKNORRS KNICKERBOCKERS
BCCEIIIJSSTTUV SUBJECTIVISTIC
BCCHINOOOPRSST BRONCHOSCOPIST
BCCILNOOSSSUUY SUBCONSCIOUSLY
BCDEEEEILRRSTT STREET-CREDIBLE
BCDEEHHNOORSUU BOUCHES-DU-
  RHONE
BCDEEHILLLOOTW WHITE BLOOD CELL
BCDEEIILNRSTTU INDESTRUCTIBLE
BCDEELOORRSSSU DOUBLE-CROSSERS
BCDEEMOOOPPRTT COPPER-
  BOTTOMED
BCDEGILNOORSSU DOUBLE-CROSSING
BCDEIIIILRRTUY IRREDUCIBILITY
BCDEIIILPPRSTU PUBLIC-SPIRITED
BCDEIILNRSTTUY INDESTRUCTIBLY
BCDEILLNNOORSS COLOR BLINDNESS
BCEEEEFKNOORRS REFERENCE BOOKS
BCEEEHILMNOPRS COMPREHENSIBLE
BCEEEIILNOPRSWY EYEBROW PENCILS
BCEEFIIILPRTTY PERFECTIBILITY
BCEEGIIILLLNNPU BLUE-PENCILLING
BCEEGIMNNNOSSU UNBECOMINGNESS
BCEEHIILNOPRSY HYPERBOLIC SINE
BCEEHILMNOPRSY COMPREHENSIBLY
BCEEIIIILPPRTTY PERCEPTIBILITY
BCEEIILMNNOSTU BIOLUMINESCENT
BCEEIILMNOPRSS INCOMPRESSIBLE
BCEEILNOORRTTV CONTROVERTIBLE
BCEEIMNNPRSTUU SUPERINCUMBENT
BCEFHIKLOOOSTT LICK THE BOOTS OF
BCEFHIMNOOOSTT FINE-TOOTH
  COMBS
BCEFJMOOORRSST JOB'S COMFORTERS
BCEIIILNORTTVY CONVERTIBILITY
BCEIIILPSSTTUY SUSCEPTIBILITY
BCFGIIMMNNOORS COMBINING FORMS
BCGIIILMOOORST MICROBIOLOGIST

BCIIILOPRRTTUY CORRUPTIBILITY
BCIIMNOORSSTTU OBSTRUCTIONISM
BCIINOORSSTTTU OBSTRUCTIONIST
BCIKMNNOPRTUUY COUNTRY BUMPKIN
BDDEEEELNNORTU DOUBLE ENTENDRE
BDDEEEIILNOOPRX PEROXIDE BLONDE
BDDEEIILNOOPRSX PEROXIDE BLONDS
BDDEFFIINORRTU FORBIDDEN FRUIT
BDDEFGIIINNORSS FORBIDDINGNESS
BDEEEFGILNOSTT FEEDING BOTTLES
BDEEEGIJLLNOSU GOLDEN JUBILEES
BDEEEGIMMNOSTU DISEMBOGUEMENT
BDEEEHHIIMNSTT BEHIND THE TIMES
BDEEEHINORTTTT TO THE BITTER END
BDEEEIINNNORTZ DINITROBENZENE
BDEEEILMMNOSTW DISEMBOWELMENT
BDEEFILMNPRRSU PLUMBER'S FRIEND
BDEEGGHILMNOST THE MIND BOGGLES
BDEEGIIIILLNSVY DISBELIEVINGLY
BDEEGIIILLMNOSW DISEMBOWELLING
BDEEGILLNRSTUW TUNBRIDGE WELLS
BDEEIMNOOORRTW ON BORROWED
  TIME
BDEELOOPRRSSSU BLOOD PRESSURES
BDEGHHINOOORSU NEIGHBOURHOODS
BDEGHIILNNNSST NIGHT BLINDNESS
BDEGIIINRRSTTU REDISTRIBUTING
BDEIIIILMQRSUU DISEQUILIBRIUM
BDEIIIILNSSTTY DISTENSIBILITY
BDEIIILNNOSSSU LIBIDINOUSNESS
BDEIIILNPSSTUY SUSPENDIBILITY
BDEIIILRSTTUVY DISTRIBUTIVELY
BDEIIINORRSTTU REDISTRIBUTION
BDGIILNNOOOOPS BLOOD POISONING
BDHIILLOORSTTY BLOODTHIRSTILY
BDIIIIILNSTVY INDIVISIBILITY
BEEEEHLNOOPSTX TELEPHONE BOXES
BEEEELMNORSTUV BOULEVERSEMENT
BEEEFFGIINNRST FRINGE BENEFITS
BEEEFFGIKNOOST GET OFF ONE'S BIKE
BEEEGGIIINNNOR BIOENGINEERING
BEEEHHLNOOOPTT TELEPHONE
  BOOTH
BEEEHILLMMNSST EMBELLISHMENTS
BEEEHILORRRSTW WHORTLEBERRIES
BEEEIIJLLRSSUV SILVER JUBILEES
BEEEIILLNORSSU REBELLIOUSNESS
BEEEIMMNRRSSTU REIMBURSEMENTS
BEEEINRSSSSUVV SUBVERSIVENESS
BEEELLNOOOSSTT LOSE ONE'S BOTTLE
BEEGHIILNNORSS NEIGHBORLINESS
BEEGIIILLLNNTU UNINTELLIGIBLE
BEEGIIOOPRSTTU PETIT BOURGEOIS
BEEGIOOPRSTTUY PETTY BOURGEOIS

BEEHHHILMNTTTU HUNT THE
THIMBLE
BEEHLOOOORRSTTU TROUBLESHOOTER
BEEIILNOSSTVWY LIVE BY ONE'S WITS
BEEIILNPPRSSSU INSUPPRESSIBLE
BEEIILOPRSSTVX VISIBLE EXPORTS
BEEIIMNSSSSSUV SUBMISSIVENESS
BEEIKMNNOSSSUY MONKEY BUSINESS
BEEIMNOOPPRSTU OPPOSITE NUMBER
BEEINOOQSSSSUU OBSEQUIOUSNESS
BEEINOORSSSSTU BOISTEROUSNESS
BEELMNORSSSSUU SLUMBEROUSNESS
BEELOOPRRSSTUY OBSTREPEROUSLY
BEFFGINNORRSTU BURNT OFFERINGS
BEFGILNRSSTTUY FLYING BUTTRESS
BEGGIIILSSTTUY SUGGESTIBILITY
BEGGILNOORSTTT GLOBETROTTINGS
BEGHNOOOORRSTTU ROTTEN
BOROUGHS
BEGILNORSSSUUU LUGUBRIOUSNESS
BEHHIKNOOPSTTU PUT THE KIBOSH ON
BEHIIINOSSTTX EXHIBITIONISTS
BEIIIILMPRSSTY PERMISSIBILITY
BEIIIILLORRSTUY IRRESOLUBILITY
BEIIIILMOPRSSTV VISIBLE IMPORTS
BEIIIILNOPRSSTY RESPONSIBILITY
BEIINOQSSSTUUU UBIQUITOUSNESS
BELOPRRSSSSTUU BRUSSELS SPROUT
BGIILLMMNNOOUU IMMUNOGLOBULIN
BHIIIIMNOOPRST PROHIBITIONISM
BHIIIINOOPRSTT PROHIBITIONIST
CCCDEEEEENRRSSU RECRUDESCENCES
CCCDEEHIIOOPRT CERCOPITHECOID
CCCDGILOOORRTU GLUCOCORTICORD
CCCEEEFIMNRRSU CIRCUMFERENCES
CCCEEEHHHIINNR CHINCHERINCHEE
CCCEEEIIINRSTT ECCENTRICITIES
CCCEEFIIINNOST SCIENCE FICTION
CCCEHHINOPSSTY PSYCHOTECHNICS
CCCEIIILMRSSSU CIRCUMSCISSILE
CCCEIIILORSSUV VICIOUS CIRCLES
CCCEIIMMNOOORS MICROECONOMICS
CCCEIIMNOPRSTU CIRCUMSPECTION
CCCIIIMORRRTUY MICROCIRCUITRY
CCCIILMNOORTUU CIRCUMLOCUTION
CCCILMOORRTUUY CIRCUMLOCUTORY
CCCILNNOOSTUUY COUNTY COUNCILS
CCDDEEEELLMNNOS CONDEMNED CELLS
CCDDEEILNNOSTY DISCONNECTEDLY
CCDEEEIILLRST DIESEL-ELECTRIC
CCDEEEFFILNNOS SELF-CONFIDENCE
CCDEEEHIINPRST INDIRECT SPEECH
CCDEEEIINNNNOV INCONVENIENCED
CCDEEEIINPRSVY VICE-PRESIDENCY

CCDEEENNOOPRRS CORRESPONDENCE
CCDEEGIIILNNRV DRIVING LICENCE
CCDEGIILNNOOOR ENDOCRINOLOGIC
CCDEGINNNOORST CONNECTING RODS
CCDEHHILLNOORS SCHOOLCHILDREN
CCDEHIIORRSTTU SHORT-CIRCUITED
CCDEIIINPRRTTU PRINTED CIRCUIT
CCDEIIMNNOOSTU SEMICONDUCTION
CCDEIINNNOOSST DISCONNECTIONS
CCDEIIOOORRSTT CORTICOSTEROID
CCDEIMNOORSSTU SEMICONDUCTORS
CCDENOOPRRSTUU SUPERCONDUCTOR
CCDGIIIMOOOPSS SIGMOIDOSCOPIC
CCDHHHOOOORRTUX ORTHODOX
CHURCH
CCDHNOOOOOPRTTU
PHOTOCONDUCTOR
CCEEEEEJNNRSUV REJUVENESCENCE
CCEEEEFHIITUVX CHIEF EXECUTIVE
CCEEEEFNNNORSW NEWS CONFERENCE
CCEEEEFNORRRSS CROSS-REFERENCE
CCEEEEMMMNNORT
RECOMMENCEMENT
CCEEEFIIOPRSST STEREOSPECIFIC
CCEEEGJLNNORTU CONCRETE JUNGLE
CCEEEHILMORRTT THERMOELECTRIC
CCEEEHILMORSTT ELECTROCHEMIST
CCEEEIIKLNORTT ELECTROKINETIC
CCEEEIINNNNOSV INCONVENIENCES
CCEEEIMNORRSTX CONCRETE MIXERS
CCEEEINSSSSSUV SUCCESSIVENESS
CCEEFFIILOOPRS POLICE OFFICERS
CCEEFFIILOORST CORIOLIS EFFECT
CCEEFHIINOPRST CHIEF INSPECTOR
CCEEFLNSSSSSUU SUCCESSFULNESS
CCEEGHHHINNOSU CHECHENO-
INGUSH
CCEEGIIILLOOSST ECCLESIOLOGIST
CCEEHHHIMNOSTTY CHEMOSYNTHETIC
CCEEHHIINORTTTY THEOCENTRICITY
CCEEHHILOOPRSTU HEROIC COUPLETS
CCEEHIMNNORRSY CHIMNEY CORNERS
CCEEHINOPRSSTY PYROTECHNICSES
CCEEIINNOSSTTU CONSTITUENCIES
CCEEILLMOORSTT COLLECTOR'S ITEM
CCEEILLNNOOTUV COLLECTIVE NOUN
CCEEILNOORSTTU ELECTROCUTIONS
CCEEINNOOPPRST PRECONCEPTIONS
CCEEINOOOORRSTT CORTICOSTERONE
CCEEINOOPRRSUW OWNER-OCCUPIERS
CCEEINOOPRSSSU PRECOCIOUSNESS
CCEEINORRSTTUV RECONSTRUCTIVE
CCEGHIIKNNPRSS SPRING CHICKENS
CCEGIILNNRRSTU TURNING CIRCLES

CCEGINNORRSTTU RECONSTRUCTING
CCEHHIIKOSSSTW SCOTCH WHISKIES
CCEHHIINOPRSSZ SCHIZOPHRENICS
CCEHHIOOPSSUYZ SCHIZOPHYCEOUS
CCEHIIIMOORSTT STOICHIOMETRIC
CCEHIIMMORRSTY MICROCHEMISTRY
CCEHIMMNOSTTUY COMMUNITY
CHEST
CCEHIMOOSSTUYZ SCHIZOMYCETOUS
CCEHINOOPRSTUY PSYCHONEUROTIC
CCEIILLNNOSUVY INCONCLUSIVELY
CCEIIMNNOOPSST MISCONCEPTIONS
CCEILNORSTTUVY CONSTRUCTIVELY
CCEILOOORRSSTU STERCORICOLOUS
CCEIMMOOPRRSTU MICROCOMPUTERS
CCEIMOOOPRRRSS MICROPROCESSOR
CCEIMORRRSTTUU MICROSTRUCTURE
CCEINNOOPRRSST PRINCES CONSORT
CCEINNOORRSTTU RECONSTRUCTION
CCEINOORRSSSTU CROSS-COUNTRIES
CCEIOOPPRRSSSTT SPECTROSCOPIST
CCGHIILOOPSSTY PSYCHOLOGISTIC
CCGIILNNNNOUVY UNCONVINCINGLY
CCHIINOOOPRRTT CORTICOTROPHIN
CCHIIOPRRRTVYY PYRRHIC VICTORY
CCIIIJJNNOSTTUV CONJUNCTIVITIS
CCIIIILPRSSTTUU PISCICULTURIST
CCIILMNOORTUUV CIRCUMVOLUTION
CCIILNOOPRRUVY PRIVY COUNCILOR
CCIIMNORSSTTUV CONSTRUCTIVISM
CCIINORSSTTTUV CONSTRUCTIVIST
CCILMOORRTUUVY CIRCUMVOLUTORY
CCINNOORSSTUUY COUNTRY COUSINS
CDDDEEHLLOORSU COLD SHOULDERED
CDDEEEFLRSSTTU SELF-DESTRUCTED
CDDEEEELLMNOTUW WELL-
DOCUMENTED
CDDEEEILNNOSTTY DISCONTENTEDLY
CDDEGHIIILOPRS CHILD PRODIGIES
CDDEHIILMOORSU SODIUM CHLORIDE
CDDEILNOOOSTUY DICOTYLEDONOUS
CDEEEEEINNQSUV QUEEN'S EVIDENCE
CDEEEEHOPPRRST REPORTED SPEECH
CDEEEEILNPRSTT PRESIDENT-ELECT
CDEEEEIORSTTTV STORE DETECTIVE
CDEEEEIQRSSTUZ CREDIT SQUEEZES
CDEEEENNPSSTUX UNEXPECTEDNESS
CDEEEFGILLNNSU SELF-INDULGENCE
CDEEEFILORRTTT LETTER OF CREDIT
CDEEEFIMNNOPRS PRESENCE OF MIND
CDEEEGILNNORUV OVERINDULGENCE
CDEEEIIMMNOOSX MIXED ECONOMIES
CDEEEIINNRRSSV DINNER SERVICES
CDEEEEILOOPRSTT ELECTRODEPOSIT

CDEEEINRRSSSTT RESTRICTEDNESS
CDEEEELNNNOOORT NOLO
CONTENDERE
CDEEENNNOQRUUW UNCROWNED
QUEEN
CDEEFGHINNRRSS FRENCH DRESSING
CDEEFHHILNOPRS FRENCH POLISHED
CDEEFIIILLNPSS SELF-DISCIPLINE
CDEEFLLLNOORST SELF-CONTROLLED
CDEEGGINNOSSSU SECOND-GUESSING
CDEEHILNNORSSW CHINLESS WONDER
CDEEHLLLOORSUY HYDROCELLULOSE
CDEEIIINNSSTVV VINDICTIVENESS
CDEEIIINOPPRST EDITIO PRINCEPS
CDEEIINRSSSSUV DISCURSIVENESS
CDEEIILLNOOPTUY POLYNUCLEOTIDE
CDEEILMOOPPSUX OEDIPUS COMPLEX
CDEEIMNNNOSTTT DISCONTENTMENT
CDEEINNOORSSSU INDECOROUSNESS
CDEEINOPRSSTUV PRODUCTIVENESS
CDEEKKLNRSSTUU KNUCKLE-DUSTERS
CDEENNOOPRRSST CORRESPONDENTS
CDEFIIIMMMOSSU FIDEICOMMISSUM
CDEFOOOOPRRSSS FOOD PROCESSORS
CDEGHHIIILNPPR HIGH-PRINCIPLED
CDEGHHILLOORUY HIGHLY
COLOURED
CDEGHHNOOSSTTU SECOND
THOUGHTS
CDEGIIINNNOORT RECONDITIONING
CDEGINOOPRRSSW WORD PROCESSING
CDEHILMNNOOPTT HOLD IN
CONTEMPT
CDEHINOOORRSTY HYDROCORTISONE
CDEIIIILRSTTUV DIVERTICULITIS
CDEIIILORSSTUV DIVERTICULOSIS
CDEIIINNNSSSTT INDISTINCTNESS
CDEIILNNOOPRTU PRODUCTION LINE
CDEIILNORSSSSUU RIDICULOUSNESS
CDEIINNOORRTTU REINTRODUCTION
CDEIINNOPRSSUU UNDER SUSPICION
CDEIINNOPRSTUU SUPERINDUCTION
CDEIINOPRSTUWW PICTURE WINDOWS
CDEIINORSSTTTU DESTRUCTIONIST
CDEILOORSSTUUY DISCOURTEOUSLY
CDEINOOOPRRTUV OVERPRODUCTION
CDEINOORSSSTTU DISCOUNT STORES
CDEOOOOPRRRSSSW WORD PROCESSORS
CDFIINNOOOOTTU OUT OF CONDITION
CDGIILMNOOPSSY DISCOMPOSINGLY
CDHHILLLOOOPRY CHLOROPHYLLOID
CDHINOOOPRSSTT PROSTHODONTICS
CDIIJJNNNNOOSTU NONDISJUNCTION
CDIILMMNOOOSUY INCOMMODIOUSLY

CDIILNOORRTTUY INTRODUCTORILY
CEEEEFFLNRSTVY EFFERVESCENTLY
CEEEEFILNRSSTV REFLECTIVENESS
CEEEEFNPPRRSTT PRESENT PERFECT
CEEEEGIILNNORT ELECTIONEERING
CEEEEHLNPSSSSS SPEECHLESSNESS
CEEEFFGHIOPRSU FIGURE OF SPEECH
CEEEFFGIIORRST REGISTER OFFICE
CEEEFFGILNRSVY EFFERVESCINGLY
CEEEFFLLPRSSTU SELF-RESPECTFUL
CEEEFGILNPRSST SELF-RESPECTING
CEEEFGLLNNSSTU NEGLECTFULNESS
CEEEFIIOPRRSTV IRRESPECTIVE OF
CEEEFIMNNORRST REINFORCEMENTS
CEEEFINORRSTTU COUNTERFEITERS
CEEEFLNPRSSSTU RESPECTFULNESS
CEEEFNOORSSTUV VOTES OF CENSURE
CEEEGGINORRSTU GEIGER COUNTERS
CEEEGIILNNRSV CIVIL ENGINEERS
CEEEGIILLNNNTU UNINTELLIGENCE
CEEEGIIMNOPRST SPERMIOGENETIC
CEEEGILNORRTTV COVERING
  LETTER
CEEEGLORRRSTUY ELECTROSURGERY
CEEEHIKNNOPPSU KEEP ONE'S CHIN UP
CEEEHIMNOPRSSV COMPREHENSIVES
CEEEHIMORSSTTY HYSTERECTOMIES
CEEEHKMNNORSWY MONKEY
  WRENCHES
CEEEHLMNOORRTT
  THERMOELECTRON
CEEEHNOORRTTUV OVER THE
  COUNTER
CEEEIIKNNPRSST PERNICKETINESS
CEEEIIMMOORRTT MICROMETEORITE
CEEEILMMNOPRST COMPLEMENTISER
CEEEILMMNOPRTZ COMPLEMENTIZER
CEEEILMNNOPSST INCOMPLETENESS
CEEEIMMNNOPRTV PINCER MOVEMENT
CEEEINOPRSSTTV PROTECTIVENESS
CEEEIOPRRSSTTV RETROSPECTIVES
CEEEKOOPRRRSSU PRESSURE COOKER
CEEELNNOQSSSUU QUEEN'S COUNSELS
CEEEMNNORRSTUU COUNTERMENSURE
CEEENNOPPPRRRT PEPPERCORN RENT
CEEFFFIILNSSTU SELF-SUFFICIENT
CEEFFGIIORRSTY REGISTRY OFFICE
CEEFGIINNORTTU COUNTERFEITING
CEEFGINORRRRSS CROSS-REFERRING
CEEFHIILMNNOSU ICHNEUMON FLIES
CEEFIILNOSSSTU FELICITOUSNESS
CEEFIILORRSSST CROSS-FERTILISE
CEEFIILORRSSTZ CROSS-FERTILIZE
CEEFIINNOSSSTU INFECTIOUSNESS

CEEFIINOPRSSTT PERFECTIONISTS
CEEFILNOOPRSTT SELF-PROTECTION
CEEFINOOOOPSTV TOP OF ONE'S VOICE
CEEFINOORSSSUV VOCIFEROUSNESS
CEEGHINNOPPRST SHOPPING CENTRE
CEEGIILNNORRTY NITROGLYCERINE
CEEGIIMMNNOSTU IMMUNOGENETICS
CEEGIINNNPRRST SCREEN PRINTING
CEEGILLLLNOOSU LIGNOCELLULOSE
CEEGILLNORSSSV LEVEL CROSSINGS
CEEHHIMNOSSSTY CHEMOSYNTHESIS
CEEHHMOOORRSTU
  HETEROCHROMOUS
CEEHHNOOPPRSST PHOSPHORESCENT
CEEHHNORSSSTTU HORSE CHESTNUTS
CEEHIILMOPRRTY PYRHELIOMETRIC
CEEHIIMOPRSTYZ PIEZOCHEMISTRY
CEEHIIOOPRRTTY ERYTHROPOIETIC
CEEHIMMOPSSSTY METEMPSYCHOSIS
CEEHIMNNOOPRSS COMPREHENSIONS
CEEHIMNNORSSTT ETHNOCENTRISMS
CEEHIMOPRRSTTY PETROCHEMISTRY
CEEHNOPRSSTTUW PUT THE SCREWS
  ON
CEEIIIILMRSSSSU CRUISE MISSILES
CEEIIIMPPRTTVY IMPERCEPTIVITY
CEEIIINNORSSST SENIOR CITISENS
CEEIIINNORSSTZ SENIOR CITIZENS
CEEIIILLMNORSTT SCINTILLOMETER
CEEIIILMORRSTUY MERETRICIOUSLY
CEEIIILNNNNOTVY INCONVENIENTLY
CEEIIILNNOSSSTU LICENTIOUSNESS
CEEIIILNORSSTTW WINTER SOLSTICE
CEEIIILPPRRSTVY PRESCRIPTIVELY
CEEIIINNOPRSSSU PERNICIOUSNESS
CEEIIINNORRSTTV NONRESTRICTIVE
CEEIIOOPPPRRTV PROPRIOCEPTIVE
CEEIKLNOORSTTT SILK-COTTON TREE
CEEIKNORRRRSTT TERROR-STRICKEN
CEEILLLNOORSTU NITROCELLULOSE
CEEILMMORSSSTU SUMMER SOLSTICE
CEEILMNOPSSSUV COMPULSIVENESS
CEEILMNOSSSTUU METICULOUSNESS
CEEILNORRSSTTU INTERLOCUTRESS
CEEILNORRSSUYY YOURS SINCERELY
CEEIMMOOPRRRTY MICROPYROMETER
CEEIMMNOOOPRRST RECEPTION ROOMS
CEEINNOORSSSSU CENSORIOUSNESS
CEEINNOSSSSTUU INCESTUOUSNESS
CEEINOOOPRRTTV OVERPROTECTION
CEEINOOPRSSSTU PRECIOUS STONES
CEELLNOORSSSSU COLOURLESSNESS
CEEMNNNOOPRSTU
  PRONOUNCEMENTS

CEEPRRRSSTTUUU SUPERSTRUCTURE
CEFFFGIILNORSY FLYING OFFICERS
CEFFIIILLNNOST SELF-INFLICTION
CEFFIIILNNSTUY INSUFFICIENTLY
CEFGHIMNOORSUZ GNOMES OF ZÜRICH
CEFGIIKLLNORST STOCKING-FILLER
CEFHMMNOOOOSSU HOUSE OF
COMMONS
CEFIIINOSSSTTU FICTITIOUSNESS
CEGGHHHHILNOOTY HIGH
TECHNOLOGY
CEGGIINNNORSTU COUNTERSIGNING
CEGHIJNOOPRSTU HOUSING PROJECT
CEGHIMMNPRSSTU SPRECHSTIMMUNG
CEGHINNOOSSTUU COUNTINGHOUSES
CEGIIIILNOORSST CORELIGIONISTS
CEGIIKNNNORSTU COUNTERSINKING
CEGIIMNOPRSTUV MOVING PICTURES
CEGIINNOOPRSTU COUNTERPOISING
CEGIINNORSTTTU RECONSTITUTING
CEHHIIMORSSTTY HISTOCHEMISTRY
CEHHIMMNOOOOPPR
MORPHOPHONEMIC
CEHHIMOOPRSTTY PHOTOCHEMISTRY
CEHHINOOPSTTTY PHOTOSYNTHETIC
CEHHOOOOOPPPRSS PHOSPHOROSCOPE
CEHIINOPRRSTTT STREPTOTHRICIN
CEHIJMNNOORTTU THERMOJUNCTION
CEHIKNOORRRRST HORROR-STRICKEN
CEHILMMOOPRSUY MYRMECOPHILOUS
CEHILMOORSSSST SCHOOLMISTRESS
CEHIMMMNOOSTUY COMMUNITY
HOMES
CEHLNOOOOORSSSW SHOW ONE'S
COLORS
CEHINOOPRSSSUY PSYCHONEUROSIS
CEHLNOORRSSSSUY NURSERY SCHOOLS
CEIIIINOSSTTVV VIVISECTIONIST
CEIIILNOOSTTUV EVOLUTIONISTIC
CEIIIMPPRRRSSTV PRESCRIPTIVISM
CEIIINORRSSTTT RESTRICTIONIST
CEIIIPPRRSSTTV PRESCRIPTIVIST
CEIIJNOOPRSSTT PROJECTIONISTS
CEIILLOPRSSUUY SUPERCILIOUSLY
CEIILNNNOSSTTY INCONSISTENTLY
CEIILNOORRRSTT TRINITROCRESOL
CEIILNOOSSSSTU SOLICITOUSNESS
CEIIMMNNNOORTU
INTERCOMMUNION
CEIIMNNOOOPSSU PNEUMOCONIOSIS
CEIIMNOOPRSTTU MOTION PICTURES
CEIINNOORSTTTU RECONSTITUTION
CEIINOOPRSSTTT PROTECTIONISTS
CEIINOORSSSTUV VICTORIOUSNESS

CEIINOPPRRSSTU SUPERSCRIPTION
CEIINOPRSSSSTU PERCUSSIONISTS
CEIINOPSSSSSUU SUSPICIOUSNESS
CEILLMNOOSTUUY CONTUMELIOUSLY
CEILNOPRRSTUUV PROVENTRICULUS
CEILNORRSSSSUU SCURRILOUSNESS
CEIMMMMOOORTTY COMMIT TO
MEMORY
CEKLMOOPRSTTUU MOCK TURTLE
SOUP
CELMNOOPSTTUUY CONTEMPTUOUSLY
CELNOPRSSSSUUU SCRUPULOUSNESS
CFFHIILMNOSTTU FIFTH COLUMNIST
CFFIKKLORRSTTU FORKLIFT TRUCKS
CFIILLORRSTTUU FLORICULTURIST
CFIINOOQRRTUUY COURT OF INQUIRY
CFIMNNNOOOORSST NONCONFORMISTS
CGHHIIIMMNOOSS HIGH COMMISSION
CGHIIKNOOSSSTT SHOOTING STICKS
CGHIILNOPSSTUY PSYCHOLINGUIST
CGHILOOOOOPSTYY PHYTOSOCIOLOGY
CGIIIKNNOPSSTT STICKING POINTS
CGIIIILMNOORSST CRIMINOLOGISTS
CGIIIILNNRSTUYZ SCRUTINIZINGLY
CGIIIILNOOOPSST OLIGOPSONISTIC
CGIIMMMNNOOPRSU UNCOMPROMISING
CHHKNOORSSTTUW NOT WORTH
SHUCKS
CHHLLLOOOOPRSUY CHLOROPHYLLOUS
CHIILORRSTTTUU HORTICULTURIST
CHIINOPRRSSTTU INSTRUCTORSHIP
CHIIOOORSSTTXY THYROTOXICOSIS
CHILMOOORSTTUY TRICHOTOMOUSLY
CIIILLRSSTTUUV SILVICULTURIST
CIINNNOOORSSTTT CONTORTIONISTS
CLLNOPRSSUUUUY UNSCRUPULOUSLY
DDDEEGGILNNOSW GOLDEN WEDDINGS
DDEEEEEGNRRSWY DYER'S-
GREENWEED
DDEEEEIMNNRSST DETERMINEDNESS
DDEEEEINNNPRTT INTERDEPENDENT
DDEEEELMMNOSSS MEDDLESOMENESS
DDEEEIIKLMNNSS LIKE-MINDEDNESS
DDEEEIILMNNSSV EVIL-MINDEDNESS
DDEEEIINQSSSTU DISQUIETEDNESS
DDEEEIMNNNOPSS OPEN-MINDEDNESS
DDEEEIMNNNORTU UNDERMENTIONED
DDEEGHHIIMNNSS HIGH-MINDEDNESS
DDEEGIIILMSSSU GUIDED MISSILES
DDEEGIILLMNNSY SINGLE-MINDEDLY
DDEEGIILNRSSVW SILVER WEDDINGS
DDEEGILNNNOSSW LONGWINDEDNESS
DDEEHINNORRSUU UNDERNOURISHED
DDEEIIJNNOSSST DISJOINTEDNESS

DDEEIILNORRSSSS DISORDERLINESS
DDEEEINNOPSSSSUW UPSIDE-DOWNNESS
DDEGGHINNOSTUW SHOTGUN
WEDDING .
DDEGHLMOOOORUUY GOOD-
HUMOUREDLY
DDEGIINNORSSWW WINDOW DRESSING
DDEGILMNNORSTY STRONG-MINDEDLY
DDEHIILNOPSSSS SLIPSHODDINESS
DDEHIMNNOPSTUW DOWN IN THE
DUMPS
DEEEEFFGIRRRSZ FRIDGE-FREEZERS
DEEEEFILNRSSTT SELF-INTERESTED
DEEEEGHHNORTTT TO THE NTH
DEGREE
DEEEEGINNRSSSV EVENING DRESSES
DEEEEHMNORRRTV REVEREND
MOTHER
DEEEEILLMMOSSS MESDEMOISELLES
DEEEEIMNPRRRST PREDETERMINERS
DEEEEIMNPRRSST MISREPRESENTED
DEEEEINRSSTTTV VESTED INTEREST
DEEEELMNOPRSTV REDEVELOPMENTS
DEEEENNRRSSSUV UNRESERVEDNESS
DEEEFFGOORRSST DEGREES OF FROST
DEEEFIIINNNSST INDEFINITENESS
DEEEFILNRRSSSS FRIENDLESSNESS
DEEEFNOORSSSTU SUREFOOTEDNESS
DEEEGIIKLNNNTT KNITTING NEEDLE
DEEEGIIMNNPRRT PREDETERMINING
DEEEGILNOOPRVV OVERDEVELOPING
DEEEGIOPRRSSTT REGISTERED POST
DEEEHHLOORSTTT THREE-TOED
SLOTH
DEEEHHPPRRSSSU SHEPHERD'S-PURSE
DEEEHLLMOOOPPS OLD PEOPLE'S
HOME
DEEEEHLMNNOOSWY HONEYDEW
MELONS
DEEEIIMNPRRSTT MISINTERPRETED
DEEEIIMNRSSTTV DIVERTISSEMENT
DEEEIINORRSSVV REVISED VERSION
DEEEILNPRRSSTY INTERSPERSEDLY
DEEEINNNPRSTTU SUPERINTENDENT
DEEEINOQSSTUVX VEXED QUESTIONS
DEEELLNNORRSSU ENROLLED NURSES
DEEEMNNORSSSTU TREMENDOUSNESS
DEEFFFINORRSST FIRST OFFENDERS
DEEFFIIIMNNRST INDIFFERENTISM
DEEFFIIINNRSTT INDIFFERENTIST
DEEFGHILLNSSTU DELIGHTFULNESS
DEEFGHINOORSTW THE WRONG SIDE
OF
DEEFGIIMNRSSTU DISFIGUREMENTS

DEEFIIIILMOPRSV OVERSIMPLIFIED
DEEFIILNNNRSSU UNFRIENDLINESS
DEEFIINOPRSSSU PERFIDIOUSNESS
DEEFILOORRSTUY DO-IT-YOURSELFER
DEEFLOORRRTTUW FOUR-LETTER
WORD
DEEGHILLNOSSUW DWELLING HOUSES
DEEGIIILMOOPST EPIDEMIOLOGIST
DEEGIINNNOSSSU INDIGENOUSNESS
DEEGIINNNPRSTU SUPERINTENDING
DEEGILMNNRSTTU DISGRUNTLEMENT
DEEGLNNORSSSSU GROUNDLESSNESS
DEEHHIOOPPRRSW HERO WORSHIPPED
DEEHNNOORRSSSU HORRENDOUSNESS
DEEIIILMRSTUV VERISIMILITUDE
DEEIIIILNOPRSTV VESPERTILIONID
DEEIIILNOORSTUV REVOLUTIONISED
DEEIIILNOORTUVZ REVOLUTIONIZED
DEEKNOOPPRRSTV DNEPROPETROVSK
DEENNOOOOOPRSST ON ONE'S
DOORSTEP
DEENNOPSSSSTUU STUPENDOUSNESS
DEFFIIIILNOOSSV FIELDS OF VISION
DEFHILLNOQTTUU NOT THE FULL QUID
DEGHHIIILMNOTT THE MIDNIGHT OIL
DEGHHIIKLRSTTU TURKISH DELIGHT
DEGHHILORSSTTY SHORTSIGHTEDLY
DEGHILNOORSSYY HYDROGENOLYSIS
DEGIILNNNOOSSV LOVING KINDNESS
DEGIILNNOORRSS SOLDERING IRONS
DEGIILNNOSSUUY DISINGENUOUSLY
DEGIINOOPRSSSU PRODIGIOUSNESS
DEGILNOORSSTUY SOUL-DESTROYING
DEHIIMOOOOPPRST PHOTOPERIODISM
DEHIMMOOPPRSSU PSEUDOMORPHISM
DEHINOOPPRSSWW WINDOW-SHOPPERS
DEIIINOOPPRSST PREDISPOSITION
DEIILOOPPRRSTY POOR-SPIRITEDLY
DEIIMNNNRSTTUW WIND INSTRUMENT
DEILMNOOOPSSTU DIPLOSTEMONOUS
DEILNNNOPRSSUU SUN IN SPLENDOUR
DEILNORSSSSTUU STRIDULOUSNESS
DEINNNOSSSTTUU STUDENTS' UNIONS
DFGGHINNOOOOORT GOOD-FOR-
NOTHING
DGGHIIIINNSSTU DISTINGUISHING
DGGHINNNORSTUU HUNTING
GROUNDS
DGGINNNOOPRRSUV PROVING GROUNDS
DGHIINNOOPPSWW WINDOW-SHOPPING
DGIIIILLNNOSSU DISILLUSIONING
DHINOOOOPRSSTTT PROSTHODONTIST
DIIIINNOOPSSST INDISPOSITIONS
EEEEEFINPRRRST FREE ENTERPRISE

EEEEEKMNOPPRST KEEP ONE'S TEMPER
EEEEELPRSTTTTY TELETYPESETTER
EEEEFHINNOORTY ONE IN THE EYE FOR
EEEEFILPRRRSSV LIFE PRESERVERS
EEEEFIMNORRRTT INTERFEROMETER
EEEEGHILNRSSTW STEERING WHEELS
EEEEGINRRSSSSV REGRESSIVENESS
EEEEGJLLORRSUW JEWELLER'S ROUGE
EEEEHKLLRRSSTT HELTER-SKELTERS
EEEEIINPRSSTTV REPETITIVENESS
EEEEIMNPRRRSST MISREPRESENTER
EEEEINNPRSSTVV PREVENTIVENESS
EEEEINPRRSSSSV REPRESSIVENESS
EEEEINPRSSSSVX EXPRESSIVENESS
EEEELLNNRSSSST RELENTLESSNESS
EEEEELMNOOPRSST LOSE ONE'S TEMPER
EEEFFLNORSSSST EFFORTLESSNESS
EEEFGLMNNORSTV SELF-GOVERNMENT
EEEFIMNORRRTTY INTERFEROMETRY
EEEFLLMMNOPSTY SELF-EMPLOYMENT
EEEFLLNORRSTTU FORTUNE-TELLERS
EEEFLMNORRSSSU REMORSEFULNESS
EEEFLNNNSSTUUV UNEVENTFULNESS
EEEGGINSSSSTUV SUGGESTIVENESS
EEEGHILNSSSSTW WEIGHTLESSNESS
EEEGIIMNOPRSSS SPERMIOGENESIS
EEEHHIILNPRSTW THREE-LINE WHIPS
EEEHHILMOPPSST MEPHISTOPHELES
EEEHIINPRSSTVY HYPERSENSITIVE
EEEHINNOSSTTTX SIXTEENTH NOTES
EEEIILMNOPSSST IMPOLITENESSES
EEEIILMNPRSSTT SIMPLE INTEREST
EEEIIMNPRRRSTT MISINTERPRETER
EEEIIMNPRSSSSV IMPRESSIVENESS,
  PERMISSIVENESS
EEEILMNOSSSSTV MOTIVELESSNESS
EEEILNOPRSSSSX EXPRESSIONLESS
EEEIMNOPPRRSST PEREMPTORINESS
EEEINNOPRSSSSV RESPONSIVENESS
EEEINNPSSSSSUV SUSPENSIVENESS
EEEINOPPRSSSSV OPPRESSIVENESS
EEEINOPSSSSSSV POSSESSIVENESS
EEEJLLLMOPRTUY PETROLEUM JELLY
EEEMMMMNNOOSTVW WOMEN'S
  MOVEMENT
EEEOPRRRSSSSTU TROUSER PRESSES
EEFFGGHIIORSTU FIGURES OF EIGHT
EEFGGHINOOSTTT NOT THE FOGGIEST
EEFGGIIIKLNNNS SINKING FEELING
EEFGHINNOORRST FORESHORTENING
EEFGIINNOPRSTZ FREEZING POINTS
EEFGINOORRRRST REIGNS OF TERROR
EEFHIIINNORRST IRONS IN THE FIRE
EEFHILNRSSSSTT THRIFTLESSNESS

EEFHNNORRSTTUU FORTUNE HUNTERS
EEFIIILNRRTTTY INTERFERTILITY
EEFILNOOPSSSSS SELF-POSSESSION
EEFLNOPPRSSSUU PURPOSEFULNESS
EEGGHHIILNNSTT SHEET LIGHTNING
EEGGHIILLNNNTY ENLIGHTENINGLY
EEGGIILNNNSTTT STINGING NETTLE
EEGGHHIIILLMNTT IN THE LIMELIGHT
EEGGHHIILOPSSVX HIGH EXPLOSIVES
EEGGHIILNNNPSSW SPINNING WHEELS
EEGGHIIMNNSTTUX EXTINGUISHMENT
EEGGHIKNRRRSSTU HUNGER STRIKERS
EEGGHILLMNORVWY OVERWHELMINGLY
EEGGHINOOPPRRTY PORPHYROGENITE
EEGGHLNOOORSTUY HETEROGONOUSLY
EEGIILMNORTTUU ULTIMOGENITURE
EEGIILMOOPSSTT EPISTEMOLOGIST
EEGIILNNPRRSTY ENTERPRISINGLY
EEGILMOOORSSTT METEOROLOGISTS
EEGILNOOPRRVWY OVERPOWERINGLY
EEGINNOOPRRSSV NONPROGRESSIVE
EEGINNOPPSSSTT STEPPING-STONES
EEGINOPRRSSTTU INTEREST GROUPS
EEGINORSSTTTUW TONGUE TWISTERS
EEGINPRRSSSSTU PURSE STRINGSES
EEGOPPRRRSSSUU PRESSURE GROUPS
EEHHHILNOORSTWW WORTH ONE'S
  WHILE
EEHHILNORSSTWW WORTHWHILENESS
EEHHIMMOOPRRST HETEROMORPHISM
EEHHLLOOPRSTUY HETEROPHYLLOUS
EEHHLLOORSTTUY YOUTH HOSTELLER
EEHIILMNNQRSTU RELINQUISHMENT
EEHIILNOPPRSTY PYELONEPHRITIS
EEHIINOOPSSSTT PHOTOSENSITISE
EEHIINOOPSSTTV PHOTOSENSITIVE
EEHIINOOPSSTTZ PHOTOSENSITIZE
EEHIIOOPRRSSTY ERYTHROPOIESIS
EEHILLOORSSSTT TORTOISESHELLS
EEHIMOOPRRRSTU MOTHER SUPERIOR
EEHINNOORSSTTW NOTEWORTHINESS
EEHINNOPRRTTTU THREE-POINT TURN
EEHINNORSSSTWW NEWSWORTHINESS
EEHINOOPPQSTTU POP THE QUESTION
EEHINOPQSTTTUU PUT THE QUESTION
EEHLMNOOORSTUY
  HETERONOMOUSLY
EEHLMNOORSTUYY
  HETERONYMOUSLY
EEHLMNORSSSSUU HUMOURLESSNESS
EEHMOOOPPRRTTY PYROPHOTOMETER
EEIIIMMNPRRSST PRIME MINISTERS
EEIILMNNRTTTTY INTERMITTENTLY
EEIILNOORRSTUV REVOLUTIONISER

EEIILNOORRTUVZ REVOLUTIONIZER
EEIILNPRSSSSST SPIRITLESSNESS
EEIIINNOPRSTUVY OPEN UNIVERSITY
EEIINOPRSSSSTX EXPRESSIONISTS
EEILLMOPRSSTTU MULTIPLE STORES
EEILMNNOOSSSST MOTIONLESSNESS
EEIMNORSSSSTUY MYSTERIOUSNESS
EEINOOPPRSSSSS PREPOSSESSIONS
EEINOPPRRSSSTU PRESSURE POINTS
EEINOPRRSSSTUV PROTRUSIVENESS
EELOOPPRRSSTUY PREPOSTEROUSLY
EEMNORSSSSTUVY NERVOUS SYSTEMS
EENNOOOOPPRRSST PERSON-TO-PERSON
EENNOOPRSSSTTU PORTENTOUSNESS
EENOOPPRRSSSSU PROSPEROUSNESS
EENOORRSSSSTTU STERTOROUSNESS
EFFGHHLOORTTUU FORETHOUGHTFUL
EFFGIIJLNSSTUY SELF-JUSTIFYING
EFFILNNRSSTUUU UNFRUITFULNESS
EFGGIIINNNPRRT FINGERPRINTING
EFGHHINORRSSTT FORTHRIGHTNESS
EFGHHLNOSSTTUU THOUGHTFULNESS
EFGHLNOOORSTWY GLORY-OF-THE-
SNOW
EFGILNOPPRSSTU SELF-SUPPORTING
EFHILNOPRSSSUW WORSHIPFULNESS
EFHIOOPPRRSSSS PROFESSORSHIPS
EFHMMNOORSTTTU MOMENTS OF
TRUTH
EFINOORSSSTTUU FORTUITOUSNESS
EGGHHIINPRRSSU HIGH-PRESSURING
EGGIILMNNOORRS MORNING GLORIES
EGHHILNNOOOTTT LONG IN THE
TOOTH
EGHHILNNORRSTT NORTHERN LIGHTS
EGHHILNORSSTTU SOUTHERN LIGHTS
EGIIIINNOQRSTU REQUISITIONING
EGIIILMNNRTTTY INTERMITTINGLY
EGIIILNNNRTTWY INTERTWININGLY
EGIINNPRRSSSSU SURPRISINGNESS

EGILNOPPRRSSTU SPLINTER GROUPS
EHHINOOOPPPRST PHOSPHOPROTEIN
EHHINOOPSSSTTY PHOTOSYNTHESIS
EHHNNOORRSTTTW NORTH-
NORTHWEST
EHHOOSSSTTTUUW SOUTH-
SOUTHWEST
EHIILNNOOOPRRTT TRINITROPHENOL
EHILMNOPSSSTYY POLYSYNTHESISM
EHINNOOPRSSTTU PUT ONE'S SHIRT ON
EHLNOPRSSSSUUU SULPHUROUSNESS
EHMOOOOPPRRTTYY
PYROPHOTOMETRY
EIIIMNOPRSSSST IMPRESSIONISTS
EIIINNOOPRSSTT INTERPOSITIONS
EIILNOQRSSTTUV VENTRILOQUISTS
EIIINNORSSSTTUU NUTRITIOUSNESS
EIINOOPPPRSSTU PRESUPPOSITION
EIINOOPPRSSSTU PROPITIOUSNESS
EIKNNNNOOOOSSW KNOW ONE'S
ONIONS
EILMNNOOSSSUUV VOLUMINOUSNESS
EIMNNOOOOPPRRTT PROPORTIONMENT
EIMNOPRSSSSTTU STIR ONE'S STUMPS
EINNOOPQRRSTUU NON PROSEQUITUR
ELMNOSSSTTUUUU TUMULTUOUSNESS
ELMOPPRSSTUUUY PRESUMPTUOUSLY
ELNOOPSSSTUUUV VOLUPTUOUSNESS
EMNNNOOSSSSUYY SYNONYMOUSNESS
FGHHLLOOORSTUW FOLLOW-
THROUGHS
FGHIILLMNOOSTT MOONLIGHT FLITS
GHHIIILNOOPPSZ PHILOSOPHIZING
GHIILNOOORSSTT ORNITHOLOGISTS
GIIINNOOOPPRST PROPOSITIONING
GIIKMMNNRSSTUW SWIMMING TRUNKS
GILOOOOOPRSTTZ PROTOZOOLOGIST
HHINOOOOOPPRSSU SIPHONOPHOROUS
IIIIINNOQSSTTU INQUISITIONIST
IIINOOPRRSSSTV PRISON VISITORS

FIFTEEN-LETTER WORDS

AAAAACDEHHMMRRS MAD AS A
MARCH HARE
AAAAADDEGINSTTV AT A
DISADVANTAGE
AAAABBDIKKLNORR KABARDINO-
BALKAR
AAAABCEILLNOOPT PALAEOBOTANICAL

AAAABGHKKNNOORR NAGORNO-
KARABAKH
AAAACCDIIKLLLSY LACKADAISICALLY
AAAAACCEHHLNNOPT
ACANTHOCEPHALAN
AAAACCILLLLPRTY
PARALLACTICALLY

AAAACDEGILRRUWY DUAL
CARRIAGEWAY

AAAACEFFMORSTTT AS A MATTER OF
FACT

AAAACEGHILLOPPR PALAEOGRAPHICAL

AAAACEILLMNNRTY ALIMENTARY
CANAL

AAAACFGHHILMNSU HALF AS MUCH
AGAIN

AAAACGHILLPPRRY PARAGRAPHICALLY

AAAAEIILMNNPRRT PARLIAMENTARIAN

AAAAFIIMNRRSSST RASTAFARIANISMS

AAAABBCEILNNPRSU BANANA REPUBLICS

AAAABBDDIIILNNQZ INQILAB ZINDABAD

AAABCEEHINRRTTT
TETRABRANCHIATE

AAABCHIILOPPRTY APPROACHABILITY

AAABCIIILNNNOTZ CANNIBALIZATION

AAABDGHHKNNOORS GORNO-
BADAKHSHAN

AAABDHIMOPRSSSS AMBASSADORSHIPS

AAABEGHHINOTTUV HAVE A THING
ABOUT

AAABEGIIILMRRTY MARRIAGEABILITY

AAABEHIILNOPSTT ALPHABETISATION

AAABEHIILNOPTTZ ALPHABETIZATION

AAABEIILLMNPRRS PRIMA BALLERINAS

AAABIILLNRSTTTY TRANSLATABILITY

AAABILNNRSSTTTU TRANSUBSTANTIAL

AAACCDEEILOPSSU ASCLEPIADACEOUS

AAACCDHIMMNOPRY
PHARMACODYNAMIC

AAACCEEFHILMRRW CHEMICAL
WARFARE

AAACCEEGHIKNRRY HACKNEY
CARRIAGE

AAACCEEINORRSSU SARRACENIACEOUS

AAACCEFHILLPTTY PATHETIC FALLACY

AAACCEFIIRRRRRT AIRCRAFT CARRIER

AAACCEMOPPRRSTU
CARPOMETACARPUS

AAACCGHILLMOOPR
PHARMACOLOGICAL

AAACCHIILLNRSTY ANARCHISTICALLY

AAACCIIILMNOSTT ACCLIMATISATION

AAACCIIILMNOTTZ ACCLIMATIZATION

AAACCILLLOPPTYY APOCALYPTICALLY

AAACDEEEMMNRSTU AMUSEMENT
ARCADE

AAACDEEFFGHIRRS CHARGÉ D'AFFAIRES

AAACDEFGIORRRRW CARRIAGE
FORWARD

AAACDEFJKLLORST JACK-OF-ALL-
TRADES

AAACDEGIILLMNTY DIAMAGNETICALLY

AAACDEILLMNORYY
AERODYNAMICALLY

AAACDEILLMORSUY
AMARYLLIDACEOUS

AAACDEIMNNOORTT ANIMATED
CARTOON

AAACDFGIILMNORR AFRICAN
MARIGOLD

AAACDIIINOORTTV RADIOACTIVATION

AAACDIILLNOOORT
RADIOLOCATIONAL

AAACEEGILLNPRTY PARAGENETICALLY

AAACEEHIMMMSTTT
METAMATHEMATICS

AAACEFHHIILMRRS AIR CHIEF
MARSHAL

AAACEFILLLMNOWY FAMILY
ALLOWANCE

AAACEGILMNOPRTY
MALACOPTERYGIAN

AAACEHIILMRRSSV AIR VICE-
MARSHALS

AAACEHIIMNNPRSS SPANISH-AMERICAN

AAACEHIMPPRSTTY PARASYMPATHETIC

AAACEIIIMNNORST AMERICANISATION

AAACEIIIMNNORTZ AMERICANIZATION

AAACEIKLMMNORTX EXCLAMATION
MARK

AAACGGHIJKLNSSU LAUGHING
JACKASS

AAACHIIMNOORTTZ
ACHROMATIZATION

AAACIILLLMNOSTY ANOMALISTICALLY

AAACIILNORSSTUV VASCULARISATION

AAACIILNORSTUVZ VASCULARIZATION

AAACILLNORSTTUY ASTRONAUTICALLY

AAADDDEEEELSTUVX VALUE-ADDED
TAXES

AAADDEGINOSSTUV DISADVANTAGEOUS

AAADDIINNORSSTT STANDARDISATION

AAADDIINNORSTTZ STANDARDIZATION

AAADEEEEHIIKLSV A HEAD LIKE A
SIEVE

AAADEEEILLRTVWY ELEVATED RAILWAY

AAADEEGNNOOSTTV TO ONE'S
ADVANTAGE

AAADEFHHOOPRTTT AT THE DROP OF
A HAT

AAADEIILNNRSTUV VALETUDINARIANS

AAADGHILLMNRRSY MARSHALLING
YARD

AAADGHILMNRRSSY MARSHALING
YARDS

AAADGHIOOPRRTUY
AUTORADIOGRAPHY
AAAEEFHMMNNNORV MANNA FROM
HEAVEN
AAAEEGGHILMNTTU
HAEMAGGLUTINATE
AAAEEGINNPRSSTU SEPTUAGENARIANS
AAAEEGLMMNNRSTT GENTLEMAN-AT-
ARMS
AAAEEGMNRRSSSTT SERGEANTS-AT-
ARMS
AAAEFIILMNNOSTT MANIFESTATIONAL
AAAEGGHIINNRSTT AGAINST THE
GRAIN
AAAEGHLNOOPPRTY
PALAEONTOGRAPHY
AAAEGIINNNQQRUU
QUINQUAGENARIAN
AAAEGINORSSTTVW STARVATION
WAGES
AAAEGLMOPRRSSSU MASSAGE
PARLOURS
AAAEGNNNOOPRRST PERSONA NON
GRATA
AAAEHILMNNNOSTT NATIONAL
ANTHEMS
AAAEIIILMNQRSTU EQUALITARIANISM
AAAEIIILNORRSTT ARTERIALISATION
AAAEIIILNORRTTZ ARTERIALIZATION
AAAEILMNNPRRTUY
UNPARLIAMENTARY
AAAEMORRSSSTTTU
TARSOMETATARSUS
AAAFFIKMMNNRRTU FRANKFURT AM
MAIN
AAAFIIIILMNORST FAMILIARISATION
AAAFIIIILMNORTZ FAMILIARIZATION
AAAGIINNOORSTTV
ASTRONAVIGATION
AAAHIIIMMNNRSTU
HUMANITARIANISM
AAAHIIIMNNRSTTU HUMANITARIANIST
AAAIIIILLMMNOSST MALASSIMILATION
AAAIIILMNORSTTT TOTALITARIANISM
AAAIIILNNNOOSTT NATIONALISATION
AAAIIILNNNOOTTZ NATIONALIZATION
AABBCGHIIILLOPR BIBLIOGRAPHICAL
AABCCCELMOORSUU COOL AS A
CUCUMBER
AABCCDEEHILLNSY HENDECASYLLABIC
AABCCDEELNNORTU
COUNTERBALANCED
AABCCDEGHHLMNNO MONCHEN-
GLADBACH

AABCCDEKKLLNOST BLOCK AND
TACKLES
AABCCEELNNORSTU
COUNTERBALANCES
AABCCEELORRRSUV
CEREBROVASCULAR
AABCCEEMNOORSST CRAB SOMEONE'S
ACT
AABCCEGIILLOORT BACTERIOLOGICAL
AABCCEGIILMNRUV CIRCUMNAVIGABLE
AABCDEEEHLLLNSY HENDECASYLLABLE
AABCDEEHORSTTUY CATHODE RAY
TUBES
AABCDEEIKRRSSTV BACK-SEAT DRIVERS
AABCDEGIKLNRRST BLANK
CARTRIDGES
AABCDEIILNOORST ANABOLIC STEROID
AABCDEIINNOORST DECARBONISATION
AABCDEIINNOORTZ
DECARBONIZATION
AABCDEILNOORTXY
DECARBOXYLATION
AABCDGIIILLOOOR RADIOBIOLOGICAL
AABCDGILLMNNOOR BALLROOM
DANCING
AABCDHIILLMRTYY
DITHYRAMBICALLY
AABCEEEFKLRRTVW BLACKWATER
FEVER
AABCEEEKKLMRRST BLACK
MARKETEERS
AABCEEFFIIILNTY INEFFACEABILITY
AABCEEGGIIMNNRT MAGNETIC
BEARING
AABCEEGHIILNTXY EXCHANGEABILITY
AABCEEGHILNNRTY
INTERCHANGEABLY
AABCEEGHLNORSUX LABOUR
EXCHANGES
AABCEEHINSSTTUU EUSTACHIAN
TUBES
AABCEEINOQRSSTU SESQUICARBONATE
AABCEFHKLOORRTY THE BACK OF A
LORRY
AABCEGGHIILOOPR BIOGEOGRAPHICAL
AABCEGHHIIMNNST BATHING
MACHINES
AABCEGHIOOPRSTU
BACTERIOPHAGOUS
AABCEGILMNOPSUU
PLUMBAGINACEOUS
AABCEILLLMOPRTY PROBLEMATICALLY
AABCEILLLMORSTY MEROBLASTICALLY
AABCFIIILLNOSTY SYLLABIFICATION

AABCGHKLLNNOOTY NOT BY A LONG CHALK

AABCHIILLLNRTYY LABYRINTHICALLY

AABCHILLLLOOSTY HOLOBLASTICALLY

AABCIIIILLNPPTY INAPPLICABILITY

AABCIIIILMNOPRTY INCOMPARABILITY

AABCIIINOORSSTTU BIOASTRONAUTICS

AABDDDGGILNNOOR BOARD AND LODGING

AABDDEEIMNNORST ONE-ARMED BANDITS

AABDDEFIIOPRRSS BIRDS OF PARADISE

AABDEEEHILNNNRS BANNER HEADLINES

AABDEEFFHIORRST BIRDS OF A FEATHER

AABDEEGHINORRTW WEATHERBOARDING

AABDEIIILNORSTT DETRIBALISATION

AABDEIIILNORTTZ DETRIBALIZATION

AABDEIIILNOSSTT DESTABILISATION

AABDEIIILNOSTTZ DESTABILIZATION

AABDHILMNOSSSUY BUSMAN'S HOLIDAYS

AABEEEEFIKLMNOR MAKE A BEELINE FOR

AABEEEELNNORSSST TREASONABLENESS

AABEEFHILNNOSSS FASHIONABLENESS

AABEEFLNNORSSUV UNFAVORABLENESS

AABEEGHIILRTTTY A TIGER BY THE TAIL

AABEEGHIKLNRRTY HEARTBREAKINGLY

AABEFGIIILRRRTY IRREFRAGABILITY

AABEFIILNRRSTTY TRANSFERABILITY

AABEFLNORRTTUZZ BURNT TO A FRAZZLE

AABEGHHMOOPRRRT THERMOBAROGRAPH

AABEGHIILMNOORU HAEMOGLOBINURIA

AABEGHIIOOPRSTU AUTOBIOGRAPHIES

AABEIIILMMRSTUY IMMEASURABILITY

AABEIILMNORTUVY MANOEUVRABILITY

AABEKMRRRRSSTWY STRAWBERRY MARKS

AABGGIIILLNTTUY AGGLUTINABILITY

AABIILNOPRSSTTY TRANSPOSABILITY

AACCCCEIILNRRTT ANTARCTIC CIRCLE

AACCDEEHHLOOPRT CEPHALOCHORDATE

AACCDEEKNORTTTU COUNTERATTACKED

AACCDEGHIILOORS OLIGOSACCHARIDE

AACCDEGIILLLOOT DIALECTOLOGICAL

AACCDEGIIMNRTUV CIRCUMNAVIGATED

AACCDEHHILMNORY HYDROMECHANICAL

AACCDEIIILLMRTY ACIDIMETRICALLY

AACCDEILMOORSST SOCIAL DEMOCRATS

AACCDEIMNPPRRSS SCRIMP AND SCRAPE

AACCDGILMMNOOTY ACCOMMODATINGLY

AACCDHIIMOOSSST SADOMASOCHISTIC

AACCDHILNOOPRST ACHONDROPLASTIC

AACCDIILLOOPRSY RADIOSCOPICALLY

AACCEEEGILNPRRT GENERAL PRACTICE

AACCEEGHILMMNOT MAGNETOCHEMICAL

AACCEEHIIOPPRST ARCHIEPISCOPATE

AACCEEHILMNORSV SERVOMECHANICAL

AACCEEHILORSSTT THE COAST IS CLEAR

AACCEEILLNNOPRT PRECANCELLATION

AACCEEILLNORTTY ELECTROANALYTIC

AACCEEILNNOPSTT PENTATONIC SCALE

AACCEEILNNRSSTU NATURAL SCIENCES

AACCEEINNNORSSS RECONNAISSANCES

AACCEEKNORRTTTU COUNTERATTACKER

AACCEELNORRRSTU NUCLEAR REACTORS

AACCEFIILOOPRSU CAPRIFOLIACEOUS

AACCEGGHINRRRSY CARRYING CHARGES

AACCEGHIIMNOPRT CINEMATOGRAPHIC

AACCEHHILMNOOPT PHOTOMECHANICAL

AACCEHIILLMNSTY MECHANISTICALLY

AACCEHIILLRSTUY EUCHARISTICALLY

AACCEHILLLLMNOY MELANCHOLICALLY

AACCEHILLMORTTY TACHOMETRICALLY

AACCEHILLMRTTYY TACHYMETRICALLY

AACCEHILLRRTTUY ARCHITECTURALLY

AACCEIIILLMNRST ANTICLERICALISM

AACCEIILLMNOSTY ENCOMIASTICALLY

AACCEIILLNRRTUV INTERCLAVICULAR

AACCEILRRRRTUUX EXTRACURRICULAR

AACCFFFGHKLOOOT GO OFF AT HALF-COCK

AACCFIIILNOSSST CLASSIFICATIONS

AACCFNNORSTTTUU TURF ACCOUNTANTS

AACCGHHIMOOPRRT CHROMATOGRAPHIC

AACCGHIMMNOORRT CHRONOGRAMMATIC

AACCGHIMNOOPRST PHARMACOGNOSTIC

AACCGIIMNORRTUV CIRCUMNAVIGATOR

AACCGINNOSSSTUV SAVINGS ACCOUNTS

AACCHHIINNRRTUU UNITARIAN CHURCH

AACCHHIIOOPPRTT HIPPOCRATIC OATH

AACCHIIILNOOSTT CATHOLICISATION

AACCHILLNOPSTYY SYCOPHANTICALLY

AACCIIILLLOSSTY SOCIALISTICALLY

AACCIIILNORRSTU CIRCULARISATION

AACCIIILNORRTUZ CIRCULARIZATION

AACCIIILPRRSTTU PARTICULARISTIC

AACCIILLMNORTUV CIRCUMVALLATION

AACCIILLMNOSSTU MISCALCULATIONS

AACCILLLOPRTTUY PLUTOCRATICALLY

AACDDEEEEHLNRSS CLEAR-HEADEDNESS

AACDDEEEGNSSTUU AN EDUCATED GUESS

AACDDEEILOSSTVV DEVIL'S ADVOCATES

AACDDHIKMNORRTY TOM, DICK, AND HARRY

AACDEEEEGIORSST ASSOCIATE DEGREE

AACDEEEHNPRRSTV CHAPTER AND VERSE

AACDEEGIILLNPPS SPECIAL PLEADING

AACDEEGIILLNRST LEADING ARTICLES

AACDEEHIKLMMNRS HAMMER AND SICKLE

AACDEEHIMNNOTUU HUMANE EDUCATION

AACDEEHKKNRRSTY THE KNACKER'S YARD

AACDEEIILNPRSTU UNDERCAPITALISE

AACDEEIILNPRTUZ UNDERCAPITALIZE

AACDEEIILOPRSTV OVERCAPITALISED

AACDEEIILOPRTVZ OVERCAPITALIZED

AACDEEIIMNNOTTV DECONTAMINATIVE

AACDEEILNNSSTTU INDECENT ASSAULT

AACDEGIIIKKLNNV ALIVE AND KICKING

AACDEGIIMNNNOTT DECONTAMINATING

AACDEHOORRSSSTT AT THE CROSSROADS

AACDEIIILLMORTUY AUDIOMETRICALLY

AACDEIILMMNOSST DOMESTIC ANIMALS

AACDEIILNOSSTTU EDUCATIONALISTS

AACDEIIMNOORSTT DEMOCRATISATION

AACDEIIMNOORTTZ DEMOCRATIZATION

AACDEILLMORRTTU COURT-MARTIALLED

AACDEILNNOOSSTT SEA ISLAND COTTON

AACDFIIINOSSSTT DISSATISFACTION

AACDFIIORSSSTTY DISSATISFACTORY

AACDHIILLNOOPRY RADIOPHONICALLY

AACDIIIILNNPRSS DISCIPLINARIANS

AACDIIILNORSTTU DISARTICULATION

AACDIILNOPQRTUU QUADRUPLICATION

AACEEEFGHNORSTX RATE OF EXCHANGES

AACEEEFHORRSTTW WEATHER FORECAST

AACEEEGIPPRRSTT CIGARETTE PAPERS

AACEEEILLRSSTUV RELATIVE CLAUSES

AACEEEILNRSSSST SALES RESISTANCE

AACEEENNQRRTTUY QUATERCENTENARY

AACEEFFHIMNNRST AFFRANCHISEMENT

AACEEFGHLMNORRT FARM THE LONG ACRE

AACEEFHINNOSTTT AT THE INSTANCE OF

AACEEFIILLMNRSU NUCLEAR FAMILIES

AACEEFIINOORSST FREE ASSOCIATION

AACEEGHHLNOPPRY ENCEPHALOGRAPHY

AACEEGHILLLPRTY TELEGRAPHICALLY

AACEEGHIMNOPRRT CINEMATOGRAPHER

AACEEGHLLLNORWY YELLOW ARCHANGEL

AACEEHIINORTTTZ CATHETERIZATION

AACEEHILLMORTTY THEOREMATICALLY

AACEEHILLNPRTTY PARENTHETICALLY

AACEEHILLPRTTUY THERAPEUTICALLY

AACEEHMNOPRRTWW COME THE RAW PRAWN

AACEEIIILLPPRTTY PERIPATETICALLY
AACEEIIILNNORSTV NATIONAL SERVICE
AACEEIILLNNPRSTU INTERNAL CAPSULE
AACEFFINORRRSTW WARRANT
OFFICERS
AACEFHHIMRRSSTT FATHER
CHRISTMAS
AACEFILOOPRSSSU PASSIFLORACEOUS
AACEGGHINNORRST GREGORIAN
CHANTS
AACEGHHIIMNNSSW WASHING
MACHINES
AACEGHHMOOPRRRT
CHROMATOGRAPHER
AACEGHIJKRSSTTT STRAIGHTJACKETS
AACEGHILLOPRRXY
XEROGRAPHICALLY
AACEGHILOOPSTTT COTTAGE
HOSPITAL
AACEGIIMNORSSTV MOVING STAIRCASE
AACEHILLNOPRTUY NEUROPATHICALLY
AACEHILLOOPSTTY OSTEOPATHICALLY
AACEHLMORSSTUUW WALRUS
MOUSTACHE
AACEIIILMNOPPSS EPISCOPALIANISM
AACEIIILNOPSSST SPECIALISATIONS
AACEIIILNOPSSTZ SPECIALIZATIONS
AACEIIILPRRSTTU PARTICULARITIES
AACEIIIMNNOPSTT EMANCIPATIONIST
AACEIIILLLMNSTTY MENTALISTICALLY
AACEIIILLLPRSTTY PERISTALTICALLY
AACEIILLMNNRSTY MANNERISTICALLY
AACEIILMNOPRRTT MALPRACTITIONER
AACEIIILNNPRSSTU PURITANICALNESS
AACEIIILNOPRSTTU RECAPITULATIONS
AACEIIILPPPRSSTT PAST PARTICIPLES
AACFGILNORRSTUV VULGAR
FRACTIONS
AACFIIINNOORSTT FRACTIONISATION
AACFIIINNOORTTZ FRACTIONIZATION
AACFIIINORSSTTT STRATIFICATIONS
AACGGHILLNOOPRY
PHARYNGOLOGICAL
AACGHHILLLOOPRY
HOLOGRAPHICALLY
AACGHIIILMNORTT ANTILOGARITHMIC
AACGHIILLLMORTY
ALGORITHMICALLY, LOGARITHMICALLY
AACGHILLLOPPRYY POLYGRAPHICALLY
AACGHILLMNOOPRY
MONOGRAPHICALLY, NOMOGRAPHICALLY
AACGHILLNOOOPRT
ANTHROPOLOGICAL
AACGHILLOOPPRTY TOPOGRAPHICALLY

AACGHILLOPPRTYY TYPOGRAPHICALLY
AACGHILMOOPRSST
PHARMACOLOGISTS
AACGIIILNPRRTUZ PARTICULARIZING
AACGIILMNORRTTU COURT-
MARTIALING
AACGIINNOPRRSTT PROCRASTINATING
AACGILLMNOORSTY
GASTRONOMICALLY
AACGILNNOORSTTU
CONGRATULATIONS
AACGILNOORSSTUY
AGRANULOCYTOSIS
AACGIMMNOOPRRSU
MACROSPORANGIUM
AACHIIIINNOPSST HISPANICISATION
AACHIIIINNOPSTZ HISPANICIZATION
AACHIILLMNORSTY HARMONISTICALLY
AACHILLLMOOPSTY
HOMOPLASTICALLY
AACHILLOPPRSTYY SAPROPHYTICALLY
AACHILLOPPSSTTY STAPHYLOPLASTIC
AACIIILLLRSTTUY RITUALISTICALLY
AACIIIMNNOORSTT ROMANTICISATION
AACIIIMNNOORTTZ
ROMANTICIZATION
AACIILLLMOPSTUY POLITICAL
ASYLUM
AACIILLNORSSTTY CRYSTALLISATION
AACIILLNORSTTYZ CRYSTALLIZATION
AACIILMMNNOOSTU
COMMUNALISATION
AACIILMMNNOOTUZ
COMMUNALIZATION
AACIILMNOOSSSTY ANCYLOSTOMIASIS
AACIILMOOPSTTTU AUTOMATIC PILOTS
AACIILNNOPRRSTT TRANSCRIPTIONAL
AACIINNOOPRRSTT PROCRASTINATION
AACIKMNNOPRTTUU PUNCTUATION
MARK
AACILLLLMOPSTYY PLASMOLYTICALLY
AACILLMMOPSTTYY
SYMPTOMATICALLY
AACLLRRRSTTTUUU
ULTRASTRUCTURAL
AADDDEINNNORSST
NONSTANDARDISED
AADDDEINNNORSTZ
NONSTANDARDIZED
AADDDELMNNPPSUY SUPPLY AND
DEMAND
AADDEHILNOOSTWW WHITE
SANDALWOOD
AADDEIILNOPRSTU SUPERADDITIONAL

AADEEEEEILNRSSV VENEREAL DISEASE
AADEEEELMNOPRTV DEVELOPMENT
AREA
AADEEEFHHLNRSST HALF-
HEARTEDNESS
AADEEEFHIMNOOST AHEAD OF ONE'S
TIME
AADEEEGKMNRRRST MARKET
GARDENERS
AADEEEGLMOOPSTX SET A GOOD
EXAMPLE
AADEEEHLRRRSSSS DRESS REHEARSALS
AADEEEHMNRRSSTW WARM-
HEARTEDNESS
AADEEEILMNPRSTT DEPARTMENTALISE
AADEEEILMNPRTTZ DEPARTMENTALIZE
AADEEEMNPRSTTTT STATE
DEPARTMENT
AADEFGGIKMNNRRT MARKET
GARDENING
AADEEGHILOPRRTY
RADIOTELEGRAPHY
AADEEGIIMNNOSTT
DEMAGNETISATION
AADEEGIIMNNOTTZ
DEMAGNETIZATION
AADEEHIIIMNRRST HEREDITARIANISM
AADEEIILNOSSTUX DESEXUALISATION
AADEHIIOPRRSSTT RADIOTHERAPISTS
AADEIIKLRSSSTTW SIDEWALK ARTISTS
AADEIIILNOPSSSTY DISPASSIONATELY
AADEIILNORRRTXY EXTRAORDINARILY
AADEIIMOPPPRRST MISAPPROPRIATED
AADEILMNNOORSTT
DEMONSTRATIONAL
AADEINPRRSSSSTT STARS AND STRIPES
AADELLOPSSSTTTU SLOTTED SPATULAS
AADELMPRRSSSTTU MUSTARD
PLASTERS
AADELNOPRSTTUUY
POLYUNSATURATED
AADEMNOOPRRTTUW PORTMANTEAU
WORD
AADFGHIORRRSTTW
STRAIGHTFORWARD
AADFHMNNOOSSTUY A MONTH OF
SUNDAYS
AADFIIILNNORSTY DISINFLATIONARY
AADGHHIMNPRSSTU
DRAUGHTSMANSHIP
AADGIIINNOORSST DISORGANISATION
AADGIIINNOORSTZ DISORGANIZATION
AADIIILNORSSTTT TRADITIONALISTS
AADIIIMNNORSSTT ADMINISTRATIONS

AADIIMMNSSTTTUU MUTATIS
MUTANDIS
AAEEEEEHNOPRTWY A WEATHER EYE
OPEN
AAEEEFGLMMNNRRT GENTLEMAN
FARMER
AAEEEGILLNNRRTT ETERNAL
TRIANGLE
AAEEEGLMMNNRSTT GENTLEMEN-AT-
ARMS
AAEEEILMNNPTTTU ANTEPENULTIMATE
AAEEEELLMMNPRTTY
TEMPERAMENTALLY
AAEEEFFINOORRSTT REAFFORESTATION
AAEEEFGIMNNRRSST FRAGMENTARINESS
AAEEEFHILRSSTTVV HARVEST FESTIVAL
AAEEEFIIILMRSSSZ LAISSEZ-FAIREISM
AAEEEFILMNNOSTX SELF-EXAMINATION
AAEEEFLLNOPRSTXY SELF-EXPLANATORY
AAEEEGGIIINNRSTV NEGATIVE-RAISING
AAEEEGHHINRRSTTT
EARTHSHATTERING
AAEEEGIILNNORSST GENERALISATIONS
AAEEEGIILNNORSTZ GENERALIZATIONS
AAEEEGILMNRTTUVY
ARGUMENTATIVELY
AAEEEHINOPRRSTVY AVERSION
THERAPY
AAEEEHINORSSTTTW WEATHER
STATIONS
AAEEEHMNOPRSSTTU APARTMENT
HOUSES
AAEEEIILNNORSTTX EXTERNALISATION
AAEEEIILNNORTTXZ EXTERNALIZATION
AAEEEIINNOOPRSTU EUROPEANISATION
AAEEEIINNOOPRTUZ EUROPEANIZATION
AAEEEILNNOPRRSST PROLETARIANNESS
AAEEEIMNPRSSTTTV PAVEMENT
ARTISTS
AAEEEINOPPPRRSST APPROPRIATENESS
AAEEELLNPRRRTTUY PRETERNATURALLY
AAEEENNNPRRSSSTT TRANSPARENTNESS
AAEEFLLNOPRRRSUU FUNERAL
PARLOURS
AAEEGHILLLLNOTTTU LET IT ALL HANG
OUT
AAEEGIIILNNOSTTV INVESTIGATIONAL
AAEEGIIKNNNPSSST PAINSTAKINGNESS
AAEEGIILNNOORRTT
INTERROGATIONAL
AAEEGIILNNRRSTTT TRANSLITERATING
AAEEGIIMNNPRSSTY PRAYING MANTISES
AAEEGILLNOOOPSTT PALAEONTOLOGIST
AAEEGILLOOOOPSTZ PALAEOZOOLOGIST

AAEGIMMNNNOSSSU
MAGNANIMOUSNESS
AAEHIILORTTTUVY AUTHORITATIVELY
AAEHILLMNOPSSTT MENTAL HOSPITALS
AAEIIIILMMNPRST ANTI-IMPERIALISM
AAEIIIILMNPRSTT ANTI-IMPERIALIST
AAEIIILMMNOORST MEMORIALISATION
AAEIIILMMNOORTZ
MEMORIALIZATION
AAEIIILMNNNORTT INTERLAMINATION
AAEIIILNNNORSTT INTERNALISATION
AAEIIILNNOORTTZ ORIENTALIZATION
AAEIIILNPRSSSTT ANTIPERISTALSIS
AAEIIILLMNNRSTTU TRANSILLUMINATE
AAEIIILLNNNORTTY INTERNATIONALLY
AAEIILMORRRRTTY TERRITORIAL
ARMY
AAEIILNNOOPRSST PERSONALISATION
AAEIILNNOOPRSTZ PERSONALIZATION
AAEIILNNORRSTTT TRANSLITERATION
AAEIILNNOSSSSTT SENSATIONALISTS
AAEIILNOPPPRRTY INAPPROPRIATELY
AAEIIMNOSSSTTTY SYSTEMATISATION
AAEIIMNOSSTTTYZ SYSTEMATIZATION
AAEIINNPPRRSSTT ANTIPERSPIRANTS
AAEILLLMNNNPSTT INSTALLMENT
PLAN
AAEILMNPRRSSTUU SUPERNATURALISM
AAEILNNNOSSTTUY INSTANTANEOUSLY
AAEILNPRRSSTTUU SUPERNATURALIST
AAEINNNNOPSSSTT ANTS IN ONE'S
PANTS
AAELMNSSSSSTTYY SYSTEMS ANALYSTS
AAENNORRSSSTUUY
TYRANNOSAURUSES
AAFGGGIILMNNSSY MAGNIFYING GLASS
AAFGIINNORRSTTU TRANSFIGURATION
AAFIIIILMNRSTTU FUTILITARIANISM
AAFIILLNORRTTTU ULTRAFILTRATION
AAFIILMNOORRSTU FORMULARISATION
AAFIILMNOORRTUZ
FORMULARIZATION
AAFIMNNOORRSSTT
TRANSFORMATIONS
AAGIIILNNORSSTU SINGULARISATION
AAGIIILNNORSTUZ SINGULARIZATION
AAGIILNORSTTTUU GUTTURALISATION
AAGIILNORTTTUUZ GUTTURALIZATION
AAHHHLOPPRRSTYY
STAPHYLORRHAPHY
AAHHIINOOPPSSTT PHOSPHATISATION
AAHHIINOOPPSTTZ PHOSPHATIZATION
AAHIIILNOOPSSTT HOSPITALISATION
AAHIIILNOOPSTTZ HOSPITALIZATION

AAIIIIMNNORSTTU MINIATURISATION
AAIIIIMNNORTTUZ MINIATURIZATION
AAIIILMMNOORSTT IMMORTALISATION
AAIIILMMNOORTTZ
IMMORTALIZATION
AAIIILMNOOPRSTV IMPROVISATIONAL
AAIIJLNOOPSTTUX JUXTAPOSITIONAL
AAIIILLNNORTTUVY INVOLUNTATARILY
AAIILNNOOPRSSTT TRANSPOSITIONAL
AAIIMNNOOPRSSSTY TRYPANOSOMIASIS
AAIINNOOPSTTTU SATURATION POINT
ABBCCEFIIMNNORU FIBONACCI
NUMBER
ABBCEEEFFKLOOOT COFFEE-TABLE
BOOK
ABBDDEEELLLORRU DOUBLE-
BARRELLED
ABBDEEELNORSSTU REDOUBTABLENESS
ABBDEGHILORRTYY DAYLIGHT
ROBBERY
ABBDELNORRRSTWY STRAWBERRY
BLOND
ABBEEIIILLMORRS MOBILE LIBRARIES
ABBEEIIILLNTUVY UNBELIEVABILITY
ABBEIIIILMOPRST IMPROBABILITIES
ABCCCDEIIILNORU RIBONUCLEIC ACID
ABCCEEFHILNOSST CHIEF CONSTABLES
ABCCEEIIKRRRSTU CIRCUIT BREAKERS
ABCCEEILLNOOPST POLICE CONSTABLE
ABCCEFIIIJNOOTT OBJECTIFICATION
ABCCEFIIILLPSSUY SUBSPECIFICALLY
ABCCEGHINOPRSST BATCH PROCESSING
ABCCEIIIILNSSTY INACCESSIBILITY
ABCCEIIIILLNORTY RECONCILABILITY
ABCCEIILMNOPPSU PUBLIC COMPANIES
ABCCEIILNNPSSUU PUBLIC NUISANCES
ABCCIIILNORTTTY CONTRACTIBILITY
ABCCIIKLMNNOOOT COMBINATION
LOCK
ABCDEEEEGHLORRS BACHELOR'S
DEGREE
ABCDEEELLOOORST COLORADO
BEETLES
ABCDEEHIIILPRTY DECIPHERABILITY
ABCDEEIILORRRRS RECORD LIBRARIES
ABCDEELMNORRSUU CONSUMER
DURABLE
ABCDEGHIKNNORTU IN THE
BACKGROUND
ABCDEGIIILPRSTY CREDIBILITY GAPS
ABCDEIILLLOQTUY QUODLIBETICALLY
ABCDEIILMOOPSTY DECOMPOSABILITY
ABCDEIIMOOSSTUY BASIDIOMYCETOUS
ABCEEEIIILLNOSTV CABLE TELEVISION

ABCEEEIILNNOPTUX UNEXCEPTIONABLE
ABCEEGHIKLOORST GLOBE ARTICHOKES
ABCEEGHINORSSTT TOSSING THE CABER
ABCEEHHLMNNOOPR RHOMBENCEPHALON
ABCEEILMMNNORSU INCOMMENSURABLE
ABCEEILMNNNOOOU ONCE IN A BLUE MOON
ABCEEILNNOPTUXY UNEXCEPTIONABLY
ABCEELNNNOOPRUU UNPRONOUNCEABLE
ABCEGIIILNORTYZ RECOGNIZABILITY
ABCEGIILOORSSTT BACTERIOLOGISTS
ABCEIIIILLNPTXY INEXPLICABILITY
ABCEIIIILNRTTXY INEXTRICABILITY
ABCEIIILLMMRSTYY BISYMMETRICALLY
ABCEIIILLNOPRSTU PUBLIC RELATIONS
ABCGIIILLNOOOTTY GNOTOBIOTICALLY
ABCIIIILMNOPTTY INCOMPATIBILITY
ABCIIIILLNNOOSTY INCONSOLABILITY
ABCIIILMMNOTTUY INCOMMUTABILITY
ABCIIILMNOPTTUY INCOMPUTABILITY
ABCIIILNNOORSUV BINOCULAR VISION
ABCIILLLMOSSTYY SYMBOLISTICALLY
ABDDDEEIMNNORSS BROADMINDEDNESS
ABDDDEEHLNNOORTU BLOOD-AND-THUNDER
ABDDEEEHNOORSUW BONDED WAREHOUSE
ABDDEEIIJLMNOSU DIAMOND JUBILEES
ABDDEEELMNOORSSW WARM-BLOODEDNESS
ABDEEEEHILLLSSTW WELL-ESTABLISHED
ABDEEEEHKLNORRTY BROKEN-HEARTEDLY
ABDEEEIIILMRRTY IRREDEEMABILITY
ABDEEEILNORRTVY BEYOND RETRIEVAL
ABDEIIILMNOPRTY IMPONDERABILITY
ABDEIIILPRSTTUY DISREPUTABILITY
ABDEIIILMNORSTTY DEMONSTRABILITY
ABDEIIILNNORSTUY INSUBORDINATELY
ABDEILLMNNOPSTU PLATINUM BLONDES
ABDFIIILNOOOORSV DIVISION OF LABOR
ABDIIIIILMNSSTY INADMISSIBILITY
ABDIIIIILNPSTTUY INDISPUTABILITY
ABDIIINNNOORSTU INSUBORDINATION
ABEEEEGIKLNSTVV VEGETABLE KNIVES
ABEEEEILNNPRRTT INTERPENETRABLE

ABEEEELNNPRSSST PRESENTABLENESS
ABEEEFHHLMORSTT STAR-OF-BETHLEHEM
ABEEEFHOPRRTTTT THE BETTER PART OF
ABEEEGHHHLNOSTW THE WHOLE SHEBANG
ABEEEHKNNORRSST HEARTBROKENNESS
ABEEEHILMNORSSTW BLAMEWORTHINESS
ABEEIILNNORSTUV LABOUR-INTENSIVE
ABEEIIMNPRRSSTY PRESBYTERIANISM
ABEEINNSSSSTTUV SUBSTANTIVENESS
ABEGHHIMNOORSTT SMOOTH BREATHING
ABEHIIIILMPRSTY IMPERISHABILITY
ABEHIILMORSTTTY THERMOSTABILITY
ABEHILMNOOOORRTT TRIBROMOETHANOL
ABEIIIILLNNRTUVY INVULNERABILITY
ABEIIIILLORRSTVY IRRESOLVABILITY
ABEIIILLMNOPTUYY UNEMPLOYABILITY
ABEINOOOPRSSTTV OBSERVATION POST
ABFIIIILNOPRTTUY UNPROFITABILITY
ABFILMMNOOOORSTY SYMBOL-FORMATION
ABHNNOOOORTTTTUW NOT WORTH A BUTTON
ACCCCEGHIKNNOTU CHECKING ACCOUNT
ACCCDDKLLNOOOUU CLOUD-CUCKOO-LAND
ACCCDEEEEEHKRRR CHECKERED CAREER
ACCCEEGIILLLOOS ECCLESIOLOGICAL
ACCCEEHILLNORSV VICE-CHANCELLORS
ACCCEEIIIILMSSST ECCLESIASTICISM
ACCCEEILOORSTTU ELECTROACOUSTIC
ACCCEFIIKNNOOTY COCKNEYFICATION
ACCCEHHIILMOPSY PHYSICOCHEMICAL
ACCCEHHILNOPSTY PSYCHOTECHNICAL
ACCCEIIILMMORST COMMERCIALISTIC
ACCCEIILNOPSTTU CONCEPTUALISTIC
ACCCEILOOPRSTUU ACOUSTIC COUPLER
ACCCENNORRSTTUU CURRENT ACCOUNTS
ACCCHIOOPSSSTUY PSYCHOACOUSTICS
ACCCIILLMOOPRSY MICROSCOPICALLY
ACCDDDEKLOOOOOS COCK-A-DOODLE-DOOS

ACCDDEEINNNOSTU
DISCOUNTENANCED
ACCDDEIMMNNNOOS SECOND-IN-
COMMAND
ACCDEEEEEHQRRRU CHEQUERED
CAREER
ACCDEEHILLLPSYY PSYCHEDELICALLY
ACCDEEHINOOOPSU
CHENOPODIACEOUS
ACCDEEILMNOPSST COMPLICATEDNESS
ACCDEEILMNORSTY
ELECTRODYNAMICS
ACCDEFFFGHKLOOO GO OFF HALF-
COCKED
ACCDEFGHHLNNORU CHURCH OF
ENGLAND
ACCDEHINORSSSUW SANDWICH
COURSES
ACCDEIIILMNNSTU INCIDENTAL MUSIC
ACCDEINOOPSSTTU DEPOSIT
ACCOUNTS
ACCDEIOPPRRSTTU PICTURE POSTCARD
ACCDFHIIINNOORT CHONDRIFICATION
ACCEEEFIMNORSST MASTER OF
SCIENCE
ACCEEEGILMNORTT
ELECTROMAGNETIC, MAGNETOELECTRIC
ACCEEEHKLRRSSTV TRAVELER'S
CHECKS
ACCEEEIINORSTVV ON ACTIVE SERVICE
ACCEEENNOPSSTUX EXPENSE
ACCOUNTS
ACCEEFHIIINOPST SPEECHIFICATION
ACCEEFIIILNORTT ELECTRIFICATION
ACCEEFIILMNRRTU CIRCUMFERENTIAL
ACCEEFILLMORSTV COLLECTIVE FARMS
ACCEEFINNOOOSSS SENSE OF
OCCASION
ACCEEGILLORRSTU ELECTROSURGICAL
ACCEEHHIMOORRTT
HETEROCHROMATIC
ACCEEHILOORRSTT ATHEROSCLEROTIC
ACCEEIIMMNOTUVX
EXCOMMUNICATIVE
ACCEEIINNOORSSS CONCESSIONAIRES
ACCEEILNORTTXYY
OXYTETRACYCLINE
ACCEFFGIIILNRSS SELF-SACRIFICING
ACCEFGIIIPRSTVY SPECIFIC GRAVITY
ACCEFHHMMNOSSUU MUCH OF A
MUCHNESS
ACCEGHIIILNNORT ANTICHOLINERGIC
ACCEGHIIMNNPRRS PRINCE
CHARMINGS

ACCEGHILLLNOOTY
TECHNOLOGICALLY
ACCEGHILLNOPSYY PSYCHOGENICALLY
ACCEGIIILMMNORZ
COMMERCIALIZING
ACCEGIILNNOPRSS PELICAN CROSSING
ACCEGIILNNOPTUZ CONCEPTUALIZING
ACCEGIIMMNNOTUX
EXCOMMUNICATING
ACCEGIKLLNOOSTU COCKTAIL
LOUNGES
ACCEGILLLNOOSYY SYNECOLOGICALLY
ACCEHHILLMNOOPR
CHLORAMPHENICOL
ACCEHIIILPRRTYY HYPERCRITICALLY
ACCEHIILNORSSTT INTERSCHOLASTIC
ACCEHIIMNOPRSTY PSYCHOMETRICIAN
ACCEHILLMNOORTY
HOMOCENTRICALLY
ACCEHILLMOOPRTY
CHEMOTROPICALLY
ACCEHILMMNOPSST
ACCOMPLISHMENTS
ACCEHINNOOPRRTT
ANTHROPOCENTRIC
ACCEIIKNNORSSTW STICK IN ONE'S
CRAW
ACCEIILMRRTUUUV CURRICULUM
VITAE
ACCEIILNNOPRSUY INSURANCE POLICY
ACCEIILOPPRSSUY PERSPICACIOUSLY
ACCEIIMMNNOOTUX
EXCOMMUNICATION
ACCEIIMMNNOTUUV
UNCOMMUNICATIVE
ACCEIIOORRSSSTV VICTORIA CROSSES
ACCEILMOOPRRSTU
ULTRAMICROSCOPE
ACCELLNOOOSUUVV
CONVOLVULACEOUS
ACCFIMMNNOOORST COMMON
FRACTIONS
ACCGHIIILLOOOST STOICHIOLOGICAL
ACCGHILLLNOOORY
CHRONOLOGICALLY
ACCGHILLLOOPSYY PSYCHOLOGICALLY
ACCHHILMOOOPPST
OPHTHALMOSCOPIC
ACCHIILNNOORTTY
THYROCALCITONIN
ACCIKLLMOOOOTTV MOLOTOV
COCKTAIL
ACDDEEEELNNPSTU DEPENDENT
CLAUSE

ACDDEEEHHIKNSST THICKHEADEDNESS
ACDDEEEHILMSSTU DUTCH ELM
DISEASE
ACDDEEEHLNORSST COLD-
HEARTEDNESS
ACDDEEGILNNNORS ENDOCRINE
GLANDS
ACDDEEHIILLRSUY DIESEL-HYDRAULIC
ACDDEEMNNOORRSY SECONDARY
MODERN
ACDDEFLMOOORSSW SWORD OF
DAMOCLES
ACDDIIIIILNSTUV INDIVIDUALISTIC
ACDEEEEEGGHLRRT THREE-LEGGED
RACE
ACDEEEEFILMNTTV MENTAL
DEFECTIVE
ACDEEEEILNNORTT ENTENTE
CORDIALE
ACDEEEFHILLNORS HALL OF RESIDENCE
ACDEEEFIIILNRTT DEFINITE ARTICLE
ACDEEEGHILORRTT CIGARETTE
HOLDER
ACDEEEIIMNNPSTT PATENT MEDICINES
ACDEEEINNORSSST CONSIDERATENESS
ACDEEEMNOOPRSTV
OVERCOMPENSATED
ACDEEFHORRSSSTW CHESTS OF
DRAWERS
ACDEEFILNORRRTU FUNERAL
DIRECTOR
ACDEEFLMNNORRRT CLERMONT-
FERRAND
ACDEEFMMNNOORSY COMEDY OF
MANNERS
ACDEEGGHIINPRRS GRAPHIC DESIGNER
ACDEEGHHIINORTU HIGHER
EDUCATION
ACDEEGHIIMNNNSV VENDING
MACHINES
ACDEEGHILOOSSSW WILD-GOOSE
CHASES
ACDEEGIIIILLMOOP EPIDEMIOLOGICAL
ACDEEGIINORSSTT STAGE DIRECTIONS
ACDEEGIMNORSSTU
DISCOURAGEMENTS
ACDEEGKLMNNOSTW
ACKNOWLEDGMENTS
ACDEEGMOOPRRRSU PROGRAMED
COURSE
ACDEEHIILNOOPRT RADIOTELEPHONIC
ACDEEHILLMNORTY
ENDOTHERMICALLY
ACDEEIIILNNORSTY INCONSIDERATELY

ACDEEIIMMOORRRT
RADIOMICROMETER
ACDEEIINNOORRST RECONSIDERATION
ACDEEILLNPPRRUY PERPENDICULARLY
ACDEEIMMNNOORST
RECOMMENDATIONS
ACDEEIMNNOSSTWW CASEMENT
WINDOWS
ACDEELMOORRSSTU
SCLERODERMATOUS
ACDEEMNNNOORSTY STAND ON
CEREMONY
ACDEENORRSSSSTY SECONDARY STRESS
ACDEFGIKNNOORSY DAYS OF
RECKONING
ACDEFIIIIMNNNOT INDEMNIFICATION
ACDEFIIIINNORTT DENITRIFICATION
ACDEFIIIINORSTV DIVERSIFICATION
ACDEFIIIINORTTV DEVITRIFICATION
ACDEFIIIILMNOSTU DEMULSIFICATION
ACDEFIIIILNNOTTY CONFIDENTIALITY
ACDEGIKNOOPSSTT SPIGOT AND
SOCKET
ACDEGILNNNOSTTU CONSENTING
ADULT
ACDEGINORSTTTUY COTTAGE
INDUSTRY
ACDEHIIIILNPSSTU DUAL CITISENSHIP
ACDEHIIILNPSTUZ DUAL CITIZENSHIP
ACDEHIILLMOSTTY METHODISTICALLY
ACDEHIINOPSSTTU UNSOPHISTICATED
ACDEHIKLORRSSTU HARD LUCK
STORIES
ACDEHLOOOPPRSSV APPROVED
SCHOOLS
ACDEHMNNOOORSTU
ENCHONDROMATOUS
ACDEIIIILMNNOORT OMNIDIRECTIONAL
ACDEIIIILNORRSTY DISCRETIONARILY
ACDEIIIINNNOORST INCONSIDERATION
ACDEIIIINNORRSTY INDISCRETIONARY
ACDEIIILLMNORSTY MODERNISTICALLY
ACDEIIILLMNPRSTU PNEUMATIC DRILLS
ACDGHIMNNOOPRRY
GYNANDROMORPHIC
ACDGIIIINNNOORT AIR-CONDITIONING
ACDHIIILLMOOPRY IDIOMORPHICALLY
ACDHIIIMNOOOSTT
DICHOTOMISATION
ACDHIIIMNOOOTTZ
DICHOTOMIZATION
ACDIIIILLNNNOSST DISINCLINATIONS
ACDIIIINRSSTUVY VICISSITUDINARY
ACDIIINNNOOSTTU DISCONTINUATION

ACDIILLNNNOOTUY
UNCONDITIONALLY
ACEEEEELNOPSSUV ACE UP ONE'S
SLEEVE
ACEEEEGILLNNORT GENERAL
ELECTION
ACEEEEGILNORTTV ELECTRONEGATIVE
ACEEEEHHILNRSTW CATHERINE
WHEELS
ACEEEFGGHINNORX FOREIGN
EXCHANGE
ACEEEFGILNNOPRR PEREGRINE FALCON
ACEEEFHIMNNNRST
ENFRANCHISEMENT
ACEEEGIILLNORTT INTERCOLLEGIATE
ACEEEGIMMOSSTTT COMMITTEE
STAGES
ACEEEGIMNOPRSTT SPERMATOGENETIC
ACEEEHHHLNOOPRX
HEXACHLOROPHENE
ACEEEHHIPPRSSTT SPEECH THERAPIST
ACEEEHILLMNRTUY
HERMENEUTICALLY
ACEEEHILNNNRSST CHINESE LANTERNS
ACEEEHNORRSSSTU TREACHEROUSNESS
ACEEEIILLLNSTTU INTELLECTUALISE
ACEEEIILLLNTTUZ INTELLECTUALIZE
ACEEEILNNOPSSTX EXCEPTIONALNESS
ACEEEILNORRSSTV CORRELATIVENESS
ACEEEILNPSSSTUV SPECULATIVENESS
ACEEEIMMNOPRSSU
MENISPERMACEOUS
ACEEEMNORRSSTUU
COUNTERMEASURES
ACEEENOPPRSSSTY PAY ONE'S RESPECTS
ACEEFHHMNOOOORRT REACH FOR THE
MOON
ACEEFHLNOPRRSSU REPROACHFULNESS
ACEEFIIILMNOPTX EXEMPLIFICATION
ACEEFIINNORRSTT CONFRATERNITIES
ACEEFILMPRRSSTU SIMPLE FRACTURES
ACEEGGIILLNNORT TRAINING COLLEGE
ACEEGHINNOOPRTT
ANTHROPOGENETIC
ACEEGIILLMOOPST EPISTEMOLOGICAL
ACEEGIINNNORSTT TRACTION ENGINES
ACEEGIINORRSTTT GASTROENTERITIC
ACEEGILLLNOPTYY POLYGENETICALLY
ACEEGILLNOORSTY OESTROGENICALLY
ACEEHHIIKNNOTTT TAKE IT ON THE
CHIN
ACEEHHIMNOORRTT
HETEROCHROMATIN
ACEEHHINOOPPRST PHOSPHOCREATINE

ACEEHIILLLLNSTY HELLENISTICALLY
ACEEHIINPPPRSST APPRENTICESHIPS
ACEEHILOORRSSST ATHEROSCLEROSIS
ACEEHIMMNORSSSV
SERVOMECHANISMS
ACEEIIINQSSSTUV ACQUISITIVENESS
ACEEIILLLMNSTTU INTELLECTUALISM
ACEEIILLLNSTTTU INTELLECTUALIST
ACEEIILLLNTTTUY INTELLECTUALITY
ACEEIILLMOPRTYZ PIEZOMETRICALLY
ACEEIILMNOPRSVY LIVERY COMPANIES
ACEEIILNNNOOSTV CONVENTIONALISE
ACEEIILNNNOOTVZ
CONVENTIONALIZE
ACEEIILNNNOQSTU INCONSEQUENTIAL
ACEEIINORSSSTTV SERVICE STATIONS
ACEEILLLMNOSSUY MISCELLANEOUSLY
ACEEILLNOORSTTY ELECTROLYSATION
ACEEILMMNRSSSTY SYMMETRICALNESS
ACEEINOOPRSSTVV PROVOCATIVENESS
ACEEINORRRRSTUY RESURRECTIONARY
ACEELMNOOQRRSUU LOURENÇO
MARQUES
ACEEMNNOOOPRSTU
CONTEMPORANEOUS
ACEFFGIJLMNOPPU JUMPING-OFF PLACE
ACEFIIIINNNOSTT INTENSIFICATION
ACEFIIILMNNOOST SOLEMNIFICATION
ACEFIIINNOOPRST PERSONIFICATION
ACEFIILORRSTTUV ARTICLES OF VIRTU
ACEFINOOPPRRRST PROPER FRACTIONS
ACEFINRRRSSTTUU INFRASTRUCTURES
ACEGHHIMNOOSSTT SHOOTING
MATCHES
ACEGHIIIKMNNNTT KNITTING
MACHINE
ACEGHILLLOOPPSY PSEPHOLOGICALLY
ACEGHIMMOOPRRTT
PHOTOGRAMMETRIC
ACEGHLLOOPSUYYZ
ZYGOPHYLLACEOUS
ACEGIILLMMNNOUY
IMMUNOGENICALLY
ACEGIILLMNOOORT
TERMINOLOOGICAL
ACEGIINOOPRSTTV PROGNOSTICATIVE
ACEGILLNORRSUUY NEUROSURGICALLY
ACEGILMNNOOORST
CONGLOMERATIONS
ACEGILNOPRSSSTU PLASTIC SURGEONS
ACEHHIILLMNPTTY PLATYHELMINTHIC
ACEHHIKNORTTUVW HAVE NO TRUCK
WITH
ACEHHINNPSSSTTU SPANISH CHESTNUT

ACEHHINOPPRSTTU PITHECANTHROPUS
ACEHHIOPPRSSTTY PSYCHOTHERAPIST
ACEHIILLLOOPRTY HELIOTROPICALLY
ACEHIILLOPRRSTY PREHISTORICALLY
ACEHIILOOPSTTTY PHOTOELASTICITY
ACEHIIMMMOPSTTY
SYMPATHOMIMETIC
ACEHILLMNOOPRXY
XENOMORPHICALLY
ACEHILLMOOPRTTY
PHOTOMETRICALLY
ACEHILOPSSTUXYY PSYCHOSEXUALITY
ACEHINOPRRSTUYY NEUROPSYCHIATRY
ACEHMNOOPRSSTUY
PROSENCHYMATOUS
ACEIIILLMPSSSTY PESSIMISTICALLY
ACEIIIMMNOORSSS COMMISSIONAIRES
ACEIIILLORSTUVYY VOYEURISTICALLY
ACEIILMNNNOOSTV
CONVENTIONALISM
ACEIILNNNOOSTTV CONVENTIONALIST
ACEIILNNNOOTTVY
CONVENTIONALITY
ACEIILNNOOPRSTT INTROSPECTIONAL
ACEIILNNOORSTTU INTEROSCULATION
ACEIIMNNOORSSTV CONSERVATIONISM
ACEIIMNOOPRSTTU COMPUTERISATION
ACEIIMNOOPRTTUZ
COMPUTERIZATION
ACEIINNOORSSTTV CONSERVATIONIST
ACELNOOOPPRRSTU
COUNTERPROPOSAL
ACELPRRRSSTTUUU SUPERSTRUCTURAL
ACEOOPPRRSSSSTU AT CROSS-PURPOSES
ACFGIIIILNNNSTY INSIGNIFICANTLY
ACFIIIILMNOPSST SIMPLIFICATIONS
ACFIIMNNOOOSTTY COMITY OF
NATIONS
ACFIMNOOORSSTTT COMFORT
STATIONS
ACGGIINNOOPRSTT PROGNOSTICATING
ACGHHIIIOOPRRST HISTORIOGRAPHIC
ACGHHIMOOOOPPRRT
MICROPHOTOGRAPH,
PHOTOMICROGRAPH
ACGHHINOOOOPPRTZ
PHOTOZINCOGRAPH
ACGHHLLMNNOPSUU PLOUGHMAN'S
LUNCH
ACGHHLOOOPPSTYY
PSYCHOPATHOLOGY
ACGHILLLMOOOPRY
MORPHOLOGICALLY
ACGIIIILLLNNSTTY SCINTILLATINGLY

ACGIIINNNNOOTTX
NONINTOXICATING
ACHHMOOOOPRRSTU
CHROMATOPHOROUS
ACHIIIMOOSSSSST SCHISTOSOMIASIS
ACHIINNNOORSSTY SYNCHRONISATION
ACHIINNNOORSTYZ
SYNCHRONIZATION
ACHIIOPRSSSSTTY ASTROPHYSICISTS
ACHIKLNNOOPPTTY
PHYTOPLANKTONIC
ACHILLLORRTTUUY HORTICULTURALLY
ACIIIILNNOPQTTUU QUINTUPLICATION
ACIILMMNOOOOPSST
COSMOPOLITANISM
ACIILMNNOOSSTUY SANCTIMONIOUSLY
ACIILNNOOSSTTTU CONSTITUTIONALS
ADDDDEGIIMNNOSW DIAMOND
WEDDINGS
ADDDEEEHNNNRSSU
UNDERHANDEDNESS
ADDDEEFHILMOORT MIDDLE-OF-THE-
ROAD
ADDEEEEEFHLLNSSV LEVEL-HEADEDNESS
ADDEEEEEHLNRRTTY
TENDERHEARTEDLY
ADDEEEGHHILNSST LIGHT-HEADEDNESS
ADDEEEGHNNORSSW
WRONGHEADEDNESS
ADDEEEHIKNNRSST KIND-
HEARTEDNESS
ADDEEGHHINNRSST RIGHT-
HANDEDNESS
ADDEEGHINNOORTY
DEHYDROGENATION
ADDEEGNNOORSSTU GOOD-
NATUREDNESS
ADDEEHHNNORSSST SHORT-
HANDEDNESS
ADDEEILLMMNNSSS SMALL-
MINDEDNESS
ADDEEINNNORSSWY NINE DAYS'
WONDERS
ADDEGHIIKNRRSTW WITH KIND
REGARDS
ADDEIMNNNOPQSSS MIND ONE'S P'S
AND Q'S
ADDGIIIIILNNUVZ INDIVIDUALIZING
ADEEEEEGHHORTVV HAVE THE EDGE
OVER
ADEEEEGILLNRRVY GENERAL
DELIVERY
ADEEEEHHNRRTTUW UNDER THE
WEATHER

ADEEEEHNNOPRSST
OPENHEARTEDNESS
ADEEEEFGHINORSTU UNDER THE AEGIS
OF
ADEEEFHNORSSSTT SOFTHEARTEDNESS
ADEEEGHHMNPRRSS GERMAN
SHEPHERDS
ADEEEGHINNRSSST NEARSIGHTEDNESS
ADEEEGILMNNNSTT
DISENTANGLEMENT
ADEEEGILNNOOPRS OLD AGE
PENSIONER
ADEEEHIMNNRSSTT
DISHEARTENMENTS
ADEEEIIINNNSSST SEINE-SAINT-DENIS
ADEEEIILMNNSSTT SENTIMENTALISED
ADEEEIILMNNSTTZ SENTIMENTALIZED
ADEEEMNNRSSTTTU
UNDERSTATEMENTS
ADEEEMNOPRRSTTT DEPARTMENT
STORE
ADEEFFFHHLLNOTY FLY OFF THE
HANDLE
ADEEFFGIIINNRTT DIFFERENTIATING
ADEEFFIIINNORTT DIFFERENTIATION
ADEEFILNSSSSTTU DISTASTEFULNESS
ADEEGIIMNNRSTTU UNDERESTIMATING
ADEEHILNNOORSTW LET ONE'S HAIR
DOWN
ADEEHINPRSSSTTW SHARP-WITTEDNESS
ADEEIIINNOSSSTT DESENSITISATION
ADEEIIINNOSSTTZ DESENSITIZATION
ADEEIIILOPRRSSTV PRIVATE
SOLDIERS
ADEEIIMNNOPRTTU
UNPREMEDITATION
ADEEIIMNNORSTTU
UNDERESTIMATION
ADEEIIINNNOOPSST OPINIONATEDNESS
ADEEILMNOPRRSTU MENSTRUAL
PERIOD
ADEEILMNORSTTVY
DEMONSTRATIVELY
ADEEIMNNORSTTUV
UNDEMONSTRATIVE
ADEFFGHINNORSTU FOUNDING
FATHERS
ADEFFHINNOSSSST STANDOFFISHNESS
ADEFGHIMOORRSTY FAIRY
GODMOTHERS
ADEFGIIILLNQSTU SELF-LIQUIDATING
ADEGHLLMORRTUYY
HYDROMETALLURGY
ADEGIIIOPRRSTTT PRESTIDIGITATOR

ADEHHIIMMOPRRST
HERMAPHRODITISM
ADEHILMNOOPSTTU PENTOTHAL
SODIUM
ADEHIMOOPRSSTTY
DERMATOPHYTOSIS
ADEIIIIILMRSSST DISSIMILARITIES
ADEIIIINORSSSTTT DISSERTATIONIST
ADEIIJLNPRRSTUU JURISPRUDENTIAL
ADEIILNORRSSTTX SINISTRODEXTRAL
ADEIILNORRSTTVY DORSIVENTRALITY
ADEIIMNNOPPSSTT DISAPPOINTMENTS
ADEILMOPSTTUUUY
PSEUDOMUTUALITY
ADGGIMNNOPRSSTU STAMPING
GROUNDS
ADGHIINNNOSTTTW
NOTWITHSTANDING
ADGIIIILNNRSTUZ INDUSTRIALIZING
ADGIIILNNOPPSTY DISAPPOINTINGLY
AEEEFHIIKNNNOSV HAVE ONE'S KNIFE
IN
AEEEFHOORRRSTWW THE WORSE FOR
WEAR
AEEEFIILNPRRTTY PREFERENTIALITY
AEEEFLLLLORRTVW FELLOW
TRAVELLER
AEEEFLLLORRSTVW FELLOW
TRAVELERS
AEEEGGGIMNNNRST ENGAGEMENT
RINGS
AEEEGGILLORRSSU ROGUES' GALLERIES
AEEEGGLNNOORRRV GOVERNOR-
GENERAL
AEEEGHHILNORTTT IN THE
ALTOGETHER
AEEEGHINNOPRSST PARTHENOGENESIS
AEEEGIILNNRSSTT LARGE INTESTINES
AEEEGILLMNNNSST GENTLEMANLINESS
AEEEGILMNNNSSSS MEANINGLESSNESS
AEEEGILNNPPRRST SLEEPING PARTNER
AEEEGILNNRSSSTV EVERLASTINGNESS
AEEEGIMNOPRSSST SPERMATOGENESIS
AEEEHHILMNOPPST MEPHISTOPHELEAN
AEEEHIIMMNORRST IMMERSION
HEATER
AEEEHIIMNPPRSSV MISAPPREHENSIVE
AEEEHILORSTTUXY HETEROSEXUALITY
AEEEHORRRSSTTUW WEAR THE
TROUSERS
AEEEIILMMNPRSTX EXPERIMENTALISM
AEEEIILMNPRSTTX EXPERIMENTALIST
AEEEIIMNNOPRTTX EXPERIMENTATION
AEEEIINNNSSTTTV INATTENTIVENESS

AEEEIILNPRSSSTUV SUPERLATIVENESS
AEEEIMNOPRRSSTX EXTEMPORARINESS
AEEEIMNPRRRSSUU SUPERNUMERARIES
AEEEINNOPRRSSTT REPRESENTATIONS
AEEELMNOQRRSSSU
QUARRELSOMENESS
AEEELNOOPRRSSST PERSONAL STEREOS
AEEELOPRRRSSSTW LESSER SPEARWORT
AEEFGGHILNRSSTT FLIGHT SERGEANTS
AEEFGHIMNNORRTT THE MORNING
AFTER
AEEFGHINOOPRRTW
WEATHERPROOFING
AEEFGIMNNRRSTTU
TRANSFIGUREMENT
AEEFHILLLLOTVYY LILY OF THE VALLEY
AEEFIILNNRSTTTU FIRST LIEUTENANT
AEEFNNNOPRSSTTU
UNFORTUNATENESS
AEEFNOOOPRRTTWY POWER OF
ATTORNEY
AEEGGHHOOPPRRTY
PHYTOGEOGRAPHER
AEEGGHLORRSSTTW LET THE GRASS
GROW
AEEGGHHILNORSSSY ROYAL HIGHNESSES
AEEGGHHLOOPPRTTY
PHOTOTELEGRAPHY, TELEPHOTOGRAPHY
AEEGGHHLORSSSTUU
SLAUGHTERHOUSES
AEEGHIKLOPRRTTW TIGHTROPE
WALKER
AEEGHINNOOPRSST ANTHROPOGENESIS
AEEGHLLMNOOSSTZ THOMSON'S
GAZELLE
AEEGIILNORRTTVY INTERROGATIVELY
AEEGIINOORRRSTT INTERROGATORIES
AEEGIINORRSSTTT GASTROENTERITIS
AEEGIMNOPRSSTTY OPERATING
SYSTEM
AEEHHHILLNNOPPT
PHENOLPHTHALEIN
AEEHHHIJNOSSSTVW JEHOVAH'S WITNESS
AEEHIILMOOPSTTU EPITHELIOMATOUS
AEEHIIMNNOPPRSS MISAPPREHENSION
AEEHIKLNNOPRTUY
PHENYLKETONURIA
AEEHILMMNOOPRRY HOLY ROMAN
EMPIRE
AEEHINPPPPRRSSW WHIPPERSNAPPERS
AEEIIILMMMMORST TIMES
IMMEMORIAL
AEEIIINOORRSTTX EXTERIORISATION
AEEIIINOORRTTXZ EXTERIORIZATION

AEEIIILLMNNSSSTT SMALL INTESTINES
AEEIIILMNNSSSTTT SENTIMENTALISTS
AEEIIILNNOPPRTTY PLENIPOTENTIARY
AEEIILNOORRSTUV REVOLUTIONARIES
AEEIIMNNOPRSSTT PRESENTATIONISM
AEEIIMNOOPRSTTX EXTEMPORISATION
AEEIIMNOOPRTTXZ
EXTEMPORIZATION
AEEIINNOPRRSTTT INTERPRETATIONS
AEEIINNOPRSSTTT PRESENTATIONIST
AEEILLMMNOOOPSS OIL SOMEONE'S
PALM
AEEILLMNNNORTVY
ENVIRONMENTALLY
AEEILLMNPPRSTUY SUPPLEMENTARILY
AEEILMNNOOPPRUU
PLEUROPNEUMONIA
AEEILMNNOPPSTTU SUPPLEMENTATION
AEEILNNOOPRRTUV RELATIVE
PRONOUN
AEEILNNOPSSSSSS PASSIONLESSNESS
AEEILNORRSSTTUU RUSSIAN ROULETTE
AEEIMNOQRSSSTTU QUESTION
MASTERS
AEEIMPRRRSSSSTY PRIMARY STRESSES
AEEINOQRRSSSSTU QUARTER SESSIONS
AEENNNOOPSSSSTU SPONTANEOUSNESS
AEFGGHJLOORRTUU GO FOR THE
JUGULAR
AEFIIIILLMNNSTY INFINITESIMALLY
AEFIILLLNNOOPST SELF-POLLINATION
AEFIILMNOOPRSSS PROFESSIONALISM
AEFIILNOOPRSSST PROFESSIONALIST
AEFIILNORSSSTTU FLIRTATIOUSNESS
AEFILLMNOPRSTTY SELF-IMPORTANTLY
AEGGHILLNOORSTY SHOOTING
GALLERY
AEGGIILNNORRTTY INTERROGATINGLY
AEGGILNNRRSSSTY TRANSGRESSINGLY
AEGHHIIMNNRSSST NIGHTMARISHNESS
AEGHHIIOOPRRRST HISTORIOGRAPHER
AEGHIINNOPRSSTW WITHIN ONE'S
GRASP
AEGIIINNNOORSTT NITROGENISATION
AEGIIINNNOORTTZ NITROGENIZATION
AEGIIINNNRSSTTT INTRANSIGENTIST
AEGIILNOORRRTTY INTERROGATORILY
AEGILLNOOOPSSTT PALEONTOLOGISTS
AEGILLNOPSTTUXY EXPOSTULATINGLY
AEHHIIMNOPRRSTT
THERIANTHROPISM
AEHHIIOPPRRSSTY PHYSIOTHERAPIST
AEHIIJJMNOORTTY JOIN THE
MAJORITY

AEHIIMMNNOOPRST
ENANTIOMORPHISM
AEHIMNOOOPRRSTTT
ANTHROPOMETRIST
AEIIILMMMNNRSSX MARXISM-
LENINISM
AEIIILMNNRSSTTX MARXIST-LENINIST
AEIIJLNNORSSTUV UNIVERSAL JOINTS
AEIILLNOOOPPRSTY PREPOSITIONALLY
AEIILLNOORRTUVY REVOLUTIONARILY
AEIILMMNNRSSTTU INSTRUMENTALISM
AEIILMMNOOPRSTT
METROPOLITANISM
AEIILMNNRSSTTTU INSTRUMENTALIST
AEIILMNNRSTTTUY INSTRUMENTALITY
AEIILNNNORSSTUV INVOLUNTARINESS
AEIILNOOPRSSTTY PROSELYTISATION
AEIILNOOPRSTTYZ PROSELYTIZATION
AEIIMNNNORSTTTU
INSTRUMENTATION
AEIILNOOOPPRRTTY PROPORTIONATELY
AELNNNOOOPPRRSU PERSONAL
PRONOUN
AFFGHNNOOSSSTUW SAWN-OFF
SHOTGUNS
AFFHILLORSTUUYY YOURS FAITHFULLY
AFGGIIMNNORRSTY
TRANSMOGRIFYING
AFGHLMOOOOPRRTU
PHOTOFLUOROGRAM
AFGIIILLNNOSSTT FILLING STATIONS
AFGIIKMNNNOOPRT NON-PROFIT-
MAKING
AGHHHILOOOPPRTT
PHOTOLITHOGRAPH
AGHHIILLLLNSSYY SHILLY-SHALLYING
AGHHIIMNOOPSSTT
OPISTHOGNATHISM
AGHHILLMOOOPSTT
OPHTHALMOLOGIST
AGHHINOOOPSSTTU
OPISTHOGNATHOUS
AGHHOOOOPPPRTTY
PHOTOTOPOGRAPHY
AGHHOOOOPPPRTTYY
PHOTOTYPOGRAPHY
AGHIILMNOOOSTTY
MYTHOLOGISATION
AGHIILMNOOOTTYZ
MYTHOLOGIZATION
AGHILNOOOOPRSSTT
ANTHROPOLOGISTS
AGIIINNNORRSSTTZ TRANSISTORIZING
AGIIILLNNOOPSSTT POLLING STATIONS

AGINOPPPRRSSTTU SUPPORTING PARTS
AHHIILNOPPRSSTT PHILANTHROPISTS
AHIJLMNOOOPRSTU
PHOTOJOURNALISM
AHIJLNOOOOPRSTTU PHOTOJOURNALIST
AHINOOOOPRRSSTTT
PHOTOTRANSISTOR
AIIIILLNOQRSTUY INQUISITORIALLY
AIIINNNOOSSTTUW NO-WIN
SITUATIONS
AIILLLMNOPSSUUY PUSILLANIMOUSLY
AIILNOOOOPPRRTTY PROPORTIONALITY
AIKNNNNOQTTUUWY UNKNOWN
QUANTITY
BBBBEEFGIIILRTT FLIBBERTIGIBBET
BBBDEEHLLLMNOOS BLONDE
BOMBSHELL
BBCEEKKLOORRSTT STOCKBROKER
BELT
BBCGIKLLMNOSSTU STUMBLING
BLOCKS
BBCHIIIIILLOPST BIBLIOPHILISTIC
BBDEIIIILNOOSSV DIVISION LOBBIES
BBDIMOORRRSTUUY DORMITORY
SUBURB
BBEHILMMMOOORST
THROMBOEMBOLISM
BCCDEEIIJNORSTT INDIRECT OBJECTS
BCCEEEEGILRSTTU ICEBERG LETTUCES
BCCEEEIILMNNOSU BIOLUMINESCENCE
BCCEEEIMNNPRSUU SUPERINCUMBENCE
BCCEEILNORRSTTU RECONSTRUCTIBLE
BCCEEINOPRSSSTU SUBSISTENCE CROP
BCCEGHIMNNNRRUU NUMBER-
CRUNCHING
BCDDDEELLNOOOSS COLD-
BLOODEDNESS
BCDEEEIMMNNRSTU
DISENCUMBERMENT
BCDEEHILLLOOSTW WHITE BLOOD
CELLS
BCDEGIIILNOSTUY BUILDING SOCIETY
BCDEIIILOPRRTUY REPRODUCIBILITY
BCDEIIILRSTTTUY DESTRUCTIBILITY
BCDEILLNNOORSSU COLOUR
BLINDNESS
BCEEEEFFGILNORTY BENEFIT OF CLERGY
BCEEEFGHIIOPRTT TIP OF THE ICEBERG
BCEEEFIIKNNSSST SICKNESS BENEFIT
BCEEEILNPSSSSTU SUSCEPTIBLENESS
BCEEFFIOOOPSSTX POST OFFICE BOXES
BCEEHILLOOPRSSS PHLEBOSCLEROSIS
BCEEIIILMPPRRST IMPRESCRIPTIBLE
BCEEINORSSSTTUV OBSTRUCTIVENESS

BCEGHIILNOOOSTT BIOTECHNOLOGIST
BCEHIIIIINOSTTX EXHIBITIONISTIC
BCEHIILNOPPRSUW PUBLIC OWNERSHIP
BCEIIILMNOPTTTY CONTEMPTIBILITY
BCEIIILMOPRSSTY COMPRESSIBILITY
BCGHIILOOOPSSTY PSYCHOBIOLOGIST
BCGIIIIILNORRTY INCORRIGIBILITY
BCGIIILMOOORSST MICROBIOLOGISTS
BCGIINNNNOORTTU
  NONCONTRIBUTING
BCIINOORSSSTTTU OBSTRUCTIONISTS
BCINNNOOORRTTUY
  NONCONTRIBUTORY
BDDEEEELNNORSTU DOUBLE
  ENTENDRES
BDDEEEILNOOPRSX PEROXIDE BLONDES
BDDEEFLLLNOOSSU FULL-
  BLOODEDNESS
BDEEFIIIILNNSTY INDEFENSIBILITY
BDEEFILMNPRRSSU PLUMBER'S FRIENDS
BDEGIIIIILNSTTY INDIGESTIBILITY
BDFFIIILMNNORUU INFUNDIBULIFORM
BDIIIILLNOSSTUY INDISSOLUBILITY
BEEEEFILNNNOOSS FEEL IN-ONE'S
  BONES
BEEEGGILNSSSSTU SUGGESTIBLENESS
BEEEIINNNORRTTZ TRINITROBENZENE
BEEEILNNOPRSSSS RESPONSIBLENESS
BEEELMNOORSSSTU
  TROUBLESOMENESS
BEEGHHIILLNOOTW THE WHOLE
  BOILING
BEEGHIILNNORSSU NEIGHBOURLINESS
BEEHIIINOPRSSTV PROHIBITIVENESS
BEEHILNOOPSTTUW UP TO THE
  ELBOWS IN
BEEHINOORRSSSUV HERBIVOROUSNESS
BEEHLOOOORRSSTTU
  TROUBLESHOOTERS
BEEIIIIILNNSSST INSENSIBILITIES
BEEIIIILNNSTTXY INEXTENSIBILITY
BEEIIIILRRRSTVY IRREVERSIBILITY
BEEIMNOOPPRSSTU OPPOSITE NUMBERS
BEEINNORSSSTUUV UNOBTRUSIVENESS
BEFHHLMOOOOTTUY THE BLOOM OF
  YOUTH
BEGIIIIILLLNTTY INTELLIGIBILITY
BEIIIIILMRRSSTY IRREMISSIBILITY
BEIIIIILRRSSTTY IRRESISTIBILITY
BEIMNORSSSSTUUU RUMBUSTIOUSNESS
BELLLORSSTUUWYY SLOWLY BUT
  SURELY
BELOPRRSSSSSTUU BRUSSELS SPROUTS
BFILLNOPPSTUUUY BOUNTIFUL SUPPLY

BHIIIINOOPRSSTT PROHIBITIONISTS
CCCDEEEIIMNOSST DOMESTIC SCIENCE
CCCDEEFIIKNNORT CONFIDENCE TRICK
CCCEEEHHIKNRSS CHINESE CHECKERS
CCCEEEIMNNNOOSY CONSCIENCE
  MONEY
CCCEEEHLMOOSTTYY
  CHOLECYSTECTOMY
CCCEEIIILMNOORRT
  MICROELECTRONIC
CCCEIILNORSTUUY SECURITY COUNCIL
CCCIIIMNOPRRSTU CIRCUMSCRIPTION
CCCIILMNOORSTUU
  CIRCUMLOCUTIONS
CCDDDEHHILNOOOS SECOND
  CHILDHOOD
CCDEEEFFNOORRTT CONCERTED
  EFFORT
CCDEEEFINNNOOOV CONVENIENCE
  FOOD
CCDEEEIIMORSSTV DOMESTIC SERVICE
CCDEEEENNNNORSSU
  UNCONCERNEDNESS
CCDEEEENNNNOSSTU
  UNCONNECTEDNESS
CCDEEGIIILNNRSV DRIVING LICENCES
CCDEEINOPRSTUUV SUPERCONDUCTIVE
CCDEELLNORSTTUW WELL-
  CONSTRUCTED
CCDEGIILNNORSTY DISCONCERTINGLY
CCDEIIINPRRSTTU PRINTED CIRCUITS
CCDEINNOOPRSTUU
  SUPERCONDUCTION
CCDENOOPRRSSTUU
  SUPERCONDUCTORS
CCDHIIKLLOSUWWW CHUCK-WILL'S-
  WIDOW
CCDHINNOOOOPTTU
  PHOTOCONDUCTION
CCEEEEFNNNORSSW NEWS
  CONFERENCES
CCEEEEFNNOPRRSS PRESS CONFERENCE
CCEEEEFNORRRSSS CROSS-REFERENCES
CCEEEEHHINQRSSU CHINESE CHEQUERS
CCEEEEILMMOSTTT SELECT
  COMMITTEE
CCEEEFFILOSTTVY COST-EFFECTIVELY
CCEEEFIINNOORST CONFECTIONERIES
CCEEEGJLNNORSTU CONCRETE
  JUNGLES
CCEEEHHNOOPPRSS
  PHOSPHORESCENCE
CCEEEHILOOPRRTT ELECTROPHORETIC
CCEEEIIKLNORSTT ELECTROKINETICS

CCEEFFFIILNSSUY SELF-SUFFICIENCY
CCEEFHIINOPRSST CHIEF INSPECTORS
CCEEGIINNNNNNOV INCONVENIENCING
CCEEHIIILNORTTY HELIOCENTRICITY
CCEEHIINNORTTTY ETHNOCENTRICITY
CCEEHNORRSTTTUU
TECHNOSTRUCTURE
CCEEIIINNNOSSST INCONSISTENCIES
CCEEIIILOPRRTTYY PYROELECTRICITY
CCEEIINNNNOORTT
INTERCONNECTION
CCEEILLMOORSSTT COLLECTOR'S
ITEMS
CCEEILLNNOOSTUV COLLECTIVE
NOUNS
CCEEIMMNNORTTUY COMMUNITY
CENTRE
CCEEINNOPRRSSSW CROWN PRINCESSES
CCEFILLNOOSSSUY SELF-CONSCIOUSLY
CCEHIIMMOOPSTTY
PSYCHOTOMIMETIC
CCEHIMMNOSSTTUY COMMUNITY
CHESTS
CCEIILLNOOORSSU COLLISION COURSE
CCEIIILNNOOSSTUY CONSCIENTIOUSLY
CCEIMOOOOPRRRSSS MICROPROCESSORS
CCEINNNOOSSSSUU UNCONSCIOUSNESS
CCEINNOOPSSSSUU CONSPICUOUSNESS
CCEINNOORRSSTTU
RECONSTRUCTIONS
CCGHIIINORRSTTU SHORT-CIRCUITING
CCGIIIILNOOSSTU SOCIOLINGUISTIC
CCIIINNOOORSTTT CONTORTIONISTIC
CCIIINNOOPRSSTT CONSCRIPTIONIST
CCIILLNOOPRRUVY PRIVY COUNCILLOR
CCIILNNOOPSSUUY INCONSPICUOUSLY
CCIILNOOPRRSUVY PRIVY COUNCILORS
CCIIMNNOORSSTTU
MISCONSTRUCTION
CDDEEEEEINNNPRT INTERDEPENDENCE
CDDEEEEELNNPRTUY
UNPRECEDENTEDLY
CDDEEFIIILLNPSS SELF-DISCIPLINED
CDDEEFIIINNORRT DIRECTION FINDER
CDDEFNNOOOOPSTU FOOT-POUND-
SECOND
CDDEGHILLNOORSU COLD-
SHOULDERING
CDDEINNOOPRRTUU
UNDERPRODUCTION
CDEEEEEINNQSSUV QUEEN'S EVIDENCES
CDEEEEFLNNRSSST SELF-CENTREDNESS
CDEEEEINNNPRSTU SUPERINTENDENCE
CDEEEEIORSSTTTV STORE DETECTIVES

CDEEEFILORRSTTT LETTERS OF CREDIT
CDEEEHHILPRSTUW WHITED
SEPULCHRE
CDEEEHNNORRTTUU UNDER-THE-
COUNTER
CDEEEIINNPRRSWW WINDSCREEN
WIPER
CDEEEIINPRSSSTV DESCRIPTIVENESS
CDEEEIMNNPRSTUU
SUPERINDUCEMENT
CDEEEINNNPRSTUY SUPERINTENDENCY
CDEEEINRSSSTTUV DESTRUCTIVENESS
CDEEELLMMNOOPSW COMMON
SPEEDWELL
CDEEFFILLNNOSTY SELF-CONFIDENTLY
CDEEFGILNRSSTTU SELF-DESTRUCTING
CDEEFIILNORSTYY FRIENDLY SOCIETY
CDEEFIILORRSSST CROSS-FERTILISED
CDEEFIILORRSSTZ CROSS-FERTILIZED
CDEEFILLPRSSTUY DISRESPECTFULLY
CDEEFILNORSSTTU SELF-DESTRUCTION
CDEEHIIKNSSTTTW THICK-WITTEDNESS
CDEEHILNNORSSSW CHINLESS
WONDERS
CDEEIIIIMNNRSTT INDETERMINISTIC
CDEEIIIINNSSSTTV DISTINCTIVENESS
CDEEIIKNQSSTTUW QUICK-WITTEDNESS
CDEEILMNNOOPTWY ENDOWMENT
POLICY
CDEEILNNORSSSUU INCREDULOUSNESS
CDEEINOOQRSSSTU CROSS-
QUESTIONED
CDEGIILNNOOORST
ENDOCRINOLOGIST
CDEGILNNOOPRRSY
CORRESPONDINGLY
CDEIIIINNNOSSTTU DISCONTINUITIES
CDEIIIJNNOSSSUU INJUDICIOUSNESS
CDEIILNNOOPRSTU PRODUCTION LINES
CDHIILNOPRSTUUU PULCHRITUDINOUS
CDIILNNOOSSTUUY DISCONTINUOUSLY
CDIINNOOPRTTUVY
NONPRODUCTIVITY
CEEEEELOOPRSSTT TELESTEREOSCOPE
CEEEEFFIINNSSTV INEFFECTIVENESS
CEEEEFHORRRRSSU REFRESHER COURSE
CEEEEGIIMNNRSSS ÉMINENCES GRISES
CEEEEKLNNOOPSSU KEEP ONE'S
COUNSEL
CEEEFFGHIOPRSSU FIGURES OF SPEECH
CEEEFFGIIORRSST REGISTER OFFICES
CEEEFIIMNORRRTT INTERFEROMETRIC
CEEEFLNORRSSSUU RESOURCEFULNESS
CEEEGGILNNOOSSU GLUCONEOGENESIS

CEEEGHILORRSSTU GLOUCESTERSHIRE
CEEEEGILNORRSTTV COVERING LETTERS
CEEEHIIMNNOPRSV INCOMPREHENSIVE
CEEEHILMNOPRSVY COMPREHENSIVELY
CEEEHILOOPRRSST ELECTROPHORESIS
CEEEHIMORRSSTTY STEREOCHEMISTRY
CEEEIIILLNNOSUUV NOUVELLE CUISINE
CEEEIILOOPRSTTV ELECTROPOSITIVE
CEEEIIMNOPSSTTV COMPETITIVENESS
CEEEIIMOORRSSTT STEREOISOMETRIC
CEEEIINRRSSSTTV RESTRICTIVENESS
CEEEILOPRRSTTVY RETROSPECTIVELY
CEEEIMMNNOPRSTV PINCER
  MOVEMENTS
CEEEIMNNOORSSSU CEREMONIOUSNESS
CEEEINPQRSSSTUU PICTURESQUENESS
CEEEKOOPRRRSSSU PRESSURE
  COOKERS
CEEENNOPPPRRRST PEPPERCORN
  RENTS
CEEFFGIIORRSSTY REGISTRY OFFICES
CEEFHIIIKMNNOTT IN THE NICK OF
  TIME
CEEFIIIILLNOSTTU FEUILLETONISTIC
CEEFINNOPRRSSTU PERFUNCTORINESS
CEEGHIILNNORSST CROSSING THE LINE
CEEGHINNOPPRSST SHOPPING CENTRES
CEEGIIIKMOSSTTV GIVE IT SOME
  STICK
CEEGLLLNOOPPRYY PROPYLENE
  GLYCOL
CEEHHIMMORRSTTY
  THERMOCHEMISTRY
CEEHIIMNNNOOPRS
  INCOMPREHENSION
CEEHIIMNOSSSSUV MISCHIEVOUSNESS
CEEHIINOPRRSSTT HISTORIC PRESENT
CEEHILLNOORRSXY
  HEXYLRESORCINOL
CEEHIMNOORRSTTU MOTHER
  COUNTRIES
CEEIIINOPRSSSTX EXPRESSIONISTIC
CEEIIILNOPRSTTVY INTROSPECTIVELY
CEEIIMNNOPSSSUU IMPECUNIOUSNESS
CEEIIMNORRRSSTU RESURRECTIONISM
CEEIINOPPRSSSTU PRECIPITOUSNESS
CEEIINORRRSSTTU RESURRECTIONIST
CEEIINPSSSTTUUV INTUSSUSCEPTIVE
CEEIKNOPRRSTTVY POVERTY-STRICKEN
CEEILMNNOORSUUY
  UNCEREMONIOUSLY
CEEIMNNNOOOOSTW COME INTO
  ONE'S OWN
CEEINNNOOSSSTTU CONTENTIOUSNESS

CEEINNOOQRRSSTU CORONER'S
  INQUEST
CEEINOOQRRSSSTU CROSS-QUESTIONER
CEEINOPPRSSSSUU PERSPICUOUSNESS
CEELLMNOOPPRSTU COLOR
  SUPPLEMENT
CEEPRRRSSSTTUUU SUPERSTRUCTURES
CEFGHHIILNNOPRS FRENCH POLISHING
CEFGHIILNNNNSSU UNFLINCHINGNESS
CEFGIIKLLNORSST STOCKING-FILLERS
CEGHIJNOOPRSSTU HOUSING PROJECTS
CEGIIKMNNNORSSS MORNING SICKNESS
CEGIIMMMNOSSTUW SWIMMING
  COSTUME
CEGILNOOPPSSSTY SYNOPTIC GOSPELS
CEGINNNOORSSSUU
  INCONGRUOUSNESS
CEGINOOOPRRSSTY CROSSOPTERYGION
CEHHIMMNOOOPPRS
  MORPHOPHONEMICS
CEHIIMMMNORSTUY
  IMMUNOCHEMISTRY
CEHLNOOOORSSSUW SHOW ONE'S
  COLOURS
CEHNNNOORSSSSUY
  SYNCHRONOUSNESS
CEIIIIMNOPRSSST IMPRESSIONISTIC
CEIIIINOSSSTTVV VIVISECTIONISTS
CEIILNNOPSSSTUU PUNCTILIOUSNESS
CEIINNNOPSSSTTUU INTUSSUSCEPTION
CEIMMNNNOOOOPSST NON COMPOS
  MENTIS
CEIMNOOPRSSSSUU PROMISCUOUSNESS
CEIMNOPRSSSSTUU SCRUMPTIOUSNESS
CEKLLNOOPPSSSUU PULL ONE'S SOCKS
  UP
CFFHIILMNOSSTTU FIFTH COLUMNISTS
CFGHHHLOOOOSTTU SCHOOL OF
  THOUGHT
CFGHHIIILNNOOSS FINISHING SCHOOL
CFHILMNOOOORRRT
  NITROCHLOROFORM
CFIINOOOQRRSTUUY COURTS OF
  INQUIRY
CGHHIIIMMNOOSSS HIGH
  COMMISSIONS
CHHHINNOORRSTUY
  ORNITHORHYNCHUS
CHILLMOOOPPRRSY
  MICROSPOROPHYLL
DDDEEEHLNOORRSUU ROUND-
  SHOULDERED
DDEEEFHILMNOORW MIDDLE OF
  NOWHERE

DDEFGHLNOOOPSSU SLOUGH OF DESPOND

DDEGGHINNOSSTUW SHOTGUN WEDDINGS

DDEGHIIINNSSTUU UNDISTINGUISHED

DEEEEGINRRRSSTU REGISTERED NURSE

DEEEEHMNORRRSTV REVEREND MOTHERS

DEEEEINRSSSTTTV VESTED INTERESTS

DEEEELMNOOPRTVV OVERDEVELOPMENT

DEEEFGHINORSSST FORESIGHTEDNESS

DEEEFLLOPSSSSSY SELF-POSSESSEDLY

DEEEHLLMOOOPPSS OLD PEOPLE'S HOMES

DEEEIILLNNNOTTW WELL-INTENTIONED

DEEEIILMMNRRSTU DELIRIUM TREMENS

DEEEIINOPSSSTUX EXPEDITIOUSNESS

DEEEINNNOSSSTTU TENDENTIOUSNESS

DEEEINNNPRSSTTU SUPERINTENDENTS

DEEEELMMNNOPRTUY UNDEREMPLOYMENT

DEEHIINOOPSSSTT PHOTOSENSITISED

DEEHIINOOPSSTTZ PHOTOSENSITIZED

DEEHIMOORRSTTTU RIDE OUT THE STORM

DEEILNNPRRTTUUY UNINTERRUPTEDLY

DEFFIILLNNORSTY FLY INTO FLINDERS

DEFGGHIIKLNNORT FORKED LIGHTNING

DEFHHLLNOOOSTUW FOLLOW THE HOUNDS

DEFHIIMNNOORSTU FOURTH DIMENSION

DEFILNRSSSSTTUU DISTRUSTFULNESS

DEGHHIIILNRRSVW WHIRLING DERVISH

DEGHHIINNNORSTU HUNTINGDONSHIRE

DEIIIILLMNNOSSTU DISILLUSIONMENT

DEIIINOOPPRSSST PREDISPOSITIONS

DEIIMNNNRSSTTUW WIND INSTRUMENTS

DEIINNORSSSSTUU INDUSTRIOUSNESS

DEIINNRRSSSTUUY SUNRISE INDUSTRY

EEEEGILNPSTTTTY TELETYPESETTING

EEEEGNNNOORSSTV GET ON ONE'S NERVES

EEEEHLLNOOPSSTT TELEPHOTO LENSES

EEEEHNOPQSTTUUZ PUT THE SQUEEZE ON

EEEEIINNNPSSSVX INEXPENSIVENESS

EEEEELMNORRSSSSS REMORSELESSNESS

EEEEMNNORSSSTUV VENTURESOMENESS

EEEFFIINNNOSSSV INOFFENSIVENESS

EEEFHIILLNOSSSUW HOUSEWIFELINESS

EEEFHNNOOOORRSTW NONE THE WORSE FOR

EEEFILMMNOPRSTV SELF-IMPROVEMENT

EEEGHMNNOOOSSSU HOMOGENEOUSNESS

EEEGIILLMOSTVWY GIVE IT SOME WELLY

EEEGIIMNNPRRSST MISREPRESENTING

EEEGIINNOPRSSTV PROGENITIVENESS

EEEGILORRRSSTVY RETROGRESSIVELY

EEEIIIILNNOPRSTV VESPERTILIONINE

EEEIIMMOORRSSST STEREOISOMERISM

EEEIINOPRSSSTTU REPETITIOUSNESS

EEEEILLLMNOPPRWY YELLOW PIMPERNEL

EEEILNNOOPPRSTT POISON-PEN LETTER

EEEEIMNPPRSSSTUV PRESUMPTIVENESS

EEEINNNOSSSSTTU SENTENTIOUSNESS

EEEINNOPRSSSTTU PRETENTIOUSNESS

EEELNOPPRSSSSSU PURPOSELESSNESS

EEEMNOPSSSSTTUU TEMPESTUOUSNESS

EEFFFHILNOORSST SHIFT FOR ONESELF

EEFGHILLORSSTUY SELF-RIGHTEOUSLY

EEFGHNOORRSTTTW TOWER OF STRENGTH

EEFGIOOPRRRSSSU REGIUS PROFESSOR

EEFHMMNOOPRSTTU SPUR-OF-THE-MOMENT

EEFILLLMNOSSSUU MELLIFLUOUSNESS

EEFLNOPRSSSSUUU SUPERFLUOUSNESS

EEFMMNOORRSSTTT FROM STEM TO STERN

EEGGIILNNNSSTTT STINGING NETTLES

EEGHHLNOSSSSTTU THOUGHTLESSNESS

EEGHIMNOORSSSTY MOOG SYNTHESISER

EEGHIMNOORSSTYZ MOOG SYNTHESIZER

EEGIIIJNNNNNPSS SPINNING JENNIES

EEGIIIMNNPRRSTT MISINTERPRETING

EEGIINNORSSSTUV VERTIGINOUSNESS

EEGIINNPPRRSSST PRINTING PRESSES

EEGIINOPRSSSSTU PRESTIGIOUSNESS

EEHHILNOORTTTWW THROW IN THE TOWEL

EEHHLLOORSSTTUY YOUTH HOSTELLERS

EEHIKNOOPRRSTUY KEEP YOUR SHIRT ON

EEHILNNOOORSSST LOSE ONE'S SHIRT ON

EEHIMOOPRRRSSTU MOTHER SUPERIORS

EEHINNNOPRRSTTTU THREE-POINT TURNS

EEEHLNOPRSSSSUUU SULPHUREOUSNESS

EEIIIINNQSSSTUV INQUISITIVENESS

EEIIIMNNNORSTTV INTERVENTIONISM

EEIIINNNORSTTTV INTERVENTIONIST

EEIILNNOORRTTTU TRINITROTOLUENE

EEIINNNNNOORTTV NONINTERVENTION

EEILNNOPRSTTUUY UNPRETENTIOUSLY

EEINNNNOOPPRSSTU INOPPORTUNENESS

EFGIIIILMNOPRSVY OVERSIMPLIFYING

EFIIIIILNNPSTTV SPLIT INFINITIVE

EFILMNRSSSSTTUU MISTRUSTFULNESS

EGGHIIIKLNNRSTT LIGHTNING STRIKE

EGHHIILLMNOOSTT HELMINTHOLOGIST

EGHHIINOOPPRRSW HERO-WORSHIPPING

EGHHILLNOOSTTUY YOUTH HOSTELLING

EGHHILNOOPRSTTT PLIGHT ONE'S TROTH

EGHIIIKLNNORSTV SHRINKING VIOLET

EGHILNOOOPRSUYY NEUROPHYSIOLOGY

EGIIIILNNOORTUVZ REVOLUTIONIZING

EHHINOOPPRSSUYY NEUROHYPOPHYSIS

EHIIIKLMMOOPRST POIKILOTHERMISM

EHIILLMOOPPRTTU PHOTOMULTIPLIER

EHILOOPRSSTTTUW WHISTLE-STOP TOUR

EHINORRSSSTTTUW TRUSTWORTHINESS

EIIIMNOOPPRSSTU SUPERIMPOSITION

EIILOPRRSSTTUUY SURREPTITIOUSLY

EIILOPRSSSTTUUY SUPERSTITIOUSLY

EIINOOPPPRSSSTU PRESUPPOSITIONS

FFGHIINNORSSSTU SOFT FURNISHINGS

FGHHIIIKLNNSTUW WISHFUL THINKING

FGHIINNNNOOOSWW NO SHOW OF WINNING

▬ SIXTEEN-LETTER WORDS ▬

AAAAACDDEELLPPSS CALL A SPADE A SPADE

AAAAACEEEKMNNPPR MAKE AN APPEARANCE

AAAAACGILLMMMNRTY ANAGRAMMATICALLY

AAAABBDGGILNORTT RAGTAG AND BOBTAIL

AAAABCEHILLLNPTY ANALPHABETICALLY

AAAACCHILLLNPTYY ANAPHYLACTICALLY

AAAACDEGILRRSUWY DUAL CARRIAGEWAYS

AAAACDEHHLNPRRSU ARUNACHAL PRADESH

AAAACDGIILLMMRTY DIAGRAMMATICALLY

AAAACDGIIILLMPRTY PARADIGMATICALLY

AAAACEEHILMMMTTT METAMATHEMATICAL

AAAACEELLNOPPRST TO ALL APPEARANCES

AAAACEILLMNNRSTY ALIMENTARY CANALS

AAAADEGHIIRSSSTT AS STRAIGHT AS A DIE

AAAAEHIIMNNOSTTT ANATHEMATISATION

AAAAEHIIMNNOTTTZ ANATHEMATIZATION

AAAAEIILMNNPRRST PARLIAMENTARIANS

AAABBDDEEFKNRSST BED AND BREAKFASTS

AAABCCEILLRRTUUY BUREAUCRATICALLY

AAABCDDHHMNNOOTT HAND-TO-HAND COMBAT

AAABCDEGGIIILORR REGGIO DI CALABRIA

AAABCEEGHHILNNNT HANG IN THE BALANCE

AAABCEEKKLLNRSTT BLACK
RATTLESNAKE
AAABCEFILLMNOORT AMERICAN
FOOTBALL
AAABCGHIILOOPRTU
AUTOBIOGRAPHICAL
AAABEEEKPPRSSTTW WASTEPAPER
BASKET
AAABEEGGLLMNSSUY ASSEMBLY
LANGUAGE
AAABEINNRSSTTTTU
TRANSUBSTANTIATE
AAACCCFHIIINORST
SACCHARIFICATION
AAACCDHIMMNOPRSY
PHARMACODYNAMICS
AAACCDIIILLLRSTY RADICALISTICALLY
AAACCEEGHIKNRRSY HACKNEY
CARRIAGES
AAACCEEHHHIKKRRSS KARACHAI-
CHERKESS
AAACCEEHHILLMNPT
THALAMENCEPHALIC
AAACCEEIIILNOPSSU
CAESALPINIACEOUS
AAACCEFIIRRRRRRST AIRCRAFT
CARRIERS
AAACCEGHILLLOORY
ARCHAEOLOGICALLY
AAACCEHIINNPQSTU
ACQUAINTANCESHIP
AAACCEHIINORRSTT
CHARACTERISATION
AAACCEHIINORRTTZ
CHARACTERIZATION
AAACCEHILLMPRTUY
PHARMACEUTICALLY
AAACCFIIILLNOSST CLASSIFICATIONAL
AAACCGHIILLLLPRY
CALLIGRAPHICALLY
AAACCHILLOPRSTTY
CATASTROPHICALLY
AAACCIILLORRSTTY
ARISTOCRATICALLY
AAACDEEEMMNRSSTU AMUSEMENT
ARCADES
AAACDEEFFGHIRRSS CHARGÉS
D'AFFAIRES
AAACDEGINORRRSTU REARGUARD
ACTIONS
AAACDEILLLMMORTY
MELODRAMATICALLY
AAACDEIMNNOORSTT ANIMATED
CARTOONS

AAACEEEILMNNOPRT AMERICAN
ANTELOPE
AAACEEGGILLMNOTY
AGAMOGENETICALLY
AAACEEGHIMMNORST
ARCHAEOMAGNETISM
AAACEEHHLLMNNOPT
THALAMENCEPHALON
AAACEEKLLNOORRTW LOCAL AREA
NETWORK
AAACEFHHIILMRRSS AIR CHIEF
MARSHALS
AAACEGHILLMNOPRY
ANEMOGRAPHICALLY
AAACEGHILNOOPPRT
PALAEONTOGRAPHIC
AAACEGHINNOPRTTY
ACANTHOPTERYGIAN
AAACEGIILLMMPRTY
EPIGRAMMATICALLY
AAACEGILLLNOOOPT
PALAEONTOLOGICAL
AAACEGILLLOOOOPZ
PALAEOZOOLOGICAL
AAACEHIILLNPTTTY
ANTIPATHETICALLY
AAACEHILLLMNPRUY
ALPHANUMERICALLY
AAACEHILLMPRSTTY
METAPHRASTICALLY
AAACEIIILNOPRSTT RECAPITALISATION
AAACEIIILNOPRTTZ
RECAPITALIZATION
AAACEIKLMMNORSTX EXCLAMATION
MARKS
AAACEINNORTTTTTT ATTRACT
ATTENTION
AAACFHIIILLNSSTT ATLANTIC SAILFISH
AAACGHILLLNOPPRY
PLANOGRAPHICALLY
AAACGHILLNOPPRTY
PANTOGRAPHICALLY
AAACGIILLNNOSTTY
ANTAGONISTICALLY
AAACIILLLNRSTTUY
NATURALISTICALLY
AAACILLMMOPSTTYY
ASYMPTOMATICALLY
AAACILLMNNOOSTTY
ANTONOMASTICALLY
AAACILLMNOOPRSTY
PARONOMASTICALLY
AAADDDEEKLNNRSSS SNAKES AND
LADDERS

AAADDEEFHLMOPRRY
PARAFORMALDEHYDE

AAADEEEEILLRSTVWY ELEVATED
RAILWAYS

AAADEEGNNOSSSTUV
ADVANTAGEOUSNESS

AAADEEIMNOPRRSST DRAMATIS
PERSONAE

AAADEFJLMMNOSSTT FLOTSAM AND
JETSAM

AAADEGHIMPPRRSSY DIAPHRAGM
PESSARY

AAADEGIILNNORRTT
INTERGRADATIONAL

AAADEIILNNORSTTU
DENATURALISATION

AAADEIILNNORTTUZ
DENATURALIZATION

AAADGHILLMNRRSSY MARSHALLING
YARDS

AAADIILMMNORRSTT
MALADMINISTRATOR

AAAEEEEGLNRSSTTT REAL ESTATE
AGENTS

AAAEEEEHHKMRTVWY MAKE HEAVY
WEATHER

AAAEEEGLMNPRRSTY PAYMASTER
GENERAL

AAAEEEJLNNNPRSST JAPANESE
LANTERNS

AAAEEFLLMMNNNORS ALL MANNER
OF MEANS

AAAEEGIILNOQRTUU EQUATORIAL
GUINEA

AAAEEHIINNOSSTTT
ANAESTHETISATION

AAAEEHIINNOSTTTZ
ANAESTHETIZATION

AAAEEIIMNNOPPRTX EXAMINATION
PAPER

AAAEILLMNNOOPSYY MALAYO-
POLYNESIAN

AAAFILMNNOORRSTT
TRANSFORMATIONAL

AAAGIILLNNOORSTY
ORGANISATIONALLY

AAAGIILLNNOORTYZ
ORGANIZATIONALLY

AAAGIILMNNORRSTT
TRANSMIGRATIONAL

AAAHIIIMNNORRSTTU
AUTHORITARIANISM

AAAIIILNNOORSSTT
RATIONALISATIONS

AAAIIILNNOORSTTZ
RATIONALIZATIONS

AAAIILLMNNORSTTU
ULTRANATIONALISM

AAAIILLNNORSTTTU
ULTRANATIONALIST

AAAIILMNNOPRSSTU
SUPRANATIONALISM

AABBDDELNNOPSSUY BY LEAPS AND
BOUNDS

AABBEIIILLMOTTYZ METABOLIZABILITY

AABCCDEIIIMNNOOZ AMINOBENZOIC
ACID

AABCCEEGGLLOORRT GARBAGE
COLLECTOR

AABCCEEHHMORRRST CHAMBER
ORCHESTRA

AABCCEGILNNNORTU
COUNTERBALANCING

AABCCIIIILMPRTTY IMPRACTICABILITY

AABCCIILMMNORTUU
CIRCUMAMBULATION

AABCCILMMORRTUUY
CIRCUMAMBULATORY

AABCDEEIIMNNOORW AMERICAN
WOODBINE

AABCDEIILNOORSST ANABOLIC
STEROIDS

AABCDGILMNOOPTUY GUNBOAT
DIPLOMACY

AABCEEEILLMMNSST
EMBLEMATICALNESS

AABCEEHILNNRSSTU
UNCHARITABLENESS

AABCEFGILLMNORRU AMERICAN
BULLFROG

AABCEHIIILMNPTUY
UNIMPEACHABILITY

AABCEIIIILLMRRTY IRRECLAIMABILITY

AABCGIILNORSSTUU
SUBCARTILAGINOUS

AABCIILLMNOOORST
COLLABORATIONISM

AABCIILLNOOORSTT
COLLABORATIONIST

AABCILLLLLOPSYYY POLYSYLLABICALLY

AABCILLLLMNOOSYY
MONOSYLLABICALLY

AABCINNOOORSSSTT
CONTRABASSOONIST

AABDDEEFGIKNRSTW WEDDING
BREAKFAST

AABDEEEEFFNNRTWW FEW AND FAR
BETWEEN

AABDEEEEGILNRSSS DISAGREEABLENESS
AABDEEEIMNOORRRT ANEROID
BAROMETER
AABDEEFHILLSTWYY FALL BY THE
WAYSIDE
AABDEEIMMNRRSSST
DISEMBARRASSMENT
AABDEFGIIIILNTTY INDEFATIGABILITY
AABEEEGHLLLMNOWW WHOLE NEW
BALL GAME
AABEEEGLMORRSTVW VEGETABLE
MARROWS
AABEEELNNNORSSSU
UNREASONABLENESS
AABEEELNNNOSSSSU
UNSEASONABLENESS
AABEEFGHIKLNRSST ENGLISH
BREAKFAST
AABEEFLNNORSSUUV
UNFAVOURABLENESS
AABIIILNNNNOTTTU
TINTINNABULATION
AABIIILNNSSTTTUY
INSUBSTANTIALITY
AABIILNNSSTTTUUY
UNSUBSTANTIALITY
AABIILNOPRRSTTTY
TRANSPORTABILITY
AACCCDEFIILNOORR AFRICAN
CROCODILE
AACCCDEHIINNORTW IN
ACCORDANCE WITH
AACCCDIIINORRSTY
IDIOSYNCRACRATIC
AACCCEEIILLLSSTY ECCLESIASTICALLY
AACCCEHIKMRRRSST CHRISTMAS
CRACKER
AACCCIILLLNOOSTY
ICONOCLASTICALLY
AACCDEEHHIILPRTT TEREPHTHALIC
ACID
AACCDEEILNNOORTU
DEUTEROCANONICAL
AACCDEFGHKLNORRT GRANDFATHER
CLOCK
AACCDEFIIILNOSST DECLASSIFICATION
AACCDEFIILLOPTTY FILLED TO
CAPACITY
AACCDEGILLLNNOST LONGDISTANCE
CALL
AACCDIIINNNOORTT
CONTRAINDICATION
AACCEEFGIKNNOOTZ TAKE
COGNIZANCE OF

AACCEEHILLMORTTY
TACHEOMETRICALLY
AACCEEILLORSTTTY
STEREOTACTICALLY
AACCEEKNORRSTTTU
COUNTERATTACKERS
AACCEELLNOOSSTTW COALS TO
NEWCASTLE
AACCEEMNOPRRSTYY COMPANY
SECRETARY
AACCEGHHILLOPRTY
HECTOGRAPHICALLY
AACCEGHIIMMPSTTY SYMPATHETIC
MAGIC
AACCEGHILLNOPRSY
SCENOGRAPHICALLY
AACCEGIKNNORTTTU
COUNTERATTACKING
AACCEGILLLNRSTUU INTEGRAL
CALCULUS
AACCEHHHILNNOPRY
RHYNCHOCEPHALIAN
AACCEHHIIIMNPRSV VICE-
CHAIRMANSHIP
AACCEHIILMNSSSST SCHISMATICALNESS
AACCEHLLOOPRSUYY
CARYOPHYLLACEOUS
AACCEIILLLNORTVY
INTERVOCALICALLY
AACCFILOOPRRRSTU PROCURATOR
FISCAL
AACCGGIIIMNNRTUV
CIRCUMNAVIGATING
AACCGHIILLMNOOST ANGLO-
CATHOLICISM
AACCGHIILLMOPRRY
MICROGRAPHICALLY
AACCGHILLOPRRSTY
CRYSTALLOGRAPHIC
AACCGIIIMNNORTUV
CIRCUMNAVIGATION
AACCHHILLOPPSTYY
PSYCHOPATHICALLY
AACCHIIILLNSTUVY CHAUVINISTICALLY
AACCHIIINNNORSST
ANACHRONISNISTIC
AACCHIILMMNOORST ROMAN
CATHOLICISM
AACCHILLLOPPRTYY
PROPHYLACTICALLY
AACCIILLMNRSTTUY
CIRCUMSTANTIALLY
AACCILLOOPRSSTUY
STAUROSCOPICALLY

AACDDEEIILNPRSTU
UNDERCAPITALISED
AACDDEEIILNPRTUZ
UNDERCAPITALIZED
AACDDEGHLNOOSSTT GOODS AND
CHATTELS
AACDDEHLLNNOOOTT NOT HOLD A
CANDLE TO
AACDDHILLMNORYYY
HYDRODYNAMICALLY
AACDEEEEGIORSSST ASSOCIATE
DEGREES
AACDEEEELORRSSUY DAY RELEASE
COURSE
AACDEEEIMNNNORRT MAINTENANCE
ORDER
AACDEEFGILLNORTT FLAGRANTE
DELICTO
AACDEEGHIILOPRRT
RADIOTELEGRAPHIC
AACDEEGIILMRRRST MEDICAL
REGISTRAR
AACDEEHIIOPRRTTU
RADIOTHERAPEUTIC
AACDEEIILNNNQRTU
QUADRICENTENNIAL
AACDEEIILNNORSTT
DECENTRALISATION
AACDEEIILNNORTTZ
DECENTRALIZATION
AACDEEILNNSSSTTU INDECENT
ASSAULTS
AACDEELLNNNRSTTY
TRANSCENDENTALLY
AACDEFIILMNNSTTU
FUNDAMENTALISTIC
AACDEHHIILNPRSST
CHRISTADELPHIANS
AACDEHIIKKMNNRST KITCHEN-SINK
DRAMA
AACDEIILLLMORTTY
DILATOMETRICALLY
AACDEINOPRSSSSST SCISSORS-AND-
PASTE
AACDFIIIILNOQSTU DISQUALIFICATION
AACDGHHILLOPRRYY
HYDROGRAPHICALLY
AACDIIIILMNNORST
DISCRIMINATIONAL
AACDIIIILNORSTTT TRADITIONALISTIC
AACDIIIILNNORSTTU INDUSTRIAL
ACTION
AACEEEEGLNRRRSTY SECRETARY-
GENERAL

AACEEEFHORRSSTTW WEATHER
FORECASTS
AACEEEHHHLNOORTX
HEXACHLOROETHANE
AACEEEIINPPRSSTV APPRECIATIVENESS
AACEEEFFMNORSSTTT MATTER-OF-
FACTNESS
AACEEEFHKNNOORTTV ARK OF THE
COVENANT
AACEEGHILLMNPSST
PHLEGMATICALNESS
AACEEGIILLLNNPTY
PALINGENETICALLY
AACEEGIILLLNSTVY EVANGELISTICALLY
AACEEGILLNPRSSTT LAST RESTING
PLACE
AACEEGLMNOOPRTUU ANALOGUE
COMPUTER
AACEEGNOOPRRTTUV AGENT
PROVOCATEUR
AACEEHILLNNRSTUY
NEURASTHENICALLY
AACEEHILMNOPRSST
METAPHORICALNESS
AACEEHIMOPRSSTTU
MASSOTHERAPEUTIC
AACEEIIILNNPSTTV CAPITAL-INTENSIVE
AACEEIIIMNNRSSST NECESSITARIANISM
AACEEIIILLRRSTTTV VERTICILLASTRATE
AACEEIIILMNRRSSSU MACLAURIN'S
SERIES
AACEEIIILNNRSSTTU INARTICULATENESS
AACEEIKMNNNOORSTV MAKE
CONVERSATION
AACEEIILLNNORSTTU NATURAL
SELECTION
AACEEIILLNOOPRTUV PALACE
REVOLUTION
AACEEIILMMNOPRSTT
COMPARTMENTALISE
AACEEIILMMNOPRTTZ
COMPARTMENTALIZE
AACEEIILMNSSSSTTY
SYSTEMATICALNESS
AACEEKNNNORSSSTU
CANTANKEROUSNESS
AACEFFIILNOSSSTT SELF-SATISFACTION
AACEFGILLNRRTTUU
ULTRACENTRIFUGAL
AACEFIINORSSSSTT SATISFACTORINESS
AACEGHHIILNOPSTT TEACHING
HOSPITAL
AACEGHHILLNOPRTY
ETHNOGRAPHICALLY

AACEGHILLOPPRRTY
PETROGRAPHICALLY
AACEGHILOOPSSTTT COTTAGE
HOSPITALS
AACEGHLLOPRRRSTY
CRYSTALLOGRAPHER
AACEGIIILNOPRTVZ OVERCAPITALIZING
AACEGIIMNORSSSTV MOVING
STAIRCASES
AACEHHIILLNOPRTY
HIEROPHANTICALLY
AACEHIILLNSSTTUY ENTHUSIASTICALLY
AACEHIILLOORSTTU LOCAL
AUTHORITIES
AACEHIILLPPRRSTY PERIPHRASTICALLY
AACEHIILMNNORRTV HARMONIC
INTERVAL
AACEHILLMORSTTTY
THERMOSTATICALLY
AACEHLMORSSSTUUW WALRUS
MOUSTACHES
AACEIIILLLLRSTTY LITERALISTICALLY
AACEIIILLLRSTTVY RELATIVISTICALLY
AACEIIILMNORRSTU
MERCURIALISATION
AACEIIILMNORRTUZ
MERCURIALIZATION
AACEIIILNNOOSSTT SECTIONALISATION
AACEIIILNNOOSTTZ
SECTIONALIZATION
AACEIIILNNOSSSTT SENSATIONALISTIC
AACEIIILNOOPRSTT
OPERATIONALISTIC
AACEIIINNNOORSTT
CONTAINERISATION
AACEIIINNNOORTTZ
CONTAINERIZATION
AACEIIINNNORRSTT
REINCARNATIONIST
AACEIIILLLRRSSTUY SURREALISTICALLY
AACEIIILNORRRTTUV
ATRIOVENTRICULAR
AACEIIMNNOORSSTX CROSS-
EXAMINATION
AACEILLLMNNOPRTY
PLANNOMETRICALLY
AACEILLMNOOOOPTY
ONOMATOPOEICALLY
AACEILLNNOORSTVY
CONVERSATIONALLY
AACEILNNNNORSTTT
TRANSCONTINENTAL
AACELOOOPRRSTUVY SUPER ROYAL
OCTAVO

AACFIIIILNNOOSTT FICTIONALISATION
AACFIIIILNNOOTTZ FICTIONALIZATION
AACGHHIILLLOPRTY
LITHOGRAPHICALLY
AACGHHILLLMOOOPT
OPHTHALMOLOGICAL
AACGHHILLOOPPRTY
PHOTOGRAPHICALLY
AACGHHILLOOPRRTY
ORTHOGRAPHICALLY
AACGHIIILNNPRSTY PHYSICAL
TRAINING
AACGHILLLOPRSTYY
STYLOGRAPHICALLY
AACGHILLNOOPPRRY
PORNOGRAPHICALLY
AACGIIINNNOPPRTT
NONPARTICIPATING
AACGIILLMNORRTTU COURT-
MARTIALLING
AACHHHILOPPRRSTY
STAPHYLORRHAPHIC
AACHIIIINNORSSTT CHRISTIANISATION
AACHIIIINNORSTTZ CHRISTIANIZATION
AACHIILLMNOPRSTY
MISANTHROPICALLY
AACHILLNOOPTTUYY
AUTOHYPNOTICALLY
AACIIIILLLMRSTTY MILITARISTICALLY
AACIIIILMNNOPSTU MUNICIPALISATION
AACIIIILMNNOPTUZ
MUNICIPALIZATION
AACIIILLLMNOPTTU
MULTIPLICATIONAL
AACIIILLNOOPRRSTY
CONSPIRATORIALLY
AACIKMNNOPRSTTUU PUNCTUATION
MARKS
AACILNNORRSTTTUU
TRANSCULTURATION
AADDDDEEEGILMPRS MIDDLE AGED
SPREAD
AADDEEEGILMMMNNT MIDDLE
MANAGEMENT
AADDEEGHHKLNNOSS GOLDEN
HANDSHAKES
AADDEEIIKMPRRSST MAKE RAPID
STRIDES
AADDFGIILNNORSTV STANDARD OF
LIVING
AADEEEEEILNRSSSV VENEREAL
DISEASES
AADEEEELMNOPRSTV DEVELOPMENT
AREAS

AADEEEFFGIILNRRT DIFFERENTIAL
GEAR
AADEEEFHINNRSSTT FAINT-
HEARTEDNESS
AADEEEGHHNRSTTUW THE GREAT
UNWASHED
AADEEEHILMORRRSTT
TETARROHEDRALISM
AADEEHLNNOOPRSVY OVERPLAY
ONE'S HAND
AADEEIIKNRSTTTTU STRIKE AN
ATTITUDE
AADEEIILNRSSTTTU INDUSTRIAL ESTATE
AADEFFIIILNOORRT AFFILIATION
ORDER
AADEFFIINOORSSTT DISAFFORESTATION
AADEIIIILMNORSTT DEMILITARISATION
AADEIIIILMNORTTZ DEMILITARIZATION
AADEIIIILNOORSTT EDITORIALISATION
AADEIIIILNOORTTZ EDITORIALIZATION
AADEIIILMNRSTTVY
ADMINISTRATIVELY
AADEMNOOPRRSTTUW
PORTMANTEAU WORDS
AAEEEFGOOPPPRRRS GREASEPROOF
PAPER
AAEEEGLNNORRSTTY ATTORNEY
GENERALS
AAEEEILNNOPRRSTT
REPRESENTATIONAL
AAEEEILRRRRSTTTX
EXTRATERRESTRIAL
AAEEFFHIIIMNRTTV IN THE
AFFIRMATIVE
AAEEFHILRSSSTTVV HARVEST FESTIVALS
AAEEFHLMNOOPRTUY POLYURETHANE
FOAM
AAEEGHHIILMNSTVY TIME HANGS
HEAVILY
AAEEGHIJNNOPRRTU EUROPEAN
NIGHTJAR
AAEEGHILLNOOPSTT
PALAEETHNOLOGIST
AAEEGILOOPRRRTVY ROYAL
PREROGATIVE
AAEEGPPRRRRSSTUY SPARE-PART
SURGERY
AAEEIIIILNNNORSTT INTERNATIONALISE
AAEEIIIILNNNORTTZ
INTERNATIONALIZE
AAEEIIILNNOPRRTTT
INTERPRETATIONAL
AAEEIIILNNORSSTTX
EXTERNALISATIONS

AAEEIILNNORSTTXZ
EXTERNALIZATIONS
AAEEIIILORRRRTTTX
EXTRATERRITORIAL
AAEEEILMNPRRRSTTU
PRETERNATURALISM
AAEEILMNPRRTTUWY MANUAL
TYPEWRITER
AAEELNNPRRSSSTUU
SUPERNATURALNESS
AAEEFFHOOOPRSSTTV HAVE A SOFT
SPOT FOR
AAEFHIIILLNNNOST SELF-
ANNIHILATION
AAEGGIIILNOSTTUV
ISOAGGLUTINATIVE
AAEGIIIILMNOSTTT LEGITIMATISATION
AAEGIIIILMNOTTTZ
LEGITIMATIZATION
AAEGIILNNORSSTTT
GASTROINTESTINAL
AAEIIILMNNNORSTT
INTERNATIONALISM
AAEIIIILMNNOOOSTT
EMOTIONALISATION
AAEIIIILMNNOOOTTZ
EMOTIONALIZATION
AAEIIIILNNNORSTTT
INTERNATIONALIST
AAEIIIILNNNORTTTY
INTERNATIONALITY
AAEIIIILNNORSSTUV UNIVERSALISATION
AAEIIIILNNORSTUVZ
UNIVERSALIZATION
AAEIIKNNOORRSTTW SANITATION
WORKER
AAEIIILNNORRSSTTT
TRANSLITERATIONS
AAEEILNOPRRSSSSYY SENSORY PARALYSIS
AAELOOPQRRRSTUUY SUPER ROYAL
QUARTO
AAFGIINNORRSSTTU
TRANSFIGURATIONS
AAGGIIILNNOOSTTU
ISOAGGLUTINATION
AAGHHOOOOPPRRSTTY
ASTROPHOTOGRAPHY
AAGIIIMNOPPPRRST MISAPPROPRIATING
AAIIIIILNOPRSSTTU SPIRITUALISATION
AAIIIILNOPRSTTUZ SPIRITUALIZATION
AAIIILLNNOQRSTTU
TRANQUILLISATION
AAIIILLNNOQRTTUZ
TRANQUILLIZATION

AAIIIMNOOPPPRRST
MISAPPROPRIATION
AAIILLMNNORRSTTU
TRANSILLUMINATOR
AAIIMNNORSSTTTTU
TRANSMUTATIONIST
ABBBCDEEIKNRSTTU BEST BIB AND
TUCKER
ABBCDDEEGHIKMPRU HUMPBACKED
BRIDGE
ABBCDEIIIILNRSTY INDESCRIBABILITY
ABBCEEEFFKLOOOST COFFEE-TABLE
BOOKS
ABBCEHLNOORSSTTU BACHELOR'S-
BUTTONS
ABBCEIIIJLNOOTTY OBJECTIONABILITY
ABBDEEEGMNRRTTUW BADEN-
WURTTEMBERG
ABBDEELNORRRSTWY STRAWBERRY
BLONDE
ABBDELNORRRSSTWY STRAWBERRY
BLONDS
ABBEEEEINNNNOOST A BEE IN ONE'S
BONNET
ABBEIIILMPRRTTUY IMPERTURBABILITY
ABBIIILSSTTTTUUY SUBSTITUTABILITY
ABCCDKLLNOORSTUY COCK-AND-
BULL STORY
ABCCEEEIKLLNRSTT ELECTRIC
BLANKETS
ABCCEEHILNOPRSTY HYPERBOLIC
SECANT
ABCCEEILLNOOPSST POLICE
CONSTABLES
ABCCEFIIIJNOSTTU SUBJECTIFICATION
ABCCEGHIILLNOOOT
BIOTECHNOLOGICAL
ABCCEIIIILNNOTVY INCONCEIVABILITY
ABCCGHIILLOOOPSY
PSYCHOBIOLOGICAL
ABCCIIKLMNNOOOST COMBINATION
LOCKS
ABCCILLOOOPRSSTY
STROBOSCOPICALLY
ABCDDEEEMNOORTTT BOTTOM DEAD
CENTRE
ABCDEEEEGHLORRSS BACHELOR'S
DEGREES
ABCDEEEHHHLLOOOTW THE WHOLE
CABOODLE
ABCDEEGILNNORSSU CUDGEL ONE'S
BRAINS
ABCDEEHIMNNOPRRS DOBERMAN
PINSCHER

ABCDEELMNORRSSUU CONSUMER
DURABLES
ABCDEGIILLNOSSTT DISCLOSING
TABLET
ABCDEGKNNOOOORSW GO BACK ON
ONE'S WORD
ABCDEIIILNNNOSTY
INCONDENSABILITY
ABCDEIIIILNPRTTUY UNPREDICTABILITY
ABCEEEEFILNRRRRY REFERENCE
LIBRARY
ABCEEEEHRRRRSSTT STRETCHER-
BEARERS
ABCEFFIINOOOPRRT PROBATION
OFFICER
ABCEFGIIILLNNORY FIBRINOGENICALLY
ABCEHIILLNOSTTYY
BIOSYNTHETICALLY
ABCEHIMNNNOOOPRU
BRONCHOPNEUMONIA
ABCEIIIILLLMSSST BALLISTIC MISSILE
ABCEIIILNNOSTTTY INCONTESTABILITY
ABCEIMNNORSSSTUU
RAMBUNCTIOUSNESS
ABCFIILMNNOORTUY
UNCONFORMABILITY
ABDDEEEHNOORSSUW BONDED
WAREHOUSES
ABDDEEEIMNNNSSST ABSENT-
MINDEDNESS
ABDDEHLNNNOOOOSS BLOOD ON
ONE'S HANDS
ABDEEEFIIILNNSST IDENTIFIABLENESS
ABDEEEFIOOPSSSTX SAFE-DEPOSIT
BOXES
ABDEEEILNPRSSSTU DISREPUTABLENESS
ABDEEFIIMNNORRST FIRE-AND-
BRIMSTONE
ABDEEFIOOPSSTTXY SAFETY-DEPOSIT
BOX
ABDEEGGILMNPRRSU GINGERBREAD
PLUMS
ABDEEGIIILLNNRRS LENDING LIBRARIES
ABDEEHIILMNSSSTT DISESTABLISHMENT
ABDEEKNNOORRSUVW NERVOUS
BREAKDOWN
ABDEFIIIIILRSTVY DIVERSIFIABILITY
ABDEGHIMNOOSSTTU DOUBTING
THOMASES
ABDEIIIIILLLMTTY LIMITED
LIABILITY
ABDEIIIILNNPSSTY INDISPENSABILITY
ABDFIIILNOOORSUV DIVISION OF
LABOUR

ABDFILNNOOORSSTU BLOOD
TRANSFUSION

ABEEEFILNNRRSSTT ENFANTS
TERRIBLES

ABEEEGLNNNORSSUV
UNGOVERNABLENESS

ABEEEIIILMMPRSTY SEMIPERMEABILITY

ABEEEIILMNNNRSST
INTERMINABLENESS

ABEEEIILNPRRSTTY REPRESENTABILITY

ABEEEILNNOQSSSTU
QUESTIONABLENESS

ABEEGHIIILNNSTUX INEXTINGUISHABLE

ABEEGIIMPRRRTTUZ
PIETERMARITZBURG

ABEEHILMNNNOOOORT HONORABLE
MENTION

ABEEIIIILRRRTTVY IRRETRIEVABILITY

ABEEIIILNPRRTTTY INTERPRETABILITY

ABEELMNNORSSSTUU
SURMOUNTABLENESS

ABEFGIIIILNRRRTY IRREFRANGIBILITY

ABEHIIIILNSTTUXY INEXHAUSTIBILITY

ABEHILOORRSSSTTY
ERYTHROBLASTOSIS

ABEINOOOOPRSSSTTV OBSERVATION
POSTS

ABIIIILMNRSSSTTY TRANSMISSIBILITY

ACCCCCEEEILNNOSSU CONSCIENCE
CLAUSE

ACCCCCEGHIKNNOSTU CHECKING
ACCOUNTS

ACCCDDHHIILOORRY HYDROCHLORIC
ACID

ACCCDEEILLLNOPYY
ENCYCLOPEDICALLY

ACCCDFHHLNOORSTU CHURCH OF
SCOTLAND

ACCCEEEGHILLLNOT TECHNICAL
COLLEGE

ACCCEEEILNOSSSUV CONCESSIVE
CLAUSE

ACCCEEGHHILLORTU COLLEGIATE
CHURCH

ACCCEEHIIINNRSST CHRISTIAN SCIENCE

ACCCEEIIIILLNOPST POLITICAL SCIENCE

ACCCEEILOORSSTTU
ELECTROACOUSTICS

ACCCEHHIIINNOPSTY
PSYCHOTECHNICIAN

ACCCEILOOPRSSTUU ACOUSTIC
COUPLERS

ACCCIILMOOPRRSTU
ULTRAMICROSCOPIC

ACCDDEIMMNNNOOSS SECONDS-IN-
COMMAND

ACCDEEEMNNOOPRRT PROMENADE
CONCERT

ACCDEEFHIIMMNNOR COMMANDER
IN CHIEF

ACCDEEHHIKLLNRTY LATCHKEY
CHILDREN

ACCDEFHIKLOOOSVW FIVE O'CLOCK
SHADOW

ACCDEFMNOOPRRTUU COMPOUND
FRACTURE

ACCDEGIINNNNOSTU
DISCOUNTENANCING

ACCDEHHIILLMOOPS
DOLICHOCEPHALISM

ACCDEHIIMOOSSTTY
HOMOSCEDASTICITY

ACCDEIOPPRRSSTTU PICTURE
POSTCARDS

ACCEEEEFIILNPSTX LIFE
EXPECTANCIES

ACCEEEEGLLLLOORT ELECTORAL
COLLEGE

ACCEEEELLMOPRSTX ELECTRA
COMPLEXES

ACCEEEFFIIILORRV OFFICIAL RECEIVER

ACCEEEFHIINOOPTT PIECE OF THE
ACTION

ACCEEEFIMNORSSST MASTERS OF
SCIENCE

ACCEEFMOORRRSTTU CREATURE
COMFORTS

ACCEEHIILLLNORTY
HELIOCENTRICALLY

ACCEEHILLNNORTTY
ETHNOCENTRICALLY

ACCEEHLMNORSSTUY
SCLERENCHYMATOUS

ACCEEIILOORRRSTT
ARTERIOSCLEROTIC

ACCEEIIMMMNNORTTU
INTERCOMMUNICATE

ACCEEIKNOOPRRTTT PROTECTION
RACKET

ACCEEIILLOOPRSSTY
STEREOSCOPICALLY

ACCEEIMNNOPRSSTY COPERNICAN
SYSTEM

ACCEFIIILLLNNSTUY UNSCIENTIFICALLY

ACCEGIILNNNOPRSS PELICAN
CROSSINGS

ACCEHIINOPRRSTUY
NEUROPSYCHIATRIC

ACCEHILLMOOPRSTY
THERMOSCOPICALLY
ACCEHILLMOPRSTYY
PSYCHOMETRICALLY
ACCEIIILLNOOSTTV
COLLECTIVISATION
ACCEIIILLNOOTTVZ
COLLECTIVIZATION
ACCEIIILOSSSTTTX LEXICOSTATISTICS
ACCEIILLMNORRSTY
MICROCRYSTALLINE
ACCEIILLNOOPRSTY
RETINOSCOPICALLY
ACCEIIMMNNOOSTUX
EXCOMMUNICATIONS
ACCEIINOORSSTTVV
VASOCONSTRICTIVE
ACCFILLLOOOPRSUY
FLUOROSCOPICALLY
ACCGHHIILLLOOTYY
ICHTHYOLOGICALLY
ACCGIILLMMOOORTY
MICROCLIMATOLOGY
ACCHHIIOOPRRSTTY
ORTHOPSYCHIATRIC
ACCIINNOOORSSTTV
VASOCONSTRICTION
ACCIKLLMOOOOSTTV MOLOTOV
COCKTAILS
ACDDDEFILNNOOSTU CONSOLIDATED
FUND
ACDDEEEELNNPSSTU DEPENDENT
CLAUSES
ACDDEEMNNOORRSSY SECONDARY
MODERNS
ACDDEFHIIIIMNOTU
DEHUMIDIFICATION
ACDDEGHILLNOSSTW SWADDLING
CLOTHES
ACDDGHIIMNPRSSTU CHRISTMAS
PUDDING
ACDDHHJNNOPSUUWY PUNCH-AND-
JUDY SHOW
ACDEEEEEGGHLRRST THREE-LEGGED
RACES
ACDEEEEFILMNSTTV MENTAL
DEFECTIVES
ACDEEEEHIMNNRTUV
UNDERACHEIVEMENT
ACDEEEEIIKMNNOST TAKE ONE'S
MEDICINE
ACDEEEEIIPRTTTVV PRIVATE DETECTIVE
ACDEEEEINRRRSSTU
UNDERSECRETARIES

ACDEEEFHILLNORSS HALLS OF
RESIDENCE
ACDEEEFIIILNRSTT DEFINITE ARTICLES
ACDEEEFIINOQRRSU RADIO
FREQUENCIES
ACDEEEFLLOORRUVV FOUR-LEAVED
CLOVER
ACDEEEGHILNRSSST CLEAR-
SIGHTEDNESS
ACDEEEGHILORRSTT CIGARETTE
HOLDERS
ACDEEEGHKLPSTTUU TAKE UP THE
CUDGELS
ACDEEEIIILNPRSTV VICE-PRESIDENTIAL
ACDEEEIILLLNSTTU INTELLECTUALISED
ACDEEEIIMNPRSSSV MANIC-
DEPRESSIVES
ACDEEEILNNNOSTTU SECOND
LIEUTENANT
ACDEEENNNNRSSSTT
TRANSCENDENTNESS
ACDEEFHIIMNNRSST
DISFRANCHISEMENT
ACDEEFHINORRTTUU FURTHER
EDUCATION
ACDEEFIIMNNOORST
CONFEDERATIONISM
ACDEEFIINNOORSTT
CONFEDERATIONIST
ACDEEFILNORRRSTU FUNERAL
DIRECTORS
ACDEEFINNOPRSTUU
SUPERFECUNDATION
ACDEEGGHIIINPRRSS GRAPHIC
DESIGNERS
ACDEEGINNOORRRTU RECREATION
GROUND
ACDEEGMMOOPRRRSU PROGRAMMED
COURSE
ACDEEHIILMNOPRTY
DIACETYLMORPHINE
ACDEEIILLMNOSTUY
EUDEMONISTICALLY
ACDEEIILMNNORSTU
RADIOLUMINESCENT
ACDEEIILNPPRRTUY
PERPENDICULARITY
ACDEEJKLNOORSSVY DAVY JONES'S
LOCKER
ACDEFIIIIMNNNOST INDEMNIFICATIONS
ACDEFIILNNNORTTT CONTINENTAL
DRIFT
ACDEFINNOOORSTUU FOUNDATION
COURSE

ACDEGHIILMNNOOPS HOLDING
COMPANIES
ACDEGHILLLMOOOTY
METHODOLOGICALLY
ACDEGIIIKNNRSSTT STRIKING
DISTANCE
ACDEGIILMOPRSTTU DIGITAL
COMPUTERS
ACDEGILNNNOSSTTU CONSENTING
ADULTS
ACDEGMNOOPRRSSTU SOUND
SPECTROGRAM
ACDEHILLMOPSTTUY SHUTTLE
DIPLOMACY
ACDEIIIILMNNRSTY INDISCRIMINATELY
ACDEIIILLMNORTTU
MULTIDIRECTIONAL
ACDEIILMNORRSTTU
ULTRAMODERNISTIC
ACDEIINORRSTTTTY DISTRICT
ATTORNEY
ACDEILOOPRSSSTUY
PERISSODACTYLOUS
ACDIIIIIMNNNORST INDISCRIMINATION
ACDIIIILMNORRSTY
DISCRIMINATORILY
ACEEEEEFFFMNORRR FRAME OF
REFERENCE
ACEEEEGILLNNORST GENERAL
ELECTIONS
ACEEEEHLLQRRSTUV TRAVELLER'S
CHEQUE
ACEEEFGILNNOPRRS PEREGRINE
FALCONS
ACEEEGGHIILRRTTT CIGARETTE
LIGHTER
ACEEEGHKLNOPSSTU GET ONE'S
HACKLES UP
ACEEEGIIINPRRRSV VIRGINIA CREEPERS
ACEEEGILMMNORSTT
ELECTROMAGNETISM
ACEEEGINNOOPRSTU
COUNTERESPIONAGE
ACEEEHHILNNPRSTY
CHRYSELEPHANTINE
ACEEEHHIPPRSSSTT SPEECH THERAPISTS
ACEEEHIIILLMRSTUY
EUHEMERISTICALLY
ACEEEHIPRRRSSTTT STRETCHER
PARTIES
ACEEEHLLMNOORSTY ELEMENTARY
SCHOOL
ACEEEIILLLNRSTTU INTELLECTUALISER
ACEEEIILLLNRTTUZ INTELLECTUALIZER

ACEEEIILNNNQSSTU
SESQUICENTENNIAL
ACEEEILLMNPPRRST SCARLET
PIMPERNEL
ACEEFGINORRSTTVY CENTRES OF
GRAVITY
ACEEFHILLNNNOSTT CONTINENTAL
SHELF
ACEEFIIILMNOPSTX EXEMPLIFICATIONS
ACEEFIKNOOPRSTWY NASTY PIECE OF
WORK
ACEEGGIILLNNORST TRAINING
COLLEGES
ACEEGHHILOOPPRTT
PHOTOTELEGRAPHIC,
TELEPHOTOGRAPHIC
ACEEGHIIILNOSTTY
HISTOGENETICALLY
ACEEGHILLLOOPRTY
HERPETOLOGICALLY
ACEEGHILLMNNOOOP
PHENOMENOLOGICAL
ACEEGHILLNOORTTY
ORTHOGENETICALLY
ACEEGHILLNOPTTYY
PHYTOGENETICALLY
ACEEGHIMMNORSTTY
MAGNETOCHEMISTRY
ACEEGIIILLNOORRST SOLICITOR
GENERAL
ACEEGIILNORSSSSU SACRILEGIOUSNESS
ACEEGIIMNORSTTTV
MAGNETOSTRICTIVE
ACEEGIMNNOOPRSTV
OVERCOMPENSATING
ACEEGLMMNOOPRTTV GLOVE
COMPARTMENT
ACEEHHIINNOPPRTT
PITHECANTHROPINE
ACEEHHIMMOORRSTT
HETEROCHROMATISM
ACEEHHIOOPPRTTTU
PHOTOTHERAPEUTIC
ACEEHIILMNORSTVV THERMIONIC
VALVES
ACEEHIINORSSTTUV
OVERENTHUSIASTIC
ACEEHILLMMORRTTY
THERMOMETRICALLY
ACEEHILLNOOPRSTY
STEREOPHONICALLY
ACEEIIILLOPPSSTVX PLASTIC EXPLOSIVE
ACEEIILNNNNORTTT
INTERCONTINENTAL

ACEEIILNNOQSTTUY
CONSEQUENTIALITY
ACEEIILOORRRSSST ARTERIOSCLEROSIS
ACEEIMNNOOOPRSTV
OVERCOMPENSATION
ACEEINNOOPPRSTTY PRESENTATION
COPY
ACEELMNOOPPRRSTU PERSONAL
COMPUTER
ACEEMNOOOPRRSTVY
OVERCOMPENSATORY
ACEFFGIJLMNOPPSU JUMPING-OFF
PLACES
ACEFIIINNOOPRSST PERSONIFICATIONS
ACEFIIMNOOPPRRRT IMPROPER
FRACTION
ACEFLLMNNOORTUWY FELLOW
COUNTRYMAN
ACEGGHILLMOOOOPR
GEOMORPHOLOGICAL
ACEGHHIILLLMNOOT
HELMINTHOLOGICAL
ACEGHHIILLLOPRYY
HIEROGLYPHICALLY
ACEGIIKLNPRSSSTT STICKING PLASTERS
ACEGIILNNOORSSST
CONGRESSIONALIST
ACEGIIMNNOORSTTT
MAGNETOSTRICTION
ACEGILNNNOOSSUUY
CONSANGUINEOUSLY
ACEHHILLMOOPRTTY
PHOTOTHERMICALLY
ACEHHILMOOPPRSXY
CHEMOPROPHYLAXIS
ACEHHILMOOPRSSST
SCHOOLMASTERSHIP
ACEHHIOPPRSSSTTY
PSYCHOTHERAPISTS
ACEHIIKLLNOOPTTY
PHOTOKINETICALLY
ACEHIIKMNNNOORRS CHINK IN ONE'S
ARMOR
ACEHIIILLLOPSTTYY POLYTHEISTICALLY
ACEHIIILLMNOOSTTY
MONOTHEISTICALLY
ACEHIILMOPRSTTTY
THERMOPLASTICITY
ACEHILLLLOPPTYYY
POLYPHYLETICALLY
ACEHIMNNOOPRRSTT
ANTHROPOCENTRISM
ACEIIIKKNNRSSTTW KNICKERS IN A
TWIST

ACEIIIINNOPSSSSUU INAUSPICIOUSNESS
ACEIILLLMOPRTUVY
PLUVIOMETRICALLY
ACEIILLNNNOQTTTU CONTINENTAL
QUILT
ACEIILMNOOOOPRSTY
COPOLYMERISATION
ACEIILMNOOOOPRTYZ
COPOLYMERIZATION
ACEIILMNOORRSSTV
CONTROVERSIALISM
ACEIILNNOOOOPRSST CONSOLATION
PRISE
ACEIILNNOOOOPRSTZ CONSOLATION
PRIZE
ACEIILNOORRSSTTV
CONTROVERSIALIST
ACEIINNOORSSSTTV
CONSERVATIONISTS
ACEIKNNOOPRSSSTT STOP IN ONE'S
TRACKS
ACEILLNOPRSSTTUY PERSONALITY
CULTS
ACFGIIIMNNOORSTU
CONFIGURATIONISM
ACFGIIINNOORSTTU
CONFIGURATIONIST
ACFIIIILLNNOSTTU NULLIFICATIONIST
ACGHHHILMOOOPRRT
CHROMOLITHOGRAPH
ACGHHIMOOOPPRRTY
MICROPHOTOGRAPHY,
PHOTOMICROGRAPHY
ACGHHINOOOPPRTYZ
PHOTOZINCOGRAPHY
ACGHIILLLNOOORTY
ORNITHOLOGICALLY
ACGHIILLMNOOPSYY
PHYSIOGNOMICALLY
ACGIINNOOOPRSSTT
PROGNOSTICATIONS
ACHHIOOOOPPRTTTU
PHOTOAUTOTROPHIC
ACHIILLORRSTTTUU
HORTICULTURALIST
ACIIIILLOPSSTTVY POSITIVISTICALLY
ACIIIMNNNOOPRSTU
MISPRONUNCIATION
ACIILLLMNOOOPSTY
MONOPOLISTICALLY
ACIILLNNOOOOPRSST CROSS-
POLLINATION
ACIILLNNOOSTTTUY
CONSTITUTIONALLY

ACIILNNNOOSTTTUU
UNCONSTITUTIONAL

ADDDDEEEEHLMNSSU MUDDLE-
HEADEDNESS

ADDEEEEFIILMNSTX EXTENDED
FAMILIES

ADDEEEEIMNNNNPST INDEPENDENT
MEANS

ADDEEGINNOOORRRT RIO GRANDE
DO NORTE

ADDEEIIIKKLLNSSS LIKES AND DISLIKES

ADDEEIMMMMNRSSSU MIDSUMMER
MADNESS

ADDEEIMNNNORRSSW NARROW-
MINDEDNESS

ADDEGIIMNNNRSSTU
MISUNDERSTANDING

ADEEEEFHHLOORSTU LEADER OF THE
HOUSE

ADEEEEHHLNORSSTW
WHOLEHEARTEDNESS

ADEEEEIIMNPRRTTV
PREDETERMINATIVE

ADEEEFGHMNOORTUY YEOMEN OF
THE GUARD

ADEEEFGIIILNNRTT DEFINITE INTEGRAL

ADEEEGGIINORSSTT
DESEGREGATIONIST

ADEEEGHILNOOPRRT GARDEN
HELIOTROPE

ADEEEGILNNOOPRSS OLD AGE
PENSIONERS

ADEEEHIILMNNORST THREE-
DIMENSIONAL

ADEEEHNNORSSSTTY STONY-
HEARTEDNESS

ADEEEHNORSSSTTTU
STOUTHEARTEDNESS

ADEEEIIMNNOPRRTT
PREDETERMINATION

ADEEEINNNRRSSSTU
UNRESTRAINEDNESS

ADEEEMNOPRRSSTTT DEPARTMENT
STORES

ADEEFFIIINNORSTT
DIFFERENTIATIONS

ADEEGGGHIILNNRST GREASED
LIGHTNING

ADEEGHHINPRSSSST SHARP-
SIGHTEDNESS

ADEEGIILNNOQSSTU LEADING
QUESTIONS

ADEEGILNNOPPRRTY
PREPONDERATINGLY

ADEEHHHHIINRRTTT HITHER AND
THITHER

ADEEHHILMMNRRRUU MULHEIM AN
DER RUHR

ADEEHIINNNOORSST A THORN IN
ONE'S SIDE

ADEEILMNOPRRSSTU MENSTRUAL
PERIODS

ADEFHINOOOORRTTUY OUT OF THE
ORDINARY

ADEFINNNOOOSSTTU FOUNDATION
STONES

ADEGGGHIOORSSSTY SHAGGY-DOG
STORIES

ADEGIIIINOPRSTTT PRESTIDIGITATION

ADEHHHINOOPPSSYY
ADENOHYPHOPHYSIS

ADEIIIINORSSTTVY RADIOSENSITIVITY

ADEIIMNOPRRRTTTX DOT-MATRIX
PRINTER

ADEIINOOOPPRRSTT
DISPROPORTIONATE

ADELLNOOORSSSWWW SWALLOW
ONE'S WORDS

ADFGIIIKNNNNORTU DRINKING
FOUNTAIN

ADGHHIIIINNOOPSTT
DIPHTHONGISATION

ADGHHIIIINNOOPTTZ
DIPHTHONGIZATION

ADGHIMMNNOOPRRSY
GYNANDROMORPHISM

ADHHINOPRSSSTTTY SHORTHAND
TYPISTS

AEEEEFGLMMNNRRST GENTLEMEN
FARMERS

AEEEEFIMNNRSSTTV
FERMENTATIVENESS

AEEEEHHIKLNOPSTW A SPOKE IN THE
WHEEL

AEEEEHINNPPRSSSV APPREHENSIVENESS

AEEEEIINNPRRTTTV
INTERPENETRATIVE

AEEEEINNPRSSSTTV PRESENTATIVENESS

AEEEFFFHLMOORSTT FLAME-OF-THE-
FOREST

AEEEFHILNNNNPPSY PENNY-
HALFPENNIES

AEEEFILNOPRRSSTV SELF-
PRESERVATION

AEEEFLLLLORRSTVW FELLOW
TRAVELLERS

AEEEGGIIILLLMNOR REGGIO
NELL'EMILIA

AEEEGGINNORSSSST SEASON'S GREETINGS

AEEEGGLNNOORRRSV GOVERNORS-GENERAL, GOVERNOR-GENERALS

AEEEGHIINNNRRTWY RING IN THE NEW YEAR

AEEEGHIMNOOOSSVW GIVE SOMEONE A SHOW

AEEEGHNOPRRRSTUY OPEN-HEART SURGERY

AEEEGILNNPPRRSST SLEEPING PARTNERS

AEEEHHILMNNPRTTY TRIPHENYLMETHANE

AEEEHIILMMNNOPPS EPIPHENOMENALISM

AEEEHIILMNNOPPST EPIPHENOMENALIST

AEEEHIIMMNNORRSST IMMERSION HEATERS

AEEEIINNNOPRRTTT INTERPENETRATION

AEEEELMNOOPRSTUXY EXTEMPORANEOUSLY

AEEFGHIILLNNTTTU FLIGHT LIEUTENANT

AEEFIILMNNOOPRSSS SEMIPROFESSIONAL

AEEFIILNNRSSTTTU FIRST LIEUTENANTS

AEEFNOOOPRRSTTWY POWERS OF ATTORNEY

AEEGGHHHIILTTVWY LIGHT HEAVYWEIGHT

AEEGGIIILMNNNRST MINISTERING ANGEL

AEEGGLNOOOORRSTTY GASTROENTEROLOGY

AEEGHIKLOPRRSTTW TIGHTROPE WALKERS

AEEGHMMMNOOPRSTY SPHYGMOMANOMETER

AEEGIIILMNNNSTTZ SENTIMENTALIZING

AEEGIIJKMNNORSSV KING JAMES VERSION

AEEGIMNOPRSSSTTY OPERATING SYSTEMS

AEEHIIMNNOPPRSSS MISAPPREHENSIONS

AEEHIINOPRRSSSTW PRAISEWORTHINESS

AEEHMNOORSSSTTTU SOUTHEASTERNMOST

AEEIIIILNSSSTTTX EXISTENTIALISIST

AEEIIIILNOPQTTTUY EQUIPOTENTIALITY

AEEIIIILORRRTTTXY EXTERRITORIALITY

AEEIIILLNNQSSTTUY QUINTESSENTIALLY

AEEIIILMMNNNORSTV ENVIRONMENTALISM

AEEIIILMNNNORSTTV ENVIRONMENTALIST

AEEIIMNNRSSSSSTV TRANSMISSIVENESS

AEEIIMNOOPRSSTTX EXTEMPORISATIONS

AEEIIMNOOPRSTTXZ EXTEMPORIZATIONS

AEEILMNNOSSSSTUU SIMULTANEOUSNESS

AEEILNNOOPRRSTUV RELATIVE PRONOUNS

AEELNOOPPPRRRSTY PERSONAL PROPERTY

AEFFGIILLNORRSSU SELF-RAISING FLOUR

AEFGIILLMNNOPRRT MORNING-AFTER PILL

AEFHIOPPRSSSTTTT FIRST PAST THE POST

AEFIIKMNOOOOPRRSV MAKE PROVISION FOR

AEFIIILLNOOPPRSTY PELLITORY OF SPAIN

AEFIILMNORSSSTUU MULTIFARIOUSNESS

AEFIILNNNOOOPRRT NONPROLIFERATION

AEFILLNNOOPRSSUY UNPROFESSIONALLY

AEGHIILLNNORTTWW WRITING ON THE WALL

AEGHILNOOOPRSTTU NEUROPATHOLOGIST

AEGHIMMOOPRRSTTT PHOTOGRAMMETRIST

AEHHIIOPPRSSSTTY PHYSIOTHERAPISTS

AEHHIMNOOOPPRRST ANTHROPOMORPHISE

AEHHIMNOOOPPRRTZ ANTHROPOMORPHIZE

AEHIIMNNNOORSSSU INHARMONIOUSNESS

AEIIIILLLMMNORTU MULTIMILLIONAIRE

AEIIIILNNOSSTTTU INSTITUTIONALISE

AEIIIILNNOSTTTUZ INSTITUTIONALIZE

AEIIILMNNRSSSTTX MARXIST-LENINISTS

AEIIILLNOPPRSSTTY SPLIT PERSONALITY

AEIIILMNNRSSSTTTU INSTRUMENTALISTS

AEIIMNNOOPRSSSSU
PARSIMONIOUSNESS
AEINOQRRSTTUUVYY QUANTITY
SURVEYOR
AELNNNOOOPPRRSSU PERSONAL
PRONOUNS
AFILLMOOOOPPRRSTT FROM PILLAR TO
POST
AGGIILMMMNOPRRTU
MULTIPROGRAMMING
AGGILLNOOOOORSTTY
OTOLARYNGOLOGIST
AGHHHILOOOPPRTTY
PHOTOLITHOGRAPHY
AGHHILLMOOOPSSTT
OPHTHALMOLOGISTS
AGHHILOOOPPSTTTY
PHYTOPATHOLOGIST
AHHIIIILNOOOPPSST PHILOSOPHISATION
AHHIIIILNOOOPPSTZ
PHILOSOPHIZATION
AHHIMMNOOOOPPRRST
ANTHROPOMORPHISM
AHHIMNOOOPPRRSTT
ANTHROPOMORPHIST
AHHMNOOOOPPRRSTU
ANTHROPOMORPHOUS
AIIIILMNNOSSTTTU INSTITUTIONALISM
AIIIILNNOSSTTTTU INSTITUTIONALIST
AKKLMMMNOOOORSSU
KOMSOMOLSK-ON-AMUR
BBBBEEFGIIILRSTT FLIBBERTIGIBBETS
BBBCEGHINRRSSSUU SCRUBBING
BRUSHES
BBCEEKKLOORRSSTT STOCKBROKER
BELTS
BBCEKLNOOOOOOPSTY BLOT ONE'S
COPYBOOK
BBCIIIILMNOSTTUY INCOMBUSTIBILITY
BBDEEEEINNORRSTVY INVERTED
SNOBBERY
BBEEHHNNOOOORSSY ON ONE'S
HOBBYHORSE
BBEHHIILMOOPRSTT
THROMBOPHLEBITIS
BCCDEEIILNOORUXY
DEOXYRIBONUCLEIC
BCCEEHIILNOOPRSY HYPERBOLIC
COSINE
BCCEEIIILORRTTTY TRIBOELECTRICITY
BCCEEINOPRSSSSTU SUBSISTENCE
CROPS
BCCEILOOPPRRSTUU PUBLIC
PROSECUTOR

BCCEINNOOSSSSSUU
SUBCONSCIOUSNESS
BCCIIIIILNNNOTVY INCONVINCIBILITY
BCDDEEGKNOOOORTTW GET DOWN
TO BEDROCK
BCDDEGHIILNNPTUU IN THE PUDDING
CLUB
BCEEEHIILMNNOPRS
INCOMPREHENSIBLE
BCEEEELMOOOOPRRSTT
SPECTROBOLOMETER
BCEEFINNNNOOOOTT BONE OF
CONTENTION
BCEEHIILMNNOPRSY
INCOMPREHENSIBLY
BCEEIIIILMPPRTTY IMPERCEPTIBILITY
BCEEIILMNNORSTTU
TRIBOLUMINESCENT
BCEEIILNNOORRTTV
INCONTROVERTIBLE
BCEIIIILNNORTTVY INCONVERTIBILITY
BCEIIIILNPSSTTUY INSUSCEPTIBILITY
BCEIIIILPPRRSTTY PRESCRIPTIBILITY
BCEIILNNOORRTTVY
INCONTROVERTIBLY
BCIIIILNOPRRTTUY INCORRUPTIBILITY
BDDDEEILMNNOOSSY BLOODY-
MINDEDNESS
BDDEEEEEEFILMNNSS
FEEBLEMINDEDNESS
BDEEGIINNOPRSSSU SUSPENSION
BRIDGE
BDEHIILNOORSSSTT
BLOODTHIRSTINESS
BEEEEELNQRRRSSUUY QUEENSBERRY
RULES
BEEEGHILNORSTTTU TEETHING
TROUBLES
BEEEGIIOOPRSSTTU PETIT BOURGEOISES
BEEEGIOOOPRSSTTUY PETTY
BOURGEOISES
BEEEHIIILNPRRSTY REPREHENSIBILITY
BEEEENOOPRRSSSSTU
OBSTREPEROUSNESS
BEEFGILNRSSSTTUY FLYING BUTTRESSES
BEEIIIILNOPRSSST RESPONSIBILITIES
BEEIIIILNPRSSTXY INEXPRESSIBILITY
BEEIIIILPRRRSSTY IRREPRESSIBILITY
BEEIIIILNOPRSSTVX INVISIBLE EXPORTS
BEIIIIILMMPRSSTY IMPERMISSIBILITY
BEIIIILMNOPRSSTV INVISIBLE IMPORTS
BEIIIILNOPRRSSTY IRRESPONSIBILITY
CCCDEEFIIKNNORST CONFIDENCE
TRICKS

CCCEEEINNNNOOOSS ON ONE'S
CONSCIENCE
CCCEEIILMNOORRST
MICROELECTRONICS
CCCEEIKLNOORSTUW
COUNTERCLOCKWISE
CCCHLNNOOOORRSTYY
SYNCHROCYCLOTRON
CCDEEEFFINNOOOTV VOTE OF
CONFIDENCE
CCDEEEFINNNOOOSV CONVENIENCE
FOODS
CCDEEHIILORRTTYY
HYDROELECTRICITY
CCDIINOOPRTTUVYY
PYROCONDUCTIVITY
CCEEEEFNNOPRRSSS PRESS
CONFERENCES
CCEEEEILMMOSSTTT SELECT
COMMITTEES
CCEEEELOOPPRSSTT
TELESPECTROSCOPE
CCEEEFIILORRRTTY FERROELECTRICITY
CCEEEHIILMMNNSTU
CHEMILUMINESCENT
CCEEEHILMORRSTTY
ELECTROCHEMISTRY
CCEEEIIILOPRTTYZ PIEZOELECTRICITY
CCEEHIILOOPRTTTY
PHOTOELECTRICITY
CCEEIILNNNOSSSUV
INCONCLUSIVENESS
CCEEIILNOORRSTTT
ELECTROSTRICTION
CCEEIMMNNORSTTUY COMMUNITY
CENTRES
CCEEINNOOPRSSSSU
PRECONSCIOUSNESS
CCEEINNORSSSTTUV
CONSTRUCTIVENESS
CCEHIIIOPRRRSTVY PYRRHIC
VICTORIES
CCEIIILLNOOORSSSU COLLISION
COURSES
CCGHIIIILNOPSSTUY PSYCHOLINGUISTIC
CCGIIIILNOOSSSTU SOCIOLINGUISTICS
CCIIILLNOOPRRSUVY PRIVY
COUNCILLORS
CCIIMNNOORSSSTTU
MISCONSTRUCTIONS
CDDDEEEEILORRRVY RECORDED
DELIVERY
CDDEEEEHILMNOPRY HYPODERMIC
NEEDLE

CDDEEEINNNOSSSTT
DISCONTENTEDNESS
CDDEEFIIINNORRST DIRECTION
FINDERS
CDDEGHIIILRRSTTT RED-LIGHT
DISTRICT
CDDEGHLNNOOOORRY
DENDROCHRONOLOGY
CDEEEEINNOPRSTUX INDECENT
EXPOSURE
CDEEEFHIMNOORSTW DEMISE OF THE
CROWN
CDEEEHHILPRSSTUW WHITED
SEPULCHRES
CDEEEIINNPRRSSWW WINDSCREEN
WIPERS
CDEEEILMOOPPSSUX OEDIPUS
COMPLEXES
CDEEEINOPRRSSTUV
REPRODUCTIVENESS
CDEEELLMNOOOORRTT REMOTE-
CONTROLLED
CDEEHIIJOPRTTUUW WITHOUT
PREJUDICE
CDEEIMNNOOPRSTTU COMPOUND
INTEREST
CDEEINOORSSSSTUU
DISCOURTEOUSNESS
CDEFFGIILNOOOOPR COOLING-OFF
PERIOD
CDEGIIKLMMNNOOTU UNTIL
KINGDOM COME
CDELLNOOOOPSTUYY
POLYCOTYLEDONOUS
CDELMNNOOOOOSTUY
MONOCOTYLEDONOUS
CEEEEEFFGHNORSTU GREENHOUSE
EFFECT
CEEEEEFFMNORRRST TERMS OF
REFERENCE
CEEEEEKKNOPPPRSU KEEP ONE'S
PECKER UP
CEEEEFHORRRRSSSU REFRESHER
COURSES
CEEEEHHLNOPPRSTU THE UPPER
ECHELONS
CEEEEJLLMORSTUWY COSTUME
JEWELLERY
CEEEFFINNOORSTUV
COUNTEROFFENSIVE
CEEEGGIIIILNNNRV CIVIL ENGINEERING
CEEEGIIKLNNPSSSS SLEEPING SICKNESS
CEEEHHMMOOOORRST
HETEROCHROMOSOME

CEEEHLOOOPPRTTTY
PHOTOELECTROTYPE

CEEEHMOORRRTTTYY
ERYTHROCYTOMETER

CEEEIIMNORRSSSTU
MERETRICIOUSNESS

CEEEIINOPRRSSSTV PRESS INTO
SERVICE

CEEFFGIINNORRRTU RETURNING
OFFICER

CEEFLOOORSTTTTUU SETTLE OUT OF
COURT

CEEGIILLLNNOPPPR PROPELLING
PENCIL

CEEGILMMOOOOORRTY
MICROMETEOROLOGY

CEEHHLNOOPPRSSTY
PHOSPHORESCENTLY

CEEHILMNNOOPSTTU
PHOTOLUMINESCENT

CEEHMOORRRTTTYYY
ERYTHROCYTOMETRY

CEEIILNOPRSSSSUU SUPERCILIOUSNESS

CEEIINOPPRRSSSTV PROSCRIPTIVENESS

CEEINOOQRRSSSSTU CROSS-
QUESTIONERS

CEELLMNOOPPRSSTU COLOR
SUPPLEMENTS

CEELLMNOOPPRSTUU COLOUR
SUPPLEMENT

CEFGIIILNORRSSTZ CROSS-FERTILIZING

CEGHHIIIMMNOORSS HIGH
COMMISSIONER

CEGHIMNNOOPRSTYY
CHYMOTRYPSINOGEN

CEGIIILNNORRRTTY
TRINITROGLYCERIN

CEGIIMMMNOSSSTUW SWIMMING
COSTUMES

CEGIINNOOQRSSSTU CROSS-
QUESTIONING

CEIIINNOOPRSSTTT
INTROSPECTIONIST

CEIIINNORRSSSTTU INSURRECTIONISTS

CELNNOPRSSSSUUUU
UNSCRUPULOUSNESS

CFGHHHLOOOOSSTTU SCHOOLS OF
THOUGHT

CFGHHIIILNNOOSSS FINISHING
SCHOOLS

CGGHLLNOOOOORTTY
GLOTTOCHRONOLOGY

CGHHILOOOPPSSYYY
PSYCHOPHYSIOLOGY

CGHIILOOOOPSSTTY
PHYTOSOCIOLOGIST

CGIIIMMNNOOORSSV ROVING
COMMISSION

CGIILMMNNOOPRSUY
UNCOMPROMISINGLY

CHIIMNOOOOOPPSTT
PHOTOCOMPOSITION

DDEEEEILNNNPRTTY
INTERDEPENDENTLY

DDEEEELMNNOPRTUV
UNDERDEVELOPMENT

DDEEEGHINOOPRRXY HYDROGEN
PEROXIDE

DDEEEGIILMNNNSSS SINGLE-
MINDEDNESS

DDEEEIILMMNNPSSS SIMPLE-
MINDEDNESS

DDEEGGGGHIILLPYY HIGGLEDY-
PIGGLEDY

DDEEGIMNNNORSSST STRONG-
MINDEDNESS

DDEEHIKNNOPRRSZZ
DNEPRODZERZHINSK

DDEEHILOORRSSSUY DISORDERLY
HOUSES

DDEGHIIKNOPRRSUY YORKSHIRE
PUDDING

DEEEEEGMNNORRSTY GREEN-EYED
MONSTER

DEEEEGINRRRSSSTU REGISTERED
NURSES

DEEEEINNNRSSSTTU
UNINTERESTEDNESS

DEEEHILLNORRSTVW SELL DOWN THE
RIVER

DEEEHIMMNOSSSTVW SWEDISH
MOVEMENTS

DEEFFILNOOORRSTU SOLDIER OF
FORTUNE

DEEGGIKKLNNOORWW WORKING
KNOWLEDGE

DEEGHHIIINPRSSST HIGH-
SPIRITEDNESS

DEEGHHILNOPRSTUY HYDROGEN
SULPHITE

DEEGHHINORSSSSTT
SHORTSIGHTEDNESS

DEEGHLMOOOOORRTYY
HYDROMETEOROLOGY

DEEGHNNOOOOSSSTT HONEST-TO-
GOODNESS

DEEGIINNNOSSSSUU
DISINGENUOUSNESS

DEEHILLNOORRSSTW
OTHERWORLDLINESS
DEEHIMMNOOORSSTT MONTESSORI
METHOD
DEEHIMNNNORRSTUU
UNDERNOURISHMENT
DEEILLNOOOPPRRTW WELL-
PROPORTIONED
DEFFIIIIMNSTUUVX DIMINUTIVE SUFFIX
DEHIIINNOOOORRTTY
TRIIODOTHYRONINE
EEEEEEGHINOSTTVY GIVE ONE'S
EYETEETH
EEEEEHHILNNRTTVW REINVENT THE
WHEEL
EEEEEHLLMMORSTTU MEURTHE-ET-
MOSELLE
EEEEGHINNOOSTTTT GET ONE'S
TEETH INTO
EEEEHINNPPRRRSTU
ENTREPRENEURSHIP
EEEEINNPRSSSSUVX UNEXPRESSIVENESS
EEEFGHIIINRRSTUX FIRE EXTINGUISHER
EEEFGIILNNOORRTW OIL OF
WINTERGREEN
EEEGHHIIMMPSTTUV IT GIVES ME THE
HUMP
EEEGHHMMOOOORRSTY MOTHER
GOOSE RHYME
EEEHIIMPPRRSSTUV HEIRS
PRESUMPTIVE
EEEIILLNOPRSSSSXY EXPRESSIONLESSLY
EEEEILNNOOPPRSSTT POISON-PEN
LETTERS
EEENOOPPRRSSSSTU
PREPOSTEROUSNESS

EEFGHNOORRSSTTTW TOWERS OF
STRENGTH
EEFHHIILOOPRTTWW WIPE THE FLOOR
WITH
EEFHIILMNNNOTTTY FLY IN THE
OINTMENT
EEFIIILMMNNOPRST LIFE
IMPRISONMENT
EEGHHHHIOPRSTTTU PERISH THE
THOUGHT!
EEGHINOOPPSTTTTY
PHOTOTYPESETTING
EEGHLLMNOOOOPRSY
SELENOMORPHOLOGY
EEHMNNOORRSSTTTW
NORTHWESTERNMOST
EEHMNOORSSSTTTUW
SOUTHWESTERNMOST
EEMNOPPRSSSSTUUU
PRESUMPTUOUSNESS
EFFGIILLNORRSSSU SELF-RISING
FLOURS
EFIIIILLNNPSSTTV SPLIT INFINITIVES
EGGHHILNNOOPRSTU HOUGHTON-LE-
SPRING
EGGHIIIKLNNRSSTT LIGHTNING
STRIKES
EGHIIIKLNNORSSTV SHRINKING
VIOLETS
EGHIIINNOOPSSTTZ
PHOTOSENSITIZING
EHIIINOOPSSTTTVY
PHOTOSENSITIVITY
EHILOOPRSSSTTTUW WHISTLE-STOP
TOURS
EIINOOPPSSSSSTUU SUPPOSITIOUSNESS

SEVENTEEN-LETTER WORDS

AAAAABDEGLMORRSST AMBASSADOR-
AT-LARGE
AAAAABDDEGHIINRRRV DRIVE A HARD
BARGAIN
AAAAABDELNRSSTTTUY ASSAULT AND
BATTERY
AAAACCDEIIKLLNSSS
LACKADAISICALNESS
AAAAACDGHIILLMPRTY
DIAPHRAGMATICALLY

AAAACEEHIIMMMNTTT
METAMATHEMATICIAN
AAAACEEINNNPPPRTU PUT IN AN
APPEARANCE
AAAAFIIILMNNPRRSS
INFRALAPSARIANISM
AAAAGIILMNORSSTTV GRAVITATIONAL
MASS
AAABCEEFLMNNOPSTY BALANCE OF
PAYMENTS

AAAABCEEHIILLLMNRT
LAMELLIBRANCHIATE

AAABCEFGIILLOORRW BIOLOGICAL
WARFARE

AAABCHIIILNOPPRTY
INAPPROACHABILITY

AAABEEEKPPRSSSTTW WASTEPAPER
BASKETS

AAABEEGGLLMNSSSUY ASSEMBLY
LANGUAGES

AAABEEHLNNOOOPTTY
PALAEOETHNOBOTANY

AAACCCIIILLLMNTTY
ANTICLIMACTICALLY

AAACCCIILLLMMORTY
MACROCLIMATICALLY

AAACCDEHHKLNOSSST SACKCLOTH
AND ASHES

AAACCEEEIIKLLLMNS SICKLE-CELL
ANAEMIA

AAACCEGHILLNOOPRY
OCEANOGRAPHICALLY

AAACCEHIINORRSSTT
CHARACTERISATIONS

AAACCEHIINORRSTTZ
CHARACTERIZATIONS

AAACCHIILLNNORSTY
ANACHRONISTICALLY

AAACDEEGGILNNORRR GREGORIAN
CALENDAR

AAACDEIINOQQRTTUU QUADRATIC
EQUATION

AAACEEEEKNPPPPRSU KEEP UP
APPEARANCES

AAACEEGHILLLNOOPT
PALAEETHNOLOGICAL

AAACEEIIIMNNOPRSU PERNICIOUS
ANAEMIA

AAACEEKLLNOORRSTW LOCAL AREA
NETWORKS

AAACEFFIIIMNORTTV AFFIRMATIVE
ACTION

AAACEFIILLNOSSTTU SELF-
ACTUALISATION

AAACEFIILLNOSTTUZ SELF-
ACTUALIZATION

AAACEGGHIJKLNSSSU LAUGHING
JACKASSES

AAACEGILLLMOOOPTY
PALAEOCLIMATOLOGY

AAACEIIILLLMRSTTY
MATERIALISTICALLY

AAACEIIILLLNPRSTTY
PATERNALISTICALLY

AAACEIILNNNNORSTU NATIONAL
INSURANCE

AAACGGILLLMMOORTY
LOGOGRAMMATICALLY

AAACIIIILNNNOSTTT
ANTINATIONALISTIC

AAACIIILLLNNOSTTY
NATIONALISTICALLY

AAACIIILLLNORSTTY
RATIONALISTICALLY

AAACIIIILNOPRRSTTU
PARTICULARISATION

AAACIIIILNOPRRTTUZ
PARTICULARIZATION

AAADDEGILNOSSTUVY
DISADVANTAGEOUSLY

AAADEFJLMMNOSSSTT FLOTSAM AND
JETSAMS

AAADEIIILMNNRSTUV
VALETUDINARIANISM

AAADEIIILNNNOOSTT
DENATIONALISATION

AAADEIIILNNNOOTTZ
DENATIONALIZATION

AAADGHINNORRRSTTW STRAIGHT
AND NARROW

AAADIIIILMNNRSTTU
LATITUDINARIANISM

AAADIIILMMNNORSTT
MALADMINISTRATION

AAAEEEGLMNPRRSSTY PAYMASTER
GENERALS

AAAEEIIMNNOPPRSTX EXAMINATION
PAPERS

AAAEHIILLNNSSSTTY IN THE LAST
ANALYSIS

AAAEIIKLNNPRSSSTY SPINNAKER
STAYSAIL

AAAEILNNNOPRSSSSTT PERSONAL
ASSISTANT

AABBCDDEEKNORRSVW BEND OVER
BACKWARDS

AABCCEEGGLLOORRST GARBAGE
COLLECTORS

AABCCEEHHMORRRSST CHAMBER
ORCHESTRAS

AABCCEELNNNOSSTUU
UNACCOUNTABLENESS

AABCDDEHIKNORSSST SHORT BACK
AND SIDES

AABCDEEEEHLNRRSST REDRESS THE
BALANCE

AABCDEEILNORSSTUU SUBORDINATE
CLAUSE

AABCDEIMNNNSSSTUU IN SUM AND
SUBSTANCE
AABCEEEGHHIILNNTW WEIGH IN THE
BALANCE
AABCEHIIILOPRRRTY
IRREPROACHABILITY
AABCEIIILNNOPRSTU
REPUBLICANISATION
AABCEIIILNNOPRTUZ
REPUBLICANIZATION
AABCIILLNOOORSSTT
COLLABORATIONISTS
AABCIINNNOOSSTTTU
CONSUBSTANTIATION
AABDDEEFGIKNRSSTW WEDDING
BREAKFASTS
AABDEEEIMNOORRRST ANEROID
BAROMETERS
AABEEEIKLMNRRSTTT TIMBER
RATTLESNAKE
AABEEFGHIKLNRSSST ENGLISH
BREAKFASTS
AABIIILNNNNOSTTTU
TINTINNABULATIONS
AACCCDEIMNOPRSTTU CUSTOM AND
PRACTICE
AACCCEEEHILLMNORT
ELECTROMECHANICAL
AACCCEEEILNRRSTUY SECURITY
CLEARANCE
AACCCEHIILLNORTTY
ARCHITECTONICALLY
AACCCEHIKLNOOOORRT ORIENTAL
COCKROACH
AACCCEHIKMRRRSSST CHRISTMAS
CRACKERS
AACCCEIMNNNOOPRTT
CONCENTRATION CAMP
AACCCIIILLLMMORTY
MICROCLIMATICALLY
AACCDEEGILMOORRRT
ELECTROCARDIOGRAM
AACCDEEIOOPPRRSTU
DIPTEROCARPACEOUS
AACCDEFGHKLNORRST
GRANDFATHER CLOCKS
AACCDEGILLLNNOSST LONGDISTANCE
CALLS
AACCDEIIILNNOOSTT
OCCIDENTALISATION
AACCDEIIILNNOOTTZ
OCCIDENTALIZATION
AACCDEIIKLLLOOPSY
KALEIDOSCOPICALLY

AACCDHILLMNOPSYYY
PSYCHODYNAMICALLY
AACCDIIILLNORSTYY
IDIOSYNCRATICALLY
AACCDIIINNNOOORSTT
CONTRAINDICATIONS
AACCEEILLLORSTTTY
ELECTROSTATICALLY
AACCEGHHILLOOPRRY
CHOREOGRAPHICALLY
AACCEGHIILLLLOPRXY
LEXICOGRAPHICALLY
AACCEGHILLMOOPSTY
METAPSYCHOLOGICAL
AACCEHILOOPRRSSUU
SCROPHULARIACEOUS
AACCEIIILMMNOORST
COMMERCIALISATION
AACCEIIILMMNOORTZ
COMMERCIALIZATION
AACCEIILNNOOPSTTU
CONCEPTUALISATION
AACCEIILNNOOPTTUZ
CONCEPTUALIZATION
AACCEINNOORRTTTTU
COUNTERATTRACTION
AACCFILOOPRRRSSTU PROCURATOR
FISCALS
AACCGHHILLOPPRSYY
PSYCHOGRAPHICALLY
AACCGHILLOPPRRTYY
CRYPTOGRAPHICALLY
AACCHILLMMNOOOORTY
MONOCHROMATICALLY
AACCHILLMOOPSSTYY
PSYCHOSOMATICALLY
AACCIIILMNRSTTTUY
CIRCUMSTANTIALITY
AACCIIIMNNORSTTTU
CIRCUMSTANTIATION
AACDEEEELNOPRSSUV A CARD UP
ONE'S SLEEVE
AACDEEEELORRSSSUY DAY RELEASE
COURSES
AACDEEEIMNNNORRST
MAINTENANCE ORDERS
AACDEEHIMMNOORRTY
AEROTHERMODYNAMIC
AACDEEIINORRTTTUY TERTIARY
EDUCATION
AACDEEILMMNOPRSTT
COMPARTMENTALISED
AACDEEILMMNOPRTTZ
COMPARTMENTALIZED

AACDEEILMNNNRSSTT
TRANSCENDENTALISM
AACDEEILNNNRSSTTT
TRANSCENDENTALIST
AACDEEILNNNRSTTTY
TRANSCENDENTALITY
AACDEGHINNNORSSTTT NO STRINGS
ATTACHED
AACDEGIIILNNPRTUZ
UNDERCAPITALIZING
AACDEHIIKKMNNNRSST KITCHEN-SINK
DRAMAS
AACDEHILLMMNORTYY
THERMODYNAMICALLY
AACDEHILNNNPSTUVY PENNSYLVANIA
DUTCH
AACDFIIIILNOQSSTU
DISQUALIFICATIONS
AACEEEEFHORRRSTTW WEATHER
FORECASTER
AACEEEEGLNRRRSSTY SECRETARY-
GENERALS
AACEEEEINNQRRSTTU
QUATERCENTENARIES
AACEEEHLPPPRSTTTU UPSET THE
APPLECART
AACEEFHHIMRRSSSTT FATHER
CHRISTMASES
AACEEGGILLNNOORTY
ORGANOGENETICALLY
AACEEGHILLLNOPRSY
SELENOGRAPHICALLY
AACEEGHINOOPRRTTU
ORGANOTHERAPEUTIC
AACEEGLMNOOPRSTUU ANALOGUE
COMPUTERS
AACEEHIILNOPPRTTV HEPATIC PORTAL
VEIN
AACEEHIILNOPRSTTU
AUSTRALOPITHECINE
AACEEIILLNOOPRSTUV PALACE
REVOLUTIONS
AACEEILNNOORSTTTT EASTERN
COTTONTAIL
AACEEILNORRSTTUVV
ULTRACONSERVATIVE
AACEEINOPRRSTTVVY CONSERVATIVE
PARTY
AACEFFIIILNNNNOOS A NAIL IN ONE'S
COFFIN
AACEGGHILLOOOPRYZ
ZOOGEOGRAPHICALLY
AACEGGIILMNNOORST
CONGREGATIONALISM

AACEGGIILNNOORSTT
CONGREGATIONALIST
AACEGGIILRRRRSSTU SURGICAL
REGISTRAR
AACEGHHIILNOPSSTT TEACHING
HOSPITALS
AACEHIILMNNPPSTTU CAPITAL
PUNISHMENT
AACEHLOOOPPRRRSTY PREPARATORY
SCHOOL
AACEIIIILLLMPRSTY IMPERIALISTICALLY
AACEIIILNORRSSTTY
RECRYSTALLISATION
AACEIIILNORRSTTYZ
RECRYSTALLIZATION
AACEIILNNOORSSTTV
CONVERSATIONALIST
AACEIILNPRRSSTTUU
SUPERNATURALISTIC
AACEIIMNNOORSSSTX CROSS-
EXAMINATIONS
AACEILMNOOORRTUVY
MACROEVOLUTIONARY
AACGGILLLNOOOORTY
OTOLARYNGOLOGICAL
AACGHHIILLOOOPSTT
HISTOPATHOLOGICAL
AACGHHILLOOOPPTTY
PHYTOPATHOLOGICAL
AACGHHIOOOPPRRSTT
ASTROPHOTOGRAPHIC
AACGHIIILNNPRSSTY PHYSICAL
TRAININGS
AACGHILLLNOOOPRTY
ANTHROPOLOGICALLY
AACGHILLMNNOOOOPTY
PATHOGNOMONICALLY
AACHHIILLLNOPPRTY
PHILANTHROPICALLY,
PHILANTRHOPICALLY
AADDDEHILLLNNOPUW UP HILL AND
DOWN DALE
AADDEEGHINNORRSSU ROUGH-AND-
READINESS
AADDEEGHINPRRSTUU
UNDERGRADUATESHIP
AADDFGIILLNNORSSTV STANDARDS OF
LIVING
AADDIIIIILNNOSTUV
INDIVIDUALISATION
AADDIIIIILNNOTUVZ
INDIVIDUALIZATION
AADEEEFFGIILNRRST DIFFERENTIAL
GEARS

AADEEEFFHIINRRRTW FAIR-WEATHER
FRIEND
AADEEEGILNOORSSTT SANTIAGO DEL
ESTERO
AADEEEHIMMNOPRTTX
DEXTROAMPHETAMINE
AADEEEHLLNORTZZZZ ON THE
RAZZLE-DAZZLE
AADEEEHORSSTTTTYY STEADY STATE
THEORY
AADEEEILMNNPRRTTT
INTERDEPARTMENTAL
AADEEGHILLLLNOTVY ALL THE
LIVELONG DAY
AADEEGHIMRRTTUWWY GET AWAY
WITH MURDER
AADEEGIILNNOORTTT TRENTINO-
ALTO ADIGE
AADEEIIILMNPQSSSU
SESQUIPEDALIANISM
AADEEIIILNNNORSTT
INTERNATIONALISED
AADEEIIILNNNORTTZ
INTERNATIONALIZED
AADEEIIIMNNPRRSST
PREDESTINARIANISM
AADEEIIINNOPRSSTT
PEDESTRIANISATION
AADEEIIINNOPRSTTZ
PEDESTRIANIZATION
AADEEIIKNNOPRSSSS PARKINSON'S
DISEASE
AADEEIILNNOOPRSST
DEPERSONALISATION
AADEEIILNNOOPRSTZ
DEPERSONALIZATION
AADEEIILNRSSSTTTU INDUSTRIAL
ESTATES
AADEEIINNOPSSSSST
DISPASSIONATENESS
AADEEIINNORRRSSTX
EXTRAORDINARINESS
AADEFFIIILNOORRST AFFILIATION
ORDERS
AADEFGIMNNNOORTTU FOUNDATION
GARMENT
AADEIIILMMNNNOOST
DENOMINATIONALISM
AADEIIILMNNNOOSTT
DENOMINATIONALIST
AADFGHILORRRSTTWY
STRAIGHTFORWARDLY
AADIIIILNNORSSTTU
INDUSTRIALISATION

AADIIIILNNORSTTUZ
INDUSTRIALIZATION
AADIIIILLNPSSTUUVY VISUAL DISPLAY
UNIT
AAEEEEIIKLMMORSVY A MEMORY LIKE
A SIEVE
AAEEEGIMNNRSSTTUV
ARGUMENTATIVENESS
AAEEEGLMNOPRRSSTT POSTMASTER
GENERAL
AAEEEHHHLLMNNPTTY
METHYLNAPHTHALENE
AAEEEELNNPRRRSSTTU
PRETERNATURALNESS
AAEEGHHILNRRSTTTY
EARTHSHATTERINGLY
AAEEHIINORSSTTTUV
AUTHORITATIVENESS
AAEEIILORRRRSTTTW TERRITORIAL
WATERS
AAEEIINNOPPPRRSST
INAPPROPRIATENESS
AAEEILLMNOPPRRTTU
LUMPENPROLETARIAT
AAEEINNNNOSSSSTTU
INSTANTANEOUSNESS
AAEFGGGIILMNNSSSY MAGNIFYING
GLASSES
AAEFGHINNOOOORRSTT A FROG IN
ONE'S THROAT
AAEGHHMMMMOOOPRRTY
MAMMOTHERMOGRAPHY
AAEGIIIKNNOORRSTV VIRGINIA
SNAKEROOT
AAEGIIKMNNNOORRRTT
INTERROGATION MARK
AAEIIIILMNNOOPRSST
IMPERSONALISATION
AAEIIIILMNNOOPRSTZ
IMPERSONALIZATION
AAEIIILNNNORSSTTT
INTERNATIONALISTS
AAEIIKNNOORRSSTTW SANITATION
WORKERS
AAEIIILNNOORRTTUVY
ANTIREVOLUTIONARY
AAFIIIIMMNNORRSTU
UNIFORMITARIANISM
AAHHILLNOOPPRSTUY NATURAL
PHILOSOPHY
AAIIIILLMNNNORSTTU
TRANSILLUMINATION
AAIIIILMNNNOOOPRST
PRONOMINALISATION

AAIIIILMNNNOOOOPRTZ
PRONOMINALIZATION
AAIIIIMNOOPPPRRSST
MISAPPROPRIATIONS
ABBCDDEEEGHIKMPRSU HUMPBACKED
BRIDGES
ABBDEEIKLLMNOOOOS MAKE ONE'S
BLOOD BOIL
ABBDEELNORRRSSTWY STRAWBERRY
BLONDES
ABCCCCEEEFHMMMOORR CHAMBER
OF COMMERCE
ABCCEEIILMMNNORTU
INTERCOMMUNICABLE
ABCCEIIIIILLNORRTY
IRRECONCILABILITY
ABCCEIIIIJLLOSTTVY OBJECTIVISTICALLY
ABCCIIIIILMMNNOTUY
INCOMMUNICABILITY
ABCDEEEEEGGRRRSTT GREAT
CRESTED GREBE
ABCDEEEHIIIIILNPRTY
INDECIPHERABILITY
ABCDEEIIIILPRSSTTY
DISRESPECTABILITY
ABCEEEEFGMNOORSST ESSENCE OF
BERGAMOT
ABCEEEEEILNNOPSSTX
EXCEPTIONABLENESS
ABCEEEEFLNOQRSTUUY ABSOLUTE
FREQUENCY
ABCEEEGIKMMNNNRRRS KING'S
REMEMBRANCER
ABCEEGHILNNOPRTTY HYPERBOLIC
TANGENT
ABCEEGHOPRRRRSTUU
TURBOSUPERCHARGER
ABCEEGKKLNRSSTUUY KENTUCKY
BLUEGRASS
ABCEEIIINPRRSSTTY
PRESBYTERIANISTIC
ABCEFFIINOOOPRRST PROBATION
OFFICERS
ABCEIIIILLLLMSSSST BALLISTIC
MISSILES
ABCIILLLNNOORTTUY
UNCONTROLLABILITY
ABDDEFFGGIIILNNNN EFFING AND
BLINDING
ABDEEEGHIOORRSTTT SABRE-
TOOTHED TIGER
ABDEEFFIIIILNRTTY DIFFERENTIABILITY
ABDEEGHHILLNRSTUU LIGHT UNDER
A BUSHEL

ABDEEKNNOORRSSUVW NERVOUS
BREAKDOWNS
ABDEGHIIIILNNSSTU
INDISTINGUISHABLE
ABDEIILNOOOPPRRST
DISPROPORTIONABLE
ABDFILNNOOORSSSTU BLOOD
TRANSFUSIONS
ABDGHIIIILNNSSTUY
INDISTINGUISHABLY
ABEEEEHHNRRSSTTTU HUNTER'S
HARTEBEEST
ABEEEFGGILNNNOOSS A SENSE OF
BELONGING
ABEEHILMNNNOOORTU
HONOURABLE MENTION
ABEIIIILMNOPRSSTY
IMPRESSIONABILITY
ABEIIILNNOQSTTUUY
UNQUESTIONABILITY
ABIIIILMNNORSTTUUY
INSURMOUNTABILITY
ABIIIILNOOOPPRRTTY
PROPORTIONABILITY
ACCCCEEEILNNOSSSU CONSCIENCE
CLAUSES
ACCCDIIMMNNOOORTU
COMMUNICATION CORD
ACCCEEEGHILLLNOST TECHNICAL
COLLEGES
ACCCEEEILNOSSSSUV CONCESSIVE
CLAUSES
ACCCEHHILMOOPPRTY
CHEMOPROPHYLACTIC
ACCCEHIKKLNNOOTTU TECHNICAL
KNOCKOUT
ACCCEIIILLMNOOOOSY
SOCIOECONOMICALLY
ACCCEILLOOPPRSSTY
SPECTROSCOPICALLY
ACCCEILMNNOOOOSTU COME TO A
CONCLUSION
ACCCFIINOOOPPRRRT TROPIC OF
CAPRICORN
ACCCGIIIILLMMOOORT
MICROCLIMATOLOGIC
ACCDDEEEEFIIINSSY DEFICIENCY
DISEASE
ACCDEEEEEIINPRSST PIECE DE
RÉSISTANCE
ACCDEEEIILMNNORSU
RADIOLUMINESCENCE
ACCDEEEMNNOOPRRST PROMENADE
CONCERTS

ACCDEEFHIIMMNNORS COMMANDERS IN CHIEF

ACCDEEGIIINRRTTTU INTEGRATED CIRCUIT

ACCDEEHILLLORRTYY HYDROELECTRICALLY

ACCDEEIIMMNNORTTU INTERCOMMUNICATED

ACCDEFIILNNOORSTT SELF-CONTRADICTION

ACCDEFILNOORRSTTY SELF-CONTRADICTORY

ACCDEFMNOOPRRSTUU COMPOUND FRACTURES

ACCDEIIILMNOOORRT MINERALOCORTICOID

ACCDEIIINNORSTTTV CONTRADISTINCTIVE

ACCDHHIIILOPRSTUU THIOSULPHURIC ACID

ACCDIIINNNOORSTTT CONTRADISTINCTION

ACCEEEEEFHIJOPSTTU JUSTICE OF THE PEACE

ACCEEEEGLLLLOORST ELECTORAL COLLEGES

ACCEEEFFGILNNNOOV FLAG OF CONVENIENCE

ACCEEEFFIIILORRSV OFFICIAL RECEIVERS

ACCEEEFIILPPPRRTT PERFECT PARTICIPLE

ACCEEEFILLLORRRTY FERROELECTRICALLY

ACCEEEHIILLMNOPTY ENCEPHALOMYELITIC

ACCEEEHIKKORRSTTV KICK OVER THE TRACES

ACCEEEIIILLLOPRTYZ PIEZOELECTRICALLY

ACCEEEIINNOOPRSTV CONVERSATION PIECE

ACCEEFGIIIIPRSSTV SPECIFIC GRAVITIES

ACCEEGHILLNOPSTYY PSYCHOGENETICALLY

ACCEEGHILLNRRTTUU THE CULTURAL CRINGE

ACCEEHHIOPPRSTTUY PSYCHOTHERAPEUTIC

ACCEEHIINOOORSSTT RISE TO THE OCCASION

ACCEEHILLLOOPRTTY PHOTOELECTRICALLY

ACCEEIIILLLNSTTTU INTELLECTUALISTIC

ACCEEIIILNNOPRSSU INSURANCE POLICIES

ACCEEIILMMNNOOTTU TELECOMMUNICATION

ACCEEIINOPPRSSSSU PERSPICACIOUSNESS

ACCEEIKNOOPRRSTTT PROTECTION RACKETS

ACCEHHIILLNOPRSYZ SCHIZOPHRENICALLY

ACCEHIIKLLNOPSTYY PSYCHOKINETICALLY

ACCEEIIKMMNOOTTTTU COMMUTATION TICKET

ACCEEIIMMNNOORRTTU INTERCOMMUNICATOR

ACCEEILLNOPRRSTTYY CRYPTOCRYSTALLINE

ACCGHHIIMOOOPPRRT MICROPHOTOGRAPHIC, PHOTOMICROGRAPHIC

ACCGHIIKMNORSSSTT CHRISTMAS STOCKING

ACCGHIILLOOOOPSTY PHYTOSOCIOLOGICAL

ACCHIILLNNORSSTYY SYNCHRONISTICALLY

ACCIJKMNNOOOOPSTTY JOINT-STOCK COMPANY

ACDDEEEEEHNNNTTTY DENY THE ANTECEDENT

ACDDEEEEILNNNPSTU INDEPENDENT CLAUSE

ACDDGHIIMNPRSSSTU CHRISTMAS PUDDINGS

ACDDHHJNNOPSSUUWY PUNCH-AND-JUDY SHOWS

ACDEEEEIIPRSTTTVV PRIVATE DETECTIVES

ACDEEEFIIIILNNRTT INDEFINITE ARTICLE

ACDEEEFIMMNNOORSS COMEDIES OF MANNERS

ACDEEEFLLOORRSUVV FOUR-LEAVED CLOVERS

ACDEEEHJOOOPRRRTV OVERHEAD PROJECTOR

ACDEEEIINNNORSSST INCONSIDERATENESS

ACDEEEILNNNOSSTTU SECOND LIEUTENANTS

ACDEEENORRSSSSSTY SECONDARY STRESSES

ACDEEFHIINOORSTTT AT THE
DISCRETION OF

ACDEEGIINORSSTTTU COTTAGE
INDUSTRIES

ACDEEGINNOORRRSTU RECREATION
GROUNDS

ACDEEGMMOOPRRRSSU
PROGRAMMED COURSES

ACDEEHHIMMOOOORRTY
HAEMORRHOIDECTOMY

ACDEEHHHLNNOORTTTW NOT
WORTH THE CANDLE

ACDEEIIIMNOOSSTTU SITUATION
COMEDIES

ACDEEIINOOORRRRTT INTERIOR
DECORATOR

ACDEENNNORRSTTUWY COUNTRY
AND WESTERN

ACDEFINNOOORSSTUU FOUNDATION
COURSES

ACDEGGILLNNOOPRRY LONG-PLAYING
RECORD

ACDEGHNNOORSSSSTU NOUGHTS
AND CROSSES

ACDEGIIIKNNRSSSTT STRIKING
DISTANCES

ACDEHIILLOOOPPRTY
PHOTOPERIODICALLY

ACDEIIIILNNPRRSTY
INTERDISCIPLINARY

ACDEIILNNNNOOSSTU
UNCONDITIONALNESS

ACDEIINNNNOOOORST ON NO
CONSIDERATION

ACDEIINORRSSTTTTY DISTRICT
ATTORNEYS

ACDEIMMMNNNOOOORT COMMON
DENOMINATOR

ACDGHIIINNORSSTTU
CONTRADISTINGUISH

ACDHLMOPRRSSTUUYY MUSCULAR
DYSTROPHY

ACDIIIILLMNPRSTUY
MULTIDISCIPLINARY

ACEEEEEFFFMNORRRS FRAMES OF
REFERENCE

ACEEEEEGHHLNNOPTX TELEPHONE
EXCHANGE

ACEEEEFILNQRRTUVY RELATIVE
FREQUENCY

ACEEEEGHIIMMNNRTW GREENWICH
MEAN TIME

ACEEEEGHILLNORTTY
HETEROGENETICALLY

ACEEEEHLLQRRSSTUV TRAVELLER'S
CHEQUES

ACEEEFFFGGGILLOTU LEFT LUGGAGE
OFFICE

ACEEEFFIILNOOPTTX EXPECTATION OF
LIFE

ACEEEGGHIILRRSTTT CIGARETTE
LIGHTERS

ACEEEGIILLMNNOPPS SLEEPING
POLICEMAN

ACEEEGIILNORTTTVY
ELECTRONEGATIVITY

ACEEEGLLLMORRTTUY
ELECTROMETALLURGY

ACEEEGLMNNNNORRTTV CENTRAL
GOVERNMENT

ACEEEHIILLMNOPSTY
ENCEPHALOMYELITIS

ACEEEHLLLMNOORSSTY ELEMENTARY
SCHOOLS

ACEEEIILNPPPRRSTT PRESENT
PARTICIPLE

ACEEEILLLMNNOSSSSU
MISCELLANEOUSNESS

ACEEEEILLMNPPRRSST SCARLET
PIMPERNELS

ACEEEILNORRSSTUUX SEXUAL
INTERCOURSE

ACEEELNNNOPSTTUWY NEWCASTLE-
UPON-TYNE

ACEEFGIIIINNSSSTV
SIGNIFICATIVENESS

ACEEGHHILOOPPRRST
SPECTROHELIOGRAPH

ACEEGIIILLLNNSTTU
INTELLECTUALISING

ACEEGIIILLLNNTTUZ
INTELLECTUALIZING

ACEEGIILLNOORRSST SOLICITORS
GENERAL

ACEEGLMMNOOPRSTTV GLOVE
COMPARTMENTS

ACEEHHLLNNOOOPPRT
PENTACHLOROPHENOL

ACEEHIJMNNOORTTUW NAME TO
CONJURE WITH

ACEEIIILNNNOOSTTV
CONVENTIONALITIES

ACEEIIILLNNNOQSTUY
INCONSEQUENTIALLY

ACEEIIILLOPPSSSTVX PLASTIC
EXPLOSIVES

ACEEIILNNOPRRSTTT
TELETRANSCRIPTION

ACEELMNOOPPRRSSTU PERSONAL
COMPUTERS
ACEFFFHIINNOOOSST CONFESSION OF
FAITH
ACEFFIIIJLNOSSTTU
SELF-JUSTIFICATION
ACEFIIMNOOPPRRRST IMPROPER
FRACTIONS
ACEGHHIMOOOPPRRRT
PHOTOMICROGRAPHER
ACEGHHLLMNNOPSSUU
PLOUGHMAN'S LUNCHES
ACEGIILLLMNOOORTY
TERMINOLOOGICALLY
ACEGIILLMNOORRTTY
TRIGONOMETRICALLY
ACEHHIILLNOOPPSSS
PHILOSOPHICALNESS
ACEHIIKMNNNOORRSU CHINK IN
ONE'S ARMOUR
ACEHIIKNNOORSSTTT STICK IN ONE'S
· THROAT
ACEHIINOPRRSSTTUY
NEUROPSYCHIATRIST
ACEHLLMNOOOPPRRUY
POLYMORPHONUCLEAR
ACEIIILLLMNORTTUY
MULTICOLLINEARITY
ACEIIILMNNNOORTTU
INTERCOLUMNIATION
ACEIIINNOORRRTTTU
COUNTERIRRITATION
ACEIIILLNNNOQSTTTU CONTINENTAL
QUILTS
ACEIILMMNNRSSTTUU MUSICAL
INSTRUMENT
ACEIILNNNNOOTTUVY
UNCONVENTIONALITY
ACEIILNNOOOPRSSST CONSOLATION
PRISES
ACEIILNNOOOPRSSTZ CONSOLATION
PRIZES
ACEIIMNNNOOSSSSTU
SANCTIMONIOUSNESS
ACGHHHILMOOOOPRRTY
CHROMOLITHOGRAPHY
ACGHHILOOOPPSSTTY
PSYCHOPATHOLOGIST
ACHHIIOOPRRSSTTTY
ORTHOPSYCHIATRIST
ACHIIJLNOOOPRSTTU
PHOTOJOURNALISTIC
ACHIILLORRSSTTTUU
HORTICULTURALISTS

ACIIILMNNOOSSTTTU
CONSTITUTIONALISM
ACIIILNNOOSSTTTTU
CONSTITUTIONALIST
ACIIILNNOOSTTTTUY
CONSTITUTIONALITY
ACIILNNNNOOOSTTTU
NONCONSTITUTIONAL
ADDEEEEEHNNRRSSTT
TENDERHEARTEDNESS
ADDEEEFFIIINNORTT
DEDIFFERENTIATION
ADDEEGHIINNOORSTY
DEHYDROGENISATION
ADDEEGHIINNOORTYZ
DEHYDROGENIZATION
ADDEGHHIIMNNOORTU DIAMOND IN
THE ROUGH
ADDEGIIMNNNRSSSTU
MISUNDERSTANDINGS
ADEEEFIILMNNORSTT SELF-
DETERMINATION
ADEEEGGMMNNOORTTW
ENDOWMENT MORTGAGE
ADEEEHHINNORRTTTU THEATER IN
THE ROUND, THEATRE IN THE ROUND
ADEEEINOOPRRRRSTV PRESERVATION
ORDER
ADEEFIIMMNOPPRRVX VERMIFORM
APPENDIX
ADEEGHIILMNNPPRSY
MISAPPREHENDINGLY
ADEEGHILNOORRTTUY RING OUT
THE OLD YEAR
ADEEHIILMPRSSTTTY METHYLATED
SPIRITS
ADEEHIINOORRSSTUV AUTHORISED
VERSION
ADEEHIINOORRSTUVZ AUTHORIZED
VERSION
ADEEIINOPPRRRSSTU DRAINPIPE
TROUSERS
ADEIIIILMNNORSTTY
TRIDIMENSIONALITY
ADEIIIILNNOSSTTTU
INSTITUTIONALISED
ADEIIIILNNOSTTTUZ
INSTITUTIONALIZED
ADEIIILMNNOOSTTWY TWO-
DIMENSIONALITY
ADEIIMNOPRRRSTTTX DOT-MATRIX
PRINTERS
ADFGIIIKNNNNORSTU DRINKING
FOUNTAINS

ADGIIIILNNOOOOQTTU GO INTO LIQUIDATION

AEEEEFHHLLORTTTTW THE LETTER OF THE LAW

AEEEEIIMNPRRSSTTV MISREPRESENTATIVE

AEEEEIINPPRRRSSTTV PRIVATE ENTERPRISE

AEEEEELLNNOPRTTTYZ PENTYLENETETRAZOL

AEEEFGHINNOOOORTTV ONE FOOT IN THE GRAVE

AEEEFGIINPRRSSTUV PREFIGURATIVENESS

AEEEFHIILLLLLOSTVY LILIES OF THE VALLEY

AEEEEFHILLLLLMOTWW HAIL-FELLOW-WELL-MET

AEEEGHIIMNNOORSST GET IN SOMEONE'S HAIR

AEEEGILMNNNORRTTV INTERGOVERNMENTAL

AEEEHHIJNOSSSSTVW JEHOVAH'S WITNESSES

AEEEIIILNNOPPRSTT PLENIPOTENTIARIES

AEEEIIMNNOPRRSSTT MISREPRESENTATION

AEEFFIIIILLNORSSTT SELF-FERTILISATION

AEEFFIIIILLNORSTTZ SELF-FERTILIZATION

AEEFGHIILLNNSTTTU FLIGHT LIEUTENANTS

AEEFGHLLLNOSTTUUW FULL TO THE GUNWALES

AEEFHHHIIKLNNOPTT IN THE PINK OF HEALTH

AEEGGHHHIILSTTVWY LIGHT HEAVYWEIGHTS

AEEGGHIILLNOORSST SHOOTING GALLERIES

AEEGGIIILMNNNRSST MINISTERING ANGELS

AEEGMNOOOORRSSTTTY GASTROENTEROSTOMY

AEEHIIILNNOPRRSTT INTERRELATIONSHIP

AEEHIKNNNOPRRSSTW SPANNER IN THE WORKS

AEEIIIIILNSSSSTTTX EXISTENTIALISISTS

AEEIIIMNNOPRRSTTT MISINTERPRETATION

AEEIIILMNNNORSSTTV ENVIRONMENTALISTS

AEEIIILNNNNNOORTTV NONINTERVENTIONAL

AEEINNOOOPPRRSSTT PROPORTIONATENESS

AEFGIIILLMNNOPRRST MORNING-AFTER PILLS

AEFILLNOPPRRRSSTU FIRST PERSON PLURAL

AEGGHHHIILNNRSTTU THRUSH NIGHTINGALE

AEGHHHILOOOPPRRTT PHOTOLITHOGRAPHER

AEIIIILLLMMNORSTU MULTIMILLIONAIRES

AEIIKNNNNOQSTTUUW UNKNOWN QUANTITIES

AEINOQRRSSTTUUVYY QUANTITY SURVEYORS

AFGHHLOOOOPPRRTUY PHOTOFLUOROGRAPHY

AHHIMNOOOOPPRRSST ANTHROPOMORPHOSIS

BBDEEEILMNNOOPRTV RIBBON DEVELOPMENT

BCCCEEEIIILNNNOPUV PUBLIC CONVENIENCE

BCCDDEEEIIIILNOSV CIVIL DISOBEDIENCE

BCCEEEIILMNNORSTU TRIBOLUMINESCENCE

BCCEEILMOOOPRRSTT SPECTROBOLOMETRIC

BCCEILOOPPRRSSTUU PUBLIC PROSECUTORS

BCDEEEIIILRRSTTTY STREET-CREDIBILITY

BCDEEGIIIILNOSSTU BUILDING SOCIETIES

BCDEIIIILNRSTTTUY INDESTRUCTIBILITY

BCEEHIIILMNOPRSTY COMPREHENSIBILITY

BCEIIIILMNOPRSSTY INCOMPRESSIBILITY

BDDEEEEEILLPRSSWY BIRD'S-EYE SPEEDWELL

BDDEEHILMNOSSTTUW TWIDDLE ONE'S THUMBS

BDEEGIINNOPRSSSSU SUSPENSION BRIDGES

BDEEGINNOOSSSTTUW GET DOWN TO BUSINESS

BEEHHILOOPSTTTUWW UP TO THE ELBOWS WITH

BEEHIIIMMMRRSSTTU BRITISH
SUMMER TIME
CCCCEEEEHIILMMNNSU
CHEMILUMINESCENCE
CCCEEEHILLLOOPRTT PHOTOELECTRIC
CELL
CCDEEEEEFLNORRSTT LETTERS OF
CREDENCE
CCDEEEFFINNOOOOSTV VOTES OF
CONFIDENCE
CCDEEEILLLNOORTVY COLLECT ON
DELIVERY
CCDEEGHIKNNOSSTTT NIGHT-
SCENTED STOCK
CCDEEINOOPRRTTUUV
COUNTERPRODUCTIVE
CCDEEIOOPRSTTTUVY PROTECTIVE
CUSTODY
CCDEIINOPRSTTUUVY
SUPERCONDUCTIVITY
CCDHIINOOOPTTTUVY
PHOTOCONDUCTIVITY
CCEEEEFFINOSSSTTV COST-
EFFECTIVENESS
CCEEEHIILMORRTTTY
THERMOELECTRICITY
CCEEEHILMNNOOPSTU
PHOTOLUMINESCENCE
CCEEEHILOOOPPRSST
SPECTROHELIOSCOPE
CCEEEILLNOORSTUVV
ELECTROCONVULSIVE
CCEEFILNNOOSSSSSU SELF-
CONSCIOUSNESS
CCEEGINNNORRSTUUY
COUNTERINSURGENCY
CCEEIIMMNNOOSSSSSU
SEMICONSCIOUSNESS
CCEEIINNNOOSSSSTU
CONSCIENTIOUSNESS
CCEIINNNOOPSSSSUU
INCONSPICUOUSNESS
CCGHIIILNOPSSSTUY
PSYCHOLINGUISTICS
CCIJLMNNOOOPSSTUU JUMP TO
CONCLUSIONS
CDDEEEEIIMNNNNOPT INDEPENDENT
INCOME
CDDEEEFIILNNOORTX CONDITIONED
REFLEX
CDDEEFIILNOORTTUY DERELICTION
OF DUTY
CDDEGHIIILRRSSTTT RED-LIGHT
DISTRICTS

CDEEEEFHILNNNRTUU UNDER THE
INFLUENCE
CDEEEFIIILNORSSTY FRIENDLY
SOCIETIES
CDEEEGIIKNNNRSTUV TURN KING'S
EVIDENCE
CDEEEIILMNNOOPSTW ENDOWMENT
POLICIES
CDEEEIILNOOOPRSTT
ELECTRODEPOSITION
CDEEGHIIIMNNPSSST DISPENSING
CHEMIST
CDEEGILNNOOPRTUVY DEVELOPING
COUNTRY
CDEEINNNOOPRSSTUV
NONPRODUCTIVENESS
CDEFFGIILNOOOOPRS COOLING-OFF
PERIODS
CEEEEGIILLMNNOPPS SLEEPING
POLICEMEN
CEEEEGIIMMNNORSTTT STEERING
COMMITTEE
CEEEEHHHKNORRTTTU TURN THE
OTHER CHEEK
CEEEEHHINPRSSSSTY SPEECH
SYNTHESISER
CEEEEHHINPRSSSTYZ SPEECH
SYNTHESIZER
CEEEEINOPRRSSSTTV
RETROSPECTIVENESS
CEEEFFINNOORSSTUV
COUNTEROFFENSIVES
CEEEFGHHINQRRUVYY VERY HIGH
FREQUENCY
CEEEHHHILLNOORRTTY
TRICHLOROETHYLENE
CEEEHILMMNNORSTTU
THERMOLUMINESCENT
CEEEHMOOOPPRRSTTT
SPECTROPHOTOMETER
CEEEIMNNNOORSSSUU
UNCEREMONIOUSNESS
CEEFFGIINNORRRSTU RETURNING
OFFICERS
CEEGHHIIILLNOSSSTW SCHLESWIG-
HOLSTEIN
CEEGHIIIPPRRRSTTV PRESCRIPTIVE
RIGHT
CEEGHILLOOOPRSTYY
ELECTROPHYSIOLOGY
CEEGIILLLNNOPPPRS PROPELLING
PENCILS
CEEHMOOOPPRRSTTTY
SPECTROPHOTOMETRY

CEEIIILLLMOPRSSSTU MULTIPLE
SCLEROSIS
CEEILNNOOOORRTTUUV COUNTER-
REVOLUTION
CEELLMNOOPPRSSTUU COLOUR
SUPPLEMENTS
CEFIIJKNOOOOOPRSTY JOCKEY FOR
POSITION
CEGHHIIIMMNOORSSS HIGH
COMMISSIONERS
CEIINOPRRSSTTTUUU COITUS
INTERRUPTUS
CGIIIMMNNOOORSSSV ROVING
COMMISSIONS
DDEEEEIINNRSSSSTT
DISINTERESTEDNESS
DDEGHIIKNOPRRSSUY YORKSHIRE
PUDDINGS
DEEEEHIMNORRSUUYY HERE'S MUD
IN YOUR EYE
DEEFFILNOOOORRSSTU SOLDIERS OF
FORTUNE
DEEHIIMNNOOOPSTTU THIOPENTONE
SODIUM
DEEIIINNRRSSSSTUU SUNRISE
INDUSTRIES
DEHHIIIMOOOOSTTYY HIDEYOSHI
TOYOTOMI
DEIILMNNOSSSTTUUU
MULTITUDINOUSNESS
EEEEIIMNNNOPRRSTT RETIREMENT
PENSION

EEEELLLNOOPRSSSUV ROLL UP ONE'S
SLEEVES
EEEFGHIIINRRSSTUX FIRE
EXTINGUISHERS
EEEFGHILNORSSSSTU SELF-
RIGHTEOUSNESS
EEEGHHMMOOOORRSSTY MOTHER
GOOSE RHYMES
EEEGINNOPPRSSSSSS
PREPOSSESSINGNESS
EEEINNNOPRSSSTTUU
UNPRETENTIOUSNESS
EEFIIILMMNNOPRSST LIFE
IMPRISONMENTS
EEHHILNOOOOPPRSSST PHILOSOPHER'S
STONE
EEHIIIMMNPPRRSST PRIME
MINISTERSHIP
EEIINOPRRSSSSTTUU
SURREPTITIOUSNESS
EEIINOPRSSSSSTTUU
SUPERSTITIOUSNESS
EGHHIIKNOOPRSSTWY WORKING
HYPOTHESIS
EGHIILNOOOOPRSSTUY
NEUROPHYSIOLOGIST
EIIIMMNOOPPRSSSST
POSTIMPRESSIONISM
EIIIMNOOPPRSSSSTT
POSTIMPRESSIONIST

EIGHTEEN-LETTER WORDS

AAACDEEIIILMNNOSST ESSENTIAL
AMINO ACID
AAAACEEILLMNNORTTWY MATERNITY
ALLOWANCE
AAADEEEEHHMMNNORTVV MOVE
HEAVEN AND EARTH
AAAAEFHIIILLNNNSSTY IN THE FINAL
ANALYSIS
AABCCEEEHIILMNPRST SPLICE THE
MAINBRACE
AACCCDEEFFHINOPRSTT CHAPTER OF
ACCIDENTS
AACCEEEEFIKMNNNOOV MAKE A
CONVENIENCE OF

AACCEEGIILLNNNORTT
CONTINENTAL GLACIER
AACDDDEEEHHIKNQTTU THE QUICK
AND THE DEAD
AACDDEEHILNOOPRSTT DENTAL
ORTHOPAEDICS
AACDEEKNNNNOOORRVYY EVERY
NOOK AND CRANNY
AACDEGHILNOPRRSSTY PLAY ONE'S
CARDS RIGHT
AACEEEFFHHMORTTTTT THE FACT
OF THE MATTER
AACEEEFIMOOPRRRSTV FARMERS'
COOPERATIVE

AACEEELNOPPPRSSTTU UPSET ONE'S
APPLECART
AACEEFGHHILMOORTTU MALICE
AFORETHOUGHT
AACEGIIIKNNNOPSSSU A SNEAKING
SUSPICION
AADDEEEGGINORSTWWY GET A
WORD IN EDGEWAYS
AADHILMMOPRSSTTWWY
WITHDRAWAL SYMPTOMS
AAEEEHKMMNOORSTTUW MAKE
ONE'S MOUTH WATER
AAEEHIKNNNOPRRSSTW A SPANNER
IN THE WORKS
ABBEEEHLNOPRRRTUUY
POLYURETHANE RUBBER
ABCCCEEHILNOOPRSTY HYPERBOLIC
COSECANT
ABCCDEGHIKNOOOORTT
ACCORDING TO THE BOOK
ABCEEEEEMMNNQRRRSU QUEEN'S
REMEMBRANCER
ABCEEIIKMNNOOPRSSS PICK
SOMEONE'S BRAINS
ABEEFHHMMOOORTTTY THE
BOTTOM OF MY HEART
ACCEEEFHKLNOOORSST COCKLES OF
ONE'S HEART
ACDDEEIINNNOORRSTU UNDER
CONSIDERATION
ACDEEEEINNRSSTTTUV TURN STATE'S
EVIDENCE
ACDEEEFHINOPRSSTUU UNDER THE
AUSPICES OF
ACDEEEGLLOOORRSSSS ROSE-
COLORED GLASSES
ACEEELMNOOOSSTTUWY OUTSTAY
ONE'S WELCOME
ADDEEEEEGLLMNPRRSW GERMANDER
SPEEDWELL

ADDEEEFIIIKLLPRRSW SPREAD LIKE
WILDFIRE
ADEEEEHIMNOORSTTTT NOT THE
REMOTEST IDEA
ADEEEFGIIIILNNNRTT INDEFINITE
INTEGRAL
ADGGHHIIINNNNOOOTT ON A
HIDING TO NOTHING
AEEEHIILLMNORSTTTT TELL IT TO
THE MARINES
BBDDEFHIIMMNOOOSTU BOMBED
OUT OF HIS MIND
BBEFGINOOOOOORSSTT TOO BIG FOR
ONE'S BOOTS
BDEEEHMMNNOORSSTUU UNDER
SOMEONE'S THUMB
BEELMNNOOOPRSTTUWW BLOW
ONE'S OWN TRUMPET
CCEEEEIILPRRRTTTWY ELECTRIC
TYPEWRITER
CCEEEHIJKLORSSTTTU CLERK TO THE
JUSTICES
CCEEFGILNNNOOOORSU FOREGONE
CONCLUSION
CDDEEHILMNNOOORTWW COME
DOWN IN THE WORLD
CDEEEEEINNNQRSTUUV TURN
QUEEN'S EVIDENCE
CDEEGIILMNOOOPRRSS MELODIC
PROGRESSION
CEEEEHIMNOOPQRSSTU QUEER
SOMEONE'S PITCH
CEEEIIJNNNOOSSTUWW STEW IN
ONE'S OWN JUICE
CEFIINNNNOOOOPSSSU CONSENSUS
OF OPINION
DEEEEEEEEKLNOPPSSY KEEP ONE'S
EYES PEELED
EEEEHHHIILLNSSTWWW WHEELS
WITHIN WHEELS

NINETEEN-LETTER WORDS

AAAAEIIILLNQSSTTUVY QUALITATIVE
ANALYSIS
AAABCEEEEGHHLMORRRR CEREBRAL
HAEMORRHAGE
AAACCEIIIILLLNOORTTV VOCALIC
ALLITERATION

AAACEGHHMOOPPPRRRTY PAPER
CHROMATOGRAPHY
AAADDDGHHHIILNOSSYY HIGH DAYS
AND HOLIDAYS
AAAEEEIIILMNNNOPRRTT
INTERNATIONAL AMPERE

AABCDEGKNOORSSSTTTW GET
DOWN TO BRASS TACKS

AACCEEGHIMNNNOOPPST CATCH
SOMEONE NAPPING

AACEEEEHIKKLMNORSSS MAKE ONE'S
HACKLES RISE

AADEEGIIKMNNNORSTTV NOT GIVE
A TINKER'S DAMN

AAEEEEGGLLMMNNNNSTT
GENTLEMAN'S GENTLEMAN

AAEEGGHLLMNNNOPSTTU
TUNGSTEN-HALOGEN LAMP

ABCCEEGHILNNOOPRTTY
HYPERBOLIC COTANGENT

ABCDEEGGIINOOPRRSTT TO BEGGAR
DESCRIPTION

ABEEEEFHHHLOORSTTTW THE
BOWELS OF THE EARTH

ABEEHIILNNNNOOORSTT
HONORABLE INTENTIONS

ABEIILLLLOOPRSTTTWW BITTER PILL
TO SWALLOW

ACCEEEEEHKNNOQSSTTU TAKE THE
CONSEQUENCES

ACCEEEEFGILNOPRRSTT REFRACTING
TELESCOPE

ACCEEEEGGHIIILMNNNR CHEMICAL
ENGINEERING

ACDEEEEEFLNNPRRSSTU UNDER FALSE
PRETENCES

ACDEEEGLLOOORRSSSSU ROSE-
COLOURED GLASSES

ACDIIIJMMNORRSSTUUY SUMMARY
JURISDICTION

ACEEEELMNOOORSSTVWY OVERSTAY
ONE'S WELCOME

ACEEEFFHIMNNNOQRSTTU AFFIRM
THE CONSEQUENT

ACEGHIIMNNNOOOPRRRSS HARMONIC
PROGRESSION

ADDEEEEELNNOPPRSTXYY EXPANDED
POLYSTYRENE

AEFGIILNNOPRRRSSSTU FIRST PERSON
SINGULAR

BBBEEEEGGLNNOOSSTYY LET
BYGONES BE BYGONES

BCDDEEEELLMNOOOORSSU CURDLE
SOMEONE'S BLOOD

BDEEEIILLNNNOOSTTWW NEW WINE
IN OLD BOTTLES

BDEEILLLNOOOORSSTUV BLOODLESS
REVOLUTION

CCEEEEEFGILLNOPRSTT REFLECTING
TELESCOPE

CDEEHIIILLPPRRRSSVW PHILLIPS
SCREWDRIVER

DEEEEEEIKKNNNOPSSSY KEEP ONE'S
EYES SKINNED

DEEEGGHIIILNNOOPRTW NIGGER IN
THE WOODPILE

DEEEGHINNNOOORSSTTT NOSE TO
THE GRINDSTONE

DEEEHILLNNOOPSTTWYY LOW-
DENSITY POLYTHENE

EEEEFGHLLLNOOPRSTTU PULL
ONESELF TOGETHER

EEEHILLLOORRSSTTTTU
TORTOISESHELL TURTLE

TWENTY-LETTER WORDS

AAAAABCEIKKLLNNRSSTU
AUSTRALIAN BLACKSNAKE

AAAAEIIILNNQSSTTTUVY
QUANTITATIVE ANALYSIS

AAACDEILMNNORRSSSUUX ALARUMS
AND EXCURSIONS

AAADEEILLLMNNSSTTTTW LAST
WILL AND TESTAMENT

AABBDDEEEELNRRRTTTTU BREAD-
AND-BUTTER LETTER

AACCGHHLMMNOOOPRRTUY
COLUMN CHROMATOGRAPHY

AACDDEEIILLMOOPPRSTY
DIAMETRICALLY OPPOSED

AACEEEHIKKMMNOOSSTTW WHAT
MAKES SOMEONE TICK

ABCCDEEEIIKKLNNPSSTT TEN-SPINED
STICKLEBACK

ABEEHIILNNNNOOORSTTU
HONOURABLE INTENTIONS

ACCEEEEHHINNRSSTTTUW CHINESE
WATER CHESTNUT

ACCEHIIKNNNOORSSSSSU KRISHNA
CONSCIOUSNESS

ACDEEFGHIKNOORRSSTTW WRONG
SIDE OF THE TRACKS
ACEEGHHHILNOOPPRRSTY
SCHLIEREN PHOTOGRAPHY
ADEEEEFHHHNORRSSTWWY THE
WHYS AND WHEREFORES
ADEEEEHLMNNOORSSSTTU STEAL
SOMEONE'S THUNDER

ADEEGHNOOOPRTTTTTUWW PUT
TWO AND TWO TOGETHER
BCCEEEFFFHHHKNORSTTUY BY THE
SCRUFF OF THE NECK
DDEEEFGHILOOPRSSSSTT LESSER
SPOTTED DOGFISH
DEEEGHHHIILNNNOPSTTYY HIGH-
DENSITY POLYTHENE

TWENTY-ONE-LETTER WORDS

AAAACCDFHIIILNORRSSTV HARVARD
CLASSIFICATION
AAAAACCEEEFHIKMNNNOQTTU MAKE
THE ACQUAINTANCE OF
AAACDEEIIILMNNNNOOSST
NONESSENTIAL AMINO ACID
AAAAEEHIIILLMMNNSSTTTUY IN THE
ULTIMATE ANALYSIS
AACCEEEEGGHIIILMNNNNR
MECHANICAL ENGINEERING
AACDEEEFFIKLNNOOOORRTT TAKE
ON A DIFFERENT COLOR
AACDEEIIIKNNNOOOORSTTT TAKE
INTO CONSIDERATION
AADEEFGGHHINOORRRTTUW GO
THROUGH FIRE AND WATER
ABCCEEMOOOPPRRSSSSTUY
MÖSSBAUER SPECTROSCOPY
ABCDEEEHIKLNNOOPRSTTU
SKELETON IN THE CUPBOARD
ABCEILLMNOOPRRSSTUUUY
PULMONARY TUBERCULOSIS

ACCCDEEEELLOOOPRRSSST ROSE-
COLORED SPECTACLES
ACCEEEEGGGIIILLNNNRRT
ELECTRICAL ENGINEERING
ACCEEEEFHHKLNOOORSSTT THE
COCKLES OF ONE'S HEART
ACDEEEGIIMNOPRRTTTUVY
PRODUCTIVITY AGREEMENT
ACDEEHHIILNNOORRTTTUW
WITHOUT LET OR HINDRANCE
ADEEEGHMNOOOOORRRTTWY
HERE TODAY, GONE TOMORROW
BBCEEEEFGHINOOOORRSST TOO BIG
FOR ONE'S BREECHES
BCCEEFFKKKLMNNOOOOOSS
KNOCK SOMEONE'S BLOCK OFF
CCCDEEEENNOOOPRRRSSSU
CORRESPONDENCE COURSES
DEEFHIILNNNOOOPPSSUWY PENNY-
WISE, POUND-FOOLISH

TWENTY-TWO-LETTER WORDS

AABCDDEEEHHIKLLNOOOTTW THE
WHOLE KIT AND CABOODLE
AABEEEEGGIKLLNNNOOSSST ALL
ONE'S EGGS IN ONE BASKET
AACDEEEFFIKLNNOOOORRTTU TAKE
ON A DIFFERENT COLOUR
AADEEEGHIILLNNNOORTVVV IRON
HAND IN A VELVET GLOVE

ABCCDEEEEHIIKKLNPRSSTT THREE-
SPINED STICKLEBACK
ABCDEEGINNNOOOORSSSTTW A
SECOND STRING TO ONE'S BOW
ABCEEHIIKKLMOORSSTTTUU STICK
OUT LIKE A SORE THUMB
ACCCCDDEEEIIMNNRRSSTUU IN
REDUCED CIRCUMSTANCES

ACCCDEEEELLOOOPRRSSSTU ROSE-
COLOURED SPECTACLES
ACDEEHIILNNOOPRSSSSTUY
HYDROELASTIC SUSPENSION

ACEEEFHILMMNNOOOPSSSTT
COMPLIMENTS OF THE SEASON

TWENTY-THREE-LETTER WORDS

AAAAABDDEIMNOORRRRSSTXY
AMBASSADOR EXTRAORDINARY
AAAAACEIILLLNNNNOOORSTTT
CONSONANTAL ALLITERATION
AAACEEEEGGIIILNNNNORRTU
AERONAUTICAL ENGINEERING

AABBCDDEEEHHLNNNORSTTTU
BURN THE CANDLE AT BOTH ENDS
AADEEIILLNNNOOPPRSSSTTTU TO
ALL INTENTS AND PURPOSES

TWENTY-FOUR-LETTER WORDS

ABCDEEEEEEFFFHLLNNOORSTT THE
NOBLE ART OF SELF-DEFENCE
ABCEEEEEFHHHOOPRRRSTTTTU
PUT THE CART BEFORE THE HORSE
ABDEEEEEEFFFHLLNNOORSSTT THE
NOBLE ART OF SELF-DEFENSE

ACCCEEFGIINNNOOOOORSSTUV
COURAGE OF ONE'S CONVICTIONS
ACCEEEEHILLNOOPRRSTTUVVY
ELECTROCONVULSIVE THERAPY

TWENTY-FIVE-LETTER WORDS

AAAABDEEIILMNNOOPPRRSSTTY
AMBASSADOR PLENIPOTENTIARY

AEEEGHHHHHIKMOOORSTTTTUW
TAKE THE ROUGH WITH THE SMOOTH

TWENTY-SIX-LETTER WORDS

AAABCDEEEEHNNOOPRRSSSTTTUW
CAST ONE'S BREAD UPON THE WATERS

TWENTY-EIGHT-LETTER WORDS

AAAEEEEEEFGHHHMOOPPRRSSSTTTT
SEPARATE THE SHEEP FROM THE GOATS